By Authority.

OFFICERS DIED IN THE GREAT WAR 1914-1919.

PART I.
OLD AND NEW ARMIES.

PART II.
TERRITORIAL FORCE.

LONDON:
PRINTED AND PUBLISHED BY
HIS MAJESTY'S STATIONERY OFFICE.

To be purchased through any Bookseller or directly from
H.M. STATIONERY OFFICE at the following addresses:
IMPERIAL HOUSE, KINGSWAY, LONDON, W.C. 2, and
28 ABINGDON STREET, LONDON, S.W. 1;
37 PETER STREET, MANCHESTER;
1 ST. ANDREW'S CRESCENT, CARDIFF;
23 FORTH STREET, EDINBURGH;
or from E. PONSONBY, LTD., 116 GRAFTON STREET, DUBLIN.

1919.

Printed & bound by Antony Rowe Ltd, Eastbourne

PREFACE.

These rolls have been compiled in the Officers' Casualties Branch of the War Office from reports coming to the notice of the Military Secretary.

They are published to enable information, which has from time to time been circulated during the war, to be available in one volume.

In Part I the names are tabulated alphabetically, while in Part II they are arranged by Ranks. Any other method has been found impracticable.

It has not been possible to give the number of the Battalion in every case, as officers changed battalions so rapidly that the Army List was not always a guide, and in the notifications of casualties battalions were not always given.

Attention is invited to the matters at the end of the book; these additions and amendments have arisen during the time the book has been in the press.

The rolls of missing, and missing believed killed, contain the names of those whose cases were or are held in abeyance in deference to the wishes of their next of kin.

Nothing whatever contained in these rolls is to be quoted or made use of in any representation which it may be desired to make on the subject of rank, decoration, nature or date of casualty, or anything consequent upon any casualty.

OCTOBER, 1919.

ABBREVIATIONS.

K. in A.	... ...	Killed in action.
D. of W.	... ...	Died of wounds.
Killed	... ...	Killed, other than in action.
Died...	... ...	From natural causes, etc.

Attention is invited to the note at the foot of the "Commands and Staff" Section on this page.

The number of officers serving on the staff whose names appear under their units amounts approximately to one hundred and fifty-one, but this figure possibly would not include officers temporarily attached to the Staff during a specific operation.

Regimental Rolls of Officers who Died in the War.

Part I—Old and New Armies.

Commands and Staff.

Kitchener of Khartoum, The Rt. Hon. Horatio Herbert, "Earl," K.G., K.P., G.C.B., O.M., G.C.S.I., G.C.M.G. G.C.I.E., Field-Marshal, drowned, 6/6/16 (Secretary of State for War).

V.C. Roberts, The Rt. Hon. Frederick Sleigh, "Earl," K.G., K.P., G.C.B., O.M., G.C.S.I., G.C.I.E., V.D., Field-Marshal, died, 14/11/14 (Col. Commdt. R.A., Col. Ir. Gds.).

Broadwood, Robert George, C.B., Lt.-Gen., d. of w., 21/6/17 (Staff G.O.C. 57/Divn.).

Grierson, Sir James Moncrieff, K.C.B., C.V.O., C.M.G., A.D.C., Lt.-Gen., died, 17/8/14 (Staff, late R.A.).

Lomax, Samuel Holt, C.B., Lt.-Gen., d. of w., 10/4/15 (Staff).

Maude, Sir Frederick Stanley, K.C.B., C.M.G., D.S.O., Lt.-Gen., died, 18/11/17 (Staff, G.O.C.-in-Chief, M.E.F.).

Benson, Sir Frederick William, K.C.B., Major-Gen., died, 19/8/16 (Res. of Off., Remount Ser.).

Capper, Sir Thompson, K.C.M.G., C.B., D.S.O., Major-Gen., d. of w., 27/9/15 (Staff, G.O.C. 7/Divn.).

Davies, Richard Hutton, C.B., Major-Gen., died, 9/5/18.

Feetham, Edward, C.B., C.M.G. Major-Gen. (Tp.), k. in a., 29/3/18 (Commdg. 39/Divn.).

Hamilton, Hubert Ian Wetherall, C.B., C.V.O., D.S.O., Major-Gen., k. in a., 14/10/14.

Heath, Henry Charles Newport, C.B., Major-Gen., died, 22/7/15 (Commdg. South Midland Divn.).

Holmes, William, C.M.G., D.S.O., V.D., Major-Gen., k. in a., 2/7/17 (Spec. List Staff, Aust. Div. H.Q., late A.I.F.).

Ingouville-Williams, Edward Charles, C.B., D.S.O., Major-Gen., k. in a., 22/7/16 (Commdg. 34/Div.).

Wing, Frederick Drummond Vincent, C.B., Major-Gen., k. in a., 2/10/15 (R A.).

Baldwin, Anthony Hugh, Col. (T/Brig.-Gen.), k. in a., 10/8/15 (H.Q. Staff 38/Inf. Bde.).

Bulkeley-Johnson, Charles Bulkeley, A.D.C., Brig.-Gen., k. in a., 11/4/17 (8/Cav. Bde.).

Cole, Arthur Willoughby George Lowry, C.B., D.S.O., Col. (T/Brig.-Gen.), d. of w., 9/5/15 (25/Inf. Bde.).

De Gex, Francis John, C.B., C.M.G., Brig.-Gen., died, 2/4/17 (Base Commdt., Rouen).

Fitton, Hugh Gregory, C.B., D.S.O., A.D.C., T/Brig.-Gen., d. of w., 20/1/16 (Staff, 101/Inf. Bde.).

V.C. Fitzclarence, Charles, Brig.-Gen., k. in a., 12/11/14 (Staff).

Gosling, Charles, C.M.G., Col. (T/Brig.-Gen.), k. in a., 12/4/17 (Staff).

V.C. Gough, John Edmond, A.D.C., K.C.B., C.M.G., Brig.-Gen., d. of w., 21/2/15 (Staff).

Greenfield, Richard Mentieth, C.B., Brig.-Gen., died, 25/4/16 (Gen. Staff, Irish Command).

Heyworth, Frederick James, C.B., D.S.O., T/Brig.-Gen., k. in a., 9/5/16 (Commdg. 3/Gds. Bde.).

Holland, Gerald Edward, C.B., C.M.G., C.I.E., D.S.O., T/Brig.-Gen., died, 26/6/17 (R.E., I.W.T.).

Jacson, Mainwaring George, Col. (T/Brig.-Gen.), died, 2/6/15 (Res. of Off.).

V.C. Kenna, Paul Aloysius, D.S.O., A.D.C., Brig.-Gen., d. of w., 30/8/15 (3/Mounted Bde.).

Longford, Thomas Earl of, K.P., M.V.O., Brig.-Gen., k. in a., 21/8/15 (H.Q.S. 2/Mounted Bde.).

McKerrell, Augustus De Segar, C.B., T/Brig.-Gen., died, 24/4/16 (Commdg. Tay Defences).

Matthews, Godfrey Estcourt, C.B., C.M.G., T/Brig.-Gen., d. of w., 13/4/17 (198/Inf. Bde., R.M.L.I.).

Morrison, Colquhoun Grant, C.M.G., T/Brig.-Gen., died, 23/5/16 (President Claims Commission).

Napier, Henry Edward, T/Brig.-Gen., d. of w., 27/4/15 (88/Bde.).

Nickalls, Norman Tom, T/Brig.-Gen. (Col.), k. in a., 26/9/15 (Bde. Staff).

Nugent, George Colborne, M.V.O., Col. (T/Brig.-Gen.), k. in a., 3/5/15 (Staff).

Peake, Malcolm, C.M.G., T/Brig.-Gen., k. in a., 27/8/17.

Pratt, Ernest St. George, C.B., D.S.O., Brig.-Gen., died, 24/11/18 (Inspector of Infantry).

Riddell, James Foster, Brig.-Gen., k. in a., 26/4/15 (Staff).

Scott-Moncrieff, William, Brig.-Gen., k. in a., 28/6/15 (Commdg. 156/Bde.).

Tanner, John Arthur, C.B., C.M.G., D.S.O., Brig.-Gen., d. of w., 23/7/17 (Staff, 7/Corps).

Adye, Walter, C.B., Col., died, 3/9/15 (G.S.O.I., War Office).

Dickinson, William Vicris, C.M.G., Col., died, 28/10/17 (Staff A.A.G., G.H.Q. 3/Ech.).

Dunn, Robert William Henry, Col., died, 8/1/17 (13/Res. Inf. Bde. Comdr.).

Kerr, Frederick Walter, D.S.O., Col., k. in a., 31/10/14 (Staff).

Norie, Evelyn William Meadows, A.D.C., Col., died, 29/8/15 (Staff, A.M.S., War Office, Half-pay).

Page, Robert Burton, Col., died, 11/11/14 (Staff).

Panton, John Gerald, C.M.G., Col., died, 7/12/15 (Staff, Ret. Pay, Res. of Officers).

Holloway, James Clinton, Lt.-Col., died, 11/1/17 (Staff).

St. Aubyn, The Hon. Edward Stuart, Major, k. in a., 30/12/15 (Staff).

Stuart-French, C. H., Major, died, 23/12/16 (D.A.Q.M.G. 1/Mounted Divn.).

Walter, William Frederick, Major, k. in a., 11/8/15 (53/Divn. G.S.O.).

Berkeley, Thomas Mowbray Martin, Bt.-Lt.-Col., k. in a., 20/5/16 (Staff, D.A.Q.M.G.).

NOTE.—Officers who are borne on the Cadre of units, etc., will be found in the rolls of such units.

Royal Flying Corps.

Adamson, W. C., Capt. (Tp.), k. in a., 5/9/15.

Barfield, John Claude Horsey, 2/Lt., killed, 29/6/15.

Barrington-Kennett, Basil Herbert, Bt.-Maj., killed, 18/5/15 (Gren. Gds.).

Bayly, Charles George Gordon, Lt., k. in a., 20/8/14 (R.E.).

Bewes, Reginald Charles Hope, Lt., k. in a., 23/5/15 (L'pool Regt.).

Blood, Bindon, Capt., killed, 29/9/15 (4th Hussars).

Boles, Hastings Fortescue, 2/Lt., d. of w., 24/5/15 (17th Lancers).

Braithewaite, M. L., Lt., killed, 17/5/15.

Browne, Arthur Richard Howe, Lt., killed, 5/12/15.

Caws, Stanley Winther, Lt., k. in a., 21/9/15.

Chinnery, Esme Fairfax, Capt., killed, 18/1/15 (Cold. Gds.).

Cholmondeley, Reginald, Capt., killed, 12/3/15 (Rif. Bde.).

Cleaver, Digby Crunden, 2/Lt., k. in a., 29/12/15.

Crean, Theodore, Capt., killed, 26/10/14 (North'n Regt.).

Croft, Cyril Talbot Burnley, 2/Lt., killed, 8/12/15 (9th Som. L.I.).

Cockerell, Samuel Pepys, 2/Lt., died, 20/3/15.

Corbett-Wilson, Denys, Lt., k. in a., 10/5/15.

Dryden-Smith, Henry Dalby, Capt. (Tp.), killed, 14/12/15.

Fleming, Henry Roland, 2/Lt., killed, 24/11/14.

Fox, Alan Geoffrey, Capt., k. in a., 9/5/15 (R.E.).

Fulton, John Duncan Bertie, C.B., Major (Tp. Lieut.-Col.), died, 11/11/15 (R.A.).

Gallie, Charles, 2/Lt., k. in a., 22/8/15 (R. S. Fusrs.).

Gardner, Maurice Leigh, 2/Lt., killed, 19/1/15.

Gay, J., 2/Lt., k. in a., 10/10/15.

Glen, David Alexander, 2/Lt., k. in a., 28/12/15 (Manch. Regt.).

Harvey, Gerald Franklyn, Lt., k. in a., 8/11/15 (R.F.A.).

Head, Mark, 2/Lt. (Tp.), k. in a., 28/12/15.

Hobbs, Alan Victor, 2/Lt. (Tp.), k. in a., 15/12/15 (Gen. List).

Hobbs, Geoffrey Bryan, Lt. (Tp.), killed, 7/9/15 (10th North'd Fus.).

Hosking, Cyril Gordon, Lt., killed, 26/10/14 (R.F.A.).

Hyland, F. H., 2/Lt., k. in a., 23/5/15 (Yorks Regt.).

Irving, Aubrey Gordon, Lt., k. in a., 10/3/15 (R.E.).

James, Baron Trevinnen, Lt. (Tp. Capt.), k. in a., 13/7/15 (R.E.).

Kane, John Francis Aloysius, Capt., killed, 22/3/15 (Devon Regt.).

Kelway-Bamber, Claude Herschell, 2/Lt., k. in a., 11/11/15 (Gen. List).

Lascelles, John Frederick, Lt., k. in a., 31/7/15 (Rif. Bde.).

Lawrence, William George, 2/Lt., k. in a., 23/10/15 (Ox. & Bucks L.I.).

Le Bas, Owen Vincent, Lt., k. in a., 7/11/15 (R. W. Surr. Regt.).

V.C. Liddell, John Aidan, Capt., d. of w., 31/8/15 (A. & S. Hrs.).

Lumsden, Henry Tailyour, Capt., killed, 21/6/15 (Cam. Highrs.).

McConnochie, William Jamieson, 2/Lt., k. in a., 8/11/15.

Macdonnell, Herbert Creagh, Capt., d. of w., 24/5/15 (Roy. Ir. Regt.).

Mapplebeck, Gilbert William, D.S.O., Lt. (Tp. Capt.), killed, 24/8/15 (L'pool Regt.).

Marks, C. H., Lt. (Tp. Capt.), k. in a., 23/10/15, (Middx. Regt.).

Monckton, Marmaduke Henry, Lt., k. in a., 9/7/15 (R.G.A.).

V.C. Moorhouse, William Barnard Rhodes, Lt., k. in a., 26/4/15.

Morgan, Albert Ernest, Capt., killed, 10/3/15 (Roy. Fus.).

Morkill, Ronald Falshaw, Lt., killed, 23/6/15 (1st W. Yorks. Regt.).

Mullins, John Ollis, 2/Lt., killed, 30/3/15 (Middx. Regt.).

Newton, Arthur Victor, Capt., killed, 20/10/15 (3rd Som. L.I.).

7961. Wt.18035/520/P.P.3114. 5,000 10/19. S.O.,Rd.

Nixon, W. H., 2/Lt., k. in a., 19/9/15 (Roy. Lanc. Regt.).
Parker, John, 2/Lt., k. in a., 21/7/15 (Roy. Lancs. Regt.).
Perry, Evelyn Walter Copland, 2/Lt., killed, 16/8/14.
Picton-Warlow, Wilfrid, Capt., k. in a., 20/12/14 (Welsh Regt.).
Pike, Robert Maxwell, Capt. (Tp.), k. in a., 9/8/15.
Pitt, George Llewellyn, 2/Lt. (Tp.), killed, 28/12/15 (York. & Lancs.).
Playfair, Lambert, Lt., k. in a., 6/7/15 (R. Scots).
Polehampton, Frederick William, 2/Lt., killed, 26/4/15.
Porter, Gavin Alexander, Lt. (Tp. Capt.), died, 6/12/15 (R.F.A.).
Raleigh, George Hebden, Bt. Major, killed, 20/1/15 (Essex Regt.).
Reed, Paul Maurier, 2/Lt., died, 27/12/15 (8th Som. L.I.).
V.C. Read, Anketell Moutray, Capt., k. in a., 25/9/15 (North'n Regt.).
Rich, Christopher Stiles, Capt., killed, 22/3/15 (R.F.A.).
Roche, Hyacinth Joseph Albert, Capt., killed, 19/1/15 (Roy. Mun. Fusrs.).
Rodney, The Hon. William Francis, 2/Lt., killed, 9/5/15 (Rif. Bde.).
Rogers, William Frederick, 2/Lt., killed, 28/12/15.
Skene, Robin Reginald, 2/Lt., killed, 12/8/14.
Soames, Arthur Henry Leslie, Capt. (Tp. Lt.), died, 7/7/15 (3rd Hussars).
Spence, Charles Bennett, Lt., killed, 9/5/15 (R.F.C.).
Smith, Norman Gordon, 2/Lt., k. in a., 19/12/15 (High.L.I.).
Tudor-Jones, Charles Edward Tudor, 2/Lt., killed, 15/12/15 East Lancs. Regt.).
Vachell, Richard Tanfield, Capt., d. of w., 1/8/15 (North'd Fus.).
Wallace, William Middleton, Lt., k. in a., 22/8/15 (5th Rif. Bde.).
Warrand, Alastair St. John Munro, Lt., killed, 18/3/15 (Royal Hrs.).
Washington, Jonathan Noel, 2/Lt., d. of w., 2/10/15 (Manch. Regt.).
Waterfall, Vincent, 2/Lt., killed, 22/8/14 (3rd East Yorks.).
West, Percy Charles Warren, Lt. & Q.M., died, 29/7/15.
Woodiwiss, Isaac Newton, 2/Lt., k. in a., 10/5/15 (Lincoln Regt.).
Yule, Louis William, 2/Lt., k. in a., 29/9/15.
Abbott, Victor Stephen Henry, 2/Lt., killed, 15/9/16.
Adams, Ralph Newton, M.C., Capt., k. in a., 10/10/16 (7th Roy. Fus.).
Adie, Harry M. Ellis, 2/Lt. (Tp.), k. in a., 1/5/16.
Aimer, George Vernon, 2/Lt., killed, 20/6/16.
Allan, John, 2/Lt., d. of w., 4/11/16 (Gen. List).
Allen, Geoffrey May, 2/Lt., k. in a., 2/9/16 (Gen. List).
Allport, Morton, 2/Lt., died, 10/11/16.
Amor, Ernest John, 2/Lt. (Tp.), k. in a., 15/5/16 (14th Middlx. Regt.).
Archer, Albert Erskine Carson, 2/Lt., k. in a., 9/2/16 (E. Kent Regt.).
Arnold, Herbert Edward, 2/Lt., died, 26/12/16 (Gen. List).
Atkinson, Noel Mitford Henson, 2/Lt. (Tp.), killed, 27/12/16 3/East Lancs.).
Backhouse, Gerald Lovell, 2/Lt., killed, 2/8/16 (Norfolk Regt.).
Bacon, Douglas Haviland, Lt., k. in a., 16/11/16.
Bailey, John Winckworth, 2/Lt., killed, 31/3/16.
Bainbridge, Eric, Lt., k. in a., 5/9/16 (Gen. List.).
Baker, Harold Carl, 2/Lt., killed, 8/10/16.
Barr, Herbert Carrick, 2/Lt. (Tp.), k. in a., 11/12/16 (Gen. List).
Barrett, Ernest William, Capt. (Tp.), k. in a., 29/5/16.
Barrington-Kennett, Victor Annesley, Major (Tp.), k. in a., 13/3/16.
Barton, Robert, 2/Lt., k. in a., 12/1/16.
Bassett-Smith, Thurstan Francis, 2/Lt. (Tp.), died, 23/11/16.
Battye, Cyril Wynard, Lt., killed, 13/3/16 (Roy. Berks).
Bavin, Geoffrey Wynne, 2/Lt., killed, 1/4/16 (Lincoln Regt.).
Beatson, Walter William Gordon, 2/Lt., killed, 18/7/16.
Beatty, Carl John, 2/Lt. (Tp.), k. in a., 15/9/16.
Begg, Henry Berners, 2/Lt., k. in a., 23/11/16.
Bennett, Trevor Moutray, M.C., Lt. (Tp.), k. in a., 10/11/16 (10th R. Ir. Rif.).
Bentham, George Andrew, 2/Lt., k. in a., 3/11/16 (7th East Surr. Regt.).
Bentley, George Greenwood, Lt., d. of w., 17/9/16 (Gen. List).
Berry, Eustace Carlton, 2/Lt., killed, 5/7/16 (R.F.A.).
Bertram, Cyril Robertson, 2/Lt., killed, 18/6/16 (King Edward Horse).
Bidie, George Maxwell Vereker, Lt., killed, 8/7/16 (Royal Scots).
Bidmead, Charles Hugh, 2/Lt. (Tp.), k. in a., 10/11/16 (Gen. List).
Bird, Eric Hinckes, Lt., d. of w., 27/6/16 (1st R. Fusrs.).
Bolitho, Geoffrey Richard, 2/Lt., died, 25/10/16.
Bowen, Eynon George Arthur, Lt., died, 8/9/16 (R.G.A.).
Bowerman, Arthur James, Lt., k. in a., 9/9/16.
Bowman, William Powell, Lt., k. in a., 17/10/16 (19th West Yorks).
Bowyer, Fritz, 2/Lt., k. in a., 25/7/16 (Gen. List).
Brereton, Herbert, Lt. (Tp.), k. in a., 21/12/16 (Gen List).
Brooke, Arthur Goulbourn, 2/Lt. (Tp.), killed, 10/12/16.
Brooke-Murray, Kenneth Algernon, Capt. (Tp.), d. of w., 23/9/16 (A.S.C.).
Brooking, Walter Arthur, 2/Lt., k. in a., 19/1/16 (R.A.).
Brophy, J. B., 2/Lt., killed, 24/12/16
Brown, Claude Algernon Felix, Lt (Tp.), k. in a., 26/12/16 (Gen. List).
Brown, John, 2/Lt. (Tp), d. of w., 11/8/16 (R.F.A.).
Brown, James Alfred, 2/Lt., k. in a., 25/7/16 (S.R.).
Browning-Paterson, Norman Alexander, Capt., k. in a., 21/7/16 (R.A.).
Bruno, Carlo, Lt. (Tp.), k. in a., 29/4/16.
Buchanan, William Archibald, Lt., killed, 2/6/16 (Connaught Rangers).
Burgess, Reginald, Lt. (Tp.), died, 7/7/16 (P. of W.) (A.C.C.).
Burke, Edward William, 2/Lt., k. in a., 14/9/16.
Butterworth, H. W., 2/Lt., killed, 15/7/16.
Byers, Henry Elliott, 2/Lt., killed, 12/11/16 (3rd D.C.L.I.).
Byrne, Patrick Anthony Laugan, D.S.O., 2/Lt., k. in a., 17/10/16 (R.F.A.).
Callaghan, Eugene Cruess, 2/Lt., k. in a., 27/8/16.
Cameron, John Gilmour, 2/Lt., k. in a., 9/11/16 (Cam. Highrs.).
Carlyle, William Mackay, 2/Lt., k. in a., 26/10/16.
Carre, Edward Mervyn, Lt. (Tp.), k. in a., 16/10/16 (8th Linc. Regt.).
Carryer, Charles Ivan, 2/Lt., killed, 18/8/16.
Cave, Eric Arthur, 2/Lt., k. in a., 13/2/16.
Chamberlain, James Russell, Lt., killed, 2/6/16.
Chancellor, Geoffrey Ellis, 2/Lt., k. in a., 9/7/16 (3rd R.W. Surrey).
Charles, Leslie Stafford, Capt., died, 30/7/16 (6th Worcs. Regt.).
Clarke, Donald, 2/Lt. (Tp.), k. in a., 26/8/16 (Gen. List).
Clayton, George, 2/Lt., k. in a., 17/10/16 (1st West Yorks.)
Clover, Harwood Linay, Lt. (Tp.), died, 25/12/16 (7th R. Dub. Fus.).
Coller, Bernard Tarrant, Lt., k. in a., 26/9/16 (Gen. List).
Cooke, John, 2/Lt. (Tp.), died, 20/6/16 (Dur. L.I.).
Cooper, Clarence Edwards Nooth, Lt., k. in a., 16/9/16 (3rd Lincolns).
Cooper, Herbert Ambrose, Capt. (Tp.), k. in a., 21/6/16.
Cooper, Jack Oliver, Capt. (Tp.), k. in a., 23/7/16.
Corbold, H. M., Lt., died, 26/8/16.
Cotton, William Martin Vernon, 2/Lt., k. in a., 21/12/16 (Gen. List).
Cousans, Guy Newson, 2/Lt. k. in a., 9/9/16.
Cowan, Sidney Edward, M.C., Capt. (Tp.), k. in a., 17/11/16.
Coxe, Cecil Henry, 2/Lt., k. in a., 1/7/16.
Crawford, William Charlton, 2/Lt. (Tp.), k. in a., 17/11/16 (Gen. List).
Creey, Cuthbert John, 2/Lt., k. in a., 20/10/16.
Cropper, Alexander, 2/Lt., d. of w., 22/10/16 (Wilts Regt.).
Crowther, Leslie Oakes, Capt. (Tp.), k. in a., 6/12/16 (Gen. List).
Cruickshank, Andrew John Tuke, 2/Lt., k. in a., 7/7/16 (R.G.A.).
Cruickshank, G. L., D.S.O., M.C., Capt., k. in a., 15/9/16.
Cunningham, James Campbell, 2/Lt., k. in a., 14/3/16.
Dampier, Glenny William, 2/Lt., k. in a., 11/12/16.
D'Arcy, Lionel George, 2/Lt., k. in a., 20/12/16.
Davidson, Alexander Bonn, 2/Lt., killed, 26/9/16 (S.R.).
Davies, Alan Wilmot, Lt., killed, 23/4/16 (R.F.A.).
Davis, Hugh Courtenay, 2/Lt., k. in a., 5/8/16 (3rd R. Berks).
Davis, Reginald, 2/Lt., k. in a., 20/10/16 (Gen. List).
Davy, John Alfred, Lt., killed, 8/11/16 (Gen. List).
De Bruyn, Douglas Bayly, 2/Lt., killed, 27/5/16 (K.O.R. Lancs.).
De Frece, Cyril, 2/Lt. (Tp.), killed, 10/8/16.
Dendrino, Stephen, 2/Lt., died, 27/9/16.
Dennistoun, James Robert, Lt., d. of w., 9/8/16 (N. Ir. Horse, P. of W.).
Dobbyn, Robert Newport, 2/Lt. (Tp.), killed, 23/11/16 (Gen. List).
Donnell, Arthur Patrick, 2/Lt., killed, 5/12/16 (North'd Fus.).
Doughty, George, 2/Lt. (Tp.), k. in a., 20/11/16 (13th Royal Scots).
Douglas, Archibald, 2/Lt., killed, 16/10/16 (R.F.A.).
Drewery, Arthur Bancroft, 2/Lt., k. in a., 20/10/16.
Earle, Wallace Sinclair, 2/Lt. (Tp.), k. in a., 16/4/16 (Gen. List).
Echlin, Frederick St. John Ford North, Lt. (Tp.), k. in a., 27/9/16 (5th Roy. Fus.).
Edwards, George, 2/Lt. (Tp.), died, 24/9/16 (Gen. List).
Ellis, Philip Challinor, Lt., k. in a., 17/10/16 (14th H.L.I.).
Evans, Frank Dudley, 2/Lt., killed, 9/6/16 (R. Warwicks).
Evans, Henry Cope, D.S.O., 2/Lt., k. in a., 4/9/16 (Gen. List).
Farie, Claude Allen Gilbert Lindsay Hamilton, Capt., d. of w., 15/3/16 (1st H.L.I.).
Fawkner, Leslie Charles, 2/Lt., k. in a., 26/10/16.
Fenwick, William Cecil, 2/Lt., died, 7/10/16.
Fincham, George Edmund Heygate, 2/Lt. (Tp. Capt.), k. in a., 9/3/16.
Firbank, Godfrey Benjamin Joseph, 2/Lt., k. in a., 11/9/16.
Fisher, Arthur James, 2/Lt., k. in a., 25/10/16 (Gen. List).
Fiske, Harold, Lt., k. in a., 20/12/16.
Flinn, Edgar Wormald, 2/Lt., k. in a., 13/11/16 (R.F.A.).
Floyd, Hayden, 2/Lt. (Tp.), d. of w., 11/7/16 (Gen. List, P. of W.).
Fowler, William, 2/Lt., killed, 16/11/16.
Fraser, William, 2/Lt., k. in a., 25/10/16.
Freeman, James Edward Hutton, 2/Lt., k. in a., 24/4/16 (7th R. W. Surr. Regt.).
Fullerton, William Francis Hannan, 2/Lt., k. in a., 22/10/16 (Gen. List).
Gale, John Hugh, 2/Lt., k. in a., 14/9/16.
Gardner, James, 2/Lt., killed, 27/11/16.
Garlick, Frank Arthur, 2/Lt., k. in a., 20/2/16.
Garner, Frank Leslie, 2/Lt. (Tp.), killed, 20/12/16.
Garnett, William Herbert Stuart, Lt. (Tp.), killed, 21/9/16 (Gen. List).
Giles, George Edward, Lt. (Tp.), killed, 11/11/16.
Girod, Milton, 2/Lt., killed, 19/3/16 (3rd Ches. Regt.).
Glenday, Ferdinand Goncalves, Capt., k. in a., 15/9/16 (12th North'd. Fus.).

Glew, Aubrey Edward, 2/Lt., k. in a., 8/9/16 (24th Sqd.).
Glorney, Ernest Edward, 2/Lt., killed, 25/10/16.
Glover, Brian Edward, 2/Lt. (Tp.), died, 13/3/16 (Gen. List).
Godfrey, Oliver Cyril, 2/Lt., died, 23/9/16.
Godlee, John, 2/Lt. (Tp.), k. in a., 19/7/16.
Goodrich, Frank Edward, M.C., Capt. (Tp.), k. in a., 12/9/16.
Gordon, Bernard Vernon, 2/Lt., killed, 14/12/16.
Gray, Douglas Huon, Lt., k. in a., 3/7/16 (Gen. List).
Gunton, John Welby, 2/Lt., k. in a., 9/8/16 (9th Som. L.I.).
Haarer, Philip McLellan, 2/Lt., k. in a., 28/11/16.
Hake, Osmond George, 2/Lt., killed, 14/5/16 (Gen. List).
Hakewill, Thomas George, 2/Lt. (Tp.), killed, 11/2/16 (11th N. Staff.).
Halcrow, John William, 2/Lt. (Tp. Lt.), k. in a., 7/7/16 (3rd Dorset).
Hall, Edward Henry, Lt. (Tp.), killed, 27/11/16.
Hall, Fred., 2/Lt., k. in a., 22/9/16 (Dorset Regt.).
Hall, Gilbert Sudbury, 2/Lt., d. of w., 30/11/16 (P. of W.).
Hall, Gordon William, 2/Lt., killed, 21/8/16 (Gen. List).
Hann, Cecil Collins, 2/Lt., k. in a., 22/10/16 (Gen. List).
Hanning, James Talmage, 2/Lt., k. in a., 27/11/16.
Hardman, Cecil William, Lt. (Tp.), k. in a., 21/9/16 (23rd Manch. Regt.).
Hart, Clifford John, Capt. (Tp.), k. in a., 9/8/16 (Worcs. Regt.).
Hathaway, Sidney, 2/Lt. (Tp.), k in a., 12/1/16.
V.C. Hawker, Lanoe George, D.S.O., Major (Tp.), died, 23/11/16 (R.E.).
Hayne, Moreton, 2/Lt., died, 10/10/16 (Lancs Fus.) (P. of W.).
Hayward, Charles Oswald, Lt. (Tp.), k. in a., 17/1/16 (7th Lincs. Regt.).
Haywood, Sydney, Lt. (Tp.), killed, 26/10/16.
Hedderwick, Guy, 2/Lt, k. in a., 22/9/16 (1st Res. Cav.).
Hele-Shaw, Henry Rathbone, Lt., k in a., 19/7/16 (Gen. List).
Hewson, Charles Victor, 2/Lt., k. in a., 9/7/16.
Higgins, Claude D., 2/Lt., k. in a., 22/9/16.
Hildreth, Ernest, 2/Lt. (Tp.), killed, 18/10/16 (14th Yorks Regt.).
Hodges, John Cyril, Lt., killed, 17/9/16 (R.G.A.).
Hollingsworth, Frank Edwin, 2/Lt., k. in a., 15/9/16.
Holtom, John Nicholson, 2/Lt., died, 22/10/16.
Hopwood, Robert Gerald, Capt., k. in a., 24/8/16 (Rif. Bde.).
Hugill, Valentine Francis Herbert, 2/Lt., k. in a., 16/10/16 (16th R. Fus.).
Hynes, Ernest Stanley Patrick, 2/Lt., k. in a., 10/11/16 (E. Kent Regt.).
Irvine, William Henry, 2/Lt. (Tp.), killed, 25/10/16.
Jacques, Geoffrey Plateras Lawson, 2/Lt., killed, 5/10/16.
Jack, Henry Claude, 2/Lt., killed, 1/9/16 (H.L.Inf.).
Jenkins, Cyril Donald Thomas, Lt., killed, 2/11/16 (3rd Bn. R.W. Fusrs.).
Jenkins, Richard Borlase 2/Lt, d. of w., 17/1/16 (S.W.B.).
Jervis, John Cedric Lt. (Tp), k. in a., 26/10/16.
Johnson, Harold Richard, Lt., killed, 19/1/16.
Johnston, Herbert Augustus, 2/Lt., k. in a., 4/3/16.
Jones, George Alfred Prime, Capt., killed, 28/5/16 (8th Bn. E. Kent Regt.).
Jordon, William, 2/Lt. (Tp.). k. in a., 8/11/16 (Gen List).
Jowett, Eric Craven, Lt, d. of w., 9/7/16 (Gen. List).
Kane, Frederick Paul, 2/Lt., k. in a., 1/11/16 (Gen. List).
Kemp, Ernest Charles, 2/Lt., k. in a., 6/9/16 (9th Yorks Regt.).
Kenny, John Mary Joseph, Lt (Tp.), k. in a., 23/9/16 (A.S.C.).
Kidd, Leonard Cameron, M.C., Lt., k. in a., 12/10/16.
King, Cyril Henry Marshall, 2/Lt., k in a., 30/9/16 (Gen. List).
King-Harman, Lawrence Hope, Capt., killed, 26/10/16 (R.H.A.).
Kingdon, Leonard, 2/Lt, k. in a., 12/1/16 (Worcs. Regt.).
Knight, A.G., D.S.O., M.C., Capt. (Tp.), k. in a., 20/12/16.
Knox, William, Capt., died, 20/2/16 (Cameron Hrs.).
Law, Henry Merrick Burrell, 2/Lt., k. in a., 8/8/16.
Lamb, Francis Cardno, 2/Lt., killed, 7/9/16.
Lawledge, Francis Mott, 2/Lt., k. in a., 10/10/16 (R.E.).
Leigh, Henry Clifford, Capt., killed, 24/10/16.
Le Sauvage, Ernest Davies, 2/Lt., killed, 30/5/16 (Dorset Regt.).
Lewis, Donald Swain, D.S.O., Lt.-Col. (Tp.), k. in a., 10/4/16 (R.E.).
Lillywhilte, Robert John, Capt. (Tp.), killed, 26/11/16.
Lonnen, Leslie Edgar John, Lt., killed, 16/8/16.
Lotan, William Desmond Guthrie, 2/Lt. (Tp.), killed, 10/12/16.
Lowe, Henry Griffith Pagan, 2/Lt. (Tp.), k. in a., 8/11/16 (Gen. List).
Lucas, Frederick Richard, 2/Lt., killed, 21/10/16.
McKisack, Lawrence Hill Willson, Lt., killed, 13/11/16 (5th Lancers).
MacNamara, Kerin Parnell, 2/Lt., k. in a., 29/6/16.
McNeill, Donald Augustus, 2/Lt., k. in a., 16/11/16.
Main, Percy Rowland, 2/Lt., killed, 28/9/16 (15th Hants Regt.).
Malcolm, George John, Major (Tp.), k. in a., 9/7/16 (R.A.).
Mann, Stanley Walter, 2/Lt., k. in a., 1/11/16.
Marchant, Francis George Wake, 2/Lt., d. of w., 25/10/16 (R.W. Kent).
Martin, Harry Edward, 2/Lt., k. in a., 16/11/16.
Mathewson, Kenneth, Lt., k. in a., 3/8/16.
Milner, John, Lt., k. in a., 26/4/16.
Mitchell, Erik Harrison, Capt. (Tp.), k. in a., 29/4/16 (R.A.).
Mitchell, James, 2/Lt. (Tp.), k. in a., 26/4/16 (Gen. List).
Mitchell, Joseph Spencer, 2/Lt., d. of w., 5/10/16.
Molineux, Albert Ward Spencer, 2/Lt., killed, 28/7/16.

Monckton, Christopher, 2/Lt., k. in a., 1/7/16 (R. Ir. Fus.).
Morgan, Cyril Edward, 2/Lt. (Tp.), killed, 4/12/16 (Gen. List).
Morison, John Sinclair, 2/Lt. (Tp.), killed, 13/10/16 (Gen. List).
Morris, Lionel Bertram Frank, 2/Lt., d. of w., 17/9/16 (3/R.W. Surr.) (4th Sqd.).
Mowat, Morden Maxwell, 2/Lt., d. of w., 16/5/16 (P. of W.).
Nason, John William Washington, Capt. (Tp.), k. in a., 26/12/16 (Gen. List).
Newman, Robert, 2/Lt., killed, 27/5/16.
Newton, Henry Joseph, 2/Lt., died, 2/8/16 (Ches. Regt.).
Nichol, John, Capt., killed, 5/4/16 (R.S. Fus.).
Nicholson, George Crosfield Norris, Capt., killed, 11/3/16.
Niven, William Adam Mackie, 2/Lt., k. in a., 28/10/18.
Nixon, Oswald, 2/Lt., k. in a., 17/9/16 (Essex Regt.).
Nops, Thomas Waldegrave, 2/Lt. (Tp.), k. in a., 21/10/16 (Gen. List).
Oakes, Robert Claude, 2/Lt., k. in a., 19/7/16 (R.F.A.).
O'Brien, Terence Donough, 2/Lt., k. in a., 3/3/16 (16th Lancers).
Oliver-Jones, Alfred Vernon, Lt. (Tp.), died, 23/7/16 (R.F.A.).
Ormrod, Oliver Hugh, Capt. (Tp.), killed, 12/9/16 (R.F.A.).
Osmaston, Robert Shirley, M.C., 2/Lt., k. in a., 24/9/16 (3rd R. Sussex).
Palfreyman, George Alexander, 2/Lt., k. in a., 26/10/16 (3rd E. Kent).
Palmer, Charles Walter, 2/Lt., died, 29/3/16 (Gen. List) (P. of W.).
Parker, Cecil William Hannington, Lt., k. in a., 27/12/16 (Worcs. Regt.).
Parker, George Alec, Capt., k. in a., 27/11/16.
Parsons, Forrest Gale, 2/Lt., k. in a., 26/10/16.
Pashley, Herbert Dudley, 2/Lt., killed, 25/12/16.
Paterson, David William Stewart, 2/Lt., died, 20/6/16.
Patterson, Arnott Andrew, 2/Lt. (Tp.), d. of w., 9/11/16 (6th Border Regt.).
Patterson, Aubrey Frederick Albert, 2/Lt. (Tp.), d. of w., 25/9/16 (Gen. List) (P. of W.).
Pearman, Humphrey, Lt. (Tp.), killed, 13/8/16 (2nd Leinster Regt.).
Peck, Roland Henry, Lt. (Tp.), k. in a., 5/3/16.
Pemberton, Alan John MacDonald, M.C., Capt., died, 3/11/16 (Leinster Regt.).
Pemberton, C. Warren, 2/Lt., killed, 25/4/16.
Penn-Gaskell, Leslie Da Çosta, Major (Tp.), killed, 4/2/16 (Norf. Regt.).
Phillips, Fenton Ellis Stanley, 2/Lt., k. in a., 12/10/16 (3rd Devons).
Pinsent, Philip Ryland, 2/Lt. (Tp.), d. of w., 24/9/16.
Pomeroy, Norman Ransch, 2/Lt., k. in a., 20/10/16 (Gen. List).
Porter, Leslie, Capt., died, 24/10/16.
Powell, Lindsay Carlton, 2/Lt. (Tp.), k. in a., 31/5/16 (7th R.S. Fus.).
Powell, William Uniacke Perry, Lt. (Tp.), died, 20/10/16.
Power, William Boyle, 2/Lt., killed, 17/7/16.
Preston, Rudolph Arthur, Lt., k. in a., 15/9/16.
Price, Graham, 2/Lt. (Tp.), k. in a., 9/3/16 (Gen. List).
Prickett, Lancelot, Capt., killed, 2/6/16 (R.G.A.).
Proctor, Charles Gordon, 2/Lt. (Tp.), killed, 20/2/16 (10th E. Surr. Regt.).
Pulleyn, James Lewis, 2/Lt. (Tp.), k. in a., 17/10/16 (6th Dorset Regt.).
Quinlan, John Francis Pembroke Boxwell, 2/Lt., k. in a., 3/7/16 (R.A.).
Radcliffe, Ernest John, 2/Lt. (Tp.), killed, 20/2/16 (Gen. List).
Radford, Basil Hallam, Capt. (Tp.), k. in a., 20/8/16.
Randall, Geoffrey Victor, 2/Lt., k. in a., 20/7/16.
Rebbeck, Edward William Wise, 2/Lt. (Tp.), killed, 24/4/16 (K.R.R.C.).
Reed, John Sleeman, 2/Lt., died, 31/3/16 (E. Kent Regt.).
Rees, Tom, Lt., k. in a., 17/9/16 (14th R.W. Fus.).
Reeves, Charles d'Arcy Edmund Wentworth, Capt. (Tp.), killed, 18/7/16 (Suffolk Regt.).
Reid, John Lawrie, 2/Lt. (Tp.), d. of w., 16/7/16.
Ridley, Stewart Gordon, 2/Lt. (Tp.), died, 18/6/16.
Rippon, Gilbert Harold Earle, 2/Lt., killed, 7/6/16.
Roberts, Eric James, 2/Lt., k. in a., 23/9/16.
Robertson, Norman McLeod, Lt., k. in a., 17/10/16 (Gen. List).
Rogers, Clarence Elias, 2/Lt., k. in a., 18/6/16.
Rogers, George Stanley, 2/Lt., killed, 10/8/16.
Ross, Alaistair, 2/Lt., killed, 17/1/16.
Ruck, John Arthur, 2/Lt. (Tp.), killed, 25/5/16 (Gen. List).
Russell, Lawrence Dobree, 2/Lt., d. of w., 2/9/16.
Ryckman, Edward Gurney, 2/Lt., k. in a., 4/5/16.
Samuels, George Bernard, 2/Lt., k. in a., 22/10/16 (21st Durham L.I.).
Sanders, James Donald Gerhardt, Capt., k. in a., 5/1/16 (R.F.A.).
Saundby, William Spencer Fitz-Robert, 2/Lt., k. in a., 17/11/16.
Savage, John Raymond Boscawen, 2/Lt., k. in a., 18/6/16.
Scaife, Thomas Earle Gordon, 2/Lt., k. in a., 26/9/16 (6th Drag. Gds).
Scott, Nigel Dennistoun, 2/Lt., killed, 19/4/16 (R.W. Surr. Regt.).
Settle, Reginald William, 2/Lt. (Tp.), k. in a., 23/7/16 (Gen. List).
Sharpe, Maurice, 2/Lt., k. in a., 28/10/16 (Gen. List).
Sheffield, Edward Frederick, 2/Lt (Tp.), killed, 17/5/16 (Gen. List).
Shepherd, Arthur Lindesay Moore, Lt. (Tp.), died, 3/11/16 (6th K.R.R.C., P. of W.)

Shepherd, Richard Malcolm Sisnett, 2/Lt., k. in a., 9/8/16 (4th R. Irish Regt.).
Sherwell, Rex, 2/Lt., k. in a., 3/7/16 (3rd Linc. Regt.).
Shives, Robert Kilgour, Capt. (Tp.), killed, 29/9/16.
Simpson, Henry Richard Deighton, Lt. (Tp.). killed, 20/12/16 (6th Drag. Gds.).
Simpson, James Alexander, Lt. (Tp.), d. of w., 22/10/16 (Gen. List).
Simpson, John Clark, 2/Lt., k. in a., 1/7/16.
Smith, Ernest Frederick William, 2/Lt. (Tp.), d. of w., 27/12/16 (1st Leinster Regt.).
Smith, John Fletcher, Lt. (Tp.), died, 28/7/16 (19th Sherwood Foresters).
Smith, Reginald, Lt., k. in a., 20/12/16.
Smyth, Philip Joseph, 2/Lt. (Tp.), d. of w., 16/9/16 (6th Connaught Rangers).
Spanner, Herbert, Capt. (Tp.), k. in a., 28/12/16.
Steenekamp, Petrus Andries, 2/Lt., killed, 23/5/16.
Stewart, James Aitchison, Lt. (Tp.), d. of w., 12/10/16 (Gen. List).
Steytler, Edward Dickinson, 2/Lt., k. in a., 25/7/16 (South Lancs).
Stileman, Cecil Herbert, 2/Lt. (Tp.), k. in a., 29/2/16 (R. Fusrs.).
Stobart, William, Lt. (Tp.), k. in a., 24/8/16 (10th Durh. L.I.).
Stoddard, Ralph Cyril, 2/Lt., k. in a., 3/7/16 (South Lancs).
Strauss, Victor Arthur, Lt., k. in a., 27/11/16 (A.S.C.).
Stuart, David Aymery, 2/Lt. (Tp.), killed, 29/10/16 (7th Cameron Highrs.).
Stubbs, Reginald Arthur, 2/Lt., k. in a., 8/6/16 (4th Munster Fus.).
Sturrock, Thomas Gibbs Gordon, 2/Lt. (Tp.), d. of w., 16/10/16 (17th R. Scots).
Summers, William Assheton, Capt., k. in a., 1/8/16 (18th Hussars).
Summers, Alfred Spencer Mason, Capt., died, 15/9/16 (19th Hussars, P. of W.)
Sweet, Leonard Herbert, Capt. (Tp.), k. in a., 22/6/16 (Hants Regt.).
Taylor, Douglas John, 2/Lt., killed, 29/12/16.
Taylor, Denis Percival Beauchamp, M.C., Lt., k. in a., 14/3/16, (3rd Hussars).
Taylor, Henry Arthur, M.C., 2/Lt. (T/Capt.), k. in a., 27/9/16 (R. West Kents).
Talbot, Reginald Fitzroy, 2/Lt., k. in a., 27/8/16.
Teale, Guy Neville, 2/Lt. (T/Capt.), k. in a., 20/7/16.
Thierry, Frederick George, 2/Lt., k. in a., 17/9/16 (Gen. List).
Thomas, Cyril Llewellyn Seymour, 2/Lt., k. in a., 6/9/16 (3rd Border R.).
Thomas, Maurice Wotton, Lt., k. in a., 5/8/16 (R.F.A.).
Thomas, William Norman, 2/Lt., k. in a., 8/4/16 (Gen. List).
Thompson, Hector, 2/Lt., d. of w., 18/9/16 (P.O.W.).
Thompson, John, Lt., k. in a., 16/10/16 (Gen. List).
Thornley, Maurice, 2/Lt. (Tp.), killed, 3/12/16 (Northants R.).
Thornton, James, 2/Lt., killed, 9/11/16 (R. Scots).
Thouless, Archibald Cecil, 2/Lt. (Tp.), killed, 26/4/16 (10 Norfolks).
Thuell, William Johnson, 2/Lt. (Tp.), k. in a., 22/10/16 (Gen. List).
Thunder, Michael Hubert, 2/Lt., k. in a., 23/9/16.
Tidswell, Cecil Robert, Capt., k. in a., 16/10/16 (R. Dragoons).
Tollemache, Arthur Henry William, 2/Lt., k. in a., 19/7/16 (R.E.).
Tower, Hugh Christopher, Capt., k. in a., 19/9/16.
Turk, Herbert Henry, M.C., 2/Lt., k. in a., 3/11/16.
Turner, James Clifford, Lt., k. in a., 3/8/16 (R.F.A.).
Turner, Ralph Pool 2/Lt. (Tp.), died, 9/3/16 (Gen. List).
Tweedie-Smith, Douglas, Lt. (Tp.), died, 10/4/16 (Gen. List).
Unwin, Ernest Frederick, Major (Tp.), died, 22/3/16 (A.S.C.).
Vaisey, Charles Thomas Hilton, 2/Lt., d. of w., 30/6/16.
Vaughan-Lewes, Martyn Tulloch, Lt., d. of w., 22/7/16 (3 Welsh R.).
Vernon, Leslie Godfrey Harcourt, 2/Lt., k. in a., 11/9/16.
Vernon-Inkpen, Robert Cecil, 2/Lt. (Tp.), killed, 21/10/16 (12 R. Warwick).
Wade, Oliver John, 2/Lt. (Tp.), k. in a., 22/10/16 (9 R.W. Kent R.).
Wadham, Vivian Hugh Nicholas, Capt., k. in a., 17/1/16 (Hampshire R.).
Waldron, Francis Fitzgerald, Major (Tp.), died, 3/7/16 (19 Hussars).
Wallis, Harold Legh, Lt., killed, 2/7/16 (Gen. List).
Warn, Wallace Gordon, Lt , d. of w., 23/9/16 (10 R. Suss. R.).
Watts, Wilfrid, 2/Lt. (Tp.), k. in a., 17/1/16 (Gen. List).
Webb, Gilbert Watson, Capt., died, 1/7/16 (3 R. Irish Rifs.).
Welsford, Geoffrey Joseph Lightbourn, 2/Lt., k. in a., 30/3/16 (Middx. R.).
Welsford, George Keith, 2/Lt. (Tp.), k. in a., 20/10/16.
White, Charles Douglas, Lt. (Tp.), died, 10/5/16 (12 K.R.R.C.).
Whitehead, John Robert Gobertus, 2/Lt. (Tp.), killed, 3/8/16.
Whitty, John Leo, M.C., Capt., k. in a., 8/7/16 (Leinster R.).
Wiglesworth, Godfrey, 2/Lt., k. in a., 8/7/16.
Williams, Cyril, Lt., k. in a., 30/7/16 (60 Sqd.) (High. L.I.).
Williams, Stanley Norman, 2/Lt. (Tp.), died, 25/10/16 (Gen. List).
Williamson, H. A., 2/Lt., k. in a., 2/7/16 (3 Manch. R.).
Wilson, David, Lt. (T/Capt.), k. in a., 30/7/16.
Wilson-Browne, Rowland Murray, 2/Lt., died, 21/7/16 (P.O.W.).
Wilson-Walker, Alan Alexander, Lt., killed, 20/3/16.
Wright, Percy Andrew, 2/Lt. (Tp.), killed, 21/12/16 (Gen. List).
Wynn, Arthur Ernest, 2/Lt. (Tp.), d. of w., 1/11/16 (Gen. List) (P.O.W.).
Yates, R., 2/Lt., killed, 11/2/16.

Abbott, Thomas Walker, 2/Lt., k. in a., 18/8/17 (11th Sqd., Gen. List).
Adams, Fred, 2/Lt., killed, 12/5/17 (53rd Sqd., Gen. List).
Adams, John Percy Fitzherbert, Lt., k. in a., 14/10/17 (20th Sqd., 4th Dur. L.I.).
Adams, Valentine Harold, 2/Lt., d. of w., 5/5/17 (70th Sqd.).
Addis, Henry Dansey, 2/Lt., killed, 24/1/17 (43rd Sqd., Gen. List).
Adeney, Robert Edward, 2/Lt., died, 11/4/17 (48th Sqd., 3rd R.W. Sur. Regt.).
Aimger, Herbert Cecil, Lt., k. in a., 4/10/17 (19th Sqd., 3rd R. Scots).
Airth, Rennie Alexander, Lt. (Tp.), k. in a., 29/7/17 (7th Sqd., 8th Bedfords.).
Albury, Norman Howard, 2/Lt. (Tp.), d. of w., 15/9/17 (24th Sqd., Gen. List).
Alexander, John Petrie, 2/Lt. (Tp.), died, 14/5/17 (4th Sqd., Gen. List).
Alger, George Crosbie, 2/Lt. (Tp.), killed, 7/6/17 (Gen. List).
Allcock, William Thomas Lloyd, Capt., k. in a., 5/6/17 (40th Sqd.).
Allen, Albert Alexander, 2/Lt., k. in a., 11/10/17 (46th Sqd., Gen. List).
Allen, Melville Richard Howell Agnew, Lt., died, 21/3/17.
Allen, Owen Augustus Ellis, Lt. (Tp.), killed, 3/11/17 (Gen. List).
Allinson, Fred, M.C., 2/Lt. (Tp.), died, 27/3/17 (70th Sqd., Gen. List).
Anderson, Francis Brian Hallam, 2/Lt. (Tp.), killed, 8/9/17 (Gen. List).
Anderson, Herbert Norman Scott, 2/Lt. (Tp.), killed, 24/12/17 (Gen. List).
Anderson, Patrick Alexander, 2/Lt. (Tp.), killed, 19/10/17 (Gen. List).
Anderson, Richard William Laurence, 2/Lt. (Tp.), died, 12/6/17 (1st. Sqd., Gen. List).
Andrew, James Lionel, 2/Lt., killed, 13/12/17.
Andrews, Frederick Seymour, 2/Lt. (Tp.), d. of w., 29/4/17 (13th Sqd., Gen. List).
Andrews, William James Morrison, 2/Lt. (Tp.), killed 4/6/17 Gen. List).
Angood, Percival George, 2/Lt., killed, 12/9/17.
Anne, Crathorn Edward Isham Charlton, Major (Tp.), drowned, 15/4/17 (Gen. List).
Applin, Richard, 2/Lt, k. in a., 29/4/17 (19th Sqd., Gen. List).
Arbery, Ernest Edward, 2/Lt. (Tp), k. in a., 6/6/17 (Gen. List).
Armitage, Eric, 2/Lt., d. of w., 4/10/17 (46th Sqd.).
Armitage, George Jones, 2/Lt., k. in a., 17/6/17 (4th Sqd., Gen. List).
Armstrong, Hilliard Mark, 2/Lt. (Tp.), killed, 14/11/17.
Arthur, William Herbert, 2/Lt. (Tp.), killed, 13/12/17 (Gen. List).
Asher Ronald Stuart, 2/Lt., k. in a., 21/9/17 (46th Sqd., Gen. List).
Aston, Leonard Hugh, 2/Lt. (Tp.), killed, 6/9/17 (Gen. List).
Bailey, Clive Maxwell, 2/Lt. (Tp.), k. in a., 3/8/17 (Gen. List).
Bailey, John Bodley, 2/Lt., k. in a., 20/9/17 (7 Sqd., 1st E. Yorks.).
Bailey, Louis John, 2/Lt. (Tp.), k. in a., 17/6/17 (41 Sqd., Gen. List).
Baines, George, 2/Lt. (Tp.), d. of w., 3/6/17 (48 Sqd., Gen. List).
Baines, Jack Gordon Barrymore, 2/Lt., k. in a., 25/2/17 (R. Warwick.).
Baker, Arthur Forbes, Lt. (T/Capt.), k. in a., 11/4/17 (52 Sqd., 3 D.C.L.I.).
Baker, Arnold Rennie, 2/Lt., k in a., 16/8/17 (27 Sqd., Gen. List).
Baker, Lawrence Edgar, 2/Lt. (Tp.), killed, 1/5/17 (Gen. List).
Bakewell, George John, 2/Lt. (Tp.), d. of w., 16/11/17 (21 Sqd., Gen. List).
Ball, Arthur, 2/Lt., killed, 19/2/17 (3 R Lancs.).
Ball, Oswald Frederic Grevatte, 2/Lt. (Tp.), k. in a., 5/4/17 (13 Sqd., Gen. List).
Ballantyre, Allen James, 2/Lt. (Tp.), d. of w., 10/11/17 (46 Sqd., Gen. List).
Bamford, Joseph Lamont, 2/Lt., k. in a., 20/8/17 (17 Sqd., R. Scots. Fus.)
Bannatyne, Edgar James, D.S.O., Lt. (T/Major), killed, 11/9/17 (19 Huss.).
Barber, Bradley King Bell, 2/Lt. (T/Capt.), k. in a., 4/9/17 (9th Sqd., 1 N'd. Fus.).
Barbour, Hastings Duncan, 2/Lt., k. in a., 21/10/17 (10 Sqd., Gen. List).
Barlow, Charles Alfred, 2/Lt. (Tp.), d. of w., 17/8/17 (4 Sqd., R. Suss. R.).
Barlow, Harold Carver, Lt., k. in a., 18/6/17 (9th Sqd., 20 Lancs Fus.).
Barlow, John Lancashire, 2/Lt. (Tp.), k. in a., 23/9/17 (40 Sqd., Gen. List).
Barnard, Edward Armstrong, 2/Lt., k. in a., 29/9/17 (10 Sqd., R.F.A.).
Barne, Seymour, M.C., Capt., k. in a., 23/4/17 (35 Sqd., 20 Huss.).
Barnes, David John, 2/Lt. (Tp.), killed, 25/4/17 (Gen. List).

Barnes, Eric Earle, Capt., k in a., 7/11/17 (102 Sqd., R.E.).
Barnett, William Augustus, 2/Lt. (Tp.), d. of w., 15/11/17 (21 Sqd.).
Barr, John William, 2/Lt. (Tp.), killed, 14/11/17 (Gen. List).
Barron, John George, 2/Lt. (Tp.), killed, 25/5/17.
Barry, Cecil, Lt., k in a., 21/8/17 (57 Sqd., R. Irish R.).
Barton, Clarence Harry, 2/Lt. (Tp.), k. in a., 26/10/17 (6 Sqd., Gen. List).
Bascombe, Cecil Reginald 2/Lt. (Tp.), killed, 10/10/17.
Bate, George Beaumont, 2/Lt. (Tp.), k. in a., 29/4/17 (18 Sqd., L.N. Lancs).
Bates, Allan Harold, 2/Lt., k. in a., 13/4/17 (25 Sqd., S.R.).
Batson, Henry Thomas, 2/Lt. (Tp.), k. in a., 11/9/17 (48 Sqd., 10 R. W. Surr. R.).
Baumann, Maximilian Otto, 2/Lt., k. in a., 13/7/17 (70 Sqd., Gen. List).
Baylis, Charles John, 2/Lt., died, 6/6/17 (Gen. List).
Beatty, Benjamin George, 2/Lt., k in a., 28/7/17 (45 Sqd., Gen. List).
Beaumont, Charles Leslie, 2/Lt. (Tp.), killed, 20/5/17 (Gen. List).
Bell, Elvis Albert, 2/Lt. (Tp.), k. in a., 22/9/17 (22 Sqd., Gen. List).
Bell, John, Capt., d. of w., 27/12/17 (68 Sqd.).
Bell, Norman, 2/Lt., k. in a., 18/8/17 (57 Sqd., 10 Ches. R.).
Bennett, Robert Davis, 2/Lt. (Tp.), k. in a., 7/12/17 (Gen. List).
Bennie, Robert Smith, 2/Lt., killed, 5/6/17 (45 Sqd.) (S.R.).
Bentley, George Warwick, 2/Lt. (Tp.), died, 13/1/17 (3 Sqd.) (Gen. List).
Berridge, Victor Arnold, 2/Lt. (Tp.), k. in a., 6/3/17 (34 Sqd.) (Bedford R.).
Berry, Oswald William, 2/Lt., k. in a., 8/4/17 (48 Sqd.) (K.O.S.B.).
Berwick, Robert George, 2/Lt. (Tp.), killed, 7/7/17 (Gen. List).
Bevan, Francis Harry Vaughan, Capt. (Tp.), k. in a., 19/4/17 (14 Sqd.) (Gen. List).
Bevan, Wilfrid, 2/Lt., k. in a., 3/12/17 (20 Sqd.) (Gen. List).
Bibby, Gerald Maurice Gosset, 2/Lt. (Tp.), k. in a., 6/3/17 (16 Sqd.) (Gen. List).
Billings, David Kitto, 2/Lt., killed, 15/9/17.
Billings, Hugh Bradish, 2/Lt. (Tp.), died, 9/8/17 (29 Sqd.) (S.R.).
Biner, Frank Amsden, 2/Lt. (Tp.), k. in a., 3/12/17 (22 Sqd.) (Gen. List).
Binns, John Houghton, 2/Lt. (Tp.), died, 4/9/17 (29 Sqd.) (Gen. List).
Birkin, Thomas Renard Chetwynd, 2/Lt., k. in a., 12/6/17 (25 Sqd.) (7 D. Gds.).
Bishop, Frank Ernest, 2/Lt. (Tp.), k. in a., 12/7/17 (57 Sqd.) (Gen. List).
Bishop, William Reason, 2/Lt., k. in a., 2/10/17 (Gen. List).
Bispham, David Charles, 2/Lt. (Tp.), killed, 4/11/17 (Gen. List).
Bissicks, Francis, 2/Lt. (Tp.), killed, 2/1/17 (Gen. List).
Black, David, 2/Lt. (Tp.), killed, 3/10/17 (Gen. List).
Black, James Somerville, 2/Lt. (Tp.), k. in a., 29/4/17 (16 Sqd.) (Gen. List).
Black, Maurice Adam, Major, k. in a., 11/2/17 (5 Drgn. Gds.).
Blackburn, Harry Dudley, Lt., k. in a., 5/4/17 (1st R. Berks R.) (43 Sqd.).
Blake, James Edward, 2/Lt., k. in a., 6/4/17 (45 Sqd.) (R.E.).
Blythe, Harold, 2/Lt. (Tp.), died, 10/2/17 (32 Sqd.) (Gen. List).
Bond, William Arthur, M.C., T/Lt. (T/Capt.), k. in a., 22/7/17 (40 Sqd.) (Yorks L. Inf.).
Bonner, Augustine, 2/Lt. (Tp.), k. in a., 30/4/17 (13 Sqd. (Gen. List).
Boor, Alaric Pinder, Lt. (Tp.), d. of w., 31/10/17 (Gen. List).
Boorne, George Howard, 2/Lt. (Tp.), killed, 28/3/17.
Booth, John Thomas, 2/Lt. (Tp.), d. of w., 19/11/17 (Gen. List).
Booth, William, 2/Lt. (Tp.), d. of w., 28/12/17 (17 Sqd.) (Rifle Bde.).
Booth, William Albert, 2/Lt. (Tp.), k. in a., 23/11/17 (8 Sqd.) (Gen. List).
Bouie, Jean Auguste André, 2/Lt. (Tp.), killed, 24/3/17 (Gen. List).
Boultbee, Arthur Elsdale, Lt., k. in a., 17/3/17 (25 Sqd.) (Northants R.).
Bourne, Gerald Hugh Temple, 2/Lt. (Tp.), k. in a., 18/3/17 (4 Sqd.) (K.R.R.C.).
Bowden, Horace George Cecil, 2/Lt. (Tp.), k. in a., 11/3/17 (45 Sqd., 9 Wing).
Bower, Frank, 2/Lt., d. of w., 31/3/17 (60 Sqd.) (North'd. Fus.).
Bowling, Victor Macdonald, 2/Lt., k. in a., 4/3/17 (29 Sqd.) (S.R.).
Bowyer-Bower, Eldred Wolferstan, Capt., k. in a., 19/3/17 (59 Sqd.) (E. Surrey R.).
Boyd, Philip Bentinck, 2/Lt., k. in a., 13/4/17 (59 Sqd.) (Gordon Hrs.).
Bracey, Victor Charles Edelsten, 2/Lt. (Tp.), killed, 23/9/17.
Bradford, George William Bathurst, 2/Lt., k. in a., 4/2/17 (15 Sqd.) (Gen. List).
Bradley, George Page, 2/Lt., k. in a., 27/10/17 (43 Sqd.) (Gen. List).
Bramley, Samuel Leslie John, 2/Lt., k. in a., 23/9/17 (57 Sqd.) (S.R.).
Brandon, Edgar Thomas Colin, Lt., k. in a., 3/4/17 (11 Sqd.).
Brasington, Frederick Thomas, 2/Lt. (Tp.), k. in a., 9/10/17 (9 Sqd.) (Gen. List).
Brewis, John Arthur Gardner, Lt., k. in a., 29/4/17 (40 Sqd.).
Brink, Johannes Hieronymus, Lt., d. of w., 11/4/17 (14 Sqd.) (R.F.A.).
Briscoe, Mervyn Whitby, Lt. (Tp.), k. in a., 23/7/17 (6 Sqd.) (R.F.A.).
Britton, William Kerr Magill, 2/Lt., killed, 23/5/17 (29 Sqd.) (1 R. Munster Fus.).
Broadhurst, Thomas Clifford, 2/Lt., killed, 28/9/17 (Gen. List).
Brooks, Charles Alfred, Capt., k. in a., 8/7/17 (Wilts R.).
Brooks, Francis Cyril, 2/Lt., killed, 17/8/17 (R.A.).
Brotherhood, Frank Ridgway, 2/Lt. (Tp.), k. in a., 15/9/17 (55 Sqd.) (Gen. List).
Brown, Arthur Roberts, 2/Lt., k. in a., 6/4/17 (2 Sqd.) (R.F.A.).
Brown, Edward John, 2/Lt., k. in a., 17/8/17 (45 Sqd.).
Brown, Lionel George Henry, 2/Lt., died, 8/12/17 (52 Sqd.) (Gen. List).
Brown, Sidney Frederick, 2/Lt., died, 21/7/17 (21 Sqd.) (S.R.).
Browne, William Angus, Lt., k. in a., 21/9/17 (53 Sqd.) (8 R. Innis. Fus.).
Browning, Oakley Alsop, 2/Lt., killed, 11/8/17 (Gen. List).
Browning, Stanley Forrester, Capt. (Tp.), k. in a., 3/5/17 (41 Sqd.) (Gen. List).
Bruce, Charles William, Capt., killed, 22/11/17 (Gordon Hrs.).
Bruce, Robert Stuart Malcolm, 2/Lt. (Tp.), killed, 17/8/17 (Gen. List).
Buckeridge, Guy Dennis, Lt. (Tp.), killed, 21/8/17 (Gen. List).
Budd, Eric Frank Corydon, Lt. (Tp.), k. in a., 11/9/17 (52 Sqd.) (R.E.).
Buntine, Walter Horace Carlyle, M.C., 2/Lt., killed, 19/6/17 (4 N. & D.R.).
Burdon, Rowland, Capt. (Tp.), killed, 10/1/17 (Gen. List).
Burlton, Arthur Vivian, Capt., killed, 30/8/17.
Burnand, Geoffrey Chasmore, Lt., k. in a., 7/4/17 (48 Sqd.) (S.R.).
Burt, Owen Lyndon, Lt. (Tp.), k. in a., 23/7/17 (6 Sqd.) (Gen. List).
Burton, Sidney Rex, 2/Lt. (Tp.), killed, 11/9/17 (Gen. List).
Busby, Harry Eldred, 2/Lt. (Tp.), killed, 11/9/17 (Gen. List).
Bush, James Cromwell, M.C., Lt., k. in a., 7/10/17 (Dorset R.) (22 Sqd.).
Bush, John Stewart de Lisle, Capt., died, 25/8/17 (Somerset L.I.) (41 Sqd.).
Butler, Harry, 2/Lt., k. in a., 25/3/17 (70 Sqd.).
Caffyn, Chalenor McCrae Humphrey Mannington, 2/Lt. (T/Lt.), k. in a., 28/3/17 (60 Sqd., E. Surrey R.).
Calder, Alexander, Lt., k. in a., 10/8/17 (57 Sqd., 8/Ox. & Bucks. L.I.).
Caldwell, Anthony Steel, 2/Lt. (Tp.), killed, 4/5/17 (Gen. List).
Callaghan, Stanislaus Cruess, Lt. (T/Capt.), killed, 28/6/17 (Gen. List).
Cameron, Charles Wilson, 2/Lt. (Tp.), k. in a., 18/12/17 (21 Sqd.) (Gen. List)
Cameron, Percy Grant, Lt, k. in a., 14/8/17 (10 Sqd.) (R.G.A.).
Cameron, Robert, 2/Lt. (Tp.), d. of w, 4/6/17 (16 Sqd.) (Gen. List).
Cameron, Robert Campbell, 2/Lt., d. of w., 2/4/17 (8 Sqd.) (Gen. List).
Campbell, Alexander Findlay, 2/Lt. (Tp.), killed, 22/9/17 (Gen. List.).
Campbell, Charles Bruce, 2/Lt. (Tp.). died, 29/11/17 (49 Sqd.) (Gen. List).
Campbell, Colin St. George, 2/Lt., k. in a., 6/4/17 (45 Sqd.) (S.R.).
Campbell, Ian Dermid, 2/Lt., k. in a., 30/11/17 (24 Sqd.) (Gen. List).
Campbell, John Kennedy, 2/Lt. (Tp.), k. in a., 28/7/17 (29 Sqd.) (Gen. List).
Campbell, William, Lt., k. in a., 6/7/17 (2 Sqd.) (R.F.A.).
Capper, Bass Durant, Capt. (Tp.), killed, 6/12/17.
Carey, Allan Stewart, 2/Lt. (Tp.), killed, 27/5/17 (45 Sqd.) (Gen. List).
Carse, William Kenric, 2/Lt. (Tp.), k. in a., 13/2/17 (3 Sqd.) (Gen. List).
Carson, Thomas, 2/Lt., k. in a., 31/7/17 (4 Sqd.) (Gen. List).
Carter, Bernard Robert Hadow, 2/Lt. (Tp.), killed, 7/11/17 (Gen. List).
Carter, Frank Leslie, Lt., k. in a., 22/4/17 (3 Sqd.) (E. Surrey R.)
Carter, George Augustine, 2/Lt. (Tp.), k. in a., 5/12/17 (13 Sqd.) (Gen. List)
Carter Henry William, 2/Lt. (Tp.), k. in a., 2/7/17 (59 Sqd.) (Spec. List).
Carter, Seton Rodney, 2/Lt. (Tp.), k. in a., 14/4/17 (52 Sq.) (17 Lancs Fus.).
Carter, Wilfred Arthur Douglas, 2/Lt., killed, 23/5/17 (Dorset Regt.).
Cass, William Edward, 2/Lt. (Tp.), killed, 4/6/17 (Gen. List).
Casswell, Eric Denison Seymour, Capt., k. in a., 7/11/17 (6/Rifle Bde.).
Castle, Errington Edward, Lt. (Tp.), killed, 12/8/17 (Gen. List).
Cathie, Archibald James, 2/Lt. (Tp.), killed, 11/7/17 (Gen. List).
Cato, Geoffrey Maidens Walter Gaven, 2/Lt. (Tp.), k. in a., 6/11/17 (Gen. List, 6 Sqd.).
Cattell, Frank Douglas Bernard, 2/Lt. (Tp.), killed, 22/10/17 (Gen. List).
Caulfield, Toby St George, 2/Lt., k. in a., 16/6/17 (45 Sqd.).
Caunter, John Charles Ashford, Capt., k. in a., 28/10/17 (1/Welsh Rgt., 60 Squad).
Cawson, George Adrian, 2/Lt. (Tp.), k. in a., 30/11/17 (Gen. List, 56 Sqd.).
Cayford, George Everett, 2/Lt. (Tp.), killed, 16/7/17 (Gen. List)

Chambers, Percy Wilmot, Capt. (Tp.), d. of w., 13/8/17 (Gen. List, 22 Sqd.) (P of W.).
Chandler, Henry Leonard, 2/Lt. (Tp.), killed, 30/10/17.
Chapman, Alfred John, 2/Lt. (Tp.), died, 18/9/17 (Gen. List, 41 Sqd.).
Chapman, Charles Meredith Bouverie, M.C., Lt. (T/Major), d. of w., 1/10/17 (E. Kent Regt., 29 Sqd.).
Chapman, Lewis Carlton, 2/Lt. (Tp.), died, 16/4/17 (60 Sqd.) (Gen. List).
Chapman, William Wetheral, Lt., k. in a., 7/10/17 (E. Kent Regt.).
Charlesworth, Alick Thomas Bentall, 2/Lt. (Tp.), killed, 30/5/17 (Gen. List).
Chatterton, Arthur Measures, 2/Lt. (Tp.), killed, 30/7/17 (Gen. List).
Chaworth-Musters, Roger Michael, 2/Lt., k. in a., 7/5/17 (Leic. Regt., 56 Sqd.).
Cheatle, Charles Chesterfield, 2/Lt. k. in a., 5/5/17 (Gen. List, 23 Sqd.).
Chivers, Wreford, 2/Lt., k. in a., 17/8/17 (32 Sqd., Gen. List).
Chown, Francis Jack, 2/Lt. (Tp.), k. in a., 20/9/17 (1 Sqd., Gen. List).
Christie, Robert Francis Sanderson, 2/Lt. (Tp.), killed, 15/10/17 (Gen. List).
Churcher, Edgar, Lt. (Tp.), k. in a., 14/7/17 (32 Sqd., 3/Rif. Bde.).
Chuter, Harry Athelstan, Lt., k. in a., 25/3/17 (70 Sqd., 2/R. Fusrs.).
Clark, Eric Foster, Tp. Lt., k. in a., 1/1/17 (E. Kent Regt.).
Clark, Ernest Vaughan, 2/Lt., k. in a., 29/11/17 (20 Sqd.).
Clark, Frank Nelham), 2/Lt., killed, 29/4/17 (Gen. List).
Clark, John, 2/Lt. (Tp.), killed, 6/8/17 (Gen. List).
Clark, Reginald Burton, 2/Lt., d. of w., 1/5/17 (60 Sqd.).
Clark, Walter Llewellyn, T/2/Lt. (T/Capt.), k. in a., 23/5/17 (6 Squad.) (Gen. List).
Clarke, Francis Charles Erlin, Lt., d. of w., 11/10/17 (5 Squad., 3/Worc. Regt.).
Clarke, Harry Charles, Lt. (Tp.), k. in a., 6/7/17 (48 Squad.).
Clarke, Nathaniel Fuhrmann, 2/Lt. (Tp.), killed, 1/6/17 (Gen. List).
Clarke, Nicholas Vincent, Tp. 2/Lt., killed, 19/6/17 (Gen. List).
Clarke, Sidney Herbert, M.C., Lt. (T/Capt.), k. in a., 2/9/17 (3/Wilts Regt.).
Clayphan, George Alfred, 2/Lt. (Tp.), k. in a., 4/12/17 (12 Sqd., Gen. List).
Cleary, Robert Ernest, 2/Lt. (Tp.), killed, 18/12/17 (Gen. List).
Cleaver, Eric Arnold, Lt. (Tp.), d. of w., 3/7/17 (Gen. List).
Clegg, Robert Leslie, Lt., k. in a., 3/9/17 (45 Sqd.) (4/Lancs. Fus.).
Cleland-Hollamby, Douglas MacDonald, 2/Lt. (Tp.), killed, 22/8/17 (R. W. Kent Regt.).
Clement, Carleton Main, Capt., k. in a., 19/8/17 (22 Squad.) (Gen. List).
Clifford, William James, 2/Lt., k. in a., 25/4/17 (48 Squad.) (Gen. List).
Clifton, George Leake Cecil, Lt., died, 22/7/17 (2/Aircraft Depot).
Clifton, William Gerard Talbot, 2/Lt., k. in a., 31/3/17 (3/Ox. & Bucks. L.I.) (11 Squad.).
Coates, Sydney, 2/Lt. (Tp), k. in a., 27/5/17 (52 Squad.) (Gen. List).
Cobb, John Elbridge, 2/Lt. (T/Lt.), d. of w., 14/8/17 (21 (Squad. (R.A.S.C.).
Cobb, Reginald John Preston, 2/Lt., k. in a., 11/10/17 (56 Squad., W. Rid. Regt.).
Cock, John Herbert, 2/Lt., k. in a., 14/4/17 (60 Squad., Gen. List).
Cody, Samuel Franklyn, 2/Lt. (Tp.), k. in a., 23/1/17 (41 Squad., Gen. List).
Cole, Maxwell Gerard, 2/Lt. (Tp.), k. in a., 18/5/17 (1/Squad., Gen. List).
Cole-Hamilton, Con William Eric, Capt., killed, 2/7/17 (20 Squad., R. Scots).
Collett, Clive Franklyn, Lt. (T/Capt.), killed, 23/12/17 (70 Squad).
Collins, Arthur Duppa, 2/Lt. (Tp.), d. of w., 1/4/17 (52 Squad., Gen. List).
Collins, Harold George, Lt. (Tp.), k. in a., 9/4/17 (48 Squad., R.A.S.C.).
Collinson, Geo. Edward Cleather, Lt., killed, 13/4/17 (Cameron Highrs.).
Conran, Owen Mostyn, Major, k. in a., 29/7/17 (10 Sqd.) (R. Lancs. Regt.).
Constable, Arthur Leslie, 2/Lt., k. in a., 17/3/17 (43 Squad).
Cook, Alfred Burton, Capt. (Tp.), k. in a., 20/11/17 (57 Squad.) (Gen. List).
Cooksey, Kenneth Bassano, 2/Lt., k. in a., 8/4/17 (3/R.W. Kent Regt.).
Cooper, Cyril Ashley, 2/Lt. (Tp.), killed, 29/6/17 (Gen. List).
Cooper, Clifford Edward Gordon, 2/Lt. (Tp.), killed, 26/11/17 (Gen. List).
Cooper, Horace Charles Henry, 2/Lt. (Tp.), killed, 15/4/17 (Gen. List).
Cooper, John Stephen, Lt. (Tp.), k. in a., 25/3/17 (70 Sqd., Gen. List).
Coppard, Stuart Benjamin Hayes, 2/Lt. (Tp.), k. in a., 20/11/17 (57 Sqd.).
Corbishley, Ronald Heathcote, 2/Lt., k. in a., 28/7/17 (57 Squad., 8/Devon Regt.).
Cornford, Ross, Lt., k. in a., 17/8/17 (22 Squad., Gen. List).
Cornish, William Oliver, 2/Lt. (Tp.), k. in a., 20/9/17 (32 Squad., Gen. List).
Cosgrove, Gordon Sallnow, 2/Lt. (Tp.), killed, 4/11/17 (Gen. List).
Cotterill, Harold Gordon Knight, Lt., died, 6/6/17 (35 Squad., R.F.A.).
Coupland, John Charles Gerald, Lt., k. in a., 6/5/17 (2 Squad., R.F.A.).
Coutts, Walter Gordon, 2/Lt. (Tp.), killed, 2/12/17 (Gen. List).
Cowie, George, 2/Lt., k. in a., 22/10/17 (54 Squad.) (Gen. List).
Cox, Arthur George, 2/Lt. (Tp.), k. in a., 15/12/17 (42 Squad., Gen. List).
Cox, Clarence Rupert, Capt. (Tp.), d. of w., 13/4/17 (12 R. Sussex Regt.).
Cox, Derek Percy, 2/Lt., k. in a., 21/8/17 (27 Squad., Gen. List).
Cox, Hugh Bertram Hamilton, 2/Lt., killed, 29/1/17 (R.F.A.).
Cragg, Sydney Bolton, 2/Lt. (Tp.), k. in a., 9/11/17 (25 Squad., Gen. List).
Craig, George Roberts, M.C., Lt., killed, 19/8/17 (E. Lancs. Regt.).
Craig, Hedley William, 2/Lt. (Tp.), k. in a., 15/4/17 (R.E.).
Cramb, Wilfred Brown, 2/Lt., k. in a., 14/4/17 (9 Squad., 4/A & S. Hrs.).
Cranswick, George Alec., 2/Lt., k. in a., 18/11/17 (23 Squad., Y. & Lancs. Regt.).
Crapp, Cyril Frederick, 2/Lt. (Tp.), 22/5/17 (Gen. List).
Cravos, Cyril Stephen, 2/Lt. (Tp.), k. in a., 2/3/17 (5 Squad., Gen. List).
Creasey, Arthur Andrew, 2/Lt., k. in a., 14/7/17 (22 Squad., 1/Beds. Regt.).
Cremetti, Max Arthur Eugene, 2/Lt. (Tp.), killed, 14/8/17 (Gen. List).
Cremonini, James Henry, 2/Lt. (Tp.), k. in a., 18/10/17 (66 Squad.).
Crerar, Malcolm Charlton, 2/L., killed, 3/8/17 (R.F.A.).
Crewe, Clifford Whatley, 2/Lt. (Tp.), killed, 13/8/17 (Gen. List).
Crisp, Harold Dudley, 2/Lt., k. in a., 6/11/17.
Croager, Norman Eustace Sassoon, 2/Lt. (Tp.), killed, 8/11/17 (Gen. List).
Croft, Herbert Arthur, 2/Lt., k. in a., 14/2/17 (2 Squad., Gen. List).
Crooke, Walter, 2/Lt. (Tp.), killed, 12/11/17 (Gen. List).
Crosbie, John Colin, Lt., d. of w., 7/9/17 (70 Squad, R.G.A.).
Crow, Charles Maurice, 2/Lt., k. in a., 23/4/17 (16 Squad.).
Crow, Norman Howard, 2/Lt., k. in a., 14/9/17 (56 Squad., Gen. List).
Crowther, Stanley Lorne, 2/Lt., k. in a., 20/9/17 (29 Squad.).
Cruickshank, Kenneth George, 2/Lt., died, 12/7/17 (32 Squad., Gen. List).
Cryer, Harold James, 2/Lt. (Tp.), killed, 13/10/17 (Gen. List).
Cull, Arthur Tulloch, Capt., k. in a., 11/5/17 (48 Squad., 1/S'fth. Highrs.).
Cumming, Alfred Lionel, 2/Lt. (Tp.), k. in a., 7/6/17 (15 Squad., Gen. List).
Cunningham, Joseph Francis Crowley, 2/Lt. (Tp.), killed, 28/11/17 (Gen. List).
Cunningham, James Nelson, Lt. (Tp.), d. of w., 19/10/17 (56 Squad., Gen. List).
Curphey, William George Sellar, M.C., Capt. (Tp.), died, 15/5/17 (32 Squad., Gen. List).
Curtis, Frank Warren, 2/Lt., k. in a., 14/8/17 (9 Squad.).
Curtis, Henry Neville, 2/Lt. (Tp.), k. in a., 25/7/17 (45 Squad., Gen. List).
Curtis, Ralph Luxmore, 2/Lt. (Tp.), died, 21/9/17 (48 Squad, Gen. List) (P.O.W.).
Cushing, Geoffry Edgar, 2/Lt., killed, 29/12/17.
Cutler, Stuart le Geyt, Lt. (T/Capt.), k. in a., 9/8/17 (21 Squad., R.A.S.C.).
Cutler, William Reynolds, 2/Lt. (Tp.), k. in a., 18/11/17 (70 Squad., Gen. List).
Daniel, Fleetwood Earnscliffe, 2/Lt. (Tp.), killed, 20/12/17 (Gen. List).
Dann, Henry Norman Groves, 2/Lt. (Tp.), k. in a., 15/9/17 (55 Squad., Gen. List).
Darnell, Charles Verdon, 2/Lt., k. in a., 25/4/17 (25 Squad., Conn. Rngrs.).
Davey, Roland Alfred, 2/Lt. (Tp.), killed, 8/8/17 (Gen. List).
Davey, Wilfrid Charles, Lt. (Tp.), d. of w., 21/11/17 (15 Squad., R.A.S.C.).
Davidson, Donald Alastair Leslie, Capt., k. in a., 30/4/17 (9 Squad.).
Davidson, William, 2/Lt., k. in a., 31/10/17 (10 Squad., Gen. List).
Davies, Albert, 2/Lt. (Tp.), killed, 19/6/17 (Gen. List).
Davies, David Benyon, Lt., k. in a., 11/8/17 (52 Squad., Gen. List).
Davies, David Evan, 2/Lt., k. in a., 29/4/17 (12 Squad., Gen. List).
Davies, Robert William Marengwyn, 2/Lt. (Tp.), k. in a., 6/4/17 (52 Squad., 22/N'land. Fusrs.).
Davis, Basil Raymond, Lt., k. in a., 20/9/17 (45 Squad.).
Davis, Horace John, 2/Lt., k. in a., 6/2/17 (15 Squad., 3/Lincs. Regt.).
Davis, Lawrence Alan, 2/Lt. (Tp.), k. in a., 23/6/17 (4 Squad., Gen. List).
Dawson, Harold William, 2/Lt. (Tp.), k. in a., 4/10/17 (19 Squad., Gen. List).
Day, Herbert James, 2/Lt., d. of w., 8/8/17 (11 Squad., Glouc. Regt.).

Day, John Charles, 2/Lt., k. in a., 9/5/17 (52 Squad., 3/R. Sussex Regt.).
Day, William Leonard, Lt., k. in a., 6/4/17 (59 Squad., Border Regt.).
Dean, Arthur Le Roy, 2/Lt., killed, 9/8/17.
Deberigny, Charles Etienne, 2/Lt., d. of w., 29/4/17 (43rd Sqd.).
De Lacey, John Matthew, 2/Lt., k. in a., 23/9/17 (57th Sqd.) (18th W. Yks.).
De Lisle, Alexander Charles Nicholas March Phillipps, Lt. (Tp.), k. in a., 20/11/17 (Gen. List, 21st Sqd.).
Dennett, Stephen Hepworth, 2/Lt. (Tp.), killed, 11/5/17 (8th K. Shrop. L.I.).
d'Erf Wheeler, Percival Francis Crommelin, Capt., killed, 24/7/17 (3rd Dorset R.).
De Rochie, Curtis Matthew, 2/Lt., k. in a., 14/7/17 (27th Sqd.).
De Ross, Adam Gower Sutherland, 2/Lt. (Tp.), k. in a., 14/2/17 (Gen. List, 3rd Sqd.).
De Teissier, Aubrey, 2/Lt. (Tp.), killed, 12/10/17 (Gen. List).
Devenish, George Weston, Lt., k. in a., 6/6/17 (R.F.A., 35th Sqd.).
Diamond, Julius, M.C., Lt., k. in a., 8/10/17 (K.O. Sco. Bord., 7th Sqd.).
Dickie, Edward Gordon, Lt. (Tp.), k. in a., 30/11/17 (Gen. List, 84th Sqd.).
Diment, Harry Stanley, 2/Lt. (Tp.), k. in a., 23/5/17 (Gen. List, 6th Sqd.).
Dixon, Cecil Hargreave, Lt. (Tp.), k. in a., 28/11/17 (Gen. List, 9th Sqd.).
Dixon, Charles Penrose, 2/Lt., d. of w., 25/10/17 (9th Sqd.).
Dixon, Henry Eric, Capt. (Tp.), killed, 19/8/17 (Gen. List., 62nd Sqd.).
Dobson, Arthur Edward John, 2/Lt. (Tp.), k. in a., 7/6/17 (Gen. List, 45th Sqd.).
Docking, Robert James, Lt. (Tp.), d. of w., 10/2/17 (9th E. Kents, 43rd Sqd.).
Dodd, Walter De Courcy, Lt., died, 31/10/17 (In German hands; 5th R. Mun. Fus., 11th Sqd.).
Dow, Allan Gladstone, 2/Lt. (Tp.), killed, 17/8/17 (Gen. List).
Downing, George Guy Barry, Lt., killed, 4/9/17 (Gen. List).
Downing, Herbert George, M.C., 2/Lt., k. in a., 6/11/17 (29th Sqd., Gen. List).
Draper, Mark Denman, 2/Lt. (Tp.), killed, 7/2/17 (Gen. List).
Drey, Adolphe, M.C., Lt., Tp., killed, 9/5/17 (58 Res. Sqd. R.A.S.C.).
Duerden, Henry, 2/Lt., Tp., killed, 27/7/17 (Gen. List).
Duggan, Joseph Henry William, 2/Lt., k. in a., 6/11/17 (20th Sqd., Glos. R.).
Dunford, Ernest Thubron, 2/Lt., Tp., d. of w., 23/4/17 (12th Sqd., Gen. List) (P. of W.).
Dunnett, Raymond Frederick, M.C., Lt., killed, 17/11/17 (5th Worc. R.).
Dunstan, Hedley, 2/Lt., Tp., k. in a., 18/8/17 (55th Sqd. Y. and L.R.).
Durrad, Francis Albert, Capt., k. in a., 8/11/17 (22nd Sqd. R.A.S.C.).
Dusgate, Richard Edmund, 2/Lt., Tp., died, 19/12/17 (46th Sqd. R.E.) (P. of W.).
Dutton, Richard, 2/Lt., Tp., died, 19/8/17 (48th Sqd., Gen. List).
Duxbury, Herbert Cecil, 2/Lt., Tp., died, 11/5/17 (54th Sqd., Gen. List).
Dyer, Herbert Arthur, 2/Lt., k. in a., 7/12/17 (65th Sqd., Gen. List).
Eberlin, Frederick Harold Maden, 2/Lt., killed, 25/7/17 (3rd K.O.Y.L.I.).
Eccles, Charley Gordon, T/Capt., k. in a., 25/5/17 (41st Sqd., Gen. List).
Eccles, David Roderick, 2/Lt., Tp., killed, 5/12/17 (Gen. List).
Edmunds, Vivian Spence, 2/Lt., Tp., killed, 6/9/17 (Gen. List).
Edwards, Arthur Webb, 2/Lt., k. in a., 10/10/17 (41st Sqd., Gen. List).
Edwards, Donald William, M.C., Capt., k. in a., 6/4/17 (45th Sqd. R.A.S.C.).
Egerton, Robert, M.C., Capt., T/Major, k. in a., 23/12/17 59th Sqd., 2nd R. Ir. Fus.).
Eliot, Geoffrey Lionel, 2/Lt., Tp., killed, 2/7/17 (Gen. List).
Elliott, Clifford Wilfrid, 2/Lt., k. in a., 12/8/17 (23rd Sqd.).
Elliott, Eric Cuthbert John, Lt., Tp., k. in a., 22/11/17 (27th Sqd., Gen. List).
Ellis, Bryan Grogan Langley, 2/Lt., T/Capt., k. in a., 13/10/17 (R. Guernsey Militia).
Ellis, Guy Stuart, 2/Lt., Tp., k. in a., 12/7/17 (57th Sqd., Gen. List).
Ellis, Reginald Walter, Lt., Tp., k. in a., 18/6/17 (9th Sqd., Gen. List).
Elphinstone, Montague, Major, Tp., k. in a., 22/3/17 (R.A.S.C.).
Elwood, Robert Vernon, 2/Lt., Tp., killed, 17/11/17 (Gen. List).
Erlebach, Arthur Woodland, 2/Lt., Tp., k. in a., 5/7/17 (57th Sqd., Gen. List).
Erlebach, Edward Eustace, 2/Lt., k. in a., 7/2/17 (45th Sqd.).
Esdale, Robert Blair, 2/Lt., Tp., killed, 13/11/17 (Gen. List).
Etches, Alfred Joseph Edward, Lt., Tp., k. in a., 11/4/17 (52nd Sqd., Gen List).
Evans, Bernard, Lt., Tp., died, 8/4/17 (55th Sqd., Gen. List).
Evans, Frederick Woodham, 2/Lt., Tp., d. of w., 26/5/17 (20th Sqd., 21st Middx. R.).
Evans, Hugh William, 2/Lt., Tp., killed, 30/8/17 (Gen. List).
Evans, Philip, 2/Lt., Tp., killed, 24/1/17 (Gen. List).
Everingham, Guy, 2/Lt., Tp., k. in a., 8/4/17 (16th Sqd., Gen. List).
Eyton-Lloyd, John Wathen, 2/Lt., Tp., k. in a., 24/6/17 (10th Sqd., Gen. List).
Ezard, Herbert Henry, 2/Lt., Tp., killed, 30/5/17 (24th R.S.).
Falck, Jack Randell, 2/Lt., killed, 7/12/17 (Gen. List).
Falkiner, Frederick Baldwin, M.C., 2/Lt., k. in a., 21/8/17 (57th Sqd., 15th R. Ir. Rifs.).
Falkner, William Harold, 2/Lt., k. in a., 20/10/17.
Farnes, Henry Charles, 2/Lt., Tp., k. in a., 6/7/17 (48th Sqd., Gen. List).
Farrer, Fred., 2/Lt., killed, 28/11/17.
Farrow, Eric Tom, 2/Lt., T/Capt., killed, 7/2/17 (Gen. List).
Featherstone, Walter, 2/Lt., died, 3/10/17 (Gen. List).
Felts, Percival Claude, 2/Lt., Tp., k. in a., 23/7/17 (6th Sqd., Gen. List).
Fendall, Denis John, 2/Lt., k. in a., 7/8/17 (R.F.A., 4th Sqd.).
Fenn, Roland Pitt, 2/Lt., k. in a., 25/3/18 (18th Sqd., Gen. List).
Fennelly, James Philps, 2/Lt., Tp., killed, 24/12/17 (Gen. List).
Ferguson, Charles Edgar, 2/Lt., k. in a., 18/10/17 (22nd Sqd., Gen. List).
Ferguson, James, 2/Lt., Tp., killed, 12/3/17 (Gen. List).
Ferriman, Frederick Samuel, 2/Lt., Tp., k. in a., 7/6/17 (25th Sqd., Gen. List, 6th Ox. & Bucks.).
Findlay, Lorimer, Capt., Tp., killed, 14/6/17 (Gen. List, H.L.I.).
Findlay, Ronald James, 2/Lt., Tp., killed, 24/12/17.
Finlayson, Alexander Cunningham, 2/Lt., d. of w., 9/4/17 (4th Sqd.).
Fitzgerald, William Wilks, 2/Lt., Tp., k. in a., 27/7/17 (25th Sqd., Gen. List).
Fitzherbert, Wyndham Waterhouse, Capt., k. in a., 7/7/17 (55th Sqd., 13th R Suss. R.).
Fleet, Leonard, 2/Lt., Tp., killed, 27/10/17 (Gen. List).
Fleming, Wilfrid Allan, M.C., Capt., k. in a., 10/8/17 (56th Sqd., Devon. R.).
Fleming, James Wellington, 2/Lt., k. in a., 12/7/17 (29th Sqd.).
Fletcher, Arthur Henry Felix, 2/Lt., killed, 22/5/17 (13th Huss.).
Fletcher, George Herbert, 2/Lt., k. in a., 2/6/17 (4th Sqd., W. Yks., R.).
Fletcher, Leslie Morley, 2/Lt., Tp., killed, 5/7/17 (Gen. List).
Flower, Frederick Godfrey, 2/Lt., Tp., k. in a., 18/12/17 (21st Sqd., Gen. List).
Flynn, John Hoskins, 2/Lt., Tp., k. in a., 30/9/17 (60th Sqd., Gen. List).
Fogarty, Gerald Joseph, Lt., k. in a., 26/8/17 (9th Sqd., 3rd R. Ir. R.).
Follit, Reginald William, 2/Lt., d. of w., 28/4/17 (13th Sqd., Gen. List).
Foot, David Victor, 2/Lt., Tp., killed, 4/5/17 (Gen. List).
Foreman, Granado Walter, 2/Lt., k. in a., 14/7/17 (22nd Sqd.).
Forbes, Gordon William, 2/Lt., died, 18/10/17 (24th Sqd.; in German hands).
Forsaith, Hugh John, 2/Lt., k. in a., 18/8/17 (55th Sqd.).
Forsyth, Roy Anderson, 2/Lt., k. in a., 28/11/17 (7th Sqd., R.F.A.).
Foster, Frank Hawley, 2/Lt., Tp., k. in a., 3/6/17 (45th Sqd., Gen. List).
Foster, Franklin James, 2/Lt., Tp., k. in a., 23/8/17 (11th Squad., Gen. List).
Foubister, John Leask, 2/Lt., killed, 8/10/17 (Gen. List).
Fowler, David Dennys, 2/Lt., k. in a., 16/3/17.
Fowler, John Orr, 2/Lt., k. in a., 19/8/17 (45th Sqd., Gen. List).
Franklin, Benjamin Lester, Lt., Tp., k. in a., 4/5/17 (70th Sqd., 12th Mdx. R.).
Franklin, Rodney Vernon, Lt., Tp., killed, 24/6/17 (16th Sqd., Gen. List).
Freemantle, Ronald Percy Cowen, 2/Lt., k. in a., 30/4/17 (9th Sqd.).
French, Thomas Hugo, 2/Lt., Tp., killed, 13/1/17 (Gen. List).
Fry, Horace Charles, 2/Lt., killed, 24/2/17 (10th R.W. Kent R.).
Fry, John Libby, 2/Lt., killed, 20/2/17.
Fuller, Charles Stephen, M.C., 2/Lt., Tp., k. in a., 11/11/17 (1st Sqd., Gen. List).
Gagne, John, 2/Lt., k. in a., 24/5/17 (43rd Sqd., Gen. List).
Gallinger, George Harry, 2/Lt., Tp., k. in a., 31/10/17 (Gen. List).
Galloway, Frederick Philip, Lt., Tp., d. of w., 12/11/17 (27th Sqd.).
Game, Hubert John, Lt., Tp., killed, 8/6/17 (R.F.A.).
Gardner, Wm. Sutton, 2/Lt., k. in a., 6/3/17 (57th Sqd., R.F.A.).
Garnett, William Patrick, Lt., d. of w., 30/3/17 (3rd R. Bks. R.).
Garratt, Reginald Horatio, 2/Lt., k. in a., 29/9/17 (1st Sqd., Gen. List).
Garrett, Hyde Tregillas, 2/Lt., k. in a., 20/5/17 (Gen. List).
Gartside-Tippinge, Francis, 2/Lt., k. in a., 6/11/17 (19th Sqd., Gen. List).
Gates, Horace John, 2/Lt., Tp., k. in a., 19/11/17 (E. Kent R.).
Gay, Frederick Hollington, 2/Lt., d. of w., 25/3/17.
Geddes, Alastair Cosmo Burton, M.C., T/Major, k. in a., 19/4/17 (Gen. List).
Gee, Geoffrey Richard Dudley, 2/Lt., k. in a., 4/6/17 (21st Sqd., 3rd R. Suss. R.).
Geeson, Leslie Frederic, 2/Lt., Tp., killed, 15/6/17 (Gen. List).
George, Herbert Duncan King, Lt., died, 6/4/17 (2nd R. Dub. Fus.) (P. of W. in German hands).
George, Thomas William, T/2/Lt., killed, 18/10/17 (Gen. List).

Gibbes, Frederick William, 2/Lt., Tp., died, 13/10/17 (54th Squad., Gen. List).
Gibbs, Cecil Charles, 2/Lt., Tp., k. in a., 27/3/17 (14th Sqd., Gen. List).
Gibbon, John Taylor, T/2/Lt., killed, 6/2/17 (20th Sqd., Gen. List).
Gibson, Albert Fisher, 2/Lt., k. in a., 24/3/17 (4th Sqd., 4th Lein. R.).
Gibson, Edgar Daniell, T/2/Lt., k. in a., 9/10/17 (2nd Sqd., Gen. List).
Gibson, Ivor Griffith, 2/Lt., Tp., d. of w., 11/8/17, (6th Sqd., 11th W. Yks.).
Gilbert, Archibald Holmes, 2/Lt., Tp., k. in a., 21/9/17 (22nd Sqd., Gen. List).
Gilson, Alexander Ivan, 2/Lt., k. in a., 17/3/17 (Gen. List).
Glasson, Donald Havelock, 2/Lt., d. of w., 12/3/17 (47th Sqd.).
Gleed, John Victor Ariel, 2/Lt., died, 7/7/17 (45th Sqd.).
Gloster, Francis Beresford, Lt., k. in a., 3/12/17 (20th Sqd., R.A.S.C.).
Glover, Alexander Milligan Thomson, Lt., k. in a., 17/8/17 (70th Sqd., K.O.S.B.).
Glynn, Bernard James, 2/Lt., k. in a., 29/5/17 (84th Sqd.).
Goodban, Montague Sidney, 2/Lt., Tp., k. in a., 19/5/17 (22nd Sqd., E. Surr. R.).
Goodden, Frank Widenham, Lt., T/Major, killed, 28/1/17.
Goode, George Mortlock, Lt., k. in a., 24/5/17 (43rd Sqd., Gen. List).
Goodman, John Everatt, 2/Lt., Tp., k. in a., 14/8/17 (53rd Sqd., Gen. List).
Goodwin, Norman William, 2/Lt., k. in a., 16/9/17 (1st Bn. Mdx. R.).
Goodyear, Duncan Matheson, Lt., Tp., k. in a., 29/6/17 (57th Sqd., Gen. List).
Gordon, Albert William, 2/Lt., d. of w., 12/8/17 (32nd Sqd.).
Gordon-Kidd, Arthur Lionel, D.S.O., Lt., T/Capt., d. of w., 27/8/17 (4th Drag. Gds.).
Gould, Walter Harvey Russell, Lt., k. in a., 26/9/17 (70th Sqd., Gen. List).
Gowar, Lancelot John, 2/Lt., Tp., killed, 1/5/17 (Gen. List).
Grace, Alfred Alexander Gordon, T/2/Lt., killed, 26/6/17 (Gen. List).
Graham, Robert Lynedoch, Lt., k. in a., 16/9/17 (Gen. List).
Grandin, Richard John, 2/Lt., k. in a., 18/5/17 (60th Sqd., R.A.S.C.).
Grant, Robert, 2/Lt., Tp., k. in a., 13/6/17 (29th Sqd., Gen. List).
Grattan-Bellew, William Arthur, 2/Lt., T/Major, d. of w., 24/3/17 (29th Sqd., Conn. Ran.).
Graves, Evelyn Paget, Capt., T/Major, k. in a., 6/3/17 (60th Sqd., R.F.A.).
Gray, Alexander Allen, M.C., T/2/Lt., killed, 3/2/17 (Gen. List).
Gray, George Robert, Lt., Tp., d. of w., 31/10/17 (84th Sqd., Gen. List) (P.O.W.).
Gray, Geoffrey Thomas, 2/Lt., k. in a., 24/3/17 (8th Sqd., R.E.).
Green, Charles Layton, 2/Lt., Tp., k. in a., 9/6/17 (53rd Sqd., Gen. List).
Green, Herbert John, 2/Lt., Tp., k. in a., 4/3/17 (43rd Sqd., Gen. List).
Green, Thomas Seaman, Lt., Tp., k. in a., 13/2/17 (3rd Sqd., Gen. List).
Greenhous, Ernest Brereton, Lt., Tp., k. in a., 26/8/17 (9th Sqd.) (1st R. Scots Fus.).
Greenhow, Denys Edward, 2/Lt., Tp., k. in a., 6/3/17.
Greenwood, John Exley, 2/Lt., Tp., died, 11/9/17 (Gen. List).
Greg, Arthur Tylston, Capt., k. in a., 23/4/17 (55th Sqd., 3rd Ches. R.).
Grevelink, Edward Jas Yzenhoed, Lt., died, 6/6/17 (3rd Sqd., 3rd Wing, W. Rid. R.).
Grieve, James, Lt., Tp., killed, 21/2/17 (3rd S. Lancs Regt.).
Griffin, Cecil Scott James, Capt., killed, 11/10/17 (Gord. Hdrs.).
Griffiths, Gwyn Arthur, Lt., Tp., k. in a., 2/6/17 (35th Sqd., 15th Welsh Regt.).
Griffith, Henry Hall, Capt., Tp., killed, 2/11/17 (45th Sqd.).
Grimwood, Bertie Constantine Ruffell, M.C., Lt., k. in a., 7/11/17 (R. A.).
Grose, Albert George, 2/Lt., died, 9/11/17 (4th Sqd., Gen. List, P.O.W.).
Grosvenor, Thomas, Lt., Tp., k. in a., 17/9/17 (57th Sqd., 7th Linc. Regt.).
Grossart, Robert Dykes, 2/Lt., Tp., killed, 9/2/17 (18th Welsh Regt.).
Gubbin, John Richard Francis, 2/Lt., d. of w., 20/11/17 (47th Sqd.) (P.O. War).
Gunn, Murray Grant, 2/Lt., k. in a., 7/12/17 (23rd Sqd.).
Gunner, William Henry, M.C., 2/Lt., k. in a., 29/7/17 (60th Sqd., Gen. List).
Gunnery, Cedric Leopold, 2/Lt., Tp., k. in a., 22/5/17 (46th Sqd., Gen List).
Hahn, Benno Oscar Linsengen, 2/Lt. (Tp.), killed, 13/10/17 (Gen. List).
Haist, Orville Dwight, 2/Lt. (Tp.), killed, 5/7/17 (Gen. List).
Hall, Charles Sidney, 2/Lt. (Tp.), k. in a., 7/4/17 (60 Sqd., Gen. List).
Hall, George Henry, 2/Lt. (Tp.), killed, 24/12/17.
Hall, George Wilfred, 2/Lt., k. in a., 20/11/17 (Gen. List).
Hall, William Teesdale, 2/Lt., k. in a., 19/5/17 (24 Sqd.).
Haller, Edward Denison, 2/Lt. (Tp.), k. in a., 3/6/17 (45 Sqd.) (Gen. List).
Halley, Clifford Richard Brice, 2/Lt. (Tp.), k. in a., 2/10/17 (Gen. List).
Halliday, Morrice Frederick John, 2/Lt., k. in a., 7/6/17 (Glouc. R.).
Halligan, Matthew, Lt., k. in a., 18/11/17 (R. Dub. Fus.).
Halliwell, Eric John, Lt., k. in a., 11/9/17 (57 Sqd., R.F.A., S. R.).
Halse, Clive Harold, 2/Lt., k. in a., 24/4/17 (70 Sqd.) (Gen. List).
Ham, Frederick William, 2/Lt. (Tp.), died, 6/5/17 (Gen. List).
Hamar, Alfred John, Lt., d. of w., 8/4/17 (55 Sqd., 9 Wing).
Hamer, Harold, Lt. (Tp.), died, 6/6/17 (56 Sqd.) (Gen. List).
Hamilton, Eric, 2/Lt. (Tp.), k. in a., 15/2/17 (54 Sqd.) (Gen. List).
Hanafy, Sydney Reginald, 2/Lt. (Tp.), d. of w., 24/11/17 (46 Sqd.) (Gen. List).
Hardie, David Whyte, 2/Lt. (Tp.), k. in a., 18/11/17 (48 Sqd.) (S.R.).
Harding, Sydney Allen, 2/Lt. (Tp.), d. of w., 3/9/17 (S.R.).
Hardwick-Terry, Leonard Alfred, T/Lt. (A/Capt.), k. in a., 31/8/17 (24 Sqd.) (R.E.).
Hare, Edward John, 2/Lt. (Tp.), k in a., 24/3/17 (15 Sqd.) (Gen. List).
Hare, John Alfred, 2/Lt. (Tp.), killed, 1/3/17 (10/Suff. R.).
Harel, Louis Octave, 2/Lt., k. in a., 18/8/17 (11 Sqd.) (Gen. List).
Hargrave, Ernest Lawton, 2/Lt. (Tp.), killed, 22/9/17 (Gen. List).
Hargreaves, Cyril Augustus, 2/Lt. (Tp.), d. of w., 15/8/17 (43 Sqd.).
Harman, John Augustus, Lt. (Tp.), killed, 18/11/17.
Harms, William, 2/Lt. (Tp.), k. in a., 4/3/17 (N. Fus.).
Harries, Wyndham Trevor, 2/Lt. (Tp.), killed, 21/8/17 (Gen. List).
Harriman, Charles Henry, 2/Lt. (Tp.), k. in a., 29/10/17 (43 Sqd.) (Gen. List).
Harris, Percy George, 2/Lt. (Tp.), k. in a., 11/8/17 (21 Sqd.) (17/R.W. Fus.).
Harris, Roland Milton, 2/Lt., k. in a., 7/6/17 (60 Sqd.) (2/York. R.).
Harryman, Sydney, 2/Lt. (Tp.), d. of w., 24/3/17 (8 Sqd.) (Glouc. R.) (P. of W.).
Harston, William Harvey, 2/Lt., k. in a., 23/11/17 (52 Sqd.) (Northants R.).
Hart-Davies, Ivan Beauclerk, Lt., killed, 27/7/17 (S.R.).
Hartigan, Edward Patrick, 2/Lt. (Tp.), k. in a., 20/11/17 (57 Sqd. (R. Mun. Fus.).
Hartley, James Harold, 2/Lt., k. in a., 22/7/17 (45 Sqd.) (R. Mun. Fus.).
Hartnett, Michael Charles, Lt., k. in a., 19/9/17 (R. Mun. Fus.).
Harvey-Kelly, Hubert Dumsterville, D.S.O., Capt. (T/Major), k. in a., 29/4/17 (R. Ir. Regt.).
Hawes, Frederick Maxwell, 2/Lt., killed, 14/9/17 (R.G.A.).
Haslam, Herbert, 2/Lt., k. in a., 16/9/17 (6 Sqd.) (14 Manch. R.).
Hawley, Cyril, 2/Lt. (Tp.), killed, 23/7/17 (Gen. List).
Hawtrey, John James Alexander, 2/Lt., died, 17/9/17 (60 Sqd.) (Gen. List) (P. of W. in German hands).
Hay, John, 2/Lt., k. in a., 23/1/17 (40 Sqd.) (S.R.).
Hay, Roger Bolton, M.C., Lt., d. of w., 17/7/17 (48 Sqd.) (3/W. Yorks R.) (P. of W. in German hands).
Hayes, Reginald, 2/Lt., k. in a., 22/7/17 (45 Sqd.) (Gen. List).
Headley, Herbert Marshall, 2/Lt. (Tp.), k. in a., 11/3/17 (18 Sqd.) (R.F.A.).
Heald, Thomas Penrose, 2/Lt. (Tp.), k. in a., 13/10/17 (6 Sqd.) (Gen. List).
Hearn, Edward Thomas Hills, 2/Lt., k. in a., 11/9/17 (R.F.A.).
Heathcote, William Godfrey, 2/Lt. (Tp.), k. in a., 23/11/17 (29 Sqd., Gen. List).
Hefferman, William, 2/Lt. (Tp.), killed, 25/10/17 (Gen. List).
Hemming, William Norman, 2/Lt. (Tp.), died, 15/11/17 (65 Sqd.) (Gen. List).
Hemphill, Richard Patrick, 2/Lt. (Tp.), died, 24/3/17 (6/Lein. R.).
Henderson, Eric Joseph, M.C., 2/Lt. (T/Capt.), k. in a., 25/3/17 (70 Sqd.) (S.R.).
Herald, Thomas, 2/Lt. (Tp.), killed, 20/10/17 (Gen. List).
Hesketh, James Ernest Bytheway, 2/Lt. (Tp.), k. in a., 22/4/17 (11 Sqd.) (Gen. List).
Heywood, Aubrey Talley, Lt., k. in a., 3/9/17 (45 Sqd.) (Gen. List).
Hickie, Charles Sinclair, Lt., d. of w., 1/10/17 (6 Sqd.) (S.R.).
Hicks, Harry Ronald, 2/Lt., k. in a., 12/10/17 (19 Sqd.) (Gen. List).
Higginbottom, Frederick, 2/Lt. (Tp.), died, 6/4/17 (23 Sqd.) (9/Ches. R.).
Higginson, Ernest George, 2/Lt. (Tp.), killed, 4/10/17 (Gen. List).
Higginson, John Thomas Gordon, 2/Lt. (Tp.), killed, 1/11/17 (Gen. List).
Higginson, William Clifton Vernon, 2/Lt. (Tp.), k. in a., 20/11/17 (3 Sqd.) (Gen. List).
Higgs, Lucien Herbert, 2/Lt. (Tp.), killed, 8/6/17 (S.R.).
Hill, Beresford Winnington, Lt. (Tp.), k. in a., 4/3/17 (Gen. List) (10/Rif. Bde.).
Hill, Henry Oswald William, M.C., Capt. (Tp.), died, 21/10/17 (52 Sqd.) (Gen. List).
Hillebrandt, Frederick Edmund, 2/Lt. (Tp.), killed, 22/3/17 (5 Wing) (Gen. List).
Hills, William Frederick Waller, Lt. (Tp.), k. in a., 6/3/17 (Gen. List).
Hinchliff, Cyril Stanley, 2/Lt. (Tp.), killed, 4/9/17 (Gen. List).

Hinckley, Douglas Roy, 2/Lt., k. in a., 13/1/17 (5 Sqd.) (Y. & L.R.).
Hobart-Hampden, George Miles Awdry, 2/Lt., killed, 17/9/17 (O. & B.L.I.).
Hodgson, Albert Hodgson, 2/Lt. (Tp.), k. in a., 22/1/17 (52 Sqd.) (Gen. List).
Hodgson, George Bailey, Capt. (Tp.), k. in a., 13/4/17 (59 Sqd.) (Gen. List).
Hodkinson, Leonard, 2/Lt. (Tp.), k. in a., 14/9/17 (53 Sqd.) (15 R. Welsh Fus.).
Hoey, Fredk. Cyril, 2/Lt. (Tp.), killed, 7/6/17 (Gen. List).
Hofmeyr, Richard, Lt. (Tp.), died, 11/9/17 (1/K.O.Y.L.I.).
Hogben, Leslie Thomas, 2/Lt. (Tp.), killed, 23/10/17.
Holdsworth, Ernest, 2/Lt. (Tp.), k. in a., 23/9/17 (29 Sqd.) (Gen. List).
Holm, Frank Diederick, T/2/Lt., T/Lt., k. in a., 14/5/17 (27 Sqd.) (R.E.).
Holman, Cecil Graham, 2/Lt., d. of w., 5/9/17 (K.O.S.B.) (8 Sqd.).
Holman, Gerald Chaplin, Lt., k. in a., 17/9/17 (41 Sqd.) (Gen. List).
Holmes, Thomas George, Lt., k. in a., 6/5/17 (100 Sqd.) (S.R.).
Holroyde, John Sheffield, 2/Lt., k. in a., 10/5/17 (55 Sqd.) (E. Yorks R.).
Holt, Hubert Granville, M.C., Lt. (Tp.), k. in a., 6/10/17 (9 Sqd.) (Gen. List).
Homer, Charles William, 2/Lt. (Tp.), killed, 27/10/17 (Gen. List).
Honeyman, Herbert Tom Allan, 2/Lt., k. in a., 10/12/17 (15 Sqd.) (R. Scots Fus.).
Hood, Ronald Paton, 2/Lt., k. in a., 28/9/17 (43 Sqd.) (Gen. List).
Hope, Herbert Alfred, 2/Lt. (Tp.), d. of w., 28/7/17 (25 Sqd.).
Hopper, Raymond, 2/Lt. (Tp.), k. in a., 11/1/17 (60 Sqd.) (Gen. List).
Horn, Edmund Eric, 2/Lt. (Tp.), k. in a., 4/3/17 (8 Sqd.) (Mdx. R.).
Horncastle, Leonard Harry, M.C., Capt., k. in a., 20/5/17 (11 Sqd.) (1/Wilt R.).
Horsfall, George Rowland, 2/Lt. (Tp.), k. in a., 20/11/17 (48 Sqd.) (14/Y. & L.R.).
Horsley, Wilfred Palmer, M.C., Capt. (Tp.), k. in a., 2/7/17 (53 Sqd.) (Gen. List).
Hoskins, George Chandos, 2/Lt. (Tp.), k. in a., 11/3/17 (2 Sqd.) (Gen.. List).
Hoskins-Abrahall, Christopher Henry, 2/Lt., killed, 22/12/17 (R.F.A.).
Howard, Eric Stanley, 2/Lt. (Tp.), k. in a., 18/5/17 (60 Sqd.) (R.E.).
Howells, George James, 2/Lt., k. in a., 23/11/17 (8 Sqd.) (Gen. List).
Howells, Hugh, 2/Lt. (Tp.), killed, 10/4/17 (Gen. List).
Hudson, Leslie Sidney, 2/Lt., killed, 28/10/17 (3/Glouc. R.).
Hudson, Thomas James, 2/Lt., k. in a., 20/5/17 (11 Sqd.) (Gen. List).
Huggan, Thomas, 2/Lt. (Tp.), killed, 24/7/17.
Hughes, Eric, 2/Lt., killed, 14/11/17 (S.R.).
Hughes, Edward Phillip, 2/Lt. (Tp.), killed, 27/7/17.
Hughes, John Lawrence, Lt. (Tp.), k in a., 1/10/17 (25 Sqd.) (17/Welsh R.).
Hughes, Robert Baskerville, 2/Lt. (Tp.), killed, 31/5/17 (Gen. List).
Hume, Ronald, Lt., k. in a., 6/4/17 (20 Sqd.) (20/R. Fus.).
Humphries, Leslie Glendower, 2/Lt. (Tp.), k. in a., 16/9/17 (4 Sqd.) (Gen. List).
Hunstone, George Neil, 2/Lt. (Tp.), k. in a., 28/6/17 (11 Sqd.).
Hunt, Alfred Stanley, 2/Lt., killed, 20/8/17 (Gen. List).
Hunt, Edward Wallace Alleyne, 2/Lt., k. in a., 1/5/17 (18 Sqd.) (Gen. List).
Hunt, Geoffrey Albert, 2/Lt. (Tp.), killed, 6/9/17 (Gen. List).
Hunter, Harry, 2/Lt. (Tp.), d of w., 5/11/17 (Gen. List).
Hunter, Patrick Colin, 2/Lt. (Tp.). d. of w., 16/10/17 (N. Staff. R.).
Hunter, Thomas Vicars, Capt., k. in a., 5/12/17 (66 Sqd.) (Rif. Bde.).
Hutchinson, Cecil Dunbar, Lt. (Tp.), d. of w., 12/8/17 (57 Sqd.) (7/S. Staff. R.) (P. of W., in German hands).
Hyde, Cyril, 2/Lt., k. in a., 1/12/17 (35 Sqd.) (R.G.A.).
Hyslop, Ninian Steele, 2/Lt. (Tp.), killed, 30/10/17.
Ideson, Joseph Henry, 2/Lt. (Tp.). killed, 13/3/17 (12 Training Bn.).
Inchbold, Gerald, Lt., k. in a., 31/5/17 (55 Sqd.) (4/N. & D.R.).
Inglis, Robert Anderson, 2/Lt. (Tp.), k. in a., 21/9/17 (19 Sqd.) (Gen. List).
Inglis, Sidney Herbert, 2/Lt. (Tp.), d. of w., 5/6/17 (16 Sqd.) (Gen. List).
Ironside, James Paul, 2/Lt. (Tp.), d. of w., 29/10/17 (28 Sqd.) (Gen. List).
Jackson, Arthur, 2/Lt. (Tp.), killed 7/2/17 (24 Sqd.) (Gen. List).
Jackson, Cedric Arthur, Lt. (Tp.), killed, 5/11/17 (12/Y. & L.R.).
Jackson, Harold, Capt. (Tp.), k. in a., 7/6/17 (41 Sqd.) (Gen. List).
Jackson, Herbert Meynell, 2/Lt (Tp.), k in a., 18/6/17 (53 Sqd.) (Gen. List).
Jackson, John Bell, Lt., k. in a., 7/6/17 (43 Sqd.) (R. Scots).
Jacot, Conrade William, 2/Lt. (Tp.), killed, 23/6/17 (Gen. List).
Jakins, Walter Vosper, 2/Lt. (Tp.), killed, 10/7/17 (Gen. List).
Jameson, Harold, M.C., 2/Lt., k. in a., 5/1/17 (6 Sqd.) (S.R.).
Jardine, Robert Gordon, 2/Lt., k. in a., 20/7/17 (56 Sqd.) (S.R.).
Jardine, Ronald James, 2/Lt., killed, 13/9/17 (2/Dragoons).
Jarvie, Thomas Russell, 2/Lt (Tp.), killed, 10/9/17.
Jeffery, Ronald Edward, 2/Lt., k. in a., 25/5/17 (55/Sqd.) (Gen. List).
Jenkins, Christopher Hutchinson, Lt. (T/Capt.), d. of w., 22/5/17 (45 Sqd.) (3/R. Suss. R.).
Jenkin, Louis Fleeming, M.C., Capt., k. in a., 11/9/17 (1 Sqd.) (Gen. List).
Jenkins, Ralph Conway, 2/Lt. (Tp.), killed, 2/12/17 (Gen. List).
Jenkins, William Edwin, 2/Lt., k. in a., 23/11/17 (60 Sqd.) (E. Surr. R.).
Jenner, Russell John, 2/Lt., killed, 21/12/17 (Gen. List).
Jennings, Alexander, Lt. (T/Capt.), died, 7/4/17 (29 Sqd.) (R.F.A.).
Jessopp, Augustus John, Lt (Tp.), k. in a., 12/5/17 (Gen. List).
Jickling, Frank, 2/Lt (Tp.), killed, 23/10/17 (Gen. List).
Johnson, Hubert Alfred, 2/Lt. (Tp.), k. in a., 27/2/17 (Gen. List).
Johnson, Pieter Cedric Earlam, 2/Lt., k. in a., 28/1/17 (Gen. List).
Johnson, Russell Lowell, 2/Lt. (Tp.), killed, 12/11/17 (Gen. List).
Johnson. Stanley Morrell, 2/Lt. (Tp.), killed, 25/5/17 (Gen. List).
Johnston, Andrew, 2/Lt., k. in a., 30/10/17 (R.F.A.).
Johnston, Alfred Roy, 2/Lt. (Tp.), k. in a., 24/4/17 (Gen. List).
Johnston, Gilbert Henderson, 2/Lt. (Tp)., killed, 15/12/17 (Gen. List).
Johnstone, Melville, 2/Lt., k. in a., 16/7/17 (S.R.).
Jones, George James, Lt. (T/Capt.), k. in a., 7/4/17 (Gen. List).
Jones, Harold Edward, 2/Lt. (Tp.), k. in a., 22/11/17 (41 Sqd.) (Gen. List).
Jones, Harry Edward, 2/Lt., died, 12/10/17 (22 Sqd.).
Jordan, Hugh Stewart Latimer, 2/Lt., killed, 20/8/17 (R.F.A.).
Joseph, John Rhys, 2/Lt., died, 23/4/17 (Gen. List).
Kann, Edward Henry, Lt. (Tp.), k. in a., 21/10/17 (102 Sqd.).
Kay, George Pollard, 2/Lt., d. of w., 29/6/17 (46 Sqd.).
Kay, Maurice Alfred, 2/Lt., k. in a., 30/4/17 (56 Sqd.) (Gen. List).
Keast, William Reginald, 2/Lt., k. in a., 21/8/17 (66 Sqd.) (S.R.).
Keeble, John Harold, 2/Lt. (Tp.), killed, 27/10/17 (Gen. List).
Keevil, Cecil Horace Case, Capt. (Tp.), k. in a., 13/6/17 (18/W. York. Regt.).
Keir, Edward Hugh, 2/Lt. (Tp.), k. in a., 28/10/17 (16 Sqd.) (Gen. List).
Kellett, William, 2/Lt. (Tp.), k. in a., 22/1/17 (10 Sqd.). (8/Som. L.I.).
Kelly, Oscar Raphael, 2/Lt. (Tp.), killed, 2/5/17 (53 Sqd.) (Gen. List) (N. Fus.).
Kent, Ernest, Lt. (Tp.), d. of w., 8/4/17 (24 Sqd.) (2/Essex Regt.).
Keyser, Richard Norman, Lt., killed, 22/8/17 (3/E. Lanc. Regt.).
Kidder, Milton Ellory, 2/Lt. (Tp.), killed, 19/5/17 (Gen. List).
Kilgour, Arthur Wilson, T/Lt., Capt., killed, 27/7/17 (S.R.).
Kimbell, Richard Evison, 2/Lt., k. in a., 16/4/17 (60 Sqd.) (14/Hussars).
King, Berry, 2/Lt. (T/Lt.), k. in a., 3/5/17 (25 Sqd., 3/York L.I.).
King, Ebenezer, M.C., 2/Lt., killed, 17/3/17 (3/K.O.S.B.).
King, Wilfred Frank, 2/Lt. (Tp.), killed, 4/11/17 (Gen. List).
Kinkead, Thompson Calder, 2/Lt. (Tp.), killed, 4/9/17 (Gen. List).
Kirby, Frederick William, 2/Lt. (Tp.), k. in a., 21/9/17 (19 Sqd.) (Gen. List).
Kirkness, Thomas Robert, 2/Lt., k. in a., 18/8/17 (32 Sqd.) (Gen. List).
Kirkpatrick, John Crighton, Lt. (Tp.), k. in a., 10/12/17 (20 Sqd.) (Gen. List).
Kitchin, Francis Leslie, Lt. (Tp.), killed, 11/4/17 (4 Sqd., Glouc. Regt.).
Kither, James Frederick, 2/Lt. (Tp.), killed, 12/12/17 (Gen. List).
Kneale, John Francis, 2/Lt. (Tp.), killed, 21/12/17 (Gen. List).
Knight, George Harold, 2/Lt. (Tp.), k. in a., 6/10/17 (11 Ball. Coy.) (Gen. List).
Knowlson-Williams, Henry William, 2/Lt. (Tp.), killed, 11/7/17 (Gen. List).
Knox, Charles Duncan, 2/Lt., k. in a., 17/3/17 (43 Sqd.) (Suff. Regt.).
Laing, John Darg, 2/Lt. (Tp.), k. in a., 24/10/17 (19 Sqd.) (Gen. List).
Laird, Homer Warring, 2/Lt. (Tp.), k. in a., 8/10/17 (Gen. List).
Langwill, Trevor, 2/Lt., died, 17/4/17 (60 Sqd.) (Gen. List).
Lascelles, Harold Leslie, Lt. (Tp.), killed, 11/3/17 (Gen. List).
Latham, Edgar Retief, 2/Lt. (Tp.), killed, 20/1/17 (72 Sqd.) (Gen. List).
Laverton, Frederick King, 2/Lt., Lt. (Tp.), killed, 19/12/17 (3 Glouc. R.).
Law, James Kidston, Capt., k. in a., 21/9/17 (60 Sqd.) (R. Fus.).

Lawrence, George Aubrey Kennedy, D.S.O., Capt. (T/Lt.-Col.), killed, 28/1/17 (R.A.).
Lawrence, Norman Alan, 2/Lt., k. in a., 30/4/17 (16 Sqd.) (R. Fus.).
Leal, George, Lt., k. in a., 7/8/17 (9 Sqd.) (R.F.A.).
Leask, John, 2/Lt. (Tp.), killed, 26/3/17 (Gen. List).
Leckie, Graham, 2/Lt. (T/Lt.), k. in a., 7/7/17 (21 Sqd.) (R.G.A.).
Ledger, Harold Partington, 2/Lt. (Tp.), k. in a., 20/11/17 (3 Sqd.) (Gen. List).
Leduc, John Charles Romuald, 2/Lt. (Tp.), killed, 7/11/17 (Gen. List).
Lee, Herbert Malachi, 2/Lt. (Tp.), killed, 26/9/17 (Gen. List).
Leech, William Frederick, D.S.O., 2/Lt. (Tp.), d. of w., 18/8/17 (9 Sqd.).
Leeson, Alexander Neve, D.S.O., Lt., k. in a., 22/10/17 (R.H.A.).
Legallais, Reginald Walter, Lt. (Tp.), killed, 15/9/17.
Leighton, John Burgh Talbot, M.C., Capt. (T/Major), d. of w., 7/5/17 (23 Sqd.) (Scots Gds.).
Lennard, Edward Stuart Russell, 2/Lt. (Tp.), k. in a., 14/9/17 (9 Sqd.) (Gen. List).
Leventon, Raymond Sylvester, 2/Lt. (Tp.), drowned, 5/11/17 (Gen. List).
Lewington, George Longley, 2/Lt. (Tp.), killed, 23/12/17 (Gen. List).
Lewis, Edward Pugh, 2/Lt., k. in a., 6/10/17 (9 Sqd.) (Gen. List).
Lewis, Granville Vernon Loch, 2/Lt. (Tp.), killed, 5/10/17.
Liddell, John Robert Hugh, 2/Lt. (Tp.), killed, 10/11/17 (Gen. List).
Lillis, Martin Michael Arthur, Lt. (Tp.), k. in a., 11/4/17 (3 Sqd.) (R. Ir. R.).
Lindsay, George Walter Thomas, Capt., killed, 26/6/17 (R.F.A.).
Litchfield, Frederick George, Lt. (Tp.), killed, 24/9/17.
Littler, Tom, 2/Lt. (Tp.), k. in a., 3/7/17 (1 Sqd.) (Gen. List).
Lloyd, David Rhys Cadogan, Lt. (Tp.), k. in a., 16/6/17 (Gen. List).
Lloyd, Richard Serjeantson, 2/Lt., k. in a., 18/6/17 (1 Sqd.) (Gen. List).
Lockwood, Frank, 2/Lt. (Tp.), killed, 4/11/17 (Gen. List).
Lomer, Henry Charles, T/Capt., k. in a., 5/5/17 (10 Sqd.) (Gen. List).
Long, Charles Percy, 2/Lt. (Tp.), k. in a., 13/4/17 (46 Sqd.) (R.E.).
Long, John Thomas, 2/Lt., killed, 10/10/17 (53 Sqd.) (17 Mdx. R.).
Longton, John, Lt., k. in a., 31/7/17 (4 Sqd.) (R.A.S.C.).
Lovell, Leslie Graham, 2/Lt. (Tp.), k. in a., 11/4/17 (48 Sqd.) (Gen. List).
Lovell, William Leslie, 2/Lt., k. in a., 27/7/17 (25 Sqd.) (R.W. Kent R.).
Low, Eustace Bertram, 2/Lt. (Tp.), k. in a., 24/3/17 (4 Sqd.) (Gen. List).
Lowe, Maurice, Lt., k. in a., 27/6/17 (19 Sqd.) (Gen. List).
Lowery, Allan Maxwell, Capt. (Tp.), d. of w., 24/3/17 (70 Sqd.) (Gen. List).
Lownds, Reginald Herbert, 2/Lt. (Tp.), died, 17/3/17 (43 Sqd.) (Gen. List).
Lowson, Courtenay Patrick Flowerdew, Lt., killed, 3/11/17 (1 Rif. Bde.).
Lubbock, The Hon. Eric Fox Pitt, Capt (Tp.), k. in a., 11/3/17 (45 Sqd.) (Gen. List).
Lucas, Albert James, 2/Lt. (Tp.), d. of w., 16/5/17 (66 Sqd.) (Gen. List).
Lucas, Thomas Charles Harvey, Lt., k. in a., 6/2/17 (20 Sqd.) (Suff. R.).
Lucas, Thomas Farquhar, Lt., k. in a., 16/6/17 (3/R. War. R.).
Luchford, Harry George Ernest, M.C., Capt., k. in a., 2/12/17 (20 Sqd.).
Lukis, Leofwin Collings Fellowes, 2/Lt., k. in a., 6/1/17 (27 Sqd.) (Essex R.).
Lukyn, Stanley Edward, M.C., 2/Lt., died, 10/4/17 (3/R.W. Surr. R.).
Lyle, James Vernon, 2/Lt. (Tp.), k. in a., 23/1/17 (Gen. List).
McArdle, Hugh Francis, Lt., k. in a., 18/9/17 (K. Edw. Horse) (41 Sqdn.)
McArthur, John, Temp. Capt., k. in a., 27/2/17 (Gen. List, 12 Sqdn.).
McBrayne, David Cecil Hope, Temp. 2/Lt., d. of w., 21/6/17 (In Ger. Hands) (Gen. List, 11 Sqdn.).
McCormick, Edward John, Lt. (Tp.), k. in a., 14/5/17 (7 R. Innis. Fus.).
McCracken, Henry Joy, 2/Lt., died, 17/10/17 (Gen. List, 111 Sqdn.).
McCulloch, Alexander Fenton, 2/Lt. (Tp.), killed, 16/8/17 Gen. List).
McCulloch, Frederick James, 2/Lt., k. in a., 8/11/17 (R.G.A., 53 Sqdn.).
MacDaniel, James, 2/Lt., k. in a., 18/8/17 (3/R. Dub. Fus., 57/Sqdn.).
MacDonald, Alexander Lindsay, M.C., Lt. (T/Capt.), k. in a., 26/8/17, (Rl. Hldrs., 9/Sqdn.).
McDonald, Henry Rhodes, Temp. 2/Lt., killed, 22/12/17, (Gen. List).
MacDonald, Wilfred Ferguson, Temp. 2/Lt., k. in a., 23/5/17 (Gen. List, 18/Sqdn.).
MacFarlane, Harold Embleton, Temp. 2/Lt., k. in a., 14/7/17 (55/Sqdn.).
McFerran, Thomas Malcolm, 2/Lt. (Tp.), k. in a., 21/6/17 (Gen. List, 1/Sqdn.).
McGavin, Peter Liddell, 2/Lt., k. in a., 14/8/17 (25 Sqdn.) (Gen. List).
McGill, Douglas, Temp. 2/Lt., killed, 27/10/17 (Gen. List).
MacGregor, Donald Argyle Douglas Ian, Temp. Lt., k. in a., 30/11/17 (Gen. List, 41/Sqdn.).
MacGregor, Thomas Charles Stuart, Temp. 2/Lt., k. in a., 8/6/17 (Gen. List, 53/Sqdn.).
MacHaffie, John, Temp. 2/Lt., k. in a., 21/9/17 (Gen. List).
McJanet, Arthur William, Temp. 2/Lt., k. in a., 31/10/17 (Gen. List).
MacKain, Henry Fergus, Temp. 2/Lt., k. in a., 27/2/17 (Gen. List).
McKay, Alfred Edwin, Capt., k. in a., 28/12/17 (S.R.).
MacKay, John Alexander, 2/Lt., k. in a., 11/9/17.
McKay, James Ivan, 2/Lt. (T/Capt.), k. in a., 5/10/17 (W. Rid. Regt.).
McKenna, Justin Morell, Lt. (Tp.), k. in a., 2/10/17 (Gen. List).
MacKenzie, Adrian Somerset, 2/Lt. (Tp.), k. in a., 1/4/17 (Gen. List, 15 Sqd.).
McKenzie, Gordon William, 2/Lt. (Tp.), k. in a., 20/9/17 (Gen. List).
MacKenzie, Ivan Emilio Mario, Capt. (Tp.), killed, 12/10/17.
MacKenzie, John, 2/Lt., k. in a., 1/12/17 (Gen. List).
MacKenzie, Keith Ingleby, 2/Lt., k. in a., 8/4/17 (A. & S. Hldrs.).
McKergow, Robert Dudley Wilson, 2/Lt. (T/Lt.), k. in a., 21/9/17 (5/Dgn. Gds.).
Mackey, Edward Reeves, Lt., killed, 15/3/17.
McKimmie, Alexander, 2/Lt. (Tp.), k. in a., 23/5/17 (Gen. List).
Mackintosh, Charles, 2/Lt. (Tp.), k. in a., 5/4/17 (Gen. List).
McLaren, Frederic Monteath, 2/Lt., k. in a., 12/8/17 (Gen. List).
McLaren, The Hon. Francis Walter Stafford, 2/Lt. (Tp.), killed, 30/8/17 (Gen. List).
McLaren, William Somerville, 2/Lt., d. of w., 19/11/17 (Gen. List).
Maclean, Frederick William, 2/Lt. (Tp.), d. of w., 14/6/17 (Gen. List).
McLean, Thomas William, 2/Lt., k. in a., 21/9/17 (Gen. List).
MacLennan, Roderich Ward, 2/Lt. (Tp.), k. in a., 23/12/17 (Gen. List) (60/Sqdn.).
McLeod, Elmer George, 2/Lt. (Tp.), d. of w., 23/11/17 (Gen. List)) (46/Sqdn.).
McMillan, John Casely, 2/Lt. (T/Capt.), d. of w., 6/2/17 (R. Scots Fus.) (4/Sqdn.).
MacMillan, Thomas, 2/Lt., killed, 12/2/17 (Gen. List).
MacMurchy, Ian Ure, 2/Lt. (Tp.), k. in a., 9/10/17 (Gen. List) (9/Sqdn.).
McNamara, Joseph Charles, 2/Lt., k. in a., 2/6/17 (Gen. List) (4/Sqdn.).
McNaughton, Norman George, M.C., Capt., k. in a., 24/6/17 (57/Sqdn.).
Macpherson, Henry Douglas, 2/Lt. (Tp.), k. in a., 14/10/17 (29/Sqdn.).
McPherson, Leonard Alfred, 2/Lt. (Tp.), k. in a., 28/7/17 (Gen. List) (43/Sqdn.).
McRae, William Gordon, 2/Lt., k. in a., 26/10/17 (Gen. List) (19/Sqdn.).
McWha, Archibald John, 2/Lt., killed, 2/1/17.
Maddison, Walter, 2/Lt., died, 24/11/17.
Maguire, Matthew Laurence, M.C., 2/Lt. (T/Lt.), k. in a., 28/4/17 (1/Con. Rgrs.).
Mahaffy, Henry Irwin, 2/Lt. (Tp.), killed, 22/10/17.
Maitland, Arthur James, 2/Lt. (Tp.), killed, 22/9/17 (Gen. List).
Malcolm, Geoffrey Cooper, 2/Lt. (Tp.), killed, 27/9/17 (3/K.O. Y.L.I.).
Manley, John, 2/Lt. (T/Capt.), k. in a., 18/9/17 (19/Sqdn.).
Mann, William George, 2/Lt., k. in a., 28/11/17 (Gen. List) (7/Sqdn.).
Mansell, William Stanley, 2/Lt., k. in a., 11/9/17 (E. Surr. Regt.) (22/Sqdn.).
Manuel, Vane Carrington, 2/Lt. (Tp.), killed, 18/12/17 (Gen. List).
March, William Francis George, 2/Lt., d. of w., 24/10/17 (in Ger. hands) (Gen. List).
Margetson, Emil Alexander, 2/Lt., killed, 16/6/17 (Gen. List).
Marks, Craig Royston, 2/Lt. (Tp.), killed, 3/5/17 (Gen. List).
Marsh, Zacheus Stanley, 2/Lt. (Tp.), k. in a., 10/10/17 (Gen. List) (52/Sqdn.).
Marshall, Bernard Sanderson, M.C., Lt., k. in a., 7/6/17 (Gen. List) (20/Sqdn.).
Marshall, Donald Ewan, 2/Lt., k. in a., 8/8/17 (W. Works R.) (18/Sqdn.).
Marshall, Harry Cecil, 2/Lt. (Tp.), killed, 23/12/17 (Gen. List).
Marshall, Herbert William Hare, Lt. (Tp.), killed, 26/8/17 (Gen. List).
Marshall, Louis, 2/Lt., k. in a., 23/11/17 (Gen. List) (65/Sqdn.).
Marshall-Lewis, Frank, Lt. (Tp.), k. in a., 13/9/17 (Gen. List) (43/Sqdn.).
Martin, Fairlie Russell, 2/Lt., k. in a., 29/6/17 (R. Scots Fus.) (57/Sqdn.).
Martin, George Ernest, 2/Lt. (Tp.), killed, 29/11/17 (Gen. List).
Martinson, Karl Ludwig, Lt. (Tp.), k. in a., 1/6/17 (R.F.A.).
Marvin, Henry Leslie, 2/Lt., k. in a., 27/10/17 (Gen. List) (6/Sqdn.).
Mason, Arthur Walton, 2/Lt. (Tp.), k. in a., 11/5/17 (Gen List) (7/Sqdn.).

Mason, George, 2/Lt. (Tp.), killed, 4/5/17 (Gen. List).
Matheson, Alexander Percival, Lt., k. in a., 13/7/17 (Gen. List) (55/Sqdn.).
Matheson, Harry Mackay, 2/Lt., died, 24-26/12/17.
Mathews, George, 2/Lt., k. in a., 2/10/17 (R.F.A.) (55/Sqdn.).
Matthews, Frank Arthur, Lt. (Tp.), k. in a., 24/4/17 (10/R. Suss. Regt.) ((9/Sqdn.).
Matthews, Henry, 2/Lt., k. in a., 15/1/17 (47/Sqdn.).
Maule, Edward Barry, Lt. (Tp.), k. in a., 6/2/17 (18/H.L. Inf.) (20/Sqdn.).
Mayberry, Richard, Lt., k. in a., 15/11/17 (3/R. Scots. Fus.) (70/Sqdn.).
Maybery, Richard Aveline, M.C., Lt., k. in a., 19/12/17 (21/Lancers) (56/Sqdn.).
Mayne, Denis John Heriot, 2/Lt., killed, 12/10/17 (R. Irish Rfls.).
Mearns, Angus Hughs, Lt., died, 24/6/17 (9/Blk. Watch) (57/Sqdn.).
Medlen, Leslie Lashbrook, 2/Lt. (Tp.), k. in a., 22/12/17 (Gen. List) (16/Sqdn.).
Mevdell, Colin Grant, 2/Lt., k. in a., 10/8/17 (43/Sqdn.).
Merchant, Arthur Douglas Mount-Stephen, 2/Lt. (Tp.), killed, 13/5/17 (Gen. List).
Meredith, Owen Watkin Wynn Harding, 2/Lt. (Tp.), d. of w., 20/11/17 (in Ger. hands) (Gen. List) (64/Sqdn.).
Meyer, Herbert Frederick, 2/Lt., killed, 15/10/17 (Gen. List).
Miall-Smith, George Eric, M.C., Lt., k. in a., 25/9/17 (3/Norf. R.).
Middleton, James Russell, Lt. (Tp.), d. of w., 21/6/17 (in Ger. hands) (Gen. List) (11/Sqdn.).
Middleton, Leonard William, 2/Lt. (Tp.), k. in a., 8/11/17 (Gen. List) (53/Sqdn.).
Mighell, Philip, 2/Lt. (Tp.), d. of w., 12/10/17 (Gen. List) (5/Sqdn.).
Miles, George Henry, 2/Lt., k. in a., 13/9/17 (R.W. Kent Regt.) (6/Sqdn.).
Miller, Archibald William Buchanan, Lt., died, 13/7/17 (in Ger. hands) (1/K.O.S.B.).
Miller, Bertram Charles St. Clair, 2/Lt., killed, 29/11/17 (R.E.).
Miller, George Blair, 2/Lt. (Tp.), k. in a., 1/5/17 (H.L.I.) (18/Sqdn.).
Miller, Robert Goldie, 2/Lt., k. in a., 17/3/17 (4/A. & S. Hldrs.) (5/Sqdn.).
Milliship, William Griffin, 2/Lt. (Tp.), k. in a., 7/6/17 (Gen. List) (1/Sqdn.).
Mills, George Carlton, Lt., killed, 4/11/17.
Mills, Gerald Desmond, Capt. (T/Maj.), k. in a., 19/5/17 (N. & D. Regt.) (19/Sqdn.).
Mills, Kenneth Le Gai, 2/Lt. (Tp.), d. of w., 11/11/17 (Gen List) (10/Sqdn.).
Mills, William Longley, 2/Lt., k. in a., 9/5/17 (R.A.) (43/Sqdn.).
Milne, William, M.C., Capt. (T/Maj.), killed, 13/4/17 (N. Lanc. R.) (25/Sqdn.).
Minot, Laurence, Capt., k. in a., 28/7/17 (57Sqdn.).
Mitchell, John Patrick Cameron, 2/Lt., k. in a., 21/4/17 (4/H.L.I.) (16/Sqdn.).
Mitchell, Leslie James, 2/Lt. (Tp.), killed, 22/12/17 (Gen. List).
Mitton, Harold, Lt., k. in a., 29/7/17 (R.A.) (10/Sqdn.).
Moody, Charles Angelo, 2/Lt., k. in a., 21/8/17 (Gen. List) (1/Sqdn.).
Moore, Albert James, 2/Lt. (Tp.), killed, 11/11/17 (Gen. List).
Moore, Beaufoi John Warwick Montressor, M.C., Lt. (T/Capt.), k. in a., 10/6/17.
Moore, Cuthbert Alex, 2/Lt., died, 25/9/17.
Moore, Clive Goulding, Lt., k. in a., 15/8/17 (Gen. List) (43/Sqdn.).
Moore, Frederick, 2/Lt. (Tp.), k. in a., 3/7/17 (Gen. List) (4/Sqdn.).
Moore, Reginald John, 2/Lt. (Tp.), killed, 7/11/17 (Gen. List).
Morgan, Alan Bertram, 2/Lt., died, 22/4/17.
Morgan, Brinley Arthur, 2/Lt., k. in a., 4/3/17 (R.F.A.).
Morgan, Joseph Anthony, Lt. (Tp), k. in a., 30/5/17 (Shrop. L.I.).
Morgan, Ronald Charles Wybrow, 2/Lt. (T/Lt.), d. of w. 27/7/17 (3/S. W. Bdrs.).
Morgan, Wilfrid Gilbert, 2/Lt. (Tp.), d. of w., 23/10/17 (Gen. List) (P. of W.).
Morris, Charles Herbert, Lt., k. in a., 13/4/17 (R. Welsh Fus.).
Morris, Eyre Percival, T/2/Lt., k. in a., 1/5/17 (E. Kent R.).
Morris, Ellis Wayman 2/Lt. (Tp.), k. in a., 9/11/17.
Morris, Francis St. Vincent, 2/Lt., d. of w., 29/4/17 (3/N. & Derby R.).
Morris, Mansell John, 2/Lt., k. in a., 3/5/17.
Morrison, Lindsay, 2/Lt., killed, 28/7/17 (Gen. List).
Morrison, Norman Walter, 2/Lt. (Tp.), k. in a., 14/4/17 (Gen. List).
Morrison, Walter Scott, 2/Lt. (Tp.), killed, 18/3/17 (Gen. List).
Morse, Christopher Charles, 2/Lt. (Tp.), k. in a., 14/11/17 (Gen. List).
Moss, William Thomas Gregory, 2/Lt. (Tp.), killed, 5/7/17 (Gen. List).
Mott, Jacob Ernest, 2/Lt. (Tp.), k. in a., 23/12/17 (1/R. Ir. Fus.) (21/Sqdn.).
Mott, Lewes Woodham, 2/Lt. (Tp.), k. in a., 23/4/17 (9/Essex Regt.).
Mouritzen, Roy Walter, 2/Lt. (Tp.), killed, 5/6/17 (Gen. List).
Mowat, John MacLellan, 2/Lt. (Tp.), killed, 5/1/17 (N. Staff. R.).
Mowat, Sydney Alexander, 2/Lt. (Tp.), killed, 2/7/17 (Gen. List).
Muir, James Hunter, 2/Lt., k. in a., 7/4/17.
Muir, Stanley Keith, M.C., T/2/Lt. (T/Capt.), killed, 12/9/17 (Gen. List).
Muirhead, John 2/Lt. (Tp.), k. in a., 16/3/17 (Gen. List).
Mulock, Henry Collister, Lt. (Tp.), k. in a., 15/2/17 (Gen. List).
Munn, Leslie Vincent, 2/Lt. (Tp.), died, 16/2/17 (Gen. List).
Munro, Donald Rice, 2/Lt., killed, 28/7/17.
Munro, Guy Horace, 2/Lt., (Tp.), killed, 18/8/17 (Gen. List).
Munro, James Donald Sutherland, 2/Lt., killed, 17/7/17.
Murphy, A. G., Capt. Qr.-Mr., died, 14/6/17 (Gen. List).
Murphy, Allen Ingham, 2/Lt., killed, 30/3/17.
Murray, Joseph Leonard, 2/Lt. (Tp.), k. in a., 29/5/17 (Gen. List).
Murray, William Roland, 2/Lt. (Tp.), k. in a., 11/11/17 (Gen. List).
Mutch, George, T/Lt., k. in a., 6/7/17 (Gord. Hldrs.) (4/Sqdn.).
Myburgh, John Adrian, 2/Lt. (Tp.), d. of w., 10/4/17 (Gen. List).
Myers, Francis Michael, M.C., Temp. 2/Lt., k. in a., 14/2/17 (Gen. List).
Needham, Joseph Walter David, 2/Lt. (Tp.), d. of w., 12/11/17 (48/Sqdn.).
Needs, Charles Richard, 2/Lt., killed, 27/2/17.
Neill, Rolfe Mayne, 2/Lt., k. in a., 3/6/17 (70/Sqdn.).
Neily, Frederick Ernest, 2/Lt. (Tp.), k. in a., 22/12/17 (Gen. List) (16/Sqdn.).
Nelson, Graham, 2/Lt. (Tp.), killed, 30/8/17 (Scot. Rfls.).
Neser, Frank Charles, 2/Lt. (Tp.), died, 30/9/17 (Gen. List).
Neville, Henry George, 2/Lt. (Tp.), d. of w., 10/5/17 (Gen. List) (20/Sqdn.).
Nichols, Stanley Lawrence, 2/Lt., k. in a., 12/8/17 (Gen. List) (19/Sqdn.).
Nicholson, Geoffrey Arnold, 2/Lt. killed, 19/5/17 (Gen. List).
Nicholson, Geoffrey Alec. Shield, 2/Lt. (Tp.), d. of w., 22/8/17 (Gen. List) (6/Sqdn.).
Nicholson, Maurice, 2/Lt., k. in a., 18/8/17 (Gen. List) (11/Sqdn.) (A.C.C.).
Nixon, Arthur William Lennox, 2/Lt. (Tp.), k. in a., 1/6/17 (Gen. List) (16/Sqdn.).
Nixon, William Eric, Capt., k. in a., 7/5/17 (K.O.S.B.) (40/Sqd.).
Noakes, Harold Thomas, 2/Lt. (Tp.), k. in a., 23/7/17 (Gen. List) (32/Sqdn.).
Noble, Harold Taylor, 2/Lt. (Tp.), k. in a., 28/9/17 (Gen. List) (20/Sqdn.).
Nolan, Howard Stanley, 2/Lt. (Tp.), killed, 27/7/17 (Gen. List).
Norris, Colin Chad Armstrong, 2/Lt. (Tp.), killed, 26/12/17 (Gen. List).
Norris, Harold Aubrey Blurton, 2/Lt. (Tp.), k. in a., 24/7/17 (Gen. List) (57/Sqd.) (9/Wing).
Norris, Leslie Archibald, Lt. (Tp.), k. in a., 25/3/17 (R.E.) (70/Sqd.).
Norton, Hugh, Lt. (Tp.), k. in a., 24/3/17 (Gen. List) (8/Sqdn.).
Noss, Arthur Rex Hurden, M.C., 2/Lt. (Tp.), d. of w., 15/9/17 (Gen. List) (48/Sqdn.).
Nosworthy, Claude William Michelin, Lt., d. of w., 6/12/17 (R.F.A.) (10/Sqd.).
Nowell, Roger Emmett, 2/Lt., k. in a., 22/9/17.
Nunnerley, Willson Kenwick, 2/Lt. (Tp.), k. in a., 5/12/17 (Gen. List) (13/Sqdn.).
Nutter, Alan Charles, 2/Lt., d. of w., 15/9/17 (40/Sqdn.).
O'Beirne, John Ingram Mullanniffe, 2/Lt., k. in a., 3/4/17 (25th Sqd.) (R War. Regt.).
O'Giollagain, John Gabriel, 2/Lt. (Tp.), killed, 5/9/17 Gen. List).
Oldman, Harold Victor, 2/Lt. (Tp.) killed 29/10/17.
Oliver, Frank Lambton, 2/Lt., k. in a., 13/7/17 (55th Sqd.) (Som. L.I.).
Oliver, Siddartha John, 2/Lt., k. in a., 10/8/17 (66th Sqd.) (Gen. List).
Oliver, Thomas Alfred, Capt., k. in a., 14/8/17 (Gen. List).
Olivier, Henri, Lt. (Tp.), d. of w., 11/10/17 (Gen. List).
O'Longan, Paul Charles Stacpoole, 2/Lt., k. in a., 1/6/17 (R. Ir. Regt.).
Ormerod, Andrew, 2/Lt. (Tp.), k. in a., 13/4/17 (59th Sqd.).
Orrell, John Turton, 2/Lt., k. in a., 2/12/17 (57th Sqd.) (Gen. List).
Osborn, Edward Stanley, 2/Lt. (Tp.), killed, 29/11/17 (Gen. List).
O'Sulivan, John Anthony, 2/Lt. (Tp.), k. in a., 27/5/17 (1st Sqd.) (Gen. List).
Ottey, Raymond Gascoyne, 2/Lt., k. in a., 28/7/17 (32nd Sqd.) (3rd Leic. R.)
Ottley, Reginald Benade Glendower, 2/Lt., k. in a., 23/12/17 (59th Sqd.) (9th N. Staffs.).
Owen, Herbert Ernest Malcolm, 2/Lt. (Tp.), killed, 18/7/17 (Gen. List).
Owen, Iorwerth Roland, 2/Lt. (Tp.), d. of w., 7/5/17 (13th Sqd.) (Gen. List).
Owen, Thomas John, 2/Lt., k. in a., 8/4/17 (29th Sqd.).
Oxley, Malcolm Guy Macdonald, 2/Lt., k. in a., 19/9/17 (43rd Sqd.) (Gen. List)
Page, Dudley Alfred, 2/Lt. (Tp.), d. of w., 14/8/17 (56th Sqd.) Ches. Regt.) (in German hands).
Paget, Gerald Lewis, Lt., k in a., 13/7/17.
Palmer, Lewis Arthur, 2/Lt. (Tp.), killed, 9/11/17 (Gen. List).
Palmer, Percy Eric, 2/Lt., k. in a., 17/7/17 (29th Sqd.).
Palmer, Percy Rogers, M.C., 2/Lt, k in a., 25/5/17 (55th Sqd.) (10th Leicester Regt.).
Palmer, William Samuel Hudson, 2/Lt (Tp.), killed, 15/9/17 (Gen. List)
Parker, Leonard, Maj., k in a., 7/1/17 (52nd Sqd.) (15th Huss.).

Parker, William Lefevre Oxley, Lt., k. in a., 31/10/17 (13th Sqd.) (11th Huss.).
Parsons, Beresford Frank 2/Lt. (Tp.), killed, 23/1/17 (Gen. List).
Pascoe, Eric John, 2/Lt., k. in a., 14/4/17 (29th Sqd.) (Gen. List).
Pascoe, Frank Guy Buckingham, 2/Lt. (Tp.), k. in a., 2/7/17 (53rd Sqd.) (9th R. Irish Fus.).
Pashley, Eric Clowes, 2/Lt., k. in a., 17/3/17 (24th Sqd.).
Pasley, George Gerald, 2/Lt. (Tp.), killed, 19/12/17.
Pateman, Henry Lewis 2/Lt., k. in a., 6/2/17 (15th Sqd.) (Gen. List).
Pater, Hugh, 2/Lt., killed, 17/4/17 (3rd W. Yorks).
Paton, David Moir, Lt., k. in a., 24/9/17 (66th Sqd.) (Gen. List).
Paton, Henry Forsyth, 2/Lt. (Tp.), died, 4/6/17 (21st Sqd.) (Gen. List).
Patterson, Hugh Cecil, Lt., k. in a., 30/4/17 (48th Sqd.) (4th Bedford Regt.).
Payne, Cecil Brandon, 2/Lt., k. in a., 20/8/17 (21st Sqd.) (R.F.A.).
Payne, Cecil McKenzie, 2/Lt. (Tp.), k. in a., 22/9/17 (16th Sqd.) (Gen. List).
Payne, Wilfred Stuart Lane, M.C., Lt., k. in a., 4/9/17 (7th Sqd.) (R.G.A.).
Peach, Crugar Stanley, 2/Lt., killed, 24/4/17 (1st W. Yorks).
Peacock, Alfred Walter, 2/Lt. (Tp.), k. in a., 9/9/17 (24th Sqd.) (R. Scots).
Peacock, William Hubert, 2/Lt. (Tp.), killed, 7/4/17 (Gen. List).
Pears, Charles Martin, 2/Lt (Tp.), k. in a., 23/11/17 (52nd Sqd.) (Gen. List).
Pearson, Arthur John, M.C., 2/Lt., k. in a., 9/3/17 (29th Sqd.) (N'hants Regt.).
Pearson, Francis Gilbert, Lt. (Tp.), d. of w., 10/7/17 (10th Sqd.) (Gen. List).
Pearson, Gerald, 2/Lt. (Tp.), k. in a., 29/10/17 (45th Sqd.).
Pearson, James Alan, 2/Lt. (Tp.), killed, 9/12/17.
Pearson, Oliver Charles, 2/Lt., k. in a., 10/9/17 (70th Sqd.) (Gen. List).
Pell, Harry Saxon, 2/Lt., k, in a., 6/4/17 (40th Sqd.).
Pember, Edward Horace, Lt., k. in a., 30/9/17 (5th Sqd.) (R.F.A.).
Pemberton, Frederick Despard, Capt., k. in a., 21/8/17 (59th Sqd.) (R.F.A.).
Pender, William Gordon, M.C., Capt., k. in a., 15/8/17 (40th Sqd.).
Perkins, Thorold, 2/Lt., k. in a., 31/5/17 (41st Sqd.).
Perney, Erland Dauria, 2/Lt., k, in a., 23/11/17 (11th Sqd.).
Perry, William Charles, 2/Lt. (Tp.), k. in a., 30/12/17 (Gen. List).
Phalen, Ralph Uriel, 2/Lt., k. in a., 28/5/17 (60th Sqd.).
Phear, Norman Carlyon, 2/Lt. (Tp.), d. of w., 20/11/17 (27th Sqd.) (Gen. List).
Philip, Edgar Thomas, 2/Lt. (T/Lt.), k. in a., 18/6/17 (9th Sqd.) (R.F.A.).
Phillippo, Arthur James Cecil Eyre, Lt., k. in a., 7/6/17 (6th Sqd.) (R.A.S.C.).
Phillips, Cecil Ivor, 2/Lt., k. in a., 27/10/17 (45th Sqd.) (Glos. Regt.).
Phillips, Joseph Leo, 2/Lt. (Tp.), killed, 20/7/17 (Gen. List).
Phillips, Norman Arthur, 2/Lt., k. in a., 25/3/17 (54th Sqd.).
Phillips, Ralph Aberdeen, 2/Lt (Tp.), killed, 16/8/17.
Phipps, Christopher Leckonby, Lt., k. in a., 14/8/17 (7th Ball. Co., R.G.A.).
Pickstone, Charles, 2/Lt., k. in a., 3/9/17 (1st Sqd.) (Gen. List).
Pierson, Christopher Frank Kershaw, 2/Lt. (Tp.), k. in a., 10/10/17 (52nd Sqd.) (Gen. List)
Pile, Cyril John, 2/Lt., d. of w., 29/4/17 (12th Sqd.).
Pilkington, John Oscar, Lt. (Tp.), k in a., 6/9/17 (20th Sqd.).
Pilling, Walter, 2/Lt. (Tp.), killed, 3/4/17 (5th Res. Sqd.) (Gen. List).
Pillow, Henry Montgomery Scott, 2/Lt. (Tp.), k. in a., 8/8/17 (7th Sqd.).
Pinnock, Carey, 2/Lt. (Tp.), killed, 30/11/17.
Pinson, Ivan Lapworth, 2/Lt. (Tp.), d. of w., 4/5/17 (70th Sqd.) (Gen. List).
Pitt, Bevan William, 2/Lt., k. in a., 10/5/17 (55th Sqd.).
Pittman, Cecil Frederick, Lt., killed, 20/7/17 (14th Sqd.).
Platt, Charles Henry Morris, 2/Lt. (T/Lt.), k. in a., 23/11/17 (52nd Sqd.) (Royal Warwick Regt.).
Platt, Lionel Sydney, Capt., k. in a., 13/4/17 (57th Sqd.) (17th Lancers).
Pope, Edwin Albert, 2/Lt. (Tp.), k. in a., 27/2/17 (8th Sqd.) (Gen. List).
Porter, Stanley Fitzherbert, 2/Lt., died, 6/6/17 (Gen. List).
Portlock, Alfred Edgar, 2/Lt. (Tp.), killed, 6/12/17 (R. Fus.).
Poundall, William Arthur Lloyd, M.C., Capt. (Tp.), k. in a., 31/10/17 (53rd Sqd.) (S. Lancs Regt.).
Powell, Edward Watson, 2/Lt., k. in a., 31/10/17 (84th Sqd.).
Powell, Patrick John Gordon, Lt., k. in a., 2/4/17 (R.A.S.C.).
Powell, Thomas Henry Norman, 2/Lt., killed, 24/4/17.
Power, Henry Richard, Lt., k. in a., 22/8/17 (48th Sqd.) (3rd R. Ir. Rfls.).
Power-Clutterbuck, James Edward, 2/Lt. (Tp.), k. in a., 25/6/17 (52nd Sqd.) (R.F.A.).
Powers, Bernard Alexander, Lt., k. in a., 25/9/17 (19th Sqd.) (Middx. Regt.).
Powney, Arthur John, 2/Lt. (Tp.), d. of w., 15/9/17 (9th Sqd.) (Gen. List).
Prentice, James, 2/Lt. (Tp.), killed, 4/11/17.
Price, Victor William, Lt. (Tp.), killed, 7/11/17 (11th Worcs. Regt.).
Primeau, Cecil Willibrod, 2/Lt., k. in a., 27/10/17 (70th Sqd.) Gen. List).
Prince-Smith, Donald St. Patrick, Lt. (Tp.), k. in a., 24/10/17 (16th Sqd.) (R. Dub. Fus.).
Prismall, Merrick Orville, Lt., killed, 20/12/17 (R.F.A.).
Pritchard, Charles Frederick, 2/Lt., k. in a., 17/9/17 (57th Sqd.) (Gen. List).
Pritchard, Thomas Bradley, M.C., 2/Lt. (Tp.), killed, 5/12/17.
Pritchard, Thomas Thompson, 2/Lt. (Tp.), killed, 30/8/17 (Gen. List).
Prothero, Phillip Bernard, Lt. (T/Capt.), k. in a., 26/7/17 (51st Sqd.) (4th A. & S. Hlrs.).
Protheroe, William Bertram, Lt. (Tp.), k. in a., 12/6/17 (53rd Sqd.) (Gen. List).
Proud, John Reginald Stanhope, Lt. (Tp.), d. of w., 6/4/17 (Gen. List) (P. of W.).
Pryke, Edgar, 2/Lt. (Tp.), k. in a., 30/11/17 (3rd Sqd.) (Gen. List).
Pullan, John Aynsley, 2/Lt. (T/Lt.), k. in a., 28/11/17 (9th Sqd.) (Dur. L. I.).
Purvis, John William, 2/Lt. (Tp.), killed, 2/5/17 (Gen. List).
Pycroft, Arthur Percival, 2/Lt. (Tp.), killed, 16/6/17 (Gen. List).
Radcliffe, George Amyas, Lt., k. in a., 25/4/17 (Arg. & Suth. High.).
Rainboth, Lawrence John, 2/Lt. (Tp.), killed, 24/12/17 (Gen. List).
Raine, George Stevenson, 2/Lt. (Tp.), killed, 15/3/17 (26th R. Fus.).
Ralphs, Arthur, 2/Lt. (Tp.), k. in a., 23/4/17 (12th Sqd.) (Gen. List).
Randall, Sidney Walter, 2/Lt. (Tp.), died, 31/10/17 (11th Sqd.) (Gen. List).
Raney, Paul Hartley, 2/Lt., k. in a., 21/8/17 (66th Sqd.).
Ransom, Hubert William, 2/Lt., k. in a., 27/3/18 (70th Sqd.) (Gen. List).
Ransome, John Edwin, 2/Lt. (Tp.), killed, 12/12/17 (Gen. List).
Ravenscroft, Alan Paddock, Lt. (Tp.), killed, 16/1/17 (R.F.A.).
Rawbone, Charles Robert, 2/Lt. (Tp.), killed, 18/12/17 (Gen. List).
Ray, Philip Oliphant, 2/Lt. (Tp.), died, 13/4/17 (59th Sqd.) (8th B. Watch).
Rayner, Charles Oliver, 2/Lt. (Tp.), k. in a., 1/10/17 (25th Sqd.) (Gen. List).
Rayner, Noel Roderick, Lt., k. in a., 27/7/17 (57th Sqd.) (W. York. Regt.).
Read, Charles Stanley, 2/Lt., k. in a., 6/12/17 (52nd Sqd.) (Gen. List).
Redman, Wilfred George, 2/Lt. (Tp.), killed, 8/11/17 (Gen. List).
Reeve, Charles Frederick, 2/Lt. (Tp.), d. of w., 13/5/17 (2nd Sqd.) (Gen. List).
Reid, Alexander William, 2/Lt. (Tp.), k. in a., 4/3/17 (43rd Sqd.) (6th K.O.S.B.).
Reid, Guy Patrick Spence, M.C., Capt. (Tp.), killed, 16/10/17 (1st Seaforth High.).
Reincke, Leo Frederick, Capt. (Tp.), k. in a., 17/8/17 (48th Sqd.) (10th W. Riding R.).
Reynell, Frederick Henry, 2/Lt. (Tp.), k. in a., 23/4/17 (35th Sqd.) (Gen. List).
Rhude, Foster Weston, 2/Lt., k. in a., 30/11/17 (43rd Sqd.) (Gen. List).
Rhys-Davids, Arthur Percival Foley, D.S.O., M.C., 2/Lt., k. in a., 27/10/17 (56th Sqd.).
Rice, Arnold Hamilton, 2/Lt. (Tp.), k. in a., 29/11/17 (19th Sqd.) (Gen. List).
Richards, Henry Scotson, 2/Lt. (Tp.), d. of w., 3/4/17 (25th Sqd.) (15th N. & D. Regt.).
Richardson, Lancelot Lytton, Capt., k. in a., 13/4/17 (25th Sqd.).
Richardson, William Quintus Newsom, 2/Lt., killed, 6/10/17.
Rickards, Arthur Traherne, Lt. (T/Capt.), k. in a., 13/9/17 (43rd Sqd.) (R.G.A.).
Rickards, Hew Wardrop Brooke, Lt., k. in a., 28/7/17 (57th Sqd.) (R.F.A.).
Rider, Clifford Ernest, 2/Lt. (Tp.), killed, 10/10/17.
Riggs, Roy Robertson, 2/Lt., k. in a., 22/7/17 (19th Sqd.).
Rimer, James Cook, 2/Lt., k. in a., 17/3/17, (43rd Sqd.).
Ripley, Eris Richard, 2/Lt. (Tp.), k. in a., 31/10/17 (53rd Sqd.) (Gen. List).
Rishworth, Keith, 2/Lt. (Tp.), killed, 6/8/17 (Gen. List).
Risteen, Clifford Fraser, 2/Lt., k. in a., 26/9/17 (45th Sqd.) (Gen. List).
Ritter, William Henry, Lt. (Tp.), k. in a., 2/6/17 (15th Sqd.) (Gen. List).
Roadley, Thomas Stanley, Lt., k. in a., 17/8/17 (8th Sqd.) (4th S. Staffs.).
Roberts, Arthur Doricourt, M.C., Lt. (Tp.), killed, 31/8/17 (Gen. List).
Roberts, Elwyn, 2/Lt. (Tp.), k. in a., 10/2/17 (10th Sqd.) (Gen. List).
Roberts, Gavesen Brooke, 2/Lt., k. in a., 26/9/17 (Gen. List).
Robertson, Alexander, 2/Lt., d. of w., 17/8/17 (34th Sqd.) (R.F.A.).
Robertson, Archibald Garden, 2/Lt., k. in a., 8/6/17 (66th Sqd.) (B. Watch).
Robertson, Charles Eric, 2/Lt. (T/Capt.), k. in a., 12/7/17 (11th Sqd.).
Robertson, Duncan Alexander, 2/Lt. (Tp.), killed, 11/11/17 (Gen. List).
Robertson, David Norman, 2/Lt., died, 16/4/17 (60th Sqd.) (P. of W.).
Robertson, John Keith Grant, Lt. (Tp.), k. in a., 1/1/17 (Gen. List).
Robinson, Edward, Lt., killed, 6/12/17.
Robinson, Eustace Dixon Sharper, 2/Lt., k. in a., 4/9/17 (25th Sqd.) (Gen. List).

Rodocanachi, Paul John, 2/Lt. (Tp.), k. in a., 27/7/17 (53rd Sqd.).
Rogers, Cecil Victor De Burgh, 2/Lt., k. in a., 21/4/17 (29th Sqd.) (Gen. List).
Rook, Frederick William, 2/Lt., k. in a., 21/7/17 (40th Sqd.).
Rosenthal, Arthur, 2/Lt., k. in a., 23/11/17 (65th Sqd.) (Gen. List).
Roskelly, Wilfred Menadue, Lt., k. in a., 29/7/17 (52nd Sqd.).
Ross, Arthur Claude, 2/Lt., d. of w., 6/12/17 (10th Sqd.) (R. Scots Fus.).
Ross, Arthur Justin, D.S.O., Maj., killed, 2/8/17 (R.E.).
Ross, Claude Murray, 2/Lt., k. in a., 10/8/17 (45th Sqd.).
Ross, James Kenneth, 2/Lt. (Tp.), died, 9/4/17.
Ross, Peter Cunningham, 2/Lt. (Tp.), d. of w., 26/6/17 (Gen. List).
Rouquette, Douglas George, 2/Lt., k. in a., 26/9/17 (Gen. List).
Roux, Frank, 2/Lt. (Tp.), died, 26/4/17.
Rowat, Robert, 2/Lt., k. in a., 16/9/17 (Gen. List).
Rowden, Reginald Colin George, Lt. (Tp.), k. in a., 30/11/17.
Rowe, Benjamin Franklin, Lt., k. in a., 1/6/17 (R. Fus.).
Rowlands, Arthur William, Lt. (Tp.), killed, 15/8/17.
Rowles, Stanley Walter, Lt. (Tp.), d. of w., 13/12/17 (R.A.S.C.).
Runnels-Moss, Cyril Gower Vincent, 2/Lt., died, 5/12/17 (Gen. List).
Russell, Francis Gerald, 2/Lt., k. in a., 28/1/17 (R.F.A.).
Russell, John Hepburn, 2/Lt. (Tp.), killed, 12/11/17.
Rutter, Donald Campbell, Capt., k. in a., 7/6/17 (43rd Sqd.) (R. Sussex R.).
Ryan, John Henry, 2/Lt., d. of w., 2/5/17 (57th Sqd.).
Ryder, Reginald Victor, 2/Lt. (Tp.), d. of w., 28/6/17 (4th Sqd.) (Glos. Regt.).
Sage, Douglas Michael, 2/Lt., k. in a., 18/12/17 (65 Squad.) (Gen. List).
Saines, Charles Edward, 2/Lt. (Tp.), killed, 22/10/17 (Gen. List).
Salmon, Wilfred Graham, 2/Lt., k. in a., 7/7/17.
Salter, John Henry Raymond, 2/Lt. (Tp.), k. in a., 13/10/17 (54 Squad.) (Gen. List).
Samuels, Wilfred Templeton, 2/Lt. (Tp.), died, 14/7/17 (Gen. List).
Sanders, John Henry, 2/Lt. (Tp.), d. of w., 27/10/17 (59 Squad.) (Gen. List).
Sandys, William Edwin, Lt. (Tp.), k. in a., 5/9/17 (32 Squad.) (Gen. List).
Sant, Edward Medley, 2/Lt., k. in a., 1/9/17 (19 Squad.).
Savage, William Leslie, 2/Lt. (Tp.), killed, 16/6/17 (Gen. List).
Sayer, Charles Melville, 2/Lt. (Tp.), k. in a., 17/6/17 (4 Squad.) (Gen. List).
Sayer, Hubert Lionel, 2/Lt., k. in a., 17/8/17 (7 Squad.) (R.F.A.).
Sayer, James Herbert, 2/Lt., k. in a., 3/4/17 (15 Squad.).
Schofield, John Douglas Price, 2/Lt. (Tp.), killed, 26/5/17
Scott, Charles Lindsay Murray, Capt., k. in a., 15/2/17 (Gen. List).
(54 Squad.) (3/N. Staff Regt.).
Scott, Douglas Gordon, 2/Lt. (Tp.), killed, 13/12/17.
Scott, David Harden, M.C., Lt., k. in a., 12/11/17 (65 Squad.) (Gen. List).
Scott, Eric Douglas, 2/Lt., k. in a., 30/10/17 (1 Squad.) (Gen. List).
Scott-Miller, Walter Dudley, 2/Lt., killed, 22/6/17 (R. Fusrs.).
Segrave, William Henry, Lt. (Tp.), killed, 12/2/17 (Gen. List).
Sellers, Philip, 2/Lt., killed, 23/3/17 (Worcs. Regt.).
Senior, Joseph, Lt. (Tp.), d. of w., 9/5/17 (45 Squad.) (Gen. List).
Seguin, Ubalde Hornidas, 2/Lt., k. in a., 6/4/17 (16 Squad.).
Severs, Alfred George, 2/Lt., k. in a., 28/3/17 (25 Squad.) (Gen. List).
Sharland, Frederick James, 2/Lt., k. in a., 24/10/17 (23 Squad.).
Sharpe, Henry Norman, 2/Lt., killed, 26/1/17 (3/Leic. Regt.).
Sharples, Norman, Lt. (Tp.), k. in a., 20/9/17 (7 Squad.).
Sheehan, Cornelius, 2/Lt. (Tp.), killed, 8/8/17 (6/Muns. Fus.).
Sheehan, Desmond Joseph, 2/Lt. (Tp.), died, 10/5/17 (66 Squad.).
Shellington, Percy Gordon, 2/Lt. (Tp.), killed, 26/8/17.
Shepherd, Alfred Seymour, D.S.O., M.C., 2/Lt., k. in a., 20/7/17 (29 Squad.).
Shepherd, James Montague Edward, Capt., k. in a., 15/2/17 (1 Squad.) (Rifle Bde.)
Sheppard, Asa Frederick, 2/Lt. (Tp.), killed, 23/2/17 (27 Squad.) (Gen. List).
Sheppard, Lewis Charles Burford, 2/Lt., k. in a., 21/4/17 (32 Squad. (3/Som. L.I.).
Sherman, Palton, 2/Lt., k. in a., 30/4/17 (Gen. List).
Sherwood, William Bernard, Lt., k. in a., 27/10/17.
Shields, William, Lt. (Tp.), k. in a., 5/9/17 (14/Manch. Regt.).
Shone, Geoffrey Beville, Lt., d. of w., 19/10/17 (1/S. Staff. Regt.).
Sidney, Leicester Philip, 2/Lt., k. in a., 2/10/17 (17/K.R.R.C.).
Sillem, Stuart Charles, 2/Lt., k. in a., 12/8/17 (Gen. List).
Simmonds, Richard George, Temp. 2/Lt., died, 4/7/17 (Gen. List).
Simpson, Claude Battwell, 2/Lt., k. in a., 6/11/17 (Gen. List).
Simpson, Frank William Harris, Capt., k. in a., 16/2/17 (R.G.A.).
Simpson, George Kenneth, M.C., Lt. (Tp.), d. of w., 7/3/17.
Sinclair, Douglas Monteith Farquhar, Lt., k. in a., 30/3/17 (40th Sqd.) (Gen. List).
Sinclair, Herbert Spencer, 2/Lt. (Tp.), killed, 24/12/17.
Sisley, Arthur Jackson Smith, 2/Lt., k. in a., 10/9/17 (Gen. List).
Skeffington, Herbert Neville Southwell, 2/Lt., k. in a., 28/7/17 (57 Squad.).
Skelton, Francis, 2/Lt. (Tp.), k. in a, 21/10/17.
Slattery, Duncan Vincent, 2/Lt, killed, 3/3/17 (Hants Regt.).
Sleeman, William Fraser, 2/Lt. (Tp.), k. in a., 31/5/17 (55 Squad.) (Gen. List).
Sloan, Cyril Rennie, 2/Lt, died, 13/5/17 (29 Squad.).
Sloley, Robert Hugh, 2/Lt., k. in a., 1/10/17 (56 Squad.) (R.G.A.).
Smart, George Orme, 2/Lt. (Tp.), k. in a., 7/4/17 (Gen. List).
Smeeth, William Sutton, 2/Lt. (Tp.), killed, 17/7/17 (9/R. Irish Rifles).
Smith, Allan Higson, M.C., Capt., k. in a., 21/8/17 (Gen. List) (21 Sqd.).
Smith, Colin, 2/Lt. (Tp.), killed, 11/3/17 (Gen. List).
Smith, Charles Emanuel Webb, 2/Lt. (Tp.), killed, 28/7/17 (Gen. List).
Smith, Eric St. Clare, Lt., killed, 2/7/17 (R.F.A.).
Smith, Geoffrey Cholerton, M.C., 2/Lt. (T/Lt.), k. in a., 31/7/17 (R.A.S.C.)
Smith, Gordon Keith, M.C., Capt., k. in a., 21/8/17 (Gen. List).
Smith, Horace Claudian, 2/Lt. (Tp.), k. in a., 11/9/17.
Smith, Joseph Cecil, Lt., k. in a., 28/7/17.
Smith, Peter, Lt. (Tp.), k. in a., 28/4/17 (R.E.).
Smith, Roland, 2/Lt., k. in a., 6/4/17 (3/K.O.Y.L. Inf.).
Smith, Sidney Harold, 2/Lt (Tp.), killed, 23/10/17.
Smith, Thomas Edmund, 2/Lt., k. in a., 14/7/17 (Gen. List).
Smith, Victor Sidney, 2/Lt., k. in a., 6/10/17 (R.F.A.).
Smith, William Reginald Sturston, 2/Lt., died, 22/10/17 (Gen. List)
Smither, Harold, 2/Lt. (Tp.), k. in a., 6/7/17.
Smithett, Graeme Cecil East, 2/Lt., k. in a., 12/10/17 (1/N'thants Regt.).
Smyth, James, 2/Lt., k. in a., 12/3/17.
Sneddon, Andrew Beattie, 2/Lt, k. in a., 3/10/17 (Gen. List).
Snelgrove, Herbert Davys Bernard, 2/Lt., k. in a., 15/8/17.
Snowden, Harold Jackson, Lt, d. of w., 11/8/17 (2/S. Lancs Regt.)
Sogno, George Frank, 2/Lt., d. of w, 9/10/17 (R. Sussex Regt.).
Solly, Arthur Norbury, Capt. (Tp.), k. in a., 11/8/17 (Gen. List).
Solomon, Herbert Philip, 2/Lt., killed, 20/10/17.
Spear, Norman Victor, 2/Lt. (Tp.), killed, 29/8/17.
Spence, Alec William, 2/Lt. (Tp.), killed, 25/4/17 (Gen. List).
Spence, William Samuel, Temp. Lt., k. in a., 26/4/17 (Gen. List).
Spicer, Edmund Daniell, 2/Lt., k. in a., 1/2/17.
Spooner, Raymond Wilberforce, 2/Lt., k. in a., 8/6/17.
Spurway, Sidney Macdonald, 2/Lt. (Tp.), k. in a., 21/9/17.
Stacey, Douglas William, 2/Lt. (Tp.), d. of w., 20/6/17 (20 Squad.).
Stafford, Frederick John Ewart, 2/Lt., d. of w., 22/4/17 (8 Squad.)
Stanley, Sidney Edgar, 2/Lt. (Tp.), died, 19/10/17 (11 Squad.).
Steele, Alfred Harmer, 2/Lt. (Tp.), d. of w., 5/2/17 (16 Squad.) (Gen. List).
Stephen, James Pedraza, 2/Lt., k. in a., 23/5/17 (46 Squad.).
Stephens, Llewellyn, 2/Lt. (Tp.), killed, 12/6/17.
Steuart, Walter Willox, 2/Lt. (Tp.), d. of w., 5/3/17 (46 Squad.) (18/H. L.I.).
Stevens, Edward Henry, Lt., d. of w., 16/6/17 (25 Squad.) (E. Lancs Regt.)
Stevens, John Michael Stanislaus Gregory, 2/Lt., d. of w., 14/7/17 (1 Squad.)
Stevenson, Douglas Baptiste, 2/Lt., k. in a., 11/3/17 (45 Squad.) (D.C.L.I.).
Stevenson, James, 2/Lt. (Tp.), killed, 1/5/17 (Gen. List).
Stevenson, Walter Henry, 2/Lt. (Tp.), k. in a., 5/6/17 (29 Squad.).
Steward, Arthur Amyor, 2/Lt., k. in a., 6/10/17 (11 Balloon Coy., R.F.A.).
Stewart, Alister Douglas, Lt. (Tp), killed, 13/10/17 (Gen. List).
Stewart, Vernon Radcliffe, Lt., killed, 5/12/17 (19 Squad.) (R.A.S.C.).
Stockhausen, Ivan Lancelot, 2/Lt., k. in a., 3/10/17 (Brit. W. Indies Regt.).
Stone, Herbert John, 2/Lt. (Tp.), d. of w., 15/11/17, (19 Squad.).
Stonier, William John, Lt., k. in a., 27/4/17 (2 Squad.) (2/Beds Regt.).
Strachan, Benjamin, 2/Lt. (Tp.), k. in a., 18/5/17 (12 Squad.) (Gen. List).
Street, Cyril, Lt. (Tp.), k. in a., 26/6/17 (1 Squad.) (Gen. List).
Strettell, William Michael Dashwood Stirling, Capt., k. in a., 28/11/17 (4/H L.Inf.).
Stretton, Sidney, Lt. (Tp.), k. in a., 27/3/17 (15 Squad.) (Gen. List).
Stringer, William Charles, 2/Lt., died, 14/6/17.
Stuart, James, Capt., k. in a., 13/4/17 (59 Squad.) (1/R. Innis. Fus.).
Stuttard, Harold Pierce, 2/Lt. (Tp.), killed, 30/10/17 (Gen. List).
Sulman, Geoffrey, 2/Lt., killed, 20/6/17 (51 Squad.) (Gen. List).
Sutcliffe, Sydney, 2/Lt., k. in a., 2/10/17 (11 Squad.) (R. Welsh Fus.).
Swann, Gerald Huddart, 2/Lt. (Tp.), k. in a., 18/10/17 (41 Squad.) (Gen. List)
Swann, George William, Lt., d. of w., 24/3/17 (70 Squad.) (R.A.S.C.).
Swinfen, Percy Courtney, 2/Lt., killed, 20/9/17 (Gen. List).

Sworder, Hubert Pelham, Lt., k. in a., 2/4/17 (57 Squad.) (Roy. W. Surrey Regt.).
Sykes, Harold Keith, Lt., d. of w., 29/6/17 (42 Squad.) (Gen. List).
Symonds, Spencer Leslie Hatten, 2/Lt., k. in a., 12/11/17 (7 Squad.) (Gen. List).
Tagent, Harold, 2/Lt., k. in a., 24/3/17 (8th Sqd.) (4th R. Ir. Fus.).
Tailford, John Wilson, M.C., Capt., killed, 22/5/17 (Border R.).
Talbot, Arthur Sydney, Lt. (Tp.), killed, 27/9/17.
Tallent, Albert Cecil, 2/Lt. (Tp.), killed, 4/11/17.
Tanfield, Arthur Horace, 2/Lt., k. in a., 13/4/17.
Tardugno, Ray, 2/Lt. (Tp.), k. in a., 7/7/17 (57th Sqd.) (17th R. Fus.).
Tatham, Ion Mordaunt, 2/Lt. (Tp.), killed, 11/7/17 (Gen. List).
Taylor, Edmund, 2/Lt. (Tp.), d. of w., 26/9/17 (23rd Sqd.).
Taylor, Robert Edward, 2/Lt., k. in a., 17/9/17 (41st Sqd.).
Taylor, Vicat Scott, 2/Lt., killed, 14/1/17 (Gen. List).
Taylor, William Alexander, Lt. (Tp.), killed, 10/8/17 (Gen. List).
Taylor-Loban, Gustavus, Capt. (Tp.), killed, 7/6/17 (Gen. List).
Tennant, Henry, 2/Lt., k. in a., 27/5/17 (52nd Sqd.) (2nd Drags.).
Terry, John Elliott, 2/Lt., died, 16/10/17.
Tew, Percy, 2/Lt. (Tp.), killed, 16/6/17.
Thayre, Frederic James Harry, M.C., Lt. (T/Capt.), killed, 9/6/17.
Theron, Lucas Cornelius, 2/Lt. (Tp.), killed, 15/7/17 (Gen. List).
Thierry, Leon Hubert, 2/Lt., k. in a., 10/12/17 (Gen. List).
Thomas, Cecil Rees, 2/Lt. (Tp.), d. of w., 17/8/17 (57th Sqd.) (Gen. List) (P. of W.).
Thomas, Robert Newton, T/Capt., k. in a., 23/7/17 (Gen. List).
Thompson, Harold Victor, 2/Lt., k. in a., 26/9/17 (29th Sqd.) (Gen. List).
Thompson, J., Lt. (Tp.), k. in a., 11/3/17 (45th Sqd.) (Gen. List).
Thompson, Jonah George, 2/Lt., killed, 19/5/17.
Thompson-McLaughlin, Lee, 2/Lt., killed, 19/4/17 (4th W. Yks.).
Thomson, Wardlaw Ivor, 2/Lt. (Tp.), killed, 6/6/17 (Gen. List).
Thorne, Guy Stafford, 2/Lt. (T/Capt.), died, 18/3/17 (13th Sqd.).
Thornton, Cyril, 2/Lt. (Tp.), killed, 5/10/17 (Gen. List).
Thornton, Harold James, 2/Lt., died, 25/9/17.
Thwaytes, John, 2/Lt., k. in a., 18/3/17 (4th Sqd.) (Bdr. R.).
Tiddy, Hector Kingsley Portus, 2/Lt. (Tp.), k. in a., 26/7/17 (7th Sqd.) (Gen. List).
Tobin-Willis, John Galbraith, 2/Lt., k. in a., 17/8/17 (7th Sqd.) (R.A.S.C.).
Todd, Alick, M.C., Lt., d. of w., 16/4/17 (18th Sqd.) (4th D.L.I.) (P. of W.).
Todd, James William, 2/Lt. (Tp.), killed, 28/9/17 (Gen. List).
Tolhurst, Alfred Wilfred, 2/Lt. (Tp.), killed, 6/10/17 (Gen. List).
Tolhurst, Bernard Joseph, Lt., d. of w., 22/4/17 (11th Sqd.) (11th W. Rid. R.) (P. of W.).
Tomkies, Henry Lea, 2/Lt., k. in a., 25/4/17.
Tomlin, Harry Francis, 2/Lt. (Tp.), k. in a., 28/9/17 (20th Sqd.) (Gen. List).
Tomlinson, Hugh, M.C., Lt., died, 2/4/17.
Topham, Michael, 2/Lt., k. in a., 13/4/17 (27th Sqd.).
Torry, Arthur James Dashwood, M.C., Lt., k. in a., 9/10/17 (R.G.A.).
Townsend, Douglas, 2/Lt., k. in a., 16/8/17 (7th Sqd.) (Gen. List).
Townsend, Joseph Ernest, 2/Lt. (Tp.), killed, 2/1/17 (1st Worc. R.).
Treadwell, Robert Naylor, M.C., Lt. (Tp.), d. of w., 9/9/17 (22nd Sqd.) (Gen. List).
Trollope, William Kennedy, 2/Lt., d. of w., 3/5/17 (13th Sqd.).
Tucker, Donald Cecil, 2/Lt., k. in a., 24/3/18, (41st Sqd.) (Gen. List).
Turnbull, Alexander Miller, 2/Lt., k. in a., 25/4/17 (12th Sqd.) (Gen. List).
Turnbull, William, 2/Lt. (Tp.), k. in a., 12/6/17 (53rd Sqd.).
Turner, Frederick Harry, M.C., Lt. (Tp.), killed, 10/1/17 (Gen. List).
Turner, Herbert Deacon, 2/Lt., k. in a., 20/8/17 (70th Sqd.) (Gen. List).
Turner, Herbert Duncan Bruce, Lt., died, 9/8/17 (R.F.A.).
Turner, Richard George, 2/Lt., killed, 4/5/17.
Turner, Warren Geoffrey Dalton, Lt., k. in a., 24/5/17 (11th Sqd.) (Gen. List).
Twidale, Elfric Ashby, 2/Lt., k. in a., 22/4/17 (R.F.A.).
Underwood, George Milne, 2/Lt., k. in a., 6/3/17 (16th Sqd.) (Gen. List).
Vaile, Lawrence Edward Stuart, 2/Lt. (Tp.), killed, 29/8/17 (Gen. List).
Valentine, James, D.S.O., Capt. (T/Major), died, 7/8/17.
Vangoetham, Henry Edward, Lt. (T/Capt.), killed, 11/7/17.
Vavasour, Rudolph Dunstan, 2/Lt. (T/Lt.), died, 16/1/17 (R.F.A.).
Veacock, Stanley John, T/Lt., d. of w., 17/10/17 (20th Sqd.) (Hamps. R.).
Venables, Alfred Ernest, 2/Lt., killed, 4/4/17.
Venn, Bertram Joseph, 2/Lt. (Tp.), killed, 11/7/17 (R.E.).
Vernham, Noel Mark Hodson, 2/Lt. (Tp.), k. in a., 4/2/17 (16th Sqd.) (Gen. List).
Vessey, John Arthur, 2/Lt. (Tp.), killed, 12/6/17 (45th Sqd.).
Vick, Kenneth Jesson, 2/Lt. (Tp.), killed, 5/7/17 (Gen. List).
Villiers, Henry Lister, 2/Lt., k. in a., 4/2/17 (11th Sqd.) (6th Innis. Drags.)
Vince, William John Douglas, 2/Lt., killed, 22/5/17.
Wadlow, Harry, Capt. (Tp.), killed, 1/5/17 (Gen. List).
Wagner, Ethelbert Godwin Stockwell, 2/Lt., k. in a., 7/1/17 (32nd Sqd.) (R. Warwicks).
Wakeford, Robert Scott, 2/Lt. (Tp.), died, 22/2/17.
Wale, Alan Ernest, 2/Lt. (Tp.), killed, 23/11/17 (Gen. List).
Walker, George Henderson, Lt., k. in a., 28/7/17 (45th Sqd.) (Gen. List).
Walker, Frederick Leslie, 2/Lt. (Tp.), killed, 28/12/17.
Walker, James Hope, 2/Lt., killed, 16/3/17 (Gen. List).
Wall, Arthur Geoffrey Nelson, 2/Lt. (Tp.), killed, 6/8/17.
Waller, Charles Raymond, 2/Lt. (Tp.), killed, 9/6/17 (Gen. List).
Waller, John Raymond, 2/Lt. (Tp.), killed, 18/5/17 (Gen. List).
Walsh, Herbert, 2/Lt. (Tp.), k. in a., 30/12/17 (46th Sqd.).
Walter, Stephen Reginald Parke, Lt., k. in a., 31/7/17 (32nd Sqd.) (R.W. Surr. R.).
Walthew, John Syers, 2/Lt., k. in a., 19/9/17 (4th Sqd.) (Gen. List).
Walton, Oswald Thomas, 2/Lt. (T/Lt.), k. in a., 12/4/17 (18th Sqd.) (3rd S. Lancs R.).
Waner, Gerald Richard Francis, 2/Lt. (Tp.), d. of w., 2/3/17 (25th Sqd.) (R.E.).
Warburton, George Augustus Lowe, 2/Lt. (Tp.), killed, 1/10/17 (Gen. List).
Ward, George Bernard, M.C., T/2/Lt. (T/Maj.), k. in a., 21/9/17 (10th Sqd.) (Gen. List).
Ward, Percy Harry Bavister, 2/Lt., k. in a., 19/5/17 (22nd Sqd.) (Gen. List).
Ward-Price, Leonard Stanley, Lt., k. in a., 25/3/17 (70th Sqd.) (2nd Life Gds. Res.).
Warter, Joseph Gordon, 2/Lt., k. in a., 30/9/17 (Wilts R.).
Wasey, Cyril Walter Carleton, Capt., k. in a., 28/10/17 (16th Sqd.) (R. War. R.).
Waters, John Patrick, 2/Lt. (Tp.), k. in a., 18/11/17 (56th Sqd.).
Wates, Leslie Charles, 2/Lt. (Tp.), k. in a., 9/10/17 (29th Sqd.).
Watlington, Henry Joseph, 2/Lt., k. in a., 6/7/17 (70th Sqd.) (Gen. List).
Watson, Alfred William, 2/Lt. (Tp.), k. in a., 1/5/17 (10th Sqd.) (Gen. List).
Watson, William John, 2/Lt., killed, 26/5/17 (Gen. List).
Watt, George Macdonald, 2/Lt., k. in a., 17/3/17 (16th Sqd.).
Watt, Norman Lindley, 2/Lt., d. of w., 27/7/17 (K. Edward's Horse).
Watt, Robert Sherwin, 2/Lt., k. in a., 12/6/17 (45th Sqd.) (Gen. List).
Watts, Albert Edward, 2/Lt., died, 6/3/17 (16th Sqd.).
Wattson, Cyril Beaven, 2/Lt., k. in a., 8/10/17 (7th Sqd.).
Waud, Ernest Henry, Lt., k. in a., 16/8/17 (North. Fus.).
Wear, Albert Edward, 2/Lt. (Tp.), k. in a., 11/9/17 (20th Sqd.).
Webb, Noel William, M.C., Capt., k. in a., 16/8/17 (20th Sqd.).
Webb, Trevor, 2/Lt., k. in a., 10/5/17 (55th Sqd.) (Gen. List).
Weekes, Reginald Penkivil Olive, 2/Lt. (Tp.), k. in a., 7/5/17 (10th Sqd.) (Gen. List).
Weiss, Edward Stanley, 2/Lt. (Tp.), k. in a., 22/11/17 (41st Sqd.).
Welch, Eric Arthur, 2/Lt. (Tp.), k. in a., 23/4/17 (16th Sqd.) (Gen. List).
Wells, James Ritchie, T/2/Lt., killed, 17/11/17 (1st R. Hdrs.).
Wenden, George, Lt. (T/Capt.), k. in a., 16/3/17, (35th Sqd.) (Border R.).
West, Mortimer Sackville, 2/Lt. (Tp.), k. in a., 11/11/17 (11th Sqd.).
West-Thompson, Maurice, 2/Lt. (Tp.), k. in a., 23/11/17 (60th Sqd.).
Westlake, John Howard, 2/Lt. (Tp.), d. of w., 7/5/17 (12th Sqd.). (Gen. List).
Whitaker, Victor John, Lt., k. in a., 6/4/17 (2nd Sqd., 3rd Lincs R.).
Whitaker, William, 2/Lt., k. in a., 6/12/17 (23rd Sqd.) (Gen. List).
White, Francis Reginald, 2/Lt., d. of w., 23/1/17 (10th Sqd., R.E.).
White, Basil Walwyn, 2/Lt., k. in a., 8/4/17 (55th Sqd., Liv. R.).
White, Lewis Scott, M.C., T/Capt., killed, 29/9/17.
White, Melville Arthur, 2/Lt. (Tp.), k. in a., 23/4/17 (3rd Sqd.).
Whitehead, Geoffrey Nield, 2/Lt. (Tp.), k. in a., 15/10/17 (11th Balloon Coy.).
Whitehead, Reginald Maurice, 2/Lt., k. in a., 22/11/17 (41st Sqd.).
Whitfield, Lewis Hayes, 2/Lt. (Tp.), d. of w., 30/10/17 (21st Sqd.).
Whiting, James Oliver, Lt., k. in a., 22/9/17 (60th Sqd.).
Whittall, Noel Charles, 2/Lt. (Tp.), k. in a., 13/9/17 (6th Sqd., R. Fus.).
Whyte, George Henry, T/2/Lt., k. in a., 4/12/17 (49th Sqd.).
Whytehead, Hugh Holton, 2/Lt., k. in a., 12/7/17 (Gen. List).
Wightman, John Francis, 2/Lt., k. in a., 4/9/17 (11 Sqd.) (Gen. List).
Wilcox, Percy William, 2/Lt. (Tp.), killed, 31/12/17.
Wilkinson, David Stanley, Lt. (Tp.), died, 26/8/17 (56th Sqd.) (Gen. List).
Wilkinson, Eric Russell, M.C., Lt., (Tp.), d. of w., 7/10/17 (47th Sqd.) (Gen. List).
Wilkinson, Geoffrey Miles, 2/Lt., k. in a., 10/10/17 (56 Sqd.) (D.C.L.I.).
Wilkinson, Harold Reid, Lt. (Tp.), d. of w., 10/9/17.

Will, John George, Lt. (Tp.), k. in a., 25/3/17 (29 Sqd.) (Gen. List).
Willard, Kenneth Hugh, 2/Lt., died, 12/10/17 (York & Lanc.) (P. of W.).
Williams, Arthur Courtenay, 2/Lt. (Tp.), killed, 18/9/17.
Williams, Arthur Trevor, 2/Lt. (Tp.), d. of w., 4/9/17 (25 Sqd.) (R. Welsh Fus.).
Williams, Collingsby Philip, 2/Lt., k. in a., 26/8/17 (Gen. List).
Williams, Roderick Mathafar, Capt., k. in a., 12/8/17 (2 Garr. Bn. R. W. Fus.).
Williams, Roland Vaughan, 2/Lt. (Tp.), k. in a., 5/6/17 (32 Sqd.).
Williams, Vaughan Floyer, 2/Lt., k. in a., 3/4/17 (60 Sqd.) (Gen. List).
Williams, William George Bransby, M.C., Capt., k. in a., 12/5/17 (19 Sqd.).
Williams, William Harold Trant, 2/Lt. (Tp.), died, 22/8/17 (29 Sqd.) (P.O.W.).
Wilson, Alexander Philip, Lt., k. in a., 14/4/17 (2 Sqd.).
Wilson, Cecil Eustace, 2/Lt. (Tp.), k. in a., 16/4/17 (7 Sqd.) (Gen. List).
Winser, Frank Edward, 2/Lt., k. in a., 20/8/17 (43 Sqd.) (Gen. List).
Wodehouse, Francis John Ashburnham, 2/Lt., k. in a., 26/8/17 (9 Sqd.) (D.C.L.I.).
Wollen, Douglas Charles, 2/Lt., k. in a., 13/4/17 (25 Sqd.) (Gen. List).
Wood, Geoffrey, 2/Lt., k. in a., 6/5/17 (2 Sqd.) (Gen. List).
Wood, Philip Lovel, 2/Lt., k. in a., 4/3/17 (43rd Sqd.).
Woodcock, Victor Joseph, Lt. (Tp.), k. in a., 30/9/17 (3 Sqd.).
Woodley, Stanley William, 2/Lt. (Tp.), k. in a., 22/1/17 (10 Sqd.) (Gen. List).
Workman, Charles Service, M.C., 2/Lt. (T/Lt.), k. in a., 20/7/17 (70 Sqd.) (Scottish Rifs.).
Wormull, Charles Frederic, Lt. (Tp.), killed, 5/10/17 (Gen. List).
Worstenholm, John, 2/Lt., k. in a., 25/9/17 (Gen. List).
Wray, Thomas Ernest, 2/Lt. (Tp.), k. in a., 4/9/17 (7 Sqd.).
Wright, Frederick Adams, 2/Lt. (Tp.), k. in a., 19/9/17 (9 Sqd.) (D.C.L.I.).
Wright, Stanley, M.C., 2/Lt., k. in a., 24/10/17 (R.E.) (21 Kite Balloon Sect.).
Wylie, Alan Lindsay, M.C., 2/Lt. (Tp.), k. in a., 20/11/17 (Gen. List).
Yates, John Edwin, 2/Lt. (Tp.), k. in a., 1/11/17.
Youdale, Alfred Clarence, M.C., 2/Lt. (T/Capt.), k. in a., 23/12/17 (S.R.).
Young, Arthur Cyril, 2/Lt., k. in a., 2/4/17 (8 Sqd.).
Young, David William Laird, 2/Lt. (Tp.), k. in a., 6/1/17 (53 Sqd.) (Gen. List).
Young, Francis Chisholm, 2/Lt., k. in a., 14/2/17 (3 Sqd.).
Young, George James Taylor 2/Lt. k. in a., 20/11/17 (15 Sqd.).
Young, Harold Farquhar, 2/Lt., k. in a., 20/8/17 (43 Sqd.) (3 N. and Derby Regt.).
Young, Harold Victor, 2/Lt., d. of w., 8/12/17 (54 Sqd.).
Young, John Edward Rostron, 2/Lt. (Tp.), killed, 7/7/17.
Young, Stanley James, Lt., killed, 23/12/17.
Young-Fullalove, George, 2/Lt. (Tp.), k. in a., 13/8/17 (55 Sqd.).

Adams, Briggs Kilbwin, 2/Lt. (Tp.), k. in a., 14/3/18 (18 Sqd.).
Aitken, Andrew Ramsey, 2/Lt. (Tp.), killed, 2/3/18.
Akrill-Jones, Edward Trevor, Lt., killed, 18/3/18 (4/N. & Derby.).
Allen, Cyrus, 2/Lt., k. in a., 13/3/18.
Anstey, Alexander Burgess, 2/Lt. (Tp.), killed, 22/2/18.
Armstrong, John, 2/Lt. (Tp.), killed, 27/3/18.
Armstrong, Sydney, 2/Lt., k. in a., 17/2/18 (R.F.A.).
Atha, Leonard Edward, 2/Lt. (Tp.), k. in a., 5/3/18.
Bailey, Felix Charles, 2/Lt. (Tp.), d. of w., 28/3/18.
Bailey, Wilson Rhodes, 2/Lt. (Tp.), killed, 19/1/18.
Baker, Eric Trezier, 2/Lt., k. in a., 19/1/18.
Balfour, Alan Scott, 2/Lt., k. in a., 13/1/18 (R.F.A.).
Ball, Arthur, 2/Lt. (Tp.), killed, 17/3/18.
Banfield, Cyril Barnet, 2/Lt., k. in a., 21/3/18.
Bark, Robert Charles, 2/Lt. (Tp.), killed, 28/3/18.
Barlow, Harry Loftus, Lt. (Tp.), killed, 18/3/18 (R.E.).
Barlow, Leonard Monteagle, M.C., Lt. (T/Capt.), killed, 5/2/18 (S.R.).
Barnes, Edmund, 2/Lt. (Tp.), killed, 27/1/18.
Barwell, Humphrey Eames, 2/Lt. (Tp.), k. in a., 3/2/18.
Barwell, Hugh William E., M.C., Capt., k. in a., 25/3/18.
Batt, Francis Joseph, Lt. (Tp.), k. in a., 13/3/18.
Batten, John Hardman, 2/Lt. (Tp.), killed, 18/2/18.
Beamer, Archie Mainland, 2/Lt. (Tp.), k. in a., 4/2/18.
Beck, Herbert Musgrove, 2/Lt. (Tp.), k. in a., 22/1/18
Beer, William John, 2/Lt. (Tp.), k. in a., 21/2/18.
Beeton, Robert Henry, 2/Lt. (Tp.), killed, 1/2/18.
Bennett, John Blake, 2/Lt. (Tp.), k. in a., 21/3/18.
Black, Donald Walter Bryce, 2/Lt. (Tp.), killed, 3/1/18.
Black, John Montgomery, 2/Lt. (Tp.), killed, 5/2/18.
Blackeby, Joseph Edward, 2/Lt. (Tp.), k. in a., 21/2/18.
Bloomfield, Gerald Arthur, 2/Lt. (Tp.), killed, 13/2/18.
Blyth, Edward John, 2/Lt., k. in a., 26/3/18.
Bodycomb, George Thomas, 2/Lt. (Tp.), killed, 18/2/18.
Bonyun, Frank Vernon, 2/Lt. (Tp.), k. in a., 2/1/18.
Borthistle, William John, 2/Lt., k. in a., 29/1/18 (R. Muns. Fus.).
Brendel, John Daniel George, 2/Lt. (Tp.), killed, 27/1/18.
Brennan, Lester Luke, 2/Lt. (Tp.), killed, 25/2/18.
Broadbent, Sidney, Capt. (Tp.), k. in a., 18/2/18
Brook, Charles William, 2/Lt., killed, 26/3/18 (3/West Riding Regt.).
Brookes, Ronald Baines, 2/Lt., k. in a., 13/3/18.
Brown, James Leonard, 2/Lt., killed, 29/3/18.
Brown, Reginald Charles, 2/Lt. (Tp.), k. in a., 21/2/18.
Browne, George Edwin, Lt. (Tp.), d. of w., 21/1/18.
Buchan, William Erskine, 2/Lt. (Tp.), killed, 9/3/18.
Bulteel, Thomas Edward, Lt., killed, 24/2/18 (R.F.A.).
Bush, Victor George Anderson, Capt. (Tp.), killed, 8/2/18.
Buss, Hilary Thomas, 2/Lt. (Tp.), killed, 21/1/18.
Butler, Desmond George, Lt., killed, 17/3/18 (Leinster R.).
Butler, Harold, 2/Lt. (Tp.), k. in a., 22/2/18.
Butler, John Ormond, 2/Lt., died, 11/4/18 (P.O.W.).
Butt, Alfred, 2/Lt., k. in a., 4/1/18 (Bedford R.).
Cadzow, Robert, 2/Lt. (Tp.), killed, 22/1/18.
Caldwell, John Hay, Lt., k. in a., 24/1/18 (Cameron Hrs.).
Calverley, Geoffrey Walter, D.S.O., Lt., killed, 7/1/18 (R. Irish Rifles).
Cameron, Donald, 2/Lt. (Tp.), k. in a., 25/3/18 (3 Sqd.).
Cameron, Robert Barton, Lt. (Tp.), k. in a., 7/1/18.
Campbell, Charles Duncan Mile, M.B.E., Major, died, 9/3/18.
Cann, Leonard, 2/Lt., k. in a., 13/3/18.
Carpenter, Charles McElroy, 2/Lt. (Tp.), killed, 21/3/18.
Cartland, Arthur Edward, 2/Lt. (Tp.), killed, 25/2/18.
Cartwright, Ronald William St. George, 2/Lt. (Tp.), k. in a., 26/2/18.
Castle, Vernon William Blyth, Lt. (T/Capt.), killed, 15/2/18.
Chance, Eric Godwin, 2/Lt. (Tp.), k. in a., 19/1/18.
Chapman, Charles Dudley, 2/Lt. (Tp.), killed, 19/1/18.
Chappell, Stanley, Lt., killed, 2/3/18.
Chatterton, Roden Latham, Capt., k. in a., 28/3/18 (Leinster Regt.).
Cheesman, John Frederick, 2/Lt., killed, 25/1/18.
Cheshire, Edgar Murray, 2/Lt. (Tp.), killed, 6/3/18.
Clark, Eric Alan, 2/Lt., killed, 20/3/18.
Clarke, Claude Hamilton Law, 2/Lt., died, 22/3/18.
Clarke, Wilfrid Randall, Lt. (Tp.), killed, 4/2/18 (R.F.A.).
Cleaver, Horace Gregory, 2/Lt. (Tp.), killed, 17/3/18.
Clementz, Denis Murray, 2/Lt. (Tp.), k. in a., 6/3/18.
Cobb, Francis Walker, 2/Lt., died, 28/3/18.
Coldwell, Herbert David, 2/Lt. (Tp.), killed, 11/3/18.
Coley, Allen Cowen. Lt. (Tp.), killed, 6/3/18.
Collier, Reginald John, 2/Lt. (Tp.), killed, 12/2/18.
Collins, Robert Simpson. 2/Lt. (Tp.), k. in a., 9/3/18.
Colwell, Albert Edward, 2/Lt., killed, 23/2/18.
Connelly, Montagu Edward, Lt., died, 14/1/18.
Cook, Earl Allen, 2/Lt. (Tp.), killed, 22/3/18.
Cook, Francis Richardson, Lt. (Tp.), killed, 22/2/18.
Corbet, John Hugh, 2/Lt. (Tp.), k. in a., 13/1/18 (K.S.L.I.).
Cornforth, Norman Leslie, 2/Lt. (Tp.), k. in a., 18/1/18.
Costa, Luigi Gausche, 2/Lt. (Tp.), killed, 19/3/18.
Cotman, R. A., Lt. (Tp.), k. in a., 26/3/18.
Coward, John Bayman, 2/Lt., killed, 26/3/18.
Cowell, Jocelyn Gore, 2/Lt., killed, 28/1/18 (R. Fus.).
Craig, George Barton, 2/Lt., k. in a., 21/2/18.
Croft, George Wheeler, Lt. (Tp.), k. in a., 16/2/18 (Lincoln Regt.).
Crowley, Frederick Augustus, 2/Lt. (Tp.), killed, 26/2/18.
Cumberland, Andrew John, 2/Lt. (Tp.), killed, 3/1/18.
Cumming, James Leslie, 2/Lt. (Tp.), killed, 24/3/18.
Cummings, Ralph Michael, 2/Lt., killed, 15/1/18.
Cunningham, Edward, 2/Lt., k. in a., 28/1/18.
Cunningham, Lyman Holden. 2/Lt., killed, 14/1/18.
Curley, Alfred, 2/Lt. (Tp.), killed, 5/3/18.
Curtis-Beals, Harold, 2/Lt. (Tp.), killed, 15/3/18.
Dale, Alfred Parks. 2/Lt (Tp.), killed. 15/3/18
Davenport, Edmund Sharrington, 2/Lt. (Tp.), died, 3/1/18 (P. of W.).
Davies, Arthur Peter, 2/Lt. (Tp), killed, 22/3/18.
Davies, Benjamin Daniel Rowland, 2/Lt. (Tp.), killed, 11/3/18.
Davis, Joseph, 2/Lt. (Tp.), killed, 20/1/18.
Dawson, Arthur, 2/Lt (Tp.), killed, 21/1/18.
Dawson, Harold Percy, 2/Lt. (Tp.), killed, 9/3/18.
Dempster, Ian MacKay, 2/Lt., k. in a., 24/2/18.
Denham, Wm. Malcolm, 2/Lt., killed, 3/1/18.
Dennett, William Charles, 2/Lt., k. in a., 27/3/18 (3/Sqd.).
Denovan, Allan McNab, 2/Lt., k. in a., 26/3/18.
Dickens, Maurice Wilfred, Lt., k. in a., 27/2/18.
Donnelly, James Alexander, 2/Lt., d. of w., 31/3/18.
Dodson, H. L. M., Lt, died, 25/8/18 (R.A.S.C.).
Doughty, Robert Cecil, 2/Lt. (Tp.), killed, 26/2/18.
Doyle, Michael William, 2/Lt., killed, 22/3/18.
Drysdale, Alexander, 2/Lt. (Tp.), killed, 25/3/18.
Duncan, James Athol Gordon, 2/Lt. (Tp.), killed, 15/2/18.
Edmonds, Edward Peregrine Pell, 2/Lt., died, 18/3/18 (P. of W.).
Edwardes, Henry Arthur, 2/Lt. (Tp.), killed, 16/2/18.
Edwards, Ernest Victor, 2/Lt., killed, 16/2/18.
Egner, Frederick Albert, 2/Lt., k. in a., 6/1/18.
Erskine Ralph, Capt. (Tp.), died, 1/1/18 (P. of W.).
Evans, Alfred Henry Courtenay, 2/Lt. (Tp.), killed, 22/3/18 (11/E. Lanc. R.).
Evans, Edward Tilney, 2/Lt. (Tp.), killed, 19/2/18.
Evans, Francis Bernard, 2/Lt. (Tp.), killed, 17/2/18.
Evans, Forrest Dinnett. 2/Lt., killed, 27/3/18.
Ewart, Keith Penicuik, 2/Lt., k. in a., 4/1/18.
Fear, Robert Stanley, 2/Lt. (Tp.), d. of w., 5/3/18 (Worc. Regt.).
Fenn-Smith, Warren Kemp, 2/Lt. (Tp.), k. in a., 18/1/18.
Fernald. Van D., Lt., died, 23/7/18 (3/R.W. Surr. R.).
Ferrie. Robert Leighton Moore, M.C., 2/Lt., k. in a., 3/1/18.
Folliott, Charles Russell Hastings, Lt., k. in a., 10/3/18.
Field, A. W., Capt., k. in a., 9/1/18.

Finnemore, Henry James, 2/Lt. (Tp.), d. of w., 27/3/18 (R. Sussex R.).
Fitzgibbon, Harold, 2/Lt. (Tp.), k. in a., 27/3/18.
Fitzmaurice, Archibald Hamilton, Lt., k. in a., 12/3/18.
Fleming, Robert John, 2/Lt. (Tp.), killed, 29/1/18.
Foster, Reginald, 2/Lt (Tp.), killed, 3/1/18.
Francis, William George, 2/Lt., k. in a., 10/3/18.
Fraser, Arthur Cecil, 2/Lt. (Tp.), killed, 22/1/18.
Fudge, Alfred, T/Lt., d. of w., 22/2/18 (9/Suff. R.).
Gaisford, Robert Sandeman, Lt., k. in a., 30/1/18 (R.F.A.).
Galbraith, Alfred Hugh, 2/Lt. (Tp.), killed, 24/2/18.
Galbraith, William Thomas, 2/Lt. (Tp.), killed, 26/2/18.
Garbett, Ronald Vivian, 2/Lt. (Tp.), k. in a., 5/1/18.
Garnett, Ewanda Berckeley, 2/Lt. (Tp.), killed, 27/1/18.
Gaskell, Lawrence Norris, 2/Lt. (Tp.), d. of w., 1/3/18.
Gauld, Gordon Smith Mellis, M.C., Lt., killed, 25/3/18 (R.F A.).
Gavaghan, Colin, 2/Lt, k. in a., 13/3/18.
Gee, Donald, 2/Lt. (Tp.), killed, 31/1/18.
Gerow, Albert, 2/Lt. (Tp.), killed, 28/2/18.
Gibson, John Thomas, 2/Lt. (Tp.), killed, 10/2/18.
Gill, Hugh Goddard, Lt, k. in a., 12/3/18 (13/W. Yorks R.).
Giovanetti, Albert Harcourt, 2/Lt. (Tp.), killed, 3/2/18.
Glen, Donald Roy, 2/Lt. (Tp.), killed, 12/2/18.
Gopsill, Kenneth Lloyd, T/Lt., k. in a., 15/2/18 (E. Surr. R.).
Gordon, Cecil Philip George, Capt., killed, 21/3/18 (4/S. Staff. R.).
Gordon, Douglas Stanley, 2/Lt., k. in a., 21/2/18 (R.F.A.).
Gornall, George, 2/Lt., k. in a., 27/3/18.
Grattan, George Harry, 2/Lt. (Tp.), killed, 4/3/18.
Gray, Edward Leadbetter, 2/Lt. (Tp.), killed, 22/3/18.
Greathead, John Harding, 2/Lt. (Tp.), killed, 11/1/18.
Green, Alan Herbert, 2/Lt. (Tp.), d. of w., 25/2/18 (R.E.).
Green, G. W. Ashdown, 2/Lt., k. in a., 8/3/18 (R.F.A.).
Greene, Aldrich Wells, 2/Lt., k. in a., 17/2/18.
Gregory, John Sheridan, Capt. (Tp.), k. in a., 19/2/18 (R.A.S.C.).
Gregory, Robert, M.C., Lt. (T/Major), k. in a., 23/1/18 (Conn. Rgrs.).
Gresley-Cox, Edward Louis, 2/Lt. (Tp.), killed, 22/2/18.
Gross, Robert John, 2/Lt. (Tp.), killed, 26/2/18.
Guest, Ernest William, 2/Lt., k. in a., 26/2/18 (R. Lanc. R.).
Hainsby, Fernley Winter, 2/Lt., k. in a., 26/3/18.
Hall, Durham Donald George, M.C., 2/Lt. (T/Capt.), d. of w., 27/3/18 (York. Regt.).
Hall, Ralph Gordon, 2/Lt. (Tp.), killed, 23/1/18.
Hamel, H. P. J. G., 2/Lt. (Tp.), k. in a., 10/1/18.
Hamilton, D. R., 2/Lt. (Tp.), killed, 23/1/18.
Hamilton, John Percy, Temp. 2/Lt., killed, 8/3/18.
Hancock, John Maurice, 2/Lt. (Tp.), k. in a., 7/3/18.
Hardie, John, 2/Lt. (Tp.), killed, 7/2/18.
Harding, George Helliwell, 2/Lt., k. in a., 27/3/18.
Hargreaves, Willoughby Frankland, 2/Lt. (Tp.), k. in a., 21/2/18.
Harold, John Peter Bevan, Lt., d. of w., 16/2/18 (R.F.A.).
Harrison, Bernard Percy Bartlan, 2/Lt. (Tp.), killed, 6/1/18.
Hartley, Herbert Henry, 2/Lt. (Tp.), k. in a., 14/3/18.
Hazell, Dudley Howard, Lt., k. in a., 27/9/18 (2/R. Lanc. R.).
Heasman, George Harry, Lt. (Tp.), killed, 20/1/18.
Heigham-Plumptre, L. G., 2/Lt., d. of w., 4/6/18 (Bedford R.).
Hendershot, Charles Cecil, 2/Lt. (Tp.), killed, 6/2/18.
Hewett, Harold, Capt., k. in a., 4/1/18 (R. Berks R.).
Highton, Harold Victor, 2/Lt., k. in a., 25/3/18.
Hodges, Albert Rowland Cortis, 2/Lt., killed, 20/3/18 (Middx. R.).
Holland, C., Capt., killed, 25/1/18 (8/Sqdn.).
Holmes, Archibald, 2/Lt., k. in a., 4/2/18.
Holt, John Leonard, 2/Lt., k. in a., 16/3/18.
Howe, James Ashwell, Tp. 2/Lt., killed, 13/2/18.
Howells, Edmund Sydney, Lt. (Tp.), killed, 27/3/18.
Hudson, Francis Reginald, Lt. (T/Capt.), killed, 21/3/18.
Hughes, T. McKenny, Lt. (Tp.), k. in a., 5/2/18 (K.R.R.C.).
Hull, Edwin Charles, 2/Lt. (Tp.), killed, 17/3/18.
Humphrey, Ernest Graham, 2/Lt., d. of w., 29/3/18.
Hurst, Aubrey Clive, 2/Lt., d. of w., 22/1/18.
Hyatt, Valentine, 2/Lt., k. in a., 24/3/18.
Ikin, Alfred Edward, 2/Lt. (Tp.), k. in a., 11/3/18.
Irvine, William Magnus, 2/Lt., k. in a., 22/3/18 (Northd. Fusrs.) (12/Sqdn.).
Jarvis, Ralph Himsworth, M.C., Lt. (T/Capt.), killed, 27/2/18.
Jenkins, Charles, 2/Lt. (Tp.), killed, 21/3/18.
Johnson, Horace Samuel, 2/Lt. (Tp.), killed, 9/3/18.
Johnstone, Godfrey Gleeson, 2/Lt. (Tp.), k. in a., 30/1/18.
Jones, Harry Reynolds, 2/Lt. (Tp.), k. in a., 17/3/18.
Jones, Walter George Cottrell, 2/Lt. (Tp.), killed, 17/3/18.
Jull, Leslie Hubert, Lt., killed, 3/1/18 (N. Staffs. R.).
Kavanagh, John William, 2/Lt., died, 11/3/18.
Kay, Stanley Burnett, Capt., died, 28/1/18 (Yorks Regt.).
Keefe, Cecil Henderson, Capt. (Tp.), killed, 5/2/18.
Kempe-Roberts, John Archer Clinton, 2/Lt., k. in a., 10/3/18.
Kennard, Terence Evelyn, Lt., k. in a., 26/2/18 (R.F.A.).
Kennedy, Douglas Stewart, Capt., k. in a., 12/3/18.
Kennedy, Rolf Darab, 2/Lt. (Tp.), k. in a., 27/3/18 (23rd Sqd.).
Kent, Peter Francis, 2/Lt., k. in a., 6/2/18 (3rd Sqd.).
Kent, William Morley, 2/Lt., k. in a., 21/2/18.
Kilkelly, John George Joseph, Capt., k. in a., 24/3/18 (Roy. Mun. Fus.).
Knaggs, Kenneth John, 2/Lt., k. in a., 16/3/18 (R. Warw. Regt.).
Kneller, Frederick Kneller, 2/Lt., k. in a., 21/3/18.
Knox, William, 2/Lt., k. in a., 24/3/18.
Kohnstamm, Norman Mortimer Joseph, Capt., k. in a., 22/3/18 (Manch. Regt.).
Krohn, Edmund Otto, 2/Lt., k. in a., 1/3/18.
Kynoch, Alexander Bruce, Capt. (Tp.), killed, 8/3/18.
Kynoch, Alfred Stewart, 2/Lt. (Tp.), k. in a., 13/3/18.
Lapp, Austin Ross, 2/Lt. (Tp.), killed, 9/3/18.
Last, Leslie Sydney, 2/Lt., killed, 21/2/18 (R.F.A.).
Law, Charles Arkley, 2/Lt. (Tp.), killed, 19/2/18.
Lay, Harold Frank Douglas, 2/Lt., killed, 7/3/18.
Lee, J. W., 2/Lt., killed, 31/3/18 (S.W. Bdrs.).
Lees, Robert Milne, 2/Lt. (Tp.), k. in a., 21/3/18.
Lemessurier, Thomas, 2/Lt. (Tp.), killed, 30/1/18.
Lewis, Frank Arthur, 2/Lt. (Tp.), killed, 28/3/18.
Lewis, Francis Alexander, 2/Lt., k. in a., 5/2/18 (53rd Sqd.).
Lilico, Percy, 2/Lt. (Tp.), killed, 16/2/18.
Livingstone, Frederick James, 2/Lt. (Tp.), killed, 12/1/18.
Lovell, Robert Clifford, 2/Lt. (Tp.), k. in a., 26/1/18.
Lumley, H.R., 2/Lt., k. in a., 11/3/18.
Lytton, Percy Arthur Bertram, 2/Lt., k. in a., 4/2/18 (R. Ir. Regt.) (58th Sqd.).
Maasdorp, C. R., 2/Lt. (Tp.), died, 28/3/18 (P. of W.).
Macaulay, John Shaw, 2/Lt., d. of w., 4/1/18.
McConnell, Frederick James, 2/Lt. (Tp.), died, 10/3/18.
McCudden, John Anthony, 2/Lt., k. in a., 18/3/18.
McDonald, Lachlan, Lt. (Tp.), killed, 19/1/18.
McDonnell, George Oscar, Lt., d. of w., 18/3/18 (R.G.A.).
McDowall, Archibald, 2/Lt., killed, 12/1/18 (3rd E. Lancs. Regt.).
McGillivray, Charles Allister, 2/Lt. (Tp.), killed, 14/2/18.
McGinn, Wilfrid J., 2/Lt. (Tp.), killed, 18/2/18.
MacIlwaine, Julian M., Capt., k. in a., 22/3/18 (12 Sqd.) (Roy. Ir. Rifles).
McKin, John Nelson Burdette, 2/Lt., k. in a., 10/3/18.
McLean, Donald Gordon, Lt. (Tp.), k. in a., 4/2/18.
McLintock, John Lawrie, Lt., k. in a., 26/2/18.
McNair, Robert Schemehorn, 2/Lt. (Tp.), killed, 17/3/18.
McNeil, Francis George, 2/Lt., k. in a., 8/3/18.
McNiff, F. J., 2/Lt., k. in a., 13/3/18 (North'd Fus.).
McPherson, Allen Ross, 2/Lt. (Tp.), killed, 26/1/18.
McRae, Ronald Gwynnyd Montague, 2/Lt. (Tp.), k. in a., 28/1/18.
Madeley, Claude Neville, 2/Lt., k. in a., 19/1/18.
Manley, Terence Wood, 2/Lt. (Tp.), killed, 6/3/18.
Martin, Ronald Hutton, Capt., k. in a., 24/3/18 (Munster Fus.).
Maxwell, William Stewart, 2/Lt., k. in a., 21/3/18.
Mealing, Maurice Edmund, 2/Lt., k. in a., 24/3/18 (K.S.L.I.).
Medlicott, Harold William, 2/Lt., killed, 21/5/18.
Mellish, Roy Thompson, 2/Lt. (Tp.), k. in a., 7/3/18.
Melville, David Charles, 2/Lt. (Tp.), killed, 21/1/18.
Middleton, George North, 2/Lt. (Tp.), killed, 22/2/18.
Miller, Frederick David, 2/Lt. (Tp.), d. of w., 4/2/18.
Miller, George, 2/Lt., d. of w., 31/3/18 (P. of W.).
Miller, James Arthur, 2/Lt. (Tp.), k. in a., 28/3/18.
Millett, James Noble Layton, 2/Lt., died, 13/3/18.
Milligan, Frank Joynt, 2/Lt. (Tp.), d. of w., 13/3/18.
Milne-Henderson, John Milne, 2/Lt., k. in a., 28/1/18.
Mitchell, William George, 2/Lt., killed, 23/3/18.
Money, Duncan Goff, 2/Lt., k. in a., 16/2/18 (4th Sqd.).
Moore, Ronald, 2/Lt. (Tp.), k. in a., 8/3/18.
Morey, Alan Wilson, M.C., Lt., k. in a., 24/1/18.
Morgan, Arthur, 2/Lt. (Tp.), killed, 27/2/18.
Morgan, Ashton, Lt. (Tp.), killed, 4/2/18.
Morgan, Oswald William, Lt. (Tp. Capt.), killed, 3/2/18 (R.F.A.).
Morris, Arthur Cukelyn, Lt. (Tp.), k. in a., 17/2/18 (R. Welsh Fus.).
Morris, John Herbert, Lt., k. in a., 6/3/18 (R.H.A.) (49th Sqd.).
Murray, William Douglas Gillespie, 2/Lt., k. in a., 3/1/18.
Musgrave, John James, 2/Lt. (Tp.), killed, 27/2/18.
Muspratt, Keith Knox, M.C., 2/Lt. (T/Capt.), killed, 19/3/18 (Dorset Regt.).
Naylor, Frank, 2/Lt., k. in a., 23/3/18 (L.N. Lancs).
Neale, Robert Edward, 2/Lt., k. in a., 18/3/18.
Nelson, Herbert, 2/Lt. (Tp.), killed, 19/3/18.
Nelson, Harold Griffith, 2/Lt., killed, 22/1/18.
Neve, Rupert Ernest, Lt. (Tp.), killed, 26/1/18.
Newton, Cecil Herbert, 2/Lt. (Tp.), killed, 11/3/18.
Nicholls, Ernest, 2/Lt. (Tp.), killed, 10/3/18.
Nickson, John Reginald, 2/Lt. (Tp.), killed, 2/1/18.
Norris, Edward Fraser, Lt. (Tp. Capt.), killed, 15/3/18.
Nutkins, Vernon William, Lt., killed, 19/2/18 (R. Scots Fus.).
O'Hanlon, Sydney Esmond, M.C., Lt. (Tp.), killed, 3/2/18.
Oldridge, Peter Henry, 2/Lt. (Tp.), killed, 26/1/18.
Orcutt, Marcena Hitchcock, 2/Lt. (Tp.), k. in a., 1/3/18.
Park, George Alexander, 2/Lt. (Tp.), k. in a., 18/1/18.
Parker, Charles Allen, M.C., 2/Lt., killed, 19/2/18 (R.F.A.).
Parker, George Harvey, 2/Lt., killed, 24/3/18.
Parker, Percy Dolph, 2/Lt., killed, 4/1/18 (4th Res. Cav.).
Parrish, George Lewis, 2/Lt., killed, 11/1/18.
Patten, Francis Hope, 2/Lt., killed, 15/1/18.
Paul, Arthur Reginald, 2/Lt., k. in a., 22/1/18.
Payne, Albert, 2/Lt., killed, 13/1/18.
Payne, Horace Abram, 2/Lt., k. in a., 18/3/18.
Payne, Henry William, 2/Lt. (Tp.), killed, 12/3/18.
Peacocke, Evelyn Jeffreys, 2/Lt. (Tp.), killed, 4/2/18.
Pentecost, Charles Gordon, 2/Lt., k. in a., 27/3/18 (25th Sqd.).
Perkins, Jukes Ford Rumsey Irving, 2/Lt., k. in a., 8/3/18.
Perry, Cullen Hay, Lt. (Tp.), killed, 3/2/18 (R. Fusrs.).
Perryman, Arthur Charles, 2/Lt., killed, 7/1/18 (Middlx. Regt.) (16th Sqd.).
Phillips, Azariah, 2/Lt. (Tp.), killed, 12/1/18.
Philpott, John Reginald, M.C., T/Capt., died, 15/1/18 (P. of W.).

Pickup, William Heys, 2/Lt. (Tp.), killed, 12/3/18.
Pitt, John, 2/Lt. (Tp.), killed, 7/2/18.
Pohlmann, Reginald Peel, 2/Lt., k. in a., 5/2/18.
Poole, Bernard Goldsmith, 2/Lt. (Tp.), k. in a., 22/3/18 (53rd Sqd.).
Porter, George Anthony Gordon, 2/Lt. (Tp.), killed, 9/3/18.
Porter, Wilson, 2/Lt., k. in a., 24/3/18 (R.F.A.) (56 Sqd.).
Poulter, Wilfred Forman, 2/Lt., died, 6/3/18.
Proudfoot, Thomas John Anderson, 2/Lt. (Tp.), k. in a., 23/2/18.
Pullen, Frederick John Edward, 2/Lt. (Tp.), killed, 26/3/18.
Purser, Norman Frederick, 2/Lt. (Tp.), k. in a., 28/2/18.
Quelch, Arthur Francis, 2/Lt. (Tp.), killed, 15/1/18.
Radcliff, Robert Sussex Francis Derwentwater, 2/Lt., k. in a., 26/3/18 (80th Sqd.).
Raggett, Bertram Robert, 2/Lt., k. in a., 5/1/18 (R.G.A.).
Ramsay, William James, Lt., k. in a., 27/3/18 (R. Wel. Fus.).
Read, George Chisholm, 2/Lt., k. in a., 4/1/18 (R.E.).
Reade, Arnold Baillie, 2/Lt., Tp., k. in a., 21/2/18.
Reading, Vernon Jack, 2/Lt., k. in a., 26/3/18.
Reay, Stanley, 2/Lt., k. in a., 28/1/18.
Reeves, Harry Gosford, T/Capt., k. in a., 24/1/18.
Reynish, Horace John Cook, 2/Lt., k. in a., 23/3/18.
Rigby, Thomas Frank, 2/Lt., k. in a., 27/3/18 (3rd Sqd.).
Riley, Leslie, 2/Lt., Tp., killed, 5/2/18.
Robb, Russell Edwin, 2/Lt., Tp., died, 5/1/18.
Roberts, Laurie Paterson, T/2/Lt., k. in a., 23/2/18.
Robertson, John Henry, T/Lt., d. of w., 11/3/18.
Robinson, Fred, 2/Lt., k. in a., 26/1/18.
Robinson, Henry Awtry, 2/Lt., Tp., killed, 18/2/18.
Rooke, Claude Eugène, 2/Lt., killed, 21/1/18 (K.O.S.B.).
Ross, Douglas William, T/2/Lt., k. in a., 11/1/18.
Ross, James Wilson, T/Lt., killed, 26/3/18.
Rowat, Maurice Alexander, T/Lt., k. in a., 12/2/18.
Rowley, Charles Edgar, 2/Lt., Tp., killed, 19/1/18.
Russell, Glen., 2/Lt., k. in a., 18/3/18.
Sanborn, William Reginald, T/2/Lt., killed, 7/2/18.
Saunders, Ferdinand Ward, 2/Lt., k. in a., 25/1/18.
Saunders, George, T/2/Lt., killed, 30/3/18.
Saville, Robert, T/Capt., killed, 16/3/18.
Scott, Maurice Douglas Guest, M.C., Lt., T/Capt., killed, 17/3/18 (3rd L.N. Lancs).
Scott, Victor William, Lt., k. in a., 16/3/18 (E. Surr. R.).
Scudamore, Robert Capel, M.C., T/Capt., k. in a., 26/2/18.
Seaholme, Max, 2/Lt., Tp., k. in a., 30/3/18.
Seater, Thomas Rendall, T/2/Lt., killed, 21/1/18.
Selous, Frederick Hatherley Bruce, M.C., Capt., k. in a., 4/1/18 (R.W. Surr. R.).
Sharples, Evelyn Horace Guy, T/Capt., killed, 19/1/18.
Shaw, Arthur James, 2/Lt., killed, 1/2/18.
Shaw, John Fyffe, T/2/Lt., killed, 19/2/18.
Shaw, Thomas Gordon, 2/Lt., k. in a., 17/3/18.
Shelton, Kenneth, Lt., T/Capt., d. of w., 14/2/18 (E. Kent R.).
Shephard, Gordon Strachey, D.S.O., M.C., Brig.-Gen., k. in a., 19/1/18 (Roy. Fus.).
Shephard, Stuart Norman, 2/Lt., Tp., killed, 17/2/18.
Sherwood, Robert, T/2/Lt., k. in a., 26/2/18.
Simson, Herbert, Lt., died, 12/1/18.
Sinclair, William Everitt, 2/Lt., Tp., killed, 15/3/18.
Sisley, Donovan Laurier, 2/Lt., k. in a., 6/3/18.
Skinner, William Edward, 2/Lt., Tp., killed, 4/3/18.
Smallwood, William Spencer, T/2/Lt., k. in a., 25/1/18.
Smeddle, Geo. Robert Graham, Lt., Tp., killed, 11/3/18.
Smith, Frederick George, T/2/Lt., killed, 8/2/18.
Smith, Reston Alexander, 2/Lt., Tp., k. in a., 25/1/18.
Smith, Wm. Chas., 2/Lt., died, 8/2/18.
Smith, Walter Sydney, 2/Lt., Tp., k. in a., 9/1/18.
Somerville, Henry Arthur, M.C., 2/Lt., k. in a., 28/3/18 (R. Suss. Regt.).
Sondheim, Walter, 2/Lt., Tp., killed, 4/3/18.
Speechly, Thomas Martindale, 2/Lt., Tp., killed, 8/2/18.
Spragg, Westley Neal, Lt., k. in a., 1/1/18.
Stanton, Victor George, 2/Lt., died, 29/3/18 (P. of W.).
Starfield, Baron, 2/Lt., Tp., k. in a., 19/1/18.
Stern, Sydney Lionel, 2/Lt., Tp., killed, 22/2/18.
Stevens, Douglas Alfred Stephen, 2/Lt., Tp., k. in a., 9/3/18.
Stewart, Guy Somerville, 2/Lt., k. in a., 28/3/18.
Stobbart, Roland Walter, 2/Lt., Tp., killed, 6/3/18.
Stream, John Harvey, Lt., Tp., k. in a., 19/2/18 (Linc. Regt.).
Sykes, Leslie Gordon, 2/Lt., killed, 22/3/18 (R.F.A.).
Tancock, Osborne George, M.C., Lt., k. in a., 17/3/18 (5th Sqd., R.F.A.).
Tatham, Lawrence Castell Stanley, 2/Lt., Tp., k. in a., 10/1/18.
Tattersall, Percival John, 2/Lt., Tp., killed, 9/1/18.
Taylor, Arthur Rowland, 2/Lt., Tp., killed, 19/1/18.
Taylor, Thomas, 2/Lt., Tp., k. in a., 26/3/18.
Teunon, James M., 2/Lt., died, 30/12/18 (R.F.A.).
Thomas, David Cecil Sandby, 2/Lt., killed, 16/2/18 (Welsh Regt.).
Thomas, Francis Stephen, Capt., k. in a., 16/2/18.
Thomas, John Boaz, Lt., k. in a., 23/1/18.
Thomas, John Dobson, 2/Lt., Tp., killed, 20/3/18.
Thompson, James Reginald Walter, 2/Lt., Tp., d. of w., 22/3/18.
Thompson, Philip, Capt., k. in a., 23/3/18.
Thorowgood, Leslie Vernon, T/Capt., killed, 22/3/18
Thorp, Henry Thomas, Lt., Tp., k. in a., 21/2/18.
Tilbury, Robert William, 2/Lt., died, 18/3/18.
Tilney, Leonard Arthur, M.C., Major, k. in a., 9/3/18 (R. Horse Gds.).
Todd, Frederick George, 2/Lt., Tp., k. in a., 12/2/18 (Glos. Regt.).
Tufts, George Henry, 2/Lt., Tp., killed, 26/1/18 (K.R.R.C.).
Turnbull, Arthur Francis, 2/Lt., Tp., killed, 9/2/18.
Turnell, Robert Douglas, 2/Lt., Tp., k. in a., 27/3/18.
Tyson, Eric James, D.S.O., M.C., Major, Tp., d. of w., 11/3/18.
Urwin, Thomas Alexander, 2/Lt., Tp., d. of w., 15/1/18 (P. of W.)
Van Duzer, Harry Norman, T/2/Lt., died, 25/3/18.
Veale, Allan Adolphus, 2/Lt., Tp., k. in a., 22/1/18.
Vickers, Godfrey Raymond, 2/Lt., Tp., k. in a., 6/1/18.
Vinson, Albert Higgs, Lt., T/Capt., killed, 22/3/18.
Wade, Richard Curtis, 2/Lt., k. in a., 26/2/18.
Ward, Andrew Rushworth, 2/Lt., Tp., killed, 21/1/18.
Warren, Albert, 2/Lt., Tp., k. in a., 17/3/18 (Leic. Regt.).
Wastell, Kenneth, 2/Lt., Tp., killed, 23/3/18.
Watson, George William Annakin, 2/Lt., Tp., k. in a., 7/3/18.
Watson, Thomas, 2/Lt., Tp., k. in a., 26/3/18.
Webster, George Alexander Malcolm, 2/Lt., k. in a., 28/2/18 (S. Lanc. Regt.).
West, Percy Francis, 2/Lt., died, 24/3/18.
Westlake, Albert Neave, M.C., 2/Lt., k. in a., 4/1/18 (N. Staff. R.).
Westmoreland, Ernest, 2/Lt., d. of w., 19/2/18.
Wheelock, Charles Herbert, 2/Lt., Tp., died, 19/3/18.
White, Ritchie David, 2/Lt., Tp., d. of w., 24/2/18.
Whitehead, Eric Alfred, 2/Lt., k. in a., 13/3/18.
Whitehead, Eric Wilfred, 2/Lt., Tp., killed, 17/2/18.
Wilkes, Henry James Trevor, 2/Lt., k. in a., 28/2/18.
Wilkinson, Charles Bliss, 2/Lt., k. in a., 28/3/18 (R.F.A.).
Willcox, Alan George, 2/Lt., Tp., killed, 14/2/18.
Williamson, Gerald Douglas, 2/Lt., Tp., d. of w., 1/1/18.
Wilson, H. H., 2/Lt., Tp., k. in a., 19/2/18.
Winter, James, 2/Lt., Tp., k. in a., 28/2/18.
Wise, Francis Harry Varney, Lt., Tp., killed, 13/1/18.
Witt, Cecil, 2/Lt., Tp., k. in a., 28/2/18 (K.R.R.C.).
Wood, Joseph Clark, 2/Lt., Tp., killed, 13/1/18.
Wood, Richard Shaw, 2/Lt., Tp., killed, 17/3/18.
Woodhouse, Percy Wilfred, 2/Lt., k. in a., 28/3/18.
Woodman, Douglas, 2/Lt., Tp., k. in a., 11/3/18.
Worrall, Ernest Arthur, T/Capt., killed, 20/3/18.
Worsley, Reginald Eric Milne, 2/Lt., Tp., k. in a., 8/3/18.
Wray, John Leonard, 2/Lt., Tp., killed, 13/2/18.
Wyatt-Smith, John Drummond, 2/Lt., Tp., k. in a., 17/3/18.
Wylie, Arrol Edmiston, 2/Lt., k. in a., 18/1/18.
Yell, Reuben Harold, 2/Lt., Tp., k. in a., 9/3/18.
Young, George Cooper, 2/Lt., Tp., k. in a., 17/3/18
Young, John Stevenson, 2/Lt., Tp., killed, 3/2/18.

Territorial Officers Attached Royal Flying Corps.

Adam, Alexander Russell, Lt., k. in a., 3/7/17 (6/S'forth Hrs.).
Adams, T. D., Capt., k. in a., 7/11/15 (R.F.A.).
Allan, Lawson Ellis, Lt., k. in a., 26/4/17 (Westmoreland & Cumb'd Yeo.).
Allen, Richard Gerrard Ross, 2/Lt., k. in a., 16/11/16.
Anderson, Edward Kerr, Capt., killed, 16/3/18 (5/H.L.I.).
Angus, Robert E., Lt., k. in a., 20/11/17 (Ayrshire Yeo.).
Anthony, John Richard, Capt., d. of w., 25/5/17 (6/R. Welsh Fus.).
Armstrong, John Lewis Pasteur, 2/Lt., k. in a., 22/6/16 (R.A.S.C.).
Ashton, Hardric Grey, Lt., d. of w., 11/3/18 (11/London Rgt.).
Bacon, Edward Sivewright, Lt., k. in a., 31/8/17 (R.F.A.).
Bailey, Clifton Frederick, Lt., k. in a., 6/4/17 (7/London Regt.).
Balaam, Augustus Orland, Lt., k. in a., 24/10/17 (5/Suffolk Regt.).
V.C. Ball, Albert, D.S.O., M.C., Capt., k. in a., 7/5/18 (7/Notts & Derby Regt.).
Barltrop, Eric Arthur, Lt., k. in a., 23/4/17 (R.E.).
Basden, Maurice Duncan, 2/Lt., k. in a., 20/5/16 (16/London Regt.).
Battersby, Philip Worsley, Lt., k. in a., 7/7/17 (West Som. Yeo.).
Bayley, Edward Vincent, 2/Lt., killed, 24/2/17 (6/S. Staffs Regt.).
Bean, Bevis Heppel, Lt., k. in a., 18/6/17 (6/Roy. Welsh Fusrs.).
Bean, William Stuart, Lt., k. in a., 21/1/18 (R.E.).
Beck, Donald Coker, Lt., killed, 21/9/16 (R.F.A.).
Beckton, William, Lt., killed, 23/3/18 (5/R. Welsh Fus.).
Bell-Irvine, William, 2/Lt., killed, 28/10/15 (10/R. Scots).
Bentham, Richard, Capt., killed, 8/11/16 (7/Manch. Regt.).
Bertie, Claude Peregrine, Capt., k. in a., 19/3/17 (R.F.A.).
Best, Douglas Kenneth, Lt., k. in a., 16/8/17 (6/Essex Regt.).
Best, Francis Behrens, Lt., k. in a., 29/7/17 (R.A.S.C.).
Biederman, Harry Edward, 2/Lt., k. in a., 10/8/17 (Oxford Yeo.).
Bird, Dudley Joseph de Auguld, Lt., k. in a., 27/6/17 (R.F.A.).
Birdwood, Herbert Frederick, Lt., k. in a., 2/3/16 (20/Lon. Regt.).
Bishop, Bernard Bennett, 2/Lt., k. in a., 9/9/17 (5/D. of Corn. L.Inf.).
Bisset, Edgar George William, 2/Lt., d. of w., 7/1/17 (5/Gordon Hrs.).
Boag, Alfred, 2/Lt., killed, 29/4/16 (7/Lon. Regt.).
Bond, Hubert Samuel Emery, Lt., killed, 17/6/17 (7/Welsh Regt.).
Boon, Arthur, 2/Lt., killed, 29/3/17 (7/Manch. Regt.).
Bottomley, Edwin Rhodes, 2/Lt., k. in a., 2/6/17 (R.F.A.).
Boustead, Harry Atheling Russell, Lt., d. of w., 5/4/17 (8/Middlx. Regt.).
Bowman, Leslie Spencer, Lt., k. in a., 25/6/17 (4/K.O.R. Lanc. Regt.).

Brayshay, William Stead, Capt., k. in a., 6/4/17 (R.A.S.C.).
Brodie, Charles Gordon, Lt., k. in a., 23/5/17 (5/London
Brooks, Leonard William, 2/Lt., k. in a., 6/7/17 (8/Hamps. Regt.).
Brown, George Trevor, Lt., killed, 12/2/17 (6/Welsh Regt.).
Brown, William Joseph, Lt., killed, 21/2/18 (1/Co. of Ldn. Yeo.).
Brufton, Howard Charles, 2/Lt., k. in a., 9/7/17 (20/Rifle Bde.).
Brunwin-Hales, Greville Oxley, Capt., k. in a., 24/3/17 (8/Essex Regt.).
Burleigh, Robert, Lt., k. in a., 29/8/16 (R.E.).
Burney, Geoffry Asteley, Capt., k. in a., 7/7/16 (Scottish Horse).
Busk, Edward Teshmaker, 2/Lt., died, 5/11/14 (R.E.).
Butler, Archibald Stanley. 2/Lt., k. in a., 16/8/16 (R.F.A.).
Butler, Charles, Capt., killed, 27/8/17 (R.E.).
Butterworth, Norman, 2/Lt., k. in a., 9/5/17 (5/Manch. Regt.).
Buxton, George Barclay, 2/Lt., k. in a., 28/7/17 (5/Norfolk Regt.).
Byrne, Edward, 2/Lt., k. in a., 12/3/17 (4/Gordon Hrs.).
Campbell. John Santiago, Capt., k. in a., 28/9/17 (9/A. & S. Hrs.).
Campbell, William Archibald, Lt., d. of w., 21/9/17 (7/W. Yorks Regt.).
Cameron, George Grant, 2/Lt., k. in a., 16/10/17 (4/Gordon Hrs.).
Cantle, Leonard Heath, Lt., k. in a., 8/4/17 (Surrey Yeo.)
Capper, Edward Walter, Lt., k. in a., 14/4/17 (Montgomery Yeo.).
Churchward, Hubert Alan, 2/Lt., k. in a., 16/8/17 (2/London Yeo.).
Clark, Norman, Lt., k. in a., 18/3/18 (R.F.A.)
Clark, William Henry, 2/Lt., k. in a., 6/7/17 (8/Middlx. Regt.).
Cleghorn, Herbert Stuart, Capt., k. in a., 2/9/17 (R.E.).
Cobbold, Edgar Francis Wanklyn, Lt., k. in a., 12/1/16 (7/Cheshire Regt.).
Coddington, Charles Ernest, 2/Lt., k. in a., 4/12/17 (10/L.-pool Regt.).
Coles, Rowland Humphrey, Lt., k. in a., 9/5/17 (W. Som. Yeo.).
Collier, Sidney, M.C., Lt., k. in a., 28/3/18 (6/Manch. Regt.).
Collins, William Henry, Lt., killed, 7/3/18 (Yorks. Hussars).
Colomb, Mervyn William, 2/Lt., d. of w., 11/5/15 (4/Lond. Regt.).
Coomber, Horace Bertram, Capt., k. in a., 12/10/17 (8/Manch. Regt.).
Cooke, George Josiah, 2/Lt., k. in a., 23/11/17 (2/Lond. Regt.).
Corry, Frank Moring, 2/Lt., d. of w., 13/12/17 (8/Notts & Derby Regt.).
Coupe, Thomas Harold, Lt., died, 26/7/17 (4/E. Lanc. Regt.).
Cowan, Philip Chalmers, Capt., k. in a., 8/11/17 (8/Manch. Regt.).
Crafter, James, M.C., Lt., died, 7/7/17 (20/Lon. Regt., in Ger. hands).
Crompton, Henry Dent, 2/Lt., k. in a., 4/12/16 (R.F.A., T.F.).
Cronhelm, Arthur Geoffrey, Lt., killed, 6/9/17 (22/Lond. Regt.).
Curling, Edward Thomas, Lt., killed, 15/2/18 (22/Lond. Regt.).
Cutler, Herbert Cecil, Lt., k. in a., 10/5/17 (Worc. Yeo.).
Darrington, Harold Edgar, Lt., d. of w., 20/11/17 (9/Middlx. Regt.).
Davidson, Arthur Gerrard, 2/Lt., k. in a., 9/9/17 (4/Gordon Highrs.).
Davies, Gwynonfryn Albert Hayden, 2/Lt., k. in a., 7/6/17 (3/Mon. Regt.).
Davies, Llewelyn Crighton, M.C., 2/Lt., killed, 16/3/18 (3/Sco. Rifles).
Davies, Rhys Beynon, 2/Lt., k. in a., 1/5/17 (4/N'land. Fus.).
Dennett, Thomas Frank Preston Thwaites, 2/Lt., d. of w., 5/8/17 (4/R.W. Surrey Regt.).
Dennis, Charles Cowley, 2/Lt., k. in a., 25/9/18 (19/Lond. Regt.).
Dennis, Edward, 2/Lt., k. in a., 22/3/18 (7/Notts & Derby Regt.).
Desborough, Laurence Vernon, Lt., k. in a., 30/11/17 (R.F.A.).
Devlin, Henry Little, Lt., k. in a., 19/9/17 (5/Arg. & Suth. Highrs.).
Donaldson, Cleweth, Thomas Lee, 2/Lt., k. in a., 14/4/17 (Glasgow Yeo.).
Donaldson, Herbert Graham, 2/Lt., killed, 16/2/18 (20/Lon. Regt.).
Driver, Percy Scott, Lt., k. in a., 26/3/18 (A.S.C.).
Duncan, Harold Forrester, M.C., Lt., d. of w., 29/3/17 (5/H.L.I.).
Elgey, Eric, 2/Lt., k. in a., 19/3/17 (R.F.A.).
Emmerson, Alfred, 2/Lt., d. of w., 4/4/17 (5/Leic. Regt.).
Evans, Stewart Nicholson, Lt., killed, 9/7/17 (6/Suffolk Regt.).
Exley, George Allan, 2/Lt., k. in a., 14/1/17 (5/K.O. Yorks L. Inf.).
Fair, James Gerald, 2/Lt., k. in a., 19/3/17 (Duke of Lanc. Yeo.).
Fidler, Canel Watt, 2/Lt., d. of w., 19/5/17 (7/Arg. & Suth. Highrs.).
Field, Norman, Lt., k. in a., 14/8/17 (5/Manch. Regt.).
Fletcher, Herbert Phillips, Major, died, 3/8/16 (1/County of London Yeo.).
Fry, Horace Charles, 2/Lt., died, 24/2/17 (5/R.W. Kent Regt.).
Fryer, William Basil, 2/Lt., killed, 26/12/16 (5/S. Staffs Regt.).
Fuller, Leonard Arthur, Lt., k. in a., 17/5/17 (8/D.L.I.).
Furniss, Kevin Robert, 2/Lt., d. of w., 29/4/17 (Staffs Yeo.) (in Ger. hands).
Gadsden, Crawford Cunningham, Lt., d. of w., 16/10/17 (4/R.W. Surrey Regt.).
Gamon, Sidney Percival, Capt., killed, 23/3/18 (5/Chesh. Regt.).
Gaskain, Cecil Stanley, Lt., k. in a., 7/5/17 (R.F.A.).
Gaskell, Reginald Robinson, Lt., killed, 15/12/16 (R.E.).
Gimingham, Charles Henry, Capt., k. in a., 9/11/17 (1/Herts Regt.).
Gaulter, Cuthbert Vivian, Lt., k. in a., 7/5/17 (5/K.O.R. Lanc. Regt.).
Gibson, John, 2/Lt., k. in a., 19/6/16 (7/Devon Regt.).
Gilbert, John Driffield, Lt., k. in a., 18/10/17 (Sussex Yeo.).
Gillespie, Gordon Wood, 2/Lt., k. in a., 13/4/17 (9/Middlx. Regt.).
Glendinning, James Graham, 2/Lt., d. of w., 16/12/17 (3/Mon. Regt.) (in Ger. hands).
Golding, Edgar, Lt., k. in a., 19/9/17 (R.A.S.C.).
Goodison, Frank Bowler, Lt., d. of w., 26/5/17 (5/S. Staffs Regt.).
Gordon, Douglas, Lt., k. in a., 14/8/17 (7/Arg. & Suth. Highrs.).
Gordon, George Strachan, 2/Lt., k. in a., 19/8/17 (7/Scots Rfls.).
Guy, Christopher Godfrey, Capt., d. of w., 12/8/17 (4/Northants Regt.) (in Ger. hands).
Hall, David Sidney, M.C., Capt., k. in a., 20/11/17 (9/Arg. & Suth. Highrs.).
Hampson, Harold Norman, 2/Lt., d. of w., 8/4/17 (4/S. Lanc. Regt.).
Hampton, George William Betts, 2/Lt., k. in a., 11/3/17 (4/Suffolk Regt.).
Hardy, Alan Herbert, 2/Lt., killed, 14/10/15 (R.E. Kent Yeo.).
Hargreaves, Norman, Lt., k. in a., 23/11/16 (4/E. Lanc. Regt.).
Harley, Frederick William, 2/Lt., k. in a., 3/6/17 (7/R. Highrs.).
Herman, R. D., 2/Lt., died, 22/9/16 (5/S. Lanc. Regt.) (in Ger. hands).
Harvey, William Anthony, Lt., died, 7/11/17 (4/Norfolk Regt.).
Hatch, George John, Lt., k. in a., 6/4/17 (17/Lon. Regt.).
Hay, Donald Yalden, Lt., k. in a., 11/8/17 (5/R.W. Kent
Holaway, Charles Edmund, 2/Lt., k. in a., 11/8/17 (Cheshire Yeo.).
Holt, William Parkinson, Capt., k. in a., 24/6/17 (R.A.S.C.).
Homersham, Arthur Jones, Lt., k. in a., 18/2/18 (25/Lon. Regt.).
Honer, Douglas James, Lt., died, 4/6/17 (R.F.A.).
Hood, John, Lt., k. in a., 18/8/17 (8/Arg. & Suth. Highrs.).
Hope, Humphrey Brian Thompson, Lt., k. in a., 26/4/17 (4/Northants Regt.).
Horne, Herbert George McMillan, 2/Lt., k. in a., 13/4/17 (19/Lon. Regt.).
Horner, Karl Christian, 2/Lt., d. of w., 4/4/17 (8/W. Yorks Regt.).
Howard, James Kelvey, Lt., k. in a., 11/2/17 (5/Notts & Derby Regt.).
Hoyles, Arthur Harry Child, 2/Lt., died, 2/12/17 (5/High'd L.I.).
Hutchinson, Ambrose, Lt., k. in a., 19/1/18 (6/K. L'pool Regt.).
Hutton, William Wallace, 2/Lt., k. in a., 28/10/17 (7/Lon. Regt.).
Inglis, William Logan, 2/Lt., k. in a., 2/10/17 (4/R. Scots Fus.).
Jack, Robert Lawrence Munro, 2/Lt., d. of w., 27/2/17 (5/Gordon Hrs.).
Jackson, George William, 2/Lt., k. in a., 7/5/17 (7/North'd Fus.).
James, Burnet George, Lt., k. in a., 26/9/15 (R.F.A.).
Jarvis, Alan Bishop, Capt., k. in a., 10/8/17 (10/Middlx. Regt.).
Jenkins, Arthur Lewis, Lt., killed, 31/12/17 (4/D.C.L.I.).
Jenkins, David Roy, Capt., killed, 21/1/17 (R.F.A.).
Johnson, Derrick Sivewright, 2/Lt., k. in a., 4/12/16 (Home Counties Div'l. Cyclists).
Johnston, Thomas Peacock, Lt., k. in a., 20/5/17 (Shrops. Yeo.).
Kearley, Harold, 2/Lt., k. in a., 3/2/18 (15/Lon. Regt.).
Kebblewhite, Fred Edgar, 2/Lt., k. in a., 14/8/17 (8/Notts & Derby Regt.).
Kember, Walter, 2/Lt., k. in a., 1/9/17 (7/Lancs Fus.).
Kirk, Percival Gordon, Capt., k. in a., 13/8/17 (Camb. Regt.).
Kirkup, Philip Austin, M.C., T/Major, killed, 11/4/17 (7th Durham L.I.).
Knight, Osbert Richmond, Lt., k. in a., 6/4/17 (4/R.W. Surrey Regt.).
Knox, John Vesey, Lt., killed, 4/1/18 (18/Lon. Regt.).
Laird, Andrew Clark, 2/Lt., k. in a., 22/11/16 (5/R. Highrs.).
Langrishe, Hercules R., Lt., killed, 16/2/17 (Montgomery Yeo.).
Lansdale, Ernest Conway, Lt., died, 30/9/16 (R.A.S.C.) (in Ger. hands).
Lawrence, Walter, Capt., killed, 2/1/15 (7/Essex Regt.).

Lee, Richard Henry Driffield, Capt., killed, 23/6/17 (6/Norfolk Regt.).
Leete, Sydney John, 2/Lt., k. in a., 28/7/17 (8/Worc. Regt.).
Leggatt, Matthew, 2/Lt., k. in a., 26/3/18 (5/Lancs Fusrs.).
Lennox, Alexandra Dick, 2/Lt., k. in a., 18/10/17 (5/R. Scots Fus.).
Lewis, Edmund Llewellyn, 2/Lt., k. in a., 26/12/16 (7/Essex Regt.).
Ley, Christopher Francis Aden, Capt., killed, 16/3/18 (S. Notts Hus.).
Liardet, F. C. E., Lt., d. of w., 13/12/17 (5/Devon Regt.).
Lidsey, William John, 2/Lt., d. of w., 22/3/17 (4/Ox. & Bucks L. Inf.).
Lindley, Ernest William, 2/Lt., died, 18/2/17 (9/Manch. Regt.) (in Ger. hands).
Livock, Eric Stuart, Lt., k. in a., 8/11/17 (4/R.W. Surrey Regt.).
Lockhart, George Barclay, Capt., k. in a., 14/4/17 (High. Cyc. Bn.).
Long, Alfred Pocock, Lt., killed, 23/3/17 (7/Middlx. Regt.).
Loyd, Alwyne Travers, Capt., k. in a., 28/9/17 (5/E. Kent Regt.).
Lucas, Lord Aberon Thomas, Capt., k. in a., 3/11/16 (Hants Yeo.).
Lucas, Keith, Capt., killed, 5/10/16.
Macandrew, Colin Geen Orr, 2/Lt., k. in a., 2/10/17 (Ayr. Yeo.).
McArthur, Lawrence William, Capt., k. in a., 27/5/17 (H.A.C.).
McCash, John Watson, Lt., k. in a., 22/11/16 (6/R. Highrs.).
McCutcheon, Hugh Edward, 2/Lt., k. in a., 3/9/16 (7/Worc. Regt.).
McDonald, Kenneth William, Lt., d. of w., 4/9/17 (R.E.) (in Ger. hands).
Mackay, Hamish Strathy, Lt., k. in a., 9/9/16 (R.G.A.).
Mackay, Harry William Mackintosh, Lt., k. in a., 6/3/18 6/Gordon Hrs.).
McLeay, Duncan Matheson, 2/Lt., k. in a., 23/3/17 (6/Arg. & Suth. Hrs.).
McMaking, Oscar Lennox, 2/Lt., k. in a., 11/9/17 (Lincs Yeo.).
McMurray, Stuart, 2/Lt., k. in a., 7/8/17 (2/Lon. Regt.).
MacNicol, Douglas Oswald, Lt., k. in a., 5/1/18 (4/R.W. Kent Regt.)
MacNiven, Alister Orr, Lt., k. in a., 5/9/17 (7/H.L. Inf.).
MacQueen, Alexander Norman, 2/Lt., k. in a., 25/3/17 (6/Gord. Hrs.).
MacRae, Charles Eric, 2/Lt., k. in a., 10/11/16 (4/Seaforth Highrs.).
Malcomson, Thomas Stuart, Capt., k. in a., 10/12/17 (R.F.A.).
Manfield, Neville Phillip, Lt., k. in a., 9/9/16 (4th Northants).
Margerison, Thomas, 2/Lt., k. in a., 13/4/17 (Hunts Cyc.).
Margoliouth, Alfred Henry, 2/Lt., k. in a., 2/4/17 (5th K.O. Yorks L.I.).
Marnham, Hugh Cecil, 2/Lt., k. in a., 22/8/16 (Sussex Yeo.).
Marshall, Harold Sanders, 2/Lt., killed, 31/1/18 (6th N. Staffs).
Marshall, John Arthur, Lt., k. in a., 6/4/17 (Hunts Cyc.).
Martin, Robert, Lt., k. in a., 4/9/17 (Scot. Horse).
Messervy, Ernest Dyce, Capt., k. in a., 20/7/17 (21st Lond. Regt.).
Miers, Richard Henry Probyn, Capt., killed, 12/12/17 (Glam. Yeo.).
Miller, Walter Douglas, 2/Lt., k. in a., 2/10/16 (R.G.A.).
Mills, Robert Nicholas Fenwick, Capt., k. in a., 21/9/17 (A.S.C.).
Monk, Ernest William, Capt., k. in a., 29/3/18 (4th Lond. Regt.).
Montague, Paul Denys, Lt., k. in a., 29/10/17 (20th Rifle Bde.).
Moore, Lionel William Bentinck, Lt., k. in a., 30/1/18 (R.F.A.).
Morgan, Vernon Leslie, 2/Lt., k. in a., 21/9/16 (4th E. Kents).
Morse, Gerald Ernest, 2/Lt., killed, 31/10/17 (4th R. Welsh Fus.).
Morris, George Tod, Lt., k. in a., 11/4/17 (R.F.A.).
Muller, John Herman, Lt., k. in a., 31/10/17 (9th Middx.).
Murray, Percival William, Lt., d. of w., 2/2/17 (in German hands) (6th Dur. L.I.).
Mountford, Gordon, Capt., k. in a., 12/6/17 (5th N. Staffs Regt.).
Neale, John Everard Digby, Capt., killed, 23/8/17 (4th Leics. R.)
Nelson, Graham, Lt., killed, 30/8/17 (5th Scot. Rfs.).
New, Hedley Bruce, Lt., k. in a., 31/10/17 (4th Essex R.).
Newton, Murray Edell, Lt., k. in a., 18/6/17 (17th Lond. R.).
Nickalls, Hugh Quihampton, Lt., k. in a., 29/7/17 (1st R. Devon Yeo.).
Nisbet, Frederic William, 2/Lt., k. in a., 14/2/17 (Yorks Drag.).
Noon, Gilbert, 2/Lt., k. in a., 29/11/17 (6th Notts & Derby Regt.).
O'Beirne, Arthur James Lewis, 2/Lt., d. of w., 28/7/17 (Oxford Yeo.).
O'Sullivan, Fergus, 2/Lt., k. in a., 23/4/17 (6th N. Staffs).
Patch, Henry, Capt., d. of w., 19/10/17 (4th S. Lancs) (in German hands).
Paton, Malcolm David Rutten, 2/Lt., d. of w., 12/6/17 (22nd Lond. R.).
Pearson, Cecil William, Lt., k. in a., 3/1/18 (4th North'd Fus.).
Peden, Josef Kormendy Von Ikreny, Lt., k. in a., 28/3/18 (R F.A.).

Pettigrew, Gilbert Thomas Richardson, Lt., killed, 12/9/17 (Hereford Regt.).
Phillips, Benjamin Wynford, Lt., killed, 14/11/17 (R.G.A.).
Pickering, Charles Leigh, Lt., k. in a., 15/4/17 (6th Ches. Regt.).
Pitman, Arthur Frederick Edward, Capt., k. in a., 3/1/18 (5th Seaforths).
Pizey, Noel Martin, Lt., d. of w., 27/7/17 (N. Devon Yeo.).
Pollard, George Herbert, 2/Lt., d. of w., 7/6/17 (in German hands) (9th Arg. & Sth. Highrs.).
Porkess, Walter Henderson, Lt., k. in a., 10/2/17 (Notts Yeo.).
Potts, William Janson, M.C., Lt., k. in a., 21/9/17 (R.F.A.).
Preston, Thomas Frederick, Lt., k. in a., 24/1/17 (Norfolk Yeo.).
Prestwich, Joseph, Lt., d. of w., 7/2/16 (A.S.C.).
Prior, Leslie Percy, Capt., d. of w., 7/6/17 (10th Lond. Regt.).
Pullen, Charles Tease, Lt., k. in a., 4/9/17 (R.G.A.).
Purgold, Louis Joseph, Lt., killed, 20/8/17 (R.F.A.).
Raper, Sydney Ernest, 2/Lt., k. in a., 17/8/17 (6th Seaforth Highrs.).
Read, Harry Esmond, Capt., k. in a., 10/8/17 (Lincoln Yeo.).
Reeder, Robert, Capt., k. in a., 6/1/18 (10th Manch. Regt.).
Reed-Harding, Clarence Henry, Lt., killed, 15/2/18 (5th Som. L.I.).
Rentoul, Alexander, Lt., k. in a., 27/3/18 (Yorks Huss.).
Richardson, Douglas Birch, Capt., k. in a., 29/7/16 (R.E.).
Richardson, John Lowick, 2/Lt., k. in a., 21/8/17 (4th Gloucs.).
Richardson, Robert Harold, 2/Lt., k. in a., 6/11/17 (18th Lond. R.).
Robertson, James Leslie, 2/Lt, k. in a., 6/9/16 (4th Yorks Rgt.).
Robertson, John Ross, Lt., k. in a., 13/5/17 (Fife & Forfar Yeo.).
Robertson, Norman McLeod, Lt., k. in a., 17/10/16 (R.F.A.).
Robertson, Ralph 2/Lt., killed, 11/5/17 (8th Hamps. R.).
Rooper, William Victor Trever, Capt., k. in a., 9/10/17 (Denbigh Yeo.).
Roxburgh, Alan Cameron, Lt., d. of w., 28/11/17 (Notts Yeo.).
Russell, Patrick Alfred, 2/Lt., k. in a., 2/4/17 (Lovats Scts.)
Russell, Peter Currie Stuart, Lt., d. of w., 19/12/15 (5th Scots Rfs.)
Ryder, William Harold, Lt., k. in a., 6/7/17 (Yorks Huss.).
Sadler, Ferrebee, 2/Lt., k. in a., 21/4/17 (9th Dur. L.I.).
Saidler, William Tweeddale, Lt., k. in a., 26/3/18 (R.G.A.).
Saint, William Bell, Lt., d. of w., 15/9/16 (10th R. Scots).
Salvesen, Cristian Raymond, Lt, died. 22/5/15 (7th R. Scots).
Saunders, Reginald Arthur, Lt., k. in a., 14/3/16 (R.F.A.).
Sewell, William Allan, Lt., k. in a., 12/11/17 (4th Border R.).
Shackell, Frank Charles, Lt., k. in a., 23/5/17 (A.C.C.).
Shimmin, Thomas Edward, 2/Lt., killed, 22/4/17 (North'd Div. Cyc.).
Shirley, Archibald Vincent, 2/Lt, k. in a., 8/6/17 (Welsh Horse).
Shorter, William John, Lt, k. in a., 24/3/18 (8th Essex R.).
Sinclair, Donald, 2/Lt., d. of w., 18/12/17 (7th H.L.I.).
Skinner, Alfred, Capt., k. in a., 31/8/16 (4th S. Lancs).
Smith, Arthur Leslie, Lt., killed, 22/8/17 (4th Sea. High.).
Smith, James Bonner, 2/Lt., k. in a., 15/8/17 (6th R. High.).
Smith, Leonard Hale Lt., killed, 3/11/17 (6th Essex Rgt.).
Sotham, Ralph Clifford, Lt., k. in a., 9/1/18 (5th R.W. Kent R.).
Southin, Charles Alec, M.C., 2/Lt., killed, 15/2/18 (21st Lond.).
Speer, Alfred Henry, Lt., k. in a., 9/7/16 (R.F.A.).
Spencer, James Michael Jeslyn, Lt., k. in a., 3/11/16 (4th North'd Fus.).
Stacey, John Harold, 2/Lt., k. in a., 4/12/17 (5th E. Surr. Rgt.).
Stalker, Robert Macallan, Lt., k. in a., 8/9/15 (5th Sea. Hrs.).
Staniforth, William Moorwood, 2/Lt., killed, 23/3/17 (Yorks Drag.)
Stead, John Kenneth, Capt., d. of w., 4/2/17 (4th Yorks Regt.).
Stevens, Donald Eustace, Lt., k. in a., 13/3/18 (5th Manch. Regt.).
Stewart, John Charles Miller, 2/Lt., k. in a., 3/7/16 (7th W. Yorks).
Stewart, Nathaniel William, Lt., k. in a., 23/1/17 (7th R. Scots).
Stewart, Vernon Forster, 2/Lt., k. in a., 13/5/17 (8th Dur. L.I.).
Stout, George Ronald Yorston, 2/Lt., k. in a., 30/4/17 (8th Arg. & Sth. Hlrs.).
Stross, David, 2/Lt., died, 12/3/17 (R.F.A.).
Stroud, Henry Clifford, Capt., killed 7/3/18 (R.E.).
Tallentire, Arthur Tom, 2/Lt., killed, 20/10/15 (28th Lond. Regt.).
Tapp, Harold Donesthorpe, Lt., d. of w., 25/1/17 (R.E.) (in Ger. hands).
Tayler, John Edgar, 2/Lt., killed, 1/2/17 (R.E.).
Taylor, John Yates, 2/Lt., k. in a., 6/7/17 (4th E. Lancs).
Tetlow, Cyril Lawson, Lt., k. in a., 22/8/16 (A.S.C.).
Thomas, Frank William Henry, M.C., Lt., d. of w., 5/1/18 (Staff. Yeo.).
Thomas, James Leonard, Capt., killed, 28/2/17 (3rd Lond. Regt.).
Thompson, William George, Lt., k. in a., 14/7/17 (5th Suffolk Regt.).
Thomson, Thomas, Lt., k. in a., 24/4/17 (7 Arg. & Suth. High.).
Thorburn, James, Capt., k. in a., 11/2/17 (R.G.A.).
Thorndike, Francis Herbert, Lt., d. of w., 17/8/17 (Linc. Yeo.).

Thorp, Frederick Horace, 2/Lt., d. of w., 31/3/18 (10th Manch. Regt.).
Tillard, Thomas Atkinson, Lt., k. in a., 6/12/16 (Norfolk Yeo.).
Tillett, Reginald Alfred William, 2/Lt., k. in a., 24/3/17 (Gloucs. Hus.).
Tillie, Arnold Reid, Capt., k. in a., 11/5/16 (8th Scot. Rfs.).
Tipping, Frank Blamphin, Lt., k. in a., 19/8/17 (R.G.A.).
Tipton, Richard James, Capt., d. of w., 12/3/18 (R.F.A.).
Titchener, Leonard Raymond, Lt., k. in a., 3/12/17 (5th R. Lancs Regt.).
Tootell, Bernard, 2/Lt., k. in a., 23/6/17 (7th Notts & Derby).
Townsend, Arthur Eric, 2/Lt., k. in a., 15/2/17 (5th Dur. L.I.).
Tozer, Harold Percy, 2/Lt., killed, 16/12/16 (9th D.L.I.).
Trollope, Cyril Harvey, 2/Lt., killed, 4/5/17 (14th Lond. Regt.).
Troup, John Guthrie, 2/Lt., k. in a., 13/5/17 (5th Scot. Rfs.).
Truscott, Francis George, M.C., Lt., d. of w., 6/4/17 (6th Suff. R.).
Turnbull, David Stevens, Lt., killed, 15/4/17 (6th R. High.).
Tyrer, John Rawsthorne, 2/Lt., k. in a., 8/10/17 (7th Manch. R.).
Tyzack, Eric Delaney, 2/Lt., k. in a., 15/9/17 (R. Eng.).
Urquhart, Alesander, 2/Lt., k. in a., 17/8/17 (9th High. L.I.).
Vane-Tempest, Charles Stewart, Lt., d. of w., 25/3/17 (5th Durh. L.I.) (in German hands).
Vaughan, Francis Seymour, Lt., killed, 17/3/18 (5th R.W. Kent R.).
Vaughan-Jones, Gerald, Lt, k. in a., 26/2/17 (R. Engineers).
Wakeman, Frank Trevor, Lt., k. in a., 30/10/17 (5th R. War. R.).
Walsh, Albert, 2/Lt., d. of w., 8/8/17 (5th E. Lancs).
Ward, Edward Arthur Hunter, Lt., k. in a., 11/8/17 (6th W. Yorks).
Waters, Eric Gordon, 2/Lt., k. in a., 24/1/17 (Hamps. Yeo.).
Watt, James, 2/Lt., killed, 2/5/17 (4th R. Scots).
Wedderspoon, John Henry Butcher, Lt., k. in a., 6/4/17 (R.F.A.).
Wedgwood, William Armstrong, 2/Lt., k. in a., 9/7/16 (R.E.).
Welch, Hugh, Lt., k. in a., 28/3/17 (R.F.A.).
Wells, Henry Maurice Watkins, Lt., k. in a., 15/9/16 (4th R. Berks).
Wells, William Lewis, Capt, d. of w., 6/5/18 (8th Middx. R.).
West, Theodore, 2/Lt., k. in a., 24/9/16 (R.E.).
White, Harold Tom, 2/Lt., killed, 27/2/17 (R.E.).
White, John Gardner, Lt., k. in a., 26/8/17 (5th Scot. Rfs.).
White, Spencer John Meadows, Capt., k. in a., 15/1/17 (4th Norfolk Regt.).
Whitehead, Alfred Gordon, Lt., k. in a., 29/1/18 (6th W. Yorks Regt.).
Whiteman, Harold Ernest, 2/Lt., killed, 23/10/16 (8th Hants Regt.).
Wilkinson, Eyre Spencer, Lt., k. in a., 12/1/16 (1st Lond. Regt.).
Williams, Norman Ernest, 2/Lt., k. in a., 9/11/17 (10th Lond. Regt.).
Williamson, Charles Harry, M.C., Capt., k. in a., 27/3/17 (7th Manch. Regt.).
Williamson, John Alexander, Lt., killed, 10/4/17 (R. East Kent. Yeo.).
Wilson, Gordon Ivor, 2/Lt., killed, 12/2/17 (Yorks Drag. Yeo.).
Wilson, John Cooper, 2/Lt., k. in a., 17/10/16 (4th R. Hrs.).
Wilson, John Robert, Capt., k. in a., 20/10/17 (R.E.).
Wilson, Marshall Meredith, Lt., killed, 29/1/18 (4th Border Regt.).
Winnicott, Russall, M.C., 2/Lt., k. in a., 6/12/17 (5th Devon Regt.).
Wood, Maurice Herbert, Lt., k. in a., 13/4/17 (4th Lincoln Regt.).
Wood, Philip John, 2/Lt., k. in a., 25/5/17 (4th R. W. Sur.).
Wood, Walter Bertram, M.C., Lt., killed, 11/11/17 (8th Hamps. Regt.).
Wordsworth, Joseph Charles Ditch, 2/Lt., k. in a., 6/4/17 (8th Dur. L.I.).
Wylde, Thomas Edgar, Lt., d. of w., 27/6/17 (4th Norfolk R.).
Young, James Hill, 2/Lt., d. of w., 17/1/18 (14th Lond. Rgt.) (in Ger. hands).

1st Life Guards.

Cavendish, Lord John Spencer, D.S.O., Major, k. in a., 20/10/14.
Closebrooks, John Charles, Lt., k. in a., 30/10/14.
Collins, Frederick William, 2/Lt. (Tp.), died, 29/4/16.
Cook, Edwin Berkeley, M.V.O., Lt.-Col., d. of w., 4/11/14.
Emmet, Robert, 2/Lt., died, 30/10/15.
Fellowes, Hon. Coulson Churchill, Capt., died, 22/10/15.
Grosvenor, Lord, Hugh Williams, Capt., k. in a., 25/10/14.
Hulton-Harrop, Hugh de Lacey, Lt., k. in a., 12/5/15 (Res. of Off.).
Kelly, Edward Denis Festus, Capt., k. in a., 30/10/14.
Levinge, Sir Richard William, Bart, Lt., k. in a., 24/10/14 (Res. of Off., att.).
Portal, Oldric Spencer, Lt. (T/Capt.), k. in a., 3/5/17 (att. Household Btn.).
St. George, Harold Avenel Blight, 2/Lt., k. in a., 15/11/15.
Smith, Algernon Lindsay Eric, Lt., k. in a., 31/11/14.
Sutton, Sir Richard Vincent, Bart., M.C., Capt., died, 29/11/18 (att. Gds. M.G. Bn.).
Trafford, Geoffrey Thomas, Lt., k. in a., 23/7/18 (att. 9th Tank Bn.).
Ward, Hon. Gerald Ernest Francis, M.V.O., Capt., k. in a., 30/11/14.
Wyndham, Hon. William Reginald, Lt., k. in a., 6/11/14.

2nd Life Guards.

Barran, Roland Noel, Lt., died, 19/3/19.
Blofield, Frank d'Arcy, 2/Lt., k. in a., 13/5/15.
Butler, Edmund William, M.C., T/Lt. (T/Major), d. of w., 18/4/18 (att. 8th Glouc. Regt.).
Dawney, Hon. Hugh, D.S.O., Major, k. in a., 6/11/14.
Duff, Sir Robert George Vivian, Bart., Lt., k. in a., 16/10/14 (Res. of Off.).
Ferguson, Victor John, Lt., k. in a., 21/8/18 (att. 2nd Gds. M.G. Rgt.).
Gale, Arthur Witherby, D.S.O., Capt. (Tp.), k. in a., 10/4/16 (Res. of Off.) (att. R.F.A.).
Gunther, Charles Emil, Lt. (Tp.), k. in a., 24/9/18 (att. Gds. M.G. Regt.).
Hobson, Alwyne Chadwick, Lt., k. in a., 13/5/15.
Lovell, John Anthony, 2/Lt. (Tp.), k. in a., 22/1/16.
Murray-Smith, Arthur George, Lt., d. of w., 2/11/14.
O'Neill, Hon. Arthur Edward Bruce, Capt., k. in a., 6/11/14.
Pemberton, Francis Percy Campbell, Capt., k. in a., 19/10/14.
Torrie, Thomas, George Jameson, Lt.-Col. (Tp.), k. in a., 18/11/16 (att. 7th E. Lancs).
Townsend, Sidney John, 2/Lt., k. in a., 13/5/15.
Vandeleur, Alexander Moore, Capt., k. in a., 30/10/14.

Royal Horse Guards. (The Blues.)

Binning, George, Lord, Bdr.-Gen., died, 12/1/17 (1st Mtd. Bde.).
Bowlby, Geoffrey Vaux Salvin, Capt., k. in a., 13/5/15.
Brassey, Harold Ernest, Lt.-Col. (Tp.), k. in a., 15/7/16 (att. 8th Sth. Lancs Regt.).
Breese, W. Laurence, 2/Lt., killed. 14/3/15.
Compton, Lord Spencer Douglas, Lt., k. in a., 13/5/15.
Crichton, Henry William, Viscount, M.V.O., D.S.O., Major, k. in a., 31/10/14.
Davson, Thomas Gordon, Lt., k. in a., 13/5/15.
Hanbury-Tracy, Hon. Algernon Henry Charles, C.M.G., Major (Tp.). died, 3/12/15.
Heath, Percy Voltelin, Lt., d. of w., 1/9/15.
Hughes, Guy Ferguson, Lt., died, 21/12/15 (H.P. Indian Army (Emp. Cyc. Co., Gds. Div.), att. R.H.G.).
Ingestre, Charles John Alton Chetwynd, Viscount, M.V.O., Capt., died, 8/1/15.
Lambton, Hon. Francis, 2/Lt., k. in a., 25/10/15.
Mackintosh, Angus Alexander, Capt., died, 14/10/18.
Naylor-Leyland, George Vyvyan, Lt., d. of w., 21/9/14.
Phillips, Hon. Colwyn Erasmus Arnold, Capt. (Tp.), k. in a., 13/5/15.
Pullen, Guy Harper, 2/Lt., k. in a., 13/5/15.
Sale, Richard Lander, Lt. (Tp.), d. of w., 15/1/18.
Tilney, Leonard Arthur, M.C., Major, k. in a., 9/3/18 (att. R.F.C.).
Wendover, Albert Edward Charles Robert, Viscount, Lt., d. of w., 19/5/15.
Wilson, Gordon Chesney, M.V.O., Lt.-Col., k. in a., 6/11/14.
Wilson, Herbert Hayden, D.S.O., Capt. (Tp.), k. in a., 11/4/17
Worsley, Charles Sackville, Lord, Capt., k. in a., 30/10/14.

Household Battalion.

Beachcroft, Cyril Shakespear, Lt. (Tp.), k. in a., 12/10/17.
Bird, John Woodall, 2/Lt. (Tp.), k. in a., 21/12/17.
Boddington, Cecil, Herbert, Capt. (Tp.), k. in a., 11/4/17.
Bolitho, Victor Ayling, 2/Lt. (Tp.), d. of w., 9/4/17.
Bonham-Carter, Norman, 2/Lt. (Tp.), k. in a., 3/5/17.
Bower, Thomas Geoffrey, 2/Lt. (Tp.), k. in a., 3/5/17.
Bridgeman, Humphrey Herbert Orlando, Lt., k. in a., 11/5/17.
Godfrey, Arthur Pole, Lt. (Tp.), k. in a., 11/4/17.
Lowrie, John Edward, 2/Lt. (Tp.), k. in a., 18/6/17.
Pember, Henry Cecil, Capt. (Tp.), k. in a., 3/5/17.
Rice, Cecil, Vincent, 2/Lt., k. in a., 11/5/17.
Scott, Leslie, Lt. (Tp.), k. in a., 12/10/17.
Stockwood, Lawrence Francis, 2/Lt. (Tp.), d. of w., 12/10/17.
Tyrwhitt-Drake, D'urban John, 2/Lt., k. in a., 3/5/17.
Wakefield, Oliver, 2/Lt. (Tp.), k. in a., 12/10/17.
Wanklyn, William Hibbert, 2/Lt. (Tp.), k. in a., 11/5/17.
Whitelaw, Geoffrey Lacy, 2/Lt. (Tp.), died, 14/4/18.
Whitelaw, Robert Hilary Lockart, 2/Lt. (Tp.), d. of w., 28/5/17.
Williams, Stuart Duncan, 2/Lt., k. in a., 3/5/17.

1st (King's) Dragoon Guards.

Cheape, Leslie St. Clair, Capt., k. in a., 23/4/16 (Adj. Worces. Yeo.).
Denny, Leon Serena, Capt., k. in a., 13/5/15 (Res. of Off.).
Hawkins, Lionel Hope, Lt., k. in a., 31/10/14.
Renton, William Gerald Forrester, Capt., k. in a., 2/6/15 (att. 2nd D.G.).
Ward, Reginald Ibotson, Lt., d. of w., 26/5/19.
White, Lynton Woolmer, Lt., d. of w., 10/9/14 (att. 2nd D.G.).

2nd Dragoon Guards (Queen's Bays).

Barclay, David Frederick, Lt., k. in a., 1/4/18.
Biddulph, Robert Assheton, 2/Lt., died, 19/11/16.
Browning, James Alexander, Major, k. in a., 31/10/14.
Champion de Crespigny, Claude Norman, Lt., k. in a., 1/9/14.
Chance, Edward Seton, Capt. (Bt.-Major), k. in a., 29/5/18 (att. 6th Leics. Regt.).

Etherington, Herbert Field, 2/Lt., d. of w., 8/1/16.
Gray, Maurice, Lt. (A/Capt.), k. in a., 8/8/18 (M.G.C.).
Herron, Cyril Douglas, 2/Lt., k. in a., 13/5/15.
McGrath, Noel George Scott, Lt., d. of w., 5/11/14.
Paul, Gavin, 2/Lt., k. in a., 30/10/14.
Pinching, Minden Charles Cardigan, D.S.O., Major, died, 20/4/17.
Single, Frederick Alexander, M.C., Capt., d. of w., 30/3/18.
Springfield, George Patrick Osborn, Capt., k. in a., 12/9/14.
Waddell, David Bruce, 2/Lt., k. in a., 21/3/18.
Yeatherd, Raymond Gilbert Hooker, Lt., k. in a., 15/9/16.

3rd (Prince of Wales's) Dragoon Guards.

Brown, Valentine Oakley, Lt., k. in a., 9/10/18.
Chapman, Edward Wynne, Lt., d. of w., 17/11/14.
Chibnall, George William Russell, 2/Lt. (T./Lt.), k. in a., 26/8/18 (att. 9th W. Riding R.).
Cliff, Grosvenor Talbot, Major, died, 10/2/18.
Clifford, Anthony Clifford, 2/Lt., k. in a., 2/6/15 (Res. of Off.).
Coles, Edgar Ralph, Capt., k. in a., 12/5/15.
Dulson, Matthew Harvey, 2/Lt., k. in a., 11/4/17.
Hodgkinson, John Francis, Capt., d. of w., 10/11/14.
Holroyd-Smyth, Charles Edward Ridley, D.S.O., M.C., Capt. (T/Lt.-Col.), d. of w., 23/9/18 (att. 15th Dur. L.I.).
Katinakis, Francis Beresford, M.C., Lt., d. of w., 27/3/18.
Kent, Percival Naylor, Major (A/Lt.-Col.), died, 8/4/18.
King, Norman Toynbee, Lt., k. in a., 22/3/18.
Mason, Philip Granville, D.S.O., Major, k. in a., 26/9/15.
Neville, Thomas Villiers Tuthill Thacker, Capt., k. in a., 13/5/15.
Newton-Deakin, Charles Humphrey, Lt., k. in a., 11/4/17.
Sabler, Gerald Gloag, Capt., died, 1/11/14.
Smith, Charles Theodore, 2/Lt., d. of w., 22/5/15.
Stork, William Henry, 2/Lt., d. of w., 11/1/18.
Talbot, Humphrey Richard, Lt., d. of w., 13/11/14.
Wright, Edwin, Capt., k. in a., 17/11/14.

4th (Royal Irish) Dragoon Guards.

Boosey, Rupert George, 2/Lt., k. in a., 22/5/15.
Elmslie, Kenward Wallace, Lt., k. in a., 4/11/14.
Delmege, James O'Grady, 2/Lt. (T/Lt.), died, 27/5/15.
Fitzgerald, Gerald Hugh, Capt., k. in a., 13/9/14.
Gordon-Kidd, Arthur Lionel, D.S.O., Lt. (T/Cpt.), d. of w., 27/8/17 (att. R.F.C.).
Green, Harold Stewart, D.C.M., 2/Lt., k. in a., 4/4/18.
Greenhill, Thomas Watson, Lt., k. in a., 11/2/16.
Holman, John, Lt., d. of w., 29/10/14.
Herron, Walter Fitzroy, Lt. (Tp.), died, 3/4/16.
Oldrey, Robert John Blatchford, Capt., k. in a., 29/10/14.
Powell, Harold Osborne, 2/Lt., k. in a., 31/10/14.
Ramsay, Norman, Lt., d. of w., 3/11/14 (att. Res. of Off.).
Warter, Henry De Grey, Capt., k. in a., 20/11/17.
Wyllie, Hugh Tweed Walford, Capt., k. in a., 24/5/15.

5th (Princess Charlotte of Wales) Dragoon Guards.

Ansell, George Kirkpatrick, Lt.-Col., k. in a., 1/9/14.
Black, Maurice Adam, Major, k. in a., 11/2/17 (& R.F.C.).
Blackburne, Charles Harold, D.S.O., Capt. and Bt.-Lt.-Col., drowned, 10/10/18.
Crawshay, Mervyn, Capt., k. in a., 31/10/14.
Denny, Leon Serena, Capt., k. in a., 13/5/15.
Isham, John Vere, 2/Lt., died, 3/6/16.
Jordan, James, M.C., Lt., k. in a., 8/8/18.
McGergow, Robert Dudley Wilson, 2/Lt. (T/Lt.), k. in a., 21/9/17 (& R.F.C.).
V.C. Norwood, John, Capt., k. in a., 8/9/14 (R. of Off.).
Oswald, William Digby, D.S.O., Lt. (T/Major), d. of w., 15/7/16 (att. W. York. R.).
Partridge, Robert Charles, Capt., k. in a., 8/9/14.
Patteson, J. D., 2/Lt., k. in a., 13/10/14.
Pooley, Charles, M.C., Lt. (T/Capt.), k. in a., 9/8/18.
Wilson, Cyril Frederick, Lt., k. in a., 13/5/15.

6th Dragoon Guards (Carabiniers).

Anstruther, John Arnold St. C., Lt., k. in a., 26/12/14 (att. 2/Life Gds.).
Bovill, John Eric, 2/Lt., k. in a., 23/1/16.
Gwyer, Alexander Grant, Capt., k. in a., 22/10/14 (R. of Off.).
Harrington, George Christmas, 2/Lt., died, 30/10/17.
Home, Walter Gabriel, Major, d. of w., 13/11/14.
Kidd, John Newman, Capt., k. in a., 19/1/16.
Langford, Claude Charles, 2/Lt., died, 23/2/18.
Lee, Michael Philip Edward, M.C., Lt., k. in a., 26/3/18.
Lemon, Adrian Leigh, Lt., k. in a., 29/11/17 (4 M.G.C.).
Marsh, Douglas Charles Earle, 2/Lt., d. of w., 8/4/18.
Mitchell, Charles Richard Gerald, Lt., k. in a., 1/4/18.
Scaife, Thomas Earle Gordon, 2/Lt., died, 26/9/16 (& R.F.C.).
Watson, William Ernest, D.S.O., Major, k. in a., 31/10/14.

7th (Princess Royal's) Dragoon Guards.

Birkin, Thomas Richard Chetwynd, 2/Lt., k. in a., 12/6/17 (& R.F.C.).
Bryce, Samuel, 2/Lt., k. in a., 21/12/14.
Hartley, D'Arcy John Joseph, Lt., k. in a., 14/7/16 (att. M.G.C.).
Lane, Charles Willington Tremayne, M.C., Capt. (A/Major) d. of w., 4/4/18.
Lempriere, Henry Anderson, D.S.O., Lt.-Col., k. in a., 23/12/14.
Persse, Cecil De Burgh Gordon, 2/Lt., d. of w., 19/7/15 (att. Ir. Gds.).
Pope, Henry William, Capt., k. in a., 24/3/18 (att. 21 M.G. Bn.).
Reid, George Leslie, 2/Lt., k. in a., 1/12/17.
Ross, Lawrence George, 2/Lt., (Tp.), d. of w., 30/5/17.

1st (Royal) Dragoons.

Atkinson, William Henry Jepson St. Leger, Capt., k. in a., 12/5/15.
Browne, Charles Nicholas Foster, 2/Lt., k. in a., 13/5/15.
Burn, Arthur Herbert Rosdew, 2/Lt., k. in a., 29/10/14.
Beit, Theodore Hamilton, 2/Lt., died, 26/1/17.
Chapman, Alister Hillyar Darby, Capt., k. in a., 27/9/15.
Charrington, Arthur Craven, Capt., d. of w., 21/10/14.
Cubitt, Hon. William Hugh, Lt., d. of w., 24/3/18.
Dorington, Thomas Philip, Major, k. in a., 12/11/14.
V.C. Dunville, John Spencer, 2/Lt., d. of w., 25/6/17.
Edwardes, George D'Arcy, Major (Tp.), k. in a., 10/7/16 (att. 13/Welch Regt.).
Grenfell, The Hon. Julian Henry Francis, D.S.O., Capt., d. of w., 26/5/15.
Helme, Robert Barnard, Lt., k. in a., 25/6/17.
Lambert, Henry McLaren, Capt., k. in a., 13/5/15.
Leckie, John Harvey, Lt., k. in a., 13/5/15.
McNeile, Henry Donald, Lt.-Col., killed, 20/12/15.
Nairne, Lord Charles Mercer, M.V.O., Major, k. in a., 30/10/14.
Newcombe, William, T/Lt., k. in a., 3/7/16 (att. 8/Bn. S. Lanc. R.).
Ratcliffe, Frederick, Lt. (A/Capt.), d. of w., 30/3/18 (att. 6/M.G. Sqd.).
Sandbach, Hugh Handley, Capt., k. in a., 4/11/14 (late R. Drag. Gds. and E. African Forces).
Scott, Charles Brough, Lt., d. of w., 20/11/17.
Steele, George Frederick, C.M.G., Lt.-Col., d. of w., 22/5/15.
Tidswell, Cecil Robert, Capt., k. in a., 16/10/16 (& R.F.C.).
Waterhouse, Alfred William, M.C., Capt., k. in a., 12/1/16.

2nd Dragoons (Royal Scots Greys).

Baillie, Sir Gawaine George Stuart, Bart., 2/Lt., k. in a., 7/9/14.
Bowlby, Lionel Henry Salvin, Lt., d. of w., 5/6/16.
Filmer, Vivian Reginald Royal, 2/Lt., k. in a., 25/11/17.
Forster, Alfred Henry, Lt., d. of w., 10/3/19.
Jardine, Ronald James, 2/Lt., killed, 13/9/17 (att. R.F.C.).
Long, Walter, C.M.G., D.S.O., T/Brig.-Gen., k. in a., 28/1/17 (Commdg. 56 Inf. Bde.).
May, Peter Langton, 2/Lt., k. in a., 13/2/16 (Spec. Res.).
Pickering, Francis Alexander Umfreville, D.S.O., Major (T/Lt-Col.), k. in a., 23/12/17 (att. 9/Rif. Bde.).
Swetenham, Foster, Major, k. in a., 26/8/14.
Tennant, Henry, 2/Lt., k. in a., 27/5/17 (att. R.F.C. 52 Sqd.).
Weymouth, John Alevander (Viscount), 2/Lt., k. in a., 13/2/16.

3rd (King's Own) Hussars.

Barr, Samuel Tudor, Lt. (Tp.), k. in a., 23/2/15.
Brooks, Colin Robert Percy, M.C., Lt., d. of w., 2/4/18 (and 4 M.G.C.).
Crabbe, Hubert Lyon Bingham, 2/Lt., k. in a., 15/5/18 (and R.A.F.).
Dilberoglue, Augustus, 2/Lt., k. in a., 1/4/18.
Dobie, James Jardine, D.S.O., M.C., Capt., k. in a., 30/9/18.
Gath, Charles Henry, 2/Lt., k. in a., 30/10/14.
Kettle, Rupert Arthur, Lt., k. in a., 26/3/18.
Leechman, Colin Barclay, Lt., k. in a., 26/9/14.
Sherlock, Gerrard Loundes Edward, Lt., k. in a., 25/8/14 (and Nigerian R. W.A.F.F.).
Soames, Arthur Henry Leslie, Lt., (T/Capt.), died, 7/7/15 (and R.F.C.).
Taylor, Denis Percival Beauchamp, M.C., Lt., died, 14/3/16 (and R.F.C.).

4th (Queen's Own) Hussars.

Bell, Adam Dickson, Major, died, 8/4/18.
Blood, Bindon, Capt., killed, 29/9/15 (and R.F.C.).
Buddicom, Walter Digby, Lt., died, 6/6/18.
Darley, John Evelyn Carmichael, Lt.-Col., k. in a., 31/3/18.
Greville, George Gordon Francis, Lt., d. of w., 31/3/18.
Hogg, Ian Graham, D.S.O., Lt.-Col., d. of w., 2/9/14.
Howell, Philip, C.M.G., T/Brig.-Gen., k. in a., 7/10/16 (Staff).
Levita, Francis Ellison, Lt., k. in a., 12/10/14.
Lonsdale, James Raymond McLlintock, Lt., died, 29/10/14.
Morrison, James William Sutton, M.C., Lt., k. in a., 19/10/18
North, Kenneth Croft., Lt., k. in a., 31/10/14.
Quinlan, Harold Daniel, Lt., k. in a., 26/3/18.
Schuster, Alfred Felix, Lt., k. in a., 30/11/14 (S.R.).
Smith, Fereday Fisher, Lt., k. in a., 28/11/17.
Smith, Henry Thomas Bayard, 2/Lt., k. in a., 25/3/18 (and 9/Tank Corps).
Sowerby, Frank Douglas, 2/Lt., d. of w., 1/8/16 (att. 18/Lanc. Fus.).
Sword, James Hubert, 2/Lt., k. in a., 10/9/14.
Watkin, Henry George, Major, k. in a., 21/8/15 (Staff, 2 Mounted Bde.).

5th (Royal Irish) Lancers.

Blair, Duncan James Nugent, Capt., died, 10/1/17 (Res. of Off.) (att. R.F.A.).
Coulter, William Hugh, Lt., k. in a., 22/2/15.
Fowler, John Dudley, 2/Lt., k. in a., 30/11/14.

Gibson, Gerald Dudley, 2/Lt., d. of w., 16/8/18.
Hunter, Godfrey Jackson, 2/Lt., killed, 26/4/16.
Juler, George Critchett, Lt., k. in a., 31/8/14.
McKisack, Lawrence Hill Wilson, Lt., killed, 13/11/16 (& R.F.C.).
Maddick, Herbert, Capt., d. of w., 28/10/15.
Martin, Edward Nugent Meredyth, 2/Lt., k. in a., 30/9/16 (Res. of Off.) (att. M.G.C.).
Rice, John Arthur Talbot, M.C., Capt., d. of w., 14/4/18 (in German hands).
Robinson, Edwin Winwood, Lt., killed, 25/10/14.
Thackray, William Hesling, 2/Lt., d. of w., 26/3/18.
Wordsworth, John Lionel, Lt., k. in a., 6/11/14.

6th (Inniskilling) Dragoons.

Bridgewater, Clement Joseph Bentley, Capt., k. in a., 1/12/17.
Campbell, John Argentine, Lt. (Tp.), d. of w., 2/12/17.
Carver, Basil Armitage, 2/Lt., k. in a., 21/8/16.
Dunne, Arthur Sydney, Lt., k. in a., 2/7/17.
Herringham, Geoffrey Wilmot, Capt., k. in a., 31/10/14 (att. 5th D.G.).
Magawly Cerati Decalry, Valerio Awby, D.S.O., Capt. (T/Lt.-Col.), k. in a., 10/8/17 (att. 7th Batt. Rifle Bde.).
Simpson, Henry Richard Deighton, Lt. (Tp.), killed, 20/12/16 (& R.F.C.).
Synnott, Walter Pierre, 2/Lt., died, 11/10/18.
Villiers, Henry Lister, 2/Lt., k. in a., 4/2/17 (att. R.F.C., 11th Sqd.).

7th (Queen's Own) Hussars.

Bates, Stanes Geoffry, Capt., k. in a., 13/5/15.
Hallowes, John Chaworth, Lt., A/Capt., k. in a., 28/10/18.
Holland, Vivian Ernest, Capt., d. of w., 8/11/18.
Mason-Macfarlane, Carlyon Will, Capt., k. in a., 5/9/16 (att. 18/Imp. Camel Corps).
Prothero, Rowland John, Lt., d. of w., 8/11/18.

8th (King's Royal Irish) Hussars.

Broadbent, Edgar Richards, M.C., Major, died, 31/10/18.
Clowes, Warren Peter, Lt., k. in a., 30/3/18.
Dudgeon, Frederick Charles, 2/Lt., k. in a., 28/10/18.
Hartley, William Holliday, M.C., Lt., d. of w., 22/3/18.
Jennings, Francis Montgomery, Capt., died, 11/11/18.
Osborne, Marcus Stuart, Lt., k. in a., 24/4/18 (att. 8th Btn. M.G.C.).
Pinfield, Guy Vickery, Lt. (Tp.), killed, 24/4/16.
Ryder, Robert Nathaniel Dudley, Hon. Major, k. in a., 30/11/17.

9th (Queen's Royal) Lancers.

Abadie, Eustace Henry Egremont, D.S.O., Major, k. in a., 30/11/15.
Allfrey, Frederick de Vere Bruce, Lt., k. in a., 6/9/14.
Archdale-Porter, John Grey, D.S.O., Capt. (A/Maj.), d. of w., 22/11/17.
Brooke, Victor Reginald, C.I.E., D.S.O., Major, died, 29/8/14.
Chisenhale-Marsh, Harold Atherton, Capt., k. in a., 28/9/18 (& Staff Div. H.Q.).
Court, William Hubert Roylance, Capt., k. in a., 24/5/15.
Durant, Hugh, 2/Lt., k. in a., 20/1/16.
Edwards, Arthur Noel, Capt., d. of w., 24/5/15
Foster, Charles Finch, Lt., k. in a., 27/3/18.
Garstin, Charles William North, 2/Lt., d. of w., 24/8/14.
V.C. Grenfell, Francis Octavius, Capt., k. in a., 24/5/15.
Harvey, Douglas Lennox, 2/Lt., k. in a., 2/11/14.
Harvey, Frank Lennox, Lt., k. in a., 30/10/14
Hunter, Martin, Lt., d. of w., 11/4/18
Kerr, Henry Grace, 2/Lt., d. of w., 1/7/17.
Kevill-Davies, William Albert Somerset Herbert, Lt., d. of w., 15/5/15.
Lucas-Tooth, Douglas Keith Lucas, D.S.O., Capt., k. in a., 13/9/14.
Stapleton-Bretherton, Osmund Frederick, Lt., k. in a., 22/3/18.
Stephenson, Cyril Seymour, 2/Lt., died, 6/12/16.
Taylor Whitehead, George Edward, 2/Lt., k. in a., 29/9/14.
Wood, Herbert Frederick, Major, died, 11/12/18 (& R.A.F.).

10th (Prince of Wales's Own Royal) Hussars.

Annesley, Hon. Arthur, Capt., k. in a., 15/11/14.
Armstrong, William Maurice, M.C., Capt., k. in a., 23/5/17 (att. 86th Bde. H.Q.).
Cadogan, Hon. William George Sidney, Major, k. in a., 14/11/14.
De Tuyll, Maurice Arthur, Capt., k. in a., 13/5/15.
Dawson-Damer, The Hon. George Seymour, 2/Lt., d. of w., 12/4/17.
Drake, Robert Flint, Lt., k. in a., 17/11/14.
Ferris, Samuel Bernard Clutton, 2/Lt., died, 6/4/15 (att. 11th Res. Cav. R.).
Field, Reginald George, 2/Lt., d. of w., 6/4/18.
Hardwick, Philip Edward, D.S.O., Lt.-Col., d. of w., 9/6/19.
Hughes-Onslow, Arthur, Major, died, 17/8/14 (R. of O.).
Mitford, Hon. Clement Bertram Ogilvy, D.S.O., Major, k. in a., 13/5/15.
Mowatt, Osmond, Lt. (Tp.), d. of w., 22/4/17.
Peto, Clement Henry, Capt., k. in a., 17/11/14.
Rose, Sir Frank Stanley (Bart), Capt., k. in a., 26/1/15.
Shearman, Eustace Robert Ambrose, Lt.-Col., k. in a., 13/5/15.
Stewart, Gerald Charles, Capt., k. in a., 13/5/15
Turnor, Christopher Randolph, Lt., k. in a., 26/10/14.

11th (Prince Albert's Own) Hussars.

Ainsworth, John Stirling, Lt., k. in a., 14/10/14.
Arkwright, Frederick George Alleyne, Capt., killed, 14/10/15.
Bannatyne, James Fitzgerald, Major (Tp.), d. of w., 14/5/16 (att. 23rd Manch. Regt.).
Bell-Irving, William Ogle, M.C., Capt., k. in a., 29/11/17.
Coote, Charles Gartside Eyre, Lt., k. in a., 22/3/18.
De Gunzberg, Baron Alexis George, 2/Lt., k. in a., 6/11/14 (att. R. Horse Gds.).
Gunter, Francis James, Lt., k. in a., 24/5/15.
Halliday, John Alexander, Capt., died, 13/11/14.
Kenrick, Herbert William Mascall, Capt., died, 24/3/19 (Res. of Off.).
Lawson, Arthur Bertram, D.S.O., Bt.-Major (A/Lt.-Col.), k. in a., 24/6/18 (att. 2/5th Gloucs. Regt.).
Lumley, Richard John, 2/Lt., k. in a., 17/10/14.
MacKirdy, Charles David Scott, Lt., d. of w., 22/3/18 (in German hands).
Marshall, George Garth, Lt., k. in a., 4/11/14.
Mills, John Richard, Lt. (Qr.-Mr.), d. of w., 7/5/18.
Paget, Albert Edward, M.V.O., Capt. (Bt.-Lt.-Col.), died, 2/8/17.
Parker, William Lefevre Oxley, Lt., k. in a., 31/10/17 (att. R.F.C. 13th Sq.).
Poole, Hugh Edward Algernon, 2/Lt., d. of w., 2/6/15.
Vansittart, Arthur Bexley, 2/Lt., d. of w., 12/5/15.

12th (Prince of Wales's Royal) Lancers.

Beerbohm, Clarence Evelyn, Lt. (A/Maj.), k. in a., 26/9/17 (att. R.F.A. 162 Bde.).
Brown, George Miller, M.C., Lt., k. in a., 28/11/17.
Crawley, Eustace, Major, k. in a., 2/11/14.
Eden, John, Lt., k. in a., 17/10/14
Gordon, Geoffrey, Lt., k. in a., 30/4/15.
Hammond, Anthony Edgar, 2/Lt., k. in a., 28/11/17.
Lamb, Harold Alfred, 2/Lt., killed, 9/7/18 (and R.A.F.).
Leatham, Edward Hubert, Lt., k. in a., 31/10/14.
Michell, John Collorgan, Capt., k. in a., 28/8/14
Murray, Fanr Wright Stapleton, Capt., k. in a., 30/11/14.
Nicholson, Eric N., Capt., died, 20/6/17.
Palmer, Herbert, Lt., k. in a., 2/10/18.
Wood, Ronald Beaumont, Capt. (A/Lt.-Col.), k. in a., 21/8/18 (att. Tanks).
Wormald, Frank, C.B., Lt.-Col. (T/Brig.-Gen.), k. in a., 3/10/15.
Wroughton, Musgrave Cazenove, 2/Lt., d. of w., 31/10/14.
Yeatherd, Montagu Locke, Capt., k. in a., 11/4/17.

13th Hussars.

Clarkson, John Osborne Price, 2/Lt., k. in a., 10/3/17.
Eve, William Henry, Capt., k. in a., 5/3/17.
Fletcher, Arthur Henry Felix, 2/Lt., killed, 22/5/17 (and R.F.C.).
Hamilton-Grace, Raymond Sheffield, Capt. (Bt.-Major), died, 4/8/15.
Kennard, Willoughby Arthur, D.S.O., Capt., died, 30/10/18.
Lawson-Smith, Thomas Edward, Lt., k. in a., 1/11/14.
Lynch-Staunton, Geoffrey, 2/Lt., k. in a., 5/3/17.
Macdonald, H., M.C., Lt., k. in a., 14/7/19.
Munster, John Francis, Lt., k. in a., 4/2/17.
Newton, Horace Gerard Townsend, Capt., died, 25/4/17.
Neill, Norman, Capt., k. in a., 6/11/14.
Robinson, Stephen Owen, Capt., k. in a., 5/11/17 (att. 5th Drag. Gds.).
Rolfe, Ernest Victor, 2/Lt. (Tp.), k. in a., 5/3/17.
Symondson, Vernon F., Capt., killed, 13/11/18 (and R.A.F.).

14th (King's) Hussars.

Astley, Alexander Gifford Ludford, Capt., k. in a., 5/3/17.
Austen, Ernest, 2/Lt., died, 25/8/16.
Bruce, Thomas Robert, Capt., died, 8/2/17.
Campbell, William Robinson, D.S.O., Major, k. in a., 13/5/15.
Deakin, Cedric Guy, 2/Lt., k. in a., 20/5/16.
Hewitt, Robert Westbrooke, D.S.O., Major (T/Lt.-Col.), d. of w., 30/9/17.
Kimbell, Richard Evison, 2/Lt., k. in a., 16/4/17 (and R.F.C.).
Mewburn, Simon William Richard, Capt., k. in a., 20/5/16.

15th (The King's) Hussars.

Arnott, John, M.C., Capt., k. in a., 30/3/18.
Cubitt, Hon. Alick George, Lt., k. in a., 24/11/17.
Gaselee, Alec Mansel, 2/Lt., k. in a., 24/5/15.
Hardinge, Hon. Edward Charles, D.S.O., Lt., d. of w., 18/12/14.
Hoare, Charles Morgan, Lt., k. in a., 24/8/15.
Jackson, Henry Hall, M.C., Capt., died, 28/11/18.
Kindersley, Lionel Nassau, 2/Lt., k. in a., 25/11/17.
Livingstone-Learmonth, Nigel James Christian, Capt., k. in a., 22/8/15 (att. Dorset Yeo.).
Muir, Mathew Andrew, Capt. (Tp.), died, 18/7/16 (att. K. Afr. Rif.).
Nugent, Hon. William Andrew, Capt., d. of w., 29/5/15.
Osborne, Brian, Lt., k. in a., 11/11/14.
Parker, Leonard, Major, k. in a., 7/1/17 (att. R.F.C.) (52nd Sqd.).
Tylee, Jervis Moore, Lt., k. in a., 24/8/14.
Walker, Oswald Bethell, Capt., k. in a., 23/8/14.
Whittle, Cyril Herbert Spencer, Lt., k. in a., 24/8/14.

16th (The Queen's) Lancers.

Allen, John Edric Russell, Lt., d. of w., 8/4/18.
Arbuthnot, Maurice Armitage, M.C., Lt. (T/Capt.), died, 14/10/18.
Arbuthnot, Ronald George Urquhart, Lt., killed, 3/12/18 (and R.A.F.).

Beech, Rowland Aurio James, Lt., k. in a., 21/2/15.
Campbell, Charles Lionel Kirwan, C.B., C.M.G., Bt.-Lt.-Col. (T/Brig.-Gen.), died, 31/3/18 (5th Cav. Bde.) (2nd Cav. Div.).
Cross, David Ronald, Lt., k. in a., 21/2/15.
Dixon, Clive MacDonnell, Major, k. in a., 6/11/14.
Holland-Martin, Geoffrey Robert, 2/Lt., k. in a., 26/3/18.
King, Nathaniel Walter Ryder, Lt., k. in a., 21/2/15.
Macarthur-Onslow, Arthur William, Capt., k. in a., 5/11/14.
Macneill, William Mackinnon, 2/Lt., k. in a., 12/10/14.
Nash, Edward Radcliffe, Capt., k. in a., 21/2/15.
Neave, Arundell, Major, d. of w., 21/2/15.
O'Brien, Terence Donough, 2/Lt., k. in a., 3/3/16.
Perceval-Maxwell, Richard Nigel, Lt., k. in a., 30/3/18.
Prosser, John, Lt., died, 28/12/17.
Stephen, John Stephen, Lt., k. in a., 23/3/18.
Tempest-Hicks, Charles Edward Henry, M.C., Capt., d. of w., 9/8/18.
Watson, Sir John, Bart., 2/Lt., k. in a., 23/3/18.
Wodehouse, Hon. Edward, M.C., 2/Lt., k. in a., 30/3/18.

17th (Duke of Cambridge's Own) Lancers.

Black, George Balfour, M.C., Lt. (T/Capt.), d. of w., 23/8/18 (att. 13 Tank Corps).
Boles, Hastings Fortescue, 2/Lt., d. of w., 24/5/15.
Carden, Ronald James Walter, Lt.-Col. (Tp.), k. in a., 8/7/16 (att. 16 R. Welsh Fus.).
Dubs, Charles Edward Douglas, Capt., died, 6/11/18.
Egerton, Edward Brassey, Capt. (Tp.), d. of w., 1/9/16.
Hay, Charles Edward Erroll, Lt., d. of w., 9/8/18.
Lacaita, Francis Charles, M.C., Lt. (T/Capt.), k. in a., 3/4/18 (att. 1 M.G.C.).
Malcolm, Alan Alexander, Lt., k. in a., 17/5/18 (and R.A.F.).
Muir, John Huntly, Major, d. of w., 11/4/18 (att. 1 K.O.S.B.).
Platt, Lionel Sydney, Capt., k. in a., 13/4/17 (att. R.F.C.) (57 Sqd.).
Thorley, Horace William, 2/Lt., d. of w., 8/10/18.

18th (Queen Mary's Own) Hussars.

Childe-Pemberton, Edward William Baldwin, 2/Lt. (Tp.), d. of w., 13/4/17 (att. 11th).
Corbett, Charles Harold, Major, k. in a., 13/5/15.
Denroche-Smith, Archibald John, Lt., k. in a., 13/9/14.
De Pentheney-O'Kelly, Henry Arundel, Capt., d. of w., 19/5/15 (Res. of Off.).
Horner, Edward William, Lt., d. of w., 21/11/17.
Hulbert, George Dodson, 2/Lt., k. in a., 9/8/18.
King, Alexander Duncan Campbell, 2/Lt., k. in a., 24/5/15 (Spec. Res.).
Lyon, Edward Lycett, Major (Tp.), d. of w., 17/9/16 (att. 7 Som. L.I.).
Mitchell, Frederic McLellan, M.C., Lt. (A/Capt.), k. in a., 2/5/18 (att. Worc. Yeo.).
Nicholson, Arthur Knight, 2/Lt., k. in a., 31/10/14.
Parker, Arthur Charles, Lt., died, 11/9/18 (13 Tank Corps.).
Pedder, Edward Boynton, Lt., k. in a., 17/1/16 (Spec. Res.).
Pilter, Charles, Lt., d. of w., 30/5/15.
Summers, William Assheton, Capt., k. in a., 1/8/16 (and R.F.C.).
Taylor, Charles Tyerman, Lt., k. in a., 24/8/14.
Taylor, Edward, 2/Lt., T/Lt., k. in a., 13/5/15.
Wood, Collingwood Lindsay, Capt., k. in a., 24/5/15.
Wood, John Lockhart, D.S.O., Capt., d. of w., 11/6/15 (Res. of Off.).

19th (Queen Alexandra's Own Royal) Hussars.

Bannatyne, Edgar James, D.S.O., Lt. (T/Major), killed, 11/9/17 (and R.F.C.).
Birtwistle, Norman, M.C., Lt., k. in a., 8/10/18.
Bolitho, William Torquill Macleod, Lt., k. in a., 24/5/15.
Bonham-Carter, Guy, Capt., d. of w., 15/5/15 (att. Oxford Yeo.).
Cook, Godfrey Bruton, Lt., d. of w., 29/3/18 (in Ger. hands).
Davidson, Edward Gordon, M.C., Capt., d. of w., 2/4/18.
Egerton, George Algernon, Major, d. of w., 13/5/15.
Egerton, Philip de Malpas Wayne, Lt. (A/Capt.), k. in a., 8/10/18.
Franks, George Despard, C.M.G., D.S.O., Lt.-Col., k. in a., 8/10/18.
Fry, Leslie Harrington, Lt., k. in a., 9/8/18.
McClure, Charles Russell, Major, k. in a., 21/10/14.
Mitchell-Innes, Gilbert Robert, Lt., d. of w., 13/5/15.
Murray, Eric Dennys, 2/Lt., k. in a., 16/10/14.
Platt, Henry Evelyn Arthur, Capt., k. in a., 15/5/16 (att. 1 Cld. Gds.).
Settle, Reginald Henry Napier, D.S.O., M.C., Lt.-Col. (Tp.), k. in a., 24/3/18 (att. 21 M.G.C.).
Summers, Alfred Spencer Mason, Capt., died, 15/9/16 (P.O.W.) (and R.F.C.).
Waldron, Francis Fitzgerald, Major (Tp.), died, 3/7/16 (and R.F.C.).

20th Hussars.

Barne, Seymour, M.C., Capt., k. in a., 23/4/17 (and R.F.C.) (35 Sqd.).
Bion, R. E., Lt., k. in a., 9/4/18 (and R.A.F.).
Carew, Francis Ludovis, 2/Lt., k. in a., 30/10/14.
Cawley, John Stephen, Major, k. in a., 1/9/14.
Christy, S. H., D.S.O., Capt., k. in a., 27/8/14 (Spec. Res.).
Cook, George Trevor Roper, C.M.G., D.S.O., Lt.-Col., k. in a., 26/3/18.
Jackson, Donald Fisher, Lt., k. in a., 11/10/18.
Jeffery, George Reginald, 2/Lt. (Tp.), k. in a., 13/2/16.
Mann, Charles Julian, Lt., k. in a., 3/10/18.
Ogilvy, William Wickham, Lt., d. of w., 23/3/18.
Ralli, Lionel Peter, Lt., d. of w., 14/11/18.
Silvertop, William Alexander, M.C., Capt., k. in a., 27/11/17.
Soames, Harold Martin, Lt., k. in a., 11/9/14.
Woolf, Cecil Nathan Sidney, 2/Lt., d. of w., 30/11/17.

21st (Empress of India's) Lancers.

Anderson, Percy Hume Aufrey, Capt., k. in a., 5/9/15.
Blake, St. John Lucius O'Brien Acheson French, M.C., Major (Tp.), k. in a., 19/4/17 (att. Worc. Yeo.).
Gardner, George, Capt., k. in a., 21/8/15 (att. Bucks Yeo.).
Hollings, John Herbert Butler, Lt., k. in a., 30/10/14.
Learoyd, Geoffrey Ernest Douglas, Capt., died, 29/10/18.
Maybery, Richard Aveline, M.C., Lt., k. in a., 19/12/17 (att. R.F.C., 56 Sqd.).
Payne-Gallwey, Philip Francis, Lt., k. in a., 30/10/14.
Pirie, Arthur Murray, D.S.O., A/Lt.-Col., k. in a., 21/11/17 (att. Berks Yeo.).
Scriven, John Barclay, Lt.-Col., k. in a., 5/9/15.
Sanders, G. H. E., 2/Lt., died, 15/5/19.
Thompson, Neville Rudd, Lt., k. in a., 5/9/15.
Tringham, Llewellyn Watkins Howell, Capt., died, 22/11/18 (att. R.G.A., 51/Bde. H.Q.).

Reserve Regiment of 1st Life Guards.

Ecclestone, James, 2/Lt. (Tp.), died, 14/5/17.

Reserve Regiment of 2nd Life Guards.

Ward-Price, Leonard Stanley, Lt., k. in a., 25/3/17 (att. R.F.C., 70/Sqd.).

1st Reserve Regiment of Cavalry.

Hearson, Richard Philip, Lt. (Tp.), k. in a., 23/3/18 (att. 5 Lancers).
Hedderwick, Guy, 2/Lt., k. in a., 22/9/16 (and R.F.C.).
Scott, J. V., Lt., d. of w., 26/7/18 (P. of W.) (att. 10 R. W. Surrey R.).

2nd Reserve Regiment of Cavalry.

Jay, Arthur Palmer, 2/Lt. (Tp.), k. in a., 21/3/18 (att. 7 Bor. R.).
Mason, John Norman, M.C., Lt. (Tp.), d. of w., 13/10/18 (att. Dorset Yeo.).
Moss, Herbert Stanley, 2/Lt. (Tp.), died, 4/8/18 (att. 1 Co. of Lond. Yeo.).
Myers, Arthur Francis, Lt. (Tp.), k. in a., 31/3/18 (att. 4 Huss.).
O'Neill, Thomas, 2/Lt., died, 29/5/19 (att. 1/1 Dor. Yeo.).
Russell, Marcus Ralph, Lt. (Tp.), k. in a., 22/3/18 (att. 8 Huss.).

3rd Reserve Regiment of Cavalry.

Cooper, Cecil Davey, 2/Lt. (Tp.), d. of w., 29/1/18 (att. 6th Wilts Regt.).
Harrison, George Frederick Whitby, 2/Lt. (Tp.), d. of w., 30/9/17 (att. Wilts Yeo.) (att. 6th Batt. Wilts).
Harter, John Collier Foster, 2/Lt. (Tp.), k. in a., 28/11/17 (att. Notts Yeo.).
Marshall, Sydney James, 2/Lt. (Tp.), k. in a., 8/8/18 (att. 15th Huss.).

4th Reserve Regiment of Cavalry.

Hepton, William, Lt. (Tp.), died, 9/11/18 (att. 5 D. Gds.).
Miles, Guy Ralph, M.C., Lt. (Tp.), d. of w., 10/3/18 (att. 5th D. Gds.).
Parker, Percy Dolph, 2/Lt., killed, 4/1/18 (and R.F.C.).
Parkinson, Alfred Louis, 2/Lt. (Tp.), died, 3/6/18 (att. 2nd D. Gds.).
Thomlinson, John Robert, 2/Lt. (Tp.), k. in a., 8/8/18 (att. 2nd D. Gds.).

5th Reserve Regiment of Cavalry.

Bagshawe, Geoffrey Hamilton, 2/Lt., k. in a., 13/5/15 (att. 1st Drag. Gds.).
Hall, T. P. M., 2/Lt. (Tp.), died, 12/12/18.
Ireland, Arthur George, 2/Lt. (Tp.), d. of w., 19/10/17 (att. 1/1st N'thmb. Hus.).
Jarvis, George Frederick Jervaulx, M.C., Lt. (Tp.), d. of w., 28/9/18 (att. 9th W. Yorks Regt.).
Norman, Charles, Capt., died, 12/2/17.
Perret, Gerald Henry, Lt., k. in a., 9/8/18 (att. 10th Huss.).
Turner, Kenneth Leigh 2/Lt. (Tp.), k. in a., 2/5/18 (att. Worcs. Yeo.).
Willis, Raymond, Lt. (Tp.), k. in a., 25/3/18 (att. 18th Huss.).

6th Reserve Regiment of Cavalry.

Atack, Percy, 2/Lt. (Tp.), k. in a., 4/7/18 (att. Tank Corps.).
Bales, Theodore Alfred Herbert, 2/Lt. (Tp.), d. of w., 13/10/18 (att. 7th Drag. Gds.).
Horne, John Austen, 2/Lt. (Tp.), died, 2/11/18.
Herrison, Roger Orme, Lt.-Col., died, 18/9/17 (att. 4th Aust. F. A. Bde.).
Kittle, Ernest Arthur Lewis, Lt. (Tp.), d. of w., 10/10/18 (and 3rd D. G.).

Lyall, George William, 2/Lt., died, 7/12/17.
Main, Eric Arthur, 2/Lt., died, 26/2/18 (att. N. Som. Yeo.).
Massey-Lynch, Wilfrid John, 2/Lt. (Tp.), k. in a., 4/4/18 (att. 3rd D. Gs.).
Reynolds, Richard Frederick, Lt. (Tp.) (A/Capt.), k. in a., 2/10/18 (att. 15th Btn. Hamps. Regt.).
Savile, Francis Ewart, Lt. (Tp.), died, 9/2/16 (att. 9th Lancers).
Shone, Harold Lonsdale, 2/Lt. (Tp.), died, 9/7/18.

Remount Service.

Britten, Spencer, Major (Tp.), died, 18/8/18.
Christie, Herbert Bertram, Lt. (Tp.), died, 9/12/16.
Cockrell, William Archer, Lt., died, 11/11/17.
McLaughlin, Hubert James, D.S.O., Lt.-Col., died, 25/3/15.
Mansel, John Delalynde, Col., died, 15/12/15.
Purdey, M. Sefton, Major (Tp.), died, 25/5/16 (late 18th Huss.).
Hadden, Frank John, Lt. (Tp.), died, 5/5/16.
Wood, John William Massey, M.V.O., Lt.-Col., died, 9/12/16.

North Irish Horse.

Coombe, Samuel Barbour, Lt., died, 1/10/14.
Dennistoun, James Robert, Lt., d. of w., 9/8/16 (P. of W.) (and R.F.C.).
Kellock, Harold Plumer, Lt., d. of w., 6/10/18 (att. R.F.A.).
Saunderson, Samuel Treherne, Capt., killed, 22/4/18 (and (R.A.F.).
Vesey, George Walter, M.C., Capt., d. of w., 26/3/18 (att. 9th R. Ir. Fus.).
Waring, Holt, Major, d. of w., 15/4/18 (att. R. Ir. Rfs.).
Wise, Lancelot Charles, Lt., died, 2/5/17.

South Irish Horse.

Brewster, Richard Gardiner, 2/Lt., k. in a., 21/3/18 (att. 7th R. Irish Regt.).
Colvill, George Chaignian, Capt., k. in a., 30/11/17 (att. 7th R. Irish Regt.).
Conyngham, Victor George Henry Francis (Marquis), Lt., died, 9/11/18.
Dignan, Albert Guy, Lt., k. in a., 21/3/18 (att. 7th R. Irish Regt.).
Fogarty, William Joseph, Capt., k. in a., 21/3/18 (att. 7th R. Irish Regt.).
Morton, Thomas Edward, Capt., d. of w., 26/3/18 (att 7th R. Irish Regt.).
V.C. **West**, Richard Arnsley, D.S.O., Major, k. in a., 2/9/18 (att. Tanks).

King Edward's Horse (The King's Oversea Dominions Regiment).

Addison, Noel Goodricke, M.C., Lt., k. in a., 9/4/18.
1 **Bell**, William Henry Dillon, Capt. (Tp.), k. in a., 31/7/17.
Bertram, Cyril Robertson, 2/Lt., killed, 18/6/16 (and R.F.C.).
Cooper, Henry Mark Hugh, Lt., d. of w., 29/7/15.
Fisher, Edward Henry, 2/Lt., k. in a., 9/4/18.
Ham, Frank Livingstone, 2/Lt., died, 13/2/16.
Hermon, Edward William, D.S.O., Lt.-Col. (Tp.), k. in a., 9/4/17 (Com. 24th North'n Fus.).
Kennedy, William, Hon. Maj. & Qr.-Mr., died, 29/5/15.
Ling, Fergus Graham, Capt., died, 16/12/18.
2 **Lucas**, Algenon, 2/Lt., killed, 28/4/16.
McArdle, Hugh Francis, Lt., k. in a., 18/9/17 (and R.F.C., 41st Sq.).
O'Halloran-Giles, Robert, 2/Lt., d. of w., 26/4/18 (In German hands).
Pinckney, John William, Lt., k. in a., 9/4/18.
Shaw, Charles Athelstan, Capt., d. of w., 9/1/16.
Watt, Norman Lindlay, 2/Lt. (T/Lt.), d. of w., 27/7/17 (and R.F.C.).
2 **Worswick**, Henry Worsley, 2/Lt., killed, 28/4/16.

Royal Regiment of Artillery (R.H.A. and R.F.A.).

Abiss, Frederick Thomas Lee, Lt., d. of w., 27/10/17 (76 Bde.).
Abbott, Thomas Aveling, Capt. & Adjt., k. in a., 24/5/15.
Adam, John Isabel, Lt. (Tp.), k. in a., 10/5/18 (307 Bde.).
Adam, Norman MacLeod, M.C., Capt., A/Major, k. in a., 28/8/18 (9 Bde.).
Adam, Ronald William, M.C., 2/Lt., died, 11/9/17 (13/56 Bde.).
Adams, Henry Frederick Reginald, Lt., d. of w., 20/10/17 (A/159 Bde.).
Adams, Ord, 2/Lt. (Tp.), k. in a., 20/3/16.
Adams, Robert Sefton, Lt., A/Capt., k. in a., 5/10/17 (35 Bde.).
Agar, Richard St. George Tracy, Lt., k. in a., 29/9/18 (16 Bde. H.Q.).
Aiken, James Douglas, 2/Lt., died, 9/11/16 (att. Y. 14 T.M.B.).
Ainley, Hefford William Ernest, Lt., died, 4/2/17 (168 Bde.).
Ainslie, Walter Gordon, 2/Lt., k. in a., 10/11/16 (att. X. 33 T.M.B.).
Aitken, John Malcolm, 2/Lt. (Tp.), d. of w., 12/10/18 (D/82 Bde.).
Albrecht, John Ernest, 2/Lt., k. in a., 1/8/17 (33 Bde.).
Aldwinckle, Bernard, Lt., d. of w., 3/11/18 (421 How. Bty.).
Alexander, James Edward, 2/Lt., k. in a., 19/9/17 (277 Army Bde.).
Alexander, Robert, Lt., d. of w., 3/11/17 (26 Bde.).
Allan, Arthur Gordon, 2/Lt., d. of w., 8/12/18 (108 Bde.).
Allard, Philip Hayward, Lt (A/Capt.), k. in a., 23/6/17 (45 Bde.).
Allen, John Thomas, Lt., died, 18/2/16.
Allen, Percy, 2/Lt., k. in a., 4/10/17 (59 Bde.).
Allenby, Horace Michael Hynman, M.C., Lt., d. of w., 29/7/17 (14 Bde.) (R.H.A.).
Allinson, Athelstan John William Ward, Lt., k. in a., 9/4/18 (121 Bde.).
Almack, Edward Poulton, Capt., k in a., 25/1/16 (85 Bde.).
Alston, Rowland Evelyn, 2/Lt., k. in a., 17/8/16 (52 Bde.).
Amoroso, Michele, Lt. (Tp.), k. in a., 3/7/16 (D/96).
Amos, Frank Edward, 2/Lt. (Tp.), k. in a., 20/9/18 (230 Bde.).
Amos, John Vince, Lt., died, 13/2/17 (37 D.A.C.).
Anderson, Frederick Henry, M.C., 2/Lt., died, 15/5/18 (50 Bde.).
Anderson, Francis Sainthill, M.C., Capt. (A/Major), k. in a., 25/8/18 (15 Bde.).
Anderson, James Morton, 2/Lt., k. in a., 1/5/17 (70 Bde.).
Anderson, Robert Coventry, 2/Lt., d. of w., 4/11/17 (282 Bde.).
Anderson, William Wallace, 2/Lt., k. in a., 10/11/16 (15 Bde.).
Anderton, Albert, M.C., Lt (A/Maj.), d. of w., 5/4/18 (110 Bde.).
Anderton, William Frederick, 2/Lt. (Tp.), k. in a., 31/3/17.
Andrews, Archibald, T/Lt. (A/Capt.), d. of w., 30/5/17 (23 D.A.C.).
Appleby, Eric, 2/Lt., d. of w., 28/10/16 (48/2 Bde.).
Archdale, Theodore Montgomery, D.S.O., Lt.-Col., drowned, 10/10/18.
Armitage, Edward Stoney, 2/Lt., k. in a., 29/8/18 (76 Bde.).
Armstrong, Sydney, 2/Lt., k. in a, 17/12/18 (att. R.F.C.).
Arnold, Bernard William, Lt. (A/Capt.), k. in a., 21/3/18.
Arnold, Edward Gladwin, Lt., k. in a., 21/3/18 (232 Army Bde.).
Arthur, Henry Bartle Compton, Major, k. in a., 10/8/16 (5 Bde.).
Ashworth, L. T, Lt.-Col., died, 22/3/18.
Askwith, Thomas Nowelle, 2/Lt. k. in a., 24/10/17 (250 Bde.).
Aspinall, Francis Clifford, 2/Lt., k. in a., 17/9/18 (70 Bde.).
Atherstone, George Henry, Capt., died, 21/2/18.
Atherton, Francis Wright, Lt., killed, 15/5/18 (and R.A.F.).
Atkin, Charles Percy, M.C., Lt. (A/Major), k. in a., 23/11/17 (70 Army Bde.).
Atkin, Richard Walter, Lt., k. in a., 14/8/17 (92 Bde.).
Atkinson, Frederick Batty, 2/Lt., k. in a., 25/9/18 (87 Bde.).
Atkinson, Surtees, M.C., Capt (A/Maj.), died. 7/2/18.
Atkinson, William, M.C., Lt., d. of w., 18/7/17 (25 D.A.C.).
Atlay, Hugh Wordsworth, D.S.O., Major, k. in a., 11/4/15.
Aulton-Smith, Montague W., 2/Lt. (Tp.), k. in a., 4/11/15.
Auret, Ben, Capt. (Tp.), k. in a., 21/9/16.
Austen, Arthur Neville, M.C., Capt. (A/Maj.), d. of w., 28/3/18 (A/51 Bde.).
Austin, Vernon James, Lt., k. in a., 26/1/15.
Ayers, George Mansfield, Lt., k. in a., 31/7/17 (38 Bde.).
Ayre, Stanley Fawcett, 2/Lt., k. in a., 30/11/17 (170 Army Bde.).
Baddeley, Percy Kynnersley, 2/Lt. (Tp.), k. in a., 29/6/16.
Badelow, George, 2/Lt., d. of w., 27/12/15 (6 Div. Am. Col.).
Bailey, Allan Richard, 2/Lt., d. of w., 15/6/17 (88 Bde.).
Bailey, Guy Horsman, M.C., Lt. (A/Maj.), k. in a., 28/2/17 (15 Bde.) (R.H.A.)
Bailey, Herbert, Lt., died, 24/5/15.
Bailey, Philip Gerald, T/Capt. (A/Maj.), k. in a., 26/4/17 (36 Bde.).
Bailey, Roland Henry, Lt., died, 4/1/19.
Baillie, George, Major, k. in a., 18/11/14.
Baily, Arthur Alexander Russell, 2/Lt., k. in a., 4/11/18 (17 T.M.B.).
Baird, Louis Latham, Lt. (Tp.), d. of w., 11/4/16 (66 Bde.).
Baker, Joseph Leffler, 2/Lt., d. of w., 14/12/15.
Baker, Kingsley, M.C., Lt., d. of w., 30/3/18 (A/51 Bde.).
Baker, Waldeman John, 2/Lt., k. in a., 25/10/17 (83 Bde.).
Balcombe-Browne, William Edward, 2/Lt., k. in a., 29/6/15.
Balderson, Eric Francis Richard, 2/Lt., k. in a., 28/3/16.
Balderston, Chester Thomas, 2/Lt., died, 26/6/17 (C/58 Bde.).
Baldwin, Herbert Donald, Lt. (Tp.), d. of w., 18/7/16 (156).
Balfour, Alan Scott, 2/Lt., k. in a., 13/1/18 (and R.F.C.).
Balfour, John Melville, M.C., Capt. (A/Maj.), k. in a., 6/10/17 (91 Bde.).
Ball, Arthur Sherley, M.C., Lt., k. in a., 16/8/17 (A/186 Bde.).
Ball, Howell Thomas, 2/Lt., k. in a., 26/4/17 (36 Bde.).
Ball, T. H., Lt., died, 22/1/18 (25 D.A.C.).
Ballard, Charles Naesmyth Bruere, Lt.-Col., died, 11/2/15.
Ballard, Oliver Charles, 2/Lt., d. of w., 17/10/18 (21/2 Bde.).
Balmain, Roy Frederick, M.C., T/Lt. (A/Capt.). d. of w., 1/10/18 (51 Bde.).
Banham, William Henry, M.C., 2/Lt., d. of w., 8/9/18 (119 Bde., A. Bty.).
Banks, William John, Capt. (Tp.), k. in a., 30/7/16 (15 Bde.).
Bannerman, Robert Gilroy, Lt. (Tp.), k. in a., 25/7/16 (157 Bde.).
Barber-Starkey, William Henry Joseph, Capt., d. of w., 11/9/15 (P.O.W.).
Barbor, R. C., Lt., died, 25/5/15.
Barker, Paul Studholme, M.C., T/Lt. ((A/Capt.), k. in a., 26/10/17 (78 Bde.).
Barlow, Cecil George, 2/Lt., d. of w., 18/5/17 (B/156 Bde.).
Barnard, Dudley Henry Lionel, 2/Lt., died, 10/2/15.
Barnard, Edward Armstrong, 2/Lt., k. in a., 29/9/17 (and R.F.C. 10 Sq.).
Barnard-Smith, William Woodthorpe Barnard, 2/Lt. (Tp.), k. in a., 21/10/16 (38 Bde.).
Barnes, John Backham, 2/Lt., k. in a., 9/5/17 (87 Bde.).
Barnet, D. G., Lt., died, 31/10/18 (and R.A.F.).
Barnett, Harry Mortimer Stacey, 2/Lt., k. in a., 6/4/16 (23 Bde.).
Barr, John Lyle, 2/Lt. (Tp.), d. of w., 26/7/16 (D/159 Bde.).

Barrett, Cecil Roy, M.C., 2/Lt., d. of w., 25/6/17 (C/113 Bde.).
Barrett, Herbert Victor, M.C., 2/Lt., d. of w., 22/4/18 (D/110 Bde.).
Barrett, Knox Gordon, 2/Lt. (A/Lt.), k. in a., 20/9/17 (2/20 T.M.B.).
Barrow, Geoffrey Selwyn, O.B.E., Lt. (T/Capt.), died, 26/12/18.
Barton, Arthur Everard Hale, Lt. (Tp.), k. in a., 25/9/15.
Barton, Vivian Alfred, 2/Lt., k. in a., 22/9/17 (162 Bde.).
Bartram, Harry Brocklesby, Capt., died, 16/9/14.
Bastow, William Henry, 2/Lt. (Tp.), died, 26/11/15 (C/66 Brig.).
Bateman, Bernard Montague Basil, M.C., Lt., d. of w., 24/7/15.
Bateson, John, M.C., Lt., k. in a., 14/10/18 (A/28 Bde.).
Battersby, Charles Fremoult Preston, Capt., k. in a., 4/11/14.
Battersby, James Wilfred, Capt., k. in a., 24/10/16 (38 Bde.).
Baumer, Derek Edward Lewis Venn, Lt., d. of w., 21/10/17 (32 Bde.).
Baxendale, John Thompson, 2/Lt., k. in a., 18/7/17 (30 D.A.C. att. 149 Bde.).
Baxter, Cecil Hubert, 2/Lt., k. in a., 1/2/17 (A/55 Bde.).
Baxter, Leonard Arthur, 2/Lt., k. in a., 8/3/17 (23 Army F.A. Bde.).
Baxter, Leslie William, Lt., k. in a., 28/5/18 (95 Bde.).
Bayliss, John Edwin, M.C., T/Lt. (A/Maj.), d. of w., 29/9/17 (76 Army Bde.).
Bayly, Charles Ramsay, Lt. (Tp.), k. in a., 29/3/18 (29 Bde.).
Bazley, Ernest Edward, 2/Lt., k. in a., 4/10/17 (A/298 Bde.).
Beachcroft, W. F., Lt., died, 21/7/18 (and R.A.F.).
Beak, Frank Leslie, Lt. (Tp.), k. in a., 9/4/18 (att. 3 Co. Spec. Bde. R.E.).
Beal, Henry Benjamin, Lt., died, 23/6/19.
Beall, Roy Dixon, Lt., k. in a., 4/6/15.
Beanland, John Everard, 2/Lt., k. in a., 26/5/18 (161 Bde. att. X. 32 T.M.B.).
Beatson, Charles Ellis Stewart, M.C., Capt. (A/Maj.), d. of w., 3/10/17 (22 Bde.).
Beattie, William Francis, M.C., Lt., d. of w., 3/10/18 (73/5 Bde.).
Beck, Herbert Charles, 2/Lt. (Tp.), d. of w., 19/10/18 (152 Bde.).
Beever, Johnathan Holt, Lt., k. in a., 25/3/18 (17 Bde.).
Belas, George Henry, Capt. (Tp.), k. in a., 3/6/17 (4th D.A.C.).
Belcher, Frederick Percy, T/Capt. (A/Maj.), d. of w., 5/8/18 (C/92 Bde.).
Belcher, Harold Thomas, D.S.O., Lt.-Col., k. in a., 8/7/17 (52 Bde.).
Belcher, Raymond Douglas, D.S.O., M.C., T/Capt. (A/Maj.), d. of w., 7/12/17 (C/63 Bde.).
Bell, George Russell, M.C., 2/Lt., d. of w., 4/12/18 (C/124 Bde.).
Bell, James Clifford Aveling, Lt., d. of w., 30/5/18 (175 Bde.).
Bell, John Dobree, Lt., died, 30/10/18 (19 Corps H.Q. att. Intell.).
Bell, John Mercer Grimshaw, Lt., d. of w., 11/10/18 (and R.A.F.).
Bell, Sydney Parker, Capt., k. in a., 26/9/15.
Bellamy, John James, 2/Lt., k. in a., 24/4/17 (B/116 Bde.).
Bellingham, Robert Charles Noel, Capt., died, 4/3/15.
Bemand, George Edward Kingsley, 2/Lt. (Tp.), k. in a., 26/12/16 (Y/5 T.M.B.).
Benbow, E. L., M.C., Capt., killed, 3/5/18 (and R.A.F.).
Benham, Frank Benham, Capt., d. of w., 23/8/16 (C/81).
Benham, John Russell, 2/Lt., d. of w., 4/5/15.
Benham, Walter Edward, 2/Lt., died, 3/11/18 (A/245 Bde.).
Beningfield, John Philip, 2/Lt., d. of w., 27/4/15.
Bennell, Donald, Lt., k. in a., 16/4/17 (315 Bde.).
Bennett, Henry Richard, Lt., died, 4/1/18 (3 Cav. Div. R.A.).
Berrill, Frank Gale, Lt., died, 28/9/18 (57 Bty. 45 Bde.).
Berry, Claud Vincent Cameron, 2/Lt., k. in a., 27/7/17 (112 Bde.).
Berry, Eustace Carlton, 2/Lt., killed, 5/7/16 (att, R.F.C.).
Berry, George Herbert, 2/Lt., d. of w., 9/10/17 (315 Army Bde.).
Best, Arthur Horris, 2/Lt., d. of w., 25/3/18 (165 Bde.).
Beuttler, Charles Brereton Oakley, 2/Lt., d. of w., 24/12/16 (94 Bde.).
Bevan, Oliver Lewen, 2/Lt., d. of w., 25/10/18 (25 Army Bde.).
Beveridge, David Alexander, 2/Lt. (Tp.), died, 14/9/15 (H.Q. 54 Bde.).
Bevington, William Joseph, A/Capt., k. in a., 5/11/16 (39 Bde.).
Bevir, Cyril Edward Francis, Lt., k. in a., 29/10/15.
Bewick, Norman, 2/Lt., k. in a., 22/1/18 (157 Bde.).
Bewsher, Francis Alexander, Lt., d. of w., 18/4/18 (C/255 Bde.).
Bezuidenhout, Pieter Hendrik Schalk, M.C., 2/Lt., k. in a., 24/12/16 (94 Bde. Spec. Res.).
Bickmore, Bertram George, 2/Lt., k. in a., 21/3/18 (A/232 Bde.).
Biddulph, Leonard Shrapnell, Capt., d. of w., 29/12/16 (att. Nigerian R.).
Bingham, Harold, 2/Lt., k. in a., 15/9/18 (78 Bde.).
Bird, Henry Tattersall, 2/Lt., k. in a., 27/3/18 (160 Bde.).
Birnie, Gerald, Lt., d. of w., 4/11/18 (46/39 Bde.).
Black, Norman Annandale, Capt. (Tp.), k. in a., 23/5/16 (105 Bde.).
Blackden, Arthur Worsley, 2/Lt., k. in a, 28/9/16 (189 Bde.).
Blacklaws, Alec Stuart, M.C., 2/Lt., k. in a., 7/1/18.
Blair, George Young, 2/Lt (Tp.), d. of w., 24/7/15.
Blair, Robert Hannay, 2/Lt., k. in a., 21/3/18 (79 Bde).
Blair, William Kenneth Playfair, Major, d. of w., 14/5/15
Blake, Charles Edwin Norman, M.C., Lt. (A/Major), k. in a., 30/7/18 (70 Bde.).
Blakemore, John Edward, M.C., T/Capt. (A/Major), d. of w, 5/10/17 (42 Bty., 24 Bde).
Blandy, Claude Milberne Capt. (Tp.), died, 8/4/16.
Blanford, Charles Edward, Major, d. of w., 11/7/15 (30 Mountain Bty.).
Blathwayt, Gerald Wynter, Capt., k. in a., 14/9/14.
Blathwayt, Henry Wynter, Major, d. of w., 30/11/17 (A/74 Bde.).
Bleazard, Fred, 2/Lt., k. n a., 21/3/18 (169 Army Bde.).
Bligh, Frederick Arthur, Major (Tp.) (Capt., Ret.), died, 15/11/15.
Bligh, Jack Frederick, M.C., A/Major, k. in a., 1/7/17 (D/121 Bde).
Bliss, Francis Kennard, 2/Lt. (Tp.), k. in a., 28/9/16 (59 Bde.).
Block, Maurice William Palmer, Col., died, 5/3/19.
Blois, Dudley George, Lt.-Col., d. of w., 14/7/16 (84 Bde.).
Bloor, William Henry, T/Lt. (A/Capt.), k. in a., 3/1/18 (149 Bde.).
Blount, Greville Hubert Robins, Capt., d. of w., 23/9/14.
Blumer, John, 2/Lt. (Tp.), d. of w., 26/9/16 (283 Bde.).
Board, William John, 2/Lt., d. of w., 22/9/18 (130 Bde., att. 31 Bde.).
Body, Edward Upton, T/Capt (A/Major), k. in a., 4/11/18.
Bolster, George Emil, Major, d. of w., 23/10/14.
Bolster, Richard M.C, Capt (A/Major), k. in a., 4/6/17 (28 Bde.).
Bolton, John Ritso Nelson, Lt, d. of w., 27/9/15.
Bond, Frank Bertram, 2/Lt. (Tp.), k. in a., 24/10/18.
Bond, Frederick Hamilton Bligh, 2/Lt., d. of w., 13/5/15.
Bond, Gustave Samuel, 2/Lt., k. in a., 9/4/18 (B/276 Bde.).
Bone, Albert Edward, Capt., d. of w., 3/11/18 (242 Bde.).
Boone, Henry Griffith, D.S.O., Major, d. of w., 5/9/17 (94 Bty.).
Booth, Joseph William, 2/Lt., d of w., 8/10/18 (B/Bty., 93 Bde.).
Booth, Lawrence Elliot, M.C., Capt. (A/Major), k. in a., 13/4/18 (38 Bde).
Booth, Patrick Dick, D.S.O., M.C., T/Capt., d. of w., 2/12/17 (Div. T.M. Officer).
Boothby, John Henry, Lt., k. in a., 23/7/16.
Borain, Harold Goldsmith, 2/Lt., d. of w., 5/11/17 (22 Bde.).
Boscowen, Hon. George Edward, D.S.O., Major, d. of w., 7/6/18 (116 S.B.)
Bosher, Alfred Henry Bruce, 2/Lt., k. in a., 16/8/17 (45 Bde.).
Bostock, Neville Stanley, 2/Lt., k. in a., 22/4/17 (162 Bde.).
Botham, Arthur Frederick, 2/Lt., d. of w., 18/6/17 (D/106 Bde.).
Bourke, Patrick Miller, 2/Lt., k. in a., 25/7/16 (28 Bde.).
Bourne, Cecil Alfred, M.C., Capt. (A/Major), died, 11/12/18 (411/126 Army Bde.).
Bourne, Ralph, 2/Lt., k. in a., 10/9/17 (158 Bde.).
Bowels, James Arthur, Lt., k. in a., 26/8/14.
Bowen, George Eustace Summers, M.C., Capt., d. of w., 26/7/17.
Bowles, Edgar Branson, 2/Lt., k. in a., 31/3/18 (23 Army Bde.).
Bowles, James Arthur, Lt., k. in a., 26/8/14.
Bowles, Percy William, M.C., 2/Lt., k. in a., 10/9/18 (C/219 Bde.).
Bowman, Anthony Harvey, 2/Lt., d. of w., 20/5/16 (37 Bty.).
Bowman, Robert Moore, 2/Lt. (Tp.), k. in a., 5/8/16 (81 Bde.).
Boyd, James Duncan, M.C., Lt., k. in a., 25/9/18 (27 Bde.).
V.C. Bradbury, Edward Kinder, Capt., k. in a., 1/9/14.
Bradshaw, Ernest Edwin, Lt. (Tp.), k. in a., 30/9/17 (148 Bde.).
Bradshaw, William Douglas, 2/Lt., k. in a., 31/10/16 (88 Bde.).
Bragg, Robert Charles, 2/Lt. (Tp), d. of w., 2/9/15.
Braithwaite, James Leslie, 2/Lt., k. in a., 22/7/16 (Q Bty.).
Brayshaw, Percy St. Quentin, 2/Lt., died, 14/1/18.
Bressey, Denys John, 2/Lt., k. in a., 14/10/17 (35 Bde.).
Brewer, Reginald England, 2/Lt. (Tp.), k. in a., 10/10/16 (24 Bde.).
Brewitt, William Sydney, 2/Lt. (Tp.), k in a., 29/6/16.
Bridger, Herbert John, 2/Lt., k in a., 1/11/18 (307 Bde.).
Brien, Frederick George, Lt. (Tp.), k. in a., 30/4/18 (45 T.M.B.).
Briggs, Harley Knollys, 2/Lt., k. in a., 26/7/16.
Brims, James Sutherland, Lt (Tp.), k. in a., 8/11/16 (79 Bde.).
Brink, Johannes Hieronymus, Lt., d. of w., 11/4/17 (and R.F.C.).
Briscoe, Mervyn Whitby, Lt. (Tp.), k. in a., 23/7/17 (and R.F.C., 6 Sqd.).
Britten, Charles Edward, Lt. (Tp.), d. of w., 20/7/16 (5th D.A.C.).
Britten, Charles Wells, T/Lt. (A/Major), k. in a., 26/4/17 (D.T.M.O.)
Britton, Herbert Edward, 2/Lt., d of w., 15/10/16 (62 Bde.).
Broad, Richard Blunson, Lt. (A/Major), died, 6/11/18 (Anti-Aircraft Bty.).
Broadhurst, Gerald Henry, Lt., died, 8/5/15.
Broadrick, Frederick Benjamin Dumaresq, Major, died, 19/4/18.
Bromet, John Neville, Lt., k. in a., 30/11/17 (63 Bde.).
Bromley, John Edouard Marsden, D.S.O., T/Capt. (A/Major), k. in a., 7/6/18 (41 Bde.).
Brooking, Walter Arthur, 2/Lt., k. in a., 19/1/16.
Brooks, Leonard Samuel, Lt. (Tp.), k. in a., 9/5/18 (50 Bde.).
Brooks, Francis Cyril, 2/Lt., killed, 17/8/17 (and R.F.C.).
Brooks, Reginald St. George, 2/Lt. (Tp.), k. in a., 26/9/15 (97 Bde.).

Brough, John, C.M.G., M.V.O., Lt.-Col., died, 29/7/17 (H.Q. 61 Div.).
Brown, Arthur Roberts, 2/Lt., k. in a., 6/4/17 (and R.F.C.).
Brown, John, 2/Lt. (Tp.), d. of w., 11/8/16.
Brown, John Edward, Lt. (A/Capt.), k. in a., 14/9/18 (113 Bde.).
Brown, James William, 2/Lt., d. of w., 2/11/14.
Brown, Reg. Roy, M.C., Lt. (A/Major), died, 31/10/18 (14 Army Bde.).
Browne, Lord Alfred Eden, D.S.O., A/Lt.-Col., k. in a., 27/8/18 (H.Q. 186 Bde.).
Browning, Charles Hunter, Capt., k. in a., 26/8/14.
Browning-Paterson, Norman Alexander, Capt., k. in a., 21/7/16 (and R.F.C.).
Bruce, Alexander Angus, 2/Lt., k. in a., 24/6/18 (156 Bde.).
Bruce, James, 2/Lt. (A/Capt.), k. in a., 25/7/17 (256 Bde.).
Brufton, Wilfred Eustace, 2/Lt., d. of w., 3/9/18 (119 Bty. 27 Bde.).
Bryant, Alfred Francis, Major, d. of w., 26/11/17 (att. Ayrshire R.).
Bryett, Lewis Henry Frederick, 2/Lt., d. of w., 25/10/18 (307 Bde.).
Bryson, James Harvey, 2/Lt. (Tp.), k. in a., 20/10/18 (X 24 T.M.B.).
Buchan, Leslie Alexander, 2/Lt. (Tp.), d. of w., 30/7/16 (40 Bde.).
Buchan, Roy Eric Victor, 2/Lt. (Tp.), k. in a., 27/3/16.
Buchanan-Dunlop, Colin Napier, D.S.O., Major, k. in a., 14/10/15.
Buckle, Archie Stewart, Brig.-Gen. (Tp.), died, 18/8/16 (17 Div.).
Buckle, Harry, Capt., d. of w., 4/10/14 (P. of W.).
Bucknell, William Wentworth, Lt., k. in a., 10/8/17 (103 Bde.).
Bucknill, Llewellyn Morris, Major, d. of w., 18/5/15.
Budge, Philip Prideaux, D.S.O., Bt. Lt.-Col., d. of w., 11/9/18 (323 Bde.).
Bugg, Herbert, 2/Lt., k. in a., 19/7/18 (D/106 Bde.).
Bulteal, Sam Dominic, Capt. (A/Major), k. in a., 5/4/17 (45 Bde.).
Bulteel, Thomas Edward, Lt., killed, 24/2/18 (att. R.F.C.).
Bunbury, Hugh St. P., 2/Lt. (Tp.), d. of w., 25/8/16 (B/70 Bde.).
Bunbury, T. St. P., Capt., k. in a., 31/8/18 (and R.A.F.).
Burdekin, Sydney, 2/Lt., k. in a., 28/9/15.
Burdge, Reginald John, 2/Lt., d. of w., 9/10/17 (C/58 Bde.).
Burgoyne, John Heywood, 2/Lt., k. in a., 31/10/16 (88 Bde.).
Burke, Osborne Samuel, 2/Lt. (Tp.) (A/Capt.), k. in a., 25/9/16 (77 Bde.).
Burkinshaw, Francis William, Capt. (Tp.), d. of w., 30/3/16 (9 Bde. 19 Bty.).
Burne, Edward Robert, D.S.O., Lt.-Col., k. in a., 1/10/18 (15 Bde.).
Burnett, Leslie Cecil James, 2/Lt., k. in a., 14/3/18.
Burnyeat, Hugh Ponsonby, Major (A/Lt.-Col.), k. in a., 30/10/18 (65 Army Bde.).
Burridge, Guy Biddulph, M.C., Lt., k. in a., 4/5/18 (42 Bde.).
Burrows, Edward William Montague, Lt., k. in a., 26/8/16 (2 Bde.).
Burt, Theodore Charles Arthur, Lt. (Tp.), k. in a., 15/7/16.
Burton, Arthur Richard, Capt., k. in a., 31/1/16.
Burton, Francis Charles Deane, Major, died, 3/2/15.
Burton, Louis, Lt. (A/Major), died, 0/6/17 (70 Bde.).
Busby, Frederick William Merewether, 2/Lt., d. of w., 11/2/17 (165 Bde.).
Butcher, Frederick, Major (Actg.), k. in a., 22/5/18 (A/92 Bde.).
Butcher, Henry Townsend (Bt. Col.), k. in a., 20/9/15.
Butler, Bernard Arnold Barrington, D.S.O., Lt.-Col., d. of w., 23/10/18 (156 Bde.).
Butler, Cyril Frank, 2/Lt., d. of w., 8/6/18 (112 Bde.).
Butler, Francis Mourilyan, Lt. (A/Capt.), k. in a., 8/10/17 (93 Army Bde.).
Butler, John Leslie, Capt., d. of w., 17/5/19 (Staff).
Butters, Henry Augustus, 2/Lt. (Tp.), k. in a., 31/8/16 (109 Bde.).
Button, Charles Augustus, 2/Lt., k. in a., 27/5/18 (45 Bde.).
Byng, Percy Howard, 2/Lt., died, 25/9/16 (44 Bty.).
Byrne, Patrick Anthony Laugan, D.S.O., 2/Lt., died, 17/10/16 (and R.F.C.).
Byrne, Ralph Eugene, 2/Lt., k. in a., 4/4/18 (C/180 Bde.).
Caiger, Frederick Howard Stewart, 2/Lt., k. in a., 11/11/16 (17th Bde.).
Cairnes, Charles Beresford, 2/Lt., k in a., 22/4/17 (146th Bde.).
Calder, Kenneth William, 2/Lt. (Tp.), d. of w., 21/12/15.
Caldwell, James Robert McDonald, 2/Lt. (Tp.), k. in a., 26/10/18 (403 Howitzer Bde.).
Calthrop, Everard Ferguson, Major (T/L.-Col.), k. in a., 19/12/15.
Cambridge, William Kenneth, 2/Lt., k. in a., 26/3/18 (331st Bde.).
Cameron, Cyril Henry, 2/Lt., k. in a., 12/3/15.
Cameron, Ewen Arthur, Lt., k. in a., 16/12/15 (49th Bde.).
Cameron, Henry Robley, Lt. (Tp.), died, 6/6/17 (1st B. Res. Bde.).
Cameron, James Macdonald, 2/Lt., k. in a., 10/5/15.
Campbell, Colin Archibald Heron, Major, k. in a., 29/9/17 (C/296th Bde.).
Campbell, Charles Frederick, M.C., Capt. (A/Major), k. in a., 18/9/18 (14th A.F.A Bde.).
Campbell, Colin Palmer, 2/Lt., d. of w., 10/10/17 (94th Bde.).
Campbell, John Davies, Lt., k. in a., 1/9/14.
Campbell, William, Lt., k. in a., 6/7/17 (and R.F.C., 2nd Sq.).
Cane, Maurice, 2/Lt. (Tp.), k. in a., 4/8/17 (153rd Bde.).
Cannan, Horatius James, D.S.O., Capt. (Tp.), d. of w., 2/11/16.
Cansfield, Victor Morton, 2/Lt. (Tp.), k in a., 24/2/16.
Cape, George Augustus Stewart, C.M.G., T/Lt.-Col. (T/Brig.-Gen.), k. in a., 18/3/18 (39th Div. Arty.).
Capper, John Beausire Copeland, M.C., 2/Lt., k. in a., 26/9/16 (70th Bde.).
Cardell, Edmund Powne, M.C., Major, k. in a., 21/3/18 (46th Bde.).
Cardew, John Haydon, M.C., Lt. (A/Capt.), d. of w., 5/10/17 (5th Army Bde.).
Carey, Frederick, Capt., died, 22/1/16 (att A.O.D., India).
Carmichael, Archibald, 2/Lt., d. of w., 22/5/18 (C/108th Bde.).
Carnegie, David Alexander, 2/Lt., k. in a., 2/4/17 (122nd Bde.)
Carpenter, John Philip Morton, Lt (Tp.), k. in a., 15/9/16.
Carr, James, 2/Lt., k. in a., 21/3/18 (296th Bde.)
Carrick, James Douglas, 2/Lt., k. in a., 11/9/18 (X. 42 T.M.B.).
Carson-Packer, Gaythorne Raymond Robertson, 2/Lt. (Tp.), d. of w., 5/10/15
Carter, Edward, 2/Lt., killed, 25/9/15.
Carter, Ernest, 2/Lt., k. in a., 15/6/18 (240th Bde.).
Carter, J., 2/Lt., killed, 30/10/18 (and R.A.F.).
Cartwright, Donald Read, T/Lt. (A/Capt.), d. of w., 5/10/18 (C/153 Bde.).
Carver, Christian Creswell, Lt., d. of w., 23/7/17 (A/83rd Bde.).
Cary-Elwes, Douglas George, Lt., k. in a., 25/11/17.
Cashin, James, 2/Lt. (Tp.), k. in a., 13/10/17 (102nd Bde.).
Caslon, Thomas White, 2/Lt., k. in a., 25/11/15 (97th Bde.).
Cathcart, Francis John, 2/Lt. (Tp.), k. in a., 3/6/18 (A/55th Bde.).
Catling, Bernard, M.C., Lt. (A/Capt.), d. of w., 20/10/18 (52/15 Bde.).
Caton, Norman Newton, M.C., Lt., k. in a., 21/4/18 (124th Bde.).
Cavanagh, Frank, M.C., Capt. (A/Major), d. of w., 26/9/18 (88/14th Bde.).
Cavendish, Hugh Crawford, Major, k. in a., 1/8/16.
Chaddock, John Glover, 2/Lt., k. in a., 30/3/18 (86th Army Bde.) (Sig. Sub. Sect. R.E.).
Chalker, Eric, Lt., k. in a., 19/7/16.
Chamberlayne, Thomas Edmond Onslow, Lt. (Tp.), k. in a., 18/8/16 (73rd Bde.).
Chamberlin, Eric Valentine George, 2/Lt., k. in a., 31/12/17 (179th Army Bde.).
Chambers, William Trant, Major, d. of w., 2/6/15.
Chance, Andrew Ferguson, Capt., k. in a., 3/10/15.
Chantrill, Reginald Percy, Lt. (Tp.), k. in a., 26/10/17 (78th Bde.).
Chapman, Albert Charles, Capt. (Tp.), k. in a., 20/8/16 (29th Trench Mortar Schl.).
Chapman, Henry Ernest, M.C., Capt., d. of w., 22/3/18 (G. Bty. 17th Bde.).
Chapman, Perceval Christian, Capt., d. of w., 1/5/15.
Charles, Angus Alan Macgregor, Capt., k. in a., 20/12/14.
Chaventre, Alfred, 2/Lt., k. in a., 1/9/18 (H.A.C. 126th A. Bde.).
Chaworth-Musters, Philip Mundy, M.C., Lt. (T/Capt.), k. in a., 18/7/17.
Chenevix-Trench, Francis Maxwell, Major, k. in a., 31/10/14.
Chesterton, Frank Sidney, 2/Lt., d. of w., 11/11/16 (92nd Bde.).
Chestnut, John Albon, Lt., d. of w., 20/12/15.
Chetwynd-Stapylton, Henry Miles, Capt., k. in a., 14/11/15 (107th Bde.).
Chisholm, Edward Alexander, M.C., Major (Tp.), k. in a., 7/11/18. (161st Bde.).
Chisholm-Batten, John de Haviland, Capt. (A/Major), k. in a., 7/8/17.
Chittenden, Arthur George, 2/Lt., k. in a., 21/8/17.
Cholmely, Hugh Ralph, 2/Lt., d. of w., 14/6/15.
Christie, Dugald Roderick, 2/Lt., k. in a., 24/2/16 (66th Bty.).
Christie-Murray, Maurice, M.C., Lt. (Tp.), d. of w., 9/9/16 (112th Bde.).
Clapham, Graham Windyer, 2/Lt., d. of w., 10/5/17 (71st Bde.).
Clare, Horace Townshend, Lt. (A/Major), k. in a., 29/4/18 (245th Bde.).
Clark, Basil Vyse, Lt., k. in a., 24/7/18 (121 Bde.).
Clark, Charles, M.C., Lt. (A/Major), k. in a., 25/4/18 (295th Bde.).
Clark, Clifford Stanley, Lt., died, 30/5/19 (465th Bty.).
Clark, R. A. Ronaldson, Lt., died, 19/10/18 (and R.A.F.).
Clarke, Alexander Norwall, 2/Lt., k. in a., 24/8/18 (317th Bde.).
Clarke, Charles Basil, 2/Lt., k. in a., 21/4/16 (66th Bde.).
Clarke, Francis Herbert, M.C., 2/Lt., k. in a., 1/11/18 (28th Army Bde.).
Clarke, Geoffrey D'almaine Campbell, Lt. (Tp.), k. in a., 11/1/16 (att. T.M.B.).
Clarke, George Thomas, Lt. (Tp.), d. of w., 18/9/18 (C. Bty. 114th Bde.).
Clarke, Henry Hugh Franklyn, 2/Lt. (Tp.), k. in a., 24/9/17 (87th Bde.).
Clarke, J. E. L., Lt., k. in a., 14/9/14.
Clarke, Robert George, 2/Lt., k. in a., 9/9/18 (72nd Bde.).
Clarke, Roland Harwood, Lt. (Tp.), drowned, 21/2/17 (20th Bde.).
Clarke, Wilfrid Randall, Lt. (Tp.), killed, 4/2/18 (and R.F.C.).
Clayton, James Edward, M.C., Lt. (A/Major), k. in a., 24/6/18 (155th Bde.).
Clayton, Norman, Lt., d. of w., 13/4/18 (att. Portuguese Corps).
Cleeve, Frederick John Stewart, Col. (Brt.), died, 13/10/16 (10th D.G.C.).
Clery, John Cosney Lewis, 2/Lt., k. in a., 1/5/17 (78th Bde.).
Clery, Noel Cairns, Capt. (Tp.), k. in a., 24/7/16 (Div. H.Q.).
Clibborn, Cuthbert John Hamilton, Capt., k. in a., 14/12/15.

Cliff, Cecil Robson, L., died, 3/10/18 (161 Bde.).
Clifton, Ralph, 2/Lt., d. of w., 22/5/17 (att. H.Qrs., 14th Divn.).
Clow, Oswald William, 2/Lt., k. in a., 25/4/18 (156th Bde.).
Clutterbuck, Bernard Valentine, 2/Lt., k. in a., 13/7/17 (att. Z., 29th Trench Mort. Bty.).
Clutterbuck, David, Lt. (Tp.), d. of w., 6/5/17 (126th Bty., 28th Bde.).
Coate, Alfred Melbourne, 2/Lt. (Tp.), k. in a., 28/8/18 (36th Bde.).
Coates, George Washington Tate, 2/Lt., k. in a., 10/3/15.
Cobbold, Charles Townsend, 2/Lt., k. in a., 3/10/16 (32nd Bde.).
Cobbold, Robert Towshend, 2/Lt. (Tp.), k. in a., 25/9/15.
Cochrane, Donald James, Capt., k. in a., 8/5/15.
Cochrane, Reginald, 2/Lt., k. in a., 18/8/17 (282nd Bde.).
Cockaday, Aubrey George, 2/Lt., d. of w., 31/10/18 (10/147th Bde.).
Cocker, Thomas Edge, Lt. (A/Capt.), k. in a., 21/3/18 (Y 36, T.M.B.).
Coghlan, William Humphrey, 2/Lt., k. in a., 26/8/14.
Colbeck, L. G., 2/Lt., died, 3/1/18 (C/59th Bde.).
Colborn, Albert George, Lt., died, 10/10/18.
Coldwells, Charles Albert, 2/Lt. (Tp.), k. in a., 28/9/15.
Coles, Frederick George, M.C., 2/Lt., k. in a., 25/9/17 (att. Y/16 T.M.B.).
Coles, Thomas Wallace, Lt., d. of w., 1/5/16 (A/184.).
Colfox, Thomas David, 2/Lt., k. in a., 14/6/18 (42nd Bde.).
Colley, Philip Wellesley, 2/Lt., died, 31/10/18 (A/156th Bde.).
Collins, Charles Edwin, Lt., k. in a., 21/3/18 (24th Bde.).
Colmer, Arthur Cecil, 2/Lt., k. in a., 1/7/16 (96th Bde.).
Compton, William Horace Gordon, 2/Lt., d. of w., 17/6/17 (B. 186th Bde.).
Compton, William Walter, 2/Lt., k. in a., 25/4/18.
Condon, Thomas, 2/Lt., killed, 28/5/16.
Conlin, Bernard Francis, 2/Lt., d. of w., 9/10/16 (28th Bde.).
Connal, Arthur William Campbell, Lt., k. in a., 24/10/16 (38th Bde.).
Connell, William Patrick, Lt. (A/Capt.), killed, 24/11/18 (55th Bde.).
Connor, James Patrick, M.C., 2/Lt., k. in a., 7/6/17 (B/119 Army Bde.).
Cook, Harold Joseph Bede, Lt., d. of w., 28/5/18 (46th Bde.).
Cooke, Arthur Francis, 2/Lt., k. in a., 4/3/17 (29th Bde.).
Coombs, James Roy, 2/Lt., k. in a., 24/3/18 (93rd Army Bde.).
Cooney, Albert George, Lt., k. in a., 12/5/17 (291st Bde.).
Cooper, Cecil Bernard, 2/Lt., k. in a., 9/8/17 (38th Bde.).
Cooper, Cecil Fletcher, Major, died, 5/9/16 (D/121 Bde.).
Cooper, Leonard Russell, 2/Lt. (Tp.), drowned, 23/10/15.
Cooper, Ronald, 2/Lt., d. of w., 16/6/17 (119th Bde.).
Corbally, Lewis, Capt., d. of w., 6/5/15.
Corbett, Frank Harvey, M.C., Capt. (Tp.) (A/Major), k. in a., 5/5/18 (75th Bde.).
Coren, Edward Walker, 2/Lt., d. of w., 15/6/15.
Corfield, Egerton Anson Frederick, 2/Lt. (Tp.), d. of w., 17/6/17 (153rd Bde.).
Cormack, Sidney, M.C., 2/Lt., d. of w., 19/11/17 (D/15th Bde.).
Cormac-Walshe, Henry, Capt., d. of w., 7/11/17 (29th Bde.).
Cory, Cyril Noel, Capt., k. in a., 31/10/16 (att. T.M.B.).
Cotterill, Harold Gordon Wright, Lt., d. of w., 6/6/17 (att. R.F.C., 35th Sqd.).
Cotton, John, 2/Lt. (Tp.), d. of w., 1/7/16.
Counsell, Henry Cecil, 2/Lt., k. in a., 27/5/18 (45th Bde.).
Count, William Charles, Lt. (A/Capt.), k. in a., 5/7/17 (14th Bde.).
Coupland-Smith, Frederick Vyvyan, Lt. (Tp.), k. in a., 2/7/17 (173rd Bde.).
Covell, Howard Charles, 2/Lt. (Tp.), died, 26/6/16 (C/69th Bde.).
Cowan, A. A., 2/Lt., died, 16/7/18 (and R.A.F.).
Cowan, Henry Vivian, C.B., C.V.O., Col., died, 24/1/18.
Cowell, Henry Pulleine John, Major, d. of w., 9/8/15.
Cowland, Herbert Samuel, 2/Lt., k. in a., 15/4/17 (291st Bde.).
Cox, Hugh Bertram Hamilton, Lt. (Tp.), killed, 29/1/17 (and R.F.C.).
Coxe, Arthur Nelson, 2/Lt., d. of w., 3/11/14.
Crampton, William, M.C., Lt., died, 17/2/19.
Crampton, William, M.C., Lt., died, 17/2/19.
Craven, Brian Thornthwaite, 2/Lt. (Tp.), k. in a., 1/7/16.
Crawford, John Cane, 2/Lt., k. in a., 31/8/16 (14th Bde.).
Crawford, Reginald Waring Lindsay, 2/Lt., d. of w., 13/7/16 (63rd Bde.).
Creagh, O'Moore Charles, Lt., k. in a., 23/4/18 (108th Army Bde.).
Creasy, Robert Leonard, M.C., Lt. (A/Major), d. of w., 22/10/18 (D/190th Bde.).
Cree, William Cecil Holt, Capt., died, 24/10/14.
Crear, Malcolm Charlton, 2/Lt., died, 3/8/17 (and R.F.C.).
Crippin, Harry William, M.C., Capt., k. in a., 8/9/16 (56th Div. H.Q.).
Crisp, Stanley Searle, A/Major, d. of w., 8/12/17 (63rd Anti Aircraft Sec. S. Bty.).
Croft, E., M.C., Lt. (T/Capt.), died, 17/1/18.
Croll-Jones, Eustace Alvanley, 2/Lt., k. in a., 15/4/18 (9/38th Army Bde.).
Crook, Ernest Richard, 2/Lt. (Tp.), d. of w., 13/10/16 (59th Bde.).
Cropper, Thomas Andrew, Lt., d. of w., 19/4/18 (75th Bde.).
Cross, James, d. of w., 3/9/17 (41st D.A.C.).
Cross, Leslie, Lt., d. of w., 30/9/15.
Cross, Thomas Edward Kynaston, Capt., k. in a., 13/7/17.
Crouch, Clarence Cecil, M.C., 2/Lt., d. of w., 22/10/17 (A/50th Bde.).
Cruickshank, Eric, T/Capt. (A/Major), d. of w., 26/9/18 (87th Bde.).
Cruickshank, Ernest Alec Watson, Lt., k. in a., 21/8/18 (36th Bde.).
Cudmore, Milo Massey, Lt. (Tp.), k. in a., 27/3/16 (31st T. H. Bty.).
Cumming, Colin Edward, Lt., d. of w., 25/2/15.
Cunningham, Archibald John, Lt., k. in a., 24/3/18.
Cunningham, Stuart Gordon, 2/Lt., k. in a., 22/10/17 (35th Bde.).
Curle, William Sydney Noel, M.C., Major, d. of w., 23/3/18 (in German hands, B/107).
Curtice, Frederick Russell, Lt., d. of w., 17/11/16 (79th Bde.).
Cuthbertson, Hugh, 2/Lt., k. in a., 14/4/18 (275th Bde.).
Cuttle, G., 2/Lt., died, 9/5/18 (and R.A.F.).
Dacre, John Kenneth, M.C., Lt., d. of w., 30/9/16 (71st Bde.).
Dagge, Albert Lima, 2/Lt., k. in a., 1/7/16.
Dale, Robert Clunie, 2/Lt., k. in a., 18/8/16 (109th Bde.).
Dale, Rayner William, Major, died, 25/8/16.
Dalgleish, George Walter, Lt.-Col., died, 17/2/19.
D'Alton, James George, 2/Lt., k. in a., 27/10/17 (162nd Bde.).
Dannahy, William, 2/Lt. (Tp.), k. in a., 25/10/16 (92nd Bde.).
Dardier, Leonard Henry, 2/Lt. (Tp.), d. of w., 4/10/15.
Darts, William, 2/Lt., k. in a., 8/3/17 (66th Bde.).
Davey, A. V. P., 2/Lt., killed, 2/6/18 (and R.A.F.).
Davidson, Norman Randell, D.S.O., Major (Bt.-Lt.-Col.), d. of w., 5/10/17 (H.Q., 4th Div.).
Davidson, William Leslie, C.B., Col., died, 3/8/15 (4th Gen. Base Depot).
Davies, Aldborough Henry, 2/Lt., d. of w., 18/4/16.
Davies, Alan Wilmot, Lt., killed, 23/4/16 (att. R.F.C.).
Davies, Graham, Lt. (Tp.), d. of w., 27/7/17 (A/121 Bde.).
Davies, Harry Llanover, Lt., d. of w., 25/10/14.
Davies, Richard Harry Seymour, Lt. (Tp.), d. of w., 29/7/16 (88th Bde.).
Davies, Thomas Llewelyn, M.C., Major, killed, 16/9/18 (att. R.A.F.).
Davies, T. W. E., Lt. (A/Capt.), died, 20/5/18 (No. 1 Depot, R.F.A.).
Davies, Valentine Clements, M.C., Capt. (Tp.), d. of w., 10/7/16 (40th Bde.).
Davies, Wilfred John, Lt., k. in a., 5/11/16 (70th Bde.).
Davis, Cyril Arthur Ernest, 2/Lt. (Tp.), k. in a., 31/7/17 (108th Bde.).
Dawkins, Frederick Clifton, M.C., 2/Lt., d. of w., 2/9/17.
Dawson, Alfred, M.C., Major, k. in a., 20/5/17 (14th Bde.).
Dawson, Herbert Henry Mawson, 2/Lt. (Tp.), k. in a., 19/7/16 (148th Bde.).
Day, Charles Spencer, 2/Lt., d. of w., 25/4/18 (59th Bde.).
Day, Dennis Ivor, 2/Lt. (Tp.), d. of w., 7/10/15 (106th Bty.).
Day, George Francis Hermitage, 2/Lt., k. in a., 11/9/16.
Day, Henry James, 2/Lt., k. in a., 7/7/17 (71st Bde.).
Day, Leslie Terrett, Lt. (Tp.), k. in a., 1/7/16 (att. T.M.B.).
Deacon, Charles, M.C., Lt. (A/Major), d. of w., 14/5/18 (113th Bde.).
Dean, George Frederick, 2/Lt., k. in a., 16/10/17 (162nd Bde.).
Deane, Richard John, 2/Lt., killed, 18/7/17 (26th Bde.).
Deeks, Frederick William, 2/Lt., d. of w., 13/9/15 (69th Bty., 28th Div.).
Delamain, Frank Gun, 2/Lt., k. in a., 21/9/16 (104th Bde.).
De Lisle-Smith, Frank, 2/Lt., died, 31/10/18.
Deller, Harold James, 2/Lt., k. in a., 30/7/17 (104th Bde.).
Denison, Harry, D.S.O., Major, d. of w., 28/8/17.
Denman, Frank Christopher, 2/Lt., k. in a., 17/8/17 (84/11th Bde.).
Dennes, Wilfred, M.C., T/Capt. (A/Major), k. in a., 21/3/18 (82nd Bde.).
Dennis, James Owen Cuninghame, Lt., k. in a., 24/10/14.
Denny, Leonard George, 2/Lt., died, 21/4/17 (133rd Bde.).
De Pierres, Eric Noel, 2/Lt., d. of w., 16/9/17 (C/190th Bde.).
Deprez, Austin Edward, Capt., k. in a., 12/11/15 (62nd Bde.).
De Saumarez-Brock, Ranulf Steinthal, Lt. (Tp.), k. in a., 24/5/17 (Y/23. T.M.B.).
De Stacpoole, Roderick Algernon Antony, 2/Lt., k. in a., 11/3/15.
Devenish, Arthur Henry Noel, Major, died, 5/10/16.
Devenish, George Weston, Lt., k. in a., 6/6/17 (and R.F.C., 35th Sqd.).
Dewar, Robert Johnman, 2/Lt., d. of w., 3/10/18 (153rd Bde.).
Dibb, William Reginald, M.C., Lt., d. of w., 27/5/18 (37th Div. Trench Mortar Bty.).
Dicketts, George Humphrey, Lt., d. of w., 21/7/18 (24th Bde., 3rd Bty.).
Dickson, Sigurd Ayton, 2/Lt., k. in a., 1/2/17 (102nd Bde.).
Dinan, Francis Arthur, 2/Lt., k. in a., 31/7/17 (113rd Bde.).
Dixon, Charles Howard, Lt., d. of w., 12/9/17.
Doake, Samuel Henry, D.S.O., Capt. (A/Major), k. in a., 30/3/18 (52nd Army Bde.).
Dobb, Robert Alan, Capt., died, 22/12/17 (30th Bde.).
Dobson, Montague Charles, Major, killed, 26/9/15.
Dodd, Ernest John, 2/Lt. (T/Lt.), k. in a., 17/7/17.
Dodd, Westgarth John, 2/Lt., d. of w., 19/9/18 (X. 38th Med. T.M. Bty.).
Dolphin, Vernon Ommanney, Major, k. in a., 7/6/17 (17th Bde.).

Donaldson, Norman, Lt., k. in a., 10/3/15.
Donnally, Robert Charles, Lt. (Tp.), k. in a., 21/10/16 (147th Bde.) (97th Bty.).
Dooner, John Graham, D.S.O., Lt.-Col., k. in a., 31/7/18 (Staff. Div. H.Q.)
Dootson, Herbert, 2/Lt., d. of w., 5/11/17 (66th Bty.).
Doran, Edward Sheridan, 2/Lt., k. in a., 1/11/16.
V.C. Dougall, Eric Stuart, M.C., Lt. (A/Major), k. in a., 14/4/18 (88th Bde.).
Douglas, Archibald, 2/Lt., killed, 16/10/16 (and R.F.C.).
Douglas-Jones, William Eric Vyvian, 2/Lt., died, 15/1/15.
Douglass, George Percival, M.C., Lt., d. of w., 25/8/18 (157th Bde.).
Doyle, Eric Douglas, M.C., Lt., k. in a., 29/7/17 (190th Bde.).
Doyle, John Francis Innes Hay, C.M.G., D.S.O., Brig.-Gen., died, 19/2/19 (att. Staff).
Drake, Walker, 2/Lt., k. in a., 26/6/16.
Drake-Brockman, Ralph Zouch, M.C., 2/Lt., d. of w., 29/9/17 (46th Bde.).
Draper, Dudley, Lt., died, 21/2/18.
Drayson, John Douglas, M.C., T/Lt. (A/Capt.), k. in a., 10/4/17 (93rd Bde.).
Dresser, Bruce William, M.C., Lt., d. of w., 20/9/18 (27th Bde.).
Drought, George Thomas Acton, Major, d. of w., 14/6/15.
Drury, Alfred Aloysius, 2/Lt. (Tp.), k. in a., 16/11/16 (161st Bde.).
Drysdale, Alexander Icely, Major, k. in a., 28/7/16.
Du Buisson, John Edmund, 2/Lt., died, 11/10/16 (99th Bde.).
Du Cane, Hubert John, C.B., M.V.O., T/Brig.-Gen., died, 15/6/16 (Gen. Staff, Southern Army).
Duckett, William Garnard, M.C., 2/Lt., k. in a., 27/3/18 (300th Bde.).
Duerden, Edgar, Lt., d. of w., 17/8/17 (150th Bde.).
Duff, Guy Leith Assheton, Capt., d. of w., 2/9/16.
Duggan, Frederick, Capt., k. in a., 21/3/16.
Dunbar, Arbuthnot John, Capt., k. in a., 17/3/15.
Duncan, Edward Henry, 2/Lt., d. of w., 24/3/18 (93rd Army Bde.).
Dundas, George, M.C., Lt., d. of w., 2/9/18 (161st Bde.).
Dunlop, William, M.C., M.M., 2/Lt., k. in a., 30/10/18 (39th Bde.).
Dunlop, William James, 2/Lt. (Tp.), k. in a., 21/9/16.
Dunn, John, 2/Lt., k. in a., 20/9/18 (56th Bde.).
Dunn, John Hubert Malcolmson, 2/Lt., k. in a., 25/9/16 (18th Bde.).
Dupe, Cyril Harry, 2/Lt., d. of w., 21/3/18 (30th D.A.C., att. C/149th Bde.).
Durno, Ronald Walpole, 2/Lt., k. in a., 24/2/17 (att. Y.41 Trench Mortar Bty.).
Durrant, Alec William, Lt. (Tp.), k. in a., 13/11/16 (184th Bde.).
Dutton, John Gordon, M.C., T/Capt. (A/Major), d. of w., 5/4/18 (D. 107th Bde.).
Dutton, Joseph Issacher, 2/Lt., k. in a., 21/3/18 (82nd Bde.).
Eagar, Denis Geoffray, 2/Lt., k. in a., 28/9/18 (160th Bde.).
Eagar, Francis Russell, 2/Lt., k. in a., 9/5/15.
East, Lionel William Fellow, C.M.G., D.S.O., Col. (T/Brig.-Gen.), k. in a., 6/9/18 (Staff) (Comm. XIII. C. Hvy. Arty.).
Eastwood, Frederick Arthur Jervis, T/Lt. (A/Capt.) d. of w., 6/6/17 (103rd Bde.).
Edgington, William, 2/Lt., k. in a., 8/5/15.
Edwards, Bert, Lt., k. in a., 2/9/18 (281st Bde.).
Edwards, Frank Glencairn De Burgh, Lt., k. in a., 12/10/14.
Edwards, George Percy, M.C., Lt., d. of w., 2/10/18 (D/155th Bde.).
Edwards, George Richard Owen, D.S.O., T/Major, d. of w., 17/6/17 (C/173rd Bde.).
Edwards, John Hugh Evan Lloyd, 2/Lt., k. in a., 20/9/17 (139th Bde.).
Edwards, John Llewelyn, 2/Lt., k. in a., 7/9/17 (75th Bde.).
Eggleton, Frank, Lt., k. in a., 21/10/17 (17th Bde.).
Eggleton, Robert, 2/Lt. (T/Lt.), d. of w., 15/11/17 (33rd Bde.).
Eicke, Owen Macaulay, M.C., Lt. (Tp.), k. in a., 5/11/16 (62nd Bde.).
Elderkin, John Victor, 2/Lt. (A/Lt.), d. of w., 23/9/17 (59th Bde.).
Ellerby, Harry, 2/Lt. (Tp.), k. in a., 11/9/18 (122nd Bde.).
Ellershaw, Wilfrid, Brig.-Gen. (Tp.), drowned, 6/6/16.
Elliot, John, Lt., k. in a., 3/8/17 (108th Bde.).
Elliott, Edward, Lt., d. of w., 25/10/18 (B/181 Bde.).
Elliott, Frederick William, 2/Lt., k. in a., 19/7/16.
Elliott, Vere Arthur Edmonstone, Lt. (A/Capt.), k. in a., 25/3/18 (165th Bde.).
Ellis, David Ithel, M.C., Major, d. of w., 9/4/18 (285th Bde.).
Ellis, George Barker. Lt. (Tp.), k. in a., 21/7/16 (51st Bde.).
Emerton, Harry Burton, M.C., T/Lt. (A/Major), k. in a., 27/9/18 (B/178th Bde.).
Ellis, John Chute, 2/Lt., d. of w., 6/6/17 (106th Bde.).
Ellison, William Ronald, 2/Lt., d. of w., 20/6/15.
Elton, Frederick John, 2/Lt. (Tp.), d. of w., 11/9/15.
England, Raymond, Major, k. in a., 26/8/14.
Enright, Anthony Basil, 2/Lt., d. of w., 11/5/17 (D/17th Bde.).
Etheridge, Eckley Oxtoby, 2/Lt., k. in a., 12/7/17 (149th Bde.).
Evans, Albert Illtyd, 2/Lt., k. in a., 17/8/17 (85th Bty., att. 92nd Bde.).
Evans, Herbert Theodore Penrhys, Lt., k. in a., 4/10/16.
Evans, Noel Everard, 2/Lt., d. of w., 11/11/18 (121st Bty., 27th Bde.).
Evans, Percival Richard, T/Lt. (A/Major), d. of w., 6/9/17 (D/74th Bde.).
Faber, Stanley Colt, Major, k. in a., 30/3/17 (47th Bde.).
Fair, Arthur Edward Balfour, Major, k. in a., 16/8/17 (122nd Bde.).
Fairbairns, Joseph Maurice, 2/Lt., k. in a., 20/8/17 (8th Div. Amm. Col.).
Farmer, James Douglas, 2/Lt., k. in a., 4/11/14.
Farquhar, W. R., Lt., died, 23/3/18.
Farran, George Francis, Major, k. in a. 18/7/16 (98th Bde.).
Farrer, Henry Wyndham Francis Blackburn, M.C., Capt. (A/Major), k. in a., 30/10/18 (39th Bde.).
Fausset, Robert Clifford, Lt. (Tp.), d. of w., 16/11/16 (C74).
Fell, David Malcolm, 2/Lt., k. in a., 17/7/16.
Fellows, Mervyn, 2/Lt., d. of w., 25/8/17 (C/173rd Bde.).
Fendall, Charles Magrath, Lt. (Tp.), k. in a., 14/12/15.
Fendall, Denis John, 2/Lt., d. of w., 8/8/17 (and R.F.C., 4th Sqd.).
Fenwick, Percival Fenwick, 2/Lt., k. in a., 1/7/16.
Ferguson, Philip Hew, M.C., Capt. (A/Major), k. in a., 22/10/17 (152nd Bde.).
Ffrench, Evelyn Wilson, Capt., killed, 23/12/18 (and R.F.C.).
Field, Arthur Roland, M.C., 2/Lt., k. in a., 17/9/18 (70th Bde.).
Field, Linwood, D.S.O., M.C., Capt. (A/Major), k. in a., 26/10/17.
Figgures, Douglas Lionel, 2/Lt., d. of w., 15/10/18 (C/46th Bde.).
Filtness, John, Lt., d. of w., 22/5/18 (161st Bde.).
Findlay, Neil Douglas, C.B., Brig.-Gen., k. in a., 10/9/14.
Finn, Francis William, Lt., k. in a., 5/10/17.
Fisher, Edmund Montague Prinsep, 2/Lt., died, 31/3/18 (36th D.A.C.).
Fisher, Henry Mornington, M.C., 2/Lt., k. in a., 31/10/18 (att. 7/31st T.M.B.).
Fiske, Dudley, Lt., d. of w., 22/8/18 (86th Bde.).
Fitch, Douglas, 2/Lt., k. in a., 16/10/17 (162nd Bde.).
Fitch-Jones, Owen Edward, Lt. (Tp.), k. in a., 13/5/17 (13/275th Bde.).
Fitze, Gerald Gadsden, Lt., k. in a., 25/11/14.
Fitzwilliams, John Kenrick Lloyd, M.C., Major, k. in a., 30/8/18 (Z. 5th "A" Bde.).
Flecknoe, Percy James Deane, Lt., d. of w., 25/11/17 (64th Bde.).
Fleet, Aylmer Louis Elliot, M.C., Capt. (A/Major), k. in a., 10/9/18 (56th Bde.).
Fleming, Ernest Cole, M.C., Major, k. in a., 18/7/17 (C/121st Bde.).
Fletcher, Henry Mungles, 2/Lt., k. in a., 7/6/17 (att. Y. 30 T.M.B.).
Fletcher, Reginald William, 2/Lt., k. in a., 31/10/14.
Flinn, Edgar Wormald, 2/Lt., k. in a., 13/11/16 (34th Bde. and R.F.C.).
Fluke, Arthur Charles, 2/Lt., k. in a., 10/1/15.
Fooks, Edward Luckham, 2/Lt., k. in a., 31/10/16 (129th Bde.).
Forbes, Noel Edmund, 2/Lt., d. of w., 12/5/15.
Ford, Alfred Winn, M.C., 2/Lt., k. in a., 18/9/18 (42nd Bde.).
Ford, Richard, 2/Lt., k. in a., 3/2/17 (177th Bde.).
Forsdike, Charles William, 2/Lt., d. of w., 13/6/18 (129/42nd Bde.).
Forshall, John, Lt., k. in a., 12/4/18 (123rd Bde.).
Forster, Christopher Jack, Lt. (Acting), k. in a., 21/7/17 (att. 3rd Co., Spec. Bde., R.E.).
Forster, Frederick Richard, M.C., 2/Lt., d. of w., 3/10/17.
Forster, William Edward Blake, 2/Lt., died, 12/6/15.
Forsyth, John Cusack, Lt., k. in a., 22/9/14.
Forsyth, Roy Anderson, 2/Lt., k. in a., 28/11/17 (att. R.F.C., 7 Sqd.).
Forsyth, Samuel Sanford, Lt., k. in a., 25/9/15 (43rd Tr. How. Bty.).
Forsyth, William Allan, Capt., k. in a., 27/6/18 (and R.A.F.).
Foster, Alfred, 2/Lt., k. in a., 14/4/17 (32nd Bde.).
Foster, George, 2/Lt. (Tp.), k. in a., 16/5/17 (102nd Bde.).
Fouldes, Thomas John, Capt., k. in a., 25/6/18.
Fowler, Kenneth Ryeland, 2/Lt. (Tp.), k. in a., 3/6/15.
Fox, George, 2/Lt., d. o w., 24/5/15.
Fox, George Herbert, 2/Lt., k. in a., 23/4/16 (G.H.Q. Intelligence).
Fox, Thomas Herbert, Lt., A/Capt.), k. in a., 31/3/18 (41st Bde.).
Franklin, Edgar John, Lt. (T/Capt.), drowned, 17/4/17 (C/58th Bde.).
Franklin, Leslie Willoughby, Lt., d. of w., 16/10/18 (147th Bde.).
Fraser, James, 2/Lt., d. of w., 20/5/18 (330th Bde.).
Fraser-Tytler, Patrick Seton, Capt. (Tp.), k. in a., 3/8/16.
Frayling, Michael Stapleton, 2/Lt., k. in a., 16/9/16.
Freeman, Frank Ernest Allien, 2/Lt., k. in a., 21/3/18 (18th D.A.C., att. 83rd Bde.).
Freeman, Noel William, M.C., T/Capt. (A/Major), k. in a., 21/3/18 (68th/14th Bde.).
Freeman-Cowen, Cecil, 2/Lt., k. in a., 23/6/16.
French, Hon. Edward Fulke, 2/Lt., died, 13/11/18 (in German hands) (296th Bde.).
Frend, John Arthur Edward, 2/Lt., k. in a., 17/1/17 (281st Bde.).
Frew, James Robertson, T/Lt. (A/Capt.), d. of w., 23/11/16 (63rd Bde., 12th Div.).
Friend, Charles Philip, Lt., died, 15/10/18.
Frizelle. Archibald, 2/Lt., k. in a., 1/5/16 (75th Bde.).
Frost, Colin Blomfield, Lt. (Tp.), k. in a., 24/7/18 (44th Bde.).

Frost, Cyril Haddon, Lt. (Tp.), k. in a., 26/10/18 (403rd How. Bty.).
Frost, Ronald William, Lt., k. in a., 10/10/17 (94th Bde.).
Fry, Charles Edward, Lt., k. in a., 17/11/17.
Fryer, Stanley Phillipps, 2/Lt., k. in a., 27/10/18 (39th Bde. Y. 1st T.M.B.).
Fuller, John Severn, Lt. (T/Capt.), died, 15/3/19 (177th Bde.).
Fulton, John Duncan Bertie, C.B., Major (T/Lt.-Col.), died, 11/11/15 (and R.F.C.).
Furness, Montague Smith, 2/Lt., k. in a., 29/6/17 (3rd Bty. 45th Bde.).
Furse, Edmund William, Lt.-Col., killed, 19/5/18 88th Bde.).
Furse, George Armond, Capt., d. of w., 16/9/14.
Gage, Brenton Albert Hamilton, Lt. (T/Capt.), d. of w., 29/5/15.
Gaisford, Robert Sandeman, Lt., k. in a., 30/1/18 (att. R.F.C.).
Galbraith, James Robert, 2/Lt., died, 20/9/17 (A. 64th Bde.).
Gaillie, O. E., D.S.O. & M.C., Capt., k. in a., 7/12/17.
Gamblin, John Louis, 2/Lt., k. in a., 8/5/15.
Game, Hubert John, Lt. (Tp.), killed, 8/6/17 (and R.F.C.).
Garden, Charles Robert John, 2/Lt., died, 5/5/16.
Gardner, Frederick George Benjamin, 2/Lt. (Tp.), k. in a., 25/7/16.
Gardner, William Sutton, 2/Lt., k. in a., 6/3/17 (and R.F.C., 57th Sqd.).
Garland, George Harry Charles, 2/Lt., died, 4/3/17 (113th Bty., 25th Bde.).
Garnett, Kenneth Gordon, M.C., Lt. (Tp.), d. of w., 22/8/17.
Garnett, Laurence Henry, Lt. (Tp.), k. in a., 7/6/17.
Garvan, Edmund William, Lt., k. in a., 23/4/17.
Gates, Alan Ferrier, 2/Lt., d. of w., 20/8/17 (307th Bde.).
Gauld, Gordon Smith Mellis, M.C., Lt., killed, 25/3/18 (and R.F.C.).
Gayford, William George, 2/Lt. (Tp.), d. of w., 26/9/15 (69th Bde.).
Gee, Thomas, Lt., died, 13/11/17 (B/122nd Bde.).
Geere, Douglas Joseph, 2/Lt., k. in a., 23/2/16.
Gell, James Bainton Stowell, 2/Lt. (Tp.), k. in a., 9/10/18 (56th Bde.).
Gent, George Edward, 2/Lt., k. in a., 14/9/17 (379th Bde.).
Gerrard, John Maurice Harold, 2/Lt., d. of w., 28/8/18 (74th Bde.).
Gibson, Arthur, 2/Lt., d. of w., 6/7/17 (att. Y. 29th T.M.B.).
Gibson, Ollyett Archibald M., 2/Lt., d. of w., 27/8/16.
Giffard, Edmund Hamilton, Lt. (Act. Major), d. of w., 10/11/18 (2nd Bde.).
Giffard, Robert, Capt., d. of w., 1/11/14.
Giffard, Sydney, Lt., k. in a., 3/5/15.
Gilbert, Kenneth Nigel Wilson, M.C., Capt. (Act.), died, 15/10/18 (and R.A.F.).
Gill, Erold Waring, Lt. (Tp.), d. of w., 25/7/16 (86th Bde.).
Gilligan, John Joseph, 2/Lt., k. in a., 25/4/18 (123rd Bde.).
Gillman, Angus George, M.C., Major, k. in a., 29/4/17 (15th Bde.).
Gilpin, Robert, Lt., d. of w., 3/7/15.
Gimblett, Raymond John, 2/Lt., died, 20/2/19.
Girdlestone, H. W., Lt., killed, 30/4/18 (and R.A.F.).
Gliddon, Maurice, M.C., Lt. (Tp.) (Act. Capt.), d. of w., 16/8/17 (108th Bde.).
Glover, Leonard James, 2/Lt., d. of w., 1/11/17 (B/82nd Bde.).
Goddard, William Thomas, 2/tL., d. of w., 13/10/17 (12th Bty., 35th Bde.).
Godfrey, John Leslie, 2/Lt., d. of w., 7/5/18 (113th Bde.).
Godman, Lawrence, D.S.O., Major (Act. Lt. Col.), d. of w., 30/9/17 (46th Bde.).
Godson, William Curry, Lt. (Tp.), k. in a., 3/5/17 (46th Bde.).
Godwin, George, 2/Lt., k. in a., 28/9/18 (17th Bde.).
Goldie, Mark Leigh, D.S.O., M.V.O., Major, died, 5/3/15.
Goldsmith, Bertie, Lt., d. of w., 13/10/18 (30/39 Bde.).
Goodall, Edward Orme Clement, Lt. (Tp.), d. of w., 9/11/17 23rd Bde.).
Goodall, Harold Armitage, 2/Lt., k. in a., 22/3/18 (Z. 16th T.M.B.).
Goodfellow, Eric Hector, Lt. (Tp.), k. in a., 9/3/16.
Goodfellow, Hugh Douglas, Capt. (Tp.), d. of w., 17/12/15.
Goodwin, Cecil Herbert, 2/Lt., d. of w., 13/10/18 (D/189th Bde.).
Goodwin, Cecil Stanley, Capt. (Tp.), k. in a., 31/8/16.
Goodwin, Dudley Fletcher, 2/Lt. (Act. Capt.), d. of w., 7/3/17 (157th Bde.).
Goold, Louis, 2/Lt., d. of w., 11/5/18 (122/52/Bty.).
Gordon, Charles Cecil, Capt. (Act. Major), k. in a., 4/6/17 (110/Bde.).
Gordon, Douglas Stanley, 2/Lt., k. in a., 21/2/18 (and R.F.C.).
Gordon, Roland Elphinstone, M.C., Capt. (Act. Major), d. of w., 30/8/18 (C. Bty., 251st Bde.).
Gorst, James, 2/Lt., died, 20/5/17 (42nd Bde.).
Gosse, William Hay, M.C., Capt. (Tp.) (Act. Major), k. in a., 5/4/18 (79th Bde.).
Gossett, William Beresford, 2/Lt., k. in a., 1/11/14.
Gough, John Bloomfield, Lt., k. in a., 9/9/14.
Gough, John Noel, 2/Lt., k. in a., 8/3/18 (att. V. 29th T.M.B.).
Gough, Rupert, M.C., 2/Lt., d. of w., 28/10/17 (71st Bty.).
Gould, Clifford, M.C., Lt., k. in a., 24/8/18 (14th Bde.).
Gould, Chalkley Vivian Lt. (Tp.) (Act. Major), k. in a., 9/6/17 (25th Bde.).
Gould, Henry Charles Hamerton, 2/Lt., d. of w., 15/4/17 (32nd Bde.).
Grace, Frank, Lt. (Act. Capt.), d. of w., 5/11/17 (19th Bty.).
Graham, Francis, D.S.O. & M.C., Capt. (Act. Major), k. in a., 28/3/18 (71st Bde.).
Graham, John Frederick, Major (Tp.), k. in a., 1/7/16 (150th Bde.).
Graham, John Robertson, M.C., 2/Lt., d. of w., 22/9/16 (C/96th Bde.).
Granet, Edward John, C.B., Brig. Gen. (Tp.), died, 22/10/18.
Grant, Humphrey de Butts, Capt., k. in a., 3/10/15.
Grant, Ian Alan William, Lt., k. in a., 24/4/17 (70th Bde.).
Grant, Noel, 2/Lt., k. in a., 25/5/17 (156th Bde.).
Grant-Suttie, Archibald Ronald, Lt., d. of w., 23/7/17 (L/15th Bde.).
Grassick, William Henderson, 2/Lt., died, 9/2/19.
Graves, Evelyn Paget, Capt. (T/Major), k. in a., 6/3/17 (att. R.F.C., 60th Sqd.).
Gray, Cecil Edward Patrick, 2/Lt., d. of w., 11/10/17 (att. Bde. R.H.A.).
Gray, John Parnwell, 2/Lt., died, 13/9/18 (14 D.A.C., D/47th Bde.).
Gray, Norman McNeil, Major, d. of w., 9/2/16.
Gray, Patrick Walworth, 2/Lt., d. of w., 9/5/17 (153rd Bde.).
Gray, Roderick Hubert, M.C., 2/Lt., d. of w., 2/12/17 (7th Bde.).
Grayson, Ambrose Dixon Holdrege, Capt., k. in a., 13/10/14.
Grayson, George, 2/Lt., d. of w., 24/12/18 (155th Army Bde.).
Greatwood, Harold, 2/Lt., d. of w., 20/10/17 (36th Bde.).
Green, Arthur Knowles, 2/Lt., k. in a., 30/9/17 (146th Bde.).
Green, G. W. Ashdown, 2/Lt., k. in a., 8/3/18 (att. R.F.C.).
Greenfield, Gerald Henry, 2/Lt., d. of w., 17/8/17 (242nd A.F.A. Bde.).
Greenop, Garnet Arthur Claude, 2/Lt., k. in a., 9/7/16 (172nd Bde.).
Greenslade, Francis Harold, 2/Lt., k. in a., 31/5/18 (52nd Bde.).
Greensted, Walter, 2/Lt., d. of w., 22/10/18 (50th Bde.).
Greenwood, Charles Norman, M.C., 2/Lt., d. of w., 5/9/18 70th Bde.).
Gresley, Roger, M.C., Lt. (Act. Major), d. of w., 6/9/18.
Gribbell, Arthur Frank, Capt. (Tp.), died, 13/3/16.
Grieve, James Ross, M.C. (Tp.) (Capt.) (Act. Major), k in a., 4/4/18 (C/107/Bde.).
Griffin, Reginald Herbert, 2/Lt. (Act. Capt.), d. of w. 7/7/17 (Empld. R.G.A., 21st S.B.).
Griffith, Oswald, 2/Lt., k. in a., 27/2/15.
Griffith, Trevor Llewelyn, Lt. (Act.), k. in a., 30/10/17 (82nd Bde.).
Griffiths, Allen Rhys, 2/Lt. (Tp.), k. in a., 9/8/15.
Griffiths, David George, M.C., Lt., d. of w., 15/12/18 (84th Army Bde.).
Griffiths, John Herbert, 2/Lt., d. of w., 29/5/18 (B/175 Bde.).
Grimwood, Bertie Constantine Ruffell, M.C., Lt., k. in a., 7/11/17 (att. R.F.C.).
Groome, Robert Edward Charles, 2/Lt., d. of w., 4/3/15.
Grosvenor, the Hon. Richard Eustace, Capt., k. in a., 13/10/15.
Guilding, Sidney Cecil, 2/Lt., died, 4/11/18 (106th Bde.).
Gunn, Wilfred Herbert, 2/Lt., k. in a., 26/3/18 (331st Bde.).
Gutmann, Walter, 2/Lt., d. of w., 7/5/17 (71st Bde.).
Gye, Denison Allen (Tp.), Lt. (Act. Capt.), k. in a., 28/2/17 (15th Bde.).
Hadden, Nigel Clement Charles, Capt. (Tp.), d. of w., 9/4/16 (14th Bty.).
Haeffner, Frederick Wilfred, 2/Lt., w. in a., 9/7/16 (149th Bde.).
Hague, Harold William, 2/Lt., k. in a., 16/6/18 (47/Bde.).
Haines, Stephen Gilbert, 2/Lt., d. of w., 4/5/17 (70th Bde.).
Hall, Charles William, Lt., d. of w., 10/8/17 (65th Bde.).
Hall, Harold Platt, M.C., 2/Lt., d. of w., 9/11/18 (C/83 Bde.)
Hall, James Muir, 2/Lt., d. of w., 23/4/17 (51st Bde.).
Hall, Luther, 2/Lt. (Tp.), k. in a., 22/9/16 (22nd Bde.).
Hall, Roger Holinsworth (Tp.) Lt. (Actg. Capt.), d. of w., 11/7/17 (Anti-aircraft Group).
Hall, Thomas Kershaw, 2/Lt., k. in a., 9/10/17 (6/241/Bde.).
Hallett, Arthur Mapleton, Capt., k. in a., 2/6/16 (125th Bde.).
Halley, Edward Harland, Lt. (Tp.), k. in a., 26/11/17 (att. 12th T.M.B.).
Halliday, Charles Walter Alexander, 2/Lt., d. of w., 17/11/16.
Hallward, Basil Murray, Lt. (Tp.), k. in a., 9/4/18.
Halliwell, Eric John, Lt., k. in a., 11/9/17 (and R.F.C., 57th Sqd.).
Hame, Arthur Willam, Lt. (Act. Capt.), k. n a., 21/5/18 (att. X. 21. T.M.B.).
Hamilton, Andrew Douglas, Lt., died, 26/4/19 (310th Bde.).
Hamilton, Harry Austin, Major, k. in a., 25/1/16.
Hamilton, Robert Gordon, 2/Lt., k. in a., 27/9/16 77th Bde.).
Hammond, Richard Martin, Lt., d. of w., 20/5/18 (X/66. T.M.B.) (P. of W.).
Handfield-Jones, Neville Montague, 2/Lt., k. in a., 25/9/15.
Hannam, Sydney Philip, Lt., k. in a., 11/7/16 (161st Bde.).
Harbord, Stephen Gordon, M.C., Lt. (Actg. Capt.), k. in a., 14/8/17 (153rd Bde.).
Harder, John Charles Victor, 2/Lt., d. of w., 26/4/18 (50th Bde.).
Harding, Francis Edward Basil, Capt., d. of w., 1/12/15.
Harding, James Golding, Lt., k. in a., 30/10/17 (21st T.M. Bty.).
Hardy, Walter John, 2/Lt., died, 21/8/17 (15th Bde., L. Bty.).
Hare, Alexander Balfour, 2/Lt., k. in a., 31/10/16 (2nd Bde.).
Harger, Frank Eric, 2/Lt. (Tp.), k. in a., 16/12/15.
Hargreaves, James Pater, 2/Lt., k. in a., 9/10/17 (126th Bde.).
Harker, George Ernest, 2/Lt. (Tp. Lt.), k. in a., 19/5/17 (40th Bde.).

Harker, Herbert Charles, 2/Lt., d. of w., 25/3/18 (393rd Bde.).
Harman, John Bower, 2/Lt., k. in a., 26/8/14.
Harman, William, 2/Lt., k. in a., 27/3/18 (106th Bde.).
Harold, J. P. B., Lt., d. of w., 15/2/18 (att. R.F.C.).
Harper, Alan Gordon, 2/Lt. (Tp.), k. in a., 1/6/17 (187th Bde.).
Harris, Frederick T., 2/Lt., d. of w., 19/9/15.
Harris, Hugh Ripley, Lt., died, 20/11/18 (att. 1st T.M.B.).
Harrison, A. H., Major, died, 3/11/18.
Harrison, Charles Hibbert, Lt., k. in a., 31/7/17.
Harrison, Halford Claude Vaughan, Major (Tp.) Lt. Col., died, 1/4/16.
Harrison, Roland Damer, D.S.O., Major, k. in a., 16/9/17.
Hart, George Washington, Lt. (Tp.) (Act. Major), k. in a., 15/3/17 (189th Bde.).
Hartley, Norman Curtis, 2/Lt., d. of w., 20/1/18 (19th D.A.C.).
Harvey, Gerald Franklyn, Lt., k. in a., 8/11/15 (and R.F.C.).
Harvey, Kenneth Watson, Lt., d. of w., 27/9/15 (19th Anti-Air-craft Section).
Harvey, William Henry, 2/Lt. (Tp.), k. in a., 23/10/18 (88th Bde.).
Harvey, William Reginald, Lt. (Tp.), d. of w., 23/9/17 B/95th Bde.).
Harvie, James, 2/Lt., d. of w., 8/6/16 (D/93).
Hassard, Edward John, M.C., Lt., died, 7/11/18 (B/110 Bde.).
Hawkins, Alexander Edward, Capt. (Act. Major), d. of w., 12/12/17 (B/181 Bde.).
Hawkins, Charles Francis, Major, k. in a., 25/4/15.
Hawkins, Humphry Cæsar, M.C., 2/Lt., k. in a., 23/4/18 (121 Bde.).
Hawks, Albert John Everdale, 2/Lt., d. of w., 15/6/17 (79th Bde.).
Hawksley, John Plunkett Verney, D.S.O., Lt. Col. (Tp.), k in a., 8/8/16 (110th Bde.).
Haworth, Philip Theodore, 2/Lt., d. of w., 3/5/17 (D/86th Bde.).
Haydon, Edgar Frederick Bewes, 2/Lt., k. in a., 19/7/16.
Haydon, George Francis, 2/Lt., k. in a., 19/8/16 (C/175th Bde.).
Haylett, Newman, 2/Lt. (Tp.), d. of w., 19/8/16 (166th Bde.).
Hayter, Eric Francis Seafourth, 2/Lt., k. in a., 21/3/18 (87th Bty., 27th Bde.).
Hayward, Bertram Richard, 2/Lt., k. in a., 6/6/15.
Hayward, Kenneth Alfred, Capt., died, 22/11/18.
Hayward, Edward Ronald, 2/Lt., k. in a., 20/12/16 (99th Bty.).
Hay-Webb, Charles Robert Forbes, Capt. (Tp.), k. in a., 28/12/16 (235th Bde.).
Head. Arthur, M.M., 2/Lt., d. of w., 6/9/18 (44th Bde.).
Headley, Herbert Marshall, 2/Lt., k. in a., 11/3/17 (att. R.F.C.).
Heale, Arthur George, M.C., Lt., d. of w., 23/4/18 (41/42nd Bde.).
Heape, Brian Ruston, Lt. (Act. Capt.), k. in a., 16/5/17 (162nd Bde.) (A Bty.).
Hearn, Edward Thomas Hills, 2/Lt., k. in a., 11/9/17 (and R.F.C., 57th Sqd.).
Hearsch, Edward, 2/Lt., died, 28/6/15.
Heath, Edmund Griffith, Capt., k .in a., 25/9/15.
Heath-Caldwell, Martin Frederick, 2/Lt., k. in a., 16/5/15.
Hebblethwaite, Abraham Rhodes, 2/Lt. (Tp.), k. in a., 3/10/15.
Hebblethwaite, John Christopher, Lt. (Tp.), k. in a., 26/6/16.
Hemsley, Godfrey Hamilton, 2/Lt., k. in a., 12/10/17 (255th Bde.).
Hemsley, James Mortimer, 2/Lt., died, 28/7/17 (att. R.G.A. Derajet Mtn. Bty.).
Hemstead, John, 2/Lt., k. in a., 16/4/17 (106th Bde.).
Hemus, Cyril Harcourt, M.C., 2/Lt., d. of w., 27/3/18 (B/87th Bde.).
Henderson, Charles Edward Piercy, Capt., k. in a., 17/11/16 (71st Bde.).
Henley, Anthony Warton, 2/Lt., d. of w., 21/1/17 (156th Bde.).
Henman, Richard Mox, M.C., Lt. (Act. Major), died, 3/11/18.
Henney, Herbert Norman, 2/Lt., k. in a., 25/4/17 (17th Bde.).
Henry, Walter, 2/Lt. (Tp.) (Act. Capt.), k. in a., 8/10/16 (W.40 T.M.B.).
Hepburn, Reginald, Lt., died, 14/6/19.
Herbert, Owen William Eugene, 2/Lt., k. in a. about 27/10/14.
Hermon-Hodge, George Guy, Capt., d. of w., 7/7/16 (165th Bde.).
Hesketh, William Cecil, Lt. (Tp.), k. in a., 9/10/16 (199th Bde.).
Hess, Augustus George, 2/Lt., d. of w., 25/2/15.
Heveningham, Lionel Joseph, 2/Lt., k. in a. 7/10/18 (158th Bde.).
Hewat, Bertie Barron, M.C., 2/Lt., k. in a., 1/12/17 246th Bde.).
Hext, Francis John, D.S.O., M.C., Capt. (Act. Major), d. of w., 9/5/18 (41st Bty., 42nd Bde.).
Heynes, Dudley Hugo, 2/Lt., k. in a., 16/5/18 (14th Army Bde.).
Hibbert, Arthur James, 2/Lt. died, 14/8/17 (79th Bde.).
Hicklenton, Donald Stuart, 2/Lt., k. in a., 24/8/18 (86th Bde.).
Hickman, John George, 2/Lt., k. in a., 4/10/17 (50th Bde.).
Hickman, William Christie, 2/Lt., k. in a., 1/7/16 (175th Bde.).
Higginbotham, Robert Edward, 2/Lt., k. in a., 29/9/18.
Higginson, John Herbert, 2/Lt., k. in a., 30/11/17 (att. 5th Bde., R.H.A.).
Higgon, Archibald Bellairs, Major, k. in a., 10/9/15.
Hilary, Henry Jephson, 2/Lt., d. of w., 3/6/17 (17th Bde.).
Hildage, Harry, 2/Lt., k. in a., 15/4/17 (27th Bde.).
Hilditch, Charles Henry, 2/Lt., k. in a., 23/10/18 (27th Bde.).
Hill, Alan Purdie Dunlop, Capt. (Tp.), died, 8/2/19 (att. R.A.F.).
Hill, Leonard Coulthard, M.C., Lt. (Act .Capt.), died, 10/10/18 (att. 4th Army Art School.
Hill, Leonard Grenville, 2/Lt., k. in a., 9/11/16 (48th Bde.).
Hill, Reginald Percy, 2/Lt., d. of w., 25/8/18 (72nd Bde.).
Hill, William, Lt. (Tp.), k. in a., 30/10/17 (86th Army Bde.).
Hind, Reginald Charles, 2/Lt., k. in a., 6/2/18 (160th Bde.).
Hindle, Alfred Herbert, 2/Lt., k. in a., 12/5/18 (17th Bde.).
Hindle, Harold Burn, Lt. (Tp.), k. in a., 27/3/18 ("G" Bty., R.H.A.).
Hindson, Leslie Reginald Probyn, Lt., k. in a., 10/6/17 (187th Bde.).
Hindson, Reginald Gordon, 2/Lt., died, 13/9/14.
Hines, Harold William, M.C., 2/Lt., k. in a., 7/10/17 (113th Army Bde.).
Hinton, Godfrey Bingham, C.M.G., Lt.-Col., k. in a., 21/3/18 (26th Army Bde.).
Hitchings, Richard Gordon, Lt. (Act. Capt.), k. in a., 10/7/17 (38th D.A.C.).
Hoare, Eric Sutherland, 2/Lt., d. of w., 11/11/16 (2nd Bde.).
Hoare, Percy James, 2/Lt. (Tp.), k. in a., 18/9/18 (117th Bde.).
Hocking, E. C., 2/Lt., killed, 28/10/18 (and R.A.F.).
Hodgkinson, Geoffrey Still, Lt., k. in a., 24/7/17 (277th Bde.).
Hodgson, Reginald Drury, Capt. (Tp.), k. in a., 21/3/18 (82nd Bde.).
Hodgson, William Hope, Lt. (Tp.), k. in a., 17/4/18 (11th Army Bde.).
Hogarth, Archibald McDonald, Lt., d. of w., 9/7/16 (A/104).
Hogge, Thomas Henry, Lt., k. in a., 5/10/17 (24th Bde.).
Holland, Cyril, Capt., k. in a., 9/5/15.
Holland, Charles Stewart, Major, k. in a., 24/8/14.
Holland, Charles Trevenent, Lt., k. in a., 9/5/15.
Hollis, Victor William, M.C., 2/Lt., k. in a., 22/8/17 (281st Bde.).
Hollom, Ernest Albert Bruce, Lt. (Tp.), k. in a., 24/7/16 (53rd Bde.).
Holmes, Bryan Hanby, 2/Lt., died, 9/11/18 (5th Bde.).
Holmes, Thomas Gerald, 2/Lt., k. in a., 27/3/18 (A/16. Bde.).
Holt, Geoffrey Vesey, 2/Lt., k. in a., 2/9/17 (91st Bde.).
Holton, John Arthur, 2/Lt., k. in a., 4/10/17 (103rd Bde.).
Hone, Gilbert Bentoit, 2/Lt., k. in a., 18/8/17 (121st Bde.).
Hooper, Stuart Huntly (Hon.), Lt.-Col., died, 31/5/15 (D.A.A.G.).
Hoops, Guy Staveley, 2/Lt. (Tp.), died, 27/2/17.
Hopkins, Edward Favill George, 2/Lt., k. in a., 30/3/17 (181st Bde.).
Hore, Cecil William, 2/Lt., k. in a., 26/4/17 (47th Bde.).
Hornbeak, George Henry, 2/Lt., k. in a., 2/10/17 (22nd Bde.)
Horncastle, Cyril Charles Shubert, Lt., died, 8/1/19.
Hornung, John Peter, 2/Lt. (Tp.), d. of w., 20/2/16.
Horton, Victor John, 2/Lt., k. in a., 3/12/17 (161st Bde.).
Hosking, Cyril Gordon, Lt., killed, 26/10/14 (and R.F.C.).
Hoskyns-Abrahall, Christopher Henry, 2/Lt., killed, 22/12/17 (att. R.F.C.).
Howard, Dennis Brook, M.C., 2/Lt. (Tp.) (Act. Capt.), k. in a., 22/10/17 (35th Bde.).
Howarth, Frederick Ewart, 2/Lt., k. in a., 31/5/18 (74 Bde. X. Gds., T.M.B.).
Howe. Frederick Norman, 2/Lt., k. in a., 25/4/18 (84/11 Bde.).
Howells, John Hubert, 2/Lt., k. in a., 9/10/17 (att. 15th Bde. R.H.A.).
Howfield, John Arthur, M.C., 2/Lt., k. in a., 1/9/18 (75th Bde.).
Howse, Basil Thomas, 2/Lt., died, 18/9/16.
Howson, John Frederick, Lt., died, 18/10/18.
Hoyland, Godfrey Algernon, M.C., Lt. (Act. Capt.), d. of w., 3/10/18 (36th Bde.).
Hudson, Jocelyn Hope, Lt. (Tp.), d. of w., 12/1/16 (C. Bty., 49 Bde.).
Hudson, Robert Dennis, 2/Lt. (Tp.), k. in a., 25/1/16.
Hughes, Harold, 2/Lt., d. of w., 23/4/17 (27th Bde.).
Hughes, Myrddin McKelvie, M.C., Lt., k. in a., 16/5/18 (14th Army Bde.).
Hughes, W., 2/Lt., killed, 19/11/18 (and R.A.F.).
Hughes-Gibb, Charles Pomery, Capt., d. of w., 25/7/16 (158th Bde.).
Hughes-Gibb, Harold Francis, Lt. (Tp.), k. in a., 18/4/17.
Hughesdon, Arthur Hamilton, Lt., k. in a., 27/9/18 (59th Bde.).
Huleatt, Francis Hugh, M.C., Capt. (Act. Major), d. of w., 28/2/17 (C/83rd Bde.).
Hull, Edward Cecil Gordon, Lt., d. of w., 26/8/17 (30/39th Bde.).
Hulley, Arthur Henry Booth, Lt. (Tp.), died, 4/12/18.
Hulme, Clarence Waller, M.C., 2/Lt., k. in a., 16/9/18 (317th Bde.).
Humphreys, John Alan, 2/Lt., k. in a., 31/8/17 (C/64th Bde.).
Humphreys, Spencer Noel, M.C., 2/Lt., k. in a., 10/2/17 (116th Bde.).
Humphreys-Jones, Shon Theodore, Lt., k. in a., 14/11/17 (86th Army Bde.).
Hunt, Alfred John, 2/Lt., d. of w., 28/11/14.
Hunt, Alfred Thomas, Lt., died, 31/10/18.
Hunt, Claude Holdsworth, Capt. (Tp.), d. of w., 2/4/17 (att. 18 Corps HQ.).
Hunt, Frederick Arthur Lt., died, 21/11/18.
Hunt, James Charles Marjoribanks, Lt., k. in a., 10/8/16.

Hunt, Roger Victor Cecil, 2/Lt. (Tp.), d. of w., 1/10/18 (B/155th Army Bde.).
Hunter, Johnston Shaw Kirker, 2/Lt., k. in a., 30/6/16 (157th Bty.).
Hunter, Thomas William, M.C., Lt., d. of w., 24/10/18 (113th Bty., 25th Bde.).
Hurst, Herbert William, 2/Lt., d. of w., 10/10/17 (C/295th Bde.).
Hurst-Brown, Dudley, 2/Lt., d. of w., 15/6/15.
Hutson, William Cecil, 2/Lt., k. in a., 21/3/18.
Hyde, Leslie Arthur, 2/Lt., died, 26/10/15.
Iddon, Harold, 2/Lt., d. of w., 23/8/18 (D/173 Bde.).
Iles, John Francis, Lt. (Tp.), k. in a., 2/6/17 (165th Bde.).
Ince, Hugh Ethelred McCarthy, Lt. (Act. Major), k. in a., 4/11/16 (2nd Bde.).
Innes, James Stuart d'Auvergne, M.C., Lt., k. in a., 5/8/17 (189th Bde.).
Ireland, Albert, 2/Lt., d. of w., 9/7/16 (D. 50).
Ireland, Arthur William, 2/Lt., k. in a., 23/11/17 (256th Bde.).
Ireland, James, 2/Lt., died, 24/7/18.
Ireland, Robert Clifford, 2/Lt., d. of w., 7/11/16 (133rd Bde.).
Ironside, William Stewart, D.S.O., M.C., Lt. (Act. Major), k in a., 2/11/18 (24th Bde.).
Irvine, Edward White, 2/Lt., k. in a., 27/3/18 (186th Bde.).
Irvine-Watson, John, 2/Lt., k. in a., 14/8/17 (B/110).
Irving, Archibald Denys, 2/Lt., d. of w., 16/9/18 (82nd Bde.).
Ivatts, Selwyn, M.C., 2/Lt., k. in a., 8/10/17 (B/93rd Bde.).
Ives, Henry James Mansfield, 2/Lt., d. of w., 28/4/17 (255th Bde.).
Jack, James Charles, D.S.O., M.C., Major, d. of w., 31/5/18 (D/150/Bde.).
Jackson, Arthur Lloyd, Lt. (Tp.) (Act. Capt.), k. in a., 24/4/18.
Jackson, Martin de Carle, 2/Lt., k. in a., 5/11/16.
Jackson, Robert Raimes, M.C., Capt., d. of w., 1/11/17 (105/29th Bde.).
Jackson, Sidney Douglas, 2/Lt., k. in a., 3/5/17 (31/35/Bde.).
Jacobson, Lyonel Hugh, M.C., Lt. (Tp.), k. in a., 29/4/17 (D. Bty. 50th Bde.).
Jaggers, William John, 2/Lt., k. in a., 20/9/17 (277 Army Bde.).
James, Edward Scott, Capt. (Tp.), died, 19/8/17 (B/102 Bde.).
Jaques, George. 2/Lt., k. in a., 25/9/17 (B. 236/Bde.).
Jarvis, Arthur Bernard, 2/Lt. (Tp.), k. in a., 3/8/17 (177th Bde.).
Jebb, Arthur Beresford, 2/Lt. (Tp.), k. in a., 17/6/16 (X. 16 T.M.B.).
Jeffery, Tom Forbes, 2/Lt., d. of w., 17/4/18 (156th Bde.).
Jenkins, Ernest, 2/Lt., k. in a., 2/9/18 (40th Bde.).
Jenkins, Garrett Primrose, 2/Lt., k. in a., 7/9/17 (C/75th Bde.).
Jennings, Alexander, Lt. (Tp.), Capt., died, 7/4/17 (attd. R.F.C. 29th Sqd.) (P. of W.).
Jennings, H. W. McIvor, 2/Lt. (Tp.), died, 29/2/16.
Jephson, William Jermy, 2/Lt. (Tp.), k. in a., 26/9/18 (175th Bde.).
Jerrett, Sidney, 2/Lt., d. of w., 8/5/17 (28th Bde.).
Johns, Owen Llewellyn, 2/Lt. (Tp.), k. in a., 28/6/16 (T.M. Bty.).
Johnson, Arthur Graham, Major (Tp. Lt.-Col.), k. in a., 17/9/17 (33rd D.A.C.).
Johnson, Cyril Goode, 2/Lt., k. in a., 7/6/17 (149th Bde.).
Johnson, Edward Fielder, Capt. (Tp.), k. in a., 7/12/17 (B/310 Bde.).
Johnson, Frederick Stansfield, 2/Lt. (Tp.), k. in a., 4/11/18 (92nd Bde.).
Johnson, Joseph John Claud, 2/Lt., d. of w., 5/4/18 (48th Army Bde.).
Johnson, Ronald Lindsay, Lt. (Tp.) (Act. Capt.), k. in a., 29/5/17 (H.Q. Div. T. Mortars).
Johnston, Hugh Bertie Henriques, Major, d. of w., 27/10/16.
Johnston, Paul Headley, 2/Lt., d. of w., 11/6/18 (C/74th Bde.).
Johnston, Richard George Mann, Major, k. in a., 25/8/16.
Johnston, Stuart, Lt. (Tp.), k. in a., 12/8/16 (70th Bde.).
Johnstone, Gilbert Lumley, Capt. (Tp.) (Act. Major), k. in a., 4/10/16 (96th Bde.).
Johnstone, Henry Archer, Capt. (Tp.) (Act. Major), k. in a., 21/3/18 (152nd Bde.).
Johnstone John Andrew, Lt., k. in a., 20/5/18.
Johnstone, James Henry Walter, Major, k. in a., 15/9/14.
Johnstone. Robert Brown Whylock, 2/Lt., k. in a., 19/7/18 (51st Bde.).
Johnstone, William McCall, 2/Lt. (Tp.), k. in a., 13/2/16 (152nd Bde.).
Joice, Reginald John, Lt. (Tp.), k. in a., 30/4/17 (60th Bde.).
Jones, Evan Harries, M.C., 2/Lt., k. in a., 25/4/18 (87th Bde.).
Jones, Harold Garfield, 2/Lt., k. in a., 8/10/18 (att. A. Bty. 286th Bde.).
Jones, Hugh Ivor 2/Lt., died, 22/6/18 (B. 51st Bde.).
Jones, John Daniel. Lt., died, 21/2/16.
Jones, Robert Arthur, Capt., k. in a., 10/9/14.
Jones, Sydney Douglas Selborne, 2/Lt., k. in a., 2/9/16 (26th Bde.).
Jones, Thomas. 2/Lt., k. in a., 31/7/17 (161st Bde.).
Jones, Thomas John, M.C., Lt. (Tp.) (Act. Capt.), d. of w., 22/4/18 (122nd Bde.).
Jones, Wallace, M.C., Lt. (Act. Major), d. of w., 15/10/18 (C/174th Bde.).
Jones-Bateman, Llewelyn, Capt., d. of w., 19/3/16 (103rd Bde.).
Jordan, Hugh Stewart Latimer, 2/Lt., killed, 20/8/17 (att. R.F.C.).
Judge, William Spencer, 2/Lt., d. of w., 26/7/10.
Kane-Smith, James, M.C., Lt., k. in a., 27/5/18 (110 Bde.)
Kay, George Philip. 2/Lt., died, 21/10/18 (172 Bde.).
Kay, Noel Rawstone Wilkinson, Lt., d of w., 5/7/18 (15 Bde., L Bty.).
Kay-Shuttleworth, The Hon. Lawrence Ughtred, A/Capt., k. in a., 30/3/17 (11 Bde.)
Keating, Thomas Joseph, T/Lt. (A/Capt.), k. in a., 14/6/18.
Kedgley, Alfred Edmund, 2/Lt., k. in a., 17/10/18 (83 Bde.).
Keeling, Charles Henry, 2/Lt., died, 28/10/18 (H Bty., 15 Bde.).
Kehoe, William Charles, 2/Lt., d of w., 24/4/17 (70 Bde.).
Kellagher, Sydney Arthur, M.C., Lt., d. of w., 4/8/17 (34 Bde.).
Kellett, Richard Henry Villiers, 2/Lt, killed, 21/8/16 (B/74.).
Kellie, Leslie Lawrence, 2/Lt., k. in a., 1/2/17 (102 Bde.).
Kelsall, John Lindsay, T/Lt., k. in a., 28/8/17 (86 Bde.).
Kelsey, William, Lt. (Tp.), d. of w., 23/9/16
Kempster, Alec Albert Dresden Lt., k in a., 25/9/15.
Kennard, Arthur Molloy, D.S.O., Temp. Lt. Col., died, 2/1/17.
Kennard, Terence Evelyn, Lt., k. in a., 26/2/18 (and R.F.C.).
Kennedy, Charles, Temp. Lt., d. of w., 16/11/16 (D/102 Bde.).
Kennedy, Thomas Christian, 2/Lt., k. in a., 25/11/15.
Kennedy, Tristram Gervias, Lt., d. of w., 28/3/18 (301 Bde.).
Kent, Harold, 2/Lt., d. of w., 16/11//17 (A/50 Bde.).
Kent, William John, 2/Lt., k. in a., 12/3/15.
Kentish, Ernest George, 2/Lt., died, 27/2/18 (late B Bty., R.H.A.).
Kerr, Daniel Eugene, Lt., k in a., 10/6/18.
Keyes, Cleveland, M.C., T/Capt. (A/Major), d. of w., 24/3/18 (C83 Bde.) (in German hands).
Keyms, Thomas Booth, 2/Lt., k. in a., 19/7/16.
Kidd, Guy Egerton, D.S.O., Major, k. in a., 26/9/16 (70 Bde.).
Kiddle, Geoffrey, Capt., died, 29/7/16 (7 Bty.).
Kilgour, Charles David Winton, 2/Lt (Tp.), d. of w., 4/11/18 (23 Army Bde.).
Kilkelly, Edward Charles Randolph, M.C., Lt. (A/Major), k. in a., 26/6/17 (186 Bde.).
Kilpin, Thomas Bennett, Temp. 2/Lt., d. of w., 15/6/17 (att. Y/25 T.M.B.).
King, Albert, Temp. Lt., k. in a., 23/8/16.
King, Alfred Nelson, Temp. Lt., k. in a., 10/5/16.
King, Edward Westcott, 2/Lt., d. of w., 20/10/18 (B/79 Bde.).
King, Henry Arthur, M.C., 2/Lt., k. in a., 1/7/17.
King, Henry Frederick Irwin, Lt., died, 5/11/18 (D/165 Bde.).
King, John David, 2/Lt., died, 30/6/18 (242 Army Bde., att. Sig. Sub-Section).
King-Harman, Lawrence Hope, Capt., killed, 26/10/16 (att. R.F.C.).
Kingdon, Robert Claude Hawker, 2/Lt., k. in a., 9/4/17.
Kington, Edwin, Lt., d of w., 17/9/16
Kinnear, Charles Annesley, 2/Lt., k. in a., 16/10/16 (50 Bde.).
Kirkley, Frank Robson, M.C., Lt., died, 13/11/18 (102 Bde.).
Knaggs, Victor St. George, Lt., d. of w., 12/8/18 (5 Army Bde.).
Knight, James Matthew, 2/Lt., k. in a., 20/5/18 (168 Bde.).
Knight, John Peake, D S.O., Temp. Capt., k. in a., 31/8/16.
Knight-Bruce, Algernon James Lewis, 2/Lt., k. in a., 10/3/15.
Knowles, Arthur Yalden, Lt., d. of w., 26/8/17 (2 Reinf. Co., 5th Army).
Kyle, John, M.C., Lt., d. of w., 22/5/18 (D/123 Bde.).
Lacy, Thomas Joseph, 2/Lt., k. in a., 7/4/18 (48 A. Bde.).
Laidlaw, William Simpson, 2/Lt., k. in a., 30/8/18 (250 Bde.).
Lamb, C. W., Temp Capt., died, 15/11/15.
Lamb, Joseph, 2/Lt., d. of w., 16/8/17 (153 Bde., 36 D.A.C.).
Lamb, John McNair, 2/Lt. (Tp.), k. in a., 4/11/18 (82 Bde.).
Lambert, Cyril John Noel, M.C., Lt., k. in a., 2/9/18 (40 Bde.).
Lane-Mullins, James Brendan, 2/Lt., k. in a., 14/6/17 (att. 29 D.A.C.).
Langford, Colin Cecil, Capt. (A/Major), d. of w., 9/4/18 (295 Bde.).
Langler, John Bickford, M.C., Lt., died, 31/10/18.
Langstone, Frederick Herbert, Lt., k. in a., 17/4/18 (19 D.A.C.).
Langtree, Charles Henry Lt., d. of w., 3/8/16 (159 Bde.).
Lapthorn, Owen Heckford, 2/Lt., k. in a., 29/5/17 (102 Bde.).
Large, Charles Edward, Lt., k. in a., 27/5/18 (45 Bde.).
Laslett, Henry Clinton, Temp. 2/Lt., d. of w., 2/8/16 (D/149 Bde.).
Last, Arthur James, 2/Lt., d. of w., 9/12/18.
Last, Leslie Sydney, 2/Lt., killed, 21/2/18 (att. R.F.C.).
Latta, Alexander James Jobb, 2/Lt., k. in a., 5/8/16 (62 Bde.).
Lattey, James Cumming, Major, k. in a., 5/5/18 (att. R.G.A., 1/1 Welsh H B.).
Lawder, Arthur William Charles, 2/Lt., d. of w., 15/4/17 (155 Bde.).
Lawrence, George Aubrey Kennedy, D.S.O., Capt. (T/Lt.-Col.), killed 28/1/17 (and R.F.C.).
Lawrence, Lawrence Arthur, 2/Lt., k. in a., 16/8/17 (83/122 Bde.).
Laxton, Archer Benjamin, 2/Lt., d. of w., 21/7/17 (C/110 Bde.).
Leach, Gordon Pemberton, Capt., k. in a., 20/8/15.
Leach, William Alfred, 2/Lt., died, 5/3/19.
Leadbetter, Alan Edmonstoun Greenshields, Lt. (A/Major), k. in a., 4/8/17 (L Bty., 15 Bde.).
Leadbetter, Duncan, 2/Lt, d. of w., 6/8/18 (82 Bde.).
Leahy, Noel Edward Joseph, Lt., k. in a., 10/8/18 (5 Bde.).
Leal, George, Lt., k. in a., 7/8/17 (att. R.F.C., 9 Sqd.).
Leathes, Robert Herbert de Mussenden, 2/Lt., k. in a., 18/4/17 (62 Bde.).
Lebish, Frank Roland, 2/Lt, d. of. w., 25/7/17 (D/173 Bde.).
Lechertier, Jacques Alfred, 2/Lt., k. in a., 4/11/18 (D/211 Bde.).
Lee, Bernard George, Temp. Lt, d of w., 22/3/18 (D/180 Bde.).
Lee, Henry Duncan, 2/Lt., k in a., 5/8/17 (5 Army Bde.).

Lee, Kenneth Willoughby, M.C., Capt., d. of w., 27/9/16.
Lee, Philip Warburton, Lt. (A/Major), k. in a., 11/10/17 (3/Imp. Div. Arty.).
Lee, William Melbourne, 2/Lt., k. in a., 21/3/18 (298 Army Bde.).
Leeson, Alexander Neve, D.S.O., Lt., k. in a., 22/10/17 (and R.F.C.).
Lefaux, John Faulkner, 2/Lt., d. of. w., 15/10/18 (15 Bde.).
Lefroy, Frazer Kent, 2/Lt., d. of w., 8/4/17 (11 Bde.).
Leggatt, Ashley Gordon Scott, Temp. 2/Lt., k. in a., 16/9/16 (47 Bde.).
Leggett, Eric Henry Goodwin, D.S.O., Major, died, 30/7/16 (188 Bde.).
Leggott, Joseph Parkinson, Temp. Lt., d. of w., 16/8/17 (14 Bde.).
Lewis, Arthur Ralph Pollard, 2/Lt., k. in a., 23/3/18 (93 Army Bde., Sig. Sub-Sec.)
Lewis, Brinley Richard, T/Lt. (A/Major), k. in a., 2/4/17 (122 Bde.).
Lewis, Trefor, 2/Lt., d. of w., 27/5/18 (X/37 T.M.B.).
Lewis, Walter Henry, Lt., d. of w., 4/8/17 (D/107 Bde.).
Liberty, John Ince, Lt., k. in a., 28/11/17 (38 Army Bde.).
Lindsay, Claud Frederic Thomas, Capt., k. in a., 31/3/18 (33 Bty.).
Lindsay, George Walter Thomas, Capt., killed, 26/6/17 (and R.F.C.).
Linklater, William Irvine, 2/Lt., k. in a., 5/4/18 (77 Army Bde.).
Lister, John Curtis, Temp. 2/Lt., k. in a., 20/5/17 (17 Bde.).
Littledale, Arthur Charles, Major, d. of w., 9/5/15.
Livingstone, Harold Gordon, 2/Lt., k. in a., 1/5/15.
Livsey, William Mylrea, 2/Lt., drowned, 2/6/17 (5 Res. Bde.).
Llewellyn, John Horace, Temp. Lt, d. of w., 9/10/17 (Anti-Aircraft Bty.).
Llewellyn, Thomas Edward, M.M., 2/Lt., k. in a., 27/10/18 (39 Bde.).
Lloyd, Alan Scrivener, Temp. Lt., k. in a., 4/8/16 (78 Bde.).
Lloyd, Edward Stanley, M.C., Lt., died, 23/11/18 (H.Q. 312 Bde.).
Lloyd, William Merrick Ellis, 2/Lt., k. in a., 19/5/17 (40 Bde.).
Lock, James Palmer, 2/Lt., d. of w., 2/2/18 (63 Bty.).
Loewe, Leopold, Temp. Capt., k in a., 6/4/16 (23 Bde.).
Long, Francis William, 2/Lt., d. of w., 28/6/16 (P. of W.).
Longman, Valentine Sandford, T/Lt. (A/Major), k. in a., 1/9/18 (9 Bde.).
Lough, Frederic George, 2/Lt., k. in a, 21/3/18 (38 Bde.).
Lovett-Thomas, Richard Sackville, M.C., 2/Lt., d. of w., 12/3/17 (165 Bde.).
Lowry-Corry, Frederick Henry, Temp. Lt., d. of w., 30/9/15.
Lucas, Robert, Capt., died, 1/11/18 (52/15 Bde.).
Lucas, Wilfrid, 2/Lt., k. in a., 23/12/16 (100 Bde.).
Lumb, Herbert, Temp 2/Lt., died, 8/10/15.
Lunn, Ralph William, 2/Lt., d. of w., 17/6/17 (B/15 Bde.).
Lush-Wilson, Herbert Geoffrey, Major, k. in a., 21/7/16 (15 Bde.).
Lutyens, Charles John Lionel, Lt., d. of w., 3/10/17 (156 Bde.).
Lutyens, Lionel Gallwey, M.C., Capt. (A/Major), d. of w., 6/1/18 (123/28 Bde.).
Lyburn, John Jardine, 2/Lt., died, 13/10/16 (116 Bde.).
Lynch, John, 2/Lt, k. in a., 3/5/15.
Lynch-Staunton, Reginald Kirkpatrick, D.S.O., Bt.-Lt.-Col., d. of w., 7/11/18 (220 Bde.).
Lyon, Claude Edward, Temp. 2/Lt., k. in a., 27/5/16.
Lyon, Claude Stuart, M.C., Lt (A/Major), k. in a., 21/3/18 (53 Bty., 2 Bde.).
Lywood, Kenneth Primrose Gifford, Lt, k. in a., 24/3/18 ("O" Bty.).
Maasdorp, Norman, Capt. (Tp.), d. of w., 28/8/16.
McAndrew, Charles Arthur Worthington, 2/Lt., k. in a., 26/4/17 (24 Bde.)
McBain, John Mortimer, 2/Lt., d. of w., 9/7/16.
McBride, Joseph, Lt. (A/Major), k. in a., 23/4/17 (27 Bde.).
McCaig, George Mann, 2/Lt., d. of w., 18/10/18 (306 Bde., 61 D.A.C.).
McCall, Eric Hutchison, 2/Lt., died, 7/9/16 ("V" Bty.).
McConnel, Merrick Hugh, Major, d. of w., 14/9/17 (B/295 Bde.).
McConnell, Primrose, M.C., Capt. (Tp.), k. in a., 18/9/18 (D Bty., 101 Bde.).
McCorquodale, Archibald, Lt., d. of w., 25/7/16 (att. Anti-Aircraft Bty.).
McCulloch, John Allan, 2/Lt., k. in a., 21/12/17 (52 Div. Med. T.M.B.).
McCulloch, Robert Maxwell, Temp. Lt., k. in a., 19/4/17 (106 Bde.).
MacDonald, Charles Hodgson Barrington, 2/Lt., k. in a., 23/3/15
McDonald, John Patrick, Capt. and Qr.-Mr., died, 25/3/15.
Macdonald, Ronald Duncan, 2/Lt., k. in a., 31/10/17 (82 Bde.).
McFadyen, John Craig, 2/Lt., k. in a., 6/6/17 (11 D.A.C.).
Macfarlane, Alexander, 2/Lt, k. in a., 2/12/17 (91 Bde.).
McGarvie, Hector Archer, 2/Lt., k. in a., 8/7/17 (52 Bde.).
Macgeough-Bond, Ralph Shelton, 2/Lt., d. of w., 22/8/17 (46 Bde., "D" Bty.).
Macintyre, Charles Frederick Davis, 2/Lt. (Tp.), k. in a., 6/11/18 (27 Bde.)
Maciver, Ian, Lt., k. in a., 11/8/16 (5 Bde.).
Mackenzie, Donald Stanford Forth, Lt., d. of w., 31/7/17 (177 Bde.).
Mackenzie, Eric James Bethune, Capt., k. in a., 8/7/16.
McKinstry, Ronald William, Temp. 2/Lt., k. in a., 23/9/16.
Mackworth, Francis Julian Audley, Major, k. in a., 1/11/14.
McLachlan, Berry, M.C., Lt., d. of w., 11/10/18 (C/4 Bde.).
McLaren, Thomas James, 2/Lt., k. in a., 25/1/16.
MacLean, James Acheson, M.C., Lt., k. in a., 30/9/17 (148 Bde.).
McLean, Robert Drysdale, 2/Lt., k in a., 26/10/17 (64 Army Bde.).
Macleod, Alastair Roderick, Lt., k. in a., 25/4/15.
McLeod, Daniel Edward, 2/Lt., k. in a., 1/12/16 (86 Bde.).
Macleod, Donald Kerr, 2/Lt., k. in a., 18/10/17 (86 Bde.).
McLeod, Douglas Keith, 2/Lt., d. of w., 21/10/18 (43 Bty. 24 Bde.).
Mc Lernon, Robert William, 2/Lt., k. in a., 8/5/15.
Maclure, Gordon Stanley, 2/Lt., d. of w., 16/6/16 (32 T.M.B.).
McMaster, Hugh, D.S.O., M.C., Major, d. of w., 2/12/17 (A/46 Bde.).
McMillan, Kenneth Gregor, 2/Lt., k. in a., 16/8/17 (33 Bde.).
MacNab, Alexander, 2/Lt., d. of w., 24/10/18 (186 Bde.).
McNab, Alexander, 2/Lt., d. of w., 27/4/18 (147 Bde.).
McNaughton, Hamish Ian, 2/Lt., k. in a., 24/4/17 (E. Bty. 100 Bde.).
MacNeece, James Douglas Gaussen, Capt., k. in a., 16/8/16 (39 Bde.).
McNeil, John Fraser, 2/Lt., d. of w., 9/9/15 (D/256 Bde.).
MacNicol, Angus John Bayne, Lt. (Tp.), d. of w., 18/4/17 (D/50 Bde.).
Macpherson, Ewen Fergus Lord, 2/Lt., k. in a., 10/8/16 (5 Bde.).
Macpherson, Hugh Bannerman, M.C., Lt., k. in a., 27/9/18 (95 Bde.).
Macrae, Kenneth Matheson, M.C., Temp. Major, k. in a., 1/11/18 (28 Army Bde. 124 Bty.).
Macrosty, Henry Hugh, Temp. Lt., k. in a., 19/12/15.
McWhae, John Wilson, Lt., k. in a., 21/6/17 (189 Army Bde.).
Madders, Hubert Franklin, 2/Lt., k. in a., 1/7/16 (168 Bde.).
Magrath, Meyrick Magrath, D.S.O., Capt. (A/Major), k. in a., 2/8/18 (291 Bde.).
Maidlow, John Southern, Major d. of w., 23/8/14.
Mail, Frank Oswald, 2/Lt., k. in a., 9/10/18 (78 Bde.).
Maitland, Keith Andrew Ramsay, M.C., Lt. (A/Major), k. in a., 4/10/17 (76 Army Bde.).
Malcolm, Henry Alexander Drummond, 2/Lt., d. of w., 17/2/17 (Z/33 T.M.B.).
Malcolm, George John, T/Major, k. in a., 9/7/16 (att. R.F.C.).
Mallock, Charles Herbert, D.S.O., Major, d. of w., 5/11/17 (23 Bde.).
Manders, George Benjamin, Temp. Lt., d. of w., 24/4/16 (66 Bty.).
Manifold, William Herbert, 2/Lt., k. in a., 26/4/17 (36 Bde.).
Manly, Eric Cecil John, Lt., k. in a., 18/7/17 (B/82 Bde.).
Mann, Henry William, Lt., k. in a., 30/3/18 (178 Bde.).
Mann, Theadore John Lewis, 2/Lt., d. of w., 28/4/18 (173 Bde.).
Mansel-Pleydell, John Morton, Temp. 2/Lt., d. of w., 22/9/16 (107 Bde.).
Mansfield, Reginald Horace, 2/Lt., d. of w., 1/10/18 (121/27 Bde.).
Marchetti, Eustie, 2/Lt., k. in a., 8/11/16 (149 Bde.).
Marchment, William James, Lt. (A/Capt.), k. in a., 4/11/18 (X/32 T.M.B.).
Mare, Arthur Llewellyn, T/Lt. (A/Major), k. in a., 27/5/18 (33 Bde.).
Marks, Horace Owen, T/Lt., k. in a., 29/10/16 (111 Bde.).
Marr, Frederick Sidney, M.C., T/Lt. (A/Capt.), k. in a., 30/8/17 (47 Bde.).
Marriott, Arthur Pelham, M.C., Lt. (A/Capt.), k. in a., 7/4/17 (11 Bde.).
Marsh, Henry Sidney, 2/Lt., k. in a., 13/11/16 (78 Bde.).
Marsh, John Theodore Templeman, 2/Lt., d. of w., 28/6/18 (D/15 Bde.).
Marshall, Albert, 2/Lt., died, 12/6/19.
Marshall, John Percival, Lt., d. of w., 4/11/17 (B/282 Bde.).
Marshall, Duke, 2/Lt., d. of w., 22/2/19 (A. 159 Bde.).
Martin, Algernon, 2/Lt., k. in a., 30/7/18 (70 Bde.).
Martin, Douglas Bain, 2/Lt., d. of w., 9/10/18 (C/52 Bde.).
Martin, Ernest, 2/Lt., k. in a., 18/7/16 (306 Bde.).
Martin, Herbert, 2/Lt., d. of w., 26/5/15.
Martin, James Martin, 2/Lt., k. in a., 24/4/18 (96 Bde.).
Martin, James Nelson, 2/Lt., k. in a., 21/3/18 (61 T.M.B.).
Martin, Sidney Grant, 2/Lt., d. of w., 18/4/17 (17 Bde.).
Martin, Thomas Dick, 2/Lt., d. of w., 18/6/18 (119 Bty. 27 Bde.).
Martinson, Karl Ludwig, Temp. Lieut., d. of w., 1/6/17 (att. R.F.C.).
Mash, Oswald Nelson, M.C., T/Lt., k. in a., 1/6/18 (174 Bde.).
Maskell, William Charles, D.S.O., M.C., Lt. (A/Maj.), d. of w., 15/12/17 (C/189 Bde.).
Massey, George Hocken, 2/Lt., k. in a., 27/6/16.
Massey, John Hamon, Capt., k. in a., 27/5/18 (45 Bde.).
Massy-Beresford, John Clarina, Lt., k. in a., 28/8/18 (310 Bde.).
Mathews, George, 2/Lt., k. in a., 2/10/17 (att. R.F.C. 55/Sqdn.).
Mathews, Hubert Victor, 2/Lt., k. in a., 26/8/16 (32 Bde.).
Mathewson, James Kenneth, 2/Lt., k. in a., 14/9/18 (113 Bde.).
Matthews, Henry Arthur, 2/Lt., d. of w., 25/10/17 (65 Bde.).
Maxwell, James McCall, Lt., k. in a., 1/6/16 (118 Bde.).
Maxwell, Power MacMurrough, M.C., Capt. (A/Maj.), d. of w., 1/10/17 (95 Bde.).
Mayne, Augustus Blair, Major, died, 4/12/17 (3 D.A.C. late Central India Horse).
Mayne, Jasper Moone, 2/Lt., k. in a., 9/5/15.
Mays, Frederick William, 2/Lt., died, 20/7/17 (A/69 Bde.).
Mead, [illegible] Hallard, Temp. 2/Lt., k. in a., 24/7/16 (72 Bde.).
Medlicott, Sidney Neville, Temp. 2/Lt., d. of w., 6/10/15.
Meeson, Fitzalan Ridware, Lt., d. of w., 4/11/18 (13/17 Bde.).
Megeney, Horace William, Lt. (A/Capt.), k. in a., 21/9/18, (72 Bde.).
Mellor, John Lewis, 2/Lt., k. in a., 26/6/16 (att. T.M.B.).

Melvill, Melvill Leopold, 2/Lt., k. in a., 31/10/17 (23 Bde.).
Mendel, Reginald William Wynn, 2/Lt., died, 19/9/17.
Menzies, Alexander Lawrence, 2/Lt., d. of w., 21/9/16 (48 Bde.).
Mercer, Alfred Stephen, Temp., 2/Lt., k. in a., 13/3/17 (155 Bde.).
Meredith, John Collins, 2/Lt., k. in a., 23/9/18 (24 Bde.).
Merrick, Thomas, D.S.O., M.C., Lt. (A/Maj.), died, 8/11/18 (87 Bde.).
Merriman, Gordon Holland, Capt., k. in a., 12/5/15.
Merritt, Frederick Charles, Lt. (A/Maj.), k. in a., 17/6/17 (15 Bde.).
Messenger, L. W., 2/Lt., died, 4/7/18 (and R.A.F.).
Messervy, Gerald, M.C., Capt. (A/Maj.), k. in a., 9/10/18 (16/41 Bde.).
Metson, Herbert Frank, 2/Lt., d. of w., 9/8/16 (70 Bde.).
Michelsen, Arthur Conrad, 2/Lt., k. in a., 18/10/17 (B/64 Bde.).
Millard, Albert Wardle, Lt., d. of w., 25/2/18 (A/64 Bde.).
Millard, Henry Albert, Lt., d. of w., 16/9/16 (58 Bty.).
Milligan, George Berry, Lt., k. in a., 24/3/18 (152 Bde.).
Mills, Harry Forster, Capt., k. in a., 21/3/18 (46 Bde.).
Mills, William Langley, 2/Lt., k. in a., 9/5/17 (and R.F.C., 43 Sqdn.).
Mills, William Robert Granville, 2/Lt., k. in a., 16/2/17 (103 Bde.).
Millwood, Frederick James, Temp. 2/Lt., k. in a., 23/10/18 (186 Bde.).
Milne, George William, Temp. Lt., d. of w., 22/10/17 (22 Bde.).
Milner, John Lewis, 2/Lt., k. in a., 9/5/15.
Milton, George Herbert, 2/Lt., k. in a., 25/10/16 (2 Bde.).
Misquith, Joan Charles, 2/Lt., d. of w., 4/2/17 (A/102 Bde.).
Mitchell, Erik Harrison, T/Capt., k. in a., 29/4/16 (att. R.F.C.).
Mitchell, James Lawson, Major, k. in a., 16/3/16.
Mitchell, Lawrence Adams, M.C., Lt. (T/Capt.), k. in a., 22/10/18 (123 Bde.).
Monie, Roy Douglas John, Temp. Lt., k. in a., 18/4/17 (282 Bde.).
Monks, Charles Phatean, Lt., k. in a., 17/6/15.
Monson, Edward Charles Sutton, M.C., Lt., d. of w., 15/6/18 (A/321 Bde.).
Montgomery, Edward Henry, 2/Lt., k. in a., 16/10/16 (X/9 T.M.B.).
Montgomery, Ralph Noel Vernon, D.S.O., Lt., died, 1/4/19.
Moore, Harold Thomas Pelham, M.C., Lt., k. in a., 4/11/18 (210 Bde.).
Moore, Richard Henry, 2/Lt., d. of w., 21/3/18 (6 Div. Amm. Col.).
Moore, William Ernest, M.C., 2/Lt. (A/Capt.), k. in a., 14/11/17 (86 Army Bde.).
Moore, William Joseph, 2/Lt., k. in a., 21/3/18 (2 Bde.).
Moreton, Edgar, M.C., Lt. (A/Maj.), k. in a., 25/8/18 (27 Bde.).
Morgan, Brinley Arthur, 2/Lt., k. in a., 4/3/17 (and R.F.C.).
Morgan, Edward Compton, M.C., Temp. Capt. (A/Maj.), d. of w., 29/9/17 (76 Bde.).
Morgan, Edward Leslie, 2/Lt., d. of w., 9/11/17 (23 Bde.).
Morgan, Frederick Harold Lewis, Capt., k. in a., 4/5/15.
Morgan, John James, 2/Lt., k. in a., 7/4/17 (77 Bde.).
Morgan, John Parkinson, 2/Lt., k. in a., 27/5/18 (112 Bde.).
Morgan, Lewis Edward, 2/Lt., k. in a., 16/9/18 (275 Bde.).
Morgan, Oswald William, Lt. (T/Capt.), killed, 3/2/18 (and R.F.C.).
Morgan, William, Lt., died, 19/11/18.
Morris, Harold Henry, Lt., d. of w., 22/7/17 (150 Bde.).
Morris, John Herbert, Lt., k. in a., 6/3/18 (and R.F.C. 49 Sqd.).
Morrison, Douglas St. George, Lt., died, 3/9/17 (att. "R" A.A. Bty.).
Morrison, Richard Fielding, M.C., Capt. (A/Maj.), d. of w., 25/4/18 (51 Bde.).
Morse, Gurth Stephen, Lt., d. of w., 9/12/14.
Mortimer, Charles Gordon, Temp. Lt., died, 21/10/16 (att. 24th Anti-Aircraft).
Moses, Vivian Sylvester, 2/Lt., k. in a., 4/6/17 (11 D.A.C.).
Moss, Thomas John, M.C., Lt. (A/Maj.), k. in a., 21/3/18 (307 Bde.).
Mousley, Alfred Charles, 2/Lt., d. of w., 30/9/17 (162 Bde.).
Mowbray, John Leslie, D.S.O., Major, k. in a., 24/7/16 (41 Bde.).
Muir, Andrew Reid, 2/Lt., d. of w., 7/11/17 (233 Bde.).
Muirhead, Langdon, 2/Lt., k. in a., 29/9/18 (59 Bde.).
Muirhead, Phillips Quincy, Temp. Lt., k. in a., 18/7/16 (25 Bde.).
Muncie, Daniel McBeth, 2/Lt., k. in a., 3/12/17 (2 Bde.).
Mundy, Lionel Frank Hasting, Lt., d. of w., 3/9/14.
Munro, Colin Cameron, Temp. 2/Lt., d. of w., 23/4/16 (A/122 Bde.).
Munro, William Pearce, 2/Lt., d. of w., 5/9/18 (70 Bde.).
Murchland, Charles, Temp. Lieut., k. in a., 26/5/15.
Murdoch, James Hunter George, 2/Lt., k. in a., 4/7/16 (95 B.).
Murphy, John, Lt. (T/Capt.), d. of w., 17/8/17 (62 Bde., D. Bty.).
Murray, George Anthony, M.C., Lt. (A/Maj.), d. of w., 4/4/18 (47 Bde.).
Murray, Patrick Hallam, Capt., k. in a., 25/9/15.
Murray, William, 2/Lt., killed, 30/7/18 (and 17 Trench M. Bty.).
Musson, Harold Methuen, M.C., 2/Lt., d. of w., 26/9/17 (D/149 Bde.).
Nairn, George, 2/Lt., d. of w., 28/9/16 (70 Bde., 15/Divn.).
Nathan, Robert Percy, M.C., Lt. (A/Capt.), d. of w., 22/3/18 (and 36 Trench M. Bty.).

Neame, Geoffrey, M.C., Temp. Capt. (A/Maj.), k. in a., 2/4/18 (190 Bde.).
Neate, Alan Burnaby, 2/Lt., d. of w., 23/4/17 (62 Bde.).
Neilson, William, 2/Lt., k. in a., 30/5/18 (87 Bde.).
V.C. Nelson, David, Lt. (A/Maj.), d. of w., 8/4/18 (D/59 Bde.).
Nevill, Hugh Lewis, D.S.O., Major, k. in a., 7/8/15.
Niccol, George McLaughlan, Capt., died, 30/10/18.
Nicholl, Alan Hope Smith, 2/Lt., k. in a., 21/3/18 (24 Bde.).
Nicholls, George Arthur, 2/Lt., k. in a., 9/4/17 (15 Bde.).
Nicholls, William Montague, Temp. Lt., k. in a., 26/9/15.
Nicholson, John Anthony, Lt., d. of w., 5/10/18 (48/36 Bde.).
Nicolson, Walter Adams, Major (Temp. Lt.-Col.), k. in a., 4/9/17 (104 Army Bde.).
Nixon, Gerald Ferrers, Lt., k. in a., 24/10/14.
Noble, Marc Andrew Patrick, 2/Lt., d. of w., 1/7/17 (122 Bde.).
Noble-Smith, John, 2/Lt., k. in a., 9/4/18 (165 Bde.).
Nodder, Frederick May, 2/Lt., k. in a., 14/8/16 (48 Bde.).
Nolan, Philip John, Lt., died, 7/4/18 (and R.A.F.).
Norris, Sydney Frank, 2/Lt., died, 28/4/19.
Norton, Frederick John, Lt., k. in a., 23/3/18 (D/187 Bde.).
Norton, Richard Conyers, Lt., k. in a., 23/3/18 (E Bty.).
Nottidge, Edward, Capt., k. in a., 8/11/16 (79 Bde.).
Nowell, Wilfrid James, 2/Lt, k. in a., 9/4/17 (460 How. Bty.).
Nugent, Raymond Henry, 2/Lt., k. in a., 25/11/17 (70 Bde.).
Nunn, John Henry, Major, d. of w., 1/4/17 (149 Bde.).
Oakes, James Edwards Brooks, M.C., Lt., k. in a., 10/7/17 (att. Z/1st T.M.B.).
Oakes, Robert Claude, 2/Lt., died, 19/7/16 (att. R.F.C.).
O'Brien, Aubrey Ulick Marshall, Capt., k. in a., 1/11/14.
O'Brien, Hugh Rivers Hamilton, Temp. Capt., k. in a., 1/6/16 19 A.A. Bty).
O'Brien, Timothy John Aloysius, Lt., k. in a., 7/8/16 (27 Bde.).
O'Callaghan, John Charles, M.C., T/Capt. (A/Maj.), k. in a., 4/4/18 (190 Bde.).
O'Connell, Maurice James, Lt., died, 30/7/18 (222 Bde., T.M.B.).
O'Donnell, Percy, 2/Lt., d. of w., 6/5/16 (5 Bde.).
O'Dwyer, Robert Martin, Temp. 2/Lt., d. of w., 18/10/15.
O'Ferrall, Brendan Hynds, 2/Lt, k. in a., 16/8/17 (A/76 Bde.).
O'Keeffe, Marcus Menus, M.C., Lt. (A/Maj.), k. in a., 2/4/18 (48 Army Bde.).
O'Keefe, William Henry, Temp. Lieut., k. in a., 19/5/17 (40 Bde.).
O'Kelly, Patrick Joseph, Lt. (Tp.), k. in a., 26/9/16 (58 Bde.).
Oliver, George Baxter, 2/Lt. (Tp.), k. in a., 17/6/16.
Oliver, Guy Bertram, Major, d. of w., 29/9/16 (189 Bde.).
Oliver-Jones, Alfred Vernon, Temp. Lt., died, 23/7/16 (att. R.F.C.).
Olver, John Denis Circuit, M.C., 2/Lt. (A/Lt.), k. in a., 27/4/17 (28 Bde.).
Orde, John Barwick, M.C., Capt. (T/Maj.), d. of w., 12/2/17 (99 Bde.).
Ormerod, Andrew, Temp., 2/Lt., k. in a., 13/4/17 (att. R.F.C., 59/Sqdn.).
Ormrod, Oliver Hugh, Temp. Capt., killed, 12/9/16 (att. R.F.C.).
Orpin, Ralph Ernest, 2/Lt., d. of w., 6/8/17 (92 Bde.).
Orr, Edward Farquharson Burkitt, Lt., k. in a., 23/3/18 (H.Q. 173 Bde.).
Osgood, Thomas William, Lt. (Tp.), k. in a., 19/7/16.
Osler, Edward Revere, 2/Lt., d. of w., 30/8/17 (A/59 Bde.).
Ostler, Alan, 2/Lt., killed, 16/9/18 (and R.A.F.).
Owen, Evan Richard, T/L. (A/Capt.), k. in a., 28/4/17 (86 Bde.).
Owen, Norman Moore, 2/Lt., k. in a., 13/9/14.
Oxlet, Alan Hayes, 2/Lt., k. in a., 10/12/17 (149 Bde.).
Packard, Henry Norrington, D.S.O., Lt.-Col., k. in a., 12/4/16.
Packman, Thomas Alfred, Lt., k. in a., 10/9/16 (att. T.M.B.).
Padley, Percy, 2/Lt., k. in a., 4/11/18 (112 Bde.).
Page, Vernon, M.C., 2/Lt., d. of w., 23/9/17 (D/315 Bde., A F.A.).
Parbury, Frederick Nigel, Major, k. in a., 9/5/15.
Pargiter, William Herbert, T/Lt., k. in a., 12/10/16 (24 Bde.).
Park, Adam St. John Lloyd, M.C., Major, k. in a., 21/4/17 (38 Bde.).
Parker, Charles Allen, M.C, 2/Lt., killed, 19/2/18 (att. (R.F.C.).
Parker, John Bradbery, Lt. (A/Capt.), died, 19/11/18 (D/84 Bde.).
Parker, Ronald Elphinstone, Lt., k. in a., 9/9/14.
Parks, William, Lt. (A/Capt.), died, 22/12/18 (263 Bde.).
Parrott, Lionel Overton, 2/Lt., k. in a., 7/8/18 (19 Bty.).
Parry, Claude Frederick Pilkington, D.S.O., Lt.-Col., k. in a., 20/8/18 (34 Bde.).
Parry, Donald George de Courcy, Lt. (A/Maj.), k. in a., 5/4/18 (78 Bde.).
Parry, Wilfred Seaton Bagott, 2/Lt. (Tp.), k. in a., 24/11/15.
Parson, Ernest Edward, M.C., Temp. Lt., d. of w., 1/6/17 (124 Bde.).
Parsons, Algernon George, Major, k. in a., 26/4/18 (149 Bde.).
Parsons, Maurice Harry Donne, Temp. Capt., k. in a., 18/7/16 (5 Bde.).
Pask, Isaac Arthur James, D.S.O., M.C., Capt., k. in a., 1/9/16 (28 Bde.).
Parteur, William Raymond, M.C., Lt. (Act. Maj.), k. in a., 10/7/17 (102 Bde.).
Paterson, Norman Keith, T/Lt., k. in a., 29/6/16.
Paterson, Robert Sanderson, 2/Lt., k. in a., 11/3/15.
Paterson, Walter Edward Wadbrook, 2/Lt. (Tp.), died, 26/11/18.
Patterson, Alan, Capt., k. in a., 14/3/16 (71 Bde.).

Patterson, George Beatty, 2/Lt., d. of w., 22/6/18 (168 Bde. 32/Divn.).
Patterson, Kenneth Scott, 2/Lt., d. of w., 6/12/17 (in Ger. hands) (92 Bde.).
Pattisson, John Howell, Major, k. in a., 28/4/15.
Pattullo, Hugh James, Lieut., d. of w., 30/9/18 (28 Bde.).
Paul, Courtenay Talbot Saint, D.S.O., Major (Act. Lt.-Col.), d. of w., 31/7/17 (45 Bde.).
Paul, Laird Irvine Cassan, M.C., Capt. (A/Maj.), d. of w., 12/8/17 (D/82 Bde.).
Payne, Harold, 2/Lt., k. in a., 30/11/17 (93 Army Bde.).
Payne, John Robert, 2/Lt., d. of w., 4/11/17 (82 Bde. D. Bty.).
Peake, Malcolm, C.M.G., Brig.-Gen., k. in a., 28/8/17 (R.A. & Staff).
Pearce, George, Lt. (Tp.), k. in a., 28/1/16.
Pearce, Walter Harry, 2/Lt., d. of w., 24/4/18 (in Ger. hands) (X/39 T.M.B.).
Pearse, Raymond Stanley, Temp. 2/Lt., k. in a., 23/8/16 (71 Bde.).
Pearse, Walter Josiah, M.C., 2/Lt., k. in a., 9/4/17 (5 Bde.).
Pearson, Cyprian Thomas, 2/Lt., d. of w., 6/10/17 (A/91 Bde.).
Pearson, Edward John, 2/Lt., k. in a., 2/8/17 (83 Bde.).
Pearson, Harry, 2/Lt., d. of w., 1/10/18 (A/Bty. 14 Bde.).
Peel, Robert Lloyd, M.C., Lt., d. of w., 3/9/17 (A/58 Bde.).
Peerless, Charles Stephen, 2/Lt. (Tp.), k. in a., 14/8/16 (166 Bde.).
Peile, John Selby Chadwick, Lt., k. in a., 2/6/17 (190 Bde.).
Pember, Edward Horace, Lt., k. in a., 30/9/17 (att. R.F.C. 5/Sqdn.).
Pemberton, Fredrick Despard, Capt., k. in a., 21/8/17 (att. R.F.C. 59/Sqdn.).
Penlington, Arthur Berkeley, M.C., 2/Lt., k. in a., 6/10/17 (15 Army Bde.).
Perkins, Frank Bailey, Lt. (A/Capt.), k. in a., 19/5/17 (40 Bde.).
Perry, Cecil Victor, M.C., 2/Lt., k. in a., 23/4/17 (27 Bde.).
Perry, George Hugh, 2/Lt., k. in a., 31/3/18 (41 Bde.).
Perston, George Fortescue, 2/Lt., k. in a., 12/2/17 (B/99 Bde.).
Persse, Edward Aubrey, Capt., k. in a., 14/10/18 (47 Bde.).
Phear, Henry John, Lt., d. of w., 17/10/17 (14 A. Bde.).
Philbrick, E. H., Lt., died, 6/11/18 (395 Bty.).
Philip, Edgar Thomas, 2/Lt. (T/Lt.), k. in a., 18/6/17 (att. R.F.C. 9/Sqdn.).
Philip, John Alexander, 2/Lt., d. of w., 7/5/18 (D/122 Bde.).
Phillips, Edward Hawkin, D.S.O., Major, d. of w., 6/11/14.
Phillips, Maurice Aldcroft, Capt., k. in a., 21/5/15.
Phillpotts, Louis Murray, C.M.G., D.S.O., T/Brig.-Gen., k. in a., 8/9/16 (Staff 56 Divn.).
Philp, Richard William Manning Haigh, Temp. Capt., k. in a., 5/10/16 (91 Bde.).
Pickering, Albert Edwin, M.C., 2/Lt., k. in a., 28/9/18 (165 Bde.).
Pickering, Robert Hackney, Lt., k. in a., 30/11/17 (N. Anti-Aircraft Bty.).
Pickering, William James, 2/Lt., d. of w., 7/6/17 (113 Army Bde.).
Pickrell, Leslie John, 2/Lt., k. in a., 29/3/18 (29 Bde.).
Pickthall, William Roy, 2/Lt., k. in a., 16/9/18 (26 Army Bde.).
Pidcock, Frank, Lt., died, 17/2/19 (296 Bde.).
Pierce, John Beresford Hudson, Temp. 2/Lt., d. of w., 27/4/17.
Pierrepoint, James H., Temp. Lt., drowned, 4/5/17.
Piggott, Gerald Wellesley, 2/Lt., d. of w., 14/5/15.
Pilcher, Gerald Aubrey, 2/Lt., d. of w., 26/10/17 (159 Bde.).
Pile, Cyril John, 2/Lt., d. of w., 29/4/17 (att. R.F.C. 12/Sqdn.).
Pilliner, Rupert Colerick Leybourne, 2/Lt., k. in a., 4/11/14.
Pilling, Edgar, 2/Lt., k. in a., 23/4/17 (15 Bde.).
Pim, Thomas, Lt., killed, 28/8/18 (and R.A.F.).
Pinhey, Kenneth Fleetwood Gordon, Lt., k. in a., 2/8/17 (83 Bde.).
Pinniger, Wilfred James, 2/Lt., k. in a., 4/10/17 (91 Bde.)
Pitt, Stanley Robert, M.C., Temp. 2/Lt., k. in a., 23/10/16 (2 Bde.).
Platt, Claud Lucien Francis, 2/Lt., k. in a., 27/5/18 (25/-D.A.C.).
Playfair, The Hon. Lyon George Henry Lyon, Capt., k. in a., 20/4/15.
Plunket, Cedric John, Lt., k. in a., 5/8/17 (123 Bde.).
Pockett, Walter Harold, 2/Lt., k. in a., 24/4/18 (96 Bde.).
Poer, Hubert Piers Beresford, Capt. (A/Maj.), k. in a., 24/4/18 (91 Bde.).
Pohl, Frederick Alfred, Lt., died, 22/10/18 (A/161 Bde.).
Pointer, Henry John, Lt., died, 13/12/17 (130 Bde.).
Pollard, Geoffrey Blemell, Lt., killed, 24/10/14.
Pollard, Stanley Madel, Temp. 2/Lt., d. of w., 12/4/18 (att. Ayrshire Bty.).
Poore, Roger, Lt. (Tp.), k. in a., 19/9/15.
Pope, Philip Gladstone, Lt., k. in a., 16/10/17 (35 Bde. H.Q.).
Porter, Gavin Alexander, Lt. (T/Capt.), died, 6/12/15 (att. R.F.C.).
Porter, W., 2/Lt., died, 28/2/19 (att. R.A.F.).
Porter, Wilson, 2/Lt., k. in a., 24/3/18 (att. R.F.C. 56/-Sqdn.).
Porterfield, Leonard W., Temp. Lt., died, 1/11/18.
Potter, Kenneth Mitchell, D.S.O., Major, k. in a., 8/7/17 (52 Bde.).
Potter, William Robert McCall, 2/Lt., k. in a., 17/9/18 (70 Bde.).
Powell, Eric Limbery, Temp. Lt., k. in a., 6/4/18 (174 Bde.).
Powell, John Harold Slade, Major, died, 8/2/15.
Powell, Maurice, Temp. Lt., k. in a., 5/7/17 (14 Bde.).
Powell, Richard, Temp. Lt., d. of w., 22/8/17 (153 Bde.).
Powell, Richard Oversby, T/Capt. and Adjt., k. in a., 16/7/16 (33 Bde.).
Power-Clutterbuck, James Edward, Temp. 2/Lt., k. in a., 25/6/17 (att. R.F.C. 53/Sqdn.).
Pownall, Allen Claude Morrison, 2/Lt., k. in a., 27/3/18.
Praetorius, Alfred, 2/Lt., k. in a., 27/5/18 (C/155 Army Bde.).
Pratt, Aylwin Murray, 2/Lt., k. in a., 21/8/17 (186 Bde.).
Pratt, Ernest Victor, 2/Lt., k. in a., 25/9/17 (C/277 Army Bde.).
Pratt, Geoffry Cowper Spencer, Lt., d. of w., 27/11/15.
Preeston, Philip Southwell, 2/Lt., k. in a., 28/3/18 (1/Bty.).
Prescott, Ernest Twiss, 2/Lt., d. of w., 26/2/18 (34 Bde.).
Preston, Herbert William Lawson, Lt., died, 19/8/17.
Price, James Thirkell, Capt., k. in a., 21/4/16 (C/77 Bde.).
Priest, Benjamin, M.C., 2/Lt., d. of w., 26/4/18 (72/38 Bde.).
Primrose, Nigel, M.C., Temp. Lt., died, 25/10/18 (64 Bde.).
Prior, Leslie Montague Sidney, Temp. 2/Lt., k. in a., 26/7/16.
Prismall, Merrick Orville, Lt., killed, 20/12/17 (att. R.F.C.).
Pritchard, John Eric Stirling, 2/Lt., d. of w., 27/10/17 (52 Bty.).
Pritchard, Wilfred Dryden, Capt., d. of w., 25/9/15.
Proctor, James Adolphus, 2/Lt., d. of w., 18/9/18 (14 Bde.).
Pugh, Cyril Webster, Lt., k. in a., 21/8/18 (Div. Bn. M.G.C.).
Pulleine, Robert Percy, 2/Lt., k. in a., 4/9/16.
Pulley, Charles, Major, d. of w., 26/7/15.
Purchas, Ernest Charles, Lt., d. of w., 4/3/15.
Quarry, Herbert, Temp. Lt., k. in a., 2/8/16 (F/8 T.M.B.).
Quiller-Couch, Bevil Brian, D.S.O., M.C., Act. Major, died, 6/2/19.
Quin, Francis John, 2/Lt., d. of w., 2/5/18 (50 Bde.).
Quinlan, John Francis Pembroke Boxwell, 2/Lt., died, 3/7/16 (att. R.F.C.).
Quinn, William Henry Corry, 2/Lt., k. in a., 21/4/18 (70 Bde.).
Radcliffe, Arthur Philip Joseph, Lt. (A/Capt.), d. of w., 18/8/17 (71 Bde.).
Radcliffe, Samuel Roberts, D.S.O., Major, died, 30/4/18 (172 Bde.).
Rae, John Cairns, M.C., Lt. (A/Capt.), k. in a., 10/4/17 (86 Bde.).
Rait-Kerr, Sylvester Cecil, Capt., k. in a., 13/5/15.
Rait-Kerr, William Charles, D.S.O., Capt., k. in a., 10/11/14.
Ralph, Henry Bertie, 2/Lt., d. of w., 12/10/18 (255 Bde.).
Ralphs, Walter Joel, Lt. (Tp.), d. of w., 15/7/16.
Ramsay, John Richard, Major, k. in a., 6/1/17 (160 How. Bty.).
Ramskill, William Bliss, 2/Lt., d. of w., 16/9/18 (A/119 Bde.).
Randall, Charles Barton, Lt. (Tp.), k. in a., 31/7/17 (A/74 Bde.).
Rankin, John Hall, 2/Lt., died, 2/3/16.
Ratcliff, Sidney Arthur, 2/Lt., k. in a., 31/3/17 (59 Bde.).
Rattray, David, 2/Lt., d. of w., 21/9/18 (D/23 Bde.).
Ravenscroft, Alan Paddock, Lt. (Tp.), died, 16/1/17 (and R.F.C.).
Rawe, Charles Henry, 2/Lt., k. in a., 24/4/18 (att. R.G.A., 309 S.B.).
Rayner, James Ernest Robert, M.C., 2/Lt. (T/Lt.), d, of w., 10/5/18 (91 Bde.).
Rayson, William Humphrey Ronald, T/Lt. (A/Capt.), d. of w., 27/3/18 (in German hands) (47 Bde.).
Read, Phillips Towter, 2/Lt., k. in a., 23/10/16 (2 Bde.).
Reading, Harold Leslie, 2/Lt., k. in a., 5/11/17 (108 Bde.).
Redgate, Bernard Allan, 2/Lt., k. in a., 29/4/18 (15 Bde.).
Reed, John Charles, M.C., 2/Lt., died, 14/12/18 (D. Bty. 280 Bde. 56 Div.).
Reed, William Percy, 2/Lt., k. in a., 15/9/17 (232 Army Bde.).
Rees, Ernest Llewellyn, 2/Lt. (Tp.), k. in a., 22/10/18 (113 Bde.).
Reeves, Leslie Leonhardt, Capt., died, 14/2/19.
Reid, George, Lt., k. in a., 25/8/18 (27 Bde.).
Reid, Reginald Harper, Lt. (A/Capt.), k. in a., 14/9/18 (153 Bde.).
Relton, Douglas Edward Lloyd, Lt., d. of w., 4/6/18 (23 Bty.).
Rendel, Andrew James, M.C., Capt. (A/Major), d. of w., 29/6/17 (5 Bde.).
Rennie, James Francis, 2/Lt., k. in a., 31/7/17 (B/70 Bde.).
Renny, Gerald Mercer, Lt., k. in a., 15/4/17 (92 Bde.).
Repen, Frederick, Capt., died, 13/6/19.
Reynolds, Alfred Slater, 2/Lt., k. in a., 25/7/17 (70/34 Bde.).
V.C. Reynolds, Douglas, Major, died, 23/2/16.
Reynolds, Robert Reynold, 2/Lt., k. in a., 31/5/18 (41/Bde.).
Rhodes, Henry, Capt. (Tp.), k. in a., 17/9/17 (33 D.A.C.).
Rich, Charles Bayard, Major, k. in a., 16/8/17 (45 Bde.).
Rich, Christopher Stiles, Capt., died, 22/3/15 (att. R.F.C.).
Rich, Cyril Shirston, 2/Lt., k. in a., 7/8/16 (164 Bde.).
Rich, Ernest Evelyn, D.S.O., Major, d. of w., 1/12/17 (U Bty.).
Richards, Arthur William, Lt., k. in a., 28/3/18 (62 Bde.).
Richards, Bruce Carlton, Lt., k. in a., 11/7/17.
Richards, James Thomas, Lt. (Tp.), d. of w., 27/9/16 (180 Bde.).
Richardson, Sidney Athelstone, 2/Lt. (Tp.), d. of w., 3/11/17 (266 Bde.).
Richardson, Thomas William, M.C., D.C.M., 2/Lt., k. in a., 28/3/18 (32 Bde.).
Rickards, Hew Wardrope Brooke, Lt., k. in a., 28/7/17 (R.F.C.).
Ricketts, James Stuart, 2/Lt., d. of w., 3/10/18 (122 Bde. A Bty.).
Ridout, Gaspard Alweed Evelyn, 2/Lt., k. in a., 21/3/18 (331 Bde.).
Riecke, Arnold Francis, Major, died, 19/6/19 (307 Bde.).
Riley, Albert Victor, Lt. (Tp.), k. in a., 20/8/17 (A Bty. 155 Bde.).
Riley, Thomas, Capt., d. of w., 5/8/16 (158 Bde.).
Roberts, Cecil Quinlan, 2/Lt., k. in a., 16/5/15.

Roberts, George Peskett, Lt. (Tp.), d. of w., 26/4/16 (61 How. Bty.).
Roberts, Harry Leslie, 2/Lt. (Tp.), d. of w., 10/9/16.
Roberts, Ivon L'Esterre, Major, k. in a., 8/6/15.
Roberts, John, M.C., Lt., died, 11/11/18 (S/158 Bde.).
Roberts, John Herbert, Lt., killed, 24/9/18 (and R.A.F.).
Robertson, Alexander, 2/Lt., d. of w., 17/8/17 (and R.F.C. 34 Sqd.).
Robertson, Charles Boyd, 2/Lt., k. in a., 16/10/17 (165 Bde.).
Robertson, Edmund John Macrory, Lt., k. in a., 22/5/15.
Robertson, Herbert Charles, Lt., k. in a., 1/11/18 (32 Bde.).
Robertson, John Struan Carmichael, 2/Lt., k. in a., 31/3/18 (46 Bde.).
Robertson, Norman Bethune, D.S.O., Major, k. in a., 30/11/17 (2 Bde.).
Robin, Cecil, 2/Lt., d. of w., 24/5/18 (86 Army Bde.).
Robinson, Alec, Major, d. of w., 16/4/18 (177 Bde.).
Robinson, Alexander Joseph, 2/Lt., d. of w., 8/8/17 (26/Bde.).
Robinson, Frederick Winwood, Major (T/Lt.-Col.), d. ot w., 18/4/17 (40 Bde.).
Robinson, Sidney Furness, 2/Lt., died, 10/3/15.
Robson, Edward Fawcett, 2/Lt., d. of w., 18/5/18 (79 Bde.).
Robson, William Friend, 2/Lt., k. in a., 3/5/17 (296 Bde.).
Rochfort-Boyd, Henry Charles, Major (T/Lt.-Col.), d. of w., 4/12/17 (16 Bty. 4 Cav. Div.).
Rodgers, A. H., Lt., died, 7/11/18 (4 Res. Bde.).
Rodney-Ricketts, Stewart Arthur, M.C., T/Lt. (A/Capt.), k. in a., 31/10/17 (82 Bde.).
Roe, John Windsor, Major, d. of w., 7/8/16 (R.A. Bde., Indian E.F.), C/185.
Rogers, Charles Hunter, 2/Lt., d. of w., 9/11/14.
Rogers, Denys Stutely, 2/Lt., k. in a., 21/3/18 (189 Army Bde.).
Rogers, Francis Lyttelton Lloyd, 2/Lt. (Tp.), k. in a., 7/1/16 (75 Bde.).
Rogers, Gerald, 2/Lt., k. in a., 1/9/18 (AAC. 126, A. Bde.).
Rogers, Richard Henry Lyster, Lt., k. in a., 4/10/17 (32 Bde.).
Rogers, Wilfrid Frank, D.S.O., Capt. (A/Major), k. in a., 19/5/17.
Rosa, Herbert Charles, 2/Lt., k. in a, 31/7/17 (8 Div. Amm. Col.).
Rose, Hugh Alexander Leslie, D.S.O., Major, k. in a., 18/4/18 (Staff Div. H.Q.).
Ross, Donald Neil Campbell, 2/Lt., d. of w., 3/11/17 (46 Bde.).
Rotheram, Walter Sutton, 2/Lt., k. in a., 29/9/17 (83 Bde.).
Rous, Thomas, 2/Lt., d. of w., 22/3/18 (296 Bde.).
Rowatt, David, 2/Lt. (Tp.), k. in a., 1/7/16.
Rowland, John Walter Bruce, 2/Lt., k. in a., 1/11/18 (175 A. Bde.).
Rowley, Reginald Frederick, Lt., k in a., 21/3/18 (A/179 Bde.).
Rowntree, Lawrence Edmund, 2/Lt, k. in a., 25/11/17.
Runnels-Moss, Eric Cross Arnold, 2/Lt., died, 9/7/18 (2 Bde.) (P. of W.).
Rushby, Frank, Capt., died, 26/2/15.
Russell, Francis Gerald, 2/Lt., k. in a, 28/1/17 (and R.F.C.).
Russell, John, Lt. (Tp.) (A/Capt.), k. in a., 10/4/17 (B/76 Bde.).
Russell, Noel John Gilbert, 2/Lt., d. of w., 27/9/18, (A/26 Bde.).
Russell, Walter Edward, 2/Lt. (A/Lt.), k. in a., 11/5/17 (129/42 Bde.).
Russell, William Edward, 2/Lt. (A/Lt.), k. in a., 13/7/17 (att. X. 29 T.M.B.).
Ruston, Frederick Augustus, Lt., d. of w., 21/3/18 (94 Bde.).
Rutherfoord, David Geoffrey Corry, Capt., k. in a., 17/4/16.
Rutledge, Joseph Ward, Lt., k. in a., 31/7/17 (B. 103).
Samuels, Lesser Joseph, M.C., T/Lt. (A/Major), k. in a., 29/9/17 (83 Bde.).
Sanders, James Donald Gerhardt, Capt., k. in a., 5/1/16 (and R.F.C.).
Sanderson, Eric Harvard, 2/Lt, k. in a., 24/9/18 (D/149 Bde.).
Sanderson, Harry, Temp. Capt. (A/Major), k. in a., 23/4/17 (63 Bde.).
Sanderson, Ronald Harcourt, Major (A/Lt.-Col.), k. in a., 17/4/18 (148 Bde.).
Sants, Herbert Walter, Lt., died, 24/12/17 (att. A.O.C.).
Saulez, Arthur Travers, A/Major, k. in a., 22/4/17 (64 Bde.).
Saunders, Clement, 2/Lt., d. of w., 11/2/17 (66 Bty.).
Saunders, Robert Stratford Howard, Lt., d. of w., 12/4/18 (D/330 Bde.).
Savage, Alfred, 2/Lt, died, 7/10/17 (4 Bde., D.A.C.).
Savage, Henry Osborne, Lt., k. in a., 26/10/16.
Savile, William Henry Bouchier, Temp. Capt., k. in a., 14/8/16.
Sayer, Hubert Lionel, 2/Lt, k. in a., 17/8/17 (and R.F.C., 7 Sqd.).
Sayle, George Randall Fysh, Lt., d of w., 10/5/15.
Saywood, Charles, 2/Lt, k. in a 5/7/16.
Schreiber, Owen Reginald, M.C., Capt. (A/Major), d. of w., 22/10/17 (106 Bty., 22 Bde.).
Scott, Alan Dale Wyndham, M.C., Temp. Lt., d. of w., 26/10/16 (92 Bde.).
Scott, Clifford, 2/Lt, k. in a., 2/8/17 (83 Bde.).
Scott, Desmond, 2/Lt, k. in a., 25/10/16 (39 Bde.).
Scott, G. G. D, Lt., died, 22/4/18 (157 Bde.).
Scott, Harold Donald, 2/Lt, k. in a., 16/10/18 (45 Bde.).
Scott, John Murray, 2/Lt., k in a., 2/4/18 (295 Bde.).
Scott, Ralph, 2/Lt., k. in a., 12/4/18 (256 Bde.).
Scott-Deakin, Reginald, Lt., k. in a., 31/7/17 (74 Bde.).
Searle, Valentine Lang Stuart, 2/Lt., d of w., 22/6/16 (76 Bde.).
See, Sydney Matthews, 2/Lt., k. in a., 10/10/16 (A/71 Bde.).

Selwyn, George Vincent Carus, Lt., d. of w, 25/10/18 (106 Bde.).
Semple, Robert Edward Watson, M.C., Capt., d. of w., 5/11/18 (att. Gds. Div. T.M.B.).
Senior, Harold Frank, M.C., T/Capt. (A/Major), d. of w., 13/4/18 (A/75 Bde.).
Sewell, Harry Kemp, Lt., died, 20/8/17.
Sewell, Herbert Victor, Temp. 2/Lt, k. in a., 13/11/16 (186 Bde.).
Shakerley, Arthur Cecil, 2/Lt., k. in a., 22/4/17 (64 Bde.).
Shand-Kydd, William, 2/Lt., k. in a., 16/5/17 (51 Bde.).
Shannon, Robert Mortimer, M.C., 2/Lt., d. of w., 29/4/18 (50 Bde.).
Shapland, Herbert George, 2/Lt., d. of w., 2/3/18 (36 Bde.).
Sharp, Arthur Granville, M.C., Lt., k. in a., 23/8/18 (72 Army Bde.).
Sharp, Frederick Arthur Hamilton, Lt., k. in a., 30/10/18 (att. Staff).
Sharp, Frederick Leonard, C.M.G., Lt.-Col., k. in a., 13/8/16 (39 Bde.).
Shaw, Randolph Albert, Major, d. of w., 14/11/16.
Shaw, William Maxwell, D.S.O., Major, k. in a., 29/5/17 (102 Bde.).
Shelley, Philip John, 2/Lt., k in a., 31/7/17 (83 Bde.).
Shepard, Bernard Anthony, 2/Lt. (Tp.), d. of w., 26/5/17 (att. Z. 24 T.M.B.).
Shepard, Norbert Gerald, Temp. Lt., d. of w., 2/8/16.
Sherman, John James, Lt., k. in a., 20/10/17 (36 Bde.).
Sherrard, Bertram, 2/Lt., k. in a., 22/5/18 (D/92 Bde.).
Short, William Ambrose, Lt.-Col., k. in a., 21/6/17 (286 Bde.).
Sibold, Sidney Sparkling Moverley, M.C., Lt. (A/Capt.), d. of w., 12/4/18 (C/165 Bde.).
Sidley, John Witherington, Temp. 2/Lt., d. of w., 2/8/16 (41 Bde.).
Siedle, Karl Otto, M.C., T/Capt. (A/Major), d. of w., 30/5/18 (B/174 Bde.).
Sillem, Augustus Charles Herman, Temp. 2/Lt., k. in a., 18/7/16.
Simmonds, Austin Gundry, 2/Lt., drowned, 2/6/17 (5A. Res. Bde.).
Simmons, William Aubrey, Temp. Lt., d. of w., 3/11/18 (B/88 Bde.).
Simpson, Brian George Casson, 2/Lt., d. of w., 29/7/15.
Simpson, Colin, 2/Lt., k. in a., 7/8/16.
Sims, Thomas Augustus, Hon. Capt. & Ridg. Mr., died, 19/5/15.
Simson, David Henry Ainsworth Cranstown, 2/Lt., k. in a., 18/9/18 (24 Bde.).
Simson, Ronald Francis, Lt., k. in a., 15/9/14.
Sinclair, Colin Johnston, 2/Lt., died, 30/11/16 (27/32 Bde.).
Sinclair, John Norman, D.S.O., Major, A/Lt.-Col., k. in a., 24/3/18.
Sinclair, R. B., Lt., died, 22/3/19 (att. R.A.F.).
Sinton, Edwin, M.C., Lt., A/Capt., k. in a., 21/8/18 (att. R.E., 4/Lt., Rly. Op. Coy.).
Skipwith, Granville Arthur, 2/Lt., k. in a., 16/6/15.
Skrine, Sholto Herries, Lt. (Tp.), d. of w., 19/9/17 (B/95 Bde.).
Slade, Robert Gordon, Lt., k. in a., 18/4/18 (19 D.A.C.).
Slade, Wilfrid Adolphus, 2/Lt., k. in a., 23/4/17 (70 Bde.).
Slaney, John Cobley, Lt., k. in a., 17/2/16.
Slinger, George Nicholas, Temp. 2/Lt., k. in a., 28/11/16.
Smillie, George Sinclair, 2/Lt., d. of w., 13/8/17 (C/121 Bde.).
Smith, Cecil Owen, 2/Lt., k. in a., 20/8/17 (36/33 Bde.).
Smith, Clifford Thomas, 2/Lt., k. in a., 30/7/17 (B/122 Bde.).
Smith, Edmund Percival, Col., k. in a., 2/5/15.
Smith, Eric St. Clare, Lt., killed, 2/7/17 (and R.F.C.).
Smith, Godfrey Michael, M.C., Temp. 2/Lt., d. of w., 28/10/18 (D/256 Bde.).
Smith, Headford, 2/Lt., d. of w., 14/9/18 (119 Army Bde.).
Smith, Harold Heyworth, 2/Lt. (Tp.), k. in a., 13/2/16.
Smith, James Albert, 2/Lt., k. in a., 21/3/18 (30 D.A.C.).
Smith, John Hobson, 2/Lt., died, 24/11/18 (78 Bde.).
Smith, Reginald John, 2/Lt., d. of w., 1/4/18 (291 Bde.).
Smith, Victor Sidney, 2/Lt., k. in a., 6/10/17 (and R.F.C.).
Smith, William Hammond, Capt., A/Major, k. in a., 12/4/17 (A/52 Bde.).
Smith, William Henry, 2/Lt., k. in a., 23/4/17 (281 Bde.).
Smith, William Robson, Lt., A/Capt., died, 19/11/18 (X/31 T.M.B. 2nd Army).
Smith-Rewse, Henry Bingham Whistler, Major, d. of w., 21/11/14.
Snell, Stanley Saxon, 2/Lt., d. of w., 6/5/18 (B/159 Bde.).
Snow, Charles Foote, 2/Lt., k. in a., 30/6/16.
Snowball, John Hearn, 2/Lt., d. of w., 15/9/16 (108 Bde.).
Soames, Maurice Gordon, Major, d. of w., 24/9/16 (A/48 Bde.).
Souness, Thomas, 2/Lt., k. in a., 7/9/18 (116/26 Bde.).
Spaull, Ernest Mayall Vaughan, 2/Lt., k. in a., 26/3/18.
Spence, Charles Bennett, Lt., killed, 9/5/15 (att. R.F.C.).
Spence, David Stuart, 2/Lt., k. in a., 13/12/15.
Spencer, Charles Herbert Slingsby, 2/Lt., k. in a., 5/10/18 (330 Bde.).
Spencer, James Sturtevant, 2/Lt., k. in a., 2/9/16 (26 Bde.).
Spreat, Leicester Hulke, M.C., 2/Lt., d. of w., 8/10/16 (91 Bde.).
Squire, Basil Brett, Lt., A/Capt., k. in a., 23/4/17 (15 Bde.).
Squires, Charles Arthur, 2/Lt., k. in a., 25/4/18 (162 Bde.).
Stacey, Brian John, 2/Lt., d. of w., 26/4/17 (B/63 Bde.).
Stafford, Kenneth James, M.C., Lt, d of w., 14/11/18 (37/27 Bde.).
Stainbank, Arthur Reeve, 2/Lt., k. in a., 20/7/17 (113 Bde.).
Stainbank, William Dering, 2/Lt., died, 8/4/16.
Staley, Edward Vernon, Lt., k. in a., 18/9/18 (290 Bde.).
Stalker, Daniel, Temp. Lt., d. of w., 12/4/18 (169 Bde.).

Stapylton, Granville Joseph Chetwynd, Major, k. in a., 25/8/14.
Staveley, Miles, M.C., Capt., A/Major, d. of w., 29/9/18 (44 Bde.).
Stenning, Sidney Nelson, 2/Lt., k. in a., 21/3/18 (189 Bde.).
Stephen, Adnian Consett, M.C., Lt., A/Major, k. in a., 14/3/18.
Stephen, Kenneth Travers, M.C., Lt., A/Capt., d. of w., 22/4/18 (X/2 T.M.B.).
Stephens, Cecil Hubert, Lt., k. in a., 23/10/18 (24 Bde.).
Stephens, Dudley Eric, 2/Lt., d. of w., 29/3/18 (B/70 Bde.).
Stephens, Henry French, D.S.O., M.C., Temp. Major, d. of w., 14/10/18 (86 Bde.).
Stephenson, Derek Charles, D.S.O., M.C., Major, k. in a., 23/3/18 (Z. Bty.).
Stephenson, Ernest Cooper Apperly, 2/Lt., k. in a., 21/3/18 (18 D.A.C., att. 83 Bde.).
Sternberg, Rupert Oswald, 2/Lt., d. of w., 1/7/16 (83 Bde.).
Stevens, Frederick Charles, Capt. (Tp.), k. in a., 31/7/16 (158 Bde.).
Steward, Arthur Amyot, 2/Lt. k. in a., 6/10/17 (11 Balloon Coy., R.F.C.).
Stewart, Charles Edward, Temp Lt.-Col., k. in a., 31/8/16 (190 Bde.).
Stewart, James Henry, 2/Lt., killed, 21/12/17 (302 Bde.).
Stewart, Mungo, Lt., d. of w., 7/2/17 (H.Q. Staff, 55 Bde.).
Stewart, Osmer Noel, M.C., 2/Lt., k. in a., 31/7/17 (71 Bde.).
Stewart, Samuel George, M.C., Lt., Act. Major, k. in a., 27/10/18 (30/39 Bde.).
Steyn, Stephanus Sebastian Lombard, Lt. (Tp.), k. in a., 8/12/17 (B/117 Bde.).
Stickland, William Alban, Lt., k. in a., 23/5/16.
Stokes, Guy Lennard, 2/Lt. (Tp.), k. in a., 5/7/17 (D/174 Bde.).
Stone, Tom Pearse Griffith, Temp. Lt., d. of w., 5/2/17 (66 Bde.).
Stopford, Heneage Frank, Major, k. in a., 15/9/16.
Storer, Patrick George Rawlings, 2/Lt., d. of w., 16/6/18 (3 D.A.C.).
Stormont, William Lundie, 2/Lt., k. in a., 31/8/18 (5 A. Bde.).
Stovin, Lewis John Elliott, Lt., died, 22/8/17 (127 Bty.).
Strachan, Aubrey Causton, Lt., k. in a., 28/3/18 (70 Bde.).
Straker, Frank, Temp. 2/Lt., d. of w., 16/7/16 (Z. 39 T.M.B.).
Strang, John Traquair, 2/Lt., k. in a., 18/5/18 (79 Army Bde.).
Street, Harold Edward, C.M.G., Lt.-Col., k. in a., 25/8/17 (106 Bde. Gen. Staff).
Stroud, Sydney Hill, Lt., A/Capt., killed, 20/10/18.
Stuart, George Douglas Gordon, Lt., k. in a., 23/9/17 (24 Bty., 11 Army Bde.).
Sutherland, Anderson, M.C., T/Lt., Act. Major, d. of w., 7/11/18 (51/39 Bde.).
Sutherland Andrew Ernest, Temp. Lt., k. in a., 3/10/16 (67 Bde.)
Sutton, Cyril John, Temp. 2/Lt., k. in a., 1/7/16
Sutton, George Nathaniel, 2/Lt., died, 14/10/16.
Swaine, S. W., 2/Lt., killed, 4/4/18 (and R.A.F.).
Sweet-Escott, William Arthur, Lt., d. of w., 14/10/18 (H.Q., 50 Bde.).
Sweetnam, Richard Rodney Stephen, Temp. Capt., k. in a., 1/7/16 (125 Bty.).
Swift, Allen Richard, 2/Lt., k. in a., 10/11/17
Swinton, Ernest, 2/Lt., d. of w., 28/5/15
Syers, Thomas Scott, M.C., Capt., A/Major, died, 14/11/18 (D/157 Bde.).
Sykes, Leslie Gordon, 2/Lt., killed, 22/3/18 (and R.F.C.).
Sykes, William, Lt., died, 4/4/18 (112 Bty., 6 Div.).
Symons, Hubert, Major, d. of w., 22/3/18 (D/47 Bde.), in German hands.
Talbot, Eric Lawrence, Lt., d. of w., 23/10/14.
Talbot, Leonard Lane, M.C., Capt., d. of w., 24/4/17 (27th Bde.).
Talbot, Rimell Smith, 2/Lt., k. in a., 23/4/18 (121st Bde.).
Talbot, Theophilus Edwin, 2/Lt., d. of w., 21/3/18 (C/160th Bde.).
Tancock, Osborne George, M.C., Lt., k. in a., 17/3/18 (att. R.F.C., 5th Sqd.).
Tanner, Thomas George, Lt. (Tp.), k. in a., 14/10/17.
Tarras, John Rae, 2/Lt., k. in a., 16/10/16 (X 9 Trench Mortar Batt.).
Tate, Herbert Lloyd, 2/Lt. (Tp.), k. in a., 12/6/16.
Tatem, Rolland James, M.C., Lt., k. in a., 27/9/18 (42nd Bde.).
Tavener, Harold Tait, 2/Lt., d. of w., 12/4/18 (B/88th Bde.).
Taylor, Brook Wilbraham, D.S.O., Major, d. of w., 2/4/16.
Taylor, Charles Christopher Vassel, Lt. (Tp.), k. in a., 26/12/17 (301st Bde.).
Taylor, Charles Matheson, 2/Lt., d. of w., 20/4/17 (121st Bty.).
Taylor, Ernest Albert Isaac, Capt. (Tp.), d. of w., 23/7/18 (B/98th Bde.).
Taylor, Ezra Dolphin, 2/Lt., k. in a., 30/4/15.
Taylor, Geoffrey England, 2/Lt., d. of w., 26/9/18 (Y. 33 T.M.B.).
Taylor, George Milburn, Lt. (Tp.), d. of w., 25/5/16 (161st Bde.).
Taylor, George William, Lt., d. of w., 9/11/17 (A/150 Bde.).
Taylor, Robert William, M.C., Lt., d. of w., 24/10/17 (83rd (8th Bty.).
Taylor, Stanley Gordon, 2/Lt., k. in a., 21/10/16 (38th Bde.).
Taylor, William Currie, Lt. (A/Capt.), died, 7/11/18 (14th D.A.C.).
Teare, John Stewart, M.C., Lt. (Tp.), k. in a., 3/8/17 (108th Bde.).
Teeling, Luke Joseph, Lt. (A/Major), d. of w., 8/11/18 Bde.).
Terrell, Claud Romako à Beckett, M.C., 2/Lt. (A/Capt.), d. of w., 10/6/17 (15th Bde.).
Thackeray, Frederick Rennell, Col., died, 15/10/15 (75th Bde. Guards Div.) (Ret. Pay, late R.A.).
Thesiger, The Hon. Frederic Ivor, 2/Lt., d. of w., 8/5/17 87th Bde.).
Thomas, Cyril Vaughan, 2/Lt., k. in a., 18/7/17 (2nd Bde.).
Thomas, Sir Godfrey Vignolles, Bart., C.B., C.B.E., D.S.O., B/Gen., died, 17/219.
Thomas, Geoffrey Lynn, M.C., Capt., k. in a., 6/6/18 (95th Bde.).
Thomas, Hugh, Lt. (Tp.), k. in a., 2/3/17 (att. Y. 1st T.M.B.).
Thomas, Maurice Wotton, Lt., k. in a., 5/8/16 (and R.F.C.).
Thompson, Francis Clement, Lt., d. of w., 3/10/17 (B/59th Bde.).
Thompson, Harold Blundell, Lt., k. in a., 2/10/17 (Staff Lt., H.Q. Div. Art.).
Thompson, Harold Eustace, 2/Lt., d. of w., 7/10/16 (23rd Div. X. 22. T.M.B.).
Thompson, Joseph, M.C., T/Lt. (A/Capt.), k. in a., 25/10/18 (121st Bde.).
Thompson, Robert Lloyd, Lt. (A/Major), k. in a., 1/12/17.
Thonemann, Emil Howard, 2/Lt., k. in a., 3/5/17.
Thornton, G. St. Leger, D.S.O., Major, died, 4/2/18.
Thorp, Thomas Tudor, 2/Lt., k. in a., 16/8/17 (D/83rd Bde.).
Threlfall, Herbert Edward, 2/Lt. (T/Lt.), d. of w., 4/11/17 (266th Bde.).
Tidswell, Wm. Framcis Howard, Lt., k. in a., 31/10/16 (88th Bde.).
Tiernan, Edwin Lawrence, 2/Lt., d. of w., 29/9/16 (240th Bde.).
Timmins, Frank, 2/Lt. (Tp.), d. of w., 19/12/17 (265th Bde.).
Tindal, Archibald Arthur, 2/Lt., k. in a., 8/9/16 (177th Bde.).
Tinkley, Horace Arthur, 2/Lt., d. of w., 1/4/18 (C/75th Bde.).
Tolson, James Martin, 2/Lt., d. of w., 20/10/18 (A/74th Bde.).
Tombs, Joseph Simpson McKenzie, 2/Lt., d. of w., 11/9/15.
Tomkins, Frederick Allen, Capt. (Tp.), d. of w., 14/7/16 (att. T.M.B.).
Tongue, Andrew Leslie, 2/Lt., k. in a., 28/5/18 (175th Bde.).
Tovey, Harry Turner, Lt. (T/Major), d. of w., 22/4/18 (A/88th Bde.).
Towell, Gerald Wyman, M.C., Lt. (A/Capt.), d. of w., 8/8/18 (N/Bty.).
Trapp, Andrew, Lt., k. in a., 23/4/18 (41st Bty.).
Trease, R. E., D.S.O., M.C., Lt., died, 5/12/18 (28th Bde.) (124th Bty.).
Trebilcock, John Archibald, M.C., Major, d. of w., 21/5/18 (76th Army Bde.).
Trenchmann, Friedrich Otto, 2/Lt. (Tp.), d. of w., 15/10/16.
Treglown, Charles Henry, Lt. (Tp.), k. in a., 30/3/17 (47th Bde.).
Trench, Derrick Le Poer, D.S.O., M.C., Major, k. in a., 28/8/17.
Trenchard, Frederick Alfred, Lt., k. in a., 24/5/15.
Trevenen, Sydney Vyvyan, Capt., d. of w., 10/6/18 (40th Bde.).
Trevithick, Robert Percy, 2/Lt., k. in a., 23/4/17 (232nd Bde.).
Trimming, Henry William Noel, 2/Lt., killed, 15/5/15.
Trorery, George Alan, 2/Lt., d. of w., 21/3/18 (177th Bde.).
Trustram, Raymond Prince, M.C., Lt., d. of w., 28/8/18 (121/27th Bde.)
Trouton, Desmond Gardner, Capt. (Act.), k. in a., 13/10/17 (B/102.).
Tucker, Albert Ruthven, 2/Lt., d. of w., 16/5/17 (162nd Bde.).
Tucker, John Ayre, 2/Lt., k. in a., 1/11/14.
Tudsbery, Lancelot, 2/Lt., k. in a., 22/8/17 (70th Bde.).
Tudor, Percival Bradbury, 2/Lt., died, 1/11/18 (26th Jacobs Mtn. Bty.).
Turner, Charles Rushton, 2/Lt., died, 30/10/15 (3rd C. Res. Bde.).
Turner, Edward Percy, T/Lt. (A/Capt.), k. in a., 19/3/17 (2nd Bde.).
Turner, Frederick Richard, 2/Lt., k. in a., 15/1/17 (100th Bde.).
Turner, Herbert Duncan Bruce, Lt., died, 9/8/17 (att. R.F.C.).
Turner, James Clifford, Lt., k. in a., 3/8/16 (and R.F.C.).
Turner, Thomas Alfred, Lt. (Tp.), k. in a., 29/4/17 (50th Bde.).
Tweedie, Leslie Kinloch, 2/Lt. (Tp.), k. in a., 17/1/16.
Twidale, Elfric Ashby, 2/Lt., k. in a., 22/4/17 (att. R.F.C.).
Tyler, John Collett, 2/Lt., k. in a., 18/4/15.
Underwood, Edward James, 2/Lt., d. of w., 8/6/17 (X/47th T.M.B.).
Upfill, Thomas Henry, M.C., Lt., killied, 18/10/18 (& R.A.F.).
Uridge, Edgar John Gibbons, 2/Lt., k. in a., 26/6/17 (147th Bde.).
Usborne, Alfred James, Capt. (Tp.), (A/Maj.), k. in a., 29/4/17 (50th Bde.).
Uzielli, Valentine Leslie Douglas, 2/Lt. (T/Lt.), k. in a., 21/7/17.
Vaisey, Roland Maddison, Capt., k. in a., 7/9/18.
Vallange, Lancelot William, 2/Lt., k. in a., 31/10/16 (2nd Bde.).
Vaucour, Awdry Morris, Major, killed, 16/7/18 (& R.A.F.).
Vaughan, Edward Wilmot, 2/Lt., k. in a., 15/7/16.

Vaughan, Harold, Lt. (Tp.), k. in a., 31/7/17 (74th Bde.).
Vaughan, Henry Humphreston Scott, Major, k. in a., 24/4/16.
Vavasour, Rudolph Dunstan, 2/Lt. (T/Lt.), died, 16/1/17 (att. R.F.C.).
Veraguth, G. F., 2/Lt., died, 18/3/18 (19th Bde.).
Versfield, Vernon Ferris, 2/Lt., k. in a., 3/4/18 (B/190th Bde.).
Vick, Donald Benjamin, Lt. (Tp.), d. of w., 8/7/16 (C/162nd Bde.).
Villiers, Edgar Fyfe, Lt., died, 13/11/18 (68th Bde. att. Sch. of Instruct., Zeitoun).
Vincent, Austin Ears, Lt., k. in a., 7/11/18 (att. Z/91/Bde.).
Vizard, Harold Talbot, M.C., Lt. (A/Capt.), k. in a., 1/9/18 (A/Bty. 71 Bde.).
Vorley, W. K., Lt. (Tp.), died, 30/11/16 (12/A.A./Batt.).
Vyvyan, Beresford Houghton, Capt. (Tp.), d. of w., 18/8/17 (A. Bty., 121 Bde.).
Wadsworth, Wilfred Howard, 2/Lt., d. of w., 22/3/18 (X. 16 T.M.B.).
Wager, Arthur Howell, Lt., d. of w., 17/7/16 (C/85).
Waldegrave, Edmund John, 2/Lt., k. in a., 10/8/18 (286th Bde.).
Wale, Adie, Capt., d. of w., 30/5/18 (186th Bde. X 39 Trench Bty.).
V.C. Walford, Garth Neville, Capt., k. in a., 26/4/15.
Walker, George Stafford, Lt., d. of w., 20/11/17.
Walker, Harry Brampton, Lt. (Act. Capt.), died, 24/9/17.
Walker, James Robert, M.C., Lt. (Act. Major), k. in a., 20/3/17 (62nd Bde.).
Walker, Stanley, Capt., k. in a., 20/5/18 (246th Bde.).
Wall, Richard Ralph Baldwin, Major, k. in a., 8/6/17 (378th/169th Bde.).
Wallace, Henry Gilmour, 2/Lt., k. in a., 3/8/17 (86th Bde.).
Wallace, William Thwaites, M.C., Lt. (Tp.), k. in a., 12/4/17 (B. 160/Bde.).
Wallis, Nevill Hampton, 2/Lt., d. of w., 25/5/18 (C. 50/Bde.).
Walrond, Victor, Capt. (Act. Major), k. in a., 26/4/17 (36th Bde.).
Walsh, Archibald Charles Mark, 2/Lt., d. of w., 18/3/15.
Walsh, Frank, 2/Lt., k. in a., 29/9/18 (44th Bde.).
Walter, Bertram, D.S.O., Major, d. of w., 16/9/16 (106th Bty. 22nd Bde.).
Walton, Harold Arthur Gordon, Lt., died, 2/5/17 (33rd D.A.C.).
Wanklyn, John Sudell, Lt., k. in a., 29/5/18 (29th Bde.).
Wanklyn, Kenneth, Lt., died, 15/11/18 (98th Bty.).
Warburton, Fred Eric, 2/Lt., k. in a., 15/10/17 (3rd Div. Art. Anzac Corps Troops).
Ward, Charles Francis, Capt., k. in a., 15/5/15.
Ward, Charles Wilson, M.C., Capt., k. in a., 29/4/18 (Staff, R.G.A.).
Ward, Cecil Wellesley, 2/Lt., k. in a., 11/9/17 ("A"/148/Bde.).
Ward, Edward John, 2/Lt., k. in a., 2/10/17 (C/50/Bde.).
Ward, George Duval, (Tp.) Capt. (Act. Major), k. in a., 18/5/17 (181st Bde.).
Ward, Ernest, M.C., 2/Lt., died, 19/10/18 (A/56th Bde.).
Ward, Percival Arthur, 2/Lt., d. of w., 16/5/18 (50th Bde.).
Warr, William Charles Samuel, 2/Lt., k. in a., 1/7/16 (22nd Bde.).
Warrington, Francis Arnold, Lt. (Tp.), k. in a., 7/10/16 (148th Bde.).
Watkin, Ben Gerald Noel, 2/Lt., d. of w., 25/1/15.
Watson, George Edmund Borlase, D.S.O., M.C., Major, k. in a., 29/8/18 (5th Army Bde.).
Watson, Joseph James, D.C.M., 2/Lt., k. in a., 16/8/18 (T. Bty., 1 T.M. Bde.).
Watson, Norman John, 2/Lt., k. in a., 27/5/18 (246th Bde.).
Watson, Vesey Clayhills, Capt., k. in a., 11/4/17 (19th Bty.).
Watson, William Baikie, M.C., Lt., d. of w., 30/9/18 (C/95th Bde.).
Way, Roderick Norman, 2/Lt., k. in a., 13/1/16.
Wayte, Samuel Wilfred, M.C., 2/Lt., d. of w., 7/10/17 (103rd Bde.).
Webb, Herbert Percy, 2/Lt., d. of w., 26/4/17 (71st Bde.).
Webb, Richard Howard, 2/Lt, d. of w., 10/10/16 (A/237th Bde.).
Weeitch, James John, 2/Lt., d. of w., 8/10/17 (82nd Bde.).
Weekes, Cyril Warner, M.C., Capt., k. in a., 16/9/18.
Weinel, Edward Eugene, 2/Lt. (A/Lt.), k. in a., 7/6/17 (Y/30 T.M.B.).
Weir, Charles William, 2/Lt., k. in a., 28/10/17 (261st Bde.).
Weir, P., 2/Lt., d. of w., 15/8/15.
Weiss, Thomas Jessop, 2/Lt. (Tp.), d. of w., 27/6/16.
Welch, Walter George Frederick, Lt., k. in a., 30/10/14.
Weld, Edward Joseph, 2/Lt., d. of w., 27/9/15.
Weldon, Geoffrey, Capt., d. of w., 25/9/16 (D/48th Bde.).
Weldon, William Joseph, 2/Lt., k. in a., 4/6/17 (38th Bde.)
Wells, Maurice Godfrey, 2/Lt., k. in a., 28/3/18 (211th Bde.).
Wells, William Leslie, 2/Lt (Tp.), k. in a., 21/5/16.
Wells-Cole, Neville William, Major, k. in a., 6/1/18 (28th Bde.).
Welsh, Cyril Clifton, Capt., k. in a., 17/7/17 (256th Bde.).
Wentworth, John, 2/Lt., k. in a., 4/7/18 (179th Bde.).
West, Archibald Stewart, M.C., Major, k. in a., 23/3/18 (93rd Bde.).
West, Henry Cave, Capt., k. in a., 22-24/11/15.
West, John Preston Sackville, 2/Lt., k. in a., 14/6/17 (189th Bde.).
Westerberg, George Herbert, 2/Lt., k. in a., 5/9/16 (106th Bde.).
Wheatly, Edward Richard, 2/Lt., d. of w., 10/10/17 (156th Bde.).
Wheeler, John Piggott, M.C., Lt. (A/Major), k. in a., 30/10/17 (82nd Bde.).
White, Cecil William Keane, M.C., Lt. (A/Capt.), d. of w., 29/7/17 (X/Bty., 17th/Bde.).
White, Frederick George, 2/Lt., k. in a., 4/9/17 (64th Bde.).
White, Herbert Beresford, Lt., killed, 13/4/17 (230th Bde.).
White, Robert Stewart, 2/Lt., died, 4/11/18.
White, Roger Wingate, Major, k. in a., 18/5/15.
Whitehead, George Stanley, 2/Lt., k. in a., 2/12/17 (D/153rd Bde.).
Whitehead, George William Edendale, Lt., killed, 17/10/18 (and R.A.F.).
Whitehead, Henry, 2/Lt., k. in a., 13/6/16.
Whitehouse, Charles Thomas, 2/Lt., d. of w., 15/1/15.
Whiteside, William Leslie, 2/Lt. (Tp.), k. in a., 5/7/15.
Whittard, Harold Alfred, 2/Lt., k. in a., 13/8/17 (22nd Bde.).
Whyte, Alexander Cumming, Capt. (Tp.), died, 11/4/16 (159th Bde.).
Wiggin, Noel Holme, Lt. (Tp.), k. in a., 11/1/17 (36th Bde. Amm. Col.).
Wilcher, Leslie Reginald Victor, 2/Lt., died, 8/5/19 (113th Bde.).
Wilcox, Percy Stracey, 2/Lt., k. in a., 23/3/18 (174th Bde.).
Wilder, Frank, 2/Lt., k. in a., 31/3/16 ("Q" Bty.).
Wilkinson, Charles Bliss, 2/Lt., k. in a., 28/3/18 (att R.F.C.).
Wilkinson, Charles Harold, M.C., 2/Lt., died, 13/10/18 (42nd Bde.).
Wilkinson, Clarence Loftus Mason, Lt. (Tp.) (A/Capt.), d. of w., 6/11/16 (165th Bde.).
Wilkinson, James Fisher, M.C., Major, d. of w., 29/10/18 (39th Bde.).
Willats, Harry Ashley, 2/Lt., died, 12/2/17.
Williams, George Trevor, T/Lt., died, 19/4/18 (38th Bty., 9th Bde.).
Williams, John Herschell, 2/Lt., k. in a., 17/6/17 (84th Bde.).
Williams, Justus Harold, 2/Lt., k. in a., 9/7/16 (Guards T.M.B.).
Williams, Martin Floyer, Lt. (Tp.), k. in a., 11/8/16 (65th Bde.).
Williams, Selwyn Coldham, Lt. (Tp.), k. in a., 18/1/17 (189th Bde., "B" Bty.).
Williams, William, 2/Lt., k. in a., 29/8/18 (281st Bde.).
Williamson-Napier, Alfred Maxwell, Lt., k. in a., 12/12/18 (75th Bde.).
Willoughby, Stanley Nelson, Lt., k. in a., 1/8/17 (70th Bde.).
Wills, John Godfrey, 2/Lt., k. in a., 27/9/18 (A/93rd Bde.).
Wilshaw, Eric James, 2/Lt., died, 23/12/18 (A/233rd Bde.).
Wilson, Arthur Walker, 2/Lt., d. of w., 22/8/18 (251st Bde.).
Wilson, Cornelius William, 2/Lt., died, 25/11/18 (A/7/6 Bde.).
Wilson, Henry, M.C., 2/Lt., k. in a., 9/5/18 (28th Army Bde.).
Wilson, Robert Armstrong, Capt. (Tp.), k. in a., 18/10/15.
Wilson, Thomas James, 2/Lt., k. in a., 21/3/18 (295th Bde.).
Winbush, Edward Thomas, 2/Lt., k. in a., 24/9/17 (33rd D.A.C.).
Wing, Vincent Sladen, 2/Lt., k. in a., 10/8/17 (65th Bty., 28th Bde.).
Wingfield, Richard James Trench, 2/Lt. (Tp.), killed, 27/4/16 (28th Bty.).
Winmill, Thomas George Peyton, Capt., k. in a., 11/6/18 (16th Bde.).
Winser, Percy Ralph, 2/Lt., k. in a., 23/4/17 (149th Bde.).
Winwood, Thomas Ralph Okeden, M.C., Tp. Lt. (Act. Capt.), d. of w., 28/4/17 (B/199th Bde.).
Wise, Colin Walter, 2/Lt. (Tp.), k. in a., 31/7/17 (74th Bde., "A" Bty.).
Wissman, John Rudolph, Lt., k. in a., 15/9/14.
Witt, Leonard Stanley, 2/Lt., d. of w., 2/5/17 (A/104th Bde.).
Wolseley, William Bertie, Temp. Lt., d. of w., 5/7/16 (160 Bde.).
Wood, Donald Theodore, M.C., 2/Lt., d. of w., 25/8/18 (77 Bde.).
Wood, Ernest James Vivian, 2/Lt., d. of w., 9/11/18 (36 Bde.).
Wood, Tom, 2/Lt., died, 17/7/17 (att. R.A.O.C.).
Woodhouse, Alfred James, Capt., k. in a., 30/10/14.
Woodhouse, Gordon Stafford, Temp. 2/Lt., d. of w., 14/10/15.
Woodland, Leslie Frank, 2/Lt., k. in a., 21/3/18 (180 Bde.).
Woods, Alfred Marcus, 2/Lt., k. in a., 26/2/17 (C/78 Bde.).
Woods, Leslie, M.C., Capt., died, 25/2/19 (15 D.A.C.).
Woods, William Thornley Stoker, 2/Lt., d. of w., 27/10/16 (62 Bde.).
Woodward, Leslie Collins, D.S.O., Major, d. of w., 3/9/18 (63 Bde.).
Woollacott, Cedric Percy, 2/Lt., k. in a., 22/4/17 (64 Bde.).
Woolnough, George Morton, 2/Lt., k. in a., 7/4/17 (159 Bde.).
Worthington-Eyre, Lionel George, Lt., k. in a., 14/7/17 (78 Bde.).
Wright, John Major Stanley, 2/Lt., k. in a., 24/2/17 (157 Bde.).
Wright, Neil James Robert, 2/Lt., k. in a., 15/9/14.
Wright, Peter, Major, k. in a., 11/1/18 (B/186 Bde.).
Wright, William, 2/Lt., k. in a., 8/8/18 (175 Army Bde.).
Wrinch, Harry Durrill, Temp. Lt., d. of w., 20/8/16 (B/Bty., 115 Bde.).
Wynne, Maurice Okeover Mostyn, Lt., d. of w., 28/8/15.
Wynter, Hugh Talbot, Major, k. in a., 15/9/14.
Young, Charles Alan, 2/Lt., k. in a., 14/10/18 (256 Bde.).
Young, George Arnold, Lt., k. in a., 4/10/17 (50 Bde.).
Young, Marcus Ernest, 2/Lt., k. in a., 21/3/18 (X/58 T.M.B.

Royal Garrison Artillery.

Abbott, Joseph Octavius, 2/Lt., k. in a., 28/7/17 (179 S.B.).
Adams, Dudley, Capt. (Act.), k. in a., 21/3/18 (130 H.B.).
Adams, Frederick Leslie, 2/Lt., k. in a., 15/9/18 (232 S. B.).

Adamson, Alan John, 2/Lt. (A/Capt.), k. in a., 20/9/17 (69 S.B.).
Adamson, Harry, 2/Lt., k. in a., 15/4/18 (6 S.B.).
Auler, Henry George Vergettini, 2/Lt. (A/Major), k. in a., 21/6/17 (184 S.B.).
Ainscough, Thomas, 2/Lt., k. in a., 25/1/18 (303 S.B.).
Alcock, Richard Evans, Capt., died, 1/3/17 (99 Coy., Malta Garr.).
Aldridge, Evelyn, O.B.E., Major, A/Lt.-Col., died, 30/3/19.
Allan, George A., Temp. 2/Lt., k. in a., 16/1/16.
Allcock, Joseph, 2/Lt., k. in a., 16/10/18 (att. R.E. Sig.).
Anderson, Reginald D'Arcy, Major, died, 14/8/17 (A.O.D., 384 S.B.).
Anderson, W., M.C., 2/Lt., killed, 21/9/18 (and R.A.F.).
Anderson, William Henry, Lt., died, 4/12/18.
Andrews, Geoffrey Fleetwood, 2/Lt. (Tp.), d. of w., 16/9/18 (499 S.B.).
Andrews, George Leonard, Capt. (Tp.), k. in a., 3/5/18 (76 S.B.).
Arden, Humphrey Warwick, 2/Lt., d. of w., 6/6/17 (156 H.B.).
Arnison, Edward Burra, 2/Lt., d. of w., 18/8/18 (115 S. B., 14 Bde.).
Ashby Howard Dudley, M.C., Major, died, 7/4/19 (A.A. Bty.).
Aste, Norman Henry, 2/Lt., d. of w., 5/8/16 (23 H.B.).
Atchison, Harold Vivian, 2/Lt., d. of w., 26/8/18 (19 S. B.).
Atkinson, Harry, 2/Lt., k. in a., 28/9/17 (155 S.B.).
Attwood, Langley Latton, 2/Lt., k. in a., 12/8/17 (333 S.B.).
Bagnall, Richard Gordon, 2/Lt., k. in a., 1/7/16 (114 H.B.).
Baker, Charles, 2/Lt., k. in a., 22/10/17 (27 S.B.).
Baker, George Arthur, 2/Lt., k. in a., 29/11/17 (342 S.B.).
Baker, Joseph Franklin, 2/Lt., d. of w., 16/11/18 (185 S.B., 79 Bde.).
Baker, Thomas, Lt. (A/Capt.), k. in a., 28/7/17 (203 S.B.)
Ball, Arthur Hugh, M.C., 2/Lt. (A/Capt.), d. of w., 30/10/17 (186 S.B.).
Banks, A. B., Lt., died, 6/3/19.
Banks, Cyril D'Albini Sykes, M.C., Capt. (A/Major), died, 4/11/18 (226 S.B.).
Bannister, William George, Lt., k. in a., 28/3/18 (405 S.B.).
Barber, Frank William, Lt., k. in a., 30/6/15.
Barker, Arthur, 2/Lt., died, 20/12/18 (150 H.B.).
Barker, Holroyd Birkett, Lt., died, 15/8/17 (134 S.B.).
Barker, William Harold, Capt., d. of w., 5/11/15 (H.Q., 24 S.A.B.).
Baron, William, 2/Lt., d. of w., 19/10/17 (203 S.B.).
Barr, William Arthur, 2/Lt., k. in a., 27/8/18 (328 S.B.).
Barstow, Michael William, 2/Lt., k. in a., 3/6/17 (203 S.B.).
Bartley, Stanhope Cole, Capt., k. in a., 12/3/16.
Barton, James, 2/Lt., k. in a., 17/8/18 (11 S.B.).
Baskott, James Edward, 2/Lt., d. of w., 11/12/17 (193 S.B.).
Baugh, Bertram Percival, 2/Lt., k. in a., 16/6/18.
Baynes. Denman Lambert Henry, M.C., A/Capt., k. in a., 14/10/18 (115 S.B.).
Beaton, Grover Cleveland, M.C., 2/Lt., d. of w., 30/9/18 (143 S.B.).
Bedford, Edward Terence Bertyn, Lt. (A/Capt.), k. in a., 28/5/17 (34 S.B.) (1 Anzac Corps Troops).
Beer, Edward Albert, 2/Lt., k. in a., 22/9/17 (298 S.B.).
Begg, Robert Henderson, Capt., k. in a., 24/12/15 (att. Staff, 6 Div.).
Begg, William Pollock, Capt. (Tp.), k. in a., 9/4/18 (157 S.B.).
Bell, William James Knox, M.C., 2/Lt., k. in a., 5/4/18 (9 S.B.).
Bengough, Charles William, 2/Lt., k. in a., 21/3/18 (277 S.B.).
Bennett, Harold Stanley, 2/Lt., killed, 25/4/15.
Bennett, John Nicoll, 2/Lt., k. in a., 19/5/17 (121 S.B.).
Bennett, William Pyt, Major, k. in a., 15/7/16 (att. R.F.A., 162 Bty.).
Beveridge, Alan Primrose, M.C., Lt. (A/Maj.), k. in a., 16/9/18 (35 H.B.).
Bewlay, Thomas Henry, 2/Lt. (A/Capt.), d. of w., 21/5/17 (36 S.B.).
Beynon, Ian William Arthur, 2/Lt., d. of w., 27/9/18 (27 S.B.).
Bidgood, Thomas Aylmer Tattnall, Lt., d. of w., 28/10/17 (96 Bty. Group).
Bill, Rodney Edward, 2/Lt., k. in a., 26/8/18 (38 H.B.).
Binns, Christopher, 2/Lt., k. in a., 26/9/17 (154 S.B.).
Bishop, Ernest Eldred, 2/Lt. (A/Lt.), k. in a., 14/3/17 (att. Y/6 T.M.B.).
Bishop, Keith Ford, 2/Lt., k. in a., 8/8/16.
Bland-Hunt. Ernest Sydney de Vere, Major, k. in a., 4/9/15.
Blumfield, William George, 2/Lt., d. of w., 21/3/18 (186 S.B.).
Blunt, Ernest Lindsay, Lt. (A/Capt.), k. in a., 2/11/18 (24 S.B.).
Boal, James Spence, 2/Lt., d. of w., 29/1/17 (109 S.B.).
Bodenham, S. W. 2/Lt., died, 25/10/18 (117 H.B.).
Bois, Dudley Gillespy, Lt., died, 4/10/15.
Bolster, Francis Julian, Lt. (A/Capt.), d. of w., 4/4/17 (31 S.B.).
Bonney, James Patterson, 2/Lt., k. in a., 6/10/17 (351 S.B.).
Bonsey, Edwin Kenneth, 2/Lt., d. of w., 2/7/18 (99 S.B.).
Bowater, George William, 2/Lt., died, 20/2/17.
Bowen, Eynon George Arthur, Lt., died, 8/9/16 (and R.F.C.) (P. of W.).
Bowie, Allan Stuart Hunter, 2/Lt., d. of w., 8/5/18 (23 S.B.).
Bowler, Sydney, 2/Lt., k. in a., 21/10/17 (S/237 Bde.).
Bowler, Thomas George, 2/Lt., k. in a., 30/6/17 (6 S.B.).
Bowling, Arthur Henry, 2/Lt., died, 29/9/18 (160 S.B.).
Boyle, John Antonio Saochey, 2/Lt., k. in a., 30/11/17 (2/1 Lanc. H.B.).
Boyton, Victor Henry Thompson, 2/Lt., k. in a., 31/5/17 (289 S.B.).
Bradley, Augustus James Hector, 2/Lt., k. in a., 23/4/18 (129 H.B.).
Brain, William Henry Oliver, 2/Lt., k. in a., 10/6/17 (90 H.B.).
Brancker, James Donaldson Dulany, D.S.O., Major, k. in a., 1/5/17 (116 S.B.).
Bransbury, John Eric Cecil, 2/Lt., died, 1/4/16.
Brazier, Charles Henry, Lt., died, 17/2/16.
Breed, John Bennington, 2/Lt., k. in a., 31/7/17 (236 S.B.).
Brett, William Frank, 2/Lt., d. of w., 15/10/17 (24 S.B.).
Brian, Herbert Cecil, 2/Lt., k. in a., 9/5/15.
Brodbelt, Arthur Dell, Lt., d. of w., 18/4/18 (264 S.B.).
Bromfield, William Henry, 2/Lt., d. of w., 31/10/18.
Brown, Archie Maynard, 2/Lt., k. in a., 6/4/18 (126 H.B.).
Brown, Charles, 2/Lt. (A/Capt.), k. in a., 25/4/18 (242 S.B.).
Brown, Charles James Wilkins, 2/Lt., d. of w., 22/4/18 (73 S.B.).
Brown, Ernest Albert, Lt., died, 23/11/18 (188 S.B.).
Brown, Frank Frederick, M.C., Lt., died, 21/2/19.
Brown, John Samuel, 2/Lt., k. in a., 18/5/17 (61 S.B.).
Brown, William Charles, Lt., died, 7/11/18.
Bruce, John Elliot Lidderdale, Major, k. in a., 29/5/15.
Buckton, Arthur Scott, T/Lt. (A/Capt.), d. of w., 9/4/17 (100 S.B.).
Bullough, Charles Berthold, D.S.O., Major, k. in a., 25/4/18 (117 H.B.).
Bullough, Frederick William, 2/Lt., k. in a., 8/11/17 (152 S.B.).
Bunch, Charles Walter, 2/Lt., k. in a., 13/11/16 (128 S.B.).
Burchell, Lawrence, M.C., 2/Lt., died, 31/12/18 (153 S.B.).
Burke, John Laurence, 2/Lt., k. in a., 30/4/16 (Z/25 Trench M.B.).
Burles, Thomas John, 2/Lt., k. in a., 24/6/17 (21 S.B.).
Burtt, William John, 2/Lt., d. of w., 23/3/18 (286 S.B.).
Butt, William Frederick Reginald, 2/Lt., d. of w., 29/5/18 (202 S.B.).
Cable, James Sydney, Lt., died, 5/9/18 (46 S.B.).
Cairn-Duff, Norman, 2/Lt., k. in a., 25/4/18 (242 S.B.).
Caldecott, John Leslie, Lt., k. in a., 9/9/14.
Cameron, Charles Peter Gwydyr, M.C., Capt., d. of w., 30/4/18 (att. Staff, 9/Corps H.Q.).
Cameron, Percy Grant, Lt., k. in a., 14/8/17 (and 10 Sqd., R.F.C.).
Campbell, Duncan, 2/Lt., died, 27/11/18 (att. 4 Army Gun Park).
Campbell, Duncan Donald Heron, M.C., Capt., k. in a., 7/6/17 (att. R.F.A.).
Campbell, John Guy, 2/Lt., d. of w., 30/4/17 (125 S.B.).
Campbell, Robert William Procter, Major, k. in a., 15/11/15.
Campbell, Thomas, Capt., d. of w., 3/8/16 (19 S.B.).
Campbell, William John, 2/Lt., died, 25/5/15.
Campion, Raoul Rene, Temp. Lt., k. in a., 17/2/17 (att. 73 (S.R.) S.B. Hvy.).
Capell, Bruce Lorence, M.C., 2/Lt., k in a., 7/6/18 (2/1 North Mid. Hvy. Bty.).
Carr, Basil Alderson, 2/Lt, k. in a., 25/7/17.
Carr, Victor Francis, Lt. (A/Capt.), k. in a., 21/5/18 (108 H.B.).
Carroll, James Charles, Lt., d. of w., 26/3/18.
Carson, Robert, Major, d. of w., 21/8/16 (71 H.B.).
Carter, Audsley Ralph, Major, d. of w., 28/8/18 (and R.A.F.).
Carter, Richard Thellusson, M.C., Capt. (A/Major), d. of w., 18/8/18 (11 S.B., 14 Bde.).
Castle, Edward William, 2/Lt., d. of w., 25/8/18 (126 S.B.).
Chadwick, Richard Markham, Lt., d. of w., 12/5/15.
Challinor, Frederick William, 2/Lt., k. in a., 22/5/17.
Challis, Thomas Holt, 2/Lt., d. of w., 28/4/17 (256 S.B.).
Chambers, Charles Colhoun, Capt., k. in a., 10/7/16 (12 S.B.).
Chaplin, Frederick Hardress, Major, died 27/5/16 (154 H.B.).
Chapman, Ben Fletcher, Temp. 2/Lt., k. in a., 19/4/17 (1 Mtn. Bty., Hong Kong, Singapore).
Chappell, Ernest Rowland, 2/Lt., d. of w., 30/9/18 (C. Bty. A.A.).
Chellew, John Maurice, 2/Lt., d. of w., 26/5/17.
Chrystie, John, Major, k. in a., 17/11/14.
Churchill, Clarence Harold, 2/Lt., k. in a., 15/12/17.
Claremont, Frederick Victor Leszynski, 2/Lt., k. in a., 14/8/17 (184 S.B.).
Clark, George, 2/Lt., k. in a., 3/11/17 (189 H.B.).
Clark, John Ryder, 2/Lt., k. in a., 20/10/17 (196 S.B.).
Cleall, Ernest Harry, Temp. Capt., drowned, 4/5/17.
Coates, Clifford Marsh, 2/Lt., k. in a., 3/5/17 (174 S.B.).
Coates, James Ernest, 2/Lt., d. of w., 22/8/18 (336 Bde.).
Cock, Hubert Charles Langslow, Major, k. in a., 22-24/11/15 (17 Bde., att. Staff).
Cockfield, Charles Francis, 2/Lt., k. in a., 27/8/16.
Cohen, Cecil Hope, Lt., died, 18/11/18 (Sig.).
Cole, Cecil Clark, 2/Lt., d. of w., 13/10/17 (149 Bde.).
Collier, Ernest Stebbing, 2/Lt., k. in a., 2/4/18 (9 Bde.).
Collier, Reginald Charles, 2/Lt., died, 17/11/18 (196 S.B.).
Collings, Harry Colston, 2/Lt., k. in a., 19/9/18 (284 S.B.).
Collingwood, Gordon Francis, Temp. Lt., d. of w., 28/3/18 (405 S.B.).
Collins, Maurice, Lt., k. in a., 11/9/18 (305 S.B.).
Collins, Percy Robert Murdoch, D.S.O., Capt. (A/Major), d. of w., 25/6/17 (13 S. Bty.).
Colson, Cecil, M.C., Capt. (A/Major), k. in a., 14/12/16 (21 S.B.).

Connal, Alexander Campbell, 2/Lt., k. in a., 9/4/18 (99 S.B.).
Cooke, Thomas, Lt., died, 30/5/17 (att. 18 H.A.C.).
Cooksey, Joseph Arnold, 2/Lt., k. in a., 1/5/17 (116 S. Bty.).
Cooper, Cyril Henry, 2/Lt., k. in a., 6/4/16.
Corbin, Christopher, Lt., k. in a., 5/6/17 (141 H.B.).
Cottrell, George Frederick, 2/Lt., k. in a., 11/5/15.
Courtenay, Michael Hudson, Lt.-Col., d. of w., 4/1/16.
Cowen, Henry Walter, 2/Lt., k. in a., 29/9/18 (6 S.B.).
Cox, Albert Henry, 2/Lt., k. in a., 24/7/16.
Cox, Cecil John, 2/Lt., d. of w., 24/4/18 (331 S.B.).
Cramp, George Herbert, 2/Lt., d. of w., 18/11/18 (301 S.B.).
Crane, Lancelot, 2/Lt., died, 15/3/18 (159 H.B.).
Craymer, Douglas Charles, 2/Lt., k. in a., 15/9/18 (232 S.B.).
Creery, Ronald Hulbert, M.C., 2/Lt., d. of w., 23/4/17 (121 S.B.).
Crittenden, Frederick, 2/Lt., died, 7/9/17 (170 S.B.).
Croger, Nathaniel William, 2/Lt., d. of w., 25/9/18 (434 S.B.).
Crosbie, John Colin, Lt., d. of w., 7/9/17 (and R.F.C.).
Crosher, William John, 2/Lt., d. of w., 20/5/17 (239 S.B.).
Crouch, Frederick Charles, Lt. (A/Major), d. of w., 2/11/17 (113 H.B.).
Crouch, William Ballard, 2/Lt., k. in a., 13/4/17 (270 S.B.).
Cruickshank, Andrew John Tuke, 2/Lt., k. in a., 7/7/16 (att. R.F.C.).
Crumpton, Thomas, 2/Lt., k. in a., 17/4/18 (6 S.B.).
Cruttwell, Hugh Lockwood, 2/Lt., k. in a., 12/10/17 (118 S.B.).
Cummins, Ian Ashley Marsham, Major, died, 20/7/18.
Curry, William Leonard, Temp. Capt., d. of w., 9/11/16 (87 S.B.).
Curwen, William Lynedoch, M.C., Temp. Lt., d. of w., 30/10/17 (att. 27 Mt. B., I.A.S.R.).
Cushing, Robertson Macaulay, 2/Lt., d. of w., 30/4/18 (190 S.B.).
Cuthbertson, Eric Ian, 2/Lt., k. in a., 23/10/17 (327 S.B.).
Darbishire, Arthur Dunkinfield, 2/Lt., died, 26/12/15.
Darker, Ernest Naismith, 2/Lt., d. of w., 10/9/17 (262/Sge. Bty.).
Davenport, Harold, 2/Lt., k. in a., 21/3/18 (122/S.B.).
Davey, Ernest Charles, 2/Lt., died, 1/11/18, (210/S.B., 98/Bde.).
Davidson, David Adams, 2/Lt., killed, 28/7/17 (179/S.B.).
Davidson, James Eadie, D.S.O., Capt. (Tp.), (Act. Major), d. of w., 16/10/18 (19/S.B.).
Davidson, Thomas Andrew, 2/Lt., d. of w., 9/4/18 (12 S.B.).
Davies, David Claude Graham, 2/Lt., d. of w., 15/5/15.
Davies, Edward Thomas, 2/Lt., k. in a., 13/10/18 (140/S.B.).
Davies, William John, Lt., d. of w., 14/10/18 (140/S.B.).
Davis, Charles, 2/Lt., k. in a., 4/10/17 (210/S.B.).
Dawes, Sidney Francis, 2/Lt., k. in a., 9/10/18 (236 S.B.).
Day, Charles Norris, 2/Lt., k. in a., 1/5/18 (298 S.B.).
Dean, Cyril Edward Brietycke, 2/Lt, k. in a., 15/9/16.
De Beer, Bendix Hallenstein, 2/Lt., k. in a., 10/7/17.
De La Bere, Charles Edward, 2/Lt. (Act. Capt.), k. in a., 10/9/18 (66/Bde.).
Dell, Stephen Arthur Hayton, 2/Lt., d. of w., 5/10/17.
Dennison, James, 2/Lt., k. in a., 9/9/18 (101 S.B.).
Digby, Charles, 2/Lt., k. in a., 10/7/18 (123 S.B.).
Dinwiddy, Conrad Hugh, 2/Lt. (Act. Capt.), d. of w., 26/9/17 (13 S.B.).
Disney, Brabazon Thomas, Capt. (Act. Major), k. in a., 17/10/17 (166 S.B.).
Dixon, Ernest Edward, 2/Lt., k. in a., 9/6/17 (168/S.B.).
Dixon, Henry Oliver, 2/Lt., k. in a., 6/9/17.
Dobbin, Robert Alexander Sheridan, Lt., k. in a., 25/9/15.
Dodgson, David Scott, Lt., k. in a., 13/11/14.
Doherty, Joseph, 2/Lt., k. in a., 3/7/16.
Donaghy, Robert Andrews, 2/Lt., k. in a., 28/5/18 (N. Riding H.B.).
Douglas, Ian Victor, 2/Lt., k. in a., 25/10/17 (180/S.B.).
Douglass-James, William, Lt., d. of w., 25/9/15.
Down, Charles Boileau, Major, died, 10/5/19.
Doyle, James Charles, M.C., Capt., k. in a., 27/5/18.
Drape, Norman, 2/Lt., d. of w., 15/7/17 (28 S.B.).
Drewe, Abrian, Tp. 2/Lt. (Act. Capt.), k. in a., 12/7/17 (262/S.B.).
Dudgeon, Arthur, Lt. (Tp.), died, 19/11/18 (att. R.E., 4/Fld. Survey Coy.).
Duff, James, 2/Lt., d. of w., 9/4/17 (167/S.B.).
Duke, Valentine Gordon, Capt., k. in a., 10/7/16 (26/S.B.).
Dunlop, John Francis Logan, Lt., d. of w., 7/5/18 (139/H.B.).
Dyer, Charles, 2/Lt., k. in a., 7/3/17 (150/S.B.).
Dyer, William Oscar, 2/Lt., d. of w., 28/10/17.
Dyke, George Bewsey, Lt. (Tp.), k. in a., 26/4/16.
Dyke, Walter Ball, Capt. (Tp.), k. in a., 10/4/18 (155 S.B.).
Easton, Jack Leslie, 2/Lt., k. in a., 21/3/18 (277 S.B.).
Edlmann, Ernest Elliot, D.S.O., Major, d. of w., 17/4/15 (23/Mtd. Bty.).
Edward, Borlase, Major, k. in a., 18/3/17 (247/S.B.).
Ella, Alfred Newsam, 2/Lt., died, 18/11/18 (180/H.B.).
Ellen, Arthur Charles, 2/Lt., d. of w., 6/6/17 (156 H.B.).
Elliott, Henry Ernest, M.C., A/Capt., died, 2/3/19.
Elliott, William, Lt. (Act. Capt.), d. of w., 3/9/18 (374/att. 309 S.B.).
Ellis, Herbert Dudley, 2/Lt., k. in a., 25/9/15.
Erskine, Walter Augustus, Capt., k. in a., 24/5/15.
Evans, Ernest, 2/Lt., d. of w., 21/9/18 (att. 91 S.B.).
Everitt, Rupert Edward, 2/Lt., k. in a., 24/6/17 (299 S.B.).
Everton, Robert Frederick, Lt., died, 8/4/19.
Eyden, H., Lt., killed, 7/4/18 (and R.A.F.).
Ezra, David, Lt., k. in a., 6/8/18 (192/S.B.).
Fairgrieve, Robert, 2/Lt., d. of w., 24/11/17 (86 S.B.).
Fane, Octavius Edward, D.S.O., M.C., Capt. (Act. Major), d. of w., 18/9/18 (128 H.B.).
Farmer, Cyril, D.S.O., M.C., Major, d. of w., 3/8/17 (183 Bty., 53 Bde.).
Farnham, Frank Jefferson, 2/Lt., killed, 15/4/17 (239 S.B.).
Farrier, Douglas Towry, 2/Lt., k. in a., 1/10/17 (219 S.B.).
Faunch, Ernest Alfred, 2/Lt., k. in a., 4/5/17 (212 S.B.).
Fawcett, John Bellars, 2/Lt., k. in a., 21/3/18 (233 S.B.).
Field, Kenneth Douglas, D.S.O., Lt.-Col., k. in a., 30/11/17 (38 S.B.).
Fillingham, Reginald John, Lt. (Act. Major), d. of w., 29/9/18 (41 S.B.).
Finnis, William Frank, 2/Lt., d. of w., 2/5/17 (250/S.B.).
Fishbourne, Derrick Haughton Gardiner, 2/Lt., k. in a., 6/5/17 (99 S.B.).
Fisher-Brown, Douglas Gordon, 2/Lt., d. of w., 28/6/18 (2/Army, A.A. Section).
Fitch, Cecil Alexander Gordon, 2/Lt., d. of w., 18/9/18 (260/S.B.
Fitz-Gibbon, John Augustus, Tp. Major, died, 25/1/16.
Flack, William Arthur, 2/Lt., d. of w., 19/12/15.
Fleming, Frederick Nelson, 2/Lt., died, 22/6/18 (231 S.B.).
Fleming, Thomas, 2/Lt. (Tp.), d. of w., 20/10/18 (71st Bty., 21st Bde.).
Flitcroft, J., 2/Lt., died, 2/11/18.
Footner, Harry Erlegh, Tp. Capt., k. in a., 1/8/16.
Forster, Francis Arthur, 2/Lt., died, 6/4/19 (443 S.B.).
Foulsham, Arthur Percy, 2/Lt., k. in a., 20/7/17 (245 S.B.).
Fowler, Frank Archibald, 2/Lt. (Act. Capt.), k. in a., 28/7/17 (295 S.B.).
Fox, Sidney Thomas, 2/Lt., k. in a., 21/9/17 (230/S.B.).
Frankland, Thomas Pemberton, 2/Lt. (Tp.), k. in a., 29/7/16.
Fraser, Arthur Leslie, 2/Lt., d. of w., 1/7/17 (27 S.B.).
Freeland, Hugo Wharncliffe, Lt., k. in a., 14/8/16.
Freeman, James, 2/Lt., k. in a., 20/8/17 (25 S.B.).
Freeman, Peter, 2/Lt., d. of w., 19/9/18 (284 S.B.).
Fripp, Tom Olphert, 2/Lt., k. in a., 30/6/18 (177 S.B.).
Frith, William Wesson, Lt. (Act. Capt.), k. in a., 3/11/17.
Fulcher, Oliver Arthur, 2/Lt., died, 29/6/16.
Furnell, Cecil Herbert Michael, Capt., d. of w., 30/4/16 (128 H.B.).
Galbraith, Arthur Hugh Courtney, Lt., d. of w., 9/9/18 (285 S.B., 83 Bde.).
Gall, William John Reid, 2/Lt., d. of w., 18/4/18 (346 S.B.).
Galway, Reginald Hugh, Major, d. of w., 15-17/2/15.
Gamman, Edward, 2/Lt., k. in a., 26/10/17 (306 S.B.).
Gardiner, Robert Edward, 2/Lt., k. in a., 26/7/17 (285 S.B.).
Gardner, Leonard Clement, Lt., d. of w., 2/6/18 (139 H.B.).
Garnett, Claude Lionel, Capt., d. of w., 31/12/15 (86 H.B.).
Garrioch, John Thomas, Lt. (Act. Major), d. of w., 3/4/18 (173 S.B.).
Garvie, Peter Thomas, Tp. Lt. (Act. Capt.), k. in a., 25/6/17 (13 S.B.).
Gee, Ernest Desmond Farrell, Major, k. in a., 25/4/18 (263 Sge. Bty.).
Gibson, Franklin Reginald, Lt. (Tp.), died, 20/9/18 (80 Bde.).
Gibson, John Auchenlosh, 2/Lt., k. in a., 27/5/18 (116 S.B.).
Giles, Walter, Lt., k. in a., 13/7/16 (32 S.B.).
Gillett, Edward Francis, 2/Lt. (Tp.), d. of w., 29/9/15 (53 Bde.).
Glover, John Bertram, 2/Lt., k. in a., 16/6/18 (309 S.B.).
Goldie-Taubman, Gerald, Capt. (Tp.), died, 15/9/15 (Comdt. Detn. Bks.).
Gooch, Geoffrey Fulthorpe, Tp. Lt. (Act. Capt.), k. in a., 19/9/18 (25 S.B.).
Goodwin, Harold James, 2/Lt., k. in a., 24/4/17 (135 S.B.).
Gordon, A. E., Major, died, 19/12/16.
Gotch, Geoffrey William, Lt., died, 22/10/18 (and R.A.F.).
Gould, Frederick James, 2/Lt., died, 12/12/18 (143 H.B.).
Graham, Archibald Foster, 2/Lt., k. in a., 11/11/15.
Gratton, Albert, 2/Lt., k. in a., 20/11/17.
Gray, David, 2/Lt. (Act. Capt.), k. in a., 6/6/17 (234 S.B.).
Greaves, Reginald, Lt., died, 22/2/19.
Green, Charles Arthur, M.C., 2/Lt., k. in a., 13/7/17 (2/1 Lowland H.B.).
Green, Thomas, 2/Lt., d. of w., 28/10/16 (10 S.B.).
Greenwell-Lax, Anthony William, Capt., k. in a., 11/10/16 (43 S.B.).
Gregory, Alfred John Reginald, D.S.O., Major, died, 4/12/18 (120 H.B.).
Greig, Hugh Irwin, Major, k. in a., 2/11/17.
Grellier, Gordon Harley, 2/Lt. (Tp.), k. in a., 31/10/18 (51 S.B.).
Griffiths, Royston Swire, Lt. (Tp.) (Act. Major), died, 17/3/17 (123 S.B.).
Grigg, George Irving, 2/Lt., d. of w., 21/7/17 (234 S.B.).
Gunn, Edmond Alan, 2/Lt., died, 13/2/19.
Gunson, Leslie Robert Schrader, Lt. (Tp.), k. in a., 18/7/16.
Hack, John Frederick Charles, Lt., k. in a., 26/9/16.
Hall, George Elliott, 2/Lt., d. of w., 29/5/18 (196 S.B.).
Hall, Henry Leonard, Lt., k. in a., 27/10/18 (14 S.B.).
Hall, Sidney, Lt. (Act. Capt.), d. of w., 21/3/18 (146 Bty.).
Hallpike, Christopher George, 2/Lt., k. in a., 6/4/18 (68 S.B.).
Halsey, Francis William, 2/Lt. (Tp.), k. in a., 14/11/15 (3rd Trench Mtr. Bty.).
Hamilton, Claud William, Tp. 2/Lt. (Act. Capt.), d. of w., 6/11/17 (287 S.B.).
Hammond, Thomas Percival, 2/Lt., d. of w., 15/6/18 (137 S.B.).
Hammond, William Walter, Major, k. in a., 5/5/18 (139 H.B.).
Hands, Reginald Harry Myburgh, Tp. Capt. (Act. Major), d. of w., 20/4/18 (att. South Afr. H. Art., 73 S.B.).
Harding, Lional Cox, Lt., d. of w., 18/6/15.
Harker, E. K., 2/Lt., d. of w., 18/4/18 (and R.A.F.).

Harland, Richard, 2/Lt., k. in a., 16/6/18 (254 S.B.).
Harland, Sidney, 2/Lt., k. in a., 25/5/18 (214 S.B.).
Harris, Eric Wallace, Lt., d. of w., 4/11/17 (213 S.B.).
Harrison, Edward, 2/Lt., k. in a., 28/4/17 (158 S.B.).
Harrison, George Carmichael, Lt. (Tp.) (Act. Capt.), d. of w., 10/1/17 (6/Bty., 24 H.A.G.).
Hart, Cornelius Henry, 2/Lt., k. in a., 17/10/18 (130 S.B.).
Hartley, Alfred, Lt., d. of w., 9/10/18 (263 S.B.).
Hartree, Cyril, 2/Lt., k. in a., 29/5/18 (201 S.B.).
Harvey, George, Lt. (Tp.), (Capt.), k. in a., 21/6/17 (336 S.B.).
Hatch, Jesse, M.C., M.M., Lt., d. of w., 23/10/18 (95 S.B.).
Hawdon, Rupert Ayrton, Tp. Lt. (Act. Capt.), k. in a., (35 S.B.).
Hawkes, Gerald Arthur, 2/Lt., d. of w., 3/7/18 (att. 521 S.B.).
Hayes, Herbert Henry, Tp. Capt. (Act. Major), k. in a., 1/10/18 (409 S.B.).
Hayes, Willie, 2/Lt., d. of w., 25/9/18 (143 S.B.).
Hedderwick, James Alexander, Lt., died, 6/11/18 (56 A.A. Coy.).
Henderson, Arthur Percy, 2/Lt., d. of w., 19/6/17 (49 S.B.).
Henderson, James Sowers, 2/Lt., k. in a., 22/3/18 (33 S.B.).
Henman, Herbert Cecil, 2/Lt., d. of w., 25/9/17 (att. 18/Corp H.Q. 3/S.B.).
Hepburn, Arthur Jacobs, 2/Lt., k. in a., 30/3/18 (173 S.B.).
Herne, David Joseph, 2/Lt., k. in a. 27/5/18 (116/S.B.).
Heseltine, William Wasney, Lt., d. of w. (gas), 20/10/18 (284 S.B.).
Hicks, William Goss, 2/Lt., d. of w., 3/7/17 (260 S.B.).
Hill, Alan Purdie Dunlop, Capt., died, 8/2/19 (and R.A.F.).
Hill, Alfred Saunders, 2/Lt., k. in a., 20/11/17.
Hill, James, 2/Lt., died, 21/10/16 (16/H.B.).
Hill, Richard Alexander, Lt. (Tp.), k. in a., 10/4/17 (138 H.B.).
Hill, Thomas Edward, 2/Lt., d. of w., 21/4/18 (156 B., 47 H.A. Bde.).
Hillyer, James Excelsior, 2/Lt., k. in a., 27/10/17 (186 S.B.).
Hinckley, John, 2/Lt., k. in a., 27/3/18 (24 S.B.).
Hirst, Stanley Ewart, 2/Lt., k. in a., 24/10/17 (200 S.B.).
Hoare, George Henry, 2/Lt., d. of w., 1/6/17 (93 S.B.).
Hobden, Charles Frank, 2/Lt. (Tp.), died, 16/9/15.
Hobden, Ernest, 2/Lt., k. in a., 20/10/18 (328 S.B.).
Hodges, John Cyril, Lt., killed, 17/9/16 (att. R.F.C.).
Holland, Ralph Lingard, 2/Lt., k. in a., 8/2/17 (255 S.B.).
Hollins, Herbert Francis, Tp. Major, died, 19/8/17 (157 H.B.).
Hollis, Percival Claude, 2/Lt., k. in a., 21/3/18 (146 S.B.).
Holmes, Akehurst Wilson, 2/Lt., d. of w., 28/7/17 (295 S.B.).
Holt, Arthur Edward, 2/Lt., d. of w., 25/10/17.
Hood, John William, Lt., died, 15/11/18 (39 S.B.).
Hooper, Ronald Morley, Lt., k. in a., 21/3/18 (3/Fld. Survey Coy.).
Hope, William Henry Webley, C.M.G., Lt.-Col., died, 13/5/19.
Hopley, Thomas Henry, 2/Lt., k. in a., 10/10/18 (132 H.B.).
Horner, William Jackson, 2/Lt., d. of w., 15/7/17 (att. V/39 T.M.B.).
Hoskyns-Abrahall, Bennet Edmund, 2/Lt., d. of w., 25/4/18 (242 S.B.).
Hoult, Alfred John, Lt. (Act. Major), died, 2/11/18 (181 H.B.).
Howard, William George, 2/Lt., d. of w., 20/12/17 (119 S.B.).
Howe, George Herbert, 2/Lt., k. in a., 28/3/18 (151 S.B.).
Hudson, Harry, 2/Lt., d. of w., 25/4/18 (177 S.B.).
Hughes, John Hugh Edward, 2/Lt., k. in a., 10/7/17.
Huitt, Richard Henry William, 2/Lt., died, 13/12/17.
Hunter, Wilfred Cleaver, 2/Lt., k. in a., 29/12/15.
Husk, Frederick John, 2/Lt., d. of w., 21/3/18 (301 S.B.).
Hutt, Walter Beresford, 2/Lt., d. of w., 29/9/18 (527 S.B.).
Hutton-Squire, Robert Henry Edmund, D.S.O., Major, d. of w., 8/4/17 (att. 85 Bty. R.F.A.).
Hyde, Cyril, 2/Lt., k. in a., 1/12/17 (and R.F.C. 35th Sqd.).
Hyett, Frank, 2/Lt., k. in a., 30/11/17 (52nd H.A.G.).
Ingham, Clarence, 2/Lt., k. in a., 21/8/18 (65 Sge. Bty.).
Ingham, Robert John Fitzgerald, D.S.O., Major, A/Lt.-Col., d. of w., 1/7/17 (58/H.A.G., H.Q.).
Innes, Patrick McLeod, 2/Lt., k. in a., 30/4/17 (111 Sge. Bty.).
Irvine, Fred Catterson, 2/Lt., k. in a., 19/5/18.
Isaac, George Duncan, A/Capt., died, 13/12/17.
Izard, Francis Vallance, Capt., k. in a., 17/2/15.
Jackson, Harry, 2/Lt., died, 25/10/18 (4/S.A.R. Bde.).
Janes, Edmund, 2/Lt., k. in a., 13/5/18 (161 Sge. Bty.).
Jebson, George James, 2/Lt., k. in a., 23/1/17 (113 Hvy. Bty.).
Jenkins, William Charles, 2/Lt., k. in a., 4/10/17 (66 Sge. Bty.).
Jervois, Philip Harding, Lt., d. of w., 28/10/17 (177 Sge. Bty.).
Johns, Bradley Cooper, 2/Lt., died, 23/10/18.
Johnson, Robert Blissett Powell, M.C., Lt. (Tp.), killed, 19/9/18 (109 Hvy. Bty.).
Johnson, Rayner Harvey, M.C., Lt. (A/Major), k. in a., 26/9/18 (122/Hvy. Bty.).
Jones, Arthur Leslie Gwynne, 2/Lt., k. in a., 4/5/18 (252 Sge. Bty.).
Jones, Cyril Hammond Montague, Lt., A/Capt., died, 14/11/18.
Jones, Edwin, 2/Lt., d. of w., 14/4/18 (1/1 N. Midland H.B.).
Jones, Thomas Mozart, 2/Lt., died, 6/7/18 (262 Sge. Bty.).
Keates, Richard John, M.C., 2/Lt. (A/Capt.), k. in a., 20/8/18 (23/Bde. H.Q.).
Kiddier, Ernest, 2/Lt., k. in a., 17/9/18 (244/Sge. Bty.).
Kilpin, Franklin James, 2/Lt., k. in a., 16/4/18 (250/Sge. Bty.).
King, Kerry, D.C.M., 2/Lt., d. of w., 25/9/18 (7/Bty., 3/Bde. Mtn. Arty.).
Kirby, Richard Elston, Lt. (T/Capt.), killed, 1/6/18 (att. Staff).
Kirkus, Cuthbert Hayward, 2/Lt. (A/Capt.), k. in a., 31/7/17 (283/Sge. Bty.).
Kitchener, Cecil, Lt., died, 30/10/18 (94th Coy.).
Kurten, Gaston Peter, T/Lt. (A/Major), k. in a., 24/4/18 (291 Sge. Bty.).
Lake, William Martin, 2/Lt., d. of w., 28/6/16 (T.M.B.).
Lamb, Francis James Ongley, 2/Lt., died, 24/7/18 (att. Army Amm. Park.).
Lamb, Patrick James, Lt. (Tp.), d. of w., 31/7/18 (14 Div. Amm. Column).
Lane, Sydney Henry, T/Lt. (A/Capt.), k. in a., 5/4/18 (38 Hvy. Bty.).
Langdon, William Chappell Croeder, T/Lt., d. of w., 10/3/17 (att. 3/Fld. Survey Co., R.E.).
Laurie, Alfred William, 2/Lt., d. of w., 22/11/16 (42 Sge. Bty.).
Lawrenson, Harold, 2/Lt., k. in a., 25/5/18 (214 Sge. Bty.).
Lawson, George McFarquhar Kelly, 2/Lt., k. in a., 9/8/17 (5 Sge. Bty.).
Leckie, Graham, 2/Lt., T/Lt., k. in a., 7/7/17 (and R.F.C., 21 Sqd.).
Lee, Arnold Thomas, 2/Lt., k. in a., 1/9/18.
Lee, Charles Harold, 2/Lt., k. in a., 20/9/17 (249 Sge. Bty.).
Leggett, Wilfred Noel, Major, k. in a., 14/7/16.
Leigh, Percy Lempriere, Capt., d. of w., 29/8/16 (29 Sge. Bty.).
Lenz, William Adolph Philip, 2/Lt., k. in a., 6/11/17 (148 Sge. Bty.).
Leonard, Francis, 2/Lt., died, 4/7/15.
Leslie, William, Capt., k. in a., 12/1/16.
Light, George Joseph, 2/Lt., k. in a., 8/11/17 (142 Sge. Bty.).
Linden, Samuel McCullagh, 2/Lt., k. in a., 31/7/17 (90 H.A.G.).
Littlejohn, Stanley William, 2/Lt., k. in a., 23/9/17 (142 Sge. Bty.).
Lockton, George Woodhams, Temp. Capt., d. of w., 21/10/17 (153 Sge. Bty.).
Lockwood, Albert, 2/Lt., k. in a., 7/10/18 (93 Sge. Bty.).
Lodge, John, 2/Lt., d. of w., 18/3/18 (190 Sge. Bty.).
Logsdail, Hugh, 2/Lt., k. in a., 19/9/18 (99 Sge. Bty.).
Long, William Herbert Berkeley, 2/Lt., d. of w., 31/5/18 (261 Sge. Bty.).
Lovell, Clarence John, 2/Lt., k. in a., 19/10/17 (274 Sge. Bty.).
McBride, William Wilson, 2/Lt., d. of w., 5/12/17 (229 Sge. Bty.).
McClure, Hugh Cecil, 2/Lt., k. in a., 23/10/18 (146 Sge. Bty.).
McCrea, Alexander, 2/Lt., k. in a., 27/6/17 (58 Sge. Bty.).
McCullogh, Frederick James, 2/Lt., k. in a., 8/11/17 (and R.F.C., 53 Sqd.).
Macdonald, John, 2/Lt., k. in a., 27/5/18 (286 Sge. Bty.).
Macdonald, Neil, M.C., 2/Lt., k. in a., 25/4/18 (263 Sge. Bty.).
McDonell, G. O., Lt., d. of w., 18/3/18 (att. R.F.C.).
McElroy, George Edward Henry, Capt., k. in a., 31/7/18 (and R.A.F.).
Macfarlane, Ronald Wallace, 2/Lt., k. in a., 3/9/16 (152 Hvy. Bty.).
McGaffin, Robert Clanrye, 2/Lt., d. of w., 5/7/16 (10 H.S. Bty.).
McGildowny, William, D.S.O., Temp. Major, d. of w., 27/5/17 (124 Sge. Bty.).
McGillewie, Malcolm, T/Lt. (A/Capt.), died, 24/5/18 (390 Sge. Bty.).
MacGregor, Ralph Alexander Montgomery, Lt., d. of w., 26/9/18 (136 Sge. Bty.).
McHardy-Young, James William, Temp. 2/Lt., k. in a., 19/8/15.
McIntosh, Daniel, 2/Lt., d. of w., 20/5/18 (297 Sge. Bty.).
Mackenzie, John, 2/Lt., k. in a., 28/10/17 (11 Sge. Bty.).
McKinley, James Gordon, 2/Lt., d. of w., 3/6/15 (att. R.E.).
Maclean, Moira Francis Allan, Capt., k. in a., 17/2/15.
McMaster, John Wallace, Lt., d. of w., 11/9/18 (att. 35 Sge. Bty.).
Macneill, Andrew Duncan, Capt. (Tp.), k. in a., 29/7/17 (21 Hvy. Bty.).
McPhail, Alexander Banks, M.C., Lt., A/Capt., d. of w., 31/10/18 (2 Sge. Bty.).
McPhee, Douglas, 2/Lt., died, 21/2/19.
Magrane, George Fairfield, 2/Lt., k. in a., 7/6/17 (261 Sge. Bty.).
Mahoney, Herbert James, M.M., Lt., A/Capt., d. of w., 24/10/18 (184 Sge. Bty.).
Malcolm, Stuart Renton, Lt., died, 22/11/18 (38 Sge. Bty.).
Mansfield, John Roy, 2/Lt., k. in a., 18/6/17 (121 Hvy. Bty.).
Marden, Arthur Cecil, 2/Lt., died, 11/12/17 (117 Hvy. Bty.).
Marshall, Arthur Raymond, 2/Lt., A/Capt., d. of w., 2/2/18 (34 H.A.G.).
Marshall Cecil Clyde, 2/Lt., k. in a., 24/6/17 (21 Sge. Bty.).
Martin, Ernest, 2/Lt., died, 16/12/17 (15 H. Bty.).
Martin, John, 2/Lt., k. in a., 19/12/17 (229 Sge. Bty.).
Martin, Henry, D.C.M., 2/Lt., died, 22/10/18.
Mason, George, 2/Lt., k. in a., 16/9/18 (late B.S.M., 444 Sge. Bty.).
Massie, John Hamon, D.S.O., Major, d. of w., 15/11/14.
Masson, James Alexander, 2/Lt., d. of w., 8/5/17 (38 Hvy. Bty.).
Mathews, Walter Vivanti Dewar, Major, d. of w., 9/12/17 (102 Sge. Bty.).
Matthew, Frank Henry, 2/Lt., k. in a., 9/10/15.
Matthews, Thomas, M.B.E., Lt., A/Capt., d. of w., 27/6/18 (521 Household Sge. Bty.).

Matthews, William Henry, 2/Lt., k. in a., 28/9/18 (2/1 Lowland Hvy. Bty.).
Maughan, Alfred William, 2/Lt., k. in a., 24/6/17 (285 Sge. Bty.).
Maunsell, Reginald Harcourt Proctor, 2/Lt., k. in a., 27/4/18 (128 Sge. Bty.)
May, George Neville, Capt. (Tp.), d. of w., 29/5/18 (243 Sge. Bty., att. 87 Sge.).
Maynard, Frederick Creber, Lt., d. of w., 20/9/18 (119 Hvy. Bty.).
Menzies, William Alan, 2/Lt., d. of w., 14/6/17 (163 Sge. Bty.).
Meyer, Alan Wallace, 2/Lt., died, 11/3/18 (289 Sge. Bty.).
Miller B., M.C., 2/Lt., killed, 29/5/18 (S.R. and R.A.F.).
Miller, James Brand Scott, 2/Lt., k. in a., 14/3/18.
Mills, Henry Valentine, 2/Lt., k. in a., 25/6/17 (321 Sge. Bty.).
Milne-Home, David W., Lt.-Col., died, 27/7/18.
Milton, Ernest Edward, Lt., k.,in a., 23/1/17 (113 Hvy. Bty.).
Mitchell, John Horsley, 2/Lt., k. in a., 19/5/17 (305 Sge. Bty.).
Monckton, Marmaduke Henry, Lt., k. in a., 9/7/15.
Moore, Frederick Henry, 2/Lt., T/Capt., died, 17/5/17 (att. A.O.D.).
Moore, George William, 2/Lt., k. in a., 28/3/18 (288 Sge. Bty.).
Moreton, Cecil Harry, 2/Lt., k. in a., 17/9/18 (22 Hvy. Bty.).
Moriarty, James Henry, Lt., killed, 12/10/15.
Morin, John Archibald Scott, Capt., died, 4/11/18 (149 Sge. Bty.).
Morris, George Henry, 2/Lt., A/Capt., d. of w., 3/6/17 (T.M.B.).
Morris, Robert Cochrane, Major, T/Lt.-Col., died, 25/3/17.
Morris, William James, Lt., died, 28/3/17.
Morrison, Arthur Stanley, Lt., k. in a., 23/8/18 (336 Sge. Bty.).
Mortimer, Edmund Alfred, 2/Lt., k. in a., 4/7/18 (114 Hvy. Bty.).
Moses, Frank Samuel, Lt. (Tp.), d. of w., 31/8/18 (1/1 Welsh R.).
Moss, Herbert Frank, 2/Lt., k. in a., 30/8/18 (132 Hvy. Bty.).
Muggeridge, William, 2/Lt., k. in a., 14/5/17 (112 Sge. Bty.).
Mulhall, Frank Reginald, 2/Lt., d. of w., 15/10/18 (25 Hvy. Bty.).
Mullaly, Dennis Joseph St. Claire, Lt., k. in a., 17/10/15.
Mullis, George Edwin, Lt., A/Capt., k. in a., 30/9/16 (14 Hvy. Bty.).
Munro, Frederick John, 2/Lt., d. of w., 11/8/17 (4 S.B.).
Murphy, Christopher Trevor Elias, Lt., d. of w., 8/5/18 (216 S.B.).
Murray, Charles, 2/Lt., k. in a., 16/10/18 (115 S.B.).
Murray, Robert McDiarmid, Lt. (Tp.), d. of w. (25/2/16 (7 S.B.).
Nelson-Cookes, Henry, Capt., died, 23/10/18.
Neville, William Sim, 2/Lt., k. in a., 25/9/16.
Newbiggin, John Prentice, Lt., died, 12/12/18.
Nicholson, Henry William, 2/Lt., k. in a., 3/11/17 (171 S.B.).
Nixon, William Henry, 2/Lt., killed, 24/8/17 (298 S.B.).
Nixon-Eckersall, Frederick Eckersall, Major, k. in a., 10/11/17.
Noden, Frank Hull, 2/Lt., died, 3/12/18 (319 S.B.).
Norman, Percy William, 2/Lt., died, 21/5/15.
Norvill, Frederick Henry, 2/Lt., d. of w., 24/7/17 (81 S.B.).
O'Connor, Edward, 2/Lt., d. of w., 12/5/18 (29 S.B.).
Ofield, Charles Henry, 2/Lt., d. of w., 22/8/18 (139 H.B.).
Ollivier, Guy Lancelot, Capt., A/Major, died, 20/1/18.
O'Rourke, Daniel, Lt., k. in a., 30/7/18 (170 S.B.).
Orr, James Henry, T/2/Lt., A/Capt., k. in a., 30/11/17 (210 S.B.).
Orton, Cecil Alfred, Major, died, 30/9/17 (22 S.B.).
O'Sullivan, Horace Alexander, 2/Lt., k. in a., 22/4/17 (41 S.B.).
Paget, John Christopher, Lt., A/Capt., k. in a., 26/4/17 (157 S.B.).
Paine, James Henry, D.S.O., Lt.-Col., k. in a., 25/7/18 (76 Bde.).
Palmer, John Arthur Stuart, 2/Lt., k. in a., 16/12/17.
Paris, Harold Graham, M.C., Major, k. in a., 6/10/18 (138 H.B.).
Parker, Herbert John, 2/Lt., k. in a., 27/10/17 (1/1 Welsh Hvy. Bty.).
Patterson, Charles William Ernest, Lt., died, 12/2/19 (503 S.B.).
Paul, Ernest Kenneth Montcrieff, M.C., 2/Lt., d. of w., 18/4/18 (242 S.B.).
Pawley, R. J., 2/Lt., died, 28/11/18.
Paxton, Robert Michael Mill, 2/Lt., k. in a., 1/1/17 (155 S.B.).
Payne, Richard William, Lt., k. in a., 19/8/15.
Payne, Wilfrid Stuart Lane, M.C., Lt., k. in a., 4/9/17 (att. R.F.C., 7 Sqd.).
Pearson, David Easson, 2/Lt., d. of w., 4/9/18 (112 S.B.).
Pease, Joseph Robinson, Major and Hon. Lt.-Col., died, 17/5/15 (late Yorks R., F. Res. A.).
Pemberton, Vivian Telfer, M.C., Capt., k. in a., 7/10/18 (216 S.B.).
Penrose, Claude Quayle Lewis, M.C., Major, d. of w., 1/8/18 (245 S.B.).
Pepper, William Bramwell, Capt., d. of w., 4/8/16 (3 S.B.).
Perram, George Terrence Clements, Capt. (A/Major), k. in a., 3/8/17 (att. 177 Bde., R.F.A.).
Perry, Arthur Ernest Cecil, 2/Lt., d. of w., 20/6/18 (245 S.B.).
Phillips, William Ernest, 2/Lt., d. of w., 29/9/18 (283 S.B.).
Philpot, Godfrey, Capt., k. in a., 1/9/16 (25 S.B.).
Phipps, Christopher Leckonby, Lt., k. in a., 14/8/17 (att. R.F.C.).
Pickering, Frank Wells, 2/Lt., d. of w., 20/9/17 (287 S.B.).
Pickthall, Henry Clement Vaughan, Capt., died, 8/12/18 (320 S.B.).
Pierson, Charles Frederick Leonard, Capt., k. in a., 2/11/14.
Pittman, Frederick John, 2/Lt., died, 20/8/18 (att. 14 Mtn. Bty.).
Pond, Frederick George, 2/Lt., k. in a., 5/9/18 (144 S.B.).
Pope, Harold Edward, M.C., T/Lt. (A/Capt.), k. in a., 24/8/18 (21 Bde.).
Porter, Hugh Gordon, 2/Lt., k. in a., 6/11/16.
Powell, Thomas Clark, 2/Lt., d. of w., 15/7/17 (H.B.).
Preddy, Edward Fred Spencer, Lt., A/Capt., k. in a., 8/12/17 (36 S.B.).
Price, Paul Adrian Edward, 2/Lt., k. in a., 23/4/17.
Prickett, Lancelot, Capt., killed, 2/6/16.
Priestley, Charles Henry Ryland, Temp. Lt., died, 19/6/18 (120 H.B.).
Pugh, George Morris, 2/Lt., d. of w., 2/9/18 (91 S.B.).
Punchard, R. Hugh, Lt., died, 31/10/18.
Purcell, Richard Guy, M.C., Capt., A/Major, d. of w., 28/3/18 (31 H.B.).
Purdie, Peter Robertson, 2/Lt., d. of w., 17/8/17 (14 H.B.).
Purnell, Alfred William Howard, 2/Lt., d. of w., 20/11/17 (Corps H.A.) (P. of W.).
Putnam, Edmund, 2/Lt., died, 16/4/18 (383 S.B.).
Quaife, Eric John, 2/Lt., A/Capt., k. in a., 30/6/17 (294 S.B.).
Quinn, James, 2/Lt., d. of w., 29/7/16.
Raggett, Bertram Robert, 2/Lt., k. in a., 5/1/18 (att. R.F.C.).
Rathbone, George Benson, Lt., died, 28/5/19.
Ratton, Joseph Holroyd, Major, k. in a., 2/9/17 (163 S.B.).
Rattray, James Alec, 2/Lt., k. in a., 23/9/17.
Reed, Walter Nelson, M.C., Temp. Lt., k. in a., 27/10/16.
Reeves, Hugh Charles, Major, died, 29/1/15.
Reeves, Stafford Reichel, Major, died, 26/3/19.
Reid, Bruce Simpson, 2/Lt., k. in a., 6/8/18 (192 S.B.).
Reid, Fergus Hamilton, Capt., k. in a., 16/5/15.
Remington, Felix George, 2/Lt., k. in a., 11/5/17 (3 H.A.G.).
Rennie, E. C., Lt., d. of w., 16/6/18 (and R.A.F.).
Revene, Howard, Lt., died, 25/8/17 (72 H.B.).
Richardson, Archer Stuart, 2/Lt., k. in a., 25/6/17 (13 S.B.).
Richardson, Henry, 2/Lt., d. of w., 21/5/17 (36 S.B.).
Rickards, Arthur Traherne, Lt., T/Capt., k. in a., 13/9/17 (and R.F.C., 43 Sqd.).
Rieple, Leopold Anthony, Temp. 2/Lt., died, 30/10/18 (51 S.B.).
Riggs, John Stephenson, 2/Lt., d. of w., 19/12/17 (239 S.B.).
Ripman, Helmut Armstrong, 2/Lt., d. of w., 16/5/18.
Robinson, Albert Alexander, Temp. Lt., k. in a., 20/7/16.
Robinson, Francis Victor, Lt., died, 29/7/18 (383 S.B., 59 Hvy. Group).
Robinson, Harold Robert, 2/Lt., k. in a., 13/10/18 (19 S.B.).
Robinson, Raymond Cecil, 2/Lt., d. of w., 19/10/18 (270 S.B.).
Rochfort, Arthur D'Oyly, Lt., died, 31/10/18 (and R.A.F.).
Rolston, Leslie Hicks, Lt., d. of w., 1/4/18 (182 S.B.).
Roper, Douglas Wingfield, 2/Lt., d. of w., 11/11/17 (279 S.B.).
Rowland, Cecil Fred, 2/Lt., k. in a., 21/3/18 (321 S.B.).
Rowlett, George Thomas, 2/Lt., k. in a., 30/7/16 (137 H.B.).
Rowley, Charles Pelham, Major, killed, 29/10/16.
Ruby, Joseph Bennett, 2/Lt., killed, 4/9/18 (att. R.G.A. Base Depot, Havre).
Salter, Donald Sowerby, 2/Lt., d. of w., 22/3/18 (126 S.B.).
Saltren-Willett, Archibald John, Lt.-Col., k. in a., 11/10/17.
Sampson, Ronald Henry, 2/Lt., k. in a., 30/8/18 (122 S.B.).
Samson, Oswald Massey, 2/Lt. (A/Lt.), d. of w., 17/9/18 (143 S.B.).
Samuelson, William Denys, Lt. (A/Capt.), d. of w., 31/12/17 (113 S.B.).
Sandall, James Hosking, 2/Lt. (A/Capt.), d. of w., 23/7/17 (229 S.B.).
Sanders, Leslie Yorath, 2/Lt. (Tp.), k. in a., 10/3/17.
Sanderson, Roy Broughton, 2/Lt., d. of w., 17/4/18.
Sargeaunt, Herbert Gaussen, Major (Act. Lt.-Col.), k. in a., 15/6/17 (16 H.A.G.).
Satchwell, Ralph William, 2/Lt., k. in a., 31/1/17 (76 S.B.).
Saunders, Albert James, 2/Lt., k. in a., 27/6/17 (58 S.B.).
Savage, John Geoffrey, Temp. 2/Lt., k. in a., 24/7/16.
Savage, T. A., Capt., died, 26/6/19 (att. 10 I.M.A. Bde.).
Saxon, Fredk. Thomas., 2/Lt., k. in a., 8/12/17 (143 S.B.).
Scallan, Richard Talbot, 2/Lt., killed, 31/5/18 (Labour Cps., Escort Offr., 90/P. of W. Co.).
Schall, Henry Frederick, 2/Lt., d. of w., 24/9/16.
Schell, Frederick Stanley, 2/Lt., k. in a., 22/8/18 (130 H. Bty.).
Scholefield, Cyril Hamilton Reid, Capt .(Act. Major), k. in a., 28/3/18 (69 S.B.).
Scobie, K. McD., 2/Lt., killed, 27/10/18 (and R.A.F.).
Scott, Elvin Alfred, Temp. Lieut., k. in a., 8/4/16 (111 H.B.).
Scott, Edward Claud, 2/Lt., k. in a., 21/11/14.
Scott, Frank Edward, 2/Lt., d. of w., 4/4/18 (405 S.B.).
Scott, Robert Edward Leslie, M.C., Lt., k. in a., 14/9/18 (129 H.B.).
Seddon, Edward MacMahon, D.S.O., Lt.-Col., k. in a., 24/6/17 (45 H.A.G.).
Sellon, Marmaduke Heckford, 2/Lt., k. in a., 15/6/18 (att. 1/1 War H.B.).
Sewell, Edward John, 2/Lt., d. of w., 10/4/18 (217 S.B.).
Sewell, Francis Brooke, Lt., k. in a., 15/5/18 (126 H.B.).
Shand, John James Fraser, 2/Lt., k. in a., 6/8/17 (185 H.B.).
Shea, Richard Thomas, Lt., died, 12/11/18.
Shedden, Graham Percival, Capt., d. of w., 31/10/14.
Sheppard, Gordon, 2/Lt., d. of w., 3/11/17 (309 S.B.).

Sheppard, Percy Howard, 2/Lt., d. of w., 28/5/18 (119 S.B.).
Shorten, Henry, 2/Lt., k. in a., 16/10/18 (19 S.B.).
Sidey, William Hepburn, 2/Lt., d. of w., 13/10/17 (62 S.B.).
Sidgwick, Arthur Hugh, 2/Lt. (A/Capt.), d. of w., 17/9/17 (157 S.B.).
Silver, Thomas Samuel Harper, 2/Lt., k. in a., 16/4/18 (80 S.B.).
Silverton, Ernest George, 2/Lt., k. in a., 26/7/17 (303 S.B.).
Simmons, Richard Ernest, 2/Lt., k. in a., 5/12/17.
Simonds, John De Luze, D.S.O., Capt. (A/Major), k. in a., 21/4/17 (136 S.B.).
Simpson, Ernest Herbert, 2/Lt., d. of w., 2/10/17 (att. G. Bty., A.A. Anzac Cp.).
Simpson, Frank William Harris, Capt., k. in a., 16/2/17 (and R.F.C.).
Simpson, James Ashton, 2/Lt., d. of w., 25/7/16.
Simson, Noel Charles Spicer, Capt., d. of w., 26/9/15 (21 Anti-Aircraft Sec.).
Simson, Roderick Alexander, 2/Lt., died, 11/11/18 (259 S.B.).
Sisson, George, Lt., d. of w., 20/12/17 (71 H.B.).
Skrimshire, Herbert Eric, 2/Lt., d. of w., 28/3/18 (116 S.B.).
Slicer, Philip Sydney, Lt., d. of w., 30/9/18 (319 S.B.).
Sloan, Harold Alexander, 2/Lt., k. in a., 21/1/17 (Hvy. Cps.).
Sloley, Robert Hugh, 2/Lt., k. in a., 1/10/17 (att. R.F.C., 56 Sqd.).
Smith, Cedric Harry, M.C., 2/Lt. (A/Capt.), k. in a., 31/10/17 229 S. B.).
Smith, Charles Randolph, 2/Lt., k. in a., 22/4/17 (244 S.B.).
Smith, Frederick Herbert Corbett Douglas, 2/Lt., k. in a., 10/12/17 (52 S.B.).
Smith, Isham Percy, D.S.O., Capt. (A/Major), k. in a., 30/11/17 (102 S.B.).
Smith, James William, 2/Lt., d. of w., 30/11/18 (251 S.B.).
Smith, Leslie Phillips, 2/Lt., died, 6/3/15.
Smith, Sidney, Lt., k. in a., 8/12/15 (113 Bty.).
Smith, Thomas Emanuel, 2/Lt., k. in a., 23/4/17 (263 S.B.).
Smithers, Harold, Temp. Major, k. in a., 4/11/16.
Smyth, Richard Alexander Noel, Capt., d. of w., 8/11/14.
Smythe, Andrew Graham Cowan, Major, k. in a., 7/9/17 (140 S.B.).
Smythe, Ralph Conran, Major, d. of w., 22/11/15 (2 S.B.).
Springmann, Ralph Thomas James, 2/Lt., d. of w., 21/9/18 (169 S.B.).
Squire, Wright Thomas, 2/Lt., k. in a., 30/6/18 (78 S.B.).
Squires, Francis William, 2/Lt., k. in a., 10/11/16.
Stainfield, Walter George, Lt., died, 18/11/18 (115 S.B.).
Stannard, Alexander Jewell, Lt., (A/Major), k. in a., 20/8/17 (29 S.B.).
Stephens, Alexander Augustus, A/Capt., and Adjt., died, 25/11/18.
Stevenson, Arthur, 2/Lt., k. in a., 27/4/18 (152 S.B.).
Stevenson, Samuel Bristow, 2/Lt., died, 29/9/16 (138 S.B.).
Stevenson, William, M.C., 2/Lt., k. in a., 18/9/18 (147 H.B.).
Stewart, Henry Warburton, 2/Lt., died, 11/2/19 (77 S.B.).
Stokes, William Henry, 2/Lt., k. in a., 18/4/18 (101 S.B.).
Strain, John London, Lt. (A/Capt.), k. in a., 31/7/17 (214 S.B.).
Stribling, Lewis James, 2/Lt., d. of w., 16/11/17 (329 S.B.).
Stringer, Henry Francis Godfrey, 2/Lt., d. of w., 3/5/17 (36 S.B.).
Stuart, Vernon Douglas, M.C., Lt., k. in a., 29/9/18 (180 S.B.).
Stuart-Russell, Cecil Henry, Lt. (Tp.), k. in a., 7/9/16.
Stubbs, Lewis Robert, M.C., 2/Lt., d. of w., 29/3/18 (123 S.B.).
Summers, John Collings, 2/Lt., k. in a., 13/8/18 (120 H.B.).
Sutcliffe, George Mitchele, 2/Lt., k. in a., 21/10/17 (237 S.B.).
Sutton, John William Wellesley, M.C., 2/Lt., k. in a., 29/6/17 (att. 28 Bde., R.F.A.).
Sutton, Percy Turner, Lt., k. in a., 24/8/18 (283 S.B.).
Swain, Charles Douglas Downs, Lt., k. in a., 29/9/17 (186 S.B.).
Swan, Joseph, 2/Lt., k. in a., 29/9/17 (186 S.B.).
Sykes, Oliver John, Temp. Capt., d. of w., 17/10/16 (23 S.B.).
Tanner, Charles Cyril Pontin, Capt., died, 5/10/18 (157 H.B.).
Taylor, Adam, 2/Lt., d. of w., 22/3/18 (210 S.B.).
Taylor, Cecil Salusbury, Lt.-Col., d. of w., 6/11/16 (28 H.A.G.).
Taylor, Kenneth, 2/Lt., d. of w., 17/6/17 (184 S.B.).
Tee, Clifford Vernon, 2/Lt., d. of w., 11/8/18 (153 S.B.).
Terrey, Harry Leslie, Lt. (A/Major), d. of w., 22/3/18 (126 S.B.).
Terry, William Gregory, Capt., died, 28/10/16 (36 Div. Art.).
Thaanum, James Conrad, Temp. 2/Lt., d. of w., 12/8/15.
Thatcher, George Robin, Lt., d. of w., 1/4/18 (M. Anti-Aircraft Bty.).
Thicknesse, Francis William, D.S.O., Capt. (A/Major), d. of w., 19/10/17 (122 H.B.).
Thomas, Arthur Crichton, Act. Major, k. in a., 16/11/17.
Thomas, Harry Reid, Capt., k. in a., 25/12/15 (34 S.B.).
Thomas, Philip Edward, 2/Lt., k. in a., 9/4/17 (244 S.B.).
Thomas, Reginald Ernest, 2/Lt., k. in a., 13/9/18 (193 S.B.).
Thompson, Ernest Edward, 2/Lt., d. of w., 16/10/18 (228 S.B.).
Thompson, Hubert Roberts, 2/Lt., d. of w., 30/6/18 (99 S.B.).
Thomson, James, Major, died, 26/11/17 (130 S.B.).
Thomson, William Robinson Ketchen, 2/Lt., k. in a., 16/10/17 (23 H.B.)
Thornton, George Rowland Hart, 2/Lt., k. in a., 9/4/18 (16 H.B.).
Thorp, Austin, C.M.G., D.S.O., Lt.-Col., k. in a., 30/10/18 (att. R.F.A., 82 Bde.).
Tilston, John, 2/Lt., k. in a., 18/10/18 (291 S.B.).
Todd, Charles Bernard, 2/Lt., k. in a., 11/6/17 (184 S.B.).
Tomlinson, Herbert Cecil, 2/Lt., d. of w., 21/3/18 (39 S.B.).
Topham, Charles Henry, 2/Lt., d. of w., 21/10/16 (115 H.B.).
Toppin, Sidney Miles, M.C., Major, d. of w., 27/9/17 (151 H.B.).
Torry, Arthur James Dashwood, M.C., Lt., k. in a., 9/10/17 (att. R.F.C., 9 Sqd.).
Traherne, George Gilbert, Capt., k. in a., 6/8/16.
Trenchard, John Wilfrid Hugh, Lt., d. of w., 3/10/17 (122 H.B.).
Trerise, Robert, 2/Lt., d. of w., 13/6/18 (237 S.B.).
Turnbull, Robert Duncan, 2/Lt., k. in a., 5/9/18 (144 S.B.).
Turton, Ernest Francis, Lt. (A/Capt.), k. in a., 27/10/17 (117 H.B.) .
Tyrrell, Gerald Ernest, D.S.O., Lt.-Col., died, 17/5/17 (64 H.A.G.).
Upson, Humphrey Cyril, Temp. Capt., k. in a., 29/7/16.
Van Eeghen, Esme Charles, 2/Lt., k. in a., 20/7/17 (324 S.B.).
Varley, William, 2/Lt., k. in a., 24/3/18 (2/1 Lanc., H.B.).
Vaughan, Percy Cecil, 2/Lt., k. in a., 26/9/17 (294 S.B.).
Vessey, Frank Court, M.C., M.M., Lt., died, 25/10/18 (353 S.B.).
Veysey, Stanley, 2/Lt., d. of w., 21/9/17 (119 S.B.).
Vickers, William Burnell, Temp. 2/Lt., k. in a., 21/6/17 (184 S.B.).
Voysey, Alfred Ebenezer, 2/Lt., k. in a., 29/7/17 (21 H.B.).
Wade-Gery, Robert Hugh, Capt., d. of w., 17/7/16.
Wadlow, Harold, Major, k. in a., 24/7/16.
Wahl, Matthew Daniel, 2/Lt. (A/Major), k. in a., 21/6/17 (294 S.B.).
Wakeford, Owen, M.C., Major, d. of w., 21/3/18 (76 S.B.).
Walker, Harry, 2/Lt., k. in a., 28/7/17 (295 S.B.).
Wallace, Stuart Annesley, Lt., k. in a., 31/5/17 (156 S.B.).
Ward, Walter Granby, Lt., k. in a., 3/9/18 (171 S.B.).
Wardley, Geoffrey Charles Norton, Temp. Lt., d. of w., 24/7/16.
Warne, William Millar, Lt., k. in a., 22/5/15.
Warren, William Edward, A/Major, d. of w., 29/3/18 (81 S.B.).
Watson, Francis Shuldham, D.S.O., Major, d. of w., 2/5/18 (276 S.B.).
Watts, Francis John, 2/Lt., k. in a., 17/7/17 (9 S.B.).
Weaver, Cecil Vivian Rupert, 2/Lt., d. of w., 9/8/18..
Webb, Albert William, 2/Lt., k. in a., 24/7/16.
Webb, Henry, 2/Lt., k. in a., 26/4/18 (9 H.B.).
Webb-Ware, Kenneth Charles, 2/Lt., k. in a., 21/3/18 (77 S.B.).
Welby, Davis, 2/Lt., died, 23/10/18.
Welch, Arthur Sidney, 2/Lt., k. in a., 29/9/17 (149 S.B.).
West, Arthur Eustace Lockley, 2/Lt. (A/Capt.), d. of w., 28/4/17 (213 S.B.).
West, James Stafford, 2/Lt., d. of w., 20/7/16.
Westwood, James, 2/Lt., k. in a., 25/6/17 (321 S.B.).
Whale, William John, Lt. (A/Capt.), d. of w., 14/6/17 (163 S.B.).
Wheadon, James Hansford, 2/Lt., d. of w., 11/3/17.
Wheatcroft, George Hanson, Temp. 2/Lt., k. in a., 13/8/15.
Wheway, Frank Reginald, 2/Lt., d. of w., 14/11/17 (183 S.B.).
Whitaker, Owen, Temp. 2/Lt., k. in a., 29/8/15.
White, Ernest William, M.C., 2/Lt., died, 20/10/18 (290 S.B.).
Whitehead, Edgar Joseph William, Lt., died, 17/2/19 (att. R.E.).
Whitehouse, Arthur Leslie, 2/Lt., k. in a., 10/9/16.
Whitehouse, Eric, 2/Lt., d. of w., 5/9/18 (144 S.B.).
Wilkinson, Norman Cecil, 2/Lt., d. of w., 24/8/17 (332 S.B.).
Wilkinson, Samuel William, 2/Lt., d. of w., 9/4/18 (237 S.B.).
Williams, Christopher Manners, Capt. & Adjt., k. in a., 24/3/18 (H.Q., 66 Bde.).
Williams, Edward Emanuel Montague, 2/Lt., k. in a., 10/12/17.
Williams, Timothy Davies, 2/Lt., d. of w., 5/4/18 (248 S.B.).
Williams, William Harold, Lt., k. in a., 9/11/18 (326 S.B.).
Williamson, Robert Hamilton, Lt., d. of w., 27/12/14.
Wills, Alfred James, 2/Lt., k. in a., 18/10/18 (182 S.B.).
Wilmot, Sachevarel Darwin, Capt., died, 14/10/18.
Wilson, George Andrew, 2/Lt. (A/Capt.), k. in a., 12/7/17 (262 S.B.).
Wilson, Herbert Stanley, Capt., d. of w., 13/5/15.
Wilson, John, 2/Lt., k. in a., 22/3/18 (120 H.B.).
Wilson, James Miller, 2/Lt., k. in a., 25/7/17 (333 S.B.).
Wilson, Lawrence Trench, Temp. 2/Lt., d. of w., 9/8/15.
Winkworth, Edwin John, 2/Lt., d. of w., 6/12/17 (219 S.B.).
Winton, Ernest Walter, 2/Lt., k. in a., 15/12/17.
Wiseman-Clarke, Charles Francis Ralph., Lt., k. in a., 20/2/16.
Woodcock, Frederick, M.C., Capt., killed, 31/10/18 (and R.A.F.).
Woodthorpe, Arthur John, 2/Lt., k. in a., 9/10/18 (276 S.B.).
Woodward, Henry Joseph, Major, d. of w., 22/8/18 (336 S.B.).
Woodward, Robert William, 2/Lt., d. of w., 30/8/17 (145 S.B.).
Wright, Cecil Laurence, 2/Lt., k. in a., 7/7/17 (287 S.B.).
Wright, John Shilvock, 2/Lt., k. in a., 7/11/18 (219 S.B.).
Wright, Walter Whitmore, 2/Lt., k. in a., 23/8/17 (276 S.B.).
Wrigley, James, 2/Lt., k. in a., 29/9/17 (289 S.B.).
Wynne, Charles Wyndham, Temp. 2/Lt. (A/Capt.), d. of w., 26/6/17 (182 S.B.).
Young, Alan Edward Frushard, 2/Lt., k. in a., 25/7/17.
Ziani de Ferranti, Basil, M.C., T/Lt. (A/Major), d. of w., 12/7/17 (21 S.B.)

Corps of Royal Engineers.

Adamson, Daniel, Lt., died, 7/6/19 (att. 2 S. and M.).
Akerman, Charles Savidge Annard, Major, died, 26/9/15.
Alderson, Arthur Roy, Lt. (Tp.), k. in a., 22/3/16 (87 F Co.).
Aldin, Dudley Cecil, 2/Lt., k. in a., 15/5/16 (105 F. Co.).
Allen, Cuthbert George Llewellin, 2/Lt. (Tp.), d. of w., 3/11/15.
Almond, Rowland Latimer, Lt., k. in a., 28/10/14.
Anderson, Goldie Fraser, Lt., k. in a., 19/7/16.
Anderson, Martin Alan, M.C., Capt., d. of w., 9/5/17 (211 Fld. Co.).
Anderson, William, Lt. (Tp.), d. of w., 27/3/18 (217 Coy.).
Andrew, Harry Townsend, 2/Lt. (Tp.), k. in a., 25/6/16.
Andrews, Eric Cauty, 2/Lt. (Tp.), k. in a., 12/10/16 (9 Fd. Co.).
Andrews, Percy Heath, Lt., d. of w., 28/3/18 (73 Fd. Co.).
Ansell, Arthur George, 2/Lt. (Tp.), d. of w., 25/4/18 (1 Fd. Survey Co.).
Appleyard, John Ernest, M.C., Lt., k. in a., 26/4/18 (222 Fd. Co.).
Archbold, William Heslehurst, 2/Lt. (Tp.), d. of w., 21/10/18 (228 Fd. Co.).
Arbuthnot, Aliser Dare Staveley, Capt., k. in a., 8/3/16.
Archibald, M. S. E., 2/Lt., d. of w., 12/5/18 (and R.A.F.).
Armitage, Ernest George, 2/Lt. (Tp.), k. in a., 14/7/18 (4 Spec. Co.).
Armstrong, John Nicholas Fraser, Major (Tp.), k. in a., 5/7/16 (128 Fd. Co.).
Armstrong, Michael Richard Leader, 2/Lt. (Tp.), k. in a., 22/4/16.
Ashcroft, Edward Davey, Capt., d. of w., 30/11/17 (7 Fld. Co.).
Atkinson, Owen Dayott, M.C., Capt., A/Major, d. of w., 27/10/18 (200 Fd. Bde.).
Atock, Arthur George, M.C., 2/Lt. (Tp.), k. in a., 13/9/18 (155 Fd. Coy.).
Avery, Frederick Graeme, M.C., Capt., k. in a., 13/4/18 (Div. Sig. Coy.).
Ayris, Norman, Lt. (Tp.), k. in a., 31/12/15.
Bacon, Charles Vallance, Lt. (Tp.), died, 4/11/18.
Baile, George Frederick Cecil, Lt. (Tp.), d. of w., 9/11/17.
Baile, Robert Carlyle, 2/Lt. (Tp.), k. in a., 16/10/15 (76 Fd. Co.).
Baker, Douglas Stanley, Lt., d. of w., 23/7/16 (87 Fd. Coy.).
Baker, Edward Carleton, Capt., d. of w., 19/9/16.
Baker, Neville Ernest, Lt. (Tp.), d. of w., 31/7/17 (att. Tank Cps.).
Baker, Percy Gordon, 2/Lt. (Tp.), d. of w., 9/6/18 (81 Fd. Co.).
Balcombe, Charles Percy Lionel, M.C., T/Capt., A/Major, d. of w., 29/10/18 (11 Fd. Co.).
Baldwin, William Frederick, M.C., T/Lt., A/Major, k. in a., 27/5/18 (7 Fd. Co.).
Ball, Mark Christopher, Lt., d. of w., 9/4/18 (231 Fd. Co.).
Bamberger, Cecil David Woodburn, Capt., k. in a., 20/12/17.
Bannerman, G. G., Lt., killed, 8/6/19 (att. R.A.F.).
Barclay, Allen, 2/Lt., k. in a., 24/4/15.
Barclay, Peter, 2/Lt. (Tp.), k. in a., 15/11/18 (180 Co.).
Barker, Christopher James, T/Lt. (A/Capt.), d. of w., 12/4/18 (att. H.Q., 30 Div.)
Barker, Thomas Chesman, 2/Lt., k. in a., 3/11/18 (218 Fd. Co.).
Barlow, Harry Loftus, Lt. (Tp.), killed, 18/3/18 (and R.F.C.).
Barnes, Eric Earle, Capt., k. in a., 7/11/17 (and R.F.C., 102 Sqd.).
Barney, Montagu Mydelton, 2/Lt. (Tp.), k. in a., 27/4/16 (253 T. Co.).
Barstow, John Baillie, Major, k. in a., 31/8/14.
Bartlett, Lionel Arthur, Capt., d. of w., 14/10/15.
Baskcomb-Harrison, Arthur Montague Mattison, 2/Lt. (T/Lt.), d. of w., 27/10/15.
Bates, Arthur James Edmund, 2/Lt. (Tp), d. of w., 30/7/17 (90 Fd. Co.).
Bates, Harold Christopher, T/Lt. (2/Lt.), k. in a., 18/8/15 (Spec. Res.).
Bates, Percy Joseph, 2/Lt. (Tp.), k. in a., 28/3/17 (179 Coy.).
Batho, John, Lt., d. of w., 30/9/15 (54 Fd. Co.).
Baxter, Gavin Hector, M.C., T/Lt., d. of w., 23/3/18 (157 Fd. Co.).
Baylay, George Frederick, Lt., k. in a., 23/3/18 (1 Cav. Fd. Sq.).
Bayly, Brian Brock, M.C., T/Lt. (A/Capt.), d. of w., 30/10/17 (254 L. Co.).
Bayly, Charles George Gordon, Lt., k. in a., 20/8/14 (att. R.F.C.).
Beck, Percy Latham, 2/Lt., k. in a., 6/3/15 (R. Monmouths., Spec. Res.).
Beckett, Frank Shaw, 2/Lt. (Tp.), k. in a., 31/5/18 (Spec. Coy.).
Beech, John, T/Lt. (A/Capt.), k. in a., 12/5/18 (4 Fd. Surv. Co.).
Bell, John Scott, 2/Lt., k. in a., 1/8/17 (15 Fd. Co.).
Bell, William, 2/Lt. (Tp.), d. of w., 26/7/16.
Bellamy, James Thomas Reynell, 2/Lt., died, 14/11/18.
Bennett, James, 2/Lt. (Tp.), k. in a., 28/11/16 (129 Fd. Co.).
Bennett, Vivian Wilfred, Lt., k. in a., 21/10/17 (209 Fd. Co.).
Beresford, William, Lt. (Tp.), died, 30/3/17 (I.W.T.).
Bernard, George Robert, M.C., 2/Lt. (Tp.), k. in a., 8/4/17 (254 Co.).
Berridge, Jesse Dell, M.C., Lt. (Tp.), k. in a., 24/5/18 ("J" Spec. Co.).
Bertlin, Hugh Anthony, 2/Lt. (Tp.), killed, 12/7/15.
Best, Arthur Stephen Middleton, Lt. (Tp.), k. in a., 23/2/17 (71 Fd. Co.).
Best, James Henry, 2/Lt. (Tp.), k. in a., 25/6/16.
Bethell, Charles Francis Ithel, 2/Lt., k. in a., 22/2/16 (70 Coy.).
Bevan, Thomas William, T/Lt. (A/Capt.), died, 22/10/18.
Bigelow, Braxton, Capt., k. in a., 23/7/17 (170 Tun. Coy.).
Billington, Whitworth Leonard, 2/Lt. (Tp.), k. in a., 17/5/17 ("Z" Spec. Co.).
Black, Thomas Lloyd, 2/Lt. (Tp.), k. in a., 2/6/15.
Blad, Kenneth Sven, 2/Lt. (Tp.), died, 26/11/18 (4 Tank Cps.).
Bladwell, Leonard Joseph, 2/Lt. (Tp.), k. in a., 14/10/18 (237 Fd. Co.).
Blair, Claud Leslie, M.C., Lt. (Tp.), k. in a., 16/6/17.
Blake, Geoffrey Stuart, Lt., k. in a., 5/9/17 (203 Fd. Co.).
Blake, James Edward, 2/Lt., k. in a., 6/4/17 (and R.F.C., 45 Sqd.).
Blyth, Dennis Carleton, 2/Lt. (Tp.), k. in a., 28/8/15.
Bogle, George Stafford, 2/Lt. (Tp.), d. of w., 15/10/15 (68 Coy.).
Boileau, Edmund Kenyvett, Lt., A/Capt., k. in a., 18/10/17.
Boileau, Frank Ridley Farrer, Col., d. of w., 26/8/14.
Boothby, Charles Geoffrey, 2/Lt. (Tp.), k. in a., 28/4/16.
Boulton, Charles Valentine, 2/Lt. (Tp.), k. in a., 9/11/17 (314 Rd. Constr. Co.).
Bourdillon, James Imbert Fulton, Lt., k. in a., 15/7/16 (222 Fd. Co.).
Bovet, William, Major, T/Lt.-Col., d. of w., 5/7/18 (12 Div.).
Bowen, Ivor, Lt., died, 25/2/17 (207 Fd. Co.).
Bowles, John Campbell, Capt., k. in a., 19/2/15.
Boxall, Alfred, M.C., 2/Lt. (Tp.), d. of w., 25/10/17 (262 Rly. Coy.).
Boyd, Gavin, 2/Lt. (Tp.), k. in a., 13/7/16 (4th Bn.).
Boyd-Carpenter, Victor Charles Douglas, Lt. (Tp.), k. in a., 29/8/16 (89 Fd. Co.).
Boys, Edward Percival, 2/Lt. (Tp.), k. in a., 22/3/18 (5 Army Sig. Co.).
Bradbury, Harry, Lt. (Tp.), died, 3/12/18.
Bradley, Reginald Ernest, 2/Lt. (Tp.), d. of w., 25/12/16.
Bradshaw, Henry Herbert, 2/Lt. (Tp.), k. in a., 22/7/17 (74 Fd. Coy.).
Bradstreet, Gerald Edmund, 2/Lt. (T/Lt.), k. in a., 7/12/15 (Spec. Res.).
Braithwaite, Humphrey Layland, 2/Lt. (Tp.), k. in a., 10/7/16.
Brand, Robert, M.C., 2/Lt. (Tp.), k. in a., 8/5/18 (40 Fd. Coy.).
Brander, Robert Brander, 2/Lt., died, 27/9/17.
Bremner, George, D.S.O., M.C., T/Capt. (A/Major), k. in a., 23/3/18 (80 Fd. Coy.).
Bressey, Sydney Herbert, 2/Lt. (Tp.), k. in a., 21/9/18 (74 Div. Sig. Co.).
Brisco, Richard Brown, M.C., Capt. (Tp.), k. in a., 9/4/17 (172 T. Coy.).
Broadway, Hugh Alexander, 2/Lt., d. of w., 30/3/15.
Brothers, Arthur Stanley, Capt. (Tp.), k. in a., 2/7/16 (178 T. Coy.).
Brown, Austin Hanbury, D.S.O., M.C., Major, k. in a., 27/3/18 (2 Fd. Coy.).
Brown, Benjamin Albert, Lt. (Tp.), d. of w., 4/10/17 (253 Fd. Co.).
Brown, Foss Hunter, 2/Lt., k. in a., 31/7/17 (76 Fd. Co.).
Brown, George Alexander, Capt., died, 6/6/16.
Brown, Richard Clerke, 2/Lt. (Tp.), k. in a., 20/8/16 (103 Fd. Co.).
Brown, Stewart Patrick, 2/Lt. (Tp.), d. of w., 31/12/17 (248 Fd. Coy.).
Brown, Thomas Muirhead, Lt. (Tp.), d. of w., 16/4/18 (9 Obs. Gp., 1st Fd. Survey Co.).
Brown, William George Charteris, Lt.-Col., died, 26/5/19.
Browne, Frederick MacDonnell, D.S.O., Major, d. of w., 1/10/15 (38 Fd. Co.).
Bruce, Christopher Yule, 2/Lt. (Tp.), k. in a., 28/3/18 (176 Tunn. Co.).
Breul, Oswald George Frank Justies, 2/Lt. (Tp.), died, 16/10/17 (5 Corps H.Q.).
Brunner, Francis Wilfred, Major, k. in a., 11/8/15.
Bryant, George Herbert, O.B.E., Hon. Major, k. in a., 1/8/18.
Brydon, Thomas Edward, 2/Lt. (Tp.), d. of w., 1/2/17 (88 Fd. Coy.).
Buck, Arthur, Lt. (Tp.), killed, 9/9/18 (att. 67 Bde., R.G.A.).
Budd, Eric Frank Corydon, Lt. (Tp.), k. in a., 11/9/17 (and R.F.C., 52 Sqd.).
Bull, Joseph William, 2/Lt. (Tp.), d. of w., 1/10/16 (98 Fd. Co.).
Burgess, Robert Balderston, Capt. (Tp.), d. of w., 10/12/15.
Burt, Lewis H., 2/Lt., killed, 31/10/17 (Reinf., att. Works Directorship, Basra.).
Bury, Eric Lindsay, M.C., T/2/Lt. (T/Capt.), died, 9/11/18 (att. R.F.A. H.Q., 2 Cps.).
Busby, V., Capt., died, 8/6/18 (and R.A.F.).
Bussey, Frank, Capt. (Tp.), d. of w., 15/8/17.
Butler, R. A., Lt., died, 20/7/18 (and R.A.F.).
Buttle, Bertram Haward, T/2/Lt., d. of w., 1/10/17 (att. 5 Army H.Q., "Z" Spec. Co.).
Cadell, Richard Lewis, 2/Lt., d. of w., 28/5/18 (in Ger. hands) (98/Fld. Coy.).
Cadman, Charles Joseph, M.C., Temp. Lt., k. in a., 26/1/17 (Div. Sig. Co.).

Calvert, Lionel, Temp. 2/Lt., k. in a., 30/1/17 (175 Tunn. Co.).
Cam, Alan Noel, Temp. 2/Lt., k. in a., 16/8/17 (150/Fld. Co.).
Cameron, Charles Munnis, Temp. 2/Lt., k. in a., 12/6/16 (173 T. Coy.).
Campbell, Cecil Awdry, Lt., drowned, 4/10/18 (250/Fld. Co.).
Campbell, John King, Temp. 2/Lt., k. in a., 21/4/16 (253 Coy.).
Campbell, Norman Phillips, T/Lt. (A/Capt.), k. in a., 3/5/17 (189 Coy. Spec. Bde. O. sp. Co.).
Campbell, Thomas Callender, Lt. (Tp.), d. of w., 8/10/15 (86 Coy.).
Cardew, Edward Bellasis, Capt., k. in a., 26/9/15.
Carnduff, Kenneth McLeod, Capt., d. of w., 11/1/16.
Carnelley, Joseph Arthur, Lt. (Tp.), d. of w., 16/6/16 (173 Tun. Co.).
Carr, Arthur Clunes Hooper, Lt., d. of w., 15/2/15.
Carr, Cyril, M.C., Lt. (Tp.), k. in a., 11/4/18 (224 Fld Co.).
Carr, Hugh, 2/Lt. (Tp.), d. of w., 23/1/16 (172 Coy.).
Carr-Harris, Ernest Dale, Capt., k. in a., 3/11/14.
Carrs, Stuart, Temp. Lt., d. of w., 28/7/16 (212 Fld. Co.).
Carruthers, E. S., Major, died, 16/5/17.
Carruthers, William, 2/Lt., k. in a., 24/4/17 (154 Fld. Co. from 3/Royal I. Rifles).
Carter, Desmond Patrick Webb, Lt., died, 12/12/16 (1/Fld. Sig. Co.).
Carter, Richard Ivens, 2/Lt. (Tp.), d. of w., 12/11/15.
Carter, William Leonard, Temp. Lt., died, 4/7/17.
Case, Elliott Dryden, Lt., k. in a., 27/7/15 (2/N'brian Fld. Coy.).
Cassels, Frank Lionel, Temp. Lt., k. in a., 20/7/16.
Caton, Frederic William, Temp. 2/Lt., k. in a., 28/6/16.
Cator, Edward Philip Douglas, Lt. (A/Capt.), k. in a., 11/4/18 (69 Fld. Coy.).
Chaplin, Rowland Edward Ernest, Temp. 2/Lt., k. in a., 22/4/17 (7/Fld. Coy.).
Chapman, Charles George, Lt. (Tp.), d. of w., 17/4/16.
Chappell, Edwin Francis, 2/Lt. (Tp.), k. in a., 3/2/16.
Chase, Archibald Alderman, D.S.O., Capt. & Bt.-Major, d. of w., 11/3/17 (att. R. Sussex Regt.).
Chidgey, Percy Harold, Temp. 2/Lt., d. of w., 12/4/18 (200 Fld. Coy.).
Christie, Richard Colin, Lt., d. of w., 15/12/15.
Churchill, Herbert Payn, 2/Lt. (Tp.), died, 20/10/15.
Cleaver, Frank, Temp. 2/Lt., d. of w., 3/10/18 (R.O.D. Survey Coy.).
Cleeve-Edwards, Cecil, Temp. 2/Lt., k. in a., 16/10/18 (2/Fld. Coy.).
Clegg, Richard B., Lt., k. in a., 18/7/16 (15 Fld. Co.).
Clements, Francis Carey, 2/Lt., d. of w., 11/1/17 ("F" Corps Sig. Co.).
Clews, Robert, M.C., Temp. Lt., d. of w., 28/4/18 (235 Army Troop Coy.).
Clough, E., Temp. 2/Lt., died, 14/10/18 (97 Fld. Coy.).
Cloutman, Wolfred Reeve, Lt. (Tp.), k. in a., 22/8/15.
Coates, Percy, 2/Lt. (Tp.), k. in a., 15/4/16 (180 Co.).
Coghlan, Joseph Patrick, M.C., Lt., k. in a., 20/9/17 (228 Fld. Co.).
Coleman, John Roberts, Temp. 2/Lt., died, 26/11/18 (Spec. Bde.).
Collins, Arthur Edward Jeune, Capt., k. in a., 11/11/14.
Collins, Charles Bury, C.M.G., D.S.O., Lt.-Col. (T/Col.), died, 1/3/17.
Collyns, Robert Henry, M.C., Temp. Lt., d. of w., 1/6/18 (97 Fld. Co.).
Comrie, Alexander, 2/Lt. (Tp.), died, 15/8/16 (257 Coy.).
Connor, Isaac Joscelyn, Major, k. in a., 5/7/16 (101/F. Coy.).
Cook, Alfred John, Lt., died, 8/6/19 (att. 1st S. and M.).
Cook, B. E., 2/Lt., died, 7/11/18.
Cook, Geoffrey Bruce, Lt. (Tp.), k. in a., 1/10/18 (I.W.T. att. 1/5 L.N. Lan. Regt.).
Cook, Horace Herbert, Temp. 2/Lt., k. in a., 25/3/18 (430 Coy.).
Cooke, John Irwin, Lt., d. of w., 3/9/17 (4/Sect. L. R.O.D.).
Cooksey, Maurice Wilfrid, Temp. 2/Lt., d. of w., 13/4/17 (B. Spec. Co.).
Cooper, Astley de Borde, 2/Lt. (Tp.), d. of w., 7/7/15 (1 Sig. Co.).
Cooper, Corin Henry Benedict, Temp. Lt., d. of w., 20/11/16 (178/F. Coy.).
Cooper, Frederick William, Lt. (Tp.), k. in a., 17/4/18 (105 Fld. Coy.).
Cooper, G. C. M., A/Capt., died, 23/11/18 (R. Anglesey).
Corry, John Beaumont, D.S.O., Major, k. in a., 5/11/14.
Coules, Eric Allan Gifford, 2/Lt, k. in a., 28/10/17 (129 Fld. Coy.).
Coull, Andrew Mearns, Temp. 2/Lt., k. in a., 3/7/17 (178 Tun. Coy.).
Cowan, Adam, Temp. Lt., k. in a., 18/11/16 (82 Fld. Coy.).
Cowdell, Charles Joseph Morton, Temp. 2/Lt., k. in a., 12/9/17 (212 Fld. Co.).
Cox, Edgar William, D.S.O., Major (A/Brig.-Gen.), drowned, 26/8/18 (Staff G.H.Q., 1st Ech.).
Cox, William George, 2/Lt. (Tp.), died, 22/9/18.
Craig, Hedley William, Temp. 2/Lt., k. in a., 15/4/17 (and R.F.C.).
Craig, Isaac Murray, Act. Capt., k. in a., 22/8/18 (66 Fld. Coy.).
Cranston, William Weir, Temp. Lt, k. in a., 18/12/17 (173 Coy.).
Crawford, Daniel David Dunlop, Lt., died., 10/12/17 (att. 25 Rlwy. Corps, S & M).
Crofton, Edward Vivian Morgan, Lt., k. in a., 14/7/17 (61 Fld. Coy.).
Crompton, Nigel George, Lt. (Tp.), k. in a., 5/11/15.
Crooke, Hugh Neville, 2/Lt., k. in a., 10/12/16.
Crowther, Ernest, 2/Lt. (Tp.), k. in a., 25/10/18 (92 Fld. Co.).
Crowther, Philip Townsend, Temp. Lt., k. in a., 5/5/17 (211 Fld. Co.).
Cunnack, George James, M.C, T/Lt. (A/Capt.), d. of w., 17/10/18 (180 Tunn. Co.).
Curley, Francis, Lt., k. in a., 25/9/15 (R. Anglesey).
Currie, Clarence Algernon, Lt. (Tp.). d. of w., 19/12/15.
Curtis, Henry Edward, 2/Lt., drowned, 21/2/17 (117 Constn. Coy. Rlwy.).
Cutts, Leonard Edwin, Lt (Tp), died, 11/10/18 (256 Tunn. Co.).
Dadd, Ivor Llewellyn, Temp., 2/Lt. died, 17/7/17 (I.W.T.).
Dain, Sidney Edward, 2/Lt. (Tp.), died, 7/12/18 (Postal Sect.).
Daintith, James, Temp. 2/Lt., k. in a., 13/8/17 (150 Fld. Co.).
Dance, Charles Edward, Lt.-Col, died, 23/7/18.
Darton, Edward John, 2/Lt., died, 30/4/15 (80 Fld. Co.).
Davies, Kenneth George, Temp. Lt., k. in a., 19/5/17 (H. Cable Sect.).
Davies, Richard Cecil, Major, died, 17/5/17.
Davies, Robert Lloyd, Temp. Lt., k. in a., 12/4/17 (129 Fld. Co.).
Davies, T. H., Lt. (Tp.), died, 26/10/18.
Davies, Tom Llewelyn, 2/Lt., k. in a., 26/5/17 (I.W.T.).
Davison, Guy Middleton, Capt. (Tp), died, 30/11/18 (I.W. & D. Construct. Sect.).
Daw, William Westaway, 2/Lt (Tp). died, 12/11/18 (171 Tunn. Co.).
Dawkins, Frank, Lt., died, 11/10/18 (and R.A.F.).
Dawson-Scott, John Kearsley, Capt., k. in a., 29/11/14.
Day, Walter Evan, Capt., k. in a., 5/6/16.
Deane-Oliver, Richard Edward, Temp. Lt., k. in a., 8/9/16 (75 Fld. Coy.).
De la Haye, Cyril, 2/Lt. (Tp.), d. of w., 23/5/18 (N. Spec. Co.).
De Vere, Roger, T/Lt. (T/Capt.), died, 1/12/18 (att. Staff G.H.Q.).
Dewar, Alexander, Lt., d. of w., 21/12/14.
Dewing, Robert Edward, D.S.O., Capt. (Act. Lt. Col.), k. in a., 4/4/18 (att. 8/R. Berks Regt.).
Dickson, Edward John Quayle, M.C., Temp. Capt., k. in a., 26/10/17 (255 Tunn. Coy., Corps 1st).
Digby-Jones, Charles Kenelm, Capt. (Tp.), died, 25/9/18.
Dixon, George, 2/Lt. (Tp.), k. in a., 6/8/15.
Dixon, James W., 2/Lt., k. in a., 5/8/17 152 Fld. Co.).
Dobbs, George Eric Burroughs, Capt. & Bt.-Major (A/Lt.-Col.), d. of w., 17/6/17 (A.D Signals).
Dobell, Caleb Clifford, Lt., died, 17/11/18 (256 Tunn. Co.).
Dobinson, Thomas William, Capt. (Tp.), died, 1/12/18 (183 Tunn. Co.).
Doherty-Holwell, Raymond Vernon, D.S.O., Major, k. in a., 9/1/17 (A.D. Sigs Corps, H.Q.).
Domeleo, Robert Frearson, Lt. (Tp.), died, 10/12/18 (R.O.D.).
Don, Alexander Duff Brownlee, Lt., k. in a., 21/10/16 (2 Coy.).
Douglas, William Sholto, Major, d. of w., 14/11/14.
Dowse, Thomas William, 2/Lt. (Tp.), d. of w., 7/9/16 (34 Div. Sigs.).
Drummond, John Grey, Temp. 2/Lt., k. in a., 13/10/15 (176 Tunn. Co.).
Du Boulay, Arthur Housse Mayne, D.S.O., Major and Bt.-Lt.-Col., died, 25/10/18 (A.Q.M.G., 3rd Army).
Duggan, Herrick Stevenson, Lt. (Tp.), d. of w., 21/10/15 (70th Coy.).
Duncan, J. M., 2/Lt. (Tp.), died, 6/6/18 (I.W.T.).
Dunhill, Carlos Miguel Guillermo, Capt., k. in a., 1/12/15 (att. 17 Coy. Sprs. and Minrs.).
Dunn, Hugh Aubrey Fairfield, 2/Lt., drowned, 21/5/16.
Dunn, Ralph John, 2/Lt., k. in a., 25/9/15.
Dunnachie, William James Nimmo, Lt., k. in a., 15/4/16.
Durrant, Arthur Michael, M.C., Temp. Lt. (A/Capt.), k. in a., 5/12/16 (257 Tun Co).
Dusgate, Richard Edmund, Temp. 2/Lt., died, 19/12/17 (and R.F.C., 46 Sqd.) (P. of W.).
Dutton, Alfred Laurence, Temp. 2/Lt., k. in a., 11/4/17 (95 Fld. Coy.).
Dyer, Percy Maitland, Lt., k. in a, 1/9/17 (208 Fld. Coy.).
Dyer, Ralph Gibb, Temp. 2/Lt., k. in a., 23/2/17 (92 Fld. Coy.).
Earnshaw, Oscar, 2/Lt (Tp.), k. in a., 2/6/16.
Edwards, Oswald James, 2/Lt. (Tp.), died, 10/12/18 (456 Field Coy.).
Edwards, Charles O'Reilly, Capt., k. in a., 13/12/15.
Egerton, Brian Raleigh, Lt., k. in a., 23/10/18 (87 Fld. Coy.).
Egerton, Robert Randle, Lt., k. in a., 15/11/14.
Elliott, Henry Christopher, Temp. 2/Lt., d. of w., 20/12/17 (150 Fld. Co.).
Ellis, George Frederick, 2/Lt., k. in a., 30/3/15.
Ellis, James Graves St. John, 2/Lt. (Tp.), d. of w., 11/10/15.
Ellis, Shirley Duncan, M.C., Temp. 2/Lt., died, 19/3/16 (173 Coy.).
Elworthy, Edward Pearce, 2/Lt., k. in a., 11/8/15.
Emery, Ewart Arthur Edwin, 2/Lt. (Tp.), k. in a., 23/3/18 (16 Sig. Coy.).
Evans, Charles Edward, Major, k. in a., 6/8/18 (82 Fld. Coy.).
Evans, David, 2/Lt., killed, 14/9/16.
Evans, Emrys, 2/Lt. (Tp.), k. in a., 29/4/16 (253 Tun. Co.).
Evans, James Reginald, 2/Lt. (Tp.), died, 19/10/18 (3/Res. Batt.).
Faithfull, Sidney Leigh, 2/Lt. (Tp.), died, 15/8/16 (256 Tunn. Co.).
Farrin, Stuart Thomas, 2/Lt., d. of w., 7/12/17 (263 Rly. Co.).
Fayle, Gerald Leigh Bleeck, Lt., k. in a., 22/7/16.
Featherstone, Marshall Breckon, 2/Lt. (Tp.), k. in a., 2/9/17 (2 Spec. Coy.).
Fennemore, George Charles, 2/Lt. (Tp.), died, 3/11/18.

Ferguson, David Raeside, Lt. (Tp.), k. in a., 17/11/17 (135 Army Trps. Coy.).
Field, John Archibald, Capt., k. in a., 13/7/16 (92 Fld. Co.).
Findon, Robert, Lt. (Tp.), k. in a., 18/4/18 (9 Fld. Co.).
Finnimore, David Keith, Lt., died, 10/5/17 (2 Pontoon Pk.).
Fishbourne, Charles Eustace, Lt., died, 10/6/15.
Fisher, Cecil Eric Haig, 2/Lt., d. of w., 24/7/15.
Fisher, Harold, Lt. (Tp.), d. of w., 14/4/18 (184 Tunn. Co.).
Fitzmaurice, Maurice Alexander Ross Geraldine, Lt., k. in a., 5/8/15.
Fletcher, Arthur Philip, 2/Lt. (Tp.), k. in a., 1/10/15.
Flint, Robert Bradford, D.S.O., Lt., d. of w., 23/1/15.
Fogerty, John Frederick Cullinan, Lt., k. in a., 25/9/17 (Fld. Co. 227).
Fogg, Thomas Holt, Lt. (Tp.), k. in a., 26/3/18 (288 Army Trps. Co.).
Forbes, Arthur, 2/Lt. (Tp.), k. in a., 27/9/17 (11 Fld. Co.).
Forbes, Fergus Robert, Lt. (Tp.), k. in a., 25/9/15.
Forbes, James, 2/Lt. (Tp.), k. in a., 12/12/15.
Ford, Frederick Austin, 2/Lt., k. in a., 27/8/18 (Div. Sig. Co.).
Ford, N., 2/Lt., killed, 5/4/18 (and R.A.F.).
Formby, Richard William, Lt., k. in a., 16/2/17.
Foster, George Haslewood, 2/Lt. (Tp.), k. in a., 21/3/18 (179 Tunn. Co.).
Fowle, William Meade, Capt., d. of w., 16/3/16.
Fox, Alan Geoffrey, Capt., k. in a., 9/5/15 (att R.F.C.).
Foyster, Philip Tillard, Lt. (T/Capt.), d. of w., 11/12/16 (85 Fld. Co.).
France, Arthur Alderson, 2/Lt. (Tp.), d. of w., 7/10/16.
Francis, Hugh Gordon, M.C., T/Lt. (A/Capt.), k. in a., 22/3/18 (104 Coy.).
Fraser, Donald, Capt. (Tp.), k. in a., 1/7/16.
Fraser, William Alan, Capt. (Tp.), died, 7/7/17 (26 Div. H.Q.).
Freeman, John William, 2/Lt. (T/Lt.), k. in a., 24/9/17 (X Cps. Sig. Co.).
French, P. H., Capt., died, 12/11/14.
Gale, Henry John, M.C., M.M., 2/Lt. (Tp.), k. in a., 7/6/18.
Gale, Ralph Goulstone, 2/Lt. (Tp.), k. in a., 26/3/18 (B. Spec. Co.).
Gandy, Clement Joseph, M.C., 2/Lt., k. in a., 31/7/17 (234 Fld. Co.).
Gardiner, Alec, Major, k. in a., 20/12/14.
Gardiner, Stanley Tysol, 2/Lt. (Tp.), k. in a., 27/6/16.
Gardner, Burnett Gilroy Craufurd, 2/Lt., died, 7/5/15.
Garrett, Arthur Dale, 2/Lt., k. in a., 17/4/18 (456 Fld. Co.).
Garrett-Smith, Louis, 2/Lt., d. of w., 31/7/15 (Spec Res.).
Gates, Arthur Noel, 2/Lt. (Tp.), k. in a., 1/3/17 (176 Tunn. Co.).
Gates, Henry, 2/Lt. (Tp.), k. in a., 18/10/18 (23 Fld. Co.).
Gattens, Charles, Lt., killed, 15/6/19 (R.A.F.).
Gayford, Thomas Frederick Marter, 2/Lt., k. in a., 23/11/17 (203 Fld. Co.).
Gee, Frank Lionel, 2/Lt. (Tp.), k. in a., 5/9/17 (203 Fld. Co.).
Gelme, Reginald William, 2/Lt. (Tp.), died, 27/7/16.
George, Edward Royston, T/Lt. (A/Capt.), died, 12/8/17 (264 Co.).
Gerds, Frederick Niven, 2/Lt. (Tp.), k. in a., 1/6/15.
Gibbins, Gwynn Gilbert, Lt. (Tp.), k. in a., 26/7/17.
Gibbs, Walter William, 2/Lt. (Tp.), k. in a., 22/4/18 (1 Fld. Sur. Co.).
Gill, Francis Edwin, Capt., died, 28/2/15.
Gillespie, William, T/Capt. (A/Major), d. of w., 9/4/18 (218 Fld. Co.).
Gillott, Oswald Cronek, 2/Lt. (Tp.), k. in a., 7/6/17 (68 Fld. Co.).
Gilmour, G. L., 2/Lt. (Tp.), died, 12/8/17 (I.W.T.).
Gladstone, Ralph Oscar, 2/Lt. (Tp.), k. in a., 2/11/17 (421 W. Lancs Fld. Co.).
Glasgow, William James Nesbitt, Capt. (Tp.), d. of w., 7/10/16 (Fld. Co. 93).
Glenday, Alexander Goncalves, Capt., k. in a., 8/8/15.
Glyn, Guy Godfrey, T/Lt., died, 16/8/15 (109 Co. Rly. Cons. Sect.).
Goodbody, Owen Frederick, 2/Lt. (Tp.), died, 20/10/15 (72 Fld. Co., 13 Div.).
Goodeve, T. E., O.B.E., T/Capt. (A/Major), killed, 26/1/19.
Gordon, Alec William, M.C., Capt. (A/Major), k. in a., 6/8/18 (56 Fld. Co.).
Gornell, Noel Christopher, 2/Lt. (Tp.), k. in a., 21/3/18 (157 Fld. Co.).
Grant, George Campbell, Lt. (Tp.), d. of w., 14/10/15 (96 Fld. Co.).
Grant, Ronald Cameron, Lt. (Tp.), died, 16/10/16.
Gray, Geoffry Thomas, 2/Lt., k. in a., 24/3/17 (R.F.C. 8 Sqd.).
Gray, Julian Frederick, M.C., Capt., d. of w., 10/7/17 (att. 1 S.M.).
Green, Alan Herbert, 2/Lt. (Tp.), d. of w., 26/2/18 (att. R.F.C.).
Greene, Robin, Capt. (Tp.), died, 21/9/18 (Postal Serv.).
Greenfield, Thomas Bevil, 2/Lt. (Tp.), k. in a., 19/9/15.
Greig, Ronald Henry, D.S.O., Major, k. in a., 28/8/16 (54 Fld. Co.).
Greswell, H. G., Capt., d. of w., 18/8/16 (154 Fld. Co.).
Griffith, George Herbert, Col., died, 20/9/17 (Depty. Dir. of Works).
Griffiths, Christopher William, Lt. (Tp.), d. of w., 7/11/18 (123 Fld. Co.).
Griffiths, Hugh, 2/Lt. (Tp.), died, 1/12/18 (310 Rd. Cons. Co.).
Grindley, Herbert Taylor, Lt., k. in a., 19/10/15.
Grist, Henry Noel, 2/Lt. (Tp.), k. in a., 27/5/17 (173 Tunn. Co.).
Grogan, Gerald Forman, Lt. (Tp.), k. in a., 8/1/18 (183 Co.).
Grote, Arthur Lloyd, Capt. (Tp.), died, 9/7/18 (I.W.T.).
Guthrie, Arthur Calderwood, 2/Lt., killed, 9/8/18 (and R.A.F.).
Gwynne-Griffith, Gilbert Digby Mansel, T/Lt. (A/Capt.), d. of w., 2/7/18 (att. S. Persia Rifs.).
Hackett, William, Lt. (Tp.), died, 15/11/18 (Late 8 S. Staff. R.).
Haig, Ernest Herman, Lt.-Col., died, 28/12/14.
Haigh, Arthur Gordon, 2/Lt. (Tp.), k. in a., 15/2/16 (172 Coy.).
Halford, Edward F., Lt. (Tp.), died, 10/10/18.
Hall, Aubrey Frederick, Lt. (Tp.), k. in a., 8/8/18 (92 Fld. Co.).
Hall, George Foden Rooking, 2/Lt. (Tp.), k. in a., 28/6/17 (103 Fld. Co.).
Hall, Peveril Austin, 2/Lt., died, 5/11/18.
Halley, James Mitchell, M.C., T/Capt. (A/Major), k. in a., 24/10/18 (62 Fld. Co.).
Halliday, Charles Graham Rivers, 2/Lt., k. in a., 13/6/17 (225 Fld. Co.).
Hamblin, William Ebb, Lt., k. in a., 24/5/16.
Hamilton, Arthur Donald, 2/Lt. (Tp.), k. in a., 20/10/17 (101 Fld. Co.).
Hamilton, A. G., Capt., died, 15/2/19.
Hamilton, William, Lt. (A/Capt.), died, 13/8/17 (183 Tunn Co.).
Hamilton, William Lees, 2/Lt. (Tp.), k. in a., 20/9/17 (237 Fld. Co.).
Hammonds, Denys Huntingford, D.S.O., M.C., Capt. (A/Major), k. in a., 30/3/18 (225 Fld. Co.).
Hancock, John Henry, Lt. (Tp.), k. in a., 9/6/17 (129 Fld. Co.).
Hands, Frederick, A/Capt., k. in a., 27/5/17.
Hardie, Norman, 2/Lt. (Tp.), k. in a., 27/3/17 (2 Fld. Co.).
Hardman, Robert Taylor, 2/Lt. (Tp.), k. in a., 1/7/16.
Hardman, William Frederick Kerr, M.C., 2/Lt. (Tp.), d. of w., 28/10/17 (171 Co.).
Hardwick-Terry, Leonard Alfred, T/Lt. (A/Capt.), k. in a., 31/8/17 (and R.F.C. 24 Sqd.).
Hardy, Edgar Leslie, T/Lt., d. of w., 7/10/18.
Harger, Edwyn Oscar, 2/Lt. (Tp.), d. of w., 23/9/18 (171 Tunn. Co.).
Harland, Hugh Baxter, 2/Lt. (Tp.), died, 28/10/17 (Base Dep.).
Harper, Frederick Henry, T/Lt., d. of w., 20/4/18 (11 Fd. Co.).
Harris, Henry Lionel, 2/Lt. (Tp.), d. of w., 1/12/15 (105 Co.).
Harrison, Edward Frank, C.M.G., D.S.O., Lt.-Col. (Tp.), died, 4/11/18.
Hartnoll, Herbert Nicholas, Lt. (Qr.-Mr.), died, 28/5/16.
Haselden, Cyril Gerrard, T/Lt., died, 27/11/18 (att. Aust. Cps. H.Q.).
Haslam, Bernard John, D.S.O., Major, k. in a., 26/8/18.
V.C. Hawker, Lanoe George, D.S.O., Major (Tp.), died, 23/11/16 (and R.F.C.).
Hawthorn, William, 2/Lt. (Tp.), d. of w., 31/12/15 (172 Tunn. Co.).
Hawtrey, Ralph, Lt. (Tp.), k. in a., 3/9/16 (179 Tunn. Co.).
Haydon, Alan, Lt. (Tp.), died, 28/12/18 (71 Fld. Co.).
Hayes-Sadler, Edwin John Berkeley, Lt., k. in a., 28/10/14.
Hayman, William Muir, D.S.O., Major (Tp.), d. of w., 13/7/17 (92 F. Co.).
Hebden, Robert Coke, Capt. (Tp.), died, 25/2/16.
Hedley, Gerald Montague, Capt. (Tp.), died, 4/10/18.
Henderson, Henry May, Major (A/Lt.-Col.), k. in a., 10/3/17 (18 Div.).
Henderson, Walter, Lt. (Tp.), died, 29/10/18.
Henman, Sydney, T/Lt., k. in a., 10/8/17 (86 Fld. Co.).
Hepburn, George, Lt. (Tp.), k. in a., 22/3/18 (98 Fld. Co.).
Hepburn, Roger Paul, M.C., 2/Lt. (Tp.), d. of w., 3/8/17 (30 Div. Sig. Co.).
Hewison, Charles Runciman, Lt. (Tp.), drowned, 4/5/17.
Higgins, Thomas, M.C., T/Lt., d. of w., 15/11/16 (130 F. Co.).
Hill, John Robertshaw, 2/Lt. (Tp.), k. in a., 6/5/17 (P. Spec. Co.).
Hill, Michael, 2/Lt. (Tp.), k. in a., 19/7/16 (3 Sig. Co.).
Hingston, Edward, Major, k. in a., 28/3/15.
Hingston, George Bennett, Lt.-Col., d. of w., 16/6/15.
Hislop, Robert Wallace, T/Lt. (A/Capt.), k. in a., 22/7/17 (251 Co.).
Hodgson, John, Lt. (Tp.), died, 16/11/18.
Hodgson, John Joseph, 2/Lt. (Tp.), k. in a., 13/8/17 (184 Tunn. Co.).
Hodson, Robert Charles, 2/Lt. (Tp.), k. in a., 8/5/17 (279 Rly. Co.).
Hogg, Clement Stuart, 2/Lt. (Tp.), d. of w., 6/4/17 (Z Spec. Co.).
Holbrow, Thomas Leonard Stanley, M.C., Capt., k. in a., 28/3/18 (156 Fld. Co.).
Holm, Frank Diederick, T/Lt., k. in a., 14/5/17 (and R.F.C., 27 Sqd.).
Holms, Andrew Stuart, T/Lt., k. in a., 1/7/16 (177 T. Co.).
Holt, Herbert Wilfred, 2/Lt., k. in a., 23/8/14.
Hopkinson, Hugh James Pearson, Lt. (Tp.), d. of w., 6/11/15.
Hopkinson, Rudolf Cecil, Lt., d. of w., 9/2/17 (12 Div. Cyc. Coy.).
Hopwood, Alan Clement, 2/Lt. (Tp.), d. of w., 18/9/18 (152 Fld. Co.).
Hopwood, Frederick Ernest, Lt. (Tp.), died, 26/10/18 (R.O.D.).
Hornby, Joseph Henry, Lt., k. in a., 7/11/18 (94 Fld. Co.).
Houston, William Wylie, 2/Lt. (Tp.), k. in a., 17/8/17 (226 Fld. Co.).
Howard, Eric Stanley, 2/Lt. (Tp.), k. in a., 18/5/17 (and R.F.C., 60 Sq.).

Howard, Frederic George, M.V.O., D.S.O., Major (T/Lt.-Col.), k. in a., 19/10/15.
Howard, John Turner, Lt. (Tp.), died, 18/6/18.
Huddleston, Purefoy Gauntlett, Capt., k. in a., 25/3/16.
Hughes, Owen, 2/Lt. (Tp.), k. in a., 30/11/15 (54 F. Co.).
Hunter, Nigel Duncan Ratcliffe, M.C., Capt., k. in a., 26/3/18 (228 F. Co.).
Hunter, Peter, 2/Lt. (Tp.), k. in a., 17/4/16.
Hutchinson, Edwin Octavius, Lt. (Tp.), d. of w., 21/9/18 (78 Fld. Co.).
Hutton, George Adolph, Lt., drowned, 19/9/14.
Inches, Robert Kirk, D.F.C., 2/Lt., k. in a., 26/8/18 (and R.A.F.).
Inglis, Alexander Alves, 2/Lt., k. in a., 26/9/16 (att. 126th F. Co.).
Inglis, John Alfred Pigon, Lt., k. in a., 26/9/15.
Ings, John Walter, Lt., k. in a., 18/9/18 (56th Field Co.).
Inman, Desmond Hague, Lt. (Tp.), k. in a., 17/2/17 (80th Field Co.).
Irvine, Francis Duncan, Major, k. in a., 1/5/15.
Irving, Aubrey Gordon, Lt., k. in a., 10/3/15 (att. R.F.C.).
Isherwood, Norman George, 2/Lt. (Tp.), k. in a., 8/10/15 (174 Tunnelling Co.).
Izat, Alan, M.C., Capt., k. in a., 2/1/17 (103rd Field Coy.).
Jackson, Alexander Maclean, M.C., Lt., d. of w., 27/4/17 (12th Fld. Coy.).
Jackson, M., Lt. and Qr.-Mr., died, 23/5/18 (3rd Army) (Spec. Coy.).
James, Baron Trevinnen, Lt. (T/Capt.), k. in a., 13/7/15 (att R.F.C.).
Jameson, Harold Gordon, 2/Lt., k. in a., 16/8/15.
Jenkins, Edward Tuberville Llewellin, Lt., d. of w., 25/7/16 (59th F. Co.).
Jenks, Alan Robert Constantine, M.C., T/Lt. (A/Major), k. in a., 31/7/17 (61st Field Co.).
Jervis, Robert Norrie, Lt. (Tp.), k. in a., 5/1/16 (83 Fd. Co.).
Jewell, Dudley Mark Hayward, 2/Lt. (Tp.), k. in a., 20/1/16 (att. 18th R. Fus.).
Johns, Arthur, 2/Lt. (Tp.), k. in a., 25/9/17 (183rd Tun. Coy.).
Johns, Stephen, 2/Lt. (Tp.), k. in a., 14/3/16 (255th Co.).
Johnson, Alfred William, M.C., T/Lt. (A/Capt.), d. of w., 17/4/18 (1st Fld. Survey).
V.C. Johnson, Frederick Henry, T/Cpt. (A/Maj.), d. of w., 26/11/17 (231 Field Co.).
Johnson, Richard Colling, Lt. (Tp.), k. in a., 31/7/17 (Spec. Coy.).
V.C. Johnston, William Henry, Major, k. in a., 8/6/15.
Jones, David John, M.C., 2/Lt. (Tp.), died, 4/12/16 (178th Tunn. Coy.).
Jones, Percy Griffith, 2/Lt., killed, 2/7/18 (and R.A.F.).
Jones, Watkin Morgan, Lt., k. in a., 29/3/18 (258th Tun. Co.).
Joseph, Jack Ben, 2/Lt. (Tp.), k. in a., 8/1/17 (185th Tun. Co.).
Joseph, Stewart Hugh, Lt. (A/Maj.), d. of w., 18/8/17 (227th Fld. Co.).
Jotcham, Fred, 2/Lt. (Tp.), d. of w., 27/9/18 (4 Spec. Coy.).
Keating, Harold Francis Amboor, Lt., k. in a., 28/6/18.
Keeble, Arthur Theodore, 2/Lt. (Tp.), d. of w., 28/6/17 (8th Sig. Co.).
Keiller, George William, Capt., died, 9/3/19
Kelly, Harry Holdsworth, Capt., k. in a., 24/10/14.
Kent, George Herbert Stanton, Capt., k. in a., 24/3/18 (490th Fld. Co.).
Kentish, Harold Edward, Capt., k. in a., 30/3/18 (281 Army Troops Coy.).
Keogh, Thomas, 2/Lt. (Tp.), died, 16/12/18 (I.W.T.).
Ker, Thomas Darling, 2/Lt., killed, 1/6/16.
Kerr, Alexander Crerar, 2/Lt. (Tp.), k. in a., 1/1/17 (91st Fd. Coy.).
Key, Douglas Polson, Lt., d. of w., 25/8/15.
Kidd, Alastair Wilson, Lt. (Tp.), died, 26/10/18 (1st Base Park Coy.).
Kidd, Cecil Christian, Capt. (Tp.), drowned, 28/2/18.
Killen, Edward Osborne Brice, Lt. (Tp.), k. in a., 15/1/17 (71st Fld. Co.).
Kimpton, Frank, T/Capt., died, 14/3/19.
King, Daniel Arthur, Lt. (Tp.), died, 22/7/17 (I.W.T.).
King, Victor Reginald, Lt. (Tp.), d. of w., 13/5/18 (att. R.E. Sig.).
King, William Albert de Courcy, D.S.O., Major (A/Lt.-Col.), k. in a., 27/5/17 (Div. Hqrs.).
Kinloch, James Moncrieff Thompson, 2/Lt., k. in a., 11/7/15.
Kirkaldy, John Givens, Capt., drowned, 13/8/18.
Knowles, V., Hon. Lt. & Q.-M., died, 14/10/15.
Knox, Andrew Ronald, 2/Lt. (Tp.), k. in a., 12/12/15 (185th Tunn. Coy.).
Kyle, David Logan, 2/Lt., k. in a., 19/5/15.
Labdon, Percy Miller, 2/Lt. (Tp.), k. in a., 26/9/17 (469th Fld. Co.).
Laidlaw, Walter Sibbald, Lt. (Tp.), k. in a., 23/11/17 (203rd Fld. Co.).
Lamb, John, 2/Lt. (Tp.), d. of w., 17/10/17 (179th Tunn. Coy.).
Lambert, Arnold Stuart, M.C., Lt. (A/Maj.), died, 25/12/18 (459th Fld. Co.).
Lamond, George Alexander Walker, Lt.-Col. (Tp.), died, 25/2/18 (I.W.T.).
Landrey, Cecil Thorpe, Lt. (Tp.), k. in a., 21/4/18 (251st Coy.).
Langdon, John Stafford, 2/Lt. (Tp.), died, 24/10/18 (I.W.T.).
Larking, Ronald Guy, M.C., Capt., killed, 1/4/18.
Latham, Arthur James, 2/Lt. (Tp.), died, 4/2/16 (185th Tun. Coy.).
Laurie, Donald Saunders, O.B.E., Capt., died, 11/2/19.
Lawledge, Francis Mott, 2/Lt., k. in a., 10/10/16 (att. R.F.C.).
Lawton, William Victor, Lt. (Tp.), died, 8/7/18 (No. 7 Pontoon Park).
Layard, Arthur Austen McGregor, Major, died, 5/6/17.
Leach, Walter John, 2/Lt. (Tp.), k. in a., 11/10/18 (4th Field Sur. Btn.).
Leak, Charles Henry, Capt. & Qr.-Mr., died, 24/9/17.
Learoyd, Digby Guy, Lt. (Tp.), died, 13/12/17 (I.W.T.).
Leckie, Walter Alan, Lt. (Tp.), d. of w., 21/2/16 (90th F.C.).
Lee, Charles Stuart, 2/Lt., k. in a., 30/12/15.
Lee, Leonard Bernard, 2/Lt., k. in a., 30/11/17 (83rd Fld. Coy.).
Leeming, James Arthur, O.B.E., Lt. (Tp.), died, 4/10/18.
Le Feuvre, Walter Tom, Lt. (Tp.), died, 8/1/17 (late 2nd Home Counties R.E., T.F.).
Lefroy, Francis Percival, 2/Lt., k. in a., 28/4/16.
Legg, Charles, 2/Lt. (Tp.), died, 15/9/18 (203rd Fd. Co.).
Leventhorpe, John Algernon, Lt., k. in a., 22/1/15.
Lewis, Alfred Drysdale, Lt. (Tp.), k. in a., 24/3/18 (62nd Fld. Co.).
Lewis, Cuthbert Preston, 2/Lt. (Tp.), k. in a., 8/6/17 (2 Spec. Coy.).
Lewis, Donald Swain, D.S.O., Lt.-Col. (Tp.), k. in a., 10/4/16 (and R.F.C.).
Lewis, Henry William, 2/Lt. (Tp.), k. in a., 12/10/18 (154th Fd. Co.).
Lewis, Wallenstein Ryan, M.C., Capt. (Tp.), d. of w., 25/3/18 (284th A.T. Co.).
Leyland, Herbert Edward, 2/Lt. (Tp.), d. of w., 17/10/17 (179th Tun. Coy.).
Liddell, John, Lt. (Tp.), k. in a., 30/3/18 (144th Army Troops Co.).
Limb, Harry, Lt. (Tp.) (A/Capt.), died, 23/10/18 (I.W.T.).
Lindsay, Alexander Cuthbert, Lt. (Tp.), died, 10/2/18 (I.W.T.).
Lindsay, Archibald Thurston Thomas, Lt., k. in a., 26/3/18 (R. Mon. R.E.) (7th A.T. Coy.).
Little, John, M.C., Capt., d. of w., 17/10/18 (90th Fld. Co.).
Littlewood, Charles William Stephen, M.C., 2/Lt., k. in a., 10/7/17 (7th Fd. Co.).
Livingstone, Robert, Lt. (Tp.), died, 10/11/16.
Lloyd, Wynell Hastings, 2/Lt. (Tp.), killed, 17/4/18 (123rd Fld. Co.).
Loam, Ernest Harold, 2/Lt. (Tp.), k. in a., 7/5/18 (56th Fld. Co.).
Long, Charles Percy, 2/Lt. (Tp.), k. in a., 13/4/17 (and R.F.C. 46th Sq.).
Lott, John English, M.C., 2/Lt. (Tp.), d. of w., 21/8/17 (4th Fld. Sur. Coy.).
Lovell, Charles Ernest, Lt. (Tp.), d. of w., 21/3/17 (62nd Fld. Co.).
Low, John Jackson, M.C., 2/Lt. (Tp.), k. in a., 3/12/17 (F. Spec. Coy.).
Lowson, Norman Coutie, M.C., Capt. (Tp.), d. of w., 6/3/17 (7th Div.).
Lundie, Robert Charles, D.S.O., Capt. (A/Maj.), k. in a., 15/10/18 (93rd Fld. Co.).
Lutener, George Arthur, 2/Lt. (Tp.), k. in a., 31/1/17 (15th Fld. Co.).
McAllister, Angus, Capt. (Tp.), died, 29/8/17.
McCahon, Robert, Lt., d. of w., 30/3/18 (69th Fld. Co. S.R.).
McClure, John Richard Smyth, T/Lt. (A/Capt.), died 29/10/18 (250th Tunn. Co.).
McCutchan, Frank Marsh, 2/Lt. (Tp.), d. of w., 14/5/17 (212 Fld. Co.).
McEnery, John Aloysius, Capt., killed, 26/10/14.
McFarlane, Robert George, 2/Lt. (Tp.), d. of w., 6/3/16 (177th Co.).
MacInnes, Duncan Sayre, C.M.G., D.S.O., Brig.-Gen., died, 23/5/18.
McIntyre, Frederick Malcolm, 2/Lt. (Tp.), d. of w., 2/5/16 (176th T. Co.).
McKay, Alexander Matheson, M.C., Lt. (Tp.), d. of w., 18/5/18 (179th Tun. Co.).
McKay, Henry Marshall, Capt., k. in a., 13/11/14.
Mackay, John Mitchell, 2/Lt. (Tp.), k. in a., 10/8/17 (130th Fld. Co.).
McKenzie, Arthur Murdo, M.C., T/Lt. (A/Capt.), died. 8/9/18 (6th Div. Sig. Coy.).
Mackreth, John, Lt. (Tp.), k. in a., 15/9/16.
McLaren, Samuel Bruce, Lt. (Tp.), d. of w., 13/8/16 (35th Div. Sig. Coy.).
MacLean, Alec Clarkson, Lt. (Tp.), k. in a., 9/4/18 (296th Rly. Coy.).
McLean, Robert, Lt. (Tp.), k. in a., 11/7/16 (76th Fld Co.).
McLeod, Roderick, Patterson, 2/Lt. (Tp.), died, 14/12/18.
McMurtrie, John, M.C., T/Capt. (A/Maj.), k. in a., 26/7/17 (151st Fld. Co.).
McNamara, Vincent, 2/Lt. (Tp.), died, 29/11/15.
Macnaught, Frederick Clement, Lt. (Tp.), k. in a., 25/9/15 (91st Fd. Co.).
McNeill, Alan Gordon, M.C., Capt. & Brev.-Maj., d. of w., 10/1/17 (2/2 W. Lanc. Fld. Coy.).
McShane, John Chesterton, 2/Lt. (Tp.), d. of w., 28/7/16 (229th Fd. Co.).
Maddox, Edward Harry, Temp. Lt., k. in a., 27/8/18 (18 Div. Sig. Co.).
Madore, William Douglas, 2/Lt. (A/Capt.), d. of w., 10/2/17 (254 Tunn. Co.).
Maguire, Henry, Temp. 2/Lt., d. of w., 15/7/16 (124 Coy.).
Main, John Alexander, M.C., Temp. Lieut., k. in a., 27/3/18 (278 Coy.).
Mainprise, Bertie Wilmot, Major, k. in a., 12/3/16 (att. H.Q. Bde.).

Mair, John Gordon, Temp. 2/Lt., d. of w., 5/8/18 (150 Fld. Co.).

Mais, Herbert Roxburgh, Temp. Lt., d. of w., 30/11/17 (70/Fld. Co.).

Malcolm, John Evelyn, Lt. (A/Capt.), died, 19/2/19 (271 Rail Co.).

Malcolm William Noel, 2/Lt., d. of w., 12/6/15.

Malloch, David, Temp. Lt., killed, 14/9/16 (Spec. Bde.).

Manisty, Henry Scott, M.C., Lt., k. in a., 1/10/17 (H.Q.).

Manley, John Dundas, 2/Lt., k. in a., 26/9/14 (Spec. Res.).

Mann, Arthur Longbottom, Temp. Capt., k. in a., 30/3/18 (328 Coy.).

Manners, James Herbert, Temp. 2/Lt., died, 28/6/17.

Manning, Robert Charles, D.S.O., M.C., Temp. Major, d. of w., 6/9/18 (170 Tunn. Co.).

V.C. Mannock, Edward, D.S.O., M.C., Major, k. in a., 26/7/18 (and R.A.F.).

Manser, William Edward, Major, died, 8/4/17.

March, Arthur John Jethro, Temp. 2/Lt., died, 24/10/18 (50 Div. Sig.).

Marriott, Stanley George, 2/Lt. (Tp.), k. in a., 21/10/16.

Marris, Horace Frost, M.C., Temp. Lt., d. of w., 12/12/17 (76 Fld. Coy.).

Marshall, Laurance Herbert, Temp. 2/Lt., d. of w., 22/4/18 (9/Fld. Coy.).

Marston, Guy Eric Millett, Temp. Lt., d. of w., 9/2/18 (130/Fld. Coy.).

Martin, Francis Henry, 2/Lt., k. in a., 24/11/17 (84 Fld. Coy.).

Martin, Rankin, Temp. 2/Lt., died, 12/7/18 (176 Coy.).

Martin, Reginald Poole, Temp. Lt., died, 2/12/18.

Mason, Wilfrid Howard, Temp. 2/Lt., k. in a., 9/3/17 (72 Fld. Coy.).

Mathew, C. V. D. Waynflete, Temp. 2/Lt., k. in a., 21/8/17 (48 Div. Sig. Coy.).

Mathewson, George Gillespie, Temp. Lt., k. in a., 27/3/18 (5/Fld. Sqd.).

Matthews, Mervyn, Lt., d. of w., 28/1/15.

Maxwell-Stuart, Edmund Joseph, Temp. Lt., k. in a., 26/4/16.

Mead, John Robert, Capt., died, 15/12/17 (335 Road Cons. Co.).

Meadowcroft, James. Temp. 2/Lt., died, 7/11/18 (476 Fld. Coy.).

Merts, Walter Scott, Temp. 2/Lt., died, 28/7/16.

Mettham, John Arthur, T/Lt. (A/Capt.), died, 12/11/18.

Meyer, James Leopold, Major, died, 22/6/17.

Micklewright, James, Temp. 2/Lt., k. in a., 3/11/18 (178 Tun. Coy.).

Miller, Bertram Charles St. Clair, 2/Lt., killed, 29/11/17 (and R.F.C.).

Miller, George Gibbs, Temp. Lt., died, 17/11/18.

Miller, Godfrey Lyall, 2/Lt., k. in a., 14/9/14.

Mills, Mansfeldt Charles Nightingale, 2/Lt. (Tp.), k. in a., 29/12/15.

Mitchell, Gordon. T/2/Lt., d. of w., 17/8/17 (96 Fld. Co.).

Mitchell, Patrick James, Temp. 2/Lt., d. of w., 17/8/17 (83 Fld. Coy.).

Mitchell, William, Temp. Lt., k. in a., 24/3/18 (41 Div. Sig. Co.).

Mitchison, William Anthony, Lt., k. in a., 20/9/17 (19/Div. Sig. Coy.).

Mitton, Thomas Ewart, Temp. Lt., killed, 24/12/17 (G.H.Q. Sig.).

Moakes, John Curtis, T/Lt., k. in a., 5/9/16 (155/Fld. Coy.).

Moffat, John Alexander, Temp. 2/Lt., d. of w., 11/8/18 (69 Fld. Coy.).

Moir, Reginald, Lt., died, 9/11/15 (Spec. Res.).

Molesworth, Ernest Kerr, Major, killed, 31/1/15 (att. 2/Sappers and Miners).

Momber, Edward Marie Felin, D.S.O., M.C., Capt., d. of w., 20/6/17 (177 Tun. Coy.).

Monteith, Matthew Rankin, 2/Lt., k. in a., 15/7/16.

Moore, Douglas Owen Milner, Capt., died, 23/4/18 (att. Railway Corps).

Moore, John O'Hara, Capt., d. of w., 28/12/14.

Moore, John William, Temp. Lt., k. in a., 27/8/18 (183 Fld. Coy.).

Moore, William Webb, A/Lt., d. of w., 12/6/18 (Z/Spec. Coy.).

Moores, Clive Guise, Capt., d. of w., 30/11/14.

Mordue, Alfred George, Temp. 2/Lt., d. of w., 8/7/17 (268 Coy.).

Morgan, Joseph, Temp. Lt., died, 6/10/18 (I.W.T.).

Morgan, James Melvin, Temp. 2/Lt., k. in a., 4/3/17.

Morgan, William Donal, Temp. 2/Lt., k. in a., 13/10/15.

Morley, John Killand Gulson, Lt., d. of w., 15/5/18 (E. Spec. Coy.).

Morse, Christopher, Temp. Lt., k. in a., 7/12/17 (178 Tun. Coy.)

Morton, William Ross, Col., died, 21/11/17.

Moseley, Henry Gwyn Jeffreys, Temp. 2/Lt., k. in a., 10/8/15.

Moss, John Stephen Noel, 2/Lt., died, 24/11/16 (57 Fd. Coy.).

Moss, Samuel Foden, M.M., Temp. 2/Lt., d. of w., 28/3/18 ("J" Spec. Coy.).

Mowbray, Maurice Charles, M.C., Lt., k. in a., 23/8/17 (89 Fld. Coy.).

Murly-Gotto, James, Lt. (Tp.), d. of w., 20/8/16 (70/F. Coy.).

Murphy, Philip Frederick, Temp. 2/Lt., k. in a., 2/7/16.

Murray, George Angus, Temp. Lt., k. in a., 4/10/18.

Musgrave, Herbert, D.S.O., Major, k. in a., 3/6/18 (Staff, 11/Cps. H.Q.).

Neville, Lionel John Neville, Capt., d. of w., 17/12/14.

Newcombe, John Carr, Temp. 2/Lt., k. in a., 21/3/18 (12/Fld. Coy.).

Newell, Charles, Temp. Capt., d. of w., 24/3/18 (3 Pontoon Park).

Newland, Arthur Kenyon, Temp. 2/Lt., d. of w., 21/11/17 (12/Coy.).

Niblett, Arthur Hilton, Temp. 2/Lt., d. of w., 21/9/16.

Nicholson, Winter, Temp. 2/Lt., d. of w., 16/3/17 (224 Coy.).

Nicklin, William, Temp. 2/Lt., d. of w., 24/8/16.

Niven, James, Temp. 2/Lt., k. in a., 3/5/17 (253 Tunn. Coy.).

Noad, P. H., Temp. Capt., died, 3/7/18.

Nolan, Maurice Edward, Temp. 2/Lt., d. of w., 25/9/15.

Norman, Edward John, Temp. 2/Lt., k. in a., 30/3/18 (156/Coy.).

Norman, Isaac Thomas Victor, 2/Lt., d. of w., 28/3/18 (121 Fld. Coy.).

Norris, Leslie Archibald, Temp. Lt., k. in a., 25/3/17 (att. R.F.C., 70/Sqd.).

North, Charles Napier, Major, k. in a., 1/11/14.

Norton, Frederick William, Temp. Capt., died, 14/10/16.

Nudds, Ronald Charles, Temp. 2/Lt., d. of w., 30/11/17 (219 Fld. Coy.).

Nuttle, James Edward, Temp. 2/Lt., died, 6/7/16.

Oakes, George Frederick Thomas, Capt., d. of w., 15/7/16 (130 Fld. Coy.).

Oakes, Samuel, Temp. 2/Lt., k. in a., 6/5/17 (Spec. Bde., "Z" Spec. Coy.).

Oates, Walter, M.C., Temp. 2/Lt., k. in a., 3/11/18 (218 Fld. Coy.).

O'Brien, William Bartholomew Stevenson, Temp. Lt. died, 18/6/18.

O'Brien, Walter Hubert, Major, killed, 7/2/17 (I.W.T.).

Odling, Eric Robert Meade, Lt., killed, 25/3/15.

O'Field, Alfred, Temp. 2/Lt., d. of w., 11/11/17 (10 Cps. Sigs.).

Oldham, Leslie William Searles, Major, k. in a., 28/7/15.

Olphert, Frederick John. Lt., d. of w., 19/5/18.

Ommanney, Rupert, Capt., killed in a., 31/10/14.

Orr, Alexander Thomas, T/Capt., died, 3/1/19.

Osborn, Gordon Chadwick, 2/Lt., k. in a., 18/4/15.

Osmaston, Oswald Camplyon Hutchinson, M.C., Lt., k. in a., 26/8/17 (12/Fld. Coy).

O'Sullivan, Thomas George, Temp. Lt., k. in a., 21/8/18 (4 Lt. Rly. Op Coy.).

Ouchterlony, John Palgrave Heathcote, D.S.O., Major, k. in a., 7/6/17 (102 Fld. Coy.)

Overton, Charles, 2/Lt., drowned, 20/5/17 (I.W.T.).

Owens, William Brabazon, Temp. 2/Lt., died, 25/6/16 (56 Fld. Coy.).

Painter, Albert Ernest, Temp. 2/Lt., d. of w., 14/4/17 (171 Tun. Coy.).

Palmer, David, Lt., died, 26/2/18 (I.W.T.).

Palmer, Geoffrey, Temp. 2/Lt., k. in a., 19/11/15.

Palmer, Herbert John, Lt. (Tp.), d. of w., 21/12/16 (121 Fld. Co.).

Pank, Adalbert Daniell, Lt., d. of w., 18/6/15 (22/Fd. Sqd.).

Panton, Arthur William, 2/Lt., k. in a., 3/9/16 (234 Fld. Coy.).

Papworth, Alfred Wyatt, Temp. 2/Lt., k. in a., 2/4/17 (129 Fld. Coy.).

Parkes, James Eric, 2/Lt., k. in a., 20/7/17 (69/Fld. Coy.).

Parkin, Joseph Henry, Temp. 2/Lt., k. in a., 18/6/17 (529 Fld. Coy).

Parkinson, Richard Frank, M.C., Capt., died, 7/11/18.

Parry, S., 2/Lt., killed, 3/5/18 (and R.A.F.).

Parsons, Douglas Montgomery, 2/Lt., k. in a., 10/3/15.

Paterson, William, Temp. 2/Lt., k. in a., 10/8/17 (92 Fld. Coy.).

Paterson, Wallace Campbell, 2/Lt. (Tp.), k. in a., 17/2/16.

Paton, John Marvin. 2/Lt., k in a., 21/3/18 (Div. Sig. Coy.)

Payn, Reginald Wallace, Capt., k. in a., 28/3/18 (253 Tun. Coy.).

Paynter, John, Temp. 2/Lt., k. in a., 8/10/15.

Peache, William Wynter, Lt., died, 3/12/14

Peacock, John Luddington, Lt. (Tp.), k. in a., 1/7/16 (150 Fld. Coy.).

Peacock, William Webster, Lt. (Tp.), k in a., 16/8/16 (224 Fld. Coy.).

Pearce, Henry Goold, M.C., T/Lt. (A/Capt.), k. in a., 15/7/17 (171 Tun Coy.)

Pearse, Samuel, Lt.-Col., died, 19/11/18.

Pelmore, Bernard Julius, Temp. Lt., k. in a., 18/7/17 (247 Fld Coy.).

Pengelley, Rowland Donald, Temp. 2/Lt., k. in a., 19/8/17 (153 Fld. Coy.)

Pengelly, Edgar Ambrose, Capt., d of w. 31/3/18 (213 Army Tps Coy.).

Pepper, Alwyn Tayton, Capt., died, 6/11/18 (22/Divn.).

Perrin, Thomas Frederick, Temp. Capt., died, 24/7/17 (I.W.T.)

Pettit, William Vaughan, Temp. 2/Lt., k. in a., 29/6/16 (173 T Coy.).

Phillips, Ernest James, Temp. 2/Lt., k. in a., 15/8/17 (170 Tun. Coy.).

Phillpotts, Brian Surtees. D.S.O., Major (A/Lt.-Col.), d. of w., 4/9/17 (38 Divn.).

Philpot, John, Temp. 2/Lt., k. in a., 25/2/16 (253 Coy.).

Picker, Herbert Francis, Lt., died, 23/5/17 (Sig. Coy.).

Pike, William Edward, Temp. 2/Lt., k. in a., 31/1/17 (77 Fld. Coy.).

Pitot, Maurice Leon, 2/Lt. d. of w., 8/10/18 (and R.A.F.).

Plant, Herbert Stanley, 2/Lt., died, 18/2/18 (181 Tun. Coy., 52/Inf. Bde.).

Pollard, Herbert Edward. Temp. Lt., k. in a., 26/6/17 (134 Army Tps. Coy).

Poole, John Evered. Temp. 2/Lt., d. of w., 22/8/17 (33/Fld. Coy.).

Potterton, William Hubert, Temp. Lt., k. in a., 24/7/16.

Pottinger, Charles Evan Roderick, Lt., d. of w., 11/5/15.

Potts, Henry Herbert, Temp. 2/Lt., d. of w., 31/7/17 (254 Tunn Coy.).
Poulter, Hugh Douglas Michael. 2/Lt., k. in a., 15/7/16 (68/Fld. Coy.).
Powell, Edward Darley, D.S.O., M.C., Major, k. in a., 1/9/18 (468 Fld. Coy.).
Powney, Joseph Thomas, Major, died, 18/12/14.
Pretyman, Maurice William, 2/Lt., k. in a., 12/8/15 (10 Sig. Coy.).
Priestman, Kenneth Mallorie, Temp. 2/Lt., k. in a., 31/8/16 (105 Fld. Coy.).
Procter, Herbert, Temp. 2/Lt., died, 11/11/17.
Quail, Henry Charles, Temp. 2/Lt., k. in a., 18/2/18 (124 Fld. Coy.).
Raine, Hubert, Temp. Lt., k. in a., 23/3/18 (202 Fld Coy.).
Rankin, William, Temp. Lt., k. in a., 18/2/18 (H.Q., VII. Cps.).
Raven Frederick Gifford. 2/Lt. (Tp.), d. of w., 24/3/17.
Rawlins, Guy Vernon Champion, T/Lt., died, 30/1/19 (att. Tank Cps.).
Rayment, Edward, Lt. (Tp.), died, 6/4/17 (I.W.T.).
Read, George Chisholm, 2/Lt., k. in a., 4/1/18 (att. R.F.C.).
Rebbeck, William Henry, M.C., Temp. Lt., died, 4/11/18 (50/Divn.).
Reece, F. B., Capt., d. of w., 20/4/18 (and R.A.F.).
Rees-Mogg, Louis Leyson, Lt., k. in a., 11/8/15.
Reeves-Smith, Denys, 2/Lt., k. in a., 2/10/15.
Reid, John Lindsay, T/2/Lt. (A/Capt.), d. of w., 18/10/17 (179 Tunn. Coy.).
Reid, Robert Logan, Temp. 2/Lt., k. in a., 8/8/15.
Reid, Robert Robertson, 2/Lt., d. of w., 13/7/16 (130 Co.).
Renny-Tailyour, Henry Frederick Thornton, 2/Lt., k. in a., 11/11/14.
Richardson, Charles Frederick James, Temp. Lt., k. in a., 23/3/18 (80 Fld. Coy.).
Richardson, Ernest Benbow, Temp. 2/Lt., died, 28/10/15 (67 Fld. Coy.).
Richardson, John Stanley, Capt., k. in a., 28/10/14.
Richardson, Thomas Charles, T/Major, d. of w., 4/2/16 (185 Tun. Coy.).
Ridley, Alfred Edwin, Temp. 2/Lt., died, 25/7/18 (I.W.T.).
Roach, Matthew, Temp. Capt., k. in a., 2/7/16 (255 Tun. Coy.).
Roberts, George Jewell, Temp. 2/Lt., d. of w., 17/6/16 (250 Coy.).
Roberts, Samuel, Hon. Capt., died, 6/12/14.
Robertson, Archibald Watson, Temp. 2/Lt., k. in a., 9/6/18.
Robinson, Arthur Gordon, 2/Lt. (Tp.), k. in a., 9/1/17 (Spec. Coy.).
Robinson, Arthur Linnell, T/2/Lt., d. of w., 25/2/16 (173 Tun. Coy.).
Robinson, Isaac Vincent, 2/Lt. (Tp.), k. in a., 14/7/17 (67/Fld. Coy.).
Robinson, Louis Francis Woodward, Lt. (Tp.), k. in a., 25/5/17.
Robson, Ralph George Griffiths, Capt., k. in a., 23/12/14.
Rodger, W., Lt., died, 1/11/18 (57th Fld. Coy.).
Rodwell, William Albert, M.C., 2/Lt. (Tp.), k. in a., 9/11/17 (171 Coy.).
Rogers, Edward, M.C., Capt. (A/Major), d. of w., 8/12/16 (67th Fld. Coy.).
Rogers, James Archibald, Lt., k. in a., 26/2/18.
Rogers, Maurice Croston, 2/Lt., d. of w., 25/2/15.
Rogers, Percy Arden, 2/Lt. (Tp.), k. in a., 27/5/18 (170th Tunn. Coy.).
Rohde, John Haughton, Lt., k. in a., 28/10/14.
Rooney, Richard James, Capt. (Tp.), d. of w., 19/9/17.
Rose, Launcelot St. Vincent, Major, k. in a., 27/11/14.
Ross, Arthur Justin, D.S.O., Major, killed, 2/8/17 (& R.F.C.).
Ross, John Alexander, 2/Lt. (Tp.), k. in a., 13/8/16 (178th T. Co.).
Rowley, Harold George, Lt., died, 17/3/16 (61st Fld. Coy.).
Rudd, Arnold. 2/Lt. (Tp.), k. in a., 27/3/18 (63rd Fld. Coy.).
Ruse, Edward Wallace, Lt., killed, 31/12/15.
Russell, Henry, 2/Lt., k. in a., 12/7/16 (7th Fld. Coy.).
Russell, Walter, Col., died, 4/4/17.
Saint, James Harcourt, 2/Lt. (Tp.), k. in a., 4/6/17 (428/Fld. Co.).
Sandeman, Charles Vaughan, 2/Lt. (Tp.), k. in a., 4/7/16 (184th T. Co.).
Sanders, Arthur Richard Careless, C.M.G., D.S.O., Major (Tp. Brig.-Gen.), k. in a., 20/9/18 (50/Inf. Bde.).
Sanders, Charles Phillips, 2/Lt. (Tp.), died, 15/9/18.
Sanderson, Clement Oliver St. John, M.C., Lt. (Tp.), k. in a., 27/4/18 (58th Inf. Bde.).
Sanderson, Francis William, Lt. (Tp.), k. in a., 2/9/16 (Spec. Bde.).
Sands, John William, M.C., Lt., killed (acc.), 20/5/18 (Sig. Coy.).
Sargeaunt, Arthur Frederick, Lt.-Col., k. in a., 31/7/15.
Sassoon, Hamo, 2/Lt. (Tp.), d. of w., 1/11/15.
Savage, Donaldson Lizars, 2/Lt., d. of w., 15/11/16 (56th Fld. Co.).
Savage, Edward Hugh Noel, Lt., k. in a., 29/6/18.
Sawyer, Frederick William Campion, Lt. (Tp.), d. of w., 4/4/17 (218/Fld. Co.).
Sayer, William Thomas, 2/Lt. (Tp.), k. in a., 5/6/16 (180/Fld. Co.).
Schneider, Herbert Hugo, Lt., k. in a., 5/12/14.
Scobie, John Angus Nicholson MacEwen, Lt., k. in a., 29/7/16.
Scott, Andrew Holmes, M.C., Capt., k. in a., 31/7/17.
Scott, Eric Bertrand Ralph, Lt. (Tp.), k. in a., 10/7/16 (25th S. Co.).
Scott, George Klaassen, Lt. (Tp.), k. in a., 24/2/17 (237 Fd. Co.).
Scott, James, 2/Lt. (Tp.), drowned, 26/2/18 (I.W.T.).
Scott, Lionel Keith, Lt. (Tp.), died, 4/7/16 (225 Fd. Co.).
Scott-Holmes, Henry Favil, 2/Lt. (Tp.), k. in a., 1/7/16 (208 Fd. Co.).
Scott-Smith, Eric Henry, 2/Lt., died, 29/10/15.
Scovell, Reginald Herbert, Capt., k. in a., 16/8/15.
Sealy, E. M. W., Capt., died, 25/12/15.
Searle, Alec, 2/Lt. (Tp.), k. in a., 23/4/17 (202 Fd. Co.).
Secker, Charles, Lt. (Tp.), d. of w., 4/11/18 (3 Spec. Co.).
Sellers, Thomas, 2/Lt. (Tp.), k. in a., 22/4/17 (173 Tunn. Co.).
Sellwood, John Dorey, 2/Lt., k. in a., 26/3/18 (2 Fd. Co.).
Selous-Jones, Jeffrey Fryer, 2/Lt. (Tp.), d. of w., 26/8/16.
Semple, Henry Spencer, M.C., Lt. (A/Major), k. in a., 5/9/17 (203 Fd. Co.).
Shannon, Cyril Richmond, Capt., k. in a., 4/10/15.
Shaw, Herman, Lt., d. of w., 26/4/17 (248 Fd. Co.).
Shaw, William Lindsay, M.C., T/Lt. (A/Major), k. in a., 16/4/18 (228 Fd. Co.).
Shenton, Austin Kirk, M.C., T/Lt. (A/Capt.), died, 26/7/18 (12 Sig. Co.).
Sibeth, Charles George Augustine, 2/Lt., k. in a., 9/8/15.
Sillars, Hugh, Lt., died, 19/2/19.
Simms, Alexander, Capt., drowned, 13/9/18.
Simon, Victor Herman, M.C., Major, k. in a., 5/6/17 (3 Fd. Sqd.).
Simonds, Charles Henville, M.C., Lt., d. of w., 29/4/18 (126 Fd. Co.).
Simpson, Douglas Richard, 2/Lt. (Tp.), k. in a., 28/9/18 (att. R.F.A., 108 Bde.).
Simpson, Jas. Cowie, 2/Lt. (Tp.), k. in a., 4/12/16 (174 Coy.).
Simpson, James Marsden, 2/Lt. (Tp.), k. in a., 9/5/16 (173 Coy.).
Sladen, C. St. B., Major, died, 2/9/17.
Slattery, Francis James, Lt. (A/Capt.), died, 9/1/19 (8 Fd. Co.).
Slight, William Hubert, 2/Lt. (Tp.), k. in a., 26/9/17 (212 Fd. Co.).
Smeathman, Julian Missenden, Lt., k. in a., 24/10/14.
Smith, Arthur Gilliat, Lt., k. in a., 1/11/14.
Smith, Cecil Ramsden, 2/Lt. (Tp.), k. in a., 12/6/17 ("M" Spec. Co.).
Smith, John Grant, Lt., died, 27/2/19.
Smith, Peter, Lt. (Tp.), k. in a., 28/4/17 (and R.F.C.).
Smith, Percy Kirk, 2/Lt. (Tp.), k. in a., 12/9/17 (212 Fd. Co.).
Smith, Ralph John, Lt. (Tp.), died, 31/7/18 (I.W.T.).
Smith, Wallace, 2/Lt. (Tp.), k. in a., 23/11/17 (129 Fd. Co.).
Smith, William Travers, 2/Lt., k. in a., 20/11/17 (174 Tunn. Co.).
Smythies, Ernest Dudley, Capt. (Tp.), died, 16/7/18.
Somerville, Richard Newman, 2/Lt. (T/Lt.), k. in a., 9/10/15 (94 Fd. Co.).
Soutar, Alexander Henderson, M.C., Lt. (A/Major), d. of w., 28/5/18 (98 Fd. Bty.).
Sparrow, Frank Edward, Lt. (Tp.), d. of w., 13/8/16 (129 Co.).
Starr, Philip Comfort, Lt., k. in a., 20/2/18 (154 Fd. Co.).
Steadman, William Milton, Capt. (Tp.), killed, 10/10/17 (I.W.T.).
Stephens, Thomas Alexander, 2/Lt. (Tp.), d. of w., 22/9/17 (250 Tunn. Co.).
Stephens, William Leslie, 2/Lt. (Tp.), died, 19/6/17 (143 Army Troop Coy.).
Stevens, Albert Charles, Capt. and Qr.-Mr., died, 21/5/17.
Stocker, Thomas Fuller, 2/Lt., k. in a., 19/5/15.
Stokes, Herbert George, 2/Lt. (Tp.), k. in a., 25/3/18 (77 Fd. Co.).
Stokes-Roberts, Edward Rowland Bennett, C.B., Brig.-Gen., died, 22/11/17 (H.Q., Baghdad).
Stoney, Francis George Duncan, Lt. (Tp.), d. of w., 25/8/16.
Story, George Ernest, Lt. (Tp.), died, 9/9/17 (297 Fd. Co.).
Stourton-Langdale, Edward Francis Joseph, Lt. (Tp.), k. in a., 5/10/16 (233 Fd. Co.).
Strachan, William Stead, Capt. (Tp.), k. in a., 18/2/18.
Strong, Cecil Verge, M.C., Lt. (A/Maj.), k. in a., 10/3/17 (15 Fd. Co.).
Strong, Edward George, 2/Lt., k. in a., 27/5/18 (15 Fd. Co.).
Sutton, Eustace Martin, Lt. (Tp.), k. in a., 24/3/18 (35 Div. Sig. Co.).
Swinburne, Thomas Anthony Stewart, D.S.O., Capt. (A/Major), k. in a., 1/4/18 (2 Fd. Co.).
Sydney, Herbert, Lt., died, 26/5/17 (I.W.T.).
Symons, Charles Leslie, 2/Lt., d. of w., 23/4/18 (63 Fd. Co.)
Tannett-Walker, Frederick William, Col., died, 6/3/17.
Tart, Cyril James, 2/Lt., k. in a., 1/7/16 (219 Fd. Co.).
Tayler, H. F., Lt. (Tp.), died, 8/11/18.
Taylor, Harry, T/Lt., k. in a., 27/2/16 (98 Fd. Co.).
Taylor, John, 2/Lt. (Tp.), d. of w., 13/5/17 (233 Fd. Co.).
Taylor, Philip Gustave Adolphe, 2/Lt. (Tp.), k. in a., 25/7/17 (171 Coy.).
Taylor, Robert Henry, 2/Lt. (Tp.), d. of w., 13/6/17 (102 Fd. Co.).
Terry, Harold Millard, 2/Lt. (Tp.), k. in a., 28/6/17 (4 Spec. Co.).
Theodore-Smith, Dennis, 2/Lt., k. in a., 30/8/15.
Thirlwell, Thomas Albert, Lt. (Tp.), d. of w., 1/10/17 (170 Fd. Co.).
Thomas, David Lewis, Lt. (Tp.), k. in a., 30/3/18 (253 Fd. Co.).
Thomas, Frank Hender, 2/Lt. (Tp.), k. in a., 1/10/15.
Thompson, Frederick Vivian, D.S.O., Major (T/Lt.-Col.), d. of w., 14/10/17 (att. 9 Essex R.).
Thomson, Ronald, 2/Lt. (Tp.), d. of w., 27/1/17 (185 Tunn. Co.).
Thorne. Charles Evered, M.C., T/2/Lt., d. of w., 16/8/17 (150 Fd. Co.).

Thornton, Francis Arthur, Capt. (Tp.), died, 18/11/17 (171 Tunn. Co.).
Thornton, John McLaren, T/Lt., k. In a., 20/1/16.
Tollemache, Arthur Henry William, 2/Lt., died, 19/7/16 (and R.F.C.).
Tomblings, E. H. G., Lt. (Tp.), died, 21/1/16.
Tongue, Walter Edward, Lt., died, 1/5/18.
Torin, Richard Maynard, Lt., k. in a., 24/4/15.
Tottenham, Charles Gordon Loftus, Capt., d. of w., 30/3/15.
Towlson, Albert John, 2/Lt. (Tp.), k. in a., 16/10/18 (122 Fd. Co.).
Townend, Francis William, Capt., d. of w., 29/3/15.
Trevor, Gruffydd Vaughan, Lt. (Tp.), died, 5/11/18 (256 Tunn. Co.).
Trevor, Harry Spottiswoode, Lt., k. in a., 15/8/15.
Trewby, Arthur, Lt., d. of w., 17/5/15.
Treweeke, Frank Lesley, 2/Lt. (Tp.), died, 7/11/16.
Tully, Thomas Michael, 2/Lt. (Tp.), died, 9/10/18 (I.W.T.).
Turner, William Rowland, M.C., Lt. (Tp.), d. of w., 10/11/17 (254 Tunn. Co.).
Tweedy, William Wildman, 2/Lt. (Tp.), k. in a., 27/5/18 (Workshops).
Twiss, Arthur Montague, Capt., k. in a., 17/11/14 (att. 3 Sap. and Min.).
Tyler, Albert, Lt., k. in a., 12/11/14.
Tyler, Alfred Herbert, Major, k. in a., 11/11/14.
Vallans, Thomas, 2/Lt., died, 28/4/19 (I.W.T.).
Vardy, Harold Henry, 2/Lt., died, 22/8/18.
Venn, Bertram Joseph, 2/Lt. (Tp.), killed, 11/7/17 (and R.F.C.).
Vernon, William Walter, 2/Lt., d. of w., 11/10/16 (90th Fld. Co.)
Verschoyle, Francis Stuart, 2/Lt., k. in a., 25/4/15 (R. Anglesey).
Vigers, Lancelot Leslie, 2/Lt. (Tp.), k. in a., 1/7/16 (30th Fld. Coy.).
Walcot, Basil, D.S.O., Major, died, 14/9/18.
Walford, W.G., Capt., k. in a., 4/11/18 (and R.A.F.).
Walker, Arthur Dunbar, Lt.-Col., k. in a., 26/3/18 (24th Div. H.Q.).
Walker, Percy Richard Samuel, 2/Lt., k. in a., 5/8/18 (103rd Fld. Coy.).
Walker, Reginald, Major, d. of w., 5/9/16 (105th F. Co.).
Walker, Reginald Selby, D.S.O., Lt.-Col., k. in a., 30/9/18 (VI. Corps H.Q.).
Wallace, William Edwin, 2/Lt. (Tp.), k. in a., 31/7/17 (254th Tun. Coy.).
Waner, Gerald Richard Francis, 2/Lt. (Tp.), d. of w., 2/3/17 (and R.F.C., 25th Sq.).
Ward, Henry Ernest, Lt., died, 13/12/18.
Ward, William Arthur Bayford Kirivan, Lt. (Tp.), d. of w., 2/8/15 (Sig. Ser.).
Ware, John Wilson, 2/Lt., k. in a., 10/7/16 (74th F. Co.).
Waterer, Michael Anthony, 2/Lt., d. of w., 11/10/18 (and R.A.F.).
Waterlow, Clive Maitland, Major (T/Lt.-Col.), killed, 20/7/17 (att. R.N.A.S.).
Watson, Douglas Christian, Capt. (Tp.), died, 16/6/16.
V.C. Watson, Thomas Colclough, Lt.-Col., died, 15/6/17.
Watt, Colin Robert Jamieson, 2/Lt. (Tp.), d. of w., 14/8/16 (212 Fld. Co.).
Webb, Philip Edward, 2/Lt. (Tp.), k. in a., 25/9/16 (59th F. Co.).
Weeks, Stephen Frederick, Lt. (Tp.), k. in a., 10/7/16 (130th F. Co.).
Wells, Guy Francy, Capt., d. of w., 15/6/15.
Wheater, Kenneth Ronald Maclaren, 2/Lt. (Tp.), k. in a., 6/5/17 (4th Spec. Bn.).
White, Francis Reginald, 2/Lt., d. of w., 23/1/17 (R.F.C., 10th Sq.).
Whitehead, Percy Neil, M.C., Capt., k. in a., 21/3/18 (174th Tunn. Co.).
Whitehouse, John Walter Glendenning, Lt., k. in a., 21/3/18 (156th Fd. Co.).
Whiteley, Edward Claude, Capt., k. in a., 14/4/15.
Whitfield, John Burrows, Lt., d. of w., 20/1/16.
Whitfield, Richard Houlbrook, Lt. (Tp.), k. in a., 12/5/16 (104th Fd. Coy.).
Whyte, John Francis, Capt., died, 20/10/18 (I.W.T.).
Wigfield, Joshua Biram Crossley, Lt., d. of w., 21/9/18 (74 Div. Sigs.).
Wildgoose, Ernest Henry, 2/Lt., k. in a., 22/3/18 (104 Co.).
Wilkinson, John Bright, Lt. (Tp.), d. of w., 23/6/16.
Wilkinson, John Laurence, 2/Lt. (Tp.), k. in a., 30/6/16 (173 T. Co.).
Wilkinson, Maurice Hewson, M.C., T/Lt. (A/Major), k. in a., 31/7/17 (177 T. Co.).
Williams, Albert Stanley Gabriel, T/Lt., k. in a., 28/10/17 (171 Tunn. Co.).
Williams, George Gabriel, Lt., died, 21/2/19 (Anti-Gas Sch., Etaples).
Williams, Raymond Burke, M.C., Capt. (Tp.), k. in a., 19/9/16 (176 Tunn. Co.).
Williamson, Andrew, Major, k. in a., 21/3/18 (12 Fld. Co.).
Williamson, Charles Percival, Lt., k. in a., 12/3/17 (56 Fld. Co.).
Willis, Justin Charles, M.C., Major, d. of w., 7/8/18 (18 Div. Sig. Co.).
Wills, Robert George, M.C., 2/Lt., died, 3/12/18.
Wilson, Allan, Lt. (Tp.), died, 25/8/15 (79 Fld. Co.).
Wilson, Geoffrey Hutton, Lt., died, 23/12/18.
Wilson, John Furnevall, T/Lt., k. in a., 29/9/16 (9 Fld. Co.).
Wilson, Thomas, M.C., T/Lt., k. in a., 29/6/17.
Wingate, Malcolm Roy, D.S.O., M.C., Capt., Bt.-Major, k. in a., 21/3/18 (459 Co.).
Wilson, Wilfred Gordon, M.B.E., Capt. (Tp.), died, 10/12/18.
Winter, Wilfred Ormond, D.S.O., Capt. (A/Major), died, 30/11/18.
Wintersgill, Gerald Walker, Lt., died, 26/11/18.
Wise, Arnold Vincent Denys, M.C., Lt. (A/Capt.), k. in a., 15/5/17 (2 Fld. Co.).
Woods, Alexander Richard Rolleston, Lt., k. in a., 6/7/15.
Wraith, Alfred Osborn, T/Lt. (A/Major), d. of w., 13/6/17 (254 Co.).
Wright, Stanley, M.C., 2/Lt., k. in a., 24/10/17 (att. R.F.C.).
V.C. Wright, Theodore, Capt., k. in a., 14/9/14
Wrigley, Ralph Mortimer, Lt., died, 6/11/18 (R. Mon. Eng.).
Wroughton, John Henry Theodore, Lt., d. of w., 9/5/18 (136 Co.).
Wynne-Jones, Morys, Lt., k. in a., 29/10/14.
Yearsley, Hubert Abram, 2/Lt., k. in a., 9/4/18 (79 Fld. Co.).
Young, James, Lt., k. in a., 5/4/18 (258 Co.).
Young, Sydney Vernon, 2/Lt., d. of w., 25/9/15.
Yule, George Udney, D.S.O., Lt.-Col., died, 22/12/18.

Grenadier Guards.

4 Abbey, Noel Roland, Lt., k. in a., 12/4/18.
2 Adams, Charles John Norman, 2/Lt., d. of w., 14/11/18.
1 Alexander, Harry, 2/Lt., k. in a., 17/10/15 (Spec. Res.).
1 Anderson, Alec David, 2/Lt., k. in a., 6/11/18.
3 Anson, Arthur, Lt., k. in a., 8/10/15.
1 Antrobus, Edmund, Lt., k. in a., 24/10/14.
2 Arbuthnot, Gerald Archibald, Lt., k. in a., 25/9/16 (Spec. Res.).
2 Arbuthnot, John, Lt. (Tp.), d. of w., 18/9/16.
3 Asquith, Raymond, Lt., d. of w., 15/9/16 (Spec. Res.).
Ayles, F. P., Lt., died, 1/6/18 (and R.A.F.).
Bailey, Hon. Gerald Sergison, 2/Lt., k. in a., 10/8/15 (att. 2nd Bn.) (Spec. Res.).
1 Baker, Cecil Douglas, Lt., k. in a., 29/7/17 (Spec. Res.).
1 Barber, George Edward, 2/Lt., k. in a., 24/8/18.
Barrington-Kennett, Basil Herbert, Bt.-Major, killed, 18/5/15 (att. R.F.C.).
2 Beaumont-Nesbitt, Wilfrid Henry, M.C., Lt. (A/Capt.), k. in a., 27/11/17.
Bentley, Frederick Donald, 2/Lt., k. in a., 30/11/17 (att. 1 Gds. M.G.C.).
1 Biddy, John Pengelly, Lt., k. in a., 12/10/17.
1 Bird, H., Lt., died, 12/4/19 (att. K.A.R.).
3 Bowes-Lyon, Gavin Patrick, Lt., k. in a., 27/11/17.
Boyton, Henry James, Lt., k. in a., 14/12/16.
Bradbourne, Wyndham Wentworth (Lord), Capt., k. in a., 11/3/15 (Spec. Res.).
4 Burke, John Bernard Mary, M.C., Capt., d. of w., 1/12/17.
Burnand, Cyril Francis, 2/Lt., k. in a., 11/3/15 (Spec. Res.).
Burton, John Stanley, 2/Lt., k. in a., 16/5/16 (att. 2nd Bn.) (Spec. Res.).
2 Bury, Harold Sterndale Entwisle, 2/Lt., k. in a., 25/1/15 (Spec. Res.).
1 Byng, Leonard Gustav, M.C., Lt., d. of w., 24/8/18.
1 Carson, Richard Hartley, 2/Lt., d. of w., 4/9/17.
1 Carter, James Shuckburgh, Lt. (A/Capt.), k. in a., 27/9/18.
2 Cecil, George Edward, 2/Lt., k. in a., 13/9/14.
2 Cecil, Hon. William Amherst, Capt., k. in a., 16/9/14.
Chamberlain, Norman Gwynne, Lt., k. in a., 1/12/17.
4 Chapman, Michael, M.C., Lt., k. in a., 12/4/18.
1 Chapple, James Walter, 2/Lt., d. of w., 31/7/17.
Charteris, Hon. Ivo Alan, 2/Lt., k. in a., 17/10/15 (att. 1st Bn.) (Spec. Res.).
4 Chitty, James Malcolm, 2/Lt., k. in a., 1/12/17.
Cholmeley, Hugh Valentine, 2/Lt., k. in a., 7/4/16 (Spec. Res.).
2 Cholmeley, Bart., Sir Montague Aubrey Rowley, Capt., k. in a., 24/12/14 (Res. of Off.).
1 Clive, Percy Archer, ~~D.S.O.~~, Lt.-Col. (Tp.), k. in a., 5/4/18 (att. 1/5 Lan. Fus.).
1 Colby, Laurence Robert Vaughan, Major, k. in a., 24/10/14.
Congleton, Henry Bligh Fortescue (Lord), Lt., k. in a., 10/11/14.
4 Constable, Douglas Oliphant, Lt., k. in a., 25/9/16 (Spec. Res.).
2 Corkran, Reginald Seymour, 2/Lt., d. of w., 15/6/15 (Spec. Res.).
1 Corry, Armar Valentine Lowry, M.C., Lt., k. in a., 12/9/16.
Cottle, Walter Edward Worsdale, Lt., k. in a., 31/7/17 (att. 1 Gds. Bde. M.G. Coy.).
3 Crabbe, Campbell Tempest Eyre, Lt., k. in a., 27/9/15.
Creed, Charles Odell, 2/Lt., d. of w., 2/6/15 (Spec. Res.).
Crisp, Francis Edward FitzJohn, 2/Lt., k. in a., 5/1/15.
2 Cuninghame, Alfred Keith Smith, Capt. (Tp.), k. in a., 25/9/16.
Darby, Maurice Alfred Alexander, Lt., k. in a., 11/3/15.
1 Dashwood, Wilfred James, Lt., d. of w., 2/8/17.
4 Dawson-Greene, Charles John, 2/Lt., d. of w., 23/4/18.
4 Denman, Richard Charles, Lt., k. in a., 1/12/17.
4 Derriman, Gerard Lysley, Capt., d. of w., 7/8/15 (Res. of Off.).
Des-Voeux, Frederick William, Lt., k. in a., 14/9/14.
1 Douglas-Pennant, Hon. Alan George Sholto, Lt., k. in a., 29/10/14.
Douglas-Pennant, Hon. George Henry, Capt., k. in a., 11/3/15 (Res. of Off.).
1 Drury-Lowe, William Drury, D.S.O., Lt.-Col. (Tp.), k. in a., 25/9/16.
1 Duberly, Grey William, Major, k. in a., 13/3/15 (Res. of Off.).
3 Dunlop, Brian John, 2/Lt., k. in a., 31/7/17.
3 Durban, Percy, 2/Lt., k. in a., 25/3/18.
4 Ellice, Andrew Robert, Lt., d. of w., 29/9/16 (Spec. Res.).

Ethelston, Herbert Wicksted, Lt., k. in a., 14/3/15.
4 Farquhar, Rupert, M.C., Lt., d. of w., 17/9/17.
4 Filmer, Sir Robert Marcus, Bart, Capt. (Tp.), d. of w., 27/1/16.
3 Filmer-Strangeways-Rogers, Arthur Edmund, 2/Lt., d. of w., 4/11/18.
2 Finch, Hugh Adair, 2/Lt., k. in a., 27/8/18.
1 Fisher-Rowe, Laurence Rowe, Lt.-Col., d. of w., 12/3/15.
1 Fleet, William Alexander, 2/Lt., k. in a., 18/5/18.
2 Fletcher, Gareth Hamilton, 2/Lt., k. in a., 25/1/15 (Spec. Res.).
4 Flower, Alfred Chegwin, Lt., k. in a., 25/9/16 (Spec. Res.).
Foster, Arthur Cedric, 2/Lt., d. of w., 12/3/15 (Spec. Res.).
Fraser, John Courtenay, M.C., Lt., drowned, 9/9/18 (att. Gds. M.G.C.).
2 Gardner, Cyril Gower, Lt., k. in a., 14/9/16.
1 Gascoigne, Ivo Clifton, Lt., d. of w., 12/4/18.
4 Gault, Robert Anderson, Lt., k. in a., 16/9/16 (Spec. Res.).
Gelderd-Somervell, Roger Frederick Churchill, 2/Lt., d. of w., 13/3/15 (Spec. Res.).
Gordon-Lennox, Lord Bernard Charles, Major, k. in a., 10/11/14.
4 Goschen, Christopher Gerard, Capt. (Tp.), k. in a., 25/9/16 (Spec. Res.).
Gosselin, Alwyn Bertram Robert Raphael, D.S.O., Capt., k. in a., 7/2/15.
1 Graham, Alexander Cecil, Capt., k. in a., 10/9/16 (Spec. Res.).
1 Grant, Alexander, 2/Lt., k. in a., 27/9/18.
3 Greenhill, Frederick William Ridge, Lt., k. in a., 10/10/17.
3 Gunnis, Geoffrey George, M.C., Capt. (Tp.), d. of w., 13/10/16.
2 Gunnis, Ian Fitzgerald Stuart, 2/Lt., k. in a., 4/7/17.
3 Gunther, Geoffrey Robert M.C., 2/Lt., k. in a., 4/11/18.
2 Gwyer, Cyril, Lt., k. in a., 27/8/18.
1 Hall-Watt, Richard, 2/Lt., k. in a., 13/10/17.
1 Hamilton, George Edward Archibald FitzGeorge, 2/Lt., k. in a., 18/5/18.
Hamilton-Temple-Blackwood, Lord Ion Basil Gawen Temple, Lt., died, 4/7/17 (P. of W.).
2 Harbord, Philip Anthony Aschton, M.C., Lt., d. of w., 1/12/17.
1 Hargreaves, Sydney Jasper, 2/Lt., d. of w., 19/5/18.
Harter, Herbert Hatfield, Lt., k. in a., 9/10/17 (att. 2 M.G. Gds.).
2 Harvard, Kenneth O'Gorman, Lt., k. in a., 1/8/17.
1 Harvard, Lionel de Jersey, Lt. (A/Capt.), k. in a., 30/3/18.
2 Harvey, Douglas, Lt. (Tp.), k. in a., 27/3/18.
Hasler, Algernon, 2/Lt., d. of w., 18/9/16 (att. 2nd Bn.) (Spec. Res.).
Higginson, Thomas Cecil, Lt., k. in a., 15/9/16 (M.G.C.) (Spec. Res.)
1 Hoare, Edward, 2/Lt., k. in a., 9/5/16 (Spec. Res.).
Hope, George Everard, M.C., Lt.-Col., k. in a., 10/10/17 (att. 1/8 Lancs Fus.).
Hopley, Geoffrey William Vanderbyl, 2/Lt., d. of w., 18/5/15 (Spec. Res.).
4 Houstoun-Boswall, Sir George Reginald, Bart., Capt., k. in a., 27/9/15 (Res. of Off.).
4 Hubbard, Bertram John, M.C., 2/Lt., k. in a., 1/12/17.
1 Hughes, Geoffrey, Lt., d. of w., 5/8/18.
3 Jackson, George Dewar, 2/Lt., k. in a., 14/9/16.
1 Johnson, Harold George, Lt., k. in a., 7/8/17.
4 Joicey-Cecil, John Francis James, Lt., k. in a., 25/9/16.
1 King, Eric George Lauder, Lt., k. in a., 22/7/17.
2 Knatchbull-Hugessen, Maurice Astley, M.C., Lt., k. in a., 25/9/16 (Spec. Res.).
1 Lamont, Geoffrey Simpson, D.S.O., 2/Lt., k. in a., 5/11/18.
Lang, Arthur Horace, 2/Lt., k. in a., 25-26/1/15.
2 Langley, Francis Jasper, 2/Lt., k. in a., 27/8/18.
2 Lawrence, Guy Francis, Lt., k. in a., 27/8/18.
2 Lawson-Johnston, Arthur McWilliam, M.C., Lt., d. of w., 22/2/17.
Lee-Steers, John Henry Gordon, Lt., k. in a., 17/11/14.
Leeke, Charles, Lt., d. of w., 11/4/16 (M.G. Coy., Spec. Res.).
2 Lloyd, Marteine Kemes Arundel, Capt., k. in a., 15/9/16 (Spec. Res.).
2 Lubbock, Hon. Harold Fox Pitt, Lt., k. in a., 4/4/18.
4 Ludlow, Ernest, M.C., Capt., killed, 16/2/18.
4 Lyon, Francis Charles, Lt., k. in a., 13/4/18.
2 Macdougall, Ian, Capt., k. in a., 13/9/14.
Mackenzie, Alan Keith, Capt., d. of w., 16/9/16.
4 Maclear, Basil George Hope, 2/Lt., k. in a., 26/7/16.
1 Malcolm, Pulteney, Lt. (A/Capt.), k. in a., 25/8/18.
Manners, Hon. John Neville, Lt., k. in a., 1/9/14.
Marshall, Frederick Guy, Lt., k. in a., 22/3/15.
1 Mays, Cecil Clarence, 2/Lt., k. in a., 30/3/18.
2 Miller, Frederick William Joseph MacDonald, Lt., k. in a., 24/10/14.
1 Miller, Walter Roy, 2/Lt., k. in a., 15/9/18 (att. 4 Gds. M.G.R.).
Montgomerie, George Frederick Molyneux, Major, k. in a., 22/10/15 (Res. of Off.) (att. 3rd Bn.).
1 Morris, Alfred Ashurst, Lt., k. in a., 27/9/18
5 Murray, William Raymond Croft, Capt., died, 25/2/17.
2 Napier, Rupert George Carrington, Lt., d. of w., 2/8/17.
1 Neale, Guy Dalrymple, 2/Lt., d. of w., 18/5/18.
Nevill, John Henry Caxthorne, 2/Lt., k. in a., 24/12/14 (Spec. Res.).
Nicol, Wilfred Edward, D.S.O., Major, d. of w., 1/10/15.
2 Oliver, Roderick Magrath, Lt., k. in a., 27/8/18.
2 Orriss, Walter Gerald, Lt., d. of w., 29/3/18.
3 Osborne, Brian Riversdale, M.C. 2/Lt. (Tp.), k. in a., 4/11/18
3 Parker, Ralph Windsor, Capt., d. of w., 28/3/18.
Parnell, William Alastair Damer, M.C., Hon. Lt., k. in a., 25/9/16 (att. 2nd Bn.) (Spec. Res.).
4 V.C. Paton, George Henry Tatham, M.C., Lt. (A/Capt.), k. in a., 1/12/17.
3 Pauling, George Francis, M.C., Lt., k. in a., 25/3/18.
4 Payne-Gallwey, Maurice Hilton Frankland, Lt., k. in a., 25/9/16 (Spec. Res.).
Payne-Gallwey, William Thomas, M.V.O., Capt., k. in a., 14/9/14.
4 Pearce, Nathaniel Arthur, Lt., k. in a., 25/11/17.
2 Pearson, Stephen Hetley, 2/Lt., k. in a., 1/12/17.
4 Penn, Eric Frank, 2/Lt. (T/Capt.), k. in a., 18/10/15.
Phillipps, Reginald William, 2/Lt., k. in a., 26/10/15 (Spec. Res.) (att. 1st Bn.).
2 Pickersgill-Cunliffe, John Reynolds, 2/Lt., k. in a., 14/9/14.
4 Pixley, John Nicol Fergusson, Lt. (A/Capt.), k. in a., 12/10/17.
Ponsonby, Hon. Cyril Myles Brabazon, M.V.O., Major, k. in a., 27/9/15.
2 Ponsonby, Michael Henry, Lt., d. of w., 27/8/18.
4 V.C. Pryce, Thomas Tannatt, M.C., Capt., k. in a., 13/4/18.
Radcliffe, Dering John Jasper, Lt., killed, 31/10/17.
3 Ramney, Reginald Van Taerling, Lt., d. of w., 28/3/18.
4 Richardson, Raymond Driver, 2/Lt., d. of w., 26/4/18.
Rennie, Guy, Capt., k. in a., 26/10/14.
1 Rocke, Charles Owen, 2/Lt., k. in a., 23/8/18.
4 Rolfe, Raymond Harold, Lt., k. in a., 23/4/18.
3 Roper, William Horace Stanley, 2/Lt., d. of w., 11/10/17.
Sartorius, Euston Francis Frederick, Capt., d. of w., 5/4/15.
1 Shelley, Ernest Bowen, Lt. (A/Capt.), k. in a., 12/9/18.
1 Sim, Lancelot George Earle, 2/Lt., k. in a., 14/9/16 (Spec. Res.).
4 Sloane-Stanley, Humphrey Henry, M.C., Lt. (A/Capt.), k. in a., 13/4/18.
Smith, Charles Jervoise Dudley, 2/Lt., k. in a., 16/6/15.
Smith, Wilfred Robert Abel, C.M.G., Lt.-Col., d. of w., 19/5/15.
1 Somerset, Norman Arthur Henry, 2/Lt., k. in a., 25/10/14.
3 Stainton, Walter Adam, Lt., k. in a., 14/9/16.
3 Stanhope, Hon. Richard Philip, Capt., k. in a., 16/9/16 (Spec. Res.).
2 Stephen, Douglas Clinton Leslie, Capt., d. of w., 10/9/14.
Stewart, Howard William, 2/Lt., k. in a., 27/8/18 (att. 4 Gds. M.G. Rgt.).
Stewart, William Alfred Lindsay, M.C., Capt., k. in a., 25/9/16 (att. 4th).
2 Stocks, Michael George, Lt., k. in a., 10/11/14.
2 Stratford, Herbert Douglas, 2/Lt., d. of w., 13/4/18.
1 Stucley, Humphrey St. Leger, Major, k. in a., 30/10/14
2 Symes-Thompson, Cholmeley, Capt., k. in a., 17/11/14.
4 Tennant, Hon. Edward Wyndham, Lt., k. in a., 22/9/16.
3 Tetley, John Christopher Dodsworth, Lt., k. in a., 9/10/17.
Thomas, Oscar Clifford, Lt., k. in a., 1/12/17 (att. 1 Gds. Bde. M.G.C.).
Thompson, Ronald Fawcett Carrier, 2/Lt., k. in a., 11/9/16 (Spec. Res., att. 4 Bn.).
Thorne, Thomas Fleetwood Joseph Nicol, Capt., k. in a., 27/9/15.
1 Thrupp, Maurice, Lt., k. in a., 31/7/17.
Tompson, Alan Hawtree, 2/Lt., k. in a., 27/9/15 (Spec. Res., att. 4 Bn.).
2 Tudway, Hervey Robert Charles, Lt., d. of w., 18/11/14.
Tufnell, Carlton Wyndham, Lt., k. in a., 6/11/14.
Trotter, Edward Henry, D.S.O., Lt.-Col. (Tp.), k. in a., 8/7/16 (att. 18 L'pool R.).
Van Neck, Philip, Lt., k. in a., 26/10/14.
2 Vereker, Robert Humphrey Medlicott, 2/Lt., k. in a., 25/8/14.
Vernon, Herbert Douglas, Lt., k. in a., 15/9/16 (M.G.C.).
Wakeman, Edward Offley Rouse, 2/Lt., k. in a., 15/5/15 (Spec. Res., att. 1st Bn.).
Walter, Sydney, 2/Lt., k. in a., 25/10/14.
1 Warner, Arnold Ashton Justice, 2/Lt., k. in a., 24/8/18.
3 Webster, Godfrey Vassall George Augustus, Lt., k. in a., 4/8/17.
Welby, Richard William Gregory, Lt., k. in a., 16/9/14.
1 Weld-Forester, Hon. Arthur Orlando Wolstan Cecil, M.V.O., Major, d. of w., 1/11/14.
Wellesley, Lord Richard, Capt., k. in a., 30/10/14.
2 White, Hugh, 2/Lt., k. in a., 27/8/18.
Williams, Edward Gordon, Lt., k. in a., 12/8/15 (Spec. Res., att. 2nd Bn.).
Williams, Robert, 2/Lt., k. in a., 8/10/15 (Spec. Res., att 3rd Bn.).
4 Windeler, Herbert Wheelwright, Lt., k. in a., 28/11/17.
3 Worsley, Evelyn Godfrey, 2/Lt., d. of w., 17/9/17.
3 Worsley, John Fortescue, Lt., k. in a., 27/11/17.
3 Wynne, Edward Henry John, Lt., d. of w., 16/9/16.

Coldstream Guards.

3 Abrahams, Arthur Charles Lionel, Lt., k. in a., 13/4/18.
1 Adeane, Henry Robert Augustus, Capt., k. in a., 2/11/14.
1 Agar-Robartes, Hon. Thomas Charles Reginald, Lt. (Tp.) (A/Capt.), d. of w., 30/9/15.
Armstrong, George Carlyon, 2/Lt., k. in a., 25/1/15 (att. 1/Bn.).
3 Babington, Ralph Vivian, 2/Lt., k. in a., 9/10/17.
Banbury, Charles William, Capt., k. in a., 16/9/14.
1 Baring, Hon. Guy Victor, T/Lt.-Col., k. in a., 15/9/16.
1 Barnsley, Thomas Kenneth, Capt., k. in a., 31/7/17.
Barttelot, Sir Walter Balfour (Bart.), D.S.O., Major (Bt.-Lt.-Col.), killed, 23/10/18.
Beauchamp, Edward Archibald, 2/Lt., d. of w., 22/12/14.
Bentinck, Henry Duncan, Major (Brevet), d. of w., 2/10/16.
Berkeley, Christopher, Lt., killed, 30/1/19 (and R.A.F.).
Bewicke-Copley, Redvers Lionel Calverly, Capt., k. in a., 21/12/16.
Bingham, David Cecil, Lt., k. in a., 14/9/14.

Blacker, John Robin, 2/Lt., k. in a., 28/9/15.
Bonvalot, Edward St. Laurent, 2/Lt., d. of w., 9/10/15 (att. 2/Bn.).
Boscawen, Hon. Vere Douglas, 2/Lt., k. in a., 29/10/14.
1 Bovill, Charles Harry, Lt., d. of w., 24/3/18.
2 Boycott, Harold Charlton, Lt., d. of w., 21/3/18.
Brabazon, Hon. Ernest William Maitland Molyneux, D.S.O., Capt., k. in a., 17/6/15.
2 Brassey, Gerard Charles, 2/Lt., k. in a., 27/8/18.
4 Brenchley, John, M.C., 2/Lt., k. in a., 12/10/17.
2 Brocklebank, Bertram Vincent, Lt., k. in a., 1/8/17.
Brown, Gordon Hargreaves, Capt., k. in a., 29/10/14.
Browne, Hon. Maurice Henry Dermot, Lt., k. in a., 29/9/15.
2 Burn, Hugh Henry, M.C., Capt. (Tp.), d. of w., 16/9/16.
1 Burton, Stephen John, Major, k. in a., 28/7/17.
2 Butler, John Henry Rippon, 2/Lt., d. of w., 16/9/16.
2 Buxton, Hon. Denis Bertram Sydney, 2/Lt., k. in a., 9/10/17.
2 Caldwell, Gavin Ralston Mure, Lt., k. in a., 9/10/18.
Campbell, Allan William George, Lt., d. of w., 20/9/14.
Campbell, Donald, Lt., k. in a., 19/7/16.
Campbell, Geoffrey Arthur, Lt., k. in a., 29/10/14.
Campbell, Hon. John Beresford, D.S.O., Capt., k. in a., 25/1/15.
Carter-Wood, Joseph Alan, Lt., k. in a., 1/2/15.
Chance, Eustace George St. Clair, 2/Lt., k. in a., 27/9/18.
Chinnery, Esme Fairfax, Capt., killed, 18/1/15 (and R.F.C.).
1 Christy, Basil Robert Francis, 2/Lt., d. of w., 3/10/16.
1 Clark, Neville Arthur, Lt., d. of w., 28/11/17.
2 Clerke, Francis William Talbot, Lt., k. in a., 21-26/9/16.
Clifton, Harold Norton, 2/Lt., d. of w., 1/2/15.
1 Coleridge, Luke Frederick Rennell, 2/Lt., k. in a., 22/12/14.
Corbet, Sir Roland James (Bart.), Lt., k. in a., 15/4/15.
Cottrell-Dormer, Charles Melville, D.S.O., Lt., d. of w., 8/2/15.
2 Cromie, Samuel Osborne, Lt., d. of w., 17/11/16.
1 Crosse, Edward Arthur Willson, 2/Lt., k. in a., 27/9/18.
3 Cubitt, Henry Archibald, Capt., k. in a., 15/9/16.
Dawson, Richard Long, Capt., k. in a., 20/11/14.
De Winton, Walter, 2/Lt., k. in a., 6/9/14.
1 Dilberoglue, Richard Nicholas, Lt., k. in a., 15/9/16.
3 Dillwyn-Venables-Llewelyn, John Lister, Capt., k. in a., 10/7/17.
1 Dixson, Thomas Storie, Lt., killed, 8/12/16.
Douglas-Pennant, Hon. Charles, Lt., k. in a., 29/10/14.
2 Drummond, Robert Charles Crosbie, 2/Lt., k. in a., 28/11/17.
2 Edmonstone, William George, k. in a., 14-16/9/16.
Egerton, Arthur George Edward (Tp. Lt.-Col.), Major, k. in a., 29/9/15.
1 Fair, James Conroy, 2/Lt., k. in a., 25/9/15.
Farquhar, Francis Douglas, D.S.O., Lt.-Col., k. in a., 20/3/15 (att. Princess Pat. Can. L.I.).
2 Fielding, Hon. Henry Simon, Lt. (Act. Capt.), d. of w., 9/10/17.
Fellowes, Rupert Caldwell Butler, Lt. (Act. Capt.), k. in a., 21/8/18.
Fergusson, Robert Allan Arklay, Lt. (Act. Capt.), k. in a., 14/9/16.
Fisher-Smith, Alan Archibald, Lt., k. in a., 1/8/17 (att. 1/Gds. Bde., M.G.C.).
Follett, Gilbert Burrell Spencer, D.S.O., M.V.O., Bt.-Lt.-Col. (T/Brig.-Gen.), k. in a., 27/9/18 (3rd Gds. Bde. H.Q.).
Freeman-Thomas, Hon. Gerald Frederick, 2/Lt., k. in a., 14/9/14.
Fuller-Maitland, William Alan, Capt., d. of w., 19/9/14.
1 Gamble, Ralph Dominic, M.C., Lt., k. in a., 22/8/18.
1 Gladstone, William Herbert, M.C., Lt. (Act. Capt.), k. in a., 27/9/18.
Gordon-Ives, Victor Maynard Gordon, Lt., d. of w., 16/9/14.
Graves-Sawle, Richard Charles, Lt., k. in a., 2/11/14.
1 Gregge-Hopwood, Edward Byng George, D.S.O., Major (Act. Lt. Col.), k. in a., 20/7/17.
3 Greene, Quincey Shaw, Lt. (Act. Capt.), k. in a., 28/3/18.
1 Grissell, Francis, Lt., k. in a., 15/9/16.
Hamilton, Hon. Leslie d'Henin, M.V.O., Major, k. in a., 29/10/14.
Hamilton, William Robert, 2/Lt., k. in a., 12/10/17 (att. 4th M.G. Gds.).
2 Handley, Guy Frederick Beckham, M.C., Lt., k. in a., 27/8/18.
3 Hardy, Guy John Meredith, Lt., d. of w., 1/8/17.
Hartley, Charles Fletcher, 2/Lt., k. in a., 27/11/17 (2nd Gds. Bde. M.G.C.).
3 Harvey, George Denis, 2/Lt., k. in a., 9/10/17.
Hawarden, Robert Cornwallis (Viscount), Lt., d. of w., 26/8/14.
2 Hayes, John Carolin, M.C., Lt., died, 19/11/18.
2 Heath, Gerard Bower, 2/Lt., d. of w., 22/5/18.
Heathcote, James Shirley, 2/Lt., d. of w., 28/8/17.
1 Helme, Guy Masterman, Lt., d. of w., 30/10/17.
Hoblyn, Walter Frederick, 2/Lt., d. of w., 1/10/15 (att. 4th Bn).
Ipswich, William Henry Alfred Fitzroy (Viscount), Lt., killed, 23/4/18 (and R.A.F.).
1 Jackson, Bertram Rolfe, Capt. (Tp.), k. in a., 15/9/16.
Jackson, Claude Stewart, Capt., k. in a., 9/10/17.
2 Laing, Ivan, M.C., Lt., k. in a., 30/11/17.
3 Laird, William, 2/Lt., k. in a., 1/12/17.
Lambton, Geoffrey, Lt., k. in a., 1/9/14.
2 Lane, George Ronald, Capt. & Adjt., k. in a., 16/9/16.
4 Lane, Jocylyn Henry Cambridge, 2/Lt., died, 16/10/18.
1 Lawrence, Michael Charles, Capt. (Tp.), d. of w., 16/9/16.
2 Leggatt, Logie Colin, 2/Lt., k. in a., 31/7/17.
Legge-Bourke, Nigel Walter Henry, Lt., k. in a., 30/10/14.
2 Leigh-Bennett, Arthur, D.S.O., Capt., k. in a., 3/10/15.
1 Leigh-Bennett, Olliph Spencer, Lt., d. of w., 17/11/18.
2 Leveson-Gower, Ronald Charles Granville Gresham, Lt., d. of w., 1/8/17.
1 Leveson-Gower, William George Gresham, Lt., k. in a., 9/10/18.
Lockwood, Richard William Mark, 2/Lt., k. in a., 14-15/9/14.
3 Loyd, Reginald Percy, M.C., Lt. (Act. Capt.), k. in a., 1/12/17.
3 Lundie, Eric Balfour, 2/Lt., k. in a., 12/9/17.
3 Lutyens, Cyril Arthur George, Lt., k. in a., 9/10/17.
2 MacGregor, John Atholl, 2/Lt., k. in a., 21-26/9/16.
Mackinnon, Lionel Neil Alexander, Capt., k. in a., 6/11/15 (and W.A.E.F.).
Marker, Raymond John, D.S.O., Lt.-Col., died, 13/11/14 (Staff).
Markham, Ronald Anthony, Major, d. of w., 26/10/14.
3 Martin, Claude, 2/Lt., k. in a., 1/12/17.
2 Martin, Frank Henry, M.C., 2/Lt., k. in a, 28/3/18.
1 Maxwell-Stuart, Alfred Joseph, 2/Lt., d. of w., 24/8/18.
3 Maxwell-Stuart, Henry Joseph Ignatius, 2/Lt., k. in a., 9/10/17.
1 Maynard, Hugh Charles, Lt., k. in a., 15/9/16.
3 Meakin, Herbert Percy, (Capt.) (Tp.), k. in a., 25/9/16 (Gds. T.M.B.).
Mills, Charles Gordon, 2/Lt., k. in a., 26/1/15.
Monck, Hon. Charles Henry Stanley, Capt., k. in a., 21/10/14.
2 Montgomery, Norman Stevenson, 2/Lt., k. in a., 17/6/16.
1 Moore, Edward Patrick Aylett, M.C., 2/Lt., k. in a., 4/11/18.
Murray, Charles John, Lt., k. in a., 25/10/14.
Northland, Thomas Uchter Caulfield (Viscount), Capt. (Tp.), k. in a., 2/2/15.
O'Conor, Ronald Ramsay, 2/Lt., died, 30/11/18.
1 Peake, Raymond, Lt., d. of w., 30/9/16.
1 Pease, Ronald Herbert Pike, Lt., k. in a., 15/9/16.
1 Perry, Kenneth William, 2/Lt., d. of w., 8/12/17.
Petre, Lionel George Carroll (Lord), Lt. (Tp. Capt.), d. of w., 30/9/15.
Pollock, Frederick Robert, Lt., k. in a., 22/10/14.
Porritt, Thomas Handly, M.C., 2/Lt., d. of w., 31/7/17.
Rail, Richard Augwin, Lt., k. in a., 9/10/17.
1 Ritchie, Henry Deacon, 2/Lt., d. of w., 27/9/18.
1 Roderick, John Victor Tweed, Lt., k. in a., 27/8/18.
Rodgers, Joseph Edward, 2/Lt., d. of w., 25/1/15.
Rooke, Douglas Giles, Capt., died, 2/11/18.
2 St. Leger, William Brett, M.C., Lt., k. in a., 27/4/18.
Samuelson, Geoffrey Bernard Fitzroy, M.C., Lt., k. in a., 27/11/17.
2 Saunders, James Renault, Lt., k. in a., 4/11/18.
1 Scott, Sidney Maurice, Lt., k. in a., 15/9/16.
Senhouse, Oscar William Pocklington, 2/Lt., k. in a., 19/6/15.
Smith, Granville Keith Falconer, Lt., k. in a., 29/10/14.
Smith, Godfrey Leveson, 2/Lt., k. in a., 29/9/15.
2 Spinney, Ronald Henry, Lt., d. of w., 2/7/16.
Stanton, Roydon Ross, Lt., died, 18/10/18.
2 Starr, Dillwyn Parrish, 2/Lt., k. in a., 14-16/9/16.
2 Steel, Alan Ivo, Lt., k. in a., 8/10/17.
1 Stewart, Geoffrey, Capt., k. in a., 22/12/14.
2 Stewart-Richardson, John Lauderdale, 2/Lt., k. in a., 17/5/16.
Sturt, Hon. Gerald Philip Montagu Napier, Capt., d. of w., 11/11/18.
3 Tabuteau, Rupert Rochefort Moliere, Lt., k. in a., 28/3/18.
Tapp, Theodore Arthur, M.C., Capt., d. of w., 21/10/17 (and M.G.C.).
Taylor, Seymour George Frederick, Capt., k. in a., 20/10/15.
1 Thewlis, Frank, M.C., Lt., k. in a., 15/9/16.
2 Thompson, Henry Cedric St. John, D.S.O., Lt. (Act. Capt.), d. of w., 30/11/17.
Tollemache, Bevil Douglas, 2/Lt., k. in a., 22/12/14.
4 Treffry, Dormer Kierulff de Bretton, 2/Lt., k. in a., 15/9/16.
Tritton, Alan George, Capt., k. in a., 26/10/14.
Trotter, Archibald, Lt., k. in a., 31/12/14.
3 Tufnell, Carleton Edward, Capt., k. in a., 15/9/16.
Tyrrell, Francis Chichester, Lt., d. of w., 15/2/15.
3 Vaughan, George Edward, M.C., Major, k. in a., 15/9/16.
Verelst, Harry Wilson, M.C., Capt. (Act. Major), k. in a., 26/9/16.
1 Vincent, Charles Issam Francis, 2/Lt., k. in a., 16/10/18.
Wallis, Henry Digby, Lieut., k. in a., 21/10/14.
1 Walpole, Horatio Spencer, Lt., k. in a., 9/4/18.
2 Watson-Smyth, Edward Jeffray, Capt., k. in a., 27/8/18.
3 Whetstone, Walter Hugh, Lt., k. in a., 28/3/18.
Whidborne, George Ferris, Lt., d. of w., 24/10/15.
Williams-Wynn, Charles Walkin, 2/Lt., k. in a., 29/10/14.
1 Williamson, Hugh Henshall Clifford, Lt., k. in a., 15/9/16.
3 Wilmot-Sitwell, Jacinth Sacheverell, Lt., d. of w., 9/7/16.
1 Wilson, Robert Gerald Aldin, 2/Lt., k. in a., 13/3/17.
Windsor-Clive, Hon. Archer, Lt., k. in a., 25/8/14.
1 Woods, John Russell, Capt. (Tp.), d. of w., 16/9/16.
Wyndham, Percy Lyulph, Lt., k. in a., 14/9/14.

Scots Guards.

2 Ambler, Edward Sharp, Lt., k. in a., 8/5/18.
Armstrong, Guy Spearman, 2/Lt., k. in a., 28/9/15 (att. 1st Bn.).
2 Bagot-Chester, Greville John Massey, Capt. and Bt.-Major, k. in a., 28/11/17.
2 Balfour, Evan Murray Macgregor, M.C., 2/Lt. k. in a., 24/8/18.
Balfour, John, M.C., Capt., k. in a., 21/3/18 (att. Div. Sig. Coy.).
Balfour, Robert Frederick, Capt., k. in a., 28/10/14.
1 Barclay, David Stuart, Lt., d. of w., 24/4/17.
Barne, M., D.S.O., T/Major, k. in a., 17/8/17.

1 Bartholomew, Claude, Capt. (Tp.), k. in a., 15/9/16 (att. M.G.C.).
1 Brand, David Halyburton, M.C., Lt. (A/Capt.), k. in a., 29/3/18.
1 Broughton-Adderley, Peter Handcock, M.C., 2/Lt. (A/Capt.), d. of w., 16/10/18.
Bulkeley, C. S. Rivers, Capt., k. in a., 16/5/15.
2 Bulkeley, Thomas Henry Rivers, C.M.G., M.V.O., Capt., k. in a., 22/10/14.
Campbell, Colin Frederick Fitzroy, Capt., k. in a., 29/10/14.
Carpenter-Garnier, John Trefusis, Major, k. in a., 14/9/14.
2 Chamberlain, Rupert Maurice, 2/Lt., d. of w., 20/5/18.
1 Champion, Reginald James, Lt., d. of w., 18/7/17 (att. T.M.B.).
2 Chapman, Arthur Frederick, 2/Lt., k. in a., 25/9/16.
2 Chapman, David Archibald James, 2/Lt., k. in a., 15/9/16.
1 Coats, Eric Robert, Lt., k. in a., 17/5/18.
Coghill, Norman Harry, Lt., d. of w., 28/3/18 (att. M.G.C.).
Compton-Thornhill, Richard Anthony, Lt., k. in a., 16/9/14.
1 Cordes, Hugh de Bary, M.C., 2/Lt., k. in a., 27/9/18.
Cottrell-Dormer, Clement, Lt., k. in a., 27/10/14.
Cuthbert, James Harold, D.S.O., Capt., d. of w., 27/9/15.
2 Daniels, Russell John, Lt., died, 29/8/18.
Dawkins, Guy Stacey, 2/Lt. (Tp.), d. of w., 25/9/16 (att. 2nd Btn.).
De la Pasture, Charles Edward, Capt., k. in a., 29/10/14.
Douglas-Dick, Archibald William John Joseph, Lt., k. in a., 11/11/14.
Drummond, David Robert, Lt., k. in a., 3/11/14.
1 Drummond, Harvey Gerald Binns, M.C., Lt., k. in a., 3/9/18.
1 Dundas, Henry Lancaster Neville, M.C., Lt. (A/Capt.), k. in a., 27/9/18.
Dyer, Sir John Swinnerton, Bart., M.C., Capt., k. in a., 31/7/17 (D.A.Q.M.G., Guards Div.).
Egerton-Warburton, John, Capt., d. of w., 30/8/15.
2 Elliot, The Hon. Gavin William Esmond, Lt., d. of w., 6/8/17.
2 Femner, Cyril Frederick Hamilton, 2/Lt., k. in a., 24/9/16.
2 Ferryman, William Edward, Lt. (A/Capt.), d. of w., 12/10/18.
2 Fletcher, Jack Haslip, 2/Lt., k. in a., 20/10/18.
Fraser, The Hon. Hugh Joseph, M.V.O., Major, k. in a., 28/10/14.
Garforth, William Godfrey Willoughby, Lt., k. in a., 16/5/15 (att. 2nd Btn.).
Gibbs, R.C.M., 2/Lt., d. of w., 29/10/14.
Gipps, Reginald Nigel, Lt., k. in a., 7/11/14.
Gladwin, Ralph Hamilton Fane, Lt., k. in a., 26/10/14.
2 Gold, Percy, 2/Lt., k. in a., 19/7/16.
2 Green, Herbert William, 2/Lt. (Tp.), k. in a., 12/10/17.
Hamilton, Cecil Fife Pryce, Capt., d. of w., 27/10/14.
2 Hamilton, George, Lt., d. of w., 26/11/17.
Hanbury-Tracy, The Hon. Felix Charles Herbert, Lt., k. in a., 19/12/14 (Res. of Off.).
Hepburne-Scott, Alexander Noel, 2/Lt., k. in a., 16/5/15.
1 Hill-Trevor, Hillyer George Edwin, Lt., k. in a., 21/12/14.
Holbech, William Hugh, Lt., d. of w., 1/11/14 (Res. of Off.).
1 Holland, Edward, 2/Lt., k. in a., 13/9/16.
1 Holmes, Reginald Eden, Lt. (A/Capt.), k. in a., 4/6/18.
Houldsworth, William Gillbert, Lt., d. of w., 23/9/14.
Hulse, Sir Edward Hamilton Westrow (Bart.), Capt., k. in a., 13/3/15.
Inigo-Jones, Henry Richmond, Lt., k. in a., 4/9/14.
Jarvis, Louis Archibald, Lt., k. in a., 16/5/15.
1 Johns, Graham, Lt., k. in a., 27/9/18 (att. T.M.B.).
1 Jones, Arthur Mervyn, Lt., d. of w., 21/11/16.
1 Kinnaird, The Hon. Arthur Middleton, M.C., Lt., k. in a., 27/11/17.
Kinnaird, Hon. Douglas Arthur (Master of Kinnaird), Capt., k. in a., 24/10/14.
Lawson, William Bernard Webster, Lt., k. in a., 22/10/14.
1 Leach, Grey de Léche, 2/Lt., died, 3/9/16.
2 Lechmere, Nicholas George Berwick, Lt., k. in a., 17/10/15.
Leighton, John Burgh Talbot, M.C., Capt. (T/Major), d. of w., 7/5/17 (and R.F.C., 23/Sqd.).
1 Lloyd, Ernest Alfred Collyer, Lt., k. in a., 31/7/17.
Loyd, Geoffery Archibald, Lt., d. of w., 13/11/14.
MacDonald, Hon. Godfrey Evan Hugh, Lt., d. of w., 2/11/14.
Mackensie, James, Lt., k. in a., 16/5/15 (att. 2/Bn.).
1 Mackinnon, Duncan, Lt., k. in a., 9/10/17.
1 Maclay, Eben, Lt., d. of w., 11/4/18.
2 Maby, Lionel Bruce, 2/Lt., k. in a., 12/9/18.
2 Mahomed, Claude Atkinson Etty, Lt., k. in a., 31/7/17.
Markham, Montagu Wilfred, 2/Lt., k. in a., 29/8/17.
Marsham-Townsend, Ferdinand, 2/Lt., k. in a., 16/5/15 (att. 2/Bn.).
1 Martindale, Warine Frederic, Lt., k. in a., 15/9/16.
Menzies, Alastair Graham, Lt. (Tp.), k. in a., 1/1/15.
2 Menzies, Archibald Rudge Wilson, Lt., k. in a., 25/11/17.
2 Mills, Hon. Charles Thomas, 2/Lt., k. in a., 6/10/15.
2/1 Milne, John Archibald Dickie, 2/Lt., k. in a., 12/10/17.
Monckton, Francis Algernon, Lt., k. in a., 8/11/14.
Monckton, Geoffrey Valentine Francis, Lt., k. in a., 25/1/15.
2 Murdoch, Louis Farde Campbell, 2/Lt., d. of w., 19/9/16.
3 Nicol, Donald Ninian, Lt. (Tp.), died, 29/12/15.
1 Norman, Lionel, M.C., Capt. (Tp.), k. in a., 15/9/16.
Nugent, Richard Francis Robert, 2/Lt., k. in a., 18/12/14.
Ogilvy, Sir Gilchrist Nevill (Bart.), Lt., k. in a., 29/10/14.
Orr, Arthur Roxboroughe, Capt., k. in a., 17/11/15.
Orr-Ewing, Ernest Pellew, Capt. (Tp.), k. in a., 15/9/16 (att. 1/Bn.).
Ottley, Geoffrey Claude Langdale, D.S.O., Lt. (Tp.), d. of w., 21/12/14.
2 Prettyman, Frank Remington, Lt., k. in a., 4/7/17.
1 Schiff, Martin Noel, Lt., k. in a., 17/6/16.
Shelley, Cecil William Charles, Lt. (Tp.), k. in a., 17/10/15.
1 Shortt, William Edward Dudley, Lt., k. in a., 12/10/17.
Smith, Bernard Ridley Winthrope, Lt., d. of w., 15/11/14.
Smyth, John Fairfax, 2/Lt., k. in a., 22/7/17.
Stephen, Albert Alexander Leslie, D.S.O., Capt., d. of w., 31/10/14.
Stephenson, Denys George, Lt., k. in a., 16/5/15.
Stirling, Gordon, M.C., Lt., k. in a., 15/9/16 (att. M.G.C.).
Stirling-Stuart, James, Lt., d. of w., 9/11/14.
Stracey, Reginald George, Capt., k. in a., 1/1/15.
Taylor, Hugh, Capt., k. in a., 19/12/14.
Tennant, Mark, Lt., k. in a., 16/9/16 (and M.G.C.).
Thompson, John Cecil Caster, 2/Lt., k. in a., 25/1/15.
Thorpe, John Somerled, M.C., Major, k. in a., 15/9/16 (att. 2/Bn.).
1 Trower, Alfred Bence, 2/Lt., k. in a., 29/5/18.
Truss, George Marquand, 2/Lt., k. in a., 25/9/16 (att. M.G.C.).
Weld, Hugh Edward, 2/Lt., k. in a., 25/1/15 (att. Artists Rifles).
Wickham, William Joseph, Capt., k. in a., 31/10/14.
Wilson, Arthur Wesley, 2/Lt., k. in a., 30/7/17 (att. 3rd Bde. M.G. Coy.).

Irish Guards.

Allen, Thomas, 2/Lt., k. in a., 25/2/15 (Spec. Res.)
2 Armfield, Archie Seaward, 2/Lt., k. in a., 31/7/17.
1 Bailie, Thomas Manbourg Douglas, Major, k. in a., 15/9/16.
Bain, Andrew Lusk, Lt., k. in a., 4/11/18.
1 Baldwin, Hugh Reginald, Lt., k. in a., 27/8/18.
2 Bayly, Noel Douglas, Lt., k. in a., 27/11/17.
2 Bellew, Richard Courtenay, 2/Lt., d. of w., 21/8/17.
Berners, Hamilton Hughs, Capt., k. in a., 14/9/14.
Blacker-Douglass, Robert St. John, Lt., k. in a., 1/2/15.
Blake, Valentine Charles J., Capt., k. in a., 28/1/16 (S.R.) (att. 1/Bn.).
1 Boyd, George Pratt, 2/Lt., d. of w., 3/9/17.
Brew, Cyril Huleatt, Lt., d. of w., 12/10/16 (Spec. Res.).
Brooke, George, Lt., d. of w., 2/10/14 (Spec. Res.).
1 Budd, Edward, M.C., Lt. (A/Capt.), k. in a., 8/5/18.
Butler, Noel, 2/Lt., k. in a., 15/9/16 (Spec. Res., att 1/Bn.).
1 Butler-Stoney, Thomas, Lt., d. of w., 1/10/17.
1 Carey, Thomas Augustus, 2/Lt., k. in a., 5/12/17.
1 Carver, Lionel Henry Liptrah, 2/Lt., k. in a., 26/5/18.
2 Cary-Elwes, Wilfred Gervase, Lt., k. in a., 27/11/17.
2 Cassidy, Michael Bernard, 2/Lt., k. in a., 13/4/18.
Christy, Stephen Edmund Fell, Lt., k. in a., 12/7/16.
Clifford, Walter Francis Joseph, 2/Lt., k. in a., 27/9/15 (Spec. Res., att. 2/Bn.).
1 Close, Barry Samuel, Lt., k. in a., 27/9/18.
Coke, Langton Sacheverell, Lt., k. in a., 31/10/14 (Res. of Off.).
Connolly, Hugh Aloysius, 2/Lt., k. in a., 27/8/18 (att. 4/Bn. Gds. M.G. R.).
Crichton, Hubert Francis, Major, k. in a., 1/9/14.
2 Dame, John William Malvern, 2/Lt., k. in a., 27/11/17.
2 Dent, Edgar Dent, Capt., k. in a., 12/4/18.
1 Durant, Noel Henry Colin Fairfax, Lt., k. in a., 30/11/17.
Eiloart, Cyril Howard, 2/Lt. (Tp.), k. in a., 26/9/18 (att. 4/Gds. M.G.R.).
1 Eyre, Henry Joseph Bagshawe, Lt., d. of w., 14/7/17.
Fallows, Ernest Hamilton, 2/Lt., k. in a., 25/3/18 (Gds. Div., M.G. Batt.).
1 Fanshawe, Harvey Vernon, 2/Lt., d. of w., 11/10/17.
1 Fitzgerald, Lord Desmond, Major and Adjt., died, 3/3/16.
2 Fitzgerald, Maurice Robert, Lt., died, 19/4/18 (in German hands).
Fox, Victor William Darwin, Lt., k. in a., 18/5/15 (Spec. Res.).
1 French, Victor James Somerset, 2/Lt., k. in a., 10/10/18.
French-Brewster, Robert Abraham, Major, died, 17/2/17 (S.R.).
1 Gore-Langton, Montague Vernon, M.C., Capt., k. in a., 9/10/15.
Gough, Eric John Fletcher, Capt., k. in a., 30/12/14.
Greer, Eric Beresford, M.C., Major (A/Lt.-Col.), k. in a., 31/7/17.
2 Greer, Francis St. Ledger, M.C., Lt., died, 1/2/17.
1 Greer, James Kenneth, M.C., Lt., d. of w., 3/10/16.
Guernsey, Heneage Greville Finch, Lord, Capt., k. in a., 14/9/14.
Guthrie, John Noel, Capt., k. in a., 18/5/15.
Hamilton, Arthur John, Lord, Capt., k. in a., 6/11/14 (Spec. Res.).
2 Hamilton, Archibald James Rowan, Lt., d. of w., 21/10/15 (Spec. Res., att.).
1 Hanbury, Claude Everard Robert, Capt., k. in a., 9/10/17.
Hay, Lord Arthur Vincent, Capt., k. in a., 14/9/14.
Hargreaves, Leopold Reginald, M.C., Capt., d. of w., 25/9/16.
2 Harmsworth, The Hon. Harold Alfred Vyvyan St. George, M.C., Capt., d. of w., 12/2/18.
Hepburn-Stuart-Forbes-Trefusis, The Hon. John Frederick, D.S.O., Brig.-Gen., d. of w., 24/10/15 (20 Inf. Bde.).
Herbert-Stepney, Herbert Arthur, Major, k. in a., 7/11/14.
Hine, Godfrey Valentine Brooke, Lt., k. in a., 6/10/15 (Spec. Res.) (att. 2/Bn.).
Hope, William Edward, Lt., k. in a., 6/11/14 (S.R.).
2 Hudson-Kinahan, Daniel Dickinson, Lt., k. in a., 9/4/16 (Spec. Res.).
Hunt, Arthur George, 2/Lt., k. in a., 4/11/18 (att. 4 Gds. M.G.R.).
2 Hyne, Charles Godfrey Haggas Cuteliffe, Lt., d. of w., 21/11/16 (att. T.M.B.).
James, Gwynne Lewis Brodhurst, Lt., k. in a., 18/7/17 (Trench How. Bty.).
Keating, Henry Sheehy, Lt., killed, 20/1/15.

King, Norman, 2/Lt., d. of w., 26/5/18 (att. 4/Gds. M.G.R.).
Kipling, John, Lt., k. in a., 27/9/15.
Law, Thomas Pakenham, 2/Lt., d. of w., 27/8/15 (Spec. Res.) (att. 2/Bn.).
Lee, Frederick Henry Norris, Lt., d. of w., 4/7/16 (Spec. Res.) (att. 1/Bn.).
Lee, Lennox Cleland, 2/Lt., k. in a., 1/2/15 (Spec. Res.).
2 Leby, Maitland Benn, M.C., Capt. (Actg.), k. in a., 12/4/18.
1 Lord, Eustace Charles Gabriel, 2/Lt., k. in a., 8/5/18.
Madden, Gerald Hugh Charles, Major (T/Lt.-Col.), d. of w., 12/11/15.
2 Maher, John Charles, Lt., k. in a., 14/4/18.
Maitland, Graham Macdonell, 2/Lt., k. in a., 26/1/16.
Marion-Crawford, Harold Francis, 2/Lt., killed, 16/4/15.
V. C. Marshall, John Neville, M.C., Lt. (A/Lt.-Col.), k. in a., 4/11/18 (att. 16/Lanc. Fus.).
Mathieson, Kenneth Ronald, Lt., k. in a., 1/11/14.
1 Montgomery, Hugh, Lt., k. in a., 13/9/16.
Morris, Hon. George Henry, Lt.-Col., k. in a., 1/9/14.
Mulholland, The Hon. Andrew Edward Somerset, Capt., d. of w., 1/11/14.
Musgrave, Thomas, Lt., k. in a., 6/2/15 (Spec. Res.).
Mylne, Edward Graham, Capt., d. of w., 12/6/15.
2 Mylne, Euan Louis, M.C., Lt., d. of w., 15/9/16.
1 Nash, James Haran, Lt., k. in a., 27/3/18.
1 O'Brien, Charles Stuart, M.C., 2/Lt., d. of w., 27/9/18.
1 O'Farrell, Archibald Hugh, 2/Lt., k. in a., 27/9/18.
1 Ogilvy, The Hon. Patrick Julian Harry Stanley, M.C., A/Capt., k. in a., 9/10/17.
2 Parsons, Desmond Clere, Lt. (T/Capt.), k. in a., 15/9/16.
Pease, Cuthbert, Lt., d. of w., 18/9/16.
Purcell, Charles Francis, Lt., k. in a., 15/9/16 (att. M.G.C.).
Pusch, Frederick Leopold, D.S.O., Lt., k. in a., 27/6/16 (att. 1/Bn.) (Spec. Res.).
2 Pym, Claude John, Lt., died, 27/3/17.
2 Pym, Francis Leslie Melville, Lt., k. in a., 2/7/16.
1 Rodakowski, Raymond Juzio Paul, Lt. (A/Capt.), k. in a., 9/10/17.
Rosse, William Edward, Earl of, Major, d. of w., 10/6/18.
Shears, Edward Hornby, Lt., k. in a., 4/7/17.
Stafford-King-Harman, Edward Charles, Capt., k. in a., 6/11/14.
Stewart, John Maurice, 2/Lt., k. in a., 1/4/15 (S. Res.).
1 Stoney, Thomas Samuel Vesey, 2/Lt., k. in a., 9/10/17.
2 Synge, Allen Francis, Lt., k. in a., 27/11/17.
Synge, Francis Patrick Hamilton, M.C., Lt. (A/Capt.), k. in a., 29/7/17 (S.R.).
Tisdall, Charles Arthur, Major, k. in a., 1/9/14.
1 Tisdall, Charles Richard, M.C., 2/Lt., k. in a., 15/9/16.
2 Tomkins, Albin George, 2/Lt., k. in a., 13/9/16.
2 Vaughan, Kenelm Cuthbert, 2/Lt., k. in a., 13/9/16.
1 Walker, Thomas Kynaston, Lt., k. in a., 24/4/16.
Walters, Graham Yuille Laundy, Lt., d. of w., 15/9/16 (M.G.C.).
1 Ward, Jebusa Newton, Lt., k. in a., 27/8/18.
1 Wells, Alfred Langton, 2/Lt., k. in a., 9/10/17.
Whitefoord, Lionel Cole, Lt., k. in a., 15/9/16 (M.G.C.).
2 Wilson, Tom Benholt, 2/Lt., k. in a., 18/7/17.
Woodroffe, Neville Leslie, Lt., k. in a., 6/11/14.
Wynter, Cecil Domville, Lt., d. of w., 5/10/15 (att. 2/Bn.).
1 Young, George Edward Savill, Major, d. of w., 31/3/17.
RIC attd. Buried, Rose Town Cemetery

The Welsh Guards.

Bagot, Edward Luke Henry, 2/Lt., k. in a., 10/9/16.
1 Ballard, Charles Penfold, 2/Lt., k. in a., 10/3/18.
1 Borough, Alaric Charles Henry, Lt., k. in a., 1/12/17.
Bromfield, Harry Hickman, D.S.O., Major, k. in a., 10/9/16.
1 Byrne, Thomas Edmund, 2/Lt., k. in a., 9/3/18.
Cazalet, Edward, 2/Lt., k. in a., 10/9/16.
1 Clive, Percy Robert (Viscount), Capt., d. of w., 31/10/16.
1 Crawford-Wood, Guy, Lt., k. in a., 1/7/16.
1 Davies, Evan James, 2/Lt., k. in a., 28/3/18.
1 Foot, Victor Edward, 2/Lt., died, 25/11/18.
Hargreaves, Ralph Walter, Lt. (Tp.), k. in a., 1/12/17.
1 Howard, The Hon. Philip Granville James Fitzalan, Lt., d. of w., 24/5/18.
1 Insole, George Claude Latham, M.C., Lt., A/Capt., k. in a., 12/4/18.
1 Jones, Reginald Rees, D.S.O., 2/Lt., d. of w., 25/8/17.
1 Kearton, James Linton Graham, Lt., d. of w., 3/12/17.
1 Lewis, John Walter, Lt., k. in a., 6/6/16.
Mawby, Edwin George, Lt., k. in a., 27/9/15.
1 Newall, Nigel, Lt., k. in a., 12/10/17.
Newborough, William Charles, Lord, T/Lt., died, 19/7/16.
Osmond-Williams, Osmond Traharn Deudraith, D.S.O., Capt., d. of w., 27/9/15.
Palmer, Arthur Percy D.S.O., Capt., k. in a., 27/9/15.
1 Powell, William Edward George Pryce Wynne, 2/Lt., k. in a., 6/11/18.
Power, John Wethered, Lt., k. in a., 10/9/16.
Randolph, Julien, Lt. (Tp.), k. in a., 27/9/15.
1 Roderick, Hume Buckley, A/Capt., Lt., k. in a., 1/12/17.
Smith, Ralph, 2/Lt., k. in a., 27/9/15.
Sutton, Hubert Joselin, Lt., k. in a., 27/9/15.
1 Tennant, George Christian Serocold, 2/Lt., k. in a., 3/9/17.
1 Trotter, Henry Baron, M.M., 2/Lt., d. of w., 10/9/18.
1 Upjohn, William Moon, Lt., k. in a., 24/8/18.
1 Webb, Thomas Henry Basil, 2/Lt., k. in a., 1/12/17.
Wernher, Alexander Pigott, 2/Lt., k. in a., 10/9/16.
1 Whitehouse, Cyril Duncan, 2/Lt., k. in a., 26/5/18.
1 Williams-Bulkeley, Richard Gerard Wellesley, M.C., Major, died, 28/3/18.

Guards Machine Gun Regiment.

1 Cottle, Walter Edward Worsdale, Lt., k. in a., 31/7/17 (Gren. Gds.).
Fallows, Ernest Hamilton, 2/Lt., k. in a., 25/3/18 (Irish Gds.).
2 Ferguson, Victor John, Lt., k. in a., 21-22/8/19 (2nd Life Gds.).
Fisher-Smith, Alan Archibald, Lt., k. in a., 1/8/17 (Cold. Gds.).
Fraser, John C., Lt., drowned, 9/9/18 (Gren. Gds.).
Gunther, Charles Emil, Lt. (Tp.), k. in a., 24/9/18 (2nd Life Gds.).
4 Hamilton, William Robert, 2/Lt., k. in a., 12/10/17 (Cold. Gds.).
2 Harter, Herbert Hatfield, Lt., k. in a., 9/10/17 (Gren. Gds.).
4 Hunt, Arthur George, 2/Lt., k. in a., 4/11/18 (Irish Gds.).
4 Stewart, Howard William, 2/Lt., k. in a., 27/8/18 (Gren. Gds.).
Sutton, Sir Richard Vincent (Bart.), M.C., Capt., died, 29/11/18 (1st Life Gds.).
9 Trafford, Geoffry Thomas, Lt., k. in a., 23/7/18 (1st Life Gds.).

The Royal Scots (Lothian Regiment).

Adam, George, 2/Lt., k. in a., 22/10/17 (att. 16/Bn.).
13 Adamson, Robert Thorburn Adamson, Lt. (Tp.), k. in a., 23/4/17.
12 Ainslie, John Elliott, 2/Lt. (Tp.), k. in a., 28/9/15.
3 Ainger, Herbert Cecil, Lt., k. in a., 4/10/17 (and R.F.C.).
2 Anderson, Charles Ogilvy, Lt., d. of w., 2/10/15 (att. 3/Bn.).
2 Anderson, Francis, Major, d. of w., 28/1/17 (att. 12/Bn.).
3 Anderson, John Macnabb, Lt., k. in a., 17/6/15 (att. 2/Bn.).
2 Anderson, Robert, 2/Lt., d. of w., 23/3/18.
1 Appleby, Robert Charles Alfred, Lt., d. of w., 28/6/16 (att. 13/Bn.).
12 Arend, Ronald Sydney, 2/Lt., k. in a., 23/3/18.
16 Armit, Napier, Capt., k. in a., 4/8/16.
11 Baker, Alfred Parkes, Lt. (Tp.), d. of w., 1/12/15.
14 Balfour, Isaac Bayley, Lt., k. in a., 28/6/15.
17 Barclay, Marshall Stuart, Lt. (Tp.), k. in a., 28/3/18.
3 Barclay, Robert Stephen, 2/Lt., k. in a., 21/3/18 (att. 16/Bn.).
3 Barnett, Gerald, 2/Lt., k. in a., 3/11/15.
17 Barry, Robert Cooke, Capt., k. in a., 18/7/16.
3 Baxter, Andrew, 2/Lt., k. in a., 22/10/17 (att. 16/Bn.).
11 Bell, Alfred Herbert, Capt., k. in a., 25/9/15.
11 Bell, James, 2/Lt. (Tp.), k. in a., 11/1/17.
11 Bellamy, Howard Claxson, Lt. (Tp.), k. in a., 2/1/17.
14 Bennett, Walter James, 2/Lt. (Tp.), k. in a., 4/7/16 (att. 12/Bn.).
17 Bennie, Andrew, 2/Lt. (Tp.), k. in a., 30/9/18.
2 Berry, David Douglas Anderson, A/Capt., k. in a., 26/9/17.
Bidie, George Maxwell Vereker, Lt., killed, 8/7/16 (also R.F.C.).
11 Bogle, Andrew Blyth McCulloch, 2/Lt. (Tp), k. in a., 14/7/16.
Bowie, George, 2/Lt. (Tp.), k. in a., 12/10/17 (att. 11/Bn.).
Brady, C., Lt. (Tp.), died, 15/8/15.
1 Bremner, James, Lt. (Tp.), d. of w., 24/6/17.
15 Brodie, Walter Hamilton, 2/Lt. (Tp.), k. in a., 9/4/17.
Broome, Louis George, 2/Lt., d. of w., 5/6/15.
15 Brough, James Lindsay, 2/Lt. (Tp.), k. in a., 1/7/16.
16 Brown, Alexander, 2/Lt. (Tp.), k. in a., 28/4/17.
13 Brown, David Douglas, 2/Lt. (Tp.), killed, 27/9/15.
3 Brown, Douglas Crow, Lt., d. of w., 13/9/17 (att. M.G.C.).
11 Brown, Ian Macgregor Knox, 2/Lt., k. in a., 25/9/15.
11 Brown, James William, M.C., Capt., k. in a., 21/3/17.
13 Bruce, Bethune Duncan, Capt. (Tp.), k. in a., 27/9/15.
3 Bruce, Honble. Henry Lyndhurst, Capt., k. in a., 14/12/14.
15 Bruce, John Russel, Major (Tp.), k. in a., 1/7/16.
14 Bryce, William Hulton, 2/Lt. (Tp.), k. in a., 2/3/16.
13 Buchanan, Fraser Campbell, 2/Lt., k. in a., 9/4/17.
12 Budge, Hubert Lionel, Lt.-Col. (Tp.), d. of w., 13/7/16.
Byres, James Hope, 2/Lt. (Tp.), k. in a., 27/8/17 (att 13/Bn.).
11 Caird, Ernest Thomson, 2/Lt. (Tp.), k. in a., 24/3/18.
15 Cairns, William Anderson, Lt. (Tp.), k. in a., 30/9/18 (att. 17/Bn.).
3 Callender, Gerald Claude, Lt., k. in a., 26/4/18.
Campbell, Neil Leslie, 2/Lt. (Tp.), k. in a., 8/8/15 (att. 1/5 Bn.).
Caseby, William Robert Brown, M.C., 2/Lt. (Tp.), k. in a., 25/4/17 (att. 1/Lancs Fus.).
11 Chapman, Geoffrey Arthur, 2/Lt. (Tp.), k. in a., 28/3/16.
Chisholm, John Oliver, Lt. (Tp.), d. of w., 23/7/18 (att. 1/8 Bn.).
3 Chisholm, Alastair Edward, Lt., k. in a., 25/9/15 (att. R.S.F.).
Chree, George William Johnstone, Capt. (Tp.), k. in a., 14/7/16.
17 Coats, William Evans, 2/Lt. (Tp.), d. of w., 4/11/17.
3 Coffin, Sebright Edward, 2/Lt., d. of w., 20/12/15 (att 2/Bn.).
Cole-Hamilton, Con William Eric, Capt., killed, 2/7/17 (and R.F.C., 20 Sqd.).
16 Coles, Lionel George, Capt. (Tp.), k. in a., 1/7/16.
3 Collins, Lionel Drummond Kyrle, 2/Lt., k. in a., 11/5/16.
2 Cooper, Frank Douglas Towers, 2/Lt., k. in a., 22/7/16.
Copeland, William Alan, 2/Lt., k. in a., 25/4/15.
3 Cowan, Charles John Alexander, Capt., d. of w., 15/3/18.
3 Cowan, John Orr Craig, Capt., k. in a., 14/7/16.
3 Cowan, Robert Craig, 2/Lt., k. in a., 24/10/14.
13 Cowie, William, 2/Lt. (Tp.), d. of w., 28/9/16.
13 Crabbe, John, 2/Lt. (Tp.), d. of w., 6/5/16.
17 Craig, Edmund Robert, 2/Lt. (Tp.), d. of w., 1/6/16.
3 Craig, James Glen, M.C., 2/Lt., k. in a., 23/4/18.
3 Cromb, David Rankin, 2/Lt. (Tp.), k. in a., 23/4/17.
3 Crombie, William Lauder, 2/Lt., k. in a., 1/7/16.
3 Crossman, Richard Douglas, M.C., Lt., A/Capt., k. in a., 27/9/18.
12 Cunningham, Hugh Rose, 2/Lt., k. in a., 26/4/16.

17 **Currie, Adam, Capt. (Tp.), k. in a., 28/3/18.**
2 **Cuxson, Basil Pryce, 2/Lt., k. in a., 14/7/15.**
Dalziel, John Morrison, 2/Lt. (Tp.), k. in a., 14/11/18 (att. 2/10 Bn.).
2 Darker, Neil Campbell, 2/Lt., k. in a., 3/5/17.
12 Davidson, Ronald Riach, Capt. (Tp.), k. in a., 27/3/16.
13 Davies, Gilbert Vere Faithfull, Lt. (Tp.), k. in a., 23/4/17.
Daws, Edwin, 2/Lt. (Tp. Lt.), k. in a., 2/11/17.
3 Dawson, Reginald Todd, 2/Lt., k. in a., 13/11/16.
15 Devine, John Ross, M.C., Lt., k. in a., 26/8/17.
3 Dickinson, John, 2/Lt., k. in a., 28/8/17.
12 Donaldson, William, 2/Lt. (Tp.), k. in a., 5/6/17.
15 Dougal, John Braes, 2/Lt. (Tp.), k. in a., 1/7/16.
13 Doughty, George, 2/Lt. (Tp.), k. in a., 20/11/16 (also R.F.C.).
Drysdale, William, D.S.O., Bt.-Lt.-Col., k. in a., 29/9/16.
Duncombe-Shafto, Arthur, D.S.O., Capt., k. in a., 12/9/14.
1 Durward, Ronald Gibson Stewart, Lt., k. in a., 11/8/18.
3 Edwards, Alfred Joseph, 2/Lt., d. of w., 10/4/16 (att. 6/L.N. Lancs).
15 Elder, Alexander, 2/Lt. (Tp.), k. in a., 1/7/16.
13 Elder, James, Capt., k. in a., 29/12/17.
Elliot, James Brown, 2/Lt. (Tp.), k. in a., 22/11/17.
2 Elmslie, Ernest George, 2/Lt. (Tp.), k. in a., 26/9/17.
11 Evans, Willie Herbert, Major (Tp.), k. in a., 14/8/15.
Eykyn, Gilbert Davidson Pitt, Capt., k. in a., 25/4/15.
3 Falcomer, William Meek, 2/Lt., k. in a., 13/5/16.
14 Farmer, William McDowall, Lt., k. in a., 9/4/16 (att. 8/R. Welsh Fus.).
Farquharson, Lewis Shaw, Capt., k. in a., 12/5/18.
2 Ferguson, Alexander Crichton, Capt., died, 12/2/19.
13 Ferguson, Ian Alexander Grant, Capt. (Tp.), k. in a., 11/5/16.
13 Ferguson, Leonard, 2/Lt. (Tp.), d. of w., 20/7/16.
11 Fernie, Andrew John, 2/Lt. (Tp.), k. in a., 12/10/17.
Fitch, Matthew Craig, M.C., Lt., died, 9/12/18 (att. 10/Bn.).
11 Fleming, James, M.C., Lt., k. in a., 21/3/17.
13 Forbes, Duncan, 2/Lt. (Tp.), k. in a., 28/3/18.
12 Forsyth, Andrew Alexander, 2/Lt. (Tp.), k. in a., 12/10/18.
16 Fortune, Rutherford Lamond, 2/Lt. (Tp.), d. of w., 15/1/17.
3 Francis, Basil Hugh, 2/Lt., k. in a., 4/2/15 (att. H.L.I.).
13 Francis, Christopher Thomas, Capt. (Tp.), d. of w., 26/5/16.
12 Francis, William Pollock, 2/Lt (T/Lt.), k. in a., 22/10/17.
17 Fraser, Herbert Ross, 2/Lt. (Tp.), k. in a., 24/8/16.
13 Fulton, Alexander, 2/Lt. (Tp.), k. in a., 19/8/16.
3 Furley, Wolseley Haig, Lt., k. in a., 26/4/18.
3 Fyson, Geoffrey, Lt., k. in a., 4/9/18 (att. 1/Bn.).
3 Fyvie, William, 2/Lt., k. in a., 26/8/17.
3 Gall, Grant, Lt., k. in a., 21/3/18 (att. 3/Fd. Sur. Co.).
15 Gee, George Edward, Capt. (Tp.), d. of w., 27/7/16.
13 Gellatly, Robert, 2/Lt., k. in a., 23/4/17.
14 Gibson, William, 2/Lt., k. in a., 1/7/16.
12 Glendinning, Arthur William Frederick, 2/Lt. (Tp.), k. in a., 14/7/16.
12 Gordon, David Elder, 2/Lt., k. in a., 15/7/16.
11 Grant, Charles William, T/Lt., A/Capt., d. of w., 12/10/17.
15 Grant, John, 2/Lt. (Tp.), k. in a., 1/7/16.
11 Grant, John Mann, 2/Lt. (Tp.), k. in a., 9/4/17.
2 Grimmond, Alfred, 2/Lt., k. in a., 14/7/16.
Grindlay, Alexander Brown, 2/Lt. (Tp.), died, 24/3/17 (att. 11/Bn.).
13 Guthrie, Charles Wilford, 2/Lt., k. in a., 1/8/17.
1 Halcrow, Thomas Tulloch, 2/Lt., k. in a., 3/5/17.
16 Hamilton, George John, 2/Lt. (Tp.), k. in a., 9/6/17.
16 Harrower, Peter, M.C., 2/Lt. (Tp.), k. in a., 17/10/18.
Hedderwick, Charles Stuart, 2/Lt., k. in a., 28/2/15.
16 Hendry, James, Capt. (Tp.), d. of w., 6/9/16.
11 Henry, John Allan, Capt. (Tp.), k. in a., 14/7/16.
Hewat, Anthony Morris Coates, Capt., k. in a., 8/9/14.
3 Hewitt, William George, 2/Lt., k. in a., 14/10/14.
13 Higgins, Hugh Stevenson, 2/Lt., k. in a., 28/3/18.
15 Hislop, John Hogben, 2/Lt. (Tp.), d. of w., 11/4/17.
1 Hobbs, John, 2/Lt., d. of w., 28/6/15.
15 Hodgson, Charles, 2/Lt. (Tp.), d. of w., 9/8/16.
15 Hole, William Arthur, Lt. (Tp.), k. in a., 1/7/16.
16 Hope, John Angus, 2/Lt., k. in a., 22/10/17.
17 Houston, Hugh, Lt. (Tp.), k. in a., 24/10/17.
Houston, William Houston, Capt. (Tp.), d. of w., 28/3/16, att. 12th (att. R.S.F.).
3 Howie, George Francis, 2/Lt., k. in a., 21/3/18.
Hudson, Harry, 2/Lt. (Tp.), k. in a., 21/9/18 (att. 1/4 Bn.).
2 Hunter, James Williamson, 2/Lt., d. of w., 14/11/16.
16 Ingles, Robert Adam, 2/Lt., k. in a., 21/3/18.
3 Inman, Leslie Yardley, 2/Lt., d. of w., 5/4/16 (att. Wilts R.).
Innes, Robert Prentice, 2/Lt. (Tp.), k. in a., 21/9/18 (att. 1/7 Bn.).
Jack, Gavine, 2/Lt., k. in a., 25/9/15.
Jackson, John Bell, Lt., k. in a., 7/6/17 (and R.F.C., 43 Sqd.).
13 Jardine, Charles Hunt, Lt. (Tp.), k. in a., 3/5/18 (2/2 K.A.R.).
Johnston, Edward John Farquharson, Capt., k. in a., 12/4/15.
11 Johnston, Charles Wright, 2/Lt. (Tp.), k. in a., 12/10/17.
11 Keen, Aubrey Owen, Lt. (Tp.), d. of w., 4/8/18.
11 Kennedy, Alexander, M.C., T/2/Lt., A/Capt., k. in a., 26/3/18.
3 Kerr, David Anselm, 2/Lt., k. in a., 14/10/14.
13 Kincaid, James Brown, Lt. (Tp.), k. in a., 23/4/17.
11 Lane, Harold Frank, 2/Lt., k. in a., 14/10/15.
15 Lawrence, James Linton, Capt. (Tp.), d. of w., 3/7/16.
11 Lemmy, Frederick George, Lt. (Tp.), k. in a., 14/7/16.
16 Linn, Peter, 2/Lt., k. in a., 22/10/17.
3 Lockhart, John Sutherland, Lt., k. in a., 10/5/16.
16 Lodge, Richard Cuthbert, Lt. (Tp.), k. in a., 27/8/17.
13 Logan, John Hastie, M.C., 2/Lt. (A/Capt.), k. in a., 1/8/17.
13 Loudon, Robert, Lt. (Tp.), k. in a., 13/9/18.
16 **Low, David Finlay, 2/Lt., k. in a., 26/10/17.**
15 **Lowe, George Alexander, 2/Lt. (Tp.), k. in a., 4/12/16.**
Lumsden, Alfred Forbes, D.S.O., Brig.-Gen., k. in a., 24/6/18 (Staff, 46 Inf. Bde. H.Q.).
3 Lunn, Herbert Charles, Lt., k. in a., 22/3/17.
3 Lyell, James Francis Ronaldson, Lt., killed, 25/11/17.
3 McColl, Ednor Ernest, 2/Lt. (A/Lt.), d. of w., 24/10/17.
13 Macdonald, Andrew Moffat, Capt. (Tp.), k. in a., 11/5/16.
11 Macdonald, Hugh Ferguson, 2/Lt. (Tp.), died, 20/5/18.
16 Macdonald, John, Capt. (Temp.), d. of w., 11/4/17.
Macfadyen, Walter, Lt., k. in a., 7/5/17.
13 McFarlane, Ronald Aitchison, Lt., k. in a., 25/9/15.
McGill, George Thomas, M.C., Lt. (A/Capt.), k. in a., 3/5/17.
11 Macgregor, James, M.C., 2/Lt. (Tp.), k. in a., 10/4/18.
16 McHoul, James Stewart, 2/Lt. (Tp.), d. of w., 26/8/17.
11 Macintosh, Thomas Gordon Gall, 2/Lt. (Tp.), k. in a., 18/8/18.
1 MacIver, Robert Troutbeck, 2/Lt., k. in a., 11/9/15.
McIntosh, William Alexander, 2/Lt., k. in a., 26/9/17.
3 McKay, A. S., 2/Lt., k. in a., 10/4/18.
Mackenzie, Edward Forbes, 2/Lt., k. in a., 14/12/14.
16 Mackenzie, James Graham, Lt., k. in a., 4/8/16.
13 Mackenzie, Thomas Graham, 2/Lt. (Tp.), d. of w., 31/8/17.
12 McKinley, Samuel Brown, M.C., Capt., d. of w., 7/2/19.
17 McKnight, Samuel, Capt. (Tp.), k. in a., 29/9/18.
13 Maclean, Kemp, 2/Lt. (Tp.), k. in a., 28/3/18.
12 MacMeeken, Guy Steel Peebles, M.C., Tp./Lt., A/Capt., d. of w., 5/5/18 (P. of W.).
12 McMurray, John, Capt., k. in a., 12/10/17.
2 McNaught, James, 2/Lt. (Tp.), k. in a., 7/1/17.
12 Macouat, John, 2/Lt. (Tp.), k. in a., 12/4/17.
13 Macpherson, George Denis, Major, k. in a., 27/9/15.
2 Malcolm, Robert James, Capt. (Tp.), d. of w., 15/7/16.
12 Maloney, Francis Joseph, Act. Capt., d. of w., 20/7/16.
13 Martin, William Murdoch, 2/Lt., k. in a., 22/8/17.
11 Mason, Cecil Wyatt, 2/Lt. (Tp.), k. in a., 8/4/17.
2 Matthews, Bertram Cash, Lt. (Tp.), k. in a., 24/3/17.
2 Maxwell, Richard, T/Lt., (A/Capt.), k. in a., 23/10/18.
11 Maybin, James Johnstone, Capt. (Tp.), k. in a., 14/7/16.
13 Mitchell, Jas. Thomas Rankin, D.S.O., T/Major (A/Lt.-Col.), d. of w., 1/4/18 (att. A. & S.H.).
Mitchell, Norman R., Lt., died, 6/6/18 (and R.A.F.).
3 Molson, Eric Elsdale, Lt., k. in a., 2/4/15.
16 Molloy, Wilfred Cyril, 2/Lt., d. of w., 10/5/18 (P.O.W.).
11 Moncur, William George, 2/Lt. (Tp.), d. of w., 25/12/17 (P.O.W.).
3 Morrison, Archibald, 2/Lt., d. of w., 9/4/17.
2 Morton, John Sydney, Lt. (Tp.), k. in a., 25/4/17.
11 Mullett, W. S., Lt. & Qr.-Mr., died, 31/1/18.
15 Munro, Donald, 2/Lt., k. in a., 28/4/17.
13 Munro, Claud Bruce, Lt. (Tp.), k. in a., 27/9/15.
11 Murray, Robert Davidson, 2/Lt. (Tp.), d. of w., 2/10/18.
1 Mulligan, Herbert Butler, 2/Lt. (Tp.), k. in a., 4/7/16.
3 Nisbet, John, 2/Lt., k. in a., 15/4/15.
15 Noble, William Smyth Jackson, 2/Lt. (Tp.), k. in a., 21/3/18.
3 Nye, Reginald Rayner, Capt., k. in a., 17/12/15.
13 Ogston, James, 2/Lt. (Tp.), d. of w., 15/9/16.
3 Owen, William Vandeleur, 2/Lt., died, 12/11/18.
15 Pagan, Gavin Lang, Capt., k. in a., 28/4/17.
2 Parsons, Herbert, 2/Lt. (Tp.), k. in a., 14/7/16.
11 Paton, Leslie, 2/Lt., k. in a., 21/3/17.
15 Paxton, James William, 2/Lt., k. in a., 21/3/18.
Peacock, Alfred Walter, 2/Lt. (Tp.), k. in a., 9/9/17 (and R.F.C., 24 Sqd.).
3 Pecker, Henry Cyril, 2/Lt., k. in a., 20/4/15.
13 Penney, Ian Campbell, Capt. (Tp.), k. in a., 27/9/15.
Pickett, F. C., 2/Lt., died, 6/1/15.
15 Pinkerton, Eric Mitchell, 2/Lt. (Tp.), k. in a., 1/7/16.
Playfair, Lambert, Lt., k. in a., 6/7/15 (att. R.F.C.).
Povah, Frank, Capt., k. in a., 16/6/15.
Price, Charles Lempriere, D.S.O., Capt., k. in a., 16/9/14.
Rainie, James Wilson McTurk, k. in a., 27/3/16.
16 Rawson, Harry William, Capt., died, 22/4/18 (P.O.W.).
15 Reid, Robert, Lt. (Tp.), k. in a., 1/7/16.
12 Reilly, James Miller, 2/Lt. (Tp.), k in a., 20/9/17.
13 Renwick, Gideon Andrew Forrest, 2/Lt., k. in a., 22/8/17.
Ritchie, Frank Robert, 2/Lt., k. in a., 15/8/15 (att. H.L.I.).
12 Ritchie, John Mearns, 2/Lt. (Tp.), k. in a., 15/7/16.
13 Robertson, Gilbert Swale, Capt. (Tp.), k. in a., 27/9/15.
2 Robinson, Max Louis, 2/Lt., k. in a., 22/7/16.
Robson-Scott, Thomas Selby, Lt., k. in a., 14/12/14.
3 Ross, Cecil Goodall, M.C., 2/Lt., k. in a., 23/4/17 (att. T.M.B.).
16 Ross, Peter, Capt. (Tp.), k. in a., 1/7/16.
Ross, Ronald Campbell, 2/Lt., k. in a., —/9/14.
3 Ruddiman, William, 2/Lt., k. in a., 13/11/16.
16 Russell, George Smith, 2/Lt. (Tp.), k. in a., 1/7/16.
2 Russell, James Galloway, 2/Lt., k. in a., 3/5/17.
14 Russell, William Black, Lt., k. in a., 19/6/15.
11 Sandilands, John George, 2/Lt. (Tp.), k. in a., 21/3/17.
3 Sandison, Eric William, 2/Lt., died, 18/11/16.
Saward, Harry Douglas, Capt., k. in a., 23/3/15.
16 Scarlett, Robert Stubbs, 2/Lt. (Tp.), k. in a., 20/12/17.
3 Scott, Campbell Lowe, Lt. (Tp.), k. in a., 2/9/18 (att. T.M.B.).
3 Scott, James Francis, 2/Lt., k. in a., 23/4/17.
1 Scott, John Michael Corse, Major, died, 29/3/17.
12 Scott, Munro Briggs, 2/Lt. (Tp.), k. in a., 12/4/17.
17 Scougal, Alec Graham, M.C., Major (A/Lt.-Col.), k. in a., 18/9/18.
2 Shearman, Valentine, Lt. (A/Capt.), d. of w., 25/3/18.
13 Sim, Alexander Taylor, 2/Lt. (Tp.), k. in a., 12/5/16.
3 Sim, James Robertson Gould, 2/Lt., k. in a., 5/6/17.
12 Skinner, William, M.C., Capt. (Tp.), k. in a., 25/4/18.

1 Smith, Duncan Robertson Moir, 2/Lt. (Tp.), d. of w., 27/8/17.
14 Smith, George Pringle, Lt. (Tp.), k. in a., 12/4/17.
11 Smith, John Alexander Hay, 2/Lt. (Tp.), k. in a., 14/8/15.
11 Smith, Percy George Cecil, 2/Lt. (Tp.), k. in a., 18/8/18.
13 Smith, Thomas, 2/Lt., k. in a., 16/5/18.
3 Snead-Cox, Richard Mary, 2/Lt., k. in a., 28/10/14.
2 Spafford, Alfred Douglas Dale, 2/Lt., A/Capt., k. in a., 13/11/16.
3 Spence, William Kenneth Mackay, 2/Lt., k. in a., 23/4/17.
2 Spinney, Frank, 2/Lt. (Tp.), d. of w., 2/10/16.
13 Stell, J., 2/Lt., died, 19/6/18 (and R.A.F.).
16 Stewart, John Walcot, M.C., Lt. (Tp.), k. in a., 21/3/18.
2 Stewart, Norman Sinclair, Capt., k. in a., 30/9/15.
15 Stocks, Harris Lawrence, D.S.O., Major, k. in a., 1/7/16.
17 Struth, James Scotland, 2/Lt. (Tp.), k. in a., 16/9/17.
12 Strutt, Richard Neville, 2/Lt. (Tp.), k. in a., 25/9/15 (att. 2/Bn.).
17 Sturrock, Thomas Gibbs Gordon, 2/Lt. (Tp.), d. of w., 16/10/16 (and R.F.C.).
2 Sutherland, James, 2/Lt. (Tp.), k. in a., 9/4/17.
3 Thomas, Howard Victor Fraser, M.C., Lt., k. in a., 22/10/18.
1 Thompson, George Masterman, Lt., k. in a., 22/8/14 (Gold Coast R., W. Afr. Frontier Force).
12 Thomson, Archibald Walton, Lt. (Tp.), k. in a., 3/5/17.
12 Thorburn, Edward Francis, Capt., k. in a., 23/3/15.
Thornton, James, 2/Lt., killed, 9/11/16 (and R.F.C.).
15 Tod, William Lennox, Capt. (Tp.), d. of w., 29/4/17.
13 Tomlinson, David Mitchell, Major (Tp.), d. of w., 13/5/16.
3 Tredgold, John Clarkson, M.C., 2/Lt., k. in a., 12/4/17.
14 Tresidder, Thomas Arthur, Capt., k. in a., 28/6/15.
3 Trotter, Alexander Nigel, Lt., d. of w., 12/10/14.
16 Turnbull, George, 2/Lt. (Tp.), k. in a., 14/4/18.
11 Turner, Ernest Gilbert, D.S.O., 2/Lt. (T/Capt.), k. in a., 12/4/17.
2 Turner, James Alexander, D.S.O., M.C., Lt. (T/Lt.-Col.), k. in a., 26/7/18.
16 Urquhart, Francis Clement, Lt., d. of w., 13/4/18.
11 Waddell, James Hamilton, 2/Lt., k. in a., 5/6/17.
11 Walker, George Ernest, Lt. (Tp.), k. in a., 6/6/17.
Walker, Norman Reginald, Lt., k. in a., 23/8/18 (att. K.O.S.B.).
12 Watkinson, Arthur, 2/Lt. (Tp.), d. of w., 3/8/16.
15 Watson, Frank Fairweather, 2/Lt. (Tp.), k. in a., 4/8/16.
16 Watson, John, 2/Lt. (Tp.), k. in a., 7/4/17.
17 Watson, John, 2/Lt., k. in a., 27/4/18.
3 Watt, Alexander, 2/Lt., k. in a., 18/8/18.
Webster, Bruce, 2/Lt., k. in a., 5/9/18 (att. 1/9 Bn.).
3 West, William Anderson, M.C., 2/Lt., k. in a., 21/6/18.
3 Westwater, Frederick, 2/Lt., k. in a., 28/4/17.
3 Whitley, Benjamin Heywood, 2/Lt., k. in a., 17/7/16.
12 Whittaker, Charles Brown, Lt., k. in a., 22/7/16.
2 Whyte, Robert, Lt., k. in a., 12/4/18.
3 Wight, William Stewart Balmain, 2/Lt., k. in a., 9/4/17.
15 Wilson, Allan Clark, 2/Lt., k. in a., 28/4/17.
13 Wilson, Andrew, 2/Lt., k. in a., 16/7/18.
Wilson, Ralph Edwyn, Lt., d. of w., 28/9/15.
Winterton, William, 2/Lt., k. in a., 27/9/15.
2 Wood, Robert Smith, 2/Lt. (Tp.), d. of w.. 24/11/17.
Woltherspoon, James, 2/Lt., k. in a., 2/10/18 (att. 5/6 Bn.).
2 Worthington-Wilmer, Hugh Ferdinand Mansfield, Capt., k. in a., 11/5/16.
12 Young, Claude Norman, 2/Lt. (Tp.), d. of w., 14/7/16.
Young, Norman Mitchell, Lt., k. in a., 25/4/15.
13 Yule, Charles Whitehead, Capt. (Tp.), k. in a., 11/5/16.

The Queen's (Royal West Surrey Regiment).

7 A'Bear, Hedley John, A/Capt. (Tp. 2/Lt.), k. in a., 10/7/17.
1 Abercrombie, Alexander Ralph, D.S.O., M.C., Capt., died, 31/12/18.
10 Adams, Caleb Henry, 2/Lt. (Tp.), k. in a., 20-22/9/17.
7 Adams, James Scovell, 2/Lt. (Tp.), d. of w., 8/8/18.
3 Adenet, Robert Edward, 2/Lt., died, 11/4/17 (P. of W., and R.F.C., 48 Sqd.).
3 Albinson, William Arthur, 2/Lt., k. in a., 26/4/18.
3 Alderson, Albert Evelyn, Lt. (A/Capt.), drowned, 11/3/18 (att. 1/Y.L.I.).
Allan, Alwyn Munton, M.C., Capt., d. of w., 21/4/18.
10 Andrews, Leslie Ernest, M.C., Tp. Capt. (A/Major), k. in a., 20/9/17.
9 Anthony, George Adam Moriarty, Lt., k. in a., 24/1/16, W.A.F.F.
11 Apted, Eardley, Lt., k. in a., 1/8/17.
Armitage, Alfred Cecil, 2/Lt., killed, 21/7/15.
6 Ashton, Alexander Leslie, 2/Lt. (Tp.), k. in a., 1/7/18.
6 Aspden, Ernest Harold, 2/Lt. (Tp.), k. in a., 9/4/17.
6 Aspden, Frank Hartley, Lt. (Tp.), d. of w., 20/9/18.
9 Attfield, Sidney Hunrich, Lt., k. in a., 19/4/17 (att. Hamps.).
Austin, Cyril Frederic, 2/Lt., k. in a., 10/3/15.
11 Baker, Lionel Charles Edwin, M.C.. 2/Lt. (A/Capt.), k. in a., 1/10/18.
7 Batchelar, Robert Thomas, 2/Lt., k. in a., 23/3/18.
10 Batson, Henry Thomas, Tp. 2/Lt., k. in a., 11/9/17 (and R.F.C., 48 Sqd.).
1 Baynes, William H., 2/Lt., died, 12/10/18.
7 Bearman, Cecil Laurence, 2/Lt. (Tp.), k. in a., 23/8/18.
Bennett, Eric Fairfax, M.C., T/Lt. (A/Capt.), k. in a., 18/9/18.
7 Bennett, Ivan Provis Wentworth, T/Capt., k. in a., 14/7/16.
9 Bennett, Lawrence Ernest, 2/Lt. (Tp.), k. in a., 24/8/16.
2 Bennett, Maurice Porter, 2/Lt., d. of w., 6/10/17.
10 Bessell, Mowbray, Capt. (Tp.), k. in a., 15-17/9/16.
1 Bethell, Edward Walter, Capt., k. in a., 21/9/18.
3 Birch, Edward Cecil, Lt., died, 26/1/19 (and R.A.F.).
10 Bird, Edwy Harold, T/Capt., k. in a., 24/2/17.
Bird, John Greville Hobart, Lt., k. in a., 25(Abt)/10/14.
1 Blagden, Maurice Bernard, 2/Lt., k. in a., 21/9/18.
7 Blewchamp, Ernest John, 2/Lt. (Tp.), k. in a., 14/7/16.
Bottomley, Harry Roderick, Lt.-Col., d. of w., 18/5/15.
6 Bourne, Cyprian, 2/Lt. (Tp.), d. of w., 11/4/17.
11 Bowden, Eric Gordon, M.C., Major (Tp.), k. in a., 22/7/18.
1 Bower, Gerard Rimington, 2/Lt., k. in a., 15/7/16.
Bradshaw, Arthur William Archibald, 2/Lt., k. in a., 25/9/15.
2 Brocklehurst, Thomas Pownall, Capt. (Tp.), k. in a., 1/7/16.
2 Brown, Arthur Lyster (Tp.) 2/Lt., k. in a., 25/9/15.
1 Brown, Keith Andrews, Lt. (T/Capt.), d. of w., 22/9/18.
Budge, Preston Frederick, T/Lt., k. in a., 8-9/5/17 (att. R. Berk. R.).
8 Burgess, Philip Gulson, 2/Lt. (Tp.), d. of w., 14/10/15.
1 Burghope, Gerald Harry Vernon, 2/Lt., k. in a., 23/4/17.
11 Burnaby, Hugo Beaumont, D.S.O., Lt.-Col., k. in a., 8/9/16.
3 Burnett, John David Napier, 2/Lt., k. in a., 25/2/16.
1 Burton, Alfred, Lt., k. in a., 11/1/16.
7 V.C. Bushell, Christopher, D.S.O., Capt., T/Lt.-Col., k. in a., 8/8/18.
3 Butterworth, Walter Cecil, 2/Lt., k. in a., 21/7/16.
3 Calkin, Brian Penry Bernard, Lt., k. in a., 10/7/18.
9 Campbell, John Dundas, T/2/Lt., k. in a., 24/8/16.
6 Castle, Tudor Ralph, T/2/Lt., k. in a., 31/8/16.
2 Cawston, George, 2/Lt., died, 29/10/18 (att. R.A.F.).
3 Chancellor, Geoffrey Ellis, 2/Lt., k. in a., 9/7/16 (att. R.F.C.).
2 Chapman, Theodore Victor, M.C., Lt. (A/Capt.), k. in a., 12/5/17.
1 Charlwood, William Roger, T/2/Lt., k. in a., 18/7/17.
9 Chatterton, Harold Montagu Newnham, 2/Lt. (Tp.), d. of w., 18/6/16.
6 Christie, James Allan, T/2/Lt., d. of w., 6/11/17.
6 Chubb, Geoffrey, Capt., k. in a., 12/7/15.
Churcher, B. T., Lt.-Col., died, 31/12/18.
8 Clark, John MacTaggart, Capt., died, 18/11/18.
8 Cleef, Henry Victor, T/2/Lt., k. in a., 6/12/17.
7 Cloudesley, Hugh, T/Lt., k. in a., 1/7/16.
1 Colebrook, Geoffrey Bathurst, 2/Lt., k. in a., 27/7/15.
1 Collings, Eric D'Auvergne, 2/Lt., k. in a., 23/8/16.
11 Conway, Guy, 2/Lt. (Tp.), k. in a., 29/9/18.
11 Cook, Humphrey Noel Felix, T/2/Lt., k. in a., 26/6/17.
8 Cook, Cyril Annesley, Capt. (Tp.), k. in a., 25-26/9/15.
11 Cooke, John Valentina, M.C., T/Lt. (A/Capt.), k. in a., 1/10/18 att. T.M.B.).
7 Cooper, Percy Valentine, T/2/Lt. (A/Capt.), k. in a., 8/8/18.
6 Coppin, Richard Alfred, T/Capt., k. in a., 11/4/17.
2 Crees, William, 2/Lt., k. in a., 1/7/16.
8 Cressy, Charles Howard, 2/Lt. (Tp.), k. in a., 25/9/15.
1 Crichton, Arthur James, 2/Lt. (Tp.), k. in a., 15/7/16.
Crook, Leslie Arthur, M.C., T/Lt. (A/Capt.), k. in a., 25/9/17.
1 Crompton, Thomas, Lt., k. in a., 13/4/18.
11 Crozier, Thomas Alexander, M.C., Lt. (Tp.), k. in a., 23/3/18.
10 Curtis, Robert Henry, T/2/Lt., k. in a., 20/9/17.
7 Daly, Cyril Francis St. Felix, T/2/Lt., k. in a., 14/10/17.
7 Damer, Wilfred Percy, T/2/Lt., k. in a., 18/11/16.
Dandridge, George Sidney, T/2/Lt., k. in a., 1/7/16.
11 Darlington, Tom, Lt., k. in a., 1/10/18.
De Rougemont, Maurice Henry, 2/Lt., k. in a., 16/5/15.
3 Dimmock, James Bolton, 2/Lt., d. of w., 16/5/17.
2 Driver, Bernard Henry, M.C., A/Major (2/Lt.), k. in a., 4/10/17.
Eastwood, Frank Molyneux, Lt., d. of w., 30/10/14.
10 Eaves, Alfred Thomas, Lt. (Tp.), k. in a., 3/10/16.
6 Edwards, Eric Wilson, M.C., T/Lt. (A/Capt.), k. in a., 30/11/17.
11 Edwards, Roland Frederick, M.C., Lt., (Tp.), d. of w., 8/10/18.
1 Elliott, Clarence William, 2/Lt. (Tp.), k. in a., 14/4/18.
1 Eltham, Charles William, Lt., k. in a., 3/11/16.
9 Esten, Gerald Philip, Lt. (Tp.), k. in a., 6/8/15 (att. Essex R.).
3 Evans, Frank Montague, 2/Lt., k. in a., 4-5/4/16 (att. 9/R. War. R.).
Eyres, H. T., 2/Lt., died, 9/11/18 (and R.A.F.).
10 Fairclough, Eric Montague, T/2/Lt., d. of w., 25/2/17.
8 Fairtlough, Frederick Howard, C.M.G., Hon. Col. (Tp. Lt.-Col.), k. in a., 25-27/9/15.
7 Farren, John, 2/Lt., k. in a., 13/11/16 (att. Suff. R.).
Fernald, Van D., Lt., k. in a., 23/7/18 (att. R.A.F.).
Field, Charles Abel, T/2/Lt., d. of w., 12/11/18 (att. 8/Bn.).
10 Field, Vincent Alfred, 2/Lt., k. in a., 20/9/17.
2 Fitch, Alfred Cyril, T/2/Lt., k. in a., 2/4/17.
6 Fitch, Conrad William, Lt. (Tp.), k. in a., 3/7/16.
6 Flanagan, George Anton, T/2/Lt., k. in a., 30/6/18.
6 Flint, Ralph Stacey, 2/Lt., k. in a., 27/3/18.
2 Foord Kelsey, John Mordaunt, 2/Lt., k. in a., 1/7/16.
2 Ford, Lawton Stephen, 2/Lt., k. in a., 1/7/16.
11 Ford, Norman Stanley, M.C., 2/Lt., killed, 19/7/18 (and R.A.F.).
Fowler, Cecil Dashwood Melman, Lt., k. in a., 25/9/15.
1 Fowler, Norman John, T/2/Lt., k. in a., 23/4/17.
Fox, Michael Stanley, T/2/Lt., k. in a., 20/11/17 (att. 6/Bn.).
Foy, Martin Victor, Capt., k. in a., 13/10/14.
7 Freeman, James Edward Hutton, 2/Lt., k. in a., 24/4/16 (att. R.F.C., 29 Sqd.).
3 Freeman, Noel, 2/Lt., k. in a., 5/4/18.
7 Friend, Stanley John, 2/Lt., d. of w., 22/4/18.
Fuller, William Blyth, Capt., k. in a., 16/5/15.
2 Furze, Nevil Ford, 2/Lt., k. in a., 14/3/17.
3 Garnier, John Warren, Capt., d. of w., 29/5/15.
6 Giles, William James, T/2/Lt., k. in a., 6/4/18.

2 Gillies, James, 2/Lt. (Tp.), k. in a., 1/7/16.
Godwin Williams, Frederick James, Hon. Capt., died, 23/11/18.
3 Goldberg, Frederick William, 2/Lt., k. in a., 3/10/16 (att. R. Dub. Fus.).
3 Goldberg, Herbert Walter, 2/Lt., d. of w., 31/7/15.
7 Golding, Harold, T/2/Lt., d. of w., 25/8/17.
9 Grant, Alan Francis Montague, 2/Lt. (Tp.), d. of w., 18/6/16.
2 Green, Charles Taylor, 2/Lt., k. in a., 26/10/17.
1 Green, Eric De Wilde, T/2/Lt., d. of w., 15/4/18.
8 Green, Thomas Claud Erskine, 2/Lt., (Tp.), k. in a., 31/7/17.
9 Greenlees, Charles Fouracres, T/2/Lt., k. in a., 1/7/16.
2 Griffin, Charles John, T/2/Lt. (A/Capt.), k. in a., 1/9/16.
1 Gross, William Henry Bright, 2/Lt., k. in a., 3/11/16.
Haddon Smith, Walter Basil, Capt., k. in a., 16/5/15.
Haigh, Charles Roderick, Lt., k. in a., 7/11/14.
10 Hale, Alfred Llewellyn, Tp. Capt., k. in a., 8/7/18.
6 Hall, Clifford Sheppard, T/2/Lt., k. in a., 3/7/16.
Hamilton, Arthur Percival, T/Lt.-Col., k. in a., 15/9/16.
3 Hamilton, Guy Stanley Gerald, T/Lt. & Adj., k. in a., 1/8/17.
3 Harding, Reginald, M.C., 2/Lt., k. in a., 28/3/18 (att. 6/Bn.).
10 Hart, James Wilson, M.C., Capt., k. in a., 24/3/18.
7 Harvey, John Albert, T/2/Lt., k. in a., 4/4/18 (att. T.M.B.).
Hayes, William, D.S.O., Capt., died, 20/10/18.
Heath, Maurice Gordon, Lt.-Col., k. in a., 25/9/15.
Heath, Raymond Leopold Greig, Capt., k. in a., 25/9/15.
7 Hebeler, Roland Stuart, T/Capt., d. of w., 16/9/15.
11 Hedley, William Tames, T/Lt. (A/Capt.), k. in a., 7/6/17.
7 Henderson, James Fuller, T/Lt. (A/Capt.), k. in a., 26/4/18.
Henriques, Ronald Lucas Quiand, Lt., k. in a., 14/9/14.
9 Henwood, John Edwin, T/2/Lt., d. of w., 1/7/16.
7 Herbert, Ronald Crouch, T/2/Lt., k. in a., 1/7/16.
1 Higgs, Reginald Frank, T/2/Lt., k. in a., 22/9/18.
3 Hiller, Alan Menzies, 2/Lt., k. in a., 16/5/15.
10 Hine, Claude Annesley, T/2/Lt., d. of w., 16/10/16.
2 Hobbs, Eric, 2/Lt., k. in a., 1/7/16.
Hodgson, Charles Basil Mortimer, Capt., d. of w., 1/4/18.
3 Hoggard, Ernest John, 2/Lt., k. in a., 5/11/16 (att. M.G.C.).
10 Hoggett, Frank Reginald, T/2/Lt., d. of w., 18/7/16.
Holmes, Thomas Symonds, 2/Lt., k. in a., 12/11/14 (att. E. Kent R.).
7 Hook, Valentine, Capt. (Tp.), k. in a., 3/5/17.
8 Hoole, Ronald Herbert, T/2/Lt., k. in a., 21/8/16.
8 Hopgood, John Lambert, T/2/Lt., d. of w., 17/8/16.
2 How, John Christian, 2/Lt., k. in a., 2/4/17.
7 Howard, Lyulph Walter Mowbray, Tp. Lt., k. in a., 15/9/15.
Howell, Maurice Ives Berthon, 2/Lt., k. in a., 25/9/15.
Howells, James, 2/Lt. (Tp.), k. in a., 21/3/18 (att. 8th).
Humphreys, Dudley Francis, 2/Lt., d. of w., 16/5/15.
8 Humphrey, T. A., 2/Lt., k. in a., 3/5/18 (and R.A.F.).
Ingram, Gerald Sclater, Lt., k. in a., 21/10/14.
Ive, David, 2/Lt., k. in a., 23/10/14.
1 Jackman, Osbert William, M.M., 2/Lt. (Tp.), d. of w., 7/11/18.
Jacques, David Wright, 2/Lt., d. of w., 1/12/16.
10 Javes, Robert Charles, T/2/Lt., k. in a., 15-17/9/16.
8 Johnson, Eric Guildford, 2/Lt., k. in a., 25-26/9/15.
3 Johnson, Philip Walter, 2/Lt., d. of w., 18/5/15.
2 Jones, Charles Taylor, 2/Lt. (Tp.), k. in a., 25/9/15.
3 Jones, Hywel Herbert Saunders, 2/Lt., k. in a., 4/3/17.
11 Kelly Thomas, M.C., Major (Tp.), k. in a., 26/6/17.
1 Kemp, Charles George, 2/Lt. (Tp.), k. in a., 24/9/17.
9 Kingston, Harold William Fellemans, Lt., k. in a., 21/8/15.
7 Kitchin, Anthony Walter Brook, T/2/Lt., k. in a., 24/9/15.
6 Knight, John Owen Coldhan, T/2/Lt., k. in a., 30/11/17.
Koebel, Charles Edward, Capt., d. of w., 24/8/15 (att. Lan. Fus.).
10 Laing, James Alexander, 2/Lt. (Tp.), k. in a., 14/10/18.
3 Lambert, Arthur Frere, Major (Tp. Lt.-Col.), k. in a., 2/11/17 (att. Lond. R.).
8 Lane-Nichols, Douglas William, T/Capt., k. in a., 20/8/16.
Lang-Browne, John Agnew, Capt., k. in a., 16/5/15.
1 Laughlin, Philip Herbert, Lt. (Tp.), d. of w., 21/12/17.
3 Leader, Benjamin Eastlake, Capt., k. in a., 12/10/16.
Le Bas, Owen Vincent, Lt., k. in a., 7/11/15 (and R.F.C.).
7 Legge, David St. Clan, 2/Lt., k. in a., 14/7/16.
Lessels, Robert Murray, 2/Lt., k. in a., 29/7/18.
2 Lewis, Hugh Frederick, Capt., k. in a., 19/10/14.
3 Limbrick, Arthur William Wentworth, 2/Lt., k. in a., 14/3/17.
6 Lippiatt, William George, 2/Lt. (Tp.), k. in a., 10/8/18.
1 Lloyd, Reginald Conway, T/2/Lt., k. in a., 3/11/16.
8 Long, Arthur William Emanuel, T/2/Lt., k. in a., 24/8/16.
3 Longbourne, Hugh Richard, D.S.O., Capt., k. in a., 3/5/17.
3 Lukyn, Stanley Edward, M.C., 2/Lt., killed, 10/4/17 (and R.F.C.).
McCabe, Albert Peter Patrick, 2/Lt., k. in a., 16-17/5/15.
8 McDermott, Lawrence Alphonsus, 2/Lt. (Tp.), k. in a., 11/10/18.
8 Mackenzie, Boyce Mackey Scobie, T/Lt. (A/Capt.), k. in a., 22/3/18.
11 McKenzie, Alexander, T/Lt., k. in a., 7/6/17.
3 McWhinnie, Charles Routledge, Lt., d. of w., 1/7/18.
Mahony, James, T/Lt., d. of w., 4/3/17.
6 Maisey, Alfred George, 2/Lt., k. in a., 12/5/17.
10 Mance, Henry Eric, 2/Lt., k. in a., 15/9/16.
2 Mapleson, Gerald Horsley (Tp.) 2/Lt., k. in a., 26/4/17.
7 Marshall, Henry, Tp. 2/Lt., k. in a., 1/8/18.
7 Marston, Arthur Bright, T/2/Lt., d. of w., 14/7/16.
7 Martin, Henry Lloyd, T/Capt., k. in a., 28/9/16.
6 Martin, Alfred Stanley, 2/Lt. (Tp.), d. of w., 26/10/18.
11 Martin, Trice, 2/Lt. (Tp.), k. in a., 7/6/17.
7 Mason, Charles Harold, 2/Lt. (Tp.), k. in a., 6/7/17.
Messom, Harold, 2/Lt., k. in a., 16/5/15.
3 Millard, David Edward Hall, 2/Lt., k. in a., 23/4/17.
8 Millard, Edgar John, 2/Lt. (Tp.), d. of w., 31/7/17.
7 Miller, Francis John, 2/Lt., k. in a., 1/7/16.
3 Morris, Lionel Bertram Frank, 2/Lt., d. of w., 17/9/16 (and R.F.C., 4 Sqd., whilst P. of W.).
1 Mundye, Arnold, 2/Lt. (Tp.), killed, 29/7/16.
2 Musson, John Henry, 2/Lt., k. in a., 19/7/15.
6 Newman, Cecil Harold, 2/Lt. (Tp.), k. in a., 12/5/17.
Nicholls, E. C. H. R., Lt., k. in a., 20/9/18 (and R.A.F.).
Oldfield, Guy Christopher Ottley, Lt., k. in a., 5/9/14 (and King's Af. Rifs.).
3 Osborne, Albert John Francis, 2/Lt., k. in a, 10/7/17.
6 Oswell, Percy Vincent, 2/Lt. (Tp.), k. in a., 20/9/18.
1 Parnell, Geoffrey Brooke, Major (Tp.), k. in a., 15/7/16.
16 Parsons, William Douglas Reynolds, 2/Lt., k. in a., 26/5/18.
9 Passmore, Arthur William, 2/Lt., k. in a., 4/4/16.
Peake, William Francis Copson, Lt. (Tp.), d. of w., 9/7/16.
9 Peet, John Edward Grimston, 2/Lt., killed, 27/2/15.
Pell, Beauchamp Tyndall, D.S.O., Lt.-Col., d. of w., 4/11/14.
Pemble, Clarence Arthur Lyon, 2/Lt., k. in a., 1/8/18.
11 Penman, Geoffrey Evans, Lt. (Tp.), k. in a., 9/5/17 (att. M. G. Corps).
8 Penrose, George Alwyn, Capt. (Tp.), k. in a., 9/4/17.
7 Penrose-Fitzgerald, Maurice J., Lt. (Tp.), d. of w., 26/7/16.
1 Perkins, Leonard, 2/Lt. (Tp.), k. in a., 3/11/16.
2 Perry, Sidney, M.C., M.M., 2/Lt. (A/Capt.), k. in a., 7/8/18.
10 Philips, Henry Charles, 2/Lt. (Tp.), k. in a., 7/12/17.
Pilleau, Henry Charles, D.S.O., Lt.-Col., d. of w., 21/9/14.
Plant, Frederic George, 2/Lt. (Tp.), k. in a., 25/9/15.
10 Pope, William Archer, Capt. (Tp.), d. of w., 7/10/16.
9 Poulton, Frederick James, Lt. (Tp.), k. in a., 2/11/17 (att. Hamps.).
Pound, Murray Stuart, 2/Lt., d. of w., 7/11/14.
8 Powell, Allan Wentworth, 2/Lt. (Tp.), k. in a., 21/8/16.
7 Power, John James, 2/Lt. (Tp.), k. in a., 19/9/18.
3 Pratt, George Leslie, 2/Lt., k. in a., 16/5/15.
Pringle, Robert Scott, Lt., d. of w., 14/9/14.
1 Purchas, Geoffrey Thomas, 2/Lt., k. in a., 26/9/17.
6 Pym, John Scarlett, 2/Lt. (Tp.), k. in a., 5/12/16.
8 Ratcliffe, Frederick Frank, 2/Lt. (Tp.), d. of w., 10/9/17.
Rawlings, Thomas William, 2/Lt. (Tp.), died, 8/10/18 (att. R. Fus.).
8 Reynolds, Francis Daniel, M.C. 2/Lt. (Tp.), died, 9/9/17.
3 Richards, Henry Heaton, 2/Lt., k. in a., 2/4/17.
Ricketts, Harold Edwin, 2/Lt. (Tp.), d. of w., 14/7/16 (att. M.G.C.).
7 Roberson, Frank Hubert Langhorne, 2/Lt., d. of w., 12/8/17.
6 Roberts, Frederick John, Major (Tp.), d. of w., 17/10/15.
2 Roberts, James Thursby, 2/Lt., d. of w., 20/7/16.
3 V.C. Robertson, Clement, A/Capt., Lt. (Tp.), k. in a., 4/10/17 (att. Tank Corps).
3 Robinson, William Alfred Layton, 2/Lt., k. in a., 26/6/17.
10 Robson, Albert Frank, Capt. (Tp.), k. in a., 24/3/18.
7 Rogers, Cecil Walter, 2/Lt. (Tp.), d. of w., 28/12/17.
10 Ronaldson, James Gray, 2/Lt. (Tp.), k. in a., 20/9/17 (att. T.M.B.).
9 Rope, John Arthur, 2/Lt. (Tp.), k. in a., 24/8/16.
7 Roskilly, Alfred, 2/Lt. (Tp.), k. in a., 3/5/17.
1 Rouquette, John Hector, 2/Lt., k. in a., 17/7/16.
7 Russell, Joseph Eric, 2/Lt., k. in a., 23/11/16.
6 Rutherford, Ralph Baillie, Capt. (Tp.), k. in a., 3/7/16.
2 Rutter, Frank Lionel, 2/Lt. (Tp.), k. in a., 14/7/16.
11 Ryan, Alfred Eric, 2/Lt. (A/Capt.), k. in a., 23/3/18.
7 Saltmarshe, Oliver Edwin, Lt. (Tp.), k. in a., 1/7/16.
7 Savory, Ernest Harley, 2/Lt., k. in a., 8/8/17.
2 Schult, Edgar, 2/Lt. (Tp.), d. of w., 28/10/17.
3 Schunck, Roger Henry, 2/Lt., died, 31/10/14.
6 Schwage, Sidney Philip, 2/Lt. (Tp.), k. in a., 7/9/18.
7 Scott, George Henry Hall, Capt. (Tp.), k. in a., 1/7/16.
Scott, Nigel Dennistoun, 2/Lt., killed, 19/4/16 (and R.F.C.).
10 Seeds, William Albert, 2/Lt. (Tp.), k. in a., 6-7/7/17.
2 Sells, Archibald Jenner, Lt. (Tp.), k. in a., 26/10/16.
Selous, F. H. B., M.C., Capt., k. in a., 4/1/18 (and R.F.C.).
7 Servante, Alfred William, 2/Lt. (Tp.), k. in a., 18/9/18.
9 Shaw, Edward Lockhart, 2/Lt. (Tp.), k. in a., 5/8/16.
7 Sheppard, Joseph Henry, 2/Lt. (Tp.), k. in a., 24/8/18.
Slatter, Roland Percy, Capt. (Tp.), k. in a., 15/7/16.
11 Smith, Alexander Joseph, 2/Lt., k. in a., 31/7/17.
2 Smith, Godfrey Garrett, 2/Lt., k. in a., 11/5/17.
11 Smith, Thurston Boyd, 2/Lt. (Tp.), k. in a., 7/6/17.
2 Stanfield, Alfred Vivian, 2/Lt., k. in a., 16/8/16 (att. R. Fus.).
Stanley Creek, Robert Forbes Stanley, D.S.O., Capt., k. in a., 29/10/14.
Stenhouse, Herbert Wilson, D.S.O., Major, k. in a., 26/6/16 (G.S.O., Div. H.Q.).
8 Stevens, Percival Charles, 2/Lt., k. in a., 6/4/17.
Stevenson, John Connell, 2/Lt. (Tp.), k. in a., 23/8/18.
11 Strawson, Frank Gordon, 2/Lt. (Tp.). k. in a., 1/10/18.
Strong, Howard Bertie, Lt., k. in a., 29/10/14.
2 Stovold, Percy Angel, Capt., k. in a., 1/9/16.
Strudwick, John Meredith Ker, 2/Lt., d. of w., 21/4/18.
Sweet Henry George, 2/Lt. (Tp.), k. in a., 25/9/18 (att. 2/4 Bn.).
7 Swindall, Arthur Cecil, 2/Lt. (Tp.), k. in a., 11/10/17.
Sworder, Hubert Pelham, Lt., k. in a., 2/4/17 (and R.F.C.).
7 Taylor, Arthur George, 2/Lt., d. of w., 26/4/18.
Thomas, Alma Cyril, Lt., d. of w., 8/11/14.
3 Thompson, Charles William, 2/Lt., k. in a., 29/6/18 (att. E. Kent R.).
Thornycroft, John Ralph Mylton, Capt., k. in a., 21/10/14.
6 Tollemache, John Eadred, Lt. (Tp.), k. in a., 21/8/16.
7 Towes, Norman Henry, 2/Lt. (Tp.), k. in a., 4/11/18.
1 Trench, Percy Richard Oliver, Lt. (T/Capt.), k. in a., 25/1/17 (att. R. W. Fus.).
1 Tucker, Frederick Dennis, 2/Lt., k. in a., 25/9/17.

1 Tweedie-Smith, Alan, 2/Lt. (Tp.), k. in a., 13/10/15.
6 Varndell, Charles Henry Essex, Lt. (Tp.), k. in a., 13/3/16.
6 Wadson, Stanley Parker, 2/Lt., k. in a., 10/8/18.
2 Walch, James Bernard Millard, 2/Lt. (Tp.), k. in a., 25/9/15.
8 Waldie, Charles Percival, 2/Lt., k. in a., 26/9/15.
1 Wallis, George Herbert, Capt. (and Q.M.), d. of w., 20/9/18.
7 Walpole, John Robsart, Capt., k. in a., 1/7/16.
Walter, Joseph Stanley, Capt. (Tp.), killed, 21/5/18.
Walter, Stephen Reginald Parke, Lt., k. in a., 31/7/17 (att. R.F.C.).
7 Ward, Allen Dudley Walter, 2/Lt. (Tp.), died, 23/7/17.
3 Warrell-Bowring, Walter John, 2/Lt., k. in a., 30/7/16 (att. 6/Bn.).
Warren, Dawson, Lt.-Col., k. in a., 17/9/14.
10 Webb, Gordon Arthur, Lt. (Tp.), k. in a., 20/9/17.
Weeding, Thomas, Major, k. in a., 26/8/17.
West, Stanley James, 2/Lt., died, 20/11/17.
1 Whittaker, Herbert Leonard Charles, Lt., k. in a., 21/9/18.
7 Whittet, Gilbert, 2/Lt. (Tp.), k. in a., 14/7/16.
9 Wilcox, Kenneth Theodore Dunbar, 2/Lt. (Tp.), k. in a., 8/11/15.
10 Wilders-Lewis, Henry Charles, T/2/Lt. (A/Capt.), k. in a., 31/7/17.
Williams, Hubert Cracroft, Lt., killed, 18/10/15.
Williams, Maurice Dingwall, 2/Lt., k. in a., 22-24/10/14.
Wilson, Charles Edward, Capt., k. in a., 17/9/14.
Wilson, David Rex, Lt., d. of w., 30/10/14.
3 Wilson, Raymond Ernest, 2/Lt., k. in a., 10/3/17 (att. 7/Bn.).
3 Woods, Frank Cecil, Lt., k. in a., 2/4/17.
10 Woodward, Ernest Harold Hamley, 2/Lt. (Tp.), k. in a., 24/12/16.
8 Woollatt, Claud Humpston, Capt. (Tp.), k. in a., 21/8/16.
7 Woollatt, Philip Reginald, 2/Lt., k. in a., 14/7/16.
6 Wooster, Clarence Daniel Henry, M.C., Capt., k. in a., 9/8/18.
6 Wright, Edmund, Capt., k. in a., 3/7/16.
9 Wright, Norman George, 2/Lt. (Tp.), k. in a., 13/7/16.

The Buffs (East Kent Regiment).

Adcock, Harold Norman, 2/Lt. (Tp.), k. in a., 8/10/18.
3 Allen, Charles St. Vincent, 2/Lt., died, 16/2/17 (att. M.G.C.).
Allen, Geoffrey Charles, Lt. (Tp.), d. of w., 5/4/18.
7 Amos, William Hope, 2/Lt. (Tp.), k. in a., 14/10/16.
Anderson, Donald Knox, M.C., Temp. Lt.-Col., k. in a., 3/12/17 (Div. M.G. Officer).
3 Andrews, Edward Norman, 2/Lt., d. of w., 22/8/18.
Archer, Albert Erskine Carson, 2/Lt., k. in a., 9/2/16 (and R.F.C.).
Archer, John William Butts, Lt., d. of w., 16/2/15.
3 Asprey, Maurice, Capt., k. in a., 12/8/16 (att. T.M.B.).
7 Baddeley, John Frederick, 2/Lt. (Tp.), k. in a., 1/7/16.
6 Bainbridge, Carlyle, 2/Lt. (Tp.), k. in a., 13/10/15.
Baker, Frank Bernard, 2/Lt. (Tp.), d. of w., 17/9/16 (att. R. West Surrey Regt.).
1 Baly, Cyril James Price Tyson Sugar, Lt., k. in a., 15/9/16.
7 Bambridge, Bertram Stacpoole, 2/Lt. (Tp.), k. in a., 19/11/16.
3 Barham, Wilfred Saxby, Temp. Capt., d. of w., 10/10/15.
Batson, Leonard Henry, 2/Lt. (Tp.), k. in a., 3/7/16.
1 Bayard, Reginald Aubrey Richard, Lt., k. in a., 17/5/16.
Bilton, Lewis Edward Albert Samuel, 2/Lt. (Tp.), k. in a., 23/4/17.
3 Blackall, Charles Walter, Capt., k. in a., 24/3/18 (att. 4 S. Staff. Regt.).
3 Blackwell, Basil Bernard, 2/Lt., k. in a., 3/9/16.
2 Booth, Frederick Atkins, 2/Lt. (Tp.), k. in a., 27/9/15.
Bowles, Bernard Geoffrey, 2/Lt. (Tp.), k. in a., 3/9/16.
Bracher, Guy, 2/Lt., k. in a., 3/7/16.
Brodie, Hugh William, Capt. (Tp.), killed, 13/10/15.
3 Brown, Theodore Anthony, M.C., 2/Lt., k. in a., 15/4/17.
Budds, P. H., Lt., died, 29/10/18 (and R.A.F.).
Burnside, Eustace Bruce Caldecott, Temp. Capt., k. in a., 12/10/17.
Burton, Geoffrey Walter Melvin, Lt., k. in a., 3/7/16.
3 Butler, James William, 2/Lt., k. in a., 3/5/17.
Buttanshaw, Edward Henry Underwood, Lt., k. in a., 27/4/15.
Caney, Charles, M.C., 2/Lt., d. of w., 29/8/18.
3 Carman, Leslie Guy, 2/Lt., k. in a., 4/10/16.
1 Carter, Hugh Harry, Lt., k. in a., 8/10/18.
1 Cattley, Cyril Francis, M.C., T/Major, k. in a., 30/11/17 (att. 6/Bn.).
Chapman, Charles Meredith Bouverie, M.C., Lt. (Temp. Major), d. of w., 1/10/17 (and R.F.C., 29 Sqd.).
Chapman, William Wetheral, Lt., k. in a., 7/10/17 (and R.F.C.).
Cheeseman, Anthony Alfred, Temp. Lt., k. in a., 5/5/17.
3 Chichester, Edmund Basil, Capt., d. of w., 7/11/14.
Chill, John Metcalfe, 2/Lt., k. in a., 8/11/16.
Church, Geoffrey William, M.C., 2/Lt., k. in a., 3/5/17.
Clark, Eric Foster, Temp. Lt., k. in a., 1/1/17 (and R.F.C.).
1 Clark, Laurence Fraser, Temp. 2/Lt., d. of w., 7/12/17.
Cole, Nigel Edwin Fitz Roy, 2/Lt. (T/Lt.), k. in a., 5/10/17.
Collison-Morley, Harold Duke, Major (Temp. Lt.-Col.), k. in a., 25/9/15.
6 Combridge, Leslie Ernest, 2/Lt. (Tp.), k. in a., 22/8/18.
Cooper, Frederick William Harvey, 2/Lt. (Tp.), k. in a., 9/3/18.
8 Corner, Edward Franklin, Temp. 2/Lt., k. in a., 25/9/15.
Cox, Henry George, 2/Lt., k. in a., 3/7/16.
Craighead, John Marr, Temp. 2/Lt., killed, 25/9/17.
3 Cramer-Roberts, Edward Herbert, 2/Lt., k. in a., 10/8/15.
Cresswell, Alfred Sackville, Capt., k. in a., 13/3/15.
3 Cronk, William Guy, 2/Lt., k. in a., 26/10/14 (att. K.R.R.C.).
Dann, W. S., 2/Lt., killed, 16/5/18 (and R.A.F.).
6 Davidson, Cristopher Edmund Grant, Capt., k. in a., 13/10/15.
1 Davis, Percy Warren Theo, 2/Lt., k. in a., 30/3/17.
Davis, William Richard, Temp. Capt., k. in a., 28/9/15.
3 Derrick, L. J., 2/Lt., killed, 3/5/18 (and R.A.F.).
3 Dinsmore, John Hastings, 2/Lt., k. in a., 3/5/17.
Docking, Robert James, Temp. Lt., d. of w., 10/2/17 (and R.F.C., 43 Sqd.).
Donelan, William Lawrence, Temp. 2/Lt., k. in a., 5/4/17.
1 Drake-Brockman, Paris Villiers, 2/Lt., k. in a., 18/7/18.
1 Dungey, Francis Herbert, 2/Lt. (Tp.), k. in a., 3/5/17.
7 Dyson, Hubert Archibald, Lt. (A/Capt.), k. in a., 18/11/16.
Earle, Noel Vansittart, Lt., died, 9/3/16 (att. Notts and Derby Regt.)
Evans, Hubert William, Temp. 2/Lt., d. of w., 24/5/17.
Figgis, Lenox Paton, M.C., T/Lt. (A/Capt.), k. in a., 27/8/18.
Firminger, Thomas, 2/Lt. (Tp.), k. in a., 3/9/16.
3 Forde, Kenneth Rowley, Lt., k. in a., 23/7/15.
1 Forster, Ralph Louis Francis, 2/Lt., k. in a., 3/5/17.
Fort, Lawrence, Capt., k. in a., 16/2/15.
Foxell, Edward William Lanchester, T/Capt., died, 11/6/17 (att. 3 Army Gas School).
Freedman, Phineas, Temp. 2/Lt., k. in a., 3/10/17.
Friend, George Burton Taddy, Capt. (Tp.), k. in a., 25/7/15.
Furley, Bernard Edward, Major (Tp.), k. in a., 13/10/15.
Gates, Horace John, Temp. 2/Lt., k. in a., 19/11/17 (and R.F.C.).
Geddes, Augustus David, Lt.-Col., k. in a., 28/4/15.
Glyn, R. S., Lt., k. in a., 20/10/14.
Goss, Edward Herbert Allan, Temp. Lt., k. in a., 1/7/16.
Green, Herbert Walter, D.S.O., Major (Bt.-Lt.-Col.), d. of w., 31/12/18 (att. R. West Surrey Regt.).
1 Greiffenhagen, Norman, 2/Lt. (Tp.), d. of w., 24/12/18.
Greig, James Gordon Hamilton, 2/Lt. (T/Lt.), d. of w., 13/8/15.
3 Gulland, Alexander Falkland, Lt., d. of w., 16/6/17.
Gullick, Arthur Louis, Lt. (Tp.), k. in a., 3/10/15.
Hall, Charles, 2/Lt., k. in a., 28/3/17 (att. T.M.B.).
Hall, Percy Shene Bernard, Capt., k. in a., 9/8/16.
Hammond, Douglas William, 2/Lt., k. in a., 24/5/15.
Hanmer, Alexander John, M.C., 2/Lt., d. of w., 7/10/16.
3 Harnett, Donald Alfred, 2/Lt., k. in a., 7/10/16.
Hasler, Julian, Brig.-Gen., k. in a., 26/4/15.
Hatch, Philip Randall, Temp. Lt., k. in a., 7/10/16.
Hayfield, Allan Sydney, Temp. 2/Lt., d. of w., 6/10/16.
2 Haythornthwaite, Rycharde Mead, 2/Lt., k. in a., 24/5/15.
Hedley, William Alexander Cosgrove, Temp. Lt., d. of w., 19/7/18.
3 Hess, Ivan Henry, 2/Lt., k. in a., 15/11/16.
3 Hewitt, H.D., Lt., d. of w., 27/10/18 (and R.A.F.).
3 Heywood, Robert Myles, Lt., d. of w., 15/2/15.
Hilder, Harold Sutton, 2/Lt., k. in a., 3/5/17.
Hill, Douglas Agar Worsley, Temp. Lt., d. of w., 14/8/18.
1 Hills, Malcolm Arthur, Temp. 2/Lt., k. in a., 15/9/16.
Hine, Herbert Josiah, M.M., Temp. 2/Lt., k. in a., 25/8/18.
Hinkley, Siegfried Thomas, Temp. 2/Lt., k. in a., 3/7/16.
3 Hirst, H. D., Lt.-Col., died, 16/5/18.
Hoare, Evelyn Melville Shovell, 2/Lt. (Tp.), k. in a., 28/3/18.
1 Hollis, Charles Frederick Griffith, M.C., Lt., k. in a., 2/8/18.
Hollist, Anthony May Capron, Capt., k. in a., 25-27/9/15.
Homan, Ralph William, T/Capt. (Lt.), d. of w., 11/8/15.
Howard, William, Capt. (Tp.), d. of w., 8/10/15.
Hubbard, Adrian George, Temp. 2/Lt., d. of w., 30/8/16.
3 Hunt, Harold Montague, 2/Lt., d. of w., 27/8/18.
1 Hunter, Herbert, M.C., Lt., d. of w., 23/10/18.
Hynes, Ernest Stanley Patrick, 2/Lt., k. in a., 10/11/16 (and R.F.C.).
Jackman, Henry Croome, 2/Lt. (Tp.), died, 28/11/15.
Jackson, Wilfred George, Lt., k. in a., 27/4/15.
James, George Millais, Capt., k. in a., 3/11/14.
Jelf, Charles Gordon, 2/Lt. (Tp.), k. in a., 13/10/15.
3 Johnston, Sinclair Beatty, 2/Lt., died, 27/5/17.
8 Jones, George Alfred Prime, Capt., killed, 28/5/16 (att. R.F.C.).
Kekewich, John, Capt., k. in a., 25/9/15.
Kelsey, Pryce Atwood Clive, Temp. Capt., d. of w., 26/7/15.
Kesby, Thomas Herbert, Temp. Capt., k. in a., 15/9/16 (att. M.G.C.).
3 Kingham, George William Ambrose, 2/Lt., died, 9/11/17 (W.A.F.F.).
3 Kirkpatrick, Athol, 2/Lt., k. in a., 3/5/17.
Kirkpatrick, Harry Fearnley, D.S.O., Act. Lt.-Col., d. of w., 27/3/18 (att. R.N. Div., "Anson").
Kitchin, John Buchanan, Lt., A/Capt., d. of w., 5/5/17.
Laing, Charles William, 2/Lt., k. in a., 24/4/15.
Lambe, Percy, Temp. Lt., k. in a., 7/11/15.
Lambert, Douglas, Temp. 2/Lt., k. in a., 13/10/15.
Laurie, John William, T/Lt., A/Capt., k. in a., 12/8/18.
Lea-Smith, Leslie Arthur, Temp. Lt., k. in a., 7/7/16.
Leigh, John Charles Thomas, Temp. Capt., k. in a., 3/7/16.
Little, Henry James, Temp. 2/Lt., k. in a., 20/9/17 (att. S. Lancs).
McColl, William Laurence, 2/Lt. (Tp.), d. of w., 18/7/16.
McDougall, Ronald, Lt., k. in a., 20/10/14.
3 Major, Stanley, Temp. 2/Lt., k. in a., 3/3/17.
Marsh, Charles Walter Brockwell, Temp. Lt., k. in a., 13/10/15.
Mathias, Charles Arthur Stirling, Temp. 2/Lt., k. in a., 3/5/17.
Malton, Michael Innes, Temp. 2/Lt., k. in a., 22/8/18.
Mead, Ralph Edward Culverhouse, Temp. 2/Lt., k. in a., 29/9/17.
Millard, John Barnard, Temp. 2/Lt., k. in a., 25/6/17.
3 Moke-Norrie, Geo. Stuart, 2/Lt., k. in a., 7/10/16 (att. 6 Bn.).

3 Money, Roy Granville Kyrle, 2/Lt., k. in a., 9/4/17.
1 Moody, Thomas Lewis Vyvian, 2/Lt., k. in a., 21/3/18.
Morley, Frank William, Temp. 2/Lt., d. of w., 9/10/18.
Morley, Harold Lisle, M.C., Temp. 2/Lt., A/Capt., d. of w., 2/12/17 (P. of W.).
Morris, Eyre Percival, Temp. 2/Lt., k. in a., 1/5/17 (and R.F.C.).
Morse, Eric Victor, M.C., Temp. 2/Lt., k. in a., 23/10/18.
3 Moss, Reginald Barnes Newton, Temp. 2/Lt., k. in a., 7/10/16.
Mount, Allan, Temp. 2/Lt., k. in a., 18/9/18.
Neame, Gerald Tassell, Temp. Capt., k. in a., 1/7/16.
Nesbit, Henry George, 2/Lt., k. in a., 23/3/15.
Nettleton, Roy, Temp. Lt., d. of w., 9/10/18 (att. T.M.B.).
2 Neve, Walter Gregory, 2/Lt., k. in a., 25/8/17.
Newcomb, Charles Stuart, Lt., d. of w., 5/4/18.
1 Newington, Percy Wilmott, Lt., k. in a., 21/3/18.
Noble, William McDonald, Temp. 2/Lt., d. of w., 31/12/16 (att. R.E. Div. Sig.).
Noott, Mervyn, 2/Lt., k. in a., 20/10/14.
7 Norbury, Philip Giesler, Temp. Lt., k. in a., 1/7/16.
1 Norsworthy, Harold Milford, Temp. 2/Lt., k. in a., 18/3/17.
3 Northcote, Douglas Horace Gilbert, Lt., k. in a., 12/3/15 (att. Wilts Regt.).
3 Ommanney, Alfred Erasmus Stuart, 2/Lt., k. in a., 7/10/16.
3 Palfreyman, George Alexander, 2/Lt., k. in a., 26/10/16 (and R.F.C.).
Parsons, Leo Bernard, 2/Lt. (Tp.), k. in a., 12/8/16.
Peacock, William James Leonard, 2/Lt. (Tp.), k. in a., 18/8/16.
Pearce, Dudley George, Temp. Capt., k. in a., 3/9/16.
2 Pennington, Thomas, 2/Lt. (Tp.), k. in a., 28/9/15.
6 Peters, Charles Frederick, 2/Lt., k. in a., 18/3/18.
Peters, Charles Walter, 2/Lt., k. in a., 21/3/18.
Phillimore, Jasper Prescott, Lt. (Tp.), k. in a., 13/10/15.
3 Phillips, Reginald Gurwen, 2/Lt., k. in a., 26/1/17.
Phillips, Joseph Douglas, Lt., k. in a., 20/10/14.
Pickering, Basil Horace, 2/Lt., Temp. Lt., d. of w., 1/12/15.
Porter, Edgar George, Temp. 2/Lt., k. in a., 20/9/18.
3 Prior, Charles Ronald, 2/Lt., k. in a., 22/8/19.
3 Ramsey, Arthur William, Lt., k. in a., 12/4/15 (att. R. Innis. Fusrs.).
Randall, Stanley, 2/Lt. (T/Lt.), died, 31/12/18 (and Gold Coast Regt.).
Redshaw, Walter Geoffrey, Temp. 2/Lt., k. in a., 6/3/16.
Reed, John Sleeman, 2/Lt., died, 31/1/16 (and R.F.C.).
1 Reid, George Robert, Temp. 2/Lt., k. in a., 15/9/16.
Richardson, Arthur Gordon, Temp. 2/Lt., d. of w., 19/9/18.
3 Ricketts, Frederick, 2/Lt., k. in a., 18/9/18.
6 Robinson, Edgar Francis, 2/Lt., k. in a., 20/6/18.
Robinson, The Hon. Hercules Edward Joseph, Temp. 2/Lt., d. of w., 26/9/15.
Romer, Frederick Charles, C.B., C.M.G., Hon. Col., Temp. Lt.-Col., k. in a., 26/9/15 (late Lancs Fusrs.).
1 Ronca, Edward Henry, Temp. 2/Lt., k. in a., 17/10/18.
Ronald, James McBain, Capt., k. in a., 23/4/15.
Routley, Ernest George, M.C., Temp. 2/Lt., k. in a., 7/10/16.
3 Russell, John, 2/Lt., k. in a., 9/8/17.
3 Sankey, C. M., M.C., 2/Lt., killed, 15/5/18 (and R.A.F.).
Saunder, George Bertram, 2/Lt. (Tp.), k. in a., 15/4/17.
1 Sayer, Harry, 2/Lt., d. of w., 24/10/15.
Score, William Thomas, Temp. 2/Lt., k. in a., 27/3/18.
3 Selby, Millin, 2/Lt., d. of w., 29/9/15.
Sewell, Geoffrey Edward, 2/Lt., d. of w., 2/9/17.
Shafto, John Stanley Horsfall, Temp. 2/Lt., k. in a., 12/8/16.
Shelton, Kenneth, Lt., T/Capt., d. of w., 14/2/18 (and R.F.C.).
8 Shervington, Thomas Robert Munro, Capt., d. of w., 25/9/15.
3 Slacke, Roger Cecil, Major, k. in a., 16/5/15 (att. R.W. Surrey Regt.).
Smith, Edward Thompson, T/2/Lt., k. in a., 19/10/15.
1 Smith, Ernest Kennedy, 2/Lt., d. of w., 22/12/15.
Smith, Geoffrey Herbert, Temp. 2/Lt., d. of w., 22/9/16
Soames, Alfred, D.S.O., Temp. Major, k. in a., 13/10/15.
Spencer, H. M., 2/Lt. (Tp.), k. in a., 12/10/17.
3 Spicer, Filmer Blake, 2/Lt., d. of w., 6/10/16 (att. M.G.C.).
Stallworthy, Arthur Renolds, 2/Lt., k. in a., 30/11/17 (att. S. Lancs Regt.).
3 Stanfield, Charles Cecil, Capt., died 31/5/17 (att. 1 Garr. Northants R.).
1 Steinman, Bernard Puckle, Capt., died, 26/4/16.
3 Stephen, J., Lt., k. in a., 14/10/18 (att. Indian Army).
1 Stevens, Edward Alfred Murtagh, M.C., 2/Lt., k. in a., 16/6/18.
Stock, Hubert Reginald, 2/Lt., k. in a., 25/10/14.
1 Strauss, Bernard Lewis, M.C., A/Major, k. in a., 1/12/17.
Studd, Francis Cyril Rupert, D.S.O., Major, Temp. Lt.-Col., k. in a., 13/4/18.
3 Swayne, Stephen Cormack, Lt., k. in a., 30/9/15.
3 Taylor, Cedric Charles Okey, Lt., k. in a., 3/12/16 (att. T.M.B.).
3 Taylor, Douglas Merwyn, 2/Lt., k. in a., 4/10/16
1 Taylor Harold James, 2/Lt., k. in a., 17/10/18.
7 Taylor, Stanley Waterman, Temp. Lt., k. in a., 21/3/18.
3 Taylor, William Frederick, Lt., k. in a., 7/6/15.
Thompson, Harold, Temp. 2/Lt., k. in a., 29/9/18.
Thornhill, George Robert, Lt., k. in a., 22/10/14.
Thornley, John Dales, Temp. 2/Lt., k. in a., 24/10/18.
Trueman, Arthur Philip Hamilton, Major, Temp. Lt.-Col., died, 26/11/18.
7 Trowles, Frederick Herbert, Temp. 2/Lt., d. of w., 13/9/18.
Underhill, Thomas William, 2/Lt. (Tp.), k. in a., 19/8/16.
Wallis, Frederick George, Lt. (Tp.), k. in a., 30/11/17.
Wanstall, Elton Cyril, 2/Lt., d. of w., 25/9/15.
Ward, Robert Oscar Cyril, Temp. Major, k. in a., 20/11/17 (att. Tank Corps).
Warnington, Charles, 2/Lt., k. in a., 3/5/17.
Welldon, James Hoste, 2/Lt., k. in a., 30/11/17.
1 Wellesley-Miller, John Leslie, 2/Lt., k. in a., 15/9/16.
3 Wells, Walter Neave, Capt., k. in a., 27/10/14 (att. 1/K.R.R.C.).
Wheeler, Harry Lloyd, Temp. 2/Lt., d. of w., 26/12/15 (att. 6/R. West Kent).
3 Wood, Noel Ernest, 2/Lt., k. in a., 27/9/15.
Wood, Reginald Ewart, 2/Lt., d. of w., 3/8/18.
1 Worster, Alexander Frederick, M.C., 2/Lt. (A/Capt.), d. of w., 23/11/17.
Worthington, Claude Arthur, Major, Temp. Lt.-Col., k. in a., 28/9/15.
1 Wyatt, Geoffrey Wilfred Penfold, 2/Lt., k. in a., 15/9/16.
Zeigler, Philip Harold, Temp. 2/Lt., d. of w., 23/9/16.

The King's Own (Royal Lancaster Regiment).

Abbot-Anderson, Francis Wyatt, Lt.-Col., died, 1/1/16.
Adams, Auriol Charles Andrew, 2/Lt. (Tp.), k. in a., 16-18/8/16.
Adie, Arthur, D.C.M., 2/Lt., k. in a., 3/5/18.
Aitchison, Ronald Andrew Colquhoun, Lt., d. of w., 14/12/14.
Aldwinckle, Ralph, 2/Lt., k. in a., 15/11/16 (att. L.N. Lancs.).
Allam, Percy John, 2/Lt., d. of w., 22/5/18 (att. T.M.B.) (P. of W.).
Ashley, James, 2/Lt., k. in a., 2/5/18.
Austin, Cyril John, 2/Lt. (Tp.), k. in a., 16/5/18.
Backhouse, Horace Heptonstall, M.C., Lt. (Tp.), k. in a., 23/8/18.
Bailey, Arnold, 2/Lt. (Tp.), k. in a., 24/3/18.
3 Ball, Arthur, 2/Lt., killed, 19/2/17 (and R.F.C.).
3 Ballard, Dennis Arthur, Capt., k. in a., 12/12/17.
Barclay, George Eric, Capt., k. in a., 24/1/17 (att. 4/Nigeria Regt.).
Barnes, Edmund Lyndon, Capt. and Adj. (Tp.), k. in a., 3/4/16.
Barnwell, George Woodruffe, 2/Lt. (Tp.), k. in a., 13/4/18 (att. K.O.Y.L.I.).
Bayliss, Percy James, 2/Lt., k. in a., 27/9/18.
Beachcroft, Gerald William, 2/Lt., k. in a., 31/7/17.
Beard, Valentine Edward, 2/Lt., d. of w., 24/11/17.
Bellamy, Thomas Bilbous, 2/Lt. (Tp.), d. of w., 13/1/17.
Beswick, John Charles, 2/Lt., died, 22/4/17 (P. of W.).
1 Binks, Basil Henry, 2/Lt. (Tp.), k. in a., 23/10/16.
Black, John, Capt., died, 26/9/17.
Bland, Braithwaite, 2/Lt. (Tp.), d. of w., 31/8/16.
Bone, Quintin, Capt. (Tp.), k. in a., 19/9/18.
Bonner, W., 2/Lt., killed, 19/6/18 (and R.A.F.).
Bowden, Reginald Charles, 2/Lt. (Tp.), d. of w., 3/3/16.
1 Bower, William Carroll, 2/Lt., died, 9/8/16.
Bradbury, Dennis John Freeland, 2/Lt. (Tp.), d. of w., 15/11/16 (att. L.N. Lancs. Regt.).
3 Bridson, Charles Edward Ridgway, Capt., d. of w., 4/4/16.
Brierley, Vincent, M.C., Temp. 2/Lt., d. of w., 28/5/18.
Briggs William Lonsdale, 2/Lt. (Tp.), d. of w., 14/9/17 (att. Lancs. Fusrs.).
1 Brocklebank, Lawrence Seymour, 2/Lt., k. in a., 26/8/14.
1 Bromilow, John Nisbet, Major, k. in a., 1/7/16.
3 Brown, Archibald Dimock Montagu, Capt. (Tp.), k. in a., 23/10/16.
Carnegy, Richard Lloyd, Major, k. in a., 10/8/15 (Retd. Ind. Army).
Clegg, Percy, Temp. 2/Lt., k. in a., 1/7/16.
Clerk, Ronald Malcolm, Capt., k. in a., 9/4/17.
Clue, Henry May, Temp. 2/Lt., k. in a., 30/7/16.
Clutterbuck, Henry, Capt., k. in a., 31/8/—, 2/9/14.
Conheeny, Gerald, M.C., 2/Lt. (Tp.), killed, 5/12/18.
Conran, Owen Mostyn, Major, k. in a., 29/7/17 (and R.F.C.).
Conway, Joseph Michael, Temp. 2/Lt., k. in a., 7/7/16.
3 Cook, Leonard N., M.C., 2/Lt., k. in a., 7/7/17.
1 Coombes, George Wilson, Temp. 2/Lt., k. in a., 3/5/17.
Court, Richard, 2/Lt. (Tp.), k. in a., 9/4/18.
Crofts, Charles Howard, M.C., 2/Lt. (Tp.), k. in a., 20/7/18 (att. K.O.Y.L.I.).
Crone, Bertram, 2/Lt. (Tp.), d. of w., 13/9/16.
Crowley, Philip, Temp. Lt., k. in a., 7/7/17.
1 Cursham, Geoffry, Lt., k. in a., 12/10/17.
Dalrymple-Willes, Patrick, Lt., died, 29/9/18 (and R.A.F.).
Daniels, Thomas Harold Rayner, 2/Lt., k. in a., 9/4/16.
Dartnall, Albert John, Temp. 2/Lt., k. in a., 20/11/17.
Davies, Walter, 2/Lt. (Tp.), k. in a., 18/9/18.
De Bruyn, Douglas Bayly, 2/Lt., died, 27/5/16 (and R.F.C.).
Delaney, James Alfred Leo, Temp. 2/Lt., k. in a., 10/6/17 (att. T.M.B.).
De La Rue, Thomas, Capt., died, 28/7/17.
Denne, Vincent Alured, Temp. 2/Lt., died, 5/1/17.
3 Denwood, Thomas William, 2/Lt., died, 22/10/18 (att. 2/6 Sussex Regt.).
3 De Trafford, Reginald Francis, Lt., d. of W., 9/5/15 (att Glouc. R.).
1 Dovey, William Edward, 2/Lt., k. in a., 23/10/16.
Duxbury, Arthur, 2/Lt. (Tp.), k. in a., 9/4/18.
1 Dykes, Alfred McNair, Lt.-Col., k. in a., 26/8/14.
Eardley, George Arthur, Temp. 2/Lt., k. in a., 27/11/17 (att. K.O.Y.L.I.).
Eastwood, Leslie, 2/Lt. (Tp.), died, 19/9/15.
Eccles, John Vivian William, Temp. 2/Lt., drowned, 4/5/17.
Ellis, Harry, Temp. 2/Lt., k. in a., 9-12/4/17.
1 Elworthy, Thomas, Temp. 2/Lt., k. in a., 3/5/17.
Evans, Fisher Arthur Haslett Freke, T/Lt., A/Capt., k. in a., 11/1/17.
Fairbairn, Maurice, Temp. 2/Lt., k. in a., 7/7/17.
Farquharson, Norman Kenneth, Temp. 2/Lt., k. in a., 29/8/18.
Farrant, George, Temp. 2/Lt., k. in a., 9/2/17.
Fielden, Gilbert Sutcliffe, Temp. 2/Lt., died, 18/7/17.
Fielder, Edgar John, Temp. 2/Lt., k. in a., 9-12/4/17.
Flemming, Douglas Sidney, Temp. 2/Lt., d. of w., 1/6/17.

Forwood, Thomas Brittain, Capt., k. in a., 8/5/15.
Frame, Robert, Temp. 2/Lt., k. in a., 28/3/18.
Gilbert, Gilbert Garnet, Temp. 2/Lt., k. in a., 18/3/18.
Goldring, Frank Carter, Temp. Lt., k. in a., 13/11/16.
1 Graham, Charles Hamilton Malise, Lt., k. in a., 12/4/17.
Greaves, Frederic, Temp. 2/Lt., k. in a., 1/6/18 (att. L.N. Lancs. Regt.).
Greenwood, Charles, 2/Lt., k. in a., 22/3/18 (att. 6/Wilts Regt.).
Greenwood, John Francis, Lt., k. in a., 2/5/15.
Guest, Ernest William, 2/Lt., k. in a., 26/2/18 (att. R.F.C.).
1 Hablutzel, George Rudolph, 2/Lt., k. in a., 1/7/16.
Haigh, Allen Mortimer, Temp. 2/Lt., k. in a., 13/4/18 (att. 1/4 K.O.Y.L.I.).
6 Hall, Thomas Storey Inglis, 2/Lt., k. in a., 9/4/16.
3 Haly, Andrew Stuart, 2/Lt., d. of w., 8/7/15 (att. E. Lancs. Regt.).
7 Hammond-Chambers, Henry Borgnis Baret, Temp. Capt., k. in a., 21/7/16.
Harford, George Lawrence, Lt., k. in a., 17/2/15.
1 Harris, Albert James, 2/Lt., k. in a., 17/10/16.
11 Hart, William Cecil Frederick Nicol, Lt., k. in a., 1/4/18 (and R.A.F.).
3 Harvey, Thomas, 2/Lt., died, 29/4/17.
3 Hathaway, Thomas Hervey, 2/Lt., k. in a., 17/2/15.
Hawling, Thomas Albert, 2/Lt. (Tp.), k. in a., 4/11/17 (att. 9/Y.L.I.).
Hay, James Duncan, 2/Lt. (Tp.), d. of w., 15/12/17.
2 Hazell, Dudley Howard, Lt., killed, 27/9/18 (and R.F.C.).
Heaney, Paul, 2/Lt., k. in a., 21/10/14.
1 Henderson, James Graeme, Temp. 2/Lt., k. in a., 3/12/17 (att. 1/5).
8 Hewetson, Arthur, Temp. 2/Lt., k. in a., 24/3/18.
6 Higgins, Herbert Edward Powell, Capt., k. in a., 10/8/15.
Higham, Wilfred, Temp. 2/Lt., k. in a., 27/9/18 (att. 2/5 Bn.).
8 Higson, William Marsh, Temp. 2/Lt., d. of w., 9/4/17.
Hildyard, Robert Aubrey, 2/Lt., k. in a., 20/12/16.
10 Hodkinson, Harold Hale, Temp. 2/Lt., k. in a., 8/8/16.
Holland, Clarence Jennings, 2/Lt. (Tp.), k. in a., 14/8/18 (att. 1/4 Bn.).
9 Hollins, Edward Ralph Lambert, Temp. Capt., d. of w., 3/3/16.
6 Holmes, Robert, 2/Lt. (Tp.), died, 16/2/18.
9 Honey, George Ronald, M.C., Lt. (Tp.), d. of w., 25/9/18.
3 Howarth, Norman, Capt., died, 6/9/18 (and R.A.F.).
1 Howson, George Rowland Paget, 2/Lt. (Tp.), k. in a., 9/4/17.
1 Hudson, Arthur Henry William, 2/Lt., k. in a., 1/7/16.
7 Humphreys, Laurence Olsen, 2/Lt. (Tp.), d. of w., 13/11/15.
3 Jamieson, John Prior, Capt., d. of w., 13/10/17.
8 Jay, William Oak, Lt., k. in a., 25/4/17.
Jewell, Frank Ernest, Temp. 2/Lt., k. in a., 15/12/17 (att Y.L.I.).
9 Johnson, John Frederic, 2/Lt., k. in a., 9/4/16.
6 Jurgens, Sydney George, Temp. Lt., d. of w., 17/8/15.
3 Kent, George Edward, Lt., k. in a., 24/3/18.
8 Knox, George, 2/Lt., k. in a., 9/4/16.
2 Lamb, Launcelot Rupert, Temp. Lt., k. in a., 25/5/17.
8 Landers, George Maxwell, 2/Lt., k. in a., 28/3/18.
3 Lendon, Penry Bruce, M.V.O., Capt., k. in a., 21/10/14.
6 Lloyd-Williams, David Gray, 2/Lt., k. in a., 10/8/15.
11 Long, Basil Andrew, Temp. Capt., died, 10/2/17.
3 Long-Innes, Selwyn, Lt., k. in a., 4/8/15.
1 Lugard, E. M., 2/Lt., killed, 30/7/18 (and R.A.F.).
7 Lyons, Henry James, Temp. 2/Lt., k. in a., 23/9/17.
8 Lyons, William Thomas, Temp. Capt., k. in a., 19/7/16.
Lysons, Nigel Lucius Samuel, Major, k. in a., 21/10/14.
McFarlane, Walter, Temp. 2/Lt., d. of w., 15/1/17. (att. 38/M.G.C.).
3 Mack, Arthur Stanley, Lt., k. in a., 9/4/17.
Macklin, John James Malcolm, Lt. (Tp.), k. in a., 12/3/18 (att. 12/Lancs Fusiliers).
MacWalter, Charles Christopher, 2/Lt., k. in a., 1/7/16.
10 McConnell, Robert Wallace, Temp. Lt., k. in a., 9/4/16.
8 Madan, Nigel Cornwallis, Temp. Lt., k. in a., 3/3/16.
10 Mann, Osric Alwyn, Temp. Lt., k. in a., 5/4/16.
1 Marker, Thomas Maxwell, 2/Lt., k. in a., 1/10/17.
Martin, Aylmer Richard Sancton, Lt.-Col., k. in a., 9/5/15.
10 Mawdsley, John Edmund, Temp. 2/Lt., k. in a., 24/4/17 (att. 6/Bn.).
1 Meadows, Christopher Bentley, M.C., Temp. 2/Lt., k. in a., 19/5/18.
Melly, Hugh Peter Egeston Mesnard, 2/Lt., k. in a., 2/7/16.
6 Mere, Colin Leigh, Temp. Lt., k. in a., 10/8/15.
2 Minor, Ronald, 2/Lt., k. in a., 1/7/16.
8 Moffat, Hugh Francis Baillie, M.C., Temp. 2/Lt. (A/Capt.), d. of w., 27/9/18.
10 Mohan, Harry Deacon, Capt., k. in a., 11/4/16.
Morrar, John Henry, Major, k. in a., 18/10/14.
Morris, Anthony George Attwood, Lt., k. in a., 13/10/14.
6 Morrison, Donald, Temp. Capt., d. of w., 31/8/15.
Muchall, George William Stuart, 2/Lt., k. in a., 10/5/15.
1 Naper, Frank Cornewall, Capt., k. in a., 3/5/17.
Niven, Alan Scott, Temp. 2/Lt., k. in a., 4/11/17 (att. 9/Y.L.I.).
Nixon, W. H., 2/Lt., k. in a., 19/9/15 (and R.F.C.).
8 O'Ryan, Francis Joseph, Temp. 2/Lt., d. of w., 23/8/18.
10 Paine, Walter Lionel, Temp. Capt., k. in a., 4/6/15 (att. Lancs Fusiliers).
Parker, John, 2/Lt., k. in a., 21/7/15 (and R.F.C.).
3 Patch, Aubrey Melchior William, 2/Lt., k. in a., 16-18/8/16.
1 Pearce, Norman, Temp. 2/Lt., k. in a., 12/10/17.
3 Perfect, Cyril St. Lawrence, 2/Lt., d. of w., 13/10/15 (att. 1/R.W. Surrey Regt.).
Phillips, Christian Gibson, Major, k. in a., 10/7/16.
6 Pickup, George, M.C., A/Capt., killed, 20/8/18.
4 Place, Frank Clarke, M.M., 2/Lt., k. in a., 22/9/18.
1 Prichard, Thomas James, M.C., Temp. Capt., k. in a., 28/3/18.
Pryor, Robert Selwyn, 2/Lt., k. in a., 1/5/15.
Quartley, Thomas Warner, 2/Lt., k. in a., 15/1/15 (att. S. Lancs Regt.).
Raeside, George Forrest, M.C., Temp. 2/Lt., k. in a., 9/4/18 (att. 1/4 Bn.).
Rawlinson, Leonard Hugh, Lt., k. in a., 10/5/15.
Robinson, Reginald Humphries, Temp. 2/Lt., k. in a., 4/10/18 (att. 1/4 Bn.).
Ross, Ralph Morison Forbes, 2/Lt., k. in a., 20/2/15.
1 Rowley, Joseph, 2/Lt., k. in a., 1/7/16.
8 Rushton, Arthur, 2/Lt., k. in a., 27/7/18.
7 Rutherford, Norman Edwin, 2/Lt. (Tp.), d. of w., 21/7/16.
Salter, John Henry Clavell, 2/Lt., k. in a., 9/4/18 (att. 1/5 Bn.).
6 Sandbach, William, Temp. Major, k. in a., 10/8/15.
8 Sansom, Walter Edwin Hammond, Temp 2/Lt., k. in a. 16-18/8/16.
6 Saunders, Alfred, Temp. Capt., d. of w., 16/12/16.
8 Saxon, Harry, Temp. Lt., k. in a., 30/11/16.
6 Scholfield, Richard Denham, Temp. 2/Lt., k. in a., 10/8/15.
Scott, Thomas Rennie, Capt., k. in a., 9/5/15.
3 Scott-Miller, Edward, Lt., k. in a., 14/5/18.
Scudamore, George Prince Mountford, 2/Lt., k. in a., 8/5/15.
11 Shipley, Harold, Temp. Lt.-Col., died, 2/10/18 (11/B.W.I.R.).
Smallwood, George Baxter, M.M., 2/Lt., died, 2/11/18 (att. M.G.C.).
10 Smith, Herbert James, Temp. 2/Lt., d. of w., 29/4/16 (att. R. Dublin Fusiliers).
Smith, Robert, 2/Lt., k. in a., 20/11/17 (att. 1/4 Bn.).
3 Sommerville, George Little, Capt., k. in a., 16-18/8/16.
Sparenborg, Hans Robert, Capt., k. in a., 26/8/17.
8 Sparks, James Frederick, Temp. Lt., k. in a., 9/4/17.
Steele-Perkins, Cyril Steele, Lt., k. in a., 31-8-2/9/14.
11 Sternberg, Edgar Adolph Joseph, Temp. 2/Lt., k. in a., 16/10/16 (att. 2 Bn.).
10 Stewart, John Stanley, Temp. 2/Lt., k. in a., 17/10/16.
Stokes, Haldane Day, M.V.O., Lt., k. in a., 17/2/15.
Stone, Robert Claude, 2/Lt., T/Lt., k. in a., 8/4/17 (att. M.G.C.).
Stowell, Robert Cuthbert, 2/Lt. (Tp.), k. in a., 20/11/17.
3 Swinburne, Matthew, 2/Lt., d. of w., 5/9/18 (P. of W.).
3 Tanner, Raymond Stuart, 2/Lt., k. in a., 31/8/16.
8 Tatam, L. C., 2/Lt., k. in a., 19/5/16
3 Taylor, Ernest George, 2/Lt., k. in a., 2/5/15 (att. 2 Bn.).
Theobald, Frederick George, Capt., k. in a., 2/9/14.
11 Thomas, Walter Joseph Charles, Temp. 2/Lt., d. of w., 22/4/17.
2 Thorne, William Anthony Laroque, Capt., died, 7/8/18.
Thornycroft, Edward Gerald Mytton, Lt., k. in a., 15/9/14 (and K. Afr. Rifles).
1 Todd, Valentine Otto, Capt., k. in a., 9/4/17.
Toovey, Kennedy St. Clair Hailton, 2/Lt., died, 15/10/18 (att. 166/T.M. Bty.) (P. of W.).
Trew, John McCammon, Temp. Capt., died, 28/3/18.
Tucker, Clifford Francis, 2/Lt., k. in a., 9/4/18 (att. 1/5 Bn.).
10 Tyrrell, Arthur James, 2/Lt., k. in a., 7/3/17.
10 Vaughan, Horace William Henry, Lt., k. in a., 4/6/15 (att. R. Fus.).
Walker, Jack Bertram, 2/Lt., d. of w., 8/3/18 (att. 1/5 Bn.).
1 Walker, James Edward, 2/Lt., k. in a., 3/5/17.
Wallis, Edward Percy, Temp. Capt., k. in a., 17/10/16 (att. 8/R. Sussex R.).
Waterhouse, Arved, 2/Lt., k. in a., 13/10/14.
3 Weatherhead, Andrew, 2/Lt., k. in a., 1/7/16.
Weatherhead, George Ernest, Capt., k. in a., 8/5/15.
3 Weber, Harry Percy, 2/Lt., k. in a., 15/11/16.
9 Whiks, Charles, Temp. 2/Lt., k. in a., 10/10/15.
3 Whittaker, Norman, 2/Lt., k. in a., 12/5/18.
7 Wickham, John Seville Deacon, Temp. 2/Lt., k. in a., 31/7/17
7 Wigley, Herbert Henry, Temp. Lt., k. in a., 31/7/17.
Wilding, Godfrey James, 2/Lt., k. in a., 20/12/16.
8 Wilkinson, Frederick James, Temp. 2/Lt., k. in a., 9-12/4/17.
3 Willes, Patrick Dalrymple, Lt., died, 29/9/18 (and R.A.F.).
8 Williams, Charles Aubrey, Temp. 2/Lt., k. in a., 3/4/16.
8 Williams, Charles Oswald Nicholson, Temp. Major, k. in a., 2/12/15.
8 Williams, Harold Garnett, 2/Lt., k. in a., 27/9/18.
Wilson, Horace Hayman, Major, drowned, 30/12/15.
10 Wood, Peter Norris, Temp. 2/Lt., d. of w., 19/1/17.
Woodgate, Lionel Streatfield, Lt., k. in a., 8/9/14.
10 Woods, James, Temp. 2/Lt., k. in a., 23/10/16.
Woodward, Reginald Rupert, Temp. 2/Lt., k. in a., 1/12/17 (att. 1/5 Bn.).
6 Worthington, Noel Trevor, Lt., d. of w., 8/8/15.
Yorke, David, 2/Lt., T/Lt., k. in a., 17/2/15.
3 Young, John Ferrers Harington, Lt., T/Capt., k. in a., 1/7/16 (att. 1 Bn.).

The Northumberland Fusiliers.

Ablett, Leslie Wallace, 2/Lt. (Tp.), k. in a., 15/10/17 (Res. att. 11 Bn.).
Adams, Stanley, 2/Lt. (Tp.), d. of w., 9/9/17 (att. 9 Bn.).
Adamson, Charles John Henry, Capt. (Tp.), k. in a., 22/9/17 (att. 11 Bn.).
Adamson, John Conway, Lt., k. in a., 4/10/17 (att. 1/Lincs.).
13 Agnew, Graham, Capt. (Tp.), k. in a., 26/9/15.
9 Aikman, William Saunders, 2/Lt. (Tp.), k. in a., 23/4/17.
9 Allen, John Stanley, M.C., Temp. Major, k. in a., 11/4/18.
13 Allen William Maxey, Lt. (Tp.), k. in a., 26/9/15.
11 Alexander, James, 2/Lt., k. in a., 7/7/16.

20 Andrew, John James, 2/Lt. (Tp.), d. of w., 29/4/17.
1 Apps, Jack Harry Mason, 2/Lt. (Tp.), k. in a., 20/11/17.
1 Archer, Ronald Hedley, 2/Lt. (Tp.), d. of w., 27/12/17.
25 Arden, John Henry Morris, D.S.O., Lt.-Col., died, 22/7/18 (and R.A.F.).
20 Arkle, Norman Armitage, 2/Lt. (Tp.), k. in a., 1/7/16.
21 Armatage, Robert, 2/Lt. (Tp.), d. of w., 6/6/17.
Armstrong, Charles Arthur, Temp. Lt.-Col. (Major), k. in a., 1/10/15.
21 Armstrong, Harold, 2/Lt., k. in a., 14/11/16.
15 Armstrong, John Norman, Temp. Lt., d. of w., 16/1/17 (att. 8 Bn.).
12 Armstrong, Sydney John, 2/Lt., k. in a., 26/9/15.
13 Armstrong, Thomas Herbert, T/Lt., A/Capt., died, 15/5/17.
8 Arnold, Hugh, Lt. (Tp.), k. in a., 11/8/15.
25 Arthur, Alexander, M.C., M.M., 2/Lt. (Tp.), d. of w., 1/10/18.
8 Ash, William Behne, Capt. (Tp.), k. in a., 16/8/17.
15 Ashley, Claude, 2/Lt. (Tp.), k. in a., 1/7/16 (att. 2 Bn.).
23 Ashworth, Fred, 2/Lt. (Tp.), d. of w., 10/4/17.
13 Atkinson, John Ismay, Lt. (Tp.), k. in a., 29/6/16.
16 Avery, William Ernest, 2/Lt., k. in a., 1/7/16.
25 Ayling, Arthur Henry, 2/Lt. (Tp.), k. in a., 28/4/17.
21 Baillie, George, 2/Lt. (Tp.), k. in a., 5/6/17.
29 Bainbridge, Thomas Emery, 2/Lt. (Tp.), k. in a., 9/4/17 (att. 21 Bn.).
24 Baker, Douglas James, 2/Lt. (Tp.), k. in a., 28/4/17.
Ball, William Linnington, 2/Lt., k. in a., 5/11/18.
10 Band, George Laidman, Capt. (Tp.), k. in a., 20/6/17.
1 Barber, Bradley King Bell, 2/Lt. (T/Capt.), k. in a., 4/9/17 (att. R.F.C., 9 Sqd.).
Barkworth, Humphrey Robertson, Capt., d. of w., 3/7/16.
3 Barnes, Benjamin King, 2/Lt. (Tp.), died, 28/6/18 (att. 9/R. Fus.).
1 Barnes, Harry Scott, Lt. (Tp.), k. in a., 9/4/17.
12 Barnett, Victor Baron, Lt. (Tp.), k. in a., 25-27/9/15.
13 Barr, William, 2/Lt. (Tp.), k. in a., 11-18/7/16.
Barrett, Lindsay Alfred, Major (Tp.), k. in a., 17/3/16 (att. 1/4 Yorks Regt.).
14 Bava, Camille Bernard Colin, 2/Lt., k. in a., 26/9/15.
Beahan, Arthur, 2/Lt. (Tp.), k. in a., 15/6/18 (Res., att. 11 Bn.).
3 Beales, George Ninian, 2/Lt., k. in a., 21/3/18 (att. 22 Bn.).
25 Beattie-Brown, William, Capt. (Tp.), k. in a., 9/4/17.
26 Beavon, John Leonard, 2/Lt., k. in a., 1/7/16.
22 Begg, Alexander James Bartlett, M.C., Lt. (Tp.), k. in a., 21/3/18.
Belchem, Howard Matthew, 2/Lt., d. of w., 19/3/15.
12/13 Bell, Walter Stanley, 2/Lt., k. in a., 16/4/18.
11 Bell, William Robert, 2/Lt. (Tp.), k. in a., 12/10/17.
Bentley, Harry, 2/Lt., drowned, 10/10/18.
22 Bibby, David Houghton, Capt. (Tp.), k. in a., 13/4/18.
13 Bigham, William, 2/Lt. (Tp.), died, 19/9/15.
20 Binns, Clement Stanley, 2/Lt. (Tp.), k. in a., 1/7/16.
Birch, S. C., Capt., died, 1/8/17.
11 Blackden, Wilfred Worsley, Temp. Major (Capt.), died, 10/1/16.
27 Blight, Ernest James, 2/Lt. (Tp.), k. in a., 11/3/17.
24 Blott, Thomas Watkin, T/Lt., A/Capt., k. in a., 9/4/17.
23 Bolton, Henry Albert, Temp. Capt., k. in a., 1/7/16.
11 Bolton, Robert Frederick, 2/Lt. (Tp.), d. of w., 10/6/17.
3 Borland, George McPhearson, 2/Lt., k. in a., 14/4/18 (att. 9 Bn.).
12 Borrell, Lancelot, 2/Lt. (Tp.), d. of w., 10/7/16.
14 Bostock, Archibald Thomas, Capt. (Tp.), d. of w., 30/9/15.
Bower, Frank, 2/Lt., d. of w., 31/3/17 (and R.F.C., 60 Sqd.).
3 Bowman, Clive Septimus, Lt., k. in a., 18/9/17 (att. 11 Bn.).
Bowman, Edward Oliver, 2/Lt. (Tp.), k. in a., 31/10/18 (att. 9 Bn.).
Boyd, Edward Fenwick, Lt., k. in a., 19/9/14.
15 Bradshaw, Peter Dennison, 2/Lt. (Tp.), d. of w., 14/7/16 (att. 13 Bn.).
1 Brewis, Alfred Percy, Lt. (T/Capt.), d. of w., 1/6/17 (att. 1/5 E. Lancs.).
27 Brockbank, Herbert, 2/Lt. (Tp.), k. in a., 28/4/17.
12 Brodie, Mitchell Miller, M.C., Temp. Lt., d. of w., 14/7/17.
10 Brown, Allan George, Lt. (Tp.), k. in a., 27/10/18.
18 Brown, George Russell, Lt. (Tp.), k. in a., 11/2/18.
32 Browne, Langford Kyffin, 2/Lt. (Tp.), k. in a., 9/4/17 (att. 25 Bn.).
Brownlow, Wilfred Herbert Cecil, Capt., k. in a., 28/5/18 (att. 12/13 Bn.).
Brownlow, William Lionel, 2/Lt., k. in a., 9/5/15 (att. R. Highrs.).
20 Browning, Reginald Arthur, M.C., 2/Lt. (Tp.), d. of w., 10/4/17.
22 Brounger, William Henry Prescott, 2/Lt. (Tp.), k. in a., 9/4/17.
11 Bruty, Edward Douglas, 2/Lt. (Tp.), k. in a., 15/10/17.
Bryson, John, 2/Lt. (Tp.), d. of w., 14/10/17 (att. 21 Bn.).
Buck, William Pallister, 2/Lt. (Tp.), d. of w., 24/10/18 (att. 4/R. Fus.).
8 Buckley, Felix George, M.C., Temp. Capt., d. of w., 17/8/17.
Bucknall, Walter Harry Corfield, Lt., k. in a., 3/5/17.
12 Buglass, Cyril, 2/Lt. (Tp.), d. of w., 23/3/18.
12 Bumpus, Bernard Ebenezer, 2/Lt. (Tp.), k. in a., 3/7/16.
3 Burdon-Sanderson, Guy Askew James, 2/Lt., d. of w., 21/2/17 (att. 9 Bn.).
23 Burge, Montague, Major (Tp.), k. in a., 1/7/16.
10 Burgess, Harold, 2/Lt. (Tp.), k. in a., 27/10/18.
27 Burluraux, John Rene Cornelius, 2/Lt. (Tp.), k. in a., 1/7/16.
Burn, James, 2/Lt. (Tp.), k. in a., 17/10/17 (att. 23 Bn.).
14 Burrows, Charles Selss, M.C., Capt. (Tp.), k. in a., 28/5/18.
9 Burrows, Leonard Righton, 2/Lt. (Tp.), k. in a., 2/10/15.
24 Byrne, Louis Frederick, 2/Lt. (Tp.), k. in a., 1/7/16.
27 Byrne, William, 2/Lt. (Tp.), d. of w., 26/9/16.
8 Calder, Alexander Scott, Temp. 2/Lt., k. in a., 25/9/16 (att. 10 Bn.).
22 Calkin, John Ernest, Temp. 2/Lt., k. in a., 9/4/17.
23 Campbell, Ian Stuart, Temp. 2/Lt., k. in a., 30/6/16.
2 Carr-Ellison, Oswald Fenwicke Clennall, Lt., k. in a., 5/10/18.
Carruthers, William Alexander, M.C., Temp. Lt., d. of w., 3/9/18 (att. 1/Royal Scots).
14 Carss, Herbert Crosley, Temp. 2/Lt., d. of w., 8/10/17.
Carter, Henry, 2/Lt., k. in a., 16/6/15.
8 Carter, Henry Gordon, 2/Lt. (Tp.), k. in a., 19/8/15.
Catnach, Thomas Burnett, Temp. 2/Lt., d. of w., 19/4/17 (att. 26 Bn.).
23 Catto, William Basil, Temp. 2/Lt., k. in a., 11/9/16.
20 Chalmers, John Cyril, Temp. 2/Lt., k. in a., 15/10/16.
8 Chapman, Sydney Victor, Temp. 2/Lt., k. in a., 11/0/17.
25 Charlesworth, Thomas Stephens, 2/Lt. (Tp.), d. of w., 10/7/16.
21 Charlton, John Macfarlan, Capt. (Tp.), k. in a., 1/7/16.
11 Charlton, Norman Ewart, Temp. 2/Lt., k. in a., 15/6/18.
16 Chevreau, Louis Raymond, Temp. 2/Lt., k. in a., 22/3/18 (att. 1/4 Bn.).
10 Clifford, Wigan, D.S.O., Major (Temp. Lt.-Col.), k. in a., 20/6/17.
25 Coates, Donald Newton, 2/Lt., k. in a., 21/3/18.
22 Coates, Frederick Noel, Temp. 2/Lt., d. of w., 4/4/17.
15 Coats, Lawrence Armstrong, 2/Lt. (Tp.), k. in a., 28/10/15 (att. 8 Bn.).
20 Coleman, Arthur, 2/Lt. (Tp.), k. in a., 1/7/16.
3 Coles, D. M., Lt., k. in a., 25-27/10/14 (att. 1 Bn.).
31 Collier, Bertram, Temp. 2/Lt., d. of w., 5/11/16 (att. 25 Bn.).
16 Collings, Frank Reginald, 2/Lt., k. in a., 3/12/17.
8 Collings, William Norman, Temp. Lt., k. in a., 6/10/18.
12/13 Collins, Alexander Kilpatrick, Temp. 2/Lt., k. in a., 29/5/18.
18 Collins, Claude Henry James, Temp. 2/Lt., d. of w., 16/4/18.
1 Colton, Stanley Edmonds, M.C., 2/Lt., k. in a., 28/3/18.
Condon, David, Lt., died, 23/7/17 (in Ger. hands).
10 Constable, Ralph, Temp. Capt., k. in a., 25/9/16.
22 Constantine, Frank Iveson, 2/Lt. (Tp.), d. of w., 20/8/18 (att. 2/Lincs).
18 Coombs, Henry Whitaker, Temp. Lt., d. of w., 2/7/16.
20 Cope, George Eric, Temp. Lt., k. in a., 1/7/16.
15 Corke, Guy Harold, Temp. 2/Lt., k. in a., 17/9/16 (att. 22 Bn.).
9 Cornell, Arthur George, Temp. 2/Lt., k. in a., 7/7/16.
22 Cosgrove, Albert Bruce, 2/Lt. (Tp.), d. of w., 31/5/16.
Coulson, Arthur, 2/Lt., k. in a., 27/3/18 (att. 1/5 Bn.).
32 Cowper, Leonard Harris, 2/Lt. (Tp.), d. of w., 7/11/16 (att. 20 Bn.).
25 Cox, Percy Cyril, 2/Lt., k. in a., 28/4/17.
Coxon, William Basil, 2/Lt., k. in a., 11/4/18.
Coy, John Christopher, Capt., k. in a., 27/9/18 (Garr. Bn.).
9 Craig, Robert Hunter, 2/Lt. (Tp.), k. in a., 21/3/18.
Cramsie, Arthur Butler, Lt., k. in a., 8/5/15.
3 Cree, James Fleming, 2/Lt., k. in a., 3/9/18 (att. 22 Bn.).
23 Cubey, Joseph Berkeley, Temp. Capt., k. in a., 1/7/16.
3 Cull, Percival Stuart, 2/Lt., k. in a., 14/4/18 (att. 1 Bn.).
23 Daggett, Cedric Hunton, Capt., k. in a., 11/2/17.
Dalbiac, Charles James Shelley, 2/Lt., k. in a., 16/6/15.
9 Dallas, Raymond Vivian Leslie, M.C., Capt. (Tp.), k. in a., 13/4/18.
9 Dashwood, Claude Burrand Lewes, Temp. Major, d. of w., 26/4/16.
David, William Jenkin, 2/Lt., k. in a., 27/5/18 (Res., att. 6 Bn.).
20 Davidson, Roland Cooper, Temp. Lt., k. in a., 1/7/16.
Davidson, James, 2/Lt. (Tp.), d. of w., 27/5/18 (att. 15/D.L.I.).
12/13 Davies, A. E., 2/Lt., k. in a., 28/5/18.
19 Davies, Reginald Charles, 2/Lt. (Tp.), k. in a., 1/6/16.
22 Davies, Robert William Marengwyn, Temp. 2/Lt., k. in a., 6/4/17 (and R.F.C., 59 Sq.).
19 Davies, William Robert, Lt. (Tp.), k. in a., 1/11/18.
24 Dawson, Dan Magill, Lt. (Tp.), d. of w., 8/9/16.
12 Deeming, Frank Tetlorr, T/Lt. (A/Capt.), k. in a., 21/3/18.
9 Dexter, E. I., Lt., died, 4/5/18 (and R.A.F.).
14 Dickinson, Arthur Frowde, Temp. Lt., k. in a., 22/3/18.
12/13 Dickinson, Henry Waite, Lt., d. of w., 9/8/18 (P. of W., German hands).
3 Dignen, George William, 2/Lt., k. in a., 24/10/18 (att. 1 Bn.).
2 Dingle, John, Lt., k. in a., 10/9/16.
26 Dixon, Henry Philip Norman, Temp. 2/Lt., k. in a., 4/9/17.
13 Dixon, John George, Temp. 2/Lt., k. in a., 16/6/17.
20 Dobson, Harold Percy, T/Lt., A/Capt., k. in a., 16/10/17
12 Dodds, Cave Bradburne, 2/Lt., k. in a., 25/9/15.
13 Dodds, Robert William Lee, Lt., k. in a., 25/9/15.
8 Dodds, Walter Milbourne, Capt. (Tp.), d. of w., 14/10/18 (P. of W.).
20 Dodds, William Henry, 2/Lt. (Tp.), k. in a., 6/11/16.
12/13 Doman, George Herbert Ryder, 2/Lt., d. of w., 11/6/18 (in German hands).
24 Donald, Robert, M.C., Temp. Lt., k. in a., 28/4/17.
20 Donaldson, John, Temp. 2/Lt., k. in a., 1/7/16.
Donnell, Arthur Patrick, 2/Lt., killed, 5/12/16 (and R.F.C.).
21 Dougal, Robert Joseph, Lt., Temp., k. in a., 1/7/16.
26 Dowend, John Middleton, 2/Lt., A/Capt., k. in a., 24/11/17.
18 Draper, Arthur Reginald Olley, Lt and Qr.-Mr., d. of w., 16/4/18.
9 Drummond, Francis, 2/Lt. (Tp.), k. in a., 5/7/16.
18 Drury, Philip Blackett, Capt. (Tp.), died, 15/7/16.
13 Duncan, John Donald Parland, 2/Lt., k. in a., 16/6/17.
1 Dunglinson, William, 2/Lt. (Tp.), d. of w., 21/8/18.
23 Dunn, Frederick Oswald, Temp. Lt., killed, 19/3/16.
22 Dunn, Malcolm, 2/Lt. (Tp.), k in a., 9/4/18.
25 Edmond-Jenkins, William Hart, Major (Tp.), d. of w., 1/7/16.
11 Edwards, Griffith Oliver, M.C., Temp., 2/Lt., k. in a., 20/9/17.

Elderfield, Henry, 2/Lt. (Tp.), died, 11/11/18 (att. 163 Chinese L.C.).
31 Elias, Hywel James, Temp. 2/Lt., k. in a., 5/6/17.
12/13 Elliott, John William, 2/Lt., k. in a., 21/3/18.
10 Ellis, Francis Bevis, Temp. Capt., k. in a., 25/9/16.
22 Elphinstone, Arthur Percy Archibald, Temp. Lt.-Col., k. in a., 1/7/16.
27 Ervine, Charles James, 2/Lt (Tp), d. of w., 6/4/16.
26 Esmonde, Geoffrey, 2/Lt., k. in a., 7/10/16.
13 Evans, Albert Aylward, Temp. Capt., k. in a., 16/6/17.
Evans, David, Temp. 2/Lt., d. of w., 24/9/17 (att. 1 Bn.).
27 Evered, Henry Robert Hastings, Temp. 2/Lt., k. in a., 1/7/16.
13 Ewens, Thomas William, Temp. 2/Lt., k. in a., 30/3/17.
11 Exley, A. T., 2/Lt., killed, 22/4/18 (and R.A.F.).
16 Falconer, Robert Whitfield, Lt. (Tp.), k. in a., 1/7/16.
23 Falcy, Humphrey Ned, M.C., 2/Lt. (Tp.), k. in a., 21/11/16.
30 Falkons, Robert, Temp. Capt., k. in a., 1/7/16 (att. 27 Bn.).
Farwell, John Edmund, Temp. 2/Lt., k. in a., 30/5/18 (att. 4 Bn.).
19 Fawcus, Walter, M.C., Temp Capt., k. in a., 25/3/18.
11 Fearnley-Whittingstall, George Herbert, Lt. (Tp.), k. in a., 3/8/16.
12/13 Feggetter, John Halifax, M.C., Temp. Lt., k. in a., 4/10/17.
12 Field, Gordon Stewart, Temp. 2/Lt., k. in a., 16/6/17.
27 Fields, Edward Cotman, 2/Lt. (Tp.), d. of w., 22/6/16.
1 Finch, Philip Gerard, M.C., Lt., k in a., 28/3/18.
12 Findlay, James, Temp. 2/Lt., k. in a., 16/6/17.
26 Finlay, John Cuthbert, Capt., k. in a., 23/11/16.
8 Fishbourne, Charles Edward, Temp. Lt.-Col., d. of w., 6/10/16.
Fisher, Raymond Wadhams, Capt. (Tp.), k. in a., 13/9/16.
Fisher, Herbert, 2/Lt., k. in a., 11/4/18 (att. 1/5 D.L.I.).
26 Fitzgerald, Gerald, 2/Lt., k. in a., 1/7/16.
26 Fleming, John Joseph, Temp. Capt., k. in a., 13/10/17.
Fletcher, Roland Sackville, Capt., k. in a., 1/11/14.
26 Flint, Charles William, 2/Lt. (Tp.), k. in a., 1/7/16.
25 Flynn, Joseph Michael, Temp. 2/Lt., d. of w., 11/5/18.
25 Foley, John, Capt. (Tp.), k. in a., 1/7/16.
3 Foreman, Harry Clennell Temp. Lt., k. in a, 24/10/18 (att. 9 Bn.).
22 Forster, John Percival, Temp. Capt., k. in a., 1/7/16.
1 Fox, Douglas Charles, 2/Lt., k. in a., 23/7/16.
12/13 France, William, Temp. 2/Lt., k. in a., 8/10/18.
1 Fraser, Peter Campbell, 2/Lt., d. of w., 23/7/16.
23 Freeman, John Roland, Temp 2/Lt., d. of w., 12/2/17.
Friend, Joshua, Temp. 2/Lt., k. in a., 9/9/17 (att. 20 Bn.).
26 Fromant, Herbert Dudley Sands, Temp 2/Lt., k. in a., 29/4/17.
11 Frost, James John Temp. Lt., k. in a., 7/7/16.
22 Fryer, James Whaley, 2/Lt., k. in a., 1/7/16.
21 Furse, William Henry, Temp. 2/Lt., k. in a., 1/7/16.
1 Futers, Norman Ratcliffe, Lt. (A/Capt.), k. in a., 27/9/18.
3 Gameson, George Henry Molyneux, 2/Lt., d. of w., 14/3/17 (att. 8 Bn.).
Garrard, William Garth Blackall, Lt., killed, 19/10/17.
13 Garry, Kenneth Temp. 2/Lt., d. of w., 18/6/17.
23 Gaskin, Robert Bertram, Temp. 2/Lt., k. in a., 9/9/17.
Gatehouse, Richard Francis, Capt., k. in a., 13/9/14.
30 Gay, John, Temp. Capt., died, 29/5/16.
17 Germain, Harry Gordon, 2/Lt., k. in a., 12/7/16.
12/13 Gertson, Frederick, 2/Lt., k. in a., 16/4/18.
12/13 Gibbon, Frederic, Temp. 2/Lt., k. in a., 8/10/18.
1 Gibbon, Frederick William, Temp. 2/Lt., k. in a., 25/8/18
22 Gibson, Arthur Douglas, Temp. 2/Lt., k. in a., 9/4/17.
2 Gilchrist, Ivan Hamilton Learmouth, 2/Lt., k. in a., 2/10/15.
Gledstone, Herbert Reginald, A/Capt., k. in a., 25/5/18.
12 Glenday, Ferdinand Goncalves, Capt., k. in a., 15/9/16 (att. R.F.C.).
13 Godber, Hugh Gerald, Temp. Capt., k. in a., 11-18/7/16.
3 Goosey, H., 2/Lt., killed, 8/8/18 (and R.A.F.).
Gordon-Steward, Charleton William, Temp. Major, k. in a., 12/4/17 (Staff, Res. of Off., Brig.-Maj., 198/Inf Bde.).
Gowans, William Ireland, Temp. 2/Lt., k. in a., 13/10/17 (att. 25 Bn.).
16 Graham, Percy Gordon, Capt. (Tp.), k. in a., 1/7/16.
1 Grantham, Edward Rodney Hasluck, 2/Lt., d. of w., 31/3/17.
14 Gray, George Ernest Marshall, 2/Lt (Tp.), k. in a., 14/7/16.
1 Greener, Arthur Stephen, M.C., Lt. (A/Capt.), d. of w., 18/4/18.
12/13 Greenwell, John, Temp. 2/Lt., k. in a., 24/10/18.
12/13 Gregory, Percy John, Temp. 2/Lt., k. in a., 4/10/17.
15 Grey, Patrick Riddle, 2/Lt. (Tp.), k. in a., 26/9/16.
21 Grice, Lawrence Victor, Temp. Lt., k. in a., 13/4/18.
15 Griffiths, John Llewelyn, Temp. 2/Lt., k. in a., 26/6/16 (att. 12 Bn.).
24 Grossman, Victor David, 2/Lt. (Tp.), k. in a., 17/9/16.
1 Gunner, Benjamin George, M.C. (T/Capt.), Lt., k. in a., 7/10/15.
29 Haggarty, John Joseph, Temp. 2/Lt., d. of w., 11/9/16 (att. 22 Bn.).
21 Hall, John McRobb, Temp. 2/Lt., k. in a., 1/7/16.
19 Hall, John Pearson Herbert, Temp. 2/Lt., k. in a., 1/11/18.
15 Hall, Kenneth Stuart, Temp. Lt., k. in a., 25/1/16 (att. A.C.C.).
23 Hall, Percy George, Temp. 2/Lt., k. in a., 30/6/16 (att. 26 Bn.).
10 Hallam-Botham, G., Temp. Major, k. in a., 3/8/16.
26 Hamer, Samuel, Temp. 2/Lt. (A/Capt.), k. in a., 14/4/17.
12 Hamilton, Herbert Otho, Lt., k. in a., 25/9/15.
23 Hammond, Kenneth Lowton Charles, Temp. 2/Lt., k. in a., 22/3/18.
15 Hampton, F. A. F., 2/Lt., died, 23/8/18 (and R.A.F.).
14 Hancock, William, 2/Lt. (Tp.), k. in a., 28/9/17.
Handyside, Arthur John, Temp. 2/Lt., k. in a., 24/10/18 (att. 4/Royal Fusiliers).
Hanson, William Edward, Temp. 2/Lt., k. in a., 28/4/17 (att. 26 Bn.).
11 Harding, John Samuel, Lt. (Tp.), k. in a., 8/11/15.
22 Hardy, Charles Edwin, Temp. Capt., k. in a., 13/4/18.
3 Hardy, Frederick, 2/Lt., k. in a., 9/9/17 (att. 21 Bn.).
21 Harms, William, Temp. 2/Lt., k. in a., 4/3/17 (and R.F.C., 59 Sq.).
3 Harrison, Tom Marriott, Temp. Capt., died, 3/4/17 (att. 13 Bn.).
12 Harrower, Alan Pat, Temp. Lt., d. of w., 26/3/18 (in German hands).
Hart, Arthur Charles, Capt., k. in a., 7/5/15.
Harvey, William, 2/Lt., d. of w., 14/10/16 (att. 27 Bn.).
9 Harvie, Patrick Joseph, Temp. Lt., k. in a., 16/4/17.
9 Haslam, Arthur Dixon, Temp. Lt., d. of w., 2/11/18.
20 Hawes, Ernest Harington, Temp. 2/Lt., k. in a., 5/6/17.
12 Hay, James Lyle, Temp. 2/Lt., k. in a., 3/7/16.
11 Haynes, James, 2/Lt., k. in a., 29/3/16.
20 Head, Albert Everest, Temp. Lt., k. in a., 1/7/16.
14 Henderson, John Easton, Temp. Lt., died, 26/4/18 (in German hands).
21 Henderson, James Percy, Temp. 2/Lt., k. in a., 11/9/17.
11 Henri, Frank, Temp. Capt., k. in a., 15/6/18.
23 Hewitson, John, 2/Lt. (Tp.), k. in a., 11/11/17.
Hewitt, Cedric Atkinson, Lt., k. in a., 27/10/18 (att. 11 Bn.).
9 Hewson, Wilfrid John, Temp. Lt., d. of w., 25/10/18.
2 Hill, James Macgregor, Temp. 2/Lt., d. of w., 10/11/16.
14 Hills, Arthur Edward, Temp. Capt., k. in a., 28/5/18.
3 Hoard, Henry Herbert Hoare, 2/Lt., k. in a., 9/9/17 (att. 21 Bn.).
10 Hobbs, Geoffrey Brian, T/Lt., killed, 7/9/15 (att. R.F.C.).
Hobbs, H. E., 2/Lt., k. in a., 25/5/15.
18 Hodgkinson, John, 2/Lt. (Tp.), k. in a., 17/4/18.
28 Hodgson, Oswald Arthur, Temp. 2/Lt., k. in a., 16/4/17 (att. 9 Bn.).
20 Holloway, Leonard, Temp. 2/Lt., k. in a., 9/4/17.
26 Hopper, James Arthur, M.C., 2/Lt. (Tp.), k. in a., 10/4/17.
25 Hopps, William Leonard, Temp. 2/Lt., d. of w., 22/5/16.
29 Horne, David Douglas, Temp. Capt., k. in a., 1/7/16 (att. 21 Bn.).
24 Horrox, Henry M., Temp. 2/Lt., k. in a., 1/7/16.
1/2 Houston, John Cunningham, 2/Lt. (Tp.), k. in a., 14/10/18 (att. M.G.C.).
25 Howard, Harry Elsmore, 2/Lt. (Tp.), d. of w., 8/4/17.
24 Howard, Louis Meredith, Temp. Lt.-Col., d. of w., 2/7/16.
9 Howes, Edward, 2/Lt., k. in a., 2/8/16.
12 Howkins, George Addington, 2/Lt. (Tp.), k. in a., 25-27/9/15.
3 Hughes, Frederick Gordon, 2/Lt., k. in a., 26/6/16 (att. 12 Bn.).
23 Hunter, Albert Richmond, M.C., Lt., died, 11/2/19.
26 Hunter, Norman Archbold, 2/Lt. (Tp.), k. in a., 3/9/17.
25 Huntley, John Fenwirk, Lt. (Tp.), k. in a., 9/4/17.
Husband, William, 2/Lt. (Tp.), d. of w., 25/6/18 (att. 15/D.L.I.).
12/13 Hutchinson, William Stanhope, M.C., Temp. 2/Lt. (A/Capt.), d. of w., 8/9/18.
26 Hutchinson, Hugh Maxwell, 2/Lt. (Tp.), d. of w., 29/11/17.
26 Hynam, Walter William, 2/Lt., k. in a., 1/7/16.
24 Innes, James David, 2/Lt. (Tp.), d. of w., 5/8/17.
Irvine, William Magnus, 2/Lt., k. in a., 22/3/18 (att. R.F.C., 12 Sq.).
Jackson, Herbert William, Lt., k. in a., 20/1/18 (att. 12/13 Bn.).
13 Jackson, Henry Teasdale, Temp. 2/Lt., k. in a., 8/10/17 att. 8/Leics.).
8 James, Archibald Hugh, D.S.O., Act. Lt.-Col., k. in a., 26/3/18 (att. 8/W. Yorks Regt.).
24 James, Henry John, Temp. 2/Lt., k. in a., 9/4/17.
13 James, Herbert Walter, Temp. 2/Lt., k. in a., 4/10/17 (att. 9/Yorks L. Infantry).
23 Jamieson, John, 2/Lt., k. in a., 29/4/18.
1 Jaques, Joseph, 2/Lt., k. in a., 26/9/17.
20 Jarman, Andrew Hatch, Temp. 2/Lt., k. in a., 1/7/16.
20 Jeffreys, Alexander Harry, A/Capt., k. in a., 6/11/16 (from 19 Bn.).
1 Jenkins, Edward Geoffray, 2/Lt. (Tp.), d. of w., 26/10/18.
Jenkins, William Edwin, Capt., k. in a., 1/10/15.
14 Jennings, Harold Victor Edgar, 2/Lt., k. in a., 29/5/18.
10 Joicey, The Honble. Sidney James Drever, Temp. Capt. & Adjt., k. in a., 20/3/16.
1/2 Jones, M G., M.C., Lt., killed, 12/6/18 (and R.A.F.).
3 Jung, Henry Adolph, 2/Lt., died, 9/5/15 (att. 1 Bn.).
Keatinge, Eustace Gabriel Lawrence, Lt., k. in a., 13/4/18.
18 Keenlyside, Thomas Edward, Lt., d. of w., 21/4/18.
26 Kelly, William Peter, Temp. Capt., d. of w., 12/11/16.
2 King, Herbert Garner, Temp. 2/Lt., k. in a., 10/9/16.
16 King, Herbert Grenfell, M.C., Capt., k. in a., 22/3/18.
2 King, Humphrey Stuart, M.C., T/Lt. (A/Capt.), k. in a., 4/10/18.
23 King, Soloman, Temp 2/Lt., k. in a., 13/10/16.
26 Kinnaird, David, Temp. 2/Lt., k. in a., 5/12/17.
22 Kinrade, Edward, 2/Lt. (Tp.), k. in a., 23/10/18 (att 2/-Lincs).
16 Klean, Michael Graham, Temp. 2/Lt., k. in a., 1/7/16.
9 Knott, Henry Basil, Capt. (Tp.), d. of w., 7/9/15.
12 Knott, Ralph Leonard, Lt. (Tp.), k. in a., 25/9/15.
28 Knott, Robert Cecil, Temp. Capt., d. of w., 14/8/16 (att. 20 Bn.).
13 Laing, Alexander Torrance, Temp. Capt., d. of w., 24/7/16.
22 Laing, Dudley Ogilvie, Temp. Capt., k. in a., 1/7/16.
20 Laing, Gerald Ogilvie, Temp. Capt., k. in a., 5/6/17.
Laird, Louis Wilfred, 2/Lt. Tp.), k. in a., 2/9/18 (att. 23 Lanc. Fusrs.).
Lakeman, John Pearce, Temp. 2/Lt., d. of w., 20/4/17 (att. 20 Bn.).
3 Lamb, Everard Joseph, Capt., k. in a., 1/11/14 (att. Yorks L.I.).

22 Lamb, Walter, Temp. Lt., k. in a., 1/7/16.

25 Lambert, John Henry, Temp. Capt., d. of w., 9/8/16.

3 Lambert, John Mounsey, Capt., k. in a., 28/10/14 (att. 1 Bn.).

25 Lambert, Percy Gerald, 2/Lt. (Tp.), k. in a., 21/3/18.

26 Laughton, Geoffrey, Temp. 2/Lt., k. in a., 5/12/17.

10 Lawrence, Edward, M.C., D.C.M., Lt. (A/Capt.), k. in a., 28/3/18.

Laws, Alfred Victor, 2/Lt., k. in a., 25-27/10/14.

3 Leather, Christopher, Lt., k. in a., 25-27/10/14 (att. 1 Bn.).

27 Leather, Ernest Arthur, Temp. Major, k. in a., 10/2/16.

26 Leckenby, Harold, Temp. 2/Lt., k. in a., 9/4/17.

Legard, Geoffrey Philip, Lt., k. in a., 8/5/15.

24 Lennard, Richard Granger, Temp. 2/Lt., died, 6/5/17 (P. of W.).

12/13 Lethbridge, William Henry, Temp. 2/Lt., k. in a., 4/10/17.

21 Levin, C. N., M.C., Capt., k. in a., 21/3/18 (att. 102/T.M. Bty.).

24 Lewis, Harold Lockwood, Temp. 2/Lt., k. in a., 23/10/17.

15 Limont, William Eric, Temp. 2/Lt., k. in a., 14/7/16 (att. 12 Bn.).

23 Lindsay, James, 2/Lt. (Tp.), k. in a., 12/4/18.

27 Lister, Thomas Frederick, Temp. 2/Lt., k. in a., 28/4/17.

3 Lloyd, Mervyn, Capt., d. of w., 15/3/15.

10 Lock, James Alexander, 2/Lt., k. in a., 25/9/16.

12/13 Lockie, James, M.C., Capt., k. in a., 22/3/18 (att. 2/Lincs Regt.).

8 Lofting, Charles Edgar, Temp. 2/Lt., d. of w., 10/1/17.

13 Long, Horace Victor, Temp. 2/Lt., d. of w., 28/6/17.

Longhurst, C. R., Major (Tp.), died, 8/3/18.

3 Lord, Roland, Capt., k. in a., 8/10/18 (att. 1 Bn.).

Lovatt, Charles, M.C., 2/Lt. (Tp.), k. in a., 12/4/18 (att. 4/-Bedfords).

1 Low, John James, 2/Lt., k. in a., 3/8/17 (att. 13/Bn.).

12/13 Lowth, John Leslie, Temp. 2/Lt., k. in a., 4/10/17.

27 Lumley, Frederick William, 2/Lt., k. in a., 10/4/17.

2 Lumsden, Joseph Charles, 2/Lt. (Tp.), k. in a., 11/10/18.

23 Lyle, William, Temp. Lt.-Col., k. in a., 1/7/16.

11 Lyone, Alexander Martin, M.C., Temp. 2/Lt., d. of w., 26/9/17.

27 McClarrence, Stanley, Temp. 2/Lt., k. in a., 10/4/17.

18 McCormick, Frank Pockell, 2/Lt. (Tp.), d. of w., 9/8/18.

27 McCormack, John Joseph, Temp. Capt., k. in a., 28/4/17.

22 Macdonald, Hugh, Temp. 2/Lt., k. in a., 5/6/17.

29 McDonald, John, 2/Lt., died, 21/11/16 (att. 22 Bn.).

23 Macdonald, Roderick, Temp. 2/Lt., k. in a., 1/7/16.

8 McDonald, Ronald Graham, M.C., T/Lt. (A/Capt.), d. of w., 16/8/17.

23 Macdonald, Simon, Temp. Lt., k. in a., 1/7/16.

24 McDonnell, Frank J., Temp. Lt., died, 26/5/18 (att. 9 Bn.).

1/2 McDonnell, Thomas John, Temp. 2/Lt., k. in a., 1/11/17 (att. 26 Bn.).

26 McGillicuddy, John. Lt. (Tp.), k. in a., 1/7/16.

16 McIntosh, John, 2/Lt., k. in a., 22/3/18 (att. 1/5 Bn.).

23 McIntosh, William, Lt. (Tp.), d. of w., 6/7/16.

16 MacIntyre, Thomas, Lt., k. in a., 1/7/16.

1 McKenna, Reginald Talkington, 2/Lt., k. in a., 10/10/18 (att. 8 Bn.).

1 Mackenzie, Archibald, Capt. (Tp.(, d. of w., 4/6/18.

8 Mackenzie, John, Temp. Lt., k. in a., 26/9/16.

24 Mackenzie, Kenneth, Temp. Capt., k. in a., 1/7/16.

3 McKie, Douglas Hamlin, 2/Lt., d. of w., 11/4/17 (att. 27 Bn.).

8 Maclean, Alfred Knowles, 2/Lt. (Tp.), k. in a., 27/9/18.

MacMeeken, James, Temp. 2/Lt., k. in a., 27/5/18 (Res. att. 5 Bn.).

McMurdo, John Hamilton, Temp. 2/Lt., k. in a., 27/5/18 (Res. att. 5 Bn.).

8 Macnab, James, Temp., 2/Lt., k. in a., 19/8/15.

21 McNeill, Robert Archibald, 2/Lt., k. in a., 9/4/17.

24 McNiff, Francis Joseph, Temp. 2/Lt., k. in a., 13/3/18 (att. R.F.C.).

15 McShane, Vincent, Temp. Lt., k. in a., 21/8/15 (att. 2/South W. Borderers).

20 McSorley, Frederick William, 2/Lt., k. in a., 5/4/17.

1 Mallony, John Charles, Temp. 2/Lt., k. in a., 9/4/17 (att. 26 Bn.).

Manger, John Kenneth, 2/Lt., k. in a., 8/5/15.

16 Mann, Lawrence John, Temp. 2/Lt., k. in a., 12/7/17.

10 Manners, Lord Robert William Orlando, C.M.G., D.S.O., Lt.-Col., k. in a., 11/9/17.

12 Marchant, Sydney, Temp. 2/Lt., d. of w., 6/7/16.

1 Marjoribanks, Marmaduke Edward, 2/Lt., k. in a., 21/11/17.

Markham, Walter Henry James, Temp. 2/Lt., d. of w., 27/3/18 (att. 1/5 Bn.) (in German hands).

12 Marsh, William Bernard, Temp. 2/Lt., k. in a., 21/3/18 (att. 1/Lincs Regt.).

27 Marshall, John Woodall, Temp. Lt., k. in a., 1/7/16.

Martin, Douglas Francis de Renzy, 2/Lt., k. in a., 13/4/17.

8 Martin, George Patrick Winfield, Temp. Lt., k. in a., 2/10/18.

17 Martin, G. W., Temp. Major, k. in a., 17/9/18.

Mason, Vernon, Temp. 2/Lt., k. in a., 1/4/18 (att. 9 Bn.).

12 Mather, C. H., Temp. 2/Lt., d. of w., 18/3/16.

Matthews, John Herbert, Capt., k. in a., 13-14/9/14.

17 Maughan, William Douglas, Temp. 2/Lt., k. in a., 19/11/17.

Mayfield, Leonard Augustus, Temp. 2/Lt., k. in a., 27/9/18 (att. 1 Bn.).

23 Menzies, Harry, 2/Lt., k. in a., 29/4/17.

15 Michie, Henry George, Lt., k. in a., 26/9/16 (att. 8 Bn.).

24/27 Middlemis, Herbert, 2/Lt., k. in a., 23/10/17.

3 Miller, John Eric Hale, 2/Lt., k. in a., 11/1/16 (att. 1 Bn.).

20 Mills, William John, 2/Lt., d. of w., 4/9/18 (and R.A.F.).

26 Miln, William Wallace, Temp. Lt., k. in a., 24/5/18 (att. 4/Bedford Regt.).

Milne, Eric Sutcliffe, 2/Lt., k. in a., 28/10/17 (att. 12/13 Bn.).

Milne, John Vincent Percy, 2/Lt., k. in a., 25/9/16 (att. 10 Bn.).

13 Milton, Edward Thomas, Temp. Capt., k. in a., 26/9/15.

13 Milton, John Munro, 2/Lt., k. in a., 25/9/15.

14 Mitchell, Thomas, Temp. 2/Lt., died, 4/11/18 (att. G.H.Q., Lewis G. Sch.).

25 Mitchell, William, 2/Lt., k. in a., 28/4/17.

Molineux, George King, Lt. (T/Capt.), k. in a., 5/5/15.

1 Morant, William Hedley, Temp. 2/Lt., k. in a., 25/10/16 (att. 4 Bn.).

15 Morgan-Brown, Nigel Martin, Temp. 2/Lt., died, 31/10/15 (att. 8 Bn.).

Morris, Albert Evelyn, 2/Lt., k. in a., 27/5/18 (Res., att. 4 Bn.).

18 Morton, G., Temp. Lt., died, 23/11/18.

15 Mouck, Ernest, Capt., k. in a., 7/8/15.

26 Mullally, Brian Desmond, Temp. Capt., k. in a., 1/7/16.

30 Murphy, Albert, Temp. 2/Lt., k. in a., 3/10/16 (att. 24 Bn.).

12 Murray, Graham Dunmore, Temp. 2/Lt., k. in a., 26/1/16.

25 Murray, Patrick Austin, Temp. Capt., k. in a., 1/7/16.

12/13 Mustard, Robert William, 2/Lt., k. in a., 31/3/18.

8 Neill, Robert Kirkpatrick, Temp. 2/Lt., k. in a., 16/8/17 (Reserves att.).

Nettleship, Thomas, Temp. 2/Lt., k. in a., 22/3/18 (att. 1/5 Bn.).

1 Nichol, Anthony Thomas, 2/Lt., d. of w., 16/4/17.

Nicholls, Henry Lewin Faulconer, Capt., k. in a., 25/2/15.

Nicholls, Horace William, M.C., 2/Lt., k. in a., 24/8/18 (att. 1/East Yorks Regt.).

13 Nicholson, Bernard George Maurice, Temp. Lt., died, 29/10/18.

25 Nicholson, Thomas Edward, Temp. Lt., k. in a., 1/7/16.

1 Nimmo, William Leslie, 2/Lt., k. in a., 26/7/18.

21 Niven, Allan Graham, Temp. Major, k. in a., 1/7/16.

20 Nixon, William, Capt., k. in a., 1/7/16.

10 Noble, John Wilson, Temp. 2/Lt., k. in a., 25/9/16.

20 Noble, Thomas Gilson, Temp. Major, k. in a., 1/7/16.

19 Noyes, Talbot Ronald Arthur Herbert, Temp. Capt., k. in a., 11/7/16.

3 Nunneley, Charles Francis, Lt., k. in a., 25-27/10/14 (att. Yorks L.I.).

3 O'Dowd, Maurice Vernon, 2/Lt., k. in a., 25/5/15 (att. 2 Bn.).

8 Oliver, William Steele, 2/Lt. (Tp.), k. in a., 7-11/8/15.

2 Parish, Robert, 2/Lt., k. in a., 10/9/16.

26 Park, Andrew, 2/Lt. (Tp.), k. in a., 14/7/16.

26 Parker, James, Temp. Lt., k. in a., 1/7/16.

1 Parkinson, Gilbert Maurice, Capt., died, 14/11/18.

1 Partington, Leigh, Capt., k. in a., 28/3/18.

1 Passingham, Edward George, M.C., Lt., k. in a., 3/5/17.

9 Patten, M. G., M.C., Capt., k. in a., 14/4/18.

23 Patterson, John Hylton, Temp. Lt., k. in a., 1/7/16.

8 Paton, George Alexander Lechmere, T/Capt. (2/Lt.), k. in a., 7-11/8/15.

25 Paul, Thomas Guthrie, 2/Lt., k. in a., 9/4/17.

17 Pears, Maurice Loraine, C.M.G., T/Lt.-Col., died, 20/10/16.

25 Peckston, Cuthbert Joseph, 2/Lt., k. in a., 22/3/18.

11 Penney, Reginald Harper, Temp. 2/Lt., k. in a., 9/11/17.

Percival, Alfred Jex Blake, D.S.O., Lt.-Col. (Tp.), k. in a., 31/11/14.

16 Peyton, Montagu Frank, Temp. 2/Lt., k. in a., 12/7/17 (Res.).

1 Phelan, Albert Edward, M.C., T/Lt. (A/Capt.), k. in a., 20/11/17.

23 Philp, David Carswell, 2/Lt., k. in a., 29/4/17.

Phillips, Edward, 2/Lt. (Tp.), d. of w., 27/5/18 (att. 5 Bn.).

33 Pinnington, Victor, 2/Lt., k. in a., 5/11/16 (att. 23 Bn.).

Place, Philip Whiteley, 2/Lt., k. in a., 19/8/18 (att. 12 Norfolk Rgt.).

24 Pleasance, Charles Joseph, Temp. 2/Lt., k. in a., 31/7/17.

11 Pomfret, John William, M.C., Temp. 2/Lt., k. in a., 27/10/18.

15 Popple, George Marsden, Temp. 2/Lt., d. of w., 26/6/16 (att. 16 Bn.).

Porritt, John Ernest, Temp. 2/Lt., k. in a., 27/5/18 (att. 5 Bn.).

1 Powys, Geoffrey Mappleton, Temp. Lt., k. in a., 19/6/17 (Gar. Bn., att. 8 Bn.).

26 Price, Harold, Temp. Capt., k. in a., 26/6/16.

3 Price, Joseph William James, 2/Lt., d. of w., 22/4/17 (att. 26 Bn.).

12 Pridham, William Albert Stanley, Temp. Lt., drowned, 5/1/16.

19 Priestman, George Aloysius, Temp. Lt., d. of w., 15/5/18.

Priestnall, William Eustace, 2/Lt., k. in a., 27/5/18 (att. 5 Bn.).

24 Prior, John Peter, Temp. 2/Lt., k. in a., 9/4/17.

14 Pritchard, Ralph Broomfield, D.S.O., M.C., Capt. (Tp.), d. of w., 26/4/18.

1 Probert, Arthur James, Temp. 2/Lt., k. in a., 9/4/17 (att. 25 Bn.).

25 Prudham. Thomas Pearson, Temp. 2/Lt., k. in a., 28/4/17.

Pryor, Arthur Henry, Temp. 2/Lt., k. in a., 10/4/17.

30 Pugh, Edward Rhodes, Capt., died, 2/12/18 (att. 1/K.R.R.C.).

25 Pullein, Thomas Harold, 2/Lt., k. in a., 21/3/18.

21 Purnell, Stanley George Hardy, Temp. 2/Lt., k. in a., 5/6/17.

13 Quarrell, Charles Hubert, Temp. 2/Lt., k. in a., 16/6/17.

12 Queen, John. 2/Lt., k. in a., 17/6/17.

3 Quin, Leslie William Whitworth, M.C., T/Lt. (A/Capt.), k. in a., 24/4/17 (att. 27 Bn.).

21 Raines, Leslie Robinson, Temp. Lt., k. in a., 1/7/16.

12/13 Ramsey, Charles Owen, 2/Lt., k. in a., 21/3/18 (Res.).

21 Rand, Charles Herbert Sidney, Temp. 2/Lt., k. in a., 18/9/18 (att. 2/Lincs Regt.).

8 Raw, Rupert George, D.S.O., Capt., k. in a., 7/8/15.

1 Rea, Frank Melton, 2/Lt., k. in a., 27/3/16.

1 Redpath, Harold Edwin, 2/Lt., k. in a., 15/7/16.

1 Regan, James Herbert, Temp. 2/Lt., k. in a., 27/9/18.

Remmer, Fred, 2/Lt., k. in a., 12/4/18.

Richards, John, Temp. 2/Lt., d. of w., 30/3/18 (in Ger. hands).

Richardson, John, 2/Lt. (Tp.), d. of w., 9/9/17 (Res., att. 23 Bn.).
26 Richardson, John Sherbrooke, 2/Lt. (Tp.), k. in a., 9/4/17.
12/13 Richardson, Thomas William Taylor, 2/Lt., k. in a., 21/3/18.
11 Ridley, Joseph, Temp. 2/Lt., k. in a., 15/6/18.
12/13 Ridley, Thomas, 2/Lt., k. in a., 23/3/18.
1 Riley, Sydney, Temp. 2/Lt., k. in a., 20/9/18.
15 Robertson, Douglas Forbes, Temp. 2/Lt., d. of w., 28/9/16 (att. 8 Bn.).
21 Robertson, George, Temp. Capt., k. in a., 1/7/16.
8 Robertson, John Johnston, Temp. 2/Lt., k. in a., 27/9/18.
9 Robertson, William Ford, Capt. (Tp.), k. in a., 17/10/17.
14 Robinson, Frank, Temp. Lt., d. of w., 7/7/16.
8 Robinson, John Hunter, Temp. 2/Lt., d. of w., 17/9/18 (att. 12 Bn.).
9 Robinson, Percy Douglas, Temp. Capt., k. in a., 7/7/16.
8 Robinson, William, Temp. 2/Lt., k. in a., 22/8/18 (att. 12/13 Bn.).
8 Robinson, William Ewart, 2/Lt. (Tp.), k. in a., 19/8/15.
1 Roblin, Lewis George, 2/Lt., k. in a., 5/5/18.
18 Robson, Charles, Temp. 2/Lt., d. of w., 2/12/18.
1 Rochell, Alfred, Lt. (T/Capt.), d. of w., 14/4/18.
3 Roddam, Robert Collingwood, Capt., k. in a., 16/6/15 (att. 1 Bn.).
27 Rodham, Robert, 2/Lt. (Tp.), k. in a., 17/10/17 (att. 9 Bn.).
Rogers, Leonard Neville, Capt. (Tp.), d. of w., 11/4/17 (Res., att. 18 Bn.).
3 Rose, Stewart Alan, Lt., k. in a., 28/3/18.
1 Routledge, John Frederick, Lt. (Tp.), k. in a., 23/9/17.
19 Rutherford, William Cecil, 2/Lt., died, 10/3/19.
20 Sanby, William Worthington, Temp. 2/Lt., k. in a., 1/7/16.
16 Saunders, Kenneth, 2/Lt., killed, 31/12/14.
10 Savage, Cuthbert Farrar, Lt., d. of w., 20/6/17.
21 Scattergood, Tom Victor, 2/Lt. (Tp.), d. of w., 6/6/17.
14 Sced, Henry Forbes, Lt. (Tp.), k. in a., 24/9/17.
13 Schafer, Thomas Sydney, Lt., k. in a., 26/9/15.
8 Scott, Archibald MacDonald, 2/Lt. (Tp.), k. in a., 16/8/17.
2 Scrutton, Hugh Urquhart, Temp. Capt., d. of w., 10/9/16 (P. of W.).
Selby, Beauchamp Henry, Capt., k. in a., 20/9/14.
3 Sellers, John Harrison, 2/Lt., k. in a., 24/5/15 (att. 2 Bn.).
16 Serginson, Harold, Temp. 2/Lt. (A/Capt.), k. in a., 27/2/18 (att. 96/T.M.B.).
26 Shackleton, William Launcelot Collier, Lt. (Tp.), d. of w., 24/4/17.
3 Shann, Kenneth, 2/Lt., k. in a., 8/5/15 (att. 2 Bn.).
23 Shapley, Alfred Edward, Lt. (Tp.), k. in a., 1/7/16.
13 Shaw, Robert Henderson, Temp. 2/Lt., k. in a., 18/9/16.
27 Showell, Harold George, 2/Lt. (Tp.), k. in a., 16/7/17.
12 Shufflebotham, John, Temp. 2/Lt., k. in a., 25-27/9/15.
1 Sibbit, George Bertrand, Temp. Lt., k. in a., 27/9/18.
22 Sibbit, Henry, Temp. Major., k. in a., 1/7/16.
20 Sillery, Charles Cecil Archibald, Temp. Lt.-Col., k. in a., 1/7/16.
3 Simms, J. B. P., 2/Lt., killed, 4/6/18 (and R.A.F.).
1 Simpson, James Jamieson, Temp. 2/Lt., k. in a., 28/3/18.
27 Simpson, Thomas, Temp. Lt., k. in a., 1/7/16.
22 Simson, William Kingsbury, 2/Lt. (Tp.), k. in a., 5/6/17.
12 Sinclair, L., Temp. 2/Lt., k. in a., 28/9/16.
12 Singlehurst, Robert Bruce, Temp. 2/Lt., k. in a., 30/4/16.
12/13 Sisterton, Norman Hele, 2/Lt., k. in a., 16/4/18 (att. 1/Lincs Regt.).
Slack, John Barnett, Temp. 2/Lt., k. in a., 27/5/18 (R., att. 5 Bn.).
Sloper, Gerard Orby, M.C., Capt., died, 8/2/19 (att. 5 Bn.).
Smallwood, Robert Henry, Lt., d. of w., 27/5/18 (in German hands).
22 Smith, Edward John, Temp. Capt., k. in a., 5/10/18.
10 Smith, George Lawrence, Temp. 2/Lt., k. in a., 19/7/17.
28 Smith, John Adams, M.C., Temp. 2/Lt., d. of w., 28/4/17 (att. 20 Bn.).
32 Smith, John Richard Gutteridge, Temp. 2/Lt., d. of w., 30/12/16 (att. 8 Bn.).
21 Smith, Norman McNeill, Temp. 2/Lt., k. in a., 1/7/16.
18 Smurthwaite, Oscar, Temp. Lt., k. in a., 17/4/18.
26 Sprenger, Oliver Howard, 2/Lt. (Tp.), k. in a., 5/6/17.
23 Stancer, John William, Temp. 2/Lt., d. of w., 17/4/18.
9 Stephenson, Charles Lindsay, 2/Lt. (Tp.), k. in a., 28/11/17.
16 Stephenson, John Roberts, 2/Lt. (Tp.), k. in a., 7/8/17.
11 Sterling, George Pomeroy, D.S.O., M.C., Temp. Capt., k. in a., 27/10/18.
10 Stewart, Andrew, M.C., 2/Lt. (Tp.), k. in a., 20/9/17.
26 Stewart, George, T/Lt. (A/Capt.), k. in a., 5/6/17.
18 Storar, Robert Archibald, Temp. 2/Lt., killed, 16/12/15.
8 Straughan, T. A., Temp. Lt., died, 5/1/18.
1 Studdy, Melvin Leslie, Temp. 2/Lt., d. of w., 22/10/16 (att. 8 Bn.).
12 Summers, Archibald Young, 2/Lt., k. in a., 22/3/18 (att. 11 Leicesters).
24 Sutcliffe, Herbert Richard Charles, Temp. 2/Lt., k. in a., 1/7/16 (att. T.M.B. 5/24).
2 Swift, Sydney Reginald, Temp. 2/Lt., d. of w., 4/12/16 (att. 8 Bn.).
13 Swinney, Norman Atkinson, Temp. 2/Lt., k. in a., 28/4/16.
16 Tanner, Arthur Edward, 2/Lt. (Tp.), d. of w., 10/7/17.
Tate, Andrew, Temp. 2/Lt., k. in a., 20/1/18 (att. 24/27 Bn.).
14 Tate, John Martin, Temp. Capt., k. in a., 27/5/18.
23 Taylor, Archibald Cameron, 2/Lt. (Tp.), k. in a., 29/4/17.
9 Taylor, Frederick George, 2/Lt. (Tp.), died, 21/7/17.
8 Taylor, Henry William, 2/Lt. (Tp.), d. of w., 29/5/17.
11 Taylor, Ronald Woodhouse, Temp. 2/Lt., k. in a., 7/7/16.
11 Teale, John Arthur, Temp. 2/Lt., d. of w., 27/9/16.
21 Telford, Hilton Roberts, Capt., d. of w., 9/9/17.
Thomas, Walter Saunders, Temp. Capt., died, 15/9/17 (att. 11 Gr. Bn.).
24 Thompson, Arthur, Temp. Capt., k. in a., 1/7/16.
Thompson, Arthur, 2/Lt., k. in a., 23/10/17.
3 Thompson, Charles Milburn, 2/Lt., k. in a., 26/8/17 (att. 24/27 Bn.).
1 Thompson, Charles John McKinnon, Lt., d. of w., 27/3/16.
12/13 Thompson, J. W., 2/Lt., d. of w., 8/8/18.
3 Thompson, Matthew Arnold, 2/Lt., k. in a., 21/3/18 (att. 12 Bn.).
3 Thorp, Robert Oakley Vavasour, M.C., 2/Lt., •k. in a., 22/3/18 (att. 64 T.M.B.).
Tibbs, Thomas, 2/Lt., k. in a., 22/3/18 (att. 1/4 Bn.).
23 Todd, John George, Temp. Capt., k. in a., 1/7/16.
3 Todd-Thornton, J. H. B., Major, died, 12/1/18 (Gar. Bn.).
2 Tonge, Harry, Temp. Lt., died, 25/10/18 (Gar. Bn.).
Toppin, Harry Stanley, Capt., d. of w., 13/9/14.
Tottie, Eric Harold, 2/Lt., d. of w., 22/9/14.
12 Trechmann, Kuno Griffith, 2/Lt., k. in a., 2/7/16.
20 Tucker, Lionel Louis Clérici, 2/Lt. (Tp.), k. in a., 1/7/16.
3 Tuke, Arthur Harold Seymour, 2/Lt., k. in a., 7/5/15 (att. 2 Bn.).
11 Tulloch, Ernest St. Clair, Lt. (Tp.), k. in a., 7/7/16.
8 Tully, Henry Robson, 2/Lt., d. of w., 27/5/18 (att. 4 Bn.).
12/13 Tunnell, Oliver, Temp. 2/Lt., k. in a., 24/10/18.
3 Twigge, Francis, 2/Lt., d. of w., 9/4/17 (att. 1 Bn.).
22 Tytler, William Boyd, Lt. (Tp.), k. in a., 1/7/16.
Vachell, Richard Tanfield, Capt., d. of w., 1/8/15 (and R.F.C.).
Van Neck, Charles Hylton, Lt., k. in a., 20/10/14
20 Venus, Frederick Arthur, Temp., 2/Lt., killed, 1/7/16.
26 Vernon, Frederick Lewis, 2/Lt., k. in a., 1/7/16.
Verrill, William Gibson, Temp., 2/Lt., k. in a., 26/10/17 (Res., att. 1/5 Bn.).
23 Viner, Frank Hillidge, 2/Lt., d. of w., 12/9/18 (att. 2/7 K. Liv. Regt.).
16 Wager, Willson Stanley, 2/Lt., k. in a., 12/7/17.
16 Waggott, Garibaldi Matthewson, 2/Lt., k. in a., 11/4/18 (att. 1/6 Bn.).
12/13 Waistell, Walter Edmund, Temp. 2/Lt., k. in a., 4/10/17.
27 Wallace, Harry Herbert, Temp. 2/Lt., d. of w., 21/1/17.
21 Waller, Herbert William, M.C., Temp. Capt., k. in a., 10/4/17.
14 Walker, John, Temp. 2/Lt., k. in a., 1/7/16.
1 Walker, Samuel Richard Ernest, 2/Lt., d. of w., 11/10/18.
3 Walker, William Francis, 2/Lt., k. in a., 9/4/18 (att. 9 Bn.).
14 Wallace, Cyril John George, Lt., died, 9/9/18.
2 Waller, Thomas Jenkinson, 2/Lt., d. of w., 28/9/18 (att. 4 Bedford Regt.).
27 Walton, Harold Foster, 2/Lt., d. of w., 11/4/17.
9 Wand, Wilfred Ernest, Temp. Lt., k. in a., 7/7/16.
21 Ward, Thomas, Temp. Lt., k. in a., 11/6/16.
Watkin, Frank Ernest, Capt., k. in a., 3/1/15
Watmough, John Cyril, 2/Lt., k. in a., 10/7/15 (att. 2 Bn.).
23 Watson, James Laverick, Temp. 2/Lt., k. in a., 29/4/17.
10 Watson, John Frederick, Temp. 2/Lt., d. of w., 23/10/17.
8 Watson, Raymond Victor, Temp. 2/Lt., k. in a., 16/8/17.
Waud, Ernest Henry. Lt., k. in a., 16/8/17 (att. R.F.C.).
22 Waugh, Thomas Hall. M.C., Capt. (Tp), k. in a., 6/6/17.
8 Wedgwood, Allen, 2/Lt., k. in a., 19/8/15.
8 Weedon, Dudley Harry, Temp. 2/Lt., d. of w., 20/11/17.
Weeks, Francis Mathwin, Capt., k. in a., 11/4/18 (att. 8 D.L.I..
33 Wells, Arthur Scott, Temp. Lt., k. in a., 26/9/16 (att. 8 Bn.).
11 West, Henry Meldrum Pelham, Temp. Capt., k. in a., 20/9/17.
27 Westhorp, William Hast, 2/Lt. (Tp.), k. in a., 28/4/17.
16 Wheeldon, Thomas Victor, 2/Lt., k. in a., 12/7/17.
25 Wheeler, Hugh Graham, 2/Lt., k. in a., 28/4/17.
20 White, Bernard Charles de Boismaison, Temp. Lt., k. in a., 1/7/16.
23 White, Cecil Hayhoe, M.C., Temp. 2/Lt., d. of w., 24/9/17.
26 White, Herbert Thomas, Temp. 2/Lt. (A/Capt.), d. of w., 4/10/16 (att. 103 T.M.B.).
29 White, Nathan, Temp. 2/Lt., k. in a., 1/7/16 (att. 21 Bn.).
13 White, Samuel Walton, Temp. 2/Lt., k. in a., 16/6/17.
21 White, Stewart Alexander, Capt. (Tp.), k. in a., 3/7/16.
30 Whitlock, Tom Oliver, Temp. 2/Lt., k. in a., 29/8/16 (att. 22 Bn.).
3 Whittaker, William Gaylard, 2/Lt., k. in a., 22/10/17 (att. 23 Bn.).
24 Whitworth, Arthur George Richard, 2/Lt., d. of w., 30/3/18 (att. 19 Bn.).
15 Wickham, Charles Frederick Onslow, Temp. 2/Lt., d. of w., 26/6/16 (att. 16 Bn.).
Wild, Henry M.C., Lt., k. in a., 21/8/18 (att. 1/Lincs).
Wilkin, William White, 2/Lt., k in a., 26/10/17 (att. 1/5 Bn.).
15 Wilkins, Frank Trevor, Temp. 2/Lt., d. of w., 3/7/16 (att. 1/Border Regt.).
2 Wilkins, Geoffrey, Temp. 2/Lt., d. of w., 4/10/15.
10 Wilkinson, Marcus Leonard, Temp. 2/Lt., d. of w., 8/7/17.
19 Williams, Brinley Jenkyn, Temp. 2/Lt., k. in a., 20/5/16.
8 Williams, Edward Ernest, D.S.O., Temp. Major, k. in a., 19/8/15.
23 Williams, Howard Oscar, 2/Lt., k. in a., 11/4/18.
23 Williams, Leslie, Temp. 2/Lt., k. in a., 1/7/16.
25 Williams, Meredyth Robert Owen, Temp. 2/Lt., k. in a., 14/3/17.
19 Williams, Ralph Eustace, 2/Lt., k. in a., 29/6/18 (att. R.E.).
Willans, Robert St. John, Lt., k. in a., 9/11/14.
20 Wilmot, Ben, M.C., T/Lt. (A/Capt.), k. in a., 6/6/17.
2 Wilson, James Boyd, Lt., k. in a., 18/10/18.
9 Winton, John Hubert, Temp. 2/Lt., k. in a., 7/7/16.
13 Woodbridge, Stanley George, M.C., Capt., d. of w., 19/12/18.
21 Woodcock, Leonard Albert, 2/Lt. (Tp.), d. of w., 10/4/17.

9 Woods, Harold Ernest, Temp. 2/Lt., d. of w., 1/5/17 (P.O.W.).
8 Wooll, George, Temp. Hon. Lt. & Qr.-Mr., k. in a., 19/8/15.
Wreford-Brown, Claude Wreford, D.S.O., Capt., k. in a., 25/5/15.
9 Wreford-Brown, Oswald Eric, Temp. Capt., d. of w., 7/7/16.
18 Wright, John, 2/Lt., k. in a., 4/11/18.
1 Yatman, Dennistoun Hamilton, Lt., k. in a., 11/4/18.
16 Young, Arthur Cecil, Temp. Capt., k. in a., 6/7/16.
Young, John Haddow, 2/Lt., d. of w., 9/6/18 (att. 5 Bn.).
Young, Frank Irwin, 2/Lt., k. in a., 24-25/7/16.
11 V.C. Youll, John Scott, 2/Lt., k. in a., 27/10/18.

The Royal Warwickshire Regiment.

Achurch, William Henry, 2/Lt. (Tp.), d. of w., 6/12/17 (att. 2/5.).
3 Adams, Arthur Joseph, Lt. (Tp./Capt.), k. in a., 30/8/18.
14 Addenbrooke, Arthur, Capt. (Tp.), d. of w., 5/10/16.
14 Allchin, Walter John, 2/Lt. (Tp.), k. in a., 26/10/17.
14 Allen, Norman, Capt. (Tp.), k. in a., 14/4/18.
9 Anderson, Arthur, 2/Lt. (Tp.), k. in a., 29/3/17.
10 Arnold, Arthur Douglas, 2/Lt. (Tp.), k. in a., 9/4/16.
2 Arnott, David William, Lt., k. in a., 3/9/16.
16 Aspinall, Frank Toole, 2/Lt. (Tp.), k. in a., 1/8/16.
2 Aucutt, Donald, 2/Lt. (A/Capt.), k. in a., 9/10/17.
Baines, Jack Gordon Barrymore, 2/Lt., k. in a., 25/2/17 (and R.F.C., 23 Sq.).
9 Baker, Herbert Shorey, Capt. (Tp.), k. in a., 4-5/4/16.
15 Barrett, Bernard Thomas, 2/Lt. (Tp.), k. in a., 12/4/18.
12 Barrett, George, Lt. (Tp.), k. in a., 6/8/15 (att. 2/Hamp. R.).
4 Barrow, Edmund Sprotson Knapp, 2/Lt., k. in a., 8/5/17 (att. 14/Batt.).
Bastin, Eric Charles, 2/Lt. (Tp.), k. in a., 4/10/17 (att. 1/8 Bn.).
Batchelor, Percival Horace, 2/Lt. (Tp.), d. of w., 10/4/18 (P. of W.) (att. 2/6 N. Staff. R.).
Bates, Lewis George, 2/Lt. (Tp.), d. of w., 24/5/17 (att. 6/E. Lanc. R.).
Baxter, Charles Arthur, 2/Lt. (Tp.), d. of w., 8/10/17 (att. 15/Bn.).
15 Beard, Philip Lee, Lt. (Tp.), d. of w., 9/9/16.
10 Beaufoy, Clive Marston, 2/Lt. (Tp.), k. in a., 25/9/18.
Bennett, George Arthur, 2/Lt. (Tp.), k. in a., 3/12/17 (att. 6/Bn.).
Bentley, Charles Arthur Campbell, Capt., k. in a., 23/10/14.
Bernard, Bernard Frederick Paul, 2/Lt., k. in a., 21/12/14.
9 Berthon, Leonard Tinne, Capt. (Tp.), k. in a., 25/1/17.
2 Biden, Lawrance Trouse Gregory Vernon, Lt., d. of w., 10/10/17.
Billingsley, Harold Hinton, 2/Lt. (Tp.), k. in a., 30/4/17 (att. 6/E. Lanc. R.).
10 Bird, George Brown, Capt. (Tp.), k. in a., 30/7/16.
4 Black, Francis Henry, Lt. (T/Capt.), k. in a., 25/4/15 (att. 1/Bn.).
3 Blair, Sidney Barclay, 2/Lt., k. in a., 16/5/15 (att. 1/Bn.).
4 Blandy, Gerald Castleton, 2/Lt. (A/Capt.), k. in a., 9/10/17 (att. 2/Bn.).
3 Blenkinsop, Edward Winnington, 2/Lt., d. of w., 26/9/15 (att. 2/Bn.).
1 Blomfield, Charles George Massie, Major, k. in a., 9/6/15.
10 Bostock, Clifford, 2/Lt. (Tp. Lt.), k. in a., 20/9/17.
11 Boucher, Alec Edward, M.C., Lt. (Tp.), k. in a., 18/11/16.
1 Bowden, Percival John, 2/Lt., k. in a., 15/4/18.
Bowen, Roger Frederick, Lt., d. of w., 1/9/18 (att. 9/Batt P.O.W.).
14 Braithwaite, Ernest, 2/Lt., k. in a., 22/7/16.
Brazier, Albert Edward, 2/Lt. (Tp.), k. in a., 20/9/17 (att. 10/Bn.).
12 Brearley, Norman Blackburn, 2/Lt (Tp.), k. in a., 17-19/4/16 (att. 9/Bn.).
1 Breene, Thomas Frederick, Lt. (Tp.), k. in a., 1/7/16 (att. M.G.C.).
Brewis, Robert Henry Watkin, Major, T/Lt.-Col., k. in a., 18/12/14.
14 Brinkworth, Arthur Robert, 2/Lt., d. of w., 7/9/16.
1 Briscoe, Edward Villiers, Lt., d. of w., 27/8/16 (att. 10/Bn.).
12 Browne, John Hazell, 2/Lt. (Tp.), k. in a., 20/4/16 (att. 9/Bn.).
Brownfield, Reginald John, Capt., k. in a., 18/12/14.
14 Bryson, Lauder W., Capt. (Tp.), k. in a., 30/7/16.
Burdin, Frank Amesbury, Lt., k. in a., 16/5/15.
4 Burley, Charles Frederick, 2/Lt., k. in a., 18/11/16 (att. 10/Bn.).
10 Burningham, Ralph Horace, 2/Lt. (Tp.), k. in a., 22/3/18.
2 Burrell, Frederick George, 2/Lt., k. in a., 4/5/17.
4 Campbell, Brabazon, 2/Lt., k. in a., 18/12/14.
4 Cartwright, George Crellin, Capt., k. in a., 25/9/15 (att. 2/Bn.).
13 Carty, William George, 2/Lt. (Tp.), k. in a., 25/3/16 (att. 10/Bn.).
10 Chambers, Percival Arthur, 2/Lt. (Tp.), d. of w., 10/4/16 (att. 9/Bn.).
11 Chambers, Stanley Walter Graham, Capt., k. in a., 24/11/17.
2 Chepmell, John Dobree, Lt., k. in a., 10/4/18 (att. 14/Bn.).
Cheshire, Raymond Russell, 2/Lt. (Tp.), k. in a., 4/10/17.
16 Child, Philip Herbert, 2/Lt. (Tp.), k. in a., 23/8/18 (att. 16 Batt.).
Christie, William Charles, Major, k. in a., 13/10/14.
Clarke, Arthur Cecil Grafton, 2/Lt. (Tp.), k. in a., 28/5/18 (att. 2/6 Bn.).
10 Clarke, George Edward, 2/Lt., k. in a., 23/7/16.
3 Clement, Herbert, T/Lt. (A/Capt.), k. in a., 10/10/17 (att. 14/Bn.).
1 Coatsworth, Alfred Henry, 2/Lt. (Tp.), d. of w., 8/9/16 (att. M.G.C.).
Cockburn, John, 2/Lt., k. in a., 25/4/15.
15 Coldicott, Arden Cotterell, M.C., Capt., k. in a., 16/8/18.
3 Collier, John Thomas, 2/Lt. (Tp.), k. in a., 2/11/17 (att. 1/4 Norf. R.).
17 Cooper, Frank Penley, 2/Lt. (Tp.), k. in a., 26/9/16 (att. 16/Bn.).
1 Cooper, Richard, 2/Lt., k. in a., 8/6/17 (att. 10/Bn.).
4 Cooper, Sydney Gordon, 2/Lt., d. of w., 17/9/15 (att. 1/Bn.).
1 Cooper, Victor Travers, 2/Lt. (Tp.), k. in a., 22/6/17.
Costeker, John Henry Diver, D.S.O., Bt.-Major, k. in a., 25/4/15.
1 Cox, Francis Henry, 2/Lt., k. in a., 23/10/16.
1 Cox, George Walker, Capt., k. in a., 3/5/17.
15 Crisp, Ernest Geoffrey, 2/Lt. (Tp.), d. of w., 16/12/15.
16 Crisp, Frederick George, 2/Lt. (Tp.), k. in a., 9/10/17 (Res.).
11 Critchley, John, 2/Lt. (Tp.), k. in a., 11/7/16.
4 Croft, John Arthur Christopher, 2/Lt., k. in a., 18/4/15 (att. W. Rid. R.).
Crowe, William Maynard Carlisle, Capt., k. in a., 11/11/14 (att. North'n. R.).
4 Crowley, Cedric Hugh, Lt., k. in a., 25/4/15 (att. 2nd Bn.).
14 Curtis, Keith Saxby, 2/Lt. (Tp.), k. in a., 26/10/17 (Res.).
Cuthbertson, Edward Hadley, Lt., died, 24/7/17.
15 Danvers, Charles, 2/Lt., k. in a., 9/4/17.
Davenport, Barnabas Tom Wilcox, 2/Lt., k. in a., 15/12/17 (att. 1/4 Norf. R.).
Davies, Harold Bellamy, 2/Lt. (Tp.), k. in a., 3/11/17 (att. Essex R.).
Davies, John, 2/Lt., k. in a., 30/3/18.
2 Davies, John Hickman, 2/Lt. (Tp.), k. in a., 9/10/17.
9 Davies, Ralph Howell, Lt. (Tp.), k. in a., 9/4/16.
14 Davis, Charles Edwin, 2/Lt. (Tp.), drowned, 15/9/18 (Res.).
14 Davis, Percy Hill, 2/Lt. (Tp.), d. of w., 26/10/17 (Res.).
12 Day, Reginald Harry, Lt. (Tp.), k. in a., 4-5/4/16 (att. 9/Bn.).
4 Dean, Rosser Fellowes Marriott, 2/Lt., k. in a., 1/7/16 (att 93/M.G.C.).
Deane, Denis, 2/Lt., k. in a., 23/10/14.
Dear, Roy Evers, 2/Lt. (Tp.), k. in a., 30/4/17 (att. 6/E Lanc. R.).
4 Devis, Francis, 2/Lt., k. in a., 11/4/17 (att. 2/Bn.).
14 Douglas, Alfred William, 2/Lt., d. of w., 3/9/16.
9 Drakeley, Reginald Kenneth, 2/Lt. (Tp.), d. of w., 19/4/16
1 Edinger, Walter Mark Valentine, 2/Lt. (Tp.), k. in a. 23/8/18 (att. 4/Bn.).
Edwards, Arthur Joseph, 2/Lt. (Tp.), k. in a., 27/9/18 (att. 16/Bn.).
3 Edwards, Harold Ethelstan, Lt., k. in a., 25/9/15 (att. 2/Bn.).
15 Edwards, Percival Charles, D.C.M., Major (Tp.), k. in a., 27/9/18.
3 Elderton, Fothergill Rex, Lt., k. in a., 25/9/15 (att. 2/Bn.).
1 Elliott, Herbert John, 2/Lt. (T/Lt.), k. in a., 2/11/17 (Garr. Bn.) (att. 1/4 Northampton R.).
2 Elliott, James Harold, 2/Lt., k. in a., 29/11/16.
Evans, Frank Dudley, 2/Lt., killed, 9/6/16 (and R.F.C.).
4 Evans, Horace Thomas Royston, 2/Lt., k. in a., 8-9/5/17 (att 15/Bn.).
1 Evezard, George, Lt. (A/Capt.), d. of w., 9/5/17.
15 Farley, William, 2/Lt. (Tp.), k. in a., 15/6/16.
9 Farquhar, Ronald George, 2/Lt. (Tp.), k. in a., 29/3/17.
2 Fawdry, Alfred George, 2/Lt., k. in a., 4/5/17.
Fetherstonhaugh-Frampton, Philip Tregonwell, Lt., k. in a., 3/5/15 (att. E. Kent. R.).
2 Firth, John Stanley, 2/Lt., k. in a., 9/10/17 (att. 3/Bn.).
Fisher, William Hroace Arthur, 2/Lt., k. in a., 4/10/17.
2 Forbes, Alec, Capt., k. in a., 3/9/16.
Forster, George Norman Bowes, D.S.O., Brig.-Gen., k. in a., 4/4/18 (att. Staff 42 Inf. Bde.).
15 French, Allan George, 2/Lt., k. in a., 23/5/16.
1 Gamble, James Frederick, 2/Lt., k. in a., 24/6/16.
4 Garwood, Gerald Dennis, 2/Lt., k. in a., 13/11/16 (att. 15/Bn.).
2 Gaunt, Kenneth MacFarlane, 2/Lt., k. in a., 25/9/15 (att. 4/Bn.).
15 George, Alan Lee, 2/Lt. (Tp.), d. of w., 14/4/18.
4 Gibson, Charles Sydney, 2/Lt., k. in a., 1/7/16 (att. M.G.C.).
2 Gildea, J. A. Knox, 2/Lt., k. in a., 11/7/16.
Giles, William Stanley, 2/Lt. (Tp.), k. in a., 2/11/17 (att. 1/4 Norf. R.).
Gilliat, Cecil Glendower Percival, Capt., d. of w., 14/10/14.
1 Glyka, Anthony Isidore, 2/Lt., k. in a., 12/10/16.
12 Gorman, Gerald Francis, 2/Lt., k. in a., 30/7/16.
10 Gott, Albert Ernest, 2/Lt. (Tp.), k. in a., 18/11/16.
15 Gough, Roland Ivor, D.S.O., Capt. (Tp.), d. of w., 14/10/16.
11 Graham, Francis Noel, Capt. (Tp.), d. of w., 16/11/16.
14 Greenwood, Harold Sutcliffe, 2/Lt. (Tp.), k. in a., 22/7/16.
16 Grew, Walter Ernest, 2/Lt. (Tp.), k. in a., 7/10/17 (Res.).
1 V.C. Gribble, Julian Royds, Capt., died, 25/11/18 (P. of W.) (att. 10/Bn.).
9 Grigson, Francis Henry, 2/Lt. (Tp.), k. in a., 9/8/15.
9 Grundy, George Edward, Lt., k. in a., 22/7/15.
Hallam, Howard, 2/Lt. (Tp.), k. in a., 4/10/17 (att. 1/6 Bn.).
3 Hamilton, Tom Knox, Lt., k. in a., 1/6/15 (att. 1/Bn.).
Hankey, Donald William Alers, 2/Lt., k. in a., 12/10/16.
16 Hardy-Smith, Arnold, Capt., died, 16/5/19.
12 Harris, Vernon, 2/Lt. (Tp.), k. in a., 9/4/16 (att. 9/Bn.).
1 Harrison, Maurice Cazalet, Capt. (Tp.), k. in a., 12/10/16.
2 Harrowing, John Stanley, M.C., Lt. (Tp.), k. in a., 4/5/17 (from R.A.S.C.).
3 Hart, Richard George, 2/Lt., k. in a., 30/7/16 (att. 10/Bn.).
2 Haseler, Maurice Noble, Lt. (Tp.), d. of w., 4/7/16.
2 Hayes-Sadler, Gerard Ralph, Lt., k. in a., 3/9/16.
2 Heatherington, Eric, 2/Lt., k. in a., 4/5/17.
16 Heaven, George Frederick Victor, Capt. (Tp.), k. in a., 25/1/16.
10 Henderson, Albert N., Major, k. in a., 23/7/16.

Herbert, Edward Grafton, M.C., 2/Lt. (A/Capt.), k. in a., 9/4/18 (and M.G.C.).
10 Hewett, Herbert Arthur, Capt. (Tp.), d. of w., 20/10/18.
19 Hewett, Stephen Henry Philip, 2/Lt., k. in a., 22/7/16.
Hill, Bertram Gilbert, 2/Lt., k. in a., 25/9/15.
Hill, Henry Tavener, 2/Lt., k. in a., 18/10/14.
15 Hobson, Edgar Charles, 2/Lt. (Tp.), d. of w., 20/5/17 (P. of W., in Ger. hands).
14 Hodes, Francis Percy, 2/Lt. (Tp.), d. of w., 24/7/16.
2 Hodgkinson, Alan, Lt., k. in a., 1/7/16.
3 Hodgson, Christopher Anthony Rowlandson, Capt., k. in a., 18/12/14.
Holland, George Percival, 2/Lt. (Tp.), k. in a., 18/3/18 (att. 7/Norf. R.).
3 Hollick, Percy Hood, 2/Lt. (and A/Capt., k. in a., 8-9/5/17 (att. 15/Bn.).
16 Holme, James Edward, Capt., k. in a., 9/10/17.
Horner, Frederick Julian, M.C., T/Lt. (A/Capt.), d. of w., 15/4/18 (att. 2/Ches. R.).
14 Hughes, Charles Walter, Capt. (Tp., d. of w., 1/10/18.
3 Hughes, Harold Bickley Drewe, Capt., k. in a., 16/5/15 (att. H.L.I.).
4 Hughes, John, M.C., Lt., k. in a., 9/10/17 (att. 16/Bn.).
3 Hunt, Ronald Francis, 2/Lt., k. in a., 25/4/15.
4 Hunter, Norman Frederick, Lt., d. of w., 16/6/15 (att. 4/R. Fus.).
16 Hyde, Herbert Walter, 2/Lt. (Tp.), d. of w., 20/5/16.
Hyde, William Frederick, 2/Lt. (Tp.), k. in a., 8/11/18 (att. 2/Linc. R.).
2 Hyde, William Nelson, Capt. & Q.-M., d. of w., 16/10/16.
16 Iles, Percy Henry, 2/Lt., k. in a., 11/4/17 (att. 1/Bn.).
Ingram, Edgar Charles, 2/Lt., k. in a., 27/3/18 (att. 7/Norf. R.).
1 Irvine, Gerard Foster, Capt. (Tp.), d. of w., 24/10/16.
Izon, Edgar Godfrey, Capt. (Acting), k. in a., 27/9/18 (att. 14/Bn.).
3 Jackson, Edward Phillips, 2/Lt., k. in a., 9/5/15 (att. S.W. Bord.).
15 Jackson, Leonard, 2/Lt., k. in a., 22-23/7/16.
14 Jacobi, Walter Thomas, 2/Lt. (Tp.), d. of w., 21/10/16.
4 Jeffrey, Reginald Harry, 2/Lt., k. in a., 11/4/17 (att. 1/Bn.).
Jenkins, Edgar Ernest, M.C., T/Lt. (A/Capt.), k. in a., 25/3/18 (att. 1/5 Lanc. Fus.).
3 Johnson, John Chapman, 2/Lt., k. in a., 8/7/15 (att. 1/Bn.).
Jones, Alfred Roy, 2/Lt., k. in a., 23/3/18 (att. 2/7 Bn.).
10 Jones, Charles Edward Coursolles, Capt. (Tp.), k. in a., 4/7/16.
15 Jones, Richard Archibald, Major (Tp.), k. in a., 21/5/16.
10 Jones, William Edgar, Lt., k. in a., 10/4/18.
14 Joseph, Alan Edward, Lt. (Tp.), d. of w., 10/5/17.
Jowitt, Arthur, Lt., k. in a., 25/4/15.
12 Kay, Laurence Herbert, 2/Lt. (Tp.), k. in a., 18/11/15 (att. 9/Bn.).
Keller, R. L., 2/Lt., killed, 15/8/18 (att. R.A.F.).
9 Kemp, Alfred Greatrex, 2/Lt. (Tp.), k. in a., 10/8/15.
11 Kemsey-Bourne, Frank Leonard, 2/Lt. (Tp.), k. in a., 11/7/16.
1 Kingston, Nugent Arthur, 2/Lt (Tp.), k. in a., 1/4/18.
4 Knaggs, K. J., 2/Lt., k. in a., 16/3/18 (att. R.F.C.).
Knapton, Odber Augustus, Lt., k. in a., 18/9/14.
12 Knight, Alexander William, 2/Lt. (Tp.), d. of w., 14/10/15 (att. 9/Bn.).
4 Locon, Sidney John Boileau, Capt. (T/Major), k. in a., 12/4/18 (att. R.A.S.C.).
Lancaster, John Cecil, Major, k. in a., 8/5/15.
15 Landon, John Robert, Lt. (A/Capt.), k. in a., 3/9/16.
9 Large, Harold Bowater, 2/Lt. (Tp.), k. in a., 10/3/17.
15 Larkins, John Colin, Lt. (Tp.), k. in a., 4/6/16.
9 Leere, Henry Alan, Lt., died, 29/5/15.
Lefroy, Bertram Percival, D.S.O., T/Lt.-Col. (Major), d. of w., 27/9/15.
Legge-Wilkinson, Benjamin Claude, 2/Lt. (Tp.), died, 4/1/16 (Garr. Bn.).
16 Leith, John, 2/Lt. (Tp.), k. in a., 23/8/18 (att. 14/Bn.).
2 Lister, Herbert Henry Holden, 2/Lt., k. in a., 4/5/17.
16 Littleboy, Wilfrid Evelyn, Lt. (Tp.), k. in a., 9/10/17.
9 Lomax, John Herbert, Capt. (Tp.), d. of w., 22/11/15 (att. 9/Bn. E. Kent R.).
2 Loring, Charles Michael, 2/Lt., k. in a., 3/9/16.
2 Loring, Walter Latham, Lt.-Col., k. in a., 23/10/14.
1 Lovelace-Taylor, Arthur George, 2/Lt. (Tp.), k. in a., 9/10/16.
1 Lowder, Noel Reginald, 2/Lt., k. in a., 3/5/17.
3 Lucas, Thomas Farquhar, Lt., k. in a., 16/6/17 (and R.F.C.).
Lucie-Smith, Evan, Lt., k. in a., 25/4/15.
1 Lukey, Charles Ximis, 2/Lt., k. in a., 24/6/16.
11 Lush, Charles William, 2/Lt. (Tp.), k. in a., 14/11/16.
14 Lythgoe, Jeffrey Wentworth, 2/Lt. (Tp.), k. in a., 22/7/16.
4 McCormick, John Hugh Gardiner, Capt., k. in a., 19/10/14 (att. 2/Bn.).
14 MacIntosh, John, 2/Lt. (Tp.), k. in a., 23/7/16.
3 MacLagan, Gilchrist Stanley, Lt., k. in a., 25/4/15 (att. 1/Bn.).
17 Maddocks, John Onslow, Lt. (Tp.), k. in a., 4/6/16 (att. 15/Bn.).
12 Malet, Frank Louis, Lt. (Tp.), k. in a., 4/6/15 (att. 2/Hamps. R.).
16 Mansell, Charles Paul, 2/Lt. (Tp.), k. in a., 3/9/16.
Mansergh, John Loftus Otway, Lt., k. in a., 25/9/15 (att. 2/Bn.).
9 Marshall, Evelyn Saffery, Capt. (Tp.), d. of w., 6/4/16.
9 Marson, Eric Newton, 2/Lt. (Tp.), k. in a., 10/8/15.
10 Marston, Felix William, 2/Lt. (Tp.), d. of w., 24/7/16.
Martin, Eldred Joseph, Lt., k. in a., 1/7/16.
3 Martin, Frederick Nathaniel, 2/Lt., k. in a., 24/10/18.
10 Martin, Felix William, 2/Lt., d. of w., 24/7/16.
16 Martin, Marcel James, Capt. & Adjt., k. in a., 9/5/17.
10 Martineau, Clement, Capt., d. of w., 5/5/18 (in German hands).

Marwood, Charles Philip Lysaght, Capt., d. of w., 24/11/15 (att. Nigeria R.).
1 Mason, Hubert Harry Leslie, 2/Lt., d. of w., 12/10/17.
Matear, Norman Hirst Lawrence, Capt. (Tp.), k. in a., 25/9/15.
14 Mathews, Hugh Spencer, Capt., k. in a., 22/7/16.
Matthews, Leslie Herbert, 2/Lt., k. in a., 28/3/18 (att. 2/6).
3 Maunsell, Herbert Stofford, Lt., d. of w., 1/9/15.
Methuen, Cameron O'Bryen Harford, Capt., k. in a., 20-21/10/14.
Monk, George Bertram, 2/Lt., k. in a., 18/12/14.
13 Moor, Edward Lewis, 2/Lt. (Tp.), d. of w., 27/1/17 (att. 9/Bn.).
14 Moore, George Alexander, 2/Lt., k. in a., 2/5/18.
10 Morrall, John Bernard, 2/Lt., d. of w., 23/3/18.
16 Morrison, John Woodley, 2/Lt. (Tp.), d. of w., 30/12/16.
1 Morriss, John Septimus, Lt., k. in a., 5/10/17.
13 Mosse, Philip Godfrey, 2/Lt. (Tp.), k. in a., 18/4/16 (att. 6/E. Lancs. R.).
1 Mould, David, 2/Lt. (Tp.), k. in a., 13/6/16 (att. T.M.B.).
4 Mould, Ernest Kingston, 2/Lt., k. in a., 2/9/18 (att. 16/Bn.).
Murphy, George, Lt. (Tp.), k. in a., 6/9/17 (Res.).
10 Needham, Pascall, 2/Lt., k. in a., 18/11/16.
2 Newsome, Theodore Edward, 2/Lt. (Tp.), k. in a., 25/9/15.
15 Nichols, Thomas Leslie, 2/Lt. (Tp.), k. in a., 8-9/5/17.
Nicolai, Ronald Claud, Lt., k. in a., 25/4/15.
3 Nutting, Ernest Ralph, 2/Lt., k. in a., 18/11/16 (att. 10/Bn.).
O'Beirne, John Ingram Mullanniffe, 2/Lt., k. in a., 3/4/17 (att. R.F.C., 25 Sqd.).
14 O'Dwyer, Alfred Stanhope, 2/Lt. (Tp.), k. in a., 29/7/16.
10 O'Neill, Douglas Quirke, 2/Lt., k. in a., 26/4/18.
11 Onslow, Arthur Denzel, 2/Lt., k. in a., 13/8/16.
3 Owen, Arthur Adrian, 2/Lt., k. in a., 13/3/15.
9 Page, John Kenneth Samuel, M.C., Lt., d. of w., 21/8/18.
Paget, Colin, Lt., k. in a., 1/9/18 (att. 9/Bn.).
9 Palfrey, Reginald, 2/Lt. (Tp.), k. in a., 4-5/4/16.
15 Parker, Wilfrid Ernest, 2/Lt. (Tp.), k. in a., 8-9/5/17.
16 Parry, Francis Alexander, M.C., Major, k. in a., 27/9/18
1 Partington, Cyril, 2/Lt., killed, 30/8/18 (att. R.A.F.).
4 Payne, John Oswald, Lt., k. in a., 25/4/15 (att. 1/Bn.).
14 Payton, Ralph Stuart, Lt. (Tp.), k. in a., 22/7/16.
Pearce, Geoffrey Vincent, 2/Lt., d. of w., 18-19/12/14.
13 Pearman, James O'Hara, 2/Lt. (Tp.), k. in a., 25/1/17 (att. 9/Bn.).
Pearson, Alfred Christopher, Capt. (Tp.), killed, 4/4/19.
14 Pearson, Charles Thornhill, 2/Lt., d. of w., 29/8/18.
4 Pearson, Frederick George, 2/Lt., k. in a., 20/10/18 (att. 16/Bn.).
10 Pearson, John, 2/Lt., d. of w., 11/4/18.
12 Pearson, Stanley Osborne, 2/Lt. (Tp.), k. in a., 30/7/16 (att. 10/Bn.).
9 Peel, Robert John De Neuville, 2/Lt. (Tp.), k. in a., 29/3/17.
10 Pegg, William John, 2/Lt. (Tp.), killed, 18/3/18.
Pennington, John, Lt., k. in a., 25/9/15.
15 Phillips, Richard Hill, 2/Lt. (Tp.), k. in a., 25/9/16.
15 Phillips, William David, 2/Lt., d. of w., 28/9/18.
10 Pinsent, Richard Parker, 2/Lt. (Tp.), k. in a., 9/10/15.
15 Plant, Herbert, 2/Lt. (Tp.), d. of w., 20/12/16 (att. 14/Bn.).
Platt, Charles Henry Morris, 2/Lt. (T/Lt.), k. in a., 23/11/17 (att. R.F.C., 52 Sqd.).
14 Pocock, Charles Arthur, 2/Lt. (Tp.), k. in a., 8/5/17.
14 Poole, John Richard, 2/Lt. (Tp.), k. in a., 30/7/16.
10 Potter, Edward, Lt. (Tp.), died, 10/11/18.
16 Potter, Robert William, Lt. (Tp.), k. in a., 8/10/18 (att. 1/N. Fus.).
Pownall, Hubert Joseph, 2/Lt., k. in a., 23/7/16.
Poynton, John, 2/Lt. (Tp.), k. in a., 4/10/17 (att. Res. 1/6 Bn. G.H.Q.).
4 Preedy, Lawrence Jack, 2/Lt., k. in a., 31/3/18 (att. 1/Bn.).
2 Purcell, Albert Joseph, 2/Lt., k. in a., 14/7/16.
11 Pusch, Ernest John, 2/Lt., k. in a., 8/8/16.
4 Rainbow, Albert Edward, 2/Lt., k. in a., 23/7/16 (att. 10/Bn.).
2 Raphæl, Norman Henry, 2/Lt., d. of w., 8/6/16.
Ratcliff, John Edward, Lt., k. in a., 20/10/14.
9 Reade, Reginald William, Lt. (Tp.), k. in a., 4-5/4/16.
4 Rees, Leofric, Lt., d. of w., 4/10/17 (att. 1/Bn.).
4 Ricard, Frank, 2/Lt., k. in a., 25/4/15 (att. 1/Bn.).
10 Richards, Ewart Wilfred, 2/Lt. (Tp.), d. of w., 10/5/18.
2 Richardson, Richard Francis, Lt., d. of w., 30/9/15.
1 Riley, Stanley James, Capt. (Tp.), k. in a., 12/10/16.
3 Ring, Norman Augustus Manders, Lt., k. in a., 4/5/17 (att. 2/Bn.).
2 Roberts, Cecil Llewellyn Norton, 2/Lt. (A/Capt.), k. in a., 9/10/17.
11 Roberts, Llewellyn Hilton, 2/Lt., k. in a., 13/8/16.
Rodgers, Henry Frederick, 2/Lt. (Tp.), k. in a., 4/10/17 (Res.).
10 Rogers, Esmond Hallewell, 2/Lt. (Tp.), k. in a., 3/7/16.
Rooke, Sidney Austin Harold, 2/Lt., d. of w., 20/9/18 (att. 2/7 Bn.).
16 Rowland, Rowland Evan Basil, 2/Lt., k. in a., 27/7/16.
Ruane, John Patrick, 2/Lt. (Tp.), k. in a., 2/11/17 (att. 1/5 Norfolk R.).
3 Rudell, Emil Arthur, 2/Lt., d. of w., 27/9/18 (att. 16/Bn.).
Ryan, Patrick Joseph, 2/Lt., k. in a., 21/3/18 (att. 6/N. Staff. R.).
14 Salisbury, Cecil Roland, 2/Lt. (Tp.), k. in a., 7/5/17.
Salter, Albert Leonard, 2/Lt., k. in a., 21/3/18 (att. 2/6 N. Staff. R.).
4 Samuel, Cecil Valentine, 2/Lt., d. of w., 6/10/17.
16 Sanders, George Ernest, Lt., k. in a., 9/10/17.
16 Sangster, Frederick Charles, Lt. (Tp.), d. of w., 6/9/16.
14 Sansome, Howard Victor, 2/Lt., k. in a., 26/10/17.
16 Sayers, Leslie, M.C., Capt. (Tp.), k. in a., 23/8/18.
Schooling, Eric Charles, Capt., k. in a., 31/10/14.

1 Seaman, Leonard James Cameron, Lt., k. in a., 30/8/18.
9 Sharp, A. G., Major (Tp.), k. in a., 10/8/15.
Shaw, Albert Thomas, 2/Lt. (Tp.), d. of w., 13/6/18 (att. 1/7 Batt.).
10 Shaw, Henry Lynn, Capt. (Tp.), k. in a., 3/7/16.
Shaw, Ralph, D.S.O., Lt., k. in a., 28/4/17 (S.R.) (att. 11/-Bn.).
Shine, Edward, D.C.M., 2/Lt., k. in a., 20/10/18 (att. 15/-Bn.).
Silvester, William Hugh, 2/Lt. (Tp.), d. of w., 3/11/18 (att. 2/7 Batt.).
Simpson, Anthony Henry, Lt., died, 1/2/15 (S.R.).
10 Smart, Eric Douglas, 2/Lt., k. in a., 18/11/16.
Smetham, James Eric, 2/Lt., k. in a., 14/11/16 (No. 3 M.G.C.).
14 Smith, Eric Arthur, 2/Lt. (Tp.), k. in a., 22/7/16.
14 Smith, John Basil, 2/Lt. (Tp.), d. of w., 19/8/17.
1 Spencer, Richard Martin, Lt., k. in a., 22/1/16.
2 Stable, Russell Colin, 2/Lt., k. in a., 9/10/17.
1 Stafford, Arthur Darrell, Lt. (Tp.), d. of w., 20/5/18.
Stainforth, Richard Terrick, Lt., d. of w., 19/10/14.
Standring, Benjamin Arthur, 2/Lt., d. of w., 19/12/14.
11 Stalker, James Johnston Harris, T/Lt. (A/Capt.), k. in a., 28/4/17.
4 Stehn, Arthur Edward, Capt., k. in a., 8/11/18 (att. 10/Bn.).
Stevens, A. J., 2/Lt., k. in a., 21/9/18 (att. R.A.F.).
15 Streater, John Wenban, 2/Lt. (Tp.), d. of w., 22/7/18
3 Stretton, John de Courcy, 2/Lt., k. in a., 11/5/18 (att. 1/Bn.).
3 Stretton, William Stapleton de Courcy, Lt., d. of w., 4/9/16.
2 Surgey, Henry Norris, Capt., k. in a., 3/1/17 (att. Arab Rifles).
Talbot, Frank Henry, 2/Lt. (Tp.), d. of w., 15/7/16 (att. 1/Bord. R.).
16 Tasker, Field Pass, 2/Lt. (Tp.), d. of w., 6/10/17.
15 Tatlow, Archibald Henry, Capt. (Tp.), k. in a., 4/6/16.
Taylour, George Ryfield, Capt., k. in a., 19/10/14.
Thain, William Skinner, 2/Lt. (Tp.), drowned, 15/9/18 (Res. att. 15/Bn.).
Thomson, Henry George Allen, Major, d. of w., 28/3/17 (Staff 15 Div.).
3 Thornhill, Geoffrey Holland, Lt., died, 10/5/17 (att. 3/Lab. Cps.).
11 Thorowgood, Rowland William Theodore, T/Lt., k. in a., 7/8/18.
Tillyer, Richard Bateson Blunt, Lt., k. in a., 25/4/15.
14 Townley, Felix Lionel, 2/Lt. (Tp.), k. in a., 26/10/17.
15 Treadway, Harold Ligonier, 2/Lt. (Tp.), k. in a., 8-9/5/17.
1 Trerisc, Walter Thomas Llewelyn, 2/Lt. (Tp.), k. in a., 15/4/18.
Tucker, Alan Robert Lloyd, 2/Lt., k. in a., 18-20/12/14.
13 Tullidge, Robert Milton 2/Lt. (A/Capt.) d. of w., 25/1/17 (att. 9/Batt.).
14 Turner, Bernard, T/Lt. (A/Capt.), k. in a., 8/5/17.
13 Turner, George Herbert, 2/Lt. (Tp.), d. of w., 14/6/16 (att. 15/Bn.).
3 Turner, John Percival, 2/Lt., k. in a., 26/10/17 (att. 14/Bn.).
15 Tyrer, Christopher St. John, 2/Lt. (Tp.), d. of w., 24/7/16.
4 Vacher, George Herbert, 2/Lt., k. in a., 11/11/14 (att. 2/Bn.).
2 Vardy, Albert Theodore, 2/Lt., k. in a., 4/7/16.
12 Vernon-Inkpen, Robert Cecil, 2/Lt. (Tp.), killed, 21/10/16 (R.F.C.).
4 Vigor, William Petter, 2/Lt., k. in a., 13/8/16 (att. 11/Bn.).
14 Vince, William Lang, T/Lt., k. in a., 8/5/17.
11 Vokins, Kean Esse, 2/Lt. (Tp.), k. in a., 11/7/16.
11 Voss, Ernest William Thomas, 2/Lt. (Tp.), k. in a., 24/9/17.
Wagner, E. G. S., 2/Lt., k. in a., 7/1/17 (R.F.C., 32 Sqd.).
Walker, Henry John Innes, Capt., k. in a., 25/4/15.
Wallis, Reginald Robert, 2/Lt., k. in a., 26/3/18 (att. 7/Norf. R.).
Walmisley-Dresser, Henry Joseph, Major (Tp.) (A/Lt.-Col.), d. of w., 17/9/16 (att. E. Surr. R.).
10 Ward, Charles Sanford, T/Lt., k. in a., 7/1/16.
11 Ward, Norman John, 2/Lt. (Tp.), k. in a., 11/8/16.
Ward, Samuel Leonard, M.C., 2/Lt., k. in a., 22/3/18 (Res.) (att. 2/6 Bn.).
Wasey, Cyril Walter Carleton, M.C., Capt., k. in a., 28/10/17 (att. R.F.C., 16 Sqd).
4 Waters, Reginald Rigden, A/Capt., d. of w., 24/10/16 (att. 1/Bn.).
4 Welch, Stafford Leslie, 2/Lt., died, 20/7/17 (att. 1/Bn.).
3 Weston, John Spencer Theodore, Lt. (T/Capt.), k. in a., 20/8/15 (att. R. Berks R.).
10 Westwood, Alfred Herbert, Capt., k. in a., 21/9/18 (att. 6/Northants).
14 Whitbread, Basil, 2/Lt., k. in a., 22/7/16.
White, Denis Atholl Pheaneas Terence, 2/Lt. (Tp.), d. of w., 23/11/17.
10 Whitworth, Ernest Stanley, T/Lt., k. in a., 20/12/15.
12 Williams, Donald Mattieu, 2/Lt. (Tp.), k. in a., 9/4/16 (att. 9/Bn.).
3 Williams-Freeman, Harry Peere, Lt. (A/Capt.), k. in a., 8/8/18 (att. 1/5 Bn.).
10 Williamson, Cyril George, 2/Lt. (Tp.), k. in a., 2/7/16.
10 Wilson, Edwin Thomas, 2/Lt., k. in a., 23/3/18.
10 Wilson, Fred, 2/Lt., died, 13/11/18.
Wilson, Robert Victor, Lt., d. of w., 13/4/18 (att. 2/7 Bn.).
11 Wilson, Tristram William Jourdain, 2/Lt. (Tp.), k. in a., 24/11/17.
4 Windeler, Charles Francis, Lt., k. in a., 10/5/15.
14 Wood, Leslie John, 2/Lt., k. in a., 4/10/17.
10 Woodbridge, Stephen Antony Ruston, 2/Lt. (Tp.), d. of w., 15/9/16.
10 Wright, Victor Albert, 2/Lt., k. in a., 15/4/18.

The Royal Fusiliers (City of London Regiment).

26 Adams, Ernest Frederick, 2/Lt. (Tp.), k. in a., 22/6/17.
7 Adams, Ralph Newton, M.C., Capt., k. in a., 10/10/16 (att. R.F.C., 23 Sq.).
26 Addis, David Malcolm, 2/Lt., d. of w., 9/6/17.
26 Aldrick, Charles Pelham, 2/Lt., k. in a., 7/10/16.
8 Allen, Archibald Stafford, Lt. (Tp.), k. in a., 3/10/15.
Anderson, William Francis, Capt., d. of w., 10/12/15.
16 Andrews, Alan Charles Findlay, 2/Lt., k. in a., 29/6/15.
10 Andrews, John Leonard, M.M., 2/Lt. (Tp.), d. of w., 19/5/18.
Anketell, C. E., 2/Lt., killed, 11/5/18 (and R.A.F.).
8 Annesley, Albemarle Cator, D.S.O., Lt.-Col. (Tp.), d. of w., 8/7/16.
Anstice, John Spencer Ruscombe, Lt., k. in a., 2/5/15.
13 Anthony, Clarence Case, Capt. (Tp.), d. of w., 15/12/15.
23 Aris, Thomas Arthur, Lt. (Tp.), k. in a., 16/4/17.
14 Armstrong, Christopher, 2/Lt., k. in a., 9/4/16 (att. 6/N. Lan. R.).
10 Armstrong, John Owen, 2/Lt., k. in a., 15/7/16.
18 Arnold, A. C. P., 2/Lt. (Tp.), k. in a., 7/7/16.
4 Arnould, Derek Clement, Lt., died, 7/5/18 (att. R.T.E.).
5 Aspden, Ronald William, 2/Lt., d. of w., 8/8/17.
Astley, Aston Giffard, Major (Tp.), k. in a., 1/10/16 (att. M.G. Corps).
26 Astwood, Edward Leicester Stuart, 2/Lt. (Tp.), d. of w., 20/9/16.
Attwood, Algernon Foulkes, Capt., k. in a., 8/10/14.
4 Ayres, Victor Albert, 2/Lt., k. in a., 1/9/18.
16 Ayrton, Frank Frederick Joseph, Capt., k. in a., 28/6/15.
8 Backlake, Brian Ashber, Lt. (Tp.), k. in a., 3/5/17.
20 Badenoch, Ian Forbes Clark, 2/Lt. (Tp.), died, 19/3/17.
17 Baker, Bertram Reginald, 2/Lt. (Tp.), k. in a., 3/5/16.
8 Baker, John Bartrup Harwood, 2/Lt. (Tp.), k. in a., 1/9/1[illegible]
23 Balbirnie, John Victor Elphinstone, 2/Lt. (Tp.), k. in a 7/9/18.
10 Bambridge, Rupert Charles, D.S.O., M.C., M.M., Capt. (Tp.), d. of w., 23/5/18.
24 Bambridge, William Herbert, Lt. (Tp.) (A/Capt.), k. in a. 19/8/17.
Banister, Charles Wilfred, 2/Lt., k. in a., 16/6/15.
2 Banks, Edward Francis, 2/Lt., k. in a., 28/2/17.
13 Bantock, Arthur Thomas, 2/Lt. (Tp.), d. of w., 23/11/15.
16 Barber, George, 2/Lt. (Tp.), k. in a., 3/10/16.
6 Barker, Hugh Edwin, 2/Lt., died, 31/1/18.
5 Barnes, Edward James, 2/Lt., d. of w., 4/5/18.
24 Barnes, Vincent Kendall, 2/Lt., k. in a., 29/4/17.
10 Barnes, Wilfred Oliver, 2/Lt. (Tp.), k. in a., 18/11/16.
11 Barnett, Bret Hercules, 2/Lt., k. in a., 10/8/17.
26 Barnett, Herbert William, 2/Lt. (Tp.), k. in a., 20/9/17.
11 Barrell, Victor Henry, 2/Lt. (Tp.), k. in a., 22/8/18.
2 Barrett, Keith Joy, Lt. (Tp.), d. of w., 16/4/17.
8 Barrow, Hector Henry, 2/Lt., k. in a., 20/10/15.
8 Barten, Donald, 2/Lt., k. in a., 30/11/17.
Barton, Frank Hubert, 2/Lt. (Tp.), k. in a., 5/11/18 (att T.M.B.).
9 Barton, Kenneth Cyril, 2/Lt. (Tp.), k. in a., 7/10/16.
1 Barton, Stanley Ernest, 2/Lt., k. in a., 31/7/17.
13 Batty-Smith, F. C., Lt. (Tp.), k. in a., 4/6/16.
9 Baugh, Charles, 2/Lt. (Tp.), d. of w., 5/4/18.
12 Bayly, Harry Ayrton, 2/Lt. (Tp.), k. in a., 14/6/17.
13 Bayley, Reginald John, 2/Lt., k. in a., 29/4/17.
17 Beale, Ernest Frederick, 2/Lt. (Tp.), k. in a., 28/4/17.
Beausire, Herbert Arthur William, 2/Lt., k. in a., 16/3/15.
2 Bentley, Howard Lidyard, 2/Lt. (Tp.), k. in a., 28/2/17.
6 Berrill, Bernard Francis Gotch, Lt., k. in a., 17/3/15.
8 Berry, A. L., 2/Lt., k. in a., 7/7/16.
12 Bescoby, Edgar Laurence, 2/Lt. (Tp.), d. of w., 18/6/17.
12 Bettesworth, Tom, 2/Lt. (Tp.), d. of w., 3/11/15 (att. R.E., 172 Fld. Coy.).
26 Betts, Henry Lee, 2/Lt. (Tp.), k. in a., 20/9/17.
10 Bevir, R., 2/Lt. (Tp.), k. in a., 15/7/16.
8 Bingham, Frank Oldfield, 2/Lt. (Tp.), d. of w., 14/9/18.
Birchall, Arthur Percival, Capt. (T/Lt.-Col.), k. in a., 24/4/15 (att. Can. Div.).
9 Bird, Clement Eustace, 2/Lt. (Tp.), d. of w., 28/6/17.
1 Bird, Eric Hinckes, Lt., d. of w., 27/6/16 (att. R.F.C., 25 Sq.).
13 Bishop, Charles Frederick, 2/Lt. (Tp.), k. in a., 4/4/18.
22 Black, George Dudley Austin, Lt. (Tp.), k. in a., 21/6/16.
4 Blackwell, Charles, 2/Lt., k. in a., 20/7/15.
16 Blackwell, Cyril, 2/Lt. (Tp.), k. in a., 1/7/16.
8 Blackwell, William Gordon, Lt. (Tp.), k. in a., 5/10/16.
13 Bleaden, Lionel, Lt. (Tp.), k. in a., 6-9/7/16.
9 Boddy, G. G. D., 2/Lt. (Tp.), k. in a., 27/3/16.
7 Bolland, Frederick William Henry, 2/Lt., k. in a., 7/6/17.
26 Bond, William Henry Hugh, 2/Lt. (Tp.), k. in a., 22/6/17.
6 Booth, John, 2/Lt., k. in a., 7/10/16.
9 Bott, William Ernest, Capt. (Tp.), k. in a., 18/9/18.
2 Bourne, Leonard Cecil, M.C., 2/Lt. (Tp.), d. of w., 14/8/17.
8 Bourne, S. M., Lt. (Tp.), k. in a., 4-5/4/16 (att. 8/R W. Fus.).
Bowden-Smith, Walter Ardrian Carnagie, Capt., d. of w., 28/8/14.
20 Bower, Frederic William, Capt. (Tp.), k. in a., 8/3/18.
24 Bracey, Frederick Sidney, Lt. (Tp.), k. in a., 13/11/16.
Brand, Ernest Stanley, Capt., k. in a., 8/10/14 (and W.A. Rifs.).
Brandreth, Lyall, Major, k. in a., 4/6/15.
32 Bray, George Thomas, 2/Lt. (Tp.), d. of w., 26/10/17.
Brickland, Charles Hampton, 2/Lt., k. in a., 25/3/15.
6 Bridgman, William Louis, 2/Lt., d. of w., 20/9/17.
32 Bright, Francis John, 2/Lt., k. in a., 20/9/17.
15 Broad, A. M., Lt. (Tp.), k. in a., 12/7/16 (att. M.G.C.).
17 Brodie, Sidney Edward, 2/Lt. (Tp.), d. of w., 17/4/17.
7 Brown, Frederick Arthur, 2/Lt. (Tp.), k. in a., 13/11/16.
Brown, John Gordon, M.C., Capt., k. in a., 5/10/18 (att. 47 Div., Arty. H.Q.).

1 Bruce, Wallace Edward, Lt., k. in a., 31/7/17.
1/4 Buckland, C. J., 2/Lt., died, 19/8/18 (and R.A.F.).
16 Bulbeck, Henry Edmund, Lt. (Tp.), k. in a., 6/11/16.
6 Bull, Percival John, 2/Lt., k. in a., 7/10/16.
26 Bullock, Robert, Lt. (Tp.), k. in a., 20/9/17.
Bullock, William Acton, 2/Lt., died, 25/10/18 (att. 2/17 Lond. R.).
9 Bungey, Gerald Edwards, 2/Lt. (Tp.), k. in a., 4/8/16.
9 Burdett, C. P. B., 2/Lt. (Tp.), k. in a., 7/7/16.
1 Burdett, William Allan, M.C., A/Capt., k. in a., 31/7/17.
6 Burgess, Eric Archibald, 2/Lt., k. in a., 17/2/17.
23 Burgess, Reginald Charles, 2/Lt., k. in a., 3/5/17.
15 Burnham, Andrew William, 2/Lt. (Tp.), k. in a., 13/11/16.
6 Burton, Charles William Gordon, 2/Lt., k. in a., 22/11/17.
7 Bushell, R. H. C., 2/Lt., k. in a., 27/7/16.
31 Butchard, Robert Archibald, Lt. (Tp.), k. in a., 5/11/16.
9 Butterworth, Edward Cyril, 2/Lt. (Tp.), d. of w., 21/11/17.
Byng, Arthur Maitland, Capt., k. in a., 14/9/14.
11 Calthrop, Alfred Gordon, 2/Lt., k. in a., 10/8/17.
9 Calwell, Theophilus Legate, M.C., Lt. (Tp.), k. in a., 7/10/16.
11 Campbell, Charles, 2/Lt. (Tp.), d. of w., 20/4/18.
17 Campbell, Frederick Charles, 2/Lt. (Tp.), k. in a., 24/3/18.
10 Campbell, Ronald Walter Francis, Capt. (Tp.), d. of w., 11/8/16.
20 Cane, Leonard Dobbie, Capt. and Adj. (Tp.), k. in a., 24/1/16.
32 Carey, Francis Ambrose, 2/Lt., k. in a., 15/9/16.
Carey, Leicester William le Marchant, Capt., k. in a., 17/10/14.
3 Carmichael, David Arthur, Lt., k. in a., 17/4/18 (att. M.G. Corps).
23 Carpenter, Clarence, 2/Lt. (Tp.), k. in a., 17/2/17.
23 Carr, James Walter, M.C., D.C.M., Lt., died, 16/11/18 (att. 99 T.M.B.).
13 Carter, Ernest Lionel, M.M., 2/Lt., k. in a., 24/10/18.
5 Case, Joseph, Lt., d. of w., 15/11/18 (att. 1/Bn.).
26 Chambers, Alfred Ernest, M.C., Lt. (Tp.), d. of w., 29/10/18.
5 Champion, Sydney George, Lt. (Tp.), d. of w., 17/3/17 (att. 2/K. Afr. Rifs., P.O.W.).
8 Chapman, Donald John Stuart, 2/Lt. (Tp.), d. of w., 13/7/16.
8 Chard, Robert Alexander Farmer, Capt. (Tp.), k. in a., 8/7/16.
10 Chatham, George Henry, 2/Lt., k. in a., 23/11/16.
8 Chell, Harold, Lt. (Tp.), d. of w., 10/8/15.
4 Cheshire, Eric Colveroy, Lt., k. in a., 3/5/17.
32 Christie, Murray Inglis, D.S.O., 2/Lt. (Tp.) (A/Capt.), d. of w., 24/3/18.
2 Chuter, Harry Athelstan, Lt., k. in a., 25/3/17 (and R.F.C., 70 Sq.).
32 Clapton, Arthur, 2/Lt., k. in a., 5/9/16.
8 Clark, Arthur James Richard, Lt., d. of w., 9/10/16.
7 Clarke, Edward George, Lt. (T/Capt.), k. in a., 13/11/16.
8 Clifford, Watling Wallis, 2/Lt. (Tp.), d. of w., 12/10/17.
6 Coates, W. F., Capt., d. of w., 30/4/15 (att. 1/Bn.).
17 Cocker, Arthur Wilfred Kingsley, 2/Lt., k. in a., 30/11/17.
20 Coggin, Algernon Oswald, Lt. (Tp.), k. in a., 27/10/16.
12 Cohen, Edward, M.C., 2/Lt. (Tp.), k. in a., 31/7/17.
Cole, Mowbray Lyster Stanley Owen, Capt., died, 14/9/14.
25 Cole, Wilfred Samuel, Lt. (Tp.), died, 11/5/16.
5 Coley, Joseph Alfred, 2/Lt. (A/Capt.), k. in a., 22/3/18 (att. 4/Bn.).
11 Collings, Sydney Walter, 2/Lt. (Tp.), k. in a., 20/4/18.
11 Collis-Sandes, Maurice James, Capt., k. in a., 17/2/17.
6 Combe, Boyce Anthony, Lt., k. in a., 11/11/14 (att. 4/Bn.).
12 Compton, Harold William, Lt.-Col. (Tp.), d. of w., 7/7/17.
17 Consterdine-Chadwick, Robert Thompson Consterdine, Lt. (Tp.) (A/Capt.), k. in a., 4/10/18 (att. 3/Bn.).
9 Cook, Arthur Basil Kemball, 2/Lt. (Tp.), k. in a., 7/7/16.
32 Cook, Cyril Frank, 2/Lt. (Tp.), k. in a., 5/8/17.
26 Cooper, Frederick Edmund, Lt. (Tp.), d. of w., 18/12/18.
7 Cooper, Henry Weatherley Frank, 2/Lt. (Tp.), d. of w., 28/4/17.
12 Cooper, William, 2/Lt. (Tp.), k. in a., 31/7/17.
22 Coppack, Charles Richard Stewart, 2/Lt., d. of w., 24/3/18 (att. 24/Bn.).
24 Coppard, William John, 2/Lt. (Tp.), d. of w., 23/3/18.
26 Corben, Victor Leslie, 2/Lt., died, 22/7/18.
11 Core, Charles Gooch, 2/Lt., k. in a., 10/8/17.
3 Corlett, Douglas Stephen, T/Lt. (A/Capt.), d. of w., 12/11/18.
11 Cornaby, George Ernest, M.C., Capt. (Tp.), d. of w., 23/9/18.
23 Cornes, Henry Percy Griffiths, 2/Lt. (Tp.), k. in a., 27/9/17 (att. 99/T.M.B.).
Coull, Frederick, 2/Lt. (T/Lt.), k. in a., 30/9/18 (att. 23/Bn.).
20 Coventry, Eric, 2/Lt. (Tp.), k. in a., 20/7/16.
Cowell, J. G., 2/Lt., killed, 28/1/18 (att. R.F.C.).
10 Cowie, Gerald James Hardwicke, 2/Lt. (Tp.), k. in a., 23/4/17.
2 Cowie, Lionel Jack Hardwicke, 2/Lt. (Tp.), k. in a., 24/4/17.
26 Cox, Cecil Arthur, Capt. (Tp.), d. of w., 16/10/16.
12 Cox, Henry Jack, Capt. (Tp.), k. in a., 31/7/17.
9 Coxhead, Maurice Edward, Capt. (T/Major), k. in a., 3/5/17.
4 Crabb, Thomas Henry, 2/Lt., d. of w., 18/3/16.
5 Crampton, Edgar Walter, 2/Lt., k. in a., 9/10/17 (att. 2/Bn.).
Croal, Kenneth McFarlane, 2/Lt. (Tp.), k. in a., 19/10/18 (att. 2/10 R. Scots).
10 Crook, William George, 2/Lt. (Tp.), k. in a., 9/3/18.
24 Crookes, Ronald Orme, 2/Lt. (Tp.), k. in a., 4/6/16.
3 Crost, Chirstopher Edric Percy, Lt., k. in a., 4/10/18.
Crowe, Hugh Barby, Lt., drowned, 28/10/15.
6 Curwen, Wilfred John Hutton, Capt., k. in a., 9/5/15 (att. 3/Bn.).
29 Cuthbert, David, Capt. (Tp.), k. in a., 7/10/16 (att. 8/Bn.).
7 Dadd, Reginald John, 2/Lt. (Tp.), k. in a., 5/4/18.
7 Daines, Allan Edward, 2/Lt., k. in a., 30/12/17.
32 Daines, Roland Lewis, 2/Lt. (Tp.), k. in a., 3/8/17.
6 Daniell, George Francis Blackburne, 2/Lt., k. in a., 24/4/17 (att. 2/Bn.).

2 Darker, Richard Owen, 2/Lt., k. in a., 12/4/18.
25 V.C. Dartnell, Wilbur, Lt. (Tp.), k. in a., 3/9/15.
22 Davies, Donald Frederick, 2/Lt. (Tp.), k. in a., 15/4/18 (att. 23/Bn.).
3 Davies, Roland Arthur Llewlwyn, Lt. (Tp.), k. in a., 4/10/18.
13 Davies, William, 2/Lt. (Tp.), k. in a., 10/4/17.
23 Davis, George Leith Blakeman, 2/Lt. (Tp.), k. in a., 27/9/18.
5 Davison, Robert Charles, 2/Lt., d. of w., 19/5/17 (att. 4 Bn.).
11 Dawson, Frederick Charles Blakeman, 2/Lt. (Tp.), k. in a., 3/5/17 (att. R.A.C.).
Day, Frederick Charles, Capt., k. in a., 31/7/17 (att. 12/Bn.).
11 Day, Hubert Francis, 2/Lt. (Tp.), k. in a., 10/8/17.
13 Day, Hubert Victor, 2/Lt. (Tp.), k. in a., 9/4/17.
4 V.C. Dease, Maurice James, Lt., k. in a., 23/8/14.
23 De Beck, George Clifford, 2/Lt. (Tp.), k. in a., 18/2/17.
De Trafford, Ralph Edric Galfrid Antony, Lt., k. in a., 25/4/15.
De Trafford, Thomas Cecil, Capt., k. in a., 10/11/14.
8 Dilnutt, Eric William, Lt. (T/Capt.), k. in a., 2/3/16.
9 Disney, Arthur William, 2/Lt. (Tp.), k. in a., 30/11/17.
26 Dixon, Robert William, M.M., 2/Lt. (Tp.), k. in a., 5/9/18.
Docker, George Arthur Murray, Capt., k. in a., 17/11/14.
6 Done, Neville Savage, 2/Lt., k. in a., 10/3/17 (att. 22/Bn.).
12 Doudney, Hugh Denham, A/Capt., k. in a., 31/7/17.
5 Douglas-Crompton, Sidney Harold Lionel, 2/Lt., k. in a., 7/6/17.
4 Downing, Ernest Gillespie, Lt. (Tp.), k. in a., 3/5/17.
2 Drinkill, Frederick Maurice, Lt., d. of w., 1/7/16.
17 Drummond, Samuel Frederick, 2/Lt., k. in a., 29/7/17.
10 Dudley, Leonard Thomas, M.C., Lt., d. of w., 8/10/18.
4 Dudley, Walter Joseph, Lt. (Tp.), k. in a., 16/6/15.
Du Maurier, Guy Louis Busson, D.S.O., Lt.-Col., k. in a., 10/3/15.
7 Dunnington-Jefferson, Wilfred Mervyn, 2/Lt., k. in a., 22-29/4/15 (att. 3/Bn.).
5 Dunwell, Frederick Leslie, 2/Lt., k. in a., 4/1/16.
9 Dupres, Ernest Cruzick, T/Lt. (A/Capt.), k. in a., 29/8/18.
14 Dutch, Ernest James, 2/Lt. (Tp.), d. of w., 6/1/17 (att. 25/7 Bn.).
Eagar, Rowland Tallis, 2/Lt., k. in a., 8/8/18 (att. 9/Bn.).
7 Eames, William Stanley, Lt., d. of w., 16/2/16 (att. 12/Bn.).
24 Eathorne, Francis John, 2/Lt. (Tp.), k. in a., 31/7/16.
32 Eborall, John Arthur, 2/Lt. (Tp.), d. of w., 25/2/17.
5 Echlin, Frederick St. John Ford North, 2/Lt., d. of w., 27/9/16 (and R.F.C.).
11 Ede, Edwin William, M.C., 2/Lt. (Tp.), A/Capt., k. in a., 30/8/18.
26 Edwards, Albert John, 2/Lt., T/Lt., k. in a., 2/8/17.
24 Edwards, Guy Thulkeld, Capt. (Tp.), k. in a., 31/7/16.
6 Edwards, Leslie Edward, M.C., Capt. (Tp.), d. of w., 6/12/17 (att. 8/Bn.).
17 Edwards, Wilfred William, M.C., 2/Lt. (Tp.), d. of w. 22/1/17.
7 Elliott, Walter, 2/Lt., k. in a., 13/11/16.
8 V.C. Elliott-Cooper, Neville Bowes, D.S.O., M.C., Lt.-Col. (Tp.), d. of w., 11/2/18 (in German hands).
4 Enderby, Arthur Aaron, Lt. (Tp.), d. of w., 2/8/17.
17 Etheridge, Hugh Dimsdale, M.C., M.M., 2/Lt. (Tp.), d. of w., 2/10/18.
20 Evans, James Bansall, Lt. (Tp.), k. in a., 20/8/16.
6 Evans, Lawrence Picton, Lt., k. in a., 21/8/18 (att 4/Bn.).
26 Farquharson, Peere William Nesham, 2/Lt., k. in a., 7/10/16.
8 Featherstonhaugh, Harry, Capt. (Tp.), k. in a., 8/7/16.
6 Fergusson, Robert Arthur, 2/Lt., k. in a., 15/4/17 (att. 17/Bn.).
7 Ferrier, Gilbert Colin Cunninghame, 2/Lt., k. in a., 11/11/14 (att. 4/Bn.).
Fetherstonhaugh, George Rupert Alexander, 2/Lt., k. in a., 25-27/10/14.
14 Field, Arthur Clarence Henley, 2/Lt. (Tp.), d. of w., 4/4/16. (att. 4/S.W. Borderers).
1 Field, William James, M.C., 2/Lt., k. in a., 31/7/17.
Fielding, Alexander, M.C., 2/Lt. (Tp.), d. of w., 26/10/18 (att. 124/L.T.M.B.).
22 Fisher, Percy Watkins, 2/Lt., k. in a., 12/9/16.
1 Fitch, Louis Cifford, 2/Lt. (Tp.), k. in a., 28/7/18.
7 Fitton, Norman, 2/Lt., k. in a., 14/11/16 (att. 22/Bn.).
Fitzclarence, Augustus Arthur Cornwallis, Capt., k. in a., 28/6/15.
Flack, Wilfred George, M.C., Lt., d. of w., 7/9/17.
13 Fletcher, Arthur Joseph, 2/Lt. (Tp.), k. in a., 23/4/17.
14 Fletcher, Robert Henry, Lt. (Tp.), k. in a., 27/7/16.
Ford, A., 2/Lt., k. in a., 9/5/15.
25 Ford, John, 2/Lt. (Tp.), died, 16/6/16.
Ford, Richard Nagle, M.C., Capt. (T/Major), k. in a., 6/1/18.
Forster, Frederick Albert, Capt., d. of w., 23/8/15.
Forster, Herbert Cyril, Capt., k. in a., 25/5/15.
7 Forster, John, M.C., Capt. (A/Major), d. of w., 2/10/18.
8 Forsyth, Gordon Amhurst, 2/Lt., k. in a., 27/8/16.
10 Foster, Edward, 2/Lt. (Tp.), k. in a., 23/4/17.
22 Fowler, Charles Jefford, 2/Lt. (Tp.), d. of w., 1/6/16.
16 Fox, Charles Joseph, 2/Lt., k. in a., 29/6/16 (att. 2/Bn.).
11 Francis, William Joseph, 2/Lt., k. in a.,22/3/18.
Franklin, Francis, 2/Lt., k. in a., 3/5/15.
8 Franklyn, Henry, Capt. (Tp.), k. in a., 8/7/16.
5 Fraser, Donald Charles, 2/Lt., k. in a., 3/5/17 (att. 9/Bn.).
5 Freston, Charles Albert Edward, 2/Lt., d. of w., 25/3/18 (att. 23/Bn.).
3 Friedberger, William Sigismund, Capt., k. in a., 24/5/15 (att. 5/Bn.).
12 Fripp, Joseph, 2/Lt. (Tp.), died, 12/3/18.
23 Fugeman, William Alfred, Capt. (Tp.), k. in a., 1/12/17.
11 Fuller, Dunstan Milley, M.C., Capt. (Tp.), k. in a., 10/8/17.

10 Fuller, Morris Richard, 2/Lt. (Tp.), k. in a., 11/4/17.
17 Gaddum, Russell Charles Sydney, 2/Lt. (Tp.), k. in a., 10/9/16.
Gardiner, C. T., 2/Lt., d. of w., 1/6/15.
14 Gardiner, Kenneth Edward MacAlpine, 2/Lt. (Tp.), 17/10/15 (att. 8/Bn. Lond. Rgt.).
12 Garnons-Williams, Richard Davie, Lt.-Col., k. in a., 25/9/15.
14 Garrad, Edward Victor, 2/Lt. (Tp.), k. in a., 22/4/16 (att. 6/N.Lan.R.).
32 Garratt, Leslie Thomas, 2/Lt. (Tp.), d. of w., 3/7/16.
13 Gibson, Pendarves Christopher Foll, Lt. (Tp.), k. in a., 10/4/17.
25 Gilbert, Edward Burton, 2/Lt. (Tp.), k. in a., 21/3/18.
24 Gilbert, John Ewart, Capt. (Tp.), died, 6/11/18.
13 Gilbert, L. S., 2/Lt. (Tp.), k. in a., 4/4/16 (att. 8/R.W. Fus.).
12 Gill, Colin, 2/Lt., k. in a., 31/7/17.
5 Gjems, Albert Ole Möller, 2/Lt., k. in a., 8/8/17 (att. 2/Bn.).
4 Goddard, Frederick Sidney, 2/Lt., k. in a., 15/12/17.
11 Goddard, Philip Henry Thomas, 2/Lt. (Tp.), k. in a., 26/9/16.
4 Godfrey, Frederick, 2/Lt. (T/Capt.), k. in a., 16/8/16.
14 Goff, Alfred Laurence, 2/Lt. (Tp.), k. in a., 16/1/17 (att. 6/L.N. Lancs).
10 Goldthorp, Guy, Capt. (Tp.), k. in a., 23/4/17.
13 Goodman, P. N., Capt. (Tp.), k. in a., 3/3/16.
6 Goolden, Donald Charles, 2/Lt., k. in a., 15/8/16 (att. 4/Bn.).
Gonne, M. E., M.C., Capt., killed, 7/8/18 (and R.A.F.).
Gordon, Alexander Maurice, Lt., k. in a., 23/1/16.
5 Gordon, Gerald Montague, Capt. (Tp.), k. in a., 9/6/17 (att. 12/Bn.).
6 Gordon, S. E. L., Lt., k. in a., 13/3/15 (att. 4/Bn.).
1 Gorst, E. W., 2/Lt., k. in a., 25/10/14.
32 Gosling, Frederick Horace, 2/Lt., k. in a., 7/6/17.
Grady, Walter Henry, 2/Lt., killed, 22/4/15 (att. 3/Bn.).
7 Granville, Basil Rayond, 2/Lt. (A/Capt.), k. in a., 23/4/17.
11 Gray, Hubert McKenzie, A/Capt., k. in a., 10/8/17.
17 Gray, John Hunter Wood, T/Capt. & Qtm., died, 17/11/18.
9 Greathead, Alan, T/Capt., k. in a., 20/11/17.
9 Green, Henry Morris, Capt. (Tp.), k. in a., 4/8/16.
6 Green, Leslie Alan, 2/Lt., k. in a., 13/11/16 (att. 23/Bn.).
11 Greenwood, Charles Stuart, 2/Lt., died, 21/7/16.
15 Gregory, Stanley Harris, 2/Lt. (Tp.), k. in a., 13/11/16 (att. 24/Bn.).
Griffith, Rupert Varden De Burgh, Lt., k. in a., 12/3/15.
7 Griffiths, Charles Ridley, 2/Lt. (Tp.), d. of w., 1/5/17.
24 Griffiths, Leon David, 2/Lt. (Tp.), d. of w., 29/4/17 (att. 5/T.M.B.).
11 Grisot, Reginald, 2/Lt. (Tp.), k. in a., 6/8/18.
16 Gudgeon, Frederick Gustavus, Capt. (Tp.), k. in a., 28/6/15 (att. 2/Bn.).
Gush, William George, 2/Lt. (Tp.) (A/Capt.), k. in a., 23/4/17.
2 Guyon, George Sutherland, Lt.-Col., k. in a., 1/7/16.
15 Gwynne-Vaughan, Kenneth Duncan, 2/Lt. (Tp.), k. in a., 6/9/16 (and 33/M.G.C.).
11 Haddon, Vernon, 2/Lt., k. in a., 10/8/17.
9 Hall, Geoffrey, M.C., Lt. (Tp.), k. in a., 20/11/17.
5 Hall, William Ernest, Lt., k. in a., 23/5/15.
26 Hamilton, Albert Edward, 2/Lt. (Tp.), k. in a., 18/8/17.
26 Hammond, Robert Whitehead, Capt. (Tp.), d. of w., 30/9/17.
8 Hanna, David Wishart, 2/Lt. (Tp.), d. of w., 24/6/16.
Harding, Charles Egerton Hugh, Capt. (Bt.-Major), died, 10/12/17.
13 Harding, Donald Stanley, M.C., 2/Lt. (Tp.) (A/Capt.), k. in a., 10/4/17.
4 Hardman, Adrian Thomas, Lt., d. of w., 30/3/16.
Hardman, Frederick McMahon, 2/Lt., k. in a., 29/10/14.
2 Hardy, Ferdinand H., Lt. (Tp.), k. in a., 4/9/16 (att. 22/-M.G.C.).
9 Harrup, Frederick Charles Leonard, M.C., 2/Lt. (Tp.), k. in a., 21/9/18.
Harter, Clements Jesse, Lt., k. in a., 16/6/15.
9 Harvey, Albert Henry, 2/Lt. (Tp.), k. in a., 7/10/16.
17 Harvey, R. W., 2/Lt., died, 22/10/18 (and R.A.F.)
26 Havelock, Ernest Wilfrid, Lt (Tp.), d. of w., 18/9/16.
10 Haviland, John Doria, Lt. (Tp.), d. of w., 16/7/16.
7 Hawkins, Kenneth Edwards, M.C., Lt. (A/Capt.), k. in a., 22/3/18.
15 Hawkridge, Joseph Arnold, 2/Lt. (Tp.), d. of w., 6/11/16 (att. 9/Suss. R.).
6 Haycraft, Alan Montague, Lt., k. in a., 1/7/16 (att. 2/Bn.).
1 Hayes, Claude Julian Patrick, Capt. (A.), k. in a., 9/8/16.
23 Hayward, Cecil Bernard, Capt. (Tp.), k. in a., 27/7/16.
5 Hayward, Edward John, 2/Lt., k. in a., 12/11/15 (att. 2/Bn.).
10 Heathcote, Martin Arthur, 2/Lt. (Tp.), d. of w., 18/7/16.
8 Heaver, Douglas Cams, 2/Lt. (Tp.), k. in a., 4/8/16.
20 Heinemann, John Walter, Capt. (Tp.), d. of w., 6/3/16.
23 Helmore, S. T. J., 2/Lt., killed, 14/5/18 (and R.A.F.).
Hendriks, Augustus Mark, Capt., k. in a., 25/5/15.
9 Hendry, Charles Arthur, 2/Lt., k. in a., 27/3/18.
20 Henley, Frederick, 2/Lt. (Tp.), k. in a., 27/10/16.
9 Hersee, Charles Patrick Allen, 2/Lt. (Tp.), k. in a., 3/3/16.
4 Hicks, Frank Alan, M.C., Lt., k. in a., 21/8/18.
8 Hicks, Walter Gerald, 2/Lt. (Tp.), d. of w., 12/8/15.
4 Hiddingh, Stephen Van Der Poel, Lt. (A/Capt.), k. in a., 3/5/17.
5 Hilder, Maurice Lake, M.C., Lt. (T/Capt.), k. in a., 3/5/17 (att. 23/Bn.).
9 Hill, William Ernest, Lt. (Tp.), k. in a., 8/8/18.
20 Hine, T. C., 2/Lt., k. in a., 20/7/16.
6 Hinton, Norman Charles, 2/Lt., d of w., 4/4/18.
11 Hoare, Walter John Gerald, D.S.O., Capt. (Tp.), k. in a., 25/10/16.
Hobbs, Frank Matthew, 2/Lt., k. in a., 16/9/14.
10 Hodding, James Douglas, 2/Lt. (Tp.), d. of w., 10/7/16.
Hodges, Charles Edward, 2/Lt., k. in a., 16/6/15.
Hodges, Sydney Howard, 2/Lt., k. in a., 17/10/14.
Hodgson, Michael Reginald Kirkman, Capt., k. in a., 17/3/15 (att. York L.I.).
32 Hogbin, Raymond, 2/Lt. (Tp.), k. in a., 20/9/17.
Holdcroft, Eric Crane, 2/Lt. (Tp.), k. in a., 4/10/17 (Res., att. 13/Bn.).
22 Holland, Jack Harold, 2/Lt., died, 16/6/18 (and R.A.F.).
7 Hollands, Wilfrid George, 2/Lt., k. in a., 12/10/16 (att. 4/Bn.).
4 Honeywill, Stanley Ross, 2/Lt., k. in a., 8/10/18.
Hope-Johnstone, Henry Murray, M.C., Capt. (A/Major), d. of w.), 31/7/17 (att. 12/Bn.).
Hope-Johnstone, William Gordon Tollemache, Lt., k. in a., 25/10/14.
5 Hosegood, Henry Arnold, 2/Lt., k. in a., 24/2/15.
11 Houghton, William, 2/Lt. (Tp.), k. in a., 9/4/16 (att. 15/Bn.) (att. 8/R.W. Fus.).
4 Howard, Leslie Rayner, Lt. (Tp.), k. in a., 27/3/16.
Howells, David Geoffrey, 2/Lt. (Tp.), died, 1/12/18.
Hudson, Arthur Cyril, Major (Tp.), d. of w., 2/10/16 (att. 11/Bn.).
23 Hughes, Sidney Russell, 2/Lt. (Tp.), k. in a., 30/9/18 (att. 11/Bn.).
17 Hugill, Edwin Abbott, Capt. (Tp.), died, 25/9/17.
16 Hugill, Valentine Francis Herbert, 2/Lt., k. in a., 16/10/16 (and R.F.C., 42 Sq.).
20 Hume, Ronald, Lt. (Tp.), k. in a., 6/4/17 (and R.F.C., 20 Sq.).
3 Humphreys, William Thomas, Lt. (T/Capt. & Qr.-Mr.), k. in a., 4/10/18.
20 Humphrys, Stewart Francis, 2/Lt. (Tp.), k. in a., 26/8/16 (14/Bn. att.).
9 Hunter, Arthur Lawrence, 2/Lt. (Tp.), k. in a., 8/8/18.
9 Hyams, Alec Hallenstein, Lt., k. in a., 3/5/15 (att. 3/Bn.).
5 Illing, Francis, 2/Lt., d. of w., 8/5/18 (att. 13/Bn.).
33 Inglis, W. R., Col., died, 30/3/16.
26 Ireland, Joseph Knowles, Capt., k. in a., 7/10/16.
9 Isaacs, Vincent Harcourt, 2/Lt., k. in a., 21/9/18.
23 Jackson, Arthur Rushton, 2/Lt. (Tp.), k. in a., 25/4/18.
26 Jackson, John, 2/Lt. (Tp.), k. in a., 20/9/17.
4 Jacob, Arthur Henry Augustus, Lt., d. of w., 16/7/16.
1 Jacobs, John Harry, M.C., A/Capt., k. in a., 11/10/18.
22 Jeffcoat, Stanley Ferns, 2/Lt. (Tp.), d. of w., 29/4/17.
13 Jeffreys, Hubert Leslie, 2/Lt., k. in a., 29/4/17.
14 Jepson, Norman Richard, 2/Lt. (Tp.), k. in a., 15/10/15 (att. 2/Bn.).
15 Johnson, Newton Farring, 2/Lt. (Tp.), k. in a., 16/8/16 (att. 26/Bn.).
23 Johnson, Robert Deane, Capt. (Tp.), k. in a., 6/7/16.
5 Judge, Wilfred Justice, 2/Lt., d. of w., 21/8/16 (att. 1/Bn.).
7 Juniper, John Harvey, 2/Lt., k. in a., 30/4/17.
26 Kay, Albert, 2/Lt. (Tp.), k. in a., 1/8/17.
5 Kaye, Frank Leon, 2/Lt. (Tp.), d. of w., 11/4/17 (att. 9/Bn.).
23 Kentfield, Edwin Nelson, 2/Lt. (Tp.), k. in a., 17/2/17.
1 Kerry, Albert, 2/Lt., k. in a., 22/3/18.
5 Kilmister, Harold Howard Linsdell, M.C., Lt., k. in a., 22/8/18 (att. 9/Bn.).
23 Kinahan, James, 2/Lt. (Tp.), d. of w., 8/10/18.
9 King, Alan Howard, 2/Lt. (Tp.), k. in a., 22/8/18.
9 Knight, Arthur George, Lt., k. in a., 29/6/15.
11 Knott, Charles Singleton, 2/Lt., k. in a., 23/3/18.
6 Lamb, Harold George Wellesley, 2/Lt., k. in a., 8/10/18 (att. 10/Bn.).
Lambert, George, 2/Lt., k. in a., 22/4/15.
Lambert, Leonard Walter, 2/Lt. (Tp.), k. in a., 28/3/18 (att. 4/Bn.).
6 Larcombe, Henry Reginald Reader, 2/Lt., k. in a., 2/9/17.
7 Large, Ronald Murray, Lt. (A/Capt.), k. in a., 4/11/18.
Law, James Kidston, Capt., k. in a., 21/9/17 (and R.F.C., 60 Sq.).
9 Lawford, Herbert Martin Benson, Capt. (Tp.), k. in a., 7/10/16.
11 Lawrence, John James, 2/Lt. (Tp.), k. in a., 23/10/18.
Lawrence, Norman Alan, 2/Lt., k. in a., 30/4/17 (and R.F.C., 16 Sq.).
11 Leatherland, Frederick Arthur, 2/Lt. (Tp.), k. in a., 7/8/18.
7 Lecky, John Rupert Frederick, Capt., k. in a., 28/9/15 (att. Norf. R.).
7 Lee, William Robert Charles Paul, 2/Lt., k. in a., 10/7/15 (att. R. Welsh Fus.).
6 Leeming, Alfred Johnson, 2/Lt. (A/Capt.), k. in a., 31/7/17.
Legge, Hugo Molesworth, Lieut., k. in a., 5/5/15.
17 Lelievre, Albert Frederic Henry, 2/Lt. (Tp.), d. of w., 4/8/16.
6 Le Marchant, S. H., 2/Lt., d. of w., 25/5/15 (att. 3/Bn.).
7 Lenton, Harold Bertram, 2/Lt., k. in a., 30/10/17.
8 Lethbridge, Cecil Augustus, Lt., k. in a., 3/5/17.
Leslie, Frank King, Capt., k. in a., 25/4/15.
9 Levi, Harry, 2/Lt. (Tp.), k. in a., 30/11/17.
2 Lewis, David Jacob, 2/Lt. (Tp.), k. in a., 28/2/17.
8 Ling, Frederick William, Capt. (Tp.), k. in a., 27/6/17.
12 Linstead, Douglas Walter, 2/Lt. (Tp.), k. in a., 6/5/16.
5 Lipp, Vernon Robertson, 2/Lt., k. in a., 17/6/16 (att. 12/Bn.).
23 Lissaman, Arthur John, Lt. (Tp.), k. in a., 13/4/17.
11 Little, Norman James Richard, Lt. (Tp.), k. in a., 13/3/17.
9 Long, William Charles, M.C., 2/Lt. (Tp.), d. of w., 31/8/18.
Longman, Frederick, Lt., k. in a., 18/10/14.
Lowe, George Stanley, 2/Lt., k. in a., 18/9/18 (att. 9/Bn.).
17 Lucas, John, 2/Lt. (Tp.), d. of w., 28/12/17.
Lupton, Frank William, 2/Lt. (Tp.), k. in a., 4/8/16.
1 Macartney, Hussey Burgh George, Capt., k. in a., 24/6/15.

4 McCallum, Rae Bruce, 2/Lt. (Tp.), k. in a., 2/9/17 (att. 9/Bn.).
13 McCarthy, Alexander, 2/Lt. (Tp.), k. in a., 23/8/18.
22 Macdougall, Allen, Capt. (Tp.), k. in a., 4/8/16.
10 McIntyre, James Lennie, 2/Lt. (Tp.), d. of w., 14/5/18.
7 Mackadam, Harold James, 2/Lt. (Tp.), k. in a., 30/12/17.
2 McGregor, Ian Alexander, 2/Lt. (Tp.), k. in a., 10/9/16 (att. 2/N'd. Fus.).
24 Mackay, Angus, 2/Lt. (Tp.), d. of w., 10/5/18.
26 Mackay, Alexander William, M.C., Capt. (Tp.), d. of w., 28/9/17.
McMahon, Norman Reginald, D.S.O., Brig.-Gen., k. in a., 11/11/14 (H.Q. 10 Inf. Bde.)
12 McNaught, Ernest Henry, 2/Lt., k. in a., 18/7/16.
Maclean, Donald Frederick Durant, Major (Tp.), died, 10/12/17.
Magnay, Philip Magnay, Capt. (T/Lt.-Col.), k. in a., 13/4/17 (att. 12/Bn. Manch. R.).
Maguire, Edward Alphonsus, 2/Lt. (Tp.) k. in a., 8/10/18 (att. 4/Bn.).
16 Malcolm, Albert Victor Sadler, 2/Lt. (Tp.), k. in a., 17/2/17 (att. 11/Bn.).
9 Manson, John Cochrane, 2/Lt. (Tp.), k. in a., 7/7/16.
13 Marquard, John, Lt. (Tp.), A/Capt., k. in a., 23/8/18.
5 Marsh, Harold, 2/Lt., k. in a., 4/10/18.
6 Marshall, Dudley, 2/Lt., k. in a., 26/9/17 (att. 4/Bn.).
6 Marsland, Eric Forbes, 2/Lt., k. in a., 7/10/16 (att. 8/Bn.).
4 Martin, Bertram Charles, 2/Lt. (Tp.), k. in a., 13/4/17.
12 Martin, Harold, Lt. (Tp.), k. in a., 31/7/17.
7 Mason, Arthur Edward Wright, Capt., k. in a., 2/3/16 (att. 8/Bn.).
5 Mason, Royston Alfred Robson, 2/Lt., d. of w., 20/11/17 (att. 2/Bn.).
1 Massey, Louis Oger, 2/Lt., k. in a., 21/8/16.
5 Masters, Charles William, 2/Lt., k. in a., 30/8/17 (att. 8/Bn.).
9 Masters, Geoffrey, 2/Lt. (Tp.), k. in a., 9/4/17.
9 Masterton, Frank, 2/Lt., k. in a., 5/4/18.
1 Matthews, Charles Henry, 2/Lt., d. of w., 22/3/18.
Maude, Gervase Henry Francis, 2/Lt., d. of w., 9/4/17 (att. 8/Bn.).
6 Mawdsley, Norman Hargreaves, Lt., died, 17/6/18.
Mayer, Frank, Lt. (Tp.), k. in a., 3/10/18 (att. 4/Bn.).
Mead, Bernard Wallace, 2/Lt., d. of w., 2/6/15.
Mead, Joseph Frederick, 2/Lt., k. in a., 23/8/14.
8 Mead, Robert John, 2/Lt. (Tp.), d. of w., 2/8/15.
19 Meares, Cecil Stanley, Capt. (Tp.), k. in a., 30/7/16 (att. 24/Bn.).
12 Mears-Devenish, John Augustus, 2/Lt. (Tp.), d. of w., 22/3/18 (att. 1/Bn.).
5 Measures, William Henry, M.C., 2/Lt. (Tp.), k. in a., 22/8/18 (att. 11/Bn.).
15 Mellor, Harold Welton, Capt. (Tp.), died, 28/5/18 (att. 2/K.A.R.).
17 Menzies, Alastair Forbes, D.S.O., Lt. (Tp.) (A/Capt.), k. in a., 4/5/18.
6 Mepham, Horace Leslie, 2/Lt., k. in a., 11/4/18 (att. 2/Bn.).
32 Meredith, Eric Duntee, 2/Lt. (Tp.), k. in a., 4-10/10/16.
11 Meyricke, Robert James Francis, T/Major (A/Lt.-Col.), k. in a., 17/2/17.
11 Miall-Smith, Ralph A., Lt. (Tp., k. in a., 26/9/16.
11 Michell, Noel Burgess, Capt. (Tp.), k. in a., 22/3/18.
7 Miles, John Harris, 2/Lt., k. in a., 27/9/15 (att. 4/Bn.).
6 Miles, Leonard Percy, 2/Lt., k. in a., 7/10/16 (att. 8/Bn.).
6 Millson, Alvan Ewen, Capt. (Act.), k. in a., 9/4/17.
10 Milway, Edwin Horace, 2/Lt. (Tp.), k. in a., 8/10/18.
11 Minchin, William Smith, M.C., Capt. & Qr.-Mr., k. in a., 20/4/18.
26 Monkman, Fred Kerbey, 2/Lt. (Tp.), d. of w., 28/9/17.
Morgan, Albert Ernest, Capt., killed, 10/3/15 (att. R.F.C.).
7 Morgan, F. J., 2/Lt., d. of w., 16/5/18 (and R.A.F.).
13 Morgan, William Alfred, 2/Lt. (Tp.), k. in a., 23/4/17.
9 Morris, Collin Dwight, 2/Lt. (Tp.), k. in a., 14/3/16.
9 Mortimer, Leonard James, Lt. (Tp.), d. of w., 24/11/17.
26 Mortlock, Percy George, 2/Lt., k. in a., 20/9/17.
Moscrop, William N. J., M.C., 2/Lt. (A/Capt.), k. in a., 27/5/18 (att. 5/Durh. L.I.).
24 Mott, Francis Stanley, 2/Lt. (Tp.), d. of w., 23/7/16.
11 Mount, Edward Alfred, 2/Lt. (Tp.), k. in a., 4/1/16.
4 Moxon, Gerald John Mortimer, Capt. (Tp.), k. in a., 27/3/16.
9 Mullane, Bernard Patrick, 2/Lt. (Tp.), d. of w., 1/4/18.
2 Mundey, Lionel Clement, Lt., k. in a., 6/6/15.
7 Munds, Percy, 2/Lt. (Tp.), d. of w., 8/10/18.
1 Murless, Herbert Reginald, M.C., Lt. (Tp.), d of w., 7/2/17 (att. 12/Bn.).
1/4 Murphy, Harry Eustace, Lt., killed, 22/4/18 (and R.A.F.).
6 Murray-Smith, Geoffrey, Lt., k. in a., 29/9/15 (att. 3/Bn.).
Nathan, William Sylvester, 2/Lt., k. in a., 14/6/16 (att. 12/Bn.).
11 Neate, Nelson Rayner, M.C., Capt., k. in a., 3/5/17 (att. H.A.C.).
24 Neate, William, 2/Lt., k. in a., 24/3/18.
14 Neely, Clive William, 2/Lt. (Tp.), died, 20/6/16.
4 Neighbour, Walter Bayard, 2/Lt. (Tp.), d. of w., 16/8/16.
12 Newcomb, Cyril, 2/Lt. (Tp.), k. in a., 25-28/9/15.
24 Newland, Edward Albert, 2/Lt. (Tp.), k. in a., 23/10/18.
Newnham, Alfred Geoffrey, 2/Lt., k. in a., 11/11/14.
5 Nicholls, John Watson, Lt., k. in a., 1/7/16.
9 Nicholson, Albert, 2/Lt. (Tp.), k. in a., 8/8/18.
6 Nicholson, Bruce Hills, 2/Lt., k. in a., 3/5/17 (att. 4/Bn.).
Nicholson, Edward Hills, D.S.O., Major, A/Lt.-Col., k. in a., 4/10/18 (att. East Surr. R.).
11 Nield, Wilfred Herbert Everard, Lt. (Tp.), k. in a., 1/7/16.
6 Noel, Honble. Robert Edmund Thomas More, Capt., died, 2/2/18 (att. 1/Nigerian R.).
26 Norman, Garnet, 2/Lt. (Tp.), d. of w., 2/4/18.
26 Norris, Cyril Norman, 2/Lt. (Tp.), d. of w., 19/8/17.
5 Norwell, Herbert, 2/Lt., k. in a., 12/4/18 (att. 2/Bn.).
7 Notcutt, Leonard Ernest, Lt., k. in a., 3/5/17 (and 27/M.G.C.).
24 Nyren, Dudley Richard, 2/Lt. (Tp.), k. in a., 24/3/18.
3 O'Connor, Bernard Joseph, Lt. (Tp.), k. in a., 4/10/18.
Ohlmann, Gerrard Alexander Louis, 2/Lt., k. in a., 29/9/15.
23 Oliver, Edgar Alexander, 2/Lt. (Tp.), k. in a., 27/7/16.
Orbell, Ivan Scott, 2/Lt., k. in a., 25/10/17.
Osborn, Ernest John, M.C., Lt. (Tp.), A/Capt., d. of w., 13/4/18 (att. 5/T.M.B.).
27 Osborne, H. C. B., Major (Tp.), died, 28/6/16.
14 Osborne, Robert Lionel, 2/Lt. (Tp.), k. in a., 7/7/16 (att. 9/Bn.).
Ottley, Glendower George, Major (Tp.), k. in a., 3/9/16.
Ozanne, Edward Graeme, Capt., d. of w., 16/2/15.
4 Paddock, William Francis, 2/Lt., d. of w., 9/4/17.
26 Page-Green, Reginald Sebastian, M.C., 2/Lt. (Tp.), k. in a., 22/6/17.
15 Paiba, Ellis James Alfred, Lt. (Tp.), k. in a., 20/10/15 (att. 2/Bn.).
8 Palling, William Lionel, 2/Lt. (Tp.), k. in a., 15/3/16.
13 Palmer, Edward Charles Maxwell, 2/Lt., k. in a., 23/4/17 (att. 111/T.M.B.).
20 Palmer, John Henry, Lt. (Tp.), k. in a., 20/7/16.
Parker, Walter Henry, Lt., A/Capt., k. in a., 15/6/17 (att. 2/4 Lon. R.).
9 Parkes, Robert Lionel, 2/Lt. (Tp.), k. in a., 7/10/16.
4 Parr, Wilfred Alexander, 2/Lt., k. in a., 3/5/17.
11 Parr-Dudley, John Huskisson, 2/Lt. (Tp.), k. in a., 1/7/16.
9 Parr-Dudley, Walter, 2/Lt., k. in a., 5/4/18.
24 Parry, William Henry Liddon, 2/Lt. (Tp.), d. of w., 29/11/16.
4 Parsons, Alfred Ernest, 2/Lt., k. in a., 3/5/17.
Parsons, George Jonathan, 2/Lt., d. of w., 31/8/18 (att. 4/Bn.).
12 Patman, Harold George, 2/Lt., k. in a., 31/7/17.
Pattinson, H. L., Capt. & Adj., k. in a., 4/8/15 (att. 9/Bn.).
22 Payne, William Henry, 2/Lt. (Tp.), k. in a., 17/2/17.
14 Pearson, Angus John William, 2/Lt. (Tp.), k. in a., 1/7/16.
8 Pearson, John Ashworth, Lt. (Tp.), k. in a., 4/8/16.
5 Pearson, Neil M., 2/Lt., k. in a., 17/8/16 (att. 1/Bn.).
1 Peaston, Leslie Gordon, 2/Lt., k. in a., 21/3/18.
9 Peecock, Edward Gordon, 2/Lt. (Tp.), k. in a., 7/7/16.
1 Pennington, Harold Cocking, Lt. (Tp.), d. of w., 20/6/17.
2 Penny, Bernard Willoughby, 2/Lt., d. of w., 18/8/17.
14 Penny, Stanley, 2/Lt. (Tp.), d. of w., 28/7/16.
12 Penrose, Harold, 2/Lt. (Tp.), d. of w., 27/3/17 (att. 8/Bn.).
4 Penrose, Harold Wesley, 2/Lt., k. in a., 26/3/18.
4 Penwarden, William Francis, 2/Lt., k. in a., 31/8/18.
22 Perraton, Frank Mayvour, 2/Lt., k. in a., 29/4/17.
4 Perrier, William Samuel, 2/Lt. (Tp.), k. in a., 27/3/16.
Perry, Cullen Hay, Lt. (Tp.), died, 3/2/18 (and R.F.C.).
2 Persse, Henry Wilfred, M.C., Capt., A/Major, d. of w., 28/6/18.
9 Phillipps, The Honble. Rowland Erasmus, Capt. (Tp.), k. in a., 7/7/16.
12 Phillips, Sydney, Capt., k. in a., 25/10/15.
4 Pickop, James Taylor Greer, 2/Lt., d. of w., 21/6/17.
4 Pickop, William Bannister Augustus, Lt., d. of w., 24/10/18.
9 Pilgrim, Hugh Thomas, M.C., Capt., k. in a., 25/8/18.
32 Pincombe, Lionel John, 2/Lt. (Tp.), k. in a., 20/9/17.
1 Pinney, John Charles William Adderley, Lt., k. in a., 1/12/17 (att. 38 Horse).
26 Pitt, Geoffery Stanhope, T/Capt., died, 11/2/19.
17 Pollak, Otto Dennis, Lt., k. in a., 8/7/16.
11 Porter, Robert Ernest, 2/Lt. (Tp.), d. of w., 10/8/17.
Portlock, Alfred Edgar, 2/Lt. (Tp.), killed, 6/12/17 (att. R.F.C.).
24 Potts, Ernest Alexander, M.C., 2/Lt. (Tp.), d. of w., 15/10/18 (att. 10/Bn.).
20 Powell, Eric Layton, 2/Lt. (Tp.), k. in a., 16/4/17.
23 Pratt, William George James, 2/Lt. (Tp.), k. in a., 28/9/17.
Price, Harold Strachan, 2/Lt. (Tp.), k. in a., 24/5/15.
20 Price, John Thomas, 2/Lt. (Tp.), k. in a., 20/7/16.
18 Price-Edwards, Owen, Capt., k. in a., 22/6/16.
8 Pride, A. R., 2/Lieut. (Tp.), k. in a., 3/5/17.
1/4 Prior, H. L., 2/Lt., died 3/7/18 (att. R.A.F.).
8 Procter, Alexander Duncan Guthrie, 2/Lt. (Tp.), k. in a., 7/7/16.
4 Prynne, Edgar George Fellowes, T/Lt., A/Capt., k. in a., 16/9/16 (att. 1/23 Lond. R.).
26 Pugh, Geoffrey Arthur, 2/Lt., k. in a., 10/10/16.
Puzey, Arthur Kenneth, Capt., k. in a., 11/11/14.
5 Pye, Francis John, Capt., k. in a., 15/12/16 (att. Gold Coast Rgt.).
2 Quin, James Davidson, 2/Lt., k. in a., 19/8/18.
24 Radcliffe, David, Lt. (Tp.), k. in a., 18/3/16.
3 Radford, Francis Buckley, 2/Lt., k. in a., 25/3/18 (att. 13/Bn.).
26 Raine, George Stevenson, 2/Lt. (Tp.), killed, 15/3/17 (att. R.F.C.).
5 Ralfs, Francis Arthur, Lt., d. of w., 16/9/16 (att. 9 Lancs Fus.).
5 Ramsay, A., Lt., died, 28/4/15.
29 Ramsbottom, Reginald, 2/Lt. (Tp.), k. in a., 29/7/16 (att. 17/Bn.).
7 Randall, Edwin Walter, Lt., k. in a., 23/4/17.
23 Ranken, Dudleigh Chalmers, Capt. (Tp.), k. in a., 27/7/16.
7 Rattigan, Cyril Stanley, Capt., k. in a., 13/11/16.
23 Rattray, David Lindsay, Capt. (Tp.), k. in a., 17/2/17.
9 Rawlins, Gerald Edmund Adair, Capt., k. in a., 7/7/16.
20 Rawson, Stuart Milner, Lt. (Tp.), k. in a., 20/7/16.
8 Reed, James Richard, 2/Lt. (Tp.), k. in a., 24/11/17.
1 Reed, Russel Walter, 2/Lt., k. in a., 11/10/18.
6 Rees, Eric Montague, 2/Lt., k. in a., 8/10/18 (att. 13/Bn.).

9 Reeve, Herbert, 2/Lt. (Tp.), k. in a., 30/11/17.
24 Remington, Wallace, 2/Lt. (Tp.), k. in a., 23/3/18.
Rennie, Donald Williamson, 2/Lt., k. in a., 11/11/14.
10 Richards, Percival Morgan, 2/Lt. (Tp.), k. in a., 15/7/16.
16 Richards, Roland, Lt. (Tp.), k. in a., 7/12/15 (att. 7/R. Mun. Fus.).
6 Richardson-Jones, Charles Harry, 2/Lt., k. in a., 11/6/16.
6 Righton, Richard Harry, 2/Lt., k. in a., 27/9/18 (att. 7/Bn.).
Roberts, Arthur Colin, C.M.G., D.S.O., Brig.-Gen., died, 17/5/17 (80 Inf. Bde. H.Q.).
3 Roberts, Frederick Norman, 2/Lt. (Tp.), d. of w., 19/11/18.
20 Roberts, Francis, 2/Lt. (Tp.), k. in a., 27/10/16.
Roberts, William Arthur, Lt. (Tp.), died, 20/8/17 (30 T.R.B.).
4 Robertson, Barrie Dow, 2/Lt. (Tp.), A/Capt., k. in a., 22/8/18.
8 Robertson-Walker, Arthur Murdoch Maxwell, Capt. (Tp.), k. in a., 7/7/16.
25 Robinson, Arthur Henry, 2/Lt. (Tp.), k. in a., 11/6/17.
Robinson, Thistle, M.C., Lt. (Tp.), k. in a., 25/10/18 (att. 26/Bn.).
11 Roe, William Richard, 2/Lt. (Tp.), died, 11/5/17 (att. H.A.C.), in German hands.
6 Rogers, Benjamin Richard Corlay, 2/Lt., k. in a., 17/10/18 (att. 3/Bn.).
4 Rogers, Sheffield Digby Kissane, Lt., k. in a., 14/6/15 (att. North'd Fus.).
2 Roope, Charles Francis, 2/Lt. (Tp.), k. in a., 1/7/16.
17 Roper, Eric Walter, Lt. & Adj. (Tp.), d. of w., 12/9/16.
11 Roper, William Frank, M.C., 2/Lt. (Tp.), k. in a., 29/9/18 (att. 54/T.M.B.).
22 Roscoe, Richard Lang, M.C., Capt. (Tp.), d. of w., 4/2/17.
7 Rose, Theodore William Frank, 2/Lt., k. in a., 4/4/18.
Rowe, Benjamin Franklin, Lt., k. in a., 1/6/17 (and R.F.C.).
4 Royer, Harold Ernest, 2/Lt. (Tp.), k. in a., 27/9/18.
4 Royle, Dennis Carlton, M.C., Capt. (Tp.), k. in a., 21/8/18.
Rumball, George Thomas Sydney, M.C., 2/Lt. (Tp.), k. in a., 13/4/18 (att. 2/Bn.).
25 Ryan, Martin, Capt. (Tp.), A/Major, k. in a., 18/10/17.
11 Sampson, Bertram George, 2/Lt. (Tp.), k. in a., 12/2/17.
12 Sandall, Horace Cecil Blandford, 2/Lt. (Tp.), k. in a., 9/3/18 (att. 10/Bn.).
23 Sanders, Frederick John, 2/Lt. (Tp.), d. of w., 6/8/18.
11 Savage, William Howard, 2/Lt. (Tp.), k. in a., 1/7/16.
6 Savours, Arthur William, Lt., k. in a., 2/8/18 (att. 11/Bn.).
22 Saward, Ralph, 2/Lt., k. in a., 29/4/17.
17 Sayer, Leonard Charles, 2/Lt. (Tp.), d. of w., 4/7/16.
11 Sayer, Robert Bramwell, 2/Lt. (Tp.), d. of w., 19/2/17.
14 Schofield, Cuthbert, Lt. (Tp.), k. in a., 25/9/15 (att. 12/Bn.).
7 Scott, Arthur Ernest Mortimer, Lt., k. in a., 7/11/16 (att. 4/Bn.).
26 Scott, William David, 2/Lt. (Tp.), k. in a., 3/8/17.
Scott-Miller, Walter Dudley, 2/Lt., killed, 22/6/17 (att. R.F.C.).
Scudamore, John Venables, Lt., k. in a., 25/4/15.
7 Sealy, Charles Frederic Noel Prince, 2/Lt., k. in a., 24/5/15.
25 Selous, Frederick Courteney, D.S.O., Capt. (Tp.), k. in a., 4/1/17.
7 Seward, Stanley Richard, Lt. (A/Capt.), k. in a., 30/10/17 (att. 7/R. Sco. Fus.).
32 Seymour-Ure, William Bruce, 2/Lt. (Tp.), k. in a., 4-10/10/16.
Shafto, Thomas Duncombe, Capt., k. in a., 2/5/15.
4 Shannon, Richard Bernard, Earl of, 2/Lt., k. in a., 13/4/17.
11 Sharp, Humphrey, Lt. (Tp.), k. in a., 5/10/15.
25 Sharpe, Sydney William, 2/Lt. (Tp.), d. of w., 25/3/18.
5 Shaw, Hugh James, Capt., killed, 11/11/14 (att. 1/Bn.).
16 Shaw, Max Joseph, Lt. (Tp.), k. in a., 15/9/16 (att. 26/Bn.).
5 Shaw, Raymond Pugh, Lt. (T/Capt.), k. in a., 28/11/15 (att. 2/Bn.).
Shaw, Walter Douglas, M.C., Lt. (Tp.), d. of w., 8/11/18 (att. 1/10 Manch. R.).
Shephard, Gordon Strachy, D.S.O., M.C., Brig.-Gen., k. in a., 19/1/18 (and R.F.C.).
17 Sherwood, Clement Walter, 2/Lt. (Tp.), k. in a., 28/11/17.
1 Shoesmith, Edward James, 2/Lt., k. in a., 7/6/17.
2 Shillingford, Stanley Charles, Lt., k. in a., 16/6/18 (att. R.A.F.).
26 Shorrock, Thomas Dudley Ralph, 2/Lt. (Tp.), k. in a., 20/9/17.
10 Shurey, Charles, Capt. (Tp.), d. of w., 21/7/16.
9 Sidwell, Albert Edward, M.C., Lt. (Tp.), k. in a., 7/7/17.
9 Simonds, Ernest Hugh, 2/Lt. (Tp.), k. in a., 28/3/18.
11 Simmons, Robert George, 2/Lt. (Tp.), k. in a., 22/3/18.
22 Simons, Leon, M.C., Capt., k. in a., 17/2/17.
26 Simpson, Christopher Byron, Capt. (Tp.), k. in a., 7/10/16.
5 Simpson, John Parker Norfolk, 2/Lt., d. of w., 27/5/15 (att. 3/Bn.).
4 Sims, Heber Harold, 2/Lt. (Tp.), d. of w., 1/9/18.
Sinclair, Frank, Lt. (Tp.), drowned, 3/10/18 (att. Nigeria Rgt.).
8 Skelton, Harry, 2/Lt. (Tp.), d. of w., 12/10/16.
32 Skinner, Stephen William, 2/Lt., k. in a., 4/10/16.
23 Smith, Arthur William, 2/Lt. (Tp.), k. in a., 7/9/18.
4 Smith, Dugald, 2/Lt. (Tp.) (A/Capt.), d. of w., 8/10/18.
Smith, Everard Cecil, Lt., k. in a., 23/8/14.
4 Smith, James Clement, 2/Lt., k. in a., 27/3/16.
26 Smith, Sydney John, 2/Lt. (Tp.), k. in a., 20/9/17.
9 Smith, Walter Wyville, 2/Lt. (Tp.), k. in a., 18/10/15.
4 Snaith, William Ernest, 2/Lt. (Tp.), k. in a., 3/5/17.
7 Snelling, Frederick John, 2/Lt. (Tp.), k. in a., 30/10/17.
2 Solomon. L. B., Lt. (Tp.), k. in a., 12/4/18.
20 Soro, William, 2/Lt. (Tp.), k. in a., 16/4/17.
Sparks, James Elliot, Lt., k. in a., 21/7/16.
2 Sparks, Robert Lionel, 2/Lt., k. in a., 22/11/17.
Speakman, Alan Edwards, 2/Lt. (Tp.), k. in a., 5/9/18 (att. 2/Bn.).
9 Spence, Bertram, 2/Lt. (Tp.), k. in a., 21/9/18.
17 Spicer, George Henry, 2/Lt. (Tp.), k. in a., 6/6/18.
Spooner, George Piercy, 2/Lt. (Tp.), k. in a., 20-23/9/17 (att. 26/Bn.).
5 Stables, Harold Rolleston, Lt., k. in a., 15/11/14 (att. Chesh. R.).
24 Stafford, Cyril Francis, 2/Lt., d. of w., 14/4/17.
9 Stanley, Lawrence Aston, 2/Lt., k. in a., 30/11/17.
Stapleton-Bretherton, Wilfred Stanislaus, Capt., k. in a., 8/11/14.
Stearns, Eric Gordon, 2/Lt. (Tp.), d. of w., 7/8/15.
Steele, Frederick Wilberforce Alexander, Lt., d. of w. 25-27/10/14.
5 Stephens, Geoffrey Duncan, 2/Lt., k. in a., 9/7/16 (att. 1/Bn., att. T.M. By.).
10 Stephenson, Rennie, Lt. (Tp.), k. in a., 16/11/16.
9 Stevens, Arthur Reginald Ingram, Lt. (Tp.), k. in a., 4/8/16.
22 Stevenson, Frederick, 2/Lt., k. in a., 29/4/17.
Stileman, Cecil Herbert, 2/Lt. (Tp.), k. in a., 29/2/16 (and R.F.C., 5 Sq.).
8 Stiles, Arthur James, 2/Lt., k. in a.. 3/8/16.
28 Still, Reginald Sidney Hewitt, 2/Lt., k. in a., 7/10/16 (att. 9/Bn.).
5 Stirling, Richard Kellock, Lt., k. in a., 21/8/15 (att. 1/Bn.).
28 Stocker, Frederick Luff, Lt. (Tp.), k. in a., 23/8/18 (att. 20/Bn.).
5 Stollery, John Cecil, 2/Lt., k. in a., 24/5/15 (att. Warwicks).
3 V.C. Stone, Walter Napleton, A/Capt., k. in a., 30/11/17 (att. 17/Bn.).
11 Stovold, Grosvenor Henry, 2/Lt. (Tp.), k. in a., 10/8/17.
4 Stoyle, A. P., Lt., died, 27/2/19 (att. R.A.F.).
9 Street, Frank, Lt. (Tp.), k. in a., 7/7/16.
26 Stringer, John, 2/Lt. (Tp.), k. in a., 7/10/16.
6 Stuart, J., 2/Lt. (Tp.), died, 24/4/18.
7 Sykes, Ronald Arthur, Lt., d. of w., 28/4/17.
23 Symonds, Arthur, 2/Lt., k. in a., 17/2/17.
5 Symons, Charles Handley Lanphier, 2/Lt., k. in a., 20/11/17 (att. 8/Bn).
17 Tardugno, Ray, 2/Lt. (Tp.), k. in a., 7/7/17 (att. R.F.C., 57 Sqd.).
Tate, William Lewis, Lt., k. in a., 13/3/15.
7 Taylor, Arthur George Ernest, Lt. (A/Capt.), d. of w., 26/5/17.
17 Taylor, Clives Wailes, M.C., 2/Lt., d. of w., 25/2/17.
Taylor, Eric Francis Howard, 2/Lt. (Tp.), k. in a., 27/7/16.
10 Taylor, Francis Maurice, Lt. (Tp.), k. in a., 15/7/16.
Taylor, Maurice, 2/Lt., k. in a., 23/3/18 (att. 11/Bn.).
6 Tealby, Harold Edgar William, 2/Lt. (A/Capt.), k. in a., 5/4/18 (att. 7/Bn.).
2 Templar, John Franklin Hopwood, Capt., died, 8/2/19.
4 Thoday, Albert Eric, 2/Lt., k. in a., 3/5/17.
Thomas-O'Donel, George O'Donel Frederick, Capt. & Adjt., k. in a., 16/6/15.
Thompson, Albert Martin, 2/Lt. (Tp.), k. in a., 21/12/15 (att. 1/15 Lond R.).
11 Thompson, Richard Henry Vaughan, Capt. (Tp.), k. in a., 26/9/16.
14 Thomson, Spencer, M.C., Lt. (Tp.), k. in a., 24/4/17 (att. 2/Bn.).
32 Thorburn, John Morgan, Capt. (Tp.), d. of w., 7/8/17.
4 Thornton, Robert West, Lt., k. in a., 16/6/15.
10 Thorp, Leslie, 2/Lt., k. in a., 16/11/16.
12 Tiffany, Harry Waddington, M.C., 2/Lt., k. in a., 15/11/16.
20 Toller, Edward Northcote, Capt. (Tp.), k. in a., 20/7/16.
4 Tothill, Géoffrey Ivan Francis, 2/Lt., k. in a., 27/3/16.
Tower, Bertie Christopher Butler, M.C., Capt. (A/Major), d. of w., 22/8/18.
Tristram, Eric Barrington, 2/Lt. (T/Lt.), k. in a., 6/9/17. (att. 1/5 Lan. Fus.).
13 Troup, Frank Monck Mason, Lt. (Tp.), k. in a., 10/4/17.
10 Tupper, Harold, 2/Lt., d. of w., 22/7/18.
6 Turney, Leonard William, Major, k. in a., 3/5/17 (att. 8/Bn.).
4 Twigg, Ellis, 2/Lt. (Tp.), k. in a., 18/9/18.
10 Twyman, Percy Gedge, 2/Lt. (Tp.), d. of w., 15/4/17.
24 Ullman, Douglas Maurice Jaques, 2/Lt. (Tp.), k. in a., 23/4/17.
4 Umney, Basil Charles Lovell, 2/Lt., k. in a., 22/7/16.
17 Underwood, Edmund Poole, 2/Lt. (Tp.), k. in a., 30/7/16 (att. 29/Bn.).
Undery, John Alfred, 2/Lt., k. in a., 29/10/14.
1 Uphill, Reginald William James, 2/Lt., k. in a., 22/3/18
10 Usher, Arthur Norman, M.C., 2/Lt., k. in a., 4/11/18.
1 Van Gruisen, Wilfred, M.C., Lt., d. of w., 1/11/16.
Vaughan, John Montgomery, 2/Lt., d. of w., 25/5/15.
14 Veresmith, Evelyn Henry, 2/Lt. (Tp.), d. of w., 9/7/16 (att. 9/Bn.).
13 Vincent, George Samuel, 2/Lt. (Tp.), k. in a., 4/10/17
12 Waddell, James Douglas, Capt., k. in a., 25/9/15.
Waddell-Dudley, Robert Rowland, Lt., k. in a., 15/4/15.
9 Wade, Lawrence Frank, 2/Lt., k. in a., 28/8/18.
8 Waghorn, Percy William, 2/Lt., k. in a., 7/10/16.
12 Waley, Aubrey John, Lt. (Tp.), k. in a., 31/7/17.
20 Walker, Alfred English, Lt. (Tp.), k. in a., 22/8/16.
6 Waller (Bart.), Francis Ernest (Sir), Capt., k. in a., 25/10/14 (att. 4/Bn.).
5 Waller, Richard Alured, 2/Lt., died, 1/11/17.
20 Wallwork, Herbert, Lt. (Tp.), k. in a., 20/7/16.
22 Walsh, John, Major (Tp.), d. of w., 19/2/17.
10 Ward, Eric, 2/Lt., d. of w., 27/2/18.
6 Warde, Brian Edmund Douglas, Lt., k. in a., 16/6/15 (att. 4/Bn.).
22 Wardley, Miles Edward, 2/Lt. (Tp.), k. in a., 29/4/17.
8 Wardrop, John, 2/Lt. (Tp.), k. in a., 3/8/16.
9 Wason, Cyril Ernest, 2/Lt. (Tp.), k. in a., 30/11/17.
11 Watt, Robert, 2/Lt., k. in a., 10/8/17.
4 Weare, Frederick John, 2/Lt., d. of w., 9/10/18.
24 Webb, George Tudor, 2/Lt. (Tp.), k. in a., 21/4/16.
25 Webb, R. B., Major (Tp.), died, 26/7/16.

23 Wells, Frederick Bennett, 2/Lt., d. of w., 10/10/18.
2 Wells, Hurlestone Vesey, Capt., k. in a., 12/4/18.
2 Westaway, Leslie Thomas, 2/Lt. (Tp.), k. in a., 1/7/16.
11 Whiteman, Ormonde Charles, Capt. (Tp.), k. in a., 22/11/17.
Whitworth, James Frederick, Capt., k. in a., 21/3/18 (from W. York.).
7 Whittall, Noel Charles, 2/Lt. (Tp.), k. in a., 13/9/17 (att. R.F.C., 6 Sq.).
Whyte, Mark Gilchrist, 2/Lt., k. in a., 19/8/18.
Wickham, Cyril Henry, Capt., d. of w., 15/1/15.
15 Wiggen, Robert Harrison, M.C., 2/Lt. (Tp.), k. in a., 17/2/17 (att. 23/Bn.).
13 Wilcock, Maurice Nettleton, Lt., k. in a., 18/9/18.
2 Willett, Nelson Herbert, 2/Lt., k. in a., 11/4/18.
Williams, Idris Havard Joseph, Capt., d. of w., 3/6/15.
9 Williams, Rowland, 2/Lt., k. in a., 23/10/18.
7 Williams, Trevard Lewis, 2/Lt., k. in a., 30/10/17.
17 Williams, William Frederick, 2/Lt., k. in a., 27/9/18.
29 Wilmshurst, Edwin Roy, Lt. (Tp.), d. of w. 1/12/16 (att. 20/Bn.).
6 Wilshin, J. H., 2/Lt., d. of w., 25/4/18 (att. 1/Bn.).
4 Wilson, Arthur Hone, Lt., d. of w., 18/11/16 (att. 7/Bn.).
5 Wilson, Frederick Thomas Austen, 2/Lt., k. in a., 12/3/18 (att. 2/Bn.).
6 Withall, John, 2/Lt., k. in a., 7/10/16 (att. 8/Bn.).
38 Wolfe, Bernard, Lt. (Tp.), died, 20/7/18.
32 Wood, Hector Frederick, M.C., Capt., k. in a., 20/9/17.
19 Wood, Henry, 2/Lt. (Tp.), d. of w., 2/1/16.
5 Wood, Paul Barnard, Lt., k. in a., 23/4/17.
10 Woodcock, Cecil William Napier, 2/Lt., k. in a., 14/9/18.
6 Woodville-Morgan, Eric Theodore, 2/Lt., k. in a., 20-23/9/17 (att. 26/Bn.).
10 Wright, Cecil Keith Foyle, 2/Lt., k. in a., 21/8/18.
20 Wright, Eric Tracey, Capt. (Tp.), k. in a., 13/3/16.
1 Wright, George Bertram, 2/Lt., k. in a., 11/10/18.
26 Wright, Norman Stanley, 2/Lt, (Tp.), k. in a., 15/9/16.
Wright, Richard Bertram, 2/Lt., k. in a., 8/7/18 (att. 1/6 W. Yorks R.).
19 Wright-Ingle, Cecil Hubert, 2/Lt. (Tp.), k. in a., 30/4/16 (att. 2/Lein. R.).
13 Yandle, Thomas, 2/Lt. (Tp.), k. in a., 10/4/17.
Yellen, Cyril Francis, 2/Lt. (Tp.), k. in a., 30/11/17 (att. 17/Bn.).
7 Young, James Cecil, 2/Lt., k. in a., 6/4/18.
13 Young, Rowdon Morris, 2/Lt. (Tp.), k. in a., 11/8/16.

The King's (Liverpool Regiment).

18 Adam, Arthur de Bels, Capt. (Tp.), k. in a., 1/7/16.
12 Ainslie, Montague Forwood, Lt. (Tp.), d. of w., 17/5/16.
14 Anderson, Max Edward Alwyn, Temp. Capt., d. of w., 13/9/16.
4 Andrews, Frederick George, Lt., k. in a., 21/10/14 (att. S. Lan. R.).
13 Arundel-Smith, Harold Edward, 2/Lt., k. in a., 23/7/16.
13 Ashburner, Daniel, Temp. 2/Lt., k. in a., 10/12/16.
17 Ashcroft, Edward Stanley, Lt. (Tp.), d. of w., 12/5/18 (P. of W.).
Ashcroft, Frederick, 2/Lt. (Tp.), k. in a., 9/4/17 (att. 18/Bn.).
19 Ashcroft, William, Lt. (Tp.), k. in a., 22/3/18.
4 Aslachsen, Hector Shields, 2/Lt. (Tp.), k. in a., 23/4/17.
4 Atkin, George Dawson Hope, 2/Lt., d. of w., 16/7/16.
1 Atkinson, Fred., M.C., Temp. Capt., k. in a., 27-30/9/18 (att. 9th).
17 Averill, Thomas Hanson, 2/Lt. (Temp.), k. in a., 30/8/17.
4 Back, Louis William Alexander, 2/Lt. (Tp.), k. in a., 23/4/17.
11 Bailey, Ernest, 2/Lt. (Tp.), k. in a., 28/10/16.
15 Baillon, Gerald Wolstan, 2/Lt. (Tp.), k. in a., 25/9/15.
3 Baines, Kenneth James Mackenzie, 2/Lt., k. in a., 2/1/16.
1 Baird, William, 2/Lt. (Tp.), k. in a., 15/9/18.
3 Baker, Edward Benjamin, Lt., k. in a., 26/10/14.
18 Baker, Harry Leslie, M.C., T/Lt., k. in a., 8/11/18.
4 Ballinger, Francis Allan, 2/Lt., k. in a., 22/5/15.
17 Band, Lawrence, 2/Lt. (Tp.), k. in a., 28/4/17.
Bannatyne, William Stirling, Lt.-Col., k. in a., 24/10/14.
Bargh, George, 2/Lt., k. in a., 10/5/15 (att. Suffolk).
13 Barlow, Lovel Hardwick, Temp. 2/Lt., k. in a., 16/8/16.
19 Barlow, Percy, 2/Lt. (Tp.), k. in a., 15/11/17
18 Barnard, Norman Arthur Southard, 2/Lt. (Tp.), k. in a., 8/7/16.
17 Barnes, Aubrey, 2/Lt. (Tp.), k. in a., 22/3/18.
22 Barnes, Francis, 2/Lt. (Tp.), d. of w., 1/7/16.
13 Barratt, John Leslie, 2/Lt. (Tp.), k. in a., 27/9/17.
Batten, John Henry Strode, Capt., k. in a., 25/10/14.
17 Beaumont, Eric Paton, M.C., Temp. Lt., d. of w., 2/4/18.
3 Beck, Bernard, Temp. Capt., k. in a., 18/8/16.
1 Beesley, Edwin, M.C., T/2/Lt. (A/Capt.), k. in a., 27/9/18.
11 Bennett, Henry Ryan, Capt. (Tp.), k. in a., 23/3/18.
1 Bennett, William Frank, 2/Lt. (Tp.), k. in a., 23/4/17.
17 Berry, James Frederick Williamson, Lt. (Tp.), died, 22/11/18.
Bewes, Reginald Charles Hope, Lt., k. in a., 23/5/15 (and R.F.C.).
18 Bigg, Albert Charles, 2/Lt. (Tp.), k. in a., 31/7/17.
20 Black, David Hammond, 2/Lt., k. in a., 8/5/18.
15 Blake, Francis Seymour, T/Capt., k. in a., 1/7/16 (att. 2nd South Wales Borders.).
Blake, Reginald Howard, 2/Lt. (Tp.), k. in a., 1/6/18.
3 Bland, Percy Richard, Capt., k. in a., 3/5/17.
15 Blease, Harvey, T/Capt., k. in a., 7/8/15 (att. 7th Bn. Lan. Fus.).
13 Blinch, Wilfrid Joseph Hastings, 2/Lt., k. in a., 16/8/16.
Bloom, Bertram, 2/Lt. (Tp.), died, 30/6/18.
17 Bloore, Ronald Henry, T/Lt. (A/Capt.), k. in a., 28/4/18.
22 Bolton, Cecil Rawley, T/Capt., k. in a., 22/2/17.
19 Booth, Arthur Wilfred, 2/Lt. (Tp.), k. in a., 22/3/18.
17 Boundy, Frank Everard, T/Lt., d. of w., 30/7/16.
Bourke, James Gay Shute, 2/Lt. (Tp.), k. in a., 15/4/18 (att. 1st R. Warwicks.).
13 Bowman, Henry Arthur, 2/Lt., k. in a., 28/3/18.
Bowring, Frank Harvey, Major (Tp.), k. in a., 28/8/18 (att. 9th Bn.).
13 Bramley, Harry Brian, 2/Lt. (Tp.), d. of w., 15/7/18.
3 Broadhurst, Cecil Howard, 2/Lt., d. of w., 1/12/17.
18 Brockbank, Charles Norman, Capt. (Tp.), k. in a., 1/7/16.
2 Bulkley, Edmund Burke Mabbot, Capt., died, 13/11/16.
13 Burns, Percival Fossey Thackaberry, 2/Lt. (Tp.), d. of w., 21/3/17.
16 Burt, Frederick Stanley, T/Lt., d. of w., 21/2/17 (att. 6th N. Lancs.).
20 Butcher, Richard Norman, 2/Lt. (Tp.), d. of w., 5/8/16.
15 Calcott, Charles David, T/Lt., k. in a., 23/4/17.
14 Callaghan, Arthur Nickson, T/Lt., k. in a., 30/8/17.
12 Carefull, John Holt, Temp. Capt., k. in a., 21/3/18.
Carline, Thomas, Temp. 2/Lt., k. in a., 30/9/18 (att. 15th Lan. Fusiliers).
Carr, John Cory, Capt. & Qr. Mr., k. in a., 21/10/18 (att. 2/5th Bn.).
13 Carter, William Henry Seaman, T/Lt., k. in a., 14/7/16.
19 Carver, Harold Quinan, Lt. (Tp.), k. in a., 30/7/16.
13 Challener, Percival Crawley, T/2/Lt., k. in a., 12/12/17.
12 Charsley, Reginald Burton, T/Major, k. in a., 30/11/17.
17 Chavasse, Aidan, Lt., k. in a., 4/7/17.
11 Christie, Cedric Pasche, Temp. 2/Lt., d. of w., 16/12/15.
13 Clark, Archibald Strachan, Temp. 2/Lt., k. in a., 8/10/18.
Clery, Carleton Lumley St. Clair, 2/Lt., k. in a., 12/3/15.
13 Coates, Harold Edward, T/Major, k. in a., 3/5/17.
20 Cockey, John Edmund Percy, 2/Lt., k. in a., 30/7/16.
12 Collin, Kenneth Glenfield, 2/Lt. (Tp.), k. in a., 12/10/16.
16 Cook, Arthur Clifford, T/2/Lt., k. in a., 16/8/16.
12 Cooke, Harold Esmond, Capt., k. in a., 30/11/17.
3 Cooper, Edward George, Capt., k. in a., 4/8/16 (att. 1st King's Afr. Rifles).
18 Copland, George Harold, Temp. 2/Lt., k. in a., 31/7/17.
4 Corbridge, Arthur, M.C., Temp. 2/Lt., k. in a., 20/5/17.
12 Corish, Thomas Power, Temp. 2/Lt., k. in a., 16/9/16.
13 Corrigan, Francis Stanislaus, Lt. (Tp.), k. in a., 31/8/18.
17 Crook, Harry, 2/Lt., d. of w., 20/4/18.
1 Crosby, John Claude Parry, 2/Lt. (Tp.), d. of w., 21/1/18.
1 Cross, Alfred, 2/Lt., k. in a., 13/11/16.
1 Crowder, Harry, 2/Lt., k. in a., 14/3/17.
11 Crundwell, Alan, Lt., k. in a., 23/3/18.
3 Curlett, Patrick Alexander, Lt., k. in a., 3/7/15.
18 Davies, Lindsay Ramsay, 2/Lt. (Temp.), d. of w., 5/7/16.
4 Davies, Robert Glynne, Capt. (Temp.), k. in a., 14/8/16.
12 Davison, Robert, M.C., Lt., d. of w., 8/10/16.
18 Dawson, Gerald Moore, Lt. (Temp.), k. in a., 1/7/16.
13 Dawson, Norman Currey, Lt. (Temp.), k. in a., 28/3/18.
14 Day, Norman Leslie, 2/Lt. (Temp.), k. in a., 14/9/16.
20 Dean, Thomas Albert Wray, 2/Lt., d. of w., 8/5/18.
Denny, Barry Maynard Rynd, 2/Lt., d. of w., 26/10/14.
1 De Segundo, Robert Charles Edward Stewart, 2/Lt., k. in a., 17/2/17.
11 Dickson, Robert Maxwell, 2/Lt. (Temp.), k. in a., 22/3/18 (att. 8th Bn. The Rifle Brigade).
17 Dimond, Francis Robert, 2/Lt., k. in a., 31/7/17.
13 Dines, Joseph, 2/Lt. (Temp.), k. in a., 27/9/18.
Dinnen, Campbell Hackwood, Capt., k. in a., 4/3/18 (and W. Afr. R.).
17 Dixon, James Galloway, 2/Lt. (Temp.), k. in a., 12/10/16.
Doll, Philip Walter Rudolph, Lt., k. in a., 31/10/14.
12 Dow, John, 2/Lt. (Temp.), k. in a., 25/3/18.
17 Draper, Arnold Inman, T/Major, k. in a., 21/10/17.
13 Dundon, Sydney Jack, 2/Lt., k. in a., 16/8/16.
12 Dunn, Herbert Harman, Temp. Lt., k. in a., 26/9/16.
22 Eaton-Jones, Stafford Thomas, 2/Lt. (Temp.), k. in a., 28/10/16.
14 Eddison, Tom Denton, Lt., k. in a., 30/7/16.
Edwards, Frederick Thomas, M.C., 2/Lt. (Temp.), k. in a., 20/10/18.
12 Edwards, Harry, 2/Lt., k. in a., 7/10/16.
3 Edwards, James Tudor, 2/Lt., k. in a., 13/9/15.
11 Elliot, Hugh, Major, killed, 26/7/15.
1 Elliot, Hugh, Lt., died, 21/6/16 (att. 14th).
1 Erskine, Neil, 2/Lt., d. of w., 23/8/18.
1 Evans, Douglas Osmond, 2/Lt., k. in a., 8/8/16.
18 Ewing, Harold Gordon, Temp. 2/Lt., k. in a., 9/4/17.
17 Faris, Sturton Johnston, 2/Lt. (Temp.), k. in a., 30/7/16.
Feneran, Frank Edward, Capt., k. in a., 10/3/15.
2 Fieldhouse, Walter Benjamin, Temp. 2/Lt., died, 1/11/18.
12 Ford, Arthur Llewelyn, 2/Lt. (Temp.), k. in a., 27/9/15.
13 Foster, Leslie Arthur Clifford, Temp. 2/Lt., k. in a., 12/4/18.
1 Fraser, Campbell Robertson, 2/Lt., k. in a., 17/4/18.
19 Fraser, Wallace, T/Capt., k. in a., 30/7/16.
15 Freedman, Bertie, Temp. 2/Lt., k. in a., 3/7/17 (att. 1/9th Man. Regt.).
15 French, Bertram St. George, T/Capt.), k. in a., 1/7/16 (att. R. Innis. Fusiliers).
17 Friend, James Bertie, Temp. 2/Lt., k. in a., 21/8/18.
18 Fritzbrown, Eric, 2/Lt. (Temp.), k. in a., 1/7/16.
19 Furlong, Philip James, Temp. 2/Lt., k. in a., 30/7/16.
Furneaux, Phillip Templer, Lt., k. in a., 26/10/14.
4 Galloway, Graeme Stuart Montgomerie, Temp. 2/Lt., k. in a., 4/7/16.
Garland, Cecil William Robert, 2/Lt., k. in a., 20/2/18 (att. 1/7 Battn.).
3 Gaulter, Charles Pendrick, 2/Lt., k. in a., 18/8/16.
16 Gee, Herbert, Lt., k. in a., 10/7/15.
3 Gibb, George Calder, 2/Lt., k. in a., 17/4/18 (att. 4th Bn.).
13 Gibbons, Alfred St. Hill, Temp. Lt.-Col., d. of w., 15/7/16.
17 Gill, Rowland, M.C., M.M., 2/Lt., k. in a., 19/4/18.
1 Goff, Charles Edward, M.C., Lt.-Col., k. in a., 8/8/16.

18 Golds, Gordon Brewer, Temp. 2/Lt., k. in a., 1/7/16.
Goldspink, Edward Newell, Temp. 2/Lt., k. in a., 31/7/17.
13 Gollin, Edgar Bearman, Temp. 2/Lt., d. of w., 14/5/17.
4 Goodman, Claude Pendarvis, 2/Lt., k. in a., 18/8/16.
18 Graham, William James, Temp. 2/Lt., k. in a., 31/7/17.
3 Gray, Vivian, 2/Lt., k. in a., 18/8/16.
3 Green, Daniel Abbott, 2/Lt., k. in a., 13/11/16 (att. 1st Bn.).
20 Green, Robert Edward, 2/Lt., k. in a., 21/3/17.
15 Greenhalgh, Maurice Lomax, 2/Lt. (Temp.), k. in a., 25/9/15.
12 Gregory, Henry Vincent, Lt., k. in a., 15/3/17.
20 Grennan, Gerald Lismore, Temp. 2/Lt., k. in a., 12/10/16.
13 Grierson, John, Temp. 2/Lt., k. in a., 21/3/18.
18 Griffin, Douglas Morley, Temp. 2/Lt., d. of w., 16/7/16.
11 Griffiths, John Joseph, Temp. 2/Lt., k. in a., 23/3/18.
14 Haines, Ernest Edward, M.C., 2/Lt. (Temp.), died, 11/2/17.
3 Hampson, Frank, 2/Lt., k. in a., 30/11/17.
16 Handyside, John, Temp. 2/Lt., d. of w., 18/10/16.
1 Hannah, John George, 2/Lt., d. of w., 30/11/17.
3 Hannon, John Coulson, 2/Lt., k. in a., 18/8/16.
11 Hardman, Tom Walker, 2/Lt. (Temp.), k. in a., 18/7/17.
4 Harper, Gordon Phillip, 2/Lt., k. in a., 29/9/18.
Harrison, Frank Cyril, Temp. 2/Lt., d. of w., 4/5/18 (att. 1/5th Battn.).
3 Harrison, George Victor, M.C., Lt., d. of w., 26/8/18 (att. 1st Battn.).
17 Harrop, Tom, Temp. 2/Lt., k. in a., 28/4/18.
3 Harvey, William, 2/Lt., k. in a., 25/9/15.
Hawksworth, Stanley Harcourt, Temp. 2/Lt., k. in a., 20/9/17.
16 Haworth, Arthur, Temp. 2/Lt., k. in a., 19/7/16 (att. Machine Gun Corps).
3 Hayes, Leo John, 2/Lt., k. in a., 10/10/18.
Hayes-Newington, Harold May, 2/Lt., k. in a., 10/3/15.
3 Head, Raymond Evelyn, M.C., Lt. (A/Capt.), died, 24/11/18.
12 Heatley, Leonard, Capt. (Temp.), d. of w., 17/8/17.
17 Henry, Norman, M.C., Temp. Capt., k. in a., 8/5/18.
12 Hepworth, Henry James Jephson, 2/Lt., k. in a., 16/8/17.
18 Herdman, George Andrew, Temp. 2/Lt., k. in a., 1/7/16.
18 Hewett, Ernest Arthur Frederick, 2/Lt., k. in a., 28/3/18 (att. 2nd Essex Regt.).
19 Hick, Harold Crispen, 2/Lt. (Temp.), k. in a., 12/7/16.
17 Higgins, George Frederick, Major (Temp.), k. in a., 10-12/7/16.
Higgins, Stanley, Temp. 2/Lt., k. in a., 28/9/18.
14 Hilditch, Richard, Temp. Lt., k. in a., 14/9/16.
13 Hillyer, Philip Charles, Temp. 2/Lt., k. in a., 31/8/18.
3 Hirst, Gerald William, 2/Lt., k. in a., 26/2/17.
4 Hodgson, Richard Everleigh, Lt., k. in a., 16/9/18 (and R.A.F.).
13 Hollins, James P., Temp. Lt. & Qr.-Mr., died, 3/2/16.
4 Horbury, George Squire, Temp. 2/Lt., k. in a., 21/5/16
17 Hornby, William, Temp. 2/Lt., k. in a., 12/10/16.
15 Horner, Walter A., 2/Lt., died, 24/3/15.
17 Horser, Stanley Cottrell Seymour, T/Capt., k. in a., 12/10/16.
12 Horsfall, Robert Elcum, Capt. (Temp.), k. in a., 20/11/17.
3 Horton, Frank, M.C., 2/Lt., drowned, 10/10/18.
19 Hough, Eric Bernard, Capt., k. in a., 29/4/18.
Howson, C. J., Lt., died, 5/7/18 (and R.A.F.).
3 Hubble, Harry Ronald, 2/Lt., k. in a., 20/5/17 (att. 4th Batt.).
Hudson, Charles Herbert, 2/Lt., k. in a., 16/5/15.
Hughes, Albert Edward, 2/t., k. in a., 4/8/18 (att. 1/9th Batt.).
3 Hughes, Edward John, M.C., Lt., k. in a., 20/10/18 (att. 13th R.W. Fus.).
12 Hughes, William George, 2/Lt. (Temp.), k. in a., 23/7/18.
3 Hulme, Wilfred, Lt., died, 14/11/18 (att. 6th T.M.B.).
14 Humphrey, Idwal Ben, 2/Lt. (Temp.), d. of w., 14/9/16.
4 Hutchings, Kenneth Lotherington, Lt., k. in a., 3/9/16.
1 Hutchison, William Murray, Capt., d. of w., 27/4/16.
13 Innes, Alfred James, 2/Lt., k. in a., 3/5/17.
17 Ireland, Samuel James, Temp. 2/Lt., k. in a., 12/10/16.
3 Irving, Thomas Henry, 2/Lt., k. in a., 19/8/16.
4 James, Frederick, Temp. 2/Lt., k. in a., 20/5/17.
1 Jefferson, E. B. B., Capt., killed, 15/5/19 (att. R.A.F.).
14 Jennison, Alfred Denzil, Temp. 2/Lt., died, 17/9/16.
3 Jervis, Arthur Cyril, Lt. (T/Capt.), k. in a., 3/7/18 (att. K.A. Rif.).
12 Johnston, Alexander Vyvyan, Temp. Lt., k. in a., 18/8/17.
17 Johnston, William Holden, 2/Lt., k. in a., 30/7/16.
19 Jones, Hugh M., T/Lt., k. in a., 30/7/16.
17 Joseph, John Herbert, Temp. Capt., k. in a., 1/8/17.
20 Jowett, William Hall, Temp. 2/Lt., d. of w., 28/6/16.
Kenyon, John De Winton, 2/Lt., k. in a., 16/5/15.
14 King, Frank Radcliffe, Temp. 2/Lt., k. in a., 14/9/16.
1/2 Kinnear, J. L., D.S.O., M.C., Major, killed, 28/4/18 (and R.A.F.).
Kyrke-Smith, Arthur Kyrke, Capt., d. of w., 23/9/14.
19 Laird, Colin, T/Lt. (A/Capt.), k. in a., 20/9/17.
18 Lane, Frank Ashton, Temp. 2/Lt., k. in a., 31/7/17.
Last, Ernest Reginald, M.C., Capt., k. in a., 24/3/18.
1 Lauder, George Gordon, 2/Lt., k. in a., 30/7/16.
20 Laughlin, James Courtney, Temp. 2/Lt., k. in a., 1/7/16.
18 Lawson, Joseph, T/Lt. (A/Capt.), k. in a., 22/3/18.
13 Leak, Reginald, Temp. 2/Lt., d. of w., 14/7/16.
Leatherland, Percy John, 2/Lt. (Temp.), drowned, 10/10/18 (att. 3rd Bn.).
18 Lee, Robert Carswell, 2/Lt. (Temp.), k. in a., 4/11/18 (att. 10th Lan. Fus.).
19 Lloyd, Richard Glyn, Lt., k. in a., 13/9/16.
Lloyd, Robert Arthur, 2/Lt., k. in a., 27/4/15.
4 Lomas, John Henry, Temp. 2/Lt., k. in a., 30/8/16 (att. 98th T.M.B.).
1 Long, Frederick Edward, M.C., T/Capt., k. in a., 24/8/17.
15 Longley, Leslie Gordon, Temp. 2/Lt., k. in a., 12/7/16 (att. 19th Lanc. Fus.).
4 Lumsden, David Aitken, Capt., k. in a., 1/5/15.
15 Lunt, Arthur Towers, Temp. 2/Lt., d. of w., 17/8/16.
McCarthy, David, M.C., Lt., k. in a., 7/10/18.
13 McDonald, Alexander, Temp. 2/Lt., k. in a., 14/7/16.
19 McHale, John Richard Jarlath, Lt. (Temp.), k. in a., 24/3/18.
19 Mackie, Frank James, Temp. 2/Lt., k. in a., 29/5/17.
12 Mackie, James, T/Capt., k. in a., 10/4/16.
13 McVicker, John William, Temp. 2/Lt., k. in a., 14/7/16
Madden, Thomas Hylton, 2/Lt., k. in a., 10/3/15.
20 Maddick, Sidney Alfred, T/Lt., died, 1/12/18 (att. K. Af. Rif.).
3 Makinson, Frederick, 2/Lt., k. in a., 14/4/18.
1 Mansergh, Harry Read, T/Lt., d. of w., 12/11/16 (att. 9th Bn.).
Mapplebeck, Gilbert William, D.S.O., Lt. (T/Capt.), killed, 24/8/15.
16 Marsh, Nicholas Clayton, Temp. 2/Lt., k. in a., 25/9/15.
Marshall, Francis, Capt., d. of w., 30/9/14.
19 Mason, George William, T/Lt., k. in a., 9/4/17.
Marshall, H., Temp. 2/Lt., d. of w., 5/11/18 (att. 1/5th Battn.).
11 Marshall, William Cornelius, Temp. 2/Lt., k. in a., 29/9/18.
20 Mather, Robert, Temp. 2/Lt., k. in a., 27/3/18.
20 Melly, Reginald Ernest, Lt., k. in a., 30/7/16.
18 Merry, Ralph Valentine, T/2/Lt., k. in a., 1/7/16.
19 Milliken, Frank Stevens, Temp. 2/Lt., d. of w., 4/5/17.
13 Mitchell, Clement Alexander, T/Capt., k. in a., 13/10/16.
3 Mitchell, Guy Spencer, Temp. Major, k. in a., 15/5/17
13 Molony, Charles Albert, T/Capt., k. in a., 14/7/16.
1 Morgan, Victor Harold, Temp. Lt., k. in a., 6/9/17 (Garr. Bn.).
17 Morris, George Mackelvey, Temp. 2/Lt., d. of w., 7/9/16.
16 Morris, William Oliver Ernest, Temp. 2/Lt., k. in a., 17/6/16.
1 Morrison, Leslie, Capt., k. in a., 25/3/18 (att. 1/7th Lanc. Fus.).
Morten, Galbraith, 2/Lt., k. in a., 16-19/5/15.
11 Mulroy, Thomas Bernard, Temp. 2/Lt., died, 23/1/16.
21 Murdoch, Ronald Hamilton William, Temp. 2/Lt., k. in a., 28/10/16 (att. 4th Bn.).
20 Musker, Joseph Walter, Temp. 2/Lt., k. in a., 30/7/16.
12 Myers, Wilfrid Herman, Temp. Capt., died, 10/4/16.
Nelson, William Jackson, Temp. 2/Lt., k. in a., 27-30/9/18 (att. 9th Bn.).
4 Nichols, Arthur Robert, M.C., Capt., k. in a., 23/10/18.
4 Nickalls, Edward Gilbert, Temp. 2/Lt., k. in a., 18/8/16.
20 Nickel, George Gaston, Temp. 2/Lt., k. in a., 31/7/17.
19 Nickson, William, Capt., k. in a., 30/7/16.
O'Donoghue, Humphrey Patrick, 2/Lt., k. in a., 10/3/15.
1/2 Openshaw, Fred, Temp. 2/Lt., d. of w., 8/10/18 (att. 8th Bn.).
20 Orford, Ernest Charles, Temp. Capt., k. in a., 30/7/16.
18 Orme, Alfred Lyth, 2/Lt. (Temp.), k. in a., 31/7/17.
16 Ormesher, William, Temp. Lt., d. of w., 7/12/15 (att. 2nd R. Fus.).
Parkin, Thomas Henry, Lt. (T/Capt.), d. of w., 4/10/18.
Parberry, Ernest, 2/Lt., k. in a., 27/9/18 (att. 1st North. Fus.).
Parkinson, Albert, 2/Lt., k. in a., 9/4/18 (att. 1/5th Battn.).
12 Parle, John Audley, M.C., 2/Lt. (A/Capt.), k. in a., 30/11/17.
15 Parry, John Stanley, 2/Lt. (Temp.), k. in a., 14/7/16.
20 Paterson, Robert Denzil, Lt. (Temp.), k. in a., 12/10/16.
1 Patey, Robert Thomas, M.C., Lt. (A/Capt.), k. in a., 20/5/17.
12 Pearson, Evelyn Henry Malcolm, Capt. (Temp.), killed, 8/1/16.
12 Percy, Raymond, Lt. (A/Capt.), d. of w., 12/8/18.
17 Peters, Cyril Aubrey, Temp. 2/Lt., k. in a., 4/7/17.
13 Phillips, Joseph Alexander, Lt., k. in a., 3/5/17.
Phipps, Constantine James, D.S.O., M.C., Lt. (T/Capt.), died, 19/2/19.
4 Pocock, Thomas Guy, 2/Lt., d. of w., 3/4/15.
17 Porritt, Edward Radcliffe, Temp. 2/Lt., k. in a., 30/7/16.
3 Pratt, John Armstrong, M.C., Lt., k. in a., 23/8/18.
Profit, Lodwig Tudor, Temp. 2/Lt., d. of w., 20/6/18 (att. 2/6th Battn.).
13 Purdon, Robert Gordon, 2/Lt., k. in a., 16/8/16.
11 Pye-Smith, Phillip Howson Guy, T/Lt., k. in a., 15/5/17.
18 Ravenscroft, Guy, T/Capt., k. in a., 18/10/16.
4 Reid, John, Temp. 2/Lt., k. in a., 18/8/16.
1/2 Reid, Robert, 2/Lt., d. of w., 14/5/17.
12 Rice-Jones, Alfred Theodore, T/Capt., d. of w., 23/3/18.
3 Rich, John Stanser, Lt., k. in a., 16-19/5/15.
16 Riddell, David Moore, 2/Lt. (Temp.), died, 23/9/17.
3 Roberts, Frederick John, Temp. Capt., k. in a., 28/9/15.
Roberts, John, Temp. 2/Lt., k. in a., 14/9/18.
4 Ross, John Edgar, Capt., d. of w., 25/4/16.
Ryan, James Henry Aloysius, Lt. (T/Capt.), k. in a., 25/9/15.
17 Ryder, Charles Ernest, Hony. Lt. & Qtr.-Mtr. (Temp.), died, 6/11/15.
19 Salisbury, Robert Cecil, T/Capt., k. in a., 22/3/18.
13 Scoones, Earl Foster, Temp. 2/Lt., k. in a., 23/11/16.
17 Scott, Dudley Holme, T/Lt., d. of w., 2/7/16.
Seddon, Frank Augustus, 2/Lt., k. in a., 30/11/17 (att. 1/8th Battn.).
13 Segal, Marcus, 2/Lt. (Tp.), k. in a., 19/6/17.
19 Sergiades, John Nicholas, Lt., k. in a., 30/7/16.
3 Sharpe, Anthony Herbert, Lt. (A/Capt.), k. in a., 25/9/17.
19 Sharples, George Woods, T/2/Lt. (A/Lt.), k. in a., 7/6/17.
Shaw, Charles Salisbury, 2/Lt. (Tp.), d. of w., 30/9/18.
Shaw, Gerald Alan Santor, 2/Lt. (Tp.), k. in a., 1/7/17.
18 Sheard, Fraser Morton, M.C., Capt. (Tp.), d. of w., 2/4/18 (P. of W.).
13 Simkin, Horace John, Capt. (Tp.), d. of w., 14/7/16.
4 Simmance, Allan James Spencer, Capt. (Tp.), k. in a., 18/8/16.
18 Sinclair, William, 2/Lt. (Tp.), k. in a., 18/10/16.
16 Slaughter, Arthur Charles, 2/Lt. (Tp.), d. of w., 23/8/16.
20 Small, Hugh Alexander, 2/Lt. (Tp.), k. in a., 10/7/16.

12 Smethurst, John, 2/Lt. (Tp.), k. in a., 16/9/16.
19 Smith, Herbert Leslie, Capt. (Tp.), k. in a., 24/3/18.
15 Smith, Jas. Norman, 2/Lt. (Tp.), k. in a., 31/7/16.
Smith, John, 2/Lt. (Tp.), k. in a., 20/7/18 (att. 5/Devon R.).
17 Smith, Ralph Henry, 2/Lt. (Tp.), k. in a., 30/7/16.
4 Soden, Harold Corbet, Lt., k. in a., 22/5/16.
18 Sparks, Robert William, M.C., 2/Lt. (Tp.), k. in a., 29/4/18.
12 Spears, Alexander, 2/Lt. (Tp.), k. in a., 18/8/17.
17 Sproat, James McCosh, 2/Lt., k. in a., 17/7/16.
13 Stainforth, George, 2/Lt. (Tp.), k. in a., 14/7/16.
18 Statton, Percival Graham, 2/Lt. (Tp.), d. of w., 18/4/17.
22 Stewart, James, 2/Lt., k. in a., 28/10/16.
19 Sutton, Geoffrey Storrs, M.C., Capt. (Tp.), k. in a., 23/3/18.
1 Swallow, John Reginald, 2/Lt., k. in a., 8/8/16.
3 Sweet-Escott, Murray Robertson, Lt., k. in a., 20/9/14.
Tanner, Ralph Eyre, Capt., d. of w., 23/9/14.
1 Tarran, Reginald Stuart, M.C., 2/Lt., k. in a., 24/3/18.
19 Taylor, Norman Leopold, 2/Lt. (Tp.), d. of w., 18/9/16.
12 Taylor, Robert Leslie, 2/Lt., k. in a., 30/11/17.
4 Tharratt, George Vanes, Lt., drowned, 17/11/15.
13 Thomas, Bryn Atherton Brodie, 2/Lt. (Tp.), k. in a., 16/8/16.
12 Thompson, Arthur Ernest, 2/Lt. (Tp.), k. in a., 3/9/16.
1 Thompson, Aubrey Lloyd Sinclair, M.C., Lt. (A/Capt.), died, 14/11/17.
12 Thompson, George Eric, 2/Lt (Tp.), k. in a., 3/9/16.
11 Thomson, George Frederick Maynard, 2/Lt. (Tp.), d. of w., 19/5/17.
1 Tisdall, John Theo. St. Clair, 2/Lt, k. in a., 8/8/16 (att. 11/Bn.).
1 Tomlinson, Dan, 2/Lt. (Tp.), k. in a., 10/8/18.
18 Tomlinson, Robert Henry, 2/Lt. (Tp.), d. of w., 19/7/16.
2 Towers, Grainger Malcolm, Lt., d. of w., 20/1/16.
Tripp, Arthur William Howard, Brev.-Col., died, 6/5/17.
14 Turton, Thomas Charles, 2/Lt. (Tp.), k. in a., 8/5/17.
18 Twenlow-Allen, William Alfred, 2/Lt. (Tp.), k. in a., 18/10/16.
1/2 Urinowski, Alexander, 2/Lt., d. of w., 25/8/18 (and R.A.F.).
4 Varndell, Leslie John, 2/Lt. (Tp.), d. of w., 18/9/16.
3 Vaughan, Donald, 2/Lt., k. in a., 30/10/17.
20 Vaughan, John, 2/Lt. (Tp.), k. in a., 30/7/16.
19 Vaughan-Roberts, Richard William, Lt. (Tp.), k. in a., 30/7/16.
Vick, Sidney Francis, 2/Lt. (Tp.), k. in a., 20/9/17.
18 Villar, Robert Peter, Capt., k. in a., 22/3/18.
12 Vince, Arthur Neville, Lt.-Col., k. in a., 21/3/18.
17 Wainwright, Henry Carrey, Lt. (Tp.), d. of w., 5/2/16.
15 Wakeley, William Norman, 2/Lt., k. in a., 8/5/17 (att. M.G.C.).
18 Walker, Turner Russell, 2/Lt. (Tp.), d. of w., 2/7/16.
3 Wallace, Harold Bruce, 2/Lt., k. in a., 26/10/14.
18 Wane, Hayward, 2/Lt. (Tp.), k. in a., 18/10/16.
Warburton, Gergoe Harold Edmonson, M.C., Lt. (A/Capt.), k. in a., 17/4/18.
Ward, Arthur, 2/Lt., k. in a., 17/10/14.
Ware, Denys C., Capt. killed, 20/9/18 (and R.A.F.).
11 Wareing, William Robert Alexander, Capt., k. in a., 23/3/18.
21 Watson, Arthur Paton, 2/Lt. (Tp.), d. of w., 13/10/16.
3 Watson, Henry Trelss, Capt., d. of w., 6/3/15 (att Manch. R.).
17 Watson, William Erskine, 2/Lt., k. in a., 24/3/18.
3 Webb, Horace Maitland Turner, Lt., k. in a., 10/3/15.
3 Webster, Sidney Herbert, 2/Lt., k. in a., 30/11/17.
3 Wheeler, Henry Thornton Camden, Capt., died, 30/10/16 (Commd. Gold Coast).
Wheen, John, Capt., k. in a., 15/5/15.
White, Basil Walwyn, 2/Lt. (Tp.), 8/4/17 (att. R.F.C., 35 Sqd.).
1 Whiteside, Robert Parkinson, 2/Lt (Tp.), k. in a., 28/4/17.
Whiting, Reginald Cunningham, 2/Lt. (Tp.), d. of w., 31/5/17.
20 Whiting, Thomas, Capt. (Tp.), k. in a., 30/7/16.
13 Whitley, William George, 2/Lt. (Tp.), k. in a., 16/8/16.
4 Whitrod, Roper Henry, 2/Lt., k. in a., 28/5/18.
12 Whittington, George Edgar, 2/Lt., k. in a., 30/11/17.
20 Wilkinson, Geoffrey Ellison, 2/Lt. (Tp.), k. in a., 30/7/16.
1 Williams, Gordon Percy, 2/Lt., k. in a., 16/4/18.
4 Williams, John Victor, 2/Lt., k. in a., 26/9/17.
Williams, Joseph Stephenson, M.C., Lt. (A/Capt.), k. in a., 25/9/17.
1 Williams, Thomas Langley, 2/Lt., k. in a., 1/9/18.
Williams, William Henry, 2/Lt., k. in a., 22/3/18 (att. 1/7 Bn.).
3 Williams, Walter Patrick, 2/Lt., k. in a., 17/4/18 (att. 4/Bn.).
19 Willmer, Walter, Capt. (Tp.), k. in a., 13/7/16.
3 Wilson, Ernest Albert, 2/Lt., k. in a., 6/9/18 (att. 1/Bn.).
3 Wilson, Frank, 2/Lt., k. in a., 3/6/16 (att. 1/Bn.).
18 Withy, Basil, Lt. (Tp.), d. of w., 2/7/16.
12 Wolley-Dod, Douglas Kirk, Lt. (Tp.), k. in a., 25/9/15.
20 Woodin, Walter Guise, 2/Lt. (Tp.), k. in a., 30/7/16.
12 Woods, Eric Evelyn, 2/Lt., d. of w., 18/5/18.
Wright, Frederick John, 2/Lt. (Tp.), d. of w., 4/8/17.
13 Wynne, Arnold, 2/Lt. (Tp.), k. in a., 8/4/17.
Young, Philip Mortlock, Lt., k. in a., 10/3/15.

The Norfolk Regiment.

Abel, Frederick, 2/Lt. (Tp.), drowned, 30/12/17.
8 Adams, Ernest Geoffrey, 2/Lt. (Tp.), d. of w., 26/6/18.
Adams, William John, 2/Lt., drowned, 30/12/17.
10 Alexander, John William Ewart, 2/Lt., died, 14/4/16.
7 Allen, Merwyn Richard William, 2/Lt. (Tp.), k. in a., 2/8/17.
Armstrong, Gwin Henry, Lt., died, 28/10/18 (att. Nigeria R.).
8 Attenborough, John Haddon, 2/Lt. (Tp.), k. in a., 1/7/16.
8 Ayre, Bernard Pitts, Capt. (Tp.), k. in a., 1/7/16.
Backhouse, Gerald Lovell, 2/Lt., killed, 2/8/16 (and R.F.C.).
Balders, Arthur William, Capt., k. in a., 27/11/15 (att. W.A.F.F., Nigeria R.).
7 Barton, George Frank, 2/Lt. (Tp.), k. in a., 10/4/17.
9 Barton, Hugh Fabian, 2/Lt. (Tp.), k. in a., 12/2/16.
9 Bashforth, John Francis Cuthbert, 2/Lt. (Tp.), k. in a., 15/9/16.
1 Bates, Arthur William, 2/Lt., k. in a., 30/3/16.
Bell, Francis de Beauvoir, Major, d. of w., 24/4/15.
8 Benn, Bertie William, 2/Lt. (Tp.), k. in a., 19/7/16.
7 Benn, Walter Horace, 2/Lt. (Tp.), k. in a., 2/8/17.
1 Benton, Sydney, 2/Lt. (Tp.), k. in a., 27/10/17.
10 Bice, William Francis, 2/Lt. (Tp.), k. in a., 4/9/16.
Bickmore, David Francis, D.S.O., Lt. (A/Lt.-Col.), k. in a., 19/7/18.
10 Bird, Percy Charles Hilton, 2/Lt. (Tp.), k. in a., 5/4/16 (att. 6/L.N. Lanc. R.).
10 Blagden, Robert, 2/Lt. (Tp.), d. of w., 15/5/16 (att. 7/Bn.).
3 Boast, Thomas, 2/Lt., killed, 29/9/18.
10 Bollond, John Wulstan Charles, 2/Lt. (Tp.), k. in a., 9/4/17.
7 Bonham, William Daniel, 2/Lt. (Tp.), k. in a., 14/10/17.
Boosey, Frederick Cecil, Lt., k. in a., 22/11/15.
Bowlby, Thomas Rupert, Capt., k. in a., 17/9/14.
1 Bradshaw, Harold James, 2/Lt. (Tp.), d. of w., 18/5/17 (P. of W.).
9 Bray, Reginald Boydon, 2/Lt. (Tp.), k. in a., 23/10/18.
Briard, Ernest Felix Victor, Capt., k. in a., 24/8/14.
1 Brown, Edwin Percival Wildman, Lt., k. in a., 4/9/16.
1 Brown, Thomas, 2/Lt., k. in a., 4/9/16.
3 Brown, W. J. H., Capt., k. in a., 4/9/16.
Brownrigg, John Huleath, Lt., k. in a., 14/4/15.
3 Brumbley, Walter James, M.C., 2/Lt., k. in a., 27/3/18 (att. 7/Bn.).
9 Brunger, Robert, D.S.O., Capt., k. in a., 8/10/18.
3 Buckell, Christopher James Allardyce, 2/Lt., k. in a., 19/4/17.
7 Buckland, Thomas Adrian, Lt. (Tp.), k. in a., 18/10/15.
8 Bunting, William, M.C., Capt. (Tp.), k. in a., 11/8/17.
1 Burlton, George Philip, Lt., k. in a., 5/6/16.
Butler, Owen James, 2/Lt. (Tp.), k. in a., 16/10/18.
8 Byrne, Hugh Vyvian Edward, M.C., Capt. (Tp.), k. in a., 15/4/18.
9 Cadge, William, Lt. (Tp.), k. in a., 26/9/15.
3 Cameron, Hume Smith, Capt., k. in a., 4/9/16.
7 Carley, Henry Victor, 2/Lt. (Tp.), d. of w., 14/10/15.
2 Carr, Dudley Reed, Lt., k. in a., 23/2/17.
10 Carter, George Thomas, 2/Lt. (Tp.), k. in a., 10/3/16.
7 Case, Frederick Marcus Beck, 2/Lt. (Tp.), k. in a., 10/8/16.
8 Case, John Wyatt, 2/Lt. (Tp.), k. in a., 21/10/16.
7 Chaland, Maurice L., M.C., Lt. (Tp.), d. of w., 1/12/17.
7 Charlton, Arthur Nesbit, M.C., Lt. (T/Capt.), k. in a., 30/11/17.
10 Chilvers, Reginald Cuthbert, 2/Lt. (Tp.), k. in a., 19/4/17.
1 Clarke, Francis Arthur, 2/Lt. (Tp.), k. in a., 31/7/16.
3 Clarke, George Henry, 2/Lt., k. in a., 22/4/18 (att. 1/Bn.).
3 Clements, Louis Walter, A/Capt., k. in a., 9/10/17.
10 Coath, Leonard Charles, 2/Lt., k. in a., 4/9/16 (att. 1/Bn.).
1 Cocksedge, Robert James, 2/Lt., k. in a., 25/9/18.
3 Coleman, Eric, 2/Lt., k. in a., 31/7/17 (att. M.G.C.).
3 Coleman, Fred Creighton, 2/Lt., k. in a., 23/4/17 (att. 1/Bn.).
7 Collins, William Geoffrey, Lt., d. of w., 21/1/18 (P. of W.).
Cooke, Sydney Philip, 2/Lt., died, 4/11/18.
Cresswell, Francis Joseph, Capt., k. in a., 24/8/14.
7 Curwen, Henry Stanley, 2/Lt. (Tp.), k. in a., 13/10/15.
8 Cutbill, Bernard, Capt. (Tp.), died, 24/3/18 (P. of W.).
3 Davis, Herbert Gough, Lt., k. in a., 14/2/15.
9 De Caux, William, T/Capt., k. in a., 15/9/16.
1 Dickinson, Leslie Alfred, 2/Lt. (Tp.), d. of w., 17/11/17.
7 Digby, John Kenelm, Lt., k. in a., 4/8/15.
9 Dye, George Harry Gordon, Lt. (Tp.), d. of w., 21/11/17.
1 Edwards, Leo, 2/Lt., died, 8/6/16
Entwistle, Frederick, 2/Lt., k. in a., 9/10/17.
9 Everett, William Wallis, Capt. (Tp.), k. in a., 9/10/18
9 Failes, Gerald Watson, D.S.O., M.C., Capt (Tp.), k. in a., 15/4/18
Farebrother, Harcourt Sutcliffe, Capt. (Tp.), d. of w., 24/7/16.
2 Farquharson, Hugh Joseph, 2/Lt. (Tp.), died, 27/8/16
9 Faulke, William James, Lt. (Tp.), k in a., 21/3/18
10 Flagg, Allston, Capt. (Tp.), k. in a., 26-27/9/15 (att. 1st 58/Rifles).
Foley, Thomas Algernon Fitzgerald, Lt., k. in a, 25/10/14.
1 Fox, Harry Norton, 2/Lt. (Tp.), k. in a., 23/4/17.
Fox, James John, 2/Lt. (Tp.), k. in a., 11/9/18 (att 12/Bn.).
9 Frederick, Thomas, M.C., Capt. (Tp.), d. of w., 14/12/17.
7 Gielgud, Henry Lex Francis Adam, M.C., Major (A/Lt.-Col.), k. in a., 30/11/17.
9 Glanfield, Gordon, 2/Lt (Tp.), k in a., 12/11/15.
Glanville West, Herbert, 2/Lt. (Tp.), k. in a., 19/8/18 (att. 12/Bn.).
7 Goddard, Alex Spencer, 2/Lt, k. in a., 30/11/17.
9 Goddard, John Lister, Lt. (Tp.), k. in a., 15/9/16.
9 Goodman, Basil Harris, 2/Lt., k. in a., 25-27/9/15
7 Goosens, Adolphe Antony, Lt., d. of w., 17/8/16.
7 Graham, Duncan Charles, Capt., k. in a., 28/4/17.
7 Green, Arthur Percival, Lt. (Tp.), k. in a., 6/7/16.
Griffiths, Lewis Herbert, 2/Lt. (Tp.), k. in a., 11/9/18 (att. 12/Bn.).
Grissell, Bernard Salwey, D.S.O., Major (T/Lt.-Col.), k. in a., 19/4/17 (att. 1/5 Bn.).
7 Haig-Smellie, Herbert Hamilton, 2/Lt. (Tp.), d. of w., 26/4/17
1 Hall, Geoffrey Evans, 2/Lt. (Tp.), k. in a., 25/4/17.
2 Hall, Humphrey Evans (T/Capt.) Lt., k. in a., 27/11/15.
3 Hampton, William Orr, 2/Lt., k. in a., 1/7/16 (70/M.G.Co.).
9 Hancock, John Eliot, D.S.O., Capt. (Tp.), k. in a., 21/3/18.
Hayter, Arthur Cecil Thomas, Lt., d. of w., 1/11/14.
3 Hewitt, Arthur Kidman, 2/Lt. (Tp.), k. in a., 20/9/17 (att. 1/8 K. L'pool. R.).

7 Hewitt, Thomas, 2/Lt., k. in a., 27/3/18.
9 Hill, John Edward, Capt. (Tp.), d. of w., 24/3/18 (P. of W.).
1 Hoare, Frank William, 2/Lt., k. in a., 23/4/17.
7 Hogben, Frank, 2/Lt. (Tp.), k. in a., 12/10/16.
3 Hood, Percy Charles 2/Lt., d. of w., 20/9/18 (att. 1/5 Bn.).
Hullett, William Ernest. 2/Lt. (Tp.), d. of w., 7/12/17 (att. 7/Batt.).
8 Inch, Robert Stuart Mark, M.C., Lt. (Tp.), k. in a., 22/10/17.
7 Izard, George Henry, 2/Lt. (Tp.), k. in a., 10/8/18 (att. 35 L.T.M.B.).
10 Jephson, Edward Jermy, Capt. (Tp.), k. in a., 15/9/16.
7 Johnson, Geoffrey Barham, Capt. (Tp.), k. in a., 23/11/15.
9 Jones, Cyril Gordon, Lt. (Tp.), k. in a., 20/11/17.
7 Jones, Walter Joseph, Lt. (Tp.), d. of w., 15/10/17.
1 Jones-Bateman, Lloyd Newton, C.M.G., Lt.-Col., died, 25/7/17.
Joyce, Alexander Hugh Sinclair, M.M., 2/Lt. (Tp.), d. of w., 20/8/18 (att. 12/Batt.).
9 Kendall, Locke Francis William Angerstein, Lt. (Tp.), d. of w., 22/11/17 (att. 11/M.G. Sqd.).
3 Kerkham, Francis Leslie, 2/Lt., k. in a., 14/10/17 (att. 7/Bn.).
3 King, Edward Roly Capt., d. of w., 23/4/18.
7 Lancaster, Robert, 2/Lt. (Tp.), k. in a., 28/4/17.
Lane, Shales Frederick, Capt. (Tp.), k. in a., 18/9/18 (att. 9/Batt.).
Last, Leonard Walter, 2/Lt., k. in a., 22/8/18.
Lawrence, John George, 2/Lt., died, 15/2/18 (att. 2/West India R.).
9 Lewington, Frank Samuel, 2/Lt. (Tp.), k. in a., 21/3/18.
8 Lewton-Brain, James Andrew, 2/Lt. (Tp.), d. of w., 14/8/17.
9 Lightbody, Wilfred Petre, Lt. (Tp.), k. in a., 26/9/15.
3 Ling, Leonard Simpson, 2/Lt., k. in a., 23/4/17.
3 Longfield, John Percival, M.V.O., Capt., k. in a., 30/9/15.
1 Lorimer, John Scott, M.C., 2/Lt. (T/Capt.), k. in a., 5/11/17 (att. 95/Trench Mortar Bty.).
Luard, Charles Elmhirst, D.S.O., Major, k. in a., 15/9/14.
8 Macnicol, Harry Mansfield, Lt. (Tp.), k. in a., 19/7/16.
7 Maddison, Geoffrey, 2/Lt. (Tp.), k. in a., 28/8/18.
1 Magnay, John Christopher Frederick, Lt., k. in a., 23/4/17.
Maltby, Charles Thomas, 2/Lt. (Tp.), d. of w, 27/3/18 (att. 7/Bn. Suff. R.).
7 Manners, Henry Fairholm, 2/Lt. (Tp.), k in a., 28/4/17.
8 Marsh, Harry Victor, 2/Lt (Tp.), d. of w., 22/10/16.
1 Martin, Ernest William, 2/Lt (Tp.), k. in a., 27/7/16.
1 Martin, Rowland Hill, C.B., C.M.G., C.I.E., Bt. Col., died, 31/1/19 (Garr. Bn.).
Megaw, William Cecil Kennedy, Capt., k. in a., 31/3/15.
9 Meire, Walter Herbert Geoffrey, 2/Lt. (Tp.), k. in a., 26/9/15.
3 Miall-Smith, George Eric, Lt., k. in a., 25/3/17 (and R.F.C., 11 Sqd.).
10 Mitchley, Sydney Robert, 2/Lt. (Tp.), k. in a., 12/10/16.
Molloy, Joseph G., M.C., 2/Lt. (Tp.), k. in a., 2/9/18.
8 Morgan, Walter Chapman, 2/Lt. (Tp.), k. in a., 19/7/16.
9 Nancarrow, William Thomas, 2/Lt. (Tp.), k. in a., 15/4/18.
7 Nash, Charles Frederic Wybrow, M.C., Capt., killed, 27/3/18.
Northcote, George Barons, Capt., d. of w., 4/12/15.
Norton, Richard Legge, 2/Lt., k. in a., 18/9/18 (att. 9/Bn.).
1 O'Connor, Arthur Cathal, Capt. (Tp.), k. in a., 27/7/16.
Openshaw, Harold Michael, Lt., d. of w., 28/8/14.
Orr, John Boyd, D.S.O., Major, d. of w., 24/8/14.
Otter, Robert John Charles, Capt., d. of w., 15/2/15.
9 Page, John Canler, 2/Lt., k. in a., 18/10/16.
9 Page, Thomas Spencer, 2/Lt. (Tp.), k. in a., 19/10/16 (att. 71 T.M.B.).
7 Parish, William Harry, 2/Lt. (Tp.), k. in a., 30/11/17.
3 Peden, George Edward, 2/Lt., k. in a., 25/3/17 (att. 133 M.G.Co.).
Penn-Gaskell, Leslie Da Costa, Lt. (T/Major), died, 4/2/16 (and R.F.C.).
7 Peyton, John Algernon Wynward, Lt., k. in a., 22/8/18.
9 Phelps, Wilfred John, Lt., k. in a., 15/9/16.
7 Preston, Philip Chamberlayne, Capt. (Tp.), k. in a., 13/10/15.
7 Procter, Charles Edgecumbe, Lt. (Tp.), k. in a., 2/8/15.
9 Randall, Frank Horace, 2/Lt. (Tp.), k. in a., 18/7/17.
Read, Terrance Capon, 2/Lt. (Tp.), d. of w., 22/4/17 (att. 1/5 Bn.).
10 Riches, Percy William, 2/Lt. (Tp.), died, 6/12/15.
3 Ritchie, Richard Ayres, Lt., k. in a., 22/11/15 (att. 2/Bn.).
9 Robinson, Charles Surtees, Capt. (Tp.), d. of w., 13/9/16.
10 Row, Leslie Joseph, 2/Lt. (Tp.), k. in a., 4/6/16.
Rushbrook, Sydney Herbert, 2/Lt., k. in a., 6/7/15 (att. Cyc. Corps).
3 Russel, Arthur Richard, Lt., k. in a., 25/12/15.
10 Sarsby, Reginald Ambler, 2/Lt. (Tp.), k. in a., 21/12/15.
9 Selfe, Edgar Donald, Capt. (Tp.), k. in a., 7/8/18.
3 Sharp, Christopher Harold, 2/Lt., died, 26/9/18 (and R.A.F.).
9 Shaw, Albert, 2/Lt. (Tp.), k. in a., 12/10/16.
8 Shelton, Charles, Capt., k. in a., 21/10/16.
7 Shepherd, Charles Arthur, 2/Lt. (Tp.), k. in a., 12/10/16.
7 Sizeland, Charles, 2/Lt. (Tp.), k. in a., 12/10/16.
3 Smith, Bernard Alfred, 2/Lt., d. of w., 16/4/18.
7 Smith, Harold, 2/Lt., k. in a., 12/10/16.
Soddy, James, 2/Lt. (Tp.), k. in a., 23/4/17.
8 Spencer, Gerald William Suckling, 2/Lt. (Tp.), d. of w., 24/2/16.
9 Sprott, Maurice William Campbell, M.C., Capt. (Tp.), k. in a., 21/3/18.
4 Steward, J. H., Major, died, 10/5/15.
Stone, Frank Ablett, 2/Lt. (Tp.), k. in a., 20/9/17 (att. 1/8 K. L'pool R.).
8 Symonds, Frederick George, 2/Lt. (Tp.), k. in a., 22/10/17.
Teeling, Ambrose Mary Anthony Twibide de Lone, Lt., k. in a., 24/9/14.
7 Thorn, Humphrey, 2/Lt., d. of w., 13/10/16.
10 Thouless, Archibald Cecil, 2/Lt. (Tp.), k. in a., 26/4/16 (and R.F.C.).
7 Tilley, John, Capt. (Tp.), k. in a., 28/11/16.
3 Todd, Alexander Findlater, Capt., d. of w., 21/4/15.
1 Trafford, Edmond Thyrkel, Lt. (Tp.), died, 10/5/16 (Garr. Batt.).
10 Tucker, Edwin George, 2/Lt. (Tp.), k. in a., 13/10/15.
Tucker, Samuel William Joseph Brocklehurst, 2/Lt. (Tp.), d. of w., 13/9/18 (att. 2/5 K.O.R.L.R.).
Turton, Zouch Austin, Lt., k. in a., 23/4/15 (att. E. Yorks).
Tyler, Guy Cromwell, T/Lt. (A/Capt.), k. in a., 22/8/18.
1 Walsha, Albert Arthur, Lt., k. in a., 18/9/18.
Ward, Arthur Edward Martyr, Capt., k. in a., 12/8/15.
9 Webber, Frederick Henry, M.C., 2/Lt., d. of w., 24/10/18.
9 Wellesley, Edmund Ernest Charles, Capt. (Tp.), k. in a., 30/4/16.
1 West, Edward Lynn, Capt. (Tp.), k. in a., 31/7/16.
8 Wharton, Sidney Alfred, 2/Lt. (Tp.), d. of w., 1/7/16 (att. Trench Mortar Bty.).
9 White, Cecil Wilson Morton, 2/Lt. (Tp.), k. in a., 26/9/15.
3 Whitmore, Harry Cyril, 2/Lt., killed, 8/8/18 (att. 94 T.M.B.).
8 Whitty, Thomas, 2/Lt., k. in a., 5/10/16.
8 Williamson, Wilford Robert, M.C., Lt. (Tp.), d. of w., 14/8/17.
3 Wilson, Laurence Cecil, 2/Lt., d. of w., 12/8/15.
9 Wright, William Sidney, 2/Lt., k. in a., 21/3/18.
Wroughton, Herbert, 2/Lt. (Tp.), k. in a., 8/12/17.
Wynn, Richard Alexander, 2/Lt., k. in a., 14/4/15.

The Lincolnshire Regiment.

2 Abbott, Clifford Hewson, 2/Lt. (Tp.), d. of w., 7/5/17.
1 Allan, Wallace, Capt., died, 29/6/16 (Garr. Bn.).
Anderson, Bernard Gordon, M.C., Lt. (Tp.), d. of w., 8/8/16.
6 Andrews, J. A. R., 2/Lt., killed, 14/4/18 (and R.A.F.).
Andrews, Leigh Courtney, 2/Lt. (Tp.), k. in a., 3/7/16.
2 Anstee, Joseph, 2/Lt., k. in a., 1/7/16.
1 Applin, Geoffrey Walter Henry, 2/Lt. (Tp.), k. in a., 1/7/16.
3 Askey, Cecil Henry Leonard, 2/Lt., d. of w., 5/4/18.
Baines, Arthur Edward Carrow, Lt., k. in a., 9/4/16 (att. R. Welsh Fusrs.).
Baines, John Hugh, 2/Lt. (Tp.), k. in a., 3/7/16.
Baker, Tom, Capt. (Tp.), k. in a., 1/7/16.
10 Bannister, Henry William, 2/Lt. (Tp.), k. in a., 14/6/17.
Barlow, Cuthbert Charles Lambert, Major, k. in a., 1/11/14.
Barnes, Eric, 2/Lt., k. in a., 1/11/14.
3 Barnicot, John Livingston, 2/Lt., k. in a., 22/12/16.
1 Barrett, Jack Harper Phillip, Lt., died, 1/11/18 (and R.A.F.).
Barrett, Thomas Cyril, 2/Lt. (Tp.), d. of w., 4/7/16.
1 Bartram, William Elliott, Lt., d. of w., 1/5/17.
Battle, Arthur Newsum, 2/Lt. (Tp.), k. in a., 10/11/15 (att. R. Lanc.).
Bavin, Geoffrey Wynne, 2/Lt., killed, 1/4/16 (att. R.F.C.).
Beaver, Leslie Arnold, 2/Lt. (Tp.), k. in a., 21/9/18.
10 Bellamy, Charles Henry, Capt. (Tp.), d. of w., 23/7/16.
Black, Eric Osborne, Lt., k. in a., 9/5/15.
3 Bloomer, Arnold Grayson, Lt., d. of w., 3/8/17.
2 Bloomer, Guy Howard Walmesley, 2/Lt. (Tp.), k. in a., 5/9/18.
8 Bosworth, Arthur Wright, 2/Lt., k. in a., 26/9/15.
8 Bosworth, Philip Charles Worthington, Lt., k. in a., 26/9/15.
Bott, Charles Stuart, 2/Lt., k. in a., 17/4/17.
3 Bowen, Leslie Harold, Lt., k. in a., 22/12/15.
Bowlby, George Elliott Lowe, T/Capt., k. in a., 15/3/16.
Box, Philip John Murray, Lt. (Tp.), k. in a., 7/8/15.
Boxer, Hugh Edward, D.S.O., Major, k. in a., 16/6/15.
Branfoot, Clayton, 2/Lt. (Tp.), k. in a., 25/8/17.
3 Bransbury, Vernon Dudley Bramsdon, Lt., k. in a., 25/10/14.
Brice-Smith, John Kenneth, 2/Lt. (Tp.), d. of w., 11/9/15.
1 Brock, Percy Douglas, 2/Lt., k. in a., 29/5/18.
1 Brown, Arthur, 2/Lt. (Tp.), d. of w., 5/10/17.
Brown, Benjamin Ewart, A/Capt., k. in a., 9/9/16 (att. R. Mun. Fus.).
Brown, Francis, M.C., 2/Lt. (Tp.), k. in a., 5/4/18 (att. T.M.B.).
Brown, Frederick William Archer, 2/Lt. (Tp.), k. in a., 25/4/18.
Brown, George West, Lt., died, 23/2/18 (Garr. Bn.).
Brown, Phillip Kentish, 2/Lt., k. in a., 13/10/15.
Browne, Percival Leathley, Capt., k. in a., 9/8/15.
2 Budibent, Cecil, 2/Lt. (Tp.), k. in a., 25/9/15.
Buller, Lesley Montague, Lt., k. in a., 24/8/14.
Burton, Alfred Henry Wellesley, Capt., k. in a., 23/10/16.
2 Bush, Alfred John, Temp. 2/Lt., k. in a., 31/7/17.
Busher, Denis John Bryan, Temp. 2/Lt., k. in a., 24/4/17.
Butler, George Victor, Lt. (Tp.), k. in a., 23/3/18.
Carr, Robert Meredith, Temp. Lt., k. in a., 29/5/18.
8 Carre, Edward Mervyn, T/Lt., k. in a., 16/10/16 (att. R.F.C.).
1/2 Chambers, William Geoffrey, Capt., k. in a., 15/5/18 (and R.A.F.).
Childerhouse, Francis James, Temp. 2/Lt., k. in a., 23/9/16 (att. E. York. Regt.).
Clifford, Hugh Gilbert Francis, Lt., k in a., 1/7/16.
1 Clough, Walter, 2/Lt., k. in a., 18/9/18.
Coates, Harold, Capt., k. in a., 25/9/15.
3 Cocks, Willard Fleetwood, T/Lt., d. of w., 9/4/17.
3 Cooper, Clarence Edwards Nooth, Lt., k. in a., 16/9/16 (and R.F.C.).
2 Coneybeare, Herbert William, Temp. 2/Lt., d. of w., 24/10/16.
Cordiner, Roy Grote, M.C., Temp. Capt., k. in a., 4/10/17.
Cook, Robert Leslie, 2/Lt., k. in a., 7/8/15.
Corke, Frederick William, 2/Lt., k. in a., 10/4/18.
8 Courtice, Reginald Leyster, Temp. 2/Lt., k. in a., 2/7/16.

Cowan, Basil Terence Reilly, Lt., k. in a., 6/8/15 (att. Manch. Regt.).
Cowie, Arthur William Spring, Temp. 2/Lt., k. in a., 8/7/16.
Crabtree, William, 2/Lt., died, 10/2/15.
Cragg, John Francis, 2/Lt. (Tp.), k. in a., 1-3/7/16.
Crawley, Albert, 2/Lt. (Tp.), d. of w., 9/5/17.
Croft, George Wheeler, Lt. (Tp.), k. in a., 16/2/18 (and R.F.C.).
Crouch, Augustus Barton, Temp. 2/Lt., k. in a., 27/4/17.
10 Cummins, Leslie, Temp. 2/Lt., k. in a., 1/7/16.
1 Currie, William George, 2/Lt., k. in a., 22/3/18.
Davey, Charles Richard, M.C., M.M., Temp. 2/Lt. (A/Capt.), d. of w., 30/10/18.
3 Davis, Horace John, 2/Lt., k. in a., 6/2/17.
Dawson, Herbert Edward, Capt., k. in a., 14/9/14.
2 Day, Gerald Philip, Lt., d. of w., 26/9/16.
2 De Cann, Harold John, Temp. 2/Lt., k. in a., 29/7/16.
De Houghton, Vere, Capt., k. in a., 11-13/10/15.
Denis-Marklew, Leslie Ernest, 2/Lt., d. of w., 12/10/17.
Denning, John Edward Newdigate Poyntry, 2/Lt. (A/Capt.), d. of w., 26/10/16.
Dickinson, George Sidney, T/Capt., k. in a., 2/7/16.
2 Dickinson, Hubert John, 2/Lt., k. in a., 20/9/16.
Dickinson, Walter Stanley, Temp. 2/Lt., k. in a., 23/4/17.
Dickson, Edwyn David, Lt., k. in a., 28/4/17.
Downes, Gilbert George, T/Capt., d. of w., 11/8/15.
1 Drake, Robert Edward, Capt., d. of w., 8/9/14.
Drought, Charles Frederick, Capt. (Tp.), d. of w., 31/12/15.
2 Drysdale, Joseph Dudley, Lt. (Tp.), k. in a., 23/10/16.
Dunn, William, 2/Lt. (Temp.), k. in a., 24/3/18.
Du Plergney, Victor Wilder, 2/Lt., d. of w., 18/4/18.
1 Depuis, Alfred, 2/Lt., d. of w., 8/8/16.
Eadie, Robert Allan, 2/Lt. (Tp.), k. in a., 6/8/16.
Eason, Raymond Praed, Lt. (Tp.), d. of w., 1/7/16.
3 Edmondson, Kenneth James, T/Capt., k. in a., 4/6/16.
1 Edwards, Edward, M.C., A/Capt., k. in a., 21/3/18.
Edwards, Lancelot, Major, d. of w., 15/4/15.
2 Eld, Arthur William, T/Lt., k. in a., 19/4/17.
Elsom, Harold, 2/Lt., k. in a., 28/4/17.
3 Fairweather, Leslie John Edgar Cuthbert, Lt. (Tp.), d. of w., 19/3/16.
Falkner, Leonard, Lt., k. in a., 25/9/15.
Farrar, Fred, Temp. 2/Lt., d. of w., 4/10/17.
Fenwick, Anthony Lionel, T/Lt. (A/Capt.), k. in a., 16/2/18.
2 Fergusson, Kenneth Mountney James, Lt., k. in a., 31/7/17.
10 Finnerty, Wilfrid Edward, 2/Lt., k. in a., 22/3/18.
1 Fisher, John, 2/Lt., d. of w., 17/4/18.
Forge, Arthur Fyfe, Temp. 2/Lt., k. in a., 4/10/17.
Foster, John Cecil, M.C., T/Capt., k. in a., 20/8/17.
Fraser, D'Arcy McKenzie, Major (Tp.), k. in a., 7-11/8/15.
3 Fripp, John Trude, 2/Lt., k. in a., 13/10/15.
1 Gale, Henry James, 2/Lt., k. in a., 21/3/18.
Gaul, Ernest, Temp. 2/Lt., k. in a., 23/10/18 (att. Leic. Regt.).
Gayer, Edward John, 2/Lt., k. in a., 4/10/17.
Gibson, Walter Reginald, 2/Lt., k. in a., 4/10/17.
Graham, John Arthur, Temp. Major, k. in a., 20/3/16.
3 Grantham, E. M., Capt., k. in a., 27/2/15.
2 Grantham, Richard Aubrey Fuge, Temp. 2/Lt., k. in a., 4/3/17.
Green, Frank Clifford, 2/Lt., k. in a., 16/6/15.
2 Griffin, Basil Walker, 2/Lt. (Tp.), d. of w., 2/12/17.
7 Grosvenor, T., Temp. Lt., k. in a., 17/9/17 (and R.F.C.).
2 Gwyn, Reginald Augustine Jerome, 2/Lt., d. of w., 3/3/16.
Hadrill, Arthur William, Temp. Lt., k. in a., 12/8/15 (att. R. Mun. Fus.).
Hall, Harold, Temp. 2/Lt., k. in a., 15/2/16.
Hanning, James Henry Rowland, 2/Lt., k. in a., 26/9/15.
Harper, John Boughton, Temp. 2/Lt., k. in a., 12/10/17.
Harris, Joseph Walter, Lt., k. in a., 2/6/15.
3 Harrison, Herbert William, 2/Lt., d. of w., 9/6/17.
Harrison, John Henry, Temp. 2/Lt., killed, 31/8/16.
7 Hayward, Charles Oswald, T/Lt., k. in a., 18/1/16 (and R.F.C.).
10 Hendin, Harold Percival, Lt., k. in a., 28/4/17.
1 Herapath, Randolph Fitz Roy Boehm, Lt. (A/Capt.), k. in a., 3/7/16.
Hewart, Gordon Morley, Temp. 2/Lt., k. in a., 9/5/15.
1 Hills, Laurance Clifford, Temp. 2/Lt., k. in a., 3/7/16.
1 Hilton, Fawcett, Temp. 2/Lt., k. in a., 3/7/16.
Hirons, William John, Temp. 2/Lt., k. in a., 21/3/18.
Hodgson, Hamilton, Capt., k. in a., 6/5/15 (att. Hants Regt.).
1 Holmes, Cecil Crampton, Lt. (T/Capt.), d. of w., 26/8/14.
Hooper, Henry Hoskin, Temp. 2/Lt., k. in a., 28/8/18.
Hornsby, Ridiard Lionel, 2/Lt. (Tp.), k. in a., 7-11/10/15.
1 Hoskyns, Henry Charles Walter, D.S.O., Major, k. in a., 25/9/15.
1 Howley, Jasper Joseph, D.S.O., Major, k. in a., 11/3/15.
Hunter, William Stuart, 2/Lt. (Tp.), k. in a., 31/7/17.
Huntington, Nigel Jocelin Searanche, Lt., k. in a., 17/11/14.
1 Impey, John Eugene, Lt., k. in a., 27/3/16 (att. M.G.C.).
2 Ingersoll, James Hamilton, 2/Lt., k. in a., 29/9/16.
Ingle, Roland George, Temp. 2/Lt., k. in a., 1/7/16.
Inman, Edwin, Lt., k. in a., 1/7/16.
Jacobs, Henry Houston, 2/Lt., k. in a., 25/9/15.
Jarvis, William Simpson, 2/Lt. (Tp.), k. in a., 8/11/18.
Jeudwine, Spencer Henry, Capt., k. in a., 1/7/16.
1 Jeynes, Harry, M.C., M.M., 2/Lt. (Tp.), k. in a., 22/3/18.
1 John, Lennox William McClure, 2/Lt., d. of w., 24/9/16.
Jolley, John Andrew Benjamin, 2/Lt. (Tp.), k. in a., 11/10/15.
Jones, Alfred Cotton, M.C., Capt. (Tp.), k. in a., 2/7/16.
Jones, Douglas Llewellyn, T/Lt., k. in a., 22/8/17.
Jones, Gwilym, 2/Lt. (Tp.), k. in a., 10/9/18.
2 Jones, Lawrence Bertram, 2/Lt., k. in a., 23/10/16.

Kimber, Basil Liddon, 2/Lt. (Tp.), k. in a., 10/7/16.
King, Robert Neal, Capt., k. in a., 1/11/14.
3 Kirk, Gerard Arthur, Lt., d. of w., 20/7/16.
Knell, William, Hon. Major Qtr.-Mstr., died, 22/7/17.
9 Labbett, John William Hooper, Temp. 2/Lt., k. in a., 25/1/17.
1 Larkin, James, 2/Lt., k. in a., 25/12/16.
Lavender, John Elliott, 2/Lt., k. in a., 28/4/17.
8 Lee, Holdsworth, Temp. 2/Lt., d. of w., 31/5/17.
1/2 Letts, John Herbert Towne, Capt., killed, 11/10/18 (and R.A.F.).
1 Levi, Frederick Joseph, 2/Lt., k. in a., 21/3/18.
Lewis, John Thorpe, T/Capt., k. in a., 9/8/15.
1 Ley, Maurice Aden, Lt., k. in a., 1/11/14 (att. E. Kent Regt.).
3 Lish, John Robertson, 2/Lt., k. in a., 4/10/17.
Lluellyn, Raymond Chester, T/Capt., k. in a., 13/8/18.
Lockyear, Horace, 2/Lt., k. in a., 20/5/18.
3 Losh, James Norman Merryweather, 2/Lt., k. in a., 4/10/17.
Love, Ronald Barclay, Temp. 2/Lt., k. in a., 15/3/16.
3 Lucking, Frank Horatio, 2/Lt., k. in a., 28/4/17.
Lummis, Ralph, 2/Lt., k. in a., 4/10/17.
Lyall, Charles Genie, Capt., killed, 18/10/14.
2 McAndrew, George Burbury, Lt.-Col., k. in a., 14/3/15.
McClay, Samuel Whitfield, 2/Lt., d. of w., 4/10/17.
McKellar, Frederick Charles Marshal, M.C., Temp. 2/Lt., k. in a., 21/8/18.
Margetts, Percy Alexander, Temp. 2/Lt., k. in a., 5/12/15.
3 Marshall, George Leonard, Lt., d. of w., 26/9/15.
Maulkinson, Harry Young, Temp. 2/Lt., d. of w., 4/6/17.
Manterfield, John Thomas, 2/Lt., k. in a., 21/9/18 (att. M.G.C.).
2 Meyer, Constant Clifford William, Lt., d. of w., 3/7/16.
2 Monat-Biggs, Eric, 2/Lt., k. in a., 3/5/16.
Montague, Felix David, Lt., k. in a., 10-16/3/15.
Moody, Henry Fred, 2/Lt., k. in a., 5/4/18.
3 Morris, William Harold, 2/Lt., died, 23/11/17.
1 Moss, Leonard George, 2/Lt., k. in a., 21/3/18.
Mulcuck, Daniel Henry, 2/Lt., k. in a., 11/10/17.
10 Murphy, Hugh Palmer, T/Lt., k. in a., 6/8/16.
Nainby, William, 2/Lt., k. in a., 27/5/18 (att. 62 L.T.M.B.).
7 Naylor, Cyril Doughty, M.C., Temp. 2/Lt., k. in a., 25/8/18.
2 Needham, Benjamin Llewellyn, Temp. Capt., k. in a., 1/7/16.
3 Neilson, Douglas Francis, D.S.O., M.C., Lt. (A/Capt.), k. in a., 16/4/18.
Nevile, Bernard Philip, Capt. (Tp.), k. in a., 11/2/16.
1 Newland, Herbert Basil, Temp. 2/Lt., d. of w., 18/3/16.
Nightingale, Frank Leslie, Temp. 2/Lt., k. in a., 19/12/15.
Nisbett, Robert Douglas Morton, Lt., k. in a., 9/5/15.
O'Reilly, Gerald Joseph, 2/Lt. (Tp.), d. of w., 30/11/16.
Ormesher, Herbert, Lt. (Tp.), k. in a., 4/10/15.
Overton, Thomas Darwin, Temp. Lt., k. in a., 30/7/15.
3 Owen, Ernest Haddon, 2/Lt., k. in a., 21/12/14 (att. S. Wales Bdrs.).
Parker, Gerrard William, Lt. (Tp.), d. of w., 29/9/15.
Parker, Rupert Hardy, Lt., k. in a., 2/12/17.
Parkin, Thomas Gregory, 2/Lt. (Tp.), k. in a., 9/8/15.
Parkinson, James Herring, Temp. 2/Lt., k. in a., 2/7/16.
Parsloe, William Henry, M.C., Temp. Capt., k. in a., 8/11/18.
Peadon, Percy Hewitt, 2/Lt. (Tp.), d. of w., 7/4/18.
Peake, Cecil Gerald Wyatt, Lt. (T/Capt.), k. in a., 10/3/15.
Peake, Kenneth John Wyatt, Lt., k. in a., 9/8/15.
Pearson, Reginald Oswald, 2/Lt., k. in a., 16/6/15.
Peddie, Alexander William Ponsonby, Capt., k. in a., 13/9/14.
3 Peel, Walter Sidney, M.C., Lt., killed, 27/9/18. (and R.A.F.).
2 Penfold, Edward Norman, Lt., k. in a., 29/5/18 (att. Leic. Regt.).
Penn, Thomas, 2/Lt., k. in a., 15/4/18.
Phillips, John Noel, Capt., d. of w., 18/4/15.
1 Pippet, John Gilbert, M.M., 2/Lt., k. in a., 29/5/18.
Pitt, William Neville, T/Major, d. of w., 20/8/16.
Prangley, Charles Dean, 2/Lt., k. in a., 25/9/16.
Pratte, Arthur Williams Staples, T/Lt., k. in a., 6/8/16.
7 Pritchard, Francis James, Temp. 2/Lt., k. in a., 15/11/17.
Rahles-Rahbula, Arnold James, T/Capt. (2/Lt.), k. in a., 28/4/17.
Rankin, John, 2/Lt. (Tp.), k. in a., 23/4/17.
6 Read, Cyril de Lacy, Lt. (Tp.), died, 5/3/19.
Renshaw, Percy Connaught, Temp. 2/Lt., d. of w., 24/7/18 (att. Lanc. Fus.).
2 Ritchie, Frank Johnstone, Temp. 2/Lt., k. in a., 23/10/16.
Roberts, Charles Edward, 2/Lt., d. of w., 10/10/16.
Roberts, David, M.C., Capt. (Tp.), d. of w., 23/4/17.
2 Robertson, William Maxwell, Lt., died, 28/6/15.
3 Robilliard, Francis Humphrey John, 2/Lt., k. in a., 4/10/17.
3 Robinson, Frederick Henry, M.C., Lt., k. in a., 30/9/17 (att. Nigerian Regt.).
Robinson, John Edward, Temp. 2/Lt., k. in a., 3/11/16.
Ross, Douglas Stuart, Lt., k. in a., 1/7/16.
Rushton, William Henry, Lt. (A/Capt.), k. in a., 25/9/16.
Shankster, Stanley, 2/Lt., k. in a., 3/7/16.
Sharp, Leon Owen, Temp. 2/Lt., k. in a., 1/7/16.
10 Sharpe, Robert, M.C., 2/Lt., d. of w., 12/9/18 (att. 2nd Batt.).
1 Shaw, Clarence Gordon, Lt., k. in a., 1/7/16.
2 Shaw, George, Temp. 2/Lt., k. in a., 12/4/18.
1 Shaw, Harold Lee, Temp. 2/Lt., k. in a., 9/6/16.
2 Shearman, Herbert Henry, Lt., d. of w., 5/7/16.
3 Sherwell, Rex, 2/Lt., k. in a., 3/7/16 (and R.F.C.).
Shorter, Vernon Banbury, Capt., d. of w., 28/9/17 (att. R.W. Surr. Regt.).
Simons, George Henry, 2/Lt. (Tp.), k. in a., 26/8/17.
Slidel, Sydney Robert, Temp. (2/Lt.), d. of w., 20/4/18.
1 Smith, Albert Edward, 2/Lt., k. in a., 22/3/16.
2 Sowerby, Victor Holgate, 2/Lt. (Tp.), d. of w., 31/7/17.
2 Spicer, Cecil Wilfred, Temp. 2/Lt., k. in a., 23/11/16.

Stephens, Ernest Stanley, 2/Lt. (Temp.), k. in a., 6/7/17.
1 Stephenson, Urban Arnold, Lt., k. in a., 23/3/18.
3 Stevens, George Kellner, 2/Lt., k. in a., 4/6/16.
Stockdale, Norman Henry, Temp. 2/Lt., k. in a., 18/9/16.
Storer, John Young, Major, k. in a., 25/9/15.
7 Stream, John Harvey, T/Lt., k. in a., 19/2/18 (and R.F.C.).
Stromquist, Sydney Goodwin, Temp. Capt., k. in a., 26/9/15.
Swann, Humphrey Nisbet, Capt., died, 4/4/17 (Staff, 15th Corps).
Swift, William, Temp. 2/Lt., k. in a., 1-3/7/16.
1 Tapsell, William Algernon, D.C.M., M.M., 2/Lt., d. of w., 18/9/18.
7 Taylor, Ernest, Temp. 2/Lt., d. of w., 7/9/18.
3 Taylor, James Irvine, M.C., 2/Lt., k. in a., 28/4/17.
Tedder, Oswald Stanley, 2/Lt., k. in a., 27/4/18.
Thomas, John Simons, Temp. 2/Lt., k. in a., 27/8/17.
Thompson, Herbert Balfe, T/Capt., k. in a., 18/9/16.
Thruston, Bertie John, D.S.O., Capt. (T/Maj.), died, 22/11/18 (att. W. Afr. Regt.).
Tilbury, Herbert Walter, Temp. 2/Lt., k. in a., 5/9/18.
3 Tillett, John Edward, Lt., k. in a., 8/10/18.
3 Tindall, Richard Frederick, 2/Lt., k. in a., 25/9/15.
1 Tollemache, Leo De Orellana, Capt., k. in a. 1/11/14.
Toller, George Reginald, Temp. Lt., died, 27/7/17 (Gar. Btn.).
2 Toolis, James Hollingworth, Lt., k. in a., 1/7/16.
8 Topham, James, Capt. & Adjt., k. in a., 26/9/15.
2 Truby, George Edward, 2/Lt. (Tp.), k. in a., 31/7/17.
Von Poellnitz, Herman Walter, Capt. (T/Maj.), killed, 11/5/18 (and R.A.F.).
Wade, Samuel Shorten Arthur, 2/Lt., k. in a., 8/12/14.
Wade, Sidney, 2/Lt. (Tp.), died, 26/10/18.
Waldron, Cecil Hamersley, T/Lt., k. in a., 2/3/16.
Walley, George John, 2/Lt., d. of w., 25/8/18.
Wallis, Walter Kelburne, Lt., died, 17/7/18 (att. E Lancs. Regt.).
8 Walter, Harold Ernest, Capt. (T/Lt.-Col.), d. of w., 29/9/15 (P. of W.).
Ward, George Arthur Ernest, 2/Lt., k. in a., 20/10/18.
Webb, Edward Charles Harry, 2/Lt., k. in a., 10/3/15.
6 Webber, Lynden, T/Lt., k. in a., 9/8/15.
1 Webster, Henry Hellyer, 2/Lt., k. in a., 14/4/18.
Weekes, Walter, Temp. 2/Lt., k. in a., 23/4/17.
8 Welch, John Eric Haddon, 2/Lt., k. in a., 25/9/15.
1 Welchman, Eric Hewelyn, Lt., k. in a., 24/8/14.
2 Wellesley, Cyril Gerald Valercan, Capt., k. in a., 14/3/15.
1 Wells-Cole, William Francis, 2/Lt., k. in a., 31/7/17.
Wensley, Frederic Martin, Temp. 2/Lt., k. in a., 5/8/16.
1 Wensley, Harold William, 2/Lt., died, 15/11/18.
3 Westoby, Reginald Herbert, 2/Lt., k. in a., 4/10/17.
Whinney, Frederich Stoddart, M.C., Capt., died, 17/3/19.
3 Whitaker, Victor John, Lt., k. in a., 6/4/17 (att. R.F.C.).
White, John Robert, Temp. 2/Lt., k. in a., 23/4/17.
Wickham, John Dobree Durrell, Capt., d. of w., 22/6/15.
6 Wickham, Lister Darell, T/Capt., k. in a., 3/7/16.
3 Williams, Leonard Charles, 2/Lt., d. of w., 10/11/17.
Williams-Freeman, Anthony Peere, Capt., d. of w., 4-5/4/16.
3 Wipf, John Jacob, 2/Lt., k. in a., 8/10/18.
Wiseman, Willingham Franklin Gell, Capt., k. in a., 1/7/16.
Woodiwiss, Isaac Newton, 2/Lt., k. in a., 10/5/15 (att. R.F.C.).
10 Worthington, Frederick, Temp. Capt., k. in a., 28/4/17.
Wright, Thomas, Temp. 2/Lt., k. in a., 13/10/15.
Wroe, Wilfred Dent, Lt. (Tp.), k. in a., 13/10/15.
3 Wyatt, Arthur Thomas Elford, Capt., died, 19/2/17.
Wylie, Arthur William, Lt., k. in a., 10-16/3/15.
3 Young, Frederick Henry, M.C., Lt. (A/Capt.), 25/8/18.

The Devonshire Regiment.

1 Abell, Albert Reginald, 2/Lt. (Tp.), died, 10/6/17 (P. of W.).
9 Adamson, Travers Farrant, 2/Lt. (Tp.), k. in a., 1/7/16.
Ainslie, Denys Alfred Lafone, Lt., k. in a., 24/10/14.
Allen, Frederick John, 2/Lt. (Tp.), k. in a., 25/9/15.
Anderson-Morshead, Rupert Henry, D.S.O., Capt. (A/Lt.-Col.), k. in a., 27/5/18.
Andrews, James Alfrey, Capt., k. in a., 1/7/16.
Anstey, George Alexander, Capt., k. in a., 24/6/15 (att. Cheshire Regt.).
2 Archer, Harry, D.S.O., Lt. (A/Major), k. in a., 25/11/17.
Arnold, Henry, 2/Lt., d. of w., 10/10/18 (att. 9 Bn.).
8 Ashcroft, Ernest, Lt. (Tp.), k. in a., 25/9/15.
9 Austen, George Alan, 2/Lt., k. in a., 26/10/17.
Balderson, Henry Leslie Paxton, 2/Lt. (Tp.), k. in a., 23/7/16 (att. Glouc. Regt.).
2 Bates, Reginald Plumptre, Lt., k. in a., 10/3/15.
2 Baxter, Gordon Eyre, 2/Lt. (Tp.), k. in a., 8/10/18.
1 Bazalgette, William Thomas Arnold, 2/Lt., k. in a., 9/5/17.
Beaumont, John Barrie, 2/Lt. (Tp.), k. in a., 20/10/18.
2 Beddow, Cecil Victor, 2/Lt. (Tp.), k. in a., 1/7/16.
9 Bedford, Rowland, M.C., Temp. Lt., k. in a., 13/9/18.
9 Bell, Cuthbert Patrick, Lt. (Tp.), d. of w., 23/2/18.
Bellamy, David Humphrey, T/Lt. (A/Capt.), k. in a., 2/4/17.
8 Bellwood, Frank, Temp. Capt., k. in a., 14/7/16.
Besly, Barton Hope, Capt., k. in a., 25/10/14.
1 Blake, John Morgan, 2/Lt., k. in a., 4/10/17.
1 Blunt, Duncan Hamilton, D.S.O., Major (Temp. Lt.-Col.), k. in a., 3/10/17.
Boyd, Robert Colin, Lt. (T/Capt.), k. in a., 14/7/16.
Bragg, Frederick John, 2/Lt. (Tp.), d. of w., 25/9/17 (att. King's L'pool Regt.).
9 Bridgewater, Arthur Sidney, M.C., 2/Lt. (Tp.), k. in a., 8/10/18.
8 Bridson, John Paul Ridgway, 2/Lt., k. in a., 25/9/15.
2 Bristowe, Robert Owen, Lt., k. in a., 10/3/15.
Brock, Algernon Bertram, 2/Lt., d. of w., 26/10/17.
Brock, Cecil Howard, Temp. Lt., d. of w., 4/11/18.
Brutton, Eric West, M.C., Lt., k. in a., 14/4/18 (and M.G.C.)
Butt, George, Lt. & Qr.-Mr. (Hon.), died, 6/6/17.
1 Bush, Frederick Charles, 2/Lt., d. of w., 9/5/17.
Caleb, Clement Daryl Nicoll, Temp. 2/Lt., k. in a., 2/4/17.
Carden, Henry Charles, D.S.O., Major, k. in a., 25/9/15.
Cardew, Richard Cornelius Arthur, 2/Lt., k. in a., 24/4/18.
2 Carey, Leonard Arthur, 2/Lt. (Tp.), k. in a., 1/7/16.
Carlton, Claude Gray, 2/Lt., k. in a., 26/10/17.
Carrick, Richard Hamilton, Temp. 2/Lt., k. in a., 2/4/17.
Carter, Alfred John, Temp. 2/Lt., k. in a., 13/5/17.
Carter, Walter James Coe, Temp. 2/Lt., k. in a., 14/7/16.
2 Carthew, Sydney George, 2/Lt., k. in a., 26/3/18.
Carver, Frank Maitland, Lt. (Tp.), k. in a., 25/9/15.
2 Carver, George Sholto Douglas, 2/Lt., k. in a., 1/7/16.
Cary, Launcelot Sulyarde Robert, Temp. 2/Lt., k. in a., 20/7/16.
3 Chichester, Henry Arthur, Capt., k. in a., 20/10/14.
11 Clark, Henry Featherstone, T/2/Lt. (T/Lt.), k. in a., 3/5/17 (att. 2/6 Glouc. Regt.).
1 Clifton, Hubert Everard, M.C., 2/Lt., d. of w., 4/10/16.
Clough, Ernest Rowan Butler, 2/Lt., d. of w., 27/6/16 (att. 11/D.L.I.).
Cohen, John Icely, Temp. Capt., d. of w., 11/8/17.
2 Coldwells, Francis Baker, 2/Lt., k. in a., 1/7/16.
9 Cole, Humphrey Portevs, 2/Lt. (Tp.), d. of w., 3/4/16.
3 Cook, Reginald William, M.C., 2/Lt., k. in a., 1/9/18.
Copner, Arthur Bruce, Lt., k. in a., 25/9/15.
Corbett, Harry, 2/Lt., k. in a., 23/7/16 (att. Glouc. Regt.).
8 Corbishley, Ronald Heathcote, Temp. 2/Lt., k. in a., 28/7/17 (and R.F.C., 57 Sq.).
Cornelius, Frank Stuart, M.C., Temp. 2/Lt., k. in a., 3/10/17.
Cottle, Sidney Joseph, Temp. Lt., k. in a., 31/7/17 (att. M.G.C.).
3 Cox, Eustace Richard Alan Calthrop, M.C., Capt., died, 18/3/17.
Croxson, Sidney, Temp. 2/Lt., died, 16/9/16.
Cumming, Lionel George, Temp. 2/Lt., k. in a., 9/5/17.
Dale, Arthur, 2/Lt., k. in a., 25/9/16.
Davidson, Robert Henry Walter, Temp. 2/Lt., k. in a., 1/7/16.
Davies, Maurice Albert Mervyn, Temp. 2/Lt., k. in a., 25/9/15.
2 Davis, Eugene, 2/Lt. (Tp.), k. in a., 28/3/18.
1 Dawe, Richard Henry O'Neill, 2/Lt., k. in a., 13/9/16.
Dines, Percy John Francis, Temp. 2/Lt., d. of w., 1/7/16.
Ditmas, Thomas Owen Bulteel, Lt., k. in a., 14/1/15.
Dodgson, Kenneth Vernon, Temp. Lt., k. in a., 25/9/15.
2 Drake, Wilfred Wallace, 2/Lt. (Tp.), d. of w., 16/8/17 (att. T.M.B.).
Dunn, Harold Black, 2/Lt. (Tp.), k. in a., 30/8/18.
Dunsterville, Graham Eardley, Lt., k. in a., 30/10/14.
2 Eales, Charles Wilfred, Lt., k. in a., 27/9/18.
Elliot, Henry Gratten, Capt., k. in a., 20/9/14.
Esdaile, Arthur James, Lt., k. in a., 7/11/18.
Evans, John Ewart, 2/Lt., k. in a., 27/9/18
Farrar, Ernest Bristow, 2/Lt., k. in a., 18/9/18.
Featherstone, Reginald Benjamin, Capt., k. in a., 18/12/14.
Fenwick, Maurice Edward Edmonds, Temp. 2/Lt., k. in a., 2/4/17.
2 Ferard, George Deas, Lt., k. in a., 21/2/18
Finnemore, Percival Edward, Lt., k. in a., 26/10/17.
Fischer, Alexander William, Temp Lt., d. of w., 12/5/16.
Fleming, Wilfrid Allan, M.C., Capt., k. in a., 10/8/17 (and R.F.C., 56 Sq.).
Floyd, Howard Grimley, Temp. 2/Lt, k. in a., 9/4/18.
1 Frazer, John Gordon, Lt.-Col., died, 1/8/16 (Gar. Bn.).
Gainey, Henry Charles, Temp. 2/Lt., k. in a., 14/7/16.
Galton, Francis William Joseph, Lt., k. in a., 23/4/17.
Gethin, Percy Francis, 2/Lt., k. in a., 28/6/16.
8 Girvan, Frederick William, Lt. (A/Capt.), k. in a., 26/10/17.
Glossop, Bertram, Temp. Lt, k. in a., 4/9/16.
1 Gloster, Gerald Charles Edward, Lt., k. in a., 6/11/17.
Goldsmith, H. M., Lt., k. in a., 9/5/15 (att. Lincs. Regt.).
Goodman, Harold Harry, 2/Lt. (A/Capt.), k. in a., 16/8/17.
Gould, Eric Melville, 2/Lt., k. in a., 1/7/16.
2 Grant, Alexander George William, Lt.-Col., k. in a., 25/9/15 (and W. Afr. R).
Grant, Harold Duncan, 2/Lt., died, 27/3/19.
Gribbell, Leslie Terrell, Temp. 2/Lt., died, 31/3/16.
Grigson, Lionel Henry Shockforth, 2/Lt, k. in a., 9/5/17.
1 Hambly, Alan Gordon, 2/Lt., d. of w., 22/5/17.
1 Hamilton, Ronald Eric, 2/Lt., k. in a., 23/4/17.
Hancock, Ralph Escott, D.S.O., Lt., k. in a., 26/10/14.
3 Hannah, Charles William Cooper, 2/Lt., k. in a., 28/9/16 (att. 2/Bn.).
1 Hardwick, Oswald William, 2/Lt. (Tp.), k. in a., 9/5/17.
Harris, Walter Lewis, 2/Lt., k. in a., 10/2/17.
Hart, John Harcourt Welby, Temp. Lt., k. in a., 20/9/18 (att. Manch. Regt.).
Hay, Robert, Temp 2/Lt, k. in a., 28/7/18.
Higgs, Marcus Webb, Temp. 2/Lt., k. in a., 23/10/18.
Hirst, Cecil Pollock, Temp. 2/Lt., k. in a., 1/7/16.
Hodgson, William Noel, Temp. Lt., k. in a., 1/7/16.
Holcroft, Raymond Boycott, Temp. 2/Lt., k. in a., 1/7/16.
Holdsworth, Charles John, Temp. 2/Lt., k. in a, 8/5/17.
Hollingworth, Leonard, Temp. 2/Lt., k. in a., 28/9/16.
Hosegood, Gilbert, 2/Lt., k. in a., 10/9/16.
Hounson, George James, 2/Lt. (Tp.), died, 20/9/17.
Hudson, Edward Stanley, 2/Lt. (Tp.), d. of w., 13/2/17.
Hughes, N. L., 2/Lt., k in a., 26/9/19 (att. Ox. & Bucks L.I.).
Huish, Francis, 2/Lt (Tp), k. in a., 28/7/18.
Hulm, Wynne Odyerne, Lt (Tp.), d. of w., 25/9/15.
3 Hussey, Harold Edward, 2/Lt. (Tp.), k. in a., 25/3/17 (att. 1/Manch. Regt.).
9 Inchbald, John Chantry Elliot, A/Capt. (Temp. Lt.), k. in a., 2/4/17.
Jacks, Edmund Cecil, 2/Lt., k. in a., 25/10/16

2 Jacob, Cecil Otway Reed, Capt., k. in a., 29/11/17.
Jago. Edward Arthur, 2/Lt., k. in a., 1/7/16.
2 Jago, Henry Harris, M.C., Lt. (A/Capt.), k. in a., 24/4/18.
Jameson, John, 2/Lt., k. in a., 30/8/18.
Jeeves, Charles Anthony Victor, Temp 2/Lt., k. in a., 20/9/17 (att. K. L'pool Regt.).
Jeffreys, Darell Richard, Capt., k. in a., 11/7/15.
8 Johnson, Laurence Frederick, Temp. 2/Lt., k. in a., 16/6/17.
Joseph, Horace, 2/Lt., k. in a., 20/7/16.
2 Joy, Thomas Cyril Bruce, T/Capt. (Lt.), k. in a., 11/12/15 (att. Dorset Regt.).
Jupe, Charles Eric, A/Capt., k. in a., 26/10/17.
Kane, John Francis Aloysuis, Capt., killed, 22/3/15 (att. R.F.C.).
Karslake Harry Howard, Temp. 2/Lt., k. in a., 23/4/17 (att. D.C.L.I.).
8 Kekewich, Arthur St. John Mackintosh, Capt., k. in .a, 25/9/15.
King, Charles Frederick, 2/Lt, k. in a., 20/9/17 (att Liv. Regt.).
10 Kirby, James Sabey 2/Lt., k. in a., 10/2/17.
Lafone, Claude Alexander D.S.O., Capt., k. in a., 14/3/15.
Leat, Frederick Charles, 2/Lt., k. in a., 27/5/18 (att. 2 Bn.).
Legge, Ronald George, Capt., k. in a., 18/12/14.
2 Lethbridge, Fred, D.C.M., 2/Lt., k. in a., 24/4/18.
3 Lewis, John Walter, 2/Lt, d. of w., 15/7/16.
Lewis, Richard Percy, Major (Act. L.-Col.), k. in a., 8/9/17 (att. Manch. Regt.).
3 Ley, Geoffrey Arthur Henry, 2/Lt., k. in a., 30/7/17.
Ley, Maurice Carew, 2/Lt., k. in a., 1/7/16.
2 Lloyd, Francis Burrows, Temp. 2/Lt., k. in a., 3/10/16.
Lockyer, Felix Courtenay, 2/Lt., k. in a., 12/2/17.
Lord, Frank Samuel, 2/Lt. d. of w., 12/3/15.
Lord, Hugh Cecil, 2/Lt., k in a., 26/10/17.
Lovett, Owen, Capt., k. in a., 24/4/17.
3 McGowan, John Spence, 2/Lt., k. in a., 1/7/16
1 Malone, Brian Wilmot L'Estrange, Lt., k. in a., 23/4/17.
Mansel-Carey, Spencer Lort Maunsel, Temp. 2/Lt., d. of w., 24/2/16.
Marchant, Harold Edgar, Temp. 2/Lt., k. in a., 5/6/16.
9 Martin, Duncan Lenox, Temp. Capt., k. in a., 1/7/16.
Martin, Marshall, Temp. Lt., died, 18/2/19 (Gar. Bn.).
Mathews, Anthony Edward, Temp. 2/Lt., k. in a., 19/7/16 att. Glouc. Regt.).
Maton, Leonard Evelyn Leigh, M.C., Capt., k. in a., 9/5/17.
1 May, Paul Archer, 2/Lt., k. in a., 15/4/17.
Miller, Robert Fordyce, 2/Lt., k. in a., 4/9/16.
Miller, William Reginald Francis, Temp. Lt., k. in a., 24-25/4/17.
Mitchell, George James, Temp. 2/Lt., k. in a., 19/7/16 (att. Glos. Regt.).
Monk, Alan, Lt., k. in a., 26/10/17.
Moon, Leonard James, Lt. (Tp.), died, 23/11/16.
Moore, Francis William, M.C., Temp. Capt., d. of w., 26/4/17.
3 Mortimore, Owen John, Capt., k. in a., 22/11/15 (att. 2/Dorset Regt.).
Muntz, Joseph Oscar, Temp. Capt., d. of w., 4/9/18.
Neilson, Somerville Montgomerie, 2/Lt., k. in a., 14/4/17.
Noel, Francis Methuen, 2/Lt., k. in a., 26/10/17.
2 Noon, Alfred Lewis, Lt., d. of w., 2/4/18.
1 Norrish, Thomas Theodore, 2/Lt., k. in a., 13/9/16.
Oliver, Charles Gordon, 2/Lt., d. of w., 14/10/15 (att. York Regt.).
Osborne, Trevor Leonard, Lt., k. in a., 30/9/18 (and R.A.F.).
Paramore, Robert Edward Pynsent, Lt., k. in a., 23/7/16.
Partridge, Wilfred Issell, Lt., k. in a., 24/4/17.
Pearcy, Albert, 2/Lt., k. in a., 30/11/17 (att. 7 Som. L.I.).
Pells, Cyril Elmore, 2/Lt. (Tp.), k. in a., 27/5/18.
Perkins, Audley St. John, Lt., k. in a., 2/4/17.
2 Perry, William Everard Hill, Temp. 2/Lt., k. in a., 14/4/17.
Peters, William John, M.C., Lt., k. in a., 23/4/17.
3 Phillips, Fenton Ellis Stanley, M.C., 2/Lt., k. in a., 13/10/16 (and R.F.C.).
Port, William Garfield, 2/Lt., k. in a., 4/10/17.
3 Preedy, Alban, Temp. Capt., k. in a., 1/7/16.
Pritchard, Richard, Temp. 2/Lt., d. of w., 22/8/16.
10 Prynne, Norman Fellowes, 2/Lt., k. in a., 24-25/4/17.
Puddicombe, Frank Cecil, Temp. Lieut., k. in a., 28/10/18.
1 Pugsley, John Frederick, 2/Lt., k. in a., 30/8/18.
3 Quicke. Edward Owen St. Ayres Godolphin, Capt., k. in a., 25/10/14.
Radcliffe, Jasper Fitzgerald, D.S.O., Lt.-Col., k. in a., 31/1/16 (att. Essex Regt.).
9 Raffin, Archibald Franklin, M.C., Temp. Lieut. (A/Capt.), died, 30/11/18.
Rainey, Victor Thomas James, 2/Lt., k. in a., 30/9/17.
Rayner, Harold Leslie, Temp. 2/Lt., k. in a., 1/7/16.
9 Read, Edward Macartney, 2/Lt. (Tp.), k. in a., 2/4/17.
Reed, Robert, 2/Lt., k. in a., 24/5/15.
Reed, William John, 2/Lt. (Tp.), d. of w., 28/10/17 (P.O.W.).
9 Rendle, Anthony Darley Russell, 2/Lt. (Tp.), k. in a., 10/10/17.
3 Rennie, John Archibald, 2/Lt., d. of w., 25/7/16.
8 Renton, Stanley, M.C., A/Capt. (Lt., Temp.), k. in a., 6/5/17.
9 Revington, John Huleatt, 2/Lt., k. in a., 4/9/16.
8 Rew, John Frederick George, 2/Lt. (Tp.), k. in a., 1/7/16.
Rice, Ernest John, 2/Lt. (Tp.), k. in a., 20/11/17 (att. 7 Som. L.I.).
1 Richards, John Leslie Hill, Temp. Lt., d. of w., 15/4/18.
11 Riddell, William, Temp. 2/Lt., k. in a., 1/7/16.
1 Roberts, Charles William, 2/Lt., k. in a., 28/12/17.
2 Rodd, Charles Bouchier, 2/Lt., k. in a., 30/10/16.
1 Rogers, Sidney Gilbert, 2/Lt., k. in a., 4/10/17.
1 Ross, Richard, M.C., 2/Lt., k. in a., 25/9/16.
8 Rundle, Horace Liberty, 2/Lt., k. in a., 20/7/16.
9 Sandoe, Montague William Augustus, 2/Lt. (Tp.), k. in a., 8/5/17.
Sanford, Walter Henry, 2/Lt., died, 11/2/19 (att. 2/4 Bn.).
2 Sayes, John, Temp. 2/Lt., k. in a., 31/10/18.
3 Scarbrough, Reginald John, Capt., d. of w., 2/11/17 (att. 8/Hamps. Regt.).
1 Schuh, Rudolf Oscar, M.C., Lt., died, 8/11/18.
Sheepshanks, Charles John Harcourt, Capt. (Tp.), k. in a., 17/3/16.
Shepard, Cyril Harry, Temp. 2/Lt., k. in a., 1/7/16.
9 Silk, Thomas William, Lt., k. in a., 26/10/17.
1 Simpson, Stanley Ashe, Temp. 2/Lt., k. in a., 28/9/18.
Skardon, Herbert John, Temp. Lt., d. of w., 31/10/18.
Skewes, Arthur Courtis, Temp. 2/Lt., k. in a., 19/7/16 (att. 2/6 Glos. Regt.).
Skinner, Edward Howard, 2/Lt., k. in a., 25/9/16.
2 Smith, Arthur Herbert, A/Capt., k. in a., 6/10/16.
Smith, Gordon Hamilton, Temp. 2/Lt., k. in a., 9/5/17.
Smith, John Henry, 2/Lt., k. in a., 28/8/18 (att. 7 Som. L.I.).
10 Smith, Sidney John Howard, 2/Lt., k. in a., 10/2/17.
Spencer, Charles James, Capt., k. in a., 18/12/14.
Stephens, Sidney Thompson, M.C., 2/Lt., k. in a., 9/10/17.
1 Studholme, Paul Francis William, 2/Lt., k. in a., 3/10/17.
2 Sunderland, Alfred Joseph Elton, Major (Temp. Lt.-Col.), k. in a., 31/7/17.
2 Taylor, Arthur Martin, 2/Lt. (Tp.), k. in a., 1/8/17.
9 Teape, Charles Lewarne, Temp. 2/Lt., k. in a., 4/9/16.
Teglio, Max, Temp. 2/Lt., k. in a., 11/4/17 (att. Worcs. Regt.).
10 Thorne, Sydney Charles, 2/Lt., k. in a., 24/4/17.
1 Thornhill, Hubert Burrington, Lt. (A/Capt.), died, 25/3/19 (T.M.B., att. 2 R.W. Kent R.).
1 Thorp, Edward Henry Courtenay, Lt. (A/Capt.), k. in a., 21/8/18.
2 Thuillier, George Fleetwood, M.C., Lt. (A/Capt.), k. in a., 26/3/18.
Tillett, Alexander, D.S.O., M.C., Lt. (Act. Lt.-Col.), d. of w., 3/12/17.
2 Tindall, Louis Nicolas Lindsay, M.C., Lt., k. in a., 27/5/18.
1 Tomlinson, Thomas Harry, 2/Lt., d. of w., 23/7/16.
3 Toms, Arthur Woodland, Lt., killed, 27/11/14 (att. Sco. Rif.).
Tozer, Sidney Prout, Temp. Lt., k. in a., 8/10/18.
9 Tracey, Geoffrey Eugene, Temp. Lt., k. in a., 25/9/15.
8 Tregelles, Geoffrey Philip, Temp. Capt., k. in a., 1/7/16.
Trotman, Francis Henry Lionel, Temp. 2/Lt., k. in a., 7/11/18.
9 Tremlett, Elias, M.C., T/Lt., d. of w., 23/5/17.
1 Twining, Richard Wake, 2/Lt., k. in a., 1/7/16.
9 Underhill, George, Lt. (Tp.), k. in a., 6/9/16.
Vaughan, Guy Carleton, Capt. (Tp.), k. in a., 20/7/16.
2 Vesey-Fitzgerald, William Herbert Leslie, 2/Lt., k. in a., 14/8/16.
2 Vinnicombe, Leslie, Lt., died, 25/10/18 (att. R.T.E.).
Walker, Frederick Cecil Banes, 2/Lt., k. in a., 9/5/15.
Wallington, Charles Harold, 2/Lt. (Tp.), k. in a., 20/9/17 (att. K. L'pool Regt.).
9 Walter, Cecil, T/Lt. (A/Capt.), k. in a., 8/10/17.
3 Watkins, Eustace Arundel De St. Barbe Sladen, Capt., d. of w., 31/1/15.
Webber, Leonard Alexander, Temp. 2/Lt., d. of w., 9/7/16.
Weeks, John, Temp. 2/Lt., drowned, 13/8/15 (att. Hamps. Regt.).
Whipple, Herbert Connell, Capt., d. of w., 24/11/14.
8 White, Edwin Gordon, M.C., Lt. (A/Capt.), d. of w., 7/5/18.
3 Williams, Sir Burton Robert, Bart., Lt., k. in a., 3/10/17.
Willis, Frederick, Lt., k. in a., 30/9/18.
2 Willy, John Howard Cole, Temp. 2/Lt., k. in a., 25/11/17.
10 Wilson, William James, 2/Lt., k. in a., 24/4/17.
Wilson, William Keates Harrison, Temp. Capt., died, 12/4/16 (Gar. Bn.).
8 Windle, Michael William Maxwell, Temp. Lt., k. in a., 25/9/15.
Windsor, Mark Gilham, 2/Lt., d. of w., 10/3/15.
Wollocombe, Francis. Temp. 2/Lt., d. of w., 10/9/16.
3 Wonnacott, Thomas Henry, 2/Lt., k. in a., 9/5/17.
1 Woollocombe, John Morth, Major. k. in a., 3/2/17.
Worner, Percival Seymour, Temp. 2/Lt., k. in a., 4/9/16.
Wreford, Bertram William Heyman, Lt. (A/Capt.), k. in a., 23/4/17.
Wright, George Clinton, 2/Lt., k. in a., 10/3/15.
8 Wyatt, William John. Temp. 2/Lt., d. of w., 26/10/17.
3 Wyndham, George Heremon, 2/Lt., k. in a., 24/3/15 (att. North'd Fus.).
Yaxley, Charles William, 2/Lt. (Tp.), d. of w., 23/4/17.
Yeatman, Bernard Pym, Lt., k. in a., 23/10/18.
Yonge, Geoffrey Bowen, 2/Lt., d. of w., 21/11/18.

The Suffolk Regiment.

7 Abbs, Bertie Edward, 2/Lt. (Tp.), k. in a., 26/3/18.
Ablett, Frank Ellis, 2/Lt., k. in a., 20/9/17 (att. 1/8 K. L'pool R.).
11 Alderwick, Ernest Ewart Gladstone, 2/Lt. (Tp.), k. in a., 26/8/17.
1 Allanson, Henry Peter, 2/Lt., k. in a., 20/7/16.
3 Allison, Cyril Hugh, 2/Lt., k. in a., 13/11/16.
10 Anderton, James Devereux 2/Lt. (Tp.), k. in a., 13/11/16.
Arnold, Karl Ferdinard Franck William, Capt., k. in a., 23/4/15.
3 Ashworth, George Bertram, 2/Lt., d. of w., 10/8/16.

7 Ashworth, John Percival Curtis, M.C., 2/Lt. (T/Lt.), k. in a., 28/4/17.
9 Askham, Sydney Thomas, 2/Lt. (Tp.), k. in a., 21-22/8/16.
Attree, Francis William Wakeford Town, Capt., k. in a., 10/5/15.
2 Baldwin, Austin Provost, 2/Lt. (Tp.), k. in a., 27/9/18.
3 Balls, Frank William, Lt., died, 1/7/18 (and R.A.F.).
7 Bamkin, Harold Picton, 2/Lt., k. in a., 19/7/15.
2 Barnard, Albert, 2/Lt. (Tp.), k. in a., 1/10/18.
12 Barnard, Arthur Wilson, 2/Lt. (Tp.), d. of w., 29/3/18.
2 Barton, Reginald Frederick, Lt., k. in a., 17/6/17.
2 Baylis, Alfred Keppel, 2/Lt. (Tp.), d. of w., 24/4/18.
2 Bennett, Sydney Garnet, 2/Lt., k. in a., 20/7/16.
3 Berkeley, Thomas Berkeley Hartman, Lt., died, 7/11/18 (att. M.G.C.).
3 Bevan, Clement Beckford, A/Capt., k. in a., 20/7/16.
3 Black, David Smith, M.C., 2/Lt. (T/Capt.), k. in a., 27/3/18.
7 Blackwell, Thomas, 2/Lt. (Tp.), k. in a., 27/3/18
11 Bolton, Edward Trevor, Lt. (Tp.), k. in a., 10/4/18.
2 Bond, Charles Reginald, 2/Lt., k. in a., 26/9/17.
2 Bradley, James, 2/Lt., k. in a., 21/7/16.
Bradley, Shephin, Lt., k. in a., 25/5/15.
1 Bradon, Harry, 2/Lt., k. in a., 16/11/16.
2 Brett, Charles Arthur Hugh, D.S.O., Lt.-Col., k. in a., 26/8/14.
7 Brooke, Gerald Douglas, Capt., k. in a., 3/7/16.
11 Brown, Osbert Harold, D.S.O., M.C., Capt. (Tp.), k. in a., 1/11/16.
7 Bryant, Richard Leslie Algernon, 2/Lt., d. of w., 23/5/17 (att. T.M.B.).
11 Buckoke, Oswald Lee, 2/Lt. (Tp.), k. in a., 8/7/17.
2 Bunbury, Patrick Stanney St. Pierre, 2/Lt., k. in a., 19/12/16.
2 Burgess, William Frederick, 2/Lt., k. in a., 18/8/16.
9 Byrne, Samuel Hubert, Capt. (Tp.), k. in a., 13/9/16.
2 Campbell, David Wylie, 2/Lt. (Tp.), d. of w., 28/9/18.
12 Carey, Richard Cyril, 2/Lt. (Tp.), d. of w., 8/7/16.
7 Catchpole, Charles Edward, 2/Lt. (Tp.), k. in a., 12/10/16.
3 Cautley, William Oxenham, D.S.O., Major, k. in a., 9/5/15.
3 Chalk, Theodore Wilson, 2/Lt., k. in a., 3/7/16.
2 Chalmers, Ralph, Capt., k. in a., 10/5/15.
8 Chibnall, Ronald Stanley, Lt. (Tp.), k. in a., 31/7/17.
12 Chippington, Horace Leonard, 2/Lt. (Tp.), d. of w., 23/8/18 (att. 16/War. R.).
Clarke, Percy Thomas, 2/Lt. (Tp.), k. in a., 19/8/18.
11 Claughton, Ian Drummond, Lt. (Tp.), k. in a., 2/3/16.
2 Clifford, Henry Frederick Hugh, Brig.-Gen. (Tp.), k. in a., 11/9/16 (att. Staff, 149 Inf. Bdn.).
7 Cobbold, Charles Augustus, Capt. (Tp.), k. in a., 13/10/15.
3 Collins, Norman Cecil, 2/Lt., k. in a., 9/8/16.
3 Collis, Bert Humphrey, Lt., d. of w., 20/12/15.
11 Cook, Richard Edward, 2/Lt. (Tp.), d. of w., 13/4/18.
Cotton, William John Stanley, 2/Lt. (Tp.), d. of w., 23/8/17.
7 Cowper, Frank Neville, 2/Lt., k. in a., 12/10/16.
3 Cox, Douglas Weld, 2/Lt., d. of w., 17/5/15.
11 Creagh, Henry James Perceval, M.C., T/Lt. (A/Capt.), d. of w., 23/11/18.
7 Cunningham, James Michael, T/Lt. (A/Capt.), d. of w., 28/3/18.
7 Currey, Vere Fortrey, Major, k. in a., 13/10/15.
3 Danvers, Robert William Ford, 2/Lt., k. in a., 26/8/17.
11 Darley, Desmond John, 2/Lt., k. in a., 1/7/16.
2 Davall, Cecil George, 2/Lt. (Tp.), k. in a., 23/8/18.
3 Dawes, Hubert James, 2/Lt., k. in a., 8/5/18 (att. 2/Yorks).
3 De Castro, James Vivian Reynell, Capt., k. in a., 1/10/15.
2 Deck, Richard Frank, 2/Lt. (Tp.), k. in a., 30/9/15.
7 Deighton, Gerald William, Capt., k. in a., 3/7/16.
2 Devas, Bertrand Ward, Lt. (Tp.), k. in a., 13/11/16.
Dingley, William, 2/Lt. (Tp.), d. of w., 29/4/17.
10 Dixey, Edmund Harry, 2/Lt. (Tp.), d. of w., 3/7/16.
11 Duddy, George Lionel Alfred, 2/Lt. (Tp.), k. in a., 10/4/18.
3 Dunn, John. 2/Lt., d. of w., 1/2/18.
11 Durtnell, Richard Neville, 2/Lt., (Tp.), k. in a., 28/4/17.
7 Eagle, Gerald Charles, 2/Lt. (Tp.), k. in a., 12/10/16.
2 Elkington, Thomas Garrett, 2/Lt. (Tp.), d. of w., 4/3/16.
2 Evans, Arthur Leslie, 2/Lt., k. in a., 20/7/16.
9 Fallowes, John Tyrrell Champion, Lt. (Tp.), k. in a., 15/9/16.
7 Fish, John Leslie, 2/Lt. (Tp.), k. in a., 3/7/16.
Forbes, Donald Keith, Lt., k. in a., 15/2/15.
11 Foster, Robert Clow, 2/Lt. (Tp.), k. in a., 10/4/18.
2 Francis, Vere, 2/Lt. (Tp.), d. of w., 20/4/17.
2 Franks, Harold Cooper, 2/Lt. (Tp.), k. in a., 15/6/18.
7 Frost, George Jesse, 2/Lt. (Tp.), d. of w., 9/9/15.
10 Frost, Robert Wall, 2/Lt., k. in a., 3/7/16.
9 Fudge, Alfred, Lt. (Tp.), d. of w., 22/2/18 (att. R.F.C.).
9 Gardiner, Godfrey Dernan, 2/Lt. (Tp.), k. in a., 13/9/16.
1 Gates, Douglas Leslie, 2/Lt., k. in a., 1/10/15.
7 Gedge, Peter, Lt. (Tp.), k. in a., 13/10/15.
7 Gilson, Leo Herbert, T/Lt., d. of w., 29/7/16.
11 Gilson, Robert Quilter, T/Lt., k. in a., 1/7/16.
Glen, David, 2/Lt., d. of w., 24/4/17.
9 Goatcher, Fred, T/Lt., d. of w., 31/10/17.
2 Gomme, Edward Elfred Coote, T/Lt. (A/Capt.), k. in a., 18/6/17.
11 Grand, Hugh Stevenson, 2/Lt. (Tp.), k. in a., 28/4/17.
12 Griffiths, Arthur Ivor, 2/Lt. (Tp.), k. in a., 3/8/17.
8 Grimble, Henry, 2/Lt. (Tp.), k. in a., 28/9/16.
3 Grose-Hodge, Dorrien Edward, 2/Lt., k. in a., 24/4/15.
12 Habershon, Sidney Heathcote, 2/Lt., k. in a., 8-13/4/18.
2 Hall, Francis Edward Charles, 2/Lt., k. in a., 16/8/16.
1 Hall, Norman de Haviland, 2/Lt. (Tp.), d. of w., 7/10/16.
11 Hall, Wilfred Rodenhurst, M.C., Lt. (Tp.), k. in a., 21-22/3/18.
12 Hamblin, John Edward, Lt. (Tp.), k. in a., 24/3/18.
8 Hannan, George Giles, 2/Lt. (Tp.), d. of w., 17/8/17.
Hare, John Alfred, 2/Lt. (Tp.), killed, 1/3/17 (and R.F.C.).
2 Harmsworth, Cecil John, 2/Lt., d. of w., 9/1/17 (att. 3/Mdx. R.).
Harris, Percy Cuthbert, Capt., k. in a., 17/2/15.
11 Harrison, Wilfred Ernest, M.C., Capt. (Tp.), d. of w., 10/4/18.
7 Hartopp, Charles William Liddell, 2/Lt., k. in a., 13/10/15.
Harwood, Gerald, Lt., killed, 1/5/19 (and R.A.F.).
7 Hearn, John Stanley, 2/Lt. (Tp.), k. in a., 12/10/16.
Hempson, Claude Dawson, D.S.O., Capt. (Tp.), k. in a., 8/3/17 (att. 6/R. Lanc. R.).
3 Henry, George Cecil, 2/Lt., d. of w., 9/12/17.
7 Henty, George Herbert, Major, k. in a., 30/11/17.
Hepworth, Laurence Frederic, Capt., died, 9/3/17 (P. of W.).
7 Hewlett, Harry Campbell, 2/Lt. (Tp.), k. in a., 28/4/17.
2 Hills, Cyril, M.C., 2/Lt. (Tp.), k. in a., 30/8/18.
3 Hood, Thomas, 2/Lt., k. in a., 12/10/16.
Hornby, Geoffrey Phipps, 2/Lt., k. in a., 10/5/15.
Horsnell, Alick George, 2/Lt. (Tp.), k. in a., 1/7/16.
8 Hubbard, Alfred, 2/Lt. (Tp.), k. in a., 17/2/17.
11 Hunt, John William Reynolds, 2/Lt., k. in a., 28/4/17.
1 Isaacs, Francis Harold, 2/Lt. (Tp.), k. in a., 30/9/18 (Garr. Bn.) (att. 11/Bn. R. Scots. Fus.).
7 James, Arthur Ling, Capt., k. in a., 8/8/16.
11 Johnson, Owen Bennett Goold, 2/Lt. (Tp.), k. in a., 9/4/17.
2 Johnson, Stanley, 2/Lt. (Tp.), k. in a., 20/7/16.
3 Joscelyne, Clement Percy, 2/Lt., d. of w., 10/10/17 (att. 11/Bn.).
Jourdain, Ernest Nevill, Capt., k. in a., 16/2/15.
8 Keats, Frederick Thorold, Lt. (Tp.), k. in a., 25/5/16.
10 Kell, Waldegrave Frank Sydney, 2/Lt., d. of w., 23/7/17.
3 Kemble, Cyril Stewart, 2/Lt., k. in a., 27/5/18 (att. 2/4 R. Berk. R.).
2 Kemble, Henry Noel, Lt., k. in a., 20/7/16.
10 Kenny, Laurence Henry, 2/Lt. (Tp.), k. in a., 26/6/16.
1 Kilner, Charles Ussher, 2/Lt. (Tp.), d. of w., 8/10/16.
7 Kinder, Thomas Harry, Capt., k. in a., 3/7/16.
3 King, George, 2/Lt., k. in a., 12-13/2/17 (att. 9/Bn.).
2 Kirby, William Howard Lee, T/Lt., died, 11/12/16 (Garr. Bn.).
Knox, Charles Duncan, 2/Lt., k. in a., 17/3/17 (and R.F.C., 43 Sqd.).
8 Lack, John Westlake, T/Capt., d. of w., 26/7/16.
3 Landon, William Henry Fitz Roy, Capt., k. in a., 15/2/15 (att. Bedf. R.).
2 Law, Charles Lindsay Qwyder, 2/Lt. (Tp.), k. in a., 30/9/15.
3 Lawes, Thomas Eric, 2/Lt., k. in a., 18/6/17.
7 Le Cheminant, Cyril, 2/Lt. (Tp.), k. in a., 9/8/17.
3 Lee, Herbert Victor, 2/Lt., d. of w., 17/11/16 (att. 1/Bn.).
10 Lee, Richard, 2/Lt. (Tp.), k. in a., 13-16/10/15 (att. 7/Bn.).
2 Llarena, Eustace Fernando, 2/Lt., k. in a., 18/6/15.
2 Llewellyn-Jones, Vivian Bruford, Lt., k. in a., 4/5/15 (att. 1/Welsh R.).
2 Locke, Robert Douglas, 2/Lt. (Tp.), k. in a., 2/3/16.
3 Locket, George Eimer, 2/Lt., k. in a., 28/6/18.
7 Logan, Crawford Raudolph, Capt., k. in a., 3/7/16.
8 Long, Guy Steer, 2/Lt. (Tp.), k. in a., 28/9/16.
Looker, Arthur Donald, 2/Lt. (Tp.), k. in a., 8/10/18 (1 Garr. Bn.) (att. 15/Essex R.).
Lucas, Thomas Charles Henry, Lt., k. in a., 6/2/17 (and R.F.C., 20 Sq.).
9 Mack, Arthur Paston, T/Lt.-Col., k. in a., 15/9/16.
Mack, Isaac Alexander, T/Lt., k. in a., 1/7/16 (Trench Mortar Bty.).
3 MacKinnon, Neil Alexander, Lt., k. in a., 19/9/18.
11 McGain, Ashley Waterson, 2/Lt. (Tp.), k. in a., 1/7/16.
11 McLean, Atholl Archibald, 2/Lt. (Tp.), k. in a., 1/7/16.
1 Marshall, Charles Samuel, 2/Lt. (Tp.), d. of w., 2/4/18 (Garr. Bn.).
3 Marshall, William Robert, 2/Lt., k. in a., 12/10/16 (att. 7/Bn.).
8 Mason, Stanley Hopkins, 2/Lt. (Tp.), k. in a., 26/9/16.
11 Mason, Vere Karsdale, 2/Lt. (Tp.), k. in a., 3/8/16.
11 Maxwell, John Duncan, 2/Lt. (Tp.), d. of w., 18/7/17.
Maycock, Frederick William Orby, D.S.O., Major, k. in a., 25/5/15.
11 Miller, Dudley Melville, Lt. (Tp.), k. in a., 28/4/17.
7 Morbey, Charles Frederick William, Capt. (Tp.), k. in a., 9/8/17.
11 Morton, Philip Francis, Major (Tp.), d. of w., 11/8/16.
2 Moss, C. J., 2/Lt., died, 19/8/16.
2 Mowbray, Kenneth John Wharton, 2/Lt., k. in a., 9/4/17 (att. 7/Bn.).
Myddleton, Edward Geoffrey, 2/Lt., k. in a., ?/9/14.
5 Neely, Hugh Bertram, 2/Lt., k. in a., 25/4/15.
Newman, Albert, 2/Lt. (Tp.), k. in a., 20/9/17 (att. 1/9 K. L'pool R.).
Newstead, George Pope, Lt.-Col., d. of w., 4/3/15 (W.A.A.F.).
7 Nicholls, Douglas William Arthur, M.C., Capt. (Tp.), k. in a., 10/4/17.
12 Nisbet, Cecil Andrew, Capt. (Tp.), d. of w., 21/6/16.
7 Nock, Geo. Goodwin Rudgard, 2/Lt. (Tp.), k. in a., 5/9/18 (att. 1/1 Cambridge R.).
1 Nowell, Ernest Harold, 2/Lt., k. in a., 1/9/15.
9 Packer, Bertram Frith, 2/Lt. (Tp.), k. in a., 19/10/17.
7 Page, Donald Frederick Vincent, Lt., k. in a., 21/9/18 (att. R.A.F.).
8 Page, Arthur Herbert, 2/Lt. (Tp.), k. in a., 19/7/16.
Pargiter, Reginald Amherst, 2/Lt., k. in a., 10/5/15.
12 Passman, Kenelm Granby, Lt., k. in a., 30/8/18.
10 Paterson, Hugh Trevor, 2/Lt. (Tp.), died, 13/5/16.
Payne, George Herbert, Lt., died, 26/8/14.
8 Peck, Edwin Robert Richmond, M.C., 2/Lt. (Tp.), k. in a., 3/5/17.
12 Pedrick, George Richard, 2/Lt., k. in a., 22/3/18.
2 Platts, Arthur Leslie, Capt., k. in a., 20/7/16.
3 Pollock-Hodsall, G. B., Capt., killed, 9/11/14.
12 Postlethwaite, Christopher Joyce, Lt. (Tp.), d. of w., 9/1/18.

3 Prentice, John Ridley, 2/Lt., k. in a., 18/6/15.
1 Prestidge, John Vernon Fitz Gerald, Lt., d. of w., 2/5/17.
9 Price, Sidney James, 2/Lt., k. in a., 15/9/16.
Prichard, Rowland George, Lt., k. in a., 24/4/15.
2 Pryke, Arthur, M.C., 2/Lt., k. in a., 11/4/17.
1 Pulverman, Oscar Percy, 2/Lt. (Tp.), d. of w., 1/9/15.
7 Ranby, Harvey, Lt., k. in a., 9/8/17.
7 Rash, Ralph Reginald, 2/Lt. (Tp.), k. in a., 12/10/16.
11 Reed, Horace Alfred, M.C., Lt. (Tp.), d. of w., 9/4/18.
Reeve, Charles d'Arcy Edmund Wentworth, Capt. (Tp.), killed, 18/7/16 (and R.F.C.).
Reid, Edward Harington, Capt., k. in a., 30/4/15.
7 Riches, George William, 2/Lt. (Tp.), k. in a., 8/10/17.
Roberts, James Roderick Trethowan, 2/Lt., d. of w., 3/3/15.
8 Row, John Eric, 2/Lt. (Tp.), k. in a., 29/10/16.
11 Roxbrough, William Henry, 2/Lt. (Tp.), d. of w., 13/4/18.
7 Rush, Ernest William, 2/Lt., k. in a., 28/4/17.
3 Rushbrooke, Bartle Davers, Capt., k. in a., 25/5/15.
Ryley, Harold Buchanan, Lt. (Tp.), k. in a., 15/12/17 (att. 1/5 Bn.).
8 Sanctuary, Charles Lloyd, M.C., Capt. (Tp.), d. of w., 15/11/16.
7 Saul, Herbert Lepard, 2/Lt. (Tp.), k. in a., 24/10/18.
8 Savage, Alfred Charles, 2/Lt. (Tp.), k. in a., 31/7/17.
1 Savory, Henry Lawrence Scott, 2/Lt., d. of w., 26/4/18 (Garr. Bn., att. 3/Worc. R.).
7 Sawyer, Herbert, 2/Lt., k. in a., 12/10/16.
12 Schiff, Mortimer Edward Harold, Capt., k. in a., 26/9/17.
Schroder, Francis Thomas, Lt., k. in a., 24/3/15.
1 Scott, Leonard, 2/Lt. (Tp.), k. in a., 24/3/18 (Garr. Bn.).
3 Shapter, Lewis Henry, Capt., k. in a., 31/1/15 (att. Bedf. R.).
7 Shears, Arthur Cecil, 2/Lt., k. in a., 3/7/16.
11 Sheen, Cyril, 2/Lt. (Tp.), d. of w., 3/5/17.
7 Silver, Walter Laurence Conningham, T/Lt., k. in a., 12/10/16.
12 Smith, C. F., 2/Lt., k. in a., 9/4/18 (att. 121 T.M.B.).
Smith, Charles Francis Bateman, Lt., k. in a., 15/2/15.
7 Smith, Donald Claud, 2/Lt. (Tp.), d. of w., 13/10/15.
Smith, Edward Corrigan, Capt., k. in a., 30/9/15.
9 Smith, Robert Gardner Paget, 2/Lt., k. in a., 15/9/16.
7 Smith, Sydney Newman, 2/Lt., k. in a., 9/8/17.
7 Sorley, Charles Hamilton, Capt. (Tp.), k. in a., 13/10/15.
Speyer, Frederick William Heurick, 2/Lt. (Tp.), k. in a., 14/6/17 (att. 2/Bn.).
3 Stantial, Frank Evered, 2/Lt., d. of w., 4/5/15.
7 Stapley, Lawrence D'Arcy, 2/Lt., k. in a., 12/10/16.
3 Steel, Douglas Graham, M.C., 2/Lt., (A/Capt.), k. in a., 13/11/16.
9 Stevens, Thomas Tearle, T/Lt., k. in a., 26/9/15.
7 Stotherd, Sidney Boyle, Major, d. of w., 19/10/15.
7 Sworder, Charles Frederick, 2/Lt., k. in a., 3/7/16.
11 Tallon, Moses, 2/Lt., k. in a., 4/8/16
Taylor, Albert Cecil, 2/Lt., k. in a., 20/7/16.
10 Taylor, Alfred Francis, T/Lt., k. in a., 9/8/16 (att. 7/Bn.).
7 Taylor, George Henry Recknett, Capt., k. in a., 30/11/17.
Taylor, Thomas Owen, Lt., d. of w., 4/11/17 (att. 5/Bn.).
Temple, Arthur Hilliard William, Capt., k. in a., 14/12/14.
7 Terry, Walter John, Major (Tp.), k. in a., 1/10/15.
3 Theobald, Reginald, M.C., Lt., k. in a., 10/4/18.
Thill, John Joseph, Lt., k. in a., 30/9/15.
Thomas, Henry Evan, Major, k. in a., 18/4/18.
11 Thomas, Sydney, 2/Lt. (Tp.), k. in a., 1/7/16.
9 Throssell, Horace Claude Sharman, 2/Lt., k. in a., 17/3/17.
7 Todd, Harold George Winslow, Lt. (Tp.), k. in a., 12/10/16.
10 Trask, Sydney Robert, 2/Lt. (Tp.), k. in a., 8/8/16.
Turner, Charles Hampden, Major (Tp.), k. in a., 30/9/15.
3 Venning, Edwin Gerald, Capt., k. in a., 6/8/15.
10 Vincent, William Morris 2/Lt. (Tp.), k. in a., 26/3/17 (att. 1/4 Essex R.).
Wainwright, Geoffrey Harry, Lt., d. of w., 8/9/18.
11 Waitt, Reginald Charles, 2/Lt., k. in a., 27/8/17.
2 Walford, Alexander Ellis, Lt. (Tp.), k. in a., 16/8/16.
Walford, George Henry, Major, k. in a., 19/4/15.
8 Walker, Frederick Charles, 2/Lt. (Tp.), k. in a., 25/11/15.
2 Walne, Horace George, 2/Lt., k. in a., 11/4/17.
7 Waters, George Thorold, Capt., d. of w., 29/3/18.
13 Weston, John Douglas, 2/Lt., k. in a., 1/7/16.
8 Whatling, Harold Wilfred, 2/Lt. (Tp.), k. in a., 26/6/16.
9 Whillier, Leonard Alfred, Lt. (Tp.), k. in a., 15/9/16.
12 Whymark, William Emerson, 2/Lt. (Tp.), d. of w., 27/11/17.
3 Wilder, Reginald Connor Philip, 2/Lt., k. in a., 18/11/14.
1 Wiles, John Davenport, 2/Lt., k. in a., 4/10/16.
9 Williamson, Alexander, 2/Lt. (Tp.), k. in a., 31/1/16.
9 Wilson, Fred, 2/Lt. (Tp.), k. in a., 15/9/16.
2 Windsor, Leslie St. Lawrence, 2/Lt. (Tp.), k. in a., 11/6/15.
8 Winkworth, Kenneth John, 2/Lt. (Tp.), k. in a., 12/8/17.
3 Winn, Arthur, Capt., k. in a., 9/9/14.
Winton, Harry George Denys, Lt., k. in a., 3/5/15.
7 Wood, Geoffrey Dayrell, Lt. (Tp.), k. in a., 13/10/15.
Wood, Oswald Ireland, Lt., k. in a., 3/10/15.
Woodgate, Arthur Horace, T/2/Lt. (A/Lt.), k. in a., 9/4/17 (T.M.B.).
Wood-Martin, Francis Winchester, Capt., k. in a., 17/2/15.
10 Woods, William John Peirce, 2/Lt. (Tp.), k. in a., 3/7/16.
3 Woodward, William Thomas, 2/Lt., k. in a., 14/6/17.
3 Wortley, Maurice Lester, 2/Lt., k. in a., 3/10/15.
11 Wootton, John Wesley, Capt. (Tp.), d. of w., 11/10/17.
7 Wright, Edwin Stanley, 2/Lt. (Tp.), k. in a., 3/7/16.
Wrinch, Stanley, 2/Lt., k. in a., 8/5/15.
13 Wrixon, Arthur Henry, Lt. (Tp.), k. in a., 2/6/16 (att. 11/Bn.).

Prince Albert's (Somerset Light Infantry).

3 Abecasis, Arthur Philip, 2/Lt. (Tp.), k. in a., 9/4/17.
6 Adams, Philip Rockey, T/2/Lt., k. in a., 27/5/18 (att. 2/Devon R.).
7 Armstrong, Henry Louis Winthrop, 2/Lt. (Tp.), k. in a., 29/11/15.
3 Auslin, Percy Edward, 2/Lt., d. of w., 24/10/18.
1 Backlake, Denis Ives, 2/Lt. (Tp.), k. in a., 19/10/16.
8 Bailey, Hugh Gardner, Lt., died, 31/1/19 (att. 1/4 Bn.).
8 Bailey, Robert Humphrey David, Lt., k. in a., 3/5/17.
8 Baker, Harold Glasspool, M.C., Capt., (Tp.), d. of w., 5/4/18.
8 Baker, Sidney, Capt. (Tp.), d. of w., 28/5/17.
8 Baker, Silvanus Wilfred, 2/Lt. (Tp.), k. in a., 26/9/15.
8 Baker, Wilfred Harry, Lt. (Tp.), k. in a., 2/7/16.
3 Barnes, Arthur Randall, 2/Lt., k. in a., 4/10/17.
8 Basker, Reginald Hugh, 2/Lt. (Tp.), k. in a., 26/9/15.
6 Beck, Theodore David Vodden, 2/Lt., k. in a., 16/9/16.
6 Benham, Ralph George, 2/Lt. (Tp.), k. in a., 11/9/18.
9 Benn, Oliver Williams, Capt., k. in a., 6/6/15.
6 Berridge, William Eric, 2/Lt. (Tp.), d. of w., 20/8/16.
7 Berry, Samuel George, Lt. (Tp.), k. in a., 22-23/3/18.
7 Betteley, William Lawrence, M.C., 2/Lt. (Tp.), k. in a., 25/6/17.
6 Birrell, Stuart Erskin, Capt. (Tp.), d. of w., 11/7/16.
6 Black, John Neill, Capt. (Tp.) (A/Major), k. in a., 9/4/17.
3 Bond, Charles Nesbit, Lt., d. of w., 30/6/16 (att. 1/4 Linc. R.).
Bone, Thomas William, Lt. (Tp.) (A/Capt.), died, 6/8/18.
3 Boucher, Henry Mason, M.C., Lt. (T/Capt.), k. in a., 23/4/18.
1 Bower, Alfred Percy, 2/Lt. (Tp.), k. in a., 1/11/18.
6 Bradney, Philip Edwin, Capt. (Tp.), k. in a., 31/7/15.
Bradshaw, Frank Seymour, Capt., k. in a., 19/12/14.
Braithwaite, Valentine Ashworth, 2/Lt., k. in a., 2/7/16.
8 Briggs, Orriell, Lt. (A/Capt.), k. in a., 4/11/18.
8 Brooks, Horace William, 2/Lt. (Tp.), k. in a., 4/11/18.
7 Buckland, John Arnold, 2/Lt., k. in a., 1/3/17.
Bullivant, Robert Walter, 2/Lt., d. of w., 1/5/17 (att. 8/Bn.).
3 Bush, John Stewart de Lisle, Capt., died, 25/8/17 (and R.F.C., 41 Sqd.) (P. of W.).
7 Butler, Stanley Reginald, M.M., 2/Lt., k. in a., 27/3/18.
Button, Norman Frederick, Lt. (Tp.), k. in a., 4/11/17 (att. T.M.B.).
1 Card, Stormont Hays, 2/Lt., k. in a., 10/4/17.
3 Caulfield, Gordon, 2/Lt., k. in a., 30/11/17 (att. 7/Bn.).
8 Chalmers, John Robert Thorburn, 2/Lt. (Tp.), k. in a., 1/7/16.
1 Chambers, George Alfred, 2/Lt., k. in a., 22/8/17 (att. 6/Bn.).
3 Chippindall, Bertrand Thorold, 2/Lt., k. in a., 16/11/16.
1 Codner, Christopher Cardew, 2/Lt. (A/Capt.), k. in a., 3/5/17.
9 Colville, Harold Linklater, 2/Lt. (Tp.), d. of w., 6/7/16.
3 Cox, Ernest, 2/Lt., d. of w., 8/12/17 (att. 7/Bn.).
1 Crabtree, Walker, M.M., 2/Lt. (Tp.), k. in a., 21/8/18.
9 Croft, Cyril Talbot Burney, 2/Lt. (Tp.), killed, 8/12/15 (and R.F.C.).
8 Dalrymple, Hew, 2/Lt. (Tp.), k. in a., 1/7/16.
3 Darwall, Gordon Cecil, Capt., died, 31/3/17 (and A. Cy. C.).
1 Daubeny, Charles John Odinel, Lt. (A/Capt.), d. of w., 16/6/17.
1 Davies, James Thomas, Lt. (Tp.), d. of w., 14/4/18.
3 Davies, Wallis Rowland Henry Rochfort, 2/Lt., died, 8/3/16.
6 Davy, William James, 2/Lt., k. in a., 7/7/16.
9 Dawes, Arthur Irwin, Capt. (Tp.), died, 22/6/17 (att. 10/Gurkhas).
6 Denton, Brian Maurice, Lt. (Tp.), k. in a., 19/8/16.
1 De Ritter, Victor Frank, 2/Lt. (Tp.), d. of w., 9/8/16.
1 Dickinson, Hugh Carey, Capt. (T/Lt.-Col.), died, 18/12/18 (att. 2/3 The King's Afr. Rifs.).
Dodington, Thomas Marriott, Lt., k. in a., 2/7/16.
8 Drakeford, Harold Arthur, 2/Lt. (Tp.), k. in a., 5/4/18.
6 Dudley, Herbert Edward, 2/Lt. (Tp.), k. in a., 23/8/17.
1 Dunn, Ralph Ellis, 2/Lt. (Tp.), d. of w., 1/7/16.
8 Ealand, Frederick John Arthur, 2/Lt. (Tp.), k. in a., 26/9/15.
1 Elliott, Charles Arthur Boileau, 2/Lt., d. of w., 12/4/17.
3 Elliott, Horace William, 2/Lt., k. in a., 13/11/17.
8 Emms, Harry, 2/Lt. (Tp.), k. in a., 6/8/16.
1 Fair, George Patrick Conroy, 2/Lt., k. in a., 1/7/16.
Fear, Edgar Leslie Brinsdon, 2/Lt. (Tp.), d. of w., 11/4/18.
Filleul, Leonard Amaurie, 2/Lt., k. in a., 21/10/14 (att. Ox. & Bucks L.I.).
8 Fitzmaurice, Lindsay, Lt. (Tp.) (A/Capt.), k. in a., 18/11/16.
7 Foley, Geoffrey Robert, 2/Lt. (Tp.), d. of w., 17/5/17.
1 Ford, Clement Charles, Lt. (T/Capt.), k. in a., 2/7/16.
9 Foster, James Sloman, 2/Lt. (Tp.), drowned, 13-14/8/15.
Fox, Thomas Noel, 2/Lt. (T/Lt.), died, 12/12/18 (att. M.G.C.).
1 Foy, Ernest Reginald, 2/Lt., k. in a., 11/4/17.
8 Friend, Henry John, 2/Lt. (Tp.), k. in a., 4/10/17.
6 Fuge, Frederick Henry, Lt. (Tp.), k. in a., 13/8/16.
1 Gardiner, Ashley James, 2/Lt. (Tp.), d. of w., 24/10/18
3 Gardner, Eric Mawdsley, 2/Lt., k. in a., 10/4/17.
9 George, Laurence Edgar, Capt., k. in a., 28/6/15.
8 Gibbs, Gilbert Fincher, 2/Lt. (Tp.), k. in a., 28/4/17.
Glossop, E. E., 2/Lt., d. of w., 4/5/15.
3 Gordon, Charles Campbell Boswell, 2/Lt., k. in a., 28/4/17.
9 Griffiths, Harry James, 2/Lt. (Tp.), d. of w., 9/8/16 (att. 1/Bn.).
9 Gunton, John Welby, 2/Lt., k. in a., 9/8/16 (att. R.F.C., 70 Sq.).
2 Hall, Arthur Henry, M.C., Lt. (Tp.) (A/Capt.), k. in a., 19/11/16.
5 Hannaford, William Allan, 2/Lt. (Tp.), k. in a., 23/11/17.
8 Hardyman, John Hay Maitland, M.C., Major (Tp.), k. in a., 24/8/18.
9 Hart, Frank Arthur Squire, 2/Lt. (Tp.), k. in a., 16/9/16.
8 Hatt, Arthur Beach, Capt. (Tp.), k. in a., 1/7/16.

7 Hatt, Edward Beach, Capt. (Tp.), k. in a., 26/8/16.
3 Hayes, Reginald Pole, 2/Lt., killed, 12/3/16.
3 Hayward, Marcus Henry Hugh, 2/Lt., d. of w., 26/3/18 (att. 7/Bn.).
6 Heath, Roger Meyrick, 2/Lt. (Tp.), k. in a., 15/9/16.
3 Hellard, John Alexander, 2/Lt., k. in a., 2/7/16.
6 Hensley, Wilfrid Henry, Capt., k. in a., 21/3/18.
Henson, Stanley Benskin, 2/Lt., k. in a., 19/12/14.
1 Herapath, Norman Finnis, 2/Lt., k. in a., 11/4/17.
3 Hind, Henry Basil Lindsay, Lt., k. in a., 22/11/15 (att. Ox. & Bucks L.I.).
6 Hobhouse, Paul Edward, Capt., k. in a., 21/3/18.
3 Holmes, Leslie Stuart, 2/Lt., died, 14/12/18.
8 Hopkins, Lewis, 2/Lt. (Tp.), k. in a., 26/9/15.
6 Hornsby, William, 2/Lt. (Tp.), k. in a., 21/8/17.
8 Howard, Lewis Charles, D.S.O., Lt.-Col. (Tp.), k. in a., 23/12/15.
3 Hucker, Wilfred Thomas, 2/Lt., d. of w., 23/12/17 (att. 8/-Bn.).
8 Humphreys, Frederick Charles, M.C., Capt. (Tp.), k. in a., 4/10/17.
12 Jenkins, Francis Howard, 2/Lt. (Tp.), k. in a., 2/9/18.
3 Johnson, Laurence Bertrand, 2/Lt., d. of w., 15/4/18.
3 Johnston, James Annandale, 2/Lt., k. in a., 2/7/16.
8 Joscelyne, Frank Henry Tremlett, Lt. (Tp.) (A/Capt.), k. in a., 19/11/16.
7 Joscelyne, Lawrence Arthur, M.C., 2/Lt. (Tp.), d. of w., 1/10/17.
8 Kellett, William, 2/Lt. (Tp.), k. in a., 22/1/17 (att. R.F.C., 10 Sq.).
Kennedy, John Horace, 2/Lt., k. in a., 10/1/15 (att. Scottish Rifs.).
Kenworthy, Donald, Lt. (T/Capt.), k. in a., 17/5/17.
7 Kinsey, Albert Thornley, 2/Lt. (Tp.), k. in a., 16/8/17.
3 Kitchen, George Rowland, 2/Lt., k. in a., 9/4/18.
Knight, Philip Clifford, 2/Lt., k. in a., 1/7/16.
9 Lalonde, Lionel Victor Pollock, 2/Lt., died, 31/3/16.
Leacroft, Ronald John Ranulph, Capt., k. in a., 1/7/16.
8 Leathley, William George, 2/Lt. (Tp.), k. in a., 1/7/16.
3 Leche, Arthur Victor Carlton, 2/Lt., k. in a., 1/7/16.
Le Peton, Desmond Alexander, 2/Lt., d. of w., 9/8/16
8 Lewis, John Emrys, 2/Lt. (Tp.), k. in a., 1/7/16.
3 Macbryan, Edward Crozier, Lt., k. in a., 2/7/16 (att. 1/Bn.).
6 Manson, Gerald Patrick, M.C., Capt. (Tp.), k. in a., 24/8/17.
Marler, Wilfred Earlstone, 2/Lt., d. of w., 4/5/17.
8 Marsh, Alford Stanley, Capt. (Tp.), k. in a., 6/1/16.
3 Marshall, Ernest William, M.C., Lt. (A/Capt.), k. in a., 22/4/18.
Massie, Sidney Edward, 2/Lt., k. in a., 8/5/17.
8 Mason, Arthur Pelham, 2/Lt. (Tp.), k. in a., 22/8/18.
Maud, Charles Carns, D.S.O., Capt., k. in a., 19/12/14.
7 Melhuish, Ian Vaughan Brenridge, 2/Lt. (Tp.), k. in a., 27/10/15.
Mills, Frank Symons, Capt., k. in a., 5/8/17 (att. 7/Bn.).
1 Moore, Douglas Lewis, Lt., k. in a., 22/4/18.
Moore, Roger Ludovic, Lt., d. of w., 20/12/14.
3 Munden, John Arnold, 2/Lt., k. in a., 27/8/16 (att. 6/Bn.).
7 Nepean, Francis Molyneux Yorke, Capt., k. in a., 16/9/15.
1 Neville, George Henry, Capt. (Tp.), k. in a., 2/7/16.
Newton, Arthur John, 2/Lt. (Tp.), k. in a., 30-31/7/18.
3 Newton, Arthur Victor, Capt., killed, 28/10/15 (att. R.F.C.).
8 Nichols, Walter Henry, Major (Tp.), died, 15/10/15.
Oliver, Frank Lambton, 2/Lt., k. in a., 13/7/17 (att. R.F.C., 55 Sqd.).
3 Orr, Robert Clifford, Capt., k. in a., 19/12/14.
8 Owen, Augustus Charles, M.C., Lt. (Tp.), k. in a., 6/8/18.
6 Pain, Edward Davy, Capt. (Tp.), k. in a., 18/8/16.
Parr, George Roworth, Lt., k. in a., 19/12/14.
Parsons, Alfred Cyril, Lt., k. in a., 29/3/18.
1 Paul, Edgar, M.C., Capt. and Adjt., d. of w., 10/9/18.
1 Pearse, Frank Arthur, 2/Lt. (Tp.), k. in a., 2/7/16.
3 Pepper, Cedric William, 2/Lt., died, 21/10/15.
8 Plant, Verner Lovelace, Lt., k. in a., 5/4/18.
1 Powell, Roland Rice, 2/Lt., d. of w., 29/8/18.
7 Powell, Wilfred Guy, 2/Lt., k. in a., 26/3/18 (att. 61/T.M.B.).
3 Price, Herbert Allen, M.C., 2/Lt. (Tp.), d. of w., 30/11/17 (att. M.G.C.).
Prideaux, Geoffrey Arthur, M.C., Capt. (Tp.), k. in a., 19/1/17.
11 Prowse, Charles Bertie, D.S.O., Brig.-Gen. (Tp.), d. of w., 1/7/16 (11th Inf. Bde.).
3 Pullen, Alan Collier, 2/Lt., d. of w, 19/8/16.
Purkis, John Nottage, 2/Lt. (Tp.), k. in a., 25/9/15 (att. 6/Bn.).
6 Randall, Frederick Percival, 2/Lt., k. in a., 16/9/16
62 Rawling, Cecil Godfrey, C.M.G., C.I.E., D.S.O., Brig.-Gen. (Tp.), k. in a., 28/10/17 (62 Inf. Bde.).
Read, Arthur Beddome, 2/Lt, k. in a., 16/9/14.
6 Reader, Bertram Edward, 2/Lt. (Tp.), k. in a., 22/10/17.
8 Reed, Paul Maurice, 2/Lt. (Tp.), died, 27/12/15 (att. R.F.C.).
8 Robinson, Edward Colston, 2/Lt. (Tp.), k. in a., 26/9/15.
9 Rogers, Herbert George, 2/Lt., k. in a., 28/12/15.
9 Roseveare, Ronald Chard, 2/Lt. (Tp.), k. in a., 8/8/16.
Samuda, Cecil Markham Annesley, Major, d. of w., 2/7/17.
3 Sargeant, Ralph Leslie, 2/Lt., killed, 25/3/17.
6 Scammell, Sydney John Alfred, 2/Lt., k. in a., 16/9/16.
8 Scott, William Francis, 2/Lt. (Tp.), k. in a., 1/7/16.
6 Selwyn, Colin Redgrave, 2/Lt., k. in a., 22/8/17.
Sharp, Stanley Ernest, 2/Lt., died, 20/10/18.
3 Sheppard, L. C. B., 2/Lt., k. in a., 21/4/17 (att. R.F.C., 32 Sqd.).
7 Shufflebotham, Guy Mynors, Lt. (Tp.), T/Capt., k. in a., 3/9/16.
6 Skrine, Henry Langton, Capt. (Tp.), k. in a., 25/9/15.
3 Smerdon, John Geoffrey, 2/Lt. (Tp.), k. in a., 20/9/17 (att 2/5 Lancs Fus.).
8 Smith, Henry James, 2/Lt. (Tp.), k. in a., 4/10/17.
7 Spiller, Arthur James, 2/Lt. (Tp.), k. in a., 17/9/16.
3 Springfield, Arthur Lincoln, 2/Lt. (Tp.), k. in a., 9/4/17.
2 Spurway, Richard Popham, 2/Lt. (Tp.), drowned, 13/8/15 (att. Hamp. R.).
3 Staight, Ralph Neville, 2/Lt., k. in a., 24/3/17.
Stead, Aubrey Arthur, 2/Lt., k. in a., 9/4/17 (att. T.M.B.).
3 Steer, Gordon Pemberton, Capt., d. of w., 26/12/15 (att. 2/Wilts R.).
3 Stocken, Kenneth Edger, 2/Lt., k. in a., 30/8/18 (att. 1/Devon R.).
8 Stone, Harold George, 2/Lt. (Tp.), k. in a., 5/4/18.
1 Strong, Oswald Lucking, 2/Lt. (Tp.), d. of w., 5/8/17 (att. T.M.B.).
9 Sully, Donovan Ernest, 2/Lt. (Tp.), d. of w., 9/8/16.
3 Swabey, Alan Maurice Eustace, 2/Lt., k. in a., 20/4/15 (att. York. L.I.).
! Swayne, Cecil Walter Harris, Lt., died, 25/5/17.
6 Talbot, Claude Eustace Chetwynd, 2/Lt. (Tp.), k. in a., 25/9/15.
1 Tanner, Hubert John, 2/Lt. (Tp.), A/Capt., k. in a., 9/4/17.
7 Tawney, Robert Lionel, 2/Lt., A/Lt., d. of w., 30/11/17.
1 Thicknesse, John Audley, Lt.-Col. (Tp.), k. in a., 1/7/16.
9 Thompson, Edward Homer Boxwell, Lt. (Tp.), drowned, 13/8/15 (att. Hamps. R.).
3 Thompson, Reginald Paul, 2/Lt., d. of w., 9/8/16.
Thoyts, Francis Gordon Grant, Major, d. of w., 26/8/14.
3 Trask, Charles William Trevor, 2/Lt. (Tp.), k. in a., 18/8/18 (att. 24/Welsh Regt.).
1 Treasure, William Herbert, 2/Lt., k. in a., 1/7/16.
8 Vernon, Roger, 2/Lt. (Tp.), k. in a., 14/5/16.
Wallington, Frank Courtneay, 2/Lt., k. in a., 6/8/18 (att. 1/5 Sth. Lancs R.).
1 Wallington, Nigel Hugh, 2/Lt., killed, 21/6/17.
12 Wallis, Thomas Francis, Capt., k. in a., 2/9/18.
6 Walrond, George Basil Stuart, Capt. (Tp.), killed, 19/3/16.
8 Warden, Walter George, Capt. (Tp.), k. in a., 1/7/16.
6 Warre-Cornish, Gerald, Major, k. in a., 16/9/16.
1 Wasborough, Spencer Vere, Capt., k. in a., 12/4/17.
Watson, William, Major (T/Lt.-Col.), k. in a., 3/5/17 (att 5/York. L.I.).
Webber, Harold Victor, 2/Lt., k. in a., 5-7/7/15.
7 Whall, Walter Edward, M.C., Capt., k. in a., 6/5/18.
1 Whitgreave, Henry Egerton, 2/Lt. (Tp.), k. in a., 1/7/16.
7 Whitworth, Herbert Clifford, Lt., k. in a., 26/3/18.
9 Whitworth, James Melville, 2/Lt., k. in a., 6/6/15 (att. Essex R.).
7 Wild, Lionel Tudor, Capt., k. in a., 30/11/17.
9 Willett, John Arnold, 2/Lt., k. in a., 2/7/15.
Williams, Theodore Edward, 2/Lt., k. in a., 1/7/15.
3 Wills, Thomas George Francis, 2/Lt., k. in a., 2/9/18.
3 Willstead, Grahame Ernest Lord, Lt. (A/Capt.), k. in a., 24/3/18.
1 Winstanley, George Clement, 2/Lt. (Tp.), k. in a., 2/7/16.
8 Withers, Frank Dean, 2/Lt. (Tp.), k. in a., 1/7/16.
1 Wright, Aislabie Harcourt Nelson, 2/Lt., k. in a., 2/9/18.
7 Wright, Edwin George Englesby, 2/Lt. (Tp.), k. in a., 16/6/16.
9 Young, James Vincent, 2/Lt. (Tp.), k. in a., 1/7/16.
1 Young, Lucian Albert, 2/Lt., d. of w., 26/10/18

The Prince of Wales's Own (West Yorkshire Regiment).

8 Abé, Frank, 2/Lt. (Tp.), k. in a., 23/7/18.
21 Adamson, Henry Bardell, Capt. (Tp.), d. of w., 30/10/16.
13 Adlington, Ernest Mason, 2/Lt. (Tp.), k. in a., 14/9/16 (att. 9th Bn.).
18 Akam, James Rhodes, Lt., k. in a., 1/7/16.
10 Allen, Humphrey Decius, T/Lt., k. in a., 1/7/16.
10 Allen, Percivall Knight, Capt. (Tp.), k. in a., 23/4/17.
4 Altoft, George Herbert, 2/Lt., k. in a., 17/7/17.
10 Anderson, Archibald Joseph, Capt. (Tp.), k. in a., 1/7/16.
13 Anderson, Percival Robert, 2/Lt. (Tp.), k. in a., 12/10/15.
10 Andrews, Charles William, 2/Lt. (Tp.), k. in a., 13/4/17.
14 Andrews, Hector George Robert Frank, Lt., k. in a., 28/6/15.
15 Appelbee, Thomas, 2/Lt. (Tp.), k. in a., 20/8/16
12 Appleyard, Harry Elston, 2/Lt. (Tp.), k. in a., 14/7/16.
1 Armitage, Francis Arthur William, D.S.O., Major (A/Lt.-Col.), k. in a., 22/4/18 (att. 1st Hants. Regt.).
16 Armitage, Geoffrey Ambler, Capt. (Tp.), k. in a., 27/2/17.
2 Arnold, Alfred Huntriss, Capt., d. of w., 30/12/16.
Asprey, Bernard Noel, Lt., k. in a., 24/2/15.
1 Ayrton, John, 2/Lt., d. of w., 29/4/17.
Backhouse, William Henry, 2/Lt. (Tp.), k. in a., 13/3/18.
4 Bailey, Cecil Arthur, Lt., k. in a., 5/5/15 (att. 2nd W Riding R.).
18 Baker, Frederick Gerald, 2/Lt. (Tp.), k. in a., 17/4/18.
11 Baker, Ward, 2/Lt. (Tp.), d. of w., 21/9/17.
10 Barker, Frederick Ernest, 2/Lt. (Tp.), k. in a., 13/10/17.
Barlow, Charles Leslie, D.S.O., Lt.-Col. (Brevet), k. in a., 5/8/18 (att. 1/5th Argyll & Suth. Hldrs.).
1 Bartlett, Ernest Jack, 2/Lt. (Tp.), k. in a., 16/4/17.
2 Bartley, Edward Hall, Lt. (A/Capt.), k. in a., 31/7/17.
3 Bastow, Frank, Capt., k. in a., 27/5/18.
3 Bastow, Norman, Lt., k. in a., 23/10/16 (att. 23 Trench Mortar Battery.).
12 Beaumont, Leslie, 2/Lt. (Tp.), k. in a., 17/8/16.
Bedford, Alan William, 2/Lt. (Tp.), k. in a., 20/11/17 (att. 2/6th Battn.).
9 Benn, Alfred Maurice, Lt., k. in a., 27/9/16.
Bennett, Alfred Charles, D.S.O., Lt.-Col., died, 16/1/15.
10 Berkley, John Humphrey, Capt., d. of w., 8/4/16.
Berry, Harry, 2/Lt. (Tp.), k. in a., 1/11/18.

15 Bickersteth, Stanley Morris, Lt. (Tp.), k. in a., 1/7/16.
Biggar, William Francis Wilson, 2/Lt., died, 20/10/18.
10 Blackburn, Geoffrey Gaskell, Capt. (Tp.), k. in a., 1/7/16.
1 Blackburn, Harry Clement, 2/Lt. (Tp.), killed, 23/3/18 (att. 1/7th Battn.).
10 Blatherwick, Robert Hugh, 2/Lt., k. in a., 1/7/16.
15 Blease, Richard Morris Stanley, Capt. (Tp.), k. in a., 3/5/17.
Booth, Frederick Arthur, D.C.M., 2/Lt. (Tp.), k. in a., 11/10/18 (att. 1/7th W. Rid. Regt.).
12 Booth, Herbert, 2/Lt. (Tp.), d. of w., 3/5/17.
15 Booth, Major William, 2/Lt. (Tp.), k. in a., 1/7/16.
9 Boston, Lawrence, T/Lt., died, 6/5/16.
21 Boulnois, Edmund, T/Capt., k. in a., 23/10/16.
19 Bowman, William Powell, Lt., k. in a., 17/10/16 (att. R.F.C.).
Bowran, Robert Orton, 2/Lt., k. in a., 9/10/17 (att. 1/8th).
Bradbury, William Rowland, 2/Lt. (Tp.), k. in a., 7/9/18 (att. 10th E. Yks.).
Bray, Sidney Herbert, 2/Lt. (Tp.), k. in a., 20/7/18 (att. 8th Battn.).
Brooke, Percy, T/Lt. (A/Capt.), k. in a., 28/3/18 (att. 9th T.M.B.).
4 Brooks, Leslie, Lt., k. in a., 25/9/15 (att. Lincs. Regt.).
2 Brophy, Ernest Gordon, 2/Lt. (Tp.), k. in a., 1/7/16.
1 Brotherton, Vincent, 2/Lt. (Tp.), d. of w., 14/10/16.
15 Burbridge, Frederick, 2/Lt. (Tp.), d. of w., 28/8/18
1 Burke, Martin, 2/Lt., k. in a., 18/9/16.
9 Burnley, Ernest Sidney, 2/Lt. (Tp.), k. in a., 5/11/18.
11 Busher, Charles Joseph, T/Lt., d. of w., 30/1/16.
4 Buttenshaw, Leonard Horace, Lt., k. in a., 27/6/18.
1/2 Butterworth, F., 2/Lt., killed, 14/9/18 (and R.A.F.).
2 Campbell, Robert Alexander Rankine, 2/Lt., k. in a., 1/7/16.
Carew, Jasper, 2/Lt., k. in a., 14/10/14.
9 Carnell, Frederick Harry Wright, Capt. (Tp.), k. in a., 9/6/18.
11 Cave, Joseph, Temp. 2/Lt., d. of w., 21/9/17.
4 Chalcraft, George Arthur, Lt., d. of w., 7/5/15 (att. 2nd Bn. W. Rid. Rgt.).
3 Charlton, Robert Arthur, Lt., k. in a., 21/3/18.
1 Chart, Eric Nye, Lt., k. in a., 25/9/16.
Cheesbrough, Harold, Temp. 2/Lt., k. in a., 4/9/18 (att. 10th E. Yorks.).
2 Cholmeley, Eric Randolph, Lt., k. in a., 1/7/16.
12 Clapham, Robert Sydney, Temp. 2/Lt., d. of w., 28/9/17.
Clarkson, Amos, M.C., T/Lt., d. of w., 24/10/18 (att. 8th Bn.).
2 Clayton, Benjamin Chipchase, M.C., A/Capt. (T/2/Lt.), k. in a., 16/8/17.
1 Clayton, George, 2/Lt., d. of w., 24/10/16 (and R.F.C., 11 Sqd.).
3 Cliff, Herbert Theodore, Major, k. in a., 13/10/14.
16 Clough, Alan, Temp. Capt., k. in a., 1/7/16.
18 Clough, Morris, Capt., k. in a., 25/4/18.
Clothier, John Keith, Capt., k. in a., 7/12/14.
17 Cohen, Adolph Broadfield, T/Lt., d. of w., 22/7/17.
18 Colley, Harold, 2/Lt., k. in a., 1/7/16.
Colley, Harry Leonard, M.C., 2/Lt., k. in a., 4/11/18 (att. 2nd Yorks. L.I.).
Colvin, Robert Alexander, Capt., k. in a., 10/3/15.
Compston, John Milton, Temp. 2/Lt., k. in a., 8/10/18.
Consterdine, Arthur Edward, Temp. Capt., k. in a., 26/12/16 (att. 9th Bn.).
Cooper-King, Reginald Garret, Major, d. of w., 10/12/14.
1 Corp, Benjamin, T/Capt., k. in a., 18/9/16.
Costin, Bruce Duffus, Lt., T/Capt., d. of w., 24/10/14.
9 Court, Robert Ambrey, Temp. Capt., k. in a., 26/4/17 (att. 8th W. Rid. R.).
9 Coyne, Cecil Thomas, Temp. Capt., k. in a., 27/8/17.
Crabtree, Lawrence, 2/Lt. (Tp.), k. in a., 24/4/18.
2 Craven, Frank, 2/Lt., k. in a., 28/3/18.
17 Crawford, Alexander Basil, Capt. (Tp.), k. in a., 10/5/16.
2 Cropper, Edward Percival, M.C., Lt., k. in a., 25/3/18.
2 Crosland, William Philip, Temp. 2/Lt., k. in a., 16/8/17.
18 Cross, Ronald Sydney, Capt. (Tp.), k. in a., 27/7/16.
3 Culshaw, Ronald Henry, 2/Lt., k. in a., 14/7/18.
9 Curtis, Horace, Lt., k. in a., 7/8/15.
9 Cuthell, Algernon Hubert, T/Maj., k. in a., 22/8/15.
18 Dalton, Richard Gregory, T/2/Lt., k. in a., 31/8/17.
2 Dashwood, Robin Henry Lyndsay, Lt., A/Capt., k. in a., 27/5/18.
15 Davidson, George Wilson, Temp. 2/Lt., d. of w., 27/12/17.
1 Davies, Harold Blakeney, 2/Lt., k. in a., 23/4/16.
9 Davison, Charles William Joseph, 2/Lt. (Tp.), k. in a., 14/9/16.
13 Davison, Henry James Goddard, 2/Lt. (Tp.), k. in a., 4/6/15 (att. 3 Lan. Fusrs.).
13 Dawson, Leonard, 2/Lt. (Tp.), k. in a., 4/6/15 (att. Lan. Fus.).
15 Day, Francis Thomas Pressland, Capt. (Tp.), d. of w., 25/3/18.
17 Day, Oliver, 2/Lt., d. of w., 3/9/17.
3 Day, Samuel Albert, 2/Lt., k. in a., 10/11/16 (att. 15th Bn.).
12 Daysh, Maurice, 2/Lt. (Tp.), k. in a., 23/4/18.
Dean, Hedley, 2/Lt. (Tp.), k. in a., 21/3/18.
18 De Lacey, John Matthew, 2/Lt., k. in a., 23/9/17 (and R.F.C., 57 Sqd.).
18 Derwent, Robert Ivor, 2/Lt. (Tp.), k. in a., 1/7/16.
14 Deverell, Richard Seddon, 2/Lt. (Tp.), died, 4/11/16 (att. 15th Bn.).
15 De Pledge, Edward Karl, T/Capt., k. in a., 3/6/16.
15 Dimery, George Wentworth, 2/Lt. (Tp.), died, 4/4/17.
Dore, William Hayward, 2/Lt., k. in a., 25/9/16.
11 Doyle, Edward Percival, 2/Lt. (Tp.), d. of w., 5/7/16.
Drake, Francis, 2/Lt. (Tp.), k. in a., 27/3/18 (att. 2/4th K.O.Y.L. Inf.).
18 Duckitt, Charles Stanley, T/Capt., k. in a., 3/5/17.
1 Edwards, Robert Amor, Lt., d. of w., 14/7/18.
Eliot, William Lawrence, Lt., k. in a., 20/9/14.
3 Elvidge, Jabez Gordon, 2/Lt., k. in a., 17/11/17 (att. 1/7th Bn.).
13 English, Eric, 2/Lt. (Tp.), k. in a., 7/8/15 (att. Man. Regt.).
9 Evans, Frederick Henry, Lt. (Tp.), k. in a., 9/10/17 (att. 15th Bn.).
11 Evans, Harry, Lt. (Tp.), k. in a., 26/3/18.
3 Evans, Rupert Ancrum, 2/Lt., died, 25/1/16.
15 Everitt, John Paxman, T/2/Lt., k. in a., 1/7/16.
9 Evers, Bertram Saxelbys, T/Capt., k. in a., 14/9/16.
2 Farrar, John Frederick, T/2/Lt., A/Capt., died, 2/11/18.
10 Faulder, Eric Amyas Wareing, 2/Lt., k. in a., 18/9/18.
3 Ferrill, Tom Archibald, 2/Lt., k. in a., 16/8/17 (att. 2nd Bn.).
14 Field, Edwin Arthur, 2/Lt. (Tp.), k. in a., 14/9/16 (att. 9th Bn.).
14 Fippard, Richard Clift, Capt. (Tp.), k. in a., 4/6/15 (att. Lan. Fus.).
12 Firth, Fred, T/Lt., k. in a., 24/8/18 (att. 10th Bn.).
Fisher, Mortimer, Capt., k. in a., 20/9/14.
Fletcher, George Herbert, 2/Lt., k. in a., 2/6/17 (and R.F.C., 4th Sqd.).
18 Foizey, Harold Egbert, Lt. (Tp.), k. in a., 1/7/16.
Forrest, Henry Dacre, Temp. 2/Lt., k. in a., 7/4/18 (att. 5th W. Rid. Regt.).
7 Foster, John Bowden, Temp. 2/Lt., k. in a., 11/10/18.
15 Foster, Leonard, 2/Lt. (Tp.), d. of w., 13/8/16.
11 Fox, David, Temp. 2/Lt., k. in a., 15/10/17.
21 Fox, Lawrence Anselm Storrs, T/Lt., d. of w., 27/4/18.
9 Fraser, Thomas Francis, Capt. (Tp.), k. in a., 7-11/8/15.
4 Freeman, Frederick John, 2/Lt., d. of w., 3/7/16 (att. 2nd Bn. W. Yorks Regt.).
13 Fyffe, John James, Temp. 2/Lt., k. in a., 14/9/16.
Gardner, Willie, Temp. 2/Lt., d. of w., 17/10/17 (att. 1/8th).
9 Geary-Smith, Alexander, Capt., k. in a., 7/8/15.
1 Gell, Christopher Stowell, 2/Lt., k. in a., 18/9/16.
9 Gent, Frank Ernest, Lt., k. in a., 7/8/15.
Getty, James Houghton, Capt., k. in a., 3/5/17.
12 Gibbon, Oliver Vernon, T/2/Lt., k. in a., 3/4/16.
2 Gibson, George Henry, 2/Lt., k. in a., 27/8/17 (att. 9th Bn.).
11 Gibson, Ivor Griffiths, Temp. 2/Lt., d. of w., 11/8/17 (and R.F.C., 6 Sqd.).
18 Gill, Daniel, T/2/Lt., k. in a., 24/10/16.
2 Gill, Frank Hubert, T/2/Lt., k. in a., 16/8/17.
13 Gill, Hugh Goddard, Lt., k. in a., 12/3/18 (att. R.F.C.).
11 Gill, John Ignatius, T/2/Lt., k. in a., 7/6/17.
15 Glenn, Archibald Patrick, T/2/Lt., k. in a., 14/9/16.
21 Grange, James Burness, Temp. 2/Lt., k. in a., 20/4/18.
18 Gray, John, 2/Lt., died, 26/11/18.
2 Greaves, George Harold, Temp. 2/Lt., k. in a., 5/3/17.
10 Grell, Louis George Neville, Lt., died, 5/6/18.
21 Green, Allan, Temp. 2/Lt., k. in a., 19/8/17.
Green, Geoffrey George Miers, T/2/Lt., k. in a., 28/3/18 (att. 5th York. L.I.).
10 Green, John James, Hon. Capt. & Qr.-Mr., died, 9/12/17.
4 Green, Philip Louis Samuel, 2/Lt., k. in a., 18/9/16 (att. 1st Bn.).
16 Greville, David Onslow, 2/Lt., k. in a., 3/5/17.
15 Griffith, John Herbert, 2/Lt., k. in a., 27/3/18.
9 Grose, Guy Charles George, 2/Lt., k. in a., 9/10/17.
1 Haddock, William, M.C., T/Lt., k. in a., 24/9/18.
17 Hadow, Erlan Godfrey, M.C., T/Capt., k. in a., 29/5/17.
14 Hall, M. E. A., 2/Lt., died, 27/3/15.
Hamer, Maurice, T/Lt., k. in a., 27/3/18 (att. K.O.Y.L.I.).
Hanson, James Arthur, 2/Lt., k. in a., 14/4/18 (att. 1/5th Batt.).
9 Hanson, Norman, M.M., 2/Lt., d. of w., 12/10/18.
Hardy, Edgar Leslie, T/Lt., d. of w., 7/10/18 (att. R.E.).
2 Harkness, Percy Yarborough, Capt., k. in a., 1/7/16.
4 Harris, Reginald Arthur, 2/Lt., k. in a., 9/10/17 (att. 9th Bn.).
4 Harris, Reginald William, T/Lt., k. in a., 3/9/16 (and Z1, T.M.B.).
Hartley, Noel Thomas, Temp. Capt., k. in a., 5/11/18 (att. 9th Bn.).
11 Haselden, Edgar Adolphus, T/Capt., d. of w., 9/7/16.
Hawkins, John Henry, Temp. 2/Lt., d. of w., 8/2/18 (att. 8th Bn.).
3 Hay, Roger Bolton, M.C., Lt., d. of w., 17/7/17 (and R.F.C., 48 Sq., P.O.W.).
15 Hazzard, William, M.C., T/2/Lt., d. of w., 28/3/18.
10 Henderson, William Lewis, T/Capt., d. of w., 3/5/16.
Hesketh, John, Temp. 2/Lt., k. in a., 14/10/18 (att. 1/6th Bn.).
1 Heslop, Fred, Temp. 2/Lt., k. in a., 26/4/18.
Hewitt, James Gordon, T/2/Lt., died, 14/11/18 (att. 2/7th Bn.).
13 Hicking, Francis Joseph, 2/Lt. (Tp.), k. in a., 1/7/16 (att. 1st Bn.).
11 Hill, Henry Hamp, T/Capt. d. of w., 8/3/16.
15 Hinchliffe, George William, 2/Lt., k. in a., 26/6/18 (att. 93 T.M.B.).
Hirst, William Henry, Temp. 2/Lt., k. in a., 1/8/18 (att. 10th Bn.).
17 Hitchen, Stanley Lucas, Temp. 2/Lt., k. in a., 6/6/16.
Hobday, Victor Maitland, 2/Lt., T/Capt., k. in a., 7/6/17.
12 Hogben, William Iggulden, 2/Lt., k. in a., 18/8/16.
10 Holland, William Rawlinson Garside, M.C., Temp. 2/Lt., d. of w., 18/9/17 (att. 50th T.M. Bty.).
18 Holt, Wilfrid, 2/Lt., k. in a., 3/5/17.
Horsford, Thomored Edward O'Bryen, Lt., d. of w., 14/3/15.
12 Houghton, George, 2/Lt. (Tp.), k. in a., 27/8/18 (att. 6th Dorsets).
2 Hoult, Robert Percy, 2/Lt. (Tp.), k. in a., 16/8/17.
22 Howe, Edward, Lt., died, 4/1/17.

2 Hoyle, Frederick Harold, 2/Lt. (Tp.), d. of w., 20/4/18.
Hucklebridge, Sidney Eames, Lt., died, 7/3/19.
18 Hummel, Raymond, T/2/Lt., k. in a., 19/5/16.
15 Humphries, Thomas, 2/Lt. (Temp.), k. in a., 1/7/16.
18 Humphries, Walter Rawleigh, 2/Lt. (Tp.), k. in a., 27/7/16.
16 Hyde, Charles Stuart, T/2/Lt., k. in a., 1/7/16.
3 I'Anson, John Francis, Capt., k. in a., 20/9/14.
10 Ibbitson, William Beveridge, T/2/Lt., k. in a., 1/7/16.
2 Ingham, Horace, M.C., T/Lt., A/Maj., k. in a., 24/4/18.
Ingham, Major, 2/Lt. (Tp.), k. in a., 13/4/18 (att. 1/7th Bn.).
Ingles, Alexander Wigton, Major, k. in a., 20/9/14.
1 Jackson, Robert William, M.C., 2/Lt. (Tp.), k. in a., 23/10/18 (att. 16th Bn.).
15 Jackson, William Hickin, T/2/Lt., k. in a., 3/5/17.
15 James, Clement Wilbraham, 2/Lt., k. in a., 1/7/16.
12 Jaques, Arthur, Capt. (Tp.), k. in a., 27/9/15.
12 Jaques, Joseph Hodgson, Major, k. in a., 27/9/15.
10 Jarvis, Charles Edward, T/Lt., k. in a., 18/7/17.
11 Jaye, Harold Conway, T/2/Lt., d. of w., 9/7/16.
14 Jennings, Basil Spencer, 2/Lt. (Tp.), d. of w., 7/11/15 att. 6th).
15 Jennison, James Leonard, 2/Lt., k. in a., 3/5/17.
Jewitt, Joseph, 2/Lt. (Tp.), k. in a., 1/11/18 (att. 1/7th Bn.).
10 Jones, Reginald George, 2/Lt. (Tp.), k. in a., 20/10/18.
13 Jones, Robert Henry, T/2/Lt., k. in a., 29/9/16 (att. 18th Bn.).
18 Keevil, Cecil Horace Case, T/Capt., killed, 13/6/17 (and R.F.C.).
10 Keighley, William Munkley, T/Lt., k. in a., 1/7/16.
18 Kennard, Maurice Nicholl, T/Lt.-Col., k. in a., 1/7/16.
13 Kent, William James, Capt., k. in a., 7/8/15 (att. Manch. R.)
4 Kiddle, Cyril Frank, 2/Lt., k. in a., 25/4/18 (att. 1/5th Bn.).
15 King, Gilbert Stewart, T/Capt., k. in a., 3/4/17.
18 King, John Rose, M.C., Lt. (Tp.), k. in a., 22/4/18 (att. 10th Bn.).
9 Kirk, Leslie Christiern, T/Capt., k. in a., 9/10/17.
14 Knight, Walter Foster, T/Lt., k. in a., 27/2/17 (att. 16th Bn.).
10 Knott, James Leadbitter, D.S.O., T/Major, k. in a., 1/7/16.
1 Knowles, Harry, M.C., 2/Lt., T/Lt., k. in a., 8/6/17 (att. 11th Bn.).
17 Lachlan, Cecil George, T/2/Lt., k. in a., 31/8/17.
4 Lamb, John Albert, 2/Lt., k. in a., 14/10/18 (att. 13th Bn. W. Rid. Regt.).
Lawson-Smith, John, Lt., k. in a., 20/10/14.
16 Laxton, Reginald Earl, T/2/Lt., k. in a., 10/6/16.
Legard, Reginald John, Lt., d. of w., 9/5/15.
15 Lintott, Evelyn Henry, T/Lt., k. in a., 1/7/16.
15 Lisle, John Wynne, 2/Lt., k. in a., 3/5/17.
2 Littlejohn, John, T/2/Lt., k. in a., 26/10/16.
15 Liversidge, Albert, T/2/Lt., d. of w., 2/7/16.
16 Long, Bernard Wilfrid, T/2/Lt., k. in a., 16/8/17.
15 Long, Cyril Edwin Arnold, Capt., k. in a., 27/3/18.
9 Long-Price, Cecil Evelyn, Capt., k. in a., 7/8/15.
Loveband, Arthur Reginald, T/Capt., k. in a., 6/12/14.
2 Lowry, Auriol Ernest Eric, D.S.O., M.C., Capt., A/Lt.-Col., k. in a., 23/9/18.
2 Lowry, Cyril John Patrick, Lt., k. in a., 25/3/18.
Luck, John Lewis, 2/Lt. (Tp.), d. of w., 6/9/18 (att. 1/7th Bn.).
Lund, Gilbert William, T/2/Lt., k. in a., 9/10/17 (att. 1/7th Bn.).
9 Lupton, Reginald, T/Capt., d. of w., 22/8/15.
10 Lynch, Denis, T/2/Lt., k. in a., 23/3/18.
1 Macdonald, John Alexander, T/Lt., k. in a., 30/11/17.
14 Macdonnell, Francis William Joseph, T/Major, died, 4/10/15 (att. 9th Bn.).
21 Mackay, James Bruce, T/Capt., d. of w., 3/5/17.
4 Mackridge, Ralf Leslie, 2/Lt., k. in a., 26/4/18 (att. 1st Bn.).
2 Mclaren, Richard Juson, Major, d. of w., 2/8/17.
3 Maguire, John Reginald, T/2/Lt., k. in a., 18/8/16 (att. 12th Bn.).
13 Maitland, Arthur Dudley, T/Lt., k. in a. 1/7/16.
18 Mansfield, Harold Lawrie, 2/Lt., d. of w., 3/5/17.
2 Mangin, Reuben Addison, T/2/Lt., d. of w., 7/5/18.
Marshall, Donald Ewan, 2/Lt., k. in a., 8/8/17 (and R.F.C., 18 Sqd.).
10 Marshall, Herbert, T/2/Lt., k. in a., 13/4/17.
15 Marshall, John, T/Lt., k. in a., 18/9/18.
1 Marten, Charles Peter, T/Lt.-Col., k. in a., 15/9/16.
Matthews, George, T/2/Lt., d. of w., 2/7/18 (in German hands) (att. 1/6th Bn.).
2 Maude, Robert Henry Ernest, 2/Lt., died, 12/9/16 (Gar. Bn., att. 3rd N. Staff.).
11 Maufe, Statham Broadbent, T/Major, d. of w., 5/7/16.
2 May, Wilfred John, M.C., T/2/Lt., d. of w., 1/8/17.
3 Meautys, Denzil Hatfield, Lt., d. of w., 7/5/17 (att. 12th Bn.).
Meautys, Thomas Gilliat, Lt., k. in a., 26/9/14.
4 Metcalfe-Smith, Bertram Cecil, Lt., d. of w., 22/4/18 (att. 21st Bn.).
Mettam, Athol Roy, 2/Lt., k. in a., 16/8/17 (att. 217th M.G.C.).
Millar, James, 2/Lt., d. of w., 25/4/18 (Res., att. 1/6th Bn.).
11 Miller, Charles Wilde, 2/Lt., k. in a., 7/6/17.
11 Mills, George Charles, 2/Lt., k. in a., 10/7/16.
3 Minogue, John O'Brien (C.M.G.), Lt.-Col., died, 26/10/16 (att. 9th Bn.).
1 Moorhouse, Walter, T/2/Lt., k. in a., 22/11/17 (att. 2/6th Bn.).
16 Morant, Gerald Alexander Mackay, M.C., T/Capt., k. in a., 15/4/18 (att. 2/5th Bn.).
1 Morkill, Ronald Falshaw, Lt., killed, 23/6/15 (att. R.F.C.).
12 Morland, Leonard Mark, T/Lt., d. of w., 3/5/16.
12 Morris, William, T/Lt., d. of w., 14/4/17.
18 Moulson, Samuel, T/2/Lt., k. in a., 4/9/18.
Murgatroyd, Ellison, D.C.M., T/Capt., k. in a., 26/3/18.
15 Neil, Stanley Thomas Arthur, T/Capt., k. in a., 1/7/16.
12 Newall, William Osborne, Lt., k. in a., 12/12/17.
16 Newlands, Sydney Barron, T/2/Lt., k. in a., 1/7/16.
4 Newman, Vernon William, 2/Lt. (T/Capt.), k. in a., 25/9/15 (att. 1st N. Lancs.).
1 Newton, Charles Thomas Kemp, 2/Lt., k. in a., 3/6/16.
10 Newton, Walter Kilshaw, 2/Lt., k. in a., 31/3/18.
12 Norris, William James George, Capt., k. in a., 25/9/15.
18 Nowell, Francis Percival, T/2/Lt., d. of w., 2/7/16.
12 Nuttall, Eric John, 2/Lt., k. in a., 21/3/18 (att. 59th M.G.C.).
1 Oakes, Gerard Edmund Roseingrave, Lt., d. of w., 19/4/18.
8 Oddy, Alfred Edward, T/2/Lt., k. in a., 27/9/18.
15 O'Land, Valentine, T/2/Lt., k. in a., 1/7/16.
12 Oliver, Cyril Francis Harrison, T/Capt., k. in a., 14/7/16.
12 Osborne, Hugh Corry, T/2/Lt., k. in a., 23/7/16.
11 Ostler, Thomas, T/2/Lt., k. in a., 7/6/17 (att. 69th T.M.B.).
13 Owens, Charles Arnold, T/Lt., d. of w., 10/1/17 (att. 10th Bn.).
21 Padgett, James Philip, T/2/Lt., k. in a., 5/5/17.
Palmer, Albert Edgar, 2/Lt., k. in a., 27/9/18 (att. 8th Bn.).
3 Palmes, John Philip, M.C., Capt., k. in a., 1/8/17 (att. 2nd Bn.).
1 Parker, A. F., 2/Lt., killed, 31/5/18 (and R.A.F.).
13 Parker, Edward Thompson, 2/Lt. (Tp.), k. in a., 4/6/15 (att. 1st Bn. Lan. Fus.).
Parker, John Norman, Temp. 2/Lt., k. in a., 8/9/17 (att. 2/6th Bn.).
Parker, John Womersley, T/2/Lt., d. of w., 13/11/17 (att. 1/5th Bn.).
10 Parker, William, T/2/Lt., d. of w., 31/12/17.
15 Parkin, Absalom Sydney, 2/Lt., k. in a., 3/5/17.
12 Parkin, George Frederic, T/2/Lt., k. in a., 9/4/17.
3 Pater, Hugh, 2/Lt., killed, 17/4/17 (and R.F.C.).
1 Paul, William, D.S.O., M.C., Lt. (A/Capt.), d. of w., 1/12/17.
16 Paus, Oscar Lionel, T/2/Lt., d. of w., 29/7/17.
Peach, Crugar Stanley, 2/Lt., killed, 24/4/17 (and R.F.C.).
2 Pearce, James, D.C.M., M.M., 2/Lt., died, 13/11/18.
9 Pearkes, Andre Mellard, Capt., k. in a., 7/8/15.
15 Peek, Alfred Taylor, 2/Lt., k. in a., 3/5/17.
14 Pennington, William Henry, 2/Lt., died, 2/3/15.
12 Perham, Edgar, T/Capt., k. in a., 23/7/16.
2 Perkins, George, 2/Lt. (Tp.), k. in a., 1/7/16.
2 Perry, George Herbert Gresley, Lt. (T/Capt.), d. of w., 15/3/15.
10 Peters, Lionel Gordon, Capt., k. in a., 25/3/18.
Petty, Robert Leach, 2/Lt., k. in a., 31/8/18 (att. 7th N. Staff. R.).
13 Pierce, Ronald Hugh MacGregor, T/2/Lt., k. in a., 14/9/16.
Pighills, John Arthur, 2/Lt., d. of w., 29/5/18 (att. 11th Lanc. Fus.) (in German hands).
2 Pimm, Victor Lionel, 2/Lt., k. in a., 10/11/16.
16 Platnauer, Leonard Maurice, 2/Lt., d. of w., 3/5/17.
11 Porter, George Francis Lambert, 2/Lt. (T/Capt.), k. in a., 8/6/17.
3 Price, Hugh, 2/Lt., k. in a., 11/10/18 (att. 1/7th W. Rid. R.).
21 Pridmore, George Harry, 2/Lt. (Tp.), k. in a., 31/8/18 (att. 1st Essex R.).
16 Pringle, Robert William Hay, T/Capt., k. in a., 1/7/16.
1 Procter, Harry Mettam, 2/Lt., k. in a., 27/8/17 (att. 9th Bn.).
4 Pyne, Ernest Sydney, 2/Lt., d. of w., 12/10/17 (att. 9th Bn.).
16 Ransome, Cecil Talbot, T/Lt., k. in a., 1/7/16.
10 Ratcliffe, Alfred Victor, T/Lt., k. in a., 1/7/16.
Rayner, Noel Roderick, Lt., k. in a., 27/7/17 (and R.F.C., 57 Sqd.).
15 Rayner, Roy Balfour Hodgson, T/Lt., d. of w., 24/5/16.
10 Reed, Bernard, T/Lt., k. in a., 12/4/18 (att. 15th Bn.).
15 Reed, Bertram, Lt., k. in a., 12/4/18.
2 Reese, Arnold, M.C., 2/Lt., k. in a., 1/8/17.
10 Reynolds, Victor Eustace, T/Capt., k. in a., 4/5/16.
10 Richardson, Arthur Douglas, 2/Lt., died, 12/1/15.
3 Richardson, Roger Bryer, 2/Lt., k. in a., 27/5/18.
16 Robb, John, 2/Lt. (Tp.), k. in a., 21/7/17.
Roberts, Birdsell, 2/Lt. (Tp.), k. in a., 9/10/17 (Res., att 9th Bn.).
12 Robinson, Charles, Temp. Lt. (A/Capt.), k. in a., 14/7/18.
13 Robinson, Cecil Beaumont, T/Lt., k. in a., 14/9/16 (att. 9th Bn.).
15 Robinson, Donald, Lt. (Tp.), k. in a., 3/5/17.
18 Robinson, Frank Victor, Lt. (Tp.), k. in a., 3/5/17.
16 Robinson, John Holdsworth, 2/Lt., k. in a., 1/7/16.
3 Rogerson, Noel, 2/Lt., k. in a., 28/2/18 (att. 2/4th K.O.Y.L.I.).
17 Roscoe, E., 2/Lt., died, 26/6/15.
17 Rose, Alexander Daniel, M.C., 2/Lt., k. in a., 31/8/17.
17 Rose, John Alexander, Capt. (Tp.), k. in a., 9/3/17.
Row, William Burnett, T/2/Lt., d. of w., 15/4/18 (att. 1/5th Bn.) (in German hands).
Royley, Joseph Holt, 2/Lt., k. in a., 25/4/18 (att. 1/5th Bn.).
10 Rudd, Kenneth Sutherland, T/Capt., k. in a., 10/10/18.
16 Russell, Henry, Capt. (Tp.), d. of w., 10/6/16
2 Ruttledge, John Forrest, T/Capt., k. in a., 1/7/16.
Salmons, Harry, T/2/Lt., d. of w., 1/4/18 (in German hands).
Sanders, Clive, A/Capt., k. in a., 27/5/18 (att. 2nd Bn.).
Sanderson, Wilfrid, T/2/Lt., d. of w., 15/4/18 (att. 1/7th Bn.).
Sankey, Thomas, 2/Lt. (Tp.), k. in a., 13/12/17.
15 Saunders, Charles, T/2/Lt., k. in a., 1/7/16.
3 Scarborough, Haydn, 2/Lt., k. in a., 17/9/18.
12 Scarr, Reginald Graham, T/2/Lt., k. in a., 14/7/16.
15 Scholes, Fredk. W., 2/Lt., k. in a., 3/5/17.
2 Scott, George Trotter, T/2/Lt., d. of w., 6/5/17.
4 Senior, George Fairburn, 2/Lt., k. in a., 17/11/17 (att. 1/7th Bn.).
12 Sewill, Arnold Waterlow, T/2/Lt., k. in a., 23/7/16
10 Shann, John Webster, Lt. (Tp.), k. in a., 1/7/16.
3 Sharp, Cyril Robert, Capt. (Tp.), k. in a., 14/7/16.

Shaw, Bernard Henry Gilbert, Lt., k. in a., 18/12/14.
3 Shaw, Joshua Harold, 2/Lt., d. of w., 1/5/18 (att. 1st Bn.).
12 Shaw, Sydney Thomas, T/2/Lt., d. of w., 11/5/16 (att. 10th Bn.).
Shuttleworth, Ernest Hebden, T/2/Lt., k. in a., 20/7/18 (att. 8th Bn.).
12 Skeet, William Celington, Capt. (Tp.), k. in a, 9/4/17.
2 Skett, Arthur Edwin Pye, 2/Lt., k. in a., 11/11/16.
4 Slade, Charles Godfrey Mitford, Major, k. in a., 8/11/14 (att. N. Lancs R.).
18 Sleigh, William Ward, Lt. (Tp.), k. in a., 25/2/17.
2 Smailes, George, T/2/Lt., k. in a., 22/10/16.
4 Smart, George Henry, Capt., k. in a., 22/12/14 (att. N. Lancs R.).
16 Smith, Donald, Temp. Capt., k. in a., 1/7/16.
1 Smith, Frederick William, Temp. Capt., k. in a., 25/4/16.
15 Smith, Harold, M.C., Temp Capt., d. of w., 28/3/18.
18 Smith, John Taylor, Temp. 2/Lt., d. of w, 29/3/18 (att. 2 Bn.).
10 Smith, Matthew Frederick, M.C., Temp. Capt., k. in a., 18/9/18
12 Smith, Percy Lloyd, 2/Lt. (Tp.), k in a., 3/5/17.
1 Soames, Gilbert Horsman, Major, k. in a., 9/6/17.
17 Sowry, Alfred Allan 2/Lt. (Tp.), k. in a., 31/8/17.
9 Spencer, John Aldersley Craven, 2/Lt., k. in a., 9/8/15.
12 Squires, Edward Constable, M.C., Temp. Capt., k. in a., 18/8/16.
2 Stagg, Arthur John, Temp. 2/Lt., k. in a., 27/5/18.
12 Stananought, Richard Frederick, T/Lt. & Adjt., d. of w., 5/9/16.
16 Stead, Ralph, 2/Lt. (Tp.), k. in a., 1/7/16.
17 Stead, Willie Wouldhave, Temp. Lt., k. in a., 25/8/16.
2 Stewart, Alexander James, M.C., Lt. (A/Major), d. of w., 30/4/18 (att. M.G.C.).
Stockdale, Guy Nelson, M.C., Major, k. in a., 21/3/18 (att. 11/Essex).
4 Stott, Philip Harle, 2/Lt., k. in a., 25/4/18 (att. 1/5 Bn.).
Street Richard, 2/Lt. (Tp.), k. in a., 24/4/17 (att. M.G.C., 86 Coy.).
3 Studley, Charles Carr, 2/Lt., k. in a., 9/10/17 (att. 1/8 Bn.).
9 Surtees, William Beverley, Temp. Capt., d. of w., 28/9/16.
4 Sussex, Reginald Arthur, 2/Lt., d. of w., 20/3/17 (att. 1/York & Lancs Regt.).
16 Sutcliffe, Robert, 2/Lt., d. of w., 5/7/16.
Swaby, Sydney Thomas, Temp. Lt., d. of w., 31/8/18 (att. 2/4 K.O.Y.L.I.).
Swift, William, Temp. 2/Lt., k. in a., 11/10/18, (Res. att. 1/7 W. Rid. Regt.).
16 Symonds, Frank James, Temp. 2/Lt., k. in a., 1/7/16.
1 Taylor, Charles Edward, Lt., k. in a., 1/11/15.
10 Taylor, Charles Harry, Lt., drowned, 17/11/15.
12 Taylor, Francis Galloway, 2/Lt., k. in a., 23/7/16.
Temple, Edgar, 2/Lt. (T/Lt.), k. in a., 10/9/17 (att. 12/Yorks Regt.).
Temple, Ernest Nelson, Temp. 2/Lt., d. of w., 8/4/18 (att. 2/7 Bn.).
Tennent, Oswald Moncreiff, 2/Lt., k. in a., 16/6/15.
3 Thomas, Frederick James, 2/Lt., k. in a., 21/9/17 (att. 11 Bn.).
15 Thomas, James Shepherd, Temp. 2/Lt., k. in a., 3/5/17.
Thompson, Offley Charles Wycliffe, Lt., k. in a., 20/9/14.
4 Thompson-McLaughlin, Lee, 2/Lt., died, 19/4/17 (and R.F.C.).
10 Thornsby, Harold Stansfield, Temp. 2/Lt., k. in a., 24/8/18.
4 Titley, Anthony Graham, 2/Lt., k. in a., 13/4/17.
15 Tolson, Robert Huntries, 2/Lt., k. in a., 1/7/16.
18 Tooke, Bernard, Temp. Capt., k. in a., 3/5/17.
11 Town, Charles Aubrey, M.C., Temp. Capt., k. in a., 20/9/17.
12 Townsend, John, Temp. 2/Lt., k. in a., 14/7/16.
12 Townsley, Bryan Hill, Temp. 2/Lt., k. in a., 14/9/16 (att. 9 Bn.).
15 Townson, H. J., 2/Lt., k. in a., 21/4/18 (and R.A.F.).
1 Trafford-Rawson, John Henry Edmund, Temp. Capt., k. in a., 18/9/16.
4 Tugwell, Oswald Norman, 2/Lt., d. of w., 22/4/17 (att. 1 Bn.).
Tunnah, William, Temp. 2/Lt., died, 28/4/18 (att. 1/6 Bn.) (In German hands).
1/2 Turner, F. E., 2/Lt., died, 27/9/18 (and R.A.F.).
Turner, Francis Ignatius, Temp. 2/Lt., killed, 27/9/18 (att. 8 Bn.).
12 Turner, Herbert Norman, Temp. Lt., k. in a., 14/7/16.
13 Tweedale Eric, 2/Lt. (Tp.), k. in a., 1/7/16 (att. 16 Bn.).
12 Underhill, Charles Bertram, Lt. (Tp.), k. in a., 27/3/16.
12 Vann, Arthur Harrison Allard, Capt. & Adjt., k. in a., 25/9/15.
15 Vause, John Gilbert, Lt. (Tp.), k. in a., 1/7/16.
Vose, Thomas, 2/Lt. (Tp.), k. in a., 13/12/17 (att. 12 Bn.).
4 Waite, Charles, 2/Lt., d. of w., 28/3/18 (att. 2/8 Bn.).
Wakefield, Thomas Butler, Temp. 2/Lt., k. in a., 8/9/17 (att. 2/6 Bn.).
18 Walton, Francis John George, 2/Lt. (Tp.), k. in a., 1/7/16.
1 Walton, Percy Jackson, Temp. 2/Lt., k. in a., 8/3/17.
12 Walton, Reginald Frederick William, Temp. 2/Lt., k. in a., 26/9/17.
15 Ward, Albert, 2/Lt., k. in a., 28/6/18.
15 Ward, Alec, 2/Lt., k. in a., 28/6/18.
15 Wardle, James Kenneth, Temp. Lt., d. of w., 30/4/16.
18 Warner, William James, 2/Lt., k. in a., 3/5/17.
4 Warren, Fred Langford, 2/Lt., k. in a., 1/7/16 (att. 2 Bn.).
10 Waterhouse, Irvin Preston, Temp. 2/Lt., k. in a., 8/11/16.
18 Watson, Frank, Lt., k. in a., 1/7/16 (att. 93 T.M.B.).
13 Webster, Michael Harold, Lt. (Tp.), k. in a., 1/7/16 (att. 16 Bn.).
1 Welchman, Edward Theodore, D.S.O., Capt., d. of w., 26/10/14.
9 Wells, Leonard Frank, M.C., 2/Lt., k. in a., 11/10/18.
9 Westcott, Edgar, M.C., Capt., d. of w., 4/11/18.
4 Weston, Kingsley Vale, 2/Lt., d. of w., 10/4/18 (att. M.G.C.).
1 Wheelton, William, 2/Lt., k. in a., 29/3/18 (att. 1/7 Bn.).
2 Whelan, George, M.C., 2/Lt., k. in a., 16/8/17.
11 Whitaker, Arthur Cecil, Temp. Capt., k. in a., 1/1/16.
15 Whitaker, George Clifford, Temp. Capt., k. in a., 1/7/16.
11 Whitby, Harry Alden, Temp. Capt., k. in a., 10/7/16.
Whitteron, Claude, 2/Lt., k. in a., 25/4/18 (att. 1/6 Bn.).
3 Wilkinson, Arthur Wilfrid, Capt., d. of w., 18/4/18.
4 Wilkinson, W. S., 2/Lt., died, 6/9/15.
15 Willey, Thomas Arthur Raymond Robert Ellicott, Temp. 2/Lt., k. in a., 1/7/16.
Williams, Aubrey, 2/Lt., k. in a., 25/4/18 (att. 1/6 Bn.).
18 Williams, Eric, Lt., k. in a., 27/3/18 (att. 2 Bn.).
Wilson, Eric Western, 2/Lt., k. in a., 20/9/14.
4 Winch, Edmond Arthur, 2/Lt., k. in a., 19/10/15 (att. 2 Bn.).
11 Winser, Frederick Herbert, Temp. 2/Lt., k. in a., 7/10/16.
11 Wood, Gordon, 2/Lt. (T/Lt.), d. of w., 9/6/17.
9 Wood, Maxmilian, David Francis, Major, d. of w., 22/8/15.
Woodcock, Arthur Douglas, 2/Lt. (Tp.), k. in a., 16/8/17 (Res., att. 10 Bn.).
Woodd, Alex. Bethune Peter, 2/Lt., d. of w., 24/8/18 (Res. att. 10 Bn.).
9 Woods, Eric Joseph, 2/Lt. (T/Lt.), k. in a., 9/10/17.
12 Wooler, Charles Armytage, 2/Lt. (Tp.), d. of w., 20/7/16.
12 Wooler, Herbert Sykes, Temp. 2/Lt., d. of w., 28/3/16.
12 Wooler, Rupert Basil, Lt., d. of w., 3/5/17.
Worrall, Herbert, 2/Lt., k. in a., 25/4/18 (att. 1/6 Bn.).
9 Worsnop, Edgar, Temp. Lt., d. of w., 7/8/15.
18 Worsnop, John William, 2/Lt., k. in a., 30/6/16.
1 Wright, Walter Horace, 2/Lt., k. in a., 21/3/18.

The East Yorkshire Regiment.

Abbott, Alfred, 2/Lt., d. of w., 26/4/18 (att. 9/Yorks L.I.).
Addey, George, 2/Lt. (Tp.), k. in a., 2/9/18 (Res. att. 7 Bn.).
10 Addy, James Carlton, Capt., k. in a., 3/5/17.
Addyman, Oscar James, Lt., k. in a., 4/2/15.
7 Alcock, Randal Arthur, 2/Lt. (Tp.), k. in a., 1/9/18.
1 Allchorn, Edward Walter, 2/Lt. (Tp.), d. of w., 5/11/17.
10 Andrew, Ernest John, Lt., k. in a., 23/3/18.
Andrew, Frederick, 2/Lt. (T/Lt.), k. in a., 27/2/15 (W. Afr. Regt.).
1 Anson, Stanley Edmund, 2/Lt. (Tp.), k. in a., 4/6/16.
7 Ashington, Henry Sherard Osborn, T/Lt. (A/Capt.), d. of w., 31/1/17.
Bailey, John Bodley, 2/Lt., k. in a., 20/9/17 (and R.F.C., 7 Sqd.).
Ball, Henry, Lt., k. in a., 13/1/16 (R.E., 180 Coy.).
7 Bambridge, Harry Liddall, M.C., 2/Lt., k. in a., 31/3/18.
9 Banbury, Ralph Frontenac, 2/Lt. (Tp.), died, 8/1/16.
7 Barker, Gordon, 2/Lt. (Tp.), d. of w., 23/10/18.
Barnett, Thos. William, 2/Lt., died, 17/1/19 (att. R.A.F.).
12 Beckh, Robert Harold, 2/Lt. (Tp.), d. of w., 15/8/16.
13 Beechey, Frank Collett Reeves, 2/Lt. (Tp.), d. of w., 14/11/16.
13 Bell, Harold, 2/Lt., k. in a., 13/11/16.
1 Benson, Richard Erle, Lt.-Col., d. of w., 27/9/14.
8 Bibby, Joseph Morton, 2/Lt., k. in a., 3/5/17.
Billing, John, 2/Lt. (Tp.), k. in a., 2/9/18 (att. 5/K.O.Y. L.I.).
13 Binning, Albert Huteson, 2/Lt. (Tp.), k. in a., 13/11/16.
Blagbrough, George Stanley, Major (Tp.), k. in a., 11/12/16 (att. 16/W. Yorks Regt.).
8 Blake, Norman Pilkington, Capt. (Tp.), k. in a., 14/7/16.
1 Bolton, Gordon Wallace, Capt., k. in a., 24/4/18.
1 Boncker, Barry Robert, 2/Lt., k. in a., 1/7/16.
Bottomley, Thomas Reginald, Lt., k. in a., 23/9/14.
Bowman, Alexander White, 2/Lt., k. in a., 25/9/16 (att. M.G.C.).
9 Brogden, Frederick Newman, 2/Lt., k. in a., 3/5/17 (att. 8/T.M.B.).
9 Brook, Cecil Frederick, 2/Lt. (Tp.), died, 5/4/16.
13 Brooke, Clarence, 2/Lt. (Tp.), k. in a., 31/3/18.
7 Brooke, Harold William, Temp. Capt., k. in a., 24/4/17.
13 Brown, Frederick David, 2/Lt., k. in a., 8/3/17.
7 Buckley, Humphry Paul Stenneth, Capt., d. of w., 29/7/17.
13 Burbidge, Howard Churchill, 2/Lt. (Tp.), d. of w., 13/9/16.
1 Butt, John George, 2/Lt. (Tp.), d. of w., 18/9/18.
Callard, Stanley Edwin, 2/Lt., k. in a., 23/4/15.
Campion, William Ernest, Major, k. in a., 28/10/14.
Canty, Frederick William, Temp. 2/Lt., d. of w., 29/6/18 (Res. att. 2/Y. & Lanc. Regt.).
1 Capper, George William, Major, died, 7/1/19 (Garr. Bn.).
Carew, Cyril Joseph Theodore, 2/Lt., d. of w., 29/4/15.
10 Carlisle, Reginald, T/Lt. (A/Capt.), k. in a., 3/5/17.
12 Carrall, John Edwin, 2/Lt., k. in a., 3/5/17.
12 Carroll, William, M.C., A/Capt., k. in a., 3/5/17.
12 Cattley, William, M.C., 2/Lt. (A/Capt.), k. in a., 3/5/17.
Cart de Lafontaine, Alfred Edwin Cecil, Capt., k. in a., 9/7/16.
1 Case, Albert Robert, M.C., T/Lt. (A/Capt.), k. in a., 26/8/18.
1 Cemery, Arthur Frank, Capt., k. in a., 19/7/17.
3 Chalmers, Francis, 2/Lt., k. in a., 25/9/16.
10 Clark, William Sowerby, M.C., Temp. Capt., killed, 10/7/17.
8 Clarke, Cyril George, Temp. Lt., d. of w., 26/9/15.
3 Cleminson, Robert, 2/Lt., k. in a., 25/9/16.
11 Clift, Marcus Henry, Temp. 2/Lt., k. in a., 8/11/17.
Clutterbuck, Peter, Lt., k. in a., 20/10/14.
1 Coles, James Hugh, D.S.O., Capt. (Act. Lt.-Col.), k. in a., 24/4/18.
7 Collcutt, Philip Martin Blake, Temp. Lieut., k. in a., 12/5/17.
Collen, Norman Owen, 2/Lt. (Tp.), k. in a., 25/9/16.
Cookson, Bernard, Temp. 2/Lt., k. in a., 10/4/17 (Res., att. 1 Bn.).

7 Cooper, Harold Leslie, 2/Lt. (Tp.), k. in a., 31/3/18.
1 Corrie, William Ronald, 2/Lt., d. of w., 23/4/17.
Cosens, Harold Stanley Frederick, Lt., k. in a., 27/10/14.
6 Coultas, Thomas Bestwick, Temp. Lt., k. in a., 26/9/16.
11 Cowley, Frank Wheatley, M.C, Lt (Tp.), d. of w., 9/8/18 (att. T.M.B.).
8 Cox, Arthur Johnson, Temp. 2/Lt., k. in a., 3/5/17
18 Crabtree, Stephen Mark, Lt., k. in a.. 28/6/16.
3 Cracroft, Robert Brian, Lt., k. in a., 10/7/16.
1 Crane, Reginald Hooper, Temp. 2/Lt., k. in a., 4/10/17.
8 Crocker, Francis George, Temp. 2/Lt., k. in a., 14/7/16.
8 Cubitt, Bryan Barton, Temp. Lt., k. in a., 26/9/15.
1 Cutcliffe, John, Lt. (Tp.), k. in a.. 26/8/18 (att. 9/W. Riding Regt.).
8 Cuttle, George William, 2/Lt., k. in a., 4/6/17.
8 Dalton, Horace Montague, Temp. 2/Lt., k. in a., 3/5/17.
9 Davis, Owen Mazzinghi, 2/Lt. (Tp.), k. in a., 27/6/16.
Dean, Harry, Temp. 2/Lt., k. in a., 11/4/18.
8 Diment, William James Gregory, 2/Lt. (Tp.), k. in a., 26/9/17.
6 Dingle, Arthur James, Temp. Lt., k. in a., 22/8/15.
13 Dorman, Anthony Godfrey, M.C., Lt. (Tp.), k. in a., 13/11/16.
7 Douglas, Percy, Temp. 2/Lt., died, 25/5/17.
9 Drew, Frederick William, 2/Lt. (Tp.), k. in a., 5/11/16.
12 Drewett Charles, 2/Lt. (Tp.), d. of w., 29/6/16
10 Dugdale, Daniel, Capt. (Tp.), k. in a., 28/9/18.
1 Eames, Arthur Horwood, 2/Lt., k. in a., 1/7/16.
7 Edwards, Arthur Ernest, 2/Lt. (Tp.), k. in a., 1/9/18 (late 8 Bn.)
6 Edwards, Charles, 2/Lt., k. in a.. 29/1/17.
Edwards, Eric Lea Priestley, Capt., k. in a., 20/9/14.
3 Ekins, Willingham Richard, 2/Lt., k. in a., 3/5/17.
12 Elford, Arthur Douglas, Temp. Lt., k. in a., 13/11/16.
8 Elliott, Eustace Trehane, Temp. 2/Lt., k. in a., 9/4/17.
1 Ellwood, Francis James, Lt., k. in a., 4/10/17.
9 Elmhirst, William, Temp. Capt., k. in a., 13/11/16.
Elrington, Gerard Gordon Clement, 2/Lt., k. in a., 2/11/14.
3 Estridge, Edward Wilfred, 2/Lt., k. in a., 13/11/16.
Evans, J., 2/Lt, died, 29/10/18 (and R.A.F.).
1 Ewing, Arthur Harold, M.C., Lt. (A/Capt.), d. of w., 8/9/18.
12 Faker, Frank Leonard, 2/Lt. (Tp.), k. in a., 13/11/16.
7 Fenner, John Prebble, Temp. 2/Lt., d. of w., 8/8/17.
7 Field, Francis Morgan, T/Lt. (A/Capt.), k. in a., 31/3/18.
10 Flintoff, Randolp Alex, Lt. (Tp.), k. in a., 25/6/16.
1 Foster, Heaton, 2/Lt., k. in a., 16/4/18.
10 Fricker, Albert Charles, Temp. 2/Lt., k. in a., 27/2/17.
12 Frizoni, Oscar Lorenzo, Lt., k. in a., 13/11/16.
6 Garrett, Henry Fawcett, Temp. Capt., k. in a., 22/8/15.
6 Garrett, Hubert Frederick, Lt., k. in a., 4/6/15.
3 Gatrell, Reginald James Hurst, Lt., k. in a., 1/7/16.
8 Geraghty, Thomas, 2/Lt., k. in a., 26/9/17.
7 Giles, Thomas William, Temp. 2/Lt., d. of w., 14/12/17.
7 Goldthorpe, Arthur Francis, Temp. 2/Lt., k. in a., 12/5/17.
1 Gosset, Rene Frankland, A/Capt., k. in a., 25/9/16.
1 Green, William Wesley, 2/Lt., k. in a., 9/4/17.
7 Groves, Ernest, 2/Lt., k. in a., 31/3/18.
12 Habershon, Leonard Osborne, Temp. Capt., k. in a., 13/11/16.
1 Hall, John Francis A., 2/Lt., k. in a., 14/8/18 (att. R.A.F.).
12 Hall, Joseph Stanley, 2/Lt., k. in a., 5/5/17.
13 Hamm, William George, M.C., Temp. 2/Lt., k. in a., 2/5/17.
11 V.C. Harrison, John, M.C., 2/Lt., k. in a., 3/5/17.
8 Hartert, Joachim Charles, Temp. Lt., k. in a., 28/10/16.
8 Hartley, Richard, Temp. 2/Lt., killed, 11/11/16.
3 Haswell, Frederick, 2/Lt., d. of w., 23/4/15.
3 Hawkins, Oliver Luther, 2/Lt., d. of w., 26/4/15.
8 Hayes, Mortimer Frederick, Temp. Lt, k. in a., 10/7/16.
7 Heathcock, Thomas, Temp. Capt., k. in a., 10/7/16.
12 Heathcote, Ralph Noel, Temp. 2/Lt., d. of w., 17/11/16.
Hill, Lional George, Capt., k. in a., 17/2/15.
Hind, Frank, Capt.. d. of w., 29/10/14 (P. of W.).
Hinings, Frederick William Crowther, Capt., k. in a., 25/9/16.
1 Holmes, George, 2/Lt., k. in a., 9/4/17.
7 Holroyd, Lister, Temp. Capt., d. of w., 12/9/16.
Holroyde, John Sheffield, 2/Lt., k. in a., 10/5/17 (and R.F.C., 55 Sqd.).
11 Hopkins, William Jones, Temp 2/Lt., d. of w., 8/10/16.
13 Horn, John Cyril, 2/Lt (Tp.). k. in a., 29/4/17.
1 Horrocks, John, Hon. Lt. & Q.M., died, 23/10/15.
6 Hosken, Wilfrid, 2/Lt., k in a., 21/8/15.
8 Hough, Topham Becher Dabridgecourt, Temp. 2/Lt., k. in a., 17/1/16.
10 Houghton, Albert William, 2/Lt., d. of w., 31/3/18.
12 Hoult, Arthur, Temp. 2/Lt., died, 17/11/16.
1 Howe, Robert Ernest, 2/Lt., k. in a., 4/10/17.
8 Hoyle, William, 2/Lt. (Tp.), k. in a., 9/4/17.
Hubbert, Francis Stanley William, 2/Lt., k. in a., 23/5/15.
6 Huggard, Hewitt, Lt., k. in a., 7/8/15.
1 Huntriss, Cyril John, Temp. Capt., k. in a., 1/7/16.
11 Hutchinson, Benjamin, M.C., 2/Lt., k. in a., 3/5/17.
Hutchinson, Basil Stewart Cayley, Lt., k. in a., 20/9/14.
10 Hutchinson, Leslie Gwynne, Lt. (Tp.), k. in a., 10/9/18.
13 Hutchinson, Tom Macintosh, Temp. 2/Lt., k. in a., 13/11/16.
2 Illingworth, Frank, Temp. 2/Lt., k. in a., 15/12/16.
6 Jalland, Stephen, Lt., k. in a., 9/8/15.
3 Jalland, Boswell Victor, 2/Lt., k. in a., 9/4/17.
11 James, Rupert Frederick, Lt., k. in a., 27/3/18.
3 Jenner, George Reginald, 2/Lt., d. of w., 2/8/16 (att. 1 Bn.).
10 Johnston, Alexander, 2/Lt., k. in a., 25/3/18.
13 Johnston-Stuart, Cyril George, Lt., k. in a., 16/4/18.
10 Jones, Arthur Godman, Temp. 2/Lt., d. of w., 1/7/17.
8 Keith, Malcolm, Temp. 2/Lt., k. in a., 26/0/17.
1 Kennard, Patrick Noel, Capt., k. in a., 14/7/16.
7 King, Bertie Allen, Temp. 2/Lt., d. of w., 29/4/17.
7 Kippax, Arthur Hadden, Temp. 2/Lt., k. in a., 1/7/16.
1 Krog, Eustace John, M.C., Lt. (Tp.), k. in a., 7/0/18.
7 Laing, Ernest Edward, Temp. 2/Lt., k. in a., 29/7/17.

Lawrence Bertram, Capt., k. in a., 27/10/14.
10 Leech, Norman Black, 2/Lt. (Temp. Capt.), d. of w., 10/5/17.
15 Lewis, Norman Victor, Temp. Lieut., k. in a., 13/11/16.
7 Lightley, Albert, 2/Lt., k. in a., 31/3/18.
7 Lindley, Foster, 2/Lt., d. of w., 5/9/18.
12 Livsey, Ernest Claude, Temp. 2/Lt., k. in a., 13/11/16.
9 Lowrie, James Harold, Temp. 2/Lt., d. of w., 25/1/17 (att. 7 Bn.).
3 Macaulay, George Cecil Gordon, 2/Lt., killed, 2/5/17.
10 McDermott, Edward, M.C., 2/Lt. (Tp.), k. in a., 12/4/18.
8 McIntyre, Francis, Temp. 2/Lt., k. in a., 3/5/17.
11 McIntyre, Robert William, M.B.E., 2/Lt. (Tp.), k. in a., 25/7/18.
9 McKenzie, Kenneth Nowell, 2/Lt., k. in a., 4/6/15.
11 McReynolds, John Bernard, Hon. Lt. & Qr.-Mr., k. in a., 12/11/16.
7 Major, Cyril Birdee, 2/Lt., k. in a., 5/11/16.
3 Manley, George Sydney, 2/Lt., died, 30/11/18.
Markham, John Addis, Capt., k. in a., 7/5/15.
12 Marriott, Herbert Norman, Temp. Capt., k. in a., 13/11/16.
10 Marshall, Andrew Fairlie Wilson, 2/Lt., died, 26/9/18 (P.O.W.).
Maxwell, Peter Benson, Capt., d. of w., 24/9/14.
6 Mee, George Hamilton, Temp. Lieut., k. in a., 22/8/15.
Meller, Arthur William, 2/Lt., k. in a., 29/1/16.
1 Micklethwaite, Harold Chandos, Temp. 2/Lt., d. of w., 25/3/18.
3 Millar, Walter Gordon, Capt., k. in a., 8/7/16.
3 Miller, Henry Thornton, Lt., k. in a., 6/5/15 (att. 2/W. Rid. Regt.).
8 Mills, Thomas Henry Lewis, Temp. Capt., k. in a., 14/7/16.
3 Mintoft, Henry Stephen, 2/Lt., k. in a., 4/10/17.
11 Mitchell, Henry, 2/Lt., d. of w., 3/4/18.
9 Moncrieff, Charles George C., Temp. 2/Lt., d. of w., 24/11/16.
6 Montgomerie-Fleming, James Brown, Temp. Major, d. of w., 18/8/17.
6 Moore, Henry Glanville Allen, Temp. Lt.-Col., k. in a., 11/8/15.
12 Moore, Percy, Temp. 2/Lt., d. of w., 5/5/17.
12 Morgan, Richard G., Temp. 2/Lt., k. in a., 13/11/16.
7 Morice, Norman Archibald, Temp. Lt., d. of w., 11/3/16.
1 Morrison, Ronald MacDonald, 2/Lt., k. in a., 9/4/17.
11 Muir, Harry, Temp. 2/Lt., killed, 18/4/16.
1 Nevill, Wilfred Percy, Capt. (Tp.), k. in a., 1/7/16 (att. 8 E. Surrey Regt.).
6 Newman, John Sherwood, Temp. 2/Lt., k. in a., 7-11/8/15.
Nielson, William Christian, Temp. 2/Lt., k. in a., 2/9/18 (att. 5 Yorks L.I.).
12 Officer, Arnold Vincent, 2/Lt. (Tp.), died, 10/5/17.
11 Oliver, Arthur Harold, 2/Lt. (Tp.), k. in a., 8/11/17.
Ottley, Algernon Glendower, Capt., d. of w., 22/5/15.
10 Palmer, Derek William Onslow, Temp. Lt., k. in a., 4/6/16.
8 Pappa, Armaud Francis, 2/Lt., k. in a., 5/5/17.
Payne, Henry Drummond, 2/Lt., k. in a., 20/3/15.
Pease, Mark Robinson, Lt., k. in a., 20/12/14.
1 Peregrine, John Pryor Puxton, Lt., k. in a., 1/7/16.
7 Perry, Claude William, Temp. 2/Lt., k. in a., 1/7/16.
13 Peters, Ashley, 2/Lt., k. in a., 13/11/16.
3 Petersen, Aaron, 2/Lt., k. in a., 3/9/18 (and R.A.F.).
10 Pierson, Leslie D., Lt., k. in a., 30/10/16.
8 Pinn, Tyrrell Steventon, 2/Lt. (Tp.), d. of w., 12/10/15.
8 Price, Wilfred, Temp. 2/Lt., d. of w., 3/5/17.
Prichard, Frederic Giles, Lt., d. of w., 9/8/15.
8 Prince, Frederick Harold, Temp. 2/Lt., k. in a., 9/4/17.
6 Pringle, Norman Douglas, Temp. Capt., k. in a., 7-11/8/15.
13 Puddicombe, Donald Ramsay, Temp. 2/Lt., d. of w., 24/7/16.
11 Purll, William Albert George, 2/Lt., k. in a., 3/5/17.
13 Ransom, Richard Edward Croft, Temp. Capt., d. of w., 21/7/16.
15 Read, Stephen Tucker, Temp., Lt., died, 11/12/18 (and K.A.R.).
3 Redfern, Wilfrid, A/Capt., k. in a., 22/3/18 (att. 7 Bn.).
8 Reeder, Edward, Temp. Lt., k. in a., 26/9/15.
11 Reeve, Ernest William, Capt., k. in a., 3/5/17.
3 Rerrie, Errol Seymour, M.C., Lt., k. in a., 12/5/17 (att. 7 Bn.).
3 Reynard, Charles Frederick, Capt., died, 16/6/18.
10 Rice, Bernard Neville, Capt. (Tp.), died, 9/7/17.
Richardson, Frank Arnold, 2/Lt., killed, 25/4/18 (att. 11 Bn.).
Rippingille, Frank Alexander, 2/Lt., k. in a., 11/11/14.
Roberts, John Harry, Temp. 2/Lt., d. of w., 11/4/18 (Res. att.).
7 Robertson, Harold Hay, M.C.. Temp. 2/Lt., d. of w., 11/9/18.
3 Robins, George Upton, Capt., d. of w., 7/5/15.
6 Rogers, Alan Stanley Clark, Capt. (Tp.), k. in a., 7/8/15.
9 Russell, Charles, Lt., k. in a., 22/11/17 (att. 2/10 Gurkhas).
2 Russell, Francis George, Temp. 2/Lt., d. of w., 17/4/18.
10 Rutherford, William McConnell, Temp. 2/Lt., d. of w., 19/4/18.
1 Ruthven, William Logan, Major, k. in a., 3/12/17 (att. 2/6 Glos. Regt.).
7 Rutledge, John Bedell, Temp. Capt., k. in a., 1/7/16.
Saillard, Phillip, 2/Lt. (T/Lt.), k. in a., 22/8/17.
7 Salmon, Reginald Thomas, 2/Lt. (Tp.), k. in a., 12/5/17.
8 Samuel, Gerard Stuart, Temp. 2/Lt., d. of w., 14/7/16.
10 Sanger, Henry Keith, Temp. 2/Lt., k. in a., 13/4/18.
Saunders, Harold Cecil Rich, D.S.O., Capt. (A/Major), k. in a., 30/5/18.
Sasse, Frederick Hugh, Capt., d. of w., 8/5/15.
11 Saville, Clifford Allen, Capt., k. in a., 8/11/17.
13 Sawdon, Arthur Tindale, 2/Lt. (Tp.), k. in a., 28/6/17.
8 Sawyer, Charles Quinton, Temp. Capt., k. in a., 14/7/16 (att. T.M.B.).
6 Sawyer, William Robert, 2/Lt. (Tp.), d. of w., 8/10/17.

1 Scott, Edward Richard, 2/Lt., k. in a., 19/2/18.
Scott, Richard Thomas Folliott, Lt., k. in a., 16/3/15.
1 Sheffield, Harold Welford, Lt., k. in a., 23/3/18.
6 Sieber, John Frederick Louis, Temp. 2/Lt., d. of w., 4/10/16.
8 Simon, Norman, Temp. 2/Lt., k. in a., 14/7/16.
Sissons, Norman Lea, Temp. Lt., k. in a., 9/9/16.
11 Skevington, William Percy, Temp. 2/Lt., k. in a., 8/9/18.
Smith, Arthur Charles Vaughan, Temp. 2/Lt., k. in a., 9/10/17.
1 Smith, Percy Claude Jacomb, 2/Lt., k. in a., 1/7/16.
1 Smith, William Arthur Heseltine, 2/Lt., k. in a., 27/5/18.
8 Snell, Norris, Temp. Capt., k. in a., 14/7/16.
10 Southern, Mathew, 2/Lt. (Tp.), k. in a., 12/9/17.
10 Spink, Cecil Cooper, Temp. 2/Lt., k. in a., 4/6/16.
Stamp, Douglas Blatspiel, Lt., d. of w., 10/4/16.
Staveley, Frederick Simpson, Capt., killed, 15/3/15 (att. W. Riding Regt.).
11 Staveley, Hugh Sheardown, Temp. Lt., k. in a., 3/5/17.
6 Steele, Arthur Joseph, Temp. Lt., k. in a., 22/9/15.
3 Stevenson, George Arthur, 2/Lt., d. of w., 9/5/15.
Stockley, Philip George, Capt. (Tp.), died, 12/2/17.
1 Stow, Montague Bruce, Lt.-Col. (Tp.), d. of w., 2/7/16.
3 Strickland-Constable, Frederick Charles, Lt.-Col., died, 20/12/17 (and Staff.).
10 Stringer, Dudley, 2/Lt., k. in a., 3/5/17.
3 Tate, Gerald Charles, 2/Lt., d. of w., 21/3/15.
2 Tatham, Basil Owen, Capt., k. in a., 23/4/15.
8 Taylor, Conrad Paul, Temp. Capt., k. in a., 28/10/16.
12 Taylor, Richard Neville, Temp. 2/Lt., k. in a., 26/5/16.
7 Thomas, William Edgar, D.S.O., M.C., T/Major (Act./Lt.-Col.), k. in a., 20/10/18.
7 Thornton, Frank, Temp. 2/Lt., k. in a., 1/7/16.
11 Tomey, Donald Stuart, Temp. Lt., k. in a., 25/3/18.
7 Tonkin, Frederick Cuthbert, D.S.O., M.C., Lt., T/Capt., d. of w., 4/11/18.
1 Townsend, Thomas, Temp. 2/Lt., k. in a., 4/6/16.
10 Traill, Colin Balfour, M.C., Temp. Major, k. in a., 28/6/18.
2 Trier, Norman Ernest, 2/Lt. (Tp.), d. of w., 6/10/15.
7 Tuke, Ottley, Temp. Lt., k. in a., 17/10/18 (att. 1/K.O.Y.L.I.).
8 Turner, David Fotheringham, Temp. 2/Lt., k. in a., 26/9/15.
8 Tyrrell, John McIntosh, Temp. 2/Lt., k. in a., 9/4/17.
8 Tyrrell, Launcelot Adrian Hope, 2/Lt (Tp.), k. in a., 13/11/16.
7 Urry, Robert Alexander, 2/Lt., died, 27/4/18.
7 Vale, Andrew Walter, Temp. 2/Lt., k. in a., 9/2/17.
Vickers, Noel, Lt., k. in a., 24/3/18.
1 Wadsworth, Percy, 2/Lt., k. in a., 22/3/18.
9 Wales, Harold Robert, Temp. 2/Lt., k. in a., 14/7/16.
3 Walker, Edgar Wilmer, Capt., k. in a., 27/10/14.
12 Walker, Sydney Stratton, Capt. (Tp.), k. in a., 19/7/16.
Wallace, Robert, Capt., died, 6/5/15.
11 Wallis, Francis Herbert Guy, Capt., d. of w., 17/5/18.
1 Walter, Arthur, 2/Lt., k. in a., 21/3/18.
8 Ward, Arthur Bowsher, 2/Lt., k. in a., 15/8/18.
Warren-Swettenham, Thomas Robert Eaton Wybault, Major, k. in a., 6/2/15.
3 Waterfall, Vincent, 2/Lt., killed, 22/8/14 (att. R.F.C.).
7 Watkins, Frederick Augustus, 2/Lt., k. in a., 24/3/18.
7 Watkins, Reginald Noel, Lt., k. in a., 31/3/18.
3 Watson, John Peirson, 2/Lt., k. in a., 29/7/17.
Watson, Walter, 2/Lt., k. in a., 27/5/18 (att. 4 Bn.).
13 Watt, Robert Stapleton, Temp. 2/Lt., d. of w., 20/11/16.
6 Watts, Henry Rowland, Temp. 2/Lt., k. in a., 7/6/17.
7 Westerby, James Thomas, 2/Lt., d. of w., 5/6/18.
6 Wheatley, Rutland Villiers, 2/Lt. (T/Lt.), k. in a., 29/11/17.
8 White, Joseph Wetherall, Temp. 2/Lt., k. in a., 26/9/15.
11 Whittington-Ince, Ralph Piggott, M.C., Lt., d. of w., 11/11/18.
3 Wigfall, William Edmund Clare, M.C., Lt., d. of w., 29/8/16.
2 Wigginton, Arthur, Temp. 2/Lt., k. in a., 30/7/16.
Wilkinson, Osborn Cecil, Capt., d. of w., 5/2/15.
7 Willats, Horace Lennan, Capt., died, 17/12/16.
Wilson, Arthur Henry, Capt., k. in a., 18/10/14.
Wilson, Evelyn Seppings, Temp. Capt., k. in a., 29/9/15.
6 Wilson, Robert Philip, 2/Lt., k. in a., 7/8/15.
Wood, Cecil Strachan, Capt., d. of w., 3/12/14.
13 Wood, John, Temp. 2/Lt., k. in a., 13/11/16.
Woodmass, Kenrick Talbot, Capt., k. in a., 23/4/15.
Wookey, Guy Richard Penny, Lt., d. of w., 10/5/15.
8 Wright, Arthur Samuel, 2/Lt., k. in a., 15/8/18.
1 Wyatt, William Herbert, 2/Lt., T/Lt., k. in a., 4/5/16.
1 Yates, Richard, 2/Lt., k. in a., 24/4/18.
8 Young, George Walter, Capt., k. in a., 27/5/18.

The Bedfordshire Regiment.

2 Abbott, Sidney Herbert, 2/Lt., k. in a., 4/11/18.
1 Ackroyd, Thomas, 2/Lt., k. in a., 23/4/17 (att. 9/Bn.).
10 Adair, John Thomas, Lt. (Tp.), d. of w., 22/8/15 (att. 1/Bord. R.).
3 Agate, Sydney Herbert, 2/Lt., k. in a., 13/11/16 (att. 4/Bn.).
8 Airth, Rennie Alexander, Lt. (Tp.), k. in a., 29/7/17 (and R.F.C., 7 Sq.).
Allen, Stephen Dexter, 2/Lt. (Tp.), k. in a., 27/8/18 (att. 4/Bn.).
8 Ambridge, William, 2/Lt. (Tp.), k. in a., 7/4/18 (att. 6/Batt.).
Anderson, Wilfred Cruttenden, Lt., k. in a., 30/10/14.
3 Angas, Lionel George, 2/Lt. (Tp.), k. in a., 3/5/17 (att. 7/Bn.).
4 Anns, Frederick, 2/Lt., k. in a., 6/11/15 (att. 2/Bn.).
8 Ash, John Cuxton, Lt. (Tp.), k. in a., 2/7/18 (att. 2/Bn.).
4 Ashmead-Bartlett, Francis George Coningsby, Capt., k. in a., 13/11/16.

7 Baden, Reginald, 2/Lt. (Tp.), k. in a., 26/6/16.
6 Bailey, Tom Esmond Geoffrey, Capt., k. in a., 2/4/19.
Baird, William Frank Gardiner, Capt., d. of w., 5/11/14.
2 Baldwin, Frederick Charles, 2/Lt., d. of w., 11/5/18.
3 Balfour, Percy, D.S.O., Major (T/Lt.-Col.), k. in a., 12/12/17 (att. 2/7 Worc. R.).
2 Ballard, Robert Francis Cooper, 2/Lt. (Tp.), k. in a., 30/7/16.
3 Banyard, James Hirst, 2/Lt., k. in a., 3/9/16 (att. 1/Bn.).
Bastard, William, Lt., k. in a., 27/10/14.
8 Beck, Edmund Wallis, Lt. (Tp.), d. of w., 9/1/16.
Bell, Charles Ockley, 2/Lt., k. in a., 12/10/14.
6 Bellamy, Frank William, 2/Lt. (Tp.), d. of w., 8/10/18 (att. 4/Bn.).
Berridge, Victor Arnold, 2/Lt. (Tp.), k. in a., 6/3/17 (and R.F.C., 34 Sqd).
6 Bignell, Gurth, Capt., k. in a., 15/7/16.
6 Binns, George Alfred, 2/Lt. (Tp.), k. in a., 8/4/18.
10 Bird, William Henry, 2/Lt. (Tp.), k. in a., 12/10/16 (att. 2/Bn.).
Blackburn, Reginald Herbert, 2/Lt., died, 5/11/18.
3 Blake, Christopher, 2/Lt., k. in a., 4/9/16.
8 Body, Frank Lydford, Capt. (Tp.), d. of w., 18/6/17.
2 Boys, Richard Harvey, Lt. (Tp.), k. in a., 13/11/16 (att. 4/Bn.).
4 Brawn, Mark, D.C.M., Lt. & Q.M., k. in a., 1/9/18.
3 Bridges, William Robert, 2/Lt., d. of w., 23/4/17 (att. 4/Bn.).
4 Brodie, John, 2/Lt., k. in a., 13/11/16.
9 Buch, Charles Justus, 2/Lt. (Tp.), k. in a., 14/9/16 (att. 8/Bn.).
7 Bull, Wilfred Herbert, Capt. (Tp.), k. in a., 3/5/17.
1 Burton, Henry Patrick Claude, Lt. (A/Capt.), k. in a., 27/7/16.
Butt, Alfred, 2/Lt., k. in a., 4/1/18 (att. R.F.C.).
4 Candy, Douglas Bowhill, 2/Lt., d. of w., 25/9/16 (att. 1/Bn.).
8 Cartwright, Charles, 2/Lt. (Tp.), k. in a., 19/4/16.
10 Casswell, Frederick Charles, 2/Lt. (Tp.), drowned, 13/8/15 (att. 1/Essex R.).
4 Cecil, Rupert Edward Gascoyne, 2/Lt., (T/Lt.), k. in a., 11/7/15 (att. 1/Bn.).
2 Chadwick, Francis Joseph, 2/Lt. (Tp.), k. in a., 12/10/16.
2 Chamen, Harold Ashcombe, Lt., d. of w., 1/8/16.
4 Charlton, St. John Alan, Lt., k. in a., 26/10/14 (att. 1/Bn.).
4 Childs, George Willmot, 2/Lt., d. of w., 22/1/18.
1/2 Christie, Paul Norman Jones, 2/Lt., k. in a., 9/10/17.
6 Colchester, Bernard Valentine, 2/Lt. (Tp.), k. in a., 25/4/17.
2 Collisson, Evelyn Ernest Arnold, 2/Lt. (Tp.), k. in a., 23/2/16.
4 V.C. Collings-Wells, John Stanhope, D.S.O., Capt. (A/Lt.-Col.), k. in a., 27/3/18.
9 Collymore, Hubert Aubrey, Lt., k. in a., 17/4/18 (att. 25/Bn. M.G.C.).
1 Cook, Charles Adam, 2/Lt. (Tp.), k. in a., 11/3/16.
9 Cooper, Maurice Stanley Charles, 2/Lt. (Tp.), d. of w., 10/8/16 (att. 6/Bn.).
1 Cornelius, Herbert Walter, 2/Lt. (Tp.), k. in a., 20/7/18.
1 Cotchin, Joseph, 2/Lt., k. in a., 9/10/17.
1 Cothill, William Henry Thomas, 2/Lt. (Tp.), k. in a., 23/10/18.
Courtenay, Hugh, D.S.O., M.C., Bt.-Major (A/Lt.-Col.), d. of w., 23/8/18.
4 Courthope, William George, Lt., died, 21/10/18 (and R.A.F.).
Coventry, William St. John, Lt., k. in a., 22/10/14.
7 Craig, Gordon Robert, 2/Lt. (Tp.), d. of w., 3/4/18.
Creasey, Arthur Andrew, 2/Lt., k. in a., 14/7/17 (and R.F.C., 22 Sq.).
3 Croockewit, Alexander Edward, 2/Lt., d. of w., 26/10/17 (att. 1/Bn.).
1 Cropley, Reginald John, 2/Lt. (Tp.), d. of w., 22/9/18.
2 Cross, Dennis Patrick, M.C., Lt. (A/Capt.), k. in a., 24/8/18.
6 Cunningham, Harold John, M.C., Capt. (Tp.), d. of w., 4/10/17.
9 Cunningham, James, 2/Lt. (Tp.), k. in a., 1/7/16 (att. 7/Bn.).
1 Curry, Vernon Edward, 2/Lt. (Tp.), k. in a., 23/4/17.
6 Dann, Ernest, 2/Lt. (Tp.), d. of w., 22/11/15.
10 Dawson, John Leonard, 2/Lt. (Tp.), died, 6/5/16.
Denham, Aubrey Crawshaw, Lt., died, 1/4/15 (att. 10/Bn.).
Denne, William Henry, D.S.O., Major, d. of w., 21/2/17.
4 Despicht, Leonard Terry, M.C., Lt., k. in a., 11/2/17.
4 Dickenson, Lawrence Aubrey Fiennes Wingfield, Lt., d. of w., 10/5/15 (att. R. Ir. Rif.).
8 Dolman, Leonard, 2/Lt. (T/Lt.), d. of w., 31/12/17.
3 Downes, Villiers Chermocke, Lt., d. of w., 18/10/14.
8 Draisey, Edwin Rowland Watts, Lt. (Tp.), k. in a., 15/9/16.
7 Duplock, Marten Cave, Lt. (Tp.), k. in a., 2/4/18.
1 Eaton, Alexander Robert Charles, Lt. (Tp.), k. in a., 23/8/18.
3 Edwards, Edwin Allen James, Lt., d. of w., 31/12/14 (att. 1/Bn.).
4 Ellis, Ernest, Lt. (Tp.), k. in a., 27/9/18.
4 Fawcett, Robert Heath, 2/Lt., k. in a., 26/4/15 (att. 1/Bn.).
7 Ferguson, John James Moore, Capt. (Tp.), died, 19/11/18 (att. 2/Bn.).
Fernandes, Dudley Luis De Tavora, 2/Lt., k. in a., 23/10/14.
2 Fink, Lawrence Alexander Lewis, M.C., 2/Lt. (A/Capt.), k. in a., 5/10/17.
1/2 Fleming, Harold Winning, 2/Lt., k. in a., 6/10/17.
1 Fletcher, Thomas Murray Kilpin, 2/Lt. (Tp.), k. in a., 23/4/17.
4 Flory, Percival James, 2/Lt. (Tp.), k. in a., 22/8/18.
2 Forward, Charles Arthur, 2/Lt., k. in a., 25/9/15.
Foster, Harold John Brittain, Capt., k. in a., 14/4/17 (att. 1/Essex R.).
1 Fox, Frank Herbert, 2/Lt. (Tp.), k. in a., 23/8/18.
4 Fox, Leslie Herbert, 2/Lt., k. in a., 11/7/16.
4 Freear, Eric Charles, 2/Lt. (Tp.), k. in a., 13/4/17.
4 Frere, Bartle Laurie Stuart, Lt., k. in a., 13/11/16.
4 Fynn, Robert Charles, 2/Lt. (Tp.), k. in a., 25/3/18.
2 Fyson, Harold George, 2/Lt., k. in a., 12/10/16.
Garnett-Botfield, Charles Sidney, Capt., d. of w., 14/12/14.

10 Gate, Leslie Charles Thomas, 2/Lt., k. in a., 30/10/17.
9 Gaussen, David Newbold, 2/Lt. (Tp.), k. in a., 31/7/16 (att. 1/Bn.).
8 Gibson, John Seear, 2/Lt. (Tp.), d. of w., 15/10/16.
3 Gibson, Robert Bowness, Lt., k. in a., 11/7/16 (att. 2/Bn.).
4 Gilbertson, Graham Sydney, 2/Lt., k. in a., 28/11/17 (att. 7/Bn.).
Gledstanes, S. A., Capt., d. of w., 9/5/15.
3 Graves, Walter Francis, Lt., k. in a., 9/11/14 (att. 1/Bn.).
1 Green, Reginald Cumberland, Lt., d. of w., 18/5/16.
2 Greenwood, Arthur Donald, 2/Lt. (Tp.), k. in a., 30/8/18.
8 Gretton, Rupert Harold, Capt. (Tp.), k. in a., 17/12/15.
6 Griffin, John James Wahal, 2/Lt. (Tp.), k. in a., 15/11/16.
1/2 Hague, Sydney George, M.C., Lt. (Tp.), d. of w., 21/9/18.
Hall, Arthur Gordon, Capt., k. in a., 26/10/14.
13 Hall, Percy Mark, Capt., died, 4/1/19.
7 Halsey, Frederick, 2/Lt., k. in a., 10/8/17.
10 Hamilton, Wallace Bernard, 2/Lt. (Tp.), k. in a., 9/8/16 (att. 6/Bn.).
4 Harding, Robert Denis Stewart, Lt., k. in a., 9/11/14 (att. 1/Bn.).
4 Harris, Antrobus Taft, 2/Lt., k. in a., 19/3/16 (att. Linc. R.).
3 Hart, Percival Frank, Lt., d. of w., 3/5/17 (att. 1/Bn.).
Harvey, Herbert Alexander, Lt. (Tp.), k. in a., 12/10/16 (att. 1/Essex R.).
9 Hasler, Gordon Beverley, 2/Lt. (Tp.), k. in a., 26/7/16 (att. 7/Bn.).
7 Haward, Hereward Warren, 2/Lt. (Tp.), d. of w., 1/7/18 (att. 2/Bn.).
3 Hayes, Arthur, 2/Lt., k. in a., 25/3/18.
1 Hayhoe, Alfred Charles, 2/Lt., k. in a., 27/7/16.
Heigham-Plumptre, L. G., 2/Lt., d. of w., 4/6/18 (and R.A.F.).
4 Hill, Thomas Hooton, 2/Lt., k. in a., 13/11/16.
8 Hislop, John, M.C., T/Lt. (A/Capt.), k. in a., 22/9/17.
6 Hobson, Owen Ellis, Capt. (Tp.), k. in a., 27/9/18 (att. 4/-Batt.).
8 Hodges, Archibald Gordon, Lt. (Tp.), k. in a., 15/9/16.
1 Holland, Archibald Clare, 2/Lt., k. in a., 27/7/16.
6 Holt, Percy James, 2/Lt. (Tp.), d. of w., 6/9/18 (att. 1/1 Hert. R.).
1 Hood, Douglas Edward, 2/Lt., k. in a., 14/4/17.
3 Hopkins, Eric Arthur, 2/Lt., k. in a., 5/5/15 (att. 1/Bn.).
Horsford, Thomas Gavin Moor, Lt., k. in a., 16/6/15.
3 Howard, Addison James, Lt., k. in a., 4/9/16 (att. 1/Bn.).
7 Howard, Cedric Stewart, 2/Lt. (Tp.), k. in a., 28/9/16.
10 Hudson, Harold Baldwin, 2/Lt. (Tp.), k. in a., 13/11/16 (att. 4/Bn.).
8 Hughes, William, M.C., 2/Lt. (Tp.), d. of w., 14/9/18 (att. 2/Batt.).
6 Hunston, John Norman, 2/Lt. (Tp.), d. of w., 15/7/16.
10 Hunston, Robert Donald, 2/Lt. (Tp.), k. in a., 28/9/16 (att. 7/Bn.).
Huntriss, Harold Edward, Capt., k. in a., 17/5/15.
1 Hutchinson, Herbert, 2/Lt., k. in a., 27/9/18 (att. 3/Bn.).
2 Hutchinson, James Walter, Lt. (T/Capt.), d. of w., 25/9/15.
1 Illingworth, Fred Donald Roberts, Lt. (Tp.), k. in a., 23/4/17.
1/2 Inch, George, 2/Lt., k. in a., 22/9/17 (att. 6/Bn.).
4 Ingram, Arthur Charles, Lt. (A/Capt.), k. in a., 26/3/18 (att. 4/E. Lan. R.).
6 Jesson, Arthur, 2/Lt., k. in a., 16/11/16.
7 Johnson, Evelyn Walter James, 2/Lt. (Tp.), d. of w., 20/7/16.
7 Keep, Douglas Scrivener Howard, M.C., Capt. (Tp.), k. in a., 14/7/17.
Kellie, Esmond Lawrence, 2/Lt., k. in a., 19/4/15.
Ker, Cecil Howard, Capt., k. in a., 15/9/14.
2 Kerr, George Augustus L'Estrange, 2/Lt., k. in a., 30/6/18.
7 Kingdon, Oliver, M.C., Capt. (Tp.), k. in a., 24/4/18.
6 Kirk, Charles Edmund, 2/Lt., k. in a., 6/8/17.
Kirsh, Charles Sidney, 2/Lt., k. in a., 19/4/15.
3 Knight, Richard Brodnax, Capt., d. of w., 5/9/18 (att. 4/Bn.).
Kuhn, Alfred Edgar, Lt., d. of w., 18/5/15.
3 Kydd, Chester Bishop, 2/Lt. (Tp.), k. in a., 3/5/17 (att. 7/Batt.).
9 Lardner, Dion Albert, 2/Lt. (Tp.), k. in a., 4/9/16.
1 Laughton, Joseph Thornton, 2/Lt. (Tp.), d. of w., 29/9/18.
7 Lawrence, Charles Alfred, M.C., Lt. (Tp.) (A/Capt.), k. in a., 24/4/18.
1 Lawder, Noel Wilfred, Major (Tp.), k. in a., 4/9/16.
10 Leland, Walter Alfred, 2/Lt., k. in a., 4/6/15.
6 Le Messurier, Cecil Cooper, 2/Lt. (Tp.), k. in a., 15/11/16.
2 Lenton, Gerald, 2/Lt. (Tp.), d. of w., 27/7/17.
8 Lethbridge, Brian Hugh Bridgeman, Lt. (Tp.), d. of w., 19/7/17.
Levi, Albert, 2/Lt., d. of w., 12/6/19.
8 Leys, Colin McLaren, 2/Lt. (Tp.), k. in a., 15/9/16.
6 Lilley, Edmund Arthur Howe, Lt. (Tp.), k. in a., 31/7/18 (att. 112 T.M.B.).
7 Lingwood, Edward St. Hilary, 2/Lt. (Tp.), k. in a., 3/5/17.
Lithfield, John, 2/Lt., k. in a., 22/10/14.
1 Loe, Harold Charles, M.C., 2/Lt. (Tp.) (A/Capt.), k. in a., 27/9/18.
6 Lucas, Frederic Gerald Bazalgette, M.C., Capt. (Tp.), d. of w., 10/8/17.
9 Luscombe, Gridland John, 2/Lt. (Tp.), k. in a., 3/5/19 (att. 7/Bn.).
Lyddon, Ernest Hugh, Capt., k. in a., 31/10/14.
McCloughin, Robert James, Capt., d. of w., 18/9/14.
3 MacGregor, James Hamilton, 2/Lt. (T/Lt.), k. in a., 10/1/17 (att. M.G.C., 132 Coy.).
2 McJannet, Walter Guy, 2/Lt., d. of w., 24/8/18.
1 V.C. MacKenzie, John, Major, k. in a., 17/5/15.
4 McKirdy, Gillies, 2/Lt. (Tp.), (A/Capt.), k. in a., 11/2/17.
9 McEwan, George Edward, 2/Lt., k. in a., 15/11/16.
8 McMichael, Douglas William, 2/Lt. (Tp.), d. of w., 17/4/16.
1 Marshall, Arthur Norris, 2/Lt., k. in a., 31/7/16.
4 Mathieson, William, 2/Lt., k. in a., 25/5/18.
1 Mattey, Charles Percival, 2/Lt. (Tp.), died, 22/1/17 (in German hands).
Maw, Harry, 2/Lt. (Tp.), k. in a., 22/8/18.
9 Merchant, Herbert George, 2/Lt. (Tp.), k. in a., 28/9/16 (att. 7/Bn.).
1 Millais, Geoffrey de Carteret, T/Lt. (A/Capt.), d. of w., 21/8/18.
4 Millson, Edgar G. Butlin, 2/Lt., k. in a., 18/6/16.
8 Mitchell, Edward Noel, T/Lt., k. in a., 15/2/16.
3 Mitchell, Walter Victor, 2/Lt., k. in a., 27/11/15 (att. T.M.B.).
Monteith, John Cassels, T/Lt.-Col., k. in a., 1/10/15.
3 Morris, Charles Alan Smith, Capt. (A/Major), died, 7/5/17 (as Prisoner in German hands).
Moxly, John Hewitt Sutton, 2/Lt., k. in a., 13/3/15.
1 Moyse, John Jenkins, Capt. (A/Major), d. of w., 8/2/17.
4 Muir, Horace Wellesley, 2/Lt., k. in a., 24/4/17.
3 Mulligan, Sidney Gerald, 2/Lt., k. in a., 23/4/17.
1 Naifer, Edgar Ivan Fitzroy, Lt., k. in a., 23/8/18.
Ness, James Charles Alexander, Lt., k. in a., 27/6/15.
8 Nixon, Noel Charles Frederick, Capt., k. in a., 24/3/18 (att. 4/Bn.).
4 Nunneley, George Paterson, M.C., Capt. (A/Major), k. in a., 27/3/18.
3 O'Neill, H. Dubois, M.C., Capt. (T/Major), died, 2/6/18.
3 Orlebar, Basil John, Capt., k. in a., 15/1/15 (att. 1/Bn.).
Paine, William Thomas, 2/Lt. (Tp.), k. in a., 23/8/18.
Patterson, John Agar, 2/Lt., k. in a., 30/11/14.
4 Patterson, Hugh Cecil, Lt., k. in a., 30/4/17 (att. R.F.C., 48 Sqd.).
2 Pawle, Malcolm Gerald, Capt. (Tp.), died, 27/6/17 (Garr. Bn.).
Pearson, Terence Charles, 2/Lt., k. in a., 26/9/15.
1 Peel, Ambrose Ethelstone, 2/Lt., k. in a., 27/4/18.
6 Peel, Geoffrey, T/Lt. (A/Capt.), k. in a., 17/7/17.
3 Perham, William Francis George, Lt., d. of w., 10/3/18 (att. 1/Bn.).
7 Potts, Henry, 2/Lt. (Tp.), d. of w., 1/10/16 (att. 1/Essex R.).
2 Pratt, Arthur, 2/Lt. (Tp.), d. of w., 2/7/18 (att. 6/Northamptonshire R.).
4 Primrose-Wells, James Bowen, Lt., d. of w., 4/4/18 (in German hands).
Punchard, Edmund Elgood, Lt., k. in a., 29/10/14.
8 Quilter, Roy Molyneux, Capt. (Tp.), k. in a., 19/4/16.
10 Rae, James Albert, 2/Lt. (Tp.), died, 4/9/15.
7 Ransom, Robert Cyril Starling, 2/Lt. (Tp.), d. of w., 19/10/17.
7 Rawes, Joscelyn Hugh Russell, Lt. (Tp.), k. in a., 1/7/19.
1 Ray, Frederick Lee, 2/Lt., k. in a., 16/5/18.
8 Reed, Guy Baron, Lt., d. of w., 23/8/18 (att. 2/Batt.).
1 Rendell, Leonard Wyndham, 2/Lt., d. of w., 19/10/14.
1 Reynolds, Harold Henry, 2/Lt. (Tp.), k. in a., 4/10/17.
4 Reynolds, Thomas Josceline Gordon, 2/Lt., d. of w., 11/10/10 (att. 2/Bn.).
9 Riddell, Frederick James, Lt. (Tp.), drowned, 13/8/15 (att. Essex R.).
3 Roeber, David Arnold, 2/Lt., k. in a., 14/8/16 (att. 7/Bn.).
6 Rose, Ronald Henry Evan Lt. (Tp.), k. in a., 28/4/17.
7 Ross-Taylor, Ian Henry Munro, 2/Lt. (Tp.), k. in a., 27/9/16.
6 Rycroft, Nelson Wynne, 2/Lt. (Tp.), k. in a., 25/9/17.
Ryde, John Titcombe, 2/Lt., d. of w., 8/5/17 (Res.).
1 Sanders, Vincent Stanton, 2/Lt., k. in a., 4/9/16.
1/2 Searle, Thomas George, 2/Lt., k. in a., 20/9/17.
9 Sharpin, Frank Lloyd, 2/Lt. (Tp.), d. of w., 14/10/16, att. 8/Bn.).
3 Shaw, Charles Henry, 2/Lt., d. of w., 1/8/17.
2 Shekury, Cecil, M.C., Lt. (Tp.), k. in a., 16/4/18.
1 Sherry, Gerald, 2/Lt., d. of w., 26/7/16.
7 Sherwell, Ferdinand Nigel, Lt. (Tp.), k. in a., 13/6/17.
9 Shervington, William Hugh Byam, 2/Lt. (Tp.), k. in a., 18/7/16.
3 Shippey, Cyril Shaw, 2/Lt., d. of w., 21/12/15 (att. 8/Bn.).
Shippey, James Reginald, 2/Lt., d. of w., 14/10/14.
8 Simeons, Edward Emil, Capt. (Tp.), d. of w., 17/2/16.
3 Smith, Clement Roy Blackshaw, 2/Lt., k. in a., 28/4/17 (att. 6/Bn.).
1 Smith, Leslie Morgan, Major (Tp.), died, 20/12/17 (Garr. Bn.).
Smith, Walter Thomas, 2/Lt., k. in a., 3/3/17.
6 Smith-Masters, George Arthur, 2/Lt. (Tp.), k. in a., 19/8/15.
Snell, Eric Aylmer Goldney, Major (Tp.), k. in a., 16/11/17 (att. 4/King's African Rifs.).
4 Soames, Oliver Jack, 2/Lt. (Tp.), k. in a., 27/3/18.
6 Solomon, Harry M., Lt., died, 5/12/18 (and R.A.F.).
4 Sprunt, Alexander Dalzell, 2/Lt., d. of w., 17/3/15.
10 Squier, Harry Anderton, 2/Lt. (Tp.), k. in a., 19/4/16 (att. 8/Bn.).
6 Stables, Leonard Theodore Drury, Lt., k. in a., 23/10/18 (att. Northants R.).
Stafford, Claude C., Lt., k. in a., 13/10/14 (Res. of Off.).
Stapleton, William Howell, 2/Lt. (Tp.), k. in a., 26/8/18 (att. 5/R. Berks).
Stares, Robert Percy, Major, k. in a., 30/10/14.
2 Stephenson, Kenneth Langton, 2/Lt. (Tp.), k. in a., 26/9/15.
2 Stonier, William John, Lt., k. in a., 27/4/17 (att. R.F.C., 2 Sqd.).
4 Stonor, Hon. Howard Carew, Lt., k. in a., 10/3/15 (att. S. Staffs.).
1/2 Strange, Reginald Sydney, 2/Lt. (Tp.), k. in a., 17/10/18 (att. 1/Northampton. R.).
7 Taylor, Leon Eric, 2/Lt., k. in a., 17/2/17 (att. 54 T.M.B.).
4 Tee, Albert Edward, 2/Lt., k. in a., 30/10/17.

9 Telfer, Leslie Groom, 2/Lt. (Tp.), d. of w., 12/5/16.
10 Tennant, John Amherst, Capt. (Tp.), d. of w., 23/8/15 (att. Bord. R.).
9 Thomas, Honoratus Leigh Murron, 2/Lt. (Tp.), k. in a., 15/9/16.
7 Thompson, Frederic George, 2/Lt. (Tp.), k. in a., 10/4/17 (att. 6/Bn.).
2 Thompson, Herbert Richard, Lt. (Tp.), died, 3/5/18 (2 Garr. Bn.).
Thomson, Donald Godrid Campbell, Lt., k. in a., 31/10/14.
Timmins, George Oswald, 2/Lt. (Tp.), k. in a., 23/10/18 (att. 1/Northants R.).
13 Toovey, Arthur Wilfred, Capt. (Tp.), died, 1/12/18.
Traill, John Murray, Major, k. in a., 30/10/14.
7 Tremeer, Sidney Charles, 2/Lt. (Tp.), d. of w., 17/5/17.
Timberlake, Roy, Lt. (Tp.), k. in a., 27/7/17 (att. 4/Bn.).
3 Turnbull, Laurence, 2/Lt., k. in a., 16/6/15 (att. 2/Bn.).
4 Turnbull, Wm. Arthur, T/Lt., k. in a., 13/11/16.
3 Tyler, Cornelius George, Capt., d. of w., 11/7/16.
6 Vander-Linde, Simon, 2/Lt. (Tp.), d. of w., 18/10/17.
10 Vaulkhard, John Vincent, 2/Lt. (Tp.), k. in a., 15/9/16 (att. 8/Bn.).
4 Vincent, Leslie Arthur Walter, 2/Lt., d. of w., 31/3/18 (in German hands).
8 Vipond, Sidney James, 2/Lt. (Tp.), d. of w., 20/4/16.
10 Walker, George, Lt. (Tp.), d. of w., 28/11/15 (att. W.A.F.F.).
Walker, Lawrence Hale, 2/Lt., k. in a., 12/10/16.
Walker, Walter Arthur Beaumont, 2/Lt., d. of w., 30/10/14.
4 Wareing, Cecil Hooten, Lt., d. of w., 1/11/17.
3 Watt, Kenneth Murray, 2/Lt., d. of w., 1/10/17 (P. of W.).
8 Webb, Ernest Charles, 2/Lt., k. in a., 17/2/18 (att. 4/Bn.).
1 Wemyss, Norman Douglas, 2/Lt., k. in a., 27/7/16.
4 West, Herbert John, M.C., Capt., d. of w., 22/8/18.
7 Whatmoor, Donald Gurney, 2/Lt. (Tp.), k. in a., 17/1/16.
6 Whitbourn, Walter, M.C., 2/Lt., k. in a., 22/8/18 (att. 2/Bn.).
2 White, William, M.C., Lt., k. in a., 12/10/16.
1 Whittemore, Frederick, Lt., k. in a., 29/3/16.
4 Wilkinson, Leslie Stuart, 2/Lt., d. of w., 21/11/16.
8 Williams, Charles James, Lt. (Tp.), d. of w., 19/12/15.
7 Wilson, Thomas Percy, 2/Lt. (Tp.), k. in a., 28/9/16 (att. 7/Bn.).
1 Winmill, Westropp Orbell Peyton, Lt., k. in a., 22/3/18.
1 Wodehouse, Evelyn Charles Bradley, T/2/Lt. (T/Lt.), k. in a., 4/10/17 (att. 10/Bn.).
10 Woolnough, Charles Walter Fyffe, 2/Lt. (Tp.), k. in a., 22/3/16 (att. 69/Bde., M.G.C.).
1 Wright, Donald Samuel, 2/Lt. (Tp.), d. of w., 25/4/17 (att. 8/Bn.).
Wright, George Drennan Cron, 2/Lt., k. in a., 23/10/14.
6 Wright, R. K., M.C., Lt. (A/Capt.), k. in a., 29/9/18 (att. 2/Worc. R.).
Younghusband, Harold, D.S.O., Lt.-Col. (Tp.), k. in a., 20/4/16 (att. 7/Glouc. R.).

The Leicestershire Regiment.

7 Abbott, Lionel Pilkington, T/Lt., k. in a., 14/7/16.
8 Alexander, John, 2/Lt. (Tp.), k. in a., 15/7/16.
10 Allberry, Cecil Charles, Capt. (Tp.), k. in a., 25/9/16 (att. 9th Bn.).
2 Ames, Robert Henry, T/Capt., k. in a., 6/1/16.
1/2 Asher, Albert, 2/Lt. (Tp.), k. in a., 24/9/18 (att. 1/5th Bn.).
1/2 Ashton, Frederick James, 2/Lt. (Tp.), k. in a., 21/3/18 (att. 11th Bn.).
8 Astle, Albert George, T/Lt. (A/Capt.), k. in a., 3/5/17.
1 Atter, Christopher Francis, Lt., k. in a., 21/3/18.
8 Baldwin, David Aitken, Lt. (Tp.), died, 31/8/15.
7 Bam, Cyril Turpin, 2/Lt. (Tp.), k. in a., 14/7/16.
8 Barling, Harold, 2/Lt. (Tp.), k. in a., 15/6/16.
1/2 Barrett, Arthur Lennard, 2/Lt., k. in a., 1/10/17 (att. 8th Bn.).
1/2 Barrowcliff, Cyril Herbert Ford, 2/Lt. (Tp.), k. in a., 27/10/17.
Bayfield, Herbert Lockington, Lt, d. of w., 15/3/15.
11 Baxter, William, 2/Lt. (Tp.), k. in a., 22/3/18.
11 Benger, Alfred Horace, Major (Tp.), d. of w., 17/4/17.
9 Bennett, Arthur Shirley, T/Lt., k. in a., 14/7/16.
9 V.C. Bent, Philip Eric, D.S.O., T/Lt.-Col., k. in a., 1/10/17.
Bettles, Joseph, 2/Lt. (Tp.), k. in a., 7/11/18 (att. 5th Bn.).
9 Billings, Herbert, 2/Lt. (Tp.), k. in a., 6/4/16 (att. 6th Bn.).
9 Boucher, Alan Estcourt, T/Capt., d. of w., 25/7/16.
8 Bowell, Archibald Gordon Edward, 2/Lt. (Tp.), k. in a., 15/7/16.
Bowley, Thomas Henry, 2/Lt., k. in a., 26/10/14.
2 Brakes, Bert, Lt., died, 5/1/18 (att. M.G.C., 210th Bde.).
1 Brounsworth, Edmund Arthur, 2/Lt., d. of w., 27/5/16.
1 Brown, Albert Edward, 2/Lt. (Tp.), k. in a., 9/10/18.
6 Brown, David Westcott, Capt., k. in a., 17/7/16.
Brown, Harold Atherton, 2/Lt., k. in a., 15/5/15.
2 Brown, Miles Wheelton, Lt., k. in a., 25/9/15.
1 Burford, Francis Emery, 2/Lt., k. in a., 4/6/18.
9 Burn, Cuthbert John, Lt., k. in a., 1/10/17.
1 Burnett, John, 2/Lt. (Tp.), d. of w., 15/9/16.
7 Burnett, Noel Compton, Lt. (Tp.), k. in a., 14/7/16.
1/2 Callison, Robert William, Lt., k. in a., 24/3/18 (att. 8th Bn.).
7 Carr, Frank Henry, 2/Lt. (Tp.), d. of w., 23/3/18.
6 Champneys, John Dalrymple, Lt., d. of w., 22/11/15.
3 Charlesworth, Walter Alexander, T/2/Lt., k. in a., 7/2/17 (att. 1st Bn.).
Chaworth-Musters, Roger Michael, 2/Lt., k. in a., 7/5/17 (and R.F.C., 56 Sq.).
1/2 Christy, John George, T/2/Lt., k. in a., 3/10/18 (att. 1/5th Bn.).
7 Clarke, Arthur Aubrey, M.C., Lt., k. in a., 1/10/17.
1 Cooke, Archibald Ernest, 2/Lt., d. of w., 1/5/18.
3 Cox, Frederick Percy, 2/Lt. (T/Capt.), k. in a., 3/5/17 (att. 9th Bn.).
Cox, John James, 2/Lt., d. of w., 29/5/15.
9 Cresswell, Frank, 2/Lt. (Tp.), k. in a., 18/5/16.
Crosse, Ewins Charles Marlborough, Lt., d. of w., 16/5/15.
6 Curtis, Frank William, T/Lt., k. in a., 4/11/17 (att. Shrop. L.I.).
8 Davenport, Vyvyan Hope Lancelot, 2/Lt., k. in a., 14/7/16.
7 Dickinson, Frederick William, 2/Lt., k. in a., 17/3/18.
10 Dixon, Claude Dudley, 2/Lt. (Tp.), d. of w., 28/7/16 (att. 6th Bn.).
Dods, William Henry Gordon, Lt., k. in a., 21/10/14.
3 Dolby, Horace Adams, Lt., k. in a., 7/5/17 (att. 1st Bn.).
Dooley, Thomas, 2/Lt., k. in a., 1/5/15.
10 Douglas, Alexander Gawain, T/Lt., k. in a., 15/8/16 (att. 1st Bn.).
Dowding, Lionel, 2/Lt., k. in a., 7/1/16.
11 Dudman, David, Lt. & Qr.-Mr., died, 26/4/19.
9 Eales, Francis Daw Sherbrooke, 2/Lt., k. in a., 3/5/17.
11 Eaton, Charles William, T/Capt., d. of w., 9/8/17.
8 Edey, Sydney, 2/Lt. (Tp.), k. in a., 28/4/18.
Ellingham, Victor Edward, 2/Lt. (T/Lt.), k. in a., 1/10/17.
Ellwood, Geoffrey Thomas Lovick, T/Lt., k. in a., 17/7/16.
1/2 Elson, George Henry, M.M., 2/Lt. (Tp.), died, 8/12/18 (att. 14th Bn.).
10 Emmerson, Henry Hetherington, T/Major, k. in a., 25/9/16.
9 Emmet, Frederick Herbert, T/Capt., k. in a., 14/7/16.
3 Farrar, Herbert Ronald, 2/Lt., k. in a., 24/12/14 (att. Manch. R.).
1 Faulks, Levi, T/2/Lt., k. in a., 14/4/18.
1 Fidoe, Norman Godfrey, T/2/Lt., k. in a., 21/3/18.
9 Flint, Harvey Priestman, 2/Lt., k. in a., 27/5/18 (att. 8th Bn.).
2 Foister, Percy Reuben, 2/Lt., k. in a., 13/1/16.
10 Freer, John William, Lt., d. of w., 29/6/15.
Gandy, George Joseph, 2/Lt., k. in a., 15/5/15.
1/2 Gardner, Francis Henry, T/2/Lt., d. of w., 17/10/18.
1 Gardner, William James, 2/Lt., d. of w., 26/9/16 (att W York. R.).
1 Geddis, Samuel, T/Lt., k. in a., 19/9/18.
7 Gifford, Norga Ernest, T/Capt., k. in a., 14/7/16.
9 Gilbart, William Stuart, T/2/Lt., d. of w., 26/9/16.
6 Gillett, George Maurice Gerald, T/Capt., k. in a., 26/9/16.
6 Gladstone, John Ravenhill, T./Capt., k. in a., 23/8/18.
Grant, Hubert Anthony, Capt., k. in a., 24/11/14.
8 Greenway, Frederick Charles Garton, 2/Lt. (Tp.), k. in a., 14/7/16.
3 Gribble, Charles Ethelburt, M.C., Lt., A/Capt., d. of w., 15/10/18 (att. 7th Bn.).
3 Gristwood, George Harry, 2/Lt., d. of w., 16/9/16 (att. 1st Bn.).
Gruchy, Francis Le Maistre, Capt., k. in a., 22/10/14.
11 Grundtvig, Humphrey Halgrim, M.C., T/Lt., d. of w., 22/3/18.
10 Gutteridge, Eric Lancelot, T/2/Lt., k. in a., 14/7/16.
3 Guy, Norman Glass, 2/Lt., k. in a., 27/5/18 (att. 7th Bn.).
2 Gwyther, Guy Llewelyn, 2/Lt. (Tp.), k. in a., 6/1/16.
1 Hackett, David Frederick Mackness, Lt., k. in a., 22/8/18.
8 Haines, Frank Percy, Lt., k. in a., 15/6/17.
3 Hall, Edwin Lincoln, M.C., 2/Lt., k. in a., 22/4/17 (att. 2nd Bn.).
11 Hall, Ernest Louis, 2/Lt. (Tp.), d. of w., 6/11/17.
1 Harbottle, John, Lt. (A/Capt.), k. in a., 21/3/18.
Harcourt, Joseph, 2/Lt., d. of w., 5/10/18 (att. 12th N. Staff. Regt.).
1/2 Harding, Lionel Henry Powys, M.C., 2/Lt., k. in a., 23/10/18 (att. 6th Bn.).
1 Harper, Owen Tannett, 2/Lt., k. in a., 22/3/18.
3 Harrison, Christopher Rene, Lt., d. of w., 23/5/15 (att. 2nd Bn.).
3 Harrison, Eric, Lt., k. in a., 30/6/15 (att. 1st Bn.).
2 Hatter, Bernard, 2/Lt., k. in a., 25/9/15 (att. 3rd Bn.).
Hawes, Robert Frank, Capt., d. of w., 23/9/14.
7 Hawkes, John Aubrey, 2/Lt. (Tp.), d. of w., 11/9/18.
1/2 Hearn, Albert Henry, 2/Lt., k. in a., 1/10/17 (att. 8th Bn.).
2 Hebden, George Spencer, 2/Lt. (Tp.), k. in a., 22/4/17
2 Henderson, Everard Francis Scott, Major, k. in a., 6/7/16.
1 Herbison, Charles William, T/Capt., d. of w., 17/9/16.
11 Hicks, Arthur Leslie, T/Lt., died, 4/4/18.
1 Hill, James Alfred, Lt., T/Capt., k. in a., 17/4/18.
6 Hill, Mark Carr, T/Lt., k. in a., 17/7/16.
6 Hind, Frank Farmer, T/2/Lt., k. in a., 16/7/16 (att. Trench Mortar, 110 Bde.).
6 Hoggarth, Norman Scott, 2/Lt. (Tp.), d. of w., 30/5/18 (P.O.W.).
7 Hollis, John Gordon, T/Lt., k. in a., 14/7/16.
6 Hopewell, James Handley, Lt., k. in a., 14/7/16.
3 Hornabrook, Leonard Charles, 2/Lt., d. of w., 21/5/18 (att. 1/4th Bn.).
2 Howell, Aubrey Hamilton, Lt., k. in a., 6/1/16.
Hutchinson, Henry William, 2/Lt. (Tp.), k. in a., 13/3/17.
Hutton, Richard, 2/Lt., k. in a., 7/11/14.
7 Ibbotson, Tom, T/2/Lt., k. in a., 25/9/16.
6 Jalland, Robert Miles, 2/Lt. (Tp.), k. in a., 26/8/18.
3 Jennings, Francis William, T/Lt., killed, 26/3/16.
Johnson, William, 2/Lt., d. of w., 16/5/15.
10 Joyce, George Edgar, T/Lt., k. in a., 20/9/16 (att. 7th Bn.).
1 Kennedy, John Gilbert, T/2/Lt., k. in a., 14/9/16.
9 King, Henry Frederick, T/2/Lt., d. of w., 7/5/17.
Knatchbull, Reginald Norton, D.S.O., Lt.-Col., died, 24/7/17.
1 Lancaster, Charles Edward, Lt. (Tp.), k. in a., 21/3/18.
3 Lancaster, Howard Vincent, T/2/Lt., d. of w., 21/11/17 (att. 1st Bn.).
8 Lawson, Arthur James, T/Lt., A/Capt., k. in a., 22/3/18 (att. 110th T.M.B.).
7 Lazarus, Cyril Henry, Lt., k. in a., 27/5/18.
8 Lea, John, T/2/Lt., d. of w., 15/7/16.

9 Lee, Audley Andrew Dowell, M.C., T/Capt., k. in a., 1/10/17.
Lewin, John Wesley, 2/Lt., k. in a., 24/9/18.
6 Lindley, Harry, Lt. and Qr.-Mr., died, 27/1/16.
3 Lloyd, Valentine, M.C., Lt., k. in a., 23/10/18 (att. 11th Bn.).
Lodge, Ronald Edward Somerville, Lt., k. in a., 25/9/15.
Longcroft, Thomas Roy, Lt., k. in a., 25/9/15.
1/2 Lord, A. J. H., 2/Lt., k. in a., 18/9/18 (att. 7th Bn.).
Murphy, William, 2/Lt., k. in a., 10/3/15.
7 McLaren, Malcolm Colquhoun, M.C., T/Lt., k. in a., 22/10/18.
1/2 McLay, Archibald, M.C., 2/Lt., A/Capt., k. in a., 21/3/18 (att. 6th Bn.).
1 Mansfield, George, 2/Lt., k. in a., 22/3/18.
2 Mansfield, Oscar Marshall, T/2/Lt., k. in a., 14/3/17.
10 Marner, George Lionel Stuart, Lt., k. in a., 8/4/17.
Marshall, Wilfred, Lt., k. in a., 4/6/15.
6 Martin, Chas. Stanley, T/2/Lt., k. in a., 4/10/17.
9 Martin, Henry Yarde, T/2/Lt., d. of w., 14/9/16 (att. 9th E. Lan. R.).
7 Mason, Allan Edward Glendinning, T/2/Lt., d. of w., 30/6/16.
Meakin, Thomas, T/2/Lt., k. in a., 21/10/18 (att. 11th Bn.).
3 Medcalf, Edwin Francis, T/2/Lt., d. of w., 11/6/17 (att. 8th Bn.).
8 Mercer, George Enos, T/2/Lt., k. in a., 3/10/18 (att. 1/4th Bn.).
8 Mignon, Jephson George, Temp. Lt.-Col., k. in a., 15/7/16.
1/2 Miles, Roger Thomas William, T/2/Lt., k. in a., 1/10/17 (att. 7th Bn.).
11 Millward, Charles, T/2/Lt., k. in a., 22/3/18.
10 Mitchell, James Thornburn, A/Capt., died, 16/3/17 (att. 7th Bn.).
9 Moll, Tobias Mortimer, T/2/Lt., k. in a., 15/7/16.
3 Morgan, Stephen Beverley, 2/Lt., k. in a., 14/5/15 (att. 1st Bn.).
3 Morton, John William, T/Lt., k. in a., 10/4/17 (att. 9th Bn.).
1 Morton, Leicester Charles, T/2/Lt., d. of w., 19/5/17.
8 Moss, Frederick Walter, T/2/Lt., k. in a., 28/5/18 (att. 98th Fld. Co., R.E.).
Mosse, John, T/Lt.-Col., died, 17/6/16 (Commdg. Depot).
Murgatroyd, Hugh Lester, M.C., Lt., A/Capt., d. of w., 27/9/18 (att. 1/7th Lan. Fus.).
7 Newton, Leslie Abbott, T/2/Lt., k. in a., 14/7/16.
9 Nolan, William Henry, T/Lt., k. in a., 14/7/16.
8 Norman, Arthur John, T/2/Lt., d. of w., 29/9/16.
3 Norton, William, Lt., k. in a., 23/3/18 (att. 7th Bn.).
8 Oliver, Frederick Ruddall, Lt., k. in a., 3/5/17.
3 Olphert, Hugh Montgomery Archdale, 2/Lt., k. in a., 9/9/16 (att. 7th Bn.).
3 Ottey, Raymond Gascoyne, 2/Lt., k. in a., 28/7/17 (att. R.F.C.).
10 Palmer, Percy Rogers, M.C., 2/Lt., k. in a., 25/5/17 (and R.F.C., 55th Sqd.).
9 Papprill, Frederick Ernest, T/2/Lt., k. in a., 3/6/17 (att. 1/4th E. Lancs.).
Pegg, Conrad, 2/Lt., d. of w., 2/6/18.
3 Pegg, Kenneth Hugh Lt., k. in a., 20/2/16 (att. 2nd Bn.).
2 Phillips, Hubert Henry, Lt., d. of w., 4/10/15 (att. 3rd Bn.).
10 Phillips, Sydney Vernon, T/2/Lt., k. in a., 14/8/16 (att. 7th Bn.).
6 Pickard, Donald Johnson, 2/Lt. (Tp.), k. in a., 17/7/16.
10 Pickering-Clarke, John Norman, T/2/Lt., k. in a., 14/7/16 (att. 7th Bn.).
2 Pickin, William Thomas, T/Lt., k. in a., 25/9/15.
3 Pinder, Albert Humphrey, Lt., k. in a., 14/9/16 (att. 1st Bn.).
3 Pitts, Francis Burton, 2/Lt., d. of w., 17/5/17 (att. 8th Bn.).
Plummer, John Scott, 2/Lt., k. in a., 17/8/17 (att. 1/5th Bn.).
8 Popham, John Francis Watson, T/Capt., d. of w., 3/10/16.
6 Powell, Charles Swan, T/2/Lt., k. in a., 17/7/16.
Prain, Theodore, Lt., k. in a., 21/10/14.
8 Pratley, Joseph Edward, 2/Lt., k. in a., 3/5/17.
2 Privett, Arthur Bellman, T/2/Lt., d. of w., 8/1/16.
Puckle, Thomas Norman, Capt., k. in a., 30/8/14.
1 Purdy, Archer Kershaw, T/2/Lt., d. of w., 20/11/17.
1 Quayle, Rupert Charles, T/2/Lt., k. in a., 4/10/18 (att. 1/4th Bn.).
7 Reed, Charles Sydney, T/2/Lt., k. in a., 14/7/16.
9 Rennie, Cyril Thomas, T/2/Lt., k. in a., 25/9/16.
3 Reynolds, William Kingsley, Lt., k. in a., 10/9/15 (att. 1st Bn.).
11 Richardson, Harold Stewart, Lt., (Tp.), d. of w., 24/4/17.
1 Roberts, George Alfred, 2/Lt., k. in a., 21/3/18.
1/2 Roberts, John Lambert, M.C., Lt., k. in a., 21/3/18 (att. 6th Bn.).
Robinson, William George, 2/Lt. (Tp.), k. in a., 1/10/17 (att. 8th Bn.).
Rolph, Charles Colwyn, Capt., k. in a., 15/10/15.
2 Romilly, Francis Henry, D.S.O., Capt., k. in a., 25/9/15.
3 Rowley, Walter Austin, 2/Lt., k. in a., 16/7/17 (att. 8th Bn.).
2 Royce, David Costa, Lt., k. in a., 7/1/16.
Russell, Leonard William Edward, T/2/Lt., died, 14/11/18 (att. 2/4th Bn.).
10 Salisbury, Percy Harold, T/2/Lt., k. in a., 27/8/16 (att. 11th Ches. R.).
9 Sargeant, Arthur Percival, 2/Lt., k. in a., 14/7/16.
10 Sartoris, Charles Frederick, Lt., k. in a., 24/6/15 (att. 7th Bn.).
9 Sayers, Charlie Ronald, 2/Lt. (Tp.), k. in a., 13/4/17.
9 Scott, Frederick, M.C., Capt., k. in a., 27/5/18.
9 Scott, James Thompson, T/Lt., d. of w., 5/10/17.
Seton-Browne, Montague William, Lt., k. in a., 24/11/14.
7 Shackleton, James Ernest, T/2/Lt., k. in a., 21/3/18.
3 Sharpe, Henry Norman, 2/Lt., killed, 26/1/17 (and R.F.C.).
Shaw, Alfred 2/Lt. (Tp.), k. in a., 1/10/17 (att. 8th Bn.).
11 Shrubsole, Arthur Edward, T/2/Lt., k. in a., 13/4/17.
1 Simmons, Frederick William, T/2/Lt., k. in a., 27/5/18 (att. 7th Bn.).
7 Simpson, Cyril Woodhouse, Lt. (Tp.), k. in a., 14/7/16.
1 Sims, Douglas Henry, M.C., T/2/Lt., d. of w., 10/10/18.
7 Smart, Eustace Fowler, T/Lt., k. in a., 8/2/16.
Smeathman, Cecil, Lt., d. of w., 24/10/14.
8 Smith, Alfred William, T/2/Lt., d. of w., 4/10/17 (att. 8th Lincs.).
10 Smith, Arthur Howard, T/2/Lt., k. in a., 14/7/16.
1/2 Smith, Charles Arthur, D.C.M., T/2/Lt., k. in a., 19/9/18.
7 Smith, George Morley, T/2/Lt., dw. of w., 6/10/17.
1 Smith, Herbert Stoney, D.S.O., Lt.-Col., k. in a., 22/10/15.
7 Spencer, Herbert, 2/Lt., k. in a., 11/7/16.
11 Spencer, John Clive, Capt., k. in a., 22/3/18.
8 Spencer-Smith, Henry, Capt. & Qr.-Mr., k. in a., 21/3/18.
2/4 Springate, Arthur Stephen, T/2/Lt., k. in a., 25/3/18.
9 Stephens, William Head, T/2/Lt., k. in a., 14/7/16.
1 Stevens, Alfred Leslie, Lt., k. in a., 18/4/17.
11 Stevenson, William Henry, 2/Lt., k. in a., 21/3/18.
2 Swindells, Charles Geoffrey Rupert, 2/Lt., k. in a., 9/1/17.
3 Tayler, Jervoise Graham, 2/Lt., k. in a., 15/5/15 (att. 2nd Bn.).
9 Taylor, Arnold Bradley, T/2/Lt., k. in a., 12/7/16.
11 Taylor, Gerard Bardsley, T/2/Lt., k. in a., 24/9/18 (att. 9 Dur. L.I.).
6 Thirlby, Stuart Longston, 2/Lt., k. in a., 22/3/18.
1 Thomas, William Hope, 2/Lt., k. in a., 11/4/18 (att. 6th T.M.B.).
1/2 Thomason, Herbert James Bateman, T/2/Lt., k. in a., 26/9/17.
11 Thornton, Frank Cecil, T/2/Lt., killed, 15/7/16.
11 Thornton, Sidney Percy, T/Capt., d. of w., 5/12/16.
Tollemache-Tollemache, L. S. D. O. Frandati-Filius Tollemache-Tollemache de Orellana Plantagenet, Capt., died, 20/2/17.
Tristram, Lancelot Barrington Crofte, Capt., k. in a., 31/10/14.
9 Trotter, Alexander William Lewis, Major (Tp.), k. in a., 12/7/16.
11 Trotter, Bertram Freeman, 2/Lt. (Tp.), k. in a., 8/5/17.
10 Underwood, John, T/2/Lt., d. of w., 16/4/17.
3 Vandeleur, John Beauclerk, Lt., k. in a., 7/11/14 (att. Worc. Rgt.).
3 Vernall, Arthur Humphrey, 2/Lt., d. of w., 23/8/18 (att. 6th Bn.).
Vine, Christian Courtenay, 2/Lt., d. of w., 25/9/16.
Viney, Philip Ernest. Capt., d. of w., 17/12/14.
7 Wakeford, Edward Kingsley, Lt. (Tp.), k. in a., 14/7/17.
3 Walker, Gervaise Mapletoft, Lt., k. in a., 15/4/18 (att. 1st Bn.).
8 Warner, Thomas Lovell, D.S.O., Major (Tp.), died, 27/12/17.
Warren, Albert, T/2/Lt., k. in a., 17/3/18 (and R.F.C.).
Wateridge, Edgar Leake, Lt., k. in a., 20/11/14.
1/2 Watson, Joseph Harold, 2/Lt., d. of w., 3/10/18 (att. 1/4th Bn.).
3 Webb, Alfred Henderson, 2/Lt., died, 4/5/16.
3 Webb, Duncan Vere, M.C., Capt., d. of w., 16/10/18 (att. 1st Bn.).
7 Webb, Ernest, T/2/Lt., d. of w., 14/7/16.
3 Webb, John Clifford, 2/Lt., k. in a., 14/9/16 (att. 1st Bn.).
2 Wells, William, 2/Lt., k. in a., 13/1/16.
9 West, George, 2/Lt., k. in a., 22/3/18.
6 Wetenhall, William Thornton, T/Capt., k. in a., 17/7/16.
8 White, Charles Kirbell, 2/Lt., k. in a., 1/9/18 (att. 110 T.M.B.).
3 Wilde, Edwin Joseph, Lt., k. in a., 1/9/18 (att. 110 T.M.B.).
2 Wilkinson, Ernest Alexander, 2/Lt., k. in a., 25/9/15.
Wilkinson, William Jefferson, 2/Lt., k. in a., 25/9/15.
Woodburn, Cecil George, 2/Lt., k. in a., 25/9/15.
7 Wright, Charles James Stewart, T/Capt., k. in a., 14/7/16.
7 Wright, George William, 2/Lt., k. in a., 24/3/18.
9 Wright, William Joseph, T/2/Lt., k. in a., 17/5/16.

The Royal Irish Regiment.

5 Adrian, William Kearns, 2/Lt., k. in a., 24/8/16 (att. 1st Irish Rif.).
3 Anderson, Alan James Ramsay, 2/Lt., k. in a., 20/10/14 (att. 2nd Bn.).
Anderson, Mervyn Kebble, 2/Lt. (Tp.), d. of w., 11/5/15.
3 Anderson, Philip Maurice Ramsay, 2/Lt., d. of w., 24/2/15.
2 Arbuckle, Hubert Hugh, 2/Lt. (Tp.), k. in a., 2/9/18.
Barry, Cecil, Lt., k. in a., 21/8/17 (and R.F.C., 57 Sqd.).
3 Bell, Robert William Popham, Capt., k. in a., 5/7/16 (att. 2nd.).
1 Bennett, John Edgar, Capt., k. in a., 3/9/16.
3 Bick, Percy Arthur, 2/Lt., k. in a., 3/9/16 (att. 2nd Bn.).
6 Broderick, Thomas Joseph, Lt. (Tp.), k. in a., 15/4/16.
Brown, Hubert William, Lt., d. of w., 19/9/14.
1 Burke, Charles James, D.S.O., Major (A/Lt.-Col.), k. in a., 9/4/17 (att. East Lancs).
6 Byrne, Leo Francis, 2/Lt. (Tp.), k. in a., 21/8/16.
6 Carruth, Matthew, 2/Lt., k. in a., 9/9/16 (att. 6th Connaught Rangers).
2 Carson, Sidney Thomas, 2/Lt. (Tp.), k. in a., 2/9/18 (att. 1st Royal Munster Fus.).
5 Caruth, James Gordon, 2/Lt., k. in a., 25/9/15 (att. 2nd Bn.).
4 Chirstie, James Hugh, Capt. (Tp. Major), k. in a., 24/5/15.
4 Cockburn, Henry Howard, 2/Lt., k. in a., 1/4/17 (att. 2nd Royal Innis. Fus.).
4 Considine, Heffernan James, M.C., Capt., k. in a., 27/10/16 (att. 2nd Bn.).
5 Costello, Gabriel Patrick, 2/Lt. (Tp.), k. in a., 16/8/15.
4 Cross, Philip Frederick, Lt., k. in a., 9/9/16.

2 Curran, Nevil William, M.C., Lt., k. in a., 4/10/16 (att. 3rd Bn.).
6 Curzon, Fitzroy Edmund Penn, Lt.-Col., k. in a., 9/9/16.
3 Dalton, George Henry, 2/Lt., d. of w., 14/8/16 (att. 4th Bn. Oxford & Bucks L.I.).
Daniell, Edward Henry Edwin, D.S.O., Major (Tp.) (Lt.-Col.), k. in a., 20/10/14.
6 Day, John Edward, T/Capt., d. of w., 6/4/17.
4 D'Alton, Thomas Joseph, 2/Lt., d. of w., 9/6/17.
Deane, Arthur Denman, 2/Lt. (Tp.), k. in a., 14/7/17.
Dixon, Charles George, Lt., k. in a., 9/5/15 (att. Royal Irish Rif.).
4 Dickson, Robert Adair, 2/Lt., k. in a., 2/8/17 (att. 6 Bn.).
3 Downing, James, 2/Lt., k. in a., 3/9/16 (att. 6 Bn.).
5 Duggan, John Rowswell, Lt., k. in a., 16/8/15.
5 Dunlop, James Wilkie, Lt. (Tp.), died, 5/3/17.
1 Eaves, Frederick William D., 2/Lt., k. in a., 21/3/18 (att. 7 Bn.).
3 Eberli, John Frederick, 2/Lt., d. of w., 16/8/17 (att. 2 Bn. att. T.M.B.).
Ekins, Franklin George, M.C., Lt., died, 27/1/19.
3 Fairbairn, Andrew Hubert, 2/Lt., died, 5/6/15 (att. 2 Bn.).
3 Fausset, Charles Reginald, 2/Lt., k. in a., 3/5/15 (att. 1 Bn.).
3 Finlay, George Guy, Lt., k. in a., 14/7/18 (att. 2 Bn.).
6 Fitzgibbon, Brian Normanby, T/Lt., k. in a., 21/8/16.
3 Fogarty, Gerald Joseph, Lt., k. in a., 26/8/17 (att. R.F.C., 9 Sqd.).
1 Forbes, Hon. Fergus George Arthur, Capt., d. of w., 23/8/14 (in German hands).
2 Forbes, George Francis Reginald, Lt.-Col., d. of w., 17/3/15.
Ford, Royston Dearmer, 2/Lt., k. in a., 15/3/15.
3 Forster, Thomas Burton, 2/Lt., k. in a., 10/6/16 (att. 2 Bn.).
3 Fottrell, Brendan Joseph, 2/Lt., k. in a., 15/3/15 (att. 1 Bn.).
French, Claude Alexander, Capt., d. of w., 1/6/15.
George, Ion Barry, Major, died, 5/5/18.
2 Gore, William Frederick, M.M., Temp. 2/Lt., k. in a., 27/9/18 (att. 1/R. Muns. Fus.).
Gordon-Ralph, Philip James Gordon, Capt., k. in a., 6/8/17.
2 Grant, Stanley Chadwick, 2/Lt. (Tp.), k. in a., 3/9/16.
2 Graves, Robert James, Lt. (Tp.), died, 28/1/17 (H.S. Gar. Bn.).
6 Grayson, John Henry, Lt. (Tp.), k. in a., 20/11/17.
6 Hackett, Eric Adrian Nethercote, 2/Lt. (Tp.), k. in a., 9/9/16.
Harvey-Kelly, Hubert Dunsterville, D.S.O., Capt. (T/Major), k. in a., 29/4/17 (and R.F.C.).
2 Hayden, Leo Anthony, 2/Lt., d. of w., 14/1/17.
3 Heffernan, William Patrick, 2/Lt., k. in a., 9/5/15 (att. 1/Glos. R.).
3 Hegarty, Edward, M.C., A/Capt., k. in a., 3/9/16 (att. 2 Bn.).
3 Henna, John Ramsey, 2/Lt., k. in a., 9/9/16 (att. 6 Bn.).
3 Hewitt, Robert Edward Talbot, 2/Lt., k. in a., 7/6/17 (att. 6 Bn.).
2 Hodges, Eric Colpoys, 2/Lt., d. of w., 15/7/16.
5 Hodson, Bertie John, Lt. (Tp.), k. in a., 21/3/18 (att. R. Irish Rifles).
Homan, Arthur Douglas, Capt. (A/Major), d. of w., 9/5/17 (att. 7/Ox. & B. Lt. Inf.).
Howard, Percy Edward Napier, 2/Lt., k. in a., 27/10/14.
Irwin, James Ross, 2/Lt. (Tp.), k. in a., 2/9/18 (att. 7 Bn.).
3 Jackson, Samuel, Lt., k. in a., 20/3/18 (att. 2 Bn.).
4 Jones, Herbert Joaquin, 2/Lt., d. of w., 29/3/18 (in German hands) (att. 7 Bn.).
1 Kelly, Philip Edward, Lt.-Col. (Tp.), k. in a., 10/10/18.
4 Kenealy, John William Kierman, 2/Lt., died, 21/8/15.
3 Kenny, Cecil John, Lt., k. in a., 24/3/18 (att. M.G.C.).
2 Kerr, Finlay, 2/Lt., k. in a., 4/7/16.
Knox, Alexander William Coningham, Capt., k. in a., 19/10/14.
Laing, David Patrick, Lt., k. in a., 20/10/15.
Leary, Eric, Lt., d. of w., 21/6/15.
6 Le Page, George William, Major (Tp.), k. in a., 26/1/16.
Lillie, Frederick Sutherland, Major, k. in a., 15/3/15.
Lillis, Martin Michael Arthur, Temp. Lt., k. in a., 11/4/17 (and R.F.C., 3 Sqd.).
Lipsett, Louis James, C.B., C.M.G., T/Major-Gen., k. in a., 14/10/18 (Staff Div. H.Q. 18/1). Goc 4 Div
6 Lloyd, Charles Edward, Major & Hon. Lt.-Col., died, 8/10/15.
6 Lloyd, Harvey Richard, Temp. Capt., d. of w., 6/9/16.
4 Lloyd, Robert Courtois, 2/Lt., k. in a., 22/8/18 (att. 7 Bn.).
Locke, Harold, Capt., drowned, 10/10/18.
2 Lowry, Joseph Ewart, Temp. Lt., k. in a., 25/8/18.
2 Luckett, John Spokes, Lt., d. of w., 24/5/15.
2 Lyons, William Barry, Capt. & Bvt.-Major, d. of w., 4/9/16.
Lytton, Percy Arthur Bertram, 2/Lt., k. in a., 4/2/18 (att. R.F.C., 58 Sqd.).
5 MacAndrew, Ronald, Temp. Lt., k. in a., 16/8/15.
4 McBrinn, John Charles, 2/Lt., k. in a., 3/9/16.
5 MacDonald, Thomas, Hon. Lt. & Qr.-Mr., died, 23/11/14.
MacDonnell, Herbert Creagh, Capt., d. of w., 24/5/15 (and R.F.C.).
3 McGrane, Peter Leo, 2/Lt., k. in a., 20/5/17 (att. 1/Innis. Fusrs.).
6 Magill, Thomas Edmund, 2/Lt., k. in a., 3/9/16.
2 Mahoney, Thomas, M.C., Capt. & Qr.-Mr., died, 10/1/18.
6 Malcomson, Hubert, T/Lt. & Adjt., d. of w., 16/9/16.
2 Mark, James Wilson, 2/Lt., d. of w., 7/8/17.
3 Marlow, John, Major, died, 29/2/16.
2 Mellor, Walton, Capt., k. in a., 23/8/14.
Mockler, Francis George Ross, Capt., k. in a., 1/7/16 (and M.G.C.).
Moore, Henry Geoffrey Hamilton, 2/Lt., k. in a., 19/5/15.
2 Moriarty, Redmond George Sylverius, Lt.-Col., k. in a., 24/5/15.
3 Mouatt-Biggs, J. A., Lt., d. of w., 22/3/18 (att. 2 Bn.) (in German hands)
4 Nealon, Cedric Dunnill, 2/Lt., k. in a., 16/8/17 (att. R. Innis. Fusrs.).
Newton-King, Alexander Reginald, 2/Lt., d. of w., 12/4/15.
4 Nolan, Bevan John, 2/Lt., k. in a., 3/9/16.
1 Nolan, Maurice Herbert William, 2/Lt., d. of w., 9/12/16 (att. 10/R. Irish Rifles).
3 North, Francis Wilson, 2/Lt., k. in a., 9/9/16 (att. 6/Conn. Rangers).
3 North, Harry Lonsdale, Lt., k. in a., 27/9/18 (att. 2 Bn.).
4 O'Brien, Jeremiah, Capt., k. in a., 10/3/18 (att. 1 Bn.).
4 O'Brien-Butler, Capel Desmond, M.C., Capt., k. in a., 7/6/17 (att. 6 Bn.).
2 O'Callaghan, Gerard Arthur, Capt., d. of w., 24/5/15.
O'Longan, Paul Charles Stacpoole, 2/Lt., k. in a., 1/6/17 (att. R.F.C., 41 Sqd.).
3 Owen, Godfrey Felix, Temp. Lt., died, 21/10/18.
2 Panter-Downes, Edward Martin, Capt. & Brev.-Major, d. of w., 26/8/14.
5 Penrose-Welsted, Samuel Richard, Capt., k. in a., 17/7/18 (and R.A.F.).
4 Phillips, Charles Ernest, M.C., Lt., k. in a., 22/10/18 (att. 7 Bn.).
2 Phillips, Edward George Dunscombe Masters, Lt. (A/Capt.), k. in a., 13/11/16 (att. 6 Bn.).
Pigott, Eric John Keefe Pemberton, Lt., k. in a., 24/6/15.
8 Powell, Thomas, D.C.M., Temp. Capt., died, 1/7/18.
1 Price, Charles Leslie, 2/Lt., d. of w., 15/3/18.
3 Price, Ernest Dickenson, Lt., d. of w., 19/3/16.
3 Ramsay, Alan Livingstone, Lt. (T/Capt.), k. in a., 24/4/16.
6 Redmond, William Hoey Kearney, Major (Tp.), d. of w., 7/6/17.
3 Rennison, Walter Martyn, Lt., k. in a., 30/12/16 (att. 6 Bn.).
Rushton, Frederick Hornby Lever, Lt., k. in a., 15/9/14.
3 Ruxton, W. H., Lt., died, 29/8/18 (and R.A.F.).
4 Sanderson, William Howard, Lt., d. of w., 28/9/18.
5 Scott, John Davie, D.S.O., Capt. (A/Lt.-Col.), k. in a., 21/3/18 (att. 2 Bn.).
4 Shepherd, Richard Malcolm Sisnett, 2/Lt., died, 9/8/16 (and R.F.C.).
2 Shine, John Denis, 2/Lt., died, 25/8/14.
4 Smithwick, James Arnold, Capt., died, 9/11/15 (att. 2 Bn.).
Smyth, Donald Seymour, 2/Lt., k. in a., 19/10/14.
3 Smyth, John Ross, 2/Lt., k. in a., 20/10/14 (att. 2 Bn.).
Stacpoole, George Eric Guy, Lt., k. in a., 27/1/15.
4 Stoker, Edward Alexander, M.C., Lt., d. of w., 12/9/16 (att. 6 Bn.).
4 Stone, Charles Douglas Felgate, 2/Lt., k. in a., 9/9/16 (att. 6 Conn. Rangers).
6 Stovin, John Thomas, 2/Lt., k. in a., 28/1/18.
Tandy, Archdale Maurice Stratford, Lt., k. in a., 20/10/14.
3 Taylor, Charles, Capt. (T/Major), k. in a., 5/8/17.
2 Tighe, James Patrick, Lt. (Temp. Capt.), k. in a., 15/7/16.
6 Toohey, James Thomas, 2/Lt. (Tp.), k. in a., 18/1/17.
2 Usher, Isaac William, Lt., k. in a., 4/7/16.
3 Wall, Michael Thomas, 2/Lt., k. in a., 7/6/17 (att. 6 Bn.).
6 Warmington, Alfred Ernest, Temp. Capt., k. in a., 24/5/16.
2 White, Gerald John Davis, 2/Lt., k. in a., 6/7/16.
White, William Hawtrey, Major, k. in a., 15/2/15.
2 Williamson, John George Joseph, 2/Lt., k. in a., 2/9/18 (att. 7 Bn.).
Wookey, Frederick Maurice, 2/Lt., d. of w., 19/3/15.

Alexandra, Princess of Wales's Own (Yorkshire Regiment).

2 Acomb, Horace, 2/Lt. (Tp.), k. in a., 21/8/16 (att. 2/Devon R.).
Alexander, Walter Lorenzo, Lt.-Col., k. in a., 14/5/15.
6 Appleyard, Benjamin Sydney, 2/Lt. (Tp.), k. in a., 29/9/18 (att. 2/Batt.).
6 Appleyard, William, Lt. (Tp.), k. in a., 22/8/15.
9 Armitage, William Harold, Lt. (Tp.), k. in a., 22/5/16.
9 Atkey, Freeman Archibald Haynes, Capt. (Tp.), k. in a., 5/7/16.
6 Bailey, Tom Esmond Geoffrey, Capt., k. in a., 2/4/19.
3 Bale, Thomas Henry Thriscutt, Lt., k. in a., 24/4/18 (att. 2/Bn.).
10 Ball, Oliver Herbert, 2/Lt. (Tp.), k. in a., 28/9/16.
10 Ball, Walter William, 2/Lt. (Tp.), k. in a., 24/11/15.
7 Banner, Frederick William, 2/Lt. (Tp.), k. in a., 12/5/17.
2 Barber, Willard, 2/Lt. (Tp.), killed, 5/1/18.
6 Barnett, Lionel, Lt. (Tp.), died, 6/2/17.
7 Bartrum, H. L., Capt. (Tp.), died, 8/7/18.
10 Bass, Charles Brodie, 2/Lt., k. in a., 25/9/15.
10 Bass, Harold, M.C., Capt. (Tp.), k. in a., 24/4/18 (att. 2/W. York. R.).
13 V.C. Beal, Ernest Frederick, 2/Lt. (Tp.), k. in a., 22/3/18.
9 Beckett, Victor Louis Sydney, Major (Tp.), d. of w., 19/7/16.
9 V.C. Bell, Donald Simpson, 2/Lt. (Tp.), k. in a., 10/7/16.
8 Bell, Henry, 2/Lt., d. of w., 17/10/17.
2 Bennett, Geoffrey Ernest Layton, 2/Lt. (Tp.), k. in a., 1/7/16.
9 Bennison, Miles, 2/Lt., k. in a., 1/10/17.
3 Bentley, Arthur Webb Butler, 2/Lt. (Tp.), died, 2/12/18.
15 Berryman, John William, 2/Lt. (Tp.), d. of w., 27/11/17 (att. 2/4 K.O.Y.L.I.).
11 Bethell, Richard Carrington, 2/Lt. (Tp.), d. of w., 22/5/16 (att. 9/Bn.).
1 Bicknell, Herman Bysshe Bagshaw, 2/Lt., k. in a., 28/5/18.
8 Binns, Raymond Louis, 2/Lt. (Tp.), k. in a., 10/7/16.
2 Birch, William Claud Kennedy, M.C., Capt. (A/Major), killed, 5/1/18.
12 Bloom, Henry, Lt. (Tp.), k. in a., 14/2/17.
12 Bocking, Bernard, M.C., 2/Lt. (Tp.), k. in a., 21/8/18.
Bradford, Cecil Aubrey, Capt., drowned, 24/4/17 (att. Nigeria R.).

Brooke, Cecil Berjew, D.S.O., 2/Lt., k. in a., 1/7/16.
Brooksbank, Hugh Geoffrey, 2/Lt., d. of w., 16/12/14.
3 Brooksbank, Stamp, Lt., k. in a., 26/9/15.
Broun, Ernest Scott, Capt., k. in a., 30/10/14.
Brown, James Herbert, 2/Lt. (Tp.), d. of w., 8/10/17 (Res. att. 2/Bn.).
7 Brown, John William, 2/Lt., k. in a., 16/10/17.
Brown, John William, M.C., 2/Lt. (Tp.), d. of w., 1/8/17 (Res. att. 2/Bn.).
10 Brown, John William, M.M., 2/Lt., d. of w., 11/4/18 (att. 5/Bn.).
6 Bruce, Norman Martin, Lt. (Tp), k. in a., 7/8/15.
8 Buckle, William, 2/Lt. (Tp.), d. of w., 7/6/17.
3 Bullock, William, 2/Lt., d. of w., 12/5/18.
9 Bunker, Harold John, 2/Lt. (Tp.), k. in a., 28/9/17.
2 Burkett, William Peter, 2/Lt., killed, 23/4/18.
2 Camm, Bertram Cunliffe, M.C., A/Capt., killed, 7/1/18.
2 Campbell, John Greenbank, 2/Lt., k. in a., 8/5/18.
3 Casebourne, Rowland Telford, Lt., k. in a., 2/7/16 (att. 5/Bn. W. York. R.).
6 Casley, Hugh de Chastelai, Lt., k. in a., 7/8/15.
12 Champney, Harold D'Arcy, 2/Lt., d. of w., 29/4/18 (in German hands).
6 Chapman, Edward Henry, Lt.-Col. (Tp.), k. in a., 7/8/15.
6 Chapman, Wilfred Hubert, Capt. (Tp.), k. in a., 7/8/15.
10 Charteris, Thomas, Capt. (Tp.), k in a., 27/9/15.
9 Child, Joseph Alfred, 2/Lt., k. in a., 7/6/17 (att. 69/T.M.B.).
12 Clark, George Milburn, 2/Lt. (Tp.), k. in a., 14/7/18 (att. 1/W. York. R.).
Clarke, James Henry Fisher, 2/Lt. (Tp.), k. in a., 1/7/16.
1 Clidero, Herbert, 2/Lt. (Tp.), k. in a., 1/9/18 (att. 8/W. York. R.).
10 Cliff, Frank Pearce, Lt. (Tp.), k. in a., 4/10/17.
7 Coates, Harold Brearley, 2/Lt. (Tp.), k. in a., 1/7/16.
8 Cole, Ernest, 2/Lt. (Tp.), d. of w., 8/8/16.
7 Collett, Thomas Theodore, 2/Lt., d. of w., 15/2/17.
1/2 Cook, William Edwin, 2/Lt. (Tp.), d. of w., 27/4/18 (att. 4/Bn.).
9 Cooper, Claude Huntley, 2/Lt. (Tp.), drowned, 17/1/18.
10 Cornaby, Hubert Arthur, 2/Lt. (Tp.), k. in a., 15/7/16.
7 Crabtree, Fred Walmseley, Lt. (Tp.), k. in a., 15/8/15.
3 Crapper, Charles, M.M., 2/Lt., d. of w., 26/4/18 (att. 5/Bn.).
2 Cressey, George Ernest Lister, Lt., k. in a., 26/9/15.
7 Croft, Randal William Shuckburgh, Capt. (Tp.), k. in a., 12/5/17.
Crosse, M. E. B., 2/Lt., k. in a., 13/3/15.
2 Cunningham, David, 2/Lt. (Tp.), died, 27/10/17.
6 Currey, George Grafton, Capt. (Tp.), k. in a., 22/8/15.
10 Cust, Bertram Mitford, 2/Lt. (Tp.), k. in a., 9/11/15.
Cuttle, Geoffrey, 2/Lt., k. in a., 14/3/15.
3 Daglish, James Wilson, 2/Lt., k. in a., 14/2/16.
8 Darling, Alan Heppell, 2/Lt. (Tp.), k. in a., 10/7/16.
7 David, Lionel Adolf David, 2/Lt. (Tp.), k. in a., 1/7/16.
2 Dean, Harold, M.C., 2/Lt. (Tp.) (A/Capt.), killed, 5/1/18.
9 Dean, Thomas Walton, 2/Lt. (Tp.), k. in a., 7/6/17.
1 Delap, John Follansbee Bredin, 2/Lt., k. in a., 18/10/16.
2 Denman, Percy Darrell, 2/Lt., k. in a., 1/7/16.
10 Dent, Wilfred Harry, Major (Tp.), k. in a., 27/9/15.
6 Derrick, John Leslie, Capt. (Tp.), k. in a., 27/8/17.
11 Dickinson, Edward, Capt., k. in a., 28/6/15.
9 Dixon, Harry, Lt. (Tp.), k. in a., 6/10/18.
10 Dobinson, Stanley Raine, Lt. (Tp.), k. in a., 31/3/18.
8 Dodgson, Francis, Capt. (Tp.), k. in a., 10/7/16.
10 Douglas, John Charles Edward, Major (Tp.), d. of w., 18/12/15.
2 Drake, Godfrey Ward, 2/Lt. (Tp.), d. of w., 1/8/17.
3 Eade, Aylmer, 2/Lt., k. in a., 9/10/17 (att. 2/Bn.).
6 Eadon, Alfred Mitchell, 2/Lt., d. of w., 21/8/15.
1/3 Eames, Fred, 2/Lt., k. in a., 19/9/18 (att. 1/5 Bn. The Essex R.).
9 Edwardes-Crate, Ian Ronald, M.C., 2/Lt. (Tp.), d. of w., 10/10/18.
6 Evers, Leslie Montague, 2/Lt., k. in a., 30/3/18.
1/2 Eyre, Thomas Herbert, 2/Lt. (Tp.), k. in a., 17/7/17 (att. 7/Bn.).
10 Fairbairns, Arnold, T/Lt. (A/Capt.), k. in a., 14/10/18 (att. 13/W. Rid. R.).
3 Fawcett, John, 2/Lt., k. in a., 8/5/18 (att. 2/Bn.).
8 Fenton, William Vernon, 2/Lt. (Tp.), d. of w., 16/9/15.
2 Field, Robert Alister, M.C., Lt. (A/Capt.), k. in a., 2/4/17.
4 Fife, Alexander John, Lt.-Col., died, 7/2/17 (att. M.G.C.).
6 Firth, Harold, Lt., k. in a., 9/10/17.
2 Firth, Percy, 2/Lt., d. of w., 28/7/18 (att. 8/W. York. R.).
3 Fish, Frank Edward, Capt., k. in a., 17/5/15 (att. 2/Bn.).
Fisher, Edward Humbert, 2/Lt., k. in a., 19/5/15.
2 Forsyth, Cusack Grant, D.S.O., Lt.-Col. (Tp.), k. in a., 14/9/16 (att. 6/Bn.).
10 Fowler, Valentine, Major (Tp.), k. in a., 2/6/17.
6 Frank, Edward, 2/Lt. (Tp.), k. in a., 7/8/15.
3 Fraser, Henry Hubert, Lt., k. in a., 27/5/18 (att. 5/Bn.).
2 Freeland, John Buchan, 2/Lt., k. in a., 26/7/17.
7 Freeston, Cecil James, 2/Lt. (Tp.), k. in a., 18/9/17.
1/2 Galtry, Raymond, 2/Lt. (Tp.), k. in a., 9/10/17 (att. 6/Bn.).
9 Gamble, Walter Rayes, M.C., Capt. (Tp.), d. of w., 12/6/17.
9 Gibson, John, Lt. (Tp.), k. in a., 5/7/16.
Gill, Basil Every, Capt., k. in a., 18/10/16.
7 Goldsmith, Lewis Wilberforce, Capt. (Tp.), k. in a., 5/11/16.
7 Goodall, Arthur Charles, 2/Lt. (Tp.), k. in a., 6/11/16.
7 Goodway, James, 2/Lt. (Tp.), k. in a., 27/12/17.
Gorton, George Herbert, 2/Lt. (Tp.), k. in a., 10/7/16.
1/2 Graham, Hugh Colborne, 2/Lt. (Tp.), k. in a., 1/10/17 (att. 9/Bn.).
3 Graham, Malcolm Hewley, Lt., k. in a., 15/6/15 (att. 2/Bn.).
13 Graves, Horace Jocelyn, M.C., Lt. (Tp.), d. of w., 14/10/18 (att. 8/W. York. R.).
8 Gregery, James Langdale, 2/Lt. (Tp.), k. in a., 13/5/17 (att. 101 F. Co., R.E.).
3 Griffiths, Frank Calvert, 2/Lt., d. of w., 14/2/17 (att. 7/Bn.).
14 Grimsley, William Henry, Lt. (Tp.), k. in a., 6/10/18 (att. 9/Bn.).
9 Groom, Noel, Lt. (Tp.), k. in a., 20/9/17.
10 Hadow, Arthur de Salis, Bt.-Col., k. in a., 27/9/15.
2 Hadow, Gerald Francis, Lt., k. in a., 15/6/15.
Hall, Durham Donald George, M.C., 2/Lt. (T/Capt.), d. of w., 27/3/18 (att. R.F.C.).
2 Halliday, John, 2/Lt., k. in a., 8/5/18.
Hallifax, John Dampier, Lt., k. in a., 17/5/15.
9 Halliwell, Wilfrid Newbold, 2/Lt. (Tp.), d. of w., 21/9/16.
12 Harris, John Anthony, Capt., k. in a., 26/11/17.
Harris, Roland Milton, 2/Lt., k. in a., 7/6/17 (and R.F.C., 60 Sqd.).
3 Harrison, Francis Harold, Lt, k. in a., 2/9/16 (85/Bn., Spec Bde., R.E.).
13 Hart, Edgar Oswald, 2/Lt. (Tp.), k. in a., 10/7/16 (att. 9/Bn.).
Hatton, Frederick Charles, 2/Lt., k in a., 30/10/14.
6 Haynes, William Harold, Capt., killed, 26/9/18 (and R.A.F.).
Heatly, Henry Francis, Lt., k. in a., 22/2/15.
9 Helms, Percy, 2/Lt (Tp.) d of w., 5/10/18.
9 Hermiston, Frank, Lt. (Tp.), k. in a., 5/7/16.
6 Hildersley, Stanley Kentfield Edwards, 2/Lt. (Tp.), k. in a., 12/9/16
14 Hildreth, Ernest, 2/Lt. (Tp.), killed, 18/10/16 (and R.F.C.).
8 Hiley, Frank, Capt (Tp.), killed, 13/2/18.
3 Hill, Richard, Major, died, 17/2/15.
2 Hill, William Henry Ostler, 2/Lt, d. of w., 25/9/15.
11 Hillman, Harold Alexander Moore, Lt. (Tp.), k. in a., 1/7/16 (att. 7 Bn.).
Hodgkinson, George Cedric, Lt. (Tp.), d. of w., 4/7/16 (att. Yorks and Lancs R.).
Hollingshead, Amos, Lt. and Q.M., died, 26/7/17.
10 Hornby, Gerald Barford, 2/Lt. (Tp.), k. in a., 12/7/16.
7 Hornsby, Harold Gibson, 2/Lt (Tp.), k. in a., 1/7/16.
2 Howarth, Norman, 2/Lt., k. in a., 22/3/18.
3 Howells, Courtney Philip, 2/Lt. (Tp.), k. in a., 30/9/18 (att. 5/K.O.Y.L.I.)
3 Hubbard, William Dickenson, Lt., k. in a., 8/7/16 (att. 2/Bn.).
7 Huffington, Thomas, A/Capt., d. of w., 8/2/17.
8 Hume-Wright, Maurice Gabriel, Lt. (Tp.), k. in a., 10/7/16.
9 Hunnybun, Gerald Norman, Major (Tp.), k. in a., 23/10/18
11 Hurst, Charles Ernest, 2/Lt. (Tp.), k. in a., 14/9/16 (att. 6/Bn.).
6 Hurst, Henry Cubbin, 2/Lt. (Tp.), k. in a., 28/9/16.
12 Hutton, Stanley Fell, 2/Lt. (Tp.), k. in a., 9/11/18.
Hyland, F. H., 2/Lt., k. in a., 23/5/15 (and R.F.C.).
10 Hyslop, Thomas Anderson, M.C., 2/Lt. (Tp.), k. in a., 22/3/18 (att. 4/Bn.).
7 James, Arthur, Lt., k. in a., 3/1/17.
Jeffery, Claud Gifford, Capt., d. of w., 23/10/14.
Jeffries, Herbert, Lt. (Tp.), d. of w., 20/9/18 (and M.G.C.).
6 Jelley, William Frederick, M.C., 2/Lt., d. of W., 2/11/17.
13 Jennings, Charles Francis, 2/Lt (Tp.), k. in a., 8/4/17.
7 Jolly, Benton Ord, 2/Lt. (Tp.), d. of w., 9/2/17.
7 Jones, Loftus Edward Percival, Capt. (Tp.), k. in a., 3/8/15.
1 Jones, William Henry, 2/Lt., k. in a., 27/5/18 (att. 4/Batt.).
12 Jowett, Sydney Ferguson, 2/Lt., k. in a., 27/5/18 (att. 5/Bn.).
Kay, Stanley Burnett, Capt., died, 28/1/18 (and R.F.C.).
9 Kemp, Ernest Charles, 2/Lt., died, 6/9/16 (and R.F.C.).
10 Kemp-Welch, Maurice, 2/Lt. (Tp.), k. in a., 11/4/17.
4 Kent, Ralph E. Dawson, Lt.-Col., k. in a., 27/5/18 (and 81 Train. Reserve Bn.).
Kidd, Philip Chabert, 2/Lt, k. in a., 30/10/14.
King, Charles Arthur Cecil, Col., k. in a., 30/10/14
11 Kingcombe, Alexis Randolph, Lt., d. of w., 28/6/15.
10 Kinnach, Samuel James, 2/Lt. (Tp.), k. in a., 15/7/16.
Kirkwood, William John, 2/Lt. (Tp.), k. in a., 11/11/15 (att. 6/Bn.).
Knights, Henry Thorne, Capt. (Tp.), k. in a., 19/10/16 (and T.M.B.).
9 Knott, Frederick William, 2/Lt. (Tp.), k. in a., 7/6/17.
3 Knowles, George Clarence, 2/Lt., d. of w., 10/6/17 (att. 9/Batt.)
3 Laird, Hugh Blackhall, 2/Lt, k. in a., 8/7/16.
3 Lambert, Eric Noel, M.C., Capt. (Tp.), d. of w., 7/6/17 (att. 8/Bn.).
6 Lambert, Maurice Borington, Lt. (Tp.), k. in a., 7/8/15.
10 Lawson, George William, 2/Lt., k. in a., 11/4/18 (att 5/Batt.).
2 Leatham, Bertram Henry, D.S.O., Major (T/Lt.-Col.), k. in a., 26/9/15 (att. Wilts R.).
3 Leather, Edward Wilberforce, Capt., k. in a., 18/4/15 (att. Y.L.I.).
Ledgard, Frank Cooper, Lt., k. in a., 23/10/14.
2 Leonard, Denis, M.M., 2/Lt. (Tp.), k. in a., 6/11/18.
1 Le Sueur, Ernest Geoffrey Carrington, Lt. (T/Capt.), k. in a., 26/7/17.
1/2 Lewis, Herbert Owen Roland, M.C., 2/Lt. (Tp.), k. in a., 1/10/17 (att. 9/Batt.).
2 Lloyd-Jones, John, Capt. (Tp.), died, 11/3/16.
3 Lodge, John William, Col. (Hon.), died, 23/8/17 (att. 2 (H.S.) Garr. Bty., Yorks R.).
12 Lord, Albert Edward, 2/Lt. (Tp.), d. of w., 29/4/18.
10 V.C. Loudon-Shand, Stewart Walter, Major (Tp.), k. in a., 1/3/17.
Lowther, William, 2/Lt., k. in a., 27/5/18.
10 Lynch, Joseph Edward, Capt (Tp.), k. in a., 26/9/15.
13 McBain, Frederick Thomas, 2/Lt. (Tp.), k. in a., 9/4/18.
McCarthy, Noel Fisher, 2/Lt., k. in a., 18/10/16.
11 MacFarlane, Ian Cameron, 2/Lt. (Tp.), k. in a., 14/9/16 (att. 6/Bn.).
15 MacIntyre, George Duncan, Lt. (Tp.), k. in a., 10/7/16 (att. 7/Bn.).

11 McIntyre, John Caldwell, 2/Lt. (Tp.), d. of w., 5/10/15 (att. 2/Bn.).
2 Maddison, Bertram Lionel, Lt.-Col. (Tp.), k. in a., 1/7/16 (att. 8/Y. & L.R.).
Maddox, Cyril Percy, 2/Lt. (Tp.), k. in a., 20/11/17 (att. 2/4 K.O.Y.L.I.).
10 Margerrison, James, 2/Lt. (Tp.), d. of w., 14/4/18 (att. 150 T.M.B.).
Marlowe, Cecil Arthur, 2/Lt. (Tp.), d. of w., 18/10/18 (att. 1/7 W. York. R.).
13 Mason, Richard, T/Lt. (A/Capt.), k. in a., 23/11/17.
1 Mathews, Avard Yuill, 2/Lt., d. of w., 26/10/18 (whilst P.O.W., att. 1/W. York. R.).
9 Matthews, Richard Malcolm, 2/Lt. (Tp.), k. in a., 20/9/17.
3 Maude, Michael Day Wade, Capt., d. of w., 14/10/17 (att. 9/Bn.).
5 Melhado, Owen Stirling, 2/Lt. (Tp.), d. of w., 7/12/15 (att. 11/Bn.).
1/2 Melhuish, Leslie, 2/Lt. (Tp.), k. in a., 27/11/17 (att. 2/5 K.O.Y.L.I.).
6 Messenger, Henry Frederick Roy, 2/Lt., k. in a., 22/8/15.
14 Miles, Gordon, Lt. (Tp.), k. in a., 7/10/16 (att. 9/Bn.).
7 Milholland, Frederick Raymond, Capt. (Tp.), d. of w., 26/2/18 (att. 6/Batt.).
3 Millar, Audley Charles Hyde, M.C., Capt. (Tp.), d. of w., 16/10/17 (att. 9/Bn.).
12 Millar, Duncan Crerar Reeve, Lt., d. of w., 10/4/18 (att. T.M.B.).
3 Miller, Alan, 2/Lt., d. of w., 14/10/16 (att. 2/Bn.).
3 Mills, William Checkley, 2/Lt., k. in a., 23/7/16.
11 Mitchell, Thomas James, 2/Lt. (Tp.), k. in a., 10/7/16.
2 Moir, Douglas Dana Drew Kinnaird, 2/Lt., k. in a., 23/7/16.
2 Morant, Norman, 2/Lt., d. of w., 27/3/18 (in German hands).
6 Morgan, John Cecil, Capt., k. in a., 7/8/15.
6 Morris, Sydney, 2/Lt. (Tp.), k. in a., 7/8/15.
7 Mowat, John Farquhar, 2/Lt. (Tp.), d. of w., 15/5/17.
11 Murray, Robert Henry, Capt. (Tp.), k. in a., 7/7/16 (att. Mun. Fus.).
6 Myers, John Flesher, Capt. (Tp.), k. in a., 9/10/17.
Nevile, Guy Lister, Capt., k. in a., 15/6/15.
9 Nicholson, Lancelot, 2/Lt. (Tp.), k. in a., 20/9/17.
Nilsson, Geoffrey Burbank, 2/Lt. (Tp.), k. in a., 18/9/18 (att. 7/E. York R.).
10 Noyes, Ralph Elliot, Major, k. in a., 27/9/15.
Oakes, Orbell, Capt., killed, 13/3/15.
15 Oakley, Reginald, 2/Lt. (Tp.), k. in a., 25/8/16 (att. 8/Bn.).
11 Oppé, Henry Sigismund, Lt. (Tp.), k. in a., 6/11/15 (att. 6/Bn.).
6 Osmond, Charles Frederick Squire, 2/Lt. (Tp.), k. in a., 28/11/17.
Parker, Frank Bryan, Capt. (Tp.), killed, 23/3/19 (att. 6/Bn.).
12 Peach, Bertie Charles, Lt. (Tp.), k. in a., 9/4/18.
1/2 Pearson, Robert, 2/Lt., d. of w., 7/8/18 (P.O.W., att. 8/W. York. R.).
2 Perkins, Cecil Howard, Lt., k. in a., 22/7/18 (att. 21 Trench Mortar Bty.).
3 Perry, John, 2/Lt., k. in a., 23/7/16.
Phayre, Richard Herbert, Lt., k. in a., 26/10/14.
13 Phillips, Frank Stewart, 2/Lt. (Tp.), k. in a., 23/11/17.
2 Phillips, Herbert, 2/Lt., k. in a., 13/10/16.
13 Phillips, Percy Montague, Lt. (Tp.), k. in a., 25/9/16.
2 Pickup, Alfred James, 2/Lt. (Tp.), k. in a., 26/9/15.
8 Player, Eric Noel, Capt. (Tp.), k. in a., 6/8/16.
6 Plumpton, Robert, 2/Lt., died, 25/12/18.
9 Pomfrey, James Arthur, 2/Lt. (Tp.), d. of w., 4/10/18
10 Pratt, John Selby, Lt. (Tp.), k. in a., 11/4/17.
3 Pritchard-Barrett, John Oscar, Lt., k. in a., 15/6/15 (att. 2/Bn.).
3 Pyman, Allan, Lt., k. in a., 15/6/15 (att. 2/Bn.).
3 Raley, William Henry George, Capt., k. in a., 15/6/15 (att. 2/Bn.).
6 Randerson, Robert, Capt. (Tp.), k. in a., 7/8/15.
13 Ransome, Geoffrey Cyril, Lt. (Tp.), d. of w., 15/1/18.
1/2 Read, Charles, Lt. (Tp.), k. in a., 5/10/18 (att. 9/Bn.).
2 Richardson, Evan John, Capt., k. in a., 25/9/15.
6 Richardson, George Alvarez, 2/Lt., k. in a., 27/9/16.
3 Rigby, James Richard Anderton, Lt., k. in a., 26/9/15 (att. 2/Bn.).
6 Roberts, Archibald, Major, d. of w., 22/8/15.
11 Robinson, Thomas Edward, Lt., k. in a., 18/10/16 (att. 2/Bn.).
3 Roper, Geoffrey Stapylton Rowe, M.C., 2/Lt. (Tp.), k. in a., 12/5/17 (att. 7/Bn.).
8 Rowley, Newton, 2/Lt. (Tp.), k. in a., 10/7/16.
7 Rudge, Reginald Theodore, 2/Lt. (Tp.), k. in a., 5/11/16.
6 Rushworth, Frederick Arthur, 2/Lt., k. in a., 29/9/16.
6 Rutherford, Thomas Wood, 2/Lt. (Tp.), k. in a., 22/8/15.
9 Selch, Frederick William, 2/Lt. (Tp.), k. in a., 4/11/18 (att. 7/E. York. R.).
2 Shann, Albert, 2/Lt., k. in a., 8/5/18.
Sheay, William, 2/Lt., d. of w., 16/5/15.
6 Shepherd-Turneham, Thomas Percy, Capt. (Tp.), k. in a., 28/9/16.
6 Shipley, Arthur Hammond Butler, 2/Lt. (Tp.), k. in a., 27/9/16 (A. Coy., 11 Div.).
13 Shorthouse, Algernon Geoffrey, 2/Lt. (Tp.), died, 5/6/18.
1 Simonet, Kenneth William Lee, Capt., k. in a., 21/1/16.
13 Simpkin, Arthur Wilson, Capt. (Tp.), k. in a., 30/9/18 (att. 8/Batt. W. York. R.).
13 Simpkin, Harry Hargreaves, Capt. (Tp.), k. in a., 22/3/18.
8 Simpson, Clifford Sandford, Capt. (Tp.), k. in a., 10/7/16.
3 Smart, William Ellis, 2/Lt., k. in a., 11/10/18 (att. 7/W. York. R.).
Smith, Gilbert Parker, 2/Lt., killed, 5/1/18.
1 Stafford, Thomas Colegrave, Capt. (Tp.), died, 2/4/16 (Garr. Bn.).
13 Stanfield, Thomas William, 2/Lt. (Tp.), k. in a., 23/11/17.
Stansfeld, H. A., Hon. Major, died, 8/12/14.
2 Stembridge, Jim, 2/Lt. (Tp.), k. in a., 29/9/18.
13 Storch, Herbert, M.C., 2/Lt. (Tp.), d. of w., 24/8/18 (att. 1/E. York. R.).
3 Strathern, Tom Dalrymple, 2/Lt., k. in a., 8/7/10.
2 Strugnell, Alfred Charles, 2/Lt., k. in a., 1/7/16.
6 Stout, George Frederick, 2/Lt. (Tp.), k. in a., 30/9/16.
Studley, Logan, 2/Lt., k. in a., 25/10/14.
8 Summerville, Joseph, M.C., 2/Lt. (Tp.), k. in a., 29/10/18.
8 Swain, Thomas, 2/Lt. (Tp.), d. of w., 25/7/16.
14 Swain, William, 2/Lt. (Tp.), k. in a., 22/9/16 (att. 8/Bn.).
7 Sykes, Tom, 2/Lt. (Tp.), k. in a., 29/6/17.
2 Symon, John, 2/Lt. (Tp.), killed, 5/1/18.
11 Tanner, Edward Joseph Selby, 2/Lt. (Tp.), k. in a., 8/7/16 (att. M.G.C.).
15 Taylor, William Bruce, 2/Lt. (Tp.), d. of w., 17/4/17 (att. 9/Batt.).
7 Thacker, William Alfred, 2/Lt. (Tp.), k. in a., 12/5/17.
Thorpe, Albert Edward, 2/Lt. (Tp.), died, 6/12/18 (att. 11/E. York. R.).
Thwaites, Marmaduke, Lt. (T/Capt.), k. in a., 30/9/15.
8 Tilly, John, M.C., Capt. (Tp.), k. in a., 8/6/18.
3 Tozer, Horace Gordon, 2/Lt., k. in a., 1/10/15 (att. 2/Bn.).
13 Tune, Charles Walter, 2/Lt. (Tp.), k. in a., 23/11/17.
2 Turner, Hubert Samuel Alston, 2/Lt., k. in a., 1/8/17.
3 Tweddell, Thomas, Lt., d. of w., 28/6/18 (att. 7/Batt.).
14 Venables, Charles Edward, 2/Lt. (Tp.), d. of w., 12/10/16.
11 Vick, Arnold Oughtrad, Lt., k. in a., 27/9/18 (att. 6/Bn.).
13 Vickers, Noel Muschamp, Lt. (Tp.), k. in a., 3/8/16.
11 Walker, Arthur John, Capt. (Tp.), k. in a., 7/8/15 (att. 6/Bn. Manch. R.).
Walker, Wilfred Bertram, Major, k. in a., 29/10/14
3 Walmesley, Richard, Lt., k. in a., 23/10/14.
2 Walton, Herbert Parlby, Lt., d. of w., 7/12/17.
13 Walton, Harold William, Lt., d. of w., 24/11/17.
2 Watson, William Wallace, 2/Lt. (Tp.), k. in a., 13/10/16.
2 Webb, Cyril Francis, Lt., k. in a., 25/9/15.
3 Welford, Frederick, 2/Lt. (Tp.), k. in a., 9/10/17 (att. 6/Bn.).
8 Wellesley, Eric George, 2/Lt., k. in a., 21/12/15.
7 Weston, Charles Guy, Lt. (Tp.), k. in a., 1/11/15.
2 Whaley, Frank, 2/Lt. (Tp.), k. in a., 31/3/17.
11 White, Edward Beadon, 2/Lt. (Tp.), d. of w., 1/7/16 (att. M.G.C.).
6 White, John Finlayson, 2/Lt. (Tp.), d. of w., 7/8/15.
1/2 Whitley, Harry, 2/Lt., k. in a., 27/3/18 (att. 2/Batt. W. York. R.).
1/2 Whitwell, P. H., 2/Lt., killed, 25/4/18 (and R.A.F.).
6 Whitworth, Charles Edward, 2/Lt., d. of w., 22/8/15.
9 Wilkins, Bernard Ivan, 2/Lt. (Tp.), d. of w., 6/1/16.
3 Wilkinson, Bernard Jocelyn, 2/Lt., k. in a., 8/7/16.
9 Wilkinson, William Thomas, Capt. (Tp.), k. in a., 5/7/16.
Wilson, Humphrey Worthington, Lt. (T/Capt.), k. in a., 4/10/15.
6 Wilson, Ian McLean, Lt., k. in a., 7/8/15.
Wilson, Edwin, 2/Lt., k. in a., 4/11/18 (att. 9/West Rid. R.).
15 Wilton, Richard Birkenhead, 2/Lt., k. in a., 1/10/17 (att. 9/Bn.).
9 Wolstenholme, George Mellor, M.C., Lt., k. in a., 5/10/18.
9 Wood, Thos. Theodore, 2/Lt. (Tp.), d. of w., 14/7/16.
6 Woosnam, Richard Bowen, Lt., k. in a., 4/6/15 (att. 4/Bn.).
Wray, Harry, 2/Lt. (Tp.), k. in a., 29/12/17 (att. 10/Batt.).
2 Wright, Herbert Melville, 2/Lt. (Tp.), k. in a., 2/4/17.
3 Wright, Noel Tracey, Lt. (T/Capt.), d. of w., 1/10/15 (att. 2/Bn.).
9 Wyld, Cyril Garnet, 2/Lt. (Tp.), k. in a., 5/7/16.

The Lancashire Fusiliers.

16 Abraham, Frederick Henry, 2/Lt. (Tp.), k. in a., 2/10/18.
Adams, George Stopford, Major, k. in a., 11/5/15.
10 Adcock, Harold Meredyth, Capt. (Tp.), k. in a., 5/7/16.
15 Aird, James Gilbert, Temp. 2/Lt., k. in a., 1/7/16.
17 Allin, Harold Arthur, 2/Lt. (Tp.), k. in a., 23/10/17.
3 Almon, Harold Pryor, 2/Lt., k. in a., 31/7/17 (att. 11 Bn.).
4 Anderson, Arthur Ferneaux Dalgairno, 2/Lt., k. in a., 1/7/16 (att. 1 Bn.).
1 Anderson, William, Capt. (Tp.), died, 25/7/18.
3 Anderton, Frank Westall, 2/Lt., k. in a., 1/7/16 (att. 1 Bn.).
Anderton, George Eric Asquith, Lt., k. in a., 22/3/18 (att. M.G.C.).
Andrew, Malcoln, Lt. (Tp.), k. in a., 4/11/18 (att. 104/T. M.B.).
12 Armstrong-Dash, Arthur, Lt., k. in a., 22/4/18.
11 Ash, Edwin Alexander Rays, Lt. (Tp.), d. of w., 26/4/18 (att. 10 Bn.).
Ashby, Leslie, 2/Lt. (Tp.), k. in a., 20/10/18 (att. 2/5 Bn.).
1/2 Ashcroft, John, 2/Lt. (Tp.), k. in a., 2/10/18 (att. 16 Bn.).
9 Ashton, Edward Deakin, 2/Lt. (Tp.), k. in a., 1/7/16 (att. 19 Bn.).
17 Aspden, Fred, M.C., 2/Lt. (Tp.), k. in a., 14/10/18.
13 Audaer, Ernest Clifford, 2/Lt., k. in a., 1/7/16.
10 Bache, Harold Godfrey, 2/Lt. (Tp.), k. in a., 15/2/16.
20 Backwell, Charles William, 2/Lt. (Tp.), k. in a., 22/6/17 (att. X35 T.M.B.).
12 Baker, William Frank, 2/Lt. (Tp.), k. in a., 15/5/16 (att. 11 Bn.).
10 Barber, George Ernest, 2/Lt., k. in a., 7/7/16.
20 Barker, Albion Mitchell, 2/Lt. (T/Lt.), d. of w., 19/7/17 (att. 2/5 Bn.).
1 Barker, Harry, 2/Lt. (Tp.), k. in a., 4/9/18.
16 Barlow, Harry Archibald, 2/Lt. (Tp.), k. in a., 10/7/17.

20 Barlow, Harold Carver, Temp. Lt., k. in a., 18/6/17 (and R.F.C., 9 Sqd.).
3 Barnett, Ralph Thurlby, 2/Lt., k. in a., 12/10/16 (att. 2 Bn.).
10 Barratt, Geoffrey Ravenscroft, 2/Lt., k. in a., 7/7/16.
11 Barrett, Reginald, 2/Lt. (Tp.), k. in a., 15/5/16.
10 Barrow, Alfred James, M.C., Capt., d. of w., 24/6/18 (in Ger. hands).
4 Barnsley, Alan, Capt., k. in a., 25-27/10/14 (att. North'd Fus.).
Bass, Charles Harold, Capt., k. in a., 27/8/14.
Bassett, George Sidney, 2/Lt. (Tp.), d. of w., 6/7/17 (Res., att. 10 Bn.).
10 Batson, Robert Evelyn, 2/Lt. (Tp.), k. in a., 11/10/16 (7 Bde. T.M.B.).
Battye, Reginald, 2/Lt. (Tp.), k. in a., 23/10/18 (att. 1/7 Bn.).
12 Beardsell, Richard Ernest, 2/Lt., k. in a., 22/4/18.
16 Bell, Cecil Charles, 2/Lt., k. in a., 28/11/17.
11 Bernstein, Maurice Leon, M.C., 2/Lt. (Tp.), k. in a., 10/4/18.
19 Berry, Alexander James, 2/Lt. (Tp.), k. in a., 22/8/16 (att. 20 Bn.).
V.C. Best-Dunkley, Bertram, Capt. (Temp. Lt.-Col.), d. of w., 5/8/17.
4 Billington, Leslie Charles, 2/Lt., 9/7/15 (att. 2 Bn.).
3 Bingham, Bentinck Aglionby, 2/Lt., k. in a., 12/5/17 (att. 10 Bn.).
11 Blackwell, Julian Victor, 2/Lt. (Tp.), k. in a., 11/4/18.
Blakeney, Leslie St. Leger, Lt., drowned, 28/3/15 (and Gold Coast Regt.).
18 Bowe, Stanley Gordon, Lt. (Tp.), d. of w., 15/5/18.
2 Bowen, Geoffrey Grenside, M.C., Lt. (T/Capt.), k. in a., 2/9/18.
11 Bowyer, Joseph, M.C., Hon. Lt. & Qr.-Mr., k. in a., 9/6/17.
Boyle, David Erskine, Lt., k. in a., 26/8/14.
4 Brewer, Cecil Harold, 2/Lt., k. in a., 4/10/17 (att. 7 Bn.).
Brierley, Charles Leonard, Major, d. of w., 16/9/15.
9 Brierley, Horace James, Lt. (Tp.), k. in a., 7/8/15.
V.C. Bromley, Cuthbert, Temp. Major, drowned, 13/8/15.
17 Brookes, Harry, 2/Lt. (Tp.), d. of w., 12/4/18.
16 Brooman, Edward James, M.C., Temp. 2/Lt. (A/Lt.), k. in a., 1/4/17.
3 Brown, S. V., 2/Lt., died, 9/11/18.
12 Brundle, Henry Carlton Bulman, Lt. (T/Capt.), k. in a., 9/10/17.
1 Buchan, Charles, 2/Lt. (Tp.), d. of w., 2/12/17 (att. 15 Bn.).
12 Budden, Harold William, 2/Lt. (Tp.), k. in a., 14/9/16.
4 Butler, Geoffrey Lewis, Lt., k. in a., 15/5/17 (att. 11 Bn.).
2 Butler-Bowden, Basil Joseph Bernard, 2/Lt., k. in a., 28/3/18.
11 Carruthers, George MacLellan, Temp. 2/Lt., k. in a., 10/8/17.
17 Carter, Seton Rodney, Temp. 2/Lt., k. in a., 14/4/17 (and R.F.C., 52 Sqd.).
19 Cartmell, Thomas, Temp. 2/Lt., d. of w., 8/5/16.
20 Cartwright, Joseph Harry, Temp. 2/Lt., d. of w., 2/6/18.
2 V.C. Cassidy, Bernard Matthew, Temp. 2/Lt., k. in a., 28/3/18.
1/2 Challis, Ivor James, 2/Lt., k. in a., 14/4/18 (att. 11 Bn.).
19 Chambers, Edward Chandos Elliot, Temp. 2/Lt., k. in a., 1/7/16.
16 Chamberlayne, Arthur, 2/Lt., d. of w., 10/4/17.
Charleston, Frederick, 2/Lt. (T/Lt.), d. of w., 7/7/15.
15 Chester, Lewis Charles Bagot, Temp. 2/Lt., k. in a., 4/4/18.
2 Chilton, Hubert, Temp. 2/Lt., k. in a., 23/4/18.
1/2 Chorley, Charles Leonard, M.C., Temp. 2/Lt., k. in a., 26/4/18 (att. 2/5 Bn.).
2 Clark, Charlie, Temp. 2/Lt., k. in a., 9/4/18 (att. 5 Bn.).
Clark, Ellis, 2/Lt., k. in a., 1/5/15.
3 Clarke, Alfred Lord, 2/Lt., k. in a., 27/3/18.
10 Clay, Vernon Harcourt, M.C., Temp. 2/Lt., d. of w., 26/10/16.
Clayton, Harold Robert, Capt., k. in a., 4/6/15.
13 Clegg, Alexander, 2/Lt., k. in a., 1/7/16.
4 Clegg, Robert Leslie, Lt., k. in a., 3/9/17 (and R.F.C., 45 Sqd.).
10 Comyn, David Charles Edward ffrench, Major, k. in a., 12/5/17.
2 Concannon, James, 2/Lt., k. in a., 3/5/17.
1 Conran, Percy Wogan Drysdale, Capt., d. of w., 12/4/18.
4 Corkill, Ernest, 2/Lt., k. in a., 28/2/17.
1/2 Cotter, Harold Cecil, 2/Lt., k. in a., 10/4/18 (att. 11 Bn.).
1/2 Crank, Harry, Temp. 2/Lt., k. in a., 22/10/17 (att. 17 Bn.).
15 Crossley, Cyril, 2/Lt., k. in a., 1/7/16.
Cunliffe, Thomas Henry Withers, Capt., k. in a., 4/6/15.
Daley, Richard, 2/Lt. (Tp.), k. in a., 25/10/18 (att. 2/5 Bn.).
2 Davenport, Robert, 2/Lt., k. in a., 3/5/17.
20 Davis, Hugh Courtney, 2/Lt. (Tp.), k. in a., 25/7/16.
21 Dean, Arthur, Temp. 2/Lt., k. in a., 8/11/16 (att. 10 Bn.).
1 Dickens, William Castle, 2/Lt. (Tp.), k. in a., 13/10/18 (att. 10 Bn.).
15 Dilling, John Francis, Lt. (Tp.), k. in a., 10/8/18.
19 Dixon, Alfred Charles, 2/Lt., k. in a., 4/2/16.
18 Dobbyn, William Augustus Nelson, Temp. 2/Lt., killed, 4/1/17.
18 Dobinson, William, M.C., 2/Lt. (Tp.), k. in a., 22/10/17.
1 Dodd, James Forrest, 2/Lt., k. in a., 28/2/17.
17 Doidge, Reginald Chamberlain, Temp. Capt., killed, 2/3/16.
15 Doncaster, Robert Ivan, Temp. 2/Lt., k. in a., 1/7/16.
17 Drummond, Harry, 2/Lt. (Tp.), k. in a., 31/10/18.
20 Duckworth, William, 2/Lt. (Tp.), k. in a., 25/3/18 (att. 18 Bn.).
20 Duckworth, William Henry, 2/Lt. (Tp.), d. of w., 21/4/16.
11 Dunn, Frederick Charles Robert, Temp. Lt., k. in a., 9/7/16.
2 Dunne, Walter Edwin, 2/Lt. (T/Lt.), died, 18/10/15.
4 Dussee, Arthur Norman, 2/Lt., k. in a., 1/7/16 (19 Bn.).
10 Dutton, Charles, 2/Lt. (Tp.), k. in a., 7/7/16.
18 East, Kingsley Dunmore, Lt. (Tp.), k. in a., 27/5/16.
15 Edghill, Ashley Gay, M.C., Lt. (A/Capt.), d. of w., 15/4/18 (att. 96 T.M.B.).
11 Edwards, William Ian, M.C., T/Capt. and Adjt., k. in a., 5/8/17.
17 Esson, Alfred Charles, Temp. 2/Lt., d. of w., 23/10/17.
1/2 Evans, Eric Ben, Temp. 2/Lt., k. in a., 11/11/17 (att. 2/8 Bn.).
18 Evans, Edward Herbert Sandford, Lt. (T/Capt.), k. in a., 22/7/16.
2 Faragher, Edward Sayle, 2/Lt., k. in a., 9/10/17.
12 Farrar, Julian Gordon Knowles, Capt. (Tp.), k. in a., 14/9/16.
17 Farrar, Valentine Anstruther, Lt. (Tp.), d. of w., 15/3/16.
4 Farrow, Brian, 2/Lt., k. in a., 1/7/16 (att. 2 Bn.).
1 Fielding, Frank, Temp. 2/Lt., k. in a., 4/10/17 (att. 7 Bn.).
1/2 Fitton, W., 2/Lt., killed, 19/8/18 (and R.A.F.).
Foggo, Watson Henry, Temp. Lt., died, 20/5/18.
10 Forbes, John Donald, 2/Lt. (Tp.), d. of w., 29/9/15.
Forshaw, George Leslie Fresson, Temp. 2/Lt., k. in a., 19/11/17 (att. 3/5 Bn.).
3 Fortescue, William Aubrey, Lt., k. in a., 12/10/16 (att. 2 Bn.).
1 Francis, Ainslie, M.C., M.M., 2/Lt., d. of w., 30/4/18.
19 Freeman, Francis Hubert, Temp. 2/Lt., k. in a., 1/7/16.
4 Fryer, Eric Hamilton, Lt., k. in a., 3/8/16.
2 Gamon, Maurice Partridge, Temp. Capt., k. in a., 1/7/16.
Ganly, Roger, M.C., Capt., k. in a., 29/9/16 (att. 11 Bn.).
10 Garment, Leonard Charles, Temp. 2/Lt., k. in a., 21/3/18.
3 Garnet, Grosvenor, 2/Lt., k. in a., 9/10/17.
20 Gibbons, Edward Ingram, Lt., k. in a., 29/4/17.
10 Gibbs, Lawrence Henry, M.C., T/Lt., A/Capt., k. in a., 18/9/18.
1/2 Glass, Leonard George, 2/Lt., k. in a., 9/10/17.
1/2 Goddard, William Neale, Temp. Lt., k. in a., 13/6/17.
13 Gorfunkle, Isaac, Temp. Lt., k. in a., 12/8/18 (att. 1 Bn.).
Granger, Ernest Every Wyatt, Temp. Capt., k.in a., 16/8/17.
1 Grant, Henry Norman, 2/Lt., k. in a., 1/7/16.
15 Greenhill, Reginald Fowler, Capt., d. of w., 1/1/18.
19 Greenwood, James Barton, Lt., k. in a., 13/10/18 (att. York & Lanc. Regt.).
19 Gregory, Frank, Temp. Lt., k. in a., 16/4/18.
Grellier, Arthur Bertean, 2/Lt., k. in a., 26/3/18 (att. 2/7 Bn.).
13 Griffiths, George Clement, Capt. (Tp.), k. in a., 28/6/15 (att. 1 Bn.).
1 Griffiths, Walter, 2/Lt., k. in a., 21/11/17.
17 Grime, Joseph Crookes, 2/Lt., k. in a., 26/3/18.
3 Grimwade, Edward Ernest, 2/Lt., k. in a., 17/9/16 (att. 9 Bn.).
3 Guthrie, Hector MacLennan, Lt., k. in a., 4/6/15 (att. 1 Bn.).
11 Halfpenny, W. H., 2/Lt., died, 24/11/18 (and R.A.F.).
1/2 Halsall, Donald Court, 2/Lt. (Tp.), k. in a., 9/10/17 (att. 3/5 Bn.).
10 Hamilton, James Montgomery, M.C., Temp. 2/Lt. (A/Capt.), d. of w., 19/9/18.
17 Hamilton, James Russell, Temp. 2/Lt., k. in a., 22/10/17.
15 Hampson, Edgar, Temp. Lt., k. in a., 1/7/16.
4 Hardie, William, 2/Lt., d. of w., 18/4/17 (att. 13 Bn.).
1 Harper, Rennie, Temp. 2/Lt., k. in a., 14/10/18.
1/2 Harper, Tom, Temp. 2/Lt., k. in a., 4/6/17 (att. 7 Bn.).
4 Harrison, John 2/Lt., k. in a., 31/7/17 (att. 11 Bn.).
10 Harriss, Reginald Edmund, Temp. Capt., k. in a., 12/5/17.
20 Hartley, Bernard Harold, Temp. Lt., k. in a., 4/11/16.
2 Hartley, Edmund, Lt., k. in a., 18/5/18.
12 Haslam, Robert, Temp. 2/Lt., died, 29/3/18.
10 Hastings, Joseph Lorton, Temp. 2/Lt., k. in a., 12/5/17.
Hayne, Moreton, 2/Lt., died, 10/10/16 (and R.F.C.) (P.O.W.).
15 Heald, Geoffrey Yates, Capt. (Tp.), k. in a., 1/7/16.
1 Heard, Robert James Bannatyne, Capt., d. of w., 5/5/15.
10 Hebblethwaite, George, Temp. 2/Lt., k. in a., 7/7/16.
2 Hemelryk, Eugene John Vincent, 2/Lt., k. in a., 23/4/18.
2 Heron, James, Temp. 2/Lt., k. in a., 28/3/18.
11 Hetherington, Stephen Owen, Temp. 2/Lt., k. in a., 29/9/16.
16 Higginson, George Neale, Temp. Lt., k. in a., 23/11/16.
16 Higson, Richard Henry, 2/Lt., k. in a., 23/10/16.
11 Holden, Leonard Neil, Temp. Lt., k. in a., 9/7/16.
9 Hook, Duncan, T/Lt., k. in a., 7/8/15.
9 Hook, Robin, 2/Lt. (Tp.), k. in a., 9/8/15.
3 Hoskins, George, 2/Lt., k. in a., 5/11/16 (att. 10 Bn.).
4 Hoyland, John Fraser, Capt., k. in a., 26/9/16 (att. 9 Bn.).
16 Hubbard, Percy William, 2/Lt. (Tp.), k. in a., 6/6/18.
20 Hughes, Rhys, 2/Lt. (Tp.), d. of w., 1/8/16.
16 Hulton, Cecil Harry Joy, M.C., Temp. 2/Lt. (A/Capt.), k in a., 4/11/18.
2 Humfrey, William Knox, Lt., k. in a., 26/8/14.
1 Hutchings, Thomas Clifton, Capt. (Tp.), d. of w., 19/7/17.
3 Hutchinson, Bert, 2/Lt., d. of w., 12/8/18 (att. 15 Bn.).
4 Ingleton, Hubert John, Lt., d. of w., 2/11/18 (att. 1/8 Bn.).
1/2 Irving, Herbert Rufus Evelyn, M.C., 2/Lt. (Tp.), k. in a., 31/10/18 (att. 17 Bn.).
1/2 Jackson, Charles, 2/Lt., k. in a., 10/10/18.
3 Jackson, Ernest, 2/Lt., k. in a., 1/7/16.
10 Jackson, Harold James, 2/Lt. (Tp.), k. in a., 4/6/18.
1 Jagger, Harry, 2/Lt., k. in a., 10/6/18.
9 Jamieson, John, 2/Lt. (Tp.), k. in a., 3/4/18 (att. 16 Bn.).
11 Jewell, Edward Herbert, Temp. 2/Lt., k. in a., 15/5/16.
10 Jobling, Joseph Higgin, Temp. Lt., k. in a., 1/12/17.
1 Johnson, Norman Alfred Power, 2/Lt. (Temp. Capt.), k. in a., 27/11/15.
11 Jones, Arthur, 2/Lt., k. in a., 27/5/18.
10 Jones, F. D., Lt., k. in a., 7/7/16.
Jones, Frederick S. C., 2/Lt., k. in a., 30/11/16 (att. M.G.C.).
9 Joyce, James, 2/Lt. (Tp.), k. in a., 22/8/15.
11 Kay, John Calvert, 2/Lt., k. in a., 15/7/16.
3 Keigwin, Henry David, 2/Lt., k. in a., 20/9/16 (att. 19 Bn.).
Kenderdine, Tom Herbert Gordon, Temp. Lt., k. in a., 9/9/16 (att. 2/5 Bn.).
2 Kenion, Hugh Cyril, Temp. 2/Lt., k. in a., 1/7/16.
20 Kennedy, Andrew Macpherson, 2/Lt. (Tp.), k. in a., 26/3/18 (att. 18 Bn.).

1 Kerr, Peter Campbell, 2/Lt. (Tp.), k. in a., 18/8/18 (att. 1/7 Bn.).
13 Kershaw, Ellis, Temp. 2/Lt., k. in a., 1/7/16 (att. 1 Bn.).
Kershaw, Thomas James, Temp. 2/Lt., d. of w., 23/1/17.
16 Kinna, James Eckersley, Temp. Lt., died, 12/9/17.
1 Kirby, George, Lt. (Tp.), d. of w., 8/5/18.
Kirkpatrick, Samuel, 2/Lt. (Tp.), died, 30/9/18 (att. 2/5 Bn.) (P.O.W.).
19 Kydd, John William Albert, 2/Lt. (Tp.), d. of w., 26/3/18.
16 Law, Alan Hugh, 2/Lt. (Tp.), k. in a., 4/11/18.
1 Law, Cecil Edward, 2/Lt. (Tp.), k. in a., 30/9/18.
17 Layman, Douglas Arthur Campbell, Temp. 2/Lt., d. of w., 22/2/16.
Leake, Eric Larkin Wheadon, Lt., k. in a., 4/6/15.
11 Leete, William John Hurthwaite, Temp. Capt., k. in a., 21/1/16.
17 Leigh, Harvey Tunstill, 2/Lt., k. in a., 14/10/18.
4 Lewis, Graham Lawson, Lt., d. of w., 9/7/16 (att. 2 Bn.).
1/2 Lewis, Harold Nicholson, Temp. 2/Lt., k. in a., 18/10/17 (att. 17 Bn.).
16 Lines, Thomas, M.C., D.C.M., 2/Lt. (Tp.), d. of w., 5/4/18.
11 Littler, John Edward, 2/Lt. (Tp.), d. of w., 4/5/18.
16 Livingston, Frederick Maurice, 2/Lt. (Tp.), d. of w., 4/11/18.
11 Lockley, Henry James, 2/Lt. (Tp.), k. in a., 22/3/18.
1 Lodge, K. A., 2/Lt., died, 5/11/18.
3 Lodge, Ralph Nesbit, 2/Lt., k. in a., 1/7/16.
9 Longworth, Eustace Counsellor, Temp. Capt., k. in a., 26/9/16.
Lowther, Thomas Beresford, Lt., k. in a., 4/6/15.
20 Lynch, Thomas, 2/Lt., d. of w., 29/4/17.
McCulloch, James Arthur, Capt. (Tp.), k. in a., 27/9/18.
McCulloch, Robert Arthur Douglas, 2/Lt., k. in a., 3/5/15.
11 McFarlan, Arthur Keith, 2/Lt., k. in a., 15/5/16.
17 McGiveney, Philip, D.S.O., 2/Lt. (Tp.), d. of w., 2/6/18.
17 McInnes, Robert Donald, 2/Lt. (Tp.), d. of w., 30/3/18.
4 MacIver, Reginald Squarey, Lt., k. in a., 1/7/16.
11 MacKinnon, Ronald Fullerton, M.C., Temp. Lt., k. in a., 21/10/16 (att. 9/L.N. Lancs Regt.).
15 Maclaren, Ernest Cecil, Capt., k. in a., 1/7/16.
3 Maddox, John Mortimer, 2/Lt., k. in a., 12/8/16 (att. 10 Bn.).
1/2 Magniac, Meredith, D.S.O., Major (Temp. Lt.-Col.), k. in a., 25/4/17.
Mahony, Norman, Temp. 2/Lt., d. of w., 23/6/18 (att. 1/2 Bn.).
19 Mahony, Thomas George, Temp. 2/Lt., k. in a., 13/7/16.
2 Mansell, William Du Pra, Temp. Capt., k. in a., 12/10/16.
Manoukian, Zavern, Temp. 2/Lt., k. in a., 3/9/18, att. 2/5 Bn.).
Marshall, Douglas Cargill, Lt., k. in a., 28/6/15.
15 Marshall, Harry, Temp. Lt., k. in a., 30/9/18.
Martindale, John Ball, Temp. Lt., d. of w., 1/8/18 (att. L.N. Lanc. Regt.).
9 Masterman, Robert Chauncey, Lt. (Tp.), k. in a., 1/7/16.
Matthey, Edward Granville, Capt., k. in a., 1/7/16.
Maunsell, Thomas Bowyer Lane, Capt., k. in a., 1/5/15.
Mercer, Eric Cameron, 2/Lt., k. in a., 13/10/14 (att. Indian Army).
10 Mercer, Eric Dawson, Temp. 2/Lt., d. of w., 2/5/17.
16 Merryweather, Charles Walter, Temp. Major, k. in a., 23/11/16.
Miller, Thomas Peacock, Temp. 2/Lt., k. in a., 26/3/18 (att. 6 Bn.).
16 Milligan, Herbert Ward, Temp. Lt., k. in a., 21/11/17 att. 1 Bn.).
Moffatt, Cecil Henry, Temp. 2/Lt., d. of w., 1/8/16.
2 Moffatt, Stanley L., Temp. 2/Lt., d. of w., 13/8/16.
Moody, Rowland Harry Mainwaring, Capt., k. in a., 26/8/14.
Morris, Hubert Marmaduke, Temp. 2/Lt., d. of w., 13/8/18 (att. 15 Bn.).
16 Morris, Joseph, Temp. 2/Lt., d. of w., 4/11/18.
4 Morris, William Sydney, Lt. (T/Capt.), k. in a., 1/6/18 (att. 18 Bn.).
19 Morrison, Stanley, Temp. 2/Lt., k. in a., 9/7/16.
Needham, George Geoffrey, Lt., d. of w., 22/8/15.
1 Newton, Thomas, M.C., T/Lt. (A/Capt.), d. of w., 5/8/18.
22 Noble, Bertram, Temp. Lt., died, 26/8/16 (att. 1/Army School).
2 Norris, Bertie, Temp. 2/Lt., k. in a., 3/5/17.
15 North, Samuel Frost, Temp. 2/Lt., k. in a., 2/11/18.
15 Noyes, Claude Robert Barton, Temp. 2/Lt., k. in a., 1/7/16.
1/2 Orford, Charles Robert Hadfield, 2/Lt. (Tp.), d. of w., 18/7/17 (att. 16 Bn.).
2 Orpen, Walter Selwyn, 2/Lt., k. in a., 6/7/16 (att. 10 Bn.).
9 Osborne, Leslie Hall, Lt. (Tp.), k. in a., 7/8/15.
9 Osborne, William John, 2/Lt. (Tp.), d. of w., 9/8/15.
3 Paget, Michael Theodore, 2/Lt., k. in a., 17/8/17.
9 Parke, Allan, M.C., Capt., k. in a., 27/9/18 (att. 1/8 Bn.).
2 Parry, Thomas Ellis, 2/Lt. (Tp.), k. in a., 23/10/16.
20 Parry, Robert Stephenson, Temp. 2/Lt., d. of w., 23/10/17.
Patterson, C., Capt., died, 20/1/15.
Paulson, John Sydney, 2/Lt., k. in a., —/9/14.
Petty, Nelson, Lt., k. in a., 28/6/15.
16 Pledger, Earnest Charles, 2/Lt., k. in a., 10/10/17.
10 Pollard, Thomas Whittaker, Temp. Lt., k. in a., 16/5/17.
Porter, Alwyne Morton Francis Worsley, Lt., k. in a., 25/4/15.
16 Powell, Sidney Lewis, Temp. Capt., k. in a., 12/7/17.
Pownall, Edward, Temp. 2/Lt., k. in a., 9/10/17 (att. 8 Bn.).
18 Prescott, Reginald Julius, 2/Lt., k. in a., 15/4/17.
4 Price, Leonard Charles, 2/Lt., k. in a., 25/4/18 (att. 16 Bn.).
Priestley, Douglas Bernard, Temp 2/Lt., k. in a., 31/7/17.
18 Pritchett, George Edgar Kenyon, Temp. 2/Lt., d. of w., 3/6/18.
Proctor, George, Temp. Lt., k. in a., 17/4/18 (att. 19 Bn.).
9 Raw, Rowland, 2/Lt. (Tp.), k. in a., 7/8/15.
18 Rayner, Cyril Hood, 2/Lt. (Tp.), k. in a., 24/2/17.
Riley, Paul, 2/Lt. (Tp.), k. in a., 10/10/17 (att. 8 Bn.).
4 Roberton, Charles Drinnan, 2/Lt., k. in a., 1/7/16.
20 Robertson, Frederick Percival, Temp. Lt., k. in a., 4/3/16.
15 Robinson, Harold Fletcher, Temp. Lt., k. in a., 1/7/16.
Robinson, James Norman, Temp. 2/Lt., d. of w., 22/7/18 (att. 13 Bn., E. Lanc. R.).
1 Robinson, James Vernon, Temp. Lt., d. of w., 13/8/18 (att. 16 Bn.).
9 Robinson, Leonard, Temp. Capt., k. in a., 22/8/15.
2 Rogers, Albert Edward, 2/Lt., k. in a., 3/5/17.
3 Roe, Harold, 2/Lt., k. in a., 4/9/18 (att. 2/5 Bn.).
2 Roffey, Harold Bowyer, D.S.O., Major (Temp. Lt.-Col.), k. in a., 15/4/18 (att. 2/5 Linc. Regt.).
1/2 Rose, Eric William, M.C., Temp. 2/Lt., k. in a., 5/4/18 (att. 1/2 Bn.).
4 Roughton, Thomas Hende, M.C., Lt. (A/Capt.), d. of w., 24/3/18 (att. 2 Bn.).
1/2 Routledge, Joseph, 2/Lt. (Tp.), k. in a., 14/9/17 (att. 15 Bn.).
9 Rowley, Charles Ronald, Temp. 2/Lt., k. in a., 10/7/16 (att. 1 Bn.).
11 Rowson, Stanley, 2/Lt., k. in a., 29/9/16.
11 Rufus, Thomas, M.C., Temp. Capt., k. in a., 14/4/18.
4 Rushmore, Ernest Reginald, 2/Lt., k. in a., 6/9/17 (att. 11 Bn.).
2 Ruston, Allan Maxwell, M.M., 2/Lt., k. in a., 23/4/18.
16 Rylands, Harold Bertram, Temp. 2/Lt., k. in a., 23/11/16.
2 Salt, Walter Petit C., Temp. Capt., k. in a., 24/10/16.
17 Sanders, John Emerton, 2/Lt., k. in a., 25/8/16.
10 Sands, Leslie Kelham, Temp. Capt., d. of w., 28/4/16.
Sayres, Hugh Wingfield, Capt., k. in a., 1/7/16.
21 Schill, Edward Melland, Temp. Lt., d. of w., 25/8/16 (att. 17 Bn.).
V.C. Schofield, John, Temp. 2/Lt., k. in a., 9/4/18 (att. 2/5 Bn.).
13 Schooling, Paul Sydney Bedford, Temp. Lt., k. in a., 26/9/16.
15 Schroder, Henry Dudley, 2/Lt., k. in a., 2/12/17.
16 Scott, John George Alec, Temp. 2/Lt., d. of w., 15/3/16.
2 Sharp, James Calrow, 2/Lt., k. in a., 12/10/16.
16 Sharratt, Robert Weetman, Lt. (Tp.), k. in a., 10/3/16.
Shaw, Harold, Major, k. in a., 4/6/15.
20 Shaw J. T., Capt., died, 8/5/18.
4 Shepherd, John Cuthbert, Lt., k. in a., 25/8/18 (att. 10 Bn.).
18 Short, Andrew David Aitkin, 2/Lt., k. in a., 26/3/18.
1/2 Shuttleworth, Henry, Temp. 2/Lt., k. in a., 2/10/18 (att. 16 Bn.).
9 Shuttleworth, R. W., 2/Lt., died, 15/8/18 (and R.A.F.).
2 Sidebottom, Robert Yardley, Capt., k. in a., 26/8/14.
4 Simpson, Reginald Henry 2/Lt. k. in a., 7/7/15 (att. 2 Bn.).
11 Skelton, Henry, Temp. 2/Lt., k. in a., 2/10/18.
20 Slater, John, Temp. 2/Lt., d. of w., 26/3/18 (att. 17 Bn.).
1/2 Smart, William, Temp. 2/Lt., k. in a., 29/8/18 (att. 8/K.O.R. Lan. Rgt.).
10 Smith, Alec, Temp. 2/Lt., k. in a., 8/7/16.
19 Smith, Geoffrey Bache, Temp. Lt., d. of w., 3/12/16.
1/2 Smith, Herbert Dudley, Temp. 2/Lt., k. in a., 17/3/18 (att. 2/7 Bn.).
20 Smith, Harry Norman, Temp. 2/Lt., k. in a., 23/11/17.
1/2 Smith, Norman Edward, Temp. 2/Lt., k. in a., 20/7/18.
1 Smith, Percy, Temp. 2/Lt., d. of w., 13/5/18 (att. 2/5 Bn.).
13 Smith, Quintin Livingstone, Temp. 2/Lt., k. in a., 1/7/16.
15 Smith, Robert John, Temp. Capt., k. in a., 6/5/16.
3 Smyth, James, Capt., k. in a., 9/7/15 (att. 2/Bn.).
4 Sneyd, Thomas Humphrey, Capt., k. in a., 2/11/14 (att. 2 Bn.).
3 Solly, William Buckle, M.C., Lt., d. of w., 19/10/18 (101/T.M.B.).
Spafford, Arthur Langworthy, Capt. & Adjt., k. in a., 7/8/15 (att. 6 Bn.).
10 Speke, Hugh, Temp. Major, k. in a., 12/8/15.
1 Spencer, James Hilary, L. (A/Capt.), d. of w., 16/7/18 (in German Hands).
17 Sproson, William Wilson, 2/Lt., killed, 7/8/18 (and R.A.F.).
1 Stange, George Nugent, M.C., Temp. Lt., k. in a., 27/10/18 (att. 2 Bn.).
4 Stanley, John William, 2/Lt., k. in a., 7/6/17 (att. 11 Bn.).
Stanwell, William Alexander, 2/Lt., d. of w., 6/7/15.
Steele, William, 2/Lt., d. of w., 27/9/18 (att. 1/7 Bn.).
1 Stelfox, George Henry, 2/Lt. (Tp.), k. in a., 9/10/17.
11 Stephens, Arnold Melvill, Temp. 2/Lt., d. of w., 30/12/15.
1/2 Stevens, Cyril Geoffrey, A/Capt., k. in a., 9/10/17 (att. 3/5 Bn.).
10 Stockdale, Edward Leslie Johnson, Temp. Lt., k. in a., 7/7/16.
15 Stone, Arthur, D.S.O., Temp. Lt.-Col., k. in a., 2/10/18.
Stott, James, Temp. 2/Lt., k. in a., 11/10/18 (att. 2/5 Bn.).
17 Strang, James Buchanan, Temp. 2/Lt., k. in a., 30/7/16.
18 Strong, James William, Temp. Lt., k. in a., 11/6/16.
Stuart, Cecil Edgar, Lt., k. in a., 13/9/14.
1/2 Swallow, Bertie, Temp. 2/Lt., k. in a., 31/10/18 (att. 18 Bn.).
Talbot, Ainslie Douglas, Capt., k. in a., 3/6/15.
4 Tankard, William Joseph, 2/Lt., k. in a., 31/8/18 (att. 5 Bn.).
15 Taylor, Herbert, 2/Lt. (Tp.), k. in a., 1/4/17.
1 Templeman, John Watson, 2/Lt., k. in a., 25/3/18.
Tennant, Alexander Smith, Temp. Lt., k. in a., 27/9/18 (att. 1/7 Bn.).
4 Thicknesse, Raymond Samuel, 2/Lt., k. in a., 10/10/17 (att. 2 Bn.).
15 Thomas, Alfred Henry, T/2/Lt., k. in a., 21/6/16 (att. 96 T.M.B.).
Thomas, Aubrey Jocelyn Nugent, Capt., k. in a., 1/5/15.

19 Thomas, Geoffrey Owen, 2/Lt., k. in a., 25/4/18.
15 Thomas, Robert Alfred, Temp. Major, died, 3/6/16.
17 Thompson, Alfred Mussali, Temp. 2/Lt., died, 31/7/17 (in German hands).
20 Thompson, Cyril, Temp. 2/Lt., k. in a., 1/6/18 (att. 18 Bn.).
13 Tomlinson, James Ashworth, Temp. 2/Lt., d. of w., 22/11/15 (att. 1 Bn.).
15 Tonge, John Richard, Temp. Lt., k. in a., 16/12/17.
1/2 Townsend, Joseph Leslie, Temp. 2/Lt., k. in a., 2/10/17 (att. 3/5 Bn.).
11 Trimingham, Wentworth Gray, Temp. 2/Lt., died, 4/1/18.
2 Trimmer, George Ernest, Lt., died, 16/11/18 (att. R.E.).
18 Turnbull, Robert Henry, M.C., Temp. 2/Lt., d. of w., 4/6/18.
1 Uren, Philip, 2/Lt., k. in a., 18/5/10.
9 Vasey, Sydney, M.C., 2/Lt., k. in a., 10/8/18 (att. 16 Bn.).
Vores, Geoffrey Bernard, 2/Lt., k. in a., 4/6/15.
2 Walden, Rand Edwin John, Temp. 2/Lt., k. in a., 16/11/17.
10 Walker, Thomas Campbell, Temp. 2/Lt., k. in a., 14/2/16.
15 Walters, David, Temp. 2/Lt., d. of w., 22/5/17.
9 Wand-Tetley, Charles Ernest, Lt., k. in a., 22/8/15.
12 Warburton, Stanley, Temp. 2/Lt., k. in a., 14/9/16.
2 Ward, Arthur Claud, D.S.O., Capt., k. in a., 26/8/14.
1/2 Ward, J. G., 2/Lt., died, 7/5/18 (and R.A.F.).
11 Ward, Maurice Arthur, M.C., Capt., d. of w., 10/4/18.
11 Ward, Percy Duncan, Capt. (Tp.), d. of w., 11/10/16.
1 Waters, Reginald William, 2/Lt., k. in a., 12/8/18.
2 Watson, Francis George Stuart, 2/Lt., A/Capt., k. in a., 23/10/16.
17 Watt, William, 2/Lt., d. of w., 10/4/18.
3 Wells, Leslie Howard Elliott, 2/Lt., died, 4/5/15 (att. 2 Bn.).
1/2 Wells, Norman, Temp. 2/Lt., d. of w., 25/9/17 (att. 16 Bn.).
9 Welstead, Harry Marrion, Temp. Lt.-Col., k. in a., 17/8/15.
3 Whittam, Francis Joseph, 2/Lt., k. in a., 1/7/16 (att. 1 Bn.).
17 Wiggins, Thomas, 2/Lt., k. in a., 27/6/18 (and R.A.F.).
4 Wilcox, Frederick Herbert Cumberland, Capt., k. in a., 14/1/17.
Wilkinson, James Rendell, 2/Lt., died, 20/5/16 (P.O.W.).
3 Willans, Guy Russell, 2/Lt., d. of w., 29/3/18 (att. 2 Bn.).
19 Willett, Joseph Cyril, 2/Lt. (T/Lt.), k. in a., 15/5/17 (att. M.G.C.).
18 Williams, George Henry Spence de Meaker, Temp. Capt., k. in a., 13/5/16.
18 Williams, James, Temp. Capt., d. of w., 22/7/16.
Williamson, John Stanley, 2/Lt., k. in a., 1/5/15.
Wilson, Archibald, 2/Lt., k. in a., 27/3/18 (att. 6 Bn.).
15 Wilson, John, 2/Lt. (Tp.), k. in a., 1/4/17.
10 Winser, Basil Charles, Temp. Capt., k. in a., 15/2/16.
18 Wolfe, Sidney George, Temp. Lt., k. in a., 22/10/17.
15 Wood, Alfred Lee, Temp. Capt., k. in a., 1/7/16.
1 Wood, Frank, 2/Lt., k. in a., 30/9/18.
1 Wood, Geoffrey Kershaw Pemberton, 2/Lt., k. in a., 31/10/18.
10 Wood, James Buckley, Capt., k. in a., 26/3/18.
18 Wood, Matthew Rodney, M.C., Temp. Capt., k. in a., 22/10/17.
2 Woodman, James Edward Somerville, D.S.O., Major, k. in a., 25-27/9/15 (att. 12/N'land Fus.).
12 Wormald, Guy, Temp. Capt., k. in a., 14/9/16 (14 Bn.).
Worsley, Harold Rapley, 2/Lt., k. in a., 1/9/18 (att. 10 Bn.).
15 Wright, Clarence Haries, Temp. Lt., k. in a., 1/7/16.
15 Wrong, Harold Verschoyle, Lt., k. in a., 1/7/16.
3 Yorke-Lodge, Bryant Wynne, M.C., 2/Lt., k. in a., 14/9/16. (att. 12 Bn.).
15 Younger, John Ramsay, Temp. 2/Lt., k. in a., 6/5/16.

The Royal Scots Fusiliers.

6 Adam, Walter William, Capt. (Tp.), killed, 14/12/15.
8 Adamson, Charles Young, Capt. & Qr.-Mr. (Tp.), k. in a., 17/9/18.
Adamson, Maurice L., 2/Lt., k. in a., 1/7/16 (attd. 10th R. Irish Rifs.)
3 Alexander, Archibald Charles Edward, Lt., k. in a., 11/3/15 (attd. 2 Bn.).
6 Allan, Marshall Thomson, Lt. (Tp.), k. in a., 26-29/9/15.
8 Allan, Lewis Davidson, Lt. (Tp.), k. in a., 27/9/18.
9 Allan, John Steele, 2/Lt. (Tp.), k. in a., 12/10/16 (attd. 2 Bn.).
7 Allenby, Augustus Heathcote, Lt.-Col., k. in a., 7/8/15.
Alston, Claude McCaul, 2/Lt., k. in a., 25/10/14.
Anderson, Ernest Lionel Lane, 2/Lt., k. in a., 10/11/14.
Angus, William John, 2/Lt. (Tp.), k. in a., 29/10/16 (att. 1st Scottish Rifs.).
2 Ashton, Roger Hay, 2/Lt., k. in a., 30/7/16.
8 Atkins, Herbert Lonsdale, 2/Lt., k. in a., 30/7/16.
1 Atkinson, James, M.C., 2/Lt. (Tp.), k. in a., 2/9/18.
Bamford, Joseph Lamont, 2/Lt. (Tp.), k. in a., 20/8/17 (and R.F.C., 17 Squad).
Barrett, Charles John Chard, Capt., k. in a., 13/11/14.
Barton, Harold William Ferguson, 2/Lt., k. in a., 18/10/14.
Bell, Alexander Murray MacGregor, Capt., d. of w., 28/4/15.
Benson, Thomas Brooke, Lt., k. in a., 13/3/15.
1 Bissett, George, D.S.O., M.C., Lt. (A/Major), d. of w., 18/10/18.
9 Black, Ernest Charteris, 2/Lt. (Tp.), k. in a., 22/11/15 (att. 7th Bn.).
2 Blackman, George Hugh Willoughby, Lt. (Tp.), k. in a., 30/7/16.
Blackwood, Walter Lennox, Lt. (Tp.), k. in a., 31/7/17.
2 Boyd, John, 2/Lt. (Tp.), k. in a., 12/4/18.
Boyle, Hon. James, Capt., k. in a., 18/10/14.
7 Boyle, Thomas Houston, 2/Lt., k. in a., 12/10/16 (att. 2nd Bn.).
Briggs, George Clark, Capt., k. in a., 15-16/10/14.
8 Brindley, Charles Stuart, 2/Lt. (Tp.), k. in a., 23/4/16 (att. 4th Bn.).
6 Brodie, John, Capt., d. of w., 26/9/15.
3 Brown, Christopher Wilkinson, Capt., k. in a., 1/5/16 (att. 1st Bn.).
2 Brown, Joseph Jackson, Lt. (Tp.), k. in a., 5/8/18.
3 Brown, George Sydney Robert Johnston, 2/Lt., d. of w., 22/5/15 (att. 1st Bn.).
1 Brown, William Robertson, 2/Lt. (Tp.), d. of w., 30/9/17.
6 Buchan, Alastair Ebenezar, T/Lt., d. of w., 9/4/17.
7 Burr, Frederick Godfrey, Capt. (Tp.), k. in a., 26/9/15.
Bush, John Wheler, 2/Lt. (Tp.), k. in a., 25/9/15.
3 Charlton, John, 2/Lt., k. in a., 2/9/18 (att. 1st Bn.).
3 Chrystie, James Alexander, 2/Lt., k. in a., 30/11/14 (att. 2nd Bn.).
Clark, Andrew Scott Duncan, T/2/Lt., d. of w., 22/4/17 (att. 1/4th Bn.).
3 Clark, William Frederick Hunter, 2/Lt., d. of w., 23/2/16.
1 Cochrane, William, T/2/Lt., k. in a., 26/9/17.
9 Colquhoun, Robert Clark, T/2/Lt., d. of w., 3/7/16 (att. 2nd Scot. Rifs.)
Connell, Alfred Hamilton, Capt. (T/Major), k. in a., 28/9/15.
3 Cozens-Brooke, John Gilbert Somerset, Lt., k. in a., 18/10/14.
Crawford, Robert Stobo, 2/Lt., k. in a., 17/5/15 (Res. of Off.).
8 Crawshaw, Charles Neville, M.C., Capt. (Adjt.), k. in a., 19/9/18.
3 Cruickshank, Harold Arthur, Lt., d. of w., 28/9/15 (att. 2nd Bn.).
1 Currer, Thomas Russell, 2/Lt., k. in a., 26/9/17.
8 Currie, John Eugene Havelock, 2/Lt. (Tp.), k. in a., 11/9/15 (att. 1st Bn.).
1 Davidson, Gordon Parsons, 2/Lt., k. in a., 3/5/17.
3 Duncan, George Balfour, 2/Lt., k. in a., 30/7/16.
Fairlie, Frank, Capt., k. in a., 23/10/14.
1 Fairley, Gilbert, 2/Lt., k. in a., 9/4/17.
1/2 Fairley, William Kerr, T/2/Lt., k. in a., 12/8/18 (att. 12th Bn.).
1 Ferguson, Robert George, M.C., T/2/Lt. (A/Capt.), died, 11/6/18 (in Ger. hands).
3 Findlay-Hamilton, John Eric, Lt., k. in a., 16/6/15 (att. 2nd Bn.).
6 Fisher, John Campbell, A/Capt., d. of w., 6/5/17.
7 Fleming, George, T/Lt., d. of w., 18/7/16 (att. 1st Bn.).
6 Foulkes, George Boyd, T/Capt., k. in a., 12/8/16.
6 Fraser, Hugh Crawford, Capt. (Tp.), k. in a., 5/8/15.
2 Freeman, Arthur Cyril Bruce, Lt., k. in a., 27/9/18.
3 Fry, Leslie, M.C., 2/Lt., d. of w., 9/11/18 (and M.G.C.).
Gallie, Charles, 2/Lt., k. in a., 22/8/15.
7 Gardner, John, M.C., T/Capt., d. of w., 27/9/17.
3 Geddes, Alistair Alexander Francis, 2/Lt., k. in a., 16/6/15 (att. 2nd Bn.).
3 Gillies, Halliday Gordon, 2/Lt., k. in a., 13/11/16 (att. 1st Bn.).
2 Godfrey, Victor, 2/Lt., k. in a., 1/7/16.
6 Goodeve, Lionel, Major (Temp.), k. in a., 26/8/15.
1/2 Gooding, William Thomas, 2/Lt., k. in a., 22/3/18 (att. 6/7th Bn.).
6 Gordon, Alistair Campbell Miller, T/2/Lt., d. of w., 1/3/17.
9 Graham, Hugh Christison, 2/Lt. (T/Lt.), k. in a., 9/6/17 (M.G.C., 33rd Coy.).
1 Grant, Alan, 2/Lt., d. of w., 3/9/18.
Greenhous, Ernest Brereton, T/2/Lt., k. in a., 26/8/17 (and R.F.C., 9th Sq.).
3 Grierson, John Livingstone Hailes, T/2/Lt., k. in a., 1/7/16.
3 Grieve, Nicholas Harrington, 2/Lt., k. in a., 13/11/16 (att. 1st Scots. Fus.).
3 Hadden, Cyril Martin, A/Capt., k. in a., 28/3/18 (att. 1st Bn.).
2 Harris, William Lawson, M.C., Lt., k. in a., 30/7/16.
7 Hay, Frank Tochetti, T/Lt., k. in a., 26/9/15.
9 Heggie, David Alexander, 2/Lt., k. in a., 3/8/15 (att. 1st Bn.).
1 Henderson, Angus, 2/Lt., k. in a., 3/5/17.
Henderson, Norman William Arthur, Lt., k. in a., 10/11/14.
6 Hodge, William Bardo, Lt. (Tp.), died, 4/11/18 (att. 11th Bn.).
Honeyman, Herbert Tom Allan, 2/Lt., k. in a., 10/12/17 (att. R.F.C., 15 Sqd.).
1 How, William Alexander, 2/Lt., k. in a., 12/4/18.
Hurt, Seymour Frederick Auckland Albert, Capt., k. in a., 18/10/14.
7 Hutcheon, Thomas, 2/Lt. (Tp.), d. of w., 12/8/16.
6/7 Hutchison, William Ramsay, Capt. (Temp.), k. in a., 22/3/18.
6 Hutt, Ernest Reginald, 2/Lt., k. in a., 25/9/15.
3 Irving, David Piercy, 2/Lt., k. in a., 30/7/16.
3 Johnston, Thomas McKinnon, 2/Lt., k. in a., 13/11/16 (att. 1st Bn.).
Kennedy, Charles Noel Jardine, Capt., k. in a., 30/7/16.
2 Kennedy, David Hew, M.C., T/2/Lt., k. in a., 31/7/17.
2 Kennedy, Horas Tristram, T/Lt., k. in a., 6/6/17.
Kennedy, Nigel, Lt., k. in a., 22/10/14.
1/2 Kennedy, Norman, 2/Lt., d. of w., 31/10/17.
2 Kennedy, Robert, 2/Lt., d. of w., 10/7/16 (att. 3rd Bn.).
9 Ker, Laurence Arthur, 2/Lt., died, 4/4/15.
7 Kerr, David, T/2/Lt., k. in a., 12/8/16.
3 Kerr, John Murdoch, 2/Lt., k. in a., 13/11/16 (att. 1st Bn.).
6 Kerr, William, Lt. (Tp.), k. in a., 2/9/18 (att. M.G.C., 4th Bn.).
1 Kincaid, John Brown, 2/Lt., k. in a., 3/5/17.
9 King, William Galbraith, T/2/Lt., k. in a., 7/7/16.
1 Laing, William McClymont Black, 2/Lt., d. of w., 21/6/16.
3 Laird, William Allan, Lt., d. of w., 18/9/15 (att. 1st Bn.).
1 Lambart, Gerald Edgar Oliver Fortescue, Capt (A/Major), d. of w., 28/3/16.
1 Lambroughton, Hugh, 2/Lt. (Tp.), d. of w., 12/4/18.
1 Lawson, William, 2/Lt. (Tp.), k. in a., 19/9/18 (att. 8th Bn.).
3 Lindsay, William, 2/Lt., k in a., 31/7/17 (att. 2nd Bn.).

1 Lindsay-Young, Laurence Hingston, Capt., d. of w., 25/12/18 (and R.A.F.).
9 Lockhart, Robert Hamilton, T/2/Lt., k. in a., 11/11/15 (att. 7th Bn.).
Loftus, William, M.C., Lt. (Tp.) (Capt. & Adj.), d. of w., 25/4/17 (att. 11th Bn.).
1 Logan, John Francis, 2/Lt. (Tp.), k. in a., 12/4/18.
3 Lomax, William Sinnott, Lt., k. in a., 30/7/16 (att. 7th Bn.).
2 Low, George Alexander, 2/Lt., k. in a., 28/9/18.
Lyon, Charles James, Lt., k. in a., 13/1/14.
1 McArthur, William Bell, M.C., T/2/Lt., k. in a., 9/4/17.
3 McCall, Alfred Ward, 2/Lt., k. in a., 30/9/18 (att. 11th Bn.).
1 McConaghey, Maurice Edwin, D.S.O., Major (A/Lt.-Col.), k. in a., 23/4/17.
1 McCracken, James Henderson, T/2/Lt., k. in a., 26/9/17.
3 McDonald, James Vallance, 2/Lt., d. of w., 17/4/18 (att. 6/7th Bn.).
Macgregor-Whitton, Percy William Thomas, Capt. (Tp.), k. in a., 9/7/16.
2 McEwan, James Robt. Dundas, Lt., k. in a., 12/10/16.
3 Mackay, Arnold Langley, 2/Lt., d. of w., 31/10/16 (att. 2nd Bn.).
Mackenzie, Cortlant Graham Gordon, Lt., k. in a., 25/10/14.
McMillan, John Casely, 2/Lt. (T/Capt.), d. of w., 6/2/17 (and R.F.C., 4 Sqd.).
1 McMutrie, Robert Lindsay, T/Lt. (A/Capt.), k. in a., 21/8/18.
7 Macqueen, Roderick Reid, Capt. (Tp.), k. in a., 15/5/16.
1 Markus, Eugene Bernays, M.C., 2/Lt., d. of w., 5/4/17.
Martin, Fairlie Russell, 2/Lt., k. in a., 29/6/17 (att. R.F.C., 57 Sqd.).
Masson, J., H/Major & Qr.-Mr., died, 1/5/15.
3 Mayberry, Richard, Lt., k. in a., 15/11/17 (att. R.F.C., 70 Sqdn.).
3 Mercier, Y. W., 2/Lt., k. in a., 25-27/9/15 (att. 1st Bn.).
Millar, James Ainslie, 2/Lt., k. in a., 25/9/15.
1 Milne, Irvine McKenzie, T/2/Lt., k. in a., 31/8/17.
Moffett, John Leeson, 2/Lt., k. in a., 11/3/15.
2 Morrison, Albert Victor, 2/Lt., k. in a., 30/7/16.
7 Moyna, Edwar Gerald James, T/Capt., k. in a., 26/9/15.
9 Mudie, James, T/2/Lt., k. in a., 30/9/16 (att. 1st R. Scots).
3 Murray, Anthony Hepburn Poore, Lt., k. in a., 9/4/17 (att. 1st Bn.).
8 Murray, Ronald Alexander, T/Capt., d. of w., 19/9/18.
9 Neill, Thom. W. R., T/2/Lt., d. of w., 3/7/16.
3 Nepean, Evan Cecil, Lt., k. in a., 4/10/18 (att. 3rd R. Fus.).
3 Ness, Gordon Stuart, Lt., k. in a., 10/11/14 (att. 1st Bn.).
3 Newbigging, Alexander Tweedie, 2/Lt., k. in a., 3/5/17 (att. 1st S. Fus.).
Nichol, John, Capt., killed, 5/4/16.
6 Nicolson, William, T/2/Lt., k. in a., 13/8/16.
8 Nimmo, Stuart Henry, T/Lt., k. in a., 19/9/18.
2 Nisbet, John Andrew, T/2/Lt. (A/Capt.), k. in a., 28/9/18.
Nutkins, Vernon William, Lt., killed, 19/2/18 (att. R.F.C.).
9 Paterson, Gavin, 2/Lt, died, 21/1/15.
9 Paton, George Cyril Olquin, Lt. (Tp.), killed, 20/6/16.
8 Paul, William Edgar, T/Capt., k. in a., 31/7/17.
6 Peck, C. W., Lt., k. in a., 29/9/15.
1 Petter, Harold Rupert, 2/Lt., d. of w., 3/5/17.
Pollock, Max Kenneth, Capt. (Tp. Lt.), k. in a., 25/9/15.
8 Pooley, Richard Sibthorpe, T/2/Lt., k. in a., 23/4/17 (att. 1st Bord. R.).
7 Powell, Lindsay Carlton, T/2/Lt., k. in a., 31/5/16.
6 Purves, George Gordon de Burgh, T/Capt., d. of w., 8/11/15.
3 Riddell, Walter, M.C., 2/Lt., k. in a., 29/4/18 (att. 2nd Bn.).
1 Robertson, Neil Wallace, M.C., 2/Lt., k. in a., 2/9/18.
1/2 Robertson, William, 2/Lt., d. of w., 3/5/17.
2 Robinson, Alfred Elliot, 2/Lt., k. in a., 16/6/15.
Rose, Thomas Allen, D.S.O., Capt., k. in a., 23/8/14.
Ross, Arthur Claude, 2/Lt., d. of w., 6/12/17 (and R.F.C., 10 Sq.).
6/7 Ross, George James, T/2/Lt., killed, 30/1/18.
Ross-Thompson, Alexander, Lt., k. in a., 30/11/14.
6 Roxburgh, John, Capt., k. in a., 26/9/15.
9 Russell, Walter Nicol, T/2/Lt., d. of w., 26/8/16.
7 Scandrett, John Jackson, T/2/Lt., k. in a., 15/5/16.
3 Scott, Arnold Charles, Lt., d. of w., 9/6/18 (att. 1st Bn.).
7 Scott, David, 2/Lt. (Tp.), k. in a., 7/4/17.
2 Scott, Herbert Lawson, 2/Lt., died, 6/6/17.
1 Scott, John Kemp, T/2/Lt., k. in a., 14/7/16.
7 Sharer, George Short, T/2/Lt., k. in a., 26/9/15.
1/2 Sherriff, Alexander, T/2/Lt., k. in a., 22/3/18 (att. 6/7th Bn.)
3 Shutt, Herbert Cecil, Lt., k. in a., 13/11/16 (att. 1st Bn.).
7 Skipworth, Frank Peyton, Major, k. in a., 25/9/15.
2 Smith, Herbert Fyfe, 2/Lt. (Tp.), k. in a., 23/4/17.
2 Smith, Robert, 2/Lt. (Tp.), k. in a., 15/12/17.
6 Smith, Thomas, T/Major, k. in a., 23/1/17.
1 Smith, William Strain, M.C., A/Capt., T/2/Lt., d. of w., 23/3/17.
7 Smylie, Robert Stewart, T/Lt., k. in a., 14/7/16 (att. 1st Bn.).
2 Spears, John, 2/Lt., k. in a., 23/4/17.
7 Spencer, Richard Isaac Barre, T/2/Lt., k. in a., 14/7/16.
6 Staples, Osric Orsmund, T/2/Lt., k. in a., 25/9/15.
3 Sterling, John Lockhart, 2/Lt., k. in a., 28/9/15 (att. 2nd Bn.).
3 Sterling, Robert William, Lt., k. in a., 24/4/15 (att. 1st Bn.).
7 Stewart, Robert Taylor, T/2/Lt., d. of w., 27/9/15.
Stevenson, Thomas Kerr, T/2/Lt., A/Lt., k. in a., 28/1/17 (att. 45 T.M.B.).
Stewart, Henry Ernest, T/Lt., killed, 19/11/17 (55 Tr. Res. Bn.).
Stirling-Cookson, Samuel Baillie, Capt., k. in a., 17/5/15.
2 Stiven, Albert, 2/Lt. (Tp.), k. in a., 24/1/17.
Stiven, Ronald Walter Sutherland, Capt., d. of w., 15/9/15.
6 Stuart, Andrew John, Visc., T/Lt., k. in a., 25/9/15.
6 Strang, Robert Brown, T/2/Lt., d. of w., 12/8/16 (att. 7th Bn.).
3 Stuart, Robert Noel, 2/Lt., k. in a., 16/5/15 (att. 2nd Bn.).
Stuart, Robert Sheffield, Visc., Lt., k. in a., 2/11/14.
3 Sturrock, Andrew, Lt., k. in a., 14/7/16 (att. 1st Bn.).
1 Swales, George, A/Capt., Lt., k. in a., 26/9/17 (att. 8/1 T.M.B.).
1 Swan, George Henry, T/2/Lt., k. in a., 14/7/16.
Sweet, John Lemon Leslie, 2/Lt., k. in a., 16/6/15.
6/7 Sykes, Edward Burton, 2/Lt. (Tp.), k. in a., 31/7/17.
3 Symons, Frederick Gordon, Lt., k. in a., 22/5/16.
2 Tait, William Bell, 2/Lt. (Tp.), k. in a., 15/12/17.
1/2 Teacher, Norman McDonald, D.S.O., Major, A/Lt.-Col., d. of w., 26/9/17.
1 Templeton, James Russell, 2/Lt., k. in a., 19/9/18 (att. 8th Bn.).
1 Thompson, Harold, D.S.O., T/Lt.-Col., d. of w., 22/4/17 (att. 1/4 Bn.).
Thomson, Kenneth Clarke, Lt., d. of w., 31/12/14.
3 Thomson, Sydney James Kerr, 2/Lt., d. of w., 12/10/15 (att 1st Bn.).
1 Tinley, James, 2/Lt., A/Capt., k. in a., 20/7/16.
1 Torrance, Kenneth, T/2/Lt., k. in a., 2/9/18.
2 Towers-Clarke, John William, Lt., k. in a., 1/7/16.
Tullis, John Drysdale, Capt., d. of w., 18/11/14.
Tullis, William, Capt., k. in a., 1/7/16.
1 Walker, John Alexander, 2/Lt., k. in a., 26/8/18 (att. 1/4 K.O.S.B.).
Wallace, John Roger, 2/Lt., k. in a., 23/4/15.
7 Warnock, Robert, T/2/Lt., k. in a., 12/8/16.
7 Watson, John Eben, T/2/Lt., k. in a., 26/9/15.
6 Watson, Thomas, T/Capt., k. in a., 11/4/17.
8 Watson, Stanley John, T/2/Lt., d. of w., 28/11/15 (att. 2nd Bn.).
Webster, George William, 2/Lt., k. in a., 15/6/15.
3 White, George Anderson, 2/Lt., d. of w., 30/3/18 (att. 1st Bn.).
6 Whitelaw, James Weir, 2/Lt., k. in a., 11/4/17.
2 Wilson, James Gilmour, T/2/Lt., d. of w., 15/2/17.
1 Wolstencroft, William Herbert Beau, 2/Lt., k. in a., 12/4/18.
1 Wood, Edwin Leonard, 2/Lt., k. in a., 26/9/17.
Wyllie, Alexander, Capt., died, 18/4/17 (att. Egypt. Army).
Young, John Erskine, Capt., k. in a., 24/8/14.
3 Young, William Nicholas, 2/Lt., k. in a., 9/9/16.

The Cheshire Regiment.

11 Abell, John Lloyd Williams Howard, Capt., k. in a., 3/7/16.
1 Aldersey, Mark, 2/Lt., k. in a., 1/11/17.
3 Anderson, Archibald John Scott, 2/Lt., k. in a., 27/8/16 (att. 11/Bn.).
3 Anderson, Gerard Rupert Laurie, 2/Lt., k. in a., 9/11/14 (att. 1st Bn.).
2 Andrews, Charles Raymond, Capt., k. in a., 24/5/15.
11 Aspinall, Robert Lowndes, D.S.O., T/Lt.-Col., k. in a., 3/7/16.
Austin, Edward Gerrard, 2/Lt. (Tp.), k. in a., 18/9/18 (att. 2/24 London Regt.).
Austin, Edgar William, 2/Lt. (Tp.), k. in a., 23/7/18 (att. 4th Ryl. Sussex Rgt.).
15 Austin, George Frederick, 2/Lt. (Tp.), k. in a., 19/7/16.
3 Bailey, John William, 2/Lt., drowned, 30/12/17.
9 Barnes, Arthur William, Temp. Lt., k. in a., 11/4/18.
11 Barton, George Rawson, Capt., k. in a., 9/4/18.
14 Baskett, Roger Mortimer, 2/Lt. (Tp.), d. of w., 14/11/16 (att. 16 Bn.).
13 Bates, Ernest Harold, 2/Lt. (Tp.), k. in a., 13/5/16.
10 Bell, Norman, 2/Lt. (Tp.), k. in a., 18/8/17 (and R.F.C. 57 Sqd.).
10 Bell, Robert Stephen, 2/Lt. (Tp.), d. of w., 17/4/18.
3 Bellis, Cecil Magnus, 2/Lt., d. of w., 9/7/16 (att. 13 Bn.).
Bennett-Dampier, John Tudor, 2/Lt., k. in a., 2/3/15 (att. Notts & Derby Regt.).
Blackaby, Arthur, 2/Lt., k. in a., 17/5/15.
1 Blain, Charles Victor, 2/Lt., k. in a., 3/9/16.
8 Boote, Charles William, T/Capt., k. in a., 4-5/4/16.
10 Bostock, Joseph, 2/Lt., k. in a., 21/3/18.
3 Brien, Desmond Cecil Bagge, 2/Lt., k. in a., 2/10/15 (att 2 Bn.).
3 Brocks, Archibald William, 2/Lt. (Tp.), d. of w., 10/3/18 (att. 16th Devon Regt.) (P. of W.).
8 Broughton, Hugo Delves, Capt. (Tp.), k. in a., 4-5/4/16.
14 Brown, Richard Stanley, 2/Lt., died, 9/2/16.
Bruce, Jasper, Lt., died, 17/2/19 (att. Remounts).
14 Burrows, Arthur Cecil, 2/Lt. (Tp.), d. of w., 5/6/16 (att. 8th)
11 Bushe, Gervase Gray, 2/Lt. (Tp.), d. of w., 4/6/16.
Campbell, Charles Arthur, Lt., k. in a., 24/8/14.
14 Chamberlain, George Herbert, 2/Lt. (Tp.), k. in a., 4/10/16
17 Chandler, James Cook, 2/Lt. (Tp.), k. in a., 11/7/16 (att. 11 Bn.).
3 Chaplin, Humphrey Marmaduke, Lt., k. in a., 11/5/15 (att 1st Bn.).
2 Clark, Egbert Douglas, Lt., d. of w., 15/2/17.
11 Clarke, David, 2/Lt. (Tp.), k. in a., 22/3/18.
9 Clayton, William Ernest Albert, 2/Lt. (Tp.), d. of w., 22/4/16
12 Clegg-Hill, The Hon. Arthur Reginald, D.S.O., Lt.-Col. (Tp.) k. in a., 18/9/18.
3 Cole, Leslie Stewart, 2/Lt., k. in a., 3/10/15 (att. 2 Bn.).
13 Cotton, Arthur Edward, 2/Lt., k. in a., 7/7/16.
3 Crowther, Norman, 2/Lt., k. in a., 14/10/18 (att. 15th Suffolk Rgt.).
8 Cullimore, John, Lt. (Tp.), d. of w., 16/4/16.
12 Curry, William Gordon, 2/Lt. (Tp.), k. in a., 7/6/17 (att. 13 Bn.).
11 Curtis, Thomas Britt, 2/Lt. (Tp.), d. of w., 25/10/17.
1 Daniels, James, 2/Lt. (Tp.), k. in a., 28/9/18.

9 Davey, William Aubrey Carthew, 2/Lt. (Tp.), k. in a., 21/8/18.
1 David, Edward Harold, 2/Lt. (Tp.), k. in a., 5/11/18.
18 Davy, William Edward, Capt. & Adjt. (Tp.), k. in a., 7/7/16.
2 Dawson, Walter Henry Mountiford Westropp, 2/Lt., k. in a., 24/5/15.
13 Dean, John Henry Ellis, M.C., Capt. (Tp.), k. in a., 27/5/15 (att. 10 Bn.).
12 Denyer, Horace Frederick, Lt. (Tp.), k. in a., 13/7/17.
11 Dewar, Harold Ernest, 2/Lt. (Tp.), d. of w., 12/7/16.
13 Dickin, Albert Edward, 2/Lt. (Tp.), k. in a., 21/10/16.
15 Dickinson, Colin James Henry, 2/Lt. (Tp.), k. in a., 28/7/16.
15 Done, Robert, Lt., d. of w., 13/10/18.
Downes, Arthur Chernocke, 2/Lt., d. of w., 20/11/14.
11 Dowse, William Arthur Clarence, Lt., k. in a., 3/7/16.
1 Dresser, Harry Jex, Capt. (A/Major), k. in a., 2/6/18 (att. 15 Bn.).
1 Duckworth, Bernard, 2/Lt., k. in a., 28/7/16.
11 Dunlop, Launcelot Lindsay Brook, 2/Lt. (Tp.), k. in a., 3/7/16.
16 Earle, Charles Edward, Lt.-Col., died, 11/8/17.
Earle, Walter Colby, Capt., died, 7/4/15.
3 Easterbrook, William Reginald, Lt., d. of w., 17/7/18.
3 Edwards, Edward Ernest, 2/Lt. (Tp.), k. in a., 17/12/17 (att. 1/4th Ryl. Sussex Regt.).
10 Ellerton, Charles Fleetwood, Capt. (Tp.), k. in a., 21/5/16.
16 Elliott, James Dunsmore, 2/Lt. (Tp.), k. in a., 22/10/17.
13 Ellis, Douglas Wilmshurst, Lt. (Tp.), k. in a., 24/5/17.
9 Evans, William Ashton, 2/Lt. (Tp.), d. of w., 16/11/16.
11 Ford, Kenneth George Haslam, Lt. (Tp.), d. of w., 1/12/15.
Forster, Lionel Archibald, Capt., died, 4/11/14 (P. of W.).
3 Frost, Kingdon Tregosse, Lt., k. in a., 4/9/14.
Frost, Thomas Lawrence, Capt., k. in a., 28/3/15.
9 Fulton, George Koberwein, D.S.O., T/Capt. (A/Lt.-Col.), k. in a., 14/4/18.
9 Gadsdon, Frank Bannatyne, T/2/Lt., k. in a., 7/6/17.
3 Gell, Philip, 2/Lt., died, 5/9/17 (att. 217 Inf. Bn.).
3 Girod, Milton, 2/Lt., died, 19/3/16 (and R.F.C.).
3 Gledsdale, Irving, Lt., k. in a., 13/7/17 (att. 15 Bn.).
1 Gleed, George Alfred, Lt., d. of w., 6/9/16.
10 Goss, Hubert John, M.C., 2/Lt., k. in a., 15/7/16.
Gosset, Claude Butler Gosset, Major, died, 16/2/16 (att. Royal Engineers).
13 Gould, Arthur, 2/Lt. (Tp.), k. in a., 13/5/16.
15 Grace, Joseph, 2/Lt., k. in a., 19/8/17.
1 Gray, Cyril Seaton, 2/Lt., d. of w., 21/4/17.
13 Green, Gilbert Pitcher, 2/Lt. (Tp.), d. of w., 25/10/16.
Greenhalgh, James Arthur, 2/Lt., k. in a., 22/10/14.
3 Greg, Arthur Tylston, Capt., k. in a., 23/4/17 (and R.F.C.).
3 Gresson, John Edward, 2/Lt., k. in a., 24/5/15 (att. 2 Bn.).
8 Greswell, E. W., Lt., killed, 9/6/18 (and R.A.F.).
13 Hall, Frederick Grainger, T/Capt., k. in a., 7/7/16.
10 Hampson, Alfred Eric, 2/Lt. (Tp.), k. in a., 8/7/16 (att. 7th T.M.B.).
Hand, Maurice William, Lt., k. in a., 25/6/15.
15 Hanford, Albert William, Lt. (Tp.), k. in a., 23/4/18.
3 Harper, James, 2/Lt., k. in a., 28/6/18 (att. 1st Bn.).
3 Harris, Frank, 2/Lt., k. in a., 15/7/16 (att. 10 Bn.).
3 Harry, Alfred Edward, Capt., k. in a., 3/1/16 (att. 1st Bn.).
Hartford, Hugh Leving St. John, Capt., k. in a., 22/10/14.
2 Hartley, William Edwin, 2/Lt. (Tp.), k. in a., 2/10/15.
3 Hartill, John Harry, Capt. (Tp.), died, 25/1/16.
Hayes-Newington, Charles Wetherell, Capt. (Tp.), k. in a., 11/5/15.
10 Hesketh, William, 2/Lt. (Tp.), d. of w., 9/6/17.
2 Hill, Arthur Rowland, Major, k. in a., 3/10/15.
15 Hodson, Edward Hutchinson, Lt. (Tp.), k. in a., 24/3/18.
9 Holmes, Duncan McPherson Studdert, 2/Lt. (Tp.), k. in a., 4/3/16.
14 Hunter, Archibald, 2/Lt. (Tp.), k. in a., 2/7/16 (9th).
10 Hunter, William, 2/Lt., d. of w., 10/10/16.
9 Jackson, Thomas Leslie, Capt. (Tp.), k. in a., 2/7/16.
16 Joice, Philip Sidney, 2/Lt. (Tp.), d. of w., 1/12/17.
Jones, Ernest Rae, Capt., k. in a., 2/9/14.
11 Jones, George William, 2/Lt. (Tp.), k. in a., 15-16/5/16 (att. 6th South Wales Borderers).
1 Jolley, Robert James, 2/Lt., d. of w., 22/8/18.
Keating, George, 2/Lt., k. in a., 17/2/15.
Keating, John, Lt., killed, 17/2/15.
Kennedy, R. B. C., 2/Lt. (T/Lt.), died, 10/8/17.
14 Kerr, Daniel, Lt., k. in a., 6/7/15.
15 Kidd, Claude Bernard, M.C., Capt. (Tp.), k. in a., 24/3/18.
8 King, Gordon Wick, 2/Lt., k. in a., 9/4/16.
17 Lacey, Edred Severs, 2/Lt., k. in a., 21/10/16 (att. 11th Bn.).
10 Langdon, Wilfrid Max, Capt. (Tp.), k. in a., 21/5/16.
16 Lawrenson, Raymond Fitmaurice, Lt., d. of w., 5/9/17.
9 Laws, Selwyn Vernon, 2/Lt. (Tp.), d. of w., 25/5/18.
9 Lees, William Henry, 2/Lt., died, 25/6/19.
Leftwich, Nigel George, Lt., k. in a., 15/4/18 (att. 2nd Bn.).
Lloyd, A., Lt., died, 4/2/18.
Lloyd, Frank Lewis, Capt., k. in a., 1-4/10/15.
Loder-Symonds, Robert Francis, Capt., died, 3/3/15.
10 Longster, William Ernest, 2/Lt. (Tp.), k. in a., 28/7/16.
1/2 McArdle, Peter Paul, 2/Lt. (Tp.), k. in a., 26/4/18 (att. 1/4th York. and Lancs.).
9 McCall, Robert Alfred, 2/Lt. (Tp.), k. in a., 25/9/15.
14 McCullagh, Edwin Samuel, 2/Lt. (Tp.), k. in a., 7/6/17 (att. 13th Bn.).
16 McCullough, Robert James, 2/Lt. (Tp.), k. in a., 22/10/17.
3 McGregor, Marcus, 2/Lt., k. in a., 3/10/15 (att. 3 Bn.).
2 McGregor, Ronald Malcolm, 2/Lt., k. in a., 24/5/15.
16 MacLaren, Robert 2/Lt. (Tp.), d. of w., 24/7/16.
McLaren, Robert John, Capt., k. in a., 1/7/16 (att. 2nd South Wales Borderers).
Mahony, Frederick Henry, Capt., d. of w., 22/10/14.
Maitland-Addison, Arthur Creighton, 2/Lt., d. of w., 27/10/14.
Mallinson, Richard, Capt., k. in a., 1/8/17.
13 Malone, William Adolph, 2/Lt., k. in a., 16/5/17.
3 Manning, John Carlton, 2/Lt. (Tp.), d. of w., 17/2/17 (att. 10th Bn.).
1 Mansfield, Harold, 2/Lt. (Tp.), d. of w., 12/4/16.
3 Maquire, Maurice, 2/Lt., k. in a., 21/8/18.
12 Marsh, Charles Frederick William, A/Capt., k. in a., 22/9/18.
11 Martin, George Ernest, Capt., k. in a., 2/8/17.
14 Mathews, Arnold, Lt. (Tp.), d. of w., 14/4/16.
13 Maxwell, Henry, 2/Lt. (Tp.), k. in a., 10/10/16.
8 Melland, Edward Guy, Lt., k. in a., 30/6/15 (att. W. Yorks.).
10 Merry, Norman Cuthbert, Capt. (Tp.), k. in a., 15/7/16.
13 Metcalfe, John Chaytor, Major (Tp.), k. in a., 7/7/16.
4 Miller, George Frederick, 2/Lt., k. in a., 23/3/18.
3 Miller, James, Lt., k. in a., 14/10/18 (att. 11/Bn.).
16 Milm, George Gordon, M.C., Capt. (Tp.), k. in a., 22/4/18 (att. 15/Bn.).
1 Milner Archibald Donald, Lt. (A/Capt.), k. in a., 23/3/18 (att. 9/Bn.).
3 Molyneux, Benjamin, M.C., Lt., d. of w., 8/11/18 (att. 11/Bn.).
3 Moore, John Rushton, M.C., Lt. (A/Major), k. in a., 20-23/3/18 (att. M.G.C.).
11 Morgan, Thomas Cyril, 2/Lt. (Tp.), k. in a., 12/8/17.
12 Morris, Arthur, Capt., k. in a., 18/9/18.
Morris, Leslie Tounsend, 2/Lt. (Tp.), k. in a., 1/6/18 (att. 5/S. Wales Borderers).
13 Mountain, Cyril Robert Wightman, T/2/Lt. (A/Capt.), k. in a., 5/8/17.
11 Munro, Alexander Douglas, 2/Lt. (Tp.), k. in a., 2/9/18 (att. 1/Bn.).
11 Murray, Thomas, Capt., k. in a., 3/7/16.
3 Musker, John Henry, 2/Lt., k. in a., 1/11/17 (att. 1/Bn.).
Napier, Maurice Alexander, Major (Tp.), k. in a., 27/5/16 (att. 10/Welsh R.).
9 Naylor, John, 2/Lt. (Tp.) (A/Capt.), k. in a., 11/4/18.
14 Newell, Matthew Banks, 2/Lt. (Tp.), k. in a., 4-5/4/16.
3 Newell, Thomas Stanley, 2/Lt., d. of w., 5/7/15 (att. 2/Bn.).
3 Newson, Norman A., Lt., k. in a., 18/2/15.
17 Newstead, Rupert Randolph, 2/Lt. (Tp.), k. in a., 7/7/16.
Newton, Henry Joseph, 2/Lt., died, 2/8/16 (and R.F.C.).
2 Nicholson, Hugh Hathorn, 2/Lt., k. in a., 24/5/15 (att. 3/Bn.).
Nicholson, Huntly Warwick, Lt., k. in a., 17/11/14.
11 Nicholson, Richard Le Brun, M.C., T/Capt. (A/Major), k. in a., 31/8/18 (att. 1/6 Bn.).
12 Ninis, Francis Aubrey, M.C., Lt. (A/Capt.), d. of w., 19/9/18.
10 Noble, Archibald Francis, T/Capt. & Adjt., k. in a., 21/5/16.
Nosworthy, Philip Chorlton, 2/Lt., k. in a., 11/5/15.
1 O'Brien, William Vincent, 2/Lt. (Tp.), k. in a., 20/9/16.
13 O'Callaghan, James, 2/Lt. (Tp.), k. in a., 21/10/16.
1/2 Oliver, Edward Cole, 2/Lt., k. in a., 22/10/17 (att. 16/Bn.).
10 Oliver, George Frank, 2/Lt. (Tp.), k. in a., 15/7/16.
9 Owen, Herbert Morris, 2/Lt. (Tp.), d. of w., 25/3/18.
10 Owens, Edward, D.C.M., 2/Lt., k. in a., 27/6/18.
Page, Dudley Alfred, 2/Lt. (Tp.), d. of w., 14/8/17 (in Ger. hands) (att. R.F.C., 56 Sq.).
14 Parker, William Brabazon Hallowes, Lt. (Tp.), d. of w., 25/4/16 (att. 8/Bn.).
1 Patterson, Charles Cox, Capt., k. in a., 21/10/16.
3 Peake, Arthur, Lt., k. in a., 24/10/17 (att. 11/Bn.).
16 Philipps, Ivor John Douglas, Capt. (Tp.), died, 8/3/15.
10 Pickersgill, John Henry, M.C., Lt., k. in a., 28/8/18 (att. 1/6 Bn.).
3 Prout, William Thomas, 2/Lt., k. in a., 28/7/16 (att. 1/Bn.).
10 Pumphrey, Hubert, 2/Lt. (Tp.), k. in a., 26/4/18.
10 Reynolds, Eric Hindle, 2/Lt., died, 26/12/17 (att. 120 P.O.W. Coy.).
11 Rhodes, Charles Frederick Stanley, 2/Lt. (Tp.), k. in a., 7/6/17.
Rich, William Suttor, Capt., d. of w., 9/11/14.
3 Rimington, Ernest Cameron Waterfield, 2/Lt., k. in a., 2/10/15.
10 Robbins, John Laurence, Lt. (Tp.), k. in a., 26/3/18 (att. Staff, 26 Div.).
14 Roberts, Robert James, 2/Lt. (Tp.), k. in a., 10/10/16 (att. 13/Bn.).
3 Roberts, Thomas, 2/Lt., k. in a., 25/5/15 (att. 2/Bn.).
1 Roberts, Thomas Wilson, 2/Lt. (Tp.), d. of w., 1/9/16.
3 Robertson, Herbert Neville, 2/Lt., d. of w., 30/4/18 (att. 10/Bn.).
Routh, John Cyril, Capt., k. in a., 6/5/15.
10 Rowe, Harvey Wilfrid Warwick, M.C., Lt. (Tp.) (A/Capt.), k. in a., 20/8/17.
3 Saltmarsh, John Henry T., 2/Lt. (Tp.), d. of w., 30/12/17 (att. 2/22 Lon. R.).
12 Sampson, T. F., 2/Lt., k. in a., 18/9/18.
16 Scholefield, Richard Powell, 2/Lt. (Tp.), d. of w., 25/7/16.
15 Schultz, George Edward, Capt. (Tp.), d. of w., 12/8/17.
Scott, Arthur de Courcy, Lt.-Col., k. in a., 6/5/15.
11 Scott, Kenneth William Laing, 2/Lt., k. in a., 21/10/16.
3 Scott, Samuel Lackland, 2/Lt. (Tp.), k. in a., 8/8/18 (att. 11/Bn., att. Mach. Gun Corps).
9 Sernberg, Allan, Capt. (Tp.), k. in a., 2/7/16.
13 Shaw, Bernard Hudson, 2/Lt. (Tp.), k. in a., 22/1/17.
9 Shaw, Rowan, 2/Lt. (Tp.), k. in a., 22/2/16.
3 Sheard, Geoffrey Senior, 2/Lt., died, 26/6/17.
14 Silcock, Percy Bryan, 2/Lt. (Tp.), d. of w., 11/8/17 (att. 16/Bn.).
14 Simcock, Gilbert Alexander, 2/Lt., k. in a., 9/4/14. 9/4/16 X
10 Simpson, Eric Hadley, 2/Lt. (Tp.), k. in a., 11/4/18.
3 Simpson, George Ricardo, Lt., d. of w., 30/8/18 (att. 1/Bn.).
Smith, Sydney Ferrar, 2/Lt., k. in a., 7/5/15.
13 Somerset, Fitz Roy Aubrey, Lt. (Tp.), k. in a., 7/7/16.

Stead, Geoffrey Henry, M.C., Lt. (Tp.), d. of w., 22/7/18.
12 Stephenson, Claudius, Capt. (Tp.), d. of w., 2/11/16.
13 Stevenson, Henry Fitzroy, Lt. (Tp.), k. in a., 7/7/16.
13 Stewart, Douglas Alexander, 2/Lt. (Tp.), k. in a., 7/7/16.
Stone, Arthur Brabazon, Major, k. in a., 10/5/15.
13 Stringer, Gerald Moffatt, 2/Lt., killed, 15/3/15
9 Stubbs, William Norman, 2/Lt. (Tp.), k. in a., 23/10/18.
16 Styles, Alfred Cornwall, Lt. (Tp.), k. in a., 19/7/16.
1 Sweeney, Gilbert Martin, 2/Lt. (Tp.), k. in a., 5/10/17.
14 Tapp, George Norman, 2/Lt. (Tp.), d. of w., 28/3/16.
10 Thrift, Sydney Henry, 2/Lt., k. in a., 15/7/16.
8 Tierney, Herbert Stanislaus, 2/Lt., k. in a., 9/4/16.
16 Thurgood, Ernest Fuller, Capt. (Tp.), k. in a., 31/5/18.
11 Trayes, Frederic Kenneth Jackson, 2/Lt., k. in a., 22/3/18.
Turner, Herbert Guy, Capt., k. in a., 2-3/3/15.
3 Turner, Roger Bingham, Lt., k. in a., 9/4/16.
15 Tyson, William Noel, T/Lt., k. in a., 29/9/18.
3 Vance, Charles Richard Griffin, 2/Lt., k. in a., 10/3/15.
12 Vigors, Charles Henry, M.C., Capt., k. in a., 18/9/18.
15 Wainwright, Harry Arnold, 2/Lt., k. in a., 16/7/18.
2 Walford, Alfred Sanderson, Lt. (A/Capt.), died, 19/1/19.
3 Walker, Arnold Henry, Lt., d. of w., 17/9/18 (att. 8th Bn.).
12 Wallis, Noel Veder, 2/Lt. (Tp.), k. in a., 10/4/17.
Walsh, Geoffrey Christian Lansdale, 2/Lt., k. in a., 22/6/17 (att. 13/Bn.).
10 Walter, Raymond, 2/Lt. (Tp.), k. in a., 15/7/16.
10 Watson, Charles John, Lt. (Tp.), d. of w., 26/1/17.
11 Watson, Geoffrey William, 2/Lt. (Tp.), k. in a., 1/8/17.
14 Watt, John Vade, 2/Lt. (Tp.), died, 30/10/15.
13 Webb, Denys Stubbs, 2/Lt. (Tp.), k. in a., 21/10/16.
9 Welch, Richard Sydney, 2/Lt., k. in a., 24/3/18.
14 Welsby, Sydney Walter Humfrey, 2/Lt. (T/Lt.), k. in a., 30/4/17.
13 White, Gilbert Clement Whit, Lt. (Tp.), d. of w., 6/10/15.
13 Willmore, William Albert, 2/Lt., k. in a., 26/4/18 (att. 10/Bn.).
Winnington, Charles, 2/Lt., k. in a., 14/10/18 (att. 1/7 Bn.).
15 Wolstenholme, Richard Francis, Capt. (Tp.), k. in a., 28/11/16.
16 Wood, Thos. Leonard, 2/Lt., d. of w., 26/6/17.
16 Worthington, Ralph, Major (Tp.), k. in a., 17/5/17.
3 Wright, Charles, M.C., Lt., k. in a., 27/5/18 (att. 11/Bn.).
10 Young, Leonard George Birmingham, 2/Lt., k. in a., 19/5/16.

The Royal Welsh Fusiliers.

3 Ackerley, Ronald Hermann, Lt., k. in a., 16/5/15 (att. 1/Bn.).
Ackland-Allen, Hugh Thomas, Lt., k. in a., 23/10/14.
9 Acton, Charles Annesley, Major (Tp.), k. in a., 25/9/15.
11 Adams, John Bernard Pye, Lt. (Tp.), d. of w., 27/2/17 (12).
17 Allen, Alfred James Benedict, 2/Lt. (Tp.), k. in a., 3/3/16.
8 Allies, Alfric Evan, Lt., k. in a., 16/8/15.
3 Allison, Harry, Lt., k. in a., 27/8/18 (att. 13/Bn.).
Alltree, Charles Derek, Lt. (Tp.), d. of w., 27/3/18 (in German hands) (att. 9/Bn.).
19 Andrews, Glyndwr Levi, Capt. (Tp.), k. in a., 21/8/18 (att. 16/Bn.).
14 Apsimon, Arthur Injwerm, Lt. (Tp.), d. of w., 4/8/17.
12 Aubertin, William Aldworth, Major, died, 20/2/19.
13 Ayer, Leonard Stuart, Capt. (Tp.), d. of w., 15/7/16.
Ball, Samuel George, 2/Lt., k. in a., 20/3/18.
12 Bancroft, Stanley Fleming, Lt. (Tp.), k. in a., 19/8/16 (att. 10/Bn.).
2 Banks, Arthur Chaplin, 2/Lt., k. in a., 22/6/16.
Barker, Randle Barnett, D.S.O., Brig.-Gen. (Tp.), k. in a., 24/3/18 (Major, R. of Off.).
Barker, Richard Vincent, Capt., k. in a., 31/10/14.
Barrett, Adrian Hamilton Silverton, 2/Lt. (Tp.), k. in a., 10/7/16 (att. 14/Bn.).
18 Bartle, George, 2/Lt. (Tp.), k. in a., 2/11/16 (att. 9/Bn.).
14 Bartley, John, M.C., 2/Lt. (Tp.), k. in a., 31/10/18.
9 Baxter, Ian Alexander, M.C., Capt. (Tp.), k. in a., 30/5/18.
1 Baynes, R. H. B., Lt., k. in a., 14/7/16.
16 Bennett, Herbert, 2/Lt. (Tp.), k. in a., 22/4/18.
16 Bevers, Isaac Gwilyn, 2/Lt (Tp.), d. of w., 2/8/17.
10 Binny, Steuart Scott, D.S.O., Lt.-Col. (Tp.), k. in a., 3/3/16 (R.O., 19 Hus.).
12 Birch, Howard, 2/Lt. (Tp.), k. in a., 9/4/16 (att. 8/Bn.).
10 Blake, George Penderell, Capt. (Tp.), k. in a., 20/7/16.
11 Bone, Victor Arnold, Capt. (Tp.), k. in a., 18/9/18.
3 Bottomley, Frederick, 2/Lt. (Tp.), drowned, 4/5/17.
15 Bowes, Roy, M.C., T/Lt. (A/Capt.), d. of w., 5/8/17.
3 Bowles, Reginald Julian Albany, Lt., d. of w., 20/7/16.
3 Brennan, John Henry, Capt., k. in a., 19/10/14.
1 Brocklebank, Ralph Royds, 2/Lt., d. of w., 16/5/17.
3 Brodie, William Alan, 2/Lt., d. of w., 13/5/18.
3 Brown, John, 2/Lt. (Tp.), drowned, 4/5/17 (Garr. Bn.).
10 Broxup, John William, 2/Lt. (Tp.), d. of w., 24/4/17.
3 Brunt, Henry John Francis, Lt., k. in a., 25/9/15 (att. 1/Bn.).
1 Cadogan, Henry Osbert Samuel, Lt.-Col., k. in a., 30/10/14.
2 Camies, Ernest Arthur, 2/Lt. (Tp.), k. in a., 15/7/16.
Campbell, Victor Robert Wilkie, 2/Lt. (Tp.), k. in a., 7/9/18 (3/Garr. Bn.) (att. 23 Ches. R.).
10 Capell, Arthur Edward, 2/Lt. (Tp.), k. in a., 13/11/16.
2 Casson, Randal Alexander, 2/Lt., k. in a., 26/9/17.
8 Cawley, Robert, Lt. (Q.M.), died, 30/6/18.
Chance, Guy Ogden de Peyster, Lt., k. in a., 19/10/14.
Chapman, Herbert, 2/Lt. (T/Lt.), d. of w., 29/5/15.
14 Charles, George Harold, 2/Lt., k. in a., 31/10/18.
Childe-Freeman, John Arthur, M.C., Capt., k. in a., 25/9/15.
Coles, Herbert Stonehouse, Capt., k. in a., 16/5/15.
3 Colquhoun, Ernest Forbes Campbell, 2/Lt., k. in a., 26/9/17 (att. 2/Bn.).
2 Conning, Thomas Rothsay, M.C., Lt., k. in a., 27/5/17.
1/2 Coster, Ernest, M.C., T/2/Lt. (A/Capt.), k. in a., 26/9/17.
9 Cowie, William Anderson, M.C., Lt. (A/Capt.), k. in a., 30/5/18.
10 Cree, Adrian Victor, 2/Lt. (Tp.), k. in a., 17/2/16.
Crosland, John Herbert, Lt., died, 13/4/19 (att. K. Afr. Rifs.).
2 Crosland, Trevor Allington, 2/Lt., k. in a., 22/6/16.
10 Curran, Henry, 2/Lt., k. in a., 25/4/17.
11 Curtis, Harry Reginald, Major (Tp.), k. in a., 18/9/18.
1 Dadd, Edmund Halton, Capt. (Tp.), k. in a., 3/9/16.
17 Daniel, Ralph Picton, Capt. (Tp.), k. in a., 31/7/17.
22 Daniel, Thomas George, Lt. (Tp.), k. in a., 23/11/17 (att. 19/Bn.).
Darwell, Thomas Walter, 2/Lt., k. in a., 18/9/18 (att. 14/Bn.).
10 Davies, David, 2/Lt. (Tp.), k. in a., 13/11/16.
10 Davies, David Ethelstone, Lt. (Tp.), k. in a., 18/6/17.
15 Davies, Evan, Major (Tp.), k. in a., 27/7/17.
19 Davies, Ernest Glyn, Capt. (Tp.), k. in a., 5/7/16.
8 Davies, Joseph Ithel Jehu, 2/Lt. (Tp.), d. of w., 3/9/16 (att. 1/Batt.).
16 Davies, John Wesley, Lt. (Tp.), k. in a., 26/3/16.
18 Davies, John Charles, 2/Lt. (Tp.), d. of w., 12/4/17.
16 Davies, John Morris, 2/Lt. (Tp.), k. in a., 8/10/18.
13 Davies, Robert Humphrey, 2/Lt. (Tp.), k. in a., 23/8/18.
9 Davies, Sydney George, 2/Lt. (Tp.), k. in a., 31/7/17.
13 Davies, William Lloyd, 2/Lt. (Tp.), k. in a., 31/7/17.
2 Davis, Thomas Edward George, 2/Lt. (Tp.), k. in a., 27/5/17.
2 Diggle, Joseph, 2/Lt. (Tp.), k. in a., 23/8/18.
10 Dixon, Ernest, 2/Lt., k. in a., 19/8/16.
1 Dobell, Colin Macpherson, Lt., d. of w., 30/5/18 (att. 9/Bn.).
2 Dolling, Caledon Robert John Radcliffe, 2/Lt. (Tp.) (A/Capt.), k. in a., 20/8/16.
1 Dooner, Alfred Edwin Claud Toke, Lt., k. in a., 30/11/14.
V.C. Doughty-Wylie, Charles Hotham Montagu, C.B., C.M.G., Lt.-Col., k. in a., 28/4/15.
1 Dove, Etienne Howard, 2/Lt. (Tp.), k. in a., 30/3/17.
8 Dunn, Philip Morgan, Capt. (Tp.), k. in a., 3/2/17.
8 Dyche, John, Lt. (Tp.), d. of w., 28/1/17.
18 Edmunds, Gwynne Rhys, Lt., k. in a., 20/7/16.
23 Edridge-Green, Henry Allen, 2/Lt., died, 5/11/18 (and R.A.F.).
17 Edwards, Algernon Stuart, Lt. (Tp.), k. in a., 31/7/17.
3 Edwards, Henry Laidley Garland, Lt., d. of w., 16/5/15 (att. 1/Bn.).
3 Edwards, John Francis Coster, Lt. (A/Capt.), d. of w., 10/11/18 (att. 24/Batt.).
2 Edwards, John Ivor Jones, 2/Lt. (Tp.), k. in a., 31/10/18 (att. 24/Batt.).
13 Edwards, Kenneth Grenville, Lt. (Tp.), k. in a., 8/5/18.
1 Egerton, Rowland Le Belward, 2/Lt., k. in a., 30/10/14.
3 Elliott, George Keith, Lt., k. in a., 8/9/18 (att. 25/Bn.).
15 Ellis, Ceredig, 2/Lt. (Tp.), d. of w., 19/7/16.
1/2 Ellis, Hughie Lodwick Maldwyn, 2/Lt. (Tp.), d. of w., 5/5/17.
19 Ellis, Robert Thomas Hugh, 2/Lt., k. in a., 13/10/17.
13 Evans, Bertram Trevor, 2/Lt. (Tp.), k. in a., 22/4/18.
3 Evans, David Edward, 2/Lt., k. in a., 26/8/18.
17 Evans, David Owen, Lt. (Tp.), k. in a., 12/2/16.
1/2 Evans, David William, 2/Lt. (Tp.), k. in a., 8/10/18 (att. 14/Batt.).
1 Evans, John, 2/Lt., k. in a., 19/9/18.
17 Evans, Norman Edward, 2/Lt. (Tp.), k. in a., 4/11/18.
8 Evans, Oscar James, 2/Lt. (Tp.), k. in a., 5/1/16.
Evans, Richard Parry, 2/Lt. (Tp.), k. in a., 14/5/17.
Evans, Thomas Richard, D.S.O., T/Major (A/Lt.-Col.), k. in a., 3/10/18 (att. 1/6 N. Staff. R.).
3 Evans, William Edwards, 2/Lt., k. in a., 1/5/17 (13).
Farren, William Ignatius George, Lt., died, 29/3/18.
3 Fenn, Edward Gerald Palmer, 2/Lt. (Tp.), k. in a., 19/9/18 (Garr. Bn.) (att. 1/5 Essex R.).
15 Fleming, Reginald Henry, 2/Lt. (Tp.), k. in a., 11/7/16.
9 Fletcher, Horace William, 2/Lt. (T/Lt.), d. of w., 26/3/17 (att. 7/Bn.).
Fletcher, Joseph Harold, Capt. (Tp.), k. in a., 25/11/17 (att. 19/Bn.).
Fletcher, Walter George, 2/Lt., k. in a., 20/3/15.
13 Flower, Oswald Swift, Lt.-Col. (Tp.), d. of w., 12/7/16.
10 Follit, Charles Albert Roy, D.S.O., Capt. (Tp.), d. of w., 20/8/16.
Foxall, Thomas William, 2/Lt. (Tp.), k. in a., 2/10/18 (3/Garr. Bn.) (att. 25/Garr. Bn. K. L'pool R.).
10 Freeman, Edward, Major (Tp.), k. in a., 3/3/16.
3 French, Robert Mason Jackson, Capt., d. of w., 19/2/16.
Gabbett, Richard Edward Phillip, Lt.-Col., k. in a., 16/5/15.
3 Gannon, John Howard, 2/Lt. (Tp.), killed, 9/10/17 (att. 11/Bn.).
9 Garvin, Samuel, 2/Lt., k. in a., 27/3/17 (att. 1/7 Bn.).
16 George, Thomas, 2/Lt. (Tp.), k. in a., 27/8/18.
3 Gladstone, William Glynne Charles, Lt., k. in a., 13/4/15.
10 Godfrey, Leonard George, 2/Lt., k. in a., 20/7/16.
3 Gore, Gerard Ribton, 2/Lt., d. of w., 20/12/14 (att. 2/Bn.).
1 Green, George Binch, 2/Lt. (Tp.), k. in a., 11/6/18 (att. 7/Shrop. L.I.).
2 Griffith, Arthur Charles Fleming, Lt., k. in a., 8/10/18 (att. 17/Bn.).
15 Griffith, William Henry, M.C., 2/Lt. (Tp.), d. of w., 5/7/17.
1 Griffiths, William George, 2/Lt. (Tp.), k. in a., 9/3/18 (att. 5/Bn.).
10 Griffiths, William Percival, Capt. (Tp.), k. in a., 30/3/16.
3 Groser, Arthur Hugh, 2/Lt., k. in a., 22/9/16 (att. 1 Bn.).
10 Hale, William John Douglas, Capt. (Tp.), k. in a., 28/4/17.
16 Hancock, Harold, 2/Lt. (Tp.), k. in a. 19/9/18.
9 Handley, Walter, 2/Lt. (Tp.), k. in a., 25/3/18.
19 Hargreaves, Frank, Lt. (Tp.), k. in a., 12/7/16.
18 Harries, Howard Lock, 2/Lt. (Tp.), k. in a., 13/11/16 (att. 10/Bn.).
1 Harris, Arthur Harold, 2/Lt., d. of w., 4/7/18 (att. 16/Bn.).
Harris, Charles Henry, 2/Lt., d. of w., 19/9/18 (att. 11/Bn.).

9 Harris, Nathan Leonard, Capt. (Tp.), k. in a., 28/8/18.
17 Harris, Percy George, 2/Lt. (Tp.), k. in a., 11/8/17 (and R.F.C., 21 Sqd.).
16 Harris, William Handel, 2/Lt. (Tp.), k. in a., 26/8/18.
14 Harrison, Brian, 2/Lt. (Tp.), k. in a., 10/7/16.
8 Hay, Archibald, Major (T/Lt.-Col.), k. in a., 3/2/17.
3 Heastey, George Rodney, 2/Lt., k. in a., 20/7/16.
16 Heatly, Charles Frederick, 2/Lt. (Tp.), d. of w., 17/4/18.
13 Heaton, Harold Sinclair, 2/Lt. (Tp.), k. in a., 22/4/18.
Heaton, Lionel James, 2/Lt., k. in a., 29/8/18 (att. 17/Batt.).
8 Herington, Percy Godfrey, 2/Lt. (Tp.), k. in a., 15/2/17.
2 Heycock, Edwin, 2/Lt. (Tp.), k. in a., 27/8/18 (att. 14/Bn.).
Hill, Hugh, M.V.O., D.S.O., Bt.-Lt.-Col., k. in a., 10/9/16 (Staff).
8 Hill, William, Hon. Lt. & Qr.-Mr., died, 11/10/15.
12 Hills, Ernest Leslie, Lt. (Tp.), d. of w., 26/11/15 (att. N. Nigeria R.).
15 Hinds, William Pugh, Lt. (Tp.), d. of w., 2/2/16.
15 Hodkinson, Leonard, 2/Lt. (Tp.), k. in a., 14/9/17 (and R.F.C., 53 Sqd.).
9 Hogg, Lewis Stephen, Capt. (& Adjt., Tp), k. in a., 25/9/15.
3 Hollingbery, Raymond Archibald Robert, Lt., k. in a., 6/7/16.
12 Holme, Bertram Lester, Lt. (Tp.), d. of w., 25/4/16.
19 Hope-Evans, Timothy Idwal, Capt. (Tp.), k. in a., 23/11/17.
Hoskyns, Edwin Cecil Leigh, Lt., k. in a., 20-21/10/14.
17 Howell, George Woodbourne, 2/Lt., k. in a., 22/6/18 (att. 1/2 Bn.).
9 Hoyle, Basil William Edmond, Capt. (Tp.), k. in a., 25/9/15.
8 Hubbard, Alfred William, 2/Lt. (Tp.), k. in a., 25/1/17.
1 Hughes, Horatio Clement, 2/Lt. (Tp.), k. in a., 18/9/18 (att. 11/Bn.).
3 Hughes, Hugh Darrell, 2/Lt., k. in a., 14/1/17 (att. 8/Bn.).
10 Hughes, John Edwyn, 2/Lt. (Tp.), d. of w., 19/8/16.
20 Hughes, John Gwilym, Lt. (Tp.), killed, 3/11/16 (att. 9/Bn.).
20 Hughes, Maurice Thomas, 2/Lt. (Tp.), k. in a., 30/5/16 (att. 13/Bn.).
10 Hughes, Tegerin, Capt. (Tp.), d. of w., 1/4/16.
10 Hughes, William, 2/Lt. (Tp.), k. in a., 3/3/16.
Hughes, William Francis, M.C., M.M., 2/Lt. (Tp.), d. of w., 7/9/18.
19 Humphrey-Jones, Cecil, Capt. (Tp.), k. in a., 24/11/17.
14 Hunkin, William Burrows Clement, M.C., Lt. (Tp.), k. in a., 3/11/18.
13 Hutchins Frederick Charles, 2/Lt. (Tp.), k. in a., 22/4/18.
10 Huxley, Joseph, 2/Lt. (Tp.), k. in a., 22/4/18 (att. 14/Bn.).
1 Jackson, Dudley William Gerald, Capt., d. of w., 13/4/16.
2 Jackson, James Battle, 2/Lt. (Tp.), k. in a., 23/4/17.
9 Jagger, Arthur Stannus, 2/Lt. (Tp.), d. of w., 1/10/18.
10 James, Albert John Stanley, D.S.O., M.C., T/Major (A/Lt.-Col.), k. in a., 28/3/18 (att. 8/Bn., K.O.R.L.R.).
14 James, Enoch Lewis, 2/Lt. (Tp.), k. in a., 18/2/17.
13 James, Gwilym, 2/Lt. (Tp.), d. of w., 8/10/18.
James, Vivian Gwynne, Lt., k. in a., 26/3/17 (att. 7/Bn.).
13 James, William David M.M., 2/Lt., k. in a., 8/10/18.
3 James Walter Ibbe, Lt., k. in a., 25-27/9/15.
19 James, Wilfred Sydney, 2/Lt. (Tp.), k. in a., 24/11/17.
3 Jenkins, Cyril Donald Thomas, Lt., killed, 2/10/16.
3 Jenkins, Sidney Oswald, 2/Lt., k. in a., 22/8/18 (att. 10/K. Shrop. L.I.).
20 Jennings, Gouldbourne Hayward, 2/Lt., k. in a., 10/8/16 (att. 10/Bn.).
10 Johns, Bernard Digby, Capt. (Tp.), k. in a., 17/2/16.
14 Jones, Arthur Lloyd, M.C., Capt. (Tp.), d. of w., 3/9/18.
15 Jones, Clifford, 2/Lt. (Tp.), k. in a., 2/8/17.
11 Jones, Cecil Hughes, Capt. (Tp.), k. in a., 18/9/18.
3 Jones, Daniel Thomas 2/Lt., k. in a., 4/5/17.
8 Jones, Ernest Kerrison, Capt. (Tp.), k. in a., 3/7/16.
12 Jones, Evelyn Llewellyn Hustler, 2/Lt., k. in a., 26/3/17 (att. 5/Bn.).
3 Jones, Edwin Tudor, Capt., k. in a., 3/9/16 (att. 1/Bn.).
2 Jones, Francis Leonard Clarence, M.C., M.M., 2/Lt., k. in a., 1/9/18.
10 Jones, Hugh, 2/Lt. (Tp.), k. in a., 3/9/16.
17 Jones, Harold Madoc, Lt. (Tp.), k. in a., 31/7/17.
10 Jones, Henry Myrddin, 2/Lt. (Tp.), k. in a., 13/11/16.
13 Jones, Harold Vivian, Lt. (Tp.), k. in a., 10/7/16.
1 Jones, John Harold, 2/Lt. (Tp.), k. in a., 1/10/17.
3 Jones, Leonard, 2/Lt., k. in a., 16/5/15 (att. 1/Bn.).
14 Jones, Stanley, 2/Lt. (Tp.), d. of w., 25/2/17.
Jones, Stanley, Capt., k. in a., 16/5/15.
1/2 Jones, Thomas Stephen, 2/Lt., k. in a., 26/9/17 (att. 10/Bn.).
13 Jones-Bateman, Francis, Capt., k. in a., 4/11/18.
Jones-Savin, John Savin, 2/Lt. (Tp.), k. in a., 27/3/17.
Jones-Vaughan, Evan N., Capt., k. in a., 26/10/14.
3 Keepfer, William Robert Cyril, 2/Lt., k. in a., 4/11/16 (att. 2/Bn.).
9 Kilvert, Harry, 2/Lt. (Tp.), d. of w., 1/8/17.
15 King, David, 2/Lt. (Tp.), k. in a., 31/7/17.
Kington, William Miles, D.S.O., Capt., k. in a., 20/10/14.
13 Lack, Reginald Walter, 2/Lt., k. in a., 29/9/16 (att. 1/Bn.).
Law, Harry, Lt., d. of w., 7/7/15.
9 Lawes, Charles Gilbert, Lt. (Tp.), k. in a., 27/10/16.
1 Lewis, Arthur Starkey, Lt. (Tp.), k. in a., 4/5/17 (Garr. Batt.).
16 Lewis, David Elwyn, 2/Lt., d. of w., 18/9/18.
17 Lewis, Joseph Henry, T/2/Lt. (A/Capt.), k. in a., 8/10/18 (att. 1/7 Ches. R.).
17 Lewis, Llewelyn, 2/Lt., (Tp.), k. in a., 1/-12/7/16.
1 Lewis, Thomas William, 2/Lt. (Tp.), d. of w., 27/10/17.
3 Lindsley, George Vincent, 2/Lt., d. of w., 16/3/17 (att. 2/Bn.).
16 Linton, Frederick Tom, 2/Lt. (Tp.), k. in a., 22/4/18.
Llewellyn, Edward Thomas, Lt. (Tp.), d. of w., 18/5/18 (4/Garr. Bn., att. 9/Bn.).
14 Llewellyn, Vivian, 2/Lt. (Tp.), k. in a., 3/11/18.
10 Lloyd, Charles Gordon, Lt., died, 9/6/15.
13 Lloyd, Frank Stuart, Major (Tp.), d. of w., 5/9/17.
1/2 Lloyd, James Percival, 2/Lt. (Tp.), k. in a., 25/7/17 (att. 16/Batt.).
Lloyd, M. E., Capt., k. in a., 23/10/14.
Lloyd, Robert Love, Major, d. of w., 9/12/15.
8 Lloyd, Walter, Capt., k. in a., 7/8/15.
15 Lloyd, William Robert, 2/Lt. (Tp.), k. in a., 12/7/18.
3 Lord, Arthur George, 2/Lt., k. in a., 20/7/16.
10 Lord, Charles Henry, Major (Tp.), died, 30/12/14.
Lynch, Harold Francis, 2/Lt., k. in a., 16/5/15.
10 Lyons, William Thomas, Capt. (Tp.), k. in a., 3/3/16.
McIntosh, Joseph Francis, Lt. (Tp.), drowned, 10/10/18 (att. 2/Bn.).
1 McKay, Frederick, Lt., d. of w., 28/2/17.
McBean, Donald, Lt. (Tp.), k. in a., 15/3/16 (att. 10/Bn.).
9 McCammon, Charles Duncan, 2/Lt., k. in a., 3/7/16.
1 Madley, Lewis George, 2/Lt. (Tp.), k. in a., 14/5/17.
9 Madocks, Henry John, Lt.-Col. (Tp.), k. in a., 25/9/15.
3 Mair, George Hay, Lt., died, 14/12/18 (att. R. Sussex R.).
9 Manders, S. G., Capt., died, 9/12/18 (and R.A.F.).
2 Mann, John Charles, M.C., A/Capt., k. in a., 26/9/17.
3 Mann, Robert Leonard, 2/Lt., k. in a., 9/10/14 (att. 16/Bn.).
9 Manwaring, Jack Lancaster, M.C., 2/Lt. (Tp.), died, 15/11/16.
3 Martin, William Howard, 2/Lt. (Tp.), k. in a., 31/7/17 (att. 2/Bn.).
11 Meecham, David Jeffreys, 2/Lt. (Tp.), k. in a., 27/3/17.
Miller, Reginald de Hochepied Marillier, 2/Lt. (Tp.), d. of w., 27/10/18 (3 Garr. Bn.).
14 Mills, Robert Henry, Major (Tp.), k. in a., 10/7/16.
15 Morgan, Emlyn Thomas, Lt. (Tp.), d. of w., 7/2/16.
19 Morgan, George Hamilton, Capt. (Tp.), k. in a., 23/11/17.
1 Morgan, Geoffrey Penney, 2/Lt. (Tp.), k. in a., 14/7/16.
Morgan, Guy Williams Stuart, Capt., k. in a., 25/9/15.
Morgan Herbert Glyn Rhys, 2/Lt. (Tp.), d. of w., 31/7/17.
1/2 Morgan, John Towlson, Capt., k. in a., 29/10/18 (and R.A.F.).
1 Morgan, Wilfrid, 2/Lt. (Tp.), k. in a., 18/9/18 (att. 11/Bn.).
Morris, Arthur Cukelyn, Lt. (Tp.), k. in a., 17/2/18 (att. R.F.C.).
Morris, Charles Herbert, Lt., k. in a., 13/4/17 (and R.F.C.).
Morris, John Torrington, 2/Lt., k. in a., 16/5/15.
9 Moss, Enoch Frank, 2/Lt. (Tp.), d. of w., 17/9/16.
Naylor, Rowland Edmund, Lt., k. in a., 16/5/15.
1 Newton, Vivian Frederic, 2/Lt., d. of w., 15/9/16.
14 Nicholls-Jones, Thomas Cyril, Lt. (Tp.), k. in a., 1/8/17.
3 Orme, Edward Leslie, Lt., k. in a., 27/5/17 (att. 1/Bn.).
Orme, Francis Reginald, 2/Lt., k. in a., 7/11/14.
1 Ormrod, Lawrence Moreland, M.C., Capt., died, 25/8/17.
14 Ormsby, Harold Sydney, T/Lt. (A/Capt.), d. of w., 18/2/17.
15 Osborne-Jones, Noel, 2/Lt., k. in a., 8/5/16.
16 Owen, Henry James, 2/Lt. (Tp.), k. in a., 24/8/18.
2 Owen, John Morris, T/Lt. (A/Capt.), k. in a., 23/4/17.
3 Owen, Thomas John, 2/Lt., d. of w., 19/2/17 (att. 8/Bn.).
13 Owen, Thomas Starr, 2/Lt. (Tp.), k. in a., 8/10/18.
9 Owen, Vernon Elias, 2/Lt (Tp.), d. of w., 29/11/15.
16 Owen, William, 2/Lt., d. of w., 27/8/18.
15 Owens, Arthur Owen, 2/Lt., k. in a., 22/4/18 (att. 16/Bn.).
10 Page, Henry, 2/Lt., k. in a., 20/7/16.
Palfreyman, A., 2/Lt., d. of w., 9/10/18 (att. 16/Bn.).
Parker, Colin, 2/Lt., died, 25/10/18 (3/Garr. Bn. (whilst P.O.W. in enemy hands).
Parkes, Horace Frederick, 2/Lt., k. in a., 12/3/15.
10 Parry, James Hywell, Lt. (Tp), d. of w., 5/9/17.
9 Payne, Edward Geoffrey, Capt. (Tp.), k. in a., 25/9/15.
Penson, Thomas Edward, 2/Lt., k. in a., 18/9/18 (att. 25/Bn.).
17 Perrett, Fred Leonard, 2/Lt., d. of w., 1/12/18.
2 Phillips, Arthur, 2/Lt., k. in a., 23/4/17.
9 Phillips, James Williams, Capt. (Tp.), k. in a., 30/5/18.
Phillips, Ralph Noel, Capt., d. of w., 27/12/14.
1/2 Pickard, Harry Lawson, M.C., 2/Lt., k. in a., 20/10/18 (att. 9/Bn.).
3 Pilling, William, M.C., 2/Lt., died, 22/10/18 (att. 2/Bn.).
20 Porter, Graham Hawksworth, Lt. (Tp.), k. in a., 3/10/16.
8 Powell, Scott, Capt. (Tp.), d. of w., 4-5/4/16.
3 Pritchard, T. L., Capt., d. of w., 9/11/14 (att. 2/Bn.).
1 Pritchard, David, 2/Lt., k. in a., 19/3/16.
Pritchard, Henry, 2/Lt. (Tp.), k. in a., 7/4/18 (att. Hood Bn.).
13 Pritchard, John, 2/Lt., k. in a., 4/9/17.
1/2 Raby, William Donald, 2/Lt. (Tp.), k. in a., 8/10/18.
15 Radcliffe, Ernest Charles Derwentwater, 2/Lt. (Tp.), k. in a., 31/7/17.
Ramsay, William James, Lt., k. in a., 27/3/18 (and R.F.C.).
1 Rees, Albert Lloyd, Lt. (Tp.), k. in a., 6/11/17.
Rees, Edward Davies, 2/Lt. (Tp.), k. in a., 13/6/17 (att 16/Bn.).
19 Rees, Edgar George, 2/Lt., k. in a., 23/11/17.
16 Rees, Henry Hugh Tregarthen, 2/Lt. (Tp.), k. in a., 11/7/16.
3 Rees, Edris, 2/Lt., d. of w., 27/10/17 (att. 1/Bn.).
Rees, John Trevor, 2/Lt., k. in a., 22/1/15.
15 Rees, Roland Gwyn, Lt. (Tp.), k. in a., 10-11/7/16.
14 Rees, Tom, Lt., k. in a., 17/9/16 (and R.F.C.).
1 Richardes, Roderick Alexander William Pryse, 2/Lt., d. of w., 18/9/18 (whilst P. of W. in Bulgarian hands).
14 Richards, Gwilym Owen, 2/Lt. (Tp.), d. of w., 23/4/18.
16 Richards, John, 2/Lt. (Tp.), k. in a., 15/3/18.
17 Richards, Llewelyn Thomas, 2/Lt. (Tp.), k. in a., 4/9/15.
1 Richardson, Mervyn Stronge, Capt. (Tp.), d. of w., 19/3/16.
14 Roberts, Alan Sheriff, 2/Lt. (Tp.), k. in a., 10/7/16.
9 Roberts, Cadwalader Glyn, Lt. (Tp.), k. in a., 3/7/16.
1 Roberts, Frederick Sheriff, 2/Lt., k. in a., 28/8/18 (att. 9/Bn.).

14 Roberts, Howel Dilwyn, 2/Lt. (Tp.), k. in a., 31/10/18.
17 Roberts, Henry Sheriff, Capt., k. in a., 27/8/17.
17 Roberts, Idris, 2/Lt. (Tp.), d. of w., 3/9/18.
Roberts, Thomas Owen, 2/Lt., k. in a., 18/9/18 (att. 14/Bn.).
3 Robertson, Helenus MacAulay, Capt., k. in a., 26/1/16 (att. 2/Bn.).
Robinson, James Thompson, Lt. (Tp.), k. in a., 7/9/18 (att. 24/Batt.).
3 Rowland, Stanley Jackson, Lt., k. in a., 2/11/17 (att. 1/8 Sco. Rifs.).
Rowland, William Henry, 2/Lt., died, 22/2/19 (att. 26/Bn.).
10 Rowlands, Charles William, 2/Lt. (Tp.), k. in a., 26/9/17.
9 Ruck-Keene, Ralph Edgar, Lt. (Tp.), killed, 16/1/16.
12 Rudd, William Ferris, Capt., k. in a., 13/11/16.
2 Samson, Arthur Legge, Capt., k. in a., 25/9/15.
13 Samuel, James Frederick, 2/Lt. (Tp.), k. in a., 22/4/18.
Saunders, Gwilyn Essex, 2/Lt. (Tp.), k. in a., 18/9/18 (att. 16/Bn.).
Savage, John Brown, 2/Lt., d. of w., 16/5/15.
10 Scale, George Devereux, Capt. (Tp.), k. in a., 20/7/16.
19 Shankland, Llewelyn Ap Tomas, Lt. (Tp.), d. of w., 25/11/17.
20 Singleton, William James, Lt. (Tp.), drowned, 10/10/18 (att. 3/Bn.).
8 Sinnett-Jones, Gilbert Lloyd, Capt. (Tp.), k. in a., 4/4/16.
3 Sinnett-Jones, James Victor, 2/Lt., k. in a., 10-12/7/16 (att 17/Bn.).
Snead-Cox, Geoffrey Phillip Joseph, 2/Lt., k. in a., 20/10/14.
11 Spooner, Ronald Alan, Capt. (Tp.), d. of w., 23/9/16.
Stable, Lascombe Law, Capt., k. in a., 26/10/14.
12 Stanley, Robert Oliver, 2/Lt., k. in a., 9/4/16.
11 Stockdale, Frank, Capt. (Tp.), d. of w., 19/9/18.
Stone, Ellis Robert Cunliffe, 2/Lt., k. in a., 26/10/14.
17 Styles, Arthur Horatio, Lt. (Tp.), d. of w., 26/7/16.
Sutcliffe, Sydney, 2/Lt., k. in a., 2/10/17 (and R.F.C., 11 Sqd.).
13 Swain, Robert Ernest, 2/Lt. (Tp.), d. of w., 8/7/16.
3 Sweetland, Rupert Girard, 2/Lt., d. of w., 26/1/17.
9 Symons, Charles Fleming Jelinger, Lt. (Tp.), k. in a 25/9/15.
1 Syrett, Alfred Montague, 2/Lt. (Tp.), k. in a., 4/5/17.
11 Taggart, Herbert, 2/Lt., k. in a., 8/5/16 (att. 15/Bn.).
16 Tanner, David Thomas, Lt. (Tp.), k. in a., 31/8/16.
1 Taylor, Guy Collins Vernon, Lt., k. in a., 2/10/17.
15 Thomas, Basil Llewellyn Boyd, Lt. (Tp.), k. in a., 9/4/17 (att. 27/M.G.C.).
Thomas, David Arthur, 2/Lt. (Tp.), k. in a., 4/5/17.
3 Thomas, David Cuthbert, 2/Lt., d. of w., 18/3/16.
15 Thomas, David John, 2/Lt. (Tp.), k. in a., 22/4/18 (att. 13/Bn.).
10 Thomas, George, 2/Lt. (Tp.), k. in a., 13/11/16.
2 Thomas, George Oliver, Capt., k. in a., 26/9/15.
3 Thomas, Herbert Gordon, 2/Lt., k. in a., 13/11/16.
1 Thomas, Noel Lavender, 2/Lt., k. in a., 18/9/18 (att. 11 Bn.).
9 Thomas, Richard Nixon, 2/Lt. (Tp.), d. of w., 23/8/15.
Thomas, Reginald Spenser Dudley, 2/Lt., k. in a., 18/9/18 (att. 25/Bn.).
16 Thomas, Rufus William, 2/Lt. (Tp.), k. in a., 9/5/18 (att. 113 T.M.B.).
19 Thomas, Tudor, 2/Lt. (Tp.), k. in a., 25/11/17.
16 Thomas, Thomas, 2/Lt. (Tp.), k. in a., 10/1/16.
17 Thomas, Thomas Oliver, 2/Lt. (Tp.), k in a., 10-12/7/16.
14 Thompson, Arthur George, 2/Lt. (Tp.), k. in a., 2/6/16.
3 Thompson, Edward James Vibart Collingwood, 2/Lt., d. of w., 10/9/14.
3 Thompson, Walton Downing, Lt., d. of w., 2/9/18 (att. 1/6 H.L.I.).
Tobias, Leslie Mark, Capt., died, 25/2/19 (2/Garr. Bn.).
1/2 Tyrrell, Walter, 2/Lt. (Tp.), d. of w., 4/9/18 (att. 17/Batt.).
3 Vaughan-Jones, Edward, Lt., k. in a., 11/5/18 (att. 11/Bn.).
14 Venmore, James Frederick, Lt. (Tp.), k. in a., 11/7/16.
10 Vernon, Leonard Patrick, M.C., Lt. (Tp.), k. in a., 18/6/17.
Vyvyan, William Geoffrey, Capt., d. of w., 24/10/14 (In German hands).
10 Walker, John Arthur, Capt. (Tp.), k. in a., 19/2/16.
14 Webb, Joseph Gilbert, Lt., died, 9/5/18.
Webb-Bowen, Hugh Ince, Capt., d. of w., 23/5/15.
12 White, John Stephen Grantham, Lt. (Tp.), d. of w., 31/7/17.
3 Wilding-Jones, Hugh Wynn, Lt., d. of w., 22/9/18 (att. 11/Bn.).
13 Williams, Arthur Ivor Meakin, Capt., d. of w., 9/10/18.
10 Williams, Arthur Owen, 2/Lt. (Tp.), k. in a., 16-19/8/16.
15 Williams, Arthur Trevor, 2/Lt. (Tp.), d. of w., 4/9/17 (att. R.F.C.).
17 Williams, Bleddyn, Capt., k. in a., 22/1/16.
10 Williams, Evan, 2/Lt. (Tp.), k. in a., 10/4/17.
10 Williams, E. G., 2/Lt., d. of w., 13/5/17.
12 Williams, Gwilym, 2/Lt. (Tp.), d. of w., 21/5/16 (att. 17/Bn.).
Williams, Howell, 2/Lt. (T/Lt.), died, 21/2/17 (att. Gold Coast R.).
17 Williams, Hywel, Capt. (Tp.), k. in a., 10-12/7/16.
14 Williams, Hugh Powell, Capt. (Tp.), k. in a., 5/6/16
1/2 Williams, Idwal, 2/Lt., k. in a., 26/9/17.
19 Williams, John, Capt. (Tp.), k. in a., 30/6/17.
Williams, James Griffith, Lt., k. in a., 27/8/18 (att. 17/Bn.).
19 Williams, James Morgan, 2/Lt., k. in a., 9/5/18 (att. 17/Bn.).
10 Williams, Lewis, 2/Lt. (Tp.), k. in a., 18/8/16.
10 Williams, Peter, 2/Lt. (Tp.), k. in a., 13/11/16.
19 Williams, Philip Ernest, M.C., Capt. (Tp.), d. of w., 24/11/17.
17 Williams, Richard, 2/Lt., d. of w., 2/4/18 (att. M.G.C.).
10 Williams, Richard Henry, 2/Lt. (Tp.), k. in a., 13/11/16.
9 Williams, Reginald Joseph, 2/Lt. (Tp.), k. in a., 25/9/15.
17 Williams, Richard Lloyd, Capt. (Tp.), d. of w., 2/8/17.
Williams, Roderick Mathafar, Capt., k. in a., 12/8/17 (2/Garr. Bn.) (R.F.C., 32 Sqd.).
3 Williams, Thomas Benjamin, 2/Lt., k. in a., 27/5/17 (att. 2/Bn.).
15 Williams, Vivian Pedr., 2/Lt., k. in a., 22/4/18.
3 Williams, William, 2/Lt., died, 27/2/17 (att. 1/Bn.).
17 Williams, William George, Capt. (Tp.), d. of w., 29/8/17.
9 Williams, William Henry, 2/Lt. (Tp.), k. in a., 6/11/17 (att. 7/Bn.).
1 Williams, William Ifor, 2/Lt., d. of w., 18/3/18 (att. 16/Bn.).
16 Williams, William James, M.C., 2/Lt., k. in a., 19/9/17.
14 Williams, William John, Lt. (Tp.), k. in a., 25/2/17.
3 Williams, William James Minister, 2/Lt., k. in a., 7/2/16 (att. 2/Bn.).
Williams-Meyrick, Edmund Oswald Griffith, Lt. (Tp.), died, 7/5/16 (Garr. Batt.).
3 Wilson, Neville Inchbold, M.C., Lt., k. in a., 6/4/18 (att. 4/Bn.).
3 Wilson, Philip Stanley, 2/Lt., k. in a., 20/8/16 (att. 2/Bn.).
13 Winter, Thomas Barron, 2/Lt., k. in a., 22/4/18.
3 Wolff, Gustav Frederick, A/Capt., k. in a., 21/3/18 (att. M.G.C.).
Wood, Charles Edmund, Capt., k. in a., 11/3/15.
15 Wood, William Leslie, 2/Lt. (A/Capt.), k. in a., 7/5/17.
Woodward, Charles Francis, Lt., d. of w., 20/5/15.
17 Wright, William Clifford, Lt. (Tp.), k. in a., 10-12/7/16.
10 Wynne-Williams, Humphrey Evan, 2/Lt. (Tp.), k. in a., 30/3/16.

The South Wales Borderers.

4 Addams-Williams, Donald Arthur, 2/Lt. (Tp.), k. in a., 13/8/18.
3 Allaway, Trevor Rhys, Capt., d. of w., 29/6/16 (att. Welsh R.).
9 Allen, Lionel Raymund Whateley, Lt., k. in a., 27/3/18 (12th Div. Bn., M.G.C.).
2 Arnold, Hedley Graham, 2/Lt., k. in a., 11/4/18.
8 Kane, Augustine George, 2/Lt., Msg., Bld. Kld., 24/6/18 (and R.A.F.).
4 Austin, Thomas Carnelly MacDonald, Capt. (Tp.), k. in a., 9/4/16.
2 Beardshaw, Reginald Dudley, 2/Lt. (Tp.), d. of w., 21/10/16.
Bedbrook, Ernest Arthur St. George, T/2/Lt. (Act. Major), died, 1/5/18.
Behrens, Robert Philip, Lt., d. of w., 26/4/15.
4 Bell, Aveling Francis, 2/Lt. (Tp.), k. in a., 12/8/15.
5 Bence-Trower, Edward, M.C., Major, k. in a., 30/5/18.
1 Bennett, Herbert Sydney, Lt. (Tp.), d. of w., 18/10/18 (att. 9th Bn.).
Bill, John Francis, Capt., d. of w., 29/3/15.
4 Birch, Frederick William, Major, k. in a., 17/4/16.
Blackall-Simonds, George Prescott, Lt., k. in a., 26/9/14.
4 Blaxland, John Bruce, Capt., k. in a., 24/1/17.
2 Bowyer, George Henry, T/2/Lt., k. in a., 1/7/16.
3 Bradly, John Frank, Lt., d. of w., 2/7/15.
9 Bricknell, Ernest Thomas Samuel, 2/Lt. (Tp.), d. of w., 20/10/16 (att. 2nd.).
9 Budd, Wrinch Joseph Charles, Lt., k. in a., 28/6/15.
11 Bullock, Gervas Frederick, 2/Lt., k. in a., 31/7/17.
Bunce, George, 2/Lt., k. in a., 12/5/15.
3 Burmester, Charles Mansel, Capt. (Tp.), d. of w., 8/10/18.
3 Burrell, Percy Edmund, 2/Lt., k. in a., 21/8/15 (att. 2nd Bn.).
3 Byrne, Edward James Widdrington, Capt., k. in a., 29/4/16 (att. 2nd. Bn.).
3 Cass, Hugh Launcelot, 2/Lt., k. in a., —/6/15.
3 Chamberlain, John, M.C., Capt., k. in a., 13/5/17 (att. 1st Welsh Rgt.).
10 Charlton, George Fenwick Hedley, Capt., k. in a., 6/10/16.
2 Clarke, Horace Yelverton Chatfield, 2/Lt., k. in a., 23/4/17.
Coker, John Cadwallader, Lt., d. of w., 26/9/14.
1 Cole, Richard Harry, 2/Lt., k. in a., 25/7/16.
4 Cooper, Leonard Gosse, 2/Lt. (Tp.), k. in a., 9/8/15.
4 Cracroft-Wilson, Clive Winthorpe, Lt. (Tp.), died, 12/11/18.
Crawford, Gerald Shakespear, Major, d. of w., 10/8/17.
11 Cullimore, Smart, T/Capt., k. in a., 20/2/16.
Curgenven, William Charles, Capt., k. in a., 21/10/14.
10 Darby, Ernest, 2/Lt., died, 4/6/15.
11 Davies, Bengiman Evan Stedman, T/Capt., k. in a., 31/7/17.
3 Davies, Benjamen Jones, Capt., k. in a., 19/5/17.
4 Davies, Glyn Lloyd, T/2/Lt., k. in a., 15/2/17.
3 Davies, Harry Harding, 2/Lt., k. in a., 10/11/17.
1 David, Arthur Walter, 2/Lt., k. in a., 14/9/18.
David, Frederick John Louis, 2/Lt. (Tp.), d. of w., 18/9/18 (att. 15th Bn. Welsh Rgt.).
7 Davies, Charles Albert, 2/Lt., k. in a., 22/9/18.
2 Davies, George Price, 2/Lt. (Tp.), k. in a., 29/9/18.
2 Davies, William, Capt., k. in a., 11/4/18.
6 Davies, William Thomas, Lt., d. of w., 13/4/18.
Davis, James Waldon Fortune McNaught, Lt., k. in a., 17/1/15.
6 Deane, Lancelot Colin William, D.S.O., M.C., T/Major (A/Lt.-Col.), k. in a., 29/5/18.
3 De Freyne, Arthur Reginald French, Lord, Capt., k. in a., 9/5/15 (att. 1st Bn.).
7 Dick, Watson Tullock, M.C., Capt. & Adjt., k. in a., 18/9/18.
2 Dickinson, Digby Cecil Cales, 2/Lt., k. in a., 18/8/18.
2 Dickinson, Francis John Twysden, Lt. (T/Capt.), k. in a., 17/9/18.
11 Dixon, Leonard Frederick, 2/Lt. (Tp.), k. in a., 21/5/18 (att. 2nd Bn.).
2 Earland, Reginald John, T/2/Lt., d. of w., 30/1/17.
12 Edwards, Eric, 2/Lt. (T/Lt.), k. in a., 22/11/17.

2 Edwards, Hywell, 2/Lt., d. of w., 22/11/17.
Elgee, Hugh Francis, Capt., k. in a., 6/7/15 (att. Egypt. Army).
10 Evans, Arthur John, T/Lt. (A/Capt.), k. in a., 2/7/18.
8 Evans, Frew Ferguson, T/2/Lt., k. in a., 13/2/17 (att. 4th Bn.).
2 Evans, Humphrey Pennefather, Lt. (Tp.), k. in a., 1/7/16.
1 Evans, Norman, 2/Lt., k. in a., 25/7/16.
3 Evans, Neville Vernon, 2/Lt., k. in a., 16/8/17.
9 Evans, Raymond, T/2/Lt., k. in a., 12/1/17 (att. 4th Bn.).
9 Evans, Roy Galloway, Lt. (Tp.), k. in a., 26/8/18 (att. 2nd).
13 Everton, Maryon Jeffreys, T/2/Lt., k in a., 9/7/16 (att. 10th Bn.).
4 Fairweather, Joseph, Capt. (T/Major), k. in a., 15/1/17.
Farrier, Archibald, 2/Lt., d. of w., 29/12/14.
4 Farrow, Jack, T/Capt., k. in a., 9/4/16.
13 Field, John Alan Francis, T/Lt.-Col., died, 23/4/18.
11 Fletcher, Arthur Stanley, 2/Lt. (Tp.), k. in a., 11/7/16.
1 Forster-Morris, Herbert Gloyne Forster, 2/Lt., d. of w., 10/10/15.
2 French, The Hon. Ernest Aloysius, Lt., d. of w., 16/8/17.
3 French, Hon. George Philip, Lt., k. in a., 9/5/15 (att. 1st Bn.).
Garnett-Botfield, Alfred Clulow Fitzgerald, Lt., k. in a., 9/5/15.
Garnett, Harold Gwyer, Capt. (A/Major), k. in a., 3/12/17.
Garnons-Williams, A. A. C., M.C., Capt., died, 14/5/18 (and R.A.F.).
4 Gillespie, Franklin Macaulay, Lt.-Col. (Tp. Major), k. in a., 9/8/15.
7 Gotelee, Geoffrey Harris, T/Lt. (A/Capt.), k. in a., 18/9/18.
Gould, Ralph Bohn, T/2/Lt., d. of w., 20/12/16.
Graham, Eric Montrose, Lt., d. of w., 2/4/15.
12 Green, Harold Syddal, 2/Lt., d. of w., 1/5/17.
11 Griffiths, Edwin Arthur, T/Lt., k. in a., 27/2/18 (att. 115th T.M.B.).
7 Griffiths, Nicholas, T/2/Lt., k. in a., 10-11/7/16.
5 Hall, Clarence Espent Lyon, T/Lt., k. in a., 7/7/16.
3 Hall, John Edward Kenyon, 2/Lt., d. of w., 22/9/15 (att. 2nd Bn.).
11 Hamer, Thomas Pryce, T/Lt., k. in a., 7/7/16.
3 Harford, John Henry, Lt., k. in a., 25/10/16.
3 Harmood-Banner, Walcot, T/Capt., k. in a., 30/8/15 (att. 1st Bn.).
3 Harries, John Elvet, 2/Lt., k. in a., 23/4/17.
8 Haydon, Geoffrey Miles, T/Lt. (A/Capt.), k. in a., 16/8/17.
Heal, Charles Henry, 2/Lt., d. of w., 9/5/15.
4 Hemingway, Stewart, T/Lt., d. of w., 6/4/16.
8 Heslop, W., Lt., died, 5/4/18.
4 Hillman-Miller, James, T/Lt., d. of w., 10/8/15.
6 Hillier, Sidney Napier, T/2/Lt., k. in a., 25/3/18.
5 Holden, Norman, 2/Lt. (Tp.), d. of w., 29/10/18.
Homfray, John Richard, Lt., k. in a., 11/11/14.
12 Hooper, Ernest Jesse Joseph, Lt. (Tp.), d. of w., 24/11/17.
2 Hopkins, Daniel Idwal, 2/Lt., k. in a., 23/4/17.
10 Hornsby, John Philip Skipworth, T/Capt., k. in a., 2/9/18.
4 Huggett, William Wyndham, T/2/Lt., d. of w., 24/4/16 (att. 10th Bn.).
2 Hughes, Alexander Arbuthnot, Capt., k. in a., 1/7/16.
10 Hughes, William Price, 2/Lt. (Tp.), k. in a., 24/8/18.
3 Inglis, Rupert Charles, Lt., d. of w., 29/6/15.
3 James, Frank, Lt., k. in a., 1/11/18 (att. 1st Bn.).
3 James, Gwilym Christopher Bowring, Lt., d. of w., 23/11/17 (att. 2nd Bn.).
6 Jenkins, Aneurin, 2/Lt., k. in a., 13/4/18.
11 Jenkins, Cyril Frank Bingham, T/Capt., d. of w., 13/10/17.
12 Jenkins, John Ernest, T/Capt., d. of w., 25/11/17.
Jenkins, Richard Borlase, 2/Lt., d. of w., 17/1/16 (att. R.F.C.).
Jewell, William John, 2/Lt. (Tp.), k. in a., 1/9/18 (att. 10th Bn.).
3 John, Iorwerth Glyndwr, 2/Lt., k. in a., 24/2/16 (att. 1st).
Johnson, Mervyn-Taylor, Lt., d. of w., 17/10/14.
3 Jones, Barham Ivor Lewis, 2/Lt., k. in a., 22/6/15.
3 Jones, David, 2/Lt. (Tp.), k. in a., 24/7/18 (att. 1st K.S.L.I.).
10 Jones, David, 2/Lt., k. in a., 8/10/18.
3 Jones, Emyr Griffiths, M.M., 2/Lt., d. of w., 18/9/18 (att. 7th Bn.).
10 Jones, William Orlando, Major, k. in a., 26/8/17.
Jones, Geoffrey Brian, 2/Lt. (Tp.), k. in a., 18/9/18 (att. 13th Bn. Welsh R.).
3 Jones, Herbert Thomas, 2/Lt., k. in a., 4/11/18 (att. 10th Bn.).
5 Jones, Ivor Dryhurst, T/Lt., k. in a., 10/4/18.
10 Jones, James Arthur, Capt. (Tp.), k. in a., 8/10/18.
6 Jones, Rhys Harris, T/Lt., k. in a., 8/10/18.
3 Jones, Robert Carl Molsch, 2/Lt., d. of w., 13/11/16 (att. 5th Bn.).
Jones, Tom Wason, 2/Lt. (Tp.), k. in a., 8/10/18 (att. 15th Bn. Welsh Rgt.).
9 Jordon, John, Lt., d. of w., 19/6/15 (att. 2nd Bn.).
3 Joyce, Frederick George, Lt., k. in a., 29/9/17 (att. 2nd Bn.).
8 Kane, Augustine George, 2/Lt., k. in a., 24/6/18 (att. R.A.F.).
8 Kane, James Gabriel, 2/Lt. (Tp.), k. in a., 22/10/18 (att. 10th Bn.).
9 Karran, John Bowler, T/2/Lt., k. in a., 1/7/16 (att. 2nd Bn.).
3 Kent, Harold, 2/Lt., k. in a., 4/8/17 (att. 8th Bn.).
3 Kent, Lionel Victor, 2/Lt. (T/Lt.), d. of w., 31/7/17.
6 Kerley, Bertram Frederick, 2/Lt., k. in a., 10/9/17.
1 Keyzor, Herbert Louis Abraham, 2/Lt. (Tp.), k. in a., 9/3/18 (att. 25th R.W. Fus.).
1 King, Robert, 2/Lt. (Tp.), k. in a., 29/9/18.
9 Kirk, Arthur, T/2/Lt., d. of w., 12/8/16 (att. 4 R. Scots Fus.).
6 Kitchen, Fred Tudor, 2/Lt., k. in a., 28/5/18.
2 Lake, John Stephen Raymond, Capt., k. in a., 16/6/16 (att. 3rd Bn.).
3 Langlands, Alan, 2/Lt., k. in a., 9/5/15 (att. 1st Bn.).
Lawrence, William Lyttleton, D.S.O., Major, k. in a., 31/10/14.
2 Lee, John William, 2/Lt., killed, 31/3/18 (att. R.F.C.).
5 Le Thicke, Gerald Mann, 2/Lt., died, 23/7/15.
3 Lewis, Arthur Glanmor, 2/Lt., k. in a., 11-13/10/15 (att. 1st Mon. R.).
11 Lewis, Charles Vernon, T/Lt., died, 18/8/15 (att. 3rd Dor. R.).
11 Lewis, Lawrence Reddrop, T/Capt., k. in a., 11/7/16.
5 Lewis, Trevor Edward, T/Capt., killed, 28/8/15.
5 Livesay, George Augustus Bligh, Lt., k. in a., 28-29/5/16.
2 Llewellin, William Mervyn Johnes, 2/Lt., k. in a., 17/8/18.
8 Llewellyn, Harold Alfred, T/Lt., killed, 14/6/16.
1 Lloyd, Ewan Christian, 2/Lt., d. of w., 5/10/18.
11 Lloyd, Llewellyn, T/2/Lt., d. of w., 1/8/17.
1 Loch, Alex. Arthur Francis, Capt., k. in a., 22/7/16.
3 Lowe, Arthur Denis Worsley, M.C., 2/Lt., k. in a., 4/10/17.
10 Loxton, Lionel D'Estelle, 2/Lt. (Tp.), k. in a., 29/8/18.
4 Lucas, Clifton Malet, T/2/Lt., k. in a., 10/7/16 (att. 15th Welsh R.).
2 Lucas, Ernest, Lt., k. in a., 18/9/18 (att. 7th Bn.).
McCowan, James, 2/Lt. (Tp.), k. in a., 16/6/18.
MacGregor, Cortland Richard, Lt., k. in a., 5/5/15.
Malins, Edward Francis, T/2/Lt., d. of w., 12/4/18.
Margesson, Edward Cuminghame, Major, k. in a., 25/4/15.
1 Martin, Harry Forster, 2/Lt., k. in a., 29/9/18.
1 Matthews, William Frederick, Capt., k. in a., 18/8/18 (att. 1st E. Lan. R.).
3 Maxwell, Ian Bouverie, Capt., k. in a., 31/1/14 (att. 1st Bn.).
1 Maxwell, Walter, T/2/Lt., died, 11/2/18.
1 Mayne, Victor Charles Moore, Lt., k. in a., 19/2/16.
11 Miller-Hallet, Stewart Alexander, T/2/Lt., k. in a., 11/7/16.
8 Montague, Reginald Marcus, 2/Lt., k. in a., 8/5/17.
5 Moore, Alexander Holland, T/Lt., k. in a., 26/3/18.
10 Morgan, Alfred, M.C., T/2/Lt., d. of w., 28/4/18.
12 Morgan, Frederick Ernest, M.C., T/2/Lt., k. in a., 23/11/17.
11 Morgan, I. A., T/Capt., k. in a., 17/4/18.
4 Morgan, Matthew, Lt., died, 8/11/18 (att. 4th Mon. Regt.).
3 Morgan, Ronald Charles Wybrow, 2/Lt., T/Lt., d. of w., 27/7/17 (and R.F.C.).
12 Morgan, William Hugh, 2/Lt., k. in a., 11/4/18 (att. Welsh Regt.).
9 Morgan, William Rich, T/2/Lt., k. in a., 2/4/16 (att. 1st).
4 Morgan-Owen, John Guith, T/2/Lt., k. in a., 9/4/16.
Morris, Edward Alan, 2/Lt., d. of w., 1/12/17 (att. 25th R.W. Fus.).
12 Morris, Oscar David, T/Capt., k. in a., 21/4/17.
2 Morris, William Henry, T/2/Lt., k. in a., 3/2/18.
12 Moss, George Percival, T/2/Lt, d. of w., 22/12/17.
2 Murray, John Claude, 2/Lt., k. in a., 9/7/16.
4 Napier, Sir William Lennox (Bart.), T/Major, k. in a., 13/8/15.
2 Nethercleft, Hugh Kirk, T/2/Lt., d. of w., 25/12/17.
Nevile, Hugh George, Lt., k. in a., 21/8/15.
12 Newman, Alfred, Lt. (Tp.), d. of w., 1/7/16.
Nightingale, William Bryant, T/2/Lt., d. of w., 27/4/17.
3 Nisbet, Douglas Guille, Lt., k. in a., 10/6/16 (att. 5th).
12 Osborn, Arthur Guy, Capt., k. in a., 6/5/17.
11 Owen, Griffith Christmas, T/2/Lt., k. in a., 31/7/17.
3 Owens, Charles Percy, Capt., Act., k. in a., 14/4/17 (att. 2nd).
5 Oxley, Harry Chamberlain, T/Major, d. of w., 18/4/18 (att. 17th N. Fus.).
Palmer, Roland Gaskell, Capt., k. in a., 25/4/15.
1 Parker, Leslie Rowland, 2/Lt., k. in a., 29/9/18.
9 Parry-Davies, David Christopher, 2/Lt. (Tp.), d. of w., 10/5/16 (att. 2nd Bn.).
Paterson, Charles James, Capt., d. of w., 1/11/14.
Peel, Alan Ralph, Capt., k. in a., 17/11/14.
3 Phillips, Cyril Gordon, 2/Lt., k. in a., 10/11/17 (att. 1st).
4 Phillips, Owen Sherwood, 2/Lt. (Tp.), k. in a., 21/8/15.
2 Phillips, Reginald, 2/Lt., k. in a., 23/4/17.
3 Pierson, William Henry Maxwell, M.C., Lt., A/Capt., k. in a., 21/11/17 (att. 2nd).
14 Platten, Walter Henry, T/2/Lt., k. in a., 10/9/16 (att. 10th Wel. Fus.).
Playford, Antony Boydell, 2/Lt., k. in a., 28/9/15.
3 Pollock, Martin Viner, Lt., k. in a., 9/5/15 (att. 1st Bn.).
Prance, Arthur Christopher Norman, M.C., Lt., k. in a., 29/5/18.
12 Price, Gordon William Bassett, T/Lt., k. in a., 23/11/17.
12 Pritchard, Charles Meyrick, T/Capt., d. of w., 14/8/16.
Prickard, Gerald Thornton, 2/Lt., k. in a., 4/6/15.
Pryce-Jenkin, Richard Douglas, 2/Lt., k. in a., 31/12/14.
3 Pugh, Henry Loyn, 2/Lt., d. of w., 11/9/16.
12 Reed, Charles Napier, T/Lt., k. in a., 24/11/17.
12 Rees, Henry Charles, T/Major, k. in a., 5/8/16.
Rees, John Oswald, 2/Lt. (Tp.), d. of w., 8/11/17 (att. 24th Welsh R.).
3 Reid, John Shute, 2/Lt., d. of w., 17/8/17 (87 T.M.B.).
Renwick, H. A., Lt., killed, 19/8/18 (and R.A.F.).
8 Rice, Fred, T/2/Lt., k. in a., 1/7/16.
6 Richards, John Hywell, M.C., T/Lt., d. of w., 19/4/18.
10 Roberts, David Charles, T/2/Lt., k. in a., 19/7/16.
7 Roberts, William, 2/Lt., k. in a., 22/9/18.
9 Robertson, George Arthur Norris, T/Capt., k. in a., 16/8/17.
7 Robinson, Claude Gladstone, 2/Lt. (Tp.), k. in a., 20/10/15.
3 Robinson, John, 2/Lt., k. in a., 1/7/16 (att. 2nd).
Ross, Willie, Lt., A/Capt., k. in a., 16/8/17.
3 Rowlands, Franklyn Theodore Rowland, 2/Lt., k. in a., 21/11/17 (att. 2nd Bn.).
7 Royle, John Bedward, Major (Tp.), k. in a., 15/1/17.
5 Rumbelow, Albert, 2/Lt., k. in a., 16/4/18.
2 Rundle, Cubitt Noel, 2/Lt., k. in a., 19/5/15.
11 Salathiel, Ewart Gladstone, T/2/Lt., d. of w., 17/7/16.
3 Sandys-Thomas, Walter Jones, 2/Lt., k. in a., 4/2/17.
1 Saunders, Louis Desormeaux, T/2/Lt., k. in a., 26/9/15.

Scott, William, T/2/Lt., d. of w., 8/10/18 (att. 13th Wel. Regt.).
10 Seager, William Henry, T/2/Lt., k. in a., 7/2/16.
12 Sharpe, Stanley Arthur, T/Lt., A/Capt., k. in a., 23/11/17.
2 Sherer, Stephen Frank, T/2/Lt., k. in a., 29/9/18.
10 Silby, Thomas Stanley, M.C., T/Lt., k. in a., 12/9/18.
Silk, Norman Galbraith, Lt., k. in a., 9/6/15.
Sills, Charles Caldwell, 2/Lt., k. in a., 26/9/14.
Simpson, George, M.C., T/2/Lt., k. in a., 12/9/18 (att. 10th).
Skinner, Hilary Francis Cleveland, 2/Lt., k. in a., 25/7/16.
4 Smith, Roger, 2/Lt. (Tp.), k. in a., 25/1/17.
3 Sparrow, George Lewis, Lt., d. of w., 23/12/15 (att. K.O.S.B.).
3 Spartali, Michael, 2/Lt., k. in a., 15/6/15.
8 Spence, Geoffrey Shalders, T/2/Lt., died, 15/4/17.
Stanborough, Walter Thomas, 2/Lt., d. of w., 13/5/15.
9 Stephens, Godfrey Gwilyn Brychan, T/2/Lt., k. in a., 7/7/16.
1 Taylor, Edward Roy, M.C., T/Capt., k. in a., 23/10/18.
11 Thomas, Cyril Raymond, T/2/Lt., k. in a., 18/8/18 (att. 2nd.).
2 Thomas, Evan David, T/2/Lt., d. of w., 20/4/18.
3 Thomas, Reginald Ivor Victor Clifford, 2/Lt., k. in a., 24/11/17.
11 Thomas, Reginald Percy, T/Lt., k. in a., 24/8/18 (att. 10th).
Towler, F. S., 2/Lt., died, 5/10/18 (and R.A.F.).
Travers, Hamilton Henry, Lt., d. of w., 28/3/15.
3 Turner, Noel Price James, Lt., d. of w., 10/5/15 (att. 1st).
3 Turner, Percy Herbert, 2/Lt., k. in a., 6/7/15 (att. 2nd Bn.).
3 Walshe, Francis Weldon, M.C., T/Capt., k. in a., 25/8/16 (att. 1st Bn.).
1 Ward, Thomas Pryce, 2/Lt., d. of w., 10/10/18 (att. 1/1st Hereford Rgt.).
1 Ward-Jones, Frederick Vivian, M.C., 2/Lt., k. in a., 17/7/16 (att. 9th).
1 Watkins, David John George, 2/Lt., k. in a., 21/4/18.
Watkins, Horace Holmes, 2/Lt., k. in a., 21/10/14.
2 Weeks, Herbert Ward Meredith, T/Lt., d. of w., 23/11/17.
Welby, Glynne Everard Earle, Major, k. in a., 27/9/14.
2 Wells, Thomas William Maurice, 2/Lt., k. in a., 1/7/16.
Wernet, William Edward, A/Capt., killed, 30/7/18 (att. T.M.B.).
7 Whitehorn, William Joseph, Lt., k. in a., 18/9/18.
2 Wileman, Gerald Watkins Brett, 2/Lt. (A/Capt.), k. in a., 8/9/16.
10 Wilkinson, Sidney John, D.S.O., T/Lt.-Col., k. in a., 7/7/16.
7 Williams, Charles Ellicombe, Lt. (T/Capt.), d. of w., 27/5/17.
1 Williams, David Aubrey, T/2/Lt., k. in a., 25/7/16.
2 Williams, Edward Herbert, T/2/Lt., k. in a., 31/8/16.
3 Williams, Leonard, Lt., d. of w., 11/9/15 (att. 1st).
7 Williams, Leonard Vincent, T/Capt., k. in a., 26/5/17.
Williams, Walter Frank, 2/Lt., k. in a., 12/9/18 (att. 10th).
3 Wilton, Charles Innes, 2/Lt., k. in a., 21/10/16 (att. 2nd Bn.).
7 Wingard, Hume Saunders, T/2/Lt., d. of w., 20/9/16 (att. 12th Bn.).
8 Wood, Charles Harold, 2/Lt., d. of w., 25/8/16 (att. 8th Bn., K.R.R.C.).
3 Woodward, Robert, Capt., k. in a., 9/5/15 (att. 1st Bn.).
3 Woolley, William Lawton, 2/Lt., d. of w., 18/9/18 (att. 7th).
Yeatman, Marwood Edwards, Capt., died, 15/9/14.
12 Yorath, Glynne Lougher, T/Lt., k. in a., 23/11/17.
1 Young, Arthur John, 2/Lt., d. of w., 10/3/18 (att. 7th Bn.).
3 Zacharias, Francis Herbert, 2/Lt., k. in a., 25/9/16.

The King's Own Scottish Borderers.

6 Adamson, George Addis, 2/Lt. (Tp.), k. in a., 12/10/17.
2 Addis, Ronald Forrester, Lt. (A/Capt.), k. in a., 3/9/16 (att. Mach. Gun Corps).
7 Allan, John Love Strathearn, 2/Lt. (Tp.), k. in a., 25/9/15.
3 Allan, William Lewis Campbell, Hon. Major, k. in a., 12/10/14.
1 Aitchison, Andrew Leslie, 2/Lt., d. of w., 3/11/16.
6 Ainslie, George, M.C., Capt. (Tp.), d. of w., 21/8/18.
Ainslie, John Archibald, Capt., k. in a., 19/5/17.
2 Allan, Robert Gregor, 2/Lt., k. in a., 9/4/17.
7/8 Allan, William Halliday, 2/Lt. (Tp.), k. in a., 31/7/17.
3 Amess, Frederick Thomas, 2/Lt., d. of w., 22/7/17.
Amos, Gilbert Stratton, 2/Lt., k. in a., 4/9/14.
2 Anderson, James, 2/Lt. (Tp.) (A/Capt.), k. in a., 25/9/16.
6 Anderson, Matthew, 2/Lt. (Tp.), k. in a., 11/6/17.
Antrobus, Charles Alexander, Capt., k. in a., 25/4/15.
6 Archer, Thomas, Lt., k. in a., 25/4/18.
8 Ardill, Ivan Roy, 2/Lt., k. in a., 25/9/15.
3 Bagshawe, Leonard Vale, Capt., k. in a., 16/6/15 (att. 1/North'd. Fus.).
Bark, N., Lt., k. in a., 1/10/18 (and R.A.F.).
3 Barrie, Walter, 2/Lt., k. in a., 7/6/17 (att. 6/Border R.).
3 Bartlett, Cedric Drummond, 2/Lt., died, 1/12/15.
Bayley, George Baird, 2/Lt., k. in a., 26/10/14.
Becher, Maurice Andrew Noel, Capt., k. in a., 26/4/15.
1 Bent, Percy Temple, 2/Lt., k. in a., 1/7/16.
Berry, Oswald William, 2/Lt., k. in a., 8/4/17 (and R.F.C., 48 Sqd.).
6 Birrell, Andrew Smith, 2/Lt. (Tp.), k. in a., 9/4/17.
7/8 Black, James, 2/Lt. (Tp.), d. of w., 19/8/17.
3 Bland, Charles Ernest William, D.S.O., Capt., k. in a., 23/4/15 (att. 2/Bn.).
1/2 Bonnin, Ronald Homfray, Lt., k. in a., 24/8/18.
9 Bradshaw, Percival Challon, 2/Lt. (Tp.), k. in a., 1/5/16 (att. 6/Bn.).
1 Brameld, John Neville, 2/Lt. (Tp.), d. of w., 19/9/15.
8 Brigstocke, Hugh Fraser, Lt. (Tp.) (A/Capt.), k. in a., 9/1/17.
7 Brown, Alexander Russell, Capt. (Tp.), k. in a., 18/8/16.
6 Brown, Charles William, 2/Lt. (Tp.), d. of w., 23/5/17.
6 Brown, David Hepburn, Capt. (Tp.), k. in a., 25/9/15.
3 Brown, James Macpherson Gordon, Lt., k. in a., 6/5/15 (att. 2/Bn.).
3 Brown, Thomas Elliot Thorburn, Lt., d. of w., 20/9/18.
6 Bryce-Smith, Norgrave Ingram, Lt. (Tp.), k. in a., 25/4/18.
3 Caird, John Roberts, Capt., k. in a., 23/4/15 (att. 2/Bn.).
1/2 Caldwell, Thomas, M.M., 2/Lt. (Tp.), k. in a., 3/10/18 (att. 1/4 Bn.).
1 Campbell, Aubone Charles, D.S.O., Capt. (T/Major), d. of w., 3/4/18 (att. 11/R. Scots).
Campbell, Robert Charles Cowburn, Capt., d. of w., 19/5/15.
6 Canning, Edward, 2/Lt., k. in a., 6/7/16.
6 Carmichael, Andrew, 2/Lt. (Tp.), k. in a., 12/10/17.
1 Carson, Frederick Glover, 2/Lt., k. in a., 30/11/17.
7/8 Causley, Frederick George, 2/Lt. (A/Capt.), k. in a., 31/7/17.
Cheatle, Walter John North, Lt., k. in a., 25/4/15.
8 Clark, Richard, 2/Lt. (Tp.), k. in a., 15/5/15 (att. 7/Bn.).
6 Cobb, Frederick Charles, Capt. (Tp.), k. in a., 25/9/15.
1 Collier, Harry Ronald, M.C., Lt. (A/Capt.), k. in a., 17/4/18.
1/2 Common, Henry Alder, 2/Lt., d. of w., 4/10/18 (att. 1/4 Bn.).
2 Cook, Robert Alexander, 2/Lt. (Tp.), k. in a., 30/6/16.
Cooper, Alexander Stewart, Capt., d. of w., 25/4/15.
1 Cooper, Howard Frank Byrne, 2/Lt., k. in a., 1/7/16.
2 Cooper, William Ferguson, 2/Lt., d. of w., 28/6/18.
7 Cowley, Victor Travers, Lt. (Tp.), k. in a., 23/7/18.
3 Cox, George Henry, Lt., k. in a., 30/10/14 (att. 2/Bn.).
3 Crichton-Browne, Cecil Harold Verdin, M.C., Capt. (A/Major), died, 13/12/18.
Crofts, Edmund Cyril Iveson, 2/Lt., d. of w., 28/4/18 (P. of W.).
1 Cruickshank, Harold Thomas, Capt. k. in a., 25/9/15.
7/8 Deans, Harold Mackenzie, Capt., k. in a., 17/9/18.
Deighton, Frederick Hamilton, Lt., d. of w., 18/6/15.
3 Dempster, David Burns, M.C., Lt. (A/Capt.), k. in a., 26/10/17 (att. 2/Border Rgt.).
7/8 Dennis, Michael Frederick Beauchamp, D.S.O., Major (T/Lt.-Col.), k. in a., 19/5/18.
Dering, Rupert Cholmeley Yea, Capt., d. of w., 19/4/15.
Diamond, Julius, M.C., Lt., k. in a., 8/10/17 (and R.F.C., 7th Sqdn.).
1 Doughty, Gordon Gray, 2/Lt. (Tp.), k. in a., 11/4/18.
7/8 Douglas, Ronald Ross, 2/Lt. (Tp.), d. of w., 30/8/17.
3 Douglas, William Campbell, 2/Lt., d. of w., 17/8/17 (att. 1/Bn.).
8 Drummond, Patrick Campbell, 2/Lt. (Tp.), k. in a., 25/9/15.
1 Dryburgh, Joseph, 2/Lt. (Tp.), d. of w., 26/6/18 (att. 7/8 Bn.).
7 Duirs, Mearns William, 2/Lt. (Tp.), k. in a., 25/9/15.
1/2 Duncan, Daniel McFie, 2/Lt. (Tp.), k. in a., 2/10/18.
2 Dunn, James Shannon, 2/Lt. (Tp.), k. in a., 4/10/17.
6 Dunn, William John, 2/Lt. (Tp.), k. in a., 17/7/16.
6 Durward, Andrew, M.C., Lt. (T/Capt.), k. in a., 16/10/18.
3 Edgell, Richard Fayrer Arnold, Lt., k. in a., 5/5/15 (att. 2/Bn.).
6 Ellicott, Frederick Arthur John, 2/Lt., k. in a., 8/7/16.
1 Farish, Samuel, Lt. (Tp.), k. in a., 24/4/17.
3 Ferguson, Duncan MacIntyre Grant, Lt., d. of w., 14/5/15 (att. 2/Bn.).
6 Findlay, John, 2/Lt. (A/Capt.), k. in a., 25/4/18.
7 Forbes, Gordon Stewart Drummond, C.M.G., D.S.O., Major, d. of w., 21/7/15.
3 Forbes, Henry James, 2/Lt., k. in a., 18/8/18 (att. 1/Bn.).
1 Ford, James Ernest, T/2/Lt., A/Capt., k. in a., 4/10/17.
9 Forret, David James, 2/Lt. (Tp.), d. of w., 28/12/15 (att. 1/Bn.).
8 Forster, Hugh Murray, Capt. (Tp.), d. of w., 28/9/15.
3 Forsyth, William James Samuel, 2/Lt., k. in a., 12/5/17.
6 Franklin, William Hyslop, Lt. (Tp.), k. in a., 25/9/15.
6 Gall, Campbell McKenzie, Lt., k. in a., 18/8/18.
2 Garvie, James Alexander, M.C., Lt., k. in a., 21/8/18.
Gibson, Robert, Lt., k. in a., 5/5/15.
Gillespie Thomas Cunningham, 2/Lt., k. in a., 18/10/14.
7 Gilmour, Archibald Keltie, Capt. (Tp.), k. in a., 16/8/16.
1 Glennie, John Herbert, 2/Lt., k. in a., 1/7/16.
7 Glenny, Thomas Alexander, Major, k. in a., 25/9/15.
Glover, Alexander Milligan Thomson, Lt., k. in a., 17/8/17 (and R.F.C., 70 Sqd.).
3 Gordon, Henry, Lt., d. of w., 19/12/15 (att. 2/Bn.).
9 Gow, James Lightfoot, 2/Lt. (Tp.), k. in a., 1/7/16 (att. 1/Bn.).
1 Gracie, John James, M.C., Lt., k. in a., 17/9/18 (att. 7/8 Bn.).
6 Graham, John Hamilton Thom, Lt. (Tp.), k. in a., 6/7/16.
9 Graham-Clarke, John Altham Stobart, 2/Lt., k. in a., 1/7/16 (att. 6/Border R.).
1 Grant, Douglas, Lt., k. in a., 30/11/17.
6 Greener, Noel Hindmarsh, Lt. (Tp.), k. in a., 25/9/15.
Grogan, James Colin, Lt., k. in a., 4/6/15.
7 Haddon, Walter, 2/Lt. (Tp.), d. of w., 27/9/15.
3 Haining, William John, 2/Lt., k. in a., 28/1/17 (att. 1/Bn.).
7 Hamilton, Archibald Charteris, Capt., k. in a., 28/6/15.
7 Hamilton, Henry McCartney, 2/Lt. (Tp.), k. in a., 14/5/16.
Hamilton-Dalrymple, John Raphael, Lt., d. of w., 23/4/15.
2 Hamilton-Johnston, Ewen Colquhoun Richardson, Lt., k. in a., 1/9/18 (att. 1/4 Bn.).
Hammond, Gilbert Philip, 2/Lt., k. in a., 10/9/14.
Harle, Richard John Patterson, M.C., 2/Lt. (T/Lt.), died, 26/4/17 (att. 2/Suth. Hrs.).
Hartley, John Bernard, Capt., k. in a., 4/6/15.
1 Hay, Andrew Peter, 2/Lt. (Tp.), k. in a., 29/4/16.
Henderson, Neil Emslie Nelson, 2/Lt., k. in a., 11/4/18.
8 Herbertson, William Gray, 2/Lt. (Tp.), k. in a., 25/9/15.
2 Heygate, Reginald, 2/Lt., k. in a., 11/6/18.
6 Hillier, Maurice, 2/Lt., k. in a., 9/4/17.
6 Hodges, John Percy, 2/Lt., k. in a., 25/4/18.
Holman, Cecil Graham, 2/Lt., d. of w., 5/9/17 (and R.F.C., 8 Sqd.).

Holme, Ronald Henry Paull, Lt., d. of w., 9/11/14.
7 Hopkins, Gerald Broughton, Lt. (Tp.), k. in a., 17/9/18.
7 Horne, Cyril Henry Morton, Capt. (Tp.), k. in a., 27/1/16.
6 Hosley, William James Seymour, Major, k. in a., 25/9/15.
7 Howard, William Aloysius, 2/Lt. (Tp.), k. in a., 24/4/17.
1 Hunter, Hugh Swinterton Forsyth, 2/Lt. (Tp.), k. in a., 29/4/16.
7 Hutt, Francis Rodes, Capt. (Tp.), k. in a., 25/9/15.
3 Hutton-Balfour, Archibald Gibson, 2/Lt. (Tp.), d. of w., 22/3/18 (att. 6/Bn.).
6 Innes-Brown, Ambrose Robin, C.M.G., D.S.O., T/Major, A/Lt.-Col., k. in a., 10/4/18.
6 Jackson, George Conway, Lt. (Tp.), k. in a., 25/9/15.
6 Janes, Willis, 2/Lt. (Tp.), d. of w., 22/1/17.
Jardine, William, Sir, Bart., Major (Tp.), died, 13/12/15.
Jarvie, John, T/2/Lt., d. of w., 17/4/17.
7 Jarvis, James Warden, Lt. (Tp.), d. of w., 26/9/15.
3 Johnstone, George Smith, Lt., k. in a., 26/8/18 (att. 2/Bn.).
3 King, Ebenezer, M.C., 2/Lt., killed, 17/3/17 (att. R.F.C.).
Kirkpatrick, Hugh Cunningham Bruce, D.S.O., M.C., Capt., T/Major, k. in a., 1/10/18 (Staff, G.H.Q.).
2 Kirkwood, Robert Patrick, Lt., k. in a., 5/10/17 (att. 1/G.B. North Staffs R.).
Kirton, Ralph Imray, 2/Lt., died, 22/11/18 (and R.A.F.).
2 Knipe, Edward Arthur, 2/Lt., d. of w., 26/9/16.
Koe, Archibald Stephen, Lt.-Col., d. of w., 25/4/15.
1 Laird, Ninian Parker, 2/Lt. (Tp.), k. in a., 26/3/18 (att. 7/8 Bn.).
7 Lamont, John, 2/Lt., k. in a., 11/5/16.
7 Lang, Graeme Gordon, 2/Lt. (Tp.), k. in a., 11/4/17.
Lang, James Corbet, Capt., k. in a., 12/7/15.
3 Laurie, Wilfrid Walter, Lt. (A/Capt.), k. in a., 19/5/17 (att. 2/Bn.).
6 Laurie, James Alexander, Lt., k. in a., 3/5/17.
3 Law, Charles John, Lt., k. in a., 19/4/17.
3 Lawrie, James Hunter, 2/Lt., k. in a., 9/8/16 (att. 7/Bn.).
1/2 Lawson, James McKercher, 2/Lt. (Tp.), k. in a., 1/7/17.
7 Lees, Robert Wallace, 2/Lt. (Tp.), k. in a., 3/9/16 (att. 2/Bn.).
Leigh, Chandos, Major, died, 29/8/14.
7 Lethbridge, Patrick Lionel, T/Capt. and Adj., k. in a., 25/9/15.
1 Lewis, Alfred John, 2/Lt. (Tp.), k. in a., 1/8/18 (att. 7/8 Bn.).
Little, John Russell, 2/Lt., k. in a., 3/5/17 (att. 6/Bn.).
8 McAlpin, James Montgomerie, 2/Lt. (Tp.), k. in a., 11/4/17.
8 McClelland, Samuel George, 2/Lt., k. in a., 25/9/15.
6 MacCombie, William John, Capt. (Tp.), k. in a., 17/7/16.
6 McConnell, Reginald Bryan, 2/Lt. (Tp.), k. in a., 22/1/17.
3 McDiarmid, Kenneth, Capt., k. in a., 18/4/15 (att. 2/Bn.).
9 Macfarquhar, Murdo Mackenzie, 2/Lt. (Tp.), k. in a., 15/9/16 (att. 7/8 Bn.).
6 McGillewie, Nigel, 2/Lt. (Tp.), k. in a., 12/10/17.
Macgregor, Kenneth Cortlandt, 2/Lt., k. in a., 26/2/15.
3 Mackay, Philip Storrs, 2/Lt., k. in a., 14/4/17 (att. 1/Bn.).
9 Mackenzie, William Alexander, Lt., k. in a., 17/5/17 (att. M.G.C.).
Mackinnon, Gordon, M.C., Lt., k. in a., 8/11/17 (att. 1/5 Bn.).
1 McLaren, Donald, Lt., k. in a., 3/5/17 (att. 6/Bn.).
6 McLaren, James, 2/Lt. (Tp.), d. of w., 12/1/17.
1 Maclean, Archibald, 2/Lt. (Tp.), k. in a., 18/8/18.
3 Macleod, Donald Angus, 2/Lt., d. of w., 5/10/17.
9 Macleod, George Calder, 2/Lt. (Tp.), k. in a., 19/4/17 (att. 1/7 R.W. Fus.).
8 Macleod, James Herbert Negnoe, Lt. (Tp.), k. in a., 29/6/16.
7/8 McMillan, John Mackie, 2/Lt., k. in a., 1/8/18.
3 Macrae, Ivor Alexander, 2/Lt., d. of w., 15/10/14 (att. 2/Bn.).
9 McDonald, Alexander, 2/Lt. (Tp.), k. in a., 30/7/16 (att. 2/Bn.).
McGeoch, William, 2/Lt. (Tp.), k. in a., 13/10/16 (att. Trench Mortar Bty.).
6 McNeil, Robert, 2/Lt. (Tp.), k. in a., 6/2/16.
9 Mahood, Charles Cleland, 2/Lt. (Tp.), d. of w., 16/9/16.
Main, George Ernest, Lt., k. in a., 12/10/17 (att. 6/Bn.).
Malet, Hugh Arthur Grenville, Lt., k. in a., 18/4/15.
1 Malcolm, Archibald Hugh, 2/Lt. (Tp.), k. in a., 16/5/17.
1 Marsh, Robert Neville Caldicot, 2/Lt., k. in a., 3/7/16.
Marrow, Edward Armfield, Capt., k. in a., 25/4/15.
6 Marsters, John Victor Harold, Lt. (Tp.), k. in a., 25/9/15.
6 Martin, Ernest Ivor, 2/Lt. (Tp.), k. in a., 18/8/18.
6 Maxwell, Ronald Erskine Wilford, T/Major, k. in a., 25/9/15.
1 Meikle, William Reginald Dempster, 2/Lt., k. in a., 30/11/17.
3 Middlemass, Robert McGregor, 2/Lt., d. of w., 29/9/16 (att. 8/Bn.).
2 Miles, Herbert Francis, 2/Lt. (Tp.), A/Capt., k. in a., 3/9/16.
3 Mill, James Drysdale, 2/Lt., k. in a., 15/10/15 (att. 1/Bn.).
9 Millar, Robert Given, 2/Lt. (Tp.), d. of w., 16/8/16.
3 Miller, Andrew Richard Stuart, 2/Lt., d. of w., 21/4/18.
Miller, Archibald William Buchanan, Lt., died, 13/7/17 (and R.F.C.) (in Ger. hands).
Miller, Thomas Alexander Grant, Lt., k. in a., 27/4/15.
7 Miller, Thomas Murray, 2/Lt. (Tp.), k. in a., 27/1/16.
1 Milroy, Peter, 2/Lt., k. in a., 30/11/17.
6 Montgomery, Frederick, 2/Lt. (Tp.), k. in a., 19/10/16.
9 Morley-Brown, Alastair James, 2/Lt. (Tp.), k. in a., 29/4/16.
9 Muir, Christison, 2/Lt. (Tp.), d. of w., 27/10/18 (att. 1/Bn.).
1/2 Munro, James John, 2/Lt. (Tp.), k. in a., 31/10/18 (att. 1/5 Bn.).
Murray, Archibald, Capt. and Qr.-Mr., d. of w., 13/9/14.
9 Murray, Charles Robinson, 2/Lt. (Tp.), k. in a., 18/9/16 (att. 7/8 Bn.).
1 Nettleship, Mark, 2/Lt. (Tp.), k. in a., 1/9/18 (att. 1/4 Bn.).
6 Newbould, Henry James Frank, Capt. (Tp.), k. in a., 2/8/15.
7 Newton, Percy, Capt. (Tp.), k. in a., 25/9/15.
6 Nicol, Andrew, Lt. (Tp.), k. in a., 22/5/16.
Nixon, William Eric, Capt., k. in a., 7/5/17 (and R.F.C., 40 Sqd.).
3 Noel, Tom Cecil, M.C., Lt., killed, 22/8/18 (and R.A.F.).
1 Pasley, Thomas Edward Sabine, 2/Lt., k. in a., 11/4/18.
9 Paterson, Frank, 2/Lt. (Tp.), k. in a., 1/7/16.
3 Paterson, William Paterson, Capt. (Tp.), k. in a., 30/7/16 (att. 2/Bn.).
7 Penfold, Jeffery Bradley, Lt. (Tp.), d. of w., 28/1/16.
9 Petrie, Henry Lawson, 2/Lt. (Tp.), k. in a., 30/7/16 (att. 2/Bn.).
6 Philps, Andrew Christie, 2/Lt. (Tp.), k. in a., 17/7/16.
1/2 Pither, S. E., Capt., d. of w., 11/6/18 (and R.A.F.).
Pollard, Edward Branch, Lt. (Tp.), d. of w., 26/7/15 (att. R.E.).
1 Pollard, Harold Ernest, 2/Lt. (Tp.), d. of w., 4/8/16.
6 Porteous, Douglas Simpson, 2/Lt. (Tp.), k. in a., 20/10/16.
2 Price, Lenard John Joliffe, 2/Lt. (Tp.), d. of w., 15/8/16.
6 Pringle, Walter Gerald, 2/Lt. (Tp.), k. in a., 12/10/17.
3 Randall, Guy Philip, M.C., Lt. (A/Capt.), k. in a., 18/9/18.
7 Ranken, Ernest Ford, 2/Lt. (Tp.), d. of w., 25/3/16.
Redpath, James Thomas, 2/Lt., k. in a., 25/4/15.
6 Reid, Alexander William, 2/Lt. (Tp.), k. in a., 4/3/17 (att. R.F.C., 43 Sqd.).
9 Reid, Gordon, 2/Lt., k. in a., 3/5/17 (att. 6/Bn.).
9 Reid, Robert, 2/Lt. (Tp.), k. in a., 1/7/16 (att. 1/Bn.).
9 Reid, Thomas Mayne, 2/Lt., k. in a., 3/5/17 (att. 6/Bn.).
1 Roberts, Noel Humphreys, 2/Lt., k. in a., 23/4/17.
1 Robertson, Douglas Hill, 2/Lt. (Tp.), k. in a., 14/4/17.
9 Robertson, Laurence Grant, 2/Lt. (Tp.), k. in a., 30/7/16.
1 Robertson, Robert Sergius, 2/Lt., d. of w., 20/7/16 (att. 3/Bn.).
Robertson, Sydney, 2/Lt. (Tp.), k. in a., 29/7/18 (att. 1/5 Bn.).
3 Robinson, Harry Stanley Shepley, Lt., d. of w., 9/6/15 (att. 2/Bn.).
1/2 Robinson, William, 2/Lt. (Tp.), k. in a., 1/8/18 (att. 1/5 Bn.).
9 Rogers, Robert Maxtone, 2/Lt. (Tp.), k. in a., 25/9/16 (att. 2/Bn.).
8 Rolland, Frederick James Gordon, Lt. (Tp.), k. in a., 25/9/15 (att. 6/Bn.).
Rooke, Claude Eugene, 2/Lt., killed, 21/1/18 (and R.F.C.).
3 Rooke, Henry Clive, Lt., k. in a., 11/4/18 (att. 1/Bn).
9 Rooney, Bruno Martin, Lt., k. in a., 25/6/15.
9 Ross, Robert Simmie, 2/Lt. (Tp.), k. in a., 3/9/16 (att. 2/Bn.).
1 Routledge, John, 2/Lt. (Tp.), k. in a., 16/4/17.
Sanderson, Archibald James, Capt., d. of w., 2/5/15.
Sanderson, Philip Noel, Lt. (T/Capt.), d. of w., 25/4/15.
1 Saxton, Arthur Cyril, 2/Lt. (Tp.), k. in a., 30/7/16 (att. 2/Bn.).
1 Scott, Ian Archibald Sawers, 2/Lt., k. in a., 1/7/16.
7 Scott, James, Lt. (Tp.), k. in a., 25/9/15.
Scott, Norman Sawers, 2/Lt., k. in a., 23/4/15.
9 Scott, Thomas McCreary, 2/Lt. (Tp.), k. in a., 3/9/16 (att. 2/Bn.).
7 Sellar, John Mill, Lt. (Tp.), k. in a., 25/9/15.
1 Shaw, Alexander James Mackintosh, Capt. (Tp.), k. in a., 9/7/16.
7/8 Shannon, Jeremiah, 2/Lt., k. in a., 1/8/18.
1 Short, William Innes, 2/Lt., k. in a., 11/8/15.
7 Skinner, Thomas Arnold, 2/Lt. (Tp.), d. of w., 10/8/17.
6 Skinner, William, 2/Lt. (Tp.), k. in a., 25/9/15.
8 Smith, Hubert Hector, Capt., k. in a., 25/9/15.
2 Smith, William Spencer, 2/Lt., k. in a., 23/7/16.
8 Snowie, George, 2/Lt. (Tp.), k. in a., 15/9/16.
1 Solomon, Leonard, 2/Lt. (Tp.), k. in a., 23/4/17.
9 Soulsby, Henry Stanley, 2/Lt., k. in a., 6/7/16.
2 Stark, James Duncan, 2/Lt. (Tp.), d. of w., 3/9/18 (P. of W. in German hands) (att. 6/Bn.).
1 Stewart, Robert, 2/Lt. (Tp.), k. in a., 1/7/16.
6 Stocker, Edward, 2/Lt., k. in a., 29/5/15.
Stoney, George Butler, D.S.O., Major (T/Lt.-Col.), k. in a., 15/10/15.
6 Stoney, Thomas Ramsay, 2/Lt., k. in a., 10/4/18.
9 Sulley, Alan Hereford, 2/Lt., (Tp.), k. in a., 3/9/16 (att. 2 Bn.).
3 Swinley, Gordon Noel Balfour, Lt., k. in a., 22/6/15 (att. 2 Bn.).
6 Taylor, Robert Thomson, 2/Lt. (Tp.), k. in a., 22/10/17.
3 Telfer, Robert Harold Cecil, 2/Lt., k. in a., 26/9/16 (att. M.G.C.).
7 Tod, Frederick Masefield Cockburn, 2/Lt. (Tp.), k. in a., 25/9/15.
Turnbull, Hugh Vincent Corbett, Capt., k. in a., 13/11/14.
6 Tweedie, Cunningham Burnside, M.C., Capt. (Tp.), d. of w., 17/4/17.
8 Ure, James Mitchell, 2/Lt. (Tp.), d. of w., 16/8/16.
7 Verner, George de Wet, Lt.-Col., d. of w., 10/10/15 (ret. pay).
3 Wallace, Charles Arthur Phin, 2/Lt., k. in a., 22/3/18 (att. 6 Bn.).
8 Walmsley, James Blair, 2/Lt. (Tp.), k. in a., 8/8/16.
6 Watson, William Norman, Capt. (Tp.), died, 29/5/16.
1/2 Welchman, Patrick Elliot, Capt., d. of w., 28/11/18 (and R.A.F.).
3 Wedderburn-Maxwell, James, 2/Lt., k. in a., 30/9/18.
1 Wheeler, Harold Ernest, 2/Lt., k. in a., 3/9/16.
3 Wildman-Lushington, Percy John, 2/Lt., k. in a., 3/5/17 (att. 6 Bn.).
1 Willock, Neville Gore, Lt., (A/Capt.), d. of w., 22/11/17.
1 Wingate, Thomas Paterson, Capt., k. in a., 18/4/15.
Woollcombe, Charles Stephenson, 2/Lt., k. in a., 12/10/14.
6 Wright, William, Lt. (Tp.), k. in a., 7/7/16.
7/8 Wyper, James, 2/Lt., k. in a., 23/7/18.
8 Wyper, James Stewart, Lt. (Tp.), d. of w., 8/9/16.

2 Yarrow, Henry Edwin Goodwin, 2/Lt., k. in a., 30/7/16.
7 Young, Martin Cortlandt de Bude, 2/Lt. (Tp.), d. of w., 26/9/15.
Young-Herries, Alexander Dobree, Capt., k. in a., 22/7/16.

The Cameronians (Scottish Rifles).

3 Alston, John Douglas, Lt., k. in a., 10/3/15 (att. 2 Bn.).
3 Anderson, Abdy Fellowes, Capt., k. in a., 23/4/15 (att. K.O Sco. Bord.).
10 Anderson, William, Lt. (Tp.), k. in a., 25/9/15.
2 Ansell, Thomas, A/Capt., k. in a., 23/10/16.
4 Ashcroft, John Robson, M.C., Lt. (T/Capt.), k. in a., 23/3/18 (att. 9 Bn.).
10 Baillie, Alan La Touche, Capt. (Tp.), k. in a., 29/10/15.
10 Baillie, Evan Henry, Temp. Capt., k. in a., 25/9/15.
12 Bain, John Meikle, 2/Lt. (Tp.), k. in a., 14/7/16 (att. 9 Bn.).
1 Baker, John Kildour, Capt. (Tp.), k. in a., 9/10/18.
Becher, Harry Owen Dabridgecourt, Capt., k. in a., 13/3/15.
2 Bellew, Alexander, 2/Lt., k. in a., 23/10/16.
3 Bibby, Francis Stephen, 2/Lt., k. in a., 20/7/16.
2 Bibby, John Patrick, Temp. Lt., k. in a., 10/3/15.
11 Bilsland, James, 2/Lt. (Tp.), k. in a., 9/6/16 (att. 10 Bn.).
2 Bliss, Wilfrid Marryat, Lt.-Col., k. in a., 10/3/15.
Blue, Dougall, Capt., d. of w., 11/5/15 (att. 2 Bn.).
12 Boyd, Reginald Russell, 2/Lt. (Tp.), d. of w., 4/5/17.
11 Boyle, William Scott, Lt. (Tp.), k. in a., 4/1/17.
1/2 Braidwood, Robert Simpson, D.C.M., 2/Lt. (Tp.), k. in a., 31/10/18 (att. 1/8 Bn.).
8 Bramwell, Charles Guy, Capt. & Adjt., k. in a., 28/6/15.
3 Brickmann, Noel, Temp. Capt., k. in a., 29/10/16 (att. 1 Bn.).
9 Briggs, Arthur Desmond, Capt. (Tp.), k. in a., 25/9/15.
12 Brough, Alexander, 2/Lt. (Tp.), k. in a., 18/11/15 (att. 6/York & Lanc.).
9 Brown, Hugh Alexander, 2/Lt. (Tp.), k. in a., 14/7/16.
11 Brownlie, John Reid, 2/Lt. (Tp.), k. in a., 29/6/16 (att. 1 Bn.).
9 Browse, Reginald, 2/Lt. (Tp.), k. in a., 25/4/18.
11 Bruce, Robert Lloyd, Temp. Lt., k. in a., 19/11/16.
Buchan, James Wilson, Temp. 2/Lt., k. in a., 23/4/17 (att. Border Regt.).
3 Burgess, William Henry Langdon, Capt., k. in a., 20/7/16 (att. 1 Bn.).
9 Carlyon, Lionel George, Temp. 2/Lt., k. in a., 3/5/17.
12 Carnaghan, James, 2/Lt. (Tp.), k. in a., 23/10/16.
10 Carswell, John Jamieson, 2/Lt. (Tp.), k. in a., 25/9/15.
Cathro, James Grant, Temp. 2/Lt., k. in a., 24/10/18.
4 Christie, Harold Reginald Morris, 2/Lt., k. in a., 16/7/16 (att. 1/Bn.).
3 Clark, Alan Glover, 2/Lt., k. in a., 21/9/18 (att. 1 Bn.).
Clerk, Robert Vere, Capt. & Adjt., k. in a., 28/6/15.
3 Cole, Herbert William, 2/Lt., k. in a., 14/4/18.
3 Collier, Guy Cecil, Lt., k. in a., 23/7/18 (att. 10 Bn.).
4 Cox, John Lennox, Lt., k. in a., 19/9/18 (att. 11 Bn.).
4 Cox, Thomas Henry, 2/Lt., k. in a., 21/6/17.
Craig, William Tait, T/Lt. (A/Capt.), k. in a., 21/9/18.
4 Crookston, William John, 2/Lt., k. in a., 12/4/18 (att. 8/Border Regt.).
12 Cunningham, Charles Albert Glentworth, Capt., k. in a., 6/6/15
3 Cunnison, Alan Watson, 2/Lt., k. in a., 29/10/16.
1/2 Currie, Harold Maxwell, Temp. 2/Lt., k. in a., 1/8/17 (att. 10 Bn.).
4 Dale, Robert Percy, M.C., Lt. (T/Capt.), k. in a., 25/10/18 (att. 9 Bn.).
11 Dangerfield, William Cecil Hay, Temp. Lt. & Adjt., killed, 26/12/16.
2 De Blaquiere, The Hon. John, Lt., k. in a., 10/3/15.
10 Delarue, Francis, 2/Lt. (Tp.), d. of w., 23/7/18.
9 Dewar, William, Capt., k. in a., 22/3/18.
2 Dodd, Percy Reed, Capt., k. in a., 10/3/15.
11 Doull, Gilbert Laurie, Temp. 2/Lt., d. of w., 11/3/17.
9 Dow, Samuel Hugh, Temp. 2/Lt., k. in a., 30/12/16.
4 Drew, Alan Appleby, Lt., k. in a., 10/3/15.
10 Duncan, John Francis, T/Capt. (& Adjt.), k. in a., 25/9/15.
2 Dunn, Thomas Edward Doncaster, Lt., d. of w., 21/12/14.
9 Edmonds, Walter, 2/Lt. (Tp.), k. in a., 14/7/16.
2 Ellis, George Adams, Major, k. in a., 10/3/15.
1 Evans, David, M.C., Capt., k. in a., 20/7/16.
Ewing, Douglas Ramsay, Major, died, 31/5/17 (att. 66 Brig. H.Q.).
3 Fenton, Douglas Annand, Lt., k. in a., 9/9/16.
4 Ferguson, John, 2/Lt., k. in a., 23/10/16 (att. 2 Bn.).
10 Fisher, Alexander McEwan, Temp. 2/Lt., k. in a., 24/4/17.
3 Fleming, George, 2/Lt., k. in a., 29/5/18.
10 Flynn, George Axen Wallace, 2/Lt. (Tp.), k. in a., 25/9/15.
4 Forbes, Leslie Alexander, 2/Lt., k. in a., 27/5/17 (att. 1 Bn.).
9 Forsyth, Maxwell Hanton, D.S.O., M.C., Temp. Major, d. of w., 11/3/18.
1 Foster, Douglas Cameron, Capt., k. in a., 14/4/17.
2 Fraser, Malcolm Goulding, 2/Lt., k. in a., 1/7/16.
Garrety, J. F., Temp. 2/Lt., k. in a., 21/9/18 (att. 1 Bn.).
9 Gathorne-Hardy, Alfred Cecil, Capt. (Tp.), k. in a., 25/9/15.
Gilkinson, Donald Stewart, Capt., k. in a., 20/9/14.
Gilhespy, John William, Temp. 2/Lt., k. in a., 20/7/16 (att. 1 Bn.)
13 Gilmour, William, Temp. 2/Lt., k. in a., 4/12/16 (att. 6/K.O. Lancs.).
10 Glegg, Cuthbert Kemp, Temp. Capt., k. in a., 19/5/16.
4 Glen, John Todd, 2/Lt., k. in a., 27/11/15 (att. 1/R. Mun. Fusrs.).
Gordon, John Frederic Strathearn, Capt., d. of w., 19/11/14 (att. R. Scots Fusrs.).
9 Goudie, Alexander Currie, Temp. 2/Lt., k. in a., 20/9/17.
3 Gourlay, Alexander Smith Forrest, 2/Lt., k. in a., 24/3/18 (att. 2 Bn.).
Graham, Richard, 2/Lt., k. in a., 10/1/15.
2 Graham, Thomas Eric, M.C., 2/Lt., k. in a., 24/3/18.
10 Grant, John Cardross, Capt. (Tp.), k. in a., 27/1/16.
3 Gray, Magnus Nigel, Lt., d. of w., 21/6/15 (att. 1 Bn.).
2 Gray-Buchanan, Walter Bruce, Capt., k. in a., 10/3/15.
2 Grice, Howard Thomas, 2/Lt., k. in a., 25/3/18.
3 Grice, Thomas Gerald, Capt. (T/Major), d. of w., 15/6/16 (att. 2 Bn.).
4 Gunner, Frank, Lt., k. in a., 14/4/18 (att. 12 Bn.).
4 Guthrie, Willie Forrester, Lt., k. in a., 26/4/18 (att. 9 Bn.).
9 Hannan, George Madder, Temp. Major, died, 13/10/15.
10 Hardinge, Patrick Robert, Temp. Major, d. of w., 17/6/16.
12 Hay, William, Temp. 2/Lt., d. of w., 1/4/16 (att. 1/R. Sco. Fusrs.).
2 Hayes, Ernest de Launoy, Major, k. in a., 10/3/15.
12 Henderson-Hamilton, Charles Campbell, Capt. (Tp.), k. in a., 21/8/15 (att. 1/K.O.S.B.).
4 Hepner, Herman, 2/Lt., k. in a., 8/5/17 (att. 11 Bn.).
Hewitt, James Francis, Lt., k. in a., 26/10/14.
2 Hopkins, Charles Randolph Limes, Lt., k. in a., 18/12/14.
Howat, George, 2/Lt. (Tp.), k. in a., 26/8/18 (att. 2 K.O. Sco. Bdrs.).
2 Humphrys, Edward Thomas, T/Capt., died, 3/5/16 (Garr. Bn.).
10 Hunter, William Scott, 2/Lt. (Tp.), k. in a., 1/8/17.
9 Hutcheson, Andrew Guy, Capt., (Tp.), k. in a., 14/7/16.
12 Jameson, Francis John, Lt. (Tp.), k. in a., 25/9/15 (att. 9 Bn.).
1 Johnston, Donald Clark, Capt., d. of w., 13/9/18 (att. 1/8 Bn.).
Kennedy, John, 2/Lt., k. in a., 23/4/17 (att. 7/Border Regt.).
2 Kennedy, John Pitt, Capt., k. in a., 10/3/15.
4 Kennedy, James Wallace, A/Capt., k. in a., 27/5/17 (att. 1 Bn.).
10 Kerr, John William, Temp. 2/Lt., k. in a., 28/3/18.
2 Kerr, William John, Lt., d. of w., 10/3/15.
Laidlaw, James Clelland, Temp. 2/Lt. (A/Capt.), k. in a., 6/11/17.
9 Laing, George, Temp. 2/Lt., d. of w., 10/4/17.
4 Laing, Robert MacLeod, 2/Lt., k. in a., 20/7/16.
3 Lambert, William Fairlie, 2/Lt., k. in a., 22/3/16 (att. 9 Bn.).
1 Lawrie, Francis Allan, Capt. (Tp.), died, 25/9/18 (G. Bn., att. Manch. Rgt.).
12 Lawson, Gavin. Temp. 2/Lt., k. in a., 4/8/16.
2 Lawson, James Burnett, Lt. (Tp.), k. in a., 27/3/18.
12 Leitch, George Fraser, Temp. 2/Lt., k. in a., 26/4/16 (9 Bn.)
10 Lindsay, Douglas Alexander, Temp. 2/Lt., k. in a., 25/9/15.
2 Lipp, Frank, 2/Lt., d. of w., 30/5/16 (att. 8/R.W. Fusrs.).
2 Lloyd, Hesperus David Watkins, Major, k. in a., 12/3/15.
2 Loder-Symonds, Thomas Lenthall, Lt., k. in a., 9/5/15.
10 Lovell, John Cuthbert, Temp. Lieut., k. in a., 1/8/17.
10 Low, Alexander Sturrock, Temp. 2/Lt., k. in a., 23/6/17.
Mabon, John Craig Ferrie, 2/Lt. (Tp.), k. in a., 14/10/18 (att. 1/8 Bn.).
12 Macaulay, Colin Alexander, Temp. 2/Lt., k. in a., 9/4/16.
10 McCall, Gavin, M.C., D.C.M., A/Capt., k. in a., 28/3/18.
10 McCallum, Donald, Temp. 2/Lt., k. in a., 25/9/15.
Macdonald, Archibald Hillcoat, Temp. 2/Lt., d. of w., 5/3/16 (att. 1 Bn.).
12 McDonald, Donald Alexander, Temp. 2/Lt., k. in a., 25/8/15 (att. 5 Bn. R. Scots.).
9 Macfarlane, D. McI., Temp. 2/Lt., killed, 18/4/18 (and R.A.F.).
9 Macfarlane, Keith Dix Lewis, Temp. Lt., k. in a., 14/4/17.
11 McGhee, Harry, Temp. Capt., k. in a., 8/5/17.
Macgilvary, Alexander Renfrew, Temp. 2/Lt., k. in a., 29/11/17 (att. 1/7 Bn.).
3 Macharg, Ebenezer Maitland, Capt., k. in a., 23/10/16 (att. 1 Bn.).
4 Mackenzie, Albert James, M.C., 2/Lt., d. of w., 13/12/17 (att. 2 Bn.).
9 Mackenzie, Henry Pierce, Temp. Capt., k. in a., 25/9/15.
3 Mackillop, Donald, Lt. (Tp.), k. in a., 20/7/16.
10 Macleod, Victor Charles Augustus, Temp. 2/Lt., k. in a., 18/7/17 (att. 1/8 Bn.).
4 Macrae, John Harold, 2/Lt., k. in a., 25/8/16 (att. 18 Bn.).
4 Mactavish, Hugh, 2/Lt., k. in a., 22/3/18 (att. 8/Border Regt.).
4 Maguire, Cecil Augustine, 2/Lt., k. in a., 31/7/17 (att. 2 Bn.).
3 Marshall, Alexander Balfour, 2/Lt., k. in a., 14/4/16 (att. Conn. Rangers).
1 Marriott, John Douglas, 2/Lt., k. in a., 26/9/17.
16 Martin, Herbert Ernest, Temp. 2/Lt., k. in a., 14/10/18 (att. 1/8 Bn.).
10 Maskell, George, Lt. & Qr.-Mr., k. in a., 21/3/18.
Maunsell, Wilfrid Innscent, Capt., k. in a., 8/2/15.
3 Maxwell, Richard Henry Perceval, Lt., k. in a., 23/7/18 (att. 10 Bn.).
4 Miller, Cyril Rowland Eyre, Lt., d. of w., 25/11/14 (att. K.O. Sco. Bordrs.).
3 Miller, Kenneth Steven, 2/Lt., k. in a., 1/8/17.
3 Miller, Robert, Lt., d. of w., 25/4/17 (att. 10 Bn.).
Misell, William, Temp. 2/Lt., k. in a., 20/10/18 (att. 10 Bn.).
11 Mitchell, John Marshall, Temp. Lt., k. in a., 9/5/17.
10 Moll, Albert Donald Campbell, Temp. Lt., k. in a., 25/9/15.
Morris, Hugh, Lt., d. of w., 14/7/15 (att. 2 Bn.).
12 Morrison, G., Temp. 2/Lt., d. of w., 25/10/15 (att. 10 Bn.).
12 Morrison, John Stewart, Temp. 2/Lt., d. of w., 14/5/17.
9 Mosscrop, Allan, M.C., Temp. 2/Lt., d. of w., 11/9/17.
10 Munro, Alexander, Temp. 2/Lt., d. of w., 5/11/16.
10 Myles, William Whitson, Temp. 2/Lt., d. of w., 20/9/16 (and T.M.B.).

Neale, Aubrey Charles, Temp. 2/Lt., k. in a., 1/8/17 (att. 10 Bn.).
Nelson, Graham, 2/Lt., killed, 30/8/17 (att. R.F.C.).
9 Nicol, George Moffat, Temp. Lt., k. in a., 25/9/15.
4 Oppé, Thomas Armin, 2/Lt., k. in a., 20/5/17 (att 1 Bn.).
Ormesby, Horatio Nelson, Lt., k. in a., 4/6/15.
Orton, Ernest Henry, 2/Lt., k. in a., 9/5/15.
10 Paisley, Thomas, Temp. 2/Lt., k. in a., 25/9/15.
10 Paton, William George, Capt. (Tp.), k. in a., 14/6/16.
12 Peacock, Robert Archibald, 2/Lt. (Tp.), k. in a., 27/1/16 att. 10/Bn.).
4 Peck, Reginald Geoffrey, Lt., d. of w., 29/2/16 (att. 10 H.L.I.).
3 Percy, George Clark, M.C., Lt. (A/Capt.), k. in a., 31/7/17 (att. 2 Bn.).
4 Phillips, Arthur Cornwallis, 2/Lt., d. of w.. 22/5/17 (att. 1 Bn.).
2 Pontifex, Dudley Allen, Capt., k. in a., 31/7/17.
1 Porter, Robert, 2/Lt. (A/Capt.), k. in a., 25/11/17.
12 Pratt, Alexander Stewart, Temp. 2/Lt., k. in a., 24/3/17 (att. 10 Bn.).
12 Prentice, Alexander Reid, Temp. Capt., k. in a., 9/11/17 (att. 10 Bn.).
10 Pringle, Arthur Stanley, Temp. Capt., k. in a., 25/9/15.
4 Reid, James, 2/Lt., k. in a., 23/10/16 (att. 2 Bn.).
3 Raynes, Frank Arthur, M.C., 2/Lt., k. in a., 27/3/18 (att. 17/Royal Scots).
3 Reid, William George, 2/Lt., d. of w., 23/2/17.
9 Rennie, F. Robert, Temp. 2/Lt., k. in a., 9/2/16.
Reynolds, John James, 2/Lt. (T/Capt.), d. of w., 31/12/15.
11 Ritch, William Robertson, Temp. Capt., k. in a., 23/3/18.
Ritchie, Alexander, 2/Lt., d. of w., 28/4/17 (att. T.M.B.).
Ritchie, Arthur Gerald, Capt., d. of w., 22/11/14.
1 Ritchie, Francis James Dickson, 2/Lt., k. in a., 20/7/16.
11 Ritchie, The Hon. Harold, D.S.O., T/Major (A/Lt.-Col.), d. of w., 28/10/18 (att. 1/R. W. Surrey Regt.).
1 Ritchie, Robin Blackwood, Lt. (A/Capt.), k. in a., 20/7/16.
9 Ritchie, Robert Richard, T/Capt., k. in a., 3/5/17.
3 Robb, Alexander Gentle, M.C., Lt., d. of w., 20/5/18 (P.O.W.).
10 Robb, Ralph George Campbell, Lt. (Tp.), k. in a., 25/9/15.
4 Robertson, David Hunter Henderson, Lt., k. in a., 10/3/15.
Robertson, John Barclay, 2/Lt. (Tp.), killed, 13/11/17 (att. 2 Bn.).
10 Robertson-Durham, William Hugh, Temp. Capt., k. in a., 25/9/15.
4 Rodger, Matthew Freer, Lt., k. in a., 23/10/16 (att. 2 Bn.).
10 Rodgers, Edward Joseph, Temp 2/Lt., k. in a., 24/4/17.
Rogerson, John Lilly, Temp 2/Lt., k. in a., 5/10/18.
12 Ronaldson, Alexander, Temp. 2/Lt., k. in a., 9/6/16 (att. 10 Bn.).
Rooke, Charles Douglas Willoughby, Lt., k. in a., 19/6/15.
Rose, Ronald Hugh Walrond, Capt., k. in a., 22/10/14.
9 Ross, Robert Stewart, 2/Lt. (Tp.), d. of w., 24/9/17.
3 Salmon, Claude Garrett, Capt., k. in a., 9/5/15 (att. 2 Bn.).
10 Sanders, Joseph Henry, 2/Lt. (Tp.), k. in a., 23/6/17.
10 Scott, James Hall, Temp. Major, k. in a., 25/9/15.
4 Scott, Thomas, M.C., 2/Lt., d. of w., 21/5/17.
11 Scougal, Francis William, M.C., Temp. Major, k. in a., 19/9/18.
Seath, Douglas Ambrose, Temp. Lt., k. in a., 24/4/17.
11 Selbie, Colin Mackenzie, Temp. 2/Lt., k. in a., 14/7/16 (att. 9 Bn.).
4 Shearburn, Frank Alan, 2/Lt., k. in a., 14/9/16 (att. 10 Bn.).
Sim, Herman Alexander Coysgarne, Lt., k. in a., 9/5/15.
Simpson, Brian, 2/Lt. (T/Lt.), k. in a., 9/5/15.
10 Simpson, George Paterson, Temp. 2/Lt. (A/Capt.), d. of w., 2/8/18.
13 Sinclair, John Mitchell, Temp. 2/Lt., k. in a., 6/12/15 (att. 5/Conn. Rangers).
10 Slater, Charles Hugh Hope, Lt. (Tp.), k. in a., 31/7/17.
Smith, James Douglas, Lt. (A/Capt.), k. in a., 27/9/18 (att. 1/7 Bn.).
12 Smith, John Macdonald, Temp. 2/Lt., k. in a., 12/5/16.
Somervail, William Fulton, D.S.O., M.C., Capt., k. in a. 4/10/18.
10 Spring, Harold Albert Arden, Temp. 2/Lt., k. in a., 15/9/16.
10 Steedman, Arthur Haldane, Temp. 2/Lt. (A/Capt.), d. of w., 30/3/17.
9 Steele, Allan Robert, Temp. Capt., d. of w., 6/4/18.
10 Stenhouse, Andrew, Temp. Lt., d. of w., 27/9/15.
Stirling, Colin Robert Hoste, D.S.O., M.C., Capt. (A/Lt.-Col.), d. of w., 29/5/18 (att. 2/R. Berks Regt.).
3 Stirling, James, Capt., k. in a., 2/1/15 (att. 1 Bn.).
1 Stormouth-Darling, John Collier, D.S.O., Temp. Lt.-Col., k. in a., 1/11/16 (att. H.L.I.).
10 Struthers, Andrew Craig, Temp. 2/Lt., k. in a., 14/9/16.
3 Sussex, Edgar William, M.C., Lt. (A/Capt.), k. in a., 25/8/17.
10 Tait, Henry Forsyth, Temp. 2/Lt., k. in a., 1/9/16 (att. 12 Bn.).
4 Taylor, Peter, 2/Lt., k. in a., 8/8/16 (att. 2 Bn.).
Thomson, Haldane, Lt., k. in a., 4/6/15.
3 Thurburn, Eric James Ptolemy, 2/Lt., k. in a., 9/4/17 (att. 16/Royal Scots).
10 Tronton, Frederick Thomas, Temp. Capt., k. in a., 25/9/15
3 Tudhope, Thomas, 2/Lt., k. in a., 25/9/15 (att. 9 Bn.).
4 Turner, Frederick Whitecross, Temp. 2/Lt., k. in a., 9/4/17 (att. 10 Bn.).
1 Walker, William Cleland, Lt., k. in a., 16/4/18 (att. 19 T.M.B.).
3 Wayet, Frank Merewether, Lt., k. in a., 27/9/15 (att. 1 Bn.).
3 Wedderburn, Robert Hamilton Maclagan, 2/Lt., k. in a., 3/2/15.
4 White, Robert Edward, 2/Lt., died, 18/3/15.
4 White, William Kenneth, 2/Lt., k. in a., 31/7/17.
Williamson, Frank Alfred, 2/Lt., d. of w., 4/6/15.
✓3 Williamson, Stephen de Thierry, Lt., k. in a., 10/3/15.
9 Wilson, Archibald Field, Temp. Capt., k. in a., 25/9/15.
3 Wilson, Charles George Gordon, 2/Lt. (Tp.), k. in a., 9/4/17 (att. 9 Bn.).
Workman, Charles Service, M.C., 2/Lt. (T/Lt.), d. of w., 20/7/17 (att. R.F.C., 70 Sqd.).
1 Wyatt, Alfred John, Lt., k. in a., 23/10/18 (att. 8 Bn.).
3 Young, Andrew, 2/Lt., k. in a., 27/12/16 (att. 13/Royal Scots).
13 Young, Andrew Yates, Temp. 2/Lt., k. in a., 30/9/15 (att. R. Scot. Fusrs.).
10 Young, David Goldie, Temp. Lt., k. in a., 25/9/15.

The Royal Inniskilling Fusiliers.

6 Acheson, Vincent Andrews, Capt. (Tp.), k. in a., 10/9/16 (att. 7th).
5 Aitchison, Scott McDiamid, Lt. (Tp.), k. in a., 22/3/18 (att. 1st Bn.).
9 Anderson, Albert Stewart, 2/Lt. (Tp.), died, 1/2/17.
Aplin, Kenneth Sharland, 2/Lt., k. in a., 1/11/14 (att. 2nd Bn.).
3 Armstrong, William Arthur, 2/Lt., d. of w., 26/10/18.
Auchinleck, Daniel George Harold, Capt., k. in a., 20/10/14.
2 Aylmer, Gerald Hans, Hendrick, Lt., k. in a., 16/4/17.
6 Baillie, George Richard Lancelot, Lt., k. in a., 3/10/18.
11 Ballintine, Joseph, Capt., k. in a., 1/7/16.
Barton, Albert Thomas Lionel, 2/Lt., k. in a., 7/11/14.
6 Barton, Charles Geoffrey, M.C., Capt. (Tp.), k. in a., 17/10/18.
9 Barton, William Edgar, 2/Lt., k. in a., 22/3/18.
12 Beale, Oscar Child, 2/Lt. (Tp.), k. in a., 4/10/16 (att. 10th Bn.).
4 Berry, William Herbert Stuart, Lt., k. in a., 24/5/15 (att. 2nd R. Ir. Rgt.).
1/2 Best, Thomas Andrew Dunlop, D.S.O., Major (T/Lt.-Col.), k. in a., 20/11/17.
2 Beverland, Charles Ferris, 2/Lt. (Tp.), k. in a., 4/12/16.
8 Boardman, Thomas Henry, D.S.O., T/Lt.-Col., d. of w., 5/8/17.
12 Bogle, Albert, 2/Lt. (Tp.), k. in a., 10/8/17 (att. 10th Bn.).
2 Bogle, David Morrow, 2/Lt., d. of w., 1/9/18.
Boyd, Harold Alexander, 2/Lt., k. in a., 19/9/14.
9 Boyd, William Gaston, T/2/Lt., d. of w., 13/10/16.
2 Broadley, Harry, T/Capt., k. in a., 6/8/17.
4 Brooman-White, Ronald George, 2/Lt., d. of w., 15/5/15 (att. R. Ir. Fus.).
8 Brown, Lawrence Crawford, 2/Lt. (Tp.), k. in a., 16/8/17.
8 Browne, William Angus, T/Lt., k. in a., 21/9/17 (and R.F.C., 53 Sqd.).
12 Brunt, John Jarvis, 2/Lt., k. in a., 24/3/18 (att. 10th).
3 Buckworth, Alan Benjamin, 2/Lt., k. in a., 16/8/17.
Buckworth, Wallace Alfred, 2/Lt., k. in a., 8/5/15.
3 Caird, Frank Clagget, 2/Lt., d. of w., 22/11/16 (att. 2nd).
11 Carlile, Thomas, T/2/Lt., k. in a., 16/8/17.
7 Carroll, Frederick Stanley, 2/Lt. (Tp.), k. in a., 21/11/16.
8 Carrothers, John Samuel, 2/Lt., k. in a., 16/8/17.
1 Cathcart, Richard Robert, 2/Lt., k. in a., 16/8/17.
10 Cinnamond, Francis, T/2/Lt., died, 13/11/18 (att. 2nd) (in Ger. hands).
11 Clements, Thomas Lipton, T/2/Lt., k. in a., 23/3/18 (att. 9th).
11 Clements, William Hunter, 2/Lt., k. in a., 16/8/17.
5 Coghill, Sinclair Baxter, 2/Lt. (Tp.), k. in a., 9/9/16 (att. 8th).
6 Collen, William Stewart, 2/Lt. (Tp.), k. in a., 7-10/8/15.
5 Collins, Newton Henry, 2/Lt. (Tp.), k. in a., 27/4/16.
Collis, William Henry, T/Capt., k. in a., 9/5/17.
4 Corscaden, James Noel, 2/Lt., k. in a., 17/10/18 (att. 6th Bn.).
3 Costello, Edward William, Lt., k. in a., 1/7/16 (att. M.G.C.).
11 Craig, John Arnott Taylor, 2/Lt. (Tp.), k. in a., 1/7/16.
3 Crawford, Edward, Lt., d. of w., 27/5/15 (att. 2nd).
10 Crawley, Eric, T/Lt., died, 26/2/17.
12 Crockett, Charles Love, 2/Lt. (Tp.), k. in a., 28/4/16.
Crofton, Hugh Lefroy, Capt., k. in a., 22/5/15.
7 Crowe, Cecil Alexander, T/2/Lt., k. in a., 9/9/16.
9 Crozier, William Magee, Lt., k. in a., 1/7/16.
9 Cruickshank, Philip, T/Capt., k. in a., 1/7/16.
2 Cundall, Cecil, M.C., Lt. (A/Capt.), k. in a., 30/11/17.
3 Cupples, William, Capt., k. in a., 25/9/15.
8 Dalzell-Walton, Hubert Pulteney, T/Lt.-Col., k. in a., 9/9/16.
3 Despard, Marcus Carden, 2/Lt., k. in a., 19/7/17.
1 Dick, Arthur James Seaber, Lt., k. in a., 22/3/18.
6 Dickson, William Tillie, Lt., d. of w., 9/7/16.
Dolan, Stephen Christopher, 2/Lt., k. in a., 16/8/17 (and 49 T.M.B.).
10 Drennan, James Wilson, T/Lt., d. of w., 12/8/17.
3 Duff, John, 2/Lt., d. of w., 25/8/18 (att. 1st).
Dunlop, Charles, 2/Lt., d. of w., 22/10/14.
Edden, Henry Stewart, Capt., k. in a., 21/8/15.
9 V.C. Emerson, James Samuel, T/2/Lt., k. in a., 6/12/17.
6 Fagan, James Edward, 2/Lt. (Tp.), d. of w., 5/10/16 (att. 8th).
3 Farley, George Herbert, 2/Lt., k. in a., 16/8/17.
9 Fawcett, Joseph John, 2/Lt., k. in a., 23/3/18.
4 Fearn, Charles Frederick, 2/Lt., k. in a., 4/7/15 (att. 2nd Muns. Fus.).
4 Field, Sydney Hubert, 2/Lt., d. of w., 9/8/16 (att. 1st).
5 Finn, Thomas, 2/Lt., died. 20/11/18.
Finney, J., M.C., 2/Lt., died, 8/2/19.
3 Fletcher, George William, 2/Lt., d. of w., 9/8/16 (att. 1st).
11 Fluke, Samuel, T/Lt. (A/Capt.), k. in a., 16/8/17.
9 Fox, Francis Parker, T/2/Lt., k. in a., 1/7/16.

11 Fox, James Joseph, T/2/Lt., k. in a., 1/9/18.
9 Gage, John Stewart Moore, 2/Lt., k. in a., 1/7/16.
11 Gallaugher, Henry, D.S.O., Capt., k. in a., 7/6/17.
Geoghegan, James Randolph, Capt., k. in a., 7/11/14.
2 Geoghegan, William George Richard, 2/Lt., d. of w., 13/4/17.
12 Gibson, Albert Henry, T/2/Lt., k. in a., 1/7/16 (att. 9th).
9 Gibson, John Anthony, 2/Lt., d. of w., 27/8/18 (in German hands).
5 Gillett, Richmond Edward, T/2/Lt., d. of w., 29/4/16.
Gilliland, William Miller Major, Lt., k. in a., 28/4/15.
9 Gilmour, Robert Wallace, T/2/Lt., k. in a., 21/3/18.
9 Graham, James Lawson, T/Lt., d. of w., 30/9/18.
7 Graves, Algernon Frederick Charles, T/Capt., d. of w., 26/8/17 (P.O.W.).
12 Gray, John Purves, T/2/Lt., d. of w., 1/10/18 (att. 1st).
9 Green, Percy Harold, T/2/Lt., k. in a., 26/3/18.
12 Green St. John, 2/Lt. (Tp.), k. in a., 6/12/17 (att. 9th).
9 Greene, Richard Ernest, 2/Lt., d. of w., 3/2/19.
10 Griffiths, William Charles, T/Lt., k. in a., 21/10/18.
5 Grubb, Donald James, 2/Lt. (Tp.), k. in a., 15/8/15.
6 Gunning, Frank Douglas, 2/Lt., k. in a., 1/7/16 (att. 11th).
5 Hall, Malcolm Wilfrid Forrester, Lt., k. in a., 20/5/17.
3 Hamilton, Hector Macdonald, 2/Lt., k. in a., 22/3/18 (att. 1st).
11 Hamilton, John, 2/Lt., k. in a., 1/7/16.
10 Hamilton, Thomas, T/2/Lt., k. in a., 8/12/17.
3 Harbord, George Alfred Lionel, Lt., k. in a., 1/7/16 (att. 1st).
1 Harrison, Samuel Dunlop Henderson, T/Lt., d. of w., 29/10/18 (att. 11th).
9 Harvey, John Forsyth, T/Capt., k. in a., 23/3/18.
4 Hawksley, George, Lt., k. in a., 22/3/18 (att. 7/8th).
1 Henderson, Duncan Frank, Capt., k. in a., 8-9/8/16.
5 Hermges, Arthur Cyril Gustave, 2/Lt. (Tp.), d. of w., 19/5/17.
Hester, Edgar Hazel, Capt., k. in a., 16/8/17.
9 Hewitt, William Arthur, T/2/Lt., k. in a., 1/7/16.
6 Hicks, Charles Albert, T/2/Lt., k. in a., 3/10/18.
Hinds, Ralph William Gore, Lt., k. in a., 16/5/15.
Holmes, Frederick, 2/Lt., d. of w., 10/5/15.
7 Holmes, O. W., 2/Lt., k. in a., 16/8/17.
Hornby, Hugh Langton, Hon. Capt., d. of w., 5/6/18 (late 8th Bn.).
9 Houston, Arthur Oswald, T/2/Lt., k. in a., 26/3/18.
4 Hunter, William Mortimer, 2/Lt., k. in a., 29/6/17.
Huskinson, Frederick John, Capt., k. in a., 1/7/16.
Ingram, Eric Talbot Allan, M.C., Lt., k. in a., 4/11/18 (att. X/32 T.M.B.).
1 Irvine, Charles Wallace, 2/Lt. (Tp.), k. in a., 14/10/18.
12 Irvine, Robert, 2/Lt., k. in a., 1/9/18 (att. 7/8th Bn.).
9 Irwin, Frederick, 2/Lt. (Tp.), k. in a., 16/8/17.
12 Jackson, William John Humphrey, 2/Lt., d. of w., 26/3/18 (att. 6th Bn.).
1 Jones, Francis George, Lt.-Col., d. of w., 9/5/15.
3 Jordon, Percy Thomas, Lt., k. in a., 21/8/15 (att. 15th Bn.).
7 Justice, George Hercules, A/Capt., d. of w., 31/7/17 (att. 7th N. Lancs. R.).
12 Johnston, Thomas James, 2/Lt. (Tp.), k. in a., 21/3/18 (att. 7/8th).
10 Kemp, Albert, 2/Lt., k. in a., 1/7/16.
6 Kennedy, James Joseph, Lt. (Tp.), d. of w., 17/10/18 (att. 11th Bn.).
8 Kennedy, Thomas James, T/Lt., k. in a., 9/9/16.
7 Kerr, Robert Goodman, M.C., T/Major, A/Lt.-Col., k. in a., 11/7/18 (att. 9th R. Ir. Fus.).
4 Knight, Geoffrey St. John, Lt., d. of w., 10/9/18 (and Tank Corps).
7 Knox, John Stanley, T/2/Lt., d. of w., 11/7/16.
4 Lavelle, William James, 2/Lt., k. in a., 21/3/18 (att. 1/8).
1 Lee, Henry, Lt., d. of w., 22/11/17.
12 Leech, James Alexander, 2/Lt. (Tp.), k. in a., 10/10/18 (att. 5th).
3 Lendrum, Charles James William Kane, A/Maj., d. of w., 13/11/16.
8 Leonard, Francis Patrick Mapletoft, Lt. (Tp.), d. of w., 29/4/16.
8 Le Peton, Clive Alfred, Lt., k. in a., 15/8/17 (att. 7th).
7 Linde, Henry Eyre, T/2/Lt., d. of w., 24/6/17.
Lloyd, Edward Raymond, Capt., k. in a., 3/12/14.
1 Long, Arthur Trevor D'Arcy, Lt., k. in a., 21/8/15.
9 Love, Ronald Andrew, 2/Lt., d. of w., 1/11/18.
9 Lowden, Norman, 2/Lt., k. in a., 21/3/18 (109th T.M.B.).
1 Ludlow, John Coape, A/Capt., d. of w., 15/12/16.
9 McCarter, John Wylie, T/2/Lt., k. in a., 6/12/17.
12 McClatchie, Edward Alexander, T/2/Lt., d. of w., 10/8/17.
5 McCormac, Herbert Hood, T/Lt., k. in a., 15/8/15.
7 McCormick, Edward John, T/Lt., k. in a., 14/5/17 (and R.F.C.).
10 McCracken, Benjamin Brayshan Victor, T/2/Lt., d. of w., 23/8/17.
11 McCullagh, Alexander Henry, T/2/Lt., k. in a., 16/8/17 (109th T.M.B.).
4 McDonald, Mark William, 2/Lt., drowned, 2/8/15.
Macdougald, Llewellyn George Duncan, T/2/Lt., k. in a., 16/8/17.
9 McFall, Thomas Lamont, T/2/Lt., k. in a., 7/8/17.
4 McHugh, Edward James, Lt., died, 31/10/18 (att. 1st).
12 McKenny, Edward Richard, 2/Lt. (Tp.), k. in a., 18/10/18 (att. 6th).
10 McKnight, Thomas, T/2/Lt., k. in a., 21/2/17.
9 Maclean, Henry Chevers, T/Capt., k. in a., 1/7/16.
9 McNamee, John Joseph, T/Lt., d. of w., 1/9/18.
12 McCarter, John Wylie, 2/Lt., k. in a., 6/12/17 (att. 9th).
2 McKinstry, James McNeil, T/2/Lt., d. of w., 2/12/16.
10 McClure, Ernest, Lt., k. in a., 1/7/16.
9 Marshall, Edward Leslie, M.C., T/Capt., d. of w., 1/9/18.
6 Martin, Sidney Todd, Lt., k. in a., 1/7/16.
Miller, Inglis Francis Rowley, Lt., d. of w, 13/9/14.
11 Miller, Stanley, 2/Lt., k. in a., 1/7/16.
7 Milligan, Frederick Albert, T/2/Lt., died, 29/4/16.
3 Mitchell, R. W. H., Capt., died, 9/5/17.
5 Montgomery, Arthur Samuel, Lt. (Tp.), died, 21/6/16.
Mordaunt-Smith, Lionel St. George, 2/Lt., k. in a., 15-16/5/15.
Morgan, John Joseph Lee, 2/Lt., d. of w., 16/5/15.
7 Morgan, William, T/2/Lt., k. in a., 9/9/16.
2 Moriarty, Denis, 2/Lt., k. in a., 1/9/18.
7 Murray, Randolph Noel, T/Lt., d. of w., 28/4/16.
5 Nelis, James Edward Thornhill, T/Lt., k. in a., 15/8/15.
8 Newell, Charles Edward, T/Lt., d. of w., 25/5/16.
11 Norwood, John Norton, 2/Lt., d. of w., 22/7/16.
3 Osman, Eric Edward, 2/Lt., k. in a., 20/5/17.
V.C. O'Sullivan, Gerald Robert, Capt., k. in a., 21/8/15.
Patterson, Arthur Henry, Lt., k. in a., 14/10/18 (att. 109th T.M.B.).
11 Peak-Garland, George, 2/Lt. (Tp.), k. in a., 7/6/17.
9 Pelly, William Francis Henry, Capt. (Tp.), k. in a., 1/7/16.
Penrose, Algernon Fane Keane, Lt., k. in a., 10/5/15.
2 Phillips, Edwin Mann, Lt., d. of w., 29/9/18.
Pierce, Robert Campbell, T/Lt.-Col., k. in a., 1/7/16.
Pike, William, Capt., k. in a., 21/8/15.
Ponsonby, Gerald Maurice, Capt., d. of w., 31/8/14.
6 Porter, William, T/2/Lt., k. in a., 1/7/16 (att. 1st).
11 Pratt, Audley Charles, D.S.O., Capt., Tp. Lt.-Col., d. of w., 16/8/17.
10 Proctor, James Claude Beauchamp, T/Capt., k. in a., 1/7/16.
6 Purdy, Richard Shaw, T/2/Lt., d. of w., 11/9/16 (att. 8th).
4 Quaile, Robert Ernest Browne, 2/Lt., k. in a., 3/10/18 (att. 6th).
8 Quinlan, Louis, T/2/Lt., k. in a., 27/4/16.
Raymond, Edward Wetherall Hunter, Lt., d. of w., 29/5/15.
9 Reilly, Alexander Maxwell, T/2/Lt., A/Capt., d. of w., 26/11/16.
7 Ritty, John, M.C., T/Capt., k. in a., 9/9/16.
7/8 Robbins, Arthur Hodder, Capt. and Adj., k. in a., 21/3/18.
Roberts, Anthony Gerald Malpas, 2/Lt., k. in a., 20/10/14.
10 Robertson, Maxwell Alexander, Capt., k. in a., 1/7/16.
11 Robertson, John Gilfillan, 2/Lt., k. in a., 7/6/17.
4 Robinson, Charles Arthur, Lt., k. in a., 9/4/17 (att. M.G.C.).
5 Robinson, Reginald William, T/Capt., k. in a., 15/8/15.
Roe, Samuel George, Capt., k. in a., 20/10/14.
2 Sadlier, Francis Arthur, 2/Lt., k. in a., 14/10/18.
8 Seaver, Charles, T/Capt., d. of w., 3/10/16.
11 Sewell, William Tait, T/Capt., k. in a., 1/7/16.
7 Shaw, Thomas Herbert, Lt., k. in a., 8/8/17.
12 Saunders, F. W., Capt., died, 29/4/18.
Shubrick, Richard Brian, Lt., T/Capt., d. of w., 28/4/15.
5 Smyth, Irvine Johnston, 2/Lt., k. in a., 3/9/15.
10 Smyth, Ross Acheson, Major, died, 27/9/17.
1 Somers, Cyril Dermott Fouace, 2/Lt., d. of w., 20/5/17.
Somerville, Stafford James, Major, T/Lt.-Col., d. of w., 16/8/17 (att. 9th R. Ir. Fus.).
Spalding, Albert, T/2/Lt., k. in a., 1/7/16 (att. 10th).
10 Speares, Harold Thorne, 2/Lt. (Tp.), k. in a., 16/8/17.
3 Stacey, Cyril Robert William, 2/Lt., k. in a., 8-9/8/16 (att 1st Bn.).
Stacke, Oliver George Norman, Lt., k. in a., 17/5/15.
11 Starr, Arthur James, T/Lt., k. in a., 22/3/18 (att. 9th Bn.).
Stewart, John Houghton, Lt., k. in a., 24/5/15.
9 Stevenson, Leonard William Hugh, M.C., Lt. (Tp.), k. in a., 1/7/16.
11 Stewart, William McEwan Henderson, 2/Lt. (Tp.), k. in a., 16/8/17.
6 Stewart-Moore, Henry, T/Lt., k. in a., 10/9/16 (att. 7th).
1 Stonor, Cuthbert Anthony, 2/Lt., k. in a., 1/7/16.
1 Stuart, James, Capt., k. in a., 13/4/17 (and R.F.C., 59 Sq.).
13 Summerhayes, John Alexander, T/2/Lt. (A/Capt.), k. in a., 27/8/18.
9 Sutherland, George Hay, T/Lt., d. of w., 2/11/18.
7 Sutton, Richard Thomas, T/Lt. (A/Capt.), d. of w., 3/10/18.
1 Tarbet, Arthur Kenneth, 2/Lt., k. in a., 21/8/15.
Tarbet, Edmund Alex., 2/Lt., k. in a., 21/8/15.
9 Taylor, Samuel Alexander, T/2/Lt., k. in a., 16/8/17 (109th T.M.B.).
Thomas, James Grant Brandon, 2/Lt., d. of w., 17/11/14.
2 Thompson, Cecil Cuthbert, Capt., k. in a., 14/7/16 (att. 4th).
9 Thompson, Henry Norman, 2/Lt., k. in a., 22/3/18 (att. 12th Bn.).
3 Thompson, Philip Aloysius Xavier Murray, 2/Lt., k. in a, 21/8/15 (att. 1st).
6 Thompson, William John, T/2/Lt., k. in a., 26/3/18.
Tillie, Charles Gordon, Lt., T/Capt., d. of w., 23/8/15.
6 Topp, Richard William, 2/Lt., d. of w., 1/7/16 (att. 11th Bn.).
2 Tottenham, Arthur Henry, 2/Lt., k. in a., 27/6/16.
12 Trimble, Noel Desmond, 2/Lt. (Tp.), d. of w., 29/4/16.
3 Trouton, Edmund Arthur, Lt., k. in a., 1/7/16.
Uniacke, Robie Fitzgerald, Major, T/Lt.-Col., killed, 28/5/15.
5 Vanrenen, Arthur Saunders, T/Lt.-Col., k. in a., 15/8/15.
9 Verner, James Hamilton, T/Capt., k. in a., 5/12/17.
5 Vernon, Charles Edward Granville, T/Capt., k. in a., 15/8/15.
2 Walker, Claud Arthur Leonard, Lt., k. in a., 10/7/18.
7 Walker, Cornwall Nathaniel Brownlow, Lt., k. in a., 16/8/17.
4 Washington, Frederick, M.C., 2/Lt., k. in a., 22/8/18 (att. 1st Bn.).
5 Watson, Benjamin, T/2/Lt., d. of w., 17/6/16 (att. 7th Bn.).
3 Watson, James Norman, 2/Lt., d. of w., 10/8/16 (att. 1st).
9 Weir, John, T/Capt., k. in a., 1/7/16.
9 West, Wilfrid Thomas, 2/Lt., k. in a., 25/3/18.
8 Wheltop, Daniel, T/2/Lt., d. of w., 29/4/16.

2 White, Leslie Charles Walter, 2/Lt., d. of w., 29/9/18.

5 Whitsitt, John Reginald, T/Lt., d. of w., 16/8/15.

3 Whittington, William James, 2/Lt., k. in a., 16/5/15 (att. 2nd Bn.).

4 Wilkinson, William Andrew, 2/Lt., k. in a., 21/3/18.

12 Williams, Gerald Leopold, M.C., 2/Lt., k. in a., 15/10/18.

12 Wilson, Alexander Gordon, 2/Lt., k. in a., 27/8/18 (att. 13th Bn.).

9 Wilson, Frederick William, Lt., k. in a., 24/3/18.

3 Wilson, Victor John Frackleton, Lt., k. in a., 17/10/18 (att. 6th).

9 Wintle, Armar Lowry Corry, M.C., Lt., d. of w., 22/8/17.

9 Woods, James Edwin, Lt., k. in a., 6/12/17.

4 Worth, Stanley Seymour, 2/Lt. (Tp.), k. in a., 1/12/17 (att. 14th M.G.C.).

5 Wray, Cormac Patrick James, T/2/Lt., k. in a., 15/7/16 (att. 8th).

1/2 Wynne, Maurice St. Clair Patrick, D.C.M., Lt., d. of w., 11/10/18.

7 Young, Herbert Nugent, D.S.O., Major, A/Lt.-Col., k. in a., 25/10/18 (att. 11th N. & D.R.).

The Gloucestershire Regiment.

18 Alcock, Alfred, 2/Lt., k. in a., 21/8/16.

10 Alford, Allen Charles George, 2/Lt., k. in a., 3/9/16 (att. 3rd Worc.).

8 Allen, Harry, Capt. (Tp.), d. of w., 16/1/18.

12 Allison, Thomas McGregor, T/Major, k. in a., 30/5/18.

3 Andrews, Frank Henry, M.C., 2/Lt., k. in a., 11/8/18.

Aplin, Elphistone D'Oyly, Lt., d. of w., 13/5/15.

1 Arnot, C., 2/Lt. (Tp.), k. in a., 22/3/18.

3 Back, H. A., 2/Lt., k. in a., 22/9/16 (att. 1st).

1 Bailey, Donald William, 2/Lt. (Tp.), k. in a., 4/10/17 (att. 12th Bn.).

15 Baines, Henry Parkyns Bridge, 2/Lt. (Tp.), k. in a., 3/2/17 (att. 7th).

1 Baker, Sydney Harold, Major (Tp.), k. in a., 23/3/18.

3 Baker, Walter, M.C., Lt., A/Capt., d. of w., 23/10/17 (att. 14th).

Bamberger, William Ewart Woodburn, 2/Lt., k. in a., 16/8/17.

14 Barber, Henry Cecil, 2/Lt. (Tp.), drowned, 9/11/17 (W.A.F.F.).

7 Barnes, John Edward Templeman, T/2/Lt., A/Capt., k. in a., 3/2/17.

9 Barratt, Harold Charles Edward, 2/Lt. (Tp.), d. of w., 18/5/17.

Basdell, Frank George, 2/Lt., drowned, 4/5/17.

3 Baynes, Nigel William Francis, Major, died, 19/3/15 (att. 1st).

1 Beale, Robert Anthony, 2/Lt., k. in a., 15/3/17.

12 Beer, Robert Alexander, 2/Lt. (Tp.), k. in a., 5/10/17.

10 Bell, L. H., 2/Lt., died, 26/9/18 (and R.A.F.).

13 Bennett, Reginald, 2/Lt., k. in a., 3/9/16.

7 Bernard, Henry Claude, 2/Lt. (Tp.), k. in a., 3/9/16.

8 Bloomfield, Arthur Herbert, 2/Lt., k. in a., 9/7/17.

Blyth, Reginald Crommelin Popham, Capt., k. in a., 4/6/15 (att. R. Fus.).

1 Bosanquet, Graham Bromhead, Major, k. in a., 1/7/16.

8 Boulton, Arthur Vane, 2/Lt., d. of w., 25/2/17.

11 Boulton, Wallace Dawson, 2/Lt. (Tp.), k. in a., 20/4/16 (att. 7th).

Bowyer-Smith, Cedric Gray, Capt., k. in a., 4/11/15 (att. W. Afr. Front. Fce.).

3 Bradbury, Ernest Alfred, 2/Lt., died, 2/5/17 (att. 12th).

3 Brenan, Byron Edward, 2/Lt., k. in a., 18/4/15.

3 Bridges, Fleming Hardy, 2/Lt., k. in a., 10/4/18 (att. 8th).

8 Britten, Arthur, M.C., Lt. (Tp.), k. in a., 14/4/18.

Brodigan, Francis John, Capt., killed, 9/5/15.

1 Brown, Alan Francis Donald, 2/Lt. (Tp.), k. in a., 8/9/16.

Brown, James Ferguson, 2/Lt. (Tp.), k. in a., 24/4/17 (att. 1/6th Res. Bn.).

3 Brown, Laurence Clerke, Lt., k. in a., 11/10/15 (att. 1st).

11 Browning, Edwin Ormonde, T/2/Lt., k. in a., 20/4/16 (att. 7th).

1 Bryant, Alan, D.S.O., Major and T/Lt.-Col., k. in a., 17/10/17.

3 Burges, Walter Travers, 2/Lt., k. in a., 8/5/17 (att. 12th).

7 Burnaby, Eustace Hotham, Capt., k. in a., 5/8/15.

14 Burton, Charles Arthur, 2/Lt. (Tp.), k. in a., 23/3/18.

3 Bush, Hugh Godfrey de Lisle, M.C., Lt., d. of w., 17/1/17.

14 Butt, Harry Alfred, Capt. (Tp.), k. in a., 8/6/16.

10 Butt, Charles Edward, 2/Lt., k. in a., 4/4/18.

8 Byers, Richard Knight, Capt. (Tp.), k. in a., 20/7/16.

Calcutt, Albert Birch, 2/Lt., k. in a., 30/3/18.

1 Canning, Ernest Harold, 2/Lt., killed, 5/10/18 (and R.A.F.).

10 Carnegy, Frederick Alexander, Lt. (Tp.), k. in a., 13/10/15.

7 Caunter, Robert Lawrence Luscombe, T/2/Lt., d. of w., 18/12/16.

10 Caws, Ronald Newton, M.C., T/Capt., d. of w., 31/7/17.

8 Childe, Charles Murray, T/Capt., d. of w., 21/3/16.

1 Clairmonte, George Egerton, 2/Lt., k. in a., 25-26/9/15.

1 Clayton, Charles Cam Thackwell, 2/Lt., d. of w., 19/7/17.

1 Cockett, Edward Allan, 2/Lt. (Tp.), d. of w., 9/9/16.

11 Codd, Stephen Arthur Herbert, 2/Lt. (Tp.), k. in a., 9/9/16.

8 Colcutt, Thomas Mills, 2/Lt. (Tp.), k. in a., 9/9/18.

3 Colgate, Roger Edward, 2/Lt., k. in a., 18/11/16 (att. 8th).

8 Collett, Arthur Leigh, 2/Lt. (Tp.), d. of w., 18/11/16.

3 Collins, William, 2/Lt., k. in a., 30/7/16 (att. 8th).

14 Colthurst, Arthur Beadon, T/Capt., k. in a., 25/10/16.

Conner, Richard, Major, d. of w., 7/9/15.

Conyers, Harold Cater, 2/Lt. (Tp.), k. in a., 22/9/18 (att. 8th).

3 Cook, Arthur Thomas, 2/Lt., d. of w., 9/8/16 (att. 8th).

10 Corke, Hubert William, T/2/Lt., k. in a., 19/4/16.

Cowley, Frederick John Bodenham, 2/Lt. (Tp.), k. in a., 11/8/18.

8 Cox, Harleigh, Capt., k. in a., 3/7/16 (Res.).

1 Cox, Lupton James, 2/Lt. (Tp.), k. in a., 18/4/18.

14 Crawley-Bowey, Thomas Russell, T/Capt., d. of w., 30/8/16.

Croft, Robert John, 2/Lt., k. in a., 21/3/15.

8 Crooke, Elliot Hampden, Capt. (Tp.), k. in a., 3/7/16.

7 Cross, Frank Alan, T/2/Lt., k. in a., 25/2/17.

1 Culpin, Charles Henry, T/2/Lt., d. of w., 15/5/17 (att. 10th).

2 Cure, Basil Alfred Capel, Capt., d. of w., 1/10/16.

14 Dainton, Howard Hillier, 2/Lt. (Tp.), d. of w., 5/4/18 (att. 7th R.W. Kent R.).

1 Danckwerts, Richard William, Lt., k. in a., 21/12/14.

3 Dann, Wilfred, 2/Lt., d. of w., 30/10/17 (att. 12th).

3 Danne, Arthur William Brian, Lt., k. in a., 30/3/18 (att. 13th).

10 Darch, Stanley Percival, T/2/Lt., k. in a., 22/4/16.

Day, Herbert James, 2/Lt., d. of w., 8/8/17 (R.F.C., 11th Sqd.).

10 Deacon, Stanley Alfred, T/2/Lt., k. in a., 28/2/17.

10 De la Bere, Cyril John Baghot, T/Lt., k. in a., 18/8/16.

14 Dewdney, Clifford Mostyn French, Capt., k. in a., 4/4/18 (att. 7th R.W. Kent R.).

10 Dickinson, Herbert, M.C., Lt., A/Capt., k. in a., 27/5/18 (att. 2nd Middx. Regt.).

11 Drake, Percy Albert, 2/Lt. (Tp.), k. in a., 13/10/16.

3 Drew, Richard William, 2/Lt., k. in a., 25/6/18 (att. 12th).

Duggan, Joseph Henry William, 2/Lt., k. in a., 6/11/17 (and R.F.C., 20th Sq.).

Duncan, Stuart, Capt., k. in a., 13/11/14 (Res. Off. List).

1 Durant, Norman, Lt., k. in a., 12/3/16.

8 Eastwood, Benjamin, M.C., T/Capt., k. in a., 30/5/18.

13 Eaton, Harold, T/2/Lt., k. in a., 31/7/17.

8 Edwards, Harold Welleson Hurst, 2/Lt., A/Capt., k. in a., 18/11/16.

11 Ellis, Edward Charles, Lt. (Tp.), k. in a., 7/8/15.

9 Evans, Edward Juson, 2/Lt. (Tp.), k. in a., 3/7/16 (att. 8th).

8 Evans, Lewis, Lt. and Qr.-Mr., died, 28/10/18.

3 Farrington, George William, 2/Lt., k. in a., 28/6/18 (att. 12th).

10 Field, George Walton, 2/Lt. (Tp.), k. in a., 25/9/15.

12 Fitzgerald, Roy James, Lt., k. in a., 1/7/18 (att. R.A.F.).

8 Fitzgerald, Thomas David, 2/Lt. (Tp.), k. in a., 30/7/16.

11 Forrest, Evelyn Arthur Atherley, Lt. (Tp.), died, 9/12/15 (att. 7th).

Foster, Herbert Knollys, 2/Lt., k. in a., 30/10/14.

1 Fowler, George Edward, T/2/Lt., k. in a., 28/10/17 (att. 12th).

13 Frampton, John Reginald, T/2/Lt., k. in a., 3/7/17.

1/2 Frye, Lionel Henry, 2/Lt., k. in a., 16/6/18 (att. 1/5th Bn.).

11 Fyson, George Dumill, T/2/Lt., k. in a., 20/4/16.

8 Gadney, Gilbert Sims, T/2/Lt., k. in a., 3/7/16.

Gardner, Robert MacGregor Stewart, Major, killed, 31/10/14.

1/2 Garland, John Jeffrey, T/2/Lt., d. of w., 9/7/18.

2 Garnier, Denys Keppel, Capt., d. of w., 7/12/16.

10 George, Eric Coe, 2/Lt. (Tp.), died, 15/9/15.

3 George, William King, Capt., k. in a., 25/1/15.

10 Gibbs, Ivan Richard, Capt. (Tp.), k. in a., 25/9/15.

10 Gleave, Fergus, 2/Lt., k. in a., 22-23/7/16.

11 Goldie, Amyas Leigh, Lt. (Tp.), k. in a., 6/8/15 (att. 4th Worc.).

1 Gosling, Gerald Noel, M.C., Lt., k. in a., 7/7/19.

1 Granger, Frederick Collins, M.C., T/2/Lt., d. of w., 30/3/17.

10 Grant, Percy Victor, 2/Lt., k. in a., 3/4/18 (att. 9th Rif. Bde.).

Greenland, Charles Stirling Walter, Lt., k. in a., 9/5/15.

10 Griffin, Leslie Stuart Herbert, T/Lt., k. in a., 18/8/16.

9 Griffiths, Walter Edward Lambourn, T/Capt., k. in a., 26/4/17.

3 Hackforth-Jones, Arthur, Lt., k. in a., 8/8/18 (att. 7th R.W. Kent).

13 Hague, Leonard, 2/Lt., k. in a., 26/4/18.

Halliday, Morrice Frederick John, 2/Lt., k. in a., 7/6/17 (and R.F.C.).

12 Halse, Lionel William, T/2/Lt., died, 17/10/18.

2 Hammond, H. J., T/Lt., A/Capt., died, 23/3/18.

4 Harding, Arthur Dennis, Lt., d. of w., 30/10/14 (att. 1st).

1 Harman, Cecil Rochfort, 2/Lt., k. in a., 10/11/17.

7 Harris, William Gregory, 2/Lt. (Tp.), k. in a., 3/2/17.

3 Harrison, Henry Malcolm, Lt., d. of w., 19/3/15 (att. 2nd).

13 Harryman, Sydney, T/2/Lt., d. of w., 24/3/17 (and R.F.C., 88 Sqd.).

13 Harvey, Henry Burnett, T/2/Lt., k. in a., 30/3/18.

1 Hart, Reginald Munro, Lt., d. of w., 25/7/16.

Haslock, John Charles Simeon, 2/Lt. (Tp.), d. of w., 2/11/15. (att. 7/Bn.).

8 Hastings, Noel Henry Bruce, T/Capt., k. in a., 7/6/17.

8 Hawker, Albert Victor, T/Lt., died, 23/12/18 (att. 9th).

8 Hawker, Frederick James, T/2/Lt., d. of w., 16/7/16.

8 Hawkins, Walter Elmslie, 2/Lt. (T/Lt.), d. of w., 8/6/17.

1 Heath, William Rufus Kennard, 2/Lt., k. in a., 25/2/16.

1 Heppenstall, George Percival, 2/Lt., k. in a., 24/4/18 (att. 2nd Mdx. R.).

Herbert, Malcolm Cavagnari Norton, Lt., d. of w., 2/1/15.

11 Hewetson, Charles Herbert, Major, k. in a., 23/7/16.

3 Hickling, Edward Robert Eyre, 2/Lt., d. of w., 27/10/14 (att. N. Lanc. R.).

13 Hillier, Geoffrey Stuart Drummond, T/Capt., k. in a., 30/3/18.

Hippisley, Harold Edwin, 2/Lt., k. in a., 23/10/14 (Special Res.).

Holme, Alexander Charles, Lt., k. in a., 6/9/14.

12 Hosegood, Ralph, T/2/Lt., k. in a., 23/7/16 (and T.M.B.).

13 Howman, Henry Roger, Major (Tp.), k. in a., 25-26/4/18.

11 Huddy, Edward, T/2/Lt., k. in a., 30/7/16.

3 Hudson, Godfrey Burnside, 2/Lt., k. in a., 18/4/18 (att. 1st Bn.).

3 Hudson, Leslie Sydney, 2/Lt., killed, 28/10/17 (att. R.F.C.).

1/2 Humphrey, Joseph Herbert, 2/Lt. (Tp.), k. in a., 20/9/17 (att. 8th).
Hussey, Charles Francis, 2/Lt. (Tp.), k. in a., 5/10/18 (att. 1/5th).
3 Hyman, Ezra Herbert, 2/Lt., d. of w., 1/11/18 (att. 11th S. Lancs).
Ingram, Arthur Herbert, Lt., k. in a., 6/9/18 (att. 8th Bn.).
1 Ireland, James Balleny, T/Lt., k. in a., 5/5/17 (att. 7th).
9 Irwin, Richard Nynian, T/Lt.. k. in a., 6/3/17.
8 Jackson Arthur Thomas, 2/Lt. (Tp.), d. of w., 8/11/18 (att. 1/5th Bn.).
1 Jackson, Daniel Talbot, 2/Lt. (Tp.), k. in a., 30/9/18 (att. 2/5th).
8 James, Samuel Forest, T/2/Lt., k. in a., 18/11/16.
9 Jeune, Hugo St. Helier, T/Capt., d. of w., 12/5/17.
7 Johnson, Geoffrey Robert, 2/Lt. (Tp.), d. of w., 7/8/15.
10 Jones, Charles Lambert, T/Lt., killed, 15/6/16.
13 Jones, Hugh, M.C., T/Capt., died, 10/11/18.
1 Kearns, Arthur Clark Rose, Lt., died, 7/6/16 (att. Worc. R.).
Kershaw, Milton, 2/Lt., k. in a., 7/11/14 (Spec. Res.).
10 Kilby, John, T/2/Lt., d. of w., 21/8/16 (7th T.M.B.).
8 Kimber, Reginald Ernest, T/2/Lt., k. in a., 20/9/17.
10 Kirby, George Ernest, T/2/Lt., k. in a., 23/7/16.
Kitchin, Francis Leslie, T/Lt., k. in a., 11/4/17 (and R.F.C., 4 Sqd.).
10 Lammert, Rennie Dean, 2/Lt. (Tp.), k. in a., 23/3/18 (att. 8th Bn.).
Langdon, J. H., M.C., Lt., killed, 5/6/18 (and R.A.F.).
3 Laverton, Frederick King, 2/Lt., T/Lt., killed, 19/12/17 (and R.F.C.).
3 Lawrence, Frank Helier, 2/Lt., k. in a., 9/5/15.
10 Leary, George Godfrey Whitney, T/Lt., k. in a., 25/9/18.
12 Leicester, Donovan Nicolas, T/2/Lt., k. in a., 8/5/17.
Le Mottee, Edward D'Albert, Major, k. in a., 25/9/15 (Div. Staff).
3 Leslie, William Robert Norman, 2/Lt., k. in a., 25/1/15.
8 Lightbourn, Robert, T/2/Lt., k. in a., 26/7/17.
Lloyd, James, M.C., Lt., T/Capt., d. of w., 21/4/18 (att. 8th).
1 Look, John Leopold, T/Lt., d. of w., 1/9/18 (att. 5th Devons).
1 Lovett, Alfred Crowdy, C.B., T/Brig-Genrl., died, 27/5/19.
3 McBride, John Gordon, 2/Lt., killed, 8/10/18 (and R.A.F.).
McLeod, Archibald, Alastair, Capt., k. in a., 2/11/14.
1 Mainstone, James Francis, 2/Lt., A/Capt., k. in a., 4/10/17 (att. 12th).
1 Mallett, Phillip Henry John, M.C., Lt., A/Capt., d. of w., 12/11/18.
8 Mason, William John, Capt. (Tp.), k. in a., 3/7/16.
3 May, Leo Cuthbert, 2/Lt., k. in a., 27/6/18 (att. 12th).
10 Maybrey, Arthur James, 2/Lt., k. in a., 22/7/16.
1/2 Merrell, Arthur Walter, 2/Lt., k. in a., 8/5/17 (att. 12th).
2 Measdy, Thomas Percy, 2/Lt., k. in a., 30/9/16.
11 Miles, Allan Oswald, T/2/Lt., k. in a., 30/6/16.
1/2 Miles, Jesse Samuel, 2/Lt., d. of w., 19/6/18 (att. 1/6th Bn.).
1 Mills, William Henry, 2/Lt., k. in a., 5/10/17 (att. 12th Bn.).
10 Moss, Edward Hampton, Capt., k. in a., 25/9/15.
10 Naish, Edwin Athelstan, T/2/Lt., k. in a., 22-23/7/16.
10 Neems, Percy Vincent Nigel, T/2/Lt., died, 9/10/15.
11 Negus, Ralph Albert, T/2/Lt., k. in a., 18/4/16.
2 Nixon, Philip Henry, 2/Lt., d. of w., 18/12/16.
3 Olds, Cyril Austin, 2/Lt., k. in a., 16/4/16.
16 Painter, Henry Septimus, T/2/Lt., k. in a., 29/7/16.
1 Parnell, John Atherton Parnell, T/Lt., k. in a., 8/9/16.
12 Parr, Wilfred Wharton, M.C., Capt., k. in a., 8/5/17.
1/2 V.C. Parsons, Hardy Falconer, T/2/Lt., k. in a., 21/8/17 (att. 14th Bn.).
3 Peate, John, Lt., k. in a., 8/9/16 (att. 2nd).
1/2 Phelps, Leslie James, 2/Lt., died, 3/11/18 (att. 8th).
Phillips, Cecil Ivor, 2/Lt., k. in a., 27/10/17 (att. R.F.C., 45th Sqd.).
7 Phillpotts, Fitzroy Charles, T/Lt., d. of w., 9/8/18.
7 Pickering, Thomas, T/2/Lt., died, 1/11/15.
11 Preston, John Abe Stanley, Lt., d. of w., 6/10/16.
1 Priestley, Charles Lacey, 2/Lt., A/Capt., d. of w., 11/11/17.
8 Priestley, Stanley Noel, Lt., k. in a., 23/7/16.
Pritchett, Walter Penrose, Capt., d. of w., 26/12/14.
3 Quint, Henry John, T/2/Lt., k. in a., 24/9/18 (att. 5th Leic. R.).
11 Rathbone, Guy Benson, T/Capt., k. in a., 21/4/16 (att. 7th).
1 Rawlings, Chas. William Ernest, 2/Lt. (Tp.), d. of w., 28/9/17.
12 Richards, Norman Frederick Kynaston, T/2/Lt., k. in a., 24/7/16.
Richmond, Harold Christopher, Capt., k. in a., 25/1/15.
Ridgway, Richard Harry James Willis, 2/Lt., k. in a., 6/12/16 (att. 1st T.M.B.).
Rising, Robert Edward, D.S.O., Major, died, 7/11/14.
14 Roberts, Gerard Chip-chase, T/Lt.-Col., k. in a., 8/6/16.
7 Robertson, Eustace James, T/2/Lt., d. of w., 2/3/17.
12 Robinson, Eric Arthur, T/Capt., d. of w., 10/9/16.
10 Robinson, Geffrey Wathen, T/Lt., k. in a., 25/9/15.
15 Rogers, Alfred Morris, T/2/Lt., k. in a., 18/7/16.
1 Rogers, Godfrey Marcus, Lt., d. of w., 27/4/18 (att. 12th).
8 Ross, Gwilliam Emanuel Henry, T/2/Lt., k. in a., 3/7/16.
Ross-Jenkins, Maurice, 2/Lt., k. in a., 16/6/18 (and R.A.F.).
7 Ruck, John Egerton, T/Maj., k. in a., 8/8/15 (Capt., Glos. Rgt.).
Russell, Harley Raymond, Lt., k. in a., 13/10/15.
13 Ryder, Reginald Victor, T/2/Lt., d. of w., 28/6/17 (and R.F.C., 4 Sqd.).
10 Sale, Edward Hanson, T/Capt., k. in a., 25/9/15.
11 Scamell, Reginald Frank, T/Capt. k. in a., 20/4/16.
Scott, Roger Douglas, Capt., A/Major, k. in a., 13/10/15.
1 Scroggie, Vallentine, M.C., T/2/Lt., k. in a., 4/11/18 (att. 5th).
3 Sellman, Edgar Nevill Newmark, 2/Lt., k. in a., 4/4/18 (att. 5th O. & B.L.I.).
1 Shipway, Guy Maxwell, Capt., k. in a., 28/8/14.
8 Silver, Keith, T/2/Lt., k. in a., 18/11/16.
8 Slocombe, Arthur Douglas, 2/Lt., k. in a., 30/7/16.
3 Smith, Wilfred Vincent, 2/Lt. (T/Lt.), k. in a., 8/8/17 (att. 8th).
11 Solomon, Kenneth Maurice Halpen, T/2/Lt., d. of w., 18/9/15.
7 Squire, Stanley Charles, T/Lt., k. in a., 9/8/15.
11 Stagg, Alfred Charles, T/2/Lt., k. in a., 19/7/16.
14 Stagg, Edward Christopher, T/2/Lt., k. in a., 18/7/16.
Stanway, Frank, T/2/Lt., k. in a., 29/3/17 (att. 1st).
Stephenson, Eric Seymour, D.S.O., Capt., died, 6/5/15 (att. Egypt. A.).
Stewart, Adrian Harry, Lt., k. in a., 29/8/14 (and Nigeria Regiment).
8 Stileman, Frederic William Cheere, Capt., k. in a., 23/7/16.
7 Stone, Frederick James, T/Lt., A/Capt., d. of w., 29/12/16.
3 Swanwick, Russell Kenneth, Lt., k. in a., 15/9/14.
10 Symons, Clement Aubrey, T/Lt., k. in a., 25/9/15.
Taylor, Robert Fowler, 2/Lt., d. of w., 23/6/18 (Res., att. 3rd Bn.).
Temple, William Arthur Mould, Capt., d. of w., 23/10/14.
1 Templer, Claude Frank Lethbridge, Lt., A/Capt., k. in a., 4/6/18.
8 Terrell, Frank William, Lt., k. in a., 3/9/16 (att. 3rd Worc.).
8 Thomas, Hugh Gareth, T/2/Lt., k. in a., 30/7/16.
11 Thornton, Leonard Neville, 2/Lt., k. in a., 22/7/16.
1 Till, Henry, 2/Lt. (Tp.), k. in a., 4/10/17.
Todd, Frederick George, T/2/Lt., k. in a., 12/2/18 (and R.F.C.).
7 Tomkins, Frank Savell, T/Lt., k. in a., 8/8/15.
10 Tongue, John William Collis, T/Capt., k. in a., 25/9/15.
14 Tratman, Francis Victor, T/2/Lt., k. in a., 25/8/17.
7 Tresidder, Charles Tolmie, Capt., d. of w., 22/4/16.
1 Tulloh, George Swinton, Lt.-Col., k. in a., 10/5/15.
1 Vaisey, Guy Maddison, 2/Lt., d. of w., 19/4/18.
7 Vassall, Phillip Saumarez, Capt., k. in a., 7/8/15 (Res. of Off.).
7 Venables, Charles John, D.S.O., Major, k. in a., 8/8/15 (Res. of Off.).
8 Vick, Edward, T/2/Lt., k. in a., 9/7/17.
8 Vincent, Basil Britton, 2/Lt. (Tp.), k. in a., 23/7/16.
12 Vincent, Lionel Charles Henry, 2/Lt (Tp.), k. in a., 3/9/16.
10 Voller, Herbert William, T/2/Lt., k. in a., 6/12/16.
1 Wakeley, John Eric Stanley, 2/Lt. (Tp.), d. of w., 9/9/16.
14 Walker, Victor, 2/Lt., k. in a., 4/4/18 (att. 7th R.W. Kent).
14 Waller, Thomas Henry Whalley, T/Lt., k. in a., 22/10/17.
8 Walters, Ernest Beauchamp, T/Lt., k. in a., 30/7/16.
3 Walters, Edward Charles, 2/Lt., k. in a., 22/12/14 (att. 1st).
11 Warner, Thornton Sparr, Capt., k. in a., 23/7/16.
3 Warren, Ivan John, 2/Lt., d. of w., 8/3/18 (att. 1st).
12 Webb, Jack Purnell, Capt., d. of w., 22/8/18.
Webster, Frank Augustus, M.C., 2/Lt., k. in a., 1/11/18.
10 Whiffin, Hartley Allen, T/Lt., k. in a., 25/9/15.
8 Whyatt, Albert Allen, 2/Lt., k. in a., 30/5/18.
Wiggin, Douglas Holme, 2/Lt., d. of w., 23/12/14.
7 Willoughby, Edwin Charles, Capt., d. of w., 8/8/15.
3 Womar, Frederick, 2/Lt., k. in a., 22/10/17.
8 Wood, David Cardale, 2/Lt., k. in a., 23/7/16.
8 Wood, William Bryan, 2/Lt., k. in a., 23/7/16.
15 Woodford, Charles Basil Stanley, 2/Lt., k. in a., 22/8/16.
1 Woodward, Sydney Forest, M.M., 2/Lt., d. of w., 19/10/18 (att. 5th).
8 Wookey, William Nehemiah, T/Capt., k. in a., 26/7/17 (att. 11th T.M.B.).
8 Wright, Joseph Herbert, M.C., Capt., k. in a., 25/3/18.
Yalland, William Stanley, Lt., k. in a., 23/10/14.
8 Yaneske, Walter, T/2/Lt., k. in a., 30/7/16.

The Worcestershire Regiment.

4 Acton, Norman Frederick, 2/Lt. (Tp.), k. in a., 23/4/17.
1/2 Adams, Arthur Charles Henry, 2/Lt., k. in a., 21/3/18 (att. 2/8th Bn.).
Aitken, James, 2/Lt. (Tp.), k. in a., 3/10/18 (1st Garr. Bn., att. 11th Som. Lt. Inf.).
12 Aldana, Juan Manuel, Lt. (Tp.), k. in a., 21/4/17.
1 Aldrich, Arnold, 2/Lt. (Tp.), died, 1/5/18 (att. 1/8th Bn.).
13 Allen, John Hugh, Lt., k. in a., 13/6/15.
12 Amphlett, Edward Maylie, Capt., k. in a., 4/6/15 (att. Roy. Fus.).
2 Aplin, Eric Scott, Lt. (A/Capt.), d. of w., 11/3/18.
6 Arnold, Oliver Vaughan, 2/Lt., d. of w., 11/8/16 (att. 2nd Bn.).
6 Atkins, Kenneth Croydon, 2/Lt., d. of w., 30/5/18 (att. 6th).
5 Atkinson, Geoffrey J. Buddle, Lt., k. in a., 19/6/15.
Attwell, Ernest, 2/Lt. (Tp.), k. in a., 15/6/18 (att. 1/7th Bn.).
12 Austin, Harold Lunn Ferrier, T/2/Lt., k. in a., 6/1/16 (att. 9th).
Bacon, Basil Kenrick Wing, Major, k. in a., 13/12/14.
1 Baird, Andrew Augustus Dering, 2/Lt., k. in a., 8/7/15.
Baird, Gilbert Campbell, 2/Lt. (Tp.), k. in a., 28/7/17 (229th Co., M.G.C.).
3 Banks, Charles Hunter Donaldson, 2/Lt., d. of w., 1/7/15.
4 Bannister, Samuel, Capt., d. of w., 15/4/17.
Barfoot, George Allan, 2/Lt., killed, 20/6/15.
9 Barker, William, Capt., T/Major, d. of w., 15/8/18.
6 Barling, William Bingham, 2/Lt., k. in a., 12/3/15 (att. 3rd).
6 Barnes, George Gaylor, Lt., k. in a., 16/7/16 (att. 3rd).
5 Barnett, Guy, 2/Lt., k. in a., 11/3/15.
1/2 Barton, Bernard, T/Maj., k. in a., 11/8/18.

14 Bateman, Hubert Harry, 2/Lt. (Tp.), k. in a., 23/4/17 (att. 4th).
Battle, Edward Charles Vulliamy, 2/Lt., k. in a., 21/10/14.
9 Beard, Frederick Gerald Vesey, T/Lt., k. in a., 4/7/16 (att. 4th).
Beauchamp, Penrith Sutton, T/2/Lt., k. in a., 25/1/17.
10 Benbow, Sidney, 2/Lt. (Tp.), k. in a., 29/9/18 (att. 2nd).
Beningfield, Maurice Victor, 2/Lt., k. in a., 10/3/15.
5 Bennett, Theodore John, Lt., k. in a., 7/9/18 (att. 17 Ind. Inf.).
10 Bennett, Ralph, 2/Lt. (Tp.), k. in a., 4/9/18 (att. 1 Heref. R.).
9 Bidlake, Herbert Cooper Keith, T/2/Lt., A/Capt., k. in a., 25/2/17.
13 Birch, John, 2/Lt., k. in a., 5/7/15.
4 Bird, Eric James, 2/Lt. (Tp.), d. of w., 25/4/17.
1 Birtles, Roland Powell, T/Lt., A/Capt., k. in a., 4/3/17.
Biscoe, Frederick Crozier Frazer, Capt., d. of w., 19/5/15.
2 Bishop, Charles Dudley, 2/Lt., A/Capt., k. in a., 17/4/18.
3 Bomber, Jeffrey Allan, Lt. (Tp.), k. in a., 14/4/18.
6 Booth, Francis Hardinge Follett, A/Capt., k. in a., 26/9/17 (att. 1st).
9 Bourne, John Callander, 2/Lt., k. in a., 18/7/15.
4 Bowden, Richard Thomas, 2/Lt. (Tp.), k. in a., 16/8/17.
9 Boyd-Moss, Ernest William, D.S.O., Major, k. in a., 10/8/15.
10 Brake, Frederick Carlton James, 2/Lt. (Tp.), k. in a., 21/3/18.
3 Brampton, Harry Lee, 2/Lt. (Tp.), k. in a., 7/6/17.
5 Brock, Edgar Nathaniel Loftus, Capt., k. in a., 21/5/15 (att. 3rd).
1 Brooksbank, Hugh Freeth Gilbert, 2/Lt. (Tp.), k. in a., 8/7/16.
11 Brown, George Congdon, 2/Lt. (Tp.), d. of w., 8/5/17.
4 Brunskill, John Jesmond, T/2/Lt., k. in a., 23/4/17.
6 Buckler, Eric Wilson, Capt., k. in a., 16/6/15 (att. 3rd).
6 Bruton, Thomas, M.M., 2/Lt., k. in a., 1/9/18 (att. 4th).
1 Budden, Ronald Anderson, 2/Lt., k. in a., 31/7/17.
2 Bullock, Albert Edward, 2/Lt. (Tp.), k. in a., 26/10/18.
1 Burns, William Beaumont, 2/Lt., k. in a., 8/7/16.
Burr, Frederick Bonham, 2/Lt., k. in a., 12/3/15 (Res. off. List).
4 Bush, Walter Donald, Capt., k. in a., 4/6/15.
12 Busby, William Baldwin, T/2/Lt., k. in a., 15/2/17 (att. 9th).
5 Cale, Sidney, 2/Lt., d. of w., 29/8/17 (att. 4th).
9 Callender, George Wilfred, T/Lt., A/Capt., k. in a., 25/1/17.
3 Campbell, John William Ronald, M.C., Lt., k. in a., 14/4/18.
Carr, Martin Raymond, Capt., k. in a., 18/9/14.
Carter, Walter James, T/2/Lt., d. of w., 29/8/18 (att. 1/7th Bn.).
✓1 Cartland, James Bertram Falkner, Capt., A/Major, k. in a., 27/5/18.
6 Charles Leslie Stafford, Capt., died, 30/7/16 (and R.F.C.).
6 Chaytor, Alban Kingsford, 2/Lt., d. of w., 26/5/15 (att. 3rd).
3 Chignell, Hugh, 2/Lt., k. in a., 26/4/18.
Christie, Albert William Ernest, 2/Lt., killed, 27/9/15.
Clarke, Francis Charles Erlin, Lt., d. of w., 11/10/17 (and R.F.C., 5th Sqd.).
6 Clarke, Frederick John Noel, 2/Lt., k. in a., 29/6/15.
Clarke, Mordaunt Edward Leonard Hannam, Lt., k. in a., 26-27/8/14.
5 Clarke, William Hamilton, 2/Lt., k. in a., 12/3/15.
10 Clee, Thomas Howard, 2/Lt., died, 7/11/18 (att. 23rd Lanc. Fus.).
5 Cocks, Edward James Trist, 2/Lt., k. in a., 5/8/18.
1 Collins, Ernest Stanley, 2/Lt., k. in a., 31/7/17.
9 Compton, Neville George, 2/Lt. (Tp.), k. in a., 20/4/16.
1 Conybeare, Edward Bruce, Capt., k. in a., 5/4/16.
3 Cook, Robert Guy, T/2/Lt., k. in a., 9/2/17.
2 Cooper, William Marsden, 2/Lt., k. in a., 17/2/17.
11 Corbin, Charles Robert Peel, T/Lt., d. of w., 21/10/16.
Cotgrave, Christopher Russell Farmar, Capt., died, 29/12/17 (att. 100th T.M.B.).
12 Couldridge, Jack Oswald, 2/Lt., k. in a., 6/11/16 (att. 2nd).
13 Court, Eric McClintock Wathen, T/Capt., k. in a., 6/8/16 (att. 4th).
5 Cowherd, John, M.C., 2/Lt. (Tp.), k. in a., 29/9/18 (att. 4th).
6 Cox, John Ramsay, Capt., k. in a., 11/3/15.
14 Crane, Lucius Francis, 2/Lt. (Tp.), k. in a., 8/10/18.
4 Crawley, Henry Thomas, 2/Lt., d. of w., 6/5/18.
Crawley, Thomas Henry Ouseley, Capt., k. in a., 6/5/15.
9 Crofton, Charles Woodward, Major, k. in a., 10/8/15 (Res. of Off., N. Staffs.).
2 Croydon-Fowler, Hilgrove, T/Lt., k. in a., 12/10/18 (1st Garr. Bn.).
5 Curtler, Frederick G. Watkin Oldham, Lt., k. in a., 21/10/14.
12 Dane, Wilfred Spencer, T/2/Lt., k. in a., 18/11/16 (att. 10th).
Darby, Frederick, 2/Lt., k. in a., 29/11/14.
6 Daubeney, George Henry James, Lt., k. in a., 26/9/15 (att. 2nd).
4 Daw, Frederick Pole, Lt., A/Capt., k. in a., 18/10/16.
12 Day, Gerald Harlow, 2/Lt., k. in a., 24/4/17 (att. 7th R. Bks.).
1 Deakin, William Ewart, T/2/Lt., k. in a., 4/3/17.
4 Deans, Geoffrey Chase, Capt., k. in a., 6/5/15.
Denham, Francis Bardon, Lt., k. in a., 7/7/16.
1 Denley, Herbert Owen, 2/Lt. (Tp.), k. in a., 30/3/18 (att. The Camel Cps.).
5 Dickson, George Arthur Hamilton, M.V.O., Major, died, 16/2/18 (The Labour Cps.).
6 Dingley, Norman Oliver, T/Lt., d. of w., 5/5/17 (M.G.C., 93rd Coy.).
3 Dixon, Frederick, 2/Lt. (Tp.), k. in a., 18/9/18.
3 Dixon, Sidney Thomas, 2/Lt. (T/Lt.), d. of w., 20/11/17 (att. 4th).
9 Dobson, Harold Pierce, Capt., k. in a., 5/4/16.
4 Downes, Donald Litt, 2/Lt., d. of w., 5/10/18.
Drake, Gerald Edward, 2/Lt. (Tp.), d. of w., 26/1/18 (att. 10th).
2 Dudley, Arthur Walter, 2/Lt. (Tp.), k. in a., 30/3/18 (att. 8th).
12 Dunkley, Alexander, 2/Lt., k. in a., 9/4/16 (att. 9th).
5 Dunnett, Raymond Frederick, M.C., Lt., killed, 17/11/17 (and R.F.C.).
13 Durant, Christopher Gilbert, 2/Lt. (Tp.), k. in a., 18/10/16 (att. 4th).
5 Durlacher, Eric Alexander Ogilvie, 2/Lt. (A/Capt.), k. in a., 20/5/17.
10 Dwyer, Charles Henry, T/Capt., k. in a., 17/11/16.
5 Edwards, Clement Edward Alexander, 2/Lt., died, 5/12/18 (att. 11th).
4 Edwards, Edward, T/2/Lt., k. in a., 30/5/17.
Eliott, Hugh Russell, Capt., k. in a., 12/10/14.
3 Elliott, Frederick Guy, T/Lt., k. in a., 22/3/18.
Entwistle, John Maurice Binley, Capt., died, 2/12/18.
6 Eyles, Harold Morley, Lt., k. in a., 6/11/16.
12 Falcon, Francis, Capt., k. in a., 6/8/15.
1/2 Farmer, Frederic Stanley, T/2/Lt., d. of w., 20/7/17 (att. 14th).
Fear, Robert Stanley, T/2/Lt., d. of w., 5/3/18 (att. R.F.C., 15 Sqd.).
12 Featherstone, Thomas, M.C., T/2/Lt., k. in a., 25/4/17 (att. 11th).
12 Fell, Sidney Fitzroy, 2/Lt. (Tp.), k. in a., 10/7/16.
12 Ferguson, William, T/Capt., k. in a., 1/11/16.
5 Field, Cyril Decimus, 2/Lt., k. in a., 4/6/15.
Field, Howard, Lt. (T/Capt.), k. in a., 6/8/15.
10 Fish, Jack, 2/Lt. (Tp.), k. in a., 22/7/16.
12 Flux, Leonard Taylor, 2/Lt. (Tp.), k. in a., 1/11/16 (att. 2nd).
Ford, Richard Jellard, Capt., k. in a., 9/5/15.
1 Forsyth, James Corson, T/2/Lt., k. in a., 31/8/17.
10 Foster, George Major Solloway, 2/Lt. (Tp.), k. in a., 3/7/16.
10 France, Errol Martin, T/2/Lt., k. in a., 30/7/16.
10 Franklin, William Ernest, T/2/Lt., k. in a., 1/4/18.
6 Freeman, Tristram, Lt., k. in a., 12/3/15.
2 Frost, Arthur, 2/Lt., d. of w., 23/3/18 (att. 8th).
4 Gallaugher, Robert Rankin, T/2/Lt., died, 23/2/17.
Galton, Theodore Hugh, 2/Lt., k. in a., 21/10/14 (att. 3rd).
4 Gamlen, Robert Arthur Winnington, Lt., A/Capt., k. in a., 30/11/17.
✓1 Gardner, Maurice Reginald George, 2/Lt., k. in a., 27/5/18.
Gerald, Harold, T/2/Lt., k. in a., 2/12/17 (att. 2/8th Bn.).
11 Gibbs, Archibald Edward, T/2/Lt., k. in a., 25/4/17.
14 Gibbs, Percy Roland, T/2/Lt., died, 17/3/16.
3 Gibbs, William Beresford, T/Lt.-Col., k. in a., 3/9/16.
Gilmour, Herbert James Graham, Lt., k. in a., 19/9/14.
3 Ginn, Harold Etridge, 2/Lt. (Tp.), k. in a., 8/7/16.
10 Glynn, Martin, T/2/Lt., k. in a., 29/9/18 (att. 2nd).
5 Goddard, Kenneth Aquinas McKenzie, 2/Lt., k. in a., 11/7/16.
Goldsmid, Sidney Alexander, 2/Lt., died, 7/11/14.
Gotch, Duncan Hepburn, 2/Lt., k. in a., 11/3/15.
6 Graham, Alec George Malcolm, Capt., k. in a., 22/12/14 att. N. Lan. Rgt.).
3 Grant, Theodore, M.C., Capt., k. in a., 28/5/18 (Capt., S. Af. Def. Force).
13 Gray, Leslie Austin, 2/Lt. (Tp.), k. in a., 12/10/16 (att. 4th).
Green, Arthur Dowson, D.S.O., Major, k. in a., 28/9/14.
3 Greenhill, Campbell, M.C., T/Lt., k. in a., 10/8/17.
13 Greenway, Douglas Howard Wilson, 2/Lt. (Tp.), k. in a., 17/10/15 (att. 4th).
13 Greenway, Kenneth, 2/Lt. (Tp.), k. in a., 27/11/15 (att. 4th).
4 Grogan, Hubert Lawrence, M.C., Lt., A/Capt., k. in a., 6/5/18.
6 Gunston, Frederic John Dover, M.C., Lt., A/Capt., d. of w., 14/7/18 (in German hands).
10 Hadley, Cyril Vernon, 2/Lt., k. in a., 3/7/16.
2 Hale, William, T/2/Lt., d. of w., 9/8/18.
6 Hall, William, M.C., 2/Lt., k. in a., 21/3/18.
13 Halley, Jack J., T/Lt., k. in a., 26/7/16 (att. M.G.C.).
3 Hallward, Kenneth Leslie, T/Lt., k. in a., 28/5/16.
1 Hammond, Edward William, 2/Lt., died, 2/10/18.
Hardy, Leonard Basil, Lt., k. in a., 11/2/15.
13 Harley, John, Lt., k. in a., 4/6/15.
5 Harrington, Philip William, 2/Lt., k. in a., 13/1/17.
Harrison, Cyril Cazalet, Lt., k. in a., 19/9/14.
Hart, Clifford John, T/Capt., k. in a., 9/8/16 (and R.F.C.).
6 Hart, Robert Arthur, 2/Lt., d. of w., 1/8/17 (att. 1/Bn.).
10 Hartley, Reginald, T/Lt., killed, 26/10/15.
Hartnoll, Hugh Peter, Lt., k. in a., 12/12/14.
Hastings-Medhurst, F. L., 2/Lt., k. in a., 17/10/14.
1 Haynes, John Eustace Tarleton, 2/Lt., k. in a., 23/3/18 (att. 2/8th).
1 Hedworth, Thomas Hedworth, 2/Lt., drowned, 10/10/18.
Hemingway, Kenneth Stanley, Lt., A/Capt., k. in a., 21/3/18 (att. 10th).
5 Hemming, Frank James, M.C., Lt., k. in a., 13/4/18 (att. 2nd).
3 Hemus, Donald George, T/Lt., k. in a., 22/3/18.
14 Hennell, Arthur, T/2/Lt., k. in a., 3/1/18.
Henry, Claude, Lt., k. in a., 19/9/14.
Henry, Cyril Charles, Lt., k. in a., 26/9/15 (att. 2nd).
Hewett, George Edward, Capt., k. in a., 12/3/15 (Res. of Off., att. 6th Bn.).
2 Heyes, William, 2/Lt., k. in a., 27/2/17.
10 Heyworth, Peter George, 2/Lt., d. of w., 12/5/17 (att. T.M.B., 57th Co.).

9 Hiscock, Ernest Henry, T/Capt., k. in a., 25/1/17.
9 Hiscock, Leonard Ernest, 2/Lt. (Tp.), k. in a., 10/8/15.
4 Holland, Edward Hugo, T/2/Lt., k. in a., 23/4/17.
2 Holland, Edward Matthew, Lt., k. in a., 6/11/16.
3 Hollowell, Francis John, 2/Lt., k. in a., 7/7/16.
5 Honey, Alexis Cowper, 2/Lt., d. of w., 10/2/18 (att. 4th).
Horsfall, Cuthbert, 2/Lt. (Tp.), d. of w., 17/2/18 (att. 2/8th Bn.).
3 Houghton, Arthur, 2/Lt. (Tp.), k. in a., 22/3/18.
3 Hudson, Alban John Benedict, M.C., Lt., k. in a., 7/6/17.
5 Hudson, Aubrey Wells, Lt., d. of w., 20/9/14.
1 Hudson, Frank Hobbs, 2/Lt. (Tp.), d. of w., 26/4/18.
Hughes, Thomas Hector, Capt., k. in a., 15/10/14.
13 Hull, Joseph Laurence, T/2/Lt., d. of w., 19/10/16.
13 Irvine, Harold, T/Lt., d. of w., 29/6/15.
5 Isaac, Arthur Whitmore, 2/Lt., k. in a., 7/7/16.
1 Jackson, Stewart Spiers, M.C., 2/Lt., k. in a., 21/3/18 (att. 2/8th Bn.).
1 James, Merridith Charles Clifton, T/2/Lt., d. of w., 27/10/16.
12 Jenkinson, John Wilfred, Capt., k. in a., 4/6/15 (att. Roy. Fus.).
6 Jennings, Henry Arthur, 2/Lt., k. in a., 29/4/16 (att. 3rd).
10 Jennings, Richard William, T/Lt., d. of w., 3/7/16.
6 Johnson, Anthony, M.C., 2/Lt., k. in a., 13/4/18 (att. 2nd Bn.)
6 Jones, Douglas Grainger, 2/Lt., k. in a., 4/6/15 (att. 4th).
6 Jones, Francis Maynard Harvey, M.C., 2/Lt., d. of w., 18/6/17.
6 Jones, Joseph Maurice, 2/Lt., k. in a., 15/2/17 (att. 9th).
1/2 Jones, Penry, T/2/Lt., k. in a., 20/9/17 (att. 10th Bn.).
6 Jones, Russell, 2/Lt., k. in a., 3/9/16 (att. 3rd).
Jotcham, Walter Morse, 2/Lt., k. in a., 19/8/17 (att. 8th).
3 Kauntze, Cedric Ernest Wheldon, Lt., k. in a., 1/10/15.
11 King, Harry, T/2/Lt., A/Capt., k. in a., 3/9/16 (att. 3rd).
King, Harold Dudley, 2/Lt., k. in a., 6/10/18 (att. 1/8th Bn.)
Kingdon, Leonard, 2/Lt., k. in a., 12/1/16 (and R.F.C.).
9 Kittermaster, Arthur Noel Colley, T/Capt., k. in a., 4-5/4/16 (att. 12th).
5 Knott, Sydney James, 2/Lt., d. of w., 8/7/16 (att. 3rd).
14 Ladd, Alfred Caldier, Major, k. in a., 25/3/18.
1 Lambert, George, 2/Lt. (Tp.), k. in a., 29/9/18 (att. 2nd).
10 Lambert, Maurice Gustave Louis, 2/Lt., k. in a., 5/1/17 (att. 7th Berk. R.).
9 Lancaster, James Norman, T/2/Lt., k. in a., 10/8/15.
4 Lang, Henry Astell, Major, k. in a., 9/6/15.
3 Langford, Albert Frederick, 2/Lt., k. in a., 10/7/16.
2 Laughton, Hubert Henry Schomberg, T/Lt., died, 25/11/18 (att. M.G.C.).
Lea, Gerald Ernest, Capt., k. in a., 16/9/14.
1 Leach, Eric Thomas, 2/Lt., d. of w., 14/10/18.
12 Leacroft, Richard Frederick, T/2/Lt., k. in a., 10/11/15.
13 Lester, Eric Peter, T/2/Lt., k. in a., 13/10/15 (att. 2nd).
3 Lett, John Millard, T/2/Lt., A/Capt., k. in a., 22/3/18.
4 Lewis, Edward Richard Hampton, T/2/Lt., d. of w., 25/4/17.
1 Lewis, Reginald Walter Morton, T/Lt., died, 3/10/18 (att. 9th).
4 Linton, Charles Strangways, D.S.O., M.C., Major, A/Lt.-Col., k. in a., 20/11/17.
1/2 Lloyd, Ira Cyril, 2/Lt. (Tp.), died, 24/11/18.
Loos, Cecil George Bertram, Lt., k. in a., 13/3/15.
5 Loring, Robert Nele, 2/Lt., k. in a., 16/6/15 (att. 3rd).
Lowe, Henry Shanten, Lt., d. of w., 21/10/14.
6 Luby, Thomas William, 2/Lt., k. in a., 5/10/16 (att. 3rd).
11 Luckmann, Harold John, M.C., 2/Lt. (Tp.), k. in a., 10/4/18 (att. 10th).
10 Lushington, Cecil Henry Gossett, Lt., k. in a., 3/7/16.
5 McClellan, Greville Edward Gordon, Capt., k. in a., 20/10/15 (att. 2nd).
McCormick, James Gardiner, 2/Lt., k. in a., 16/5/15.
3 Macdonald, Sylvester Patrick Joseph, M.C., 2/Lt., A/Capt., k. in a., 7/6/17.
Mackay, Claude Lysaght, 2/Lt., d. of w., 7/6/15 (att. Manch. R.).
4 McNally, William Wright, M.C., 2/Lt., k. in a., 8/10/17.
5 McMichael, John Douglas Wield, 2/Lt., k. in a., 23/5/16.
1 Marrs, Frederick Mallinson, 2/Lt., k. in a., 4/3/17.
13 Martin, Basil Cuthbert Danvers, 2/Lt., k. in a., 4/6/15.
10 Masterson, Christopher John, 2/Lt., k. in a., 2/9/17.
6 Meade, Wakefield Waldo, 2/Lt., k. in a., 20/6/15 (att. 3rd).
4 Meredith, Malcolm Hereward, 2/Lt., k. in a., 10/11/15.
Merrifield, Percy, 2/Lt., k. in a., 21/3/18 (att. 2/8th Bn.).
Metcalfe, Ian Morehouse, Lt., d. of w., 1/11/17 (in German hands).
1/2 Midgley, Albert, T/2/Lt., d. of w., 18/6/18.
14 Miles, W. N., 2/Lt., died, 24/7/18 (and R.A.F.).
Molyneux Eric Seymour, A/Capt., k. in a., 30/11/17 (111th Cyc. Cps.).
Moon, Wilfrid James, 2/Lt., k. in a., 17/8/15.
Moore, Charles Frederick, 2/Lt., k. in a., 12/3/15.
1/2 Morgan, Daniel Phillips, 2/Lt., k. in a., 26/9/17.
3 Mould, James, D.S.O., M.C., A/Capt., k. in a., 3/9/16.
6 Muir, Basil, 2/Lt., k. in a., 16/6/15 (att. 3rd).
5 Muller, Carl Wilhelm Albert, 2/Lt., k. in a., 5/10/16.
3 Munro, John Clegg, T/2/Lt., died, 10/11/18.
Murphy, M. J., 2/Lt., k. in a., 12/3/15.
3 Muspratt, Terence Petty, M.C., Capt., d. of w., 29/5/18.
Myddleton-Gavey, Francis, Capt., k. in a., 26/9/15.
Myer, Denzil Grenville Alex, T/2/Lt., k. in a., 25/2/17.
6 Nash, George, 2/Lt., d of w., 29/6/15 (att. 3rd).
10 Neale, Christopher Ernest, T/2/Lt., k. in a., 29/9/18 (att. 2nd).
Neilson, Malcolm Arthur, Lt., k. in a., 9/4/17 (A/Maj., 2nd Can. Inf.).
Nesbitt, Arnold Stearns, Capt., k. in a., 7/11/14.
5 Newcombe, Clark Charles Upham, 2/Lt., k. in a., 17/8/17 (att. 10th).
1 Nicholls, Edwin Jesse, M.C., T/2/Lt., k. in a., 18/10/18.
4 Nicholson, Geoffrey Douglas Lothian, 2/Lt., k. in a., 23/4/17.
2 Nicklin, Harry John, M.C., 2/Lt., k. in a., 16/4/18.
Northey, Alfred, Lt., k. in a., 12/10/14.
9 Nunn, Mervyn Henry, Lt.-Col., k. in a., 10/8/15 (Maj., Res. of Off.).
1 O'Brien, Francis Joseph, 2/Lt. (A/Capt.), k. in a., 31/7/17.
Oldham, Llewellyn Haslope, T/2/Lt., k. in a., 26/9/15.
4 Paddison, Henry Jepson, M.C., 2/Lt. (A/Capt.), k. in a., 16/8/17.
√1 Page, Lionel, 2/Lt., k. in a., 27/5/18.
1 Palmer, Edward Anderson, 2/Lt., k. in a., 14/10/18.
Palmer, Cecil Howard, Major, k. in a., 27/7/15 (T/Lt.-Col., att. 9th R. Warw. R.).
2 Pandfield, William Godridge, 2/Lt., k. in a., 21/8/16.
Parker, Cecil William Hannington, Lt., k. in a., 27/12/16 (and R.F.C.).
Parker, Harold James, 2/Lt., k. in a., 15/4/18 (att. 2/8th).
3 Parker, William Harold, M.C., Lt., k. in a., 26/4/18.
6 Parkes, Henry Gordon, 2/Lt., k. in a., 4/6/15 (att. 4th).
5 Parsons, Edgar Vincent Peter, 2/Lt., d. of w., 26/4/18 (att. 2nd).
1 Peacock, Thomas Harold, 2/Lt., k. in a., 27/6/18 (att. 14th Bn.).
9 Pearson, George Turney, T/Lt., k. in a., 12/8/15.
2 Pepys, Reginald Whitmore, Capt., d. of w., 21/9/14.
Perham, Ernest Noble, 2/Lt. (Tp.), d. of w., 1/8/17.
3 Perks, Wilfred Lawson, 2/Lt., k. in a., 24/8/16.
4 Peto, James Archibald, Lt., k. in a., 23/8/15.
12 Phillips, Leonard Harry Perrins, Lt. (Tp.), k. in a., 6/11/16.
6 Pickersgill-Cunliffe, John Cunliffe, Capt., k. in a., 4/6/15 (att. 1st Bn.).
0 Pigg, Bernard William, 2/Lt., k. in a., 3/7/16.
4 Pine, Albert Arthur, Lt., k. in a., 16/1/17.
3 Ping, Alan Roy, 2/Lt., k. in a., 21/7/17.
3 Piper, Lawrence, T/2/Lt. (T/Lt.), k. in a., 10/6/17.
9 Polack, Benjamin James, 2/Lt. (Tp.), k. in a., 9/4/16.
4 Pollock, Douglas William, Capt., k. in a., 6/5/15.
5 Pope, Cyril Montague, Lt., d. of w., 24/10/14 (att. 2nd Bn.).
5 Potter, Percy Walter, 2/Lt., d. of w., 21/5/17 (att. 2nd Bn.).
3 Powell, Reginald Walter, 2/Lt. (Tp.), k. in a., 10/7/16.
6 Pownall, John, 2/Lt., k. in a., 30/10/16 (att. 2nd).
1 Price, Victor William, Lt. (Tp.), killed, 7/11/17 (att. R.F.C.).
1 Prosser, Arthur Edward, T/Capt., died, 23/10/18 (in German hands).
Prosser, Albert Victor, T/Lt., k. in a., 26/11/16 (att. Bord. R.).
10 Rainbow, Thomas Welford, T/2/Lt., k. in a., 18/11/16.
3 Randle, Thomas Henry, 2/Lt., d. of w., 11/8/17.
5 Ranson, Leslie Edward, Lt., k. in a., 29/9/18 (att. 2nd).
9 Rawle, Charles William Forbes, T/2/Lt., k. in a., 5/4/16.
Ray, Archibald Douglas Hussey, Capt., k. in a., 30/4/15.
1 Read, Arthur Herbert, T/Lt., d. of w., 28/4/18.
11 Reid, John Gardner, T/Capt., k. in a., 8/9/16.
12 Richards, Arthur Gough, T/Lt., k. in a., 24/4/17.
4 Roberts, D'Arcy Granville St Clair, M.C., T/Capt., k. in a., 26/4/18 (att. 1st)
5 Robertson, George Seaborn Hyssett, 2/Lt., k. in a., 18/11/16 (att. 10th).
12 Robertson, Frank, Capt., d. of w., 25/6/15.
V.C. Robinson, W. Leefe, Capt., died, 31/12/18 (and R.A.F.).
Rolph, George William, Capt., k. in a., 10/8/15 (att. 9th).
12 Romanes, Edmund Giles Radcliffe, Lt., d. of w., 7/6/15 (att. R. Fus.).
Rose, Joseph Harold, 2/Lt. (Tp.), d. of w., 28/12/17 (Res., att. 2/8th Bn.).
1 Rosling, Alan Percy, 2/Lt., k. in a., 4/3/17.
3 Ross, David George, 2/Lt., k. in a., 5/9/15.
1 Ross, Ronald Maynard, 2/Lt., k. in a., 4/3/17.
4 Round, Edward, 2/Lt. (Tp.), k. in a., 21/4/17.
3 Round, William George, M.C., T/Lt., k. in a., 1/5/18.
Rouse, Albert Charles, Lt., d. of w., 20/3/16 (att. R.E.).
Rowden, Cuthbert Roger, Major, killed, 20/4/18 (and R.A.F.).
Ruck, Laurence Humphrey, Lt., k. in a., 14/3/15.
13 Ruddock, Edgar Herbert Montague, Capt., k. in a., 22/6/15.
4 Russell, Henry Freeman, 2/Lt., k. in a., 6/8/15.
11 Ryder, Leonard Charles, 2/Lt. (Tp.), k. in a., 25/4/17 (att. 12th).
6 Scott, Alister Will Henderson, Capt., d. of w., 16/5/15 (att. 2nd).
5 Scott, John Crossfield, 2/Lt., k. in a., 16/10/16 (att. 4th).
Scougall, Alan Muir, 2/Lt. (Tp.), d. of w., 7/10/15.
Sellers, Philip, 2/Lt., died, 23/3/17 (att. R.F.C.).
Senior, Thomas Hugh Sandford, T/Lt., k. in a., 11/6/16.
10 Short, Oliver James, 2/Lt. (Tp.), d. of w., 3/4/18 (P.O.W., in German hands).
Simpson, Eric Maudsley, Capt., died, 2/5/16.
Slater, Ronald Mortimer, Lt., d. of w., 21/11/14.
10 Smart, Claude Edward, T/Lt., k. in a., 24/7/17.
6 Smith, Frederick Neville Cowran, A/Lt., d. of w., 27/8/16 (att. 100th T.M.B.).
1/4 Smith, T. E., 2/Lt., died, 11/6/18 (and R.A.F.).
2 Smith, William Leslie, Lt. (A/Capt.), d. of w., 15/4/18.
2 Smyth, William Henry, Lt. (Tp.), k. in a., 17/4/18.
Smyth-Osborne, Wilfred, Lt., k. in a., 29/8/15.
Smythe, Frederick Fleming, 2/Lt., k. in a., 18/9/14.
4 Sneade, Charles George, M.C., Lt., k. in a., 14/10/18.
Snowden, Jasper Whitfield, Lt., k. in a., 25/2/17.
1 Steele, Ben Harry, 2/Lt., k. in a., 20/11/17.
Stephens, Howell Charles, 2/Lt., k. in a., 31/7/17.
10 Steven, Archibald, 2/Lt. (Tp.), k. in a., 25/10/16 (att. 8th Glos. R.).
5 Stevens, Montague, Lt., k. in a., 7/7/16.
1 Stone, Noel Herbert, M.C., Lt. (A/Capt.), k. in a., 27/4/18.
Street, Norman Kingsley, Capt., k. in a., 10/8/15.
2 Sudbury, John Allen, Lt. (Tp.), k. in a., 29/9/18 (1st Gar. Bn.).

2 Sudlow, Horace Stanley, 2/Lt. (Tp.), k. in a., 30/3/18 (att. 8th Bn.).
5 Surr, Rudolph Vincent, 2/Lt. (A/Lt.), k. in a., 31/10/16.
6 Sweetman, Michael James Joseph, Major, d. of w., 27/11/15 (att. Dor. R.) (Bt.-Maj., Res. of Off.).
Sykes, John Spencer, 2/Lt., k. in a., 3/12/17 (att. 2/7th Bn.).
9 Sykes, William Ernest, Major (T/Lt.-Col.), died, 8/1/15.
4 Talbot, John Lionel Pemberton, 2/Lt., d. of w., 14/10/18.
10 Tasker, Richard Greaves, T/Capt., k. in a., 3/7/16.
9 Taylor, Charles Harry, 2/Lt. (Tp.), k. in a., 25/1/17.
Taylor, Robert Leslie, 2/Lt. (Tp.), d. of w., 11/9/18 (1st Gar. Bn., att. 11 S.L.I.).
12 Taylor, Sidney Arnold Turner, T/2/Lt., d. of w., 17/4/17 (att. M.G.C.).
10 Thomas, Alexander Reginald, Capt. (Tp.), k. in a., 3/7/16.
4 Thomas, Robert Stanley, M.C., T/2/Lt., k. in a., 24/3/18.
Tongue. Claude Leslie, T/2/Lt., died, 26/10/18 (1st Res. Gar. Bn., att. L.C.B. Depot).
Townsend, Josph Ernest, T/2/Lt., killed, 2/1/17 (att. R.F.C.).
9 Tree, Charles James. Lt., d. of w., 20/7/15.
10 Tree, Warren Francis, T/Capt., killed, 22/7/16.
Tristram, John Hutchinson, Lt., k. in a., 11/3/15.
10 Tucker, Frederick St. George, Major (Tp.), k. in a., 3/7/16.
6 Tullidge, Bernard Henry, A/Capt., k. in a., 27/8/17 (att. 13th).
Underhill, William Annesley, Capt., k. in a., 21/10/14.
3 Vaile, Edward Ernest, 2/Lt., k. in a., 5/10/15.
Veasey, John Sherard, Lt., k. in a., 12/3/15.
7 Vigors, Philip Wilson, M.V.O., Capt., died, 2/4/17.
6 Vinter, Robert Bagster Wilson, M.C., 2/Lt., k. in a., 31/10/16.
4 Voyce, Henry Eugene, T/2/Lt., k. in a., 6/8/15.
6 Wainman, Philip Stafford Gordon, Capt., Bt. Maj., k. in a., 26/9/15 (att. 2nd).
12 Walford, Hamilton Stewart, Lt., k. in a., 27/5/18 (att. 1/4 Wel. R.).
12 Walker, Oscar Robert, Capt., k. in a., 4/6/15 (att. R. Fus.).
10 Wallace, Houston Steward Hamilton, T/Capt., k. in a., 22/7/16.
Walton, Frederick Maxwell, 2/Lt., died, 21/2/19 (att. 1/8 Bn.).
5 Ward, William, 2/Lt., k. in a., 4/3/17 (att. 1st).
11 Warlow, Edmund Jarvis Leith, T/Lt., k. in a., 6/11/16 (att. 2nd).
5 Warren, Martin, 2/Lt. (A/Capt.), k. in a., 24/3/18 (att. 1st).
5 Warriner, Thomas Andrew Latimer, 2/Lt., k. in a., 10/10/16.
Watson, Louis Talbot, Capt., k. in a., 11/3/15.
2/1 Watson, Thomas Hovenden, D.S.O., M.C., A/Lt.-Col., k. in a., 23/3/18 (att. 1st N. & D.R.).
6 Watt, John Heigh, 2/Lt., k. in a., 12/4/18 (att. 4th).
13 Watts, Ronald William Ailsa, M.C., T/2/Lt., d. of w., 12/11/16 (att. 2nd).
4 Weatherhead, Stanley Ernest William, 2/Lt., k. in a., 23/4/17.
11 Welby, John Arthur, T/Capt., d. of w., 17/3/17.
3 Wevell, William Henry, Lt., k. in a., 14/5/16.
1 Whitehurst, Albert Percival, 2/Lt., k. in a., 25/3/18.
1 Whittingham, Leonard Buxton, 2/Lt., d. of w., 26/4/18 (att. 3rd).
Whittle, Walter Victor Patrick Charles, 2/Lt., k. in a., 13/4/15.
11 Williams, Harold, Lt. (T/Capt.), k. in a., 25/4/17.
3 Williams, Henry Vincent, 2/Lt., k. in a., 26/5/16.
Williams, Owen Edgar, 2/Lt., k. in a., 19/4/17 (att. 1/4th Welsh R.).
6 Willmott, John Dyott, Lt., k. in a., 3/7/15 (att. 2nd).
4 Wills, Alfred Leslie, Lt., k. in a., 23/4/17.
2 Wilmot, Thomas Norbury, M.C., 2/Lt., d. of w., 25/8/16.
1 Wilson, William Clement, T/2/Lt. (T/Lt.), k. in a., 25/9/15.
1 Winnington, John Francis Sartorius, D.S.O., Lt.-Col., d. of w., 22/9/18.
Wodehouse, Ernest Charles Forbes, D.S.O., Lt.-Col., k. in a., 10-13/3/15.
Woodward, George Ernest, 2/Lt., k. in a., 29/9/18 (att. 2nd).
2 Worster, Frank Copeland, M.C., Lt. (A/Capt.), d. of w., 30/5/18.
Wrenford, Arthur Leonard, Capt. (A/Lt.-Col.), k. in a., 21/3/18 (att. 4th E. Lancs).
Wythes, Claude Aspinall, Capt., k. in a., 28/4/15.

The East Lancashire Regiment.

3 Allen, Percy Herman Charles, Lt., k. in a., 9/5/15 (att. 2/Bn.).
3 Allen, William Frederick, 2/Lt., k. in a., 9/10/17 (att. 2/4 Bn.).
Allison, Charles A., Lt. (Tp.), k. in a., 12/3/15.
1 Argyle, Percival Edgar, 2/Lt. (Tp.), k. in a., 9/4/17.
Arnott, Kenneth Hugh Lowden, D.S.O., M.C., Capt. (Lt.-Col.) (Tp.), k. in a., 30/5/18 (att. 7/K.S.L.I.).
12 Atkinson, Guy Cheselden Renell, 2/Lt. (Tp.), d. of w., 30/10/16.
3 Atkinson, Noel Mitford Henson, 2/Lt. (Tp.), died, 27/12/16.
Aubin, Alfred Charles, Capt., k. in a., 30/8/14.
10 Backhouse, St. John Salmon, 2/Lt., k. in a., 3/4/18 (att. R.A.F.).
Baker, Roger Dyke, Major, d. of w., 13/8/15 (Staff 38 Inf. Bde.).
3 Barr, David Buik, Capt., d. of w., 13/7/19.
11 Barrett, William, 2/Lt. (Tp.), k. in a., 11/8/16.
6 Bartlett, Robert Nigel Oldfield, Capt. (Tp.), d. of w., 6/4/16.
10 Beacall, Arthur, 2/Lt. (Tp.), k. in a., 1/7/16 (att. 11/Bn.).
7 Bearman, Frank, Lt. (Tp.), died, 5/8/17.
11 Beaumont, George Joseph, Lt. (Tp.), died, 18/1/17.
Beaumont, Sydney, M.C., 2/Lt. (Tp.), d. of w., 28/3/18 (att. 2/4 Bn.).
Belchier, Frank Elliot, Capt., k. in a., 20/5/15.
8 Bell, Albert, 2/Lt. (Tp.), k. in a., 27/3/18 (att. 11/Bn.).
8 Billinger, Hector Fussell, 2/Lt. (Tp.), k. in a., 23/11/16.
10 Bishop, John Edmund, Capt. (Tp.), k. in a., 18-19/4/16 (att. 6/Bn.).
1 Blake, Reginald Joseph Albert, Lt. (Tp.), k. in a., 13/4/18 (att. 11/Bn.).
3 Bligh, Eric, Lt., k. in a., 9/5/15 (att. 2/Bn.).
8 Brash, John, 2/Lt. (Tp.), k. in a., 25/8/18 (att. 1/5 Bn.).
3 Brown. Harold Montague, 2/Lt., k. in a., 9/4/16.
3 Brown, Norman Watson, 2/Lt. (T/Lt.), d. of w., 1/5/17 (att. M.G.C., 103 Coy.).
10 Brown, Tom, 2/Lt. (Tp.), k. in a., 13/11/16 (att. 7/Bn.).
7 Browning, George Howard, 2/Lt. (Tp.), k. in a., 13/3/18 (att. 1/Bn.).
3 Buckley, Godfrey, Lt., killed, 15/8/17 (att. 9/Bn.).
6 Bull, Henry Spencer, D.S.O., Major (Tp.), died, 30/7/18.
Burmann, Robert Moyle, D.S.O., M.C., Capt., k. in a., 27/10/18.
3 Burnett, Ian Alistair Kendale, Capt., k. in a., 31/5/17 (att. 8/Bn.).
3 Butcher, Francis Percival Herbert, 2/Lt., k. in a., 30/8/16 (att. 1/Bn.).
Cane, Lionel Alfred Francis, Capt., k. in a., 7/11/14.
Canton, Herbert Westrup, Lt. (T/Capt.), k. in a., 13/5/15.
13 Carter, Harold Major, 2/Lt. (Tp.), d. of w., 28/8/18.
Chisholm, William Malcolm, Lt., d. of w., 27/8/14.
2 Chorlton, Herbert Bichonall, 2/Lt., k. in a., 26/3/18 (att. 4/Bn.).
9 Chowne, Gerard Henry Tilson, Capt. (Tp.), d. of w., 2/5/17.
11 Clarke, Leonard William, 2/Lt. (Tp.), d. of w., 14/11/16.
Clayhills, George, D.S.O., Capt., k. in a., 2/11/14.
10 Clifton, Hubert Arthur, 2/Lt. (Tp.), d. of w., 6/4/16.
2 Coar, Edward Roland, 2/Lt. (Tp.), d. of w., 8/1/18.
6 Cole-Hamilton, Arthur Richards, Lt.-Col. (Tp.), d. of w., 10/8/15.
7 Corfield, Hubert Vernon Auchitel, 2/Lt. (Tp.), k. in a., 6/7/16.
Coventry, Edgar Ernest, Capt., k. in a., 1/11/14.
Craig, George Robert, M.C., Lt., killed, 19/7/17 (and R.F.C.).
2 Cranwill, Valentine Arthur Butler, M.C., Lt. (A/Capt.), 24/4/18.
11 Cronshaw, Thomas Edgar, 2/Lt. (Tp.), d. of w., 8/3/17.
1 Currall, Norman Frank, 2/Lt., k. in a., 18/10/16.
1/2 Davenport, Allen Arthur Orme, Lt., d. of w., 24/3/18 (att. 4/Bn.).
3 Davey, Herbert, 2/Lt., k. in a., 18/4/17 (att. 6/Bn.).
10 Davies, Harry Noel, 2/Lt. (Tp.), k. in a., 1/7/16 (att. 11/Bn.).
Daw, Thomas Herbert, Capt. (Tp.), k. in a., 9/5/15.
10 Day, Douglas Knowles, 2/Lt. (Tp.), d. of w., 19/11/15 (att. 6/Bn.).
6 Debenham, Herbert, Lt. (Tp.), k. in a., 9/8/15.
2 Delmege, Eyre Bolton Massy, M.C., Capt., k. in a., 23/10/16.
3 Dickinson, George Bairnsfather, Lt., k. in a., 3/5/15.
2 Donley, David C. B., 2/Lt., d. of w., 3/9/17.
3 Douglas, David Tocher, 2/Lt. (Tp.), d. of w., 1/11/17.
Dothie, Elvery Ashton, 2/Lt., killed, 9/5/15.
7 Duggan, Thomas Alphonsus, 2/Lt. (Tp.), k. in a., 13/11/16.
Dugdale, James, D.C.M., 2/Lt. (Tp.), d. of w., 7/7/18 (att. 1/Bn.).
12 East, William Frederick Ernest, 2/Lt. (Tp.), k. in a. 16/11/16 (att. 8/Bn.).
1 Edmondson, Frank, Capt., k. in a., 11/4/17 (att. 8/Bn.).
2 Ellen, Eric Adrian, T/Lt. (A/Capt.), k. in a., 30/1/17.
2 Ellison, Samuel, 2/Lt. (Tp.), d. of w., 25/3/18.
7 Emmott, Rennie, 2/Lt., k. in a., 31/7/17.
3 Fisher, Edmund, 2/Lt., k. in a., 16/11/16 (att. 8/Bn.).
11 Evans, Alfred Henry Courtenay, 2/Lt. (Tp.), killed, 22/3/18 (att. R.F.C.).
2 Farthing, Leonard, M.C., Lt. (A/Capt.), k. in a., 16/11/16
8 Fawcett, Bertram James Acton, Capt., d. of w., 24/4/17.
1 Fisher, Thomas Edward Coney, Lt., k. in a., 1/7/16.
8 Fitzhugh, Harold, 2/Lt. (Tp.), k. in a., 31/7/17.
8 Forman, Moses, Lt. (Tp.), d. of w., 11/4/17.
3 Forster, Walter Johnson, Capt., k. in a., 31/5/17 (att. 8/Bn.).
2 Frampton, William John Goulbourn Shipdern, Capt., k. in a., 24/4/18.
Gallagher, William Augustine, Capt., k. in a., 12/3/15.
11 Gardner, Sidney, 2/Lt. (Tp.), k. in a., 27/3/18.
6 Gayer, Alexander Edward, Capt. and Adj., died, 23/11/18.
2 Gittings, Charles, 2/Lt. (Tp.), k. in a., 21/3/18 (att. 2/5 Bn.).
10 Glennon, Francis Henry, 2/Lt. (Tp.), k. in a., 16/11/16 (att. 8/Bn.).
3 Goodall, George Mortimer Langdon, 2/Lt., k. in a., 9/5/15 (att. 2/Bn.).
7 Goulding, George Percival Kimber, 2/Lt. (T/Lt.), d. of w., 31/7/17.
1 Gray, Charles Dixon, Lt., k. in a., 9/9/18.
7 Griffiths, Iorwerth, 2/Lt. (Tp.), k. in a., 5/7/16.
0 Guest, Cyril Stuart, 2/Lt. (Tp.), d. of w., 5/8/16 (att. 10/S. Staff. R.).
7 Halfhide, Charles Edward Nelson, Lt. (Tp.) (A/Major), k. in a., 24/5/18 (att. Div. M.G.C.).
2 Hambley, Francis William, 2/Lt. (Tp.), k. in a., 31/7/17.
8 Hammond, Paul, Capt. (Tp.), d. of w., 25/2/16.
1 Hannaford, Stanley John, Lt., k. in a., 5/10/17.
Harston, Frank Northey, M.C., Lt. (T/Capt.), k. in a., 22/4/18 (and Staff, 11 Inf. Bde.).
1 Hart, John Sidney, 2/Lt., d. of w., 18/4/18 (att. 1/5 Bn.).
1 Heard, Charles Miller, 2/Lt., k. in a., 10/4/17 (att. 8/Bn.).
8 Hewson, Joseph Edward, 2/Lt. (Tp.), k. in a., 10/7/16.
7 Hilton, Murray Venables (Bt.-Col.), T/Col., k. in a., 20/10/15.
10 Hitchon, James Foldys, Lt., k. in a., 1/7/16 (att. 11/Bn.).
3 Hoare, Percival Hugh Trench, Lt., d. of w., 8/1/15 (att. 1/Bn.).

Hodges, James William, 2/Lt. (Tp.), k. in a., 21/3/18 (att. 5/Bn.).
Hodgson, Philip Ormiston, 2/Lt., d. of w., 13/3/15.
3 Hollinshead, Shadrach, 2/Lt., k. in a., 27/3/18 (att. 11/Bn.).
3 Holles, Frederick Tetherley Noel, 2/Lt., died, 11/9/16.
7 Holloway, Henry, 2/Lt. (A/Capt.), k. in a., 11/4/18 (att. 9/Welsh R.).
3 Hooper, David Ernest, 2/Lt., k. in a., 30/4/15 (att. 2/Bn.).
10 Hopwood, Edwin John, Lt. (Tp.), k. in a., 9/4/16 (att. 6/Bn.).
Hornby, Cecil Geoffrey, O.B.E., M.C., Major (T/Lt.-Col.), died, 30/12/18 (att. W.A.F.F.).
1 V.C. Horsfall, Basil Arthur, 2/Lt., k. in a., 27/3/18 (att. 11/Bn.)
Howell, Herbert Edgar, 2/Lt., k. in a., 9/5/15.
Hughes, Frederick Deeton, Lt., k. in a., 21/10/14.
6 Hughes, Thomas, 2/Lt. (Tp.), died, 14/12/18.
1/2 Hunwick, Edward Noel, 2/Lt. (Tp.), k. in a., 30/8/18.
10 Hunt, James, 2/Lt. (Tp.), k. in a., 16/11/16 (att. 8/Bn.).
3 Hutchinson, Cecil Leigh, 2/Lt., k. in a., 31/7/17 (att. 2/Batt.).
Ilsley, Alfred Lewis, 2/Lt. (Tp.), died, 23/11/17.
11 Inman, Richard Hugh, Lt. (Tp.), k. in a., 28/6/18.
2 Irish, Edwin Charles, 2/Lt., k. in a., 26/12/17.
9 James, Richard Arthur Brodie, Capt. (Tp.), k. in a., 13/9/16.
11 James, Richard Walter, 2/Lt. (Tp.), k. in a., 8/5/17.
10 Jarintzoff, Dmitri, T/Lt. (A/Capt.), k. in a., 8/10/17 (att. 6/Bn.).
1 Jones, Kenneth Champion, 2/Lt. (Tp.), k. in a., 1/7/16.
Jones, Maurice, Lt. (Tp.) d. of w., 27/9/18 (att. 14/War. R.).
3 Julius, Cecil Herbert, 2/Lt., k. in a., 9/4/16 (att. 6/Bn.).
3 Keyser, Richard Norman, Lt., killed, 22/8/17 (and R.F.C.).
3 Knight, Frederick Thornton, 2/Lt., k. in a., 13/5/15 (att. 1/Bn.).
3 Knight, Hugh Eric Coleraine, Capt., k. in a., 11/4/18 (att. 1/Bn.).
11 Kohn, Wilfred Arthur, 2/Lt. (Tp.), k. in a., 1/7/16.
Lane, Hector Allan, Lt., k. in a., 13/5/15.
Larkins, Edward Arthur Malcolm, Lt., k. in a., 18/7/15.
7 Laverick, Frederick Gordon, 2/Lt. (Tp.), k. in a., 23/7/17.
11 Leach, Errol William Carlisle, Act. Lt., k. in a., 15/5/17.
Leake, George Dalton, Capt., k. in a., 13/5/15.
1 Le Marchant, Louis St. Gratieu, D.S.O., Lt.-Col., k. in a., 14/9/14.
10 Litton, Reginald, 2/Lt. (Tp.), k. in a., 8/9/16 (att. 2/Bn.).
11 Livesey, Harry, Capt. (Tp.), k. in a., 1/7/16.
3 Lott, John Cyprian, M.C., 2/Lt., k. in a., 13/4/18 (att. 11/Bn.).
7 Lowe, William, Lt. (Tp.), k. in a., 5/7/16.
6 Lutyens, Charles Grae, Capt., d. of w., 8/8/15.
1/2 Lyons, Edward Thomas, 2/Lt. (Tp.), k. in a., 4/10/17.
3 McDowall, Archibald, 2/Lt., killed, 12/1/18 (att. R.F.C.).
MacLear, Harry, D.S.O., Lt.-Col., k. in a., 15/3/16 (att. 13/R. Scots).
2 McMillan, George, 2/Lt. (Tp.), k. in a., 31/7/17.
8 MacQueen, Thomas Malcolm, Lt. (Tp.), k. in a., 15/7/16.
8 Magrath, Beauchamp Henry Butler, Major, (Tp.), k. in a., 2/6/16.
1 Mallett, Eric Sydney, 2/Lt., k. in a., 1/7/16.
11 Mallinson, Charles Heathcote, Capt., d. of w., 26-27/6/18 (whilst P.O.W. in German Hands).
2 Manktelow, Walter Stanley, 2/Lt. (Tp.), k. in a., 21/3/18 (att. 2/5 Bn.).
8 Marshall, John Hamilton, 2/Lt. (Tp.), k. in a., 23/10/16.
Marshall, Augustus de la Pere, 2/Lt., k. in a., 9/5/15.
2 Martin, Cecil Hampson, Capt., k. in a., 2/10/16.
3 Mathews, Robert Arthur Cecil, Lt., k. in a., 18/10/16 (att. 1/Bn.).
Mathews, Thomas Hugh, Lt., k. in a., 2/11/14.
3 Mauleverer, Richard De Burgh, 2/Lt., d. of w., 13/11/17 (att. 2/Bn.).
10 May, Percy William, 2/Lt. (Tp.), k. in a., 13/11/16 (att. 7/Bn.).
10 Mellor, Francis Rigby, Lt. (Tp.), d. of w., 15/1/17 (att. 6/Bn.).
3 Minnaar, Charles William Rorich, 2/Lt., k. in a., 16/11/16 (att. 8/Bn.).
12 Mitchell, Bertram Earnshaw, 2/Lt. (Tp.), died, 4/2/17 (att. 7/Bn.).
11 Mitchell, Henry Harrison, Lt. (Tp.), d. of w., 23/2/16.
Moloney, Bertram Weldon, Capt., k. in a., 28/2/15.
8 Moorhouse, Arthur, 2/Lt., k. in a., 16/11/16.
3 Morkel, Daniel Johannes Cecil, 2/Lt., k. in a., 16/11/16.
7 Morris, William Reginald, 2/Lt. (Tp.), k. in a., 25/9/15.
1 Naylor, Herbert William Eastwood, Lt., Qr. Mr., k. in a., 17/2/17.
8 Needham, Arthur Charles, Capt. (Tp.), k. in a., 16/11/16.
1 Neve, Harold, 2/Lt., k. in a., 27/5/18 (att. 7 Bn.).
1 Newcombe, Richard, Lt. (Tp.), k. in a., 1/7/16.
10 Nicolson, William Alexander, Capt., died, 20/7/16.
Norton, A. G., 2/Lt., k. in a., 9/5/15.
Nutcombe, Thomas Arthur, 2/Lt., killed, 2/8/18 (and R.A.F.).
3 O'Meara, Leon Alfred, 2/Lt., k. in a., 6/2/17 (att. 6/Batt.).
2 Osborne, Edward Bertram, 2/Lt. (Tp.), d. of w., 1/4/18 (att. 5/Bn.) (in German hands).
2 Owen, Herbert, 2/Lt. (Tp.), d. of w., 23/3/18.
3 Parkinson, Oswald Wright, 2/Lt., k. in a., 1/2/17 (att. 6/Batt.).
1 Penny, Arthur Hugh, Capt., d. of w., 1/7/16.
10 Phillips, Patrick Tewan, 2/Lt. (Tp.), k. in a., 4-5/4/16 (att. 6/Bn.).
1 Pickup, William, 2/Lt., k. in a., 25/3/18.
8 Pocock, Raglan Lionel Alfred, 2/Lt. (Tp.), k. in a., 25/8/17.
8 Pointer, Reginald James, 2/Lt., k. in a., 21/3/18 (att. 4/Bn.).
Pollard, Frank, 2/Lt. (Tp.), d. of w., 21-22/3/18.
7 Potter, Fred, 2/Lt., d. of w., 22/9/17.
10 Prescott, Robert Stewart, 2/Lt. (Tp.), k. in a., 1/7/16.
3 Preston, Thomas Haworth, Capt., k. in a., 17/11/14.
9 Purves, Walter Douglas Laidlaw, T/Lt. (A/Capt.), k. in a., 28/4/17.
8 Raeburn, Gordon Peter, 2/Lt. (Tp.), d. of w., 11/4/17.
7 Raphael, Henry George, 2/Lt., k. in a., 31/7/17.
7 Redden, Herbert, M.C., 2/Lt. (T/Capt.), k. in a., 7/6/17.
7 Redding, John Wills, 2/Lt. (Tp.), k. in a., 24/4/18 (att. 2/Bn.).
3 Reichardt, Paul, 2/Lt., k. in a., 31/7/17.
2 Richardson, Walter Fairfax, Capt., k. in a., 9/5/15.
7 Ridgway, Harold Edwin, Lt. (Tp.), k. in a., 7/6/17.
11 Riley, Henry Davison, Capt. (Tp.), k. in a., 1/7/16.
3 Ritchie, Thomas Arthur, 2/Lt., k. in a., 18/10/16 (att. 1/Bn.).
12 Robinson, Isaac, 2/Lt. (Tp.), k. in a., 23/10/16 (att. 2/Bn.).
Rose, William Samuel, 2/Lt. (Tp.), k. in a., 2/12/17 (att. 2/5 Bn.).
Russell, Leonard, Major, k. in a., 9/5/15.
Rutter, Eustace Frederick, Major, k. in a., 13/5/15.
2 Ryan, Patrick Cornelius, 2/Lt. (Tp.), k. in a., 13/10/18.
10 Sadler, Charles Edward, 2/Lt. (Tp.), k. in a., 1/7/16.
Sanders, Alvin Augustus, Major, k. in a., 12/3/15.
11 Saunders, Harold Macleod, 2/Lt. (Tp.), k. in a., 25/6/18.
10 Saunders, Roy Llewellyn, 2/Lt. (Tp.), k. in a., 9/4/16 (att. 6/Bn.).
Seckham, Gerald Adair, Lt., k. in a., 6/1/15.
Sedgwick, Joseph, 2/Lt. (Tp.), k. in a., 9/10/17.
13 Sefton, Percy, 2/Lt. (Tp.), k. in a., 22/8/18.
3 Shann, Reginald Arthur, Lt., k. in a., 21/3/18 (att. 4/Bn.).
7 Sims, Charles Henry, 2/Lt. (Tp.), k. in a., 24/4/18. (att. 2/Bn.).
12 Slinger, William, Lt. (Tp.), k. in a., 23/7/17 (att. 1/Bn.).
2 Small, Alexander Couper, M.C., 2/Lt. (Tp.), k. in a., 23/10/16.
11 Smith, W., 2/Lt., killed, 2/4/18 (and R.A.F.).
2 Smith, William Harold Vyvyan, 2/Lt., k. in a., 31/7/17.
12 Standring, William Shuttleworth, 2/Lt., k. in a., 30/7/16.
Stanley, George Hopkins, 2/Lt., k. in a., 31/10/14.
2 Stanworth, Joseph, 2/Lt. (Tp.), d. of w., 11/7/17.
1 Stead, Brian Desmond Howland, Lt., k. in a., 21/3/18.
Stevens, Edward Henry, Lt., d. of w., 16/8/17 (att. R.F.C., 25 Sq.).
8 Stock, James Mulock Thompson, Lt. (Tp.), k. in a., 16/11/16
11 Stonehouse, Charles, Lt. (Tp.), k. in a., 1/7/16.
3 Swift, Neville Cropley, D.S.O., M.C., Lt. (A/Major), d. of w., 28/3/18 (att. 2/Bn.).
11 Tarrant, Percival John, Capt. (Tp.), k. in a., 25/6/18 (att. 11/Bn.).
3 Taylor, Charles Livingstone, Lt. (A/Capt.), k. in a., 24/3/18 (att. 8/Bn.).
1 Thomas, Heinrich William Max, Capt. (Tp.), k. in a., 1/7/16.
1/2 Thomas, William, M.M., 2/Lt. (Tp.), died, 7/11/18 (att. 1/5 Bn.).
8 Thompson, Cecil Victor, 2/Lt. (Tp.), k. in a., 6/2/17.
10 Thompson, Herbert William, 2/Lt., k. in a., 1/7/16.
2 Thompson, Reginald, Lt. (Tp.), k. in a., 23/10/16 (late 7/Bn.).
10 Thompson, Walter Albert, 2/Lt., died, 8/9/17.
7 Thomson, Charles, M.C., Capt., k. in a., 2/9/18 (att. 2/Bn.).
1/2 Thornhill, William Ewart, 2/Lt. (Tp.), k. in a., 4/10/17.
Tinling, George Evelyn, M.C., Lt. (A/Capt.), k. in a., 4/10/17.
10 Tompkins, Harold Arthur, 2/Lt., d. of w., 1/7/16.
1 Tosswill, Walter Roy, Capt., d. of w., 12/8/16.
11 Tough, Arnold Bannatyne, Capt. (Tp.), k. in a., 1/7/16.
Townsend, Ivan Vesey, Lt., k. in a., 3/2/15.
6 Treadwell, George Reuben, Capt. (Tp.), k. in a., 5/2/17.
6 Trimmer, Edmund Howard, Lt. (Tp.), d. of w., 10/8/15.
Tudor-Jones, Charles Edward Tudor, 2/Lt., killed, 15/12/15.
7 Tyser, George Beaumont, Major (Tp.), k. in a., 5/7/16.
1 Vandome, Joseph John, 2/Lt., k. in a., 4/10/17.
1 Vella, Arthur Henry, 2/Lt., k. in a., 28/4/17 (att. R. Ir. Fus.)
2 Wakeford, Walter Thomas, 2/Lt., k. in a., 7/7/16.
8 Walker, Vernon Lee, 2/Lt. (Tp.), k. in a., 29/5/17.
Warner, Herbert Moline, Lt., d. of w., 16/11/14.
1 Watson, Charles Edward Stephen, 2/Lt., k. in a., 1/7/16.
3 Watson, Cyril Pennefather, 2/Lt., k. in a., 1/7/16.
6 Watson, Thomas Palmer, M.C., Capt. (Tp.), k. in a., 7/3/17.
Watterson, Gerald, 2/Lt., k. in a., 13/3/18 (att. 1/Bn.).
Waud, Lionel Douglas, Lt., k. in a., 8/11/14.
11 Wayland, Richard Bunster, 2/Lt. (Tp.), d. of w., 22/9/16.
7 Webster, Hugh Maxwell, 2/Lt. (Tp.), k. in a., 5/7/16.
1 West, George Arnold, 2/Lt., d. of w., 8/8/18 (att. M.G.C.).
1 Wheate, Arthur, 2/Lt. (Tp.), d. of w., 5/4/16.
7 White, Thomas Herbert, M.C., 2/Lt. (Tp.), died, 24/1/19 (and R.A.F.).
10 Wighton, George Edwin, 2/Lt. (Tp.), d. of w., 11/3/16 (att. 11/Bn.).
10 Winder, Harold, 2/Lt., k. in a., 15/5/17.
8 Winser, Arthur Cecil, Lt. (Tp.), d. of w., 22/2/16.
Wolseley, William Joseph, 2/Lt., k. in a., 11/3/15.
6 Wood, Cecil Gordon, Lt. (Tp.), d. of w., 20/9/15.
2 Wood, Clement Percy, 2/Lt., k. in a., 21/11/17.
7 Wyllie, Hugh William, Lt. (Tp.), k. in a., 26/10/16.

The East Surrey Regiment.

1 Abbiss, John Lee, Lt., died, 25/7/18 (att. M.G.C.).
8 Ackerley, Peter Roger, Lt. (Tp.), k. in a., 7/8/18.
3 Adams, George Allsop, 2/Lt., k. in a., 9/4/17 (att. 7 Bn.).
11 Armitage, George Duncan, 2/Lt. (Tp.), k. in a., 6/8/15 (att. 2/Hants Regt.).
7 Armstrong, Harry William Thomas, 2/Lt., d. of w., 14/7/15.
3 Arnold, Thomas Sorrell, 2/Lt., d. of w., 11/10/17 (att. 2/7 Lanc. Fusrs.).

8 Astington, Thomas Jeffery, 2/Lt. (Tp.), k. in a., 28/2/17.
7 Ayres, Stanley Frank, Capt. (Tp.), k. in a., 20/11/17.
12 Bailey, Herbert Packer, M.C., 2/Lt., k. in a., 31/7/17.
3 Ball, Frank Granville, 2/Lt., k. in a., 16/8/16 (att. 9 Bn.).
8 Barber, Harry Mason, 2/Lt. (Tp.), k. in a., 8/8/18.
8 Barder, Sam Gerald, 2/Lt. (Tp.), k. in a., 30/9/16.
9 Barnett, Charles Edward, Capt. (Tp.), d. of w., 1/10/15.
9 Barnett, Harold Thornton, 2/Lt. (T/Lt.), d. of w., 21/10/15
8 Bartrum, Arthur Allan, 2/Lt. (Tp.), k. in a., 30/9/16.
9 Bate, Eric Raoul Hender, 2/Lt., k. in a., 25/9/15.
2 Bayne, Edward Gordon, Lt. (Tp.), k. in a., 4/10/17 (att. 1 Bn.).
4 Beatty, Desmond Henry, 2/Lt., d. of w., 21/2/15.
3 Becker, Charlie Hereward, Lt. (T/Capt.), killed, 8/8/18 (att. Royal Fusrs.).
Becker, Jonathan Otto Gustavus, Lt., k. in a., 12/3/15.
3 Begbie, S. C. H., Lt., died, 22/4/18 (and R.A.F.).
8 Bell-Irving, Kenneth, Capt., d of w., 22/10/17.
3 Benning, Murray Stuart, Lt., d. of w., 1/11/14.
Benson, John Peurice, Capt., k. in a., 23/8/14.
7 Bentham, George Andrew, 2/Lt., died, 3/11/16 (and R.F.C.).
4 Bigger, John Alfred Whittard, 2/Lt., k. in a., 8/5/17 (att. 1 Bn.).
9 Birch, Charles Richard Eli, Lt. & Qr.-Mr., died, 12/8/17.
3 Birch-Reynardson, Edward Vere, Lt., k. in a., 25/12/15 (att. 1 Bn.).
Birnie, Edward John Wilfrid, 2/Lt., k. in a., 14/2/15 (Spec. Res.).
9 Birt, Wilfrid Beckett, Capt., died, 18/4/16 (in Ger. hands).
1 Blackman, William, 2/Lt. (A/Capt.), k. in a., 8/5/17.
7 Board, George William, Lt., k. in a., 30/11/17.
9 Bogue, Patrick Yule, 2/Lt. (Tp.), k. in a., 23/7/17.
3 Bowyer-Bower, Eldred Wolferstan, Capt., k. in a., 19/3/17 (and R.F.C., 59 Sqd.).
7 Brasnett, Thomas John Grose, 2/Lt. (Tp.), k. in a., 13/10/15.
Bridgland, Neville Linton, Lt., k. in a., 22/10/14 (att. 1 Bn.).
4 Britts, Charles William Gordon, 2/Lt., killed, 6/11/15 (att. 9 Bn.).
8 Brown, Harold Vernon, 2/Lt. (Tp.), k. in a., 3/5/17 (att. 11 Bn.).
1 Brown, Leonard James, 2/Lt., k. in a., 19/8/18 (att. 2/Royal Fusrs.).
13 Buckland, Ernest Blas, T/Lt., k. in a., 5/10/16.
12 Buckman, James Leslie, Temp. Capt., k. in a., 15/9/16.
1 Burdett, Glanville, 2/Lt., k. in a., 4/10/17.
Burn, Arthur George McCausland, Capt., k. in a., 29/10/14.
Caesar, George Theodore, Lt., d. of w., 2/5/18 (att. Tank Corps).
Caffyn, Chalenor McCrae Humphrey Mannington, 2/Lt., T/Lt., k. in a., 28/3/17 (and R.F.C., 60 Sqd.).
9 Campbell, Alexander Charles Penn, Lt. (Tp.), k. in a., 26/9/15.
8 Canfor, Arthur Reginald, Temp. 2/Lt., k. in a., 23/3/18.
3 Card, John Victor, Lt., k. in a., 25/3/19.
13 Carey, Loyd Carleton, 2/Lt. (Tp.), k. in a., 4/9/16 (att. 1 Bn.).
Carter, Frank Leslie, Lt., k. in a., 22/4/17 (and R.F.C., 3 Sqd.).
9 Carter, George Sidney, M.C., 2/Lt., d. of w., 28/11/17.
1 Carter, Malcolm Russell, Lt., A/Capt., k. in a., 23/3/18 (att. 8 Bn.).
7 Case, Lionel Trevor Elliott, Temp. Capt., k. in a., 30/11/17.
11 Chambers, Wilfrid John, Temp. Lt., k. in a., 18/8/16.
Chandler, Charles Robert, 2/Lt. (Tp.), k. in a., 29/9/15.
Chapman, Arthur Thomas, Capt., k. in a., 26/4/15 (att. Hamps. Regt.).
12 Chesters, John Richards, Temp. Lt., k. in a., 15/9/16.
3 Cheers, Donald Heriot Anson, 2/Lt., killed, 17/4/18 (and R.A.F.).
1 Clark, Oscar William, 2/Lt. (Tp.), k. in a., 22/7/16.
Clarke, Booth Frederick, 2/Lt., k. in a., 26/1/17.
11 Clarke, Cyril, 2/Lt. (Tp.), d. of w., 16/6/16 (att. 8 Bn.).
1 Clay, Henry George Walter, 2/Lt., k. in a., 29/7/16.
1 Colin, Felix Augustus, 2/Lt., k. in a., 3/5/17 (att. 7 Bn.).
9 Collinson, Arthur Amery, Capt., k. in a., 25/9/15.
Combe-Ceaton, Frank, 2/Lt. (Tp.), k. in a., 14/10/18 (att. 12 Bn.).
Cook, Albert Edward, Temp. 2/Lt., k. in a., 20/2/18 (att. 2/22 Lon. Regt.).
9 Corley, William Raymond, 2/Lt. (Tp.), k. in a., 27/3/18.
9 Coutts, Norman Vawdrey, 2/Lt., d. of w., 26/9/15.
4 Covington, Edwin Thornton, 2/Lt., k. in a., 9/3/17 (att. 6th N. Lan. Regt.).
Crabb, Leonard George Bruce, 2/Lt., k. in a., 12/3/15.
13 Crocker, Edward, Temp. Capt., k. in a., 24/4/17.
9 Cuthbert, Charles Louttit, Temp. 2/Lt., d. of w., 18/8/16.
3 Davy, Reginald, 2/Lt., k. in a., 21/10/18.
12 Davis, Cyril York, Temp. Capt., k. in a., 15/9/16.
8 Dawson, Frederick Albert, M.C., Temp. 2/Lt., k. in a., 7/8/18.
1 Darrell, Albert, 2/Lt., k. in a., 25/12/15.
9 Dealtry, Herbert Arthur Berkeley, Capt., k. in a., 26/9/15.
3 D'Albertanson, Ronald, 2/Lt., d. of w., 8/8/16 (att. 6/Dorset Regt.).
4 Davis, Wilfred Allen, 2/Lt., k. in a., 21/4/15 (att. 1 Bn.).
De Buriatte, John Philip, 2/Lt., k. in a., 12/3/15.
9 De la Fontaine, Henry Victor Mottet, D.S.O., Major (T/Lt.-Col.), k. in a., 5/8/17.
7 Deslandes, Denis George, 2/Lt. (Tp.), k. in a., 27/11/16.
8 Dix, Cyril Bernard, 2/Lt. (Tp.), k. in a., 9/8/17.
7 Dixon, Cuthbert Stuart, 2/Lt. (Tp.), k. in a., 3/5/17.
9 Douglass, Archibald Henry, Temp. Lt., d. of w., 8/4/18.
8 Dove, Edward Maddison, M.C., Lt. (Tp.), k. in a., 23/3/18.
12 Duncan, Alick Thomas, 2/Lt., k. in a., 2/3/17.
1/2 Dunkley, Henry Newman, Temp. 2/Lt., k. in a., 21/9/17 (att. 12 Bn.).
4 Eccles, Arthur John Tolcher, M.C., Lt., died, 26/11/18 (att. R.E.).
1 Edwards, Colin Hyde, 2/Lt., d. of w., 22/5/17.
Emmett, Charles Percival, Lt., A/Capt., d. of w., 28/6/18 (att. 8 Bn.).
9 Elverson, Ronald Whidborne, Lt., k. in a., 25/9/15.
4 England, John Kenneth, 2/Lt. (Tp.), d. of w., 5/9/18.
7 Evans, Douglas Houghton, 2/Lt., k. in a., 13/8/16.
1 Evans, George Edwin, 2/Lt. (Tp.), k. in a., 26/3/18.
8 Evans, Tudor Eglwysbach, 2/Lt., k. in a., 1/7/16.
8 Fairbank, Stanley Reginald, Temp. 2/Lt., k. in a., 4/4/18.
8 Falcon, Geoffrey William Lockhart, Lt. (Tp.), k. in a., 6/8/15.
3 Fardell, Hubert George Henry, Lt., k. in a., 23/4/15 (att. 2/Bn.).
4 Farey, Cecil Victor, M.C., 2/Lt., d. of w., 11/8/17 (att. 7 Bn.).
7 Farquharson-Roberts, Donald, M.C., Temp. Capt., k. in a., 20/11/17.
8 Fearn, Herbert, Temp. 2/Lt., k. in a., 12/10/17.
3 Featherstone, Cecil Frederick, Lt., k. in a., 25/4/15 (att. 2 Bn.).
4 Fisher, Charles Heath, M.C., 2/Lt., k. in a., 14/10/18 (att. 12 Bn.).
Fitz-Gerald, Alfred Edward, Lt.-Col. (Tp.), d. of w., 13/7/16 (att. 15/D.L.I.).
8 Flatau, A. Theodore, Capt. (Tp.), k. in a., 1/7/16.
12 Fox, Cecil Croker, Temp. Lt., k. in a., 15/9/16.
8 Franks, Rolland Sutton, 2/Lt., k. in a., 12/10/17 (att. 1 Bn.).
11 Franklin, William Joseph, Temp. 2/Lt., k. in a., 5/10/16 (att. 7/Sussex Regt.).
9 Frischling, Geoffrey Hepworth, Temp. 2/Lt., k. in a., 14/8/18 (att. 12 Bn.).
1 Gashion, Stanley Michael, 2/Lt., k in a., 8/5/17.
7 Gennings, Cecil, 2/Lt., k. in a., 13/8/16.
3 Gibbons, Percy James, Temp. 2/Lt., k. in a., 7/10/16 (att. 1 Bn.) (att. 11/R.W. Kent R.).
7 Gibson, Malcolm Reginald, Lt. (Tp.), k. in a., 8/10/15.
9 Goddard, Gordon Cecil, Temp. 2/Lt., k. in a., 16/10/18.
11 Golds, Frank, Temp. 2/Lt., k. in a., 5/10/16 (att. 7/R. Suss. Regt.).
7 Golds, Ingram Thomas, A/Capt., k. in a., 30/11/17.
Goodban, Montague Sidney, Temp. 2/Lt., k. in a., 19/5/17 (and R.F.C., 22 Sqd.).
Gopsill, Kenneth Lloyd, Temp. Lt., k. in a., 15/2/18 (att. R.F.C.).
9 Grant, Stanley Kenneth, Temp Lt., k. in a., 26/3/18.
9 Grantham, Ernest Russell, Temp. 2/Lt., k. in a., 27/11/17.
Greener, Francis Pemberton, 2/Lt., k. in a., 15/2/15.
1 Grigg, Lionel Francis, Temp. 2/Lt., k. in a., 29/7/16.
3 Gripper, Walter Vincent Thomas, Capt., k. in a., 24/7/16 (att. 1 Bn.).
3 Gurrin, Reginald Wells, 2/Lt., d. of w., 5/8/17 (att. 12 Bn.).
9 Hadenham, Lawrence George, Temp. 2/Lt., d. of w., 18/7/16.
11 Haines, Ernest Andrade, Temp. 2/Lt., k. in a., 3/9/16 (att. 9 Bn.).
8 Hall, Albert Loader, Temp. Capt., k. in a., 4/4/18.
3 Haller, John Henry Lyle, Capt., k. in a., 12/3/15.
4 Handford, Frederick Stanley, 2/Lt., k. in a., 27/1/16 (att. 9 Bn.).
11 Harding, Clive Scotland, Lt., k. in a., 6/8/15 (att. 2/Hants Regt.)
12 Harding, Frederick John, 2/Lt. (Tp.), d. of w., 22/9/17.
8 Harrison, Frank Talbot, 2/Lt. (Tp.), k. in a., 3/5/17.
3 Hartley, Frederick Lynn, 2/Lt., k. in a., 23/8/18 (att. 1 Bn.).
3 Hartnell-Sinclair, St. John Leslie, 2/Lt., k. in a., 25/9/15 (att. 2/Welsh Regt.).
3 Haskins, Victor Bradshaw, 2/Lt., k. in a., 20/11/15 (att. 5/Shrop. L.I.).
7 Hastings, Aubrey Joseph, 2/Lt. (Tp.), k. in a., 5/10/15.
11 Hawes, Herbert, Temp. Lt., k. in a., 20/10/18 (att. 1 Bn.).
1 Hearn, George Harold, 2/Lt., d. of w., 12/5/17 (in German hands).
1 Henderson, Cecil Ivanhoe, Temp. 2/Lt., k. in a., 26/11/17 (att. 13 Bn.).
Hewitt, The Hon. Archibald Rodney, D.S.O., Capt., k. in a., 25/4/15.
14 Holgate, Harold Arthur, Temp. 2/Lt., k. in a., 25/9/16 (att. 1 Bn.).
Hopkinson, Charles Reginald Thompson, Capt., k. in a., 6/9/14
Hovenden, Arthur Lester, 2/Lt., k. in a., 3/5/17 (att. 7 Bn.).
4 Howard, Victor Charles, 2/Lt., drowned, 15/4/17.
9 Howell, Wilfred Symonds, Temp. 2/Lt., k. in a., 25/4/16.
12 Howitt, Adam Gordon, M.C., Temp. Capt., k. in a., 5/8/17.
4 Housecroft, Harold, 2/Lt., k. in a., 19/11/14 (att. 1 Bn.).
4 Howard, The Hon. Robert Henry Palmer, 2/Lt., k. in a., 9/5/15 (att. 2 Bn.).
4 Humphreys, Stanley Howard, 2/Lt., k. in a., 20/11/17 (att. 7 Bn.).
12 Hutcheson, James McLeod, 2/Lt. (Tp.), k. in a., 21/9/17.
4 Huth, Austin Henry, Capt., k. in a., 20/4/15.
9 Ingrams, Frank Ridley, Temp. 2/Lt., k. in a., 3/9/16.
8 Jacobs, Alan Edward Aflalo, 2/Lt., k. in a., 7/8/16.
Jenkins, William Edwin, 2/Lt., k in a., 23/11/17 (and R.F.C., 60 Sqd.).
3 Jennings, Sidney James, 2/Lt., k. in a., 30/3/18 (att. Fld. Survey, R.E.).
12 Jessop, Frederic Devereux, M.C., Temp. Capt., k. in a., 16/9/16.
4 Johnson, Malcolm Thomas, 2/Lt., killed, 16/11/17 (att. 12 Bn.).
7 Johnson, William Stanley, Temp. 2/Lt., d. of w., 17/3/17.
13 Johnston, Foster Crampton, 2/Lt., d of w., 23/4/17.
Jollie, Francis Ormonde Holden, Capt., k. in a., 25/4/15.
3 Jolly, Trevor Blake, 2/Lt., k. in a., 20/9/17.
2 Jones, Lawrence, Capt., k. in a., 4/10/17.
7 Jones, Llewellyn James, Capt., d. of w., 16/3/16.
7 Jordan, Edward, 2/Lt., k. in a., 9/4/18.
4 Joseland, Arthur Noel, Lt., k. in a., 22/9/17 (att. Nigeria Regt.).

9 Keep, Douglas William, 2/Lt. (Tp.), k. in a., 16/10/18.
10 Kelly, Percy Patrick, Temp 2/Lt., k. in a., 1/7/16.
7 Kemp, Eric Arthur, Temp. 2/Lt., k. in a., 30/11/17.
8 Killick, Sydney Howard, 2/Lt., died, 16/5/18 (att. M.G.C.).
7 King, Percy, Temp 2/Lt., d. of w., 5/8/17.
4 King, Thomas Shirley, Capt., k. in a., 3/5/17 (att. 7 Bn.).
Kirtland, John, 2/Lt., k. in a , 12/3/15.
7 Knapp, Valentine Powell, Temp. 2/Lt., killed, 18/7/16.
11 Kyd, Frank Proctor, Temp 2/Lt., k. in a., 18/8/16 (att. Warwick Regt.).
3 Lasenby, Searlin, 2/Lt., k. in a., 20/9/17 (att. 1 Bn.).
1 Law, John Gordon, 2/Lt. (Tp.), k. in a., 20/10/18.
3 Lawrence, Joseph Reginald Mark, 2/Lt., k. in a., 16/8/16 (att. 9 Bn.).
2 Lawton, Edward Gerald, Capt., d. of w., 12/4/18.
Leach, Edward Savory Wykeham, Capt., k. in a., 3/5/17.
Le Fleming, Lawrence Julius, Bt. Lt.-Col., k. in a., 21/3/18 (att. 9 Bn.).
4 Lester, William Owen Ernest, 2/Lt., k. in a., 4/4/18 (att. 8 Bn.).
4 Lewis, George Hardy, Lt. (T/Capt.), d. of w., 28/9/15 (att. 2nd Bn.).
12 Libby, Alfred Thomas, Temp. Lt., k. in a., 20/9/17.
9 Lindsay, William Henry, M.C., Capt. (Tp.), k. in a., 3/9/18.
4 Macan, Hugh O'Donoghue, Lt. (A/Capt.), d. of w., 1/9/18.
12 McCallum, Duncan, Temp. Capt., k. in a., 22/9/17.
3 McEvoy, Frank Osmond, Temp. 2/Lt., k. in a., 9/4/17 (att. 7 Bn.).
MacLean, Andrew De Vere, Capt., k. in a., 19/9/14.
Manning, George, 2/Lt., k. in a., 28/1/16.
Mansell, William Stanley, 2/Lt., k. in a., 11/9/17 (and R.F.C.).
9 Marchant, Richard Henry, 2/Lt., k. in a., 26/1/16.
Marks, Charles Bernard, M.C., Temp. 2/Lt., k. in a., 23/10/18 (att. 8 Bn.).
9 Marshfield, Harold William, Temp. 2/Lt., k. in a., 14/8/18 (att. 10/R. W. Surrey Regt.)
7 Martin, Alfred John, Temp. 2/Lt., d. of w., 2/8/16.
1 Marshall, Thomas Frederick, Temp. 2/Lt., k. in a., 30/10/17.
3 Mason, James Philip, 2/Lt., k. in a., 9/4/17 (att. 7 Bn.).
9 Matheson, Homer Lindsay, Temp. 2/Lt., k. in a., 16/8/16.
9 Matthews, Alfred Apsley, Temp. 2/Lt., d. of w., 12/9/16.
12 Matthews, Frank Reginald, Lt., d. of w., 23/3/18.
3 Mazengart, George Richard Bostock, 2/Lt., k. in a., 29/7/16 (att. 1 Bn.).
4 Mead, Christopher, Lt., k. in a., 28/9/15 (att. 2 Bn.).
12 Meadows, Reginald Melville, Temp. Lt., k. in a., 4/9/18.
13 Merryfield, Leopold Reginald, Temp. Capt., d. of w., 28/8/16.
11 Metcalfe, Wilfred Charles, T/Lt., d. of w., 19/8/16.
4 Milburn, Richard Gerald, 2/Lt., d. of w., 10/2/15.
1 Millar, Ion Keith, Temp. 2/Lt., k. in a., 27/7/16.
9 Willard, Alfred George, Temp. 2/Lt., d. of w., 7/8/17.
13 Mills, Trevor Blake, Temp. 2/Lt., died, 24/5/17 (in German hands).
4 Mitchell, William Holford, Lt., drowned, 15/4/17.
1 Mobbs, Edward Thomas, 2/Lt., k. in a., 7/5/17.
7 Moffatt, Durward Forbes, 2/Lt., k. in a., 30/11/17.
12 Morgan, Sidney Herbert, Temp. 2/Lt., k. in a., 4/4/17 (att. 122/T.M.B.).
Morritt, William Graveley, Capt., killed, 27/6/17.
9 Murray, Kenneth Desmond, 2/Lt., k. in a., 25/9/15.
8 Musgrove, George Henry Stuart, Temp. Lt., k. in a., 1/7/16.
4 Nash, James, 2/Lt., k. in a., 3/4/15 (att. 1 Bn.).
3 Newington, John, Lt., k. in a., 22/5/15 (att. Ches. Regt.).
8 Newland, Henry John, Temp. 2/Lt., k. in a., 18/2/17.
Nichols, Cyril Robert, Lt., k. in a., 23/9/18 (att. 5/T.M.B.).
3 Nichols, Harold, 2/Lt., d. of w., 7/8/18 (att. 8 Bn.).
3 Norman, Albert Edmund, Capt., d. of w., 11/5/15.
4 Norton, Tom Edgar, 2/Lt., k. in a., 20/4/15 (att. 1 Bn.).
10 O'Brien, Francis Pat, Temp. 2/Lt., k. in a., 16/8/16 (att. 9 Bn.).
3 O'Hara, Patrick Gilbert Warwick, 2/Lt., k. in a., 14/8/16 (att. 1/4 R. Berks Regt.).
Osborn, Alfred Herbert, 2/Lt., k. in a., 23/10/18 (att. 8 Bn.).
7 Parker, Sidney, Temp. 2/Lt., k. in a., 30/3/17.
Paterson, Walter Herbert, Temp. Lt.-Col., k. in a., 20/4/15.
9 Patterson, John Keppel Priuli, Temp. Lt., d. of w., 26/12/17.
10 Paul, John Andrew Bowring, M.C., Temp. 2/Lt., k. in a., 10/10/16 (att. 7 Bn.).
13 Peacock, Reginald Howard Trees, Lt., k. in a., 9/4/18.
8 Pearce, Charles Stanley, Capt., k. in a., 1/7/16.
11 Pearse, Kenneth Herbert, Temp. 2/Lt., k. in a., 6/8/15.
8 Pegg, Hallam William, 2/Lt. (Tp.), d. of w., 3/7/16.
9 Picton, James Allanson, M.C., Temp. Lt., k. in a., 23/7/17.
1 Pocock, Charles Clarke, T/2/Lt., killed, 14/3/16.
3 Potter, Harold, 2/Lt. (T/Lt.), k. in a., 9/4/17 (att. 7th).
9 Pratt, Arthur Victor, T/2/Lt., k. in a., 21/3/18.
10 Proctor, Charles Gordon, T/2/Lt., killed, 20/2/16 (and R.F.C.).
Pullinger, Harold Bessant, T/2/Lt., k. in a., 1/9/18 (att. 8 Bn.).
3 Rae, Reginald Wilson, 2/Lt., k. in a., 30/3/15 (att. S. Staff. Regt.).
Reeve, Charles Simms, Capt., k. in a., 14/2/15.
1 Reid, Alex John, 2/Lt., k. in a., 26/4/16.
3 Relton, Gerald Lyons, 2/Lt., d. of w., 17/9/14.
1/2 Richardson, Edward Earle, 2/Lt., k. in a., 9/11/18 (att. R.A.F.).
4 Riddett, Norman Lock, 2/Lt., k. in a., 12/10/17 (att. 8th).
Riordan, Hubert De Burgh, Capt., k. in a., 10/5/15 (att. 2nd).
9 Rivers, George Claude, T/2/Lt., k. in a., 21/8/16.
12 Roberts, Leslie, M.C., T/2/Lt., k. in a., 24/8/18 (att. 6th R. W. Surr. R.).
Robinson, Archibald, D.S.O., Major (T/Lt.-Col.), d. of w., 11/5/17 (att. 7th Ox. & Bucks. L. I.).
3 Robinson, Gerald Duckworth, Capt., d. of w., 26/9/16 (att. 1st).
Robinson, Leonard Herbert Frank, T/Lt., d. of w., 18/3/16 (att. T.M.B.).
Roe, Edward Allan, M.C., T/Lt. (T/Capt.), k. in a., 2/9/18 (att. 2/4th R. W. Surr. R.).
1 Roe, Heriot Baker, T/2/Lt., k. in a., 23/8/18
3 Rottman, Richard Charles Lt., k. in a., 24/4/15 (att. 2nd).
4 Rumbold, Christian Franklyn Hales, Major, k. in a., 22/11/15 (att. 2nd Norf. R.).
12 Ryan, Edward St. John Norwood, M.C., T/Capt., k. in a., 22/10/18.
4 Sadler, William Douglas 2/Lt., d. of w., 3/8/17.
8 Santler, William Amos, T/2/Lt., k. in a., 13/6/16.
Savage, George Henry, M.M., T/2/Lt., k. in a., 21/10/18 (att. 12th).
9 Schooling, Peter Holt, 2/Lt., d. of w., 30/3/16.
3 Scott, Ralph Quintus, Lt., k. in a., 16/4/17 (att. 20th R. Fus.).
Scott, Victor William, Lt., k. in a., 16/3/18 (att. R.F.C.).
4 Scurfield, Bryan, M.C., Lt., died, 30/9/18.
3 Seater, Percival John, 2/Lt., k. in a., 3/5/17.
9 Sharp, George Benjamin, 2/Lt., k. in a., 21/3/18
Shone, Robert Francis, 2/Lt., k. in a., 14/2/15.
8 Shrapnel, Victor George Fleetwood, T/Lt. (A/Capt.), k. in a., 23/3/18.
3 Simpson, William Herbert Mostyn, Lt., d. of w., 19/12/14 (att. 1st).
7 Smith, Herbert James, 2/Lt., k in a., 9/4/18 (att. 13th).
3 Smith, Sydney, Capt., k. in a , 19/5/18 (att. 1st).
8 Soames, Robert Eley, T/Lt , k. in a., 1/7/16.
10 Spurling, Henry Stephen, T/2/Lt., d. of w., 21/8/16 (att. 9th).
8 Stacey, John Brewer, T/2/Lt., k. in a., 19/11/16.
3 Staley, Frederick Alexander, 2/Lt., k. in a., 25/10/18 (att. 8th).
4 Stedman, Raymond Cecil, 2/Lt., d. of w., 20/5/18 (att 1st).
10 Stimson, Montague Adolph, 2/Lt , k. in a., 30/9/16 (att 8th).
1 Streatfield-James, Ralph, D.S.O., Capt., d. of w., 7/10/16.
7 Striegler, Henry William, 2/Lt., k in a., 12/8/16.
Strong, Harold, 2/Lt., k. in a , 13/3/15.
1 Strong, Oliver Arthur, 2/Lt., k. in a. 8/5/17.
4 Sulivan, Eugene Gilbert, Capt., died, 8/5/17 (att. 1st Bn.).
Tagg, Charles Hirch, 2/Lt., k in a., 15/2/15.
9 Taylor, Forster, T/2/Lt., k. in a., 16/10/18.
11 Thomas, Alec Vaughan, T/Capt., k. in a., 6/8/15 (att. 2nd Bn., Hamps R.).
8 Thorne, Cornelius, T/Capt., k in a., 30/9/16
8 Thorne, Marlborough, 2/Lt., k. in a., 28/9/15.
4 Todd, Alfred Guy Eric, 2/Lt., k. in a., 23/4/17.
4 Todd, Herbert Stanley, M.C., Lt., A/Capt., k. in a., 18/9/18 (att. 8th).
7 Tomkins, Vigor, T/Capt., k in a., 13/10/15.
9 Trench, Nugent Charles Le Poer, T/2/Lt., k. in a., 16/1/17.
3 Tripp, Harold, Lt. (A/Capt.), k. in a., 16/8/17 (att. 1/4th Berks R.).
3 Upton, Ralph Hamon Weeley, 2/Lt., k. in a., 3/5/17.
11 Urban, Oscar Arthur, 2/Lt. (Tp.), k. in a., 3/9/16.
4 Vaughan, John Lindhurst, Capt. (Tp.), k. in a., 15/8/16 (att. 9th).
4 Vernham, Noel Marshall, 2/Lt., k. in a., 28/7/16.
2 Walliker, Lester Charles, 2/Lt., d. of w., 15/5/15.
3 Warland, Frederick Leslie, 2/Lt., k. in a., 25/3/18 (att. 12th).
11 Walton, Joseph Frank, 2/Lt., d. of w., 12/11/16 (att. 12th).
7 Ward, Harold Frederick, M.C., T/Capt., k. in a., 30/11/17.
Ward, Neville Lascelles, 2/Lt., k. in a., 23/8/14.
3 Watson, Francis, Lt., k. in a., 9/5/15 (att. 2nd Bn.).
3 Watson, Geoffrey Launcelot, Capt., k. in a., 20/4/15 (att. 1st Bn.).
4 Webb, Henry Stanley, 2/Lt., k in a., 21/3/18 (att. 9th Bn.).
9 Welch, Howard Vyse, T/Major, died, 4/10/15 (whilst P. of War).
Wells, Cyril Edward Elliott, Lt., k. in a., 10/3/15.
1/2 Wells, Reginald William, 2/Lt., d. of w., 3/10/17.
3 Wentzel, Eric Francis, Lt. (A/Capt.), k. in a., 23/3/18.
1/2 West, Charles Frederick Arthur, 2/Lt., k. in a., 4/10/17.
Whish, John Kenneth Tulloch, Capt., d. of w., 8/9/14.
7 White, Douglas Archibald, 2/Lt., k. in a., 23/3/18 (att. 8th).
12 White, Ralph Ernest, 2/Lt., d. of w., 28/9/17.
1/2 Whitehead, Charles James, T/2/Lt., k. in a., 4/10/17.
4 Whitehead, Henry Montagu, Lt., k. in a., 14/4/15.
13 Whiteway, Edward Victor, M.C., Capt., d. of w., 28/4/18 (att. 122nd Bde. H.Q.).
11 Wicks, Harry Valentine Inwood, T/2/Lt., k. in a., 14/4/17 (att. 11th Coy. M.G.C.).
8 Wightman, James, D.S.O., M.C., Major, d. of w., 9/4/18.
1 Wigston, Geoffrey Herbert, Capt., k. in a., 9/9/16 (att. 2nd Sussex).
7 Willcox, Hugh Patterson, 2/Lt., k in a., 30/11/17.
3 Williams, Francis Christopher Dallas, 2/Lt., k. in a., 19/7/16 (att. Roy. Berks R.).
3 Williams, William Hutton, Capt., k. in a., 18/5/15 (att. Bedf. R.).
3 Wilson, Alan Mowbray, 2/Lt , k. in a , 19/11/16 (att. 8th Bn.).
3 Wix, Geoffrey Arthur Gibson, Lt., k. in a., 12/10/17 (att. R. Berks R.).
3 Wright, Alan Austin, Capt., k. in a., 6/9/18 (att. 12th Bn.).
Wynter, Philip Cecil, Capt., d. of w. 20/4/15.
Wynyard, Damer, T/Capt., k. in a., 20/4/15.
9 Youngman, John Marshall, M.C., T/Lt., k. in a., 23/6/16.

The Duke of Cornwall's Light Infantry.

1 Arbery, Frederick James, Capt. (Tp.), d. of w., 9/10/17.
6 Armitage, George, 2/Lt. (Tp.), k. in a., 16/9/16.
6 Aston, Frederick Marriner, Temp. Capt., k. in a., 30/7/15.
Aston, Ronald Moseley, Lt., k. in a., 14/3/15.
9 Atkinson, William Edward, Capt., k. in a., 6/8/15.
3 Baker, Arthur Forbes, Lt. (Temp. Capt.), k. in a., 11/4/17 (and R.F.C., 52/Squad.).

Baker, George Stanley Charles, 2/Lt., killed, 23/9/16.
1 Baldwin, Harry Sandford, 2/Lt. (Tp.), k. in a., 23/7/16.
1 Ball, J., M.C., Capt., died, 23/1/18.
9 Barnes, Herbert George, 2/Lt. (Tp.), k. in a., 16/9/16 (att. 7 Bn.).
6 Barnett, Carew, Major, k. in a., 12/8/15.
Batson, Alfred William, Lt., k. in a., 14/3/15.
9 Bawden, Leslie John, 2/Lt. (Tp.), d. of w., 1/10/16 (att. 6 Bn.).
6 Beckingsale, John Elgar, 2/Lt. (Tp.), k. in a., 23/8/17.
3 Beckerleg, Stephen Trevor, Lt., k. in a., 15/10/15 (att. 2 Bn.).
1 Bell, Walter Albert, 2/Lt., k. in a., 13/4/18.
7 Benford, Charles George, 2/Lt. (Tp.), killed, 5/1/18.
6 Bennett, Arthur Hugh, 2/Lt. (Tp.), k. in a., 18/8/16.
Bennett, Victor Cyril Wentworth, Lt., died, 13/10/18.
6 Birch, William Elric Hawthorn, 2/Lt. (Tp.), k. in a., 31/7/15.
Blagrove, Richard Coore, Lt., (and Adj.), k. in a., 12/8/15 (att. 6 Bn.).
Blanchard, Frederick Wilson, Capt., d. of w., 26/1/18 (att. 2/5 R. War. Regt.) (in Ger. hands).
3 Blair, Herbert Samuel Penny, 2/Lt. d. of w., 31/10/16.
3 Bosanquet, Armytage Percy, M.C., Capt., k. in a., 25/1/17.
Boswell, Denis St. George Knox, Capt. (Tp. Major), died, 28/9/18 (att. M.G.C., 82nd).
7 Brandon, William George, 2/Lt. (Tp.), died, 13/7/18.
Bree, Edward Russell, Lt., k. in a., 18/9/18.
9 Brett, Ernest Hugh William, 2/Lt. (Tp.), d. of w., 2/8/16 (att. 5 Bn.).
7 Brett, Hugh Corthorn, Temp. Capt., k. in a., 29/7/16.
10 Brian, Arthur Gerald, Temp. Lt., d. of w., 16/10/17.
9 Brookes, Gordon Byron, Capt. (Tp.), k. in a., 16/9/16 (att. 6 Bn.).
3 Bucknall, Marc Antony, 2/Lt., d. of w., 6/3/17 (att. 10 Bn.).
Burrows, George William Cruttwell, Lt. (Tp.), k. in a., 25/8/18 (att. 7 Leic. Regt.).
3 Burton, Henry Reginald, 2/Lt., k. in a., 11/9/18 (att. 10 Bn.).
1 Byard, Hubert, 2/Lt., k. in a., 6/11/17.
3 Byers, Henry Elliott, 2/Lt., killed, 12/11/16 (and R.F.C.).
3 Byfield, Arthur Thomas Stoneman, Lt., died, 24/3/15 (att. 2 Bn.).
6 Byrne, Edward, Temp. 2/Lt., k. in a., 23/8/17.
1 Cantan, Henry Thomas, C.M.G., Lt.-Col., k. in a., 16/4/16.
2 Carne, Maxwell Halford, 2/Lt. (Tp.), d. of w., 23/12/16.
6 Carter, John Allen, Temp. Lt., died, 2/4/17 (in Ger. hands).
6 Challoner, Alan Crawhall, 2/Lt., k. in a., 30/7/15.
7 Chard, Thomas Norman, Temp. 2/Lt., k. in a., 23/4/17.
1 Chilcott, Gilbert George Cardew, 2/Lt, k. in a., 18/4/17.
7 Chilwell, Eric Robert, Temp. 2/Lt., k. in a., 16/9/16.
3 Church, Walter Harry, 2/Lt., k. in a., 23/7/16 (and Trench Mortar Bty.).
8 Clarke, Gerald Foulkes, Temp. 2/Lt., d. of w., 6/10/17 (att. 1 Bn.).
6 Clarke, Gordon Elstone, M.C., Temp. 2/Lt., k. in a., 28/8/16.
1 Cobbett, Arthur Irvin Brooke, 2/Lt., d. of w., 23/8/18.
3 Cocking, Frank Kenneth, Lt., k. in a., 23/7/16.
Colley, Archibald, 2/Lt., k. in a., 14/3/15.
1 Collins, Alfred John, 2/Lt., k. in a., 29/9/18.
6 Collins, Percival George, Lt. (Tp.), k. in a., 18/8/16.
1 Coombe, Leslie Clarence, 2/Lt. (Tp.), k. in a., 25/3/18.
7 Coombe, William John, Temp. Lt., k. in a., 1/10/16.
Crane, Charles Edward. 2/Lt., d. of w., 18/9/14.
10 Crouch, Foster Brooke, Lt. (Tp.), k. in a., 23/3/18.
1 Crouch, George Percy, Temp. 2/Lt., d. of w., 4/10/17.
6 Cruddas, Sandwith George Peter, 2/Lt. (Tp.). k. in a., 20/9/15.
Daniell, Neville Reay, D.S.O., Capt. (Tp. Lt.-Col.), k. in a., 4/10/17 (att. Yorks. L.I.).
7 Davies, Ernest Frank, Temp. 2/Lt., k. in a., 24/8/16.
Delepine, Helenus George Sheridan, 2/Lt., k. in a., 17/4/15.
Dennis, John Edmund William, Lt., k. in a., 23/8/14.
Dickinson, Francis Arthur, Major, d. of w., 11/4/15.
11 Dryerre, Robert Henry, 2/Lt. (Tp.), k. in a., 1/10/16 (att. 7 Bn.).
7 Eary, Frederick Charles, M.C., Temp. Capt., k. in a., 24/3/18.
6 Edwards, Albert Campbell, 2/Lt. (Tp.), k. in a., 24/3/18 (att. 7 Bn.).
3 Edwardes, Henry Frederick Edgcumbe, 2/Lt., k. in a., 6/3/17 (att. 1 Bn.).
7 Edwards, John Rathbone, 2/Lt., k. in a., 6/7/16.
Edye, Charles Vivian de Grete, Lt., k. in a., 30/10/14.
Elliott, Phillip Lloyd, 2/Lt., k. in a., 21/10/14.
8 Evans, Henry Robert Noel, 2/Lt. (Tp. Capt.), k. in a., 16/8/17 (att. 7 Bn.).
1 Evans, John Henry Grant, 2/Lt., d. of w., 7/2/17.
7 Feild, John Forbes, 2/Lt., k. in a., 16/9/16.
7 Follis, Thomas, 2/Lt., d. of w., 24/2/17.
3 Forbes, William Alexander Stanhope, 2/Lt., k. in a., 3/9/17.
1 Forestier, Walter Waldorf, M.C., Temp. Capt., k. in a., 12/3/18 (att. 4 Bn.).
6 Fowler, Ralph, 2/Lt., k. in a., 16/9/16.
9 Francis, Alan Buller, Temp. 2/Lt., k. in a., 24/8/16 (att. 7 Bn.).
1 Frayling, Herbert Joseph, Temp. 2/Lt., k. in a., 30/8/18.
9 Freeman, Eric Allen, Temp. Lt., k. in a., 18/8/16.
6 Fuller, Percy D., 2/Lt., k. in a., 18/8/16.
1 Gard, Frederick, Temp. Lt., k. in a., 28/6/18.
Garsia, Oliver Dunham Melville, Lt., d. of w., 18/9/14.
6 Gay, Edgar Percy, Temp. 2/Lt., d. of w., 6/1/17.
9 Girling, Stephen Eastough, Temp. Lt., k. in a., 29/9/18 (att. 7 Bn.).
1 Graham, Edwin Michael, 2/Lt. (Tp.). k. in a., 4/10/17.
1 Gray, John James Enslie, 2/Lt., killed, 18/3/17.
1 Hailstone, Dudley William, Temp. 2/Lt., k. in a., 7/7/18.
10 Hall, Henry Guy Fitzwilliam, Lt. (Tp.), k. in a., 13/11/16.
Hamilton, H. J., Capt., died, 13/6/18 (and R.A.F.).
9 Hamlyn, Alfred Ernest, Temp. 2/Lt., k. in a., 16/7/16.
6 Hamlyn, Wilfrid Stephen, Temp. 2/Lt., k. in a., 24/8/17.
1 Hammans, Arthur John Spencer, M.C., Capt. (Act. Major), k. in a., 3/7/17.
8 Hammond, William Cecil, Capt., k. in a., 24/4/17.
2 Hanwright, Thomas, 2/Lt., k. in a., 3/10/16.
10 Hardwick, Nathaniel Charles, 2/Lt., d. of w., 15/9/17.
Harrison, Henry Neville Baskcombe, M.V.O., Capt., d. of w., 16/3/15.
6 Hearn, Leonard Webb, 2/Lt. (Tp.), k. in a., 18/10/17.
1/2 Heath, William Charles, Temp. 2/Lt., k. in a., 22/5/18 (att. 10 Bn.).
9 Herbert, William Alfred, 2/Lt., k. in a., 1/10/16 (att. 8/Y.L.I.).
9 Hichens, William Thomas, 2/Lt., k. in a., 3/9/16 (att. 1 Bn.).
6 Higman, Michael, Temp. 2/Lt., k. in a., 18/8/16.
7 Hill, William Alfred, Tp. Lt. (Act. Capt.), k. in a., 23/3/18 (att. 61 T.M.B.).
6 Hill, Wilfrid James, Temp. 2/Lt.. d. of w., 17/9/16.
Hingston, Frank Leonard, Capt., k. in a., 26/4/15.
1 Hocking, Herbert Victor, Lt., Act. Capt., k. in a., 13/4/18.
Holder, T. S., Capt. (Tp.), died, 26/11/18.
10 Hollis, Arthur Reginald, Tp. Lt., k. in a., 12/9/18.
2 Howden, George Bruce, 2/Lt., died, 8/5/16.
6 Hulton-Sams, Frederick Edward Barwick, Tp. Lt., k. in a., 30/7/15.
1 Humphries, Cecil Frederick George, D.S.O., M.C., D.C.M., Tp. Capt. (Act. Lt.-Col.), d. of w., 22/8/18 (att. 1 Norf. R.).
6 Hyman, Robert Leslie, 2/Lt. (Tp.), k. in a., 23/8/17.
7 Jackson, Theophilus Rudolph, Capt. (Tp.), d. of w., 25/3/18.
2 Jenkins, Edgar Kynnersley, Tp. Capt., d. of w., 23/9/16.
1/2 Jenkins, W. W. L., 2/Lt., d. of w., 25/6/18 (and R.A.F.).
6 Jessup, William Henry Gray, D.S.O., Capt. (Hon.), d. of w., 24/12/18.
8 Jones, Arthur, 2/Lt. (Tp.), k. in a., 23/8/18 (att. 3 M.G.C.).
6 Jones-Parry, John Jeffreys Bulkeley, Temp. Major, k. in a., 30/7/15.
Kelynack, Richard Henry, Temp. 2/Lt., k. in a., 4/10/17.
6 King, William, 2/Lt. (Tp.), d. of w., 26/6/18 (att. 7 Bn.) (in Ger. hands).
3 Kirkpatrick, Robert Buist, 2/Lt., k. in a., 23/6/18.
3 Kitson, Edward Gerard Templeman, 2/Lt., d. of w., 3/9/16.
7 Lailey, Eric Lillywhite, Temp. 2/Lt., k. in a., 29/2/16.
1 Langdon, Douglas Eckley, 2/Lt., A/Capt., k. in a., 23/4/17.
3 Largen, Edward Charles, 2/Lt., k. in a., 23/7/16.
3 Lawrance, John Henry, 2/Lt., k. in a., 20/8/17 (att. 2 Bn.).
7 Lewin, Kenneth Robert, Temp. Lt., k. in a., 9/3/16.
1 Liversidge, Harold, 2/Lt., k. in a., 23/7/16.
Lloyd, Hugh Clifford Chetwode, Lt., Tp. Capt., died, 25/2/16.
3 Lomax, John, 2/Lt., k. in a., 18/8/16 (att. Rl. War. R.).
7 Lonsdale, Thomas Wilkes, Temp. Capt., d. of w., 5/6/16.
Lunnon, George John, 2/Lt., k. in a., 27/4/15.
7 McGregor, Charles, 2/Lt. (Tp.), k. in a., 24/3/18.
6 McIntyre, Sidney Colin, 2/Lt., d. of w., 25/3/18 (att. 10 Bn.).
7 MacMillan, James Bonthron, D.S.O., Temp. Major, k. in a., 30/11/17.
1 Madden, William Thomas, Temp. Lt., k. in a., 14/4/18.
1 Malton, Paul Locock, 2/Lt., d. of w., 3/9/18 (in Ger. hands).
7 Marriott, John Francis Laycock, 2/Lt., died, 26/1/15.
Marshall, John Edward, Capt., k. in a., 30/3/15.
9 Martin, Eric Tomlinson, Temp. 2/Lt., k. in a., 1/10/16 (att. (8 K.O.Y.L. Inf.).
7 Martin, Walter Percival, Temp. 2/Lt., k. in a., 24/8/16.
1 Maywood, James Henry, Lt., Tp. Capt., k. in a., 23/8/18.
10 Miles, Harold Gordon, Temp. 2/Lt., k. in a., 4 or 5/8/16.
7 Milward, Etienne Geoffrey, Temp. Capt., d. of w., 2/9/16.
1 Molesworth, Hon. Charles Willoughby Murray, 2/Lt., d. of w., 15/4/17.
Morris, Henry Gage, 2/Lt., killed, 23/4/15.
2 Morrison, Edwin Walter, M.C., Temp. Lt., died, 10/12/18.
3 Morse, Anthony Philip, Lt., died, 5/6/15 (att. 2 Bn.).
2 Murphy, Lewis William, Capt., k. in a., 9/4/16.
7 New, Brian Brooke, 2/Lt., k. in a., 16/8/17.
7 Nicholas, Walter Wynne, Temp. 2/Lt., k. in a., 29/3/16.
2 Norway, Frederick Hamilton, 2/Lt., d. of w., 4/7/15.
9 Oates, John Stanley, Tp. Lt., Act. Capt., d. of w., 11/12/17 (att. 6 Bn.).
3 O'Callaghan, Duncan McKay McDonald, 2/Lt., k. in a., 14/3/15 (att. 2 Bn.).
Oldham, Joseph Haslope, 2/Lt., k. in a., 18/4/15.
3 Olivier, Jasper George, 2/Lt., k. in a., 16/9/16 (att. 7 Bn.).
Olivier, Robert Harold, Capt., k. in a., 14/9/14
7 Oudin, L'Eugene, Capt., d. of w., 24/8/16.
1 Outram, John, 2/Lt., k. in a., 6/11/17.
6 Paddison, George Mitford, Tp. Lt., k. in a., 30/7/15.
Passy, Logan Deare, Capt., k. in a., 21/10/15.
8 Paterson, Arthur Stanley, Lt., d. of w., 2/10/18
6 Paull, Henry Baynham, Tp. 2/Lt., d. of w., 21/8/16.
3 Peacock, J. T., 2/Lt., killed, 16/7/18 (and R.A.F.).
1 Pearson, Harold, 2/Lt., k. in a., 22/5/18 (att. 7 Bn.).
3 Pinhey, Hammett Eardley, 2/Lt., k. in a., 19/4/15 (att. 2 Bn.).
1 Pole-Carew, Wymond Nicholas Richard, Lt., k. in a., 6/11/17.
3 Puckridge, Christopher Francis Hewitt, Act. Capt., k. in a., 28/3/17 (att. 7 Bn.).
7 Rae, James Edmond Pringle, T/Capt. (Act. Major), k. in a., 30/11/17.
Rawlinson, William Gray, Lt., k. in a., 14/3/15.
3 Reay, Thomas Stanley, Lt., d. of w., 1/3/18 (att. 10 Bn.).
6 Reep, Alfred Mills, Temp., 2/Lt., k. in a., 16/9/16.
Rendall, Francis Holden Shuttleworth, D.S.O., Temp. Lt.-Col., d. of w., 9/7/16 (att. 5 Yorks and Lancs Regt.).
8 Rendall, Robert Alexander, M.C. Tp. Lt. (Act. Capt.), k. in a., 18/9/18.
1 Rendle, Arthur Edward, 2/Lt., k. in a., 6/11/17.

3 Richards, William Beresford. Lt., k. in a., 30/11/17 (att. 7 Bn.).
3 Roberts, William Thomas, 2/Lt., k. in a., 28/9/18 (att. 1 Bn.).
Rogers, Francis Caryer Campbell, M.V.O., Capt., k. in a., 15/2/15
Romilly, Arthur Hovell Capt., k. in a., 21/10/14.
7 Rooke, William Albert, Temp. 2/Lt., k. in a., 29/7/16.
3 Rosling, Charles Holbrook, Lt (Act. Capt.), d. of w., 22/10/18 (att. 7 Bn.).
1 Sandoe, Charles Frederick, M.C., 2/Lt. (Act. Capt.), k. in a., 30/8/18.
Saunders, Arthur Courtenay, Capt., k. in a., 14/3/15.
5 Scobey, Richard Campbell, 2/Lt., k. in a., 23/8/17.
10 Schlotel, Charles Henry Cooper, M.C., Capt., died, 21/3/19.
9 Simpson, Henry Gordon, 2/Lt., k. in a., (about) 16/6/15 (att. 1 Bn., R. Innis. Fus.).
3 Slee, John Balhatchet, Lt., k. in a., 24/3/18.
7 Smith, James Bowman, Temp. 2/Lt., k. in a., 28/6/18.
Southey, Robert George Melvill, Lt., k. in a., 23/7/16.
7 Sowell, Arthur Donald, Lt. (Tp.), k. in a., 24/8/16.
1 Stephenson, Hubert Victor, 2/Lt. (Tp.), k. in a., 8/5/17.
Stevenson, Douglas Baptiste, 2/Lt., k. in a., 11/3/17 (and R.F.C., 45 Sqd.).
6 Stoer, Fred Charles, 2/Lt. (Tp.), k. in a., 17/3/16.
10 Stratton, George Bernard, Temp. Major, k. in a., 10-11/8/17.
1 Strevens, George William, M.C., Lt. (Act. Capt.), d. of w., 27/9/18
6 Swainson, Joseph Leonard, D.S.O., Temp. Lt.-Col., d. of w., 9/8/16.
1 Taylor, Alfred Cecil, M.M., Temp. 2/Lt., k. in a., 23/10/18.
1 Taylor, Bruce Mitchell, M.C., Major, k. in a., 6/11/17.
6 Taylor, Harold Victor, Temp 2/Lt., k. in a., 23/8/17.
7 Thomas, Arthur Lanham, 2/Lt. (Tp.), k. in a., 11/4/16.
3 Tonking, David Wilson, 2/Lt., d. of w., 29/5/17 (att. 10 Bn., R. War. Regt.).
1 Trelawny, Henry Wallace, Lt., k. in a., 23/10/18.
3 Tremellen, Donald Hargreaves, 2/Lt., k. in a., 23/4/17 (att. 1 Bn.).
3 Trevor, Frederick Pelham, 2/Lt., k. in a., 8/5/15 (att. 2 Bn.).
3 Turner, Harcourt Charles, Lt., k. in a., 23/8/17.
6 Tyack, Richard Henry, Temp. Capt., d. of w., 4/11/18.
Vincent, William, Capt., k. in a., 30/10/14.
6 Vine, Christopher Nithsdale Vincent, 2/Lt. (Tp.), k. in a., 18/8/16.
Vowler, Edward Maxwell, 2/Lt., k. in a., 14/3/15.
7 Ward, George Matthews, 2/Lt (Tp.), k. in a., 24/8/16.
7 Watson, Frederick John, 2/Lt., k. in a., 24/3/18.
1/2 Widdows, Archibald, Lt., died, 6/10/18 (att. 8 Bn., Ches. Regt.).
10 Wilkins, John Christopher Martin Lt., k. in a., 24/3/18.
Wilkinson, Geoffrey Miles, 2/Lt., k. in a., 10/10/17 (and R.F.C., 56 Sqd.).
9 Williams, Guy Grenfell, Temp. 2/Lt., k in a., 6/6/16.
1 Williams, Lloyd Allison, Temp 2/Lt., k. in a., 20/7/16.
1 Willis, Raymond Maurice, 2/Lt. (Tp.), k. in a., 6/11/17.
1 Willis, William Francis Bucknote, Temp. 2/Lt, k. in a., 23/7/16.
Wills, Percy, 2/Lt., d. of w., 19/4/15.
3 Wodehouse, Francis John Ashburnham, 2/Lt., k. in a., 26/8/17.
Woodham, Charles Burnett, D.S.O., Capt., k in a., 15/6/15.
7 Woolnough, Arthur Stanley, Temp. 2/Lt., d. of w., 1/12/17 (in German hands).
Wright, Frederick Adams, Temp. 2/Lt., k. in a., 19/9/17 (att. R.F.C., 9 Sqd.).
6 Yeo, Hubert Claud Cater, 2/Lt. (Temp.), k. in a., 24/8/17.

The Duke of Wellington's (West Riding Regiment).

9 Adderley, William Harris, 2/Lt., d. of w., 27/10/18 (and R.A.F.).
9 Amesbury, Frank Cholmondely Dering, Major, died, 7/2/18 (Ind. Army, ret.).
Anderson, William James, Major, k. in a., 19/10/15 (H.Q. Staff, 9/Army Cps.).
9 Armitage, Laurie Ritchie, M.C., 2/Lt. (Tp.), d. of w., 25/11/16.
1/2 Babb, Royland Nettleton, 2/Lt. (Tp.), died, 15/10/18.
9 Barran, Alfred Rawson, 2/Lt. (Tp.), d. of w., 31/3/18.
9 Barry, William Patrick, 2/Lt. (Tp.), k. in a., 25/8/18.
2 Beard, Frederic Whiteley, 2/Lt. (Tp.), k. in a., 10/10/16.
11 Beattie, Thomas, Lt., k. in a., 27/10/18.
9 Beckhuson, Donald Frederic, 2/Lt. (Tp.), k. in a., 2/3/16.
9 Benjamin, John Alfred, Capt. (Tp.), k. in a., 5/7/16.
9 Bentham, Harley, 2/Lt. (Tp.), d. of w., 16/9/18.
8 Best, Thomas Edward, Lt., k. in a., 9/8/15.
Best, Wilfred Robert, 2/Lt. (Tp.), d. of w., 27/8/18.
11 Bladen, Eustace Clement, 2/Lt. (Tp.), d. of w., 4/11/15 (att. 8/Bn.).
1/2 Bouchier, Charles Arthur, 2/Lt. (Tp.), k. in a., 4/11/18 (att. 9/Bn.).
2 Bowes, Cyril Hulme, 2/Lt. (Tp.), k. in a., 1/7/16.
3 Braine, William Thomas Coker, 2/Lt., k. in a., 9/10/16 (att. 2/Bn.).
10 Brinsley-Richards, Roland Herbert Wyndham, 2/Lt., k. in a., 30/7/16.
3 Brook, Charles William, 2/Lt., killed, 26/3/18 (and R.F.C.).
1/2 Cameron, William George, 2/Lt. (Tp.), k. in a., 4/9/18 (att. 1/5 Lanc. Fus.).
10 Carpenter, Herbert Montagu Soame, Capt. (Tp.), k. in a., 5/7/16.
1 Carruthers, Gordon, 2/Lt. (Tp.), d. of w., 27/11/18 (att. 5/Bn.).
8 Carter, John Wilfred, 2/Lt. (Tp.), k. in a., 7/8/15.
Cartwright, George Arthur, 2/Lt. (Tp.), d. of w., 28/11/17 (att. 2/7 Bn.).
2 Cheetham, Alan Humphrey, Lt., k. in a., 16/12/16.
Cobb, Reginald John Preston, 2/Lt., k. in a., 11/10/17 (att. R.F.C., 56 Sqd.).
2 Coldwell, Norman Goodman, M.C., 2/Lt. (Tp.), d. of w., 16/5/18.
10 Crawford, George Rainier, C.B., Col., died, 22/8/15, (Ind. Army, retd.).
9 Culling, Harold William, 2/Lt. (Tp.), k. in a., 7/7/16.
2 Cunningham, Edward Malcolm, Lt. (T/Capt.), k. in a., 4/8/17 (att. 9/Bn.).
Cunningham, Kenneth Edward, Capt., d. of w., 3/5/17 (P. of W.).
9 Dacre, Brian, Capt. (Tp.), k. in a., 12/10/18.
3 Davis, Reginald Noel, Capt. (Tp.), k. in a., 12/10/16 (att. 2/Bn.).
Denman-Jubb, Cyril Oswald, Capt., k. in a., 24/8/14.
De Wend, Douglas Fenton, Lt., k. in a., 11/11/14.
3 Duncanson, Roy, 2/Lt., k. in a., 7/7/16 (att. 9/Bn.).
9 Dunn, Gwynne Morgan, 2/Lt. (Tp.), d. of w., 23/2/17.
1/2 Dunshee, Ernest Rowland, 2/Lt. (Tp.), d. of w., 11/8/18 (att. 5/Bn.).
9 Edwards, Geoffrey Otto Charles, 2/Lt., k. in a., 7/7/16.
8 Edwards, Gordon Stafford, Capt., (Tp.), k. in a., 28/9/16.
Egerton, Charles Caledon, Lt., k. in a., 18/4/15.
3 Elliott, Geoffrey Edmund, 2/Lt., k. in a., 12/10/16 (att. 2/Bn.).
Ellis, Thomas Martin, Capt., k. in a., 18/4/15 (att. W. York R.)
8 Elmhirst, Ernest Christopher, 2/Lt., k. in a., 7/8/15.
2 Elmitt-Browne, Austin, 2/Lt. (Tp.), d. of w., 15/6/16.
11 Ewart, Archibald John, 2/Lt. (Tp.), k. in a., 28/9/16 (att. 8/Bn.).
9 Ferguson, Alan, Lt. (T.), d. of w., 4/7/16.
11 Franks, Braham Alfred, 2/Lt. (Tp.), k. in a., 24/10/15 (att. 8/Bn.).
3 Gardner Norman, 2/Lt. (Tp.), k. in a., 2/10/18 (att. 16/Lanc Fus.).
Gatacre, Edward George, Capt., d. of w., 20/2/16.
9 Gelder, George Douglas, Capt. (Tp.), k. in a., 4/11/18.
11 Gilbert, Christopher Choaler, Lt. (Tp.), k. in a., 28/9/16 (att. 8/Bn.).
10 Glover, Samuel Lawrence, 2/Lt. (Tp.), died, 12/1/16.
10 Graham, Robert Main, 2/Lt. (Tp.), k. in a., 4/10/16.
Greaves, Victor, 2/Lt. (Tp.), d. of w., 28/11/17 (att. 2/5 Bn.).
Grevelink, Edward James Yzenhoed, Lt., k. in a., 6/6/17 (and R.F.C., 3 Sqd.).
2 Gunn, Arthur, 2/Lt. (Tp.), k. in a., 5/5/15.
2 Hadwen, Noel Waugh, Capt., k. in a., 1/7/16.
10 Halstead, Arthur, M.C., Lt. (Tp.), died, 1/8/17.
8 Hamilton-Cox, Cecil Francis, 2/Lt. (Tp.), k. in a., 27/8/17
10 Hammond, Leonard, Lt. (Tp.), k. in a., 5/7/16.
1/2 Harper, Harold Raymond, 2/Lt. (Tp.), k. in a., 4/11/18 (att. 2/4 Bn.).
8 Harriman, Horace William, M.C., Capt. (Tp.), k. in a., 1/9/18 (att. 9/Bn.).
12 Harris, Ernest Charles, Capt. (Tp.), k. in a., 23/10/16.
10 Harris, Henry, Lt. (Tp.), k. in a., 4/10/16 (att. North'n Regt.).
11 Harris, Robert Hugh, 2/Lt., k. in a., 28/9/16 (att. 8/Bn.).
3 Hart, Charles Crowther, 2/Lt. (T/Lt.), k. in a., 14/11/17 (att. K. A. Rifles).
3 Hart, Cecil Lyon, Capt., k. in a., 1/7/16.
Hart, James, M.C., Lt. (A/Capt.), k. in a., 1/11/18 (att. 1/6 Batt.).
8 Haseldine, Frederick, Hon. Lt. & Qr.-Mr., died, 2/12/14.
10 Heale, George Reginald Charles, Capt., d. of w., 3/5/17.
11 Henderson, James Hugh, 2/Lt. (Tp.), k. in a., 7/11/15 (att. 8/Bn.).
2 Henderson, Patric Gordon, 2/Lt. (Tp.), d. of w., 2/5/18.
3 Heskett, John, 2/Lt., k. in a., 15/4/18 (att. 2/Bn.).
8 Hird, Christopher, 2/Lt. (Tp.), k. in a., 19/4/17 (att. 1/4 Northants R.).
2 Hodge, Jack Wheaton, Lt., k. in a., 12/10/16.
2 Horsfall, Alfred Garnett, D.S.O., Major (A/Lt.-Col.), k. in a., 9/10/17.
8 Horsfall, John Joseph, Capt. (Tp.), d. of w., 19/1/17.
2 Hughes, John William, M.C., Lt. (Tp.), k. in a., 15/4/18.
10 Hunt, Benjamin Owen, 2/Lt. (Tp.), d. of w., 23/5/17.
9 Huntriss, William, Lt. (Tp.), died, 23/10/18 (att. Gold Coast R.).
3 Inchley, William, Lt., k. in a., 19/12/15 (att. 9/Bn.).
Jackson, Harry, 2/Lt. (Tp.), k. in a., 9/10/17 (att. 1/7 Bn.).
8 Johnson, Horace James, Lt.-Col., k. in a., 7/8/15.
8 Jones, Charles David, 2/Lt. (Tp.) (A/Lt.), died, 7/3/18 (att. British Portuguese Mission).
1/2 Jones, Rowland, 2/Lt. (Tp.), d. of w., 13/10/18 (att. 9/Bn.)
8 Kidd, Vivian Norval, Major (Tp.), died, 21/3/17 (Staff).
3 Kitchen, Harold Rosslyn, Lt., k. in a., 27/9/16 (att. 8/Bn.).
2 Lambert, Philip Felix, 2/Lt., k. in a., 3/5/17.
2 Larcombe, Archibald Herbert, 2/Lt. (Tp.), died, 26/10/18 (P. of W.).
10 Lavarack, Adolph Keith, Lt. (Tp.), k. in a., 5/7/16.
2 Leece, Francis Ballantyne, 2/Lt., k. in a., 12/10/16.
3 Lees, Clifford, M.C., Lt., d. of w., 5/11/18 (att. 15/Lanc. Fus.).
11 Lister, John Raymond, 2/Lt. (Tp.), k. in a., 15/12/15 (att. 8/Bn.).
10 Lyon, Donald Halliday, 2/Lt., k. in a., 20/9/17.
1/2 Lyon, Eric, 2/Lt. (Tp.), k. in a., 4/11/18 (att. 15/Lanc. Fus.).
3 Mackay, James Ivan, 2/Lt. (T/Capt.), k. in a., 5/10/17 (and R.F.C.).

3 MacNamara, Joseph Bernard, 2/Lt., k. in a., 19/10/16 (att. 2/Bn.).
9 Maitland, John Dalrymple, 2/Lt. (Tp.), k. in a., 22/2/16.
3 Mallinson, Eric, Lt., k. in a., 7/7/16 (att. 9/Bn.).
Maples, William Evelyn, Major (A/Lt.-Col.), k. in a., 14/12/16 (att. 6/N. Lanc. R.).
11 Marks, Isidor David, 2/Lt. (Tp.), k. in a., 10/7/16.
1/2 Marriott, K. M. H., Lt., k. in a., 28/9/18 (and R.A.F)
3 Marsden, H., 2/Lt., died, 5/6/18.
8 Marriott, Osborne Delano, T/Lt. (A/Capt.), k. in a., 27/8/17.
8 Mawhood, Claude George, 2/Lt. (Tp.), k. in a., 14/9/16.
8 Middleton, John, Tp. Capt., d. of w., 2/10/17.
2 Middlewood, Albert, 2/Lt., k. in a., 3/5/17.
3 Milbank, Robert Charles Alfred Paslo Edmund, Capt., d. of w., 10/5/15 (att. 2/Bn.).
2 Millican, John Stamper, 2/Lt. (Tp.), d. of w., 3/7/16.
9 Moss, Hamilton, M.C., Capt. (Tp.), k. in a., 31/5/18.
3 Morris, John Clarke, Lt., killed, 13/1/19 (att. R.A.F.).
11 Narey, Vincent Gerald, Lt. (Tp.), d. of w., 15/10/16 (att. 8/Bn.).
8 Nathan, Leopold Charles, 2/Lt. (Tp.), k. in a., 14/9/16.
3 Owen, Rowland Hely, Lt., k. in a., 18/4/15 (att. 2/Bn.).
10 Palmer, Geoffrey Raymond, 2/Lt. (Tp.), k. in a., 30/7/16.
11 Parsons, Ernest, 2/Lt. (Tp.), died, 23/7/16 (att. 1/Welsh Regt.).
10 Pass, Alfred Ernest, 2/Lt., k. in a., 26/8/18.
10 Pereira, Adrian O'Donnell, Capt. (Tp.), k. in a., 20/9/17.
10 Perks, Robert Clement, D.S.O., T/Capt., k. in a., 27/10/18.
Phripp, Arthur Thornton, 2/Lt. (Tp.), k. in a., 19/10/17.
11 Pickles, Harry Thornton, 2/Lt. (Tp.), k. in a., 26/4/16 (att. 9/Bn.).
3 Plumb, Edward Stephen, Lt. (Tp.), d. of w., 8/9/17.
1/2 Potts, Richard Harold Urwin, 2/Lt. (Tp.), d. of w., 2/12/18 (att. 16/Lanc. Fus.).
8 Power, Joseph Leo, 2/Lt. (Tp.), k. in a., 14/2/18 (att. 9/Bn.).
9 Quinn, Thomas Joseph, 2/Lt. (Tp.), d. of w., 18/6/18.
3 Raine, Charles William, 2/Lt., k. in a., 3/11/18 (att. 16/Lanc. Fus.).
Reincke, Leo Frederick, Capt. (Tp.), k. in a., 17/8/17 (att. R.F.C., 48/Sqd.).
1/2 Roch-Austin, Sidney Leslie, Lt. (Tp.), d. of w., 4/11/18 (att. 1/4 Bn.).
9 Roebuck, Alfred Eric Eaton, Capt. (Tp.), k. in a., 8/9/18.
9 Rowland, William Charles Roche, Lt. (Tp.), k. in a., 4/11/18.
9 Russell, John William Binfield, Lt. (Tp.), k. in a., 7/7/16.
Russell, Lawrence Edward, Lt., k. in a., 24/8/14.
3 Rycroft, Robert, 2/Lt., k. in a., 11/10/18.
1/2 St. Hill, Ashton Alexander, D.S.O., Lt.-Col. (Tp.), k. in a., 27/10/18 (att. 11/N. Fus.).
9 Savory, Maurice Jeffery, Capt. (Tp.), d. of w., 3/2/17.
1 Scaife, Joseph, 2/Lt., k. in a., 21/3/18.
2 Scott, Arthur George, 2/Lt., k. in a., 23/12/15.
3 Simkins, Walter Francis, 2/Lt., k. in a., 9/10/16 (att. 2/Bn.).
Simpson, Anthony Bean Tracey, 2/Lt., k. in a., 6/5/15.
9 Simpson, Percy William, Lt. (Tp.), k. in a., 1/11/16.
11 Skipworth, Philip John, Lt. (Tp.), k. in a., 7/8/15 (att. 5/Bn. Manch. R.).
8 Smith, Edward James, Lt. (Tp.), k. in a., 28/9/16.
10 Snell, Christopher, 2/Lt. (Tp.), d. of w., 14/7/16.
10 Stafford, Henry Herbert Owen, 2/Lt. (Tp.), k. in a., 4/10/16.
1/2 Stent, Harold Rudolph, 2/Lt., k. in a., 20/7/18.
3 Stocks, Tom Dixon, 2/Lt. (Tp.), d. of w., 16/4/18.
Strafford, Percy Belcher, Major, k. in a., 24/8/15.
3 Stuart, Joseph Joachim Maxwell, Lt., k. in a., 2/3/16 (att. 9/Bn.).
3 Sugden, Guy Hatton, Lt., k. in a., 12/10/16 (att. 2/Bn.).
1/2 Sugden, John, 2/Lt. (Tp.), k. in a., 29/3/18 (att. 1/5 Bn.).
2 Taylor, Albert Edward, 2/Lt., k. in a., 9/4/17.
Taylor, Ernie Rumbold, Capt., k. in a., 18/4/15 (att. E. York. R.).
10 Taylor, Walter Douglas, 2/Lt. (Tp.), k. in a., 5/7/16.
10 Tetley, Arthur Calvert, 2/Lt. (Tp.), k. in a., 7/6/17.
Thackeray, Frederick Rennel, Lt., k. in a., 18/4/15.
3 Thelwell, Harry Rowland, 2/Lt., d. of w., 8/7/16 (att. 2/Bn.).
2 Thomas, Eric Hand, 2/Lt. (Tp.), died, 18/1/18 (P.O.W. in enemy hands).
Thompson, John Henry Louis, Lt., d. of w., 17/9/14.
1/2 Thomson, James Stein, 2/Lt. (Tp.), k. in a., 22/7/18 (att. 1/7 Lanc. Fus.).
8 Thurlow, Arthur Geoffrey, 2/Lt. (Tp.), d. of w., 29/8/15.
1/2 Tidmarsh, J. M., Lt., died, 3/9/18 (and R.A.F.).
10 Tindall, Lawrence, 2/Lt., k. in a., 21/6/18.
Tolhurst, Bernard Joseph, Lt., d. of w., 22/4/17 (in German hands) (att. R.F.C., 11/Sqd.).
8 Travers, Hugh Price, Major, k. in a., 7/8/15.
Tyndall, William Ernest Marriott, D.S.O., Bt.-Lt.-Col., d. of w., 1/8/16.
3 Vicat, Frederick Holland, 2/Lt., k. in a., 8/12/17 (att. 2/Bn.).
2 Vile, Herbert Leslie, 2/Lt., k. in a., 3/5/17.
1/2 Walker, Adolphus, 2/Lt., d. of w., 15/4/18.
Walker, Arthur, Lt., k. in a., 10/8/18 (att. M.G.C.)
3 Ward, John, 2/Lt., k. in a., 30/8/18 (att. 2/Bn.).
1 Watkin, Harry, Lt., died, 21/10/18.
2 Watmough, Oscar Oswald, 2/Lt., k. in a., 1/9/18.
3 Watthews, Harold, Lt., k. in a., 8/6/17 (att. 10/Bn.).
9 Weatherby, Thomas, Capt., died, 8/5/15.
3 Whitaker, Charles Frederick, Lt., k. in a., 5/5/15 (att. 2/Bn.).
8 Whittam, Matthew John Goldsborough, Lt. (Tp.), d. of w., 11/8/15.
11 Wilkinson, Edward Wilson, 2/Lt. (Tp.), k. in a., 7/7/16.
8 Willbourn, Horace Haynes, 2/Lt., k. in a., 8/5/18.
3 Williamson, George, Lt., d. of w., 12/11/14 (att. 2/Bn.).
Wilson, John Hutton Bowes, Lt.-Col., k. in a., 7/6/17 (att. 9/Y. & L.R.).
2 Wolfenden, Laurence, 2/Lt., k. in a., 24/10/18.
8 Wood, Claude Ernest, Capt. (Tp.), k. in a., 14/9/16.
9 Wood, Eric Arthur Walton, 2/Lt. (Tp.), k. in a., 25/2/16.
9 Wood, Ralph Miles, 2/Lt. (Tp.), d. of w., 9/11/16.
3 Wood, Wilfred Thomas, 2/Lt., k. in a., 9/8/17.
1/2 Woodhouse, Henry, 2/Lt., k. in a., 4/11/18 (att. 9/Bn.).
8 Wright, Samuel King, Lt. (Tp.), k. in a., 7-11/8/15.
3 Young, Colin Turner, Capt., k. in a., 24/4/17 (att. Welsh R.).

The Border Regiment.

3 Abram, Robert, 2/Lt. (A/Capt.), k. in a., 26/10/17.
2 Adamson, Francis Douglas, Lt., k. in a., 16/11/15.
1 Ainscough, Henry, 2/Lt., k. in a., 11/4/18.
8 Aldous, Alan Edward, 2/Lt. (Tp.), k. in a., 5/7/16.
8 Allen, John William Anderson, M.C., 2/Lt., d. of w., 10/4/18.
Allen, William Lynn, D.S.O., Major, killed, 28/10/14.
6 Allured, Will, 2/Lt. (Tp.), k. in a., 14/9/16.
1 Ampt, Norman Crosland, 2/Lt. (Tp.), d. of w., 22/8/15.
7 Andrew, Frank, 2/Lt., k. in a., 23/4/17.
Andrews, Charles George Williams, Capt., k. in a., 28/10/14.
Arber, Archibald Guy, 2/Lt. (Tp.), k. in a., 21/10/15 (att. 1/7th High. L. Inf.).
Armer, Arthur, 2/Lt. (Tp.), k. in a., 5/9/17 (att. 11th Bn.).
3 Armstrong, Leonard William, 2/Lt., k. in a., 19/5/17 (att. 1st Border Regt.).
10 Ashby, Samuel, Lt. & Qr.-Mr., died, 13/2/16.
Askew, Henry Adam, Capt., k. in a., 19/12/14.
Bales, Keith, 2/Lt., k. in a., 16/5/15.
8 Barnes, John Christopher Craven, Capt. (Tp.), k. in a., 29/5/16.
11 Barnes, William Sibson, Lt. (Tp.), k. in a., 5/6/16.
10 Barron, Louis, Lt. (Tp.), k. in a., 19/7/16 (att. 2/6th Warwick Rgt.).
Bartholomew, William George, 2/Lt. (T/Lt.), died, 26/4/15.
1 Baxendine, John Young, 2/Lt. (Tp.), k. in a., 1/7/16 (att. 5th R. Scots).
1 Beattie William Lindsey, 2/Lt., k. in a., 27/1/17.
2 Beaty-Pownall, George Ernest, D.S.O., Major (A/Lt.-Col.), d. of w., 10/10/18 (att. 1st K.O.S.B.).
3 Beaty-Pownall, Thomas Trelawny, 2/Lt. (A/Capt.), k. in a., 24/3/17 (att. 2 Bord. Regt.).
2 Beaumont, Wilfrid Newton, 2/Lt., k. in a., 25/9/15.
Beckett, John, 2/Lt., k. in a., 28/6/15.
7 Belchamber, Ernest Henry, 2/Lt. (Tp.), k in a., 23/4/17.
10 Bell, Francis Richard Lowry, 2/Lt. (Tp.), k. in a., 22/2/16.
Bell, John, 2/Lt. (Tp.), k. in a., 27/5/18 (att. 8th Bn.).
8 Bell, James Ernest Kirkham, Lt. (Tp.), d. of w., 5/8/16.
Bell, William Arundel, 2/Lt. (Tp.), k. in a., 14/6/17 (att. 8th Bn.).
11 Benson, Isaac, T/Lt. (A/Capt.), k in a., 2/12/17.
1 Beves, Trevor Howard, Capt., k. in a., 1/7/16.
7 Birch, Leonard, Capt., k. in a., 23/4/17.
8 Birnie, Edward D'Arcy, D.S.O., M.C., T/Lt. (A/Capt.), d. of w., 22/3/18.
Bishop, Wilfrid, 2/Lt. (Tp.), d. of w., 6/7/17 (att. 11th Bn.).
1 Bowyer, Douglas Michael, 2/Lt., k. in a., 23/8/16.
3 Bradshaw, Bartle, 2/Lt., k. in a., 11/6/15.
10 Bremner, David, 2/Lt. (Tp.), d. of w., 9/7/16 (att. 11th Bn.).
Brett, Ernest Edward, 2/Lt., k. in a., 23/4/17 (att. 7th Bn.).
3 Briggs, Frederick Clifton, Col. (Bvt.), died, 30/12/16.
6 Broadrick, George Fletcher, Lt.-Col., k. in a., 22/8/15.
Brooke, George Cecil, Major, k. in a., 28/4/15.
11 Brown, Colin Selwyn, Capt., k. in a., 1/7/16.
11 Brown, Gilfrid Elliott, 2/Lt. (Tp.), k. in a., 18/11/16.
1 Bunting, Henry, M.C., T/Lt. (T/Capt.), died, 5/2/18.
Byng, Harry Gustave, 2/Lt., d. of w., 18/5/15.
8 Cameron, Archie, M.M., 2/Lt., k. in a., 11/4/18.
7 Campbell, W. C., 2/Lt., k. in a., 23/4/17.
Carr, Donald Nevill, M.C., Lt. (T/Capt.), died, 26/11/18 (att. S. Persia Rifles).
Cassels, Wilfrid Gardiner, T/Capt, k. in a., 13/7/16.
6 Caulfield, Algernon Montgomerie, D.S.O., Major, k. in a., 7/8/15.
3 Chetham-Strode, Edward Randall, Capt., k. in a., 1/10/17 (att. 2nd Bn.).
1 Cheverton, Stanley Campbell Lt., k. in a., 27/1/17.
Chisholm, William Dempster, 2/Lt. (Tp.), d. of w., 23/3/18 (att. 5th).
3 Cholmeley, Harry Lenin, Lt., k. in a., 1/7/16.
Cholmondeley, Charles Almeric John, Capt., k. in a., 28/10/14.
Clancey Trevor John, 2/Lt., k. in a., 28/10/14.
Clapp, Leonard Bishop, 2/Lt. (Tp.), d. of w., 2/10/17 (att. 1st Bn.).
1 Clark, Alick Morton, 2/Lt., k. in a., 27/1/17.
7 Clarke, Eric Groby, 2/Lt. (Tp.), k. in a., 23/4/17.
6 Clegg, Frank Cecil, Capt (Tp.), k. in a., 22/8/15.
Coe, George, 2/Lt. (Tp.), k in a, 1/7/16.
6 Collingwood, George Albert, 2/Lt (Tp.), k. in a., 10/8/15.
7 Constantine, William, M.C., Lt. (Tp.), k. in a., 18/9/18.
Cooch, Charles Rollo, Lt., k. in a., 17/12/14.
10 Cook, Frederick James, T/2/Lt. (T/Capt.), d. of w., 30/11/15 (att. 1/4 R. Scots).
11 Corbett, Alfred Edward, T/Capt., k. in a., 1/7/16.
Corley, Frederick Charles, 2/Lt., k in a., 12/4/18 (att. 8th Bn.).
6 Cowan, Reginald Percival, 2/Lt. (Tp.), died, 15/8/15.
1 Coward, Henry, T/Lt., d. of w., 20/4/17.
8 Coxon, Percy Hunter, M.C., Capt. (Tp.), k. in a., 13/4/18.
7 Crompton, Arthur Harold, 2/Lt. (Tp.), k. in a., 3/7/16.
7 Crosse, Thomas Latymer, Capt. (Tp.), k. in a., 3/7/16.
6 Cuningham, Charles Arthur, Capt., k. in a. 10/8/15.
10 Cruickshank, Donald Edward, 2/Lt., k. in a., 9/4/16 (att. 5th Wilts).
2 Cumpston, Basil Lancelot, 2/Lt. (Tp.), d. of w., 10/5/17.
8 Curteis, Lancelot, 2/Lt., k. in a., 4/7/16.
1 Daffurn, Oswald, M.C., 2/Lt, k. in a., 1/4/18.

Darvell, Frederick William, M.C., 2/Lt., k. in a., 27/5/18 (att. 8th Btn.).
6 Darwell, Claude Randall, 2/Lt. (Tp.), k. in a., 10/8/15.
2 Davis, Charles Henry, 2/Lt., k. in a., 24/5/15 (att. 5th Btn.).
Davidson, John, 2/Lt. (Tp.), d. of w., 15/10/17 (att. 8th Btn.).
Day, William Leonard, Lt., k in a., 6/4/17 (and R.F.C., 59 Sqd.).
1 Dick, Andrew Robertson, 2/Lt. (Tp.), k. in a., 18/7/18.
6 Dickie, William, 2/Lt., k. in a., 1/7/16 (att. 9/K.O.S.B.).
Dinwiddie, James Travers Blount, Lt. (T/Capt.), d. of w., 13/9/15.
6 Dixon, James Alfred, Lt. (Tp.), k. in a., 10/8/15.
Dobson, Nathaniel George, Lt. (Tp.), d. of w., 17/11/18 (att. 1/Cam.).
8 Donohue, Thomas, 2/Lt. (Tp. Lt.), d. of w., 8/2/17.
2 Dothie, John Howard, 2/Lt. (Tp.), k. in a., 27/6/16.
3 Dove, Charles Bertram, Capt., k. in a., 21/3/18 (att. 8th Bord. Regt.).
3 Dowdell, Ernest George, M.C., 2/Lt., k. in a., 22/3/18 (att. 8th Bord. Regt.).
7 Duley, Edwin Joseph, 2/Lt. (Tp.), k. in a., 2/11/16.
11 Dunstan, Guy Pierce, 2/Lt. (Tp.), k. in a., 1/7/16.
Egerton, Phillip John, Lt., d. of w., 17/10/14.
Evans, Charles Heyland, 2/Lt., k. in a., 26/10/14.
Ewbank, John Walter, M.C., Lt. (T/Capt.), k. in a., 30/11/17.
Fentiman, Frederick William, 2/Lt., d. of w., 24/3/18 (att. 8th Bn.).
8 Foss, Gilbert Harry, 2/Lt. (Tp.), k. in a., 3/7/16.
1 Fraser, Arthur William, D.S.O., 2/Lt. (Tp.), k. in a., 1/7/16.
3 Fraser, Geoffrey Norris, 2/Lt., k. in a., 12/3/15.
8 Fryer, John Percival, 2/Lt. (Tp.), k. in a., 22/3/18.
1 Gamon, John Lionel Percival, Lt., killed, 4/6/18 (att. N'thmb. Fus.).
11 Gayes, Thomas Samuel, 2/Lt. (A/Capt.), k. in a., 10/4/18.
Gerrard, Harry Vernon, Lt., k. in a., 2/11/14.
6 Gilbanks, Richard Parker, Lt. (Tp.), k. in a., 10/8/15.
3 Gillespie, Daird Andrew, 2/Lt., d. of w., 24/1/17 (att. 2/Bord.).
3 Goodall, Frank Basil, Lt., k. in a., 21/8/15.
11 Goodwin, Stuart Wycliffe, M.C., 2/Lt. (Tp.), k. in a., 31/3/18.
8 Gordon, Donald Jervis, 2/Lt. (Tp.), k. in a., 3/7/16.
Gordon, Robert Norman, Capt., k. in a., 28/10/14.
11 Gordon, Thomas Seton, 2/Lt. (Tp.), d. of w., 22/1/16.
2 Graham, Cecil Erskine, Capt., k. in a., 1/7/17 (att. 5th N. Staffs.).
12 Graham, Ernest William, 2/Lt., k. in a., 18/10/16 (att. 1st E. Lancs Rgt.).
11 Gray, James Cook, M.C., A/Capt., k. in a., 22/12/17.
8 Gruby, Thomas William, 2/Lt. (Tp.), d. of w., 19/7/16.
3 Hall, John Martindale, 2/Lt., k. in a., 28/8/16 (att. 8/Bord.).
7 Halstead, John James, 2/Lt. (Tp.), k. in a., 21/3/18.
7 Hamilton, Harold Gerard Hans, Capt. (Tp.), d. of w., 27/7/17.
3 Hamlett, George Froude, 2/Lt., k. in a., 13/8/17 (att. 1/Bord.).
3 Harding, Joseph, 2/Lt., k. in a., 6/10/17 (att. 2/Bord.).
2 Harper, Arthur, 2/Lt., d. of w., 1/4/17.
11 Harrison, Brian Charles, Capt. (Tp.), d. of w., 12/8/18 (att. 5/Bord.).
3 Hawkesworth, Francis Henry Stanley, 2/Lt., k. in a., 25/1/15 (att. Welsh Regt.).
Head, Reginald, Capt., k. in a., 28/4/15.
6 Healy, Edward, Lt. (Tp.), k. in a., 7/6/17 (att. 8th Bn.).
7 Heath, Sidney Stuart, 2/Lt., k. in a., 23/4/17.
3 Hellier, Leonard Gordon, 2/Lt. (Tp.), d. of w., 16/12/17 (att. 11/Brd.).
2 Helm, Henry Paul Dundas, Capt., died, 6/11/18 (and R.A.F.).
6 Hill, Henry William, 2/Lt. (Tp.), k. in a., 10/8/15.
2 Hinton, Walter Reginald, 2/Lt. (Tp.), k. in a., 14/7/16.
Hodgson, George William Houghton, Lt., d. of w., 6/11/14.
1 Hodgson, Isaac Harvey, Lt. (Tp.), d. of w., 20/4/16.
10 Hodgson, John Charles, Capt., k. in a., 28/6/15.
3 Holliday, Henry Lowther, 2/Lt., k. in a., 15/12/17 (att. 9/Bord. R.).
8 Hook, Gerald Francis, 2/Lt., k. in a., 13/4/18.
3 Horsley, John, Capt. (Tp.), k. in a., 16/5/15 (att. 2nd Btn.).
1 Hume, Robert Anseley Cuthbert, Lt.-Col., d. of w., 1/5/15.
2 Inkpen, Wilfred, 2/Lt. (Tp.), k. in a., 26/10/17.
1 Ireland, Herbert, Lt. & Q.M., died, 13/11/18 (att. M.G.C.).
Irving, Ernest, 2/Lt. (Tp.), k. in a., 5/10/17 (att. 2nd Btn.).
7 Jackson, Arthur, 2/Lt. (Tp.), k. in a., 2/11/16.
6 Jackson, Ernest Alexander, 2/Lt., k. in a., 27/5/18 (att. 8th Btn.).
1 Jackson, Lancelot, 2/Lt., k. in a., 1/7/16.
6 James, Charles Kenneth, D.S.O., A/Lt.-Col., k. in a., 19/5/18.
James, Douglas Attwood, Lt., k. in a., 25/4/15.
1 Jessup, Francis Reginald, T/Capt., k. in a., 1/7/16.
3 Johns, Hubert Hilditch, 2/Lt., died, 29/5/17.
3 Johnson, Sidney Frederick, Lt. (T/Capt.), k. in a., 10/1/17 (att. 2nd Bord. R.).
2 Johnson, Wilfrid Lloyd, 2/Lt. (Tp.), k. in a., 19/4/16.
6 Johnston, James Tait, Lt. (Tp.), k. in a., 28/9/16.
7 Joyce, Frank Postlethwaite, Lt. (Tp.), k. in a., 29/5/17.
1 Keeliher, William John, 2/Lt., k. in a., 25/7/18.
3 Kelly, Edward Rowley, 2/Lt., k. in a., 7/7/15 (att. Lancs Fus.).
3 Kemp, Godwin Francis, Lt., k. in a., 23/4/17 (att. 1/Bord. R.).
Kennedy, John, 2/Lt. (Tp.), k. in a., 20/4/18 (att. 15/Durham L. Inf.).
2 Kerr, William, D.S.O., M.C., Capt. (A/Lt.-Col.), k. in a., 3/5/18.
8 Keys, Malcolm, 2/Lt. (Tp.), d. of w., 31/8/16.
10 Kirby, Sidney Henry, 2/Lt. (Tp.), k. in a., 19/12/15 (att. 5th Btn. High. L.I.).
Krohn, Nicholas Adolf, 2/Lt., k. in a., 16/5/15.
3 Lait, Wilfrid Francis James, 2/Lt. (Tp.), k. in a., 3/8/17 (att. 8th Btn. Bord. Rgt.).
3 Lake, James Louis Engelbert Rey, 2/Lt., d. of w., 24/8/15 (att. 1st Btn.).
Lamb, Cameron, D.S.O., Capt., d. of w., 29/12/14.
1 Lane, Henry Clarence Horsburgh, 2/Lt. (Tp.), k. in a., 10/7/17.
Langworth, Harold Samuel, 2/Lt. (Tp.), d. of w., 9/9/17 (att. 8th).
1 Layard, Frank Stanley, M.C., 2/Lt., k. in a., 19/5/17.
6 Leach, Gerald Kimball, Lt. (Tp.), k. in a., 10/8/15.
7 Lee, John Mitchell, 2/Lt., k. in a., 27/9/15.
Lees, Edmund Hastings Harcourt, Capt., k. in a., 28/10/14.
10 Lester, Ernest Charles, Lt., k. in a., 3/7/15 (att. 1st Bn.).
7 Linzell, Harold Harding, 2/Lt. (Tp.), k. in a., 3/7/16.
2 Logan, David Herbert Hosken, 2/Lt., k. in a., 1/7/16.
Logie, James Paton, 2/Lt. (Tp.), k. in a., 1/10/18 (att. 1st Btn. Gordon High.).
Lowe, Thomas Henry, 2/Lt. (Tp.), k. in a., 23/4/17 (att. 7th).
2 Lowson, Matthew Stewart, 2/Lt., k. in a., 14/7/16.
2 Lucas, Percival Drewett, 2/Lt. (Tp.), d. of w., 6/7/16.
1 Lyall, Francis Gerald, 2/Lt., k. in a., 9/12/16.
6 McAuley, Bernard, Capt., k. in a., 7/8/15.
3 McCarthy, William Ronald Ware, 2/Lt., k. in a., 2/11/17 (att. P. of W. Camp).
3 McCauce, Finlay, 2/Lt., d. of w., 22/5/15 (att. 2nd Btn.).
6 McCausland, Arthur John Kennedy, 2/Lt. (Tp.), k. in a., 10/8/15.
8 McCulloch, John Wyndham Hamilton, Capt. (Tp.), d. of w., 21/10/15.
3 Machell, Humphrey Gilbert, 2/Lt., died, 12/6/18.
11 Machell, Percy Wilfrid, C.M.G., D.S.O., Lt.-Col. (Tp.), k. in a., 1/7/16.
McIntyre, Walter, 2/Lt. (Tp.), d. of w., 21/8/18 (att. 1st Btn.).
Mackenzie, John Kincaid, 2/Lt. (Tp.), k. n a., 27/5/18 (att. 8th Btn.).
Macleod, Donald, M.C., 2/Lt. (Tp.), k. in a., 1/7/17 (att. 1st Btn.).
Macrae, Joseph Nixon, 2/Lt. (Tp.), k. in a., 18/2/18.
7 MacWilliam, Frank, 2/Lt. (Tp.), k. in a., 2/6/18.
2 Mahoney, Frank, M.C., 2/Lt., k. in a., 6/10/17.
2 Malkin, James Andrew, 2/Lt. (A/Capt.), k. in a., 4/9/16
1/2 Malley-Martin, J., M.C., 2/Lt., killed, 30/10/18 (and R.A.F.).
11 Margerison, Caleb Walden, Lt. (Tp.), d. of w., 6/7/16.
6 Marsh, Frederick Courtney, Major, k. in a., 7/8/15 (Res. of Off., att. 6th Bn.).
11 Martin, Peter McEwan, A/Capt., k. in a., 2/12/17.
2 Martindale, Stanley, 2/Lt., k. in a., 4/9/16.
11 Matthews, Wilfrid Vernon, M.C., 2/Lt. (Tp.), k. in a., 1/10/18 (att. 1/5 Bn.).
6 May, Claude Boyle, M.C., Capt. (Tp.), k. in a., 19/11/17.
3 Middleton, Thomas Stanley, 2/Lt., k. in a., 19/5/17 (att. 1st Bord. Rgt.).
8 Miller, Tom Drysdale, M.C., Capt. (Tp.), k. in a., 21/10/16.
Mitchell, E. P. H., 2/Lt., killed, 7/5/18 (and R.A.F.).
Moffatt, Archibald Shirving Woolery, Lt.-Col., k. in a., 16/5/15.
Molyneux-Seel, Louis Edmund Harington, Capt., d. of w., 6/1/15.
11 Monkhouse, Alfred Ernest, 2/Lt. (Tp.), k. in a., 1/7/16.
3 Moore, John, 2/Lt. (A/Capt.), k. in a., 26/10/17 (att. 2nd Bord. Regt.).
1 Moore, Reginald Henry Hamilton, Capt., k. in a., 11/6/15.
7 Morrall, Egar Percy Basil, T/Capt. (A/Major), k. in a., 28/7/17.
Morris, Frank George Grier, D.S.O., Major (A/Lt.-Col.), k. in a., 17/8/17 (att. 16th Middlesex).
Morton, Gerald Arthur, Capt., k. in a., 4/5/15.
Muriel, Sidney Herbert Foster, Capt., k. in a., 30/4/15.
Nash, W. F., D.S.O., Lt.-Col. (Tp.), died, 28/12/15 (Major, Res. of Off.).
7 Nasmith, Arthur Plater, D.S.O., Capt. (Tp.), k. in a., 23/4/17.
3 New, Paul, Lt., k. in a., 19/5/17 (att. 1 Btn. Bord. Rgt.).
3 Newdigate, Richard Francis, Capt., k. in a., 4/9/16 (att. 1st Btn. Bord. Rgt.).
1 Olden, Sidney Montague, 2/Lt. (Tp.), k. in a., 4/5/18.
6 Oliver, Robert, 2/Lt., k. in a., 20/3/18.
9 Ogilvie, William Edmond, 2/Lt. (Tp.), k. in a., 27/9/15.
3 Owen, Hugh, Lt., k. in a., 16/5/15 (att. 2nd Btn.).
6 Oxland, Nowell, Lt. (Tp.), k. in a., 10/8/15.
Park, Herbert Sidney, 2/Lt. (Tp.), k. in a., 26/10/17 (att. 1st).
11 Parker, John Caird, 2/Lt. (Tp.), k. in a., 1/7/17.
1 Paterson, Douglas William, 2/Lt., d. of w., 31/3/18.
11 Paton, Walter Storie, 2/Lt. (Tp.), k. in a., 1/7/16.
6 Patterson, Arnott Andrew, 2/Lt. (Tp.), d. of w., 9/11/16 (att. R.F.C.).
Pawle, Derek Weatherall, Capt., k. in a., 29/4/15.
2 Paynter, Reginald, 2/Lt., k. in a., 26/10/17.
Perry, Francis Ina Lowre, Lt., k. in a., 2/5/15.
8 Phillips, Eric Sutherland, Capt. (Tp.), d. of w., 21/2/17.
3 Pirrie, Robert Bourn, Lt., k. in a., 9/8/15 (att. Shrop. L.I.).
10 Pitt, Bernard, 2/Lt. (Tp.), k. in a., 30/4/16 (X 47 T.M.B.).
8 Preston, William Carter, 2/Lt., k. in a., 10/4/18.
3 Pyman, James, Capt., killed, 18/11/14 (att. Manch. Regt.)
Radcliffe, Miles, Capt. (Tp.), k. in a., 12/12/14 (att. R. Scots Fus.).
3 Rawlinson, Robert, 2/Lt., k. in a., 25/9/15 (att. 2nd).
8 Reed, Gerald Francis Woolterton, Lt. (Tp.), k. in a., 21/3/18.
8 Renton, Francis Wallace Home, Lt. (Tp.), k. in a., 30/8/16.
1 Rettie, William Philip, 2/Lt., k. in a., 1/7/16.
10 Rhodes, John Kenneth, 2/Lt. (Tp.), d. of w., 17/7/16 (att. 8th Bn.).

3 Richardson, Daryl Stewart, Lt., k. in a., 16/5/15 (att. 2nd).
3 Richardson, Robert Cecil, 2/Lt., k. in a., 2/12/17 (att. 11th Bord.).
7 Richardson, Wilfrid Frank, M.C., Capt. (Tp.), died, 27-28/9/17.
Ridgway, William Thomas, 2/Lt., k. in a., 2/12/17 (att. 11th Btn.).
6 Roberts, Griffith Evans, 2/Lt. (Tp.), k. in a., 7/6/17.
3 Robertson, Fergus, 2/Lt., died, 3/12/18 (att. 1/5th Bord. Rgt.) (in German hands).
2 Robertson, Walter Raymond, 2/Lt. (Tp.), k. in a., 1/7/16.
11 Robinson, Arthur Gabriel, 2/Lt. (Tp.), k. in a., 9/3/16.
3 Robinson, Walter de Horne, M.C., Lt. (A/Capt.), k. in a., 27/1/17.
1 Ross, William Stuart, Lt. (Tp.), k. in a., 23/7/17.
0 Rupp, Frederick Albert, Lt., k. in a., 1/7/16.
7 Rusack, Louis Amrhein, Lt. (Tp.), k. in a., 4/7/16.
1 Rutherford, Alfred Fletcher Corrie, Capt., k. in a., 10/8/15 (att. 6th).
1 Ruxton, William Stewart Mitchell, M.C., Lt., k. in a., 12/4/18.
10 Salusbury, N. H. P., 2/Lt. (Tp.), k. in a., 1/12/15 (att. 1/7th High. L.I.).
11 Sandeman, Albert Fitzroy, T/Lt. (A/Capt.), k. in a., 2/12/17.
7 Sanderson, John Topping, 2/Lt. (Tp.), k. in a., 18/12/15.
1 Sanderson, Walter Kerr, 2/Lt. (Tp.), k. in a., 1/7/16.
7 Saunders, Noel Martyn, Capt. (Tp.), k. in a., 20/10/18.
Seward, Robert Francis, 2/Lt. (Tp.), k. in a., 25/10/16 (att. 2nd E. Lancs Rgt.).
Seymour-Isaacs, Maurice, 2/Lt., k. in a., 26/10/17.
7 Simpson, John Watt, 2/Lt. (Tp.), killed, 8/12/16.
Simpson, William Ronald Carde, 2/Lt., k. in a., 16/5/15.
6 Sinton, William, 2/Lt. (Tp.), k. in a., 30/11/17.
11 Smith, Raymond, Capt. (Tp.), k. in a., 1/7/16.
Smith, Robert, 2/Lt., d. of w., 9/8/17 (att. 8th Bn.).
9 Sorge, Ivan Percival Campbell, 2/Lt. (Tp.), d. of w., 15/10/16 (Pioneers).
11 Spring-Rice, Gerald, Lt. (Tp.), k. in a., 26/5/16.
2 Stephen, James Anderson, 2/Lt. (Tp.), d. of w., 28/10/17.
Stevenson, William, 2/Lt., k. in a., 11/6/18 (att. 10/N. & Derby R.).
8 Stewart, John Ebenezar, M.C., Capt. (Tp.), k. in a., 26/4/18 (att. S. Staffs Regt.).
11 Story, Tom, 2/Lt. (Tp.), k. in a., 18/11/16.
Surtees, Charles Gordon Villiers, Lt., k. in a., 26/10/14.
7 Sykes, Douglas Collett, M.C., Lt. (Tp.), d. of w., 26/7/17.
Tailford, John Wilson, M.C., Capt., killed, 22/5/17 (att. R.F.C.).
6 Taylor, Harold St. George, 2/Lt. (Tp.), died, 15/4/16 (att. 11th Bord. Regt.).
Taylor, Richard Booksbank, Capt., k. in a., 30/4/15.
1 Taylor, William John Macdonald, 2/Lt. (Tp.), k. in a., 19/12/15.
3 Thomas, Cyril Llewellyn Seymour, 2/Lt., died, 6/9/16 (and R.F.C.).
Thwaytes, John, 2/Lt., k. in a., 18/3/17 (att. R.F.C., 4 Sq.).
7 Tombs, James Douglas, 2/Lt. (Tp.), died, 18/2/16.
3 Turnbull, Maxwell, M.C., Capt. (Tp.), died, 18/10/18 (att. 8th Bn.).
Tweedy, Gerald Vincent, 2/Lt. (Tp.), k. in a., 13/4/17 (att. 11th Bn.).
11 Twynam, Godfrey, 2/Lt., d. of w., 18/11/16.
Vaughan, Charles Davies, D.S.O., Major, k. in a., 25/4/15.
8 Warren, Archibald Alexander, Lt. (Tp.), k. in a., 20/1/16.
Warren, John Booker Brough, Lt., k. in a., 28/10/14.
3 Warren, William Stanley, 2/Lt., died, 10/10/17 (att. 2 Bn.).
8 Watson-Thomas, Walter Patrick, 2/Lt. (A/Capt.), k. in a., 21/10/16.
3 Weber, Victor Joseph, Lt., killed, 15/12/18 (and R.A.F.).
7 Welsh, Robert Milne Ballantyne, Lt. (A/Capt.), k. in a., 23/4/17.
Wenden, George, Lt. (Tp.), k. in a., 16/3/17 (att. R.F.C., 35 Sq.).
11 West, Sidney, 2/Lt. (Tp.), k. in a., 1/4/17.
7 Whiteside, Carrol Herbert Marston, Lt. & Adjt., d. of w., 1/11/16.
8 Williams, Frank Leonard, Lt. (A/Capt.), d. of w., 30/5/18 (att. 25 M.G.C.).
Wilson, Charles Wyndham, Lt., k. in a., 12/3/15.
11 Wilson, Stanley Wright, 2/Lt., k. in a., 18/11/16.
1 Wood, Lewis Ironside, C.M.G., Lt.-Col., k. in a., 16/5/15.
6 Wood, Robert Basil, 2/Lt. (Tp.), k. in a., 12/10/16.
3 Woolf, Walter Richard, 2/Lt., d. of w., 26/9/15 (att. 2nd Bn.).

The Royal Sussex Regiment.

3 Adams, Joseph, 2/Lt., k. in a., 23/7/16 (att. 2 Bn.).
8 Addison, Frank, 2/Lt. (Tp.), died, 22/3/16.
Adkin, Frederick Edward, M.M., 2/Lt. (Tp.), k. in a., 24/9/18 (att. 2 Bn.).
Aldridge, Reginald John Petty Devenish, Capt., k. in a., 7/10/14.
Alexander, Gordon Reuben, 2/Lt. (Tp.), k. in a., 24/4/17 (att. 2 Bn.).
13 Andrews, Bertram John William, 2/Lt. (Tp.), d. of w., 31/7/17.
10 Arkcoll, Frederick Thomas, 2/Lt. (Tp.), k. in a., 30/6/16 (att. 7 Bn.).
9 Armitage, Douglas William, 2/Lt., k. in a., 25/9/15.
Ashby, Thomas Philip, Temp. 2/Lt., k. in a., 3/9/18.
2 Atkinson, Lewis de Burgh, Lt. (Tp.) (A/Capt.), k. in a., 16/8/16.
Austin, Oliver, 2/Lt., k. in a., 9/5/15.
Baddeley, Alfred James, Lt., k. in a., 23/10/18 (and T.M.B.).
7 Ballard, Charles William, M.C., Capt. (Tp.), k. in a., 25/11/17.
9 Banham, Joseph John, Major (Tp.), k. in a., 27/3/18.
11 Barlow, Charles Alfred, Temp. 2/Lt., d. of w., 17/8/17 (and R.F.C., 4 Sqd.).
Barnes, Hugh Cecil, M.C., Lt., k. in a., 21/7/18 (att. 2/T.M.B.).
14 Barrow, Frederick William, 2/Lt., k. in a., 3/9/16 (att. 13 Bn.).
10 Barrow, Lawrence Alfred Howard, 2/Lt. (Tp.), k. in a., 1/9/16 (att. 11 Bn.).
Barthropp, Sidney Alfred Nathaniel Shafto, 2/Lt., k. in a., 29/1/15.
13 Bartlett, Cyril, M.C., Major (Tp.), d. of w., 14/11/17.
11 Battley, Frederick Walter, Temp. 2/Lt., k in a., 21/4/16.
2 Baxter, Ralph Frederick, 2/Lt., k. in a., 25/9/15.
10 Bazeley, Roland Arthur, 2/Lt., Tp., k. in a., 28/1/16 (att. 9 Bn.).
7 Beale, Clifford William, Lt. (Tp.), k. in a., 3/3/16 (att. 36/-T.M.B.).
13 Bennett, William Henry Pope, M.C., T/Lt. (A/Capt.), k. in a., 3/3/18.
Bird, William Edmund, 2/Lt (Tp.), d. of w., 28/4/17.
Blencowe, Charles Edward, 2/Lt. (Tp.), k. in a., 3/5/18 (att. 1/Wilts Regt.).
Boardman, Alfred, 2/Lt, k. in a., 21/9/18.
3 Botting, William Rolph, 2/Lt., k. in a., 25/9/17 (att. 11 Bn.).
12 Boyd, Alexander Charles, 2/Lt. (Tp.), k. in a., 4/6/16.
Boys, Sydney Charles, Lt. (Tp.), k. in a., 23/6/18 (att. 7 Bn.).
Bradley, James, 2/Lt. (Tp.), d. of w., 26/10/18 (att. 7 Bn.).
3 Bray, Frank Hugh, 2/Lt., killed, 28/5/18 (att. 9 Bn.).
Bright, John Leslie, 2/Lt. (Tp.), k. in a., 25/9/15.
2 Bright, Kenneth Coldwell, 2/Lt., k. in a., 18/8/16 (att. 9 Bn.).
2 Broad, Clifford Newman, 2/Lt (Tp.), d. of w., 9/4/16.
Bromley, Hugh Frederic, 2/Lt. (Tp.), k. in a., 25/9/15.
Burgess, Walter, Capt., k. in a., 13/10/15.
7 Burley, Cyril Percival, 2/Lt. (Tp.), k in a., 9/8/18.
9 Burnier, Richard, Lt., d. of w., 21/2/18.
11 Burton, Frank, 2/Lt. (Tp.), d. of w., 3/3/18.
7 Bussell, John Garrett, Capt., k. in a., 28/6/15.
8 Calvert, Eric Ruegg, Temp. 2/Lt., k. in a., 8/8/17.
Carne, John Reeves, Temp. 2/Lt., d of w., 25/7/17.
Carter, Albert, 2/Lt, k. in a., 12/4/17 (att. 9 Bn.).
13 Carter, Norman Cecil, Temp 2/Lt., d. of w., 23/7/16 (att. 14 Bn.).
7 Cass, Leonard Francis, Capt (Tp.), k. in a., 13/12/15.
8 Cater, W. H, Temp. 2/Lt., died, 16/8/18.
3 Catmur, Harry Albert Frederick Valentine, Lt., k. in a., 1/7/16 (att. M.G.C.).
Chaize, Jean Edward Gabriel, Temp. 2/Lt., d. of w., 18/8/17 (att. 13 Bn.).
8 Cheape, John de Caerick, Temp. Lt., k. in a., 3/9/16 (att. 13 Bn.).
10 Chepmell, William Dobree, Temp. Lt., k. in a., 11/4/17 (att. T.M.B.).
Child, Gilbert Richard Gregory, 2/Lt., k. in a., 9/5/15.
11 Christie, Denis Halstead, Temp. 2/Lt., k. in a., 21/9/18 (att. 16 Bn.).
2 Clark, James Tony, 2/Lt., k. in a., 9/9/16.
9 Clarke, J. Gay, Temp. Capt., k. in a., 27/9/15.
7 Clements, Reginald Francis, M.C., Temp. Lt., k. in a., 14/8/18.
2 Coleman, Herbert Edward Evatt, 2/Lt., k. in a., 9/9/16.
Collins, John Stratford, Lt., k in a., 5/4/18 (att 12 Bn.).
3 Collins, Neville Lancelot, 2/Lt., k. in a., 15/8/16 (att. 2 Bn.).
Collyer, William James, Temp 2/Lt., k. in a., 31/7/17 (att. 13 Bn.)
Compton, Guy, Temp. 2/Lt., k. in a., 27/7/17 (att. 9 Bn.).
2 Cook, Cyril Edward, Lt., d. of w., 8/7/16.
7 Cooke, Henry Frederick, 2/Lt, k. in a., 4/8/16.
Cookson, Mostyn Eden, Major, k. in a., 14/9/14.
1 Corban-Lucas, Percival Laurence, Temp. Capt., d. of w., 15/12/16 (att. 9/Worc Regt.)
13 Cornwell, Joseph, 2/Lt. (Tp.), d. of w., 29/5/16.
12 Cotton, Aubrey Nightingale, Temp. Capt., k. in a., 30/6/16.
12 Cox, Clarence Rupert, Temp. Capt., d. of w., 13/4/17 (and R.F.C.)
7 Cox, Norman John, Lt. (Tp.), k. in a., 23/8/15.
12 Coxson, Lawrence Frederick, 2/Lt., k. in a., 17/10/16.
Crawley-Boevey, Edward Martin, Capt, k. in a., 24/12/14 (att. R. Fus.).
Crispin, Hugh Trevor, Lt.-Col., k. in a., 30/10/14.
Croft, Leslie Robert, 2/Lt., k. in a., 30/10/14.
11 Cushen, Aylett Cameron, 2/Lt., k. in a., 30/6/16.
3 Dadswell, Clifford Irwin, 2/Lt., k. in a., 7/7/16 (att. 7 Bn.).
11 Davies, Sydney Francis, Temp. 2/Lt., d. of w., 15/11/17.
3 Davison, Edmund, 2/Lt., k. in a., 24/9/17 (att. 11 Bn.).
Daun, Edward Charles, Lt., k. in a., 14/9/14.
Daunt, Barry, 2/Lt., k. in a., 22/9/18 (att. 7 Bn.).
3 Day, John Charles, 2/Lt., k. in a., 9/5/17 (and R.F.C., 52 Sqd.).
3 De Wolf, George Le Blanch, Lt. (Tp.), k. in a., 14/2/16 (att. 9 Bn.).
2 Dickison, John Malcolm, Lt., d. of w., 12/6/18.
13 Diggens, Martin Charles, Capt (Tp.), k. in a., 30/6-1/7/16.
Dixon, Albert Ernest Lucas, 2/Lt. (Tp.), k. in a., 8/5/18 (att. 23/Royal Fusrs.)
Dixon, Peter Sydenham, Lt. (Tp.), k. in a., 7/8/18 (att. 7 Bn.).
11 Doogan, George William, Lt. (Tp.), k. in a., 21/10/16.
13 Dudley, Eric Whittington, 2/Lt., k. in a., 30/6/16.
Dugnolle, John Henry, 2/Lt, k. in a., 25/9/15.
3 Duke, Barry Pevensey, Lt., k. in a., 3/11/14 (att. 2 Bn.).
Du Moulin, Francis Louis, M.C., Capt. (A/Lt.-Col.), k. in a., 7/11/18 (att. 1/E. Yorks Regt.)
2 Earl, Harry Walter, 2/Lt. (Tp.), k. in a., 18/9/18 (Res.).
Eaton-Richards, Julian David, 2/Lt., k. in a., 25/9/15.
13 Elliott, George Edward, Temp. 2/Lt., d. of w., 20/5/16.
11 Ellis, Victor Richard Helps, M.C., 2/Lt. (Tp.), k. in a., 28/4/18.

Ericson, Eric Charles, M.M., 2/Lt. (Tp.), k. in a., 18/9/18 (att. 7 Bn.).
Ewing, James Robert, Capt., died, 19/5/15.
8 Fabian, Arthur Stanley, Lt. (Tp. Capt.), k. in a., 3/9/16 (att. 13 Bn.).
3 Fast, William Jack, 2/Lt. (A/Capt.), k. in a., 24/3/18 (att. 12 Bn.).
12 Fenchelle, George John, 2/Lt. (Tp.), d. of w., 30/6/16 (P. of W.).
3 Ferguson, James Arthur Ross, Lt., k. in a., 9/5/15 (att. Y.L.I.).
7 Field, John Morton, 2/Lt. (Tp.), k. in a., 11/4/16.
Finke, Richard Fenwick, Capt., k. in a., 9/5/15.
Finnemore, Henry James, Temp. 2/Lt., d. of w., 27/3/18 (att. R.F.C.).
11 Fish, Barrow Edmondson, 2/Lt. (Tp.), k. in a., 3/9/16.
10 Fisher, Percy Harold, Temp. 2/Lt., d. of w., 4/7/16 (att. M.G.C.).
3 Fisher, Wilfrid Frederick, 2/Lt., k. in a., 24/7/17 (att. 12 Bn.).
13 Fitzherbert, Harold Lancelot, Lt. (Tp.), k. in a., 30/6/16.
13 Fitzherbert, Wyndham Waterhouse, Capt., k. in a., 7/7/17 (att. R.F.C.).
3 Fitzsimons, Terence, 2/Lt., k. in a., 4/4/16 (att. 7 Bn.).
10 Flowers, John Arthur, 2/Lt. (Tp., k. in a., 1/9/16.
11 Foley, Alfred Montague, 2/Lt., k. in a., 9/9/16 (att. 2 Bn.).
3 Forder, Charles Frederick, 2/Lt., k. in a., 9/9/16 (att. 2 Bn.).
8 Foster, Alfred David, M.C., 2/Lt. (T/Capt.), k. in a., 5/5/17.
7 Foster, Percy George, 2/Lt. (Tp.), d. of w., 2/4/16.
2 Fowler, William Maurice, Temp. 2/Lt., d. of w., 26/9/18.
11 French, Albert Anthony, Temp 2/Lt., k. in a., 3/9/16.
7 Gale, Harold William, Temp. 2/Lt., k. in a., 8/8/18 (att. 5/R. Berks Regt.).
2 Garton, Arthur, Temp. 2/Lt., k. in a., 24/9/18.
3 Gee, Geoffrey Richard Dudley, 2/Lt., k. in a., 4/6/17 (and R.F.C.).
13 Gillespie, Francis Sydney, Temp. Capt., d. of w., 18/6/16.
Gillham, Reginald George William, 2/Lt., k. in a., 26/9/17 (att. 13 Bn.).
2 Goddard, Sydney George, 2/Lt., k. in a., 30/6/16.
9 Godman, Frederick Tyrell, Temp. Capt., died, 12/10/17 (in Ger hands).
10 Godwin, John Charles Raymond, Temp. 2/Lt., k. in a., 7/7/16 (att. 7 Bn.).
9 Golden, Alfred William, Temp. 2/Lt., k. in a., 25/3/18.
7 Gordon, Henry Bernard, Lt. (Tp.), k. in a., 7/7/16.
3 Gordon, Ronald Granville, 2/Lt., k. in a., 19/9/18 (att. 2 Bn.).
7 Gorringe, Edward Clifton, M.C., Temp. Capt., k. in a., 5/9/18.
3 Gramshaw, R. W. R., 2/Lt., d. of w., 27/1/15 (att. 2 Bn.).
3 Grant, John Anderton, 2/Lt., k. in a., 14/5/18 (att. 8 Bn.).
1/2 Greatwood, F. S., 2/Lt., died, 12/4/18 (and R.A.F.).
13 Green, Charles James, Lt. (A/Capt.), k. in a., 16/4/18.
Green, Cyril Mortimer, Lt., k. in a., 6/11/17.
11 Grisewood, Francis, 2/Lt., k. in a., 30/6/16.
11 Grisewood, George Maria Joseph Alphonsus, Capt., died, 27/3/16.
11 Groves, Leonard Alloway, Lt., k. in a., 3/9/15.
11 Gunner, Arthur Henry Edmund, Temp. 2/Lt., k. in a., 37/3/18.
9 Hall, Edward Lionel, Temp. 2/Lt., k. in a., 27/3/18.
12 Hanby, Francis James, 2/Lt., k. in a., 30/6/16
Harden, Arthur James Victor, 2/Lt., k. in a., 25/9/15.
2 Harvey, Rollo d'Aubigne, A/Capt., k. in a., 9/9/16.
13 Heagerty, William Thomas, Major (Tp.), d. of w., 31/1/17.
9 Heldman, Harry Randolph, Lt. (Tp.), k. in a., 27/9/15.
12 Hemsley, Ernest James, Temp. 2/Lt., k. in a., 4-5/9/18 (att. 10/R.W. Surrey Rgt.).
Herron, Reginald Maurice, 2/Lt. (Tp.), d. of w., 12/6/17 (att. 13 Bn.).
Hickman, Harry Claude, 2/Lt., k. in a., 23/3/18 (att. 13 Bn.).
9 Hill, Charles Douglas Lucas, Temp. 2/Lt., k. in a., 14/2/16.
8 Hill, Edwin Arundel, Temp. Major, d. of w., 26/10/18.
14 Hollingsworth, John Frederick, Temp. 2/Lt., d. of w., 2/10/16 (att. E. Surr. Regt.).
9 Holloway, Bernard Henry, Capt. (Tp.), k. in a., 27/9/15.
10 Hood, Oswald, Temp. 2/Lt., k. in a., 1/9/16 (att. 11 Bn.).
10 Hopwood, Marcus, 2/Lt., k. in a., 3/9/16 (att. 13 Bn.).
Howett, William, 2/Lt. (Tp.), k. in a., 18/9/18 (att. 7 Bn.).
Huggett, Sidney George, 2/Lt. (Tp.)., k. in a., 18/9/18 (att. 7 Bn.).
Hughes, William Sladen, Lt., k. in a., 14/9/14.
13 Humble-Crofts, Cyril Mitford, Temp. Capt., k. in a., 30/6/16.
2 Humphreys, William George, 2/Lt., k. in a., 9/9/16.
2 Hutchins, Alfred John Avalon, 2/Lt. (Tp.), d. of w., 22/3/18 (in Ger. hands).
Hutt, Harold Vernon, 2/Lt., k. in a., 26/1/15.
Hyde, Herbert William, 2/Lt., k. in a., 17/5/15 (att. R. Innis. Fusrs.).
Ireland, William, 2/Lt., k. in a., 25/9/15.
11 Ivens, Frank Harold Howe, 2/Lt., A/Capt.), k. in a., 21/10/16.
Jemmett-Browne, Antoney Edward, Capt., k. in a., 11/9/14.
Jenkins, Christopher Hutchinson, Lt. (T/Capt.), d. of w., 22/5/17 (and R.F.C., 45 Sqd.).
10 Johns, Arthur Hugh, Temp. Lt., k. in a., 1/9/16 (att. 11 Bn.).
3 Juckes, Thomas Roland, Lt., k. in a., 9/5/15 (att. 2 Bn.).
8 Kemp, Horace Douglas Meadows, Temp. 2/Lt., d. of w., 31/8/16.
12 Kennedy, Walter Louis, 2/Lt., k. in a., 3/9/16.
9 Kennelly, Leslie William, Lt. (Tp.), d. of w., 9/10/15.
2 Kenward, Robert, 2/Lt., k. in a., 7/7/16.
10 Kenyon, Charles Wilton, Temp. 2/Lt., k. in a., 16/3/16 (att. T.47/T.M.B.).
3 Keogh, Henry Claude, 2/Lt., k. in a., 4/4/17 (att. 13 Bn.).
2 King, Philip Douglas Atwood, 2/Lt., k. in a., 18/12/16.
2 Knifton, Charles William McKinley, 2/Lt., k. in a., 23/11/17.
3 Knifton, James McKinley, 2/Lt., k. in a., 21/7/18 (att. 2 Bn.).
7 Knox, John Laurence, Temp. 2/Lt., k. in a., 20/11/17.
Lanaway, Francis Charlton, 2/Lt. (Tp.), k. in a., 21/8/18 (att. 7/Roy. Fusrs.).
13 Langdale, Harold Carthew, Lt., k. in a., 26/9/17.
Lathan, William, 2/Lt. (Tp.), k. in a., 24/9/18 (att. 17 Bn.).
Lawrence, Thomas Edward, 2/Lt., d. of w., 22/9/18 (att. 7 Bn.).
7 Ledger, Robert John, 2/Lt., d. of w., 11/3/17.
3 Le Doux Veitch, Dallas Gerard, 2/Lt., k. in a., 4/8/16 (att. 7 Bn.).
3 Lewin, Rex Richard, Lt., k. in a., 25/9/15 (att. 2 Bn.).
9 Lias, Ronald John Mortlock, Temp. Lt., k. in a., 23/2/16.
2 Little, Harry Ewart, 2/Lt. (Tp.), k. in a., 18/9/18.
2 Loader, Ernest Stanley, 2/Lt., k. in a., 4/11/18.
14 Lott, William, Temp. 2/Lt., k. in a., 7/10/16.
Lousada, Edward Arthur, Lt., k. in a., 2/11/14.
12 Lupton, Reginald Banister, Temp. 2/Lt. (A/Capt.), k. in a., 1/8/17.
13 MacNaghton, Arthur Edward Harry, Temp. 2/Lt., k. in a., 31/7/16.
9 V.C. McNair, Eric Archibald, Temp. Capt., died, 12/8/18.
7 Manley, Hamilton Douglas, Temp. 2/Lt., k. in a., 27/3/18.
Marillier, Frederick Charles Jennens, 2/Lt., k. in a., 30/10/14.
8 Marsland, John, M.C., Temp. Lt., k. in a., 23/7/17.
2 Marten-Smith, Cecil Eugene, Temp. 2/Lt., k. in a., 13/11/17
13 Martin, George Johnston, 2/Lt., k. in a., 26/9/17.
Matthews, Frank Arthur, Temp. Lt., k. in a., 24/4/17 (att R.F.C., 9 Sqd.).
7 May, Richard Trelawney, Temp. Capt., k. in a., 7/7/16.
8 Meade, Horace Warren, Temp. Capt., k. in a., 13/7/16.
7 Mennie, James, Temp. 2/Lt., k. in a., 18/9/18.
Mitchell, Henry Theophilus Kelly, Lt., killed, 12/11/15.
1 Mitchell, Thomas, Major, d. of w., 12/4/17 (att. 8/Ches. Regt.).
11 Mole, Harold Pearce, 2/Lt., k. in a., 3/9/16.
7 Montesole, Eric Alfred, Temp. 2/Lt., k. in a., 4/3/16.
Montesole, Herbert Sarip Roy, Lt., k. in a., 16-17/5/15 (att. Beds. Regt.).
2 Montresor, Ernest Henry, Lt.-Col., k. in a., 14/9/14.
12 Moody, Leonard Leighton, Temp. 2/Lt., k. in a., 30/6/16.
Moore, Gillachrist, 2/Lt., k. in a., 7/11/14.
7 Murray, Arthur, Temp. 2/Lt., k. in a., 8/8/18.
7 Nagle, Gilbert, M.C., Temp. Capt. & Adjt., k. in a., 5/7/17.
3 Naylor, Henry Charles, 2/Lt., d. of w., 24/9/17 (att. 11 Bn.).
11 Northcote, Edward Stafford, Capt., k. in a., 3/9/16.
13 Nott, Saumarez Ewen, Temp. 2/Lt., k. in a., 9/9/17.
13 Oliver, Harry Percy Greenwood, 2/Lt., k. in a., 30/6/16.
Orme, Owen Felix, Lt. (Temp. Capt.), k. in a., 25/9/15.
14 Ormsby, Francis James, Temp. 2/Lt., k. in a., 3/9/16 (att. 13 Bn.).
3 Osmaston, Robert Shirley, M.C., 2/Lt., k. in a., 24/9/16 (att. R.F.C.).
Oxley, Fergus Richard, A/Lt., k. in a., 20/9/16.
13 Oxley, Richard Stephen, Temp. 2/Lt., k. in a., 18/4/18.
7 Palmer, Horace John, Temp. 2/Lt., k. in a., 8/8/18.
8 Peerless, C. H., 2/Lt., died, 12/5/18.
Pelham, Hon. Lyttelton, Lt., k. in a., 14/9/14.
9 Pennington, Harold Evelyn, 2/Lt. (Tp.), k. in a., 27/9/15.
11 Penruddocke, Cyril Powys, Capt., k. in a., 3/9/16.
2 Perks-Morris, Arthur Bois, 2/Lt., d. of w., 14/11/17.
11 Perry, Kenneth George, Temp. 2/Lt., d. of w., 1/11/16.
Phelps, Duncan, 2/Lt., k. in a., 29/9/18 (att. Hants Regt.)
Pollard-Urquhart, William Edward, Lt., k. in a., 18/4/15.
3 Price, W. E., Lt., died, 31/5/19 (att. 9/Bn.).
9 Prince, Claude Melnotle, Temp. 2/Lt., k. in a., 18/8/16.
9 Pring, Francis Raleigh, Lt., k. in a., 25/9/15.
13 Prior, Lewis Atkins, 2/Lt., k. in a., 30/6/16 (att. 10 Bn.).
9 Prowse, Gerald Maurice Warren, Temp. 2/Lt., k. in a., 12/4/17.
Ramsay, Duncan Gavin, 2/Lt. (T/Lt.), k. in a., 19/12/14 (att. R. W. Surrey Regt.).
3 Ramsbotham, Geoffrey Bury, Lt., k. in a., 16/5/15 (at. S. Staff Regt.).
Raynes, Albert Brainerd, 2/Lt., k. in a., 11/3/15 (att. R. Berks Regt.).
2 Reade, Charlton Leverton Ridout, 2/Lt., k. in a., 9/9/16.
9 Regan, Ernest Charles, Temp. 2/Lt., k. in a., 21/3/18.
11 Richards, Ronald Henry, Temp. 2/Lt., k. in a., 2/6/16.
3 Richards, Walter Edward, 2/Lt., d. of w., 11/12/18 (att. 16 Bn.).
8 Roberson, George Lewis, Temp. 2/Lt., d. of w., 21/3/18.
12 Robinson, Hugh Thomas Kay, D.S.O., Lt.-Col., k. in a., 26/4/18 (att. 13 Bn.).
9 Rogerson, Ernest Sidney, Temp. Capt., k. in a., 19/8/16.
3 Rousell, William Stephen, 2/Lt., k. in a., 8/8/18 (att. 7 Bn.).
9 Rumsby, R. W., Lt., d. of w., 9/5/18 (and R.A.F.).
Rutter, Donald Campbell, Capt., k. in a., 7/6/17 (and 48 Sqd., R.F.C.).
2 Sainton, Francis Charles, M.C., Lt. (A/Capt.), k. in a., 18/4/18.
12 Salberg, John Beaumont, Temp. 2/Lt., died, 30/6/16 (P.O.W.).
11 Salter, Francis Henry, Temp. 2/Lt., k. in a., 21/10/16.

Scandrett, William Frederick, Temp. 2/Lt., k. in a., 27/6/16.
Shiffner, Sir John Bridger, Bart., 2/Lt., k. in a., 24/9/18 (att. 2 Bn.).
Shaw, Cuthbert Frank, 2/Lt., k. in a., 30/10/14 (att. 2 Bn.).
Shaw, Reginald Thomas, Lt., k. in a., 9/5/15 (att. 2 Bn.).
9 Shaw, William Bernard, Lt. (Tp.), k. in a., 12/4/17.
12 Sheppard, Frederick William, 2/Lt (Tp.), k. in a., 12/6/17.
Silver, Humphrey William, Temp 2/Lt, k. in a., 7/6/18 (att 2 Bn.).
Silvester, Anson Lloyd, 2/Lt, k. in a., 1/1/15.
7 Sing, Charles Millington, 2/Lt., d. of w., 7/7/16.
Sivewright, William George, 2/Lt. (Tp.), k. in a., 26/9/17 (att. 13 Bn.).
3 Skipworth, Bernard William, M C. Lt., k. in a., 25/4/18 (att. 9/M.G.C.).
Slater, Leonard, Capt., k. in a., 14/9/14.
2 Smith, Alexander Cooper, Temp. 2/Lt., k. in a., 23/7/16.
12 Smith-Howard, Kenneth Overend, Temp. 2/Lt., k in a., 16-17/10/16.
13 Sogno, George Frank, Temp. 2/Lt., d. of w., 9/10/17 (and R.F.C.).
Somerville, H. A., M.C., 2/Lt., k. in a., 28/3/18 (and R.F.C.).
12 Sparks, Clive, Temp. Lt., k in a., 1/7/16.
9 Spurrell, Frederick John Durnford, Temp. 2/Lt., died, 19/2/15.
9 Stewart, Alan Dundas, Temp. 2/Lt., killed, 19/9/15.
8 Stewart, Henry Edward, Capt (Tp.), k. in a., 1/6/17.
2 Sunderland, Geoffrey, T/Lt. (A/Capt.), k. in a., 24/9/18.
7 Sutton, Eric Guy, Temp. Lt., k. in a. 8/4/16.
11 Swain, Basil Fitzroy, Lt. & Qr.-Mr., d. of w., 22/3/18.
3 Symington, George Charles, 2/Lt., d. of w., 1/8/17 (att. 12 Bn.).
3 Symons, T. S., Capt., killed, 29/9/18 (and R.A.F.).
12 Tate, Tom Campbell, Temp. 2/Lt., d. of w., 2/9/16.
3 Taylor, William Ernest Ewart, 2/Lt., k. in a., 27/3/18 (att. 13 Bn.).
Terry, Robert Joseph Atkinson, M.V.O., D.S.O., Major, k. in a., 3/10/15.
10 Thomas, Sydney Edwin Bailey, Lt. (Tp.), k. in a., 3/9/16 (att. 13 Bn.).
Thomas, Walter Edward, Temp. 2/Lt., k. in a., 21/9/18 (att. 16 Bn.).
1 Thorne, Foster Newton, Major (T/Lt.-Col.), k. in a., 18/4/17 (att. 6/L.N. Lancs Regt.)
Tice, Ernest William, Temp. 2/Lt., d. of w., 1/8/17 (att. 11 Bn.).
9 Tisdall, Charles Henry, 2/Lt. (Tp.), k. in a., 13/2/16.
Toye, Hubert Clarence, 2/Lt., d. of w., 15/10/15.
3 Turner, Richard Radford, 2/Lt., k. in a, 3/2/17.
2 Tuttiett, Laurence William, Capt., k in a., 2/9/16.
3 Uloth, Arthur Curtis Wilmot, M.C., Lt., d of w., 19/9/18.
12 Uppleby, Wyvil Charles Spinola, Capt., d. of w., 9/2/18.
3 Vaughan, John Muir, 2/Lt., d. of w., 18/9/18 (att. 2 Bn.).
2 Verrall, Christopher Francis, Lt., k. in a., 22/12/14.
9 Vidler, Bertram Hall, 2/Lt., k. in a., 12/4/17.
11 Vorley, Charles Archibald, 2/Lt. (Tp.), d. of w., 13/9/16 (P. of W.).
3 Wainwright, Geoffrey Lennox, 2/Lt., k. in a., 25/9/15 (att. 2 Bn.).
Ward, George Ernest (T/Capt.), 2/Lt., k. in a., 25/9/15.
10 Waring, Frederick Royden, 2/Lt., k. in a., 7/7/16 (att. 7 Bn.).
10 Warn, Wallace Gordon, Lt., d. of w., 23/9/16 (and R.F.C.).
3 Welham, Harry George, M.C., Temp. Lt., k. in a., 4/11/18.
7 Wells, Ronald Graham, Temp. Lt., k. in a., 4/3/16.
12 Wentworth, Cyril John, Temp. 2/Lt., d. of w., 3/2/17.
West, Cyril Fredk. Ernest, 2/Lt., k. in a., 28/9/18.
West, Gerald William, Lt., k in a., 25/9/15 (att. 2 Bn.).
Westall, Ronald Cameron, Lt, k. in a., 12/11/14.
2 White, John Stanley, 2/Lt., k in a., 18/9/18.
13 Whittaker, Roger D'Arcy, Capt. & Adjt., k. in a., 30/6/16.
8 Whyte, John Dudley, Temp. Capt., k. in a., 13-14/7/16.
7 Willard, Albert Ellis, Lt., k. in a., 4/7/17.
1/2 Williamson, Robert Burdett, 2/Lt., k. in a., 29/10/18 (and R.A.F.).
8 Willis, Edgar Reginald, Temp Lt., k. in a., 13-14/7/16.
3 Wilmot, Paul Dominic, Lt., k. in a., 25/3/18 (att. 12 Bn.).
3 Wood, Alexander, Major, d of w., 12/4/17.
7 Wood, Thomas Victor, Temp. 2/Lt., k. in a., 4/8/16.
7 Woodhams, Geoffrey, Temp. Capt., k. in a., 19/3/16.
2 Wright, Basil Charles, M.C., Lt., k. in a., 24/9/18.
11 Wright, John Armer, M.C., Lt., k. in a., 18/9/18 (att. 7 Bn.).
Wright, William Lake, 2/Lt., k. in a., 20/10/18 (att. 17 Bn.).
2 Young, Nevill Lindsay, 2/Lt., k. in a., 20/8/16.

The Hampshire Regiment.

1 Adams, Hugh Irving, Lt. (Tp.), k. in a., 1/7/16.
Addison, Alfred Charles, Capt., k. in a., 25/4/15.
2 Aitcheson, Thomas Charles, 2/Lt., k. in a., 19/10/16.
Alexander, Henry Talbot, 2/Lt. (Tp.), k. in a., 1/7/16.
11 Andrews, Arthur Alfred, Capt., died, 16/10/18.
2 Arnell, Douglas Carstairs, Capt., k. in a., 13/7/16.
14 Ash, Gilbert Stanley, 2/Lt., k. in a., 3/9/16.
15 Baddeley, Kenneth, 2/Lt. (Tp.), k. in a., 15/9/16.
15 Bailey, Walter George William, Capt. (Tp.), k. in a. 15/9/16.
14 Bainbridge, John Stuart, Lt. (Tp.), k. in a., 26/9/17.
13 Ball, Benedict Hanly, 2/Lt., k. in a., 3/9/16 (att. 14/Bn.).
Barton, Frederick St. John, Capt., k. in a., 24/7/15.
13 Baxter, George William, Lt. (Tp.), k. in a., 14/4/17 (att. 2/Bn.).
Beanlands, Bernard Paul Gascoyne, M.C., Capt., died, 8/5/19 (and R.A.F.).
13 Bearn, Percy Dare, 2/Lt., k. in a., 3/9/16 (att. 14 Bn.).
10 Beckett, John Douglas Mortimer, D.S.O., Major (Tp. Lt.-Col.), killed, 9/2/18.
11 Bell, Gawain Murdoch, D.S.O., Major, k. in a., 31/7/17.
3 Bell, Norman Henderson, 2/Lt., k. in a., 1/7/16 (att. 1/Bn.).
1 Bell, Richard Logsdaile, M.C., 2/Lt., k. in a., 9/4/18 (att. 5th Bn.).
10 Bell, Philip Lawrence, Lt., k. in a., 10/8/15.
10 Bench, James George, 2/Lt., k. in a., 24/4/17.
15 Bender, Alfred Courteney, Lt. (Tp.), k. in a., 20/9/17.
1 Bishop, Alfred Wedderburn, 2/Lt. (Tp.), k. in a., 12/5/17.
10 Black-Hawkins, Claude Cranstoon Ridout, Capt., k. in a., 10/8/15.
11 Bland, Charles Edward, Capt. (Tp.), k. in a., 9/9/16.
3 Bonham-Carter, Arthur Thomas, Capt., k. in a., 1/7/16 (att. 1/Bn.).
Boxall, Carze Lermithe, Capt., d. of w., 4/5/15.
1 Bramble, George Henry Joseph, 2/Lt., k. in a., 1/7/16.
15 Breslaw, Geoffrey Reynell, 2/Lt., k. in a., 7/10/16.
15 Brewin, Harry Hedley, 2/Lt. (Tp.), k. in a., 12/8/18 (att. 2/Bn.).
Bryant, Harvey, M.C., 2/Lt., k. in a., 12/9/18 (att. 2/4 Bn.).
Buckley, Arthur Dashwood Bulkeley, C.B., Col., died, 3/4/15.
11 Cade, Francis Thomas Darrel, Capt. (Tp.), k. in a., 6/9/16.
3 Cain, Alan Victor, 2/Lt., k. in a., 19/10/16 (att. 2/Bn.).
13 Calder, William Menzies Grant, 2/Lt. (Tp.), k. in a., 15/9/16 (att. 15/Bn.).
10 Calderwood, Alex Taylor, 2/Lt. (Tp.), k. in a., 21/8/15.
3 Cancellor, Desmond Bertram, M.C., Lt., k. in a., 1/11/18 (att. 1/Bn.).
1 Cane, Reginald Shapland, 2/Lt. (Tp.), k. in a., 1/7/16.
2 Carpenter-Turner, Eric Walter, Lt., d. of w., 9/8/16 (3rd).
15 Carrington, Harold Edward, Capt. (Tp.), k. in a., 15/9/16.
15 Challis, William Guy Fawcett, Lt. (Tp.), k. in a., 13/7/16.
3 Chambers, Robert Avalon Montagu, 2/Lt., d. of w., 15/10/15 (att. Glouc. R.).
10 Cheesman, George Leonard, Lt. (Tp.), k. in a., 10/8/15.
11 Chubb, Alan Travers, 2/Lt. (k. in a., 9/9/16.
14 Colebrook, Leslie Charles, 2/Lt. (Tp.), k. in a., 1/2/17.
Colyer, Wilfred Victor, 2/Lt. (Tp.), k. in a., 22/10/18 (att. 15/Bn.).
Connellan, Peter Martin, Major, k. in a., 20/10/14.
2 Cook, Charles Reynolds, 2/Lt. (Tp.), k. in a., 29/5/18.
3 Counsell, Christopher Herbert, 2/Lt., d. of w., 6/7/16 (att. 2/Bn.).
Cowan, Douglas Henderson, 2/Lt., k. in a., 26/8/14.
3 Cromie, Henry Julian, Capt. (Tp.), k. in a., 23/10/16 (att. 1/Bn.).
3 Cromie, Maurice Francis, Lt., k. in a., 4/6/15 (att. 2/Bn.).
Culley, Walter Duncan, 2/Lt. (Tp.), d. of w., 12/7/17 (att. 1/Bn.).
Cunningham, Edward Hamilton, 2/Lt. (Tp.), k. in a., 11/8/18 (att. 1/Dorsets).
Cureton, Edward Robert, Major, died, 18/5/16.
3 Currie, James Hamilton, Lt., k. in a., 25/8/18.
1 Daines, Sidney, 2/Lt. (Tp.), k. in a., 16/5/18.
Daniels, James Alfred, T/Lt. (A/Capt.), d. of w., 21/9/17 (att. 15/Bn.).
14 Davenport, Cyril Francis, 2/Lt. (Tp.), d. of w., 2/8/16.
Day, Owen Heathcote Lacy, Capt., k. in a., 6/8/15.
Deane, John Henry, Major, k. in a., 30/4/15.
2 Derry, Richard Courtnay Powell, 2/Lt. (Tp.), k. in a., 6/8/15.
Dolphin, Eric John Weston, Lt., k. in a., 7/11/14.
11 Elkington, Walter Henry, 2/Lt. (Tp.), k. in a., 22/3/18.
13 Ellis, Yvo Lempriere, Lt. (Tp.), k. in a., 29/5/16.
Fidler, Frederick, Capt., k. in a., 26/4/15.
14 Finlay, George Malcolm, Capt. (Tp.), k. in a., 5/11/17.
10 Fishlock, Albert Ernest, 2/Lt. (Tp.), d. of w., 7/9/18.
Foster, Archibald Courtenay Hays, Lt., k. in a., —/9/14 (and K. Afr. Rif.).
14 Freeman, Eric Payne, Capt. (Tp.), died, 23/3/18 (in Ger. hands).
2 Gawn, Thomas, 2/Lt., k. in a., 6/8/15.
1 German, Ivon Hector, M.C., T/Lt. (A/Capt.), died, 1/12/18.
12 Gibaud, Ernest John, 2/Lt., k. in a., 24/4/17.
14 Gilbert, Frank Charles Henry, Lt. (Tp.), d. of w., 23/4/16.
1 Girling, Charles John, 2/Lt., k. in a., 23/10/16.
Gold, George Rome, 2/Lt., k. in a., 27/5/18 (att. 2 Berks R.).
14 Goldsmith, Frank, M.C., Major (Tp.), d. of w., 27/9/17.
Goodford, Charles James Henry, M.C., Lt., k. in a., 1/7/16.
2 Gorman, D. T., M.C., Lt. (A/Capt.), d. of w., 22/6/19.
12 Graham-Montgomery, Graham John Early, Capt., k. in a., 24/4/17.
14 Green, Ernest Michael, Lt. (Tp.), k. in a., 3/9/16.
Greene, Henry Roundell, Capt., died, 27/6/18.
Griffith, Gerald, Lt., k. in a., 26/8/14.
Gunn, James Campbell, 2/Lt. (Tp.), k. in a., 27/5/18 (att. 2 R. Berks R.).
3 Gunning, William Herbert, 2/Lt., d. of w., 31/10/16 (att. 10/Bn.).
13 Hailstone, Ralph Puroglove, 2/Lt. (Tp.), k. in a., 18/10/16 (att. 2/Bn.).
3 Halcrow, Arthur Palmer, Lt., k. in a., 23/4/17 (att. 2/Bn.).
12 Hale, S. F., Lt., died, 31/5/19.
Hall, Henry Cecil, 2/Lt. (Tp.), k. in a., 4/10/17 (att. 1/Bn.).
2 Haly, William Hele, 2/Lt., k. in a., 14/10/16.
1 Harding, Henry George, M.C., Lt., k. in a., 4/10/17.
3 Harrington, Herbert Andrzey Biernaski, Lt., d. of w., 9/12/14 (att. 1/Bn.).
Harland, Reginald Wickham, Capt., k. in a., 30/10/14.
16 Harris, Henry James Lawrence, Lt. (Tp.), k. in a., 6/11/16 (att. 14/Bn.).
1 Harrison, Stanley, 2/Lt. (Tp.), k. in a., 23/10/16.
10 Hayes, Charles Bianconi, Capt., k. in a., 10/8/15.
11 Hayman, William Deacon, 2/Lt. (Tp.), k. in a., 13/8/17.
11 Hayward, Ernest Frank Walton, 2/Lt. (Tp.), k. in a., 5/10/16.
10 Hellyer, George Edgcombe, Capt. (Tp.), d. of w., 22/8/15.

2 V.C. Hewitt, Denis George Wyldborn, 2/Lt., k. in a., 31/7/17 (att. 14/Bn.).
Hicks, Frederick Richard, Lt.-Col., d. of w., 12/6/15
1 Hobson, Geoffrey Hamilton, 2/Lt., d. of w., 14/4/17.
1 Hogan, Jack Graham, 2/Lt., k. in a., 28/3/18.
1 House, Horace George, 2/Lt. (Tp.), k. in a., 28/3/18.
Howard, Arthur, 2/Lt., k. in a., 30/4/15.
Howcroft, Laurence Walter, Lt. (Tp.), k. in a., 20/11/17 (att. 2nd Bn.).
Humphrey-Davy, Darrel Norman O'Neale, 2/Lt (Tp.), k in a., 12/2/17 (att. 14 Bn.).
Hutchison, Seton Marshall, T/Lt., A/Capt., died, 8/1/18 (att. 2 W.I. Regt.).
2 Irwin, Aubrey Joseph, 2/Lt. (Tp.), k. in a., 3/9/18.
3 James, George Henry, 2/Lt., d. of w., 8/5/17 (att. 2nd Bn.).
15 James, James Wright, Capt. (Tp.), k. in a., 7/10/16.
Jarvis, Edwin Leonard, 2/Lt. (Tp.), k. in a., 4/9/18 (att. 2nd Bn.).
11 Jefferies, James Leslie, Lt. (Tp.), k. in a., 9/9/16.
15 Keep, Walter Fischer, 2/Lt. (Tp.), k. in a., 7/6/17.
Kent, Edward Montague Wayne, Lt., k. in a., 26/8/14.
4 Kingswell, Leonard William, T/Lt., A/Capt., k. in a., 26/3/18 (att. 7/Corps Reinf.).
Knocker, Arthur Paget, Lt. (T/Capt.), k. in a., 7/2/15.
15 Lacy, Wilfrid Henry, Capt. (Tp.), k. in a., 7/10/16.
Lambert, Francis Henry, Lt., d. of w., 14/6/15.
3 Lambourne, Reginald Bertram, 2/Lt., d. of w., 5/1/16 (att. 2nd Bn.).
3 Lane, Edward F., Capt., died, 3/4/19.
1/2 Lane, R. W., 2/Lt., k. in a., 9/11/18 (and R.A.F.).
14 Langdon, Lawrence, Lt. (Tp.), d. of w., 14/3/16.
Le Brun, Lewis Appleby, 2/Lt. (Tp.), k. in a., 31/10/18 (att. 11 Bn. Som. L.I.).
1/2 Leed, David, 2/Lt., k. in a., 12/8/18 (and R.A.F.).
Leedham, William, 2/Lt. (Tp.), k. in a., 4/9/18 (att. 15/Bn.).
16 Lees, Percival Booth, 2/Lt. (Tp.), k. in a., 19/7/16.
Leigh, Edward, Major, k. in a., 1/5/15.
1 Le Marchant, Edward Herbert Charlie, Lt., d. of w., 29/10/16.
3 Lloyd, Lyndsey, 2/Lt., k. in a., 9/10/17 (att. 2nd Bn.).
Lloyd, Thomas Newburn Chetwoode, Capt., died, 25/4/16.
13 Lowy, Walter Albert, Capt. (Tp.), d. of w., 3/9/18 (att 10/Bn.).
Lucas, Thomas Henry, Lt., killed, 15/5/18 (and R.A.F.).
11 McConnochie, Norman, Capt., k. in a., 29/3/18.
2 McCurdy, John, 2/Lt., d. of w., 9/8/16.
15 Main, Percy Rowland, 2/Lt., killed, 28/9/16 (and R.F.C.).
3 Man, Frederic Cecil, Lt., died, 21/2/19 (att. 3 Gurkha Rifles).
3 Manlove, Leonard Cecil Tong, 2/Lt., k. in a., 3/8/16 (att. 2nd Bn.).
15 Martin, Stanley Charley James, 2/Lt. (Tp.), d. of w., 25/7/16 (T.M.B.).
3 Mason, Gerald Francis, Lt., killed, 1/9/17 (att. M.G.C., 12 Coy.).
May, Walter Gould, 2/Lt., k. in a., 3/9/16 (1 Garr. Bn.).
Medcraft, Alexander Raymond, 2/Lt. (Tp.), k. in a., 18/9/18 (att. 12 Bn.).
15 Merrett, Arthur Edwin, 2/Lt. (Tp.), k. in a., 18/12/16.
1 Mooney, Reginald Herbert, 2/Lt. (Tp.), d. of w., 5/5/17.
Moor, Christopher, 2/Lt., k. in a., 6/8/15.
2 V.C. Moor, George Raymond Dallas, M.C., Lt., died, 3/11/18 (att. 30 Div. H.Q.).
1 Morgan, Basil Algernon Cecil, 2/Lt., k. in a., 28/3/18.
3 Morgan, Cecil Edward, Lt., drowned, 3/7/15.
13 Morgan, Walter Henry, 2/Lt. (Tp.), k. in a., 12/7/16 (att. 15 Bn.).
2 Morris, Michael Ambrose, Lt. (Tp.), k. in a., 6/8/15 (13 Bn. att.).
13 Nelder, Gordon Charles Aldridge, 2/Lt. (Tp.), k. in a., 6/8/15 (att. 2 Bn.).
15 Newman, Chafen Cecil, M.C., T/Lt., Capt., k. in a., 4/9/18 (att. Hants Yeo.).
3 Nixon, William Gerald, Lt., k. in a., 1/7/16 (11 T.M.B.).
14 O'Farrell, Howard Patrick Curtis, Lt.-Col., died, 6/12/16.
Owen, Richard Frank, 2/Lt. (Tp.), k. in a., 30/4/17 (att. M.G.C., 102 Coy.).
Pakenham, Charles John Wingfield, Lt., k. in a., 30/4/15.
Palk, Hon. Lawrence Charles Walter, D.S.O., Lt.-Col. (Tp.), k. in a., 1/7/16.
Parker, Basil Stewart, Capt., k. in a., 6/8/15.
Parker, George Hastings, Major, k. in a., 19/12/14.
Parker, Henry, 2/Lt., d. of w., 30/4/15.
15 Parry, Frank Meredith, 2/Lt. (Tp.), k. in a., 15/9/16.
15 Pasco, John Crawford Claud, 2/Lt., k. in a., 4/9/18.
14 Pearce, Charles Denison Fillis, 2/Lt. (Tp.), k. in a., 18/10/16.
12 Pearce, Maurice Leonard, Lt., d. of w., 24/9/16 (att. R. Suss. R.).
3 Peel, Colin Nevill, 2/Lt., k. in a., 3/9/16 (att. 14 Bn.).
14 Penton, Arthur Herbert, 2/Lt., k. in a., 16/4/18 (att. 1/5 Manch. R.).
Perrett, Ernest Henry, 2/Lt. (Tp.), k. in a., 4/10/17 (att. 1 Bn.).
3 Philip, Gerald Huntley, 2/Lt., d. of w., 11/11/16 (att. 15 Bn.).
1 Phippard, Dudley West, 2/Lt. (Tp.), k. in a., 4/10/17.
13 Pigott, Lancelot Boltry, Lt. (Tp.), k. in a., 6/8/15 (att. 2nd Bn.).
10 Pilleau, Arthur Langston, Major, k. in a., 10/8/15.
2 Pine, Leslie William Tattersall, 2/Lt., d. of w., 18/8/17.
3 Pite, Horace Victor Walter, 2/Lt., k. in a., 10/4/18 (att. 5 Bn.).
13 Popham, Edward Home, Capt. (Tp.), k. in a., 6/8/15 (att. 2nd Bn.).
Potter, Keith Erskine, 2/Lt. (Tp.), d. of w., 13/8/18 (att. 1st Bn).
11 Powell, John Stewart, Capt. (Tp.), k. in a., 2/7/16.
1 Price, Eric William Manning, 2/Lt., d. of w., 1/7/16.
3 Prynn, Norman, Lt. (A/Capt.), k. in a., 28/3/18 (att. 1st Bn.).
3 Quarrier, Edward John, 2/Lt., k. in a., 31/5/18 (att. 2nd Bn.).
12 Reavell, Keith Watts, Lt. (Tp.), k. in a., 9/12/16.
3 Reeves, Geoffrey Frederick John, 2/Lt., k. in a., 6/6/15.
1 Reid, Eric Archdall, 2/Lt., k. in a., 29/3/18.
Reid, George Whiteley, Capt., k. in a., 4/5/15.
Richards, Frank, 2/Lt., k. in a., 14/5/15.
2 Robertson, Norman Cairns, Capt., died, 20/6/17 (P.O.W.).
3 Robertson, Robert Hamilton, 2/Lt., k. in a., 30/11/17 (att. 2nd Bn.).
11 Robinson, Wilfred Cane, Lt., k. in a., 22/3/18.
13 Rodger, James Alexander Valentine, 2/Lt., k. in a., 3/9/16 (att. 14 Bn.).
14 Rowsell, Herbert Greaves, Capt. (Tp.), k. in a., 3/9/16.
3 Sandeman, George Amelius Crawshay, Capt., k. in a., 26/4/15.
11 Sandeman, Kenneth Charles, Lt. (Tp.), k. in a., 1/9/18 (att. 2 R. Innis. Fus.).
10 Savage, Harold Wilson, Capt., k. in a., 10/8/15.
2 Scoggin, Harry Cumming, 2/Lt., k. in a., 9/8/16.
3 Sebastian, Skinner Raymond, M.C., Lt. (Tp. Lt.-Col.), d. of w., 27/3/18 (att. 5/Ox. & Bucks L. I.).
2 Seed, James Parrott, 2/Lt., (Tp.), k. in a., 17/6/18.
Seely, Frank Reginald, 2/Lt., d. of w., 13/4/17.
15 Seers, Wilfrid, Major (Tp.), k. in a., 20/9/17.
15 Sevin, Clifford Newton, 2/Lt., d. of w., 25/3/18.
13 Sheffield, Surtees, Lt. (Tp.), k. in a., 6/8/15 (att. 2nd Bn.).
1 Shirley, John George Frederick, 2/Lt., k. in a., 22/4/18.
1 Sillence, James, M.M., Lt., d. of w., 24/4/18.
14 Skinner, Frederick Tom, T/Capt. (A/Major), k. in a., 3/9/16.
Slattery, Duncan Vincent, 2/Lt. (Tp.), killed, 3/3/17 (and R.F.C.).
Smith, Herbert Carington, Lt.-Col., k. in a., 25/4/15.
10 Smith, Sidney Arthur, 2/Lt. (Tp.), k. in a., 10/8/15.
Snyder, Lorne, 2/Lt., k. in a., 23/4/17 (att. 2nd Bn.).
3 Sparrow, Walter Burnaby, Lt., k. in a., 1/9/18 (att. 10 Bn.).
14 Sprigg, Henry Aldwin Guildford, Capt. (Tp.), k. in a., 9/5/18.
15 Stapleton, Hubert, Capt., k. in a., 15/9/16.
Stevens, Arthur Eustace, 2/Lt., d. of w., 16/7/15.
3 Stevenson, Richard John, 2/Lt., d. of w., 10/5/18 (att. 1st Bn.).
13 Stock, Charles Herbert, 2/Lt. (Tp.), died, 31/5/16 (att. 9 Worc. R.).
15 Stopford, Frederick Duncan, 2/Lt. (Tp.), k. in a., 15/9/16.
11 Sulman, Paul Loxton, M.C., Capt. (Tp.), d. of w., 28/4/18.
Sweet, Leonard Herbert, Capt. (Tp.), k. in a., 22/6/16 (and R.F.C.).
10 Tanner, John Howard, Lt. (Tp.), k. in a., 15/9/16.
Telfer, Andrew, 2/Lt. (Tp.), died, 15/11/18 (att. 10/Bn.).
1 Thompson, Fendall Powney, 2/Lt., k. in a., 1/7/16.
15 Thompson, Stanley, Capt. (Tp.), k. in a., 15/9/16.
12 Tidy, Percy Ernest, 2/Lt., k. in a., 24/4/17.
11 Tobin, Gerald Vere, 2/Lt. (Tp.), died, 15/5/17.
13 Tollemache, Horace Murray, Lt. (Tp.), k. in a., 17/7/18.
Trask, John Hedley, 2/Lt. (Tp.), k. in a., 20/11/17 (att. 14 Bn.).
13 Trattles, William Horace, 2/Lt. (Tp.), k. in a., 25/1/17 (att. 9/Worc. R.).
Trimmer, William Douglas Maclean, Lt., k. in a., 30/10/14.
3 Twining, Cecil Francis Harvey, Capt., k. in a., 3/5/15 (att. 1st Bn.).
Unwin, Lancelot Urquhart, Capt., k. in a., 27/4/15.
Veacock, Stanley John, Lt. (Tp.), d. of w., 17/10/17 (and R.F.C., 20 Sqd.).
Wadham, Vivian Hugh Nicholas, Capt., died, 17/1/16 (and R.F.C.).
Walford, Oliver Robson, 2/Lt., k. in a., 26/4/15.
Wallace, Thomas Victor Walter, 2/Lt. (Tp.), d. of w., 2/11/17 (att 8 Bn.).
2 Wallis, William Isaac, 2/Lt., d. of w., 10/10/18.
14 Warren, Frederick Robert Fulford, T/Lt. (A/Major), k. in a., 22/10/16.
3 Watson, Alec Philip, 2/Lt., d. of w., 14/4/17 (att. 2nd Bn.).
Webb, Gerald Vernon Tisdall, Capt., k. in a., 6/8/15.
11 Wellsted, George Wormall, Capt. (Tp.), k. in a., 30/6/16.
2 West, William James, M.C., 2/Lt. (A/Capt.), k. in a., 3/9/18.
1 Westmore, Lawrence Arthur, 2/Lt. (Tp.), k. in a., 1/7/16.
10 Whaley, Oswald Stanley, 2/Lt. (Tp.), k. in a., 10/8/15.
15 White, Algernon William, 2/Lt., k. in a., 9/8/18
2 White, John, Lt., k in a., 4/6/15.
12 Whitmarsh, Donald Lyle 2/Lt. (Tp.), k. in a., 22/8/17 (att. 2nd Bn.).
1 Wilde, Arthur William, 2/Lt., k. in a., 21/1/16.
1 Williams, David Ransome Vaughan, 2/Lt. (Tp.), died, 20/11/18
10 Williams, Philip Clarence, Lt. (Tp.), k. in a., 10/8/15.
12 Williams, Wilfred Cyril, Lt., k in a., 24/9/16.
2 Wilson, Belford Alexander Wallis, M.C., 2/Lt., k. in a., 26/9/17 (att. 14 Bn.).
1 Wood, Eric Horace, 2/Lt., k. in a., 23/10/16.
15 Woollven, John Humphrey, 2/Lt., k. in a., 4/9/18.
2 Yates, Frederick, 2/Lt (Tp.), k. in a., 30/11/17.

The South Staffordshire Regiment.

3 Archer-Shee, George, Lt., k. in a., 31/10/14 (att. 2/Bn.).
2 Atkinson, John, 2/Lt. (Tp.), k. in a., 24/3/18

8 Barlow, Osborn, M.C., Capt. (Tp.), d. of w., 14/4/18.
1 Barlow, Theodore Kenneth, Lt. (Tp.), d. of w., 15/7/16.
8 Barnett, William Raymond, 2/Lt. (Tp.), k. in a., 29/4/18 (att. 5/Bn.).
Bean, Charles Reginald Chamberlayne, 2/Lt., k. in a., 26/10/15.
2 Bell, Alfred Joseph, Lt. (Tp.), k. in a., 13/5/17.
2 Benson, William Roy Gwyn, 2/Lt., k. in a., 2/7/16.
4 Berry, Reginald, 2/Lt., k. in a., 30/5/16 (att. 2/Bn.).
8 Birdseye, Douglas Martin, 2/Lt. (Tp.), d. of w., 10/2/17.
8 Birrell, Thomas Yates, Lt. (Tp.), k. in a., 17/2/16.
Blakeman, Albert Victor, 2/Lt. (Tp.), k. in a., 7/10/18 (att. 1/K.S.L.I.).
1 Bone, Harry Whittenburg, 2/Lt., k. in a., 25/9/15.
Bonner, Singleton, D.S.O., Major, d. of w., 1/5/17.
8 Bourne, Austin Spencer, 2/Lt., d. of w., 23/4/17.
5 Bower, Henry Raymond Syndercombe, Lt., killed, 18-19/12/14.
Bracey, Ernest Clifford, 2/Lt., k. in a., 28/9/18 (att. 5/Bn.).
10 Brettell, Sidney Walter, Lt. (Tp.), k. in a., 10/7/16 (att. 8/Bn.).
4 Bristol, Harold James, T/Lt. (A/Capt.), d. of w., 4/5/18.
4 Brooks, Frederick Jacob, 2/Lt., k. in a., 13-15/11/16 (att. 2/Bn.).
8 Browne, Andrew Cranstoun, 2/Lt. (Tp.), k. in a., 2/7/16.
8 Browne, Alfred James Haslip, 2/Lt., d. of w., 23/4/17.
Bunn, Jack Coulson, 2/Lt. (Tp.), k. in a., 13/5/18.
1 Burke, Henry Joseph, Lt., k. in a., 25/9/15.
3 Burton, Howard, 2/Lt., d. of w., 14/10/17 (att. 1/7 R. War. R.).
10 Bussy, Cyril, 2/Lt. (Tp.), k. in a., 3/1/16 (att. 8/Bn.).
7 Bussy, Julian, 2/Lt. (Tp.), k. in a., 29/9/16.
3 Butler, William Andsley, 2/Lt., k. in a., 16/11/16 (att. 1/8 R. War. R.).
3 Calvert, Cecilius Frederick Holcombe, 2/Lt., k. in a., 14/9/15 (att. 2/Bn. E. Lanc. R.).
4 Campbell, Donald William Auchinbolck, Capt., k. in a., 23/11/14 (att. N. & D.R.).
3 Carbonell, William Charles, 2/Lt., d. of w., 1/9/16 (att. 1/Bn.).
4 Cave, Frank, 2/Lt., k. in a., 17/2/17 (att. 2/Bn.).
8 Chapman, Sidney George, 2/Lt., d. of w., 28/9/16 (att. 7/Bn.).
11 Charlton, Robert, M.C., Capt. (Tp.), d. of w., 5/10/17 (att. 7/Bn.).
2 Chipman, John Douglas, Lt. (Tp.), k. in a., 17/2/17.
7 Christian, Edward Charles, Capt. (Tp.), k. in a., 11/9/16.
3 Clements, F. C., Lt., k. in a., 6/9/15.
Coghlan, Clifford Edward Leslie, Lt., k. in a., 27/8/17 (att. 9/Bn.).
Collins, Horace Alexander, Lt. (Tp.), k. in a., 18/9/17 (att. R.F.A., 246 Bde., att. 49 Sig. Co., R.E.).
Conley, William Cockayne, M.C., Lt. (Tp.), k. in a., 26/10/17 (att. 91 T.M.B.).
1 Cooper, William, 2/Lt., k. in a., 25/9/15.
Coxe, Eric Noel, 2/Lt. (Tp.), d. of w., 9/6/17 (att. 7/Bn.).
8 Creasy, Francis Symons, 2/Lt. (Tp.), k. in a., 23/4/17.
Crousaz, Cecil Francis, Lt., k. in a., 31/11/14.
3 Curry, William Horace, D.S.O., 2/Lt. (A/Capt.), k. in a., 25/10/17 (att. 1/Bn.).
7 Daukes, Archibald Henry, Lt.-Col. (Tp.), k. in a., 7-11/8/15 (Maj. S. Staff. R.).
2 Dent, Joseph Leslie, D.S.O., M.C., Capt. & Bt.-Major, k. in a., 11/4/17.
3 De Trafford, Henry Joseph, Capt., k. in a., 25/9/15 (att. 1/Bn.).
4 Dolphin, Samuel, 2/Lt., k. in a., 24/3/18.
4 Douglas, Bruce Francis Sholto, 2/Lt., k. in a., 14/4/15 (att. 2/Bn.).
2 Douglas-Willan, Stanhope William Howard Sholto, Lt. (A/Capt.), k. in a., 17/2/17.
2 Draycott-Wood, William, 2/Lt., k. in a., 29/6/15.
3 Duddell, Arnold Leslie, Lt., d. of w., 27/9/17 (att. 6/York. R.).
Dunlop, Julian Silver Strickland, Capt., k. in a., 24/10/14.
4 Dunlop, Kenneth, 2/Lt., k. in a., 26/9/15 (att. 1 Bn.).
2 Dutton, Charles, Capt. (Tp.), d. of w., 28/7/16.
4 Dutton, Gerald Alexander, 2/Lt., died, 5/5/16.
4 Edgar, John Maxwell, Lt. (A/Capt.), k. in a., 22/3/18.
8 Edwards, Stanley Robert, Lt. (Tp.), k. in a., 24/9/15.
4 Elliott, Geoffrey Faber, 2/Lt., k. in a., 31/8/16 (att. 8/Bn.).
1 Emberton, Percival Harvey, 2/Lt. (Tp.), k. in a., 1/7/16.
Evans, Charles Wilmot, M.C., Capt., k. in a., 1/7/16.
4 Fawcett, Richard Wilfrid, 2/Lt., d. of w., 26/9/15 (att. 15/T.M.B.).
9 Ferguson, Hugh Mortimer, Capt. (Tp.), k. in a., 11/6/17.
3 Fisher, Robert, 2/Lt., k. in a., 14/11/16 (att. 10/Y. & L.R.).
3 Fitzpatrick, Dudley Thomas Francis, Lt., k. in a., 27/10/14 (att. 2/Bn.).
Foster, William Augustus Portman, Lt., d. of w., 11/11/14 (in enemy hands).
4 Fowell, John, 2/Lt., k. in a., 12/10/17 (att. 8/Bn.).
4 Fox, Walter Henry, Lt., k. in a., 16/6/15 (att. Bedf. R.).
8 Gale, Ralph George, 2/Lt. (T/Lt.), k. in a., 12/10/17.
Gething, William Gordon, 2/Lt., k. in a., 22/9/17.
11 Giles, William Charles, 2/Lt., k. in a., 12/10/17 (att. 8/Bn.).
3 Gillender, Alfred Williamson, 2/Lt., d. of w., 10/4/17 (att. 7/Linc. R.).
3 Gissing, Alexander, 2/Lt., died, 9/10/18 (att. 2/Bn.).
Glaze, Donald Stuart, 2/Lt. (Tp.), k. in a., 26/10/17 (att. 1/Bn.).
Goddard, Norman Molyneux, 2/Lt. (Tp.), d. of w., 2/7/17 (att. 9/Bn.).
2 Goodall, Clarence William, 2/Lt., k. in a., 15/11/16.
1 Goodwin, John Stanley, 2/Lt. (T/Lt.), k. in a., 28/3/17 (att. 22/Bn. Manch. R.).
4 Gordon, Cecil Philip George, Capt., killed, 21/3/18 (att. (R.F.C.).
3 Gramshaw, Hugh, 2/Lt., died, 28/2/16.
4 Grant, Harold Allan, 2/Lt., died, 27/9/18 (att. 7/N. Staffs Regt.).
Green, Charles Henry, Capt. (A/Major), d. of w., 8/11/17 (att. Nigeria Regt.).
8 Green, John Alexander, Lt. (Tp.), died, 18/8/18 (att. Anson Bn., R.N.D.).
Gwyther, Edwin Thomas, 2/Lt. (Tp.), d. of w., 28/5/18 (att. 6/Bn.).
Hall, Bruce, Lt., k. in a., 25/9/15.
Hall, Warwick, Lt., d. of w., 1/7/16.
8 Harper, Edgar Henry, Lt. (Tp.), k. in a., 10/7/16.
Harris, Jack St. Clair Gainez, 2/Lt., k. in a., 22/2/15.
3 Hatton, Horace Walter Smeathman, Lt. (A/Capt.), k. in a., 23/8/18 (att. 2/Bn.).
1 Henderson, Thomas Eric, 2/Lt., k. in a., 3/8/16.
Hewat, George Michael Fitz Gerald, 2/Lt., k. in a., 10/3/15.
10 Hewetson, John Dixon, Capt. (Tp.), d. of w., 30/5/18 (att. 1/Bn.).
8 Hider, Arthur Leslie George, 2/Lt. (T/Lt.), k. in a., 27/5/17.
2 Hind, Charles Raymond, Lt., k. in a., 30/5/16.
1 Hindsley, Eric, Lt. (Tp.), d. of w., 11/4/17.
4 Hogben, Frederick, 2/Lt., k. in a., 23/10/16 (att. 2/Linc R.).
2 Holdcroft, William Lawrence, 2/Lt. (Tp.), k. in a., 29/7/16.
1 Holdsworth, Godfrey Edward, Lt. (A/Capt.), k. in a., 24/3/18 (att. 4/Bn.).
9 Holland, Ernest, 2/Lt. (Tp.), k. in a., 19/7/17.
Holmes, Francis Lennox, Lt., k. in a., 23/10/14.
1 Hooper, William, 2/Lt. (Tp.), k. in a., 3/10/18 (att. 5/Bn.).
10 Hudspeth, Arthur, 2/Lt., k. in a., 19/9/16 (att. D.L.I.).
11 Hughes, Douglas Duncan, 2/Lt., k. in a., 10/7/16.
Hume, Charles Geoffrey, Lt., k. in a., 20/10/14.
7 Hume, Edward Archibald, Capt. (Tp.), d. of w., 27/8/15.
Hurdman, Cyril, 2/Lt., k. in a., 19/7/16 (att. War. R.).
2 Hussey, Hubert Murray, M.C., 2/Lt., k. in a., 6/8/18.
1/2 Hutchinson, Arthur George, 2/Lt. (Tp.), d. of w., 10/3/18 (att. 4/Ches. R.).
Hutchinson, Cecil Dunbar, Lt. (Tp.), d. of w., 12/8/17 (and R.F.C., 57 Sqd.) (P.O.W.).
Iles, John Owen, Lt., k. in a., 25/9/15.
Instone, Edwin Lloyd, 2/Lt. (Tp.), d. of w., 4/8/17 (att. 7/Batt.) (P.O.W.).
7 Isle, William Collinson, Lt. (T/Lt.), d. of w., 13/8/15.
1 James, Douglas Charles, 2/Lt., d. of w., 1/10/15.
8 Jennins, Harry, 2/Lt. (Tp.), k. in a., 12/11/16.
3 Johnson, Alexander Downing, 2/Lt., (T/Capt.), k. in a., 25/9/15 (att. 2/Bn.).
8 Johnson, William, 2/Lt. (Tp.), d. of w., 12/11/16.
4 Johnston, John Edwin, 2/Lt. (Tp.), k. in a., 10/7/16 (att. 10/Bn.).
11 Jones, Hugh, 2/Lt. (Tp.), k. in a., 27/9/16 (att. Leic. R.).
Jones, Horace Edwin, 2/Lt., k. in a., 21/3/18 (att. 2/6 Bn.).
Jones, Kenneth James Devison, T/Lt. (A/Capt.), k. in a., 3/5/17.
2 V.C. Kilby, Arthur Forbes Gordon, Capt., k. in a., 25/9/15.
King, Charles William, 2/Lt., k. in a., 25/9/15.
4 Kingsley, Albert Thomas, 2/Lt., k. in a., 26/4/18.
4 Kinnaird, Francis Joseph, Capt., d. of w., 6/6/15 (att. 2/Bn.).
3 Lake, William, Capt. (Tp.), k. in a., 28/7/16.
4 Laver, Francis Reynell, Lt., k. in a., 9/4/18.
1 Lee, Walter Noel Oliff, 2/Lt. (Tp.), k. in a., 25/9/15.
7 Legge, The Hon. Gerald, Capt. (Tp.), k. in a., 9/8/15.
8 Leonard, George, Lt. & Qr.-Mr. (Tp.), died, 1/9/16.
4 Lewis, George Arthur Dunally, 2/Lt., k. in a., 8/7/15 (att. R. Welsh Fus.).
1 Limbery, Charles Roy, Capt., k. in a., 1/7/16.
Loder-Symonds, John Frederick, Major, k. in a., 31/11/14.
3 Lord, Cuthbert Edwards, H/Major, d. of w., 23/6/15 (att. 1/Bn.).
3 Lycett, Lawrence Henley, 2/Lt., d. of w., 31/5/18 (att. 1/Bn).
3 MacFie, Claud William, 2/Lt., k. in a., 16/6/15 (att. 2/Bed. R).
MacGeorge, Henry Warwick, Lt. (T/Capt.), k. in a., 25/9/15.
2 McKee, John Albert, 2/Lt. (Tp.), k. in a., 1/12/17.
Mackintosh, Henry Leith, 2/Lt., d. of w., 5/3/15.
1 MacKrory, Ernest William, 2/Lt. (Tp.), k. in a., 14/7/16.
2 Malpas, John Louis, Lt., k. in a., 29/7/16.
3 Marlin, Harold James, 2/Lt., k. in a., 12/4/17 (att. 1/Linc. R.).
3 Maples, Kenneth James, Capt., k. in a., 16/5/15 (att. 2/Bn.).
7 Marshall, Claud, 2/Lt. (Tp.), k. in a., 27/7/17.
7 Marten, Harold Charles, Capt., k. in a., 7/8/15.
2 Miller, James, D.C.M., 2/Lt., k. in a., 25/3/18.
Moor-Raford, Leslie Claude, Lt., d. of w., 26/10/14.
4 Moorcroft, Alfred, 2/Lt., died, 6/11/18.
7 Moore, John Aubrey, Lt. (Tpp.), k. in a., 7-11/8/15.
3 Moores, Henry Eustace, 2/Lt., k. in a., 7/7/16 (att. E. Lanc. R.).
7 Morris, Christopher Mowbray, Capt. & Adjt., k. in a., 7-11/8/15.
3 Naylor, Eric Lewin, Lt., k. in a., 3/12/17 (att. 2/6 R. War. R.).
4 O'Connor, Roderick Stratford, 2/Lt., k. in a., 28/4/17 (att. 2/Batt.).
3 Parker, Gilbert Edmund Anthony, Lt., k. in a., 10/3/15 (att. 2/Bn.).
1 Parkes, Theodore David, T/Lt. (A/Cat.), k. in a., 5/10/17.

11 Peed, Thomas Percy, 2/Lt. (Tp.), d. of w., 10/7/16 (att. 8/Bn.).
1 Penketh, Alfred Thomas, 2/Lt. (Tp.), k. in a., 12/5/17.
4 Pepper, Enoch, 2/Lt., k. in a., 26/4/18.
Perrin, Gilbert Dennis, Lt., k. in a., 13-15/11/16.
1 Philcox, Cecil Ernest, Lt. (Tp.), died, 24/5/17.
4 Philips, Mark Hibbert, 2/Lt., k. in a., 4/10/17 (att. 1st Bn.).
4 Phipps, Robert Pickering, 2/Lt. (A/Capt.), k. in a., 13-15/11/16 (att. 2/Bn.).
4 Pollock, George Henry, 2/Lt., d. of w., 18/6/15 (att. R. War. R.).
8 Porter, Eric Henry, Lt. (Tp.), k. in a., 17/2/16.
3 Posner, Philip Ernest, 2/Lt., d. of w., 27-28/4/17 (att. 8/Linc. R.).
1 Potter, John, 2/Lt. (Tp.), d. of w., 24/7/16.
Potts, Norman Rhead, 2/Lt. (Tp.), k. in a., 19/7/17 (att. 9/Bn.).
3 Poulton, Harry Edward, 2/Lt., d. of w., 26/10/17 (att. 1/Bn.).
Powell, Henry Mitchell, Capt., k. in a., 9/12/14.
10 Powell, James Henry, 2/Lt. (Tp.), k. in a., 24/11/15 (att. 2/Bn.).
4 Poynder, Robert Hamilton, Lt., k. in a., 24/3/18 (att. 2/Bn.).
Pullen, Richard Standeford, 2/Lt. (Tp.), k. in a., 26/10/17 (att. 1/Bn.).
Ransford, Clement Gascoyen, Capt., k. in a., 26/10/14.
8 Raper, Robert George, T/Major, k. in a., 2/7/16.
4 Ratcliffe, William Henry, 2/Lt., k. in a., 1/7/16 (att. 1/Bn.).
4 Rawson, Edward Douglas, 2/Lt., k. in a., 23/8/18 (att. 2/Bn.).
1 Reynard, Henry Corner, 2/Lt. (Tp.), k. in a., 25/9/15.
3 Richardson, Ruskin John Robert, k. in a., 25/9/15 (att. 2/Bn.).
4 Roadley, Thomas Stanley, Lt., k. in a., 17/8/17 (att. R.F.C., 8 Sqd.).
4 Robinson, Augustine, Lt., d. of w., 15/3/15 (att. E. Lanc. R.).
9 Roberts, Harold, M.C., Capt. (Tp.), d. of w., 27/10/18.
3 Robinson, Francis Edward, Lt., k. in a., 27/10/14 (att. 2/Bn.).
11 Robinson, William Eardley, 2/Lt. (Tp.), k. in a., 26/9/16 (att. Leic. R.).
Routledge, Phillip Charles Lytton, Lt.-Col., k. in a., 17/5/15.
10 Savery, Roger de la Garde, Capt., k. in a., 7/8/15.
Scott, Basil John Harrison, 2/Lt., k. in a., 23/10/14.
10 Searle, B. W., 2/Lt., died, 3/10/15.
Savage-Armstrong, Francis Savage Nesbit, D.S.O., Major (T/Lt.-Col.), k. in a., 23/4/17.
Seckington, Frank, Lt., k. in a., 14/7/16.
2 Shakespear, Everard Richard, 2/Lt. (Tp.), k. in a., 23/8/18.
7 Shaw-Hellier, Arthur Joseph Bradney, Lt. (Tp.), k. in a., 9/8/15.
Sheffield, George Alfred Charles, 2/Lt. (Tp.), k. in a., 26/10/17.
Shone, Geoffrey Beville, M.C., Lt., d. of w., 19/10/17 (and R.F.C.).
8 Sifton, William Alfred, 2/Lt. (Tp.), d. of w., 25/12/15.
4 Small, John Bertram, 2/Lt. (Tp.), k. in a., 23/3/18.
4 Smalley, Robert Francis, Lt., died, 14/5/18.
8 Smith, Horace Uchtred, 2/Lt. (Tp.), k. in a., 18/1/18.
1 Smith, John Wilmhurst Grainger, A/Capt., k. in a., 31/8/16.
4 Smith, Sergius Holland, 2/Lt., k. in a., 24/11/15 (att. 2/Bn.).
8 Snowden, Reginald Wallace, Lt. (Tp.), k. in a., 10/7/16.
2 Spicer, Stanley Thomas, Lt. (Tp.), d. of w., 9/8/16.
8 Stephens, John Stanley, 2/Lt., k. in a., 23/4/17.
Stevens, Lothian Basil, 2/Lt., k. in a., 9/5/15.
Strong, Thomas William, 2/Lt. (Tp., died, 26/5/18 (att. 4/Batt.).
7 Summerton, Harold, Lt. (Tp.), k. in a., 29/7/15.
Sylvester, Charles Percival Haythorn, 2/Lt. (Tp.) k. in a., 3/10/18 (att. 1/6 Bn.).
2 Tate, Harold Glen, Capt. (Tp.), k. in a., 17/2/17.
7 Taunton, Cuthbert Andre Patmore, 2/Lt. (Tp.), k. in a., 9/8/15.
7 Taylor, Roger Cecil, Lt. (Tp.), k. in a., 4/10/17.
Teague, Cyril, 2/Lt. (Tp.), k. in a., 4/10/17 (att. 1/Batt.).
2 Thomas, Charles Herbert, Capt., d. of w., 5/11/14.
7 Thomson, Henry Thomas, Lt. (Tp.), d. of w., 26/9/15.
2 Thornton, Stanislaw Bonaventure, 2/Lt. (Tp.), k. in a., 29/7/16.
Timmins, William Benjamin, 2/Lt., d. of w., 20/5/15.
7 Tinkler, George Henry, 2/Lt. (Tp.), k. in a., 25/4/17.
Tomlinson, Ferdinand Roger John, 2/Lt., k. in a., 26/10/14.
4 Tonks, Leslie Robert James, 2/Lt., k. in a., 11/4/18 (att. 9/Bn.).
7 Townsend, Lionel George Oliver, Capt. (Tp.), k. in a., 7-11/8/15.
Trevarthen, Arthur Francis Vivyan Aubrey, Lt. (Tp.), k. in a., 28/1/16.
8 Turney, William, 2/Lt., k. in a., 10/7/16.
V.C. Vallentin, John Franks, Capt., k. in a., 7/11/14.
7 Vaughan, George William, 2/Lt. (Tp.), k. in a., 21/11/17.
Wagstaff, John Carleton, 2/Lt. (Tp.), k. in a., 12/10/17 (att. 8/Bn.).
10 Walker, Charles Nigel Gordon, Lt. (Tp.), k. in a., 7/8/15 (att. 8/Bn. Manch. R.).
Walker, Herbert Newton, 2/Lt. (T/Lt.), k. in a., 6/6/17 (att. M.G.C.).
Walters, Sidney, 2/Lt., d. of w., 4/10/18 (att. 1/6 Batt.).
3 Wansbrough, William Evelyn, Capt., k. in a., 29/7/16 (att. 2/Bn.).
1 Ward, Edward Leslie, 2/Lt., k. in a., 14/7/16 (att. 3/Bn.).
1/2 Webb, George, 2/Lt., k. in a., 5/6/18 (att. R.A.F.).
4 Webb, Henry Rees, Lt. (A/Capt.), d. of w., 7/5/18 (in German hands).
1 Webber, Stanley Albert, 2/Lt., k. in a., 1/7/16.
10 Weir, Henry Keith Crichton, 2/Lt. (Tp.), d. of w., 3/5/16 (att. 9/N. & D.R.).
4 Weitzmann, Cecil Gothet, 2/Lt., d. of w., 25/9/15 (att. 1/Bn.).
Wesley, Charles Wallace, 2/Lt. (Tp.), died, 6/2/19 (att. 1/Bn.).
3 West, George Clifford, 2/Lt., killed, 12/2/17 (att. 7/Bn.).
3 Westwood, James Henry, 2/Lt., k. in a., 12/7/16 (att. 62 Bde., M.G.C.).
Wheeler, Wilfrid Henry, 2/Lt., k. in a., 26/4/18 (att. 4/Bn.).
3 White, Cecil Augustus, 2/Lt., d. of w., 4/10/17 (att. 7/Bn.).
7 White, Edwin Victor, Lt., k. in a., 6/9/18.
1 White, George, Capt. (Tp.), k. in a., 1/7/16.
10 Whilmore-Searle, Bertram, 2/Lt. (Tp.), died, 3/10/15 (att. 4/Bn.).
9 Wickham, Bernard William Theodore, M.C., Lt. (Tp.), k. in a., 14/4/17.
Wilford, Lionel Russel, Lt., died, 8/11/18.
8 Willcock, Frederick Norman, 2/Lt. (Tp.), k. in a., 10/7/16.
Williams, David Marmaduke, Lt., k. in a., 25/9/15.
1 Williamson, John Daniel, 2/Lt., k. in a., 15/7/16 (att. 4/Bn.).
4 Wilmot, Edmund Sacheverell, 2/Lt., k. in a., 13-15/11/16 (att. 2/Bn.).
8 Wilson, John Soulsby, Lt., d. of w., 12/10/17.
10 Winter, Robert Harold, 2/Lt. (Tp.), d. of w., 17/12/15 (att. 7/Bn.).
4 Winstanley, Newnham Leibman, Lt., k. in a., 13-15/11/16 (att. 2/Bn.).
7 Worcester, Harold Paul, Capt. (Tp.), k. in a., 10/9/16.
3 Wragg, Norman John, Lt., d. of w., 18/7/16.
11 Wright, Charles James, 2/Lt. (Tp.), k. in a., 18/10/16 (att. M.G.C.).
2 Wright, William, 2/Lt., k. in a., 17/2/17.
Yeo, Leslie Farquhar, Lt., d. of w., 10/3/15.
3 Youngs, James William, Lt., d. of w., 12/4/18 (att. M.G.C.).

The Dorsetshire Regiment.

1 Agelasto, August, M.C., Lt., k. in a., 8/11/16 (att. 4th Bn.).
1 Alderman, William, M.C., Capt. & Q. Mr., k. in a., 28/8/16.
1 Algeo, William Bensley, Capt., k. in a., 17/5/16.
3 Allbon, B. C. J., Capt. (Tp.), died, 3/2/19 (att. 6th).
3 Ayres, Giles Frederick, 2/Lt., k. in a., 9/5/15 (att. Linc. Rgt.).
2 Baillie, Humphry John, Lt., k. in a., 2/3/16.
3 Baker, Gordon Lennox, Capt. (Acting), k. in a., 11/8/18.
Baker, Walter Percy, 2/Lt., k. in a., 14/7/16 (att. R. Warwick Rgt., 7th Bn.).
3 Ball, Alec Radford, 2/Lt., d. of w., 17/8/17 (att. 5th).
Bamkin, Carl Jocelyn, 2/Lt. (Tp.), k. in a., 19/8/18.
Banks, William Sykes, Major, died, 19/2/16 (Res. of Off.).
1 Barker, Cecil Noel, 2/Lt. (Tp.), k. in a., 19/11/16.
Bartlett, Tom Brensley, 2/Lt. (Tp.), k. in a., 19/9/18 (att. 8 Hamps. R.).
6 Barton, Albert Ernest, Lt. (T/Capt.), d. of w., 24/5/17.
7 Bayly, Vere Talbot, 2/Lt. (Tp.), k. in a., 8/5/16 (att. 1st).
1 Birks, Alfred Owen, 2/Lt. (Tp.), d. of w., 13/3/18.
3 Bishop, Edwin Maurice, Lt., k. in a., 18/10/14 (att. Yorks. L. Inf.).
3 Blakeway, Noel Carleton, 2/Lt., k. in a., 27/3/16 (att. 1st Bn.).
3 Blanchard, Neville, 2/Lt., died, 26/7/17 (att. 2nd Dorset Rgt.).
6 Blencowe, Ernest Cecil Blencowe, Capt. (Tp.), k. in a., 16/12/16.
1 Boileau, Edward Bulmer Whicher, Lt., k. in a., 3/10/18.
2 Boles, Noel Henry, Lt., k. in a., 11/1/16 (att. R.N.A.S.).
3 Borrough, Horace William, Capt. (Acting), d. of w., 18/8/16 (att. 1st).
3 Bowes, Stanley Ward, 2/Lt., k. in a., 29/9/15 (att. R. Fus.).
6 Broad, Alfred Evans, Lt. (Tp.), d. of w., 2/3/16.
3 Brooke, Cyril Thomthwaite, 2/Lt. (A/Capt.), k. in a., 22/8/17 (att. 6th Som. L.I.).
3 Brownlee, Wilfred Methven, 2/Lt., died, 12/10/14.
3 Budden, Henry Richard, 2/Lt. (T/Lt.), k. in a., 25/9/15 (att. 2nd Lincs. Rgt.).
2 Bull, Arthur Henry, 2/Lt., died, 14/12/18.
3 Bull, John Edward, 2/Lt., k. in a., 29/9/15 (att. R. Fus.).
1 Bullock, Thomas William Major (A/Lt.-Col.), k. in a., 11/4/18.
3 Burfoot, W. M., 2/Lt., killed, 22/5/18 (and R.A.F.).
Butcher, Charles Geoffrey, Lt., killed, 2/5/15.
1 Cansdale, Lionel, 2/Lt., k. in a., 29/3/18.
7 Carew, Coventry George Warrington, Capt. (Tp.), d. of w., 20/11/16 (att. 1st Bn.).
Carter, Wilfrid Arthur Douglas, 2/Lt., killed, 23/5/17 (and R.F.C.).
5 Caruthers-Little, Arthur William Palling, Capt., k. in a., 7-11/8/15.
3 Cave, Walter Henry Charles, 2/Lt., k. in a., 16/3/15 (att. 1st Bn.).
Cherry, Alfred Douglas, T/Lt. (A/Capt.), k. in a., 4/4/17 (att. Som. L.I.).
3 Chisholm-Batten, James Utermarck, 2/Lt., k. in a., 29/9/15 (att. R. Fus.).
3 Chown, William Leonard, 2/Lt., k. in a., 30/7/16 (att. 2nd Bn., Ox. & Bucks L.I.).
1 Clarke, Hamlet John, 2/Lt., k. in a., 21/5/18.
6 Clarke, Walter Stanley Arnold, 2/Lt., k. in a., 10/7/16.
Clayton, James Gardner, Capt. (Tp.), k. in a., 20/8/16 (att. 1st N'hampton Regt.).
3 Clift, Maurice Richard, 2/Lt., d. of w., 4/8/16 (att. 9th Devon Regt.).

1 Coley, William John, 2/Lt., k. in a., 15/7/16.
2 Corrall, Arthur, 2/Lt., d. of w., 24/12/15.
3 Courtnay, Kilcoursie Sigismond, Lt., k. in a., 11/8/18.
Cowie, Hugh Norman Ramsay, C.M.G., D.S.O., Major, d. of w., 20/5/15.
6 Cox, Robert William Talbot, 2/Lt. (Tp.), k. in a., 15/2/16.
Cushny, Donald, Lt., k. in a., 14/4/15.
5 Dancer, Alfred Christopher, M.C., T/Lt. (A/Capt.), k. in a., 4/10/17.
6 Davidson, Gerald Louis, Lt. (Tp.), d. of w., 11/7/16.
Davidson, William Thomas Chorley, Capt., k. in a., 13/10/14.
3 Davies, Francis Hugh, Lt., k. in a., 10/12/17.
7 Davis, Ralph Salway, 2/Lt. (Tp.), k. in a., 16/9/16 (att. 6th Som. L.I.).
3 Delamain, Henry Creswell, 2/Lt., died, 17/4/15.
7 D'Erf Wheeler, Geoffrey Noel Popham, 2/Lt., k. in a., 26/9/16 (att. 5th Bn.)
3 D'Erf Wheeler, Percival Francis Crommelin, Capt., killed, 24/7/17 (and R.F.C.).
3 Dixon, Harold George, 2/Lt., k. in a., 4/11/18 (and R.A.F.).
2 Dixon, Robert Archibald, 2/Lt., k. in a., 12/4/16.
5 Drysdale, Donald Roy, Lt., d. of w., 25/9/16.
Dudley, Bernard John Cherleton, Capt., k. in a., 24/1/17 (att. 3rd Nigeria R.).
3 Dunn, John Cragg, Lt., d. of w., 25/3/16 (att. 59 Trench Mortar Bty.)
6 Durrant, William Henry Gilbert, 2/Lt (Tp.), k. in a., 26/9/15 (att. 2nd Bn. Wilts).
5 Eason, Sampson, Lt. (Tp.), k. in a., 7/8/15.
5 Elliott, Wilfrid Edmund, 2/Lt., k in a., 26/9/16.
3 Farrow, Clifford Willis, 2/Lt., d. of w., 9/4/18 (att. 4th Bn.).
1 Fenton, Bede Liddell, Capt. (T/Major), k. in a., 15/7/16.
1 Few, Robert James Donald, Lt., d. of w., 27/10/18.
6 Fitch, Christopher John, Lt. (Tp.), k. in a., 16/2/16.
7 Fleming, Hugh Joseph, 2/Lt (Tp.), k. in a., 24/8/16 (att. 6th Bn.).
1 Ford, Herbert Alfred, M.C., 2/Lt., k. in a., 11/8/18.
Forde, Lionel Winnington, 2/Lt., k. in a., 8/6/18 (att. 6th Bn.)
3 Forman, Francis, 2/Lt., k. in a., 14/7/16 (att. 7th R. Warwick Regt.).
3 Fox, Owen Gurney, 2/Lt., k. in a., 6/2/17 (att. 1st Bn.).
Fraser, William Augustus Cumming, Major, died, 14/6/15.
1 Fripp, George, 2/Lt., d. of w., 4/6/18.
Gallie, Arthur Lockhart, Major, died, 23/9/15.
Gandon, Ralph, 2/Lt. (Tp.), k. in a., 26/9/16 (att. 7th Bn.).
George, Athelstan Key Durrance, Lt., d. of w., 14/9/14.
5 George, Frank William, 2/Lt. (Tp.), k. in a., 22/8/15.
Gibbons, John, 2/Lt. (Tp.), d of w., 6/6/17 (att. 6th).
3 Goddall, Cecil Clarence, 2/Lt., k in a., 7/7/16 (att. 6th).
6 Goodman, Eric George, 2/Lt. (Tp.), k. in a., 12/4/17.
3 Goodson, Harold Walter, M.C., 2/Lt. (T/Capt.), k. in a., 11/10/18 (att 6th).
Gore-Browne, Eric Anthony Rollo, Major, drowned, 3/7/18 (and 3rd King's Afr. Rfs.)
1 Green, William Eddowes, Lt., d. of w., 6/7/16.
Griffith, Allex James William, 2/Lt., k. in a., 25/3/17.
2 Hacker, Norman, Capt., killed, 26/10/17.
3 Halcrow, John William, 2/Lt. (T/Lt.), k. in a., 7/7/16 (and R.F.C.)
Hall, Fred, 2/Lt., k. in a., 22/9/16 (and R.F.C.).
6 Hambly, Dudley Charles, 2/Lt (Tp.), k. in a., 14/5/17.
6 Hamley, William Walter, 2/Lt. (Tp.), d. of w., 26/3/18.
3 Harvey, Ralph de Warenne, 2/Lt., d. of w., 7/6/16 (att. 1st King's R.R.C.)
3 Hedding, James Lawrence, 2/Lt., d. of w., 28/3/16 (att. 1st Middx. Regt.)
3 Helsdon, Harold Leofric, 2/Lt., k. in a., 26/11/16 (att. 1/7th R. Warwick Regt.)
3 Heyward, Maurice, 2/Lt., k. in a., 20/7/16 (att. 8th Btn. Devon. Regt.).
7 Hobbs, Geoffrey Harold Chapman, 2/Lt., k. in a., 16/9/16 (att. 6th Som. L. Inf.).
Hodgson, John Solomon Riddell, Lt., k. in a., 25/3/17.
6 Homan, Claude Knox, Lt. (Tp.), k. in a., 18/9/15.
5 Hooper, Leonard John, 2/Lt. (Tp.), k. in a., 26/9/16.
3 Hore, Ruthven Pomfret, 2/Lt., d. of w., 2/10/15 (att. Welsh Regt.).
5 Hughes, Aubrey Noel, 2/Lt. (Tp.), k. in a., 26/9/16.
6 Hughes-Onslow, Denzil, Major (Tp.), k. in a., 10/7/16.
3 Jackson, John, 2/Lt., k. in a., 19/8/16 (att. 2/5th Glouc. Rgt.).
3 Janasz, James George Gee, 2/Lt., k. in a., 15/6/15 (att. 2nd Bn. Wilts Rgt.).
Jenkins, William, 2/Lt. (Tp.), k. in a., 11/10/18 (att. 6th).
3 Jenks, Arthur Leslie, Lt., d. of w., 7/10/18 (att. 2nd).
Jerrard, C. F., M.C., Capt., died, 15/5/19 (Res. of Off.).
3 Johns, Edward Tregonwell, 2/Lt., d. of w., 3/4/18 (att. 6th Btn.).
3 Jones, John Victor, 2/Lt., k. in a., 14/7/16 (att. 7th R. Warwick R.).
Kendall, John Hayward, 2/Lt., k. in a., 14/4/15.
Kent, Charles Ronald, M.C., 2/Lt. (Tp.), k. in a., 20/10/18 (att. 6th Btn.).
Kestell-Cornish, Robert Vaughan, M.C., Lt. (T/Capt., d. of w., 17/6/18 (and Staff Div. H.Q.).
5 Kitcher, Henry Ernesy, Capt. (Tp.), k. in a., 7/8/16.
Law, Edward Michael Fitzgerald, 2/Lt., k. in a., 11/8/18 (att. 1st Bn.).
Leat, Edwin John, 2/Lt., d. of w., 8/6/18 (att. 6th Bn.).
5 Le Marchant, Henry Neville, Capt., k. in a., 7-11/8/15.
6 Lemon, Lionel Theodore, 2/Lt. (Tp.), k. in a., 12/4/17.
Le Sauvage, Ernest Davies, 2/Lt., killed, 30/5/16 (and R.F.C.).
5 Leslie, Richard Fitzgerald William Ferris, Major, k. in a., 22/8/15.
3 Lindow, Edwin, 2/Lt., d. of w., 11/8/16 (att. 6th Bn.).
3 Lindsey, Douglas, Lt., k. in a., 17/12/17 (att. 5th Dorset Rgt.).
3 Litster, Hugh Sinclaire, 2/Lt., d. of w., 20/4/16.
5 Lloyd, Gwion Llewelyn Bowen, Capt., k. in a., 7-11/8/15.
Maben, James Armstrong, Lt. (Tp.), k. in a., 23/8/18 (att. 6th).
6 McCaskie, John, 2/Lt. (Tp.), k. in a., 23/3/18.
Macey, Clifford James, 2/Lt. (Tp.), k. in a., 25/5/15.
3 Malpas, Reginald Arthur, 2/Lt. (T/Lt.), d. of w., 18/11/17 att. 7 Som. L.I.).
3 Mann, Horace, Lt., died, 25/12/18 (att. 1st K. Afr. Rif.).
3 Mansel-Pleydell, Edmund Morton, Lt., k. in a., 12/3/15 (att. Worc. Regt.).
1 Mansell-Pleydell, Henry Grove Morton, Lt., k. in a., 17/5/16.
2 Maxwell-Moffat, Alexander Logan Nathan, Lt., died, 21/11/14.
3 May, Harold Costwick, 2/Lt., d. of w., 27/3/15.
3 Mayo, Percy Austin, 2/Lt., killed, 9/5/16.
Mercer, Archibald Ariel, Major, k. in a., 17/11/15.
Middleton, Frank, Capt., k. in a., 17/11/14.
5 Montgomery, George Edward, Capt., k. in a., 22/8/15.
5 Moody, Ambrose, Capt., k. in a., 22/8/15.
6 Moore, Kenneth Hartley, 2/Lt. (Tp.), k. in a., 7/7/16.
6 Morley, Frederic Joseph, D.S.O., M.C., Capt. (A/Major), d. of w., 24/4/18.
6 Mortimer, C. O., 2/Lt., k. in a., 1/4/18.
2 Muspratt, Keith Knox, M.C., 2/Lt. (T/Capt.), killed, 19/3/18 (and R.F.C.).
3 Nesbitt, Terrence Beale, 2/Lt., d. of w., 24/4/16.
Northcott, Henry John, 2/Lt. (Tp.), d. of w., 18/10/18 (att. 1/5th Gloucs. R.).
3 Ogle, Thomas Burton, 2/Lt., k. in a., 23/3/16.
6 Palmer, Francis Reginald, 2/Lt. (Tp.), k. in a., 23/4/17.
Parkinson, Joe Anthony Francis, Lt., k. in a., 13/10/14.
Parrish, Harry Thorburn, M.C., 2/Lt., d. of w., 23/11/18 (att. 6th Bn.).
Pitt, James Maxwell, Lt., killed, 13/10/14.
Priestley, Archibald Bertram, Capt., d. of w., 12/9/14.
6 Pulleyn, James Lewis, 2/Lt. (Tp.), k. in a., 17/10/16 (and R.F.C.).
3 Rathbone, John Ernest Vivian, Lt., k. in a., 4/6/18 (att. 1st Bn.).
3 Rawlinson, Curwen Vaughan, 2/Lt., k. in a., 21/5/15 (att. 1st Bn.).
Reid, William Leonard, Capt., d. of w., 17/4/15.
Ritson, Francis, Capt. (Tp.), k. in a., 17/6/17 (att. 5th Bn.).
Roberts, John Henry Charles, 2/Lt., d. of w., 2/5/15.
Roe, Arthur Robert Montgomery, Capt., d. of w., 16/9/14.
Roper, Reginald Trevor, Major, k. in a., 12/10/14.
Rosher, Henry Louis, Lt.-Col., k. in a., 14/4/15.
3 Rowe, Stafford Gordon Garnet Godfrey Thomas, 2/Lt., k. in a., 10/11/17 (att. 6th Bn.).
1 Rothon, Charles Francis, 2/Lt. (Tp.), k. in a., 1/7/16.
6 Saunders, Clifford William, M.C., A/Capt. (T/Lt.), k. in a., 16/10/17.
Schulze, Hugh Lees, 2/Lt (Tp.), k. in a., 20/10/18 (att. 6th Bn.).
3 Seymour, Greville Crawford, 2/Lt., k. in a., 15/4/17.
1 Shaddick, Cecil George, 2/Lt. (Tp.), k. in a., 7/8/16.
Shannon, George Strangman, 2/Lt., k. in a., 5/5/15.
6 Shave, Leslie Harrie, 2/Lt. (Tp.), k. in a., 12/4/17.
3 Sheffield, Lancelot Hull, 2/Lt., k. in a., 25/3/17 (att. 2nd Bn.).
5 Shephard, Ernest Arthur, 2/Lt., k. in a., 11/1/17.
1 Shiel, John Hubert Trevor, 2/Lt., k. in a., 8/3/18.
3 Slater, Thomas Alexander Fletcher, 2/Lt., k. in a., 16/9/16 (att. 5th Bn.).
Smith, Thomas Sidney, 2/Lt., k. in a., 13/10/14
Smith, William James, Capt., drowned, 29/5/17 (att. Egyptian Army).
6 Sprang, Frederick Williamson, Lt. (A/Capt.), k. in a., 12/4/17.
3 Statham, Hugh Kington Llewellyn, Lt., k. in a., 6/9/17.
3 Steele, D'Arcy Walter Stewart, 2/Lt., k. in a., 1/10/16.
3 Steele, Frederick James, 2/Lt., k. in a., 13/10/15 (att. 8 R. Berks Regt.).
3 Stock, John Launcelot Walmsley, 2/Lt., d. of w., 3/5/17 (att. 6 Som. L. Inf).
5 Stockwell, George, Capt. (Tp.), k. in a., 6/10/17.
2 Strange, H. S., 2/Lt., died, 7/10/18 (and R.A.F.).
3 Taylor, Sidney Harold, 2/Lt., k. in a., 4/4/17.
3 Tennant, Charles Alan Ramsay, 2/Lt., k. in a., 9/5/15 (att. Devon Regt.).
1 Tiddy, Claude Julian, 2/Lt., k. in a., 11/8/18.
3 Turner, Crosby Russell Swanson, 2/Lt., k. in a., 27/7/16 (att. K.R.R.C.).
3 Turner, John Reginald, Lt., k. in a., 13/10/14.
7 Umney, Cecil Francis, 2/Lt. (Tp.), k. in a., 26/9/16 (att. 5th Bn.).
Utterson, Henry Kelso, D.S.O., Lt.-Col., k. in a., 10/8/18 (att. 15th Lancs Fus.).
5 Vincent, Alfred Copplestone Waldon, Capt. (Tp.), k. in a., 26/9/16.
1 Vincent, William Jefferson, 2/Lt., k. in a., 1/10/18 (att 5th Bn.).
6 Warr, Thomas Edward, 2/Lt. (Tp.), d. of w., 14/10/17.
Webster, Robert Bell, 2/Lt., killed, 28/4/16.
3 Wilkinson, Frank, 2/Lt., k. in a., 27/7/16 (att. 2/5th Glouc. Regt.).
1 Willes, William Frances George, Capt., died, 19/7/16 (att. Army Cyclist Corps).
1 Williams, Harold Sutton, Major, died, 21/3/15.
3 Witty, James Hannay, 2/Lt., k. in a., 15/4/17 (att. 1st).
1 Wolferstan, Stanley, 2/Lt., k. in a., 3/4/17.

3 Wood, Henry Stewart, Lt., k. in a., 11/8/18.
3 Wood, Theodore Herbert Henry, 2/Lt., k. in a., 13/4/15.
1 Wood, William Allan, 2/Lt., k. in a., 1/10/18.
3 Woodthorpe, Wm. Ernest, 2/Lt., k. in a., 13/10/15 (att. 8th R. Berks R.).
3 Woolnough, Frederick Ullathorne, Capt., d. of w., 22/3/18 (att. 6th Som. L. I.).

The Prince of Wales's Volunteers (South Lancashire Regiment).

2 Acheson, Joseph, 2/Lt. (Tp.), d. of w., 7/6/18
Albrecht, Charles Esmond Redlin, Lt., k. in a., 24/8/14.
Allsopp, Jerome Boileau, D.S.O., Major (Act. Lt.-Col.), k. in a., 27/5/18.
7 Anderson, Francis, Lt. (Tp.), k. in a., 18/11/16.
8 Appleby, John Gill, Lt. (Tp.), k. in a., 14/7/16.
2 Aron, Frederick Adolphus, Lt. (Tp.), k. in a., 23/8/18.
2 Badman, Raymond Clarence, 2/Lt. (Tp.), k. in a., 21/10/18.
Bagley, Frank Adams, Capt., d. of w., 2/10/15.
Barrow, Ernest Isaac, Lt. (Tp.), k. in a., 23/10/16 (att. East Lancashire R.).
9 Bayley, Charles Humphrey, Capt. (Tp.), d. of w., 7/8/17.
8 Baylis, Joseph Anno Jones, Capt. (Tp.), k. in a., 13/6/17.
6 Bayspoole, Bernard, Capt., k. in a., 9/4/16.
8 Beauchamp, Leslie Heron, 2/Lt. (Tp.), killed, 6/10/15.
7 Bell, Samuel Edward, M.C., T/Lt. (A/Capt.), d. of w., 19/11/16.
9 Beven, Thomas, 2/Lt. (Tp.), k. in a., 3/7/16 (att. 2nd Bn.).
Birdwood, Gordon Alic Brodrick, 2/Lt., k. in a., 19/9/14.
9 Bishop, Basil Frederic, M.C., Major (A/Lt.-Col.), k. in a., 18/9/18.
2 Blair, Alexander McPherson, Capt. (Tp.), k. in a., 3/7/16.
10 Blake, Charles Stanley, Capt. (Tp.), k. in a., 7/8/15.
2 Boast, John, M.C., Capt., k. in a., 22/3/18.
10 Bolton, Herbert Frederick, Lt. (Tp.), d. of w., 3/5/17 (M.G.C., 103 Coy.).
3 Bott, George Gerald Randell, Lt., k. in a., 13/4/18 (att. 8 Bord. R.).
7 Bowles, John George, 2/Lt. (Tp.), k. in a., 1/11/16.
6 Boyd, Henry Ormsby, 2/Lt. (Tp.), k. in a., 9/5/16.
3 Breckell, Edward Ryder, Lt., died, 8/2/18.
3 Breckell, Ralph Leicester, 2/Lt., k. in a., 9/7/15 (att. 2 Lanc. Fus.).
9 Brewer, John Angus, Capt. (Tp.), d. of w., 18/9/18.
Butler, Armar Somerset, Lt. (Tp.), k. in a., 16/10/17 (att. 7 Wilts.).
2 Castle, Cecil Wells, Lt., k. in a., 3/8/17.
Case, Geoffrey, Lt., k. in a., 22/3/18.
3 Case, George Ronald Ashburner, 2/Lt., k. in a., 25/9/15 (att. 2nd Bn.).
6 Cattarns, Glanvill Richards, M.C., Capt. (Tp.), k. in a., 12/2/17.
Chadwick, Norman Stuart, 2/Lt. (Tp.), k. in a., 6/11/17 (att. Som. L.I.).
11 Champion, Eric Osbourne, 2/Lt. (Tp.), k. in a., 10/6/17.
3 Charlton, Frank Tysor, 2/Lt., d. of w., 3/10/18 (att. Y. 55 T.M.B.).
3 Cheers, Ronald Anson Vlascow, 2/Lt., k. in a., 27/9/15 (att. 4th Bn.).
7 Cole, William Norman, 2/Lt., k. in a., 5/2/17.
3 Collinson, Jeffreys Lewis William, 2/Lt., k. in a., 15/7/16 (att. 2nd).
Cooper, Frederick John, 2/Lt. (Tp.), k. in a., 27/5/18.
? Coppock, Hugh Searle, Lt. (Tp.), k. in a., 10/4/18 (att 2nd Bn.).
2 Cotton, Harold Temple, D.S.O., Lt.-Col., k. in a., 3/9/16.
2 Cottrell, Harold William, 2/Lt., k. in a., 30/9/16.
10 Craig, William Colston, 2/Lt. (Tp.), d. of w., 20/1/17 (att. 6th Bn.).
Critchley, Frank, 2/Lt. (Tp.), d. of w., 10/4/18 (att. 1/4 Bn.).
8 Cumming, George, 2/Lt. (Tp.), k. in a., 9/7/16.
8 Daniels, Edwin Ambrose, T/Lt. (A/Capt.), k. in a., 21/10/16.
8 Daunt, Conrad O'Neill, 2/Lt., killed, 29/9/18 (and R.A.F.).
10 Daunt, Giles Wellacott, 2/Lt., k. in a., 9/4/16 (att. 6th Bn.).
8 Dickie, Herbert, 2/Lt., k. in a., 2/10/16.
1 Dickson, Arthur, Lt.-Col. (Tp.), k. in a., 1/7/16 (att. 10 West Yorks).
2 Dow, James Robertson, 2/Lt. (Tp.), k in a., 11/4/18.
Duff, Peter Tyrie, 2/Lt. (Tp.), k. in a., 20/9/18 (att. 5th).
Ebsworth, Alexander, M.C., Capt. (A/Lt.-Col.), k. in a., 21/9/18 (att. 9 Northd. Fus.).
8 Edwards, Llewellyn Foster, Lt. (Tp.), d. of w., 12/4/18.
2 Evans, Norman Emryn, 2/Lt. (Tp.), d. of w., 3/10/16.
Evans, Thomas George, 2/Lt. (Tp.), k. in a., 20/9/17 (att. 1/4 Bn.).
10 Finlayson, Alexander Moncrieff, 2/Lt. (Tp.), d. of w., 23/7/17 (att. 7 Bn.).
9 Firth, Richard Charles Dundas, Lt., died, 21/12/14.
Fletcher, Eric Graham, Lt., k. in a., 3/7/16 (att. 2nd Bn.).
11 Fletcher, William Guy, 2/Lt. (Tp.), d. of w., 14/10/16.
2 Franks, Spencer, Capt., k. in a., 22/3/18.
3 Fraser, Alexander Roderick, 2/Lt., d. of w., 26/4/17 (att. 6th Bn.).
Fulcher, Bernard Vincent, Lt., k. in a., 17/11/14.
11 Garton, Reginald William, Lt. (Tp.), k. in a., 1/7/16.
7 Garvin, Roland Gerrard, Capt. (Tp.), k. in a., 22/7/16.
Gates, Alfred William, 2/Lt., k. in a., 3/7/16.
Gebbie, James Francis Roy, Lt., d. of w., 4/10/14.
3 Gibson, Athol Thomas, Capt., k. in a., 21/10/14 (att. 2nd Bn.).
3 Gillespie, Rollo, 2/Lt., k. in a., 25/9/15 (att. 2nd Bn.).
3 Goldsworth, Duncan William, Lt., k. in a., 25/9/15 (att. 2nd Bn.).
3 Gourd, Percy, Capt. (Tp.), k. in a., 18/4/16.
7 Green, James, 2/Lt. (Tp.), d. of w., 21/7/16.
Green, Malcolm Charles Andrew, Lt.-Col., k. in a., 17/11/14.
2 Grieve, Alan Edward, 2/Lt., k. in a., 3/7/16.
3 Grieve, James, Lt. (Tp.), killed, 21/2/17 (and R.F.C.).
8 Grimsdell, Gerald Lucien, M.C. Capt. (Tp.), died, 6/7/18.
Hadfield, Wilfred John Mackenzie, Lt., died, 10/9/14.
9 Haddock, Wilfrid Spencer, 2/Lt. (Tp.), d. of w., 16/7/17.
3 Harrison, Charles Gordon, M.C., 2/Lt. (Tp.), d. of w., 26/9/18 (att. 2nd Bn.).
Harrison, Cyril Henry, 2/Lt (Tp.), k. in a., 6/9/17 (att. 1/5 Lancs Fus.).
3 Harvey, Oliver Colin, 2/Lt., k. in a., 4/7/16 (att. 7th Bn.).
10 Harvey, Frederick William, Lt. (Tp.), k. in a., 9/8/15 (att. 6 Lancs Fus.).
2 Hatch, Norman Claud, 2/Lt., k. in a., 21/10/16.
Hewitt, Gordon Hughes, Lt., d. of w., 24/9/14.
3 Hilliar, Gordon Edward, 2/Lt., k. in a., 26/9/15 (att. E. Lancs R.).
10 Honan, Matthew, Capt. (Tp.), k in a., 14/11/16.
7 Hopkins, Arthur Maskern, Lt. (Tp.), d. of w., 18/11/16.
7 Horsey, Cyril James, 2/Lt. (Tp.), d. of w., 22/11/16.
3 Howarth, Norman, 2/Lt., k in a., 13/7/16.
7 Hoyle, John Baldwin, Lt. (Tp.), k in a., 1/7/16.
1 Hughes, Frederick, Lt. (Tp.) k. in a., 12/10/16 (att. York and Lancaster R.).
3 Humfrey, John Edward Hampinstall, 2/Lt. (Tp.), died, 28/7/18 (att. 18 York & Lanc. R.).
Hutchinson, John Summerscales, Capt., k. in a., 3/9/14.
3 Jackson, Arthur Gordon, 2/Lt., k. in a , 25/2/17 (att. 6th Bn.).
6 Jarvis, Ernest Cory, Capt. (Tp.), k. in a., 28/8/16.
10 Jefferies, Maurice Arnold, 2/Lt. (Tp.), k. in a., 19/7/16.
3 Jefferson, Ralph James, 2/Lt., k. in a., 25/2/17 (att. 6th Bn.).
7 Jones, John Harold Ryle 2/Lt. (Tp.), k. in a., 4/7/16.
2 Jones, Richard, 2/Lt. (Tp.), k. in a., 21/10/16.
8 Jones, Simon James, Lt. (Tp.), d. of w., 5/6/18.
8 Kember, Walter Herbert, Capt. (Tp.), k. in a., 7/6/17..
8 Kew, George Richard, Capt. (Act.), d. of w., 8/11/17.
1 Killick, Sidney Herbert, Capt., d. of w., 18/11/16 (att. H.Q. Staff).
6 King, Richard, 2/Lt. (Tp.), d. of w., 18/4/16.
6 Kirwan, Laird, 2/Lt., died, 20/8/18 (and R.A.F.).
? Larsen, Hubert Victor, 2/Lt , d. of w., 23/8/18 (att. 2nd Bn.).
3 Laythorpe, Roger Marmaduke, 2/Lt., d. of w., 8/7/16 (att. 7th Bn.).
10 Lechler, Henry Nicholson, 2/Lt. (Tp.), k. in a., 4/4/16 (att. 6th Bn.).
3 Leighton, Arthur, 2/Lt., k. in a., 14/11/16 (att. 7th Bn.).
11 Lidgett, John Cuthbert, Lt. (Tp.), k. in a., 23/3/18.
Linaker, Archibald Frederick Richard, Lt. (Tp.), k. in a., 9/9/18 (att. 2 L.N. Lancs.).
Littler, Frank, 2/Lt. (Tp.), k. in a., 23/7/17 (att. 8 Bn.).
2 Lodge, Raymond, 2/Lt., d. of w., 14/9/15 (att. 3rd Bn.).
8 Lomax, Edward Harold, T/Lt. (A/Capt.), k. in a., 13/8/17.
6 Longbottom, Henry, 2/Lt., k. in a., 9/8/15.
7 McClinton, John Stuart, Capt. (Tp.), k. in a., 5/7/16.
6 McGregor, Robert Roy, 2/Lt , died, 6/10/18.
3 McIver, Donald, Lt., k. in a., 24/3/18 (att. 2/7 Bn.).
3 Macreight, Lionel Albert, Lt., killed, 22/3/18 (att. 2nd Bn.).
Marsh, Cuthbert A., 2/Lt., d. of w., 24/6/18 (and R.A.F.).
2 Marthews, Leonard Gordon, 2/Lt., d. of w., 20/4/18 (P. of W. in Ger. hands).
15 Matthews, Arthur James, Capt. (Tp.), died, 21/11/18.
7 Mellenfield, Cecil Beven, 2/Lt. (Tp.), k. in a., 23/10/16.
7 Miller, Wilfred Heard, 2/Lt., k. in a., 4/7/16.
6 Millichap, Frank Henry, Lt., d. of w., 24/4/16 (att. W. Rid. R.).
Mitchell, Eric Arthur, 2/Lt., k. in a., 27/10/14.
8 Morgan, R. T. P., 2/Lt., k. in a., 9/7/16.
6 Morgan, Walter Bassett, 2/Lt. (Tp.), k. in a., 9/8/15.
8 Morris, Noel Dyke, Lt. (Tp.), d. of w., 12/5/16.
3 Morrison, Lechlan Allan, 2/Lt., d. of w., 6/1/16 (att. 4th Bn.).
3 Morrison, Vernon MacDonald, 2/Lt., k. in a., 14/11/16 (att. 7th Bn.).
7 Murdock, James Gordon, Lt. (Tp.), d. of w., 22/9/15.
3 Nairne, William Graham, 2/Lt., d. of w., 11/7/15 (att. Lan. Fus.).
8 Negroponte, Jack, 2/Lt. (Tp.), d. of w., 29/10/16.
2 Nevill, Robert, M.C., 2/Lt. (A/Capt.), k. in a., 10/4/18.
Nicholson, Edward Francis Dale, Major, d. of w., 12/10/17.
10 Orrell, Keith Faulkner Andrew, 2/Lt., k. in a., 13/1/17 (att. 6th Bn.).
11 Parr, Edgar Brian, 2/Lt. (Tp.), d. of w., 21/10/16.
10 Paton, Morton Brown, Capt. (Tp.), k. in a., 7/8/15 (att. 5th Bn.).
8 Peacocke, Herbert Parker, 2/Lt., k. in a., 3/7/16.
Pickering, Henry Earlam, 2/Lt. (Tp.), died, 9/3/18 (att. 1/5 Bn.).
3 Porritt, William Murray, 2/Lt., k. in a., 25/9/15 (att. N. Lan. R.).
7 Porter, John Edward, 2/Lt. (Tp.), k. in a., 23/7/16.
3 Poultney, John Bernard, 2/Lt., k. in a., 18/2/17 (att. 8th Bn.).
Poundall, William Arthur Lloyd, M.C., T/Lt. (T/Capt.), k. in a., 31/10/17 (and R.F.C., 53 Sqd.).
7 Pringle, William Rennie, Lt. (Tp.), k. in a., 22/7/16.
8 Prior, Edward Robert Seymour, D.S.O., M.C., T/Major (A/Lt.-Col.), k. in a., 27/5/18 (att. 11 Chesh. R.).
3 Pugh, Herbert Elias, 2/Lt., k. in a., 22/7/16 (att. 7).
3 Rathbone, Arnold Richard, Capt., d. of w., 24/6/15 (att. 2nd Bn.).
9 Reade, Leonard Edwin, 2/Lt. (Tp.), k. in a., 30/8/17.
10 Reynolds, George Hubbard, 2/Lt. (Tp.), k. in a., 9/4/16.
3 Richardson, Maurice Lewis George, 2/Lt., k. in a., 28/2/17 (att. 7 R. War. R.).
8 Rickett, Rupert Alexis, Capt. (Tp.), k. in a., 9/7/16.

7 Ritson, John Andrew, Capt. (Tp.), k. in a., 22/7/16.
Robson, Edgar, Capt., d. of w., 3/12/14.
2 Roe, Francis Leslie, 2/Lt. (Tp.), d. of w., 7/1/16.
8 Ross, Norman Leslie, Capt. (Tp.), d. of w., 15/4/18.
3 Sadler, William Edward, 2/Lt., k. in a., 8/5/15 (att. 2nd Bn.).
Salter, Reginald Charles Falconer, Lt. (T/Capt.), k. in a., 8/6/15.
Saunders, George James Rich, Lt. (T/Capt.), k. in a., 26/9/16 (att. 7 Leic. R.).
11 Shaw, Richard Joseph, 2/Lt. (Tp.), d. of w., 26/6/17.
6 Shuffrey, Gilbert, Lt., k. in a., 9/8/15.
10 Skelton, Charles George Gordon, 2/Lt. (Tp.), k. in a., 18/11/16 (att. 17 Bn.).
2 Skottowe, Claude Mannering, 2/Lt., k. in a., 21/10/16.
Smith, Joseph Basil, 2/Lt. (Tp.), k. in a., 18/9/18 (att. 9th Bn.).
Snowden, Harold Jackson, Lt., d. of w., 11/8/17 (and R.F.C.).
1 Soloman, Edmund John, 2/Lt. (Tp.), k. in a., 2/8/17 (att. 8 Bn.).
3 Spalding, Robert Gordon, 2/Lt., d. of w., 28/9/15 (att. 2nd Bn.).
Spendlove, Gervase Thorpe, 2/Lt., d. of w., 17/11/14.
Steytler, Edward Dickinson, 2/Lt., k. in a., 25/7/16 (and R.F.C.).
Stoddard, Ralph Cyril, 2/Lt., died, 3/7/16 (and R.F.C.).
3 Stowell, Thomas Brown, M.C., 2/Lt., d. of w., 19/11/17 (att. 8th Bn.).
Stretton, Alexander Lynam De Courcy, M.C., Capt., k. in a., 16/10/17 (att. Nigeria Rgt.).
2 Strickland, James Edward Trench, Lt. (Tp.), d. of w., 8/8/16.
Sutton, Fergus Algernon, Lt., k. in a., 26/2/15.
3 Thomas, Charles Humphrey Rittsen, Lt., d. of w., 16/6/15 (att. 2nd Bn.).
2 Tickel, Ernest, 2/Lt. (Tp.), died, 13/7/18.
8 Tickner, Thomas George, Lt. (Tp.), d. of w., 1/9/16.
9 Trotter, Alick Dunbar, M.C., Lt., k. in a., 18/9/18.
7 Unsworth, Cyril Joseph, Lt. (Tp.), d. of w., 7/7/16.
2 Ventris, Alan Favel, 2/Lt., k. in a., 14/9/15.
7 Viner, Rollo Lee, 2/Lt. (Tp.), k. in a., 4/7/16.
6 Voelcker, Harold Edward, 2/Lt. (Tp.), k. in a., 20/7/16.
10 Wakeford, Harold, 2/Lt. (Tp.), k. in a., 4/4/16 (att. 6th Bn.).
Waldy, Cuthbert Temple, 2/Lt., k. in a., 20/10/14.
Wallace, David Stephenson, 2/Lt., k. in a., 19/9/14.
3 Walton, Oswald Thomas, 2/Lt. (T/Lt.), k. in a., 12/4/17 (and R.F.C., 18 Sqd.).
6 Ward, Peter Womersley, M.C., T/Capt. & Adjt., d. of w., 23/2/17.
Watson, Ernest Guthrie, 2/Lt., k. in a., 19/9/14.
3 Watson, Kenneth Charles Forrester, M.C., Lt., k. in a., 12/4/18 (att. 2/7 R. Warw. R.).
3 Watton, Stanley Victor, 2/Lt., d. of w., 27/11/16 (att. 7th Bn.).
7 Watts, Harland, 2/Lt. (Tp.), d. of w., 22/11/16.
10 Waugh, Edward Geoffrey, 2/Lt. (Tp.), k. in a., 4/4/16 (att. 6th Bn.).
7 Webber, Henry, Lt. (Tp.), d. of w., 21/7/16.
Webster, George Alexander Malcolm, 2/Lt., k. in a., 28/2/18 (and R.F.C.).
1 Wensley, George Thomas, 2/Lt., died, 31/1/18.
Wesche, Ernest Brocklesby, Capt., k. in a., 19/10/14.
Wheeler, Charles Norman, Capt., k. in a., 7/1/15.
3 Whinyates, Harold Bennet, 2/Lt., d. of w., 14/8/17 (att. 8th Bn.).
White, Geoffrey Stewart Augustus, Lt., k. in a., 10/9/14.
2 Widdowson, Alfred John Harold Ryder, 2/Lt., k. in a., 25/8/14.
1 Wilkins, Herbert Jocelyn Ussher, Capt., k. in a., 10/8/15 (att. 6th Bn.).
3 Williams, Noel Dyson, Lt., k. in a., 22/10/18 (att. 5th Bn.).
6 Willis, G. H., Lt., d. of w., 10/8/15.
2 Wilson, Alan Sydney, Lt., k. in a., 23/4/17 (51 Mach. Gun Corps).
10 Winchester, William Charles Connor, T/Lt. (A/Capt.), k. in a., 21/10/16 (att. 2nd Bn.).
3 Winterbottom, Charles Percy, 2/Lt., k. in a., 2/8/17 (att. 2nd Bn.).
9 Withers, Charles Garnet, 2/Lt. (Tp.), k. in a., 3/7/16 (att. 2nd Bn.).
Wood, Leslie William, 2/Lt., k. in a., 19/7/16 (att. R. War. R.).
10 Woodhouse, Frederick George, 2/Lt. (Tp.), k. in a., 10/7/16 (att. 8th Bn.).
Woodward, Leslie, 2/Lt., k. in a., 22/3/18 (att. 2nd Bn.).
2 Wyatt, Esdaile Frederick Burkett, Capt. (Tp.), k. in a., 8/1/16 (att. M. Gun. Sect.).

The Welsh Regiment.

16 Angus James Robert, Act. Lt.-Col., drowned, 17/9/17 (att. 11 Bn. S.W. Bdrs.).
18 Anthony, Albert Frederick, 2/Lt. (Tp.), d. of w., 10/4/18.
15 Anthony, Percy, Major (Tp.), k. in a., 10/7/16.
2 Arnott, Evan Edward, 2/Lt., d. of w., 23/9/16.
10 Avery, Joseph Francis, 2/Lt. (Tp.), k. in a., 31/7/17.
8 Baggs, Harold Frank, Lt. (Tp.), d. of w., 28/1/17.
17 Bailey, Hubert Percy Andrew, 2/Lt. (Tp.), k. in a., 24/11/17.
14 Balsom, Ernest Henry, Lt. (Tp.), k. in a., 30/8/18.
Betts, John William, 2/Lt., k. in a., 9/5/15.
1 Bewicke, Calverley George, Lt., k. in a., 26/7/16.
Birch, George Owen, Lt., k. in a., 14/9/14.
13 Bond, Charles Edward, Major (Tp.), k. in a., 10/7/16.
13 Boulton, Clifford John, M.C., Capt. (Tp.), k. in a., 30/8/18.
18 Bowen, Joseph Jones, M.C., Lt., k. in a., 9/4/18.
3 Bowen, William, 2/Lt., d. of w., 30/8/18 (att. 15 Bn.).
16 Bracher, Frank Vivian, Major (Tp.), k. in a., 1/6/18 (att. 9 Bn.).
2 Brockington, Conrad Clive, Lt., k. in a., 8/9/16.
3 Brown, Geoffrey Hubert, Lt., k. in a., 23/10/18.
11 Brownson, Alfred Reginald, Lt. (Tp.), k. in a., 18/9/18.
13 Burtonwood, Ernest, 2/Lt. (Tp.), k. in a., 1/9/18.
Caunter, John Charles Ashford, Capt., k. in a., 28/10/17 (and R.F.C., 60 Sqd.).
1 Coker, Cadwallader John, Lt., k. in a., 22/6/15.
14 Colquhoun, Ivor Kenneth, 2/Lt. (Tp.), died, 9/9/15.
9 Cooke, Reginald Charles, M.C., Tp. 2/Lt., k. in a., 7/7/16.
18 Cooper, Robert Charles, Lt. (Tp.), d. of w., 12/4/18 (att. 119 T.M.B.).
Corbet, George Frederick Francis, 2/Lt., d. of w., 25/1/16.
Corder, Hugh Gerald Annerley, Lt., k. in a., 9/5/15.
14 Corker, Francis Llewelyn, Lt., k. in a., 4/6/16.
3 Cornelius, Cecil Victor Powell, Lt., k. in a., 10/11/14.
10 Cowie, Henry Benedict, Temp. 2/Lt., k. in a., 10/7/16.
3 Crofts, George Robert Murray, Lt., k. in a., 9/5/15 (att. 2/Bn.).
13 Crossman, Guy Danvers Mainwaring, Temp. 2/Lt., k. in a., 10/7/16.
Dallas, William Frederick, Lt., k. in a., 9/4/16 (att. 6/East Lancs Regt.).
Davies, Brinley Owen, Lt., k. in a., 22/4/18 (att. 16/R. Welsh Fus.).
9 Davies, Charles Hugh, 2/Lt. (Tp.), k. in a., 17/1/16.
10 Davies, Dan, Temp. Capt., d. of w., 10/9/17.
1 Davies, Griffith, 2/Lt., k. in a., 2/10/15.
18 Davies, Geoffrey David, Temp. Lt., d. of w, 28/11/17 (att. T.M.B.).
10 Davies, James Gordon, Capt. (Tp.), d. of w., 9/2/16.
Davies, Harold Casamajor, Capt., k. in a., 26/9/14.
3 Davies, John James, 2/Lt., d. of w., 29/9/17 (att. 9 Bn.).
17 Davies, Percy Hier, Lt. (T/Capt.), k. in a., 16/8/17 (att. 15 Bn.).
1 Davies, Thomas John Carlyle, 2/Lt., k. in a., 2/10/15.
Davis, Henry William Warren, Lt., k. in a., 18/4/15.
9 Dawkins, Charles John Randle, Temp. 2/Lt., k. in a., 25/9/15.
13 De Lacy-White, Cyril, Temp. 2/Lt., died, 27/6/18.
14 Devenish, Donald Henry, Lt. (Tp.), died, 17/1/16.
8 Digges La Touche, Denis, Capt., k. in a., 8/8/15.
Ducksworth, Walter Clarence, 2/Lt. (Tp.), k. in a., 8/10/18 (att. 1 King's Shp. L. Inf.).
18 Duff, Sidney Hamilton, 2/Lt., k. in a., 13/4/18.
13 Duguid, Clarence Donald, T/2/Lt., k. in a., 18/9/18.
Dundas, Cecil Henry, Lt., d. of w., 2/3/15.
17 Dunn, Clifford Martyn, T/Capt., k. in a., 25/11/17.
18 Edmunds, David Gwym, Temp. Lt. (A/Capt.), k. in a., 25/11/17.
18 Edwards, Edward Walter, Tp. Capt., k. in a., 23/11/17.
12 Ellison, Theodore Tarleton, Temp. 2/Lt., k. in a., 14/3/16 (att. 1/6 Bn.).
17 Elmitt, Austin Joyce, M.C., A/Capt., k. in a., 24/11/17.
14 England, John Humphrey, Temp. 2/Lt., k. in a., 31/7/17.
17 Ensor, John Collin, Lt., d. of w., 26/11/17.
18 Evans, Arthur, 2/Lt., died, 31/3/15.
19 Evans, Arthur Ernest, Temp. Capt., k. in a., 24/6/17.
14 Evans, David Edgar, Lt., k. in a., 18/9/18.
13 Evans, Frederick William, 2/Lt. (Tp.), d. of w., 28/10/16.
18 Evans, Hugh Robert, 2/Lt., k. in a., 19/9/18 (att. 9 Bn.).
13 Evans, Percy Charles David, Capt. (Tp.), d. of w., 22/12/15 (114 Bde. M.G. Offr.).
15 Evans, Robert Charles, 2/Lt. (Tp.), k. in a., 24/8/18.
14 Evans, Robert Prichard, Temp. 2/Lt., d. of w., 11/4/17.
12 Eyre, William, Capt. (Tp.), d. of w., 19/8/15 (att. Lanc. Fus.).
Evan-Jones, Hilary Gresford, Lt., k. in a., 16/2/15.
Ferrar, Walter Hughes, Capt., k. in a., 2/11/14.
3 Fitzpatrick, Gabriel Roy, Capt., k. in a., 14/9/14.
14 Fox, Francis Nevil Wilson, Temp. 2/Lt., k. in a., 31/7/17
18 Franklin, Arthur John, 2/Lt., k. in a., 9/4/18.
16 Gaskell, David Lyndsay Stranack, Temp. 2/Lt., d. of w., 12/1/16.
16 Gaskell, Frank Hill, Temp. Lt.-Col., d. of w., 17/5/16.
15 George, Elmor Wright, Temp. 2/Lt., k. in a., 10/5/18.
9 Gibbs, John Angel, D.S.O., Temp. Major, k. in a., 20/9/17.
14 Godfrey, Leonard Powell, Temp. Capt., d. of w., 23/8/17.
17 Gough, Henry Percy Bright, M.C., Temp. Major, d. of w., 22/4/18.
18 Gracie, Hugh Colin Stuart, Temp. 2/Lt., d. of w., 26/11/17.
9 Green, George Owen, Capt. (Tp.), k. in a., 23/8/15.
9 Green, Oswald Robert John, Lt. (Tp.), d. of w., 5/7/16.
Griffith, William Llewelyn, Temp. 2/Lt., d. of w., 22/9/17 (att. 9 Bn.).
15 Griffiths, Gwyn Arthur, Temp. Lt., k. in a., 2/6/17 (and R.F.C., 35/Sqd.).
9 Griffiths, Reginald Hopkins, 2/Lt., killed, 17/10/18 (and R.A.F.).
17 Griffiths, William John, M.C., Capt., k. in a., 24/11/17.
18 Grossart, Robert Dykes, Temp. 2/Lt., killed, 9/2/17 (and R.F.C.).
1 Gwyer, Charles Percy, Capt., k. in a., 8/8/15 (att. 8/Bn.).
11 Hackett, Harry Osborne, 2/Lt. (Tp. Lt.), d. of w., 28/8/17.
10 Hadfield, Edgar, Temp. 2/Lt., k. in a., 22/3/17.
Haggard, Mark, Capt., d. of w., 15/9/14.
15 Hall, John Reginald, Temp. 2/Lt., k. in a., 10/7/16.
8 Harding, William Arthur, Capt., k. in a., 8/8/15.
3 Hardy, Reginald Herbert William, Lt., died, 4/11/18.
16 Harris, Lyn Arthur Philip, Temp. Capt., k. in a., 10/7/16.
13 Harvey, William Mitchell, Temp. 2/Lt., k. in a., 10/7/16.
2 Hayman, Alfred George, Capt., k. in a., 8/9/16.

14 Hazard, William Noel, Temp. 2/Lt., k. in a., 26/8/18.
Herd, Horace Falkland, Capt., k. in a., 27/12/14.
9 Herbert, Thomas William Percy, Temp. Lt. (A/Capt.), k. in a., 1/8/17.
3 Hickman, Arthur Kendrick, Lt., k. in a., 5/4/16 (att. 8 Bn.).
17 Higson, Frederic Stewart, M.C., Tp. Lt. (A/Capt.), k. in a., 31/8/17.
1 Hobbs, Arthur Harold, Capt., k. in a., 2/10/15.
17 Hobby, Grenville Howard, 2/Lt. (Tp.), k. in a., 20/10/18 (att. 14 Bn.).
Holmes, Cyril, Lt. (Tp.), died, 21/12/15 (att. 8 Bn.).
3 Howell, Richard David, M.C., 2/Lt., k. in a., 15/9/18 (att. 2 Bn.).
14 Howells, Graham, Temp. Capt., d. of w., 2/5/16.
8 Howells, William John, Temp. Capt., d. of w., 10/8/15.
16 Howill, John Edwin, 2/Lt., k. in a., 7/7/16.
Hughes, Benjamin Thomas, 2/Lt. (Tp.), k. in a., 17/3/18 (att. 13/R. Welsh Fus.).
14 Hughes, Charles Henry, 2/Lt. (Tp.), k. in a., 30/8/18.
17 Hughes, John Lawrence, Temp. Lt., k. in a., 1/10/17 (and R.F.C., 25 Sqd.).
11 Hughes, Norman Alfred, Capt. (Tp.), k. in a., 18/9/18.
11 Hughes, Percy Canynton, 2/Lt. (Tp.), d. of w., 3/10/18 (att. S. Wales Bdrs.).
Hughes, Sam, 2/Lt. (Tp.), k. in a., 6/11/17 (att. 10 Bn.).
9 Hughes-Hughes, William Montagu, Capt. (Tp.), k. in a., 25/9/15.
15 Humphreys, Percy Lloyd, Capt. (Tp.), k. in a., 31/7/17.
17 Jackman, Gerald Radcliffe, Temp. 2/Lt., k. in a., 21/4/17.
James, Charles Llewellyn, 2/Lt. (Tp.), k. in a., 10/5/18 (att. 15 Bn.)
3 James, Evan, Temp. 2/Lt., k. in a., 27/7/17 (att. 15 Bn.).
18 Jeffery, John, 2/Lt. (Tp.), k. in a., 20/9/18 (att. 9 Bn.).
13 Jeffreys, William Stanley, Temp. Lt., k. in a., 10/7/16.
10 Jenkins, Llewellyn Maynard, 2/Lt. (Tp.), d. of w., 2/12/16.
23 Jenkins, William Marenday, Temp. Lt., k. in a., 3/10/16.
3 Jenkins, Sydney Randell, Lt., d. of w., 26/9/15 (att. 2 Bn.).
9 Johns, Harold Thomas, Temp. 2/Lt., k. in a., 11/1/17.
8 Jones, Arthur Ewart, 2/Lt. (Tp.), k. in a., 8/8/15.
17 Jones, Arthur Trevor, Temp. Lt., d. of w., 19/6/17.
1 Jones, Basil Gordon Dawes, M.C., Lt., k. in a., 23/9/16.
3 Jones, Cecil Norman, 2/Lt., died, 9/11/17 (att. 15 Bn.).
10 Jones, David, Temp. Capt., k. in a., 12/7/16.
Jones, David, 2/Lt., k. in a., 18/9/18 (att. 11 R. Welsh Fus.).
9 Jones, Dan Llewellyn, Temp. 2/Lt., d. of w., 14/3/16.
13 Jones, Evan Gwilym, 2/Lt. (Tp.), d. of w., 31/8/18.
8 Jones, Ernest William, 2/Lt. (Tp.), died, 9/11/15.
10 Jones, Herbert Francis, Temp. 2/Lt., k. in a., 10/7/16.
Jones, John Arllwyd, 2/Lt., k. in a., 20/9/17 (att. 9 Bn.).
10 Jones, James Brinley, Temp. Lt., k. in a., 31/5/17 (att. 25 Lab. Bn.).
Jones, John Lewis, 2/Lt. (Tp.), died, 13/8/17.
Jones, John Owen, Temp. 2/Lt., k. in a., 6/6/17 (att. 16 Bn.).
20 Jones, John Wilfred, Temp. 2/Lt., k. in a., 16/11/16 (att. 9 Bn.).
14 Jones, John Ynys Palfrey, 2/Lt. (Tp.), k. in a., 30/8/18.
Jones, Llewellyn Price, Temp. 2/Lt., k. in a., 20/9/17 (att. 9 Bn.).
8 Jones, Sydney Everard, 2/Lt. (Tp.), k. in a., 8/8/15.
16 Jones, Trevor Benjamin, Lt. (Tp.), k. in a., 18/9/18.
Jones, Victor Trevor, 2/Lt. (Tp.), k. in a., 18/9/18 (att. 17 Bn.).
9 Jukes, Frederick, Temp. 2/Lt., k. in a., 20/9/17.
Joy, George Bruce, Lt., d. of w., 21/5/15.
14 Kelk, Arthur Frederick Hastings, M.C., Temp. 2/Lt., k. in a., 9/3/17.
Kerrich, John Herbert, Capt., k. in a., 14/9/14.
Kington, William Miles, D.S.O., Capt., k. in a., 20/10/14.
2 Knapp, Oswald Reed, 2/Lt., d. of w., 13/9/16.
3 Latham, Francis Pulsford, Major, died, 26/2/16 (att. 1/Garr. Bn. Welsh Fus.)
18 Leece, Edwin Stanley, Temp. Lt., d. of w., 24/11/17.
13 Leech, Percy Leonard, 2/Lt. (Tp.), k. in a., 27/8/18.
10 Lewis, Gordon, 2/Lt. (Tp.), d. of w., 18/4/18.
8 Lewis, John Nicholas, Lt., k. in a., 8/8/15.
18 Lewis, Leonard Glynne, M.C., Temp. 2/Lt., k. in a., 24/11/17.
Lloyd, Gerald Aylmer, Lt. (T/Capt.), k. in a., 16/2/15.
15 Lloyd, Thomas Glyn, Capt. (Tp.), k. in a., 10/5/18.
10 Lloyd, Thomas Yale, Temp. 2/Lt., k. in a., 12/7/16.
17 Lloyd-Williams, Kelyth Pierce, Temp. 2/Lt., k. in a., 17/10/16.
3 Lomax, Gerald David, 2/Lt., d. of w., 11/5/15 (att. R. Berks Regt.).
3 Lord, Arthur, Capt., d. of w., 12/2/17.
15 Lowe, George Ernest, M.C., 2/Lt., k. in a., 28/10/18.
17 Lyne, Charles Vyvyan, Temp. Capt., k. in a., 18/10/16.
McCartney, Robert Stuart, 2/Lt., d. of w., 9/1/18 (att. 17 Bn.).
10 McEwan, David Grant, Temp. 2/Lt., killed, 23/1/16 (att. T.M.B.).
10 Marsh, Henry Herbert, Temp. Lt., k. in a., 12/2/16.
8 Marson, John Charles, Temp. 2/Lt., k. in a., 8/8/15.
Martin, Arthur William, 2/Lt., died, 14/3/17.
2 Miles, Alfred Crosfield Vernor, Temp. 2/Lt., k. in a., 24/8/15.
Miles, Cyril Vernor, Capt., k. in a., 25/9/15.
15 Minshull, George Henry, M.C., Temp. 2/Lt., k. in a., 20/10/18.
1 Monk, Gerald Patrick Baillow, Capt., k. in a., 3/10/15.
3 Moore, Henry, Temp. 2/Lt., k. in a., 15/7/16 (att. 2/Bn.).
Moore, Waldo Alington Gweanap, Capt., k. in a., 31/10/14.
15 Morgan, George Elton, Temp. 2/Lt., d. of w., 19/8/17.
3 Morgan, Ralph Lewis, 2/Lt., k. in a., 14/1/17 (att. 13 Bn.).
Morgan, Thomas Augustus, Temp. 2/Lt., k. in a., 8/10/18 (att. 13 Bn.).
2 Morland, Charles Bernard, Lt.-Col., k. in a., 31/10/14.
13 Morris, Allan Duncan, Temp. Lt., k. in a., 30/8/18.
8 Morris, John Child, Temp. Lt., k. in a., 8/8/15.
12 Morris, John William Gibson, Capt., k. in a., 1/4/16 (att. 6 Bn.).
16 Neilson, Richard Clark, Temp. 2/Lt., k. in a., 27/8/17.
19 Newlyn, Walter Tessier, Temp. 2/Lt., k. in a., 11/7/16.
18 Nicholas, Thomas Glyn, Temp. 2/Lt., k. in a., 18/2/17 (att. 14 Bn.).
Nicholl, John William Harford, 2/Lt., k. in a., 29/10/14.
9 Nicholl-Carne, Osmond Whitlock, Temp. 2/Lt., k. in a., 1/8/17.
2 Nicholls, R. M., Lt., d. of w., 18/7/16.
17 O'Donnell, Hugh Neil, Temp. 2/Lt., d. of w., 4/2/17.
17 O'Malley, Charles, Lt., k. in a., 25/11/17.
14 Osmond, Cyril Thomas, Temp. Lt., d. of w., 25/8/18.
9 Owen, Meredyth, Temp. 2/Lt., k. in a., 25/9/15.
Owen, Meurig, Temp. 2/Lt., k. in a., 1/8/17 (att. 9 Bn.).
Owen, William David, Temp. 2/Lt., died, 11/10/18 (att. 15 Bn.).
9 Owen, William Henry Kenrick, Temp. Lt., d. of w., 1/10/15.
Partridge, Geoffrey Dorman, Lt., k. in a., 3/11/14.
20 Percival, Cecil Bernard, Tp. Lt. (A/Capt.), k. in a., 24/11/17 (att. 18 Bn.).
Phillips, Leslie, Capt., k. in a., 25/5/15.
Picton-Warlow, Wilfrid, Capt., died, 20/12/14 (att. R.F.C.).
Pope, Percy Paris, 2/Lt., k. in a., 1/10/15.
Pope, Reginald Thomas Buckingham, Lt., k. in a., 16/2/15.
Postlethwaite, William, Temp. 2/Lt., d. of w., 14/3/18 (att. 15 Bn.).
2 Price, David Eleazer, 2/Lt., k. in a., 8/9/16.
1 Pridham, George Frederick, Temp. Lt.-Col., died, 16/12/16 (att. 5 Bn.).
Pritchard, Osborn Brace, Lt.-Col., died, 27/11/16.
13 Purdie, Thos. Paterson, Temp. 2/Lt., k. in a., 10/7/16 (att. 20 Bn.).
15 Radmilovic, John, Temp. 2/Lt., died, 3/11/18 (att. 3 Bn.).
9 Rees, Ivor Guest, Temp. Lt., d. of w., 5/8/16.
3 Rees, John Cyril, 2/Lt. (Tp.), died, 6/11/15 (att. 8 Bn.).
13 Rees, Lawrence Sinclair, Temp. 2/Lt., k. in a., 10/7/16.
15 Reese, William, Lt. (Tp.), died, 2/2/17.
21 Reeves, Harry Charles, Temp. 2/Lt., k. in a., 24/8/16 (att. 2 Bn.).
3 Richards, John Thomas, 2/Lt. (Tp.), k. in a., 6/11/17 (att. 24 Bn.).
16 Richards, William Jenkin, Capt. (Tp.), k. in a., 27/8/17.
15 Richards, William John, Temp. Lt., d. of w., 12/10/18.
3 Roberts, Arthur Hosbury Starkey, Lt., d. of w., 4/11/18 (att. 15 Bn.).
10 Roberts, Robert Jesse Adams, D.S.O., Capt. (Tp.), d. of w., 22/9/17.
9 Roberts, Victor, 2nd Lt. (Tp.), k. in a., 19/7/17.
13 Robinson, John Singleton Henry, T/Lt., k. in a., 24/9/18 (att. 12 Bn.).
14 Roderick, Francis, Lt. (Tp.), d. of w., 31/7/17.
18 Rogers, Trevor, 2/Lt. (Tp.), k. in a., 24/11/17.
14 Rosser, Arthur, Temp. 2/Lt., k. in a., 10/7/16.
13 Rowe, Edwin Vivian, Temp. 2/Lt., k. in a., 1/9/18.
9 Salmon, Stanley Francis, 2/Lt. (Tp.), k. in a., 19/7/17.
14 Sandbrook, David Aubrey, Capt. (Tp.), k. in a., 31/7/17.
2 Sear, Eric John Cecil, 2/Lt., k. in a., 8/9/16.
Sessions, John Herford Vivian, T/Lt., d. of w., 28/9/18 (att. 13/Bn.).
14 Sheppard, Richard Bellamy, M.C., Tp. Capt., k. in a., 22/4/18.
11 Short, John, Temp. Lt., died, 28/10/18.
16 Shurey, Edward, Temp. Lt., died, 18/7/18.
16 Sillem, Thomas George, Tp. Lt. (A/Capt.), k. in a., 14/4/18.
1 Simpson, David, M.C., 2/Lt., k. in a., 2/6/17.
13 Smith, Charles Henry, Temp. 2/Lt., k. in a., 19/3/16.
Snelson, Victor Louis, Temp. 2/Lt., k. in a., 15/7/17 (att. 12 Sth. Wales Bdrs.).
8 Spencer, Alfred de Courboisier, 2/Lt., k. in a., 26/9/15 (att. 8 Bn. R. Berk. R.).
10 Stanton, Clifford, Temp. Lt., k. in a., 31/7/17.
Stanyon, Terence George, 2/Lt., d. of w., 23/7/16.
2 Stevenson, George Herbert, Major, k. in a., 25/9/15.
13 Stothert, George Mervyn, Temp. Lt., d. of w., 10/6/17.
13 Sullivan, Walter Ernest, M.C., Temp. 2/Lt., d. of w., 19/4/18 (att. 1/4 Bde., H.Q. 38/Div.).
3 Sumsion, Francis, Lt., k. in a., 4/11/18 (and R.A.F.).
2 Sutton, William Henry, Temp. Lt., k. in a., 23/10/18.
Swift, Humphrey Morris, 2/Lt., k. in a., 16/11/17 (att. 2 Bn.).
10 Tait, Wilfred Webster, Lt., d. of w., 19/12/15.
19 Taylor, Charles Frederick, 2/Lt., d. of w., 18/2/17.
16 Thomas, Albert, Temp. 2/Lt., k. in a., 30/5/18 (att. 9 Bn.).
Thomas, David Cecil Sandby, 2/Lt., killed, 16/2/18 (and R.F.C.).
13 Thomas, Eric Lawrence, Temp. Lt., k. in a., 18/9/18.
3 Thomas, John Mewrig, 2/Lt., k. in a., 22/5/18 (att. 2nd Bn.).
13 Thomas, Thomas, Temp. Capt., k. in a., 23/8/17.
Torkington, Charles Coke, Capt., k. in a., 25/5/15.
3 Torney, Thomas Frederick Hastings, Lt., k. in a., 3/9/18 (att. 13 Bn.).
16 Tregaskis, Arthur, Temp. 2/Lt., k. in a., 7/7/16.
16 Tregaskis, Leonard, Temp. 2/Lt., k. in a., 7/7/16.
9 Trehearne, Leslie Llewellyn, 2/Lt. (Tp.), d. of w., 25/9/15.
10 Trott, Henry George, 2/Lt. (Tp.), d. of w., 16/8/17.
13 Tugby, Leslie Andrew, Temp. 2/Lt., k. in a., 18/9/18.
18 Turnbull, Gerald Illtyd, Temp. Lt., d. of w., 9/4/18 (in Ger. hands).
3 Turnbull, John Oswin, Capt., k. in a., 8/9/16.
11 Turner, Edgar Harold Holmes, 2/Lt. (Tp.), d. of w., 23/10/16.
3 Tyson, Percy Eldin, 2/Lt., k. in a., 8/12/16 (att. 2 Bn.).
14 Vaughan, John David, M.C., 2/Lt., d. of w., 18/3/17.
3 Vaughan-Lewes, Martyn Tulloch, Lt., d. of w., 22/7/16 (and R.F.C.).
2 Vawdrey, Gilbert Lloyd, 2/Lt., k. in a., 10/11/17.

Vincent, James Trevor Crawley, 2/Lt., k. in a., 9/5/15.
16 Waddington, James Hubert, 2/Lt. (Tp.), d. of w., 6/7/16.
9 Warren, Frederik John, Major, died, 14/7/15.
Warren, James Lionel East, Capt., k. in a., 2/10/15.
Watkins, William, 2/Lt., k. in a., 23/7/18 (att. R.A.F.).
15 Watts, Albert Edward, 2/Lt., k. in a., 22/4/18.
1 Wavell, Arthur John Byng, M.C., Major, k. in a., 9/2/16 (att. Arab Rifles, E. Afr. Protec. Forces).
Weeding, John Richard Baggalay, 2/Lt., k. in a., 22/12/14.
1 Weeks, Henry Russell, Capt., d. of w., 23/9/18.
Wells, Frank Irving Pascoe, Lt., k. in a., 9/5/15.
1 Westby, Edmund Henry Herbert, Capt. and Adj., k. in a., 25/5/15.
3 White, Henry Thompson, Lt., k. in a., 8/9/16 (att. 1 Bn.).
10 White, Lionel, Temp. Lt., k. in a., 19/3/16.
17 Wilkie, Charles Joseph, Temp. Lt.-Col., k. in a., 18/10/16.
Williams, Arthur Jones, Temp. 2/Lt., k. in a., 3/11/17 (att. 4 Bn.).
1 Williams, Daniel Llewellyn, 2/Lt., k. in a., 15/10/18 (att. 1/1 Hereford Rgt.).
8 Williams, Gordon, Capt., died, 15/11/18.
Williams, George Shanley, Lt., k. in a., 20/10/18 (att. 14 Bn.).
16 Williams, John Lewis, Temp. Capt., d. of w., 12/7/16.
Williams, William Bernard, Lt., k. in a., 20/10/18 (att. 14 Bn.).
20 Williams, Wilfred Brynmor, Temp. 2/Lt., k. in a., 5/7/16 (att. 16 Bn.).
14 Williams, William Morley, Temp. 2/Lt., k. in a., 7/6/17.
9 Wilson, Douglas Jonathan Rogers, Temp. 2/Lt., k. in a., 25/9/15.
14 Wilson, Edward Henry, 2/Lt., k. in a., 8/10/18.
Woolf, William, Lt., k. in a., 21/9/18.

The Black Watch (Royal Highlanders).

10 Alexander, Thomas Loudon, 2/Lt., k. in a., 8/5/17.
Amery, Harold Francis Saphir, Major, d. of w., 24/11/15.
11 Anderson, David Horace, 2/Lt. (Tp.), k. in a., 22/4/16 (att. 2 Bn.).
2 Anderson, George John, 2/Lt. (Tp.), k. in a., 22/4/16.
11 Anderson, James Alexander, 2/Lt. (Tp.), k. in a., 19/10/16 (att. 8 Bn.).
Anderson, Robert Cunningham, Capt., d. of w., 27/9/15.
1 Anderson, Thomas Binnie, 2/Lt. (Tp.), d. of w., 22/11/16.
11 Anderson, William, 2/Lt. (Tp.), d. of w., 23/4/17 (att. 9 Bn.).
3 Balfour-Melville, James Elliot, 2/Lt., k. in a., 25/9/15 (att. 2 Bn.).
8 Balkwill, Albert Thomas James, 2/Lt., k in a., 17/10/16.
1 Ballantyne, William, 2/Lt. (Tp.), k. in a., 13/10/15.
1 Balmain, Walter, 2/Lt., k. in a., 18/4/18.
10 Bassett, William Frederick, M.C., Lt. (Tp.), k. in a., 27/10/18 (att. 2/Royal Scots.).
9 Bearn, Octavius Leslie, Lt. (Tp.), k. in a., 23/4/17.
Belford, Charles Roberts, 2/Lt., k. in a., 2/9/18 (att. 9 Bn.).
Bell, Arthur McLean, Lt. (Tp.), k. in a., 20/5/18.
9 Bell, John Murray, Capt. (Tp.), k. in a., 27/9/15.
11 Bell, Thomas Hector, 2/Lt. (Tp.), k. in a., 9/2/16 (att. 9 Bn.).
11 Blacklock, William, 2/Lt. (Tp.), died, 12/9/16.
3 Blackwood, John Angus, 2/Lt., died, 10/9/16.
Blair, Patrick Edward Adam, 2/Lt., k. in a., 29/10/14.
3 Boddam-Whetham, Cecil, Capt., k. in a., 14/12/14 (att. Gordon Highrs.).
Bone, George Drummond, 2/Lt., k. in a., 9/5/15.
3 Bowie, Henry, Lt., k. in a., 28/7/18 (att. 6 Bn.).
3 Bowes-Lyon, Charles Lindsay Claude, Lt., k. in a., 23/10/14 (att. 1 Bn.).
8 Bowes-Lyon, Hon. Fergus, Capt. (Tp.), k. in a., 27/9/15.
Boyd, Hugh Lennox Fleming, Capt., k. in a., 18/11/17.
Boyd, Nigel John Lawson, 2/Lt., d. of w., 12/10/14.
Bracelin, Daniel, 2/Lt. (Tp.), k. in a., 20/7/18 (att. 1/7 Bn.).
2 Brown, George James Rankine, 2/Lt. (Tp.), d. of w., 21/5/17.
3 Brown, Oswald Stanley, 2/Lt., k. in a., 22/12/15 (att. 1 Bn.).
Brown, Robert, 2/Lt., k. in a., 19/7/18 (att. 8 Bn.).
10 Browne, George Brownlie, 2/Lt. (Tp.), k. in a., 7/2/16 (att. 9 Bn.).
11 Bruce, Eric, Temp. 2/Lt., died, 17/11/16 (att. 2 Bn.).
2 Bruce, Herbert William, Temp. 2/Lt., k. in a., 17/2/17.
Buist, Kenneth, Lt., k. in a., 25/1/15.
Burn, Maurice Edward Pelham, Temp. Lt., k. in a., 9/4/17 (att. 8 Bn.).
Burns, David Chalmers, 2/Lt., k. in a., 30/9/18 (att. 8 Bn.).
3 Burt, James, 2/Lt., k. in a., 19/7/18.
9 Burton, John Lees, Temp. 2/Lt., k. in a., 24/4/17 (att. 1 Gr. Bn. H. L. Inf.).
8 Butter, Henry John, Capt. (Tp.), k. in a., 15/7/16.
9 Cameron, James Hunter, Lt., k. in a., 25/9/15.
8 Cameron, William McAdam, Temp. 2/Lt., k. in a., 14/7/16.
2 Campbell, Duncan, Capt., k. in a., 18/5/15.
8 Carswell, John Dingwall, Capt. (Tp.), k. in a., 14/7/16.
10 Carswell, William Alexander, M.C., Capt., d. of w., 21/3/18.
3 Clark, A. B., M.C., Capt., k. in a., 3/10/18 (and R.A.F.).
Clark, William Muir, Temp. 2/Lt., k. in a., 20/11/17 (att. 1/7 Bn.).
3 Clement, Hubert Arnold, 2/Lt., k. in a., 3/5/17 (att. 8 Bn.).
9 Clow, George Robert, Temp. 2/Lt., k. in a., 17/3/16.
8 Collins, John Gerrard, Temp. Major, k. in a., 27/9/15.
3 Colquhoun, Philip Leslie Campbell, M.C., Lt. (A/Capt.), k. in a., 19/9/18 (att. 1 Bn.).
8 Cook, Kenneth Richmond, Temp. 2/Lt., d. of w., 30/7/16 (T.M.B.).
3 Cooke, Denys, Capt., k. in a., 18/4/18 (att. 1 Bn.).
3 Cotterill, John Henry, 2/Lt., d. of w., 15/3/17 (att. 2 Bn.).
8 Craven, Asa, 2/Lt. (Tp.), k. in a., 19/10/16 (att. 11).
8 Crighton, John Fairweather, Lt. (Tp.), k. in a., 18/7/16.
8 Crighton, John, Lt. (Tp.), k. in a., 27/9/15.
3 Cumming, Alex Bryant, Lt., k. in a., 22/4/16.
3 Cumming, Frederick Kenneth, 2/Lt., k. in a., 23/10/18 (att. 14 Bn.).
Cumming, Lewis Robertson, 2/Lt., k. in a., 28/9/14.
3 Cunningham, Douglas Murray, 2/Lt., d. of w., 11/6/18
9 Cuthbert, David Wilson Harper, Temp. 2/Lt., d. of w., 9/4/17.
Dalglish, Charles Antoine de Guerry, Capt., d. of w., 9/9/14.
3 Dawson, James, 2/Lt., died, 2/4/17 (att. 2 Bn.).
1/2 Delmar-Williamson, George Frederick, Lt., killed, 12/7/18 (and R.A.F.).
Denison, Archibald Campbell, Capt., k. in a., 25/9/15.
10 Denniston, Jack Evelyn, Temp. 2/Lt., d. of w., 20/9/16 (att. 1 Bn.).
Dewar, James Melville, Lt. (Tp.), k. in a., 16/10/18 (att. 1/7 Bn.).
3 Dickson, Hugh Barclay, Lt., k. in a., 12/10/17 (att. 8 Bn.).
1 Dixon, Frederick John Cruse, 2/Lt. (Tp.), d. of w., 6/9/16.
10 Don, Archibald William Robertson, Lt. (Tp.), died, 11/9/16.
Don, Reginald Gilbert, 2/Lt., k. in a., 15-16/9/14.
10 Don, Robert Macpherson, Lt., k. in a., 8/4/17.
3 Douglas, Andrew, Temp. 2/Lt., d. of w., 19/2/16 (att. 2 Bn.).
3 Douglas, Alexander Stark, 2/Lt., d. of w., 28/10/18 (att. 1/6 Bn.).
9 Dow, William, Temp. 2/Lt., d. of w., 2/2/17.
3 Drummond, Alexander Gilmour, M.C., 2/Lt., d. of w., 5/4/18 (att. 6 Bn.) (P.O.W.).
8 Drummond, Henry Murray, 2/Lt. (Tp.), d. of w., 26/5/16 (att. 9 Bn.).
Edwards, William Hardinge Colvin, Temp. Capt., k. in a., 9/5/15.
3 Egerton, Philip Graham, Capt., d. of w., 18/10/18.
10 Ewart, Richard Henry Charles, Lt. (Tp.), d. of w., 16/10/18 (att. 14 Bn.).
1 Feiling, Hubert St. Lawrence, 2/Lt., k. in a., 20/11/16.
8 Fergusson, James Grant, Temp. 2/Lt., k. in a., 14/7/16.
2 Forrester, Hugh Fielding, 2/Lt., k. in a., 22/4/16.
8 Forrester, Patrick Hamilton, 2/Lt. (Tp.), d. of w., 11/10/15.
Forrester, Robert Edgar, Capt., k. in a., 16/6/15.
1 Fraser, Alexander, 2/Lt., k. in a., 13/10/15.
9 Fraser, Oswald Campbell, Temp. 2/Lt., k. in a., 9/4/17.
1 Fraser, William, 2/Lt. (Tp.), d. of w., 29/9/15.
3 Game, Reginald Francis, 2/Lt., died, 10/10/18.
8 Gawne, William Zacharias, Temp. 2/Lt., k. in a., 9/4/17.
George, William, 2/Lt., k. in a., 12/3/15.
9 Gilchrist, John, Capt. (Tp.), d. of w., 29/8/15.
2 Gillespie, Thomas, Temp. 2/Lt., k. in a., 14/3/17.
8 Gilroy, George Bruce, Temp. Capt., d. of w., 15/7/16.
Gilroy, Kenneth Reid, Lt., d. of w., 12/3/15.
Glencross, Andrew, 2/Lt., k. in a., 18/4/18 (att. 1/T.M.B.).
1 Godfrey, William John, 2/Lt., k. in a., 3/9/16.
Gordon, Charles William Eric, Brig.-Gen., k. in a., 23/7/17 (123/Inf./Bde.).
9 Graham, Andrew, Temp. Lt., k. in a., 30/12/17 (att. 44/T.M. Bty.).
9 Graham, Donald Hatt Noble, Capt. (Tp.), k. in a., 27/9/15.
3 Graham, Henry Balfour, 2/Lt., k. in a., 9/5/17 (att. 10 Bn.).
11 Grainger, James Francis Stuart, Temp. Capt., d. of w., 12/8/15 (att. K.O.S. Bdrs.).
1 Grant-Duff, Adrian, C.B., Lt.-Col., k. in a., 21/9/14.
Gray, Andrew, 2/Lt., k. in a., 9/5/15.
3 Gunn, Kenneth, Lt., k. in a., 14/4/16 (att. 1 Bn.).
1 Gunn, Marcus Sinclair, M.C., Lt., d. of w., 6/9/16.
Haig, David, Temp. 2/Lt., killed, 5/7/18 (att. 4/5 Bn.).
Hamilton, David Love, 2/Lt., k. in a., 21/3/18 (att. 6 Bn.).
Hamilton-Johnston, Douglas Charles, Capt., k. in a., 21/1/16.
8 Harper, Alexander Simpson, Temp. Lt., k. in a., 12/10/17.
Harrison, Dennis Riley, 2/Lt. (Tp.), k. in a., 3/5/17 (att. 8 Bn.).
Harrison, Ronald, Temp. Lt., k. in a., 10/11/17 (att. 1/5 A. & Suth. Highrs.).
9 Harvey, Richard Ernle, Temp. Capt. & Adjt., d. of w., 27/10/15.
Harvey, William James St. John, T/Brig.-Gen., d. of w., 1/2/16.
11 Hastings, Joseph Edward, Temp 2/Lt., k. in a., 18/7/16 (att. 8 Bn.).
11 Hay, William George, Temp Capt., died, 7/8/16 (att. 8 Bn.).
Hayes, Harry Urmston, 2/Lt., k. in a,. 13/10/15.
4 Henderson, James Richard. 2/Lt., died, 29/11/14.
9 Henderson, Michael William, Major (Tp. Lt.-Col.), k. in a., 27/9/15.
Henderson, Noel Charles 2/Lt, k. in a., 25/9/15.
9 Henderson-Hamilton, James Campbell, Lt. (Tp.), k. in a., 27/9/15.
Holland, Basil Thomas, 2/Lt., k. in a., 10/3/15
9 Howard, Richard Jackson, Temp. 2/Lt., k. in a., 17/3/16.
3 Huddlestone, Sydney Chantler, 2/Lt., k. in a., 25/1/15 (att. 2 Bn.).
3 Hunter, William Alexander Dobson, Lt., k. in a., 1/10/18 (att. 8 Bn.).
Husband, Peter Ross, 2/Lt (Tp.), k. in a., 25/9/16.
2 Hutchison, Innes Owen, Temp. 2/Lt., k. in a., 7/1/16.
8 Hutchison, Robert Hamilton, T/Lt., k. in a., 13/10/15 (att. 1 Bn.).
8 Hutton, Walter Forbes, Temp. 2/Lt., k. in a., 14/7/16 (11 Bn.).
8 Hyslop, William Douglas, 2/Lt. (Tp.), d. of w., 25/3/18.
Inglis, James Normand, Capt., k. in a., 22/4/16.
Innes, Donald McLeod, 2/Lt., d. of w., 7/10/18 (att. 14 Bn.).
9 Ireland, John Balfour, 2/Lt., k. in a., 8/9/16.
8 Jackson, David, Temp. 2/Lt., k. in a., 16/12/17.
3 Jalland, Henry Herbert, Lt., k. in a., 18/10/18 (att. 1 Bn.).

1 Johnson, Thomas, M.C., Lt., k. in a., 4/9/16.
Johnstone, Nelson Gordon, M.C., 2/Lt., k in a., 30/12/17 (44 T.M.B.).
8 Johnstone, William, 2/Lt., k in a., 30/3/16.
2 Kay, William Joseph O'Neill Beaumont, 2/Lt. (Tp.), died, 19/11/18.
Kedie, William Thomas, Capt., k. in a., 21/8/15.
3 Keith-Murray, Alastair William, 2/Lt., k. in a., 8-9/5/17.
Kincaid, Andrew Duncan, 2/Lt., d. of w., 23/3/18 (att. 8 Bn.).
1 Lawson, Alexander Sutherland, 2/Lt., k. in a., 11/11/14.
Lindsay, W. H., 2/Lt., d. of w, 30/5/19 (att. 6 Bn.).
Linning, John, Hon. Major & Qr.-Mr., died, 16/9/14.
2 Loudoun, Thomas, 2/Lt., k in a., 8/6/18.
Lyle, Thomas Basil, 2/Lt., k. in a., 9/5/15.
McAndrew, Alister, 2/Lt., k. in a., 24/12/14.
2 McArthur, Dugald, Temp. 2/Lt., d. of w., 21/4/17.
McConaghey, Charles Jack, Lt., k. in a., 22/4/16.
Macdonald, Alexander Lindsay, M.C., Lt. (T/Capt.), k. in a., 26/8/17 (and R.F.C., 9 Sqd.).
10 Macdonald, Malcolm, Temp. Lt., k. in a., 10/10/16.
9 Macdonald, Robert Brown Aitchison, Temp. 2/Lt., k. in a., 17/8/16.
3 Macdougall, Finlay Neil, Lt., k. in a., 18/8/16.
3 Macfarlane, Robert, M.C., Capt., k. in a., 21/4/17 (att. 2 Bn.).
10 McGregor, Andrew William, 2/Lt. (Tp.), k. in a., 27/2/16 (att. 9 Bn.).
8 McIntosh, Charles George Gordon, Temp. 2/Lt., d. of w., 28/9/15.
McKenzie, Leslie, Lt. (Tp.), d. of w., 2/4/18.
9 Mackenzie, Murdock, Temp. 2/Lt., k. in a., 5/11/15.
Mackenzie, Roderick Ian, 2/Lt., d of w., 11/4/15.
3 Mackinnon, Brice Bunny, M.C., Lt., died, 5/8/18 (att. 10 Bn.).
Mackintosh, Douglas Bruce, Capt., k. in a., 24/7/16 (att. K.A. Rifs., 1st Bn.).
8 Mackintosh, Edwin Hampson, Temp. Lt., k. in a., 25/9/15.
Macleod, George Charles Sholto, Capt., d. of w., 13/5/15.
Macleod, Ian Breac, Lt., k in a., 17/4/15.
8 McMillan, Hugh Dobie, Temp. Lt., k. in a., 19/7/18.
1 McMillan, Neil, T/2/Lt., d. of w., 29/11/16.
Macnaughton, Angus Charles Rowley Stuart, Lt., k. in a., 29/10/14.
McNeill, Neil, 2/Lt., k. in a., 11/11/14.
11 Macrae, John Alexander, Temp. 2/Lt., k. in a., 18/7/16 (att. 8 Bn.).
11 Macrury, Norman, Lt., k in a., 4/6/15 (att. K.O.S.B.).
3 McVeigh, Joseph, 2/Lt., k. in a., 28/3/18 (att. 9 Bn.).
McWilliam, Hamish, Lt., k in a., 29/5/16.
8 Mann, Alexander James, Temp. 2/Lt, d. of w., 10/4/17.
3 Mather, Alan William, Lt., died, 29/10/18 (and R.A.F.).
9 Mearns, Angus Hughes, Lt., k. in a., 24/6/17 (and R.F.C., 57 Sqd.).
Mercer, Andrew, 2/Lt., d. of w., 22/10/15.
9 Millar, James, Temp. 2/Lt., k. in a., 25-27/9/15.
9 Miller, John Donald Gardiner, Temp. Lt., d. of w., 15/11/15.
2 Miller-Stirling, Edward George Bradshaw, Lt., d. of w., 14/3/17.
8 Milroy, Eric, 2/Lt., k. in a., 18/7/16.
3 Mitchell, George, 2/Lt., killed, 22/7/15 (att. 1 Bn.).
Moir, Jame McMurchy, Temp. 2/Lt., k. in a., 25/9/15.
3 Monday, Joseph Cyril, 2/Lt., k in a., 3/5/17 (att. 8 Bn.).
9 Morrison, Leonard Graeme, Temp. Lt., k. in a., 23/4/17.
2 Morrison, Robert Stevenson, 2/Lt, k. in a., 7/1/16.
3 Moubbray, Percy Lionel, Capt., k. in a., 29/10/14 (att. 1 Bn.).
8 Mowbray, James Seymour Strachan, Temp. Capt., k. in a., 25/9/15.
Munro, Duncan Leitch, Temp. 2/Lt., d. of w., 13/10/17 (att. 8 Bn.).
8 Murray, Edward Douglas, Temp. Lt., d. of w., 20/7/16.
Murray, Henry Francis Farquharson, Major (A/Lt.-Col.), k. in a., 23/8/17.
Murray, James Thomas Crockatt, D.S.O., Major, d. of w., 16/2/15.
Murray-Menzies, Clive William, 2/Lt., k. in a., 25/1/15.
Murray-Menzies, Duncan Innes, M.C., Lt. (A/Capt.), k. in a., 22/8/17 (att. Tank Corps).
10 Nicol, Charles Ashmore, Capt., k. in a., 8/5/17.
3 Nolan, Raymond Philip Drummond, Lt., k. in a., 3/11/14 (att. 1 Bn.).
8 Odell, Robert Eric, Temp. Lt., d. of w., 20/12/16.
3 Parker, Alfred Ernest, Capt., k. in a., 7/11/14 (att. 2 Bn. Sea. Highrs.).
3 Paton, James Ley, 2/Lt., k. in a., 13/10/15 (att. 1 Bn.).
Paul, Philip Reid, Lt., k. in a., 1/10/18 (att. 8 Bn.).
Peel, Tom, Temp. 2/Lt., d. of w., 21/4/17 (att. 2 Bn.).
8 Pitcairn, Ellis Gledhill, Capt., died, 6/10/18.
2 Plunkett, Havelock Arthur Terence, Lt., k. in a., 7/1/16.
1 Polson, Geoffrey William, 2/Lt., k. in a., -/9/14.
9 Potter, Robert Wilson, Temp. Lt., k. in a., 11/1/18 (att. 4/5 Bn.).
Potter, Robert, M.C., Temp. 2/Lt., k. in a., 14/10/18 (att. 8 Bn.).
1 Preston, Herbert Stanley, Temp. 2/Lt., d. of w., 8/9/16.
3 Purvis, Ronald Montague, Capt., d. of w., 14/3/17.
2 Quine, Brian Howell, Temp. Lt., k. in a., 27/6/18.
2 Rawdon-Hastings, Edward Hugh Hastings, 2/Lt., died, 25/9/15.
8 Ray, Philip Oliphant, Temp. 2/Lt., died, 13/4/17 (and R.F.C., 59 Sqd.).
9 Reid, Robert William, 2/Lt., d. of w., 17/5/16.
3 Reid, Thomas Ernest, 2/Lt., d. of w., 18/4/17 (att. 9 Bn.).
8 Ritchie, Alexander Stewart, M.C., Temp Capt., k. in a., 1/10/18.
Ritchie, James Adam, Temp. 2/Lt., d. of w., 8/8/18 (att. 4/5 Bn.).
Robertson, Archibald Garden, 2/Lt., k. in a., 8/6/17 (att. R.F.C., 66 Sqd.).
3 Robertson, Herbert Johnston Graeme, Lt., k. in a., 25/9/15 (att. 1 Bn.).
9 Robertson, John Brewis, Temp. Capt., d. of w., 17/9/16.
8 Robertson, James Horan, Temp. Lt., k. in a., 18/7/16 (att. 11 Bn.).
10 Robertson, William Stewart, Temp. Lt., k. in a., 3/9/16 (att. 4/5 Bn.).
Ross, Evan Nicholas, Temp. Lt., k. in a., 27/6/18 (att. 2 Bn.)
8 Sanderson, Harold Scott, Temp. Lt., k. in a., 25/9/15.
3 Scoones, Fitzmaurice Valentine, 2/Lt., died, 18/8/16.
Scott, John Gordon, 2/Lt., k. in a., 9/5/15.
11 Scott, John Millar, Temp. 2/Lt., k. in a., 18/8/16 (att. 1 Bn.).
Shand, Alexander, 2/Lt., d. of w., 9/5/15.
9 Sharp, Andrew, Temp. 2/Lt., k. in a., 27/9/15.
8 Shaw, Philip Haldane, 2/Lt., k. in a., 25/9/15.
11 Sim, Louis St. George Leslie, 2/Lt., died, 20/12/15.
11 Sinclair, Archibald King, Temp. 2/Lt., k. in a., 5/12/16.
1 Sinclair, Gerald John, Lt. (A/Capt.), k. in a., 18/4/18
Sinclair, Robert, 2/Lt., k. in a., 9/5/15.
1 Skey, Charles Harland, Capt., k. in a., 18/8/16.
1/2 Skinner, Robert Leonard, 2/Lt., died, 3/5/18 (and R.A.F.).
9 Small, John, Temp. Lt., k. in a., 29/4/16.
1 Smith, David, M.C., D.C.M., 2/Lt., k. in a., 18/10/18.
Smurthwaite, Douglas Stuart Stirling, 2/Lt., k. in a., 26/10/14.
3 Smythe, Patrick Evelyn, Lt., died, 30/11/18 (att. 2/Bn.).
3 Soutar, Frank Henderson, 2/Lt., k. in a., 21/1/16 (att. 2 Bn.).
8 Sprake, George Harold, Temp. Lt., k. in a., 18/7/16 (3 Bn.).
Sprot, James William Lennox, Capt., k. in a., 11/11/14.
Stewart, Charles Edward, C.M.G., Temp. Brig.-Gen., k. in a., 14/9/16 (154/Inf. Bde.).
Stewart, Hon. Keith Anthony, Lt., k. in a., 9/5/15.
Stewart-Murray, Lord George, Major, k. in a., 14/9/14.
Stewart, William Debenham McLaren, Capt., k. in a., 25/9/16.
3 Stewart-Richardson (Bart.), Sir Edward Austin, Capt., d. of w., 28/11/14 (att. 1 Bn.).
Strahan, Charles Eric, Capt., k. in a., 28/11/14.
9 Strang, John S., Capt., k. in a., 28/3/18.
3 Stuart, John, 2/Lt., k. in a., 28/7/18 (att. 9 Bn.).
Stuart, Maurice Stevenson, 2/Lt., k. in a., 15/6/18 (att. 8 Bn.).
9 Taylor, James, 2/Lt. (Tp.), k. in a., 31/7/17.
14 Thomson, Ernest Anderson, Temp. 2/Lt., k. in a., 6/11/17.
3 Thomson, George Ewan Christian, 2/Lt., k. in a., 18/11/17 (att. 1 Bn.).
Tillie, John Archibald, 2/Lt., k. in a., 19/7/18 (att. 8 Bn.).
11 Tindal, David, 2/Lt., d. of w., 18/7/16 (att. 8 Bn.).
2 Topping, J., 2/Lt., k. in a., 16/9/18 (and R.A.F.).
9 Tuke, Cyril Stratford, Temp. Capt., k. in a., 25/9/15 (M.G.C.).
11 Turnbull, Thomas Russell, Temp. 2/Lt., k. in a., 11/10/16 (att. 9 Bn.).
Turner, Henry Scott, 2/Lt., died, 11/3/15.
8 Tyser, Henry Erskine, Temp. 2/Lt., k. in a., 9/4/17.
Urquhart, Edward Frederick Maltby, Capt., k. in a., 23/10/14.
11 Urquhart, William, Lt. (Tp.), k. in a., 7/8/16.
11 Waldie, John Gray, Temp. Lt., k. in a., 31/7/17 (and 25 M.G.C.).
Wallace, John, 2/Lt., k. in a., 9/5/15.
Wanliss, Alexander, Lt., k. in a., 9/5/15.
Warrand, Alastair St. John Munro, Capt., died, 18/3/15 (and R.F.C.).
9 Watson, Alastair Fisher, Temp. 2/Lt., k. in a., 23/4/17.
3 Webster, Joseph Frain, 2/Lt., k. in a., 30/10/14 (att. 1/-Gordon Highrs.).
Wells, James Ritchie, Temp. 2/Lt., killed, 17/11/17 (att. R.F.C.).
West, Harold, 2/Lt., k. in a., 9/5/15.
3 Whyte, Robert Barbour, 2/Lt., k. in a., 25/9/15 (att. 1 Bn.).
Wilson, Ewen Holmes Humphries James, Lt., k. in a., 8/9/14.
3 Wilson, John, 2/Lt., k. in a., 23/4/17 (att. 9 Bn.).
3 Young, Alexander Aytoun, 2/Lt. d. of w. 14/3/17 (att. 2 Bn.).
8 Young, James Logie, Lt., k. in a., 19/7/18.
Young, William Alexander, M.C., Capt., d. of w., 10/6/18

The Oxfordshire and Buckinghamshire Light Infantry.

5 Anderson, Basil Arthur, M.C., Capt. (Tp.), k. in a., 21/3/18.
5 Ashman, Stanley, Lt. (Tp.), k. in a., 3/5/17.
9 Bailey, Arthur William, Lt., k. in a., 4/6/15.
2 Bailey, Walter Arthur Francis, 2/Lt., k. in a., 23/3/18.
6 Baines, Athelstan Basil, Capt. (Tp.), k. in a., 3/4/17.
7 Baker, Cyril Percival, Lt., d. of w., 8/5/17.
2 Barclay, Edward Wilfred Howard, 2/Lt., k. in a., 27/1/18.
Barrington-Kennett, Aubrey Hampden, 2/Lt., d. of w., 20/9/14.
2 Bartlett, Leonard, Lt. (Tp.), k. in a., 1/10/18.
2 Beaufort, Francis Hugh, Capt., k. in a., 16/5/15.
1/2 Belgrave, James Dacre, M.C., Capt., k. in a., 13/6/18 (and R.A.F.).
6 Benson, Cyril Samuel, 2/Lt. (Tp.), k. in a., 24/4/17.
5 Berlein, Charles Maurice, Lt., k. in a., 16/6/15.
1 Bicknell, Herman Kentigern, Capt. (Tp.), died, 24/7/17.
6 Birch, Walter Robert, Capt. (Tp.), k. in a., 7/10/16.
Birt, Lascelles William, Capt. (Tp.), d. of w., 1/10/17 (att. 1/4 Bn.).
Bleeze, Frank James, 2/Lt. (Tp.), k. in a., 29/7/18 (att. 4 R. Suss. R.).
6 Blencowe, Oswald Charles, 2/Lt. (Tp.), k. in a., 7/10/16.
1/2 Blount, J. H., 2/Lt., died, 6/7/18 (and R.A.F.).

Boardman, John Hopwood, Capt. (T/Major), d. of w., 25/4/18 (in Ger. hands).
5 Bowman, John, 2/Lt. (Tp.), d. of w., 23/11/15.
5 Bradley, Gordon, 2/Lt., k. in a., 24/8/16.
Brooke, Richard Reginald Maude, Capt., k. in a., 31/5/15.
6 Brooks, Ernest William, T/Lt. (A/Capt.), k. in a., 20/9/17.
1 Brown, Fred, 2/Lt., k. in a., 11/12/15.
6 Bryant, John Evelyn, Capt. (Tp.), k. in a., 4/8/16.
Bull, Robert Edward Bristow, Lt. (Tp.), k. in a., 16/5/15.
9 Burrows, Stanley Eric, 2/Lt. (Tp.), k. in a., 30/12/15 (att. 5th Bn.).
1 Buttery, Robert Arthur, 2/Lt. (Tp.), k. in a., 15/6/18 (att. 4th Bn.).
8 Calder, Alexander, Lt. (Tp.), k. in a., 10/8/17 (and R.F.C., 57 Sqd.).
Calderon, George, Lt., k. in a., 4/6/15.
2 Calloway, Gilbert Charles, 2/Lt. (Tp.), k. in a., 28/4/17.
3 Carew-Hunt, Aubrey Noel, Capt., k. in a., 5/6/16 (att. 2nd Bn.).
Carfrae, Charles Francis Kirkpatrick, Capt., k. in a., 25/9/15 (att. 5th Bn.).
5 Clarke, Harold Frank, Lt. (Tp.), k. in a., 25/9/15.
3 Clifton, William Gerard Talbot, 2/Lt., k. in a., 31/3/17 (and R.F.C., 11 Sqd.).
6 Copeman, Herbert Guy Hele, 2/Lt., k. in a., 3/9/16.
9 Coulthard, Eustace Frank, 2/Lt. (Tp.), k. in a., 6/4/16 (att. 1st Bn.).
Courtis, John Harold, Capt., k. in a., 22/11/15.
2 Creswell, Ronald Arthur, 2/Lt., k. in a., 13/11/16.
Dancy, George, M.C., Lt. and Q.-Mr., died, 2/6/19.
Dashwood, Lionel Albert, 2/Lt. (Tp.), k. in a., 16/5/15.
Davenport, Frank Maturin, Capt., k. in a., 22/11/15.
6 Davies, Henry, 2/Lt. (Tp.), k. in a., 13/11/16 (att. 2nd Bn.).
5 Davies, Ivor Theophilus, 2/Lt., k. in a., 22/6/15.
1 Davis, Anthony Hugh, 2/Lt., k. in a., 6/4/16.
2 Dillon, H. M., D.S.O., Major, died, 13/1/18.
Drury, Gordon Vallancy, Major (Tp.), died, 19/11/17 (35 Training Reserve).
7 Durno-Steele, Frederick Arthur, Lt., k. in a., 9/5/17.
3 Eccles, Henry, 2/Lt. (Tp.), k. in a., 28/2/17 (att. 7th Bn.).
5 Edwards, Anthony Hepburn, Lt., k. in a., 1/4/18.
Evelegh, Rosslyn Curzon, Capt., k. in a., 19/9/14.
2 Fanning, Vivian Edward, Lt., A/Capt., k. in a., 14/11/16.
5 Farrer, Lyonel Henry St. George, 2/Lt. (Tp.), died, 28/10/15.
5 Fawcett, Woodford, 2/Lt. (Tp.), k. in a., 21/3/18.
Fewell, Charles William, 2/Lt. (Tp.), died, 6/11/18.
5 Finlayson, John, 2/Lt. (Tp.), k. in a., 23/3/18
1 Foljambe, The Hon. Josceline Charles William Saville, Capt. and Bvt.-Major, k. in a., 6/4/16.
Forrest, Charles Evelyn, D.S.O., Major, k. in a., 22/11/15.
5 Fremantle, Thomas Francis Halford, 2/Lt. (Tp.), d. of w., 17/10/15.
3 Fuller, Gordon Howard, 2/Lt., A/Capt., k. in a., 7/7/18 (att. 2nd Bn.).
3 Fussell, John William Hugo, 2/Lt., k. in a., 19/7/16 (att. 6th Bn.).
7 Garland, Wilfred, 2/Lt. (Tp.), k. in a., 8/5/17.
Girardot, Paul Charcowt, 2/Lt., k. in a., 17/9/14.
2 Goffe, William Reginald, 2/Lt. (Tp.), k. in a., 30/7/16.
5 Gray, George Godfrey, 2/Lt. (Tp.), d. of w., 10/4/17.
6 Green, Cecil Henry, 2/Lt. (Tp.), d. of w., 9/10/16.
1 Griffin, Sidney James, Capt., d. of w., 26/3/18.
5 Guise, James William, 2/Lt. (Tp.), d. of w., 19/8/17.
Hammick, Stephen Frederick, Capt., d. of w., 18/4/16.
2 Hanbury-Williams, Charles Ferdinand Reiss, Lt., died, 16/12/16.
Harden, Allen Humphrey, Capt., k. in a., 21/10/14.
3 Hardcastle, Sydney Philip, Capt. (Tp.), k. in a., 30/7/16 (att. 2nd Bn.).
3 Harper, Charles Croke, 2/Lt., k. in a., 3/5/17 (att. 5th Bn.).
9 Harrison, Noel Stuart, Lt. (Tp.), k. in a., 30/7/16 (att. 2nd Bn.).
3 Haynes, William Charles, 2/Lt., k. in a., 3/5/17 (att. 5th Bn.).
9 Higgins, Douglas Stanley, Lt. (Tp.), k. in a., 9/4/17 (att. 5th Bn.).
2 Hill, Nicholas Weatherby, M.C., Lieut., A/Capt., k. in a., 16/1/17.
Hobart-Hampden, George Miles Awdry, 2/Lt., killed, 17/9/17 (and R.F.C.).
2 Holland, John Dixon Cuyler, 2/Lt. (Tp.), k. in a., 13/11/16.
Holt, Follett Hallett, Lt., k. in a., 22/8/18 (att. Tank Corps).
Hughes, Edward Reginald Graham, 2/Lt., k. in a., 25/9/15.
7 Hulm, Glynn, T/Lt., A/Capt., died, 28/11/18.
3 Humfrey, Douglas Herbert Washington, Lt., k. in a., 16/5/15 (att. 2nd Bn.).
6 Hunt, Robert Lancelot Gibbs, Capt. (Tp.), k. in a., 7/10/16.
3 Huntley, Edward Kenneth, 2/Lt., k. in a., 20/9/17 (att. 6th Bn.).
Hurst-Brown, Cecil, 2/Lt., d. of w., 26/9/15.
Hyde, Arthur Clarendon, Major, k. in a., 22/11/15.
3 Ionides, Theodore Alexander, 2/Lt., d. of w., 16/11/16 (att. 2nd Bn.).
6 Ive, Frank, 2/Lt. (Tp.), k. in a., 7/10/16.
5 Jackson, John Montague Hammick, Lt. (Tp.), d. of w., 18/8/15.
Jacob, Victor Vivian, Lt., k. in a., 25/9/15.
Johnston, John Leslie, 2/Lt., k. in a., 12/5/15.
Jones, Jesse, 2/Lt., k. in a., 11/11/14.
Kearsley, John Stewart, Lt., k. in a., 22/11/15.
Kirkpatrick, Edward Hartley, Major, k. in a., 15/5/15.
3 Kite, Ralph Bertram, M.C., Capt., d. of w., 10/12/16 (att. 2nd Bn.).
5 Knighton, Gerald Godfrey, Major (Tp.), d. of w., 30/4/17.
5 Labouchere, Arthur Maxwell, D.S.O., Major (Tp.), d. of w., 30/4/18.
Lawrence, William George, 2/Lt., k. in a., 23/10/15 (and R.F.C.).
5 Lee, Lionel Shaw, 2/Lt., k. in a., 25/9/15.
2 Littledale, Willoughby John, Lt., k. in a., 23/3/18.
Lodge, Tom, M.C., 2/Lt. (Tp.), d. of w., 21/5/18.
Logan, Rowland Octavius, Capt., k. in a., 17/10/15 (att. 5th Bn.).
6 Luis, Eric George Vincent, 2/Lt. (Tp.), k. in a., 6/10/16.
2 Lyle, Geoffrey Samuel La Warre, 2/Lt., d. of w., 29/4/17.
6 Marsh, Victor Braine, 2/Lt. (Tp.), k. in a., 3/9/16.
Marshall, Jenner Stephen Chance, 2/Lt., d. of w., 21/10/14.
1 Martin, David Archibald, 2/Lt., k. in a., 25/3/18.
2 Maul, Richard Selby Lowndes, 2/Lt., k. in a., 30/7/16.
5 Mellis, Andrew Douglas John, 2/Lt. (Tp.), k. in a., 17/10/15
Middleditch, Arnold Warden, 2/Lt. (Tp.), died, 19/6/16.
Mitchell, Charles Johnstone, D.S.O., Major, died, 16/10/18 (Res. of Off.).
5 Mitchell, John McGeorge, 2/Lt., k. in a., 25/9/15.
Mockler-Ferryman, Hugh, Lt., k. in a., 16/9/14.
6 Moore, James Voaden, 2/Lt. (Tp.), k. in a., 2/12/17.
1 Moore, Thomas, 2/Lt. (Tp.), k. in a., 15/6/18 (att. 4th Bn.).
6 Morland, Kenneth Irvine Thomas, 2/Lt. (Tp.), k. in a., 3/9/16.
6 Morris, Charles Geoffrey Noel, Lt. (Tp.), k. in a., 7/10/16.
Murphy, Christopher Fowler, Lt., k. in a., 21/10/14.
Newton-King, Pierce Francis, Lt., k. in a., 25/9/15.
3 Osborne, Victor Edward, 2/Lt., killed, 7/4/18 (P. of W.) (att. M.G.C.).
3 Owen, D. G., 2/Lt., died, 23/11/16.
2 Owen, Reginald Mansfield, Major (Tp.), d. of w., 2/8/16.
Parr, Bertram Chambré, Major, k. in a., 3/9/18 (att. 2 South Staffs.).
2 Peploe, Keith, Lt. (A/Capt.), k. in a., 9/11/16.
Pepys, Francis, D.S.O., 2/Lt., k. in a., 12/11/14.
Pickford, Herbert Thomas Reade, 2/Lt., k. in a., 25/4/17.
Ponsonby, Ashley William Neville, Capt., k. in a., 8/9/15.
Priest, F., 2/Lt. (Tp.), died, 22/5/18 (att. 3rd Bn.).
9 Ramsay, Archibald Hamilton, 2/Lt. (Tp.), k. in a., 13/10/15 (att. 2nd Bn.).
3 Rawson, Hubert Wyatt Hay, Capt., k. in a., 15/11/16 (att. 2nd Bn.).
3 Rayner, Haydn Eric W., 2/Lt., k. in a., 17/3/17 (att. 2nd Bn.).
Rendel, Reginald Dacres, 2/Lt. (T/Lt.), k. in a., 16/5/15.
5 Richards, Richard John, 2/Lt. (Tp.), d. of w., 12/5/17 (in Ger. hands).
Riddle, Francis Edmund Langton, 2/Lt., k. in a., 16/5/15.
5 Royal-Dawson, Oswald Sydney, Capt. (Tp.), d. of w., 25/8/17.
3 Scott, John Hastings Folliott, 2/Lt., k. in a., 9/4/17 (att. 5 Bn.).
Seago, George William Edward, Lt. (Tp.), d. of w., 6/10/18 (att. 1/5 Glouc. R.).
2 Seale, William Henry, 2/Lt., d. of w., 14/3/18 (att. 5 T.M.B.).
Sears, Joseph Patrick, 2/Lt. (Tp.), k. in a., 20/8/18 (att. 2 Bn.).
6 Sellar, James Arthur, 2/Lt. (Tp.), k. in a., 3/4/17.
6 Shaw, Edward Alfred, Capt. (Tp.), k. in a., 7/10/16.
3 Sherwood, Charles Edward, 2/Lt., k. in a., 22/10/17.
Simpson, Rupert Victor, Major, k. in a., 28/9/15.
6 Skoulding, Alfred Cecil, 2/Lt. (Tp.), d. of w., 21/2/17.
6 Skuce, Arthur, Lt. (Tp.), d. of w., 8/10/17.
3 Slocock, Cyprian Henry Benson, Lt. (A/Capt.), d. of w., 3/4/18 (att. 2nd Bn.).
5 Smith, Augustus William, 2/Lt. (Tp.), k. in a., 2/2/16.
Smith, John Gardiner, 2/Lt. (Tp.), k. in a., 20/9/17 (att. 6th Bn.).
3 Spurge, Henry Wesley, Lt. (A/Capt.), d. of w., 17/9/17 (att. 5th Bn.).
5 Stammers, Joseph Ralph, 2/Lt. (Tp.), k. in a., 9/4/17.
5 Stevens, James, 2/Lt. (Tp.), k. in a., 9/4/17.
3 Stokes, Hugh Adrian Innys Blyth, M.C., 2/Lt., d. of w., 28/11/18.
3 Strickland, Reginald, 2/Lt., died, 25/12/15 (att. 2nd Bn.).
6 Sutherland, Hector John, Capt. (Tp.), died, 2/2/17.
5 Sweet Escott, Leslie Wingfield, Lt. (Tp.), k. in a., 25/9/18.
5 Talbot, Norman Hale, 2/Lt. (Tp.), k. in a., 24/8/16.
Theobald, Ronald John MacIver Wilson, 2/Lt., k. in a., 21/3/18 (att. 5th Bn.).
6 Thomas, Arthur Coke, 2/Lt. (Tp.), k. in a., 2/6/16.
Thomas, Ernest William Noel, 2/Lt. (Tp.), k. in a., 20/11/17 (att. 6th Bn.).
3 Truman, Alfred Holloway, 2/Lt., k. in a., 6/4/16.
3 Tuck, Duncan Johnson, Capt., d. of w., 3/7/16 (att. 6th Bn.).
3 Turbutt, Gladwyn Maurice Revell, Lt., k. in a., 21/10/14.
Tylden-Pattenson, Arthur Dagnall, Lt. (Tp.), k. in a., 5/1/15.
3 Vidall, Lancelot Andrews, 2/Lt., k. in a., 25/9/15 (att. 2nd Bn.).
5 Walrond, Francis Hillier, 2/Lt. (Tp.), d. of w., 15/8/16
2 Walter, Alfred Ernest, 2/Lt. (Tp.), d. of w., 13/5/17.
Ward, Jack Bouverie Mallam, 2/Lt., k. in a., 7/11/14.
Warde, Basil Charles Conroy, 2/Lt., k. in a., 30/7/16.
3 Warner, Cornwallis John, Lt., k. in a., 16/5/15 (att. 2nd Bn.).
3 Webster-Jones, Alfred Owen Webster, Lt., k. in a., 13/11/16 (att. 2nd Bn.).
6 West, Arthur Graeme, T/2/Lt. (A/Capt.), k. in a., 3/4/17.
5 Weston-Webb, Henry, Lt. (Tp.), k. in a., 24/8/16.
6 Whittock, Frederick Walter, 2/Lt. (Tp.), k. in a., 25/9/15.
3 Widcombe, Charles Ingleton, 2/Lt., k. in a., 6/4/16.
Williams, George Ernest, 2/Lt. (Tp.), k. in a., 20/11/17 (att. 6th Bn.).
3 Wood, Almerick Watkins, 2/Lt., d. of w., 26/9/15 (att. 5th Bn.).
Worthington, Reginald George, Lt., k. in a., 16/9/14.
Wynter, Francis Constantine Wm., Capt., k. in a., 22/11/15

The Essex Regiment.

11 Akerman, Alexander Grant, 2/Lt. (Tp.), k. in a., 17/9/18.
2 Allen, Geoffrey Austin, 2/Lt., k. in a., 1/7/16.
10 Archibald, James Duncan, Lt. (Tp.), d. of w., 20/7/16.
Avery, Clare Havill, Lt. (A/Capt.), d. of w., 11/4/17 (and 12/T.M. Bty.).
14 Baldry, William George Forsyth, 2/Lt. (Tp.), d. of w., 7/11/17 (att. 11 Bn.).
3 Balme, Edward Nettleton, M.C., Lt., d. of w., 22/4/18 (att. 11 Bn.).
1/2 Banks, F., 2/Lt., died, 2/6/18 (and R.A.F.).
2 Barker, George Frederick, 2/Lt. (Tp.), k. in a., 12/5/17.
Barrell, Philip James, 2/Lt., k. in a., 1/5/15.
3 Barratt, Kenneth Franklin, Lt., k. in a., 1/7/16 (att. M.G.C.).
13 Barrett, Jack Ainslake, 2/Lt., k. in a., 28/4/17.
Barrett, Noel Bertram, 2/Lt. (Tp.), k. in a., 29/4/18 (att. 2 Bn.).
11 Bartlett, Herbert Claude, M.C., Capt. (Tp.), k. in a., 15/9/16.
Bartom, William Sidney, 2/Lt., d. of w., 26/4/18 (att. 10 Bn.).
3 Bavin, Nigel Benjamin, Lt., k. in a., 23/5/15 (att. 2 Bn.).
9 Bearlock, Charles Henry, Lt. (Tp.), d. of w., 20/10/15.
12 Beauclerk, Nevill Alfred de Vere. Lt., k. in a., 20/6/15 (att. 2 Bn.).
11 Bedells, Cecil Arthur, 2/Lt., k. in a., 26/9/15.
14 Beevor, Vernon Saville, M.C., 2/Lt. (Tp.), k. in a., 10/3/17 (att. 10/Bn.).
1 Bell, Jack Whateley, T/Lt. (T/Capt.), k. in a., 26/3/17 (att. 4 Bn.).
2 Bennett, Alfred John, 2/Lt., k. in a., 9/8/17.
9 Bennett, John Alick, 2/Lt. (Tp.), k. in a., 22/8/18.
Bestall, E. D., Lt., k. in a., 3/7/16.
10 Binley, Percy Augustine, M.C., 2/Lt. (Tp.), k. in a., 23/8/18.
Binney, Robert Humphrey, M.C., A/Capt., d. of w., 23/3/18.
Binstead, Gerald Charles, Capt. (Temp. Major), k. in a., 8/4/15.
1 Black, Donald MacGregor, Capt., k. in a., 6/8/15.
Blyth, Herbert Russel, Major (T/Lt.-Col.), died, 17/1/18 (Gar. Bn.).
12 Bonney, Sydney Richard, 2/Lt. (Tp.), k. in a., 26/9/16 (att. 10 Bn.).
Boone, Charles Frederick de Bohun, Capt., d. of w., 23/9/14.
Brabazon, Terence Anthony Chaworth, Lt., d. of w., 3/8/16.
11 Bradbeer, Francis Henry, 2/Lt. (Tp.), k. in a., 21/3/18.
1 Brand, Eric Jermyn, 2/Lt. (Tp.), k. in a., 23/8/18.
Braun, Charles Lema, Capt. (Tp.), died, 19/6/17 (Gar. Bn.).
12 Broomfield, James Taylor, T/2/Lt., k. in a., 3/12/16 (att. 1 Bn.).
13 Brown, Charles Roydon, M.C., Capt., k. in a., 14/4/17.
10 Brown, Eric Howard, Temp. Lt., k. in a., 22/10/17.
2 Browne, Charles Eric Wyndham, 2/Lt., d. of w., 24/10/16.
Browne, Henry Arthur, 2/Lt. (Tp.), k. in a., 26/10/18 (att. 2 Bn.).
1 Browne, Herbert Maxwell, Temp. 2/Lt. (A/Lt.), k. in a., 26/3/17 (att. 5 Bn.).
12 Bunting, Robert Russell, Lt. (Tp.), k. in a., 6/8/15 (att. 1 Bn.).
Burford, Richard Ellis, 2/Lt. (Tp.), d. of w., 8/10/18.
Burmester, Maurice George, Lt. (Tp.), d. of w., 25/8/15 (att. 1 Bn.).
13 Busby, William Walter, Lt., k. in a., 13/11/16.
Cadge, Francis Edward, Lt., k. in a., 30/4/15.
2 Cadic, Lawrence William Ludovic, M.C., Capt., d. of w., 10/10/17.
9 Capper, Ernest Raphael, M.C., Temp. Capt., d. of w., 24/12/17.
1 Capron, Thomas Harvey Overbury, Temp. Lt., k. in a., 26/3/17 (att. 5 Bn.).
13 Carson, Charles Graham, Capt. (Tp.), d. of w., 28/11/16.
10 Carson, Lindsay Hubert, Temp. Capt., d. of w., 31/10/18.
Carter, Charles Oscar Percival, 2/Lt. (Tp.), k. in a., 26/4/18 (att. 10 Bn.).
10 Carter, William James, Temp. 2/Lt., k. in a., 21/9/18.
10 Chaplyn, Cyril Edward, Temp. 2/Lt., k. in a., 26/4/18.
Chappy, Athol Isdale, 2/Lt., k. in a., 24/9/18 (att. 11 Bn.).
3 Charrington, Edwin Milward, Capt., k. in a., 13/11/16 (att. 13 Bn.).
3 Chawner, Alain Percy Mark, 2/Lt., k. in a., 20/10/16 (att. 1 Bn.).
2 Chawner, Meredith Andre, Capt., k. in a., 21/5/17.
1 Cheshire, William Robert, Temp. 2/Lt., k. in a., 1/7/16.
Christy, Philip Archibald, Lt., k. in a., 10/2/15 (Spec. Res.).
11 Cleal, Harry, M.C., Temp. 2/Lt., k. in a., 10/12/17.
1 Clutterbuck, Arthur Vincent, Major, died, 31/10/16.
13 Cole, Cyril Charles, 2/Lt., died, 14/11/18 (and R.A.F.).
9 Comber, Turner, M.C., Temp. 2/Lt. (A/Capt.), k. in a., 19/9/18.
9 Constable, Archibald Thomas Wynne, Capt. (T/Major), d. of w., 16/10/15.
12 Cook, Thomas, 2/Lt., k. in a., 2/10/15 (att. 6/Linc Regt.).
12 Cooke, Leslie Frederick, Temp. 2/Lt., k. in a., 26/9/16 (att. 10 Bn.).
Cooper, Clarence Percy, Temp. Lt., d. of w., 2/4/17 (att. 1/4).
9 Cooper, Ernest Walter, 2/Lt. (Tp.), d. of w., 13/10/18.
3 Cooper-Brown, Arthur Neville, 2/Lt. (A/Capt.), d. of w., 27/10/18 (att. 2 Bn.).
9 Copeman, Robert George Henry, 2/Lt. (Tp.), d. of w., 12/1/16.
2 Corn, Frederick, 2/Lt. (Tp.), k. in a., 29/4/18.
Cousins, Charles Hope, 2/Lt., d. of w., 27/4/15.
1 Cousins, Leonard, Temp. 2/Lt., k. in a., 14/4/17.
Cox, George Pottinger, Capt., k. in a., 24/12/15.
11 Creasy, Harry William Hay, Temp Capt., k. in a., 13/6/16.
2 Croager, Lawrence William, 2/Lt., k. in a., 3/5/17.
Dale, John Ernest, Temp. 2/Lt., d. of w., 14/9/17 (att. 9 Bn.).
11 Davies, Geoffrey Boisselier, Capt. (Tp.), k. in a., 26/9/15.
11 Davies, John Llewelyn, Major (Tp.), k. in a., 25/9/15.
9 Davis, Harold Charles, 2/Lt., k. in a., 26/6/18 (and R.A.F.).
13 Davis, Herbert Pinder, 2/Lt. (Tp.), d. of w., 29/7/16.
3 Davis, John Charles Reginald, Lt., k. in a., 13/5/15 (att. 2 Bn.).
12 Davis, William, 2/Lt. (Tp.), k. in a., 18/10/16 (att. 9 Bn.).
Dawes, Morris, 2/Lt., k. in a., 26/4/18 (att. 10 Bn.).
11 Deane, George Frederic, Temp. 2/Lt., k. in a., 22/4/17 (att. 18/T.M. Bty.).
9 Derbyshire, Albert, 2/Lt., k. in a., 30/4/17.
Devas, Arthur Edward, Lt., died, 15/2/15.
11 Dickson, Walter Felix, 2/Lt. (Tp.), k. in a., 1/8/18.
Dinan, Frederick Charles, Capt., d. of w., 29/9/17.
Dixon, Charles Ralph, Capt., d. of w., 5/5/15.
10 Dodd, Herbert Robert, 2/Lt. (Tp.), k. in a., 21/3/18.
11 Duke, John, M.C., Capt. (Tp.), d. of w., 22/4/18.
13 Dunscombe, Charles William, T/Lt. (A/Capt.), d. of w., 14/3/17.
1 Edey, William John, 2/Lt. (Tp.), k. in a., 1/2/18.
11 Ellis, Frederick Alfred, 2/Lt. (Tp.), k. in a., 22/3/18.
3 English, Frederick Garnet, 2/Lt., k. in a., 13/11/16 (att. 13 Bn.).
3 Evans, Arthur, 2/Lt., k. in a., 18/10/16, (att. 9 Bn.).
2 Evans, Philip Henry, 2/Lt., k. in a., 3/5/17.
Everett, Walter Reginald, Temp. 2/Lt., d. of w., 4/9/17 (att. 11 Bn.).
1 Eyre, Sebert Henry Robert, 2/Lt., k. in a., 14/4/17.
9 Farley, Ernest Harold, 2/Lt. (Tp.), k. in a., 3/7/16.
11 Ferguson, James Duncan, Temp. Lt., d. of w., 27/10/16.
12 Finn, Bernard William, 2/Lt., k. in a., 13/11/16 (att. 13 Bn.).
Flin, Richard Valentine, 2/Lt., k. in a., 8/8/18 (att. 10 Bn.).
1 Flinn, Cyril Herbert, 2/Lt., k. in a., 14/4/17.
1 Ford, Frank Stephen, Capt. & Qr.-Mr., died, 24/3/18.
3 Forster, Eric Murray, 2/Lt., k. in a., 3/5/17 (att. 2 Bn.).
1 Footner, Arthur Henry, 2/Lt. (Tp.), k. in a., 6/8/15.
3 Francis, Francis Gustave, 2/Lt., k. in a., 6/8/15 (att. 1 Bn.).
Fraser, Thomas, Lt., k. in a., 1/7/16.
3 Fulkes, John Greville, 2/Lt., k. in a., 13/11/16 (att. 13 Bn.).
12 Gabb, Richard George, 2/Lt. (Tp.), d. of w., 6/8/15 (att. 1 Bn.).
12 Gardom, John Charles, Lt. (Tp.), k. in a., 6/8/15 (att. 1 Bn.).
3 Garbutt, Lawrence Mark, Temp. 2/Lt., d. of w., 10/8/18 (att. 9/Nflk. Regt.).
1 Garvin, William Myles, Temp. 2/Lt., k. in a., 23/9/17.
13 Gemmell, George Manners, 2/Lt., k. in a., 13/11/16.
9 Gibbs, Cecil Thomas, Temp. 2/Lt., k. in a., 9/4/17.
1 Gidley, Frederick William, Lt., k. in a., 27/3/17 (att. 4 Bn.).
2 Gilbert, Frank William, 2/Lt., k. in a., 11/10/17.
13 Ginder, Thomas Wilfred, Temp. 2/Lt., k. in a., 21/3/18.
Girardot, Markham Henry, Capt., k. in a., 30/4/15.
3 Gladden, Leslie Charles, Lt., k. in a., 20/4/18 (att. 2 Bn.).
Godfrey-Faussett, Owen Godfrey, D.S.O., Lt.-Col., k. in a., 2/5/15.
2 Goodchild, Stanley Cecil, 2/Lt., k. in a., 1/7/16.
Goodyear, Frederick, Temp. 2/Lt., d. of w., 23/5/17 (att. 2 Bn.).
Graham, Ronald McLeod, 2/Lt., k. in a., 12/3/15 (att. R. Scots. Fusrs.).
1 Grant, Arch, T/Lt. (A/Capt.), k. in a., 30/11/17.
3 Grantham, Hugo Frederick, 2/Lt., k. in a., 28/6/15.
9 Griggs, Horace Edward, Capt. (Tp.), k. in a., 5/10/15.
11 Gulliland, John Hutchison, Temp. Capt., d. of w., 18/7/16.
10 Haile, Robert, M.C., Temp. Lt., d. of w., 29/10/18.
3 Haley, Arthur, 2/Lt., k. in a., 1/6/18 (and R.A.F.).
13 Hall, Edward Charles, 2/Lt., k. in a., 30/11/17.
11 Hammond, John Martin Richard, Lt., k. in a., 25/9/15.
Hare, Robert Stuart MacLaine, Capt., k. in a., 6/8/15.
3 Harris, Howard Kilbourne, M.C., Capt., k. in a., 22/2/18 (att. 11 Bn.).
2 Hart, Ernest, 2/Lt., k. in a., 26/10/18.
Hartley, William Guest, Temp. 2/Lt., d. of w., 8/8/18 (att. 9 Bn.).
10 Harvey, Phillip, 2/Lt. (A/Capt.), k. in a., 8/8/18.
2 Hasler, Leonard Melsome, Temp. Lt., d. of w., 21/9/17 (att. 17/M.G. Corps).
10 Hawkins, Herbert Edwin, Temp. Capt., k. in a., 1/7/16.
10 Hawksworth, Henry Charles, M.C., Lt., k. in a., 21/3/18.
9 Haworth, Thomas Eldred Curwen, Temp. 2/Lt., d. of w., 2/12/17.
2 Hayhurst, John, 2/Lt., k. in a., 19/4/18.
9 Hickox, Edwin Baskerville, M.C., Temp. Major, d. of w., 15/8/17.
9 Hickson, Reginald Davies, Temp. Capt., d. of w., 30/4/17.
3 Hight, Norman Dudley John, M.C., 2/Lt., k. in a., 24/3/18 (att. 10 Bn.).
9 Hill, Jeremiah Charles Holmes, Temp. 2/Lt., d. of w., 2/5/17.
2 Hobbs, Gerald Parker, 2/Lt., d. of w., 15/10/17.
3 Hobday, Charles Frederick, A/Capt., d. of w., 1/12/17 (att. 1 Bn.).
2 Holmes, Aubrey, Temp. 2/Lt., k. in a., 1/7/16.
3 Hornung, Arthur Oscar, 2/Lt., k. in a., 6/7/15 (att. 2 Bn.).
3 Horwood, Ronald Bentall, 2/Lt., k. in a., 1/7/16 (att. 1 Bn.).
1/2 Howard, Guy Robert, D.S.O., Major, died, 23/10/18 (and R.A.F.).

7961

K 2

3 Howard, John Allan, Lt., d. of w., 9/5/18 (att. 1 Bn.).
12 Howis, Francis Thackeray, 2/Lt. (Tp.), d. of w., 8/12/15 (att. 6/Lincs. Regt.).
10 Hudson, Harold Edwin, 2/Lt. (Tp.), k. in a., 27/9/15.
3 Hughes, John Walter, 2/Lt., k. in a., 8/10/18 (att. 1 Bn.).
Hunt, Arthur Warner, 2/Lt. (Tp.), d. of w., 28/4/18 (att. 11 Bn.).
11 Hunt, Ralph Leslie, Temp. 2/Lt., k. in a., 15/10/16.
12 Hunt, Sidney William, 2/Lt. (Tp.), k. in a., 26/10/16 (att. 13 Bn.).
10 Hunt, William George Philip, M.C., Capt. (Tp.), d. of w., 15/8/17.
2 Ide, Thomas Norman, 2/Lt., k. in a., 2/7/16.
Ilieve, William Arthur, 2/Lt., k. in a., 9/10/17 (att. 2 Bn.).
12 Jarvis, Archibald Thomas, Lt. (Tp.), died, 24/9/16 (att. 1/Yorks. L. Inf.).
13 Jenns, Frank Arthur, 2/Lt. (Tp.), d. of w., 6/4/18.
Johnson, Robert Harold Jervis, 2/Lt., k. in a., 13/3/15.
Jones, Lumley Owen Williames, D.S.O., Temp. Brig.-Gen., died, 14/9/18 (Staff).
3 Keell, Herbert Alfred, 2/Lt., k. in a., 9/10/17 (att. 2 Bn.).
Kennefick, Edward Hamerton, Capt., k. in a., 8/7/16.
3 Kennefick, John George Hamerton, Capt., k. in a., 20/4/18 (att. 2 Bn.).
Kent, Ernest, Temp. Lt., d. of w., 8/4/17 (and R.F.C., 24 Sqd.).
11 Keys, Joseph Nicholas Douglas, M.C., Lt. (A/Capt.), k. in a., 21/9/17.
King, Harry Garfield, 2/Lt. (Tp.), k. in a., 26/4/18 (att. 10 Bn.).
11 Kinsley, Lawrence Millais, 2/Lt., k. in a., 15/10/16.
2 Kirk, Thomas James, 2/Lt., d. of w., 2/7/16.
1 Kortright, Mountney Coesvelt William, Lt., k. in a., 21/5/17.
Knight, William Leonard, Temp. Lt., died, 26/2/19 (att. 2 Bn.).
3 Lane, Ernest Albert, 2/Lt., k. in a., 1/9/18 (att. 2 Bn.).
10 Lawrence, Francis Alfred John, 2/Lt., k. in a., 12/4/18.
3 Lawrie, John Charles, Capt. & Hon. Major, died, 7/5/15.
Legg, Frederick William, Temp. 2/Lt., k. in a., 9/10/17.
Liddell, Robert, 2/Lt., died, 24/1/19 (att. 1/7 Bn.).
12 Linford, Ivor Hutchison, M.C., Capt. (Tp.), k. in a., 21/3/18.
11 Long, Frank Stevenson, Temp. Lt., k. in a., 26/9/15.
3 Longton, Edward John, 2/Lt., k. in a., 6/6/15 (att. 1 Bn.).
Loxley, Charles Eric Smart, T/Capt., died, 18/12/18 (att. M.G.C.).
Lukis, Leofwin Collings Fellowes, 2/Lt., k. in a., 6/1/17 (and R.F.C., 27 Sqd.).
11 Lyne, Cyril Lionel Bishop, 2/Lt., k. in a., 13/11/16.
Macaskill, George Hasken, 2/Lt., died, 4/7/18 (and R.A.F.).
1 McLean, William James, 2/Lt., d. of w., 12/8/16.
11 Macmichael, Michael William Annesley, Capt., d. of w., 16/9/16.
McMurdo, John Coke, Capt., k. in a., 25/4/15.
2 McNeill, John Charles, 2/Lt., k. in a., 3/5/17.
Mantz, Victor Frank, Temp. 2/Lt., k. in a., 25/10/18.
Markham-Rose, Kenneth, Lt., k. in a., 3/5/15 (and W. Afr. Front. Fce.).
12 Markwick, Frederick Thomas, Temp. 2/Lt., k. in a., 6/8/15 (att. 1 Bn.).
13 Mason, Douglas Howard, 2/Lt., k. in a., 28/4/17.
9 Maxwell Clyde Fairbanks, 2/Lt., k. in a., 3/7/16.
10 Mears, Edward de Quincey, Temp. 2/Lt., k. in a., 13/7/16.
12 Meynell, Hugo Charles, Temp. 2/Lt., d. of w., 27/9/15.
12 Middleditch, Archibald Milne, Lt., k. in a., 1/7/16.
2 Miller, George William, 2/Lt., k. in a., 15/12/17.
11 Moore, Andrew Douglas, Temp. 2/Lt., k. in a., 21/3/18.
3 Moore, Kenneth William James, 2/Lt., k. in a., 15/9/17 (att. 11 Bn.).
3 Morison, Alfred James, 2/Lt. (A/Capt.), k. in a., 20/11/17 (att. 1 Bn.).
9 Mott, Lewis Woodham, Temp. 2/Lt., k. in a., 23/4/17 (and R.F.C.).
Mullock, Sidney Goss, Act. Lt.-Col., k. in a., 12/4/17.
3 Munday, Edwin George Stanislaus, 2/Lt., k. in a., 20/2/17 (att. 13 Bn.).
11 Murray, Maurice Austin, Lt., k. in a, 25/9/15.
3 Nash, William Walter, 2/Lt., k. in a., 4/7/18 (att 2 Bn.).
3 Nichols, Alselan Buchanan, Lt., k. in a., 23/4/17 (att. 1 Bn., 88 T.M.B.).
Nixon, Oswald, 2/Lt., died, 17/9/16 (and R.F.C.).
12 Noble, Walter Frederick, 2/Lt. (Tp.), k. in a., 3/7/16 (att. 9 Bn.).
Northey, George Evelyn Anson, Lt., k. in a., 26/8/14.
2 Nunneley, Wilford Herbert, 2/Lt., k. in a., 24/4/18.
2 O'Halloran, Sylvester North East, A/Capt., k. in a., 9/8/17.
13 Ollett, Alfred Oscar, Temp. 2/Lt., k. in a., 27/4/16.
14 Orford, Ernest Victor Molson, 2/Lt., k. in a., 23/10/16 (att. 2 Bn.).
2 Osburn, Francis Cecil Trousdale, 2/Lt., d. of w., 17/5/17 (att. 9 Bn.).
1 Owen, Reginald Frank Leear, Lt. (T/Capt.), k. in a., 23/4/17 (att M.G.C., 88 Coy.).
13 Page, Bernard Robert, Lt., k. in a., 9/8/16
Page, Wilfred Frank, Temp. Capt., d. of w., 28/3/18 (att. 4 Bn.)
Parish, Albert Francis, 2/Lt., k. in a., 18/9/18 (att. 9 Bn.).
2 Parker, Leonard George, Capt., k. in a., 1/9/18.
3 Paterson, Leslie Arnott, 2/Lt., d. of w., 16/5/15 (att. R. Berks. Regt.).
3 Paterson, William Brown, M.C., 2/Lt., k. in a, 28/4/17 (att. 13 Bn.).
3 Payne Henry Tomkin, 2/Lt. k. in a., 6/8/15 (att. 1 Bn.).
9 Peake, Henry Arthur Wyatt, Capt., k. in a., 3/7/16.
13 Pearson, Laumarin Saxe William, Temp. 2/Lt., k. in a., 19/7/16 (att. 10 Bn.).
1 Perkins, Bernard St. George, Lt., k in a., 10/8/18 (att. 9 Bn.).
1 Peters, Frank Wesley, M.C., 2/Lt., k. in a., 18/7/17 (att. 9 Bn.).
9 Phillimore, Matthew Arden, Temp. 2/Lt., k. in a., 25/6/16 (att. R.E.).
Pierson, Roy, Temp. Lt., k. in a., 30/4/15.
10 Pochin, Arthur Campbell, Temp. 2/Lt., k. in a., 26/9/16.
1 Portway, Lionel Felix, 2/Lt., k. in a., 14/4/17.
2 Powley, Joseph, Temp. 2/Lt., k. in a., 3/5/17.
1 Preston, Sidney, Temp. Lt., k in a., 10/4/18 (98 Tr. Res. Bn. att.).
11 Radclyffe, Charles Edward, Lt.-Col., k. in a., 25/9/15.
3 Raikes, John Francis, 2/Lt., k. in a., 11/10/16 (att. 9 Bn.).
Raleigh, George Hebden, Bt.-Major, killed, 20/1/15 (and R.F.C.).
Rayner, George Biddulph, 2/Lt., k. in a., 12/5/15 (att Glouc. Regt.).
11 Raynes, Albert Herbert, Lt., k. in a., 25/9/15.
11 Read, John Frederick Cullingford, 2/Lt. (Tp.), k. in a., 28/9/15.
11 Read, Leonard St. Clair, Temp. 2/Lt., died, 20/12/16 (P. of W.).
1 Read, Lawrence William, Temp. Lt., k. in a., 9/12/16.
9 Rees, Andrew Montgomery, Lt., k. in a., 18/10/16.
12 Reeve, Gilford Montier, Capt., k. in a., 8/7/16.
1 Reid, Gordon Alexander, Temp. 2/Lt., k. in a., 8/10/18.
2 Renton, Alan John, Capt., k. in a., 2/12/17.
1 Revell, Robert Arthur, Capt., d. of w., 13/6/15.
10 Richards, Henry Stokes, 2/Lt., died, 1/8/18 (and R.A.F.).
3 Ridgwell, Sydney Causton, 2/Lt., k. in a., 2/11/17 (att. 1/7 Bn.).
10 Ridley, Christopher Mellor, Temp. Capt., k. in a., 31/10/16.
13 Ritson, Claude Wilson, Temp. 2/Lt. (A/Capt.), k. in a., 28/4/17.
11 Roberts, Edmund Percy, Temp. Lt., k. in a., 21/3/18.
Robertson, Charles Granville, Temp. 2/Lt., k. in a., 27/3/18 (att. 2/Northants Regt).
2 Robertson, Magnus Rainer, M.C., Temp. Capt., d. of w., 22/8/18 (att. 11 Bn.).
3 Rose, Arthur Hugh Percy, Capt., k. in a., 23/11/14.
13 Ross, George Harry Thornton, 2/Lt., k. in a., 9/8/16.
Round, Auriol Francis Hay, Lt., d of w., 5/9/14.
Round, James Murray, Capt., k. in a., 13/11/16.
Rowley, Joseph Albert, Temp. 2/Lt., k. in a., 26/10/18 (att. 10 Bn.).
1 Russell, Henry Branfill, Temp. Lt., d. of w., 11/7/16.
Ryan, Clement Ignatius, Major, k. in a., 8/7/16 (att. 9 Bn.).
Sammut, Herbert Joseph, Major, k. in a., 2/5/15.
3 Savage, Gerald Roderick, Lt. (Tp. Capt.), d. of w., 4/10/17.
3 Savill, Ronald John, 2/Lt., k. in a., 30/4/17 (att. 9 Bn.).
Searson, Harold William, 2/Lt., d. of w., 17/6/17.
3 Shandley, Robert Newlyn, 2/Lt., k. in a., 22/8/18 (att. 9 Bn.).
3 Shedel, Rupert Frederick, 2/Lt., k. in a., 12/10/16 (att. 1 Bn.).
3 Sheffield, George Nelson, Major, died, 1/1/18.
Shepheard, Philip, Capt., k. in a., 13/6/15.
3 Showers, St. George Swaine, Lt., k. in a., 9/8/17 (att. 2 Bn.).
9 Sievers, Nowell Johnstone, Capt. (Tp.), k. in a., 30/11/17.
3 Silver, Sidney Edwin, Temp. Lt., k. in a., 20/11/17 (att. 11 Bn.)
Skelton, Benjamin Dowell, Temp. 2/Lt., d. of w., 7/11/18 (att. 10 Bn.).
2 Smith, Leonard George, 2/Lt., k. in a., 1/7/16.
Smith-Masters, Bruce Swinton, Capt., k. in a., 1/7/16.
Songhurst, Charles Edward, Temp. 2/Lt., k. in a., 22/8/18 (Res., att. 9 Bn.).
3 Stoddart-MacLelland, Chaltair Ruaridh Alwinn Domhnuill, Capt. & Hon. Major, died, 30/11/14.
13 Stokes, Clifford, 2/Lt., k. in a., 18/2/17.
12 Straight, Marshall Stuart, Temp. 2/Lt., k. in a., 24/12/15 (att. 1 Bn.).
Strange, Lionel Cresswell, 2/Lt. (Tp.), d. of w., 22/7/17 (att. 9 Bn.).
Stroud, Stephen George, Temp. 2/Lt., d. of w., 13/10/18 (Res., att. 9 Bn.).
Sturgess, G. M., 2/Lt., killed, 5/4/18 (and R.A.F.).
3 Sweet, Frederick Gordon, Lt., k. in a., 26/3/17 (att. 4 Bn.).
2 Taber, Stacey James Hutley, 2/Lt., k. in a., 20/7/16.
2 Talbot, Arthur Charles, 2/Lt. (T/Lt.), d. of w., 17/7/15.
Taylor, Charles Stanley, 2/Lt. (Tp.), k. in a., 3/11/17.
2 Taylor, George Francis Woodland, 2/Lt., k. in a., 4/5/17.
Taylor, George Thomas, 2/Lt. (Tp.), k. in a., 2/11/17.
9 Tench, Montague Beavan, 2/Lt., k. in a., 10/3/16.
Thomas, Frederick George Byam, Lt., k. in a., 6/8/15.
3 Thompson, Walter Lincoln, 2/Lt., k. in a., 9/10/17 (att. 2 Bn.).
9 Thurburn, Augustus Edward Charlie Sedgwick, 2/Lt. (A/Capt.), k. in a., 28/5/17.
2 Tokely, Reginald Cyrus, 2/Lt., d. of w., 23/12/16.
Touche, Eric Percy Johnstone, 2/Lt., died, 17/5/18 (and R.A.F.).
Turner, Douglas William, 2/Lt., died, 15/2/19.
10 Tween, Alfred Stuart, D.S.O., Temp. Major, k. in a., 23/3/18.
Vance, James, Lt., k. in a., 21/10/14.
Vandeleur, William Mountcharles Crofton, Capt., k. in a., 26/8/14.
3 Vowles, Stephen Foster, 2/Lt., k. in a., 28/4/17 (att. 13 Bn.).
2 Waldron, Fionn Thomas, 2/Lt., k. in a., 23/10/16.
10 Walker, Clarence Howard, Temp. 2/Lt., d. of w., 28/9/16 12th Bn.).
Walton, Hector Cyril, Temp. 2/Lt., k. in a., 9/9/17 (att. 8/R.W. Kent Rgt.).
Ward, Basil Mignot, Capt., k. in a., 3/5/15.
Ward, Hubert Henry, Temp. 2/Lt., k. in a., 19/9/18 (att. 1/4 Bn.).

12 Warden, Edmund Oscar, Capt., k. in a., 28/6/15.
3 Warner, Bernard Oldershaw, Lt., k. in a., 19/5/17 (att. 1 Bn.).
Waterhouse, Gilbert, 2/Lt., k. in a., 1/7/16.
9 Watts, Henry Leonard, Temp. Capt., k. in a., 20/10/15.
3 V.C. Wearne, Frank Bernard, 2/Lt., k. in a., 28/6/17 (att. 10 Bn.).
Wearne, Keith Morris, Capt., k. in a., 21/5/17.
11 Weatherdon, Sidney George, Temp. 2/Lt., k. in a., 19/9/17.
3 Whalley, Julian Lawson, Lt. (A/Capt.), d. of w., 3/12/17 (att. 9 Bn.).
12 Wheatley, Frank Rees, Temp. 2/Lt., k. in a., 11/8/16.
3 White, Herbert Robert, 2/Lt., k. in a., 1/7/16 (att. 2 Bn.).
3 Wilcock, Henry Blamires, Lt., k. in a., 13/11/16 (att. 13 Bn.).
12 Wilkinson, Hugh Wilmot, Temp. 2/Lt., k. in a., 18/7/16 (att. 11 Bn.)
3 Willmott, John Herbert Victor, M.C., Lt. (A/Capt.), k. in a., 28/3/18 (att. 2 Bn.).
9 Wilson, John Andrew Hackett, 2/Lt., d. of w., 19/9/18.
12 Wilson, Lewis, Temp. Capt. & Adjt., died, 27/11/16 (att. 9 Bn.).
Witcombe, Henry James, 2/Lt., k. in a., 23/8/18 (att. 1 Bn.).
1 Wood, Algernon George Newcome, D.S.O., Major, k. in a., 30/10/15.
Wood, Creighton Arthur Bell, Lt., k. in a., 28/6/15.
10 Wood, James, 2/Lt., d. of w., 11/8/18.
Wright, Sydney John, 2/Lt., k. in a., 23/8/18.
12 Wright, Vivian Arthur Butler, Temp. 2/Lt., k. in a., 3/12/15 (att. 6/Lincs. Regt.).
9 Yardley, William, 2/Lt., d. of w., 30/4/17.

The Sherwood Foresters (Nottinghamshire and Derbyshire Regiment).

4 Abbott, Ernest Henry Fortescue, M.C., Lt., k. in a., 9/7/18 (att. 2nd Bn.).
4 Adams, Percy Horace, 2/Lt., k. in a., 3/10/18 (att. 1st Bn.).
2 Allen, Maurice Reginald, 2/Lt. (Tp.), k. in a., 13/9/16.
9 Allpass, Esmond Theodore, 2/Lt. (Tp.), k. in a., 21/8/15.
Anson, George Lechmere, Capt., k. in a., 20/10/14.
14 Appleyard, Richard, Lt. (Tp.), k. in a., 4/8/16 (att. 10th Bn.).
Ash, Basil Claudius, Lt., k. in a., 20/9/14.
Atkin, Jesse Marson, Lt., k. in a., 7/11/14 (att. Worcs.).
Backhouse, Hubert Edmund, Capt. (Acting), k. in a., 15/10/16 (att. 2nd Bn.).
10 Baker, Colin Claud, 2/Lt. (Tp.), d. of w., 12/5/17.
Barker, Herbert Leslie, 2/Lt., k. in a., 22/3/18 (att. 12th Bn.).
10 Barker, Robert Arnold, M.C., T/Lt. (A/Capt.), d. of w., 13/10/18.
4 Barnes, Basil Goodall, Lt., d. of w., 19/8/18.
1 Baron, Sydney Percival, 2/Lt., k. in a., 5/7/16.
11 Bartlett, Cyril Ward, M.C., Capt. (Tp.), k. in a., 9/10/18.
13 Bassano, Edward Arthur, 2/Lt. (Tp.), k. in a., 1/10/16 (att. 11th Bn.).
Bavin, William, 2/Lt. (Tp.), k. in a., 29/9/18 (att. 6th Bn.).
19 Bayzand, Alec, 2/Lt. (Tp.), k. in a., 10/10/16 (att. 16th Bn.).
1 Beal, Edward Gerald, Lt. (Tp.), d. of w., 6/11/18 (att. 8th Bn.).
2 Beanland, George Edward, 2/Lt., k. in a., 30/4/17.
Bell, Colin, 2/Lt. (Tp.), k. in a., 29/10/17 (att. 15th Bn.).
13 Bellamy, John Holland, 2/Lt. (Tp.), d. of w., 4/10/16 (att. 11th Bn.).
16 Benner, Walter, Lt. (Tp.), k. in a., 2/9/18.
3 Bennett, Vere Raymond, Lt., k. in a., 10/4/17 (att. M.G.C., 64th Coy.).
13 Bentley, Arthur Fletcher, 2/Lt. (Tp.), d. of w., 11/3/16 (att. 10th Bn.).
19 Benton, John Walford, 2/Lt. (Tp.), k. in a., 28/9/16 (att. 11th Bn.).
Bernard, Lawrence Arthur, Lt., k. in a., 20/9/14.
17 Betts, Thomas Walter, 2/Lt. (Tp.), k. in a., 31/7/17.
Bewley, Frederick Norman, 2/Lt. (Tp.), k. in a., 20/9/17 (att. 16th Bn.).
Binney, Edward Hibbert, 2/Lt. (A/Lt. & Adj.), died, 11/10/17.
1 Bion, Kenneth Norman, M.C., Lt. (A/Capt.), k. in a., 21/3/18.
11 Bird, Basil William, M.C., Capt. (Tp.), d. of w., 24/11/18.
19 Black, Tom, 2/Lt. (Tp.), k. in a., 18/9/16 (att. 17th Bn.).
9 Black, Thomas Porteous, Capt. (Tp.), k. in a., 9/8/15.
9 Blackburne, John George, Major (Tp.), k. in a., 22/8/15 (Lt., Res. of Off.).
Blagg, Sidney, 2/Lt. (Tp.), k. in a., 29/7/18.
12 Boden, Hugh Charles Wollaston, Capt. (Tp.), k. in a., 11/10/15.
Blurton, Cyril Evers, 2/Lt., k. in a., 22/10/17 (att. 15th Bn.).
17 Bolton, Geoffrey Charles, 2/Lt., k. in a., 1/8/16.
19 Bond, Bernard, Lt. (Tp.), d. of w., 2/8/16 (att. 11th Btn.).
12 Borman, George Wilson, Lt. (Tp.), d. of w., 2/1/16.
4 Boothroyd, Edwin, 2/Lt., d. of w., 21/3/18 (in German hands) (att. 26th Btn.).
9 Bosanquet, Lionel Arthur, Lt.-Col. (Tp.), k. in a., 22/8/15.
16 Bower, Charles Francis, T/Lt. (A/Capt.), k. in a., 13/9/17.
3 Bowers, Thomas James, Lt.. k. in a., 7/11/16 (att. 7th L.N. Lancs).
Boyd, Stuart, Lt., d. of w., 7/10/16 (att. 1st L.N. Lancs).
17 Bracewell, Harry, 2/Lt. (Tp.), d. of w., 21/9/17.
Bradley, W. R., Lt., died, 29/6/18 (and R.A.F.).
1 Brewer, Wilfred Aubrey, Lt. (Tp.), k. in a., 21/11/17.
15 Bridgewater, Samuel Ernest, 2/Lt. (Tp.), k. in a., 29/3/16.
3 Bright, Archibald Viccars, Lt., k. in a., 7/6/17 (att. 11th Bn.).
4 Bright, Harold Viccars, 2/Lt., k. in a., 21/9/18.
2 Brittain, Edward Harold, M.C., Lt. (T/Capt.), k. in a., 15/6/18 (att. 11th Btn.).
17 Brookfield, Sydney Freeman, Capt. (Tp.), k. in a., 3/9/16
2 Brown, Ernest, Lt. (A/Capt.), k. in a., 20/11/17.
Browne, Arthur George, 2/Lt., k. in a., 20/10/14.
17 Buck, Bertram, Lt. (Tp.), k. in a., 3/9/16.
17 Bullivant, Alfred James, 2/Lt. (Tp.), d of w., 21/7/16.
4 Buntine, Walter Horace Carlisle, M.C., 2/Lt., killed, 19/6/17 (and R F.C.).
Burdekin, Geoffrey Eric, 2/Lt., k. in a., 26/1/15 (att. N. Lancs Rgt.).
3 Burrows, Percival Ernest, M.C., Lt., k. in a., 19/9/18 (att 2nd Btn. 3rd Gurkha Rfs., I.A.).
1 Burt, Frank William, 2/Lt., k. in a., 5/7/16.
Burton, Richard, Lt., d. of w., 24/6/15.
15 Burton, Francis Hugh, 2/Lt. (Tp.), k. in a., 14/10/18.
4 Byles, Arthur Benzeville, 2/Lt. (A/Capt.), d. of w.. 11/12/17 (att. 2nd Btn.).
2 Callaway, Robert Furley, 2/Lt., k. in a., 13/9/16.
Callingham, Frank Reginald, T/2/Lt., died, 26/2/19 (att. 10 Bn.).
9 Carey, Henry Pattison, Lt. (Tp.), k. in a., 7-11/8/15.
17 Carr, Charles Frederick, 2/Lt., d. of w., 20/2/17 (att. 4th Bn.).
11 Carter, Sydney Chatterton, 2/Lt. (Tp.), d. of w., 3/7/16.
12 Carty, Bertram Samuel, 2/Lt. (Tp.), k. in a., 21/8/16.
11 Cavell, Hubert John, Lt. (Tp.), d. of w., 22/4/17.
10 Chandler, Edwin Spencer, 2/Lt. (Tp.), k. in a., 14/2/16.
16 Chappell, Francis Harold, 2/Lt. (Tp.), k. in a., 3/9/16.
Chatteris, Tom Brodie, Capt. (Tp.), k. in a., 9/8/15 (att. 2nd Bn.).
Clark, Anthony Dalzell, Capt. (Tp.), d. of w., 4/12/17.
3 Clark, Reginald William, 2/Lt. (Tp.), k. in a., 19/8/17 (att. 17th Bn.).
Clarkson, Donald James, 2/Lt., k. in a., 9/8/18 (att. 6th Bn.).
2 Cleveland, Alfred Sherwood, 2/Lt., k. in a., 16/10/16.
13 Cleveland, Ernest Herbert, 2/Lt., k. in a., 31/7/16 (att. 8th York & Lanc. Regt.).
3 Clulow, Frederick Reginald, 2/Lt., d. of w., 24/4/18 (att. 1st Bn.).
15 Collier, Frederick Herbert Mark, Lt. (Tp.), k. in a., 23/4/17.
13 Collins, Vivian Donald Berry, Lt., k. in a., 9/5/15.
2 Connor, Amos Lloyd, 2/Lt., d. of w., 30/6/17.
4 Cook, Cyril Ramsay, 2/Lt., k. in a., 9/6/17 (att. 9th Bn.).
16 Cooke, James Gore, Capt., k. in a., 8/10/16.
2 Cooke, William Henry, 2/Lt., k. in a., 9/8/15.
Cooper, Percy Newbery, Lt. (Tp.), d. of w., 6/7/16.
Copland, Dudley Charles James, 2/Lt., k. in a., 9/5/15.
2 Corless, John Stanley, 2/Lt. (Tp.), k. in a., 17-19/9/18.
3 Cotterell, B. W., 2/Lt., k. in a., 30/10/18 (att. R.A.F.).
13 Cousins, Eric Cyril, 2/Lt., k. in a., 21/3/18 (att. 2nd Btn.).
3 Cox, Charles Frederick, Lt., k. in a., 31/3/18.
10 Cox, Clarence Frederick Stuart, M.C., Lt. (Tp.), k. in a. 29/10/17.
3 Coxon, William Hugh, 2/Lt, k. in a., 11/3/15.
13 Crawford, John Russell, 2/Lt., d. of w., 27/9/16 (att. 9th Btn.).
Crellin, William Anderson Watson, D.S.O., Capt. (T/Lt.-Col.), d. of w., 8/10/18.
14 Croggan, Josiah Fenwick Sibree, Capt. (Tp.), died, 18/11/18 (att. 10th Btn.).
3 Crowther, William Osborne, 2/Lt. (Tp.), k. in a., 24/11/16 (att. 9th Bn.).
Cutts, Thomas Bernard, Capt. (Tp.), k. in a., 20/7/16.
1 Daniels, C. W., 2/Lt. (Tp.), died, 4/11/18.
13 Davidson, Charles Lingard, 2/Lt., k. in a., 6/8/15.
4 Davidson, John Whitworth, Lt., d. of w., 5/3/17 (att. 10th Bn.).
4 Davis, Wallace Heward, 2/Lt., k. in a., 1/7/17 (att. 2nd Bn.)
11 Davis, Walter Arthur, 2/Lt. (Tp.). k. in a., 1/7/16.
10 Davis, William Rhys Lancelot, T/Lt. (A/Capt.), k. in a., 23/4/17.
1 Dawson, Leonard Leslie, Lt. (Tp.), k. in a., 27/5/18.
16 Dawson, Niel Creaton, 2/Lt. (Tp.), d. of w., 12/7/16.
10 Day, Shirley Cuthbert, M.C., T/Lt. (A/Capt.), k. in a., 12/10/17.
15 Denison, William Frank Evelyn, 2/Lt. (Tp.), d. of w., 22-28/3/18.
17 Dennis, Frederick Claude, 2/Lt. (Tp.), k. in a., 1/8/16.
Dick, George Frederick Graeme, 2/Lt., k. in a., 9/5/15.
15 Dickerson, Jersey Horrex, 2/Lt. (Tp.), k. in a., 22/4/18.
12 Dickins, Wyndham Harold, Capt. (Tp.), d. of w., 28/9/15.
3 Dicksee, Lawrance Rowland Arthur, 2/Lt., killed, 2/5/16.
Dilworth, Maclean Proctor, Lt., k. in a., 20/10/14.
Dixon, Hubert Bradshaw, Capt., k. in a., 12/3/15.
15 Dixon, William Francis Trevor, 2/Lt. (Tp.). k. in a., 20/7/16.
14 Don, Daird Fairweather, 2/Lt. (Tp.), k. in a., 1/7/16 (att. 2nd Btn.) (att. S. Wales Bord.).
10 Dorrington, Percy, 2/Lt. (T/Lt.), k. in a., 12/10/17.
2 Dove, Percy Matthew, Major, k. in a., 15/5/15.
9 Downman, Bernard Vincent Ridout, (2/Lt.) (Tp.), k. in a., 21/9/16 (att. 13th Btn.).
11 Drake, Leonard, 2/Lt. (Tp.), d. of w., 5/10/16.
Dunkin, Alfred Davy Hosking, 2/Lt. (Tp.), k. in a., 3/10/18 (att. 1/8th).
3 Durrant, John, Lt. (Tp.), died, 17/10/18.
Dye, Norman Sawford, 2/Lt., k. in a., 25/3/18 (att. 16th Btn.).
Earle, John Vincent. Lt., k. in a., 20/6/15 (and W.A.F.F.).
10 Eastwood, John William, 2/Lt. (Tp.), killed, 28/1/18.
10 Ebery, Wilfred, 2/Lt. (Tp.), k in a., 14/2/16.
9 Egerton, Bertram Gustavus, 2/Lt. (Tp.), d. of w., 8/9/16.
Elleray, Robert Lincoln, 2/Lt. (Tp.), k. in a., 18/4/18.
Elly, Cyril John, 2/Lt. (Tp.), d. of w., 6/9/18 (att. 1/8th Bn.).
17 Else, William Edwin, T/Lt. (A/Capt.), k. in a., 3/1/18.
11 Evans, John William, 2/Lt. (Tp.), d. of w., 10/4/17.
9 Everard, Clement Charlie, Lt. (Tp.), k. in a., 7/9/16.
9 Ewin, Arthur, Hon. Lt. & Q.-Mr., k. in a., 7-11/8/15.
2 Eyre, Harry, 2/Lt., k. in a., 17/9/18.
14 Fellows, Richard Woodhouse, Lt. (Tp.), k. in a., 15/9/16.

9 Fielding, George Rudolf, Major (Tp.), k. in a., 24/7/15.
Fielding, S., Lt. & Qr.-Mr., died, 12/11/14.
10 Fisher, John Wilfred, D.S.O., Capt. (Tp.), d. of w., 8/7/16.
Fletcher, Tom Walter, 2/Lt., k. in a., 26/9/17 (att. 2/5th Bn.).
19 Fox, Frederick Donald, 2/Lt. (Tp.), k. in a., 5/11/16 (att. 17 Bn.).
Frend, William Reginald, Capt. k. in a., 20/9/14.
3 Furness, Godfrey Gordon, 2/Lt., k. in a., 9/2/17 (att. 2nd Bn.).
Gabriel, Allan, Lt. (Tp.), d. of w., 23/8/16 (105 Trench Mortar Bty.).
11 Garrett, William Robert, 2/Lt., died, 6/5/19.
3 Gleave, Harold Mason, Capt., k. in a., 6/3/17 (att. 1st Bn.).
3 Godwin, Leslie Wentworth, 2/Lt., k. in a., 10/10/16 (att. 16th Btn.).
Goodall, George Percy, Capt. (Tp.), k. in a., 14/2/16.
16 Grant, James, M.C., 2/Lt. (Tp.), k. in a., 23/10/18 (att. 8th R. Berks R.).
4 Graves, Francis George, 2/Lt., k. in a., 20/9/17 (att. 16th Bn.).
10 Gregory, Reuben Henry, M.C., Capt. (Tp.), k. in a., 9/6/17.
4 Grounds, Keble, 2/Lt., d. of w., 15/9/16 (att. 2nd Bn.).
3 Gunn, Ronald William Craig, 2/Lt., k. in a., 6/1/17 (att. 12th Bn.).
Hacking, Walter William, 2/Lt., k. in a., 21/3/18 (att. 2/8th Btn.).
Haddon, Harwood Albert, 2/Lt. (Tp.), k. in a., 26/9/17 (att. 2/8th Btn.).
15 Haines, Alfred Godfrey, Lt. (Tp.), d. of w., 22/4/17.
1 Hall, Harford Greville, 2/Lt. (T/Lt.), k. in a., 4/3/17.
10 Hall-Brown, John, Major (Tp.), k. in a., 7/7/16.
15 Hallam, Robert Samuel, 2/Lt., k. in a., 20/7/16.
20 Handford, John Willis, 2/Lt. (Tp.), d. of w., 24/3/18.
13 Harris, Hamilton Snow, Capt. (Tp.), k. in a., 1/7/16 (att. 11th Btn.).
Harris, Leslie George Hamlyn, 2/Lt., k. in a., 2/11/14.
5 Harrison, Lionel Joseph Briggs, Capt. (Tp.), k. in a., 27/3/18 (att. 16th Bn.).
16 Hart, Conway John, Lt. (Tp.), k. in a., 10/10/16.
1 Helmore, Ernest Creswell, 2/Lt., d. of w., 1/1/17 (att. 15th Bn.).
15 Henstock, Arthur Frank Newman, M.C., Capt., k. in a., 22/3/18.
13 Henley, Frederick Louis, 2/Lt. (Tp.), k. in a., 1/10/16 (att. 11th Bn.).
9 Hind, Jesse Francis Montague, Lt. (Tp.), k. in a., 27/9/16.
2 Hobbs, Charles James Willoughby, D.S.O., Major, d. of w., 16/10/16.
10 Hodding, Henry Ellis, M.C., Lt. (Tp.), d. of w., 8/11/18.
15 Hodgkinson, James Percival, Capt. (Tp.), k. in a., 2/11/16.
15 Hodgson, Arthur Dawson, Lt. (Tp.), k. in a., 20/7/16.
Hodgson, Maurice Kirkham, Capt., d. of w., 12/3/15.
Hofmeyr, Jan Hendrik, 2/Lt. (Tp.), k. in a., 27/10/17 (att. 1/8 Bn.).
Hogan, Arthur Alan, Lt. (Tp.), k. in a., 24/1/18 (att. 15th Bn.).
3 Holland, Frederick, 2/Lt., d. of w., 22/8/17.
15 Holmes, George Francis Edwin, 2/Lt. (Tp.), k. in a., 25/10/16.
15 Homan, Russell Charles, Lt. (Tp.), k. in a., 22/3/18.
17 Hopewell, Robert George, Capt. (Tp.), k. in a., 3/9/16.
3 Horwitz, Samuel Salmen, Lt., killed, 21/10/16 (att. L.N. Lancs. Rgt.).
11 Hotson, William Hugh McIntosh, 2/Lt. (Tp.), k. in a., 10/9/18.
16 Houghton, Noel, T/Major (A/Lt.-Col.), k. in a., 13/9/17.
1 Hovell, Mark, 2/Lt. (Tp.), k. in a., 12/8/16.
Howard, Kenneth Salwey, Lt. (T/Capt.), k. in a., 6/10/18 (att. 1st).
3 Hoyle, Geoffrey Morgan, Lt., k. in a., 9/8/15 (att. 2nd Bn.).
Hudson, Henry Erris, 2/Lt., k. in a., 18/6/18 (att. 9th Bn.).
10 Hutcheson, John, 2/Lt. (Tp.), k. in a., 8/9/15.
4 Huyton, John, 2/Lt., k. in a., 28/5/17 (att. 51 T.M.B.).
13 Hyrons, Francis Austin, 2/Lt. (Tp.), k. in a., 13/9/16 (att. 2nd Bn.).
Ideson, J. H., 2/Lt. (Tp.), killed, 13/3/17 (and R.F.C.).
4 Inchbold, Gerald, Lt., k. in a., 31/5/17 (and R.F.C., 55th Sqd.).
2 Irwin, Thomas Whitmore Crommelin, Lt., d. of w., 31/10/18.
15 Jackson, Edward Cecil, Lt. (Tp.), k. in a., 30/5/16.
11 Jackson, John William, Lt. (Tp.), k. in a., 17/10/17.
1 Johnson, Raymond Albert, M.C., Lt. (Tp.), k. in a., 24/4/18.
Jones, Oliver Saint Michael, Lt. (Tp.), k. in a., 4/10/17 (att. 9th Bn.).
10 Joyce, Frank Bernard, M.C., Capt. (Tp.), k. in a., 21/4/18.
Kay, George Alexander, 2/Lt. (Tp.), k. in a., 9/8/15.
15 Keating, John Baker, 2/Lt. (Tp.), k. in a., 20/7/16.
Kennedy, Charles Seccombe, Capt., killed, 22/8/16 (att. R.E.).
16 Kerr, Adam, Capt. (Tp.), d. of w., 3/11/18.
3 Kerrich, Henry Latham, Lt., d. of w., 27/9/17.
9 Kilner, Thomas Richard Burgess, 2/Lt. (Tp.), k. in a., 18/6/18.
King, Richard Henry, 2/Lt. (Tp.), k. in a., 27/6/17 (att. 12th Bn.).
3 Kirby, Alexander Claude, 2/Lt., k. in a., 24/7/18 (att. 1/5th Btn.).
4 Kitching, George Allenby, 2/Lt., k. in a., 22/4/18 (att. 10th Btn.).
3 Knight, Albert James, M.C., 2/Lt., d. of w., 2/6/17 (att. 11th Btn.).
17 Langford, Arthur Hector Allan, 2/Lt. (Tp.), d. of w., 1/8/16.
12 Langsdale, William Anthony, M.M., 2/Lt. (Tp.), k. in a., 22/3/18.
14 Lauria, Jack Victor, 2/Lt. (Tp.), d. of w., 18/6/16 (att. R.E.).
Laws, Casil William, Lt. (Tp.), k. in a., 27/5/18.
16 Laws, Philip Umfreville, M.C., Capt. (Tp.), k. in a., 20/9/17.
16 Lehfeldt, William Robert Alexander, Lt. (Tp.), d. of w., 11/10/16.
16 Lifetree, Ernest Henry, 2/Lt. (Tp.), k. in a., 20/5/16.
17 Littlewood, George Patrick, Capt. (Tp.), k. in a., 3/9/16.
11 Longhurst, Seaward, 2/Lt. (Tp.), k. in a., 1/7/16.
2 Loveday, Claude Godfrey, 2/Lt., k. in a., 10/10/16.
Lowcock, R. J., M.C., Major, died, 22/7/18 (and R.A.F.).
McClelland, William Alan, Major (Tp.), d. of w., 18/1/18 (att. 15th Btn.).
10 McCombe, William Joseph Pogue, 2/Lt. (Tp.), k. in a., 23/4/17.
9 McCormack, Joseph Francis, Capt. (Tp.), k. in a., 4/10/17.
15 Machutcheon, John Chisholm, 2/Lt. (Tp.), d. of w., 2/8/16.
Marriott, Geoffrey Vaughan, 2/Lt., k. in a., 22/4/18 (att. 1st Bn.).
2 Martin, Frederick Arthur, 2/Lt. (Tp.), d. of w., 7/9/15.
1 Mastin, Frank, 2/Lt. (Tp.), k. in a., 2/11/17 (1st Garr. Bn. att. 1/4th Bn. Northampton R.).
9 Mayo, William Charles, Lt. (Tp.), k. in a., 7-11/8/15.
Meads, John Arthur, M.C., Capt. (Tp.) (A/Major), k. in a., 10/10/17.
15 Medcalf, William Archer, 2/Lt. (Tp.), d. of w., 15/10/17.
Meek, William, 2/Lt. (Tp.), k. in a., 17-19/9/18.
2 Mellor, Frank Johnson, Lt., d. of w., 19/9/16.
13 Melville, Hugh Colquhoun, 2/Lt., k. in a., 14/2/16 (att. 10th Btn.).
11 Melville, Stuart Powis, 2/Lt. (Tp.), k. in a., 23/1/16.
10 Merrett, Harold Edmund, 2/Lt. (Tp.), d. of w., 17/8/18.
13 Miles, Robert William, Capt. (Tp.), k. in a., 1/6/17 (att. 11th Btn.).
Mills, Gerald Dermond, Capt. (T/Major), k. in a., 19/5/17 (att. R.F.C., 19th Sq.).
Milner, Roydenzil Pashley, 2/Lt., k. in a., 20/9/14.
3 Mitchell, George Clarkstone, 2/Lt., k. in a., 21/3/18.
Molloy, Michael Vallanery, 2/Lt., k. in a., 9/8/15.
1 Moore, Robert Frank, D.S.O., M.C., T/Lt. (A/Lt.-Col.), k. in a., 30/5/18.
3 Morris, Francis St. Vincent, 2/Lt., d. of w., 29/4/17 (and R.F.C.).
Morris, John Glynne, 2/Lt. (Tp.), d. of w., 23/9/17 (att. 16th Bn.).
2 Moult, Samuel Walker, 2/Lt., k. in a., 15/9/16.
Murray, Patrick Maxwell, Lt., k. in a., 20/9/14.
11 Napier, Henry Lenox, Major, k. in a., 17/11/15.
10 Nelson, William Horace Vere, Lt. (Tp.), d. of w., 8/7/16.
1 Neville, Charles, Capt. (Tp.), d. of w., 13/7/16.
2 Newman, Cuthbert Alan, 2/Lt. (Tp.), k. in a., 19/4/18 (att. 15th Bn.).
3 Nicholas, William John Worth, 2/Lt., drowned, 3/4/15 (and Nigeria R.).
12 Nichols, Eustace Alfred Morez, 2/Lt. (Tp.), k. in a., 20/7/16 (att. 15th Bn.).
9 Nicolls, Richard Jefferys, Capt. (Tp.), k. in a., 1/10/16.
2 Nicolson, Alexander, 2/Lt. (Tp.), k. in a., 13/5/18.
19 Norman, Gilford William, 2/Lt. (Tp.), k. in a., 25/9/16 (att. Leics. Regt.).
2 North, Robert Dudley, Lt. (Tp.), k. in a., 3/5/16 (att. 13th Bn.).
3 North-Cox, Wilfrid Herbert Marshall, 2/Lt., died, 2/3/16.
10 Oakden, Edward Ralph, Capt. (Tp.), d. of w., 22/3/17.
9 Odell, William Ward, M.C., 2/Lt. (Tp.), k. in a., 4/10/17.
Orchard, Hugh Thomas, 2/Lt. (Tp.), k. in a., 20/8/17 (att. 15th Bn.).
Paddock, Henry Leslie, Major, k. in a., 23/3/18 (att. 4th E. Lancs. Rgt.).
16 Palfree, John William Bateman, 2/Lt., d. of w., 20/9/18 (att. 8th R. Berks. R.).
2 Palmer, Roger, Lt., d. of w., 13/8/15.
10 Parr, Denis Fillingham, 2/Lt., k. in a., 7/7/16.
2 Paterson, Robert Walker, M.C., 2/Lt., k. in a., 21-23/3/18.
4 Pattinson, Ernest, 2/Lt., k. in a., 31/7/17 (att. 1st Bn.).
14 Paull, Frederick Major, 2/Lt. (Tp.), k. in a., 27/11/15 (att. 9th Bn.).
Penfold, Bernard Hugh, 2/Lt. (Tp.), k. in a., 20-23/10/17 (att. 15th Bn.).
14 Pettigrew, Douglas St. George, 2/Lt. (Tp.), d. of w., 23/10/17 (att. 17th Bn.).
14 Picot, Philip Simons, Capt., k. in a., 11/7/15.
3 Picton, F. J. L., Lt., died, 6/2/18 (att. 1st Bn.).
15 Pollard, Wilfrid Downes, 2/Lt. (Tp.), d. of w., 26/4/18.
10 Pratt, Neville Herbert, Capt. (Tp.), d. of w., 8/7/16.
15 Price, Stanley Hastings, M.C., 2/Lt. (Tp.), k. in a., 24/1/18.
10 Ramsay, David Winson, Lt. (Tp.), k. in a., 14/2/16.
9 Randall, Charles Deschamps, Capt. (Tp.), k. in a., 7-11/8/15.
17 Renshaw, Frank, 2/Lt. (Tp.), k. in a., 12/7/16.
2 Reynolds, Frank, 2/Lt. (Tp.), k. in a., 13/9/16 (att. T.M.B.).
11 Reynolds, Frank Leslie, 2/Lt. (Tp.), k. in a., 20/7/16 (att. 15th).
2 Ridley, Hector, 2/Lt., k. in a., 9/8/15.
3 Robb, Henry Alexander, Lt., k. in a., 10/7/17 (att. 1st L.N. Lancs.).
Robinson, Arthur Owen, 2/Lt., k. in a., 21/3/18 (att. 2/8th Batt.).
Roe, John George, 2/Lt., k. in a., 26/9/17 (att. 2/8th Btn.).
1 Rogers, Henry Peverell, Lt., k. in a., 5/7/16.
13 Romilly, Cosmo George, Lt. (Tp.), k. in a., 11/8/15 (att. 1st R. Inn. Fus.).
17 Rowe, Arthur Robert Reginald, 2/Lt. (Tp.), k. in a., 7/2/17.
Ruegg, Kenneth, 2/Lt., k. in a., 20/9/14.
Rundle, Raymond Wallis, Lt., k. in a., 9/5/15 (att. R. Warwick Regt.).

11 Russell, Alexander Christopher, Capt. (Tp.), k. in a., 10/10/15.
11 Russell, Edward, Lt., k. in a., 1/7/16.
Sabine, Gerald, Lt. (Tp.), k. in a., 22/10/18 (att. 15th Hants.).
3 Salmon, Cecil Gordon, Lt., k. in a., 14/6/15 (att. 2nd Bn.).
15 Sargent, Augustus Montague, 2/Lt. (Tp.), d. of w., 27/4/18.
1 Sargent, Henry Westbury, 2/Lt., d. of w., 6/7/16.
2 Saunders, Charles Frederick, 2/Lt., d. of w., 18/4/18.
Schur, Philip, Lt., k. in a., 15/6/18 (att. 9th Bn.).
9 Schweder, Archibald Alan, M.C., Capt. (Tp.), k. in a., 26/9/16.
16 Seabrook, Harry Spencer, 2/Lt., k. in a., 12/7/16.
Searle, John Arthur, 2/Lt. (Tp.), d. of w., 4/5/17.
17 Seed, Harper, 2/Lt. (Tp.), k. in a., 20/9/17.
Shacklock, George Miller, 2/Lt., k. in a., 12/3/15.
10 Shaw, Arthur Gilbey, Lt. (Tp.), k. in a., 24/12/15.
1 Shaw, Francis Joseph Marshall, 2/Lt., k. in a., 5/7/16
3 Shaw, Marmaduke Marshall, M.C., Lt. (A/Capt.), k. in a., 21/3/18 (att. 2nd Bn.).
4 Simpson, Odo Mackay, Lt., k. in a., 13/7/18.
17 Singleton, Frank Chester, Capt. (Tp.), k. in a., 3/9/16.
Smalley, William Miles, 2/Lt., k. in a., 9/12/14.
Smith, Arthur, 2/Lt. (Tp.), k. in a., 26/8/18 (att. 10th Bn.).
Smith, Eric Drummond, 2/Lt. (Tp.), k. in a., 4/10/17 (att. 6th York & Lanc. Rgt.).
Smith, Harold Andrew, 2/Lt., k. in a., 21/3/18 (att. 2/6th Btn.).
Smith, Harry Leonard Chappell, Lt., k. in a., 20/10/14.
19 Smith, John Fletcher, Lt. (Tp.), died, 28/7/16 (and R.F.C.).
Smith, Thomas Rowland, 2/Lt. (Tp.), d. of w., 30/3/18 (att. Camel Corps).
3 Sowter, Geoffrey Smart, Capt., k. in a., 14/10/18 (att. 15th Bn.).
Sowter, Unwin Henry Etches, Lt., d. of w., 22/4/17.
10 Spencer, Arthur Egerton, Lt., k. in a., 2/7/16.
4 Spencer, Francis, 2/Lt., k. in a., 26/9/17 (att. 2/7th Btn.).
9 Squires, Roger Dewar, Capt. (Tp.), k. in a., 7/8/15.
Stackhouse, William Thomas, Capt., k. in a., 12/3/15.
4 Stamper, Geoffrey, 2/Lt., killed, 25/3/18 (att. 1st Bn.).
Steggall, Hubert Henry, Lt. (Tp.), k. in a., 18/9/18 (att. 10th Bn.).
13 Stevenson, Alan, Capt. (Tp.), k. in a., 26/9/16 (att. 9th Bn.).
17 Stollard, Gordon, Major (Tp.), k. in a., 3/9/16.
Stoneham, Reginald Percy, 2/Lt., k. in a., 9/5/15.
Stranger, Richard Henry, Lt., d. of w., 13/3/15.
Straw, Alexander, Lt. (Tp.), d. of w., 3/6/18 (P. of W.).
Street, Edmund Rochfort, D.S.O., Major (Tp.), d. of w., 15/10/16.
1 Stribling, Frederick George, Lt. (Tp.), d. of w., 8/7/16.
16 Strutt, Anthony Herbert, Lt. (Tp.), d. of w., 27/4/18
15 Stubbs, Frank Percival, 2/Lt. (Tp.), d. of w., 25/11/16.
13 Sutton, Horace Josiah, 2/Lt. (Tp.), d. of w., 24/11/15 (att. 9th Bn.).
13 Swain, John George, 2/Lt. (A/Capt.), k. in a., 9/1/17 (att. 93rd Burma Inf.)
15 Talbot, Frederic Herbert, 2/Lt. (Tp.), k. in a., 20/7/16.
3 Tanner, Morris Villiers Godwin, 2/Lt. (Tp.), d. of w., 7/4/17 (att. 2/8th Bn.).
10 Taylor, Arthur Leonard, 2/Lt. (Tp.), d. of w., 16/11/18.
2 Taylor, Garth Smithies, Lt. (Tp.), k. in a., 15/10/16.
Taylor, James Wood Colin, Lt., k. in a., 9/8/15 (att 2nd Bn.).
10 Taylor, William Birrell, 2/Lt. (Tp.), k. in a., 31/7/18.
11 Teahan, John Patrick, 2/Lt., k. in a., 8/10/16.
11 Thornton, Douglas Saville, 2/Lt. (Tp.), k. in a., 1/10/16.
13 Thurlow, Geoffrey Robert Youngman, 2/Lt. (T/Lt.), k. in a., 23/4/17 (att. 10th Bn.).
2 Tombazis, James Lyell, D.S.O., M.C., 2/Lt., k. in a., 8/10/18.
11 Tomlinson, Charles Valentine, 2/Lt. (Tp.), k. in a., 1/7/16.
11 Toms, Horace James Henry, 2/Lt. (Tp.), k. in a., 9/4/17.
14 Travers, Horace Eden Kennedy, 2/Lt. (Tp.), d. of w., 8/11/16 (att. 10th L.N. Lancs Regt.).
3 Tucker, James Parke, Lt. (T/Capt.), k. in a., 23/4/17 (att. 10th Bn.).
3 Tupman, Arthur Lyon, Lt., k. in a., 22/8/18 (and R.A.F.).
15 Unwin, George Stuart, 2/Lt. (Tp.), k in a, 30/7/16 (att. 11 Bn.).
19 Upton, William Edwin, Lt. & Qr.-Mr., died, 5/3/16.
Urquhart, William Thomas Bruce, 2/Lt. (Tp.), k. in a., 6/7/17 (att. 1st Bn.).
1 Venner, George Eric, Major (Tp.), k. in a., 8/7/16 (att 3rd Bn.).
15 Vickers, Frederick, Major (Tp.), k in a., 21/4/17.
11 Vincent-Jackson, Montagu John, Lt. (Tp.), k. in a., 4/2/16.
Vowler, Darrell Francis Stephen, Major (Tp.), died, 28/2/19 (att. M.G.C.).
3 Wakefield, Montague Stephen, Lt., k. in a., 20/11/17 (att. 1st Bn.).
Walker, Harry Cullis Steele, 2/Lt., k. in a., 12/3/15.
Walsh, Geoffrey Pennell, Lt., k. in a., 9/8/15 (att. 2nd Bn.).
17 Walters, Harold Victor, Capt. (Tp.), k. in a., 3/9/16.
3 Wardle, Cyril Ernest, 2/Lt., k. in a., 3/10/18 (att. 1st Bn).
3 Waters, William Denne, 2/Lt., k. in a., 12/3/15.
17 Waterson, Frederick Paris, 2/Lt. (Tp.), k. in a., 31/7/17.
Webster, Jno. Ryrie, D.S.O., M.C., Lt.-Col., k. in a., 22/3/18.
Weigall, Richard Edward Cromwell, Lt., k in a., 12/3/15.
2 Wells, Frederick, 2/Lt., died, 1/8/15.
9 West, William, 2/Lt. (Tp.), k. in a., 7/8/15.
Weston, Maurice Sydney, 2/Lt. (Tp.), k. in a., 27/4/17 (att. 6th Bn.).
Whalley, Leonard, 2/Lt., k. in a., 26/3/18 (att. 15th Bn.).
Wheatley, John Charles, 2/Lt., d. of w., 3/10/18 (att. 1/5th Bn.).
4 Wheatley, Roland, 2/Lt., k. in a. 24/11/16 (att. 15th Bn.).
4 Whitewright, Alfred Rutherford, 2/Lt., died, 11/5/16.
11 Whyatt, Percy, M.C., Capt. (Tp.), k. in a., 18/10/17.
10 Whyatt, Raymond Selwyn, 2/Lt., k. in a., 13/10/18.
4 Wicks, William Charles, M.C., 2/Lt., k. in a., 16/9/17 (att. 10th Bn.).
3 Williams, Samuel Mervyn, 2/Lt., k. in a., 16/10/16 (att. 2nd Bn.).
16 Williams, Theodore Cecil Ormonde, M.C., Capt., d. of w., 24/3/18.
Williamson, Edward Maurice, Lt., k. in a., 1/3/15.
9 Wills, Arthur George, Lt., k. in a., 7/8/15.
10 Wilmot, Robert Coningby, Capt. (Tp.), k. in a., 29/10/17.
16 Wilson, Ernest Edwin, 2/Lt., k. in a., 4/11/18 (att. 10th Bn.).
15 Wilson, Strawson Lieveslay, Lt. (Tp.), d. of w., 21/7/16.
15 Winckley, Charles Reginald, 2/Lt (Tp.), k. in a., 20/7/16.
17 Woodhouse, Leslie Douglas, Lt. (Tp.), k. in a., 3/9/16.
Woodroffe, Charles Edward, 2/Lt, k. in a., 27/7/18 (att. 15th Bn.).
4 Wright, Robert Taylor, 2/Lt., k. in a., 1/11/17 (att. 15th Bn.).
10 Young, Arthur Webster, Major (Tp.), k. in a., 13/9/15.
3 Young, Harold Farquhar, 2/Lt., k. in a., 20/8/17 (att. 9th Bn.) (att. R.F.C., 43rd Sqd.).
17 Young, John Arthur, Capt., k. in a., 4/10/17.

The Loyal North Lancashire Regiment.

Adamson, Peter, M.C., 2/Lt. (Tp.), k. in a., 27/2/18 (att. 4th Bn.).
6 Adamson, William, Capt. (Tp.), k. in a., 24/4/16.
1 Allason, Lionel Theopilus, Capt., k. in a., 7/10/14.
1 Allen, John Francis, Capt., d. of w., 4/11/14.
2 Almond, Owen Edmund, 2/Lt., k. in a., 29/9/15.
3 Andrews, Charles Neville, 2/Lt., k. in a., 24/3/15.
10 Andrews, Robert Freeman, 2/Lt. (Tp.), k. in a., 15/11/16.
11 Appleby, Sidney Derrick, 2/Lt., k. in a., 18/7/17 (att. 8th Bn.).
Ashton, Robert Mark, D.C.M., 2/Lt. (Tp.), k. in a., 7/11/17 (att. 2/19 Lond. R.).
8 Ashworth, George, 2/Lt. (Tp.), k. in a., 2/10/16.
7 Banister, Maurice James, Lt. (Tp.), d. of w., 17/2/16.
9 Barrett, Joseph Gordon, 2/Lt. (Tp.), k. in a., 10/4/18.
Bate, George Beaumont, 2/Lt. (Tp.), k. in a., 29/4/17 (and R.F.C., 18 Sqd.).
8 Bennett, Ernest, Lt. (Tp.), died, 12/8/17.
10 Bennett, Harold Presdee, 2/Lt. (Tp.), k. in a., 15/11/16.
10 Bidwell, Claude Arthur Stephen, 2/Lt. (Tp.), k. in a., 21/9/15.
Body, Grant Trenavin, Capt., k. in a., 14/9/14.
3 Bowler, Thomas Chester, 2/Lt., d. of w., 3/10/18.
Braithwaite, Francis Joseph, Major, k. in a., 4/11/14.
9 Brown, Claude Fitzgerald Sedley, 2/Lt., k. in a., 19/10/16.
Brown, George Lothian, Lt. (Tp.), d. of w., 15/11/17 (att. 1st Bn.).
Buchan, James, 2/Lt., k. in a., 22/3/18 (att. 15th Bn.).
11 Bullough, Thomas Horrolin Stanley, 2/Lt. (Tp.), k. in a., 7/7/16 (att. 9th Bn.).
Burkinshaw, Herbert Thornton, 2/Lt., d. of w., 20/9/18 (att. 5 York & Lanc. R.).
Byrne, Walter, 2/Lt. (Tp.), k. in a., 30/9/18 (att. 4th Bn.).
Callard, Malcolm Ernest, 2/Lt., d. of w., 26/1/15.
1 Calrow, William Robert Launcelot, 2/Lt., k. in a., 7/10/14.
Carline, Norman John, 2/Lt., k. in a., 22/3/18 (att. 10 Bn.).
1 Carmichael, Thomas Sydney, 2/Lt. (Tp.), d. of w., 18/5/16.
Carter, Aubrey John, D.S.O., Major, k. in a., 4/11/14.
6 Cash, Geoffrey Edwin, Lt., k. in a., 27/8/16.
Chamberlain, Eric Dunstan, 2/Lt., k. in a., 30/11/17.
5 Chronnell, Hubert, M.C., 2/Lt. (A/Capt.), k. in a., 31/7/17.
8 Clark, George Ernest Cecil, Capt. (Tp.), k. in a., 9/1/16.
6 Collins, James Henry William, 2/Lt. (Tp.), d. of w., 6/5/17.
10 Couper, John Ralph, T/Lt. (A/Capt.), k. in a., 15/11/16.
10 Crane, Herbert Donovon, 2/Lt. (Tp.), k. in a., 22/3/18.
9 Crichton, John Drummond, Capt. (Tp.), k. in a., 22/3/18.
1 Cross, Maurice Assheton, Capt., k. in a., 18/8/16.
11 Darby-Griffith, Octavius Sidney, M.C., T/Capt. (A/Major), k. in a., 27/5/18 (att. 9th Bn.).
Dawes, Charles Edmund, 2/Lt., d. of w., 28/1/15.
7 Dawson, William Arthur, Lt. (Tp.), k. in a., 23/7/16 (11th).
8 Day, Herbert, 2/Lt. (Tp.), k. in a., 10/7/16
1 Dean, Leonard Lawson, 2/Lt., k. in a., 3/10/18.
3 De Blaby, Reginald Swithun, Capt., d. of w., 9/8/16 (att. 4th Bn.).
11 De Chazal, Robert, Lt., k. in a., 9/4/16.
6 De Fallot, Carl Clare, Capt., d. of w., 15/6/15.
10 Dennys, Richard Molesworth, Capt. (Tp.), d. of w, 24/7/16.
Dickson, A. H., 2/Lt., died, 13/10/15.
Dickson, Cyril Garlies, Lt., k. in a., 4/11/14.
9 Downing, Alfred Edward, 2/Lt., d. of w., 27/5/18.
3 Edward, Bernard Joseph, 2/Lt., d. of w., 18/4/18.
1 Edwards, Philip Arthur, Capt. (T/Major), k. in a., 18/3/16
Einem-Hickson, Samuel Vernon, Lt., k. in a., 4/11/14.
8 Emerson, Harold Theodore, 2/Lt. (Tp.), k. in a., 10/7/16.
8 Everard, Ernest Victor, 2/Lt. (Tp.), d. of w., 23/6/17.
6 Fairlie, James Gordon, Lt.-Col. (Tp.), k. in a., 22/4/16.
8 Falkner, Arthur Newstead, Capt. (Tp.), d. of w., 20/7/16.
Faulknor, Robert Sylvester John, Capt., k. in a., 25/9/15.
Fazackerley, Harold, M.C., 2/Lt. (Tp.), k. in a., 25/8/18 (att. 4th Bn.).
Fergie, Alexander Bancroft, 2/Lt. (Tp.), k. in a., 20/9/17 (att. 4th Bn.).
9 Finch-Noyes, Charles William Fabin, 2/Lt., k. in a., 3/9/16.
11 Firmin, Maurice Harold Cuffe, Lt. (Tp.), k. in a., 26/2/16.
Fisher, Wilfred, 2/Lt. (Tp.), k. in a., 9/5/15.
7 Fletcher, Herman, 2/Lt. (Tp.), k. in a., 13/11/16.
Fletcher, John, 2/Lt. (Tp.), k. in a., 28/9/18 (att. 2/4 Bn.)
8 Foote, Trevor Mawdsley, Major (Act.), k. in a., 10/7/17.
Fraser, Alexander, 2/Lt., k. in a., 30/11/17.
1/12 Fryer, Charles William, 2/Lt., d. of w., 1/8/18.
Fullerton, Frank, 2/Lt. (Tp.), k. in a., 31/7/17 (att. 1/4 Bn.).
Garrod, Basil Rahere, Lt., died, 4/2/19 (and R.A.F.).

3 Garrod, Thomas Martin, 2/Lt., d. of w., 10/5/15.

Gifford, Gordon Arthur, Lt., k. in a., 10/7/17 (att. 2 T.M.B.)

1 Gifford, Harry William, Capt. (Tp.), k. in a., 15/7/16.

Gilhespie, Charles Salkeld, 2/Lt. (Tp.), d. of w., 12/12/17 (att. 5 S. Lancs R.).

1 Goldie, George Henry, Lt., k. in a., 14/9/14.

1 Goldie, Paul Francis, 2/Lt. (Tp.), k. in a., 25/9/15.

10 Goodman, G. A., 2/Lt., k. in a., 28/10/18 (and R.A.F.).

10 Gordon, Adam Frazer, 2/Lt., d. of w., 11/8/16.

9 Green, Edward Unsworth, M.C., Capt. (Tp.), k. in a., 10/8/17.

Green, Frederick George, M.C., 2/Lt. (Tp.), k. in a., 3/10/18 (att. 1/4 Bn.).

Gregory, Arthur Skelton, 2/Lt. (Tp.), k. in a., 22/9/18 (att. 2 East Lanc R.).

Griffiths, Thomas Combes, Lt., d. of w., 8/7/19 (att. 1st Slavo. Brit. Legion).

6 Grimshaw, Geoffrey Harrison, 2/Lt. (Tp.), k. in a., 10/7/16.

3 Grundy, Edwin Bosworth, Lt. (Tp.), d. of w., 19/8/18 (att. 11 E. Lancs).

6 Guilliband, Geoffrey Peter, Lt., k. in a., 10/8/15.

3 Haggar, Harry Douglas Fox, Lt., k. in a., 17/8/16.

Hall, Edward Lawrence, 2/Lt., k. in a., 30/11/17.

Halstead, James Thornton, 2/Lt. (Tp.), k. in a., 7/12/16 (att. T.M.B.).

11 Hampson, Norman, 2/Lt. (Tp.), k. in a., 15/2/17.

Harris, Sydney Ernest, 2/Lt. (Tp.), d. of w., 15/5/18 (att. 2/4 Bn.).

1 Harrison, George Herbert, M.C., 2/Lt., d. of w., 21/8/16.

9 Harrison, William Stanford Bennett, 2/Lt. (Tp.), k. in a., 7/7/17.

Harrop, James Lawton, 2/Lt., d. of w., 13/9/18 (att. 4 Bn.).

6 Hathorn, Charles Nicholls, 2/Lt., k. in a., 10/8/15.

11 Haworth, Herbert, Lt., (Tp.), k. in a., 7/6/17 (att. 8/Bn.)

3 Hay, Geoffrey William, Capt., k. in a., 9/5/15 (att. 1st Bn.)

Helme, Harold Lutwyche, Capt., k. in a., 18/9/14.

Helme, Richard, 2/Lt., k. in a., 25/9/15.

9 Henderson, William James, Capt. (Tp.), k. in a., 6/7/16.

3 Hewetson, Richard John Philip, Capt., d. of w., 3/7/18 (P.O.W.).

1 Hibbard, Nelson Stuart, 2/Lt., k. in a., 14/7/17.

3 Hill, Wilfrid Dudley, Capt., d. of w., 13/5/15 (att. 1st Bn.)

3 Hodgkiss, Frederick, 2/Lt., d. of w., 8/10/18 (att. 4th Bn.)

8 Holden, Ernest Airlie, 2/Lt. (Tp.), d. of w., 17/10/16.

3 Holt, Laurence Guy, M.C., Capt. (Tp.), k. in a., 27/9/16.

Horn, John Bernard, 2/Lt. (Tp.), k. in a., 26/10/17 (att. 2/4 Bn.).

1 Horn, John Hetherington, 2/Lt. (Tp.), k. in a., 13/10/18 (att. 4 York & Lanc. R.).

6 Horsfall, Henry Francis Coghlan, Capt. (Tp.), d. of w., 22/4/16.

7 Hosking, Herbert John Roy, 2/Lt., k. in a., 23/7/16 (att. 3rd Bn.).

1 Howard, Albert Leonard, Lt. (Tp.), k. in a., 18/9/18.

8 Howard, Cecil Cunningham, 2/Lt. (Tp.), d. of w., 23/5/16.

1 Howard Vyse, Richard, Capt., k. in a., 14/9/14.

9 Howarth, John Dearden, 2/Lt. (Tp.), d. of w., 1/8/17.

7 Hoyle, Harold, 2/Lt. (Tp.), k. in a., 23/7/16.

7 Hughes, Cyril Rodyk, Lt. (Tp.), k. in a., 4/7/16.

10 Ibbotson, Edwin, M.C., 2/Lt., k. in a., 11/4/17.

9 James, William David, 2/Lt. (Tp.), k. in a., 23/5/18.

7 Jardine, Richard Webster, 2/Lt., k. in a., 23/7/16.

3 Jones, James Richard Tudor, 2/Lt., k. in a., 23/7/18.

8 V.C. Jones, Richard Basil Brandram, Lt. (Tp.), k. in a., 21/5/16.

2 Jourdain, Charles Edward Arthur, Lt.-Col., k. in a., 29/7/18.

10 Jude, Leo Gerald, T/Lt., A/Capt., k. in a., 15/11/16.

10 Kay, John, 2/Lt. (Tp.), k. in a., 30/9/18 (att. 1st Bn.).

9 Kemp, Louis Augustus, 2/Lt. (Tp.), d. of w., 22/3/18.

8 Kewley, George Raymond, 2/Lt. (Tp.), k. in a., 20/5/16.

6 Kewley, John Tasker, Lt. (Tp.), d. of w., 16/1/17.

Kingsley, Gerald Cecil, Lt., k. in a., 23/10/14.

Knight, Guy Cunninghame, Lt.-Col., d. of w., 11/9/14.

3 Lancaster, Joseph Clement, 2/Lt., k. in a., 29/4/18 (att. 9th Bn.).

11 Lassetter, John James Wilder, 2/Lt. (Tp.), k. in a., 8/3/17 (att. 6th Bn.).

3 Leake, Russell Madley, M.C., Lt., A/Capt., k. in a., 18/9/18 (att. 1st Bn.).

6 Leggatt, Jack, 2/Lt. (Tp.), k. in a., 5/4/16.

Leigh, William Booth, 2/Lt., k. in a., 30/11/17 (att. 1/5 Bn.).

6 Levinge, Henry George, Lt.-Col., k. in a., 10/8/15.

6 Levitt, Robert, T/Lt., A/Capt., d. of w., 7/7/17.

3 Livesey, Alan George Hilton, Lt., k. in a., 25/9/15 (att. 1st Bn.).

Lloyd, Walter Reginald, Lt.-Col., k. in a., 14/9/14.

6 Lockhart, Gerald Bevis, Lt. (Tp.), k. in a., 10/8/15.

1 Loomes, Herbert Reuben, Lt., k. in a., 14/9/14.

3 Lunt, Christopher, 2/Lt., k. in a., 10/8/17 (att. 9th Bn.).

3 McDonald, Norman, 2/Lt., d. of w., 25/12/16.

1 McIlwaine, Arthur Arnold, 2/Lt., k. in a., 5/3/16.

1 Macmahon, Charles Edward Valentine, 2/Lt., died, 9/3/16.

11 Manderson, Horace Leslie, 2/Lt., k. in a., 9/4/16 (att. 6th Bn.).

6 Mann, Horatio Gordon, Capt., k. in a., 10/8/15.

6 Mann, Horace Walpole, 2/Lt. (Tp.), k. in a., 10/8/15.

Mann, Nevill Swire, Major, d. of w., 12/4/16 (att. 6th Bn.).

Marshall, Archibald James, 2/Lt., k. in a., 26/10/17 (att. 2/5 Bn.).

3 Mason, Rowland Charles, Lt., d. of w., 30/9/14.

6 Mather, John Wilfred, Capt. (Tp.), k. in a., 10/8/15.

11 May, Stanley Harris, Lt., k. in a., 27/8/16 (att. 2 R. War. R.).

Mewha, George Henry, 2/Lt., k. in a., 20/9/17 (att. 1/5 Bn.).

Meyer-Griffith, Harold Walter Gooch, Major, k. in a., 28/5/15.

Middlehurst, John, 2/Lt. (Tp.), k. in a., 26/10/17 (att. 2/5 Bn.).

7 Milbourne, Leslie, Lt. (Tp.), d. of w., 10/7/16.

3 Miller, Ernest Cyril, Capt., k. in a., 23/10/14 (att. 1st Bn.).

Miller, Jack Humphrey, Capt., died, 25/8/17.

Milne, Clifford, 2/Lt. (Tp.), k. in a., 14/5/18 (att. 4 Bn.).

Milne, William, M.C., Capt., T/Major, killed, 13/4/17 (and R.F.C., 25 Sqd.).

9 Moses, James, 2/Lt. (Tp.), k. in a., 4/8/16.

Naylor, Frank, 2/Lt., died, 23/3/18 (and R.F.C.).

8 Nicholls, Ernest James, 2/Lt. (Tp.), k. in a., 21/5/16.

3 Nicholson, John Edward Patrick, 2/Lt., k. in a., 16/9/18 (att. 13 K.R.R. Corps).

10 O'Keefe, Joseph Richard, 2/Lt. (Tp.), k. in a., 4/5/16.

1 Palmer, Joseph Sidney Herbert, 2/Lt., d. of w., 27/9/16.

Paton, Walter, 2/Lt., k. in a., 26/10/17 (att. 2/5 Bn.).

Pearson, Frank, Capt. (Tp.), died, 5/2/18 (49 Training Reserve Bn.).

Pearson, Ignatius Gerald, 2/Lt., k. in a., 30/11/17.

9 Perks, Maurice Case, 2/Lt. (Tp.), k. in a., 26/4/17 (74 T.M.B.).

11 Perry, Roy Sinclair, 2/Lt., k. in a., 4/4/16 (att. 6th Bn.).

10 Peskett, Harry St. Hill, Capt., d. of w., 13/4/17.

1 Pettitt, William, 2/Lt., k. in a., 19/4/18.

3 Pinches, Edward Harold, 2/Lt., d. of w., 16/11/17 (att. 1st Bn.).

7 Porter, Frederick Ernest Gilchrist, Capt. (Tp.), d. of w., 3/11/16.

Potter, Reginald, 2/Lt., k. in a., 9/5/15.

Prince, Alick Lancelot, Capt., k. in a., 8/11/14.

8 Pringle, Charles Eric, 2/Lt. (Tp.), k. in a., 10/7/16 (att. 11th Bn.).

10 Proctor, William Howard, D.S.O., Capt., k. in a., 23/4/17.

9 Pullin, John Henton, Lt. (Tp.), d. of w., 21/1/16.

8 Ramsay, Stuart, D.S.O., Capt. (Tp.), d. of w., 3/6/17.

Rankin, James, 2/Lt., k. in a., 30/11/17 (att. 1/5 Bn.).

Ransdale, Alfred Charles, 2/Lt. (Tp.), k. in a., 1/9/18 (att. 15 Bn.).

9 Readman, Wilfred, T/2/Lt., A/Capt., d. of w., 30/9/18 (att. 2/4 Bn.).

1 Reid, James, Lt., d. of w., 8/10/18.

11 Reid, Robert William Kerr, 2/Lt. (Tp.), k. in a., 7/7/16 (att. 9th Bn.).

11 Rendell-Dunn, Hubert Cecil, 2/Lt. (Tp.), d. of w., 24/11/16 (att. 10 Bn.).

10 Roberts, Henry Norman, 2/Lt., k. in a., 28/4/17.

Robinson, Edgar, Lt., k. in a., 14/9/14.

2 Robinson, Harold Arthur, Major, died, 31/5/16.

9 Robinson, Ralph Duncan, Capt. (Tp.), k. in a., 7/6/17.

9 Rodwell, Hubert, 2/Lt. (Tp.), d. of w., 10/10/16 (att. 11th Bn.).

Rowell, William Cecil, Capt., died, 22/5/19 (and R.A.F.).

6 Rowley-Conwy, Geoffrey Seymour, Major, k. in a., 10/8/15.

Ryley, Herbert Frank Brownlow, Capt., k. in a., 2/11/14.

1 Sandalls, Charles, 2/Lt., k. in a., 18/9/18.

3 Saunders, Cyril Page Gore, A/Capt., k. in a., 27/9/16 (att. 1st Bn.).

3 Scott, Maurice Douglas Guest, M.C., Lt. (T/Capt.), died, 17/3/18 (and R.F.C.).

Scroggie, William Robertson, 2/Lt., k. in a., 2/12/17.

1 Shippard, Sanford William, Lt., k. in a., 10/7/17.

Shippobotton, Frank, 2/Lt. (Tp.), d. of w., 20/11/17 (att. 1/4 Bn.).

10 Smith, Alexander Cyril, 2/Lt. (Tp.), k. in a., 23/11/16.

7 Smith, Allison Gould, M.C., Capt., k. in a., 18/4/18.

1 Smith, Harry Marsden, Lt., d. of w., 27/2/17 (P. of W.).

Smith, James Salsbury, Capt., k. in a., 17/12/17 (att. 1/5 Bn.).

10 Smith, Lawrence Brumwell, 2/Lt. (Tp.), k. in a., 14/9/18 (att. 1/4 Bn.).

6 Soman, Leon Asher, 2/Lt. (T/Lt.), k. in a., 8/3/17.

11 Stevens, Walter Sydney John, 2/Lt. (Tp.), k. in a., 7/7/16 (att. 9th Bn.).

2 Stokes, Reginald George, Major, k. in a., 28/9/15.

3 Stott, Ronald Howorth, 2/Lt., k. in a., 20/9/17 (att. 7 Rif. Bde.).

9 Summerson, Herbert Walker, 2/Lt. (Tp.), d. of w., 5/6/18.

9 Swift, Harold Heyes, 2/Lt. (Tp.), k. in a., 10/8/17.

9 Tait, Robert Andrew, 2/Lt. (Tp.), k. in a., 22/3/18.

8 Taylor, Leslie Thompson, Lt. (Tp.), d. of w., 3/6/16.

7 Thomas, Matthew, Capt. (Tp.), k. in a., 30/12/15.

6 Thompson, Brian Wildman-Osborne, Capt., k. in a., 10/8/15.

Thompson, Wilfred Bernard, 2/Lt. (Tp.), k. in a., 8/10/18 (att. 1/4 Bn.).

9 Tiley, George Charles, 2/Lt. (Tp.), k. in a., 21/10/16.

11 Tottenham, Edward Lowry, 2/Lt., k. in a., 9/4/16 (att. 6th Bn.).

6 Toulmin, H., M.C., Lt., k. in a., 17/9/18 (and R.A.F.).

11 Townshend, Dudley Ryder, Capt. (Tp.), d. of w., 21/8/15 (att. Lan. Fus.).

9 Trefusis, Arthur Owen, Capt. (Tp.), k. in a., 7/7/16.

3 Tripp, Cyril Claude, 2/Lt., k. in a., 13/11/16 (att. 7th Bn.).

1 Tripp, Donald Owen Howard, D.S.O., Capt. (Tp.), k. in a., 18/8/16.

7 Turpie, McKenzie Fleming, 2/Lt., d. of w., 23/7/16.

8 Underhill, Edward Samuel, Capt. (Tp.), k. in a., 12/10/16.

3 Wadeson, Edward Yeadon, Lt., k. in a., 22/3/18 (att. 10th Bn.).

Wakley, Bertram Joseph, Major, died, 11/2/17.

2 Wale, Alick Arthur, Capt. (Act.), k. in a., 8/11/17 (att. 7th Bn.).

8 Walsh, Percival, Lt. (Tp.), d. of w., 8/7/16.

1 Wasbrough, William Lewis, 2/Lt., k. in a., 25/9/15.

10 Watson, Kenneth Clennell, Lt. (Tp.), k. in a., 11/4/17.

10 Way, Robert Edward Allen, 2/Lt. (Tp.), d. of w., 29/5/17.
3 Weber, Reginald Otho, 2/Lt., d. of w., 4/9/17 (att. 8th Bn.).
6 Wells, Norman Lancaster, Lt., k. in a., 10/8/15.
3 Wharton, Frank Hammond, Lt., k. in a., 25/9/15 (att. 1st Bn.).
2 White, Thomas, 2/Lt. (Tp.), d. of w., 8/7/16 (11th).
Wilkinson, Edmund, Hon. Lt. & Qr.-Mr., k. in a., 31/10/14.
Wilkinson, Robert Bruce, 2/Lt. (Tp.), d. of w., 12/12/17 (att. 1/4 Bn.).
7 V.C. Wilkinson, Thomas Orde Lawder, Lt. (Tp.), k. in a., 5/7/16.
3 Williams, Edward Stanley, 2/Lt., k. in a., 3/6/17 (att. 8th Bn.).
9 Willis, Richard, Lt. (Tp.), k. in a., 15/5/16.
6 Wilson, Robert Meredith, Lt., k. in a., 10/8/15.
3 Wilson, Thomas, 2/Lt., k. in a., 29/8/18 (att. 2/4 Bn.).
3 Wood, Henry George, Capt., k. in a., 25/9/15 (att. 1st Bn.).
10 Wren, Thomas Thorpe, 2/Lt. (Tp.), d. of w., 29/7/16.
6 Wright, Harold, Capt. (Tp.), d. of w., 14/9/15.
9 Wynne, Francis George, D.S.O., Major, k. in a., 10/4/18 (att. 1/Wilts R.).
9 Yates, Charles Cecil, Lt. (Tp.), k. in a., 15/5/16.

The Northamptonshire Regiment.

7 Adderley, Douglas Herbert, 2/Lt. (Tp.), k. in a., 16/6/17.
3 Airy, Arthur Langton, Lt., k. in a., 11/1/15 (att. 1st).
7 Allport, Ivor Merlin, 2/Lt., k. in a., 9/1/17.
3 Alnack, A. C. T., 2/Lt., k. in a., 27/9/16 (att. M.G.C.).
2 Alston, Ernest Alfred Brooke, Major (T/Lt.-Col.), k. in a., 10-11/8/17 (att. 10 D.C.L.I.).
Attwater, Humphrey St. John, Capt. (Tp.), k. in a., 26/6/16.
1 Badcock, Edmund Downes, Lt. (Tp.), k. in a., 22/7/16.
3 Ballard, Frank Watson, 2/Lt., k. in a., 11/10/18.
1 Barthorp, Michael Arthur Raymond, Lt., k. in a., 20/7/16.
6 Bates, Archibald Claude, M.C., Lt., d. of w., 20/10/17.
6 Batty, Geoffrey George Horn, Capt. (Tp.), d. of w., 27/9/16.
7 Beale, Norman Stuart Charles Gascoigne, 2/Lt. (Tp.), k. in a., 18/8/16.
Belding, Clare, 2/Lt., k. in a., 11/3/15.
3 Bell, Robert James, 2/Lt., k. in a., 2/11/18 (att. 1/4th N'hamp. R.).
Bentley, Geoffrey Malcolm, Capt., d. of w., 29/10/14.
Beresford, Charles Zaragoza de La Poer, Lt., k. in a., 9/5/15.
8 Bird, Walter Cyril, Lt. (Tp.), k. in a., 4/3/17 (att. 2nd N'hants. R.).
3 Blacker, George Frederick, Lt., k. in a., 9/5/15 (att. 2nd Bn.).
7 Boal, William Wainhouse, 2/Lt. (Tp.), d. of w., 10/10/18.
Boultbee, Arthur Elsdale, Lt., k. in a., 17/3/17.
3 Boulton, James Babington, 2/Lt., k. in a., 17/2/17 (att. 6th N/hamp. Regt.).
3 Brown, Claude Joseph John, Lt., died, 18/11/18 (att. 1/7th K.A.R.).
Buckle, Arthur Charles, Lt.-Col., died, 21/12/18.
2 Buckle, Christopher Galbraith, D.S.O., M.C., A/Lt.-Col., k. in a., 27/5/18.
Burke, Edward Terrence. Lt. & Qr.-Mr., k. in a., 25/4/18 (and M.G.C., 9th).
7 Burnham, Albert Frederick James, 2/Lt. (Tp.), k. in a., 28/6/16.
6 Burrows, Arnold Hayes, Capt. (Tp.), k. in a., 13/3/16.
Capell, Arthur George Coningsby, Capt., k. in a., 12/3/15.
1 Carey, Bertram Chepmell, M.C., Lt. (A/Capt.), d. of w., 22/9/18.
2 Carritt, Harry William, Capt. (Tp.), k. in a., 8/7/16.
5 Cartledge, Charles Ashforth, 2/Lt. (Tp.), k. in a., 30/7/16.
8 Cartwright, Stanley, Lt. (Tp.), k. in a., 17/8/16 (att. M.G.C.).
Catherall, William Cecil, 2/Lt., k. in a., 2/11/17 (att. 1/5 Norf. R.).
6 Chalmers, David, T/Lt. (A/Capt.), k. in a., 18/9/18.
1 Chambers, Norman Archibald, 2/Lt., d. of w., 17/8/16.
5 Chisholm, Kenneth James, Lt. (Tp.), d. of w., 18/8/16.
9 Clark, Gerald Maitland, Major (Tp.), k. in a., 14/7/16.
2 Clark, Noel, T/2/Lt. (A/Capt.), d. of w., 1/4/18.
Clarke, Arthur Henry Gilbert, 2/Lt., k. in a., 9/9/16.
7 Clarke, Charles Louis, Lt. (Tp.), k. in a., 8/10/16.
3 Close, William Collins, 2/Lt., k. in a., 20/3/17 (att. 6th Bn.).
8 Cole, Ernest Lockett, 2/Lt. (Tp.), k. in a., 27/9/16.
V.C. Colyer-Fergusson, Thomas Riversdale, 2/Lt. (A/Capt.), d. of w., 31/7/17.
1 Cooper, Donald Keith, 2/Lt. (Tp.), k. in a., 9/9/16.
6 Cooper, George Spencer, 2/Lt. (Tp.), k. in a., 17/2/17.
Cowley, Charles Selwyn, Lt., k. in a., 9/5/15.
1 Crawford, Charles Noel, 2/Lt., k. in a., 8/4/16.
Crean, Theodore, Capt., killed, 26/10/14 (and R.F.C.).
6 Cuzen, Richard, 2/Lt., k. in a., 5/4/18.
3 Davison, Ralph, Lt., k. in a., 9/5/15 (att. 1st Bn.).
3 Dawson, Roger Graham, 2/Lt., k. in a., 18/9/15 (att. 6th N'hants R.).
Dickson, Barrington Blomfield, Capt., k. in a., 9/5/15.
7 Duchesne, Richard Ernest, 2/Lt. (Tp.), k. in a., 8/10/16.
Duncan, Charles Walter, 2/Lt. (Tp.), k. in a., 22/11/17 (att. 6th).
Eden, Bernard, Lt., k. in a., 9/5/15.
Elliot, Nichol, 2/Lt. (Tp.), k. in a., 9/7/17 (att. 2nd T.M.B.).
Elston, Charles Douglas, Capt., d. of w., 22/11/17.
1 Erle, Christopher, Capt. (Tp.), died, 10/2/17 (Gar. Btn.).
6 Evans, Douglas Lane, Capt. (Tp.), d. of w., 26/9/16.
3 Farrar, John Harold, Capt., k. in a., 9/5/15.
6 Farrell, Reginald, 2/Lt. (Tp.), k. in a., 14/7/16.
8 Farrimond, Joseph, 2/Lt. (Tp.), k. in a., 21/7/16 (att. 1/5th Gloucs.).
2 Fisher, Charles John, 2/Lt., d. of w., 28/7/17.
Fletcher, Arthur Frederick, 2/Lt. (Tp.), k. in a., 12/5/18 (att. 6th Bn.).
6 Freeman, Tom, 2/Lt. (Tp.), k. in a., 17/2/17 (att. 54th T.M.B.).
6 Frend, Hugh Palliser, 2/Lt. (Tp.), k. in a., 20/3/17.
1 Fricker, Arthur Warwick, Lt. (Tp.), k. in a., 29/5/16.
2 Frost, John William, M.C., Lt., died, 23/3/19.
1 Giddy, Napier Llewellyn, 2/Lt., k. in a., 15/8/16.
Gordon, Cosmo George, 2/Lt., d. of w., 17/9/14.
Gordon, George Duff, Lt. (Tp.), k. in a., 12/3/15.
Gordon, Robert Eddington, Capt., k. in a., 15/9/14.
5 Gould, William Justin, T/Lt., k. in a., 23/8/15.
6 Grace, Handley Carleton, Capt. (Tp.), d. of w., 2/9/17 (P. of W.).
1 Greenwood, Cyril Stewart, 2/Lt. (Tp.), k. in a., 20/8/16.
2 Growse, John Hartley, Lt. (T/Capt.), d. of w., 1/4/18.
5 Gurney, Frederick Arthur, 2/Lt. (Tp.), died, 23/3/16.
7 Hadley, Peyton Sheldon, M.C., T/Lt. (A/Capt.), died, 24/10/18.
Haldane, Laurence Aylmer, D.S.O., Major (Tp.), k. in a., 2/4/16 (and Staff).
2 Hall, Robert Lane, 2/Lt., k. in a., 27/5/18.
6 Hall, William Hingston, 2/Lt., k. in a., 5/4/18.
8 Halliday, Leigh Hales, 2/Lt., k. in a., 31/7/17 (att. 7th N'hants.).
6 Hamilton, Noel Crawford, 2/Lt. (Tp.), k. in a., 14/7/16.
7 Hammond, Jack Cecil, 2/Lt. (Tp.), k. in a., 11/4/17.
3 Harper, Walter Lacon, Lt., k. in a., 1/7/18 (att. 6th N'hants.).
Harston, William Harvey, 2/Lt. (Tp.), k. in a., 23/11/17 (and R.F.C., 52nd Sq.).
8 Hartigan, Thomas Jerome, 2/Lt. (Tp.), k. in a., 18/8/16.
8 Hayward, Herbert William, 2/Lt. (Tp.), k. in a., 26/9/16 (att. 6th N'hants.).
1 Heather, Percy Arthur, Lt., k. in a., 12/7/17.
6 Heriz-Smith, Denzil Mitford Heriz, 2/Lt. (Tp.), d. of w., 17/2/17.
Higginbotham, Charles Ernest, Major, k. in a., 11/3/15.
6 Higham Percy Harrowell, M.C., 2/Lt., k. in a., 17/2/17.
Higson, John Turnbull, 2/Lt. (Tp.), d. of w., 4/8/18 (att. 2nd).
3 Hills, Frederick Mervyn, 2/Lt., k. in a., 27/7/17 (att. 7th N'hants. Rgt.).
5 Howard, Norman, Lt. (Tp.), d. of w., 1/8/15.
Hunt, George Ward, Capt., k. in a., 9/5/15.
5 Hunter, James Whitaker, 2/Lt. (Tp.), d. of w., 9/7/16.
1 Jackson, Nicholas William Goddard, 2/Lt., k. in a., 9/9/16.
1 Jacques, Edward William Rigbye, Lt., k. in a., 17/8/16.
Jarvis, Arthur Septimus Guy, 2/Lt., k. in a., 31/10/14.
2 Jarvis, Frederick Charles, 2/Lt. (Tp.), k. in a., 7/7/16.
1 Joseph, Wilfred Gordon Aron, 2/Lt. (Tp.), k. in a., 19/4/17 (Gar. Bn.) (att. 1/5th Norfolk R.).
2 Knight, Francis Ernest, T/2/Lt. (A/Capt.), k. in a., 4/3/17.
6 Knight, Philip, 2/Lt. (Tp.), k. in a., 28/5/17 (att 7th Btn. N'hants R.).
1 Knight, Robert Valentine Harold, 2/Lt., k. in a., 19/7/16.
6 Lambert, James Edward Downes, Lt. (Tp.), k. in a., 2/11/15.
3 Latham, Stephen Grey, D.S.O., Capt. (A/Lt.-Col.), k. in a., 24/4/18 (att. 2nd Bn. N'hants. R.).
6 Law, Edgar Felix, Lt., k. in a., 5/4/18.
7 Laycock, Lewis James Penard, Lt. (Tp.), k. in a., 31/7/17.
7 Lea, Maurice Bertram, 2/Lt. (Tp.), k. in a., 18/8/16.
3 Lees, Percy Beresford, 2/Lt., k. in a., 11/3/15.
1 Lidington, Norman Herbert, 2/Lt. (Tp.), k. in a., 15/9/16 (Gar. Bn.).
3 Litchfield, Thomas, 2/Lt., k. in a., 31/7/17 (att. 7th Btn. N'hants.).
5 Littledale, Robert, Capt. (Tp.), k. in a., 30/11/17.
7 Lloyd, Herbert, 2/Lt. (Tp.), k. in a., 12/8/16.
3 Lloyd, William Benjamin, 2/Lt., k. in a., 10/8/17 (att. 7 Bn N'hants.).
Lucas, Charles Lucas Clement, 2/Lt., d. of w., 30/6/17 (att. 7th Btn. N'hants. R.).
Lucy, Reginald Eric, Lt., d. of w., 20/3/15.
8 Lycett, William Bernard, 2/Lt. (Tp.), d. of w., 24/7/16 (att. 1/5th Gloucs.).
6 Lys, Francis George Bryan, 2/Lt. (Tp.), k. in a., 14/7/16.
7 McRae, Peter McKay, 2/Lt. (Tp.), k. in a., 24/12/17 (att. R.E.).
1 Marshall, Bernard Gouldsmith, 2/Lt., k. in a., 5/4/16.
3 Martin, George Henry, 2/Lt., k. in a., 26/12/17 (att. 2nd N'hants. R.).
3 Mason, Edward, 2/Lt., k. in a., 9/5/15 (att. 2nd Bn.)
3 Matthews, Edward Alexander, 2/Lt., k. in a., 14/3/15.
7 Meadway, B. W., 2/Lt., died, 4/6/18 (att. R.A.F.).
7 Millard, Harold, Capt. (Tp.) (A/Major), d. of w., 11/4/17
7 Mobbs, Edgar Roberts, D.S.O., T/Lt.-Col., k. in a., 31/7/17
3 Monro, Kenneth Edward, Lt., d. of w., 14/5/15 (att. 1st Bn.).
7 Morley, John Norris, Lt., k. in a., 25/9/15.
7 Motion, Sidney Howard, Lt. (Tp.), d. of w., 1/8/17.
Moulding, Sydney Dormer, Lt., k. in a., 22/8/15.
Myers, Thomas Wrighton, 2/Lt. (Tp.), d. of w., 19/11/17 (att. 1st Bn.).
Neale, Herbert Cecil Thubron, 2/Lt., d. of w., 1/1/16.
3 Neish, Herbert Theodore Louis, 2/Lt., k. in a., 31/8/15 (att. 1st Bn.).
Nelles, Norman Cummings, 2/Lt., k. in a., 29/1/15.
6 Neville, Frank Septimus, Capt. (Tp.), d. of w., 24/11/17.
1 Noaks, Geoffrey Vaughan, 2/Lt., d. of w., 18/8/16.
Norman, Harold Henry, Major, k. in a., 10/11/14.
7 Nott, George Vincent, Lt., (Tp.), k. in a., 18/8/16.
8 Nye, Charles, Lt. (Tp.), k. in a., 17/8/16.
O'Brien, Humphrey D. Stafford, M.C., Capt., killed, 14/9/18 (and R.A.F.).
2 Oldfield, John Burleigh, M.C., T/2/Lt. (A/Capt.), k. in a., 16/8/17.
Owen, Arthur Edmund, Lt., died, 18/10/16 (att. 2/4th Gloucs. R.).

5 Page, Alfred Cecil Dudley, 2/Lt. (Tp.), k. in a., 18/8/16.
3 Paget, George Godfrey Brandreth, Lt., k. in a., 14/9/14 (att. 1st Bn.).
3 Palmer, Eric George, 2/Lt. (Tp.), k. in a., 4/3/17 (att. 2nd Bn. N'hants. R.).
Parker, Robert Burbon, Capt., k. in a., 19/9/14.
7 Parkin, Arthur, Lt.-Col., k. in a., 25/9/15.
Peake, John Thelwal, 2/Lt., d. of w., 11/12/15.
Pearson, Arthur John, M.C., 2/Lt., k. in a., 9/3/17 (att. R.F.C., 29th Sqd.).
7 Pearson, Reginald, M.C., Capt., k. in a., 9/10/18.
7 Phipps, Lionel Lush, Lt. (Tp.), d. of w., 28/9/15.
2 Pickering, George Anthony Raymond, 2/Lt. (Tp.), k. in a., 2/11/17 (att. 1/4 Bn.).
2 Piggott, William, 2/Lt. (A/Capt.), k. in a., 24/3/18.
Pilkington, Joseph Bernard, Lt., k. in a., 20/4/18.
6 Podmore, Hubert, D.S.O., Major (Tp.), killed, 31/12/17 (att. 12th Middx.).
3 Powell, Townsend George, Capt., k. in a., 9/5/15 (att. 2nd Btn.).
Power, Herbert, Capt., killed, 12/3/15.
2 Prevel, James Alexander, M.C., Lt. (Tp.), k. in a., 29/9/18.
1 Ramsay, Herbert Cyril, Lt., d. of w., 22/4/18.
Randall, Reginald Wigmore Sancroft, 2/Lt. (Tp.), k. in a., 9/5/15.
Rastrick, Urpeth, Lt., k. in a., 14/12/14.
7 Rathbone, George Powell, Lt. (Tp.), k. in a., 21/3/18.
2 Rawlings, Leonard Justly, 2/Lt. (Tp.), k. in a., 7/11/16.
1/2 Rayner, A. S., Lt., d. of w., 15/7/18 (and R.A.F.).
V.C. Read, Anketell Moutray, Capt., k. in a., 25/9/15 (and R.F.C.).
3 Redhead, Harold Arthur, Lt., k. in a., 7/8/18 (att. 6th Btn.).
8 Renton, Charles, 2/Lt. (Tp.), k. in a., 6/3/17 (att. 1st N'hants.).
6 Ripley, George Eustace, Colonel, d. of w., 16/10/10.
Robinson, Leslie John, Capt., k. in a., 12/3/15.
Royston-Pigott, George Arthur, D.S.O., Lt.-Col. (Tp.), k. in a., 3/7/16 (att. 10th Worcs. R.).
2 Rushton, Edward Birley Leigh, Capt., k. in a., 25/9/16.
Russell, Walter Russell, Capt., k. in a., 21/10/14.
Ryan, Donald Whitmore, 2/Lt., k. in a., 9/5/15 (att. 2nd Bn.).
7 Saunders, Charles Fabian, 2/Lt. (Tp.), k. in a., 18/8/16.
Savage, John Ardkeen, Capt., k in a., 18/9/14.
6 Scales, Patrick Joseph, 2/Lt. (Tp.), k. in a., 17/2/17.
2 Selby, Millin John, Lt. (Tp.), k. in a., 7/7/16.
1 Serjeant, Cyril Lawson, Lt. (Tp.), d. of w., 21/6/16.
6 Shankster, George Lt. (Tp.), k. in a., 9/10/16.
Shaw, Guy Trevor, Major (Tp.), k. in a., 7/7/16.
2 Sheehan, Gordon Keith Patrick, Lt., k. in a., 28/8/18.
Sherriff, Alexander Nimmo, 2/Lt., k. in a., 30/10/14.
8 Shield, Frederick Dowson, 2/Lt. (Tp.), k. in a., 6/7/16 (att. 5th Bn.).
7 Shortt, Vere Dawson, Capt. (Tp.), k. in a., 25/9/15.
3 Simons, John Henry Stuart, 2/Lt., k. in a., 10/7/17 (att. 1st Bn.).
2 Smalley, Walter Herbert, 2/Lt. (Tp.), d. of w., 28/10/18.
Smith, Geoffrey Harold, 2/Lt., d. of w., 10/7/17 (att. 1st Bn.).
1 Smithett, Grame Cecil East, 2/Lt., k. in a., 12/10/17 (and R.F.C.).
Sparrow, William Gordon Morgan, Capt., k. in a., 8/7/17 (and King's Afr. Rfs.).
3 Stanfield, William Bowman, 2/Lt., d of w., 29/9/15 (att. 1st Bn.).
8 Stevenson, Elston Henry, Lt., k. in a., 16/2/16 (att. 7th Bn.).
Stocker, St. John Crichton, Capt. (Tp.), k. in a., 12/3/15.
6 Stone, William Henry, 2/Lt., k. in a., 26/9/16.
1 Swell, Albert Ernest, D.S.O., Capt. (Acting), k. in a., 17/8/16.
3 Syfret, Edward Tristram Smyth, 2/Lt., d. of w., 17/8/16 (att. 1st N'hants R.).
3 Taylor, Ralph Paton, 2/Lt., k. in a., 10/7/16 (att. S. Wales Bord.).
Tayton, Wilfrid Edward, 2/Lt., k. in a., 10/8/17 (att. 6th Bn.).
3 Thomas, Arthur Lewis, 2/Lt., k. in a., 24/4/18 (att. 2nd N'hants R.).
3 Thompson, Harold, 2/Lt., k. in a., 9/5/15 (att. 1st Bn.).
Thomson, George Burrell, Lt., d. of w., 12/7/17.
Thornely, Maurice, 2/Lt. (Tp.), killed, 3/12/16 (and R.F.C.).
Tolmie, George Lester, 2/Lt., d. of w., 19/11/18 (att. 6th Bn.).
7 Tosdevin, William Cecil, 2/Lt., k. in a., 20/11/17.
1 Trefusis, Haworth Walter, Capt., k. in a., 7/11/16.
Trevor, Herbert Edward, Capt. (T/Lt.-Col.), k. in a., 11/4/17 (att. 9th Essex).
1 Tuckey, Albert William, Lt. (Tp.), k. in a., 25/9/15.
1 Twigg, Francis William, Lt. (A/Capt.), k. in a., 24/9/18.
8 Tyrrell, Joseph Lionel Allanson, 2/Lt. (Tp.), k. in a., 3/3/16 (att. 5th N'hants R.).
7 Urquhart, James Lawrance, Lt., k. in a., 25/9/15.
Vandell, Henry Ivanhoe, Lt., k. in a., 10/11/14 (Res. of Off.).
3 Vernon, Grenville Bertie, Capt., k. in a., 25/4/18 (att. 2nd N'hants Regt.).
Viney, Cecil Henry, 2/Lt., k. in a., 9/5/15.
3 Wainwright, Geoffrey Chauner, 2/Lt., d. of w., 22/12/14.
6 Walker, Gordon Henry, 2/Lt., k. in a., 10/11/17
3 Wallace, Alexander Moultrie, Capt, k. in a., 12/3/15.
Ward, Thomas Pillans, Lt., k. in a., 31/7/17 (att. 7th Bn.).
6 Warner, Harry James, 2/Lt., k. in a., 3/6/17.
Watts, Charles Harold Reynell, Capt., k. in a., 25/12/14.
6 Webster Aubrey Herbert, 2/Lt. (Tp.), killed, 25/4/16.
White, Edward Erskine, Capt., k. in a., 14/9/14.
6 Wilcox, Frederic Alexander Cumberland, Lt. (Tp.), k. in a., 14/7/16.
2 Williams, Frederick Thesiger, Lt.-Col. (Tp.), d. of w., 12/7/16.
3 Williams, Thomas Wodehouse Lt., k. in a., 9/5/15 (att. 1st Bn. N. Lancs R.).
3 Willson, Francis George Dudley, Lt., k. in a., 24/9/18 (att. 1st N'hants R.).
1 Wilson, Charles Edward, 2/Lt (Tp.), k. in a., 16/8/16.
6 Winkworth, Henry Edward Vernon, 2/Lt. (Tp.), d. of w., 18/2/17.
3 Wood, John Gervaise, 2/Lt., k. in a., 3/10/16.
Wood-Martin, James Isidore, Capt., k. in a., 12/3/15.
6 Woulfe, Gerald Lascelles, 2/Lt. (Tp.), k. in a., 14/7/16.
3 Young, Geoffrey Abbott, 2/Lt., k. in a., 4/3/17 (and 24th T.M.B.).

Princess Charlotte of Wales's (Royal Berkshire Regiment).

Aldworth, Douglas Gilbert Hayward, 2/Lt., drowned, 10/10/18 (att. 3/Bn.).
Aldworth, Thomas Rupert, Capt., k. in a., 11/3/15.
Alison, Laughton Hassard, 2/Lt., k. in a., 15/5/15.
Apps, Reginald Denman, 2/Lt., k. in a., 17/5/15.
3 Archdale, George Mervyn, 2/Lt., d. of w., 30/4/17 (att. 1/Bn.).
3 Astley, Edward Dugdale D'Oyley, Lt. (A/Capt.), k. in a., 1/6/18 (att. 1/Bn.).
3 Atkinson, Lionel Edward Mapletoft, Lt., k. in a., 9/5/15 (att. 2/Bn.).
Austin, George Frederick, 2/Lt. (Tp.), k. in a., 11/10/17 (att. 6/Bn.).
6 Avery, Henry Norris, 2/Lt. (Tp.), k. in a., 5/6/18 (att. 1/Bn.).
1 Bacon, Arthur Robert Dick, Lt., k. in a., 25/4/17.
1 Baker, Robert Cunynhame Slade, M.C., Lt., k. in a., 9/8/17.
9 Bance, Robert Arman, 2/Lt. (Tp.), k. in a., 9/8/16 (att. 5/Bn.).
8 Barrow, James, Hon. Lt. & Qr.-Mr. (Tp.), d. of w., 1/6/16.
5 Bartlett, Leonard Percival, 2/Lt. (Tp.), k. in a., 9/4/17.
3 Baseden, Eric, Lt., k. in a., 26/10/16 (att. 2/Bn.).
5 Bath, John Euel Witherden, Capt. (Tp.), k. in a., 22/12/15.
Battye, Cyril Wynyard, Lt., killed, 13/3/16 (and R.F.C.).
3 Bayley, Norman David, M.C., 2/Lt., died, 20/10/18 (att. 2/Bn.).
5 Bayley, William Kercheval, Major, k. in a., 13/10/15.
6 Bayly, Erskine Cochrane, 2/Lt. (Tp.), k. in a., 1/7/16.
5 Beattie, Malcolm Bartlett, Lt. (Tp.), d. of w., 16/10/17.
6 Bebee, Alexander Denman, 2/Lt. (Tp.), k. in a., 30/9/16.
2 Bedford, Seaton Hall, 2/Lt. (Tp.), k. in a., 1/7/16.
2 Belcher, Basil Henry, 2/Lt., k. in a., 1/7/16.
3 Belcher, Gordon, Capt., k. in a., 15-17/5/15 (att. 2/Bn.).
1 Beresford, Spencer Charles, 2/Lt. (Tp.), k. in a., 5/6/18.
8 Berlein, Leslie Herman, Lt. (Tp.), k. in a., 25/10/15.
6 Birch, Arthur, 2/Lt. (Tp.), d. of w., 17/2/17.
9 Birkby, Henry Alexander, 2/Lt. (Tp.), d. of w., 20/4/16 (att. 5/Bn.).
Birt, Lightly Harold, D.S.O., Capt., k. in a., 5/1/15.
8 Bissley, William Howe, 2/Lt. (Tp.), k. in a., 18/8/16.
1 Blackburn, Harry Dudley, Lt., k. in a., 5/4/17 (and R.F.C., 43 Sqd.).
Blackburn, Norman Henry Gershorn, M.C., 2/Lt. (Tp.), k. in a., 23/10/18 (att. 8/Bn.).
3 Bland, C. F. R., M.C., Lt., k. in a., 7/7/19 (att. 1st Slavo-British Legion).
1 Blazey, John William Victor, 2/Lt., k. in a., 26/9/15.
Bond, Ernest Frederick, 2/Lt. (Tp.), k. in a., 26/9/18 (att. 5/Batt.).
5 Boshell, Frederick Stephen, 2/Lt. (Tp.), k. in a., 23/7/18.
Bourchier, Arthur George, 2/Lt., k. in a., 9/5/15.
1 Bowles, Alan John, Capt. (Tp.), k. in a., 10/4/16.
Brain, Francis Sydney, Lt. (Tp.), k. in a., 3/10/18 (att. 1/Dorset R.).
8 Brakspear, Ronald William, Major (Tp.), d. of w., 2/10/15.
Bridge, Donald Gerald Clive, 2/Lt, d. of w., 23/5/15.
8 Bray, Aubrey Mellish, M.C., Lt. (Tp.), d. of w., 8/8/18.
7 Bray, George William Reginald, Lt. (Tp.), d. of w., 16/8/16.
3 Brazier, Anthony David Cecil, 2/Lt. (Tp.), k. in a., 10/3/17 (att. 1/Bn.).
5 Brown, Harold Masters, 2/Lt. (Tp.), d. of w., 9/7/16.
Brown, Stanley Newman, 2/Lt. (Tp.), k. in a, 27/8/18 (att. 8/Bn.).
Buckingham, William Albert, 2/Lt. (Tp.), d. of w., 3/10/18 (Res., att. 5/Bn.).
Buckley, George William, 2/Lt. (Tp.), k. in a., 27/8/18 (att. 8/Bn.).
Burgess, William Vernon, 2/Lt. (Tp.), k. in a., 19/7/16 (att. 6/Bn.).
Burne, Thomas Oldbury, 2/Lt., k. in a., 25/3/18.
7 Butcher, Arthur Algernon Lionel Hastings, 2/Lt. (Tp.), k. in a., 4/3/17.
9 Butler, Aubrey Edward Walter, 2/Lt., k. in a., 3/7/16 (att. 5/Bn.).
Cahill, John Archibald, M.C., Capt. (Tp.), k. in a., 16/8/17.
Carswell, Malcolm Shanks, Lt. (Tp.), k. in a., 17/9/17 (att. 2/Bn.).
2 Carter, Geoffrey Herbert, Lt. (Tp.), d. of w., 12/11/16.
8 Cassels, Hugh Kennedy, Capt. (Tp.), k. in a., 25/9/15.
3 Challenor, Norman Bowen, Capt., k. in a., 31/7/15 (att. 2/Bn.).
8 Chambers, Cleveland Hugh, 2/Lt., k. in a., 3/9/16.
7 Chancellor, Richard Albert Beresford, Capt. (Tp.), d. of w., 24/12/16.
Chapman, Leonard, 2/Lt. (Tp.), d. of w., 2/9/18 (att. 5/Bn.).
7 Childs, Robert Edward, Lt. (Tp.), d. of w., 26/9/18.
3 Childs, Royden James, 2/Lt., k. in a., 27/7/16 (att. 1/Bn.).
3 Clarke, Harold Joyce, Lt., k. in a., 17/5/15 (att. 1/Bn.).
5 Cobb, Reginald, 2/Lt. (Tp.), k. in a., 13/10/16.
9 Cohen, Harold, 2/Lt. (Tp.), died, 18/7/15.

3 Colbourne, Eric Krabbe, 2/Lt., d. of w., 27/6/15 (att. 1/Bn.).
6 Collier, Samuel Robert, 2/Lt. (Tp.), k. in a., 20/7/16.
6 Collot, Thomas Alexander, 2/Lt., k. in a., 1/7/16.
8 Conyers, Walter Neville, 2/Lt. (Tp), k. in a., 13/8/16.
3 Cooper, Geoffrey Rowsell, 2/Lt., died, 8/11/16.
8 Coote, Richard Markham, Capt. (Tp.), k. in a., 13/10/15.
6 Courage, Godfrey Michell, 2/Lt. (Tp.), k. in a., 1/7/16.
Cox, William Joseph, Lt. (T/Capt.), k. in a., 16/5/15.
Cripps, Reginald Edward, 2/Lt. (Tp.), k. in a., 5/11/17 (att. 6/Bn.).
Cumbley, Reginald, 2/Lt. (Tp.), k. in a., 19/9/18 (att.. 8/Batt.).
2 Davies, Harry, 2/Lt. (Tp.), d. of w., 10/4/16.
3 Davis, Hugh Courtenay, 2/Lt., k. in a., 5/8/16 (and R.F.C.).
Day, Maurice, 2/Lt., k. in a., 9/5/15.
Deare, F. A., Lt.-Col., died, 24/1/15.
Denniss, Thomas Vivian Bartley, Capt., d. of w., 28/8/18.
3 De Vries, Harry K., 2/Lt., k. in a., 20/11/17 (att. 5/Bn.).
3 Dobbie, Herbert William, 2/Lt., k. in a., 14/11/16 (att. 1/Bn.).
Druitt, Joseph, 2/Lt., k. in a., 9/5/15.
6 Dymoke, Walter George, 2/Lt. (Tp.), d. of w., 3/10/16.
9 Eason, Alan, 2/Lt., died, 20/1/16.
8 Edens, Lionel George, 2/Lt. (Tp.), k. in a., 3/9/16.
5 Edwards, Francis Andrew Lloyd, 2/Lt. (Tp.), d. of w., 10/8/16.
3 Fellows, Basil Hamilton Abdy, 2/Lt., d. of w., 22/3/17 (att. 5/Bn.).
Field, Leslie Jack, 2/Lt. (Tp.), k. in a., 4/11/18 (att. 8/Bn.).
Finch, Frank Marshall, 2/Lt., k. in a., 22/9/18 (att. 2/Bn.).
Finch, Herbert Marshall, D.S.O., Lt.-Col., k. in a., 9/5/15.
8 Foot, Douglas Eric, 2/Lt., k. in a., 13/10/15.
Forster, Harold Thomas, D.S.O., M.C., Lt. (A/Major), d. of w., 29/5/18 (att. 2/Northants R.).
6 Fox, Andrew J., Lt. (Tp.), k. in a., 1/9/18.
6 Freeman, George Cyril, T/Lt. (A/Capt.), k. in a., 1/10/16.
3 Freston, Hugh Reginald, 2/Lt., k. in a., 24/1/16 (att. 6/Bn.).
6 Fuller, Cyril John, 2/Lt. (Tp.), d. of w., 22/7/16.
Garnett, Philip Nigel, Lt., d. of w., 11/10/14.
3 Garnett, William Patrick, Lt., d. of w., 30/3/17 (att. R.F.C.).
Getting, Eric Noel, Capt., k. in a., 28-29/9/15.
1 Gibbs, Horace Austen, 2/Lt., k. in a., 29/4/17.
Giddings, Frank, 2/Lt., k. in a., 2/12/17 (att. 2/Bn.).
9 Giles, Edward Victor, 2/Lt. (Tp.), k. in a., 3/7/16 (att. 5/Bn.).
7 Gillespie, William Robert Beauchamp, Major (Tp.), k. in a., 8/9/17.
8 Glen, David Corse, Lt. (Tp.), k. in a., 25/9/15.
2 Godfrey, Hugh, 2/Lt., k. in a., 1/7/16.
5 Gold, Cecil Argo, Lt. (Tp.), k. in a., 3/7/16.
2 Goodall, Albert James Gill, Lt. (Tp.), k. in a., 1/7/16.
8 Gordon, John Cameron, 2/Lt., k. in a., 21/3/18
9 Gouldsbury, Henry Cullen, Capt. (Tp.), died, 27/8/16 (att. 1/K.A. Rifs.).
2 Gray, John Arthur, 2/Lt., k. in a., 4/3/17.
Green, Clifford Whittington, Lt. (T/Capt.), d. of w., 27/6/15.
Gregory, Geoffrey Francis Gregory, Lt., k. in a., 25/9/15.
2 Griesbach, Claude Walter, 2/Lt., k. in a., 23/10/16.
1 Grimes, John Arthur, M.C., 2/Lt. (Tp.), k. in a., 7/3/18.
Guest-Williams, Wynne Austin, Capt., k. in a., 25/9/15.
8 Guy, Reginald Churchill, 2/Lt. (Tp.), k. in a., 24/8/18.
9 Haase, Edward George Louis, 2/Lt. (Tp.), k. in a., 3/7/16 (att. 5/Bn.).
8 Hales, William Clifford, 2/Lt. (Tp.), k. in a., 23/10/16 (att. 2/Bn.).
7 Halfacre, Cecil William, 2/Lt. (Tp.), died, 19/10/16 (att. Trench Mortar Bty.).
Hall, George Ferrier Mansfield, Lt., k. in a., 28/9/15.
3 Hamilton, Chatham Anson Shirley, 2/Lt., d. of w., 24/11/16 (att. 1/Bn.).
8 Hanna, Douglas Murray, Capt. (Tp.), k. in a., 25/9/15.
8 Harrison, Cecil George Bradford, 2/Lt. (Tp.), k. in a., 13/8/16.
8 Harvey, Stanley Alfred George, Lt. (Tp.), k. in a., 21/3/18.
3 Harvey, Richard Prentice, Major, k. in a., 9/5/15 (att. 2/Bn.).
3 Hawkes, Septimus James, Lt. (A/Capt.), died, 10/7/18.
2 Haye, Basil, Lt., drowned, 10/10/18.
3 Haye, Philip, Lt., died, 2/4/19 (att. M.G.C.).
8 Haynes, William Gray, Lt. (Tp.), k. in a., 25/9/15.
2 Heming, Maurice Ivory, 2/Lt. (Tp.), k. in a., 1/7/16.
Hewett, Harold, Capt., k. in a., 4/1/18 (att. R.F.C.).
8 Hicks, Basil Perrin, Lt. (Tp.), k. in a., 25/9/15.
Hill, Charles Glencairn, C.M.G., D.S.O., T/Lt.-Col., k. in a., 26/6/15.
Hinde, Cyril de Villiers, M.C., Lt., died, 11/1/17.
2 Hissey, Maurice Henry, Capt. (Acting), k. in a., 26/10/16.
8 Hobbs, William George, Lt. (Tp.), k. in a., 25/9/15.
Hodgson, George Graham, Lt., k. in a., 9/5/15.
Hogan, Robert Garret Roche, 2/Lt., k. in a., 12/3/15.
Holdsworth, Arthur Mervyn, Lt.-Col., d. of w., 7/7/16.
2 Hope-Lumley, Reginald Lewis, Lt. (Tp.), k. in a., 11/10/17 (att. 37 Bn. Training Res.).
Hopton, Guy William, Capt., k. in a., 27/7/15 (att. 5/Bn.).
Hopwood, Frederick William, 2/Lt., k. in a., 27/8/18 (att. 8/Bn.).
5 Horsford, Harry Curwin, Capt., d. of w., 8/4/17.
5 Howard, Lionel George, 2/Lt. (Tp.), d. of w., 12/4/17.
6 Howe, Charles Kingsley, 2/Lt. (Tp.), k. in a., 1/7/16.
3 Howse, Harold Edward, A/Capt., k. in a., 16/8/17 (att. 2/Bn.).
6 Hudson, Arthur Hensley, Capt. (Tp.), k. in a., 31/7/17.
5 Hudson, Thomas Heylyn, Capt., k. in a., 13/10/15.
9 Hughes, Gordon McGregor, 2/Lt., k. in a., 8/8/16 (att. 5/Bn.).
2 Hugo, Stephen Hofmeyr, Capt., k. in a., 21/8/16.
9 Humbert, Ernest Graham Johnston, Lt., d. of w., 8/6/15.
Humbly, William Leeuwin, Lt., k. in a., 23/8/18 (att. 1/Bn.).
2 Humphreys, Victor Richard, 2/Lt., k. in a., 24/9/16.
Hunt, Gerald Ponsonby Sneyd, C.M.G., D.S.O., Major (A/Lt.-Col.), k. in a., 23/3/18.
1 Jackson, Edward Philip, 2/Lt. (A/Capt.), k. in a., 30/11/17.
1 James, Frank Clifford, 2/Lt., d. of w., 4/5/17 (P of W.).
5 James, Joe Conquest, Capt. (Tp.), d. of w., 14/7/16.
3 Jarred, Geoffrey William, 2/Lt., died, 30/12/17.
Jeakes, John William, Lt. (Tp.), d. of w., 12/10/17 (att. 6/Bn.).
9 Jones, Leslie Philips, Lt., d. of w., 6/6/15.
Joscelyne, Arthur Kennett, 2/Lt. (Tp.), d. of w., 26/6/17 (att. 5/Bn.).
6 Joseph, William Franklin George, 2/Lt. (Tp.), k. in a., 27/5/18 (att. 2/Batt.).
8 Joy, Edward Sydney, 2/Lt. (Tp.), k. in a., 19/8/16.
5 Judd, Frank King, 2/Lt. (Tp.), k. in a., 30/11/17.
8 Keable, Harold Charles Linford, 2/Lt. (Tp.), k. in a., 25/9/15.
8 King, Eric George, 2/Lt. (Tp.), k. in a., 21/3/18.
1 Kingham, Leonard Arthur, Lt., k. in a., 11/8/17 (att. 6/Bn.).
8 Klemamtaski, Louis Arthur, 2/Lt. (Tp.), k. in a., 27/5/16.
2 Knott, Archibald Sherbrooke, M.C., 2/Lt. (Tp.), d. of w., 25/4/18.
Knott, Thomas Albert, 2/Lt., d. of w., 25/11/14.
3 Knowles, Walford Vernon, 2/Lt., k. in a., 31/12/17 (att. 2/Bn.).
1 Lane, George James, 2/Lt., d. of w., 29/6/16.
1 Lavers, Victor Alfred, M.C., 2/Lt. (Tp.), d. of w., 22/4/17.
2 Lee, James Clifford, 2/Lt., d. of w., 1/8/17.
2 Lewis, Reginald, M.C., Capt. (Tp.), k. in a., 1/7/16.
3 Lipscombe, Eric Lancelot, Lt., k. in a., 9/5/15 (att. 2/Bn.).
6 Litten, Raymond, Capt. (Tp.), k. in a., 1/7/16.
5 Lloyd, Ernest Henry, Capt. (Tp.), d. of w., 2/4/15.
Long, John, 2/Lt. (Tp.), k. in a., 4/11/18 (att. 8/Bn.).
6 Longhurst, Harold George Fairfax, T/Major (A/Lt.-Col.), k. in a., 12/10/17.
Love, Henry John, M.M., 2/Lt. (Tp.), d. of w., 2/11/18 (Res., att. 2/4 Bn.).
1 Lynes, Arthur Cecil D'Arcy, 2/Lt., k. in a., 10/7/15.
5 Lyons, Basil, 2/Lt., k. in a., 19/7/17.
2 MacGregor, Donald Alastair, Capt., d. of w., 15/8/15.
6 McLean, John Victor, 2/Lt. (Tp.), d. of w., 17/7/16.
8 Maggs, George Ernest, 2/Lt. (Tp.), d. of w., 14/7/16.
3 Mallam, Clifford Angus, M.C., Lt. (T/Capt.), d. of w., 29/10/18 (att. 5/Bn.).
5 Mathews, Joseph Henry, 2/Lt. (Tp.), k. in a., 27/3/18.
6 Matthews, St. John Bell, 2/Lt. (Tp.), d. of w., 25/11/15.
3 Maurice, Charles Henry Pryse, 2/Lt., died, 24/1/17.
Maurice, John Capel, 2/Lt., k. in a., 7/10/18 (att. 2/Bn.).
1 Maybury, Arthur, 2/Lt., k. in a., 19/7/17 (att. 5/Bn.).
2 Medlicott, Edward Morley, Lt. (Tp.), k. in a., 11/4/16.
2 Merrick, Herbert Frederick Rivers, Lt., k. in a., 3/5/17.
2 Miller, Frank Henry, 2/Lt., k. in a., 27/5/18.
3 Mills, Albert Edward, 2/Lt., k. in a., 16/8/17 (att. 2/Bn.).
Moody-Ward, Richard Guy Torrington, Capt., k. in a., 9/5/15.
5 Morgan, Edward Charles, 2/Lt., k. in a., 18/12/15.
7 Mosley, Harold Drewell, 2/Lt. (Tp.), k. in a., 16/8/16.
Moss, Charles William, 2/Lt. (Tp.), k. in a., 8/8/18 (att. 8/Bn.).
3 Mossman, Harold Alexander, M.C., 2/Lt., k. in a., 25/4/18 (att. 2/Bn.).
5 Mount, Francis, Capt. (Tp.), k. in a., 13/10/15.
3 Nicholson, L. C., D.S.O., Lt., d. of w., 2/11/14 (att. 1/Bn.).
Noble, John Stanley, Lt., d. of w., 30/3/18 (att. 5/Bn.).
Nugent, Charles, Capt., died, 19/11/18.
3 Oke, Robert William Leslie, Lt. (T/Capt.), k. in a., 25/9/15 (att. 2/Bn.).
8 Oldman, Wilfred Southey Deare, Capt. (Tp.), k. in a., 25/9/15.
2 Orr, John Compton, 2/Lt., k. in a., 28/4/17 (att. 5/Batt.).
5 Orrin, William John, 2/Lt. (Tp.), died, 12/11/18 (att. Lab. Cps.).
Paine, George Gordon, M.C., Capt., d. of w., 27/3/18 (att. 6/Bn.).
5 Palmer, Henry Edwardes, 2/Lt., d. of w., 5/4/18.
8 Paramore, Charles Gordon, Capt. (Tp.), k. in a., 25/9/15.
9 Partridge, Alec John, 2/Lt., k. in a., 3/7/16 (att. 5/Bn.).
Pashby, F. E., 2/Lt., d. of w., 13/4/18 (and R.A.F.).
2 Payne, Osmond Guy, Lt. (Tp.), k. in a., 1/7/16.
8 Peacock, Thomas Gordon, T/Lt. & Adjt., k. in a., 25/9/15.
9 Peatfield, Stanley James, 2/Lt. (Tp.), d. of w., 2/7/16 (att. M.G.C., 60 Bde.).
6 Peel, Alfred, 2/Lt. (Tp.), k. in a., 5/5/17.
Perkins, Reginald Gabriel Beale, 2/Lt., k. in a., 14/9/14.
Perrott, A. H., Lt., k. in a., 10/9/14.
6 Phillips, Eustace Edward Lovett, 2/Lt. (Tp.), k. in a., 30/10/15.
8 Pitt, Vio Douglas Wallace, 2/Lt., d. of w., 24/8/16.
5 Pollard, Roger Thompson, Lt. (Tp.), k. in a., 13/10/15.
8 Preston, Alfred James, 2/Lt. (Tp.), d. of w., 21/9/18.
8 Prout, Douglas William, 2/Lt. (Tp.), k. in a., 3/9/16.
Quarry, St. John Shandon, Major, k. in a., 14/4/18 (att. 14 R. War. R.).
Radford, Maurice Clive, D.S.O., Capt., k. in a., 28/9/15.
Randall, Charles Edwin, 2/Lt. (Tp.), k. in a., 27/5/18 (att. 2/4 Bn.).
6 Ravenor, Geoffrey Paxton, 2/Lt. (Tp.), k. in a., 2/10/16.
Rawson, Philip Colin, 2/Lt., k. in a., 25/9/15.
3 Ready, Edward Charles, 2/Lt., d. of w., 2/5/17 (att. 1/Bn.) (P. of W.).
1 Reid, James Robert, Lt., k. in a., 27/7/16.
5 Reiss, Stephen Lacy, Lt. (Tp.), k. in a., 13/10/15.
3 Roberts, Matthias Groves, 2/Lt., k. in a., 3/7/17 (att. 1/Bn.).
2 Robinson, Benjamin Stanley, 2/Lt., k. in a., 1/7/16.

Rossiter, Philip, 2/Lt., killed, 19/1/15.
1 Row, Arthur Leslie, M.M., 2/Lt., k. in a., 5/6/18.
5 Rowe, Gilbert James Burbery, 2/Lt. (Tp.), d. of w., 17/4/18.
Rowell, T., M.C., 2/Lt., died, 20/5/18 (and R.A.F.).
9 Rowley, Hugh Travers, Lt. (Tp.), k. in a., 1/7/16 (att. 2/Bn.).
Rozelaar, Samuel Louis, Lt. (Tp.), drowned, 10/10/18 (att. 2/Bn.).
Russell, Bernard, 2/Lt. (Tp.), k. in a., 25/9/15.
6 Sadler, Hereward Pattison, 2/Lt. (Tp.), d. of w., 19/7/16.
9 Salman, Clifford, 2/Lt. (Tp.), k. in a., 13/10/15 (att. 8/Bn.).
8 Sarchet, Hugh le Gallienne, M.C., A/Capt., k. in a., 4/4/18.
Saunders, Alfred Hewgill, Lt., k. in a., 10/3/15.
1 Saville, Eric, 2/Lt., (Tp.), k. in a., 8/10/18.
6 Saye, Lancelot Hugo, 2/Lt. (Tp.), d. of w., 11/7/16.
2 Schneider, Stewart Spearing, 2/Lt., k. in a., 1/7/16.
5 Sharp, John Stanley, Major (Tp.), k. in a., 17/3/17.
2 Shirreff, Francis Gordon, 2/Lt., k. in a., 1/7/16.
Shott, Henry Hammond, D.S.O., Capt., k. in a., 26/8/14.
Simmons, Russell Louis Harry, 2/Lt., k. in a., 25/9/15.
Simon, Marcel Andre, 2/Lt. (Tp.), k. in a., 29/4/17.
Smith, William Henry, 2/Lt. (Tp.,) died, 4/11/18 (Res., (att. 2/4 Bn.).
8 Snell, Francis Saxon, 2/Lt. (Tp.), k. in a., 11/7/16 (att. 9/Bn.).
6 Souper, Noel Beaumont, 2/Lt. (Tp.), k. in a., 1/7/16.
8 Spartali, Cyril, 2/Lt. (Tp.), k. in a., 13/10/15.
1 Spencer, Jack Hamlyn, M.C., 2/Lt. (Tp.,) d. of w., 5/6/18.
5 Spencer, Sydney Gurton, Capt. (Tp.), k. in a., 13/10/15.
Steele, Oliver, Capt., k. in a., 25/10/14.
5 Stewart, Humphrey, Capt. (Tp.), k. in a., 3/7/16.
3 Stidwell, Herbert Jenkins, 2/Lt., k. in a., 27/7/16 (att. 1/Bn.).
1 Stoneham, Greville Cope, 2/Lt., k. in a., 14/11/16.
3 Storey, Kenneth Cothay Bonnell, 2/Lt., (T/Lt.), k. in a., 9/4/17 (att. 5/Bn.).
1 Street, Herbert, 2/Lt. (Tp.), d. of w., 24/11/18.
9 Summers, Ranulph Augustus, 2/Lt. (Tp.), k. in a., 28/9/15 (att. 1/Bn.).
8 Sumpster, Frank Mariner, Lt., k. in a., 21/3/18.
3 Taffs, Charles Reginald, Lt., k. in a., 15/5/15 (att. 1/Bn.).
12 Talbot-Bowe, Edward, Capt. (Tp.), d. of w., 1/11/17 (att. 188 Lab. Coy.).
6 Tarrant, Henry Geoffrey Nelson, M.C., 2/Lt. (Tp.), k. in a., 31/7/17.
5 Taylor, Aucher Wilbraham, 2/Lt., k. in a., 26/9/16.
7 Thompson, Horace Brockbank, M.C., 2/Lt., k. in a., 24/4/17.
1 Thorne, Henry Cyril, Lt. (Tp.), k. in a., 27/6/16.
5 Thorns, Francis Joseph, 2/Lt. (Tp.), d. of w., 31/5/16.
6 Tigar, Geoffrey Herbert, 2/Lt. (Tp.), k. in a., 13/10/17.
Tindall, Howard Simson, Lt. (Tp.), k. in a., 31/7/17.
Todd, Charles Hatt, 2/Lt. (Tp.), k. in a., 12/10/17 (att. 6/Bn.).
1 Tomey, Wilfred, 2/Lt. (Tp.), d. of w., 9/10/18.
8 Tosetti, Douglas. M.C., Major (Tp.), k. in a., 21/3/18.
6 Traill, Kenneth Robert, Lt. (Tp.), k. in a., 1/7/16.
5 Trehern, Arthur Reginald, 2/Lt. (Tp.), k. in a., 27/7/15.
5 Trewartha-James, Derric Vernon, Lt. (Tp.), k. in a., 13/10/15.
3 Trotter, Ronald Herbert Gillet, Lt., k. in a., 25/9/15 (att. 2/Bn.).
7 Troup, Stewart Houghton, Lt. (Tp.), k. in a., 2/12/17 (att. 2/Batt.).
Tunbridge, Arthur Thomas Hornby, 2/Lt. (Tp.), k. in a., 12/10/17 (att. 6/Batt.).
3 V.C. Turner, Alexander Buller, 2/Lt., d. of w., 1/10/15 (att. 1/Bn.).
Tutton, Francis James, M.M., 2/Lt. (Tp.), d. of w., 26/8/18 (att. 5/Batt.).
Vesey, James, Lt., k. in a., 25/9/15.
5 Wace, Percival Beckwith, Capt., d. of w., 3/7/16.
2 Wacher, Walter Ronald, T/Lt. (A/Capt.), k. in a., 12/10/17 (att. 6/Bn.).
2 Wait, Herbert Alfred Vincent, 2/Lt., k. in a., 2/12/17.
5 Waite, Alfred, D.C.M., 2/Lt., k. in a., 5/4/18.
Waters, Charles Louis, M.C., Capt. (A/Major), d. of w., 19/10/17 (att. 1/Nigeria R..)
Watkins, Thomas, 2/Lt., k. in a., 9/5/15.
Watson, Cedric Gordon, Lt., k. in a., 9/5/15 (att. E. Surr. R.).
Way, Frederick Henry, Lt., k. in a., 11/9/15.
2 Webster, Edward Mackay, 2/Lt., k. in a., 1/8/16.
Wells, Louis Conrad, 2/Lt., k. in a., 31/3/18.
1 West, Nevile, M.C., Capt., k. in a., 16/2/17.
Wheeler, Charles Palliser, Capt., k. in a., 25/9/15.
5 Wickett, Thomas Pemberthy, 2/Lt. (Tp.), d. of w., 20/11/17.
8 Williams, Norman, Lt., k. in a., 21/3/18.
1 Wilson, Cecil Vere, Lt. (Tp.), d. of w., 31/7/16.
Wilson, Robert, 2/Lt., k. in a., 3/7/16.
8 Woodford, Harold Vivian, 2/Lt. (Tp.), k. in a., 13/10/15.
Wright, Thomas, 2/Lt., k. in a., 1/5/15 (att. 2/Bn.).
5 Wykes, Ernest Arthur Inns, 2/Lt. (Tp.), k. in a., 30/11/17.

The Queen's Own (Royal West Kent Regiment).

6 Abel, James Edgar, 2/Lt. (Tp.), d. of w., 22/12/17 (P. of W.).
6 Alderman, William John, D.S.O., Capt. (A/Lt.-Col.), k. in a., 20/11/17.
3 Allchin, Sidney Milton, 2/Lt. (Tp.), k. in a., 13/12/17.
Allen, George James, 2/Lt. (Tp.), d. of w., 12/10/17 (att. 7th Bn.).
Ames, William Kerr, Lt., d. of w., 16/9/14.
3 Anderson, Colin Knox, Lt., k. in a., 23/8/14.
8 Andrews, Edwin Charles, 2/Lt. (Tp.), died, 12/8/18.
8 Apperley, Basil Lang Marling, 2/Lt. (Tp.), d. of w., 19/4/17.
Arnold, Frederick Arthur, 2/Lt. (Tp.), d. of w., 13/10/18 (att. 6th Bn.).
6 Ashton, Cyril James, Temp. Lt. (A/Capt.), d. of w., 12/3/18.
11 Ashworth, Brian Wilding, 2/Lt. (Tp.), d. of w., 4/8/17.
Bain, Nicol, 2/Lt. (Tp.), k. in a., 16/10/18 (att. 8th Bn.).
Banks, Percy Abbott, M.C., 2/Lt. (Tp.), died, 22/2/19 (and R.A.F.).
8 Baring, Cecil Christopher, 2/Lt. (Tp.), d. of w., 21/3/18.
6 Barker, Charles Ivor, 2/Lt. (Tp.), d. of w., 17/3/16.
6 Barnett, Lascelles De Barry, Capt. (Tp.), k. in a., 3/7/16.
11 Barrs, Noel Coghlan, 2/Lt., k. in a., 15/9/16.
1 Bartlett, Lionel Arthur, Lt., k. in a., 22/7/16.
3 Battersby, Eric May, Capt., k. in a., 28/10/14 (att. 1st Bn.).
3 Beckett, Philip Arthur, 2/Lt., k. in a., 14/2/17 (att. 7th Bn.).
Beeman, Arthur Cecil, Capt., k. in a., 26/10/14.
8 Beer, Henry Oliver, 2/Lt. (Tp.), k. in a., 26/9/15.
3 Bennett, Charles Tudor, Capt., k. in a., 22/7/16 (att. 1st Bn.).
8 Bigsby, Edgar Arthur, 2/Lt., k. in a., 25/9/15.
3 Blew, Kynnersley, 2/Lt., k. in a., 12/4/18.
Bolton, Percy James, 2/Lt. (Tp.), d. of w., 5/11/18 (att. 7th Bn.).
6 Boucher, William Moore, Lt., k. in a., 20/11/17.
9 Bowen, Francis Moull Storer, Lt. (Tp.), k. in a., 1/7/16 (att. 1st Bn. Innis. Fus.).
9 Bowling, Edwyn Randolph, 2/Lt. (Tp.), k. in a., 4/6/16 (att. 8th Bn.).
3 Bradley, Philip Warden, Lt., k. in a., 23/4/15 (att. 1st Bn.).
1 Bristow, Cuthbert George, 2/Lt., k. in a., 17/7/17 (att. 3rd Bn.).
Broadwood, Maximilian Francis, 2/Lt., k. in a., 24/8/14.
8 Brock-Hollinshead, Laurence, Major, k. in a., 26/9/15.
6 Brown, Alexander Henry, 2/Lt. (Tp.), k. in a., 9/8/18.
Brown, E. C., Lt., k. in a., 18/10/18 (and R.A.F.).
Brown, Edwin Charles, 2/Lt., d. of w., 10/8/18 (att. 7th Bn.).
10 Brown, Frederick Peter, 2/Lt. (Tp.), d. of w., 24/5/18.
Brown, John Edward Guy, Capt., k. in a., 22/2/15 (att. R. Berks. Regt.).
3 Brown, Osmond Pickard, 2/Lt., d. of w., 31/7/17 (att. 11/Bn.).
1/2 Buckingham, P. E., 2/Lt., killed, 8/11/18 (and R.A.F.).
Buckle, Matthew Perceval, D.S.O., Major, k. in a., 27/10/14.
8 Buckle, Cuthbert Charles Corbett, 2/Lt., k. in a., 3/7/16.
3 Bullman, Haddon Robert Horsley, 2/Lt., k. in a., 30/11/17 (att. M.G.C., 71st).
Burbury, John Francis, 2/Lt., d. of w., 23/2/15.
8 Burrell, Raymond Francis Topham, 2/Lt., k. in a., 26/9/15.
8 Cadell, Assheton Biddulph, 2/Lt. (Tp.), d. of w., 19/12/16.
8 Cambrook, Horace, M.C., 2/Lt. (Tp.), d. of w., 17/10/18.
Came, Harold Charles, 2/Lt. (Tp.), k. in a., 20/9/17 (att. 11th Bn.).
1 Camplin, Ernest, 2/Lt. (Tp.), k. in a., 29/9/18 (att. 6th Bn.).
9 Carre, Gilbert Trenchard, Lt. (Tp.), k. in a., 20/11/17 (att. 6th Bn.).
7 Carter, Stephen Charles, 2/Lt. (Tp.), k. in a., 18/11/16.
7 Cathcart, David Andrew, 2/Lt., k. in a., 13/7/16.
Catt, Archibald William, M.C., 2/Lt. (Tp. Lt.), died, 9/3/18 3rd Nigerian Regt.).
7 Chapman, Henry James, M.C., 2/Lt. (Tp.), k. in a., 8/8/18.
Clark, Charles William, 2/Lt. (Tp.), k. in a., 20/11/17 (att. 6th Bn.).
3 Clarke, Roland Harry, 2/Lt., died, 23/5/18 (att. 1st Bn.).
Cleland-Hollamby, Douglas MacDonald, 2/Lt. (Tp.), killed, 22/8/17.
6 Coales, Stephen James, 2/Lt. (Tp.), d. of w., 18/9/16.
Cobb, William Ralph, M.C., Lt. (A/Capt.), d. of w., 5/10/17.
Coles, Reginald Walter, 2/Lt. (Tp.), k. in a., 12/10/17 (att. 7th Bn.).
3 Compton, Cyril Henry, 2/Lt., k. in a., 23/7/16.
3 Cooksey, Kenneth Barsano, 2/Lt., k. in a., 8/4/17 (and R.F.C.).
6 Coombs, Claude Stuart, 2/Lt. (Tp.), d. of w., 6/7/16.
Coote, George Bernard, Lt., k. in a., 27/5/18 (and M.G. Corps, 50th Bn.).
6 Copeman, Ernest Hugh, 2/Lt., k. in a., 18/3/16 (att. M.G. Corps, 37th Bn.).
7 Corley, Edward Cecil, 2/Lt. (Tp.), k. in a., 23/2/17.
1 Cornford, William Day, 2/Lt., k. in a., 22/7/16.
10 Costin, Henry William, 2/Lt., k. in a., 1/8/17.
11 Cottrell, John Prince, 2/Lt. (Tp.), d. of w., 24/8/18 (att. 7th R. Fusrs.).
Craston, John, 2/Lt., d. of w., 19/4/15 (3rd att. 1st Bn.).
2 Crocker, Percival James Wilberforce, Lt. (Tp.), died, 16/11/18 (att. 1/5th Bn.).
3 Crombie, James McHattie, 2/Lt., d. of w., 2/7/17 (att. 10th Bn.).
1 Cross, Philip Frank, 2/Lt., k. in a., 22/7/16.
Cross, Sidney William, 2/Lt. (Tp.), d. of w., 23/10/18 (att. 10th Bn.).
7 Crosse, Robert Grant, Lt. (Tp.), d. of w., 14/7/16.
Croucher, Frederick William, 2/Lt., k. in a., 27/4/15.
7 Cullerne, Alan Baird, M.C., 2/Lt. (Tp.), k. in a., 23/10/18.
11 Culley, Geoffrey Matthew George, Capt. (Tp.), k. in a., 15/9/16.
1 Daniel, Archibald Morris, 2/Lt. (Tp.), k. in a., 4/10/17.
1 Darlow, John William Edward, M.C., Lt. (Tp.), k. in a., 29/8/18 (att. 16th R. Warwicks).
3 Daubeney, Giles Robert, 2/Lt., k. in a., 23/4/15 (att. 1st Bn.).
10 Davies, Clifford Thomas, 2/Lt., k. in a., 7/6/17.
6 Dawson, William Robert Angrave, D.S.O., Capt. (Tp. Lt.-Col.), d. of w., 3/12/18

7 Desprez, Warwick Haynes, 2/Lt. (Tp.), k. in a., 24/8/18.
10 Dickinson, Bruce Norman, 2/Lt. (Tp.), k. in a., 29/6/16.
3 Dickinson, Humphrey Neville, 2/Lt., d. of w., 13/10/16 (att. 6th Bn.).
10 Dillon, Charles Edward Maxwell, 2/Lt., k. in a., 31/7/17.
7 Dix, Herbert Golden, M.C., 2/Lt. (Tp.), k. in a., 14/2/17.
3 Dobie, William Murray, Lt., k. in a., 9/4/16 (att. 1st Bn.).
Dodson, Joseph Edward, 2/Lt. (Tp.), k. in a., 10/10/18 (att. 10th East Kents).
8 Don, Valentine Grantham, Lt., k. in a., 26/8/15.
8 Dove, Sydney Ernest, 2/Lt. (Tp.), k. in a., 16/8/16.
Driffield, Herbert George, 2/Lt. (Tp.), d. of w., 1/8/17.
Dyke, Francis Hart, 2/Lt., k. in a., 27/9/17 (att. 7th Loyal N. Lanc. Regt.).
10 Edmett, Arthur William, Lt. (Tp.), d. of w., 16/3/18.
Edmonds, Leonard, 2/Lt. (Tp. Lt.), k. in a., 3/11/17 (att. 2/4th Battn.).
8 Edwards, Arthur Corbett, Capt., k. in a., 25/9/15.
6 Elliott, William James, M.C., 2/Lt., d. of w., 30/6/18.
2 Elton, Arthur Charles, Lt., k. in a., 24/7/15.
8 Everson, Harry Thomas, 2/Lt. (Tp.), k. in a., 7/11/18.
3 Ewen, William James, Lt. (A/Capt.), k. in a., 25/3/18 (att. 8/Bn.).
Farley, Harry William, Lt., k. in a., 24/4/18 (att. 8/Bn.).
Fenton, Arthur Edward, 2/Lt. (Tp.), k. in a., 14/6/17 (att. 11/Bn.).
Field, Charles Cecil, 2/Lt. (Tp.), k. in a., 30/3/16 (att. Suff.).
7 File, Harold William, 2/Lt. (Tp.), k. in a., 13/7/16.
Fisher, Frank, Capt., k. in a., 13/9/14.
1 Fleming, John Allister, 2/Lt., d. of w., 22/7/16.
8 Flowers, Herbert, 2/Lt. (Tp.), k. in a., 1/9/16.
Ford, John Ballard Berkley, Capt., d. of w., 16/2/17.
7 Forsyth, James, 2/Lt. (Tp.), k. in a., 13/7/16.
1 Fox, Charles James, 2/Lt. (Tp.), k. in a., 22/7/16.
12 Fraser, Frederick Gordon, M.C., Capt. (Tp.), k. in a., 14/6/17 (att. 11/Bn.).
3 Freeman, John Bentley, 2/Lt., k. in a., 20/9/17 (att. 11/Bn.).
7 French, Sidney Arthur, Lt. (Tp.), k. in a., 20/3/18.
7 Fricker, Edwin, 2/Lt. (Tp.), k. in a., 29/9/16.
Frost, Kenneth, 2/Lt., k. in a., 22/2/15.
10 Fry, Horace Charles, 2/Lt. (Tp.), died, 24/2/17 (att. R.F.C.).
Fuller, Bernard, 2/Lt. (Tp.), k. in a., 4/11/18 (att. 7/Bn.).
8 Gibbs, Leslie, Lt., k. in a., 26/9/15.
1 Gillett, Frederick Tremlow, 2/Lt. (Tp.), k. in a., 22/7/16.
1 Gladwell, John Henry, 2/Lt. (Tp.), k. in a., 12/10/17 (att. 7th Bn.).
7 Glover, Ben Hilton, 2/Lt. (Act. Capt.), k. in a., 1/7/16 (att. T.M.B.).
Godfrey, Edward, 2/Lt. (Tp.), k. in a., 31/7/17 (att. 10/Bn.).
Gordon-Smith, Gordon, Temp. Lt. (Act. Capt.), k. in a., 24/10/18 (att. 10/Bn.).
1 Gore, Sidney Kingston, Lt., k. in a., 28/10/14.
2 Graham, Marmaduke Whitaker, Capt., k. in a., 24/7/15.
10 Grant, Ivan Thorold, 2/Lt. (Tp.), k. in a., 9/10/16.
3 Gray, Gerald Montague, 2/Lt., k. in a., 7/10/16 (att. 6/Bn.).
1 Gray, Harry Albert, M.C., Lt. (Tp.), d. of w., 15/7/18.
11 Greenwood, James Hurst, M.C., Lt. (Tp.), d. of w., 24/7/18.
7 Gregory, Herbert Thomas, 2/Lt. (Tp.) (Act. Capt.), d. of w., 13/10/17.
Gregson, Alan Herbert, 2/Lt. (Tp.), k. in a., 19/4/17 (att. 2/4 Bn.).
7 Griffiths, Walter Harold, 2/Lt. (Tp.), k. in a., 4/10/16.
Grist, Cecil Howard, 2/Lt., k. in a., 3/5/17.
3 Grocott, Frederick William, 2/Lt., k. in a., 17/7/17 (att. 6/Bn.).
Gross, Geoffrey Yates, Capt., k. in a., 9/4/16.
10 Ground, John Kingston, 2/Lt. (Tp.), k. in a., 19/6/16.
7 Hackett, Walter Ralph, Lt. (Tp.), k. in a., 3/10/16.
6 Hall, Alexander Kilburn, Capt., k. in a., 7/10/16.
3 Hall, Harry Sydney Hopton Hadley, Capt., died, 24/10/18.
1 Hallowes, Geoffrey Blackwood, 2/Lt., k. in a., 4/9/16.
8 Hamilton, Francis William, 2/Lt. (Tp.), d. of w., 3/3/16.
10 Harding, Arthur Keith, M.C., Capt. (Tp.), k. in a., 24/10/18.
Harding, Jack Maynard, 2/Lt., k. in a., 26/10/14.
6 Harris, Herbert Cecil, Capt. (Tp.), k. in a., 3/7/16.
3 Harrison, Francis Ingleby, Lt. (Act. Capt.), d. of w., 8/5/18 (att. 1/Bn.).
3 Harrison, Edward Donald, 2/Lt., k. in a., 25/7/16 (att. 19th Manch. Regt.).
8 Harvey, Edward Byron Atkins, 2/Lt. (Tp.), k. in a., 15/4/17.
Hastings, Percy, Major, d. of w., 2/9/14.
Hayes, Gordon Stanley, 2/Lt. (Tp.), k. in a., 15/6/18 (att. 5th Glouc. Regt.).
9 Hearnden, Harry Crespin Stephens, Lt. (Tp.), k. in a., 6/8/15 (att. 2/Bn. Hants. Regt.).
Healey, Richard Elkanah Hownam, Lt., k. in a., 22/7/16.
Heatly, John Firth, 2/Lt., k. in a., 21/3/18 (att. 7/Bn.).
7 Heaton, Ivon, Lt. (Tp.) (Act. Capt.), d. of w., 14/10/17.
11 Heath, John Oswald, Lt. (Tp.), k. in a., 7/10/16.
6 Heath, Arthur George, Lt. (Tp.), k. in a., 8/10/15.
6 Hemmerde, Charles Eric, M.C., Lt., k. in a., 27/9/18.
3 Hill, Harold Belfit, Lt., killed, 6/9/18 (att. R.A.F.).
6 Hodge, Lionel Clifford, 2/Lt., k. in a., 30/11/17.
3 Hodges, Daniel Alfred, 2/Lt., k. in a., 5/5/17.
10 Holden, Vernon, D.S.O., and M.C., Major (Tp.), d. of w., 2/10/18 (att. West Surr. Regt.).
7 Holland, Ralph B., Capt. (Tp.), k. in a., 2/10/16.
3 Hougham, Bertram William, M.C., Lt. (Tp. Capt.), k. in a., 6/9/18 (att. 5th Roy. Berks).
2 Howell, Norman Bulmer, Lt., k. in a., 24/7/15.
7 Hudson, George Trevor, 2/Lt. (Tp.), k. in a., 2/10/16.
8 Hughes, John Henry, 2/Lt. (Tp.), k. in a., 3/7/16.
9 Hunter, William Samuel, 2/Lt. (Tp.), died, 1/2/16.
1 Hyde, Francis Cecil, Lt., k. in a., 9/4/17.
9 Innocent, Edward John, Lt. (Tp.), k. in a., 3/7/16.
3 Jarvis, Charles Wemyss Barron, 2/Lt. (Act. Capt.), k. in a., 30/7/16 (att. 7/Bn. R. Dub. Fus.).
3 Job, Bernard Craig Keble, 2/Lt., k. in a., 18/4/15.
3 Johnson, Norman Teasdale, 2/Lt., k. in a., 16/4/17 (att. 8th Bn.).
11 Jones, Sydney James, Lt. (Tp.), k. in a., 15/9/16.
Joslin, Francis John, Major, k. in a., 18/4/15.
Judd, Morris Stanley, 2/Lt. (Tp.), killed (acc.), 18/8/17 (att. 7th Bn.).
Keenlyside, Guy Francis Headlam, Capt., d. of w., 29/10/14.
9 Kirkham, William Laban, 2/Lt. (Tp.), d. of w., 21/10/16.
3 Knight, John Oswald, 2/Lt., k. in a., 2/11/16 (att. 11th/Bn.).
12 Knott, Donald James Vivian, 2/Lt. (Tp.), k. in a., 7/10/16 (att. 11th Bn.).
1 Kysh, Claude James Anthony, Lt., died, 27/11/18.
3 Lamb, Ernest Edwin, 2/Lt., k. in a., 26/9/16 (att. 9th Bn. Lancs Fus.).
Laskey, George, M.M., 2/Lt. (Tp.), k. in a., 16/10/18 (att. 8th Bn.).
8 Latimer, Hugh, 2/Lt., k. in a., 3/7/10.
7 Latter, Francis Robinson, Capt., d. of w., 3/5/17.
10 Laurence, Stuart, 2/Lt., k. in a., 17/9/16.
8 Lawson, Cecil David Norton, 2/Lt. (Tp.), k. in a., 26/9/15.
1 Leatherdale, Donald Ryan, 2/Lt., k. in a., 22/7/16.
Legard, George Bruce, Capt., k. in a., 27/10/14.
3 Levett, Richard Henry, 2/Lt., died, 20/8/16.
Lewin, Edward Chaloner, Lt. (Tp.), k. in a., 27/9/18 (att. 1st Bn.).
7 Lewin, Francis Harold, M.C., Capt. (Tp.), k. in a., 12/10/17.
1 Lewinstein, Harry, 2/Lt., k. in a., 22/7/16.
Littleboy, Frederick Graham, Lt. (Tp.), d. of w., 7/12/15 (att. 9th Bn. Worcs. Regt.).
10 Logan, Hubert Henderson, Capt. (Tp.), k. in a., 15/9/16.
12 Longuehaye, James Stanley, 2/Lt. (Tp.), k. in a., 7/10/16 (att. 6 Bn.).
Lovelace, Ronald Desmond Weston, 2/Lt., k. in a., 26/10/17.
Lovell, William Leslie, 2/Lt., k. in a., 27/7/17 (and R.F.C., 25th Sqd.).
1 Luck, Nelson Amos, 2/Lt. (Tp.), k. in a., 15/6/18 (att. Ox. & Bucks. L.I.).
1 McClenaghan, George Mayo, Capt., d. of w., 8/11/18.
McDonach, Patrick, 2/Lt., k. in a., 18/11/14 (att. Suff. Regt.).
11 Malpass, Charles Edward, Capt. (Act.), k. in a., 8/10/18 (att. 28th London Regt.).
8 Manley, Charles Percival Henry, M.C., 2/Lt. (Tp.), d. of w., 4/10/18.
6 Mann, Horatio Geoffrey Cornwallis, M.C., 2/Lt., k. in a., 17/7/17.
11 Mansfield, Gerald Turner, 2/Lt. (Tp.), k. in a., 15/9/16.
Marchant, Francis George Wake, 2/Lt., d. of w., 25/10/16 (and R.F.C.).
7 Marsh, Ralph Hedley, 2/Lt. (Tp.), k. in a., 12/4/18.
1 Martin, Alfred, 2/Lt. (Tp.), k. in a., 3/9/16.
6 Martyn, Edgar Spear, Capt., k. in a., 30/11/17.
3 Mason, Charles, 2/Lt., k. in a., 27/9/18.
Matheson, Roderick Kyrle, 2/Lt., d. of w., 8/9/16 (att. 20th Bn. Manch. Regt.).
7 Matthews, John Brice, Capt. (Tp.), k. in a., 14/2/17.
6 Matthews, Myles Lewis Wyan, Capt. (Tp.), k. in a., 3/7/16.
1 Meakins, Robert William Spencam, 2/Lt., k. in a., 27/8/16.
7 Michell, Arthur, 2/Lt. (Tp.), k. in a., 12/10/17.
Miles, George Henry, 2/Lt., k. in a., 13/9/17 (and R.F.C., 6th Sqd.).
3 Mills, Percy Trevenson, Capt., k. in a., 8/2/15 (att. 1st Bn.).
3 Monypenny, Phillips Burnley Sterndale Gybbon, Lt., k. in a., 28/6/18 (att. 1st Bn.).
1 Moorhouse, W., Lt., died, 22/8/18 (and R.A.F.).
10 Mothersill, James Neville, 2/Lt. (Tp.), k. in a., 7/6/17.
7 Newbold, Philip, 2/Lt. (Tp.), d. of w., 13/7/16.
Newton, Wilfrid, Capt., d. of w., 28/9/16.
3 Nicholas, Oliffe Richmond, Lt., k. in a., 17/4/16.
10 Norris, Frank Ernest Edwin, Lt. (Tp.), d. of w., 2/10/18.
Norris, Kenneth Arthur Annesley, 2/Lt., died, 16/6/16.
3 Northey, Mervyn Ackland, Lt., k. in a., 28/10/18 (att. 2nd Bn.).
Pack-Beresford, Charles George, Major, k. in a., 10/9/14.
3 Payton, Charles Mervyn, Lt., k. in a., 18/4/15 (att. 1st Bn.).
7 Peglar, Harry Sidney, 2/Lt., k. in a., 4/11/18.
Phillips, William Charles Owen, Capt., k. in a., 24/8/14.
3 Piggott, Deighton Torre, M.C., Lt., k. in a., 15/10/18 (att. 8 Bn.).
10 Pillman, Robert Lawrence, Temp. Capt., d. of w., 9/7/16.
8 Plant, Percy William, 2/Lt., k. in a., 28/9/15.
Poland, Henry Arthur, 2/Lt., k. in a., 18/4/15.
Pownall, Lionel Henry Yorke, Lt., k. in a., 21/3/15.
1 Pracy, Henry Reginald, Temp. 2/Lt., d. of w., 5/9/16.
1 Press, George William, Lt., A/Capt., k. in a., 26/10/17.
8 Preston, Leslie George, M.C., Temp. Capt., d. of w., 10/7/18 (att. 6/Dorset Regt.).
11 Prior, Henry George Redmond, Lt. (Tp.), k. in a., 7/10/16.
6 Proctor, William Harold, Temp. 2/Lt., k. in a., 9/4/17.
11 Purver, Bernard Arthur, Temp. Capt., k. in a., 7/10/16.
6 Pye, William Wakeley, Temp. 2/Lt., k. in a., 14/10/15.
3 Rapson, Harold Thomas, 2/Lt. (A/Capt.), d. of w., 23/3/18 (att. 7 Bn.) (P. of W.).
Redding, Edward Joseph, 2/Lt., k. in a., 4/10/17.
3 Revelle, Roy Cyril, 2/Lt., k. in a., 15/9/18 (and R.A.F.).
8 Richardson, Arthur Balfour, 2/Lt., k. in a., 21/3/18.
Richardson, William Arthur Ingham, 2/Lt. (Tp.), d. of w., 31/8/15.
10 Roberts, Frederick William, M.C., Capt. (Tp.), d. of w., 4/10/17 (P. of W.).
7 Roberts, Thomas William, Temp. 2/Lt., k. in a., 30/9/16.

8 Robertson-Ross, Patrick Maitland, Temp. Capt., k. in a., 26/9/15.
Robinson, Henry, 2/Lt. (Tp.), k. in a., 21/9/17 (att. 10 Bn.).
11 Rodney, Burnett William, 2/Lt. (Tp.), k. in a., 20/4/17.
8 Roscoe, Arthur, M.C., Temp. 2/Lt., d. of w., 5/9/16.
8 Ross, Walter Urquhart, Temp. Capt., d. of w., 22/2/16.
Russell, John Guy Harry Stebbing, 2/Lt., d. of w., 29/9/18 (att. 10 Bn.).
11 Sams, Charles, 2/Lt. (Tp.), k. in a., 7/6/17.
10 Samuel, Gerald George, Temp. Lt., k. in a., 7/6/17.
Sanders, Sydney Elphick, 2/Lt., k. in a., 30/11/17 (att. 6 Bn.).
7 Saveall, Garrett, Temp. 2/Lt., k. in a., 13/7/16.
1 Scott, John James, M.C., T/Lt. (A/Capt.), k. in a., 28/6/18.
V.C. Sewell, Cecil Harold, Lt., k. in a., 29/8/18 (and Tank Corps).
3 Sewell, Douglas Clifford Campbell, Lt., d. of w., 10/9/14.
7 Shattock, Harry Edward, T/Lt., A/Capt., d. of w., 7/8/17.
3 Sheppey-Greene, Napier Guy Sheppey, Lt., d. of w., 14/6/18 (att. 7 Bn.).
3 Sheriff, Kenneth, 2/Lt., d. of w., 23/6/15 (att. 2/Border Regt.).
1 Short, Francis Leslie, Capt., died, 3/6/16.
7 Skinner, Douglas Hilton, Temp. Capt., d. of w., 16/7/16.
7 Skottowe, Gordon, Temp. 2/Lt., d. of w., 12/4/18.
8 Smith, Eric, 2/Lt., died, 15/10/16.
10 Smith, George, 2/Lt. (Tp.), k. in a., 15/9/16 (att. 9th Bn.).
Smith, Harold Robert, M.C., Lt. (Tp.), k. in a., 7/11/18 (att. 8th Bn.).
8 Smith, Percival Thomas, Lt., k. in a., 26/9/15.
7 Smyth, Edwin Percy, Lt. (Tp.), k. in a., 28/6/18.
Snelgrove, Frederick Augustus, 2/Lt. (Tp.), k. in a., 24/8/18 (att. 6th Bn.).
3 Southgate, Henry Albert, 2/Lt., k. in a., 8/4/18 (att. Anson Bn.).
11 Squire, Frederick, 2/Lt. (Tp.) (Act. Capt.), k. in a., 31/7/17.
3 Stansell, Lionel Brough, 2/Lt., died, 26/10/18 (and R.A.F.).
8 Stanton, Gareth Marsh, 2/Lt. (Tp.), d. of w., 20/2/16.
1 Steele, Alfred Charles John, 2/Lt., k. in a., 23/8/18.
6 Stevens, Henry Francis Bingham, Lt. (Tp.), k. in a., 16/9/15.
7 Stevens, Percy, Lt. (Tp.), k. in a., 23/9/18.
3 Stokes, John Hill, Capt., d. of w., 22/3/15 (att. R. Berks Regt.)
9 Stones, Thomas Frederick, 2/Lt. (Tp.), k. in a., 17/9/16 (att. 10th Bn.).
3 Streatfield, Thomas Basil Maryon, 2/Lt., d. of w., 7/11/17 (att. 1/Bn.).
6 Stuart, William Esme Montague, 2/Lt., k. in a., 7/10/16.
7 Summers, Walter Gordon, Capt. (Tp.), k. in a., 28/12/15.
1 Sutherland, James Lawrence Cathcart, M.C., Lt., d. of w., 13/8/18 (att. R.A.F.).
Sutton, Vivian Charles Woolfe, 2/Lt. (Tp.), d. of w., 14/9/18 (att. 20th London).
Taylor, Henry Arthur, M.C., 2/Lt. (Tp. Capt.), k. in a., 27/9/16 (and R.F.C.).
Taylor, Thomas Jesse, 2/Lt. (Tp.), k. in a., 21/3/18 (att. 52nd T.M.B.).
10 Tennyson-Smith, John Alan, Lt. (Tp.), k. in a., 7/3/17.
Thomas, Sidney John, 2/Lt. (Tp.), k. in a., 21/9/17 (att. 10/Bn.).
Thompson, M. H., 2/Lt., d. of w., 28/11/14.
11 Thompson-Smith, Kingsley, 2/Lt., k. in a., 23/3/18.
3 Towler, Cyril John, 2/Lt., killed, 4/9/18 (and R.A.F.).
6 Towse, Clifford Henry, Tp. Capt., k. in a., 8/11/15.
11 Townshend, Arthur Fitzhenry, Temp. Lt.-Col., d. of w., 16/9/16.
Trotter, Erle Britt, M.C., D.C.M., Lt., died, 28/5/19 (att. 3rd Welsh).
3 Tuff, Cecil Thomas, Capt., k. in a., 18/4/15 (att. 1/Bn.).
3 Turner, Gilbert Austin, 2/Lt., k. in a., 17/11/16 (att. 7/Loy. N. Lanc. Rgt.).
11 Turner, Joseph Henry, M.C., 2/Lt. (Tp.), d. of w., 21/9/18 (att. 6/Bn.)
Twelvetrees, Bernard, 2/Lt. (Tp.), k. in a., 4/10/17 (att. 5th Glos. Regt.).
8 Vaughan, Richard Creswell, 2/Lt. (Tp.), k. in a., 16/4/17.
Venner, Edgar William, 2/Lt., k. in a., 9/7/16.
Vicat, Horatio John. Lt., k. in a., 18/9/14.
8 Vinicombe, Lionel Frank, 2/Lt. (Tp.), k. in a., 29/6/16.
1 Wacher, John Stewart, 2/Lt., killed, acc., 5/8/16.
9 Wade, Oliver John, 2/Lt. (Tp.), k. in a., 22/10/16 (and R.F.C.).
3 Waghorn, Leonard Pengelly, 2/Lt., k. in a., 6/11/14 (att. 1st Bn. R. Berks Regt.).
Walker, Edmund Basil, 2/Lt., k. in a., 18/4/15.
6 Walker, Maurice John Lea, 2/Lt., k. in a., 3/5/17.
8 Wallis, George Arthur Edward, M.C., 2/Lt., d. of w., 16/10/18.
Walsh, William Leopold Hampson, 2/Lt., k. in a., 9/8/18 (att. 8/Bn.).
12 Ward, Geoffrey Arthur, 2/Lt. (Tp.), k. in a., 30/9/16 (att. 7/Bn.).
6 Waterhouse, Gilbert Wilmot, 2/Lt. (Tp.), d. of w., 10/4/17.
11 Watson, Reginald, 2/Lt., k. in a., 7/10/16.
8 Watts, Dudley Haldane, 2/Lt., k. in a., 26/9/15.
Watts, Robin Kenelm, 2/Lt., k. in a., 23/8/18 (att. 7/Bn.).
3 Webb, Charles Parker, M.C., 2/Lt., k. in a., 23/7/17 (att. 11th Bn.).
3 Webb, Stanley Horace, 2/Lt., d. of w., 26/3/18 (att. 7/Bn.) (P. of W.).
3 Westmacott, Frederick Charles, 2/Lt., k. in a., 31/7/17 (att. 11/Bn.).
White, Leslie Spencer, 2/Lt., killed, acc., 15/3/15.
3 Whitehouse, Percy John, 2/Lt., k. in a., 31/10/14 (att. 1/Bn. North'n Rgt.).
8 Wigan, William Lewis, Lt. (Tp.), d. of w., 23/2/16.
6 Wilks, Sydney, Lt., k. in a., 7/10/16.
6 Williams, Ernest Thurston, Capt., k. in a., 3/5/17.
9 Wilson, Arthur Desmond Lloyd, Lt. (Tp.), k. in a., 1/7/16.
2 Wilson, Eric Crawcour, Lt., k. in a., 28/10/18.
8 Winch, Edward Nightingale, 2/Lt., d. of w., 9/10/18.
6 Wood, Basil Vaughan, 2/Lt., k. in a., 3/7/16.
8 Wood, Williams, Temp. Capt., k. in a., 31/5/16.
Woodroffe, Arthur Henry, 2/Lt. (Tp.), k. in a., 31/7/17 (att. 10/Bn.).
8 Woolley, Henry George, 2/Lt. (Tp.), d. of w., 17/4/17.
7 Wright, Cyril Paul, 2/Lt. (Tp.), killed acc., 25/5/16 (att. 55/2 T.M.B.).
3 Yates, James Stanley, 2/Lt., k. in a., 8/10/15 (att. 6/Bn.).
8 Yeo, Frederick George, 2/Lt. (Tp.), k. in a., 26/10/16.
11 Yorke, Charles Henry, 2/Lt. (Tp.), k. in a., 7/10/16.

The King's Own (Yorkshire Light Infantry).

3 Abbis, Reginald Donaldson, 2/Lt., d. of w., 2/12/17 (att. 2/Bn.).
Addenbrooke, Guy Besley, 2/Lt., k. in a., 7/5/15.
9 Alexander, N. L., 2/Lt. (Tp.), k. in a., 1/7/16.
1 Allott, Thomas Richard, 2/Lt. (Tp.), d. of w., 4/11/18.
3 Alt, George Earl, Capt., k. in a., 18/4/15.
3 Andrew, John, 2/Lt., k. in a., 1/7/16 (att. 10/Bn.).
8 Armitage, Arthur William, Capt., k. in a., 1/10/16.
10 Armstrong, Charles MacDonald, 2/Lt., k. in a., 25/9/16.
10 Asher, Kenneth John Penrith, 2/Lt. (Tp.), k. in a., 1/7/16.
11 Atherley, Christopher Ernest, Lt., d. of w., 17/6/15.
Ashworth, Frank, 2/Lt., d. of w., 29/7/18.
9 Asquith, Ernest, 2/Lt. (Tp.), k. in a., 17/9/16.
3 Asquith, G. W., 2/Lt., k. in a., 2/12/17.
8 Atkinson, Harry John, 2/Lt. (Tp.), k. in a., 17/8/16.
11 Atkinson-Jowett, James, Lt. (Tp.), k. in a., 16/9/16 (att. 6/Bn.).
6 Badcock, Arthur Lawrence, 2/Lt. (Tp.), k. in a., 13/10/15.
7 Ball-Acton, Reginald Thomas Annesley, Capt., k. in a., 22/5/16.
10 Bamber, John Walton, Lt. (Tp.), k. in a., 1/7/16.
Barker, Henry Arthur Eric, 2/Lt. (Tp.), k. in a., 20/11/17 (att. 4/Bn.).
7 Barnaby, William Gordon, Capt. (Tp.), k. in a., 23/8/16.
Barnes, Lawrence Fairbank, 2/Lt. (Tp.), k. in a., 24/7/1 (att. 10/Bn.).
10 Barrett, Alec Roland, Lt. (Tp.), k. in a., 4/10/17.
8 Barrett, Colin Frederick, M.C., Lt. (T/Capt.), d. of w., 23/9/18.
3 Battersby, Caryl Lionel Morse, 2/Lt., k. in a., 18/11/16.
6 Beatson, Roger Stewart Montresor, Lt. (Tp.), k. in a., 1/7/16.
Beaumont, Phillip Fairclough, 2/Lt. (Tp.), k. in a., 9/10/17 (att. 4/Bn.).
Bennett, Robert Granville, 2/Lt. (Tp.), k. in a., 4/10/17 (att. 9/Bn.).
3 Bentall, William Douglas, 2/Lt., k. in a., 16/9/16 (att. 6/Bn.).
10 Bethell, Christopher, Capt. (Tp.), k. in a., 20/2/16.
11 Birch, Gilbert Wilson Fitzroy, T/Lt. (A/Capt.), k. in a., 24/8/17.
9 Blakey, George, 2/Lt., k. in a., 16/9/16.
3 Bocking, John Webb, 2/Lt., k. in a., 24/4/18.
Bond, William Arthur, M.C., T/Lt. (T/Capt.), k. in a., 22/7/17 (and R.F.C., 40 Sqd.).
Boone, William Ernest, 2/Lt., k. in a., 20/4/15.
8 Boswell, Percy George, 2/Lt. (Tp.), k. in a., 1/7/16.
Bottomley, Frederick, 2/Lt. (Tp.), k. in a., 2/9/18 (att. 5/Batt.).
Bradley, Arthur, 2/Lt., k. in a., 24/8/17 (att. 6/Bn.).
1 Brasier, James Charles, Capt. & Qr.-Mr., died, 26/12/16.
7 Broughton, Thomas Dugdale, 2/Lt. (Tp.), d. of w., 10/4/17.
7 Brown, John Ambrose, 2/Lt. (Tp.), k. in a., 12/3/17.
8 Browne, William Lindsay, 2/Lt. (Tp.), d. of w., 5/7/16.
10 Butler, Charles Kingstone, Capt. & Adjt., k. in a., 1/7/16.
2 Cain, Edward, 2/Lt., k. in a., 2/12/17.
16 Calvert, Geoffrey Clifford, Lt. (Tp.), died, 15/1/19.
8 Camble, Edward Maurice Baldwin, Lt. (Tp.), k. in a., 1/7/16.
3 Carswell, Robert Nevin, 2/Lt., k. in a., 26/10/14 (att. 2/Bn.).
Carter, Herbert Francis George, M.C., Capt. (Bt. Major) (T/Lt.-Col.), died, 28/2/19.
6 Charlesworth, William Henry, Major (Tp.), k. in a., 15/9/16.
Child, Gerald Julius, Lt., k. in a., 18/4/15.
3 Chubb, Francis John MacLardie, 2/Lt., k. in a., 18/4/15 (att. 2/Bn.).
6 Clegg, Joseph, Capt. (Tp.), k. in a., 16/9/16.
11 Cockcroft, Arthur Clarence, 2/Lt. (Tp.), k. in a., 1/7/16 (att. 10/Bn.).
Collis-Browne, Alfred Ulick, Lt., k. in a., 13/4/15.
Cooil, Henry Stuart, 2/Lt. (Tp.), k. in a., 9/9/18 (att. 9/Bn.).
8 Cook, Henry James, 2/Lt. (Tp.), d. of w., 6/10/15.
2 Cook, William Edward, 2/Lt., k. in a., 12/3/17.
1 Cooke, William Harry Coleman, Capt. (Tp.), k. in a., 1/9/18 (Garr. Bn., att. 2/6 D.L.I.).
2 Copeland, John Stuart, 2/Lt. (Tp.), d. of w., 20/2/17.
3 Corcoran, Alban Thomas, 2/Lt., d. of w., 2/12/17 (att. 2/Bn.).
9 Crick, William Edward, 2/Lt. (Tp.), d. of w., 9/4/17.
11 Crompton, Cyril, 2/Lt. (Tp.), died, 17/9/15.
9 Cundall, Stanley, 2/Lt. (Tp.), k. in a., 21/4/18.
6 Davidson, Hugh Douglas, 2/Lt. (Tp.), k. in a., 28/8/16.
9 Davis, Francis Edward, 2/Lt. (Tp.), k. in a., 9/10/17 (att. 5/Batt.).
Davis, Norman, 2/Lt., k. in a., 4/10/17 (att. 9/Batt.).

Deacon, E. C. W., 2/Lt., killed, 22/4/18 (and R.A.F.).
2 Denison, Bertram Noel, Capt., d. of w., 15/9/14.
2 Dixon, O. D., Lt. (Tp.), died, 4/11/18.
8 Donahoo, Malcolmson Gardiner, M.C., Lt. (Tp.), d. of w., 31/1/17.
Drummond, John Davidson, 2/Lt., k. in a., 9/10/17 (att. 5/Bn.).
3 Drury, Harold Strickland, Lt., k. in a., 1/7/16 (att. 8/Bn.).
Drury, Leonard George, M.C., 2/Lt. (Tp.), d. of w., 11/9/18 (att. 9/Bn.).
3 Eberlin, Frederick Harold Maden, 2/Lt., died, 25/7/17 (and R.F.C.).
7 Edmanson, Joe, Lt., k. in a., 2/7/16 (att. 13/Bn.).
6 Elborough, Alfred Charles Ernest, Capt. (Tp.), d. of w., 30/7/15.
9 Ellis, Clifford Walker, 2/Lt., k. in a., 1/7/16 (att. 2/Bn.).
3 Ellis, James Norman, 2/Lt., k. in a., 2/12/17 (att. 2/Bn.).
3 England, Ernest William, Lt., k. in a., 26/9/16 (att. 7/Bn.).
Errington, A. H. P., 2/Lt., k. in a., 30-31/11/14.
10 Eversfield, Charles John, 2/Lt. (Tp.), k. in a., 25/9/16.
1 Ewinge, John George Vivian, Lt., k. in a., 3/10/18.
9 Featherstone, George Herbert, 2/Lt. (Tp.), k. in a., 1/7/16.
2 Forde, Henry Rawson, M.C., Lt. (A/Capt.), k. in a., 2/12/17.
9 Forryan, Donald, 2/Lt. (Tp.), k. in a., 16/9/16.
3 Foster, Arthur Edward, 2/Lt., k. in a., 10/4/17 (att. 7/Bn.).
10 Fountain, John Alfred Arnott, 2/Lt. (Tp.), k. in a., 1/7/16.
7 Furze, Alfred, T/Capt. & Adjt., k. in a., 16/9/16.
11 Gepp, Nicolas Melvill, T/Capt., k. in a., 6/8/15 (att. 1/Essex R.).
6 Gill, Jack Woodward, 2/Lt. (Tp.), k. in a., 19/11/15.
9 Gillard, Frederick, 2/Lt. (Tp.), k. in a., 24/8/18.
9 Golding, Frank Alf, 2/Lt. (Tp.), k. in a., 1/7/16.
3 Gosschalk, Edward Meyer, Lt., k. in a., 28/8/16 (att. 6/Bn.).
Goulding, Reginald, 2/Lt. (Tp.), k. in a., 27/9/17 (att. 2/Bn.).
Gowans, William, Major, d. of w., 2/5/15.
9 Grafton, William Salter, 2/Lt. (Tp.), k. in a., 15/8/18.
6 Gray, Martin Kenion, 2/Lt. (Tp.), k. in a., 28/8/16.
9 Green, Percy, 2/Lt. (Tp.), k. in a., 9/9/18.
7 Gribbon, John Stewart, 2/Lt., k. in a., 27/5/18 (att. 2/Rif. Bde.).
9 Griffin, George Edward, Capt. (Tp.), k. in a., 1/7/16.
7 Gripper, Edward Cutbush, Capt., d. of w., 5/12/17.
9 Gross, Herbert George, 2/Lt., k. in a., 16/9/16.
Grubb, Lawrence Ernest Pelham, 2/Lt., k. in a., 18/11/14.
8 Hack, Adrain Henry, Lt. (Tp.), k. in a., 1/7/16.
9 Hall, James Thomson, 2/Lt. (Tp.), d. of w., 9/6/17.
9 Hardman, Archibald, T/Lt., (A/Capt.), k. in a., 4/10/17.
7 Hargreave, Frederick Parker, T/Lt. (A/Capt.), k. in a., 20/11/17.
2 Harker, Lewis, 2/Lt. (Tp.), k. in a., 1/10/18.
8 Hartley, William Ismay Spooner, Lt. (Tp.), k. in a., 1/7/16.
9 Haswell, Gordon, Capt. (Tp.), k. in a., 1/7/16.
Hayward, Herbert William, 2/Lt., k. in a., 23/7/16.
9 Head, Leslie Dymoke, Capt. (Tp.), k. in a., 1/7/16.
6 Heaton-Ellis, Charles Edward Robert, Lt. (Tp.), k. in a., 19/3/16.
1 Heath, John Lionel, 2/Lt. (T/Lt.), k. in a., 2/10/15.
9 Hetherington, Arthur, Lt. (Tp.), k. in a., 22/3/18.
2 Heygate, Claud Raymond, Capt., k. in a., 1/7/16 (att. 10/Bn.).
10 Heywood, Albert Bertine, 2/Lt. (Tp.), k. in a., 4/10/17.
3 Higman, Frederick James, 2/Lt., d. of w., 17/10/18 (att. 1/Batt.).
13 Hill, John Rowland, 2/Lt. (Tp.), k. in a., 5/8/16.
1 Hill, Percy Joseph, Lt. (Tp.), k. in a., 3/10/18.
Hinchliffe, Charles Ernest, M.M., 2/Lt., k. in a., 20/7/18 (att. 4/Bn.).
Hine-Haycock, Ralph Hugh, Capt., k. in a., 3/5/17.
3 Hobbs, Arnold William, 2/Lt., k. in a., 9/4/17 (att. 10/Bn.).
Hodges, Henry Burden, 2/Lt., k. in a., 18/4/15.
Hofmeyr, Richard, Lt. (Tp.), died, 11/9/17 (and R.F.C.).
Holdroyd, Percy, 2/Lt. (Tp.), k. in a., 5/5/17 (att. 5/Bn.).
6 Holmes, Oswald Matthews, 2/Lt. (Tp.), d. of w., 25/8/17.
Hopewell, Charles, 2/Lt., k. in a., 24/3/18 (att. 64 T.M.B.).
3 Hotson, Herbert Charles, 2/Lt., k. in a., 18/11/16 (att. 2/Bn.).
9 Howlett, Charles Wilfred, 2/Lt. (Tp.), k. in a., 1/7/16.
Hughes, George William Victor, 2/Lt., k. in a., 27/11/17 (att. 2/5 Bn.).
Hughes, Henry Kent, Capt., k. in a., 9/5/15.
3 Hughes, Walter, 2/Lt., k. in a., 8/3/18 (att. 2/Bn.).
Hunter, Archibald, 2/Lt. (Tp.), k. in a., 7/11/18.
Hunter, Charles Gawain Raleigh, Lt., k. in a., 24/4/15.
Hutchinson, Harry, 2/Lt. (Tp.), k. in a., 30/9/18 (att. 3/Bn.).
Hutchinson, Tom, 2/Lt., k. in a., 18/9/18 (att. 9/Bn.).
3 Hutchison, David Fancourt, 2/Lt. (A/Capt.), k. in a., 29/8/18 (att. 2/Bn.).
10 Hutson, Harold, 2/Lt. (Tp.), d. of w., 26/3/18 (att. 9/Bn.).
Hyde, Gilbert Arthur, 2/Lt. (Tp.), k. in a., 4/10/17 (att. 9/Bn.).
2 Ilbery, Oscar Reginald, 2/Lt., k. in a., 1/7/16.
1 Iliffe, Thomas Dealtrey, 2/Lt. (Tp.), k. in a., 10/9/18 (att. 2/Bn.).
9 Jackson, Arthur Selby, 2/Lt. (Tp.), k. in a., 16/9/16.
8 Jackson, Henry Stewart, Lt. (Tp.), k. in a., 1/7/16.
9 Jones, Charles Douglas, Lt. (Tp.), k. in a., 28/10/16.
Jones, Merfin Harman Salisbury, 2/Lt. (Tp.), k. in a., 11/8/18 (att. 8/Batt.).
9 Keay, Wilfrid Farrar, T/Lt. & Adjt., k. in a., 16/9/16.
11 Kemp, Frank, 2/Lt., k. in a., 22/7/16 (att. M.G.C.).
9 Kemp, George Arnold, 2/Lt. (T/Lt.), died, 12/1/18 (att. 3/3 K.A.R.).
8 Kernaghan, Graham Hemery, Lt. (Tp.), k. in a., 1/7/16.

1 Key, William Partridge, Lt., k. in a., 11/9/15 (att. 11/Bn.).
3 King, Berry, 2/Lt. (T/Lt.), k. in a., 3/5/17 (and R.F.C., 25 Sqd.).
2 King, Charles Eustace Dickson, M.C., Capt., k. in a., 11/10/16.
6 Knapp-Fisher, Cyril Edward Holme, 2/Lt. (Tp.), d of w., 31/7/15.
Lambert, Kenneth, Capt., k. in a., 9/5/15.
9 Leason, Thomas Herbert, 2/Lt. (Tp.), d. of w., 16/9/16.
3 Levick, Arthur Lascelles, 2/Lt., k. in a., 15/9/16 (att. 6/Bn.).
Lewis, Benjamin Alfred, 2/Lt. (Tp.), k. in a., 8/11/18 (att. 2/Batt.).
Liddell, Arthur John, 2/Lt. (Tp.), d. of w., 5/10/17 (att. 8/Batt.).
9 Lillie, Frank William, 2/Lt. (Tp.), killed, 18/12/16.
10 Lister, Philip Thomas, 2/Lt. (Tp.), d. of w., 10/4/17.
10 Lockwood, George, 2/Lt. (Tp.), d. of w., 3/11/17.
Logsdon, Frank Lionel de Marche, 2/Lt., k. in a., 4/10/17 (att. 9/Bn.).
Lynch, Colmer William Donald, D.S.O., Lt.-Col. (Tp.), k. in a., 2/7/16.
McDougall, Lionel Robert, 2/Lt. (A/Capt.), k. in a., 8/4/17 (att. 97 Trench Mortar Bty.).
9 Maconachie, Arthur Delano, 2/Lt., k. in a., 1/7/16.
6 Maiden, Albert Augustus, 2/Lt. (Tp.), k. in a., 16/9/16.
11 Maitland, John Pelham Blanchard, Capt., died, 2/8/15.
9 Makin, Stanley, 2/Lt. (Tp.), k. in a., 22/3/18.
Malcolm, Geoffrey Cooper, 2/Lt. (Tp.), k. in a., 27/9/17 (and R F.C.)
3 Martin, Albert Emanuel, 2/Lt., k in a., 2/9/18 (att. 2/4).
1 Martindale, Alfred Horace, 2/Lt. (Tp.), k. in a., 1/10/15.
9 Mason, Ernest, T/Lt. (A/Capt.), d. of w., 5/10/17.
Maud, Frederick Stanley, M.C., 2/Lt. (Tp.), k. in a., 3/10/18 (att. 2/Bn.).
11 Maude, Louis Edward Joseph, 2/Lt., k. in a., 1/7/16.
2 Maybank, John Gunter, Lt. (Tp.), k. in a., 15/9/16.
5 Mayson, Frank Eric Halton, 2/Lt. (Tp.), k. in a., 28/8/16.
Milburn, Robert Norman, 2/Lt. (Tp.), k. in a., 20/7/18 (att. 2/9 Bn.).
2 Millin, Edward Job, Capt. (Tp.), k. in a., 1/7/16.
2 Mills, Samuel, 2/Lt. (Tp.), k in a., 18/11/16.
Moon, Clifford Abraham, 2/Lt., k. in a., 22/3/18 (att. 9/Bn.).
Moorcock, Frederick Arthur, 2/Lt., k. in a., 3/5/17 (att. 2/5 Bn.).
7 Moore, Francis Hirst, 2/Lt., k. in a., 7/10/16.
8 Morley, Marmaduke Robert Hood, Lt (Tp.), k. in a., 1/7/16.
8 Morris, Gilbert Willan, Lt. (Tp.), k. in a., 1/7/16.
1 Morrish, Donald Bernard 2/Lt. (Tp.), k. in a., 18/8/16 (att. Trench Mortar Bty.).
Musgrave, Kenneth, Lt., k. in a., 22/3/15.
7 Napier, Jonathan, 2/Lt., k. in a., 16/8/17.
1 Neligan, Geoffrey Hook, Lt, k. in a., 8/11/18.
8 Nelson, John, 2/Lt., k. in a., 1/7/16.
7 Newcombe, Charles Neil, Lt (Tp.), k. in a., 27/12/15.
Newton, William Henry, 2/Lt. (Tp.), d. of w., 11/8/18 (att. 2/Bn.).
9 Nicholson, Paul Cheesum, 2/Lt., k. in a., 26/4/18.
Nock, Frederick John, 2/Lt., d. of w., 3/6/17 (att. 9/Batt.).
9 Nott, Edward Ross, 2/Lt. (Tp.), d. of w., 13/7/16.
8 Oakley, Reginald William Kennedy, Lt. (Tp.), k. in a., 1/7/16
9 Oldershaw, John Joseph Fritz, 2/Lt. (Tp.), k. in a., 1/7/16.
8 Ormrod, Harry, Lt. (Tp), k. in a., 1/7/16.
9 Overman, John Gilbert, 2/Lt. (Tp), k. in a., 9/9/18 (H.Q.).
Palmes, Guy Nicholas, Lt., k. in a., 9/5/15.
Parr, Jackson Webster, 2/Lt, d. of w., 29/3/18 (att. 2/4 Bn.).
2 Pepys, John, 2/Lt., k. in a., 23/8/14.
Percival, Walter Lowe, 2/Lt., d. of w., 24/10/18 (att. 9/Bn.).
10 Perrin, Alfred John, 2/Lt (Tp.), k. in a., 4/10/17.
8 Pettinger, Harold Sidney, Lt. (Tp.), k. in a., 10/10/17 (att. H.Q., 70th Inf Bde.).
11 Philips, Arthur Maxwell, Capt. (Tp.), k. in a., 11/11/15 (att. 9/Bn., W York R.).
Plumer, William, Lt., killed, 7/2/15.
9 Porter, John Thomas, 2/Lt. (Tp.), k. in a., 25/8/18 (att. 2/4 Bn.).
8 Powell, Phillip Keith, 2/Lt. (Tp.), k. in a., 7/6/17.
Powell, Rendel, 2/Lt. (Tp.), k. in a., 20/8/18 (att. 2/Bn.).
3 Powell-Akroyd, Frank Allnutt, 2/Lt., k. in a., 24/8/18.
Pretsell, William Gardiner, M.C., 2/Lt. (Tp.), k. in a., 20/7/18 (att. 5/Bn.).
7 Prust, Henry Royston, 2/Lt. (Tp.) (A/Capt.), k. in a., 20/11/17.
Pugh, David William, 2/Lt., k. in a., 7/10/18 (att. 15/Bn.).
10 Rawlins, Hugh Penrose Cardozo, 2/Lt., k. in a., 4/10/17.
3 Reynolds, Guy Beresford Eaton, 2/Lt., k. in a., 18/11/16 (att. 2/Bn.).
3 Richmond, Thomas Herbert, Capt., d. of w., 1/11/14.
3 Riley, Nathaniel Edgar, 2/Lt., k. in a., 21/5/18 (att. 2/Bn.).
Ritchie, Archibald Frederick, Lt., k. in a., 10/9/14.
11 Roberts, Fred, Lt. (Tp.), k. in a., 23/7/16 (att. 6/Bn.).
Robinson, G. C., 2/Lt., died, 6/6/18 (and R.A.F.).
Robinson, Harold William, 2/Lt. (T/Lt.), k. in a., 30/9/17 (att. 3/Nigerians).
Robinson, John Cecil, 2/Lt. (Tp.), k. in a., 5/6/17 (att. 2/Bn.).
8 Robinson, Percival Bewman Palmer, 2/Lt., k. in a., 1/7/16.
2 Rodgers, John, Lt. (A/Capt.), d. of w., 8/3/18.
Rohan, Patrick Bernard, 2/Lt., k. in a., 16/3/15.
Rowland, Maurice, 2/Lt., killed, 4/10/17 (att. 10/Batt.).
2 Sales, N., Lt., d. of w., 30/6/18 (and R.A.F.).
11 Sayer, Thomas Errington, Capt. (Tp.), k. in a., 25/9/16 (att. 10/Bn.).
3 Scott, Francis Sherwood, Lt., k. in a., 17/10/18 (A Coy.).
7 Scott, Phillip Camm, 2/Lt., k. in a., 8/10/18 (att. 1/Batt.).
10 Sharp, Lewis Frederick, 2/Lt. (Tp.), k. in a., 1/7/16.
Short, Walter, Capt. (Tp.), k. in a., 20/7/18 (att. 5/Batt.).

3 Siddle, Joe, 2/Lt., d. of w., 14/10/17 (att. 5/Bn.).
10 Simpson, Allen Ross Fraser, 2/Lt. (Tp.), k. in a., 16/7/16.
Simpson, John Edmund, Capt., k. in a., 30/10/14.
3 Simpson, Paul James Calvert, 2/Lt., k. in a., 1/10/15.
Simpson, William Norman, Lt. (Tp.), k. in a., 31/3/18 (att. 16/Entrenching Bn.).
Singleton, Mark Rodney, Lt., k. in a., 7/5/15.
13 Skevington, Arthur Victor, 2/Lt. (Tp.), k. in a., 25/9/16 (att. 10/Bn.).
Slingsby, Henry Laurence, Capt., d. of w., 11/8/17 (att. 10/Duke C.L.I.).
Slowe, Alfred, 2/Lt. (Tp.), d. of w., 25/8/17 (att. 6/Bn.).
7 Smith, Ernest John, Major (Tp.), d. of w., 28/12/15.
7 Smith, Leslie Tildero, 2/Lt. (Tp.), k. in a., 16/9/16.
2 Smith, Robert, 2/Lt., k. in a., 1/7/16.
3 Smith, Roland, 2/Lt., k. in a., 6/4/17 (and R.F.C.).
Smith, William Byron, 2/Lt. (Tp.), d. of w., 25/10/18 (att. 9/Bn.).
8 Smith, Walter Ernest, Lt. (A/Capt.), d. of w., 5/7/17 (Training Res.).
Smithers, Reginald Cuthbert Welsford, 2/Lt. (A/Capt.), k. in a., 16/8/17 (att. 7/Bn.).
Smyth, Algernon Beresford, Capt., k. in a., 15/11/14.
10 Snaith, Henry, 2/Lt. (Tp.), k. in a., 5/4/15.
Snape, Frank William, 2/Lt., k. in a., 7/5/15.
Somerville, Stafford Dudley, 2/Lt., k. in a., 5/7/16 (Lt., 5/Bn.).
9 Spark, Archibald Graham, M.C., Capt. (Tp.), k. in a., 9/4/17.
Spelman, Henry Harington, 2/Lt., d. of w., 22/9/18 (att. 4/Bn.).
Spicer, Leonard Baker, 2/Lt., k. in a., 4/10/17 (att. 9/Bn.).
16 Squires, Reginald Alfred, Capt., died, 25/4/19 (A.P.M., 61 Div.).
Stanley, Percy Douglas, 2/Lt., k. in a., 4/10/17 (att. 9/Bn.).
7 Starkey, Vivian George, Lt. (Tp.), k. in a., 14/10/15.
2 Staveley, George Hendley, Capt., k. in a., 14/4/17.
8 Stephenson, Olaf Stephen, 2/Lt., k. in a., 1/7/16.
9 Stokes, Reginald Alexander, 2/Lt., k. in a., 24/2/17.
6 Stokoe, Henry Bertram, Capt. (Tp.), killed, 12/10/15.
Stott, William Charles Herbert Ernest, 2/Lt. (Tp.), k. in a., 29/9/18.
6 Sturridge, Ernest Arthur Leland, Capt. (Tp.), died, 30/12/15.
9 Sutcliffe, Kenneth Wilson, 2/Lt. (Tp.), k. in a., 16/9/16.
Symons, Herbert William, Capt., k. in a., 20/11/14.
3 Taylor, Stuart Campbell, D.S.O., Brig.-Gen., d. of w., 11/10/18 (att. Staff, 93 Inf. Bde.).
9 Teaz, Homer Nevin, M.C., T/Lt. (A/Capt.), k. in a., 22/3/18.
1 Telfer, Claude William, Lt. (Tp.), k. in a., 8/11/18.
Telfer, Henry Adam, Lt. (Tp.), k. in a., 1/7/16 (att. Trench Motor Bty.).
6 Tempest, Wilfred Norman, Major (Tp.), k. in a., 26/9/16.
6 Tennant, Robert Edward, Capt. (Tp.), k. in a., 28/8/16.
12 Thompson, Arthur Herbert, T/Lt. (A/Capt.), k. in a., 25/9/16 (att. 10/Bn.).
3 Thorp, Henry Guy Hanwing, 2/Lt., d. of w., 13/3/15.
10 Turner, Ernest John, 2/Lt., d. of w., 3/4/18 (att. 2/4, att. 20 Entrenching Bn.).
Turner, George Henry, 2/Lt. (Tp.), k. in a., 15/10/18 (att. 1/4 Batt.).
7 Tyson, Donald, 2/Lt. (Tp.), k. in a., 8/8/15.
1 Upton, Thomas Francis Joseph, Capt., k. in a., 8/11/18.
Vassie, Charles Edward, 2/Lt. (Tp.), k. in a., 1/7/16.
7 Wade, Arthur Norman, 2/Lt. (Tp.), d. of w., 19/9/15.
Wade, Hubert, 2/Lt. (Tp.), k. in a., 9/10/17 (att. 5/Bn.).
11 Waghorne, Harold Frederick, 2/Lt. (T/Capt.), d. of w., 21/9/16.
10 Wait, Charles Frederick Wells, Lt. (Tp.), d. of w., 15/7/16.
2 Walker, Henry Gerald, 2/Lt., k. in a., 1/7/16.
9 Walker, William, Capt. (Tp.), k. in a., 1/7/16.
6 Warlow, Theodore William, Lt. (Tp.), d. of w., 28/7/15.
10 Watts, Albert Edward, 2/Lt. (Tp.), k. in a., 25/9/16.
9 Webster, John Philip, Lt., d. of w., 24/10/18.
3 Weighell, Frank, 2/Lt., k. in a., 14/4/17 (att. 4/Bn.).
12 Welch, James Stanley Lightfoot, Lt. (Tp.), k. in a., 1/7/16.
Whitaker, Leonard, 2/Lt. (Tp.), k. in a., 16/8/17 (att. 7/Bn.).
12 White, Francis Herbert, Capt., d. of w., 16/4/18.
6 Whittaker, James Russell, T/2/Lt., k. in a., 29/8/16.
Wilcher, Harold, 2/Lt., d. of w., 5/7/16.
Wilkinson, Frank, 2L/t., d. of w., 13/9/18.
10 Wilkinson, Gordon Frederick Noble, 2/Lt. (Tp.), k. in a., 1/7/16.
11 Williams, Douglas, 2/Lt. (Tp.), d. of w., 10/7/16 (att. 9/Bn).
11 Williams, John Alfred, 2/Lt. (Tp.), k. in a., 18/11/16 (att. 2/Bn.).
Williams, Robin A. W., Lt., k. in a., 18/4/15.
2 Willington, Reginald, Lt., d. of w., 31/8/18.
10 Wingworth, Charles Henry Cecil, 2/Lt. (Tp.), k. in a., 25/9/16.
Wood, Archibald, 2/Lt., k. in a., 29/9/18.
Woodley, Charles Albert, 2/Lt., k. in a., 8/10/18 (att. 9/Bn.).
2 Woods, John William, M.C., T/2/Lt. (A/Capt.), k. in a., 14/4/17.
Woollerton, Frank, M.C., 2/Lt., k. in a., 3/10/18 (att. 2/Bn.).
9 Woollett, William Charles, Capt., k. in a., 16/9/16.
1 Wressell, Frank, 2/Lt. (Tp.), k. in a., 2/8/17.
7 Wright, Reuben, D.S.O., Capt. (Tp.), d. of w., 17/8/17.
7 Wright, William Edward Bellyse, Lt. (Tp.), k. in a., 22/9/15.
Wyley, Francis John, Capt., d. of w., 23/4/15.
V.C. Yate, Charles Allix Lavington, Major, died, 20/9/14 (in German hands).
3 Yates, Francis William, Capt., d. of w., 25/4/15 (att. 2/Bn.).
Yearwood, Carleton Douglas, 2/Lt. (Tp.), k. in a., 16/8/17 (att. 7/Bn.).

The King's (Shropshire Light Infantry).

1 Adams-Posner, Robert Cecil, 2/Lt. (Tp.), k. in a., 18/9/18.
6 Allin, Harold Wyse, Lt. (Tp.), d. of w., 13/12/17.
Allnutt, Albert, 2/Lt. (Tp.), k. in a., 27/9/18 (Res. att. 7th Bn.).
Amey, Harold, 2/Lt., k. in a., 27/9/18.
7 Artaud, Gerald Frank Deveniere, Lt. (Tp.), k. in a., 26/9/17.
Atchison, Charles Ernest, D.S.O., Major (A/Lt.-Col.), k. in a., 24/8/17.
5 Avery, Thomas, 2/Lt. (T/Capt.), k. in a., 16/6/15.
1 Bamford, Harold W., 2/Lt., d. of w., 26/11/15.
9 Barnes, John Robert Evans, 2/Lt., d. of w., 18/4/16 (att. 6th).
Battye, Clinton Wynyard, D.S.O., Major (A/Lt.-Col.), k. in a., 24/11/17.
9 Bausor, Thomas Paul, T/2/Lt., k. in a., 6/4/16 (Trench M. Battery).
Beacall, Hugh, Lt., d. of w., 14/5/15.
Beamish, John Spread Hamilton, Lt., died, 2/11/15.
5 Beaumont, Samuel George, Capt. (Tp.), k. in a., 25/9/15.
5 Bellasis, Philip Joseph, Capt. (Tp.), k. in a., 24/8/16.
7 Benbow, Walter Harold, M.M., T/2/Lt., k. in a., 23/8/18.
Biddle-Cope, Anthony Cyprian Prosper, 2/Lt., k. in a., 25/4/15 att. 2nd Bn.).
3 Bird, Francis Clifford, 2/Lt., k. in a., 2/3/15.
Blackett, Charles Robert, 2/Lt., k. in a., 25/4/15.
1 Blake, George Victor, 2/Lt. (Tp.), k. in a., 3/12/17.
8 Boardley, Harold, Lt.-Tp., k. in a., 26/9/17.
6 Boddington, Myles, T/Capt., k. in a., 1/7/16.
7 Bolt, Bertram Leslie, 2/Lt. (Tp.), d. of w., 13/5/16.
7 Boucher, Albert Adolph, 2/Lt. (Tp.), d. of w., 16/10/16 (att. 8th T.M.B.).
7 Bowie, David Drummond, M.M., T/Capt., d. of w., 31/5/18.
Brandon, Brian Lloyd, 2/Lt. (Tp.), k. in a., 4/9/18 (Res. att. 1/7 Cheshire).
Brooke, William John, Capt., d. of w., 9/4/18 (att. 21st Mdx. R.).
Bryant, Henry Grenville, D.S.O., Capt., d. of w., 1/5/15.
3 Buckley, Hubert Hyde, Lt., k. in a., 14/4/17 (att. 1st Bn.).
5 Bugden, Robert Gordon, Lt. (Tp.), k. in a., 24/8/15.
1 Burke, Thomas Edward, 2/Lt. (T/Capt.), d. of w., 14/4/17 (att. 5th).
10 Burkett, Harold, T/Capt., d. of w., 5/6/17.
3 Burns, Walter Bell, Lt., k. in a., 9/10/17 (att. 4th Glos.).
6 Burrough, Francis Thomas, T/Capt., k. in a., 1/7/16.
9 Butt, Robert Acton, 2/Lt. (Tp.), k. in a., 9/1/16 (att. 5th).
7 Ceasar, Charles Patrick, T/Lt., k. in a., 14/7/16.
Cannon, Sidney Leslie, 2/Lt., died, 14/9/18 (att. R.A.F.).
5 Chapman, Joseph Robert, T/2/Lt., k. in a., 8/4/17.
Charles, James Arthur Merriman, 2/Lt., d. of w., 10/2/15.
3 Church, John Victor, Lt., k. in a., 10/12/17 (att. 6th).
5 Clarke, Robert Shuttleworth, Capt. (Tp.), k. in a., 25/9/15.
Coakley, Charles Stewart, T/2/Lt., k. in a., 30/10/17 (att. 1/4th Bn.).
1 Colville, Henry George Coulson, Capt., k. in a., 22/9/15 (att. H.Q., 16th Inf. Bde.).
Cooke, Cecil Pybus, T/2/Lt., k. in a., 22/8/17 (att. 5th Bn.).
Corbet, John Hugh, 2/Lt., k. in a., 13/1/18 (att. R.F.C.).
Cox, Leonard Albert, 2/Lt. (Tp.), k. in a., 10/6/18.
3 Currie, Frederic Rivers, Lt., k. in a., 8/8/15 (att. 1st).
7 Dallow, William Ewart, 2/Lt., k. in a., 9/4/17.
1 Davenport, Francis Edward Alexander, 2/Lt., k. in a., 21/3/18.
3 Davies, George Herbert, Lt., k. in a., 9/8/15 (att. 1st Bn.).
1 Davies, James Gordon, 2/Lt., k. in a., 1/6/17.
Davies, James Parton, 2/Lt. (Tp.), k. in a., 26/10/18 (att. 7th Bn. Ches. R.).
7 Davies, Walter Llewelyn, 2/Lt. (Tp.), d. of w., 15/7/16.
7 Dell, Louis Michael, T/2/Lt., k. in a., 14/7/16.
8 Dennett, Stephen Hepworth, T/2/Lt., killed, 11/5/17 (and R.F.C.).
9 Dyer, Edward Arnold, Lt., k. in a., 28/6/15.
1 Dymock, Robert Townsend Vaughan, Lt., d. of w., 27/10/15.
Eakin, Robert Andrew, Capt., d. of w., 24/9/17.
Eastham, Clement Vincent, T/2/Lt., k. in a., 3/5/17 (att. 7th Bn.).
Egerton, Arthur Oswald, 2/Lt., k. in a., 25-26/9/15.
5 Elliott, Robert Chambers Macdonald, T/2/Lt., k. in a., 24/8/16.
5 Ellis, Basil Herbert, Lt., k. in a., 16/6/15.
1 Evans, Albert Ashley, 2/Lt., k. in a., 24/9/18.
6 Evans, Kenneth George Ogle, 2/Lt., k. in a., 31/3/18.
5 Faber, Walter Louis, T/Lt., k. in a., 24/8/16.
9 Fisher, Hubert Patrick, 2/Lt. (Tp.), k. in a., 9/7/16.
6 Fitzmaurice, John Herbert, 2/Lt., k. in a., 25/3/18.
Foulger, Maurice, 2/Lt. (Tp.), k. in a., 9/8/15.
3 Fox, Arthur, M.C., A/Capt., k. in a., 8/5/17 (att. 1st).
5 French, Charles John, T/Major, d. of w., 2/7/16 (att. 255th Tunn. Co., R.E.).
5 French, Valentine Douglas, 2/Lt., d. of w., 17/6/15.
Frost, Percy Causton, T/2/Lt., k. in a., 8/9/18 (att. 10th).
6 Garnett, Ivan William, T/2/Lt., k. in a., 12/2/16.
5 Gittins, Albert, M.C., T/Lt., k. in a., 25/5/17.
Goodale, Arthur William, 2/Lt., k. in a., 9/8/15.
3 Goodchild, Stewart John, 2/Lt., k. in a., 28/3/18.
9 Green, Charles Ernest, 2/Lt. (Tp.), k. in a., 14/7/16 (att. 7th
6 Green, Richmond Edward Ormond Lyttleton, 2/Lt. (Tp.), k. in a., 19/2/16.
Griffen, Harold Samuel, 2/Lt. (Tp.), d. of w., 9/4/17 (att. 5th).
Gubbins, Richard Rolls, D.S.O., Bt.-Lt.-Col., drowned, 25/1/18.

6 Hair, Donald Campbell, 2/Lt., k. in a., 3/10/16.
6 Hamer, John, T/2/Lt., k. in a., 22/3/18.
6 Hannah, Edward Meale, M.C., 2/Lt. (Tp.), d. of w., 16/8/17.
6 Hares, Vincent Colin, T/Lt., k. in a., 30/11/17.
2 Harper, Charles, 2/Lt., died, 27/11/18.
Harrop, James Allinson, T/2/Lt., k. in a., 8/10/18 (att. 1st).
Harty, William, T/2/Lt., k. in a., 30/9/18 (att. 4th).
6 Hawkins, William Percy, Lt. (Tp.), d. of w., 12/10/15.
1 Hazard, Charles Piper, 2/Lt., k. in a., 21/4/16.
Hazard, Douglas George, Lt., k. in a., 23/5/15.
1 Herbert, Edmund Widdington, T/2/Lt., k. in a., 16/10/18 (att. 1/4th Ches. R.).
Herdman, Arthur Widdrington, Lt., k. in a., 25/10/14.
Hibbard, Richard, 2/Lt., k. in a., 6/11/18 (att. 4th).
1 Higgins, Percy Clynton, Capt., k. in a., 22/9/17 (att. Nig. R.).
6 Higginson, Tom Arthur, Capt. (Tp.), killed, 19/9/15.
2 Hill, Guy Charles Dunlop, 2/Lt., drowned, 4/5/17.
1 Hitchcock, Cyril Augustus, T/2/Lt., k. in a., 21/4/16.
5 Holder, Charles Vincent, T/2/Lt., k. in a., 24/8/16.
Holman, Geoffrey, Lt., k. in a., 9/4/15.
Hornby, Cyril Blurton, 2/Lt., died, 15/4/15.
6 Howell, Norman Asquith, T/2/Lt., k. in a., 23/12/16.
7 Hughes, George, 2/Lt., killed, 12/8/17.
5 Hunt, Francis Henry Walter, Capt. (Tp.), d. of w., 27/9/15.
Isaac, Frank Philip, T/2/Lt., k. in a., 9/8/15.
Jackson, Douglas William, T/Lt., d. of w., 18/5/17 (att. 1st Bn.).
1 Jackson-Taylor, John Curzon, 2/Lt., k. in a., 21/3/18.
1 James, Eric Gwynne, D.S.O., T/Capt. and Adjt., d. of w., 15/10/16.
Jeffreys, Charles Wilfred, 2/Lt., k. in a., 17/10/17 (att. 5th
Jenings, George Pierce Creagh, Lt., k. in a., 6/11/14.
1 Johnston, Alec, T/Lt., k. in a., 22/4/16.
7 Johnston, Frank, Capt., T/Major, d. of w., 31/5/18.
7 Jones, George Frederick, M.C., T/2/Lt., A/Capt., k. in a., 28/3/18.
7 Jones, George Harold Price, Lt., k. in a., 30/5/18.
Jones, John William, 2/Lt. (Tp.), k. in a., 8/8/18 (att. Camel Cps.).
King, Edward Gordon Macgregor, 2/Lt., k. in a., 17/7/16 (att. Glos. Regt.).
2 Koch, Marcus Addison, 2/Lt. (Tp.), k. in a., 22/9/15.
5 Lawrence, Rudolph Russell, 2/Lt., k. in a., 24/8/16.
Leach, Francis James, Capt., d. of w., 26/4/15.
9 Lee, Eric Hanson, T/2/Lt., d. of w., 19/9/16 (att. 1st).
3 Lee, John Arthur, 2/Lt., k. in a., 16/9/16 (att. 5th).
Lee, Percy William, T/2/Lt., k. in a., 9/4/17 (att. 5th).
Leech, Robert Edward Holt, T/2/Lt, k. in a., 30/9/18 (att. 4th).
7 Legg, William Norman, T/Lt., d. of w., 24/3/16.
7 Leleu, Sydney Francis, T/2/Lt., d. of w., 11/4/17.
1 Lewis, Archibald Ernest, T/2/Lt., k. in a., 28/9/17.
3 Lewis, John Dunning Gaunt, Lt., k. in a., 24/9/18.
5 Llewellyn, John Herbert, T/Capt., k. in a., 24/8/16.
9 Lloyd, Francis Oswald, T/2/Lt., k. in a., 12/2/16 (att. 6th).
3 Lloyd, Gilbert Kingsley, 2/Lt., died, 21/2/16.
Lloyd, Lewis John Bevenall, Lt., k. in a., 25/4/15.
3 Lloyd, Owen Robert, M.C., 2/Lt., A/Capt., d. of w., 20/9/17 (att. 7th).
9 Lowry, John, T/2/Lt., died. 4/5/17 (att. 2nd).
Luard, Edward Bourryan, D.S.O., T/Lt.-Col., d. of w., 24/4/16.
6 Lutener, Richard Arthur Maurice, T/2/Lt., k. in a., 6/4/16.
Machell, Maurice Irving, 2/Lt., k. in a., 16/9/16.
1 Maclaverty, Colin Johnston, Capt., k. in a., 18/9/16.
Maclean, Dugald Fitzroy, 2/Lt., d. of w., 23/7/16 (att. 1/4th Glos. R.).
9 McMordie, James Wilson, 2/Lt., k. in a., 18/11/16 (att. 2 Yorks L.I.).
9 McSwiny, Claude O'C., T/2/Lt., k. in a., 14/7/16 (att. 7th).
Marindin, Henry Eden Allan, M.C., T/2/Lt., d. of w., 8/10/18 (att. 4th).
Marriott, Richard Henry, M.C., Lt., k. in a., 18/9/16.
9 Martin, William Henry, 2/Lt., died, 27/11/18 (att. 6th).
Masefield, Robert, Major, k. in a., 24/10/14.
Mealing, Maurice Edmund, 2/Lt., died, 24/3/18 (att. R.F.C.).
7 Middleton, James, M.C., T/2/Lt., k. in a., 2/9/18.
Miles, Robert Patric, Capt., d. of w., 30/12/14.
Millar, William McKay, T/2/Lt., k. in a., 18/9/18 (att. 10th).
3 Mitchell, Julian Alan Spencer, Capt., d. of w., 28/9/14.
Morgan, Joseph Anthony, T/Lt., k. in a., 30/5/17 (and R.F.C.).
7 Morgans, Thomas, T/2/Lt., d. of w., 13/4/18.
5 Mould, Charles William, T/Capt., k. in a., 25/9/15.
1 Mylius, John Kingsford, Lt., d. of w., 12/10/16.
8 Nalder, Frank Shirley, Capt., k. in a., 21/9/18.
7 Newell, W. J., Lt.-Col., died, 20/12/14.
7 Norris, Alfred James, 2/Lt., k. in a., 28/3/18.
6 O'Connor, Hubert Michael, M.C., Capt. (Tp.), d. of w., 17/8/17.
3 O'Fflahertie, Godwin Joseph Anthony Swifte, Lt., killed, 4/3/18 (att. 1 G.B. King's Liv.).
3 Onslow, Tom, 2/Lt., k. in a., 6/1/17 (att. 5th).
6 Ormiston, Robert Williams, T/2/Lt., d. of w., 25/3/18.
Owen, Arthur Bankes, 2/Lt., d. of w., 26/10/18.
9 Owen, Philip Charles, T/2/Lt., k. in a., 25/9/15 (att. 5th).
Owen, William Llewellyn, T/2/Lt., d. of w., 12/6/18 (att. 1/4th Bn.).
5 Palmer, Charles, T/Capt., died, 15/1/16.
5 Partridge, Ernest William, 2/Lt. (Tp.), k. in a., 19/11/15.
Paterson, John Jamieson, 2/Lt., k. in a., 21/9/18 (att. 10th).
7 Pecker, Francis George, A/Capt., d. of w., 18/5/17.
Pitchford, Arthur Reginald, 2/Lt., k. in a., 17/9/18.
3 Platt, Frank Lindsay, Capt., k. in a., 21/3/18 (att. 1st).
Postles, Charles Ernest, 2/Lt., d. of w., 21/8/18 (att. 1st Ches. R.).
3 Pound, John Russell, Capt., d. of w., 27/4/15 (att. 2nd).
3 Powell, Victor Edmund, T/Lt. (A/Capt.), k. in a., 26/9/17 (att. 7th).
7 Price, Arthur, T/2/Lt., k. in a., 13/11/16.
5 Price, David Leonard, T/2/Lt., k. in a., 27/3/18 (att. 7th).
8 Profeit, Leopold, T/Capt., k. in a., 25/4/17.
3 Pugh, Ronald George, 2/Lt., k. in a., 19/8/16 (att. 7th N. Staffs).
Pye, Colin, T/2/Lt., d. of w., 8/10/18 (att. 1st).
7 Randall, Herbert Ernest, T/2/Lt., d. of w., 20/5/18.
9 Ridout, Clarence Grosvenor, 2/Lt. (Tp.), d. of w., 22/12/15 (att. 1st).
7 Rigby, Edward William, T/Capt., k. in a., 14/7/16.
Robinson, Geoffrey Francis, Capt., k. in a., 21/5/15 (att. 1/4th Ghurkas).
1 Rooper, Trevor Godolphin Hungerford, 2/Lt., k. in a., 18/1/17.
Rowan-Robinson, William James, Major, k. in a., 12/5/15.
Sampson, Tom Burton, T/Lt., k. in a., 20/11/17.
Savory, Francis Richard Egerton, Capt., d. of w., 5/12/15.
Shackles, Ronald Guy, M.C., 2/Lt., k. in a., 19/9/18 (att. 10th Bn.).
Shaw, William Easterby, Lt., d. of w., 18/5/15.
3 Sherwood, Hamilton Stanley, 2/Lt., k. in a., 28/8/18 (att. 1/4th Bn.).
9 Shields, William Francis Waugh, T/Lt., k. in a., 25/9/15 (att. 5th).
Sidebotham, John Frith, T/Lt., k. in a., 12/2/16.
7 Silvester, Geoffrey Francis, T/Capt., d. of w., 17/7/16.
5 Simpson, Victor James, 2/Lt., k. in a., 24/8/16.
Skinner, James Stuart, Capt., drowned, 21/2/17.
5 Smith, Charles Cyril, 2/Lt., k. in a., 25/9/15.
6 Smith, Douglas George, M.C., T/Lt., d. of w., 6/8/17.
6 Smith, Roderic Franklyn, M.C., T/Capt., k. in a., 28/3/18.
7 Southwell, Arthur Horace Steadman, 2/Lt., k. in a., 13/11/16.
3 Sparrow, Brian Hanbury, M.C., Capt., k. in a., 26/8/18 (att. 7th N. Staffs).
Spearman, John Vanstone, T/2/Lt., k. in a., 25/8/15.
7 Spiers, Archibald Lionel Clive, T/Lt., k. in a., 26/9/17.
3 Steward, Charles, 2/Lt., k. in a., 25/5/15 (att. 2nd).
3 Symonds-Tayler, Frederick Kingsley, Capt., d. of w., 17/4/17.
1 Taverner, Arthur Frederick, 2/Lt., d. of w., 11/10/16.
5 Taylor, Ronald Francis, T/2/Lt., k. in a., 8/8/15.
Thomson, Reginald Gresham, Lt., A/Capt., d. of w., 18/9/18.
Tippett, Alexander Arnold, 2/Lt., d. of w., 19/8/15.
3 Topham, Alfred James Tudor, 2/Lt., A/Capt., k. in a. 26/9/17.
7 Townsend, Charles Victor, T/2/Lt., k. in a. 21/3/16.
5 Turner Henry Alfred, T/2/Lt., k. in a., 18/9/18 (att. 8th).
Turner, Reginald, T/2/Lt., k. in a., 20/11/17 (att. 6th).
9 Underhill, Cyril Scott, 2/Lt. (Tp.), d. of w., 21/1/16.
7 Upton, John Alberic Everard, 2/Lt., d. of w., 20/8/16.
8 Ursell, Victor George, T/2/Lt., k. in a., 3/5/17.
3 Venables, Gilbert Rowland, 2/Lt., k. in a., 7/3/15.
1 Verner, Frederick Charles, 2/Lt., k. in a., 25/10/14.
Vyvyan, Walter Drummond, Lt., k. in a., 2/3/15.
9 Walker, Eric Arthur, T/2/Lt., k. in a., 29/12/15 (att. 6th).
5 Ward, Alfred Claude, T/Capt. & Adjt., died, 18/11/15.
5 Webb, Arthur Pelham, T/2/Lt., k. in a., 8/4/17.
6 Welch, Harold Echalaz, D.S.O. & Bar, Lt.-Col., k. in a., 29/3/18.
Wellings, Henry William, T/2/Lt., d. of w., 20/6/18 (and M.G.C., 17 Bn.).
White, Arthur Ingram, 2/Lt., d. of w., 23/3/18 (att. 4th).
Whitmore, Roger Searle, M.C., Capt., k. in a., 20/11/17.
1 Wildig, G., Lt., d. of w., 6/11/18.
Wilkinson, Clement Arthur, Major, k. in a., 2/5/15.
3 Williams, Ivor Phillips, 2/Lt., k. in a., 7/1/16 (att. 4th Bn. S. Wales Bdrs.).
Wilson, Harold Algar, 2/Lt., T/Capt., k. in a., 6/1/16.
Woodland, Richard William, Lt., k. in a., 9/8/15.
3 Woolf, Walter Francis, Lt., k. in a., 27/3/18 (att. 7th).
7 Wright, Edmund Lancelot, T/2/Lt., d. of w., 16/7/16.
5 Yeomans, Walter Joseph George, 2/Lt. (Tp.), k. in a., 8/4/17.

The Duke of Cambridge's Own (The Middlesex Regiment).

4 Abell, William Henry, Major, k. in a., 23/8/14.
17 Abercromby, John Stevenson, 2/Lt. (Tp.), d. of w., 29/4/17.
13 Adam, James Robert, 2/Lt. (Tp.), k. in a., 18/8/16.
11 Adams, James Andrew, 2/Lt. (Tp.), k. in a., 17/4/18.
16 Addington, Cyril John Flinton, 2/Lt. (Tp.), k. in a., 2/7/16 (att. 24 Bn.).
Amery-Parkes, Douglas John, Lt. (A/Major), d. of w., 30/4/18 (and M.G.C.).
14 Amor, Ernest John, 2/Lt. (Tp.), k. in a., 15/5/16 (and R.F.C.).
4 Andrews, Alfred George, 2/Lt. (Tp.), d. of w., 14/10/18.
16 Andrews, Herbert George, Lt. (Tp.), k. in a., 19/4/17.
1 Anson, Henry Percy Richmond, Capt. & Adjt., k. in a., 25/5/15 (att. 8th Bn.).
23 Ash, William Claudius Casson, Lt.-Col. (Tp.), d. of w., 29/9/16.
Ash, Wilfred John, Lt., k. in a., 16/2/15.
Ashby, Henry Herbert, 2/Lt. (Tp.), k. in a., 28/9/15.
13 Ashman, Sidney John, M.C., 2/Lt. (Tp.), k. in a., 10/10/18.
Asser, Harold Edward, 2/Lt. (Tp.), k. in a., 1/7/16 (att. 16th Bn.).
24 Auckland, Ernest, 2/Lt. (Tp.), d. of w., 30/10/16 (att. 1st Bn.).
27 Austen, William Henry, 2/Lt. (Tp.), k. in a., 13/11/16 (att. 17th Bn.).
4 Backhouse, Herbert Franklin, 2/Lt. (Tp.), k. in a., 25/8/18.

20 Baines, Joseph, Capt. (Tp.), k. in a., 29/7/16.
28 Bainton, Herbert Sidney, 2/Lt., d. of w., 16/2/18.
1 Baker, George Lionel John, 2/Lt., k. in a., 23/4/17.
16 Baldwin, Harold John Taylor, 2/Lt., k. in a., 23/10/16.
Ball, George William, 2/Lt., k. in a., 25/3/15.
18 Barber, Herbert Sydney, 2/Lt. (Tp.), d. of w., 15/5/18 (att. 10 Bn.).
Barker, Edward, Capt. (T/Major), died, 2/1/16 (att. Essex R.).
Barker, Hubert Joseph, 2/Lt. (Tp.), d. of w., 28/3/18 (att. 1/8 Bn.).
16 Barker Harold William, Lt. (Tp.), d. of w., 1/7/16.
4 Barnett, Phillip, 2/Lt., k. in a., 2/7/16.
20 Barr, Percival Fowler, M.C., 2/Lt. (Tp.), k. in a., 2/3/17.
11 Bartlett, William Herbert Lionel, 2/Lt. (Tp.), k. in a., 13/5/17.
18 Baxter, Arthur Sunderland, 2/Lt. (Tp.), d. of w., 2/1/16.
6 Bays, Albert William, 2/Lt., k. in a., 10/10/17 (att. 4th Bn.).
4 Bear, Sydney James, 2/Lt., d. of w., 31/7/17.
Bedingham, Albert, 2/Lt. (Tp.), k. in a., 25/2/17 (att. 23 Bn.).
Beeman, John Neville, M.C., Lt., k. in a., 29/9/18 (att. 1st Bn.).
1 Beevor, Felix Victor, 2/Lt., k. in a., 1/7/16 (5th).
21 Beggs, James, 2/Lt. (Tp.), k. in a., 9/4/18.
Bell-Hughes, John Otto, 2/Lt. (Tp.), k. in a., 28/9/17 (att. 5 Lanc. Fus.).
3 Benham, Malcolm Erick, 2/Lt., k. in a., 29/9/15.
1 Benson, George Agar Trevor, M.C., 2/Lt., k. in a., 28/10/16.
Bentley, Gerald Wilson, Capt., k. in a., 12/10/14.
Bilby, Eustace John, 2/Lt., k. in a., 16/8/17 (att. 2nd Bn.).
6 Billman, Walter Melville, Lt., d. of w., 5/11/16 (att. 1st Bn.).
Bishop, Gerald Clement William, 2/Lt. (Tp.), k. in a., 11/8/17 (att. 16 Bn.).
13 Black, Cyril Pakenham, 2/Lt. (Tp.), k. in a., 18/8/16.
Blake, Cecil Francis John, 2/Lt., k. in a., 7/10/18 (att. 2nd Bn.).
Bobby, Arthur Lawrence, 2/Lt. (Tp.), k. in a., 20/11/17 (att. 16th Bn.).
17 Bonathan, Frank Stanley, M.C., 2/Lt., k. in a., 28/4/17.
11 Booth, Philip Eustace, 2/Lt., d. of w., 4/12/17.
18 Boreham, Harry Pendry, 2/Lt. (Tp.), k. in a., 16/4/18.
1 Bosanquet, Sidney Courthorpe, 2/Lt., d. of w., 17/12/14.
16 Bowden, Walter Horace, 2/Lt. (Tp.), k. in a., 12/4/18.
16 Bowman, Hugh James, 2/Lt. (Tp.), k. in a., 10/1/16.
18 Bradbury, Harry Claude, 2/Lt. (Tp.), k. in a., 16/4/18.
17 Bradstreet, Lionel Arthur, 2/Lt. (Tp.), k. in a., 1/6/16.
4 Branch, Albert, 2/Lt., k. in a., 1/7/16.
12 Brewerton, Augustine, 2/Lt. (Tp.), k. in a., 26/9/16.
1 Broad, Francis Boase, M.C., Lt. (A/Capt.), k. in a., 24/10/18.
Brodie, John Miller, 2/Lt. (Tp.), k. in a., 15/5/18 (att. 8th Bn.).
23 Brown, Francis Wrentmore, Lt. (Tp.), d. of w., 16/9/16.
Brown, John Cuthbert Backhouse, Lt. (Tp.), k. in a., 29/9/18 (att. 1st Bn.).
17 Brunton, Edward Benjamin Durnford, 2/Lt., k. in a., 13/11/16.
15 Bryan, Frederick Stawell, M.C., Capt. (Tp.), k. in a., 23/11/17 (att. 21 Bn.).
1 Buchanan, Harold Cyril Dudley, Lt. (Tp.), d. of w., 12/11/16.
20 Buist, George Bruce, Lt. (Tp.), k. in a., 25/9/16.
6 Burch, Charles Leonard, 2/Lt., k. in a., 18/8/16 (att. 13th Bn.).
1 Burrell, Sydney, 2/Lt., d. of w., 20/7/16 (att. 5th Bn.).
6 Burt, William James, Lt., k. in a., 18/8/16 (att. 13th Bn.).
Burton, George, 2/Lt., k. in a., 24/8/17 (att. 13th Bn.).
2 Cade, Arthur Gordon, D.S.O., M.C., Capt. (A/Lt.-Col.), k. in a., 26/4/18.
Campbell, William, 2/Lt. (Tp.), k. in a., 20/9/17 (att. 23rd Bn.).
12 Card, Arthur Henry, M.C., 2/Lt., k. in a., 26/9/16.
5 Carless, Albert William Buchan, Lt., d. of w., 27/9/15 (att. 1st Bn.).
6 Carpenter, Bernard Melville, 2/Lt., d. of w., 3/4/18 (att. 19th Bn.).
16 Carruthers, James Mein Austin, Capt. (Tp.), d. of w., 26/4/17.
5 Carter, Archibald Wren, 2/Lt., k. in a., 13/5/17 (11th).
Castberg, Francis Albert Harboe, Capt., d. of w., 13/3/15.
6 Castle, Sidney Batho, Lt., died, 4/1/16.
4 Chambers, Anthony Gerald, 2/Lt., k. in a., 1/7/16.
Chapman, Arthur Gerald, Lt. (Tp.), died, 5/5/17.
12 Chase, Philip Hugh, 2/Lt. (Tp.), d. of w., 1/7/16.
Child, Edward, 2/Lt. (Tp.), k. in a., 24/8/18 (att. 1/8th Bn.).
12 Chipperfield, Arnold Henry, 2/Lt. (Tp.), k. in a., 24/4/18 (att. 2/2 Lond.).
17 Christmas, Leslie Frederick, 2/Lt. (Tp.), k. in a., 3/11/16 (att. 14th Bn.).
4 Churchfield, Sidney Percival, 2/Lt. (Tp.), k. in a., 1/7/16.
Clachan, William James, Capt., k. in a., 6/1/18 (att. 1 K.A.R.).
6 Clark, Eric Groby, 2/Lt., k. in a., 23/4/17 (att. 1st Bn.).
16 Cloutman, Thomas Henry, 2/Lt. (Tp.), d. of w., 7/3/17.
Cochran, Herbert Philip Gordon, D.S.O., Lt.-Col., k. in a., 24/3/18 (att. 15 Ches. R.).
17 Cocks, Edward Louis, 2/Lt., k. in a., 8/8/16.
Coles, Sidney Harcourt, Lt., k. in a., 12/10/14
Cook, George Albert, 2/Lt., k. in a., 10/3/15.
11 Cooper, Albert Frederick, 2/Lt. (Tp.), d. of w., 9/5/18.
18 Cooper, Clifford, 2/Lt., (Tp.), k. in a., 22/4/18.
5 Corcoran, William James, Major, d. of w., 25/10/14.
4 Cottam, Clement John, 2/Lt. (Tp.), k. in a., 18/12/15.
1 Coughlan, Julius Edward, M.C., Capt. (Act.), k. in a., 25/10/16.
Cousens, George Edward, 2/Lt. (Tp.), k. in a., 24/8/18 (att 1/8 Bn.).
5 Coward, Leslie Graham, Capt., k. in a., 25/9/15 (att. 1st Bn.).
11 Crombie, Ian Osborne, Capt. (Tp.), k. in a., 28/7/16.
5 Cross, Ernest, 2/Lt., k. in a., 24/4/18 (att. 2nd Bn.).
5 Cutbush, Douglas, M.C., 2/Lt. (A/Capt.), k. in a., 10/4/17 (att. 4th Bn.).
28 Davies, Cecil Lloyd, 2/Lt. (Tp.), d. of w., 25/11/16 (att. 2nd R. Berks R.).
5 Davis, Charles Stewart, 2/Lt., k. in a., 1/7/16 (att. 2nd Bn.).
Dawson, Albert George, Capt. (A/Lt.-Col.), k. in a., 22/4/17.
16 Deakin, Charles Joseph John King, 2/Lt. (Tp.), d. of w., 2/7/16
5 Defries, Frederick, Lt., k. in a., 6/4/18 (att. 3 Bn.).
Deighton, Bartholomew James, Lt. (T/Capt.), k. in a., 25/9/15.
12 Dennis, Albert Claude, Capt. (Tp.), d. of w., 27/7/16.
6 De Pass, William Hugh David, Lt., k. in a., 25/3/18 (att. 13 Bn.).
23 Devereux, Frederick Herbert, 2/Lt. (Tp.), k. in a., 31/7/17.
Dewes, Bryan Osmond, 2/Lt. (Tp.), k. in a., 30/7/15.
6 Dick, Norman Brabazon, 2/Lt., k. in a., 28/4/17 (att. 17th Bn.).
6 Dickason, Reginald Percy, 2/Lt., k. in a., 14/2/17 (att. 1st Bn.).
Dixon, James, Capt., k. in a., 10/3/15.
Dobbs, William Carey, Capt., k. in a., 31/7/17.
14 Dodgson, Vernon Colville, Lt. (Tp.), d. of w., 5/3/16 (att. 11th Bn.).
11 Dore, Sidney Arthur, 2/Lt. (Tp.), k. in a., 24/4/18 (att. 1/7 Bn.).
22 Doughty, George Marbrook, Lt., k. in a., 21/8/17 (att. 17 M.G.C.).
16 Douglas, Sholto, Capt. (Tp.). k. in a., 28/1/16.
6 Down, John Eric, Lt., k. in a., 29/9/18 (att. Div. M.G. Bn.).
5 Downing, Francis Geoffrey, Lt., died, 27/10/16 (att. R.E.).
18 Drage, Arthur William, M.M., 2/Lt. (Tp.), k. in a., 26/9/18.
1 Draper, Cecil Frederick Napier, Lt., d. of w., 17/6/16.
1/4 Driscoll, D. O'Neill, Lt., died, 13/8/18 (and R.A.F.).
17 Duncan, Arthur Seymour, 2/Lt., k. in a., 9/4/18.
15 Dunman, Charles Norman Innes, 2/Lt. (T/Lt.), k. in a., 31/7/17 (att. M.G. Corps).
Dyer, Frederick Vivian Alma, Lt. (T/Capt.), k. in a., 25/9/15.
Earley, William, 2/Lt. (Tp.), k. in a., 11/10/18 (att. 13 Bn.).
Easton, Percy Thomas, Capt. & Qr.-Mr., died, 26/11/16 (att. Nigerian R.).
Eddy, Charles, 2/Lt. (Tp.), k. in a., 9/10/17 (att. 16 Bn.).
15 Edingborough, Noel Duncan, 2/Lt. (Tp.), k. in a., 1/7/16 (att. 109 M.G. Corps).
3 Elliott, Philip Maurice, 2/Lt. (Tp.), k. in a., 1/7/16.
2 Evans, Edwin, 2/Lt. (Tp.), d. of w., 22/11/16.
21 Evans, Frederick Woodham, 2/Lt. (Tp.), d. of w., 26/5/17 (and R.F.C., 20 Sqd.).
Evatt, George Raleigh Kerr, Capt., k. in a., 14/11/14.
15 Evers, Ernest William, M.C., Capt. (Tp.), k. in a., 23/11/17 (att. 21 Bn.).
15 Fall, Patrick Joseph, Lt., d. of w., 15/11/16 (att. 17 Bn.).
4 Farr, Percival Ward, Lt., k. in a., 31/7/17.
5 Fergusson, James Scott Elliott Gillon, Lt., k. in a., 27/4/15 (att. 3 Bn.).
12 Fish, Benjamin Leslie, Lt. (Tp.), d. of w., 30/10/18 (att. 18 Bn.).
6 Flaherty, John Ernest, 2/Lt. (Tp.), died, 12/7/18.
1 Flexen, Harold Augustus, 2/Lt. (Tp.), d. of w., 29/7/16.
6 Fluck, Harold Graham, 2/Lt. (Tp.), d. of w., 3/11/17 (att. 1/4 Northants.).
2 Forge, William Frederick, 2/Lt., k. in a., 1/7/16.
16 Forsyth, William Matthew, 2/Lt. (Tp.), d. of w., 20/4/17.
13 Foulkes-Winks, Oswald Woodward, 2/Lt. (Tp.), k. in a., 20/7/16 (att. T.M.B.).
12 Franklin, Benjamin Lester, Lt. (Tp.), d. of w., 4/5/17 (and R.F.C., 70 Sqd.).
4 Fraser, Lachlan Henry Veitch, Lt., k. in a., 24/2/15.
16 Frayne, Ernest, Lt. (Tp.), d of w., 17/5/18 (in German hands).
21 Freeman, Joseph, M.C., 2/Lt. (Tp), d. of w., 9/4/18.
2 Frost, Alfred Iago, 2/Lt., k. in a., 1/7/16.
25 Fulton, Ernest Alan, 2/Lt (Tp.), k. in a., 3/10/16 (att. [illegible] Bn.).
2 Gibbens, George, 2/Lt. (Tp.), d. of w., 2/4/18
Gibbons, Edward Stephen, D.S.O., Major (A/Lt.-Col.), k. in a., 19/9/18 (att. 7 High. L.I.).
5 Gibson, Percy Montague, M.C., M.M, 2/Lt., d. of w., 6/9/18 (att. 17 Lond. R.).
11 Gilfillan, Donald Roy, 2/Lt. (Tp.), k. in a., 26/2/17.
13 Gliddon, R. A, 2/Lt., killed, 9/5/18 (and R A.F.).
6 Godby, Thomas Stanley, 2/Lt. (Tp.), k. in a., 20/11/17 (att. 8 L'pool R.).
11 Godfrey, Herbert Arthur, 2/Lt. (Tp.), k. in a., 12/5/17.
2 Golding, Eric, 2/Lt., k. in a., 15/7/16.
16 Goodwin, Harold Desborough, Lt., k. in a., 1/7/16.
1 Goodwin, Norman William, 2/Lt, k. in a., 16/9/17 (and R.F.C.).
2 Gordon-Jones, Eric, 2/Lt., d. of w., 1/8/17.
23 Gore, Francis, 2/Lt. (Tp.), d. of w, 26/3/17.
Gould, Francis Hunt, Capt., killed, 6/6/15.
Goulden, William Charles, 2/Lt. (Tp.), k. in a., 12/2/18 (att. 2nd Bn.).
1 Gow, John Halley, 2/Lt. (Tp.), k. in a., 15/7/16.
Graham, George William, 2/Lt. (Tp.), k. in a., 20/9/17 (att. 5 Lancs Fus.)

Gransmore, Rodney, Capt., k. in a., 28/9/15.
Granville, Clifford Paul McGarry, Capt., k. in a., 12/5/18 (and K. Afr. Rif.)
1 Green, Edward Scott Waring, 2/Lt., k. in a., 28/8/16.
2 Green, James, 2/Lt., d. of w., 27/9/18
Green, Rupert Anthony, Lt., k. in a., 25/3/18 (att. 23rd Bn.).
15 Green, Vivian Unsworth, 2/Lt. (T/Lt.), k. in a., 26/3/17 (att. 10th Bn.).
11 Green, William Bruce, 2/Lt. (Tp.), k. in a., 29/3/18.
20 Greenhalgh, Hugh Charles, 2/Lt. (Tp.), k. in a., 5/5/17.
19 Greenstreet, E. H., 2/Lt. (Tp.), died, 15/2/19.
Grieve, William Percival 2/Lt., k. in a., 16/2/15.
20 Groves, Reginald Edward, 2/Lt. (Tp.), k. in a., 9/4/18.
6 Grundy, Cecil Boyce, 2/Lt., d. of w., 16/11/15 (att. 1st Bn.).
2 Grundy, Ronald Edwin, 2/Lt., k. in a., 1/7/16.
24 Guest, John Aloysius, 2/Lt. (Tp.), d. of w., 27/7/16 (att. 17th Bn.).
Gulbenkian, Krikor, 2/Lt. (Tp.), k. in a., 20/9/17 (att. 23rd Bn.).
23 Haig-Brown, Alan Roderick, D.S.O., Lt.-Col., k. in a., 25/3/18.
2 Hair, Eric Francis Wilson, 2/Lt. (Tp.), d. of w., 27/8/17.
2 Hall, Geoffrey, 2/Lt. (Tp.), k. in a., 23/10/16.
Hallett, Henry William Percy, Capt. (Tp.), d. of w., 12/10/18 (att. 2nd Bn.).
1 Hallett, Samuel William, Lt., d. of w., 15/7/16.
4 V.C. Hallowes, Rupert Price, M.C., 2/Lt. (Tp.), k. in a., 30/9/15.
Hamilton-Jones, Charles Nugent, 2/Lt. (Tp.), k. in a., 20/9/17 (att. 9 L'pool R.).
6 Hanby, Edward Wrey, 2/Lt., died, 30/4/17 (att. 23 Bn.).
1 Hardingham, Robert Cecil, M.C., Capt. (T/Major), d. of w., 18/9/17 (att. K. Afr. Rifs.).
5 Hardwick, William West, 2/Lt., d. of w., 11/6/15 (att. 2nd Bn.).
14 Hare, Bernard Urmston, 2/Lt. (Tp.), k. in a., 25/9/15 (att. 1st Bn.).
Hare, Evan Alfred Amyas, 2/Lt., k. in a., 10/3/15.
15 Hare, Stanley Grant, 2/Lt. (Tp.), k. in a., 19/4/17.
5 Harris, Reginald Samuel, 2/Lt., d. of w., 24/6/17.
Harvey, Charles Milne, Lt., k. in a., 25/11/14.
Hastings, George Herbert, Capt., k. in a., 5/2/15.
11 Hawkins, Harold George, 2/Lt. (Tp.), d. of w., 24/7/15.
6 Hay, Douglas Woulfe, M.C., Lt., k. in a., 29/9/18 (att. 1st Bn.).
17 Haynes, George James, 2/Lt. (Tp.), k. in a., 16/6/18.
16 Heath, Henry James, Lt., k. in a., 17/7/16.
14 Heaton, Eric Rupert, 2/Lt. (Tp.), k. in a., 1/7/16 (att. 16th Bn.).
5 Hedley, John Hunt, 2/Lt., k. in a., 8/3/18 (att. 4th Bn.).
Henderson, Alfred Roche, 2/Lt. (Tp.), k. in a., 28/4/17 (att. 17th Bn.).
17 Henderson, William Fraser, 2/Lt., k. in a., 8/8/16.
17 Hendry, William, 2/Lt. (Tp.), k. in a., 27/7/16.
5 Henry, Arthur Richard, 2/Lt. (Tp.), k. in a., 23/4/17 (att. 1st Bn.).
4 Henstock, Kenneth Parnell, Lt., k. in a., 23/8/14.
11 Henty, Arthur Frank, Capt. (Tp.), k. in a., 4/3/16.
4 Herbert, Allan Douglas, 2/Lt., d. of w., 29/9/15.
6 Hertslet, Harold Cecil, 2/Lt., k. in a., 1/7/16 (att. 16th Bn.).
16 Heslop, George Henry, Capt. (Tp.), k. in a., 1/7/16.
2 Hess, Henry, 2/Lt., d. of w., 28/10/16.
Heywood, Herbert, Capt., d. of w., 22/8/17 (att. M.G.C.).
5 Hicks, Harleigh* Lionel Adrian Oswald, 2/Lt., k. in a., 12/4/18 (att. 1/8 Bn.).
Hill, Arthur Lionel, 2/Lt. (Tp.), k. in a., 25/9/15.
13 Hill, Charles Edward, Capt. (Tp.), k. in a., 28/9/15.
18 Hill, Horace Frederick, M.C., Capt. (Tp.), d. of w., 5/9/17.
2 Hilton, Clarence Stuart, Capt., k. in a., 1/7/16.
5 Hilton, Henry Denne, 2/Lt., k. in a., 19/12/14 (att. 4th Bn.).
Hilton, Herbert Philip, Capt., k. in a., 16/2/15.
6 Hilton, Reginald Musgrave, 2/Lt., k. in a., 23/4/17 (att. 4th Bn.).
17 Hislop, Percy Robert, 2/Lt. (Tp.), d. of w., 7/12/17.
Hodges, Albert Rowland Curtis, 2/Lt., killed, 20/3/18 (and R.F.C.).
4 Hodgson, John Henry, Lt. (Tp.), k. in a., 30/4/18.
Holland, Harold Richard, 2/Lt., k. in a., 12/4/18 (att. 1/8 Bn.).
1 Holland, Richard Edward, 2/Lt. (Tp.), k. in a., 24/10/18.
11 Holman, Donald, Lt. (Tp.), k. in a., 8/8/18 (att. 7 R.W. Surr. R.).
1 Holton, Francis Keatley, Lt., killed, 27/10/17 (att. 98 T.M.B.).
Homan, Henry Leslie, Capt., k. in a., 10/3/15.
Honess, Albert Edward, 2/Lt. (Tp.), k. in a., 9/4/18 (att. 21 Bn.).
4 Hooke, Alfred Douglas, 2/Lt., k. in a., 28/4/17.
Hooper, Alfred Henry, Capt., k. in a., 10/3/15.
16 Hopwood, Robert Hervey, Lt. (Tp.), k. in a., 5/2/16.
Horn, Edmund Eric, 2/Lt. (Tp.), k. in a., 4/3/17 (and R.F.C., 8 Sqd.).
Hornby, Richard Arthur, Capt., k. in a., 9/4/18 (att. 21 Bn.).
18 Howard, William, 2/Lt. (Tp.), k. in a., 24/4/18 (att. 2 Northampton R.)
13 Hubbard, Leslie Victor, 2/Lt. (Tp.), k. in a., 31/8/16.
14 Hudlestone, Harold Robert, 2/Lt. (Tp.), d. of w., 2/7/16.
Hudspith, Walter Leonard, M.C., Lt. (Tp.), k. in a., 7/11/18 (att. 1st Bn.).
Hughes, Guy Wiley, 2/Lt., d. of w., 31/12/14.
5 Hughes, Lestocq, 2/Lt., k. in a., 26/9/16 (att. 12th Bn.).
11 Hughes-Jones, Harry Llewelyn, Lt. (Tp.), k. in a., 3/3/16.
11 Hughman, Leopold Alexander, Capt., k. in a., 5/3/16.
1/4 Hunter, Alfred James, 2/Lt., killed, 6/8/18 (and R.A.F.).
Hussey, Edmund Dobson, 2/Lt., k. in a., 9/4/18 (att. 21 Bn.).

5 Hutchins, Douglas Markham, 2/Lt., d. of w., 2/8/16 (att. 4 Ox. & Bucks.).
Jackson, Alan James, 2/Lt., k. in a., 27/4/15.
4 Jackson, Albert Leslie, 2/Lt., d. of w., 18/3/17.
13 James, Bernard Ashworth, Capt. (Tp.), k. in a., 18/8/16.
5 Johnson, Edward Francis, 2/Lt., d. of w., 7/11/18 (att. 1st Bn.).
6 Johnson, William Charles Littley, 2/Lt. (Tp.), k. in a., 30/5/17 (att. 16th Bn.).
5 Johnston, Adrian Alexander Hope, Lt., k. in a., 2/7/16 (att. 4th Bn.).
Johnston, Oct Ralph Featherston, Capt., k. in a., 1/7/16.
5 Jones, Edwin, 2/Lt., k. in a., 23/8/18 (att. 2/16 Bn. London Regt.).
4 Jones, Geoffrey Anthony St. John, Lt., k. in a., 14/6/16.
Jones, Percy Barrett, Capt., k. in a., 28/9/15.
12 Keith, Alexander James, 2/Lt. (Tp.), k. in a., 14/7/16.
12 Kelsey, Herbert Burleigh, 2/Lt. (Tp.), k. in a., 17/2/17.
2 Kemp, Frederick Owen, 2/Lt. (Tp.), k. in a., 23/10/16.
5 Kemp, William Meadows, 2/Lt., k. in a., 28/2/17 (att. 16 Bn.).
17 Kempster, Stephen Alec, 2/Lt. (Tp.), k. in a., 8/6/17.
Keogh, Alfred Alexander, 2/Lt. (Tp.), k. in a., 12/5/17 (att. 11 Bn.).
25 Kessack, James O'Connor, Capt. (Tp.), k. in a., 13/11/16 (att. 17th Bn.).
11 Kidds, George Frederick, 2/Lt. (Tp.), k. in a., 25/7/17.
2 King, Arthur Philip, 2/Lt., k. in a., 24/11/17.
11 Kingwell, Francis Robert, 2/Lt. (Tp.), d. of w., 14/10/16.
13 King, Maurice Edmund, 2/Lt. (Tp.), k. in a., 15/3/16.
4 Knowles, Jonathan Edward, Capt., k. in a., 23/8/14.
20 Ladell, John Francis, Lt. (Tp.), k. in a., 20/7/16.
Large, Herbert Edward, Capt., k. in a., 16/2/15.
Large, Philip Martin, Major, k. in a., 27/4/15.
16 Larkins, Charles Horace, 2/Lt. (Tp.), d. of w., 21/11/17.
17 Last, Basil Herbert, 2/Lt. (Tp.), k. in a., 23/4/17.
16 Launceton, Roy, M.C., Capt. (Tp.), k. in a., 24/3/18 (att. 2 Bn.).
Lawrence, Brian Lightly, 2/Lt., k. in a., 1/6/15.
20 Learoyd, Ernest Smith, 2/Lt. (Tp.), k. in a., 23/11/17.
17 Leaver, Stanley Horace, 2/Lt. (Tp.), k. in a., 9/4/18.
17 Lee, Edgar Charles, 2/Lt. (Tp.), k. in a., 1/6/16.
21 Leggott, William Evers, 2/Lt. (Tp.), k. in a., 29/7/16.
Lepper, Harper Mervyn, M.C., 2/Lt., k. in a., 9/4/16 (att. 8 R. Welsh Fus.).
6 Lewis, Cyril William Victor, Lt., killed, 3/10/17 (att. 1st Bn.).
11 Lewis, Gerald Sidney, Capt. (Tp.), k. in a., 7/7/16.
2 Lillywhite, Frederick Thomas Sherwood, 2/Lt. (Tp.), d. of w., 26/5/17.
Linsell, Johnson Hugh, 2/Lt. (Tp.), k. in a., 25/9/15.
Liversedge, Alexander Frederick, 2/Lt., k. in a., 25/3/18 (att. 2nd Bn.).
2 Livesey, Cyril Joseph Glanville, 2/Lt. (Tp.), k. in a., 4/1/18.
6 Lodge, William Wass, 2/Lt., d. of w., 17/4/18 (att. 1st Bn.).
6 Lyons, William Holmes St. G., Lt., died, 1/11/18 (att. 2/4 Ox. & Bucks.).
21 Macan, Hugh Turner, Lt. (Tp.), k. in a., 23/3/18.
6 McCulloch, Kenneth Lionel Nevill, 2/Lt., k. in a., 1/6/17.
12 McDonnell, Charles Edward, Lt. (Tp.), k. in a., 26/9/16.
McDonnell, Herbert, 2/Lt. (Tp.), k. in a., 31/7/17 (att. 4th Bn.).
5 MacFarlane, Wallace Bird, 2/Lt., k. in a., 10/3/15 (att. 2nd Bn.).
23 McGuire, Robert Blayrey, 2/Lt. (Tp.), killed, 30/4/17.
24 Mackay, Gordon, 2/Lt. (Tp.), k. in a., 16/8/17 (att. M.G. Corps).
Mackinnon, Colin Alexander John, 2/Lt., k. in a., 25/9/15.
23 McKinnon, James Beaton, 2/Lt. (Tp.), k. in a., 7/6/17.
4 V.C. McReady-D'Iarmid, Allastair Malcolm Cluny, Lt. (Tp.), A/Capt., k. in a., 1/12/17 (att. 17th Bn.).
McSweeney, Felix Joseph, 2/Lt. (Tp.), k. in a., 30/7/17 (att. 19 Bn.).
6 Maisey, Albert Henry, 2/Lt., d. of w., 16/2/17.
5 Maitland, William Renmure, 2/Lt., k. in a., 18/11/16 (att. T.M.B.).
14 Major, Harold, Lt. (Tp.), killed, 19/10/15.
13 Makeham, Eric Noel, 2/Lt. (Tp.), died, 28/8/17 (in Ger. hands).
Marks, C. H., Lt., T/Capt., k. in a., 23/10/15 (and R.F.C.).
4 Marks, Philip Moses, 2/Lt., k. in a., 29/9/15 (att. 5th Bn.).
Mason, Thomas Henry, 2/Lt., d. of w., 24/7/15.
1 Mathews, Edward Stanley, Lt. (Tp.), k. in a., 2/10/18 (att. 2nd Bn.).
2 Meeke, William Stanley, Capt., k. in a., 1/7/16.
Mellish, Richard Coppin, 2/Lt. (Tp.), k. in a., 25/9/15.
16 Michelmore, Robert Frank, 2/Lt., d. of w., 7/7/16.
5 Miers, Maurice Colin Capel, Major, Act. Lt.-Col., d. of w., 9/8/17 (att. 8 Som. L.I.).
4 Millican, Reginald Isaac, 2/Lt., d. of w., 23/3/18.
2 Mills, Henry Jackson, Lt., k. in a., 30/5/18 (att. 19 M.G.C.).
11 Mills, Tenlon Lewis, Capt. (Tp.), d. of w., 5/8/15.
6 Mitchell, Alexander Goble, Lt., killed, 30/5/18 (att. 4th Bn.).
Mitchell, Robert William Page, 2/Lt. (Tp.), d. of w., 10/10/17 (att. 16 Bn.).
16 Mitchell, Tom Illingworth, Capt., A/Major, d. of w., 12/4/18.
4 Money, George Russell, 2/Lt., k. in a., 1/7/16.
6 Moorat, Francis Ferrers, Lt., A/Capt., d. of w., 23/8/18 (att. 4th Bn.).
4 Moore, Leonard Edwin, 2/Lt., k. in a., 6/4/18.
Morgan, Alfred Ernest, 2/Lt., k. in a., 29/10/16 (att. 12 Bn.).
21 Morris, Alfred Arthur Thomas, M.C., Lt. (Tp.), d. of w., 24/10/18.

3 Morris, Henry, 2/Lt., k. in a., 28/9/15 (att. 5th Bn.).
Morrison, Robert Vernon, 2/Lt. (Tp.), k. in a., 13/5/17 (att. 11 Bn.).
Morse, Gordon T. H., 2/Lt., k. in a., 12/10/14.
Mullins, John Ollis, 2/Lt., killed, 30/3/15 (and R.F.C.).
Mundy, Jesse Ernest, 2/Lt., d. of w., 24/4/18 (att. 2/2 Lond. R.) (in enemy hands).
1 Murray, William, 2/Lt. (Tp.), k. in a., 24/4/17.
3 Neale, George Henry, Lt.-Col. (Tp.), k. in a., 28/9/15.
22 Negretti, Norman Charles Achille, 2/Lt. (Tp.), k. in a., 30/1/17.
23 Newman, Arthur Cecil, T/8/Lt., A/Capt., k. in a., 20/9/17.
20 Newsome, Clifford William, 2/Lt., k. in a., 14/7/18 (att. 26 R. Fus.).
2 Newton, Alan Herbert, 2/Lt., d. of w., 7/4/16.
23 Nixon, Lionel Philip, 2/Lt. (Tp.), k. in a., 15/9/16.
Norwood, William James, 2/Lt., k. in a., 27/3/18 (att. 2 Northampton R.).
Norquoy, James, Capt. (Tp.), k. in a., 3/4/17 (att. 13 Bn.).
23 Norris, Frederick, T/2/Lt., A/Capt., k. in a., 7/6/17.
5 Ochs, Ronald Philip, 2/Lt., k. in a., 27/9/15 (att. 4th Bn.).
2 Oddie, Francis Arthur Joseph, Lt. (Tp.), k. in a., 23/10/16.
Orlebar, Robert Evelyn, Lt., k. in a., 9/1/15.
16 Orr, James Kenneth, 2/Lt. (Tp.), k. in a., 1/7/16.
17 Parfitt, Ernest, Capt. (Tp.), d. of w., 28/5/17 (while P. of W.).
1 Parkhouse, Frank Mayfield, 2/Lt. (Tp.), k. in a., 23/4/17.
Parris, Walter Frederick, 2/Lt., k. in a., 15/3/15.
5 Pastfield, James Thomas Robinson, 2/Lt., k. in a., 21/12/14 (att. N'bld. Fus.).
5 Pastfield, Joseph Victor, Lt., k. in a., 9/9/18 (att. 13 Bn.).
Paterson, Alan Foster, Lt. (Tp.), k. in a., 1/7/16 (att. R. Fus.)
Pattrick, John Harry, 2/Lt., k. in a., 30/11/17 (att. 8th Bn.).
4 Paxton, Archibald Francis Campbell, 2/Lt., k. in a., 1/7/16.
16 Peake, John Lewis, 2/Lt., k. in a., 1/6/17.
4 Pemberton, Percy Leigh, 2/Lt., d. of w., 27/7/16.
Perryman, Arthur Charles, 2/Lt., killed, 7/1/18 (att. R.F.C., 16 Sqd.).
Pery, Cecil, 2/Lt. (Tp.), k. in a., 25/9/15.
4 Peyton, Ernest, 2/Lt. (Tp.), k. in a., 1/7/16.
12 Pointer, Arthur James, 2/Lt. (Tp.), k. in a., 22/3/18 (att. 6 N'hamp. R.).
12 Ponsonby, Spencer Lawrence, Lt. (Tp.), d. of w., 12/1/16.
4 Powell, Thomas William, 2/Lt., k. in a., 25/4/18.
Power, George Henry Fosbrooke, Lt., d. of w., 9/5/15.
Powers, Bernard Alexander, Lt., k. in a., 25/9/17 (att. R.F.C., 19 Sqd.).
12 Prebble, Cyril Edgar, M.C., 2/Lt. (Tp.), d. of w., 8/8/18 (att. 2/2 Lond. R.).
1 Preston, Stanley, Capt., A/Major, k. in a., 25/9/17.
19 Price, William Henry, Capt. (Tp.), k. in a., 24/3/18.
16 Purnell, Arthur Channing, Capt. (Tp.), k. in a., 1/7/16.
3 Purser, Philip Warburton, 2/Lt., died, 11/10/16.
23 Purves, Thomas Warren, Lt. (Tp.), k. in a., 7/6/17.
15 Pyman, Ronald Lee, Lt., k. in a., 3/5/17 (att. 12th Bn.).
Rapley, William Godfrey, 2/Lt., k. in a., 25/9/17 (att. 1st Bn.).
1 Raynham, Charles, 2/Lt., d. of w., 19/3/18.
17 Read, Stanley, M.C., 2/Lt. (Tp.), k. in a., 28/4/17.
14 Reed, Dane Baron, Capt. (Tp.), k. in a., 18/8/16 (att. 13 Bn.).
5 Reid, Archibald David, 2/Lt., d. of w., 8/8/17 (att. 4th Bn.).
12 Restall, Kenneth, Lt. (Tp.), k. in a., 26/9/16.
Ridpath, Geoffrey Lionel Chevalier, 2/Lt., T/Lt., k. in a., 1/7/16.
20 Robertson, Archibald, 2/Lt., k. in a., 9/4/18.
12 Rogers, Arthur Gerald, Lt. (Tp.), k. in a., 26/9/16.
13 Rogerson, Harold, 2/Lt. (Tp.), k. in a., 1/8/17.
13 Romer, Guy Frederick, 2/Lt. (Tp.), d. of w., 3/5/16.
15 Rothe, Sidney Ernest Orme, 2/Lt., k. in a., 13/11/16 (att. 17th Bn.).
4 Rowley, Dalbiac Thomas Cotton, Capt., d. of w., 2/7/16.
Roy, Kenneth James, Capt., k. in a., 24/8/15.
Runge, Oscar Julius Tolme, M.C., Lt., k. in a., 15/10/16 (and 18 M.G.C.).
17 Salter, William, Capt. (Tp.), k. in a., 9/8/16.
4 Sampson, Arthur Henry Winn, 2/Lt., k. in a., 1/7/16.
16 Samuel, Edgar Barnett, 2/Lt. (Tp.), k. in a., 30/1/16.
5 Sanderson, Arthur Keith, 2/Lt., k. in a., 25/9/15 (att. 7 Lond. Regt.).
2 Sandys, Edwin Thomas Falkiner, D.S.O., Lt.-Col. (Tp.), died, 14/9/16.
4 Sapte, Anthony, Capt. (Tp.), k. in a., 1/7/16.
16 Sargood, Hugh Frank, 2/Lt. (Tp.), k. in a., 10/5/17.
Sayers, Robert, 2/Lt., k. in a., 21/10/14.
Scales, E. Lionel, Capt., died, 11/11/18.
12 Scarbrough, Michael Claud, Major (Tp.), k. in a., 26/9/16.
2 Scott, Gordon, Lt., k. in a., 1/7/16.
12 Scruby, William Samuel, 2/Lt. (Tp.), k. in a., 29/6/16.
Secrett, Albert George, 2/Lt., k. in a., 28/4/17 (att. 17 Bn.).
Shackle, Frank Guy, M.C., Lt., A/Capt., k. in a., 21/11/17.
Sharpe, Charles Lancelot Arden, 2/Lt., k. in a., 26/4/15.
11 Shaw, Eyre Massey, Lt., d. of w., 30/7/16.
1 Shaw, Edward Wingfield, D.S.O., Capt., d. of w., 7/12/16.
18 Shaw, Julius Brinkley, 2/Lt., k. in a., 25/3/18 (att. 7 Northampton R.).
5 Shawyer, Maurice Arthur Pritchard, 2/Lt., k. in a., 12/10/14 (att. 1st Bn.).
23 Shoobert, Neil, Lt. (Tp.), k. in a., 31/7/17.
Sichel, Geoffrey Michael John, Lt., k. in a., 9/2/15.
Sim, Bueth Vernon, Capt., d. of w., 7/5/15 (att. 4 Bn.).
5 Simpson, Frederick John Rayner, 2/Lt., k. in a., 31/7/17 (att. 4 Bn.).
11 Sinclair, George, 2/Lt. (Tp.), k. in a., 9/4/17.
Skaife, Arthur Frederick, Capt., k. in a., 1/11/14.
17 Skerry, James Beadnell, 2/Lt. (Tp.), k. in a., 1/6/16.
Skill, Harold Jefferson, Capt. (Tp.), d. of w., 7/4/18 (att. 21st Bn.) (in Ger. hands).
Small, Arnold, 2/Lt. (Tp.), d. of w., 12/4/17.
11 Smallwood, James Fenemore, M.C., Lt. (Tp.), d. of w., 22/5/17.
Smith, Albert Victor, 2/Lt. (Tp.), k. in a., 28/8/18 (att. 20th Bn.).
1/4 Smith, D. G., 2/Lt., killed, 10/4/18 (and R.A.F.).
5 Smith, Gilbert Keppal, Lt. (Tp.), died, 13/3/16 (att. 11/Bn.).
16 Smith, Leonard Hearne, 2/Lt. (Tp.), k. in a., 11/8/17.
2 Smith, Leonard William, 2/Lt. (Tp.), k. in a., 23/10/16.
Smith, William Edward, M.C., 2/Lt., k. in a., 29/8/18.
Smith, William George Richard, 2/Lt., k. in a., 16/8/17 (att. 2nd Bn.).
Sneath, Claude Davis, Lt., k. in a., 14/10/14.
18 Sothers, Charles Gordon, 2/Lt. (Tp.), d. of w., 6/12/17.
20 Sparke, Errol, 2/Lt., k. in a., 22/3/18.
Spatz, Walter, 2/Lt. (Tp.), k. in a., 1/7/16.
Spratt, David Herbert, 2/Lt. (Tp.), k. in a., 20/9/17 (att. 6/L'pool R.).
27 Stagg, John Reginald, 2/Lt. (Tp.), k. in a., 17/9/16 (att. 17th Bn.).
17 Stansfield, Frederick Noel, 2/Lt., k. in a., 2/12/17.
15 Stanton, Oswald Wilfred, Capt. (Tp.), died, 6/11/18 (att. 10 Lond. R.).
Stead, Charles Henry, 2/Lt., k. in a., 27/4/15.
21 Steel, A. E., Lt., k. in a., 3/5/18 (and R.A.F.).
Stephens, John Herbert, 2/Lt. (Tp.), k. in a., 3/5/17 (att. 12 Bn.).
Stephenson, Eric William Rokeby, Lt.-Col., k. in a., 27/4/15.
2 Storkey, Gordon Coleman, 2/Lt. (Tp.), k. in a., 1/8/17.
18 Storr, H., D.S.O., Major, Tp. Lt.-Col., died, 15/8/18.
1/4 Strugnell, L. W., 2/Lt., killed, 16/6/18 (and R.A.F.).
2 Stuart, Karl Edwin, Lt., k. in a., 25/3/18.
20 Sturt, Douglas Elliott, Lt. (Tp.), died, 30/10/18.
12 Sturt, Ernest Guy Maclean, 2/Lt. (Tp.), k. in a., 16/8/16 (att. 6 Northampton R.).
23 Sutherland, James Lindsay, 2/Lt. (Tp.), k. in a., 31/7/17.
6 Swallow, Ernest Harold, 2/Lt., k. in a., 10/10/17 (att. 4th Bn.).
21 Symons, Arthur George, M.C., Capt. (Tp.), died, 23/10/18.
Tagg, Harold Arthur, Lt., k. in a., 12/10/14.
3 Taite, William, 2/Lt., died, 27/9/18.
14 Talbot, Cecil Melliar, 2/Lt. (Tp.), k. in a., 28/9/15 (att. 4th Bn.).
16 Tanqueray, Frederic Baron, 2/Lt., k. in a., 1/7/16.
Tedman, Basil, 2/Lt. (Tp.), k. in a., 21/3/18 (att. 13th Bn.).
3 Terrell, Arthur Clive, 2/Lt., d. of w., 20/4/17.
14 Thompson, Conway Bennett, Capt. (Tp.), died, 23/5/16.
4 Thomson, Leslie Charles, Lt. (Tp.), k. in a., 31/7/17.
Tigar, Harold Walter, Lt., k. in a., 9/5/15.
2 Tillett Albert Edward, 2/Lt., d. of w., 25/3/18.
14 Tiplady, Frank Ewart, 2/Lt. (Tp.), d. of w., 27/9/15 (att. 7 Lond. R.).
Tomkins, Charles Percy, 2/Lt., (Tp.), d. of w., 20/10/18 (att. 1 L'pool R.).
27 Towgood, Arthur Cecil Carden, 2/Lt. (Tp.), k. in a., 13/5/17.
23 Treliving, Arthur Stanley, 2/Lt. (Tp.), k. in a., 29/3/18 (att. T.M.B.).
Trewman, Athol Benedict, 2/Lt., d. of w., 22/10/14.
16 Tuck, Duncan Beresford, Capt. (Tp.), d. of w., 30/3/18.
21 Tuck, Henry Malpas, 2/Lt. (Tp.), d. of w., 26/10/18 (att. 26 R. Fus.).
13 Tuckey, James Caulfield, 2/Lt., k. in a., 31/8/16.
5 Tull, Walter David, 2/Lt., k. in a., 25/3/18.
Tulloh Cecil Falconer, Capt., k. in a., 13/10/14.
13 Turnell, Reginald Leaf, 2/Lt. (Tp.), k. in a., 23/11/17 (att. 20 Bn.).
Turner, William Joseph, 2/Lt. (Tp.), k. in a., 12/10/18 (att. 4th Bn.).
11 Underhill, Reginald, Lt. (A/Capt.), k. in a., 18/11/16 (att. 4th Bn.).
2 Van-Den-Bok, Frederick, 2/Lt., k. in a., 1/7/16.
13 Vaughan, Evan James Stanley, Capt. (Tp.), k. in a., 18/8/16.
4 Viner, George Noel, Lt. (A/Capt.), k. in a., 12/10/18.
13 Vogan, Lindsay Clarence, 2/Lt. (Tp.), d. of w., 28/4/17.
2 Von Winckler, Myles William, Lt., k. in a., 1/8/17.
17 Wade, Albert Luvian, Lt. (Tp.), k. in a., 28/4/17 (att. T.M.B.).
5 Wade, Gordon Standley, 2/Lt., d. of w., 13/11/16 (att. 17th Bn.).
13 Wadlow, Bernard Victor, 2/Lt. (Tp.), k. in a., 3/4/17.
Walker, Wilfred Harold, 2/Lt., k. in a., 3/5/17 (att. 12th Bn.).
20 Wallace, George Frederick, 2/Lt. (Tp.), k. in a., 23/5/17.
12 Wallace, Walter Mackenzie, 2/Lt. (Tp.), k. in a., 21/10/15.
6 Wallis, Charles William, 2/Lt., k. in a., 31/7/17 (att. 13th Bn.).
13 Wallond, William John, 2/Lt., k. in a., 22/3/18.
1 Ward, Bertram Edmund, Lt.-Col., died, 22/10/14.
11 Ward, James Eyre Drummond, Major, died, 20/6/16, (and R.A.O.D.).
5 Ward, Norman Hartley, 2/Lt. (Tp.), d. of w., 8/3/17 (att. 1 L.N. Lancs R.)
Warne, Bertie Joseph, 2/Lt., d. of w., 4/4/18 (att. 21 Bn.).
3 Waterman, Henry Richard, Lt., k. in a., 28/8/16.
16 Watts, Talbot Hamilton, Capt. (Tp.), k. in a., 1/7/16.
Wauchope, James Bourdillon, Lt., k. in a., 10/3/15.
16 Way, George Currey, Major (Tp.), k. in a., 28/1/16.
16 Wegg, Hugh Neville, Capt., k. in a., 25/3/18.
Welman, Noel Yvon Loftus, D.S.O., Capt., k. in a., 25/9/15.
Welsford, Geoffrey Joseph Lighthourn, 2/Lt., k. in a., 30/3/16 (and R.F.C.).
6 West, Charles Henry Raymond, Lt., k. in a., 3/6/15 (att. 4th Bn.).

13 Wheldon-Williams, Victor, Lt (Tp.), killed, 6/7/16.
1 While, Frank Richard, 2/Lt. (Tp.), k. in a., 15/7/16.
4 Whitby, Ernest Victor, 2/Lt. (Tp.), k. in a., 1/7/16.
17 White, Cyril Arthur, 2/Lt. (Tp.), k. in a., 28/4/17.
5 White, E. Norman, Lt., d. of w., 24/9/17 (att. 1st Bn.).
5 White, Hugh Reginald, 2/Lt., k. in a., 27/5/18.
4 Whiteman, John, Major, d. of w., 25/4/17 (att. Hawke Bn., R.N.D.).
Whitfield, Frederick Ashburnham Hooker, 2/Lt., k. in a., 23/4/15.
5 Widgery, Philip Henry, Lt., k. in a., 24/3/18 (att. 21st Bn.).
6 Wilkinson, Ambrose Joseph, 2/Lt. (Tp.), k. in a., 26/9/16 (att. 12 Bn.).
Wilkinson, John Rothes Marlow, Lt., k. in a., 10/9/14.
6 Wilkinson, Vaudelene Auguste Sydney, 2/Lt., died, 7/6/18.
13 Williams, Harold Osborne, 2/Lt., k in a., 21/1/17.
6 Williams, Lionel Murray, Capt., died, 9/4/17 (att. 2 Garr. Bn. Essex R.).
4 Willis, Sherlock Amyas, Lt. (T/Capt.), d. of w., 15/5/17.
23 Wilson, Henry, 2/Lt. (Tp.), k. in a., 15/9/16.
Wilson, Herbert Lawson, 2/Lt., died, 2/11/18 (att. 18th Bn.).
2 Wilson, John, 2/Lt. (Tp.), k. in a., 1/7/16.
5 Wood, Colin Richard, Capt., k. in a., 18/1/15 (att. Glouc. R.).
7 Wood, Harry Douty, 2/Lt., k. in a., 1/7/16.
3 Wood, Rowland Henry, 2/Lt. (Tp.), died, 4/7/17.
6 Wood, Wilfred John, Lt. (Tp.), k. in a., 1/7/16.
Wood, William John, 2/Lt. (Tp.), k. in a., 7/11/15. (att. 16 London R.).
Wordsworth, Alexander Gerald, Capt., k. in a., 6/12/14.
18 Wright, Frederick Charles, 2/Lt., k. in a., 14/4/18.
5 Wright, Henry Gordon, 2/Lt. (Tp.), k. in a., 9/4/17 (att. 11 Bn.).
13 Yates, Frank Dutton, 2/Lt. (Tp.), k. in a., 15/4/17.
Young, Ernest Joseph, 2/Lt., died, 7/11/18 (att. 18 Bn.).
6 Young, Phillip, Lt., d. of w., 21/8/18 (att. M.G.C., 31 Coy.).
Young, Thomas James, 2/Lt., k. in a., 24/9/17 (att. 1st Bn.).

The King's Royal Rifle Corps.

Abadie, Richard Nevile, D.S.O., Lt.-Col., k. in a., 10/7/17.
Addy, Kenneth James Balguy, 2/Lt. (Tp.), k. in a., 13/10/15.
17 Aird, Allan Muir, 2/Lt. (Tp.), k. in a., 21/10/18 (att. 18 Bn.).
Amphlett-Morton, James Fairfax, 2/Lt., k. in a., 10/1/15.
Anderson, Charles Alexander Kenneth, 2/Lt., k. in a., 10/11/14.
21 Anderson, James Skelton, 2/Lt. (Tp.), d. of w., 10/10/16.
5 Anson, Nigel Fredrick Edward, M.C., 2/Lt., k. in a., 10/7/17 (att. 2 Bn.).
7 Arnell, Reginald Brandt, 2/Lt. (Tp.), k. in a., 30/7/15.
1 Ash, Alfred William, 2/Lt., k. in a., 13/6/18 (att. 12 Bn.).
1 Ashwell, Alfred, 2/Lt. (Tp.), k. in a., 4/4/17 (att. 10 Bn.).
13 Atkinson, Fred, 2/Lt. (Tp.), k. in a., 23/4/17.
16 Atkinson, Richard Dermott, 2/Lt., k. in a., 16/7/16.
1 Austen-Cartmell, Arthur James, Lt., k. in a., 1/6/16.
16 Averdieck, Godfrey Harold, Temp. 2/Lt., k. in a., 11/3/16.
17 Bailey, Alfred John, 2/Lt. (Tp.), k. in a., 3/9/16.
5 Bailey, Anthony Yorke, 2/Lt., k. in a., 27/7/16 (att. 1 Bn.).
Baines, Frederick Athelstan Fanshawe, 2/Lt., k. in a., 25/5/15.
21 Baker, Frank Vincent, 2/Lt. (Tp.), k. in a., 22/3/18.
4 Ballance, Leslie Arthur, Capt., k. in a., 28/9/16 (att. 2 Bn.).
16 Balshaw, Newton Kesteven, Capt., k. in a., 13/4/18.
20 Banks, John Cook, M C., Capt. (Tp.), k. in a., 1/5/17.
13 Barber, Graham Brooke, Lt. (Tp.), k. in a., 25/8/18.
Barclay, Rafe Hedworth Myddleton, 2/Lt., k. in a., 14/9/14.
5 Barnes, Edward William, 2/Lt., d. of w., 10/7/17 (att. 2 Bn.).
Barnes, Herbert George, 2/Lt. (Tp.), died, 31/8/17 (att. 7 Bn.).
1 Barnet, Henry Morton, 2/Lt. (Tp.), d. of w., 23/4/18 (in Ger. hands).
Barnett, Reginald Walter, M.C., Lt. (T/Major), k. in a., 12/8/18 (att. Staff, Divl. Hqrs.).
1 Barrand, Sidney, Lt. (Tp.), k. in a., 14/8/18.
Barrett, Arthur Edward, 2/Lt. (Tp.), k. in a., 22/8/17 (att. 8 Bn.).
7 Bartholomew, Guy Wollaston, Temp. Capt., k. in a., 25/8/16.
Bashford, Charles, 2/Lt., k. in a., 20/9/17 (att. 21 Bn.).
Battenberg, His Highness Prince Maurice Victor Donald, of, K.C.V.O., Lt., k. in a., 27/10/14.
Beaver, John Denistoun Campbell, 2/Lt., d. of w., 15/5/18 (att. 13 Bn.).
1 Beck, William, Lt. & Qr.-Mr., died, 18/4/18.
Beecheno, James Herbert, 2/Lt. (Tp.), d. of w., 25/10/18 (att. 13 Bn.).
10 Bell, Robert de Houghan Mark, Lt. (Tp.), k. in a., 3/9/16.
9 Benson, Eric William, Temp. Lt.-Col., k. in a., 15/9/16.
Bentall, Ernest Hammond, 2/Lt., k. in a., 3/10/15.
15 Benton, Frank, 2/Lt. (Tp.), k. in a., 15-17/9/16 (att. 21 Bn.).
5 Bernard, Arthur Basil, Lt. (A/Capt.), d. of w., 4/5/17 (in Ger. hands) (att. 16 Bn.).
Bertie, Ninian Mark Kerr, 2/Lt., k. in a., 8/5/15.
2 Best, Edgar Harold, 2/Lt. (Tp.), d. of w., 18/9/18.
Bevan, Percival Johnstone, Lt., k. in a., 10/3/15.
Bigge, The Hon. John Neville, Capt., k. in a., 15/5/15.
2 Bircham, Humphrey Francis William, D.S.O., Temp. Lt.-Col., d. of w., 23/7/16.
7 Bird, Stanley Treadgold, 2/Lt. (Tp.), d. of w., 20/8/16.
6 Bird, William Ryder, 2/Lt. (Tp.), k. in a., 8/10/15 (att. 8 Bn.).
5 Bird, Wilfrid Stanley, Lt., k. in a., 9/5/15 (att. 2 Bn.).
7 Blackbourn, Edgar Singleton, 2/Lt. (Tp.), d. of w., 29/9/16.
10 Blake, Cecil Rodolph, Capt. (Tp.), k. in a., 4/4/17.
Blake, Maurice Frederic, Lt., k. in a., 14/9/14.
8 Blane, James Pitcairn, Capt. (Tp.), d. of w., 23/11/15.
5 Blyth, James Charles, 2/Lt., k. in a., 13/4/17 (att. 1 Bn.).
Bond, Robert Harold, Lt., k. in a., 14/9/14.
6 Boucher, Arthur Guy, 2/Lt., k. in a., 10/7/17 (att. 2 Bn.).
Bourdillon, Tom Louis, M.C., Major (Tp.), k. in a., 24/8/17 (att. 8 Bn.).
Bourke, Eustace George Walter, Capt., k. in a., 16/6/15 (att. 9 Bn.).
Bourne, Gerald Hugh Temple, Temp. 2/Lt., k. in a., 18/3/17 (and R.F.C., 4 Sqd.).
Boyd, Gavin Haddow, 2/Lt. (Tp.), k. in a., 2/12/17 (att. 16 Bn.).
Brakenberry, William Horace, M.M., 2/Lt. (Tp.), d. of w., 23/10/18 (att. 13 Bn.).
Branker, Walter Robert, M.C., 2/Lt. (Tp.), k. in a., 5/10/18 (att. 11 Notts. & Derby Rgt.).
Brocklehurst, Archibald Henry, Capt., d. of w., 29/7/16.
20 Brooks, George William, 2/Lt. (Tp.), k. in a., 29/5/18.
11 Broster, Harold Broughton, 2/Lt. (Tp.), k. in a., 30/11/17.
Brown, Edward Dell, 2/Lt. (Tp.), k. in a., 16/8/17 (att. 12 Bn.).
16 Budd, Frederick George, M.C., 2/Lt. (Tp.), d. of w., 15/10/18.
6 Bulkeley-Hughes, George Montagu Warren, T/Lt. (A/Capt.), k. in a., 27/2/17 (att. 12 Bn.).
5 Bull, Alfred George, 2/Lt., k. in a., 6/8/18 (att. 8 Bn.).
10 Bull, John Lionel Robin, 2/Lt., k. in a., 30/11/17.
Bullen, Roy Evans, 2/Lt., d. of w., 29/4/16.
18 Bullivant, Eric Claud, 2/Lt., k. in a., 24/3/18.
Burroughes, Stephen, 2/Lt., k. in a., 4/11/18 (att. 2 Bn.).
11 Bury, Edmond William, Capt. (Tp.), k. in a., 5/12/15.
13 Butcher, Norris de Gruchy, Lt. & Qr.-Mr., d. of w., 23/5/18.
17 Butcher, Arthur James Basil, 2/Lt., k. in a., 3/9/16.
7 Butler, The Hon. Brian Danvers, Temp. Lt., k. in a., 18/8/16.
V.C. Butler, John Fitzhardinge Paul, D.S.O., Capt., d. of w., 5/9/16 (att. Gold Coast Regt.).
13 Cairns, Herbert, Temp. 2/Lt., k. in a., 4/10/17.
18 Calder, William Paul, Temp. 2/Lt., k. in a., 14/6/17.
13 Campbell, Charles, Temp. 2/Lt., d. of w., 10/1/18.
10 Capern, Henry James, Temp. 2/Lt., k. in a., 22/3/18 (att. 59/T.M.B.).
12 Carnegie, Theodore Arthur, Lt., k. in a., 16/8/17.
7 Carter, Gerald Francis, 2/Lt. (Tp.), d. of w., 30/7/15.
Casey, James, Lt., k. in a., 30/10/14.
Cassidy, Cyril Martin, 2/Lt., d. of w., 17/5/15.
Cathcart, Augustus Ernest, Capt., k. in a., 14/9/14.
8 Cayley, Francis Digby Edward, Temp. 2/Lt., k. in a., 29/9/15 (att. 1 Bn.).
8 Chambers, Robert Seymour Bennet, T/Lt. (A/Capt.), k. in a., 24/12/17.
9 Chaplin, Charles Slingsby, Lt.-Col., k. in a., 30/7/15.
Charleston, Ebenezer, Temp. 2/Lt., k. in a., 20/9/17 (att. 11 Bn.).
12 Chaworth-Musters, Robert, M.C., Capt., died, 10/10/18 (att. 3rd Musk. Camp).
Chaworth-Musters, Patricius George, Lt., d. of w., 12/1/15.
13 Chester-Master, Richard Chester, D.S.O., Bt. Major (T/Lt.-Col.), k. in a., 30/8/17.
13 Chidson, Laurence Drury, M.C., T/Lt. (A/Capt.), k. in a., 24/4/17.
13 Chinnery, Harry Broderick, T/Lt., k. in a., 28/5/16.
18 Christmas, Edwin Cecil Russell, Temp. 2/Lt., d. of w., 7/10/16.
18 Clark, Douglas Scott Dalrymple, Capt., k. in a., 15/9/16 (and T.M.B.).
Claxton, Eric Abley, 2/Lt., d. of w., 31/7/17 (att. 18 Bn.).
11 Clifford, Herbert James, T/Lt. (A/Capt.), k. in a., 20/9/17.
Clinton, Walter Lawrence, Capt., died, 22/11/18.
Clowes, Charles George Edric, Lt., d. of w., 18/2/15.
15 Cobb, Kenneth Rhodes, Capt., k. in a., 1/7/15.
Coburn, Charles, 2/Lt., k. in a., 31/7/17 (att. 18 Bn.).
16 Coe, Sydney Urie Charles, Temp. 2/Lt., k. in a., 30/11/17.
2 Cockerell, Andrew Pepys, 2/Lt., k. in a., 15/8/16.
Collins, Charles, Lt., d. of w., 28/7/16.
16 Cooban, Adrian Deighton, T/Major, k. in a., 16/7/16.
18 Cook, Percy Mellows, Temp. 2/Lt., k. in a., 4/10/16.
10 Coyle, Leonard Joseph, 2/Lt. (Tp.), k. in a., 23/11/16.
6 Craggs, John James, 2/Lt., k. in a., 17/2/17 (att. 1 Bn.).
Cram, Hubert Arthur, 2/Lt. (Tp.), d. of w., 16/4/18.
Crawhall, Fritz Portmore, 2/Lt., k. in a., 10/3/15.
Croft-Smith, Edwin Spencer, 2/Lt., k. in a., 8/5/15.
12 Crooks, Edward Neilson, 2/Lt., k. in a., 22/3/18.
Cross, Samuel Allison, 2/Lt., k. in a., 14/1/18 (att. 2 Bn.).
Crossman, William Ronald Morley, 2/Lt., k. in a., 2/11/14.
14 Cruikshanks, Ernest, Capt. (Tp.), k. in a., 17/10/15 (att. 9 Bn.).
Culme-Seymour, George, Capt., k. in a., 7/5/15.
2 Cunningham, Alexander Pinman, 2/Lt. (Tp.), d. of w., 19/9/18.
18 Curwen, Cecil Neil, Temp. Lt., k. in a., 15/9/16.
10 Davies, David Guy, M.C., Temp. Capt., k. in a., 4/4/17.
6 Davies, George Llewelyn, 2/Lt., k. in a., 15/3/15 (att. Rifle Bde.).
16 Davis, Henry Christopher, 2/Lt., k. in a., 2/7/16.
Davis, Mellville Allen Duff, M.C., 2/Lt. (Tp.), died, 29/5/18 (att. 9 Bn.).
8 Davis, William Jeffery, Capt. & Adjt., k. in a., 30/7/15.
Davison, Stuart, 2/Lt., k. in a., 14/9/14.
9 Daw, Reginald Samuel, Capt. (Tp.), d. of w., 25/9/16.
13 Dawe, Alfred Henry, Temp. 2/Lt., k. in a., 11/4/17.
17 Day, Percy Oliver James, 2/Lt. (Tp.), k. in a., 19/7/16.
Dean, Frank, 2/Lt., k. in a., 31/10/14.
16 Deedes, Herbert Philip, Temp. Capt., k. in a., 16/7/16.
16 Denniss, Kenneth George, Temp. 2/Lt., k. in a., 15/7/16.
9 Dent, Arthur Evelyn, Lt. (A/Capt.), k. in a., 9/4/17.

Denton-Cardew, Warnell de Montigny, Temp. 2/Lt., k. in a., 30/11/17 (att. 12 Bn.).
De Paravicini, John Marcus, Major, k. in a., 30/11/17 (att. 11 Bn.).
1 De Satgé, Frederick Gordon, Capt., k. in a., 15/9/16 (att. 7 Bn.).
16 Devitt, Herbert John, 2/Lt., k. in a., 12/9/18 (att. 13 Bn.).
2 Dick, Andrew Campbell, 2/Lt. (Tp.), d. of w., 23/10/18.
2 Dickenson, Aubrey Greville Newton, Lt. (Tp.), d. of w., 1/7/16.
13 Dickens, Guy, Capt. (Tp.), d. of w., 17/7/16.
V.C. Dimmer, John Henry Stephen, M.C., Capt. (Temp. Lt.-Col.), k. in a., 21/3/18 (att. 2/4 R. Berks R.).
12 Dove, Tom, M.C., Temp. Capt., k. in a., 16/8/17.
7 Dowling, Geoffrey Charles Walter, Temp. Capt., k. in a., 30/7/15.
9 Dowson, Humphrey, M.C., Temp. Capt., k. in a., 15/9/16.
6 Drummond, Nigel Felton, Lt., killed, 20/12/16 (att. 1st Bn.).
9 Durnford, Richard Selby, Capt. (Temp.), k. in a., 31/7/15.
Eastman, William Viviash, Temp. 2/Lt., k. in a., 4/10/17 (att. 13 Bn.).
Eden, The Hon. William Alfred Morton, Lt., k. in a., 3/3/15.
Edgar, George Geoffrey, Lt. (Tp.), d. of w., 28/8/16.
2 Edwardes, Owen, 2/Lt., k. in a., 1/7/16.
Edwards, Lewis George, Temp. 2/Lt., k. in a., 20/9/17 (att. 11 Bn.).
8 Egerton, John Frederick, Temp. 2/Lt., d. of w., 3/4/16 (A.D.C.).
2 Egerton-Green, Charles Scroop, Lt., k. in a., 1/7/16.
2 Eldridge, John Thomas, 2/Lt. (Tp.), k. in a., 18/9/18.
5 Eley, William Arthur Derrick, 2/Lt., k. in a., 17/2/17 (att. 1 Bn.).
6 Eminson, Robert Astley Franklin, 2/Lt., k. in a., 20/7/16 (att. M.G. Cps.).
19 Erwood, Cecil Victor, Temp. 2/Lt., k. in a., 17/2/17 (att. 1 Bn.).
5 Everitt, John Wilson, 2/Lt., died, 12/4/18 (in Ger. hands).
17 Ewen, Philip Keith Somerville, Lt. (Tp.), k. in a., 3/9/16.
9 Exell, Noel Jardine, Capt. (Tp.), d. of w., 31/7/15.
6 Eyre, Charles Howard, Lt., k. in a., 25/9/15 (att. 2 Bn.).
9 Faber, Cecil Valdemar, 2/Lt. (Tp.), k. in a., 30/7/15.
7 Fairlie, Edward, T/Capt. (A/Major), k. in a., 30/3/18 (att. 17 Bn.).
5 Fardell, Gervase, M.C., Capt., k. in a., 29/9/18 (att. 1 Bn.).
7 Farmer, Charles George Edgar, Lt. (Tp.), k. in a., 18/8/16.
6 Farmer, Henry Charles Maclean, 2/Lt., k. in a., 10/5/15 (att. 4 Bn.).
Farmer, James Inglesby, 2/Lt., k. in a., 9/5/15.
9 Farran, Charles, 2/Lt. (Tp.), k. in a., 24/8/16.
Fellowes, Robert, 2/Lt., k. in a., 10/3/15.
Featherstonhaugh, Richard Collingwood, Lt., d. of w., 14/5/15.
21 Feversham (Earl of), Charles William Reginald, Lt.-Col., k. in a., 15/9/16.
5 Ffolkes, William Rupert Compton, 2/Lt., k. in a., 30/12/17 (att. 1 Bn.).
17 Fifield, Percival, Temp. 2/Lt., k. in a., 22/3/18.
15 Findlay, Arthur Bertram, Lt., k. in a., 30/7/15 (att. 7 Bn.).
12 Fisher, Leslie Benito, Lt. (Tp.), k. in a., 14/8/15.
Fleming, Ernest William, Temp. 2/Lt., k. in a., 4/11/18 (att 13 Bn.).
Foljambe, Hubert Francis Fitzwilliam Brabazon, Major, k. in a., 14/9/14.
11 Forrest, Austin Lancelot, 2/Lt. (Tp.), k. in a., 3/9/16.
16 Forrest, Laurence Bernard, 2/Lt., k. in a., 20/5/17.
Forster, John, 2/Lt., k. in a., 14/9/14.
Fowler, George Glyn, Lt., d. of w., 26/9/15.
Franks, John Fergusson, Capt. & Adjt., d. of w., 22/9/15.
2 Freeman, Frank Albert, 2/Lt., k. in a., 1/7/16.
Fryer, William Arthur, Temp. Lt., k. in a., 3/10/18 (att. 4 Bn.).
2 Gant, Alfred Claude, Temp. 2/Lt., k. in a., 17/10/18
Gantsman, Ernest, Temp. 2/Lt., k. in a., 10/11/17 (att. 9 Bn.).
16 Garrard, Reginald Herbert, Temp. 2/Lt., k. in a., 23/4/17.
9 Geen, William Purdon, 2/Lt., k. in a., 31/7/15.
Gibb, John Hardie, Temp. 2/Lt., k. in a., 31/7/17 (att. 18 Bn.).
2 Gibbs, Walter Septimus, Temp. 2/Lt., k. in a., 17/10/18.
11 Gilpin, Albert John, 2/Lt. (Tp.), k. in a., 17/9/16.
6 Glegg, Arthur Livingstone, 2/Lt., k. in a., 10/8/15 (att. 2 Bn.).
6 Glegg, Walter Scott, 2/Lt., k. in a., 15/9/16 (att. 9 Bn.).
Godman, W. W. W., 2/Lt., k. in a., 24/1/15.
18 Goldby, William Charles, Temp. 2/Lt., k. in a., 22/8/18.
12 Goffey, John Graham, 2/Lt., k. in a., 3/9/16.
16 Gonner, Edward Maurice, Temp. Capt., k. in a., 23/4/17.
1 Goodwin, John, Temp. 2/Lt., k. in a., 29/11/17.
22 Goody, Gilbert Alexander, Temp. 2/Lt., d. of w., 6/11/16 (att. 16 Bn.).
9 Goody, Geoffrey Riddel, Temp. Lt., killed, 14/7/18 (att. 10 Tr. Res. Bn.).
12 Gordon, Peter, Temp. 2/Lt., k. in a., 24/8/18 (att. 18 Bn.).
6 Gore-Brown, Harold Thomas Thirlwall, 2/Lt., d. of w., 23/8/16 (att. 7 Bn.).
11 Gough, Harold Stuart, Lt. (Tp.), k. in a., 17/6/16.
13 Gould, Gerald Oscar Alan, 2/Lt., d. of w., 25/6/16.
9 Gould, Patrick Wallace, 2/Lt. (Tp.), k. in a., 24/8/16.
Graham-Roe, Archibald Chaceley, Temp. 2/Lt., k. in a., 29/4/17 (att. 1 Bn.).
16 Grant, Edmund Henry, 2/Lt. (Tp.), d. of w., 2/8/16.
6 Grazebrook, Charles Alvery, Capt., k. in a., 10/3/15 (att. 1 Bn.).
2 Greenfield, Eric Frank, Temp. 2/Lt., killed, 13/2/17.
Grenville-Grey, Wilfred Hanbury, Lt., d. of w., 16/5/15.
Grew, Hubert, 2/Lt., k. in a., 2/7/15.
1 Griffiths, George Richards, Temp. Lt., d. of w., 15/9/16.
9 Habershon, Philip Henry, 2/Lt. (Tp.), k. in a., 25/9/15.
Hain, Edward Sydney, Temp. 2/Lt., k. in a., 21/11/17 (att. 11 Bn.).
13 Hale, Frank Ernest, Temp. 2/Lt., k. in a., 25/8/18.
Hall, Henry Lewes, 2/Lt., k. in a., 30/11/17 (att. 10 Bn.).
1 Hambro, Percival, 2/Lt., d. of w., 23/3/18.
6 Hamilton, Vyvyan Lodwick, 2/Lt., k. in a., 14/6/17 (att. 18 Bn.).
Hancock, Frank Pine, 2/Lt., k. in a., 16/8/18 (att. 2 Bn.).
Hardy, Richard Luard, Capt. (Tp.), k. in a., 24/8/17 (att. 8 Bn.).
Harman, Arthur, Capt. & Qr.-Mr., k. in a., 26/6/15.
21 Harmon, Wilfred Baldwin, Temp. 2/Lt., k. in a., 1/8/17.
12 Harries, Frederick Ebenezer Melville, Temp. 2/Lt., k. in a., 26/2/17.
2 Harvie, Stuart McLaren, 2/Lt., d. of w., 1/6/18 (att. 6 Bn.).
20 Harvey, William Clayton, Temp. Lt., k. in a., 14/7/16.
19 Hawke, Albert Edward Mountain Aysh, Temp. 2/Lt., d. of w., 11/9/16 (att. 2 Bn.).
15 Hawkins, Gilbert William, Lt. (Tp.), d. of w., 15/11/16 (att. 13 Bn.).
Hawley, Cyril Francis, Capt., k. in a., 2/11/14.
Haycroft, Frank Alexander, 2/Lt. (Tp.), k. in a., 10/8/17 (att. 10 Bn.).
5 Heberden, Arthur Clements, 2/Lt., k. in a., 10/7/17 (att. 2 Bn.).
17 Hecht, Marcus Francis, Temp. Major, k. in a., 3/9/16.
6 Henderson, Donald, 2/Lt., k. in a., 11/1/15 (att. 1 Bn.).
8 Henriques, Philip Brydges Gutterlz, Temp. 2/Lt., d. of w., 24/7/15.
Herbertson, Andrew Hunter, Lt., k. in a., 16/5/17 (att. 7 Bn. Res.).
6 Herron, Alec Rowan, 2/Lt., k. in a., 10/3/15 (att. 1 Bn.).
21 Hervey, Thomas Percy Arthur, 2/Lt. (Tp.), k. in a., 15-17/9/16.
5 Hext, Thomas Madewood, 2/Lt., k. in a., 29/4/17 (att. 12 Bn.).
16 Hichens, James Bryan, Lt. (Tp.), k. in a., 16/7/16.
6 Hill, Victor Baillie, M.C., Capt., d. of w., 15/1/18.
Hills, Walter Edward, Temp. 2/Lt., k. in a., 26/6/17 (att. 16 Bn.).
5 Hincks, Bertram, 2/Lt., k. in a., 18/12/16 (att. 10 Bn.).
Hoare, Archibald, Capt., d. of w., 27/11/17.
11 Hobbs, Reginald George, Temp. 2/Lt., k. in a., 20/9/17.
10 Hocken, Stephen Lotan, Temp. 2/Lt., k. in a., 3/9/16.
Hodges, Bernard, 2/Lt. (Tp.), d. of w., 16/4/18 (att. 16 Bn.).
6 Hodges, Harold Wardale, 2/Lt., k. in a., 9/5/15 (att. 2/Bn.).
Hodgson, Charles Edward, D.C.M., 2/Lt. (Tp.), k. in a., 2/10/18 (att. 18 Bn.).
5 Hodson, Sydney, 2/Lt., k. in a., 21/3/18 (att. 9 Bn.).
18 Holbech, David, Temp 2Lt., k. in a., 8/4/17.
16 Holborow, Frederick Bernard, 2/Lt. (Tp.), k. in a., 16/4/18
10 Hole, Michael, 2/Lt. (Tp.), k. in a., 19/9/17.
13 Holmes, Ernest Cameron, Temp. 2/Lt., k. in a., 14/11/16.
5 Holmes, Robert Bryan, 2/Lt., d. of w., 1/7/16 (att. 2 Bn.).
5 Honey, Geoffrey Henry Le Sueur, Temp. 2/Lt., k. in a., 21/10/16 (att. 17 Bn.).
11 Hopkins, Arthur Martyn, 2/Lt. (Tp.), k. in a., 28/3/18.
10 Horner, William Arthur, Lt. (Tp.), d. of w., 13/12/17.
10 Horsley, Ernest, 2/Lt. (Tp.), k. in a., 14/8/17 (att. 59 T.M.B.).
Hough, Geoffrey Goadsby, T/Lt. (A/Capt.), died, 8/9/18 (O.C., 214 P. of W. Coy.).
5 Howell, Edmund Lally, Temp. Capt., k. in a., 27/7/16 (att. 1 Bn.).
9 Howell, John, 2/Lt. (Tp.), k. in a., 25/9/15.
5 Hubbard, Archibald Charles, 2/Lt., k. in a., 8/11/17 (att. 2 Bn.).
Hughes, Peter, Capt., k. in a., 25/3/18 (att. 11 Bn.).
Hughes, T. McKenny, Temp. Lt., k. in a., 5/2/18 (att. R.F.C.).
17 Hulks, Henry John, Capt. (Tp.), k. in a., 3/9/16.
13 Humphreys, Richard Grain, 2/Lt., k. in a., 28/9/17.
Hunter, James MacMillan, 2/Lt. (Tp.), k. in a., 17/10/18 (att. 2 Bn.).
8 Huntington, George Waldeof, 2/Lt., k. in a., 24/7/16 (6th Bn.).
15 Ionides, Ambrose Constantine, Lt. (Tp.), k. in a., 16/19/15 (att. 9 Bn.).
7 Jackman, Harold, M.C., T/2/Lt. (A/Capt.), k. in a., 21/3/18.
Jackson, Bertram Washington, Lt., k. in a., 14/9/14.
6 James, Eric Samuel Pennant Kingsbury, Capt., k. in a., 17/3/15.
James, John Stephen Harvey, 2/Lt., k. in a., 16/5/15.
Jay, Frank Goldsmith, 2/Lt. (Tp.), k. in a., 29/9/18 (att. 18 Bn.).
20 Jenkins, John, M.C., T/Major (A/Lt.-Col.), d. of w., 9/10/18 (att. 1/Mon. Regt.).
Johnson, Harry Cecil, D.S.O., Bt.-Major, d. of w., 1/1/15 (P. of W.).
5 Johnson, Henry Earlam, 2/Lt., k. in a., 4/6/16.
11 Johnston, Benjamin, 2/Lt., died, 3/111/18 (in Ger. hands).
2 Johnstone, Frederick John Lawrie, Lt., d. of w., 29/8/16.
21 Jones, Philip Allsworth, Temp. 2/Lt., d. of w., 27/9/16.
Kay, Sir William Algernon Ireland, Bart., C.M.G., D.S.O, Brig.-Gen., k. in a., 4/10/18 (and 3 Inf. Bde.).
11 Kearton, Frank, Temp. 2/Lt., k. in a., 21/11/17.
Kelly, Henry John, Temp. 2/Lt., k. in a., 20/9/17 (att. 21 Bn.).
16 Kerr, Andrew Alan, 2/Lt., k. in a., 26/3/18.
Kidd, James Forrest, 2/Lt., died, 1/11/18 (and R.A.F.).
King, Frank Maxfield, Major (Tp.), k. in a., 22/3/18 (att. 9/L.N. Lancs.).

King, Lucas Henry St. Aubyn, Lt., k. in a., 8/5/15.
17 Kitchin, Ernest Harold, Capt. (Tp.), k. in a., 21/10/16 (15th Bn.).
16 Knight, Philip, 2/Lt. (Tp.), k. in a., 29/9/18.
Knowles, Richard Arthur Lees, M.C., Lt., k. in a., 25/2/18 (att. 4 Bn.).
17 Lacey, Thomas Henry, Temp. 2/Lt., d. of w., 4/9/16.
Lagden, Ronald Owen, Capt., k. in a., 3/3/15.
12 Laird, James Duncan, 2/Lt. (Tp.), k. in a., 25/3/18.
9 Lambert, Jack Fellowes, 2/Lt., k. in a., 30/7/15.
Lambert, Montague Arthur, 2/Lt. (Tp.), k. in a., 2/10/18 (att. 18 Bn.).
13 Landale, Cyril, Capt. (Tp.), k. in a., 21/8/18.
18 Langford, John Joseph, Temp. 2/Lt., k. in a., 15/9/16.
18 Langford, Wallace George, Temp. 2/Lt., d. of w., 27/6/16.
2 Langton, Arthur Henry Brodie, Lt., d. of w., 12/9/16.
6 Lawrence, Christopher Hal, 2/Lt., k. in a., 13/10/14 (att. 2 Bn.).
6 Lawrence, Malcolm Eyton, Lt., k. in a., 10/1/15 (att. 2 Bn.).
18 Laycock, Joseph Harold, 2/Lt., k. in a., 7/10/16.
11 Leadbitter, Francis John Graham, Temp. 2/Lt., k. in a., 5/3/17.
8 Lee, Noel Esmond, Temp. Capt., k. in a., 24/8/17.
5 Leech, Geoffrey Charles Martyn, Temp. Lt., d. of w., 9/4/17.
10 Leigh, John Egerton, Temp. Capt., k. in a., 4/4/17.
9 Le Mesurier, Haviland, 2/Lt., Temp., k. in a., 29/8/16.
18 Lester, John Beaumont, Capt. (Tp.), k. in a., 15/9/16.
1 Lever, Joseph, M.C., 2/Lt. (Tp.), d. of w., 1/10/18.
6 Levett, Richard William Byrd, 2/Lt., k. in a., 10/3/17 (att. 1 Bn.).
16 Levitt, Sydney Neville, 2/Lt. (Tp.), k. in a., 29/9/18.
16 Lewer, Richard Roy, Temp. Lt., d. of w., 21/7/16.
7 Lewis, Lance Will, Temp. 2/Lt., k. in a., 9/8/16 (and M.G.C.).
17 Lewis, Robert Frederick, Temp. 2/Lt., k. in a., 20/9/17 (and 117 Trench Mortar Bty.).
6 Liddell, John Henry Tandy, Lt., d. of w., 17/11/16 (att. 1 Bn.).
Lines, Herbert, Temp. 2/Lt., k. in a., 20/9/17 (att. 10 Bn.).
6 Loft, Percy Trotter, 2/Lt., k. in a., 24/3/18 (att. 18 Bn.).
7 Longbottom, Robert, Temp. 2/Lt., k. in a., 31/7/15.
6 Lonsdale, Arthur Carr Glyn, Lt., k. in a., 10/3/15 (att. 2 Bn. R. Sc. Fus.).
13 Low, John, 2/Lt., k. in a., 10/1/18.
5 Lowndes, Richard Forbes, 2/Lt., k. in a., 14/11/16 (att. 1 Bn.).
12 Loyd, Godfrey Beaumont, M.C., Capt., d. of w., 1/12/17.
12 Lycett, Timothy, D.S.O., Lt. (T/Capt.), d. of w., 5/10/18.
Lyndall, Joseph Gwynne, Temp. 2/Lt., k. in a., 3/5/17.
5 Lynes, Wynne Parr, Capt., died, 8/10/16.
20 McDonald, Angus George, Temp. 2/Lt., died, 29/12/15.
5 Macdonald-Moreton, Norman Charles Henry, Temp. Capt., k. in a., 13/10/15.
MacIver, Kenneth Mackenzie, Lt. (Tp.), killed, 30/10/18 (att. K.A.R.).
Mackay, Terence Faulkner, 2/Lt. (Tp.), k. in a., 3/10/18 (att. 4 Bn.).
9 McKecknie, Alexander, 2/Lt. (Tp.), k. in a., 21/3/18.
Mackenzie, Mark Kincaid, Lt., k. in a., 1/2/16.
McKenzie, Robert Andrew, Temp. 2/Lt., k. in a., 10/11/17 (att. 9 Bn.).
McKie, Eric, 2/Lt. (Tp.), k. in a., 24/3/18 (att. 11 Bn.).
MacLachlan, Alexander Fraser Campbell, C.M.G., D.S.O., Major (Temp. Lt.-Col.), k. in a., 22/3/18
2 McLure, David, 2/Lt. (Tp.), died, 8/3/18 (att. 4 Army Musk. School).
12 McMillan, Donald Cameron, Temp. 2/Lt., d. of w., 11/3/16.
Madeley, Sydney, 2/Lt., d. of w., 11/3/15.
11 Maggs, Eric William Bristowe, Temp. 2/Lt., k. in a., 20/8/18.
Makins, Geoffrey, M.V.O., Capt., d. of w., 23/8/15.
9 Mallalue, Maxwell, Capt., k. in a., 24/8/16.
Mann, Percy Charles, Temp. 2/Lt., k. in a., 31/7/17 (att. 17 Bn.).
8 Mansfield, Eric Oswald, Temp. 2/Lt., k. in a., 24/8/18.
Marlow, Albert Leopold Craddock, Temp. 2/Lt., d. of w, 4/4/17 (att. 10 Bn.).
12 Martin, William Gerald, Temp. Lt. (A/Capt.), k. in a., 14/1/17.
15 Mason, Gordon, Temp. 2/Lt., k. in a., 7/6/17 (att. 21 Bn.).
6 Mason, Peter, 2/Lt., k. in a., 17/2/17 (att. 1 Bn.).
18 Mathews, William Scott, Temp. Lt., k. in a., 15/9/16.
10 Maude, John William Ashley, Temp. 2/Lt., k. in a., 24/8/15.
6 May, Herbert Cecil, 2/Lt., d. of w., 29/9/18 (att. 18 Bn.).
Maynard, John Wilmot, 2/Lt., k. in a., 24/4/15.
14 Meek, Hubert Kingsley, T/Capt., k. in a., 15/9/16.
13 Meikle, James Drysdale, Temp. 2/Lt., k. in a., 4/11/18.
6 Melville, William Woodfall, Lt., k. in a., 9/5/15 (att. 2 Bn.).
11 Meredith, Gerald, M.C., Temp. Capt., died, 27/3/18.
5 Messer, Allan Ernest, Capt., d. of w., 17/2/16 (att. 1 Bn.).
16 Middlecote, E. W. A. G., 2/Lt. k. in a., 3/10/18 (and R.A.F.).
Mitchell, Norman Reid, Temp. 2/Lt., k. in a., 5/12/17 (att. 20 Bn.).
12 Molyneux, James Herbert, 2/Lt., k. in a., 16/8/17.
10 Moore, William Henry Hilme, T/Lt., killed, 19/10/15.
Morrill, George Bertie, Temp. 2/Lt., k. in a., 23/10/18 (att. 13 Bn.).
Morris, Clive Wilson, 2/Lt., k. in a., 9/5/15.
11 Morris, William Percy, Temp. Lt., died, 28/12/18.
Morrison, E. A. A., Lt., died, 13/11/18 (att. R.A.F.).
5 Morrison, Kenneth Rae, 2/Lt., k. in a., 21/9/17 (att. 18 Bn.).
Morton, Daniel, 2/Lt., k. in a., 10/5/15.
Munro, Baillie Chisholm, M.C., 2/Lt., k. in a., 10/7/17.
12 Munsey, William Frederick, 2/Lt., k. in a., 16/8/17.
9 Murray, Charles William, Temp 2/Lt., k. in a., 25/9/15.
20 Nainby, Whinfield Hamilton, Temp. 2/Lt., k. in a., 18/8/16.
20 Naish, Alfred Herbert, Temp. Lt., k. in a., 13/7/16.
Nash, Llewellyn Charles, Lt., d. of w., 29/9/15.
10 Newton, Charles Hercules Augustus Francis, Temp. Lt., k. in a., 13/3/16.
5 Nivison, Robert Butler, Temp. 2/Lt., k. in a., 15-17/9/16 (att. 21 Bn.).
6 Noble, Norris Heatley, 2/Lt., d. of w., 15/8/16 (att. 1 Bn.).
6 Norbury, Francis Campbell, Capt., k. in a., 10/1/15 (att. 1 Bn.).
21 Norris, Ernest Arthur, 2/Lt., k. in a., 22/3/18 (att. 17 Bn.).
13 Norris, Gilbert Hume, T/Capt., d. of w., 9/3/18.
21 Norton, Frank Frederick, Temp. 2/Lt., k. in a., 20/9/17.
11 Orford, Stephen Mewburn, 2/Lt., k. in a., 25/6/16.
O'Rorke, Denis Clifford, M.C., Capt., k. in a., 24/3/18.
5 Orrey, Frederick William, Temp 2/Lt., d. of w., 16/9/17 (att. 13 Bn.).
5 Osborne, Frederick William, 2/Lt., k. in a., 23/4/17 (att. 13 Bn.).
4 Oxley, Herman Grant, Temp. Lt., k. in a., 4/11/18 (att. 2 Bn.).
Paget, Desmond Otho, 2/Lt., k. in a., 21/3/18 (att. 7 Bn.).
9 Panes, Ernest Philip Morris, Temp. 2/Lt., k. in a., 25/9/15.
Parker, Cyril Edmund, 2/Lt., k. in a., 1/1/15
Parker, Frederick Neville, 2/Lt., k. in a., 28/4/15.
17 Parry, Harold, Temp. 2/Lt., k. in a., 6/5/17.
6 Paul, Edgar Newton, T/Lt. (A/Capt.), k. in a., 28/12/17 (att. 12 Bn.).
12 Paul, Herbert James, Temp. 2/Lt., k. in a., 20/11/17.
6 Paul, Jeffery William Ensor, 2/Lt., k. in a., 27/7/16 (att. 1 Bn.).
Peacocke, Eric Forrester, 2/Lt., k. in a., 20/5/17 (att. 16 Bn.).
3 Pearce, John Francis Brice, Capt., k. in a., 29/4/15.
16 Pearson, Thomas Raleigh, 2/Lt., d. of w., 2/7/16.
9 Pemberton, Leigh, 2/Lt. (Tp.), k. in a., 25/9/15 (att. 9 Bn. Rfl. Bde.).
13 Penhale, Thomas William Temp. 2/Lt., d. of w., 15/4/17.
12 Perry, Stephen Ralph, Temp. Lt., k. in a., 18/9/16.
20 Perry, William Claude, Temp. 2/Lt., d. of w., 13/7/16.
11 Pirret, James Kay, 2/Lt., k. in a., 4/4/17.
Pleydell-Bouverie, Jacob Edward, Lt., died, 1/11/14.
Poe, Charles Vernon Leslie, Capt., k. in a., 3/3/15.
Pollard, Ernest Madel, Temp. 2/Lt., d. of w., 16/8/17 (att. 12 Bn.).
11 Ponsonby, Cyril Thomas, Lt., k. in a., 23/8/16.
6 Poole, Robert Evelyn Sandford, Lt., k. in a., 4/11/18 (att. 13 Bn.).
15 Powell, George Alexander, Lt., k. in a., 28/6/15.
17 Powles-Curtis, Arthur John, Temp. Capt., d. of w., 11/9/16.
6 Preece, Henry Raymond, Lt., k. in a., 8/10/18 (att. 4 Bn.).
11 Priaulx, George Kendall, D.S.O., Major (T/Lt.-Col.), k. in a., 24/3/18.
2 Purdon, George Hardress, 2/Lt., k. in a., 23/7/16.
7 Radcliffe, John Douglas Henderson, Capt., d. of w., 30/7/15.
12 Radford, Oswald Campbell, Temp. Capt., d. of w., 26/2/16.
7 Ramsay, Keith Winton, Temp. Lt., k. in a., 3/5/16.
8 Rawes, Douglas, Lt (Tp.), d. of w., 16/8/15.
6 Rawson, Lionel Reginald, M.C., Lt. (A/Capt.), k. in a., 23/10/16.
18 Rayner, Percy Thomas, Temp. 2/Lt., k. in a., 26/8/18.
3 Reah Kenneth Hudson, Temp. 2/Lt., died, 25/11/18.
Rebbeck, Edward William Wise, Temp. 2/Lt., killed, 24/4/16 (and R.F.C.).
11 Rendall, George, 2/Lt., k. in a., 24/3/18.
9 Renton, Harry Noel Leslie, Temp. Lt., k. in a., 30/7/15.
Rice, Arthur Henry, Lt. (Tp.), k. in a., 20/9/17 (att. 17 Bn.).
11 Richardson, Frederick Edward John, 2/Lt. (Tp.), k. in a., 21/11/17.
9 Richmond, Harold Stedman, Temp. Capt., k. in a., 24/8/16.
18 Ridgway, William, 2/Lt., k. in a., 7/10/16
6 Rixon, Theodore Meredith, M.C, T/Major (A/Lt.-Col.), k. in a., 19/9/17 (att 8 Bn.).
7 Robinson, Richmond Fothergill, Temp. 2/Lt., k. in a., 30-31/7/15.
Robson, Gerald David, Lt. (Tp.), k. in a., 24/8/17 (att. 9 Bn.).
17 Robson, William, Temp. 2/Lt., died, 30/10/18.
7 Roe, Albert John Havilland, 2/Lt. (Tp.), k. in a., 9/8/15.
8 Rogers, Robert Murray, 2/Lt., k. in a., 2/7/16.
7 Romer, Mark Leman Ritchie, Temp. Capt., d. of w., 20/9/16.
5 Rowley, The Hon. George Cecil, 2/Lt., k. in a., 17/2/17 (att. 1 Bn.).
19 Royden, Thomas Utting, Temp. 2/Lt., k. in a., 14/11/16 (att. 1 Bn.).
9 Runciman, Edmund Inglis, 2/Lt. (Tp. Lt.), k. in a., 22/10/15.
18 Rushworth, Henry, Temp. 2/Lt., k. in a., 11/8/18.
18 Ryan, John Stanley, Capt. (Tp.), k. in a., 25/6/16.
18 Sadd, Philip George, Temp. Major, k. in a., 15/9/16.
7 St. Aubyn, Francis Joseph, Temp. Lt., k. in a., 10/4/17.
7 St. Aubyn, Morice Julian, M.C., Temp. Major, k. in a., 22/3/18.
St. Aubyn, The Hon. Piers Stewart, 2/Lt., k. in a., 31/10/14.
17 Saunders, Arthur Brain, Lt. (Tp.), d. of w., 4/9/16.
Sawyer, Robert Fulwell, 2/Lt., d. of w., 24/8/17 (att. 17 Bn.).
6 Schwarz, Reginald Oscar, M.C., Capt. (T/Major), died, 18/11/18 (Staff Con. of Salvage).
12 Scott, Gilbert Ernest Josiah, Capt., k. in a., 25/3/18 (att. 19 Bn.).
13 Scott, James Robinson, Temp. 2/Lt., d. of w., 23/3/18.
Scudamore, John, 2/Lt., k. in a., 25/9/15.
13 Semple, William David, 2/Lt., k. in a., 29/6/16.
7 Seymour, Francis, Temp. Lt., k. in a., 30/7/15.
4 Seymour, Harcourt, Temp. 2/Lt., d. of w., 9/11/18.
6 Shakerley, Eric Piers, Capt., k. in a., 10/3/15.

Shakerley, Geoffrey Charles, D.S.O., Major (Temp. Lt.-Col.), k. in a., 15/5/15.
Shaw, Harold Joseph, Temp 2/Lt., d. of w., 11/4/18 (att. 2 Bn.).
7 Shaw, John William, Temp. 2/Lt., k. in a. 21/3/18.
6 Sheepshanks, William, 2/Lt., k. in a., 10/7/17 (att. 2 Bn.).
Shennan, Douglas Francis Fairfax, Lt., k. in a., 8/5/15.
6 Shepherd, Arthur Lindesay Moore, Lt. (Tp.), died, 3/11/16 (and R.F.C.) (in German hands).
Sherlock, Ronald Francis, Capt., k. in a., 23/7/16.
17 Sidney, Leicester Philip, 2/Lt., k. in a., 2/10/17 (and R.F.C.).
13 Simonds, Charles Francis, T/Major, k. in a., 29/6/16.
8 Simpson, Henry Delafosse, T/Lt., k. in a., 24/8/17.
6 Simpson, John Horace, 2/Lt., k. in a., 25/9/15 (att. 2 Bn.).
18 Simpson, Rolf, 2/Lt. (Tp.), k. in a., 26/5/17.
24 Singlehurst, Reginald, Lt. (A/Capt.), k. in a., 21/3/18 (att. 9 Bn.).
Slater, Richard Henry, T/Capt., k. in a., 27/7/16.
Smith, Alexander Millar, Temp. 2/Lt., d. of w., 26/1/18 (att. 16 Bn.).
16 Smith, James Rockcliffe, M.C., Temp. Capt., k. in a., 20/5/17.
14 Snelgrove, Sidney Henry, Temp. Lt., k. in a., 30/7/15 (att. 7 Bn.).
7 Somers-Smith, Richard William, 2/Lt., k. in a., 30/6/15.
Spanton, Thomas Henry, 2/Lt., k. in a., 1/7/15.
Spilling, Charles Nathaniel Jerald, Temp. 2/Lt., k. in a., 24/8/17 (att. 8 Bn.).
17 Spinney, Kenneth Trim, Temp. Lt., k. in a., 3/9/16.
6 Spottiswoode, John, Capt., k. in a., 31/10/14 (att. 2 Bn.).
22 Spreckley, Guy Lesingham, 2/Lt. (Tp.), k. in a., 23/4/17 (att. 7 Bn.).
5 Stearns, Patrick Chillingworth, 2/Lt., k. in a., 4/12/17 (att. 7 Bn.).
6 Stephen, Alan James, 2/Lt., d. of w., 18/10/18 (att. 2 Bn.).
9 Stewart, Herbert, Temp. Lt. (A/Capt.), k. in a., 9/4/17.
Stewart, John Cecil Grahame, 2/Lt., k. in a., 25/9/15.
6 Stokes, Robert John, 2/Lt., k. in a., 20/8/16 (att. 2 Bn.).
Stone-Wootten, Frank, 2/Lt., k. in a., 21/9/17 (att. 18 Bn.).
16 Store, Albert Cash, Lt., k. in a., 25/8/16 (att. 5 Bn.).
16 Surry, Norman Frederick, Temp. 2/Lt., k. in a., 12/10/18.
Tabor, John Morton, 2/Lt. (Tp.), k. in a., 21/9/17 (att. 18 Bn.).
9 Tanqueray, Andrew Alexander Truman, Temp. Capt., k. in a., 30/7/15.
10 Tate, Frederick Herman, Capt., k. in a., 11/8/17.
9 Tatham, John Savil, 2/Lt., k. in a., 9/2/17 (att. 6 K.O.R. Lanc Regt.).
13 Taylor, Frederick Cecil, Lt. (A/Capt.), k. in a., 22/8/18.
16 Taylor, Herbert, T/Capt., died, 11/10/15.
Taylor, Leslie Francis, M.C., T/Lt., k. in a., 27/5/18 (and 8th M.G. Corps).
Tetlow, Joseph, T/Lt., k. in a., 25/8/18 (att. 12 Bn.).
16 Thomas, Charles Alexander, Capt. (Tp.), k. in a., 23/8/16.
Thomas, Kenneth, Temp. Capt., k. in a., 3/6/16.
Thompson, George Samuel Rodie, 2/Lt., k. in a., 14/9/14.
Thornton-Smith, Arthur Donald, D.S.O., T/Lt. (A/Capt.), k. in a., 16/8/17 (att. 12 Bn.).
Thursby, Arthur Delves, T/Capt., k. in a., 15/2/15.
Timmis, Richard Sutton, 2/Lt., d. of w., 10/5/15.
Tindall, Eric Vickers, 2/Lt., d. of w., 12/9/14.
8 Todd-Naylor, William Bryan, 2/Lt. (Tp.), k. in a., 24/8/16.
9 Toogood, Henry Duncan, Temp. 2/Lt., k. in a., 21/3/18.
Trench, The Hon. Frederick Sydney, Lt., d. of w., 16/11/16.
Trowsdale, Charles Robert, 2/Lt., d. of w., 2/10/18 (att. 9 Bn.).
6 Tryon, George Arthur, M.C., Capt. (A/Lt.-Col.), k. in a., 7/11/18 (att. 4 Bn.).
Tufts, George Henry, Temp. 2/Lt., killed, 26/1/18 (and R.F.C.).
11 Tunstall, James Charles Francis, 2/Lt. (Tp.), k. in a., 14/2/17.
Upton, The Hon. Eric Edward Montagu John, Capt., k. in a., 9/5/15.
9 Van Praagh, Ralp Bertram, Temp. 2/Lt. k. in a. 9/4/17.
6 Vigers, Robert Stanley Garrard, 2/Lt., d. of w., 5/4/17 (att. 10 Bn.).
5 Villiers, William Earle, Lt. (A/Capt.), k. in a., 10/11/17 (att. 9 Bn.).
7 Vincent, Frederick Charles, 2/Lt., k in a., 21/3/18.
6 Wake, Charles Baldwin Drury, 2/Lt., k. in a., 25/9/18 (att. 2 Bn.).
7 Walford, Percy Frederic, Temp. 2/Lt. k. in a., 11/4/17.
2 Walker, Frank Benjamin, 2/Lt., k. in a., 23/7/16 (att. 6 Bn.).
5 Walley, Geoffrey Stephen, Lt., d. of w., 20/8/16 (att. 2 Bn.).
Wallington, Geoffrey Stafford, 2/Lt. (T/Capt.), k. in a., 19/9/17 (att. 10 Bn.).
19 Walsh, Frederick William, 2/Lt. (Tp.), d. of w., 11/7/16 (att. 17 R Welsh Fus.).
7 Walsham, Harold, Temp. 2/Lt., d. of w., 18/9/15.
Walton, Fred, Capt. (Tp), k. in a., 15/9/16.
Walther, Kurt Albert, 2/Lt., k. in a., 4/11/18 (att. 13 Bn.).
Walton, Albert Bertie, M.M., 2/Lt., d. of w., 16/9/18 (att. 13 Bn.).
Ward, Kenneth Hilary Wodehouse, Capt., d. of w., 30/8/18.
8 Warham, Joseph, Temp. 2/Lt., d. of w., 7/5/17.
Waring, Edward Robert, 2/Lt., k. in a., 29/10/14.
21 Watson, Arthur Toward, Temp. Major, d. of w., 5/8/17.
8 Watson, Roger Wentworth, Temp. Lt., k. in a., 30/7/15.
Webb, Evelyn Maxwell, Capt., k. in a., 23/7/16.
18 Webb, Thomas Richard Henry, Temp. 2/Lt., d. of w., 31/7/17.
13 Webster, Erwin Wentworth, Temp. Capt., k. in a., 9/4/17.
17 Welter, Leslie Dingman, 2/Lt., k. in a., 18/6/17.
1 West, Harold Douglas, 2/Lt., d. of w., 25/3/18
Westerman, Harry, 2/Lt., k. in a., 11/8/18 (att. 21 Bn.).
1 Whall, Edwin Lionel, Haversham, 2/Lt. (Tp.), k. in a., 18-21/9/17.
12 White Charles Douglas, 2/Lt., died, 10/5/16 (and R.F.C.).
White, Wilfred Appleton, 2/Lt., k. in a., 3/10/18 (att. 4th Bn.).
7 Whitley, Charles, M.C., Temp. Capt., k. in a., 11/4/17.
4 Whitley, Herbert, 2/Lt., k. in a., 21/2/17.
13 Wiggett, Allan James, Temp. 2/Lt., d. of w., 15/3/16 (in German hands).
7 Wilberforce, W. R. S., 2/Lt., killed, 2/6/18 (and R.A.F.).
Wilding, Horace Holden, 2/Lt., k. in a., 13/9/18 (att. 13 Bn.).
18 Willans, William Alan Jenne, A/Capt., k. in a., 24/3/18.
7 Williams, Felix Roland, Temp. 2/Lt., k. in a., 10/4/17.
4 Williams, H. I., 2/Lt., k. in a., 18/10/18.
7 Williamson, George Hamilton, M.C., Capt. (Tp.), d. of w., 12/4/17.
7 Williamson, Kenneth Harper, Temp. 2/Lt., d. of w., 19/4/17.
6 Willmot, Robert Dyott, 2/Lt., k. in a., 17/2/18 (att. 2 Bn.).
6 Wilson, Douglas Russell, 2/Lt., k. in a., 25/10/18.
13 Wilson, James Bannerman Gartly, Temp. 2/Lt., d. of w., 30/4/17 (att. 12 Bn.).
Wingfield, Cecil John Talbot Rhys, Capt., d. of w., 29/4/15.
18 Wingfield, Glanville Harry, 2/Lt., k. in a., 12/7/16.
Witt, Cecil, Temp. 2/Lt., k. in a., 28/2/18 (and R.F.C.).
9 Wood, Thomas Anthony, Capt., died, 16/7/18.
Woodlock, Francis Joseph, Temp. 2/Lt., k. in a., 13/8/17 (att. 11 Bn.).
Woolmer, Stanley Herbert France, 2/Lt. (Tp.), k in a., 3/9/16.
16 Wyand, Edward Herbert, Temp. Capt., k. in a., 30/1/16.
21 Yeaman, Denis John, Temp. 2/Lt., k. in a., 5-10/10/16.

The Duke of Edinburgh's (Wiltshire Regiment).

6 Allen, Lawrence John Maynard, 2/Lt. (Tp.), k. in a., 2/7/16.
Anderson, Harry John, 2/Lt., k. in a., 10/4/18.
4 Armstrong, Allan, D.S.O., Lt.-Col., d. of w., 19/9/18.
1 Awdry, William Walter, Lt., d. of w., 16/4/18 (att. 6 Bn.).
1 Badgley, James Chester, 2/Lt. (Tp.), k. in a., 7/6/17.
7 Bagshaw, Arthur Samuel, 2/Lt. (Tp.), k. in a., 22/8/16.
2 Balkwill, William Horniman, 2/Lt., k. in a., 9/4/17.
7 Bartram, Harold Franc, 2/Lt., k. in a., 24/4/17.
1 Barton, Eric Percy Mervyn, 2/Lt., k. in a., 3/9/16.
5 Belcher, Austin Charles Sandham, Capt. & Adjt., k. in a., 10/8/15.
5 Belcher, Humphrey Gilbert, Lt. (Tp.), d. of w., 7/8/15.
6 Biggs, Arthur Ridley, 2/Lt. (Tp.), k. in a., 2/7/16.
3 Binns, John Eric, 2/Lt., k. in a., 9/4/16 (att. 5 Bn.).
Bishop, Charles Trevor, 2/Lt. (Tp.), k. in a., 29/3/17.
Blake, Harold Frederick, Capt., k. in a., 7/10/16 (att. 13/D.L. Inf.).
2 Bond, Charles Gordon, Capt., k. in a., 25/11/15.
2 Brewin, Harold Rowland Nelson, 2/Lt., k. in a., 19/7/16.
1 Brooke, Charles Pearson Joseph, Lt., k. in a., 3/9/16.
Brooks, Charles Alfred, Capt., k. in a., 8/7/17 (and R.F.C.).
1 Brown, Ernest Edward, Lt., k. in a., 8/5/16.
5 Brown, Eric Francis, T/Lt. (A/Capt.), d. of w., 1/4/17.
3 Brown, Gerald Dick, M.C., Lt. (A/Major), k. in a., 14/4/18.
3 Brown, Richard Walker, 2/Lt. (A/Capt.), k. in a., 9/4/17 (att. 2 Bn.).
Brown, Walter Sidney, Lt.-Col., k. in a., 6/7/16.
Browne, Gordon Stewart, Lt., d. of w., 27/11/14.
3 Burges, Eric Laurence Arthur Hart, 2/Lt., k. in a., 23/10/14 (att. 2 Bn.).
1 Butler, Eric, 2/Lt., k. in a., 25/8/16.
Cain, Ernest William, 2/Lt., k. in a., 31/7/17.
Calley, Oliver John, Lt., k. in a., 12/3/15.
3 Campbell, William Percy, 2/Lt., k. in a., 24/10/14 (att. 2 Bn.).
8 Cannon, Richard, Lt., k. in a., 5/4/16.
5 Carden, John, C.M.G., Lt.-Col., k. in a., 10/8/15.
2 Carrington, Edmund Alfred, 2/Lt., k. in a., 18/10/15.
Carter, Cleary George Molyneux, Capt., k. in a., 23/10/14.
3 Chaloner, Richard Godolphin Hume, Capt., died, 3/4/17.
Chandler, Clive, 2/Lt., k. in a., 17/11/14.
Clarke, Arthur Cyril, Temp., 2/Lt., k. in a., 9/4/17.
3 Clark, Harold Conquest, M.C., Lt., d. of w., 7/2/18 (att. 2 Bn.).
3 Clark, John Harold, 2/Lt., k. in a., 25/9/15 (att. 2 Bn.).
3 Clarke, Sidney Herbert, M.C., Lt. (T/Capt.), k. in a., 2/9/17 (and R.F.C.).
2 Clay, Vivian Hastings, Capt., k. in a., 18/10/16.
3 Clayton, Arthur Oliver, Capt., k. in a., 21/3/18.
6 Coleman, Frederick Charles, Temp. 2/Lt., k. in a., 25/9/15.
Cooper, Spencer Bruce, 2/Lt. (Tp.), d. of w., 24/4/18.
Cordon, Henry James, 2/Lt., d. of w., 17/10/16 (21/T.M.B.).
3 Cortis, John Halsted, 2/Lt., k. in a., 15/6/15 (att. 2 Bn.).
Cropper, Alexander, 2/Lt., d. of w., 22/10/16 (and R.F.C.).
3 Cruikshank, Eric Onslow, Lt., k. in a., 19/9/14.
Dakin, Albert Edward, 2/Lt. (Tp.), d. of w., 16/9/18 (att. 2 Bn.).
1 Davie, Archibald Charles, 2/Lt. (Tp.), k. in a., 19/9/18.
Davies, David Harold, 2/Lt. (Tp.), d. of w., 18/11/18 (att. 1 Bn.) (P. of W.).
Davies, Ivor Garfield, 2/Lt. (Tp.), k. in a., 8/8/18 (att. 2 Bn.).
Dawes, Walter Richard Aston, Capt., k. in a., 23/8/14.
Dehn, Thomas George Rudolph, 2/Lt., d. of w., 19/4/17.
Denham, Reginald Grainger, Lt., k. in a., 30/5/18 (att. 11/T.M.B.).
Desages, Owen Loftus, 2/Lt., k. in a., 27/5/18.

5 Dewhurst, Robert William Millington, Lt. (Tp.), d. of w., 26/4/16.
2 Doddrell, Kenneth Curling, 2/Lt., k. in a., 19/9/18 (att. 1/4 Bn.).
3 Du Boulay, Hubert Lionel Houssemayne, 2/Lt., k. in a., 3/9/16.
2 Edmonds, Harold Sylvester, M.C., Temp. 2/Lt., d. of w., 20/4/17.
3 Elwin, Frank Harold, 2/Lt., k. in a., 14/3/15.
Emanuel, Oliver, Lt., k. in a., 25/9/15.
Ferguson, Percy Grant, 2/Lt., k. in a., 10/3/15.
5 Firmin, John Eric Robert, 2/Lt. (Tp.), k. in a., 10/8/15.
Fisher, Henry Bruges, Lt.-Col. (Act.), k. in a., 3/10/16 (att. 12/Y. & Lanc. Regt.).
5 Fisher-Brown, Charles George Cranleigh, 2/Lt., k. in a., 10/8/15.
Formby, Myles Lonsdall, Capt., k. in a., 26/10/14.
Fowle, Michael Randolph, 2/Lt., k. in a., 24/11/14.
2 Friend, Frank Howard, Temp. Lt., d. of w., 29/9/15.
6 Gale, Herbert Anthony, M.C., A/Capt., d. of w., 12/8/18 (att. 2 Bn.).
2 Galliers, Richard Sidney, 2/Lt. (A/Capt.), k. in a., 31/5/18.
5 Gamman, Gilbert, 2/Lt. (Tp.), k. in a., 10/8/15.
2 Gardner, William Bristow, M.C., T/2/Lt. (A/Capt.), k. in a., 28/3/18.
8 Garlick, Charles Sidney, Temp. 2/Lt., d. of w., 16/7/16.
2 Garnett, Errol Russell, 2/Lt., k. in a., 18/10/16.
Geddes, William Murray, Capt., k. in a., 27/9/15.
3 Gee, Robert Francis McLean, 2/Lt., d. of w., 27/10/14 (att. 5 Bn.).
1 Gibson, Harold Wolfe, Lt., k. in a., 24/3/18.
3 Gibson, Samuel Archibald Gibson, M.C., 2/Lt., d. of w., 26/8/17 (att. 2/1 Bucks Bn. O. & B.L. Inf.).
1 Gosden, Dudley Walter, Temp. Lt., k. in a., 6/7/16.
Gosling, William Robert, 2/Lt., k. in a., 21/3/18.
8 Grant, Philip Thomas Wilson, 2/Lt. (Tp.), k. in a., 15/10/15 (att. 5 Bn.).
5 Greany, John Wingate, Capt., k. in a., 9/4/16.
Greene, John, 2/Lt., k. in a., 3/11/16 (att. 6 Bn.).
5 Gregory, Walter Stanley, Temp. 2/Lt., k. in a., 30/4/17.
Grimston, Horace Sylvester, Lt., k. in a., 23/10/14.
3 Gumbley, Donald Charles Beric, 2/Lt., k. in a., 3/9/16 (att. 1 Bn.).
Gunning, John Walter, 2/Lt., k. in a., 24/3/18.
Hales, Arthur Hoare, M.C., Temp. Capt., k. in a., 6/7/16.
Hall, Ernest Leslie, 2/Lt., k. in a., 21/3/18.
Hall, Henry Charles, Temp. 2/Lt., k. in a., 4/9/18 (att. 15/Hants Regt.).
Harvey, Edward George, Capt., k. in a., 16/6/15.
2 Hatton, Ernest Robert, 2/Lt., k. in a., 8/5/18.
Hayes, Richard Johnson, Temp. 2/Lt., k. in a., 4/11/18.
7 Hayward, Ernest Harold, Lt., k. in a., 24/4/17.
11 Hayward, John Stratton, Temp. 2/Lt., k. in a., 7/7/16.
3 Heal, Cecil Ambrose, 2/Lt., d. of w., 3/7/15 (att. 1 Bn.).
Healey, Arthur Wilfred, Temp. 2/Lt., k. in a., 1/9/18 (att. 1 Bn.).
3 Hern, William Stanley, Temp. Major, k. in a., 10/8/15.
2 Hicks, Lawrence Frederick, Lt., d. of w., 5/11/18.
2 Hill, Arthur James, 2/Lt., k. in a., 8/7/16.
5 Hinxman, Alfred James, Temp. Lt., k. in a., 10/8/15.
Hirschorn, Cecil, Temp. 2/Lt., died, 21/2/18.
3 Hobdell, Arthur Bert Falvey, 2/Lt. (A/Capt.), d. of w., 16/4/18 (att. 6 Bn.).
2 Hodgins, Charles Francis Burgoyne, 2/Lt., k. in a., 25/9/15.
Holman, Guy Henry Wallis, Lt., d. of w., 6/7/16.
3 Hooper, Sidney Frederick, Lt., k. in a., 12/3/15 (att. D. of C. L. Inf.).
Horncastle, Leonard Harry, M.C., Capt., k. in a., 20/5/17 (and R.F.C., 11 Sqd.).
Horton, Stanley Tom, 2/Lt. (Tp.), k. in a., 9/4/17.
House, Joseph Francis, 2/Lt. (Tp.), k. in a., 24/3/18 (att. 2/Royal Berks).
5 Huckett, Arnold Walter, Lt., k. in a., 10/8/15.
3 Hunter, Hugh Michael, Lt., d. of w., 6/4/15 (att. 2 Bn.).
6 Hunter, John Maurice, Temp. 2/Lt., k. in a., 2/7/16.
Husband, Kenneth D'Ombrian, 2/Lt., k. in a., 28/3/18.
8 Jan, Henry Gordon Hay, Temp. 2/Lt., k. in a., 15/2/17.
2 Jenkins, Samuel Clifford, 2/Lt. (Tp.), d. of w., 21/8/18.
5 Jesson, Robert Wilford Fairey, T/Capt., A/Major, k. in a., 22/2/17.
3 Johnson, Victor Reginald William, Lt., d. of w., 28/3/15 (att. 2 Bn.).
Jones, Stanley Fox Gore, Temp. 2/Lt., k. in a., 7/6/17.
6 King, Edmund Harold, Temp. 2/Lt., d. of w., 3/7/16.
King, Noel Gilbert Bryan, Lt., k. in a., 7/6/17.
3 Knubley, Robert Leavitt, Lt., A/Capt., d. of w., 9/7/16.
Langley, Alfred, 2/Lt., A/Capt., k. in a., 20/9/17 (att. 6 Bn.).
1 Law, Robert Archibald Fitzgerald, M.C., 2/Lt. (A/Capt.), d. of w., 31/10/18 (att. 7 Bn.).
6 Lock, William Absalom, Temp. Lt., k. in a., 25/9/15.
Loder-Symonds, William Crawshay, Capt., died, 30/5/18 (and R.A.F.).
3 Lyall, David Lvor, 2/Lt., k. in a., 18/10/16 (att. 2 Bn.).
McClenaghan, Arthur Bryant Phelps, 2/Lt., k in a., 16/6/15.
5 McInnes, William Miller, Temp. 2/Lt., k. in a., 25/1/17.
3 Mack, Edward Geoffrey, 2/Lt., k. in a., 27/9/15 (att. 2 Bn.).
McLean, Angus Neil, 2/Lt., k. in a., 22/6/15.
Macnamara, George, Capt., A/Major, d. of w., 25/5/17.
2 McWhannell, John, 2/Lt., d. of w., 3/7/16.
3 Magor, Arthur Curgenven, Capt., k. in a., 17/10/14 (att. 2 Bn.).
Marlow, Percy, 2/Lt., T/Capt., d. of w., 7/6/17 (att. 6 Bn.).
1 Martin, Robert Douglas, Temp. 2/Lt., k. in a., 26/8/16.
3 Martyn, Harold Henry, Capt., k. in a., 21/3/18.
1 Maybrook, Walter Richard, Temp. 2/Lt., k. in a., 24/4/16.
5 Mellish, John George, Temp. 2/Lt., k. in a., 10/3/17.
2 Merriman, Charles Henry, Temp. 2/Lt., k. in a., 9/4/17.
Monson, Cyril Archibald, 2/Lt., k. in a., 18/5/15.
Monreal, George, T/Major (Acting Lt.-Col.), d. of w., 11/4/18 (Res., att. 6 Bn.).
6 Moore, William Henry Walker, Temp. 2/Lt., k. in a., 25/9/15.
3 Morison, Douglas Rutherford, 2/Lt., k. in a., 13/3/15 (att. 2 Bn.).
Morley, George Thomas, M.M., 2/Lt., k. in a., 24/3/18.
3 Morrice, William Walter, Lt., T/Capt., k. in a., 30/12/17 (att. Lab. Corps).
3 Morris, Lionel Alfred Harry Blackmore, Lt., k. in a., 7/7/16 (att. 1 Bn.).
8 Morris, William Norman, Temp. 2/Lt., d. of w., 25/5/16 (106 M.G.C.).
6 Moulton, Charles Eric, Temp. Lt., k. in a., 16/9/15.
2 Mudge, Ernest Cecil, Capt., k. in a., 25/9/15.
2 Mumford, Frank Richard, Temp. Capt., k. in a., 8/7/16.
Nixon, Harold Percival, Temp. 2/Lt., k. in a., 26/10/18.
Northover, Neville Evelyn, Temp. 2/Lt., k. in a., 4/9/18 (att. 15/Hants Regt.).
5 O'Brien, Lucius James Francis, 2/Lt. (Tp.), d. of w., 7/4/17.
7 Osborn, George Ashby Chadwick, Temp. Capt., k. in a., 24/4/17.
Palmer, Reginald John Allen, Lt., d. of w., 22/7/16.
3 Parker, Frederick Richard, 2/Lt., k. in a., 19/7/16.
2 Parsons, Samuel Reginald, Lt., k. in a., 9/4/17.
5 Peebles, William Fleming, Temp. 2/Lt., k. in a., 30/4/17 (att. 113 M.G.C.).
Penruddocke, Charles, Lt., k. in a., 4/10/18 (att. 7 Bn.).
8 Penruddocke, Thomas, Temp. 2/Lt., k. in a., 25/4/17.
1 Pigott, Christopher Devonshire, Temp. 2/Lt., k. in a., 26/8/16.
Plowman, Charles Hugh, Lt., k. in a., 24/4/17.
8 Posener, Percy Julian, Temp. 2/Lt., k. in a., 8/7/16.
3 Powell, Eyre Burton, Lt., died, 4/8/15.
Priestley, Frederick, Lt., k. in a., 27/5/18.
5 Radcliffe, William Yonge, 2/Lt. (Tp.), d. of w., 19/8/15.
3 Reynolds, H. C., Capt., k. in a., 20/9/14.
3 Richardson, Edric Hugh Barnstey, Capt., k. in a., 15/6/15.
Roche, Thomas, Major, k. in a., 17/11/14.
Rogers, Stanley, Temp. 2/Lt., k. in a., 4/10/18 (att. 7 Bn.).
Roseveare, Harold William, 2/Lt., d. of w., 20/9/14.
Sainsbury, Charles, M.C., Lt. (Tp.), d. of w., 7/6/17.
6 Savage, Frederick Quinton, 2/Lt. (Tp.), k. in a., 20/9/17.
Schultz, Leonard Elmslie, Temp. 2/Lt., k. in a., 27/9/15.
7 Scorer, William Harold, Temp. Lt., d. of w., 6/10/18.
Seaman, Charles William Frederick, Temp. 2/Lt., k. in a., 6/11/18.
6 Shapland, Adam Francis Terrell, Lt. (Tp.), k. in a., 20/9/17.
3 Sharpe, Douglas Staveley, 2/Lt., k. in a., 7/7/16 (att. 1 Bn.).
2 Shaw, William Cobley, 2/Lt. (Tp.), k. in a., 6/9/17.
3 Skyrme, Richard Edward Elcho, 2/Lt., k. in a., 6/2/17 (att. 1 Bn.).
3 Smee, Arthur Joseph, 2/Lt., died, 28/10/18 (and R.A.F.).
6 Smith, Vivian Norman, Temp. Capt., k. in a., 13/11/16.
Spencer, Edward, Lt., k. in a., 24/10/14.
Spencer, Frederick James Edmund, Temp. 2/Lt., died, 9/11/18 (P. of W.).
Spencer, Willy Paton Berthold, Lt., k. in a., 10/3/15.
2 Stamford, Gerald Morton, 2/Lt., k. in a., 15/6/15.
Stansfeld-Smith, Lyalph, 2/Lt., killed, 12/6/15.
3 Starky, James Baynton, 2/Lt., k. in a., 6/7/16.
Stoddart, Frederick William, Capt., k. in a., 27/10/14.
Stoodley, Percy Bennett, 2/Lt., died, 9/11/16 (att. 2 Bn.).
Tanner, Gerald Russell, M.C., 2/Lt. (T/Lt.), d. of w., 8/4/18.
Terry, Sidney Frederic, Capt., k. in a., 24/3/18.
3 Thompson, James Ambrose, 2/Lt., k. in a., 18/10/16 (att. 2/Bn.).
3 Throckmorton, Richard Courtenay Brabazon, Temp. Lt.-Col., k. in a., 9/4/16.
Turner, Harold Frank Barclay, Lt., A/Capt., d. of w., 1/9/17.
3 Usher, Christopher Lancelot, Lt., d. of w., 23/4/18 (att. 1 Bn.) (P. of W.).
3 Venables, Vernon Wilson, 2/Lt., d. of w., 18/10/16.
2 Verran, Frank Nicholas, Lt., k. in a., 18/10/16.
2 Vidler, George Holbrook Eric, Lt., k. in a., 8/7/16.
3 Viner-Johnson, Percy Joseph Viner, Capt., k. in a., 12/3/15.
Virgin, William Job Farnham, 2/Lt., k. in a., 4/11/18 (att. 2 Bn.).
3 Ware, Eric Wallace, 2/Lt., k. in a., 18/10/16 (att. 2 Bn.).
3 Walker, Kenneth MacKenzie, 2/Lt., k. in a., 12/8/18 (att. R.A.F.).
8 Warland, Maurice George, Temp. 2/Lt., d. of w., 20/1/17.
Warter, Joseph Gordon, 2/Lt., k. in a., 30/9/17 (att. R.F.C., 66 Sqd.).
White, Sidney Herbert, Temp., 2/Lt., d. of w., 9/11/17.
1 Widdowson, Joseph James, Temp. Lt., d. of w., 23/10/16.
6 Williams, Herbert Henry, Temp. Capt., k. in a., 20/9/17.
3 Wilson, Geoffrey Mervyn Underhill, Lt. (T/Capt.), k. in a., 26/9/15 (att. 2 Bn.).
Wiltshire, William George Earl, 2/Lt., k. in a., 31/3/18.
Wood, James, 2/Lt., k. in a., 5/8/17.
Wood, William Bertram, M.C., 2/Lt. (A/Capt.), k. in a., 25/8/17.
3 Wyld, George Richard, Capt., k. in a., 24/12/14 (att. R. Berks Regt.).
6 Wykes, Herbert Ivie, Temp. Capt., d. of w., 30/9/15.

The Manchester Regiment.

23 Abraham, Arthur Thomas, M.C., 2/Lt. (A/Capt.), k. in a., 22/10/17.
18 Adshead, Sydney Douglas, 2/Lt. (Tp.), k. in a., 23/4/17.

12 Alderton, Colin Frederick, 2/Lt. (Tp.), k. in a., 7/7/16.
13 Allen, Kenneth Harris, Lt. (Tp.), d. of w., 11/10/18.
16 Allen, Sydney Raymond, 2/Lt. (Tp.), k. in a., 12/7/16.
24 Andrew, Harold, Lt., k. in a., 14/7/16.
18 Arnold, Joseph, 2/Lt. (Tp.), k. in a., 2/9/18 (att. 1/5th Btn.).
19 Atkinson, Arthur Wilfrid, 2/Lt. (Tp.), k. in a., 1/7/16.
13 Austin, James, 2/Lt. (Tp.), d. of w., 21/6/17.
2 Babbage, John Colston, 2/Lt., k. in a., 18/11/16.
Balshaw, Walter, 2/Lt., k. in a., 20/10/14.
2 Ball, William Charles, 2/Lt., k. in a., 27/9/18.
22 Barker, Theodore, 2/Lt. (Tp.), k. in a., 13/5/17.
Barnidge, John, 2/Lt., d. of w., 26/10/17 (att. 21st Btn.).
26 Barrat, William Topley, 2/Lt. (Tp.), d. of w., 25/4/17 (att. 13th Bn.).
Bason, Theodore Creceas, 2/Lt. (Tp.), d. of w., 29/4/18 (att. Worcs. Rgt.).
12 Bate, Harold, Lt., k. in a., 17/7/16.
11 Bates, Harry Cecil, Major (Tp.), k. in a., 7/8/15.
4 Batley, Arthur George, 2/Lt., k. in a., 27/9/18 (att. 11th Btn.).
Baxter, Paul Robert Elmhirst, Lt., k. in a., 8/3/16.
2 Bayliss, Reginald Blencowe, 2/Lt., d. of w., 18/11/16.
Beatty, Arthur Harry Wolseley, 2/Lt. (Tp.), k. in a., 31/7/17 (att. 19th Bn.).
1 Bedford, Cecil Clarke, 2/Lt. (Tp.), k. in a., 8/3/16.
14 Beer, Harold Herbert, 2/Lt. (Tp.), k. in a., 23/4/17 (att. 11th Bn.).
11 Bell, Eric Victor, 2/Lt. (Tp.), d. of w., 14/8/15.
21 Bell, James William, M.C., Capt. (Tp.), k. in a., 7/11/18.
Bellamy, Alfred Wraith, 2/Lt., d. of w., 22/10/17 (att. 23rd Bn.).
Bentley, Clarence Leslie, 2/Lt., k. in a., 28/10/14.
12 Benton, William Manstead, Capt. (Tp.), d. of w., 17/8/16.
Berry, Edward James, 2/Lt., k. in a., 28/11/17 (att. 19th Btn.).
11 Bertram, William, Major, died, 18/2/15.
12 Betts, John Hamilton, Capt. (Tp.), k. in a., 7/7/16.
19 Birley, Hugh Kennedy, Capt. (Tp.), k. in a., 23/7/16.
19 Birley, Joseph Hornby, Capt. (Tp.), k. in a., 2/9/18.
3 Blackburn, Edward, 2/Lt., k. in a., 21/3/18 (att. 7th Bn.).
Blackwell, George John Rowland, 2/Lt. (Tp.), k. in a., 30/3/18 (att. 2/6th Bn.).
22 Bland, Alfred Edward, Capt. (Tp.), k. in a., 1/7/16.
3 Blane, Sidney Taylor, 2/Lt., k. in a., 16/8/17 (att. 11th Bn.).
20 Blench, Alfred Chapman, 2/Lt. (Tp.), d. of w., 6/7/16.
12 Blythe, Norman Harry, 2/Lt. (Tp.), k. in a., 4/8/16.
18 Blythe, Percy Alfred, Capt., k. in a., 30/7/16.
21 Bouskill, Edward, 2/Lt. (Tp.), k. in a., 4/10/17.
22 Bowly, Reginald Walter, Lt. (Tp.), k. in a., 29/5/18 (att. 20th Btn.).
20 Bowsher, Williams Henry, M.C., T/Lt. (A/Capt.), d. of w., 25/10/18.
12 Box, Raymond, Lt. (Tp.), d. of w., 11/7/17.
3 Bradbeer, Alfred Harold, 2/Lt., k. in a., 21/10/16 (att. Lancs Fus., 11th Bn.).
1/2 Bramley, Arthur Henry, 2/Lt., k. in a., 8/6/18 (att. 23rd Btn.).
25 Brett, Francis Joseph, 2/Lt. (Tp.), k. in a., 30/7/16.
3 Brodribb, William Carr, Capt., killed, 26/8/14.
13 Brodrick, Edward, Lt. (Tp.), k. in a., 31/7/17.
14 Brocklehurst, John Sidney, 2/Lt. (Tp.), killed, 1/11/15 (att. 11th Btn.).
20 Brooks, Frank Smith, 2/Lt. (Tp.), k. in a., 1/7/16.
27 Brown, Arthur Horace Mortimer, 2/Lt., k. in a., 10/7/16.
12 Brown, James Sydney, 2/Lt. (Tp.), k. in a., 20/10/18.
17 Brown, Macdonald Warriner, Capt. (Tp.), k. in a., 12/10/16.
Browne, Robert Geoffrey, D.S.O., Major, died, 1/11/18.
22 Brunt, William Edward, 2/Lt. (Tp.), k. in a., 1/7/16.
Buchan, Ernest Norman, D.S.O., Capt., k. in a., 25/9/15.
4 Buckley, Robert, 2/Lt., d. of w., 9/1/17.
4 Budenburg, Donald Harlow, 2/Lt. (A/Capt.), k. in a., 25/4/18 (att. 17th Manch. Rgt.).
22 Burchill, Vivian, Lt. (Tp.), k. in a., 2/6/16.
1 Burdon, John, Lt., k. in a., 8/3/16.
3 Burgis, Edward, 2/Lt., k. in a., 16/10/17 (att. 18th Btn.).
4 Butcher, Ralph Wycombe, 2/Lt., k. in a., 14/3/17 (att. 22nd Bn.).
3 Butterworth, Benjamin, 2/Lt., d. of w., 25/3/17.
17 Callan-Macardle, Kenneth, 2/Lt., k. in a., 10/7/16.
17 Calvert, Robert Mayson, 2/Lt. (Tp.), k. in a., 9/7/16.
11 Campbell, Hugh, Lt. (Tp.), k. in a., 22/8/15.
22 Cansino, Joshua, 2/Lt. (Tp.), k. in a., 2/6/16.
Carley, Thomas Morgan, 2/Lt. (Tp.), k. in a., 27/9/18 (att. 2/9th Btn.).
11 Carr, Stanley Theodore, Lt. (Tp.), k. in a., 27/9/16.
19 Cartwright, Frank, 2/Lt., k. in a., 22/3/18.
12 Case, Charles Henry, 2/Lt., died, 29/9/18 (and R.A.F.).
Caulfield, James Crosbie, Lt., k. in a., 18/11/14.
24 Chadwick, James Henry, D.S.O., Lt.-Col. (Tp.), k. in a., 4/5/17.
23 Chaffey, Charles Russell, 2/Lt. (Tp.), d. of w., 10/3/17.
13 Chapman, Frederick Alan, Lt. (Tp.), d. of w., 29/5/18 (att. 1st Worcs. R.).
21 Chapman, John, Capt. (Tp.), k. in a., 16/7/16.
1/2 Child, James Martin, M.C., Capt., killed, 23/8/18 (and R.A.F.).
Chittenden, Arthur Grant Bourne, 2/Lt., d. of w., 9/9/14.
Clark, William, 2/Lt. (Tp.), k. in a., 27/3/17.
Clarke, John, Lt., died, 24/10/18.
23 Clarkson, Thomas, 2/Lt. (Tp.), k. in a., 22/3/18.
17 Clesham, Thomas Henry, 2/Lt. (Tp.), k. in a., 1/7/16.
3 Close-Brooks, Arthur Brooks, M.C., Capt., d. of w., 10/1/17.
14 Clough, Harry Collier, 2/Lt. (Tp.), k. in a., 30/7/16.
Code, Harold, 2/Lt. (Tp.), k. in a., 25/8/18.
21 Collier, Hubert Charles de Zoete, 2/Lt., d. of w., 4/4/17 (att. 91st T.M.B.).
24 Collins, Herbert Charles, Lt. (Tp.), died, 11/2/17.
12 Conen, James Henry, 2/Lt. (Tp.), k. in a., 25/7/18.
Connell, Sydney Dennis, Lt., k. in a., 28/11/14.
22 Conway, Brian Wiseman, T/Lt. (A/Capt.), k. in a., 4/10/17.
23 Cook, Cecil Haddon, 2/Lt. (Tp.), k. in a., 22/10/17.
12 Cook, Henry Rodham, 2/Lt. (Tp.), k. in a., 7/9/17.
14 Cooper, Arthur, 2/Lt. (Tp.), d. of w., 10/7/16
14 Cooper, Joseph, 2/Lt. (Tp.), k. in a., 26/9/16.
19 Copley, Alan, 2/Lt. (Tp.), k. in a., 2/4/17.
12 Coulter, Sidney, 2/Lt (Tp.), k. in a., 25/8/18.
21 Cowin, Henry Hampton, 2/Lt. (Tp.), k. in a., 1/7/16.
Crawhall, Neil Grant, Lt., k. in a., 7/7/16 (att. 2nd E. Lancs).
Creagh, Leo, Capt., k. in a., 20/12/14.
20 Crewdson, Theodore Wright, Capt. (Tp.), d. of w., 6/11/16.
18 Crichton, Herbert Clowe, 2/Lt. (Tp.), d. of w., 7/10/16.
Critchlow, Charles, 2/Lt. (Tp.), k. in a., 26/10/17.
18 Cunliffe, James Grimshaw, M.C., Capt. (Tp.), d. of w., 1/8/17.
21 Cunliffe, John Leonard, Capt. (Tp.), k. in a., 4/9/16.
Curtis, William, 2/Lt., k. in a., 14/3/15.
Davies, Robert Thomas, 2/Lt. (Tp.), d. of w., 2/4/17.
Davidson, Ralph Ivan Meynell, Lt., d. of w., 24/11/14.
3 Davis, Philip Henry Halton, 2/Lt., d. of w., 9/11/18.
3 Davis, Richard Christopher, 2/Lt., k. in a., 8/3/16 (att. 1st Bn.).
12 Dawson, Herbert George, 2/Lt. (Tp.), died, 29/5/18 (att. 86th Fld. Co., R.E.).
16 Dinnis, George Hugh, 2/Lt., k. in a., 28/4/18.
Dixon, George, 2/Lt., k. in a., 20/10/14.
Dixon, John William, 2/Lt. (Tp.), k. in a., 22/10/17 (att. 23rd Bn.).
12 Dixon, Thomas Herbert, M.C., Capt. (Tp.), k. in a., 25/8/18.
20 Dodge, Walter Robert, 2/Lt. (Tp.), k. in a., 2/10/17.
18 Doughty, George Harry, 2/Lt., k. in a., 25/4/17.
13 Dreschfeld, Henry Theodore, Capt., died, 19/2/15.
22 Duguid, Charles Frederick, D.S.O., M.C., Capt., k. in a., 13/5/17.
4 Duncan, Alexander, Lt., k. in a., 25/3/18 (and M.G.C., 40th Btn.).
18 Duncan, Harry, 2/Lt. (Tp.), k. in a., 23/4/17.
21 Dunderdale, William Henry, 2/Lt. (Tp.), k. in a., 11/1/17.
Dunlop, Frederick Cleave Strickland, Capt., k. in a., 8/11/14.
17 Dunscombe, George, 2/Lt., died, 6/11/18 (P. of W.).
11 Dyson, Stanley William, T/Lt. (A/Capt.), d. of w., 5/10/17.
2 Eastgate-Smith, Charles William, T/Lt. (A/Capt.), k. in a., 27/8/18.
20 Eaton, James Willcox, 2/Lt. (Tp.), k. in a., 1/7/16.
1 Elliott, Frank Phelps, 2/Lt. (Tp.), k. in a., 23/8/18.
16 V.C. Elstob, Wilfrith, D.S.O., M.C., Lt.-Col., k. in a., 21/3/18.
Elwell, Ernest Edward, 2/Lt. (T/Lt.), k. in a., 6/10/17 (att. 21st Btn.).
18 Eminton, Frederick Arthur, 2/Lt., k. in a., 23/4/17.
24 Entwistle, John Edward, 2/Lt. (Tp.), k. in a., 24/10/18.
3 Ewen, George Thomas, Capt., k. in a., 8/3/16.
Farley, Joseph, 2/Lt. (Tp.), died, 1/9/18.
13 Fazackerley, Joseph, 2/Lt., d. of w., 24/10/18.
4 Fernyhough, Samuel, Lt., died, 7/5/18 (att. 18th Manch. R.).
19 Findlay, Scott, 2/Lt. (Tp.), k. in a., 8/5/18.
Fisher, Harold, D.S.O., Capt., k. in a., 15/12/14.
17 Ford, Reginald James, Capt. (Tp.), k. in a., 2/7/16.
19 Foster, Bernard La Trobe, Lt., k. in a., 24/7/16.
Fowke, Mansergh Cuthbert, Capt., k. in a., 30/8/14.
4 Francis, Philip Arthur, 2/Lt., killed, 1/6/18.
Frith, Henry George, 2/Lt. (Tp.), k. in a., 31/7/17.
4 Gardiner, Paul Wrey, Lt., k. in a., 27/5/18 (att. 1st Worcs. Regt.).
1 Gaukroger, Hubert, 2/Lt. (Tp.), k. in a., 2/4/17.
Geddes, David Scott, 2/Lt. (Tp.), k. in a., 26/10/17.
4 Gill, Charles Treverlyn, 2/Lt., k. in a., 1/7/16.
18 Gill, Noel Brendan, 2/Lt., k. in a., 23/4/17.
Glen, David Alexander, 2/Lt., k. in a., 28/12/15 (and R.F.C.).
22 Gomersall, William Ellis, Lt. (Tp.), k. in a., 1/7/16.
Goodall, Robert Leslie, 2/Lt. (Tp.), k. in a., 18/9/18.
13 Goodwin, Eric Lindsey, Lt. (Tp.), k. in a., 12/10/16 (att. 17th Bn.).
23 Gosling, Frederick William, Capt. (Tp.), k. in a., 20/7/16.
3 Graham, Eric Clive, 2/Lt., k. in a., 9/1/17 (att. 1st Bn.).
20 Granger, Frank, 2/Lt. (Tp.), d. of w., 15/12/16.
23 Gray, Charles William, 2/Lt. (Tp.), d. of w., 4/12/17.
11 Gray, Edward Cecil, Capt. (Tp.), d. of w., 2/5/17.
4 Greenough, William Gladstone, 2/Lt., k. in a., 21/10/18 (att. 1/6th Btn.).
14 Greenwood, Tom Stanley, 2/Lt. (Tp.), k. in a., 7/7/16 (att. 12th Btn.).
Gregory, Stanley, 2/Lt. (Tp.), k. in a., 8/6/18.
Grimshaw, Harold Shrieves, 2/Lt. (Tp.), d. of w., 24/5/17 (att. 21st Btn.).
26 Grigg, Malcolm Howard, 2/Lt., k. in a., 9/7/16.
3 Gudgeon, Sidney, 2/Lt., k. in a., 14/5/15 (att. 2nd Btn.).
13 Hadfield, James Robert, Lt. (Tp.), died, 9/3/16.
26 Haldane, Colin Kennedy, 2/Lt. (Tp.), d. of w., 18/10/16 (and M.G.C.).
Hall, Sydney, Lt., k. in a., 18/10/18 (and R.A.F.).
20 Hall, William Francis, Lt. (Tp.), k. in a., 7/10/17.
11 Halliwell, Fred, 2/Lt. (Tp.), k. in a., 22/4/18.
17 Halliwell, Frederick, 2/Lt. (Tp.), k. in a., 12/10/18.
Hankinson, Richard Hooton, Lt., k. in a., 21/6/17 (att. 6th Btn.).
23 Hardman, Cecil William, Lt. (Tp.), k. in a., 21/9/16 (and R.F.C.).
13 Hardman, Wallace George, 2/Lt. (Tp.), k. in a., 9/1/17.
Harling, Tom Lough, 2/Lt. (Tp.), k. in a., 26/10/17 (att 21st Btn.).
27 Haries-Jones, Llewelyn Albert, 2/Lt., k. in a., 30/7/16
21 Harris, Aubrey, Lt. (Tp.), k. in a., 4/9/16.
25 Harryman, Geoffrey Charles, 2/Lt. (Tp.), d. of w., 8/8/16.

14 Haslam, Herbert, 2/Lt., k. in a., 16/9/17 (and R.F.C., 6th Sqd.).
Haslam, William, 2/Lt. (Tp.), k. in a., 21/3/18 (att. 2/7th Btn.).
27 Hawkins, John Noel, Capt., d. of w., 30/7/16.
18 Haworth, Percy Geoffrey du Val, Lt. (Tp.), k. in a., 30/7/16.
12 Hayward, William Hugh, 2/Lt. (Tp.), k. in a., 31/8/18 (att. 52nd T.M.B.).
3 Healey, Philip, 2/Lt., k. in a., 25/9/15 (att. 1st L.N. Lancs R.).
3 Henderson, Harold Winfred, Lt., died, 13/11/18 (att. 24th Btn.).
18 Henshall, Charles, Capt. (Tp.), k. in a., 8/7/16.
Heywood, Herbert, 2/Lt., k. in a., 25/9/15.
3 Hibbs, Richard John Walmsley, Lt., k. in a., 8/10/18 (att. 22nd Btn.).
3 Hills, Charles Herbert, 2/Lt., d. of w., 5/9/16.
16 Hilton, Robert, 2/Lt., died, 29/4/18 (and R.A.F.).
19 Hislop, John Arthur, Capt. (Tp.), died, 8/7/16.
Hitchins, Henry William Ernest, Lt.-Col., k. in a., 28/4/15.
17 Hobbs, Herbert Victor, 2/Lt. (Tp.), k. in a., 7/4/17.
Hodgkinson, Harry, 2/Lt. (Tp.), k. in a., 9/9/18 (att. 12th Btn.).
6 Holberton, Philip Vaughan, Lt.-Col. (Acting), k. in a., 26/3/18.
Holden, William Leak, 2/Lt., k. in a., 4/1/17.
Holt, Wilfred, 2/Lt. (Tp.), k. in a., 16/8/17.
Holt, William Frederick Sloane, 2/Lt. (Tp.), died, 1/7/18 (att. 19th Btn.).
16 Hook, Cyril Walter Keenan, Lt. (Tp.), k. in a., 23/4/17.
17 Hope, Charles Edward, 2/Lt. (Tp.), k. in a., 22/3/18.
4 Horn, Francis Cuthbert, Lt., d. of w., 28/5/18 (att. 2nd Bn.).
Horley, Engelbert Lutyens Rothwell, 2/Lt. (Tp.), k. in a., 4/9/17 (att. 16th Btn.).
3 Horridge, Robert, Lt., k. in a., 17/11/14 (att. 2nd Btn.)
18 Houghton, John, 2/Lt (Tp.), k. in a., 14/12/17.
2 Howard, William Hyson, 2/Lt., k. in a., 11/9/18 (att. 32nd T.M.B.).
Hudson, Frank, Lt. (Tp.), k. in a., 12/10/18.
Hulme, Arthur, 2/Lt. (Tp.), k. in a., 23/10/18.
27 Hutchison, James, 2/Lt. (Tp.), k. in a., 26/7/16.
32 Ingham, Alan, 2/Lt. (Tp.), k. in a., 14/3/17.
11 Innes, Ronald Stewart, 2/Lt. (Tp.), k. in a., 7/8/15.
Irlam, George Arthur, 2/Lt., k. in a., 21/6/17 (att. 2/8th Btn.).
Ireland, Leslie Woodhouse Cubitt, 2/Lt. (Tp.), k. in a., 12/2/17.
3 Jackson, John Cooper, 2/Lt., k. in a., 31/7/17 (att. 16th Btn.).
12 Jackson, Stanley, 2/Lt. (Tp.), k. in a., 10/11/17.
Jackson, Malcolm Race, 2/Lt. (Tp.), k. in a., 25/3/18 (att. 1/6th Btn.).
3 Jackson, William Ewart, Capt., k. in a., 9/1/17 (att. 1st Btn.).
18 James, Roy Francis, 2/Lt. (Tp.), k. in a., 2/9/18.
Jennison, Norman Lees, M.C., T/Lt. (A/Capt.), died, 30/10/18 (att. T.M.B.).
25 Jensen, Cyril Thornton, 2/Lt. (Tp.), k. in a., 10/5/16 (att. T. How. Bty).
2 Johnson, Donald Frederic Goold, Lt. (Tp.), d. of w., 15/7/16.
16 Johnson, William Morton, Capt. (Tp.), k. in a., 2/7/16.
17 Johnston, Robert London, 2/Lt. (Tp.), k. in a., 13/12/15.
12 Johnston, William Tardiff, 2/Lt. (Tp.), k. in a., 13/4/17.
11 Jones, Thomas Alex Evanson, 2/Lt. (Tp.), k. in a., 7/8/15.
17 Jones, Walter Truran, 2/Lt. (Tp.), k. in a., 12/10/16.
4 Jowett, John Sutcliffe, Capt. (Acting), d. of w., 22/9/18 (att. 1/5th Btn.).
14 Jukes, Michael Egerton Ewart, Lt. (Tp.), killed, 4/9/15.
18 Kavanagh, Edward, 2/Lt., k. in a., 30/7/16.
19 Keefe, Ronald Conray Murray, Capt. (Tp.), k. in a., 27/3/18.
21 Kemp, Charles Matthew, D.S.O., Major (Tp.), d. of w., 9/10/17.
20 Kemp, Thomas, 2/Lt. (Tp.), k. in a., 1/7/16.
17 Kenworthy, Stanley, Capt. (Tp.), k. in a., 1/7/16
Kenyon, James, 2/Lt. (Tp.), k. in a., 21/3/18 (att. 2/6th Btn.).
Kerry, Arnold John St. Ledgier, Lt., died, 14/2/18
12 King, Arthur Bernard, 2/Lt. (Tp.), k. in a., 7/7/16.
18 King, Percy Reginald, 2/Lt., k. in a., 30/7/16.
12 Kingsley, Eric, 2/Lt. (Tp.), d. of w., 7/7/16.
Knox, Hubert, Lt.-Col., k. in a., 13/10/16 (att. 16th Btn.).
Kohnstamm, Norman Mortimer Joseph, Capt. (Tp.), k. in a., 22/3/18 (and R.F.C.).
23 Kruger, Dirk Jacobus, 2/Lt. (Tp.), k. in a., 1/4/18.
Laidlaw, Andrew, 2/Lt. (Tp.), k. in a., 9/9/18.
20 Laithwaite, John, Lt. (Tp.), k. in a., 22/2/16.
Lancaster, William Oliver, 2/Lt. (Tp.), k. in a., 26/10/17 (att. 21st Btn.).
3 Lane, Eric Arthur Milner, 2/Lt., k. in a., 8/3/16.
12 Latimer, Francis, 2/Lt. (Tp.), k. in a., 7/7/16.*
Lawton, Eric Reginald, 2/Lt. (Tp.), k. in a., 10/8/17.
3 Leach, George, 2/Lt., k. in a., 28/4/18 (att. 19th Btn.).
26 Levinstein, Gerald Edward, Lt. (Tp.), k. in a., 12/10/16.
3 Lewtas, Oscar, Capt., k. in a., 9/7/16 (att. 2nd Btn.).
17 Leybourn, Frederick Percy, 2/Lt. (Tp.), died, 1/11/18.
13 Lockhart, Alan Ross, 2/Lt. (Tp.), died, 7/12/17.
Lomas, George Guest, Lt. (Tp.), k. in a., 22/3/18 (att. 2/6th Btn.).
20 Lomas, Harold, Lt. (Tp.), k. in a., 1/7/16.
26 Lord, Henry Otto, Lt. (Tp.), k. in a., 1/7/16.
18 Love, James Ellis, 2/Lt. (Tp.), k. in a., 2/9/18.
11 Lowther, Carl, 2/Lt. (Tp.), k. in a., 16/8/17.
Lowther, Ernest Frederick, 2/Lt. (Tp.), k. in a., 14/6/18 (att. 96th T.M.B.).
4 Lye, Gilbert, 2/Lt., d. of w., 27/7/16 (att. 23rd Btn.).
2 Lynch, Reginald Francis, Capt., k. in a., 8/3/16.
McAdorey, John, 2/Lt., d. of w., 5/5/18 (att. 2/10th Btn.).
14 McConnan, James, 2/Lt. (Tp.), k. in a., 20/9/16 (att. 11th Btn.).
McErvel, John Harold, Major (Tp.), k. in a., 8/8/16 (att. L'pool Regt.).
22 McEwan, William Gray, Lt. (Tp.), k. in a., 27/10/18.
12 McKean, Hugh, Capt. (Tp.), k. in a., 7/7/16.
2 McKenzie, Angus, M.C., Capt., k. in a., 4/11/18.
3 McKiever, Victor Comley, 2/Lt., d. of w., 18/5/15 (att. 2nd Btn.).
2 McLellan, Harold Noble, 2/Lt., k. in a., 9/7/16.
16 McQuinn, Wallace, M.C., 2/Lt. (Tp.), died, 6/8/18 (P. of W.).
2 McSherry, Bernard, 2/Lt., k. in a., 13/4/18.
Maden, Harold, 2/Lt. (Tp.), k. in a., 29/7/17.
Mansergh, Wilmsdorff George, Lt., k. in a., 26/8/15.
25 Marillier-Miller, Ralph, 2/Lt. (Tp.), k. in a., 30/7/16.
24 Marshall, Frank, Capt. (Tp.), k. in a., 17/3/16.
11 Marsland, Sydney Hammond, Lt. (Tp.), k. in a., 7/8/15.
Marten, Henry Humphrey, 2/Lt., k. in a., 13/8/15.
Mason, Herbert John, M.C., Lt., died, 16/12/18 (att. 23rd Btn.).
22 May, Charles Campbell, Capt. (Tp.), k. in a., 1/7/16.
20 May, Ernest Edward, 2/Lt., k. in a., 28/8/16.
Medworth, Frank Oswald, M.C., Capt. (Tp.), k. in a., 13/5/18.
16 Megson, Robert Hargraves, Capt. (Tp.), k. in a., 23/4/17.
22 Mellor, Roy, Lt. (Tp.), k. in a., 1/7/16.
20 Milne, Donald Farrow, Lt. (Tp.), k. in a., 5/11/17 (att. 1st Btn.).
Mitchell, Frank Warley, 2/Lt., k. in a., 7/6/18.
Morton, Scott Gladstone, 2/Lt. (Temp.), k. in a., 31/7/17.
23 Moore, Alfred Arnold, Lt., k. in a., 22/10/17.
12 Moorhouse, Arthur John, Major (Tp.), died, 28/11/18.
Morand-Lees, James Wright, Capt. (Tp.), died, 5/11/18 (att. B.W.I. Rgt.).
17 Morgan, Hubert Hoppin, Lt. (Tp.), k. in a., 30/3/18.
1 Morris, Charles, 2/Lt., k. in a., 8/3/16.
4 Morris, Andrew, 2/Lt., d. of w., 26/8/18 (att. 12th Manch. R.).
3 Mortiboy, William Woolley, 2/Lt., k. in a., 19/8/18 (att. 2nd Btn.)
23 Morton, Joseph Leonard Milthorp, T/Lt. (A/Capt.), k. in a., 22/10/17.
19 Moss, Gerald Alex, 2/Lt. (Tp.), k. in a., 10/8/18 (att. 2nd Btn.).
4 Motler, John Frederick, 2/Lt., k. in a., 30/7/16 (att. 18th Btn.).
Mottershall, Herbert Stanley, 2/Lt. (Tp.), d. of w., 9/10/17.
12 Moulton, William Ralph Osborne, 2/Lt. (Tp.), k. in a., 4/8/16.
Moyce, George Herbert Stanley, 2/Lt. (Tp.), d. of w., 19/4/18 (att 2/8th Btn.).
24 Murdoch, Thomas John Carson, Lt. (Tp.), k. in a., 6/2/16.
19 Murphy, Edward, 2/Lt. (Tp.), k. in a., 2/4/17.
19 Myers, James Wheatley, Capt. (Tp.), d. of w., 14/8/17.
25 Nanson, Joseph, 2/Lt. (Tp.), k. in a., 1/7/16.
21 Nash, Phillip Geoffrey, 2/Lt. (Tp.), k. in a., 5/10/17.
18 Nelson, Joseph Lawrie, 2/Lt. (Tp.), k. in a., 8/3/16.
2 Nicholas, Francis Mark, 2/Lt., d. of w., 28/9/17.
21 Nicholls, Leonard Harvey, 2/Lt. (Tp.), k. in a., 26/10/17.
19 Nicholson, Arthur Harry, 2/Lt. (Tp.), d. of w., 9/4/17.
Nisbet, Frank Scobell, Capt., k. in a., 26/8/14.
23 Norcross, Frank, 2/Lt., k. in a., 30/7/16.
Norman, Stuart Sheridan, Lt., k. in a., 23/12/14.
O'Donahue, Thomas Henderson, 2/Lt. (Tp.), k. in a., 20/4/17.
16 Oliver, John Milner, Lt. (Tp.), k. in a., 9/7/16.
Omerod, James, 2/Lt. (Tp.), died, 27/9/18 (att. 22nd Btn.).
27 Ormond, Alexander, 2/Lt. (Tp.), k. in a., 30/9/16.
24 Orr, Arthur James, 2/Lt. (Tp.), k. in a., 23/4/18.
26 Outram, Edmund, 2/Lt. (Tp.), k. in a., 1/7/16.
Owen, Arthur Percy, Capt., k. in a., 8/3/16.
3 Owen, Horre Solle, 2/Lt., k. in a., 23/11/16.
17 Palmer, Walter Harvey, 2/Lt. (Tp.), k. in a., 23/4/17.
Parker, Erasmus Darwin, Capt., k. in a., 20/3/15.
3 Parkhurst, George Henry, 2/Lt., k. in a., 3/6/18 (att. 2/8th Worcs. Rgt.).
21 Parkinson, Alfred, M.C., T/2/Lt. (A/Capt.), k. in a., 12/5/17.
11 Peacock, Frederick John, A/Capt., k. in a., 10/10/18.
14 Peak, Norman, 2/Lt., (Tp.), k. in a., 1/7/16.
3 Peirce, William Gabriel King, Capt., k. in a., 30/10/14.
25 Penn-Gaskell, William, Capt. (Tp.), k. in a., 12/10/16.
4 Percival, George Stewart, 2/Lt., killed, 13/10/18.
26 Peters, Henry, Lt. (Tp.), k. in a., 12/10/16.
21 Pickford, Howard Arthur, 2/Lt. (Tp.), k. in a., 14/7/16.
12 Pickles, Frederick Arthur, M.C., Capt., d. of w., 5/9/18.
14 Pickstone, Dick, 2/Lt. (Tp.), k. in a., 12/10/16.
4 Pickering, Freeman, 2/Lt., d. of w., 10/10/17.
4 Plested, Horace George, 2/Lt., k. in a., 30/7/16.
21 Ponting, Edward Frank, 2/Lt. (Tp.), k. in a., 5/10/18.
17 Potts, Geoffrey Fildes, Lt. (Tp.), k. in a., 23/4/17.
20 Poynter, Leslie John, 2/Lt. (Tp.), d. of w., 25/10/18.
26 Poynton, Charles Edward, Lt., k. in a., 30/7/16.
17 Prentis, Horace Taylor, 2/Lt., k. in a., 27/4/18.
4 Price, Henry Wall, Major, died, 19/6/19.
4 Price, Henry Wall, 2/Lt., k. in a., 4/7/16 (att. 2nd Bn.).
14 Price, John Esmond, 2/Lt. (Tp.), k. in a., 1/7/16.
4 Prime, Arnold, 2/Lt., k. in a., 21/3/18.
20 Pritchard, Gwynedd William Llewelyn, M.C., 2/Lt. (Tp.), k. in a., 23/10/18.
19 Purdy, Harry Wilfred, 2/Lt. (Tp.), k. in a., 23/4/17.
Rallison, Victor Edward, 2/Lt., k. in a., 7/4/17 (att. 17th Bn.).
26 Ram, Percival John, 2/Lt. (Tp.), k. in a., 1/7/16.
3 Rayner, Oliver Crossley, Lt., k. in a., 18/11/16 (att. 2nd Bn.).
Reade, John Henry Loftus, Lt., k. in a., 28/10/14.

23 Reid, William Morison, 2/Lt. (Tp.), d. of w., 26/2/16.
11 Reidy, Edmund McAyliffe, Capt. (Tp.), d. of w., 23/7/16.
18 Renshaw, Leonard, Capt. (Tp.), k. in a., 13/5/16.
21 Richards, Ernest Harry, 2/Lt. (Tp.), k. in a., 2/4/17.
22 Richardson, George Hugh, M.C., Capt. (Tp.), k. in a., 29/10/18.
2 Richardson, John Cottier, D.C.M., Capt., k. in a., 4/10/18.
3 Richardson, Rodney Francis, 2/Lt., d. of w., 31/7/17.
Roberts, George Bradley, 2/Lt., d. of w., 7/5/15 (unatt. List, Indian Army).
16 Roberts, Rupert Edward, Major (Temp.), d. of w., 26/3/18.
3 Robertson, Charles William, 2/Lt., d. of w., 22/8/16 (P. of W.).
Robinson, Arthur Hine, 2/Lt., k. in a., 26/4/15.
Robinson, Frank Wright, Lt., k. in a., 13/5/17.
22 Ross, Edward, Lt. (Tp.), d. of w., 7/10/17.
20 Ross, Frederic Gordon, 2/Lt. (Tp.), k. in a., 1/7/16.
23 Rothband, Jacob Eustace, Capt. (Tp.), k. in a., 19/7/16.
19 Royle, Frederick William, Capt. (Tp.), d. of w., 8/7/16.
Ruddy, Thomas, Lt., died, 1/7/16.
2 Rowley, John, 2/Lt., k. in a., 23/12/17.
16 Rylands, Frank, 2/Lt., d. of w., 25/4/17.
11 Rymer, John Henry, Capt. (Tp.), k. in a., 7/8/15.
25 Salmon, Bernard Bryant, 2/Lt. (Tp.), k. in a., 9/7/16.
Saportas, Herbert Arnold, Lt., k. in a., 17/7/15.
26 Sayce, George Ben, Capt. (Tp.), k. in a., 1/7/16.
Scott, Francis Gordon, M.M., 2/Lt. (Tp.), k. in a., 20/10/18.
Sharples, Norman, Capt. and Adjt., k. in a., 21/3/18 (att. 16th Btn.).
Shaw, John, 2/Lt. (Tp.), k. in a., 26/4/18.
Shields, William, Lt. (Tp.), k. in a., 5/9/17 (and R.F.C.).
1 Shipster, Walter Neville, M.C., Capt., d. of w., 20/9/18.
Shirley, Samuel Myatt, 2/Lt. (Tp.), d. of w., 1/5/17.
17 Sidebotham, James Nasmyth Wedgwood, Capt. (Tp.), k. in a., 12/10/16.
11 Sillery, John Jocelyn Doyne, Major, k. in a., 7/8/15 (Maj. Ret. In. Army).
Simmonds, Harold, 2/Lt., k. in a., 31/7/17.
23 Simpson, George Edward, Capt. (Tp.), k. in a., 22/10/17.
Smith, John Herbert Michael, 2/Lt., d. of w., 17/9/14.
Sitford, Leopold John, 2/Lt. (Tp.), k. in a., 2/9/18 (att. 1/4th Bn.).
Skinner, Edward Dudley, 2/Lt. (Tp.), k. in a., 9/9/17.
3 Smith, Albert Gower, Capt., d. of w., 20/5/16 (att. 1st Bn.)
18 Smith, Arthur Harold, 2/Lt. (Tp.), k. in a., 27/3/18.
4 Smith, Donovon Richardson McCallum, 2/Lt., d. of w., 27/5/18 (att. 1st Worcs. Rgt.).
12 Smith, Edward Frank, 2/Lt. (Tp.), k. in a., 7/7/16.
13 Smith, Henry, 2/Lt. (Tp.), k. in a., 19/10/18.
3 Smith, Herbert, 2/Lt. (Tp.), d. of w., 19/7/17 (att. 2nd Bn.).
18 Smith, William Alfred, Lt.-Col. (Tp.), d. of w., 9/7/16.
19 Smith, Willoughby Willard, 2/Lt. (Tp.), k. in a., 9/7/16 (Trench Mortar Bty.).
11 Smithers, Edward Henry Keith, Lt. (Tp.), k. in a., 9/7/16.
3 Southcomb, Edward Hamilton, 2/Lt., k. in a., 31/7/17 (att. 24th Bn.).
11 Sproat, Gerald Maitland, Lt. (Tp.), k. in a., 1/7/16.
Starkey, Francis William, 2/Lt. (Tp.), k. in a., 25/10/17 (att. 21st Bn.).
20 Stewart, Charles Edward, 2/Lt., d. of w., 10/9/16.
14 Stokoe, James Clarke, 2/Lt. (Tp.), k. in a., 11/12/15 (att. 6th L.N. Lancs Rgt.).
4 Stott, Walter Goodwin, Lt., k. in a., 19/9/18 (att. 15th Cheshire R.).
22 Street, Edmund Alger, 2/Lt. (Tp.), k. in a., 2/6/16.
1 Sturges, Roland, 2/Lt. (Tp.), k. in a., 21/3/18 (att. 2/7th Bn.).
Styles, Harold Thomas, 2/Lt. (Tp.), k. in a., 22/10/17 (att. 23rd Bn.).
27 Sutcliffe, John, Lt. (Tp.), k. in a., 12/5/16.
4 Swan, George Grieve, 2/Lt., k. in a., 1/7/16.
12 Swift, John, 2/Lt. (Tp.), k. in a., 9/1/17.
23 Tattersall, Eric, 2/Lt. (Tp.), d. of w., 26/9/17.
17 Taylor, Harry, M.C., Lt., k. in a., 22/3/18.
26 Taylor, Harry, 2/Lt. (Tp)., k. in a., 12/10/16.
18 Taylor, John Edward Middleton, 2/Lt. (Tp.), d. of w., 24/4/17.
3 Taylor, Leonard, 2/Lt., k. in a., 27/8/18.
13 Tempest, Basil, 2/Lt. (Tp.), d. of w., 25/4/17.
4 Thomas, John Baron Rittson, 2/Lt., k. in a., 18/4/18 (att. 2nd Bn.).
21 Thorniley, Percy Arthur Henry, Capt. (Tp.), k. in a., 11/1/17.
Thornley, Henry, Lt. (Tp.), d. of w., 19/12/16.
3 Tillard, Arthur George, Capt., k. in a., 20/10/14 (att. 2nd Bn.).
14 Titjen, Carsten Francis Henry, Lt., died, 12/9/16.
3 Tomblin, Harold Raymond, Lt., k. in a., 10/7/16 (att. 2nd Bn.).
17 Tonge, William Russell, 2/Lt. (Tp.), k. in a., 12/1/16.
12 Tower, Frank, Capt. (Tp.), k. in a., 13/4/17.
4 Towers, Wilfrid Goodwin, 2/Lt., k. in a., 2/4/17.
18 Townsend, Arthur Evans, 2/Lt. (Tp.), killed, 26/11/15.
21 Tresise, Richard Arthur, 2/Lt. (Tp.), d. of w., 12/10/18.
26 Trimmer, Frederick George, 2/Lt. (Tp.), k. in a., 12/10/16.
Trueman, Charles Fitzgerald Hamilton, Capt., k. in a., 26/8/14.
18 Twist, Francis Cecil Orr, 2/Lt., k. in a., 30/7/16.
Vanderspar, Edgar Roland, Lt., d. of w., 24/6/15.
3 Vaudrey, Claude Henry Slade, Capt., died, 2/5/16 (Res. of Off.).
17 Vaudrey, Norman, Capt. (Tp.), k. in a., 1/7/16.
25 V.C. Wain, Richard William Leslie, T/Lt. (A/Capt.), k. in a., 20/11/17 (Tank Corps, A. Batt.).
14 Waine, William Henry, Capt., k. in a., 6/8/15.
20 Wainman, Ernest, 2/Lt. (Tp.), k. in a., 2/3/17.
Waldron, Benson, 2/Lt. (Tp.), k. in a., 31/7/17.
7 Walker, Arthur Dight, 2/Lt., k. in a., 18/10/16.
Walker, George Stanley, 2/Lt., k. in a., 23/10/18.
Walker, Reginald Fydell, 2/Lt., d. of w., 21/10/14.
3 Walker, William, 2/Lt., k. in a., 9/1/17.
21 Wallace, George Douglas, 2/Lt. (Tp.,) k. in a., 26/10/17.
19 Walton, Charles Hindley, 2/Lt. (Tp.), k. in a., 23/7/16.
17 Ward, Philip, Lt. (Tp.), k. in a., 27/12/17.
20 Waring, John, M.C., Capt., k. in a., 6/10/18.
Washington, Jonathan Noel, 2/Lt., d. of w., 2/10/15 (and R.F.C.).
Watson, Frank, Capt. (Tp.), k. in a., 2/4/17 (att. 71st Training Reserve).
27 Watson, James, Lt. (Tp.), k. in a., 30/7/16.
24 Watson, William, Capt., d. of w., 22/8/18 (att. 1st E. Yorks).
Watts, Samuel, Lt. (Tp.), died, 28/10/18.
21 Webb, John Harold, M.C., 2/Lt., k. in a., 9/10/18.
23 Weir, William Logan, Lt. (Tp.), k. in a., 22/10/17.
Wender, Louis, D.C.M., 2/Lt., k. in a., 16/6/18.
18 Westphal, Benjamin Augustus, 2/Lt., k. in a., 23/4/17.
3 White, Harold Edward, Lt. (Tp.), d. of w., 21/4/16.
20 White, John Vernon, Capt. (Tp.), k. in a., 1/7/16.
Wickham, Thomas Strange, D.S.O., Lt., k. in a., 25/8/14 (att. Nigerian R. W.A.F.F.).
1 Wickham, William Thomas Donald, Lt., d. of w., 10/10/18 (11th Btn.).
11 Wilcox, William, 2/Lt., k. in a., 18/5/18 (att. 34th T.M.B.).
3 Wilkins, Archie Raymond, Lt., k. in a., 8/3/16 (att. 1st Bn.).
17 Wilks, Harold, 2/Lt. (Tp.), k. in a., 12/10/16.
23 Willey, Henry Lowes, Lt. (Tp.), k. in a., 22/10/17.
25 Williams, Charles Montague, 2/Lt. (Tp.), d. of w., 29/7/16 (att. 16th Manch. R.).
3 Williamson, H. A., 2/Lt., died, 2/7/16 (and R.F.C.).
Wilson, Albert Knowles, Lt., k. in a., 14/3/15.
Wilson, Fred, M.C., 2/Lt. (T/Capt.), k. in a., 25/10/17 (att. 22nd Btn.).
21 Wilson, George Frederick, 2/Lt. (Tp.), k. in a., 1/7/16.
16 Wilson, Laurence Farrer, Capt. (Tp.), k. in a., 23/4/17.
21 Wilson, Thomas Irving Ward, M.C., Capt. (Tp.), k. in a., 28/11/16.
Wilson, Thomas Lewis, 2/Lt., d. of w., 27/9/18.
Wilson, William Arnold, 2/Lt. (Tp.), k. in a., 22/10/17 (att. 23rd Btn.).
22 Wingrove, George Frederick, 2/Lt., k. in a., 15/7/16.
Wood, Alan Salisbury, Lt., d. of w., 29/3/18.
22 Wood, John Patrick Hamilton, T/Lt. (A/Capt.), k. in a., 11/1/17.
20 Woolaston, Keith Roland, Lt., k. in a., 10/10/18.
Woollen, Joseph Alfred, 2/Lt., k. in a., 27/4/18 (att. 17th Btn.).
3 Wrigglesworth, Alfred Gunn, 2/Lt., k. in a., 4/9/16.
Wright, Henry Thomas Richard Somerset, Capt., killed, 21/12/16.
18 Wyatt, Samuel John Livesley, 2/Lt., k. in a., 23/4/17.
1 Yates, William Grandage, 2/Lt., k. in a., 9/1/17.
17 Yorke-Jones, Kenrick, 2/Lt. (Tp.), k. in a., 26/12/17.

The Prince of Wales's (North Staffordshire Regiment).

8 Adams, John Hanna, 2/Lt., k. in a., 18/11/16.
Addenbrook, John Homfrey, 2/Lt. (Tp.), k. in a., 23/11/16.
Amies, Kenneth Francis, 2/Lt. (Tp.), k. in a., 23/9/17.
1 Anderson, Charles Alfred Walker, Lt.-Col. (Tp.), k. in a., 18/9/16 (att. 1/5th Royal Lanc. Regt.).
1 Anderson, Edward Darnley, D.S.O., Major (Tp.), died, 13/11/17.
4 Anderson, Edwin Frederick Spurrier, Lt., d. of w., 1/11/18.
7 Arbuthnot, Gavin Campbell, 2/Lt., d. of w., 6/8/15.
7 Armes, Raymond Linay, Capt. (Tp.), k. in a., 9/4/16.
8 Astell, Somerset Charles Godfrey Fairfax, D.S.O., Capt., died, 24/3/17 (att. 37th R. Fusrs.).
7 Atkins, Basil Elmo, 2/Lt. (Tp.) (A/Capt.), k. in a., 25/2/17.
Baker, Joseph, 2/Lt. (Tp.), k. in a., 29/6/17 (Res. att. 6th Bn.).
Baldry, Edwin James, 2/Lt., k. in a., 24/3/18.
Bear, John, Hon. Lt. & Qr.-Mr., died, 18/12/17 (258 Infty. Bn., T.R.).
2 Beauclerk, Aubrey Nelthorpe, Major, died, 22/4/16.
8 Bolton, Gilbert Benson, 2/Lt. (Tp.), k. in a., 18/11/16.
8 Boulton, Frederick Charles William, Lt. (Tp.), k. in a., 30/7/17.
8 Bourn, John, 2/Lt. (Tp. Lt.), k. in a., 31/7/17.
9 Bradley, Robert Hubert Francis, 2/Lt. (Tp.), k. in a., 25/1/17.
Brookes, Ben, 2/Lt., k. in a., 21/3/18.
3 Brown, William Sandilands, Lt. (Act. Capt.), k. in a., 14/10/18.
Bubb, Harry Wilfred, Lt. (Act. Capt.), d. of w., 1/1/17 (att. T.M.B.).
8 Bunce, Hugh Pollock, 2/Lt. (Tp.), died, 5/10/16.
4 Butcher, Gilbert Thomas, 2/Lt., k. in a., 11/6/17.
3 Caffyn, Harold Hunt, Capt., k. in a., 22/3/15 (att. 1/Bn.).
Campbell, Edward, Lt., k. in a., 18/11/16 (att. 3/Bn.).
7 Cargin, Norman, 2/Lt. (Tp.), d. of w., 1/5/16 (att. 10/Bn.).
Carnecy, James, Major, k. in a., 3/7/16 (att. 8/Bn.).
Chads, Herbert Charles, Lt., d. of w., 6/1/15.
3 Chester, Greville Arthur Bagot, 2/Lt., k. in a., 13/10/14.
3 Chew, George Douglas, M.C., Capt., k. in a., 15/11/16 (att. 11/Bn., L.N. Lancs Regt.).
7 Clark, George Reginald Heylin, Lt., k. in a., 26/8/18.
4 Cliff, Percy Jack, 2/Lt., d. of w., 16/6/17 (att. 5/Bn.).
4 Cochrane, Edwin Arthur, Lt., d. of w., 4/8/18 (att. 2/6/Bn.).
1 Conway, Arthur Septimus, D.S.O., Major, k. in a., 17/6/17.
4 Cook, Norman George, 2/Lt., k. in a., 29/6/17 (att. 6/Bn.).

Cotes, Digby Charles Bathe, Capt. (Tp.), d. of w., 15/10/18.
Cowell, John Edward, 2/Lt., k. in a., 29/11/17 (att. 2/6/Bn.).
1 Croney, Reginald Harry Talbot, 2/Lt., k. in a., 9/8/18 (att. 8/Bn.).
Dale, Arthur, 2/Lt., d. of w., 12/3/15.
Daley, Alexis, 2/Lt. (Tp.), d. of w., 14/4/17 (att. 2/York & Lancs Regt.).
Davies, Edward Stanley, Capt. (Tp.), k. in a., 10/9/18 (att. 8/Bn.).
3 Davison, Rosnell Montague Rasnell, Lt. (Tp. Capt.), d. of w., 27/1/19 (att. 8/Leics.).
8 Day, Horace Frederick, 2/Lt. (Tp.), k. in a., 5/9/16.
10 Deacon, Raymond Eric, 2/Lt., k. in a., 7/8/15 (att. 8/Lan. Fusrs.).
Dearden, Walter, Lt., k. in a., 19/12/16.
11 Dennis, John Neville, Lt. (Tp.), d. of w., 15/10/17 (att. M.G.C.).
7 Dingley, Alfred Claude, Capt. (Tp.), k. in a., 19/4/16.
8 Duffy, Alexander Noel, 2/Lt. (Tp.), k. in a., 18/11/16.
Dugmore, William Francis Brougham Radcliffe, D.S.O., Major (A/Lt.-Col.), k. in a., 12/6/17 (Res. of Offrs.).
7 Duguid, James, 2/Lt. (Tp.), k. in a., 9/4/16.
4 Duncan, Christopher William, 2/Lt. (Tp. Lt.), k. in a., 20/11/17 (att. A. Bn. Tank Corps).
4 Eaddy, Charles Thomas, 2/Lt., k. in a., 9/7/16 (att. 8/Bn.).
Edwards, William Augustus Spencer, Major, d. of w., 30/4/16 (att. 7/Bn.).
Ensor, William James Alfred, 2/Lt., k. in a., 3/10/18.
Fellowes, Cyril Walter, 2/Lt., k. in a., 21/3/18.
Fenner, Alan Thomas, 2/Lt. (Tp.), d. of w., 8/12/17 (att. 2/6 Bn.).
10 Fischer, John Bosman, Capt., k. in a., 7/8/15 (att. 8/Lancs. Fusrs.).
1 Fisher, John Joseph, 2/Lt. (Tp.), d. of w., 2/5/16.
11 Fletcher, William George, 2/Lt. (Tp.), k. in a., 3/7/16 (att. 2/Sth. Lancs. Regt.).
11 Fletcher, William Henry Anthony, 2/Lt., died, 2/7/16 (att. 7/Bn.).
3 Flindt, Leighton Harold Richard Edward, 2/Lt., d. of w., 4/10/16 (att. 8th Leics. Regt.).
Fox, Charles Alexander Newcombe, Lt., k. in a., 26/9/17 (att Worcs. Regt.).
3 Frankland, Robert Cecil Colville, Capt., k. in a., 7/8/15 (att. 8/Bn. Lanc. Fus.).
2 Franklin, George, 2/Lt. (Tp.), k. in a., 20/10/18.
11 Fraser, Patrick Neill, Lt. (Tp.), k. in a., 1/7/16 (att. 2/Bn. Border Regt.).
10 Callichan, Francis Ernest, 2/Lt., k. in a., 28/7/16 (att. M.G.C.).
4 Godfrey, William Frank, 2/Lt., k. in a., 3/9/16 (att. Trench Mortar).
Godson, Albert Bernard Lawrence, 2/Lt., k. in a., 3/8/17 (att. 9/Bn.).
Goode, Alfred, 2/Lt. (Tp.), k. in a., 29/3/17.
Gough, Horace Frederick, D.S.O., 2/Lt., k. in a., 21/9/17 (att. 8/Bn.).
9 Gracie, William James, 2/Lt. (Tp.), k. in a., 26/4/17.
7 Grail, Clifford George, Capt. (Tp.), d. of w., 23/7/15.
4 Green, Edwin Charles, 2/Lt., k. in a., 26/3/18.
7 Green, Norman, 2/Lt. (Tp.), k. in a., 25/1/17.
8 Greeves, Arthur Frederick Wellesley, 2/Lt. (Tp.), d. of w., 20/9/17.
Greville, Sydney, 2/Lt. (Tp.), k. in a., 19/4/17.
8 Gwynne, Hubert Llewellyn, 2/Lt., k. in a., 18/11/16.
11 Hakewill, Thomas George, 2/Lt. (Tp.), killed, 11/2/16 (and R.F.C.).
Harker, Robert Percy, 2/Lt., k. in a., 20/3/15.
Harley, Albert Edward, 2/Lt. (Tp.), k. in a., 15/4/18.
9 Harmer, Gerald, 2/Lt. (Tp.), k. in a., 11/8/16.
4 Harris, Charles Cecil, 2/Lt., k. in a., 13/6/17.
Harrison, Frank, 2/Lt. (Tp.), drowned, 25/4/17.
Harris, Philip Dawson, Capt., k. in a., 21/3/18.
8 Harris, Robert Edward, Lieut. (Tp.), k. in a., 4/11/18.
7 Hart, Edward Alexander, Capt. (Tp.), k. in a., 9/4/16.
Harvey, Ronald Marmaduke Dawnay, 2/Lt., k. in a., 20/4/15.
4 Harvey, Stanley, 2/Lt., k. in a., 9/4/17 (att. 9th K.O.Y.L.I.).
1 Havelock, Beresford Arthur Jardine, Major (Tp.), k. in a., 14/9/18 (att. 7/Bn.).
7 Haynes, Albert, Capt. (Tp.), died, 20/7/17.
3 Haynes, Charles Henry, 2/Lt., k. in a., 26/3/18 (att. 8/Bn.).
Hayward, Robert Edward, 2/Lt. (Tp.), k. in a., 27/3/18.
Hayward, Walter, 2/Lt., k. in a., 21/3/18.
V.C. Henderson, Edward Elers Delaval, Lt., k. in a., 25/1/17 (att. 7/Bn.).
8 Henderson, William Douglas, 2/Lt., k. in a., 18/11/16.
11 Hepple, Francis James, Lt. (Tp.), k. in a., 28/4/17 (att. M.G.C., 5th Coy.).
7 Heyworth, Heyworth Potter Lawrence, Capt., k. in a., 6/8/15.
Higgins, Claud Wilfred, 2/Lt., drowned, 25/4/17.
4 Higgitt, Leonard Henry, Lt., d. of w., 30/10/17 (att. 9/K.O.Y.L.I.).
4 Hill, Charles Percy, Capt., k. in a., 19/8/16.
3 Hill, Walter Edward, Lt., k. in a., 23/9/14.
7 Hird, Joseph William Smith, 2/Lt. (Tp.), d. of w., 26/1/17.
Hodge, Arthur Egerton, Lt., k. in a., 13/6/17.
Hodgson, Rupert Ernest, Lt., k. in a., 31/8/16
10 Hogg, Frank Alexander, 2/Lt. (Tp.), d. of w., 17/6/16 (att 1/Bn.).
Hogg, Theodore Alan, Capt. (Tp.), k. in a., 21/3/18.
1 Holdcroft, Walter Leigh, M.C., 2/Lt., k. in a., 5/8/18.
Hope, Reginald Addison, Lt. (Tp.), k. in a., 31/7/17.
4 Horsley, Claude Cressy, Lt., d. of w., 29/11/17.
Hoskins, Francis Desmond, 2/Lt., d. of w., 2/10/15.
4 Howell, Roland Basil, 2/Lt., k. in a., 2/10/15.
10 Howells, Phillip George Herbert, 2/Lt. (Tp.), k. in a. 18/11/16.
8 Hughes, Alan Stuart, 2/Lt. (Tp.), k. in a., 18/11/16.
3 Hughes, Lionel Holford, 2/Lt., k. in a., 29/10/14 (att. 1/Bn.).
4 Hughes, Lewis Reginald, 2/Lt., d. of w., 19/5/15 (att. R. Scots Fusrs.).
Hule-Kelly, George Harvey, Capt., k. in a., 20/10/14.
Jenkins, Sidney Emlyn, 2/Lt. (Tp.), k. in a., 22/4/18 (att. 16/R.W. Fusrs.).
4 Jepson, Stanley, Capt., died, 24/2/19.
Johnston, Francis Earl, C.B., Brig.-Gen. (Tp.), k. in a., 7/8/17 (3/New Zeal. Base H.Q.).
10 Jones, Evan Lewis, 2/Lt. (Tp.), k. in a., 13/11/16 (M.G.C.).
Jull, Leslie Hubert, Lt., killed, 3/1/18 (and R.F.C.).
Keble, Eustace Charles, 2/Lt., k. in a., 21/3/18
1/2 King, W. J., Lt., died 16/5/18 (and R.A.F.).
4 Knight, William Bernard, 2/Lt., k. in a., 21/4/15.
4 Kohnstam, Oscar Jacob Charles, 2/Lt., k. in a., 29/6/16 (M.G.C.).
9 Latimer, Kenneth, 2/Lt. (Tp.), k. in a., 27/2/18.
12 Lawrence, Harold Raymond, Lt., died, 28/10/18.
8 Lawton, William, 2/Lt. (Tp.), k. in a., 3-6/7/16.
Leech, Cecil Darley Farran, Lt. (T/Capt.), died, 2/3/18.
Lees, James Malcolm, Lt., k. in a., 22/8/16.
Leggett, Alan Randall Aufrere, Lt., k. in a., 30/10/14.
2 Ley, James Wickham, D.S.O., Major, died, 22/10/18.
8 Line, John Young Alexander, 2/Lt. (Tp.), d. of w., 13/3/16.
8 London, Stanhope Francis, 2/Lt. (Tp.), k. in a., 18/11/16.
Lover, Charles, Lt. (Tp.), died, 1/9/18 (att. York & Lancs Regt.).
Lovegrove, Sidney Joseph, Capt., d. of w., 14/3/16 (att. 3rd K.A. Rif.).
8 Lucas, Christopher Hollins, 2/Lt. (Tp.), k. in a., 11/4/18.
8 Lucas, William Herbert, Lt. (Tp.), d. of w., 21/1/16.
4 Loxley, Arthur Harry, 2/Lt., k. in a., 9/4/17 (att. 6/Y.L.I.).
Macdowell, Robert, 2/Lt. (Tp.), k. in a., 25/2/17.
9 McKenna, John Charles Xavier, Major (Tp.), died, 20/4/17.
3 Mackie, Thomas Sinclair, Lt., k. in a., 18/11/16 (att. 8/Bn.).
Mann, Frederick Christmas, 2/Lt., k. in a., 12/3/15.
Mapplebeck, Gordon Whitfield, Capt. (Act.), d. of w., 30/7/17 (att. 4/Bn.).
Marks, James Albert, 2/Lt., k. in a., 25/2/17.
1 Mason, George, 2/Lt., k. in a., 15/4/18.
3 Matthews, John Bredel, M.C., Lt. (Tp. Capt.), k. in a., 1/10/17 (att. 8/Bn. Leics.).
4 Meakin, Sydney Arthur, Lt., k. in a., 17/10/15 (att. 1/Bn.).
Meautys, Paul Raymond, M.C., Capt., k. in a., 16/6/17.
8 Meir, Wilfrid Ault, Lt. (Tp.) (Act. Capt.), k. in a., 11/4/18.
3 Moore, Thomas Sydney, Lt., d. of w., 30/5/18.
1 Morris, Ernest John, 2/Lt., d. of w., 17/6/16.
Mosley, Nicholas, Capt., d. of w., 1/8/15.
Mowat, John MacLellan, 2/Lt. (Tp.), killed, 5/1/17 (and R.F.C.).
Murray, Frederick Stanley, Lt., d. of w., 19/11/17 (3/2nd K. Afr. Rif.).
10 Naismith, Noel Lings, 2/Lt. (Tp.), k. in a., 11/1/17 (att. 7/Bn.).
9 Nash, Francis Henry, M.C., T/Capt., k. in a., 18/7/17.
9 Newman, Cyril Arnell, 2/Lt. (Tp.), d. of w., 28/4/17.
4 Norman, Basil Chamberlin Qu'Appella, Lt., d. of w., 30/9/18.
9 Oldfield, Fred, 2/Lt. (Tp.), k. in a., 29/6/17.
9 Ottley, Reginald Benade Glendower, 2/Lt. (Tp.), k. in a., 23/12/17 (att. R.F.C., 59th Sqd.).
Patry, Hubert Francis, 2/Lt., killed, 13/9/14.
Patterson, Philip Leslie, 2/Lt. (Tp.), k. in a., 4/6/16.
3 Peter, Alfred Edwin, 2/Lt., k. in a., 25/9/16 (att. 9/Bn. Leics. Regt.).
Pickering, Harold Crosby, 2/Lt., k. in a., 7/7/15 (S.R., att. Lancs. Fus.).
4 Pike-Stephenson, Daniel Pike, 2/Lt., d. of w., 24/5/15 (att. Ches. Regt.).
7 Pinsent, Laurance Alfred, Lt. (Tp.), d. of w., 15/8/15.
3 Plant, Holford Charles Fourdrinier, 2/Lt., k. in a., 3/5/17.
4 Potter, Reginald Funge, 2/Lt., d. of w., 24/7/16.
Powell, John Allen, 2/Lt. (Tp.), k. in a., 14/1/17 (att. York & Lancs.).
11 Powell, Robert Keal, Lt. (Tp.), k. in a., 4/10/16 (att. 2/S. Lancs. Regt.).
Pullam, Frank, 2/Lt. (Tp.), k. in a., 19/6/18.
2 Punchard, Alfred, Capt. (Act. Major), k. in a., 29/3/17.
4 Ram, George Edward, Capt., died, 25/3/16.
Ramsden, Edward, M.M., T/2/Lt., k. in a., 21/3/18.
8 Randall, Mervyn Gregory, M.C., 2/Lt. (Tp.), k. in a., 6/6/18.
1/5 Rayner, Benjamin Harold, Capt., k. in a., 14/6/17.
Reid, Eric Bruce, Capt., k. in a., 20/10/14.
3 Renwick, Donald William, Lt., d. of w., 14/6/17.
1 Ridgway, John Herbert, D.S.O., Major (Tp. Lt.-Col.), k. in a., 23/4/17 (Empld. 10/York & Lancs. Regt.).
9 Robertson, Mowbray Mitcalfe, 2/Lt. (Tp.), k. in a., 31/8/16.
1 Robinson, Harold Godfrey, Capt., k. in a., 12/6/17.
7 Robinson, John Yate, Capt. & Adjt. (Tp.), d. of w., 23/8/16.
Royle, Arthur Clegg Fanshawe, Lt., d. of w., 27/9/14.
7 Russell, Robert, 2/Lt. (Tp.), d. of w., 31/8/18.
7 Russell, Walter Oswald, Lt., k. in a., 26/8/18.
Ryley, Donald Arthur George Buchanan, Lt., k. in a., 11/2/17.
4 Ryley, Harold Buchanan, 2/Lt., k. in a., 5/9/16 (att. 1/Bn.).
7 Samuel, James Roscoe, 2/Lt. (Tp.), k. in a., 25/1/17.
8 Saunders, Alfred George, 2/Lt. (Tp.), k. in a., 29-31/7/16.
3 Scott, Charles Lindsay Murray, Capt., died, 15/2/17 (att. R.F.C., 54th Sqd.).
Selfe, Hugh Donald, Capt. (Tp.), k. in a., 9/7/17.
Sheckleton, Richard, 2/Lt., k. in a., 8/6/17.
4 Sillem, Arthur Henry, Lt., k. in a., 24/3/18.
Smith, Harold Robert, Lt., k. in a., 21/3/18.

8 Smith, Ralph Prichard, 2/Lt. (Temp.), k. in a., 5/8/17.
3 Smith, William Gerald Furness, Lt., d. of w., 5/7/15 (att. 1/Bn.).
7 Spink, Eric Minor, Lt. (Tp.) (Act. Capt.), k. in a., 14/9/18.
Stanbridge, Arthur Christian, Capt. & Adjt., k. in a., 18/11/16 (Adjt., 8/Bn.).
Steel, Ernest, 2/Lt., k. in a., 21/3/18.
Swallow, Luther James, Lt., k. in a., 31/7/17.
Tack, Eldred William, D.C.M., M.M., 2/Lt. (Tp.), k. in a., 18/9/18 (Res.).
Talbot, Stanley Alfred, 2/Lt. (Tp.), k. in a., 19/10/16 (att. L.N. Lancs Regt., 9/Bn.).
Tate, Lionel Percy, 2/Lt. (Tp.), k. in a., 4/11/18 (Res.) (att. 8th Bn.).
Tattersall, Harold Vaughan, Lt. (Tp.), died, 22/4/18 (P. of W.).
10 Tayleur, Charles Edward, Lt., k. in a., 7/8/15 (att. 8th Lancs Fusrs.).
9 Thompson, Andrew William, 2/Lt. (Tp.), k. in a., 30/5/17.
7 Thompson, Lloyd Maurice, 2/Lt., k. in a., 25/1/17.
Thompson, Peter Lettice, Lt. (Tp.), k. in a., 8/8/18 (Res.) (att. 8th Bn.).
8 Thorley, William Bowers, 2/Lt. (Tp.), d. of w., 20/4/18.
10 Tucker, Cecil Hall, 2/Lt., d. of w., 7/9/15 (att. 8 Lan. Fus.).
2 Vavasour, Lionel Ormiston, Lt., died, 24/7/15.
1 Wake, Thomas Frederick Henry, 2/Lt., d. of w., 10/4/18 (att. 8/Bn.).
4 Walker, Archdale Gillam, 2/Lt., k. in a., 17/5/15 (att. R. Scot. Fusrs.).
7 Walker, Francis Hercules, Tp. Lt.-Col., k. in a., 7/1/16.
7 Ward, Charles Cecil Brooks, 2/Lt. (Tp. Lt.), d. of w., 11/1/17.
4 Webb, Edward Melvill, Lt., d. of w., 1/5/15 (att. Yorks L.I.).
4 Webb, John Boyer, Lt., k. in a., 21/4/15 (att. Bedf. Regt.).
Webberley, Reginald Selwyn, 2/Lt. (Tp.), d. of w., 30/9/17.
8 Wedgwood, Cecil, D.S.O., Major, k. in a., 3/7/16.
2 Weldon, Arthur Steuart, Major, k. in a., 25/3/17.
Westlake, Albert Neave, M.C., 2/Lt., k. in a., 4/1/18 (and R.F.C.).
Wheatcroft, William Hands, 2/Lt. (Tp.), k. in a., 7/3/17.
4 While, Ivor Austin, 2/Lt., k. in a., 31/8/16 (att. 1/Bn.).
4 Whistler, Bertram Charles, 2/Lt., k. in a., 29/9/18.
Whitehurst, Walter Harry, 2/Lt. (Tp.), k. in a., 22/4/17 (att. York & Lancs Regt.).
1 Whiting, Arthur, 2/Lt., k. in a., 27/3/18.
9 Windridge, E. A., Lt., k. in a., about 9/6/18.
4 Woodland, Clement Arthur, Lt., died, 1/4/18 (att. 6th K.O.Y.L. Inf.).
8 Yardley, Frederick George, 2/Lt. (Tp.), d. of w., 17/9/15.

The York and Lancaster Regiment.

10 Abbott, Duncan William Sydney Elphinstone, Capt. (Tp.), k. in a., 26/9/15.
9 Addison, Arthur Joseph Berkeley, Lt.-Col. (Tp.), k. in a, 1/7/16.
3 Adsetts, William Henry, 2/Lt., d. of w., 1/10/15.
3 Allen, Percy Hampson, 2/Lt., k. in a., 20/4/16.
Ambler, Edward, 2/Lt. (Tp.), k. in a., 26/4/18.
5 Amies, Arthur George, 2/Lt. (Tp.), k. in a., 9/10/17.
6 Anderson, Frank Gordon, Capt. (Tp.), k. in a., 11/10/18.
15 Anderson, Reginald Dudley Bawawen, 2/Lt., k. in a., 1/7/16.
8 Andrews, Horace Gibson, Temp. Capt., k. in a., 7/6/17.
Angles, Robert, M.C., 2/Lt. (Tp.), d. of w., 13/11/17.
13 Ashworth, Leonard, 2/Lt., d. of w., 12/4/18.
3 Aston, Henry Norman, 2/Lt., died, 6/11/18.
Atkinson, Charles Richard, 2/Lt., k. in a., 16/10/15.
2 Atkinson, Lawrence Evans, Temp. Capt., k. in a., 20/4/16.
2 Bacchus, William Hubert Ogden, Capt., d. of w., 13/9/15.
2 Bailey, Guy Frederick, M.C., Capt., k. in a., 7/7/17.
Bakel, Frank, 2/Lt. (Tp.), k. in a., 20/5/17.
8 Baker, James Henry, 2/Lt. (Tp.), k. in a., 1/7/16.
14 Baldry, Arthur, Temp. 2/Lt., k. in a, 4/12/16.
Bamford, Edwin Scott, Capt., d. of w., 24/4/15.
Banham, Ernest, 2/Lt. (Tp.), k. in a., 29/9/18 (att. 10/E. York. Regt.).
Barber, Wilfred, 2/Lt., k. in a., 27/11/17.
12 Beal, Arnold James, 2/Lt., k. in a., 1/7/16.
1 Beales, Henry, 2/Lt. (Tp.), k. in a., 9/5/17.
6 Beck, William, 2/Lt., k. in a., 26/4/18.
Bedford, Kenneth Savile, Capt., k. in a., 12/10/16 (att. 3 Bn.).
1 Bedwell, Charles Theodore, Lt., k. in a., 12/4/18.
Bennett, George William, T/Lt. (A/Capt.), died, 29/11/18 (att. 5 Bn.).
Bentley, Basil, 2/Lt. (Tp.), k. in a., 11/9/17.
12 Berry, Reginald Douglas, Lt. (Tp.), k. in a., 12/5/17.
Beynon, Ernest John Wilson, 2/Lt. (Tp.), k. in a., 9/10/17.
Blackburn, Stanley West, 2/Lt. (Tp.), k. in a., 9/10/17.
Bodker, John George, Temp. Lt., k. in a., 20/11/17 (att. 2/6 W. Rid. Regt.).
8 Bolton, William Curtis, Temp. Lt., k. in a., 1/7/16.
11 Booth, Harold Stanley, Temp. 2/Lt., k. in a., 1/7/16 (att. 8 Bn.).
Boucher, Charles Bailey, Lt., k. in a., 9/8/15.
2 Bower, Edwin Harland, Lt., k. in a., 21/3/18.
3 Boyd, James Wilson Brack, Temp. Capt., d. of w., 16/7/16 (att. T.M.B.).
6 Brand, Stanley Oliver, T/Lt., A/Capt., k. in a., 14/6/17.
3 Breingan, Samuel Karr, 2/Lt., k. in a., 26/5/17.
Brickwood, Arthur Cyril, 2/Lt., died, 15/4/15.
3 Briscoe, Frederick John, Lt., k. in a., 11/5/15.
Broadbent, Hermann, T/Lt., A/Capt. & Adjt., k. in a., 15/2/17 (att. 10 Bn.).
8 Brodie, Duncan Smith, 2/Lt. (Tp.), k. in a., 15/6/18.
Broughton, Ernest Chamier, Lt.-Col. died, 17/12/14.
9 Bryan, Sydney Arthur, 2/Lt. (Tp.), k. in a., 1/7/16.
Buckland, John, 2/Lt., k. in a., 16/6/17 (att. 12 Bn.).
3 Buckley, Edward, Capt., k. in a., 30/9/17 (att. 2 Bn.).
13 Bufton, Edward Evan, 2/Lt. (Tp.), died, 20/11/18.
Burt, Arthur George, Lt.-Col., k. in a., 23/4/15.
Burton, Hubert, 2/Lt. (Tp.), k. in a., 9/10/17.
2 Butland, George, T/Lt., k. in a., 21/5/18.
Campbell, Willie, Temp. 2/Lt., k. in a., 4/11/18.
12 Carr, Eric Marcus, 2/Lt. (Tp.), k. in a., 1/7/16.
3 Cartwright, Samuel Francis, Lt., d. of w., 5/11/18.
8 Casswell, Colin Garth Charles William Langlois, Temp. Major, k. in a., 14/1/16.
Chamier, Cyril Kinnaird, Lt., k. in a., 23/4/15.
2 Chapman, Claude Bertram, Temp. 2/Lt., k. in a., 18/9/18.
8 Clapham, Christopher Albon, 2/Lt. (Tp.), k. in a., 10/2/16.
12 Clark, William Spenceley, Capt. (Tp.), k. in a., 1/7/16.
2 Clarke, Albert Edward, 2/Lt. (Tp.), k. in a., 20/4/16.
6 Clarke, Thomas Purcell, Lt., k. in a., 30/9/16.
2 Clarkson, Wilfred Bamforth, Temp. 2/Lt., died, 20/6/18.
2 Cole, Clarence Claridge, Temp. 2/Lt., k. in a., 8/5/18.
3 Cole, Kenneth Leonard, Lt., k. in a., 29/9/15.
12 Colley, William Arthur, Capt. (Tp.), k. in a., 1/7/16.
Colston, Harold Kelway, Major, k. in a., 23/4/15.
7 Conan-Davies, Brynmor Ivan, Hon./Lt., died, 23/11/18.
10 Corban, Joseph, 2/Lt. (T/Lt.), k. in a., 17/7/17.
3 Cottam, Hubert Frank, 2/Lt., k. in a., 23/3/18.
Cotterill, Frank, 2/Lt. (Tp.), d. of w., 11/11/18.
12 Cousin, Arthur Norman, Temp. Capt., k. in a., 7/12/17.
3 Cowing, Ralph Henry, 2/Lt., d. of w., 15/7/15.
13 Craggs, Percival, 2/Lt., k. in a., 30/9/18.
Cranswick, George Alec, 2/Lt., k. in a., 18/11/17 (and R.F.C., 23 Sqd.).
3 Creswell, Leonard Curtis, Lt., d. of w., 13/10/16.
3 Cummins, Thomas Coote, 2/Lt., k. in a., 25/3/18.
8 Cuthbert, Olaf Ranson, Capt. (Tp.), k. in a., 1/7/16.
11 Dalby, Herbert Charles, Temp. 2/Lt., k. in a., 1/7/16.
13 Dart, Hugh, Temp. Capt., d. of w., 2/7/16.
12 Davies, Frederick Anscombe, Temp. 2/Lt., k. in a., 14/5/17.
Davison, Frederick William, 2/Lt., k. in a., 17/4/18.
Dawkins, Norman Leslie, 2/Lt. (Tp.), k. in a., 14/4/18 (att. 1/5 Bn.).
8 Dawson, Sydney, Lt. & Adjt (Tp.), k. in a., 1/7/16.
De Landre-Grogan, Leon Victor St. Patrick, M.C., Temp Lt., k. in a., 13/10/18.
9 Denyer, Augustus Andrew, M.C., Temp. 2/Lt., k. in a., 7/6/17.
2 Derry, Douglas Alfred Laurie, Lt. (Tp.), d. of w., 9/10/16.
7 Dibbs, Thomas Graythwaite Burton, 2/Lt. (Tp.), k. in a., 27/8/15.
12 Dickinson, Leonard, 2/Lt (Tp.), k. in a., 11/4/18.
12 Dinsdale, Frank, 2/Lt., k. in a., 1/7/16.
Dixon, Cyril Burton, M.C., Temp. Lt., d. of w., 12/11/18.
Dixon, Frederick William, Temp. 2/Lt., k. in a., 9/10/17.
11 Dixon, Harry Yorston, 2/Lt., k. in a., 13/7/15 (att. 9/Manch. Regt.).
Dobson, Frank Rayner, 2/Lt. (Tp.), k. in a., 28/9/18
Dodwell Oscar Wilfred, 2/Lt., k. in a., 10/5/15.
Douthwaite, Robert Christopher Morris, Lt., died, 19/6/19.
6 Draper, Roger Francis, Capt. (Tp.), k. in a., 22/8/15 (att. 8/W. Rid. Regt.).
Dunstan, Hedley, Temp. 2/Lt., k. in a, 18/8/17 (and R.F.C, 55 Sqd.).
14 Durnan, Edward, Temp. 2/Lt., k. in a., 16/10/17.
8 Dyke, E. P. W., 2/Lt., killed, 30/10/18 (and R.A.F.).
Eardley-Wilmot, Theodore, D.S.O., Major (Temp. L.-Col.), k. in a., 22/3/18 (att. 12/Suffolk Regt.).
East, Hubert James, Capt., k in a., 10/5/15.
8 Edmundson, Charles Robert Eubank, Capt. (Tp.), k. in a., 1/7/16.
3 Edwards, Arthur, Temp. 2/Lt., k. in a., 17/9/17.
8 Ekin, James, 2/Lt., k. in a., 1/7/16.
12 Elam, Charles, Lt., k. in a., 1/7/16.
14 Fairley, Duncan, Lt., k. in a., 1/7/16.
3 Faulder, Harold, Lt. (T/Capt.), k. in a., 26/4/18.
5 Fawsitt, Thomas Ruby, 2/Lt., k. in a., 16/9/16 (att. 9 Bn.).
Feasby, Harold, Temp. 2/Lt., k. in a., 11/4/18 (att. 1/5 Bn.).
G 6 Fenning, Algernon Esme Hal, Major, k. in a., 6/8/15.
Fielding, Arthur William, Temp. 2/Lt., k. in a., 16/4/18 (att. 6 Bn.).
3 Findlay, Ian Caulcutt, 2/Lt., d. of w., 10/8/15.
3 Finney, Thomas, 2/Lt., k. in a., 21/3/18.
13 Firth, Ernest Hartley, Capt. (Tp.), k. in a., 1/7/16.
2 Fitzherbert, Gilbert Clare, M.C., Lt., k. in a., 18/9/18.
Flatt, Harry, Temp. 2/Lt., k. in a., 28/11/17.
Flowers, William Henry Field, Temp. 2/Lt., d. of w. 15/4/18.
3 Folker, Edgar Reginald, 2/Lt., k. in a., 20/2/15.
14 Forsdike, Harold Brooke, Lt (Tp.), k. in a., 1/7/16.
3 Forster, James Ernest, Hon. Major, k. in a., 29/9/15.
Francis, Richard John, Lt., d. of w., 31/3/15.
Furber, Gilbert George, 2/Lt., d. of w., 22/7/17.
14 Furniss, Charles Frederick, Temp. 2/Lt., d. of w., 16/4/18.
3 Garnett, Alfred Edward, 2/Lt., k. in a., 29/9/17.
3 Gaunt, Benjamin William, Lt., k. in a., 7/9/18 (att. 63/T.M. Bty.).
3 Gawan-Taylor, Francis, 2/Lt., k. in a., 9/8/15.
9 Geake, Boyd Burnet, Temp 2/Lt., k. in a., 1/7/16.
Genge, John, Temp. 2/Lt., d. of w., 24/3/18 (P. of W.).
Gibson, Henry, Temp. 2/Lt., k. in a., 30/9/18 (att. 13 Bn.).
Gilson, Edward Norman, 2/Lt., d. of w., 5/11/18 (P. of W.).
15 Godwin, Colin Harold, 2/Lt., k. in a., 1/7/16.
11 Goodwin, William Alexander Delap, Temp. Lt., k. in a., 1/7/16
Gosling, Frank, Temp. 2/Lt., k. in a., 26/4/18.
Gould, Joseph William, Temp. 2/Lt., k. in a., 13/10/18.
Gray, George Donald, Temp. Lt, died, 5/5/17.
7 Gregory, George, Temp. 2/Lt., k in a., 26/9/17.
13 Guest, Thomas Heald, Temp. Major, k. in a., 1/7/16.
10 Hall, Douglas Alexander, Lt. (Tp.), k. in a., 25/4/17.

Hallmark, Percy Harold, Temp. 2/Lt., k. in a., 2/9/18.
14 Harbord, Cecil Gordon, Temp. Lt., k. in a., 1/9/16.
Hardy, Victor Harriott, Lt., k. in a., 25/10/14 (att. Lincs Regt.).
8 Hatfield, Alfred Charles, M.C., 2/Lt. (A/Capt.), d. of w., 21/9/17.
2 Heggs, Frederick, 2/Lt., k. in a., 21/8/16.
3 Herapath, Alfred Maltravers, 2/Lt., k. in a., 1/7/16 (att. M.G.C.).
6 Hicking, George Graham, Lt. (Tp.), k. in a., 1/7/16.
3 Highfield, George Harold, 2/Lt., d. of w., 4/7/15.
11 Hill, Chas. Herbert, Capt. (Tp.), k. in a., 21/8/15 (att. 1/R. Innis. Fusrs.)
6 Hill, Frederick Thomas Cecil, Temp. Major, k. in a., 7/8/15.
5 Hilton, Arthur, Temp. 2/Lt., k. in a., 9/10/17.
Hinckley, Douglas Roy, 2/Lt., k. in a., 13/1/17 (and R.F.C., 5 Sqd.).
14 Hirst, William, 2/Lt., (Tp.), k. in a., 1/7/16.
6 Hobkinson, Charles Wilfred, 2/Lt. (Tp.), d. of w., 23/8/15.
3 Hodgson, Alec Edmund Smart, 2/Lt., k. in a., 12/10/16.
2 Holmes, Albert Edward, 2/Lt., k. in a., 18/9/18.
10 Holt, William Leslie, Temp. 2/Lt., k. in a., 23/12/17.
Houston, Frederick Neville, Capt., k. in a., 1/7/16.
Howard, Henry Charles Mowbray, Lt., k. in a., 29/9/15.
Howell, Charles Joseph, Lt., k. in a., 25/1/17.
13 Huggard, Lewis Dudley Richard, T/Lt. (A/Capt.), k. in a., 26/6/17.
Hutchinson, Albert, 2/Lt. (Tp.), k. in a., 8/10/18.
Irons, William Morley, 2/Lt. (Tp.), d. of w., 13/4/18.
Isherwood, Francis Edmund Bradshaw, Lt.-Col., k. in a., 8/5/15.
12 Jackson, Cedric Arthur, Temp. Lt., drowned, 5/11/17 (att. R.F.C.).
Jarrett, Aylmer Vivian, D.S.O., Capt., d. of w., 22/6/15.
Jenkins, George Cliffe, 2/Lt., k. in a., 3/5/17.
3 Jepson, Albert Clarence Leonard, 2/Lt., k. in a., 12/10/16.
Johnson, Arthur Ellis, Temp. 2/Lt., k. in a., 20/7/17 (att. 2 Bn.).
Jones, George William, 2/Lt., d. of w., 12/4/18.
14 Keating, David Timothy, Lt. (Tp.), d. of w., 21/4/18.
2 Kelly, Brian Edmund, Temp. 2/Lt., k. in a., 2/12/17.
6 Kingdon, Arthur Francis, Temp. Capt., k. in a., 9/10/17.
10 Kingsford, Reginald John, Temp. 2/Lt., k. in a., 1/7/16.
10 Knight, James William, Temp. 2/Lt., d. of w., 12/12/17.
14 Kirk, Charles Gordon, Capt. (Tp.), k. in a., 20/7/18.
3 Kirkby, John Nevil, 2/Lt., k. in a., 25/9/16.
3 Land, Ronald John, Lt., k. in a., 20/3/18 (att. M.G.C.).
3 Laws, Bernard Courtney, Lt., d. of w., 25/5/15.
5 Lawson, David, Temp. 2/Lt., k. in a., 9/10/17.
2 Leach, Herbert, Lt., k. in a., 22/4/17.
6 Leahy, Percy Edward, T/Major (A/Lt.-Col.), k. in a., 17/7/18.
3 Leary, Ernest Richard, 2/Lt., d. of w., 23/7/16 (and M.G.C.).
9 Lewis, Harry Arthur, Major, k. in a., 1/7/16.
8 Littlewood, Frederick William, Lt. (Tp.), k. in a., 5/3/16.
10 Loftus, Henry Gordon, Temp. Capt., k. in a., 26/9/15.
Lousada, Bertie Charles, Capt., k. in a., 9/5/15.
10 Lupton, Frank, Temp. 2/Lt., k. in a., 25/4/17.
7 McAlister, Hugh, Temp. 2/Lt., died, 17/9/17.
8 McGonagil, Charles John, M.C., Lt. and Qr.-Mr. (Tp.), died, 5/11/18.
McIntyre, Donald William, Temp. 2/Lt., k. in a., 28/6/17 (att. 14 Bn.).
McNally, Thomas Patrick, Temp. 2/Lt., k. in a., 30/9/17.
Maleham, Edgar Hubert, Temp. 2/Lt., d. of w., 29/3/18 (att. 9 Bn.).
13 Maleham, Stewart, Temp. Capt., k. in a., 1/7/16.
12 Malkin, Norman Harry, Temp. 2/Lt., d. of w., 14/5/17.
Manton, Thomas, Temp. 2/Lt., d. of w., 22/10/17.
3 Marshall, John Willoughby Hadfield, 2/Lt., k. in a., 21/3/18.
Martin, George Charles Russel, Lt., died, 12/9/18.
10 Mashiter, Thomas Alexander Greenwood, Temp. Lt., k. in a., 31/8/17 (att. 1/5 Lanc. Fusrs.).
2 Mason, George Sowersby, Temp. 2/Lt., k. in a., 8/10/18.
3 Mather, Alfred Lushington, 2/Lt., k. in a., 7/1/17
Mather, John Kearsley, Lt., k. in a., 18/2/15.
May, William John, Temp. 2/Lt., d. of w., 23/3/18.
6 Measures, John Charles, Temp. 2/Lt., k. in a., 30/9/16.
13 Midwood, Harry, 2/Lt. (Tp.), d. of w., 25/12/16.
6 Mirfin, Joseph Colin, Temp. 2/Lt., d. of w., 17/8/17.
8 Montrose-Ekin, Leslie, M.C., 2/Lt., k. in a., 1/7/16.
3 Moore, Edward Hayden, M.C., Lt., d. of w., 25/4/17.
Moorse, Harold Henry, Lt., k. in a., 18/3/15.
3 Morris, Thomas Hodgkinson, 2/Lt., k. in a., 9/8/15.
6 Mott, John Francis, Capt., k. in a., 7/8/15.
3 Mozley, Richard Inger, Lt., k. in a., 21/3/18 (att. 36/M.G.C.).
Munson, George Philip, 2/Lt., k. in a., 7/8/15.
10 Mullins, Richard Walter, Temp. Capt., k. in a., 1/7/16.
Nicholls, Alfred John, Temp. 2/Lt., d. of w., 12/4/18 (att. 1/4 Bn.).
7 Nixon, Thomas William, Temp. 2/Lt., d. of w., 26/10/18.
Nolan, Bernard, Temp. 2/Lt., k. in a., 21/3/18.
13 Normansell, John, Temp. Capt., d. of w., 10/3/17.
10 Organ, Harold Percy, T/Lt. and Adj., k. in a., 1/7/16.
7 Palmer, Frederick Edmund Corbett, Temp. Major, d. of w., 28/8/15.
3 Parfitt, Bertram Nowitt, 2/Lt., died, 17/11/18.
3 Parry, Norman Cecil, Lt., k. in a., 27/7/15.
3 Peace, Hubert Kirkby, Lt., d. of w., 18/10/14 (att. Linc. Regt.).
Penrose, Robert John Rowson, 2/Lt., k. in a., 26/4/18 (att. 1/4 Bn.).
12 Perkin, Philip Kenneth, 2/Lt., k. in a., 1/7/16.
2 Philby, Harold Payne, D.S.O., Temp. Major, k. in a., 17/5/16.
Piggott, Frederick, 2/Lt., k. in a., 28/9/18.
Pimm, Charles William, Temp. 2/Lt., k. in a., 18/5/17.
6 Pitman, Thomas Stuart, Temp. Lt., k. in a., 28/9/17.
Pitt, George Llewellyn, Temp. 2/Lt., killed, 28/12/15 (and R.F.C.).
11 Porter, Samuel, Lt. (Tp.), d. of w., 7/8/15 (att. 8/Manch. Regt.).
Powrie, William, Temp. 2/Lt., k. in a., 27/9/18 (att. 2/4 Bn.).
2 Pratt, Francis Norton, Capt., k. in a., 18/9/18.
6 Priestman, Edmund Yerbury, 2/Lt. (Tp.), k. in a., 19/11/15.
6 Prince, William, Temp. 2/Lt., d. of w., 28/8/17.
9 Pritchard, William, Temp. Capt., k. in a., 21/6/16.
1 Proctor, Maubray, Temp. 2/Lt., k. in a., 26/5/17.
Pryce-Jones, Reginald, Temp. 2/Lt., k. in a., 19/10/17.
12 Purkess, Arthur James, Temp. 2/Lt., k. in a., 27/6/18.
14 Quest, Harold, M.C., Temp. Capt., k. in a., 3/11/16.
6 Raine, Leonard, Temp. 2/Lt., k. in a., 15/8/16.
Rankin, William John, Temp. 2/Lt., k. in a., 30/6/17.
11 Richards, Peter Austin Willmott, Temp. 2/Lt., k. in a. 10/9/16.
9 Riddell, Sidney, M.C., T/Lt. (A/Capt.), k. in a., 13/10/17.
3 Rigby, George, M.C., Lt. (Tp.), k. in a., 7/6/17.
3 Rigg, George Southerton, D.S.O., 2/Lt. (T/Lt.), k. in a., 31/7/17 (att. 52/M.G.C.).
3 Ripley, Charles Roger, Lt., k. in a., 22/10/14.
Roberts, Thomas, Temp. Lt., d. of w., 11/10/18.
Robertson, Edward Craig, Major, k. in a., 29/9/15.
2/4 Robson, Joseph, Temp. 2/Lt., k. in a., 20/7/18.
10 Rockley, William Lisle, M.C., 2/Lt. (Tp.), k. in a., 10/10/17.
14 Roos, Gustav Oscar, Capt., k. in a., 1/7/16.
Rose, Ronald Madoc Tierney, Capt. (T/Major), k. in a., 18/9/16 (att. K. Afr. Rif.).
3 Rycroft, Henry Frederick, Capt., k. in a., 7/8/15.
2 Sanders, Arthur Edward, Capt., d. of w., 19/5/16.
Sandys, Mervyn Keats, Capt., k. in a., 25/10/14.
Sawyer, Maitland Lindsay, 2/Lt. (Tp.), d. of w., 27/4/17.
Sensicall, George Edwin, 2/Lt. (Tp.), k. in a., 9/10/17.
Seymour, Lewis Thievry, Lt., k. in a., 13/8/16.
13 Sharp, Stephen Oswald, Temp. Lt., k. in a., 1/7/16.
9 Sharples, Philip Edmund, Lt. (Tp.), k. in a., 7/6/17.
13 Shearer, George, T/Lt. (A/Capt.), k. in a., 24/8/18.
9 Sillar, Tom Cameron, Temp. Lt., k. in a., 30/9/15.
6 Simmons, Eric Warr, 2/Lt., k. in a., 11/8/15.
7 Simpson, Geoffrey Barnsley, Capt. (Tp.), d. of w., 12/11/15.
12 Simpson, Vivian Samuel, M.C., Capt. (Tp.), k. in a., 13/4/18.
13 Skirrow, Arthur, Lt. (Tp.), k. in a., 28/3/18.
8 Smith, Charles Henry, Major (Tp.), k. in a., 27/7/16.
13 Smith, George de Ville, Capt. (Tp.), k. in a., 1/7/16.
10 Smith, Patrick Leete, Lt. (Tp.), d. of w., 27/9/15.
15 Smith Rex Johnston, Capt. (Tp.), k. in a., 1/7/16.
Smith William James, Lt. (Tp.), k. in a., 2/10/17 (att. 8th Bn.).
15 Spencer, Arthur, 2/Lt. (Tp.), k. in a., 1/7/16.
14 Staff-Brett, Henry William, 2/Lt. (Tp.), k. in a., 24/3/18.
10 Stainton, Robert Meres, 2/Lt. (Tp.), k. in a., 1/7/16.
3 Stephenson, Erik, 2/Lt., k. in a., 1/7/16.
13 Stevenson, Harold George, 2/Lt., k. in a., 25/6/17.
8 Stewart, Robert Colin, Capt. (Tp.), k. in a., 1/7/16.
3 Straw, Frederick Walter, 2/Lt., k. in a., 7/11/16 (att. 14 Bn.).
3 Strother, John Marmaduke, M.C., 2/Lt., k. in a., 28/4/17.
9 Stroud, Reginald Gordon, 2/Lt. (Tp.), k. in a., 1/7/16.
6 Sturdy, George, 2/Lt. (Tp.), k. in a., 9/10/17.
2 Sutton, Wilfred Moschary, Lt., d. of w., 17/9/16.
3 Sykes, Arnold Walker, Capt. (Tp.), k. in a., 30/9/17.
6 Symes, Henry, 2/Lt. (Tp.), k. in a., 30/9/16.
1 Tayler, Eric Hardwick, Lt., died, 9/2/15.
10 Taylor, Frank, Major (Tp.), k. in a., 13/3/16.
3 Taylor, Norman Gawan, 2/Lt., k. in a., 24/4/17.
10 Teasdale, Samuel Bird, 2/Lt. (Tp.), k. in a., 31/7/17.
9 Thomas, Wilfred Patrick Otto, 2/Lt. (Tp.), k. in a., 1/7/16.
Thornton, John William, 2/Lt. (Tp.), d. of w., 27/3/18 (att. 2/4 Bn.).
10 Topping, Eric, 2/Lt. (Tp.), d. of w., 25/4/17.
1 Tunbridge, Gerard Charles, 2/Lt., d. of w., 27/4/18 (P.O.W.).
9 Turton, Richard Dacre, Lt. (Tp.), k. in a., 24/9/17.
10 Twentyman, Denzil Clive Tate, Capt. (Tp.), k. in a., 1/7/16.
2 Twine, Harold William, 2/Lt. (Tp.), k. in a., 13/5/16.
2 Vine, Wilfred Harold, M.C., 2/Lt. (Tp.), k. in a., 12/10/16.
2 Waller, Hardress Edmund, Capt., d. of w., 22/11/17.
Walton, Arthur James, 2/Lt. (Tp.), d. of w., 16/10/17 (att. 9th Bn.).
2 Ward, Reginald Lucian, Lt., k. in a., 21/4/16
15 Wardill, Charles Henry, 2/Lt. (Tp.), k. in a., 1/7/16.
3 Watts, Donald William Stuart, 2/Lt., k. in a., 12/10/16.
2 Wear, Arthur, T/Lt. (A/Capt.), k. in a., 4/12/17.
6 Weston, Wilfrid James, Lt. (Tp.), k. in a., 22/8/15.
2 Wheat, Harold Arthur, 2/Lt. (Tp.), k. in a., 2/12/17.
8 White, Aubrey Cecil, 2/Lt. (Tp.), k. in a., 1/7/16.
Whiteley, Clifford, 2/Lt., k. in a., 18/9/17.
6 Whitfield, Edward Hillyard Day, 2/Lt., k. in a., 7/8/15.
Willard, Kenneth Hugh, 2/Lt., died, 12/10/17 (att. R.F.C., 45 Sqd.) (in German hands).
Willats, Alton Henry, Capt. (Tp.), k. in a., 7/9/17.
Williams, Horace George, Lt., k. in a., 17/10/18.
Willis, Russell, 2/Lt., k. in a., 25/10/14 (att. Lincs R.).
12 Wilson, Fred Brookfields, 2/Lt. (Tp.), d. of w., 7/8/17.
9 Wilson, Robert, 2/Lt. (Tp.), k. in a., 30/6/17.
12 Winn, John, 2/Lt., k. in a., 23/3/18.
13 Wise, Frederick Mortimer, 2/Lt. (Tp.), k. in a., 5/9/16.
Wood, Richard Poingdestre, M.C., Capt. (A/Lt.-Col.), k. in a., 9/10/16.
12 Woodhouse, Cecil Herbert, Lt., k. in a., 6/6/18.

8 Woodstock, Walter Percy, Lt. (Tp.), k. in a., 1/7/16.
Woolman, John Gray, 2/Lt., k. in a., 2/11/18.
Wylie, William Stanley, Lt., d. of w., 10/5/15.

The Durham Light Infantry.

4 Adams, John Percy Fitzherbert, Lt., k. in a., 14/10/17 (and R.F.C.).
2 Addington, Geoffrey William, 2/Lt., k. in a., 1/12/17.
10 Adie, George Carl, 2/Lt. (Tp.), k. in a., 22/8/17.
Adie, Robert Roland, 2/Lt., k. in a., 21/4/17.
21 Allan, Frank Cecil, 2/Lt. (Tp.), d. of w., 29/9/16.
4 Allen, D. G. A., Capt., killed, 8/10/18 (and R.A.F.).
11 Applegarth, Thomas William, 2/Lt. (Tp.), d. of w., 20/3/18 (P. of W.).
2 Appleton, Richard Aidan, Lt., k. in a., 21/3/18.
15 Arkless, John William, 2/Lt. (Tp.), k. in a., 30/12/15.
12 Armstrong, Cecil, 2/Lt., k. in a., 21/9/16.
20 Armstrong, John White, 2/Lt. (Tp.), k. in a., 21/10/18.
Arnott, Frederick, 2/Lt., k. in a., 29/3/18.
15 Atkins, Herbert de Carteret, Lt. (Tp.), d. of w., 10/10/15.
13 Austin, Arthur Hyndman Piercy, Capt., k. in a., 4/8/16.
4 Bacon, Dudley Francis Cecil, 2/Lt., d. of w., 1/11/15 (att. N. Fus.).
13 Bagguley, James Lionel, Lt. (Tp.), killed, 6/12/17.
21 Baildon, Christopher Nevile, 2/Lt. (Tp.), k. in a., 3/5/17.
13 Bailey, Gerald Hinton, 2/Lt. (Tp.), d. of w., 20/10/15.
15 Baillie, John Henry, 2/Lt., k. in a., 3/5/17.
20 Ballanlyne, James Allan, 2/Lt., k. in a., 1/8/17.
20 Bamborough, Thomas Clarence, 2/Lt. (Tp.), d. of w., 25/9/17.
11 Banks, William, 2/Lt. (Tp.), d. of w., 6/4/18 (P. of W.).
Barclay, Henry, 2/Lt., k. in a., 15/10/16 (att. 2 Bn.).
Barkas, John Charles Pearson. Lt., k. in a., 15/9/16 (att. 10/Bn.).
15 Barker, Charles William Tone, M.C., Capt., d. of w., 24/3/18.
10 Batty, Charles Frederick, 2/Lt. (Tp.), k. in a., 19/1/16.
23 Baty, Bertie Cecil, Capt. (Tp.), k. in a., 16/9/16.
4 Beart, Vere Leopold Dunstan, 2/Lt., k. in a., 17/9/16 (att. 13/Bn.).
Beckley, Eric White, 2/Lt. (Tp.), d. of w., 9/6/18 (att. 36/N. Fus.).
10 Bell, Alfred Gordon, M.C., 2/Lt., d of w., 18/4/17.
19 Bell, James, 2/Lt. (Tp.), k. in a., 22/4/18.
18 Bell, William, 2/Lt., d. of w., 3/7/16.
Benton, Ronald Mackenzie, 2/Lt., k. in a., 7/6/16 (att. U.L.I.A.).
15 Beyts, Julian Falvey, D.S.O., Lt.-Col. (Tp.), k. in a., 5/10/17.
2 Birtles, Leonard, 2/Lt., k. in a., 16/9/16.
13 Bishop, Charles Harold, M.C., 2/Lt. (Tp.), d. of w., 23/10/18.
3 Black, James Ashton, 2/Lt., k. in a., 21/3/18.
Blake, Edward Algernon Cleader, Major, k. in a., 20/10/14.
19 Blake, Frank William, M.C., 2/Lt. (Tp.), k. in a., 31/10/18.
15 Blenkinsop, Frank, 2/Lt. (Tp.), k. in a., 5/5/17.
12 Blenkinsop, William Millford, Lt. (Tp.), d. of w., 7/11/18.
14 Boden, Samuel Standidge, 2/Lt. (Tp.), k. in a., 15/10/16 (att. M G.C.).
15 Bodman, Charles Walter, 2/Lt. (Tp.), k. in a., 24/8/18.
12 Bollom, Johnson, 2/Lt., k. in a., 24/9/16.
15 Boulton, Harold Webster, 2/Lt. (Tp.), k. in a., 26/9/15.
Bowe, Eric Arthur, 2/Lt. (Tp.), k. in a., 27/5/18.
2 Bowers, Arthur Hugh Mansell, Capt., k. in a., 9/8/15.
Boyson, Frank, 2/Lt., k. in a., 26/3/18.
18 Bradford, James Barker, M.C., 2/Lt. (Tp.), d. of w., 14/5/17.
V.C. Bradford, Roland Boys, M.C., Brig.-Gen., k. in a., 30/11/17 (and Staff, 186/Inf. Bde. H.Q.).
15 Brady, James, Lt. (Tp.), k. in a., 26/8/18.
3 Braidford, Percy, M.C., 2/Lt., k. in a., 21/9/17.
19 Braidford, William, 2/Lt. (Tp.), k. in a., 24/7/16.
10 Braithwaite, Richard Wilfred, Capt. (Tp.), k. in a., 31/7/15.
15 Brinkworth, Edwin John, 2/Lt. (Tp.), d. of w., 9/9/18.
20 Brittin, Edward Whicker, 2/Lt (Tp.), k. in a., 31/7/17.
19 Broad, William George, 2/Lt. (Tp.), d. of w., 28/3/18.
1/2 Brown, C. F., Lt., k. in a., 25/7/18 (att. R.A.F.).
13 Brown, Philip Anthony, Lt. (Tp.), k. in a., 4/11/15.
18 Brown, William Herbert, 2/Lt. d. of w., 19/7/18.
20 Browne, Archibald Trevor, Capt. (Tp.), k. in a., 29/9/18.
14 Bryant, Reginald Eyre, T/2/Lt. (A/Capt.), k. in a., 20/1/17.
13 Buckell, Harold Claude, M.C., 2/Lt. (T/Capt.), k. in a., 21/9/17.
14 Burkett, Francis Edgar, 2/Lt. (Tp.), k. in a., 26/9/18.
14 Burn, Arthur Roland, 2/Lt. (Tp.), k. in a., 26/3/18.
18 Busby, Reginald George Camden, 2/Lt. (Tp.), k. in a., 16/12/16.
10 Butland, William Henry, 2/Lt. (Tp.), d. of w., 31/1/16.
17 Callender, Reginald Henry, 2/Lt. (Tp.), killed, 5/10/15.
15 Campbell, Archibald Douglas Lerago, Capt. (Tp.), k. in a., 18/11/15.
20 Carmichael, John, 2/Lt. (Tp.), d. of w., 25/3/18.
29 Carter, Charles Arthur, M.C., 2/Lt. (Tp.), k. in a., 14/10/18.
15 Carter, John, 2/Lt., k. in a., 29/5/18.
Cartwright, John Digby, 2/Lt., k. in a., 9/8/15.
20 Cartwright, Nigel Walter Henry, 2/Lt., k. in a., 21/9/17.
Cash, Ernest Alfred, 2/Lt. (Tp.), d. of w., 17/6/17.
10 Cates, Geoffrey, 2/Lt. (Tp.), k. in a., 21/3/18.
1 Catford, Cyril Herbert Barclay, Lt., d. of w., 5/10/16.
1/2 Cave, Arthur Douglas, Lt., died, 10/11/18 (and R.A.F.).
2 Chamberlin, Hugh Frederick Whitmore, 2/Lt., k. in a., 15/10/16.
12 Chambers, David MacDonald, Capt. (Tp.), k. in a., 20/2/17.
10 Chapman, Henry Reynolds, Major, k. in a., 27/6/15.
Charlton, Ralph Turnbull, 2/Lt. (Tp.), k. in a., 20/9/17.
Charlton, William Godfrey, Lt. (Tp.), k. in a., 26/8/18.
10 Clappen, Wilfred Joseph, 2/Lt., d. of w., 22/9/16.
10 Clarke, Vincent Charles, 2/Lt. (Tp.), d. of w., 12/10/16.
Coddington, Hubert John, Capt., k. in a., 7/7/15.
2 Cohen, Moss, M.M., Lt. (A/Capt.), k. in a., 24/9/18.
2 Collings, L. L., 2/Lt., died, 3/10/18 (and R.A.F.).
20 Conrath, Percy Thorpe, 2/Lt. (Tp.), k. in a., 4/9/18.
22 Cook, John, 2/Lt. (Tp.), k. in a., 23/10/16.
22 Cooke, Alan Welldon Hands, Capt., k. in a., 24/3/18.
Cooke, John, 2/Lt. (Tp.), died, 20/6/16 (and R.F.C.).
15 Cormack, Reginald Ormiston, 2/Lt. (Tp.), k. in a., 1/7/16.
14 Cox, Theodore Russell, 2/Lt., k. in a., 27/9/15.
Craig, Walter George, 2/Lt., died, 5/11/18 (P. of W.).
14 Cronin, John Francis, 2/Lt., died, 10/3/17.
14 Cutler, Frank, 2/Lt., k. in a., 18/9/16.
10 Davies, Herbert Howard, Capt., k. in a., 24/8/17.
Davis, William Thomas Hadley, 2/Lt., k. in a., 21/3/18.
2 Davison, Joseph Jonathan, 2/Lt., d. of w., 23/6/17.
10 Daws, Harold, 2/Lt. (Tp.), killed, 26/12/16.
Dawson, John, 2/Lt. (Tp.), d. of w., 22/7/16.
Dean, Albert, M.C., 2/Lt. (Tp.), d. of w., 15/10/18.
De Caux, Harry, 2/Lt. (Tp.), k. in a., 15/10/18.
10 Dew, Frederick Thomas, 2/Lt. (Tp.), k. in a., 24/8/17.
13 Dodds, Cecil, 2/Lt. (Tp.), k. in a., 5/10/18.
10 Dorrell, Harold George Harcourt, 2/Lt. (Tp.), k. in a., 3/4/16.
4 Douglas-Willan, Walter Gordon, Major, k. in a., 24/3/18 (att. 1/Garr. N. Fus.).
19 Drabble, C. F., Lt., k. in a., 13/8/18 (att. R.A.F.).
14 Duckett, Vincent George, 2/Lt. (Tp.), k. in a., 23/3/18.
15 Duffy, Thomas Bryan, Capt. (Tp.), d. of w., 16/8/18.
4 Dugdale, Charles Cyril, Lt., d. of w., 27/5/18 (att. York L.I.) (P. of W.).
10 Dunn, Frank Mewborne, 2/Lt. (Tp.), k. in a., 23/9/17.
15 East, John, Capt. (Tp.), k. in a., 1/7/16.
Edwards, James Harry, Lt. (Tp.), k. in a., 7/1/17.
20 Egglestone, Ernest, 2/Lt., died, 2/6/19.
15 Ely, Denis Herbert James, Capt. (Tp.), k. in a., 1/7/16.
20 Eppstein, William Reginald, Capt. (Tp.), d. of w., 4/9/18.
10 Fairbairn, George Eric, 2/Lt., d. of w., 20/6/15.
Festing, Hubert Wogan, D.S.O., Major (T/Lt.-Col.), k. in a., 21/3/18 (att. 10/York. L.I.).
10 Fisher, Harry Laireate, 2/Lt., k. in a., 27/10/18.
23 Fitzbrown, Geoffrey, 2/Lt. (Tp.), d. of w., 24/10/16.
15 Fitzgerald, Gerald Thomas, Capt. (Tp.), k. in a., 3/12/15.
Fletcher, Noel William Scott, 2/Lt., d. of w., 7/3/17.
Folliott, John, 2/Lt., k. in a., 19/9/18.
19 Forster, George Richard, Capt. (Tp.), k. in a., 25/8/17.
20 Foster, Joseph, 2/Lt. (Tp.), d. of w., 14/10/18.
16 Foster, Laurence Talbot Lisle, Lt. (Tp.), k. in a., 5/8/15 (att. 5/Manch. R.).
4 Franklen-Evans, George Philip, 2/Lt., d. of w., 18/9/18.
10 Fraser, Kenneth John, M.C., 2/Lt. (Tp.), k. in a., 27/5/18.
11 Freeman, William Winter, 2/Lt. (Tp.), k. in a., 30/11/17.
3 Freer, Arthur Martin, 2/Lt., d. of w., 12/4/18.
16 French, Percival Vincent, 2/Lt. (Tp.), d. of w., 19/7/16.
Frere, Lionel Basil, 2/Lt. (T/Lt.), d. of w., 29/9/15 (att. 2/E. Yorks R.).
11 Galley, Ralph Rowlands, 2/Lt., k. in a., 22/3/18.
2 Gamble, John Walcote, Lt. (Tp.), d. of w., 22/5/16.
10 Gardner, William, 2/Lt. (Tp.), k. in a., 24/3/18.
2 Garfit, Thomas Noel Cheney, Lt., k. in a., 30/4/15.
21 Garland, George Arthur, 2/Lt. (Tp.), k. in a., 16/9/16.
15 Gee, Reginald Claud Moline, M.C., T/Lt. (A/Capt.), k. in a., 7/11/18.
4 George, Edward Barcroft, 2/Lt., k. in a., 16/9/16.
2 Gilpin, Ernest Henry, Capt., k. in a., 21/3/18.
Godsal, Walter Hugh, D.S.O., M.C., Major, d. of w., 26/3/18.
12 Golden, Frank Charles Allen, Lt. (Tp.), k. in a., 26/12/15.
13 Golder, William, Lt. (Tp.), k. in a., 5/10/18.
Golightly, George Frederick, 2/Lt. (Tp.), d. of w., 7/5/17.
15 Graham, Cedric Kenny Onslow, 2/Lt. (Tp.), k. in a., 16/9/16.
4 Graham, Fenton Weiss, Lt., k. in a., 4/10/15 (att. York L.I.).
10 Graham, John, 2/Lt., k. in a., 16/9/16.
15 Gray, Edmund Trevennin, 2/Lt. (Tp.), k. in a, 22/10/15.
Green, Cuthbert, 2/Lt., k. in a., 15/10/16.
13 Greenwood, Leonard Montague, D.S.O., M.C., Major (Tp.), died, 17/10/18.
2 Gregg, Robert, Lt., k. in a, 9/8/15.
Grindlay, William, 2/Lt. (Tp.), k. in a., 30/5/18.
3 Griffith-Jones, William Lionel Phillips, Lt., killed, 12/7/16.
15 Hale, Harold John, 2/Lt, k. in a., 24/3/18.
22 Hall, Cecil Charles Hatfield, Major, k. in a., 27/5/18.
12 Hall, Herbert Cecil Victor, Lt. (Tp.), k. in a., 13/6/17.
12 Hall, Norman Bodger, M.C., Lt (Tp.), d. of w., 2/11/18 (att. 68th T.M.B.)
13 Hamilton, Archibald Lindsay, 2/Lt. (Tp.), k. in a., 10/6/17.
14 Hamilton, Archibald Samuel, Lt.-Col., d. of w., 13/10/15 (Ret. List, Ind. Army).
20 Hand, Moreton, Capt., k. in a., 31/7/17.
13 Hands, Cecil, 2/Lt. (Tp.), k. in a., 12/10/17.
Hanley, Alfred, 2/Lt. (Tp.), d. of w., 24/5/18
Hare, Harry Vivian, Capt., k. in a., 20/9/14.
4 Hargreaves, Reginald Anthony, Lt., k. in a., 28/6/17.
10 Harries, Gilbert James St. Clair, 2/Lt. (Tp.), k. in a., 24/8/17.
19 Harris, Thomas William, 2/Lt., k. in a., 27/3/18.
2 Harris, William Edward, 2/Lt., d. of w., 19/12/15
10 Harrison, Douglas Roy Dilworth, 2/Lt. (Tp.), k. in a., 27/3/18.
2 Harrison, James, 2/Lt. (Tp.), d. of w., 28/5/18.
12 Harrison, Leonard Arthur, 2/Lt. (Tp.), k. in a., 17/7/16.
1 Harrison, Roland Edgar, Lt. (Tp.), k. in a., 27/2/16.
13 Hart, Hyla Padgham, Lt. (Tp.), k. in a., 5/10/18.
Harter, John George, Capt., d. of w., 3/4/16.
2 Hartshorn, Laurence Alec, Lt., d of w., 26/3/18 (att. 18/L.T.M B.).
14 Hatch, Laurence Collier, Lt., k. in a., 27/9/15.

15 Haynes, Clifford Skemp, 2/Lt. (Tp.), k. in a., 1/7/16.
20 Hebron, William, 2/Lt. (Tp.), k. in a., 25/10/18.
3 Hellier, Fred, A/Capt., k. in a., 12/10/16.
1 Henderson, William, 2/Lt., k. in a., 21/3/18.
15 Herbert, Charles Stanley, M.C., Capt., k. in a., 27/5/18.
14 Herd, Oswald Alexander, Capt. (Tp.), k. in a., 24/9/16.
10 Herries, Fred, 2/Lt. (Tp.), d. of w., 19/12/17.
13 Heselton, George Robert, Lt. (Tp.), k. in a., 2/6/17.
16 Heslop, William, 2/Lt. (Tp.), k. in a., 5/11/16 (att. 64th Trench Mortar).
12 Hetherington, Thomas William, Lt. (Tp.). k. in a., 17/7/16.
15 Heyward, Harvey Heale, 2/Lt. (Tp.), k. in a., 10/10/16.
14 Hickford, Albert, 2/Lt. (Tp.) (A/Capt.), d. of w., 10/5/17.
3 Hill, John Robertson, Lt., k. in a., 2/6/15.
4 Hill, William Reginald, M.C., Lt., died, 6/11/18 (P. of W.) (att. 12/Bn.).
10 Hines, Austin, 2/Lt. (Tp.), d. of w., 15/12/15.
3 Hoare, Wilfred Gurney, Capt., k. in a., 10/3/15 (att Wilts R.).
14 Hodgson, Clarence Mortimer, Capt. (Tp.), k. in a., 18/9/16.
12 Hodgson, John, 2/Lt. (Tp.), k. in a., 27/10/18.
Hodgson, Richard Victor, 2/Lt. (Tp.), k. in a., 20/6/17 (att. 5/D C.L.I.).
Hogg, Robert Morrison, 2/Lt. (Tp), d. of w., 1/4/18.
2 Holcroft, Gilbert Culcheth, 2/Lt., k. in a., 9/8/15.
Holmes, Andrew, 2/Lt. (Tp.), d. of w., 24/10/18.
15 Hooper, Austace Woodrow Noel, 2/Lt. (Tp.), k. in a., 7/1/18.
14 Hossack. Allan John, M.M., 2/Lt. (Tp.), d. of w., 27/4/18.
Hollman, George Leslie, 2/Lt. (Tp.), d. of w., 5/3/18.
19 Howes, Charles William, T/Capt. (A/Major), k. in a., 22/4/18.
15 Huddleston, Maurice Louis, 2/Lt. (Tp.), k. in a., 1/7/16.
2 Hughes, Edward, Capt. (Tp), d. of w., 16/9/16.
10 Hunt, Reginald Thomas Headley, 2/Lt., d. of w., 12/4/18.
18 Ineson, James Walker, 2/Lt. (Tp.), k. in a., 18/5/17.
11 Inglis, William Wiley, Lt. (Tp.), k. in a., 20/11/17.
Ingram-Johnson, Reginald James Theodore, 2/Lt., d. of w., 10/7/15 (att. E. Lancs R.).
16 Iveson, Frank Taylor, Lt., k. in a., 30/6/15.
Iveson, James Henry, T/Lt. (A/Capt.), k. in a., 23/3/18.
15 Jackson, William, M.C., 2/Lt. (Tp.), d. of w., 26/8/18.
4 Jacob, Anstey Ross, 2/Lt., d. of w., 18/9/16.
10 James, Walter, Capt., k. in a., 25/6/15.
23 James, Wilfrid Rowland, T/Lt., k. in a., 16/9/16.
22 Jarah, Charles, 2/Lt. (Tp.), d. of w., 20/6/17.
2 Jarrott, Samuel Fox Armitage, Lt. (Tp.), d. of w., 12/10/16.
Jebb, Hope Emile, 2/Lt., d. of w.. 21/3/18.
Jeffrey, Joseph Hunter, 2/Lt., k. in a., 23/10/18.
10 Jerwood, John Hugh, M.C., Major, k. in a., 21/3/18.
Johnston, Percy Ellwood, Lt. (A/Capt.), d. of w., 12/9/16 (att. 2/N. Fus.).
Jones, James, D.S.O., M.C., Major (A/Lt.-Col.), d. of w., 14/10/18.
17 Jones, John Myddleton, 2/Lt. (Tp.), k. in a., 1/7/16.
13 Kaye-Butterworth, George Saintow, Lt. (Tp.), k. in a., 4/8/16.
13 Keith-Brumby, Harry Catherall, 2/Lt., died, 31/10/16.
15 Kemp, G. H., 2/Lt., killed, 1/6/18 (and R.A.F.).
4 Kemp, Percy Vickerman, Lt. (A/Capt.), d. of w., 31/5/18.
3 Kent, James Maddison, Lt., d. of w., 5/8/15.
16 Kerridge, Oswald Alfred, 2/Lt. (Tp.), d. of w., 23/7/16.
12 Lafone, Eric William. M.C., Capt. (Tp.), k. in a., 15/6/18.
Large, Percy Francis, 2/Lt. (Tp.), d. of w., 28/6/17.
3 V.C. Lascelles, Arthur Moore, M.C., Capt. (Tp.), k. in a., 7/11/18.
1 Lawson, William, Lt. (Tp.), k. in a., 27/3/16.
Lax, Donald, 2/Lt. (Tp.), k. in a., 25/10/18.
14 Leader, Reginald John Carey, 2/Lt. (Tp.), k. in a., 28/4/16.
2 Legard, Ralph Hawksworth, Capt., k. in a., 9/8/15.
22 Legg, Horace Gordon, Lt., k. in a., 24/3/18.
10 Leveson, Rudolph Marcus, Lt. (Tp.), k. in a., 18/12/17.
16 Lockett, William Henry, 2/Lt. (Tp.), k. in a., 7/10/16.
4 Lodge, Bernard Grime, 2/Lt., k. in a., 24/8/17.
15 Logan, Edward Townshaw, D.S.O., Lt.-Col., k. in a., 25/9/15 (att. 3/Ches. R.).
18 Long, John, 2/Lt. (Tp.), k. in a., 12/4/18.
4 Longden, Frederick Cecil. Capt., k. in a., 24/8/18.
15 Lowery, Thomas, 2/Lt. (Tp.), k. in a.. 3/8/17.
10 Lucas, James Edward, T/2/Lt. (A/Capt.), k. in a., 5/5/17.
14 MacDonald, Ronald Hugh Charles, 2/Lt. (Tp.), k. in a.. 10/12/16.
4 McGibbon, William Patrick, 2/Lt., k. in a., 23/9/17.
Mack, Thomas, 2/Lt. (Tp.), k. in a., 26/1/16 (att. 9/Bn.).
4 Mackie, Alexander Mackay, 2/Lt., k. in a., 21/10/18 (att. M.G.C.).
20 McNicoll, Graham, D.S.O., Major (Tp.), d. of w., 20/9/17.
Mander. D'Arcy Wentworth, Major, k. in a., 20/9/14.
21 Mann, Charles Humphrey Dalla, 2/Lt. (Tp.), k. in a.. 30/9/16.
15 Marks, John, Lt. (Tp), k. in a., 24/10/18.
Marshall, Roger, 2/Lt., k. in a., 20/9/14.
Marston, Percy Ingram, 2/Lt. (Tp.), d. of w., 20/9/17.
10 Martin, John Kingsley, Capt. (Tp.), k. in a., 1/8/15.
14 Matheson, George Hugh, 2/Lt. (Tp.), k. in a., 3/12/17.
2 May, Richard Wallis, 2/Lt., k. in a., 9/8/15.
21 Meacock, Robert Hugh, 2/Lt. (Tp.), d. of w., 19/10/16.
4 Meikle, Robert Jardine, 2/Lt., k. in a., 15/9/16.
14 Michelson, Walter, 2/Lt., d. of w., 27/7/16.
17 Millar, Leonard, 2/Lt., d. of w.. 19/7/16.
14 Milne, Alexander, Lt., k. in a., 18/9/16.
1 Moffitt, James Prior, M.C., Capt. (Tp.), k. in a., 3/12/17.
10 Mole, William, 2/Lt. (Tp.), d. of w., 28/8/17.
18 Money, Gerald Hugh Kyrle, 2/Lt. (Tp.), k. in a., 27/7/16.
22 Morgan, Cecil Buckley, C.M.G., D.S.O., Lt.-Col. (Tp.), d. of w., 29/3/18.
15 Morley, Arthur Selwyn, 2/Lt., k. in a., 16/9/16.
4 Mortimer, William Brian, Lt., k. in a., 13/6/15.
14 Moss-Blundell, Cyril Bertram, Lt., k. in a., 27/9/15.
19 Mundy, James, Lt. (Tp.), d. of w., 26/11/16.
20 Munro, Hugh Donald, Lt., k. in a., 25/3/18.
11 Myers, John James, 2/Lt. (Tp.), k. in a., 22/10/17.
13 Naylor, Urmston Shaw, Major (Tp.), k. in a., 3/9/16.
12 Neligan, Maurice Alfred Bourke, Lt., k. in a., 13/10/15.
3 Newstead, Frederick Lisle, Capt., k. in a., 7/8/16.
Northey, William, D.S.O., Major, d. of w., 22/10/14.
Norton, Leopold Grantley, Lt., d. of w., 20/10/14.
15 Odhams, Valentine Bernand, Lt. (Tp.), d. of w., 5/10/15.
3 Osborne, Derrick, Lt., k. in a., 21/3/18.
2 Palmer, John Stanley, Lt., d. of w., 18/10/16.
15 Park, William, 2/Lt., d. of w., 21/3/18.
Parke, John Aubrey, Lt., k. in a., 25/9/15 (att. 9/R.B.).
Parke, Walter Evelyn, Lt., k. in a., 13/10/14.
Parkin, James Dowell, 2/Lt., d. of w., 27/5/18.
1/2 Paterson, Arthur Cecil, 2/Lt., k. in a., 22/4/18.
Pattinson, George Foster, 2/Lt., k. in a., 27/5/18.
Peacock, John Charles Millard, 2/Lt., k. in a., 27/5/18.
4 Pearce-Browne, Richard, 2/Lt., k. in a., 17/7/16.
17 Pearson, Ernest William, Lt. (Tp.), k. in a., 6/8/15 (att. 6/Manch. R.).
18 Peart, Leonard, 2/Lt., d. of w., 12/4/18.
15 Peek, Herbert Thain, 2/Lt. (Tp.), k. in a., 14/7/16.
Penrice, William Gordon, 2/Lt. (Tp.), k. in a., 7/6/17.
18 Phorson, Douglas Stuart, 2/Lt. (A/Capt.), k. in a., 16/12/16.
3 Pick, Alfred James, Lt., killed, 2/12/18 (and R.A.F.).
21 Player, Gilbert, 2/Lt. (Tp.), d. of w., 30/7/16.
2 Pollock, Louis, 2/Lt. (Tp.), k. in a., 17/10/18.
Pritchard, William Alwyn, 2/Lt., k. in a., 26/4/18 (att. 1/Wilt. R.).
16 Pullan, Charles Ernest Arbuthnot, 2/Lt. (Tp.), k. in a., 30/12/15.
Pullan, John Aynsley, 2/Lt., T/Lt., k. in a., 28/11/17 (att. R.F.C., 9 Sqd.).
20 Pumphrey, Arnold, D.S.O., Capt. (Tp.), k. in a., 21/9/17.
4 Pybus, Harold Robert, Lt., died, 24/7/16 (att. 2/Bn.).
16 Raine, George Kenneth, 2/Lt., d. of w., 2/7/16.
14 Raynes, Robert, 2/Lt. (Tp.), d. of w., 17/10/15.
Rees, David Melvyn, 2/Lt., d. of w., 12/4/17.
22 Richmond, Frederick Robert, 2/Lt. (Tp.), k. in a., 13/3/17.
Robb, Alexander Kirkland, Major, k. in a., 20/9/14.
Roberts, Arthur Wilmot, 2/Lt., died, 16/12/18 (P. of W.).
25 Roberts, Richard D'Esterre, Capt., died, 15/10/18.
19 Robinson, Thomas Naylor, 2/Lt. (Tp.), k. in a., 25/9/16.
Rowley, Albert George, 2/Lt. (Tp.), k. in a., 26/4/18.
15 Royley, Harry, 2/Lt., k. in a., 16/9/16.
20 Russell, Ernest, 2/Lt., k. in a., 4/9/18.
21 Samuels, George Bernard, 2/Lt., died, 22/10/16 (and R.F.C.).
15 Sanger-Davies, Llewellyn Herbert, Capt. (Tp.), k. in a., 1/7/16.
13 Sauerbeck, Charles Theodore William, Lt. (Tp.), k. in a., 11/9/17.
1 Schofield, James Humphrey Clare, Lt. (Tp.), k. in a., 26/9/16.
Scollick, Laurence Trevor, 2/Lt. (Tp.), k. in a., 26/6/17.
22 Scott, John, 2/Lt. (Tp.), d. of w., 27/3/18.
Seatter, George, 2/Lt. (Tp.), k. in a., 9/9/18.
10 Sewart, Gerald Evelyn Spuldlam, 2/Lt. (Tp.), k. in a., 8/5/16.
Sharkey, Thomas, 2/Lt., k. in a., 26/3/18.
2 Shea, Joseph Patrick Lambert, M.C., Capt. & Qr.-Mr., d. of w., 1/12/17.
Shepherd, Stanley, 2/Lt. (Tp.), k. in a., 27/9/18.
Sheriff, Wilfred, 2/Lt. (Tp.), k. in a., 10/7/17.
10 Shirtcliff, Fred, 2/Lt. (Tp.), k. in a., 9/4/18.
16 Shorter, Alfred George, 2/Lt. (Tp.), k. in a., 1/7/16.
18 Simpson, George, Lt. (Tp.), k. in a., 4/7/16.
Simpson, Thomas Liddle, M.C., 2/Lt. (Tp.), d. of w., 30/11/18 (att. 64 T.M.B.).
14 Smith, David Thorne, 2/Lt. (Tp.), k. in a., 3/12/17.
23 Smith, Frederick George, 2/Lt. (Tp.), k. in a., 8/10/16.
15 Smith, Neville Field, Capt. (Tp.), k. in a., 24/1/16.
13 Smith, Philip Golding, 2/Lt. (Tp.), k. in a., 5/10/18.
Smith, Robert Cecil, Capt. (A/Lt.-Col.), d. of w., 1/12/17 (att. 11/R.W. Surr. R.).
Smyth-Piggott, Bernard Cecil, Major (Bvt.), died, 15/4/16.
Stanuell, Charles Martin, 2/Lt., k. in a., 20/9/14.
13 Start, Lesingham Eden, 2/Lt., died, 23/2/15.
14 Stearn, John Holder, D.S.O., Lt. (Tp.), k. in a., 3/12/17.
Stephenson, Francis Leaman, 2/Lt. (Tp.), died, 6/2/18.
10 Stewart, Charles Edward, M.C., Capt. (Tp.), d. of w., 10/4/17.
10 Stewart, Frederic Arnold, Lt. (Tp.), k. in a., 16/9/16.
3 Stewart, Herbert, Lt., k. in a., 23/4/15 (att. D. of Corn. L.I.).
22 Stirland, Joseph, Lt., k. in a., 24/3/18.
10 Stobart, William, Lt. (Tp.), k. in a., 24/8/16 (and R.F.C.).
Storey, Harry Hilton, 2/Lt., k. in a., 13/10/14.
Storey, Robert William, 2/Lt., killed, 9/3/18 (att. M.G.C.).
14 Swindle, Jackson, 2/Lt., d. of w., 14/10/16.
Sullivan, Francis Joseph, 2/Lt. (Tp.), k. in a., 28/5/18.
Swetenham, Edmund, Lt., k. in a., 22/10/14.
22 Tait-Knight, Alec, Capt. (Tp.), d. of w., 27/10/16.
13 Target, Noel Alexander, Lt. (Tp.), k. in a., 4/8/16.
4 Telper, Richard Greenwell, 2/Lt., k. in a., 7/10/16.
2 Thompson, Charles Henry, 2/Lt. (Tp.), k. in a., 3/6/16.
18 Thompson, Ellis, 2/Lt. (Tp.), k. in a., 18/5/17.
17 Thompson, Norman, 2/Lt. (Tp.), d. of w., 5/8/16.
Thompson, Percy Laughorn, 2/Lt. (Tp.), k. in a., 16/6/17.
17 Thompson, Walter, Capt., k. in a., 6/8/15 (att. 6/Manch. R.).
14 Thompson, Wilfred Taylor, Lt. (Tp.), k. in a., 26/9/15.
20 Thompson-Hopper, James, M.C., Lt. (Tp.), k. in a., 30/6/16.
22 Thwaites, Robert, Capt. (Tp.), k. in a., 24/3/18.
18 Tilly, Charles Wynn, Lt.-Col. (Tp.), k. in a., 14/4/18.
4 Todd, Alick, M.C., Lt., d. of w., 16/4/17 (P. of W.).
17 Toon, Harold Phillips, 2/Lt. (Tp.), k. in a., 14/7/16.

Tootill, Edward Cecil, 2/Lt. (Tp.), k. in a., 22/8/17.
Turnbull, Francis Egerton, 2/Lt., k. in a., 27/5/18.
4 Turner, Arthur, 2/Lt., k. in a., 26/6/17.
15 Turner, Herbert Stanley, 2/Lt., k. in a., 24/3/18.
Tyler, Roper Maxwell, D.S.O., Lt.-Col., died, 26/3/19.
15 Tyrie, David, 2/Lt. (Tp.), k. in a., 18/4/18.
4 Upton, Roger Maitland, 2/Lt., k. in a., 7/6/17.
17 Ussher, Beverley William Reid, Major, died, 5/2/16.
22 Vincent, Vivian, 2/Lt., d. of w., 31/5/18.
Walton, Ernest, 2/Lt., k. in a., 27/3/18.
20 Walton, William Knott, 2/Lt. (T/Lt.), k. in a., 31/7/17.
17 Warren, Theodore Stewart Wolton, 2/Lt. (Tp.), k. in a., 17/7/16.
2 Watson, Joseph, D.C.M., Lt. & Qr.-Mr., d. of w., 30/4/18.
16 Watson, Sydney Towers, 2/Lt. (Tp.), k. in a., 1/7/16.
Waud, Harold Fenwick, 2/Lt. (Tp.), k. in a., 27/8/17.
20 Wayman, Fawcitt, M.C., Capt. (Tp.), k. in a., 31/7/17.
15 Weir, Robert, 2/Lt. (Tp.), k. in a., 9/4/17.
15 Wesselhoeft, George Henri, 2/Lt. (Tp.), k. in a., 16/9/16.
12 West, Herbert St. John Carr, Major, d. of w., 27/10/18.
Wharton, Guy FitzGerald, Lt., d. of w., 9/5/15 (att. K.O.Y.L.I.).
10 Whittle, Arthur Denton, 2/Lt. (Tp.), k. in a., 16/9/16.
14 Wild, Arthur, 2/Lt., k. in a., 18/9/16.
Wiley, Evelyn Otway Scarlett, Lt., died, 7/11/18.
Wilkinson, John George, 2/Lt. (Tp.), d. of w., 25/10/17.
2 Willis, Henry George, 2/Lt., d. of w., 22/12/15.
20 Wills, John Scott, Lt., k. in a., 4/9/18.
Wilson, Edward, 2/Lt., k. in a., 26/3/18.
15 Wilson, Lloyd, 2/Lt., k. in a., 24/3/18.
4 Wilson, Ralph Aylmer, 2/Lt., k. in a., 9/4/18.
19 Wilson, Robert Alexander, 2/Lt. (Tp.), killed, 2/5/17.
18 Wilson, William, 2/Lt., d. of w., 12/4/18.
15 Wilson, William Harrison, 2/Lt., k. in a., 21/3/18.
Winter, R. R. C., 2/Lt., killed, 9/8/18 (and R.A.F.).
13 Witherspoon, John Clarence, Lt., k. in a., 11/10/17.
12 Wolstenholme, Charles Skaife, Capt. (Tp.), k. in a., 17/7/16.
12 Woodhead, Robert Comber, Capt. (Tp.), k. in a., 17/7/16.
2 Wright, Joseph Benjamin, 2/Lt., k. in a., 21/4/16.
1 Wyllie, William Thomas, Capt., k. in a., 19/7/16.
20 Yewdall, Frederick George, Lt., died, 18/5/18.
1 Youden, Sidney Edwin, Capt., k. in a., 27/8/18 (att. 1/7 H.L.I.).
13 V.C. Youens, Frederick, 2/Lt. (Tp.), d. of w., 7/7/17.
13 Young, John, Lt., k. in a., 9/6/17.

The Highland Light Infantry.

Acklom, Spencer, D.S.O., M.C., Major (Temp. Lt.-Col.), k. in a., 21/3/18 (att. 22nd N'thd. Fusrs.).
12 Adamson, George, 2/Lt. (Tp.), k. in a., 15/9/15.
Agnew, James Watson, 2/Lt., k. in a., 21/5/15.
14 Aitchison, Thomas Andrew Jamieson, 2/Lt. (Tp.), d. of w., 9/6/16 (att. 12 Bn.).
12 Aitchison, William John, 2/Lt. (Tp.), k. in a., 23/10/15.
4 Alexander, Frank Wilson, 2/Lt., k. in a., 14/4/17 (att. 16 Bn.).
16 Alexander, James, Capt., k. in a., 2/12/17.
12 Alexander, John Alexander Elliot, Lt. (Tp.), k. in a., 16/8/15.
17 Alexander, William Mercer, 2/Lt. (Tp.), k. in a., 1/7/16.
2 Allen, Alfred, 2/Lt. (Tp.), k. in a., 31/7/16.
Alston, Robert Charles Wallace, Capt., d. of w., 18/8/15.
3 Anderson, Alexander Ronald, 2/Lt., d. of w., 8/10/15 (att. 1 Bn.).
Anderson, Charles Hamilton, Capt., k. in a., 19/12/14.
10 Anderson, David A., 2/Lt. (Tp.), k. in a., 17/8/16.
10 Anderson, John Frederick, Capt. & Adjt., killed, 14/7/15.
12 V.C. Anderson, William Herbert, T/Major (Act. Lt.-Col.), k. in a., 26/3/18.
11 Andrews, Charles Edward, Major, k. in a., 25/10/16.
1 Annand, Allan Young, 2/Lt. (Tp.), k. in a., 11/1/17.
4 Aston, Herbert Selwyn, M.C., Capt. (T/Major), d. of w., 13/7/18 (att. 9 M.G.C.).
2 Austen-Cartmell, Geoffrie Hugh, Lt. (A/Capt.), k. in a., 13/11/16.
12 Austin, Hubert Morell, 2/Lt. (Tp.), k. in a., 13/8/16.
Baird, Barrington Hope, Capt., k. in a., 21/12/14.
3 Baker, Albert Parkes, 2/Lt., k. in a., 22/8/17 (att. 10/Dur. Lt. Infty.).
1 Balfour, James Alfred, Capt. (A/Major), k. in a., 11/1/17.
Bannatyne, John Miller, 2/Lt. (Tp.), d. of w., 2/8/17 (att. 12 Bn.).
18 Barr, William Speirs, Capt. (Tp.), d. of w., 23/5/17.
17 Beckett, James Ranald, 2/Lt. (Tp.), d. of w., 4/7/16.
17 Begg, Alexander James, Lt. (Tp.), d. of w., 10/7/16.
10 Bell, John Murray, 2/Lt. (Tp.), k. in a., 24/4/17.
15 Bentley, Claud Louis, Temp. 2/Lt., killed, 23/12/16.
12 Bethune, Henry Ewart, M.C., Lt. (T/Capt.), k. in a., 30/9/18.
14 Beveridge, John Baxter, Lt. (Tp.), k. in a., 22/10/16.
1 Birney, John Gordon, Lt., k. in a., 11/1/17.
16 Blackie, Albert Ferguson, Capt. (Tp.), d. of w., 17/4/17.
3 Blair, William Alexander, 2/Lt., died, 8/12/18 (att. 2/Bn.).
16 Boquc, Robert Alexander, M.C., Lt. (Tp.), d. of w., 26/9/17.
4 Boshell, Hugh Thomas Barron, Capt., k. in a., 22/3/18 (att. 10/11 Bn.).
17 Boyd, George Vallance McKinlay, Capt. (Tp.), k. in a., 1/7/16.
1 Breslin, John, 2/Lt., died, 11/7/17.
13 Brodie, Allan, Lt. (Tp.), d. of w., 27/7/16 (att. 15 Bn.).
2 V.C. Brodie, Walter Lorrain, M.C., Act. Lt.-Col., k. in a., 23/8/18.
10 Broom, Cyril Thomas, 2/Lt., died, 15/7/15.
12 Brown, Daniel, Temp. 2/Lt., k. in a., 25/9/15.
12 Brown, John, 2/Lt. (Tp.), d. of w., 26/3/18.
16 Brown, John Arbuckle, 2/Lt. (Tp.), d. of w., 3/7/16.
16 Brown, Robert Stanley, 2/Lt., k. in a., 1/7/16.
14 Bruce, Colin, Lt. (Tp.), d. of w., 5/9/18.
17 Brunton, Hereward, 2/Lt. (Tp.), k. in a., 1/7/16.
3 Bryan, Alfred, M.C., Lt., k. in a., 23/8/18.
Bryson, Andrew, 2/Lt. (Tp.), d. of w., 19/11/18 (att. 1/5 Bn.).
10 Burns, Russell Johnstone, 2/Lt. (Tp.), k. in a., 16/9/16.
14 Burton, Alexander Brown, M.C., Capt., k. in a., 9/4/18 (att. 13th E. Surrey R.).
15 Cain, Frank Backwell, 2/Lt. (Tp.), d. of w., 13/4/18.
11 Cameron, Donald Ronald Colin, Lt. (Tp.), k. in a., 13/9/15.
Cameron, William Henry Veitch, Capt., k. in a., 20/12/14.
3 Campbell, Colin Richmond, 2/Lt., k. in a., 11/1/17.
12 Campbell, Donald George, Temp. Capt., k. in a., 13/8/16.
16 Campbell, George Wands, Temp. 2/Lt., k. in a., 18/11/16.
10 Campbell, James Henderson, M.C., Temp. 2/Lt., k. in a., 24/4/17.
12 Campbell, Kenneth Gordon, Lt. (Tp.), k. in a., 25/9/15.
Campbell, William Ulick Middleton, Capt., k. in a., 14/3/15.
3 Campbell-Irons, Arthur, Capt., k. in a., 8/3/16.
17 Carpenter, John Neilson, 2/Lt. (Tp.), k. in a., 1/7/16.
17 Cassells, Robert Wilson, Temp. Capt., k. in a., 1/7/16.
4 Catto, Thomas, Lt., k. in a., 22/8/18.
Chichester, Robert Guy Incledon, Capt., k. in a., 13/11/14.
Clague, George, 2/Lt., k. in a., 14/3/15.
Close, Max Arthur, 2/Lt., k. in a., 14/3/15.
1 Cochrane, George King Hicks, Temp. 2/Lt., k. in a., 25/3/17 (att. 1/1st Gurkhas).
4 Coghill, Hugh Bernard Mackay, Capt., k. in a., 25/9/15.
Colquhoun, Robert Fletcher, T/Lt. (A/Capt.), k. in a., 16/11/16.
11 Colquhoun, William Wallace, Capt. (Tp.), k. in a., 25/9/15.
Comrie, William Ritchie, 2/Lt., d. of w., 27/11/17 (att. 16 Bn.).
Cornish, Charles Lawson, Lt., k. in a., 13/11/14.
3 Cossar, James, 2/Lt., d. of w., 16/8/16 (att. 12 Bn.).
4 Cousin, John Denholm, Lt., k. in a., 9/4/18.
10 Cowie, Daniel MacDougall, Temp. Capt., d. of w., 17/9/16.
14 Cowper, Ronald Macphail, 2/Lt. (Tp.), k. in a., 27/4/16.
Cox, Robert Ernest, 2/Lt., k. in a., 11/3/15.
12 Crawford, Robert, 2/Lt. (Tp.), died, 15/11/18.
10 Crawford, Robert McLarg, Temp. 2/Lt., k. in a., 14/8/16.
12 Crawford, William Montgomery, 2/Lt. (Tp.), d. of w., 5/9/16.
3 Crossley, Brian, Lt., k. in a., 17/5/15 (att. 2 Bn.).
Cunningham, Peter Nesbit, 2/Lt., k. in a., 2/12/17 (att. 17 Bn.).
4 Curr, Thomas, 2/Lt., k. in a., 4/10/16 (att. 18 Bn.).
1 Dall, John, Temp. 2/Lt. (T/Capt.), died, 12/10/18.
Dalrymple, Ian Douglas, Capt., k. in a., 5/5/15.
4 Davidson, George Leslie, Capt., k. in a., 2/12/17 (att. 16 Bn.).
3 Davidson, Henry Steele, Lt., k. in a., 17/5/15 (att. 1 Bn.).
13 Davidson, John, Hon. Lt. & Qr.-Mr., died, 19/12/15.
1 Davie, Fred, Temp. Lt., k. in a., 21/4/17 (att. 7 Bn.).
3 Debenham, Keith, Lt., d. of w., 4/12/16.
10 Dent, Cornelius Costall, 2/Lt., k. in a., 20/5/16.
17 Dewar, Robert, 2/Lt. (Tp.), k. in a., 18/11/16.
15 Dick, Alexander Young, Temp. 2/Lt., d. of w., 1/10/16.
Dick, John Young Farquhar, Temp. 2/Lt., d. of w., 14/11/16
Dickson, Alan James, Lt., k. in a., 14/11/14.
4 Dickson, John Gavin, 2/Lt., k. in a., 8/3/16 (att. 1 Bn.).
18 Dobbie, Robert William, A/Capt., killed, 23/12/18 (and R.A.F.).
17 Dobson, Edward, Temp. Capt., k. in a., 10/7/17.
15 Donaldson, Stuart, 2/Lt. (Tp.), k. in a., 28/9/18.
17 Drysdale, Alexander Nicholson, M.C., T/Capt., d. of w., 15/4/17.
Duff, William, 2/Lt., k. in a., 18/11/16.
10 Duncan, John, Lt. (Tp.), k. in a., 31/7/17.
10 Easton, Arthur Aitken, 2/Lt. (Tp.), k. in a., 2/3/16.
Edmond, James, 2/Lt., k. in a., 20/8/17.
14 Ellis, Philip Challinor, Lt., died, 17/10/16 (and R.F.C.).
10 Enderbury, Frederick Albert, 2/Lt., k. in a., 9/2/16.
3 Everard, Christopher Philip, Capt., k. in a., 11/1/17.
3 Everard, John Guy, Lt., k. in a., 12/3/15.
10 Fairlie, Jno. Ogilvy, Capt. (Tp.), k. in a., 27/9/15.
10 Falconer, James Rankin, 2/Lt. (Tp.), k. in a., 25/9/15.
1 Farie, Claude Allen Gilbert Lindsay Hamilton, Capt., d. of w., 15/3/16 (and R.F.C.).
10 Ferguson, Douglas Chalmers, Temp. 2/Lt., d. of w., 26/1/17.
14 Ferguson, Henry Horatio Edward, Temp. Capt., d. of w., 23/9/17.
17 Ferguson, Henry Innes, Capt. (Tp.), k. in a., 14/7/16.
14 Ferguson, John, 2/Lt. (T/Lt.), died, 8/7/18.
Fergusson, James Adam Hamilton, 2/Lt., k. in a., 20/9/14.
16 Ferris, James, Temp. 2/Lt., k. in a., 2/12/17 (att. 97/T.M.B.).
Forbes, Alexander, 2/Lt. (A/Capt.), d. of w., 22/3/18 (att. 17 Bn.).
3 Forsyth, John, 2/Lt., d. of w., 28/3/18 (att. 17 Bn.).
Forsyth, Walter William, Temp. 2/Lt., died, 7/12/18 (att. 2 Bn.).
1 Fowlie, James Lawrence, Lt., k. in a., 23/4/17 (att. 10 Bn.).
10 Frazer, Alexander, Temp. 2/Lt., k. in a., 13/8/16.
17 Gallie, Edward Archibald, Temp. Lt., k. in a., 1/7/16.
10 Ganson, Andrew, Temp. 2/Lt., k. in a., 14/12/16.
Gardiner, Frederick Thomas, Lt. (A/Capt.), k. in a., 31/7/17 (att. 12 Bn.).
Gaussen, Arratoon William David, Capt., k. in a., 17/5/15.
12 Gemmell, John, Capt. (Tp.), k. in a., 25/9/15.
Gemmell, James Brown Richardson, 2/Lt., k. in a., 16/7/17.
16 Gemmill, John Adshead, Temp. 2/Lt., k. in a., 1/7/16.
Gerard, Gilbert Meade, Capt., died, 3/5/16.
Gibb, George Eben, T/Lt., k. in a., 25-26/10/18.
Gibson-Craig, Bart., Sir Archibald Charles, Lt., k. in a., 13-17/9/14.

4 Gillespie, Charles, Lt., d. of w., 20/9/15 (att. 2 Bn.).
Gordon, Eric Alexander, Temp. 2/Lt., k. in a., 21/3/18 (att. 10/11 Battn.).
11 Gorrie, Alexander Keith, 2/Lt. (Tp.), k. in a., 26/4/16.
Grant, Edward Macpherson, Capt., k. in a., 14-15/4/16.
Guthrie-Smith, Ronald Cameron, 2/Lt., k. in a., 19-22/12/14.
4 Hall, Gerald Percy, 2/Lt., k. in a., 13/11/14 (att. 2 Bn.).
Halswelle, Wyndham, Capt., k. in a., 1/4/15.
3 Hamilton, Arthur Leslie, Lt., k. in a., 25-26/10/18.
12 Hannah, R. L., M.C., Temp. Capt., k. in a., 25/3/18.
3 Hardman, Kenrie, Capt., k in a., 25-26/10/18.
12 Harley, George Melven, Capt. (Temp.), k. in a., 25/9/15.
14 Harrower, James, Temp. Capt., d. of w., 15/9/16.
4 Hay, Arthur Leslie, 2/Lt., d. of w., 26/4/17 (att. 10/11 Bn).
10 Hayley, Cyril William Seafort Burrell, Capt. (Tp.), d. of w., 18/9/15.
17 Henderson, George Gartly, Temp. 2/Lt., k. in a., 6/8/16.
14 Henderson, William, 2/Lt., k. in a., 9/4/18.
Hill, Charles Edward Cecil, Lt., k. in a., 17/4/16.
Hill, Thomas Wilson, Temp. 2/Lt., k. in a., 10/7/17 (att. 16 Bn.).
Hilton, Harold, 2/Lt., k. in a., 26/11/17.
15 Hogg, David Adams, Temp. 2/Lt., k. in a., 9/2/17.
10/11 Holms, William, Temp. 2/Lt., k. in a., 16/9/16.
Hooper, Charles Winsmore, Capt., k. in a., 25/9/15.
Hope, James Horatio, Major, k. in a., 18/4/16.
Howell, Douglas Bert, 2/Lt. (Tp.), k. in a., 24/3/18.
Hugo, Reginald Graeff, Lt. (Tp.), d. of w., 28/3/18.
4 Hunter, Melville Adrian Cecil, 2/Lt., d. of w., 15/11/15 (att. 7 S. Staffs).
3 Hunter, William John Kenny, 2/Lt. (Tp.), died, 26/10/17.
11 Hutcheon, Samuel Wyness, Temp. 2/Lt., d. of w., 4/9/16.
17 Hutchison, Edward, Temp. Major, k. in a., 1/7/16.
11 Hutchison, Thomas, Temp. 2/Lt., k. in a., 20/5/16.
12 Hutton, Alexander, T/Capt., k. in a., 8/7/16.
15 Hutton, Andrew Donald, T/Capt., k. in a., 3/7/16.
4 Ingle, Aubrey Charles Bertram, Capt. (Hon. Major), died, 8/1/17 (att. Sco. Rfls.).
4 Inglis, James Arthur Chetwynd, Lt., k. in a., 9/5/15 (att. Seaf. Hldrs.).
Jack, Henry Claude, 2/Lt., killed, 1/9/16 (and R.F.C.).
18 Jackson, George, Temp. Capt., k. in a., 25/8/17.
1/2 Jardine, D. G. B., Capt., died, 5/8/18 (and R.A.F.).
12 Jeff, Andrew Russell, Temp. 2/Lt., k. in a., 13/8/16.
16 Johnson, Thomas, Temp. Lt., k. in a., 1/7/16.
Johnston-Stewart, Herbert Eustace Hathorn, Capt., k. in a., 17/5/15.
Johnstone, Richard Michael, Capt. (Tp.), k. in a., 25/3/18.
4 Jones, Archibald Wilson, Lt.-Col., died, 22/2/17 (att. Remounts).
17 Jones, Frank Riddell, Temp. 2/Lt., k. in a., 18/11/16.
18 Keith, Douglas Hay, Temp. 2/Lt., k. in a., 31/8/17.
19 Kelly, Thomas Cameron, Temp. 2/Lt., k. in a., 27/3/16.
Kennedy, D. C., 2/Lt., k. in a., 16/10/14.
18 Kennedy, William, M.C., Major (Actg. Lt.-Col.), k. in a., 23/11/17 (att. 18 Welsh Regt.).
16 Kerr, David Bryce, Temp. Capt., k. in a., 1/7/16.
Kerr, Hubert Rainsford Gordon, Lt., k. in a., 21/12/14.
4 Kerr, James, 2/Lt., k. in a., 1/7/16.
1 Kilroe, Francis Joseph, 2/Lt. (Tp.), d. of w., 28/8/18.
3 Kindersley, Douglas, D.S.O., Capt., k. in a., 22/6/17 (att. K.O.S.B.).
King, Alexander Lindsay, 2/Lt. (Tp.), k. in a., 9/4/18 (att. 10/11).
1 Knox, Robert, Temp. Capt., k. in a., 17/4/16.
17 Laird, Arthur Donald, Temp. 2/Lt., k. in a., 1/7/16.
18 Lambert, William, Temp. 2/Lt., d. of w., 2/6/16
15 Laughland, George Thomson, Temp. 2/Lt., d. of w., 21/6/17.
12 Lavelle, James Delargey, Temp. 2/Lt., k. in a., 20/8/15.
Lean, Hugh Henry, M.C., Capt., k. in a., 29/7/17.
4 Lees, Jasper, 2/Lt., drowned, 28/3/15 (and W. Afr. Front. Fce).
11 Leitch, Neil, Capt. (Tp.), k. in a., 20/5/16.
Leslie, George Muir, Temp. 2/Lt., k. in a., 3/10/15.
Lewis, Graham Knight, Lt. (Tp.), d. of w., 1/11/18.
4 Lindsay, William Alexander Hewes, 2/Lt., k. in a., 31/7/16 (att. 2 Bn.).
12 Linton, Henry McEwan, Temp. Lt., d. of w., 28/9/15.
12 Lloyd, Francis Charles Aylmer, Temp. Lt., d. of w., 8/10/15 (att. 2 Bn.).
15 Logan, Richard, T/2/Lt., k. in a., 10/7/16.
Long, Charles Henry, 2/Lt. (Tp.), died, 19/2/18 (1 Gar. Bn.).
14 Lowe, William Norman, Act. Capt., k. in a., 24/11/17 (att. 13 East Surr. Regt.).
18 Lumsden, Carlos Barron, Temp. Major, died, 8/3/16.
15 Lyall, James Thomson, Temp. Lt., k. in a., 2/7/16.
15 Lyall, Archibald, Temp. Lt., k. in a., 2/7/16.
18 Lyons, Vincent Aloysius, Temp. 2/Lt., d. of w., 23/8/17.
3 McAra, Duncan, 2/Lt., d. of w., 29/4/17.
17 MacBrayne, John Burns, T/Lt., k. in a., 1/7/16.
McBride, Alfred, 2/Lt., d. of w., 1/11/14.
16 McCallum, Alexander Meikle, Temp. Capt., d. of w., 3/4/17.
10 MacCulloch, William Bruce, Temp. Capt., k. in a., 11/4/17.
13 McCurrach, George, Temp. 2/Lt., k. in a., 1/7/16.
16 MacDermid, Donald Russell, Temp. 2/Lt., k. in a., 28/6/16.
MacDonald, Evew Ronald Horatio Keith, 2/Lt., k. in a., 20/9/14.
11 McDougall, Alexander Ernest, Lt. (Tp.), d. of w., 20/2/18.
3 McEachran, N., Lt., killed, 20/5/19 (and R.A.F.).
9 McFarlane, James Arthur, Temp. 2/Lt., k. in a., 16/9/16.
15 McFarlane, Robert Speedon, 2/Lt., k. in a., 3/7/16.
15 MacFarlane, William MacCallum, D.S.O., Temp. Major, k. in a., 19/2/17 (att. 1/5 Sea. Hldrs.).
15 McGibbon, Richard Forsyth, 2/Lt. (Tp.), d. of w., 16/11/16.
15 McGillivray, David, 2/Lt.. (Tp.), k. in a., 29/9/18.
11 McGuire, Edward, Temp. Lt., k. in a., 25/9/15.
16 MacHardy, David Scott, 2/Lt. (Tp.), k. in a., 1/7/16.
McIntosh, William Matthew, Temp. Lt., d. of w., 1/7/16 (and T.M.B.).
McIntyre, Reginald John, Temp. Lt., k. in a., 25-26/10/18 (att. 1 Bn.).
13 MacKay, Alexander Rinnison, Temp. 2/Lt., k. in a., 13/3/16 (att. 15 Bn.).
Mackenzie, Colin Landseer, 2/Lt., k. in a., 20/9/14.
10 McKinlay, Robert Galloway, Temp. 2/Lt., k. in a., 25/9/15.
4 Mackinnon, Bruce, Lt., d. of w., 2/10/18 (att. 97 T.M.B.).
Mackintosh, James Lawton, 2/Lt., k. in a., 1/5/15.
13 MacLachlan, Walter Miller, 2/Lt., died, 11/7/16 (att. 6 S. Lanc. Regt.).
McLean, James Monteith, Temp. 2/Lt., k. in a., 28/4/17.
3 Maclean, William Archibald, Lt., k. in a., 12/3/15.
3 McLellan, James, 2/Lt. (Tp. Lt.), k. in a., 4/10/17 (att. M.G.C.).
14 MacPherson, Arthur Vincent Claresholm, Temp. Lt., k. in a., 25/8/15 (att. 5 Bn. Rl. Scots).
13 McQueen, John, Temp. 2/Lt., k. in a., 24/4/17.
4 McSweeny, Randal Roderick, Lt., died, 15/3/17.
3 Malcolm, Thomas, 2/Lt., d. of w., 23/10/17 (att. 18 Bn.).
17 Marr, James Scott, T/Capt., k. in a., 18/11/16.
17 Marshall, Allan Gow, Capt. (Tp.), k. in a., 12/2/17.
Martin, Cuthbert Thomas, D.S.O., T/Brig.-Gen., k. in a., 27/5/18 (Staff, 151 Inf. Bde.).
10 Matheson, John, 2/Lt. (Tp.), k. in a., 9/4/17.
18 Maule, Edward Barry, Lt. (Tp.), k. in a., 6/2/17 (and R.F.C., 20 Sq.).
Mears, James William, 2/Lt., k. in a., 12/11/14.
Medley, Bertram Anthony, 2/Lt., k. in a., 25/9/15.
15 Michie, John, 2/Lt. (Tp.), k. in a., 15/7/17.
16 Middleton, Thomas, Lt., k. in a., 1/7/16 (att. 97 T.M.B.).
16 Milholm, David Archibald, 2/Lt. (Tp.), k. in a., 18/11/16.
2 Miller, George Bell, 2/Lt., k. in a., 28/4/17.
Miller, George Blair, 2/Lt. (Tp.), k. in a., 1/5/17 (and R.F.C., 18 Sqd.).
Miller, John, 2/Lt. (Tp.), k. in a., 2/12/17 (att. 17/Bn.).
10 Miller, John, M.C., 2/Lt. (Tp.), k. in a., 1/8/17.
12 Milligan, Percy Bass, Capt. (Tp.), k. in a., 30/9/18.
10 Mills, John Coleridge, Lt. (Tp.), k. in a., 25/9/15.
Milne-Henderson, James Young, Lt. (Tp.), k. in a., 31/7/17.
4 Mitchell, Charles Douglas, 2/Lt., d. of w., 26/3/18.
Mitchell, James Marshall, Lt., k. in a., 22/3/18 (att. 2/Bn.).
16 Mitchell, James Porter, 2/Lt. (Tp.), d. of w., 29/9/18.
4 Mitchell, John Patrick Cameron, 2/Lt., k. in a., 21/4/17 (and R.F.C., 16 Sqd.).
3 Moir, Robert Bruce Oliphant, 2/Lt., k. in a., 9/4/17 (att. 12/Bn.).
17 Morland, William, 2/Lt. (Tp.), k. in a., 2/12/17 (att. 97/L. T.M.B.).
17 Morrison, James Fyfe, Capt. (Tp.), k. in a., 18/11/16.
3 Muir, Frederick Bennie, Lt., k. in a., 15/11/16 (att. 2/Bn.).
Mummery, Harry Norman Samuel, Capt., died, 6/8/18 (att. 14/Bn.) (P. of W.).
16 Murdoch, John, 2/Lt., k. in a., 1/7/16.
4 Murray, Alexander Roxburgh, 2/Lt., k. in a., 18/11/16.
Murray, Thomas Francis, Major, k. in a., 21/12/14.
12 Myles, Thomas Booth, M.C., Capt. (Tp.), k. in a., 2/8/17.
3 Mylles, James Robertson Jack, 2/Lt., k. in a., 30/7/15.
17 Neilson, Thomas, 2/Lt. (Tp.), k. in a., 18/11/16.
11 Newman, Neville, 2/Lt. (Tp.), k. in a., 27/6/16.
12 Nicoll, Francis John Lt. (Tp.), k. in a., 25/9/15.
3 Notman, William Graham, 2/Lt. (Tp.), k. in a., 13/8/16 (att. 12/Bn.).
O'Halloran, John Fernan, 2/Lt., k. in a., 26/7/16.
3 Oldershaw, Thomas Harold, 2/Lt., k. in a., 14/4/18 (att. 2/Bn.).
4 Oldfield, William Henry, 2/Lt., k. in a., 17/5/15 (att. 2/Bn.).
Orr, Hugh Brian, 2/Lt. (Tp.), k. in a., 22/3/18 (att. 10/11 Bn.).
3 Orr, William Gilmour Moore, 2/Lt., d. of w., 12/1/17.
17 Osborne, John, 2/Lt. (Tp.), k. in a., 2/12/17.
13 O'Sullivan, John Andrew Hamilton, Lt., k. in a., 28/6/15.
11 Patrick, David Balfour, 2/Lt. (Tp.), k. in a., 18/7/16 (att. 28/M.G.C.).
Payne, Charles Geraint Christopher, 2/Lt., k. in a., 12/3/15.
3 Phillips, Thomas Frederick, 2/Lt., k. in a., 29/7/16.
Pitts-Tucker, Cecil Mortimer, Lt., k. in a., 21/12/14.
12 Porteous, Harry Morton, 2/Lt. (Tp.), k. in a., 25/9/15.
4 Porter, Aubrey Blackwood, Lt., k. in a., 3/10/15 (att. 2/Bn.).
Powell, Rhys Campbell Ffolliott, 2/Lt., k. in a., 13/9/14.
14 Pringle, James, 2/Lt., died, 8/2/15.
Pringle, Lionel Graham, M.V.O., Capt., d. of w., 29/12/14.
4 Reid, Donald, 2/Lt., k. in a., 17/8/17 (att. 2/Bn.).
10 Reid, James, Capt. (Tp.), k. in a., 25/9/15.
15 Reid, James, 2/Lt. (Tp.), d. of w., 1/2/17.
15 Reid, John, Lt. (A/Capt.), k. in a., 4/4/18.
3 Reid, Robert Heslop, 2/Lt., k. in a., 2/12/17.
11 Reid, Robert Walker, Capt. (Tp.), k. in a., 13/8/16.
18 Rex, Eustace Charles, 2/Lt. (Tp.), k. in a., 3/9/16.
4 Ritchie, Richard James Wallace, Lt. (A/Capt.), k. in a., 20/5/18 (att. 18/Bn.).
17 Roberts, Alfred Frank, 2/Lt. (Tp.), k. in a., 18/11/16.
4 Robertson, James, 2/Lt., died, 9/7/17 (att. 19/Durh. L.I.).
10 Robertson, Ronald, Capt. (Tp.), died, 13/9/17.
16 Robinson, William Edwin, Capt. (Tp.), k. in a., 18/11/16.
3 Rorison, William Gilbert Don Gurdon, Capt., k. in a., 9/4/18 (att. 10/11 Bn.).
10 Rose, William, Lt. (Tp.), k. in a., 11/4/17.
Ross, Donald, Lt. (Tp.), k. in a., 13/11/16.
10 Ross, John Alexander, 2/Lt. (Tp.), k. in a., 31/8/18.
10 Rout, William Owen Nelson, Lt. (Tp.), k. in a., 25/9/15.

Rowley, Joshua Robert, Capt., k. in a., 2/11/17 (att. 5/Suff. R.).
17 Russell, James, M.C., Capt. (Tp.), died, 10/7/17.
10 Scott, Alexander, 2/Lt., k. in a., 24/4/17.
3 Scott, Hugh McLellan, Capt., k. in a., 6/9/18.
12 Shaw, Maurice, Lt. (Tp.), d. of w., 30/9/15.
Sheridan, Daniel, 2/Lt., k. in a., 24/3/18.
4 Shield, Clement Ridley, M.C., Capt., k. in a., 7/10/16.
Shipton, Cyril Herbert, 2/Lt., k. in a., 25/9/15.
10 Sibold, Foster Moverley, 2/Lt. (Tp.), k. in a., 25/9/15.
12 Sillars, David Robertson, Capt. (Tp.), k. in a., 4/5/18.
16 Simpson, George Murdoch, 2/Lt. (Tp.), k. in a., 18/11/16.
Simson, James Robert, D.S.O., Major (T/Lt.-Col.), d. of w., 9/11/17 (att. K.O.S.B.).
12 Smith, Joseph Edward, 2/Lt. (Tp.), k. in a., 15/1/16.
Smith, Norman Gordon, 2/Lt., k. in a., 19/12/15 (and R.F.C.).
17 Smith-Maxwell, Archibald Findlay, Lt. (Tp.), k. in a., 1/7/16.
2 Spence, Gilbert Chisholm Drever, M.C., Capt., k. in a., 1/10/18.
10 Stafford, Charles Edward Trevor, 2/Lt. (Tp.), k. in a., 31/7/17.
3 Starkey, Joseph Bernard Collins, Lt., k. in a., 13/11/16.
4 Steele, Francis Gardner, 2/Lt., k. in a., 18/11/16 (att. 2/Bn.).
1 Stephen, James Howie Frederic, Lt., k. in a., 11/1/17.
18 Steuart, Walter Willox, 2/Lt. (Tp.), d. of w., 5/3/17 (and 46 Sqd., R.F.C.).
14 Steven, Robert, 2/Lt. (Tp.), d. of w., 24/3/18.
1 Stevens, Alexander, Capt. (Qr.-Mr.), died, 10/4/17.
14 Stevenson, William Alexander Gibb, Capt., d. of w., 20/12/17 (in German hands).
12 Stewart, Hugh, Lt. (Tp.), k. in a., 25/3/18.
4 Strettell, William Michael Dashwood Stirling, Capt., k. in a., 28/11/17 (and R.F.C.).
18 Stuart, William Aloysius, 2/Lt. (Tp.), d. of w., 26/5/17.
11 Sutherland, James Gilbert, 2/Lt. (Tp.), d. of w., 11/8/15.
17 Symington, Percy George, Lt. (Tp.), k. in a., 1/7/16.
Tarrant, Herbert Sutton, Capt., k. in a., 27/4/15.
15 Taylor, Adrian Connell, T/Lt. (A/Capt.), d. of w., 24/9/17.
4 Taylor, Edward Graham, 2/Lt., d. of w., 23/5/17.
13 Taylor, William Crookenden, Lt. (Tp.), d. of w., 5/11/18 (att. Div. M.G.C.).
15 Teacher, William George, 2/Lt. (Tp.), k. in a., 14/5/16.
10 Thom, David, 2/Lt. (Tp.), k. in a., 14/9/16.
10 Thomson, James, Capt. (Tp.), k. in a., 25/9/15.
15 Thomson, William, M.C., 2/Lt. (Tp.), d. of w., 12/4/18.
3 Thomson, Walter Halton, 2/Lt., k. in a., 3/7/16.
15 Timony, Patrick Charles Laurence, 2/Lt. (Tp.), k. in a., 24/8/18.
Todd, James Clark, 2/Lt. (Tp.), k. in a., 27/6/17.
Tomlinson, James Freeman, Lt. (Tp.), k. in a., 24/3/18.
2 Townsend, Arthur Gordon, T/Lt. (A/Capt.), k. in a., 5/9/17.
3 Twynam, Cyril Francis Frederick, Lt., k. in a., 15/4/18.
Walker, Gavin Henry, Capt., k. in a., 14/3/15.
Ward, Frank Reginald, 2/Lt. (Tp.), d. of w., 15/10/17 (P. of W.).
18 Watkinson, John, M.C., Lt. & Qr.-Mr., died, 10/12/18.
4 Watson, Mark Sanderson, 2/Lt., k. in a., 11/1/17.
Watt, Thomas Stevenson, 2/Lt. (Tp.), k. in a., 22/9/17.
Whistler, Ralfe Allen Fuller, Capt., d. of w., 27/4/17.
1 Whiteside, Miles Bruce Dalzell, 2/Lt., died, 13/6/18 (and R.A.F.).
16 Whitfield, John, 2/Lt. (Tp.), k. in a., 2/12/17.
2 Whitson, Harold White, Lt., k. in a., 25/9/15.
Whitson, Wilfred Robert, Capt. (T/Major), k. in a., 30/11/17 (att. 9/Suff. R.).
16 Wilkie, John Stewart, Capt. (Tp.), k. in a., 14/4/17.
Williams, Cyril, Lt., k. in a., 30/7/16 (and R.F.C.).
4 Willis, Arthur Rhys, 2/Lt., k. in a., 28/7/17 (att. 20/Durh. L.I.).
11 Wilson, Lewis McIver, 2/Lt. (Tp.), d. of w., 27/3/16.
12 Winch, Edward Hadfield, Lt., k. in a., 25/3/18.
2 Wolfe-Murray, A. A., C.B., Lt.-Col., died, 7/12/18.
11 Yeo, James Frederick Jesse, 2/Lt., k. in a., 1/8/17.
17 Younger, David George, 2/Lt. (Tp.), k. in a., 1/7/16.

The Seaforth Highlanders.
(Ross-shire Buffs, the Duke of Albany's.)

Abel, John Duncan, 2/Lt. (Tp.), k. in a., 26/3/18.
2 Agar, Richard Paterson, 2/Lt., k. in a., 14/10/16.
2 Alexander, George Thomson Dickson, 2/Lt. (Tp.), k. in a., 11/4/17.
Alison, George Newdegate, Capt., k. in a., 1/7/16 (att. M.G.C.).
9 Allen, Herbert Thomas, Capt. (Tp.), k. in a, 25/9/15.
Anderson, George Whitfield, Hon. Major & Qr.-Mr., died, 31/8/15 (att. Egyptian Army).
Arbuthnot, Kenneth Wyndham, Major, k. in a., 25/4/15.
Baillie-Hamilton, Arthur Buchanan, Capt., k. in a., 9/5/15.
Baird, Charles Edward, Capt., k. in a., 1/7/16.
1 Bean, Humphrey, Lt., A/Capt., k. in a., 19/9/18.
7 Bennitt, Harry Pynson, Capt., d. of w., 7/10/15.
2 Blackwood, Miles Harry, 2/Lt., k. in a., 1/7/16.
8 Blair, William, 2/Lt. (Tp.), k. in a., 23/4/17.
Booth, John Lyon, M.C., Lt. (Tp.), A/Capt., k. in a., 18/4/18.
10 Boswall, James Donaldson, Capt., k. in a., 13/6/15 (att. Essex R.).
10 Boyd, George Francis Edward, Lt. (Tp.), died, 19/10/16 (att. Y/51 T.M.B.).
Boyd, William Noel Lawson, 2/Lt., k. in a., 23/4/15.
2 Bradford, Sir Evelyn Ridley (Bart.), Lt.-Col., k. in a., 14/9/14.
3 Brash, James, D.S.O., M.C., Lt., A/Capt., d. of w., 9/11/18 (att. 7 Bn.).
Brodie, George, 2/Lt. (Tp.), d. of w., 2/8/17.
10 Brodie, Mark Moyle, 2/Lt. (Tp.), k. in a., 7/1/16 (att. 1st Bn.).
Brodie, P. W., Lt., died, 18/11/18 (and R.A.F.).
2 Broom, Frederick Jordan, 2/Lt. (Tp.), k. in a., 1/7/16.
Brown, Alexander, Johnstone, Lt. (Tp.), d. of w., 11/4/18.
7 Bruce-Lockhart, Norman Douglas Stewart, Lt., k. in a., 25/9/15.
Buchan, William George, 2/Lt. (Tp.), k. in a., 12/10/16.
2 Buchanan, David, 2/Lt. (Tp.), k. in a., 1/7/16.
Buckworth, Charles Raymond, Lt., k. in a., 1/7/16 (att. M.G.C.).
1 Burn, Charles Scott, Lt., k. in a., 3/11/17.
Burness, Alfred Richard, Lt., d. of w., 25/4/15.
Burns, Francis, M.C., 2/Lt. (Tp.), k. in a., 31/7/17 (att. 8th Bn.).
8 Calder, George MacBeth, 2/Lt. (Tp.), k. in a., 25/9/15.
Cameron, Arthur Ian Douglas, 2/Lt., d. of w., 25/4/15.
8 Campbell, Alexander Mather, 2/Lt. (Tp.), k. in a., 22/3/18.
8 Campbell, Hon. Eric Octavius, D.S.O., Lt.-Col. (Tp.), died, 4/6/18 (Staff.).
Campbell, John, D.C.M., 2/Lt., d. of w., 20/4/18.
10 Campbell, Robert Gillies, Capt., died, 1/2/15.
2 Campion, Edward, Major, T/Lt.-Col., died, 25/2/16.
Carden, Derrick Alfred, Lt.-Col., d. of w., 25/5/15 (att. 7 A. & S. Highrs.).
2 Cargill, Duncan Campbell, 2/Lt. (Tp.), k. in a., 2/11/18.
7 Carter, William Thomas, Capt., k. in a., 12/10/16.
3 Chadwick, Edward Neale, 2/Lt., k. in a., 4/10/17.
3 Chrystal, Ian Campbell, 2/Lt., k. in a., 1/5/17 (att. 9th Bn.).
9 Clark, Alexander, Lt. & Qr.-Mr., d. of w., 13/4/18.
Conduitt, Robert Bruce, 2/Lt., k. in a., 16/4/15.
2 Conner, Frederick Attenborrow, 2/Lt. (Tp.), k. in a., 1/7/16.
Cowie, Alexander Gordon, Capt., d. of w., 6/4/16.
2 Crum, Stewart Alexander, 2/Lt., k. in a., 1/7/16.
Crum-Ewing, Alexander, 2/Lt., k. in a., 22/12/14.
1 Cull, Arthur Tulloch, Capt., k. in a., 11/5/17 (and R.F.C., 48 Sqd.).
9 Cummins, Herbert Charles Bruce, Capt. (Tp.), d. of w., 7/5/16.
8 Cuthbert, Reginald Vaux, 2/Lt. (Tp.), d. of w., 28/4/17.
Daniell, Francis Edward Lloyd, D.S.O., Lt.-Col. (Tp.), d. of w., 4/3/16 (Gen. Staff, 21 Div.).
3 Davidson, Alexander Ritchie, Lt., k. in a., 21/4/16.
Davidson, Duncan Hemelin, Capt., k. in a., 9/5/15.
Dawson, William, 2/Lt. (Tp.), k. in a., 11/4/17.
3 De Salis, Peter Fane, 2/Lt., k. in a., 22/1/17 (att. 2nd Bn.).
Dixon, W. H., 2/Lt., d. of w., 23/6/18 (and R.A.F.).
3 Dixon, William Hutton, 2/Lt., k. in a., 22/4/18.
3 Donald, Colin George Hamilton, 2/Lt., k. in a., 8/8/18.
7 Douglas, John Gordon, Lt., k. in a., 12/4/18.
7 Douglas, Kenneth Mackenzie, Lt. (Tp.), died, 9/12/18 (att. K. Af. Rif.).
9 Druitt, Charles Lambert, Lt. (Tp.), k. in a., 13/10/16.
3 Faithfull, Francis William Alexander, 2/Lt., k. in a., 3/7/15 (att. 2nd Bn.).
7 Farmer, Henry Gamul, Capt. (Tp.), d. of w., 12/11/15.
Feilden, Granville John Henry, 2/Lt., k. in a., 25/4/15.
8 Fergusson, Edward Keith Ogilvy, Capt. (Tp.), k. in a., 26/1/16.
2 Fergusson, John Wright, Lt. (Tp.), died, 9/5/17.
1 Finlayson, Bernard Stuart, 2/Lt., d. of w., 13/4/18 (att. 1/4 Bn.).
Flett, Frederick, 2/Lt. (Tp.), killed, 9/3/18.
Forbes-Robertson, Kenneth, Capt., k. in a., 8/11/14.
Ford, Alfred Murnie, 2/Lt., d. of w., 28/7/18.
7 Forrest, John William, 2/Lt. (Tp.), k. in a., 27/10/15.
4 Fowler, Sir John Edward (Bart.), Capt., k. in a., 22/6/15.
Fraser, Herbert Heron, 2/Lt. (Tp.), d. of w., 18/10/17 (att. 8th Bn.).
9 Furneaux, William Edington, M.C., Major (Tp.), k. in a., 24/3/18.
7 Gaisford, Walter Thomas, Major, Tp. Lt.-Col., k. in a., 25/9/15.
7 Galloway, Harold Bessemer, Capt. (T/Major), k. in a., 25/9/15.
Gamble, Hugh Valentine, Lt., k. in a., 3/5/17.
Gander, Leslie Stephen, 2/Lt. (Tp.), d. of w., 5/6/18 (att. 1/4 Bn.).
Gardner, Albert Abercrombie, 2/Lt. (Tp.), k. in a., 23/4/17.
8 Gardner, Wedderburn MacKenzie, 2/Lt. (Tp.), d. of w., 23/8/17.
Geddes, Donald, 2/Lt., k. in a., 5/4/16 (att. 7 Bn.).
8 Georgeson, Dan Horace, T/Lt. (A/Capt.), k. in a., 9/3/18.
7 Gilmour, Douglas, Lt. (Tp.), d. of w., 16/2/16 (att. T.M.B.).
3 Gjers, Lawrence, Capt. (Act.), k in a., 4/10/17 (att. 2nd Bn.).
Glass, James Fraser, 2/Lt., d. of w., 26/4/15.
Glass, John Meldrum, 2/Lt (Tp.), k. in a., 25/10/18.
3 Gourlay, John Norman, 2/Lt., k. in a., 1/7/16.
9 Graham, Kenneth Stuart, 2/Lt., k. in a., 24/3/18.
10 Grant, Kenneth Henry, 2/Lt. (Tp.), k. in a., 26/8/16.
7 Grant, William Hugh, 2/Lt., k. in a, 29/9/15.
3 Grierson, Stanley Virtue, 2/Lt., k. in a., 31/8/18.
2 Grove, Philip Cranston, 2/Lt., k. in a., 11/4/17.
Gunn, David, Lt. (Tp.), k. in a., 13/10/17 (att. 7th Bn.).
1 Haggart, David, Lt, k. in a., 14/6/18.
10 Haldane, Arthur Cuthbert, 2/Lt. (Tp.), k. in a., 14/8/16.
3 Harper, Hugo Alfred, 2/Lt., k. in a., 15/4/18 (att. 2nd Bn.).
2 Harvey, James, 2/Lt., k. in a., 1/7/16.
2 Harvey, James, 2/Lt (Tp.), d. of w., 26/2/17.
Harvey, John Lawrence, 2/Lt. (Tp.), k. in a., 24/4/17 (att. 4th Bn.).
9 Hay, James Henry Webster, T/Capt. & Adjt., k. in a., 30/11/15.
3 Hemingway, James, 2/Lt., k. in a., 9/5/15 (att. 1st Bn.).
Hepburn, Malcolm Arnold, 2/Lt., k. in a., 30/11/14.
Hepburn, William Duncan, Capt., k. in a., 28/4/15 (att. 5/R. Scots).

Hipkin, Henry James, 2/Lt. (Tp.), k. in a., 17/7/18.
7 Holmes, William Henry, 2/Lt. (Tp.), k. in a., 15/12/17.
4 Horn, Robert, D.S.O., M.C., Lt.-Col. (Tp.), k. in a., 18/4/18 (att. 7th Bn.).
3 Horne, Thomas Wardlaw, 2/Lt., k. in a., 22/8/17 (att. 8th Bn.).
Jackson, Edward Fergusson, M.C., Lt. (T/Capt.), d. of w., 22/9/18.
9 Jackson, Robert, 2/Lt. (Tp.), k. in a., 13/4/18
Jameson, Harry Roderick Victor, 2/Lt., k. in a., 11/4/17.
8 Jameson, Ian Herbert Sydney, Capt. (Tp.), k. in a., 23/4/17.
7 Johnston, Robert Graham, Lt., k. in a., 18/7/16.
9 Keating, William Britten, M.C., Capt. (Tp.), died, 11/10/18.
2 Kennedy, Humfrey Hays, Major (A/Lt.-Col.), k. in a., 29/7/18 (att. 8th Bn.).
8 Kennedy, John Edwin, Lt. (Tp.), k. in a., 25/9/15.
9 Kennedy, John Murray Stewart, Lt. (Tp.), k. in a., 10/8/15.
7 Kerr-Clark, St. Ruan Robertson, Capt. (Tp.), k. in a., 25/9/15.
Kirkcaldy, Charles Henry, 2/Lt., k. in a., 10/3/15.
Lambroughton, Matthew, 2/Lt. (Tp.), died, 16/11/18.
2 Lancaster, Thomas Erwin, 2/Lt., k. in a., 1/7/16.
Latta, Robert William Campbell, 2/Lt. (Tp.), d. of w., 22/10/17.
10 Lawson, John Lawson, 2/Lt. (Tp.), k. in a., 14/10/16.
Little, Adam, 2/Lt. (Tp.), k. in a., 21/7/18.
3 Logan, Robert, 2/Lt., k. in a., 12/10/17 (att. 7th Bn.).
Low, James Morrison, Lt., k. in a., 1/7/16 (and M.G.C.).
Lumsden, Bertie Noel, Capt., k. in a., 23/4/15.
Macandrew, Ian Maclean, Lt., k. in a., 25/12/14.
Macaulay, Bruce Wallace, 2/Lt., k. in a., 3/5/17.
3 Macaulay, Horace, Lt., k. in a., 25/4/18 (att. 7th Bn.).
McCallion, Frank Mungo, M.C., Lt. (Tp.), k. in a., 20/7/18.
2 MacCullock, Sigurd Harold, 2/Lt., d. of w., 20/12/15.
3 McDermott, Robert Keith, Capt., k. in a., 20/9/18 (att. 1st Bn.).
Macdonald, Hector Robert, 2/Lt., k. in a., 22/2/17.
3 Macdonald, William Francis, M.C., 2/Lt., k. in a., 1/9/18 (att. 2nd Bn.).
McDougall, Duncan Albert Herbert, 2/Lt., k. in a., 9/5/15.
9 McDougall, John MacColl, 2/Lt., k. in a., 26/3/18.
1 McEwan, George Cameron, 2/Lt. (Tp.), k. in a., 9/4/17.
10 McGibbon, Richard Forsyth 2/Lt. (Tp.), k. in a., 23/4/17.
McGillivray, John, 2/Lt., k in a., 14/7/16.
8 MacGregor, George, 2/Lt., k. in a., 25/9/15.
10 McJanet, William Robert Benjamin, Capt. (Tp.), k. in a., 14/7/16.
1 McKay, Edward Horatio, Lt., d. of w., 21/9/18.
3 Mackenzie, Alistair, 2/Lt., k. in a., 24/3/18 (att. 9th Bn.).
2 Mackenzie, Alexander Kenneth, 2/Lt., k. in a., 1/9/18.
Mackenzie, Donald Charles, Lt., d. of w., 20/1/15.
2 Mackenzie, Francis Ramsay, 2/Lt., k. in a., 1/7/16.
Mackenzie, George Laing, M.C., 2/Lt. (Tp.), d. of w., 13/4/18 (att. 1/4 Bn.).
Mackenzie, Gilbert Marshall, Capt., k. in a., 21/4/16.
10 McKenzie, James, 2/Lt. (Tp.), k. in a., 30/10/15 (att. 8th Bn.).
Mackenzie, Jack Ronald Lewes, Lt., k. in a., 21/4/17.
Mackenzie, Keith, Bethune, Capt., k. in a., 12/11/14.
Mackenzie, Murray Mitchell, 2/Lt. (Tp.), d. of w., 21/11/16.
8 Mackenzie, Richard Devon Samuels, 2/Lt. (Tp.), d. of w., 1/7/17.
1 McKenzie, William Sinclair, D.S.O., 2/Lt., k. in a., 21/4/17.
8 MacKinnon, John, 2/Lt. (Tp.), k. in a., 21/4/18.
3 V.C. Mackintosh, Donald, Lt., k. in a., 11/4/17.
MacLachlan, Kenneth Douglas Mackenzie, Capt., d. of w., 27/4/15.
7 McLaughiin, Edward Archibald Crofton, 2/Lt. (Tp.), k. in a., 9/11/15.
3 McLaughlin, Hubert Guy Bromilow, 2/Lt., d. of w., 12/10/16 (att. 7th Bn.).
3 MacLean, Raymond Alastair, 2/Lt. (Tp.), k. in a., 13/11/16 (att. 6th Bn.).
Macleod, John, Lt. (Tp.), k. in a., 6/1/16.
8 Macmillan, Cameron, T/Lt., A/Capt., k. in a., 22/8/17.
2 Macmillan, Robert Alexander Cameron, 2/Lt. (Tp.), k. in a., 11/4/17.
3 Macpherson, Maximillian, Capt., k. in a., 4/10/17 (att. 1st Bn.).
7 Macpherson, R. D. M., 2/Lt., k. in a., 25/10/15.
3 Macrae, Duncan Mackenzie, 2/Lt., k. in a., 4/10/17 (att. 2nd Bn.).
8 Macrae, Frank Laing, 2/Lt., k. in a., 25/9/15.
2 Macvicar, Neil, 2/Lt. (Tp.), d. of w., 4/5/17 (att. 1/6 Bn.).
Macwatt, Norman Ian, Lt., k. in a., 1/7/16.
3 Maitland, William Ebenezer, 2/Lt., d. of w., 24/12/14 (att. R. Hrs.).
Marion, Donald, 2/Lt., k. in a., 9/5/15.
Martin, Edward James, 2/Lt. (Tp.), d. of w., 21/12/17 (att. 1/4 Bn.).
Marvin, Donald, 2/Lt., k. in a., 9/5/15.
Matheson, Andrew Scott, 2/Lt. (Tp.), d. of w., 10/4/17.
3 Matheson, Ian Kenneth, Lt., A/Capt., d. of w., 13/5/17 (att. 2nd Bn.).
Mauchline, Allan Bryce, 2/Lt. (Tp.), k. in a., 14/10/18 (att. 9th Bn.).
3 Maxwell, Robert Greenwood, Capt. (Tp.), k. in a., 7/1/16.
3 Maxwell, William Nisbet, 2/Lt., k. in a., 12/10/16 (att. 7th Bn.).
Methven, David George, Capt., k. in a., 20/10/14.
Middleton, William Archie Arbuthnot, Capt., k. in a., 25/4/15.
8 Millar, Robert Curle, Lt. (Tp.), k. in a., 25/9/15.
2 Monteith, William Albert Robertson, 2/Lt., d. of w., 2/9/18.
9 Moodie, Harry Morton, 2/Lt., killed, 16/9/18 (and R.A.F.).
8 Moodie, John, 2/Lt. (Tp.), d. of w., 27/8/17.
7 Morrison, Samuel Alexander, 2/Lt. (Tp.), k. in a., 3/5/17.
2 Munro, Hector Charles Seymour, M.C., Capt., k. in a., 23/10/18.
8 Munro, Henry Fraser, Capt. (Tp.), d. of w., 29/9/15.
7 Munro, Thomas MacKay, 2/Lt. (Tp.), k. in a., 25/9/15.
Murchison, Kenneth Bickersteth, 2/Lt., k. in a., 22/8/17.
8 Murray, James Brash, 2/Lt. (Tp.), k. in a., 21/5/16.
Murray, John Robertson, 2/Lt. (Tp.), d. of w., 18/9/17 (att. 9th Bn.).
Murray, Rupert Auriol Conaut, Capt., d. of w., 11/3/15.
7 Murray, William Grant, 2/Lt., k. in a., 16/4/18.
7 Nichol, Robert, Lt. (Tp.), k. in a., 11/10/17.
8 Nicholson, John Maurice Leonard, 2/Lt. (Tp.), k. in a., 11/7/16.
1 Norbury, Robert Fiddes, Lt. (Tp.), d. of w., 4/10/17 (att. 2nd Bn.).
3 Orr, Jack Alexander Anderson, Lt., k. in a., 12/6/18.
7 Patterson, Douglas David John, 2/Lt., k. in a., 16/4/18.
Pettigrew, Thomas Thomson, 2/Lt., k. in a., 28/7/18.
Rae, James, 2/Lt. (Tp.), k. in a., 4/10/17 (att. 2nd Bn.).
8 Ravenhill, Aleck George, Capt. (Tp.), k. in a., 25/9/15.
Reid, Guy Patrick Spence, M.C., Lt., T/Capt., killed, 16/10/17 (and R.F.C.).
3 Reid, William Bacon Johnston, Capt., d. of w., 20/5/15 (att. Gordon Hrs.).
3 Rigby, Francis John, Capt., k. in a., 21/1/16 (att. 1st Bn.).
3 Ritchie, John Nevill, 2/Lt., k. in a., 21/4/16.
2 Robinson, George Thomas, 2/Lt., k. in a., 3/6/18.
3 Rose, Geoffrey Craig, 2/Lt., d. of w., 13/2/15 (att. Gordon Hrs.).
2 Rose, Hugh Price, 2/Lt., k. in a., 11/4/17.
Ross, James Graham, 2/Lt. (Tp.), k. in a., 30/12/17 (att. 7th Bn.).
8 Ross, James Hector, 2/Lt. (Tp.), k. in a., 23/4/17.
St. Clair, The Hon. Charles Henry Murray, Capt., k. in a., 20/12/14.
10 Scarth, James Charles, 2/Lt. (Tp.), k. in a., 14/7/16.
7 Scott, Robert Walter Theodore Gordon, 2/Lt. (Tp.), d. of w., 15/8/16.
3 Selby-Lowndes, Meyrick Edward, Lt., died, 27/10/18 (att. 2/Bn.).
Shackleford, Alfred Edgar John, 2/Lt., k. in a., 9/5/15.
7 Shaw, Robert Dykes Somerville, Capt. (Tp.), k. in a., 23/3/18.
2 Shaw, William, 2/Lt., k. in a., 1/7/16.
9 Simpson, James Kirk, M.C., Lt. (Tp.), k. in a., 11/4/18.
1 Smith, Donald, 2/Lt., died, 29/1/19.
Smith, Robert Paterson, M.C., 2/Lt. (Tp.), d. of w., 2/8/17.
Smith-Cumming, Alexander Mansfield, Lt., killed, 3/10/14.
Spencer, Hugh Maitland, Capt., k. in a., 25/4/15.
Squires, John Henry, 2/Lt. (Tp.), k. in a., 12/4/18 (att. 1/5 Bn.).
7 Squair, Robert Hay, Lt. (Tp.), d. of w., 13/10/17.
Stacey, John Charles, 2/Lt., k. in a., 10/4/18.
8 Stanford, James Vesey, Lt. (Tp.), k. in a., 25/9/15.
Stevens, Ernest, 2/Lt., d. of w., 2/2/15.
1 Stewart, Algernon Brigham Anstruther, D.S.O., Lt.-Col., k. in a., 24/5/16.
Stewart, Bryce, Lt., k. in a., 21/4/16.
3 Stewart, Ronald James, M.C., Lt., d. of w., 28/1/16 (att. 1st Bn.).
Stockwell, Charles Inglis, Major, d. of w., 21/10/14.
3 Straker, Kenneth, Lt., k. in a., 23/7/16.
7 Stuart, Alexander Davidson, M.C., Lt. (Tp.), k. in a., 12/10/17.
Sutherland, Walter Riddle, 2/Lt. (Tp.), k. in a., 4/10/18 (att. 8th Bn.).
7 Tarbet, William Duncan, 2/Lt. (Tp.), k. in a., 9/4/17 (att. M.G.C.).
2 Tarratt, Duncan McNeill Fox, 2/Lt., k. in a., 4/10/17.
8 Taylor, William John, Capt. (Tp.), died, 1/8/17.
10 Thomson, Alex, 2/Lt. (Tp.), d. of w., 21/4/16.
Thornhill, John Evelyn, D.S.O., Bt. Lt.-Col., died, 2/10/18 (att. Staff).
Thornton, George Muir, Capt. (Tp.), k. in a., 22/8/17.
Tran, David Rushton, 2/Lt. (Tp.), k. in a., 28/7/18 (att. 8th Bn.).
2 Tredennick, John Archibald St. Leger, Capt., k. in a., 23/7/18 (att. 1/5 Bn.).
8 Tremearne, Arthur John Newman, Major (Tp.), k. in a., 25/9/15.
8 Tremearne, William Crew, 2/Lt., k. in a., 26/9/15.
9 Tudor, Alan Roper, 2/Lt. (Tp.), k. in a., 5/6/17.
7 Vaughan, Charles Alvarez, 2/Lt., k. in a., 25/9/15.
9 Walker, Robert Hugh, Lt. (Tp.), k. in a., 9/4/17.
Webster, John Alexander Croone, 2/Lt., k. in a., 21/4/17.
Williamson, Alexander John Neeve, 2/Lt., k. in a., 14/9/14.
2 Williamson, John, 2/Lt., k. in a., 1/7/16.
Wilson, John Thomson, 2/Lt. (Tp.), k. in a., 28/1/17 (att. 8th Bn.).
3 Wilson, Robert Archibald Scarlyn, 2/Lt., k. in a., 12/10/16 (att. 7th Bn.).
Wilson, Robert Sym, Capt., k. in a., 8/11/14.
8 Wink, John Edward, 2/Lt. (Tp.), died, 21/9/16.
3 Wood, John George, M.C., Lt., A/Capt., k. in a., 4/10/17.
Wylie, Hamilton MacLaren, 2/Lt. (Tp.), k. in a., 7/1/16.

The Gordon Highlanders.

11 Alexander, Philip Mansell, 2/Lt. (Tp.), d. of w., 30/7/16 (att. 5/Bn.).
9 Allan, James Grant, Lt. (Tp.), k. in a., 25/9/15.
Anderson, Charles Edward, Capt., k. in a., 20/7/16 (att. 8/Bn.).
2 Anderson, George Ogilvie, 2/Lt., k. in a., 26/10/17.
Arnott, Laurian Anthony Deane, 2/Lt. (Tp.), k. in a., 25/9/15.
Arnott, Thomas John, 2/Lt., k. in a., 26/10/17.
8 Arthur, John, 2/Lt. (Tp.), k. in a., 26/9/15.

10 Bain, Alexander Neill, 2/Lt. (Tp.), k. in a., 19/5/16.
3 Bain, David McLaren, Capt., k. in a., 3/6/15 (att. 2/Bn.).
3 Balloch, Humphrey Colquhoun, 2/Lt., died, 2/6/15.
11 Barnes, Henry, 2/Lt. (Tp.), k. in a., 25/9/15 (att. 2nd Bn.).
Beattie, Charles, Lt. (Tp.), k. in a., 20/7/18 (att. 1/7 Bn.).
8 Begg, John Henderson, Capt., k. in a., 23/7/16.
Bell, Quentin David, 2/Lt., k. in a., 31/10/15.
2 Berry, John Anthony, 2/Lt. (Tp.), k. in a., 25/9/15.
3 Bentley, Freeland Martell, Lt., k. in a., 18/6/15 (att. 2/Bn.).
8 Beveridge, Walter Joseph Paterson, Lt. (Tp.) (Act. Capt.), k. in a., 23/10/18.
8 Birnie, William John Gordon, Lt., k. in a., 23/11/17 (B Bn. Tank Corps).
8 Black, Robert Alaister McGregor, Lt. (Tp.) (Act. Capt.), k. in a., 27/7/18.
Blair-Cunynghame, Ronald Ogilvy, Capt., d. of w., 5/5/15.
9 Blakely, John Douglas, 2/Lt. (Tp.), k. in a., 9/4/17.
1 Booth, Cecil Richard, 2/Lt. (Tp.), d. of w., 21/3/16.
1 Bothwell, Alec, M.C., Lt. (Tp.) (Act. Capt.), k. in a., 26/4/17.
Boyd, James Peter, Lt. (Tp. Capt.), k. in a., 25/9/15.
Boyd, Philip Bentinck, 2/Lt., k. in a., 13/4/17 (and R.F.C., 59th Sqd.).
8 Brooke, Cecil Rupert, 2/Lt. (Tp.), k. in a., 24/4/17.
2 Brooke, Henry Brian, Capt., d. of w., 24/7/16.
V.C. Brooke, James Anson Otho, Capt., k. in a., 29/10/14.
Brown, Allison, 2/Lt. (Tp.), k. in a., 26/10/17 (att. 2/Bn.).
3 Brown, Harold Halstead, 2/Lt., k. in a., 18/7/16 (att. 1/Bn.).
3 Brown, John Albert Hunter, Act. Capt., k. in a., 18/8/16 (att. 1/Bn.).
Bruce, Charles William, Capt., killed, 22/11/17 (and R.F.C.).
Buchan, David, Lt. (Tp.), k. in a., 9/4/17.
Buchanan, Adam Heaton, 2/Lt. (Tp.), k. in a., 5/10/18 (att. 5/Bn.).
1 Buchanan, Archibald Ure, 2/Lt. (Tp.), d. of w., 28/9/15 (att. 1/Bn.).
3 Buckingham, Aubrey Webster, Major, k. in a., 17/11/14 (att. 1/Bn.).
Buntine, Robert, 2/Lt. (Tp.), d. of w., 31/3/18 (att. 8/10 Bn.).
3 Carey, Arthur John Edward, 2/Lt., k. in a., 22/8/17 (att. 8/Bn.).
3 Carless, Hugh Dobbie, 2/Lt., d. of w., 24/4/17.
3 Chambers-Hunter, Charles Allardyce, 2/Lt., k. in a., 1/4/16 (att. 1/Bn.).
3 Christie, William, Lt. & Q.M., died, 8/11/17.
10 Christison, Robert Colin, Lt., k. in a., 25/9/17.
11 Clark, Hugh Reginald Stanley, 2/Lt. (Tp.), k. in a., 18/8/16.
1 Clark, Samuel Clarkson, Lt., d. of w., 17/9/18.
11 Cleghorn, Allan James, 2/Lt. (Tp.), died, 7/9/16 (att. 1/Bn.).
1 Cochran, Frances Alexander, 2/Lt., k. in a., 25/9/15.
1 Cochrane, Cyril, Lt., k. in a., 25/9/15.
9 Cowper, Gordon, Capt., died, 2/2/19.
3 Craig, Archibald, M.C., Lt. (Act. Capt.), k. in a., 23/3/18 (att. T.M.B.).
Crichton, Robert Renfrew, 2/Lt., k. in a., 20/11/17 (att. 6/Bn.).
3 Currie, William Thomson, Capt., d. of w., 31/7/18 (att. 1/5 Bn.).
11 Davidson, Andrew Pearson, 2/Lt. (Tp.), k. in a., 5/9/16.
Davidson, Archibald Randall, Capt., k. in a., 15/6/17.
Davidson, Charles, 2/Lt., k. in a., 26/10/17.
2 Davidson, William Adrian, 2/Lt., d. of w., 2/7/16.
12 Davitt, Felix William, 2/Lt. (Tp.), k. in a., 12/4/18.
11 Dawson, John, 2/Lt. (Tp.), k. in a., 25/9/15 (att. 4/Bn.).
11 Dippie, Harry Peckham, 2/Lt. (Tp.), k. in a., 18/7/16.
3 Dobbie, John Shedden, Lt., k. in a., 5/10/17.
3 Dobie, Kirkpatrick Smith, 2/Lt., k. in a., 26/10/17 (att. 2/Bn.).
Dobie, William Findlay Robertson, Lt., k. in a., 14/12/14.
1 Dove, Patrick Edward, Lt., k. in a., 14/6/17.
8 Drover, Charles Peacock, Lt. (Tp.), k. in a., 23/3/18.
Duff, John Creran, Lt., k. in a., 10/6/15.
Duthie, Bertie, 2/Lt. (Tp.), k. in a., 23/10/18.
10 Elliott, Oswald Carr Finnes, 2/Lt. (Tp.), k. in a., 14/10/16.
9 Elrington-Bisset, Water Faviere, 2/Lt. (Tp.), k. in a., 25/9/15.
10 Farquhar-Thompson, Douglas, 2/Lt. (Tp.), k. in a., 13/10/15.
2 Fearnley, William, 2/Lt., k. in a., 1/7/16.
8 Ferguson, Alexander Lundie Hunter, Lt. (Tp.), k. in a., 23/7/16.
Fiennes, John Eustace, Capt., d. of w., 18/6/17.
3 Finlay, Thomas Pretsell, Lt., k. in a., 25/9/15 (att. 2/Bn.).
Fleming, James Sword, 2/Lt. (Tp.), d. of w., 29/9/17.
Fraser, James Howie, Lt., k. in a., 29/10/14.
3 Fraser, Patrick Grant, 2/Lt., k. in a., 3/5/17 (att. 8/Royal Highrs.).
3 Fraser, The Hon. Simon, 2/Lt., killed, 29/10/14 (att. 2/Bn.).
1 Fraser, William, 2/Lt. (Act. Capt.), k. in a., 9/4/17.
1 Gammell, Henry Stobart, M.C., Lt. (Act. Capt.), k. in a., 31/8/18.
Garrard, Frederick George, M.C., 2/Lt., d. of w., 22/5/18.
2 Giles, Geoffrey, 2/Lt. (Tp.), k. in a., 1/7/16.
Gordon, Alister Fraser, C.M.G., D.S.O., Temp. Brig.-Gen., d. of w, 31/7/17 (153rd Bde. Staff).
Gordon, Bertram Gorges Reginald, D.S.O., Temp. Lt.-Col., k. in a., 20/7/16.
3 Gordon, Colin Graham, 2/Lt., k. in a., 1/7/16.
8 Gordon, Gilbert Thomas, 2/Lt. (Tp.), d. of w., 28/9/15.
Gordon, Lewis, D.S.O., Capt., d. of w., 18/10/15.
3 Gordon, Maitland Lockhart, Capt., k. in a., 7/5/17.
8 Gordon, Robert Charles Lowther, 2/Lt. (Tp.), d. of w., 30/9/15.
3 Gordon, Ronald Henry, Capt., k. in a., 18/7/16 (att. 1/Bn.).
8 Gordon, Vivian, Capt. (Tp.), k. in a., 25/9/15.
8 Gordon, William Hyde Eagleson, Lt. (Tp.), d. of w., 30/9/15.
3 Gordon-Duff, Lachlan, Capt., k. in a., 24/10/14 (att. 1/Bn.).
Graham, Archibald Stuart Bulloch, Lt., k. in a., 31/10/14.
Graham, Malcolm G., M.C., 2/Lt. (Act. Capt.), k. in a., 26/10/17.
3 Grierson, John Henry Clifford, 2/Lt., k. in a., 31/7/17.
Griffin, Cecil Scott James, Capt., killed, 11/10/17.
1 Haig, Alexander Weir, M.M., 2/Lt., d. of w., 17/10/18 (att. 1/5th Bn.).
Hamilton, Mervyn James, Capt., d. of w., 28/11/14.
3 Harrison, William, 2/Lt., d. of w., 5/7/16, (att. 2/Seaf. Highrs.).
2 Harvey, Alex Scott, Lt. (Tp.), d. of w., 29/3/18.
2 Harvie, Eric Fulton, M.C., Lt., k. in a., 15/6/18.
3 Hay, Alfred Chalmers, 2/Lt., k. in a., 9/4/17.
Henderson, Bertram Mackay, M.C., Lt. (Act. Capt.), d. of w., 7/4/18 (att. 7/Bn.) (P.O.W.).
Henderson, G. A. F., Lt., died, 4/7/18 (att. R.A.F.).
8 Herbert, Hubert Leslie, Lt. (Tp.), k. in a., 7/8/15.
3 Hill, Sydney Moir Byres, 2/Lt., k. in a., 25/9/15 (att. Cam. Highrs.).
Horsley, Oswald, Capt., killed, 19/8/18 (and R.A.F.).
Hotchkis, Gilbert, 2/Lt. (Tp.), k. in a., 23/4/17.
Howard, Herbert Arthur, 2/Lt. (Tp.), d. of w., 29/9/18 (att. 1/Bn.).
Howell, Francis Slinger, 2/Lt., k. in a., 2/8/17 (att. 8/10).
8 Hughes, Daniel, 2/Lt., k. in a., 23/7/16.
Huntly, Louis Francis, 2/Lt., k. in a., 26/4/17.
9 Hutchison, John McMaster, Lt. (Tp.), k. in a., 22/10/16.
3 Hyslop, John Wallett, 2/Lt., k. in a., 26/10/17 (att. 2/Bn.).
8 Inglis, Alexander, Lt. (Tp.), k. in a., 11/4/17.
8 Ireland, William Farquhar, 2/Lt. (Tp.), k. in a., 9/4/17.
Kay, Walter Haddow, 2/Lt. (Tp.), k. in a., 23/3/18 (att. 6/Bn.).
11 Keith, Alexander Gill, Temp. Capt., k. in a., 26/11/15 (att. 1/Bn.).
1 Kennedy, Donald, 2/Lt., k. in a., 30/8/18.
Ker, Arthur Milford, Capt., k. in a., 14/10/14.
9 Kershaw, Kenneth Robert Beresford, 2/Lt. (Tp.), k. in a., 25/9/15.
2 King, David Taylor, 2/Lt. (Tp.), k. in a., 1/7/16.
10 Knowles, Harold Leslie, 2/Lt., k. in a., 30/1/17.
Latta, Charles Keith, Lt., k. in a., 29/11/15.
1 Lawrence, Alexander, Temp. Capt. & Adjt., d. of w., 19/9/16 (att. 10/Bn. R. W. Surr. Regt.).
11 Lawson, Arthur Cresswell, 2/Lt. (Tp.), k. in a., 19/11/16 (att. Scot. Rifles).
1 Lawson, Robert Wybergh Gordon, 2/Lt. (Tp.), k. in a., 18/7/16.
3 Lee, Sidney Edward, 2/Lt., k. in a., 11/4/17 (att. 1/Bn.).
3 Letters, Thomas Arthur, Lt., k. in a., 13/3/15.
8 Little, John, 2/Lt. (Tp.), k. in a., 24/4/17.
1 Low, David Carmichael, 2/Lt., k. in a., 18/7/16.
1 Lumsden, Charles Ramsay, Capt., k. in a., 26/8/14.
1 Lyall, James, 2/Lt. (Tp.), d. of w., 14/11/16.
9 Lyle, Hedley Robert, 2/Lt. (Tp.), k. in a., 24/5/16.
Lyon, Alexander Patrick Francis, Lt., k. in a., 9/9/14.
Macbean, Duncan Gillies Forbes, Temp. Capt., k. in a., 18/6/15.
McCaskill, Kenneth, Lt. (Tp.), k. in a., 27/9/18.
2 Macdonald, George Harper, 2/Lt. (Tp.) (Act. Capt.), k. in a., 5/9/16.
10 Macdougall, Stewart, Temp. Lt.-Col., k. in a., 21/7/15.
McEwan, Fraser, 2/Lt. (Tp.), k. in a., 24/3/18 (att. 44 T.M.By.).
McGechan, George Ross, 2/Lt. (Tp.), k. in a., 28/3/18.
9 MacGregor, Colin Alexander, 2/Lt. (Tp.), k. in a., 26/9/15.
McGregor, Donald Hamilton, 2/Lt. (Tp.), k. in a., 23/8/18.
McGrigor, James Neil Grant, 2/Lt., d. of w., 7/11/14.
1 McIntosh, James, 2/Lt. (Tp.), k. in a., 13/11/16.
8 MacKay, Ian Forbes, Tp. Capt., k. in a., 25/9/15.
3 MacKay, James, Lt., k. in a., 25/9/15 (att. 1/Bn.).
3 MacKay, William Gidden, 2/Lt., k. in a., 25/9/15.
8 MacKenzie, George Arthur, 2/Lt. (Tp.), k. in a., 25/9/15.
MacKenzie, Percy Melville, Capt., k. in a., 6/10/18.
3 MacKinnon, Francis James Ogilvie, Capt., k. in a., 16-17/5/15 (att. 2/Bn.).
1 MacLean, David, 2/Lt., k. in a., 14/7/18.
1 McLennan, Farquhar John, 2/Lt. (Tp.), k. in a., 18/8/16.
3 MacLennan, Iain Donald Forrest, 2/Lt., k. in a., 12/5/17 (att. 1/Bn.).
8 MacLeod, David, D.S.O. (Tp.) Lt.-Col., died, 19/12/17.
8 McNaught, Douglas Ramson, 2/Lt. (Tp.), killed, 27/3/17.
3 McNeill, Nigel Lorne, 2/Lt., k. in a., 1/7/16 (att. 2/Bn.).
3 McPherson, Ian Charles, 2/Lt. k. in a., 25/9/15 (att. 2/Bn.).
11 MacPherson, John Cook, 2/Lt. (Tp.), k. in a., 25/9/15 (att. 1/Bn.).
8 MacPherson, Robert David, 2/Lt. (Tp.), drowned, 6/6/16 (enemy action).
McTavish, James Duncan, 2/Lt., k. in a., 23/4/17 (att. 7/Bn.).
9 MacWhirter, Thomas, M.C., Major, k. in a., 27/4/17.
MacWilliam, James Julian Gordon, Lt. (Tp.), k. in a., 14/12/14.
10 Maitland-Makgill-Crichton, Charles Julian, Major (Tp.), k. in a., 25-27/9/15.
8 Martin, John, M.C., Capt., k. in a., 9/4/17.
8 Maxwell, William Gardner, M.C., Bt. Major, died, 11/12/18 (G.S.O., attd. 3/Corps School).
Mearnes, Henry Gould, 2/Lt. (Tp.), d. of w., 20/8/16.
11 Millar, Douglas Archibald, 2/Lt. (Tp.), k. in a., 18/-/16 (att. 1/Bn.).
3 Miller, Edwin George, 2/Lt., k. in a., 23/4/17 (att. 7/Bn.).
10 Milne, George Smith Mitchell, Lt. (Tp.), k. in a., 14/10/17.
Milne, William, 2/Lt., k. in a., 27/9/15.
3 Monteith, George Michael, Capt., k. in a., 25/9/15 (att. 1/Bn.).
3 More, Eric Roy, Lt., k. in a., 27/10/18 (att. 2/Bn.).

Muir, John Hugh, Lt. (Tp.), k. in a., 26/9/17.
Mulock, Edward Ross, 2/Lt., k. in a., 11/3/15.
3 Murray, William Edward, Capt., k. in a., 17/9/14.
Mutch, George, D.S.O., Lt. (Tp.), k. in a., 6/7/17.
1/5 Napier, Egbert, Major, k. in a., 13/11/16 (Res. of Offrs.).
Nicholson, Walter Alan, 2/Lt. (Tp.), d. of w., 27/9/15.
3 Ogilvie, Andrew Maxwell, 2/Lt., k. in a., 5/10/17.
1 Oxley, Robert Duncombe (Act. Major), Capt., k. in a., 6/9/16.
3 Paton, Norman Macalister, 2/Lt., d. of w., 16/7/17 (att. 1/Bn.).
3 Pender, James Granger Gailes, 2/Lt., k. in a., 11/3/15 (att. 2/Bn.).
Pirie, Alexander, 2/Lt., d. of w., 13/12/14.
3 Plummer, John Humphrey, 2/Lt., died, 10/8/18.
3 Powell, Leonard Maurice, 2/Lt., k. in a., 17/6/15 (att. 1/Bn.).
3 Price, George Bernard Locking, 2/Lt., d. of w., 23/8/17 (att. 8/Bn.).
2 Pringle-Pattison, John Ronald Seth, 2/Lt., k. in a., 5/9/16.
3 Puntan, Herbert Forbes, 2/Lt., k. in a., 9/4/17 (att. 2/Bn.).
3 Ramsay, Louis Nail Griffitt, 2/Lt., k. in a., 21/3/15 (att. 2/Bn.).
1 Reece, Humphrey Stanley, Lt. (Tp.), d. of w., 2/4/16.
3 Reid, Hugh, 2/Lt., k. in a., 23/7/18 (att. 1/6/Bn.).
9 Reid, Robert, 2/Lt. (Tp.), k. in a., 22/5/16.
Reid, William John, 2/Lt. (Tp.), d. of w., 26/11/17.
Richardson, Angus MacDonald, 2/Lt., k. in a., 25/9/15.
Richmond, Leslie, Lt., k. in a., 10/9/14.
10 Riddell, Robert Mackie, 2/Lt. (Tp.), killed, 1/7/16.
2 Ritchie, John Waugh, 2/Lt. (Tp.), k. in a., 23/4/17 (att. 7/Bn.).
3 Roberts, Frederick Roberts, 2/Lt., d. of w., 7/9/16.
Robertson, Charles Thomas Andrews, Capt. (Act. Major), d. of w., 23/3/18 (P. of W.).
10 Robertson, Gordon, 2/Lt. (Tp.), k. in a., 17/11/15.
9 Robertson, James Duncan, M.C., Lt. (Tp. Act. Capt.), d. of w., 27/8/17.
3 Robertson, Leslie Johnston Walker, M.C., Lt., k. in a., 3/10/17.
1 Robertson, Matthew Struan, Capt. (Tp.), k. in a., 2/3/16.
11 Robertson, William George, Lt., d. of w., 15/12/17 (att. 156th M.G.C.).
Robertson, William Stewart, 2/Lt., k. in a., 31/10/14.
3 Ross, George Duncan, 2/Lt., k. in a., 9/4/17 (att. 8/Royal Highrs.).
2 Ross, Hugh Alexander, D.S.O., Major (Act. Lt.-Col.), k. in a., 27/10/18.
Ross, William Munro, Lt., k. in a., 11/3/15.
Sandeman, William Alastair Fraser, Lt., died, 19/10/14.
Sanderson, Christopher, D.S.O., 2/Lt. (Tp.), k. in a., 18/6/17.
8 Scott, Archibald, 2/Lt. (Tp.), k. in a., 25/4/17.
11 Sinclair, Luke Taylor, 2/Lt. (Tp.), k. in a., 2/3/16.
Smith, Alexander Will, M.C., 2/Lt., k. in a., 21/3/18 (att. 1/5/Bn.).
11 Smith, Campbell Lindsay, Lt. (Tp.), k. in a., 10/11/15 (att. 8/Bn.).
Smith, George Buchanan, 2/Lt., k. in a., 25/9/15 (att. 2/Bn.).
10 Smith, James, 2/Lt. (Tp.), k. in a., 9/4/17.
Smith, William Watson, 2/Lt. (Tp.), d. of w., 18/10/16.
Spark, Archibald Charles, 2/Lt. (Tp.), k. in a., 31/7/17.
Stansfield, John Raymond Evelyn, D.S.O., T/Lt.-Col. (Major), d. of w., 28/9/15.
11 Stocks, Murdoch, 2/Lt. (Tp), d. of w., 10/4/16 (att. 8/Bn.).
3 Stranack, Frederick George, Lt., k. in a., 27/7/15 (att. 1/Bn.).
4 Sutherland, Goodwin, 2/Lt., k. in a., 9/4/17.
3 Sykes, Jack A., 2/Lt., killed, 4/10/18 (and R.A.F.).
2 Terris, William, 2/Lt. (Temp.), d. of w., 3/4/17.
Thorburn, Christopher Cowan, 2/Lt. (Tp. Lt.), k. in a., 14/6/17
Tindall, Alexander George, 2/Lt. (Tp.), k. in a., 8/10/18 (att. 1/5/Bn.).
1 Trotter, James Keith, Lt., d. of w., 26/8/14.
Turnbull, Dudley Ralph, D.S.O., Br. Major (Act. Lt.-Col.), k. in a., 1/10/17 (att. 20th Manch. Regt.).
Udny, George Richard Murray, 2/Lt., d. of w., 17/5/15.
2 Uniacke, Henry Percy, C.B., Lt.-Col., k. in a., 13/3/15.
6 Usher, John Milne, 2/Lt. (Tp.), k. in a., 25/9/15.
10 Vade-Walpole, Thomas Henry Bourke, Lt. (Tp.), k. in a., 20/9/15.
Walker, Robert Jardine, Capt., k. in a., 25/9/15 (S.R.) (att. 1/Bn.).
8 Watson, Herbert Sanderson, Capt. (Tp.), k. in a., 26/9/15.
2 Watson, John Christopher, Capt., k. in a., 26/9/17
2 Watson, Sydney Fairweather, 2/Lt., k. in a., 6/9/16.
3 Watt, Douglas Gordon, 2/Lt., k. in a., 2/3/16
13 Watt, Percy Bryden, Lt., k. in a., 14/4/18 (att. 13 M.G.C.).
3 Webster, Alf. Alexander, 2/Lt., d. of w., 24/8/15 (att. 1/Bn.).
3 White, John, 2/Lt., k. in a., 1/7/16.
Williamson, John Maurice, 2/Lt., k. in a., 16/5/15.
Wilson, Charles, 2/Lt., k. in a., 9/5/17.
Wilson, Hugh Young, 2/Lt. (Tp. Lt.), k. in a., 14/6/17.
3 Wilson, James (Act. Capt.), k. in a., 15/6/18 (att. 1/Bn.).
Withey, Ralph Wallace, Lt., died, 2/1/18.
1 Wright, Harry William, 2/Lt., k. in a., 19/12/15.
2 Yule, John, M.C., Lt., d. of w., 25/12/17.

The Queen's Own Cameron Highlanders.

5 Aitken, James, 2/Lt., d. of w., 3/5/17.
3 Allan, Peter, 2/Lt., d. of w., 19/7/18 (att. 5/Bn.).
7 Anderson, David, M.C., T/2/Lt. (A/Capt.), k. in a., 23/4/17 (att. 44 T.M.B.).
Anderson, James Richard Haig, Lt., k. in a., 11/5/15.
7 Anderson, John William, 2/Lt. (Tp.), k. in a., 17/8/16.
6 Antrobus, Cecil Hugh, Capt. (Tp.), k. in a., 26/9/15.
3 Archdall, Nicholas James Mervyn, Major, k. in a., 25/9/15 (att. 5/Bn.).
Baird, Percy Thomas Charles, Major, k. in a., 15/2/15.
1 Barber, Gordon, Capt. (Tp.), k. in a., 22/7/16.
7 Barron, James, Major (Tp.), d. of w., 27/9/15.
6 Begbie, Alfred Vincent, 2/Lt. (Tp.), d. of w., 11/4/17.
6 Biggar, Kenneth, 2/Lt. (Tp.), k. in a., 26/9/15.
5 Black, Allan Maclean, 2/Lt. (Tp.), k. in a., 18/7/16.
3 Blane, Malcolm Gilbert Stewart, Lt., k. in a., 25/9/15 (att. 5/Bn.).
6 Blyth, Robert Paterson, 2/Lt., k. in a., 10/7/17.
6 Borthwick, George Williamson, 2/Lt. (Tp.), k. in a., 28/6/16
5 Boulton, Christian Harold Ernest, Lt. (Tp.), k. in a., 12/10/17 (Staff).
Bower, Donald Robert, 2/Lt. (Tp.), k. in a., 20/9/18 (Res.).
1 Boyd, Thomas Cecil, Lt., d. of w., 21/7/17.
5 Brereton, Charles MacLeod, 2/Lt. (Tp.), k. in a., 25/9/15.
3 Brodie, Douglas Edward, Capt. (Tp.), k. in a., 17/8/16 (att. 1/Bn.).
Brodie, Ewen James, Capt., k. in a., 12/11/14.
Brown, Donald Morton, Lt. (Tp.), k. in a., 17/10/18 (Res., att. 1/Bn.)
Brown, Samuel, 2/Lt. (Tp.), d. of w., 27/9/18 (Res., att. 11/Bn.).
3 Cadenhead, George, 2/Lt., k. in a., 10/5/15.
Caldwell, John Hay, Lt., died, 24/1/18 (att. R.F.C.).
3 Cameron, Archibald, Capt., k. in a., 3/5/17.
Cameron, Allan George, Capt., k. in a., 25/9/14.
7 Cameron, Francis Blake, Lt. (Tp.), d. of w., 19/8/16.
Cameron, Hector William Lovett, 2/Lt., k. in a., 14/9/14.
3 Cameron, James Alstair Gordon, 2/Lt., k. in a., 18/11/16.
Cameron, John Gilmour, 2/Lt., k. in a., 9/11/16 (and R.F.C.).
2 Cameron, Kenneth, M.C., Capt. (T/Major), k. in a., 26/9/18.
Cameron, Napier Charles Gordon, Capt., k. in a., 26/9/14.
5 Cameron, Neil Kennedy, Capt., k. in a., 25/9/15.
Cameron, Roy Douglas, Lt. (Tp.), k. in a., 26/10/15.
5 Cameron, Thomas Wright, 2/Lt. (Tp.), k. in a., 17/10/16.
1 Cameron, William, Lt., d. of w., 27/10/15.
5 Cameron, William, 2/Lt. (Tp.), k. in a., 17/6/18.
6 Cameron, Waldo Hastie, 2/Lt. (Tp.), k. in a., 11/4/17.
6 Campbell, Sir Archibald Augustus Ava (Bart.), Lt. (Tp.), k. in a., 9/5/16.
3 Campbell, C. C. K., Capt., k. in a., 28/9/15 (att. Army Cyc. Cps.).
Campbell, Claude Henry, D.S.O., Lt.-Col. (Tp.), k. in a., 14/3/16 (att. 12/W. York. R.).
Campbell, Ian Patrick, 2/Lt., k. in a., 9/5/15.
5 Campbell-Orde, J. V., Lt. (Tp.), died, 14/10/17.
6 Carmichael, Andrew Gemmell, 2/Lt. (Tp.), k. in a., 11/4/17.
6 Carrick, John, Lt. (Tp.), k. in a., 31/7/17.
7 Chapman, Samuel Eric, 2/Lt., k. in a., 25/9/15.
Coats, Thomas, 2/Lt. (Tp.), k. in a., 30/9/18.
Collinson, George Edward Cleather, Lt., killed, 13/4/17 (and R.F.C.).
7 Crawford, James, 2/Lt. (Tp.), d. of w., 19/7/16.
1 Davidson, George William Smyttan, 2/Lt., k. in a., 25/9/16.
3 Dempster, Francis Erskine, 2/Lt., k. in a., 23/7/16.
7 Denholm, Thomas Stobie, 2/Lt. (Tp.), d. of w., 5/4/18 (P. of W.).
5 Dewar, Ian Dalrymple, Capt. (Tp.), k. in a., 16/3/16.
Dickson, John Hamilton, 2/Lt., k. in a., 14/9/14.
8 Donaldson, Alexander Cleveland, Capt. (Tp.), k. in a., 6/8/15 (att. 1/Essex).
6 V.C. Douglas-Hamilton, Angus Falconer, T/Lt.-Col., k. in a., 26/9/15.
7 Douglas-Hamilton, Leslie Reginald Coventry, Capt. (Tp.), k. in a., 25/7/16 (att. Lanc. Fus.).
1 Downie, Reginald Alexander Forbes, 2/Lt., d. of w., 24/3/18 (att. 3/Bn.).
3 Drummond, Douglas Torrie, 2/Lt., d. of w., 3/5/17 (att. 5/Batt.).
6 Drummond, Robert Kenneth, M.C., Capt. (Tp.), d. of w., 24/7/18.
5 Duff, Beauchamp Patrick, 2/Lt. (Tp.), k. in a., 25/9/15.
5 Dunsmure, Colin Hamilton Terrot, 2/Lt., k. in a., 25/9/15.
Dunsmure, Henry Alexander Henderson, Lt., k. in a., 20/2/15.
5 Eadie, William, Capt. (Tp.), k. in a., 18/10/16.
5 Ellice, Alexander, Capt. (Tp.), d. of w., 18/10/16.
Elliot, Thomas Archibald Scott, 2/Lt. (Tp.), d. of w., 6/8/17 (att. 7/Bn.).
6 Farquhar, James Edward Mainwaring, Major (Tp.), k. in a., 15/9/16.
1 Fergusson, Douglas Herbert Lewin, Lt., d. of w., 2/2/16.
5 Foulis, James Bell, Capt. (Tp.), k. in a., 18/10/16.
Fowler, Alan Arthur, Capt., k. in a., 28/4/15.
2 Fraser, Andrew, M.C., Capt., d. of w., 20/4/18.
Fraser, Percy William Norman, D.S.O., Capt., k. in a., 22/2/15.
5 Fulton, James, 2/Lt. (Tp.), k. in a., 12/10/16 (att. 26 Trench Mortar Bty.).
Gammie, Herbert Forsyth, Lt. (Tp.), k. in a., 14/9/18 (att. 7/N. Staff. R.).
Gearey, Edward, 2/Lt., k. in a., 1/1/15.
3 Gemmell, Stuart Sterling, 2/Lt., k. in a., 21/3/18 (att. 7/Bn.).
3 Gibson, James Guthrie, 2/Lt., d. of w., 12/9/17 (att. 6/Bn.) (P. of W.).
2 Giffen, James, M.C., Lt. (A/Capt.), d. of w., 22/12/16.
12 Gilhespy, John William, 2/Lt. (Tp.), k. in a., 20/7/16 (att 1/Bn.).
Gordon, Arthur Forbes, 2/Lt. (Tp.), d. of w., 18/4/18.
Gordon, William, Lt., k. in a., 9/5/15.
7 Goudie, Humphrey Blaikie, 2/Lt. (Tp.), k. in a., 17/8/16.
5 Gourlay, William Norris, Capt. (Tp.), d. of w., 6/6/17.
1 Graeme, Laurence Oliphant, C.M.G., Lt.-Col. (Tp.), k. in a., 10/3/16.
Graham, John Wilfrid, Lt., k. in a., 21/12/14 (att. 3/H.L.I.).
Graham, Peter, Capt., k. in a., 30/8/18 (att. 1/K.A.R.).

Grant, D., 2/Lt., k. in a., 28/4/15.
5 Grant, William St. Clair, M.C., Capt. (Tp.), k. in a., 26/9/18.
5 Gray, David William, 2/Lt. (Tp.), k. in a., 18/7/16.
6 Guthrie, Thomas, 2/Lt. (Tp.), d. of w., 27/6/18.
3 Hardman, Hudson Beaufort, Lt., k. in a., 17/8/16.
Henderson, Benjamin Hall Blyth, 2/Lt., d. of w., 18/6/18.
3 Hendry, Archibald Thomas, 2/Lt., died, 23/10/16.
Hislop, James, M.C., T/Lt. (A/Capt.), k. in a., 31/7/17 (att. 6/Bn.).
Horne, Alexander, Capt., k. in a., 14/9/14.
7 Hosken, Ernest Dryden, 2/Lt., k. in a., 14/10/17.
5 Hunter, Archibald, M.C., Major (Tp.), died, 10/10/18.
Johnstone, Reginald Fitzroy Lewis, Lt., k. in a., 8/9/14.
1 Kennedy, James, 2/Lt. (Tp.), d. of w., 26/9/15.
8 Kerr, Henry Thomas Ross, 2/Lt., died, 3/7/16 (P. of W.).
6 Kinnear, Alexander Hope, 2/Lt. (Tp.), d. of w., 19/7/17.
3 Kinmont, John Collie, Capt., died, 18/11/17 (att. Tank Corps).
7 Kirkland, William Harrison, Capt., k. in a., 25/9/15.
Knox, William, Capt., died, 20/2/16 (and R.F.C.).
7 Lambert, George, 2/Lt. (Tp.), k. in a., 23/4/17.
5 Lee, Hector McLean, 2/Lt. (Tp.), k. in a., 18/10/16.
3 Leggat, William, 2/Lt., k. in a., 13/10/18.
8 Liebenthal, Louis George, Lt., k. in a., 4/6/15 (att. Essex R.).
Littleton, Cecil Francis Henry, Lt. (Tp.), d. of w., 6/5/17 (att. 5/Batt.).
5 Logan, Alexander Taylor, 2/Lt., k. in a., 23/3/18.
Lorimer, James Bannerman, Capt., k. in a., 3/5/17 (att. 8/Rif. Bde.).
8 Lowe, William James, 2/Lt. (Tp.), k. in a., 27/4/16 (att. T.M.B.).
Lumsden, Henry Tailyour, Capt., died, 21/6/15 (and R.F.C.).
McAuliffe, George Henry, 2/Lt., k. in a., 29/10/14.
3 McCallum, John, 2/Lt., k. in a., 15/9/16.
3 McColl, Duncan Colin, 2/Lt., k. in a., 18/10/16.
7 McCullock, James, 2/Lt. (Tp.) (A/Capt.), k. in a., 22/8/17.
6 MacCunn, John Francis, Capt. (Tp.), d. of w. 25/9/15.
7 MacDonald, Alexander Robert, 2/Lt., k. in a., 28/3/18.
3 MacDonald, Ronald Ian, Capt., The Hon., died, 17/10/18 (att. Gen. Staff).
5 MacDonald, John, Capt. (Tp.), d. of w., 23/7/16.
1 MacDonald, James Cecil, 2/Lt. (Tp.), died, 27/4/16.
7 MacDonald, Murdock Donald, 2/Lt. (Tp.), k. in a., 18/7/16.
MacDonald, Ronald Mosse, Lt., k. in a., 3/11/14.
7 McDonald, Samuel, 2/Lt. (Tp.), k. in a., 25/9/15.
3 MacDonell, Alasdair Somerled, 2/Lt., k. in a., 13/10/15.
5 McDonnell, Hon. Sir Schomberg Ken, G.C.V.O., K.C.B., Major, d. of w., 23/11/15.
6 MacDougall, Edward Greaves, Capt. (Tp.), k. in a., 26/10/15.
MacDuff, Alexander, Capt., k. in a., 24/4/15.
3 MacFadyen, Neil Douglas, 2/Lt., k. in a., 6/5/15 (att. 2/Bn.).
3 McFarlane, William Arthur, 2/Lt., died, 8/2/19.
3 McGhee, Thomas Aloysuis, 2/Lt. (Tp.), k. in a., 28/9/18.
5 McGregor, Ian Lacy, Lt. (Tp.), k. in a., 18/7/16.
McIntosh, Robert Rae, Lt., k. in a., 24/4/15 (Spec. Res.).
6 McIntyre, Malcolm, 2/Lt. (Tp.), d. of w., 21/9/16.
5 Maciver, Duncan, 2/Lt. (Tp.), k. in a., 11/10/16 (att. 26/Trench Mortar).
MacIver, Kenneth, Capt. (Tp.), k. in a., 27/3/18 (Res., att. 5/Bn.).
8 MacKay, Charles William Donaldson, 2/Lt., k. in a., 17/8/16.
7 Mackay, John William, Lt. (Tp.), d. of w., 20/8/17.
7 Mackay, Mark Sprot, 2/Lt. (Tp.), k. in a., 23/4/17.
5 McKenzie, Kenneth Fitzpatrick, Lt. (Tp.), k. in a., 25/9/15.
Mackinnon, Alexander Hood, 2/Lt., k. in a., 14/9/14.
8 Mackinnon, Lachlan, 2/Lt. (Tp.), k. in a., 30/6/16.
Mackintosh, Alastair Hugh, Capt., k. in a., 14/9/14.
MacIntyre, Ian Campbell, Lt., k. in a., 22/11/17 (att. 108 M.G.C.).
6 Maclean, Donald, 2/Lt. (Tp.), d. of w., 12/10/16.
3 MacLean, Malcolm Alexander, 2/Lt., k. in a., 13/10/15.
8 MacLeay, George Cameron, 2/Lt. (Tp.), k. in a., 17/8/16.
6 MacMaster, Donald Cameron Deford, Lt. (Tp.), k. in a., 26/9/15.
7 McNiven, Alastair, 2/Lt. (Tp.), d. of w., 1/5/17.
5 McRae, Archibald Ludovic, 2/Lt. (Tp.), k. in a., 12/10/17.
3 Mair, Edward Millett, 2/Lt., k. in a., 3/9/16.
Maitland, Hon. Alfred Henry, Major, k. in a., 19/9/14.
5 Mann, Hugh Wallace, Capt. (Tp.), d. of w., 12/11/17.
5 Martin, Norman, D.S.O., Lt., k. in a., 22/7/16 (att. 1/Bn.).
Matheson, John James, 2/Lt., d. of w., 13/8/18 (att. 7/Bn.).
Maxwell, Harley Hyslop, 2/Lt., d. of w., 24/10/18.
2 Maxwell, William Jardine, Capt., died, 26/8/16 (att. 10/Soudanese Inf., Egypt. Army).
Meiklejohn, Kenneth Forbes, Lt., k. in a., 26/9/14.
2 Methvin, Donald, Capt. (Tp.), k. in a., 12/9/18.
3 Middleton, Alexander Samuel, 2/Lt., d. of w., 30/9/18 (att. 1/Bn.).
Miers, Douglas Nathaniel Carleton Capel, Capt., k. in a., 25/9/14.
6 Miller, James, M.C., 2/Lt. (Tp.), k. in a., 11/3/18.
5 Milligan, Alastair, 2/Lt. (Tp.), d. of w., 30/4/17 (att. 1/7 A. & S. H.).
7 Mitchell, Robert Clapperton, 2/Lt. (Tp.), d. of w., 26/7/18.
7 Moir, Douglas, M.C., Lt., d. of w., 22/7/18 (att. 1/2 K.A.R.).
Montgomery, Andrew Graham, 2/Lt., k. in a., 6/9/18 (att. 3/Bn.).
3 Morison, Gerald Patrick John, 2/Lt., k. in a., 13/10/15.
5 Morrison, Alexander, Capt. (Tp.), k. in a., 25/9/15.
1 Morrison, John, Lt. (Tp.), k. in a., 24/9/18.
7 Morton, Gordon Reid, M.C., 2/Lt. (Tp.), k. in a., 9/4/17.
2 Moyes, John, Lt. (Tp.), d. of w., 14/10/17.
3 Muirhead, William, 2/Lt., k. in a., 28/3/18 (att. 44 T.M.B.).
2 Muldoon, John, Lt., k. in a., 13/9/18.
Munro, Fergus Fullerton, 2/Lt. (Tp.), k. in a., 20/9/17 (att. 5/Batt.).
Murray, Alastair John Greville, 2/Lt., d. of w., 14/9/14.
1 Murray, Randolph, Lt. (Tp.), d. of w., 27/10/17.
Napier, Lennox Robert Murray, Capt., d. of w., 28/7/16 (P.O.W.).
6 Newton, Cecil, 2/Lt. (Tp.), k. in a., 15/9/16.
Nicholson, Arthur Davidson, Major, d. of w., 25/9/15.
Nicholson, Arthur Stuart, Lt., k. in a., 4/9/14.
Nicholson, William Dukinfield, Lt., d. of w., 23/2/15.
Orr, John Arhur, Capt., k. in a., 22/10/14.
Patchett, William Ernest, Lt. (Tp.), k. in a., 25/9/15.
6 Paterson, Colin Campbell, Lt., k. in a., 11/4/17.
3 Paterson, Iain Rose, 2/Lt., k. in a., 12/10/17 (att. 6/Batt.).
7 Pearson, Maxwell Colquhoun, Lt. (Tp.), k. in a., 23/11/15.
1 Perry, Thomas, 2/Lt., k. in a., 25/9/15.
1 Pollock, D., M.M., T/Lt. (A/Capt.), k. in a., 18/9/18.
8 Pratt, Christopher, 2/Lt. (Tp.), k. in a., 18/10/16.
1 Reddy, William George, Lt., died, 4/4/19.
3 Riach, Gordon Pennington, Lt., k. in a., 24/9/18.
Riach, Walter Hamilton, Lt. (T/Capt.), d. of w., 5/5/18 (P. of W.) (att. 5/Bn.).
5 Robb, Albert Victor, 2/Lt. (Tp.), d. of w., 12/3/18.
3 Robertson, Gilbert, 2/Lt., k. in a., 25/9/15 (att. 1/Bn.).
7 Robertson, John Stoddart, Lt. (Tp.), k. in a., 21/5/16.
Robertson, Lewis, Capt., d. of w., 7/11/14.
3 Robertson, Peter, Lt., died, 16/1/19 (and R.A.F.).
3 Ronaldson, John Stein, 2/Lt., k. in a., 9/4/17.
Ross, Archibald Seymour, 2/Lt., k. in a., 9/5/15.
6 Ross, Donald Ord, 2/Lt. (Tp.), k. in a., 11/4/17.
3 Ross, Thomas Stewart, 2/Lt., d. of w., 13/11/18.
3 Seafield, James, Earl of, Capt., d. of w., 12/11/15 (att. 5/Bn.).
7 Semple, Robert Woodburn Barnard, M.C., 2/Lt. (Tp.), k. in a., 9/4/17.
Smith, John Frazer, 2/Lt. (Tp.), k. in a., 11/4/17.
Smith-Sligo, Archibald George Roderick Joseph, 2/Lt., k. in a., 14/9/14.
Sprot, Ivan Boyd, Lt., k. in a., 23/10/14.
1 Stewart, George Pemberton, 2/Lt. (Tp.), k. in a., 25/9/15.
Stewart, James, 2/Lt. (Tp.), d. of w., 25/10/18 (Res. att. 5/Bn.).
7 Stuart, David Aymery, 2/Lt. (Tp.), killed, 29/10/16 (and R.F.C.).
7 Stuart, Robert Alexander, 2/Lt. (Tp.), k. in a., 25/9/15.
Stuart, William Grant Spruell, M.C., Capt., k. in a., 23/4/17 (att. 7/Bn.).
7 Taylor, Edward Graham, 2/Lt. (Tp.), k. in a., 25/9/15.
6 Taylor, James McEwen Thomson, M.C., Lt., died, 27/2/19.
Thomson, Arthur Yalden Graham, M.C. and Bar, Capt., k. in a., 30/11/17 (att. Staff).
6 Thomson, James Pringle, Lt. (Tp.), d. of w., 15/8/16.
3 Thomson, William James, 2/Lt., d. of w., 18/11/16 (att. 1/Bn.).
6 Thorburn, James Walker, 2/Lt., d. of w., 12/3/17.
1 Traill, Sinclair George, Capt., k. in a., 24/11/16.
Trotter, Reginald Baird, Capt., k. in a., 9/5/15.
5 Veitch, James, M.C., 2/Lt., d. of w., 19/8/18.
Walkinshaw, James, 2/Lt., k. in a., 26/4/18.
3 Wallace, William, Lt., k. in a., 16/11/17 (att. 1/Bn.).
3 Watson, James Clarkson, Lt., d. of w., 31/8/17 (att. 6/Bn.).
7 Watt, Basil Harry, 2/Lt. (Tp.), k. in a., 25/9/15.
1 Watts, Graham Harman, 2/Lt., died, 11/7/18 (att. 2/King's African Rifs.).
7 Welch, Stephen Cocks, 2/Lt. (Tp.), k. in a., 29/4/16.
5 Williams, John Bromfield, 2/Lt. (Tp.), k. in a., 25/9/15.
5 Wilson, Arthur Leslie, Lt., k. in a., 18/7/18.
3 Wilson, Hugh, 2/Lt., k. in a., 17/10/18.
Wilson, James, 2/Lt., died, 12/7/18 (att. 52/T Bt., Gordon Highrs.).
6 Wilson, Joseph, M.C., Capt. (Tp.), k. in a., 30/11/17.
Wilson, Philip John Conning, Lt., k. in a., 9/5/15 (att. 1/Bn.).
3 Wylie, Robert Downie, Capt., k. in a., 23/8/17.
Young, William, Lt. (Tp.), k. in a., 22/8/17 (att. 7/Bn.).

The Royal Irish Rifles.

1 Allgood, Bertram, Capt., k. in a., 6/12/14.
7 Allison, Hazlett Samuel, Major, k. in a., 9/8/17.
2 Alston, James William, Major (T/Lt.-Col.), k. in a., 15/4/15.
9 Amy, Adolphe Barbier, 2/Lt., k. in a., 19/9/16.
15 Anderson, William, Lt. (Tp.), k. in a., 20/10/18.
15 Andrews, Francis Nicholas, 2/Lt. (Tp.), d. of w., 11/10/15.
11 Andrews, Joseph Hamilton Millar, 2/Lt., d. of w., 16/8/17.
Andrews, Robert H., 2/Lt. (Tp.), k. in a., 25/9/15.
2 Andrews, William Ernest, Lt. (T/Capt.), k. in a., 1/8/15. 1/8/15
10 Atkinson, Hugh, 2/Lt. (Tp.), k. in a., 22/11/17.
16 Baillie, Hugh Montgomery, Capt., k. in a., 21/3/18.
1 Baker, Osbert Clinton, Lt.-Col., k. in a., 9/5/15.
11 Barr, James Hamilton, Lt. (Tp.), k. in a., 1/9/18 (att. 7/8th R. Innis. Fus.).
Barrington, Noel Scott, Lt., k. in a., 10/3/15.
4 Barton, Charles Erskine, Capt., d. of w., 23/8/18.
4 Barton, Thomas Eyre, 2/Lt., k. in a., 16/7/16 (att. 2nd).
3 Bayly, Launcelot Myles, M.C., Lt. (A/Capt.), d. of w., 22/10/18.
13 Beatty, Hugh Hogg, Capt. (Tp.), k. in a., 31/3/18.
8 Beggs, Henry Parker, Lt., k. in a., 1/7/16.

10 Bennet, Trevor Moutray, M.C., Lt. (Tp.), k. in a., 10/11/16 (and R.F.C.).
18 Bill, John Alexander Patterson, 2/Lt., k. in a., 16/8/17 (att. 12th Bn.).
18 Biner, Benjamin Clive, 2/Lt., died, 21/7/18 (att. 4th E. Yorks) (P. of W.).
Biscoe, Arthur John, Capt., d. of w., 12/3/15.
2 Bland, John George, 2/Lt., d. of w., 9/7/15.
5 Boas, Ernest George, 2/Lt., k. in a., 1/7/16 (att. 13th Bn.).
11 Bond, Thomas Morgan, 2/Lt. (Tp.), k. in a., 3/5/15.
12 Boomer, Walter Charter, M.C., Capt. (Tp.), d. of w., 1/10/18.
14 Boyd, Brian, 2/Lt. (Tp.), d. of w., 7/6/17.
8 Boyd, Cecil Vincent, 2/Lt. (Tp.), k. in a., 23/11/17.
3 Boyhan, Thomas Francis, 2/Lt., d. of w., 12/9/16 (att. 7th Bn.).
2 Bridcutt, John Henry, D.S.O., Capt. (A/Lt.-Col.), k. in a., 1/10/18.
18 Briggs, John Mackay, Capt. & Adjt. (Tp.), died, 2/10/16.
18 Brown, Edward, Lt. (Tp.), k. in a., 7/8/17 (att. 2nd Bn.).
6 Brown, Hugh, 2/Lt. (Tp.), k. in a., 31/7/17.
17 Brown, John, M.C., Capt., k. in a., 21/3/18.
1 Browne, Dominick Augustus, Capt., k. in a., 1/7/16.
Browne, Maximilian Herbert, M.C., T/Lt. (A/Capt.), killed, 21/6/18.
17 Bryce, James, Lt. (Tp.), k. in a., 27/5/18.
13 Buchanan, James Robert, Lt. (Tp.), d. of w., 1/4/18.
Burges, William Armstrong, Lt., k. in a., 10/3/18.
16 Burnside, Edward Edmund, 2/Lt. (Tp.), k. in a., 21/3/18.
17 Buttle, Albert Edward, Lt. (Tp.), d. of w., 2/10/18 (att. 2nd Bn.).
3 Byrne, Vincent Cornel, 2/Lt., k. in a., 31/7/17 (att. 1st Bn.).
13 Cahill, John Nugent, Capt., k. in a., 16/8/17.
7 Cairnes, Alfred Bellingham, Major (Tp.), k. in a., 9/9/16.
Calverley, Geoffrey Walter, D.S.O., Lt., killed, 7/1/18 (att. R.F.C.).
6 Calvert, James Howard, 2/Lt. (Tp.), killed, 24/4/16.
5 Calwell, Walter Henry, Lt., d. of w., 27/8/18 (att. 2nd Bn.).
2 Campbell, Lawford Bwine, Lt. (Tp.), k. in a., 1/7/16.
9 Campbell, William Mackenzie, 2/Lt. (Tp.), k. in a., 1/7/16.
20 Capper, Adam Clarke, 2/Lt. (Tp.), k. in a., 9/9/16 (att. 7th Bn.).
15 Chiplin, William Henry, Capt., k. in a., 1/7/16.
4 Clancy, George David Louis, 2/Lt., drowned, 4/5/17 (att. 1st Leins. Rgt.).
7 Cliff-McCulloch, Walter Alexander, Lt. (Tp.), k. in a., 27/2/18.
5 Coffee, Francis Warren, 2/Lt., k. in a., 16/8/17 (att. 14th R. Ir. Rfs.).
16 Cole, David, 2/Lt. (Tp.), k. in a., 3/7/16.
8 Coote, Arthur Eyre, 2/Lt., k. in a., 1/7/16.
17 Corbett, David Bertram, 2/Lt. (Tp.), k. in a., 3/7/16.
17 Cordner, James, M.C., Lt. (Tp.), k. in a., 16/4/18.
14 Corscadden, Francis Theodore George, 2/Lt. (Tp.), d. of w., 18/6/16.
17 Craig, Charles Frederick, 2/Lt. (Tp.), k. in a., 3/7/16.
20 Craig, Eric Ericksen, 2/Lt. (Tp.), k. in a., 30/8/16 (att. 10th Bn.).
4 Daniel, Ernest, Lt., k. in a., 21/10/18 (att. 1st Bn.).
3 Darling, Claude Henry Whish, 2/Lt., k. in a., 12/12/15 (att. 2nd Bn.).
3 Darling, William Oliver Fortesque, Lt., k. in a., 16/10/15 (att. 1st Bn.).
13 Davidson, James Samuel, Capt. (Tp.), k. in a., 1/7/16 (att. M.G.C.).
5 Davis, Henry Ouseley, Capt., k. in a., 27/10/14 (att. 2nd Bn.).
Davy, Howard Samuel, 2/Lt., k. in a., 15/2/15.
3 Dean, William, 2/Lt., k. in a., 1/7/16 (att. 10th Bn.).
17 Dennis, Richard Thomas, 2/Lt. (Tp.), died, 19/12/18.
13 Dewar, James Tyrie, 2/Lt. (Tp.), k. in a., 14/2/17.
15 V.C. De Wind, Edmund, 2/Lt., k. in a., 21/3/18.
2 Dobbie, William, 2/Lt., k. in a., 7/6/17.
3 Dobbin, William Leonard Price, M.C., Lt., k. in a., 21/3/18.
Doherty, Patrick, 2/Lt. (Tp.), d. of w., 1/8/17.
14 Downey, Sydney James Livingstone, 2/Lt. (Tp.), k. in a., 7/6/17.
Drage, George T., Major, died, 19/10/18.
3 Drought, Robert Victor, M.C., 2/Lt., d. of w., 9/6/17 (att. 14th Btn.).
17 Dunwoody, Samuel, 2/Lt. (Tp.), k. in a., 5/10/18.
Eastwood, William, Major (Tp.), k. in a., 11/8/15 (att. 6 Bn.).
18 Eaton, William, 2/Lt. (Tp.), k. in a., 6/9/18.
10 Elliott, Thomas Brignall, 2/Lt. (Tp.), k. in a., 1/7/16.
1 Ellison, Frederick John Gwynn, 2/Lt., k. in a., 16/8/17 (att. 13th Btn.).
4 Elphick, Kevin, 2/Lt., d. of w., 28/9/16 (att. 2nd Btn.).
3 Empey, Simeon Robert Franks, 2/Lt., died, 17/8/16.
15 Endean, Frank Edgar, 2/Lt. (Tp.), k. in a., 24/3/18.
Ennis, Reginald Joseph, 2/Lt., k. in a., 16/8/17.
Enright, Thomas, 2/Lt., d. of w., 20/4/18.
11 Ewart, Cecil Frederick Kelso, Capt. (Tp.), k. in a., 1/7/16.
15 Falkiner, Frederick Bladwin, M.C., 2/Lt., k. in a., 21/8/17, (and R.F.C., 57th Sq.).
2 Farran, Edmond Chomley Lambert, Capt., k. in a., 16/6/15.
17 Farrell, John Leo, 2/Lt. (Tp.), k. in a., 16/3/18.
12 Fenton, Charles Edwin, 2/Lt. (Tp.), died, 19/8/17.
12 Ferris, William Small, 2/Lt. (Tp.), k. in a., 7/6/17.
2 Festing, Arthur Hoskyns, C.M.G., D.S.O., Major, k. in a., 9/5/15.
Field, John William, 2/Lt. (T/Capt.), k. in a., 20/9/15.
10 Franklin, Frederick Robert, 2/Lt., k. in a., 9/12/17.
4 Furniss, James, 2/Lt., k. in a., 31/7/17.
9 Gaffikin, George Horner, Major (Tp.), k. in a., 1/7/16.
Gardiner, James Totton, 2/Lt., d. of w., 1/11/18 (P. of W.).
10 Gatensby, Samuel, Lt. (Tp.), died, 24/11/18.
5 Gault, John Victor, 2/Lt., k. in a., 23/10/16 (att. 1st Bn.).
2 Gavin, Robert Fitzaustin, Lt., k. in a., 25/9/15.
Gibson, Matthew Henry, M.C., T/Lt. (A/Capt.), d. of w., 28/10/18 (att. 12th Bn.).
7 Giles, Victor Marshall, 2/Lt. (Tp.), k. in a., 28/6/16.
2 Gilliland, Valentine Knox, Capt., k. in a., 8/5/15 (att. 2nd Bn.).
Gilmore, Andrew, 2/Lt., k. in a., 11/3/15.
15 Gilmore, Alexander William Francis, M.C., 2/Lt., k. in a., 23/11/17.
19 Given, Robert, 2/Lt., k. in a., 27/5/18 (att. 4th E. Yorks R.).
5 Glastonbury, Harold Mynett, 2/Lt., d. of w., 1/7/16 (att. 1st Bn.).
Goulding, Frederick Ernest, 2/Lt. (Tp.), died, 5/8/18.
18 Graham, William John, 2/Lt. (Tp.), k. in a., 22/11/17.
10 Gransden, Victor Eric, 2/Lt. (Tp.), k. in a., 26/4/18.
10 Green, William Osmond, 2/Lt. (Tp.), k. in a., 1/7/16.
5 Gregg, William Henry, 2/Lt., k. in a., 1/7/16.
12 Griffiths, John, Capt. (Tp.), k. in a., 1/7/16.
18 Gurnell, Robert Matthew, 2/Lt. (Tp.), k. in a., 21/5/17.
10 Hackett, Learo Aylmer Henry, M.C., Capt. (Tp.), k. in a., 24/4/18.
20 Hadden, John Hazlett Millar, 2/Lt. (Tp.), k. in a., 31/10/16.
14 Haddock, Joseph Henry, 2/Lt. (Tp.), k. in a., 24/3/18.
10 Hall, William Charles, Major (Tp.), died, 17/12/17.
9 Halliday, Thomas Owens, 2/Lt. (Tp.), k. in a., 21/3/18.
Hamilton, Douglas, 2/Lt., k. in a., 9/5/15 (att. 1st Btn.).
91 Hamilton, Robert Victor, 2/Lt. (Tp.), k. in a., 1/7/16.
7 Hannah, Robert, 2/Lt., k. in a., 16/8/17.
13 Hardy, Harold, Capt. (Tp.), k. in a., 15/4/18.
14 Harley, Benjamin Chapman, 2/Lt., k. in a., 1/7/16.
7 Harpur, Edward Percival H., Lt. (Tp.), d. of w., 11/9/16.
10 Haslett, Thomas Sinclair, M.C., Lt. (Tp.), k. in a., 22/11/17.
13 Hatch, Nicholas Stephen, 2/Lt., k. in a., 1/7/16.
7 Hatte, Edward Stokes, 2/Lt. (Tp.), k. in a., 16/8/17.
12 Haughton, Thomas Greenwood, Lt. (Tp.), k. in a., 1/7/16.
3 Healy, John Frederick, Lt., k. in a., 1/7/16 (att. 9th Btn.).
Hellmers, Alfred, 2/Lt., d. of w., 11/5/15.
Henderson, George York, M.C., Lt., k. in a., 22/11/17 (att. 10th Btn.).
8 Henderson, Thomas, 2/Lt. (Tp.), k. in a., 6/8/17.
7 Henley, Henry Thomas, 2/Lt. (Tp.), k. in a., 8/3/17.
10 Hill, Barry, Lt., k. in a., 1/7/16.
4 Hill, Oldham Cyril Darley, 2/Lt., k. in a., 16/8/17 (att. 7th Btn.).
2 Hill, William Carlisle, M.C., Lt. (Tp.), k. in a., 7/6/17 (and 74th T.M.B.).
15 Hind, Ernest William Gayles, 2/Lt., k. in a., 1/7/16.
15 Hogg, Walter Gordon, Lt. (Tp.), k. in a., 24/5/17.
18 Hollywood, James, 2/Lt. (Tp.), k. in a., 1/7/16.
14 Hooton, Henry Hurst, Lt. (Tp.), d. of w., 5/5/16.
Hutcheson, Norman Heber, Lt., k. in a., 12/3/15.
14 Hyndman, James Valentine, Capt. (Tp.), d. of w., 7/7/16.
Innes Cross, Sydney Maxwell, 2/Lt., k. in a., 27/10/14.
Irwin, William James, 2/Lt., k. in a., 16/8/17 (att. 7th Bn.).
2 Jackson, Patrick Arthur Dudley, 2/Lt., k. in a., 4/1/17.
16 Jagoe, Charles B., 2/Lt. (Tp.), k. in a., 26/7/17.
10 Jamison, James Clawson, Capt., k. in a., 22/11/17.
4 Jeffares, Richard Thorpe, Capt., d. of w., 6/10/17 (att. 2nd Bn.).
12 Jenks, John Edward, Capt. (Tp.), d. of w., 4/7/16.
13 Johnston, Elliott, Capt., k. in a., 1/7/16.
3 Johnston, Rowland Ivan, 2/Lt., d. of w., 28/8/18.
Jones, Hubert Victor Edward, 2/Lt. (Tp.), k. in a., 25/10/18.
15 Jones, Otto Hamilton, 2/Lt. (Tp.), d. of w., 23/11/17.
3 Joy, Frederick Charles Patrick, 2/Lt., k. in a., 16/6/15 (att. 2nd Bn.).
2 Kennedy, Herbert Alexander, Capt., d. of w., 28/10/14.
14 Kennedy, Hugh Victor Strain, 2/Lt. (Tp.), k. in a., 16/8/17.
8 Kennedy, James, 2/Lt. (Tp.), k. in a., 21/3/18 (att. 1st Bn.).
3 Kerr, James, Lt., k. in a., 21/3/18.
7 Kingston, William, Lt. (Tp.), k. in a., 16/8/17.
11 Kingston-Blair Oliphant, Philip Laurence, D.S.O., Lt.-Col. (Tp.), d. of w., 8/4/18.
13 Knox, John, M.C., 2/Lt. (Tp.), d. of w., 23/10/18.
14 Kyte, Henry Edward, 2/Lt. (Tp.), d. of w., 22/11/17.
14 Lack, Reg Lambert, 2/Lt. (Tp.), d. of w., 18/7/16.
Laing, Gilbert James, 2/Lt., k. in a., 12/3/15 (U.L.I.A.).
La Nauze, George Mansfield, Lt., k. in a., 9/5/15.
4 La Nauze, William, Lt., k. in a., 16/5/15.
Lane, Charles Henry, 2/Lt., d. of w., 21/8/18 (att. 10th Btn.).
Lanyon, William Mortimer, Capt., k. in a., 5/4/15.
7 Lash, Augustus Oliver, Major, d. of w., 11/9/16.
5 La Touche, Averell Digges, Lt., k. in a., 25/9/15 (att. 2nd Btn.).
Laurie, George Brenton, Lt. Col., k. in a., 12/3/15.
13 Laverty, Joseph, 2/Lt. (Tp.), k. in a., 16/8/17.
3 Leach, Ernest Walter Vindin, Capt. (Acting), k. in a., 2/1/17 (att. 2nd Btn.).
18 Lecky, John, 2/Lt. (Tp.), k. in a., 16/7/16.
12 Lemon, Archie Dunlop, Lt. (Tp.), k. in a., 1/7/16.
4 Lennard, Edward Wood, 2/Lt., k. in a., 30/11/17 (att. 1st Btn.).
2 Lennox, Alfred James, 2/Lt. (Tp.), k. in a., 20/1/17.
6 Levis, James Henry Bruce, 2/Lt. (Tp.), k. in a., 12/8/15.
10 Lewis, Frederic Homer, 2/Lt. (Tp.), k. in a., 20/4/18.
6 Lucas, Norman Carey, 2/Lt. (Tp.), d. of w., 2/10/16.
14 Lyons, Robert Victor, 2/Lt. (Tp.), k. in a., 24/3/18.
2 McAlindon, Thomas, M.C., 2/Lt. (A/Capt.), died, 17/9/18.
12 McBride, Arthur King, Capt. (Tp.), k. in a., 7/6/17.
14 McBurney, James, 2/Lt. (Tp.), k. in a., 16/8/17.
5 McCammon, Thomas Valentine Plaisted, Lt.-Col., d. of w., 28/4/17 (att. 20th Btn.).
McCann, Bertie Joseph, 2/Lt. (Tp.), k. in a., 12/11/16.
12 McCausland, David, T/Lt. (A/Capt.), k. in a., 22/11/17.
15 McCay, James Frederick Daniel, Lt. (Tp.), k. in a., 27/3/18.
10 McCay, Thomas Fulton, 2/Lt. (Tp.), k. in a., 22/11/17.

18 McClellan, Allan John, 2/Lt., k. in a., 1/7/16 (att. 15th Btn.).
5 McClelland, Alfred, 2/Lt., d. of w., 13/10/17.
1 McConnell, Harold Jeffrey, 2/Lt., died, 31/5/18.
12 McCluggage, William, Lt. (Tp.), k. in a., 1/7/16.
8 MacColl, George Edwardes, Major (Tp.), k. in a., 5/8/17.
3 McConnell, William Clark, Lt., k. in a., 9/7/16 (att. 2nd Bn.).
8 MacDermott, Robert Wilson, 2/Lt. (Tp.), k. in a., 9/1/16.
12 McDonald, Edward Lawson, Lt. (Tp.), k. in a., 22/11/17.
2 McDonnell, Martin Joseph, 2/Lt., d. of w., 24/1/17.
7 MacFarren, Ernest, 2/Lt. (Tp.), d. of w., 8/11/16.
5 McFerran, Maurice Anderdon, M.C., 2/Lt., k. in a., 21/3/18.
8 McGilton, James, 2/Lt. (Tp.), k. in a., 23/3/18.
McGusty, George Ross, Lt. (Tp.), d. of w., 14/6/16.
MacIlwaine, Julian M., Capt., k. in a., 22/3/18 (att. R.F.C., 12 Sqd.).
2 McIntosh, James Marshall, 2/Lt., k. in a., 16/6/15.
10 McKee, Alexander, Lt. (Tp.), k. in a., 22/11/17.
3 McKee, Patrick Joseph, 2/Lt., k. in a., 10/8/17 (att. 2nd Bn.).
12 McKee, William Dickson, Lt. (Tp.), k. in a., 11/8/17.
13 McKinney, George, Lt. (Tp.), k. in a., 16/8/17.
12 McKinney, Joseph James Moore, 2/Lt., k. in a., 27/3/18.
7 MacFarren, Ernest, 2/Lt., d. of w, 8/11/16.
3 McLaughlin, Arthur, Lt., k. in a., 9/5/15 (att. 1st Btn.).
10 McLaurin, Robert, Lt. (Tp.), k. in a., 7/6/17.
4 McMahon, Patrick, 2/Lt., d. of w., 11/6/17.
7 McMaster, Charles, M.C., T/Lt. (A/Capt.), k. in a., 16/8/17 (att. T.M.B.).
14 McMinn, John, Capt., k. in a., 27/5/18.
1 Macnamara, Charles Carroll, Major, d. of w., 15/7/16.
16 Macready, Oscar Henry, Capt. (Tp.), d. of w., 3/12/17.
20 McRoberts, Thomas, 2/Lt. (Tp.), k. in a., 13/8/17.
16 Madden, William Henry, Capt. (Tp.), d. of w., 24/3/18.
3 Magenis, R. H. C., 2/Lt., k. in a., 15/9/14.
12 Magookin, William Douglas, 2/Lt., k. in a., 21/3/18.
3 Mahony, Edward Archibald, Lt., k. in a., 16/8/17.
2 Marriott-Watson, Richard Brereton, M.C., Lt., k. in a., 24/3/18.
15 Marsh, Joseph, 2/Lt. (Tp.), k. in a., 23/11/17.
Martin, John Sinclair, Lt., k. in a., 9/5/15.
6 Martyr, John Francis, Capt., d. of w., 11/8/15.
3 Masterman, Frederick Michel, 2/Lt., k. in a., 1/7/16.
2 Master, Charles Lionel, Capt., k. in a., 12/10/14. Brown's Road
8 Maxwell, Stanley Woods, 2/Lt. (Tp.), d. of w., 27/7/16.
11 May, Frederick Wilson Laughton, Capt. (Tp.), d. of w., 8/6/17.
Mayne, Denis John Heriot, 2/Lt., killed, 12/10/17 (and R.F.C.).
Mercier, H. B., 2/Lt., died, 3/11/18 (and R.A.F.).
6 Millar, Ian Arthur, 2/Lt. (Tp.), d. of w., 30/9/16.
5 Millar, James Lytton, 2/Lt., k. in a., 29/7/16 (att. 15th Btn.).
5 Miller, Joseph Ewing Bruce, Lt., d. of w., 24/5/15 (att. 1st Bn.).
11 Milliken, James, 2/Lt., killed, 31/12/18 (and R.A.F.).
5 Mitchell, Arthur Gorman, 2/Lt., k. in a., 13/5/16 (att. 2nd Bn.).
13 Moore, Archibald, 2/Lt., k. in a., 26/3/18.
Moore, Morgan Edward Jellett, M.C., Lt., d. of w., 27/3/18 (P. of W.).
17 Moore, Robert McConnell, 2/Lt., k. in a., 27/3/18.
17 Moore, Thomas George, 2/Lt., k. in a., 1/7/16.
Morgan, Samuel Valentine, Capt., k. in a., 10/8/17.
15 Morrow, Hugh Gelston, M.C., T/Lt. (A/Capt.), k. in a., 22/10/18.
10 Mortimer, Robert, 2/Lt. (Tp.), died, 27/10/18.
5 Morton, William, Lt., k. in a., 5/9/15 (att. 2nd Btn.).
3 Motherwell, John Ernest, 2/Lt. (A/Capt.), k. in a., 21/10/16 (att. 1st Bn.).
11 Moultsaid, Wesley, 2/Lt., k. in a., 12/11/16.
2 Mulcahy-Morgan, Edward Spread, Lt., k. in a., 27/10/14.
7 Mulcahy-Morgan, Francis Campion, Lt. (Tp.), k. in a., 6/9/16.
6 Murphy, Johnston, Lt., k. in a., 2/7/16.
Murphy, Robert, 2/Lt. (Tp.), d. of w., 1/10/18.
12 Murray, Charles Stephenson, Capt. (Tp.), d. of w., 1/7/16.
11 Neill, Reginald Henry, Lt., k. in a., 14/7/16.
5 Neill, Robert Larmour, Lt., k. in a., 9/5/15 (att. 1st Btn.).
13 Nicholl, Alfred Ernest, 2/Lt. (Tp.), killed, 3/2/17.
5 Nicholson, Alfred Francis James Steele, 2/Lt. (A/Capt.), k. in a., 16/8/17.
7 Oakshott, Albert Neville, Lt. (Tp.), k. in a., 16/8/17.
14 O'Brien, John Dwyer, M.C., Lt. (Tp.), d. of w., 17/8/17.
15 O'Flaherty, Douglas Hill, Capt. (Tp.), k. in a., 1/7/16.
4 O'Kane, Paul, Lt., k. in a., 21/3/18 (att. 1st Bn.).
2 O'Lone, Robert James, 2/Lt. (T/Capt.), k. in a., 11/11/15.
2 O'Lone, Walter Percy, 2/Lt., k. in a., 25/9/15.
4 O'Reilly, Herbert Wilson, 2/Lt., d. of w., 20/1/16 (att. 2nd Bn.).
4 Orr, Walter Leslie, 2/Lt., k. in a., 25/9/15 (att. 2nd Bn.).
2 O'Sullivan, Arthur Moore, Capt., k. in a., 9/5/15.
7 Owens, William, 2/Lt., k. in a., 16/8/17.
6 Parsons, Kenneth Templeton Jerrard, Capt. (Tp.), died, 14/8/17.
11 Paul, Alexander Charles, 2/Lt. (Tp.), d. of w., 2/10/17.
Paull, Bryan Dolphin, 2/Lt., k. in a., 30/9/16.
8 Pettigrew, Robert McCalmont, 2/Lt. (Tp.), d. of w, 10/6/16.
4 Pollin, Robert Kelly, 2/Lt., k. in a., 31/7/17.
13 Pollock, John, Lt., k. in a., 1/7/16.
3 Popplewell, Harry Bury, Capt., k. in a., 22/7/18 (att. 3rd King's Afr. Rfs.).
3 Power, Henry Richard, Lt., k. in a., 22/8/17 (att. R.F.C., 48th Sqd.).
3 Pryor, Ferdinand William, Lt., d. of w., 12/9/16 (att. 6th Innis. Fus.).
2 Rainey, William, 2/Lt., k. in a., 23/11/17.
15 Rankin, Robert Herbert, 2/Lt. (Tp.), k. in a., 23/11/17.
2 Raymond, Arthur Augustus, Lt., k. in a., 1/8/15.
14 Rea, Herbert Finlay, Lt., k. in a., 16/8/17.
4 Rea, Vivian Trevor Tighe, Lt., k. in a., 25/10/14 (att. 2nd Bn.).
1 Reid, Alexander Daniel, D.S.O., Major (A/Lt.-Col.), k. in a., 31/7/17.
10 Renwick, J. C., 2/Lt. (Tp.), died, 21/3/18.
Reynolds, Thomas James, Capt., k. in a., 25/10/14.
6 Richardson, Allan William, Lt. (Tp.), k. in a., 11/8/15.
14 Robb, Victor Harold, Lt. (Tp.), d. of w., 3/7/16.
15 Robson, Richard Ivan, M.C., Capt., d. of w., 6/8/17.
13 Rogers, George Murray, Lt. (Tp.), k. in a., 1/7/16.
5 Ross, Arthur J., Capt., k. in a., 16/8/17 (att. 1st Bn.).
4 Ross, Kenneth, 2/Lt., k. in a., 20/6/16.
4 Ross, Melbourne, 2/Lt., k. in a., 25/9/15 (att. 2nd Bn.).
15 Ross, William Samuel Baird, 2/Lt., k. in a., 21/3/18.
11 Samuels, Arthur Purfoy Irwin, Capt. (Tp.), d. of w., 24/9/16.
10 Scilley, James Frederick, 2/Lt., k. in a., 22/1/18.
Scollard, David, M.C., Capt., k. in a., 20/4/17 (att. 7th Bn.).
10 Scott, Walter Alexander, 2/Lt., k. in a., 22/11/17.
6 Sheen, George Edward Hayes, Capt., died, 19/2/15.
17 Sheridan, William Nicholas, 2/Lt. (Tp.), k. in a., 1/9/16.
5 Shorland-Ball, Leslie, 2/Lt., k. in a., 6/9/16.
3 Sinclair, George Stanley, 2/Lt., died, 28/5/17 (att. 1st Btn.).
14 Slacke, Charles Oven, Capt. (Tp.), k. in a., 1/7/16.
9 Smeeth, William Sutton, 2/Lt. (Tp.), killed, 17/7/17 (and R.F.C.).
13 Smiles, Samuel, 2/Lt. (Tp.), k. in a., 16/8/17.
2 Smiles, William Alan, Capt. (Tp.), k. in a., 9/7/16.
5 Smith, Samuel Douard Irvine, Lt., k. in a., 1/7/16 (att. 1st Bn.).
11 Smyth, Edmund Fitzgerald, Major (Acting), k. in a., 3/12/17.
13 Smyth, Gordon Dill Long, 2/Lt. (Tp.), k. in a., 16/8/17.
7 Smyth, George Bostall Jenkinson, Lt. (Tp.) (A/Capt.), k. in a., 22/10/18.
9 Smyth, John, 2/Lt. (Tp.), k. in a., 23/11/17.
13 Smyth, William Houghton, Capt. (Tp.), k. in a., 1/7/16.
Spedding, Charles Rodney, D.S.O., Major, k. in a., 19/9/14.
2 Stanley, John Joseph, 2/Lt., k. in a., 9/12/17.
3 Stein, John Francis, 2/Lt., k. in a., 28/9/16.
Stevens, Reginald Walter Morton, Capt., d. of w., 29/8/14.
4 Stoker, Edward Alexander, M.C., Lt., d. of w., 12/9/16 (att. 6th Bn.).
15 Stow, Basil, 2/Lt. (Tp.), d. of w., 22/10/18.
6 Strange, William Hilbert Charles, 2/Lt. (Tp.), k. in a., 31/10/16.
12 Stuart, William Bruce George, M.C., Capt. (Tp.), k. in a., 22/11/17.
10 Sugden, John Edwin, D.S.O., T/Capt. & Adjt., k. in a., 28/9/16.
Swaine, Henry Poyntz, 2/Lt., k. in a., 15/9/14.
15 Tate, Charles Bernard, Capt., k. in a., 1/7/16.
5 Thompson, John Crawford, 2/Lt., k. in a., 21/3/18.
16 Unwin, Wilfrid Peyto, 2/Lt. (Tp.), died, 16/5/16.
13 Uprichard, Henry Albert, Major (Tp.), k. in a., 1/7/16.
11 Vance, Ezekiel, Lt. (Tp.), d. of w., 15/7/16 (P. of W.).
Wale, Clifford Hardwicke, 2/Lt. (Tp.), k. in a., 19/1/16.
14 Walker, Jerome Lennie, 2/Lt. (Tp.), k. in a., 6/5/16.
14 Walker, Samuel Hugh, 2/Lt. (Tp.), k. in a., 16/8/17.
2 Walkington, Charles Edward, Capt., k. in a., 14/10/18.
8 Wallace, Kenneth Moss, Lt. (Tp.), d. of w., 31/5/16.
12 Warner, Samuel, 2/Lt., k. in a., 1/10/18.
8 Watson, Evan Philip, 2/Lt., d. of w., 28/3/18.
3 Watson, James, 2/Lt., k. in a., 7/7/16 (att. 2nd Bn.).
3 Webb, Gilbert Watson, Capt., died, 1/7/16 (and R.F.C.).
11 Webb, Oswald Brooke, Capt. (Tp.), d. of w., 3/7/16.
16 Wedgwood, Philip Egerton, 2/Lt. (Tp.), k. in a., 1/7/16.
12 Weir, Henry Leabody, 2/Lt., died, 28/10/18 (P. of W.).
2 Whelan, John Percy, Capt., k. in a., 11/12/14 ~~(att. R. Ir. Rgt.)~~
17 Whiteside, Albert, 2/Lt. (Tp.), k. in a., 6/12/17.
Whitfield, Arthur Noel, Lt., k. in a., 14/10/14.
7 Whitford, Myles, 2/Lt. (Tp.), k. in a., 29/4/16.
1 Wilkie, Alexander Buchan, 2/Lt., d. of w., 30/11/17.
2 Williams, Charles Beasley, Capt. (Tp.), k. in a., 28/8/15.
5 Williams, Ernest Joseph, Lt., k. in a., 15/10/18 (att. 2nd Bn.).
14 Willis, Samuel, Capt., k. in a., 1/7/16.
11 Willson, William Alick Parkinson, Lt., d. of w., 1/4/18.
17 Wilson, Eric Maurice, 2/Lt. (Tp.), k. in a., 1/7/16.
15 Wilson, John Wilson, 2/Lt. (Tp.), k. in a., 27/12/17.
Windus, Charles Eric, 2/Lt., k. in a., 9/5/15.
17 Witherow, Alexander Hunter, 2/Lt. (Tp.), d. of w., 3/7/16.
Witherow, John Thomas, 2/Lt. (Tp.), d. of w., 5/8/17.
5 Workman, Edward, Lt., d. of w., 26/1/16 (att. 2nd Bn.).
Wright, Allan O'Halloran, Capt., k. in a., 13/3/15.
14 Wright, Matthew John, 2/Lt. (Tp.), k. in a., 1/7/16.
18 Wright, Robert, 2/Lt. (Tp.), k. in a., 7/11/17.

Princess Victoria's.
(Royal Irish Fusiliers.)

Abbott, Edward John White, Lt., k. in a., 17/5/15.
9 Anderson, Leigh Maxwell, Lt. (Tp.), died, 1/9/15.
3 Armstrong, George Canning Staples, Lt., k. in a., 3/5/17.
1 Ashley, Maurice, 2/Lt., k. in a., 23/11/17.
Atkinson, Hon. Hector John, Capt., died, 26/5/17.
5 Atkinson, John Broadwood, Lt. (Tp.), died, 24/12/15.
9 Atkinson, Thomas Joyce, Major (Tp.), k. in a., 1/7/16.
6 Barker, Cecil Massey Arbuthnot, 2/Lt. (Tp.), k. in a., 17/8/15.
6 Beasley, James Joyce, 2/Lt. (Tp.), k. in a., 9/8/15.
Beckingsale, Beauclere Leigh, Lt. (Tp.), k. in a., 21/3/18.
3 Bird, Eric Stephen, 2/Lt., k. in a., 12/8/17 (att. 8th Bn.).
6 Birmingham, William Arthur, 2/Lt. (Tp.), k. in a., 9/8/15.
3 Boal, John Kirk, Lt., A/Capt., k. in a., 3/5/17 (att. 1st Bn.).

3 Bourke, Albert William, 2/Lt., k. in a., 9/5/15 (att. R. Ir. Rif.).
9 Boyd, William Graham, Lt., (Tp.), k. in a., 16/8/17.
1 Boyer, Sydney James, 2/Lt. (Tp.), k. in a., 12/10/16.
9 Brew, John George, Major, d. of w., 6/4/18 (P.O.W.).
Briscoe, Henry Whitby, 2/Lt. (Tp.), died, 15/4/17 (3 Garr. Btn.).
1 Brinckman, Denys, Lt., k. in a., 10/6/15.
1 Bryson, Joseph, 2/Lt., k. in a., 6/10/18 (att. 9th Bn.).
7 Buchanan, James Herbert, Lt., k. in a., 16/3/15 (att. Leinster R.).
Bull, G., T/B.-Gen., d. of w., 11/12/16 (Comdg. 8 Inf. Bde.).
Bunting, Thomas Edward, 2/Lt., k. in a., 24/8/18.
3 Bussey, Harry Marstin, 2/Lt., k. in a., 3/5/17.
4 Butler, Leonard William, 2/Lt., k. in a., 20/11/17 (att. 7th Bn.).
Carbery, Miles Bertie Cunningham, Capt., k. in a., 18/10/14.
Carr, A. W., 2/Lt., died, 6/7/18 (att. R.A.F.).
9 V.C. Cather, Geoffrey St. George Shillington, T/Lt. & Adjt., k. in a., 2/7/16.
5 Chalmers, John Leslie, M.C., Lt., A/Capt., k. in a., 27/3/18.
Clancey, John Austin, M.C., Major, died, 22/7/18 (att. M.G.C.).
5 Clarke, Neville Dutton, 2/Lt., died, 18/4/16.
3 Coghlan, Thomas Reginald, 2/Lt., d. of w., 24/10/18.
Coleman, Ernest Harold, 2/Lt., k. in a., 15/2/15.
Conyers, Charles, Major, T/Lt.-Col., d. of w., 12/5/15.
3 Cooke, Charles Ernest, 2/Lt., k. in a., 25/5/15 (att. 1st Bn.).
8 Cooke, Ernest Richard, Capt. (Tp.), k. in a., 25/4/16.
Coombes, George, 2/Lt., k. in a., 16/8/17 (att. 7/8 Bn.).
9 Cowdy, Harold Evans, 2/Lt. (Tp.), k. in a., 16/8/17.
9 Crosbie, Thomas Edward Chapman, T/2/Lt., A/Capt., d. of w., 15/4/18.
Crosley, Cecil, 2/Lt., k. in a., 16/8/15 (att. 5th Bn.).
3 Crymble, Cecil Reginald, Lt., k. in a., 20/11/14 (att. 1st Bn.).
9 Crymble, John Gordon, 2/Lt. (Tp.), d. of w., 28/12/16.
Cullen, Gerald Somerville Yeats, 2/Lt., k. in a., 11/4/17.
Cullen, James, M.C., 2/Lt., d. of w., 3/10/18.
6 Cullen, Ralph Neville, 2/Lt., k. in a., 6/12/15.
8 Cullimore, Joseph Albert, 2/Lt. (Tp.), k. in a., 23/5/16.
1 Cuming, Arthur Eric MacMorrough, M.C., Lt., A/Capt., d. of w., 26/10/18.
4 Cunningham, William, 2/Lt., k. in a., 1/10/18 (att. 1st Bn.).
4 Darling, Jack, M.C., 2/Lt., d. of w., 26/10/18.
3 Davenport, Leonard Merriott, 2/Lt., d. of w., 6/9/16.
9 Davis, Vivian Alfred, 2/Lt. (Tp.), k. in a., 4/9/18.
1 Deane, Gordon Alexander, Capt., d. of w., 11/4/18 (whilst P.O.W.).
4 Dease, Trevor Herbert Llewellyn, 2/Lt., k. in a., 12/10/16 (att. 1st Bn.).
1 Denny, James, 2/Lt. (Tp.), k. in a., 23/10/18.
9 Despard, Charles Beauclerk, D.S.O., M.C., Capt. (Tp.), k. in a., 18/4/18.
3 Dixon, William Alexander, 2/Lt., k. in a., 16/8/17 (att. 8th Bn.).
6 Dobbin, George Frederick, 2/Lt. (Tp.), k. in a., 16/8/15.
9 Dobson, James Robinson, 2/Lt. (Tp.), d. of w., 19/2/17.
Dobson, John, 2 Lt., d. of w., 4/5/17.
Domegan, Christopher Patrick, Lt., drowned, 10/10/18 (and R.A.F.).
1 Drew, Charles, T/Lt., A/Capt., k. in a., 12/4/18.
5 Duggan, George Grant, Capt. (Tp.), d. of w., 16/8/15.
10 Dunwoody, Hugh Henderson, 2/Lt. (Tp.), killed, 31 7/16 (att. 9th Bn.).
1 Dyson, William Webster, 2/Lt., k. in a., 26/8/16.
8 Eaton, Guy Wellesley, Capt. (Tp.), k. in a., 6/9/16.
Egerton, Robert, M.C., Capt., T/Major, k. in a., 23/12/17 (and R.F.C., 59 Sq.).
Elton, Gordon Daubeney Gresley, D.S.O., M.C., Capt., k. in a., 5/11/17.
5 Espie, Thomas Fletcher, Lt., died, 6/2/19.
6 Falle, Bertram Vernon, Capt. (Tp.), k. in a., 16/8/15.
Fitt, Norman Eric Lloyd, 2/Lt., died, 26/6/17 (P.O.W.).
Fitzgerald, Loftus de Vallentin, Major, Act. Lt.-Col., k. in a., 16/9/18 (att. 2 R. Innis. Fus.).
8 Fitzpatrick, Thomas Gordon, Capt. (Tp.), k. in a., 6/9/16.
Fletcher, Arthur, Capt. (Tp.), died, 14/2/18 (2 Garr. Bn.).
9 Flood, Robert Samuel, M.C., Capt. (Tp.), k. in a., 5/12/17.
Foley, William Alfred, Lt. (A/Capt.), d. of w., 1/11/17.
7 Fulton, Cecil John, Lt. (Tp.), d. of w., 29/4/16
5 Garstin, William Fortescue Colborne, Major (Tp.), k. in a., 7/8/15.
1 Gilmer, Ernest Richard, 2/Lt. (Tp.), k. in a., 12/10/16.
3 Gordon, Alexander Weston, Lt.-Col., died, 20/12/18.
9 Graham, William Rennie, Lt. (Tp.), k. in a., 1/10/18.
5 Green, Frank, 2/Lt. (Tp.), k. in a., 17/9/16.
9 Grundy, Frederick William David, 2/Lt. (Tp.), d. of w., 26/2/17.
Hall, Francis Henry, 2/Lt. (Tp.), k. in a., 30/9/18.
6 Harris, Ernest Edward, 2/Lt., died, 21/4/17.
10 Hardy, Gathorne, 2/Lt. (Tp.), d. of w., 30/4/18.
18 Harrison, Leonard John, 2/Lt. (Tp.), d. of w., 17/4/18 (att. 1st Bn.).
5 Hartley, Walter John, Capt. (Tp.), k. in a., 16/8/15.
Hatch, William Leonard Ringrose, Lt., k. in a., 25/1/15.
3 Henry, Charles Lennox, 2/Lt., k. in a., 16/8/17 (att. 7th Bn.).
5 Henry, Dermot Jepson, 2/Lt. (Tp.), k. in a., 9/7/17 (att. 1st Bn.).
1 Henry, William Ernest, Lt., k.in a., 1/5/16.
Herrick, Harry Eustace, Capt., k. in a., 11/5/17.
6 Heuston, Fred Gibson, 2/Lt., k. in a., 15/8/15.
9 Hollywood, Arthur Carson, Lt. (Tp.), k. in a., 1/7/16.
Holmes, Henry Ball, Major, d. of w., 27/11/15.
4 Hoops, Harry Albert Mostyn, 2/Lt., k. in a., 16/8/17 (att. R.I. Rifs.).
10 Hughes, William Frederick, Lt. (Tp.), k. in a., 20/11/17.
4 Hyde, Eustace Emil, Lt., k. in a., 12/10/16 (att. 1st Bn.).
4 Ibbotson, Roskell, Lt., k. in a., 2/5/17 (att. 2nd Bn.).
Inglis, James Malcolm, 2/Lt., (Tp.), d. of w., 26/10/18.
3 Irwin, Charles Patrick Michael, Lt., k. in a., 9/9/16.
7 Jestin, Martin, 2/Lt. (Tp.), k. in a., 7/6/17.
9 Johnston, Charles Moore, Capt. (Tp.), k. in a., 1/7/16.
6 Johnston, James Cecil, Capt. (Tp.), k. in a., 9/8/15.
9 Johnston, Joseph Allen, Capt. (Tp.), k. in a., 18/2/17.
3 Kavanagh, Thomas Osborne Joseph, Lt., k. in a., 24/8/18 (att. 1st Bn.).
3 Keane, William May Augustine, 2/Lt., k. in a., 4/11/10 (att. 8th Bn.).
Kernaghan, John, 2/Lt. (Tp.), d. of w., 1/10/18.
Kertland, Edwin Blow, 2/Lt., k. in a., 16/6/15. add 2 R I Rif.
1 Kiddell, George Bartam Pearce, 2/Lt., died, 27/2/17.
4 Kiely, Florence Patrick, 2/Lt., k. in a., 24/6/17 (att. 9th Bn.).
8 Kingham, Albert Edward, Lt. (Tp.), k. in a., 6/9/16.
6 Lane, John Boyd Armstrong, 2/Lt. (Tp.), d. of w., 13/9/16.
Lee, W., Lt., killed, 19/8/18 (and R.A.F.).
5 Lenny, Lancelot Arthur, Lt. (Tp.), k. in a., 20/12/17.
6 Livingston, William Montgomery, 2/Lt. (Tp.), d. of w., 15/4/17.
1 Lynden-Bell, Donald Percival, Lt., k. in a., 25/4/15.
9 Lyness, Harold, 2/Lt. (Tp.), d. of w., 2/9/16.
4 McClure, John, 2/Lt., d. of w., 24/11/17 (att. 1st Bn.).
6 McCutcheon, John Cecil, Lt. (Tp.), d. of w. (2/10/16.
6 Macdermot, Hugh Maurice, 2/Lt. (Tp.), k. in a., 7/8/15.
4 McGibney, Francis George, 2/Lt., k. in a., 3/5/17 (att. 1st Bn.).
Macgregor, Alexander Henry Campbell, Major, k. in a., 15/3/15.
4 Macmillan, Edwin James, 2/Lt., k. in a., 12/1/17 (att. 8th Bn.).
9 Malone, Briston Miniss, 2/Lt., k. in a., 16/8/17.
9 Martin, Lawrence Henry, 2/Lt. (Tp.), k. in a., 23/11/17.
4 Miles, Richard Douglas, M.C., 2/Lt., d. of w., 17/8/17 (att. 9th Bn.).
3 Millar, Arthur James, Lt., k. in a., 25/4/15 (att. 1st Bn.).
3 Miller, David Joseph, 2/Lt., k. in a., 12/4/18 (att. 9 Bn.).
10 Mitchel, Frederick David, Capt., d. of w., 24/11/17.
Monckton, Christopher, 2/Lt., k. in a., 1/7/16 (and R.F.C.).
9 Montgomery, Robert Taylor, 2/Lt. (Tp.), k. in a., 1/7/16.
Moon, Alfred Edwin, Capt. (Tp.), died, 7/6/18 (2 Garr. Bn.).
2 Moore, Richard, 2/Lt. (Tp.), died, 29/10/18.
10 Moore, William, 2/Lt. (Tp.), k. in a., 16/8/17.
9 Moran, Samuel Frederick, 2/Lt. (Tp.), d. of w., 1/10/18.
Mott, Jacob Ernest, 2/Lt. (Tp.), k. in a., 23/12/17 (and R.F.C., 21 Sqd.).
O'Hara, Osborne, Capt., k. in a., 13/2/15.
O'Toole, Daniel, 2/Lt., k. in a., 23/11/17.
1 Partridge, James Henry, M.C., 2/Lt., k. in a., 24/3/18 (att. 9 Bn.).
9 Pascoe, Frank Guy Buckingham, 2/Lt. (Tp.), k. in a., 2/7/17 (att. R.F.C., 53 Sqd.).
9 Peacock, Walter, 2/Lt. (Tp.), k. in a., 22/12/16.
Penrose, Edward John McNeill, Capt., k. in a., 25/4/15.
3 Penrose-Fitzgerald, H. J. C., Lt., k. in a., 12/10/16.
4 Pepper, Robert Forsythe, 2/Lt., k. in a., 12/10/16 (att. 1st Bn.).
Phibbs, William Griffith Baynes, Major, died, 8/11/14.
3 Pickett, Gerald Molyneux, 2/Lt., k. in a., 9/9/16.
1 Pope, John Herbert, 2/Lt., d. of w., 11/4/17.
1 Porter, Alan Grey, M.C., Lt. (A/Capt.), d. of w., 29/10/18 (att. 6/Bn.).
9 Prenter, Dalton, 2/Lt. (Tp.), k. in a., 21/3/18.
14 Radcliffe, George Kan, 2/Lt., k. in a., 1/7/16.
10 Ratcliffe, Clifford Stanley, 2/Lt., k. in a., 22/7/18.
Robson, Alexander, 2/Lt., d. of w., 8/11/17.
10 Roche, William Henry, 2/Lt. (Tp.) k. in a., 27/3/18.
Samuels, Arthur Molesworth, 2/Lt., k. in a., 13/10/14.
5 Sargaison, William Henry, 2/Lt. (Tp.), k. in. a., 6/12/15 (att. Conn. Rgrs.).
7 Sargint, Edward Eaton, M.C., Capt. (Tp.), k. in a., 16/8/17.
6 Schute, John Hartley, T/Lt., k. in a., 15/8/15.
5 Scot-Skirving, Archibald William, Capt., d. of w., 9/8/15.
9 Seggie, Alexander, 2/Lt., k. in a., 1/7/16.
Shine, Hugh Patrick, 2/Lt., k. in a., 25/5/15.
Shortridge, Arthur, 2/Lt., k. in a., 14/3/15.
10 Seymour, William Matthew, 2/Lt., k. in a., 16/8/17.
Sheridan, Henry Hamilton, 2/Lt., k. in a., 3/5/17.
9 Shillington, Thomas Graham, Capt. (Tp.), died, 18/8/17.
Silver, Walter Barrington, Major, died, 4/10/14 (Res. of Off.).
10 Skitt, Harold George, 2/Lt. (Tp.), k. in a., 1/10/18.
9 Sleator, Robert, 2/Lt. (Tp.), died, 8/5/17.
6 Snell, Philip Sidney, 2/Lt. (Tp.), k. in a., 9/8/15.
10 Stewart, William Johnston, 2/Lt., k. in a., 1/7/16.
10 Stokes, John Alan, 2/Lt. (Tp.), k. in a., 16/8/17.
9 Stronge, James Matthew, Lt., k. in a., 16/8/17.
8 Sweetnam, John Stephen, 2/Lt. (Tp.), d. of w., 27/4/16.
4 Tagent, Harold William, 2/Lt., k. in a., 24/3/17 (and R.F.C., 8 Sqd.).
5 Tate, Johnston, 2/Lt. (Tp.), k. in a., 7/11/17.
6 Taylor, Hugh Mascie, Major (Tp.), k. in a., 7/8/15.
4 Taylor, Maurice William, M.C., 2/Lt., k. in a., 12/4/18.
4 Thompson, Thomas John Chichester Conyngham, D.S.O., Capt., k. in a., 24/3/18 (att. 2 R. Irish Rifs.).
6 Tolerton, Lee, Lt. (Tp.), k. in a., 15/8/15.
10 Townsend, Richard Stepleton Barry, Lt. (Tp.), k. in a., 1/7/16.

9 Trinder, Samuel Louis, 2/Lt. (Tp.), d. of w., 17/8/17.
Tyrrell, J. M., 2/Lt., killed, 20/6/18 (and R.A.F.).
Vanston, Henry William Frederick Mortimer, Capt. died, 4/9/17.
Verschoyle, William Arthur, Capt., k. in a., 11/4/17.
Wakefield, Roger Owen Birbeck, Lt., d. of w., 28/8/14.
4 Warnock, Hugh Adolphus Hector, Lt., d. of w., 16/8/15 (att. 1 Bn.).
7 Weldon, Henry Walter Cecil, 2/Lt. (Tp.), k. in a., 26/4/16.
White, Horace Arthur, Lt., d. of w., 22/11/17.
Wilkinson, Robert John, Lt. (A/Capt.), died, 2/7/18.
3 Williams, James Alfred, 2/Lt., k. in a., 6/9/16.
9 Wood, Reginald Nixon, 2/Lt. (Tp.), k. in a., 22/2/16.
7 Wray, Percy Hugh, 2/Lt., k. in a., 7/6/17.
4 Young, Arthur Conway, 2/Lt., k. in a., 16/8/17 (att. 7/8 Bn.).

The Connaught Rangers.

Abbott, Geoffrey Dyett, Lt., k. in a., 2/11/14.
2 Abercrombie, Alexander William, Lt.-Col., died, 5/11/15 (P. of W.).
Armstrong-Lushington-Tullock, Graham de Montmorency, Lt., k. in a., 5/10/14.
4 Atwell, Robert Erskine, Lt., k. in a., 2/9/18.
Aveling, Lancelot Neville, Lt., d. of w., 29/4/15.
Barker, William Gordon Steiglitz, Capt., died, 1/12/10.
4 Battersby, Augustus Wolfe, Lt., died, 8/6/15.
3 Beater, Louis Nie Bohr, 2/Lt., died, 13/3/15.
6 Beatty, Eric Edge, Lt. (Tp.), k. in a., 29/4/16.
4 Bellemore, Raymond Alfred, Capt., d. of w., 8/6/17.
2 Benison, Robert Burton, 2/Lt., k. in a., 20/9/14.
5 Bennett, George Robert, 2/Lt. (Tp.), k. in a., 21/8/15.
3 Bethell, Frank Harry, 2/Lt., k. in a., 25/9/15.
Blacker, Cecil Francis, Lt., d. of w., 6/9/14.
5 Blake, Alfred Joseph William, Lt. (Tp.), k. in a., 21/8/15.
5 Bradshaw, William Robert, 2/Lt. (Tp.), k. in a., 19/2/17.
4 Brown, John Carolan, M.C., Lt. (A/Capt.), k. in a., 8/8/18 (and Tank Corps).
3 Browne, Arthur Davies Lang, 2/Lt., k. in a., 11/9/17.
4 Browne, Peter, 2/Lt., k. in a., 1/10/18 (att. 6 Bn.).
Buchanan, William Archibald, Lt., died, 2/6/16 (and R.F.C.).
5 Burke, John Errol, 2/Lt. (Tp.), k. in a., 21/8/15.
Burke, Robert Alfred, 2/Lt. (Tp.), k. in a., 21/7/17 (att. 2/Leins. Regt.).
1 Burrow, Edward, Lt., d. of w., 31/5/16.
3 Campbell, Montagu Irving Mitchell, M.C., Major, d. of w., 4/9/16 (att. 2/Welsh Regt.).
3 Clarke, John Kingham, 2/Lt., killed, 22/7/18 (and R.A.F.).
Cody, John, 2/Lt., k. in a., 21/8/18 (att. 2/R. Irish Rgt.).
Cooke, Hans Hendrick Anthony, Capt., k. in a., 24/1/17 (att. 3/Nigeria Regt.).
3 Crofton, Thomas Horsfall, M.C., Capt., k. in a., 21/3/18 (att. 6 Bn.).
5 Cuming, William Edward, Temp. 2/Lt., k. in a., 31/7/17 (att. R. Innis. Fusrs.).
6 Cummins, Fenton King, M.C., Lt. (A/Capt.), k. in a., 21/3/18.
Daly, Darby, 2/Lt. (Tp.), k. in a., 4/10/18.
Darnell, Charles Verdon, 2/Lt., k. in a., 25/4/17 (and R.F.C., 25 Sqd.).
De Stacpoole, Robert Andrew, 2/Lt., k. in a., 20/9/14.
4 Dignan, Joseph Patrick, 2/Lt., k. in a., 16/10/16 (att. 8/R. Innis Fusrs.).
Douglas, Brian Charles O'Driscoll, Capt., killed, 21/10/18 (and R.A.F.).
5 Elvidge, Laurence, Temp. 2/Lt., d. of w., 9/8/16 (att. R. Innis. Fus.).
3 Faithful, Eric Basil Francis, Capt., k. in a., 10/3/18 (att. 1/R. Irish Regt.).
Fenton, Geoffrey Russell, Lt., k. in a., 20/9/14.
Fox, John, Temp. 2/Lt., died, 18/11/17.
Frazer, John, Lt., k. in a., 14/9/14.
3 Garvey, Ivan Harold, Capt., d. of w., 20/2/17 (att. 6 Bn.).
George, Frederick Ralph, Lt., k. in a., 5/11/14.
4 Gilmore, Thomas Francis, M.C., Lt., k. in a., 8/11/18.
3 Goodfellow, Edward Arthur Fitzherbert, 2/Lt., k. in a., 21/2/16 (att. T.M.B.).
Gratton-Bellew, William Arthur, 2/Lt. (T/Major), d. of w., 24/3/17 (and R.F.C., 29 Sqd.).
1 Greer, Donald Allister, Lt., died, 12/7/16.
Gregory, Robert, M.C., Lt. (T/Major), k. in a., 23/1/18 (att. R.F.C.).
Hack, Charles Edward, Capt., k. in a., 5/11/14.
6 Haire, George, Temp. Lt., d. of w., 7/1/17.
3 Hamilton, Cecil Claude, 2/Lt., k. in a., 16/8/17 (att. 2/R. Irish Fusrs.).
3 Hamilton, William, Lt., k. in a., 30/9/18 (att. 1/Innis. Fusrs.).
6 Hamilton, William Arnold, Temp. 2/Lt., k. in a., 4/6/17.
3 Harrington, Charles Stanley Lawrence, Lt., died, 27/5/17.
4 Harte-Maxwell, Percival Maxwell, Lt., k. in a., 11/4/16 (att. 1/Royal Irish Rifles).
4 Hayes, Robert Harnett, 2/Lt., d. of w., 1/8/17 (att. 2/Leins. Regt.).
Henderson, Raymond Montgomerie Hume, Lt., k. in a., 20/9/14.
5 Hog, Archibald Swinton, Capt., d. of w., 20/8/15.
4 Hughes, Christopher James, Capt., died, 13/5/16.
4 Ingham, Claude Mary Leo, 2/Lt., k. in a., 19/11/16 (att. 9/Innis. Fusrs.).
Irwin, Herbert Quintus, Capt., k. in a., 26/4/15.
4 Jackson, Frederick Howard, Capt., k. in a., 28/10/14 (att. 2 Bn.).
4 Kempston, Noel Chester, 2/Lt., k. in a., 12/10/16.
5 Kenny, Francis Joseph L., Temp. 2/Lt., k. in a., 9/8/16 (att. R. Innis. Fusrs.).
4 Keoch, Frederick Bertram, M.C., Capt., k. in a., 8/8/18 (att. Tank Corps).
3 King, Joseph, 2/Lt., k. in a., 4/10/18.
Leader, Francis William Mowbray, Capt., k. in a., 26/8/14.
6 Lenox-Conyngham, John Staples Molesworth, Lt.-Col., k. in a., 3/9/16.
Lentaigne, Victor Aloysius, 2/Lt., k. in a., 14/9/14.
3 Lewin, Frederick Henry, Capt., died, 8/12/15.
5 Lewis, Stephen Henry, Lt., k. in a., 28/8/15.
4 Lynch, Francis William, 2/Lt., k. in a., 27/4/15 (att. 1 Bn.).
4 Lyons, Denis James, 2/Lt., killed, 15/11/10 (att. 6 Bn.).
3 McCarthy, John Charles Thomas, Lt., k. in a., 2/1/16 (att. T.M.B.).
1/2 McClure, T. A., 2/Lt., died, 28/5/18 (and R.A.F.).
Macdonnell, John Henry O'Connell de Courcy, Lt., d. of w., 14/10/18 (att. Leinster Regt.).
3 Macdowel, Benjamin George, Lt., k. in a., 22/9/15.
5 Mackeown, John Harold, Temp. 2/Lt., killed, 5/10/17.
McKiernan, Michael, 2/Lt., d. of w., 11/5/18.
McNally, James, Major and Qr.-Mr., died, 28/4/17.
5 Macnie, George Francis, Temp. 2/Lt., k. in a., 5/9/16 (att. 6/R. Dublin Fus.).
3 MacSherry, Dermot Joseph, 2/Lt., k. in a., 4/6/17 (att. 6 Bn.).
3 Maguire, Hugh, 2/Lt., k. in a., 9/9/16 (att. 7/Innis. Fusrs.).
Maguire, Matthew Laurence, M.C., 2/Lt., T/Lt., k. in a., 28/4/17 (and R.F.C.).
Mallins, Claude Joseph O'Conor, Lt., k. in a., 2/11/14.
6 Matthews, David, Temp. 2/Lt., k. in a., 29/5/16.
4 Meenaghan, John, 2/Lt., k. in a., 21/3/18.
6 Miles, Henry Robert, Temp. 2/Lt., k. in a., 18/7/16.
3 Montgomery, Arnulf, 2/Lt., k. in a., 22/12/14 (att. 2 Bn.).
3 Moore, John Ross, 2/Lt., k. in a., 9/9/16 (att. Innis. Fusrs.).
4 Moore, Hugh Victor, 2/Lt., k. in a., 22/3/18 (att. T.M.B.).
3 Moore, Ulick Augustus, Lt., k. in a., 22/3/18 (att. 6 Bn.).
6 O'Brien, Thomas Kevin, Temp. Capt., k. in a., 31/5/16.
3 O'Brien, William Donough, Temp. Major, d. of w., 7/6/16 (att. 20/Manch. Regt.).
4 O'Connell, Donald Charles, 2/Lt., k. in a., 9/9/16.
1 Okey, William Ewart, 2/Lt. (Tp.), k. in a., 21/1/16.
Ovens, John Roberts, Lt., k. in a., 5/11/14.
6 Parke, William Henry, Temp. Capt., k. in a., 15/10/16.
4 Prentice, Walter Lowry, 2/Lt., d. of w., 3/8/17 (att. 2/Leins. Regt.).
5 Richards, Hubert Henry Lyster, 2/Lt., k. in a., 7/12/15.
Robertson, Hugh Grant, Capt., killed, 26/4/15.
3 Russell, Arthur Henry Eric, Lt., d. of w., 22/3/18 (att. 6 Bn.).
4 Saker, Frank Harrison, Capt., k. in a., 30/10/14 (att. 2 Bn.).
Sarsfield, William Stopford, Major, d. of w., 20/9/14.
5 Shanks, Edward Ferrier, Temp. 2/Lt., k. in a., 21/10/16 (att. Innis. Fusrs.).
6 Sheridan, Henry Richards, Temp. 2/Lt., k. in a., 3/9/16.
6 Simms, Alfred George Francis, Lt., died, 30/12/17.
6 Smyth, Philip Joseph, Temp. 2/Lt., d. of w., 16/9/16 (and R.F.C.).
Spreckley, Ralph Lesingham, Lt., k. in a., 14/9/14.
Steuart, Norman Kennedy, Capt., d. of w., 15/9/16 (att. 6 Bn.).
4 Stone, Herbert William Degetan, 2/Lt., k. in a., 26/4/16.
6 Stritch, George Seymour Russell, Temp. Capt., k. in a., 7/2/16.
3 Summerscales, Claude, Lt., died, 22/7/16.
3 Tennant, Philip Eyre, 2/Lt., k. in a., 31/7/17 (att. 2/Leins. Regt.).
Thomas, Rhys Ivor, Lt., k. in a., 14/9/14.
Thompson, Gilbert, Capt., k. in a., 24/2/15.
4 Tydd, William John Stern, 2/Lt., d. of w., 22/1/17.
Vaughan, Harry Robert, 2/Lt., k. in a., 27/10/14 (att. D.L.I.).
4 Vernon, William Wood, 2/Lt., k. in a., 7/7/16 (att. R. Irish Fusrs.).
6 Waites, Charles James, 2/Lt., k. in a., 10/10/18.
3 Wallis, Duncan Boyd, Lt., d. of w., 23/7/15 (att. 2/Royal Munster Fus.).
Walsh, John Joseph, 2/Lt., k. in a., 8/10/18.
4 Wickham, Anthony Theodore Clephane, Lt., k. in a., 4/11/14 (att. 2 Bn.).
Wickham, Montagu Hill Clephane De Cristoforo De Bouillon, Capt., d. of w., 9/5/15.
6 Wirkham, Nigel John Latham, Temp. Capt., k. in a., 19/4/16.
Williamson, Edward Benjamin Bickford, 2/Lt., k. in a., 19/2/17 (att. 6 Bn.).
Winspear, Arthur, 2/Lt., k. in a., 5/11/14.
1 Wright, Stamford Walter Seppings, Lt., k. in a., 9/9/16.

Princess Louise's (Argyll and Sutherland Highlanders).

Aitken, John Christie, M.C., Capt., k. in a., 25/9/15.
3 Allan, Hugh Drummond, Lt., k. in a., 24/4/17.
3 Allan, James Stanley, 2/Lt., d. of w., 22/10/16.
14 Allison, John, 2/Lt. (Tp.), k. in a., 21/3/18.
4 Allport, Harrison Kingsley, 2/Lt., k. in a., 21/8/16.
11 Alston, James William Hamilton, Major (Tp.), died, 3/1/17.
5 Anderson, William Angus, 2/Lt., died, 8/12/18.
12 Andrew, Robert, Lt., k. in a., 8/5/17.
12 Andrews, Reginald Hugo Catchpole, 2/Lt., k. in a., 8/5/17.
Aytoun, Robert Merlin Graham, Lt., d. of w., 27/8/14.
4 Baker, Aveling John Wing, 2/Lt., k. in a., 23/3/18.
14 Bartholomew, George Hugh Freeland, T/Lt. (A/Capt.), d. of w., 2/10/17.
11 Beattie, George, M.C., 2/Lt. (Tp.), k. in a., 23/4/17.
Black, George Bennett, 2/Lt. (Tp.), k. in a., 7/10/17.
Blacklock, Algernon Haden, 2/Lt., k. in a., 21/10/14.
4 Boag, Archibald Fullarton, 2/Lt., k. in a., 23/3/16.
4 Boddam-Whetham, A. C. D.S.O., Lt.-Col., killed, 22/6/19 (att. R.A.F.).

10 Bonnyman, Edward William, D.S.O., M.C., Capt. (Tp.), d. of w., 11/8/18.

4 Brown, Archibald, M.C., 2/Lt. (Tp.), k. in a., 20/4/18.

2 Brown, Walter, 2/Lt. (Tp.), k. in a., 18/8/16.

4 Bruce, George McDonald, Lt., died, 18/2/19 (att. Cameron Highrs.).

2 Bruce, John Fryer. 2/Lt., d. of w., 28/2/18.

2 Bruce, Hon. Robert (Master of Burleigh), Capt., k. in a., 26/8/14.

Bullough, J. L., Lt., k. in a., 25/9/15.

2 Burleigh, James Emil, M.C. 2/Lt (Tp.), k. in a., 12/10/17.

3 Burnley-Campbell, Colin William, 2/Lt., k. in a., 26/6/15.

Burt-Marshall, William Marshall, Capt., d. of w., 17/11/14 (P. of W.).

3 Calder, Alexander Frazer, 2/Lt., k. in a., 19/7/16.

3 Cameron, Douglas Robert, Lt., k. in a., 31/7/17.

2 Campbell, Bruce Hutchinson, Temp. Lt., k. in a., 19/9/18.

Campbell, Henry Bethune. 2/Lt., k. in a., 23/2/15.

3 Campbell, Ivan, 2/Lt., d. of w., 8/1/16 (att. Seaforth Highrs.).

Campbell, James Archibald Lochnell, Capt., d. of w., 19/3/15.

2 Carmichael, George Clement, 2/Lt., k. in a., 18/8/16.

3 Cassie, Leith. 2/Lt., d. of w., 11/12/17.

1 Chalmers, Archibald Douglas, Temp. Lt., died, 9/12/18.

12 Chalmers, James Stewart, Temp. 2/Lt., d. of w., 7/10/16 (att. 1/Cameron Hrs.).

3 Chilton, F., Lt., k in a., 20/6/15.

10 Christison, Frederick John, Lt. (Tp.), d. of w., 4/12/15.

Clark, Marcus Broadfoot, Temp. Lt., k. in a., 25/9/17.

Clarke, John Seymour Denison, Temp. Lt., k. in a., 10/11/17.

Clarke, Montagu Christian Cuthbert, Lt., k. in a., 10/5/15.

10 Clarkson, John James, Temp. Lt., k. in a., 30/12/17.

4 Cockburn, James, 2/Lt., k. in a., 12/10/16 (att. 90/M.G. Corps.).

10 Colvin, Russell Alexander, Temp. Capt., k. in a., 1/5/17.

Cox, Reginald John Ponsonby, Major, k. in a., 27/9/15 (att. 8/Gordon Highrs.).

3 Craig, James Young, Temp. Lt., d. of w., 24/10/17 (att. K. Afr. Rifles).

4 Cramb, Wilfrid Brown, 2/Lt., k. in a., 14/4/17 (and R.F.C., 9 Sqd.).

10 Cremin, Bernard Felix Ambrose, 2/Lt., k. in a., 11/10/16 (att. T.M.B.)

13 Cullen, John, Temp. 2/Lt., k. in a., 15/9/16.

12 Cunningham, Charles Clement Francis, Capt., d. of w., 19/8/16.

3 Currie, Gilbert Heron, 2/Lt., k. in a., 12/10/16.

Davidson, Ian Sprot, 2/Lt., k. in a., 11/11/14.

10 Davidson, Robert William, Temp. Lt., k. in a., 12/10/17.

4 Davis, Alistair Ingram, 2/Lt., k. in a., 11/4/18.

1 Deas, William Darling, Temp. Lt., d of w., 30/9/15.

10 Denham, George Parsons, Temp. Capt., d. of w., 14/4/17.

Denton, Philip Sydney, 2/Lt., k. in a., 13/8/17 (att. Cameron Highrs.).

1 Dickerson, Charles Henry, Temp. 2/Lt., k. in a., 14/7/16.

11 Dickson, Walter Michael, Temp. 2/Lt., k. in a., 26/9/15.

13 Drummond, William Young. 2/Lt. (Tp.), k. in a., 11/7/16.

10 Duncan, Robert Gordon Campbell, 2/Lt., k. in a., 3/5/17.

Erskine, T. B., 2/Lt. (T/Capt.), d. of w., 20/7/15 (att. Gordon Highrs.).

11 Ewing, James Adie, Temp. 2/Lt., k. in a., 31/7/17.

Fairlie, Norman Edwin, 2/Lt., k. in a., 21/10/14.

10 Falconar-Stewart, Ian Stewart, 2/Lt., d. of w., 24/7/16.

Falconar-Stewart, Ronald Dundas, D.S.O., Capt. (Temp. Lt.-Col.), k. in a., 19/9/18.

Fallowfield, William Gordon, 2/Lt. (Tp.), k. in a., 25/9/15.

11 Farquarson, James, Temp. 2/Lt., k. in a., 23/4/17.

3 Ferguson, Peter, 2/Lt., k. in a., 28/10/18.

Fetherstonhaugh, John Lennox, 2/Lt., k. in a., 10/11/14.

Fordyce, James Dingwell, 2/Lt. (Tp.), d. of w., 27/9/15.

Fraser, Ian Catto, 2/Lt. (Tp), k. in a., 25/9/15.

Fraser, John Alexander, Capt., d. of w., 28/8/14.

11 Frost, Arthur Colin, 2/Lt. (Tp.), k. in a., 25/9/15.

12 Gardiner, Archibald Macalister, Temp. 2/Lt., d. of w., 24/5/16.

2 Gardner, Richard Pringle McKay, 2/Lt., k. in a., 18/8/16.

4 Garlick, John Munro, Lt., d. of w., 2/12/17.

Geoghegan, Stannus, 2/Lt., d. of w., 18/3/18.

Gibb, Richard, 2/Lt., k. in a., 11/5/15.

Gilchrist, Alexander Arthur, Temp. 2/Lt., k. in a., 3/9/16 (att. Cameron Highrs.).

Gilkison, James David, Lt., k. in a., 26/8/14.

4 Gillespie, Alexander Douglas, 2/Lt., k. in a., 26/9/15.

11 Gilmour, Alastair Stuart, Temp. 2/Lt., k. in a., 15/9/16.

Glasfurd, Duncan John, Temp. Brig.-Gen., d. of w., 12/11/16 (H.Q., 12 Aust. Inf. Bde.).

Gore, Robert Clements, C.B., C.M.G., Brig.-Gen., k. in a., 14/4/18 (Commdg. 101st Inf. Bde.).

Grant, Daniel Menzies, Temp. 2/Lt., d. of w., 4/8/18.

Grassick, Peter, Temp. Lt., k. in a., 25/10/18.

Gray, Charles Rutherford, Temp. 2/Lt., d. of w., 23/11/17.

4 Hamilton, Hugh Wallace, Lt. (T/Capt.), d. of w., 20/3/18.

11 Harrigan, William Piercy, Temp. Lt., died, 1/11/18 (att. K. Afr. Rifles).

4 V.C. Henderson, Arthur, M.C., 2/Lt. (A/Capt.), k. in a., 24/4/17.

Henderson, I. H. D., M.C., Capt., died, 21/6/18 (att. R.A.F.).

Henderson, William Alexander, Capt., k. in a., 10/11/14.

4 Hennel, Robert Alexander, 2/Lt., k. in a., 28/8/18.

14 Hogg, James, Temp. Capt., k. in a., 24/9/16.

4 Husband, Donald Irons, 2/Lt., k. in a., 16/8/16.

14 Humphreys, David Virgil, 2/Lt. (Tp.), k. in a. 24/4/17.

3 Ireland, James Reginald, 2/Lt., k. in a., 28/10/16.

Irvine, John Laird Gallwey, Capt., k. in a., 8/7/15.

Irwin, Horace Charles, 2/Lt. (Tp.), k. in a., 20/7/18.

11 Jackson, Geo., Lt. (Tp.), k. in a., 26/9/15.

Jamieson, Eric Liew Ellen, 2/Lt., k. in a., 22/8/17.

12 Jamieson, Robert Lindsay, Temp. 2/Lt., k. in a., 3/9/16.

13 Jardine, Graham Brymmer Thomas, 2/Lt., k. in a., 18/10/16.

Kennedy, Archibald Edward, Capt., k. in a., 26/8/14.

Kennedy, William Robert, 2/Lt. (Tp.), k. in a., 25/9/15.

Kerr, Henry, 2/Lt., k. in a., 25/9/15.

Kirk, Henry Buchanan, Temp. Brig.-Gen., died, 12/5/16 (93/Inf. Bde.).

Knowling, Francis John Dobree, M.C., Capt. (Tp.), k. in a., 8/3/18.

10 Laidlaw, John Leslie, Temp. 2/Lt., d. of w., 20/7/16.

14 Landell, William, Temp. Lt., d. of w., 22/7/17.

11 Lanstry, Reginald Redfern, Lt., d. of w., 27/9/15.

4 Law, Alan Drummond, Temp. Lt., d. of w., 3/5/17.

14 Lawson, William, Temp. Lt., k. in a., 24/4/17.

4 Leggatt, Eric Gerard, 2/Lt., k. in a., 15/7/16.

V.C. Liddell, John Aidan, Capt., d. of w., 31/8/15 (and R.F.C.).

14 McAdie, George, 2/Lt., k. in a., 22/3/18.

11 McBean, William, Temp. 2/Lt., k. in a., 12/5/16.

14 McCallum, Norman, 2/Lt., k. in a., 31/7/17.

4 MacCormick, Alexander Campbell, 2/Lt., k. in a., 11/10/16.

10 MacDonald, Claude Keith, 2/Lt., k. in a., 27/9/15.

10 MacDonald, George Anderson, 2/Lt., k. in a., 18/8/17.

4 MacFarlane, William Cargill Stuart, 2/Lt., k. in a., 27/8/16.

2 McGregor, David, Lt. (A/Capt.), k. in a., 24/9/18.

MacIntosh, Henry Maitland, Capt. (Tp.), d. of w., 26/7/18.

13 MacKay, Eric Reay, Capt., k. in a., 13/6/15.

12 MacKay, Henry Neill, Temp. 2/Lt., k. in a., 28/11/16.

14 MacKay, Ian Darrock, 2/Lt. (Tp.), k. in a., 21/3/18.

MacKenzie, Keith Ingleby, 2/Lt., k. in a., 8/4/17 (and R.F.C.).

MacLean, Alexander Harvie, Major, k. in a., 26/8/14.

MacLean, Arthur Kirkpatrick, Lt., k. in a., 26/8/14.

2 McLean, Joseph Richard Garratt, Lt., k. in a., 9/5/18.

2 McLean, William Wood, M.C., Lt., k. in a., 23/9/18.

11 MacLellan, Malcolm, Temp. Capt., k. in a., 25/9/15.

3 MacLuckie, Reginald William, Temp. Capt., k. in a, 11/8/16 (att. W. Yorks Regt.).

11 McMillan, William McLeod, Temp. Capt., k. in a., 25/9/15.

4 McNab, James Fortune, 2/Lt., d. of w., 6/4/16 (att. 1/K.O.S. Bdrs.).

11 McNeill, Malcolm, C.M.G., D.S.O., Capt., Temp. Lt.-Col., died, 3/6/17.

4 McNicol, James Percival, 2/Lt., d. of w., 20/6/18.

11 McCrone, John Milloy, Temp. 2/Lt., k. in a., 28/8/16.

2 Maitland, James Moule Hamilton, Temp. 2/Lt., d. of w., 23/4/17.

Malcolm, Sidney John, Temp. Capt., k. in a., 20/9/17.

4 Matheson, James, 2/Lt., k. in a., 26/3/16.

Mathieson, John, Temp. 2/Lt., k. in a., 5/8/18 (att. 7 Seafth. Highrs.).

14 Melville, David William, Temp. 2/Lt., k. in a., 21/3/18.

4 Millar, Robert Gordon, 2/Lt., d. of w., 11/5/17.

3 Miller, Ian MacLeilain, Lt., k. in a., 25/9/15.

4 Miller, Robert Goldie, 2/Lt., k. in a., 17/3/17 (and R.F.C., 5 Sqd.).

Miller, Walter, Temp. 2/Lt., d. of w., 30/4/17.

4 Milne, Joseph, Lt., k. in a., 29/9/18.

11 Mitchell, George Henry, Lt., k. in a., 22/8/17.

Moir, John Andrew Alexander, 2/Lt., k. in a., 16/6/15.

13 Monteith, Patrick Rankin, Temp. 2/Lt., d. of w., 13/11/16.

3 Moorhouse, Samuel, Lt.-Col., died, 11/12/18.

4 Morgan, Jeffrey Evan, Lt., k. in a., 7/9/17.

4 Mowat, John William, 2/Lt., k. in a., 21/4/17.

Murray, Andrew Buchanan, Lt., k. in a., 23/4/17.

10 Murray, Henry Berkeley, Temp. Lt., k. in a., 18/7/16.

14 Nicol, David, T/Lt. (A/Capt.), d. of w., 26/11/17.

11 Niven, Kenneth James, Temp. 2/Lt., k. in a., 22/8/17.

4 Pardy, Thomas Johnston, 2/Lt., d. of w., 7/5/17.

3 Paterson-Brown, Ian, 2/Lt., k. in a., 2/8/16.

Patten, Charles Hill, Capt., d. of w., 3/10/16.

4 Peffers, David Tweedie, 2/Lt., k. in a., 27/2/18.

Plimpton, Robert Albert, M.C., A/Capt., k. in a., 27/9/17 (att. 4/R. Hrs.).

Porteous, Dick MacDonald, D.S.O., Capt., k. in a., 10/5/15.

4 Prentice, John Robert, 2/Lt., d. of w., 17/4/18.

4 Prothero, Philip Bernard, Lt. (T/Capt.), k. in a., 26/7/17 (and R.F.C., 5 Sqd.).

2 Purves, Harry de Burgh, Capt. (T/Major), k. in a., 18/6/16.

Radcliffe, George Amvas, Lt., k. in a., 25/4/17 (att. R.F.C.).

4 Radcliffe, William Thomas, 2/Lt., k. in a., 20/7/18.

4 Rankin, James Thomson, 2/Lt., k. in a., 23/12/15 (att. 1/R. Scots).

11 Richardson, Arthur Archibald, Lt., k. in a., 26/9/15.

4 Richardson, Francis James, D.S.O., Major, died, 11/12/17.

2 Robertson, Athol, Lt., d. of w., 26/3/16.

11 Robertson, Henry William, Temp. 2/Lt., d. of w., 21/4/18.

Rose, John Charles Reginald, Lt., d. of w., 9/11/14.

2 Ross, David, D.S.O., M.C., Lt. (A/Capt.), k. in a., 6/11/18.

13 Russell, Thomas, T/2/Lt. (T/Capt.), k. in a., 12/10/16.

14 Runciman, Keith Stewart, 2/Lt. (Tp.), k. in a., 24/4/17.

Sabiston, James Anderson, 2/Lt., k. in a., 22/8/17 (att. 7/Cameron Highrs.).

3 Scott, Charles Gordon, Lt., k. in a., 28/10/16.

13 Scott, Ronald Mayne, Temp. 2/Lt., d. of w., 20/9/16.

Scratton, Geoffrey Howell, M.C., Lt. (Tp.), k. in a., 1/8/17.

4 Shaw, Alexander Jack. 2/Lt., k. in a., 12/10/16.

10 Shaw, Llewellyn William Emile, Temp. Capt., k. in a., 10/8/18.

11 Shedden-Dobbie, Robert, 2/Lt. (Tp.), d. of w., 12/4/17.

11 Shewan, Alan D., Temp. Lt., k. in a., 15/9/16.

4 Sieber, John Lonsdale, 2/Lt., k. in a., 17/10/17 (att. K. A. Rif.).

4 Sillars, Harry Frederick Lionel, 2/Lt., k. in a., 1/1/16 (att. 2/Sea. Highrs.).
4 Slingsby, Charles, 2/Lt., killed, 7/8/15.
14 Smith, George Alan Campbell, M.C., Temp. Capt., k. in a., 28/9/18.
3 Smith, George Evanston, Lt., k. in a., 25/9/15.
4 Smith, Harry Gordon, 2/Lt., k. in a., 13/3/18.
4 Smith, Hugh Stewart, Temp. Capt., k. in a., 18/8/16.
10 Smith, Reginald Iredale, Temp. 2/Lt., k. in a., 18/7/16.
Sotheby, Lionel Frederick Southwell, 2/Lt., k. in a., 25/9/15.
Speed, David, 2/Lt. (Tp.), d. of w., 2/5/17 (att. 8/R. Highrs.).
Speirs, Ronald Patrick, 2/Lt., k. in a., 23/4/17.
2 Squirl, Montague Ernest, Lt., d. of w., 15/12/18.
Steel, James Camplett, Lt., killed, 13/3/15.
11 Stevenson, Robert Dennistoun, T/Capt., k. in a., 16/5/16.
Stirling, Robert, Lt., k. in a., 19/2/15.
11 Sutthery, Dorian Melbourne, 2/Lt. (T/Lt.), d. of w., 19/5/17.
3 Taggart, Henry Rawson, 2/Lt., k. in a., 24/7/18 (att. 1/R. Highrs.).
3 Tait, Thomas Henderly, Lt., drowned, 15/4/17.
2 Taylor, Joseph Macintyre, Lt., k. in a., 24/10/18.
Teggart, Francis William Stuart, Lt., k. in a., 26/10/17 (att. Gordon Highrs.).
4 Thomas, Duncan Collison Willey, Capt., k. in a., 12/11/14 (att. 1/Gordon Highrs.).
3 Thomson, George Alastair St. Clair, Capt., d. of w., 21/7/16.
10 Thomson, Kenneth Douglas, Temp. 2/Lt., k. in a., 18/7/16.
Tyson, Alexander Baird, Lt. (A/Capt.), k. in a., 24/4/17.
Ure, John Andrew, Capt., k. in a., 21/10/14.
14 Urquhart, John, Temp. Capt., k. in a., 24/4/17.
Walker, Charles Corbould, Capt., k. in a., 26/8/14.
2 Walker, Frederick Ramsay, M.C., 2/Lt., died, 6/1/17.
11 Walker, Ralph, Temp. 2/Lt., k. in a., 21/4/17.
10 Weller, William Richard, Hon. Lt. & Qr.-Mr., k. in a., 18/7/16.
11 Whyte, Alan Hill, Temp. 2/Lt., k. in a., 9/4/17.
4 Wilkinson, John, 2/Lt., k. in a., 19/9/18.
4 Williamson, John McLeod, 2/Lt., k. in a., 12/4/18.
3 Wilson, Arthur Alexander, 2/Lt., k. in a., 23/4/17.
2 Wilson, David, 2/Lt., d. of w., 28/12/16.
4 Wilson, Evan Welldon, 2/Lt., k. in a., 23/4/17.
11 Wilson, Gavin Laurie, D.S.O., M.C., Lt.-Col., died, 16/2/19.
11 Wilson, Matthew, M.C., Capt., died, 12/10/18.
13 Wilson, Spence Ross, Temp. 2/Lt., d. of w., 13/10/16.
Wilson, William Graham, 2/Lt. (Tp.), d. of w., 24/8/17.

The Prince of Wales's Leinster Regiment (Royal Canadians).

Adams, John Gould, Capt., k. in a., 5/5/15.
3 Adcock, St. John, Major, k. in a., 9/5/15 (att. 1/Bn. R. Lanc. Regt.).
7 Ahern, Patrick Joseph, Lt. & Q.M., k. in a., 9/9/16.
Alban, Harry Chayton, Lt., k. in a., 9/2/15.
3 Algeo, Norman, Capt., d. of w., 30/11/17.
3 Andrews, Frederick Charles, 2/Lt., k. in a., 16/3/15.
Barnett, Denis Oliver, Lt. (Tp.), d. of w., 16/8/15.
5 Barnewall, The Hon. Reginald Nicholas Francis Mary, Lt., d. of w., 24/3/18.
9 Barrett, Frederick Alan, 2/Lt. (Tp.), killed, 22/4/16 (att. 8/Ches. Regt.).
Bates, William George Henry, Capt., k. in a., 26/4/15.
Blatchly, Walter John Atherton, 2/Lt. (Tp.), k. in a., 12/5/15.
4 Bliss, Arthur Joseph, 2/Lt., k. in a., 9/9/16.
6 Bowen, Thomas Henry, 2/Lt. (Tp.), k. in a., 2/8/16 (att. Innis. Fus., 11/Bn.).
Bowen-Colthurst, Robert MacGregor, Capt., k. in a., 15/3/15.
6 Brabazon, Alan, Capt. (Tp.), d. of w., 8/3/18.
4 Bren, Henry Alfred Hogarth, Lt., k. in a., 9/9/16.
3 Broad, Hubert Frederick, Lt., died, 25/10/18.
Brophy, Thomas Joseph, 2/Lt. (Tp.), k. in a., 22/3/18.
6 Brown, Francis Alfred Joseph, 2/Lt. (Tp.), k. in a., 9/9/16 (att. 8/Roy. Mun. Fus.).
Butler, Desmond George, Lt., killed, 17/3/18 (and R.F.C.).
7 Butler, William, 2/Lt. (Tp.), k. in a., 22/3/18.
4 Cartwright, Eric Percival St. George, 2/Lt., k. in a., 12/8/16 (att. M.G.C.).
Chatterton, Roden Latham, Capt., died, 28/3/18 (att. R.F.C.).
3 Coade, William Henry, Lt., d. of w., 5/11/18.
Cormac-Walshe, Edward Joseph, Capt., d. of w., 5/11/14.
7 Craig, Thomas Patrick, Lt. (Tp.), k. in a., 22/3/18.
3 Creagh, William, 2/Lt., d. of w., 7/3/17.
6 D'Arcy-Irvine, Charles William, Capt., k. in a., 6-12/8/15.
3 De Courcy, Henry Joseph, 2/Lt., k. in a., 18/1/17 (att. 6/Roy. Ir. Regt.).
Dix, Stephen Hamilton, M.C., Major (Tp. Lt.-Col.), k. in a., 4/10/17 (att. 13th North'd Fus.).
7 Downing, Henry Francis, Capt. (Tp.), k. in a., 3/9/16.
3 Dudley, Henry Pemberton, 2/Lt., k. in a., 3/9/16 (att. 2/Irish Regt.).
2 Eastwood, Edmond Patrick, 2/Lt., k. in a., 22/3/18.
Eldred, John Sturgess, 2/Lt., d. of w., 27/11/14 (att. R. Ir. Rif.).
3 Ennis, Edward Armstrong, 2/Lt., d. of w., 30/10/18.
3 Evans, George Ernest Knightly, 2/Lt., k. in a., 3/9/16 (att. 2/Roy. Ir. Rif.).
5 Evans, William, Hon. Lt. & Q.M., died, 27/5/16.
6 Figgis, Neville Johnstone, Lt. (Tp.), k. in a., 10/8/15.
Finney, Edwin Newland, 2/Lt., k. in a., 19/5/17 (att. 6/Cyc. Bn.).
4 Fletcher, Arnold Lockhart, Lt. (Tp.), d. of w., 30/4/17 (att. M.G.C.).
4 Fletcher, Donald Lockhart, 2/Lt., died, 28/4/17.
8 Flood, Dundas Charles, Lt. (Tp.), died, 27/10/18.
6 Foley, Michael Alphonsus, Lt., died, 25/4/19.
3 Foley, Thomas William Winspear, Lt., k. in a., 9/9/16.
7 Forrest, Percy Huskinson, 2/Lt., d. of w., 21/3/18 (att. 16/M.G.C.).
3 Fowler, Francis Reginald, 2/Lt., k. in a., 18/10/16 (att. 2/Roy. Ir. Rif.).
Gaitskell, Cyril Egremont, Lt., d. of w., 19/10/14.
4 Gibson, Albert Fisher, 2/Lt., k. in a., 24/3/17 (att. R.F.C., 4th Sqd.).
5 Gilliat, Reginald Horace Crosbie, Capt., k. in a., 6/4/15 (att. Conn. Rangers).
7 Girard, Geoffrey Marcus Erskine, 2/Lt. (Tp.), killed, 16/11/17.
4 Goodbody, Henry Edgar, Capt., k. in a., 12/5/15.
3 Goudie, Alexander Malcolm, Lt., d. of w., 18/8/16 (att. M.G.C.).
6 Gough, George William Blanthorne, Lt. (Tp.), k. in a., 10/8/15.
6 Griffith, Walter Stanley Currie, 2/Lt. (Tp.), k. in a., 10/8/15.
3 Handcock, Henry R., 2/Lt., k. in a., 18/8/16.
4 Hansell, Kenneth Joyce Nelson, Lt., k. in a., 21/3/18 (att. 1/Bn. R.I. Rif., att. M.G.C., 26 Bn.).
3 Harrison, Frederick Alfred, 2/Lt., k. in a., 9/9/16 (att. 6/R.I. Regt.).
Heenan, Michael Cornelius, Capt., k. in a., 12/1/16 (att. 2/Wilts).
2 Heming, Charles Leonard Parlett, Lt., d. of w., 12/2/17.
6 Hemphill, Richard Patrick, 2/Lt. (Tp.), died, 24/3/17 (and R.F.C.).
Heneker, Frederic Christian, Major, k. in a., 1/7/16 (att. 20/North'd Fusrs.).
7 Herbert, Cyril Joseph, 2/Lt. (Tp.), k. in a., 13/3/18.
2 Hickey, Denis, M.C., 2/Lt. (Tp.), died, 7/11/18.
2 Hickman, Terence, 2/Lt., k. in a., 26-27/6/16.
6 Hickson, Horace Grant, 2/Lt. (Tp.), k. in a., 6-12/8/15.
3 Higgins, Michael, Aloysius, Lt., k. in a., 31/3/17.
3 Hodge, Andrew Buckland, Lt., d. of w., 31/7/17.
7 Hodges, Harold Henry, 2/Lt. (Tp.), k. in a., 13/7/16.
7 Hodgson, Reginald, 2/Lt. (Tp.), k. in a., 27/6/16.
4 Holmes, John Alexander, 2/Lt., d. of w., 26/4/16.
3 Ireland, Herbert Richard Hall, M.C., Major, d. of w., 28/3/18 (att. R. Muns. Fus.).
5 Jameson, Edmund James, D.S.O., Lt.-Col. (Tp.), d. of w., 27/3/17 (att. 1/4th Essex Regt.).
2 Jameson, Anthony Mildmay, 2/Lt., k. in a., 1/9/16.
1 Jennings, Arnold John, Capt., k. in a., 2/2/17.
Jobling, Harold Edward 2/Lt., d. of w., 9/9/17.
2 Johnston, John Lionel Lukin, Capt. (Tp.), d. of w., 21/6/16.
7 Johnstone, John, Capt. (Tp.), k. in a., 9/9/16.
Jones, Bryan John, D.S.O., Major, k. in a., 20/10/18.
Kahn, Edgar, 2/Lt., k. in a., 5/5/15.
7 Kelly, John James, 2/Lt (Tp.), d. of w., 12/4/17.
3 Keogh, John, 2/Lt., k. in a., 22/3/18.
Keogh, William Gerald, Lt. (Tp.), died, 12/10/18.
Lane, Edward George Arthur Campbell, 2/Lt., k. in a., 30/9/18.
3 Laville, Samuel Eustace Blythe, Capt. (Tp.), k. in a., 18/8/16.
7 Lawrence, Percy, 2/Lt., killed, 9/8/18 (and R.A.F.).
Lecky, Averell, Lt., d. of w., 19/10/14.
7 Lemon, David Wardlow, M.C., 2/Lt. (Tp.), k in a., 22-23/3/18.
5 Liston, William Prosper, Lt., k. in a., 12/4/17.
1 Luger, Arthur, Lt. (A/Capt.), d. of w., 13/8/18.
7 Lynch, Palric Stephen, A/Capt., k. in a., 27/12/16.
5 McDonnell, John, Lt.-Col., k. in a., 29/9/18.
7 McGowan, William, 2/Lt (Tp.), k. in a., 9/9/16.
Mackay, George Lawrence Forbes, Lt., k. in a., 11/4/17.
Mackenzie, Ronald Angus Hugh, Lt., k. in a., 7/2/15.
Maffett, Henry Telford, Capt., k. in a., 20/10/14.
5 Maguire, Francis Patrick, 2/Lt., k. in a., 27/4/18.
Markes, John Carlon, Major, k. in a., 19/7/16.
Marsland, James Francis, Lt., d. of w., 18/8/15
Massy, Haworth Peel, Capt., died, 10/12/14 (att. Nigeria R.).
2 Mitchell, Andrew, 2/Lt. (Tp.), d. of w., 2/8/17.
Moffatt, James Robert, Capt., k. in a., 15/2/15.
4 Möllmann, Herbert Bernard, A/Capt., k. in a., 1/2/17.
Montgomerie, William Graham, Capt., d. of w., 20/10/14.
4 Moore, George Adams, 2/Lt., d. of w., 6/11/17.
3 Moore, Victor Cuthbert, 2/Lt., d. of w., 4/9/16 (att. 6/R. Ir. Regt.).
2 Moore, Geoffrey William Broadbent, Lt., k. in a., 14/10/18.
5 Mouritz, Cecil John Hastings, 2/Lt., k. in a., 5/12/16.
Murphy, Alfred, D.S.O., M.C., Bvt.-Major (A/Lt.-Col.), k. in a., 6/11/17
5 Murphy, Edwin Hale, Capt., d. of w., 6/5/15.
2 Murray, George, Capt. (Tp.), k. in a., 4/6/16.
6 Neill, G. W., Lt., killed, 8/6/18 (and R.A.F.).
5 Nugent, John Aloysius Joseph, 2/Lt., k. in a., 27/8/17.
O'Brien, Philip Anderson, 2/Lt., d. of w., 9/3/15.
3 O'Connor, Roderic Alan Edward, 2/Lt., k. in a., 1/9/16.
4 Oulton, Henry Charles, 2/Lt., k. in a., 12/4/17.
2 Pearman, Humphrey, T/Lt., died, 13/8/16 (and R.F.C.).
5 Pelton, Kenneth Kemble, M.C., 2/Lt., k. in a., 1/8/17 (att. 7/R. Ir. Rifs.).
Pemberton, Allan John MacDonald, M.C., Capt., died, 3/11/16 (and R.F.C.).
2 Plowman, James, M.C., T/Lt. (A/Capt.), d. of w., 29/4/18.
Porter, William James, Lt., d. of w., 3/8/17.
2 Power, Charles, 2/Lt., k. in a., 25/9/15 (att. 2/R. War. R.).
7 Purdon, Theodore Oscar, Capt. (Tp.), k. in a., 9/9/16.
5 Quinlan, Charles, 2/Lt., k. in a., 31/7/17.
5 Radcliff, Herbert Travers, Capt., k. in a., 15/3/15.

3 Read, George Averille, Capt., k. in a., 8/3/17.
Reeve, William Tankerville Monypenny, C.M.G., Lt.-Col., died, 28/9/15 (att. 1/Garr. Batt., Essex R.).
4 Ricketts, William Falkland Geordie, 2/Lt., k. in a., 1/4/17.
3 Robinson, George Whalley, Capt., k. in a., 15/2/15.
Rounsefell, Eric (de W.), M.C., 2/Lt., k. in a., 3/9/18.
7 Ryan, James, 2/Lt. (Tp.), killed, 13/1/18.
10 Sharpe, Robert, M.C., 2/Lt. (Tp.), d. of w., 12/9/18.
1 Shaw, Patrick, 2/Lt. (Tp.), k. in a., 30/6/15.
5 Siddons, Henry Thomas Brandon, 2/Lt., d. of w., 24/8/16.
5 Simpson, George Arnold, 2/Lt., k. in a., 2/7/16 (att. M.G.C.).
1 Smith, Ernest Frederick William, 2/Lt. (Tp.), d. of w., 27/12/16 (and R.F.C.).
5 Smith, Ernest Wilson Marshall, 2/Lt., killed, 22/3/16 (att. M.G.C.).
4 Smith, William Joseph, 2/Lt., k. in a., 31/7/17.
6 Smyth, John Hawkins, 2/Lt. (Tp.), k. in a., 12/4/17.
4 Stannus, Thomas Robert Alexander, D.S.O., Major (A/Lt.-Col.), d. of w., 17/6/17.
5 Stidston, William Popkiss, 2/Lt., d. of w., 3/8/17.
Stowell, Wilfrid, 2/Lt. (Tp.), k. in a., 22/3/18.
7 Studholme, Launcelor Joseph Moore, Capt. (Tp.), k. in a., 9/9/16.
6 Talbot, William Caithness, 2/Lt., died, 20/7/18 (and R.A.F.).
Taylor, Gordon Annesley, Capt., k. in a., 15/2/15.
6 Toomey, Archibald Roche, 2/Lt. (Tp.), k. in a., 10/8/15.
3 Trench, Frederick Power Le Poer, Lt., d. of w., 9/4/16 (att. 2/R. Dub. Fus.).
Ussher, Beverley, Capt., k. in a., 19/6/15.
3 Vowler, John Arthur Geoffrey, Lt., died, 19/7/17.
2 Ward, Albert Joseph, 2/Lt., k. in a., 13/6/18.
6 Warren, Richard Dunn, Major, k. in a., 7/4/18.
2 Webster, Jno. William, Capt., d. of w., 29/3/18.
Westmacott, Spencer Ruscombe, Lt., k. in a., 8/5/15.
Whitty, John Leo, M.C., Capt., k. in a., 8/7/16 (and R.F.C.).
Wilkie, John Hunter, 2/Lt., d. of w., 9/4/15.
6 Willington, James Vernon Yates, 2/Lt. (Tp.), k. in a., 6/8/16.
2 Young, George Neville Gardiner, Lt., d. of w., 25/7/15.
Younge, Frederick George Patrick, Lt., d. of w., 14/2/15.

The Royal Munster Fusiliers.

1 Annaheim, George Herbert, Lt. (Tp.), k. in a., 4/10/18.
Awdry, Carol Edward Vere, 2/Lt., k. in a., 27/8/14.
9 Baily, Denis Joseph, M.C., Lt. (Tp.), k. in a., 21/2/17.
8 Baldwin, Osbourne George de Courcy, Capt. (Tp.), k. in a., 26/1/16.
Banning, Percy Stuart, Lt., k. in a., 4/11/14.
Barrett, Philip Godfrey, Capt., k. in a., 27/8/14.
4 Beatty, Charles St. John, Lt., d. of w., 16/9/16.
8 Becher, Edward Richard Fane, 2/Lt. (Tp.), d. of w., 19/7/16.
4 Bennet, James Hampton, M.C., 2/Lt., k. in a., 22/9/16.
7 Bennett, Francis Evans, 2/Lt. (Tp.), k. in a., 8/8/15.
3 Bennett, John William, Lt., k. in a., 13/10/15.
8 Biggane, Francis Joseph, Lt. (Tp.), k. in a., 16/8/17 (att. 48 T.M.B.).
1 Blake, Harold Martin Joseph, Lt., d. of w., 20/11/17.
2 Boland, Michael Thomas, 2/Lt. (Tp.), k. in a., 26/2/18.
Borthistle, William John, 2/Lt., k. in a., 29/1/18 (and R.F.C.).
8 Bostock, Guy Edwin, Temp. Capt., k. in a., 30/1/16.
Britton, William Kerr Magill, 2/Lt., killed, 23/5/17 (and R.F.C., 29 Sqd.).
Brown, William, 2/Lt. (Tp.), k. in a., 1/3/18 (att. 2/R. Innis. Fusrs.).
6 Burrowes, Guy Walter, Lt. (Tp.), k. in a., 16/8/15.
4 Cahill, Patrick Leopold, Lt., k. in a., 21/3/18.
1/2 Callaghan, J. C., M.C., Temp. Major, killed, 2/7/18 (and R.A.F.).
2 Callanan, Michael, Temp. 2/Lt., k. in a., 20/12/16.
1 Carrigan, Colin Herbert, M.C., Capt., k. in a., 2/9/18.
9 Casey, Michael Francis, Temp. Capt., k. in a., 19/7/16.
5 Casserly, William Alphonse, 2/Lt., k. in a., 1/3/17 (att. 1/R. Innis. Fusrs.).
8 Chandler, Cecil William, M.C., Temp. Capt., k. in a., 30/3/18.
Charrier, Paul Alfred, Major, k. in a., 27/8/14.
Chute, Challoner Francis Trevor, Lt., k. in a., 27/8/14.
7 Clark, Norman Pickslay, 2/Lt. (Tp.), k. in a., 24/8/16.
5 Clarke, Walter Sidney, 2/Lt., k. in a., 25/6/16.
Clery, John Francis, Capt., k. in a., 16/8/17 (att. R. Irish Rif.).
8 Cobb, Sydney James, 2/Lt. (Tp.), d. of w., 20/7/16.
9 Colfer, James Richard, Temp. Lt., died, 26/2/17.
4 Comley, Edgar Cyril, M.C., Lt., killed, 27/9/18.
6 Conolly, John Henry, Temp. 2/Lt., d. of w., 1/9/16 (att. 11/Roy. Irish Rifles).
Considine, John William, Capt., k. in a., 25/9/15.
6 Conway, Edgar Philip, Major, k. in a., 10/8/15.
4 Cramer, George L'Estrange, Lt., d. of w., 16/7/15.
4 Crone, Percy Alexander, 2/Lt., k. in a., 8/9/16.
Crozier, James Cyril Baptist, 2/Lt., k. in a., 27/8/14.
7 Cullinan, Robert Hornidge, Temp. Capt., k. in a., 8/8/15.
Cunningham, Alexander Campbell, Temp. 2/Lt., k. in a., 21/8/15.
Day, Francis Innes, Major, k. in a., 21/12/14.
Dennys, Kenneth Rose, 2/Lt., k. in a., 9/5/15.
Dick, John Campbell, Capt., k. in a., 9/5/15.
2 Dilworth, Robert Kildahl, 2/Lt., k. in a., 28/12/16.
6 Dodd, John O'Connell, Lt. (Tp.), k. in a., 7/11/18.
5 Dodd, Walter de Courcey, Lt., died, 31/10/17 (and R.F.C., 11 Sq., P.O.W.).
6 Dodds, Cecil James, Capt., k. in a., 22/9/16.
1 Donnelly, Gilbert, Lt. (Tp.), k. in a., 21/3/18.
Dorman, Edward Crump, Capt., k. in a., 1/5/15.
2 Dorman, Thomas Robert Hobart, 2/Lt., d. of w., 21/2/16.
7 Dunn, John Valentine, Temp. Capt., k. in a., 15/8/15.
3 Durand, Francis William, Capt., k. in a., 21/12/14.
3 Eagar, William George Massy, Capt., k. in a., 21/8/15.
1 Ennis, Charles Francis, 2/Lt., k. in a., 20/11/17.
1 Eustace, Thomas George, Lt., k. in a., 28/6/15.
Filgate, Thomas William, Capt., d. of w., 29/9/15.
2 Fisher, Hugh Bell, Temp. Lt., d. of w., 23/11/17 (P.O.W.).
8 Fitzpatrick, John, 2/Lt., k. in a., 30/7/16.
9 Fletcher, Maurice, M.C., Temp. Capt., d. of w., 9/9/16.
5 Flynn, Percy, 2/Lt., k. in a., 10/11/17.
5 Foran, Edward Cornelius, 2/Lt., k. in a., 28/12/17.
2 Frizell, Richard Alexander, Temp. Capt., k. in a., 10/11/17.
5 Fullin, John Francis, M.C., 2/Lt., k. in a., 22/3/18.
6 Gaffney, Leon Arthur, 2/Lt. (Tp.), d. of w., 12/8/15.
Gethin, Richard Patrick Wilmot, Lt., k. in a., 25/9/15.
3 Glancy, Hugh, 2/Lt., k. in a., 30/9/18 (and M.G.C.).
8 Gleeson, John Francis, M.C., Hon. Lt., d. of w., 2/2/18.
7 Good, William Henry, 2/Lt. (Tp.), k. in a., 16/8/15.
6 Grant, Joseph Brabazon Theobald, Capt., k. in a., 16/8/15.
Grantham, Frederick William, Capt., k. in a., 9/5/15.
5 Greene, Henry Caldwell, 2/Lt., k. in a., 29/4/18 (att. 1/R. Irish Rifles).
2 Harding, James Philip, Capt., d. of w., 10/11/17.
5 Harold-Barry, John Gerard, 2/Lt., k. in a., 7/7/16.
7 Harper, Ernest Macowan, Lt. (Tp), k. in a., 9/8/15.
2 Harte, George William, 2/Lt., k. in a., 5/3/18.
Hartigan, Edward Patrick, Temp. 2/Lt., k. in a., 20/11/17 (and R.F.C., 57 Sqd.).
Hartley, James Harold, 2/Lt., k. in a., 22/7/17 (and R.F.C., 45 Sqd.).
Hartnett, Michael Charles Lt., k. in a., 19/9/17 (att. R.F.C.).
1 Harty, John Joseph, 2/Lt., d. of w., 27/9/16 (att. 10/R. Irish Rfls.).
5 Healy, Dermott Joseph, 2/Lt., k. in a., 5/8/17 (att. 74/T.M.B.).
4 Healy, Guy Rambant, Lt., k. in a., 11/3/16 (att. 3/K. Afr. Rifles).
Henderson, Eric Lockhart Hume, Capt., d. of w., 21/5/15.
3 Hepworth, Frederick Joseph, 2/Lt., k. in a., 20/5/17 (att. R. Innis. Fusrs.).
3 Hewett, William John, Capt., k. in a., 9/5/15.
3 Hewison, Geoffrey Joseph, 2/Lt., k. in a., 15/7/16.
8 Horan, Charles Robert, M.C., Lt. (Tp.), k. in a., 10/11/17.
Horsfall, Arthur Mendelssohn, 2/Lt., k. in a., 9/5/15.
3 Howe, James Roche, Lt., k. in a., 18/10/18.
Hussey, Edmund Thornbér, 2/Lt., k. in a., 7/6/17.
4 Hutchins, Richard, Capt., died, 13/5/15.
Jarrett, Charles Harry Brownlow, Major, k. in a., 25/4/15.
6 Jephson, John Noble, Major, d. of w., 29/8/15.
1 Kane, Robert Romney Godred, D.S.O., Capt. (A/Lt.-Col.), d. of w., 1/10/18.
Kearney, Arthur Joseph, Lt., k. in a., 9/9/16.
Kennedy, Gilbert, Capt., died, 11/12/18.
Kidd, William Sidney, Lt., k. in a., 21/3/18.
Kilkelly, John George Joseph, Capt., k. in a., 24/3/18 (and R.F.C.).
King, Charles Sealy, Lt., k. in a., 9/5/15.
3 Kingston, William, 2/Lt., k. in a., 16/8/17 (att. 1/Roy. Irish Rifles).
7 Laing, St. Clair King Nixon, Temp., 2/Lt., died, 2/4/17.
6 Lee, Joseph Bagnall, Temp., Lt., k. in a., 8/8/15.
5 Lefroy, Gerald, 2/Lt., k. in a., 24/8/16.
1 Ley, John Howard, 2/Lt., k. in a., 9/9/16.
6 Longfield, Charles Edmund, Capt. (Tp.), k. in a., 10/3/18.
Love, James Robert, Temp. 2/Lt., k. in a., 17/8/17.
1 MacCarthy-O'Leary, William Felix, Lt., k. in a., 6/9/16.
McCormick, Mark Huston, 2/Lt., k. in a., 23/4/17.
2 MacDaniel, Francis George Vernon, Lt., k. in a., 20/11/17.
McFarlane, Alexander Laidlaw, 2/Lt. (Tp.), d. of w., 2/9/18.
8 McMahon, Patrick Stan, 2/Lt. (Tp.), d. of w., 29/12/15.
7 McVeigh, William John, Temp. Lt., k. in a., 28/12/17.
1/2 Mahony, Brian Gerald, 2/Lt., killed, 3/9/18 (and R.A.F.).
1 Mahony, Edmund Joseph, Temp. Lt., k. in a., 27/9/18.
Male, Arthur Ernest, Temp. Lt., died, 3/7/17 (att. Conn. Rangers).
Martin, Ronald Hutton, Capt., k. in a., 24/3/18 (att. R.F.C.).
2 Maunsell, Douglas Slade, Lt., k. in a., 6/9/16.
5 Maybury, Francis Joseph, 2/Lt., d. of w., 5/10/18.
3 Meredith, William John, Lt., d. of w., 20/2/15 (att. S. Lancs Regt.).
9 Moran, Francis, Temp. Lt., k. in a., 22/8/16.
3 Morrogh-Bernard, Francis Anthony, Lt., k. in a., 12/12/17.
Morrogh, Francis Mathew Dominick, 2/Lt., k. in a., 19/6/15.
1 Mosse, William Oliver Matless, Col., drowned, 10/10/18 (Gr. Bn.) (Ret. List. Ind. Army).
5 Murphy, Bernard Joseph, 2/Lt., d. of w., 18/8/17.
9 Murphy, Christopher John, 2/Lt., k. in a., 20/7/16.
6 Noonan, Joseph Daniel, Temp. 2/Lt., k. in a., 24/8/16.
3 O'Brien, Daniel Joseph, 2/Lt., k. in a., 10/11/17.
5 O'Brien, Gerard, D.S.O., 2/Lt., k. in a., 22/3/18 (att. 1/Innis. Fusrs.).
O'Brien, Hugh Conor Henry, Capt., k. in a., 21/12/14.
2 O'Brien, John, M.C., Lt., T/Capt., k. in a., 6/10/18.
O'Brien, James Francis, Lt., k. in a., 21/12/14.
5 O'Brien, Sidney Joseph Vincent, 2/Lt., k. in a., 7/6/17 (att. 2/R. Irish Rifles).
5 O'Connor, Joseph Harris, Lt., k. in a., 10/11/17.
4 O'Donovan, Miles Henry, Capt., k. in a., 21/6/16.
7 O'Duffy, Kevin Emmet, Temp. Lieut., k. in a., 15/8/15.
9 O'Flynn, Francis Joseph, Temp. 2/Lt., k. in a., 27/4/16.
5 O'Neill, James Dominick, 2/Lt., k. in a., 24/8/16.
Page, Francis Trafford, 2/Lt., k. in a., 9/5/15.
2 Pakenham, Robert Edward Michael, Capt., d. of w., 17/1/15.
6 Panting, Arnold Clement, Temp. 2/Lt., k. in a., 13/1/17.
Parker, Wilfred Horsley, 2/Lt., k. in a., 9/5/15.
2 Pemberton, Oswald, Capt., k. in a., 21/12/14 (att. R. Dublin Fusrs.).

Perry-Ayscough, Henry George Charlie, Capt., k. in a., 25/9/15.
Phayre, Charles Frederick, 2/Lt., k. in a., 27/8/14.
Pollard, Gerald Evelyn Gustavus, Capt., k. in a., 25/4/15.
Pottinger, Robert Ormond Brabazon, Lt., k. in a., 9/5/15.
6 Prendergast, James Francis, Temp. 2/Lt., k. in a., 27/7/16.
4 Provis, Ernest Snell, 2/Lt., k. in a., 16/6/16.
2 Purdon-Stoute, Henry, Temp. 2/Lt., k. in a., 10/11/17.
Rabone, Maxwell, Temp. 2/Lt., d. of w., 22/8/15.
Redding, John Hamilton Montford, 2/Lt. (T/Lt.), died, 2/3/17.
3 Reymes-Cole, William Elmer, D.S.O., Capt., k. in a., 11/11/14.
Rickard, Victor George Howard, Temp. Lt.-Col., k. in a., 9/5/15.
Roche, Hyacinth Joseph Albert, Capt., killed, 19/1/15 (att. R.F.C.).
5 Ronayne, James Andrew, Lt., k. in a., 25/9/15.
3 Ryan, Charles M. J., M.C., Lt., k. in a., 4/10/18.
Ryan, George Julian, D.S.O., Temp. Lt.-Col., k. in a., 22/1/15.
7 Seale, Theophilus, Temp. 2/Lt., k. in a., 22/8/16.
Shaw, Gordon Thompson, M.C., Temp. Capt., k. in a., 28/8/18.
6 Sheehan, Cornelius, Temp. 2/Lt., killed, 8/8/17 (and R.F.C.).
Sheil, Charles, 2/Lt., d. of w., 22/4/18 (and R.A.F.).
Simms, George Norman, Capt., died, 27/8/14.
Sinclair, Gerald, M.C., 2/Lt., k. in a., 21/3/18 (att. R. Irish Regt.).
Smith, William Stanley, 2/Lt., k. in a., 25/6/16.
Stewart, Charles Frederick Somes, M.C., Temp. Major, k. in a., 5/4/18 (att. Northants Regt.).
3 Stewart, James Augustus, Lt., k. in a., 9/5/15.
Stokes, Oliver Chetwode, 2/Lt., k. in a., 5/3/17.
2 Stone, William, 2/Lt., d. of w., 4/11/18.
4 Stubbs, Reginald Arthur, 2/Lt., k. in a., 8/6/16 (and R.F.C.).
Styles, Frederick Ernest, Lt., k. in a., 27/8/14.
Sulivan, Philip Hamilton, 2/Lt., k. in a., 27/8/14.
Sullivan, Timothy, 2/Lt., k. in a., 4/5/15.
2 Taylor, Arthur McCutheon, 2/Lt., k. in a., 10/11/17.
Thomson, Edmund Peel, Major, k. in a., 21/12/14 (att. R. Irish Regt.).
5 Travers, Hugh Mortimer, D.S.O., Capt., k. in a., 8/11/14.
7 Travers, Spencer Robert Valentine, Temp. Lt., k. in a., 9/8/15.
4 Treacy, Michael, 2/Lt., k. in a., 21/3/18.
Tuite, Henry Mark, Lt.-Col., d. of w., 24/3/18.
6 Tynte, M. A., Temp. Major, died, 7/12/18.
5 Varian, Walter Osborne, 2/Lt., k. in a., 30/3/18.
Wace, Herbert Gordon, Temp. 2/Lt., k. in a., 21/8/15.
1 Watts, Stephen, Lt., d. of w., 6/9/16.
6 Webb, Samuel Cecil, 2/Lt., T/Capt., k. in a., 3/10/16.
1 Whateley, Stephen William, Capt., d. of w., 25/10/18.
2 Whelan, Harry George, Lt., died, 11/4/18 (P.O.W.).
Whitby, Eustace Roland, M.C., Lt., k. in a., 20/11/17 (Gr. Bn.).
5 White-Bell, John William, Capt., k. in a., 9/9/16.
9 Williams, Henry Frederick, Major, died, 2/5/16.
3 Wilson, Arthur Dominic, 2/Lt., d. of w., 10/9/16.
1 Wilson, Harry Stuart, Temp. Major and Adjt., k. in a., 9/9/16.
6 Wrong, Colin Bassett, M.C., Lt., k. in a., 28/12/17.
Young, Robert Asshelon, 2/Lt., k. in a., 21/12/14.

The Royal Dublin Fusiliers.

4 Addis, Thomas Henry Liddon, Lt., k. in a., 21/3/18.
Agnew, Andrew Eric Hamilton, Capt., died, 3/11/18.
11 Allen, Arthur Haviland, 2/Lt. (Tp.), k. in a., 4/10/17.
10 Allgood, George, 2/Lt. (Tp.), k. in a., 15/4/17.
Anderson, Denis Vipont Friend, Capt., k. in a., 25/4/15.
Andrews, William, 2/Lt., k. in a., 25/4/15.
10 Armstrong, Charles Martin, 2/Lt. (Tp.), k. in a., 8/2/17.
8 Bagley, Arthur Bracton, M.C., Capt., d. of w., 29/10/18.
3 Bankes, Edward Nugent, Capt., k. in a., 26/4/15.
11 Barre, Gerald Benedict, 2/Lt., killed, 9/8/18 (and R.A.F.).
10 Barrett, Hebron, Lt. (Tp.), d. of w., 27/3/18.
4 Bate, Alfred Francis, Lt., k. in a., 14/3/15 (att. Leinster Rgt.).
4 Beddoes, Henry Roscoe, Lt.-Col., drowned, 15/1/19 (att. 9th Bn.).
8 Belas, Reginald Charles William, 2/Lt. (Tp.), k. in a., 21/3/18.
5 Bell, Alfred Roy Lancaster, 2/Lt., d. of w., 17/5/15.
7 Bell, Lee, 2/Lt. (Tp.), k. in a., 17/10/18.
Bernard, Robert, Lt., k. in a., 25/4/15.
11 Blackwell, Walter, Lt. (Tp.), d. of w., 28/9/18.
Boles, Robert Stephen, 2/Lt. (Tp.), d. of w., 6/5/18.
2 Boulter, Jack Edward Hewitt, M.C., 2/Lt., d. of w., 15/10/18.
Bourke, Bertram Walter, Capt., k. in a., 9/5/15.
Boustead, Lawrence Clive, Lt., k. in a., 28/6/15.
5 Boyd, Frederick Ennis, 2/Lt., k. in a., 20/5/17.
9 Boyd, William Hatchell, 2/Lt., k. in a., 9/9/16.
7 Boyle, John Kennedy, M.C., Lt., died, 21/10/18 (P. of W.).
11 Bradley, John McDonald, Lt. (Tp.), d. of w., 30/9/18.
10 Brereton-Barry, William Roche, 2/Lt., k. in a., 16/8/17.
6 Broun, Richard Clive McBryde, Lt. (Tp.), k. in a., 6/12/15.
8 Burns, Robert Henry, 2/Lt. (Tp.), k. in a., 1/11/18.
Burroughs, Bernard Prendergast, 2/Lt., d. of w., 16/3/17.
11 Byrne, Edward Aloysius, 2/Lt. (Tp.), k. in a., 24/4/17.
8 Cahill, Thomas Laurence, 2/Lt. (Tp.), k. in a., 26/3/18.
9 Callear, Herbert, Capt. (Tp.), k. in a., 16/8/17.
9 Carrette, Albert Ernest, 2/Lt. (Tp.), k. in a., 27/4/16.
10 Carroll, Patrick, 2/Lt. (Tp.), k. in a., 8/2/17.
6 Carruth, John, Lt. (Tp.), d. of w., 10/10/18 (att. R. Ir. Rifs.).
Church, Frederick James, 2/Lt., k. in a., 10/5/15.
8 Clarke, George Alexander, 2/Lt. (Tp.), k. in a., 21/3/18.
5 Clarke, Wilfred John, 2/Lt., d. of w., 9/9/16.
6 Clery, Daniel Richard, Lt., k. in a., 10/8/15.
Cliff, Harold Martin, Lt.-Col., died, 1/2/17.
10 Close, Charles Paul, 2/Lt. (Tp.), d. of w., 14/11/16.
Close, H. B., Lt., died, 1/11/18 (att. 1/2 Bn.).
7 Clover, Harwood Linay, Lt. (Tp.), died, 25/12/16 (and R.F.C.).
Colles, Arthur Grove, Capt., k. in a., 12/3/15 (att. R. Ir. Rif.).
Conroy, Bernard, 2/Lt., k. in a., 5/7/15.
2 Considine, Christopher Daniel, 2/Lt., k. in a., 24/5/15.
7 Cooney, Charles Robert, 2/Lt. (Tp.), k. in a., 9/10/16 (att. R. Irish Rifs.).
9 Cooney, Edmund Luke, 2/Lt. (Tp.), k. in a., 4/6/17.
Corbet, Reginald Vincent Campbell, Lt., k. in a., 25/4/15.
Cowley, George Evelyn, Major (Tp.), d. of w., 18/6/18 (P. of W.).
9 Coyne, John Joseph Aloysius, 2/Lt. (Tp.), k. in a., 10/8/17.
1 Crawford, Sydney George, 2/Lt., drowned, 10/10/18.
7 Crichton, Aleck Godfrey, 2/Lt. (Tp.), k. in a., 16/8/15.
10 Cross, Henry Hazelock, 2/Lt. (Tp.), k. in a., 13/11/16.
Cuffey, Maurice O'Connor, Lt., k. in a., 20/5/15.
7 Cunningham, Bernard Camelis Josh, Capt. (Tp.), k. in a., 21/3/18.
4 Cusack, Reginald Ernest, 2/Lt., died, 15/4/15.
5 Daly, Arthur Charles de Burgh, 2/Lt., k. in a., 9/9/16.
2 Damiand, Walter Henry Alexander, 2/Lt., d. of w., 2/7/16.
3 Davies, Charles Bernard, Lt., k. in a., 9/6/16.
8 Davies, Noel John, 2/Lt. (Tp.), k. in a., 27/4/16.
De Lusignan, Raymond, Lt., k. in a., 25/4/15.
3 Dillon, Edeveain Charles Barclay, 2/Lt., k. in a., 13/10/16.
6 Dinan, George Albert, 2/Lt. (Tp.), k. in a., 9/9/16.
8 Doherty, John, 2/Lt. (Tp.), k. in a., 16/8/17.
2 Donovan, Cyril Bernard, M.C., Lt. (Tp.), k. in a., 25/3/18.
7 Doran, Louis Godfrey, 2/Lt. (Tp.), k. in a., 23/10/16.
1 Dowling, Frederick, Lt., k. in a., 7/8/17.
2 Doyle, Christopher J. G., 2/Lt., k. in a., 15/8/17.
6 Doyle, John Joseph, Lt. (Tp.), k. in a., 10/8/15.
8 Drury, William Symes, Lt. (Tp.), killed, 29/1/16.
Dunlop, George Malcolm, Capt., k. in a., 25/4/15.
Dunlop, John Gunning Moore, 2/Lt., k. in a., 27/8/14.
3 Dunne, John Geoffrey David Baird, Lt., died, 12/11/18.
4 Dunwoody, John Myles, 2/Lt., k. in a., 4/5/17.
4 Edwards, Brian Wallie, 2/Lt., died, 10/11/18 (and R.A.F.).
Edwards, William Victor, Capt., k. in a., 29/12/17.
3 Ellis, Robert Percy, 2/Lt., d. of w., 6/4/18 (as P. of W.).
2 Falkiner, George Stride, 2/Lt., k. in a., 16/8/17.
2 Ferguson, James Ernest, 2/Lt., k. in a., 20/4/17.
Featherstonhaugh, Edwyn, Major, d. of w., 27/4/15.
5 Finlay, Robert Alexander, Lt., k. in a., 9/5/15 (att. 1 R. Ir. Rifs.).
10 Fitzgerald, Robert William, 2/Lt. (Tp.), d. of w., 4/10/18.
10 Fitzgibbon, G. J., Lt. (T/Capt.), k. in a., 20/11/17.
7 Fitzgibbon, Michael Joseph, Lt. (Tp.), k. in a., 15/8/15.
2 Floyd, Henry Murrell, Capt., k. in a., 28/6/15.
9 Forde, John Patrick, 2/Lt., d. of w., 16/8/17.
Frankland, Thomas Hugh Colville, Brevet-Major, k. in a., 25/4/15.
6 Freeney, Patrick Joseph, 2/Lt. (Tp.), k. in a., 8/10/18 (att. 198 L.T.M.B.).
French, Charles Stockley, Lt., k. in a., 25/4/15.
3 Gaffney, James, M.C., Capt. (Tp.), k. in a., 8/10/18.
Gage, John, Capt., died, 7/11/16.
11 Gault, Arthur Alexander, 2/Lt. (Tp.), d. of w., 10/10/18.
George, Herbert Duncan King, Lt., died, 6/4/17 (and R.F.C.) (P. of W.).
2 Gibson, Henry William, 2/Lt. (Tp.), d. of w., 27/11/16.
3 Girvin, Colin Bertram, Capt. (Tp.), died, 5/11/18.
9 Good, Thomas Henry, Capt. (Tp.), d. of w., 8/9/16.
1 Gradwell, George Francis, 2/Lt., k. in a., 28/2/17.
3 Graham, Cecil Hollingsworth, 2/Lt., k. in a., 19/9/16 (att. T.M.B.).
6 Graham, George Lyons, 2/Lt. (Tp.), k. in a., 17/8/17.
4 Gray, George, 2/Lt., killed, 28/4/16.
3 Gray, Meredith, 2/Lt., k. in a., 16/8/16 (att. 10 R. Ir. Rifs.).
7 Greaves, Eric, M.C., Lt. (Tp.), d. of w., 21/11/18.
5 Green, Arthur Vivian, 2/Lt., k. in a., 17/8/17.
1 Green, Harold, 2/Lt. (Tp.), k. in a., 28/2/17.
Grimshaw, Cecil Thomas Wrigley, D.S.O., Major, k. in a., 26/4/15.
10 Guisani, St. John Joseph Vincent Anthony, 2/Lt. (Tp.), k. in a., 13/11/16.
11 Gyves, John James, 2/Lt. (Tp.), k. in a., 3/6/18.
Hackett, Henry Robert Theodore, 2/Lt., k. in a., 2/11/15.
3 Haigh, John Caleb, 2/Lt., k. in a., 2/10/18 (att. 1 R. Ir. Rifs.).
Halligan, Matthew, Lt., k. in a., 18/11/17 (and R.F.C.).
Haines, Alec C., Lt., d. of w., 8/5/15.
Hall, John Ramsay Fitz-Gibbon, 2/Lt., k. in a., 24/5/15.
8 Hamilton, Geoffrey Cecil Monck, 2/Lt. (Tp.), k. in a., 7/9/16.
4 Handyside, Thomas Fosbery, Lt., k. in a., 29/12/17.
6 Hare, Edward Henry, 2/Lt., k. in a., 23/7/19 (att. Yorks. Regt.).
7 Hare, George, Lt. (Tp.), k. in a., 27/12/17.
3 Harold-Barry, J., Capt., k. in a., 24/5/15.
11 Harty, Wilfrid, 2/Lt., k. in a., 8/8/17.
11 Harvey, John Alan, 2/Lt. (Tp.), k. in a., 20/11/17.
Head, Henry d'Esterre, Lt., d. of w., 1/6/15.
4 Heenan, Thomas George Graudon, 2/Lt., k. in a., 21/3/18.
2 Helby, John Alfred Hasler, 2/Lt., d. of w., 3/8/16.
8 Hickey, Robert Francis, 2/Lt., d. of w., 16/8/17.
7 Hickman, Poole Henry, Capt. (Tp.), k. in a., 15/8/15.
Higginson, William Frederick, Capt., k. in a., 25/4/15.
11 Howden, Francis William, 2/Lt. (Tp.), d. of w., 30/3/18.

11 Howell, Reuben Harrison, 2/Lt. (Tp.), d. of w., 29/3/18.
8 Hughes, Bryan Desmond, M.C., Capt. (Tp.), k. in a., 6/8/18.
4 Humphrey, William, M.C., 2/Lt., d. of w., 24/10/18.
Hunter, Ronald Gordon, 2/Lt., d. of w., 25/4/18 (P. of W.).
3 Inglis, Douglas Ian, 2/Lt., k. in a., 7/2/17.
2 Ingoldby, Roger Hugh, 2/Lt. (Tp.), k. in a., 1/7/16.
1 Jackson, William, 2/Lt. (Tp.), k. in a., 30/9/18 (att. 23 R. Fus.).
11 Jackson, Herbert, 2/Lt. (Tp.), k. in a., 21/3/18.
3 Johnson, Richard Digby, Major, k. in a., 24/5/15.
Jones, Samuel Victor Charles, Lt., d. of w., 23/9/16.
3 Jones-Nowlan, Thomas Chamney, 2/Lt., d. of w., 27/5/17 (att. 1st Bn.).
Judd, Frederick George Kerridge, 2/Lt. (Tp.), k. in a., 24/5/15.
7 Julian, Ernest Lawrence, Lt. (Tp.), d. of w., 8/8/15.
11 Karney, David Noel, T/2/Lt. (A/Capt.), k. in a., 21/3/18.
7 Kee, William, M.C., A/Capt., d. of w., 24/3/18 (as P. of W.).
11 Keenan, John, Capt. (Tp.), died, 26/3/17.
Kempston, Robert James, Lt., k. in a., 24/5/15.
3 Kennedy, Arthur St. Clair, 2/Lt., died, 6/3/15.
9 Kettle, Thomas Michael, Lt. (Tp.), k. in a., 9/9/16.
5 Kidson, Charles Wilfrid, Lt., k. in a., 17/10/18.
2 Killingley, Hastings Grewatt, Lt., k. in a., 23/10/16
King, Robert Anderson Ferguson Smyly, 2/Lt., d. of w., 23/5/15.
2 Lemass, Herbert Justin, 2/Lt., k. in a., 23/10/16.
Le Mesurier, Frederick Neil, Capt., k. in a., 25/4/15.
Loveband, Arthur, C.M.G., Lt.-Col., k. in a., 25/5/15.
8 Lowe, Joseph, 2/Lt. (Tp.), k. in a., 26/3/18.
9 McAllister, Charles, A/Capt., k. in a., 27/5/18.
McBrien, Hubert John, 2/Lt. (Tp.), k. in a., 4/11/18.
9 MacCarthy, Cornelius Aloysius, 2/Lt., drowned, 19/7/17.
McCreery, Mona J. M., Capt., died, 21/10/18.
10 McCusker, Patrick Joseph, Lt. (Tp.), k. in a., 13/11/16.
3 MacDaniel, James, 2/Lt., k. in a., 18/8/17 (and R.F.C., 57 Sqd.).
6 McGarry, William Frederick Cecil, 2/Lt. (Tp.), k. in a., 10/8/15.
11 McGuinness, John Norman, 2/Lt., k. in a., 21/3/18 (att. 2 R. Mun. Fus.).
McGuire, Brian, 2/Lt., k. in a., 14/9/14.
2 Maclear, Basil, Capt., k. in a., 24/5/15.
Maclear, Percy, Major, k. in a., 30/8/14.
4 McLoughlin, James Patrick, Lt., d. of w., 24/5/15 (att. R. Irish R.).
4 Macnamara, George Frederick, 2/Lt., k. in a., 17/8/16 (att. 8th Bn.).
2 Macnamara, Maccon John, 2/Lt., k. in a., 26/3/18.
5 McNulty, Michael John, Lt., k. in a., 4/9/15 (att. 9th Bn.).
11 Mallen, William James, 2/Lt. (Tp.), k. in a., 16/8/17.
9 Malone, Joseph James, 2/Lt. (Tp.), k. in a., 16/8/17.
10 Mansfield, Harold Barton, 2/Lt. (Tp.), k. in a., 13/11/16.
5 Marchant, Charles Stewart, 2/Lt., k. in a., 4/6/17.
8 Marlow, Charles Dwyer, 2/Lt. (Tp.), k. in a., 17/8/17.
6 Martin, Charles Andrew, Capt., k. in a., 6/12/15.
3 Martin, Geoffrey Clogstoun, 2/Lt., k. in a., 2/8/16.
3 Martin, Richard Archer Walcott, 2/Lt., k. in a., 16/8/17.
1 Maunsell, Edwin Richard Lloyd, Capt., k. in a., 1/7/16.
8 Maxwell, Thomas, 2/Lt. (Tp), k. in a., 9/9/16.
10 Mehegan, Daniel Joseph, 2/Lt., k. in a., 21/3/18.
11 Millar, James Roland, Capt. (Tp.), k. in a., 16/8/17.
8 Monson, William Herbert, Capt. (Tp.), d. of w., 7/9/16.
1 Mooney, Francis, 2/Lt., k. in a., 28/2/17.
9 Mooney, David George, 2/Lt. (Tp.), k. in a., 16/8/17.
1 Moore, Athelstan, D.S.O., Major (Bt.-Lt.-Col.), d. of w., 14/10/18.
5 Moran, Gerald Charles, Lt., d. of w., 26/5/15.
2 Morgan, John Walter Rees, 2/Lt., k. in a., 1/7/16.
6 Mortimer, William Lionel Gueritz, 2/Lt. (Tp.), d. of w., 10/8/15.
8 Murphy, Edward, 2/Lt. (Tp.), k. in a., 21/3/18.
5 Murphy, James Neville Herbert, 2/Lt., k. in a., 10/5/15.
9 Murphy, William Joseph, Capt. (Tp.), k. in a., 9/9/16.
10 Neilan, Gerald Aloysius, Lt. (Tp.), killed, 24/4/16.
6 Nesbitt, William Charles, 2/Lt. (Tp.), k. in a., 15/8/15.
1 Nolan, James, M.C., D.C.M., 2/Lt., d. of w., 29/9/18.
3 Nolan-Martin, Alfred John, Capt., d. of w., 22/2/17 (att. M.G.C.).
6 O'Carroll, Francis Brendon, 2/Lt. (Tp.), k. in a., 10/8/15.
O'Hara, Henry Desmond, D.S.O., Lt., d. of w., 29/8/15.
9 O'Kearney-White, Ernest Francis, 2/Lt., k. in a., 9/9/16.
5 O'Neill, Frederick, 2/Lt., k. in a., 13/11/16.
3 Palmer, David Adams, M.C, A/Capt., d. of w., 25/3/18 (att. Tank Corps).
10 Palmer, Samuel William, Lt., k. in a., 27/3/18.
Pedlow, William, M.C., A/Capt., k. in a., 12/10/18.
3 Peel, Charles William, 2/Lt., k. in a., 24/4/15.
5 Perrier, Hargrave Carroll Lumley, 2/Lt., k. in a., 8/11/18.
4 Persse, Dudley Eyre, Lt., d. of w., 1/2/15.
Philby, Denis Duncan, Lt., k. in a., 12/11/14 (att. R. Munster Fus.).
7 Pige-Leschallas, Gilbert, Capt. (Tp.), k. in a., 15/8/15.
9 Pither, Harold Francis, 2/Lt., k. in a., 6/7/16.
9 Potter, Robert John, 2/Lt. (Tp.), k. in a., 16/8/17.
8 Poulter, Henry Chapman, Capt. (Tp.), d. of w., 29/11/17.
5 Powell, Frederick William, 2/Lt., died, 20/1/17.
6 Preston, A. J. D, Capt., k. in a., 15/8/15.
Prince-Smith, Donald St. Patrick, Lt. (Tp.), k. in a., 24/10/17 (att. R.F.C, 16 Sqd.).
11 Quigley, Christopher, 2/Lt. (Tp.), k. in a., 21/3/18.
11 Quinn, John Patrick, Lt. (Tp.), d. of w., 20/6/17.
Ransome, Frederick Ronald, 2/Lt., k. in a., 27/5/18.
3 Reavie, Wilfred Laurance, 2/Lt., k. in a., 16/8/17.
3 Reid, Bernard, 2/Lt. (Tp.), k. in a., 28/6/16.
9 Richards, Leslie John, 2/Lt (Tp.), k. in a., 1/8/17.
6 Richards, William Reeves, Capt. (Tp.), k. in a., 15/8/15.
Ridley, Herbert Leslie, M.C., Lt. (A/Capt.), k. in a., 15/7/17.
1 Roberts, William John, 2/Lt., k. in a., 21/3/18.
Robertson, Eric Hume, 2/Lt., k. in a., 21/3/18 (att. 48 T.M.B.).
11 Rogers, James Joseph, 2/Lt. (Tp.), k. in a., 28/3/18.
Rooth, Richard Alexander, Lt.-Col., k. in a., 25/4/15.
4 Rose-Cleland, Alfred Middleton Blackwood Bingham, Lt., k. in a., 1/7/16.
7 Russell, Alexander James, Lt., (Tp.), k. in a., 15/8/15.
10 Russell, Thomas Wallace, 2/Lt. (Tp.), k. in a., 13/11/16.
4 Saffery, Leslie Hall, 2/Lt., k. in a., 1/7/16.
4 Salvesen, Edward Maxwell, 2/Lt., k. in a., 25/4/15.
8 Sheridan, Leonard, Capt., k. in a., 26/3/18.
8 Sheridan, Richard Brinsley, Lt. (Tp.), killed, 7/3/16.
2 Shine, James Owen Williams, Capt., k. in a., 16/8/17.
Sparrow, Francis, 2/Lt., k. in a., 25/4/15.
6 Stanford, Donovan Edward, 2/Lt., k. in a., 21/3/18.
6 Stanton, Robert, 2/Lt., k. in a., 7/8/15.
4 Stewart, Joseph, 2/Lt., k. in a., 16/8/17.
Storrar, Andrew Wynne, 2/Lt., k. in a., 16/8/17 (att. 48 T.M.B.).
7 Sutherland, William, M.M., 2/Lt. (Tp.), k. in a., 7/10/18.
2 Sutton, Robert William, 2/Lt., T/Capt., k. in a., 16/10/15.
Taylor, Adrian Aubrey Charles, Capt., k. in a., 28/6/15 (att. Egypt. Police).
Taylor, John Arthur Harold, 2/Lt., k. in a., 24/9/15.
3 Thomas, Daniel Gwyn, 2/Lt., k. in a., 25/5/15.
Thompson, Gerald Pittis Newman, Lt., k. in a., 4/5/18 (att. 8th Bn.).
7 Tippet, Charles Henry, T/Major, k. in a., 7/8/15.
7 Tobin, Richard Patrick, Capt. (Tp.), k. in a., 15/8/15.
10 Traverse, James Hector, 2/Lt. (Tp.), k. in a., 30/11/17.
11 Tumilty, Austin, 2/Lt. (Tp.), died, 10/11/17.
3 Tweedy, Cecil Mahon, Lt., k. in a. 28/2/17.
4 Tyndall, Joseph Charles, Lt., k. in a., 2/3/15 (att. R. Ir. Rif.).
9 Tyner, Thomas Goodwin, 2/Lt. (Tp.), k. in a., 9/9/16.
8 Valentine, Robert Lepper, Lt. (Tp.), d. of w., 30/4/16.
5 Vardon, Evelyn Francis Claude, 2/Lt., k. in a., 10/5/16.
9 Verley, Albert Stuart Leonard, T/Lt., k. in a., 16/8/17.
9 Vigors, Arthur Cecil, 2/Lt. (Tp.), k. in a., 9/9/16 (att. R. Munster Fus.).
Walkey, Francis Ashton, 2/Lt., k. in a., 17/10/18.
2 Walsh, Lionel Percy, Major (Tp.), d. of w., 4/7/16.
8 Walsh, Phillip James, T/2/Lt., k. in a., 30/11/17.
11 Ward, Bernard, 2/Lt. (Tp.), k. in a., 20/11/17.
4 Warner, Douglas Redston, 2/Lt., k. in a., 1/7/16.
7 Weatherill, Edward Theaker, 2/Lt. (Tp.), k. in a., 15/8/15.
4 White, William, 2/Lt., k. in a., 25/4/15.
3 Whitehead, Walter, 2/Lt., k. in a., 6/9/16.
11 Williams, John, 2/Lt. (Tp.), drowned, 22/10/17.
10 Wilson, Alexander Stewart, 2/Lt. (Tp.), k. in a., 20/4/17.
Wilson, Denis Erskine, Major (Tp.), d. of w., 24/9/16.
Wylie, J. R., 2/Lt., killed, 23/4/18 (att. R.A.F.).
Young, Mervyn Cyril Nicholas Radford, 2/Lt., d. of w., 25/5/15.

The Rifle Brigade (The Prince Consort's Own).

6 Abbott, John Gurney, 2/Lt., k. in a., 21/9/17 (att. 59 T.M.B.).
16 Abrahams, Montague, Major (Tp.), k. in a., 3/9/16.
6 Adam, Frank Dalziel, Lt., d. of w., 16/7/18.
Adam, Peter, M.C., 2/Lt., k. in a., 31/7/17.
1 Adams, Lestock Hanley, Lt. (Tp.), k. in a., 22/4/18.
1 Ainley, John Hirst, 2/Lt., k. in a., 21/[illegible]/18.
Aiton, William, 2/Lt., k. in a., 21/3/18.
Alexander, Reginald, Lt.-Col., d. of w., 29/12/14.
Allen, Valentine Francis, 2/Lt. (Tp.), k. in a., 17/11/17 (att. 16 Bn.).
7 Anstey, Henry, 2/Lt. (Tp.), k. in a., 11/4/17.
6 Anstie, Edward Basil, 2/Lt., k. in a., 23/3/18.
2 Arch, Arthur James, 2/Lt. (Tp.), d. of w., 27/5/18.
6 Armstrong, Edward William, 2/Lt., d. of w., 11/7/15 (att. 3 Bn.).
8 Ashforth, Dudley Sutton, 2/Lt. (Tp.), k. in a., 15/9/16.
10 Averdieck, George Gerald, Lt. (Tp.), d. of w., 14/9/16.
12 Ayres, Clement, 2/Lt., k. in a., 20/9/17.
1 Backus, Arthur Ronald, M.C., Capt. (Tp.), died, 23/9/17 (att. 8th Bn.).
8 Baddock, Thomas Agnew, Lt. (Tp.), d. of w., 3/12/17.
6 Bagnall, George Barry, Lt., k. in a., 23/4/17 (att. 13th Bn.).
2 Baker, Basil Howard, Lt., k. in a., 22/5/18 (att. 13th Bn.).
8 Balleine, Cuthbert Francis, Capt., k. in a., 2/7/15.
16 Banbury, William Michael Victor, Capt., k. in a., 17/8/17.
1 Barclay, Geoffrey William, Major (Tp.), k. in a., 28/7/16.
8 Barker-Mill, William Claude Frederick Vaudrey, Capt. (Tp.), k. in a., 15/9/16.
6 Barnard, Humphrey Denzil, 2/Lt., k. in a., 21/8/16 (att. 3rd Bn.).
16 Barrett, John Ambrose, 2/Lt. (Tp.), k. in a., 31/7/17.
5 Bassham, Reginald Owen, 2/Lt., k. in a., 31/5/17.
9 Bayley, Peter Ferguson, 2/Lt., k. in a., 23/3/18.
16 Beale, Cecil Charles, 2/Lt. (Tp.), d. of w., 29/1/17.
1 Beech, Robert Clyde, Capt., k. in a., 18/10/16.
1 Beever, William Henry, Capt., k. in a., 1/7/16.
Bell, Leonard, Lt. (Tp.), d. of w., 22/5/18.
Bennett, John Benson, 2/Lt. (Tp.), k. in a., 28/3/18.
9 Benson, Hugh Cecil, Lt., k. in a., 22/6/15.
5 Biddulph, Victor Roundell George, 2/Lt., k. in a., 15/9/16 (att. 8th Bn.).
5 Blackie, John Stewart, Lt., k. in a., 18/10/16 (att. 1st Bn.).
6 Blades, Laurence Turner, 2/Lt., 5/7/15 (att. 1st Bn.).
8 Blades, William Henry, 2/Lt., k. in a., 3/5/17.
5 Blair, Patrick Charles Bentley, 2/Lt., k. in a., 6/7/15.
16 Blunden, Oswald, Capt. (Tp.), k. in a., 4/7/16.

Blunt, Charles George, 2/Lt. (Tp.), k. in a., 21/3/18.
11 Blyth, James Reginald, 2/Lt. (Tp.), k. in a., 10/7/16.
Boden, Anthony Drummond, Major, k. in a., 24/9/14.
12 Bonser, Winfield Joice, Capt. (Tp.), k. in a., 25/9/15.
Booth, William, 2/Lt. (Tp.), d. of w., 28/2/17 (and R.F.C., 78 Sqd.).
13 Boothby, Ernest Brooke, 2/Lt. (Tp.), k. in a., 10/7/10.
5 Boswell, William Gerald Knox, Capt., d. of w., 28/7/16 (att. 2nd Bn.).
6 Bott, George, 2/Lt., k. in a., 9/2/17 (att. 1st Bn.).
8 Boughey, Anchital Edward Fletcher, Lt. (Tp.), drowned, 10/10/18.
6 Bourns, Charles, Lt., k. in a., 25/5/15 (att. 4th Bn.).
13 Bowyer, John William, Capt. (Tp.), k. in a., 10/4/17.
9 Bradby, Daniel Edward, Capt. (Tp.), k. in a., 9/4/17.
6 Bradley, Geoffrey Montagu, Lt., k. in a., 22/12/14 (att. Welsh R.).
12 Brand, Percy Alfred Easterling, 2/Lt. (Tp.), k. in a., 28/9/17.
1 Brandt, Douglas Robert, Lt., d. of w., 6/7/15.
2 Brooker, James, 2/Lt. (Tp.), k. in a., 2/12/17.
2 Brown, Algernon James, 2/Lt. (Tp.), d. of w., 1/12/16.
6 Brown, Anthony William Scudamore, Lt., k. in a., 18/8/16 (att. 3rd Bn.).
16 Brown, Bertram, Capt. (Tp.), k. in a., 3/9/10.
6 Brown, Frederick Henry, 2/Lt., k. in a., 29/5/18.
9 Brown, John Alexander, T/Lt. (A/Capt.), d. of w., 22/10/18 (att. 13th Bn.).
10 Brown, James McDonald, 2/Lt. (Tp.), k. in a., 21/3/18.
13 Bruce, Douglas Fraser, 2/Lt. (Tp.), k. in a., 10/7/16.
2 Bruce, Oliver, 2/Lt. (Tp.), d. of w., 9/6/18 (P. of W.).
11 Buchan, Francis Hall, 2/Lt. (Tp.), d. of w., 7/8/18.
9 Buckley, Joseph Michael, M.C., Capt (Tp.), k. in a., 23/12/17.
10 Buckworth, William, Lt. (Tp.), k. in a., 14/8/17.
Buller, Herbert Cecil, D.S.O., Lt.-Col., k. in a., 3/6/16 (P.P.C.L.I.).
2 Burnell, Arthur Coke, Capt., k. in a., 18/3/16.
Burton, Robert Cecil, Capt., d. of w., 16/3/15.
11 Butcher, Harold Thomas, 2/Lt. (Tp.), k. in a., 17/2/16.
6 Butler, Leonard Gray, Capt., k. in a., 21/8/16 (att. 3rd Bn.).
16 Butt, Lewis John Dagleish, 2/Lt. (Tp.), k. in a., 4/7/16.
9 Butterworth, Hugh Montagu, Capt. (Tp.), k. in a., 25/9/15.
6 Buxton, Andrew Richard, Lt., k. in a., 7/6/17.
5 Buxton, Hugh Forster, Lt., d. of w., 2/11/16.
6 Buxton, Jocelyn Murray Victor, 2/Lt., k. in a., 1/7/16.
10 Byng, Francis Dacre, Capt. (Tp.), k. in a., 3/9/16.
2 Byrne-Johnson, John Vivian, Capt., k. in a., 22/8/16.
5 Cable, George Pickersgill, 2/Lt., k. in a., 9/5/15 (att. 2nd Bn.).
Calvert, John Dutton, Lt., k. in a., 14/2/15.
Campbell, Evan McDonald, 2/Lt. (Tp.), k. in a., 5/10/17 (att. 13th Bn.).
9 Carmichael, Douglas, Capt. (Tp.), k. in a., 25/9/15.
1 Cartland, Guy Trevor, Capt. and Adjt., k. in a., 1/7/16.
6 Casswell, Eric Denison Seymour, Capt., k. in a., 7/11/17.
2 V.C. Cates, George Edward, 2/Lt., died, 9/3/17.
1 Chamberlain, Cyril John, Lt. (Tp.), k. in a., 6/10/17.
Chapman, David Markwell, Lt. (Tp.), k. in a., 25/3/18.
5 Chapman, Laurence Oxley, 2/Lt., k. in a., 31/7/17 (att. 3rd Bn.).
Chapman, Lawrence Vaughan, Lt. (Tp.), k. in a., 25/9/15.
10 Chapman, Montague Gerald Herbert, 2/Lt. (Tp.), k. in a., 14/8/17.
1/2 Chapman, William Henry, 2/Lt. (Tp.), k. in a., 20/9/17 (att. 11 Bn.).
Cholmondeley, Reginald, Capt., killed, 12/3/15 (and R.F.C.).
Churcher, Edgar, Lt. (Tp.), k. in a., 14/7/17 (and R.F.C., 32 Sq.).
Churchyard, Arthur Stewart, Capt. (Tp.), died, 28/1/17 (att. 1 Dub. Fus.).
5 Clark, Charles Augustus, 2/Lt., k. in a., 1/7/16 (att. 1st Bn.).
13 Clark, Colbert Walter, 2/Lt., k. in a., 26/4/18.
16 Clark, Roland Hope, 2/Lt. (Tp.), d. of w., 24/3/18.
7 Clark, Stewart, T/2/Lt., k. in a., 21/3/18.
5 Clarke, Arundel Geoffrey, 2/Lt., k. in a., 1/7/16.
6 Clarke, Harold Percival, Lt., d. of w., 9/5/15 (att. 2nd Bn.).
12 Clive-Smith, Colin Metcalfe, 2/Lt. (Tp.), k. in a., 24/3/18.
10 Coates, Basil Montgomery, 2/Lt. (Tp.), k. in a., 7/9/15.
6 Cobbold, Robert Henry Wanklyn, Lt., k. in a., 9/9/15 (att. 2nd Bn.).
Cochrane, George, 2/Lt. (Tp.), k. in a., 19/9/17.
8 Coles, Arthur Norman, Lt. (Tp.), k. in a., 24/8/16.
Coles, Herbert, 2/Lt., k. in a., 18/11/17.
Collins, George Edwin, 2/Lt. (Tp.), k. in a., 11/1/18.
7 Collins, Philip, Capt., k. in a., 30/7/15.
7 Combe, George Henry Richard, Lt. (Tp.), k. in a., 15/9/16.
V.C. Congreve, William La Touche, D.S.O., M.C., Capt. and Bvt.-Major, k. in a., 20/7/16.
Cook, Reginald Cyril, 2/Lt. (Tp.), d. of w., 11/7/18 (att. 8 Bn.).
Cooke, Charles Herbert, 2/Lt. (Tp.), k. in a., 21/9/17.
16 Cooper, Hubert, 2/Lt. (Tp.), d. of w., 30/3/18.
1 Corris, William Henry, 2/Lt., A/Capt., d. of w., 31/8/18.
7 Cossar, Norman Thomson, 2/Lt. (Tp.), k. in a., 15/5/17.
6 Cowell, Albert Victor John, Capt., died, 29/1/15 (att. 6th Bn.).
6 Craigmile, Alexander Murray, M.C., Capt., k. in a., 29/3/18.
3 Crawford-Kehrmann, Jessel, Lt., k. in a., 24/1/15 (att. S Staff. R.).
14 Creagh, Reginald Simon Macnamara, Lt. (Tp.), died, 5/12/17.
8 Crebbin, William Arthur, M.C., Capt. (Tp.), k. in a., 4/4/18.
5 Crosfield, Guy Henry G., Lt., k. in a., 26/1/18 (att. 1st Bn.).
Crouch, Alan, 2/Lt. (Tp.), k. in a., 25/8/16 (42 T.M.B.).
15 Cullis, Henry Thoreau, 2/Lt. (Tp.), k. in a., 10/12/15 (att 12 Bn.).
13 Cunliffe, Bart., Sir Foster Hugh Egerton, Major (Tp.), k. in a., 10/7/16.
6 Curnock, George Ashwin, Lt., k. in a., 14/8/17 (att. 10 Bn.).
Curtis, Jocelyn Stewart, 2/Lt., k. in a., 21/3/18.
8 Dalgoutte, George Cork, 2/Lt. (Tp.), k. in a., 3/5/17.
3 Daly, William Cecil Thomas, 2/Lt., k. in a., 18/8/16.
Daniell, Archibald Steuart Lindsey, 2/Lt., k. in a., 19/12/14.
15 Dashwood, Ronald Phillimore, T/2/Lt., k. in a., 7/10/16 (att. 12 Bn.).
6 Davenport, Arthur, Lt., k. in a., 23/8/18.
6 Davey, Thomas Kerrison, 2/Lt., d. of w., 31/3/18 (att. 1st Bn.).
9 Davies, Frederick George, 2/Lt. (Tp.), k. in a., 6/2/16.
5 Davies, Leonard, T/Lt., A/Capt., k. in a., 3/6/17 (att. 9 Bn.).
13 Davy, Philip Francis, M.C., T/2/Lt., A/Capt., k. in a., 4/11/18.
5 Dawson, Anthony, Lt., k. in a., 13/7/16 (att. 2 Bn.).
12 Denison, Gerald Evelyn Henry, 2/Lt. (Tp.), k. in a., 25/9/15.
6 Dent, Reginald Teesdale, 2/Lt., k. in a., 24/3/18.
7 Devitt, Guy Francis Ormond, 2/Lt. (Tp.), k. in a., 30/7/15.
Dewhurst, George Charnley Littleton, Lt. (Tp.), k. in a., 1/7/16.
Dimsdale, Edward Charles, Capt., k. in a., 8/5/15.
11 Donner, Eric Robert, Capt. (Tp.), k. in a., 3/9/16.
17 Doyle, Thomas Walter, 2/Lt. (Tp.), d. of w., 9/8/16.
7 Drummond, Spencer Hensage, Capt., k. in a., 30/7/15.
11 Drysdale, Ian Staveley, 2/Lt. (Tp.), k. in a., 18/9/15.
Dumaresq, Herbert William, Major, died, 14/1/16.
Duncan, Charles Eric, 2/Lt. (Tp.), k. in a., 24/11/16.
5 Dunnage, Arthur, 2/Lt., k. in a., 1/9/16.
Durham, Edward, Lt., k. in a., 26/11/14.
6 Durrant, William Blencowe, 2/Lt., k. in a., 9/5/15 (att. 2nd Bn.).
6 Dyer, Cecil MacMillan, 2/Lt., k. in a., 9/4/15 (att. 4th Bn.).
10 Edwards, Bernard Wallace, Capt. (Tp.), k. in a., 14/8/17.
3 Edwards, John, 2/Lt. (Tp.), k. in a., 22/3/18.
10 Edwards, Roy, 2/Lt., d. of w., 30/11/17.
1 Egerton-Green, John William, Capt., d. of w., 9/10/17.
9 Elliott, Walter Leonard, Lt., died, 21/11/16.
2 Ellis, Robert Charles, 2/Lt. (Tp.), died, 31/5/18 (as P.O.W.).
2 Etheridge, Cecil Norbert, Lt., k. in a., 29/3/18.
7 Eyton, Robert William, Lt. (Tp.), k. in a., 22/3/18 (att. 41 T.M.B.).
6 Fagan, Niel, 2/Lt., d. of w., 20/7/16 (att. 1st Bn.).
8 Fairweather, William Lyall, 2/Lt. (Tp.), k. in a., 22/3/18.
Fenner, Thomas, 2/Lt. (A/Capt.), k. in a., 22/3/18.
16 Fenton, Gilbert Francis Rowland, Lt. (Tp.), k. in a., 4/7/16.
12 Fergusson, Fitz-James Shillington, 2/Lt. (Tp.), k. in a., 22/3/18.
13 Ferrier, John Kinmont, 2/Lt. (Tp.), d. of w., 23/8/18.
Field, William Christian, T/2/Lt., k. in a., 31/7/17.
16 Finlay, Edward Norman Alison, 2/Lt., k. in a., 4/7/16.
Fitzherbert-Brockholes, Thomas Joseph, Capt., d. of w., 14/3/15.
6 Follett, George, 2/Lt., k. in a., 19/9/18 (att. 1/10 Lon. R.).
6 Foreshew, Henry John Hulbert, 2/Lt., k. in a., 15/4/17.
13 Forrester, James, M.C., 2/Lt. (Tp.), k. in a., 8/5/18.
12 Forster-Brown, James Cameron, Lt. (Tp.), d. of w., 27/8/16.
11 Fortescue, Greaville, Capt. (Tp.), k. in a., 4/9/15.
10 Fortune, Stanley Welsh, 2/Lt., k. in a., 13/3/16.
7 Fosdick, John Hyland, Lt. (Tp.), d. of w., 31/7/15.
10 Fox, Albert Victor, 2/Lt., k. in a., 3/9/16.
13 Fraser, George Dick, 2/Lt. (Tp.), d. of w., 3/6/18.
6 Fraser, Rowland, Capt. (Tp.), k. in a., 1/7/16 (att. 1st Bn.).
10 Frere, Gilbert Raper, T/Lt. & Adjt., d. of w., 26/10/15.
5 Frisch, Maurice, 2/Lt., k. in a., 25/8/16 (att. 2nd Bn.).
11 Gabbett-Fairfax, Thomas Oliver, 2/Lt., k. in a., 14/8/17.
Gamble, George, 2/Lt. (Tp.), d. of w., 24/9/17.
Gardiner, William MacPherson, 2/Lt. (Tp.), k. in a., 16/1/18.
14 Garrard, Stanley Charles, 2/Lt. (Tp.), k. in a., 28/8/15 (att. 8 Bn.).
Garton, Edward Clive, 2/Lt., d. of w., 2/9/18 (att. 5 Bn.).
9 Garton, Herbert Westlake, Capt. (Tp.), k. in a., 15/9/16.
Gauld, George, Lt., died, 24/6/19.
7 Gent, Thomas Samuel, 2/Lt. (Tp.), k. in a., 24/7/15.
6 Gibbs, David Angas, 2/Lt., k. in a., 24/3/18 (att. 2nd Bn.).
6 Gibbs, Bernard, M.C., 2/Lt., k. in a, 6/7/15 (att. 1st Bn.).
16 Gilbert, Herbert James, 2/Lt. (Tp.), k. in a., 22/3/18.
5 Gilbey, Eric, Lt., k. in a., 10/3/15.
1/4 Gilchrist, Archibald, 2/Lt., killed, 3/10/18 (and R.A.F.).
7 Gillespie, William Edward, 2/Lt. (Tp.), k. in a., 11/9/18.
Gilliatt, Otho Claude Skipwith, Capt., k. in a., 30/10/14.
6 Glover, George Wright, D.S.O., Lt., d. of w., 31/8/18 (att. 1st Bn.).
Godolphin-Osborne, Maurice, Capt., d. of w., 25/2/15.
7 Godsal, Alan, 2/Lt. (Tp.), k. in a., 30/7/15.
2 Godwin, Louis Vionnet, 2/Lt. (Tp.), k. in a., 23/10/16.
Gordon, Sidney George, 2/Lt. (Tp.), k. in a., 20/9/17 (att 16 Bn.).
Gracey, Horace Charles, Capt., k. in a., 18/10/16.
Gradwell, Charles Edward, Lt., k. in a., 21/3/18 (att. M.G.C.).
17 Graham, Thomas Harold, 2/Lt. (Tp.), d. of w., 25/10/16.
17 Grant, Harold Edward, 2/Lt. (Tp.), k. in a., 3/9/16.
6 Gray, Edward Jasper, 2/Lt., k. in a., 31/3/18.
2 Greathead, John Rivers, 2/Lt. (Tp.), k. in a., 23/10/16.
1 Greenfield, Ronald William, Lt., k. in a., 23/10/16.
5 Greenup, John Bertram, 2/Lt., k. in a., 12/10/17 (att. 1st Bn.).

8 Grenfell, The Hon. Gerald William, 2/Lt. (Tp.), k. in a., 30/7/15.
1 Gull, Francis William Lindley, Capt. (A/Major), k. in a., 25/8/18 (att. 13 Bn.).
12 Habershon, Kenneth Rees, Capt. (Tp.), k. in a., 12/2/16.
1 Haden, Frederick Haughton, 2/Lt., k. in a., 4/11/17 (att. 11 T.M.B.).
Hadland, Spencer Austin, Capt., k. in a., 24/3/18.
Hadwen, Charles Eugene, 2/Lt. (Tp.), k. in a., 12/9/18 (att. 13 Bn.).
Halford, Arthur Henry, 2/Lt., d. of w., 30/5/18 (att. 7th Bn.) (P.O.W.). No 7th Bn; reduced to Cadre 30/4/18
6 Haldane, James Oswald, 2/Lt., d. of w., 9/8/16.
7 Hall, John Smith, Lt., k. in a., 21/3/18.
15 Halstead, Arthur Frederick, Lt., k. in a., 28/6/15.
10 Hamilton, John Stewart, 2/Lt. (Tp.), k. in a., 21/3/18.
6 Handford, Reginald Stuart, 2/Lt., d. of w., 9/8/16.
2 Hardinge, Hon. Henry Ralph, 2/Lt., k. in a., 9/5/15.
7 Hardy, Ronald Montagu, Capt., k. in a., 23/7/15.
Hargreaves, Alan Knyveton, D.S.O., Capt., k. in a., 9/5/15.
Harman, George Malcolm N., D.S.O., Major, k. in a., 27/11/14.
Harrison, Cecil Eustace, Major, k. in a., 14/3/15.
1 Harvey, John, 2/Lt., d. of w., 10/9/18
17 Hatch, Reginald William, Lt., k. in a., 3/9/16.
6 Heald, Douglas, 2/Lt., d. of w., 6/10/17.
Heap, Wilfred Herbert, 2/Lt. (Tp.), k. in a., 25/2/17 (att. 12 Bn.)
2 Heaton-Ellis, David, M.C., Capt., k in a., 27/5/18.
Helyar, Maurice Howard, Capt., k. in a., 24/1/15.
5 Hemmant, Maurice, Lt. (Tp.), k. in a., 14/8/17 (att. 11 Bn.).
1 Henderson, Andrew William, Capt. (Tp.), k. in a., 1/7/16.
4 Henderson, James Greig Mitchell, 2/Lt., k. in a., 18/8/16.
6 Henderson, Thomas Harvey, M.C., Capt. (Tp.), k. in a., 30/11/17 (att. 10 Bn.).
9 Henn, Edward Henry Lovett, 2/Lt. (Tp.), k. in a., 25/9/15.
6 Hepburn, Andrew Munro, 2/Lt., k. in a., 3/9/16 (att. 11 Bn.).
5 Herbert-Smith, Vere, 2/Lt., k. in a., 22/3/15.
9 Hesseltine, William, 2/Lt. (Tp.), k. in a., 21/8/16.
10 Hield, John Hamer, Capt., k. in a., 3/9/16.
Hill, Walter Henry, 2/Lt. (Tp.), k. in a., 20/11/17 (att. 10 Bn.).
Hill, Wilfred Stuart, 2/Lt. (Tp.), k. in a., 31/7/17.
Hillman, Leslie Hawis, Lt, k. in a., 31/7/17.
6 Hoare, Gerard Croft, 2/Lt., died, 1/8/18.
13 Hobday, William Edward, D.C.M., 2/Lt. (Tp.), k. in a., 11/4/17.
Hogg, James, 2/Lt. (Tp.), k. in a., 2/12/17.
6 Holland, Arthur Leslie, 2/Lt., k. in a., 21/4/17 (att. 2nd Bn.).
16 Hopkin, Robert Thomas, 2/Lt. (Tp.), k. in a., 20/9/17.
Hopwood, Robert Gerald, Capt., k. in a., 24/8/16 (att. R.F.C., 70 Sqd.).
Hoste, Bart., Sir William Graham, 2/Lt., k. in a., 9/5/15.
Hosler, Albert Edward, 2/Lt (Tp.), k. in a., 26/8/17.
8 House, Malcolm Hutchinson, 2/Lt. (Tp.), k. in a., 3/5/17.
6 Howell, Augustus William, 2/Lt., k. in a., 15/4/17.
5 Huddart, Robert Edward Thorne, 2/Lt., k. in a., 30/6/16 (att. 2nd Bn.).
5 Hugh-Jones, Kenneth Herbert, 2/Lt. (A/Capt.), k. in a., 20/9/17 (att. 12 Bn.).
Hunt, Charles Francis, 2/Lt (A/Capt.), k. in a., 25/9/15.
Hunter, Thomas Vicars, Capt., k in a., 5/12/17 (att. R.F.C., 66 Sqd.).
Ingram, Henry John, 2/Lt. (Tp.), d. of w., 22/9/17 (att. 16 Bn.).
10 Irvine, Charles Knowles, Capt. (Tp.), k in a., 14/8/17.
Isaac, John Edmund Valentine, D.S.O., Capt., k. in a., 9/5/15.
Jackson, George Henry, M.C., 2/Lt., k. in a., 31/7/17.
Jackson, Geoffrey Laird, Lt. (A/Capt.), k. in a., 9/4/17.
1 Jeffery, Charles Launcelot, 2/Lt. (A/Capt.), d. of w., 23/9/17 (att. 10 Bn.).
Jeffery, William, 2/Lt. (Tp.), d. of w., 7/10/17 (att. 10 Bn.).
Jenkinson, John Banks, Capt., k. in a., 14/9/14.
13 Johnson, Fred Blacktin, 2/Lt. (Tp.), k. in a., 31/5/17.
6 Johnston, Basil, 2/Lt., k. in a., 3/9/16 (att. 11 Bn.).
5 Jones, Edward Pitcairn, 2/Lt., d. of w., 13/5/16 (att. 9th Bn.).
13 Jones, R. Colville, 2/Lt., killed, 4/11/18 (and R.A.F.).
Jones-Vaughan, Hugh Thomas Charles, Major, died, 20/11/18.
6 Juckes, George Francis, 2/Lt., k. in a., 6/7/15 (att. 1st Bn.).
14 Keele, Charles Acland, Capt. (Tp.), k. in a., 12/7/16.
8 Keesey, George Ernest Howard, Capt. (Tp.), k. in a., 24/8/16.
2 Kemp, Harold George, 2/Lt., k. in a., 21/10/15.
5 Kennedy, John Patrick Francis, Capt., k. in a., 24/4/18 (att. 2 Bn.)
2 Kennedy, Paul Adrian, Capt., k. in a., 9/5/15.
Keppell, The Hon. Albert Edward George Arnold, Lt., k. in a., 31/7/17.
Keppie, Charles Browning, 2/Lt. (Tp.), d. of w., 27/3/18.
12 Kerr, Edward Bournes, Lt. (Tp.), d. of w., 26/5/16.
King, Arthur Montague, Major, k. in a., 15/3/15.
Kingswell, Frank Alford, Lt. (Tp.), k. in a., 22/3/18 (att. 8 Bn.).
Kirkland, Frederick William, 2/Lt., k. in a., 1/7/16.
14 Knight, Alan Collingwood, Lt., d. of w., 29/6/15 (att. R. Dub. Fus.).
12 Knights-Smith, Bernard Arthur, 2/Lt. (Tp.), k. in a., 5/9/15.
5 Knowles, John Lyndon, 2/Lt., k. in a., 18/8/16.
5 Knowles, Stephen, 2/Lt., d. of w., 24/10/16.
16 Krolik, Elliot, M.C., Capt. (Tp.), k. in a., 23/10/17.
Lamb, James Scott, 2/Lt. (Tp.), k. in a., 10/9/18 (att. 2 Bn.).
Landale, Douglas Blackwood, Lt., k. in a., 23/10/14.
10 Lane, Arthur Bloomfield, Capt. (Tp.), k. in a., 20/11/17.

10 Large, Harold Emmott, Capt. (Tp.), d. of w., 9/10/15.
5 Lascelles, Guy Ernest, 2/Lt., k. in a., 24/3/18.
Lascelles, John Frederick, Lt., k. in a., 31/7/15 (and R.F.C.).
3 Latter, George Walter William, 2/Lt. (Tp.), k. in a., 11/7/16.
6 Laurence, Dudley Sydney, 2/Lt., k. in a., 23/10/16 (att. 1st Bn.).
7 Lawson, Arthur Cyril, 2/Lt. (Tp.), d. of w., 6/7/17.
7 Lawson, Reginald Hugh, Lt. (Tp.), k. in a., 24/8/16.
8 Le Blanc-Smith, Charles Ralph, Lt. (Tp.), k. in a., 27/11/15.
12 Le Blond, Robert Cecil Gamage du Plessis, Capt., died, 17/5/15.
6 Ledger, Raymond Kerwood, Lt., k. in a., 13/4/15 (att. R. Welsh Fus.).
13 Lee, Frank Stanley, Lt. (Tp.), k. in a., 22/3/18.
Leeke, Ralph Henry, Capt. (T/Maj.), died, 5/11/15 (att. 4 K. Afr. Rifs.).
5 Leetham, Reginald, Lt. (A/Capt.), k. in a., 12/10/17 (att. 1st Bn.).
2 Leigh, Edward Henry, Lt., k. in a., 9/5/15.
10 Leitch, Alexander Harold Percival, 2/Lt. (Tp.), d. of w., 22/5/18.
Leslie, Norman Jerome Beauchamp, Capt., k. in a., 19/10/14
2 Leyland, Reginald Hamilton, Lt.-Col. (Act.), k. in a., 24/9/18.
13 Lezard, Arthur Gower, Capt., k. in a., 31/1/16.
Lowson, Courtenay Patrick Flowerdew, Lt., killed, 3/11/17 (and R.F.C.).
Lynch, Bartholomew Patrick, Lt. (Tp.), k. in a., 15/9/16 (att. 9th Btn.).
8 McAfee, Lewis Alexander, Capt. (Tp.), k. in a., 30/7/15.
13 Macaulay, James, 2/Lt., k. in a., 4/11/18.
McCormick, William John, 2/Lt. (Tp.), k. in a., 8/11/17 (att. 11th Btn.).
7 McCubbin, Percy Griffith, 2/Lt. (Tp.), k. in a., 23/4/18.
9 McGee, Thomas, 2/Lt. (Tp.), k. in a., 24/4/18 (att. 2nd Bn.).
Mackenson, Christopher, 2/Lt., d. of w., 16/8/17.
9 Mackie, Harold, Lt., d. of w., 18/11/17.
Maclachlan, Ronald Campbell, D.S.O., Brig-Gen. (Tp.), k. in a., 11/8/17 (Staff, 112th Inf. Bde.).
16 McLay, Joseph, 2/Lt. (Tp.) (A/Capt.), died, 9/10/18.
16 Maclehose, James Colin, 2/Lt. (Tp.), k. in a., 14/2/17.
8 Macnaghten, Arthur Douglas, 2/Lt. (Tp.), k. in a., 15/9/16.
6 Mallinson, John Whiteley, 2/Lt., k. in a., 14/2/16 (att. M.G.C.).
12 Maltby, Charles Robert Crigaton, Lt. (Tp.), d. of w., 27/8/16.
5 Marchetti, Alexander, 2/Lt., k. in a., 15/3/16.
7 Marriott, Frederick Ernest, 2/Lt. (Tp.), k. in a., 30/7/15.
15 Marriott, Hugh Digby, 2/Lt. (Tp.), k. in a., 9/10/15.
5 Marsden-Smedley, George Futvoye, 2/Lt., k. in a., 18/8/16.
10 Martin, Gordon Eric, 2/Lt. (Tp.), k. in a., 14/8/17.
3 Martin, Wilfred Arthur, T/2/Lt. (A/Capt.), k. in a., 3/8/17.
6 Mason, Randall Stewart, 2/Lt., k. in a., 14/3/15.
Mason, William James, 2/Lt. (Tp.), k. in a., 20/9/17 (att. 11th Bn.).
5 Matheson, Claude Bruce, 2/Lt., k. in a., 23/9/17 (att. 2nd Bn.).
8 Matthews, Edward Philip, Lt (Tp.), d. of w., 16/9/16.
7 Maxwell, John, D.S.O., M.C., Capt. (A/Lt.-Col.), d. of w., 4/12/17 (8th K.R.R.C.).
13 Mayersbach, Jack Frederick, 2/Lt. (Tp.), k. in a., 4/5/18.
13 Meade, Robert Percy, 2/Lt. (Tp.), k. in a., 11/7/16.
1/4 Melvin, W. S., 2/Lt., killed, 23/8/18 (and R.A.F.).
Merewether, John Alwarth, Capt. (Tp.), k. in a., 15/9/16.
8 Merriman, William Robert Hill, 2/Lt. (Tp.), k. in a., 15/8/16.
12 Messenger, Wilfred Chaundler, Capt. (Tp.), d. of w., 16/9/17.
Meysey-Thompson, The Hon. Claude Henry Meysey, Capt., d. of w., 17/6/15.
6 Millar, Arthur Liberty, Capt., k. in a., 15/4/18 (att. 4th Bn.).
8 Milsom, Sidney, Lt. (Tp.), k. in a., 30/7/15.
7 Milward, Philip Henry, Capt. (Tp.), d. of w., 7/12/15.
Minty, Reginald, 2/Lt. (Tp.), k. in a., 22/5/18 (att. 3rd Bn.).
Moloney, Frank, 2/Lt. (Tp.), k. in a., 9/4/18 (att. 6th Som. L.I.).
6 Monteith, William Neve, Lt., k. in a., 25/9/15 (att. 2nd Bn.).
10 Moore, Robert, 2/Lt. (Tp.), d. of w., 15/8/17.
5 Moore, Ernest Francis Courtney, M.C., 2/Lt., k. in a., 24/3/18.
1/4 Moore, J. G., Lt., died, 5/7/18 (and R.A.F.).
2 Moore, Samuel Kerr, 2/Lt. (Tp.), k. in a., 25/2/18.
Morgan-Grenville, Hon. Richard George Grenville, Capt., k. in a., 19/12/14.
Morris, Garfield Hughes, 2/Lt. (Tp.), k. in a., 17/8/17.
9 Morris, Thomas Herbert Picton, M.C., Lt.-Col. (Tp.) d. of w. 18/9/16.
2 Morrison, William, 2/Lt. (Tp.), k. in a., 2/12/17.
6 Morum, James Pearse, 2/Lt., k. in a., 1/7/16 (att. 1st Bn.).
7 Moseley, Herbert James Ritchie, 2/Lt. (Tp.), k. in a., 27/6/16.
12 Munro, Murdo Simon, 2/Lt. (Tp.), k. in a., 26/4/17.
8 Newell, Arthur Francis, Capt. (Acting), d. of w., 4/4/18.
5 Nixon, M.A., Capt., died, 26/9/17.
6 Northcroft, Percival William Cordery, Lt., k. in a., 31/7/17 (att. 3rd Bn.).
8 Oakley, Henry Bernard, 2/Lt., k. in a., 3/5/17.
12 Oldfield, Laurel Cecil Francis, Capt. (Tp.), k. in a., 25/9/15.
10 Ord, Ord Ralph, Lt. (Tp.), k. in a., 18/9/16.
Paley, George, Major, k. in a., 31/10/14.
Palmer, John William, 2/Lt. (Tp.), d. of w., 25/9/17 (att. 12th Bn.).
13 Park, Alexander, 2/Lt., k. in a., 4/11/18.
Parker, William Mackworth, Capt. & Adjt., k. in a., 30/7/15 (att. 8th Bn.).
6 Parmenter, Gordon William, 2/Lt., k. in a., 26/8/16 (att. 12th Bn.).
9 Parsons, Eric King, Capt. (Tp.), k. in a., 15/9/16.
2 Pascoe, Basil Conquest, M.C., A/Capt. & Adj.), k. in a., 27/5/18 (att. 25th Inf. Bde. H.Q.).
BM 25 Bde

5 Patey, Edward, 2/Lt. (A/Capt.), k. in a., 2/8/17 (att. 3rd Bn.).
6 Patterson, Robert Arthur, 2/Lt., k. in a., 12/4/17.
8 Pawle, Bertram, Capt. (Tp.), k. in a., 30/7/15.
Pearce, Robert Swayne, 2/Lt., k. in a., 9/5/15.
Pegram, Charles Earnest, M.C., Lt. (Tp.), A/Capt., died, 9/11/18.
6 Penn, Geoffrey Mark, 2/Lt., k. in a., 11/12/15 (att. Som. L.I.).
2 Pennefather, Charles Lewis, Capt. (Tp.), k. in a., 14/6/16.
Percival, Claude Victor Noble, Major, k. in a., 14/12/14.
Persse, Rodolph Algernon, 2/Lt., k. in a., 1/1/15 (att. K.R.R.C.).
3 Peyton, Henry Sydney Charles, M.C., Lt.-Col., d. of w., 24/3/18.
1 Pickering, Cyril Aubrey, Lt., k. in a., 30/8/18.
6 Pickering, William Carrington, Lt., k. in a., 11/10/18 (att. 1st Bn.).
Pidsley, Hayward Gould, 2/Lt., d. of w., 21/5/17 (A. Coy.).
Pigot-Moodie, Charles Alfred, 2/Lt., k. in a., 14/1/15.
Pilcher, Thomas Percy, Lt., k. in a., 10/3/15.
1/4 Pink, Alan Lins, Lt., killed, 30/10/18 (and R.A.F.).
16 Pinnegar, John Arthur, M.C., Capt., k. in a., 22/3/18.
9 Plater, Richard Henry, Lt., d. of w., 3/5/17.
17 Pollak, Harry Leopold, Lt. (Tp.), k. in a., 23/10/16.
10 Ponsford, Glyn George, 2/Lt. (Tp.), k. in a., 28/8/16.
7 Pope, Ernest William, Capt. (Tp.), k. in a., 18/8/16.
9 Powell, Percival, 2/Lt., k. in a., 1/8/15 (att. 3rd Bn.).
13 Pretor-Pinney, Charles Frederick, D.S.O., Lt.-Col. (Tp.), d. of w., 28/4/17.
3 Prideaux-Brune, Edmund Nicholas, 2/Lt., k. in a., 22/5/18.
6/12 Priestley, Charles Homans, 2/Lt., k. in a., 4/9/16.
8 Prior, Edward Foss, Capt. (Tp.), k. in a., 15/9/16.
1 Prittie, The Hon. Francis Reginald Denis, Capt., k. in a., 19/12/14.
Pryce, Hugh Beauclerk Mostyn, Capt., d. of w., 19/3/15.
Purcell, Stanley Joseph, 2/Lt. (Tp.), d. of w., 26/3/17.
9 Purvis, John Ralph, Capt. (Tp.), k. in a., 25/9/15.
Quincey, Thomas Edmund De Quincey, 2/Lt., k. in a., 9/5/15.
13 Rae, Alfred Ian, 2/Lt. (Tp.), k. in a., 24/4/17.
8 Rae, Thomas Keith Hedley, 2/Lt. (Tp.), k. in a., 30/7/15.
5 Raikes, Frank Steward Waddington, 2/Lt., k. in a., 9/5/15 (att. 2nd Bn.).
2 Ramsay, John Marmaduke, Lt. (Tp.), d. of w., 14/4/17 (att. 10th Bn.).
16 Ramsay, Norman, 2/Lt. (Tp.), k. in a., 3/9/16.
6 Rapoport, John Lindsay, 2/Lt., k. in a., 27/5/18 (att. 12th Bn.).
6 Ratliff, Edward Francis, M.C., Capt., k. in a., 2/12/17 (att. 2nd Bn.).
12 Raymond-Barker, Cecil Langton, 2/Lt. (Tp.)., k. in a., 25/9/15.
6 Raynor, Harold Arthur Livingston, 2/Lt., d. of w., 7/6/18.
16 Reacher, Stanley William, Capt. (Tp.), d. of w., 4/7/16.
8 Reed, Frederick William Carlton, 2/Lt., k. in a., 3/5/17.
6 Renwick, Thomas Buchanan, Lt., k. in a., 29/4/15 (att. 3rd Bn. Middx. Rgt.).
13 Rhys, Watkin Leoline Tom, 2/Lt. (Tp.), d. of w., 24/4/17.
13 Rice, Frederick Thomas, 2/Lt. (Tp.), k. in a., 12/9/18.
Richardson, Albert Edward, Capt., died, 24/11/18 (att. M.G.C.).
Rickman, Stuart Hamilton, Major, d. of w., 26/8/14.
16 Risley, Nathan Bright, M.C., Capt. (Tp.), d. of w., 20/9/17.
9 Rissik, Bernard, 2/Lt., k. in a., 22/6/15.
6 Ritchie, Thomas Pearsall Ayres, 2/Lt., k. in a., 15/3/15 (att. 4th Btn.).
9 Roberts, Francis Bernard, Capt. (Tp.), k. in a., 8/2/16.
16 Roberts, Lionel John, 2/Lt., k. in a., 3/9/16.
6 Robertson, Keith Forbes, Lt., k. in a., 27/8/16 (att. 1st Bn.).
5 Robinson, Harry Hesketh Kay, 2/Lt. (A/Capt.), k. in a., 26/3/18 (att. 16th Btn.).
Robinson, Ralf Hubert, 2/Lt. (Tp.), d. of w., 23/8/17 (att. 2nd Bn.).
Rodney, The Hon. William Francis, 2/Lt., killed, 9/5/15 (and R.F.C.).
5 Roe, Frank Edward Mervyn, Capt., d. of w., 7/6/16 (att. 12th Bn.).
7 Rogers, Reginald, 2/Lt. (Tp.), k. in a., 15/9/16.
14 Rogers, Ronald Joseph, Capt., k. in a., 28/6/15.
16 Ronaldson, Charles Rashleigh, Lt. (Tp.), k. in a., 3/9/16.
6 Round, Harold Cecil, D.S.O., M.C., T/Lt. (A/Capt.), k. in a., 24/8/17 (att. 9th Btn.).
1 Rouse-Boughton-Knight, Thomas Andrew Greville, 2/Lt., d. of w., 18/10/16.
12 Ruddle, Reginald, M.C., 2/Lt. (Tp.), k. in a., 24/7/18.
7 Rushbrooke, William Ewart, 2/Lt., k. in a., 26/8/17.
6 Russell, Arthur Charles, Lt., d. of w., 28/10/18.
Russell, Leonard Cosmo Bolles, Capt. (Tp.), k. in a., 7/10/16 (att. 12th Btn.).
13 Sampson, Walter Bladen, Capt. (Tp.), k. in a., 10/7/16.
Savage, Thomas, 2/Lt. (Tp.), k. in a., 11/10/18 (att. 3rd Bn.).
Savill, John Edward, 2/Lt. (Tp.), k. in a., 24/8/17 (att. 9th Bn.).
1 Schiff, Alfred Sydney Borlase, 2/Lt., k. in a., 9/4/17.
9 Scholey, Charles Harry Norman, Capt. (Tp.), k. in a., 25/9/15.
5 Schuster, Christopher John Claude, 2/Lt., k. in a., 10/8/18.
3 Scott, Arthur Edward, 2/Lt. (Tp), k. in a., 21/3/18.
3 Scott, Harold Vesey, Capt., died, 1/9/15.
10 Scott, James Yuill, Lt. (Tp.), k. in a., 3/9/16.
8 Scrimgeour, Michael, Lt. (Tp.), k. in a., 30/7/15.
Selby-Smith, Miles Bury, Capt., k. in a., 15/3/15.
Sharps, Herbert Charles Valentine, 2/Lt. (Tp.), k. in a., 22/4/18 (att. 1st Bn.).
Shaw-Stewart, Neil, Lt., k. in a., 21/8/16.
Shepherd, James Montague Edward, Capt., k. in a., 15/2/17 (1st Sq., R.F.C.).
5 Sheridan, William Frederick Temple, Capt., k. in a., 25/9/15 (att. 2nd Bn.).
Sherston, Somerset Arthur, Capt., k. in a., 9/5/15.
16 Siebert, Stanley Prentice, 2/Lt. (Tp.), d. of w., 21/9/17.
10 Simmonds, Walter Sangster, 2/Lt. (Tp.), k. in a., 7/10/16.
3 Simmons, John, 2/Lt., killed, 21/8/16.
2 Simpson, Herbert William, Capt. (Acting), k. in a., 23/10/16.
16 Simpson, John Cornelius, 2/Lt. (Tp.), d. of w., 23/3/18.
13 Siordet, Gerald Caldwell, M.C., 2/Lt. (Tp.), k. in a., 9/2/17
1/4 Small, J. B., Lt., killed, 2/8/18 (and R.A.F.).
13 Smith, Geoffrey Watkins, Capt. (Tp.), k. in a., 10/7/16.
1 Smith, Hugh Francis Russell, 2/Lt., d. of w., 5/7/16 (att. 6th Btn.).
3 Smith, Jacob Hardy, D.S.O., M.C., Lt., d. of w., 29/8/16.
Smith, Lothrop Lewis de Berniere, Lt., died, 3/9/16.
9 Smith, Sidney O'Connol, 2/Lt., d. of w., 25/8/16.
6 Somerville, Martin Ashwood, 2/Lt., d. of w., 21/9/18.
9 Songer, William Arthur, 2/Lt. (Tp.), k. in a., 15/9/16 (att. T.M.B.).
1 Southgate, Charles Edward, 2/Lt. (Tp.), k. in a., 18/2/17.
13 Southwell, Evelyn Herbert Lightfoot, Lt. (Tp.), k. in a., 15/9/16.
13 Spanton, John Woodfield, 2/Lt. (Tp.), d. of w., 13/6/17.
Spencer, Arthur Max, 2/Lt., k. in a., 12/4/17.
13 Spencer, George Barton, 2/Lt. (Tp.), k. in a., 25/7/18.
8 Sproston, William Norris, M.C., 2/Lt. (Tp.), k. in a., 4/4/18.
12 Spurling, Francis Eyton, Capt. (Tp.), d. of w., 6/12/17.
2 Stanhope, Talbot Fitzroy Eden, Lt., k. in a., 9/5/15.
Stewart, James Alexander Logan, Lt., k. in a., 13/5/15.
13 Stewart, Walter Robert, D.S.O., M.C., Bt.-Major (T/Lt.-Col.), k. in a., 8/4/18.
6 Stobart, John Geoffrey, 2/Lt., k. in a., 15/3/15 (att. 4th Bn.)
6 Stokes, Philip Durham, 2/Lt., d. of w., 10/4/17.
15 Stratford, Laurence, Lt. (Tp.), k. in a., 28/3/18.
6 Sutton, Alexander Gordon, 2/Lt., k. in a., 2/1/18 (att. 2nd Bn.).
7 Talbot, Gilbert Walter Lytleton, Lt. (Tp.), k. in a., 30/7/15.
Tatham, Geoffrey Bulmer, M.C., Capt., k. in a., 30/3/18 (att. 116th Inf. Bde. H.Q. Staff).
6 Tatton-Tatton, C. H., Lt., died, 26/11/18.
6 Taylor, Maurice Llewellyn, 2/Lt., k. in a., 26/8/16 (att 12th Bn.).
Tennyson, The Hon. Alfred Aubrey, Capt., k. in a., 21/3/18
Thesiger, George Handcock, C.B., C.M.G., A.D.C., Major-Gen. (Tp.), k. in a., 26/9/15 (Staff Comm., 9th Scot. Div.).
Thistlewood, Percival, 2/Lt. (Tp.), k. in a., 28/8/17.
14 Thomas, Horace Wyndham, 2/Lt. (Tp.), k. in a., 3/9/16.
9 Thompson, Harold Francis, Capt. (Tp.), k. in a., 12/7/16.
10 Thomson, Douglas Gordon, 2/Lt., k. in a., 30/11/17.
6 Thornton, Noel Shipley, D.S.O., M.C., Lt. (T/Major), d of w., 10/4/18 (att. 7th Bn.).
12 Torry, John Shirley Archibald, 2/Lt. (Tp.), d. of w., 19/9/15.
Toynbee, Geoffrey Percy Robert, Capt., k. in a., 15/11/14.
5 Trevelyan, Wilfred, 2/Lt., k. in a., 4/5/15 (att. 4th Bn.).
6 Trevor-Jones, Evan Edward, 2/Lt., k. in a., 1/7/16.
6 Trevor-Jones, John Eric, M.C., Capt. (Tp.), k. in a., 22/4/18 (att. 1st Btn.).
6 Trotter, Kenneth Stuart, 2/Lt., k in a., 26/4/15 (att. 1st Bn.).
2 Trueman, Albert Edward, 2/Lt., k. in a., 30/5/18.
15 Tryon, Henry, Capt. (Tp.), k. in a., 15/9/16 (att. 8th Bn.).
Tryon, Richard, Capt., k. in a., 10/1/15.
13 Turnbull, Robert, M.C., 2/Lt. (Tp.), k. in a., 25/8/18.
6 Turner, Arthur Charlewood, 2/Lt., k. in a., 16/1/18.
6 Turner, Bingham Alexander, D.S.O., Capt., k. in a., 2/11/14.
2 Turnour, Arthur William Winterton, 2/Lt. (T/Lt.), k. in a., 25/9/15.
Tyndall, Arthur George, 2/Lt. (Tp.), k. in a., 18/11/17.
1 Tyrwhitt-Drake, Thomas Victor, 2/Lt., k. in a., 29/1/17.
15 Vanstone, Charles Douglas Howard, 2/Lt., died, 7/2/17 (att. T.M.B.).
10 Vanstone, Stanley Paul, Lt. (Tp.), d. of w., 29/10/15.
3 Venner, Ernest Valentine, 2/Lt., k. in a., 18/8/16.
5 Vernede, Robert Ernest, 2/Lt., d. of w., 9/4/17 (att. 12th Bn.).
8 Vickers, Eric Leslie, 2/Lt. (Tp.), d. of w., 8/1/17.
5 Vintcent, Charles Aubrey, 2/Lt., k. in a., 13/4/15 (att. 4th Bn.).
1 Volkers, Frederick Cyril, 2/Lt. (Tp.), k. in a., 1/7/16.
9 Wade, George Edward Ahern, 2/Lt., k. in a., 3/5/17.
8 Walker, Anthony Thornton, 2/Lt. (Tp.), k. in a., 30/7/15.
5 Wallace, William Middleton, Lt., k. in a., 22/8/15 (att. R.F.C.).
11 Wallis, Bertram, 2/Lt. (Tp.), d. of w., 11/7/16.
Watney, William Herbert, Lt., k. in a., 10/5/15.
15 Wegg-Prosser, Cecil Francis, 2/Lt. (Tp.), k. in a., 3/9/16.
1 Weill, Abe, 2/Lt. (Tp.), d. of w., 9/8/16.
Wellerd, George Godfrey, 2/Lt. (Tp.), d. of w., 15/4/17.
Werner, Charles Augustus, Capt., k. in a., 9/5/15.
16 Westacott, Ernest George, 2/Lt. (Tp.), d. of w., 19/5/16.
5 Whateley, Richard Herschel, Lt., k. in a., 25/8/16.
9 Wheatley, William Clarke, 2/Lt., k. in a., 3/5/17.
2 Whitaker, Harold, Capt., k. in a., 30/11/14.
5 Whitaker, Oscar Frederick, Lt. (Tp.), died, 10/11/18.
6 White, Geoffrey Wilfred, 2/Lt., d. of w., 1/4/17 (att. 10th Bn.).
6 White, Malcolm Graham, Lt., k. in a., 1/7/16 (att. 1st Bn.).
11 Williams, Hilary Evelyn Eccles, 2/Lt. (Tp.), k. in a., 30/9/15.
9 Willmer, Arthur Franklin, Capt. (Tp.), d. of w., 20/9/16.
9 Willoughby, Francis George Godfrey, Capt. (Tp.), k. in a., 9/8/15.

6 Wilson, Alan Hood, 2/Lt., k. in a., 17/3/15.
2 Wilson, Arthur Stafford, 2/Lt. (Tp.), k. in a., 25/8/16.
6 Winch, Edward Maurice, 2/Lt., d. of w., 25/3/15.
8 Wines, Walter Wheeler, 2/Lt. (Tp.), k. in a., 24/8/17.
Wollaston, Frederick Hargreaves Arbuthnot, D.S.O., Major (Act. Lt.-Col.), killed, 8/3/18 (Comm. 1/5 Suffolks).
Wolseley-Jenkins, Charles Wolseley, Capt., k. in a., 25/9/15.
1 Wood, Donald, Lt.-Col. (Tp.), k. in a., 1/7/16.
Wood, W., 2/Lt., k. in a., 8/5/15.
8 Woodroffe, Leslie, Capt. (Tp.), d. of w., 4/6/16.
6 Woodroffe, Kenneth Herbert Clayton, Lt., k. in a., 9/5/15 (att. 3rd Bn.).
8 V.C. Woodroffe, Sydney Clayton, 2/Lt. (Tp.), k. in a., 30/7/15.
Woodward, Arthur Frederick Albert, 2/Lt. (Tp.), k. in a., 19/11/17 (att. 2nd Bn.).
9 Wright, Richard Connett, 2/Lt., k. in a., 19/8/18 (att. 3rd Bn.).
Wyvill, Marmaduke Ibbetson, Major (Tp.), died, 6/3/16.

Army Cyclist Corps.

Ashton, James Ormrod, 2/Lt., k. in a., 5/7/16.
Askham, William, T/Lt. (A/Capt.), k. in a., 11/4/18.
Bristoll, Clarence, 2/Lt. (Tp.), died, 9/11/18.
Burgess, Reginald, Lt. (Tp.), d. of w., 7/7/16 (in enemy hands) (and R.F.C.).
8 Caldwell, Robert Seddon, 2/Lt. (Tp.), k. in a., 11/6/18.
Clark, Stanley Lowndes, Lt. (Tp.), k. in a., 13/4/18 (att. 13/K. L'pool R.).
16 Coate, William Henry, T/Lt. (A/Capt.), k. in a., 25/10/17.
9 Cottrell, Leonard Samuel Joscelyn, Lt. (Tp.), k. in a., 13/4/18.
Doyle, Henry, 2/Lt. (Tp.), k. in a., 17/1/17 (att. N. Fus.).
Field, Harold William, 2/Lt. (Tp.), k. in a., 27/5/18.
15 Hyder, Alfred William, 2/Lt. (Tp.), k. in a., 2/9/18.
Hall, Allan Bernard, Lt., k. in a., 3/5/17 (att. 11/E. York. R.).
Hall, William Brown, Lt., d. of w., 25/8/18 (att. 24/Lnd. R.).
6 Jobling, Edgar, A/Capt., k. in a., 23/10/18.
14 Johnson, Gilbert Ernest, T/Lt. (A/Capt.), died, 4/7/18.
Kindleysides, Charles Frederick, 2/Lt. (Tp.), d. of w., 4/10/18 (att. N. Fus.).
19 Knott, Frederick Vernon, Lt. (Tp.), k. in a., 21/3/16.
Money, Eric William, Lt. (Tp.), k. in a., 11/4/17 (att. M.G.C.).
Munro, Ian Duncan, 2/Lt. (Tp.), k. in a., 13/9/15 (9 D.C.C.).
Nicholson, Maurice, 2/Lt., k. in a., 18/8/17 (Gen. List, and R.F.C., 11 Sqd.).
Ross, George Munro, Lt. (Tp.), k. in a., 1/7/16.
14 Simmons, Benjamin Howard, Lt. (Tp.), k. in a., 29/10/18.
Smith, William George Rae, Lt. (Tp.), k. in a., 25/1/16.
9 Stewart, Alexander Charles, Capt., k. in a., 12/4/18.

Machine Gun Corps.

Abbiss, John Lee, Lt., died, 25/7/18 (1st E. Surr. R.).
4 Ablett, Arthur, 2/Lt. (Tp.), d. of w., 22/4/18.
48 Adair, Angus McPherson, Lt. (Tp.), k. in a., 21/11/17.
18 Adam, Douglas Walter, Lt. (Tp.), d. of w., 4/4/18.
212 Adams, Wilfred Evan, 2/Lt. (Tp.), k. in a., 14/5/17.
Addis, Ronald Forester, Lt., A/Capt., k. in a., 3/9/16 (2nd K.O. Scot. Bdrs.).
35 Akhurst, Norman Walter, Lt. (Tp.), d. of w., 8/6/18.
39 Aldridge, Reginald Percy, 2/Lt. (Tp.), killed, 26/3/18.
Alexander, Frank Esmond, 2/Lt. (Tp.), died, 25/7/16.
Alison, George, Capt., k. in a., 1/7/16 (Seaforth Hdrs., att.).
6 Allan, John, M.C., T/2/Lt., A/Capt., d. of w., 9/6/17 (Heavy Branch).
49 Allcock, Christian, 2/Lt., d. of w., 3/3/18.
Allen, Charles St. Vincent, 2/Lt., died, 16/2/17 (3rd E. Kent R., att.).
Allen, Lionel Raymund Whateley, Lt., k. in a., 27/3/18 (9th S. Wales Bdrs., att.).
31 Allen, William Henry, 2/Lt. (Tp.), k. in a., 12/4/18.
185 Allpass, Samuel Rosslee, Capt. (Tp.), d. of w., 21/1/17.
Almack, Alfred Christopher Turnour, 2/Lt., k. in a., 27/9/16 (3rd North. R., att.).
Almond, Henry Tristram, 2/Lt., k. in a., 31/3/16 (3rd Gordon Hdrs., att.).
Amery-Parkes, Douglas John, M.C., Lt., A/Major, d. of w., 30/4/18 (and Mdx. R.).
40 Amos, Charles Edward, 2/Lt., k. in a., 22/3/18.
Anderson, Donald Knox, M.C., T/Lt., k. in a., 3/12/17 (E. Kent R.).
73 Anderson, George Rutherford, 2/Lt. (Tp.), k. in a., 18/8/16.
212 Anderson, John Gavin, Lt., k. in a., 3/5/17.
20 Anderson, John Turnbull, 2/Lt., k. in a., 5/10/17.
1 Anderson, Vincent Tollemach, 2/Lt. (Tp.), d. of w., 13/4/18.
Anderton, George Eric Asquith, Lt., k. in a., 22/3/18 (Lanc. Fus., att.).
51 Apperley, Charles Milton, 2/Lt., k. in a., 24/3/18.
Arnold, Bernard Marcus, 2/Lt. (Tp.), d. of w., 6/2/16.
25 Ashcroft, William Worsley, T/Lt., A/Major, k. in a, 11/4/18.
199 Ashford, Isaac Dobson, 2/Lt. (Tp.), d. of w., 26/1/18 (41st Div.).
Ashton, G. Frank, T/Lt., k. in a., 20/10/18.
5 Ashworth, Edward Rose, 2/Lt. (Tp.), k. in a., 28/3/18.
25 Ashworth, Frederick Giles, 2/Lt. (Tp.), k. in a., 16/8/17.
61 Aspland, Stanley Richard, 2/Lt., k. in a., 3/10/18.
Astley, Aston Giffard, Major (Tp.), k. in a., 1/10/16 (Roy. Fus., att.).
9 Aston, Herbert Selwyn, M.C., Capt., T/Maj., d. of w., 13/7/18 (4th H.L.I., att.).
Athol, Charles Colbourne, Lt. (Tp.), k. in a., 26/8/18.
58 Attwater, Ernest, 2/Lt. (Tp.), k. in a., 22/3/18.
Auchinlech, Armar Leslie, Capt., k. in a., 17/9/16.
257 Austin, Robert George, 2/Lt. (Tp.), k. in a., 26/10/18.
28 Auterac, Robert Sames, 2/Lt. (Tp.), k. in a., 18/10/16.
147 Baddon, Wallace, T/Capt., k. in a., 3/9/16.
43 Baggs, Henry Ernest, 2/Lt., d. of w., 30/6/18 (whilst P.O.W.).
Bailey, George Haddon, 2/Lt. (Tp.), d. of w., 6/4/17.
3 Baker, Arthur Brimfield, 2/Lt., d. of w., 26/9/16.
Baird, Gilbert Campbell, T/2/Lt., k. in a., 28/7/17 (Worc. R., att.).
58 Baker, Frederick Herbert, 2/Lt., k. in a., 24/3/18.
Baker, Walter Henry, 2/Lt. (Tp.), d. of w., 20/10/18.
152 Balchin, John Richard Aubrey, M.C., Lt. (Tp.), d. of w., 14/11/16.
Ball, Gerald Harman, M.C., 2/Lt. (Tp.), k. in a., 12/4/18.
59 Bandey, George Henry, 2/Lt., died, 6/11/18 (whilst P. of W. in German hands).
176 Banks, John Howard, Lt. (Tp.), d. of w., 15/8/17.
Banks, Randolph, Capt. (Tp.), d. of w., 5/7/17.
Barclay, Eric Callender, Lt. (Tp.), k. in a., 25/9/15.
97 Barker, Osmund Vincent, 2/Lt. (Tp.), k. in a., 28/11/17.
Barker, Percy, 2/Lt. (Tp.), k. in a., 13/4/18.
162 Barnes, Herbert Charles, 2/Lt. (Tp.), k. in a., 22/12/17.
Barni, Noel Henry Louis, Lt. (Tp.), d. of w., 29/3/18 (in Ger. hands).
35 Barr, Hugh, 2/Lt. (Tp.), d. of w., 30/9/18.
Barratt, Kenneth Franklin, Lt., k. in a., 1/7/16 (3rd Essex R., att.).
120 Barrington, Allan Leslie, 2/Lt. (Tp.), killed, 29/7/16.
Barrow, Howard Cyril, Lt. (Tp.), k. in a., 20/9/17.
Bartholomew, Claude, T/Capt., k. in a., 15/9/16 (Scots Gds., att.).
103 Barton, William Bernard, 2/Lt. (Tp.), k. in a., 28/4/17.
220 Baselow, Henry Frank, 2/Lt. (Tp.), k. in a., 5/10/17.
9 Bate, Frederick Over, Lt. (Act.), k. in a., 25/9/17.
49 Bates, Thomas William, T/Lt., A/Capt., d. of w., 12/10/18.
75 Bax, George Thomas, 2/Lt. (Tp.), d. of w., 8/9/16.
Beak, Basil Charles, 2/Lt. (Tp.), died, 4/11/18.
174 Beaton, William James, 2/Lt. (Tp.), k. in a., 24/9/17.
Beard, Lewis, Digby Mansergh, 2/Lt. (Tp.), killed, 19/10/16.
5 Beck, James Fenn, 2/Lt. (Tp.), k. in a., 28/4/17.
Bell, Edward William, 2/Lt., T/Lt., k. in a., 8/12/17.
25 Belschner, William Frederick, 2/Lt. (Tp.), k. in a., 8/10/18.
29 Bennett, Edwin Herman, 2/Lt. (Tp.), k. in a., 5/5/18.
64 Bennett, Vere Raymond, Lt., k. in a., 10/4/17 (3rd N. & D., att.).
74 Berkeley, Alfred Fitzhardinge Murray, 2/Lt. (Tp.), k. in a., 7/6/17.
123 Berkeley, Philip Charles Oswald, T/Lt., A/Major, k. in a., 29/9/18.
Berkeley, Thomas Berkeley Hartman, Lt., died, 7/11/18 (3rd Suff. R., att.).
Best, Jack, T/Lt., k. in a., 15/5/18.
Bible, Geoffrey, Roskell, 2/Lt. (Tp.), k. in a., 1/7/16.
56 Bickerton, William, 2/Lt. (Tp.), k. in a., 20/9/17.
237 Bickley, George Howard, T/Lt. (A/Capt.), k. in a., 4/10/17.
Bingley, Arthur Noel, 2/Lt. (Tp.), k. in a., 14/6/16.
Binning, William Barclay, 2/Lt. (Tp.), d. of w., 24/4/16.
7 Bird, Rex William, 2/Lt. (Tp.), k. in a., 24/8/16.
2 Birdseye, Arthur Thomas, 2/Lt. (Tp.), d. of w., 25/4/18.
Bishop, Ralph Murdock, 2/Lt. (Tp.), d. of w., 15/4/18 (in German hands).
Blackman, Wilfred Ernest Arthur, T/2/Lt., died, 14/10/18.
35 Blair, James McDonald, 2/Lt. (Tp.), d. of w., 9/4/18.
73 Blech, Evelyn Lewis, 2/Lt. (Tp.), k. in a., 18/8/16.
46 Blyth, William, T/Lt., d. of w., 7/11/18.
49 Boaden, William Freeman, 2/Lt. (Tp.), k. in a., 16/4/18.
Boag, Herbert Edward, 2/Lt. (Tp.), k. in a., 31/7/17 ("B" Bn.).
14 Boden, Samuel Standidge, T/2/Lt., k. in a., 15/10/16 (14th D.L.I., att.).
49 Bodenham, Henry Edward Charles Hyacinth, Lt., k. in a., 7/9/16.
29 Bolter, Charles Albert, 2/Lt. (Tp.), k. in a., 12/4/18.
103 Bolton, Herbert Frederick, T/Lt., d. of w., 3/5/17 (10th Sth. Lan. R., and).
56 Booth, Fred, 2/Lt. (Tp.), d. of w., 24/4/18.
56 Booth, James, M.C., Lt. (Tp.), k. in a., 6/11/18.
93 Booth, Percival Edward Owen, 2/Lt., k. in a., 1/7/16.
58 Borthwick, Arthur Pollok Sym, 2/Lt. (Tp.), d. of w., 15/4/18.
Boston, Thomas, Lt. (Tp.), died, 25/12/18.
Boswell, Denis St. George Knox, Capt. (T/Major), died, 28/9/18 (D. of Corn. L.I., att.)
Bothamley, Richard Arnold, 2/Lt. (Tp.), k. in a., 9/4/18.
3 Bourner, Rowland Moody Nicholson, 2/Lt. (Tp.), d. of w., 28/3/18.
Bowden, James, 2/Lt. (Tp.), k. in a., 30/3/18.
244 Bowker, Tom, 2/Lt. (Tp.), k. in a., 9/4/18.
74 Bowler, William, 2/Lt. (Tp.), k. in a., 9/8/17.
Bowman, Alexander White, 2/Lt., k. in a., 25/9/16 (E. York R., att.).
44 Bown, William George, 2/Lt., k. in a., 31/7/17.
210 Brakes, Bert, Lt., died, 5/1/18 (2nd Leic. R., att.).
Breene, Thomas Frederick, Lt. (Tp.), k. in a., 1/7/16 (1st R. War. R., att.).
49 Brewster, Hugh P., 2/Lt., k. in a., 9/9/16.
149 Brickman, Frederick William, T/Lt., k. in a, 26/10/17.
Brierley, Harold Holland, 2/Lt., k. in a., 27/7/16.
36 Briggs-Gooderham, Ernest John Robinson, 2/Lt., k. in a., 13/12/16.
Bright, Frederick George, 2/Lt. (Tp.), k. in a., 23/8/18.
Broad, Arthur Maurice, Lt. (Tp.), k. in a., 12/7/16 (15th R. Fus., att.).
153 Broadbent, Wilfred Stuart Stidston, Lt., k. in a., 19/4/17.
29 Brock, Herbert Leslie, Lt. (Tp.), k. in a., 10/4/18.
Bromhall, John Coventry, M.C., T/Lt. (A/Maj.), k. in a., 7/8/18.

Brooks, Colin Robert Percy, Lt., d. of w., 2/4/18 (3rd Hrs., and).
37 Browett, Archibald, 2/Lt. (Tp.), k. in a., 20/11/17.
Brown, Douglas Crow, Lt., d. of w., 13/9/17 (3rd R. Scots, att.).
4 Brown, Frederick Francis, 2/Lt. (Tp.), died, 28/9/18 (Cavalry).
Brown, Eric Metcalfe, T/Lt., k. in a., 29/9/17 (A. Bty., Hvy. B.).
115 Brown, Louis Foster, Lt. (Tp.), d. of w., 15/5/18.
97 Brown, Lawrence Smith Blanche, M.C., 2/Lt. (Tp.), k. in a., 28/11/17.
Brown, Norman Watson, 2/Lt. (T/Lt.), d. of w., 1/5/17 (3rd E. Lan. R., att.).
47 Brownbridge, Herbert Edward, 2/Lt. (Tp.), died, 7/12/18.
124 Brownrigg-Jay, George Harvey, Lt. (Tp.), k. in a., 21/9/18.
8 Bruce, Edward Tyrrell, 2/Lt. (Tp.), d. of w., 9/6/18.
Bruman, Albert Victor, 2/Lt. (Tp.), d. of w., 31/5/18.
45 Brunsden, Edward James, 2/Lt. (Tp.), d. of w., 25/4/17.
Brutton, Eric West, M.C., Lt., k. in a., 14/4/18 (Dev. Rgt.).
Buckworth, Charles Raymond, Lt., k. in a., 1/7/16 (Sea. Hdrs., att.).
Bull, Lovelace Rowat, T/Lt., d. of w., 3/5/17.
Bullman, Haddon Robert Horsley, 2/Lt., k. in a., 3/11/17 (3rd R.W. Kent R., att.).
Bundey, Albert Arthur, 2/Lt. (Tp.), k. in a., 21/3/18.
Burch, Herbert Percival, 2/Lt. (Tp.). died, 20/10/16 (Motor).
Burgess, Matthew Wylie, Lt. (Tp.), k. in a., 23/7/18.
Burke, Edward Terrence, Lt. & Qr.-Mr., k. in a., 25/4/18 (North'n R., and)
97 Burns, Islay Ferrier, T/2/Lt., k. in a., 10/7/17.
Burrell, Arthur David Claypham, T/Lt., k. in a., 15/8/17.
Burrows, David, 2/Lt. (Tp.), d. of w., 3/7/16.
Burrows, William George Ritson, 2/Lt., k. in a., 3/5/17.
Bushell, Horace, T/Lt. (A/Capt.), k. in a., 6/9/18.
Caesar, George, Lt., d. of w., 2/5/18 (E. Surr. R., att. Tank Cps.).
Callaghan, Joseph Patrick Aloysious, 2/Lt., k in a., 1/7/16.
Campbell, Colin Boyd, 2/Lt., k. in a., 28/7/16.
Campbell, Guy. M.C., Capt. (Tp.), died, 26/5/17 (Motor).
207 Carley. Samuel Newman, T/2/Lt., k. in a., 25/9/17.
Carmichael, David Arthur, Lt., k. in a., 17/4/18.
143 Carnall, Ronald Gundry, Lt. (Tp.), d. of w., 29/11/16.
Carpenter, Henry Alfred Stanley. 2/Lt. (Tp.), k. in a., 2/9/16.
Carpenter, Ronald Percy Victor, Lt. (Tp.), k. in a., 6/9/18.
Carr, Frank Clifford, T/2/Lt., d. of w., 24/4/17 (while P. of W. in Turk. hands).
Cartwright, Eric Percival St. George, 2/Lt., k. in a., 12/8/16 (4th Lein. R., att.).
Cartwright, Stanley, T/Lt., k. in a., 17/8/16 (8th North. R., att.).
Catmur, Harry Albert Frederick Valentine, Lt., k. in a., 1/7/16 (3rd R. Suss. R., att.).
56 Chalkley, Thomas Henry, T/2/Lt., k. in a., 29/8/18.
6 Chapman, Alfred Reginald, T/2/Lt., k. in a., 2/12/17.
18 Charlton, John Lawther, T/2/Lt., d. of w., 15/9/18.
91 Charlesworth, Herbert, T/2/Lt., k. in a., 26/10/17.
19 Chave, John Haydon, T/Lt., d. of w., 15/4/18.
Clancey, John Austin, M.C., Major, died, 22/7/18 (R. Ir. Fus., att.).
49 Clark, Arthur Henry, T/2/Lt., d. of w., 3/5/18 (in German hands).
31 Clarke, Hilary Calvert, T/Lt., d. of w., 31/8/18.
47 Clarke, Richard Stanley, T/2/Lt., k. in a., 4/10/18.
Clarkson, Harold, 2/Lt., k. in a., 11/4/17 ("D" Batt., Hy. Br.).
35 Claughton, John Harold, 2/Lt., k. in a., 30/11/17.
59 Clement, Walter Albert, 2/Lt., k. in a., 21/3/18.
65 Clough, Gilbert Seymour, T/2/Lt., d. of w., 27/3/18.
Cobden, F. Pargeter, k. in a., 7/7/18 (att. R.A.F., 104 Sqn.).
90 Cockburn, James, 2/Lt., k. in a., 12/10/16 (4th Argyll & Suth. Hrs., att.).
64 Coldham, George Herbert, Lt. (Tp.), d. of w., 17/9/16.
Colgate, Roy, Capt. (Tp.), d. of w., 12/7/16.
8 Collier, George, T/2/Lt., d. of w., 9/8/18.
5 Collins, John Ferdinando, T/2/Lt., k. in a., 28/3/18.
18 Collinson, John Harold, 2/Lt., k. in a., 21/3/18.
25 Collymore, Hubert Aubrey, Lt., k. in a., 17/4/18 (9th Bedf. R., att.).
Coleman, Eric, 2/Lt., k. in a., 31/7/17 (3rd Norf. R., att.).
150 Commins, Arthur Edward, 2/Lt., k. in a., 23/4/17.
12 Cook, Howard Mortimer, Lt. (Tp.), k. in a., 9/8/18.
9 Cooke, William Wesley, 2/Lt. (Tp.), k. in a., 25/4/18.
18 Cooper, Percy, Lt. (Tp.), k. in a., 22/3/18.
Cooper, Thomas Gill, 2/Lt. (Tp.), died, 25/3/18.
Coote, George Bertrand, Lt., k. in a., 27/5/18 (R.W. Kent R., and)
63 Copeland, Eric Neville Van der Ben, Lt. (Tp.), k. in a., 26/3/18.
Copeman, Ernest Hugh, 2/Lt., k. in a., 18/3/16 (6th R.W. Kent. R., att.).
101 Copley, Alfred Beresford, T/2/Lt., k. in a., 26/8/17.
55 Corridon, Vesey Richard, T/2/Lt., d. of w., 8/10/16.
Costello, Edward William, Lt., k. in a., 1/7/16 (3rd R. Innis. Fus., att.).
Coster, Cecil Vincent, Lt. (Tp.), k. in a., 24/9/18.
Court, Gordon Frederick, 2/Lt., k. in a., 16/9/16.
Coutts, Paul Campbell, 2/Lt. (Tp.), k. in a., 23/8/18.
34 Craig, Robert William, M.C., 2/Lt. (Tp.), k. in a., 17/4/18.
Craike-Pickering, M.S.C., M.C., Lt. (Tp.), died, 14/4/18.
9 Crawford, Donald, 2/Lt. (Tp.), k. in a., 27/7/16.
50 Cruickshank, Alexander Douglas, M.C., 2/Lt. (Tp.), k. in a., 23/10/18.
Cuffley, Joseph Ison, M.C., T/2/Lt., d. of w., 31/3/18 (in German hands).
21 Cull, Leslie, T/Lt., k. in a., 8/11/17 (Cavy.).
33 Cullen, Thomas, 2/Lt. (Tp.), d. of w., 22/9/18.
Cullen, William Harold, 2/Lt. (Tp.), k. in a., 11/7/16.
91 Cully, Leslie, T/2/Lt., d. of w., 27/10/17.
Cummings, William Allen Wesley, 2/Lt., k. in a., 13/4/18.
37 Cunliffe, Edward Gilbert, Lt. (Tp.), k. in a., 25/3/18.
39 Cutler, Harold Arthur, Lt., k. in a., 23/3/18.
28 Cuthbert, John George Gunn, T/Lt., d. of w., 19/10/16.
30 Daly, Valentine Maurice, 2/Lt., d. of w., 20/4/18.
18 Dalzell, Thomas Frost, 2/Lt., k. in a., 21/3/18.
18 Davey, Charles Leonard, Lt. (Tp.), k. in a., 17/10/18.
Davidson, James Samuel, T/Capt., k. in a., 1/7/16 (13th R. Ir.. Rif., att.).
Davies, David James, 2/Lt., k. in a., 31/7/17 (H.B., C. Bn.).
Davies, Harold Percival, 2/Lt., k. in a., 11/4/17 (D. Bn.).
Davies, Leslie Frederick St. John, M.C., T/Capt., A/Major, died, 10/11/18.
225 Davis, Edward Bernard, T/2/Lt., k. in a., 31/7/17.
22 Dawson, Allan, 2/Lt. (Tp.), k. in a., 3/9/16.
59 Day, Harry Montague, Lt. (Tp.), k. in a., 15/4/18.
Day, Henry Julian Dunlop, Lt. (Tp.), died, 3/12/18.
93 Dean, Rosser Fellowes Marriott, 2/Lt., k. in a., 1/7/16 (4th R. War. R.).
167 Deane, Arthur Francis, T/2/Lt., k. in a., 16/8/17.
20 Dell, Reginald, Lt. (Tp.), d. of w., 8/5/18 (in German hands).
Dennis, John Neville, T/Lt., d. of w., 15/10/17 (11th N. Staff. R., att.).
14 Dewar, David, Lt. (Tp.), k. in a., 22/3/18.
122 Dewarburg, Hermann Vivian, 2/Lt. (Tp.), k. in a., 7/10/16.
93 Dingley, Norman Oliver, T/Lt., d. of w., 5/5/17.
30 Diplock, Douglas Gerard, 2/Lt. (Tp.), d. of w., 5/4/18 (in German hands).
3 Dobson, Thomas Ernest, 2/Lt. (Tp.), d. of w., 11/4/15.
63 Dodd, Francis Joseph, 2/Lt. (Tp.), died, 31/10/18.
41 Dongrey, Hayden Harry, 2/Lt. (Tp.), k. in a., 23/3/18.
101 Dore, Alfred Clarence, T/2/Lt., k. in a., 1/7/16.
17 Doughty, George Marbrook, Lt., k. in a., 21/8/17 (Middx. att.).
Douglas, Malcolm, Major (Tp.), died, 17/11/18.
23 Dredge, Stanley. Lt. (Tp.), k. in a., 15/6/18.
40 Duncan, Alexander, Lt., k. in a., 25/3/18 (4th Man. Rgt., att.).
Dunman, Charles Norman Innes, 2/Lt., T/Lt., k. in a., 31/7/17 (15th Mdx. R., att.).
Eardley-Wilmot, Gerald Howard, 2/Lt. (Tp.), d. of w., 10/3/16.
6 Eaton, George Hubert, Lt. (Tp.), k. in a., 25/3/18.
23 Edgar, Bernard Roy. T/2/Lt., k. in a., 31/7/17.
109 Edingborough, Noel Duncan, 2/Lt. (Tp.), k in a., 1/7/16 (15th Mdx. R., att.).
Edwards, Arthur Strother, Capt., died, 2/5/18 (and R.A.F.).
Edwards. Osborne Montague, Lt., Tp., k. in a., 23/8/18.
39 Ellerington, Robert, M.C., T/Lt., A/Major, d. of w., 29/3/18.
6 Ellis, Horace Nickson, M.C., 2/Lt. (Tp.), k. in a., 9/10/18.
40 Ellis, Trevor Edgar, 2/Lt. (Tp.), k. in a., 10/4/18.
8 Emerson, John Miller, 2/Lt. (Tp.), d. of w., 8/4/18 (in German hands).
Eminson, Robert Astley Franklin, 2/Lt., k. in a., 20/7/16 (6th K.R.R.C., att.).
Entwistle, Charles Herbert, Lt., Tp., k. in a., 9/4/18.
32 Evans, Harry Charles, 2/Lt. (Tp.), k. in a., 23/8/18.
Evans, Percy Charles David, T/Capt.. d. of w., 22/12/15 (att. 13th Welsh R.).
7 Fanshawe, Leighton Dalrymple, T/Lt., k. in a., 3/8/17.
87 Farrant, Archibald William, Lt. (Tp.), died, 6/11/18.
127 Ferguson, Alva John, T/2/Lt., killed, 4/8/17.
Fife, Alexander John, Lt.-Col., died, 7/2/17 (4th Yks. R., att.).
15 Finigan, Wilfred James, T/2/Lt., k. in a., 28/3/18.
9 Fisher, Henry Brean, Lt., d. of w., 24/7/16.
Fisher, Percy Harold, T/2/Lt., d. of w., 4/7/16 (10th R. Suss. R., att.).
207 Fitt, Charles William, T/Lt., k. in a., 19/5/17.
27 Fleming, Alfred, M.C., T/2/Lt., d. of w., 1/7/18.
Fletcher, Arnold Lockhart, T/Lt., d. of w., 30/4/17 (4th Lein. R., att.).
60 Foord, Charlton Willoughby Hougham, 2/Lt. (Tp.), d. of w., 19/12/16.
181 Forbes, Alexander Stewart, Lt., Tp., d. of w., 17/8/16.
16 Forrest, Percy Huskinson, 2/Lt., d. of w., 21/3/18 (7th Lein. R., att.).
47 Forster, Arthur Paul, T/Capt., A/Major, died, 24/9/18.
Forster, R., 2/Lt. (Tp.), died, 22/11/18.
Forsyth, Gordon Oliver, T/Lt., k. in a., 11/10/18.
21 Fosbery, Frank Sidney Thomas, T/2/Lt., k. in a., 21/3/18.
28 Fourmy, William Reginald, T/2/Lt., d. of w., 28/1/18.
19 Fowler, Bernard Edwin, Lt., k. in a., 22/3/18.
4 Fox, Gerald Vincent, T/Lt., k. in a., 10/7/18.
Fox, Thomas Noel, T/Lt., died, 12/12/18 (Som. L.I., att.).
75 Fraser, James Lovat Hasack, T/Lt., d. of w., 18/2/17.
47 Fraser, John, T/2/Lt., d. of w., 6/4/18.
Friend, Philip Emlyn, 2/Lt., k. in a., 7/7/16.
Fry, Leslie, M.C., 2/Lt., d. of w., 9/11/18 (3rd R. Scots Fus., att.).
88 Fry, William Henry, T/Lt., d. of w., 26/5/17.
Funnell, Harry Edward, D.S.O., T/Major, died, 10/12/18 (att. G.H.Q., Italy).
154 Furmston, Clement Barrington, T/2/Lt., k. in a., 9/4/17.
76 Gabb, Stanley Frederic, T/2/Lt., d. of w., 8/12/16.
Gallagher, Roland Henry, Capt., died, 25/6/15.
Gallichan, Francis Ernest, 2/Lt., k. in a., 28/7/16 (10th Bn. Nth. Staff. R., att.).
90 Gardiner, Evelyn Francis, Lt., k. in a., 30/7/16.
Garner, Reginald William, T/2/Lt., k. in a., 13/11/16.
Garstin, Denys Norman, D.S.O., M.C., T/Lt., T/Capt., k. in a., 15/8/18.
227 Geggie, William Millar, T/2/Lt., k. in a., 4/10/17.

12 Geddes, Robert Stirling, T/2/Lt., k. in a., 9/10/16.
Gerard, Tom Overton, T/2/Lt., k. in a., 10/7/16.
Gibson, Charles Sydney, 2/Lt., k. in a., 1/7/16 (4th R. War. R., att.).
13 Gibson, James, T/Lt., k. in a., 5/10/17.
Gilbert, Reginald William, T/2/Lt., d. of w., 21/7/16.
Gilderthorp, Ellwood, T/Lt., d. of w., 11/4/18.
89 Gillies, Forbes, T/2/Lt., k. in a., 27/8/16.
Glancy, Hugh, 2/Lt., k. in a., 30/9/18 (3rd R. Mun. Fus.).
9 Goodyear, Roland, 2/Lt., k. in a., 12/4/18.
Gordon, Robert, 2/Lt. (Tp.), d. of w., 4/12/16.
Goudie, Alexander Malcolm, Lt., d. of w., 18/8/16 (3rd Lein. R., att.).
260 Gould, James Robertson Sabiston, T/2/Lt., d. of w., 15/4/18.
73 Gourlay, George, T/2/Lt., k. in a., 14/11/17.
Gradwell, Charles Edward, Lt., k. in a., 21/3/18 (Rif. Bde., att.).
42 Graham, Arthur Thomas, T/2/Lt., k. in a., 27/3/18.
33 Graham, Hugh Christison, 2/Lt., k. in a., 9/6/17 (9th R. Scots Fus., att.).
99 Grant, Clifton Brown, Capt. (Tp.), k. in a., 27/7/16.
1 Grant, Sidney Robert, T/2/Lt., k. in a., 18/4/18.
Gray, Douglas William, 2/Lt., k. in a., 18/11/16.
Gray, Maurice, Lt., A/Capt., k. in a., 8/8/18 (2nd Drag. Gds., att.).
Graves, Adrian Hubert, M.C., T/Lt., A/Capt., k. in a., 22/3/18.
Graves, John, T/Capt., d. of w., 16/4/17.
23 Green, David, 2/Lt. (Tp.), k. in a., 1/8/17.
Greene, Godfrey Robert, 2/Lt., k. in a., 3/9/16.
122 Greenwood. Herbert, T/2/Lt., d. of w., 8/6/17.
35 Gregson, Herbert, 2/Lt., k. in a., 30/11/17.
55 Gronow, Charles David, T/2/Lt., d. of w., 18/4/18.
44 Ground, Francis William, T/2/Lt., k. in a., 25/4/17.
28 Groves, Harold Rienzi Milton, 2/Lt. (Tp.), d. of w., 14/10/17.
90 Gull, Leonard Joseph, T/2/Lt., k. in a., 24/7/17.
33 Gwynne-Vaughan, Kenneth Duncan, T/2/Lt., k. in a., 6/9/16 (15th Bn. R. Fus., and).
Haldane, Colin Kennedy, T/2/Lt., d. of w., 18/10/16 (26th Bn. Man. R., att.).
39 Hale, George Edwin, 2/Lt. (Tp.), k. in a., 22/3/18.
Halfhide, Charles Edward Nelson, T/Lt. (A/Major), k. in a., 24/5/18 (7th E. Lan. R., att.).
72 Hall, Joseph, 2/Lt. (Tp.), k. in a., 31/7/17.
150 Hall, Miles Arthur, 2/Lt., k. in a., 23/4/17.
Hall, William Hubert, T/Lt., k. in a., 19/2/17.
167 Hallewell, George Noble, T/2/Lt., d. of w., 10/10/16.
Halley, Jack J., T/Lt., k. in a., 26/7/16 (13th Worc. R., att.).
15 Hamilton, Bernard St. George, T/Lt., k. in a., 28/6/17.
Hammerton, Gilbert, T/Lt., k. in a., 4/9/16.
35 Hammond, Thomas Hill, T/2/Lt., k. in a., 31/10/18.
Hampton, William Orr, 2/Lt., k. in a., 1/7/16 (3 Norfolk).
50 Hancock, Arthur, T/2/Lt., k. in a., 17/10/18.
24 Hancock, Robert David, 2/Lt., k. in a., 21/3/18.
36 Hansell, Kenneth Joyce Nelson, Lt., k. in a., 21/3/18 (4th Lein. R., att.; 1st R. I. Rif., att.).
91 Harbottle, Stanley James, Lt., k. in a., 26/10/17.
Hardy Charles Eric, T/2/Lt., k. in a., 23/10/18 (Divl. Bn., "19" Bn.).
22 Hardy, Ferdinand H., Lt. (Tp.), k. in a., 4/9/16 (2nd R. Fus., att.).
119 Harkness, Raymond, T/Lt., k. in a., 23/11/17
Harries, William Frank Reginald, T/2/Lt., k. in a., 26/9/18 (Cavalry).
12 Harris, Alfred Edward, T/2/Lt., k. in a., 2/7/18.
Harrison, Geoffrey, T/2/Lt., k. in a., 1/7/16.
31 Harrison, John Adshead, T/2/Lt., k. in a., 12/4/18.
43 Harrison, Thomas Charles, 2/Lt., k. in a., 21/3/18.
109 Hart, Andrew Chichester, 2/Lt., k. in a., 1/7/16.
218 Hart, Neil Lancefield, T/2/Lt., k. in a., 31/7/17.
63 Hart, Thomas, T/2/Lt., k. in a., 5/4/18.
Hartley, d'Arcy John Joseph, Lt., k. in a., 14/7/16.
98 Hartshorn, Arthur William, T/Lt., d. of w., 9/1/18.
164 Harvey, Douglas Preston, M.C., T/2/Lt., k. in a., 20/11/17.
Harvey, Thomas Daniel, M.C., T/Lt., died, 17/10/18 (att. Nig. R.).
2 Harwood, Colin Crisp, T/2/Lt., died, 6/11/17.
117 Hasler, Leonard Melsome, T/Lt., d. of w., 21/9/17 (Essex R., att.).
Hastwell, Wilfrid Maurice, T/2/Lt., k. in a., 7/4/17.
Hatch, Henry Bertram William, T/2/Lt., k. in a., 18/11/16.
99 Haward, Godfrey, Lt. (Tp.), k. in a., 15/11/16.
52 Hawes, Adrian Lancelot, T/Lt., k. in a., 8/10/18.
Haworth, Arthur, T/2/Lt., k. in a., 19/7/16 (16th K. Liv. R., att.).
185 Haybittle, Richard William, Lt., d. of w., 8/1/18.
Haye, Philip, Lt., died, 2/4/19 (3rd R. Bks. R., att.).
117 Head, Arthur William George, 2/Lt. (Tp.), k. in a., 1/8/17.
33 Heath, Arthur Morris, 2/Lt., k. in a., 12/4/18.
143 Heaton, Charles Darrell, 2/Lt. (Tp.), k. in a., 26/8/17.
66 Heaven, Norman Edwin, 2/Lt., k. in a., 21/3/18.
Hedgcock, Frederick Leslie, T/2/Lt., k. in a., 30/9/18.
33 Hedgland, Charles Samuel, T/Lt., k. in a., 17/4/18.
36 Hemingway, Horace Vincent, T/2/Lt., d. of w., 2/10/18.
223 Henderson, Archibald Wright, T/2/Lt., k. in a., 30/12/17.
5 Hepple, Francis James, T/Lt., k. in a., 28/4/17 (11th Bn. N. Staff. R., att.).
Herbert, Edward Grafton, M.C., 2/Lt. (A/Capt.), k. in a., 9/4/18 (R. War. R., and).
52 Herd, James Semple, 2/Lt. (Tp.), k. in a., 16/10/17.
41 Herriott, J., M.C., T/2/Lt., died, 17/2/19.
Hetherington, John, T/Lt., died, 24/11/18.
109 Hewitt, Holt Montgomery, T/Lt., k. in a., 1/7/16.
36 Hewitt, William Taylor, T/2/Lt., d. of w., 16/4/18 (in German hands).
Heywood, Herbert, Capt., d. of w., 22/8/17 (Mdx. R., att.).
116 Higgins, Harry Vincent, 2/Lt., k. in a., 3/9/16.
Hill, Joseph, T/2/Lt., died, 23/11/18.
4 Hill, Tom Warner, 2/Lt. (Tp.), died, 14/10/17.
Hitchcock, Herbert William, T/Lt., k. in a., 13/11/16.
25 Hitchcock, Reginald Francis, 2/Lt., k. in a., 14/4/18.
175 Hobson, John Alfred, T/2/Lt., k. in a., 2/12/17.
116 Hobson, John Collinson, T/Lt., k. in a., 31/7/17.
46 Hoggan, Claude Ashley Rien, Lt., k. in a., 30/5/18.
Hoggard, Ernest John, 2/Lt., k. in a., 5/11/16 (3rd Bn. R. W. Surr. R., att.).
Holloway, James, T/2/Lt., k. in a., 27/9/18.
69 Holloway, William Robert, T/2/Lt., k. in a., 20/9/17.
Holtom, Charles Cecil, T/Lt., k. in a., 31/10/17.
66 Holwill, William Bertram, 2/Lt., d. of w., 16/5/18 (in German hands).
Money, Eric William, T/Lt., k. in a., 11/4/17 (Army Cyc. Cps., att.) (Hvy. B., D. Bn.).
14 Honeyball, Wilfred Chennell, 2/Lt., k. in a., 21/3/18.
45 Hopkins, George Henry Stanton, 2/Lt. (Tp.), k. in a., 31/7/17.
Hopkins, Henry Greenfield Berkeley, Lt. (Tp.), d. of w., 29/7/17 (H.B.).
19 Hopwood, Norman, 2/Lt. (Tp.), k. in a., 23/10/18.
122 Horler, Edwin, 2/Lt. (Tp.), k. in a., 31/7/17.
124 Horsfall, John Brown, 2/Lt. (Tp.), k. in a., 25/7/17.
86 Hosegood, Archibald Harding, 2/Lt. (Tp.), k. in a., 26/11/17.
54 Hosken, Henry Richard, 2/Lt., k. in a., 11/8/17.
Houghton, Tom Whitfield, 2/Lt., died, 21/4/19.
Houston, John Cunningham, 2/Lt., k. in a., 14/10/18 (1/2nd N. Fus., att.).
48 Howard, Walter Leslie, Lt. (Tp.), d. of w., 16/8/17.
149 Howarth, Charles Thomas, 2/Lt., d. of w., 28/5/18.
59 Howarth, Tom Hartley, 2/Lt., d. of w., 6/12/17.
49 Howarth, Wallace, 2/Lt., k. in a., 16/8/17.
215 Howlett, John Harold, 2/Lt. (Tp.), k. in a., 26/9/17.
150 Hoys, Cecil Thomas Gray, T/2/Lt., k. in a., 15/9/16.
Hudson, Godfrey, M.C., Major, k. in a., 12/4/18.
Hughes, Eric James Walrond, 2/Lt. (A/Capt.), k. in a., 20/9/17 (4th N. & D.R., att.).
25 Hughes, Ferdinand, 2/Lt. (Tp.), k. in a., 29/5/18.
197 Hughes, Harold George, M.C., Lt. (Tp.), k. in a., 4/5/17.
Hunt, William Julian, T/2/Lt., k. in a., 11/7/16.
Hunt, W. V., Lt., d. of w., 17/10/18 (and R.A.F.).
Husband, Joseph Sim, T/Lt. (A/Major), d. of w., 11/4/18.
30 Hutchinson, Anthony Christopher Campbell, Major (Tp.), died, 18/11/18.
88 Hutchinson, William John, 2/Lt. (Tp.), k. in a., 25/5/17.
41 Hutton, Lorne de Hutton, 2/Lt. (Tp.), k. in a., 24/3/18.
Huxley, John Scott, T/2/Lt., k. in a., 16/7/16.
Hyland, Herbert Bright, T/2/Lt., k. in a., 19/7/16.
220 Ibberson, Henry Joseph, 2/Lt., k. in a., 5/10/17.
Impey, John Eugene, Lt., k. in a., 27/3/16 (1st Linc. R., att.).
Ingpen, Norman Cecil, T/Capt. (A/Major), d. of w., 4/12/17.
143 Inskipp, Douglas, 2/Lt. (Tp.), k. in a., 16/4/17.
145 Inwood, Charles Hawkins, 2/Lt. (Tp.), k. in a., 16/8/17.
Ireland, Herbert, Lt. & Qr.-Mr., died, 13/11/18 (1 Border).
96 Ironside, Harold Allan, T/Major, died, 15/10/16.
41 Isaac, Dudley Charles, Capt. (Tp.), k. in a., 10/4/17.
89 Isaacs, Bernard Clifford, 2/Lt. (Tp.), d. of w., 1/8/17.
Ivory, John Arthur, Lt. (Tp.), k. in a., 27/9/18.
16 Jackson, Horace, 2/Lt. (Tp.), k. in a., 21/3/18.
233 Jackson, Robert Cameron, T/2/Lt., k. in a., 24/9/17.
10 James, Albert, Lt. (Tp.), d. of w., 28/3/18.
Jamieson, William Patterson, T/Lt., k. in a., 6/4/17.
Jeffries, Herbert, T/Lt., d. of w., 20/9/18 (York. R., att.).
15 Jeffries, Philip, Lt. (Tp.), died, 3/12/18.
20 Jenkins, Arthur Emlyn, Lt. (Tp.), k. in a., 4/12/16.
201 Jennings, Francis Henry Cuthbert, Lt. (Tp.), died, 7/2/18.
Jessopp, Walter Leverton, T/Lt., k. in a., 31/7/17.
8 Johnson, George William, Lt. (Tp.), k. in a., 24/4/18.
75 Johnson, Harold, T/2/Lt., d. of w., 14/7/16.
133 Johnson, John, T/2/Lt., k. in a., 9/1/17.
217 Johnson, Thomas, T/2/Lt., d. of w., 4/8/17.
Jones, Arthur, 2/Lt. (Tp.), k. in a., 22/8/18 (D. of C.L.I., att.).
Jones, Arthur Meredydd, M.C., Lt., d. of w., 10/4/18.
Jones, Ernest Hugh, T/2/Lt., k. in a., 26/10/17.
Jones, Evan Lewis, T/2/Lt., k. in a., 13/11/16 (10th N. Staff. R.).
Jones, Frederick S. C., 2/Lt., k. in a., 30/11/16 (Lan. Fus.).
Jones, Henry Paul Mainwaring, T/Lt., k. in a., 31/7/17.
134 Jones, William Bartholomew, 2/Lt., k. in a., 27/5/18.
4 Joyce, William Alfred, 2/Lt. (Tp.), k. in a., 28/3/18.
12 Kay, Collin Lowther, 2/Lt., d. of w., 12/10/16.
6 Keeble, Alfred Ernest, Capt. (Tp.), d. of w., 5/8/18.
Kelly, Kenneth George, Lt., k. in a., 27/5/18.
Kemp, Frank, 2/Lt., k. in a., 22/7/16 (11th Bn. Yk. L.I., att.).
25 Kemp, John Thomson, 2/Lt., k. in a., 11/4/18.
Kendall, Locke Francis William Angerstein, T/Lt., d. of w., 22/11/17 (9th Norf. and)
Kendall, Thomas Linaker, 2/Lt., k. in a., 1/8/16.
54 Kennard, Winwood Read, T/2/Lt., k. in a., 30/6/16.
Kenny, Cecil John, Lt., k. in a., 24/3/18 (3rd R. Ir. Rgt., att.).
43 Kent, Sidney, T/2/Lt., k. in a., 13/12/17.
14 Kernick, Charles Sylvester, T/Lt., d. of w., 1/12/17.
202 Kerr, James Elkin, T/Lt., d. of w., 10/9/17.
97 Kerr, Norman James, T/2/Lt., d. of w., 20/12/16.
4 Kerr, William, T/Lt., k. in a., 2/9/18 (6th R. Scots Fus., att.).

Kesby, Thomas Herbert, T/Capt., k. in a., 15/9/16 (E. Kent R., att.).
137 Kidd, Balmer, 2/Lt. (Tp.), d. of w., 19/3/18.
Killick, Sydney Howard, 2/Lt., died, 16/5/18 (8th E. Surr. R., att.).
44 King, Cuthbert, T/Major, k. in a., 11/4/17 (R.W. Surr. R.).
52 King, Cyril William, T/2/Lt., k. in a., 9/11/17.
25 King, Frederick Cross, T/2/Lt., k. in a., 23/10/16.
233 King, Victor Algernon Robert, T/2/Lt., k. in a., 29/9/17.
7 Kingham, Rolland Hill, 2/Lt. (Tp.), k. in a., 23/3/18.
10 Kingsman, Roland Walter, 2/Lt., k. in a., 12/10/17.
11 Kirby, Robert Arthur, T/2/Lt., k. in a., 11/5/17.
Kirk, John Thomas, M.C., 2/Lt., k. in a., 28/3/18.
5 Kirkby, William, T/Lt. (A/Capt.), died, 1/11/18.
233 Knight, Ernest Alexander, T/2/Lt., k. in a., 24/9/17.
Knowles, Richard Cameron, Lt. (Tp.), k. in a., 10/7/16.
Kohnstam, Oscar Jacob Charles, 2/Lt., k. in a., 29/5/16 (4th Bn. Nth. Staff. R., att.).
74 Kynaston, John Oswald Maurice, Lt. (Tp.), k. in a., 21/9/18.
1 Lacaita, Francis Charles, Lt. (Tp.), k. in a., 3/4/18 (17th Lancers, and).
25 Laing, James, MacDougall, Lt., k. in a., 23/3/18.
80 Laine, Charles Janion, T/2/Lt., k. in a., 30/7/16.
60 Lamb, Raymond Wildman, M.C., Lt. (Tp.), died, 14/11/18.
29 Lancaster, Arnold Busk, 2/Lt. (Tp.), d. of w., 11/4/18.
16 Lancaster, Ernest Randolph, T/2/Lt., k. in a., 12/10/16.
Lancaster, Percy, T/2/Lt., k. in a., 15/9/16.
Land, Ronald John, Lt., k. in a., 20/3/18 (3rd Y. & L. R., att.).
59 Lane, Edward Dion, M.C., T/2/Lt., d. of w., 8/12/17 (in German hands).
Lane-Joynt, Albert William, Lt., k. in a., 26/2/16.
Lang, Norman, Lt. (Tp.), k. in a., 24/8/18 (Div. Bn.).
36 Langton, David Elland, T/2/Lt., d. of w., 10/4/17.
Laughton, Hubert Henry Schomberg, T/Lt., died, 25/11/18 (2nd Worc. R., att.).
42 Lascelles, Francis Hope, T/Lt., k. in a., 22/8/17.
Later, Joseph Oswald, T/Lt., d. of w., 13/7/16.
58 Laurie, Eric Unwin, Lt., k. in a., 24/3/18.
41 Lawson, John Wilson, M.C., T/Lt. (A/Capt.), k. in a., 24/3/18
42 Leaman, Mark Reginald, 2/Lt., k. in a., 5/4/18
Leary, Ernest Richard, 2/Lt., d. of w., 23/7/16 (3rd Y. & L. R., and).
56 Leckie, John, M.C., T/Lt. (A/Major), d. of w., 29/8/18.
50 Lee, Thomas, 2/Lt., k. in a., 9/4/18.
148 Leech, Bernard Jack, T/2/Lt., k. in a., 9/10/17.
97 Leeson, Ian Alister, Capt., k. in a., 10/7/17.
Legge, Reginald Charles, Lt., k. in a., 16/9/16.
88 Leighton, Harold, M.C., T/Lt., d. of w., 26/5/17.
4 Lemon, Adrian Leigh, Lt., k. in a., 29/11/16 (6th D. Gds., att.).
195 Lewis, Alfred Ernest George, T/Lt., k. in a., 6/9/17.
7 Lewis, Frank, T/2/Lt., d. of w., 31/7/17.
151 Lewis, Harold, 2/Lt., d. of w., 29/4/17.
Lewis, Lance Will, T/2/Lt., k. in a., 9/8/16 (7th Bn. K.R.R.C., and).
74 Lewis, Robert George, Lt. (Tp.), k. in a., 23/9/18.
2 Lewis, Ludwig, 2/Lt. (Tp.), k. in a., 6/7/17.
Lockerbie, Herbert, 2/Lt. (Tp.), k. in a., 21/8/18.
37 Lord, Evelyn Geoffrey, Lt. (Tp.), died, 25/6/18.
54 Loveday, Charles Norton, T/2/Lt., k. in a., 12/10/17.
9 Lovell, Cyril Thomas, 2/Lt. (Tp.), k. in a., 14/6/18.
Low, James Morrison, Lt., k. in a., 1/7/16 (Sea. Hdrs., att.).
9 Lower, Neil Eustace, T/2/Lt., k. in a., 30/6/17.
Loxley, Charles Eric Smart, T/Capt., died, 18/12/18 (Essex R., att.).
63 Luff, Edgar William Guy, Lt., k. in a., 25/3/18.
Lynch, James Walker, T/2/Lt., k. in a., 31/7/17 (H.B.).
McCoull, William Sinclair, Lt., k. in a., 3/5/17 (Hvy B., D. Bn.).
235 McCredie, John Forrest, 2/Lt., k. in a., 30/11/17.
McFarlane, John Tennant, T/Lt., k. in a., 26/9/15.
38 McFarlane, Walter, T/2/Lt., d. of w., 15/1/17 (R. Lanc. R., att.).
132 McGregor, James Hamilton, 2/Lt. (T/Lt.), k. in a., 10/1/17 (3rd Bedf. R., att.).
MacIntyre, Ian Campbell, Lt., k. in a., 22/11/17 (Cam. Hrs., att.).
MacKay, Gordon, T/2/Lt., k. in a., 16/8/17 (24th, att. 16th Mdx. R., att.).
6 McKay, George Newton, T/Lt., k. in a., 24/7/18.
59 McKendrick, David, 2/Lt., k. in a., 30/11/17.
Mackenzie, William, Lt., k. in a., 17/5/17 (9th K.O.S.B., att.).
Mackie, Alexander Mackay, 2/Lt., k. in a., 21/10/18 (4th D.L.I., and).
28 McKinley, David Oliver, T/2/Lt., k. in a., 21/10/17.
10 McKinnie, Peter, T/2/Lt., k. in a., 4/10/17.
51 Mackinnon, Archibald, T/2/Lt., k. in a., 13/10/18.
Maclachlan, David Corson, T/2/Lt., died, 18/5/17 (H.B.).
McLellan, James, 2/Lt. (T/Lt.), k. in a., 4/10/17 (3rd H.L.I., att.).
55 McLellan, Joseph Taylor, T/Lt., k. in a., 21/3/18.
McMaster, Philip George, T/Lt., k. in a., 20/6/18.
Macpherson, George, T/Lt., d. of w., 15/9/16.
6 Macpherson, William Meikle, T/2/Lt., k. in a., 18/9/18.
31 Macrae, George Duncan, T/2/Lt., k. in a., 27/3/18.
42 McRae, William, 2/Lt., k. in a., 27/3/18.
McCormack, Thomas, Lt., k. in a., 15/9/16.
McDiarmid, David, T/Lt., k. in a., 10/8/16.
McKenzie, Kenneth Fitzgerald, 2/Lt., k. in a., 14/7/16.
90 Maddrell, James Keggan, T/Lt., k. in a., 23/4/17.
27 Maish, William Edward, M.C., T/2/Lt., k. in a., 12/10/17.
121 Male, Arthur Phillip, T/Lt., k. in a., 23/11/17.
Mallinson, John Whiteley, 2/Lt., k. in a., 14/2/16 (6th Rif. Bde., att.).
2 Manger, Eric, 2/Lt., k. in a., 10/7/17.
Mann, George William, T/Capt., k. in a., 24/7/17 (F. Bn., Hvy. Bde.).
52 Manners, Hugh, T/2/Lt., k. in a., 24/4/17.
25 Manning, Victor Lionel, T/2/Lt., k. in a., 23/3/18.
15 Mansell, Harry Champion, T/2/Lt., k. in a., 30/6/17.
Manterfield, John Thomas, 2/Lt., k. in a., 21/9/18 (Linc. R., att.).
2 Marsh, Robert Cecil, T/2/Lt., d. of w., 19/9/18.
214 Marsden, Morris James, T/2/Lt., k. in a., 20/9/17.
Maslin, Leonard Frank, M.C., T/Lt., died, 20/5/18.
12 Mason, Gerald Francis, Lt., died, 1/9/17 (3rd Hamp. R., att).
Mason, Robert Brereton, T/2/Lt., k. in a., 10/10/18.
8 Massey, Albert Francis, T/2/Lt., k. in a., 28/3/18.
6 Mathers, George Eric, T/Lt., k. in a., 8/10/18.
49 Matthams, Lawrence, T/2/Lt., k. in a., 13/10/18.
266 Matthews, Francis Harold, T/2/Lt., k. in a., 24/7/17.
124 Maud, Frederick, T/2/Lt., k. in a., 20/9/17.
May, Ernest Bernard, T/2/Lt., k. in a., 4/10/16.
143 May, Thomas George, T/2/Lt., k. in a., 6/8/17.
Meade, Richard Gilbert Trever, T/2/Lt., d. of w., 10/10/17.
36 Merchant, Reginald Frank, 2/Lt., k. in a., 21/3/18.
4 Merrick, Thomas Barker, M.C., T/Lt., A/Capt., k. in a. 2/9/18.
16 Merry, George William Henry, 2/Lt., k. in a., 21/3/18.
217 Mettam, Athol Roy, 2/Lt., k. in a., 16/8/17 (W. Yks. R., att.).
9 Midgley, Arthur, T/2/Lt., d. of w., 15/7/16.
Millar, Robert Bain, T/Lt., A/Capt.), k. in a., 24/7/18.
Millar, Stanley Gemmell, T/Capt., k. in a., 1/7/16.
167 Miller, John McGregor, T/2/Lt., k. in a., 8/10/16.
19 Mills, Henry Jackson, Lt., k. in a., 30/5/18 (2nd Mdx. R.).
146 Mills, Norman Hope Vandeleur, T/2/Lt., k. in a., 17/9/17.
49 Milne, William, T/Capt., d. of w., 25/7/18 (in enemy's hands).
Milner, Archibald Berry, T/2/Lt., k. in a., 4/11/18.
35 Milward, Stanley Reginald, T/2/Lt., k. in a., 11/8/16.
32 Mincer, Frank, T/2/Lt., k. in a., 23/10/18.
50 Mitchell, Frank, T/2/Lt., k. in a., 12/5/17.
66 Mitchell, Thomas Hume, T/2/Lt., d. of w., 16/4/18.
Mitchell, William Henry, T/2/Lt., k. in a., 1/11/18.
Mockler, Francis George Ross, Capt., k. in a., 1/7/16 (R. Ir. R., att.).
Mockridge, George Ewart, T/Lt., k. in a., 1/7/16.
117 Montague, Albert Cecil, 2/Lt., k. in a., 16/6/17.
208 Montford, Alfred Charles, T/2/Lt., k. in a., 3/5/17.
116 Montgomery, George, T/2/Lt., d. of w., 14/10/17.
Moon, Roy Agnew, M.C., T/Lt., d. of w., 28/4/18.
Moore, John Rushton, M.C., Lt. (A/Maj.), k. in a., 20-22/3/18 (3rd Ches. R., att.).
62 Morgan, William, T/2/Lt., d. of w., 23/7/18.
144 Morris, Philip Henry, T/2/Lt., k. in a., 9/10/17.
106 Morris, William Norman, T/2/Lt., d. of w., 25/5/16 (8th Wilt. R.).
61 Morrison, Haslett, T/Lt., A/Maj., k. in a., 23/4/18.
Moore, Dacre William, T/Lt., k. in a., 11/6/16.
99 Moritz, Oscar Frank, T/2/Lt., d. of w., 27/7/16.
51 Morrison, Robert, T/2/Lt., d. of w., 14/4/18.
30 Morrison, Thomas, 2/Lt., k. in a., 21/3/18.
Morse, Ernest Frederick, T/Lt., k. in a., 1/7/16.
59 Mortenson, Alfred, T/2/Lt., k. in a., 15/4/18.
59 Moss, Percy William, T/2/Lt., k. in a., 23/8/18.
36 Mozley, Richard Inger, Lt., k. in a., 21/3/18 (3rd Y. & L.R., att.).
123 Mulkern, Lionel Henry, T/2/Lt., k. in a., 26/9/17.
17 Mungeam, Ernest George, T/2/Lt., d. of w., 25/8/18 (Div. Bn.).
56 Murray, Andrew, Lt. (Tp.), k. in a., 19/11/16.
155 Murray, Raymond Hugh, T/2/Lt., k. in a., 12/3/18.
35 Murton, Charles Evelyn, 2/Lt., k. in a., 30/11/17.
8 Musson, Graham, T/2/Lt., k. in a., 25/3/18.
101 Neale, Percy Reginald, T/2/Lt., k. in a., 20/12/17.
Neill, James Dermot, T/Lt., k. in a., 1/7/16.
3 Neilson, Robert Rowland, T/Lt., A/Major, k. in a., 13/4/18.
Newman, Reginald Bodman, 2/Lt., k. in a., 7/9/16.
Nisbet, Edwin, T/Lt., k. in a., 6/9/18 (Divl.).
9 Noble, John, Lt., k. in a., 28/9/18.
Nolan-Martin, Alfred John, Capt., d. of w., 22/2/17 (3rd Bn. R. Dub. Fus., att.).
40 Norman, James Bertram, M.C., T/2/Lt., k. in a., 10/4/18.
154 Norman, Leonard Frank, T/2/Lt., k. in a., 21/9/17.
34 Norris, Percy Walter, T/2/Lt., k. in a., 29/7/18.
27 Notcutt, Leonard Ernest, Lt., k. in a., 3/5/17 (7th Roy. Fus., and).
14 Nuthall, John Constantine, T/2/Lt., k. in a., 3/7/17
59 Nuttall, Eric John, 2/Lt., k. in a., 21/3/18 (12th W. York. R., att.).
19 Nutter, Geoffrey Hayward Elliot, T/2/Lt., k. in a., 22/3/18.
214 Okey, Leslie Alfred, 2/Lt. (Tp.), k. in a., 15/6/17.
13 Oliver, Harry John, T/2/Lt., d. of w., 23/4/18.
Oliver-Thompson, John Herbert, T/Lt., A/Maj., k. in a., 21/3/18.
Oncken, William Gerrard, T/Lt., died, 17/2/19.
61 Orgill, Phillip Ronald, T/2/Lt., d. of w., 31/3/18 (as P. of W. in Ger. hands).
14 Orrett, Claud Cecil, T/Lt., k. in a., 25/9/18.
Osborne, Victor Edward, 2/Lt., killed, 7/4/18 (whilst P. of War) (3rd O. & B.L.I., att.).
102 Owen, Richard Frank, T/2/Lt., k. in a., 30/4/17 (Hamp. R.).
88 Owen, Reginald Frank Leear, Lt., k. in a., 23/4/17 (1st Essex R., att.).
33 Page, Gerald, T/2/Lt., d. of w., 9/6/17.
31 Palmer, John Walter Edmonde, 2/Lt., died, 11/6/18 (as P. of W. in enemy hands).

19 Pare, Charles Percy, 2/Lt., k. in a., 22/3/18.
46 Park, Alexander Crabbe, 2/Lt., d. of w., 29/9/18.
46 Park, Frederick Andrew Katchen, Lt., k. in a., 3/10/18.
50 Parsons, Herbert Mersfield, 2/Lt., k. in a., 13/4/18.
Paterson, Stuart, T/2/Lt., d. of w., 19/10/16.
54 Paton, Edward Kesson, T/2/Lt., d. of w., 3/5/17.
28 Patrick, David Balfour, 2/Lt., k. in a., 18/7/16 (11th H.L.I., att.).
76 Pattinson, William Graham, T/Lt., k. in a., 25/4/17.
Payne, Newman Hayes, 2/Lt., k. in a., 14/9/18 (Divl.).
117 Pearce, Cuthbert James, 2/Lt (Tp.), k. in a., 4/9/16.
31 Pearson, James, Lt., d. of w., 28/3/18.
60 Peatfield, Stanley James, 2/Lt. (Tp.), d. of w., 2/7/16 (9th R. Bks. R., att.).
Peden, George Edward, 2/Lt., k. in a., 25/3/17 (3rd Norf., att.).
113 Peebles, William Fleming, T/2/Lt., k. in a., 30/4/17 (5th Wilts R., att.).
Penman, Geoffrey Evans, T/Lt., k. in a., 9/5/17 (11th Bn. R.W. Surr. R., att.).
214 Penman, Rowland Arthur, T/2/Lt., k. in a., 16/6/17.
12 Penrose, Ernest, Lt., k. in a., 5/4/18
62 Pentelow, Arthur Lenton, 2/Lt., d. of w., 28/7/18.
95 Percival, Anthony, T/Lt., d of w., 15/10/17.
197 Perkins, Albert, T/2/Lt., k. in a., 4/10/17.
58 Perry, Frank Burgess, 2/Lt., k. in a., 24/4/18.
57 Phillips, Herbert Denis, T/2/Lt., k. in a., 24/10/16.
102 Pidduck, Norman Andrews, T/2/Lt., k. in a., 1/7/16.
176 Pine, Frank Youatt, T/2/Lt., k. in a., 16/8/17
215 Plummer, Frederick Charles, T/2/Lt., k. in a., 23/9/17.
21 Pope, Henry William, Capt., k. in a., 24/3/18 (7th D. Gds., att.).
Porter, John Charlton, T/2/Lt., k. in a., 24/7/17 (F. Bn., H. Br.).
149 Potter, William Rochester, T/2/Lt., d. of w., 24/4/17.
25 Potts, Robert William, T/2/Lt., d. of w., 24/3/18.
117 Pound, Cecil Davison, T/Lt., k. in a., 22/9/18.
75 Pountney, Percival, T/Lt., k. in a., 7/6/17.
Powell, David Emrys, T/Lt., k. in a. (Dvl.).
Powell, George Henry, T/2/Lt., k. in a., 29/4/17.
124 Prescott, Alec Frank Evelyn, Lt. (Tp.), k. in a., 8/10/16.
Price, Herbert Allen, M.C., T/2/Lt., d. of w., 30/11/17 (3rd Som. L.I., att.).
Price, William Henry, 2/Lt., k. in a., 23/8/17.
Prichard, Arthur Douglas, T/2/Lt., d. of w., 8/10/17.
Priestley, Dyker Stanton, 2/Lt., k. in a., 1/7/16.
Pring, Basil Crompton, T/Lt., k. in a., 1/7/16.
38 Prosser, Walter, T/2/Lt., d. of w., 9/10/18.
34 Pruden, Walter Henry, T/2/Lt., died, 27/11/18.
Purcell, Charles Francis, Lt., k. in a., 15/9/16 (Ir. Gds., att.).
19 Purches, Clifford Arthur, T/2/Lt., k. in a., 22/3/18.
111 Purkis, Harold Arthur, T/2/Lt., k. in a., 28/7/17.
56 Quirke, Amyas Septimus, M.C., T/2/Lt., d. of w., 3/11/18.
35 Radcliffe, Frederick, Lt. (Tp.), k. in a., 10/4/17.
59 Ramsay, David James, 2/Lt., k. in a., 21/3/18.
Ramsden, Emsley, T/2/Lt., k. in a., 15/9/16.
122 Raper, Frank Alexander D'Arbly, M.C., 2/Lt. (Tp.), k. in a., 11/12/17.
6 Ratcliffe, Frederick, Lt. (A/Capt.), d. of w., 30/3/18 (1st R. Drag., att.).
118 Rawlinson, Harry Raymond, T/2/Lt., k. in a., 26/9/17.
44 Rayner, Arthur Tamplin, T/2/Lt., d. of w., 6/7/16.
11 Read, Clare Moore, T/2/Lt., k. in a., 19/7/18.
Ready, Nathaniel Henry Alter, 2/Lt., d. of w., 1/8/17 ("F" Bn.).
25 Reay, William Roland, T/2/Lt., k. in a., 27/5/18.
Reed, Henry, T/2/Lt., k. in a., 30/8/18 (Divl.).
104 Reed, Sydney George Herbert, T/Lt., died, 24/12/18.
46 Rees, Thomas Stanley, T/Lt., died, 18/3/19.
247 Reeves, Frank, 2/Lt. (Tp.), d. of w., 30/12/17.
24 Rice, James Alfred, D.C.M., T/2/Lt., k. in a., 11/10/18.
189 Richards, Maurice Tom, Lt. (Tp.), d. of w., 23/9/17.
61 Richards, Paul, M.C., T/Lt. (A/Maj.), k. in a., 3/10/18.
Richardson, Albert Edward, Capt., died, 24/11/18 (Rif. Bde., att.).
Richardson, Percival Blythe, T/Capt., died, 3/11/18.
91 Richardson, Robert Scovell, Lt. (Tp.), d. of w., 1/9/16.
Richardson, William Turner, 2/Lt. (Tp.), k. in a., 1/7/16.
Ricketts, Harold Edwin, T/2/Lt., d. of w., 14/7/16 (R.W. Surr. R., att.).
26 Rider, Alonzo Ward, 2/Lt., k. in a., 12/10/17.
153 Ridge, Everard Vaughan, Lt. (Tp.), k. in a., 10/4/17.
126 Rigby, John, Capt. & Qr.-Mr., died, 21/5/18.
69 Rigby, William Geoffrey Morris, Lt. (Tp.), d. of w., 7/7/16.
52 Rigg, George Southerton, D.S.O., 2/Lt., T/Lt., k. in a., 31/7/17 (3rd Y. & L.R., att.).
204 Ritson, Eustace Blackburne, 2/Lt., k in a., 8/10/17.
1 Robertson, David McCulloch, 2/Lt., k. in a., 13/2/17.
25 Roberts, Iorworth Cynon, 2/Lt., k. in a., 10/4/18.
Roberts, Ralph Jennings, Lt. (Tp.), k. in a., 31/10/17.
Roberts, Robert John, 2/Lt., d. of w., 28/10/18 (whilst P. of W. in German hands).
218 Roberts, William, 2/Lt. (Tp.), d of w., 8/8/17.
156 Robertson, William George, Lt., d. of w., 15/12/17 (11th Bn. Gor. Hdrs., att.).
57 Robin, John, T/Lt. (A/Major), died, 29/11/18.
Robins, Charles Frederick, T/Lt., d. of w., 2/4/18 (Cav.).
Robinson, F. W., D.S.O., M.C., Major, d. of w., 29/3/18.
46 Robinson, Robert Ernest, T/2/Lt., d. of w., 12/11/18.
5 Robson, Frederick William, T/2/Lt., d. of w., 22/8/18.
50 Rodgers, Albert Henry, T/2/Lt., d. of w., 17/10/18.
36 Root, Harold Walter, Lt., d. of w., 22/3/18 whilst P. of W. in enemy hands).
59 Rostron, George, T/2/Lt., k. in a., 21/3/18.
14 Rothwell, Henry, 2/Lt. (Tp.), k. in a., 2/12/17.
61 Rowbotham, Howard Leeson, Lt., k. in a., 30/11/17.
Roxburgh, John Hewitt, M.C., T/Major, k. in a., 2/10/18 (Div. Bn.).
21 Rudkin, G. H., M.C., T/2/Lt., died, 28/10/18.
18 Runge, Oscar Julius Tolme, M.C., Lt., k. in a. 15/10/16 (Mdx. R.).
Rutherford, John Allen, T/Capt., k. in a., 24/8/16.
11 St. John, Thomas, 2/Lt., d. of w., 2/7/16.
Sandell, Robert Louis, T/2/Lt., k. in a., 22/9/16.
Sanderson, Geoffrey Evan, T/Lt., k. in a., 1/7/16.
32 Sandom, William Ernest, T/Lt., died, 10/11/18.
Sargent, Reginald William Fitzgerald, 2/Lt. (Tp.), k. in a., 5/10/17.
46 Saunders, Horace Victor Bertram, T/2/Lt., k. in a., 22/3/18.
Saunders, Robert, 2/Lt. (Tp.), k. in a., 26/10/17.
51 Savage, William Beck, Lt., k. in a., 21/3/18.
Sawyer, Aleck Makson, 2/Lt. (Tp.), d. of w., 13/12/17.
44 Schloss, Lionel Ernest, 2/Lt., k. in a., 31/7/17.
21 Scotland, David Lothian, T/Lt. (A/Capt.), d. of w., 5/10/18.
Scott, Samuel Lackland, T/2/Lt., k. in a., 8/8/18 (Ches. R., att.).
Scott-Holmes, B., 2/Lt. (Tp.), killed, 24/10/16.
58 Scott, Frank Alexander, T/2/Lt., k. in a., 18/9/18.
19 Scott, Stanley, M.C., T/Lt. (A/Major), k. in a., 6/6/18.
Scriven, Arthur Cecil, M.C., T/Lt., k. in a., 7/11/16.
16 Service, George Brown, T/2/Lt., k. in a., 30/3/18.
21 Settle, Reginald Henry Napier, D.S.O., M.C., T/Lt.-Col., k. in a., 24/3/18 (19th Hrs., and).
Seymour, Bertram, 2/Lt. (Tp.), k. in a., 31/7/17.
61 Seymour, Charles, T/2/Lt., k. in a., 13/4/18.
Shanley, Andrew, 2/Lt., k. in a., 25/9/16
61 Sharps, Robert, T/2/Lt., k. in a., 18/4/18.
39 Shaw, Charles Conway, T/Lt., k. in a., 31/8/18.
66 Shaw, Ronald Percy, T/2/Lt., k. in a., 22/3/18.
Shaw, William Hetherington, T/Lt., k. in a., 8/10/18.
3 Shepherd, Edwin Alexander, T/Lt., d. of w., 13/4/18.
55 Sherlock, Gerald, T/2/Lt., d. of w., 21/4/18.
51 Siddall, Douglas Hamblett, T/2/Lt., k. in a., 11/4/18.
76 Simmonds, Guy Bloxham, T/2/Lt., killed, 29/12/16.
Simpson, George Arnold, 2/Lt., k. in a., 2/7/16 (5 Leics. R., att.).
20 Simpson, James Francis, 2/Lt. (Tp.), d. of w., 27/10/17.
239 Sinclair, Alexander Thomson, T/2/Lt., k. in a., 10/9/17.
24 Skinner, Ernest Archibald, 2/Lt., d. of w., 26/11/17.
8 Skinner, Wilfred Henry, 2/Lt., d. of w., 27/5/18 (whilst P. of W. in Germany).
9 Skipworth, Bernard William, M.C., Lt., k. in a., 25/4/18 (3rd R. Suss. R., att.).
3 Sloper, Bruce James, M.C., T/2/Lt., k. in a., 31/8/18.
47 Small, Frank Gilbert Harrell, 2/Lt., d. of w., 9/6/18 (as P. of W.).
Smallwood, George Baxter, M.M., 2/Lt., died, 2/11/18 (R Lancs R., att.).
Smart, Walter, T/Lt., k. in a., 3/10/18.
Smellie, John Ormond, Lt., died, 8/8/17.
36 Smith, Arthur Jonathan, T/2/Lt., k. in a., 28/3/18.
97 Smith, Charles Sydney, M.C., T/Major, died, 28/11/18.
183 Smith, Edgar Ernest, M.C., Lt. (Tp.), k. in a., 3/12/17.
Smith, Ernest Wilson Marshall, 2/Lt., killed, 22/3/16 (5th Lein. R., att.).
153 Smith, Gerald Sydney, Lt. (Tp.), k. in a., 13/11/16.
68 Smith, Robert Fraser, 2/Lt., k. in a., 20/9/17.
Smith, Reginald George, T/2/Lt., k. in a., 7/10/16.
196 Smith, Robert Rutherford, 2/Lt. (Tp.), k. in a., 20/9/17
59 Smith, Sidney George, 2/Lt., k. in a., 21/3/18.
5 Smyth, John Albert Gordon, T/2/Lt., k. in a., 29/6/18.
31 Souster, Albert Edward, T/2/Lt., k. in a., 12/4/18.
104 Spankie, Dysart Watt, T/2/Lt., k. in a., 5/6/16.
Speedy, Ralph Coggin, 2/Lt., died, 4/12/18 (19 Sqd.).
Spicer, Filmer Blake, 2/Lt., d. of w., 6/10/16 (3 E. Kent R., att.).
56 Spurway, George Vyvyan, M.C., T/Lt., k. in a., 28/3/18.
15 Stagg, Harold William, 2/Lt., k. in a., 28/3/18.
24 Stampe, George Herbert, T/Major, k. in a., 27/3/18.
52 Stanbury, Lional Duncan, Lt. (Tp.), k. in a., 7/7/16.
Steele, Ernest Cecil, T/Lt., k. in a., 18/9/18 (Divl.).
34 Steinberg, George Kenneth, M.C., T/Lt., k. in a., 22/3/18 (Divl.).
Stewart, Alexander James, M.C., Lt. (A/Major), d. of w., 30/4/18 (2nd W. Yk. R., att.).
22 Stewart, Albert Lewis, D.S.O., Major (Tp.), k. in a., 4/10/17.
140 Stewart, Edward John, 2/Lt. (Tp.), k. in a., 30/11/17.
23 Stewart, William Malcolm, T/Capt., d. of w., 27/10/16.
30 Stockley, Philip Lloyd, T/Lt. (A/Capt.), k. in a., 26/4/18.
52 Stooks, Herbert Drummond Sumner, T/2/Lt., d. of w., 25/4/17.
Storey, Robert William, 2/Lt., killed, 9/3/18 (D.L.I., att.).
218 Stott, Edward Henry Hussey, 2/Lt. (Tp.), d. of w., 3/9/17.
86 Street, Richard, 2/Lt. (Tp.), k. in a., 24/4/17 (W. Yk. R., att.).
Stretch, Thomas Noel Heath, M.C., T/Lt., k. in a., 25/3/18 (R.A.S.C. and).
23 Strong, James Mortimer, 2/Lt. (Tp.), d. of w., 26/7/17.
63 Sturgess, Thomas George, M.C., T/2/Lt., d. of w., 10/11/18 (Divl.).
31 Sturrock, Arthur Hill, Lt. (Tp.), drowned, 4/5/17.
Swears, Hugh Miller, Lt., k. in a., 11/4/17.
34 Symonds, Bertram Oliver, T/2/Lt., k. in a., 21/8/18.
98 Symons, Eric Clarence, T/2/Lt., d. of w., 1/9/16.
Synnott, Walter Pierre, 2/Lt., died, 11/10/18 (6th Dns. and).
59 Tanner, Charles Patrick, Lt., A/Capt., k. in a., 30/11/17.
Tanner, Edward Joseph Selby, 2/Lt. (Tp.), k. in a., 8/7/16 (11th Yks. R., att.).
18 Tappenden, Frank William, T/2/Lt., k. in a., 2/7/18.

Tarbet, William Duncan, T/2/Lt., k. in a., 9/4/17 (7th Sea. Hdrs., att.).
166 Taylor, Bernard Arthur, 2/Lt., k. in a., 30/11/17.
169 Taylor, Eustace Edmund Marshall, T/Lt., k. in a., 1/1/17.
Taylor, Henry, T/Lt., d. of w., 9/11/17.
35 Taylor, John, M.M., T/Lt., k. in a., 29/9/18.
8 Taylor, Leslie Francis, M.C., T/Lt., k. in a., 27/5/18 (K.R. Rif. C.).
141 Taylor, Leonard William, T/Lt., A/Capt., k. in a., 19/2/18.
Taylor, Matthew Neilson, T/2/Lt., k. in a., 27/8/18 (Divl.).
Taylor, Vernon, Lt. (Tp.), k. in a., 15/9/16.
166 Taylor, William Anthony, T/Lt., k. in a., 31/7/17.
Taylor, William Crookenden, T/Lt., d. of w., 5/11/18 (13th H.L.I., att.).
92 Temperley, Jesse Hargreaves, 2/Lt. (Tp.), killed, 25/10/17.
133 Terras, James Sutherland, 2/Lt. (Tp.), k. in a., 11/1/17.
176 Thirlwell, Walter Houlden, T/2/Lt., k. in a., 16/8/17.
27 Thomas, Basil Llewellyn Boyd, T/Lt., k. in a., 9/4/17 (15th R. War. R., att.).
214 Thomas, Charles Harold Horatio, T/Lt., k. in a., 20/9/17.
51 Thomas, Thomas, Lt. (Tp.), k. in a., 3/11/16.
142 Thomas, Ivan Arthur, T/2/Lt., k. in a., 10/5/17.
118 Thomas, William Eric, 2/Lt., k. in a., 31/7/17.
8 Thompson, Morice Bell, T/Lt., k. in a., 3/5/17.
90 Thormer, Harry, 2/Lt. (Tp.), killed, 30/12/17.
69 Tight, Arthur Sidney, T/2/Lt., k. in a., 23/3/18.
Tillyard, Sidney Joseph, 2/Lt. (Tp.), k. in a., 2/3/16.
154 Tilston, John Edward, 2/Lt. (Tp.), k. in a., 23/4/17.
23 Tingle, John, 2/Lt., d. of w., 16/6/18.
62 Tiptaft, William Rutherford, 2/Lt., T/Lt., k. in a., 21/9/17.
24 Todd, Harry, T/2/Lt., died, 29/10/18.
Tomblin, James Douglas, T/2/Lt., d. of w., 13/11/15.
Torrens, Gerald Calverley, T/Capt., died, 24/12/16.
19 Torrens, James Claude, T/2/Lt., k. in a., 30/5/18.
Toshack, Thomas, 2/Lt., k. in a., 10/4/17 ("C" Bn.).
122 Towlson, William Holland, T/2/Lt., d. of w., 28/9/17.
Townsend, Harry, 2/Lt., k. in a., 19/7/16 (53 Inf. Bde.).
15 Travers-Smith, Robert Montgomery, 2/Lt., drowned, 4/10/18.
8 Tree, Philip Bevan, T/2/Lt., k. in a., 24/3/18.
62 Troman, Thomas Joseph Barnsley, 2/Lt. (Tp.), k. in a., 14/7/16.
Tuke, Cyril Stratford, T/Capt., k. in a., 27/9/15 (9th R. Hdrs.).
20 Tuke, Percy George, T/2/Lt., d. of w., 21/3/18.
Tulloch, William, 2/Lt. (Tp.), k. in a., 20/7/16 (53 Inf. Bde.).
143 Turner, Percival Eric, 2/Lt., d. of w., 5/10/17.
30 Turner, Reginald Allison, 2/Lt., k. in a., 21/3/18.
9 Turnley, John Francis, T/2/Lt., k. in a., 16/4/18.
Tyacke, Edward Humphry, T/Lt., k. in a., 29/5/18.
Tyler, William Eric, T/2/Lt., died, 28/10/18.
6 Van Someren, Claud Donald, 2/Lt., k. in a., 21/3/18.
115 Verner, Lancelot Guy, 2/Lt. (Tp.), d. of w., 27/8/16.
Vernon, Herbert Douglas, Lt., k. in a., 15/9/16 (Gren. Gds.) (att. M.G.C.).
6 Vint, William Percival, A/Capt., k. in a., 5/8/18.
Vowler, Darrell Francis Stephen, T/Major, died, 28/2/19 (Notts and Derby Regt.).
Wade, Herbert, M.C., Lt., k. in a., 2/11/18.
180 Wade, Herbert John Clark, T/Lt., d. of w., 14/11/17.
29 Wagstaff, Robert Arthur, 2/Lt., k. in a., 1/10/18.
Wakeley, William Norman, 2/Lt., k. in a., 8/5/17 (15th K. Liv. R., att.).
25 Waldie, John Gray, T/Lt., k. in a., 31/7/17 (late 11th R. Hdrs.).
Walker, Herbert Newton, 2/Lt. (T/Lt.), k. in a., 6/6/17 (11th S. Staff. R., att.).
3 Walker, Ingham, 2/Lt., k. in a., 27/9/18.
54 Wallace, William, T/2/Lt., k. in a., 29/9/16.
217 Walton, William Lees Percival, 2/Lt., k. in a., 30/11/17.
1 Wardell, William Moss, 2/Lt., k. in a., 23/3/18.
Warner, William Henry, 2/Lt., k. in a., 21/8/18 (Divl.).
88 Warre, Cecil Alberic Hardy, 2/Lt., Temp., k. in a., 24/4/17.
168 Warter, William Henry, Lt., k. in a., 9/15/17.
Warwick, Thomas Harry, M.C., 2/Lt., k. in a., 28/4/17 (3rd N. Staff. R. att., 9th Bn. att.).
152 Watney, Valentine Howell, T/Lt., d. of w., 3/2/17.
21 Watson, Charles Beaumont, M.C., Lt., d. of w., 12/7/18.
55 Watson, Frank McEwan, 2/Lt., k. in a., 3/5/17.
249 Watson, John Mowbray Walter, T/Lt., k. in a., 23/8/17.
175 Watson, James Roby, T/2/Lt., d. of w., 2/12/17.
Watson, Samuel Meredith, 2/Lt., k. in a., 1/7/16.
13 Watt, Percy Bryden, Lt., k. in a., 14/4/18 (11th Gord. Hdrs.).
88 Watts, George Leonard, T/2/Lt., k. in a., 17/10/16.
49 Watts, William John, 2/Lt., k. in a., 12/4/18.
2 Webb, Dennis Henry, T/Lt., k. in a., 10/11/17.
25 Webb, Richard Joseph, 2/Lt., d. of w., 1/6/18 (in German hands).
235 Webber, Frederick John, T/2/Lt., k. in a., 30/11/17.
21 Webster, Douglas Gordon, M.C., Lt., k. in a., 29/9/18.
203 Webster, George Thomas, T/2/Lt., d. of w., 7/12/17.
109 Wedgwood, Gilbert Colclough, Lt., Tp., k. in a., 1/7/16.
25 Weldrick, Wilfred, 2/Lt., k. in a., 12/4/18.
17 Wellings, Henry William, T/2/Lt., d. of w., 20/6/18 (Shrop. L.I.).
47 Wenborn, Harold, 2/Lt., d. of w., 24/3/18.
West, George Arnold, 2/Lt., d. of w., 8/8/18 (1st E. Lancs R., att.).
7 West, Sydney Albert, T/2/Lt., k. in a., 30/8/17.
Weston, Kingsley Vale, 2/Lt., d. of w., 10/4/18 (4th W. Yks. R., att.).
Whately, Percival Vivian Victor, T/Lt., k. in a., 27/12/17.
154 Wheatley, Lionel Frank, 2/Lt., k. in a., 22/11/17.
40 Whitaker, Sydney George, 2/Lt., k. in a., 22/3/18.
200 White, Clifford, T/2/Lt., k. in a., 26/9/17.
White, Edward Beadon, T/2/Lt., k. in a., 1/7/16 (11th Yks. R., att.).
White, Harold Norton, 2/Lt., k. in a., 6/9/18 (Divl.).
Whybrow, Harry Thomson, T/Capt., d. of w., 21/3/16.
32 Wilder, Arthur James, 2/Lt., d. of w., 23/3/18.
6 Wilkes, James Alwyn, 2/Lt., d. of w., 24/3/18 (Cav.).
Willett, Joseph Cyril, 2/Lt., T/Lt., k. in a., 15/5/17 (19th Lancs. Fus., att.).
49 Williams, Alfred Richard, T/2/Lt., k. in a.. 16/8/17.
13 Williams, Daniel John, 2/Lt., k. in a., 5/10/17.
25 Williams, Frank Leonard, Lt., A/Capt., d. of w., 30/5/18 (8th Border R., att.).
74 Williams, Kenneth George, Lt., Tp., d. of w., 21/10/16.
Williams, Richard, 2/Lt., d. of w., 2/4/18 (17th R. Wel. Fus., att.).
3 Williams, Robert John, 2/Lt., k. in a., 31/8/18 (Divl.).
25 Williamson, Harold, 2/Lt., k. in a., 27/5/18.
246 Williamson, John, 2/Lt., k. in a., 24/9/17.
25 Willson, Edgar Brian, Lt., k. in a., 27/5/18.
95 Wilshire, Laurence Stanley, 2/Lt., k. in a., 14/4/18.
51 Wilson, Alan Sydney, Lt., k. in a., 23/4/17 (2nd S. Lanc. R. att.).
88 Wilson, Charles Robert, T/2/Lt., k. in a., 24/5/17.
16 Wilson, Henry Foss, 2/Lt., k. in a., 21/3/18.
149 Wilson, Joseph Alec, T/2/Lt., k. in a., 14/11/16.
3 Wilson, William James, 2/Lt., k. in a., 28/3/18.
Winkley, Charles, M.C., T/Capt., k. in a., 30/11/17.
Withers, Victor William, T/2/Lt., d. of w., 6/7/16.
Wolff, Gustav Frederick, A/Capt., k. in a., 21/3/18 (3rd R. Welsh Fus., att.).
11 Womersley, David Norman, T/Lt., died, 1/2/17.
59 Womersley, Sinclair Patterson, 2/Lt., k. in a., 15/4/18.
21 Wood, Henry Percy, 2/Lt., k. in a., 22/3/18.
9 Wood, Richard Thomas, 2/Lt., k. in a., 25/4/18.
Woodall, John, 2/Lt., T/Lt., k. in a., 8/11/17.
124 Woodley, Charles Benjamin, T/2/Lt., k. in a., 8/10/16.
69 Woolnough, Charles Walter Fyffe, T/2/Lt., k. in a., 22/3/16 (10th Bed. R., att.)
21 Wordsworth, Osmund Bartle, 2/Lt., T/Lt., k. in a., 2/4/17.
Worth, Stanley Seymour, 2/Lt., T/Lt., k. in a., 1/12/17 (4th R. Inn. Fus., att.).
33 Wright, Arthur, T/2/Lt., k. in a., 15/9/16.
Wright, Charles James, T/2/Lt., k. in a., 18/10/16 (11th S. Staff. R., att.).
Wyatt, Esdaile Frederick Burkett, T/Capt., k. in a.. 8/1/16 (2nd S. Lanc. R., att.).
40 Wyatt, Henry Edward, T/2/Lt., k. in a., 19/1/17.
246 Yardley, Frank, T/2/Lt., k. in a., 7/8/17.
4 Yates, Alec James, D.C.M., 2/Lt., k. in a.. 28/3/18 (Divl. Bn.).
36 Yeo, Everard Lisle, T/2/Lt., d. of w., 7/10/16.
Young, Phillip, Lt., d. of w., 21/8/18 (6th Bn. Middx. R., att.).
Youngs, James William, Lt., d. of w.. 12/4/18 (3rd S. Staff. R., att.).

Territorial Officers.

Attached Machine Gun Corps.

Adam, Allan, Lt., k. in a., 1/10/18 (7/A. & S.H.).
Adam, Walter, Capt., died, 3/11/18 (E. Kent. Yeo.).
Adams, Percy Lionel, Lt., d. of w., 3/10/18 (18/Lond. R.).
Adams, Thompson, 2/Lt., k. in a., 7/10/16 (4 K.O.Y.L.I.).
Alderson, Alex George Jermyn, 2/Lt., k. in a., 19/10/16 (5 D. of C.L.I.).
Anderson, Henry McDonald, Lt., k. in a., 30/5/18 (5 N. Fus.).
Balding, Reginald Norman, Lt. (Tp.), k. in a., 30/3/17 5/Bedf. R.).
Ball, Charles Herbert, Lt., d. of w., 3/4/18 (Wilt. Yeo.).
Barnett, Edwin Bertram, Capt., k. in a., 30/10/17 (8 Lond. R.).
Barnett, Ralph Edward, Lt., k. in a., 6/9/17 (8 Lanc. Fus.).
Barns, Charles Stanley, Capt., died, 22/7/18 (17/Lond. R.).
Baxter, Alexander Carnegie, M.C., Lt., k. in a., 17/4/17 (6 Sco. Rifs.).
Bell, Guy Bayford, Lt., k. in a., 28/4/17 (5 Lanc. Fus.).
Bellamy, Geoffrey George, Capt., d. of w., 1/9/18 (7 Devon. R.).
Bennett, John Edwin, 2/Lt., k. in a., 24/7/16 (8 R. War. R.).
Bennie, Hugh Osborne, Lt., k. in a., 31/7/17 (5 H.L.I.).
Biggs, John Geoffrey, M.C., Lt., d. of w., 1/9/17 (N. Som. Yeo.).
Birch, Eric Wykeman, M.C., Lt., d. of w., 17/1/17 (4 W. Rid. R.).
Blackburn, Frank, 2/Lt., k. in a., 24/10/17 (5 E. Lanc. R.).
Blackmore, Edwin, 2/Lt., k. in a., 16/8/16 (5/D.C.L.I.).
Blackwell, Gerald Davis, Lt., k. in a., 7/6/17 (6/N. Fus.).
Blumfield, Hubert Winterbotham, Lt., k. in a., 23/2/17 (9 Mdx. R.).
Bond, Edmund, Lt., k. in a., 1/10/18 (5 West. Rid. R.).
Borthwick, Donald Walker, 2/Lt., k. in a., 28/12/16 (4 R.W. Surr. R.)
Bow, George Clark, 2/Lt., k. in a., 25/3/17 (7/A. & S.H.).
Bowles, Wilfred Spencer, 2/Lt., k. in a., 10/7/16 (5 Essex R.).
Boyce, Charles Wallace, 2/Lt., k. in a., 24/10/18 (4 Glouc. R.).
Boyne, Harry Horace, 2/Lt., d. of w., 21/7/16 (4/Suff. R.).
Brickell, Fredk. William, Lt., k. in a., 20/6/18 (5/Durh. L.I.).
Brown, Douglas Knox, M.C., Lt., k. in a., 30/11/17 (9 H.L.I.).
Brown, Sylvester Samuel, M.C., Lt., k. in a., 25/4/18 (9/Lond. R.).
Butler, Gordon Kerr Montague, Lt., died, 17/7/16 (Sco. Horse).
Cameron, Duncan, Lt., died, 5/12/18 (9/A. & S.H.).
Cave, Edward Charles, M.C., Lt., d. of w., 29/8/18 (17 Lond. R.).

Chalmers, James, M.C., Capt., k. in a., 23/3/18 (5 R. Scots).
Chapman, George Edwin, 2/Lt., d. of w., 27/9/16 (5/York. R.).
Colley, Robert Archibald, Lt., k. in a., 22/3/18 (8 Durh. L.I.).
Cotton, Ralph Charles Fairbairn, Lt., d. of w., 28/3/18 Hampshire Yeo.).
Cox, Harold, 2/Lt., d. of w., 16/4/18 (12/Lond. R.).
Craig, Arthur Francis, Capt., d. of w., 4/10/18 (4/R.W. Kent R.).
Cumming, Authony Dyson, Lt., k. in a., 6/3/17 (4/L.N. Lanc. R.).
Davey, Sydney Guy, Lt. (A/Major), k. in a., 25/3/18 (4/Norf. R.).
Davis, Edward Thomas, Lt., k. in a., 27/12/17 (24 Lond. R.).
De Candole, Alec Corry Vully, Lt., k. in a., 3/9/18 (4 Wilt. R.).
Dixon, Norman Ferguson, A/Capt., d. of w., 5/10/17 (6 R. Highrs.).
Dobson, Reginald Graham, Major, died, 4/1/18 (6 W. York. R.).
Duff-Gordon, Cosmo Leslie, Lt., k. in a., 3/9/16 (Hereford. R.).
Dunn, Ernest George, 2/Lt., k. in a., 10/6/17 (10/K. L'pool R.).
Eadie, James Albert, Lt., k. in a., 27/5/18 (9 A. & S.H.).
Elliott, Fredk., 2/Lt., d. of w., 2/8/16 (6 Sea. Highrs.).
Engall, John Sherwin, 2/Lt., k. in a., 1/7/16 (16 Lond. R.).
Faraday, Roy, Lt., k. in a., 7/6/17 (6 Lond. R.).
Fife, Alexander John, Lt.-Col., died, 7/2/17 (4 York. R.).
Fisher, Herbert Leavoyd Hammond, Lt., k. in a., 8/8/16 (8 K. L'pool R.).
Fortune, Henry George, 2/Lt., k. in a., 17/1/17 (6 Welsh Regt.).
Fradd, Kingsley Meredith Chatterton, 2/Lt., k. in a., 1/7/16 (2 Lond. R.).
Fraser, James Herbert, Lt., d. of w., 9/7/16 (2/Mon. Regt.).
Frost, Alan, Capt., k. in a., 17/10/17 (28 Lond. R.).
Gardner, Andrew Abercromby, Lt., k. in a., 6/9/18 (6 A. & S.H.).
Gatfield, Reginald Alfred, Lt., d. of w., 7/6/17 (16 Lond. R.).
Gill, Leonard Edward, 2/Lt., k. in a., 17/9/17 (7 N. & D.R.).
Goepel, Robert Mackie, Lt., k. in a., 17/9/16 (5/Sea. Highrs.).
Goldsmith, Herbert Francis, Lt., k. in a., 27/9/18 (6/Lanc. Fus.).
Gorringe, Noel Rupert, Lt., k. in a., 10/4/18 (4/Northampton R.).
Grant, John, 2/Lt., died, 24/11/18 (5 Durh. L.I.).
Green, Benjamin Cecil, Lt., k. in a., 24/4/17 (5 E. Lanc. R.).
Green, Daniel Cottle, 2/Lt., k. in a., 25/2/17 (22 Lond. R.).
Gregory, Kenneth Stuart, Lt., k. in a., 10/11/17 (7 R. Welsh Fus.).
Hanbury, Evan Robert, Major, k. in a., 24/3/18 (Leic. Yeo.).
Hansen, Carl Fredk. Vilhelm, Lt., d. of w., 31/7/17 (9 K. L'pool R.).
Hart, F. H., Lt., died, 4/7/18 (10 Manch. R.).
Hartington, John Ernest, Lt., d. of w., 13/7/17 (5/Lanc. Fus.).
Harvey, Harry Thomas, Lt., k. in a., 31/7/17 (5 Suff. R.).
Haynes, Samuel, 2/Lt., d. of w., 4/10/18 (4 Som. L.I.).
Herbert, Hon. Elidye John Bernard, Capt., k. in a., 12/11/17 (Glouc. Yeo.).
Hipwell, H. Reginald, 2/Lt., k. in a., 23/4/17 (4 Sea. Highrs.).
Hofmeyr, Robert Ernest Murray, 2/Lt., k. in a., 24/4/17 (5 York. R.).
Hopper, William Joseph, Lt., k. in a., 6/9/18 (att. 15/Durh. L.I.).
Horlick, Gerald Nolekin, Major, died, 5/7/18 (Glouc. Yeo.).
Houghton, John Reginald, Capt., d. of w., 22/3/18 (6/Manch.).
Hudson, Horace Sayer, 2/Lt., died, 17/11/18 (9 Manch. R.).
Hughes-Davies, Arthur Gwynne, M.C., Lt., k. in a., 20/9/18 (7 R. Welsh Fus.)
Hunter, George Arnold, Lt., died, 3/8/17 (Sco. Horse).
Hutchison, Andrew Levy, Lt., k. in a., 21/3/18 (7 R. Scots. R.).
Job, Ernest Dalzel, Capt., k. in a., 11/7/16 (28 Lond. R.).
Jones, Herbert Wynn, Lt., d. of w., 24/3/18 (Welsh Horse Yeo.).
Jones, Robert Nelson, Lt., k. in a., 31/7/17 (4 Northamptons).
Kay, Geoffrey Clarkson, A/Major, k. in a., 29/3/18 (5 Lanc. Fus.).
Kay, William, Lt., d. of w., 21/3/18 (8 Lanc. Fus.).
Kennedy, James Patrick, 2/Lt., k. in a., 19/6/18 (18 Lond. R.).
Kirby, Arthur Maurice, Lt., k. in a., 25/9/17 (5 Durh. L.I.).
Laing, James Gordon, Major, k. in a., 3/10/18 (28 Lond. R.).
Lockhart, R. F., 2/Lt., d. of w., 10/7/17 (13 Lond. R.).
Lowry, Vyvyan Charles, Lt., k. in a., 9/4/18 (5 E. Surr. R.).
Lyon, Robert, 2/Lt., k. in a., 17/3/17 (5/A. & S.H.).
McAlister, George Howdon, 2/Lt., k. in a., 24/8/16 (5 R. Sco. Fus.).
McAndrew, Charles Roy, 2/Lt., k. in a., 21/9/18 (War. Yeo.).
Macartney, Thomas Hendry, 2/Lt., k. in a., 7/6/17 (19 Lond. R.).
McCormick, Harry, 2/Lt., d. of w., 8/5/17 (5/E. Lanc. R.) (in German hands)
McDougall, George, M.C., Capt., k. in a., 30/3/18 (8 Manch. R.).
V.C. McGregor, David Stuart, Lt., k. in a., 22/10/18 (6/R. Scots).
Mackie, Norman Lindsay, Lt. (A/Capt.), d of w., 28/9/15 (14 Lond. R.).
MacKinnon, Alastair, Lt., died, 14/10/16 (8 A. & S.H.).
MacRae, Donald Alastair, Lt., died, 16/11/18 (5 Sea. Highrs.).
Madder, Robert, 2/Lt., k. in a., 20/7/16 (5/Glouc. R.).
Mainwaring, Frank Harry George Carver, Capt., died, 6/1/19 (3/Co of Lond. Yeo.).
Marsh, Francis Bedford, 2/Lt., d. of w., 5/10/16 (4 R.W. Surr. R.).
Matthews, R. J., Lt., died, 2/11/18 (4 Norf. R.).
Milne, S. S. B., Lt., died, 29/10/18 (5 R. Highrs.).
Mitchell, Terence Hargreaves, 2/Lt., d. of w., 6/11/16 (5/D. of Corn. L.I.).
Mollison, William Allan, Lt., d. of w., 1/10/18 (6/W. Rid. R.).
Moore, William Henry, Lt., k. in a., 8/8/16 (5 K. L'pool R.).
Mortimer, James C.M.G., Lt.-Col., k. in a., 15/9/16 (5/York. R.).
Mowat, Robert James Dugald, 2/Lt., k. in a., 24/9/18 (Hampshire Yeo.).
Neil, John, M.C., Lt., d. of w., 28/3/18 (7 A. & S.H.).
Nelson, Thomas Arthur, Capt., k. in a., 9/4/17 (Lothian & Bord. Horse Yeo.).
Nicholls, Clifford, Capt., k. in a., 31/7/17 (5/R. Welsh Fus.).
Nicol, Robert, Lt., k. in a., 17/4/18 (5 A. & S.H.).
Palliser, John Sylvester, Major, k. in a., 9/8/18 (5 York. R.).
Palmer, Leslie Stewart, Lt., k. in a., 20/9/17 (4/Dorset R.).
Peach, Ernest James, 2/Lt., k. in a., 1/7/16 (7/N. & D.R.).
Pearson, Wilfred Hearne, 2/Lt., k. in a., 29/9/18 (Northern Cyc. Batt.).
Percy-Hardman, William Henry, Capt., d. of w., 1/3/17 (4 Devon R.).
Pirie, William Shewan, D.C.M., Capt., k. in a., 19/4/17 (5/R. Scot. Fus.).
Poynting, Arthur, Lt., k. in a., 26/7/16 (6/R. War. R.).
Prankherd, Richard Percy, Lt., k. in a., 10/11/18 (War. Yeo.).
Purvis, George Bell, Capt., k. in a., 8/6/17 (5/York. R.).
Raikes, Fredk Munro, 2/Lt., k. in a., 22/2/17 (Brecknock Bn.).
Radcliffe, Percival Victor Alban, Lt., d. of w., 25/11/17 (5/York. R.).
Richards, Dudley Brookhouse, 2/Lt., d. of w., 20/9/16 (6/Glouc. R.).
Ritchie, John, 2/Lt., k. in a., 25/4/17 (6/R Highrs.).
Robbins, George Latimer, 2/Lt., d. of w., 10/6/18 (6/W. Rid. R.).
Robertson, Alexander, Lt., d. of w, 28/1/18 (6/Sea. Highrs.).
Robertson, Robert Ward Shepherd, Lt., k. in a., 27/5/17 (4/R.W. Surr. R.).
Ross, James Hamilton, 2/Lt, d. of w., 19/4/17 (5/R. Scots Fus.).
Scawin, William Neville, Lt., k. in a., 15/4/18 (5/Y. & L.R.).
Service, Alexander Cumming, Lt., k. in a., 29/5/18 (6/A. & S.H.)
Shanks, John Arthur Gordon, M.C, Capt., k. in a., 4/10/17 6/A. & S.H.).
Shepherd-Cross, Cecil, Major, d. of w., 15/10/17 (Duke of Lanc. Yeo.).
Simpson, Harry Graham, A/Major, k. in a., 27/5/18 (4/Gord-Highrs.).
Smart, Norman, Capt., k. in a., 16/10/17 (8/Lanc. Fus.).
Smith, Thomas Lawrie, Lt., k. in a., 18/9/18 (Ayr. Yeo.).
Sprott, Douglas Anderson, Capt., died, 4/1/18 (4/Bord. R.).
Standring, Fredk. John, Lt., k. in a., 6/9/18 (8 Royal Scots).
Stephens, Nassan Barrington, 2/Lt., d. of w., 1/6/16 (4/E. York. R.).
Stiles, Vincent Harcourt, Lt., k. in a., 20/9/17 (24/Lond. R.).
Stocker, Arthur Rutterford, M.C., A/Capt., died, 24/1/19 (6/Sea. Highrs.).
Stokes, Charles Leonard, Lt., k. in a., 26/9/17 (6/Hampshire R.).
Stott, Frank Gordon, Lt., d. of w., 11/7/16 (5/Ches. R.).
Strettell-Miller, Charles Wallace, Lt., k. in a., 6/10/18 (7/R. Scots).
Stross, David, 2/Lt., died, 12/3/17 (R.F.A.) (and R.F.C.).
Targett, George Henry, Lt., k. in a., 18/9/18 (10/Mdx. R.).
Taylor, Harold Richard, 2/Lt., d. of w., 17/3/17 (Surr. Yeo.).
Teasdale, Eric Henry Janson, Lt., drowned, 21/1/17 (A.S.C.) (T.F.).
Tebbutt, Arthur Brookes, Lt., k. in a., 19/4/17 (5/Norf. R.).
Thom, James Flockhart, M.C., Capt., d. of w., 27/9/18 (Ffe. & Forfar. Yeo.).
Thomas, Albert Edward, 2/Lt., k. in a., 17/2/17 (3/Mon R.).
Thomas, Lionel George Theophilus, 2/Lt., k. in a., 29/9/17 (5 Welsh R.).
Thompson, Cecil William, 2/Lt., d. of w., 6/5/17 (6/Lanc. Fus.).
Thomson, Fredk. Stanley, Capt., k. in a., 1/7/16 (14/Lond. R.).
Thomson, Stewart Armour, Lt., d. of w., 24/9/18 (S. Notts Huss.).
Thornton, Herbert Boucher, 2/Lt., k. in a., 9/7/17 (9/Lond. R.).
Thorpe, Norman John, 2/Lt., k. in a., 12/5/17 (8/Hampshire R.).
Townsend, Guy Storey, Lt., k. in a., 23/8/18 (5/York. R.).
Villiers, Algernon Hyde, Lt., k. in a., 23/11/17 (Lothian & Bord. Horse)
Wakefield, Frank Mahan, Lt., died, 2/1/18 (Dorset Yeo.).
Walker, Denham, 2/Lt., d. of w., 19/9/16 (5/E. Lanc. R.).
Warburton, Henry Heap, 2/Lt., d. of w., 9/9/16 (7/Lanc. Fus.).
Weaver, Augustus Henry, 2/Lt., d. of w., 12/4/18 (6/W. Rid. R.).
Weller, Edward Arthur Walstone, 2/Lt., d. of w., 22/10/18 7/R. War. R.).
Westoby, Frank Durrant, 2/Lt., k. in a., 7/9/16 (7/Mdx. R.).
White, Ernest, Lt., k. in a., 10/4/18 (W. Som. Yeo.).
Whiteley, Laurence, Lt., k. in a., 31/7/17 (5 R. Highrs.).
Williams, John Rowland, Lt., k. in a., 27/9/17 (2/Mon. R.).
Williams-Vaughan, John Christopher Arthur, 2/Lt., k. in a., 18/7/16 (Brecknock Batt., S.W.B.).
Wilson, Allan Stanley, 2/Lt., d. of w., 12/7/17 (5 Bord R.).

Witt, Charles, 2/Lt., k. in a., 22/9/18 (5 N. & D.R.).
Wood, Frank, 2/Lt., d. of w., 23/10/17 (8/N. & D.R.).
Wood, Llewellyn George, Capt., died, 22/11/18 (City of Lond. Yeo.).
Wright, Claude Russell, Lt., k. in a., 21/5/17 (5/Suff. R.).
Yeomans, Howard William, Capt., k. in a., 8/10/17 (Hereford R.).

Tank Corps.

Adney, George Henry, M.C., Lt. (Tp.), k. in a., 2/9/18.
2 Albertson, Armand Howard, 2/Lt. (Tp.), k. in a., 9/8/18.
Asser, Leslie, Ernest, 2/Lt. (Tp.), k. in a., 10/8/18.
10 Askew, Geoffrey, M.C., 2/Lt., d. of w., 25/3/18.
Atack, Percy, 2/Lt. (Tp.), k. in a., 4/7/18 (6th Res. Cav. Regt.).
Atkinson, Miles Linzee, 2/Lt. (Tp.), k. in a., 20/11/17.
Atkinson, William Ernest, 2/Lt. (Tp.), k. in a., 12/4/18.
Baker, Neville Ernest, T/Lt., d. of w., 31/7/17 (R.E.).
Bale, Thomas William, 2/Lt., d. of w., 10/8/18.
Ball, Joseph, 2/Lt. (Tp.), k. in a., 8/8/18.
Bates, Leonard John, M.C., T/Lt. (A/Capt.), died, 9/11/17.
Bayliss, Percival Baron, T/Lt. (A/Capt.), k. in a., 3/10/18.
7 Beaven, Charles Simeon, 2/Lt., k. in a., 14/4/18.
Begard, Michael, 2/Lt. (Tp.), k. in a., 22/3/18.
Bell, Hugh Reginald, T/Capt. (A/Major), k. in a., 3/9/18.
13 Berry, John Leslie, Lt. (Tp.), k. in a., 4/7/18.
"B." Birnie, William John Gordon, Lt., k. in a., 23/11/17 (8th Gordon Hldrs.).
13 Black, George Balfour, M.C., Lt., T/Capt., d. of w., 23/8/18 (17th Lancers).
6 Black, John, Lt. (Tp.), d. of w., 23/8/18.
Blackwell, Samuel Frederick Baker, D.S.O., Capt. (Tp.), k. in a., 20/11/17.
Blad, Kenneth Sven, 2/Lt. (Tp.), died, 26/11/18 (R.E.).
14 Bone, Charles John, 2/Lt. (Tp.), k. in a., 9/8/18.
5 Bradbury, Austen, M.C., T/Lt. (A/Capt.), k. in a., 8/8/18.
Bradney, Walter, 2/Lt., k. in a., 24/3/18.
7 Brassington, William, M.M., Lt. (Tp.), k. in a., 23/8/18.
Brown, John Carolan, M.C., Lt. (A/Capt.), k. in a., 8/8/18 (Conn. Rang.).
Brown, William Archibald Ross, 2/Lt. (Tp.), k. in a., 22/11/17.
2 Campbell, Frederick Arthur, 2/Lt., k. in a., 22/3/18.
Cartwright, Ernest Mills, 2/Lt. (Tp.), k. in a., 14/4/18.
1 Cassels, Hugh Lindesay, 2/Lt. (Tp.), k. in a., 8/8/18.
13 Challis, Thomas Archie, M.C., 2/Lt., died, 3/11/18.
2 Chambers, Philip, Carlisle, 2/Lt., k. in a., 22/3/18.
Charlton, Brian, Lt., k. in a., 27/10/18 (and R.A.F.).
Christain, Albert, 2/Lt. (Tp.), k. in a., 27/9/18.
Christopher, Richard, Lt. (Tp.), k. in a., 29/9/18.
7 Clegg, Lionel, Lt. (Tp.), k. in a., 22/8/18.
2 Coe, Herbert James, 2/Lt. (Tp.), k. in a., 8/8/18.
"B." Colley, Ernest Vincent, 2/Lt., d. of w., 23/8/17.
15 Cordner, James Henry, Lt. (Tp.), d. of w., 8/8/18.
5 Curtis, William Charles, 2/Lt. (Tp.), k. in a., 3/10/18.
Dale, Harry, 2/Lt. (Tp.), k. in a., 24/4/18.
Darrel, Richard Frederick William, 2/Lt. (Tp.), died, 26/2/19.
Dawes, William Henry George, 2/Lt. (Tp.), k. in a., 29/9/18.
De Faye, Edward Francis, 2/Lt. (Tp.), k. in a., 1/12/17.
2 De Pass, Crispin Asabel, 2/Lt., k. in a., 22/3/18.
"E." Despard, Ernest Richard, 2/Lt. (Tp.), d. of w., 26/9/17.
5 Duffell, James Henry, 2/Lt., k in a., 22/3/18.
Duncan, Christopher William, M.C., 2/Lt. (T/Lt.), k. in a., 20/11/17 (4th N. Staff. Regt.).
Eckley, Frederick George, 2/Lt., k. in a., 27/11/17.
1 Ehrhardt, John Albert, 2/Lt. (Tp.), k. in a., 26/3/18.
4 Ellis, James Clive, 2/Lt. (Tp.), died, 21/4/18 (in German hands).
"F." Emery, George William, 2/Lt. (Tp.), k. in a., 20/11/17.
Evans, John Owen, 2/Lt., k. in a., 23/11/17.
1 Evans, Leonard Austin, 2/Lt. (Tp.), died, 27/3/18.
15 Ferguson, Thomas Jenkins, 2/Lt. (Tp.), k. in a., 30/8/18.
Flanegan, Lionel Christopher, Lt. (Tp.), k. in a., 20/11/17.
13 Flux, L. G., 2/Lt. (Tp.), died, 18/6/18.
5 Fossett, Reginald Graham, 2/Lt. (Tp.), k. in a., 3/10/18.
13 Frankenstein, Cyril Joseph, 2/Lt. (Tp.), k. in a., 23/8/18.
"H." Fraser, Eldred Leslie, 2/Lt. (Tp.), k. in a., 20/11/17.
8 Galloway, Robert Herbert, 2/Lt., k. in a., 24/3/18.
11 Galsworthy, Edgar, 2/Lt. (Tp.), k. in a., 27/9/18.
13 Gatward, Frederick James, 2/Lt. (Tp.), d. of w., 25/4/18.
8 Gibson, James William, 2/Lt. (Tp.), k. in a., 9/8/18.
2 Glaister, George Frederick, Lt. (Tp.), k. in a., 1/8/18.
Glasscock, Sydney Frederick, Lt. (Tp.), k. in a., 20/11/17.
5 Godfrey, Norman Carter, 2/Lt. (Tp.), k. in a., 16/4/18.
10 Gosling, Leonard Buchanan, 2/Lt. (Tp.), died, 27/10/18.
"E." Gower, Francis John Harman, 2/Lt., k. in a., 23/11/17.
8 Gray, John, 2/Lt. (Tp.), k. in a., 24/3/18.
Green, Joseph George Airey, 2/Lt., k. in a., 23/11/17.
2 Green, Thomas William, 2/Lt. (Tp.), d. of w., 14/8/18.
16 Gregson, William, 2/Lt. (Tp.), d. of w., 18/10/18.
Grove, Charles Frederick Smith, M.C., T/Lt. (A/Capt.), k. in a., 8/8/18.
15 Gummer, Fred, 2/Lt. (Tp.), k. in a., 9/8/18.
Haining, William Stobo, 2/Lt. (Tp.), k. in a., 20/11/17.
Hall, James Herbert William, T/Lt. (A/Capt.), died, 19/10/18.
9 Hannan, James Maxwell Adair, 2/Lt. (Tp.), k. in a., 23/7/18.
Harding, Samuel Collis, 2/Lt. (Tp.), k. in a., 22/8/17.
B Haseler, William Hereward, T/Lt. (A/Capt.), k. in a., 20/11/17.
1 Hawkins, Kenneth James, 2/Lt. (Tp.), k. in a., 8/8/18.
2 Hedges, William Robert, 2/Lt., k. in a., 18/9/18.
B Henderson, Thomas, 2/Lt., k. in a., 23/11/17.
1 Hill, Brian Edward, T/Capt., d. of w., 2/10/18 (R.A.S.C.).
4 Hindle, Stephen, 2/Lt. (Tp.), k. in a., 26/3/18.
Holt, Follett Hallett, Lt., k. in a., 22/8/18 (Ox. & Bucks Lt. Inf.).
E Howells, John Edwin, 2/Lt. (Tp.), k. in a., 20/11/17.
6 Howard, Edgar Stacey, 2/Lt. (Tp.), k. in a., 9/8/18.
13 Hulton, Benjamin William, 2/Lt. (Tp.), d. of w., 5/7/18.
1 Hume, Arthur James, 2/Lt. (Tp.), d. of w., 21/5/18 (in German hands).
10 Humphreys, Noel Forbes, M.C., Capt. (Tp.), d. of w., 27/3/18.
8 Jefferies, Richard Oliver Geary, T/Lt. (A/Capt.), k. in a., 29/9/18.
8 Jefferies, Stanley Saunders, 2/Lt., k. in a., 10/8/18.
D Jones, Richard Alum, 2/Lt. (Tp.), k. in a., 20/11/17.
Keogh, Frederick Bertram, M.C., Capt., k. in a., 8/8/18 (4th Conn. Rang.).
3 Keppel-Palmer, Stuart Leslie, M.C., T/Lt. (A/Capt.), k. in a., 3/10/18 (Lt. Bn.).
11 Kingwell, Hugh Robert, Lt. (Tp.), d. of w., 24/8/18.
Kinmont, John Collie, Capt., died, 18/11/17 (3rd Cam. Hldrs.).
10 Klee, Arthur Milton, 2/Lt. (Tp.), k. in a., 8/8/18.
Knight, Geoffrey St. John, Lt.. d. of w., 10/9/18 (4th Roy. Inn. Fus.).
13 Larkins, L. H., Capt. (Tp.), k. in a., 4/7/18.
Lawrie, Andrew Ralph, Lt. (Tp.), k. in a., 22/8/17.
B Lazonby, Julian Cecil, 2/Lt., k. in a., 23/11/17.
4 Leach, Sidney, 2/Lt., k. in a., 10/8/18.
Leek, Major Frederick William, 2/Lt. (Tp.), k. in a., 20/11/17.
6 Lees, James Lowry, M.C., T/Lt. (A/Capt.), k. in a., 23/8/18.
11 Lethebe, Herbert Thomas, Lt. (Tp.), k. in a., 2/9/18.
10 Linden, Norman Eric, 2/Lt. (Tp.), d. of w., 4/9/18.
Longthorpe, Frederick, 2/Lt. (Tp.), d. of w., 20/9/18.
4 Lord, Ernest Joseph, 2/Lt. (Tp.), k. in a., 21/3/18.
McCormack, George, 2/Lt. (Tp.), died, 28/10/18.
McElroy, Frederick William, D.S.O., Lt., died, 16/11/18.
1 Macfadyn, John Dennis Goulty, M.C., Lt. (Tp.), k. in a., 8/8/18.
7 McLean, Gordon Davis, Lt. (Tp.), k. in a., 21/8/18.
15 Mansfield, Harry John, 2/Lt. (Tp.), k. in a., 27/9/18.
1 March-Phillips, Spencer Leslie, 2/Lt. (Tp.), k. in a., 20/11/17.
Marshall, Hubert Graham Hamilton, 2/Lt. (Tp.), k. in a., 2/9/18.
12 Martin, Ross, 2/Lt. (Tp.), d. of w., 25/10/18.
May, Francis Henry, 2/Lt. (Tp.), k. in a., 29/9/18.
Meugens, Geoffrey Ellsworth, Major, died, 30/10/18.
13 Millar, James, 2/Lt. (Tp.), k. in a., 24/9/18.
6 Millar, William, 2/Lt. (Tp.), k. in a., 23/8/18.
Miskin, Maurice, M.C., T/Lt. (A/Capt.), k. in a., 17/10/18.
10 Mollard, Alfred Edward, D.C.M., 2/Lt. (Tp.), died, 7/11/18.
1 Monaghan, Denis Laurence, Capt. (Tp.), k. in a., 24/11/17.
9 Morgan, Charles Joseph, 2/Lt. (Tp.), d. of w., 28/4/18.
5 Mumby, Harold Cheffings, 2/Lt. (Tp.), k. in a., 3/10/18.
Murray-Menzies, Duncan Innes, M.C., Lt. (A/Capt.), k. in a., 22/8/17 (Roy. Hldrs.).
3 Newsam, Harry Brightstone, 2/Lt. (Tp.), k. in a., 8/8/18 (Lt. Bn.).
Nichols, C., 2/Lt. (Tp.), died, 9/11/17.
Nightingale, John, Capt. (Tp.), died, 6/11/18.
Norwood, Reginald Harold, 2/Lt., k. in a., 29/9/18.
11 Ogden, Walter Frederick, 2/Lt. (Tp.), d. of w., 2/12/17.
14 O'Shea, Dermot Timothy, 2/Lt. (Tp.), k. in a., 10/8/18.
Palmer, David Adams, M.C., A/Capt., d. of w., 25/3/18 (3rd Roy. Dub. Fus.).
Parker, Arthur Charles, Lt., died, 11/9/18 (18th Hussars).
H Parker, William George John, D.C.M., 2/Lt., died, 10/10/18 (23 Coy.).
Payne, James Ralph Salisbury, Lt., k. in a., 8/8/18.
Phillips, Gilbert William, Lt. (Tp.), d. of w., 20/11/17.
13 Pilgrim, Stephen Argent Ffennell, Lt., d. of w., 24/9/18.
4 Pogue, Reginald Thomas, M.C., 2/Lt. (Tp.), d. of w., 28/9/18.
12 Porteous, Thomas Williamson, 2/Lt. (Tp.), k. in a., 23/8/18.
13 Porter, John William, 2/Lt. (Tp.), died, 11/7/18.
Powell, Thomas William, M.C., Capt. (Tp.), died, 24/11/18.
2 Power, Lawrence Henry, 2/Lt., k. in a., 22/3/18.
Punchard, R. Hugh, Lt., died, 31/10/18 (R.G.A.).
2 Purves, Thomas Henderson, 2/Lt. (Tp.), k. in a., 22/3/18.
Rawlins, Guy Vernon Champion, Capt., died, 30/1/19 (R.E.).
9 Reith, William Robertson, 2/Lt. (Tp.), died, 17/2/19.
1 Riley, James Shutt, Lt. (Tp.), k. in a., 10/8/18.
13 Roberts, Cyril Ainley, 2/Lt. (Tp.), k. in a., 25/4/18.
V.C. Robertson, Clement, A/Capt., k. in a., 4/10/17 (3rd R.W. Surr. R.).
10 Robinson, Frederick Andrew, M.C., T/Capt. (A/Major), k. in a., 4/11/18.
9 Roddan, Reginald, 2/Lt. (Tp.), k. in a., 1/10/18.
15 Russell, William, 2/Lt. (Tp.), k. in a., 27/9/18.
9 Rutherford, Mark, 2/Lt. (Tp.) (A/Capt.), k. in a., 23/7/18.
6 Ryrie, Arthur, Lt. (Tp.), k. in a., 10/8/18.
10 Sames, Gilbert Fielding, 2/Lt. (Tp.), d. of w., 25/10/18.
8 Scott, Cecil Ewart, M.C., T/Lt. (A/Capt.), d. of w., 9/9/18.
Scowen, Charles Henry, 2/Lt. (Tp.), died, 25/9/17.
6 Seddon, Henry, 2/Lt. (Tp.), k. in a., 8/8/18.
V.C. Sewell, Cecil Harold, Lt., k. in a., 29/8/18 (R.W. Kent R.).
1 Shackleton, Harold, Lt. (Tp.), k. in a., (att. 9th Bn.).
2 Sharp, Arthur Augustus Charles, 2/Lt. (Tp.), k. in a., 22/3/18.
Shaw, Harry, 2/Lt., died, 20/4/19.
"B" Simpson, Arthur Guy, 2/Lt., k. in a., 23/11/17.
2 Sinkinson, Francis Geoffrey, 2/Lt., d. of w., 8/4/18 (in German hands).
15 Slade, Stewart Harold, Lt. (Tp.), k. in a., 21/8/18.
9 Smith, Frank Harold, 2/Lt. (Tp.), k. in a., 2/9/18.

9 Smith, Henry Thomas Bayard, 2/Lt., k. in a., 25/3/18 (4 Hussars).
2 Smith, Stanley Herd, 2/Lt. (Tp.), d. of w., 27/5/18.
5 Spray, Arthur, M.C., T/Capt. (A/Major), k. in a., 5/5/18.
9 Stainsby, Thomas Cecil, 2/Lt. (Tp.), k. in a., 1/10/18.
Steven, George, Lt. (Tp.), k. in a., 24/10/16.
14 Stockley, Walter Edwin, Lt. (Tp.), k. in a., 9/8/18.
"E" Stokes, Harold, 2/Lt. (Tp.), k. in a., 20/11/17.
5 Storm, Jack Newton, 2/Lt. (Tp.), k. in a., 23/3/18.
"D" Talbot, Frederick Charles, A/Capt., k. in a., 9/10/17.
2 Tattersfield, Neville, 2/Lt. (Tp.), died, 20/11/18.
"E" Testi, George, 2/Lt. (Tp.), k. in a., 20/11/17.
9 Trafford, Geoffrey Thomas, Lt., k. in a., 23/7/18 (1 Life Gds.).
2 Tucker, Leslie Archibald, 2/Lt., k. in a., 22/3/18.
2 Turner, John, 2/Lt., d. of w., 13/4/18 (in German hands).
Vardy, Marcel, Capt., k. in a., 27/8/17.
8 Viveast, William Henry, Capt., k. in a., 9/8/18.
V.C. Wain, Richard William Leslie, T/Lt. (A/Capt.), k. in a., 20/11/17.
2 Wakefield, Sydney Clark, 2/Lt., k. in a., 22/3/18.
10 Walker, George Pybus, 2/Lt., k. in a., 9/8/18.
13 Walker, Thomas Percival Patterson, Capt., k. in a., 4/7/18.
Ward, Robert Oscar Cyril, T/Major, k. in a., 20/11/17 (E. Kent. R.).
Ward, Stephen Remson, 2/Lt. (Tp.), died, 8/12/18.
16 Way, Henry Stanley, Capt., killed, 5/5/19.
10 Weights, James Herbert, 2/Lt., k. in a., 9/8/18.
Wells, Frederick Edward, T/Lt. (A/Capt.), died, 13/10/18.
V.C. West, Richard Arnsley, D.S.O., M.C., Major, k. in a., 2/9/18 (N. Irish Horse).
9 White, William Charles, 2/Lt., k. in a., 24/10/18.
9 Wild, Basil Warren, M.C., Lt., k. in a., 1/10/18.
"E" Wilson, Thomas Reginald, 2/Lt., k. in a., 20/11/17.
13 Witter, Harold, 2/Lt., k. in a., 26/4/18.
17 Wood, Norman Clark, M.C., Lt., k. in a., 2/9/18.
Wood, Ronald Beaumont, Capt. (A/Lt.-Col.), k. in a., 21/8/18 (12 Lancers).
2 Wright, Walter Tom Crosby, Lt., k. in a., 8/8/18.

Territorial Officers.

Attached Tank Corps.

Barnett, Alan Gerrard, Lt., k. in a., 22/8/17 (7th Liv. R.).
Bown, Cyril Walter, Lt., d. of w., 1/12/17 (W. Som. Yeo.).
Davy, William Reginald, Capt., k. in a., 21/8/18 (7th Essex R.).
Edwardes, Hon. Cecil, Capt., k. in a., 20/11/17 (Scottish Horse Yeo.).
Gudgeon, T. W., 2/Lt., k. in a., 25/8/18 (5th R. Scot. Fus.).
Lakeman, Arthur Fredk., 2/Lt., k. in a., 20/11/17 (4th Royal Hdrs.).
Lister, F. W., Major, died, 24/2/19 (Worc. Yeo.).
Marchant, Francis Scott, Lt., k. in a., 22/3/18 (5th Border R.).
Muirhead, James Low, Lt. (T/Capt.), k. in a., 21/11/17 (10th R. Scots).
Robinson, Walter, 2/Lt., k. in a., 29/9/18 (5th W. Yks. R.).
Rodgers, John Richard, Lt., k. in a., 20/11/17 (8th Hamps. R.).
South, W. B. C., Lt., died, 13/10/18 (9th Mdx. R.).
Spencer, Henry Beresford, Capt., k. in a., 2/9/18 (W. Som. Yeo.).
Tripe, Alfred King, Lt., k. in a., 23/11/17 (R.G.A.).
Tuite, Mark Alan Wallace, 2/Lt., d. of w., 2/12/17 (10th Lond. R.).
Wyllie, Andrew Inglis, Capt., k. in a., 2/9/18 (4th R. Sco. Fus.).

Labour Corps.

Arthur, Hugh, M.C., T/Lt. (A/Capt.), k. in a., 29/5/18 (48 Chin. Lab. Corps).
Arthurs, Thomas Andrew, Lt. (Tp.), died, 6/12/18 (134 Chin. Lab. Corps).
Bates, William, 2/Lt. (Tp.), d. of w., 13/5/18.
5 Blewitt, Arthur, Lt.-Col. (Tp.), d. of w., 4/9/17 (late K.R.R.C.).
Bradley, George Joseph, Capt. (Tp.), died, 17/2/19 (211 Emp. Coy.).
Braybrooks, Sidney, 2/Lt. (Tp.), died, 3/2/19 (att. 17 R. Suss. R.).
177 Briddon, Charles Clark, Capt. (Tp.), d. of w., 30/9/17.
Burley, E. S., 2/Lt. (Tp.), died, 15/2/19 (112 Chin. Lab. Coy.).
111 Carter, Henry, 2/Lt. (Tp.), k. in a., 28/2/18.
10 Christie, Robert Main, Major, d. of w., 15/5/18.
25 Claughton, Wilfred, Major, died, 24/3/18.
Coakley, Joseph Lynch, Capt., died, 19/10/17.
Connor, Cleveland Alexander, Lt. (Tp.), k. in a., 23/10/18 (att. 1/8 Worc. R.).
Conroy, Hugh Tracey, 2/Lt. (Tp.), died, 28/10/18 (att. 85 Ind. Lab. Coy.).
Cooney, Patrick Augustine, 2/Lt. (Tp.), killed, 22/2/18.
93 Cox, Joseph Henry Silvanus, 2/Lt. (T/Lt.), k. in a., 30/9/17.
27 Dugdale, Joseph Warrior, 2/Lt., died, 3/1/18.
104 Dyer, Sydney Beresford Hope, 2/Lt., d. of w., 10/7/18.
731 Eckersley, Herbert, 2/Lt. (Tp.), k. in a., 15/11/17.
704 Edwards, John Roberts, 2/Lt. (Tp.), died, 15/11/18.
209 Godwin, Harold North, 2/Lt. (Tp.), d. of w., 31/7/17 (209 Empl. Coy.).
Gray, George, 2/Lt. (Tp.), died, 8/2/19.
12 Grieve, David Harley, 2/Lt. (Tp.), died, 31/10/18.
111 Griffiths, Edwin John, 2/Lt. (Tp.), k. in a., 28/2/18.
101 Hazell, Frederick Pung, 2/Lt. (Tp.), d. of w., 19/5/18.
45 Hooley, Tom Williamson, 2/Lt. (Tp.), d. of w., 3/9/17.
Hunter, Charles James, T/Lt. (A/Capt.), died, 4/11/18.
Hyatt, William Joseph, Lt., k. in a., 24/10/18 (att. Devon. R.).
17 Jobling, John Beresford, Capt. (Tp.), died, 4/11/18.
Kinnaird, John Kay, 2/Lt. (Tp.), died, 6/11/18.
Kynch, Harold Egerton Vivian, Major, died, 31/5/19.
700 Ladler, Ernest George, 2/Lt. (Tp.), died, 3/12/18.
542 Lane, John Austen, 2/Lt. (Tp.), died, 27/10/17.
159 Leigh, Bernard Henry, Lt. (Tp.), k. in a., 18/8/17.
Leigh, Henry Godfrey Thomas, 2/Lt. (Tp.), died, 11/11/18.
Lewis, Hugh Berwyn, 2/Lt. (Tp.), died, 12/2/19.
Mason, Albert Thomas, 2/Lt. (Tp.), died, 1/3/18 (att. 66 (Manipur) Ind. Lab. Co.).
64 Nickson, Edmund Reginald, 2/Lt. (Tp.), k. in a., 29/4/18.
61 O'Donnell, Ralph, 2/Lt. (Tp.), died, 25/3/18 (att. Indian).
39 Paton, Thomas Howard Moore, 2/Lt. (Tp.), died, 30/6/17.
Pearce, Richard, M.C., Lt., k. in a., 27/9/18 (att. 23 Lan. Fus.).
Ramsden, Walter Frederick Stewart, 2/Lt. (Tp.), died, 15/11/18 (att. 22 P. of W. Coy.).
Rollo, Thomas William, 2/Lt. (Tp.), died, 4/11/18.
Scholes, William Robert, Capt., died, 14/7/18.
Scott, William Henry, Lt. (Tp.), died, 20/11/17.
Sharpe, T. W., D.C.M., 2/Lt. (Tp.), died, 5/7/18.
Short, James, 2/Lt., died, 8/4/19 (att. Egyptian).
Skidmore, John Henry, T/2/Lt. (A/Capt.), died, 7/11/18 (att. 214 P. of W. Coy.).
Smith, A. H., 2/Lt. (Tp.), died, 16/8/18.
Stack, J. C., 2/Lt., killed, 30/4/18 (and R.A.F.).
Steel, Anthony, 2/Lt. (Tp.), k. in a., 11/9/18 (att. 8 K. L'pool R.).
Strachan, Albert, 2/Lt. (Tp.), died, 30/10/18 (att. Chin. Lab. Corps).
733 Taylor, George William, 2/Lt. (Tp.), killed, 1/10/17.
Taylor, Harold Harker, T/2/Lt. (A/Capt.), drowned, 11/8/18 (att. 83 C.L.C.).
Thornton, Joseph Henry Banks, 2/Lt. (Tp.), k. in a., 22/9/18 (att. 23 Lancs Fus.).
39 Tysoe, Leonard, 2/Lt. (Tp.), k. in a., 31/5/17.
101 Varley, Ernest, 2/Lt., died, 2/3/18.
152 Wellings, Charles Henry Clifford, 2/Lt. (Tp.), k. in a., 11/8/17.
Williams, Edward Albert, 2/Lt., died, 31/12/18 (and R.A.F.).
Wright, Sidney Harry, T/Lt. (A/Capt.), died, 10/2/19 (att. 114 Chin. Lab. Coy.).
Young, Edward Thomas, Capt., died, 14/3/18 (att. 6 Chin. Lab. Coy.).

New Armies.

General List.

Abel, George Fowtrell, 2/Lt., died, 20/6/18.
Addis, Henry Dansey, Temp., 2/Lt., killed, 24/1/17 (and R.F.C.).
Aitken, John Francis, 2/Lt. (Tp.), k. in a., 7/9/17 (1/6 Lancs Fus.).
Allan, John, 2/Lt., d. of w., 4/11/16 (and R.F.C.).
Allan, R., 2/Lt., killed, 22/4/18 (and R.A.F.).
Allen, Geoffrey May, 2/Lt., k. in a., 2/9/16 (and R.F.C.).
Arnaud, Frederick Cooper, 2/Lt. (Tp.), k. in a., 1/7/16 (att. T.M.B.).
Arnold, Herbert Edward, 2/Lt., died, 26/12/16 (and R.F.C.).
Arnot, A. A. McD., 2/Lt., k. in a., 12/4/18 (and R.A.F.).
Arrow, George William, Lt., died, 25/1/19.
Bailey, Charles Frederick, 2/Lt. (Tp.), k. in a., 9/5/16.
Bainbridge, Eric, Lt., died, 5/0/16 (and R.F.C.).
Bake, Noel, 2/Lt., k. in a., 10/4/18.
Ball, Theodore Hollyman, 2/Lt. (Tp.), killed, 21/1/17.
Barclay, George Reinhold, Temp. Lt., k. in a., 30/10/18.
Barker, W. J., 2/Lt., killed, 27/4/18 (and R.A.F.).
Barnard, Lewis Harold, Temp. Lt., k. in a., 25/8/16 (and T.M.B.).
Barr, Herbert Carrick, 2/Lt. (Tp.), k. in a., 11/12/16 (and R.F.C.).
Barrett, L. K. W., 2/Lt., killed, 24/4/18 (and R.A.F.).
Bartlett, James, 2/Lt., died, 6/5/18 (I.W.T.).
Barton, L. F., 2/Lt., killed, 17/5/18 (and R.A.F.).
Baskett, Edmund Graham, Temp. Capt., died, 27/10/18 (and Nigeria Regt.).
Beatty, Eric Leslie Finch, 2/Lt. (Tp.), k. in a., 23/6/16 (att. T. How. By.).
Bell, Edward Inkerman, Capt., k. in a., 24/3/18.
V.C. Bell, Eric Norman Frankland, Capt. (Tp.), k. in a., 1/7/16 (att. 109 Light T.M.B.).
Bentley, George Greenwood, Lt., d. of w., 17/9/16 (and R.F.C.).
Bidmead, Charles Hugh, 2/Lt. (Tp.), k. in a., 10/11/16 (and R.F.C.).
Bissicks, Francis, Temp. 2/Lt., killed, 2/1/17 (and R.F.C.).
Black, Maurice Charles Osborne, Lt., k. in a., 24/8/16 (and T.M.B.).
Blake, George Cyril, Temp. Lt., died, 5/11/17 (att. Recruitg. Staff).
Bobby, Sidney Fitzgerald, 2/Lt. (Tp.), k. in a., 1/7/16 (att. T.M.B.).
Bolay, A. R., 2/Lt., killed, 27/5/18 (and R.A.F.).
Bown, Edward Elms, 2/Lt. (Tp.), k. in a., 2/11/17 (att. 1/4 Northants Regt.).
Bowyer, Fritz, 2/Lt., died, 25/7/16 (and R.F.C.).
Boyd, R. H., 2/Lt., killed, 12/4/18 (and R.A.F.).
Brand, Geoffrey Jermyn, 2/Lt. (Tp.), k. in a., 1/7/16 (and 101 T.M.B.).
Brereton, Herbert, Temp. 2/Lt., T/Lt., k. in a., 21/12/16 (and R.F.C.).
Brickmann, Hugh Morton Gairn, Temp. Lt., d. of w., 1/10/16 (att. T.M.B.).

Brown, Claude Algernon Felix, Temp. Lt., k. in a., 26/12/16 (and R.F.C.).
Brown, Robin Lowis Campbell, Temp. 2/Lt., A/Lt., d. of w., 8/6/17 (att. X/8 T.M. Bty.).
Brown, W.G., 2/Lt., killed, 7/5/18 (and R.A.F.).
Bruce, George James, D.S.O., M.C., Temp. Capt., k. in a., 2/10/18.
Bryson, Thomas Harold, 2/Lt., died, 27/2/19 (207 P.O.W. Coy.).
Buchanan, Andrew MacFarlane, A/Lt., d. of w., 13/6/17 (90/T.M.B.).
Burney, Gilbert Edward, Lt. (Tp.), d. of w., 28/9/15 (and Staff).
Butcher, Cyril Arthur Mecrate, T/2/Lt. (A/Capt.), k. in a., 6/7/17 (62 T.M.B.).
Butt, F. W., 2/Lt., killed, 26/5/18 (and R.A.F.).
Campbell, K. T., 2/Lt., k. in a., 17/6/18 (and R.A.F.).
Campbell, Samuel MacDonnell, Temp. Lt., k. in a., 1/7/16 (86 T.M.B.).
Cann, P. R., 2/Lt., d. of w., 2/4/18 (and R.A.F.).
Cavanagh, John, 2/Lt., drowned, 26/2/18 (I.W.T.).
Charles, B. S., 2/Lt., died, 7/12/18 (and R.A.F.).
Clark, Arthur Vivian, Temp. 2/Lt., k. in a., 20/4/16 (att. 7/Glouc. Regt.).
Clarke, Donald, Temp. 2/Lt., k. in a., 26/8/16 (and R.F.C.).
Clarke, Peter, Temp. Lt., d. of w., 30/7/16 (T.M.B.).
Clifford, Ralph Montague Lewis, Temp. Capt., k. in a., 15/10/16 (att. T.M.B.).
Coffey, C. R., Lt., killed, 27/5/18 (and R.A.F.).
Coller, Bernard Tarrant, Lt., died, 26/9/16 (and R.F.C.).
Collins, L. E., 2/Lt., killed, 5/4/18 (and R.A.F.).
Collins, Harold Stafford, T/2/Lt., A/Capt., died, 17/11/17 (Egyptian Lab. Corps).
Colquhoun, A. S., 2/Lt., killed, 20/4/18 (and R.A.F.).
Comber-Taylor, E. H., Capt., killed, 16/6/18 (and R.A.F.).
Cotton, William Martin Vernon, 2/Lt., k. in a., 21/12/16 (and R.F.C.).
Cottrell, Percy Bagliatto, Temp. Lt., d. of w., 27/9/18.
Cowell, Charles Stanley, Lt. (Tp.), died, 13/4/17.
Coyle, Clement William, Lt., died, 19/2/19.
Craig, J., 2/Lt., killed, 11/4/18 (and R.A.F.).
Craig, R. S., 2/Lt., killed, 22/4/18 (and R.A.F.).
Crathorne, Frederick, Lt. (Tp.), k. in a., 14/1/16 (att. 252 Tun. Coy. R.E.).
Crawford, William Charlton, Temp. 2/Lt., k. in a., 17/11/16 (and R.F.C.).
Crowther, Leslie Oakes, Temp. Capt., k. in a., 6/12/16 (and R.F.C.).
Curties, Lionel Charles Alfred, Temp. Capt., k. in a., 25/10/15 (att. M.G.C.).
Dangar, Clive Colingwood, M.C., Major (Tp.), died, 4/7/18.
Davidson, S., 2/Lt., k. in a., 21/5/18 (and R.A.F.).
Davie, John, M.C., T/2/Lt., A/Capt., k. in a., 11/5/18.
Davies, Evan Walter, Temp. 2/Lt., k. in a., 26/3/17.
Davis, Reginald, 2/Lt., k. in a., 20/10/16 (and R.F.C.).
Davy, John Alfred, Lt., killed, 8/11/16 (and R.F.C.).
Dingwall, J. D., 2/Lt., killed, 21/4/18 (and R.A.F.).
Dobbyn, Robert Newport, 2/Lt. (Tp.), killed, 23/11/16 (and R.F.C.).
Doughty, E. A., 2/Lt., killed, 14/4/18 (and R.A.F.).
Duffin, Charles Francis, T/Lt. (A/Capt.), killed, 13/3/18.
Durrant, L. A., 2/Lt., killed, 6/6/18 (and R.A.F.).
Duthie, D. O., 2/Lt., k. in a., 23/8/18 (and R.A.F.).
Dyson, S. G., 2/Lt., died, 1/6/18 (and R.A.F.).
Earle, Wallace Sinclair, Temp. 2/Lt., k. in a., 16/4/16 (and R.F.C.).
Edwards, George, 2/Lt. (Tp.), died, 24/9/16 (and R.F.C.).
Emmens, Richard Reeve, 2/Lt., k. in a., 4/9/16 (T.M.B.).
Evans, Henry Cope, D.S.O., 2/Lt., died, 3/9/16 (and R.F.C.).
Evans, John Trevor Stuart, Temp. Capt., d. of w., 7/5/18 (in Ger. hands).
Evans, Philip, Temp. 2/Lt., killed, 12/1/17 (and R.F.C.).
Fausset, W. W. B., Capt., died, 6/12/18.
Fielding, Joseph, 2/Lt., died, 16/12/17 (att. I.W.T.).
Fine, S., 2/Lt., killed, 18/5/18 (and R.A.F.).
Fish, W. R., M.C., Capt., killed, 2/6/18 (and R.A.F.).
Fisher, Arthur James, 2/Lt., k. in a., 25/10/16 (and R.F.C.).
Fiske, Harold, Lt., died, 20/12/16 (and R.F.C.).
Fitch, Walter Frederick, M.C., Temp. Capt., died, 1/11/18.
Fleming, A., 2/Lt., d. of w., 29/4/18 (and R.A.F.).
Floyd, Hayden, 2/Lt. (Tp.), d. of w., 11/7/16 (and R.F.C., P. of W.).
Fordham, Charles George Harry, Lt. & Qr.-Mr., died, 29/10/17.
Fraser, R. A., 2/Lt., killed, 18/5/18 (and R.A.F.).
Fullerton, William Francis Hannan, 2/Lt., died, 22/10/16 (and R.F.C.).
Garner, Frank Leslie, Temp. 2/Lt., killed, 20/12/16 (and R.F.C.).
Garnett, William Herbert Stuart, Temp. Lt., killed, 21/9/16 (and R.F.C.).
Geidt, C. W., Lt., killed, 10/4/18 (and R.A.F.).
Gibson, Leonard, Temp. Capt., died, 1/8/18.
Gillespie, D. V., 2/Lt., k. in a., 5/4/18 (and R.A.F.).
Gimson, Walter Stanley, M.C., Temp. 2/Lt. (A/Capt.), k. in a., 16/8/17 (and 61 T.M.B.).
Glover, Brian Edward, Temp. 2/Lt., died, 13/3/16 (and R.F.C.).
Godet, L. De G., 2/Lt., k. in a., 1/6/18 (and R.A.F.).
Goodchild, Victor George, Lt., died, 31/10/18 (and R.A.F.).
Goodrick, John William, 2/Lt., drowned, 26/2/18 (I.W.T.).
Gordon, Victor Frederick, M.C., Lt., d. of w., 1/7/18 (and T.M.B.).
Gorell-Barnes, Charles Roper, D.S.O., M.C., Temp. Capt., d. of w., 21/4/18 (att 8/Rifle Bde.).
Gough, L. W., Tp. Hon. 2/Lt., died, 23/4/18.
Gray, Alexander Allen, M.C., Temp. 2/Lt., killed, 3/2/17 (and R.F.C.).
Gray, Douglas Huon, Lt., k. in a., 3/7/16 (and R.F.C.).
Gray, Francis Henry Tower, Temp. Lt., drowned, 21/7/18 (att. W.A.F.F.).
Green, Demetrius Frederick Edward Joseph, Lt., died, 15/10/18.
Greenwood, L. A., 2/Lt., d. of w., 13/4/18 (and R.A.F.).
Guerrier, Elias George, Temp. Lt., drowned, 30/11/18 (I.W.T.).
Gundry, William, Lt. & Qr.-Mr., died, 19/1/18.
Halden, Alexander, 2/Lt., drowned, 26/2/18 (I.W.T.).
Hall, G. L. D., 2/Lt., killed, 2/5/18 (and R.A.F.).
Hall, Gordon William, Temp. 2/Lt., killed, 21/8/16 (and R.F.C.).
Hamilton, Edward, Temp. Lt., k. in a., 14/4/18 (att. 9/R. Ir. Rifles).
Hamnett, Frederick George, Temp. 2/Lt., died, 15/11/18.
Hann, Cecil Collins, 2/Lt., k. in a., 22/10/16 (and R.F.C.).
Harding, Claude Stephen, Lt., died, 22/1/18 (4/4 K. Afr. Rifles).
Hargrave, W. G., 2/Lt., k. in a., 17/4/18 (and R.A.F.).
Harper, Robert Charles Middleton, 2/Lt., k. in a., 19/4/17 (att. 1/5 Norfolk Regt.).
Harris, Robert Arthur, Capt. (Tp.), drowned, 21/11/17.
Headlam, J., 2/Lt., killed, 30/5/18 (and R.A.F.).
Hele-Shaw, Henry Rathbone, Lt., k. in a., 19/7/16 (and R.F.C.).
Heyes, A. E., 2/Lt., d. of w., 14/4/18 (and R.A.F.).
Hird, Frederick, Temp. Lt., k. in a., 29/7/16 (and T.M.B.).
Hitchings, Henry Mayne, 2/Lt., k. in a., 18/8/16 (48/T.M.B.).
Hobbs, Alan Victor, Temp. 2/Lt., k. in a., 15/12/15 (and R.F.C.).
Hobson, Robert Carl, M.C., Capt. (Tp.), died, 10/11/18.
Holland, William Francis Claude, Capt. (Tp.), died, 8/11/17.
Homan, H. B., 2/Lt., killed, 4/4/18 (and R.A.F.).
Houston, Cyril Thomas, Lt., died, 22/7/18 (and R.A.F.).
Hucks, B. C., Capt., died, 7/11/18 (and R.A.F.).
Hughes, Arthur, D.C.M., T/Capt. & Qr.-Mr., died, 11/2/19.
Hughes, H., 2/Lt., k. in a., 11/4/18 (and R.A.F.).
Hunt, Percival George Havelock, Lt., k. in a., 8/11/17 (and 92/T.M.B.).
Hurd-Wood, John Grahame, Capt. (Tp.), k. in a., 4/8/16 (68 Inf. Bde. H.Q.).
Hutcheson, G. J., Lt., died, 27/5/18 (and R.A.F.).
Hutson, Harry Austen, Capt., k. in a., 28/5/18 (att. Lan Fus.).
Inglis, James, Hon. Lt. & Qr.-Mr., died, 28/11/15.
Isaacson, Colin de Slutevalle, M.C., Capt., d. of w., 11/6/17 (and Staff East Africa List).
James, Arthur Keedwell Harvey, Temp. Capt., k. in a., 15/4/17.
Jarvis, E. MacD., 2/Lt., killed, 6/6/18 (and R.A.F.).
Jeal, Walter, Temp. 2/Lt., k. in a., 1/7/16 (att. 15/R. Scots.).
Jenkins, Thomas Frederick, Temp. Major, died, 26/2/19.
Jenner-Clarke, John William, Temp. Lt., k. in a., 16/9/16 (T.M.B.).
Johnson, C. M., 2/Lt., killed, 6/6/18 (and R.A.F.).
Johnson, Stephen Henry, A/Capt., k. in a., 20/5/17 (and 19/T.M.B.).
Jones, T. B., Capt., killed, 11/4/18 (and R.A.F.).
Jordan, William, Temp. 2/Lt., k. in a., 8/11/16 (and R.F.C.).
Jowett, Eric Craven, Lt., d. of w., 9/7/16 (and R.F.C.).
Joyce, N. R., Lt., killed, 1/4/18 (and R.A.F.).
Judge, Leopold James, Temp. 2/Lt., k. in a., 3/5/17 (and T.M.B.).
Kane, Frederick Paul, 2/Lt., k. in a., 1/11/16 (and R.F.C.).
Kay-Shuttleworth, The Hon. Edward James, Capt. (Tp.), killed, 10/7/17 (late 7/Rifle Bde.).
Kelway-Bamber, Claude Herschel, 2/Lt., k. in a., 11/11/15 (and R.F.C.).
Kinder, Richard Clement, Temp. Capt., k. in a., 20/9/17 (att. 26/Royal Fusrs.).
King, Cyril Henry Marshall, 2/Lt., k. in a., 30/9/16 (and R.F.C.).
King, Maurice, Temp. 2/Lt., died, 24/6/17 (and Egyptian Lab. Corps).
King, Victor Reginald, Lt. (Tp.), d. of w., 13/5/18 (att. R.E. Signals).
Kingsbury, Edward Harrison, Temp. Lt., died, 17/8/17 (and I.W.T.).
Kinniburgh, John D., Temp. 2/Lt., k. in a., 6/11/17 (att. 14/Royal Highrs.).
Knight, J. B. C., 2/Lt., killed, 15/4/18 (and R.A.F.).
La Coste, Charles John Constable, M.C., Temp. Capt., k. in a., 9/10/17 (att. 1/8 W. Yorks Regt.).
Lamb, E. W. P., 2/Lt., killed, 24/4/18 (and R.A.F.).
Layng, George Reginald Stuart, Temp. 2/Lt., A/Lt., d. of w., 18/8/16 (att. 1/T.M.B.).
Lefebore, R. H., 2/Lt., killed, 13/4/18 (and R.A.F.).
Lillywhite, Robert John, Temp. Capt., killed, 26/11/16 (and R.F.C.).
Link, F. L. C., 2/Lt., killed, 7/6/18 (and R.A.F.).
Locheed, R. W., 2/Lt., killed, 28/5/18 (and R.A.F.).
Lowe, Henry Griffith Pagan, Temp. 2/Lt., k. in a., 8/11/16 (and R.F.C.).
Lowenstein, J. C., 2/Lt., killed, 9/5/18 (and R.A.F.).
Lubbock, Hon. Eric Fox Pitt, M.C., Temp. Capt., k. in a 11/3/17 (and R.F.C.).
Lushington, Sydney Edward James Chippendale, Temp. Lt., d. of w., 25/9/16.
MacAndrew, John McLean, Capt., died, 11/10/17.
McCrostie, Charles Hutchison, Temp. 2/Lt., k. in a., 1/7/16 (att. T.M.B.).

MacLachlan, James Menzies, M.C., T/2/Lt., A/Capt., k. in a., 2/12/17 (att. 97/L.T.M.B.).
McLean, John, Lt., killed, 16/7/18 (att. R.E., I.W.T.).
McLellan, Samuel, Temp. Lt., drowned, 16/10/17 (I.W.T.).
Macleod, Donald, Lt., drowned, 10/5/17 (att. I.W.T.).
McMillan, J. S., 2/Lt., T/Lt., died, 12/3/18 (att. K. Afr. Rifles).
McNeill, John, 2/Lt., drowned, 26/2/18 (I.W.T.).
Macrae, J. N., Capt., killed, 11/4/18 (and R.A.F.).
McTavish, I. A. B., 2/Lt., killed, 15/5/18 (and R.A.F.).
MacTavish, Roswell Murray, M.C., Temp. Capt., died, 6/2/19. (and Staff).
MacVicker, J. E. C., Lt., died, 22/7/18 (and R.A.F.).
Maden, William Henry, Temp. 2/Lt., d. of w., 4/10/17 (att. 95/T.M.B.).
Maitland, Henry Maitland, M.C., Temp. Capt., died, 10/11/18.
Maltby, A. H., 2/Lt., killed, 4/6/18 (and R.A.F.).
Mann, Robert Mathers, Major (Tp.), died, 20/11/17.
Mann, S. W., Temp. 2/Lt., k. in a., 27/3/19.
Marshall, Albert Herbert Bathurst, Temp. 2/Lt., k in a., 22/5/18 (att. 3/Rifle Bde.).
Maxwell, Alexander Edward, Lt., d. of w., 7/5/17 (att. 121/T.M. Bty.).
Mees, Ian Rudolf, Lt., killed, 14/11/18 (and R.A.F.).
Melville, Harry Taylor, T/Lt., k. in a., 31/7/18 (and R.A.F.).
Meredith, E. M., Lt., killed, 13/4/18 (and R.A.F.).
Mildmay, B. W. St. J., 2/Lt., killed, 16/4/18 (and R.A.F.).
Miller, Peter Spence, 2/Lt., drowned, 26/2/18 (I.W.T.).
Milne, James Robertson, Temp. Capt., died, 30/10/18.
Mitchell, James, Temp. 2/Lt., k. in a., 26/4/16 (and R.F.C.).
Mitchell, James Douglas, Temp. Lt., died, 9/10/18 (and K. Afr. Rifles).
Moore, G. B., M.C., Capt., killed, 7/4/18 (and R.A.F.).
Morgan, Cyril Edward, Temp. 2/Lt., killed, 4/12/16 (and R.F.C.).
Morison, John Sinclair, Temp. 2/Lt., killed, 13/10/16 (and R.F.C.).
Morrison, James Ian, Temp. Lt., d. of w., 28/9/16 (T.M.B.).
Morrison, James McGregor, M.C., Temp. Lt., died, 15/2/19 (W.A.F.F. Nig. Regt.).
Mortimer, E. G. S., 2/Lt., killed, 3/4/18 (and R.A.F.).
Napier, J., 2/Lt., killed, 7/4/18 (and R.A.F.).
Nason, John William Washington, Temp. Capt., k. in a., 26/12/16 (and R.F.C.).
Newman, Frederick Arthur, Temp. Lt., k. in a., 31/7/17 (X/37 T.M.B.).
Nicolson, Donald McDonald, 2/Lt., k. in a., 19/4/17 (att. 5/K.O.S.Bdrs.).
Nightingale, Eric, 2/Lt., k. in a., 25/6/18 (and R.A.F.).
Nops, Thomas Waldegrave, Temp. 2/Lt., k. in a., 21/10/16 (and R.F.C.).
Nugent, Gerald William, Capt., k. in a., 10/8/15 (Staff H.Q., 29 Inf. Bde.).
Oake, Douglas, M.C., T/Capt., killed, 8/8/18 (att. 92 T.M. Bty.).
O'Dwyer, John, 2/Lt. (Tp.), d. of w., 11/9/16 (and T.M.B.).
O'Hara, H. E., 2/Lt., killed, 25/5/18 (and R.A.F.).
O'Neill, Samuel, Lt., k. in a., 1/7/16 (T.M.B.).
Orford, William Kirkpatrick, Temp. 2/Lt., k. in a., 1/7/16 (att. T.M.B.).
Owen-Holdsworth, J. P., 2/Lt., killed, 12/4/18 (and R.A.F.).
Paget, Samuel James, Capt., k. in a., 26/3/18 (and Staff 149 Inf. Bde.).
Palardy, G., 2/Lt., d of w., 7/5/18 (and R.A.F.)
Palmer, Charles Walter, 2/Lt., died, 29/3/16 (and R.F.C., (P. of W.).
Panzera, Francis William, C.M.G., Col. (Tp.), died, 4/6/17.
Parker, Thomas Geoffrey Milsome, Temp. Capt., died, 3/11/18.
Parks, George Edwin Harold, Lt., d. of w., 12/10/18 (and Manch. Regt.).
Parton, Roland Thomas, Temp. 2/Lt., d. of w., 21/11/17 (att. 1/10 Lond. Regt.).
Patterson, Aubrey Frederick Albert, Temp. 2/Lt., d. of w., 25/9/16 (and R.F.C.) (P. of W.)
Pauline, V. R., 2/Lt., k. in a., 8/5/18 (and R.A.F.)
Payne, Frederick Norman, Temp. Capt., died, 14/11/17 (att. Mil. Gov., Baghdad).
Payne, S. T., Lt., died, 6/4/18 (and R.A.F.).
Peirce, G. F., 2/Lt., killed, 26/5/18 (and R.A.F.).
Perrin, Reginald Percy, M.C., Capt., k in a., 27/5/18 (att. 7 Inf. Bde. H.Q.).
Petrie, Alfred Hunt, Temp 2/Lt., k in a., 31/7/17 (att. 72 T.M.B.).
Pettigrew, John, Lt., died, 3/11/18 (att. S. Persia Rifles).
Pitt-Pitts, Walter John, Lt., died, 9/8/18 (and R.A.F.).
Piza, Daniel, A/Capt., k. in a., 9/4/17 (64 T.M.B.).
Poole, L.S.R., Lt., died, 3/12/18 (and R.A.F.).
Pomeroy, Norman Ransch, 2/Lt., k in a., 20/10/16 (and R.F.C.).
Potter, Francis John, Temp. 2/Lt., k. in a., 1/7/16 (att. T.M.B.).
Pragnell, George Frederick, Temp. Capt., k. in a., 23/7/17 (Staff, 123 Inf. Bde.).
Price, Graham, Temp. 2/Lt., k. in a., 9/3/16 (and R.F.C.).
Price, Samuel Allen, Temp. 2/Lt., died, 11/7/17 (I.W.T.).
Radcliffe, Ernest John, Temp. 2/Lt., died, 20/2/16 (and R.F.C.).
Ramsden, S., 2/Lt., d. of w., 12/4/18 (and R.A.F.).
Raphael, John Edward, Lt. (Tp.), d. of w., 11/6/17.
Rapp, Ernest James, 2/Lt (Tp.), k. in a., 9/4/17 (att. Yorks Regt.).
Rayner, Hubert William, Lt. (Tp.), d. of w., 5/11/17 (and T.M.B.).
Rayner, Leslie King, 2/Lt. (Tp.), k. in a., 18/4/17 (att. 13/R. Suss. Regt.)
Redfern, Frederick Arthur Dudley, Lt. (Tp.), died, 15/7/17 (Emp. S. Persian Rifles).
Reid, Norman Malcolm, Capt. (Tp.), died, 12/1/17.
Reynolds, J. E., 2/Lt., killed, 18/5/18 (and R.A.F.).
Robertson, Ernest Guy, Temp. Capt., died, 28/10/18.
Robertson, Norman McLeod, Lt., k. in a., 17/10/16 (and R.F.C.).
Roche, James Patrick, M.C., 2/Lt. (A/Capt.), k. in a., 7/6/17 (and 47 T.M.B.).
Rose, Phillip Vivian, Capt. (Tp.), d. of w., 25/4/17 (Bde. Staff).
Royds, T. A., 2/Lt., killed, 20/4/18 (and R.A.F.).
Ruck, John Arthur, Temp. 2/Lt., died, 25/5/16 (and R.F.C.).
Rundell, Reginald Charles, 2/Lt. (Tp.) (A/Capt.), k. in a., 3/5/17 (att. 10 T.M. Bty.).
Rushton, Cecil George, Capt., k. in a., 16/5/18 (and R.A.F.).
Rushton, Frank Gregson, Temp. 2/Lt., k. in a., 1/7/16 (att. T.M.B.).
Ruttley, Percy Kemp, Temp. Capt., died, 19/10/18.
Sampson, Richard Harry, Temp. Lt., died, 29/10/18 (att. 114 Bde. Hqrs.).
Sarchet, Leslie Lionel, Temp. Lt, k. in a., 23/10/18 (55 T.M.B.).
Satterthwaite, G. E., 2/Lt., killed, 11/6/18 (and R.A.F.).
Scott, R. J., 2/Lt., d. of w., 8/5/18 (and R.A.F.).
Scott, Robert Michael, Temp. Lt., died, 25/12/18 (att. R.E. Sigs.).
Settle, Reginald William, Temp. 2/Lt., k. in a., 23/7/16 (and R.F.C.).
Sharp, George, Temp. 2/Lt., died, 29/10/18.
Sharpe, Maurice, 2/Lt., k. in a., 28/10/16 (and R.F.C.).
Sheffield, Edward Frederick, Temp. 2/Lt., killed, 17/5/16 (and R.F.C.).
Shenkel, Frank J., Hon. Lt., d. of w., 19/11/17.
Silcox, Baylis, 2/Lt. (Tp.), k. in a., 29/12/17 (att. 7/R. Dublin Fus.)
Simpson, Eric Cograve, Capt. (Tp.), drowned, 4/5/17.
Simpson, James Alexander, Temp. Lt., d. of w., 22/10/16 (and R.F.C.).
Simpson, T. E., 2/Lt., killed, 1/6/18 (and R.A.F.).
Slaney, Albert Edward, 2/Lt. (Tp.), died, 3/10/17 (att. Lab. Corps).
Smith, E., 2/Lt., killed, 29/4/18 (and R.A.F.).
Somers-Cocks, Reginald, M.C., Capt. (Tp.), k. in a., 24/4/18 (att. 7/Som. L.I.).
Souchotte, C., 2/Lt., killed, 23/4/18 (and R.A.F.).
Spence, William Herbert John Shepherd, 2/Lt. (Tp.), died, 23/9/17 (att. I.W.T.).
Spencer, W., 2/Lt., k. in a., 10/5/18 (and R.A.F.).
Spinney, Robert Eric, M.C., Lt. (Tp.), d. of w., 1/2/17.
Stevens, R. H. B., 2/Lt., killed, 30/5/18 (and R.A.F.).
Stewart, Andrew Christie, 2/Lt. (Tp.), drowned, 19/4/18 (att. I.W.T.).
Stewart, James Aitchison, Lt. (Tp.), d. of w., 12/10/16 (and R.F.C.).
Stoddart, G. B. J., 2/Lt., killed, 10/4/18 (and R.A.F.).
Stransom, Norman G., Lt., k. in a., 10/5/18 (and R.A.F.).
Stuart, Frank, Capt. (Tp.), k. in a., 10/4/18 (att. 57 T.M.B.).
Stubbs, Herbert Edgar, 2/Lt. (Tp.), d. of w., 4/9/17 (att. 65 Chin. Lab. Co.).
Sutor, Harry C., Capt (Tp.), died, 23/9/16.
Swain, C. M., 2/Lt., killed, 4/4/18 (and R.A.F.).
Sykes, Claude, Lt. (Tp.), k in a., 2/7/16 (att. T.M.B.).
Tate, A. C. R., 2/Lt., killed, 2/5/18 (and R.A.F.).
Taylor, A. D., Capt. (Tp.), killed, 24/8/18 (and R.A.F.).
Thierry, Frederick George, 2/Lt., k. in a., 17/9/16 (and R.F.C.).
Thomas, William Norman, 2/Lt., k. in a., 8/4/16 (and R.F.C.).
Thompson, John, Lt., k. in a., 16/10/16 (and R.F.C.).
Thornton, Victor Hubert, Temp. Capt., k. in a., 24/10/18 (att. 9/N'land Fusrs.).
Thuell, William Johnson, Temp. 2/Lt., k. in a., 22/10/16 (and R.F.C.).
Topham, A. A., Temp. 2/Lt., died, 7/12/18.
Townsend, W. H., 2/Lt., d. of w., 23/4/18 (and R.A.F.).
Traunweiser, G. N., 2/Lt., killed, 15/4/18 (and R.A.F.).
Trubridge, R. W., Lt., d. of w., 6/5/18 (and R.A.F.).
Tucker, Donald Cecil, 2/Lt., k. in a., 24/3/18 (and R.F.C.).
Tucker, H. G., 2/Lt., killed, 4/4/18 (and R.A.F.).
Turner, Evelyn Victor, Lt. (Tp.), k. in a., 18/11/16 (att. 8/North Staff. Rgt.).
Turner, F. H., M.C., Temp. Lt., killed, 10/1/17 (and R.F.C.).
Turner, George Perrior, 2/Lt. (Tp.), k. in a., 30/6/16 (att. 116 T.M.B.).
Turner, Ralph Pool, Temp. 2/Lt., died, 9/3/16 (and R.F.C.).
Turpin, James Stephen, 2/Lt. (Tp.), d. of w., 21/5/16 (att. T.M.B.).
Tweedie-Smith, Douglas, Temp. Lt., died, 10/4/16 (and R.F.C.).
Tyrrell, W. A., Capt., killed, 9/6/18 (and R.A.F.).
Vandenberg, F. A., 2/Lt., killed, 20/5/18 (and R.A.F.).
Venner, William Frederick Fouracre, Lt. (Tp.), died, 5/12/16 (att. R.E.).
Walker, F. F., 2/Lt., d. of w., 14/4/18 (and R.A.F.).
Walker, J. C., 2/Lt., killed, 18/10/18 (and R.A.F.).
Walker, John Haslam, 2/Lt. (Tp.), d. of w., 22/11/17 (att. 16 R. Suss. R.).
Walker, W., Capt., killed, 8/10/18 (and R.A.F.).
Walker, William Gray Johnstone, M.C., T/Lt. (A/Capt.), k. in a., 18/7/17 (T.M.B.).
Wallace, Arthur Reginald, T/Lt., died, 18/1/19 (I.W.T.).
Wallis, Harold Leigh, Lt., killed, 2/7/16 (and R.F.C.).
Walters, H. A., 2/Lt., killed, 7/4/18 (and R.A.F.).
Ward, F. M., 2/Lt., killed, 22/4/18 (and R.A.F.).

Warwick, J. L., 2/Lt., killed, 14/6/18 (and R.A.F.).
Watts, Cyril George, Capt. (A/Bde.-Major), k. in a., 1/10/18 (Staff, 93 Inf. Bde.).
Watts, Wilfrid, 2/Lt. (Tp.), k. in a., 17/1/16 (and R.F.C.).
Wheeler, A. J. P., 2/Lt., killed, 9/5/18 (and R.A.F.).
Whittam, Frederick, 2/Lt. (Tp.), k. in a., 7/8/15 (att. 1/5 Lanc. Fus.).
Wittkugel, A. F., 2/Lt. (Tp.), d. of w., 15/2/17 (and S. Persian R.).
Wiggins, H. C., 2/Lt., killed, 1/4/18 (and R.A.F.).
Wilkes, Clifford, T/Lt. (A/Capt.), k. in a., 28/4/17 (6/T.M.B.).
Willby, Frank Richard Bagg, Lt., killed, 18/3/19 (Staff).
Willey, R., 2/Lt., killed, 20/5/18 (and R.A.F.).
Williams, John Herbert, Temp. Capt., died, 18/11/17.
Williams, Stanley Charles Howard, Temp. Lt., died, 14/10/18 (att. Nigeria Regt.).
Williams, Stanley Norman, Temp. 2/Lt., died, 25/10/16 (and R.F.C.).
Wills, Oliver Byerley Walters, Lt., died, 10/11/18 (and R.A.F.).
Wilson, Robert, Capt., died, 12/4/18.
Wilson, Theodore Percival Cameron, Lt., k. in a., 24/3/18.
Wilson, Wilfrid Gordon, Capt., died, 10/12/18 (att. R.E.).
Winton, H. B., 2/Lt., killed, 21/4/18 (and R.A.F.).
Wodehouse, Honourable Philip, Lt., died, 6/5/19.
Wordingham, Vincent Robert, Temp. 2/Lt., k. in a., 16/8/17.
Wright, Arthur William, Temp. Capt., died, 13/10/17.
Wright, Percy Andrew, 2/Lt. (Tp.), died, 21/12/16 (and R.F.C.).
Wynn, Arthur Ernest, 2/Lt. (Tp.), d. of w., 1/11/16 (and R.F.C.) (P. of W.).
Young, C., Lt., died, 20/7/18 (and R.A.F.).

The West India Regiment.

King, Frederick Harvey, Lt., k. in a., 12/10/16 (att. W. Riding Regt.).
2 Lawrence, John George, 2/Lt., died, 15/2/18 (att. Norfolk Regt.).
Lawrenson, Reginald Robert, D.S.O., Major (T/Lt.-Col.), d. of w., 27/4/18 (att. H.L.I.).
2 Martin, Albert Trever de Monteval, Major, d. of w., 10/12/17 (att. 5th Welsh R.).
Ottley, Kendal Coghill Glendower, Lt., died, 31/10/16.
Stockhausen, Ivan Lancelot, 2/Lt., k. in a., 3/10/17.
1 Thelwall, Hubert Wallace, Major, k. in a., 23/4/16 (att. 15th Notts & Derby Rgt.).
Tyndale, George Stafford Hilliard, Lt., d. of w., 13/3/15 (att. Middx. Rgt.).
Williams, Almericus John Falkiner de Courcy, 2/Lt., d. of w., 25/10/14.

Royal Army Service Corps.

Abrams, Lawrence Golding, Lt. (Tp.), died, 3/11/18.
Acheson, Percival Havelock, Major, killed, 29/4/16.
Alves, Alexander, Lt. (Tp.), k. in a., 26/5/18.
Anderson, Alexander John, Major (T/Col.), died, 11/8/18.
Anderson, D., Lt. (Tp.), died, 4/5/18.
Anderson, Gordon Wright, Capt. (Tp.), died, 20/11/18.
406 Anderson, Robert Lionel, Lt., drowned, 7/11/18.
Austin, Stephen Phillip, Lt. (Tp.), d. of w., 27/9/18 (att. 7/Lanc. Fus.).
Avery, Sir William Eric Thomas, Bart., M.C., Major, died, 20/11/18 (att. Gds. Div. M.T. Coy.).
Bagley, Thomas William Ashton, Major (Tp.), died, 14/11/15.
197 Bagshaw, Henry Kenyon, Lt. (Tp.), k. in a., 13/4/18 (H.T., att. 1/7 W. Rid. R.).
Bannerman, Stanley Cyril Forster, Lt. (T/Capt.), d. of w., 7/11/17 (375 S.B. R.G.A.).
Barnard, Laurence Claude, Major (Tp.), died, 12/1/18.
Barnard, Robert Cyril, Lt. (Tp.), d. of w., 5/9/17.
Barnet, James Knox, Lt. (Tp.), died, 2/11/18 (M.T.).
Barnett, Bertram Leeds Thomas, Capt., died, 18/4/15.
Barratt, John Roland, Lt., died, 24/1/19.
Bartlett, Allan Owen, 2/Lt. (Tp.), killed, 16/10/18.
Bartlett, Howard John, Capt. (Tp.), died, 1/12/18.
Bassett, Geoffrey Edward, Lt., k. in a., 21/3/19.
Beart, Errol George Montague, 2/Lt. (Tp.), k. in a., 31/7/17 (att. 228 S.B.).
Beatty, William John, O.B.E., Major, died, 10/2/19.
Bell, Henry Oswin, Major (Tp.), died, 30/11/18.
Bentley, Leonard Holt, 2/Lt. (Tp.), died, 30/5/18.
56 Berry, William, 2/Lt. (Tp.), died, 4/7/17 (Div. Train).
Biggs, Seward, 2/Lt. (Tp.), died, 26/11/18.
Biscoe, Archibald Fairhead, Lt., died, 22/2/19.
Bishop, Colville Jones, Lt., died, 22/4/18.
Blackstock, John, 2/Lt. (Tp.), k. in a., 6/10/18.
Blight, Horace Vincent, M.C., Lt. (Tp.), k. in a., 15/6/18 (att. 4/R. Fus.).
Blonfield, William Henry, 2/Lt. (Tp.), d. of w., 26/10/17.
Borough, George Herbert, Capt. (Tp.), died, 7/11/16 (H.T. Aux. Co., att. Ind. C. Div.).
Bourne, Rowland Hurst, 2/Lt., k. in a., 24/10/18.
Bousfield, A. S., Lt. (Tp.), died, 28/6/18.
Bower, Maurice Sydercombe, Lt., died, 13/1/19.
Bown, Cecil Bertini Watkin, Lt. (Tp.), died, 20/3/17.
Boyden, A. Kingsley, Major, died, 14/2/19.
Brass, John, 2/Lt. (Tp.), died, 28/7/18 (H.T.).
Bridges, W., Capt., died, 25/1/19.
Briginshaw, Herbert William Oswald, Lt. (Tp.), died, 30/11/18.
Bromily, James, 2/Lt. (Tp.), killed, 28/6/18 (att. 391 S.B. Amm. Col.).
Bromley, John Ledger, Lt., died, 29/9/18 (and R.A.F.).
Brooke-Murray, Kenneth Algernon, Capt. (Tp.), d. of w., 23/9/16 (and R.F.C.).
Brown, Thomas Campbell, Lt. (Tp.), died, 17/12/17.
Brownson, Roger Dawson Duffield, Capt., died, 21/10/18.
Burditt, Stanley Wilbraham, T/Lt. (A/Capt.), d. of w., 1/10/17.
Burstall, John, Capt., died, 12/4/19.
Burtt, Edward, Lt. (Tp.), drowned, 13/8/15 (att. 18/Lab. Co.).
Bush, Charles Gerald, D.S.O., Major (Tp.), died, 26/11/18.
Caffrey, Charles James, Capt. (Tp.), died, 1/7/16.
Caley, Hugh William, Capt., died, 16/9/18.
4 Carlisle, Arthur Lewis, Capt., k. in a., 29/8/18 (8/Div. Train).
Carson, Murray, Capt. (Tp.), died, 20/4/17.
Carter, Alfred Cecil, Capt., died, 15/1/19.
Catmur, Graham Gunn, Capt., k. in a., 30/6/18.
Carter, John Lovelace, 2/Lt. (A/Capt.), died, 18/4/18.
Chapman, Raleigh George Aubrey, Lt., died, 1/3/19.
Chivers, Herbert, 2/Lt. (Tp.), died, 18/6/18.
Christie, Ronald, Lt. (A/Capt.), d. of w., 12/4/18.
Christie, William Edward Tolfrey, C.M.G., O.B.E., D.S.O., Major (T/Col.), died, 22/10/18.
Clancy, William John, 2/Lt., died, 16/10/18.
Clark, Charles Inglis, Capt., died, 6/3/18 (M.T.).
170 Clarke, Henry Colin, Capt. (Tp.), died, 25/5/16.
Clarkson, Leslie Cecil Bentinck, Capt., died, 31/3/17.
Clements, William Vincent, Lt., died, 28/2/19 (M.T.).
Cobb, John Elbridge, 2/Lt. (T/Lt.), d. of w., 14/8/17 (and R.F.C., 21 Sqd.).
1 Coburn, Frederick Isaac, Lt. (Tp.), died, 4/10/17 (Supply Coy.).
Collins, Harold George, Lt. (Tp.), k. in a., 9/4/17 (and R.F.C., 48 Sqd.).
Colvin, Kenneth Colquhoun, 2/Lt. (Tp.), died, 6/9/15 (att. 348 Co.).
Cooke, John Howard, Lt. (Tp.), died, 9/10/18.
Cooper, Francis Nicholas Nooth, Lt., k. in a., 21/11/17.
Cooper, George Frederick, 2/Lt. (Tp.), k. in a., 24/2/17.
Cooper, John Bruce, Capt. (Tp.), died, 21/11/15 (Capt. A.S.C., T.F.).
Cotton, Robert Hugh Alban, 2/Lt. (Tp.), died, 12/10/18.
Coulthard, Ernest, Lt. (Tp.), died, 12/11/18.
Courtney, Edward Derek, Lt., died, 9/8/18 (M.T. Coy.).
Courthope-Munroe, John Wilfrid, 2/Lt. (Tp.), died, 24/1/16.
Cowper-Coles, S. W., Capt., killed, 14/10/18 (and R.A.F.).
Cross, George Herbert, Capt. (Tp.), k. in a., 30/9/18 (att. 9/R. Ir. Fus.).
Crowther, Percy, Capt. (Tp.), died, 14/9/16.
Cussell, Stanley James, 2/Lt. (Tp.), k. in a., 29/5/18.
Cutler, Staurt Le Guyt, Lt. (T/Capt.), k. in a., 9/8/17 (and R.F.C., 21 Sqd.).
Danes, Thomas, 2/Lt. (Tp.), died, 13/11/18.
Davey, Wilfred Charles, Lt. (Tp.), d. of w., (att. R.F.C., 15 Sqd.).
Dendy, Ralph, M.C., Capt. (Tp.), k. in a., 15/10/18 (H.T.).
De Ste Croix, Wilfred Hungerford, 2/Lt. (Tp.), died, 24/7/17.
Dewhirst, Alfred Guy, 2/Lt. (Tp.), killed, 10/8/18.
Dilliway, George Goldin, T/Lt. (A/Capt.), died, 10/10/18.
Dodson, H. L. M., Lieut., k. in a., 25/8/18 (att. R.A.F.).
Dowse, Henry Harvey, 2/Lt., died, 10/11/18 (and R.A.F.).
Dowse, Robert Joseph Gordon, Lt. (T/Capt.), died, 19/12/18.
Drey, Adolph, M.C., Lt. (Tp.), died, 9/5/17 (and R.F.C., 58 Res. Sqd.).
Driver, Graham Dudley, Lt. (Tp.), died, 5/5/15.
Duncan, Herbert Richard, Lt., died, 26/4/19.
Dunlop, Harry Holmes Kerr, Lt., died, 12/2/19.
Durrad, Francis Albert, Capt., k. in a., 8/11/17 (and R.F.C., 22 Sqd.).
Eaton, John Rodman, Lt., d. of w., 8/9/17.
Edmands, Francis Douglas, 2/Lt. (Tp.), d. of w., 1/12/17 (M.T.).
Edwards, Cuthbert, Lt. (T/Capt.), d. of w., 17/4/18 (att. 7/R.W. Kent R.).
Edwards, Donald William, M.C., Capt., k. in a., 6/4/17 (att. R.F.C., 45 Sqd.).
Edwards, William, Capt. (Tp.), d. of w., 28/3/18.
Elphinstone, Montague, Major (Tp.), k. in a., 22/3/17 (att. R.F.C.).
English, Richard Cornforth, Lt. (Tp.), died, 25/7/16.
Estall, Arthur Cecil, Capt. (Tp.), d. of w., 8/8/17.
Evans, Leslie Morier, 2/Lt. (Tp.), k. in a., 12/11/17.
Evans, Samuel Houching, Major & Qr.-Mr., died, 7/7/17.
Everton, Walter Hassell, 2/Lt. (Tp.), died, 30/5/18 (att. Camel Transport).
Fairer-Smith, Aubrey, Lt. (Tp.), k. in a., 25/4/18 (att. 182 S.B.A.C.).
Fenner, Arthur, M.C., Lt. (T/Capt.), died, 20/11/18 (H.T., 25 Div. Trn.).
Findlater, Percival St. George, Capt. (Tp.), k. in a., 28/3/18.
Flaxman, Walter James, 2/Lt., died, 27/5/17.
Foord, George Howard, 2/Lt. (Tp.), d. of w., 13/10/15.
Foster, William Leo Gorrill, Capt. (Tp.), k. in a., 2/7/18.
142 Freeman, Herbert Joseph, Capt. (Tp.), d. of w., 29/10/18 (16 Div. Train).
French, John Lawson, Lt. (Tp.), died, 26/9/17 (1 Col. G.H.Q.).
Fuller, G. H., 2/Lt., died, 26/2/15.
Gale, Robert Grafton, Lt. (Tp.), k. in a., 24/4/18 (24 D.S.C.).
28 Geddes, Arthur Alexander, Capt. (Tp.), died, 5/7/16 (Motor Amb. Convoy).
George, L., Lt., died, 12/5/18 (and R.A.F.).
Gibbs, Stanley Gordon, Major, k. in a., 20/9/17 (D.A.Q.M.G., 1 Anzac Cps. H.Q.).
Gibbs, William Henry Herbert, M.C., 2/Lt. (Tp.), k. in a., 21/8/18.

Gibson, Arthur Ferral, Lt., died, 29/10/18 (14 Divn. Train).

Gill, William Hutton Pridmore, Capt. (Tp.), died, 26/1/17.

Glenn, Cecil William, Lt. (Tp.), k. in a., 28/1/17 (att. 1/R. Innis. Fus.).

Gloster, Francis Beresford, Lt., k. in a., 3/12/17 (and R.F.C., 20 Sqd.).

Godley, Gerald Annesley George, Lt., k. in a., 26/3/18 (15 Div. Train).

Golding, Harold William, Capt. (Tp.), k. in a., 31/10/18 (att. 8/Som. L.I.).

Goodyear, Frank Percy, 2/Lt., died, 8/2/19.

Grandin, Richard John, 2/Lt., k. in a., 18/5/17 (and R.F.C., 60 Sqd.).

Grant, Percy Kenmure, Lt. (Tp.), died, 6/11/18.

Gregory, John Sheridan, Capt. (Tp.), k. in a., 19/2/18 (att. R.F.C.).

Grove, John Archibald, Major (Tp.), k. in a., 10/8/18 (H.T.).

Growse, Robert Henry, Major, died, 12/2/19.

Hallowes, Alexander Boyle, 2/Lt. (Tp.), died, 31/5/17.

Hamilton, Robert Ainslie, Lt. (Tp.), k. in a., 28/3/18.

Harrington, E., Hon. Lt. & Qr.-Mr., died, 28/7/15.

Harris, William Robert, Capt., died, 15/2/19.

Hart, Albert, Lt. (Tp.), k. in a., 30/6/18.

Harte, Michael Joseph, Capt., k. in a., 21/3/18.

Hartree, Eric Mursell, Lt. (Tp.), k. in a., 8/8/18 (att. 8 R. Berk. R.).

Hay, Robert, Lt. (Tp.), died, 9/10/18.

Haynes, George John, Capt. (Tp.), died, 30/9/17.

Hazard, Douglas, Lt. (Tp.), d. of w., 17/10/18 (att. Mdx. R.).

Hedley, James Frederic, Lt. (Tp.), died, 13/1/16.

Hett, Rolan Thorston, Lt. (Tp.), d. of w., 26/10/16.

Heyman, John Henry, Lt. (Tp.), d. of w., 18/7/17.

Heywood, F. K., Lt., killed, 1/10/18 (and R.A.F.).

Hill, Brian Edward, Capt. (Tp.), d. of w., 2/10/18 (att. 1/Tank Corps).

Hinde, William Henry Rousseau, Lt. (T/Capt.), died, 22/10/18.

Hitner, Victor Jacob, Lt. (Tp.), died, 20/7/18 (att. Lab. Cps.).

Hodges, Edward Norman, M.C., Capt. (Tp.), died, 22/6/18.

Hole, Ernest George, 2/Lt. (Tp.), died, 10/12/18.

Hooley, Arthur Wellesley, M.C., Lt., died, 9/2/19.

Hope, Percy Beckett, Lt. (Tp.), died, 25/12/17.

Horsbrugh, Boyd Robert, Lt.-Col. (Tp.), died, 11/7/16.

Hotchkiss, Henry, Lt. (Tp.), died, 19/6/18 (M.T.).

Hubble, Frederick Richard, 2/Lt. (Tp.), died, 2/8/18 (M.T.).

Hulton, Alan Edward Grey, Lt. (Tp.), d. of w., 6/5/15.

Humphrey, Vincent Ernest, Lt. (Tp.), died, 26/10/18 (3/Army E.F.C.).

Humphreys, Roy, Lt., k. in a., 4/9/18.

Hunter, George Suart, Lt. (Tp.), d. of w., 10/11/18 (att. 13/Rif. Bde.).

Hutson, Douglas Bertram, Lt., died, 23/7/18.

Hyland, Albert Clive, Lt. (T/Capt.), d. of w., 10/8/18.

Jack, Thomas Barclay, Capt. (Tp.), d. of w., 24/8/18.

Jackson, Henry Medland, 2/Lt. (Tp.), k. in a., 19/9/18.

Jackson, Hamilton Ray, 2/Lt. (Tp.), d. of w., 26/7/17 (att. 245 S.B., R.G.A.).

Jackson, Theodore Walter, Capt. (Tp.), died, 4/10/18 (H.T.).

Janes, G. F., Hon. Major (T/Qr.-Mr.), died, 13/8/18.

Jennings, Hugh Cotton, 2/Lt., d. of w., 3/5/17 (P. of W.).

Johnson, Thomas Pelham, D.S.O., Lt.-Col., died, 12/6/18.

Johnston, David Ernest, 2/Lt. (Tp.), died, 12/11/17.

Jones, Charles Arnold, 2/Lt. (Tp.), d. of w., 1/5/18.

Jones, John Thomas, M.C., Capt. (Tp), died, 28/3/18.

Jones, Thomas Luke, 2/Lt. (Tp.), d. of w., 9/10/18.

Josephi, Ernest Henry, Lt. (Tp.), died, 23/1/17.

Judd, W. B., Major (Tp.), died, 2/2/18 (15 Div. Train).

Kauffman, Albert, 2/Lt. (Tp.), died, 17/10/18.

Kean, Francis John, Lt. (Tp.), d. of w., 25/11/18.

Kelleher, Bartholomew, Lt. (Tp.), k. in a., 27/9/18.

Kemish, Charles, Lt. & Qr.-Mr., k. in a., 14/7/15 (Advanced Horse Transport).

Kemp, Kenneth Reginald Flint, 2/Lt. (Tp.), died, 18/10/18.

Kenny, John Mary Joseph, Lt. (Tp.), k. in a., 23/9/16 (and R.F.C.).

Kerr, Leslie Henry Fox, Lt. (Tp.), died, 24/11/16 (9 Div. Train).

Kipps, George Stewart, Lt. (Tp.), k. in a., 22/8/18 (att. 4/Batt. Worc. R.).

Kirwan, Theodore, 2/Lt. (A/Capt.), died, 11/6/19.

Lacey, Frank Philip Sleigh, 2/Lt. (Tp.), died, 29/3/18 (M.T.).

Lakeman, Harold Leslie, 2/Lt. (Tp.), k. in a., 22/8/18 (att. 7/Lanc. Fus.).

4 Lambert, John Lewis, Major (Tp.), died, 20/10/16 (Army Aux. Horse Co.).

Lawler, Lionel Alfred Ballantyne, 2/Lt., died, 8/3/19.

Leighton, Archibald, Capt. (Tp.), k. in a., 2/9/18 (att. 1/5 Lond. R.).

Lewis, Charles, Hon. Lt. & Qr.-Mr., died, 14/6/17.

Lewis, Cecil Hallowes, Major, died, 28/5/15.

917 Lewis, Herbert, 2/Lt., drowned, 5/5/17 (M.T. Co.).

Lindsay, Courtenay Traice, Lt. (Tp.), died, 28/4/16.

Lindsay, James Basden, 2/Lt. (Tp.), died, 8/8/18 (Base Supply Dep.).

Line, Eric Alfred Thiselton, 2/Lt. (Tp.), died, 16/12/16 (26 Div. Train).

Livingstone, Frank Darley, Capt. (Tp.), d. of w., 22/3/18.

Lloyd, Thomas Richard Beamish, 2/Lt. (Tp.), died, 20/2/16.

Longton, John, Lt., k. in a., 31/7/17 (and R.F.C., 4 Sqd.).

Louis, Gerald John, Capt. (Tp.), d. of w., 23/5/16.

Lowther, Rowland, T/Capt. (A/Major), died, 10/11/18 (M.T.).

Lucas, Sidney Richard, 2/Lt., died, 6/11/18.

Lund, William Bullen, Lt. (Tp.), drowned, 13/8/15.

Lyte, Owen Nevill, Lt. (Tp.), died, 31/10/18.

McCann, Francis, Lt. & Qr.-Mr., d. of w., 27/1/16.

McFarlane, George, Capt. & Qr.-Mr., died, 23/9/17.

MacGregor, Rhoderic, 2/Lt., d. of w., 23/7/17 (Spec. Res.).

Macrae, Charles Alexander, Lt. (Tp.), died, 22/4/16.

3 Macrae, William Charles Macintyre, Lt. (A/Capt.), k. in a., 27/9/18 (14 Div. Train.).

Manby-Colgrave, Gerard Thomas, Lt. (Tp.), d. of w., 21/4/17 (att. 221 S.B. R.G.A.).

692 Manners, Cecil Frederick, 2/Lt. (Tp.), died, 17/6/17 (M.T.C.).

Marsh, P. E. G., M.C., Capt., killed, 20/12/18 (and R.A.F.).

Mascall-Thompson, Cecil, Capt. (Tp.), died, 21/1/16.

Matheson, Archibald Angus, 2/Lt. (Tp.), died, 20/12/17.

Matteson, Leonard, Major, died, 11/4/16 (Spec. Res.).

Matthews, Henry Aylmer Vallance, M.C., T/Capt. (A/Major), died, 8/11/18 (M.T.).

Matthews, Leonard Mansfield, Lt. (Tp.), died, 25/6/18 (M.T.).

Mayne, George Rufane Talbot, M.C., Lt. (Tp.), d. of w., 10/11/18.

Mercer, William, M.B.E., Lt. (Tp.), died, 13/11/18.

Meyers, H. Deverell, Capt. (Tp.), died, 30/10/18.

Mills, John, Hon. Lt. & Qr.-Mr., died, 11/8/14.

Morgan, John William Moore, D.S.O., Lt.-Col., died, 31/3/17.

Morphy, Arthur Albert, T/Lt. (2/Lt.), d. of w., 29/11/17.

Morris, Hugh Anthony, Lt. (Tp.), died, 18/10/17.

Morris, Thomas Ernest, Lt. & Qr.-Mr., died, 9/1/16.

Moss, John Miles, 2/Lt. (Tp.), died, 6/9/15.

Mudie, Harold Bolingbroke, Capt. (Tp.), died, 6/1/16.

Muir, Burleigh Leycester, Capt. (Tp.), died, 4/11/18 (att. 3 Corps H.Q.).

3 Musgrave, Cecil David, Capt. (Tp.), died, 15/11/18 (8 Div. Train).

Nayler, Frederick Augustus, 2/Lt., died, 20/10/18.

Nelson, Richard Owen, Lt. (T/Capt.), drowned, 4/5/17.

Newbery, Gilbert Leonard, 2/Lt. (Tp.), d. of w., 12/11/17.

Noakes, Stuart Bertram, Capt., drowned, 30/12/17 (M.T.).

Norie-Miller, Claud, 2/Lt. (Tp.), drowned, 4/5/17.

Norton, Clement Edgar, 2/Lt. (Tp.), died, 10/10/18.

Noverre, Arthur Kerr, Major, died, 18/4/18 (6 Div. A/C.).

Nuttall, Harry Norbury, 2/Lt. (Tp.), d. of w., 5/7/17.

Oakeley, William Soulden, Major (Tp.), died, 11/9/18 (M.T.).

Ogilvie, Alexander Walter, Lt. (Tp.), d. of w., 30/10/18.

Olsen, Soren Bendix, Capt. (Tp.), died, 20/4/18.

Openshaw, Geoffrey Ormerod, Capt. (Tp.), d. of w., 9/8/18 (P. of W.). att 2 Devons

Ovenden, Herbert Stephen, Lt. & Qr.-Mr., died, 3/9/16.

Oxlade, Stanley, 2/Lt. (Tp.), drowned, 4/5/17.

Packham, Eric Frank, 2/Lt., d. of w., 1/11/18 (att. 2/Hampshire R.).

Partridge, Oswald, 2/Lt., died, 22/10/18.

Pavitt, Charles Frederick, Capt., died, 17/8/18.

Payne, Albert James, 2/Lt. (Tp.), died, 27/3/18.

Payne, Charles Arthur Frank, 2/Lt., died, 15/10/18.

Pearce, Arthur Carlton, Lt., k. in a., 22/7/18 (att. 5/N. & D.R.).

Pearson, Bertram Walter Mockley, Capt., died, 25/10/18.

Pearson, F. S., Lt.-Col., died, 5/9/16.

Pearson, Joseph Sykes, Lt. (A/Capt.), died, 7/11/18 (M.T.).

Penton, E. G., Lt., died, 29/5/18.

Phare, Dudley Gershom, Lt., k. in a., 28/3/18.

Philcox, Percy Vivian, 2/Lt., k. in a., 1/11/18.

Phillippo, Arthur James Cecil Eyre, Lt., k. in a., 7/6/17 (att. R.F.C.).

Pibel, Leo Maxse, 2/Lt. (Tp.), drowned, 15/4/17.

Pitcairn, Hugh Francis, 2/Lt. (Tp.), died, 3/6/17.

Posford, Benjamin Ashwell, 2/Lt., d. of w., 25/2/15.

Powell, Patrick John Gordon, Lt., k. in a., 2/4/17 (att. R.F.C.).

Proctor, L. H., Lt., killed, 17/11/18 (and R.A.F.).

Puckle, John, D.S.O., Lt.-Col., drowned, 15/4/17.

Purser, Philip Addison, Lt. (Tp.), d. of w., 30/4/16.

Rae, William Kenneth, 2/Lt. (Tp.), died, 8/11/18.

Ralli, Leonidas Lucas, Capt. (Tp.), died, 24/4/17.

Ramsay, Alexander Charles Marquis, Lt., died, 18/12/14.

Ransome, Bertram Coleby, Lt. (Tp.), died, 30/6/18 (M.T.).

Ray, Richard, 2/Lt. (Tp.), d. of w., 26/5/18 (M.T.).

Reidy, Harold St. John, Capt. (Tp.), died, 19/10/18.

Renton, Elwyn George, Lt. (Tp.), died, 29/5/18.

Reynolds, Percy Basil, Capt. (Tp.), died, 4/12/18.

Richardson, George Sydney, T/Lt. (A/Capt.), k. in a., 20/5/18.

Ricketts, Clyde Robert, Lt. (Tp.), died, 11/10/18.

Riley, George Harold, Lt., k. in a. 21/8/18.

Robb, Harold Brindley, Lt. (Tp.), died, 2/1/17.

Roger, Edward James Pringle, 2/Lt. (Tp.), k. in a., 19/7/18.

Rolfe, Philip, Capt. (Tp.), k. in a., 24/8/18 (att. 7/Norf. R.).

Rowles, Stanley Walter, Lt. (Tp.), d. of w., 13/12/17 (and R.F.C.).

Rundle, Stanley, Lt. (Tp.), d. of w., 30/4/18 (P. of W.).

Rusbridge, Robert Thomas Smith, Lt. (Tp.), died, 11/11/18 (55 Div. Supply Column).

Sampson, Hugh Delaine, 2/Lt. (Tp.), d. of w., 2/9/17.

Samuel, A. D., 2/Lt. (Tp.), died, 19/5/18.

Saner, Hubert Evelyn, Capt. (Tp.), died, 17/11/18.

Scales, Edwin Herbert, Lt., d. of w., 11/10/18.

Scott, William McDougall Woodward, Lt. (Tp.), died, 2/9/18.

Searle, Percy, 2/Lt., died, 21/2/19.

Seddon, Max Hugo, Lt. (Tp.), d. of w., 4/11/18.

Selby-Lowndes, Richard Cecil Williams, Lt. (Tp.), died, 11/7/18.

Selwyn, A. H., 2/Lt., died, 25/1/15.

Shipp, Robert Cyril, Lt., died, 11/1/18.

Simpson, Arthur Ernest, 2/Lt., T/Lt., killed, 25/1/15.

Smith, Geoffrey Cholerton, M.C., 2/Lt., T/Lt., k. in a., 31/7/17 (and R.F.C.).

Smith, Norman Spires, Lt., died, 1/2/19.

Smith, William Roy, Lt. (Tp.), killed in a., 24/3/18 (att. 8/R.W. Surr. R.).
Smyth, Arthur Hugo, 2/Lt. (Tp.), k. in a., 13/3/18.
Snyders, Emanuel Leon, 2/Lt., k. in a., 17/3/19.
Spanton, Cyril Holtby, 2/Lt. (Tp.), died, 23/11/18.
Spurgeon, Percival, Capt. (Tp.), d. of w., 18/5/18 (att. 7/R.W. Surr. R.).
Stephens, Kyrle Nalder, 2/Lt. (Tp.), died, 31/12/17.
Stewart, Vernon Radcliffe, Lt., killed, 5/12/17 (att. R.F.C., 19 Sq.).
Strauss, Victor Arthur, Lt., k. in a., 27/11/16 (and R.F.C.).
Stretch, Thomas Noel Heath. M.C., T/Lt., k. in a., 25/3/18 (and M.G.C.).
Stringer, Frederick William, Lt.-Col. (Tp.), died, 30/6/16.
Sudell, Henry James, Capt. (Tp.), d. of w., 28/8/15.
Swain, Ernest George, 2/Lt., died, 4/5/15.
Swann, George William, Lt., d. of w., 24/3/17 (att. R.F.C., 70 Sqd.)
Tarr, Henry Charles Hardman, 2/Lt., died, 2/2/19.
Taylor, Charles Manners, 2/Lt. (Tp.), k. in a., 9/4/18.
Taylor, George Stanley, 2/Lt., drowned, 4/5/17.
Taylor, Walter, 2/Lt (Tp.), died, 17/7/18.
482 Taylor, William Edward, 2/Lt. (T/Lt.), drowned, 2/6/17.
Tempest, Oswald Aldam, Lt., k. in a., 28/3/18
Thacker, Herbert Lane, 2/Lt., drowned, 15/4/17.
Thwaites, Guy, D.S.O., Major, died, 30/5/17.
Tobin-Willis, John Galbraith, 2/Lt., k. in a., 17/8/17 (att. R.F.C.).
Torbit, James, Lt. (Tp.), died, 10/9/18.
Treliving, Walter Hicks, 2/Lt. (Tp.), died, 11/10/18.
Trevelyan, Walter Raleigh, Capt. (Tp.), died, 19/4/16.
Tozer, John Henry Wallace, Lt. (Tp.), died, 3/8/17.
Trousdell, Maurice George. Capt. (Tp.), k. in a., 6/8/17 (Gds. Divl. Train.).
Truman, Thomas Archibald, 2/Lt. (Tp.), died, 17/9/18 (56 Div. Train.).
Unwin, Ernest Frederick, Major (Tp.), died, 22/3/16 (and R.F.C.).
Vincent, S., 2/Lt. (Tp.), died, 28/3/18 (M.T.).
Walker, Lewis Aubrey, 2/Lt. (Tp.), k. in a., 6/8/17.
Wallis, Bertram Henry, M.C., Capt., k. in a., 18/9/18.
Walrond, Hon William Lionel Charles, Lt. (Tp.), died, 2/11/15.
Ward, Walter Wallace, Capt., died, 28/10/18.
Warwick, Douglas Charles, M.C., Major, died, 20/1/19 (att. M.G.C.).
Watson, William Stanley, Capt., d. of w., 11/8/18
Wells, Frederick Neville, Lt., died, 7/11/18.
Wells, Herman Theodore, 2/Lt. (Tp.), died, 2/4/16 (M.T.).
Wheelhouse, George William, 2/Lt. (Tp.), died, 6/7/17.
White, Alfred William, Lt., died, 13/4/19 (M.T.).
Whiteside, Robert Borras. Capt., died, 20/4/15.
Wildblood, William Arthur, Lt. (Tp.), k. in a., 16/6/17 (24 Div. Train.).
Wilks, Percy Walter, 2/Lt., drowned, 10/10/18.
Williams, Colin Ernest, 2/Lt. (Tp.), k. in a., 17/10/17.
Williams, Richard Harte Keatings, Capt. (Bt.-Major), d. of w., 12/12/16.
Willmott, Albert McKenzie, Lt., died, 11/2/19.
Wilson, Geoffrey, Lt., died, 15/5/18 (and R.A.F.).
Wilson, William George, 2/Lt., died, 3/5/18 (M.T.).
Wilton, Ernest Parkin, Lt (Tp.), died, 5/11/18.
Worsley, Richard Stanley, D.S.O., Major (Bt.-Lt.-Col.), drowned, 4/5/17.
Wright, George Edward, M.C., 2/Lt., k. in a., 9/10/18.
Young, Frederick Sydney Newman, Capt. (A/Major), died, 1/3/18.
Young, George Minchin, Capt., died, 10/3/16.

Royal Army Medical Corps.

V.C. Ackroyd, Harold, M.C., Capt. (Tp.), k. in a., 11/8/17 (att. 6/R. Berks. R.).
Acland, John Henry Dyke, Capt. (Tp.), k. in a., 12/7/16 (att. 1/Som. L.I.).
Adams, George Gordon Crymole, Lt., died, 9/3/18.
Addey-Jibb, Arthur Harwood, Lt. & Qr.-Mr., d. of w., 12/4/18 (att. 94/F.A.).
Aitken, Robert, Capt., died, 17/1/19.
Allen, Wellesley Roe, Capt., died, 11/3/19 (att. 2 Ech.).
Almond, George Hely Hutchinson, Capt. (Tp.), k. in a., 9/8/18.
Anderson, David, Lt. (Tp.), died, 13/9/17 (37 M.A.C., att. 4 S.H.).
Anderson, George Grantham, Capt. (Tp.) (A/Major), died, 3/11/18 (att. 51 G.H.).
Alston, John, Capt., k. in a., 16/10/17.
Atkinson, Ambrose, Lt. (Tp.), died, 7/7/17 (att. 3/Suff. R.).
Atkinson, Charles Mason, Lt. (Tp.), k. in a., 9/8/17 (14/F.A., T.C.) (att. 1/Norfolk R.).
Atkinson, George Louis, Capt. (Tp.), drowned, 20-21/3/17.
Armour, Robert Stanley, Capt. (Tp.), died, 1/12/18.
Armstrong, Arthur Keith, Capt., d. of w., 15/9/14.
Armstrong, James Noble, Lt. (Tp.), k. in a., 22/8/15 (att. 2/D.L.I.).
Armstrong, Walter Seymour, Capt. (Tp.), died, 31/5/16 (att. Mhow Ind. Cav. Fd. Amb.).
Austin, John Henry Edward, Col., died, 26/4/17.
Ball, Charles Bent, Sir, Bart., Lt.-Col., died, 17/3/16.
Ball, Malcolm Edward, Lt., d. of w., 10/4/16 (att. 9/Worc. R.).
Ball, William Ormsby Wyndham, Lt., k. in a., 25/9/14.
Bampton, James Henry, Capt. (Tp.), d. of w., 25/8/17 (att. 70 Bde., R.F.A.).
Barr, George Fleet, Capt. (Tp.), died, 23/3/16 (att. 42 F.A.).
Barr, Hugh, Capt. (Tp.), died, 21/2/17 (att. 42 Amb. Tonga Train).
Bassett, Robert John, Lt. (Tp.), drowned, 10/12/18.
Batchelor, Henry Washington, Capt. (Tp.), k. in a., 24/3/18 (att. 43 F.A.).
Bateman, Arthur Cyril, M.C., Capt., k. in a., 28/3/18 (att. 7 Cam. High.).
Beattie, James Walker, Capt. (Tp.), died, 23/7/18.
Bell, Edward Augustine, Capt. (T/Hon.), drowned, 11/7/16 (att. 5/B.R.X. Hpl.).
Bell, John Cunningham, Lt. (Tp.), died, 22/11/15 (att. 7/R. Scots).
Bell, Thomas Henry Stanley, Capt., k. in a., 1/10/15 (Spec. Res.).
Berry, Percy Haycraft, Lt., drowned, 10/3/16 (att. Berks. Yeo.).
Beveridge, James O'Shaughnessy, Capt., d. of w., 22/11/17 (att. 137 F.A.).
Bingham, John Warnock, Capt., died, 10/3/19.
Birrell, William George, Major-Gen., died, 23/8/18.
Black, James Elliott, M.C., Capt., k. in a., 19/4/17 (att. 8/Bed. R.).
Blake, Cecil, Lt. (Tp.), died, 30/10/18.
Blandy, Gurth Swinnerton, M.C., Capt. (Tp.), d. of w., 24/4/17.
Bond, Cecil William, Capt., k. in a., 2/8/17 (att. 97/F.A.).
Booth, Ainslie, Lt. (Tp.), d. of w., 30/4/16 (att. 7/K.O.S.B.).
Bower, William Charles Ernest, Lt. (Tp.), k. in a., 19/10/16 (att. 1/Newfoundland R.).
Boyd, Thomas Moffatt, Lt. (Tp.), died, 25/10/18.
Boyers, Edwin, Capt. (Tp.), died, 25/10/18.
Bradley, Frederick Hoysted, D.S.O., Capt. (A/Lt.-Col.), k. in a., 22/9/18 (att. 15/F.A.).
Breen, Thomas Francis Pennefather, Capt. (A/Major), k. in a., 18/9/18 (att. 142/F.A.).
Bridges, Roland Harley, D.S.O., Major (A/Lt.-Col.), died, 22/8/18.
Brogden, Ingram Richard Rhodes, Lt. (Tp.), drowned, 15/4/17.
Brooke, Frederick Arthur John Robertson, Capt. (Tp.), k. in a., 27/5/18 (att. 1/Wilts R.).
Broughton, Norman Walford, D.S.O., Capt. (Tp.), k. in a., 9/9/16 (att. 73 Bde., R.F.A.).
Brown, Ian Macdonald, Capt. (Tp.), k. in a., 15/11/16 (att. 190/Bde., R.F.A.).
Brown, James Turner, Lt. (Tp.), drowned, 4/5/17.
Brown, John Ritchie, Lt. (Tp.), d. of w., 7/11/16.
Brown, William Elmer, Lt. (Tp.), d. of w., 18/5/18 (att. 10/F.A.).
Brown, Wilfred Stephenson, Capt., died, 27/3/19 (19 C.C.S).
Browne, Bernard Score, M.C., Capt. (Tp.), k. in a., 15/4/18.
Brownlie, William, M.C., Capt. (Tp.), k. in a., 25/3/18 (att. 13/York. R.).
Brunton, Edward Henry Pollock, Lt. (Tp.), k. in a., 8/10/15 (att. 4/Gren. Gds.).
Bulkeley, Llewelyn Alfred Henry, Capt. (Tp.), k. in a., 10/4/18 (att. 15/Chesh. R.).
Bullock, Arthur Ernest, Capt. (Tp.), k. in a., 26/9/15 (att. 4/Middx. R.).
Burges, James Alexander Stewart, Lt. (Tp.), d. of w., 23/4/17 (att. 49/F.A.).
Burke, John, Capt., died, 21/12/18.
Burnett, Maurice, Lt., k. in a., 14/4/15.
Burns, Digby, Capt. (Tp.), drowned, 10/10/18.
Burrell, Stanley Walter, Lt. (Tp.), died, 22/7/16.
Burrows, Donald, Capt. (Tp.) (A/Major), died, 7/11/18.
Butt, John Gillis, Lt., k. in a., 29/10/14.
Byatt, Harry Vivian Byatt, Capt., k. in a., 14/3/15 (att. 2/Rif. Bde.).
Campbell, Archibald Thomson, Capt. (Tp.), died, 22/2/16.
Campbell, Charles Montage Gordon, Capt., died, 19/12/18.
Campbell, Donald, Lt., k. in a., 17/2/15 (att. E. Yorks).
Campbell, William, M.C., Capt. (Tp.), k. in a., 5/9/16 (att. R.F.A.).
Carrington, Edward Worrell, Capt. (Tp.), k. in a., 27/9/15.
Carson, Herbert William, D.S.O., Capt. (A/Major), died, 12/10/18.
Carson, James Arthur Balfour, Capt., died, 9/8/18.
Cattanach, John, Lt. (Tp.), d. of w., 27/7/15 (att. 9/R. War. R.).
Cesari, Sydney Fraser McAlpine, Capt., k. in a., 3/10/15 (6th F.A.).
Chaning-Pearce, Wilfred Thomas, M.C., Capt. (Tp.), k. in a., 1/10/17 (att. 18/K. L'pool R.).
Chapman, George Martin, Lt., k. in a., 13/5/15.
Charles, John Percival, M.C., Capt. (Tp.), died, 6/10/17 (att. 1/1 Herts R.).
Chavasse, Arthur Ryland, Capt. (Tp.), died, 12/3/16.
Chissell, George Edwin, M.C., Capt. (Tp.), d. of w., 29/10/17.
Chisnall, George Henry, Lt., d. of w., 24/10/14.
Clark, Allan La Barte, Capt., k. in a., 18/9/18.
Clark, Robert, Capt. (Tp.), d. of w., 7/11/18 (att. 20/Huss.).
Clark, William Brown, Capt. (Tp.), k. in a., 12/3/17 (att. Scots Gds.).
Clarke, Austin Basil, M.C., Capt., k. in a., 23/11/17 (att. 1/9 Lond. R.).
Clarke, Ian Alexander, Capt. (Tp.), k. in a., 16/11/16 (att. 1/Dorsets).
Cleland, Frank Lee, Capt. (Tp.), d. of w., 5/7/16.
Cocks, John Stanley, Capt., died, 29/1/19.
Cohen, Aaron Simeon, Lt., k. in a., 25/9/15 (att. 8/Som. L.I.).

Cohen, Benjamin, Lt. (Tp.), d. of w., 3/7/17 (att. 122 Bde., R.F.A.).
Collins, Reginald Thomas, D.S.O., Major (T/Lt.-Col.), k. in a., 18/9/18 (att. 17/F.A.).
Compton, William Henry, Capt., died, 6/12/18.
Connell, Harry Bertram, Lt.-Col., d. of w., 16/11/16.
Connolly, James Harris, Capt. (Tp.), died, 23/10/18.
Conyngham, Cecil Allan Taylor, Capt., k. in a., 4/11/14.
Cotterill, Denis, Capt. (Tp.), died, 2/12/18 (att. 20/C.C.S.).
Cowe, Archibald, Capt. (Tp.), k. in a., 2/12/17 (att. 2/Linc. R.).
Cowper, Geoffrey Moore, Capt. (Tp.), d. of w., 3/10/18.
Craig, Thomas Forrest, Capt. (Tp.), died, 2/2/18.
Crocket, John, Lt., k. in a., 25/9/14.
Crockett, Laurence Charles, Capt., died, 17/10/18 (att. from S.L. Dental Surg.).
Crole, David Clement, Capt. (Tp.), k. in a., 23/3/18 (att. 19/Huss.).
Cropper, John, Lt. (Tp.), drowned, 21/11/16.
Cross, John, Capt. (Tp.), died, 21/7/18.
Cross, Solomon, Capt. (Tp.), k. in a., 22/3/18 (att. 11/Suff R.).
Crow, Henry Paterson, Capt, died, 9/11/18.
Crymble, William, Capt., died, 12/10/16.
Cunnington, Edward Charles, Capt. (Tp.), k. in a., 23/3/18 (att. 95/F.A.).
Curling, Edward Charles James, Lt. & Qr.-Mr., died, 2/5/17 (att. 133/F.A.).
Dalby, Herbert Ernest, Major, died, 14/10/17.
Dalton, Charles, Lt.-Col., d. of w., 18/9/14.
Daly, Thomas, C.M.G., Colonel, died, 15/4/17.
Danbridge, William Leslie, Lt., d. of w., 5/10/18 (att. 103 F.A.).
Danzig, Morris William, Lt. (Tp.), drowned, 15/4/17.
Davies, Frederick Charles, Capt. (Tp.), k. in a., 17/10/17 (att. 9/North Fus.).
Davidson, James, Capt., k. in a., 30/11/17 (att. 10/K.R.R.C.).
Deane, Ernest Cotton, M.C., Capt., k. in a., 25/9/18 (att. 2/Leic. R.).
Deans, William Wilkie, Capt. (Tp.), d. of w., 4/1/16 (att. 54 Bde., R.F.A.).
Deighton, John, Capt., d. of w., 20/9/16 (att. 5/Roy. Lanc. Regt.).
Delamere, Percy Herbert, Capt. (Tp.), died, 23/2/18.
Dewar, George, Lt. (Tp.), k. in a., 3/2/16 (att. 48 F.A.).
Dold, Cedric Lewis, M.C., Capt. (Tp.), k. in a., 5/10/18 (att. 1/S.W. Bdrs.).
Donaldson, James, Capt. (Tp.), died, 5/12/18.
Downie, James Maitland, Capt., died, 28/10/18.
Duffy, Joseph Vincent, Capt. (Tp.), died, 7/12/18.
Duggan, Charles William, Major, drowned, 10/10/18.
Duheaume, Herbert Thomas, Capt. (Tp.), died, 5/8/16.
Duncan, Emile Horace George, Capt. (Tp.), died, 28/10/16.
Duncan, Ronald Wingrave, Capt., k. in a., 9/3/16 (att. Leic. R.).
Dundon, James St. John, Lt. (Tp.), died, 17/6/16.
Dunkerley, Harold, Capt. (Tp.) (A/Major), d. of w., 23/3/18 (att. 95 F.A.).
Dunlop, George Harry Melville, Major (Tp.), died, 3/7/16.
Dunn, Arthur Gibson, Lt. (Tp.), k. in a., 5/9/17.
Dwyer, James Jameson, D.S.O., Capt., died, 19/2/19.
East, Gordon Doulton, Lt. (T/Capt.), k. in a., 30/7/17 (att. 3/Gren. Gd.).
Eccles, Horace Dorset, Capt., k. in a., 16/8/17 (att. 13/R. Ir. Rfls.).
Edmond, John Adamson, Capt., k. in a., 30/11/17 (att. 60/F.A.).
Edwards, Alfred Cecil, M.C., Capt. (Tp.), d. of w., 25/7/17 (att. 1/4 K.O.Y.L.I.).
Elliot, Edward John, Capt., k. in a., 23/5/18 (att. 10/Sty. Hpl.).
Ellison, Samuel Charles, Lt. (Tp.), died, 17/7/17.
Elmes, King, Capt. (Tp.), k. in a., 28/9/18 (att. 2/16 Lon. R.).
Enright, Thomas Louis, Capt. (Tp.), died, 19/3/18.
Esmonde, John Joseph, Capt. (Tp.), died, 17/4/15.
Evans, Edward, Lt. (Tp.), k. in a., 9/4/17 (att. 10/Roy. Welsh Fus.).
Evans, Hugh Arthur, Lt. (Tp.), died, 3/6/15.
Evans, William Jones, Capt. (Tp.), d. of w., 13/9/17 (att. 2/1 S. Mid. F.A.).
Evans, William Laurence, Lt. (Tp.), k. in a., 11/8/16 (att. 1/6 L'pool R.).
Evatt, James Millar, Capt., k. in a., 21/3/18 (att. 330/Bde. R.F.A.).
Ewing, James, Capt., d. of w., 12/4/17 (att. 8/R.W. Fus.).
Fairley, James Fairburn, Capt. (Tp.), died, 9/11/15 (att. 11/G.H.).
Farrar, William Watt, Lt. (Tp.), died, 10/8/16.
Faulks, Edgar, Lt. (Tp.), d. of w., 26/9/15 (att. 95/Bde. R.F.A.).
Fayle, Barcroft Joseph Leech, Capt., k. in a., 24/10/16 (att. 2/W. York. R.).
Fehily, Thomas, Capt. (Tp.), k. in a., 13/4/18 (att. 2/R. Fus.).
Ferguson, George Douglas, D.S.O., Capt. (Tp.), d. of w., 23/4/17 (att. 27/Bde. R.F.A.).
Ferguson, James McKee, Capt. (Tp.), k. in a., 22/12/17 (att. 6/Connaught Rangers).
Ferguson, John, Capt., k. in a., 30/11/17 (att. 12/L'pool R.).
Field, Hassel Dyer, Capt. (Tp.), d. of w., 28/9/17 (att. 134/F.A.).
Field, Stephen, Capt., died, 10/4/15 (in enemy hands).
Fischel, Claude Henry, Capt., k. in a., 14/9/18 (att. 7/Leics.).
Fisher, Arthur Maxwell, Capt. (Tp.), k. in a., 12/10/17.
Flanigan, Edmund Hughes, Lt., died, 17/6/16.
Fleming, Charles Christie, D.S.O., Col., d. of w., 24/12/17 (A.D.M.S., 51 Div. Staff).
Fleming, Charles Elphinstone, Major, died, 2/3/15.
Fleming, Geoffrey Mason, Lt., k. in a., 16/6/15.
Fletcher, Guy Verney, Lt., died, 24/4/16 (att. 19/Div. Amb.).
Foott, Alexander Boyd, Capt., died, 21/7/18 (att. 49/F.A.).
Foreman, John Eugene, Lt. (Tp.), died, 9/7/17.
Forrest, Frank, Capt., d. of w., 13/9/14.
Forrest, Thomas, Lt., died, 28/5/18 (att. Patiala Lancers).
Forrester, James David, Capt. (Tp.), k. in a., 15/11/16 (att. Roy. Naval Div.).
Fortune, John, Capt. (Tp.), died, 27/12/18 (att. 27/C.C.S.).
Foster, Norman Kessen, Capt. (Tp.), died, 2/12/18.
Fox, Arthur Clause, D.S.O., Lt.-Col., drowned, 15/4/17.
Frere, Frederick John Henry Tobias, M.C., Capt., k. in a., 10/6/17 (att. 6/Linc. R.).
Frew, Daird Thomas Crichton, Capt. (Tp.), died, 29/9/16 (att. 2/R. Ir. R.).
Frew, John William, M.C., Capt. (Tp.), d. of w., 8/10/18 (att. 2/3 W. Rid. F.A.).
Fry, John Thomas, Lt. and Qr.-Mr., died, 3/10/15.
Fry, Walter Burgess, Major, died, 17/3/15 (in Ger. hands).
Furness, James Collins, Lt.-Col., k. in a., 26/2/18.
Gage, John Munro, Capt. (Tp.), died, 29/11/18.
Garbutt, James Reston Gardiner, Lt. (Tp.), k. in a., 1/12/15 (att. 8/K. Own Sco. Bdrs.).
Gardner, Alfred Linton, Capt. (Tp.), k. in a., 9/4/18 (att. 4/N. Staff. R.).
Garrett, Dalton Gilbert Knox, Lt., k. in a., 30/9/18 (att. 133/F.A.).
Garrod, Alfred Noel, Lt. (Tp.), k. in a., 25/1/16 (att. 100/F.A.).
Gaston, James, M.C., Capt. (Tp.), d. of w., 5/11/18 (att. 4/Suff. R.).
Gatchell, James Harcourt Cecil, M.C., Capt. (Tp.), k. in a., 27/9/17.
Gaunt, Eric Thomas, Capt., k. in a., 9/10/17.
Gavin, Neil Murphy, Lt. (Tp.), died, 12/3/16.
Gavin, Noel John Hay, M.C., Capt. (Tp.), died, 2/11/17.
German, Frederic Francis, Capt. (Tp.), died, 27/3/16.
German, Hugh Bernard, M.C., Capt. (Tp.) (A/Major), k. in a., 18/9/18 (att. 17/F.A.).
Gibson, Harold, D.S.O., Capt., d. of w., 17/10/17 (att. 71/F.A.).
Gibson, Howard Greame, Major, died, 12/2/19.
Glanvill, Ernest Mure, Capt., k. in a., 2/11/14.
Glenny, Ernest Howard, Lt., died, 9/10/18.
Golding, Thomas James, Lt. (T/Capt.), k. in a., 26/9/17.
Goodden, Henry William, Lt., k. in a., 9/5/15.
Gough, Bernard Bradley, Lt. (Tp.), k. in a., 17/2/16 (att. 8/South Staffs R.).
Graham, George Stanley, Lt. (Tp.), died, 19/6/16.
Grant, George Leonard, Capt. (Tp.), k. in a., 11/10/15 (att. Lond. Scottish).
Green, Philip Sydney, Capt. (Tp.), died, 13/11/18.
Gregory, James Alfred, Lt. (Tp.), d. of w., 13/4/17 (att. 52/F.A., 12/Manch. R.).
Grier, William, Lt. (Tp.), drowned, 15/4/17.
Griffiths, John Neville, Capt. (Tp.), k. in a., 30/11/17 (att. 58/H.A.G.).
Guthrie, George Watson, Lt. (Tp.), k. in a., 13/11/16 (R.N. Div.).
Guthrie, Thomas Errol, Capt., k. in a., 3/7/16 (att. N.Z. Med. Corps).
Gwynne, John Fitzgerald, Capt., k. in a., 9/7/15.
Gyllencreutz, James Randolph, T/Major, drowned, 10/4/17.
Hairsine, Owen, M.C., Lt. (T/Capt.), k. in a., 7/6/17.
Hall, David Henry, Capt. (Tp.), d. of w., 14/5/18.
Hall, Harry Spencer, Lt., died, 14/3/15.
Hallaran, William, Col., died, 23/1/17.
Halpin, William Oswald, Capt. (Tp.), d. of w., 10/8/18 (att. 4 Huss.).
Hammond, John Maximilian, D.S.O., Lt. (Tp.), d. of w., 15/3/17 (att. 10/Devon R.).
Harding, Norman Ernest Jasper, Major (T/Lt.-Col.), died, 10/8/16 (att. 12/S.H.).
Harper, John Alexander, M.C., Capt. (Tp.), k. in a., 14/2/17 (att. 7/York. R.).
Harris, Charles Montagu, Lt. (Tp.), d. of w., 28/8/15 (att. R. Scots. Fus.).
Harris, F. W. Davie, Lt.-Col., died, 20/6/17.
Harris, Hubert Alfred, Capt. (Tp.), k. in a., 31/7/17 (att. 61/Bde., R.F.A.).
Harris, William Trengwreath, Lt., drowned, 15/4/17.
Harrison, Frank Cecil, Capt., d. of w., 13/10/18.
Harrison, Stanley Sextus Barrymore, M.C., Major (Act.), d. of w., 10/10/18 (att. 1/3 N. Mid. F.A.).
Harrison, William Sandilands, Lt.-Col., died, 12/4/15.
Harty, James Johnson, Lt. (Tp.), died, 6/3/17.
Harvey, Alfred Wallace, Capt. (Tp.), d. of w., 7/9/16 (att. 55/Bde., Am. Col., R.F.A.).
Harvey, Gilbert Aberdein, Capt., d. of w., 25/11/17 (att. 1/King's Own Royal Lancaster R.).
Hasler, Arthur Thomas, M.C., Lt. & Qr.-Mr., drowned, 4/5/17 (att. 40/C.C. Stn.).
Haverson, James Blain, Lt., d. of w., 25/6/16.
Hawes, Godfrey Charles Browne, Capt. (Tp.), drowned, 10/4/17.
Hawkes, John Cornock, Lt. (Tp.), k. in a., 30/7/15 (att. 8/K.R.R. Cps.).
Hay, William Stevenson Brown, Capt (Tp.), k. in a., 5/10/18.
Heald, William Margetson, Lt., d. of w., 8/9/18.
Heard, Geoffrey Richard, Capt. (Tp.), k. in a., 3/7/16 (att. 10/R. War. R.).

Heffernan, Francis Joseph, Lt.-Col., died, 16/7/17.
Hegarty, Andrew, Lt. (Tp.), k. in a., 16/12/15 (att. R.F.A.).
Henderson, James, Lt. (T/Capt.), died, 16/7/17.
Hewson, Falkiner Melton, Capt., died, 22/10/18.
Hill, Reginald Gordon, M.C., Lt. (Tp.), k. in a., 11/10/17 (att. 1/Cold. Gds.).
Hodgson, John Edward, O.B.E., Lt.-Col., died, 5/11/18 (att. 12/Army Corps, att. Staff).
Hodson, Thomas George Smith, Capt., drowned, 10/4/17.
Holding, Alfred William, T/Lt. & Qr.-Mr., died, 27/7/16.
Holland, Ralph, T/Lt. & Qr.-Mr., died, 21/8/16.
Holloman, Arthur, T/Lt. & Qr.-Mr., k. in a., 12/12/16.
Holmes, Charles James, Major, died, 5/4/16.
Home, Robert, Capt. (Tp.), k. in a., 23/4/17.
Hopkins, Francis Gethin, Lt. (Tp.), died, 2/2/16.
Hopkins, Herbert Leslie, Lt., k. in a., 19/9/14.
Horkins, Richard Earl, Capt. (Tp.), k. in a., 27/9/16 (att. 77/Bde., R.F.A.).
Hornsey, John Frederick, Lt., k. in a., 24/3/18 (att. 6th K.S.L.I.).
Horsley, Sir Victor Alexander Haden, Bart., C.B., Col., died, 16/7/16.
Howard, Charles Reginald, O.B.E., Capt. (Tp.), k. in a., 6/9/18 (att. K. Af. Rfls.).
Howe, Ernest, Lt. (Tp.), d. of w., 14/12/16 (att. 83/F.A.).
Huggan, James Laidlaw, Lt., k. in a., 16/9/14.
Hughes, Oscar Cecil Lawrence, Lt., k. in a., 18/8/17 (att. 2/K. Afr. Rfls.).
Hughston, Johnston, Capt. (Tp.) (A/Major), d. of w., 14/9/18 (att. 68/F.A.).
Hunter, Bentley Moore, Capt. (Tp.), k. in a., 31/7/17 (att. 1/1 Cam. R.).
Hunter, Douglas William, D.S.O., Capt. (Tp.), k. in a., 25/3/18 (att. 10/W. York. R.).
Iles, Charles Cochrane, Lt., d. of w., 19/12/14.
Inglis, Maurice Paterson, Capt. (Tp.), k. in a., 17/9/16 (att. 1/5 Border R.).
Ingram, Thomas Lewis, D.S.O., M.C., Capt. (Tp.), k. in a., 16/9/16 (att. 1/K.S.L.I.).
Irvine, Robert Charles, Capt. (Tp.) (A/Major), died, 10/11/18.
Jack, William Boyd, M.C., Capt. (Tp.), d. of w., 11/10/18 (att. 1/5 Leics. R.).
Jaffe, Joseph, Capt. (Tp.), k. in a., 1/8/18 (att. 2/4 Som. L.I.).
James, John, Capt., d. of w., 8/10/18 (att. 18/H.L.I.).
Jamieson, Leonard Foster, Lt. (Tp.), died, 27/6/18.
Jarman, Harry Love, Capt. (Tp.), k. in a., 15/1/17.
Jekyll, Arthur Cyril Albert, Capt. (Tp.), k. in a., 11/5/16.
Johnston, James MacCormac Caldwell, Lt. (Tp.), k. in a., 27/5/16.
Johnston, William Vincent, Capt. (Tp.), died, 12/12/17.
Jones, Alfred Gwilym, Capt., died, 27/1/16.
Jones, Evan Lawrence, Capt. (Tp.), k. in a., 30/9/18 (att. 2/H.L.I.).
Jones, Henry John Rutherford, Capt. (Tp.), died, 26/2/16.
Jones, John Langdale, Major, died, 14/5/17.
Jones, Raymond John, Lt. (Tp.), k. in a., 10/7/16 (att. 129/F.A.).
Jones, Thomas William, Lt. (Tp.), k. in a., 11/3/17 (att. 27/Nth'd. Fusrs.).
Keane, Edward Dawson, Capt. (Tp.), died, 31/10/18 (att. 680 Co., M.T., A.S.C.).
Keith, George Elphinstone, Capt. (Tp.), died, 6/12/18.
Kellie, Kenneth Harrison Alloa, Capt. (Tp.), k. in a., 25/6/16.
Kelly, Charles Patrick, Lt. (Tp.), k. in a., 2/7/16.
Kelly, Joseph Francis Mary, Lt.-Col., died, 22/8/16.
Kelsey, Arthur Edward, Capt., drowned, 26/2/18.
Kennedy, Ronald Sinclair, M.C., Capt. (Tp.), k. in a., 17/4/18 (att. 76/F.A.).
Kidner, Thomas Clatworthy, Capt., k. in a., 26/10/16 (att. 2 Middx. R.).
Kimbell, Harry John Sullings, Lt. (Tp.), died, 28/5/16.
King, Douglas Reid, Capt., k. in a., 7/6/17 (att. 74/F.A.).
Kinkead, Richard Crofton George Moore, Capt., k. in a., 31/10/14.
Kirkland, James Towers, M.C., Capt. (Tp.), k. in a., 18/9/18 (att. 1/Glouc. R.).
Knaggs, Francis Henry, Capt. (Tp.), died, 24/6/17.
Knowles, Henry Rylands, Capt. (Tp.), k. in a., 30/7/16 (att. 7/R. Lancs R.).
Lacey, William Stocks, Lt. (Tp.), d. of w., 11/10/16 (att. 11/R. West Kent R.).
Lambert, Ernest Charles, Lt. (Tp.), d. of w., 30/6/16.
Lambert, Francis Courtenay, Major, died, 29/3/16.
Lansdale, William Morris, Capt., k. in a., 26/8/18 (att. 5/R. Berks R.).
Latham, Thomas Jones, Lt. (Tp.), k. in a., 3/10/15 (att. R.E.).
Lawrence, Edward William, Capt. (Tp.), k. in a., 10/7/16 (att. 13/R. Welsh Fus.).
Leahy, Eugene Patrick, Capt. (Tp.), d. of w., 18/9/16 (att. 61/F.A.).
Leckie, Malcolm, D.S.O., Capt., d. of w., 29/8/14.
Lee, Robert Ernest, Capt. (Tp.), drowned, 10/10/18.
Letts, Bertram Chiene, Lt. (Tp.), died, 21/10/15.
Levick, Percy, Capt. (Tp.), killed, 15/3/18 (att. Guards D.A.C.).
Limbery, Kenneth Thomas, M.C., Capt. (Tp.), k. in a., 26/9/17 (att. 133/F.A.).
Lindsay, David Paton, Capt. (Tp.), died, 2/12/18.
Linnell, Robert McCheyne, Capt., died, 17/3/15.
Linzell, Stanley James, M.C., Capt., k. in a., 3/4/17.
Lister, William Howard, D.S.O., M.C., Capt. (Tp.), k. in a., 9/8/18 (att. 21/F.A.).
Lloyd-Jones, Percy Arnold, D.S.O., Major, d. of w., 22/12/16.
Lochrin, Michael James, Capt., k. in a., 23/10/14.
Logan, Alfred Thomas, Capt., k. in a., 16/9/16 (att. 3 Gren. Guards).
Lones, Percy East, Capt., k. in a., 28/4/17 (att. 5/F.A.).
Loy, Martin William, Lt. (Tp.), k. in a., 28/8/16.
Lucas, Reginald Blockley, Capt., k. in a., 3/7/16.
Lukyn-Williams, Herbert Temple, Capt. (Tp.), d. of w., 26/3/18.
Lunan, George Harold, Lt., k. in a., 13/5/15.
Lunn, Henry Anderson, Capt., died, 5/3/17 (att. Colaba S.H., Bombay).
Macalevey, William Francis, Capt. (Tp.), k. in a., 27/9/16 (att. 54 F.A.).
Macallan, James, Capt., d. of w., 9/2/17 (att. 6/E. Lancs. R.).
McCallum, George, Lt. (Tp.), k. in a., 31/7/15 (att. 5/D.C.L.I.).
McClatchley, Samuel Edward, Capt. (Tp.), k. in a., 25/3/18 (att. 18/Welsh R.).
McConaghy, William, D.S.O., Major, died, 4/7/18.
McConnell, William Gardiner, Capt. (Tp.), d. of w., 13/10/17 (att. 10/York. & Lancs R.).
McCormack, Campbell McNeill, M.C., Capt. (A/Major), k. in a., 22/9/18 (att. 15 F.A.).
McCosh, Thomas, M.C., Capt. (Tp.), died, 16/4/17 (att. 11/Welsh R.).
McCulloch, Thomas, Lt.-Col., died, 25/6/15.
McCurry, Walter Tennyson, Lt., k. in a., 14/3/15.
Macdonald, Walter Halli-Burton, Lt. (Tp.), died, 22/1/16 (att. No. 2 Sec. Forth Defences).
McElney, Robert Gerald, M.C., Capt., k. in a., 21/3/18 (att. 77 F.A.).
McEntire, James Thomas, Major (A/Lt.-Col.), died, 29/10/18.
Macfarland, George Adams, Capt. (Tp.), d. of w., 17/10/17 (att. 23 Stn. Hos.).
Macfarlane, Ian, Capt. (Tp.), died, 18/7/17 (att. Egyptian Hospl.).
McGillicuddy, Richard Hugh, M.C., Capt. (Tp.), (A/Major), died, 20/10/18.
McGowan, Joseph, Lt. (Tp.), died, 19/9/15.
MacGrath, Roger, M.C., Capt. (Tp.), d. of w., 5/5/18 (att. 28/F.A.).
Macgregor, Reginald Kinloch, Capt. (Tp.), killed, 23/4/16.
McKeever, Louis Lawrence, M.C., Capt. (Tp.), d. of w., 8/11/17 (att. 1/4 R. Scots Fus.).
McKenzie, John Alexander, M.C., Capt., d. of w., 10/4/18 (att. 6/D.L.I.).
Mackenzie, Henry Deedes Nutt, Capt. (Tp.), k. in a., 4/10/17 (att. 95/Bde., R.F.A.).
Mackenzie, Maurice, Lt. (Tp.), k. in a., 28/11/15 (att. 2/R. Ir. Rfls.).
McKerrow, Charles Kenneth, Capt. (Tp.), d. of w., 20/12/16 (att. 10/North'd Fus.).
Mackinnon, Duncan, Capt. (Tp.), d. of w., 12/4/18 (att. 9/H.L.I.).
Mackinnon, Frank Irvine, Capt. (Tp.), died, 30/12/18.
Mackintosh, John James, Lt. (Tp.), died, 1/4/16 (att. 1/Garr. Bn., Essex R.).
Macknight, Thomas William Finglan, Lt. (Tp.), died, 4/9/16.
Maclachlan, Peter Malcolm, M.C., Capt. (Tp.), d. of w., 26/3/18.
McLaggan, James Murray, M.C., Capt. (Tp.), k. in a., 4/10/18 (att. 3/R. Fus.).
Maclean, Dugald Black, M.C., Capt. (Tp.), k. in a., 29/8/16 (att. 8/E. Lancs R.).
Maclean, Ivan Clarkson, D.S.O., M.C., Capt. (Tp.), d. of w., 4/4/18 (in Ger. hands).
McLeod, Ian Keith Falconer, Capt. (Tp.), k. in a., 27/4/18 (att. 75 F.A.
McLeod, William, Capt., d. of w., 18/5/19.
MacMahon, John Aguila, Lt., d. of w., 12/5/15 (att. Som. L.I.).
McNicol, John Hart, M.C., T/Capt., A/Major, died, 8/10/18 (att. 86/F.A.).
McQuiban, William, Capt. (Tp.), died, 2/5/18.
MacRae, Patrick Cameron, Capt., died, 5/3/17 (80 F.A.).
McSwiney, Eugene John, Capt., died, 26/12/16.
McVicker, Edgar Harold, Lt. (Tp.), k. in a., 10/9/16 (att. 2/5 Lancs Fus.).
Maffey, Henry, Lt. & Qr.-Mr. (Tp.), d. of w., 1/5/16.
Maginness, Oscar Gladstone, Lt. (Tp.), d. of w., 15/12/15 (att. R.F.A.).
Manders, Neville, Col., k. in a., 7/8/15.
Mangin, Frederick Meredyth, Lt.-Col., died, 31/12/18.
Marks, George Frederick Handel, Lt.-Col., died, 3/5/15.
Marshall, John, Lt., drowned, 15/4/17.
Martin, Edward William Sidney, Capt. (Tp.), d. of w., 16/2/17 (att. 9/Worc. R.).
Martin, Jules Stainmetz, Capt. (Act.), died, 15/12/18 (att. 19 S.H.).
Martin, Thomas Whittle, M.C., Capt., k. in a., 9/4/17 (att. 11/R. Scots).
Massy-Miles, Henry Godfrey, M.C., Capt. (Tp.), d. of w., 26/4/18.
Matheson, James Frederick, M.C., Capt. (Tp.), d. of w., 19/4/18 (att. 7/Norf. R.).
Matheson, James McDonald, Capt. (Tp.), k. in a., 30/11/17 (att. 17/Middx.).
Mathewson, Hamilton, Capt. (Tp.), d. of w., 27/10/16.
Matthews, Samuel Wauchope, Lt. (Tp.), died, 15/9/18 (att. M.L.B.).
Maule, Geoffrey Lamb, Capt., died, 15/11/18.
Mavety, John Le Roy, Lt. (Tp.), died, 13/12/15.
Maw, George Oliver, Capt. (Tp.), d. of w., 10/7/16 (att. 13 Stat. Hospl.).
Mays, Charles Cecil Wildman, Lt., drowned, 25/1/18.

Meers, John Henry, Capt. (Tp.), d. of w., 9/10/15 (att. L.N. Lanc. R.).
Menzies, Arthur John Alexander, D.S.O., Capt. (Act. Lt.-Col.), k. in a., 9/8/18 (att. 3/Cav. F.A.).
Michell, Robert Williams, Capt. (Tp.), d. of w., 20/7/16.
Michie, John Boyd, Lt. (Tp.), died, 31/12/18.
Millar, William Linton, Capt. (Tp.), died, 23/10/18.
Miller, Albert Guy, Capt. (Tp.), k. in a., 29/12/15 (att. 12/Mddx.).
Miller, Archibald Ingram, Lt. (Tp.), k. in a., 11/3/17 (att. 47 Bde. R.F.A.).
Miller, George Sefton, Capt. (Tp.), k. in a., 8/9/16 (att. 1 F.A.).
Milligan, Donald Samuel Eccles, Lt., k. in a., 9/10/17 (att. 1/7 Worc. R.).
Milne, Patrick George, Capt. (Tp.), k. in a., 22/4/18 (att. 93 F.A.).
Mills, William Thomas, Lt. (Tp.), died, 25/10/15.
Mitchell, Francis Sidney, Lt. (Tp.), k. in a., 15/2/16 (att. 9/R. Suss. R.).
Mohan, Thomas, Capt. (Tp.), k. in a., 23/3/18 (att. 10 S.H.).
Montgomery, Raymond, Capt., k. in a., 25-29/9/15.
Moore, Henry, D.S.O., M.C., T/Capt. (Act. Lt.-Col.), d. of w., 30/5/18 (att. 16 F.A.).
Morris, Hugh Gwilym, Capt. (Tp.), k. in a., 14/7/16 (att. 54 F.A.).
Morison, Robert McKenzie, Capt., died, 8/5/19.
Morrison, William, M.C., Capt. (Tp.), d. of w., 25/10/17 (att. 54 F.A.).
Morton, Alexander, Capt. (Tp.), k. in a., 27/8/18 (att. 1/7 H.L.I.).
Mulkern, Hubert Cowell, Capt. (Tp.), k. in a., 1/7/16 (att. 9/R. Innis. Fus.).
Munro, John Sutherland, Lt., died, 16/7/17 (att. 112 F.A.).
Murphy, Matthew, Capt. (Tp.), drowned, 10/10/18.
Murray, Robert William Skinner, Capt., died, 6/5/19.
Murray, William Dunmore, Lt. (Tp.), died, 23/1/16.
Nangle, Edward Jocelyn, Capt. (Tp.), k. in a., 26/9/15 (att. 1/L.N. Lancs R.).
Naylor, Joseph, Lt. (Tp.), k. in a., 10/4/17.
Neligan, John, Lt. (Tp.), died, 13/6/17.
Nevin, Alex McDonald, Lt., died, 24/6/17 (att. 36 Gen. Hpl.).
Newbery, Richard Fenton Theodore, Lt. (Tp.), k. in a., 14/7/16 (att. 6/Bn. Northampton R.).
Newton, Eric, Capt. (Tp.), d. of w., 5/8/17 (att. Sidi Bisha Camp).
Nicholls, William Howard, Capt., died, 22/2/16 (att. Mhow Div.).
Nicol, Charles Mill, Capt., d. of w., 23/10/16 (D.A.D.M.S., 3/Div.).
Nolan, Rupert Henry, Capt., k. in a., 21/10/14.
Noyes, Harry Francis Golding, Capt. (Tp.), died, 5/9/16 (att. 17/Sty. Hospl.).
O'Brien, Henry Edward, Capt. (Tp.), d. of w., 8/9/16 (att. 99/F.A.).
O'Brien, James Vincent, Capt., k. in a., 10/8/16 (att. 5 Bde.).
O'Brien, Michael Patrick, Lt. (Tp.), died, 23/9/17.
O'Brien-Butler, Charles Paget, Capt., d. of w., 31/10/14.
O'Connell, John Forbes, Lt., k. in a., 20/9/14.
O'Connor, Richard Dominick, Capt., k. in a., 25/10/14.
O'Flynn, Dominick Thomas, Capt. (Tp.), died, 16/6/18 (att. 19 D.A.C.).
O'Flynn, Michael Joseph, Lt. (Tp.), d. of w., 24/9/18 (att. 1/Bn. Northampton R.).
O'Keefe, William Robert, Capt. (Tp.), died, 21/11/18.
O'Reilly, Patrick Joseph, M.C., Capt. (Tp.), k. in a., 11/10/18 (att. 7/E. York. R.).
O'Reilly, Patrick Stanislaus, C.M.G., Lt.-Col., died, 18/11/18.
Orme, John McCallum, M.C., Capt., died, 3/4/17.
Pagen, Wilfred Robert, Capt. (Tp.), k. in a., 7/10/16 (att. 6/E. Kent R.).
Parker, James, Capt. (Tp.), k. in a., 16/6/16 (att. 7/Som. L. I.).
Parker, Jeffery Wimpris, Lt. (Tp.), k. in a., 7/8/15 (att. 11/Manch. R.).
Parry-Jones, Owen Guy, Capt., d. of w., 29/9/16 (att. 8/Suff. R.).
Parsons, Edward Daniel, Lt. (Tp.), d. of w., 20/9/15.
Parsons-Smith, Eustace Macartney, Capt., died, 25/5/19.
Pearson, Walter, Lt. & Qr.-Mr., died, 24/5/18 (att. 41 F.A.).
Peel, Thomas Alfred, Lt. (Tp.), d. of w., 24/8/15 (att. 5/Dorsets).
Pegum, Joseph Patrick, Capt. (Tp.), k. in a., 26/9/17.
Pern, Montague, Lt., k. in a., 9/5/15.
Peter, Alexander Gordon, M.C., Capt. (Tp.), d. of w., 5/7/17 (att. 6/Seaforth Hldrs.).
Peto, Morton, M.C., Capt. (Tp.), d. of w., 22/9/16.
Pettinger, James Wilson, Capt. (Tp.), died, 6/10/17.
Philip, Andrew, Lt. (Tp.), died, 30/5/15.
Philips, Abraham Zadok, Capt. (Tp.), d. of w., 24/10/17 (att. 56 F.A.).
Phillips, Thomas McCann, Capt., d. of w., 4/11/14.
Philp, Claude Hastings George, Capt., k. in a., 28/3/18 (att. 1/7 Manch. R.).
Philson, Samuel Cowell, Col., died, 4/11/18.
Piggott, Frederick Cecil Holman, Capt. (Tp.), died, 26/6/17.
Pirie, George Stephen, Lt. (T/Capt.), k. in a., 24/7/17 (att. 9/E. Surr. R.).
Plaister, Geoffrey Ratcliffe, Capt. (Tp.), k. in a., 11/4/17 (att. 10/Y. & L. R.).
Pool, Samuel, M.C., Capt. (Tp.), k. in a., 16/6/17 (att. 8/Leic. R.).
Pope, Charles Alfred Whiting, Capt. (Tp.), drowned, 4/5/17.
Porter, Reginald Edward, Lt., k. in a., 26/10/14
Power, Pierce Michael Joseph, Lt., d. of w., 2/3/15 (att. 1/Wilts).
Preston, Richard Amyas, M.C., Capt. (Act. Lt.-Col.), d. of w., 7/6/18 (att. 58 F.A.).
Priestley, Percival Thomas, Capt. (A/Major), died 28/9/18 (att. 25/C.C.S.).
Proctor, John, Major, d. of w., 12/8/18 (att. 9/Cav. Fd. Amb.).
Proud, John Dover, M.C., Lt. (T/Capt.), d. of w., -/8/18 (att. 46/F.A.).
Proudfoot, Harold Heafford, Capt., k. in a., 2/9/16 (att. 26 Bde., R.F.A.).
Pryce, Arthur Meurig, Capt., died, 21/2/19 (35 G.H.).
Pryn, William Reginald, Lt. (Tp.), died, 27/6/15.
Rae, James, Lt. (Tp.), drowned, 13/4/17.
Randall, John Beaufoy, Capt. (Tp.), k. in a., 31/10/17.
V.C. Ranken, Harry Sherwood, Capt., d. of w., 24/9/14.
Ransome, Herbert Fullarton, Lt. (Tp.), died, 14/11/17.
Rees, Morgan James, Capt. (Tp.), d. of w., 30/10/16 (132 F. Amb.).
Reid, William Douglas, M.C., Capt. (Tp.), k. in a., 5/10/17 (att. 21/Manch. Regt.).
Richards, Francis Graham, Major, k. in a., 5/3/15.
Richardson, Martin, Lt. (Tp.), d. of w., 3/11/14.
Rintoul, David Wylie, Lt., k. in a., 21/10/14.
Rix, John Cecil, Capt. (Tp.), k. in a., 6/7/16 (att. 9/Yorks R.).
Robb-Smith, Alec, Capt. (Tp.), died, 15/12/17.
Roberts, Benjamin Richard, Lt. (Tp.), k. in a., 30/7/16 (att. 98/F. Amb.).
Robertson, Angus Burns, Capt. (Tp.), died, 8/11/18.
Robinson, Edmond, Capt., k. in a., 20/3/17.
Robinson, Henry, Hon. Lt. & Qr.-Mr., died, 3/11/15 (att. 25/Gen. Hospl.).
Robinson, Henry Ellis, Capt. (Tp.), k. in a., 25/4/18 (att. 1/6 Bn. West Yorks R.).
Robinson, Henry Harold, D.S.O., Capt. (Tp.), drowned, 4/5/17.
Robinson, Kennett, Lt. (Tp.), k. in a., 25/9/15 (att. 12/Manch. R.).
Robson, Charles Henry, Capt. (Tp.), k. in a., 1/12/17 (att. 2/4 Glouc. R.).
Rodger, Douglas, Lt. (Tp.), k. in a., 1/7/16 (att. 90 F.A.).
Rogers, Robert Carmichael, Capt. (Tp.), d. of w., 2/8/18 (att. 18 H.A.Q.).
Rogerson, William, Capt. (Tp.), k. in a., 27/8/18 att. (8/R. Berks).
Rose, Harold Emerson, Capt., d. of w., 7/7/17 (att. 2 Cold. Gds.).
Ross, Andrew Beaconsfield, Lt. (Tp.), k. in a., 6/8/17 (att. 2 R. Ir. Rifs.).
Ross, Kenneth McAlpine, Capt. (Tp.), d. of w., 17/9/18 (att. 1/5 H.L.I.).
Rowland, Sydney Domville, Major (Tp.), died, 6/3/17 (att. 26 Gen. H.).
Ruttledge, Victor John, Capt. (Tp.), died, 3/11/16 (att. 8 Mid. Brig. Fld. Amb.).
Ryley, Charles, Major, died, 4/5/17 (Staff, D.A.D.M.S., 40 Div.).
Sadler, Vyvyan Kendall, Capt. (Tp.), k. in a., 17/4/17 (att. 29 Bde., R.F.A.).
Saw, Noel Humphrey Wykeham, M.C., Capt., k. in a., 9/10/17 (att. 4 Worc. R.).
Scatchard, Thomas, Capt., k. in a., 8/9/14.
Scott, Samuel Geoffrey, Capt. (Tp.), died, 6/1/18.
Seabrooke, Alexander S., Capt. (Tp.), died, 1/7/16 (att. 2/B.G.H., Basra).
Selby, Gerrard Prideaux, Capt., k. in a., 26/9/16 (att 9/Lancs Fus.).
Senter, John Watt, Lt. (Tp.), d. of w., 9/6/18 (att. 53 F.A.).
Scudamore, Leonard George, Lt., died, 17/4/17.
Shand, William Gadrow, Capt. (Tp.), d. of w., 25/7/16.
Shannon, John James, Capt. (Tp.), k. in a., 29/11/17 (att. Lincs Yeo.).
Shannon, Percy Roy, Lt. (Tp.), d. of w., 3/11/18 (att. 11 F. Amb.).
Shegog, Richard Wellington, Capt. (Tp.), d. of w., 1/8/17 (att. 1/4 L.N. Lancs R.).
Sherlock, Charles Gregg, Capt., d. of w., 14/11/17 (D.A.D.M.S.).
Sherman, Reginald, Capt. (Tp.), d. of w., 10/10/17 (att. 4 F. Amb.).
Shields, Hugh John Sladen, Lt., k. in a., 25-26/10/14.
Simpson, Frederic, Capt. (Tp.) d. of w., 31/3/18 (att. 2/1 Lond. Fld. Amb.).
Sinclair, David Williamson, Lt., d. of w., 22/10/18 (att. 11/R. Scots).
Sinclair, James Johnston, Capt. (Tp.), died, 14/11/18.
Smith, Alfred Percy, Capt., k. in a., 23/8/15 (att. 32 F.A.).
Smith, Charles Edgar Holton, Capt. (Tp.), k. in a., 16/9/16 (att. 10/11 H.L.I.).
Smith, Douglas Wilberforce, Capt. (Tp.), k. in a., 1/7/16 (att. 20/Manch. R.).
Smith, Harry Graham, Capt. (Tp.), drowned, 10/4/17.
Smith, John Godfrey Bradley, Lt. (Tp.), drowned, 15/4/17.
Smith, William Alex, Lt. (Tp.), d. of w., 3/6/17 (att. 27 Bde., R.F.A.).
Sneath, Wilfred Archer, M.C., Lt. (Tp.), d. of w., 11/7/17 (att. 2 F. Amb.).
Spensley, Frank Oswald, Capt., died, 23/10/18 (att. R.A.F.).
Spensley, James Richardson, Lt. (Tp.), d. of w., 10/11/15 (att. 8/E. Kent R.) (P. of W.).
Spittal, Robert Haig, Capt. (Tp.), k. in a., 4/10/17 (att. 7/Lancs. Fus.).

Spoor, Herbert Mather, M.C., Capt. (Tp.), died 13/12/17.
Spurrell, Herbert George Flaxman, Capt. (Tp.), died, 8/11/18 (att. R.A.F.).
Stainsby, John Addison, Lt. (Tp.), drowned, 26/2/18.
Stanley, James Arthur, Capt. (Tp.), k. in a., 27/9/18 (att. 15/R. War. R.).
Stanton, George, Capt., d. of w., 16/8/16.
Steel, Edwin, Bedford, Major, d. of w., 23/11/14.
Steel, James, M.C., Capt., k. in a., 2/9/18 (att. 1/Som. L.I.).
Stenhouse, John Maitland, M.C., Capt. (Tp.), d. of w., 25/8/16 (att. R.F.A.).
Stephen, David James Shirres, M.C., Capt. (Tp.), d. of w., 24/10/17 (att. 54 F. Amb.).
Stephen, Lionel Henry York, Capt. (Tp.), died, 22/5/18.
Sterling, Robert, Capt., died, 16/10/17.
Stewart, Hugh, D.S.O., M.C., Major (T/Lt.-Col.), k. in a., 12/4/18 (att. 94/F.A.).
Stewart, Ronald, Lt. (Tp.), drowned, 15/4/17.
Storrie, Hugh Cochrane, Capt., k. in a., 12/9/15 (att. 2/R.W. Surr. R.).
Strain, Thomas, Capt. (Tp.), died, 16/9/16.
Stratford, Ernest, Lt., d. of w., 21/4/15.
Sturdy, Arthur Carlile, M.C., Capt., died, 1/5/19.
Sutcliffe, Archibald Alfred, Capt., died, 12/3/15.
Sykes, Harold Widdington, Capt. (Tp.), died, 11/11/18 (att. 14/C.C.S.).
Symons, Frank Albert, C.M.G., D.S.O., Lt.-Col. (T/Col.), k. in a., 30/4/17 (A.D.M.S., 9 Div. Staff).
Tanner, Harold Herbert, Capt. (Tp.), drowned, 16/8/16.
Taylor, Alfred Squire, Lt. (T/Capt.), k. in a., 31/7/17.
Taylor, Douglas, Lt., died, 26/7/18.
Taylor, Francis Mortimer, Capt., k. in a., 17/3/19.
Taylor, George, Lt. (Tp.), drowned, 30/10/17.
Taylor, Herbert Hampden, Capt. (Tp.), d. of w., 3/4/18 (att. 4/R. Welsh Fus.).
Taylor, Henry Young Cameron, Capt., died, 25/8/17.
Taylor, Raymond Brewitt, Capt. (Tp.), d. of w., 22/8/18 (att. 7/Fld Amb.).
Teggart, John Cameron Thomson, Capt. (Tp.), k. in a., 21/7/18 (att. 256 Bde. R.F.A.).
Tennent, Bernard Charles, M.C., T/Lt. (A/Major), k. in a., 22/8/18 (att. 84/Fld. Amb.).
Thatcher, Francis Geoffrey, M.C., Capt., d. of w., 1/6/18 (D.A.D.M.S., H.Q., 40 Div.).
Thomas, Rufus Haydon, Capt. (Tp.), k. in a., 24/3/18 (att. 2/R. Scots Fus.).
Thompson, William Frank, Lt. (Tp.), d. of w., 1/1/16.
Thomson, Alfred Maurice, Capt., k. in a., 7/7/16 (att. 7/R. Sussex R.).
Thornley, Arthur Lincoln, Lt. (Tp.), died, 12/4/16.
Tilbury, Arthur, Capt. (Tp.), drowned, 4/5/17.
Tough, John James, Capt. (Tp.), d. of w., 6/10/18 (att. 5 F.A.).
Traill, Anthony, Capt. (Tp.), died, 25/8/17 (att. 2/4 W. Rid. R.).
Treherne, Claude William, Lt. (T/Capt.), d. of w., 12/8/17 (D.A.D.M.S., 37/Div.).
Turnbull, Derwent Christopher, Lt., d. of w., 14/3/15 (att. Chesh. Regt.).
Underwood, Harry, Lt. and Qr.-Mr., died, 18/10/17.
Venables, Aubrey William, Capt. (Tp.), k. in a., 2/10/16 (att. 81 F. Amb.).
Waddy, John Raymond, Lt., k. in a., 17/3/15 (att. Som L.I.).
Walcott, Francis Sharpe, Capt. (Tp.), k. in a., 26/9/16 (att. 8 Nth'd. Fus.).
Walker, Arthur Nimmo, Lt.-Col., k. in a., 24/9/16.
Walker, Gideon, M.C., Capt. (Tp.), k. in a., 27/11/17 (att. 3 F. Amb.).
Walker, Stanley Arthur, Lt. (Tp.), k. in a., 14/10/16 (att. 1/5 Chesh. R.).
Walsh Stephen Barry, Lt., died, 8/9/15 (att. 1/Cav. Fld. Amb.).
Ward, William Alfred, Major, died, 30/8/18.
Wardleworth, Douglas, Lt., died, 24/10/14.
Ward, P. F., Lt., died, 12/9/15.
Watson, David Galloway, Lt., died, 5/6/15.
Watterton, William Frederick, Hon. Lt. and Qr.-Mr., died, 2/1/17.
Waugh, Arthur John, Capt. (Tp.), k. in a., 17/8/16 (att. 1/N. Staff. R.).
Wedgwood, Percy Ashworth, Lt., died, 24/1/18.
Welch, Edward Ronald, Capt. (Tp.), k. in a., 16/9/16.
Weller, Charles, Capt., k. in a., 16/8/17 (att. 1/1 Lon.).
Whincup, Frank, Lt. (Tp.), drowned, 2/7/17.
Whitaker, Frederick, Lt. (Tp.), died, 28/10/16.
Whitehorne-Cole, Arthur George, Capt., k. in a., 20/9/17.
Whittingham, Clive Alan, Capt., k. in a., 9/6/17 (att. 12/R. Fusrs.).
Whitty, Michael Joseph, Lt.-Col., died, 28/3/17.
Whitworth, Henry Parker, M.C., Capt., d. of w., 29/10/18.
Wight, Ernest Octavius, Col., d. of w., 19/12/15.
Wilcocks, James, Lt. Qr.-Mr., died, 20/10/17.
Wiley, William, Major, died, 12/2/17 (att. 42/F. Amb.).
Willis, Hugh Dudley, Capt. (Tp.), d. of w., 12/8/17 (att. 3/Worc. R.).
Wilson, Charles Edgar Andrew, Capt., d. of w., 8/4/18.
Wilson, John, Lt. (Tp.), k. in a., 9/3/16 (att. 10/W. Rid. R.).
Wilson, John, Capt., died, 30/12/18 (att. 78/Gen. H.).
Wilson, Robert Henry, Capt. (Tp.), d. of w., 15/5/17 (att. R.F.A., 34/Bde.).
Wilson, Walton Ronald, Lt. (Tp.), d. of w., 12/7/16 (att. 2/Seaf. Hldrs.).
Winter, Laurence Amos, Capt., died, 15/11/18.
Wiseley, Francis Joseph, Lt. (Tp.), d. of w., 14/9/15.
Wooderson, Douglas Henry David, Capt. (Tp.), k. in a., 6/8/16 (att. 6/K. L'pl. R.).
Woodhouse, Bernard, Capt., d. of w., 5/9/17 (att. 10/Welsh R.).
Wooster, Reginald Joseph, Capt. (Tp.), k. in a., 15/9/16 (att. 9/Rif. Bde.).
Wright, Eric Alfred, Lt. (Tp.), died, 21/6/15.
Young, Benjamin Poyntz, Capt. (Tp.), died, 6/11/16.
Young, F. H., Lt. (Tp.), drowned, 3/10/15 (att. 29/Div., Amm. Col.).
Young, George William, Capt., drowned, 26/2/18.

Royal Army Ordnance Corps.

Andrews, Charles, Capt., died, 21/7/18.
Andrews, Sidney Mottram, Capt. (Tp.), died, 8/10/18.
Beckwith, William John, O.B.E., Capt. (Hon.), died, 21/12/18.
Billington, Frank Norman, Lt., killed, 30/9/18 (and R.A.F.).
Brown, Granville Albert, Lt., died, 18/2/19.
Buckham, Norman Langley, T/Lt. (A/Capt.), died, 30/10/18.
Burdall, Albert, Lt. (Hon., ret. pay), died, 3/1/16.
Colbourne, Frederick William, Lt., died, 25/2/19.
Collins, Thomas, T/Lt. (A/Capt.), died, 23/2/10.
Downey, William Edmund, Capt., drowned, 19/7/17.
Dryden, John Thomas, Lt., died, 28/7/17.
Fitness, William John, Lt. (Tp.), died, 22/11/16.
Galloway, Reginald Edgar Charles, Capt. (Tp.), died, 11/2/19.
Grantham, Ernest Joel, Lt. (A/Capt.), died, 6/12/18.
Greenhalgh, Harold Fifield, 2/Lt. (Tp.), k. in a., 9/4/18.
Hailes, Joseph, Hon. Capt., k. in a., 1/9/15.
Handcock, Reginald Henry, Lt. (Hon.), drowned, 17/2/17.
Jones, Edward Stanley, Lt., died, 28/11/18.
King Herbert, Lt. (Tp.), d. of w., 6/10/17.
King, Sydney Robert, Hon. Capt., died, 19/11/16.
Lynam, James Michael, M.C., Lt., died, 29/12/16.
Mills, John Thomas, Capt., Hon., died, 22/12/14.
Mullin, Archibald, 2/Lt. (Tp.), killed, 16/5/17.
Newton, William Howard, Capt., died, 22/2/19.
Nicholson, T., Hon. Capt., died, 6/11/15.
O'Connor, Frederick Henry Pomeroy, Major, died, 1/2/16.
Ottey, Thomas William, Major, died, 3/12/18.
Power, William Goodlake, Capt., k. in a., 16/10/16.
Rawson, Thomas Leonard, Hon. Lieut., died, 28/6/17.
Reynolds, Arthur, Capt. (Hon.), died, 2/6/17.
Roberts, Reuben, Capt. (Tp.), k. in a., 7/7/16.
Sanders, John H., Lt. (Tp.), died, 19/1/19 (Base Dep.).
Scott, Lindsay Buchannan, Major (Tp.), died, 14/11/18.
Smith, Richard Alfred, Capt., died, 28/8/18.
Sommerville, William Henry Lionel, M.C., Lt. (Tp.), died, 3/12/18.
Stubbs, Charles Albert, T/Lt., died, 9/3/18.
Tims, Frederick, Hon. Major, ret. pay, died, 28/12/15.
Toms, William Henry, Capt., killed, 5/12/18.

Royal Army Veterinary Corps.

Anderson, Alexander Campbell, Capt., k. in a., 20/4/15.
Baines, Ellis Eylon, Capt. (Tp.), died, 7/8/18.
Blanchard, William Hutchison, Capt., died, 8/10/17 (att. 155 Bde., A.F.A.).
Bradley, John, T/Capt., died, 17/2/19 (att. R.F.A.).
Brownless, John Wilson, Lt., d. of w., 16/6/15.
Buchanan, William Arthur Irvine, Capt., d. of w., 24/7/17 (50 Mobile Vet. Div. Troops).
Campbell, Archibald Wright, Capt. (Tp.), d. of w., 13/12/17.
Carr, Frederick Wysses, Major (T/Lt.-Col.), died, 10/11/17 (att. Egyptian Army).
Clark, John Ladyman, Capt. (Tp.), died, 16/12/18.
Clapp, Alfred Henry, Lt., died, 15/5/16.
Cockburn, Robert Bowes, Capt. (Tp.), died, 27/9/18.
Cronun, William Benn, Capt. (Tp.), died, 1/2/18.
Delaine, Frederick John, Capt. (Tp.), died, 21/3/18 (att. R.F.A., 119 Bde.).
Davie, Henry William Wilson, Vet. Surgeon, drowned, 23/11/15.
Donworth, Thomas Francis, Capt. (Tp.), drowned, 28/7/16.
Doyle, Francis Hubert, Lt., d. of w., 12/10/16.
Fox, Vincent, Lt., k. in a., 26/8/14.
Hannay, David, Capt. (Tp.), died, 17/1/18 (att. R.H.A.).
Hazelton, Edwin Hills, Brig.-Gen. (Tp.), died, 25/7/16.
Higgins, Arthur Aken, Capt. (Tp.), died, 25/10/18 (att. 115 R.F.A.).
Hoskin, Alfred, Capt. (Tp.), d. of w., 4/7/17 (att. 10 Corps).
Hughes, Edward William, Lt. (Tp.), died, 30/1/18 (23 Vet. H.).
Huston, William, Capt. (Tp.), killed, 6/12/17 (att. R.A.S.C.).
Johnston, Hugh McColl, Capt., d. of w., 4/4/18 (att. 1 Royal Dragoons).
Jones, Stuart Kirby, Lt., d. of w., 17/9/14.
Kee, William John, Capt. (Tp.), died, 20/12/18 (att. 14 Army Bde., H.Q., R.H.A.).
King, James, Lt. & Qr.-Mr., drowned, 14/6/16.
Lambert, Charles Henry, Lt. (Tp.), died, 17/8/15 (att. R.F.A.).
Leach, Robert Edward, Capt. (Tp.), d. of w., 29/11/17 (att. 64 Bde., R.F.A.).
Lefebvre, Henri Homer, Lt. (Tp.), died, 15/12/17.
Lenox-Conyngham, Hubert Maxwell, D.S.O., Bt.-Lt.-Col., died, 15/3/18.
Lowry, Henry Cooke, Capt., died, 11/7/16.
Lucas, Roy Herbert Charles, Lt. (Tp.), killed, 25/12/15 (att. R.F.A.).
Macauley, William Ingham, Capt. (T/Major), killed, 14/5/17.
McHugh, Terence, Tp. Qr.-Mr. & Hon. Lt., d. of w., 20/5/18.
McMahon, Bruce, Capt., died, 3/5/19.
Morrin, William Arthur, Capt. (Tp.), died, 1/8/18 (att. R.F.A.).

O'Brien, Thomas Augustine, Lt. (Tp.), died, 6/10/18.
Pollock, Daniel, Capt. (Tp.), drowned, 15/4/17.
Roche, Francis, Capt., died, 30/6/17.
Routledge, Arthur Richard, Capt., died, 27/6/18.
Sherley, James, Capt. (Tp.), k. in a., 27/11/17 (att. 70 Bde., R.F.A.).
Shore, Walter Francis, Lt.-Col., died, 6/12/16.
Taylor, George Charles, Capt. (Tp.), d. of w., 6/9/18 (att. 26 Bde., R.F.A.).
Taylor, William Henry, Capt. & Bt.-Major (T/Major), died 11/2/19 (att. Staff).
Thexton, Percival, Capt. (Tp.), died, 20/11/18 (8 Mobile Vet. Sec., M.E.F.).
Tully-Christie. W., Capt., died, 20/2/18.
White, James Mathew, Lt. (Tp.), died, 16/3/16 (T.C., att. 126 Bde., R.A.).
Williams, Herbert Mainwaring, Major, d. of w., 23/12/17.

Royal Army Chaplains' Department.

Abbott, William David, Rev., died, 3/12/18.
Acton, Armar, Rev., d. of w., 4/11/17 (att. Border Rgt.).
Ainley, Frederick William, Rev., died, 5/12/18.
Ash, John, Rev., k. in a., 7/9/17 (att. 48 D.A.C. Div. Troops).
Baile, George William, Rev., died, 27/1/18 (att. 64th C.C.S.).
Baines, Thomas Leo., Rev., d. of w., 31/5/18 (att. 152 Bde. R.F.A.).
Baird, J., Rev., died, 13/2/19.
Barker, Edward Walter, Rev., d. of w., 18/3/18 (att. 176th T.M.B.).
Bell, Charles Henry, M.C., Rev., k. in a., 23/8/18 (att. 1st R. Berks R.).
Bennett, Arnold John, M.C., Rev., died, 26/1/18.
Bishop, George Bernard Hamilton, Rev., k. in a., 27/5/18 (att. 6th Nor. Fus.).
Black, William, Rev., died, 10/7/18.
Black, William Duncan Thomson, Rev., k. in a., 22/8/17 (att. 7th Cam. Hdrs.).
Boddington, Vincent Coke, Rev., died, 13/3/17 (att. 35th Gen. Hos.).
Buck, Cyril Bernard Wilson, Rev., k. in a., 29/9/18 (att. 5th Leic. R.).
Burdess, Matthews Forster, Rev. k. in a., 18/4/17 (att. 1/6th Glos. R.).
Burns, Joseph Dobson, Rev. d. of w., 7/6/18.
Cappell, James Leitch, Rev. died 23/1/18 (att. 1/9th R. Scots).
Carey, Timothy, Rev., died, 27/2/19.
Cheese, William Gerard, Rev., died, 7/11/18 (att. 8th Lincs).
Clarke, Stephen, Rev., k. in a., 4/10/17 (att. 7th Bn. Lanc. Fus.).
Cleveland, Frederick Walter, M.C., Rev., d. of w., 11/10/18 (att. 1/6th North Staff. R.).
Cobham, Elijah, Rev., d. of w., 19/9/17 (att. King's Afr. Rif.).
Colborne, Richard Arthur Pell, Rev., k. in a., 28/5/18 (att. 1/1st Lond. R.).
Collins, Henry Herbert John, Rev., k. in a., 9/4/17 (att. 9th R. Hdrs.).
Condie, George, Rev., died, 30/6/18.
Cowd, Arthur Martin, Rev., died, 22/12/18 (att. 81 F.A.).
Craven, George Edward, Rev., died, 7/12/18.
Creighton, Oswin, Rev., k. in a., 15/4/18 (att. 42nd Bde. R.F.A.).
Dallas, William Loraine Seymour, Rev., k. in a., 20/9/17.
Deedes, Arthur Gordon, Rev. Canon, died, 29/11/16.
De Vine, Hatton Bertram St. John, Rev., k. in a., 27/4/16.
Dickinson, Harry, Rev., k. in a., 30/10/17 (att. 1/28th Lon. R.).
Doudney, Charles Edmund, Rev., d. of w., 16/10/15.
Doyle, Denis, Rev., k. in a., 18/8/16 (att. 2nd Lein. R.).
Doyle, William Joseph, M.C., Rev., k. in a., 17/8/17.
Dugdale, Richard William, M.C., Rev., k. in a., 24/10/18 (att. 1st Bn. Norf. R.).
Duncan, Edward Francis, M.C., Rev., k. in a., 11/3/17 (att. 103rd Inf. Bde.).
Dunstan, Sidney, Rev., died, 16/7/18.
Duvall, John Richard, Rev., d. of w., 6/10/17 (att. 13th Man. R.).
East, Herbert Hinton, Rev., k. in a., 5/8/17.
Edinger, Frank Harrison, Rev., k. in a., 26/2/18.
Edwards, Evan, Rev., died, 27/11/18.
Egan, Pierce John, Rev., died, 6/4/16.
Evans, Geoffrey Maynard, M.C., Rev., k. in a., 11/8/17.
Evans-Jones, William, Rev., k. in a., 8/10/18 (att. 2nd Bn. R.W. Fus.).
Eyre-Powell, John William Alcock, Rev., k. in a., 16/4/18 (att. H.O., 27 Lab. Corps).
Falside, William James, Rev., died, 7/10/18.
Finn, William Joseph, Rev., k. in a., 25/4/15.
Fitzgibbon, John, M.C., Rev., k. in a., 18/9/18.
Fraser, Donald, D.S.O., Rev., killed, 2/6/18.
Freestone, William Herbert, Rev., k. in a., 14/12/16.
Fulford, Reginald Hardwick, Rev., k. in a., 15/12/16.
Garrett, Charles Harold, Rev., k. in a., 26/9/17.
Geare, William Duncan, Rev., k. in a., 31/7/17.
Gedge, Basil Johnson, Rev., d. of w., 25/4/17.
Gibbs, Edward Reginald, Rev., k. in a., 29/3/18 (att. 1st Gren. Gds.).
Gordon, Michael, Rev., d. of w., 27/8/17
Green, Ernest Newham, Rev., died, 26/3/16.
Green, Herbert, M.C., Rev., k. in a., 24/8/17 (att. 41st M.G.C.).
Green, Hugh James Bernard, Rev., died, 8/12/18 (att. 20th Div. Detls.).
Grobel, Peter, Rev., died, 1/1/17.
Gunson, Henry Edward, Rev., died, 23/8/18.
Guthrie, David Michall, Rev., d. of w., 21/11/16.
Gwynn, J., Rev., d. of w., 12/10/15 (att. Ir. Gds.).
Harbord, Frank Robert, Rev., d. of w., 8/8/17.
Harding, Wilfred John, M.C., Rev., k. in a., 31/10/17 (att. Drake Bn.).
Hardy, James Henry, Rev., k. in a., 5/5/18 (att. R.G.A.).
V.C. Hardy, Theodore Bayley, D.S.O., M.C., Rev., d. of w., 18/10/18 (att. 8th Linc. R.).
Hatfield, Arthur Percival, Rev., died, 9/7/18 (1st B.G.H.).
Hawdon, Noel Elliot, Rev., died, 16/11/18 (C. of E.) (att. 45 T.M.B.).
Hartigan, Jeremiah Austin, Rev., died, 16/7/10.
Heading, William Henry, Rev., died, 21/11/18.
Heath, Alfred, Rev., k. in a., 30/6/18 (att. 9th West R. Regt.).
Heggie, David, Rev., died, 23/10/17 (2/7th Roy. Scots).
Henderson, Robert Morley, Rev., died, 3/2/19.
Hewitt, Frederick Whitmore, Rev., k. in a., 28/9/15.
Hewitt, S. R., Rev., died, 16/2/19.
Holden, Oswald Addenbrooke, Rev., k. in a., 1/12/17 (att. 60th Inf. Brig.).
Hood, Charles Ivo Sinclair, Rev., d. of w., 15/4/18 (att. R.G.A., 41st Bde.).
Houlston, Edgar Charles, Rev., drowned, 4/5/17.
Howell, Thomas, Rev., k. in a., 1/12/17 (att. 6th King's Shrop. L.I.).
Inglis, Rupert Edward, Rev., k. in a., 18/9/16.
Ireland, John Thomas Craig, Rev., drowned, 4/5/17.
Jefferys, Charles Thomas Claude, Rev., died, 20/11/18.
Johnson, Ernest Edward, Rev., died, 1/12/18 (att. 15th Bn. Lanc. Fus.).
Johnson-Smyth, Edward, Rev., died, 10/2/17.
Jones, Basil, Rev., died, 25/10/18.
Jones, Thomas Glasfryn, Rev., d. of w., 12/4/17 (att. 11th S. Wales Bdrs.).
Jones, William Edgar, Rev., d. of w., 24/10/18 (att. 9th Bn. York. Regt.).
Judd, Alan Cecil, M.C., Rev., k. in a., 21/3/18 (att. 2/5 N. & Derby R.).
Kavanagh, Bernard, Rev., d. of w., 21/12/17.
Kay, William Henry, M.C., Rev., k. in a., 5/4/18 (att. 5th Dorset R.).
Kellie, John, Rev., k. in a., 1/8/17 (att. 6th Cam. Hdrs.).
Kirk, James, M.C., Rev., d. of w., 1/4/18 (att. 2nd Bn. Sea. Hdrs.).
Knapp, Simon Stock, D.S.O., M.C., Rev., d. of w., 1/8/17 (att. 2nd Bn. Ir. Gds.).
Langdon, Cecil, Rev., k. in a., 31/10/17 (att. 11th Bdr. R.).
Lawson, Henry Heaton, Rev., k. in a., 24/3/18 (att. 2nd Bn. North. R.).
Leakey, Herbert Nettleton, Rev., died, 24/7/17.
Ledbitter, Herbert Peter, Rev., died, 28/2/17 (att. A.M.T. D. Base).
Leeson, James Thomas, Rev., k. in a., 23/4/17 (att. 13th Bn. Roy. Fus.).
Lendrum, James Herbert Reginald, Rev., k. in a., 22/8/18.
Lester, Gerald James, Rev., died, 16/12/18 (att. C.M.E. Loco. Works).
Longridge, Archibald Owen Carwithen, Rev., died, 12/10/18 (att. 11th Gen. Hos., Boulogne).
Looby, Patrick, Rev., k. in a., 26/10/17.
McAuliffe, Cornelius, Rev., died, 6/10/16.
Mace, Alban Bodley, Rev., k. in a., 3/10/16.
McDonnell, John Joseph, Rev., k. in a., 9/4/18 (att. 55th M.G.C.).
McGinity, Henry Cuthbert, Rev., died, 8/11/18 (23rd Fld. Amb.).
McIlvaine, John, Rev., drowned, 26/2/18 (2/7th N. & D. Regt.).
Major, C. W. Wykeham, Rev., died, 19/3/19.
Martyn, Cecil Radcliffe, Rev., died, 3/3/19.
Matthews, Lewis Joseph, Rev., died, 26/5/16.
Meister, Charles Gustave Clark, M.C., Rev., k. in a., 18/4/18.
Millar, George, Rev., died, 26/8/17.
Mitchell, Charles Wand, Rev., d. of w., 3/5/17 (att. 8th E. Yks. R.).
Montague, Walter Philip, Rev., d. of w., 31/10/18 (att. 22nd Bde. R.G.A.).
Monteith, Robert John, Rev., d. of w., 27/11/17 (att. 70th A.F.A. Bde.).
Moore, Edgar Noel, M.C., Rev., killed, 5/1/18 (att. 20th Liv. R.).
O'Dea, Lawrence, Rev., died, 4/11/17.
O'Rorke, Benjamin Garniss, D.S.O., Rev., died, 25/12/18.
O'Sullivan, Donald, Rev., k. in a., 5/7/16.
Pardoe, George Southey, Rev., died, 15/10/18.
Peel, The Hon. Maurice Berkeley, M.C., Rev., k. in a., 14/5/17.
Plummer, Charles Benjamin, Rev., k. in a., 12/3/17.
Plumptre, Basil Pemberton, M.C., Rev., k. in a., 16/7/17 (att. 1/21st Lon. R.).
Prendergast, Matthew V., Rev., died, 16/9/18.
Ranking, George Harvey, Rev., k. in a., 20/11/17 (att. IV. Corps, Hvy. Art.).
Read, Eric Oswald, Rev., k. in a., 3/10/18 (att. 5th Dor. R.).
Reed, Clifford Hugh, M.C., Rev., k. in a., 7/6/17.
Robertson, Charles, M.C., Rev., d. of w., 3/10/18.
Roche, Francis Cavendish, Rev., died, 14/11/15.
Ruck-Keene, Benjamin Corrie, Rev., k. in a., 26/9/17 (att. 8th E. Yks. R.).
Ryan, Michael, Rev., died, 1/11/16.

Schooling, Cecil Herbert, Rev., d. of w., 21/6/17.
Shine, James, Rev., d. of w., 21/4/18 (att. 21st Bn. Mdx. R.).
Shovel, Thomas Jasper, Rev., d. of w., 5/10/18 (att. 2/2nd Wessex F.A.).
Smith, Frederick Seaton, Rev., died, 15/11/18 (att. 13th Y. & L.).
Spence, Alexander, M.C., Rev., d. of w., 31/3/18 (P.O.W. in enemy hands).
Spink, Hubert Octavius, Rev., k. in a., 9/8/16.
Staunton, Harvey, Rev., died, 14/1/18.
Stewart, James Robert, Rev., k. in a., 2/1/16 (att. 2nd Worc. R.).
Stewart, Robert Arthur, Rev., died, 3/11/17 (att. 57th C.C.S.).
Streeten, Basil Robert, Rev., died, 1/11/18 (att. 2/5th Lanc. Fus.).
Strickland, Joseph, Rev., died, 15/7/17 (12th Bde., 4th Div.).
Stuart, Alexander, Rev., k. in a., 24/10/17 (att. 12th R. Ir. Rif.).
Sullings, Stephen John, Rev., died, 21/11/15.
Tomkins, William Henry, Rev., died, 28/9/18 (att. 7th S. Staffs).
Trevor, Ernest Wilberforce, Rev., d. of w., 14/11/16 (att. 13th Rif. Bde.).
Tuke, Francis Henry, Rev., k. in a., 20/7/16.
Veryard, Albert Thomas, Rev., k. in a., 28/6/17 (att. 15th T.M.B.).
Wallace, John James, Rev., d. of w., 8/11/18 (att. 8th Nth. Staff. R.).
Watson, Charles, Rev., died, 22/7/18.
Watson, John Edmund Malone, Rev., d. of w., 10/4/18 (att. 21st Mdx. R.).
Watters, John, Rev., died, 7/11/18 (att. 115th Inf. Bde. H.Q.).
Were, Cyril Narramore, Rev., died, 9/1/18.
Whitefoord, Charles, Rev., d. of w., 30/5/18 (att. 6th Lon. R.).
Wilks, Walter Charles, M.C., Rev., k. in a., 4/10/17, Sen. Chap. NC. of E. (att. 7th Staff.).
Wood, Harold William, Rev., died, 1/11/18.
Woodhouse, Disney Charles, Rev., died, 6/10/16 (att. 12th R. Suss. R.).

Queen Alexandra's Imperial Military Nursing Service.

Armstrong, Helen, Sister, died, 20/3/19.
Barclay-Smith, J., A/Matron, died, 28/4/16.
Bates, Frances Mary, Special Probationer, died, 9/4/16.
Beaufoy, Katy, A/Matron, drowned, 26/2/18. GLENART CASTLE
Bennet, Helena Stewart, Staff Nurse, died, 18/10/18.
Beresford, R. R., Staff Nurse, drowned, 26/2/18. GLENART
Berrie, Charlotte, Sister, died, 8/1/19.
Blake, Edith, Staff Nurse, drowned, 26/2/18. GLENART CASTLE
Brace, F. E., Staff Nurse, died, 21/9/16.
Butler, S. E., Sister, died, 14/4/16.
Clough, M., Staff Nurse, died, 12/10/16.
Compton, F. D., Sister, died, 15/1/18.
Cooke, E. K., Staff Nurse, died, 8/9/17.
Croysdale, Marjorie, Military Probationer, died, 2/3/19.
Cruickshank, Isabella, Sister, drowned, 10/4/17. SALTA
Danaher, M., Staff Nurse, died, 12/10/18.
Dawson, Eveline Maud, Matron, drowned, 10/4/17. SALTA
Dewar, Margaret Smith, Staff Nurse, k. in a., 12/3/17.
Doherty, M. A., Staff Nurse, died, 5/9/16.
Donovan, B., Staff Nurse, died, 3/4/16.
Duckers, M. E., Staff Nurse, died, 16/5/18.
Duncan, Isabella Lucy, Sister, died, 1/3/17.
Edgar, Elizabeth, Staff Nurse, drowned, 26/2/18. GLENART CASTLE
Eliffe, M., Sister, died, 25/5/16.
Evans, Jane, Sister, drowned, 26/2/18. GLENART CASTLE
Farley, M., Matron, died, 1/6/18.
Ferguson, R., Staff Nurse, died, 26/6/18.
Foyster, Ellen Lucy, Sister, drowned, 10/4/17. SALTA
Garner, A. E. C., Sister, died, 12/3/17.
Gladstone, E. M., Sister, died, 24/1/19.
Gledhill, A., Sister, died, 17/10/18.
Grover, A. J., Sister, died, 6/2/19.
Gurney, Elizabeth Shepherd, Staff Nurse, drowned, 10/4/17. SALTA
Hawley, N., Military Probationer, drowned, 31/12/17.
Henry, Charlotte E., Staff Nurse, drowned, 26/2/18. GLENART CASTLE
Hilling, Sophie, Sister, died, 12/10/18.
Hobbes, Narelli, Sister, died, 10/5/18.
Hodgson, E. M., Sister, died, 21/12/18.
Jack, C., Sister, died, 22/10/18.
Jones, Gertrude Ellen, Sister, drowned, 10/4/17. SALTA
Jones, Hilda Lilian, Sister, died, 28/10/18.
Kemp., C., Staff Nurse, died, 4/7/18.
Kendall, R. E., Sister, drowned, 26/2/18. GLENART CASTLE
McAlister, Clara, Staff Nurse, drowned, 10/4/17. SALTA
Mann, Agnes Greig, Staff Nurse, drowned, 10/4/17. SALTA
Marmion, M., Sister, died, 25/1/19.
Marshall, Mary P., Staff Nurse, k in a., 12/3/17.
Mason, Fanny, Staff Nurse, drowned, 10/4/17. SALTA
Milne, Helen, Sister, died, 23/11/17.
Moreton, Ada, Staff Nurse, died, 7/9/16.
Parker, E. K., Matron, died, 16/10/16.
Pepper, Edith Dorothy, Special Probationer, died, 7/4/18.
Phillips, J., Sister, drowned, 20-21/3/17.
Radcliffe, E. B., Sister, died, 10/3/19.
Ritchie, Jessie, Staff Nurse, died, 13/8/16.
Roberts, Jane, Staff Nurse, drowned, 10/4/17. SALTA
Roberts, M. D., Staff Nurse, drowned, 31/12/17.
Robinette, C., Staff Nurse, died, 30/3/17.
Rodwell, Mary, Staff Nurse, drowned, 17/11/15.
Spindler, N., Staff Nurse, k in a., 21/8/17.
Stevens, L. M., Staff Nurse, died, 15/3/16.
Tindall, Fanny, Sister, died, 15/1/18.
Townsend, Martha, Staff Nurse, died, 21/9/18.
Turton, A. M., Staff Nurse, died, 7/5/17.
Wallace, E., Staff Nurse, died, 6/6/16.
Watson, E. H., Staff Nurse, died, 5/11/18.
Welford, Alice, Sister, died, 15/1/18.
Wilson, Christina Murdock, A/Sister, died, 1/3/10.
Wilson, M. E., Staff Nurse, died, 23/12/15.
Wright, Hannah, Elizabeth, Staff Nurse, died, 22/10/18.

Queen Mary's Army Auxiliary Corps.

Long, Violet Alice Lambton, O.B.E., Deputy-Chief Cont'r., died at sea, enemy action, 2/8/18.
Gibson, Margaret Annabella Campbell, M.M., Unit Admin'tr., died, 17/9/18.
Westwell, Mary, Asst. Admin'tr., died at sea, enemy action, 10/10/18.
Whall, Anna Marjorie, Asst. Admin'tr., died, 6/12/18.
Smyth, Mary Grace, Asst. Admin'tr., died, 22/2/19.
Martin, Margery Trail, Asst. Admin'tr., died, 17/5/18.
Stiebel, Marie Louise, Asst. Admin'tr., died, 1/12/18.
Russell, Eleanor, Asst. Admin'tr., died, 21/2/19.

Voluntary Aid.

Armstrong, Sarah Jane, Miss, died, 12/12/18.
Arnold, Margaret T., Miss, died, 12/3/16.
Baily, Wilhemina, Miss, died, 23/9/18 (St. J.A.B.).
Bain, Annie Watson, Miss, k. in a., 1/6/18 (St. J.A.B.).
Ball, Catherine, Miss, drowned, 31/12/17.
Barker, Edith Frances, Miss, died, 3/4/18.
Barrett, Sophia Violet, Nurse, drowned, 10/10/18.
Black, Eleanor Eileen, Miss, drowned, 4/6/18.
Bolus, Dorothy, Miss, drowned, 4/6/18.
Bousfield, Mary, Miss, died, 24/2/19.
Braithwaite, M. D., Miss, died, 3/3/19.
Brown, Winifred M., Miss, drowned, 31/12/17.
Bytheway, Gertrude, Miss, drowned, 31/12/17.
Chapman, M D., Miss, died, 10/8/18.
Coles, Daisy, Miss, k. in a., 30/9/17 (B.R.C.S.).
Crewdson, Dorothy Mary Lynerette, M.M., Miss, died, 13/3/19 (B.R.C.S.).
Dickson, Mary C., Miss, died, 16/2/17.
Duncanson, Una, Miss, drowned, 31/12/17.
Evans, Margaret Ellen, Miss, died, 22/7/17.
Faithfull, F. M., Miss, drowned, 15/1/18 (B.R.C.S.).
Gordon, Elizabeth Marjorie, Miss, died, 11/9/17 (St. J.A.B.).
Hackett, Venice Clementina, Miss, died, 13/10/18 (B.R.C.S.).
Hallam, Alice Violet, Miss, died, 18/12/16 (St. J.A.B.).
Ingram, Edith A., Miss, k. in a., 13-14/8/18.
Jones, Gladys Maud, Miss, died, 21/8/17 (B.R.C.S.).
Jones, L., Nurse, died, 6/6/16.
King, Nita Madeline, Miss, died, 25/5/17.
Liddell, Lily, Miss, died, 29/9/18 (B.R.C.S.).
Llewellyn, Gwenyth, Miss, died, 4/11/18 (B.R.C.S.).
Maunsell, Marian Jane, Miss, died, 7/1/19 (B.R.C.S.).
Midwood, Lilian, Miss, drowned, 31/12/17.
Neish, A., Miss, died, 18/10/18.
Richards, E., Miss, died, 14/10/18 (B.R.C.S.).
Rogers, Hermoine Angela, Miss, drowned, 31/12/17.
St. John, Esmee Barbara, Miss, died, 12/10/16.
Smith-Lee, Jeannie, Miss, died, 30/3/17.
Taylor, Nellie, Miss, died, 27/6/18 (B.R.C.S.).
Thomson, Elizabeth, Miss, k. in a., 30/9/17 (B.R.C.S.).
Tonkin, E. M., Miss, died, 14/10/18 (B.R.C.S.).
Warnock, Elizabeth MacMath, Miss, died, 5/5/18.
Williams, Jennie, Miss, died, 31/1/19.
Young, Mary Ann Eliza, died, 13/2/19.
Young, M. C., Nurse, died, 30/7/18.

Army Pay Department.

Capper, Charles Arthur, Lt. (Tp.), died, 11/3/19.
Cheese, Ernest Velmont, Lt. (Tp.), died, 30/7/16.
Clent, James Tom, Hon. Capt., died, 20/4/17.
Heselwood, George Robert Fettes, Lt., died, 15/4/15.
Hoy, William, Capt., died, 17/9/16.
Lewis, George, Lt., died, 9/12/16.
Wylie, Percival Thomas, Lt., died, 27/4/19.
Yates, George Herbert, Lt. (Tp.), died, 15/2/19 (H.Q., 4 Army).

The West African Regiment.

Andrew, Frederick, 2/Lt., T/Lt., k. in a., 27/2/15 (E. Yorks R.).
Bremner, John, T/Capt. and Qr.-Mr., died, 28/11/18.
Dinnen, Campbell Hackwood, Capt., k. in a., 4/3/18 (L'pool R.).
Fielding, Edward Fleming, Lt. (Tp.), k. in a., 24/10/15.
Grant, Alexander George William, Lt.-Col., k. in a., 25/9/15 (and Devon R.).

Channel Islands Militia (Guernsey).

1 Arnold, Frank William, 2/Lt., k. in a., 30/11/17 (R.G.L.I.).
Blanford, Frank Burrell, Capt., died, 25/4/17 (R.G.L.I.).
1 Borrett, Alfred Frank Cyril, Lt. (A/Capt.), k. in a., 24/11/17 (R.G.L.I.).
1 D'Auvergne, Francis Arthur Payne, Lt., k. in a., 12/4/18 (R.G.L.I.).
1 Davey, Archibald Henry Pingston, Major (Tp.), k. in a., 14/10/17 (R.G.L.I.).
Ellis, Bryan Grogan Langley, 2/Lt. (T/Capt.), k. in a., 13/10/17 (R.G. Mil. and R.F.C.).
1 Hamel, Robert Sydney, 2/Lt., k. in a., 12/4/18 (R.G.L.I.).
1 Johns, Herbert, 2/Lt. (A/Capt.), k. in a., 11/4/18 (R.G.L.I.).

1 Laine, Thomas de Jersey, 2/Lt. (Tp.), k. in a., 21/11/17 (R.G.L.I.).
1 Lynch, James Stewart, Lt., k. in a., 30/11/17 (R.G.L.I.).
2 Manger, Gerald, 2/Lt. (Tp.), k. in a., 21/3/18 (R.G.L.I.).
1 Mortis, Eric John, 2/Lt., k. in a., 12/4/18 (R.G.L.I.).
1 Rihoy, Stanley Alfred, 2/Lt., d. of w., 12/4/18 (R.G.L.I.).
1 Stranger, George, 2/Lt., k. in a., 11/4/18 (R.G.L.I.).
1 Stranger, Harry Easterbrook K., M.C., A/Capt., d. of w., 11/5/18 (R.G.L.I.).

Channel Islands Militia (Jersey).

Hibbs, Laurence Bosdet, 2/Lt. (Tp.), died, 21/3/16 (R. Jersey Mil., att. 7/R. Ir. Rifs.).
Johnston, George Mitchell, Capt., k. in a., 3/4/16 (R. Jersey Mil.) (7/R. Ir. Rifs.).
2 Robin, Charles Harold, Capt., k. in a., 11/5/17 (R. Jersey Mil., att. 13/Y. & L.R.).

The King's Own Malta Regiment of Militia.

1 Huber, Edgar W., 2/Lt. (Tp.), killed, 2/11/16.
Huber, H. W., Lt., k. in a., 7/1/16 (att. R. Innis. Fus.).
2 Micallef, Paolo, Capt., died, 11/12/16.
Eynaud, P. A. M., Lt., k. in a., 21/3/18 (att. R. Mun. Fus.).

Special Lists.

Agerup, H., Lt., acc. killed, 5/6/18 (and R.A.F.).
Agg, Arthur William, Lt. (Tp.), died, 2/4/10.
Allatt, Henry Thomas Ward, Col., died, 8/5/16.
Anderson, James, Lt. (Tp.), k. in a., 20/8/16 (87th T.M.B., 26/10.).
Anderson, J. L. K., 2/Lt., k. in a., about 31/5/18 (and R.A.F.).
Anderson, Robert, Lt., drowned, 29/5/18 (I.W.T.).
Arbuthnot, Lenox Stanley, Capt., killed, 1/11/18 (and R.A.F.).
Baker, James, Lt. & Q.M. (Tp.), died, 4/6/17.
Barlow, R. T., Capt., k. in a., 30/7/18 (and R.A.F.).
Barnard, Ernest Yorke, Capt. (Tp.), died, 5/3/18.
Barrie, David, Capt. & Q.R., died, 18/12/17.
Barrett, Hugh Treherne, Lt., died, 6/11/17 (Nyassaland Field Force).
Beatty, Charles Harold Longfield, D.S.O., Major (Tp.), d. of w., 17/5/17 (A.D.C., Can. Corps H.Q.).
Bennett-Goldney, Francis, Tp. Capt. (Act. Major), died, 26/7/18.
Boulton, Alec Gordon, 2/Lt. (Tp.), died, 19/2/16.
Box, G. H., Lt., killed, 25/8/18 (and R.A.F.).
Braithwaite, Sydney, Lt., died, 4/12/16.
Browning, G. S., Capt. (Tp.), died, 25/2/16.
Burge, P. S., Capt. (Tp.), k. in a., 42/7/18 (att. R.A.F.).
Burns-Begg, Robert, Col., died, 9/1/18 (Staff).
Carden, Ronald Hugh, 2/Lt., k. in a., 14/3/15 (att. Wilts Regt.).
Cooke, I. A. E., Lt k. in a., 19/7/17 (T.M.B.).
Cornock-Taylor, Gerald, O.B.E., A/Lt.-Col., died, 14/2/19.
Cotton, Willoughby Lynch, Capt., died, 6/1/18.
Craven, Austen James Arthur, Lt. (Tp.), died, 27/8/18.
Cunliffe, Robert Ellis, 2/Lt. (Tp.), k. in a., 9/5/15 (att. Royal Berks).
Curtis, H. J., Lt., k. in a., 4/11/18 (att. R.A.F.).
Dennis, L. V., T/Lt., k. in a., 31/7/18 (att. R.A.F.).
Dinsmore, Edmund, Capt. (Tp.), died, 12/11/18.
Durrant, Christopher Martin, Lt. (Tp.), killed, 31/7/18.
Durrant, T., Capt., died, 16/5/18 (and R.A.F.).
Dyer, R., M.M., Lt., died, 30/12/18.
Gregson, Francis Robert, Capt., d. of s., 15/5/17 (att. 4th Aust. Div.).
Gunter, Sir Robert Benson Nevill (Bart.), Lt.-Col., died, 16/8/17.
Gabain, William George, M.C., Capt., k. in a., 24/3/18 (att. 2nd Rif. Bde.).
Gleeson, Timothy (Capt. & Q.-M. (Tp.), died, 22/11/18 (School of Musk., Sth. Com.).
Goodman, Reginald Moon, 2/Lt., k. in a., 16/5/15 (att. Border Regt.).
Gribble, Horace Dewey, Lt. (Tp.), died, 13/7/18 (Nigeria Regt.).
Grier, Francis Nemo, Lt. & Q.-M., died, 30/4/18.
Guiney, Edward Castray, Capt., drowned, 14/2/18 (Nyassaland Field Force).
Harper, Alfred George Montague Norton, Capt. (Tp.), k. in a., 16/10/17 (att. Nigeria Rgt.).
Hawkins, John Bawtree, Capt. & Adjt. (Tp.), died, 30/8/16.
Hill, Eric Alfred, Lt. (Tp.), killed, 12/1/17.
Hill, John Newton, 2/Lt. (Tp.), died, 11/8/16 (Camel Transport Corps).
Hind, I. F., Capt., died, 12/8/18 (and R.A.F.).
Hore, Charles Owen, C.M.G., Col., died, 14/2/16.
Knight, C. R. Wentworth, Lt., died 21/6/19 (P. of W.).
Lindberg, Thomas Henry, Major (Tp.), died, 24/4/15.
Lansdown, Francis Arthur Stanley, 2/Lt. (Tp.), died, 14/8/17 (1/Bn. Brit. West Indies Regt.).
Lawson, Arthur James, 2/Lt. died, 17/12/18.
Macdonald, John Doran, Capt. (Tp.), d. of w., 18/3/16.
McKinnon, C. F., Capt., died, 14/6/19 (att. 1/6th K.A.R.).
MacMullen, George Reade, Major, died, 28/1/16.
Madge, Charles Albert (Tp.) Lt.-Col., k. in a., 10/5/16.
Maxwell-Heron, Basil Charles Montague, Capt. (Tp.), died, 22/9/16.
Molyneux-Seal, Edmund Harrington, Major, died, 6/8/15.
Norton, John Arnold, Capt. (Tp.), d. of s., 19/11/15.
Newsam, Arthur Fowler, Lt. (Tp.), d. of w., 30/3/18 (att. Imp. Camel Corps).
Proctor, Frederick William, Major (Tp.), died, 13/6/16.
Rich, Arthur, Capt., died, 29/2/16.
Sang, Alfred Frederick Joseph, 2/Lt., d. of w., 2/10/14.
Scarlett, Thomas, Capt., died, 31/1/19.
Scott, Walter Elvin, 2/Lt., k. in a., 7/5/15.
Seabrook, James Herbert, Lt., k. in a., 10/9/14.
Shuff, William Edward, Lt. & Qr.-Mr., died, 20/12/16.
Smith, Julian Martin, 2/Lt. (Tp.), died, 10/9/14.
Stalker, Francis Brown Douglas, 2/Lt. (Tp.), k. in a., 22/8/15.
Taylor, Percy Ezra, Lt., died, 30/3/19 (I.W.T.).
Thicke, Frank Vincent, Lt., k. in a., 31/10/14.
Thompson, Peter Cleasby, Lt., died, 4/3/19 (Nigerian Regt.).
Wallis, Arthur Vincent, Lt., died, 10/7/17 (Egyptian Labour Corps).
Wearing, Douglas George, Capt. (Tp.), died, 11/11/18.
Welinkar, S. K. C., Lt., k. in a., 27/6/18 (and R.A.F.).
Wellwood, Frederick Paton, Capt., died, 6/2/17.
White, Arthur Elimen, Lt., died, 22/7/17 (I.W.T.).
Whittall, Roland William, 2/Lt. (Tp.), d. of w., 6/8/15.
Watson, William, Lt. & Q.M., died, 18/6/18.
Will, Alfred William, Lt. (Act. Major), k. in a., 25/5/18 (att. S. Persia Rifles).
Willey, Duncan, Capt., k. in a., 14/7/19.
Wintour, Reginald Prince, Lt., died, 15/12/16.
Walker, Robert Sandiland Frowd, C.M.G. (Tp.), Lt.-Col., died, 16/5/17.
Wood, James, Capt., died, 14/9/18.

West African Frontier Force.

Allen, Henry Edward, Lt. (Tp.), drowned, 24/4/17 (Gen. List).
Anthony, George Adam Moriarty, Lt., k. in a., 24/1/16 (9 R.W. Surr. R., att.).
Arnold, Thomas Wilson, Lt. (Tp.), d. of w., 15/9/16 (Gold Coast R.).
Balders, Arthur William, Capt., k. in a., 27/11/15 (Norf. R., att. Nigerian R.).
Barclay, George Eric, Capt., k. in a., 24/1/17 (R. Lanc. R., att. 4/Nigerian R.).
Baskett, Edmund Graham, Capt. (Tp.), died, 27/10/18 (Gen. List, att. Nigerian R.).
Biddulph, Leonard Shrapnell, Capt., d. of w., 29/12/16 R.F.A., att. Nigerian R.).
Blakeney, Leslie St. Leger, Lt., drowned, 28/3/15 (Lanc. Fus. & Gold Coast Rgt.).
Bowyer-Smijth, Cedric Gray, Capt., k. in a., 4/11/15 (Glos. R.).
Bradford, Cecil Aubrey, Capt., drowned, 24/4/17 (Yorks R., att. Nigerian R.).
Brown, James Sutherland, Lt. (Tp.), k. in a., 30/9/17 (att. 3 Nigerian R.).
Catt, Archibald William, M.C., 2/Lt. (T/Lt.), died, 9/3/18 (3 Nigerian R., W. Kent R.).
Cooke, Hans Hendrick Anthony, Capt., k. in a., 24/1/17 (Conn. Rangers, att. 3 Nigerian R.).
Corner, Herbert Edward, Lt. (Tp.), died, 30/10/17 (Gen. List, att. Gold Coast R.).
Dudley, Bernard John Cherleton, Capt., k. in a., 24/1/17 (Dorset R., att. 3 Nigerian R.).
Earle, John Vincent, Lt., k. in a., 20/6/15 (1 N. & D.R.).
Easton, Percy Thomas, Capt., died, 26/11/18 (Middlesex R. & Nigerian R.).
Gray, Francis Henry Tower, Lt. (Tp.), drowned, 21/7/18.
Green, Charles Henry, Capt. (A/Major), d. of w., 8/11/17 (S. Staffs R., att. Nigerian R.).
Harper, Alfred George Montague Norton, Capt., k. in a., 16/10/17 (41 L. Nigerian R.).
Harvey, Thomas Daniel, M.C., Lt. (Tp.), died 17/10/18 (M.G.C., att. Nigerian R.).
Higgins, Percy Clynton, Capt., k. in a., 22/9/17 (1 Shrops. L.I., att. Nigerian R.).
Hills, Ernest Leslie, Lt. (Tp.), d. of w., 26/11/15 (12 R. Welsh Fus., att. N. Nigerian R.).
Hornby, Cecil Geoffrey, O.B.E., M.C., Major (Tp. Lt.-Col.), died, 30/12/18 (E. Lancs R., att.).
Huddart, Lindow Hereward Leofric, Lt. (Tp.), died, 5/2/17 (Gen. List, att. 1 Nigerian R.).
Huntriss, William, Lt. (Tp.), died, 24/10/18 (9 W. Rid. R., att.).
Kingham, George William Ambrose, 2/Lt., drowned, 9/11/17 (3 E. Kent. R.).
Knapp, Arthur Douglas, Lt. (Tp.), died, 27/5/17 (Nyasaland Field Force).
Joseland, Arthur Noel, Lt., k. in a., 22/9/17 (4 E. Surr. R., att. Nigerian R.).
Lees, Jasper, 2/Lt. drowned, 28/3/15 (H.L.I., att. 4th).
Lockley, Rupert, Major, died, 21/10/15 (Gordon Hrs.).
McIver, Kenneth Patrick John, Lt. (Tp.), d. of w., 26/1/16 (Nigerian R.).
Mackinnon, Lionel Neil Alexander, Capt., k. in a., 6/11/15 (Cold. Gds.).
Markham-Rose, Kenneth, Lt., k. in a., 3/5/16 (Essex R.).
Marwood, Charles Phillip Lysaght, Capt., d. of w., 24/11/15 (R. War. R., att Nigerian R.).
Massy, Haworth Peel, Capt., died, 10/12/14 (Leinster R., att. Nigerian R.).
Mesham, Robert Seymour, Lt. (Tp.), k. in a., 19/4/18.
Morrison, James McGregor, M.C., Lt. (Tp.), died, 15/2/19 (Gen. List, Nigerian Regt.).
Newstead, George Pope, Lt.-Col., d. of w., 4/3/15 (Suff. R.).
Nicholas, William John Worth, 2/Lt., drowned, 3/4/15 (3 N. & D.R. & Nigerian R.).
Noel, The Hon. Robert Edmund Thomas More, Capt., died, 2/2/18 (6 R. Fus., att. 1/Nigerian R.)
Pike, Richard Nicholson, Capt., k. in a., 8/9/15 (Nigerian R.).

Pomeroy, Granville George, Capt. (Tp.), died, 30/3/17 (Gen. List, att. Nigerian R.).
Randall, Stanley, 2/Lt. (T/Lt.), died, 31/12/18 (E. Kent R., att.).
Robinson, Frederick Henry, M.C., Lt., k. in a., 30/9/17 (3 Linc. R., att Nigerian R.).
Robertson, G. H. M., Lt. (Tp.), died, 10/3/19 (Nigerian R., Gen. List).
Robinson, Harold William, 2/Lt. (T/Lt.), k. in a. 30/9/17 (York. L.I., att. 3/Nigerian R.).
Shaw, S., Lt. (Tp.), died, 13/1/18 (Gold Coast R.)
Sherlock, Gerrard Lourdes Edward, Lt., k. in a., 25/8/14 (3 Huss. & Nigerian Rgt.).
Shields, George Hilord, Lt. (Tp.), k. in a., 3/2/17 (Gold Coast R.).
Sinclair, Frank, Lt., drowned 3/10/18 (R Fus., att. Nigerian R.).
Stewart, Adrian Harry, Lt., k. in a., 29/8/14 (Glos. R. & Niger. R.)
Strong, George Henry, 2/Lt. (T/Lt.), k. in a., 3/1/17 (Nigerian R., Gen. List).
Thompson, George Masterman, Lt., k. in a., 22/8/14 (R. Scots & Gold Coast R.).
Thompson, Peter Cleasby, Lt., died, 4/3/19 (Spec. List., att. Nigerian Regt.).
Thruston, Bertie John, D.S.O., Capt. (T/Major), died, 22/11/18 (Lincoln R.).
Walker, George, Lt. (Tp.), d. of w., 28/11/15 (10 Bedford R., att.).
Waters, Charles Louis, M.C., Capt. (A/Major), d. of w., 19/10/17 (R. Berks R., att. 1/Nigerian R.).
Wickham, Thomas Strange, D.S.O., Lt., k. in a., 25/8/14 (Manch. R., att. Nigerian R.).
Williams, Stanley Charles Howard, Lt., died, 14/10/18 (Nigerian R.).
Woods, Richard Cheetham, Lt. (Tp.), k. in a., 18/10/17 (Gold Coast R.).

The King's African Rifles.

3/2 Alcock, Frank, Lt., died, 3/9/17.
1 Angell, Benjamin Eyre, Lt., k. in a., 20/2/17.
Archdale, D. M., Lt. (Tp.), k. in a., 13/11/16.
Armstrong, Gwin Henry, Lt. (Tp.), died, 28/10/18 (Norfolk and Nigeria Rgt.).
2/2 Batchelor, T. A., Capt., d. of w., 29/11/17.
3 Biddulph, Percival Vincent, 2/Lt. (Tp.), k. in a., 19/7/17 (Gen. List).
Bird, H., Lt., died, 12/4/19 (Gren. Gds., att. K.A.R.).
Bones, A. M., Lt. (Tp.), k. in a., ——1916.
1 Booty, W. G. S., 2/Lt. (Tp.), k. in a., 30/10/16 (Gen. List).
Brand, Ernest Stanley, Capt., k. in a., 8/10/14 (Roy. Fus.).
1/2 Brown, Claude Joseph John, Lt., died, 18/11/18 (3rd N'hants Rgt.).
2 Bryant, Oliver Mackenzie Beadon, Lt., killed, 11/12/16.
3/4 Calder, William Herberton, Lt., d. of w., 22/8/17.
1/2 Caldicott, Alan, Capt. (Tp.), k. in a., 7/12/16 (Gen. List).
1 Clachan, William James, Capt., k. in a., 6/1/18 (Middx. Regt.).
1 Clark, C. B., Capt., k. in a., 3/11/16.
3 Claydon, A. W. R., Lt., died, 31/5/18.
2 Coxwell, W. S. G., Lt., d. of w., 18/10/17.
Craig, James Young, 2/Lt., d. of w., 24/10/17 (3rd Arg. and Suth. Hldrs.).
Crosland, John Herbert, Lt., died, 13/4/19 (R.W. Fus.).
Cundle, Thomas William, 2/Lt. (T/Lt.), k. in a., 27/9/17 (att. 2nd Bn.).
3 Dawson, C. C., Lt., died, 23/9/16.
2/3 Dickenson, Hugh Carey, Capt. (T/Lt.-Col.), died, 18/12/18 (1st Som. L.I.).
Douglas, Kenneth Mackenie, Lt. (Tp.), died, 9/12/18 (7th Seaforth Hld.).
2/2 Dunman, Victor William, Lt. (Tp.), d. of w., 19/9/17.
1 Dyer, Arthur Francis Rayner, T/Cpt. & Adjt., k. in a., 30/9/17 (Gen. List).
Evershed, Ernest Bernard, 2/Lt. (T/Lt.), k. in a., 27/9/17 (Gen. List).
Foster, Archibald Courtenay Hayes, Lt., k. in a., 20/9/14 (& Hamps. Rgt.).
1 Fowler, Alexander George, Capt. (Tp.), k. in a., 1/1/18.
Gardiner, Kenneth John Rattray, Lt. (T/Cpt.), died, 1/2/17 (Spec. List).
Going, C. H. B., Lt., k. in a., 18/8/17.
Graham, Peter, Capt. (Tp.), k. in a., 30/8/18 (Cam. Hldrs.).
2/2 Green, Alfred, Lt. (Tp.), k. in a., 19/9/17.
3/4 Greswolde-Williams, Francis Humphrey John, Lt., k. in a., 3/8/17.
Guiney, Edward Castray, Capt. (Tp.), drowned, 14/2/18.
Gundle, G. W., Lt., k. in a., 27/9/17.
Harding, Claude Stephen, Lt. (Tp.), died, 22/1/18 (Gen. List).
Harrigan, William Piercy, Lt. (Tp.), died, 1/11/18 (11th Arg. & Suth. Hldrs.).
Hart, Charles Crowther, 2/Lt. (T/Lt. in Army), k. in a., 14/11/17 (3rd W. Riding R.).
3 Healy, Guy Rambant, Lt., k. in a., 11/3/16 (4th R. Mun. Fus.).
1/2 Heaton, Philip Ralph, Lt. (Tp.), died, 4/1/17.
1 Hill, Ralph Grenfell, k. in a., 20/2/17.
3/2 Hodgkinson, G., Lt., d. of w., 18/10/17.
Hodgson, Frederick James, Lt. (Tp.), died, 5/5/18 (Gen. List).
3 Hoffa, J. M. G., Lt., died, 28/7/17.
4 Hudson-Kinahan, C. B., Lt. (Tp.), died, 30/12/15.
1/4 Hunt, D. A., D.S.O., Capt. (Tp.), d. of w., 30/11/17.
Hutchins, Cedric Page, Lt. (Tp.), k. in a., 14/11/17 (Gen. List).
1/3 Ireland, H. F., Lt., d. of w., 22/7/17.
Jardine, Charles Hunt, Lt. (Tp.), k. in a., 3/5/18 (13th R. Scots).
Jervis, Arthur Cyril, Lt. (T/Cpt.), k. in a., 3/7/18 (3rd L'pool R.).
3/3 Kemp, George Arnold, Lt. (Tp.), died, 12/1/18 (3rd York. L.I.
1 Kendrick, A. Percy, Lt., d. of w., 9/10/17.
4 Leeke, Ralph Henry, Capt. (T/Major), died, 5/11/15 (Rifle Bde.).
Le May, Lionel Henry, Lt. (A/Cpt.), died, 24/2/19.
1 Leslie, Leslie Francis, 2/Lt., k. in a., 20/8/17.
1/3 Lloyd, H., Lt. (Tp.), k. in a., 19/7/17.
3 Lovegrove, Sidney Joseph, Capt., d. of w., 14/3/16 (N. Staff. R.).
3 Lyonclark, Basil L., Capt. (Tp.), d. of w., 9/7/17.
3 McDonald, Archibald, Lt., k. in a., 19/7/17.
1/3 MacDougall, D. C., Lt., k. in a., 27/7/17.
McIver, Kenneth MacKenzie, Lt. (Tp.), killed, 30/10/18 (K.R.R.C.).
2/2 McGregor, R., Lt., died, 3/5/17.
4/3 McMichael, J. E., Lt., died, 12/5/17.
3/3 McMillan, J. S., Lt. (Tp.), died, 12/3/18 (Gen. List).
Maddick, Sidney Alfred, Lt. (Tp.), died, 2/12/18 (20th L'pool Rgt.).
Mann, Horace, Lt., died, 25/12/18 (3rd Dorset Rgt.).
Mellor, Harold Welton, Capt. (Tp.), died, 28/5/18 (15th R. Fus.).
Michell, James Douglas, Lt. (Tp.), died, 9/10/18 (M.G.C.).
Moir, Douglas, M.C., 2/Lt., d. of w., 22/7/18 (Cam. Hldrs.).
1 Muir, Mathew Andrew, Capt., died, 18/7/16 (15th Hus.).
3/2 Murray, Frederick Stanley, Lt., d. of w., 19/11/17 (N. Staffs Rgt.).
Oldfield, G. C. O., Lt., k. in a., 5/9/14 (R. W. Surrey Rgt.).
4 Power, R. E., Lt., k. in a., 17/4/18.
Pugh, Edward Rhodes, Capt. (Tp.), died, 2/12/18 (30th N'thumb. Fus.).
Ramsay, A. G., Capt. (Tp.), died, 6/1/19.
Read, Stephen Tucker, Lt. (Tp.), died, 11/12/18 (15th Yorks Rgt.).
Rose, Ronald Madoc Tierney, Capt., k. in a., 18/9/16 (York and Lanc.).
3/2 Russell, T. L., T/Lt. (A/Capt.), k. in a., 6/11/17.
1/4 Sheppard, A. G. E., Lt., killed, 12/11/17.
Sharp, E., Lt., died, 22/5/17.
Sieber, John Lonsdale, Lt., k. in a., 17/10/17 (4th Arg. & Suth. Hldrs.).
4 Snell, Eric Aylmer Goldney, Major (Tp.), k. in a., 16/11/17 (Bedfords Regt.).
Stern, Sidney, Lt., k. in a., 19/7/17.
1/3 Stirling, Gordon Sheffield, D.S.O., M.C., Capt., d. of w., 26/12/16 (R. of O., Arg. & Suth. Hldrs.).
Thornycroft, Edward Gerald Mytton, Lt., k. in a., 15/9/14 (Roy. Lanc. R.).
3/2 Tribe, A. L., Capt. (Tp.), d. of w., 17/11/17 (2nd Rhodesian Rgt.).
2 Trotter, C. L., Lt. (Tp.), died, 22/1/18.
Vaughan, James Henry Lionel, Major, k. in a., 12/5/18 (Gen. List).
3/4 Vetter, H. E., Capt., died, 12/1/18.
4 Walsen, C. W., Lt. (Tp.), k. in a., 4/8/17.
Watts, Grahan Harman, 2/Lt., died, 11/7/18 (Cameron Hdrs.).
3/2 Williams, G., Lt. (Tp.), d. of w., 7/8/17.
1/7 Wilson, William Alderice, Lt. (Tp.), died, 6/4/19 (Gen. List).
2 Wood, Hubert Kenneth, Lt. (Tp.), died, 16/5/17.
1/2 Woods, W. J., Lt. (Tp.), d. of w., 24/4/17.
4 Woodhouse, A. F., Lt., k. in a., 13/4/18.
2/4 Wroth, W. A., Lt., k. in a., 31/5/18.

Part II.—Territorial Forces.

Ayrshire Yeomanry.

Bell, James, Major, died, 2/3/15.
Mackie, James Logan, Lt. (A/Capt.), k. in a., 27/12/17.
Cooper, William Dermot, Capt., k. in a., 30/8/17.
Shairp, Norman, M.C., Capt., died, 13/10/18.
Angus, Robert E., Lt., k. in a., 20/11/17 (att. R.F.C.).
Bruce, J. A., Lt., died, 6/1/19 (and R.A.F.).
Smith, Thomas Lawrie, Lt., k. in a., 18/9/18 (and M.G.C.).
Weir, Herbert James, Lt., d. of w., 9/11/17.
Dunlop, Alesander Hamilton, 2/Lt., k. in a., 6/11/17.
MacAndrew, Colin Geen Orr, 2/Lt., k. in a., 2/10/17 (and R.F.C.).

Bedfordshire Yeomanry.

Dove, Lewis, Lt., d. of w., 1/4/18.
Edis, Walter Owen, Lt., k. in a., 29/3/18.
Woodhams, Eric William, Lt., d. of w., 11/12/17.
Clark, Norman Henry, 2/Lt., d. of w., 25/11/17.
Wiltshire, Charles Robert, 2/Lt., d. of w., 13/7/16.

Berks Yeomanry.

Gooch, Edward Sinclair, Major, d. of w., 21/9/15.
Wroughton, Philip Musgraven, Major (Tp.), k. in a., 19/4/17.
Thomas, William Humphrey, Capt., d. of w., 28/11/17.
Bertie, Richard Frederick Norreys, Lt., k. in a., 20/11/17.
Headington, Arthur Hutton, Lt., k. in a., 27/11/17.
Niven, William Edward Graham, Lt., k. in a., 21/8/15.
Ainger, Thomas Edward, 2/Lt., k. in a., 21/8/15.
Hewer, Richard Tuckey, 2/Lt., k. in a., 21/11/17.
Sutton, William Victor Ross, 2/Lt., k. in a., 13/11/17.

Buckinghamshire Yeomanry.

De Rothschild, Evelyn Achille, Major, d. of w., 17/11/17.
Egerton, Louis Edward William, Capt., k. in a., 1/8/17.
Grenfell, Riversdale Nonn, Capt., k. in a., 14/9/14.
Primrose, The Hon. Neil James Archibald, M.C., Capt., k. in a., 15/11/17.
Bennett, Charles Henry, M.C., Lt., drowned, 27/5/18.

Cheshire Yeomanry.

Glazebrook, Philip Kirkland, D.S.O., Major, k. in a., 7/3/18.
Aldersey, Hugh, Capt., k. in a., 10/3/18.
De Knoop, John Julius Jersey, Capt., k. in a., 7/8/16.
Lockett, Garstang Bradstock, M.C., Lt. (A/Capt.), d. of w., 4/11/18.
Edghill, Arthur Richard, Lt., k. in a., 9/10/17.
Soames, William Noel, Lt., died, 19/5/16.
Holaway, Charles Edmund, 2/Lt., k. in a., 11/8/17 (and R.F.C.).

Denbighshire Yeomanry.

James, Alyn Reginald, Capt., k. in a., 24/3/18 (and R.F.C.).
Rooper, William Victor Trevor, Capt., k. in a., 9/10/17 (and R.F.C.).
Sandbach, Gilbert Robertson, Capt., d. of w., 3/7/17.
Miller, John Kingsley, Lt., k. in a., 19/9/18.
Allison, Robert Stafford, 2/Lt., k. in a., 16/6/17.
Thomas, Llewellyn, 2/Lt., k. in a., 27/12/17.

Derbyshire Yeomanry.

Winterbottom, Guy, Major, k. in a., 9/8/17.
Gold, Charles Read, D.S.O., Capt., k. in a., 21/11/17.
Vernon, Lord George Francis Augustus, Capt., died, 10/11/15.
Gillett, Herbert Edward, Lt., died, 23/11/18.
Mansell, Leslie Wyndham, 2/Lt., k. in a., 20/4/17

Royal 1st Devon Yeomanry.

Hain, Edward, Capt., k. in a., 11/11/15.
Hawker, Reginald Sudlow, Capt., d. of w., 9/11/17.
Heathcoat-Amory, Ludovic, Capt., d. of w., 25/8/18.
Bragg, William Robyns, Lt., k. in a., 3/12/17.
Nickalls, Hugh Quihampton, Lt., k. in a., 29/7/17 (and R.F.C.).

Royal North Devon Yeomanry.

St. Hill, George Herbert, Lt.-Col., k. in a., 8/7/17.
Thynne, Algernon Cateret, D.S.O., Lt.-Col., k. in a., 6/11/17.
Bayly, John, Major, died, 26/2/18.
Greig, Morland John, Major, k. in a., 17/10/15.
Clemson, John Oliver, Lt. (T/Capt.), d. of w., 9/12/15.
Hodgson, Cyril Arthur Godwin, Capt., died, 20/3/18.
Whitfield, N. B., Capt., died, 7/7/18 (att. R.A.F.).
Crimmin, Florence, Lt., k. in a., 24/4/17.
Hancock, William Reginald, Lt., k. in a., 24/4/17.
Kelly, Robert Maitland, Lt., k. in a., 11/1/17.
Pizey, Noel Martin, Lt., d. of w., 27/7/17 (and R.F.C.).

Dorset Yeomanry.

Reeves, Victor Charles Methuen, Major, k. in a., 26/2/16.
Browne, Harold Vernon, Capt., d. of w., 7/9/15.
Hoare, Henry Colt Arthur, Capt., d. of w., 20/12/17.
Yeatman, Harry Farr, Capt., k. in a., 21/11/17.
Cross, Reginald Carlton, Lt., k. in a., 7/6/18.
Kennaway, Arthur Lewis, Lt., k. in a., 21/8/15.
Knight, George Gordon, Lt., d. of w., 17/6/18.
Lees, Sir Thomas Evans Keith, Bart., Lt., d. of w., 24/8/15.
Middleton, Ernest, Lt., k. in a., 26/2/16.
Wakefield, Frank Mahan, Lt., died, 2/1/19 (and M.G.C.).
Gray, Frederick William, M.C., 2/Lt., k. in a., 21/8/15.
Hope, Charles Bateman, 2/Lt., k. in a., 26/2/10.
Paulet, Cecil Henry, 2/Lt., k. in a., 27/2/16.
Roberts, Edgar, 2/Lt., k. in a., 31/8/18.
Ryan, Warwick John Norwood, 2/Lt., k. in a., 5/9/16.

Essex Yeomanry.

Deacon, Edmund, Lt.-Col., k. in a., 13/5/15.
Roddick, Andrew, Major, k. in a., 14/5/15.
Wedd, Edward Parker Wallman, M.C., Capt., k. in a., 13/7/18.
Herron, K. C., Lt., k. in a., 24/4/18 (and R.A.F.).
Johnston, Geoffrey Stewart, Lt., k. in a., 14/5/15.
Reid, Geoffrey Percy Nevile, Lt., k. in a., 14/5/15.
Tower, Christopher Cecil, Lt., k. in a., 4/10/15.
Woodhouse, L. M., M.C., D.F.C., Lt., k. in a., 21/3/18 (and R.A.F.).
Christy, Thomas Hill, 2/Lt., k. in a., 12/4/18.
Lingeman, John Florris, 2/Lt., d. of w., 28/4/17.
Swire, Alexander Glen, 2/Lt., killed, 14/5/15.

Fife and Forfar Yeomanry.

Osborne, George Edward Bell, Major, k. in a., 6/11/17.
Stewart, Ralph Walker, Major, k. in a., 2/9/18.
Colthart, Robert Herd, Capt., d. of w., 2/11/18.
Nairn, Ian Couper, M.C., Capt., k. in a., 2/9/18.
Thom, James Flockhart, M.C., Capt., d. of w., 27/9/18 (and M.G.C.).
Baldie, J. B., Lt., k. in a., 6/11/18 (and R.A.F.).
Ewart, William Grieve, Lt., k. in a., 30/3/18.
Darsie, George, Lt., d. of w., 31/7/18.
Johnstone, William Jeffray, Lt., k. in a., 28/12/17.
Robertson, John Ross, Lt., k. in a., 12/5/17 (and R.F.C.).

Glamorgan Yeomanry.

Prichard, Richard Gerald Mannsell, Major, d. of w., 7/6/18 (att. Central India Horse).
Abraham, Geoffrey William Pepperall, Capt., d. of w., 19/11/17.
Aylett-Branfill, Capel, Capt., died, 11/5/16.
Baskerville, Ralph Hopton, Capt., k. in a., 9/4/18.
Miers, Richard Henry Probyn, Capt., killed, 12/12/17 (and R.F.C.).
Thomas, Arthur Tuder, Capt., d. of w., 29/9/18.
Edwards, William Armino, Lt., d. of w., 1/11/17.
Morris, James, Lt., k. in a., 27/12/17.
Wakeford, Charles Herbert Stanley, Lt., k. in a., 7/9/18.
Wakeford, F. R. S., Lt., died, 25/12/18 (and R.A.F.).
Brewer, Edmund, 2/Lt., d. of w., 12/1/18.

Queen's Own Royal Glasgow Yeomanry.

Croshaw, Oswald Moseley, D.S.O., Lt.-Col., d. of w., 26/9/18.
Wardle, John Russell, Major, k. in a., 2/1/16.
Farquhar, John Oswald, Lt., k. in a., 23/3/18.
Taylor, Cecil Frederick, Lt., d. of w., 20/1/18 (and R.F.C.).
Donaldson, Cleweth Thomas Lee, 2/Lt., k. in a., 14/4/17 (and R.F.C.).
Imrie, Daniel McLachlan, 2/Lt., d. of w., 16/11/17.

Gloucestershire Yeomanry.

Clifford, Henry Francis, Major, k. in a., 9/1/17.
Horlick, Gerald Nolekin, Major, died, 5/7/18 (and M.G.C.).
Elcho, Hugo Francis (Lord), Lt. (T/Capt.), k. in a., 23/4/16 (Gloucs. Hussars).
Herbert, Hon. Elidyr John Bernard, Capt., k. in a., 12/11/17 (Machine Gun Corps).
Baker, Micheal Granville Lloyd, Capt., k. in a., 23/4/16.
Bengough, John Crosbie, T/Capt., k. in a., 26/2/16.
Anderson, Robert Graham, Lt., k. in a., 12/11/17.
Ellis, Herbert Pearce, M.C., Lt., d. of w., 1/12/17.
Guise, Reginald Edward, M.C., Lt., k. in a., 29/6/18.
Quenington, Michael Hugh, Viscount, Lt., d. of w., 23/4/16.
Gething, Hugh Bagnall, 2/Lt., k. in a., 21/8/15.
Smith, Wyndham Alexander, 2/Lt., k. in a., 23/4/16.
Tillett, Reginald Alfred William, 2/Lt., k. in a., 24/3/17.

Hampshire Yeomanry.

Gunner, John Hugh, Capt., d. of w., 9/8/18.
Lowis, John R., Capt., k. in a., 4/9/18.
Lucas, Aberon Thomas (Lord), Capt., k. in a., 3/11/16 (and R.F.C.).
Thompson, Roger Eykyn, Capt., k. in a., 12/4/18.
Bodenham, Charles James, Lt., k. in a., 9/8/18.
Cotton, Ralph Charles Fairbairn, Lt., d. of w., 28/3/18 (and M.G.C.).
Falconer, John Keith, Lt., k. in a., 31/7/17.

Seal, George Hatcher, M.C., Lt., d. of w., 29/10/18.
Wedderburn, George Herbert, Lt., k. in a., 9/8/18.
Mowat, Robert James Dugald, 2/Lt., k. in a., 24/9/18.
Sumption, Henry George, 2/Lt., d. of w., 15/10/18.
Waters, Eric Gordon, 2/Lt., k. in a., 24/1/17 (and R.F.C.).

Herts Yeomanry.

Sheppard, Samuel Gurney, Lt.-Col., d. of w., 21/8/15.
Carlile, Edward Hildred Hanbury, Capt., k. in a., 22/3/18.
Jolly, Frederick, Capt., died, 20/8/18.
Morris, Ian Russell Campbell, 2/Lt., k. in a., 7/8/15.

Royal East Kent Yeomanry.

Adam, Walter, Capt., died, 3/11/18 (and M.G.C.).
Allfrey, Hugh Lionel, Capt., k. in a., 19/9/18.
Hatfield, Charles Eric, M.C., Capt., k. in a., 21/9/18.
Segbag-Montefiore, Robert-Montefiore, Capt., d. of w., 19/11/15.
Mitchell, Ronald Walter, Lt., d. of w., 19/11/17.
Page, L. S. M., Lt., k. in a., 20/8/18 (R.A.F.).
Pavitt, Reginald James, Lt., k. in a., 9/8/18.
Williamson, John Alexander, Lt., killed, 10/4/17 (and R.F.C.).
Gunther, Norman Otto Fredick, 2/Lt., k. in a., 11/7/17.
Hardy, Alan Herbert, 2/Lt., killed, 14/10/15 (and R.F.C.).
Montague-Williams, Samuel Roger Thomas Aubon, 2/Lt., d. of w., 25/10/15.
Tuff, Frank Noel, 2/Lt., d. of w., 5/11/15.

West Kent Yeomanry.

Simpson, Roger Cordy, Capt., died, 27/2/19.
Stewart, Bertrand, Capt., k. in a., 13/9/14.
Larken, John Savage, 2/Lt., k. in a., 21/9/18.
Peter, Pomeroy John, 2/Lt., k. in a., 19/9/18.

Lanarkshire Yeomanry.

Monteith, Henry John Joseph Laurence, Major, k. in a., 27/12/15.
Brown, William Douglas, Capt., d. of w., 29/12/17.
Fawcett, Leopald George Frederick Elliot, Capt., k. in a., 6/11/17.
Greenall, J. E. D., Capt., k. in a., 31/3/18 (att. R.F.C.).
Jackson, Walter, Lt., d. of w., 8/11/17.
Forrest, Bertram Thomas Alexander, 2/Lt., k. in a., 27/12/17.
McMillan, John, 2/Lt., k. in a., 24/3/18.

Lancashire Hussars Yeomanry.

Rawstorne, Thomas Geoffrey, Major, d. of w., 31/7/17.
Edwards, John Stanley, A/Capt., d. of w., 24/4/18.
Brennan, Jeremiah, Lt., killed, 8/8/18.
Murray, Leonard, Lt., killed, 13/3/17.
Tacon, Ernest John Ballard, 2/Lt., k. in a., 9/10/17.

Duke of Lancaster's Own Yeomanry.

Bibby, Henry Leigh, Major, k. in a., 4/5/17.
Shepherd-Cross, Cecil, Major, d. of w., 15/10/17.
Crook, Philip Joseph, Lt., k. in a., 9/11/17.
Morgan, Henry Richard, Lt., k. in a., 8/11/17 (and R.F.C.).
Fair, James Gerald, 2/Lt., k. in a., 19/3/17 (att. R.F.C.).

Leicestershire Yeomanry.

Evans-Freke, Hon. Percy Charles, Lt.-Col., k. in a., 13/5/15.
Hanbury, Evan Robert, Major, k. in a., 24/3/18 (M.G.C.).
Liebert, Bernard Robert, Major, k. in a., 13/5/15.
Martin, William Francis, Major, k. in a., 13/5/15.
Blackett, William Stewart Burdett, Lt., d. of w., 25/11/14.
Brooks, Thomas Edward, Lt., k. in a., 13/5/15.
Logan, Hugh, Lt., died, 24/2/19.
Peake, Colin, Lt., killed, 13/5/15.
Sikes, Robert Gordon, Lt., died, 22/2/19.
Thomson, Samuel Pestel Donald, Lt., killed, 13/5/15.
Toulman, Philip Musgrave, Lt., k. in a., 22/6/17.
Turner, Alan Fletcher, Lt., k. in a., 13/5/15.
Wiggins, William Esmy, 2/Lt., died, 19/8/16.

Lincolnshire Yeomanry.

Hood, Edward Thesiger Franklin, Lt.-Col., d. of w., 15/5/18.
Wright, Robert, Major, k. in a., 29/11/17.
Kesteven, Thomas Carew (Lord), Capt., d. of w., 4/11/15.
Read, Harry Esmond, Capt., k. in a., 10/8/17 (R.F.C.).
King, Arthur Towers, Lt., k. in a., 17/11/17.
Paddisan, Charles Waller, Lt. & Q.M., k. in a., 29/11/17.
Wright, Charles, Lt., k. in a., 29/11/17.
Thorndike, Francis Herbert, Lt., d. of w., 17/8/17 (R.F.C.).
McMaking, Oscar Lennox, 2/Lt., k. in a., 11/9/17 (R.F.C.).

City of London Yeomanry.

Knollys, Frederick Roger Alexander Nicholas, Major, d. of w., 24/9/15.
Kekewich, George, Capt., d. of w., 28/10/17.
Wood, Llewellyn George, Capt., died, 22/11/18 (M.G.C.).
Howard, Alfred Lewis, 2/Lt., k. in a., 21/11/17.
Ridsdale, Aubrey Hayward, 2/Lt., k. in a., 22/8/15.

1st County of London Yeomanry.

V.C. Watson, Oliver Cyril Spencer, D.S.O., Lt.-Col., k. in a., 28/3/18.
Fletcher, Herbert Philips, Major, died, 3/8/16 (R.F.C.).
V.C. Lafone, Alexander Malins, Major, k. in a., 27/10/17.
Bullivant, Ritchie Pelham, Capt., k. in a., 24/9/18.
Orchardson, Charles Moxon Quiller, M.C., Capt., d. of w., 26/4/17.
Brown, William Joseph, Lt., killed, 21/2/18 (R.F.C.).
Jehu, John Howard, Lt., k. in a., 28/11/17.
Van den Bergh, Seymour Jacob, Lt., k. in a., 27/10/17.
Holton, George James Paul, 2/Lt., d. of w., 16/9/18.
Lister, Hon. Charles Alfred, 2/Lt., died, 26/8/15 (Temp. Lt., R.M.).
Blakeway, Philip John Thomas, Chap., died, 16/6/15.

2nd County of London Yeomanry.

Burdett, Halford Gay, Capt., died, 3/3/16.
V.C. Norwood, John, Capt., k. in a., 8/9/14 (att. 5th Drag. Gds.).
Hobson, Charles Cuthbert, Lt., died, 20/2/19.
Churchward, Hubert Alan, 2/Lt., k. in a., 16/8/17 (R.F.C.).
Coke, Hon. Arthur George, 2/Lt., k. in a., 21/5/15.
Fishbourne, Morgan, 2/Lt., drowned, 1/1/17.
Laurence, Bertie Standish, 2/Lt., k. in a., 9/9/15.

3rd County of London Yeomanry.

Clarke, Eric Fitzgerald, Capt., k. in a., 9/4/17.
Gregory, Fleming Clement, M.C., Capt., d. of w., 29/11/17.
Mainwaring, Frank Harry George Carver, Capt., died, 6/1/19 (and M.G.C.).
Combe, Stanley Greatrex, Lt., died, 11/10/18.
Burt, Charles Herbert, 2/Lt., died, 27/10/18.
Harris, Harold Maltby, 2/Lt., k. in a., 16/6/17.
Heriot, George Edward, 2/Lt., died, 11/12/15.

Lothians and Border Horse, Yeomanry.

Binning, George (Lord), C.B., M.V.O., Brig.-Gen., died, 12/1/17.
Nelson, Thomas Arthur, Capt., k. in a., 9/4/17 (and M.G.C.).
Villiers, Algernon Hyde, Lt., k. in a., 23/11/17 (and M.G.C.).
Younger, Charles Frierson, Lt., d. of w., 21/3/17.
Campbell, Robert Colin, 2/Lt., died, 28/11/18.
Macaulay, Maxwell Stanley, 2/Lt., k. in a., 7/5/18.
Watson, Charles Victor Macgregor, 2/Lt., k. in a., 3/10/17.

1st Lovat's Scouts.

Gilmour, Allan, Capt., died, 16/12/17.
Weld, Thomas Joseph Wilfrid, M.C., Capt., died, 18/11/18.
Forbes, Arthur John, Lt., k. in a., 21/10/17.
McDonald, A. J., Lt., died, 3/11/18.
MacGregor, Ronald, Lt., died, 1/5/17.
Anderson, William, 2/Lt., k. in a., 4/6/17.
Muir, Philip Denis Graham, 2/Lt., k. in a., 6/12/16.
Rampley, William Temple, 2/Lt., k. in a., 30/9/18.
Russell, Patrick Alfred, 2/Lt., k. in a., 2/4/17 (and R.F.C.).

2nd Lovat's Scouts.

Duff, Hugh John, M.C., Major, k. in a., 6/9/18.
Loyd, Lewis Frederick Innes, A/Major, died, 21/9/18.
Forsyth-Grant, Ivor, Lt., d. of w., 19/10/15.

Montgomeryshire Yeomanry.

Charlesworth, Frederick Raymond, Capt., d. of w., 19/9/18.
Ellis, Rae Adam, Capt., d. of w., 22/9/18.
Fitzhugh, Godfrey, Capt., k. in a., 31/10/17.
Capper, Edward Walter, Lt., k. in a., 14/4/17 (and R.F.C.).
Roberts, Harry Cureton, Lt., k. in a., 27/12/17.
Langrishe, Hercules R., Lt., killed, 16/2/17 (and R.F.C.).
Norris, William Eric, 2/Lt., killed, 14/1/18.

Norfolk Yeomanry.

Bonsor, Malcom Cosmo, Capt., k. in a., 10/3/18.
Harbord, John, Capt., d. of w., 10/7/18.
Mason, Arthur Humphrey, Capt., k. in a., 21/8/15.
Birkbeck, George, Lt., died, 19/2/15.
Buszard, Stanley George, Lt., k. in a., 8/12/17.
Plant, George Bede Hornby, M.C., Lt., k. in a., 18/9/18.
Preston, Thomas Frederick, Lt., k. in a., 24/1/17 (and R.F.C.).
Ramsbottom, Basil William, Lt., k. in a., 19/8/18.
Tillard, Thomas Atkinson, Lt., k. in a., 6/12/16 (and R.F.C.).
Clapp, William Gilbert Elphinstone, 2/Lt., d. of w., 29/4/17.
Cobon, Harold Gardiner, 2/Lt., d. of w., 24/1/18.
Ford, Cecil George, 2/Lt., drowned, 10/10/18.
Gaskell, Arnold Joseph, 2/Lt., k. in a., 2/11/18.
Goslett, John Southcote, 2/Lt., died, 11/11/15.
Jode, Gordon Robert Lovelace, 2/Lt., k. in a., 19/8/18.
Notton, Cyril George, 2/Lt., k. in a., 3/12/17.
Stone, William, M.M., 2/Lt., k. in a., 18/8/18.
Watts, Frederick Robert, 2/Lt., k. in a., 29/8/18.

Northamptonshire Yeomanry.

Cunliffe, John Brooke, Major, died, 20/4/17.
Brudenell-Bruce, James Ernest John, Lt., d. of w., 11/4/17.
Chaplin, Aubrey Fletcher, Lt., k. in a., 10/4/17.
Wartnaby, Charles Richard Arnold, Lt., killed, 11/3/15.
Pirie, George Lawrence, 2/Lt., died, 16/6/15.
Goodman, James, 2/Lt., k. in a., 11/4/17.
Humphriss, Edward Victor, 2/Lt., k. in a., 11/4/17.
Wilson, Gordon Javot, 2/Lt., k. in a., 12/3/15.

Northumberland Yeomanry.

Ridley, Charles Noel, Capt., d. of w., 7/10/15.
Smith, R. E., Capt., k. in a., 19/4/18 (R.A.F.).
Robson, William John, 2/Lt., k. in a., 30/11/17.

Nottinghamshire Yeomanry
(Sherwood Rangers).

V.C. Milbanke, Sir John Peniston (Bt.), Lt.-Col., k. in a. 21/8/15.
Heath, Leonard George, Capt., d. of w., 14/3/16.
Layton, Roland Churchill, Capt., k. in a., 30/4/18.
Birchall, Wilfred Arthur, Lt., k. in a., 28/11/17.
Porkess, Walter Anderson, Lt., k. in a., 10/2/17 (R.F.C.).
Roxburgh, Alan Cameron, Lt., d. of w., 28/11/17 (R.F.C.).
Smith, Thomas, Lt., k. in a., 28/10/18.
Stockdale, Walter Edwin, 2/Lt., k. in a., 10/9/15.

Nottinghamshire Yeomanry
(South Nottinghamshire Hussars).

Cunninghame, William John, Major, died, 19/3/19.
Coventry, Leslie Corbett, Capt., k. in a., 27/5/18.
Hanson, Sydney, Capt., drowned, 27/5/18.
Ley, Christopher Francis Aden, Capt., killed, 16/3/18 (R.F.C.).
Piggin, Frederick William, M.C., Capt., drowned, 27/5/18.
Burch, Sydney Gasking, Lt., k. in a., 13/11/16.
Coombe, William Robert, Lt., k. in a., 27/5/18.
Hunter, Jack, Lt. & Q.-Mr., drowned, 27/5/17.
Oldrey, Gerald Vivian, Lt., died, 19/2/19.
Thomson, Stewart Armour, Lt., d. of w., 24/9/18 (M.G.C.).
Repton, C. T., Lt., k. in a., 25/4/18 (R.A.F.).
Warwick, John Cedric Geoffrey, Lt., drowned, 27/5/18.
Nason, Richard Philip, 2/Lt., k. in a., 16/4/18
Proudfoot, C. D., 2/Lt., k. in a., 22/4/18 (R.A.F.).
Shaw, Alfred John, 2/Lt., drowned, 27/5/18.

Oxfordshire Yeomanry.

Scott, John Willoughby, D.S.O., Lt.-Col., k. in a., 23/4/17.
Fleming, Valentine, D.S.O., Major, k. in a., 20/5/17.
Fane, Horatio Alfred, M.C., Capt., d. of w., 11/8/18.
Molloy, Brian Charles Baskerville, Capt., k. in a., 1/11/14.
Higgs, John Phillip, Lt., d. of w., 14/4/18.
Silvertop, Francis Somerled Joseph, Lt., k. in a., 20/5/17.
Biederman, Harry Ernest, 2/Lt., k. in a., 10/8/17 (att. R.F.C.).
O'Beirne, Arthur James Lewis, 2/Lt., d. of w., 28/7/17 (att. R.F.C.).
Vernon, William Henry Lovell, 2/Lt., k. in a., 7/10/16.
Whinney, John Arthur Perrot, 2/Lt., k. in a., 22/6/17.

Pembroke Yeomanry.

Higgon, John Arthur, Major, k. in a., 20/7/16.
Hoare, Reginald Arthur, Capt., k. in a., 19/9/18.
Lambton, Edward, Capt., died, 28/3/16.
Morgan, David Lloyd Pophen, M.C., Capt., k. in a., 9/3/18.
Roch, George Powell, Capt., k. in a., 21/5/18.
Yorke, James Hamilton Langdon, M.C., Capt., k. in a., 27/12/17.
Clemetson, David Louis, Lt., k. in a., 21/9/18.
De Rutzen, Alan Frederick James, Lt., k. in a., 7/8/16.
Watkins, Howel Cyril, M.C., Lt., d. of w., 23/10/18 (in German hands).
Williams, Hugh, 2/Lt., k. in a., 28/7/18.

Scottish Horse.

Beech, John Robert, C.M.G., D.S.O., Lt.-Col., died, 6/11/15.
Aitchison, Walter, Major, k. in a., 12/7/17.
3 Hume, Arthur Sinclair Vernon, Major, died, 21/9/15.
Burney, Geoffrey Asteley, Capt., k. in a., 7/7/16 (att. R.F.C.).
Edwardes, Hon. Cecil, Capt., k. in a., 20/11/17 (and Tanks).
Grant-Peterkin, Cosmo Gordon, Capt., d. of w., 12/9/17.
Hutton, Robert, Capt., k. in a., 22/8/17.
Loring, William, Capt., d. of w., 24/10/15.
3 MacGregor, Alexander John Lindsay, Capt., d. of w., 8/10/18.
Murray, Alexander, Capt., k. in a., 14/8/17.
Myers, John Coupar, Capt., killed, 4/5/18.
Proctor, William Fife, Capt., d. of w., 27/9/15.
Rawson, Arthur, Capt., k. in a., 6/10/18.
2 Sloan, George Henry, Capt., d. of w., 16/11/15.
Armitage, Noel, Lt., k. in a., 25/4/18.
Bruce, John Gardiner, Lt., k. in a., 14/4/18.
Butler, Gordon Kerr Montague, Lt., died, 17/7/16.
Hunter, George Arnold, Lt., died, 3/8/17 (and M.G.C.).
Inglis, Robert, M.C., Lt., d. of w., 5/10/18.
Martin, Robert, Lt., k. in a., 4/9/17 (and R.F.C.).
3 Morris, Frederick, Lt., drowned, 27/5/18.
3 Parker-Smith, Wilmot Babington, Lt., d. of w., 12/9/15.
2 Rowan, Robert, Lt., killed, 22/8/18.
Bell, David, 2/Lt., k. in a., 6/10/18.
Cowan, James, 2/Lt., died, 25/10/18.
3 Ferguson, Alexander Robertson, 2/Lt., killed, 14/6/16.
Ferguson, Donald Francis, 2/Lt., k. in a., 7/5/17.
Forsyth, John Charles, 2/Lt., k. in a., 11/10/18.
Gilmour, Willis John Oberlin, 2/Lt., k. in a., 15/5/15.

Shropshire Yeomanry.

Cawley, Oswald, Capt., k. in a., 22/8/18.
Partridge, Richard Crawshay Bailey, M.C., Capt., k. in a., 28/9/18.
Tillard, Philip Algernon, Capt., k. in a., 19/11/16.
Cunningham, William John, Lt. & Qr.-Mr., died, 18/5/15.
Hopton, Edward Michael, Lt., died, 17/3/16.
Johnston, Thomas Peacock, Lt., k. in a., 20/5/17 (and R.F.C.).
Plowden, Francis Charles, Lt., d. of w., 22/8/18.
Henningsen, Cecil Eric, 2/Lt., k. in a., 30/11/17.
Muddock, Jasper Milton Preston, 2/Lt., k. in a., 30/11/17.

North Somerset Yeomanry.

Stewart, William Norman, D.S.O., Lt.-Col., k. in a., 22/3/18.
Barstow, J. E. J., Capt., killed, 27/1/19 (and R.A.F.).
English, Robert Ernest, Capt., k. in a., 13/5/15.
Gibbs, Eustace Lyle, Capt., d. of w., 11/2/15.
Liebert, Frederick Alexander Charles, Capt., k. in a., 17/11/14.
Bellot, Byson, Lt., died, 27/3/18.
Biggs, John Geoffrey, M.C., Lt., d. of w., 12/9/17 (and M.G.C.).
Davey, John Stanley, Lt., k. in a., 17/11/14.
Gaskell, Joseph, Lt. & Qr.-Mr., died, 5/4/17.
Jenkins, Kenneth Gordon, Lt., d. of w., 31/3/18.
Hill, Arthur Moberly, 2/Lt., k. in a., 9/4/17.

West Somerset Yeomanry.

Richardson, Alfred Terence Leatham, Capt., k. in a., 6/11/17.
Spencer, Henry Beresford, Capt., k. in a., 2/9/18 (and Tank Corps).
Taylor, Douglas John Bulpin, Capt., k. in a., 2/9/18.
Thomson, Cyril Ground, M.C., Capt., killed, 22/9/18.
Battesby, Philip Worsley, Lt., k. in a., 7/7/17 (and R.F.C.).
Bown, Cyril Walter, Lt., d. of w., 1/12/17 (and Tank Corps).
Checkland, Montmorency Beaumont, Lt., k. in a., 16/8/17.
Coles, Rowland Humphrey, Lt., k. in a., 9/5/17 (R.F.C.).
Watson, Dominic MacAulay, Lt., d. of w., 3/12/17.
White, Ernest, Lt., k. in a., 10/4/18 (and M.G.C.).
Smith, Herbert Bennett, 2/Lt., k. in a., 17/7/17.

Staffordshire Yeomanry.

Clowes, Henry Arthur, Lt.-Col., died, 8/3/16.
Forbes, Harry Seymour, Capt., died, 3/11/18.
Pritchard, Andrew Baden, Capt., died, 26/10/18.
Brewitt, James Leonard, Lt., d. of w., 1/12/17.
Brough, John William, Lt. & Qr.-Mr., died, 20/10/18.
Burns, William, Lt., k. in a., 21/3/18.
Furniss, Kevin Robert, Lt., d. of w., 29/4/17 (att. R.F.C., in Ger. hands).
Noakes, Frederic, Lt., k. in a., 25/11/17.
Thomas, Frank William Henry, M.C., Lt., d. of w., 5/1/18 (and R.F.C.).
White, Dixon, 2/Lt., k. in a., 29/11/17.

Suffolk Yeomanry.

Barne, M., D.S.O., Major, died, 17/9/17.
4 Brown, Eric Landon, Capt., k. in a., 18/8/15.
Brown, John Gordon, Lt., d. of w., 5/2/17.
Henderson, Jacob Johnson, Lt., d. of w., 17/10/18.
Douglas, Robert Greenshields, 2/Lt., died, 14/8/16.
Gray, Arthur Frederick, 2/Lt., drowned, 10/10/18.
Oliver, Ernest, 2/Lt., k. in a., 22/9/17 (att. Nigeria Regt.).
Wood, William Anthony, 2/Lt., k. in a., 6/11/17.

Surrey Yeomanry.

Barclay, Thomas H., Major, drowned, 4/5/17.
Cantle, Leonard Heath, Lt., k. in a., 8/4/17 (att. R.F.C.).
May, Herbert Edwin, Lt., drowned, 6/12/17.
Morley, William, Lt., k. in a., 24/3/18.
Dodgshon, John Hampson, 2/Lt., killed, 2/10/16.
Proughten, Charles Ernest, 2/Lt., k. in a., 23/5/18.
Taylor, Harold Richard, 2/Lt., d. of w., 17/3/17 (and M.G.C.).

The Sussex Yeomanry.

Kekewich, Hanbury Lewis, Major, k. in a., 6/11/17.
Blunt, Harold Ernest, Capt., died, 16/2/19.
Campbell, Alexander Boswell, Lt., d. of w., 13/9/17.
Campbell, Islay McKinnon, Lt., d. of w., 4/4/18.
Gilbert, John Driffield, Lt., k. in a., 18/10/17 (att. R.F.C.).
John, W. A., Lt., k. in a., 1/8/18 (and R.A.F.).
Penfold-Wyatt, Hugh Graystone, Lt., died, 12/11/15.
Pickard-Cambridge, Herbert Evelyn Winn, Lt., k. in a., 1/11/17.
Harker, John Gordon, 2/Lt., d. of w., 28/9/18.
Johnston, Henry Edward, 2/Lt., d. of w., 16/3/18.
Marnham, Hugh Cecil, 2/Lt., k. in a., 22/8/16 (and R.F.C.).
Taylor, Alexander John, 2/Lt., d. of w., 8/8/18.
Wiley, Donald William, 2/Lt., k. in a., 12/10/18.
Wilson, Gilbert John, 2/Lt., k. in a., 6/11/17.

The Warwickshire Yeomanry.

Wight-Boycott, Thomas Andrew, D.S.O., Brig.-Gen., died, 30/3/16.
Drake, Frederic Augustus, Capt., drowned, 27/5/18.
Glentworth, Viscount E. W. C. G. de V., Capt., died, 18/5/18 (R.A.F.).
Smith-Ryland, Henry Dennis, Capt., d. of w., 7/4/17.
Valintine, Rudolf, M.C., Capt., d. of w., 12/11/17.
Gilman, Ronald John, Lt., died, 15/7/18.
Prankherd, Richard Percy, Lt., k. in a., 10/11/18 (and M.G.C.).
Chambers, Arthur Joseph Ferguson, 2/Lt., d. of w., 11/8/16.
Lade, John Harvey, 2/Lt., d. of w., 5/10/17.
Loverock, Harold George, 2/Lt., d. of w., 5/8/16.
McAndrew, Charles Roy, 2/Lt., k. in a., 21/9/18 (and M.G.C.).
Springfield, Humphrey Osborn, 2/Lt., k. in a., 5/8/16.

Welsh Horse Yeomanry.

Roch, William Protheroe, Lt. (A/Capt.), k. in a., 11/3/18.
Thomas, Owen, Capt., died, 21/8/17.
Jones, Herbert Wyman, Lt., d. of w., 24/3/18 (and M.G.C.).
Shirley, Archibald Vincent, 2/Lt., k. in a., 8/6/17 (and R.F.C.).

Westmoreland and Cumberland Yeomanry.

Lees, Eric Brown, Major, k. in a., 31/7/18.
Lacy, Francis Prior, M.C., 2/Lt. (Tp. Capt.), k. in a., 13/8/15.
Barker, F. E., Lt., died, 13/1/19 (R.A.F.).
Allan, Lawson Ellis, Lt., k. in a., 26/4/17 (R.F.C.).
Parker, Thomas Cowper, Lt., k. in a., 12/10/17.
Pawson, G. St. V., M.C., Lt., died, 6/11/18 (R.A.F.).
Adey, William Thomas Henworth, 2/Lt., drowned, 10/10/18.
Bennett, George William, 2/Lt., k. in a., 3/12/17.

Royal Wiltshire Yeomanry.

Thynne, Lord Alexander George, D.S.O., Lt.-Col., k. in a., 14/9/18.
Awdry, Charles Selwyn, D.S.O., Major, k. in a., 24/3/18.
Poore, Roger Alvin, D.S.O., Major, k. in a., 26/9/17.
Palmer, Alen Llewellen, Major, died, 15/11/16.
Cowtan, Francis Scott, Capt., k. in a., 24-25/4/17.
Rooke, Wallace Mortimer, Capt., died, 8/10/18.
Ball, Charles Herbert, Lt., d. of w., 3/4/18 (and M.G.C.).
Collier, Simon, M.C., Lt., k. in a., 14/9/18.
Simmons, Sydney Noel, Lt., d. of w., 27/10/16.

Worcestershire Yeomanry.

Gray-Cheape, Hugh Annesley, D.S.O., Lt.-Col., drowned, 27/5/18.
Albright, Martin Chicheley, Major, d. of w., 8/11/17.
Lister, F. W., Major, died, 24/2/19 (and Tanks).
Norfolk, Harold, Major, k. in a., 23/4/16.
Cay, Albert Jaffray, Lt., k. in a., 23/4/16.
Cutler, Herbert Cecil, Lt., k. in a., 10/5/17 (and R.F.C.).
Marsh, John, Lt., died, 23/10/18 (in Turkish hands).
Wiggin, George Robert, Lt., k. in a., 23/4/16.
Edwards, John Wesley, M.C., 2/Lt., k. in a., 8/11/17.
Hatton, Bryan, 2/Lt., k. in a., 23/4/16.
Jaffray (Bart), Sir John Henry, 2/Lt., k. in a., 23/4/16.
Jewitt, Dermod Patrick, 2/Lt., k. in a., 23/4/16.
Lane, William George, 2/Lt., d. of w., 7/11/17.
Pearson, Maurice Murray, 2/Lt., k. in a., 23/4/16.
Smith, Henry, 2/Lt., drowned, 1/1/17.

Yorkshire Dragoons Yeomanry.

Clay, Lionel Pillean, Capt., k. in a., 18/2/18.
Rae, Lindsay Leon de'Cram Clement Marsham, 2/Lt., drowned, 10/10/18.
Nisbet, Frederic William, 2/Lt., k. in a., 14/2/17 (and R.F.C.).
Staniforth, William Moorwood, 2/Lt., died, 23/3/17 (and R.F.C.).
Wilson, Gordon Ivor, 2/Lt., killed, 12/2/17 (and R.F.C.).

Yorkshire Hussars Yeomanry.

Feversham, The Earl of, Lt.-Col., k. in a., 15/9/16.
Pease, Christopher York, Capt., k. in a., 9/5/18.
Walker, Roger Beverley, M.C., Capt., d. of w., 13/11/18.
Bailey, Richard Percival, Lt. & Qr.-Mr., died, 30/5/15.
Collins, William Henry, Lt., killed, 7/3/18 (and R.F.C.).
Haslam, Charles Stanley, Lt., k. in a., 10/11/17.
Rentoul, Alexander, Lt., k. in a., 27/3/18 (and R.F.C.).
Ryder, William Harrold, Lt., k. in a., 6/7/17 (and R.F.C.).
Turton, Edmund Spencer, Lt., k. in a., 1/9/15.

East Riding of Yorkshire Yeomanry.

Bailey, Robert Neale Menteith, Lt., d. of w., 1/12/17.
Bryson, William Miller, 2/Lt., k. in a., 1/9/18
Coates, John, 2/Lt., k. in a., 15/8/18
Gresham, Leonard Stanley, 2/Lt., d. of w., 7/5/17.
Spicer, Ronald Murray, 2/Lt., died, 31/5/16.

Honourable Artillery Company (Territorial Force).

Boyle, Ernest Charles Patrick D.S.O., Lt.-Col., k. in a., 7/2/17.
Lucas-Tooth, Sir Archibald Leonard Bt., Major, died, 12/7/18.
Brunton, Douglas, Capt., k. in a., 9/10/17.
Bryan, Sterry James, A/Capt., k. in a., 8/2/17.
Catley, James Thatcher, Capt., k. in a., 12/9/17.
Dyer, Charles Nettleton, Capt., died, 14/7/16.
Ellis, Edward Miller, M.C., Capt., k. in a., 7/8/18.
Harris, Claude Leslie, Capt., d. of w., 2/5/18.
Hayden, William Clarence, Capt., k. in a., 19/9/15.
Hawkins, Stanley, M.C., Capt., k. in a., 29/5/18.
Hoare, Frederick William Ernest, Capt., k. in a., 10/8/17.
Murray, Ernest Francis Hume, M.C., D.C.M., Lt. (A/Capt.), k. in a., 9/10/17.
Newton, William Savage, Capt., killed, 6/1/15 (Infantry).
Pritchard, John Harold, Capt., k. in a., 15/5/17 (Infantry).
Satchwell, Frank Henry Sandom, Capt., k. in a., 3/5/17 (Infantry).
Thorpe, George Robert, Capt., d. of w., 25/4/17.
Bazin, Geoffry Martyn, Lt., k. in a., 19/9/15.
Curties, Dudley Thomas Lees, Lt., died, 24/10/18.
Davis, Douglas Stalman, Lt., died, 27/1/10.
Norris, Arthur James, Lt., died, 10/1/17 (Infantry).
Ommundsen, Arthur Norman Victor Harcourt, Lt., k. in a., 19/9/15.
Reeve, John Stanley, Lt., k. in a., 29/6/18 (Infantry).
St. Quintin, Clifford Jack, Lt., k. in a., 15/5/17 (Infantry).
Tatham, Cautley, Lt., d. of w., 18/6/15.
Trewhitt, Eric Gerald, Lt., d. of w., 14/11/16.
Beck, Aubrey Moore, 2/Lt., k. in a., 15/5/17.
Blissett, Percy Cecil, 2/Lt., k. in a., 9/10/17.
Bockett, Harold Arthur Palmer, 2/Lt., k. in a., 3/5/17.
Bonham, Denis Pierpont, 2/Lt., d. of w., 16/11/16.
Brass, Ewart Stanley, 2/Lt., k. in a., 31/3/17.
Brown, George Easter, 2/Lt., drowned, 20/4/17.
Brown, Guy Frank Courtney, 2/Lt., d. of w., 11/5/17.
Byron, Clement John, 2/Lt., k. in a., 10/1/17.
Caudle, Cedric, 2/Lt., k. in a., 3/5/17.
Chaffey, Henry Percival, 2/Lt., k. in a., 10/8/17.
East, Sydney Clark, 2/Lt., k. in a., 9/10/17 (Infantry).
Ellis, Cyril Brooks, 2/Lt., k. in a., 13/11/16.
Ellis, Evelyn Charles, 2/Lt., k. in a., 3/5/17.
Farmiloe, George Frederick, 2/Lt., k. in a., 26/6/17.
Fedden, Raymond Henshaw, 2/Lt., k. in a., 3/5/17.
2 Flory, Robert James, M.C., 2/Lt., k. in a., 28/6/17.
2 Fraser, George Allan, 2/Lt., k. in a., 15/5/17.
2 Gandar-Dower, Leonard Francis, 2/Lt., died, 3/5/17 (in Ger. hands).
1 Goddard, Ralph Garnett, 2/Lt., k. in a., 9/10/17
Gray, Frederick Hodskinson, 2/Lt., k. in a., 1/4/17.
Hammond, Ernest William Frost, M.C., 2/Lt., k. in a., 3/5/17.
Hoare, William George, 2/Lt., k. in a., 16/6/15.
Humphrys, Leslie Palmer, 2/Lt., d. of w., 13/12/16
Jones, Arthur William, 2/Lt., k. in a., 31/3/17.
Leeds, John Stanley, 2/Lt., k. in a., 19/9/15.
Link, Horace Arthur, 2/Lt., k. in a., 9/9/16.
Meldrum, Ronald, 2/Lt., k. in a., 9/10/17 (Infantry).
Moore, Raymond Cecil Devereux, 2/Lt., k. in a., 9/10/17 (Infantry).
Newton, John, 2/Lt., k. in a., 23/4/17.
Porter, Royden Spencer Bayspool, 2/Lt., died, 6/2/17 (Infantry).
Sims, Donald Palmer, 2/Lt., k. in a., 23/10/18 (Infantry).
Smallman, Arthur Frederick Strong, 2/Lt., k. in a., 14/11/16 (Infantry).

Royal Horse and Royal Field Artillery (Territorial Force).

Lowe, Arthur Cecil, C.M.G., D.S.O., Lt.Col. (T/Brig.-Gen.), k. in a., 24/11/17.
Griffith, Frank, V.D., Col., died, 4/1/17.
Gordon, Adrian Charles, D.S.O., Lt.-Col., k. in a., 12/12/17.
Grandage, William Briggs, Lt.-Col., d. of w., 14/5/17.
Gregor, George Trevor, Lt.-Col., k. in a., 1/7/17.
Hamilton, The Hon. Ralph Gerard Alexander, Lt.-Col., k. in a., 31/3/18.
Tonge, John, Lt.-Col., d. of w., 19/4/17.
Walker, Arthur Nimmo, Lt.-Col., k. in a., 24/9/16.
West, Francis Charles Bartholomew, Lt.-Col., k. in a., 28/9/16.
Wolff, John Alfred, Lt.-Col., k. in a., 23/10/18.
Arnstrong, Forster Moore, Major, k. in a., 25/9/17.
Beck, William Crabbe, Major, k. in a., 28/3/18.
Bell-Bathurst, Basil Woodd Bambridge, Capt. (A/Major), d. of w., 23/4/17.
Bennett, Frederick Barberry, Major, d. of w., 22/10/18.
Browne, Geoffrey Dennis, Major, k. in a., 19/9/16.
Burnyeat, Norman Quayle, Major, d. of w., 6/8/17.
Chapman, Charles Lancelot, M.C., Major, d. of w., 22/8/17.
Cheverton, Thomas Bird, Major, k. in a., 24/3/18.
Cheyne, Henry, Major, k. in a., 10/7/17.
Clapperton, James Hugh, Major, d. of w., 7/5/17.
Clifton, Percy James, D.S.O., Major, d. of w., 26/8/18.
Collis, Frank Reginald, Major, k. in a., 27/9/16.
Cowell, George Edmund Maurice, Major, k. in a., 30/12/17.
Davenport, Fred, D.S.O., M.C., Major, k. in a., 25/9/17.
Davy, John Evelyn, D.S.O., Major, died, 9/12/18.
Day, Richard, M.C., Major, d. of w., 23/2/18.
De St. Paer, Louis Emile, M.C., Major, d. of w., 8/5/18.
Dickinson, William Henry Egerton de Brissac, Major, d. of w., 19/10/18.
Dickson, Ashley Gordon, Major, d. of w., 18/6/17.
Dust, Frank William, M.C., Major, k. in a., 23/4/17.
Eills, William, M.C., Major, k. in a., 9/4/18.
Gardner, George Ryding Sankey, Major, died, 26/6/16.
Geard, Walter Leslie, Major, killed, 26/6/16.
Gorell, Henry Gorell (Lord), D.S.O., Major, d. of w., 16/1/17.
Gossage, Guy Winwood, Major, died, 24/12/17.
Greenwood, Victor John, Major, k. in a., 18/4/18.
Guthe, Thomas Percival, Major, d. of w., 13/1/16.
Halcomb, Leslie Broughton, Major, k. in a., 25/10/18.
Hall, Allan Gordon, Major, k. in a., 24/4/18.
Hartnall, Archibald John, Major, died, 6/3/17.
Hatton, Robert Andrew, Major, d. of w., 23/10/18.
Hillerns, Hero Wilhelm Oswald, Major, k. in a., 14/4/17.
Jackson, Frederick Vyvyan Milbourne, Major, k. in a., 13/4/18.
Jameson, Horace Armytage, M.C., Major, k. in a., 24/3/18.
Johnson, George Bernard, D.S.O., Major, k. in a., 18/4/18.
Jones, George Worthington, M.C., Major, d. of w., 10/11/17.
Lindrea, George Patrick, Major, k. in a., 18/7/16.
Llangattock, John McLean (Lord), Major, d. of w., 31/10/16.
Malcolmson, John Joseph, Major, died, 4/6/15.
Mason, Norman George Minta, M.C., Major, killed, 13/9/18.
Melrose, James Douglas Leitch, Major, d. of w., 25/4/18.
Ness-Walker, William Percy, M.C., Major, d. of w., 31/12/17.
Newton, Arthur Douglas, Major, k. in a., 27/10/17.
Paynter, Francis Pendarvis, Major, k. in a., 10/1/16.
Porter, William Guthrie, D.S.O., Major, k. in a., 8/6/17.
Pridmore, Reginald George, M.C., Major, k. in a., 13/3/18.
Robertson, Herbert, M.C., Major, d. of w., 5/4/18.
Robinson, Noel Stafford, Major, d. of w., 2/8/18.
Simon, Henry Hemrick, Major, d. of w., 8/9/17.
Stewart, Hugh Duncan, M.C., Major, k. in a., 12/10/18.
Suffolk, Rt. Hon. Henry Molyneux Paget, The Earl of, Major, k. in a., 21/4/17.
Todd, Chester William, Major, k. in a., 9/8/17.
Torrens, Attwood Alfred, Major, k. in a., 8/12/16.
Von Treuenfels, Carl Otto, D.S.O., Major, d. of w., 24/6/17.
Whitehouse, Herbert, Major, killed, 23/3/18.
Wilkinson, Charles Leyburn, D.S.O., Major, d. of w., 7/4/18.

Willey, John, Major, k. in a., 3/4/18.
Wilson, George Henry, M.C., Lt. (A/Major), d. of w., 4/11/17.
Wilson, Sydney Cunningham, Major, died, 9/11/18.
Wilson, William John, Major, d. of w., 20/6/18.
Wiltshire, Percy, Major, d. of w., 25/4/17.
Winch, Gordon Bluett, D.S.O., Major, d. of w., 10/4/18.
Adams, Theodore Dawson, Capt., k. in a., 7/11/15 (R.F.C.).
Adamson, James, Lt. (A/Capt.), k. in a., 5/5/17 (242 Bde.).
Benn, Joseph Reginald Tankard, Capt. (Tp.), k. in a., 2/9/15.
Bertie, Claude Peregrine, Capt., k. in a., 19/3/17 (R.F.C.).
Bradley, Arthur Newsome, Capt., died, 6/11/18 (W. Riding).
Brocklebank, Thomas Geoffrey, Capt., k. in a., 5/8/16.
Brown, Arthur Anthony, M.C., Lt., A/Capt.), died, 4/3/18.
Brunner, Cecil Heywood, Capt., d. of w., 25/10/17.
Burgess, Charles, Capt., k. in a., 11/10/18.
Cattle, James Henry Nightingale, Capt., d. of w., 1/5/17.
Cawood, William Benjamin Crane, Capt., died, 24/5/15.
Chalmers, Henry Stewart, Lt., A/Capt., d. of w., 29/9/17.
Christian, Edward, M.C., Capt., d. of w., 19/10/16.
Cliff, Reginald Bertram Talbot, Capt., d. of w., 23/9/15.
Craig, John William Archibald, Capt., d. of w., 26/8/16.
Darbyshire, Graham Hirtzell, Capt., k. in a., 7/10/17.
Dawson, W. E., Capt., died, 16/9/18 (R.A.F.).
Farquhar, Bt., Sir Walter FitzRoy, Capt., k. in a., 15/10/18.
Forster, John Stanley, Capt., d. of w., 23/8/18.
Frazer, Douglas Villers, Capt., k. in a., 16/8/17.
Gallimore, Henry Burrows, Capt., k. in a., 26/5/17.
Gascoyne-Cecil, John Arthur, M.C., Capt., k. in a., 27/8/18.
Gibb, Alexander Reid, Capt., k. in a., 12/10/16.
Gordon, Alec McDougall. M.C., Capt., d. of w., 7/11/17.
Greenwood, Gerald Wyatt, Capt., died, 17/11/18.
Gudgeon, Robert Eustace, Capt., d. of w., 2/4/18 (in Ger. hands).
Hall, Henry, Capt., killed, 25/9/18.
Hannan, Stanley Livingstone, Lt., A/Capt., k. in a., 30/11/17.
Harvey, George Winfred, M.C., Lt., A/Capt., k. in a., 12/4/18.
Haslam, William Kenneth Seale, Capt., k. in a., 27/4/17.
Harrison, John German, Capt., died, 11/4/18.
Hartnoll, James, Capt., died, 20/5/17.
Hepworth, George Percy, Capt., d. of w., 27/10/18.
Hillerns, H. W. O., Capt., k. in a., 14/4/17.
Jenkins, David Roy, Capt., killed, 21/1/17 (att. R.F.C.).
Jones, Herbert Japson, M.C., Capt., d. of w., 12/11/18.
Kirsop, Conrad Robert John, Capt., died, 13/10/17.
Lenke, Ernest, Capt., died, 2/6/15.
Lindsay, Bernard Wilfred, Capt., d. of w., 22/11/18.
Longmore, Charles Gerard, Lt., A/Capt., died, 24/11/18.
Lord, Reginald Hollins, M.C., Capt., d. of w., 25/11/18.
McAuley, Francis Willmer, T/Capt., k. in a., 21/5/16.
McJannet, Hector William, Capt., died, 28/10/18.
MacPherson, Ronald Charters, Capt., d. of w., 18/4/18.
Malcomson, Thomas Stuart, Capt., k. in a., 10/12/17 (and R.F.C.).
Mellis, George Duncan, Capt., k. in a., 30/11/17.
Miller, George James, Capt., d. of w., 29/8/18.
Milne, Esmond William, Capt., d. of w., 12/8/17.
Mond, F. L., Capt., k. in a., 15/5/18 (att. R.A.F.).
Mottram, Frederick, Capt., d. of w., 9/9/17.
Nesbitt, James Thompson, Capt., d. of w., 25/3/18.
Nicholas, John Allen, Capt., died, 28/1/19.
Parker, Albert Alfred, Capt., k. in a., 25/9/17.
Phillips, Philip Roy, Capt., died, 7/5/18.
Rowe, Percy Trevelyan, Capt., d. of w., 30/11/17.
Samuel, George Christopher, Capt., d. of w., 16/8/18.
Saunders, Reginald Arthur, T/Capt., k. in a., 14/3/16.
Sinclair, Donald George, Capt., d. of w., 15/7/17.
Spence, John Robert, Capt., k. in a., 9/4/18.
Squirl-Dawson, Hugh Dawson, Capt., died, 31/1/18.
Stewart, William Beardmore, Capt., k. in a., 24/5/17.
Stone, Arthur Edward, Capt., k. in a., 24/7/15.
Tawse, James Gordon, Capt., d. of w., 15/4/17.
Triphook, Owen Leech, Lt., A/Capt., died, 6/4/19.
Tilbury, Augustus, Capt., k. in a., 8/6/17.
Tipton, Richard James, Capt., d. of w., 12/3/18 (and R.F.C.).
Vane, Hon. Henry Cecil, Capt., died, 9/10/17.
Walker, Ernest James, Capt., d. of w., 4/10/17.
Westby, Percival St. George Charles, Capt., k. in a., 23/9/17
Weyman, Henry Morton, Capt., died, 26/8/16.
White, John Peregrine Robertson, Capt., died, 7/10/16.
Whitehead, John Walton, Capt., k. in a., 1/12/17.
Wigg, Sydney Harold, Capt., k. in a., 13/10/18.
Wilson, Guy Denis, Capt., k. in a., 30/11/17.
Yeaman, Keith Sanger, Capt., died, 5/6/18.
Alcock, Empson, Lt., k. in a., 21/8/17 (N. Mid. Bde.).
Allen, William Sproston, Lt., k. in a., 14/3/18.
Allom, Charles Cedric Gordon, Lt., d. of w., 20/10/17.
Anderson, Clifford William, Lt., k. in a., 24/10/18.
Armstrong, Joseph, Lt., k. in a., 5/5/17.
Atkinson, Elwyn, Lt., d. of w., 18/5/17.
Auber, Charles St. Lo, Lt., k. in a., 29/10/16.
Bacon, Edward Sivewright, Lt., k. in a., 31/8/17 (att. R F C.).
Ball, John J. Barry, Lt., k. in a., 27/6/16.
Ballamy, Harold William, Lt., k. in a., 15/8/17.
Barr, James, Lt., d. of w., 16/10/18.
Beale, Alfred Percy Gordon, Lt., d. of w., 28/3/17.
Beck, Donald Coker, Lt., killed, 21/9/16 (and R.F.C.).
Bedford-Pim, Edward Woodley, Lt., died, 5/7/18.
Bee, William, Lt., d. of w., 24/9/17.
Beer, Arthur Henry, M.C., Lt., d. of w., 21/4/18.
Bellamy, Osmund, Lt., k. in a., 21/3/18.
Bemrose, Roderick Henry, M.C., Lt., died, 7/11/18.
Beresford, Harold, M.C., Lt., d. of w., 24/5/18.
Bethune, John, Lt., d. of w., 29/10/17.
Bird, Dudley Joseph de Anguld, Lt., k. in a., 17/6/17.
Blackwell, Aubrey Francis, M.C., Lt., k. in a., 2/6/17.
Blake, Bernard Cecil, Lt., d. of w., 9/4/18.
Blake, James Alexander Jeffrey, Lt., k. in a., 18/8/16.
Blomfield, Arthur Eustace, Lt., died, 28/10/17.
Bloor, Guy Hegan, Lt., died, 20/11/18.
Booth, John Charles, Lt., died, 30/9/16.
Bouch, John, Lt., died, 23/11/18.
Boyd, William, Lt., k. in a., 24/3/18.
Boyton, Bertram Alfred, Lt., d. of w., 9/11/17.
Bradley, Cyril Montague, Lt., k. in a., 2/4/17.
Briercliffe, Louis Bernard, Lt., k. in a., 31/3/17.
Brown, Archibald Campbell, Lt., k. in a., 27/5/18.
Bruce, Robert, Lt., d. of w., 25/9/15.
Budgen, Sidney Norman, Lt., k. in a., 4/10/17.
Bullen, Henry Stanley Tempest, Lt., k. in a., 14/4/17.
Burgh, Edward Henry, Lt., d. of w., 4/1/18.
Bury, John, Lt., k. in a., 5/7/15.
Butterworth, Harold, M.C., Lt., k. in a., 20/9/18.
Cardwell, Hugh Brodie, Lt., d. of w., 9/8/18 (256th Bde.).
Carslaw, John Howie, Lt., d. of w., 26/11/17.
Chapman, Fred Tarlington, Lt., d. of w., 18/12/17.
Chatterton, Alfred Henry Goodbarne, Lt., died, 21/7/17.
Clark, Norman, Lt., k. in a., 18/3/18.
Cockrill, Charles Whalley, Lt., k. in a., 2/2/18.
Cole, Percival James, Lt., d. of w., 22/9/16.
Coleman, Edward Charles, Lt., k. in a., 2/4/17.
Colson, Anthony Francis Douglas, M.C., Lt., k. in a., 10/11/17.
Corfield, Herbert Roy, Lt., d. of w., 5/11/17.
Couper, James Mudie, Lt., d. of w., 4/4/18.
Craig, Donald Leslie Langford, M.C., Lt., k. in a., 31/7/17.
Craven, George Alfred Senior, Lt., d. of w., 15/9/17.
Crerar, Donald Campbell, Lt., k. in a., 24/4/18.
Dale, Charles, Lt., died, 16/10/18.
Davies, Cecil James, Lt., died, 25/11/18.
Davies, Joseph Charles Gladstone, Lt., drowned, 6/1/18.
Davies, Trevor Arthur Manning, Lt., k. in a., 1/7/16.
Davoren, Ambrose Joseph Stanislaus, Lt., k. in a., 18/7/17.
Densham, Walter Henry, M.C., Lt., d. of w., 5/4/18.
Desborough, Laurence Vernon, Lt., k. in a., 30/11/17 (and R.F.C.).
De Wael, Cecil Hubert, Lt., d. of w., 6/4/18.
Dickinson, John, Lt., k. in a., 9/4/17.
Eagleton, John Ronaldson, Lt., d. of w., 3/9/18.
Earle, Ernest Clifford, Lt., k. in a., 27/5/18.
Edmondson, Percival Henry, M.C., Lt., d. of w., 28/6/18.
Elliot, Thomas Victor Guppy, Lt., d. of w., 16/10/15.
Essex, Robert Charles, Lt., d. of w., 14/5/18.
Featherstone, William Davies, M.C., Lt., k. in a., 23/3/18.
Fenner, Walter Noel, Lt., d. of w., 2/7/17.
Fitch, Philip Henry Burt, M.C., Lt., k. in a., 23/7/17.
Flowers, H. F., Lt., k. in a., 14/10/18 (R.A.F.).
Foord-Kelcey, William Beverly, Lt., k. in a., 24/9/18.
Fry, Edward Meaburn, M.C., Lt., k. in a., 23/8/18.
Fullerton, James Basil, Lt., k. in a., 9/8/17.
Gair, Thomas, Lt., k. in a., 10/9/17.
Galletley, Ian, Lt., k. in a., 3/8/16.
Gane, Wilfred Errol, M.C., Lt., d. of w., 8/12/17.
Garnett, Jerry Knowles, Lt., died, 6/11/15.
Gascoyne-Cecil, Randle William, Lt., k. in a., 1/12/17.
Gaskain, Cecil Stavley, Lt., k. in a., 7/5/17 (R.F.C.).
Gedge, Edward Leonard, Lt., k. in a., 23-24/8/16.
Gibb, Alexander, Lt., k. in a., 5/6/17.
Gibbs, Harold Walter, Lt., d. of w., 25/3/18.
Gibson, John Lancelot, Lt., k. in a., 27/5/18.
Glaisby, Kenneth, Lt., k. in a., 1/11/17.
Goodman, Geoffrey Thomas, Lt., k. in a., 1/6/17.
Griffin, Clive, M.C., Lt., d. of w., 11/11/16.
Grune, Gilbert Dennis James, Lt., k. in a., 13/3/16 (and R.F.C.).
Guthrie, Alexander, Lt., k. in a., 12/7/17.
Guthrie, Robert Gilbert, Lt., died, 7/11/18.
Hanson, Wilfred Clements, Lt., d. of w., 15/9/17.
Harman, L. W., Lt., died, 27/10/18 (R.A.F.).
Harris, Wilfred Ernest, Lt., k. in a., 15/9/17.
Harrison, Donald Howard, Lt., k. in a., 16/9/18.
Hartley, Christopher, Lt., k. in a., 1/9/17.
Hendry, Alistair, Lt., k. in a., 27/9/17.
Herbert, Ronald Young, Lt., k. in a., 23/9/17.
Heywood, Charles Clement, Lt., k. in a., 25/4/18.
Hicks, Eric Raymond, M.C., Lt., died, 25/12/18.
Hillyard, Noel Hardcastle, Lt., d. of w., 23/4/17.
Hodgson, Christopher Michael, Lt., d. of w., 17/6/17.
Honer, Douglas James, Lt., died, 4/6/17 (R.F.C.).
Howkins, Ernest, Lt., k. in a., 4/8/16.
Hunt, Reginald Frank, Lt., died, 29/5/18.
Hunter, Robert, Lt., k. in a., 5/6/17.
Hutchinson, James Gwynne, Lt., k. in a., 10/11/17.
Ironside, Oliver Dalton, Lt., died, 1/4/19.
Jackson, Herbert Percival, Lt., k. in a., 25/9/17.
James, Burnet George, Lt., k. in a., 26/9/15 (and R.F.C.).
James, Henry Vernon, Lt., d. of w., 12/4/18.
Johnson, Malcolm Johnson Williams, Lt., died, 18/2/19.
Johnson, Samuel, Lt., k. in a., 24/9/18.
Johnston, Walter Robertson, Lt., k. in a., 6/9/18.
Jones, James Melville, Lt., k. in a., 27/8/17.
Kempthorne, Harold Sampson, Lt., k. in a., 24/8/17.
Kennington, Harry, Lt., k. in a., 27/10/17.
Killby, Chester Winterbon, Lt., k. in a., 21/3/18.
Kimber, Henry Cyril Dixon, Lt., d. of w., 22/6/16.
King, Charles, Lt., d. of w., 10/5/17.
Lacey, Wilfred, Lt., k. in a., 31/3/18.
Lamont, James Kenneth, Lt., k. in a., 27/10/17.
Langley, Arthur Cecil, Lt., k. in a., 23/9/17.
Latham, Thomas Selby, Lt., d. of w., 29/11/17.
Lawson, Harry Sackville, Lt., k. in a., 5/2/18.
Legat, Andrew Ronald, Lt., k. in a., 28/3/17.
Le-May, Algernon Edward, Lt., d. of w., 24/7/17.

Levy, Arthur Herbert, Lt., k. in a., 31/7/17.
Lewthwaite, Charles Gilfred, M.C., Lt., k. in a., 29/7/17.
Long, Frederick Joseph John, Lt., k. in a., 31/7/17.
Lord, Douglas Frears, Lt., k. in a., 26/5/17.
Lord, George Hammond, Lt., killed, 30/11/17.
Lucas, Victor Carrington, M.C., Lt., k. in a., 7/6/17.
Lupton, Lionel Martineux, Lt., k. in a., 16/7/16.
McCash, John Watson, Lt., k. in a., 23/11/17 (and R.F.C.).
McCulloch, Kenneth, Lt., k. in a., 12/10/17.
McKenzie, Fredk. Thomas, Lt., k. in a., 23/3/18.
McPherson, William, Lt., k. in a., 8/5/17.
Maddison, George Lionel Temple, Lt., k. in a., 17/7/17.
Manford, Reginald Valentine, Lt., k. in a., 8/8/18.
Marrable, Edmund Douglas, Lt., died, 25/4/18 (att. R.A.F.).
Marsden, Wallis Austin Jonathan, Lt., d. of w., 20/7/17.
Marshall, Philip Spencer, Lt., k. in a., 15/8/17.
Marshall, Roger Charles, Lt., died, 7/1/18.
Marshall, William Gainer, Lt., d. of w., 19/8/15.
Melles, Gordon Frank, Lt., died, 6/11/15.
Middlemiss, Thomas Elmslie, Lt., k. in a., 17/10/17.
Miles, Francis James, Lt., d. of w., 6/11/17.
Miles, Herbert Talbot, Lt., d. of w., 16/4/17.
Miley, Miles, Lt., d. of w., 30/12/15.
Moore, John Davidson, Lt., k. in a., 22/3/18.
Moore, John Holmes Lyndon, Lt., k. in a., 9/4/18.
Moore, Lionel William Bentinck, Lt., k. in a., 30/1/18 (att. R.F.C.).
Morris, George Tod, Lt., k. in a., 11/4/17 (and R.F.C.).
Morgan, Arthur Conway Osborne, Lt., k. in a., 13/10/15.
Morton, William Cattell, M.C., Lt., d. of w., 22/7/17.
Mumford, John Houston, M.C. and Bar, Lt., k. in a., 13/8/17.
Nathan, David, Lt., k. in a., 20/8/17.
Nevill, Cuthbert St. John, Lt., k. in a., 18/4/18.
Nicholson, Basil Lee, Lt., k. in a., 24/7/15.
O'Brien, Dermot, Lt., k. in a., 26/9/17.
Palethorpe, Edwin Donald, Lt., k. in a., 9/10/17.
Parker, Victor, Lt., died, 5/3/16.
Pearse, Cecil George Lunell, Lt., died, 20/10/18.
Peden, Josef Kormendy Von Ikreny, Lt., k. in a., 28/3/18 (and R.F.C.).
Penney, Roland, Lt., k. in a., 2/4/18.
Pitt, Stanley, Lt., k. in a., 26/10/17.
Platt, John Rookhurst, Lt., d. of w., 27/3/16.
Playford, Patrick Randal, Lt., k. in a., 1/7/17.
Potts, William Janson, M.C., Lt., k. in a., 21/9/17 (and R.F.C.).
Priest, Robert Edgar Priest, Lt., killed, 15/8/17.
Pullin, Bernard John, M.C., Lt., d. of w., 21/10/17.
Purgold, Louis Joseph, Lt., killed, 20/8/17 (and R.F.C.).
Ramsey, Harry Victor, Lt., died, 5/8/18.
Richards, Arthur Stanley, Lt., k. in a., 25/6/17.
Richardson, Francis Aymer, Lt., k. in a., 27/5/18.
Rimmer, Samuel Gerard, Lt., k. in a., 4/5/16.
Robertson, Norman McLeod, Lt., k. in a., 17/10/16 (and R.F.C.).
Robinson, Leslie Fergus, M.C., Lt., k. in a., 27/9/18
Rosier, James Erle Radcliff, Lt., d. of w., 20/9/16.
Ross, Raymond Glenara, Lt., k. in a., 4/4/18.
Rouse, Alexander Ritchie, Lt., d. of w., 31/8/18.
Scott, James, M.C., Lt., d. of w., 10/3/18.
Scott, Walter, Lt., died, 23/10/15.
Sellers, Vernon Guy, Lt., died, 27/10/18.
Sharpley, Henry, Lt., d. of w., 24/3/18.
Shearer, William, Lt., k. in a., 8/6/18.
Smith, Martin Kirke, Lt., killed, 14/12/15.
Sopwith, Frank Wesley, M.C., Lt., k. in a., 27/5/18.
Sowinski, Joseph Ladislas, M.C., Lt., k. in a., 28/11/17.
Speer, Alfred Henry Templeman Loraine, Lt., k. in a., 9/7/16 (and R.F.C.).
Spencer, Shirley McTurk, Lt., k. in a., 10/10/17.
Stevens, George Percival, Lt., k. in a., 21/3/18.
Stirling, John Hunt, Lt., d. of w., 22/8/17.
Sutherland, Hugh, Lt., k. in a., 29/10/17.
Sykes, Frank William, Lt., k. in a., 14/3/18.
Taylor, George Robert Stanbury, Lt., d. of w., 30/9/17.
Taylor, Herbert William, Lt., died, 12/6/16.
Taylor, William Edward, Lt., k. in a., 31/7/17.
Tozer, William, Lt., died, 5/5/16.
Turner, Alexander Law, Lt., died, 12/3/16.
Turpin, James Knowles, Lt., k. in a., 14/8/17.
Twite, Harold Llewellyn, Lt., k. in a., 1/12/15.
Ure, William Alan, Lt., d. of w., 3/11/17.
Van den Bergh, James Henry, Lt., k. in a., 21/5/16.
Vanpraet, Francis, Lt., k. in a., 1/10/18.
Veitch, Alexander Gordon, Lt., k. in a., 23/4/17.
Veresmith, Daniel James Christopher, Lt., d. of w., 14/4/17.
Walbaum, William Frederick, Lt., d. of w., 12/9/17.
Wall, Leonard Comer, Lt., k. in a., 9/6/17.
Warnes, David Hoggett, Lt., died, 10/6/17.
Warrington, Harold Gordon, Lt., d. of w., 6/12/17.
Watkins, Eric Leopold Charles, Lt., died, 2/3/17.
Watkins, Mervyn Holmes, Lt., k. in a., 18/9/18.
Watson, Charles Challinor, Lt., d. of w., 1/6/17.
Weddell, Herbert, Lt., d. of w., 8/10/16.
Wedderspoon, John Henry Butcher, Lt., k. in a., 6/4/17 (and R.F.C.).
Weir, George, Lt., died, 5/10/18.
Welch, Hugh, Lt., k. in a., 28/3/17 (and R.F.C.).
Wheeler, Arthur Leslie Doble, Lt., k. in a., 10/8/17.
White, Thomas James, M.C., Lt., k. in a., 20/11/17.
Whittingham, Arthur William, M.C., Lt., k. in a., 10/10/17.
Williams, Leigh Roslin, Lt., k. in a., 27/5/18.
Williams, Leslie Caradoc, Lt., k. in a., 27/8/17.
Wilson, George Douglas, Lt., d. of w., 13/9/16.
Woodhouse, Robert Cecil, Lt., k. in a., 14/8/15.
Woollven, Gerald Clifton, Lt., k. in a., 11/9/18.
Worthington, Samuel, Lt., k. in a., 28/11/17.
Wyley, William Reginald FitzThomas, Lt., k. in a., 19/9/16.
Yates, John Carrington, Lt., k. in a., 21/3/18.
Young, Douglas Campbell, Lt., died, 18/9/15.
Adam, John Stewart, 2/Lt., k. in a., 11/8/18.
Adams, Henry Gordon, 2/Lt., k. in a., 5/10/17 (Stn. Mid. Bde.).
Andrews, E. B., 2/Lt., k. in a., 16/9/18 (and R.A.F.).
Appleton, Aaron, 2/Lt., k. in a., 17/3/17 (and R.F.C.).
Archbold, John, 2/Lt., k. in a., 19/6/17.
Arney, Frank Stanley, 2/Lt., k. in a., 18/4/18.
Baines, Henry Burgess, 2/Lt., d. of w., 4/6/17.
Barkby, Hartley, 2/Lt., k. in a., 1/8/16.
Barnes, Will, 2/Lt., k. in a., 2/11/18.
Barr, Ninian Horrell, 2/Lt., k. in a., 3/9/16.
Barrick, George Oliver James, 2/Lt., k. in a., 6/11/17.
Behrens, Walter Louis, 2/Lt., k. in a., 9/7/17.
Best, Norrys Aubrey, 2/Lt., k. in a., 19/7/17.
Binney, Leslie Wingfold, 2/Lt., k. in a., 15/4/18.
Blyton, Arthur Allister, 2/Lt., k. in a., 5/9/18.
Bottomley, Edwin Rhodes, 2/Lt., k. in a., 2/6/17.
Boully, Frederick Courtnay, 2/Lt., k. in a., 10/7/17.
Brocklesby, Horace Markham, 2/Lt., k. in a., 1/7/17.
Brunstrom, Waldemar, M.C., 2/Lt., k. in a., 19/8/18.
Buncle, Ronald, 2/Lt., died, 16/10/15.
Bushell, Roland, 2/Lt., d. of w., 26/9/17.
Busk, George Laurence, 2/Lt., died, 19/5/17.
Butler, Archibald Stanley, 2/Lt., k. in a., 16/8/16 (R.F.C.).
Butler, Eric Busvine, 2/Lt., k. in a., 30/9/17
Cairns, Gerge Ritchie, 2/Lt., d. of w., 4/1/16.
Carse, Robert Mercer, 2/Lt., k. in a., 12/4/18.
Chambers, James Edward, 2/Lt., d. of w., 1/10/16 (Wessex).
Clark, Eric Henry Lloyd, 2/Lt., k. in a., 1/7/16.
Clark, Lyonel Latimer, 2/Lt., k. in a., 2/8/16.
Clegg, Robert Burton, 2/Lt., k. in a., 17/2/17.
Collins, Frank Basil, 2/Lt., k. in a., 22/8/17.
Cowland, Herbert Samuel, 2/Lt., k. in a., 15/4/17.
Cox, Henry Hayr, 2/Lt., killed, 16/5/17.
Craig, John Beverley, 2/Lt., k. in a., 3/6/17.
Crompton, Henry Dent, 2/Lt., k. in a., 4/12/16 (and R.F.C.).
Cubie, Adam, 2/Lt., k. in a., 30/7/18.
Davenport, Thomas Lowe, 2/Lt., k. in a., 27/4/17.
Davies, David Daniel, 2/Lt., d. of w., 26/8/18.
Deane, Wellesley Venables, 2/Lt., k. in a., 24/9/17.
Dickinson, Geoffrey Garbutt, 2/Lt., k. in a., 2/10/17.
Dixon, John Vibart, 2/Lt., k. in a., 6/3/17.
Drinkwater, Leonard Wilfred, 2/Lt., k. in a., 3/10/17.
Duckworth, Percy Blezard, 2/Lt., k. in a., 9/4/17.
Duerden, Charles, 2/Lt., d. of w., 24/3/18.
Duffus, Gordon Charles, 2/Lt., k. in a., 16/1/17.
Elgey, Eric, 2/Lt., k. in a., 19/3/17 (R.F.C.).
Esdaile, George Augustus Churchill, 2/Lt., k. in a., 10/8/17.
Fell, George Charles Huntley, 2/Lt., d. of w., 24/7/17.
Findlay, Ernest Robert, 2/Lt., d. of w., 5/10/17.
Firth, Arnold, 2/Lt., k. in a., 15/4/17.
Fitton, Walter Verdi, 2/Lt., d. of w., 29/9/16.
Fleming, Richard Thomas Cyril Willis, 2/Lt., d. of w., 4/8/16.
Folingsby, Thomas Grueber, 2/Lt., d. of w., 23/6/16.
Frater, David George, M.C., 2/Lt., k. in a., 17/4/18.
Freakes, Alexander John, 2/Lt., d. of w., 3/9/18.
Frost, William Frank, 2/Lt., k. in a., 17/10/18.
Fyfe, Austyn James Claude, 2/Lt., k. in a., 23/3/17.
Galloway, James Blyth, 2/Lt., died, 17/11/18.
Glover, Ronald Howard, 2/Lt., k. in a., 25/9/17.
Gordon, Donald, 2/Lt., k. in a., 17/7/17.
Grice, Leslie Clark, 2/Lt., d. of w., 20/4/17.
Guthrie, William Colville, 2/Lt., died, 7/11/18.
Hall, William Holden, 2/Lt., k. in a., 26/9/17.
Hardy, Geoffrey, 2/Lt., d. of w., 27/5/17.
Harrison, Thomas Percy, 2/Lt., k. in a., 9/4/18.
Helliar, Leonard Jeffrey, 2/Lt., k. in a., 14/5/17.
Henshall, Donald Edward, 2/Lt., d. of w., 14/9/16.
Hill, Benjamin Godlonton, M.C., 2/Lt., d. of w., 5/6/17.
Holme, George Weston, 2/Lt., k. in a., 22/12/16.
Holmes, Basil Ralph Gardiner, 2/Lt., k. in a., 2/10/17.
Hughes, John Richard Hammond, 2/Lt., died, 29/6/18.
Hurstbourne, Walter Hirsch, 2/Lt., k. in a., 23/6/17.
Imrie, Arthur Leslie, 2/Lt., k. in a., 30/11/17.
Ironside, Arthur Douglas, 2/Lt., k. in a., 22/9/17.
James, Albert Hazlewood, 2/Lt., died, 20/12/18.
Jeavons, Rechab Vivian, 2/Lt., k. in a., 30/8/17.
Jobling, Henry Douglas, 2/Lt., d. of w., 22/1/18.
Johnston, Arthur Annan, 2/Lt., d. of w., 16/4/17.
Jones, Arthur Henry, 2/Lt., died, 15/3/16.
Jones, John Sydney, 2/Lt., died, 27/8/17.
Kimpton, Norman Herbert, 2/Lt., d. of w., 14/7/17.
King, Percy James Church, 2/Lt., k. in a., 24/10/17.
Kitching, Edward Allen, 2/Lt., died, 8/9/15.
Lant, Edwin, 2/Lt., k. in a., 8/9/17.
Lawther, Arthur Leonard, 2/Lt., d. of w., 23/5/16.
Laycock, Donald Stanley, 2/Lt., d. of w., 24/3/18.
Lethem, John, 2/Lt., k. in a., 1/12/17.
Lindley, John Bennett, 2/Lt., d. of w., 19/5/17.
Little, William, 2/Lt., k. in a., 24/4/18.
Loftus, Kenneth, 2/Lt., died, 9/11/18.
McCreadie, John, 2/Lt., k. in a., 21/3/18.
MacDonald, William Forbes, 2/Lt., k. in a., 23/11/17.
MacKenzie, Murdo John, 2/Lt., k. in a., 28/6/15.
McFarlane, John, M.C., 2/Lt., k. in a., 23/4/17.
MacFarlane, William Walter, 2/Lt., k. in a., 12/4/18.
MacGregor, Andrew Steven, 2/Lt., k. in a., 23/4/17.
Mackpherson, Donald, 2/Lt., d. of w., 11/11/17.
Mann, Thomas Edward, 2/Lt., k. in a., 30/7/18.
Melville, Sydney John Craig, 2/Lt., k. in a., 8/10/16.
Millar, George Inglis, 2/Lt., k. in a., 8/4/17.
Newton, Charles Ronald, 2/Lt., k. in a., 20/9/18.
Niven, John, 2/Lt., k. in a., 13/5/17.

Nuttrall, Alfred, 2/Lt., died, 11/5/16.
Ollett, Henry Wallace, 2/Lt., d. of w., 28/10/18.
O'Malley, William Joseph, 2/Lt., k. in a., 9/4/17.
Peacop, Reginald Trevor, 2/Lt., k. in a., 2/9/17.
Peterson, William Sinclair, 2/Lt., k. in a., 6/11/14. att 2 LG.
Plowes, Errol Sydney, 2/Lt., k. in a., 9/4/18.
Plum, Robert Bagshaw, 2/Lt., d. of w., 2/10/17.
Prebble, John, 2/Lt., k. in a., 21/6/17.
Pringle, Matthew, 2/Lt., k. in a., 27/8/17.
Pritchard, Douglas William Lindsay, 2/Lt., k. in a., 27/7/17.
Pullan, Charles Maxwell, 2/Lt., killed, 21/3/17.
Pye, Walter George, 2/Lt., k. in a., 24/7/17.
Robinson, Herbert Edwin, 2/Lt., k. in a, 10/7/17.
Rowe, Harold Charles, 2/Lt., k. in a., 19/7/17.
Salaman, Euston Abraham, 2/Lt., died, 18/2/16.
Sandbach, Frank Stainton, 2/Lt., k. in a., 29/7/17.
Sanderson, Fred Borthwick, 2/Lt., d. of w., 10/8/16.
Sawer, Edgar, 2/Lt., k. in a., 31/7/17.
Scott, Eric Farrow, 2/Lt., k. in a., 30/10/17.
Sloan, Arthur James, 2/Lt., k. in a., 30/8/18.
Smith, Henry Leslie, 2/Lt., k. in a., 17/8/18.
Smith, Sidney Fraser, 2/Lt., d. of w., 3/9/17.
Smith, William, 2/Lt., d. of w., 8/6/17.
Shand, Frederick Gordon, 2/Lt., d. of w., 12/10/18.
Shaw, Victor Charles, 2/Lt., died, 16/10/16.
Skinner, Frederick William Fletcher, 2/Lt., d. of w., 13/8/17.
Spence, Joseph, 2/Lt., d. of w., 8/8/17.
Sprinks, Ralph Cecil, 2/Lt., k. in a., 7/8/17.
Stevens, Frederick George, 2/Lt., d. of w., 21/10/17.
Stone, Oliver John, 2/Lt., d. of w., 22/9/16.
Stross, David, 2/Lt., killed, 12/3/17.
Suffield, Ernest, 2/Lt., d. of w., 1/5/18.
Sutton, Austin Ivor Spencer, 2/Lt., d. of w., 13/4/18.
Swan, Donald Brian, 2/Lt., k. in a, 7/3/17.
Swan, Robert John, 2/Lt., k. in a., 29/3/18.
Thomas, Stanley Meredith, 2/Lt., died, 13/12/18.
Thring, Ashton Edward, 2/Lt., died, 9/2/17.
Toye, Sydney Samuel, 2/Lt., k. in a., 10/10/18.
Underwood, John Middleton, 2/Lt., k. in a., 10/11/16.
Vickers, Robert, 2/Lt., d. of w., 10/12/17.
Watson, John Allan, 2/Lt., killed, 31/1/19.
Watson, Leslie Riley, 2/Lt., k. in a., 4/7/16.
Westwood, Walter Raymond, 2/Lt., d. of w., 26/10/16.
White, William Gurney, 2/Lt., d. of w., 23/9/16.
Whiteman, George Worley, 2/Lt., k. in a., 31/7/17.
Wildon, Edward Harold, 2/Lt., k. in a., 27/4/17.
Wilkinson, William Alfred, 2/Lt., k. in a., 2/12/17.
Willis-Fleming, Richard Thomas Cyril, 2/Lt., d. of w., 4/8/16
Wright, Percival Edward, 2/Lt., k. in a., 24/4/18.
Wrigley, Henry Neville, 2/Lt., died, 30/8/17.
Yirrell, Percy Tom Wilson, 2/Lt., d. of w., 30/3/17.
Young, Arthur Ernest, 2/Lt., d. of w., 21/5/18.

Royal Garrison Artillery (Territorial Force).

Jenkins, L., D.S.O., M.C., Lt.-Col., died, 20/11/18, R.A.F.
O'Connor, Henry, Lt.-Col., died, 1/12/15.
Richardson, Jasper Myers, Lt.-Col., d. of w., 30/3/18.
Aglionby, Hugh, M.C., Major, d. of w., 7/11/18.
Alexander, Thomas Wedderspoon, Major, k. in a., 21/3/18.
Balfour, Robert Wilson, Major, died, 6/1/18.
Barker, Harold Frederick, Major, k. in a., 29/3/18.
Blake, William Henry, Major, died, 19/5/16.
Breton, Walter Guy Nicholas, D.S.O., Major, k. in a., 14/9/17.
Challis, Arthur Bracebridge, T.D., Major, k. in a., 21/9/18.
Chaplin, Frederick Hardress, Major, died, 27/5/16.
Dargie, Arnold, Major, k. in a., 18/9/17 (Welsh Hy. Arty.).
Forbes, William Guthrie, M.C., Major, d. of w., 26/9/18.
Fownes, Henry Harley, Major, d. of w., 17/3/17.
Fry, Edwin Harries Sargood, Major, d. of w., 25/5/18.
Gordon, Reginald Glegg, D.S.O., Major, killed, 26/3/18.
Lyell, Hon. Charles Henry, Major, died, 18/10/18.
Martineau, Alfred John, Major, k. in a., 17/4/17.
Moubray, Arthur Russell St. John, M.C., Major, d. of w., 2/7/18.
Neame, Arthur, Major, died, 17/3/16.
Robertson, Alexander Winton, M.C., Major, d. of w., 23/4/16.
Robinson, Courtney Vyvyan, Major, died, 22/1/19.
Scott, Alexander, Capt. (Hon. Major), died, 12/2/15.
Sinclair-Travis, Norman Brownlie, Major, d. of w., 26/3/18.
Slade, Robert Blackmore, Major, k. in a., 10/7/18.
Treasure, James Herbert, T.D., Major, died, 3/12/18.
Turner, Harold Runciman, M.C. & Bar, Major, k. in a., 19/5/18.
Young, Cyril Rutherford Moffat, Major, d. of w., 1/7/17.
Buist, Charles Edward, M.C., Capt., d. of w., 21/10/17.
Cadic, Bernard Francis, Capt., died, 20/8/16.
Coulson, Coulson Tregarthen, M.C., Capt., d. of w., 8/9/18.
Craig, Robert Clark, Capt., k. in a., 22/7/17.
Gittins, Henry Neville, Capt., died, 20/3/17.
Harris, Edward, M.C., Capt., d. of w., 25/4/18.
Keighley, Richard Ernest Clayton, Capt., k. in a., 1/8/17.
Kersey, William Henry Myddleton, Capt., k. in a., 17/10/17.
Miller, A. C., Capt., killed, 3/10/15.
Morris, Robert Parry, M.C., Capt., k. in a., 27/10/17.
Rodgers, Robert William Christian Meyer, Capt., k. in a., 29/7/17.
Sandry, James Ralph, M.C., Capt., d. of w., 13/11/17.
Stapleton, Harold Edward Beaumont, Capt., d. of w., 26/9/17.
Thorburn, James, Capt., k. in a., 11/2/17 (and R.F.C.).
Todd, William, Capt., d. of w., 29/6/15.
Turner, Herbert Ellery, Capt., k. in a., 15/4/18.
Wheeler, John Eric, Capt., k. in a., 10/11/16.
Wormald, Drury Frank Percy, Capt., died, 4/11/18.
Young, Harry, Capt., died, 4/3/19.
Ainsley, Archie Robson, Lt., k. in a., 12/10/18.
Coomber, Harry Alan, M.C., Lt., d. of w., 29/4/18.
Cowan, Eric H., Lt., died, 28/2/16.
Field, Arthur Dudley, Lt., k. in a., 4/7/16.
Forbes, Joel Scott, Lt., k. in a., 1/4/17.
Hervey, Gerald Arthur, Lt., k. in a., 8/8/17.
Hirst, Fred Philip, Lt., died, 19/2/19.
Hort, Courtenay Randell, Lt., died, 10/5/16.
Howarth, Gilbert, Lt., k. in a., 29/3/18.
Jennings, Herbert Blake, Lt., d. of w., 25/7/17.
Jones-Parry, Ivor Norman, Lt., d. of w., 12/5/17.
Locking, Thomas Edgar, Lt., d. of w., 20/1/18.
MacDonald, David Johnston, Lt., k. in a., 29/10/17.
MacKay, Hamish Strathy, Lt., k. in a., 9/9/16 (att. R.F.C.).
McLauchlan, Alan Stewart, Lt., k. in a., 28/3/18.
Morris, Robert Crowe, Lt., k. in a., 23/9/18.
Morrison, Alexander, Lt., d. of w., 25/7/15.
Paterson, Thomas Simpson, Lt., k. in a., 10/11/16.
Peggie, Alexander Wallace Bruce, Lt., k. in a., 17/8/17.
Phillips, Benjamin Wynford, Lt., killed, 14/11/17 (and R.F.C.).
Phillips, Richard Glyndwr, Lt., k. in a., 27/8/17.
Plummer, Frederick Ryle, Lt., died, 2/11/18.
Pullen, Charles Tease, Lt., k. in a., 4/9/17 (and R.F.C.).
Rank, Sydney, Lt., d. of w., 23/10/18.
Ranken, George, Lt., k. in a., 1/11/18.
Saidler, William Tweeddale, Lt., k. in a., 26/3/18 (and R.F.C.).
Sandeman, Sydney Robert, Lt., k. in a., 22/4/15.
Sawden, William Wright, Lt., d. of w., 5/6/17 (and R.F.C.)
Seamans, Arthur Edward, Lt., d. of w., 3/12/17.
Stringer, Guy Frederick, Lt., k. in a., 17/6/15.
Tipping, Frank Blamphin, Lt., k. in a., 19/8/17 (and R.F.C.).
Tripe, Alfred King, Lt., k. in a., 23/11/17 (and Tanks)
Whitley, Alexander Fauvel, Lt., k. in a., 23/7/16.
Wright, John Crosby, Lt., k. in a., 10/4/17.
Young, Frederick Dobell, Lt., d. of w., 6/8/17.
Young, William Thomas, Lt., k. in a., 12/7/17.
Benison, Eric William, 2/Lt., died, 13/8/15.
Bly, Harold Alfred Edwin, 2/Lt., died, 17/11/18.
Bostock, Alexander Gordon, 2/Lt., died, 12/1/19.
Brown, Sidney Frederick, 2/Lt., k. in a., 15/5/18.
Carlyon, Thomas Tonkin, 2/Lt., d. of w., 28/6/18.
Drew, Frederick James, 2/Lt., k. in a., 29/3/18.
Dunn, Gerald Morton, 2/Lt., k. in a., 13/10/18.
Farthing, William Edgar, 2/Lt., died, 8/2/17.
Free, Ernest Robert, 2/Lt., died, 16/7/18.
Halley, William Carr, 2/Lt., died, 28/5/17.
Hannah, James, 2/Lt., drowned, 21-22/4/16.
Heckford, Percy James, 2/Lt., k. in a., 31/10/16.
Jones, Gwilyn Arthur, 2/Lt., k. in a., 25/10/17.
Lewis, John Clifford, 2/Lt., d. of w., 27/3/18.
McIntosh, John, 2/Lt., k. in a., 9/4/18.
Meggs, Stewart Gordon, 2/Lt., died, 3/3/17.
Miller, Walter Douglas, 2/Lt., k. in a., 2/10/16 (and R.F.C.).
Munday, Leslie William Crawford, 2/Lt., killed, 12/8/18.
Oakden, Ernest, 2/Lt., k. in a., 22/8/18.
Phillibrown, Cyril George, 2/Lt., d. of w., 15/11/17.
Royston, Basil Drage, 2/Lt., d. of w., 2/10/16.
Sharp, Reginald Archibald, 2/Lt., k. in a., 2/9/16.
Smith, Alan Joseph, 2/Lt., k. in a., 9/7/18.
Smith, Sydney Bicheno, 2/Lt., died, 1/12/18.
Syson, Leslie, 2/Lt., killed, 17/9/16.
Taunton, Percy Charles James, 2/Lt., killed, 7/8/17.
Thomson, Peter Walls, 2/Lt., k. in a., 24/7/16.
Turner, Edmund Sanctuary, 2/Lt., k. in a., 21/8/15.
Wedd, Hermann, 2/Lt., k. in a., 30/4/17.
Wellings, Thomas Fitch, 2/Lt., d. of w., 16/7/18.
Wenden, Charles Blade, 2/Lt., k. in a., 31/7/17.
White, Leonard Thomas, M.C., 2/Lt., k. in a., 21/9/18.
Whitham, John Edmund, 2/Lt., k. in a., 20/10/16.
Taylor, William, The Rev., died, 19/10/16.

Royal Engineers (T.F.).

Walthew, Ernest John, M.C., Lt.-Col., k. in a., 22/5/18.
Archibald, William, Major, d. of w., 18/6/15.
Bishop, Charles Gamble, M.C., Major, k. in a., 30/10/17.
Blogg, Edward Basil, D.S.O., Major, d. of w., 15/3/16.
Bray, Francis Patrick, Major, k. in a., 23/3/18.
Bryan, Cecil Clive, D.S.O., Major, k. in a., 11/8/17.
Butler, William Martin, Capt. (A/Major), died, 5/3/19.
Clissold, Harry, D.S.O., Major, k. in a., 28/9/17.
Colson, Douglas Fairley, D.S.O., Major, died, 3/2/19.
Ferguson, Harold Gowan, M.C., Major, died, 30/11/18.
Fisher, Frank, Major, k. in a., 26/9/17.
Gardiner, Ernest, Major, k. in a., 2/3/15.
Goodfellow, James Gordon, M.C., Lt. (A/Major), k. in a., 23/3/18.
Harvey, Sidney Lancelot, D.S.O., M.C., Major, died, 8/1/19
Hobson, Allen Faber, Major, k. in a., 28/8/16.
Hodgart, Matthew, Major, k. in a., 9/10/17.
Jackson, Ernest, D.S.O., M.C., Lt. (A/Major), d. of w., 15/4/18.
Jane, William, Major, d. of w., 24/4/18.
Lace, Walter Henry, M.C., Major, k. in a., 8/11/18.
McCraith, Bernard, Major, died, 29/1/19.
Marsh, Henry Herbert Stanley, Major, d. of w., 2/4/15.
Nell, Basil Frank, Major, died, 22/12/18.
Sewell, Sidney Davis, Major, k. in a., 18/2/15.
Tonks, Samuel William, Major, k. in a., 13/10/15.
Webster, Harold Wolstan, Major, d. of w., 12/4/18.
Weir, Thomas Henderson, M.C., Lt. (A/Major), k. in a., 8/5/18.
Whitten, Francis Robert, M.C., Major, d. of w., 18/4/18.
Anderson, Fredk. William, Capt., k. in a., 29/3/18.
Beaman, E. R. H., Capt., died, 17/12/18 (and R.A.F.).
Beit, Rupert Owen, A/Capt., d. of w., 29/7/17.
Black, Allan, Capt., k. in a., 27/5/18.
Bowers, Frederick Henry, Capt., killed, 29/5/17.

Brooke, George Townshend, Capt., k. in a., 6/5/15.
Brown, Clive Andrews, Capt., died, 7/11/18.
Butler, Charles, Capt., died, 27/8/17 (and R.F.C.).
Carver, Oswald Armitage, Capt., d. of w., 7/6/15.
Cleghorn, Herbert Stuart, Capt., k. in a., 2/9/17 (att. R.F.C.).
Danby, C. D., M.C., Capt., k. in a., 18/7/18 (and R.A.F.).
Davis, Clement John Burton, Capt., d. of w., 29/9/17.
Faber, John Benbow, M.C., Capt., k. in a., 18/9/16.
Fairtlough, Gerald Harold, Capt., d. of w., 13/6/18.
Gorringe, Wilfred Stuart, Capt., d. of w., 10/6/18.
Haldinstein, Frank Worlfe, Capt., d. of w., 7/3/17.
Hedges, William Herbert, Capt., died, 21/8/16.
Herbert, Robert Bingley, Capt., k. in a., 30/9/15.
Hillyer, William Harold, M.C., Capt., k. in a., 22/5/16.
Hinton, Charles Allan, M.C., Capt., k. in a., 22/5/18.
Jackson, Frank Wigmore, M.C., Capt., k. in a., 9/6/17.
Laird, Matthew James Donald, Capt., k. in a., 23/4/16.
MacIver, Andrew Tucker Squarey, Capt., k. in a., 24/4/15.
Mackenzie, Lynedoch Archibald, Lt. (T/Capt.), d. of w., 19/10/15.
Mackinlay, Robert Wallace, Capt., died, 6/2/19.
Marsden, James Alfred, Capt., k. in a., 21/4/18.
Maunsell, Robert George Frederick, Capt., drowned, 4/5/17.
Meston-Reid, James, Capt., died, 6/11/18.
Middleton, Henry, Capt., k. in a., 23/4/18.
Patterson, George, Capt., k. in a., 13/10/15.
Powell, Charles, M.C., Capt., d. of w., 21/3/18.
Richardson, Douglas Birch, Capt., k. in a., 29/7/16.
Salomons, David Reginald Herman Philip, Capt., drowned, 28/10/15.
Smith, Duncan Galloway, Capt., d. of w., 26/6/16.
Stroud, Henry Clifford, Capt., killed, 7/3/18 (R.F.C.).
Wills, Robert Bruce Melville, Capt., k. in a., 15/2/15.
Wilson, John Robert, Capt., k. in a., 20/10/17 (R.F.C.).
Adcock, Keith White, Lt., died, 30/10/18.
Aitken, Andrew Danskine, Lt., k. in a., 4/8/16.
Aitkens, Cyril Arthur Charles, Lt., d. of w., 10/7/16.
Ashmore, Geofrey William Paley, Lt., drowned, 4/5/17.
Ball, Gerald Wheatley, Lt., k. in a., 19/5/17.
Banks, Thomas George, Lt., k. in a., 26/4/18.
Barltrop, Eric Arthur, Lt., k. in a., 23/4/17.
Barnett, Edwin James, Lt., k. in a., 7/8/17.
Bean, William Stuart, Lt., k. in a., 21/1/18 (and R.F.C.).
Beckton, James Robson, Lt., k. in a., 18/2/18.
Board, Richard Frank, Lt., d. of w., 30/10/18.
Bostock-Smith, Claude, Lt., k. in a., 5/10/18.
Braddell, Edward Terrence, Lt., d. of w., 27/3/17.
Bruce, William George, Lt., k. in a., 25/4/18.
Bull, Godfrey John Oswald, Lt., k. in a., 8/7/15.
Burleigh, Robert, Lt., k. in a., 29/8/16 (R.F.C.).
Burns, Walter Scot, Lt., d. of w., 1/7/15.
Case, Elliott Dryden, Lt., killed, 27/7/15.
Chadwick, Percival Miller, Lt., k. in a., 22/9/18.
Challoner, Thomas, Lt., d. of w., 25/7/16.
Chapman, Douglas Collier, Lt., k. in a., 20/10/18.
Chiswell, Henry Pettit, M.C., Lt., k. in a., 25/3/18.
Colver, Edward Watkin, Lt., k. in a., 28/6/15.
Davis, George Edward, Lt., k. in a., 11-13/10/15.
Davis, Herbert Nathaniel, Lt., d. of w., 22/2/15.
Dawson, Phillip, Lt., k. in a., 26/3/18.
Dixon-Nuttall, Frederick John, Lt., k. in a., 21/5/15.
Douglas, Leslie Hall, Lt., k. in a., 9/7/15.
Eagle, Frank Water, Lt., k. in a., 6/6/16.
Emery, Burkett John, Lt., k. in a., 11-13/10/15.
Eastwood, Ronald, Lt., k. in a., 5/12/17.
Fernie, Roy Mackenzie, Lt., k. in a., 16/8/15.
Forster, James Henry, Lt., k. in a., 29/9/15.
Franklin, Cyril Edward, Lt., d. of w., 20/2/17.
Fuller, Henry Arthur, Lt., d. of w., 26/4/18.
Gaskell, Reginald Robinson, Lt., killed, 15/12/16 (att. R F C.).
Gibson, James Douglas, Lt., k. in a., 25/3/18.
Glegg, Robert, Lt., k. in a., 19/7/15.
Gosling, Douglas Edward, Lt., k. in a., 20/5/15.
Gowan, Arthur Blackmore, Lt., k. in a., 14/7/16.
Hall, Louis Sylvester, Lt., k. in a., 27/5/18.
Hall, Stanley Alexander, Lt., d. of w., 10/4/18.
Harrison, R., Lt., T/Lt., died, 17/5/18 (attd. R.A.F.)
Hayes, Cedric George, Lt., k. in a., 9/4/18.
Head, Frank William, Lt., d. of w., 17/10/18.
Hood, Andrew Smith, Lt., died, 24/7/18.
Hughes, Peter Fred'k, M.C., Lt., d. of w., 7/8/18.
Hunter, James Kenneth, Lt., k. in a., 6/9/17.
Hunter, Thomas, Lt., k. in a., 16/7/17.
Jamieson, Douglas, Lt., k. in a., 9/7/17.
Jones, Charles Henry, Lt., k. in a., 10/4/16.
Jones, David Raymond, Lt., k. in a., 17/4/18.
Jordon, Leslie Tiel, Lt., k. in a., 6/6/16.
Kelly, John Lawson, M.C., Lt., k. in a., 4/11/18.
Kemp, Alexander, M.C., Lt., d. of w., 26/7/18.
Killingback, Stanley Gordon, Lt., k. in a., 10/8/16.
Laing, Alexander Arthur, Lt., k. in a., 28/11/17.
Large, John Gerald, Lt., died, 4/6/18.
Lyon, George William, M.C., Lt., k. in a., 16/4/18.
McDonald, Kenneth William, Lt., d. of w., 4/9/17 (and R.F.C.) (in German hands).
Machregor, Amyas, M.C., Lt., d. of w., 13/10/16.
McNab, John Borrie McCulloch, Lt., k. in a., 14/2/19.
McPherson, Archibald Austin Oliver, Lt., d. of w., 26/5/18.
Manning, George Alfred, Lt., k. in a., 26/9/17.
Michaelis, Grant Moritz, Lt., k. in a., 23/9/15.
Miller, Francis Samuel, Lt., d. of w., 7/6/17.
Morton, Eric, Lt., d. of w., 26/8/18.
Munby, Ernest John, Lt., k. in a., 31/1/15.
Narracott, Ronald William, Lt., k. in a., 10/8/15.
Newton, Edwin Brierley, Lt., k. in a., 10/4/18.
Nicholson, William Herbert Hamilton, Lt., d. of w, 13/4/18.
Phillips, James, Lt., k. in a., 1/11/18.
Picker, Herbert Francis, M.C., Lt., died, 23/5/17.
Pickering, Leonard, Lt., k. in a., 9/4/18.
Poynton, Reginald James, Lt., died, 29/9/15.
Prince, George Reginald Dudley, Lt., died, 24/11/18.
Ritchie, Leonard Albany, Lt., k. in a., 24/3/18.
Roberts, David Francis, Lt., k. in a., 2/11/17.
Robertson, Glynn Cuthbert, Lt., k. in a., 15/3/16.
Robertson, William Bethune, Lt., k. in a., 25/3/18.
Rowden, Edmund Percival, Lt., k. in a., 6/9/17.
Scott, Noel Edmund, Lt., d. of w., 21/9/17.
Shorto, Martin Hubert, Lt., k. in a., 27/7/17.
Simpson, James Hawthorne, Lt., d. of w., 3/7/16.
Sinclair, Kenneth, Lt., d. of w., 12/10/18.
Stevenson, John Scott, Lt., d. of w., 9/10/18.
Stone, Henry Brassington, Lt., k. in a., 18/2/15.
Tapp, Harold Donesthorpe, Lt., d. of w., 25/7/17 (R.F.C.) (in German hands).
Taunton, Oscar, Lt., d. of w., 14/6/15.
Taylor, Alfred Thurston, Lt., k. in a., 5/10/18.
Thomas, John Vick, Lt., died, 3/12/18.
Thompson, Patrick Stapler, M.C., Lt., k. in a., 27/4/18.
Thresher, Oswald, Lt., d. of w., 2/10/18.
Tong, George, Lt., k. in a., 16/8/18.
Turner, Frederick William Robertson, Lt., k. in a., 5/8/16.
Vaughan-Jones, Gerald, Lt., k. in a., 26/2/17 (and R.F.C.).
Wallace, John Ernest Dudley, Lt., d. of w., 7/8/17.
Williams, John Ronald Watson, M.C., Lt., k. in a., 12/4/18.
Worth, Leslie, Lt., died, 16/8/18.
Wray, Ernest Warneford, Lt., k. in a., 23/8/17.
Young, William Steele, Lt., k. in a., 2/11/17.
Ainley, Kendrick Edward Denison, 2/Lt., k. in a., 9/6/15.
Allan, George McLachlan, 2/Lt., d. of w., 14/7/15.
Angus, Raymond Brocklehurst, 2/Lt., k. in a., 22/9/15.
Angus, Stewart, 2/Lt., k. in a., 2/7/16.
Arnold, Arthur Edward, M.C., 2/Lt., k. in a., 13/10/18.
Bell, John Wilson, 2/Lt., died, 18/2/17.
Bennallack, William Frederick, 2/Lt., k. in a., 17/10/18.
Birnie, William, 2/Lt., k. in a., 24/10/16.
Box, Roy Leslie, 2/Lt., k. in a., 9/10/16.
Brightman, Sidney Charles, 2/Lt., k. in a., 22/3/18.
Bruce, William, 2/Lt., k. in a., 3/12/18.
Bull, Bernard George Sheen, 2/Lt., k. in a., 4/4/15.
Busk, Edward Teshmaker, 2/Lt., died, 5/11/14.
Campbell, Oscar William, 2/Lt., d. of w., 24/6/17.
Case, Harry Ernest, 2/Lt., k. in a., 14/8/15.
Chandler, Eric Oatey, 2/Lt., k. in a., 11/4/18.
Clarke, William Mitchell, 2/Lt., k. in a., 12/11/16.
Davies, Hugh Mercer, 2/Lt., k. in a., 12/10/18.
Downes, Howard Gray, 2/Lt., k. in a., 12/3/17.
Dunbavano, Hubert, 2/Lt., k. in a., 25/8/16.
Fraser, Alan Simon, 2/Lt., k. in a., 24/3/18.
Grogan, Richard Lawrence Renny, 2/Lt., k. in a., 30/1/17.
Hanstock, John Walter, 2/Lt., d. of w., 30/10/18.
Holden, Joseph Rogers, 2/Lt., k. in a., 5/8/16.
Howarth, John, 2/Lt., d. of w., 10/9/16.
Hoy, Arthur, 2/Lt., k. in a., 3/11/16.
Hudson, Wilfred, 2/Lt., d. of w., 8/2/16.
Hughes, Alfred, 2/Lt., k. in a., 1/7/18.
Hume, George Minchin, 2/Lt., k. in a., 12/6/15.
Johnson, Charles Cuthbert, 2/Lt., killed, 9/6/15.
Johnston, John, 2/Lt., k. in a., 10/4/18.
Jones, Stanley Cottmore, 2/Lt., k. in a., 3/9/16.
Kemp, Douglas Gordon, M.C., 2/Lt., k. in a., 21/3/18
Kinsman, Cecil Henry, 2/Lt., d. of w., 28/3/16.
Lambert, Harry Redcliffe, 2/Lt., k. in a., 21/3/17.
Lathbridge, Staughton Charles Archelas, 2/Lt., d. of w., 31/10/15.
Mackinnon, Louis Charles Bowden Fuller, 2/Lt., k. in a., 21/3/18.
Maitland, Alexander McLean, 2/Lt., k. in a., 1/8/16.
Mather, Edward William, 2/Lt., d. of w., 13/10/16.
Maurice, Sterling, 2/Lt., d. of w., 11/5/15.
Medland, James Edward Percy, 2/Lt., k. in a., 23/3/18.
Moubray, Cyril Lloyd, 2/Lt., k. in a., 10/10/18.
Newbigin, George Nesbitt, 2/Lt., died, 6/4/16.
Ogilvie, James Roy, 2/Lt., d. of w., 22/8/18.
Penderel-Brodhurst, Bernard Richard, 2/Lt., k. in a., 1/10/18.
Phillips, John Harold Montague, 2/Lt., d. of w., 25/1/16.
Pink, Harold William, 2/Lt., d. of w., 7/10/16.
Pryor, Joseph Stoneman, 2/Lt., k. in a., 25/3/18.
Ramsey, George Bennett, 2/Lt., died, 27/8/15.
Rogers, Sidney Frederick, 2/Lt., killed, 31/12/17.
Scott, Henry Arthur, 2/Lt., k. in a., 8/4/17.
Smallman, Edward, 2/Lt., died, 19/11/16.
Smart, David Lorimer, 2/Lt., d. of w., 5/4/17.
Stone, George Morrison, 2/Lt., k. in a., 17/8/16.
Taylor, John Edgar, 2/Lt., killed, 1/2/17 (att. R.F.C.).
Tinniswood, Alfred, 2/Lt., k. in a., 1/10/18.
Trubshawe, Eric James, 2/Lt., d. of w., 2/2/17.
Tyzack, Eric Delaney, 2/Lt., k. in a., 15/9/17 (and R.F.C.).
Ward, Cyril Richard, 2/Lt., k. in a., 14/7/16.
Wedgwood, William Armstrong, 2/Lt., k. in a., 9/7/16 (att. R.F.C.).
West, Theodore, 2/Lt., k. in a., 24/9/16 (and R.F.C.).
Whimster, Thomas Forbes, 2/Lt., k. in a., 19/11/16.
White, Arthur, 2/Lt., k. in a., 18/1/15.
White, Eric, 2/Lt., k. in a., 6/5/16.
White, Harold Tom, 2/Lt., killed, 27/2/17 (and R.F.C.).
White, Ronald Edwin, 2/Lt., d. of w., 5/3/15.
Wilkinson, William, 2/Lt., died, 24/2/19.
Wilson, John, 2/Lt., k. in a., 9/5/15.
Woods, Basil Hamilton, 2/Lt., drowned, 17/12/14.
Wrigley, Percy Bernard, 2/Lt., k. in a., 23/3/18.

Royal Scots.

4th Battalion (Queen's Edinburgh Rifles).

(Territorial).

Dunn, Spottiswoode Robery, Lt.-Col., d. of w., 29/6/15.
Gray, James, Major, k. in a., 28/6/15.
Henderson, James Norman, Major, k. in a., 28/6/15.
Gerrard, Robert Finlay, Capt., k. in a., 18/4/17.
McCrae, George, Capt., k. in a., 28/6/15.
Mackie, Reginald Ernest, Capt., k. in a., 28/6/15
Macrorie, Roderick Douglas, Capt., k. in a., 2/11/17.
Pollock, John Dunbar, Capt., k. in a., 28/6/15.
Robertson, John, Capt., k. in a., 28/6/15.
Ross, George Alexander Sinclair, Capt., k. in a., 28/6/15.
Rutherford, Robert Witten Glendinning, Capt., k. in a., 28/6/15.
Allan, Charles Frederick, Lt., k. in a., 28/6/15.
Allan, Robert Beausire, Lt., died, 5/4/18.
Brunton, George, Lt., d. of w., 11/4/18.
Clark, George Mackay, Lt., k. in a., 12/11/17.
Considine, Patrick Francis, Lt., d. of w., 12/7/15.
Dalgleish, William, M.C., Lt., k. in a., 12/11/17.
Falconer, James Page, Lt., k. in a., 5/8/18.
Grice, Harold George, Lt., d. of w., 27/3/18.
Hawks, Aubrey Meldrum Wood, Lt., k. in a., 27/9/18.
Hoy, Andrew Burn, Lt., d. of w., 2/6/18.
Jeffrey, Ernest, Lt., k. in a., 24/3/18.
MacLean, A. P., Lt., killed, 17/9/18 (R.A.F.).
Millar, David Hopkin, Lt., d. of w., 30/5/18.
O'Hara, Thomas, Lt., died, 10/3/19.
Ritchie, Louis Malcolm, Lt., k. in a., 5/5/18 (and K.A.R.).
Turnbull, Hugh McDiamid, Lt., k. in a., 5/9/17.
Young, Archibald, Lt., k. in a., 28/6/15.
Aitchison, Thomas Donald, 2/Lt., k. in a., 28/6/15.
Alexander, James Kidd, 2/Lt., k. in a., 20/9/17.
Allan, William Alexander, 2/Lt., k. in a., 7/6/17.
Banks, Henry Crawford, 2/Lt., k. in a., 30/6/18.
Benson, Thomas Washington, 2/Lt., k. in a., 22/8/17
Brown, William Clark, 2/Lt., k. in a., 21/5/17.
Care, Graham Bristowe, 2/Lt., k. in a., 19/4/17.
Cook, Henry, 2/Lt., k. in a., 23/4/17.
Cumming, Andrew Alex. 2/Lt., died, 6/2/18.
Foster, John, 2/Lt., k. in a., 25/4/18.
Gibson, Reginald James, 2/Lt., k. in a., 28/6/15.
Haggo, Aubrey Paxton, 2/Lt., k. in a., 18/8/16.
Hanley, Bartholmew, 2/Lt., k. in a., 23/8/17.
Henderson, William James, 2/Lt., k. in a., 3/5/17.
Hewison, John Edward, 2/Lt., d. of w., 19/4/17
Hunter, James Gladstone, 2/Lt., k. in a., 14/3/17
Irvine, Charles, 2/Lt., k. in a., 24/8/18.
Jackson, James Crosby, 2/Lt., k. in a., 1/8/18.
Johnstone, William James, 2/Lt., k. in a., 28/6/15.
Kerr, David Chesne, 2/Lt., k. in a., 12/10/17.
Kerr, Harry Smellie, 2/Lt., d. of w., 25/4/18.
Lorimer, Robert, 2/Lt., k. in a., 14/3/17.
Lynch, James Meacher, 2/Lt., k. in a., 1/10/18.
McBlane, David McMurtrie, 2/Lt., k. in a., 12/10/17.
MacKenzie, William Sinclair, 2/Lt., k. in a., 28/4/17.
MacLachlan, Robert Hugh Muir Dow, 2/Lt., k. in a., 23/3/18.
Manning, Nicol Page, 2/Lt., k. in a., 6/10/18.
Matheson, John MacLean, 2/Lt., k. in a., 26/6/18.
Mitchell, Archibald, 2/Lt., k. in a., 25/4/18.
Mitchell, Francis James, 2/Lt., k. in a., 27/9/18.
Paterson, Charles, 2/Lt., k. in a., 28/6/15.
Richardson, Robert, 2/Lt., d. of w., 26/7/18.
Simpson, George Duddington, 2/Lt., k. in a., 22/10/17.
Sinclair, George Walker, 2/Lt., k. in a., 27/9/18.
Smith, Adam Davidson, 2/Lt., k. in a., 2/10/18.
Somerville, William, 2/Lt., k. in a., 25/4/18.
Speedie, John Gibson, 2/Lt., k. in a., 14/6/17.
Stewart, John Kennedy, 2/Lt., d. of w., 2/11/17.
Tait, David Borthwick, 2/Lt., k. in a., 11/8/18.
Thomson, John Murray, 2/Lt., k. in a., 21/9/18.
Turner, Thomas James, 2/Lt., k. in a., 2/9/18.
Wallace, Denis, 2/Lt., d. of w., 18/4/18 (P. of W.).
Wallace, John, 2/Lt., k. in a., 1/8/17.
Watt, James, 2/Lt., killed, 2/5/17 (and R.F.C.).

The Royal Scots.

5th Battalion (Queen's Edinburgh Rifles) (Territorial).

White, Alexander, Major, d. of w., 9/9/15.
Chalmers, James, M.C., D.C.M., T/Capt., A/Major, k. in a., 23/3/18 (and M.G.C.).
Darling, James William Kingsley, Capt., k. in a., 11/8/18.
Douglas, William Anderson, Capt., k. in a., 24/8/16.
Farquharson, Francis David, Capt., d. of w., 11/4/18.
Kemp, James Ogilvie, Capt., died, 12/12/17.
Lavelle, Patrick Joseph Aloysius, Capt., k. in a., 4/10/18
Lindsay, Douglas Alexander, Capt., k. in a., 15/5/15.
Macintosh, John Douglas, Capt., k. in a., 6/5/15.
Macrae, Alexander William Urquhart, Capt., killed, 11/8/18.
Newlands, Thomas, Capt., k. in a., 22/3/18.
Russell, William, Capt., k. in a., 5/5/15.
Bassett, William George, Lt., died, 17/12/15.
Good, William Knight, Lt., k. in a., 27/2/18.
Gordon, Charles Ewan, Lt., k. in a., 27/8/18.
Herdman, James, Lt., d. of w., 9/5/17.
Kerr, Alexander, Lt., d. of w., 30/4/15.
Lindsay, George, Lt., k. in a., 7/5/17.
Maule, Robert, Lt., k. in a., 27/5/15.
Murray, Robert Elder, Lt., k. in a., 11/8/18.
Robertson, William Moore, M.C., Lt., k. in a., 12/11/17
Smith, James Montague, Lt., k. in a., 2/5/15.
Steel, William Hendry, Lt.-Qr.-Mr., k. in a., 28/6/15.
Turnbull, William Elliot, Lt., k. in a., 28/4/15.
Whyman, Richard David, Lt. and Qr.-Mr., died, 10/3/17.
Aitchison, John Brebner, 2/Lt., killed, 10/5/15.
Cheyne, Charles Leslie, 2/Lt., d. of w., 21/4/18.
Hannah, Henry William, 2/Lt., k. in a., 10/2/17.
Harte, Joseph, 2/Lt., k. in a., 6/6/17.
Hislop, Walter Balmer, 2/Lt., k. in a., 28/4/15.
Kemp, Charles John, 2/Lt., k. in a., 25/5/15.
Lamb, John, 2/Lt., died, 28/7/17.
Merriles, John Sutherland, 2/Lt., k. in a., 19/6/15.
Nairne, Ronald, 2/Lt., k. in a., 3/4/18.
Reid, David Inglis, 2/Lt., k. in a., 25/8/15.
Simpson, William Drysdale, 2/Lt., k. in a., 3/10/15.
Veitch, Michael, M.C., 2/Lt., k. in a., 11/8/18.
Woodrow, William Davidson, 2/Lt., k. in a., 23/4/17.

Royal Scots.

6th Battalion (Territorial).

Adams, John Wood, Major, k. in a., 3/9/17.
Douglas, William Anderson, Capt., k. in a., 24/8/16.
Jackson, David, Capt., died, 3/9/15.
Barker, Nello, Lt., died, 14/3/17.
Brown, William, Lt., k. in a., 11/8/18.
Cavanagh, Patrick Felix, Lt., k. in a., 12/7/18.
Gibson, Robert Gray Nicol, Lt., k. in a., 21/3/18.
Henderson, Robert Francis Watt, Lt., d. of w., 15/10/18.
Jardine, Henry Marshall, Lt., k. in a., 23/7/16.
V.C. McGregor, David Stuart, Lt., k. in a., 22/10/18.
Neill, William Proudfoot, Lt., died, 24/12/16.
Brunton, James McLeod, 2/Lt., k. in a., 1/8/17.
Croneen, Laurence, 2/Lt., k. in a., 28/4/17.
Jack, Thomas, 2/Lt., k. in a., 9/4/17.
Low, Joseph Davidson McKenzie, 2/Lt., k. in a., 13/7/16.
Mackie, William, 2/Lt., died, 29/4/16.
Marshall, Matthew, 2/Lt., killed, 11/8/18.
Masterton, William Murray, 2/Lt., d. of w., 10/6/17.
Moyes, William Bernard, 2/Lt., k. in a., 7/4/17.
Paterson, William Charles Dawson, 2/Lt., k. in a., 25/9/16.
Robertson, David, 2/Lt., k. in a., 31/7/17.
Stewart, George Lothian, 2/Lt., k. in a., 9/4/17.

The Royal Scots.

7th Battalion (Territorial).

Dawson, John Douglas, Major, k. in a., 28/6/15.
Hamilton, John Dundas Lawrie, Major, killed (acc.), 22/5/15.
Sanderson, Arthur Watson, Major, k. in a., 28/6/15.
Mitchell, John Halliburton, Capt., d. of w., 26/10/17.
Mitchell, John Monfries, Capt., killed, 22/5/15.
Peebles, John Reid, Capt., k. in a., 28/6/15.
Pender, George, Capt., d. of w., 24/4/17.
Rogers, Arthur Norman, Capt., k. in a., 24/11/17.
Weir, Genge Gordon, M.C., Capt., drowned, 9/9/18.
Bean, Keneth Foster, Lt., d. of w., 12/4/18.
Binnie, W. H., Lt., k. in a., 22/7/18 (att. R.A.F.).
Flett, Arthur David, Lt., k. in a., 9/4/17.
Flett, John Edmund, Lt., k. in a., 15/11/15.
Galloway, Ronald Moncrief, Lt., k. in a., 28/6/15.
Herdman, Thomas Anderson, Lt., k. in a., 21/9/18.
Hutchinson, Andrew Levy, Lt., k. in a., 21/3/18 (M.G.C.).
Molyneaux, Ian Moore, Lt., d. of w., 10/7/18.
Muirhead, Lennox, Lt., k. in a., 21/9/18.
Salveson, Cristian Raymond, Lt., killed, 22/5/15.
Stewart, Nathaniel William, Lt., k. in a., 23/1/17 (R.F.C.).
Strettell-Miller, Charles Wallace, Lt., k. in a., 6/10/18 (M.G.C.).
Theobald, Arnold, M.C., Lt., died, 29/6/18.
Thomson, Alan Graham, Lt., k. in a., 26/9/17.
Thomson, Eric James, Lt., k. in a., 28/6/15.
Lyell, David, 2/Lt., k. in a., 12/7/15.
Mungall, Robert, 2/Lt., k. in a., 23/4/17.
Neill, David Taylor, 2/Lt., k. in a., 3/5/17.
Salveson, Eric Thomas Somervell, 2/Lt., k. in a., 23/4/17.
Stewart, John James Erskine Brown, 2/Lt., d. of w., 12/6/17.
Taylor, Ian Cleasby, 2/Lt., k. in a., 4/12/17.
Thomson, Francis Wishart, 2/Lt., k. in a., 28/6/15.
Wilson, John Victor, 2/Lt., k. in a., 17/11/17.

Royal Scots.

8th Battalion (Territorial).

Brook, Alexander, Lt.-Col., d. of w., 19/5/15.
Gemmill, William, D.S.O., Lt.-Col., k. in a., 25/3/18.
Stewart, Thomas, M.C. & bar, Major, k. in a., 12/9/17.
Todrick, Thomas, Capt., k. in a., 14/12/14.
Blackie, John, Lt., k. in a., 22/10/18.
Burnet, Francis Alexander, Lt., k. in a., 11/4/18.
Burt, Andrew, Lt., k. in a., 18/12/14.
Cowan, William Wilson, Lt., k. in a., 14/4/17 (and R.F.C.).
Dods, John Ballantyne, Lt., d. of w., 11/4/18.
Macdonald, Sydney, Lt., k. in a., 2/9/18.
Macfarlane, Alastair Hunter, Lt., k. in a., 12/5/15.
McKerrell, W. A. S., Lt., d. of w., 10/4/18 (att. R.A.F.).
Monilaws, Selwyn Macgeorge, Lt., k. in a., 12/8/18.
Murray, John Congreve, Lt., d. of w., 23/9/17.
Mylne, James Graham, Lt., k. in a., 2/9/18.
Reid, George, Lt., k. in a., 12/4/18.
Robertson, Alexander Stuart, M.C., Lt., k. in a., 2/9/18.
Scott, James Huggan, Lt., died, 9/11/18.
Standring, Frederick John, Lt., k. in a., 6/9/18.
Strachan, Wellesley Kendle, Lt., k. in a., 24/8/18.
Wallace, William Ernest, Lt., k. in a., 17/4/17.
Weir, Robert, Lt., k. in a., 16/11/16.
Allison, James, 2/Lt., k. in a., 20/9/17.
Bailey, Dermot Harvey, 2/Lt., k. in a., 24/5/17.

Bone, John Craigie, 2/Lt., k. in a., 28/4/17.
Cullen, William Geoffrey Langley, 2/Lt., died, 30/3/15.
Honeyman, Norman Stark, 2/Lt., k. in a., 22/10/17.
Hutchison, John William, 2/Lt., d. of w., 26/11/17.
Jameson, Robert Alexander, 2/Lt., k. in a., 21/7/18.
Lowson, William, 2/Lt., d. of w., 17/11/16.
Macfarlane, Leslie Kerr, 2/Lt., k. in a., 23/8/18.
McIver, James Noble, 2/Lt., k. in a., 25/8/17.
MacLachlan, Kenneth Gilbert, 2/Lt., k. in a., 23/4/17.
Moncur, James Melville, 2/Lt., k. in a., 17/4/17.
Muir, Alan Steele, 2/Lt., d. of w., 12/11/16.
Robertson, William Dickson, 2/Lt., k. in a., 28/7/17.
Snow, George Wilkie, 2/Lt., k. in a., 20/4/17.

The Royal Scots.
9th (Highlanders) Battalion (Territorial).

Cowan, George Deas, Major, k. in a., 23/4/18.
Blair, Patrick Alexander, M.C., Capt., k. in a., 23/4/17.
Liddle, William, Capt., died, 27/9/18.
MacKenzie, Kenneth, Capt., killed, 9/9/18.
Mountford, Stanley, M.C., Capt., k. in a., 24/3/18.
Smith-Grant, J. G. S. C., Capt., died, 30/5/18 (att. R.A.F.).
Taylor, Alexander, Capt., k. in a., 21/4/17.
Bannatyne, Douglas Alexander, Lt., k. in a., 1/8/18.
Douglas, Archibald Halliday, Lt., k. in a., 16/9/16.
Huie, Henry William Richard, Lt., k. in a., 11/8/18.
Jamieson, Crawford, Lt., k. in a., 23/4/17.
Lyon, Walter Scott Stewart, Lt., k. in a., 8/5/15.
McLean, Charles John, Lt., k. in a., 20/9/17.
Morrison, William Fleming Oliphant, Lt., k. in a., 2/9/18.
Ross, Findlay McFadyen, M.C., Lt., k. in a., 1/8/18.
Spens, Walter Thomas Patrick, Lt., died, 18/2/17.
Stevenson, Tom, Lt., k. in a., 1/8/18.
Willison, John Downie, Lt., k. in a., 25/7/18.
Adams, James Allison Wilson, 2/Lt., k. in a. 9/4/17.
Ainslie, John, 2/Lt., d. of w., 11/4/17.
Asquith, Arnold Senior, 2/Lt., d. of w., 2/10/18.
Black, James Muir, 2/Lt., k. in a., 1/8/18.
Brown, Charles Lawrie, 2/Lt., d. of w., 18/6/16.
Brown, Robert, 2/Lt., d. of w., 11/4/17.
Brunsdon, Henry George, 2/Lt., d. of w., 24/4/17.
Campbell, William, M.C., 2/Lt., k. in a., 31/7/17.
Clunie, William Halkerston, 2/Lt., k. in a., 26/4/18.
Ferguson, William Percival, 2/Lt., k. in a., 9/4/17.
Gellatly, John Stewart, 2/Lt., k. in a., 31/7/17.
Lawrie, Thomas Helm, 2/Lt., k. in a., 25/7/18.
Macdonald, John Row Mackenzie, 2/Lt., k. in a., 3/3/17
McEwen, David Campbell, 2/Lt., d. of w., 10/4/17.
Mackie, George, 2/Lt., d. of w., 12/4/17.
Philips, William Theodore Caldwell, 2/Lt., k. in a., 2/5/18.
Robertson, William Haswell, 2/Lt., d. of w., 2/8/18.
Shaw, John Donald, Lt., k. in a., 26/7/18.
Smith, Charles Hoyle, 2/Lt., k. in a., 23/4/17.
Smith, Herbert Shaw, 2/Lt., d. of w., 12/4/17.
Sutherland, John McIntyre, 2/Lt., k. in a., 23/4/17.

The Royal Scots.
10th (Cyclist) Battalion (Territorial).

Gray, Alexander Jackson, Major, k. in a., 7/11/17.
Brock, Sydney Edward, M.C., Capt., d. of w., 11/11/18.
Hutchison, Thomas Walter, Capt., died, 22/11/15.
Johnston, John Thomas, Capt., k. in a., 27/5/17.
Muirhead, James Love, Lt. (T/Capt.), k. in a., 21/11/17 (and Tanks).
Stuart, Atholl Archibald, Capt., k. in a., 12/10/17.
Wolfe, George, Capt., k. in a., 2/6/15.
Long, Austin Theodore, Lt., k. in a., 22/8/17.
Saint, William Bell, Lt., d. of w., 15/9/16 (att. R.F.C.).
Andrew, William Dickie, 2/Lt., k. in a., 22/3/18.
Bell, James Rogerson, 2/Lt., d. of w., 1/4/18.
Bell-Irving, William, 2/Lt., died, 28/10/15 (and R.F.C.).
Forsyth, William Forbes, 2/Lt., k. in a., 15/9/18.
Lindsay, Adam, 2/Lt., d. of w., 1/8/18.
Macnicol, Horatius Bonar, 2/Lt., drowned, 30/7/15.
Metcalfe, George, 2/Lt., d. of w., 12/4/18.
Petrie, Donald John, 2/Lt., k. in a., 9/9/16.
Stewart, John Morley, 2/Lt., d. of w., 21/8/18.
Thomson, George Vallance Bruce, 2/Lt., k. in a., 22/3/18.

Royal West Surrey Regiment.
4th Battalion (Territorial).

Hooke, Utten Lamont, Lt.-Col., d. of w., 21/6/17.
Beach, Lionel Hadwen Fletcher, D.S.O., Capt., died, 28/11/18
Crowley, John Cyril, Capt., k. in a., 11/9/16.
Hewett, Edmund Geoffrey, Capt., k. in a., 2/12/15.
Nicoll, Eric Stanhope, M.C., Capt., k. in a., 19/1/18.
Potter, Donald Rolls, Capt., d. of w., 21/12/17.
Reilly, Henry Duncan Ryan, Capt., d. of w., 30/5/19.
Spicer, Robert William, Capt., k. in a., 26/3/17.
Barrow, Alexander Egan, Lt., k. in a., 4/10/17.
Brodie, Peter Bellinger, Lt., died, 12/8/16.
Brydon, Alec Whitworth, Lt., k. in a., 31/8/15.
Buckell, Francis William Ashton, Lt., k. in a., 21/3/18.
Cooper, Arthur Herbert Augustus, Lt., k. in a., 4/10/17.
Dickinson, John Archibald, Lt., k. in a., 13/4/18.
Frost, Arthur Byfield. M.C., Lt., k. in a., 23/3/18.
Gadsden, Crawford Cunningham, Lt., d. of w., 16/10/17.
Hepworth, A. M., M.C., Lt., k. in a., 4/5/18.
Knight, Osbert Richmond, M.C., Lt., k. in a., 6/4/17 (R.F.C.).
Livock, Eric Stuart, Lt., k. in a., 8/11/17 (R.F.C.).
MacNicol, Douglas Oswald, Lt., k. in a., 5/1/18 (R.F.C.).
Ponter, Harry William, Lt., k. in a., 3/9/18.
Ridpath, Frederick Cecil Lacey, Lt., k. in a., 27/12/17.
Robertson, Robert Ward Shepherd, Lt., k. in a., 27/5/17 (M.G.C.).
Allen, Geoffrey Peake, 2/Lt., killed, 21/12/15.
Aldridge Archie Horace, 2/Lt., d. of w., 8/11/18.
Bennett, Leslie Punsfer, 2/Lt., d. of w., 16/2/17.
Borst, Charles Louis, 2/Lt., k. in a., 24/11/17.
Borthwick, Donald Walker, 2/Lt., k. in a., 28/12/16 (M.G.C.).
Dennett, Thomas Frank Preston Thwaites, 2/Lt., d. of w., 5/8/17 (R.F.C.).
Dorrell, Evelyn Percy, 2/Lt., d. of w., 14/10/18
Everett, William Thomas, 2/Lt., k. in a., 6/11/18.
Fuller, Ernest Paget, 2/Lt., k. in a., 20/9/17.
Goss, Edward Oliver, 2/Lt., d. of w., 14/10/18.
Harris, Cecil Alfred, 2/Lt., d. of w., 3/11/16.
Harvey, Claude Lindsay, 2/Lt., k. in a., 23/3/18.
Marsh, Francis Bedford, 2/Lt., d. of w., 5/10/16 (M.G.C.).
Nelson, Ethelbert Horatio, 2/Lt., k. in a., 18/11/16.
Parker, Thomas, 2/Lt., died, 11/12/18.
Payne, Hedley Stuart, 2/Lt., d. of w., 21/2/19.
Wood, Philip John, 2/Lt., k. in a., 25/5/17 (R.F.C.).

Royal West Surrey Regiment.
5th Battalion (Territorial).

Sladen, St. Barbe Russell, T.D., Lt.-Col., k. in a., 12/3/18.
Windham-Wright, John, Major, died, 14/2/19.
Smith, Valentine Herbert, Capt., died, 1/6/18
Cocks, Percy Frank Anderson, Lt., died, 25/5/16.
Evans, Eric Charles, Lt., k. in a., 23/3/18.
Hay, Donald Malden, Lt., k. in a., 11/8/17 (R.F.C.).
Hitchings, Francis Noel Wells, Lt., killed, 3/12/18.
Jephson, Charles Mitchell Warren, Lt., k. in a., 27/12/17.
Longbourne, William Louis Jennings, Lt., k. in a., 9/8/15.
Quin, Desmond Hilary, Lt., k. in a., 18/9/18.
Shilcock, John Winton, Lt., k. in a., 22-24/11/15.
Sotham, Ralph Clifford, Lt., k. in a., 9/1/18 (R.F.C.).
Sworder, John Perkins, Lt., d. of w., 24/7/18.
Vaughan, Francis Seymour, Lt., killed, 17/3/18 (R.F.C.).
Bowers, Frank Ewart, 2/Lt., d. of w., 31/3/18.
Bray, Gerard Theodore, 2/Lt., k. in a., 9/8/15.
Fenwick, William, 2/Lt., d. of w., 22/5/18 (In German hands).
Ford, Herbert Walter, 2/Lt., k. in a., 10/8/17.
Fry, Horace Charles, 2/Lt., died, 24/2/17 (R.F.C.).
Garden, John James, 2/Lt., k. in a., 3/5/17.
Looker, Leonard Davies, 2/Lt., k. in a., 1/8/17.
Martin, George Elvyn, 2/Lt., k. in a., 4/4/18.
Morris, Francis, 2/Lt., killed, 11/9/16.
Pickard, Lawrence Delapons, 2/Lt., k. in a., 10/8/17.
Wearne, Kenneth Martin, 2/Lt., k. in a., 20/9/17.

East Kent Regiment.
4th Battalion (Territorial).

Arfiold, Victor, Capt., k. in a., 15/1/17.
Sherren, Arthur Oswald, Capt., k. in a., 3/8/17.
Taylor, John Ogilvie, Capt., k. in a., 3/5/17.
Durdle, Reginald William, Lt., k. in a., 18/9/18.
Dyer, Laurence Charles, Lt., k. in a., 19/4/17.
Gribble, Charles Herbert, Lt., k. in a., 30/11/17.
Henderson, Edward Francis, Lt., k. in a., 27/3/18.
Hobbs, Victor William John, Lt., k. in a., 9/8/18.
Morgan, Leonard, Lt., d. of w., 1/12/17.
Naylor, Fred, Lt., k. in a., 12/4/18.
Oxley, Harry Alfred, Lt., k. in a., 21/9/18.
Ruddock, Thomas, Lt., k. in a., 7/8/18.
Sharp, Eric, Lt., died, 22/5/17 (and K.A. Rfls.).
Taylor, Frederick George, Lt., k. in a., 14/4/18.
Widdop, Arthur Norman, Lt., k. in a., 30/9/18.
Arnold, Hugo Cholmondeley, 2/Lt., d. of w., 12/6/17.
Baxter, Leonard Josiah, 2/Lt., d. of w., 12/11/18.
Beagley, Frederick Parkman, M.C., 2/Lt., k. in a., 26/8/18.
Beer, Robert Gerald, 2/Lt., k. in a., 30/11/17.
Brown, Horace Leslie, 2/Lt., d. of w., 11/3/18.
Carlos, Ernest Stafford, 2/Lt., k. in a., 14/6/17.
Coates, Stanley Harvey, 2/Lt., k. in a., 7/6/17.
Cousins, Donald Threlkeld, 2/Lt., k. in a., 10/4/17.
Crisp, Reginald, 2/Lt., k. in a., 29/3/18.
Davis, Leslie James George, 2/Lt., k. in a., 5/4/18.
Edwards, Arthur, 2/Lt., k. in a., 16/6/17.
Edwards, Spenser Ernest, 2/Lt., died, 9/3/17.
Frost, Francis Conrade Shenstone, 2/Lt., k. in a., 21/3/18.
Hardey-Mason, Harold Victor, 2/Lt., k. in a., 3/5/17.
Jack, Douglas Peacock. 2/Lt., k. in a., 18/9/18.
James, Basil Lister, 2/Lt., d. of w., 25/11/16.
James, Kenneth Lister, 2/Lt., k. in a., 3/5/17.
Lane, John Elston, 2/Lt., k. in a., 3/5/17.
Mann, John William, 2/Lt., d. of w., 22/8/18.
Morgan, Vernon Leslie, 2/Lt., k. in a., 21/9/16 (and R.F.C.).
Paige, Jack Brian, 2/Lt., k. in a., 14/6/17.
Pitt-Pitts, Edward Crewdson Pitt, 2/Lt., killed, 17/10/18.
Ruston, Cecil Harold Sowerby, 2/Lt., k. in a., 4/4/18.
Sansom, Edwin Richard. 2/Lt., d. of w., 30/10/18.
Sowter, Francis Ingle, 2/Lt., k. in a., 9/8/17.
Squire, Wallace Henry, 2/Lt., d. of w., 9/4/17.
Stevens, Douglas Harcourt, 2/Lt., k. in a., 7/8/18.
Stiles, Edgcumbe Leopold, 2/Lt., k. in a., 14/4/18.
Thomas, Heber, 2/Lt., k. in a., 12/10/17.
Vincent, Charles, 2/Lt., k. in a., 17/10/18.
Webb, Arthur Henry, 2/Lt., k. in a., 23/6/17.

East Kent Regiment.
5th (The Weald of Kent) Battalion (Territorial).

Fraser, James Scholfield, Major, k. in a., 13-14/1/16.
Adam, Alan Gordon Acheson, Capt., k. in a., 21-22/1/16

Beall, Stephen Spencer, A/Capt., k. in a., 18//9/18.
Buss, Benjamin, Capt., d. of w., 4/11/18.
Cheesman, Arthur Edwin, Capt., died, 26/9/16.
Loyd, Alwyne Travers, Capt., k. in a., 28/9/17 (and R.F.C.).
Osborne, Archibald Edward, Capt., k. in a., 21/3/18.
Skelton, Sydney, Capt., died, 20/3/18.
Baker, Guy Talbot, Lt., k. in a., 7/1/16.
Jemmett, Charles William, Lt., k. in a., 15/3/18.
Marchant, Hugh Stephen, Lt., k. in a., 7/1/16.
Scrace, J., Lt., died, 24/8/18 (and R.A.F.).
Waite, J. T., Lt., k. in a., 21/1/16.
Bone, Ronald Walter, 2/Lt., k. in a., 12/10/17.
Buss, Percy Charles, 2/Lt., k. in a., 24/6/17.
Buss, Thomas Weston, 2/Lt., k. in a., 9/4/17.
Goschen, The Hon. George Joachim, 2/Lt., d. of w., 19/1/16.
Holyman, Leslie Edward, 2/Lt., k. in a., 9/3/17.
Johnson, Howard Fife, 2/Lt., k. in a., 9/3/17.
Osborne, Henry Douglas, 2/Lt., died, 24/2/19.
Rothwell, Sidney, 2/Lt., k in a., 7/1/16.
Winch, William Haffenden, 2/Lt., d. of w., 13/1/16.

Royal Lancaster Regiment.

4th Battalion (Territorial).

Ellwood, Albert, M.C., Capt., k. in a., 14/4/18.
Hendry, John Taylor, A/Capt., died, 16/6/19.
Morrell, Ralph D'Albin, Capt., k. in a., 8/8/16.
Withey, Charles Elisha, Capt., k. in a., 20/9/17.
Wright, Alexander Allen, Capt., k. in a., 8/8/16.
Bolton, Stuart, Lt., k. in a., 17/3/18.
Bowman, Leslie Spencer, Lt., k. in a., 25/6/17.
Bradley, Richard, Lt., k. in a., 31/7/17.
Clark, Alfred Matthews, Lt., k. in a., 20/11/17.
Hatcher, Reginald Gordon, Lt., d. of w., 20/9/17.
Hewitt, Ernest Henry, Lt., k. in a., 15-16/6/15.
Johnstone, John Douglas, Lt., k. in a., 31/7/17.
Ruddock, Joseph John, Lt., d. of w., 5/6/18.
Spearing, Edward, Lt., k. in a., 11/9/16.
Walker, George Henry, Lt., k. in a., 16/6/15.
Brockman, Albert John, 2/Lt., k. in a., 8/8/16.
V.C. Collin, Joseph Henry, 2/Lt., k. in a., 9/4/18.
Glenie, George Richard, 2/Lt., k. in a., 11/9/16.
Gough, Bert Harold, 2/Lt., k. in a., 9/4/18.
Hilton, George, 2/Lt., k. in a., 8/8/16.
Howard, Edward Douglas, 2/Lt., k. in a., 20/9/17.
Hunter, Herbert, 2/Lt., k. in a., 26/4/18.
Jolly, Percy, 2/Lt., k. in a., 13/7/17.
Keighley, Linden Raynes, 2/Lt., d. of w., 3/12/17.
Lawson, Joseph Percy, 2/Lt., k. in a., 8/8/16.
Leah, Wilfred Reginald, 2/Lt., k. in a., 10/9/16.
Lincey, Charles Edgar, 2/Lt., k. in a., 31/7/16.
Metcalf, Lister, 2/Lt., k. in a., 8/8/16.
Rundle, James Robson, 2/Lt., k. in a., 20/11/17.
Thomson, Adam, 2/Lt., k. in a., 17/5/18.
Veevers, Edgar Samuel, 2/Lt., k. in a., 10/7/18.
Ward, John, 2/Lt., died, 18/12/15.
Wheatley, Arthur, 2/Lt., d. of w., 8/5/18.
White, Edwin Thexton, 2/Lt., k. in a., 20/9/17.

Royal Lancaster Regiment.

5th Battalion (Territorial).

Cadman, Edward Cadman, Lt.-Col., k. in a., 27/5/18.
Bingham, Frank Miller, Capt., k. in a., 22/5/15.
Burdett, William Edward, Capt., k. in a., 29/8/18.
Carter, William Arthur Roise, Capt., k. in a., 23/4/15.
Evans, Edward Meredyd Lloyd, Capt., k. in a., 14/3/16.
Kean, John Herdman, Capt., k. in a., 1/12/17.
Parsons, William Josiah, Capt., died, 27/10/18.
Roper, William Edward, Capt., k. in a., 31/7/17.
Satterthwaite, William Herbert, Capt., k. in a., 7/6/18.
Simpson, Charles Vernon Martin, Capt., k. in a., 31/7/17.
Baldwin, Terence Kennet James, Lt., k. in a., 20/3/18.
Barrow, Spencer Ellwood, Lt., d. of w., 16/11/15.
Bates, Stanley Knight, Lt., k. in a., 9/5/15.
Carr, Edgar Joseph Austin, Lt., d. of w., 18/5/15.
Coupland, Henry, Lt., d. of w., 24/4/15.
Deacon, William Warren, M.C., Lt., k. in a., 22/8/18.
Dickson, Angus, Lt., killed, 15/10/16.
Gaulter, Cuthbert Vivian, Lt., k. in a., 7/5/17 (R.F.C.).
Hamilton, Norman Butler, Lt., k. in a., 24/7/18.
Stevens, Fenwick Charles, Lt., d. of w., 7/9/18.
Titchener, Leonard Raymond, Lt., k. in a., 3/12/17 (R.F.C.).
Bennett, Reginald George, 2/Lt., k. in a., 26/10/17.
Bigland, George Braddyll, 2/Lt., k. in a., 15/6/15.
Brash, Wilfred, 2/Lt., k. in a., 9/3/17.
Ford, Clement William, 2/Lt., k. in a., 31/7/17.
Gardner, Robert, 2/Lt., k. in a., 5/5/15.
Goodman, Joseph, 2/Lt., k. in a., 11/4/17.
Gregg, Charles Edward, 2/Lt., k. in a., 15/6/17.
Higginson, Robert, 2/Lt., k. in a., 15/8/16.
Hinde, Kenneth, 2/Lt., k. in a., 3/2/17.
Irving, Robert, 2/Lt., k. in a., 2/8/16.
Jacobs, Henry, 2/Lt., k. in a., 6/7/18.
Kirk, Gerald, 2/Lt., d. of w., 24/4/15.
Ling, Arthur Leonard, 2/Lt., d. of w., 3/11/18.
Mackenzie, William Archibald, 2/Lt., d. of w., 29/9/18.
Notley, Albert Carr, 2/Lt., k. in a., 30/5/18.
Pinch, William, 2/Lt., k. in a., 31/7/17.
Price, John Turner, 2/Lt., k. in a., 27/5/18.
Scott, Sidney Towers, 2/Lt., d. of w., 12/4/17.
Wood, Samuel Herbert, 2/Lt., k. in a., 26/10/17.

Northumberland Fusiliers.

4th Battalion (Territorial).

Gibson, Bertrand Dees, D.S.O., Lt.-Col., k. in a., 27/5/18.
Bell, Henry Hogarth, Capt. (Tp.), k. in a., 5/9/16.
Benson, John Martin, A/Capt., k. in a., 27/5/18.
Bunbury, Wilfred Joseph, Capt., k. in a., 15/4/17.
Cox, Percival Elliot, Capt., d. of w., 23/5/17.
Davies, Geraint, M.C., Capt., d. of w., 14/4/18.
Gregory, Thomas William, Capt., d. of w., 22/3/18.
Henderson, John Thomas, Capt., k. in a., 15/9/16.
Joicey, Clive Montague, Lt. (T/Capt.), k. in a., 5/6/17.
North, Arthur Juvell, M.C., Capt., k. in a., 27/9/18.
Parker, Charles Thomas, Capt., died, 11/7/18.
Plummer, Lionel Davey, Capt., k. in a., 15/9/16.
Robinson, John Wilfred, Capt., k. in a., 15/11/16.
Turner, David Thompson, Capt., k. in a., 30/5/18.
Hope-Wallace, James, Lt., k. in a., 15/9/17.
Jones, William Saville, Lt., k. in a., 27/5/18.
Lund, Tom Clough, Lt., k. in a., 23/3/18.
Napier, John Chatt, Lt., k. in a., 29/10/18.
Pearson, Cecil William, Lt., k. in a., 3/1/18 (R.F.C.).
Simpson, Robert Arthur Abbs, Lt., d. of w., 30/10/17.
Spencer, James Michael Jeslyn, Lt., k. in a., 3/11/16 (R.F.C.).
Stroud, Arnold, Lt., k. in a., 15/9/16.
Walton, George Pears, Lt., k. in a., 22/8/18.
Bagnall, John Angus, 2/Lt., k. in a., 15/9/16.
Clements, Robert Cooper, 2/Lt., k. in a., 7/8/18.
Davies, Rhys Beynon, 2/Lt., k. in a., 1/5/17.
Davison, Charles Montague, 2/Lt., d. of w., 10/4/18.
Diack, William, 2/Lt., k. in a., 20/9/17.
Hall, Thomas, 2/Lt., k. in a., 27/3/18.
Hamilton, John, 2/Lt., k. in a., 23/3/18.
Johnson, Robert, 2/Lt., k. in a., 24/4/17.
Lees, Frank Priestman, 2/Lt., k. in a., 17/6/16.
Long, Henry Archibald, 2/Lt., k. in a., 15/9/16.
Nasby, Frank Clementine, 2/Lt., k. in a., 1/9/17.
Rayner, Ryde Guild, 2/Lt., k. in a., 26/10/17.
Roberts, John Robert Bowden, 2/Lt., k. in a., 1/2/16.
Ruddy, William, 2/Lt., k. in a., 26/10/17.
Sharp, Charles Gordon, 2/Lt., d. of w., 5/2/16.
Smith, Burns Crawford, 2/Lt., k. in a., 31/10/17.
Smith, David Arthur, 2/Lt., k. in a., 26/10/17.
Stephenson, Robert Brewis, M.C., 2/Lt., d. of w., 23/10/17.
Stobbs, Henry, 2/Lt., k. in a., 26/10/17.
Tully, Richard Latimer, 2/Lt., died, 22/7/18.
Waite, Arthur Sydney, 2/Lt., d. of w., 25/9/16.
Weir, Harold Llewellyn, 2/Lt., k. in a., 31/10/17.
Wright, Edward Frank Macer, 2/Lt., k. in a., 2/4/17.
Young, David Lindsay, 2/Lt., k. in a., 26/10/17.

The Northumberland Fusiliers.

5th Battalion (Territorial).

Hedley, John Ralph, D.S.O., Lt.-Col., died, 15/7/17.
Nash, Fountain O'Key Colbourne, Capt., T/Major, k. in a., 27/4/15.
Forrett, Percival Donald, Capt., k. in a., 5/2/16.
Graham, William George, Capt., k. in a., 24/6/15.
Lawson, Frederick Henry, Capt., k. in a., 24/5/15.
Leask, James Cunliffe, M.C., Capt., k. in a., 30/3/18.
North, Neville Marriott, M.C., Capt., k. in a., 27/5/18.
Patterson, Charles Alfred, Capt., d. of w., 8/10/16.
Anderson, Henry McDonnell, Lt., k. in a., 30/5/18 (and M.G.C.).
Armstrong, Denys, Lt., d. of w., 3/10/16.
Bainbridge, Thomas Lindsay, Lt., k. in a., 29/4/15.
Edwards, Percy Howarth, Lt., k. in a., 24/5/15.
Field, Alfred John, Lt., k. in a., 11/4/18.
Hill, Maurice Cridland, Lt., k. in a., 24/5/15.
Holloway, Robert James, Lt. & Qr.-Mr., died, 14/8/16.
Knox, Arthur Victor, Lt., k. in a., 6/6/17.
Lawson, Norman Wilfrid, Lt., k. in a., 14/11/16.
Poole, William Evelyn Stanley, Lt., k. in a., 19/9/17.
Richardson, Henry Thomas, Lt., d. of w., 23/8/15.
Sargent, Ernest Vernon, Lt., k. in a., 27/5/18.
Allen, Charles Arthur, 2/Lt., killed, 12/3/19 (and R.A.F.).
Grieves, James, 2/Lt., k. in a., 20/9/18.
Melrose, Thomas Nelson, 2/Lt., k. in a., 14/11/16.
Moorhouse, Arthur Edward, 2/Lt., k. in a., 15/11/16.
Phillips, Frederick Charles, 2/Lt., d. of w., 6/2/16.
Richmond, Cuthbert Laurence, 2/Lt., killed, 24/5/15.
Steele, Robert Kingsley, 2/Lt., k. in a., 24/5/15.
Stones, Shepherd, 2/Lt., k. in a., 3/11/16.
Willis, Oscar, 2/Lt., k. in a., 20/6/16.
Winfield, Frank, 2/Lt., d. of w., 31/5/15 (in Ger. hands).
Winkworth, Walter, 2/Lt., d. of w., 26/8/15.

The Northumberland Fusiliers.

6th Battalion (Territorial).

Charlewood, William Henry, T/Capt., d. of w., 22/7/16.
Drummond, Keaisley Mathwin, M.C., Capt., d. of w., 24/3/18.
Dunford, Roy Craig, D.S.O., Capt., d. of w., 10/11/16.
Penketh, Robert Charles, Capt., d. of w., 16/4/17.
Hunter, George Edward, Capt., k. in a., 26/4/15.
Hunter, Howard Tomlin, Capt., k. in a., 27/4/15.
Tweedy, Trevor Carlyon, Capt., k. in a., 15/9/16.
Bainbridge, Wilfred Hudson, Lt., d. of w., 15/3/16.
Blackwell, Gerald Davis, Lt., k. in a., 7/6/17 (and M.G.C.).
Bowden, Edward Ratcliffe, Lt., d. of w., 29/4/15.
Garton, Arthur Richmond, Lt., k. in a., 26/4/15.
Greenwell, Thomas William Maddison, Lt., k. in a., 19/7/18.
Guy, Ronald Litterdale, Lt., k. in a., 26/10/17.
Hall, Alan Ryder, Lt., k. in a., 30/5/18.
Leech, Arthur William, M.C., Lt., d. of w., 12/4/18.

Morpeth, Stanley, Lt., died, 22/10/18 (in German hands).
Mortimer, Edmund, Lt., k. in a., 26/4/15.
Murphy, John, Lt., k. in a., 25/8/18.
Noble, William Black, Lt., k. in a., 26/4/15.
Shaw, Philip, Lt., k. in a., 26/10/17.
Temperley, Harold Kenyon, Lt., k. in a., 26/10/17.
Tucker, Stanley Dawson Simm, Lt., k. in a., 26/10/17.
Aldrich, Francis Pelham, 2/Lt., k. in a., 6/7/17.
Benson, Henry Lawrence, 2/Lt., k. in a., 11/4/16.
Clephan, William Richmond, M.C., 2/Lt., k. in a., 7/7/17.
Collinson, William Holmes, 2/Lt., k. in a., 5/1/16.
Isherwood, Arthur, 2/Lt., killed, 8/12/16.
Jacques, George Sheriff Harkus, 2/Lt., k. in a., 27/6/16.
Lant, Thomas, 2/Lt., k. in a., 1/11/16.
Mather, Edward Noel, 2/Lt., k. in a., 26/4/15.
Mitchell, James Arthur, 2/Lt., k. in a., 27/9/18.
Ruddock, Richard Fenwick, 2/Lt., k. in a., 18/6/16.
Shaw, John Herbert, 2/Lt., k. in a., 26/10/17.
Smith, Andrew, 2/Lt., k. in a., 14/11/16.
White, Esmonde Ricarde Burke, 2/Lt., k. in a., 5/1/16.

The Northumberland Fusiliers.

7th Battalion (Territorial).

Merivale, John William, Capt., k. in a., 15/9/16.
Neville, Robert Patrick, M.C., Capt., d. of w., 27/10/17.
Brown, Fred'k. Anderson, Lt., k. in a., 26/10/17.
Burnett, Charles Guy Arobiun, Lt., k. in a., 30/6/16.
Davis, Guy Clifton, Lt., died, 11/5/18.
Davis, Wilfred Jervis, Lt., k. in a., 30/6/16.
McCreath, Andrew Berghans, Lt., d. of w., 11/12/17.
Jackson, George William, T/Lt., k. in a., 7/5/17 (and R.F.C.).
Merivale, Francis, Lt., died, 17/10/18.
Smail, Frank Weddell, Lt., d. of w., 1/12/15.
Stiles, Edgar Watson, Lt., d. of w., 13/4/18.
Strong, Arthur Penton, Lt., k. in a., 26/10/17.
Trinder, Arnold James, Lt., k. in a., 16/6/15.
Webb, Athelstan Sylvester Kenshole, Lt., k. in a., 21/3/18.
Booth, Baron Brooke, 2/Lt., k. in a., 15/9/16.
Burt, Roger Frederick, 2/Lt., k. in a., 27/3/16.
Charlton, Hugh Vaughan, 2/Lt., k. in a., 24/6/16.
Counsellor, Thomas Bell Small, M.M., 2/Lt., died, 8/12/18.
Dale, Arthur William, 2/Lt., k. in a., 1/7/16.
Derrick, Alan James, 2/Lt., k. in a., 15/11/16.
Dew, Albert William John, 2/Lt., k. in a., 10/4/17.
Donkin, Samuel Thornton, 2/Lt., k. in a., 25/12/15.
Doucet, Gerald Danby, 2/Lt., k. in a., 26/10/17.
Grey, John Ivor, 2/Lt., k. in a., 15/9/16.
Kent, Alan Williamson, 2/Lt., d. of w., 27/4/15.
Larken, Frederick James, 2/Lt., k. in a., 15/11/16.
Lawson, Edward Grey, 2/Lt., k. in a., 14/11/16.
MacLeod, Daniel MacKay, 2/Lt., died, 9/7/18.
Miller, James Archibald Montgomerie, 2/Lt., k. in a., 16/4/17.
O'Daly, Dominic Roe Dathy, 2/Lt., k. in a., 14/11/16.
Peckston, Robert Henry, 2/Lt., died, 22/10/17.
Robinson, Joseph, 2/Lt., d. of w., 11/10/16.
Smith, Alexander Noel, 2/Lt., d. of w., 26/9/16.
Straker, Albert Gray, 2/Lt., k. in a., 3/10/16.
Swinney, James Herbert Cecil, M.C., 2/Lt., k. in a., 16/4/17.
Thompson, Robert, M.C., 2/Lt., k. in a., 26/10/17.
Watson, Benjamin Alexander, 2/Lt., k. in a., 24/10/18.
Woods, Fletcher Hugh Lionel, 2/Lt., k. in a., 14/11/16.

The Royal Warwickshire Regiment.

5th Battalion (Territorial).

Banks, Leon Thomas Victor, M.C., Major, d. of w., 29/6/18.
Bindloss, Edward Alexander Morgan, Major, k. in a., 15/6/18.
Bratt, Alfred Charles, Lt., A/Capt., k. in a., 4/10/17.
Francis, John, Capt., k. in a., 2/6/15.
Grant, Stuart, M.C., Lt., A/Capt., k. in a., 3/12/17.
Lunt, Douglas Gordon, Capt., k. in a., 16/7/16.
Rabone, John Kenneth, Capt., died, 1/9/15.
Sichel, Oliver Walter, Capt., d. of w., 25/10/18.
Suckling, Cornelius Vincent, Capt., k. in a., 16/7/16.
Turner, Russell Sandon, Capt., k. in a., 4/10/17.
Edginton, Robert Walter Lawrence, Lt., k. in a., 3/6/15.
Farrington, Alfred Jack, Lt., k. in a., 27/8/17.
Hudson, John William Willoughby, Lt., killed, 30/11/15.
Keay, James Gordon, Lt., d. of w., 2/7/16.
Lamaison, Leonard William Henry, Lt., k. in a., 2/7/16.
O'Bryen, Myles Wheeler, Lt., killed, 2/10/16.
Spencer, Eliot, Lt., d. of w., 18/2/18.
Squires, Sidney Charles, Lt., k. in a., 29/10/18.
Truman, Donald George Harding, Lt., k. in a., 1/7/16.
Wakeman, Frank Trevor, Lt., k. in a., 30/10/17 (and R.F.C.).
Alabaster, Frederic Clifford, 2/Lt., d. of w., 25/8/16.
Bird, Arthur Leonard, 2/Lt., k. in a., 6/9/17.
Buttery, Henry George, 2/Lt., k. in a., 27/9/18.
Crichton, Ronald, 2/Lt., k. in a., 22/8/17.
Curtis, William Edward, 2/Lt., k. in a., 18/8/16.
Daniels, Fred, M.C., 2/Lt., k. in a., 3/12/17.
Gonner, Edward Dermot Leslie, 2/Lt., died, 2/7/18.
Goode, Thomas Lord, 2Lt., k. in a., 15/6/18.
Grove, Percival Allen, 2/Lt., d. of w., 7/7/16.
Harcourt, Howard Leslie, 2/Lt., d. of w., 18/3/17.
Huby, O. M., 2/Lt., died, 11/9/18 (att. R.A.F.).
Magness, Thomas Charles, 2/Lt., k. in a., 22/8/17.
Matts, Frank, 2/Lt., k. in a., 24/7/16.
Rose, Merton Alfred, M.C., 2/Lt., d. of w., 19/9/18.
Simpkin, Reginald John Henry, 2/Lt., k. in a., 16/7/16.
Uzzell, Francis Claude, 2/Lt., d. of w., 3/2/18.
White, Cyril William, 2/Lt., k. in a., 4/10/17.
Young, Bertrand John, 2/Lt., k. in a., 5/10/18.

The Royal Warwickshire Regiment.

6th Battalion (Territorial).

Baxter, William Hedley Bruce, Capt., k. in a., 27/8/17.
Boddington, Guy Livingston, Capt., k. in a., 19/12/16.
Davies, Cyril Thomas Morris, Capt., k. in a., 1/7/16.
Dixon, James Evelyn Bevan, Temp. Capt., k. in a., 1/7/16.
Greener, Leysters Llewellyn, M.C., Capt., k. in a., 5/12/17.
Lowe, Richard Conway, T/Capt., k. in a., 18/8/16.
Powell, Harry Stranger, M.C., Capt., d. of w., 5/10/17.
Pridmore, Percy Malin, M.C., Capt., k. in a., 21/9/17.
Rabone, Arthur Brian, Capt., k. in a., 1/7/16.
Simms, William, Capt., k. in a., 19/7/16.
Stafford, James Neilson Greenleer, Capt., k. in a., 16/4/17.
Wathes, Thomas Sidney, Capt., k. in a., 19/7/16.
Austin, George Elliott, Lt., k. in a., 27/8/17.
Bisseker, Arthur Vanderkists, Lt., k. in a., 4/10/17.
Flesher, Frederick Arthur, Lt., d. of w., 27/9/16.
Humby, Frederick Harry, Lt., d. of w., 9/11/18.
Martin, George Russell Courtney, Lt., k. in a., 1/7/16.
Orton-Smith, Geoffrey Ewing, Lt., died, 1/3/17 (in Ger. hands).
Poynting, Arthur, Lt., k. in a., 26/7/16.
Sanders, Henry Sacheverel, Lt., k. in a., 21/8/18.
Swann, Cecil Herbert, Lt., d. of w., 27/8/18.
Andrew, Herbert Leslie, 2/Lt., died, 14/10/18.
Assinder, William Alfred, 2/Lt., k. in a., 16/6/18.
Balkwill, John, 2/Lt., k. in a., 1/7/16.
Bisseker, John Wallis, 2/Lt., k. in a., 1/4/17.
Campbell, Henry Wallace, 2/Lt., k. in a., 22/6/16.
Clarke, Albert Edward, 2/Lt., d. of w., 9/7/16.
Cleave, Norman, 2/Lt., k. in a., 8/11/18.
Darvell, George William, 2/Lt., k. in a., 8/5/18.
Dawson, Wilfred Leedham, 2/Lt., k. in a., 3/12/17
Field, Henry Lionel, 2/Lt., k. in a., 1/7/16.
Gwynne, Henry Stanley, 2/Lt., k. in a., 24/11/17.
Harper, Hal, 2/Lt., k. in a., 19/7/16.
Harrison, John, 2/Lt., k. in a., 16/4/17.
Houghton, Ralph, 2/Lt., k. in a., 20/3/18.
Leedham, Richard Walter, 2/Lt., k. in a., 24/10/18.
Lilley, William Fred, M.M., 2/Lt., k. in a., 24/4/18.
Lilly, Arthur John, 2/Lt., k. in a., 4/4/17.
Lloyd, Dennis Montford Anthony, 2/Lt., k. in a., 22/3/18.
Mascord, Alfred Edgar, 2/Lt., k. in a., 6/5/18.
Packwood, William Harry, 2/Lt., k. in a., 12/4/18.
Oldham, John, 2/Lt., k. in a., 19/4/18.
Piper, Ronald Brandon, 2/Lt., d. of w., 3/4/16 (in Ger. hands).
Price, Reginald, 2/Lt., k. in a., 1/7/16.
Roberts, Edward Elwyn Lloyd, 2/Lt., d. of w., 20/9/18
Rogers, Samuel, 2/Lt., died, 24/11/17.
Rose, Reginald Vincent, 2/Lt., k. in a., 1/7/16.
Smith, Ernest Stuart, 2/Lt., k. in a., 15/5/18.
Sowerby, Isaac, 2/Lt., k. in a., 4/9/17.
Stocker, Harold Victor, 2/Lt., k. in a., 28/3/18.
Tetley, Harold Arthur, 2/Lt., k. in a., 12/4/18.
Tolson, Horace, 2/Lt., k. in a., 29/3/18.
Wheeler, William Pierce, 2/Lt., k. in a., 2/7/16.
Winkley, Sydney Joseph, 2/Lt., k. in a., 1/7/16.
Wooldridge, Albert Edward, 2/Lt., k. in a., 19/8/17.

The Royal Warwickshire Regiment.

7th Battalion (Territorial).

Knox, James Meldrum, D.S.O. & Bar, Lt.-Col., d. of w., 23/9/18.
Bethell, Thomas Henry, Capt., k. in a., 19/7/16.
Browett, Arnold Leslie Thackall, Capt., k. in a., 5/7/16.
Caley, Vernon Christopher Russell, M.C., A/Capt., k. in a., 22/8/17.
Donaldson, Geoffrey Boley, Capt., died, 19/7/16 (in German hands).
Godfrey-Payton, Arthur, Capt., d. of w., 29/8/16.
Graham, George Lionel, Capt., died, 11/4/18 (in German hands).
Kench, Leonard Sheldon, Capt., d. of w., 29/6/16.
Murray, Norman Cairns, Capt., k. in a., 30/6/16.
Crombie, W. E., M.C., Lt., k. in a., 31/8/18 (att. R.A.F.).
Edwards, Llewellyn Albert, Lt., died, 21/3/18 (in German hands).
Fowler, Edward Wareham, Lt., k. in a., 15/7/16.
Wise, George Edward Foster, Lt., k. in a., 4/6/16.
Bullock, Henry Acton Linton, 2/Lt., k. in a., 14/7/16.
Chance, Albert Henry, 2/Lt., k. in a., 22/3/18.
Edkins, Philip Eric, 2/Lt., d. of w., 16/7/16.
Greaves, John, 2/Lt., d. of w., 31/3/18.
Harris, Arthur Edward Crawford, 2/Lt., d. of w., 11/9/17.
Hill, Andrew Bruce, 2/Lt., k. in a., 27/9/18.
Imber, William Arthur, 2/Lt., k. in a., 27/8/17.
Loveitt, Alan Percy Charles, 2/Lt., k. in a., 25/7/16.
Quinlan, James Leonard, 2/Lt., d. of w., 28/12/17.
Rose, George, 2/Lt., k. in a., 28/6/18.
Tetley, Frederick Noel, 2/Lt., k. in a., 27/9/18.
Weller, Edward Arthur Walstone, M.C., 2/Lt., d. of w., 22/10/18 (att. M.G.C.).

The Royal Warwickshire Regiment.

8th Battalion (Territorial).

Innes, Edgar Arthur, C.M.G., Lt.-Col., k. in a., 1/7/16.
Beer, John Henry, Major, T/Lt.-Col., k. in a., 19/7/16. 2/4 R Berks Co
Caddick, Alfred Armstrong, T/Major, k. in a., 1/7/16.
Lefroy, Tracy Edward, Major, k. in a., 5/12/17.
Denison, Robert Charles, T/Capt., k. in a., 27/8/16.
Gibbins, Roland Bevington, Capt., k. in a., 3/12/17.
Ludlow, Stratford Walter, Capt., k. in a., 1/7/16.
Morton, William Ronald, Capt., k. in a., 4/5/17.
Parsons, Septimus Eric, Capt., killed, 14/4/18.
Pepper, Sydney Whitelock, Capt., k. in a., 27/8/17.

Richards, Joseph, Capt., k. in a., 4/11/18.
Taylor, Robert Valentine, Capt., k. in a., 29/7/18.
Turner, John, M.C., A/Capt., k. in a., 22/10/18.
Adams, Ralph, M.C. & Bar, Lt., k. in a., 1/7/16.
Fussell, James Gerald, Lt., k. in a., 1/7/16.
Hooton, Edward Cedric, Lt., k. in a., 26/6/16.
Hoskins, Cyril, Lt., k. in a., 1/7/16.
Jones, Frederick Wigan, Lt., d. of w., 21/12/16.
Procter, Arthur, M.C., Lt., k. in a., 1/7/16.
Sarjeant, Douglas Leslie, Lt., k. in a., 21/1/15.
Wareham, Frederick William, Lt., k. in a., 1/7/16.
Whiteley, Charles Taylor, Lt., d. of w., 1/7/18.
Barrett, Wilfred Varnish, 2/Lt., d. of w., 28/9/18.
Battye, Harry, 2/Lt., k. in a., 21/3/18.
Bennett, John Edwin, 2/Lt., k. in a., 24/7/16 (and M.G.C.).
Freeman, Francis Basil. 2/Lt., k. in a., 1/7/16.
Gascoyne, Francis Paul, 2/Lt., k. in a., 22/3/18.
Gilderthorp, Guy, 2/Lt., k. in a., 12/4/18.
Groutage, Joseph Harry, 2/Lt., k. in a., 29/3/18.
Guest, Reginald Victor, 2/Lt., d. of w., 28/8/16.
Hetherington, Thomas Alexander, 2/Lt., k. in a., 1/11/18.
Hussey, Frank, 2/Lt., k. in a., 4/10/17.
Huxley, Robert Charles, 2/Lt., k. in a., 7/5/18.
Key, Frederick Bertram, 2/Lt., k. in a., 1/7/16.
Love, Reyson, 2/Lt., k. in a., 3/12/17.
Morris, Reginald Harry, 2/Lt., k. in a., 28/6/18.
Pitt, Douglas, 2/Lt., k. in a., 24/3/18.
Shuttleworth, Ernest Ronald, 2/Lt., k. in a., 1/7/16
Slicer, Walter Gordon, 2/Lt., k. in a., 13/4/18.
Stone, Docksey, 2/Lt., k. in a., 21/7/16.
Weinel, George Henry, 2/Lt., died, 28/10/18.
While, Charles Victor, 2/Lt., k. in a., 26/6/16.
Winterbottom, Cyril, 2/Lt., k. in a., 14/4/18.

The King's Liverpool Regiment.

5th Battalion (Territorial).

Duncan, Henry John, Major, k. in a., 8/8/16.
Cox, Henry Bowerie, T/Capt., k. in a., 8/8/16.
Fairclough, Robert Justice, Capt., d. of w., 31/5/15.
Greig, William Ewing, Capt., d. of w., 27/5/15.
Hawkes, Percival Warburton, Capt., k. in a., 9/4/18.
Meade, Michael, M.C., Capt., k. in a., 9/4/18.
Saunders, William Gilbert, T/Capt., k. in a., 6/9/16.
Cohen, George Herbert, Lt., k. in a., 16/5/15.
Craig, William Younger, Lt., k. in a., 20/9/17.
Harding, Eric Stanley Milthrop, Lt., k. in a., 6/7/17.
Hitch, G. S., Lt., died, 9/11/18 (R.A.F.).
Hobson, Nathaniel James Fennel, Lt., drowned, 10/10/18.
Hudson, Cuthbert Newton, Lt., k. in a., 29/3/17.
Moore, William Henry, Lt., k. in a., 8/8/16.
Samson, Phillip Edward, Lt., d. of w., 21/10/18.
Walker, Frederick Clarkson, Lt., k. in a., 20/9/17.
Cartman, James Victor, 2/Lt., k. in a., 19/6/18.
Dey, Herman Francis, 2/Lt., k. in a., 31/7/17.
Dudley, Noel Montague Charles, 2/Lt., d. of w., 11/10/16.
Evans, Hugh George, 2/Lt., k. in a., 4/9/18.
Faulkner, Charles Edward Arthur, 2/Lt., d. of w., 19/9/18
Flenley, Edmund Berhard, 2/Lt., k. in a., 9/4/17.
Greenwood, Tom, 2/Lt., k. in a., 31/8/18.
Heyworth, Wilfred Alexander, 2/Lt., k. in a., 23/5/16.
Hose, Cyril Arthur Sparling, 2/Lt., k. in a., 10/9/16.
Jenkins, Richard Owen, M.C., 2/Lt., d. of w., 21/9/17.
Longbottom, Donald Hough, 2/Lt., k. in a., 8/8/16.
McHale, George Nolan, 2/Lt., k. in a., 20/9/17.
Mahon, Oswold Sydney Wilson, 2/Lt., d. of w., 14/4/17.
May, Adrian Robson, 2/Lt., k. in a., 8/9/16.
Oates, Herbert Prudent. 2/Lt., k. in a., 20/9/17.
Pilling, J. E., 2/Lt., died, 1/7/18 (and R.A.F.).
Plummer, Arthur Henry, 2/Lt., k. in a., 17/5/15.
Reeve, Harry, 2/Lt., k. in a., 18/5/16.
Rowe, Thomas, 2/Lt., k. in a., 23/5/16.
Sanders, Frederick Egerton, M.C., 2/Lt., k. in a., 10/10/18.
Scott, Frank, 2/Lt., d. of w., 8/10/18.
Stewart, John Nelson, 2/Lt., k. in a., 9/4/17.
Thomson, John, 2/Lt., k. in a., 18/6/17.
Washbrook, Harry, 2/Lt., k. in a., 22/8/18.
Webster, John Ralph Ward, 2/Lt., d. of w., 11/8/16.
Williams, Harry Benjamin, M.C., 2/Lt., k. in a., 3/5/17.
Wilson, Charles Lindsay, 2/Lt., k. in a., 8/8/16.

The King's Liverpool Regiment.

6th (Rifle) Battalion (Territorial).

Brocklehurst, Edward Henry, Capt., k. in a., 5/5/15.
Buckley, Edmund Cecil, Capt., d. of w., 5/8/16.
Eastwood, Donald, Capt., k. in a., 20/9/17.
Herschell, Ernest, Capt., d. of w., 26/9/16.
Jones, Albert, Capt., k. in a., 9/4/18.
Montgomery, William Sproat, Capt., d. of w., 13/3/15.
Barrett, Reginald James, Lt., k. in a., 21/8/18.
Burton, Geoffrey Bunnell, Lt., d. of w., 3/8/17.
Burton, Kenrick Hammond, Lt., k. in a., 16/6/18.
Collinge, Wharton Rye, Lt., d. of w., 7/8/17.
Hutchinson, Ambrose, Lt., k. in a., 19/1/18.
Jones, William James, Lt., k. in a., 28/6/16.
Phillips, Thomas, M.C., D.C.M., Lt., k. in a., 29/8/18.
Ross, G. A. B., Lt., k. in a., 1/6/18 (att. R.A.F.).
Smith, Charles Ernest, Lt., k. in a., 13/4/18.
Sutton, A. E. B., Lt., died, 4/7/18 (R.A.F.).
Wilson, Thomas Wilson, Lt., k. in a., 5/5/15.
Boult, Reginald Herbert Swinton, 2/Lt., k. in a., 8/8/16.
Buttery, Charles Henry, 2/Lt., d. of w., 1/10/16.
Colley, Douglas James, 2/Lt., k. in a., 29/11/16.
Conibear, Arthur Edward, 2/Lt., d. of w., 14/10/17.
Cowman, Frederick Gregory, D.C.M., 2/Lt.. k. in a., 28/9/18.
Fitzgerald, Herbert, 2/Lt., k. in a., 9/4/18.
Griffin, Edward Stanley, 2/Lt., k. in a., 31/7/17.
Harris, Arthur Stanley, 2/Lt., k. in a., 31/7/17.
Marsden, Harold, 2/Lt., d. of w., 14/8/17.
Milroy, Alexander Anderson, 2/Lt., d. of w., 4/7/18.
Moss, Morrice Edgar, 2/Lt., k. in a., 29/11/16.
Phillips, Norman Rutherford. 2/Lt., k. in a., 20/9/17.
Rideal, Samuel, 2/Lt., k. in a., 27/6/17.
Robinson, Harold Percival, 2/Lt., k. in a., 31/7/17.
St. George, Harold Edgar, 2/Lt., k. in a., 13/8/16.
Scarborough, E. O., 2/Lt., died, 25/5/18 (att. R.A.F.).
Shield, William James, 2/Lt., k. in a., 2/3/17.
Waln, Edward Ashton. 2/Lt., k. in a., 21/10/18.
Weld-Blundell, Robert Shirburne, 2/Lt., died, 1/1/16
Wright, George, 2/Lt., d. of w., 19/9/16.

The King's Liverpool Regiment.

7th Battalion (Territorial).

Hughes, Arthur, Major, k. in a., 16/5/15.
Brock, Eric George, M.C., Lt. (A/Capt.), k. in a., 31/7/17.
Davies, Edwin Alfred, Capt., died, 25/1/15.
Dean, Josiah Stanley, Capt., d. of w., 27/5/15.
Harvey, James, Capt., k. in a., 16/5/15.
Mackenzie, Cyril Atkinson, Capt., k. in a., 24/12/17.
Mottram, Osborne Arthur, Capt., k. in a., 8/8/16.
Shaw, Robert, Capt., k. in a., 20/9/17.
Tweedale, Maurice, Capt., k. in a., 16/5/15.
Adams, Lawrence Kingston, Lt., k. in a., 16/5/15.
Allan, William Stanley, Lt., k. in a., 17/5/15.
Barnett, Allan Gerrard, Lt., k. in a., 22/8/17 (and Tank Corps).
Bodey, Alan Ralph, Lt., k. in a., 28/6/16.
Bradbury, John Cregean, Lt., d. of w., 6/10/18.
Harrison, William, Lt., d. of w., 17/9/16.
Pittock, Percy Whittle, Lt., k. in a., 27/9/18.
Plewman, Charles Edward, Lt., k. in a., 9/4/18.
Smith, Allan Wenman, Lt., killed, 18/3/17 (and R.F.C.).
Stephenson, Arthur Thomas, Lt., k. in a., 28/6/16.
White, Stafford Charles, Lt., k. in a., 31/7/17.
Alexander, William Gemmell, 2/Lt., k. in a., 15/5/15.
Bell, Sydney James, 2/Lt., d. of w., 13/10/16.
Chalmers, Arthur Lakes, 2/Lt., k. in a., 23/9/16.
Chinnery, Reginald Charles, 2/Lt., k. in a., 31/7/17.
Cook, Bernard, 2/Lt., k. in a., 6/9/16.
Duncan, Malcolm, 2/Lt., d. of w., 21/9/17.
Elliott, Thomas Nichol, 2/Lt., k. in a., 11/4/18.
Ellis, William, 2/Lt., k. in a., 29/7/18.
Fearnhead, John Hayes, 2/Lt., d. of w., 13/8/16.
Gamble, Richard Maurice Brooks, 2/Lt., k. in a., 16/5/15
Grove, Ernest Richard, 2/Lt., k. in a., 10/2/18.
Hannon, Norman Leslie, 2/Lt., k. in a., 16/5/15.
Knox, Thomas Cowe, 2/Lt., k. in a., 19/8/18.
Lewis, Harris, 2/Lt., k. in a., 25/9/16.
McClelland, Thomas, 2/Lt., k. in a., 16/5/15.
Matthews, Edwin Harold, 2/Lt., k. in a., 8/8/16.
O'Neill, Alfred Edward, 2/Lt., d. of w., 23/9/17.
Pate, George Clarence, 2/Lt., k. in a., 18/9/18.
Patterson, George Gordon, 2/Lt., k. in a., 25/9/16.
Porter, Edgar Wardle, 2/Lt., d. of w., 22/8/16.
Prendiville, Lawrence Anthony, 2/Lt., k. in a., 31/7/17.
Riley, James Louis, 2/Lt., k. in a., 29/9/18.
Robinson, Birketh Waring, 2/Lt., k. in a., 18/9/18.
Seagrave, P., 2/Lt., k. in a., 1/11/18 (and R.A.F.).
Sharp, Beresford, 2/Lt., k. in a., 9/4/18.
Shoreman, James, M.C., 2/Lt., k. in a., 27/9/18.
Stacey, Herbert Leonard, 2/Lt., k. in a., 31/7/17.
Taylor, Edward Staveley, 2/Lt., d. of w., 19/8/16.
Thomas, Edward Palgrave, 2/Lt., k. in a., 9/8/16.
Turnbull, Henry James, 2/Lt., k. in a., 25/9/16.
Williams, Walter, 2/Lt., k. in a., 15/5/18.

The King's Liverpool Regiment.

8th (Irish) Battalion (Territorial).

Leech, Harry, Major, k. in a., 31/7/17.
Bodel, Frederick Ernest, M.C., Capt., k. in a., 31/7/17.
Brown, George, Capt., k. in a., 16-18/6/15.
Davies, Edwin Alfred, died, 25/1/15.
Duder, Harvey Steevens, Capt., k. in a., 31/7/17.
Finegan, Herbert Marion, Capt., k. in a., 16-18/6/15.
Johnson, James Alexander Campbell, Capt., k. in a., 21/8/18.
Keating, Robert Pears, Capt., k. in a., 18/7/17.
Mahon, James Harold, Capt., d. of w., 13/9/16.
Meadows, Albert Henry, Capt., k. in a., 8/8/16.
Mountfield. Robert Noel, Capt., d. of w., 5/11/17.
Ryan, Finley Francis, M.C., Capt., k. in a., 25/6/17.
Ward, Frank Saxon, Capt., k. in a., 31/7/17.
V.C. Baxter, Edward Felix, Lt., k. in a., 18/4/16.
Brewerton, Robert Henry, Lt., k. in a., 30/4/18.
Downes, Herbert Laidlow, Lt., k. in a., 15/6/15.
Duncan, Walter, Lt., died, 19/12/18.
Fenn, John Edmund, M.C., Lt., k. in a., 9/4/18.
Fisher, Herbert Learoyd Hammond, Lt., k. in a., 8/8/16 (and M.G.C.).
Gordon, Robert Hope, Lt., k. in a., 8/8/16.
Keith, Noel, Lt., k. in a., 22/5/17.
Limrick, Paul Osborne, Lt., k. in a., 12/9/16.
Lowe, Ronald Charles, Lt., d. of w., 18/8/18 (in Ger. hands).
Moyniham, Michael John, Lt., d. of w., 3/6/18.
Orchard, Ernest Frank Gordon, Lt., k. in a., 31/7/17.
Cottier, Walter Kaneen, 2/Lt., died, 23/8/18.
Daniels, George, 2/Lt., k. in a., 20/11/17.
Drake, Henry Mackay, 2/Lt., d. of w., 16-18/6/15.
Ellis, William Forrest, 2/Lt., k. in a., 9/9/16.

Lee, James Francis, 2/Lt., k. in a., 11/9/18.
Levene, Nathan Neville, 2/Lt., k. in a., 8/8/16.
Lilley, William David Hetherington, 2/Lt., d. of w., 11/8/16 (in Ger. hands).
Lunn, Frank Victor, 2/Lt., k. in a., 31/5/18.
McCabe, Daniel James Bernard, 2/Lt., k. in a., 31/7/17.
Mogridge, L., 2/Lt., k. in a., 12/4/18 (att. R.A.F.).
Moran, John, 2/Lt., died, 7/6/18.
Munro, William, 2/Lt., k. in a., 29/4/18.
Quinn, James Ewart, 2/Lt., k. in a., 5/10/18.
Richards, Charles Walter, 2/Lt., k. in a., 27/9/16.
Sharpe, John Sutton, 2/Lt., k. in a., 8/8/16.
Tipping, William. 2/Lt., k. in a., 8/8/16.
Wray, Francis Alan, 2/Lt., k. in a., 31/7/17.

The King's Liverpool Regiment.

9th Battalion (Territorial).

Bolland, Theodore Julian, Major, k. in a., 9/5/15.
Fulton, Andrew Wilfred, Major (Tp.), k. in a., 12/8/16
Owens, Fredrick Gordon, Major, died, 4/10/18.
Watts, Norman Luther, Major (Tp.), k. in a., 25/9/16.
Coupe, Albert, Capt., k. in a., 9/4/17.
Radford, Amyas Leith, Capt., k. in a., 12/5/15.
Raine, William, M.C., Capt., d. of w., 7/9/18.
Van Gruisen, Nicholas Albert Ray, Capt., k. in a., 21/8/18.
Brodbelt, Guy, Lt., k. in a., 14/4/16.
Challener, Arthur Cecil, Lt., k. in a., 25/9/16.
Chester, James Leslie, T/Lt., killed, 6/7/15.
Darling, Robert, M.C., Lt, k. in a., 16/9/18.
Fausset, Stewart Simon, Lt., k. in a., 31/7/17.
Gibson, Alexander Douglas, Lt., k. in a., 11/9/18.
Hansen, Carl Frederick Vilhelm, Lt., d. of w., 31/7/17 (M.G.C.).
Henshill-Wood, Alexander Russell, Lt., d. of w., 27/9/16
Milner, Lawrence Frank, Lt., k. in a., 25/9/15.
Nott, Charles, Lt., k. in a., 8/10/15.
Reid, William Alexander, Lt., d. of w., 27/12/17.
Tickle, Andrew Brown, Lt., k. in a., 14/7/17.
Adams, Arthur Marston, M.C., 2/Lt., d. of w., 20/9/17.
Alty, Daniel, 2/Lt., k. in a., 9/9/18.
Alty, Henry, D.C.M., 2/Lt., d. of w., 30/9/18.
Carr, Alfred Rothwell, 2/Lt., k. in a., 9/4/17.
Challiner, William Henry, 2/Lt., d. of w., 13/8/16.
Gummer, Basil Austin, 2/Lt., k. in a., 12/8/16.
Hansen, William George, 2/Lt., k. in a., 25/9/16.
Hartt, Harold, 2/Lt., k. in a., 5/5/17.
Hickson, James Ferguson, 2/Lt., d. of w., 31/7/17.
Hood-Rowan, Maxwell, 2/Lt., k. in a., 12/8/16.
Hoskyn, John Henry, 2/Lt., k in a., 20/9/17.
Hurst, Richard Henry, 2/Lt., k. in a., 29/9/18.
Jones, Eric, 2/Lt.. k. in a., 2/7/16
Lamont, Alexander, 2/Lt., drowned, 10/10/18.
Leaning, Reginald William, 2/Lt., killed, 31/5/18.
Lee, Charles Frederick. 2/Lt., d. of w., 27/4/17.
Mathvin, Douglas Gatecliffe. 2/Lt., k. in a., 9/5/15.
Podmore, Edward Glanville, 2/Lt., k. in a., 25/9/15.
Purdie, David Scott, 2/Lt., d. of w., 30/9/18.
Purdon, Harold Reginald, 2/Lt., d. of w., 28/4/18.
Richman, Alexander Woolacott, 2/Lt., d. of w., 26/9/17.
Riley, Herbert Angus, 2/Lt., k. in a., 28/6/16
Robinson, James, 2/Lt., k. in a., 20/5/17.
Simpson, John Wyckliffe, M.C., 2/Lt., k. in a., 1/8/17.
Smith, Edward Pelham, 2/Lt., k. in a., 16/8/18.
Threlfall, John Alexander, 2/Lt., d. of w.. 10/5/18.
Watson, Harry, 2/Lt., k. in a., 12/8/16.
Watts, Thomas William, 2/Lt., k. in a., 25/9/15.
Whitehead, Mark, 2/Lt., k. in a., 12/8/16.
Williams, John Tyler, 2/Lt., k in a., 21/3/18.

The King's Liverpool Regiment.

10th Battalion (Liverpool Scottish) (Territorial).

Anderson, Andrew Stewart, Major, k. in a., 16/6/15.
Cookson, Alan, Capt., k. in a., 27/6/17.
Dickinson, Alan Piele, Capt., d. of w., 1/6/18.
Dickinson, Ronald Francis Bickersteth, Capt., k. in a., 16/6/15.
Dun, Leslie Finlay, Capt., k. in a., 28/9/15.
Fox, Leslie William, Capt., k. in a., 31/7/17.
Graham, John, Capt., k. in a., 16/6/15.
Guthrie, Robert Forman, Capt., k. in a., 9/8/16.
McConnan, George, Capt. (Tp.), k. in a., 9/8/16.
McKinnell, Bryden, Capt., k. in a., 16/6/15.
Macleod, Donald, Capt., k. in a., 28/9/15.
Montgomery, Hugh Bertram, Capt., k. in a., 9/8/16.
Twentyman, Arthur, Capt., k. in a., 29/11/14.
Whitson, Henry Thomas, Capt., d. of w., 5/9/18.
William, John Rhonwy, Capt., d. of w., 13/8/16 (In German hands).
Astley, Christopher Basil, Lt., d. of w., 27/7/18.
Bruce, P. T., Lt., died, 30/5/18 (R.A.F.).
Gemmell, Kenneth Alexander, Lt., k. in a., 16/6/15.
Hobbs, Henry Bede, Lt., k. in a., 15/3/17.
MacSwiney, Joseph Ray, Lt., died, 2/11/18.
Mill, Leonard Binning. Lt., k. in a., 9/8/16.
Muir, Allan, Lt., k. in a., 15/5/19.
Ridehalgh, Harold, Lt., k. in a., 23/9/18.
Turner, Frederick Harding, Lt., k. in a., 10/1/15.
Turner, William Stewart, Lt., k. in a., 16/6/15.
Barber, John Christian, 2/Lt., k. in a., 16/6/15.
Bardswell, Hamilton Ainsworth, 2/Lt., k. in a., 30/11/17.
Blencowe, Lawrence Cave, 2/Lt., k. in a., 29/6/17.
Buck, Arch Charles Watson, 2/Lt., k. in a., 9/8/16.
Burnell, George Cuthbertson, 2/Lt., d. of w., 24/6/15.
Clark, Fred Sumner, 2/Lt., k. in a., 14/10/18.
Coddington, Charles Ernest, 2/Lt., k. in a., 4/12/17 (R.F.C.).
Craige, George, 2/Lt., died, 28/10/18.
Crighton, Harold Reginald, 2/Lt., k. in a., 10/4/18.
Davidson, John Philip, 2/Lt., k. in a., 9/8/16.
Douglas, William Robert, 2/Lt., k. in a., 5/10/18.
Duncan, Kenneth William Allen, 2/Lt., k. in a., 8/5/18.
Dunlop, Christian Dolymythe Hamilton, 2/Lt., k. in a., 16/6/15.
Dunn, Ernest George, 2/Lt., k. in a., 10/6/17 (M.G.C.).
Gledsdale, Arthur, 2/Lt., k. in a., 31/7/17.
Gray, Peter, 2/Lt., k. in a., 18/6/18.
Grossart, Archibald Campbell, 2/Lt., k. in a., 23/7/18.
Holford, Leonard Brocklesby, 2/Lt., d. of w., 20/2/19.
Jowett, Alan, 2/Lt., k. in a., 29/6/17.
Kellie, William Reid, 2/Lt., k. in a., 18/6/18.
Kendall, Percy Dale, 2/Lt., k. in a., 25/1/15.
Leitch, Vivian Bissett, 2/Lt., k. in a., 16/4/15.
McCallum, Charles, 2/Lt., died, 6/11/18.
MacLaren, Donald Graeme, 2/Lt., k. in a., 29/6/17.
MacNae, Robert, M.C., 2/Lt., k. in a., 10/10/16.
Mather, Norman, 2/Lt., k. in a., 9/8/16.
Moffat, John Everard, 2/Lt., k. in a., 9/4/18.
Myles, Alfred Thomas Charles, 2/Lt., k. in a., 2/7/18.
Paterson, Edward Labarte, 2/Lt., d. of w., 23/10/18.
Price, Thomas Joseph, M.C., 2/Lt., d. of w., 25/4/18.
Racine, Ernest Guy, 2/Lt., k. in a., 9/4/17.
Reid, John Lavens, 2/Lt., d. of w., 12/9/16.
Slocock, Lancelot Andrew Noel, 2/Lt., k. in a., 9/8/16.
Thurlow, John Kennings, 2/Lt., k. in a., 24/4/18.
White, James Pringle, 2/Lt., k. in a., 28 Ap./26/5/15.
Woodland, Herbert Lancelot, 2/Lt., k. in a., 9/8/16.

The Norfolk Regiment.

4th Battalion (Territorial).

Davey, Sydney Guy, Lt. (A/Major), died, 25/3/18 (and M.G.C.).
Hughes, Burroughs Maurice, Major, k. in a., 15/9/15.
Jewson, William Henry, T/Major, k. in a., 19/4/17.
Beck, John Stanley, M.C., Capt., k. in a., 16/8/17.
Begg, A., 2/Lt. (A/Capt.), died, 21/3/18.
Coller, Charles Mervyn, Capt., k in a., 21/3/18.
Cubitt, Terence Algernon Kilbee, M.C., Capt., k. in a., 22/8/18.
Fisher, George Kenneth Thompson, Capt., k. in a., 3/9/17.
Jennings, Thomas Edward, A/Capt., k. in a., 11/12/17.
Morgan, William Vanstone, Capt., k. in a., 19/4/17.
Page, Sydney Durrant, Capt., k. in a., 19/4/17.
Steel, Stanley Joseph, Capt., k. in a., 19/6/18.
Thurgar, Ralph William, Capt., k. in a., 19/4/17.
White, Spencer John Meadows, Capt., k. in a., 15/1/17 (and R.F.C.).
Barker, Sydney Clare, Lt., k. in a., 21/3/18.
Cole, Frederick John, Lt., k. in a., 19/4/17.
Hampton, George Kenneth, Lt., k. in a., 16/8/15.
Harvey, William Anthony, Lt., died, 7/11/17 (and R.F.C.).
Kirby, Kenneth Cameron, Lt., k. in a., 18/9/18.
Leamon, Douglas Arthur, 2/Lt. (T/Lt.), d. of w., 14/8/17.
Matthews. Robert John, Lt., died, 2/10/18.
Wylde, Thomas Edgar, Lt., d. of w., 27/6/17 (and R.F.C.).
Badcock, Harold John 2/Lt., k. in a., 18/10/16
Blake, William Lovewell, 2/Lt., d. of w., 27/3/18.
Cockrill, Alick Charles, 2/Lt., k. in a., 23/4/17.
Collison, Edgar Henry, 2/Lt., died, 26/6/16.
Cozens-Hardy, Raven, 2/Lt., k. in a., 9/10/17.
Gowing, William Lee, 2/Lt., d of w., 12/12/17.
Levy, Josiah, 2/Lt, k in a., 19/4/17.
Robarts, Henry Martyn, 2/Lt., d. of w., 26/9/17.
Scolding, George Henry, 2/Lt., k. in a., 26/3/18.
Senior, Robert Mackenzie, 2/Lt., k. in a., 27/3/18.
Sharp, William Dalton Colombo, 2/Lt., k. in a., 9/10/17.
White, Spencer John Meadows, 2/Lt., k. in a.. 15/1/17 (and R.F.C.).
Wood, Alfred Godfrey, 2/Lt., k. in a., 11/12/17.

The Norfolk Regiment.

5th Battalion (Territorial).

Proctor-Beauchamp, Sir Horace George (Bart.), C.B., Lt.-Col., k. in a., 12/8/15.
Woodwark, Ernest R., T/Major, k. in a., 21/8/15.
Archdale, Charles William, Capt., k. in a., 20/11/17.
Beck, Arthur Evelyn, M.C., Capt., k. in a., 19/4/17.
Beck, Frank Reginald, Capt., k. in a., 12/8/15.
Birkbeck, Gervase William, Capt., k. in a., 19/4/17.
Cubitt, Edward Randall, Capt., k. in a., 12/8/15.
Cubitt, Eustace Henry, Capt., k. in a., 19/4/17.
Gay, Edmund, 2/Lt. (A/Capt.), k. in a., 12/8/15.
Partridge, Robert Henry, Capt., killed, 4/9/17.
Pattrick, Arthur Deverus, Capt., k. in a., 12/8/16.
Wenn, William, Capt., d. of w., 1/4/17.
Beck, Albert Edward Alexander, Lt., k. in a., 12/8/15.
Cubitt, Victor Murray, Lt. (Tp.), k. in a., 12/8/15.
Dover, William, Lt., k. in a., 28/4/17.
Gardiner, Eric John, Lt., k. in a., 19/4/17.
Gardiner, I. J., Lt., drowned, 27/5/18 (and R.A.F.).
Hervey, Douglas Frederick, Lt., d. of w., 17/5/17.
Lambe, Frederick William, Lt. (Tp.), d. of w., 10/11/16.
Markwick, William Percival, Lt., k. in a., 5/9/18.
Norris, William Forbes, Lt.. k. in a., 25/8/15.
Parker, Samuel, Lt. & Qr.-Mr., died, 1/11/15.
Plaistowe, Richard Reeves, Lt., k. in a., 19/4/17.
Spencer, Sydney, M.C., Lt, k. in a., 24/9/18.
Tebbutt, Arthur Brookes, Lt., k. in a, 19/4/17 (and M.G.C.).
Adams, Robert, 2/Lt. k. in a., 12/8/15.
Proctor-Beauchamp, Montague Barclay Granville, 2/Lt., k. in a., 12/8/15.
Burroughes, Randall, 2/Lt., k. in a., 12/8/15.
Buxton, George Barclay, 2/Lt., k. in a., 28/7/17.

Dodson, Herbert Edwin, 2/Lt., k. in a., 28/4/17.
Oliphant, Marcus Francis, 2/Lt., k. in a., 12/8/15.
Shaw, William Henry, 2/Lt., k. in a., 2/11/17.
Smith, Clifford Day, 2/Lt., k. in a., 23/10/18.
Williams, Cecil Arthur, 2/Lt., k. in a., 21/3/18.

The Norfolk Regiment.

6th (Cyclist) Battalion (Territorial).

Coulton, Aubrey Ewan, Capt., k. in a., 20/7/16.
Fowler, Christopher George, Capt., k. in a., 6/4/17.
Lee, Richard Henry Duffield, Capt., killed, 23/6/17 (and R.F.C.).
Miles, John Guildford, Capt., k. in a., 27/6/18.
Watts, William Kenworthy, Capt., k. in a., 2/12/17.
Brewster, Basil Stockbridge, Lt., k. in a., 3/5/17.
Callingham, Stanley Breach, Lt., died, 18/1/19.
Davies, Fairfax Llewelyn, Lt., k. in a., 8/7/17.
Fison, Frank Henry, Lt., k. in a., 19/7/16.
Ireland, Cubitt Austen, M.C., Lt., k. in a., 14/10/17.
Lee, Frederick Gurdon Driffield, T/Lt., died, 1/3/16.
Lyon, Reginald Anthony, Lt., k. in a., 13/8/17.
Parkinson, George Hartley, Lt., k. in a., 13/4/18.
Wainwright, Samuel Stewart, Lt., k. in a., 11/3/17.
High, Gilbert Cecil, 2/Lt., k. in a., 14/3/17.

The Lincolnshire Regiment.

4th Battalion (Territorial).

Jessop, John William, Lt.-Col., k. in a., 4/6/15.
Ward, Harold, Major, k. in a., 21/3/18.
Ellis, Reginald Denni, Capt., k. in a., 8/6/17.
Gray, Charles Shortland, Capt., k. in a., 13/10/15.
Johnson, William Inglis, Capt., d. of w., 15/10/15.
Staniland, Meaborn, Capt., killed, 29/7/15.
Beales, Frederick Charles, Lt., k. in a., 4/11/18.
Cook, Alexander James, Lt., k. in a., 28/4/17.
Ellwood, Charles Hugh, Lt., k. in a., 2/6/15.
Harrison, Thomas Walter, Lt., drowned, 10/10/18.
Reed, Leslie Augustus, Lt., k. in a., 27/8/15.
Ward, Aubrey Parker Orde, Lt., died, 11/11/18.
Wood, Maurice Herbert, Lt., k. in a., 13/4/17 (and R.F.C.)
Anderson, Lawrence, 2/Lt., k. in a., 11/10/15.
Bain, Alec Magnus Harold, 2/Lt., k. in a., 22/3/18.
Barker, Henry Watson, 2/Lt., k. in a., 17/4/18.
Brunwin-Hales, Henry Tooke, 2/Lt., k. in a., 13/10/15.
Chase, Harold Charles, 2/Lt., k. in a., 8/6/17.
Clixby, Edward Denis, 2/Lt., k. in a., 13/10/15.
Dixon, William Stanton, 2/Lt., k. in a., 30/4/18.
Everett, Charles Alfred Stanley, 2/Lt., d. of w., 17/6/17.
Fish, Robert John, 2/Lt., k. in a., 30/9/17.
Fox, Wilfred Armstrong, 2/Lt., k. in a., 29/7/15.
Geliot, William Henry, 2/Lt., k. in a., 1/7/16.
Hirst, Wilfred Bertram, 2/Lt., d. of w., 22/4/15.
Hodge, George William, 2/Lt., k. in a., 27/4/18.
Hubble, Harry Leonard, 2/Lt., k. in a., 15/4/18.
Jacob, Donald Allen, 2/Lt., d. of w., 13/11/17.
Maskell, Wilfred Fred, 2/Lt., k. in a., 22/11/17.
Massey, William Clayton, 2/Lt., k. in a., 5/11/18.
Miller, George James, 2/Lt., k. in a., 29/9/18.
Owston, William Henry, 2/Lt., d. of w., 23/10/17.
Page, Meaburn Staniland, 2/Lt., k. in a., 21/3/18.
Pacey, George William, 2/Lt., k. in a., 15/4/18.
Rockey, Jim, 2/Lt., k. in a., 2/5/17.
Simpson, John Eric, 2/Lt., k. in a., 7/7/18.
Staniland, Geoffrey, 2/Lt., k. in a., 14/4/15.
Stephenson, Eric Lionel, 2/Lt., k. in a., 18/3/16.
Tomlinson, Ernest, 2/Lt., k. in a., 5/9/18.
Vergette, Samuel, 2/Lt., k. in a., 4/10/17.
Wood, Thomas Basil, 2/Lt., k. in a., 13/10/15.
Wright, William Richardson, 2/Lt., k. in a., 20/4/16.

The Devonshire Regiment.

5th (Prince of Wales) Battalion (Territorial).

Kilgour, Henry, Lt.-Col., died, 24/11/15.
Clark, Frank Adams, Major, d. of w., 20/11/17.
Davis, Fredk. John Stockham, Major, died, 4/11/18.
Church, Arthur Gilbert Walsh, Capt., k. in a., 20/7/18.
Spooner, Charles Norman, Capt., k. in a., 10/4/18.
Vicary, Gilbert Dake, Capt., d. of w., 10/11/17.
Allen, Stephen Henry Hammans, Lt., k. in a., 27/3/18.
Bromham, Charles Adolphus Row, Lt., k. in a., 17/10/18.
Clarke, Stanley Vingoe, Lt., k. in a., 6/5/17.
Hall, George Dorrington, Lt., d. of w., 17/9/18.
Howarth, Harold Victor, Lt., d. of w., 2/5/18.
Liardet, Fredk. Charles Evelyn, Lt., died, 13/12/17 (and R.F.C.).
Bosworthick, William Howard, 2/Lt., k. in a., 7/11/18.
McEachran, Charles, 2/Lt., k. in a., 3/2/17.
Winnicott, Russell, M.C., 2/Lt., k. in a., 6/12/17 (and R.F.C.).

The Devonshire Regiment.

6th Battalion (Territorial).

Fox, Reginald Wilson, Lt.-Col., k. in a., 8/3/16.
Bowhay, Eustace Gilbert, Capt., k. in a., 8/3/16.
Dunn-Pattison, Richard Phillipson, Capt., k. in a., 8/3/16.
Edmonds, Walter John, Lt. & Capt., died, 19/5/19.
German, William Henry, Capt., d. of w., 16/3/16.
Stranger, John Sercombe, Capt., killed, 3/3/16.
Watson, George Carr, Capt., killed, 8/3/16
Buckingham, Thomas Nock, Lt., k. in a., 26/10/17.
Heriz-Smith, Ambrose Joseph Cocks, Lt., k. in a., 8/3/16.
Reeve, Walter James, Lt., died, 29/11/18.
Wise, Henry Lupton, Lt., drowned, 30/12/17.
Barnet, Walter, 2/Lt., d. of w., 22/11/18.
Duncan, Kenneth, 2/Lt., k. in a., 9/5/17.
Finlay, Eric Lionel, 2/Lt., d. of w., 20/3/16.
Morse, Edward Hely Templeman, 2/Lt., d. of w., 8/5/17.
Pendrigh, Alexander Conrad Cuthbertson, 2/Lt., d. of w., 17/8/17.
Tizzard, George, 2/Lt., killed, 8/3/16.
Vicary, William Dallin, 2/Lt., killed, 8/3/16.

The Devonshire Regiment.

7th (Cyclist) Battalion (Territorial).

Veitch, John Leonard, M.C., Major, k. in a., 21/5/18.
Bellamy, Geoffrey George, Capt., d. of w., 1/9/18 (and M.G.C.).
Brearley, Arthur Joseph, Capt., k. in a., 20/6/16.
Grigson, Kenneth Walton, M.C., Capt., k. in a., 20/7/18.
Watts, Harold Vaughan Iremonger, Capt., d. of w., 11/8/17.
Ball, Richard Anthony, Lt., k. in a., 10/7/16.
Langworthy, William Southmead, Lt., k. in a., 4/10/17.
Relf, Thomas Joseph, Lt., k. in a., 4/10/17.
Gibson, John, 2/Lt., k. in a., 19/6/16 (and R.F.C.).

The Suffolk Regiment.

4th Battalion (Territorial).

Pell, Albert Julian, Major, died, 28/8/16.
Pretty, Harold, M.C., Capt. (A/Major), k. in a., 24/3/18.
Brown, Eric Landon, Capt., k. in a., 18/8/15.
French, Digby Manifred, Capt., k. in a., 11/9/18.
Garrett, Stephen, Capt., k. in a., 12/3/15.
Glanfield, Bernard St. John, Capt., d. of w., 31/8/16.
Turner, Herbert Kersey, T/Capt., k. in a., 15/7/16.
Turner, Maurice Arthur, T/Capt., k. in a., 16/7/16.
Brown, Horace Manton, M.C., Lt., d. of w., 14/4/18.
Burton, George Ethelbert Earnshaw, Lt., d. of w., 16/7/16.
Hebbes, Arthur Ernest, Lt., k. in a., 28/11/17.
Layard, Peter Clement, Lt., k. in a., 23/8/18.
Moorsom, Alfred Edgar, Lt., d. of w., 3/8/16.
Pretty, Donald, 2/Lt. (T/Lt.), d. of w., 11/5/15.
Shuttleworth, Kingsley Christopher, Lt., k. in a., 19/11/17.
Woods, Thomas Cecil Hardwick, Lt., k. in a., 22/3/18.
Adams, Geoffrey Henry Cadwallader, 2/Lt., k. in a., 1/11/16.
Bedwell, Victor Leopold Stevens, 2/Lt., k. in a., 18/8/16.
Blowers, Charles Paxton, 2/Lt., d. of w., 2/10/18.
Boulting, Stanley Ernest, 2/Lt., killed, 14/4/17.
Boyne, Harry Horace, 2/Lt., d. of w., 21/7/16 (and Mach.G.C.).
Centeno, Leon, 2/Lt., died, 6/7/16.
Chaplin, Herbert, 2/Lt., k. in a., 19/10/17 (and R.F.C.).
Cropley, William, 2/Lt., k. in a., 21/9/18.
Elvin, Arthur George, 2/Lt., died, 13/10/17.
Fisher, George William, 2/Lt., k. in a., 18/11/17.
Goodall, Garnett Arthur Cumberland, 2/Lt., k. in a., 20/7/16.
Gray, William Leslie, 2/Lt., d. of w., 28/9/18.
Hampton, George William Betto, 2/Lt., k. in a., 11/3/17.
Haynes, William George, 2/Lt., k. in a., 27/6/17.
Isaacs, Henry Rowland, 2/Lt., k. in a., 9/4/17.
Joyce, Eric Gordon, 2/Lt., k. in a., 31/10/16.
Mason, Kenneth Ralph, 2/Lt., k. in a., 21/6/15.
Milburn, William Hudson, 2/Lt., k. in a., 15/7/16.
Packard, Walter Herbert, 2/Lt., k. in a., 15/7/16.
Palmer, Leslie Cowper, 2/Lt., k. in a., 26/9/17.
Pawsey, Harold Charles, 2/Lt., k. in a., 18/8/16.
Row, Harry Akers, 2/Lt., k. in a., 11/3/16.
Woods, Edward Hunter Thurtell, 2/Lt., k. in a., 15/7/16.
Woods, Harold Wallace, 2/Lt., k. in a., 23/4/17.

The Suffolk Regiment.

5th Battalion (Territorial).

Armes, William Morriss, T.D., Lt.-Col., k. in a., 12/8/15.
Kendle, Robert Hastings, Major, died, 12/8/15.
Catchpole, Thomas John, Capt., d. of w., 3/11/17.
Christmas, Dudley Vivian, Lt./Staff Capt., killed, 23/10/15.
Ledward, George William, Capt., died, 12/8/15.
Nutter, Herbert Charles, 2/Lt. (Tp.), Lt. (Act. Capt.), k. in a., 16/6/17.
Wormald, Oliver Edward, Capt., died, 2/2/17.
Wyatt, Felix, Capt., k. in a., 2/7/17 (R.F.C.).
Ashton, Henry Oswald, Lt., k. in a., 29/8/18.
Balaam, Augustus Orland, Lt., k. in a., 24/10/17 (R.F.C.).
Cockle, Clarence Tapscott, Lt., k. in a., 10/9/18.
Grimwood, John Chisnell, Lt., k. in a., 3/12/17.
Haddock, William Theodore, Tp. Lt., died, 30/1/16.
Harvey, Harry Thomas, Lt., k. in a., 31/7/17 (M.G.C.).
Hattam, Harold Colin, Lt., k. in a., 26/9/17.
Haynes, Francis Edmund, Lt., killed, 20/4/18.
Thompson, William George, Lt., k. in a., 14/7/17 (R.F.C.).
Thorn, Dudley Oswald, Lt., k. in a., 7/8/18.
Wright, Claude Russell, Lt., k. in a., 21/5/17 (M.G.C.).
Alston, Garwood Kencingdale, 2/Lt., k. in a., 12/8/15.
Bunn, Ernest Walton, 2/Lt., died, 11/6/18.
Collis, Hugh Humphrey, 2/Lt., d. of w., 12/4/17
Cory, Charles Willoughby, 2/Lt., k. in a., 12/8/15.
Elvey, Charles Leslie, 2/Lt., k. in a., 9/4/17.
Fuller, Hugh William, 2/Lt., k. in a., 18/9/18.
Harris, Walter Read, 2/Lt., died, 10/10/18.
Hinnell, Thomas Squier, 2/Lt., k. in a., 12/8/15.
Norton, Eric, 2/Lt., k. in a., 18/8/16.
Rash, Arnold William, 2/Lt., k. in a., 31/7/17.
Trounce, Sydney Abel, 2/Lt., k. in a., 5/5/17.
Walters, Leslie Hadfield, 2/Lt., d. of w., 17/2/17.
Wheeler, Jack Douglas, 2/Lt., k. in a., 31/7/17.
Willson, Harold Hilton, 2/Lt., died (acc.), 10/1/17.
Wolton, Owen Biddell, 2/Lt., k. in a., 12/8/15.

The Suffolk Regiment.
6th (Cyclist) Battalion (Territorial).

Fison, James Frederick Lorimer, M.C., Lt., T/Capt., d. of w., 2/11/17.
Moseley, Geoffrey Kingdon, Capt., k. in a., 10/4/18.
Samuel, Wilfrid Gilbert, Lt., A/Capt., k. in a., 21/9/18.
Stuart, Charles Erskine, T/Capt., d. of w., 15/3/17.
Churchman, Charles Harvey, Lt., k. in a., 3/5/17.
Cockburn, George Percival, Lt., k. in a., 23/3/18.
Evans, Stewart Nickolson, Lt., killed, 9/7/17 (and R.F.C.).
Truscott, Francis George, M.C., Lt., d. of w., 6/4/17.
Brooke, John Josselyn, 2/Lt., k. in a., 4/10/17.
Westwood, Walter Peter, 2/Lt., k. in a., 26/9/17.

Prince Albert's Somerset Light Infantry.
4th Battalion (Territorial).

Cox, William Charles, Lt.-Col., died, 21/4/19.
Openshaw, Edward Hyde, Lt.-Col., died, 23/7/17.
Graves-Knyfton, Reginald Barrett, Major, died, 29/10/18.
Baker, Aubrey Halliwell, Capt., k. in a., 8/3/16.
Bartelt, F. W., Capt., died, 11/9/16.
Lewin, Cecil Charles Humphreys, M.C., Capt., k. in a., 2/11/18.
Lewis, Edgar, Capt., k. in a., 8/3/16.
Hosegood, William Leman, Lt., died, 15/8/18.
Burgess, Wilfred Charles, 2/Lt., k. in a., 22/8/17.
Buse, Philip, 2/Lt., k. in a., 23/4/18.
Ellis, William Ewart Simpson, 2/Lt., k. in a., 13/1/17.
Findlay, Cyril Olney, 2/Lt., d. of w., 17/10/17.
Gayner, William John, 2/Lt., died, 9/5/17 (att. R.F.C.).
Hagon, Charles Douglas, 2/Lt., d. of w., 3/8/17.
Haynes, Samuel, 2/Lt., d. of w., 4/10/18 (M.G.C.).
Hewitt, James Percy, 2/Lt., k. in a., 5/4/18.
Kirk, Harold Raymond, 2/Lt., k. in a., 31/7/17.
Lillington, Conrad Ivan, 2/Lt., k. in a., 8/3/16.
Maddever, Robert William Digory, 2/Lt., d. of w., 22/10/17.
Rines, Edward Thomas, 2/Lt., k. in a., 22/8/17.
Robinson, John Henry, 2/Lt., k. in a., 30/11/17.
Vaughan, Leslie Howell, 2/Lt., killed, 23/4/17.
Ward, William Leigh, 2/Lt., k. in a., 22/12/17.
Worsley, William Reginald, 2/Lt., k. in a., 1/8/17.

Prince Albert's Somerset Light Infantry.
5th Battalion (Territorial).

Brutton, Robert Hall, Major, died, 15/1/16.
Arnold, G. F., Capt., k. in a., 8/3/16.
Major, Arthur Oswald, Capt., k. in a., 23/11/17.
Crisp, Cyril Bright, Lt., k. in a., 16/8/17.
Jowers, Joseph Frank, Lt., k. in a., 24/3/18.
Reed-Harding, Clarence Henry, Lt., killed, 15/2/18 (and R.F.C.).
Staley, Francis Colin, Lt., k. in a., 8/3/16.
Bussell, Henry Richard, 2/Lt., d. of w., 17/8/17.
Cook, Charles Stanley Blannin, 2/Lt., k. in a., 15/9/16.
Harris, Cecil St. John, 2/Lt., died, 10/9/15

The Prince of Wales's Own West Yorkshire Regiment.
5th Battalion (Territorial).

Dale, Alwyn Percy, Major, k. in a., 1/3/17.
Mackay, Donald Paley, Major, k. in a., 9/10/17.
Thompson, Frederick Charles, Major, k. in a., 2/7/16.
Allen, Richard Gerrard Ross, Capt. (Act.), k. in a., 16/11/16 (R.F.C.).
Blackburn, Charles James Critchley, Lt. (Act. Capt.), k. in a., 25/4/18.
Knowles, Frank Henry, Capt., k. in a., 3/5/17.
Mandeville, Pierce, Capt., k. in a., 28/9/16.
Mossop, William Nicholson, M.C., Capt. & Adjt., d. of w., 8/5/18.
Phillips, Frederick George, Lt. (Act. Capt.), k. in a., 25/4/18.
Skirrow, Geoffrey, Lt. (Act. Capt.), k. in a., 27/8/18.
Watson, Alfred Charles, Capt., k. in a., 3/9/16.
Fretwell, Arthur Richard, Lt., d. of w., 1/4/18.
Hutchinson, Hanley, Lt., d. of w., 1/9/17.
Jameson, James Leslie, Lt., k. in a., 2/7/16.
Parsons, Herbert, Lt., k. in a., 14/4/17.
Robinson, Charles Edward, Lt., died, 25/10/18.
Stephens, Fred Orlando, Lt., k. in a., 24/4/18.
Walker, Reginald, Lt., k. in a., 25/4/18.
Wallace, Dudley Whistler, M.C., Lt., k. in a., 9/10/17.
Wright, Harold Reginald, Lt., d. of w., 16/9/18.
Airey, Henry William Sache, 2/Lt., k. in a., 11/1/17.
Airey, Norman George, 2/Lt., k. in a., 22/11/17.
Annely, Ernest George, 2/Lt., k. in a., 4/5/17.
Barraclough, William, 2/Lt., k. in a., 28/9/16.
Beech, Norman William, 2/Lt., k. in a., 9/10/17.
Bell, Joseph, 2/Lt., k. in a., 17/4/17.
Birbeck, Sidney Walker. 2/Lt., k. in a., 9/10/17.
De Ville, Charles Arthur, 2/Lt., k. in a., 20/7/18.
Donkersley, Reynold, M.C., 2/Lt., k. in a., 20/7/18.
Firth, Charles Ronald. 2/Lt, died, 9/11/18.
Fox, Geoffrey Noel Storrs, 2/Lt., k. in a., 28/3/18.
Gaunt, Edward, 2/Lt., d. of w., 28/9/16.
Gibson, Thomas Ernest, 2/Lt., k. in a., 28/11/17.
Goddard, Harold, 2/Lt., k. in a., 9/10/17.
Goodwill, Cyril, 2/Lt., k. in a., 3/9/16.
Hopper, Robert Edward, 2/Lt., k. in a., 28/4/17.
Howe, William Thomas, M.M., 2/Lt., k. in a., 4/11/18.
Hutchinson, William. 2/Lt., k. in a., 22/11/17.
Irish, Edward, 2/Lt., k. in a., 20/6/15.
Kermode, Edgar Marsden, D.S.O., M.C. and Bar, D.C.M., 2/Lt., d. of w., 27/7/18.
Lee, Arthur Basil, 2/Lt., k. in a., 2/7/16.
Lee, Ernest William, 2/Lt., k. in a., 28/9/16.
Leslie, Charles Joseph, 2/Lt., d. of w., 24/4/18.
Mason, Lancelot William Hart, 2/Lt., k. in a., 14/4/17.
Mitchell, Lewis Medcalfe, 2/Lt., k. in a., 11/8/18.
Northcote, James Fitz Gaulfield, 2/Lt., k. in a., 9/10/17.
Pearson, Reginald, 2/Lt., k. in a., 23/10/18.
Potts, William Edgar, 2/Lt., k. in a., 13/4/18.
Prest, William Charles Seagar, 2/Lt., k. in a., 17/8/16.
Robinson, Walter, 2/Lt., k. in a., 29/9/18 (Tank Corps).
Schindler, William Barron, 2/Lt., k. in a., 20/7/18.
Smith, Herbert Norman, 2/Lt., k. in a., 20/11/17.
Treleaven, Noel Houghton, 2/Lt., k. in a., 23/11/16.
Tyrrell, Leonard Collin, 2/Lt., k. in a., 9/10/17.
Walker, John Chinnery, 2/Lt., k. in a., 19-20/12/15.
Wilde, James Greaves Spencer, 2/Lt., d. of w., 1/11/18.
Wilson, Arnold, 2/Lt., k. in a., 3/5/17.

The Prince of Wales's Own West Yorkshire Regiment.
6th Battalion (Territorial).

Scott, Charles Edward, Lt.-Col., d. of w., 9/8/16.
Dobson, Reginald Graham, Major, died, 4/1/19.
Barker, Geoffrey, Capt., k. in a., 22/11/17.
Bickerdike, Robert, M.C., Capt., k. in a., 20/11/17.
Constantine, Robert Baxandall, Capt., died, 4/3/19.
Muller, Norman, Capt., k. in a., 28/7/18.
Oddy, James Leslie, Capt., d. of w., 3/9/16.
Scales, Walter Alexander, M.C., Capt., killed, 6/1/18.
Smith, Harold, M.C., Capt., k. in a., 22/11/17.
Strachan, David Livingston, Capt., died, 29/12/16.
Turner, George Corrall, Capt., k. in a., 13/9/17.
Ambler, George, Lt., d. of w., 3/8/17.
Brown, Gerald Knapton, Lt., k. in a., 3/5/17.
Charlesworth, George, Lt., k. in a., 3/5/17.
McLean, Walter, Lt., d. of w., 17/11/17.
Pells, Charles Francis Robert, Lt., k. in a., 11/4/17.
Speight, James Leslie, Lt., d. of w., 9/10/17.
Turner, Ernest Arthur, Lt., k. in a., 3/9/16.
Ward, Edward Arthur Hunter, Lt., k. in a., 11/8/17 (and R.F.C.).
Whitehead, Alfred Gordon, Lt., k. in a., 29/1/18 (and R.F.C.).
Archer, Walter Dunlop, 2/Lt., k. in a., 25/4/18.
Armistead, Tom Elsworth, M.C., 2/Lt., k. in a., 3/5/17.
Barker, Arthur, 2/Lt., k. in a., 9/10/17.
Booth, John George, 2/Lt., k. in a., 22/11/17.
Buchannan, Alexander. 2/Lt., k. in a., 21/7/17.
Dodd, Neville, 2/Lt., k. in a., 1/7/16
Fisher, John Hammond, M.C., 2/Lt., d. of w., 7/9/18.
Fletcher, Edward Stewart, 2/Lt., k. in a., 3/5/17.
Gibson, Alwyn Morland, 2/Lt., d. of w., 27/9/16.
Hall, John Gilbert, 2/Lt., k. in a., 3/5/17.
Harper, Clarence Rucil, 2/Lt., k. in a., 15/7/16.
Harris, Christopher Samuel, 2/Lt., k. in a., 27/5/17.
Haywood, Philip, 2/Lt., k. in a., 22/11/17.
Heaton, Stanley Tomlinson, 2/Lt., k. in a., 27/9/16
Hepburn, David Laughton Inkster, 2/Lt., k. in a., 25/4/18.
Higgins, Cuthbert George, 2/Lt., d. of w., 1/7/16.
Jackson, Harold Edward, 2/Lt., k. in a., 12/6/17.
Mitchell, Charles Henry, 2/Lt., k. in a., 3-4/9/16.
Moore, Richard, 2/Lt., k. in a., 15/7/16.
Potterton, Henry, 2/Lt., d. of w., 13/12/17.
Rhodes, John Arthur, 2/Lt., k. in a., 24/8/18.
Senior, Walter Talbot. 2/Lt., k. in a., 3/9/16.
Storey, Harrison Leetham, 2/Lt., d. of w., 12/9/16.
Straker, Herbert, 2/Lt., d. of w., 9/11/18.
Watson, William Vernon Crowther, 2/Lt., k. in a., 15/10/17.
Wood, James Alexander Scott, 2/Lt., k. in a., 12/6/17.
Worth, James William, M.C., 2/Lt., d. of w., 28/11/17.

The Prince of Wales's Own West Yorkshire Regiment.
7th Battalion (Leeds Rifles) (Territorial).

Walling, Ernest, M.C., Capt. (A/Major), k. in a., 25/4/18.
Calvert, Reginald Cullen, Capt., d. of w., 15/7/16.
Fender, Edward Henry, Lt. (A/Capt.), k. in a., 9/10/17.
Ling, Godfrey Frank Mackwood, M.C. & 2 Bars, Capt., k. in a., 23/5/18.
Lupton, Maurice, Capt., k. in a., 19/6/15.
Salter, Robert, Capt., k. in a., 26/8/16.
Briggs, Richard Stanley, Lt., k. in a., 29/7/15.
Brooke, George Miller, Lt., k. in a., 25/4/18.
Brown, Walter Ravenhill, M.C., Lt., k. in a., 21/11/17.
Campbell William Archibald, Lt., d. of w., 21/9/17 (and R.F.C.).
Hamilton, Thomas, Lt., k. in a., 12/5/17.
Isherwood, Samuel Guy, Lt., d. of w., 20/9/18.
Jackson, Sidney Foster, Lt., k. in a., 17/11/17.
Lambdin, John Reginald, M.C., Lt., d. of w., 24/9/18.
Learmouth, Eric Charles Allan, Lt., k. in a., 9/10/17.
Longbottom, Edward Brooke, Lt., k. in a., 9/10/17.
Parker, James Stanley, Lt., k. in a., 9/10/17.
Rogers, Percy Alexander MacKarness, Lt., k. in a., 9/10/17.
Tarr, William, Lt, k. in a., 31/10/15.
Wilson, Norman, Lt., k. in a., 14/7/16.
Brannigan, Ernest Edward, 2/Lt., k. in a., 3/9/16.
Carter, John Taylor, 2/Lt., k. in a., 9/10/17.
Coy, Alfred Reginald, 2/Lt., k. in a., 2/7/16.
Dawson, William Healey, 2/Lt., k. in a., 20/7/18.
Garritt, John Crossland, 2/Lt., k. in a., 30/5/18.
Halliday, Balfour, 2/Lt., d. of w., 4/7/17.
Harrison, Edgar Brooks, 2/Lt., d. of w., 28/9/16.
Jackson, Walter, 2/Lt., k. in a., 9/10/17.
Leresche, Alfred Sunderland, 2/Lt., k. in a., 3/9/16.
Stewart, John Charles Miller, 2/Lt., k. in a., 3/7/16 (and R.F.C.).
Swift, John, 2/Lt, k. in a., 22/11/17.
Sykes, Gerald Wolriche, 2/Lt., k. in a., 25/5/15.
Whiteley, Benjamin Eric, 2/Lt., k. in a., 28/8/18.
Wyllie, Hugh Alexander, 2/Lt., k. in a., 3/9/16.

The Prince of Wales's Own West Yorkshire Regiment.

8th Battalion (Leeds Rifles) (Territorial).

Hudson, Robert Arthur, D.S.O., Major, A/Lt.-Col., k. in a., 9/10/17.
Hess, Arthur Frank, Major, d. of w., 14/7/16.
Lupton, Francis Ashford, Major, k. in a., 19/2/17.
Appleyard, James Eric, M.C., Capt., k. in a., 20/7/18.
Callaghan, Leslie Wilfred, Capt., k. in a., 9/10/17.
Dyson, Charles, Capt., k. in a., 6/4/17.
Hartnell, Cuthbert, Lt., A/Capt., k. in a., 16/7/15.
Hossell, Leslie Cartmell, Capt., k. in a., 8/8/16.
Kinder, Geoffrey George, M.C., Capt., k. in a., 20/7/18.
Nevitt, George Rothwell, Capt., k. in a., 28/11/17.
Pearson, Sydney James, Capt., d. of w., 15/8/16.
Rigby, Arthur George, M.C., Capt., k. in a., 12/10/17.
Stead, Charles Brian, M.C., Capt., d. of w., 28/9/18.
Wilkinson, Eric Fitzwater, M.C., Capt., k. in a., 9/10/17.
Cheetham, Herbert, Lt., k. in a., 9/10/17.
Dedman, William Albert, Lt., died, 4/2/18.
Firth, Edwin Norris, Lt., died, 16/3/18.
Hobson, Andrew John Hay, Lt., k. in a., 9/10/17.
Illingworth, John, M.C., Lt., d. of w., 3/6/18.
Jessop, George Edward, Lt., k. in a., 10/4/18.
Sissons, Roland Edward, Lt., k. in a., 2/6/16.
Wilkinson, Thomas William Musgrave, Lt., k. in a., 20/7/18.
Will, George Kennedy, Lt., d. of w., 11/9/16 (in German hands).
Baker, Arthur Leslie, 2/Lt., k. in a., 9/10/17.
Bottomley, John Cecil, 2/Lt., k in a., 3/9/16.
Chadwick, John Collinge, 2/Lt., k. in a., 25/3/17.
Horner, Karl Christian, 2/Lt., d. of w., 4/4/17.
Hutchinson, George Russell, 2/Lt., k. in a., 26/11/17.
Ives, Kenneth Hill, 2/Lt., died, 9/12/14.
Middleton, Reginald, 2/Lt., k. in a., 3/9/16.
Moore, Albert Reginald, 2/Lt., k. in a., 12/4/17.
Northrop, Harold, 2/Lt., k. in a., 9/10/17.
Palmer, Harry, 2/Lt., k. in a., 27/5/18.
Penny, George, 2/Lt., k. in a., 3/9/16.
Percival, John Lee, 2/Lt., k. in a., 30/9/18.
Raistrick, John William, 2/Lt., k. in a., 19/5/17.
Richardson, Basil James, 2/Lt., k. in a., 9/10/17.
Shann, Alan Webster, 2/Lt., k. in a., 27/11/17.
Silmon, William Osman de Weld, 2/Lt., k. in a., 28/2/17.
Stimpson, John Crockett, 2/Lt., k. in a., 2/7/16.
Thornton, Claude Arthur Muir, 2/Lt., k. in a., 27/5/18.
Vause, Thomas Christopher, 2/Lt., k. in a., 3/9/16.
Waite, Hugh Conyers, 2/Lt., k. in a., 6/4/17.
Ward, George Cecil, 2/Lt., k. in a., 2/7/16.
Williams, Thomas Rix, 2/Lt., k. in a., 20/7/18.

The East Yorkshire Regiment.

4th Battalion (Territorial).

Shaw, George Herbert, Lt.-Col., k. in a., 24/4/15.
Quibell, Samuel Boyd, Major, d. of w., 5/2/16.
Theilman, Carl Erik, Major, k. in a., 24/4/15.
Easton, Cyril, M.C., Capt., k. in a., 23/4/17.
Farrell, Bede, Capt., k. in a., 24/4/15.
Ingleby, Norman Ward, Capt., k. in a., 27/5/18.
Philip, Kenneth, Capt., k. in a., 27/3/18.
Southern, Thomas William, M.C., 2/Lt. (A/Capt.), k. in a., 29/9/18.
Spragg, Charles Edward Wright, Capt., k. in a., 10/9/18.
Wilson-Barkworth, Kenneth Arthur, M.C., Capt., k. in a., 25/10/17.
Farrell, Adrian, Lt., d. of w., 23/8/16.
Ferraby, Robinson, Lt., died, 7/4/16.
Furley, Francis Edward, Lt., k. in a., 22/3/18.
Gough, Cyril, Lt., died, 8/9/18-9/11/18 (in Ger. hands).
Gresham, John Francis, Lt., died, 16/2/19.
Grummitt, Joseph Roland, Lt., died, 14/11/18.
Jackson, Harold Willows, Lt., d. of w., 14/5/17.
Judge, Charles Harland, Lt., d. of w. 17/5/15.
Knee, George Creasy, Lt., k. in a., 3/5/17.
Rishworth, James, Lt, killed, 3/5/15.
Saxelbye, Frank Norman, Lt., d. of w., 11/5/15.
Southwell, Frederick Edward Granville, Lt., d. of w., 10/4/17.
Van Oppen, Pier William, Lt., d. of w., 16/4/18.
Webster, Harold Stanley, Lt., k. in a., 7/8/17.
Wright, Harold Ivan, Lt., k. in a., 8/11/17.
Ashby, Donald Jesse, 2/Lt., k. in a., 17/7/16.
Boyle, Charles Capes, 2/Lt., k. in a., 23/4/17.
Burstall, Arthur, 2/Lt., k. in a., 24/9/18.
Burton, Percy Charles, 2/Lt., k. in a., 5/4/16.
Carlton, William Fergus, 2/Lt., k. in a., 17/6/16.
Charlton, Ernest Henry, 2/Lt, k. in a., 31/3/18.
Clapham, Alan Charles, 2/Lt., killed, 3/1/16.
Cowl, John Douglas, 2/Lt., k. in a., 23/4/17
Cranswick, Gilbert, 2/Lt., k. in a., 26/10/16.
Davie, Frank, 2/Lt., d. of w., 2/6/17.
Dean, Arthur Reginald, 2/Lt., k. in a., 4/7/17.
Drewery, George William, 2/Lt., k. in a., 22/3/18.
Drewett, Herbert Benn. 2/Lt., k. in a., 30/10/17.
Duguid, Alexander Ritchie, 2/Lt., k. in a., 3/5/17.
Earle, Cedric, 2/Lt., k. in a., 4/9/18.
Earle, Wilfrid Antony, 2/Lt., k. in a., 23/4/17.
Elvin, Sydney James, 2/Lt., d. of w., 13/4/18.
Franks, Lionel, 2/Lt., d. of w, 5/5/17.
Grainger, John Henry. 2/Lt., k. in a., 15/9/16.
Green, Norman Wilson, 2/Lt., k. in a., 23/4/17.
Green, Phillip, 2/Lt., k. in a., 28/3/18.
Gresham, Gordon, 2/Lt., d. of w., 18/6/16.
Hellyer, Sidney Hannaford, 2/Lt., d of w., 8/5/15.
Hignett, William Rowland, 2/Lt., k. in a., 3/5/17.
Homersham, R., 2/Lt., k. in a., 30/4/18 (att. R.A.F.).
Jackson, Henry Douglas, M.C., 2/Lt., k. in a., 26/10/16.
Kirk, Arthur, 2/Lt., k. in a., 28/6/18.
Lofthouse, George Hood, 2/Lt., k. in a., 23/4/17
Mansfield. George Stanley, 2/Lt., k. in a., 22/3/18.
Morley, David, 2/Lt., killed, 16/6/17.
Nicholson, Randolph Renwick, M.C., 2/Lt., k. in a., 18/9/18.
Oughtred, Harold, 2/Lt., k. in a., 23/4/17.
Peer, Edmund Faithful, 2/Lt., k. in a., 23/4/17.
Peterson, George Benjamin, 2/Lt., k. in a., 31/3/18.
Phillips. Walter Henry Sherburn, 2/Lt., k. in a., 16/9/16.
Rayner, Harold, 2/Lt., k. in a., 4/9/18.
Rendle, George, 2/Lt., k. in a., 1/10/18.
Robson, Stanley, 2/Lt, k. in a., 31/3/18.
Rosindale, Herbert, 2/Lt., k. in a., 11/10/18.
Shackles, Kenneth George, 2/Lt., d. of w., 11/5/17.
Snowdon, Ralph, 2/Lt., k. in a., 2/10/17.
Stephens, Nasson Barrington, 2/Lt., d. of w., 1/6/16 (and M.G.C.).
Temple, John Henry, 2/Lt., d. of w., 21/5/18.
Vivian, Gilbert, 2/Lt., d. of w., 22/7/16.
Waddington, Walter Charles, 2/Lt., d. of w., 3/7/18 (in German hands).
Walker, John Henry, 2/Lt., k. in a., 18/9/17.
Watson, James Stennett, 2/Lt, k. in a., 26/11/17.
Webster, Arthur Cecil, 2/Lt., k. in a., 3/5/17.
Webster, George Alan, 2/Lt., k. in a., 18/9/18.
Wood, Charles Pascoe, 2/Lt., d. of w., 18/4/18.
Woodcock, Alfred Taylor, 2/Lt., d. of w., 4/6/18 (in German hands).

The East Yorkshire Regiment.

5th (Cyclist) Battalion (Territorial).

Allen, Thomas Gordon, Lt., k. in a., 26/8/18.
Buttery, Walter, 2/Lt., k. in a., 20/8/18.
Hutchinson, Ivan, 2/Lt., k. in a., 22/8/18.
Ullyott, Cecil, 2/Lt., k. in a., 23/8/18.

The Bedfordshire Regiment.

5th Battalion (Territorial).

Baker, Charles Tanqueray, Capt., k. in a., 15/8/15.
Batten, Joseph Keith, Capt., k. in a., 27/9/18.
Cumberland, Brian Clark, Capt., k. in a., 15/8/15.
Franklin, Thomas Alderman, M.C., Capt., d. of w., 27/11/17.
McBride, Andrew Best, M.C., Capt., k. in a., 24/4/18.
Meakin, Walter Kendrick, Capt., k. in a., 15/8/15.
Smith, Frederick John, Capt., d. of w., 23/8/18.
Smythe, Rudolph Meade, Capt., d. of w., 13/9/15.
Yarde, John Tristram, M.C. & Bar, Capt., d. of w., 21/9/18.
Balding, Reginald Norman, T/Lt., k. in a., 30/3/17 (and M.G.C.).
Cronin, Harold William, Lt., d. of w., 2/12/17.
Davis, William Stanley, Lt., k. in a., 22/3/18.
Day, Geoffrey Reynolds, Lt., k. in a., 27/8/16.
Hart, Clarence Herbert, Lt., k. in a., 23/10/18.
Lydekker, Cyril Richard, Lt., k. in a., 15/8/15.
Lydekker, Gerard Owen, Lt. & Q.M., died, 14/6/17.
Nixon, Cyril John, Lt., died, 8/10/17.
Pinchin, George Harold, Lt., d. of w., 27/11/17.
Shaw, Giles Havergal, Lt., k. in a., 11/4/17.
Shoosmith, Frank Stewart, Lt., k. in a., 21/8/15.
Watson, Henry James Arthur, Lt., k. in a., 23/8/18.
Amesbury, Hugh Frederick Raleigh, 2/Lt., k. in a., 20/11/17.
Brereton, Leonard Leader, 2/Lt., d. of w., 29/4/17.
Brighten, Ralph Dalton Jarvis, 2/Lt., k. in a., 15/8/15.
Clark, Albert Victor, M.C., 2/Lt., d. of w., 2/1/18.
Connor, Samuel Maurice, 2/Lt., k. in a., 10/8/17.
Forge, Henry Noel Francis, 2/Lt., k. in a., 20/11/17.
Foskett, Herbert Edward, 2/Lt., k. in a., 28/4/17.
Fowler, Claude Oliver, 2/Lt., k. in a., 23/10/18.
Gallo, Antonio Marie, M.C., 2/Lt., k. in a., 31/7/17.
Harding, William Kesterton, 2/Lt., died, 26/6/19.
Hose, Robert Henry, 2/Lt., k. in a., 18/3/17.
Lever, Harold Brasington, 2/Lt., died, 23/10/18 (In German hands).
Macklin, David Harold, 2/Lt., k. in a., 27/3/18.
Moxon, Hugh Cecil, 2/Lt., d. of w., 19/7/17.
Pratt, Arthur, 2/Lt., d. of w., 11/2/18.
Rising, Frederick, 2/Lt., k. in a., 15/8/15.
Taylor, John Oswald, 2/Lt., k. in a., 19/4/17.
Waterton, John Edward Mary Claude Pius Augustine, 2/Lt., k. in a., 29/11/17.
Wilford, William Frederick Shirley, M.M., 2/Lt., d. of w. 25/10/18.

The Leicestershire Regiment.

4th Battalion (Territorial).

Cooper, Arthur Charles, Capt., k. in a., 16/5/15.
Corah, Leslie, Capt., k. in a., 13/10/15.
Faire, Reginald Alfred, Capt., k. in a., 14/10/15.
Haylock, Henry, Capt., k. in a., 11/5/15.
Neale, John Everard Digby, Capt., killed, 22/8/17.
Pearce, S. M., Capt., died, 19/10/18 (and R.A.F.).
Pilkington, Sam, Capt., k. in a., 2/7/17.
Wakerley, Arthur John, Capt., k. in a., 8/6/17.
Beeby, Charles Stuart, Lt., k. in a., 27/5/18.
Brice, Harry Copeland, Lt., d. of w., 11/6/15.
Forsell, Alan Richard, Lt., k. in a., 14/10/15.
Gilbert, Bertram Thomas Chesterton, Lt., k. in a., 22/4/17.
Green, Richard Scott, Lt., k. in a., 14/10/15.
Harvey, Robert Clive, Lt., k. in a., 14/10/15.
Hussey, Frank William, Lt., k. in a., 24/9/18.
Johnson, John Frederick, Lt., d. of w., 30/10/15.
Tarr, Francis Nathaniel, Lt., k. in a., 18/7/15.

Whittingham, Thomas, Lt., k. in a., 13/10/15.
Alloway, Howard George, 2/Lt., k. in a., 30/11/17
Barker, John Edward, 2/Lt., k. in a., 13/10/15.
Beckett, Ernest Whitton, 2/Lt., k. in a., 22/3/18.
Blunt, Francis Clifford, 2/Lt., d. of w., 14/10/15.
Bowes, Ellis Arthur, 2/Lt., k. in a., 12/3/18.
Cashmore, Edwin, 2/Lt., d. of w., 4/10/18.
Clarke, Ambrose Childs, 2/Lt., k. in a., 10/5/15.
Cross, Wilfrid, 2/Lt., k. in a., 22/7/16.
Emmerson, Jabez, 2/Lt., k. in a., 13/10/15.
Fergusson, William Albert, 2/Lt., d. of w., 15/5/17.
Hodgkins, James Percy, 2/Lt., d. of w., 26/9/17.
Lennard, Samuel Frederic, 2/Lt., k. in a., 30/3/16.
Leslie, Alexander William, 2/Lt., d. of w., 23/4/17.
Mogridge, Basil Fullelove West, 2/Lt., k. in a., 13/10/15.
O'Callaghan, Thomas Francis, 2/Lt., k. in a., 13/10/15.
Orson, John Tom, 2/Lt., k. in a., 21/3/18.
Parkinson, Horace James Ankers, 2/Lt., d. of w., 1/7/17.
Russell, Guy Edward Frank, 2/Lt., k. in a., 14/10/15.
Scholes, Wilfred Paul, 2/Lt., k. in a., 13/10/15.
Smith, William Gordon, 2/Lt., d. of w., 21/3/18.
Tasker, William, 2/Lt., k. in a., 27/5/18.
Turner, Walter Gregory, 2/Lt., k. in a., 8/6/17.
Waite, Frederick Maxwell, 2/Lt., k. in a., 7/6/15.
Walters, Frederick William, 2/Lt., k. in a., 14/10/15.
Whitcher, Charles Edwin, 2/Lt., k. in a., 22/4/17.

The Leicestershire Regiment.
5th Battalion (Territorial).

Chapman, John, Capt., d. of w., 30/5/15.
Farmer, Roland Devonport, Capt., k. in a., 22/3/16.
Feilden, Oswald Henry, Capt., d. of w., 29/9/17.
Jeffries, Harold John Fotheringham, Capt., k. in a., 26/9/15.
Marriott, Norman Clarke, Capt., k. in a., 17/8/17.
Rawdon-Hastings, Paulyn Charles James, Capt., k. in a., 13/10/15.
Tomson, James Wyndham, Capt., k. in a., 24/9/18.
Wynne, Edward Ernest, Capt., k. in a., 8/6/17.
Aked, George, Lt., k. in a., 5/3/15.
Carnley, Ronald, Lt., k. in a., 27/5/18.
Corah, Sydney, Lt., k. in a., 3/10/18.
Davis, Richard Samuel, Lt., k. in a., 22/3/18.
Farrer, Richard Bracken, Lt., k. in a., 8/6/17.
Langdale, Edward George, M.C., Lt., k. in a., 13/10/15.
Lawton, Robert Charles, Lt., d. of w., 16/10/15.
Measures, Percy, Lt., k. in a., 31/12/17.
Bowie, Ralph Archibald, 2/Lt., k. in a., 26/9/17.
Callard, William Kingsley, 2/Lt., k. in a., 1/7/16.
Cole, William Maurice, M.C., 2/Lt., d. of w., 29/6/18.
Emmerson, Alfred, 2/Lt., d. of w., 4/4/17 (and R.F.C.).
Moss, Howard James Harding, 2/Lt., k. in a., 13/10/15.
Robathan, Laurence, 2/Lt., k. in a., 28/9/17.
Selwyn, Christopher Wakefield, 2/Lt., d. of w., 17/5/15.
Walley, John Clifford, 2/Lt., k. in a., 23/3/18.
Watherston, Robert James Henderson Fell, 2/Lt., k. in a., 3/12/17.

The Lincolnshire Regiment.
5th Battalion (Territorial).

Robinson, Harry Ingham, Major, k. in a., 13/10/15.
Bryant, Thomas, Capt., k. in a., 11/4/17.
Dawe, Sydney Charles, M.C., Capt., killed, 13/2/18.
Finnie, Bertram Knott, Capt., k. in a., 1/10/15.
Hall, Eric Watson, Capt., k. in a., 26/9/17.
Harvey, Charles Lewis, Capt., d. of w., 10/5/17.
Hicks, Edwin Theodore, Capt., died, 12/5/17.
Hill, Gerald Leader, Capt., k. in a., 26/9/17.
Newsum, Clement Neill, Capt., k. in a., 26/9/17.
Nicholson, H. W., Capt., k. in a., 13/10/15.
Scorer, Herbert Selwyn, Capt., k. in a., 13/10/15.
Sowter, George Henry Joseph, Capt., k. in a., 13/10/15.
Street, Hewson, M.C., Capt., d. of w., 1/6/18 (in Ger. hands).
Hartley, Walter Lockwood, Lt., k. in a., 13/10/15.
Standen, Leslie James Denman, Lt., k. in a., 18/3/16.
Turner, Robert Henry, Lt., d. of w., 23/3/18.
Walcott, Lyons George Edmund, Lt., k. in a., 2/7/16.
Walker, John West, Lt., k. in a., 11/4/17.
Barton, Frederick Pembroke, 2/Lt., d. of w., 18/10/18.
Blunt, John, 2/Lt., d. of w., 15/10/15.
Coulson, Jack Baxter, 2/Lt., d. of w., 20/6/16.
Early, Egbert Edward, 2/Lt., k. in a., 13/10/15.
Gilliatt, Francis Ralph, 2/Lt., k. in a., 26/7/17.
Gouldby, James Henry, 2/Lt., k. in a., 25/8/16.
Grantham, Percy William, 2/Lt., k. in a., 26/9/17.
Harvey, Robert George Bosworth, 2/Lt., k. in a., 25/12/17.
Havers, Frederick Charles, 2/Lt., k. in a., 27/5/18.
Hyde, William Sisson, 2/Lt., d. of w., 7/11/18.
Lowe, Ernest Archer, 2/Lt., k. in a., 26/9/17.
Neighbour, Leslie Gulliver, 2/Lt., killed, 16/8/15.
Osborne, Frank Louis, 2/Lt., d. of w., 21/3/18.
Pollard, Thomas Regester, 2/Lt., died, 2/7/18.
Price, Francis Maurice, 2/Lt., d. of w., 4/6/17.
Shrewsbury, Carl Brannell, 2/Lt., k. in a., 13/10/15.
Smith, Frederick William, 2/Lt., d. of w., 11/4/17.
Stevens, Gorham Ninton, 2/Lt., died, 18/1/18.
Thimbleby, John Egremont, 2/Lt., died, 29/8/15.
Thompson, Wilfred Albert, 2/Lt., d. of w., 21/8/17.
Wright, Frederick, 2/Lt., k. in a., 12/4/17.

The Devonshire Regiment.
4th Battalion (Territorial).

Cardew, George Eric, M.C., Capt., k. in a., 9/4/18.
Cole, Henry Munroe, Capt., died, 4/12/18.
Partington, John Bertram, Capt., k. in a., 3/2/17.
Percy-Hardman, William Henry, Capt., d. of w., 1/3/17 (and M.G.C.).
Gregory, Stephen Barnes, Lt., died, 3/6/16 (in Turkish hands).
Parkhouse, Oscar, Lt., died, 19/11/18.
Smith, Reuben Hinton, Lt., killed, 10/1/18.
Sydenham, Humphrey St. Barbe, Lt., died, 8/10/16.
Webber, William Henry, Lt., died, 2/6/15.
De Dennie, Thomas Geoffrey, 2/Lt., k. in a., 4/10/17.
Hill, Alec Leslie, 2/Lt., k. in a., 26/12/17.
Hockaday, Harold Francis Henry Legg, 2/Lt., k. in a., 10/10/17.
Tall, John Jeffery, 2/Lt., k. in a., 15/2/18.
Tarbet, Victor, 2/Lt., killed, 4/10/17.
Upstone, Cedric Donovan, 2/Lt., died, 11/7/16.
White, Spencer John Meadows, 2/Lt., k. in a., 15/1/17 (and R.F.C.).

Alexandra Princess of Wales's Own Yorkshire Regiment.
4th Battalion (Territorial).

Charlton, Bernard Hedley, M.C., Lt.-Col., k. in a., 22/3/18.
Fife, Alexander John, Lt.-Col., died, 7/2/17 (M.G.C.).
Graham, Austin, Major (T/Lt.-Col.), d. of w., 11/4/18 (5th Bn.).
Matthews, Harold Carey, Major, k. in a., 25/4/15.
Bainbridge, James Scott, Capt., k. in a., 22/3/18.
Batty, William Liley, Capt., k. in a., 25/10/16.
Bowes-Wilson, George Hutton, Capt., k. in a., 17/6/15.
Constantine, Herbert Norman, M.C., Capt., k. in a., 27/5/18.
V.C. Hirsch, David Philip, Capt., k. in a., 23/4/17.
Maughan, John, Capt., k. in a., 17/2/16.
Nancarrow, John Vivian, Capt., k. in a., 25/4/15
Rowlandson, Thomas Sowerby, M.C., Capt., k. in a., 15/9/16.
Searginson, John, Capt., k. in a., 10/11/16.
Sproxton, Charles, M.C., Capt., k. in a., 19/7/17.
Spurway, Douglas, Capt., k. in a., 23/3/18.
Stead, John Kenneth, Capt., d. of w., 4/2/17 (R.F.C.).
Stiff, Charles Neville Carleton, Capt., k. in a., 22/3/18.
Tugwell, Geoffrey Arnold, Capt., k. in a., 23/4/17.
Aust, Henry Ernest, Lt., k. in a., 18/9/18.
Close, Robert William Mills, Lt., k. in a., 27/5/18.
Cummins, Herbert Waller, Lt., k. in a., 24-25/5/15.
Hale, Herbert Charles, Lt., d. of w., 2/11/17.
Harrison, H. L., Lt., died, 28/10/18 (R.A.F.).
Hutchinson, George Hanley, Lt., k. in a., 2/3/16.
I'Anson, Leonard Percy, Lt., k. in a., 25/4/15.
Scarth, Isaac Hinton, Lt., k. in a., 23/4/17.
Welsh, Anthony Reginald, T/Lt. (2/Lt.), d. of w., 19/2/16.
Abrahams, Robert Bernard, 2/Lt., k. in a., 14/9/16.
Banks, Henry, 2/Lt., k in a., 27/8/18.
Barrett, Norman Kenyon, 2/Lt., k. in a., 18/9/18.
Brown, Roland, 2/Lt., k. in a., 13/7/18.
Coates, Arthur, 2/Lt., k. in a., 27/10/16.
Cole, William Thomas, 2/Lt., k. in a., 29/7/18.
Cram, John Edwin, M.C., 2/Lt., k. in a., 30/9/18.
Darwin, Erasmus, 2/Lt., k. in a., 25/4/15.
Gray, Thomas Robert, 2/Lt., d of w., 24/11/17.
Hawdon, Cecil, 2/Lt, k. in a., 27/6/16.
Hayton, Walter James, 2/Lt., k. in a., 16/9/16.
Hutchinson, Edgar Francis, 2/Lt., d. of w., 24/5/15.
Hudson, John Burgoyne, 2/Lt., k. in a., 25/10/16.
Jones, Edward Earle, 2/Lt., d. of w., 1/8/16.
Kitching, Fred, 2/Lt., k. in a., 10/7/18.
Laing, Harry Needham, 2/Lt., k. in a., 17/9/16
Luckhurst, William, 2/Lt., k. in a., 24/4/17.
Omand, Robert Stewart, 2/Lt., d. of w., 25/9/16.
Orde-Powlett, William Percy, 2/Lt., k. in a., 17/5/15.
Pacey, Walter Ernest, 2/Lt., d. of w., 27/6/17.
Perkins, Cyril John, 2/Lt., d of w., 27/6/17.
Perris, Eric Loftus, 2/Lt., k. in a., 27/9/16.
Prior-Wandesforde, Christopher Butler, 2/Lt., d. of w., 27/6/17.
Richardson, Ewart, 2/Lt., k. in a., 27/9/16.
Scorer, Nicholas, 2/Lt., d. of w., 29/3/18.
Thomas, Harold Morris, 2/Lt., k. in a., 10/11/16.
Ward, Laurance, 2/Lt, k. in a., 10/4/18.

Alexandra Princess of Wales's Own Yorkshire Regiment.
5th Battalion (Territorial).

Mortimer, James, C.M.G., Lt.-Col., k. in a., 15/9/16 (M.G.C.).
Robson, Frederick William, D.S.O., Lt.-Col., k. in a., 28/3/18.
Thomson, James Albert Raymond, Lt.-Col., k. in a., 27/5/18.
Brown, Harold, D.S.O., M.C., Major, k. in a., 23/3/18.
Palliser, John Sylvester, Major, k. in a., 9/8/18 (M.G.C.).
Bagshawe, Edward George Clarkson, Capt., k. in a., 20/7/16.
Barber, Geoffrey Carew, Capt., k. in a., 25/4/15.
Purvis, George Bell, Capt., k. in a., 8/6/17 (M.G.C.).
Robson, Edward Moore, M.C., Capt., k. in a., 11/4/18.
Scott, George Jefferson, Capt., k. in a., 25/12/15.
Vause, Wilfrid, M.C., Capt., k. in a., 23/4/17.
Walker, Denis Henry, Capt., d. of w., 26/1/16.
Walker, Leslie Bedford, Capt., d. of w., 1/7/17.
Woodcock, Frank, Capt., k. in a., 15/9/16.
Coles, William Henry, Lt., k. in a., 27/12/17.
Danby, Francis Geoffrey, Lt., k. in a., 27/12/17.
Dufty, Thomas Ernest, Lt., k. in a., 19/5/15.
Evans, Hugh Elwyn, M.C., Lt., k. in a., 26/3/18.
Featherstone, William, Lt., k. in a., 13/9/16.
Green, Frank, Lt., d. of w., 28/12/17.
Herbert, Johnstone Erskine Galway, Lt., k. in a., 23/4/17.
Hepton, Arthur, Lt., d. of w., 13/4/18 (in German hands).
Hurworth, Charles Reginald, Lt., k. in a., 26/3/18.
Radcliffe, Percival Victor Alban, Lt., d. of w., 25/11/17 (M.G.C.).
Spofforth, Edward Reginald, Lt., k. in a., 2/3/16.
Stewart-Corry, Eberhardt George, Lt., k. in a., 26/6/17.
Thompson, Edward Medforth, Lt., k. in a., 26/2/16.
Townsend, Guy Storey, Lt., k. in a., 23/8/18.

Townsend, John Vernon, Lt., k. in a., 24/9/18.
Whitehead, Frank Brenand, Lt., k. in a., 23/4/17.
Battye, John, 2/Lt.. k. in a., 25/3/18.
Brodrick, Eric William, 2/Lt., died, 22-23/7/16 (in German hands).
Chapman, George Edwin, 2/Lt., d. of w., 27/9/16 (M.G.C.).
Fell, Matthew Henry, 2/Lt.. k. in a., 17/9/16.
Game, Walter Harold, 2/Lt., k. in a., 23/4/17.
Hall, Walter, 2/Lt., d. of w., 15/11/18.
Hofmeyr, Robert Ernest Murray, 2/Lt., k. in a., 24/4/17 (M.G.C.).
Hood, Ernest William, 2/Lt., k. in a., 25-27/9/15.
Humphrey, Richard Ronald, 2/Lt., k. in a., 31/8/18.
Jacobs, Joel, 2/Lt., k. in a., 20/7/16.
Jennings, William, 2/Lt., d. of w., 31/7/18.
Kitson, Harold, 2/Lt., d. of w.. 21/10/18.
Lambert, Henry Stuart, 2/Lt., k. in a., 11/1/16.
Lawrence, Henry 2/Lt.. k. in a., 17/1/17.
Lowson, Wilfred Robert, 2/Lt.. k. in a., 16/9/16.
McInnes, Percy Norman Leopold, 2/Lt., d. of w., 20/7/16.
Phillips, Guy Saggerson, 2/Lt., k. in a., 15/9/16.
Tatham, George Henry Riley, 2/Lt., d. of w., 11/10/18.
Turnbull, William Andrew, 2/Lt., k. in a., 17/7/16.
Watson, Lord Arthur James, 2/Lt., k. in a., 26/9/18.
Welbourn, Ernest Cecil, 2/Lt., k. in a., 21/4/17.
Wilford, Robert, 2/Lt., k. in a., 23/11/17.
Wilkinson, Arthur William, 2/Lt., k. in a., 12/7/17.

The Lancashire Fusiliers.

5th Battalion (Territorial).

Kay, Geoffrey Clarkson, A/Major, k. in a., 29/3/18 (and M.G.C.).
Bentley, Frank Mercer, M.C., Capt., k. in a., 13/10/18.
Bloy, Laurence Henry, Capt., k. in a., 29/6/16.
Bridge, John Kelly, Capt., died, 31/1/19.
Crough, Francis Harrie, M.C., Capt., k. in a., 21/3/18.
Hedley, Joseph Walton, Capt., d. of w., 13/9/16.
Holdsworth, Joseph Arthur, M.C., Lt. (A/Capt.), died, 17/6/18 (in German hands).
Hudson, Austin Patrick, Capt., k. in a., 1/9/17.
Milnes, Sydney Herbert, Capt., k. in a., 7/8/15.
Simon, Eric Conrad, Capt., d. of w., 17/8/15.
Waterhouse, Kenneth, Capt., k. in a., 9/8/16.
Wilkinson, William Charlton, Capt., k. in a., 9/4/18.
Bell, Guy Bayford, Lt., k. in a., 28/4/17 (and M.G.C.).
Collins, Stanley Thomas, Lt., d. of w., 29/4/17.
Hartington, John Ernest, Lt., d. of w., 13/7/17 (and M.G.C.).
Hawksey, Bernard Richard, Lt., k. in a., 28/9/18.
Renshaw, Alfred, Lt., d. of w., 7/6/15.
Tweedy, Francis Charles, Lt., k. in a., 9/10/17.
Young, Malcolm Henry, Lt., k. in a., 29/6/16.
Addie, Robert Leatham, 2/Lt., k. in a., 20/11/17.
Bainbrigge, Philip Gillespie, 2/Lt., k. in a., 18/9/18.
Barton, Edwin William, 2/Lt., died, 27/4/17.
Dickinson, William, 2/Lt., k. in a., 29/3/17.
Essex, Percy Clifford, 2/Lt., k. in a., 9/9/16.
Frizelle, Edwin Samuel, 2/Lt., k. in a., 3/8/15.
Godfrey, Henry, 2/Lt., k. in a., 9/9/16.
Gratton, Reginald Ernest, 2/Lt., k. in a., 31/7/17.
Hickey, Arthur Aaidan, 2/Lt., k. in a., 25/10/18.
Hinkley, Arthur, 2/Lt., k. in a., 7/8/15.
Hoyle, Humphrey King, 2/Lt., k. in a., 1//5/15.
Hunter, Alexander, 2/Lt., k. in a., 20/11/17.
Jackson, John Henry, 2/Lt., k. in a., 9/9/16.
Kemp, Norman, 2/Lt.. k. in a., 9/9/16.
Leggatt, Matthew, 2/Lt., k. in a.. 26/3/18 (and R.F.C.).
Lovell, Edward Caton, 2/Lt., k. in a., 12/11/17.
Lupton, Joseph Brookes, 2/Lt., k. in a., 20/11/17.
MacFie, Robert Alexander, 2/Lt., k. in a., 20/11/17.
Marsden, John William, 2/Lt., k. in a., 20/11/17.
Marshall, David, 2/Lt., k. in a., 13/5/18.
Morgan, James White, 2/Lt., d. of w., 10/8/18.
Partington, Harry, 2/Lt., d. of w., 25/8/18.
Ramsay, Alexander, M.M., 2/Lt., k. in a., 20/10/18.
Riggott, Robert Cyril, 2/Lt., k. in a., 20/9/17.
Ross, Harold, 2/Lt., d. of w., 8/4/18 (in German hands).
Schofield, John, 2/Lt., d. of w., 24/9/18.
Seddon, Horace, 2/Lt.. k. in a., 25/8/18.
Smith, Kenneth Leslie, 2/Lt., k. in a., 20/9/17.
Stott, William Ernest, 2/Lt., k. in a., 8/8/18.
Stott, Robert Sebastian, M.C., 2/Lt., k. in a., 12/10/18.
Tiffen, Harold Vincent, 2/Lt., k. in a., 20/11/17.
Verity, Gilbert, 2/Lt., d. of w., 31/7/17.
Walker, Richard, 2/Lt.. k. in a., 9/8/16.
Warrell, Alfred, 2/Lt., k. in a., 9/10/17.
Wells, Fred, 2/Lt., k. in a., 25/4/18.
Yapp, William Clarence, 2/Lt., k. in a., 7/8/15.

The Lancashire Fusiliers.

6th Battalion (Territorial).

Bealey, Frederick Arthur Harold, Capt., died, 17/11/18 (in enemy hands).
Cameron, James Ritchie, Capt., k. in a., 21/3/18.
Clegg, Alfred Victor, Capt., k. in a., 7/8/15.
Briggs, William Lake, Lt. (T/Capt.), k. in a., 21/7/17.
Farnham, Ralph, Capt., d. of w., 31/10/18.
Griffiths, William Henry, Capt. & Q.M., k. in a., 7/8/15.
Jones, Edwin Jones, T/Capt., k. in a., 13/6/17.
Kay, John Alexander, A/Capt., k. in a., 9/10/17.
Williams, W. H., Capt., k. in a., 3/5/18 (R.A.F.).
Baseley, Albert Lawrence, Lt., k. in a., 11/8/17.
Crofts, William, Lt., k. in a., 5/12/17.
Duckworth, Herbert Hartley, Lt., k. in a., 24/3/18.
Goldsmith, Herbert Francis, Lt., k. in a., 27/9/18 (M.G.C.).
Holden, Norman Victor, Lt., d. of w., 4/6/15.
Isherwood, Norman, Lt., k. in a., 6/9/17.
Merchant, Alfred, Lt., k. in a., 10/4/18.
O'Neill, Samuel, Lt., killed, 12/6/15.
Smith, Joshua Harold, Lt., k. in a., 12/8/15.
Stevenson, Hugh, Lt., k. in a., 9/10/17.
Taylor, Percival Harry, 2/Lt. (T/Lt.), k. in a., 13/6/17.
Wilkinson, Percy, Lt., k. in a., 4/12/17.
Bell, James Donald Allen, 2/Lt., k. in a., 21-23/3/18.
Benson, William Arthur, 2/Lt., k. in a., 21/3/18.
Briggs, Eric Mackie, 2/Lt., k. in a., 3/5/17.
Briggs, Thomas, M.C., 2/Lt., k. in a., 18/10/18.
Brink, Albert Drury, 2/Lt., k. in a., 20/9/17.
Clay, Louis John, 2/Lt., k. in a., 5/4/18.
Croker, Frederick Reginald, 2/Lt., k. in a., 27/4/17 (R.F.C.).
Duckworth, Eric, 2/Lt., k. in a., 7/8/15.
Dyer, James Edward Stanley, 2/Lt., k. in a., 9/10/17.
Jepson, Joseph Jordan, 2/Lt., k. in a., 2/10/18.
Jones, Richard Harold, 2/Lt.. k. in a., 14/1/17.
Leak, Reginald, 2/Lt., d. of w., 26/8/15.
McCabe, John Bertram, 2/Lt., k. in a., 28/3/18.
Marlow, George, 2/Lt., died, 26/8/16.
Mason, Godfrey Jackson, 2/Lt., k. in a., 30/1/18.
Mead, Edward, 2/Lt., d. of w., 22/4/18.
Morrison, Robert, 2/Lt., k. in a., 30/8/18.
Parker, George Wilson, 2/Lt., k. in a., 9/10/17.
Skene, Ian, M.C., 2/Lt., d. of w., 13/4/18 (in German hands).
Sutherland, John, 2/Lt., killed, 21/3/18.
Taylor, Thomas Ralph, 2/Lt., k. in a., 7/8/15.
Thompson, Cecil William, 2/Lt., d. of w., 6/5/17 (M.G.C.).
Thompson, George Cyril, 2/Lt., d. of w., 24/10/15.
Walker, Walker, 2/Lt., d. of w., 25/8/18.
Willett, Richard, 2/Lt., k. in a., 31/7/17.
Wilson, Herbert, 2/Lt., k. in a., 8/11/18.
Wyatt, Godfrey Louis, 2/Lt., d. of w., 24/5/15.

The Lancashire Fusiliers.

7th Battalion (Territorial).

Law, William John, T/Lt.-Col., k. in a., 19/12/15.
Cade, Reginald Henry, Major, k. in a., 27/9/18.
Humphreys, Arthur Cecil, Capt., k. in a., 10/5/15.
Waterhouse, Rennie, Capt., k. in a., 7/5/15.
Andrews, Reginald, Lt., k. in a., 31/7/17.
Burleigh, Bennett, Lt., d. of w., 15/7/15.
Heaton, Herbert Walker, Lt., k. in a., 5/9/17.
Mottram, John Elliott, Lt., k. in a., 9/10/17.
Pearson, John, Lt., k. in a., 10/10/17.
Spink, Edward Wodehouse, Lt., k. in a., 23/10/18.
Usher, Robert William Armitage, Lt., k. in a., 2/5/17.
Weyman, Percy, Lt., d. of w., 16/10/17.
Andrews, Henry George, 2/Lt., k. in a., 25/3/18.
Bowell, Ernest Philip, 2/Lt., k. in a., 20/11/17.
Bramwell, Norman, 2/Lt., k. in a., 30/3/18.
Carter, Henry John, 2/Lt., k. in a., 22/10/18.
Church, Horace Major Scrimshire, 2/Lt., d. of w., 10/2/18.
Downham, Harold, 2/Lt., d. of w., 29/9/18.
Hamilton, John Guthrie, 2/Lt., k. in a., 21/3/18.
Hartley, William Reginald, 2/Lt., d. of w., 20/12/15.
Howells, John Wesley, 2/Lt., k. in a., 23/7/17.
Jowett, Harold Crossley, 2/Lt., k. in a., 1/9/18.
Kember, Walter, 2/Lt., k. in a., 1/9/17 (R.F.C.).
Kershaw, Ryder Samuel, 2/Lt., k. in a., 11/5/17.
Knight, Edward James, 2/Lt., k. in a., 12/5/17.
Roberts, Ernest Woolley, 2/Lt., killed, 6/6/15.
Warburton, Henry Heap, 2/Lt., d. of w., 9/9/16 (M.G.C.).
Whitworth, Walter Haworth, 2/Lt., d. of w., 14/9/18
Williams, Thomas Jones, 2/Lt., k. in a., 28/12/17.
Wilson, Alexander, 2/Lt., k. in a., 21/3/18.

The Lancashire Fusiliers.

8th Battalion (Territorial).

Fallows, James Albert, T.D., Lt.-Col., k. in a., 7/6/15.
Baddeley, Edward Lawrence, Major, k. in a., 6/6/15.
Cochrane, Hugh Paterson, Major, k. in a., 20/9/17.
Alderson, Reginald, M.C., A/Capt., d. of w., 25/3/18.
Arnold, P. F., Capt., died, 8/8/18 (R.A.F.).
Bedson, Eric Hamilton, Capt., k. in a., 7/8/17.
Goodfellow, Arthur James, Capt., d. of w., 7/8/15.
Humphrey, Eric Sutherland, Capt., k. in a., 5/6/15.
Mudie, Robert Alan, Capt., k. in a., 20/9/17.
Terry, William Gregory, Capt., d. of w., 27/8/17.
Bailey, Frank, Lt., k. in a., 6/9/17.
Barnett, Ralph Edward Fulton, Lt., k. in a., 6/9/17 (M.G.C.).
Dickinson, Talbot, M.C., Lt., k. in a., 31/7/17.
Horner, Bernard, Lt., died, 5/3/17.
Johnson, Eric Hope, Lt., k. in a., 22/12/17.
Kay, William, Lt., d. of w., 21/3/18 (M.G.C.).
Littler, James Tattock, Lt., k. in a., 7/8/15.
McLaine, Donald, Lt., d. of w., 2/4/18.
Proctor, George Vincent, Lt., k. in a., 6/9/17.
Simpson, James Harper, Lt., d. of w., 12/10/17.
Smart, Norman, Lt.. k. in a., 16/10/17 (M.G.C.).
Sturt, Humphrey Morriston, Lt., died, 17/1/18.
Thorogood, Edward Linford, Lt.. k. in a., 3/9/18.
Bell, Walter Ernest, 2/Lt., k. in a., 25/4/18.
Boydell, William Vernon, 2/Lt., d. of w., 8/6/15.
Chadwick, John, 2/Lt.. k. in a., 2/11/18.
Collinge, John Chisholm, 2/Lt., d. of w., 25/10/17 (in German hands).
Duddle, William Kearsley, 2/Lt., k. in a., 20/8/17.
Eaglesfield, William James, M.M., M.S.M., 2/Lt., died, 15/11/18.
Kelly, James Sheil, 2/Lt., d. of w., 29/3/18.

Lodge, Gerald Aylmer Bleackley, 2/Lt., k. in a., 5/6/15.
Middleton, Arthur Claud, 2/Lt., d. of w., 7/6/15.
Scrivener, John Sydney, 2/Lt., k. in a., 2/12/17.
Simpson, Henry Lamont, 2/Lt., k. in a., 29/8/18.

The Royal Scots Fusiliers.
4th Battalion (Territorial).

Stewart, William, Major, d. of w., 12/7/15.
Young, Hugh Roxburgh, Major, d. of w., 21/4/17.
Jamieson, Nicol, Capt., k. in a., 13/8/15.
Kenneth, Archibald, Capt., k. in a., 12/7/15.
Logan, Arthur, Capt., k. in a., 11/6/15.
Mair, William Craig, M.C., Capt., k. in a., 22/3/18.
Orr, James Barbour, Capt., k. in a., 31/7/17.
Templeton, William Fowler, Capt., k. in a., 1/10/18.
Wyllie, Andrew Inglis, Capt., k. in a., 2/9/18 (and Tanks).
Dunlop, James, Lt., d. of w., 1/11/18.
Elsworth, Harold, Lt., k. in a., 21/8/18.
Lewis, Morgan Henry, Lt., d. of w., 20/6/15.
McQuestin, Matthew, 2/Lt. (T/Lt.), k. in a., 28/3/18.
Roxburgh, John Wood, Lt., k. in a., 19/4/17.
Sturrock, George, Lt., k. in a., 12/7/15.
Barkley, Martin Bell, 2/Lt., k. in a., 2/9/18.
V.C. Boughey, Stanley Henry Parry, 2/Lt., d. of w., 4/12/17.
Burleigh, Finlay Swan, 2/Lt., d. of w., 2/10/18.
Cameron, James Callum, 2/Lt., k. in a., 23/4/17.
Crawford, Kenneth Clark, 2/Lt., k. in a., 2/9/18.
Donaldson, Wilfred Wallace Douglas, 2/Lt., d. of w., 19/4/17.
Gilmour, Elphinstone Forrest, 2/Lt., k. in a., 28/3/18.
Glen, David Robert, 2/Lt., k. in a., 28/3/18.
Haggo, Aubrey Paxton, 2/Lt., k. in a., 18/8/16.
Inglis, William Logan, 2/Lt., k. in a., 2/10/17 (and R.F.C.).
Kean, James Rankin, 2/Lt., d. of w., 1/10/18.
Knight, Edward, 2/Lt., k. in a., 20/9/18.
Kyle, Hugh Gavin, 2/Lt., k. in a., 12/7/15.
Logan, John, 2/Lt., k. in a., 19/4/17.
McCall, Mathew Brown Wright, 2/Lt., k. in a., 12/7/15.
McGhee, William, 2/Lt., k. in a., 9/4/17.
McQuaker, George Wilson, 2/Lt., k. in a., 13/11/17.
Oatts, Eric Pearce, 2/Lt., k. in a., 3/5/17.
Paton, Robert, 2/Lt., k. in a., 23/10/18.
Ramsay, Alexander, 2/Lt., k. in a., 28/3/18.
Robertson, James, 2/Lt., k. in a., 21/8/18.
Sommervill, John, 2/Lt., d. of w., 31/10/18.
Trench, David, 2/Lt., d. of w., 23/4/17.
Woodside, David Cunningham, 2/Lt., d. of w., 26/2/16.

The Royal Scots Fusiliers.
5th Battalion (Territorial).

Cook, John Blair, D.S.O., M.C., Lt.-Col., k. in a., 24/11/17.
Russell, John, Major, k. in a., 26/8/15.
Clark-Kennedy, Archibald Douglas Hewitt, Capt., d. of w., 18/9/18.
Croall, John James, Capt., k. in a., 4/10/17.
Cunningham, Samuel Andrew, Capt., k. in a., 12/7/15.
Haddon, Hugh Reid, Capt., died, 12/7/15.
Lees, John, Capt., k. in a., 19/4/17.
McHarrie, Robert, Capt., k. in a., 9/6/18.
Miller, George Clark, Capt., k. in a., 26/8/18.
Pirie, William Shewan, D.C.M., Capt., k. in a., 19/4/17 (and M.G.C.).
Vivers, John, Capt., k. in a., 27/10/15.
Adam, M., M.C., Lt., k. in a., 7/8/18 (att. R.A.F.).
Austin, John Carson, Lt., k. in a., 29/12/15.
Austin, William Girvan, Lt., d. of w., 23/8/17.
Ewen, Edgar Hunter, Lt., killed, 1/5/17.
Fergusson, Robert Frank, Lt., k. in a., 12/7/15.
Gudgeon, Thomas Wallace, Lt., k. in a., 25/8/18.
Jackson, Thomas, Lt., k. in a., 12/7/15.
Kennedy, Walter Douglas, Lt., k. in a., 19/4/17.
McNaughton, William James, 2/Lt., T/Lt., d. of w., 31/12/15.
Merson, Marshall, Lt., k. in a., 3/5/17.
Mitchell, Andrew Neill, Lt., k. in a., 30/12/15.
Paton, Joseph Train, Lt., k. in a., 30/5/18.
Anderson, Samuel Stephen, 2/Lt., k. in a., 30/12/15.
Barnett, James, 2/Lt., k. in a., 12/7/15.
Bell, Thomas, 2/Lt., k. in a., 26/5/18.
Buchanan, Richard Brendan, 2/Lt., d. of w., 20/6/15.
Buik, Henry Douglas, 2/Lt., k. in a., 9/4/17.
Campbell, Thomas Steel, 2/Lt., k. in a., 23/4/17.
Hamilton-Grierson, James Gilbert, 2/Lt., k. in a., 12/7/15.
Hurst, Sydney Bailey, 2/Lt., k. in a., 26/8/18.
Johnstone, Arthur James, 2/Lt., k. in a., 5/4/17.
Kerr, James Melrose, 2/Lt., drowned, 4/9/16.
Leishman, Thomas, 2/Lt., k. in a., 23/4/17.
Lennox, Alexander Dick, 2/Lt., k. in a., 18/10/17 (and R.F.C.).
McAlister, George Howden, 2/Lt., k. in a., 24/8/16 (and M.G.C.).
McCowan, Robert McCaig, M.C., 2/Lt., d. of w., 1/11/18.
Mackenzie, Ronald Patrick, 2/Lt., k. in a., 19/4/17.
McLeod, John, 2/Lt., d. of w., 25/4/17.
Maxwell, John, 2/Lt., k. in a., 12/7/15.
Mill, William Henry, 2/Lt., k. in a., 12/7/15.
Montgomerie, Robert, 2/Lt., k. in a., 1/10/18.
Moore, Samuel Johnston, 2/Lt., d. of w., 18/3/17.
Neil, Robert Donald, 2/Lt., k. in a., 26/10/16.
Ross, Robert Thomas, 2/Lt., d. of w., 29/9/18.
Ross, James Hamilton, 2/Lt., d. of w., 19/4/17.
Sinclair, Eric Alexander, 2/Lt., k. in a., 23/4/17.
Smith, John Rankin Donald, 2/Lt., k. in a., 31/7/17.
Stanton, Francis Stanilaus, 2/Lt., k. in a., 27/9/18.
Steen, Thomas, 2/Lt., k. in a., 1/3/17.

Taylor, Thomas Reekie Morrison, 2/Lt., k. in a., 14/8/18.
Tweedie, David, 2/Lt., d. of w., 5/8/18.
White, Matthew, 2/Lt., d. of w., 13/4/17.

The Cheshire Regiment.
4th Battalion (Territorial).

Swindells, Geoffrey Hillier, Lt.-Col., k. in a., 1/8/18.
Prentice, Thomas Alfred, Major, k. in a., 10/8/15.
Bazett, Arthur Hugh, Capt., k. in a., 10/8/15.
Holding, James, Capt., k. in a., 1/8/18.
Sidebotham, Gerald, Capt., k. in a., 9/3/18.
Taylor, Archibald McMillan, Capt., k. in a., 10/8/15.
Wilson, George Reginald, Capt., k. in a., 10/8/15.
Dawson, Francis Rudolf, Lt., k. in a., 10/8/15.
McKeever, James Holden, Lt., d. of w., 20/9/17.
Nicholson, Alan Grifford, Lt., k. in a., 10/8/15.
Taylor, Arthur, Lt., k. in a., 10/4/18.
Anthony, Thomas Vaughan, 2/Lt., k. in a., 10/8/15.
Ashworth, Edgar, 2/Lt., k. in a., 22/9/17.
Biddulph, William, 2/Lt., k. in a., 3/9/18.
Bullock, Charles Sidney, 2/Lt., d. of w., 6/9/18.
Burrell, John Stamp Garthorne, 2/Lt., k. in a., 10/8/15.
Cotsworth, John Henry, 2/Lt., k. in a., 28/9/18.
Dale, Frank Cottrell, 2/Lt., d. of w., 26/5/18.
Greg, Robert Phillips, 2/Lt., d. of w., 3/5/18.
Holmes, Wilfred Bertram, 2/Lt., k. in a., 20/8/17.
Hughes, John Norman, M.C. and Bar, 2/Lt., d. of w., 2/8/18.
Jones, Thomas William Allen, 2/Lt., k. in a., 31/7/17.
King, Sydney William Thacker, 2/Lt., k. in a., 10/8/15.
Lester-Smith, Henry, 2/Lt., k. in a., 15/7/17.
Newton, Frederick, 2/Lt., k. in a., 15/8/17.
Norris, Fredk. George, 2/Lt., k. in a., 4/4/18.
Potts, Charles, 2/Lt., d. of w., 11/6/17.
Proctor, Frank Goodheart, 2/Lt., 2/Lt., d. of w., 2/11/17.
Rees, Kenneth David, 2/Lt., d. of w., 29/8/17.
Warwick, William Robert St. Clair, 2/Lt., d. of w., 19/12/15.

The Cheshire Regiment.
5th (Earl of Chester's) Battalion (Territorial).

Armitage, John Basil, Capt., k. in a., 17/5/17.
Fraser, Harold Reginald Drummond, M.C., Lt. (A/Capt.), k. in a., 1/8/18.
Gamon, Sidney Percival, Capt., killed, 23/3/18 (attached R.F.C.).
Bass, Phillip Burnet, Lt., k. in a., 1/7/16.
Brierley, Roger Christian, Lt., k. in a., 14/7/17.
Foster, Charles Clifford, Lt., k. in a., 29/7/18.
Heron, Ernest Stewart, Lt., k. in a., 28/3/18.
Petty, Eric Bateman, Lt., k. in a., 23/3/18.
Radhill, P. J., Lt., died, 2/6/18 (attached R.A.F.).
Stott, Frank Gordon, Lt., d. of w., 11/7/16 (and M.G.C.).
Arthur, George Stuart, 2/Lt., k. in a., 1/7/16.
Brundrett, George Fred'k., 2/Lt., d. of w., 24/8/18.
Davies, Frank Arnold, 2/Lt., k. in a., 1/7/16.
Davies, Hugh Frederick, 2/Lt., k. in a., 3/7/15.
Davies, William Edward, 2/Lt., d. of w., 29/1/16.
Dodd, Herbert, 2/Lt., k. in a., 23/10/18.
Fraser, Victor Murray Drummond, 2/Lt., d. of w., 3/6/15.
Hamilton, Ronald Millie, 2/Lt. killed, 3/6/17.
Kneath, David John, 2/Lt., d. of w., 3/8/18.
Morrison, Robert Cecil, 2/Lt., k. in a., 13/11/16.
Saniford, Noel Pendlebury, 2/Lt., d. of w., 3/4/17.
Scott, Clarence Trebor, 2/Lt., k. in a., 20/9/17.
Smallwood, Reginald, 2/Lt., k. in a., 18/4/17.
Smith, Wilbraham Fremantle, 2/Lt., d. of w., 28/9/16.
Vernon, Fredrick Travis, 2/Lt., k. in a., 30/8/15.
Walker, Basil, Scarisbrickle, 2/Lt., killed, 9/5/15.
Wilson, John Victor, 2/Lt., k. in a., 27/4/17.

The Cheshire Regiment.
6th Battalion (Territorial).

Newton, William John, Major, died, 16/2/15.
Innes, William Robert, Capt., k. in a., 13/11/16.
Kirk, Richard, M.C., Capt., k. in a., 13/11/16.
Lee, Jack, M.C., Capt., k. in a., 31/7/17.
Read, William Lister, M.C., Capt., k. in a., 10/3/18.
Rowley, Gerald, M.C. & Bar, Capt., d. of w., 15/10/18.
White, Francis, Capt., k. in a., 4/9/16.
Berry, Bernard, Lt., k. in a., 6/6/18.
Cowpe, George Bleazard, Lt., k. in a., 31/7/17.
Holmes, Vernon Raines, M.C., Lt., k. in a., 14/10/16.
Howes, Harold Edward, Lt., k. in a., 1/8/18.
Moyes, Alexander Barclay, Lt., k. in a., 27/3/18.
Pickering, Charles Leigh, Lt., k. in a., 15/4/17 (R.F.C.).
Rigby, Douglas Marshall, Lt., k. in a., 4/9/18.
Rogers, William Ewart, Lt., k. in a., 31/7/17.
Brookes, Percy, 2/Lt., k. in a., 22/11/17.
Casson, Thomas, M.C., 2/Lt., died, 17/5/17.
Chattaway, Philip Spencer, 2/Lt., k. in a., 14/10/16.
Sproston, Frederick Alvin, 2/Lt., d. of w., 30/7/18.
Storrs, James Parker, 2/Lt., d. of w., 8/8/17.

The Cheshire Regiment.
7th Battalion (Territorial).

Backhouse, Henry, T.D., Lt.-Col., drowned, 30/12/15.
Cameron, Colin Neil, Capt., k. in a., 10/8/15.
Carswell, Henry Bradshaw, Capt., k. in a., 6/10/18.
Cooke, Charles Taylor, Capt., k. in a., 10/8/15.
Furnell, Thomas, Capt., d. of w., 31/7/18.
Haddon, Thomas, Capt., d. of w., 20/4/18 (in German hands).
Heath, Geoffrey, Capt., k. in a., 10/8/15.
Kenyon, William Douglas, Capt., d. of w., 16/9/18.

Leigh, Herbert, A/Capt., k. in a., 14/10/18.
Moss, Charles, M.C., Capt., k. in a., 6/11/17.
Turner, William Tom, Capt., k. in a., 10/8/15.
Wilkinson, William Oscar, Capt., k. in a., 5/8/17.
Carpenter, Cedric Theodore Arundel, Lt., d. of w., 6/11/18.
Cobbold, Edgar Francis Wanklyn, Lt., k. in a., 12/1/16.
Claye, Geoffrey Woolley, Lt., d. of w., 29/3/17.
Crew, Denis-Meirville, Lt., k. in a., 5/7/17.
Edwards, John Kelvin, Lt., died, 28/11/18.
Foster, Norman Rae, Lt., k. in a., 26/3/17.
Gardiner, Ellis Hubert, Lt., d. of w., 7/10/18.
Gibbs, Thomas Charles, M.C., Lt., k. in a., 31/8/18.
Gough, George Henry Waldron, Lt., k. in a., 15/12/17.
McKay, Ernest. Lt., k. in a., 19/9/15.
Beck, Charles Broughton Harrop, 2/Lt., d. of w., 15/8/15.
Clayton, John Arnold, 2/Lt., k. in a., 26/3/17.
Davies, Idris Powell, 2/Lt., d. of w.. 21/8/18.
Dodd, Stanley Preston, 2/Lt., d. of w., 25/11/17.
Goodwin, George, 2/Lt., died, 19/10/17.
Gosse, Robert Buchanan Wilkes, 2/Lt., d. of w., 1/4/17.
Gregg, George Philip, 2/Lt., k. in a., 26/3/17.
Laybourne, John Oscar, 2/Lt., k. in a., 26/3/17.
Powell, Ernest Arthur, 2/Lt., d. of w., 15/9/18.
Scott, Arthur Blake, 2/Lt., k. in a., 26/3/17.
Seel, Horace Arthur, 2/Lt., k. in a., 7/12/15.
Worth, Thomas, 2/Lt., k. in a., 10/8/15.

The Royal Welsh Fusiliers.

4th (Denbighshire) Battalion (Territorial).

France-Hayhurst, Frederick Charles, Lt.-Col., k. in a., 9/5/15.
Evans, John Eric, Capt., d. of w., 9/5/15.
Howard, John Brereton, Capt., d. of w., 6/4/18.
Howe, Claude Arthur, Capt., k. in a., 20/11/17.
Minshall, Thomas Charles Wynn, Capt., d. of w., 25/3/18.
Shingler, John Stanley Marsh, M.C., Capt., d. of w., 4/9/18.
Croom-Johnson, Brian, Lt., k. in a., 9/5/15.
Evans, Francis Graham, Lt., died, 26/9/16.
Evans, Robert Cecil, Lt., k. in a., 6/4/18.
Holland, Thomas Welsby, Lt., k. in a., 18/9/18
Hughes, John Arthur, Lt., d. of w., 26/1/15.
Jones, Thomas Esmor, Lt., k. in a., 6/4/18.
Nash, Harold John, Lt., k. in a., 24/3/18.
Quicke, Henry, Lt., k. in a., 23/3/18.
Shaw, Bernard Lynton, Lt., k. in a., 23/4/17.
Walshe, James, Lt., k. in a., 6/4/18.
Bartlett, Arthur, 2/Lt., d. of w., 12/4/18 (in German hands.).
Beynon, William Charles, 2/Lt., d. of w., 3/5/17.
Blaxley, Stewart, Lenton, 2/Lt., k. in a., 23/4/17.
Brown, Ernest James, 2/Lt., k. in a., 31/7/17.
Davies, John Howard, 2/Lt., k in a., 4/7/17.
Davis, Reginald Percy, 2/Lt., d. of w., 5/10/15.
Ellis, John William, 2/Lt., k. in a., 27/5/18.
Ellis, William John, 2/Lt., k. in a., 23/3/18.
Evans, John Arthur, 2/Lt., k. in a., 27/1/17.
Evans, Rhys Trevor, 2/Lt., k. in a., 1/9/17.
Hazeldene, John Turner Clough, 2/Lt., killed, 9/5/15.
Mills, John Birchell, 2/Lt., d. of w., 16/4/17.
Morse, Gerald Ernest, 2/Lt., killed, 31/10/17 (and R.F.C.).
Phillips, David Charles, 2/Lt., k. in a., 16/8/17.
Prichard, John Walter, 2/Lt., k. in a., 18/9/18.
Welsh, Alexander Torburn, 2/Lt., k. in a., 3/5/17.

The Royal Welsh Fusiliers.

5th (Flintshire) Battalion (Territorial).

Philips, Basil Edwin, Lt.-Col., k. in a., 10/8/15.
Head, Bernard, Major, k. in a., 12/8/15.
Trickett, William Edwin, Major, died, 21/11/17.
Nichols, Clifford, Capt., k. in a., 31/7/17 (and M.G.C.).
Arnold, Frederick Marshall, Lt., k. in a., 27/3/18.
Bate, Thomas, Lt., k. in a., 26/5/17.
Beckton, William, Lt., killed, 23/3/18 (and R.F.C.).
Evans, A. F., Lt., k. in a., 30-31/10/18 (and R.A.F.).
Morris, Tom Bernard, Lt., d. of w., 23/7/17.
Thomas, Evan Llewellyn, Lt., k. in a., 26/3/17.
Tregarthen, Ernest William, Lt., killed, 18/3/18.
Williams, Hugh Osborne, Lt., d. of w., 12/8/15.
Bradley, Horace Walter, 2/Lt., k. in a., 10/2/17.
Brash, Edmund, 2/Lt., d. of w., 2/9/18.
Hayes, John Henry, 2/Lt., k. in a., 31/7/17.
Jervis, Percy William, 2/Lt., k. in a., 3/4/17.
Jones, John Humphrey, 2/Lt., k. in a., 8/10/18.
Leland, John Henry Frederick, 2/Lt., k. in a., 10/8/15.
Lovelock, Clifford Andrew, 2/Lt., died, 20/11/18.
Mocatta, Robert Menzies, 2/Lt., k. in a., 10/8/15.
Overton, John, 2/Lt., k. in a., 22/3/18.
Roberts, Arthur Howell, 2/Lt., k. in a., 20/10/18.
Synnott, Fitz Herbert Paget, 2/Lt., k. in a., 10/8/15.
Walton, Robert Clare, 2/Lt., k. in a., 10/8/15.
Woodcock, Geoffrey Herbert, 2/Lt., k. in a., 6/4/18.

The Royal Welsh Fusiliers.

6th (Carnarvonshire and Anglesey) Battalion (Territorial).

Wheeler, Augustus Henry, Major, k. in a., 10/8/15.
Anthony, John Richard, Capt., d. of w., 25/5/17 (and R.F.C.).
Craddock, Percy Frederick, Capt., k. in a., 25/2/17.
Davies, Arthur Charles, Capt., k. in a., 10/8/15.
Jones-Manley, David Henry George, Capt., k. in a., 6/11/17.
Miller, John, Capt., k. in a., 19/8/15.
Bean, Bevis Heppel, Lt., k. in a., 18/6/17 (and R.F.C.).
Foss, Frederick George, Lt., k. in a., 6/11/17.
Jones, Owen Morris, Lt., k. in a., 31/10/18.
Roberts, William, Lt., k. in a., 27/12/17.
Anson, Walter Frank Vernon, 2/Lt., k. in a., 8/11/17.
Bagnall, Philip Walter Jowett, 2/Lt., k. in a., 10/8/15.
Edwards, John Henry, 2/Lt., k. in a., 21/9/18.
Evans, G. W., 2/Lt., k. in a., 22/4/18 (att. R.A.F.).
Griffiths, Edwin Harold, 2/Lt., d. of w., 23/10/18.
Ireland, Walter Ernest, 2/Lt., k. in a., 26/3/17.
Jones, Evan, 2/Lt., k. in a., 6/11/17.
Jones, Gwilym Rhys, 2/Lt., k. in a., 10/8/15.
Parkinson, Thomas, 2/Lt., k. in a., 12/9/18.
Perry, William Johnstone, 2/Lt., killed, 21/5/16.
Rogers, Arthur, 2/Lt., k. in a., 26/3/17.
Williams, Arthur Llewellyn, 2/Lt., k. in a., 26/3/17.
Williams, George Stewart Louis Stanislaus Stevens, 2/Lt., k. in a., 8/9/18.

The Royal Welsh Fusiliers.

7th (Merioneth and Montgomery) Battalion (Territorial).

Jones, Owen Cecil, Major, d. of w., 30/12/17.
Beadon, Basil Herbert Edwards, Capt., k. in a., 10/8/15.
Beanland, Joseph Wilfred, T/Capt., k. in a., 14/8/15.
Burdett, Thomas George Deane, M.C., Capt., k. in a., 6/11/17.
Hailstone, George Rupert, Capt., k. in a., 6/11/17
Harries, Eric Guy, Capt., d. of w., 17/8/15.
Hurlbutt, Percival, M.C., Hon. Capt., died, 8/6/18.
Lloyd-Jones, Edward Wynne, Capt., k. in a., 10/8/15.
Lloyd-Jones, Ivor Thomas, Capt., k. in a., 26/3/17.
Plowden, Godfrey Bruce, Capt., died, 2/2/17.
Reed, Andrew Gordon, Capt., k. in a., 10/8/15.
Walker, Edward William, Capt., k. in a., 6/11/17.
Axtens, Harold Surridge, Lt., k. in a., 6/4/18.
Brown, Herbert James, Lt., k. in a., 6/11/17.
Goff, William Setten, M.C., Lt., k. in a., 22/4/18.
Gregory, Kenneth Stuart, Lt., k. in a., 10/11/17 (and M.G.C.).
Hughes-Davies, Arthur Gwynne, M.C., Lt., k. in a., 20/9/18 (and M.G.C.).
Jones, Titho Glynne, Lt., k. in a., 20/4/17.
Jones, Wilfrid Griffith, Lt., k. in a., 6/4/18.
Newman, Leslie Cambridge, Lt., d. of w., 27/12/17 (in German hands).
Owen, Humphrey Francis, Lt., k. in a., 24/3/18
Roberts, William Lloyd, Lt., k. in a., 6/11/17.
Thomas, Edward Geoffrey, Lt., died, 10/10/18.
Valient, James, Lt., d. of w., 28/10/17.
Williams, F., Lt., k. in a., 24/6/18 (and R.A.F.).
Buckley, Edmund Maurice, 2/Lt., d. of w., 12/8/15.
Davies, Albert Gordon, 2/Lt., d. of w., 1/8/17.
Evans, Hywel Llewellyn, 2/Lt., k. in a., 26/9/17.
Grant, Albyn Evan Powell, 2/Lt., k. in a., 14/8/15.
James, Ralph Lionel, 2/Lt., died, 3/8/17.
Jones, Ivor Wyn, 2/Lt., d. of w., 9/6/17.
Jones, Owen Gwilym, 2/Lt., k. in a., 26/3/17.
Jones, Russell Hafrenydd, 2/Lt., k. in a., 10/8/15.
Jones, Vavasor, 2/Lt., k. in a., 19/5/15.
Jones, William Hugh, 2/Lt., k. in a., 21/6/17.
Parry, Robert, 2/Lt., d. of w., 26/3/17.
Roberts, John William, 2/Lt., d. of w., 23/3/18.
Silcock, Bertram Baker, 2/Lt., k. in a., 10/8/15.
Watson, George Walker, 2/Lt., killed, 29/12/16.
Whittingham, Lewis Stuart, 2/Lt., k. in a., 28/2/17.
Wilson, John Edward Goodwin, 2/Lt., k. in a., 16/8/17.
Windsor, Harold George, 2/Lt., k. in a., 8/10/18.

The South Wales Borderers.

Brecknockshire Battalion (Territorial).

Bailey, The Hon. John Lancelot, Capt., died, 26/10/18.
Hill, Phillip Aubrey, Capt., k. in a., 23/4/17.
Powell-Jones, Percival Morgan, Capt., k. in a., 22/4/16.
Best, Frank Harrington, Lt., k. in a., 13/2/17.
Best, Stephen Wriothesley, Lt., k. in a., 30/4/17.
Lowe, Alexander, Lt., k. in a., 24/11/17.
Mitchell, Alexander Charles Oswald, Lt., k. in a., 30/4/17.
Powell, David Bernard, Lt., d. of w., 4/9/17.
Talbot, Arthur Aston, Lt., died, 29/10/18.
Moynan, Harold Otho William, 2/Lt., k. in a., 31/7/17.
Raikes, Frederick Monro, 2/Lt., k. in a., 22/2/17.
Williams-Vaughan, John Christopher Arthur, 2/Lt., k. in a., 18/7/16 (M.G.C.).

The King's Own Scottish Borderers.

4th (The Border) Battalion (Territorial).

McNeile, John, Lt.-Col., k. in a., 12/7/15.
Forrest, Walter Torrie, Major, k. in a., 19/4/17.
Herbertson, John, T.D., Major, k. in a., 12/7/15.
Jobson, McGregor, Major, d. of w., 3/5/18 (in German hands).
Cochrane, Walter Francis, Capt., k. in a., 19/4/17.
Lumgair, Robert Robertson Morrison, Capt., k. in a., 19/4/17.
Nimmo, Adam Prentice, M.C., Capt., d. of w., 17/11/17.
Wallace, Andrew, Capt., k. in a., 12/7/15.
Watson, John Mitchell, Capt., k. in a., 13/11/17.
Alexander, Thomas Mitchell, Lt., k. in a., 12/7/15.
Anderson, Robert Ballantine, Lt., k. in a., 19/4/17.
Armstrong, Henry Leslie, Lt., k. in a., 25/4/18.
Bulman, Andrew, Lt., k. in a., 12/7/15.
Carmichael, George Gordon, Lt., k. in a., 1/8/18.
Fair, George, Lt., k. in a., 1/10/18.
Gardiner, Charles, Lt., k. in a., 25/4/18.
Innes, James Brydon, Lt., k. in a., 20/7/15.
Mercer, William Malcolm, Lt., k. in a., 28/11/17.
Robertson, Leonard Dougal, M.C., Lt., k. in a., 13/11/17.
Scott, Andrew Hamilton, Lt., k. in a., 3/5/17.
Thomson, William. Lt., d. of w., 26/8/18.
Woodhead, Percival. Lt., k. in a., 12/7/15.

Ainslie, Archibald, 2/Lt., k. in a., 19/4/17.
Cairns, John Anderson Gibson, 2/Lt., k. in a., 29/12/15.
Conochie, Robert Hope, 2/Lt., k. in a., 31/7/17.
Ditchfield, Samuel Eric, 2/Lt., k. in a., 31/7/17.
Dowens, James Alexander, 2/Lt., k. in a., 17/10/18.
Farr, Charles Gordon, 2/Lt., d. of w., 25/3/18.
Henderson, Andrew Hubert Millin, 2/Lt., k. in a., 12/7/15.
Hogarth, John Scott, 2/Lt., k. in a., 25/3/17.
Kirkwood, William Lithgow, 2/Lt., k. in a., 4/10/18.
Logan, Robert, 2/Lt., k. in a., 20/10/18.
McCall, Archibald, M.C., 2/Lt., d. of w., 23/8/17.
McIntyre, John Watson, 2/Lt., died, 30/3/17.
Moore, John Clark, 2/Lt., k. in a., 19/4/17.
Patrick, John Bonthrone, 2/Lt., k. in a., 12/7/15.
Sanderson, Hugh, Capt., k. in a., 12/7/15.
Sutherland, George, 2/Lt., k. in a., 9/4/17.
Watt, Charles Cecil, 2/Lt., k. in a., 8/5/17.
Wood, John, 2/Lt., k. in a., 13/11/17.

The King's Own Scottish Borderers.
5th (Dumfries and Galloway) Battalion (Territorial).

Clark-Kennedy, Alexander Kenelm, Capt., k. in a., 19/4/17.
Dunn, Thomas, Capt., k. in a., 19/4/17.
Dykes, James Johnstone, Capt., k. in a., 12/7/15.
McGowan, Sidney, M.C., Capt., k. in a., 25/5/17.
Watson, William George Douglas, Capt., k. in a., 19/4/17.
Welsh, Tom, Capt., k. in a., 12/7/15.
Campbell, Robert Burns, Lt., k. in a., 3/5/17.
Carlyle, Thomas Johnstone, Lt., k. in a., 5/10/17.
Crombie, Stewart Phyn, Lt., k. in a., 4/12/18.
Douglas, Robert, Lt., d. of w., 15/7/15.
Henery, Hewett Walter Lewis, Lt., k. in a., 19/4/17.
MacDougall, David Graham Mather, Lt., k. in a., 27/7/17.
Maxwell, William Francis John, Lt., k. in a., 13/8/15.
Scott, Andrew Riddell, Lt., d. of w., 24/4/17.
Smith, Ernest, Lt., k. in a., 12/7/15.
Bryson, Alexander, 2/Lt., d. of w., 25/6/17.
Campbell, William Barton, 2/Lt., k. in a., 19/4/17.
Carlyle, Robert, 2/Lt., k. in a., 12/7/17.
Cranston, Archibald Lindsay, 2/Lt., d. of w., 16/8/18.
Douglas, William Millar, 2/Lt., k. in a., 19/8/17.
Gibb, Robert Andrew, 2/Lt., k. in a., 19/4/17.
Johnston, Andrew Yaill Pollok, 2/Lt., k. in a., 5/10/17.
Kerr, James, 2/Lt., k. in a., 13/11/17.
Kirk, John Alexander, 2/Lt., k. in a., 13/10/18.
MacFarlane, William Barr, 2/Lt., d. of w., 20/7/15.
Murray, John, 2/Lt., k. in a., 16/8/17.
Sanders, Archibald Morton, 2/Lt., d. of w., 9/4/17.
Sloan, John, 2/Lt., k. in a., 23/7/18.
Tweedie, Alexander, 2/Lt., k. in a., 19/4/17.
White, Alexander Blair 2/Lt., k. in a., 23/7/18 (att. 8th Bn.).
Wilson, Alexander Newbigging, 2/Lt., k. in a., 24/11/17.

The Cameronians (Scottish Rifles).
5th Battalion (Territorial).

Douglas, Robert Jeffray, Lt.-Col., k. in a., 3/7/16.
Macalister, William Grierson, Major, k. in a., 20/7/16.
Ashby-Brown, Kenneth, Capt., k. in a., 14/4/17.
Bogle, John, M.C., Capt., k. in a., 20/9/17.
Downie, Robert, D.C.M., Capt., k. in a., 6/11/18.
Gunn, Charles Mortimer Austin, Capt., k. in a., 20/5/17.
McEwan, Robert William, Capt., k. in a., 14/4/17.
Malloch, Lyon Robert MacGregor, M.C., Capt., k. in a., 18/11/17.
Russell, Thomas, Capt., k. in a., 19/4/16
Sim, William, Capt., k. in a., 13/11/16.
Davies, L. C., M.C., Lt., died, 16/3/18.
Jamieson, George William, Lt., k. in a., 28/3/18.
Kerr, Alan Graham, Lt., k. in a., 26/10/18.
McCrae, Alexander Bissett, M.C., Lt., k. in a., 18/9/18.
Mann, John Anderson, M.C., Lt., k. in a., 9/8/16.
Martin, Thomas, Lt., k. in a., 31/10/18.
Nelson, Graham, Lt., killed, 30/8/17 (and R.F.C.).
Russell, Peter Currie Stuart, Lt., d. of w., 19/12/15.
Smith, Arthur Borland, Lt., k. in a., 1/8/18.
Watson, George Douglas, Lt., d. of w., 18/10/18.
White, John Gardner, Lt., k. in a., 26/8/17 (and R.F.C.).
Barclay, Samuel Dugald, 2/Lt., drowned, 10/10/18.
Binnie, Philip, 2/Lt., k. in a., 26/9/17.
Collins, Albert Shepherd, 2/Lt., d. of w., 25/9/17.
Craig, William, 2/Lt., k. in a., 8/5/18.
Davies, Llewellyn Crighton, M.C., 2/Lt., died, 16/3/18 (and R.F.C.).
Donald, Ian Strathy, 2/Lt., d. of w., 7/8/16.
Drynan, James Hugh St. Clair, 2/Lt., k. in a., 8/5/18.
Eadie, David, 2/Lt., k. in a., 10/5/18.
Laird, James Ritchie, 2/Lt., d. of w., 22/7/16.
Logan, Walter, 2/Lt., k. in a., 13/12/16.
McCance, Robert, 2/Lt., k. in a., 21/11/17.
MacDonald, John, 2/Lt., k. in a., 29/10/16.
McKillop, James Bunting, 2/Lt., k. in a., 27/9/18.
Murchison, Donald, 2/Lt., k. in a., 14/4/17.
Owen, James, 2/Lt., d. of w., 20/5/17.
Paterson, Alexander, 2/Lt., k. in a., 13/7/18.
Peebles, John Adair, 2/Lt., k. in a., 30/4/18.
Phillips, John, 2/Lt., k. in a., 20/7/16.
Porteous, Gilbert, 2/Lt., k. in a., 22/11/17.
Riddell, Robert Anderson, 2/Lt., d. of w., 25/8/16.
Rigby, Douglas Archibald, 2/Lt., d. of w., 24/4/17.
Simpson, George Fullarton, 2/Lt., k. in a., 29/7/18.
Spiers, Graham Kinloch, 2/Lt., k. in a., 22/7/18.
Stevenson, David James, 2/Lt., k. in a. 22/6/16.
Stuart, John Charles, 2/Lt., d. of w., 23/2/17.
Troup, John Guthie, 2/Lt., k. in a., 13/5/17 (and R.F.C.).

The Cameronians (Scottish Rifles).
6th Battalion (Territorial).

Shaw, David Perston, Major, k. in a., 15-16/6/15.
Brown, James, Capt., k. in a., 15/6/15.
Campbell, Thomas Henderson, Capt., k. in a., 4/5/16.
Hamilton, James, Capt., k. in a., 3/1/17.
Lawrie, Allan James, Capt., k. in a., 16/5/15.
Lusk, James, Capt., d. of w., 28/12/15.
Main, John, Capt., d. of w., 18/8/16.
Murray, Cecil James Carruthers, Capt., k. in a., 15/6/15.
Wilson, William Scott Banks, Capt., k. in a., 19/9/18.
Young, Eric Templeton, Capt., k. in a., 28/6/15.
Baxter, Alexander Carnegie, M.C., Lt., k. in a., 17/4/17 (M.G.C.).
Brodie, William Eastdale, Lt., k. in a., 29/3/18.
Graham, Andrew James, Lt., k. in a., 26/9/17.
Keith, Patrick Hay, Lt., k. in a., 15/6/15.
Loudon, James Brugh Livingstone, Lt., k. in a., 13/4/18.
Loudon, Robert Gavin Morton, Lt., k. in a., 12/5/16.
Millar, John, Lt., k. in a., 29/7/18.
Millar, John Pitcairn, Lt., k. in a., 21/9/18.
Thorburn, Thomas Orr, Lt., k. in a., 13/4/18.
Whyte, Alexander Williamson, M.C., Lt., k. in a., 25/10/18.
Boyd, David Thomas, 2/Lt., k. in a., 3/5/17.
Boyd, John, 2/Lt., k. in a., 29/10/16.
Cheyne, Charles George, 2/Lt., k. in a., 14/4/18.
Clark, John Dormet, 2/Lt., k. in a., 27/5/17.
Downie, James Wallace, 2/Lt., k. in a., 22/10/17.
Grant, John Russell, 2/Lt., k. in a., 8/5/18.
Gray, Alexander Tudhope, 2/Lt., k. in a., 21/4/17.
Jackson, John Alfred, 2/Lt., k. in a., 4/5/16.
Kennedy, Gilbert McClelland, 2/Lt., k. in a., 16-18/6/15.
MacDonald, Charles Gordon, 2/Lt., k. in a., 15/6/15.
McDonald, Harold Stewart, 2/Lt., k. in a., 21/9/18.
MacDonald, John McPhail, M.C., 2/Lt., k. in a., 23/9/17.
MacHarg, James Anthony Boyd, 2/Lt., k. in a., 29/10/16.
MacLean, Donald, 2/Lt., k. in a., 21/9/18.
O'Connor, John McConville, 2/Lt., k. in a., 10/7/18.
Pool, James Williamson, 2/Lt., k. in a., 20/9/17.
Smith, John Horne, 2/Lt., k. in a., 23/7/18.
Stewart, Duncan John, 2/Lt., k. in a., 23/10/16.
Todd, William Drysdale, 2/Lt., k. in a., 15/9/16.
Wilson, John Barclay, 2/Lt., k. in a., 15/6/15.
Wishart, William Ferguson, 2/Lt., d. of w., 17/6/15.

The Cameronians (Scottish Rifles).
7th Battalion (Territorial).

Wilson, John Boyd, Lt.-Col., k. in a., 28/6/15.
Bird, William Thornton, Major, k. in a., 12/7/15.
Anderson, James Kirkwood, Capt., d. of w., 24/11/17.
Howatt, James, Capt., k. in a., 28/6/15.
McGuffie, Arthur John, Capt., k. in a., 29/11/17.
Meiklejohn, Robert, 2/Lt. (T/Capt.), d. of w., 15/11/15.
Neilson, William, Capt., k. in a., 21/11/17.
Sinclair, David, Capt., k. in a., 20/7/16.
Whitton, Peter Isles, Capt., k. in a., 28/6/15.
Allison, David, D.C.M., Lt., k. in a., 29/3/18.
Brown, William Wallace, Lt., k. in a., 28/6/15.
Duff, William, Lt., k. in a., 28/6/15.
Harrison, William, Lt., k. in a., 29/9/18.
Haydock, Tom, Lt., d. of w., 2/9/18.
Hourston, David William, Lt., k. in a., 11/8/18.
Martin, John Muir, Lt., k. in a., 6/11/18.
Muir, Andrew, Lt., k. in a., 16/11/15.
Smith, James Osbourne, Lt., k. in a., 2/11/17.
Souter, George, Lt., d. of w., 3/9/18.
Taylor, Daniel Martin, Lt., k. in a., 28/6/15.
Adam, William Fredk., 2/Lt., k. in a., 25/8/16.
Beattie, William, 2/Lt., k. in a., 15/4/17.
Bow, Herbert Christie, 2/Lt., k. in a., 23/3/18.
Clarke, Gilbert Roderick Bernard, 2/Lt., d. of w., 13/6/18.
Cook, Randolph, 2/Lt., k. in a., 9/4/17.
Cruickshank, James, 2/Lt., d. of w., 3/8/16.
Davidson, William, 2/Lt., k. in a., 23/3/18.
Duff, Alexander, 2/Lt., k. in a., 28/6/15.
Dunn, John, 2/Lt., k. in a., 21/6/17.
Ford, David Milne, 2/Lt., d. of w., 3/11/18.
Forret, Robert Smith Leiper, M.C., 2/Lt., d. of w., 15/5/18.
Gordon, George Strachan, 2/Lt., k. in a., 19/8/17 (and R.F.C.).
Howatt, William Howatt, 2/Lt., k. in a., 3/5/17.
Keane, Albert Graham, 2/Lt., d. of w., 8/5/17.
Leggat, William, 2/Lt., d. of w., 2/7/15.
Liddell, M. H. G., 2/Lt., died, 17/4/16 (att. R.A.F.).
MacArthur, Daniel Reid, 2/Lt., k. in a., 21/9/18.
McCallum, Malcolm Campbell, 2/Lt., k. in a., 18/11/16.
MacGilvray, Alexander Renfrew, 2/Lt., k. in a., 29/11/17.
MacGlashan, Alexander, 2/Lt., k. in a., 27/9/18.
Maclay, James Webster, 2/Lt., k. in a., 28/6/15.
Mathieson, Stanley, 2/Lt., d. of w., 16/8/18.
Michie, Christopher Young, 2/Lt., k. in a., 21/11/17.
Mitchell, J., 2/Lt., d. of w., 3/4/18 (att. R.A.F.).
Newlands, Stewart Lindsay Leighton, 2/Lt., k. in a., 27/5/17.
Riley, Thomas Dickinson, 2/Lt., k. in a., 20/9/17.
Russell, John, 2/Lt., d. of w., 21/4/17.
Steel, Angus Murray Russell, 2/Lt., k. in a., 9/6/18.
Webster, Donald Keir, 2/Lt., d. of w., 3/5/17.
White, Thomas Pate, 2/Lt., d. of w., 17/10/17.
Whyte, John Scott, M.C., 2/Lt., k. in a., 23/10/18.

The Cameronians (Scottish Rifles).
8th Battalion (Territorial).

Hannan, Henry Monteith, Lt.-Col., k. in a., 21/6/15.
Church, William Campbell, Capt., k. in a., 28/6/15.

Cree, Robert Scott, Capt., d. of w., 14/11/17.
Hannan, William David, M.C., Capt., k. in a., 14/10/18.
Harvey, Alec Wright, Capt., d. of w., 27/3/18 (in Ger. hands).
MacDougall, Archibald, Lt. (A/Capt.), k. in a., 31/10/18.
Macindoe, Cecil Alexander Dunn, Capt., k. in a., 28/6/15.
Macindoe, Ronald Christian Black, Capt., k. in a., 28/6/15.
Mowat, Charles James Carlton, Capt., k. in a., 28/6/15.
Tillie, Arnold Reid, Capt., k. in a., 11/5/16 (and R.F.C.).
Blackie, Frank Herndon, Lt., k. in a., 11/4/18.
Bowen, Henry, Lt. & Qr.-Mr., k. in a., 21/5/17.
Cairns, George Thomas, Lt., k. in a., 30/7/18.
Findlay, John Tulloch, Lt., k. in a., 28/6/15.
Gilmour, James, Lt., k. in a., 30/3/18.
Keith, Patrick Hay, Lt., k. in a., 15/6/15.
McCowan, Hew, Lt., k. in a., 28/6/15.
Moore, Gerald Alexander Clifford, Lt., d. of w., 11/7/15.
Neilson, John Towers, Lt., k. in a., 2/11/17.
Sloan, Wilfred Scott, Lt., k. in a., 28/4/17.
Stout, Jnr., Thomas, Lt., k. in a., 28/6/15.
Templeton, Archibald Douglas, Lt., k. in a., 28/6/15.
Thom, Laurence Wilson, Lt., d. of w., 21/4/17.
Watson, Laurence Stuart, Lt., k. in a., 29/7/18.
Allan, Robert, 2/Lt., k. in a., 23/4/17.
Benzie, William Gardner, 2/Lt., d. of w., 10/4/17.
Birrell, William Henry, 2/Lt., d. of w., 20/9/18.
Blair, John, 2/Lt., d. of w., 16/6/18.
Calderwood, William Sewell, 2/Lt., k. in a., 31/7/17.
Campbell, James, 2/Lt., d. of w., 23/7/18.
Conochie, Robert Pollock, 2/Lt., k. in a., 19/5/18.
Dinwoodie, David Wallace, 2/Lt., k. in a., 19/4/17.
Dow, Walter, 2/Lt., k. in a., 19/12/15.
Dunn, Herbert, 2/Lt., died, 25/10/15.
Edwards, Norman Roy, 2/Lt., k. in a., 19/4/17.
France, John Galbraith, 2/Lt., k. in a., 12/4/17.
Gemmell, Cecil Woodburn, 2/Lt., k. in a., 24/4/17.
Johnston, Robert Neilson, 2/Lt., k. in a., 22/7/16.
Lugton, George Deane, 2/Lt., k. in a., 30/11/17.
Macdonald, Charles Gordon, 2/Lt., k. in a., 15/6/15.
Mackenzie, Francis, Edgar, 2/Lt., k. in a., 23/4/17.
Maclay, William Strang, 2/Lt., d. of w., 25/6/15.
Macmillan, John, 2/Lt., d. of w., 24/9/18.
Miller, Harold Patterson, 2/Lt., d. of w., 27/4/18.
Mitchell, Frank Kinniburgh, 2/Lt., k. in a., 8/5/18.
Muirhead, John Ritchie, 2/Lt., k. in a., 20/10/18.
Murray, James McMillan, 2/Lt., k. in a., 24/6/17.
Oliver, George Eric, 2/Lt., d. of w., 31/7/17.
Palmer, Bertie William, 2/Lt., d. of w., 25/8/18.
Paterson, James, 2/Lt., d. of w., 20/9/17.
Pattison, Robert Macfie, 2/Lt., k. in a., 28/6/15.
Patton, David, 2/Lt., d. of w., 11/2/18.
Pitt, Douglas, 2/Lt., k. in a., 31/7/17.
Pryce, Alfred Owen Challoner, 2/Lt., k. in a., 14/4/18.
Robertson, Robert Bruce Hope, 2/Lt., k. in a., 28/6/15.
Scott, James Wood, 2/Lt., k. in a., 28/6/15.
Stewart, William Marshall, 2/Lt., k. in a., 24/3/17.
Vass, Thomas McKenzie, 2/Lt., k. in a., 4/5/18.
Wells, Henry Frederick, 2/Lt., k. in a., 21/9/18.
Whitelaw, Thomas Mitchell, 2/Lt., d. of w., 29/5/18.
Wilson, Michael Connal, 2/Lt., k. in a., 20/7/16.

The Gloucestershire Regiment.

4th (City of Bristol) Battalion (Territorial).

Slade, Ernest Cowper, D.S.O., M.C., Lt.-Col., k. in a., 4/5/18.
Parkinson, Leslie Gerard, M.C., Major, k. in a., 24/4/17.
Hannam, Francis John, Capt., k. in a., 5/7/16.
Hill, Stanley Fredk., M.C. & Bar, Capt., k. in a., 4/11/18.
Pratt, Ralph Lewis, Capt., k. in a., 18/10/16.
Ward, Francis Welsford, Capt., k. in a., 9/10/17.
Anderson, Alexander Douglas, Lt., k. in a., 17/7/16.
Andrews, Frederick Dudley, M.C., Lt., k. in a., 14/8/17.
Clark, Bruce, Lt., k. in a., 9/11/16.
Down, Robert Hayward, Lt., d. of w., 17/8/16.
Edmonds, Albert Henry, Lt., d. of w., 30/5/18.
Hadingham, Roy Matthew, Lt., k. in a., 22/6/16.
Haggart, William Jackson, Lt., k. in a., 31/8/18.
Hall, Frank Leslie, Lt., k. in a., 27/8/17.
Master, George Gilbert Onslow, Lt., k. in a., 25/7/16.
Matthews, Edwin Martin, Lt., k. in a., 8/11/16.
Phippen, Henry George, Lt., d. of w., 9/11/16.
Polack, Ernest Emanuel, Lt., k. in a., 17/7/16.
Ripperger, Harold Alvin Theodore, M.C., Lt., k. in a., 23/10/18.
Scrase, Reginald George, Lt., k. in a., 19/7/16.
Skemp, Arthur Rowland, Lt., k. in a., 1/11/18.
Baker, Hubert George, 2/Lt., k. in a., 17/8/16.
Beadell, Alfred George, 2/Lt., k. in a., 13/4/17.
Beavon, Donald James, 2/Lt., k. in a., 27/8/17.
Bird, Raymond, 2/Lt., k. in a., 16/8/16.
Boyce, Charles Wallace, 2/Lt., k. in a., 24/10/18 (and M.G.C.).
Chattock, Reginald Harvey, 2/Lt., k. in a., 13/3/16.
Cox, Walter Ewart, 2/Lt., k. in a., 18/5/17.
Ferris, Henry Norman, 2/Lt., k. in a., 9/10/17.
Garland, Francis Henry, 2/Lt., k. in a., 23/10/18.
Hadley, Ernest Sidney, 2/Lt., k. in a., 27/8/17.
James, Donald Croft, 2/Lt., k. in a., 19/7/16.
Lindrea, Wilfred George, 2/Lt., k. in a., 30/3/18.
MacDonnell, Colla Ion, 2/Lt., k. in a., 9/10/17.
Moore, Ernest Leonard, 2/Lt., died, 4/7/16.
Morse, Percy Lapper, 2/Lt., d. of w., 20/11/17.
Nurse, Reginald John Cecil, 2/Lt., k. in a., 25/3/18.
Organ, Harold Charles, 2/Lt., k. in a., 9/10/17.
Pears, Norman, 2/Lt., k. in a., 24/4/17.
Perry, Leslie Harold, M.C., 2/Lt., k. in a., 6/10/18.
Phillips, Gwilym, 2/Lt., k. in a., 13/10/18.
Richardson, John Lowick, 2/Lt., k. in a., 21/8/17 (and R.F.C.).
Saunders, Frank, 2/Lt., d. of w., 17/10/17.

Savile, George Keith, 2/Lt., k. in a., 20/6/15.
Shephard, Ernest Edward, 2/Lt., k. in a., 6/6/18.
Shute, George Francis, 2/Lt., died, 13/10/17 (in German hands).
Wyatt, John, 2/Lt., d. of w., 25/10/18.

The Gloucestershire Regiment.

5th Battalion (Territorial).

Badcock, Minden Francis, M.C., Capt., k. in a., 26/3/18.
Bruton, Basil Vassar, Capt., k. in a., 15/6/18.
Cole, Cyril Lawson, Capt., died, 14/3/19.
Harvey, Eric Howard, M.C. & Bar, Capt., k. in a., 30/9/18.
Rickerby, John Harold Ellerson, M.C., Capt., k. in a., 22/3/18.
Tubbs, Seymour Burnell, Capt., k. in a., 22/8/17.
Worthington, Richard FitzPatrick, Capt., d. of w., 4/5/17.
Cole, Clifford Spearing, Lt., k. in a., 19/6/16.
Chutter, George Philip, Lt., k. in a., 15/6/18.
Dodgshon, Argus John Charles, Lt., k. in a., 10/11/17.
Fream, William, Lt., k. in a., 21/7/16.
Guise, Henry George Christopher, Lt., k. in a., 6/5/15.
Lake, Noel Graham, Lt., k. in a., 25/3/18.
Moore, Lionel Watson, Lt., k. in a., 27/8/16.
Moore, Thomas Harold, Lt., k. in a., 27/9/15.
Pearce, William James, Lt., k. in a., 2/12/17.
Winterbotham, Cyril William, Lt., k. in a., 27/8/16.
Apperly, Arthur Lancelot, 2/Lt., k. in a., 27/8/16.
Barnett, Charles Frederick Robert, 2/Lt., k. in a., 20/4/15.
Brien, Charles, 2/Lt., k. in a., 27/8/16.
Davis, Sidney Alfred, 2/Lt., k. in a., 22/8/17.
Durrant, Dudley Garton, 2/Lt., k. in a., 16/8/16.
Griffiths, John Enos, 2/Lt., k. in a., 23/4/18.
Gurney, Kenneth Gerard, 2/Lt., died, 17/12/17 (in Ger. hands).
Knight, Raymond Edward, 2/Lt., k. in a., 21/7/16.
Hadder, Robert, 2/Lt., k. in a., 19/7/16 (and M.G.C.).
Meade, Cyril, 2/Lt., k. in a., 5/4/17.
Puckridge, Cyril Vincent Noel, 2/Lt., k. in a., 21/7/16.
Steel, Norman, 2/Lt., k. in a., 16/8/17.
Taylor, William, 2/Lt., k. in a., 22/9/18.

The Gloucestershire Regiment.

6th Battalion (Territorial).

Nott, Thomas Walker, D.S.O., Lt.-Col., k. in a., 18/4/17.
Coates, Cecil Evelyn, Major, k. in a., 23/7/16.
Beck, Philip Henry Harcourt, Capt., k. in a., 2/4/17.
Bird, Ernest Walter, Capt., d. of w., 27/7/16.
Castle, Cottam Harry Hunt, Capt., died, 30/10/18.
Elliott, Gerald Even, Capt., k. in a., 21/7/16.
Eyre, Henry Wright, Capt., d. of w., 29/7/16.
Fullerton, John Kenneth, Capt., d. of w., 15/8/17.
Irvine, Paget George, Capt., d. of w., 26/11/15.
Gilmore, John Kenneth, T/Capt., k. in a., 22/8/16.
Nott, Louis Cameron, M.C., Capt., k. in a., 18/4/17.
Rudman, Harold Ewart, Capt., k. in a., 19/7/16.
Titley, Richard Guy, M.C., Capt., d. of w., 13/10/17.
Briggs, Geoffrey Featherstone, Lt., k. in a., 11/7/16.
Griffin, E. W., Lt., k. in a., 16/9/18 (att. R.A.F.).
Homer, William Howard Claude, M.C., Lt., k. in a., 26/4/18.
Howard, Gilbert Gordon, Lt., d. of w., 29/10/18.
King, Leonard, M.C., Lt., k. in a., 18/4/17.
Langford, William John, Lt., k. in a., 19/7/16.
Lewis, Clifford Stanley, Lt., d. of w., 19/9/16.
Miller, Frederick Charles, Lt., k. in a., 24/4/18.
Nott, Henry Paton, Lt., k. in a., 27/4/16.
Sage, Sidney Edward Bush, Lt., d. of w., 13/9/18.
Schwalm, Charles Edward, Lt., k. in a., 22/11/17.
Stanley, Arthur Kinnaird, Lt., k. in a., 15/6/18.
Tratman, Harold Wigmore, Lt., k. in a., 3/12/17.
Wilkins, Mervyn Sydney, Lt., k. in a., 16/6/18.
Bannell, Leonard Henry, 2/Lt., k. in a., 3/12/17.
Baron, Stephen Timmis, 2/Lt., k. in a., 8/12/16.
Beecroft, William Henry, 2/Lt., k. in a., 22/7/18.
Bowland, Conrad Cloutman, 2/Lt., d. of w., 26/10/18.
Brindal, Gladstone, 2/Lt., d. of w., 24/3/16.
Dillon, George Charles Tracy, 2/Lt., k. in a., 23/7/16.
Fry, Leonard, 2/Lt., k. in a., 19/7/16.
Garnham, Percival, 2/Lt., died, 25/10/18.
Hill, Alexander Sidney, 2/Lt., k. in a., 9/10/17.
Peters, Gerard, 2/Lt., died, 24/2/17.
Richards, Dudley Brookhouse, 2/Lt., d. of w., 20/9/16.
Smith, Arthur Roughton, 2/Lt., d. of w., 22/7/16.
Young, Wilfred Henry, 2/Lt., d. of w., 30/5/15.

The Worcestershire Regiment.

7th Battalion (Territorial).

Butcher, Charles Leslie, T/Capt., k. in a., 24/7/16.
Hancocks, William, Capt., k. in a., 9/10/17.
Hoare, Robert William, Capt., k. in a., 9/10/17.
Homfray, Richard Pophin, Capt., died, 3/3/18.
Montgomery, Albert Barr, A/Capt., d. of w., 17/8/17.
Rollason, Arthur Gilbert, Capt., died, 30/7/15.
Vigors, Philip Urban, M.V.O., Capt., died, 2/4/17.
Wallace, Geoffrey Robert, M.C. & Bar, Capt., k. in a., 27/8/17.
Wood, Henry George Westmorland, D.S.O., Capt., k. in a., 3/8/18.
Beaman, William Archie, M.C., Lt., k. in a., 10/4/18.
Booker, Stanley Charles, M.C., Lt., k. in a., 10/10/16.
Gough, Norman, Lt., k. in a., 19/7/16.
Leighton, Roland Aubrey, Lt., d. of w., 23/12/15.
Lloyd, Samuel Ernest, Lt., k. in a., 16/3/16.
Stainton, Ernest, Lt., d. of w., 25/11/18.
Thomas, William Burton, Lt., k. in a., 24/10/18.
Acworth, John Arden, 2/Lt., d. of w., 13/10/17.
Beazer, Archibald Harold, 2/Lt., d. of w., 21/4/19.

Boocock, Herbert Jennings, 2/Lt., k. in a., 6/11/17.
Braggins, Albert Edwin, 2/Lt., k. in a., 29/4/18.
Bridge, George Francis Reginald, 2/Lt., d. of w., 15/4/18.
Brown, Francis Arthur Noel, 2/Lt., k. in a., 21/7/16.
Coldrick, Thomas, 2/Lt., k. in a., 21/3/18.
Constantine, Hebden Stringer, 2/Lt., d. of w., 13/5/17.
Cook, Cyril Mountfort, 2/Lt., k. in a., 27/8/17.
Edwards, Howard Joseph, 2/Lt., k. in a., 9/10/17.
Edwards, Philip Percival, 2/Lt., k. in a., 25/4/17.
Fellows, Arthur Simpson, 2/Lt., k. in a., 1/4/17.
Felton, Hubert Ratcliffe, 2/Lt., k. in a., 9/10/17.
Flower, Wilfred Joseph, 2/Lt., d. of w., 18/8/17.
Gilbert, George Hewitt, 2/Lt., k. in a., 15/6/18.
Gorrie, John William, 2/Lt., k. in a., 19/7/16.
Gould, Francis William, 2/Lt., k. in a., 9/10/17.
Green, Hubert Bishop, 2/Lt., k. in a., 13/4/18.
Horsley, Ralph Neville, 2/Lt., k. in a., 27/8/17.
Hutchinson, Arthur Norman, 2/Lt., k. in a., 21/3/18.
Ibbs, John Thomas, 2/Lt., d. of w., 20/3/17.
Johnston, Leslie, 2/Lt., d. of w., 25/7/16.
Jordan, John Edward, 2/Lt., died, 9/2/16.
Kent, Frederick Charles, 2/Lt., k. in a., 5/7/17.
Lewis, Denys Mervyn, 2/Lt., k. in a., 25/4/17.
McCutcheon, Hugh Edward, 2/Lt., k. in a., 3/9/16 (and R.F.C.).
Painter, John Sigley, 2/Lt., d. of w., 25/4/18.
Pearce, Edward Saxelby, 2/Lt., k. in a., 21/3/18.
Potter, Francis George, 2/Lt., k. in a., 24/4/17.
Reading, John Francis, 2/Lt., k. in a., 29/4/16.
Robinson, Horace Victor George, 2/Lt., k. in a., 24/10/17.
Roy, John James, 2/Lt., killed, 13/3/18.
Rumilly, Alfred Henry Robinson, 2/Lt., d. of w., 28/6/17.
Spencer, Mowbray Bertram Stovell, 2/Lt., k. in a., 4/8/15.
Tetlow, Kenneth Burgess, 2/Lt., k. in a., 21/3/18.
Turner, William Ernest, 2/Lt., k. in a., 27/8/17.
Underwood, Cyril Charles, 2/Lt., k. in a., 4/2/17.
Ward, Harold Arthur, 2/Lt., k. in a., 20/4/18.
Ward, Paul Francis Seymour, 2/Lt., k. in a., 22/3/18.
Wareham, Lawrence John, 2/Lt., k. in a., 21/7/16.
Wenham, Edward Kimber, 2/Lt., k. in a., 30/10/18.

The Worcestershire Regiment.
8th Battalion (Territorial).

Kerwood, Lionel, Major, k. in a., 21/10/16.
Benjamin, Herbert Seymour, Capt., k. in a., 9/10/17.
Blake, James Robert, Capt., k. in a., 25/3/18.
Carter, Harvey Gerald Carminow, M.C., Capt., k. in a., 8/10/18.
Evers, Hugh Lancelot, M.C. & Bar, Capt., k. in a., 1/11/18.
Hemming Francis William, Capt., k. in a., 24/4/17.
Plaistowe, Alan, A/Capt., k. in a., 24/4/17.
Pritchard, George, M.C., Capt., k. in a., 3/12/17.
Bell, Hugh Randolph Ryan, Lt., d. of w., 29/8/17.
Clutterbuck, Norman Eckstein, Lt., k. in a., 24/4/17.
Hancock, Ralph Longhurst, Lt., k. in a., 27/8/17.
Jones, Thomas Lewis, Lt., d. of w., 10/10/18.
Kerwood, Philip Malcolm, Lt., k. in a., 25/6/15.
Slater, Gilbert John Leigh, Lt., k. in a., 30/4/16.
Amphleet, Richard Ferrand, 2/Lt., k. in a., 5/4/17.
Barber, Gordon Henderson, M.C., 2/Lt., died, 20/10/18.
Beacham, Cecil James, 2/Lt., k. in a., 9/10/17.
Brown, Christopher, 2/Lt., died, 24/10/18.
Broomhall, Harry, 2/Lt., k. in a., 22/3/18.
Burton, Reginald John, 2/Lt., d. of w., 15/4/18 (in German hands).
Clutterbuck, Arthur Stanley, 2/Lt., k. in a., 14/7/16.
Dicks, Francis James Neville, 2/Lt., d. of w., 27/5/18.
Eaton, Clifford Gwatkin, 2/Lt., k. in a., 24/4/17.
Guilding, John, 2/Lt., k. in a., 18/8/17.
Hemming, Jesse Clifford, 2/Lt., k. in a., 27/8/17.
Leete, Sydney John, 2/Lt., k. in a., 28/7/17 (and R.F.C.).
Mason, George, 2/Lt., k. in a., 20/5/17.
Potter, John, 2/Lt., k. in a., 24/3/18.
Stevens, Ronald William, 2/Lt., d. of w., 31/10/17.
Swallow, Arthur Reginald, 2/Lt., k. in a., 24/4/17.
Wilson, Hugh Stanley, 2/Lt., k. in a., 14/9/15.

The East Lancashire Regiment.
4th Battalion (Territorial).

Brothers, Malam, Capt., k. in a., 28/5/17.
Norcross, Arthur, Capt., k. in a., 9/10/17.
Smith, James Tennant, Capt., k. in a., 5/6/17.
Thwaites, Robert, Capt., d. of w., 28/6/17.
Whalley, Henry Worthington, Capt., k. in a., 4/6/15.
Whalley, R. L., Capt., k. in a., 16/9/18 (R.A.F.).
Coupe, Thomas Harold, Lt., died, 26/7/17 (R.F.C.).
De Pennington, Alan, Lt., k. in a., 4/9/17.
Dewhurst, Joseph Mullineaux, Lt., d. of w., 7/11/17.
Hampshire, Stanley, Lt., k. in a., 9/10/17.
Hargreaves, Norman, Lt., k. in a., 23/11/16 (R.F.C.).
Harrop, William Henry, Lt., k. in a., 9/10/17.
Jackson, Godfrey, Lt., d. of w., 15/9/17.
Sames, William Fielding, Lt., d. of w., 31/5/15.
Taylor, John Yates, Lt., k. in a., 6/7/17 (R.F.C.).
Thompson, Richard, Lt., d. of w., 20/10/17.
Wolf, P., Lt., k. in a., 4/6/15.
Woods, Edmund, Lt., k. in a., 12/8/15.
Wright, Edward Dearden, Lt., k. in a., 21/3/18.
Anderson, John Alexander, 2/Lt., k. in a., 21/3/18.
Ashton, John Rubard Wilmot, 2/Lt., d. of w., 6/11/17.
Blake, George Morley, 2/Lt., k. in a., 21/3/18.
Camm, P., 2/Lt., died, 10/11/18 (R.A.F.).
Charlton, William, 2/Lt., k. in a., 25/3/18.
Clarke, Thomas Henry, 2/Lt., k. in a., 28/9/18.
Coles, Crewe, 2/Lt., k. in a., 4/6/15
Fyldes, Aubrey William, 2/Lt., k. in a., 9/8/15.
Heywood, Thomas Aston, 2/Lt., d. of w., 6/6/15.
Holden, John, 2/Lt., k. in a., 28/9/18.
Hornby, William Raymond, 2/Lt., k. in a., 4/6/15.
Kippax, James Elliott 2/Lt., k. in a., 22/9/18.
Pomfret, Christopher, 2/Lt., k. in a., 27/3/18.
Smith, Richard Thomas, 2/Lt., died, 3/5/15.
Sykes, Jabez, 2/Lt., d. of w., 25/6/15.
Taylor, John Birley, 2/Lt., k. in a., 24/12/17.
Trenbath, Jack, 2/Lt., k. in a., 8/9/18.
Walkden, Arthur Chamberlain, 2/Lt., k. in a., 28/4/17.
Wilding, John, 2/Lt., d. of w., 7/12/15.
Woodhouse, Earnfaunce, 2/Lt., k. in a., 15/9/17.

The East Lancashire Regiment.
5th Battalion (Territorial).

Bolton, Harry Hargreaves, Capt., d. of w., 23/5/15.
Bolton, Maurice Baldwin, M.C., Capt., k. in a., 21/3/18.
Hopkins, Arthur Emlyn, M.C., Lt. (A/Capt.), k. in a., 21/3/18.
Mackay, Samuel Francis Henderson, Capt., k. in a., 13/6/17.
Robinson, John Cyril Charles Henry, Capt., k. in a., 3/6/17.
Walmsley, Sam Harold, Capt., k. in a., 5/6/15.
Wright, Edward Martin, Capt., k. in a., 10/4/17.
Barker, John Hawksworth Jackson, Lt., k. in a., 7/8/15.
Battock, Thomas William, Lt., k. in a., 21/3/18.
Bolton, John, Lt., d. of w., 4/6/15.
Boswell, Claude Oliver, Lt., k. in a., 9/10/17.
Brown, J. S., Lt., k. in a., 20/10/18 (and R.A.F.).
Craston, Frank Marshall, Lt., k. in a., 28/8/17.
Duerden, John, Lt., d. of w., 10/6/17.
Dyson, Charles Bertram, Lt., k. in a., 25/3/18.
Rodgers, Alan Enison, Lt., k. in a., 5/6/15.
Sprake, Gilbert Edwin, Lt., k. in a., 4/6/15.
Alder, T. G. E., 2/Lt., killed, 28/7/18 (R.A.F.).
Blackburn, Frank, 2/Lt., k. in a., 24/10/17 (M.G.C.).
Bolton, John, 2/Lt., d. of w., 4/6/15.
Davenport, Robert, 2/Lt., d. of w., 20/10/18.
Edwards, Harri Willis, 2/Lt., k. in a., 28/4/17.
Farmer, George Barten, 2/Lt., k. in a., 14/6/18.
Green, Benjamin Cecil, 2/Lt., k. in a., 24/4/17 (M.G.C.).
Holmes, Cyril Ernest Jackson, 2/Lt., k. in a., 24/6/17.
Howells, Denzil, 2/Lt., d. of w., 13/4/18.
McCormick, Harry, 2/Lt., d. of w., 8/5/17 (M.G.C.) (in German hands).
Parry, David Thomas, 2/Lt., d. of w., 24/3/17.
Sachs, Rudolf Dinges, 2/Lt., k. in a., 20/10/18.
Slater, John Elwyn, 2/Lt., k. in a., 3/5/17.
V.C. Smith, Alfred Victor, 2/Lt., k. in a., 22/12/15.
Stansfield Frank, 2/Lt., k. in a., 31/5/15.
Walker, Denham, 2/Lt., d. of w., 19/9/16.
Walsh, Albert, 2/Lt., d. of w., 8/8/17 (and R.F.C.).
Washbrook, Mark Thomas, 2/Lt., d. of w., 21/11/18.
Webber, Alan Frank Augustus, 2/Lt., k. in a., 24/8/18.

The East Surrey Regiment.
5th Battalion (Territorial).

Barry, Francis Renton, Capt., k. in a., 4/9/18.
Harrison, Ernest Hesketh, A/Capt., k. in a., 18/9/18.
Nicholls, Henry King, Capt., k. in a., 4/4/18.
Trembath, Arthur Cecil, Capt., k. in a., 22/12/16.
Haworth, Montague Burgess, Lt., k. in a., 23/3/18.
Kramer, Gerald, M.M., Lt., k. in a., 31/8/18.
Lowry, Vyvyan Charles, Lt., k. in a., 9/4/18 (and M.G.C.).
Mallett, William Victor Lancelot, Lt., k. in a., 22/3/18.
Plante, Arthur Gedge, Lt., k. in a., 26/3/18.
Statham, Noel Horner, Lt., k. in a., 3/2/17.
Tod, Alexander Revell, M.C., Lt., d. of w., 18/4/18 (in German hands).
Tofts, Charles Frank, Lt., k. in a., 7/1/18.
Davies, Sydney Bruce, 2/Lt., k. in a., 26/3/18.
MacEwan, Maxwell, 2/Lt., k. in a., 5/7/17.
Stacey, John Harold, 2/Lt., k. in a., 4/12/17 (and R.F.C.).
Statham, Arthur Yates, 2/Lt., k. in a., 3/5/17.
Stenning, Bernard Clement, 2/Lt., d. of w., 26/7/17.
Wheatcroft, Frederick George, 2/Lt., d. of w., 26/11/17.

The East Surrey Regiment.
6th Battalion (Territorial).

Beaumont, George, M.C., Capt., k. in a., 9/4/18.
Lester, Frank, Capt., d. of w., 25/3/18 (in German hands).
Mortimore, Harry Limner, Lt. (A/Capt.), d. of w., 21/9/17.
Raymond, John Brannan, M.C., Lt. (A/Capt.), d. of w., 4/10/18.
Harries, James Francis, Lt., died, 30/6/18.
Hutchinson, Jack Cliffforde, Lt., k. in a., 22/3/18.
Michelmore, Jeffery Edwards Morton, Lt., k. in a., 9/4/18.
Stevens, Leonard Frank, Lt., k. in a., 25/3/18.
Barton, Conwell Paris, 2/Lt., k. in a., 27/8/16.
Bone, John Hugh, 2/Lt., k. in a., 22/7/16.
Goodyear, Raymond Norman, 2/Lt., k. in a., 24/4/17.
Kiver, Herbert William, 2/Lt., k. in a., 17/4/17.
Russell, Lionel William Bowden, 2/Lt., k. in a., 20/9/17.
Stainer, Claude Hamilton, 2/Lt., k. in a., 15/11/16.
Williams, Percy John, 2/Lt., d. of w., 17/5/17.

The Duke of Cornwall's Light Infantry.
4th Battalion (Territorial).

Rogers, John Lewis, Capt., died, 15/11/18.
Rosewarne, Ernest William, Capt., k. in a., 27/4/18.
Chappel, William Elden, Lt., killed, 4/4/17.
Heathcock, Ethelbert Agnew, Lt., d. of w., 29/9/17.
Jenkins, Arthur Lewis, Lt., killed, 31/12/17 (and R.F.C.).

Smith, Leon Walter, Lt., k. in a., 12/4/18.
Thomas, Francis Bernard Vivian, Lt., k. in a., 22/9/16.
Avery, Edward John, 2/Lt., died, 1/2/15.
Chapple, Reginald Charles, 2/Lt., k. in a., 12/4/18.
Morgan, John Hywel, 2/Lt., d. of w., 22/11/17.
Reynolds, Albert Stanley, 2/Lt., k. in a., 13/4/18.
Scott, George Ernest, 2/Lt., k. in a., 13/4/18.

The Duke of Cornwall's Light Infantry.
5th Battalion (Territorial).

Carus-Wilson, Trevor, D.S.O., Lt.-Col., d. of w., 27/3/18.
Blanchard, Frederick John, Capt., k. in a., 1/6/18.
Tyacke, Charles Noel Walker, Capt., k. in a., 23/3/18.
Alderson, Alex George Jermyn, Lt., killed, 19/10/16 (and M.G.C.).
Goldsworthy, Thomas, Lt., k. in a., 12-14/4/18.
Maddrell, John Denis Hugh, Lt., d. of w., 13/12/16.
Morcom, Percival John Hosking, Lt., k. in a., 11/4/18.
Palmer, Henry John, Lt., k. in a., 29/3/18.
Beer, Lewis Charles, 2/Lt., k. in a., 28/3/18.
Bishop, Bernard Bennett, 2/Lt., k. in a., 9/9/17 (att. R.F.C.).
Blackmore, Edwin, 2/Lt., k. in a., 16/8/16 (and M.G.C.).
Everson, Charles Percy, 2/Lt., k. in a., 7/10/16.
Mitchell, Henry William, 2/Lt., k. in a., 22/11/17.
Mitchell, Terence Hargreaves, 2/Lt., d. of w., 6/11/16.
Morcom, Frank Clifford, 2/Lt., k. in a., 8/5/17.
Ratcliff-Gayland, Eric Ronald, 2/Lt., k. in a., 20/7/16.
Rowse, Richard Sidney, 2/Lt., died, 2/9/15.

The Duke of Wellington's (West Riding Regiment).
4th Battalion (Territorial).

Andrews, Maynard Percy, Capt., k. in a., 15/8/15.
Broster, Robert Buck, A/Capt., k. in a., 11/10/18.
Clarkson, Charles, Capt., died, 12/2/17.
Grantham, William, Capt., d. of w., 30/11/18 (in Ger. hands).
Hirst, Charles, Capt., k. in a., 3/9/16.
Holt, John William, Capt., k. in a., 27/8/17.
Mander, Alfred Ernest, Capt., k. in a., 9/10/17.
Mowat, John Graham, M.C., Capt., k. in a., 27/6/17.
Scarborough, Gerald, Capt., d. of w., 12/9/18.
Sykes, Ernest Edward, Capt., k. in a., 4/7/16.
Waller, Henry Norman, Capt., k. in a., 3/7/17.
Birch, Eric Wykeham, M.C., Lt., d. of w., 17/1/17 (and M.G.C.).
Everitt, William Needham, Lt., k. in a., 3/9/16.
Lee, Ernest, Lt., k. in a., 11/7/15.
Riley, James Trevor, Lt., k. in a., 3/9/16.
Shackleton, James Sutcliffe, Lt., k. in a., 16/4/17.
Sinclair, Harold, Lt., k. in a., 17/2/17.
Skelsey, Robert Max, Lt., killed, 29/3/18.
Walton, Joseph Cyril, Lt., k. in a., 29/4/18.
Wharton, Herbert, Lt., died, 5/7/17.
Anderton, William Lyon, 2/Lt., k. in a., 21/8/15.
Appleton, Percy Robert Agnew, 2/Lt., k. in a., 3/5/17.
Battye, Charles, 2/Lt., k. in a., 13/8/18.
Bentley, Joseph Elgey, 2/Lt., k. in a., 11/10/18.
Booth, William Stanley, 2/Lt., k. in a., 8/7/16.
Chippendale, Frank Dean, 2/Lt., k. in a., 10/4/18.
Crowther, George, 2/Lt., k. in a., 28/6/17.
Fenton, David Houston, 2/Lt., k. in a., 8/9/15.
Fleming, Frederic William Oswald, 2/Lt., d. of w., 20/12/15.
Hartley, John Armitage, 2/Lt., k. in a., 19/12/15.
Hirst, Alfred Edison, 2/Lt., k. in a., 3/9/16.
Horsfall, Vernon Adams, 2/Lt., k. in a., 3/9/16.
Innes, Frederick Arthur, M.C., 2/Lt., k. in a., 3/9/16.
Jury, Reginald, 2/Lt., d. of w., 6/10/17.
Lumb, Joseph William, M.C., 2/Lt., d. of w., 30/10/18.
Maley, Frederick, 2/Lt., k. in a., 14/10/18.
Martindale, Laurence, 2/Lt., k. in a., 31/3/18.
Mee, Ernest Campbell, 2/Lt., k. in a., 3/9/16.
Patch, Vernon Lane, 2/Lt., killed, 20/11/17.
Peskett, Guy Eastcoft Harry, 2/Lt., k. in a., 3/5/17.
Priestly, Albert Edward, 2/Lt., k. in a., 3/5/17.
Rawnsley, Gerald, 2/Lt., k. in a., 21/1/17.
Stansfield, Sydney Pearce, 2/Lt., k. in a., 30/4/17.
Taylor, Ernest, 2/Lt., d. of w., 16/10/15.
Tomlinson, Charles William, 2/Lt., k. in a., 3/9/16.
Wadsworth, Ernest Hinchcliffe, 2/Lt., died, 12/3/17.
Zelland, Edward Jonathan, 2/Lt., k. in a., 15/12/16.

The Duke of Wellington's (West Riding Regiment).
5th Battalion (Territorial).

Wheatley, Arthur Nevin, Major, d. of w., 5/7/16.
Bentley, Tom, Capt., d. of w., 4/5/17.
Hanson, Harold, Capt., d. of w., 1/12/17.
McLintock, Arnold, Capt., k. in a., 3/9/16.
Pinder, Reginald Maw, Capt., k. in a., 7/10/17.
Sykes, Eric Turner, Capt., k. in a., 3/5/17.
Bond, Edmund, Lt., k. in a., 1/10/18 (and M.G.C.).
Crocker, Joseph, Lt., k. in a., 19/9/17.
Goldseller, Leon David, Lt., d. of w., 14/4/17.
Haigh, James Aspinall, Lt., d. of w., 22/11/17.
Jackson, Donald Richard Field, Lt., k. in a., 27/8/17.
Pounder, Benjamin William, Lt., k. in a., 9/10/17.
Ridgway, John Edwin, Lt., k. in a., 20/11/17.
Sharpe, Arthur Noel, Lt., k. in a., 3/9/16.
Walker, Oscar, Lt., k. in a., 3/5/17.
Wright, James William, Lt., k. in a., 10/10/17.
Alexander, Alexander John, 2/Lt., k. in a., 27/11/17.
Anson, Harris Hartis, 2/Lt., k. in a., 30/8/18.
Ashton, G. G., 2/Lt., k. in a., 23/7/18 (att. R.A.F.)
Brown, Robert Henry, 2/Lt., d. of w., 16/1/17.
Cartwright, Ernest, 2/Lt., k. in a., 1/11/18.
Crowther, Leslie Taylor, 2/Lt., k. in a., 15/6/15.
Davies, Walter Owen, 2/Lt., k. in a., 27/11/17.
Fisher, John Hylton, 2/Lt., k. in a., 29/11/16.
Gledhill, George Richard, 2/Lt., k. in a., 3/9/16.
Heaton, William, 2/Lt., k. in a., 3/5/17.
Hinchcliffe, Frank Beatson, 2/Lt., k. in a., 4/11/18.
Johnson, Sydney, 2/Lt., d. of w., 30/8/18.
Kitson, John Henry, 2/Lt., k. in a., 14/4/18.
Little, Henry Walter, 2/Lt., k. in a., 30/8/18.
Morton, Percival Clare, 2/Lt., d. of w., 13/4/18 (in German hands).
Mosley, Percy, 2/Lt., k. in a., 28/3/18.
Probyn, John William, 2/Lt., k. in a., 12/4/18.
Riley, John Reginald Newton, 2/Lt., k. in a., 3/9/16.
Rippon, Norris, 2/Lt., k. in a., 18/11/15.
Rush, Clement Ward, 2/Lt., k. in a., 3/9/16.
Whitelam, Lewis, 2/Lt., k. in a., 3/9/16.

The Duke of Wellington's (West Riding Regiment).
6th Battalion (Territorial).

Bennett, Claude Denman, Capt., d. of w., 18/7/17.
Coulthurst, Temple, Capt., k. in a., 11/10/18.
Ermen, Godfrey Henry, Capt., died, 4/5/15.
Groves, Joseph, Capt., died, 19/10/18.
Horsfall, Cedric Fawcett, Capt., k. in a., 18/9/16.
Mann, Basil Stainforth, Capt., k. in a., 27/11/17.
Melton, Arthur Francis, A/Capt., k. in a., 27/11/17.
Ogston, Kenneth, Capt., d. of w., 12/4/18.
Prince, Norman Charlesworth, Capt., k. in a., 18/4/17.
Willink, Herman James Lindale, Capt., d. of w., 5/11/18.
Clapham, Edgar, Lt., d. of w., 5/11/18.
Darragh, James Robinson, Lt., d. of w., 5/7/17.
Denison, John William, M.C., Lt., k. in a., 18/9/18.
Hazel, Dudley David Fraser, Lt., d. of w., 25/4/17.
Holland, Frank Sidney, Lt., k. in a., 27/11/17.
Jackman, J. R., Lt., k. in a., 22/7/18 (and R.A.F.).
Knowles, Hedley, Lt., k. in a., 30/5/15.
Law, Malcolm Colin McGregor, Lt., d. of w., 29/12/15.
Mollison, William Allan, Lt., d. of w., 1/10/18 (and M.G.C.).
O'Neill, Roderick, Lt., k. in a., 3/5/17.
Procter, John Norman William Atkinson, M.C., Lt., d. of w., 2/5/18.
Shackleton, Thomas Smith, Lt., k. in a., 5/5/17.
Slingsby, Anthony Edward King, Lt., k. in a., 16/7/15.
Stockdale, William, Lt., k. in a., 3/5/17.
Supple, Edward James Collis, Lt., d. of w., 22/8/15.
Varley, Leonard, Lt., k. in a., 12/11/15.
Woollard, G. F., Lt., died, 3/9/18 (att. R.A.F.).
Atkinson, Victor Rupert, 2/Lt., k. in a., 23/11/17.
Barnett, Gilbert Mortimer, 2/Lt., k. in a., 28/9/18.
Barrmclough, George William, M.C., 2/Lt., k. in a., 29/9/18.
Butler, John Goodwin, 2/Lt., d. of w., 29/3/17.
Carson, Thomas Wright, 2/Lt., k. in a., 27/12/15.
Charlesworth, George Vernon, 2/Lt., k. in a., 28/9/18.
Darragh, Matthew Sloan, 2/Lt., k. in a., 20/3/17.
Denby, Isaac Cecil, 2/Lt., k. in a., 27/6/17.
Dixon, Kenneth, 2/Lt., d. of w., 25/11/16.
Dumville, E., 2/Lt., k. in a., 26/6/18 (and R.A.F.).
Dyer, Harry Frank, 2/Lt., d. of w., 28/8/17.
Gill, Frank Brooks, 2/Lt., k. in a., 3/9/16.
Holroyd, Clifford, 2/Lt., k. in a., 3/5/17.
Hughes, George Augustus, M.C. and Bar, 2/Lt., d. of w., 4/11/18.
Key, Hart Reginald, 2/Lt., k. in a., 13/4/18.
Marlor, Eric, 2/Lt., k. in a., 3/5/17.
Naylor, William Balme, 2/Lt., k. in a., 16/9/16.
Nevey, Frank, 2/Lt., killed, 12/10/18.
Oughton, Reginald, 2/Lt., k. in a., 11/10/18.
Parkyn, William James, 2/Lt., d. of w., 12/10/18.
Robbins, George Latimer, 2/Lt., d. of w., 10/6/18 (and M.G.C.).
Rossington, Arthur, 2/Lt., k. in a., 13/9/18.
Shaw, Charles Richard, 2/Lt., k. in a., 11/4/18.
Stewart, George, 2/Lt., k. in a., 11/4/18.
Sugden, John Paget, 2/Lt., k. in a., 8/8/17.
Stott, George Whittaker, 2/Lt., d. of w., 8/11/18.
Weaver, Augustus Henry, 2/Lt., d. of w., 12/4/18 (and M.G.C.).
Whittaker, John Chalton, 2/Lt., k. in a., 28/4/18.
Whitaker, Thomas Saville, 2/Lt., killed, 7/11/15.
Wilson, Frederick Lawrence, 2/Lt., d. of w., 23/11/16.
Wright, Crossley, 2/Lt., k. in a., 21/11/17.

The Duke of Wellington's (West Riding Regiment).
7th Battalion (Territorial).

Campbell, Duncan Frederick, D.S.O., Lt.-Col., died, 4/9/16.
Hill, Ernest Hatton, Capt., died, 11/4/18.
McFarlane, William, Capt. & Qr.-Mr., died, 1/1/19.
Whitwam, Harold Ernest, Capt., k. in a., 9/10/17.
Beaumont, James Hutchings, Lt., died, 24/6/17.
Bradbury, Thomas Piers, Lt., k. in a., 26/4/18.
Chapman, Arthur Allsop, Lt., k. in a., 25/4/17.
Davies, Rudolph Ellis, Lt., d. of w., 11/8/17.
Nuttall, Albert Armitage, Lt., d. of w., 15/8/16.
Radcliffe, James, Lt., k. in a., 24/2/18.
Tetlow, Luke Mallinson, Lt., k. in a., 29/5/15.
Walker, George William Quarmby, Lt., k. in a., 7/7/16.
Berry, John Leslie, 2/Lt., k. in a., 12/10/18.
Doggett, George Patrick, 2/Lt., d. of w., 4/7/17.
Fisher-Brown, Kenneth Cuthbert, 2/Lt., k. in a., 13/11/16.
Gibson, Arthur Lionel, 2/Lt., k. in a., 8/8/15.
Goddard, Eric, 2/Lt., k. in a., 4/7/16.
Harris, Edmund George, 2/Lt., d. of w., 26/6/17.

Hick, Joseph Marsden, 2/Lt., k. in a., 17/4/18.
Hutley, Horace Abrey, 2/Lt., k. in a., 2/4/18.
Johnson, Bernard Copestake, 2/Lt., k. in a., 14/5/17.
Kaye, Eric Priestley, 2/Lt., k. in a., 3/5/17.
Mallalieu, Joseph, 2/Lt., d. of w., 7/11/17.
Marsden, Humphrey Miller, 2/Lt., k. in a., 11/10/18.
Moore, John Clifford Dawson, 2/Lt., k. in a., 20/7/18 (or d. of w.).
Newman, Cyril Brown, 2/Lt., k. in a., 3/9/16.
Nicholl, Arnold, 2/Lt., k. in a., 18/7/16.
Parsons, Walter Douglas, 2/Lt., k. in a., 13/4/18.
Preston, Wilfrid, 2/Lt., d. of w., 4/7/16.
Quarmby, Frederick, 2/Lt., k. in a., 18/9/16.
Quarmby, James Scholfield, 2/Lt., k. in a., 2/12/17.
Rapp, Reginald, 2/Lt., k. in a., 18/6/15.
Ruff, Samuel, 2/Lt., k. in a., 17/11/16.
Thorp, John Eric, 2/Lt., k. in a., 3/5/17.

The Border Regiment.

4th (Cumberland and Westmorland) Battalion (Territorial).

Sprott, Douglas Andrew, Capt., died, 4/1/18.
Sewell, William Allan, Lt., k. in a., 12/11/17 (and R.F.C.).
White, Robert Christian, Lt., d. of w., 18/9/18.
Wilson, Marshall Meredith, Lt., killed, 29/1/18 (and R.F.C.).
Blackburn, George Stanley, 2/Lt., d. of w., 30/10/18.
Buy, Kenric Ellis Godson, 2/Lt., d. of w., 1/10/18.
Clow, David James, D.C.M., 2/Lt., k. in a., 24/8/18.
English, Charles Arthur, 2/Lt., k. in a., 6/5/17.
Hamilton, James, 2/Lt., k. in a., 5/11/16.
McVittie, George Henry, 2/Lt., died, 12/3/15.
Pickles, Harry, 2/Lt., k. in a., 14/4/17.
Sharp, Albert George, 2/Lt., d. of w., 1/9/18.
Turner, Cuthbert, 2/Lt., k. in a., 23/4/17.

The Border Regiment.

5th (Cumberland) Battalion (Territorial).

Smith, Alan Francis Broadley, Major, k. in a., 16/6/15.
Bell, Henry, Capt., d. of w., 25/1/17.
Blair, Richard Curwen Richmond, D.S.O., Capt., k. in a., 21/6/16.
Glass, David William, Capt., k. in a., 18/9/16.
Thomson, James, Capt., k. in a., 31/8/17.
Webb, Henry Carlyle, Capt., k. in a., 19/9/16.
Berwick, William, T.D., Lt. & Q.M., k. in a., 11/9/18.
Coombes, John Edwin Henshaw, Lt., d. of w., 1/4/18.
Dawes, George Hugh, T/Lt., k. in a., 16/9/16.
Graham, Cyril, T/Lt., k. in a., 27/5/15.
Hamilton, Alexander Turnbull Rossell, T/Lt., k. in a., 9/5/17.
Huntington, John, M.C., Lt., d. of w., 12/8/18.
MacLagan, Philip Whiteside, Lt., k. in a., 16/4/16.
Oertling, L. J. F., Lt., d. of w., 8/8/18 (and R.A.F.).
Marchant, Francis Scott, Lt., k. in a., 22/3/18.
Pursglove, Edwin James, Lt., k. in a., 6/11/17.
Wilson, Allan Stanley, Lt., d. of w., 12/7/17.
Anderson, William Harold, 2/Lt., k. in a., 13/6/17.
Baxter, Rowland Percival, 2/Lt., k. in a., 16/9/16.
Bell, Thomas Ernest, 2/Lt., d. of w., 1/4/18.
Betteridge, James Harper, 2/Lt., k. in a., 14/4/17.
Burke, Michael Arthur, 2/Lt., k. in a., 6/11/17.
Condi, Allan George, 2/Lt., k. in a., 1/10/16.
Coulthwaite, James, 2/Lt., k. in a., 5/8/17.
Davis, Bernard Samuel, 2/Lt., k. in a., 9/4/17.
Dunlop, William Eric Brook, 2/Lt., k. in a., 19/5/17.
Ewbank, Leonard, 2/Lt., k. in a., 23/2/16.
Farmer, Arthur William, 2/Lt., k. in a., 7/6/17.
Feetham, Alan, 2/Lt., k. in a., 18/9/16.
James, Henry Stoddart, 2/Lt., k. in a., 23/4/17.
Jennings, Isaac Gaitskell, 2/Lt., k. in a., 21/3/18.
MacDuff, William Brown, 2/Lt., k. in a., 2/12/17.
MacKay, John, 2/Lt., k. in a., 23/4/17.
Mackle, Augustine Mary, 2/Lt., d. of w., 16/8/17.
McLennan, William Ross, 2/Lt., k. in a., 21/3/18.
Mitchell, James Alexander, 2/Lt., k. in a., 15/3/17.
Musgrave, William Martin, 2/Lt., d. of w., 15/4/17.
Pass, Charles Eric, 2/Lt., k. in a., 1/4/17.
Rankin, Frederick Alan, 2/Lt., k. in a., 23/4/17.
Rigg, Stanley, 2/Lt., d. of w., 21/6/18.
Storey, Fawcett, 2/Lt., k. in a., 23/4/17.
Warwick, Colin Winder, M.C., 2/Lt., k. in a., 22/3/18.
Wills, Robert Dixon, M.M., 2/Lt., k. in a., 23/4/17.

The Royal Sussex Regiment.

4th Battalion (Territorial).

Ashworth, Hugh Stirling, Lt.-Col., k. in a., 26/3/17.
Constable, Basil John Leslie Clymping, Capt., k. in a., 9/8/15.
Gray, Hubert James Stirling, Capt., k. in a., 27/3/17.
Lodger, Robert Egerton, Capt., d. of w., 29/3/17.
Reid, Stuart Keppel, M.C., Capt., d. of w., 29/7/18.
Weekes, Arthur Nelson Henry, M.C., Capt., k. in a., 29/7/18.
Fox, William Archibald, M.C., Lt., k. in a., 6/11/17.
Frank, Robert James Brownlaw, Lt., d. of w., 6/6/16.
Harwood, Percy Gregory Shelley, Lt., d. of w., 31/12/17.
Johnston, Gordon Black, Lt., died, 22/10/18 (in Turkish hands).
Lisby, Leslie Norman, Lt., d. of w., 5/11/17.
Partridge, H. T., Lt., k. in a., 14/7/18 (att. R.A.F.).
Pierssene, Frederick Andrew, Lt., d. of w., 6/9/18.
Richardson, Victor, M.C., Lt., d. of w., 9/6/17.
Tucker, Arthur Haines, Lt., k. in a., 16/10/17.
Tyrrell-Green, Dennis Noel, Lt., k. in a., 26/3/17.
Williams, Norman Stevens, Lt., k. in a., 4/11/17.
Young, Robert Percival, Lt., k. in a., 17/12/17.
Bishop, Arthur Walter, 2/Lt., k. in a., 21/3/18.
Borrer, John Maximilian, 2/Lt., died, 9/9/17.
Bostock, Edward Lyon, 2/Lt., d. of w., 5/4/17.
Charman, John Ewart, 2/Lt., d. of w., 25/9/17.
Cohen, Dudley Trevor, 2/Lt., d. of w., 20/11/17.
Dutton, Geoffrey, 2/Lt., d. of w., 8/9/17.
Fitch, Aubrey Sugden, 2/Lt., k. in a., 26/3/17.
Golby, Arthur Hugh, 2/Lt., d. of w., 13/8/17.
Harrison, George Launcelot Godwin, 2/Lt., k. in a., 7/11/17.
Harrison, Percy Day, 2/Lt., died, 12/3/17.
Squires, Charles Thomas, 2/Lt., d. of w., 30/3/18.
Tappenden, Herbert Frederick, 2/Lt., k. in a., 26/3/17.
Wixcey, Herbert Frank, 2/Lt., k. in a., 7/8/18.

The Royal Sussex Regiment.

5th (Cinque Ports) Battalion (Territorial).

Sansom, Alfred John, Lt.-Col., k. in a., 5/7/17.
Grant, Ferris Nelson, Capt., k. in a., 9/5/15.
Holmes, Albert Arundel, Capt., died, 19/5/15.
Knight, Alfred Howard, Capt., died, 10/12/15.
Langham, Cecil Richard, Capt., k. in a., 16/8/17.
Stewart-Jones, Thorold Arthur, Capt., k. in a., 9/5/15.
Ball, Arnold Harding, Lt., k. in a., 9/4/18.
Bingen, Carl Adolf Max, Lt., k. in a., 11/2/16.
Deane, Arthur Reginald, Lt., d. of w., 14/11/17.
Herbert, John William, Lt., died, 2/7/18.
Keen, James Raglan, Lt., d. of w., 19/10/17.
Ormrod, George, Lt., k. in a., 18/9/18.
Whitehead, Hugh MacGuire, Lt., k. in a., 21/3/18.
Wilkinson, Arthur Benjamin, Lt., d. of w., 14/11/16.
Alington, Geoffrey Hugh, 2/Lt., k. in a., 9/8/16.
Baker, Walter George, 2/Lt., k. in a., 14/11/16.
Blunden, Lewis, 2/Lt., k. in a., 22/7/16.
Byrne, Hubert Corbett, 2/Lt., k. in a., 2/9/18.
Dennison, Ralph Edward McKie, 2/Lt., k. in a., 9/5/15.
Fazan, Roy, 2/Lt., k. in a., 9/5/15.
Green, Herbert William, 2/Lt., k. in a., 16/8/17.
Hobart, Joseph Claud Antonie, 2/Lt., died, 3/12/16.
Lavender, Harry Richard, 2/Lt., k. in a., 28/8/18.
Powell, Richard Henry, 2/Lt., k. in a., 9/5/15.
Price, William Eric, 2/Lt., k. in a., 2/5/15.
Symons, James Antony, 2/Lt., k. in a., 18/7/16.

The Royal Sussex Regiment.

6th (Cyclist) Battalion (Territorial).

Heckroodt, Benjamin, T/Major, died, 6/10/18.
Holland, A., Capt., k. in a., 21/9/18 (and R.A.F.).
Powell, Edward Ingram, Capt., k. in a., 22/3/18.
Tuzo, John Atkinson, Capt., died, 8/4/18.
Wilson, George Andrew Glanville, A/Capt., k. in a., 31/7/17.
Davey, Reginald, Lt., k. in a., 5/5/18.
Lunn, Gilbert Alfred, Lt., died, 15/10/18.
Turton, Cecil William, Lt., killed, 4/2/16.
Miller, Gordon Stanley Reed, 2/Lt., d. of w., 24/12/16.
Paxton, G. A., 2/Lt., k. in a., 10/8/18 (and R.A.F.).
Payne, Henry James, 2/Lt., drowned, 4/5/17.
Smith, Wilfred, 2/Lt., d. of w., 9/5/17.

The Hampshire Regiment.

4th Battalion (Territorial).

Bowker, Francis Jearrad, Lt.-Col., k. in a., 21/1/16.
Brandon, Arthur Chester, Capt., k. in a., 21/1/16.
Durnford, Robert Chichester, D.S.O., Capt., k. in a., 21/6/18.
North, Hugh Frederic, Capt., killed, 21/1/16.
Savage, Harry George, A/Capt., k. in a., 20/9/17.
Simmons, Frank Wortley, Capt., k. in a., 22/11/17.
Simmons, Paul Emery May, Capt., d. of w., 24/7/15.
Swanson, George William, Capt., drowned, 10/10/18.
Brine, Everard Lindesay, Lt., died, 24/9/18.
Buckingham, Henry, Lt. & Qr.-Mr., died, 20/12/17.
Bucknill, John Charles, M.C., Lt., k. in a., 21/1/16.
Macrae, Charles Mackenzie, Lt., k. in a., 5/7/15.
Osborne, Harold John, Lt., d. of w., 4/8/15.
Rawlings, George Wilfred Harry Leslie, T/Lt., k. in a., 27/1/17.
Wilkinson, John Graham, Lt., k. in a., 20/7/18.
Collis, Percy Harold, 2/Lt., d. of w., 31/7/17.
Fairweather, Cyril John, 2/Lt., k. in a., 22/3/18.
Gilbert, Joseph Plumptre, 2/Lt., k. in a., 11/4/17.
Haddy, Stephen Edgar, 2/Lt., d. of w., 16/8/17.
Poulter, John Charles Archibald, 2/Lt., k. in a., 24/2/17.
Tunks, Edward Joseph Austin, 2/Lt., k. in a., 3/4/18.
Warren, Harry, 2/Lt., k. in a., 7/7/17.
Wilson, Cecil Fred, 2/Lt., d. of w., 27/7/18.

The Hampshire Regiment.

5th Battalion (Territorial).

Crighton, John Arthur, Major, died, 6/2/17.
Cunnell, Donald Charles, Capt., k. in a., 12/7/17 (and R.F.C.).
Needham, Robert Lawrence, Lt., k. in a., 21/1/16.
Spencer-Smith, Gilbert Seymour Worsley, Lt., k. in a., 9/4/18.
Stevenson, Sampson Donald, Lt., d. of w., 3/10/18.
Cameron, Hugh Alexander, 2/Lt., d. of w., 21/11/17.
Elton, George Kenward, 2/Lt., k. in a., 18/10/16.
Hallum, Howard George, M.C., 2/Lt., d. of w., 12/1/18.

The Hampshire Regiment.

6th (Duke of Connaught's Own) Battalion (Territorial).

Causton, Jervoise Purefoy, Capt., k. in a., 22/4/18.
Palmer, The Hon. Robert Stafford Arthur, Capt., d. of w., 21/1/16 (in Turkish hands).
Riddock, James Keppie, Capt., died, 17/10/18.
Allen, William, Lt., died, 12/10/18.

Cosser, George Alfred, Lt., died, 15/5/16.
Powers, Herbert Grendon, Lt., k. in a., 19/9/18.
Stannard, John Arnold, M.C., Lt., d. of w., 23/4/18.
Stokes, Charles Leonard, Lt., k. in a., 26/9/17 (and M.G.C.).
Alexander, Alfred Herbert, 2/Lt., k. in a., 3/12/17.
Clarke, Samuel Frank, 2/Lt., k. in a., 7/8/17.
Huskisson, Claude Alexander, 2/Lt., k. in a., 15/6/17.
Huskisson, Herbert George, 2/Lt., d. of w., 27/1/17.

The Hampshire Regiment.

7th Battalion (Territorial).

Marshall, Harold, M.C., Lt.-Col., died, 10/9/18.
Smith, Sidney George, V.D., T.D., Lt.-Col., died, 8/10/17.
Allen, Leslie John Spencer, Capt., d. of w., 15/2/17.
Cottam, Horace Charles Bowman, M.C., Capt., k. in a., 30/9/18.
Hine, Harold Bowman Egerton, Lt., died, 31/8/18.
Hawke, Ernest William, 2/Lt., k. in a., 11/5/17.
Langdon, Arthur Charles, 2/Lt., d. of w., 27/10/18.

The Hampshire Regiment.

8th (Isle of Wight Rifles) (Princess Beatrice's Battalion). (Territorial.)

Lewis, Ernest Hastings, Major, k. in a., 12/8/15.
Coke, Leigh Rigby, Capt., k. in a., 2/11/17.
Gore, Arthur Holmes, Capt., k. in a., 12/8/15.
Leybourne, Philip Edwin, M.C. & Bar, Capt., k. in a., 4/9/18.
Loader, Graham C., Capt., k. in a., 12/8/15.
Pittis, Charles Seymour, M.C., Capt., k. in a., 19/4/17.
Ratsey, Clayton, Capt., k. in a., 12/8/15.
Ratsey, Donald White, Capt., k. in a., 12/8/15.
Seely, Charles Grant, Capt., k. in a., 19/4/17.
Trevor-Roper, Charles Cadwaladr, Capt., d. of w., 3/8/17.
Villar, Clement John, Capt., k. in a., 19/9/18.
Ashworth, R. W., Lt., died, 26/4/18 (R.A.F.).
Montague, Richard Headley, Lt., killed, 21/9/17.
Pakeman, Herbert, Lt., k. in a., 19/4/17.
Potter, Charles Gordon, Lt., k. in a., 15/9/16.
Ratsey, Stephen Gilbert, Lt., k. in a., 19/4/17.
Read, Walter Felix, Lt., died, 14/9/15.
Robertson, Ralph, Lt., killed, 11/5/17 (and R.F.C.).
Rodgers, John Richard, Lt., k. in a., 20/11/17 (and Tanks).
Sheryer, Harold John, Lt., d. of w., 5/8/17.
Wood, Walter Bertram, M.C., Lt., killed, 11/11/17 (and R.F.C.).
Young, James A. Y., Lt., died, 12/8/15.
Bartlett, William Bertram, 2/Lt., k. in a., 18/8/15.
Blofeld, Robert Alban, 2/Lt., d. of w., 20/4/17 (P. of W.).
Brooks, Leonard William, 2/Lt., k. in a., 6/7/17 (and R.F.C.).
Dodson, Henry Howard, 2/Lt., k. in a., 27/6/17.
Hills, Arthur Hyde, 2/Lt., k. in a., 19/4/17.
Hytten, Edwin Christopher, 2/Lt., k. in a., 12/11/15.
King, Reginald Duncan, 2/Lt., k. in a., 19/4/17.
Latham, Percy, 2/Lt., k. in a., 20/8/15.
Raymond, Frederick Charles Motley, 2/Lt., k. in a., 21/8/15.
Shelton, John Parker, 2/Lt., k. in a., 19/4/17.
Thorpe, Norman John, 2/Lt., k. in a., 12/5/17.
Watson, Laurence Charles, 2/Lt., k. in a., 12/8/15.
Whiteman, Harold Ernest, 2/Lt., killed, 23/10/16 (and R.F.C.).
Wright, William Gerald, 2/Lt., d. of w., 8/6/17.

The Hampshire Regiment.

9th (Cyclist) Battalion (Territorial).

Ward, Walter Delay, Capt., died, 4/9/18.
Vize, Stanley Reed, Lt., died, 11/10/18.
Bennett, John Francis, 2/Lt., k. in a., 26/8/18.
Feather, Reginald Albert, 2/Lt., k. in a., 16/8/17

The South Staffordshire Regiment.

5th Battalion (Territorial).

Winstance, William Allsop, D.S.O., M.C., Lt.-Col., k. in a., 25/4/18.
Cozens, Leslie, Capt., d. of w., 14/10/15.
Eglington, Ferdinand, Capt., k. in a., 1/7/16.
Foster, John, Capt., k. in a., 23/4/17.
Hawkins, Clarence Vincent Tom, Capt., k. in a., 26/9/17.
Ivatt, Harold Alfred, M.C., Capt., k. in a., 21/5/18.
Lister, Matthew William, Capt., k. in a., 19/7/17.
Mansell, Walter Reynolds, Capt., d. of w., 16/4/18.
Meynell, Edward James Hugh, Capt., d. of w., 4/10/18.
Millner, William, Capt., k. in a., 13/10/15.
Moore, Wilfred Englebert, Capt., d. of w., 11/3/16.
Smith, Samuel Percy, Capt., k. in a., 28/2/17.
Wilkinson, John Henry Warburton, Capt., d. of w., 5/5/17.
Allday, Stanley Owen, Lt., k. in a., 13/10/15.
Choveaux, Nigel, Lt., k. in a., 14/3/17.
Cotterell, Frederick Hampson, Lt., d. of w., 16/12/16.
Devereux, Humphrey William, Lt., k. in a., 26/6/16.
Goodison, Frank Bowler, Lt., d. of w., 26/5/17 (in Ger. hands).
Hutton, John Barnabas, Lt., k. in a., 13/10/15.
Knowles, Gavin Tenison Royle, Lt., k. in a., 1/7/16.
Parr, Hugh Wharton Myddleton, Lt., killed, 15/5/15.
Smith, Alfred Archibald, Lt., k. in a., 2/4/16
Thorne, John Parry, Lt., k. in a., 1/7/16.
Whitcut, H. M., Lt., killed, 25/4/18 (and R.A.F.).
Addison, George Mellsome, 2/Lt., d. of w., 9/8/18.
Allen, Herbert, 2/Lt., k. in a., 1/7/16.
Bloor, Ronald Terrence, 2/Lt., k. in a., 23/1/18.
Broadbent, George Carvel, 2/Lt., k. in a., 21/5/18.
Buckley, Sidney James, 2/Lt., k. in a., 24/3/18.
Cotterell, Robert Victor, 2/Lt., k. in a., 23/4/17.
Craddock, Victor, 2/Lt., d. of w., 11/10/18
Davis, Sidney John, 2/Lt., d. of w., 28/3/18.
Ellison, Stanley John, 2/Lt., k. in a., 1/7/16.
Fawcett, Frank Aldridge, 2/Lt., k. in a., 1/7/16.
Fryer, William Basil, 2/Lt., killed, 26/12/16 (and R.F.C.).
Gilbert, Bernard Ryland Joseph, 2/Lt., k. in a., 1/12/17.
Green, Alan Edward, 2/Lt., k. in a., 2/10/15.
Hartley, Arthur Rowland, 2/Lt., d. of w., 9/11/17.
Hayes, Leonard Frank, 2/Lt., k. in a., 29/4/18.
Howard, George Oscroft, 2/Lt., died, 14/11/18.
Jones, George, 2/Lt., k. in a., 21/5/18.
Kendrick, Haden Mostyn, 2/Lt., killed, 18/9/16.
Kendrick, Frederick Howard, 2/Lt., d. of w., 16/10/15.
Lavender, Frank Ashley, 2/Lt., k. in a., 14/3/17.
Miller, Neville, 2/Lt., k. in a., 28/6/17.
Morton, William, 2/Lt., died, 16/11/18.
Sanger, Thomas Rudolph, 2/Lt., k. in a., 1/7/16.
Shaw, Leslie Gardner, 2/Lt., k. in a., 13/10/15.
Smith, John Samuel, 2/Lt., k. in a., 28/4/17.
Speed, Arthur Sydney, 2/Lt., k. in a., 4/6/17.
Stanway, Gerald, 2/Lt., d. of w., 5/10/17.
Swindells, Harold, 2/Lt., k. in a., 15/8/17.
Taylor, Leonard Frank, 2/Lt., k. in a., 14/3/17.
Tildesley, Harold Vaughan, 2/Lt., k. in a., 14/3/17.
Wilkes, Norman Bayley, 2/Lt., k. in a., 29/4/18.

The South Staffordshire Regiment.

6th Battalion (Territorial).

Stuart-Wortley, John, Lt.-Col., k. in a., 21/3/18.
Collisson, Edwin Read, Capt. (A/Major), k. in a., 13/10/15.
Lewis, Edwin, Major, d. of w., 30/9/18.
Astbury, Thomas Leslie, Capt., k. in a., 21/3/18.
Atkinson, Bernard Stewart, Capt., k. in a., 30/11/17.
Cresswell, Edward Arthur, Capt., k. in a., 13/10/15.
Piper, Reginald C., Capt., k. in a., 29/4/18.
Pratt (M.A.), Arthur, The Rev., died, 29/6/17.
Sankey, Sydney John, Capt., killed, 25/9/15.
Silvers, Frank Pitchford, M.C., Capt., d. of w., 27/5/18.
Teeton, Percy Randolph, M.C., Capt., d. of w., 17/10/18.
Willner, John, Capt. and Qr.-Mr., k. in a., 7/4/18.
Coape-Arnold, R. de N., Lt., died, 28/6/18 (and R.A.F.).
Harley, Arthur Darent, Lt., k. in a., 1/7/16.
Joynson, Leonard Charles Billingsley, Lt., killed, 6/5/15.
Slater, Harry, Lt., d. of w., 28/5/18.
Smith, Gerald Howard, Lt., k. in a., 29/3/16.
Bayley, Edward Vincent, 2/Lt., killed, 24/2/17 (and R.F.C.).
Bonshor, John, 2/Lt., d. of w., 26/7/18 (in German hands).
Bostock, Hugh William, 2/Lt., k. in a., 12/6/15.
Bruce, Robert James, 2/Lt., k. in a., 2/2/18.
Bushby, Joseph Bryan, 2/Lt., d. of w., 9/10/18.
Dann, Tom Vincent, 2/Lt., k. in a., 13/10/15.
Dickinson, Thomas Arthur, 2/Lt., k. in a., 1/7/16.
Embrey, Cyril Stewart, M.C., 2/Lt., k. in a., 12/10/18.
Evans, George, 2/Lt. k. in a., 3/10/18.
Flaxman, Alfred Edward, 2/Lt., k. in a., 1/7/16.
Gordon, Douglas Neave, 2/Lt., k. in a., 21/2/17.
Gribben, James Grenfell, 2/Lt., k. in a., 12/6/17.
Hickman, Philip Gregory, 2/Lt., d. of w., 31/10/17.
Iliff, Frederick John, 2/Lt., k. in a., 13/10/15.
Jeffcock, Robert Salisbury, 2/Lt., k. in a., 1/7/16.
Jephson, Howard, 2/Lt., k. in a., 23/4/17.
Johnson, William Roland, 2/Lt., k. in a., 1/7/16.
Lanham, Walter James, 2/Lt., k. in a., 21/8/18.
Motteram, Arthur William, 2/Lt., k. in a., 21/5/18.
Nelson, Walter, 2/Lt., k. in a., 13/10/15.
Nokes, William Herbert, 2/Lt., k. in a., 26/10/17.
Page, Reginald, 2/Lt., k. in a., 1/7/16.
Pearson, Charles Hugh, 2/Lt., k. in a., 19/3/16.
Rigby, John, 2/Lt., k. in a., 21/3/18.
Riley, Ernest, 2/Lt., k. in a., 26/9/18.
Smith, Joseph, 2/Lt., k. in a., 14/3/17.
Sykes, Leslie Hindle, 2/Lt., k. in a., 3/10/18.
Thornallay, Allatt, 2/Lt., k. in a., 1/7/17.

The Dorsetshire Regiment.

4th Battalion (Territorial).

Baxter, Walter Herbert, Lt.-Col., died, 18/5/17.
Crick, Walter Haliburton Routledge, A/Capt., k. in a., 9/4/18.
Matthews, Walter Franey, Capt., k. in a., 28/9/17.
Powell, Wilfred Roderick, Lt. (A/Capt.), k. in a., 9/4/18.
Symes, Charles William, Capt., died, 10/10/15.
Mims, Harold Dickman, Lt., k. in a., 27/9/18.
Palmer, Leslie Stewart, Lt., k. in a., 20/9/17 (M.G.C.).
Woodruff, Arthur Hamilton Winthrop, Lt., k. in a., 28/9/17.
Woods, Fred'k. William, Lt., k. in a., 28/8/18.
Gair, Henry Burgh, 2/Lt., d. of w., 15/5/18.
Gliddon, Ernest Frank Leslie Nevill, 2/Lt., d. of w., 5/6/18.
Graham-King, Reginald, 2/Lt., k. in a., 23/3/18.
Tillotson, John Lancelot, 2/Lt., k. in a., 23/4/17.

The South Lancashire Regiment.

4th Battalion (Territorial).

Fairclough, Egerton, Lt.-Col., k. in a., 10/4/18.
Antrobus, Norman Briggs, T/Capt., k. in a., 1/10/15.
Armstrong, William Kings, Capt., k. in a., 11/4/18.
Collingwood, Carlton, Capt., d. of w., 8/8/16.
Patch, Henry, Capt., d. of w., 19/10/17 (and R.F.C.) (in Ger. hands).
Skinner, Alfred, Capt., k. in a., 31/8/16 (and R.F.C.).
Townroe, Geoffrey Charles, Capt., k. in a., 8/9/17.
Walsh, Arthur, M.C., Capt., k. in a., 11/4/18.

Wray, Kenneth C. G., Capt., k. in a., 9/8/16.
Carter, Percy, Lt., k. in a., 9/4/18.
Fitzgerald, John Desmond, Lt., drowned, 10/10/18.
Frost, Edmund Lionel, Lt., k. in a., 16/6/15.
Jones, Arnold Seymour, Lt., d. of w., 27/3/15.
Mackenzie, Bernard Francis, Lt., k. in a., 28/6/18.
Owen, George Crompton, Lt., k. in a., 9/4/18.
Rainbow, George, Lt., k. in a., 9/10/18.
Chapman, Bertie Robert Wyand, 2/Lt., d. of w., 13/6/18.
Clarke, James Burford, 2/Lt., k. in a., 2/9/18.
Field, Samuel Hatten, 2/Lt., k. in a., 31/7/17.
Gould, Ernest William, 2/Lt., k. in a., 10/4/18.
Guest, Sidney, 2/Lt., k in a., 11/4/18.
Hampson, Harold Norman, 2/Lt., d. of w., 8/4/17 (and R.F.C.).
Hampson, James Stanley, 2/Lt., k. in a., 21/5/18.
Handyside, Arthur Cruickshanks, 2/Lt., d. of w., 17/4/18.
Holden, Leigh, 2/Lt., k. in a., 9/6/15.
Jacobs, Daryl, 2/Lt., k. in a., 10/4/17.
James, Alfred, 2/Lt., d. of w., 8/3/18.
Mills, William Edward, 2/Lt., k. in a., 8/8/16.
Pasley, William Ewart, 2/Lt., k. in a., 17/6/18
Price, Charles, 2/Lt., d. of w., 18/7/17
Shaw, Thomas, 2/Lt., k. in a., 2/4/18.
Smith, John Lancelot, 2/Lt., k in a., 9/8/16.
Stanger, Nevill Bentley, 2/Lt., d. of w., 5/10/15.
Taylor, John Tyson, 2/Lt., d of w., 17/10/18.
Todd, Charles Leslie Morgan, 2/Lt., d. of w., 4/8/16.

The South Lancashire Regiment.

5th Battalion (Territorial).

Heaton, Robert, Capt., k. in a., 25/9/17.
Smethurst, Frederick James, M.C., Lt. (A/Capt.), k. in a., 30/11/17.
Stannard, W. L., Capt., k. in a., 4/5/15.
Taylor, William Aloysius, Capt., d. of w., 11/5/15.
Wallis, Arthur Cecil, Capt., d. of w., 17/9/18.
Crippen, George Oliver, Lt., k. in a., 14/5/15.
Fink, Sydney, Lt., d. of w., 20/4/17.
Flinn, Philip Woolven, Lt., k. in a., 20/9/17.
Frodsham, William Thomas, Lt., k. in a., 9/9/16.
Gleave, Thomas Reginald, Lt., k. in a., 11/10/16.
Long, Reginald Stuart, Lt., k. in a., 9/9/16.
Robinson, Sydney Francis, Lt., k. in a., 22/7/17.
Rowed, Charles Henry, Lt., k. in a., 8/9/16.
Acton, Reginald, 2/Lt., d. of w., 9/5/15.
Barnett, Harold Walter, 2/Lt., k. in a., 30/12/17.
Beach, Joseph Norman, 2/Lt., k. in a., 31/7/17.
Brown, Eric William, 2/Lt., k. in a., 3/5/15.
Byron, Henry, 2/Lt., d. of w., 8/9/16.
Clarke, J., 2/Lt., k. in a., 18/9/18 (and R.A.F.).
Cocking, Charles Oscar John, 2/Lt., k. in a., 11/4/17.
Dawson, Frederick William, 2/Lt., k. in a., 8/9/16.
Dymond, John Jordan, 2/Lt., k. in a., 12/4/18.
Haywood, Ernest, D.C.M., 2/Lt., k. in a., 27/5/18.
Herman, R. D., 2/Lt., died, 22/9/16 (in German hands).
Jones, Herbert, 2/Lt., d. of w., 4/11/18.
Knight, Allan, 2/Lt., k. in a., 23/3/18.
Longshaw, Charles Henry, 2/Lt., d. of w., 21/7/17.
Nisbett, Frank, 2/Lt., k. in a., 30/11/17.
Pardey, William Leslie, 2/Lt., d. of w., 16/9/16.
Stead, John, 2/Lt., died, 15/11/16.
Thompson, John Oscar, 2/Lt., d. of w., 9/8/16.
Wilson, D., 2/Lt., died, 12/7/18 (att. R.A.F.).
Wilson, Wilfred Charles, 2/Lt., k. in a., 9/8/16.
Wood, John Goldsmith, 2/Lt., k. in a., 8/12/16.

The Welsh Regiment.

4th Battalion (Territorial).

Evans, Richard William Picton, Major, died, 13/9/18.
Green, Hugh Mortimer, Capt., k. in a., Aug. 15.
Howard, Alfred Heywood, Capt., k. in a., 10/8/15.
Matthyssens, Francis Alexander, T/Capt., died, 23/6/16.
Thomas, Frederick Spriggs, A/Capt., d. of w., 21/4/17.
Foster, Ethelbert Harold, Lt., k. in a., 8/10/18.
Roderick, Allan Whitlock Nicholl, Lt., k. in a., 10/8/15.
Bladon, Henry James, 2/Lt., d. of w., 1/9/18.
Bryant, Frederick James Mansell, 2/Lt., k. in a., 26/3/17.
Curtis, John Handel, 2/Lt., k. in a., 24/11/17.
Galloway, William Ernest, 2/Lt., k. in a., 6/11/17.
Graham, John Stanley, 2/Lt., k. in a., 30/8/18.
Griffiths, William Dillwyn, 2/Lt., k. in a., 18/9/18.
Hughes, Thomas, 2/Lt., k. in a., 8/10/18.
Lister, Herbert Dixon, 2/Lt., k. in a., 4/9/18.
Peadon, Harold Thomas, 2/Lt., d. of w., 27/3/17.
Roberts, Victor George, 2/Lt., k. in a., 27/7/17.
Williams, Howel Morgan, 2/Lt., k. in a., 24/6/17.

The Welsh Regiment.

5th Battalion (Territorial).

Southey, Harry Hartley Waite, Major, d. of w., 30/3/17.
Berry, Tom Cecil Hayn, Capt., k. in a., 30/8/18.
David, Thomas William, Capt., k. in a., 27/7/17.
Davies, Arthur Trevor, Capt., k. in a., 7/6/17.
Davis, Cecil, Capt., d. of w., 27/3/17.
Evans, Rees Tudor, Capt., k. in a., 10/8/15.
Phillips, Thomas Glynn Llewellyn, Capt., k. in a., 26/3/17.
Robathan, Douglas Parker, Capt., k. in a., 10/8/15.
Tremellan, Enner Thorney, Capt., died, 20/12/17.
Williams, F. E., Capt., k. in a., 7/4/18 (and R.A.F.).
Evans, Richard Stanley, Lt., k. in a., 10/8/15.
Evans, William David Russell, Lt., k. in a., 10/8/15.
Jenkins, David Lewis, Lt., k. in a., 26/9/17.
Morgan, Ernest Alfred, Lt., d. of w., 21/8/15.
Osborne, Harry Edgar, Lt., k. in a., 10/8/15.
Thomas, Trevor Sanby, Lt., k. in a., 7/4/18.
Britton, Arthur John Allan, 2/Lt., k. in a., 10/8/15.
Dowdeswell, Horace Scott, 2/Lt., k. in a., 3/11/17.
Dunn, Francis William Morgan, 2/Lt., k. in a., 10/8/15.
Dunn, John Robert Collard, 2/Lt., k. in a., 20/8/15.
Frankenstein, Oscar Reginald, 2/Lt., k. in a., 26/3/17.
Harrington, Walter, 2/Lt., k. in a., 22/6/17.
Jenkins, Ernest Stanley, 2/Lt., k. in a., 24/11/17.
Mathias, John Edmund, 2/Lt., drowned, 11/10/16.
Mathias, John Harold Tudor, 2/Lt., k. in a., 25/11/17.
Notton, Frank Gwyer, 2/Lt., k. in a., 27/8/17.
Thomas, Lionel George Theophilus, 2/Lt., k. in a., 20/9/17 (M.G.C.).

The Welsh Regiment.

6th (Glamorgan) Battalion (Territorial).

Crichton-Stuart, Lord Ninian Edward, Lt.-Col., k. in a., 2/10/15.
Thomas, Llewellyn, Major & Qr.-Mr., died, 29/11/15.
Browning, Reginald Gordon Snell, Capt., k. in a., 2/10/15.
Brown, George Trevor, Lt., killed, 12/2/17 (and R.F.C.).
Bucknell, Harry Hill, 2/Lt., k. in a., 22/7/17.
Burnie, Donald, 2/Lt., k. in a., 1/10/15.
Fortune, Henry George, 2/Lt., k. in a., 17/1/17 (and M.G.C.).
George, Frank Alfred, 2/Lt., k. in a., 17/10/18.
Morgan, L. L., M.C., 2/Lt., k. in a., 28/4/18 (and R.A.F.).
Morris, John Herbert, 2/Lt., k. in a., 21/9/16.

The Welsh Regiment.

7th (Cyclists) Battalion (Territorial).

Foot, James Stanley, Capt., k. in a., 30/7/16.
Bond, Hubert Samuel Emery, Lt., died, 17/6/17 (and R.F.C.).
More, George, Lt., d. of w., 2/10/17.
Street, B. H., Lt., k. in a., 6/8/18 (and R.A.F.).
Cook, Philip John Cecil, 2/Lt., k. in a., 14/10/18
Harris, Alfred George, 2/Lt., k. in a., 11/4/17.
Pickard, Reginald Gilbert, 2/Lt., d. of w., 2/3/17.

The Black Watch (Royal Highlanders).

4th (City of Dundee) Battalion (Territorial).

Walker, Harry, C.M.G., Lt.-Col., d. of w., 27/9/15.
Tosh, Elmslie, Major, k. in a., 25/9/15.
Air, Charles Alexander, Capt., k. in a., 25/9/15.
Boase, Edgar Leslie, Capt., k. in a., 30/7/16.
Campbell, Ernest Valentine, Capt., k. in a., 26/9/15.
Couper, Charles Miller, Capt., d. of w., 28/9/15 (in Ger. hands).
Cunningham, Robert Cocks, M.C., Capt., k. in a., 3/9/16.
Levie, Peter MacLeod, M.C., Capt., k. in a., 24/10/18.
Rorie, Thomas Handyside Baxter, Capt., k. in a., 18/8/16.
Shepherd, Edward Alexander, Capt., k. in a., 3/9/16.
Stevenson, Talbert, M.C. & Bar, Capt., k. in a., 14/11/17.
Walker, Norman Crawford, Capt., k. in a., 25/9/15.
Watson, Stanley Lee, Capt., k. in a., 25/9/15.
Watt, Alexander, Capt., d. of w., 20/6/16.
Crosbie, Walter Robert, Lt., k. in a., 12/4/18.
Dobson, George, Lt., k. in a., 11/4/18.
Duncan, William Balfour Bethune, Lt., k. in a., 3/9/16.
Kimber, John William, Lt., d. of w., 11/5/18.
Logan, Gordon Christie, Lt., k. in a., 31/7/17.
Marshall, John, Lt., k. in a., 24/10/18.
Prosser, John, Lt., k. in a., 28/9/18.
Steven, Harvey Smith, Lt., k. in a., 7/10/15.
Steven, Sidney Herbert, Lt., k. in a., 25/9/15.
Sturrock, Bernard Silvester, Lt., k. in a., 26/9/15.
Weinberg, Philip David, Lt., k. in a., 9/5/15.
Young, George William, Lt., d. of w., 8/4/18 (in German hands).
Anderson, Frederick Kinloch, 2/Lt., k. in a., 25/9/15.
Barnet, James Howieson, 2/Lt., k. in a., 1/8/18.
Brown, James Tod, 2/Lt., d. of w., 27/4/18.
Brown, William, 2/Lt., k. in a., 5/10/17.
Delahunt, Peter Godfrey, 2/Lt., d. of w., 28/8/18.
Ferrier, Robert Ernest, 2/Lt., k. in a., 15/10/16.
Fraser, James, 2/Lt., d. of w., 28/3/18.
Gibson, Charles Methven, 2/Lt., k. in a., 14/10/16.
Greenless, George Dickson, 2/Lt., k. in a., 1/12/17.
Haggart, James, 2/Lt., d. of w., 3/1/18.
Hill, William Robb, 2/Lt., d. of w., 24/8/18.
Kent, Charles Stuart, 2/Lt., k. in a., 24/10/18.
Lakeman, Arthur Frederick, 2/Lt., killed, 5/8/18 (and Tanks).
Lundie, James Edward, 2/Lt., d. of w., 29/3/18.
McGregor, Alexander, 2/Lt., k. in a., 11/4/18.
McVicar, Thomas Graham, 2/Lt., k. in a., 28/3/18.
Musgrove, John William, 2/Lt., k. in a., 19/7/18.
Paisley, George William, 2/Lt., k. in a., 27/12/17.
Peebles, Peter, 2/Lt., k. in a., 19/7/18.
Robb, William John Mechan, 2/Lt., k. in a., 20/7/18.
Sheriff, Leo Frederick David, 2/Lt., k. in ., 13/11/16.
Smith, Harold Henderson, 2/Lt., k. in a., 19/9/18.
Smith, Walter Tyrrell, 2/Lt., k. in a., 14/10/16.
Swinton, James Gibson, 2/Lt., k. in a., 25/3/18.
Wilkes, Sidney Archer, 2/Lt., k. in a., 24/8/18.
Williamson, Thomas Cockburn, 2/Lt., k. in a., 26/9/15.
Wilson, John Cooper, 2/Lt., k. in a., 17/10/16 (and R.F.C.).

The Black Watch (Royal Highlanders).

5th (Angus and Dundee) Battalion (Territorial).

Wilkie, David, Major, k. in a., 24/4/17.
Anderson, Walter Kinloch, Lt. (A/Capt.), k. in a., 22/7/18.
Brown, Aitken, Capt., d. of w., 21/4/18.

Maxwell, David, M.C., Capt., d. of w., 3/8/18.
Stuart, James Ogilvie Grant, M.C., Capt., k. in a., 30/3/18.
Taylor, Norman Robertson, M.C., Capt., k. in a., 3/5/17.
Watt, Alexander Lyle, Capt., killed, 10/3/15.
Barrie, William Cowan Ogilvy, Lt., k. in a., 14/10/16.
Blair, Alex'r. Neville, Lt., died, 13/3/17.
Gordon, James Willison Nugent, Lt., k. in a., 22/2/15.
Hollis, Basil, Lt., k. in a., 31/7/17.
Johnstone, Robert James Halliday, Lt., k. in a., 26/9/17.
Kitson, Fredk. Neil Edmonstone, Lt., d. of w., 15/8/17.
Leslie, George Constable, Lt., d. of w., 15/8/17.
Mill, Robert Cowper King, Lt., k. in a., 3/9/16.
Paterson, Isla Scott, M.C., Lt., k. in a., 1/11/17.
Whiteley, Laurence, Lt., k. in a., 31/7/17 (M.G.C.).
Whyte, William, Lt., k. in a., 28/9/18.
Barr, John William, 2/Lt., k. in a., 24/3/18.
Begg, William, 2/Lt., k. in a., 13/11/16.
Bell, William, 2/Lt., k. in a., 3/5/17.
Butler, Clifford Hicks, 2/Lt., k. in a., 23/4/17.
Cumming, Gilmour, 2/Lt., k. in a., 21/3/18.
Don, Thomas Douglas, 2/Lt., k. in a., 21/7/18.
Dunn, Martin, 2/Lt., k. in a., 16/5/17.
Grassie, John Ainslie Aymer, 2/Lt., k. in a., 21/3/18.
Laird, Andrew Clark, 2/Lt., k. in a., 22/11/16.
Leitham, Herbert Wilson, 2/Lt., d. of w., 17/10/18
MacBeth, William David, 2/Lt., k. in a., 23/4/17.
McNicoll, Godfrey Robert, 2/Lt., k. in a., 20/11/17.
Nicoll, Leonard Orrick, 2/Lt., k. in a., 26/9/17.
Quekett, John, 2/Lt., k. in a., 31/7/17.
Renny, James, 2/Lt., k. in a., 26/9/17.
Sim, William George, 2/Lt., k. in a., 14/10/18.
Watson, James Frederick, 2/Lt., died, 22/1/16.
Wilkie, George Spence McLean, 2/Lt., d. of w., 4/8/15.

The Black Watch (Royal Highlanders). 6th (Perthshire) Battalion (Territorial).

Coutts, William Ernest, Capt., k. in a., 22/3/18.
Dixon, Norman Ferguson, Capt., d. of w., 5/10/17 (and M.G.C.).
Ellis, Robert Bruce, M.C., Capt., d. of w., 21/11/16.
Ferguson, Thomas, Capt., k. in a., 13/11/16.
Guthrie, John Mack, M.C., Capt., k. in a., 28/7/18.
Hally, John, Capt., k. in a., 30/7/16.
Hewat, James Govan Argyll, Capt., d. of w., 16/4/18.
Knight, Henry James, Capt., k. in a., 21/3/18.
Macdowell, Charles Michael Vere, Capt., d. of w., 28/4/17.
Menzies, Robert John, Capt., k. in a., 31/7/17.
Wilson, John Norman, Capt., d. of w., 4/7/17.
Allison, James Stewart, Lt., died, 18/9/17.
Graves, Harry Steele, Lt., d. of w., 24/11/17.
Haldane, Robert Patrick, Lt., d. of w., 13/6/15.
McCash, John Watson, Lt., k. in a., 22/11/16 (and R.F.C.).
Thomas, Arthur John Gordon, Lt., k. in a., 31/5/16.
Turnbull, David Stevens, Lt., killed, 15/4/17 (and R.F.C.).
Cairns, George Morton, 2/Lt., k. in a., 13/11/16
Dickson, George Hubert Murray, 2/Lt., k. in a., 26/10/18
Dobbie, Alexander Middleton, 2/Lt., d. of w., 13/4/18.
Doe, Alfred Bramhill, 2/Lt., k. in a., 23/4/17.
Elder, James, 2/Lt., k. in a., 21/3/18.
Farrell, Stanley Knox, 2/Lt., k. in a., 20/7/18.
Fleet, William Henry, M.C., 2/Lt., d of w., 19/4/16.
Fyfe, Charles Clarke, 2/Lt., k. in a, 21/3/18.
Garvie, Alexander Cockburn, 2/Lt., k. in a., 23/4/17.
Glass, William, 2/Lt., k. in a., 23/4/17.
Gowans, Alexander Douglas Stuart, 2/Lt., d. of w, 27/4/17.
Hebden, Alan, 2/Lt., k. in a., 8/5/17.
Keay, Robert Naismith, 2/Lt., d. of w., 30/11/16.
McEwan, Donald Fraser, 2/Lt., k. in a., 30/7/16.
McLaren, Quentin, 2/Lt., k. in a., 26/10/16.
McLeod, Matthew Paul, 2/Lt., k. in a., 14/11/16.
Miller, Henry William Waltson, 2/Lt., k. in a., 30/7/16.
Rae, William Alexander, 2/Lt., k. in a., 31/7/17.
Robertson, Charles John, 2/Lt., k. in a., 22/3/17.
Roy, James Ferrie, 2/Lt., k. in a., 30/7/16
Ritchie, John, 2/Lt., k. in a., 25/4/17 (and M.G.C.).
Smith, John, 2/Lt., k. in a., 14/11/17.
Smith, James Bonner, 2/Lt., k. in a., 15/8/17.
Strathairn, Hubert William, 2/Lt., d. of w., 16/11/16.
Syme, David, M.M., 2/Lt., d. of w., 4/7/18.

The Black Watch (Royal Highlanders). 7th (Fife) Battalion (Territorial).

Alexander, Peter James, M.C., Capt., k. in a., 12/10/17.
Begg, Andrew Currie, Lt. (T/Capt.), k. in a., 30/7/16.
Cargill, John, Capt., d. of w., 24/4/17.
Donaldson, James, Capt., k. in a., 23/8/17.
Gillespie, James, Capt., k. in a., 30/7/16.
Playfair, Patrick Lyon, Capt., d. of w., 11/4/18.
Stevenson, Robert, Capt., k. in a., 23/8/17.
Barclay, William Kirk, Lt., d. of w., 20/6/15.
Kilgour, Alexander, Lt., k. in a., 18/4/18.
Pagan, George Hair, Lt., k. in a., 30/7/16.
Pryde, James Watson, Lt., k. in a., 5/5/18 (K.A. Rif.).
Westwood, Alexander Cleghorn, Lt., k. in a., 16/6/15.
Aitken, James Hunter, 2/Lt., died, 2/6/16.
Allen, Hugh Charles, 2/Lt., k. in a., 25/4/17.
Anderson, James Lennox, 2/Lt., d. of w., 25/5/17.
Armstrong, William Wilberforce, 2/Lt., k. in a., 27/12/17.
Beatson, Beaumont Crowther Oswald, 2/Lt., k. in a., 23/4/17.
Darney, Clarence Edwin, 2/Lt., k. in a., 2/9/18.
Fleming, Robert Alexander, 2/Lt., d. of w., 31/7/16.
Guthrie, Hugh Smith, 2/Lt., died, 31/3/18 (in German hands).
Gyle, Ernest Woods, 2/Lt., k. in a., 18/10/16.
Harley, Fredk. William, 2/Lt., k. in a., 3/6/17 (R.F.C.).
Heard, Robert Rankin, 2/Lt., k. in a., 23/4/17.
Lockhart, James Herbert, 2/Lt., k. in a., 30/7/16.
McIntosh, James Robert Hay, 2/Lt., k. in a., 22/3/18.
Mitchell, James, 2/Lt., died, 23/10/18 (in German hands).
Morris, Alexander Ramsey, 2/Lt., k. in a., 23-25/4/17.
Nelson, James Reid, 2/Lt., k. in a., 23/4/17.
Reid, Robert, 2/Lt., k. in a., 30/7/16.
Richardson, David Alexander, 2/Lt., k. in a., 21/3/18.
Robertson, James Whittingham, 2/Lt., k. in a., 23/4/17.
Thornton, Wilfred Thomas, 2/Lt., k. in a., 30/7/16.
Wallace, John Kennedy, 2/Lt., k. in a., 23/4/17.

The Oxfordshire and Buckinghamshire Light Infantry. 4th Battalion (Territorial).

Davenport, Hughes Nares, M.C., Major, k. in a., 26/3/18.
Hadden, Eustace Waller Russell, Major, died, 11/6/16.
Allan, Archibald, M.C., Capt., d. of w., 17/6/18.
Blake, Jerrold Edward, Capt., k. in a., 23/7/16.
Brooks, Bazil Benjamin Burgoyne, Capt., k. in a., 23/7/16.
Brown, Kenneth Edward, M.C. & Bar, Capt., d. of w., 12/4/18 (in German hands).
Buxton, Richard Percy, A/Capt., k. in a., 15/6/18.
Dashwood, Ernest George, Capt., k. in a., 12/5/15.
Griffin, Innes Edward, Capt., d. of w., 19/2/16.
Stockton, James Godfrey, Capt., k. in a., 22/8/17.
Treble, James Noel, Capt., k. in a., 18/10/15.
Wayman, William Ambler, Capt., k. in a., 14/8/16.
Wotherspoon, Andrew Scott, Capt., k. in a., 16/8/17.
Barton, Charles John, Lt., k. in a., 7/4/17.
Bianchi, Edward Almachilde, Lt., k. in a., 21/3/18.
Callender, John Clement, Lt., k. in a., 21/8/17.
Doyne, Philip Denys, Lt., k. in a., 29/12/15.
Hall, Theodore Newman, Lt., d. of w., 15/8/16.
Hunter, Leslie Whitaker, Lt., k. in a., 14/8/16.
Jefferson, Hamilton, Lt., k. in a., 16/8/17.
Jones, Felix Ernest, M.C., Lt., k. in a., 16/8/17.
Lake, Reginald St. George, Lt., k. in a., 17/11/16.
Lakin, Charles, Lt., d. of w., 21/8/16.
Scott, William Douglas, Lt., k. in a., 22/8/17.
Tiddy, Reginald John Elliott, Lt., k. in a., 10/8/16.
Vyner, Cuthbert Jack Sigfrid, Lt., d. of w., 24/7/15.
Wilkins, Vernon Spencer, Lt., died, 11/11/18.
Allden, Joseph Henry, 2/Lt., k. in a., 28/4/17.
Bowman, Claude Herbert, 2/Lt., k. in a., 16/8/17.
Bulmer, John Legge, 2/Lt., k. in a., 3/5/17.
Copinger, John Patrick, 2/Lt., k. in a., 10/9/17.
Coucher, George Walter, 2/Lt., k. in a., 15/4/18.
Flory, William Henry, 2/Lt., k. in a., 21/3/18.
Frieake, Gordon Minter, 2/Lt., died, 1/8/16.
Fry, Arthur Charles, 2/Lt., d. of w., 28/2/17.
Gascoyne, William Elhanan, 2/Lt., k. in a., 22/8/17.
Gefeall, George, 2/Lt., k. in a., 23/3/18.
Gibson, Herbert Edwin, 2/Lt., k. in a., 7/8/17.
Hermon-Hodge, John Percival, 2/Lt., k. in a., 28/5/15.
Hughes, Thomas Derfel, 2/Lt., k. in a., 3/5/16.
King, John Skelton Clarke, 2/Lt., k. in a., 3/5/16.
Lidsey, William John, 2/Lt., d. of w., 22/3/17 (and R.F.C.).
Lindsey, Paul, 2/Lt., k. in a., 2/6/17.
Mallett, William James, 2/Lt., k. in a., 21/3/18.
Pett, Joseph, 2/Lt., k. in a., 21/3/18.
Rawlinson, Godfrey Marshall, 2/Lt., d. of w., 16/7/16.
Salmon, Andrew Frank, 2/Lt., killed, 16/8/17.
Sutherland, George Harry, 2/Lt., k. in a., 21/3/18.
Tilley, Alan Herbert, 2/Lt., d. of w., 10/4/17.
Turrell, Henry Gifford, 2/Lt., d. of w., 3/11/17.
Zeder, Joseph Herbert, 2/Lt., d. of w., 3/7/16 (in German hands).

The Oxfordshire and Buckinghamshire Light Infantry. Buckinghamshire Battalion (Territorial).

Wright, Egerton Lowndes, M.C., Capt. (Bde. Major), k. in a., 11/5/18.
Backhouse, John William, Capt., k. in a., 10/2/16.
Birchall, Edward Vivian Dearman, D.S.O., Capt., d. of w., 10/8/16.
Bowen, Martin, M.C., Capt., d. of w., 9/10/17.
Church, Harold, Capt., k. in a., 19/7/16.
Crouch, Lionel William, Capt., k. in a., 21/7/16.
Foster, Hedley Roy, Capt., k. in a., 22/8/17.
Gregson-Ellis, Reginald George, T/Capt., d. of w., 17/4/17.
Neave, Gerald Vansitart, Capt., k. in a., 16/8/17.
Atkinson, Geoffrey William, Lt., k. in a., 19/7/16.
Bates, Eric George Henry, Lt., k. in a., 23/8/16.
Chadwick, Douglas Gordon, Lt., d. of w., 20/7/16.
Chapman, John Percy, Lt., k. in a., 21/7/16.
Dipple, Thomas Denis, Lt., died, 30/11/18.
Duxbury, Andrew Marshall, Lt., k. in a., 30/3/18.
Garlick, Vivian, Lt., k. in a., 15/6/18.
Heath, Walter Rowland, T/Lt., k. in a., 23/8/16.
Norwood, Robert Cecil, Lt., k. in a., 18/7/16.
Phipps, Charles Percy, Lt., k. in a., 19/7/16.
Abrey, Charles Gordon, 2/Lt., k. in a., 21/7/16.
Brown, Edgar Archer, 2/Lt., k. in a., 23/8/18.
Carruthers, William Keith, 2/Lt., k. in a., 3/4/17.
Furley, Robert Basil, 2/Lt., k. in a., 25/1/16.
Gill, William Rey, 2/Lt., k. in a., 21/8/17.
Hall, Charles, 2/Lt., d. of w., 13/8/16.
Hudson, Roland Burton, 2/Lt., k. in a., 19/7/16.
Hughes, Fred Micklewright, 2/Lt., k. in a., 23/3/18.
Kemp, Sydney Frank, M.C., 2/Lt., k. in a., 16/4/18.
Molloy, Henry Edward, 2/Lt., k. in a., 22/8/17.
Morten, Lewis James, 2/Lt., k. in a., 4/11/18.
Quale, Charles Philip, 2/Lt., k. in a., 15/6/16.

Rolfe, Wilfred Edwin, 2/Lt., k. in a., 22/8/17.
Taylor, Herbert Samuel, 2/Lt., k. in a., 28/4/17.
Trimmer, William Charles, 2/Lt., k. in a., 21/7/16.
Tyson, Claude Richmond, 2/Lt., k. in a., 22/8/17.
Vokes, Basil, 2/Lt., k. in a., 15/2/17.

The Essex Regiment.

4th Battalion (Territorial).

Awbery, Charles Luker, M.C., Capt., k. in a., 31/7/17.
Beddon, John Frederick Heber, Capt., k. in a., 3/11/17.
Cowan, John Grave, Capt., k. in a., 16/8/15.
Meggy, Frederick Arthur, Lt. (A/Capt.), k. in a., 31/8/18.
New, Athelstan William, Capt., died, 15/5/18.
Tyler, Harold Robert, Capt., k. in a., 18/8/15.
Barber, John, Lt., k. in a., 27/9/17.
Black, William Thomas, Lt., k. in a., 24/9/17.
Butcher, Vivian Haweis, Lt., d. of w., 27/3/17.
Clapham, Barnard Aubrey, Lt., d. of w., 27/3/17.
Harrison, William Henry, Lt. (Tp.), k. in a., 24/1/17.
King, Horace Reginald Edward, Lt., k. in a., 28/3/18.
Macadam, James Ferrier, Lt., died, 19/11/18.
Macadam, John, Lt., d. of w., 18/8/15.
Marshall, John Morice Maitland, Lt., d. of w., 23/10/15.
New, Hedley Bruce, Lt., k. in a., 31/10/17 (R.F.C.).
Thomas, William Stanley, Lt., k. in a., 15/10/16.
Todd, William Henry, Lt. & Qr.-Mr., died, 28/8/15.
Allpass, Henry Blythe King, 2/Lt., k. in a., 16/9/16.
Chambers, John Paul, 2/Lt., d. of w., 4/4/17.
Hall, Thomas, 2/Lt., d. of w., 19/6/18.
Hambleton, Walter Edwin, 2/Lt., k. in a., 21/3/18.
Hickman, Ernest John, 2/Lt., k. in a., 16/8/15.
Hodge, Leslie Richard, 2/Lt., k. in a., 17/7/17.
Lancaster, Henry Robert, 2/Lt., k. in a., 2/11/17.
Lawrence, Harry Joseph, 2/Lt., k. in a., 26/4/18.
Noble, Henry Austin, 2/Lt., d. of w., 8/10/18.
Richardson, Geoffrey Oliver, 2/Lt., k. in a., 26/3/17.
Saunders, Ernest Manners, 2/Lt., d. of w., 4/12/17.
Saunders, Samuel George Yarrow, 2/Lt., k. in a., 3/11/17.
Secker, John Devereux, 2/Lt., died, 12/12/16.
Smith, Alan Douglas Hay, 2/Lt., k. in a., 26/3/17.
Theak, Horace Leonard, 2/Lt., d. of w., 4/5/17.
Walch, Brian James Brett, 2/Lt., d. of w., 28/10/15.
Williamson, Gerald Coutts, 2/Lt., k. in a., 9/10/17.
Wiseman, Stanley, 2/Lt., k. in a., 10/3/17.

The Essex Regiment.

5th Battalion (Territorial).

Heron, John Maxwell, Major, k. in a., 26/3/17.
Bacon, Frank William, Capt., died, 4/12/18.
Chester, Harry Keppel, Capt., d. of w., 28/3/17.
Denton, Arthur, Capt., k. in a., 16/8/15.
Fordham, Reginald Frederick, 2/Lt. (A/Capt.), k. in a., 5/11/17.
Gould, Cecil Arbuthnot, Capt., k. in a., 26/3/17.
Gray, Leonard, Capt., died, 31/7/17.
Beard, Edwin Cyril, Lt., k. in a., 26/3/17.
Bartley, Frederick John, Lt., k. in a., 26/3/17.
Box, Harold Francis, Lt., k. in a., 29/10/18.
Browett, Thomas Norman, Lt., died, 30/10/18.
Compton, Rex, Lt., k. in a., 12/8/17.
Evans, William Henry, Lt., k. in a., 2/11/17.
Wilson, Charles Oscar, Lt., k. in a., 26/3/17.
Bird, Charles Edwin, 2/Lt., k. in a., 17/2/17.
Bowles, Wilfred Spencer, 2/Lt., k. in a., 10/7/16 (and M.G.C.).
Burke, Roland Edmund, 2/Lt., d. of w., 17/11/18.
Cooper-Smith, Reginald B., 2/Lt., k. in a., 10/3/17.
Edmunds, Charles Vincent, 2/Lt., k. in a., 26/3/17.
Hill, Eric Battley, 2/Lt., died, 19/11/16.
Household, Ernest Scott, 2/Lt., died, 22/7/17.
Ibbotson, Rubert, 2/Lt, k. in a., 28/4/17.
Klein, Albert John, 2/Lt., k. in a., 14/10/18.
Moore, William Addison Hone, 2/Lt., k. in a., 5/5/17.
Morgan, Clarence William Harding, 2/Lt., k. in a., 23/10/18.
Newth, Howard Rutherford, 2/Lt., k. in a., 14/4/17.
Pearson, Arthur James Balfour, 2/Lt., killed, 18/8/16.
Ransom, Frederick Charles, 2/Lt., k. in a., 9/4/18.
Rew, Douglas Jolland, 2/Lt., k in a., 28/6/17.
Sheldon, Archibald Edward, 2/Lt., d. of w., 23/8/15
Turner, Ronald, 2/Lt., k. in a., 15/8/16.
Ward, N. Loftus Moore, 2/Lt., k. in a., 15/10/16.
Wilkinson, William Donald, 2/Lt., killed, 14/11/16.

The Essex Regiment.

6th Battalion (Territorial).

Alexander, Harold Percy, Major, k. in a., 26/3/17.
Clarke, John James Gordon, A/Capt., k. in a., 28/4/17.
Fry, Charles Augustus. Capt., k. in a., 1/4/18.
Knight, Gerald Robert Frank, Capt., d. of w., 17/8/17.
Lowe, Richard Heath, Capt., k. in a., 9/10/17.
Rayner, Leonard Bramhall, Capt., k. in a., 27/3/17.
Retallach-Maloney, Henry Richard, Capt., died, 17/12/18.
Silverwood, Hugh Fletcher, Capt., k. in a., 27/3/17.
Tee, Eric William, Capt., k. in a., 27/3/17.
Beeton, Arthur Charles, Lt., k. in a., 23/8/15.
Best, Douglas Kenneth, Lt., k. in a., 16/8/17 (and R.F.C.).
Cleall, Percy Cawdell, Lt., d. of w., 26/8/18.
Clubb, Howard William, Lt., k. in a., 27/3/17.
Forbes, Leonard Noel, Lt., k. in a., 19/9/18.
Riggenbach, Frank Arthur, Lt., k. in a., 19/9/18.
Smith, Leonard Hale, Lt., killed, 3/11/17 (and R.F.C.).
Stenning, Leslie Gerald, Lt., d. of w., 1/9/15.
Taverner, Harold Percy, Lt., k. in a., 27/3/17.
Asker, Arthur Howard, 2/Lt., died, 30/1/17.
Bishop, Samuel James Webb, 2/Lt., k. in a., 3/5/17.
Parker, Leslie Walter Grosvenor, 2/Lt., d. of w., 20/7/17.
Philips, Herbert Stanley, 2/Lt., k. in a., 26/3/17.
Rayner, Cecil Arthur, 2/Lt., d. of w., 9/11/15.
Reid, Douglas Leman, 2/Lt., k. in a., 21/9/17.
Trumble, William Acton, D.C.M., 2/Lt., died, 9/10/18.

The Essex Regiment.

7th Battalion (Territorial).

Braithwaite, Matthew Woodhouse, Major, died, 9/11/18.
Alford, Edward Nicholas, Capt., died, 11/1/19.
Davy, William Reginald, Capt., k. in a., 21/8/18 (and Tank Corps).
Hetherington, Guy, Capt., k. in a., 27/3/17.
Jones, Gerald, M.C., Capt., k. in a., 2/11/17.
Lawrence, Walter, Capt., killed, 2/1/15 (and R.F.C.).
Taylor, Ernest Reginald, M.C., Capt., k. in a., 11/8/18.
Wilson, Kenneth Felix, Capt., k. in a., 2/11/17.
Bailey, Arthur MacDougall, Lt., k. in a., 22/8/18.
Barrett, Walter Ralph, Lt., k. in a., 2/11/17.
Brasted, Frederick Elliott, Lt., died, 18/8/17.
Butterworth, Stanley Woodall, Lt., died, 16/1/18.
Champ, Leonard, Lt., died, 19/3/18.
Davies, Norman Stollard, Lt., k. in a., 2/9/18.
Foxon, Harold Richard, Lt., k. in a., 28/8/18.
Pelly, Herbert Richard, Lt., k. in a., 9/10/15.
Box, Reginald George, 2/Lt., k. in a., 30/11/17.
Brooke, Herbert Leonard, 2/Lt., k. in a., 12/4/18.
Cook, Henry Vincent, 2/Lt., k. in a., 21/3/18.
Coombs, Percy Douglas, 2/Lt., k. in a., 14/4/17.
Cutler, Edward Trevor, 2/Lt., k. in a., 9/8/17.
Eden, Arthur George, 2/Lt, k. in a., 21/5/18.
Gill, William Gerald Oliver, 2/Lt., k. in a., 27/3/17.
Gould, Roy Ernest, 2/Lt., k. in a., 27/3/17.
Lewis, Edmund Llewelyn, 2/Lt., k. in a., 26/12/16 (and R.F.C.).
Lewis, William Thomas, 2/Lt., k. in a., 27/3/17.
Marchant, Frederick Louis, 2/Lt., killed, 20/11/17.
Scott, Cecil, 2/Lt., k. in a., 31/7/17.
Singer, Ernest Henry Percy, 2/Lt., k. in a., 28/3/18.
Smith, Charles Maxwell, 2/Lt, k. in a., 3/5/17
Smith, Ernest George Humphrey, 2/Lt., k. in a, 3/11/17.
Standerwick, Edwin William, 2/Lt., k. in a., 20/4/18.
Thompson, Wilfred John, 2/Lt., k. in a., 31/7/17.
Turk, George Deane, 2/Lt., d. of w., 23/6/17 (in German hands).
Tweddle, William John, 2/Lt., k in a., 16/4/17.
Vickers, Ernest Charles, 2/Lt., k. in a., 26/1/17.
Wiltshire, Healey James Armstrong, 2/Lt., k. in a., 19/4/17.

The Essex Regiment.

8th (Cyclist) Battalion (Territorial).

Brunwin-Hales, Greville Oxley, Capt., k. in a., 24/3/17 (R.F.C.).
Croome, William Hardman, Capt., k. in a., 30/11/17.
Hill, Reginald Byng Tower, Lt. (Tp. Capt.), k. in a., 3/6/17.
Neville, Stanley, Capt., died, 6/11/18.
Byrne, Leslie Noel, Lt., died, 8/11/18.
King, W. H., Lt., k. in a., 11/4/18 (R.A.F.).
Orfeur, Howard West, Lt., k. in a., 23/8/18.
Shorter, William John, Lt., k. in a., 24/3/18 (R.F.C.).
Vaughton, Guy Eglington, 2/Lt., k. in a., 20/11/17.

The Sherwood Foresters (Nottinghamshire and Derbyshire Regiment).

5th Battalion (Territorial).

Trench, Charles Reginald Chenevix, Major, k. in a., 21/3/18.
Wragg, Frederick William, Major, k. in a., 1/7/16.
Adams, Percy Ernest, Capt., k. in a., 4/4/17.
Aldous, Stewart John, Capt., k. in a., 26/3/16.
Coles, Henry James, Capt., k. in a., 30/6/17.
Harrison, Percy Pool, Capt., d. of w., 20/10/17.
Lewes, Frederick Henry Meredith, Capt., d. of w., 2/7/16.
Longden, Alfred Henry, Capt., died, 2/3/19.
Nadin, Trafford, Capt., died, 8/6/18.
Stone, Arnold, Capt., k. in a., 29/4/17.
Swan, William, Capt., k. in a., 6/10/17.
Alliban, William Beaumont, Lt., k. in a., 5/5/17.
Claye, C. G., Lt., k. in a., 5/7/18 (and R.A.F.).
Howard, James Kelvey, Lt., k. in a., 11/2/17 (R.F.C.).
Lewis, Lloyd Edward, Lt., k. in a., 24/9/18.
Mackenzie, Donald, Lt. & Q.M., k. in a., 30/9/18.
Mills, Thomas Arthur Reginald, Lt., k. in a., 26/9/17.
Stones, George Herbert Lee, Lt., d. of w., 9/12/17.
Tate, William Edward, Lt., killed, 12/8/17.
Whiston, Philip Selwyn, Lt., k. in a., 21/3/18.
Woods, John James, Lt., died, 17/10/18.
Allen, Walter Smith, 2/Lt., k. in a., 21/3/18.
Badcock, Benjamin Morley, 2/Lt., k. in a., 9/7/18.
Barber, William Geoffrey, 2/Lt., k. in a., 1/7/16.
Barrows, Maxwell Dalton, 2/Lt., k. in a., 3/10/18.
Basford, Bromley Alfred, 2/Lt., k. in a., 4/10/17.
Bates, Alfred Neville, 2/Lt., k. in a., 1/7/16.
Bemrose, Karl, 2/Lt., k. in a., 1/7/16.
Bregazzi, Edward, 2/Lt., died, 9/11/18.
Callow, Donald, 2/Lt., k. in a., 2/7/16.
Cecil, Rotherham Bagshawe, 2/Lt., k. in a., 1/7/16.
Cook, Walter, 2/Lt., k. in a., 16/4/18.
Dornton, Harold Shafto, 2/Lt., k. in a., 1/7/16.
Gent, Alfred Harry Thomas, M.C., 2/Lt., d. of w., 3/10/18.
Godfrey, Harry Frederick, 2/Lt., k. in a., 1/7/16.
Hague, Walter, 2/Lt., d. of w., 31/3/18 (in German hands).
Hibbert, Howard Morley, 2/Lt., k. in a., 1/7/16.
Hopkinson, George Silkston, 2/Lt., k. in a., 18/1/18.
Hunt, John Reginald Lilly, 2/Lt., k. in a., 1/7/16.

Hyde, James Charles, 2/Lt., k. in a., 1/7/16.
Jackson, Noel Bower, 2/Lt., k. in a., 6/12/17.
Jacques, William Gladstone, 2/Lt., k. in a., 17/10/18.
Lakeman, Reginald Noel, 2/Lt., k. in a., 3/10/18.
Loney, Robert, 2/Lt., k. in a., 1/7/17.
McInnes, John Edward, 2/Lt., k. in a., 1/7/16.
Martin, Reginald Frank, 2/Lt., k. in a., 30/6/17.
Mitchell, Thomas Frederick, 2/Lt., d. of w., 4/10/18.
Moore, Charles Arthur George, 2/Lt., k. in a., 19/4/18.
Nash, Arthur James, 2/Lt., k. in a., 13/6/18.
Palmer, Albert Leslie, 2/Lt., d. of w., 6/3/17.
Petty, Alfred Hallam, 2/Lt., d. of w., 17/7/16 (in German hands).
Plant, Robert Sydney, 2/Lt., k. in a., 17/10/18.
Smith, Arthur Hodson, 2/Lt., d. of w., 9/6/18.
Spargo, Loris Stiles, 2/Lt., k. in a., 5/8/17.
Walters, Fred, 2/Lt., k. in a., 21/3/18.
Warmsley, Frank Walter, 2/Lt., d. of w., 22/11/17.
Witt, Charles, 2/Lt., k in a., 22/9/18 (M.G.C.).
Wooldridge, Charles Reginald, 2/Lt., died, 12/10/18.

The Sherwood Foresters (Nottinghamshire and Derbyshire Regiment).

6th Battalion (Territorial).

Johnson, Cyril Benton, Lt.-Col., k. in a., 21/9/17.
Brierley, William Hunstone, Capt., k. in a., 26/9/17.
Greaves, Thomas, Capt., d. of w., 1/7/18.
Hipkins, Fredk. Wystan, M.C., Capt., k. in a., 3/10/18.
Jackson, William Brabazon Mather, Capt., k. in a., 27/4/17.
Marsden, John Horace, M.C., Capt., k. in a., 27/4/17.
Robinson, Francis Bradbury, Capt., d. of w., 3/7/16.
Stones, Francis Dawbarn, M.C., Capt., d. of w., 28/9/17.
Tolson, Joseph, Capt., d. of w., 28/10/17.
Tyler, Herbert Henry, M.C., Capt., k. in a., 17-19/9/18.
Wallis, Alfred Babbington, Capt., k. in a., 21/3/18.
Brown, Cecil Abraham, Lt., k. in a., 23/4/17.
Cree, Charles Edward Victor, Lt., k. in a., 20/7/16.
Evans, Richard, Lt., d. of w., 10/8/17.
Groves, Richard, Lt., d. of w., 24/10/17.
Jellicoe, Eric Maitland, Lt., k. in a., 1/7/16.
Rogers, Stanley Arthur, Lt., k. in a., 21/3/18.
Swale, Arthur Duncan, Lt., d. of w., 5/10/18.
Wheatcroft, Ronald Duncan, Lt., d. of w., 2/7/16.
Wilkinson, Charles Leslie, Lt., k. in a., 21/3/18.
Barlow, Geoffrey Petrie, M.C., 2/Lt., k. in a., 2/9/17.
Bennett, Albert Henry, 2/Lt., d. of w., 6/11/16.
Bewley, Edward Neville, 2/Lt., k. in a., 26/6/17.
Bimrose, Charles, 2/Lt., k. in a., 3/10/18.
Brown, William Leonard, 2/Lt., k. in a., 25/9/15.
Burrows, Leonard Victor, 2/Lt., k. in a., 2/9/18.
Cooke, Arthur, 2/Lt., died, 22/8/17.
Croucher, Cecil, 2/Lt., died, 26/2/17.
Dickinson, Lewis George, 2/Lt., k. in a., 1/10/15.
Dicksee, Reginald Frank, 2/Lt., k. in a., 8/10/18.
Dolley, Reginald Charles Francis, 2/Lt., k. in a., 30/6/17.
Dunning, Reginald Percy, 2/Lt., k. in a., 21/3/18.
Eyre, A. N., 2/Lt., k. in a., 26/9/18 (R.A.F.).
Finch, Tom, 2/Lt., d. of w., 20/10/17.
Hall, Harry Herbert, 2/Lt., k. in a., 2/12/17.
Healing, Kenneth, 2/Lt., k. in a., 27/4/17.
Holderness, William Harold, 2/Lt., k. in a., 17/4/16.
Holloway, Arthur Grayston, 2/Lt., k. in a., 24/3/18.
Johnson, Leslie Nethercote, M.C., 2/Lt., k. in a., 3/6/17.
Lake, Thomas Ashton, 2/Lt., k. in a., 13/8/18.
Noon, Gilbert, 2/Lt., k. in a., 29/11/17 (R.F.C.).
Oliver, Frederick Richard, 2/Lt., k. in a., 1/7/16.
Paine, Harry Arthur, 2/Lt., k. in a., 29/9/18.
Pollard, Arthur, 2/Lt., k. in a., 21/3/18.
Rollason, Charles Henry, 2/Lt., d. of w., 6/4/18.
Severne, Henry Francis, 2/Lt., killed, 10/5/15.
Simpson, Herbert, 2/Lt., d. of w., 7/7/16.
Smith, John Christie, 2/Lt., k. in a., 21/3/18.
Smith, Robert Yearsley Clarke, 2/Lt., k. in a., 21/3/18.
Streatfield, J. P. S., 2/Lt., died, 3/6/15.
Stubbs, William Arthur, M.C., 2/Lt., k. in a., 9/5/17.
Tomkinson, Percy Alexander, 2/Lt., k. in a., 4/10/18.
Tuft, Gerald Hugh, 2/Lt., k. in a., 27/4/17.
Wood, Joseph, 2/Lt., k. in a., 27/9/17.

The Sherwood Foresters (Nottinghamshire and Derbyshire Regiment).

7th (Robin Hood) Battalion (Territorial).

Hind, Lawrence Arthur, M.C., Lt.-Col., k. in a., 1/7/16.
Hooley, Basil Terah, M.C., Major, died, 28/10/18.
V.C. Ball, Albert, D.S.O., M.C., Capt., k. in a., 7/5/18 (R.F.C.).
Dickins, Albert Light Moody, M.C., Capt., k. in a., 21/3/18.
Dietrichsen, Frederick Christian, Capt., k. in a., 26/4/16.
Durose, Sydney Truman, Capt., k. in a., 2/4/17.
Gascoyne, Charles, Capt., d. of w., 8/5/17 (in German hands).
Gotch, Roby Middleton, Capt., k. in a., 1/7/16.
Leman, Thomas Henry, Capt., k. in a., 1/7/16.
Mellers, George Henry Reginald, Capt., k. in a., 14/10/14.
Round, William Haldane, Capt., k. in a., 1/7/16.
Walker, Herbert William, Capt., died, 12/3/19.
Walker, William Eaton Guy, Capt., k. in a., 1/7/16.
Walton, Harold Henry, M.C., Capt., k. in a., 13/10/15.
Warren, John Crosby, M.C., Capt., k. in a., 21/3/18.
Cairns, Stanley Ewart, M.C., Lt., k. in a., 30/9/18.
Catterall, Albert, Lt., k. in a., 21/3/18.
Cordeux, Edward Henry Noble, Lt., k. in a., 1/10/15.
Hawken, William Victor, Lt., k. in a., 26/4/16.
Hoyte, Raymond Wilson, Lt., k. in a., 21/3/18.
MacPherson, John, Lt., k. in a., 1/7/16.
Perry, Percy Claude, Lt., killed, 26/4/16.
Pyatt, Richard Goodwin, Lt., k. in a., 13/10/15.
Williams, Arthur Montague, Lt., k. in a., 15/6/15.
Ball, George, 2/Lt., k. in a., 21/3/18.
Barnes, James, 2/Lt., d. of w., 28/12/18.
Boyd, Charles Gordon, 2/Lt., k. in a., 3/5/17.
Brandreth, Charles Reginald, 2/Lt., k. in a., 21/3/18.
Bright, Frank Arnold, 2/Lt., k. in a., 13/10/15.
Brodbeck, Edwin Charles, 2/Lt., k. in a., 26/7/18.
Browne, Lionel Charles, 2/Lt., k. in a., 29/6/17.
Burton, Cyril Henry, 2/Lt., k. in a., 1/7/16.
Campbell, Clarence Victor, 2/Lt., k. in a., 26/10/17.
Charles, Albert, 2/Lt., k. in a., 1/7/16.
Collins, Samuel William, 2/Lt., k. in a., 21/3/18.
Cooper, James Alfred, 2/Lt., killed, 17/5/16.
Dean, William Homer, 2/Lt., k. in a., 11/10/15.
Dennis, Edward, 2/Lt., k. in a., 22/3/18 (R.F.C.).
Fletcher, John Harwood Cash, 2/Lt., k. in a., 1/7/16.
Flewitt, Edward Luke, 2/Lt., k. in a., 7/1/18.
Flint, Wilfred Ernest, 2/Lt., k. in a., 1/7/16.
Gamble, Frank Burfield, 2/Lt., k. in a., 1/7/16.
Gill, Leonard Edward, 2/Lt., k. in a., 17/9/17 (M.G.C.).
Hall, Mark Walter, 2/Lt, k. in a., 5/12/17.
Hoy, John Leonard, 2/Lt., k. in a., 21/3/18.
Inglesant, Thomas George, 2/Lt., k. in a., 20/8/16.
Jamieson, John Melvill, 2/Lt., k. in a., 28/4/17.
Jones, Cledwyn Lloyd, 2/Lt., k. in a., 21/3/18.
Langham, John, 2/Lt., k. in a., 18/9/18.
Melhuish, Alan George James, 2/Lt., k. in a., 21/3/18.
Metcalfe, Harry, 2/Lt., k. in a., 4/4/17.
Moore, Hugh Stirling, 2/Lt., k. in a., 1/10/17.
Mycock, Sam, 2/Lt., k. in a., 21/3/18.
Newbury, Sydney Eldridge, 2/Lt., d. of w., 30/6/17.
Peach, Ernest James, 2/Lt., k. in a., 1/7/16 (M.G.C.).
Popplestone, Archibald Harry, 2/Lt., k. in a., 6/12/17.
Powell, William Arthur, 2/Lt., k. in a., 5/10/18.
Reed, Gordon Vernon, 2/Lt., k. in a., 22/3/18.
Ross, Kenneth Cameron, 2/Lt., k. in a., 11/3/18.
Sheldon, Reginald Eley, 2/Lt., d. of w., 15/4/18.
Tootell, Bernard, 2/Lt., k. in a., 23/6/17 (R.F.C.).
Wilkes, Albert Victor, 2/Lt., k. in a., 24/5/18.
Wilkins, Alfred Henry, 2/Lt., k. in a., 1/7/16.
Wilson, John William, M.M., 2/Lt., k. in a., 21/3/18.

The Sherwood Foresters (Nottinghamshire and Derbyshire Regiment).

8th Battalion (Territorial).

Fowler, George Herbert, Lt.-Col., k. in a., 15/10/15.
V.C. Vann, Bernard William, M.C. & Bar, Lt.-Col., k. in a., 3/10/18.
Becher, John Pickard, D.S.O., Major, d. of w., 1/1/16.
Gearey, Albert Edward, M.C., Capt., d. of w., 17/10/18.
Handford, Henry Basil Strutt, Capt., k. in a., 15/10/15.
Huntsman, Benjamin Canning, Capt., k. in a., 7/4/17.
Moffatt, Edmund Craig Forbes, Capt., d. of w., 30/5/17.
Simonet, Harold Keith, M.C., Capt., d. of w., 29/4/18.
Warry, John Lucas, Capt., d. of w., 27/4/17.
Woolley, Thomas Hugh Corbett, Capt., k. in a., 27/4/17.
Wright, Henry Gordon, Capt., k. in a., 6/6/15.
Abrams, Reginald Arthur, Lt., k. in a., 4/3/17.
Daffen, Harold Charles, Lt., killed, 26/4/16.
Dobson, Alfred Frederic Otterbine, Lt., k. in a., 15/6/15.
Hicks, Charles Hubert, Lt., k. in a., 21/7/18.
Houfton, Charles Morley, Lt., d. of w., 12/11/15.
Jeffcock, Harold Charles Firth, Lt., d. of w., 30/5/17.
Logan, George Baillie, Lt., d. of w., 6/5/17.
MacKinnon, Kenneth, Lt., k. in a., 7/4/17.
Williams, Francis Slaney, Lt., k. in a., 20/9/17.
Bailey, Anthony Drummond, 2/Lt., k. in a., 16/12/16.
Bennett, William Henry, 2/Lt., k. in a., 11/4/17.
Bowden, N., 2/Lt., k. in a., 25/4/18 (att. R.A.F.).
Browne, Montague Bernard, 2/Lt., d. of w., 30/4/16.
Carmichael, Chalmers, 2/Lt., k. in a., 15/7/16.
Corbett, John Whitworth, 2/Lt., k. in a., 14/7/17.
Corry, Frank Moring, 2/Lt., d. of w., 13/12/17 (and R.F.C.).
Cowley, Alexander, 2/Lt., k. in a., 1/7/17.
Duff, William Peter, M.C., 2/Lt., k. in a., 23/4/17.
Eddison, John Radley, 2/Lt., k in a., 22/4/15.
Emlem, Harold, M.C., 2/Lt., k. in a., 23/4/18.
Fisher, Geoffrey Herbert, 2/Lt., d. of w., 25/10/15.
Handford, Everard Francis Sale, 2/Lt., k. in a., 15/10/15.
Hemingway, Ralph Eustace, 2/Lt., k. in a., 15/10/15.
Hollins, William Humphrey, 2/Lt., k. in a., 15/6/15.
Kebblewhite, Fred Edgar, 2/Lt., k. in a., 14/8/17 (and R.F.C.).
King-Stephens, Lionel Eustace, 2/Lt., d. of w., 20/12/16.
Strachan, Edward Stanley, 2/Lt., k. in a., 14/10/15.
Tanner, David, 2/Lt., k. in a., 30/8/17.
Viner, Alan Bertrand, 2/Lt., k. in a., 7/4/17.
Wilson, John Hardy, 2/Lt., k. in a., 7/4/17.
Wood, Frank, 2/Lt., d. of w., 23/10/17 (and M.G.C.).

The Loyal North Lancashire Regiment.

4th Battalion (Territorial).

Hindle, Ralph, D.S.O., Lt.-Col., k. in a., 30/11/17.
Nickson, Henry, Major, k. in a., 30/10/15.
Baker, Frederick William Stewart, Capt., k. in a., 20/9/17.
Brindle, John Laurence, Capt., died, 13/3/18.
Buckmaster, Ralph Nevill Lendon, Capt., k. in a., 30/11/17.
Gregson, Edward Maurice, Capt., k. in a., 28/6/16.

Harris, Arthur Lea, Capt., k. in a., 31/7/17.
Hibbert, Cyril Gordon Reuss, Capt., k. in a., 16/6/15.
Lindsay, Henry, Capt., k. in a., 8/8/16.
Peak, John Harold, Capt., k. in a., 16/6/15.
Rennard, Edward Marmaduke, Capt., k. in a., 8/8/16.
Whitfield, John Lawrence, Capt., d. of w., 23/6/15.
Best, Frank Robson, Lt., k. in a., 2/1/16.
Cumming, Anthony Dyson, Lt., k. in a., 6/3/17 (and M.G.C.).
Eddison, Richard de Paiva, Lt., k. in a., 10/8/17.
Fisher, Norman Hill, Lt., d. of w., 16/4/17.
Jump, John Herbert, M.C., Lt., k. in a., 15/9/17.
Kay, Charles William, Lt., died, 3/11/18.
Moore, Keith Hayden, Lt., k. in a., 26/11/15.
Newton, Walter Claude, Lt., k. in a., 4/7/17.
Ostreham, Duncan Haldane, Lt., k. in a., 31/7/17.
Smith, William, Lt., d. of w., 17/6/15.
Wiseman, Phillip Henry Franklin, Lt., d. of w., 27/10/17.
Balfour, Robert, 2/Lt., k. in a., 20/5/18.
Ball, John Harry, 2/Lt., d. of w., 1/9/18.
Bellingham, Alan, 2/Lt., k. in a., 26/10/17.
Boyle, William, 2/Lt., k. in a., 26/10/17.
Brooke, Leonard, M.C., 2/Lt., k. in a., 9/4/18.
Buckmaster, Henry Augustine, 2/Lt., k. in a., 28/9/18.
Cooper, William Randolph, 2/Lt., k. in a., 13/5/18.
Davis, Walter Ambler, 2/Lt., k. in a., 15/6/15.
Dickson, William Herbert, 2/Lt., k. in a., 7/6/17.
Draper, James, 2/Lt., d. of w., 10/11/18.
Duerdon, G., 2/Lt., k. in a., 10/4/18 (and R.F.C.).
Eccles, Walter, 2/Lt., k. in a., 30/5/16.
Edge, Frank Goodair, 2/Lt., d. of w., 10/8/17.
Falby, Edward Frederick, 2/Lt., k. in a., 9/9/16.
Firth, Joseph Oliver, 2/Lt., k. in a., 18/11/17.
Hague, Albert Edward, 2/Lt., k. in a., 5/8/16.
Hailwood, John, 2/Lt., k. in a., 15/10/18.
Holmes, Cuthbert Blace, 2/Lt., d. of w., 28/9/17.
Hutchinson, Peter, 2/Lt., k. in a., 11/9/18.
Johnson, William Herbert, 2/Lt., d. of w., 28/6/17.
Jones, George Morris, 2/Lt., d. of w., 14/7/18.
King, James Norman, 2/Lt., k. in a., 18/4/18.
Livesey, Joseph Harold, 2/Lt., killed, 30/11/17.
McCarthy, Thaddens Francis, M.C., 2/Lt., k. in a., 14/4/18.
Marsden, Herbert William, 2/Lt., d. of w., 11/9/18.
Meyrick, John Charles, 2/Lt., killed, 26/6/17.
Parker, Geoffrey, 2/Lt., k. in a., 11/4/17.
Pyke, William Edward, 2/Lt., k. in a., 9/9/16.
Rawsthorn, Eric, 2/Lt., k. in a., 15/6/15.
Rippin, James Harry, 2/Lt., died, 9/3/16.
Stonehouse, Robert Alfred, 2/Lt., k. in a., 28/4/17.
Walton, Leon Maitland, 2/Lt., k. in a., 17/11/16.
Westwood, Stanley Benjamin, 2/Lt., k. in a., 15/4/18.
Wissett, John Noel, 2/Lt., k. in a., 4/6/18.

The Loyal North Lancashire Regiment.

5th Battalion (Territorial).

Ainsworth, William, Major, k. in a., 16/4/17.
Ford, Robert Englefield, A/Capt., d. of w., 3/4/17.
Hoare, Allen Brodie, Capt., k. in a., 26/10/17.
Makant, Angus Virtue, Capt., d. of w., 14/3/15.
Morris, Harry, Capt., k. in a., 26/10/17.
Pilling, Percy Cunliffe, Capt., d. of w., 6/8/16.
Redfern, Samuel Lees, Capt., d. of w., 2/3/17.
Ward, Ernest Hawksworth, Capt., k. in a., 30/11/17.
Baldwin, Alan Aquilla, Lt., k. in a., 26/4/18.
Blackburn, Ernest, Lt., k. in a., 9/8/16.
Bryans, John, Lt., d. of w., 28/10/17.
Carr, John Stanley, Lt., k. in a., 31/7/17.
Carrie, Fred George, Lt., k. in a., 26/10/17.
Chapman, Alfred Reginald Beeves, Lt., k. in a., 6/6/16.
Dixon, Arthur Edward Basil, Lt., d. of w., 6/6/15.
Eastwood, Sam, Lt., d. of w., 10/5/18.
Forrest, Reginald, Lt., k. in a., 27/9/16.
Glaister, George, Lt., k. in a., 31/7/17.
Grey, Norman, Lt., k. in a., 26/10/17.
Maclagan, James Graham, Lt., k. in a., 1/8/18.
Reid, Robert Vernon, Lt., d. of w., 26/3/18.
Thornley, Reginald Tom, Lt., k. in a., 1/10/18.
Tyldesley, William Knowles, Lt., killed, 26/4/18.
Ashcroft, George, 2/Lt., k. in a., 3/7/17.
Blackburn, Edward, 2/Lt., k. in a., 9/8/16.
Farnworth, James, 2/Lt., k. in a., 9/8/16.
Forshaw, Joseph, 2/Lt., d. of w., 4/10/18 (in German hands).
Frankland, John Cecil, 2/Lt., k. in a., 10/1/17.
Gittins, Herbert, 2/Lt., d. of w., 2/6/17.
Grosart, William David, 2/Lt., d. of w., 15/4/17.
Hartley, James Ernest, 2/Lt., k. in a., 26/10/17.
Holden, Harold, 2/Lt., k. in a., 20/9/17.
Ibbotson, George Sharples, 2/Lt., k. in a., 14/5/18.
Ogden, John Herbert, 2/Lt., k. in a., 31/7/17.
Provan, David Hart, M.C., 2/Lt., died, 27/12/18.
Rice, Edgar William, 2/Lt., k. in a., 9/8/16.
Rimmer, William, 2/Lt., k. in a., 26/10/17.
Sones, Liba, 2/Lt., k. in a., 22/3/18.
Wallis, Arthur, 2/Lt., d of w., 2/10/18.
Williams, Bernard Hallett, 2/Lt., k. in a., 31/7/17.
Wolfe, Bertram, 2/Lt., d. of w., 12/7/18.

The Loyal North Lancashire Regiment.

12th Battalion (Territorial) (Pioneers).

Wilkinson, Horace, Capt., d. of w., 31/10/18.
Mather, Volney, 2/Lt., k. in a., 31/7/17.
Treacy, Eric Henry, 2/Lt., d. of w., 14/12/16.
Vernon, Frank Lawson, 2/Lt., killed, 8/11/16.

The Northamptonshire Regiment.

4th Battalion (Territorial).

Henson, Albert Cecil, Major, k. in a., 22/8/15.
Bishop, Rowland Bridgeman, Lt. (A/Capt.), k. in a., 19/4/17.
Fisher, William Sefton, Capt., k. in a., 23/3/18.
Guy, Christopher Godfrey, Capt., d. of w., 12/8/17 (in German hands) (and R.F.C.).
Murray, Robert Leslie, Capt., k. in a., 19/4/17.
Underwood, Harold Henry, Capt., k. in a., 19/4/17.
Borrow, Frederick Guy Lomer, Lt., d. of w., 22/8/17.
Crockett, Clifden James, Lt., k. in a., 18/8/16.
Gorringe, Noel Rupert, Lt., k. in a., 10/4/18 (and M.G.C.).
Heywood, James George Cross, Lt., k. in a., 30/8/15.
Hope, Humphrey Brian Thompson, Lt., k. in a., 26/4/17 (and R.F.C.).
Howell, E. I., Lt., died, 21/4/18 (att. R.A.F.).
Jones, Robert Nelson, Lt., k. in a., 31/7/17 (and M.G.C.).
Lines, Francis Leonard, Lt., k. in a., 19/4/17.
Manfield, Neville Phillip, Lt., k. in a., 9/9/16 (and R.F.C.).
Marlow, Stanley John, Lt., k. in a., 19/4/17.
Stevenson, Frank Chawn, Lt., k. in a., 22/9/17.
Anthony, Charles Stanley, 2/Lt., k. in a., 19/9/18.
Bull, Ronald Page, 2/Lt., k. in a., 30/10/18.
Barron, Vincent, 2/Lt., d. of w., 4/11/18.
Clark, Claude Frederick, 2/Lt., d. of w., 1/10/18.
Kilsby, George Alfred, 2/Lt., k. in a., 18/9/18.
Mace, Ernest, 2/Lt., k. in a., 10/8/17.
Skillington, Harry, 2/Lt., killed, 18/8/16.
Smith, Frederick Charles, 2/Lt., k. in a., 10/7/17.

Princess Charlotte of Wales's (Royal Berkshire Regiment).

4th Battalion (Territorial).

Thorne, Harold Underhill Hatton, Act. Lt.-Col., k. in a., 9/4/17.
Attride, Raymond George, Capt., k. in a., 14/8/16.
Austen-Leigh, Arthur Alexander, Capt., k. in a., 11/5/18.
Buck, Charles, Act. Capt., k. in a., 15/5/18.
Darby, John Sprake, Capt., k. in a., 28/3/18.
Down, William Oliphant, M.C., Capt., d. of w., 23/5/17.
Dowson, Oswald John, Capt., k. in a., 3/5/17.
Holland, Reginald, Capt., k. in a., 4/4/18.
Willink, George Ouvry William, M.C., Capt., k. in a., 28/3/18.
Freeth, Richard Victor Canston, Lt., k. in a., 13/7/16.
Hedges, Cuthbert Charles, M.C., Lt., k. in a., 8/10/18.
Hunt, Noel Guy, Lt., d. of w., 5/4/17.
Palmer, Ronald William Poulton, Lt., k. in a., 4/5/15.
Ridley, Lancelot Edwin, Lt., k. in a., 19/8/16.
Watson, William, Lt., k. in a., 21/3/18.
Wells, Henry Maurice Watkins, Lt., k. in a., 15/9/16 (and R.F.C.).
Abbott, George Shrubb, 2/Lt., k. in a., 19/7/16.
Bartram, Alan, 2/Lt., k. in a., 14/8/16.
Beasley, Albert William, 2/Lt., k. in a., 14/8/16.
Cecil, Charles, 2/Lt., k. in a., 16/7/16.
Clayton, Norman, 2/Lt., k. in a., 23/8/16.
Clements, Claude Casburn, 2/Lt., k. in a., 9/10/18.
Cutting, Edward James, 2/Lt., k. in a., 9/10/18.
Garside, Thomas Oughtibridge, 2/Lt., k. in a., 5/4/17.
Griffin, Hedley Saunders, 2/Lt., d. of w., 31/8/17 (in German hands)
Heppell, Harry Denby, 2/Lt., k. in a., 5/4/17.
Hill, Albert Charles Leonard, 2/Lt., k. in a., 27/5/18.
MacKinnon, John Angus, 2/Lt., k. in a., 22/8/17.
Nicholls, Harry George, 2/Lt., d. of w., 27/5/18.
Phillips, Ernest Arthur, 2/Lt., k. in a., 2/11/17.
Skene, James Henry, 2/Lt., k. in a., 14/7/16.
Sonnex, Ernest James Harvey, 2/Lt., k. in a., 24/9/18.
Tarrant, Arthur Ralph, 2/Lt., k. in a., 24/6/18
Teed, Henry Samuel, 2/Lt., k. in a., 24/7/16.
Wakeford, George Tarik, 2/Lt., k. in a., 23/7/16.
Wilmshurst, Cecil Arthur, 2/Lt., k. in a., 5/4/18.

The Queen's Own (Royal West Kent Regiment).

4th Battalion (Territorial).

Carlisle, Francis Bruce, Major, died, 31/12/14.
Craig, Arthur Francis, Capt., d. of w., 4/10/18 (and M.G.C.).
Tanner, Thomas Lanfear, Capt., k. in a., 18/9/18.
Wilson, Henry Ivan De Burgh, Capt., k. in a., 19/4/17.
Anderson, Donald Fraser, Lt., k. in a., 27/4/18.
Clough, Hugh Francis, Lt., k. in a., 14/3/17.
Evans, Norman Harden, Lt., d. of w., 19/4/17.
Haslam, Wilfred Henry Westcott, Lt., k. in a., 7/2/16.
Mitchell, Herbert Stanley, Lt., k. in a., 21/3/18.
Stilwell, Montague James, Lt., k. in a., 30/6/18.
Cambridge, Thomas, 2/Lt., k. in a., 3/11/17.
Carey, Mansell Ernest, M.C., 2/Lt., k. in a., 30/11/17.
Coggins, Wilfred George, 2/Lt., d. of w., 15/12/16.
Darlington, William Charles, 2/Lt., k. in a., 4/11/17.
Debenham, Herbert Austin, 2/Lt., k. in a., 1/11/18.
Dunn, Henry Joseph, 2/Lt., k. in a., 26/11/17.
Foster, Harry Langton, 2/Lt., k. in a., 7/6/17.
Gray, David Gordon, 2/Lt., k. in a., 31/7/17.
Green, Henry Arthur, 2/Lt., k. in a., 9/10/18.
Hickmott, Sydney Richard, 2/Lt., d. of w., 1/10/18.
Hollman, William Harold, 2/Lt., k. in a., 16/10/18.
Rudall, Bertram Allen, 2/Lt., k. in a., 17/7/17.
Stewart, John Robertson, 2/Lt., k. in a., 12/4/18.
Stubbs, Alfred Joseph, 2/Lt., k. in a., 22/10/18.
Underwood, Francis, 2/Lt., d. of w., 18/4/17.

The Queen's Own (Royal West Kent Regiment).
5th Battalion (Territorial).

Cooper, George Stanley, Capt., died, 28/6/15.
Dutton, Thomas Dutton, Capt., k. in a., 3/11/17.
Cobb, James Cassels, Lt., k. in a., 23/8/18.
Hartmann, Carl Herbert, Lt., k. in a., 2/7/18.
Hay, Donald Yalden, Lt., k. in a., 11/8/17.
Stephens, Robert Miller, Lt., k. in a., 27/9/18.
Sykes, Walter Ernest, Lt., k. in a., 20/11/17.
Curtis, Ernest John, 2/Lt., d. of w., 22/1/18.
Dodgson, John Henley, 2/Lt., k. in a., 7/6/17.
Fry, Horace Charles, 2/Lt., died, 24/2/17.
King, William Thomas, 2/Lt., k. in a., 29/8/18.
Thornton, Hedley Thomas, 2/Lt., died, 25/1/16.
Young, Alfred Gordon, 2/Lt., died, 31/12/16.

The King's Own (Yorkshire Light Infantry).
4th Battalion (Territorial).

Moorhouse, Harry, D.S.O., Lt.-Col., k. in a., 9/10/17.
Bell, Wilson, Capt., k. in a., 5/3/17.
Burrows, James Cooke, A/Capt., k. in a., 14/4/18.
Chadwick, Arthur Clarkson, Capt. & Adjt., k. in a., 29/10/15.
Chorley, Arthur Reginald, Capt., d. of w., 28/4/18.
Creswick, Wilfred Bertram, Capt., k. in a., 10/4/16.
Hirst, Harold, Capt., k. in a., 24/6/15.
Mackay, Fred'k. William, M.C., Capt., d. of w., 24/10/18.
McNicoll, Malcolm, M.C., Capt., d. of w., 21/11/17.
Moorhouse, Ronald Wilkinson, M.C., Capt., k. in a., 9/10/17.
Roberts, Guy Hepworth, Lt., A/Capt., d. of w., 22/11/17.
Blackburn, John Herbert, Lt., died, 7/2/17.
Haworth, Harold Stanley, Lt., k. in a., 13/8/16.
Horne, Leonard John, Lt., k. in a., 15/6/18.
James, Robert Kenneth, Lt., k. in a., 27/5/18.
Mosley, Arthur Roy, Lt., d. of w., 23/11/17.
Adams, Thompson, 2/Lt., k. in a., 7/10/16 (and M.G.C.).
Archer, Eli Townend, 2/Lt., k. in a., 23/7/16.
Baldock, John William, 2/Lt., d. of w., 21/7/18.
Bates, John Hayes, 2/Lt., k. in a., 31/8/16.
Bramald, John, 2/Lt., k. in a., 9/10/17.
Brierley, George Raworth, 2/Lt., d. of w., 9/5/17.
Broadbent, Cecil Hoyle, 2/Lt., died, 1/3/16.
Brown, Charles Arthur, 2/Lt., k. in a., 5/7/17.
Calvert, Francis, 2/Lt., d. of w., 19/9/17.
Carter, Sydney Robert Eric, 2/Lt., d. of w., 8/7/16.
Clayton, Norman, 2/Lt., k. in a., 14/10/18.
Fox, Ralph Talbot, 2/Lt., k. in a., 25/8/18.
Gardner, Alfred Ernest, 2/Lt., k. in a., 13/1/17.
Glover, John Grenside, 2/Lt., k. in a., 8/11/15.
Gordon, Ernest Arthur Woodhall, 2/Lt., d. of w., 29/7/17.
Green, Frank, 2/Lt., k. in a., 3/11/16.
Gwynne, Roderick Thynne Sackville, 2/Lt., d. of w., 23/5/15.
Hargreaves, Harold, 2/Lt., k. in a., 23/8/18.
Jones, Robert Roland Akrill, 2/Lt., k. in a., 9/4/17.
Jubb, James Critchley, 2/Lt., k. in a., 23/7/16.
Lamb, Thomas, 2/Lt., died, 30/6/16.
McCormick, John, 2/Lt., d. of w., 28/7/18.
Moodie, Douglas Cameron, 2/Lt., d. of w., 15/3/17.
Mountain, Allan James, 2/Lt., k. in a., 23/7/16.
Pierce, Sidney Ernest, 2/Lt., d. of w., 26/12/15.
Rhodes, William Marvell, 2/Lt., k. in a., 16/9/16.
Rickards, David Logan, 2/Lt., k. in a., 19/12/15.
Riordan, Timothy Harold, 2/Lt., d. of w., 6/7/16.
Robertson, James Leslie, 2/Lt., k. in a., 6/9/16.
Sarson, Herbert William Phillips, 2/Lt., d. of w., 20/10/15.
Scholefield, Harry, 2/Lt., d. of w., 28/4/17.
Spedding, George, 2/Lt., k. in a., 20/8/17.
Sugden, Christopher Babington, 2/Lt., k. in a., 25/5/15
Sutcliffe, Oswald, 2/Lt., k. in a., 3/11/16.
Uncles, Charles William, 2/Lt., k. in a., 9/10/17.
Walsh, Martin Oliver, 2/Lt., k. in a., 3/5/17.
Wiseman, Vincent Harvey, 2/Lt., k. in a., 9/4/17.

The King's Own (Yorkshire Light Infantry).
5th Battalion (Territorial).

Watson, William, Lt.-Col., k. in a., 3/5/17.
Bramley, Cyril Richard, Capt., k. in a., 20/2/17.
Campbell, Quentin Hewes, A/Capt., k. in a., 19/7/17.
Creyke, Edmund Ralph, Capt., k. in a., 5/7/16.
Roper, Oliver Stuart, Lt. (A/Capt.), k. in a., 27/11/17.
Sandford, Clement Richard Folliot, M.C., Capt., k. in a., 22/2/17.
Tucker, Alfred, Capt., killed, 8/8/15.
Walker, John Wickham, Capt., k. in a., 5/7/16.
Beall, Albert Ernest, Lt., k. in a., 29/9/17.
Bingham, Montague Hearfield, Lt., k. in a., 13/4/18.
Burnell, Arthur, Lt., k. in a., 20/7/18.
Clayton-Smith, Albert Butler Henkersfeldt, Lt., k. in a., 19/12/15.
Clayton-Smith, Horace Edward Henkersfeldt, M.C., Lt., k. in a., 23/7/17.
French, Ernest Shaw, Lt., k. in a., 12/9/18.
Jones, Ivor Cynric Salusbury, Lt., d. of w., 21/9/16.
Pattinson, Edwin Potter, Lt., k. in a., 3/5/17.
Wadsworth, Maurice Moxon, Lt., k. in a., 9/7/15.
Walker, Joseph Noel, Lt., k. in a., 4/7/16.
Wills, Alban Noel, Lt., d. of w., 7/3/18.
Wilson, Charles Henry, Lt., d. of w., 30/9/18.
Atchison, John Osborne, 2/Lt., k. in a., 13/7/15.
Baker, Arthur William, 2/Lt., k. in a., 28/7/16.
Bentley, Tom, 2/Lt., d. of w., 31/7/18.
Budds, Charles Walter, 2/Lt., k. in a., 8/9/18.
Cranmer, Guy Paterson, 2/Lt., k. in a., 9/10/17.
Cundall, John Ernest, 2/Lt., k. in a., 3/5/17.
Donovan, John, 2/Lt., k. in a., 26/4/18.
Emerson, Max William Pailthorpe, 2/Lt., k. in a., 5/7/16.
Exley, George Allan, 2/Lt., k. in a., 14/1/17 (and R.F.C.).
Fullard, Norman, 2/Lt., d. of w., 22/5/18.
Greenshields, John Arthur, M.C., 2/Lt., k. in a., 27/5/18.
Haigh, Edward, 2/Lt., k. in a., 19/12/15.
Harpley, Robert Ableson, 2/Lt., k. in a., 5/7/16.
Lambert, Frederick Charles, 2/Lt., k. in a., 28/3/18.
Lang, Sidney Drummond, 2/Lt., d. of w., 26/2/17.
Lord, John Frederick Wilson, 2/Lt., k. in a., 9/4/17.
Margoliouth, Alfred Henry, 2/Lt., k. in a., 2/4/17 (and (R.F.C.).
Mayne, Cecil Robert, 2/Lt., k. in a., 30/11/17.
Midgley, Ellis Reginald, 2/Lt., k. in a., 15/11/15.
Miller, Robert Fordyce, 2/Lt., k. in a., 4/9/16.
Pearson, Athelstan, 2/Lt., k. in a., 13/6/17.
Pollard, George Edward West, 2/Lt., d. of w., 3/9/18.
Prior, Herbert, 2/Lt., d. of w., 27/8/18.
Pressly, John Seymour, 2/Lt., k. in a., 15/11/15.
Royle, William, 2/Lt., k. in a., 5/7/16.
Siddall, David Henry, 2/Lt., k. in a., 16/9/18.
Smith, Stanley, 2/Lt., k. in a., 18/11/15.
Yardley, Eric Barnes, 2/Lt., d. of w., 20/7/17.

The King's Own (Shropshire Light Infantry).
4th Battalion (Territorial).

Sparrow, George William Sparrow, Capt., k. in a., 4/10/18.
Wace, Henry Edward, Capt., k. in a., 14/4/18.
Atherton, Walter, Lt., k. in a., 30/12/17.
Clarke, Leonard, Lt., d. of w., 4/10/17.
Gallimore, Hubert Thomas Keith, Lt., k. in a., 29/3/18.
Morley, Gordon Harper, Lt., k. in a., 30/12/17.
Smith, Norman Louis, Lt., k. in a., 30/12/17.
Crabtree, John Hebron, 2/Lt., k. in a., 26/9/17.
Dibben, Harold William, 2/Lt., k. in a., 30/9/17.
Hannon, Thomas James, 2/Lt., d. of w., 1/12/17.
Jones, Griffiths Vaughan, 2/Lt., d. of w., 24/4/18 (in German hands).
McAlister, Gordon Duncan, 2/Lt., k. in a., 10/4/18.

The Duke of Cambridge's Own (Middlesex Regiment).
7th Battalion (Territorial).

Oldendorff, Friedrich Henrich, Major, d. of w., 1/9/16.
Whinney, Edward, Major, k. in a., 26/9/16.
Buller, Richard Francis Montague, Capt., k. in a., 24/8/18.
Challen, Christopher Frank, Capt., d. of w., 13/11/18.
Charlesworth, Reginald, M.C., Capt., d. of w., 9/4/18.
Frost, Eric George, Capt., k. in a., 26/1/16.
Gore, Leonard Joseph, Capt., k. in a., 3/5/17.
Hanbury, Herbert Wood, Capt., k. in a., 15/11/16.
Hurd, Douglas William, Capt., d. of w., 17/9/16.
Keen, Arthur Clive, Capt., k. in a., 10/5/17.
Keen, William Allan, Capt., d. of w., 6/9/18.
Tully, James Kivas, Capt., d. of w., 19/9/16.
Woodroffe, Walter Gordon, Capt., k. in a., 16/9/16.
Adamson, Gilbert Edgar, Lt., k. in a., 25/8/18.
Chettle, Ernest Frederick, Lt., d. of w., 5/4/18.
Glendinning, Duncan Retallick, Lt., k. in a., 16/11/17.
Groser, Arthur Geoffrey, Lt., k. in a., 7/10/16.
Long, Alfred Pocock, Lt., killed, 23/3/17 (att. R.F.C.).
Moss, Hector Albert, Lt., k. in a., 7/10/16.
Prockter, Frederic, Lt., k. in a., 2/10/16.
Robson, Henry Crompton, Lt., k. in a., 12/3/18.
Scott, Reginald Eric Edward, Lt., d. of w., 13/10/15.
Smith, Frank Redfern, Lt., d. of w., 17/11/17.
Stacey, Charles Noble, Lt., d. of w., 10/5/15.
Binns, Eric Douglas, 2/Lt., k. in a., 7/10/16.
Blaxall, Harold Gurney, 2/Lt., k. in a., 8/10/17.
Clarke, Cecil Andrews, 2/Lt., k. in a., 23/4/17.
Cooper, Herbert Leonard, 2/Lt., k. in a., 16/9/16.
Cox, Richard, 2/Lt., killed, 24/8/18
Crawford, Cecil James, 2/Lt., k. in a., 23/10/17.
Curtis, Evelyn St. George, 2/Lt., k. in a., 3/5/17.
Godward, Eric James, 2/Lt., k. in a., 25/8/15.
Harris, Theodore Trevor, 2/Lt., d. of w., 4/10/16.
Hartley, Reginald Humphrey, 2/Lt., k. in a., 3/5/17.
Hatton, John Alfred, 2/Lt., k. in a., 3/5/17.
Hawke, William Baldwin, 2/Lt., k. in a., 7/10/16.
Hoade, Reginald William, 2/Lt., k. in a., 15/7/16.
Honychurch, Terence William, 2/Lt., d. of w., 22/9/16.
Hudson, Charles Edward, 2/Lt., d. of w., 18/12/16.
Lorenzen, Olto Hans Hermann, 2/Lt., d. of w., 2/7/16.
Norman, Stanley, 2/Lt., d. of w., 16/9/16.
Perry, Robert Proelss, 2/Lt., k. in a., 9/4/17.
Price, Montague Leonard, 2/Lt., k. in a., 26/6/16.
Rowe, Philip Henry, 2/Lt., d. of w., 17/9/16.
Smith, Francis Douglas Matthews, 2/Lt., d. of w., 25/1/16.
Taylor, Herbert George Brooks, 2/Lt., k. in a., 16/9/16.
Thomas, Donald James, 2/Lt., k. in a., 21/12/17.
Thomson, Robert Thoresby, 2/Lt., k. in a., 8/6/17.
Turner, John Alvey, 2/Lt., k. in a., 24/2/17.
Webster, Thomas John, 2/Lt., k. in a., 8/10/16.
Westoby, Frank Durrant, 2/Lt., k. in a., 14-16/9/16 (and M.G.C.).
Whitehead, James Edward, 2/Lt., k. in a., 16/9/16.
Whyman, William Arthur, 2/Lt., k. in a., 16/9/16.
Wright, Horace William, 2/Lt., k. in a., 3/5/17

The Duke of Cambridge's Own (Middlesex Regiment).
8th Battalion (Territorial).

Down, John Aubrey, Major, died, 28/11/18.
Ruston, Arthur Cecil, Major, k. in a., 2/5/15.
Blest, Malcolm Alexander, Capt., died, 30/12/15.
Cuthbert, Gordon, Capt., k. in a., 27/4/15.

Dumsday, Cyril Robert, Capt., k. in a., 27/4/15.
Henderson, David, Capt., k. in a., 15/9/16.
Hughman, Cecil Mackenzie, Capt., d. of w., 18/9/16.
Keeping, Claude Jeffery, Capt., k. in a., 24/8/18.
Martin, Horace Edmund, Capt., d. of w., 19/6/16.
Woodbridge, Austin Hale, Capt., died, 28/2/19.
Boustead, Harry Atheling Russell, Lt., d. of w., 5/4/17 (att. R.F.C.).
Carey, Arthur Stanley, Lt., k. in a., 15/9/16.
Johnson, James William, Lt., k. in a., 30/11/17.
Kroenig-Ryan, Alexander Charles Thomas, Lt., k. in a., 24/10/18.
Mytton, Percy, Lt., k. in a., 2/5/15.
Roughsedge, William, Lt., k. in a., 25/9/17.
Stern, Sidney, Lt., k. in a., 19/7/17.
Wells, W. L., Lt., d. of w., 6/5/18 (and R.A.F.).
Abercrombie, Robert Henry Chester, 2/Lt., k. in a., 3/5/15.
Andre, Frederick William, 2/Lt., k. in a., 16/8/17.
Askew, Cyril Horace, 2/Lt., k. in a., 9/4/17.
Attwater, Reginald Henry, 2/Lt., k. in a., 9/4/17.
Batho, Arnold Capel, 2/Lt., k. in a., 15/9/16.
Broom, Frederick John Maurice, 2/Lt., k. in a., 7/6/17.
Colcott, Ernest Harry, 2/Lt., k. in a., 11/9/16.
Clark, William Henry, 2/Lt., k. in a., 6/7/17 (att. R.F.C.).
De Salis, George Roldolph, 2/Lt., k. in a., 21/6/17.
De Salis, Jerome Joseph Fane, 2/Lt., d. of w., 3/10/15.
Duffield, Arthur Edward, 2/Lt., k. in a., 16/8/17.
Galloway, Bernard Thomas, 2/Lt., k. in a., 6/10/16.
Harvey, Leslie, 2/Lt., k. in a., 25/4/15.
Hutchins, Ralph, 2/Lt.. died, 3/6/16.
Kelly, Percy Ewart, 2/Lt., k. in a., 27/4/15.
MacDonnagh, William John, 2/Lt., k. in a., 11/9/16.
Pengelly, William Augustus, 2/Lt., k. in a., 19/5/17.
Sandford, Charles James Vavasour, 2/Lt., d. of w., 6/5/17.
Smith, John Veere, 2/Lt., d. of w., 26/7/16.

The Duke of Cambridge's Own (Middlesex Regiment).

9th Battalion (Territorial).

Cater, John White, Capt., k. in a., 9/7/17.
Hollins-Fisher, Sydney, Capt., died, 28/9/18.
Snowden, Stanley Jackson, Capt., k. in a., 26/3/17.
Blumfeld, Hubert Winterbotham, Lt., k. in a., 23/2/17 (and M.G.C.).
Darrington, Harold Edgar, Lt., d. of w., 20/11/17 (and R.F.C.).
Dicksee, Maurice John, Lt., k. in a., 14/9/18.
Muller, John Herman, Lt., k. in a., 31/10/17 (and R.F.C.).
Pope, Herbert Arnold, Lt., k. in a., 16/8/15.
South, W. B. C., Lt., died, 13/10/18 (and Tank Corps).
Wheeler, Russell Mervyn, Lt., k. in a., 30/11/16.
Coleman, John Albert David, 2/Lt., k. in a., 3/5/17.
Elson, Edwin Arthur, 2/Lt., k. in a., 9/9/16.
Gillespie, Gordon Wood, 2/Lt., k. in a., 13/4/17 (and R.F.C.).
Godwin, William Bernard, 2/Lt., k. in a., 17/2/17.
Hickling, John Christopher, 2/Lt., k. in a., 11/4/16.
Kemp, Basil Aubrey, 2/Lt., k. in a., 3/5/17.
Moorhouse, Rowland Edward, 2/Lt., k. in a., 19/4/18.
Saxby, Eric Yardley, 2/Lt., k. in a., 9/9/16.
Vincent, George Ernest, 2/Lt., k. in a., 17/2/17.
Wright, Guy Powell, 2/Lt., k. in a., 2/7/18.

The Duke of Cambridge's Own (Middlesex Regiment).

10th Battalion (Territorial).

Ball, Leslie Alfred, Capt., k. in a., 4/10/17.
Britten, Edward William, Capt., k. in a., 10/8/15.
Dolamore, Arthur William, Capt., k. in a., 14/4/17.
Foley, Michael James Aloysius, Capt., k. in a., 10/8/15.
Jarvis, Alan Bishop, Capt., k. in a., 10/8/17.
Lewis, Henry Clifford, Capt., k. in a., 4/10/17.
Norrish, William, 2/Lt. (A/Capt.), k. in a., 27/8/17.
Pride, Harry, M.C., Capt., k. in a., 23/4/17.
Sturge, Edmund, Capt., died, 8/2/19.
Watson, Robert Oke Carey, Capt., k. in a., 26/3/17.
Greenwood, Isidore Herbert, Lt., d. of w., 6/7/18.
Grinham, Philip Richard John, Lt., k. in a., 3/5/17.
Haylor, Charles Alexander, Lt., k. in a., 17/2/17.
Hogben, Henry Francis Thomas, Lt., k. in a., 22/11/15.
Hollingsworth, John Gordon, Lt., k. in a., 12/8/15.
Hotchkiss, Felix James Bishop, Lt., k. in a., 3/5/17.
Jefferys, Montague Gane, Lt., k. in a., 18/1/17.
Laughton, H. P. W., Lt., k. in a., 28/5/18 (and R.A.F.).
Parry, Henry Maysmor, Lt., d of w., 11/3/18.
Targett, George Henry, Lt., k. in a., 18/9/18.
Watson, Jack Cecil, Lt., k. in a., 5/10/17.
Bothamley, William Broughton, 2/Lt., k. in a., 25/9/16.
Burbage, Edwin Joseph, 2/Lt., d. of w., 1/4/17.
Harris, Alfred Abraham, 2/Lt., k. in a., 9/9/16
Kerr, Arthur Douglas Garnett Odell, 2/Lt., k. in a., 3/8/16.
Kibby, H. C., 2/Lt., died, 27/10/18 (and R.A.F.).
Lewis, Herbert Morise, 2/Lt., k. in a., 4/11/15.
McFadden, Robert Edgar, 2/Lt., killed, 12/10/18.
Martin, Arthur, 2/Lt.. k. in a., 28/6/16.
Nealon, John Alfred, 2/Lt., k. in a., 4/3/17.
Parsons, Gilbert Newstead, 2/Lt., k. in a., 5/3/17.
Pitty, Thomas John, 2/Lt., k. in a., 25/3/18.
Quibell, George Edwin, 2/Lt., k. in a., 26/3/17.
Rayner, John, 2/Lt., d. of w., 6/7/16.
Sharp, Fred, 2/Lt., k. in a., 3/8/18.
Smith, J. H., 2/Lt., k. in a., 9/7/18 (and R.A.F.).
Weeks, Reginald Skinner, 2/Lt., k. in a., 9/10/16.
Whisson, William Henry, 2/Lt., d. of w., 6/5/17.
Woolley, Wilfrid Edwin, 2/Lt., k. in a., 11/7/17.

The Duke of Edinburgh's (Wiltshire Regiment).

4th Battalion (Territorial).

Little, Charles Hope, Lt.-Col., died, 18/6/18.
Knight, Robert Halley, Capt., k. in a., 19/9/18.
Merewether, Christopher Kerr, Capt., d. of w., 19/12/17.
Strong, William Charles, Capt. & Qr.-Mr., died, 26/7/18.
Burkett, Harry William Bradly, Lt., k. in a., 14/4/18.
De Candole, Alec Corry Vully, Lt., k. in a., 4/9/18 (M.G.C.).
Granger, William Thomas, Lt., d. of w., 21/9/17.
Cooper, Horace Burnaby, 2/Lt., k. in a., 23/10/18.
Hall, Reginald, 2/Lt., k. in a., 8/10/18.
Loder, W. V., 2/Lt., k. in a., 10/5/18.
Palmer, Horace Lewis, 2/Lt., k. in a., 23/10/18.
Pearman, Thomas Henry, 2/Lt., k. in a., 4/11/18.
Simmons, Percy Marston, 2/Lt., k. in a., 20/10/18.
Sloper, Victor Frederick, 2/Lt., drowned, 10/10/18.
Wallis, John Buckridge, 2/Lt., drowned, 10/10/18.

The Manchester Regiment.

5th Battalion (Territorial).

Ainscough, Cyril, Lt., A/Capt., k. in a., 7/8/15.
Brown, Frederick Seddon, Capt., k. in a., 26/5/15.
Dickey, Robert George Alex, Capt., died, 14/11/18.
Dickson, Sam, M.C., A/Capt., k. in a., 20/10/18.
James, Francis Arthur, T/Capt., d. of w., 18/9/15.
Johnson, William Godfrey Easlam, Capt., d. of w., 13/10/17.
Leech, Arthur Charles, Capt., k. in a., 4-5/6/15.
Martin, Harold Young, Capt., killed, 14/4/17.
Phethean, Charles, Capt., killed, 30/3/18.
Rogers, Henry Milward, Capt., d. of w., 26/5/15.
Winterbottom, Dudley Dickson, Capt., k. in a., 7/8/15.
Brown, Gerald Brindley, Lt., died, 21/4/18.
Chaplin, Sydney Stranger, Lt., k. in a., 21/3/18.
Field, Norman, Lt., k. in a., 14/8/17.
James, George Sidney, Lt., k. in a., 4/6/15.
Johnson, Henry Norman, Lt., k. in a., 2/11/17.
Lamb, Eric Robert, Lt., died, 2/11/18.
Martin, George Styles, Lt., k. in a., 23/4/17.
Owen, Wilfred Edward Salter, Lt., k. in a., 4/11/18.
Porter, Harold James, T/Lt., d. of w., 15/8/15.
Stevens, Donald Eustace, Lt., k. in a., 13/3/18 (and R.F.C.).
Brook, Arthur Charles, 2/Lt., k. in a., 4/6/15.
Butterworth, Norman, 2/Lt., k. in a., 9/5/17.
Darby, Norman Leslie, 2/Lt., k. in a., 16/8/17.
Davis, Leo Edwin, 2/Lt., k. in a., 7/8/15.
Downer, Frederick, 2/Lt., k. in a., 2/4/17.
McGeorge, Thomas Leslie, 2/Lt., k. in a., 7/8/15.
Mather, Donald, 2/Lt., k. in a., 2/11/17.
Mellor, Richard, 2/Lt., k. in a., 16/6/17.
Pape, Edmund Rogers, 2/Lt., k. in a., 27/3/18.
Smith, William Cecil, 2/Lt., k. in a., 31/7/18.
Swift, James Herbert, 2/Lt., k. in a., 31/5/18.
Walker, Thomas Cartmel, 2/Lt., k. in a., 5/6/15.

The Manchester Regiment.

6th Battalion (Territorial).

Lee, Noel, V.D., Brig.-Gen., d. of w., 22/6/15.
Davis, Oswyn St. Leger, Lt.-Col., d. of w., 5/4/18.
Worthington, Claude Swanwick, D.S.O., Lt.-Col., d. of w., 14/10/18.
Heywood, Arthur George Percival, Major, d. of w., 12/9/18.
Vass, William, Major & Q.M., died, 23/9/17.
Whitworth, John Haworth, D.S.O., M.C., Major, d. of w., 31/3/18.
Allen, Charles Rayle, M.C., Capt., k. in a., 27/9/18.
Bazley, Walter Neville, Capt., d. of w., 23/5/15.
Bedford, Robert Harold, Capt., k. in a., 25/3/18.
Bowers-Taylor, Archibald, Capt., k. in a., 7/6/17.
Bridgford, Stanley Lyon, Capt., d. of w., 8/4/18.
Brierley, Hugh Colley, Capt., k. in a., 23/6/17.
Brooks, Archibald Buckley, Capt., k. in a., 7/10/17.
Cawley, Harold Thomas, Capt., k. in a., 23/9/15.
Collier, Samuel Francis, Capt., k. in a., 22/3/18.
Edgar, Robert Gerald, Capt., k. in a., 4/6/15.
Holt, Joseph, Capt., k. in a., 4/6/15.
Houghton, John Reginald, Capt., d. of w., 22/3/18 (M.G.C.).
Hunter, Arthur David, Capt., k. in a., 7/8/15.
Jackson, Stanley Foster, Capt., k. in a., 4/6/15.
Kessler, Edgar, Capt., k. in a., 4/6/15.
Knott, Ernest, Capt., k. in a., 22/3/18.
Milne, Alexander Nichol, Capt., k. in a., 7/8/15.
Oliver, Alfred Donald, Capt., d. of w., 24/4/17.
Pilkington, Hugh Brocklehurst, Capt., k. in a., 4/6/15.
Collier, Sidney, M.C., Lt., k. in a., 28/3/18 (R.F.C.).
Gregg, Reginald, Lt., k. in a., 1/10/18.
Horsfield, John Francis, Lt., k. in a., 26/7/17.
Lingard, John Reginald, Lt., k. in a., 21/8/15.
McDougall, Sydney, Lt., k. in a., 7/8/15.
Maitland, Edgar Francis, Lt., k. in a., 24/9/17.
Mills, Tom Rethanan, Lt., k. in a., 4/6/15.
Reiss, Willoughby Emil, Lt., d. of w., 8/8/15.
Taylor, Arthur Cuthbert Brooke, Lt., k. in a., 4/6/15.
Thorburn, Edward Francis, Lt., k. in a., 10/6/15.
Vipond, Hugh, Lt., killed, 28/7/17.
Young, Edmund Taylor, Lt., k. in a., 10/6/15.
Barber, Leonard Harry, 2/Lt., k. in a., 5/6/15.
Baugh, James Thomas, 2/Lt., d. of w., 3/11/18.
Brooks, Rowland Causer, 2/Lt., k. in a., 4/6/15.
Compton-Smith, Roger Noel, 2/Lt., d. of w., 27/5/15.
Cunliffe, Clement Wallwork, 2/Lt., k. in a., 24/9/17.
Donald, Alan James Ingram, 2/Lt., k. in a., 4/6/15.

Farrington, William Bowker, 2/Lt., k. in a., 25/3/18.
Fielding, Herbert Hilton, 2/Lt., k. in a., 28/3/17.
Harman, Arthur George, 2/Lt., k. in a., 20/10/18.
Ingram, John Aldred, 2/Lt., k. in a., 23/4/17.
Killick, Richard, 2/Lt., k. in a., 18/5/15.
Lewis, Charles, 2/Lt., k. in a., 21/3/18.
Maybury, Reginald, 2/Lt., killed, 23/4/17.
Mills, Ben Holt, 2/Lt., d. of w., 29/4/17.
Rainbow, John, 2/Lt., k. in a., 7/8/15.
Rowbottom, Joseph Arnold, 2/Lt., k. in a., 24/9/17.
Walsh, Frank, 2/Lt., k. in a., 12/5/17.

The Manchester Regiment.

7th Battalion (Territorial).

Hurlbatt, Edgar Simon, M.C., Major, k. in a., 27/3/18.
Rowbotham, John Edwin, M.C., Major, k. in a., 26/3/18.
Staveacre, James Herbert, Major, k. in a., 4/6/15.
Bentham, Richard, Capt., killed, 8/11/16 (and R.F.C.).
Bolton, Reginald Lightbown, Capt., drowned, 3/8/18.
Brown, John, Capt., k. in a., 21/3/18.
Grant, Robert William Gordon, Capt., k. in a., 24/5/17.
Rylands, Reginald Victor, Capt., k. in a., 29/5/15.
Savatard, Thomas Warner, Capt., killed, 29/5/15.
Sivewright, William John, Lt. (A/Capt.), k. in a., 2/11/17.
Tinker, Alan Hirst, Capt., k. in a., 28/3/18.
Williamson, Charles Harry, M.C., Capt., k. in a., 27/3/17 (and R.F.C.).
Bacon, Allan Harvey, Lt., k. in a., 6-7/8/15.
Cooper, Charles Morris, Lt., k. in a., 20/10/18.
Freemantle, William George, Lt., k. in a., 4/6/15.
Hamill, William, Lt., k. in a., 16/8/17.
Kay, Henry Norman, Lt., k. in a., 21/8/18.
Leake, E. G., Lt., d. of w., 31/7/18 (and R.A.F.).
Lecomber, Philip Hebdon, Lt., k. in a., 27/3/18.
Rostern, Joseph Norman, Lt., k. in a., 26/3/18.
Thewlis, Harold Darling, Lt., k. in a., 4/6/15.
Thorp, Walter Twiss, Lt., k. in a., 28/3/18.
Tyrer, John Rawsthorne, Lt., k. in a., 9/10/17 (R.F.C.).
Andrew, Frank Douglas, 2/Lt., d. of w., 31/3/18 (in German hands).
Boon, Arthur, 2/Lt., killed, 29/3/17 (and R.F.C.).
Brown, Thomas Fletcher, 2/Lt., k. in a., 30/5/15.
Campbell, William Watson, 2/Lt., k. in a., 9/1/17.
Dudley, Charles Leonard, 2/Lt., k. in a., 14/6/15.
Hague, James Herbert, 2/Lt., k. in a., 23/4/17.
Jenkins, Richard, 2/Lt., k. in a., 11/11/16.
Lomas, Frank, 2/Lt., k. in a., 4/6/15.
Ludlam, Eric Wollaston, 2/Lt., k. in a., 28/3/18.
Mitchell, Harry, 2/Lt., d. of w., 28/9/18.
Pearson, Harold, 2/Lt., d. of w., 27/9/18.
Ray, Reginald Morison, 2/Lt., k. in a., 27/9/18.
Rhead, Charles Henry, 2/Lt., k. in a., 28/3/18.
Taylor, Robert Edward, 2/Lt., k. in a., 12/10/18.
Ward, George Herbert, 2/Lt., k. in a., 4/6/15.
Whittle, Eric Thomas, 2/Lt., k. in a., 23/4/17.
Young, Leslie Duncan, 2/Lt., k. in a., 7/10/17.

The Manchester Regiment.

8th (Ardwick) Battalion (Territorial).

Heys, William George, T.D., Lt.-Col., k. in a., 4/6/15.
Ashe, Edward Neville, M.C., Capt., k. in a., 21/3/18.
Balmforth, Alfred, Capt., k. in a., 31/7/17.
Beaumont, Thomas Somerville, Capt., k. in a., 24/9/17.
Coomber, Horace Bertram, Capt., k. in a., 12/10/17 (and R.F.C.).
Cowan, Philip Chalmers, Capt., k. in a., 8/11/17 (and R.F.C.).
Forbes, Albert, Capt., k. in a., 30/8/18.
Franklin, Percival George, Capt., k. in a., 18/7/17.
Hepburn, Archibald James, Capt., k. in a., 29/5/15.
Hall, Basil Claude, Capt., k. in a., 25/8/18.
McDougall, George, M.C., Capt., k. in a., 30/3/18 (and M.G.C.).
Oldfield, Edmund George William, Capt., k. in a., 4/6/15.
Rose, Herbert John, Capt., k. in a., 4/6/15.
Standring, Dudley Hethorn, Capt., d. of w., 30/5/15.
Thody, Clarence James, Capt., k. in a., 30/8/18.
Whitworth, Henry, Capt., k. in a., 27/9/18.
Bowen, Alan, Lt., k. in a., 7/8/15.
Darwin, John Henry Bradshaw, Lt., d. of w., 5/12/17.
Deakin, Cedric Kenworthy, Lt., k. in a., 21/3/18
Donaldson, John, M.C., Lt., k. in a., 25/3/18.
Egremont, Godfrey Leonard Hobart, Lt., died, 2/5/18.
Eller, Cyrus Radcliffe, Lt., d. of w., 30/5/17.
Entwistle, Charles Egerton, Lt., d. of w., 22/3/18.
Evans, John Edward Martin, Lt., d. of w, 9/2/18.
Gough, Harry Stanley, Lt., died, 13/3/18
Hall, Samuel, Lt., k. in a., 4/6/15.
Heywood, Stanley, Lt., k. in a., 4/6/15
Ingram, William Harold, Lt., k. in a., 4/6/15.
Marsden, Reginald, Lt., k. in a., 4/6/15.
Mayer, John Stuart, Lt., k. in a., 29/1/18.
Senior, Herbert Godbert, Lt., k in a., 28/5/19.
Whitaker, Charles Warburton, M.C., Lt., d. of w., 18/9/18.
Womersley, John William, Lt., k. in a., 4/6/15.
Baldwin, W. E., 2/Lt., d. of w., 25/8/18 (att. R.A.F.).
Collier, Frederick, 2/Lt., d. of w., 11/5/17.
Davie, Sidney John, 2/Lt., k. in a., 10/10/17.
Goodrich, Walter Michael, 2/Lt., k. in a., 25/3/18
Green, John Berks, 2/Lt., k. in a., 11/1/17.
Helm, Frank, 2/Lt, k. in a., 4/6/15
Johnson, Percy Clarkson, 2/Lt., k. in a., 16/5/15.
Kemp, Reginald, 2/Lt., k. in a., 26/8/18.
MacDonald, Alan Leslie, 2/Lt., k. in a., 19/5/17.
McLauchlan, Andrew Youngson Greig, 2/Lt., k. in a., 28/9/18.
Moore, Edward Kerrnish, 2/Lt., d. of w., 25/4/18.
Moran, John, 2/Lt., k. in a., 7/6/17.
Norris, Walter, 2/Lt., k. in a., 7/8/15.
Petyt, John Edward, 2/Lt., k. in a., 27/3/18.
Scott, William James De Vere, 2/Lt., k. in a., 29/5/15.
Tuson, William, 2/Lt., killed, 27/3/18.
Westbrook, Edward Worsley, 2/Lt., d. of w., 8/11/15.
Wilkinson, John Yeardley, 2/Lt., d. of w., 23/12/17.

The Manchester Regiment.

9th Battalion (Territorial).

Cunliffe, Thomas Hathorn, Lt.-Col., died, 25/5/15.
Archbutt, W. H., Major, died, 8/2/15.
Dearnaley, Irvine, 2/Lt. (T/Capt.), k. in a., 23/11/15.
Donnelly, John Verney, A/Capt., k. in a., 9/10/17.
Grove, James Percival, 2/Lt. (T/Capt.), k. in a., 31/7/17.
Hamer, Frank, Capt., k. in a., 7/6/15.
Hartley, William Stuart, M.C., T/Capt., d. of w., 8/10/18.
Stephenson, Douglas Buchanan, M.C., Capt., k. in a., 21/3/18.
Sugden, Harold, Capt., d. of w., 20/6/15.
Wells, William Lewis, Capt., d. of w., 6/5/18 (and R.F.C.).
Wilkinson, Norman, Capt., k. in a., 21/3/18.
Barnes, Bertram Morris, Lt., k. in a., 26/4/17.
Cooke, Charles Earsham, M.C., Lt., d. of w., 24/5/17.
Dale, Robert Jacomb Norris, Lt., k. in a., 31/1/18 (and R.F.C.).
Green, Arthur, Lt., k. in a., 26/3/18.
Knight, Harold Harrison, Lt., k. in a., 27/3/18.
Leater, Henry, Lt., k. in a., 21/3/18.
Marsden, Philip Sidney, Lt., k. in a., 30/5/17.
Reeve, Garnett Norman Bray, Lt., k. in a., 1/9/18.
Ainsworth, Herbert Green, 2/Lt., k. in a., 9/10/17.
Barratt, George Herbert, 2/Lt., k. in a., 9/10/17.
Cope, Gerald Quin, 2/Lt., d. of w., 24/5/17.
Danziger, Charles William Jack, 2/Lt., d. of w., 15/5/17.
Doyle, Henry James, 2/Lt., d. of w., 11/10/17.
Gossling, Donald Foley, 2/Lt., d. of w., 10/6/17.
Hudson, Allan Harrison, 2/Lt., d. of w., 13/6/15.
Hudson, Horace Sayer, 2/Lt., died, 17/11/18 (and M.G.C.).
Jones, Fred, 2/Lt., k. in a., 24/5/15.
Lindley, Ernest William, 2/Lt., died, 18/2/17 (and R.F.C.) (in German hands).
Masson, Alex James, 2/Lt., k. in a., 23/3/18.
Paget, Leslie Herbert, 2/Lt., k. in a., 27/9/18.
Robson, John Matley, 2/Lt., died, 17/7/15.
Stringer, Albert Edward, 2/Lt., k. in a., 7/6/15.
Wade, John Mayall, 2/Lt., k. in a., 19/6/15.
Woodhouse, Percy Aspden, 2/Lt., died, 11/9/15.
Wrigley, Leonard Gordon, 2/Lt., k. in a., 9/10/17.

The Manchester Regiment.

10th Battalion (Territorial).

Clegg, John Hamer, Capt., d. of w., 4/6/15.
Maw, Arthur Rogers, Capt., k. in a., 21/3/18.
Owen, George Webster, Capt., k. in a., 6/6/15.
Reeder, Robert, Capt., k. in a., 6/1/18.
Spielman, Harold Lionel Isidore, Capt., k. in a., 13/8/15.
Clegg, James, Lt., d. of w., 25/5/15.
Cook, Frank Ecaden, M.C., Lt., k. in a., 20/10/18.
Gilliat, Robert Vincent, Lt., d. of w., 25/5/18 (in German hands).
Griffiths, Francis Noot Gifford, Lt., d. of w., 2/6/15.
Horncastle, Edward Henry, Lt., k. in a., 27/5/18.
Norris, William John, Lt., d. of w., 14/10/18.
Stott, James, Lt., k. in a., 19/6/15.
Thorley, Gordon, Lt., d. of w., 7/11/18.
Ascroft, Robert Geoffry Lees, 2/Lt., k. in a., 4/6/15.
Baxter, Gerald William, 2/Lt., k. in a., 9/10/17.
Byron, Harry, 2/Lt., k. in a., 2/9/18.
Carmichael, Gilbert, 2/Lt., k. in a., 21/3/18.
Chapman, Henry Randal, 2/Lt., k. in a., 9/10/17 (or D. of W.).
Emmott, John Barlow, 2/Lt., k. in a., 4/6/15.
Forth, Charles, 2/Lt., k. in a., 30/7/17.
Hughes, William, 2/Lt., k. in a., 26/3/18.
V.C. Kirk, James, 2/Lt., k. in a., 4/11/18.
Kirk, Joseph Lingard, 2/Lt., died, 10/2/16.
Kirk, Tom, 2/Lt., k. in a., 4/6/15.
Lee, James Denton, 2/Lt., d. of w., 22/1/18.
Nevinson, Humphrey Kaye Bonney, 2/Lt., d. of w., 5/6/15.
Stott, Philip Nicholson, 2/Lt., died, 21/3/15.
Taylor, David George, 2/Lt., k. in a., 9/9/16.
Thorp, Frederick Horace, 2/Lt., d. of w., 31/3/18.
Walters, Ernest Henry, 2/Lt., k. in a., 26/9/16.
Yates, Samuel Benjamin, 2Lt., k. in a., 22/12/17.

The Prince of Wales's (North Staffordshire Regiment).

5th Battalion (Territorial).

Boote, Charles Edward, Lt.-Col., k. in a., 1/7/16.
Burnett, William, D.S.O., Lt.-Col., d. of w., 3/7/16.
Knight, John Hall, Lt.-Col., k. in a., 13/10/15.
Bennett, Frank Dann, Capt., k. in a., 21/3/18.
Cotterill, Arthur, Capt., k. in a., 21/3/18.
Fleming, James Hamilton, Capt., k. in a., 13/10/15.
Fletcher, Gilbert Harding, Capt., k. in a., 1/7/16.
Johnson, Arnold Leslie, Capt., k. in a., 14/10/18.
Johnson, Reginald Travernor, Capt., k. in a., 13/10/15.
Mountford, Gordon, Capt., k. in a., 12/6/17 (and R.F.C.).
Ridgway, Henry Akroyd, Capt., k. in a., 13/10/15.
Scrivener, Alwyne Twyford, Capt., died, 5/7/17 (in Ger. hands).
Settle, Mellard, Capt., died, 23/12/18 (in Ger. hands).
Soame, Everard Nixon Buckworth Herne, Capt., k. in a., 21/3/18.
Wedgwood, Arthur Felix, Capt., k. in a., 14/3/17.
Wilton, Samuel Brammer, M.C., Capt., k. in a., 14/3/17.
Aked, Robert Basil Cautley, M.C., Lt., k. in a., 21/3/18.
Belcher, Wilfrid Frank, Lt., d. of w., 17/12/17.

Boddington, Oswald William, Lt., k. in a., 13/10/15.
Bowers, William Aubrey, Lt., d. of w., 3/7/16.
Bullock, G. E., Lt., k. in a., 16/7/18 (and R.A.F.).
Davies, Henry Robert Griffith, Lt., k. in a., 13/10/15.
Lindop, Herbert Cyril, Lt., k. in a., 20/9/17.
Mayer, Frank Bertram, Lt., k. in a., 13/10/15.
Robinson, Eli, Lt., k. in a., 1/7/16.
Trimble, Robert Maxwell, Lt., k. in a., 21/3/18.
Abbott, Eric Goward, 2/Lt., k. in a., 14/3/17.
Aynsley, Ronald Walker, 2/Lt., d. of w, 15/6/15.
Bishop, Nigel Fyfe Watson, 2/Lt., k. in a., 13/10/15.
Bland, Thomas Russell, 2/Lt., k. in a., 20/7/17.
Bowler, Alfred Arthur, 2/Lt., k. in a., 27/5/18.
Bridgwood, Dudley Edwards, 2/Lt., d. of w., 10/10/17.
Butterfield, Charles Williams, 2/Lt., k. in a., 11/5/17.
Chamberlain, Arthur, 2/Lt., died, 11/2/19.
Chapman, Arthur Donald, 2/Lt., k. in a., 1/7/16.
Cockayne, Arthur Edward, 2/Lt., k. in a., 1/7/17.
Craddock, Reginald, 2/Lt., k. in a., 21/3/18.
Davies, A. C. R., 2/Lt., died, 27/10/15.
Davies, Ernest Owen, 2/Lt., k. in a., 9/9/18.
Davies, Frederick, 2/Lt., k. in a., 12/9/18.
Dawes, Oswald Stephen, 2/Lt., k. in a., 8/5/17.
Derry, Daniel, 2/Lt., died, 18/4/18.
Dix, Geoffrey Stewart, 2/Lt., d. of w., 6/5/15.
Ede, Edward Dickens, 2/Lt., d. of w., 13/6/18.
Goss, Raymond George Frederic, 2/Lt., k. in a., 13/8/15.
Green, Basil, M.C., 2/Lt., k. in a., 1/7/17.
Greeves, John, 2/Lt., k. in a., 1/7/17.
Hammersley, Alan George, 2/Lt., k. in a., 14/3/17.
Hill, Alfred, 2/Lt., k. in a., 13/9/17.
Holtom, Charles Fifield, 2/Lt., d. of w., 4/8/16.
Jarrett, Herbert Horace, 2/Lt., d. of w., 6/12/17.
Jarvis, John, 2/Lt., k. in a., 21/3/18.
Krauss, Dennis Hillel, 2/Lt., d. of w., 7/4/17
Lewty, Thomas Edmund, 2/Lt., k. in a., 14/3/17.
Lowndes, Charles Arthur, 2/Lt., k. in a., 13/10/15.
Lowe, John Edmund, M.C., 2/Lt., k. in a., 1/7/17.
Loxton, Charles Edward Holden, 2/Lt., d. of w., 23/5/15.
Masefield, Charles John Beech, M.C., 2/Lt., d. of w., 21/8/17 (in German hands).
Meakin, Kenneth William Glenny, 2/Lt., d. of w., 16/5/15.
Mellard, Richard Bartlett, 2/Lt., k. in a., 1/7/16.
Mellor, Percy, 2/Lt., k. in a., 13/10/15.
Morris, Evan Price, 2/Lt., k. in a., 8/10/18.
Moss, Ernest Sumner, 2/Lt., k. in a., 1/7/17.
Murphy, James, 2/Lt., k. in a., 15/4/18.
Plant, Wilfrid, 2/Lt., k. in a., 28/9/18.
Pollard, William Marcus Noel, 2/Lt., k. in a., 11/4/17
Purslow, George, 2/Lt., k. in a., 12/10/18.
Rathbone, Thomas Ford, 2/Lt., k. in a., 26/9/17.
Smith, Herbert Evans, 2/Lt., d. of w., 18/6/17.
Stacey, Harold, 2/Lt., k. in a., 4/8/18.
Tortoishell, George Henry, 2/Lt., k. in a., 14/3/17.
Townsend, Joseph, 2/Lt., k. in a., 21/3/18.
Watkin, Alfred Charles, 2/Lt., k. in a., 1/7/16.
Wilks, Richard Harold, 2/Lt., k. in a., 30/11/17.
Wilson, Oswald, 2/Lt., k. in a., 19/3/17.
Wood, Reginald Harry, 2/Lt., k. in a., 1/4/16.

The Prince of Wales's (North Staffordshire Regiment).

6th Battalion (Territorial).

Thorne, Thomas Bezly Houghton, Lt.-Col., k. in a., 21/3/18.
Lloyd, John Francis Selby, Major, k. in a., 18/6/15.
Bamford, Oswald Joseph, Capt., k. in a., 13/10/15.
Clay, Arthur Joseph, Capt., died, 18/2/15.
Hipkins, Norman, Capt., k. in a., 28/9/18.
Jenkinson, John, Capt., k. in a., 13/10/15.
Ridgway, Edward, Capt., k. in a., 30/11/17.
Stack, John Masfen, Capt., k. in a., 1/7/16.
Waghorn, Herbert Gilmore, Capt., d. of w., 26/4/17.
Burt, Frank Eliot, Lt., k. in a., 3/10/18.
Canby, Ronald Leslie, Lt., k. in a., 8/5/17.
Evershed, Albury, Lt., k. in a., 1/7/16.
Grace, Mervyn Bruce, Lt., k. in a., 8/5/17.
Newton, William Trafford, Lt., k. in a., 1/7/16.
Shaw, Robert Ramsey Stewart, Lt., k. in a., 1/7/16.
Beaufort, Ostcliffe Harold, 2/Lt., k. in a., 13/10/15.
Blanchard, John Balsillie, 2/Lt., k. in a., 13/10/15.
Brindley, Frank Ewart, 2/Lt., d. of w., 4/10/18.
Couchman, Cyril Seymour, 2/Lt., k. in a., 8/5/17.
Fox, Andrew Stewart, 2/Lt., k. in a., 13/10/15.
Green, Arthur Fairbrother, 2/Lt., k. in a., 21/3/18.
Hartley, Horace Neville, 2/Lt., k. in a., 13/10/15.
Heath, William Hutsby, 2/Lt., k. in a., 1/7/16.
Jones, Horace Birchall, 2/Lt., k. in a., 1/7/16.
King, Alfred John, 2/Lt., d. of w., 17/6/18.
Marshall, Harold Senders, 2/Lt., killed, 31/1/18 (R.F.C.).
Marson, William Henry, 2/Lt., k. in a., 1/7/16.
Neaverson, Percy Charles, 2/Lt., k. in a., 15/4/18.
O'Sullivan, Fergus, 2/Lt., k. in a., 23/4/17 (R.F.C.).
O'Sullivan, Hugh Henry, 2/Lt., k. in a., 10/6/15.
Owens, John Philip Edmund, 2/Lt., k. in a., 13/10/15.
Plant, Hubert Arthur, 2/Lt., k. in a., 24/5/17.
Preston, Thomas Harry, 2/Lt., d. of w., 30/9/18.
Robinson, Harry, 2/Lt., k. in a., 15/4/18.
Wilkinson, Bernard, 2/Lt., d. of w., 6/6/17.
Williamson, Harold Godwin, 2/Lt., k. in a., 1/7/16.

The York and Lancaster Regiment.

4th (Hallamshire) Battalion (Territorial).

Longden, Ernest William, Major, died, 21/8/18.
Richardson, John Watson, Major, k. in a., 3/5/17.
Barber, Herbert Graham, Capt., k. in a., 7/7/16.
Barber, Maurice, Capt., k. in a., 25/11/17.
Beeby, William Sorley Marden, Capt., k. in a., 3/5/17.
Gale, William Newlyn, Capt., k. in a., 3/5/17.
Johnson, Phillip Norman, M.C., Capt., d. of w., 16/10/18.
Marsh, John Lockwood, Capt., k. in a., 16/10/15.
Rodgers, John, M.C., Capt., k. in a., 2/9/18.
Vickers, Charles Goldthorp, Capt., k. in a., 22/11/17.
Wilkins, Laurence Arnold, Capt., k. in a., 25/8/18.
Wortley, John Francis, M.C., Capt., k. in a., 14/4/18.
Conmee, John Alphonsus, Lt., k. in a., 3/5/17.
Dixon, Cyril Maxsfield, Lt., k. in a., 30/8/15.
Eddie, George Richard, Lt., died, 3/11/18.
Harrison, Charles Geoffrey, Lt., k. in a., 27/11/17.
Head, Edward Keith, Lt., d. of w., 11/12/16.
Ibbotson, Arnold, Lt., k. in a., 13/10/18.
Phillips, Stanley Cross, Lt., k. in a., 15/9/16.
Poole, William John Rowland Ernest, Lt., k. in a., 9/10/17.
Reynolds, Sidney Holdsworth, Lt., d. of w., 16/4/18.
Sanderson, Thomas Edward, Lt., k. in a., 13/4/18.
Shepherd, Tom, Lt., k. in a., 17/10/18.
Beckett, Hubert Edge, 2/Lt., k. in a., 23/7/17.
Bowyer, Edgar Raymond, 2/Lt., k. in a., 1/10/18.
Bridger, Arthur Kynaston, 2/Lt., k. in a., 19/7/17.
Clively, John Harold, 2/Lt., k. in a., 3/5/17 (or d. of w.).
Debell, Francis, 2/Lt., k. in a., 9/10/17.
Dixon, John Francis, 2/Lt., k. in a., 12/4/18.
Dyson, Harold Edward, 2/Lt., k. in a., 31/7/16.
Favell, William Reginald, 2/Lt., k. in a., 2/7/16.
Gill, Eric Longden, 2/Lt., k. in a., 30/11/17.
Hart, W., 2/Lt., k. in a. 7/6/17.
Hay, James Blackwood, 2/Lt., died, 29/10/18.
Hobson, Leslie Faber, 2/Lt., died, 12/7/15.
Jackson, Raymond Wilfred, 2/Lt., k. in a., 9/10/17.
Kerr, Robert Thomas, 2/Lt., k. in a., 23/10/16.
Koe, Philip Stephen, 2/Lt., k. in a., 31/7/16.
O'Donnell, Anthony Patrick, 2/Lt., k. in a., 12/6/17.
Reynolds, John William, 2/Lt., k. in a., 7/8/15.
Rimer, William Marshall, 2/Lt., k. in a., 1/10/18.
Robinson, Bernard Oates, 2/Lt., k. in a., 9/10/17.
Sharpe, Gerald Norman, 2/Lt., k. in a., 31/7/16.
Snow, Richard Aslin, 2/Lt., k. in a., 4/12/15.
Steel, Wilfred, 2/Lt., killed, 9/5/15.

The York and Lancaster Regiment.

5th Battalion (Territorial).

Willis, Charles Frederick, Major, k. in a., 7/3/18.
Allport, Thomas Coote, Capt., k. in a., 1/8/15.
Colver, Henry, Capt., k. in a., 19/12/15.
Goodall, Marcus Herbert, Capt., d. of w., 14/7/16.
Gummer, Stanley, Capt., k. in a., 9/10/17.
Hall, Reginald Clifford, M.C., Lt. (A/Capt.), k. in a., 20/11/17.
Hewitt, George Alfred Guest, Capt., k. in a., 27/11/17.
Smith, Stanley Fenton, Capt., k. in a., 9/10/17.
Storm, William George, M.C., Capt., k. in a., 9/10/17.
Allen, Francis Edward, Lt., k. in a., 11/4/18.
Edwardes, Thomas, Lt., k. in a., 11/4/18.
Lucas, Ernest Henry Austin, Lt., k. in a., 7/6/17.
McHattie, J. W., Lt., k. in a., 25/4/18 (att. R.A.F.).
Scawin, William Neville, Lt., k. in a., 15/4/18 (and M.G.C.).
Spencer, Stanley, 2/Lt. (T/Lt.), k. in a., 3/5/17.
Wrigley, Joseph, Lt., k. in a., 1/7/16.
Bond, Alfred Dalton, 2/Lt., died, 22/5/16.
Broad, Malcolm Percy Eyre, 2/Lt., k. in a., 9/10/17.
Cattle, Eustace Shipstone, M.C., 2/Lt., k. in a., 7/7/16.
Childe, Derrick Francis, 2/Lt., k. in a., 19/12/15.
Day, Sidney, 2/Lt., k. in a., 11/8/16.
Dodds, Herbert Alexandra Christopher, 2/Lt., died, 13/6/16.
Francis, Dudley Collins, 2/Lt., k. in a., 13/11/16.
Gibson, Cecil Mervyn, 2/Lt., k. in a., 5/5/17.
Hardaker, Harold, 2/Lt., k. in a., 19/12/15.
Longstaff, Jack Campbell, 2/Lt., k. in a., 7/7/16.
McLaren, Eustace, 2/Lt., k. in a., 22/11/17.
Otton, Gilbert Charles, 2/Lt., k. in a., 20/9/16.
Raley, Walter Hugh, 2/Lt., killed, 14/5/15.
Russell, Thomas Edward Francis, 2/Lt., k. in a., 3/5/17.
Sheard, Arthur William, 2/Lt., d. of w., 17/1/17.
Shooter, J. H., M.C., 2/Lt., k. in a., 10/4/18 (att. R.A.F.).
Taylor, William Pike, 2/Lt., k. in a., 3/5/17.
Walker, George Francis, 2/Lt., k. in a., 7/12/16.
Waring, Frank, 2/Lt., d. of w., 24/8/16.
Warner, Robert, 2/Lt., k. in a., 6/3/17.
Wells, Douglas Henry, M.C., 2/Lt., k. in a., 3/5/17.
Williams, Edgar, 2/Lt., killed, 25/1/18.
Williams, G. J., 2/Lt., died, 27/4/15.

The Durham Light Infantry.

5th Battalion (Territorial).

Biggs, Bernard George Dawson, Major, died, 1/12/16.
Herring, Horner Reginald, Capt., k. in a., 23/4/17.
Hessler, Jacob Andrew Norman, Capt., k. in a., 27/5/18.
Hessler, Jacob Kruse Muller, Capt., k. in a., 23/3/18.
Marley, William, Capt., k. in a., 23/4/17.
Pearson, Robert William, Capt., killed, 15/5/15.
Raimes, Lancelot, Capt., d. of w., 1/6/16.
Wilson, Hugh Russell, M.C., Capt., k. in a., 11/9/16.
Ashwin, Guy John Hamilton, Lt., k. in a., 7/11/16.
Brickell, Frederick William, Lt., k. in a., 20/6/18 (and M.G.C.).
Carrington, Charles Harold, Lt., k. in a., 9/4/18.
Coulson-Mayne, Eric William, Lt., d. of w., 25/4/17.
Crosby, Timothy Hugh Stowell, Lt., k. in a., 3/2/18.
Froud, Harold William, Lt., d. of w., 27/7/17.
Holmes, Eric Cecil, Lt., d. of w., 3/4/18.
Kirby, Arthur Maurice, Lt., k. in a., 25/9/17 (and M.G.C.).

Minor, Philip, Lt., killed, 29/5/18.
Muir-Mackenzie, Sir Robert Cecil, M.C., Lt., k. in a., 12/4/18.
Mullen, A. G. L., Lt., died, 15/2/19 (and R.A.F.).
Townsend, Francis Edward Steavenson, Lt., d. of w., 30/9/16.
Vane-Tempest, Charles Stewart, Lt., d. of w., 25/3/17 (in German hands) (and R.F.C.).
West, Corney, M.C., Lt., k. in a., 27/5/18.
Woolley, Charles Rupert, Lt., k. in a., 28/7/16.
Balmer, Pringle, 2/Lt., k. in a., 27/5/18.
Berry, George Wilfred, 2/Lt., k. in a., 25/8/17.
Brown, James Cartmell Dennison, 2/Lt., d. of w., 28/4/15.
Braithwaite, Arthur, 2/Lt., killed, 11/3/18.
Cowling, Frederick Watkin, 2/Lt., d. of w., 20/10/18.
Crosby, Arthur Barnard Lifford, 2/Lt., d. of w., 24/4/17
Cummings, Thomas Horsfield, 2/Lt., died, 15/7/18.
Grant, John, 2/Lt., died, 24/11/18 (and M.G.C.).
Heap, Frederick William, 2/Lt., k. in a., 23/4/17.
Hill, Cedric Lloyd Graham, 2/Lt., k. in a., 5/11/16.
Kay, Robert Roland, 2/Lt., k. in a., 23/3/18.
Lowes, Ernest Ion, 2/Lt., d. of w., 2/6/18 (in German hands).
Luke, John Norman, 2/Lt., k. in a., 9/9/18.
Newton, William Leslie, 2/Lt., k. in a., 14/4/17.
Parsons, Arthur Oscar, 2/Lt., d. of w., 26/3/18.
Plaskitt, Sydney Vernon, 2/Lt., k. in a., 5/11/16.
Reid, John, 2/Lt., k. in a., 16/9/18.
Robinson, Douglas Eric, 2/Lt., k. in a., 17/9/16.
Summerscales, Frederick David, 2/Lt., k. in a., 9/3/17.
Townsend, Arthur Eric, 2/Lt., k. in a., 15/2/17 (and R.F.C.).
Wilkinson, George, 2/Lt., k. in a., 9/4/18.
Young, James, 2/Lt., k. in a., 24/8/18.

The Durham Light Infantry.

6th Battalion (Territorial).

Badcock, Stanley Edgar, Capt., T/Major, k. in a., 26/4/15.
Aubin, John Fosbrooke Gerrard, D.S.O., M.C. & Bar, Capt., k. in a., 9/4/18.
Brock, Alfred Lawrence, Capt., k. in a., 14/4/17.
Graham, William, Capt., k. in a., 3/5/17.
Hansell, William Booth, Capt., k. in a., 27/5/18.
Kirkhouse, George, Capt., k. in a., 9/4/18.
Marley, William, Capt., k. in a., 23/4/17.
Monkhouse, Joseph Thompson, Capt., k. in a., 27/4/15.
Walton, Henry, M.C., Capt., k. in a., 27/3/18.
Brown, Andrew Norman, M.C., Lt., k. in a., 27/5/18.
Burton, Thomas John, Lt., d. of w., 27/3/18.
Charlton, Douglas Ferrier, Lt., k. in a., 24/3/18.
Gutteridge, Richard Charley, Lt., k. in a., 28/5/18.
Harris, Roland James, Lt., k. in a., 16/9/16.
Hopper, William Joseph, Lt., k. in a., 6/9/18 (M.G.C.).
Murray, Percival William, Lt., d. of w., 2/2/17 (in German hands).
Richardson, William Harold, Lt., k. in a., 14/4/17.
Scott, Douglas Brogden, Lt., k. in a., 9/4/18.
Taft, Thomas, Lt. & Qr.-Mr., d. of w., 23/12/17.
Tyerman, Cyril Laurence, Lt., k. in a., 9/4/18.
Annett, Hugh Clarkson, 2/Lt., k. in a., 15/9/16.
Applegarth, Thomas Forster, 2/Lt., k. in a., 5/11/16.
Bailes, John Thomas, 2/Lt., d. of w., 9/5/17.
Charlton, William Ferrier, 2/Lt., k. in a., 18/9/16.
Fell, Harold, 2/Lt., k. in a., 5/11/16.
Fosbrooke, Cuthbert, 2/Lt., k. in a., 19/7/17.
Greener, Henry, 2/Lt., k. in a., 14/4/17.
Hare, John Maxwell, 2/Lt., k. in a., 24/5/15.
Horwood, Archibald Alfred, 2/Lt., k. in a., 28/3/18.
Kynock, Colin Smith, 2/Lt., k. in a., 26/4/15.
Little, William, 2/Lt., k. in a., 1/10/16.
McCullough, William John, 2/Lt., k. in a., 3/2/17.
Meyer, Llewellyn, 2/Lt., k. in a., 11/6/16.
Miller, John Charles, 2/Lt., k. in a., 27/7/15.
Payne, James William, 2/Lt., k. in a., 14/4/17.
Peacock, David Ronald, 2/Lt., k. in a., 2/10/16.
Peberdy, Leonard Montague, 2/Lt., k. in a., 22/12/15.
Robertson, George Cockburn, 2/Lt., k. in a., 21/7/15.
Robson, Alfred Styan, 2/Lt., k. in a., 5/11/16.
Stuart, Kenneth Bruce, 2/Lt., k. in a., 5/11/16.

The Durham Light Infantry.

7th Battalion (Territorial).

Carswell-Hunt, William David, M.C., Major, died, 5/4/17.
Hines, Charles William, Major, k. in a., 24-25/6/15.
Kirkup, Phillip Austin, M.C., Capt. (T/Major), killed, 11/4/17 (att. R.F.C.).
Bewley, Isaac, Capt., k. in a., 10/10/18.
Dickson, Robert, A/Capt., k. in a., 27/5/18.
Errington, James, Capt., k. in a., 30/8/15.
Forster, Thomas Foreman, A/Capt., k. in a., 31/10/17.
Goodrick, Walter Robert, M.C., Capt., k. in a., 1/1/17.
Grindell, John Flint Lotherington, Capt., k. in a., 20/6/17.
Jacks, Harold, Capt., died, 27/1/19.
Morant, William Miles, Capt., k. in a., 12/4/18.
Shepherd, Norman Robinson, Capt., k. in a., 4/11/16.
Tait, James, Capt., k. in a., 16/6/17.
Thompson, Herbert, Capt., k. in a., 28/3/18.
Wawn, Frederick Middlemont, Capt., k. in a., 25/5/15.
Bannehr, Harold James Thomas, Lt., k. in a., 5/11/15.
Cree, Arthur Thomas Crawford, Lt., k. in a., 12/5/15.
Hopson, Albert Edward, Lt., k. in a., 11/4/18.
Hudson, Arthur Thomas Rawlings, Lt., k. in a., 12/4/18.
Knight, John Percival, Lt., k. in a., 26/3/18.
Little, Herbert James, Lt., k. in a., 26/3/18.
Lynch, Gilbert Edwin, Lt., k. in a., 21/3/18.
Meek, John, Lt., k. in a., 24-26/5/15.
Probert, Sydney, Lt., k. in a., 27/5/18.
Nesbitt, Frank Wallace Rowland, Lt., d. of w., 19/4/18 (in Ger. hands).
Rhodes, Arthur, Lt., k. in a., 25/5/15.
Ridoutt, William Alexander, Lt., died, 19/2/19.
Sayer, Cecil Oversley, Lt., d. of w., 7/6/15 (in Ger. hands).
Scott, John Ellison, Lt., k. in a., 27/5/18.
Tetley, John Charlton, Lt., k. in a., 11/4/18.
Tilbrook, Frank Calder, Lt., d. of w., 10/4/18.
Adamson, Robert William, 2/Lt., k. in a., 26/5/15.
Dalziel, Charles Sutherland, 2/Lt., k. in a., 8/1/17.
Forrest, William Robinson, 2/Lt., k. in a., 12/9/18.
Green, John Feetham, 2/Lt., k. in a., 5/11/16.
Hodkinson, Peter, 2/Lt., k. in a., 23/10/18.
McCann, William Robert, 2/Lt., d. of w., 11/10/16.
Macdonald, Percy, 2/Lt., k. in a., 21/4/17.
Moon-Ord, Charles Denton, 2/Lt., died, 1/12/16.
Potts, Arnold Leslie Leopold, 2/Lt., k. in a., 5/11/16.
Stockdale, Arthur William Sinclair, 2/Lt., k. in a., 24/5/15.
Tindle, Kirton, 2/Lt., k. in a., 26/3/18.
Walker, Sydney, 2/Lt., k. in a., 15/8/17.
Yeaman, Charles Henry, 2/Lt., died, 15/9/16.
Zacharius-Jessel, Victor Albert Villiers, 2/Lt., k. in a., 6/4/17.

The Durham Light Infantry.

8th Battalion (Territorial).

Curry, Ralph, Capt., d. of w., 9/4/18.
Holdsworth, Henry Bernard, Capt., k. in a., 10/4/18.
Johnson, Luther Vincent Burgoyne, Capt., k. in a., 26/4/15.
Lisle, Robert Ernest Bentham, Capt., k. in a., 30/3/18.
Atkinson, Gilbert, Lt., d. of w., 4/10/18.
Bigg, Walter, Lt., k. in a., 27/5/18.
Blair, John, Lt., d. of w., 12/10/18.
Boyd, William, Lt., k. in a., 5/11/16.
Brass, James Robson, Lt., d. of w., 26-27/4/15.
Colley, Robert Archibald, Lt., k. in a., 22/3/18.
Forster, William Oxley, Lt., d. of w., 22/9/16.
Fuller, Leonard Arthur, Lt., k. in a., 17/5/17 (R.F.C.).
Herald, James Herbert Crossland, Lt., d. of w., 24/1/15.
McLare, Alexander Vernon, M.C., Lt., k. in a., 12/4/18.
Marshall, William, Lt., killed, 27/4/15.
Twigg, Albert Ransom, Lt., k. in a., 12/4/18.
Stewart, Vernon Forster, Lt., k. in a., 13/5/17 (R.F.C.).
Watt, Hugo Burr Craig, M.C., Lt., k. in a., 24/8/18.
Banks, Bertie Charlton, 2/Lt., k. in a., 5/11/16.
Bewicke, Ralph Nathaniel, 2/Lt., k. in a., 29/9/16.
Callinan, Thomas William, 2/Lt., k. in a., 25/4/15.
Frost, Joshua, 2/Lt., d. of w., 29/9/16.
Harrison, Frederick William, 2/Lt., k. in a., 27/5/18.
Kay, Melville Herbert, 2/Lt., k. in a., 5/11/16.
Lauderdale, John Maitland, 2/Lt., k. in a., 18/9/16.
Lewis, Douglas David Raymond, 2/Lt., d. of w., 22/4/17.
Pybus, Robert, 2/Lt., k. in a., 14/7/16.
Richardson, Basil Hutton, 2/Lt., died, 31/5/15 (in German hands).
Roan, Walter Tait, 2/Lt., k. in a., 29/9/16.
Robson, George William, 2/Lt., k. in a., 5/11/16.
Russell, Walter Guthrie, 2/Lt., k. in a., 29/9/16.
Wallace, Robinson, 2/Lt., d. of w., 2/10/16.
Wordsworth, Joseph Charles Ditch, 2/Lt., k. in a., 6/4/17 (R.F.C.).

The Durham Light Infantry.

9th Battalion (Territorial).

Bettison, Mark Hedley, Capt., k. in a., 18/4/16.
Coates, George Henry, Capt., died, 25/12/15.
Rutherford, Robert, Capt., k. in a., 15/9/16.
Simpson, Claud Frank Bell, Capt., d. of w., 3/12/17.
Spencer, Harry John, Capt., died, 17/11/16.
Atkinson, Rollo Edward, Lt., k. in a., 20/2/16.
Edgar, John Hammond, Lt., d. of w., 24/2/16.
Hall, Hugh, M.C., Lt., k. in a., 15/9/17.
Haughton, Alfred John, 2/Lt., T/Lt., k. in a., 23/6/15.
Lennox, Frederick William, Lt., died, 1/11/18.
Scott, William Emiley Oscar, Lt., k. in a., 29/9/16.
Strachan, Henry, Lt., d. of w., 29/7/18.
Wylie, William Gladstone, M.C. & Bar, Lt., k. in a., 28/3/18.
Ashworth, James Francis Gordon, 2/Lt., d. of w., 25/6/16.
Bell, Arthur Walton, 2/Lt., k. in a., 28/3/18.
Bell, Robert Norman, 2/Lt., k. in a., 14/4/17.
Brown, Donald Andrew, 2/Lt., died, 22-23/7/16 (in German hands).
Dick, James, 2/Lt., d. of w., 28/10/17.
Dixon, Charles John, 2/Lt., k. in a., 22/6/17.
Field, Oliver, 2/Lt., k. in a., 18/7/15.
Frankland, Edgar, 2/Lt., k. in a., 24/10/18.
Greenland, Richard, 2/Lt., k. in a., 13/4/17
Higgin-Botham, C. E., 2/Lt., k. in a., 5/11/16.
Lawson, Alfred, 2/Lt., k. in a., 16/9/16.
Little, Andrew, 2/Lt., k. in a., 25/4/15.
Paxton, Samuel Turven, 2/Lt., k. in a., 5/11/16.
Ridley, Henry Mills, 2/Lt., d. of w., 23/5/18 (in Ger. hands).
Sadler, Ferrebee, 2/Lt., k. in a., 21/4/17 (and R.F.C.).
Slater, James, 2/Lt., d. of w., 16/11/16.
Steel, John Gordon, 2/Lt., died, 24/5/17.
Tozer, Harold Percy, 2/Lt., killed, 16/12/16 (and R.F.C.)
Tytler, James Hall, 2/Lt., d. of w., 16/9/16.
Walton, Eric Alfred, 2/Lt., k. in a., 16/9/16.
Whiteley, Hubert, 2/Lt., d. of w., 11/10/16.

The Highland Light Infantry.

5th (City of Glasgow) Battalion (Territorial).

Morrison, Frederick Lansdowne, C.B., D.S.O., Col., died, 22/12/17.
Downie, Andrew Marshall, Major, d. of w., 20/7/15.
Findlay, John Alexander, D.S.O., Major, k. in a., 8/11/17.
Jowitt, Thomas Lawrence, Major, d. of w., 17/7/15.
Thomson, Peter McLellan, T/Major, k. in a., 24/12/15.
Aiton, Alexander Hamilton, Capt., k. in a., 28/9/18.
Anderson, Edward Kerr, Capt., killed, 16/3/18 (and R.F.C.).
Buchanan, William Learmouth, Capt., d. of w., 20/11/17.
Frost, Evelyn Fairfax Meadows, Capt., d. of w., 20/12/15.
Fyfe, Thomas Alexander, M.C., Capt., d. of w., 29/8/18.
McDonald, John, Capt., k. in a., 13/7/15.
Macfarlane, Kenneth, Capt., died, 7/12/16.
Milne, James Gordon, Capt., k. in a., 8/8/17.
O'May, William Shields, M.C., Lt. (T/Capt.), d. of w., 3/4/18.
Morton, George, Capt., k. in a., 13/7/15.
Townsend, Eric Travers, Capt., k. in a., 8/11/17.
Barbe, A. E., Lt., died, 27/5/18 (and R.A.F.).
Binnie, David Willis, 2/Lt., T/Lt., k. in a., 27/5/17.
Bennie, Hugh Osbourne, Lt., k. in a., 31/7/17 (and M.G.C.).
Downie, Robert Theodore Manners, Lt., died, 24/1/16.
Duncan, Harold Forrester, M.C., Lt., d. of w., 29/3/17 (R.F.C.).
Fleming, Hugh, Lt., k. in a., 30/9/18.
Gemmell, Andrew Steveson, Lt., died, 5/3/19.
Hardy, Ralph Miller, Lt., k. in a., 4/11/18.
Legate, Francis, Lt., k. in a., 27/8/18.
MacLellan, Lewis, M.C., Lt., k. in a., 30/11/17.
Pratt, John, Lt., d. of w., 23/3/18.
Scott, William Peach, Lt., d. of w., 9/11/17.
Tinn, Farquhar Gray, Lt., died, 6/11/16.
Turner, Alan Macfarlane, 2/Lt., T/Lt., d. of w., 19/12/15.
Alston, James, 2/Lt., k. in a., 28/9/18.
Gardner, Robert Bell, 2/Lt., k. in a., 7/1/18.
Georgeson, William, 2/Lt., k. in a., 3/4/18.
Harbison, Robert, 2/Lt., k. in a., 28/9/18.
Hoyles, Arthur Henry Child, 2/Lt., died, 2/12/17 (and R.F.C.).
Johnston, Andrew Robert, 2/Lt., k. in a., 29/7/18.
MacBeth, John Duncan Gilmour, 2/Lt., k. in a., 19/4/17.
McClelland, Herbert, 2/Lt., d. of w., 2/4/17.
MacDonald, George Cockburn, 2/Lt., died, 17/11/18.
McEwen, Charles James, 2/Lt., k. in a., 18/11/16.
McKey, Hugh Aloysius, 2/Lt., k. in a., 25/3/18.
MacLellan, George Douglas, 2/Lt., k. in a., 28/4/17.
Malcolm, James Waddell, 2/Lt., k. in a., 12/7/15.
May, Ralph Edward, 2/Lt., k. in a., 12/7/15.
Nicolson, Farquhar Murchison, 2/Lt., k. in a., 19/4/17.
Rome, James, 2/Lt., k. in a., 18/11/16.
Sillars, George Alexander, 2/Lt., k. in a., 1/12/17.
Turner, Elliott Douglas, 2/Lt., k. in a., 24/8/18.
Wallace, William Douglas, 2/Lt., d. of w., 22/8/16.
Weir, Charles Sutherland, 2/Lt., k. in a., 30/5/18.

The Highland Light Infantry.

6th (City of Glasgow) Battalion (Territorial).

Easson, David Ernest Craik, Major, k. in a., 13/7/15.
Speirs, George Patrick, Major, k. in a., 1/10/18.
Coulter, Walter McFarlane, M.C., Capt., k. in a., 20/5/17.
Finlayson, Alexander, A/Capt., k. in a., 23/3/18.
Gemmell, Stewart Armour, Capt., d. of w., 22/7/15.
Main, Donald Alexander Mill, M.C., Capt., drowned. 6/9/18.
Ritchie, John. Capt., died, 28/10/17.
Tidd, Ernest George, Capt., k. in a., 13/6/15.
Aikman, William Hudson, Lt., d. of w., 27/9/17.
Boyd, Robert Mitchell Stewart, Lt., k. in a., 12/7/15.
Cooper, Oliver Henry Donald, Lt., k. in a., 8/5/17.
Cowan, Ronald, 2/Lt. (T/Lt.), k. in a., 13/7/15.
Dron, John Kent, Lt., k. in a., 13/10/18.
Harris, Frederick James, Lt., k. in a., 13/4/18.
Hitchcock, Edward Arthur, Lt., d. of w., 29/9/18.
McEwan, George Lamme, Lt., d. of w., 21/7/15.
MacNiven, Alister Orr, Lt., k. in a., 5/9/17 (R.F.C.).
Osborne, John Sydney, Lt., k. in a., 3/9/16.
Ritchie, George, Lt., died, 15/5/16.
Balfour, George James, 2/Lt., k. in a., 15/9/16.
Blair, Thomas, 2/Lt., d. of w., 21/11/18.
Broadfoot, William Allison, 2/Lt., k. in a., 13/7/15.
Brown, John Dunlop, 2/Lt., d. of w., 3/12/17.
Cameron, Macdonald, 2/Lt., k. in a., 2/12/17.
Davidson, Farquhar Biggam, 2/Lt., d. of w., 10/9/15.
Edward, James Daniel, 2/Lt., d. of w., 26/4/18 (in Ger. hands).
Fleming, Joseph, 2/Lt., k. in a., 15/9/16.
MacIntosh, John Hill, 2/Lt., k. in a., 14/4/17.
Macintosh, Kenneth Alexander, 2/Lt., k. in a., 24/8/18.
McKenney, William James, 2/Lt., died, 9/5/16.
Martin, James Adam, 2/Lt., k. in a., 12/7/15.
Melville, Joseph Thomson, 2/Lt., k. in a., 16/9/16.
Muir, Alexander, 2/Lt., d. of w., 27/7/16.
Patrick, Keith, 2/Lt., k. in a., 15/9/16.
Smith, Robert Wright, 2/Lt., k. in a., 12/2/17.
Watson, Norman Campion, 2/Lt., k. in a., 24/4/17.
Wight, John Guthrie, 2/Lt., k. in a., 1/11/16

The Highland Light Infantry.

7th (Blythswood) Battalion (Territorial).

Richardson, James, Major, died, 24/8/17.
Brown, John Rankine, Capt., d. of w., 23/4/17.
Gandy, William Hendry, Capt., k. in a., 12/7/15.
Grieve, William Robertson, Capt., k. in a., 28/4/17.
Myles, John Adam Whitson Douglas, Capt., died, 29/5/18 (and K. Afr. Rfls.).
Russell, John, Capt. & Qr.-Mr., d. of w., 6/10/18.
Weller, George Herbert, Lt., T/Capt., k. in a., 12/7/15.
Dickson, George, Lt., k. in a., 12/7/15.
Galbraith, Norman Dunlop, Lt., k. in a., 22/8/18.
Galbraith, William Brodie, Lt., d. of w., 14/7/15.
Hart, John Gordon, Lt., k. in a., 28/8/17.
Lindsay, David, Lt., k. in a., 15/4/17.
McKersie, Archibald James, Lt., d. of w., 16/7/15.
McKie, William Purdon, Lt., k. in a., 20/9/18.
Muir, James Robert Grant, Lt., d. of w., 17/9/18.
Roxburgh, William Fletcher, Lt., k. in a., 23/3/18.
Bennie, William Robertson, 2/Lt., k. in a., 2/12/17.
Cole, Reginald Price, 2/Lt., k. in a., 20/5/17.
Crombie, James, 2/Lt., d. of w., 24/6/18.
Cumming, Robert John Alfred, 2/Lt., k. in a., 27/8/18.
Galbraith. David Boyd, 2/Lt., k. in a., 20/8/15.
Graham, Lachlan Seymour, 2/Lt., d. of w., 29/8/17
Grant, Alexander, 2/Lt., d. of w., 24/4/17.
Grant, William Gordon. 2/Lt., k. in a., 17/4/17.
Irwin, William Hetherton, 2/Lt., d. of w., 12/2/17.
Johnston, James Valentine, 2/Lt., k in a., 3/4/17.
Lamb, George Ross, 2/Lt., k. in a., 20/4/17.
MacCallum, William Hay, 2/Lt., k. in a., 27/8/18.
Motherwell, William, 2/Lt., d. of w., 5/3/17.
Munro, Fred Ross, 2/Lt., k. in a., 18/11/16.
Price, Charles Thomas, 2/Lt., k. in a., 30/11/17.
Russell, Hamish Galbraith, 2/Lt., d. of w., 16/8/15.
Sinclair, Donald, 2/Lt., d of w., 18/12/17 (and R.F.C.).
Vallance, Harold Leonard, 2/Lt., d. of w., 28/9/18.
Watson, Alexander Bruce, 2/Lt., k. in a., 28/4/17.

The Highland Light Infantry.

8th (Lanark) Battalion (Territorial).

Clark, Douglas, Major, d. of w., 29/6/15.
Ancrum, J. A., 2/Lt. (A/Capt.), k. in a., 16/7/18.
Anderson, James, Capt., d. of w., 5/7/17.
Chislett, Angus Robert Joseph, Capt., k. in a., 24/4/17.
Martin, Arthur James, Capt., killed, 15/5/15.
Brown, David, Lt., died, 23/9/15.
Elliot, Alexander Shiels, Lt., k. in a., 28/6/15.
Woodburn, Leonard Holt, Lt., d. of w., 28/8/18.
Pringle, Robert Gray, 2/Lt., k. in a., 23/4/17.
Pullar, Thomas Hume, 2/Lt., k. in a., 24/8/18.

The Highland Light Infantry.

9th (Glasgow Highland) Battalion (Territorial).

Chalmers, John Stuart, Major, k. in a., 17/4/18.
McCosh, Edward, M.C., Major, d. of w., 26/9/18.
Ancrum, James Alexander, M.C., Capt., d. of w., 17/7/18.
Anderson, Mathew, Capt., k. in a., 22/8/16.
Donald, William Francis Maxwell, M.C., Capt., k. in a., 19/9/18.
Murray, Andrew Currie, Capt., k. in a., 20/5/17.
Osbourne, Robert, Capt., k. in a., 2/3/17.
Alexander, William Fairlie, Lt., k. in a., 12/10/18.
Anderson, Robertson Topping, M.C., Lt., k. in a., 24/10/18.
Baird, Charles Arthur, Lt., k. in a., 12/10/18.
Brodie, Douglas Fontaine, M.C., Lt., k. in a., 12/10/18.
Brown, Douglas Knox, M.C., Lt., k. in a., 30/11/17 (and M.G.C.).
Donaldson, Alexander Howard, Lt., k. in a., 12/10/18.
Galbraith, Donald James Findlay, Lt., k. in a., 25/1/15.
Henderson, Arthur, Lt., k. in a., 4/8/16.
Hill, Alexander, Lt., k. in a., 12/10/18.
Huggan, Robert Elliot, Lt., died, 29/5/18.
Kennedy, Duncan Cameron, Lt., k. in a., 9/9/16.
McCraken, Peter Alexander Earle, Lt., k. in a., 16/9/18.
McLelland, Robert Carrick, Lt., d. of w., 17/8/16.
Malcolm, Archibald Houlder, Lt., killed, 24/8/18
Russell, Arthur, Lt., d. of w., 23/7/16.
Spens, William, Lt., killed, 17/5/15.
Taylor, George Gall, Lt., k. in a., 29/9/18.
Bannatyne, Ian McNiven, 2/Lt., k. in a., 18/11/16.
Beattie, William Marshall, 2/Lt., k. in a., 13/4/18.
Bruce, Andrew Moffat, 2/Lt., k. in a., 29/9/18.
Cranston, John Tennent, 2/Lt., k. in a., 15/7/16.
Duckett. Harold Ager, 2/Lt., d. of w., 7/6/17.
Duckett, Kenneth Lees, 2/Lt., d. of w., 22/8/16.
Duvoisin, John Hurll, 2/Lt., k in a., 15/7/16.
Fife, Gilbert, 2/Lt., d. of w., 16/7/16.
Fletcher, Malcolm, 2/Lt., d. of w., 8/9/17.
Fulton, Hugh, 2/Lt., k. in a., 9/10/18.
Garvie, Ernest Leonard, M.C., 2/Lt., died, 15/6/18 (and T.M.B.).
Grant, Charles Bruce, 2/Lt., d. of w., 8/12/17.
Haldane, Douglas William, 2/Lt., d. of w., 9/4/17.
Henderson, Walter, 2/Lt., k in a., 8/3/18.
Johnstone, James, 2/Lt., d. of w., 17/4/18.
Kerr, James Campbell, 2/Lt., died, 30/3/19.
McGregor, James, 2/Lt., k. in a., 20/5/17.
MacIldowie, Edward John Howard, 2/Lt., killed, 1/11/16.
MacIntyre, John Taylor, 2/Lt., k. in a., 25/8/17.
Maitland, Alexander, 2/Lt., k. in a., 20/5/17.
Monro, Harold Oswald. 2/Lt., d. of w., 21/5/17.
Morrison, William, 2/Lt., k. in a., 20/5/17.
Muir, David Orrock, 2/Lt., k. in a., 20/5/17.
Nairne, James, 2/Lt, k in a., 13/4/18.
Newlove, John Francis, 2/Lt., k. in a., 25/6/17.
Ogg, William Kelly Carmichael, 2/Lt., k. in a., 15/7/16
Page, James Horn, 2/Lt., died, 7/10/17.
Paterson, William Wilson, 2/Lt., k. in a., 15/7/16.
Patrick, Keith, 2/Lt., k. in a., 15/9/16
Raeburn, Alfred Anthony Douglas, 2/Lt., k. in a., 15/7/16.

Reid, Charles Douglas, 2/Lt., k. in a., 15/7/16.
Ritchie, John James Austin, 2/Lt., k. in a., 29/9/18.
Ross, William, 2/Lt., k in a., 12/4/18.
Simpson, David Kilgour, 2/Lt., d. of w., 2/11/16.
Smith, Frederick George, 2/Lt., k. in a., 27/8/18.
Smith, John Marshall, 2/Lt., d. of w., 27/9/18.
Steel, Walter Frank Banfield, 2/Lt., k. in a., 20/10/17.
Todd, John, 2/Lt.. d. of w., 4/7/18.
Urquhart, Alexander, 2/Lt., k. in a., 17/8/17 (and R.F.C.).
Webster, John Frederick, 2/Lt, k. in a., 24/8/18.
Wilson, Conrad Blackadder, 2/Lt., k. in a., 7/2/17.
Wingate, Alexander, 2/Lt., k. in a., 13/10/15.
Woodside, Archibald Mitchell, 2/Lt., d. of w., 23/4/18.
Woodside, Hugh Marr, 2/Lt., k. in a., 15/7/16.

The Seaforth Highlanders (Ross-shire Buffs, The Duke of Albany's).

4th (Ross Highland) Battalion (Territorial).

Robertson, William John, T.D., Major, d. of w., 11/3/15.
Budge, John Henry, Capt., d. of w., 14/3/15.
Cameron, Colin MacKenzie, Capt. & Adjt., k. in a., 12/4/18.
Finch, Aubrey Malcolm Cecil, Capt., k. in a., 7/7/19.
Findlay, Robert de Cardonnel, Capt., k. in a., 11/3/15.
Fraser, Andrew Knowles, M.C., Capt., k. in a., 20/11/17.
Macdonald, Angus MacGillivray, D.S.O., A/Capt., k. in a., 21/11/17.
Macintyre, Peter Brown, Capt., d. of w., 3/8/17.
Mackenzie, Alexander Alan, Lt. (A/Capt), k. in a., 23/3/18.
Stewart, Weston, Capt., d. of w., 27/3/18 (in German hands).
Ballantyne, Philip Hugh, Lt., k. in a., 28/10/18.
Calder, John Kellick, Lt., k. in a., 22/3/18.
Coe, James George, Lt., d. of w., 1/10/18.
Finch, Ernest Wilfred Rupert, Lt., d. of w., 7/8/16.
Harris, Johnny Stringer, Lt., k. in a., 23/3/18.
McMillan, John, Lt., d. of w., 15/3/15.
Railton, Arthur Temple, T/Lt., killed, 9/5/15.
Robson, George, Lt., k. in a., 20/9/17.
Ross, James Andrew, Lt., k. in a., 26/7/16.
Smith, Arthur Leslie, Lt., killed, 22/8/17 (att. R.F.C.).
Sutherland, Noel, Lt., k. in a., 21/11/17.
Armstrong, William David, 2/Lt., k. in a., 12/10/18.
Bastian, Stanley, 2/Lt., k. in a., 9/5/15.
Boardman, William, D.C.M., 2/Lt., k. in a., 28/10/18.
Cameron, Charles Tolmie, 2/Lt., k. in a., 21/3/18.
Clark, David Ian Graham, 2/Lt., k. in a., 20/9/17.
Crichton, Norman, 2/Lt., k. in a., 16/11/16.
Christie, John, 2/Lt., k. in a., 22/7/18.
Daman, Geoffrey Windeath, 2/Lt., k. in a., 24/5/15.
Davidson, Alexander James, 2/Lt., k. in a., 8/4/17.
Dixon, Henry Edward Otto Murray, 2/Lt., d. of w., 10/4/17.
Fitzroy, Michael Algernon, 2/Lt., k. in a., 15/4/15.
Fleming, Frank, 2/Lt., k. in a., 11/4/18.
Fox, Harold Sidney George, 2/Lt., k. in a., 8/4/17.
Hipwell, H. Reginald, 2/Lt., k. in a., 23/4/17 (and M.G.C.).
Jenkins, James Temple, 2/Lt., k. in a., 20/9/17.
Leslie, Edwin Victor Downie, 2/Lt., k. in a., 8/4/17.
MacDonald, Roderick John, 2/Lt., d. of w., 20/4/17.
Mackenzie, James Alexander, 2/Lt., k. in a., 20/9/17.
MacKenzie, Simon, 2/Lt., k. in a., 7/12/16.
McLeod, Angus, 2/Lt., k. in a., 20/11/17.
MacMillan, James Alexander, 2/Lt., k. in a., 20/7/18.
McMonnies, Stuart Menzies, 2/Lt., k. in a., 20/11/17.
Macrae, Charles Eric, 2/Lt., k. in a., 10/11/16 (and R.F.C.).
MacRae, George Pitt Taylor, 2/Lt., k. in a., 9/4/17.
Masson, Alexander, 2/Lt., d. of w., 1/10/18.
Munro, John, M.C., 2/Lt., k. in a., 16/4/18.
Nixon, James Duncan, 2/Lt., k. in a., 11/4/18.
Phillips, William James, 2/Lt., k. in a., 25/7/16.
Simpson, Cecil Barclay, 2/Lt., k. in a., 7/10/17.
Tennant, Charles Grant, 2/Lt., k. in a., 9/5/15.
Thompson, Frank Arthur, 2/Lt., d. of w., 17/8/18.

The Seaforth Highlanders (Ross-shire Buffs, The Duke of Albany's).

5th (The Sutherland and Caithness Highland) Battalion (Territorial).

Corrigall, John, Lt., A/Capt., d. of w., 8/5/18.
MacDonald, William Alexander, Capt., k. in a., 23/7/18.
MacKay, Charles Alexander, Capt., k. in a., 21/3/18.
McKenzie, Ian, M.C., Capt., k. in a., 21/3/18.
Pitman, Arthur Frederick Edward, Capt., k. in a., 3/1/18 (and R.F.C.).
Sutherland, George Angus, Capt., k. in a., 27/7/18.
Clyne, Daniel Miller, Lt., k. in a., 23/7/18.
Fraser, James Carstairs, Lt., k. in a., 21/3/18.
Goepel, Robert Mackie, Lt., k. in a., 17/9/16 (and M.G.C.).
Grant, Thomas Francis, M.C. & Bar, Lt., k. in a., 11/4/18.
McCall, Gilbert Stewart, Lt., d. of w., 20/5/18.
Mackintosh, Ewart Alan, M.C., Lt., k. in a., 21/11/17.
MacRae, Donald Alastair, Lt., died, 16/11/18 (and M.G.C.).
Marks, James Ganly, Lt., k. in a., 23/3/18.
Mowat, James Dugald Lillie, Lt., k. in a., 15/6/15.
Stalker, Robert Macallan, Lt., k. in a., 8/9/15 (and R.F.C.).
Adamson, Alexander Hutton, 2/Lt., k. in a., 9/4/17.
Bartleman, Thomas Edward, 2/Lt., k. in a., 6/9/17.
Brechin, Robert Hood, 2/Lt., k. in a., 30/9/16.
Cairnie, David Dandie, M.C., 2/Lt., k. in a., 21/3/18.
Curtis, Eric Calvin, 2/Lt., k. in a., 28/7/18.
Dunnet, Donald, 2/Lt., k. in a., 15/6/15.
Eadie, James, 2/Lt., k. in a., 15/5/17.
Forsyth, William Laing, 2/Lt., k. in a., 22/3/18.
Holroyd, Benjamin, 2/Lt., k. in a., 13/11/16.
McAdie, David Alister Alexander, M.C., 2/Lt., k. in a., 22/8/17.
Mackay, Angus, 2/Lt., d. of w., 16/11/16.
Mackay, Donald, 2/Lt., d. of w., 17/11/18.
Mackenzie, Donald Lawson, 2/Lt., k. in a., 1/10/18.
Montgomery, Matthew, 2/Lt., k. in a., 20/7/18.
Moore, Clifford, 2/Lt., k. in a., 9/4/17.
Morrice, Charles Smith, 2/Lt., k. in a., 11/6/17.
Paterson, William, 2/Lt., k. in a., 20/11/17.
Reader, William Howard, 2/Lt., d. of w., 30/7/16.
Shaw, Dugald, 2/Lt., d. of w., 27/7/18.
Simpson, Donald, M.C., 2/Lt., d. of w., 19/5/17.
Sinclair, Andrew Bremmer, 2/Lt., k. in a., 10/12/17.
Taylor, Alexander Steven Bain, 2/Lt., k. in a., 23/7/18.
Tolmie, Robert, 2/Lt., k. in a., 13/10/18.
Waddell, Thomas Bryson, 2/Lt., k. in a., 8/4/17

The Seaforth Highlanders (Ross-shire Buffs, The Duke of Albany's).

6th (Morayshire) Battalion (Territorial).

Fysh, Charles Edward, D.S.O., M.C. & Bar, Major, k. in a., 28/7/18.
Johnston, Charles Ernest, D.S.O., T.D., Major, k. in a., 23/3/18.
Anderson, Eric James, Capt., k. in a., 13/11/16.
Bliss, James, M.C. & Bar, Capt., k. in a., 31/7/17.
Edwards, George Eric, D.S.O., Act. Capt., k. in a., 20/11/17.
Macgregor, Andrew Hamilton, Capt., k. in a., 13/11/16.
Mackay, James Alastair Culbard, M.C., Capt., d. of w., 22/7/16.
Mackintosh, John, Capt., k. in a., 23/7/18.
Kennedy, John Alexander, Capt., d. of w., 6/8/16.
Stewart, Gerald, Capt., k. in a., 9/4/17.
Stocker, Arthur Rutterford, M.C., Lt. (Act. Capt.), died, 24/1/19 (and M.G.C.).
Taylor, Andrew Leitch, Tp. Capt., k. in a., 12/5/17.
Wellwood, Robert Kemp, M.C., Lt., k. in a., 23/7/18.
Adam, Alexander Russell, Lt., k. in a., 3/7/17 (R.F.C.).
Brown, John, Lt., k. in a., 11/4/18.
Ferguson, Arthur Douglas, Lt., k. in a., 12/10/17.
Lendrum, Harold Bruce, Lt., d. of w., 1/8/17.
McCaskie, Roy Whyte, M.C. & Bar, Lt., died, 5/8/18.
Macbey, George Munro, M.C., Lt., k. in a., 22/3/18.
McGregor, Ronald Alexander, Lt., k. in a., 9/4/18.
Morrison, George James, M.C., Lt., d. of w., 11/4/18.
Rees, Rowland, M.C., Lt., k. in a., 25/3/18.
Robertson, Alexander, Lt., d. of w., 28/1/18 (M.G.C.).
Sellar, John, Lt., k. in a., 9/4/18.
Stewart, David, Lt., k. in a., 14/6/15.
Aitken, Frank Thompson, 2/Lt., k. in a., 20/11/17.
Bliss, Thomas, 2/Lt., d. of w., 23/12/16.
Cameron, Nathaniel, 2/Lt., d. of w., 17/12/17.
Dow, David Edward, 2/Lt., d. of w., 17/5/17.
Elliott, Frederick, 2/Lt., d. of w., 2/8/16 (M.G.C.).
French, William Alexander Smith, 2/Lt., k. in a., 12-16/5/17.
Gilbert, Reginald Herbert, 2/Lt., d. of w., 8/8/18.
Grant, Donald, 2/Lt., k. in a., 20/11/17.
Jenkins, Donald Fraser, M.C., 2/Lt., k. in a., 13/11/16.
Kennedy, Edwin Alfred, 2/Lt., k. in a., 12-16/5/17.
King, Robert Thomas, 2/Lt., k. in a., 31/7/18.
Law, Henry Milner, 2/Lt., k. in a., 9/4/17.
Lipp, Charles Napier, 2/Lt., k. in a., 31/7/17.
Mann, Alexander David, 2/Lt., k. in a., 20/11/17.
Middleton, Edwin Relfe Barrett, 2/Lt., k. in a., 9/4/18.
Murray, Kenneth Hope, 2/Lt., k. in a., 18/6/16.
Raper, Sydney Ernest, 2/Lt., k. in a., 17/8/17 (R.F.C.).
Smith, Robert James, 2/Lt., k. in a., 13/11/16.
Webster, Charles Alexander, 2/Lt., k. in a., 9/4/17.
Young, Hugh Hutchinson, 2/Lt., k. in a., 26/5/18.

The Gordon Highlanders.

4th Battalion (Territorial).

Smith, George Alexander, D.S.O., Lt.-Col., k. in a., 28/7/18.
Henderson, James, M.C., A/Major, k. in a., 11/4/18.
Simpson, Harry Graham, Major, k. in a., 27/5/18 (M.G.C.).
Brown, John, Capt., k. in a., 20/7/18.
Catto, Robert Kilgour Thom, Capt., k. in a., 4/11/16.
Crombie, John Eugene, Capt., d. of w., 23/4/17.
Drysdale, John, M.C., 2/Lt. (A/Capt.), k. in a., 11/4/18.
Dunn, Robert James Armstrong, Capt., k. in a., 23/4/17.
Gillies, James Brown, Capt., d. of w., 14/11/16.
Henderson-Begg, John Henderson, Capt., k. in a., 23/7/16.
Hopkinson, James Garland, Capt., k. in a., 25/9/15.
Murray, Herbert, Capt., k. in a., 25/7/18.
Shakle, Hugh Philip, Capt., k. in a., 21/11/17.
Strachan, James, Capt., k. in a., 11/4/18.
Anderson, David, Lt., k. in a., 23/4/17.
Campbell, Tom Catto Pirie, Lt., k. in a., 28/3/18.
Coutts, Robert Disher, Lt., k. in a., 25-27/9/15.
Davidson, Arthur Gerrard, Lt., k. in a., 9/9/17 (and R.F.C.).
Gibson, Norman James, Lt., k. in a., 21/11/17.
Henderson, Alexander Rennie, Lt., k. in a., 25/9/15.
Leith, Douglas Meldrum Watson, Lt., k. in a., 21/3/18.
Luno, Evansten Holt, Lt., k. in a., 20/7/18.
Milne, Alexander James Bolton, Lt., k. in a., 22/8/17.
Mitchell, Robert Thomas Lamont, M.C., Lt., died, 29/11/18 (in German hands).
Morrison, James, Lt., k. in a., 25-27/9/15.
Rose, Frederick Alexander, Lt., k. in a., 10/8/15.
Ross, Simon Fraser, Lt., k. in a., 23/4/17.
Stephenson, Arthur Frederick Vere, Lt., k. in a., 23/7/16.
Thomson, James Walter Stewart, Lt., k. in a., 12/4/18.
Waddell, David Adams, Lt., k. in a., 6/4/17.
Aitken, Alexander, 2/Lt., d. of w., 15/5/17.
Anderson, Henry Angus, 2/Lt., k. in a., 21/7/18.

Anderson, William Francis Outram, 2/Lt., k. in a., 23/4/17.
Angus, Norman John, 2/Lt., d. of w., 18/9/17.
Beedle, Frank Symons Bussel, M.C., 2/Lt., k. in a., 11/4/18.
Byrne, Edward, 2/Lt., k. in a., 12/3/17 (R.F.C.).
Cameron, George Grant, 2/Lt., killed, 16/10/17 (R.F.C.).
Dawson, Frank Maitland Fraser, 2/Lt., k. in a., 20/9/17.
Diack, William, 2/Lt., k. in a., 20/9/17.
Duncan, Alexander John Farquharson, 2/Lt., d. of w., 31/3/18.
Farquharson, Ian, 2/Lt., d. of w., 23/8/18.
Ferguson, Roderick Mackenzie, 2/Lt., k. in a., 13/11/16.
Foster, John Maurice, 2/Lt., k. in a., 23/7/16.
Grant, Nigel Alexander James, 2/Lt., d. of w., 24/4/17.
Gray, James Blackhall, 2/Lt., k. in a., 27/10/18.
Henderson, Robert, 2/Lt., d. of w., 16/4/17.
Henderson, William George, 2/Lt., k. in a., 23/4/17.
Henry, Douglas John Luther Martin, 2/Lt., d. of w., 25/9/17.
Herd, John, 2/Lt., d. of w., 23/9/17.
High, Robert Donald, 2/Lt., k. in a., 22/3/18.
Inkster, Walter 2/Lt., k. in a., 25/9/15.
Jones, Sidney Herbert, 2/Lt., k. in a., 28/7/18.
Kelly, Terence O'Neil William, 2/Lt., d. of w., 2/5/15.
Kemp, Alexander Gordon, 2/Lt., d. of w., 7/5/17.
King, John Alexander, 2/Lt., k. in a., 12/9/16.
Latto, William Duncan, 2/Lt., died, 21/2/18.
Ledingham, Andrew, 2/Lt., k. in a., 22/3/18.
Low, George, 2/Lt., k. in a., 25/9/15.
Lunan, James, 2/Lt., k. in a., 20/9/17.
McCormack, Edward, 2/Lt., k. in a., 1/11/18.
MacKenzie, Alex Ritchie Doughty, 2/Lt., k. in a., 22/3/18.
Manson, Richard, 2/Lt., k. in a., 1/10/18.
Mitchell, Peter Harper, M.C., 2/Lt., d. of w., 14/9/17.
Morgan, John, 2/Lt., k. in a., 22/3/18.
Morris, Alfred George, 2/Lt., d. of w., 10/6/16.
Murray, Alexander, 2/Lt., k. in a., 29/8/18.
Robinson, Frederick, 2/Lt., k. in a., 28/7/18.
Rose, George Douglas, 2/Lt., k. in a., 20/9/17.
Sangster, William John Campbell, 2/Lt., k. in a., 25/9/15.
Scobie, James, 2/Lt., d. of w., 2/8/17.
Scott, David Lyon, 2/Lt., k. in a., 9/4/17.
Silver, John Watt, 2/Lt., k. in a., 26/10/18.
Simpson, James, 2/Lt., d. of w., 21/6/15.
Stewart, Alexander Vivian, 2/Lt., k. in a., 23/4/17.
Sutherland, William Henry, M.C., 2/Lt., k. in a., 23/3/18.
Tennant, Edward Martin Cookes, 2/Lt., d. of w., 16/10/16.
Thomson, James, 2/Lt., k. in a., 22/8/18.
Webster, Alexander, 2/Lt., k. in a., 9/4/17.
Wisely, Alfred Douglas, 2/Lt., k. in a., 12/9/16.
Wishart, William Fred'k., 2/Lt., k. in a., 15/6/18.
Wood, Bryce, 2/Lt., d. of w., 10/5/18.
Wright, William, 2/Lt., k. in a., 22/3/18.

The Gordon Highlanders.
5th (Buchan and Formartin) Battalion (Territorial).

Fowlie, Charles Wilson Lawson, Major, k. in a., 30/5/15.
Lyon, Robert, Capt., k. in a., 30/7/16.
McCulloch, John, Capt., k. in a., 9/4/17.
Minty, George, Capt., k. in a., 23/11/17.
Moir, George Andrew Christie, Capt., k. in a., 7/4/17.
Stephen, William, Capt., k. in a., 13/11/16.
Bruce, Vincent Connell, Lt., k. in a., 26/3/16.
Davidson, William Mason, Lt., d. of w., 29/3/18.
Dean, George, Lt., k. in a., 13/9/18.
Forbes-Sempill, Hon. Robert Abercromby, Lt., d. of w., 2/6/15.
Fyfe, William Quentin, Lt., k. in a., 21/3/18.
Garland, James Harvey, Lt., d. of w., 12/11/15.
Guthrie, Albert John, Lt., k. in a., 30/7/16.
Irvin, Thomas William, Lt., d. of w., 20/5/16.
Lundius, James Philip, Lt., k. in a., 28/5/16.
McWilliam, Charles Thomas, Lt., k. in a., 18/3/16.
Scott, William Leslie, Lt., k. in a., 17/6/15.
Watson, John Lawrence Craig, Lt., k. in a., 9/4/17.
Anderson, William Bruce, M.C., 2/Lt., k. in a., 7/3/17.
Bisset, Edgar George William, 2/Lt., d. of w., 7/1/17 (and R.F.C.).
Chalmers, John James, 2/Lt., died, 20/11/18 (in German hands).
Collyer, Arthur Hamilton, 2/Lt., d. of w., 23/4/17.
Douglas, Robert Morrison Wilson, 2/Lt., k. in a., 29/3/18.
Ferguson, Robert William, 2/Lt., k. in a., 13/11/16.
Gordon, James Gaspar, 2/Lt., k. in a., 5/3/17.
Hall, Herbert John, 2/Lt., k. in a., 7/4/17.
Ironside, John Gladstone, 2/Lt., died, 17/12/17.
Jack, Robert Lawrence Munro, 2/Lt., d. of w., 27/2/17 (and R.F.C.).
Laird, William Weir, 2/Lt., k. in a., 4/11/16.
McIndoe, William Reid, 2/Lt., k. in a., 6/8/18.
Meldrum, George Dunds, 2/Lt., k. in a., 16/12/16.
Mellis, James, 2/Lt., k. in a., 15/6/18.
Milne, Allan Smith, 2/Lt., k. in a., 26/6/17.
Rennie, James Davidson, 2/Lt., k. in a., 9/4/17.
Riddell, John Dean, 2/Lt., d. of w., 17/4/17.
Roberts, Philip Hugh Gore, 2/Lt., d. of w., 21/8/15.
Sykes, James Martyn Strickland, 2/Lt., k. in a., 13/11/16.
Taylor, Walter, 2/Lt., k. in a., 30/7/16.
Watt, John, 2/Lt., d. of w., 14/11/16.
Wilson, John Alexander, 2/Lt., k. in a., 13/11/16.
Wishart, Edward George, 2/Lt., d. of w., 21/4/18.

The Gordon Highlanders.
6th (Banff and Donside) Battalion (Territorial).

McLean, Colin, Lt.-Col., k. in a., 13/3/15.
MacQueen, John Ellison, Lt.-Col., k. in a., 25/9/15.
Archibald, John, M.C. & Bar, Capt., d. of w., 31/3/18.
Clark, Donald Gordon, D.S.O., M.C., Capt., d. of w., 13/4/18.
Fleming, Ian Grant, M.C., Capt., k. in a., 31/7/17.
Grant, Alexander, Capt., k. in a., 13/11/16.
Laing, Harry Davidson, Capt., k. in a., 13/3/15.
Mackay, Kenneth, M.C., Capt., d. of w., 7/11/18.
Matheson, John Hugh, Capt., d. of w., 24/4/17.
Matheson, Malcolm Angus, M.C., Capt., d. of w., 27/9/18.
Moodie, Ralph Wilson, Capt., k. in a., 17/5/17.
Reid, Alexander, Capt., d. of w., 13/10/18.
Robertson, Alexander Myron, Capt., k. in a., 4/8/10.
Smith, George, Capt., k. in a., 13/3/15.
Cooper, David Cameron, Lt., k. in a., 23/7/18.
Donaldson, George, Lt., k. in a., 16/5/17.
Duffus, William, Lt., d. of w., 1/12/17.
Duncan, George Stewart, Lt., k. in a., 23/9/17.
Farquharson, Frank Lumsden, Lt., k. in a., 4/6/15.
Gloster, Henry Colpays, Lt., k. in a., 13/3/15.
Henderson, Robert Stanley, Lt., k. in a., 13/10/18.
Mackay, Harry William Mackintosh, Lt., k. in a., 6/3/18 (and R.F.C.).
Macpherson, John Symon, Lt., d. of w., 15/3/18.
Morrison, John Gray, Lt., d. of w., 19/8/17.
Scott, James, Lt., k. in a., 25/9/15.
Stephen, Fred'k Charles, Lt., killed, 25/9/15.
Wark, Hugh Alexander, Lt., k. in a., 14/3/18.
Anton, Edwin Vincent, 2/Lt., k. in a., 17/5/17.
Burn, Arthur Sidney Pelham, 2/Lt., k. in a., 2/5/15.
Clark, James Smith, 2/Lt., k. in a., 3/5/17.
Emslie, Alexander, 2/Lt., k. in a., 16-17/5/17.
Grant, John Spence, M.C., 2/Lt., k. in a., 9/4/17.
Harvey, John Alexander, 2/Lt., k. in a., 25/9/15.
Henderson, Thomas Adam, 2/Lt., k. in a., 25-27/9/15.
Inglis, Henry Montgomery, 2/Lt., k. in a., 13/3/15.
Kelly, William John, 2/Lt., k. in a., 25/9/15.
Kilborn, Leslie Bertram, 2/Lt., d. of w., 10/4/17.
Mack, Thomas Arthur, 2/Lt., k. in a., 9/4/17.
MacQueen, Alexander Norman, 2/Lt., k. in a., 25/3/17 (and R.F.C.).
Monkhouse, Robert Alexander, 2/Lt., k. in a., 9-11/4/17.
Reid, George, 2/Lt., k. in a., 9/4/17.
Sim, John Moir, 2/Lt., killed, 25/3/17.
Stevenson, Alexander, 2/Lt., k. in a., 9/12/16.
Watt, William James, 2/Lt., k. in a., 25/9/15.
Wilson, Robert Forsyth, 2/Lt., k. in a., 13/11/16.

The Gordon Highlanders.
7th (Deeside Highland) Battalion (Territorial).

Bayley, Daniel James, Capt., k. in a., 21/3/18.
Ellis, James, Capt., d. of w., 24/4/17.
Forsyth, William, Capt., d. of w., 20/10/15.
Hillas, Arthur Benedict Edward, Capt., k. in a., 23/4/17.
MacCormac, Meriotte Campbell, Capt., k. in a., 16/5/17.
Merson, William Murison Smith, Capt., k. in a., 13/11/16.
Ross, Robert, M.C., Capt., d. of w., 18/4/17.
Innes, Alexander Berowald, Lt., k. in a., 16/6/15.
McMichael, Walter Buchanan, Lt., k. in a., 26/7/16.
Meff, William Blann, Lt., d. of w., 14/11/16.
Robertson, Frederick Neal, Lt., k. in a., 11/4/18.
Robertson, Ian Gordon, Lt., k. in a., 13/11/16.
Simpson, Robert Fraser, Lt., k. in a., 21/3/18.
Strachan, George Henry, Lt., died, 24/11/18.
Alderton, Charles John Woodward, 2/Lt., k. in a., 20/11/17.
Allison, William Frederick, 2/Lt., k. in a., 23/4/17.
Boyd, John Bain, 2/Lt., k. in a., 22/3/18.
Crowther, Eric Stuart, 2/Lt., d. of w., 21/11/16.
Dickie, Robert Bruce, 2/Lt., k. in a., 1/6/18.
Hart, Samuel Edward, 2/Lt., d. of w., 30/4/17.
Hay, Edward Hutton, 2/Lt., d. of w., 11/6/17.
Higgins, Frederick, 2/Lt., k. in a., 27/7/18.
Kell, Douglas Fearn, 2/Lt., d. of w., 24/4/17.
McLeod, George MacFarquhar, 2/Lt., k. in a., 7/4/17.
Masson, James, 2/Lt., k. in a., 28/7/18.
Miller, William Donnell, 2/Lt., k. in a., 23/6/18.
Robertson, Andrew, 2/Lt., k. in a., 13/11/16.
Simpson, Douglas Alexander, 2/Lt., d. of w., 15/10/15.
Smith, Francis Johnston, M.C., 2/Lt., k. in a., 16/5/17.
Smith, James William, 2/Lt., k. in a., 21/3/18.
Sutherland, Allan Newton, 2/Lt., k. in a., 22/3/18.
Turner, John, 2/Lt., k. in a., 29/11/16.
Watt, John Grant, 2/Lt., k. in a., 27/8/18.

The Queen's Own Cameron Highlanders.
4th Battalion (Territorial).

Fraser, Alexander, V.D., Lt.-Col., k. in a., 17/5/15.
Mackay, Ian, Capt. (T/Major), k. in a., 28/3/18.
MacDonald, Ronald, T.D., Major, d. of w., 10/6/16.
Allison, Thomas, Capt., k. in a., 18/5/15.
Baillie, Ian Henry, Capt., d. of w., 22/5/15.
Campbell, John, Capt., k. in a., 17/5/15.
Carruthers, Cameron Roy, Capt., k. in a., 31/7/17.
McKay, Harry, M.C., Capt., k. in a., 10/4/18.
Mackenzie, David Ferguson, Capt., k. in a., 17/5/15.
McLaren, John Francis, Capt., k. in a., 28/9/15.
Macpherson, James, Capt., k. in a., 10/3/15.
Melville, David, M.C., Capt. (Acting), k. in a., 26/10/18.
Milne, Douglas Thwaite, Capt. (Acting), d. of w., 28/3/18 (in German hands).
Chisholm, Alexander, Lt., k. in a., 14/10/17.
Douglas, Charles Camelon, Lt., d. of w., 25/5/16.
MacDougall, Alexander, Lt., k. in a., 30/4/18.
MacRae, Archibald John, Lt., d. of w., 5/10/18.
Munro, George William, Lt., d. of w., 1/10/18.
Scott, Henry James, 2/Lt. (T/Lt.), d. of w., 29/9/15.
Urquhart, Angus, Lt., killed, 26/9/15.

Bartholomew, Benjamin James, 2/Lt., k. in a., 18/11/16.
Baxter, Angus Cameron, 2/Lt., k. in a., 31/7/17.
Bookless, James Donald, 2/Lt., d of w., 24/5/15.
Cameron, Evan Stuart, 2/Lt., k in a., 11/4/17.
Donald, William Clark, 2/Lt., k. in a., 31/7/17.
Fairbairn, Harry Lawson, 2/Lt., k. in a., 2/8/17.
Geddie, George Alexander, 2/Lt., k. in a., 19/9/16
Jenkins, Patrick Graham, 2/Lt., k. in a., 9/4/17.
Kidd, Herbert Dickie, 2/Lt., k. in a., 17/5/15.
Macdonald, Archibald Alexander, 2/Lt., d. of w., 17/4/16.
MacIver, Donald John, 2/Lt., d. of w., 14/10/15.
Mennie, John Henderson, 2/Lt., k. in a., 10/4/17.
Moran, John, 2/Lt., k. in a., 24/3/18.
Paterson, Alistair Finlay, 2/Lt., d. of w., 5/6/15.
Paterson, Walter James, 2/Lt., d. of w., 30/10/17.
Powell, Alfred Trevanion, 2/Lt., d. of w., 22/7/16.
Still, G., 2/Lt., k. in a., 3/4/18 (and R.A.F.).

Princess Louise's (Argyll and Sutherland Highlanders). 5th (Renfrewshire) Battalion (Territorial).

Campbell, Alexander John, Capt., k. in a., 29/7/18.
Chalmers, John Hunter, Capt., d. of w., 25/3/18.
Gibb, James Shirra, Capt., k. in a., 29/7/18.
Lang, William Bryner, Lt. (T/Capt.), k. in a., 12/7/15.
Leitch, Eoin, Capt., k. in a., 31/7/17.
McKirdy, Robert Fingland, Capt., k. in a., 12/7/15.
Nesmith, James, Capt., k. in a., 12/7/15.
Baxter, John, Lt., k. in a., 10/11/17.
Carmichael, Robert Henry Morris, Lt., k. in a., 12/7/15.
Crerar, John, Lt., k. in a., 31/7/17.
Devlin, Harry Little, Lt., k. in a., 19/9/17 (R.F.C.).
Fleming, Malcolm James Henderson, Lt., d. of w., 14/7/15.
Gray, John, Lt., k. in a., 21/9/18.
McGlashan, John Ewing, Lt., k. in a., 12/7/15.
Munro, Ronald, Lt., k. in a., 8/8/17.
Nicol, Robert, Lt., k. in a., 17/4/18 (and M.G.C.).
Orkney, Robert, Lt., k. in a., 20/10/15.
Rodger, Walter Washington Buchanan, 2/Lt. (T/Lt.), k. in a., 8/7/15.
Rowan, John Leck, Lt., k. in a., 12/7/15.
Smith, Allan Bertram, Lt., k. in a., 27/5/18.
Swan, George Richard, Lt., d. of w., 9/8/18.
Wilson, John, T/Lt., died, 16/10/15.
Black, Robert, 2/Lt., d. of w., 22/10/18.
Brown, Charles Tolmé, 2/Lt., k. in a., 17/3/17.
Clark, William, 2/Lt., k. in a., 23/4/17.
Cumming, Adam Smith, 2/Lt., d. of w., 20/4/17.
Dow, William John, 2/Lt., k. in a., 22/8/17.
Lyon, Robert, 2/Lt., k. in a., 17/3/17 (and M.G.C.).
McLardie, Archibald, 2/Lt., k. in a., 25/12/15.
McLean, William Macfarlane, 2/Lt., k. in a., 24/3/18.
Nicol, Alexander, 2/Lt., k. in a., 12/7/15.
Nixon, David, 2/Lt., d. of w., 29/7/18.
Ritchie, William Smail, 2/Lt., k. in a., 29/7/18.
Stewart, John Stewart, 2/Lt., d. of w., 15/7/15.
Walker, Hugh Percy Wonham, 2/Lt., k. in a., 23/4/17.
Watson, Peter Seton, 2/Lt., k. in a., 9/4/17.
Whitaker, Foster, 2/Lt., d. of w., 3/5/17.

Princess Louise's (Argyll and Sutherland Highlanders). 6th (Renfrewshire) Battalion (Territorial).

Brown, James Hardie, M.C., Capt., d. of w., 7/6/18.
Cameron, Alexander Leckie, Capt., k. in a., 21/3/18.
Lang, Fredk. Murray, Capt., d. of w., 18/12/15.
Lang, William Brymner, Capt., k. in a., 12/7/15.
Porteous, James Hunter, Capt., k. in a., 22/8/17.
Shanks, John Arthur Gordon, M.C., Capt., k. in a., 4/10/17 (and M.G.C.).
Barclay, James George, Lt., died, 23/7/17.
Clark, Jasper, Lt., k. in a., 2/10/18.
Fraser, Angus McIntyre, Lt., d. of w., 19/6/18.
Gardner, Andrew Abercromby, Lt., k. in a., 6/9/18 (and M.G.C.).
Gardner, Caldwell, Lt., k. in a., 11/9/16.
Jaffrey, William, M.C., Lt., k. in a., 23/3/18.
Lang, Arthur, Lt., k. in a., 20/8/16.
MacIntyre, Robert Cochran, M.C., Lt., killed, 30/9/18.
Millar, Robert Spiers, Lt., k. in a., 18/9/18.
Morrison, James Bough, Lt., d. of w., 13/10/18.
Murray, John, Lt., died, 30/10/17.
Service, Alexander Cumming, Lt., k. in a., 29/5/18 (and M.G.C.).
Warnock, George Moir, Lt., d. of w., 29/3/18
Young, Andrew Gardyne, Lt., killed, 13/10/17.
Clarke, Kenneth Herbert, 2/Lt., k. in a., 30/9/17.
Davies, Owen Griffith, 2/Lt., k. in a., 15/11/16.
Emslie, Herbert Robertson, 2/Lt., k. in a., 24/10/17.
Forsyth, William, 2/Lt., d. of w., 1/4/16.
Fulton, Andrew, 2/Lt., k. in a., 23/4/17.
Gibb, James Robertson, 2/Lt., k. in a., 4/11/18.
Hislop, Fredk. Laurence, 2/Lt., k. in a., 23/4/17.
Kelly, Robert Houston, 2/Lt., k. in a., 1/1/18.
McLeay, Duncan Matheson, 2/Lt., k. in a., 23/3/17.
MacNeill, Archibald, 2/Lt., k. in a., 25/3/16.
Muir, William Stewart, 2/Lt., k. in a., 25/9/16.
Purves, James Phillip, 2/Lt., k. in a., 11/4/18.
Waters, William Nisbet, 2/Lt., k. in a., 28/7/16.

Princess Louise's (Argyll and Sutherland Highlanders). 7th Battalion (Territorial).

Jones, James Forbes, Major, d. of w., 29/3/17.
King, Andrew Buchanan, Major, d. of w., 28/5/15.
Conn, James Fullerton Caldwell, Capt., d. of w., 1/5/17.
Coupar, Sydney Bell Nicoll, Capt., died, 30/12/18.
Drummond, Henry Claude, Capt., k. in a., 24/7/16.
Hunter, Archibald Smith, M.C., Capt., d. of w., 29/8/18.
McLaren, James, Capt., k. in a., 21/11/17.
Strang, Robert, Capt., k. in a., 14/11/16.
Tullis, Robert Ramsey, Capt., d. of w., 25/5/15.
Wade, Graham Hardie, Capt., k. in a., 26/4/15.
Adam, Allan, Lt., k. in a., 1/10/18 (and M.G.C.).
Barr, John Young, Lt., k. in a., 26/4/15.
Battison, William, M.C., Lt., d. of w., 13/10/18.
Bell, William, Lt., k. in a., 10/4/17.
Cameron, Frederick, Lt., k. in a., 23/4/17.
Falconer, William Keay, Lt., k. in a., 26/4/15.
Gordon, Douglas, Lt., k. in a., 14/8/17 (and R.F.C.).
Harvey, Charles Claud, Lt., d. of w., 3/4/16.
Henderson, James Angus Smith, Lt., k. in a., 25/3/18.
Horne, Robert Stevenson, Lt., died, 29/7/18.
Hume-Gore, Gustavas, Lt., k. in a., 17/10/17 (att. K.A.R.).
Hunter, Robert Gibson, Lt., k. in a., 23/4/17.
Johnston, William Saville, Lt., d. of w., 23/3/18 (in German hands).
Miller, John, Lt., d. of w., 12/11/18.
Moir, Archibald Gifford, Lt., k. in a., 26/4/15.
Neil, John, M.C., Lt., d. of w., 28/3/18 (and M.G.C.).
Sherriff, John George, Lt., k. in a., 26/4/15.
Sinclair, Eric Russell, M.C., Lt., k. in a., 13/10/18.
Thomson, Thomas, Lt., k. in a., 25/4/17.
Whyte, John, Lt., d. of w., 26/4/15.
Barras, William, M.M., 2/Lt., d. of w., 25/3/18.
Bow, George Clark, 2/Lt., k. in a., 25/3/17 (and M.G.C.).
Cartwright, Arthur, 2/Lt., k. in a., 30/9/18.
Clark, William Campbell, 2/Lt., d. of w., 27/10/18.
Cook, Taylor, 2/Lt., died, 21/3/17.
Fidler, Carrel Watt, 2/Lt., d. of w., 19/5/17.
Gemmell, Thomas, 2/Lt., d. of w., 7/5/18 (in German hands).
Gibson, Horsburgh, 2/Lt., d. of w., 22/12/16.
Graham, Duncan, D.C.M., 2/Lt., k. in a., 30/9/18.
Hayworth, Frederick, 2/Lt., k. in a., 12/5/17.
Hayworth, Harry Asher, 2/Lt., k. in a., 15/4/17.
Jenkins, William Alexander, 2/Lt., d. of w., 14/4/17.
McGrory, John Joseph, 2/Lt., k. in a., 28/9/18.
Mackay, Malcolm, 2/Lt., d. of w., 7/4/18.
McKellar, Archibald Peter, 2/Lt., d. of w., 22/7/18.
Marshall, Robert Wilson, 2/Lt., k. in a., 27/5/18.
Mavor, Robert George Innes, M.C., 2/Lt., k. in a., 23/4/17.
Munro, Hector William, 2/Lt., k. in a., 23/4/17.
Neish, Alexander Millar, M.C., 2/Lt., d. of w., 24/3/18.
Ross, Colin, 2/Lt., d. of w., 25/10/18.
Scott, James, 2/Lt., k. in a., 15/11/16.
Sloan, Thomas Ian Thompson, 2/Lt., k. in a., 23/4/17.
Spence, Henry, 2/Lt., k. in a., 13/10/18.
Stein, Colin Hunter, 2/Lt., killed, 24/5/15.
Suttie, William Campbell, 2/Lt., k. in a., 24/5/15.
Templeton, Godfrey Allan, 2/Lt., d. of w., 27/7/18.
Tuckwell, John Henry Graham, 2/Lt., k. in a., 23/3/18
Wade, George, 2/Lt., drowned, 1/1/17.
Walker, Malcolm Reid, 2/Lt., k. in a., 23/4/17.
Wilson, Thomas Douglas, 2/Lt., k. in a., 23/4/17.
Yarrow, Eric Fernandez, 2/Lt., k. in a., 8/5/15

Princess Louise's (Argyll and Sutherland Highlanders). 8th (The Argyllshire) Battalion (Territorial).

Campbell, Neill Diarmid, Lt.-Col., k. in a., 12/4/18.
MacAlpine-Downie, James Robert, Lt.-Col., d. of w., 21/3/18.
McIntyre, Alexander Cameron, M.C., Major, d. of w., 24/3/18.
Rogerson, Andrew William, Major, d. of w., 6/10/17.
Lauder, John Currie, Capt., k. in a., 28/12/16.
MacArthur, Alaster, Capt., k. in a., 13/11/16.
MacTaggart, Murdoch Archibald, Capt., k. in a., 16/5/17.
Munro, William Dawson, Lt. (A/Capt.), k. in a., 16/5/17.
Bennett, William Munro, Lt., d. of w., 18/6/16.
Hood, John, Lt., k. in a., 18/8/17.
McFarlane, William Hannah, Lt., k. in a., 27/5/18.
MacKinnon, Alastair, Lt., killed, 14/10/16 (and M.G.C.).
Munro, Hugh Adam, Lt., k. in a., 22/9/15.
Phillimore, Hugh Bouchier, Lt., d. of w., 16/6/15.
Bannerman, Eric, 2/Lt., k. in a., 20/11/17.
Brander, Alfred Ernest, 2/Lt., k. in a., 13/11/16.
Campbell, Torquil Lorne, 2/Lt., k. in a., 1/3/17.
Duncanson, Ian Ferguson, 2/Lt., k. in a., 12/10/17.
Forbes, Alexander Bruce, 2/Lt., d. of w., 29/10/18.
Forbes, Robert Struthers, 2/Lt., k. in a., 24/4/17.
Fraser-Campbell, William Baillie, 2/Lt., k. in a., 23/3/18.
MacFarlang-Grieve, Alwyn Ronald, 2/Lt., k. in a., 17/3/17.
MacGregor, Douglas, 2/Lt., k. in a., 13/11/16.
McKellar, John Thomson, 2/Lt., k. in a., 13/11/16.
Morrison, Duncan Craig, 2/Lt., k. in a., 10/4/17.
Muir, Alexander, 2/Lt., k. in a., 20/9/17.
Smith, Robert Campbell McIntyre, 2/Lt., k. in a., 20/6/16.
Stout, George Ronald Yorston, 2/Lt., k. in a., 30/4/17 (and R.F.C.).
Wilkinson, Walter Lightowler, 2/Lt., k. in a., 9/4/17.
Williamson, Alan Kennedy, 2/Lt., d. of w., 20/4/17.

Princess Louise's (Argyll and Sutherland Highlanders). 9th (The Dumbartonshire) Battalion (Territorial).

Clark, James, C.B., Lt.-Col., k. in a., 10/5/15.
Brown, Archibald Gibson, Capt., k. in a., 25/5/15.
Campbell, John Santiago, Capt., k. in a., 28/9/17 (R.F.C.).
Findlay, Robert Scott, Capt., killed, 22/5/15.
Hall, David Sidney, M.C., Capt., k. in a., 20/11/17 (R.F.C.).
Kidston, William Hamilton Campbell, Capt., died, 8/5/17.
McLellan, Thomas Ancott, Capt., k. in a., 25/9/16.
Orr, Robert Baird, Capt., k. in a., 3/7/17.

Stewart, Alexander Leitch, Capt., k. in a., 21/3/18.
Ure, Ian, M.C., Capt., killed, 2/2/18.
Allison, John, Lt., k. in a., 24/11/17.
Anderson, Andrew Douglas McArthur, Lt., k. in a., 8/5/15.
Bonnar, James Crawford, Lt., killed, 22/5/15.
Cameron, Duncan, Lt., died, 5/12/18 (M.G.C.).
Chrystal, George Gordon, Lt., k. in a., 25/5/15.
Eadie, James Albert, Lt., k. in a., 27/5/18 (M.G.C.).
Hewer, Charles William, Lt., k. in a., 22/8/17.
Hutton, Frederick Robert Hughes, Lt., k. in a., 12/5/15.
Jackson, John, Lt., killed, 22/5/15.
Orr, Robert Duncan, Lt., k. in a., 10/8/18.
Stuart, Charles, Lt., k. in a., 31/7/17.
Birrell, George Henry Gordon, 2/Lt., k. in a., 12/5/15.
Campbell, John Fyshe, 2/Lt., d. of w., 10/4/17.
Campbell, Kenneth James, 2/Lt., k. in a., 12/5/15.
Fraser, Hugh, 2/Lt., k. in a., 13/11/16.
Gibson, James, 2/Lt., k. in a., 12/10/17.
Gosley, George Andrew Hay, 2/Lt., d. of w., 16/10/16.
Humble, Robert, 2/Lt., k. in a., 7/9/15.
Inch, John, 2/Lt., k. in a., 20/6/16.
Miller, Andrew Lindsay, 2/Lt., k. in a., 12/10/17.
Pollard, Alfred Gordon, 2/Lt., k. in a., 16/5/17.
Pollard, George Herbert, 2/Lt., d. of w., 7/6/17 (in German hands) (R.F.C.).
Smith, Archibald MacBrayne, 2/Lt., d. of w., 31/7/17.
Stewart, Duncan Hinshelwood, 2/Lt., k. in a., 20/4/18.
Stewart, Walter Ross Taylor, 2/Lt., k. in a., 6/8/16.
Thomson, George, 2/Lt., k. in a., 11/9/16.
Whyte, William Boyd, 2/Lt., k. in a., 21/9/17.

The Rifle Brigade (Prince Consort's Own).

19 Bewley, Edward, Capt., died, 19/8/18.
20 Palmer, William Henry Eyre Hollingworth, Capt., died, 26/11/15.
18 Grist, Ronald, Lt., died, 15/5/18.
20 Frankau, Paul Ewart, Lt., k. in a., 2/11/17.
23 Haughton, Charles Stanley, Lt., died, 4/2/19.
20 Montague, Paul Denys, Lt., k. in a., 29/10/17 (and R.F.C.).
23 Ponter, William Crossland, Lt., died, 27/11/18.
20 Brufton, Howard Charles, 2/Lt., k. in a., 9/7/17 (and R.F.C.).
23 Hindmarsh, George Edwin, 2/Lt., died, 16/6/17.

Army Cyclist Corps.

Glendinning, Thomas Henry, T/Capt., k. in a., 19/4/17 (Lowland Div.).
McDonald, Harry Alexander, Capt., died, 5/2/18.
Schofield, Alex Traies, Capt., d. of w., 10/11/18 (Kent Cyc. Btn.).
Sturrock, Harry Douglas, M.C., Capt., died, 1/2/18 (High. Cyc. Bn.).
9 Gratwicke, Philip Charles, Lt., k. in a., 30/3/18.
Grice, Maurice Chuma, Lt., drowned, 4/7/18.
9 Henry, John, Lt., k. in a., 13/4/18.
Shackell, Frank Charles, Lt., k. in a., 23/5/17 (and R.F.C.).
Ball, George Frederick, 2/Lt., died, 6/12/18 (High. Cyc. Bn.).
Bruce, Charles James, 2/Lt., d. of w., 20/5/17 (Lowland Div.).
Carpenter, Hubert Granville, 2/Lt., d. of w., 25/2/16 (2nd London Div.).
Findlay, Struthers, 2/Lt., k. in a., 4/8/16 (Lowland Div., Cyc. Coy.).
Harry, Reginald Charles, 2/Lt., k. in a., 29/8/16 (Sth. Mid. Div.).
Herbert, Alfred James Anthony, 2/Lt., d. of w., 17/9/17 (2nd Ldn. Div.).
Johnson, Derrick Sivewright, 2/Lt., k. in a., 4/12/16 (Home Counties Div. Cyc.) (and R.F.C.).
9 Phipps, Arthur Coryn, 2/Lt., k. in a., 13/4/18.
Smith, Cecil, 2/Lt., killed, 12/10/18 (Northern Cyc. Btn.).
Winch, Harry Wilson, 2/Lt., k. in a., 2/4/17 (2nd Lond. Cyc. Coy.).

The Monmouthshire Regiment (Territorial Force). 1st Battalion.

Robinson, Charles Lawson. Lt.-Col., killed. 8/5/15.
Trump, Frederick Joseph, D.S.O., Lt.-Col., k. in a., 2/12/17.
Williams, Edward Styant, Major, k. in a., 8/5/15.
Williams, Oswald Michael, Major, k. in a., 13/10/15.
Currey, Donald Saunders, Capt., k. in a., 24/4/17.
Edwards, Harold Thomas, Capt., k. in a., 8/5/15.
James, William Maynard, Capt., k. in a., 8/10/18.
Lewis, John Charles, Capt., k. in a., 20/11/17.
Perry, Benjamin Lewis, Capt., killed, 26/4/15.
Spittle, Thomas Stanley, Capt., d. of w., 2/10/17.
Stanton, Claude Wilfred, Capt., k. in a., 8/5/15.
Darby, William Edward Cleve Augustus, Lt., k. in a., 11-13/10/15.
Evans, John Rayner, Lt., k. in a., 8/10/18.
Frampton, John Guy, Lt., d. of w., 11/10/18.
Phillips, Edward Stone, Lt., k. in a., 8/5/15.
Archer, Henry Charles, 2/Lt., k. in a., 8/10/18.
Ballinger, Henry John, 2/Lt., k. in a., 13/10/15.
Birrell-Anthony, Henry Anthony, 2/Lt., k. in a., 8/5/15.
Duncanson, Stuart Ray, 2/Lt., k. in a., 11/8/17.
Hall, Charles Stuart, 2/Lt., k. in a., 12/1/17
Howells, George Davey, 2/Lt., k. in a., 28/2/18.
Jones, Louis Gueret Walter Southwell, 2/Lt., d. of w., 20/6/17.
King, Reginald, 2/Lt., d. of w., 15/9/18.
Thompson, Ronald William, 2/Lt., k. in a., 11/4/18.
Meredith, Arthur Llewelyn, 2/Lt., d. of w., 4/6/18.
Newland, Norman Chester, 2/Lt., d. of w., 31/5/15 (in German hands).
Richards, Arthur, 2/Lt., d. of w., 27/6/17.
Richards, Stanley Earl, 2/Lt., d. of w., 29/8/16.
Smith, Louis Herbert Collin, 2/Lt., k. in a., 13/10/15.
Stewart, William Victor, 2/Lt., k. in a., 8/5/15.
Widowfield, George, 2/Lt., d. of w., 14/10/15.
Williams, David Jenkins, 2/Lt., d. of w., 20/9/17.

The Monmouthshire Regiment (Territorial Force). 2nd Battalion.

Bowden, Alfred John Hamilton, D.S.O., Lt.-Col., k. in a., 2/3/17.
Edwards, Edward, Capt., k. in a., 17/8/16.
Hockaday, Sidney Reginald, Capt., d. of w., 2/9/16.
Spencer, Francis Leslie, Capt., k. in a., 2/12/17.
Taunton, Clive Warneford, Capt., k. in a., 25/11/16.
Watkins, Vivian Holmes, Capt., d. of w., 20/2/15.
Watkins, Iltyd Edwin Maitland, Capt., k. in a., 5/5/15.
Fraser, Alexander Evan, Lt., k. in a., 2/5/15.
Fraser, James Herbert, Lt., d. of w., 9/7/16 (and M.G.C.).
Owen, Ifor Evan, Lt., d. of w., 13/4/18.
Percival, Reginald Frank, Lt., k. in a., 12/4/18.
Sankey, William Mandeville, M.C., Lt., d. of w., 23/3/18.
Taylor, John William, Lt., k. in a., 12/3/15.
Walters, Henry James, Lt., k. in a., 5/5/15.
Williams, John Rowland, Lt., k. in a., 27/9/17.
Williams, William John, Lt., d. of w., 12/5/15.
Davies, Ellerton Osborne, 2/Lt., killed, 2/4/15.
Hillier, Cyril Anthony Hudson, 2/Lt., d. of w., 27/2/15.
Lawlor, Edward Fred'k., 2/Lt., k. in a., 27/11/16.
Paton, John Edward, 2/Lt., killed, 31/12/14.
Reed, Henry William Terrent, 2/Lt., k. in a., 2/5/15.

The Monmouthshire Regiment. (Territorial Force). 3rd Battalion.

Baker, Reginald Lawrence, Capt., k. in a., 12/5/15.
Fry, Alfred Andrew, Capt., died, 27/6/19 (and R.A.F.).
Gardner, Robert Oswald, Capt., k. in a., 8/5/15.
Hodges, Harold Augustus, Capt., k. in a., 22/3/18.
Lancaster, Gerald William, M.C., Capt., d. of w., 14/9/18.
Lancaster, James, Capt., k. in a., 8/5/15.
Lewis, Nevill Graham Nuscomb Hart, Capt., k. in a., 17/9/17.
Reese, Richard Tudor, Capt., k. in a., 23-24/8/18.
Walbeoffe-Wilson, William, Capt., killed, 2/8/15.
Williams, William Henry, Capt., k. in a., 30/5/18.
Bowen, William Lloyd, M.C., Lt., d. of w., 1/9/18.
Collings, Walter, M.C., Lt., k. in a., 10/4/18.
Groves, Francis Neville, Lt., k. in a., 8/5/15.
Martin, Charles Herbert George, Lt., killed, 2/5/15.
Raymont, William Clifton, Lt., k. in a., 6/5/17.
Reed, Charles Sydney, Lt., k. in a., 8/5/15.
Rosenbaum, Laurence Braham, Lt., d. of w., 17/4/18.
Worton, John Paton, Lt., k. in a., 8/5/15.
Cruikshank, Raymond Alfred, 2/Lt., k. in a., 23/4/17.
Davies, Gwynonfryn Albert Haydn, 2/Lt., k. in a., 7/6/17 (R.F.C.).
Glendinning, James Graham, 2/Lt., d. of w., 16/12/17 (in German hands) (R.F.C.).
Hastings, George William, 2/Lt., k. in a., 1/8/17.
King, Albert, 2/Lt., k. in a., 31/5/17.
Metcalfe, Joseph Stephen, 2/Lt., k. in a., 17/1/17.
Onions, Wilfred, 2/Lt., d. of w., 25/4/15.
Palmer, William Lucius, 2/Lt., killed, 8/5/15.
Sorby, Charles Malin Clifton, 2/Lt., d. of w., 8/5/15.
Straker, Charles Constantine Lionel, 2/Lt., d. of w., 7/7/16.
Taylor, Francis Henry, 2/Lt., k. in a., 30/11/17.
Thomas, Albert Edward, 2/Lt., k. in a., 17/2/17 (M.G.C.).
Thomas, Eric Rowland, 2/Lt., k. in a., 13/6/17.
Townsend, Hugh Vere, 2/Lt., k. in a., 6/5/15.

The Cambridgeshire Regiment.

1 Saint, Edward Twelftree, D.S.O., Lt.-Col., d. of w., 29/8/18.
1 Chaplin, Arthur Hugh Bates, Major, d. of w., 21/5/17.
1 Armstrong, Arthur Sutcliffe, Capt., d. of w., 31/5/17.
1 Aston, Walter Douglas, Capt., d. of w., 2/11/17.
1 Beale, Edmund Lansdowne, Lt., A/Capt., k. in a., 22/3/18.
1 Butlin, Sir Henry Guy Trentham, Capt., k. in a., 16/9/16.
1 Corbett, Herbert Vincent, Capt., k. in a., 17/10/18.
Dunlop, Archibald Ballantine Henderson, M.C., Capt., d. of w., 20/9/18.
1 Ford Francis William, M.C., 2/Lt., A/Capt., k. in a., 26/9/17.
1 Formby, Thomas Hope, Capt., k. in a., 13/10/16.
1 Gill, K. C., M.C., Capt., d. of w., 22/10/18 (R.A.F.).
1 Graham, Lionel Lovell, Capt., k. in a., 26/9/17.
1 Gray, Arthur John, Capt., k. in a., 31/7/17.
1 Hill, Robert William, Capt., d. of w., 31/7/17.
1 Johnson, Alec, M.C., Capt., k. in a., 18/9/18.
1 Jonas, Frank Charlton, Capt., k. in a., 31/7/17.
1 Keenlyside, Cecil Alexander Headlam, Capt., k. in a., 20/7/15.
Kirk, Percival Gordon, Capt., k. in a., 13/8/17 (R.F.C.).
1 Seaton, Alexander Adam, Capt., d. of w., 4/9/15.
Sindall, Richard Edward, Capt., d. of w., 1/7/15.
Tebbutt, Oswald Nevelle, Capt., k. in a., 15/3/15.
Tebbutt, Roger Joseph, Capt., k. in a., 24/8/18.
1 Adam, Arthur Innes, Lt., k. in a., 16/9/16.
1 Bradford, Alfred Royal, Lt., k. in a., 14/10/16.
1 Clayton, Keith Herbert, Lt., k. in a., 22/8/18.
1 Cobham, Frederick George Brian, Lt., k. in a., 8/8/18.
1 Crookham, Hugh Antony Rupert, T/Lt., d. of w., 3/8/15.
1 Driver, Harry Farrant, M.C., Lt., k. in a., 28/8/18.
1 Gray, Anthony Frederick, Lt., k. in a., 26/8/18.
1 Herman, George Alfred, Lt., k. in a., 20/7/16.
1 Hopkinson, Eric Humphrey, M.C., Lt., died, 2/6/15.
1 Keating, George Henry, Lt., k. in a., 18/9/18

1 Orbell, Douglas, Lt., k. in a., 5/9/18.
1 Rayner, Donald, Lt., k. in a., 8/8/18.
1 Saunders, Edwin Walter, Lt., k. in a., 5/5/15.
1 Shaw, William, Lt., died, 27/9/16 (in German hands).
Smalley, John Douglas, Lt., k. in a., 15/3/15.
1 Smith, Francis Edwin, Lt., died, 18/11/18.
Twelvetrees, Edward Dudley, Lt., k. in a., 8/8/18.
1 West, Walter Montague, Lt., d. of w., 5/5/15
Bowyer, Edgar George, 2/Lt., k. in a., 15/10/16.
1 Carter, Bertram, 2/Lt., k. in a., 18/9/18.
1 Chambers, Henry, 2/Lt., d. of w., 11/8/18.
1 Chaplin, Charles Montague, 2/Lt., k. in a., 26/9/17.
1 Chapman, William James, 2/Lt., k. in a., 26/3/18.
1 Cowling, Alexander, 2/Lt., k. in a., 26/4/18.
1 Day, Henry Brodie, 2/Lt., k. in a., 4/2/18.
1 Hewer, Charles, 2/Lt., k. in a., 23/8/18.
1 Huckle, Henry William, 2/Lt., k. in a., 5/9/18.
1 Jameson, Alan Battersby, 2/Lt., k. in a., 21/7/16.
1 King, Robert William, 2/Lt., k. in a., 27/3/18.
McMicking, Gilbert Thomas Gore, 2/Lt., died, 11/11/18.
1 Marsh, John Edward Joseph, 2/Lt., k. in a., 24/9/17.
1 Muirhead, Alexander Hugh, 2/Lt., k. in a., 31/7/17.
Rawlinson, Guy Edward, 2/Lt., d. of w., 23/7/16.
1 Reid, James Archibald John, 2/Lt., d. of w., 16/10/16.
1 Ritchie, William Lancelot, 2/Lt., d. of w., 1/8/17.
1 Robinson, Cecil Rowland, 2/Lt., k. in a., 26/9/17.
Scott, Thomas Walter, 2/Lt., k. in a., 13/10/16.
Skinner, Ernest Henry, 2/Lt., k. in a., 21-31/3/18 (or d. of w.).
1 Vaughan, Harold John, 2/Lt., k. in a., 8/6/16.
1 Vine, Robert Saselby, 2/Lt., k. in a., 14/10/16.
1 Walker, John Croxton, 2/Lt., k. in a., 3/9/16.
Walker, S., 2/Lt., died, 14/5/18 (R.A.F.).

1st (City of London) Battalion, The London Regiment (Royal Fusiliers).

Smith, Duncan Vaughan, D.S.O., Lt.-Col., d. of w., 13/4/17.
Buck, G. S., M.C., D.F.C., Capt., k. in a., 3/9/18 (and R.A.F.).
Carr, Leslie George, M.C. & Bar, Capt., d. of w., 27/4/18.
Coleman, Sydney, Capt., d. of w., 14/10/18.
Eiloart, Frank Oswald, Act. Capt., k. in a., 3/5/17.
Glover, Richard Bowie Gaskell, Capt., k. in a., 5/11/15.
Henderson, Alec Stewart, Capt., d. of w., 25/4/15.
Houghton, John Reginald, M.C., A/Capt., k. in a., 21/3/18.
Huggins, Douglas Frank, Capt., k. in a., 29/8/18.
Kekewich, George, Capt., d. of w., 28/10/17.
Le Tall, Cyril Herbert, Capt., k. in a., 30/8/18.
Mews, John Keith, Capt., d. of w., 24/8/18.
Mouat, George Mouat Dundas, Capt., k. in a., 9-10/5/15.
Parslow, William Hunt, Act. Capt., d. of w., 10/8/18.
Petley, Hugh, Capt., k. in a., 16/9/16.
Rowland, Cyril William, M.C., Capt., k. in a., 23/8/18.
Waddams, Walter Herbert Leonard, M.C., A/Capt., d. of w., 12/4/17.
Auerbach, Albert Arthur, M.C., Lt., k. in a., 1/9/18.
Balfour, B., Lt., k. in a., 16/4/18 (and R.A.F.).
Bowen, Rowland George Breece, Lt., k. in a., 9/5/15.
Burnaby, Geoffry, Lt., d. of w., 23/10/16.
Chichester, William George Cubitt, Lt., k. in a., 15/9/16.
Collens, Edwin Theobald, Lt., d. of w., 3/9/18.
Fry, John Desford, Lt., k. in a., 15/9/16.
Mayer, Gerald Max, Lt., d. of w., 16/2/17.
Seaverns, Joel, Harrison, Lt., d. of w., 10/5/15.
Snowdon, Henry Frederick, Lt., k. in a., 6/10/16.
Stapleton, Harold Frederick, Lt., k. in a., 15/9/16
Westlake, Geoffrey Arthur, Lt., k. in a., 7-8/10/16.
Wilkinson, Eyre Spencer, Lt., k. in a., 12/1/16 (and R.F.C.).
Allender, John Harold, 2/Lt., k. in a., 7/10/16.
Andrew, Arthur, 2/Lt., k. in a., 23/11/17.
Arden, Reginald Douglas, 2/Lt., k. in a., 8/10/16.
Atkins, Leslie Gordon, 2/Lt., k. in a., 25/5/18.
Barker, Charles Haydn, 2/Lt., d. of w., 8/10/18.
Barton, William Ewart, 2/Lt., d. of w., 25/8/18.
Bell, Kenneth Frederick Hamilton, 2/Lt., k. in a., 25/9/15.
Besley, Howard Napier, 2/Lt., k. in a. 29/6/17.
Campbell, Walter Stanley, M.C., 2/Lt., k. in a., 7/10/16.
Carter, Cecil Edward, 2/Lt., k. in a., 20/9/17.
Chamberlain, John Harold, 2/Lt., d. of w., 21/11/15.
Chapman, Fred, 2/Lt., k. in a., 22/8/18
Crowe, Harold Archer, 2/Lt., d. of w., 1/6/15.
Cundall, Hubert Walter, 2/Lt., k. in a., 1/7/16.
Dickinson, Lionel St. Clair, 2/Lt., k. in a., 16/9/16.
Dowden, Reginald Stanley, 2/Lt., k in a., 16/8/17.
Harper, Reginald Alexander, 2/Lt., d. of w., 16/9/17.
Heaton, Norman Child, 2/Lt., k. in a., 3/5/17.
Hill, Gerald Stanley, 2/Lt., k. in a., 15/9/16.
Johnson, Edmund George, 2/Lt., k. in a., 24/8/18.
Long, Daniel Edward, 2/Lt., k. in a., 28/5/18.
Martin, Edwin John, 2/Lt., k. in a., 4/9/18.
Meyers, Stanley Arthur, 2/Lt., k. in a., 26/10/17.
Mockford, Joseph, 2/Lt., d. of w., 8/4/17
Mytton, Richard, 2/Lt., d. of w., 3/10/16.
Naylor, James Reginald, 2/Lt., k. in a., 26/10/17.
Newall, Leslie, 2/Lt., k. in a., 2/9/15.
Prentice, Oliver, 2/Lt., k. in a., 27/3/18.
Richards, Robert Ingram, 2/Lt., d. of w., 27/10/17.
Scott, Ronald Burrell Ind, 2/Lt., k. in a., 9/9/16.
Shail, William Archibald, 2/Lt., k. in a., 16/8/17.
Sheasby, Edwin William, 2/Lt., k. in a., 15/9/16.
Snowdon, Sidney Frank, 2/Lt., k. in a., 15/9/16.
Stevens, William Philip, 2/Lt., k. in a., 3/8/18.
Townend, Cecil Pelham, 2/Lt., d. of w., 24/9/16.
Vawser, Thomas Edmund, 2/Lt., k. in a., 21-23/3/18.
Williams, Harold Edward, 2/Lt., k. in a., 7-8/10/16
Wilson, David Oliver, 2/Lt., d. of w., 8/10/16.

2nd (City of London) Battalion The London Regiment (Royal Fusiliers).

Stacey, Gerald Arthur, D.S.O., Major, k. in a., 9/10/16.
Falkner, Clarence Beach, Capt., k. in a., 25/10/17.
Garland, James Richard, T/Capt., k. in a., 1/7/16.
Gordon, Colin, Capt., k. in a., 16/8/17.
Gretton, Horace Edward, Capt., k. in a., 16/8/17.
Handyside, Percy James Alexander, Capt., k. in a., 1/7/16.
Heaumann, Richard, Capt., k. in a., 8-10/9/16.
Jepson, Arthur George Leslie, Capt., k. in a., 16/9/16.
Long, James William, Capt., k. in a., 8-10/9/16.
Rawle, William Richard, Capt., d. of w., 8/8/18.
Symes, John Bond, Capt., k. in a., 3/5/17.
Winterbourne, Frank Thomas, Capt., drowned, 10/10/18.
Bennett, Harold Percy, Lt., k. in a., 21/3/18.
Child, David Leslie, Lt., d. of w., 11/9/16.
Coppen, William Joseph, Lt., k. in a., 2/11/17.
Henderson, Graeme Von Hope, Lt., k. in a., 16/6/17.
Keen, S. W., M.C., Lt., d. of w., 21/8/18 (and R.A.F.).
Preedy, John Benjamin Knowlton, Lt., k. in a., 26/10/17.
Richardson, John Ernest, Lt., k. in a., 7/5/15.
Skeet, John Richard, Lt., k. in a., 27/4/18.
Taylor, Philip Charton, Lt., k. in a., 15/9/16.
Williams, Henry Evan Vincent, Lt., d. of w., 22/5/17.
Buxton, Bertie Reginald, 2/Lt., k. in a., 1/7/16.
Clayton, Albert James, M.C., 2/Lt., d. of w., 24/8/18.
Cooke, George Josiah, 2/Lt., k. in a., 23/11/17 (and R.F.C.).
Farley, Frederick Albert, 2/Lt., k. in a., 1/7/16.
Fradd, Kingsley Meredith Chatterton, 2/Lt., k. in a., 1/7/16 (M.G.C.).
Grainger, John Scott, 2/Lt., k. in a., 1/7/16.
Gant, Harold Holden, 2/Lt., k. in a., 1/9/18.
Gosnell, Harold Clifford, 2/Lt., k. in a., 1/7/16.
Hammond, Frederic Robert Cyprian, 2/Lt., k. in a., 6/7/15.
Heagerty, Richard Browne, 2/Lt., k. in a., 3/5/17.
Howard, Herbert Quey, 2/Lt., k. in a., 8/8/18.
Inwards, Horatio, 2/Lt., k. in a., 15/6/17.
Lockey, Ernest William, 2/Lt., k. in a., 8-10/9/16.
McMurray, Stuart, 2/Lt., k. in a., 7/8/17 (and R.F.C.).
Martin, Stanley, M.M., 2/Lt., k. in a., 18/9/18.
Merrikin, George Houlden, 2/Lt., k. in a., 27/8/18.
Missen, Edward Roland Cecil, 2/Lt., k. in a., 4/10/18.
Murray, Cyril, 2/Lt., k. in a., 16/8/17.
Noel, Alfred, 2/Lt., k. in a., 3/5/17.
Perris, N. F., 2/Lt., k. in a., 20/7/18 (and R.A.F.).
Prince, Frederick George, 2/Lt., killed, 18/5/19 (and R.A.F.).
Rolleston, Francis Launcelot, 2/Lt., killed, 26/4/15.
Royce, Percival Francis, 2/Lt., k. in a., 10/9/18.
St. Leger, St. John Richard, 2/Lt., k. in a., 15-17/9/16.
Smoothy, Albert Victor, 2/Lt., d. of w., 9/11/18.
Solley, Bernard John, 2/Lt., k. in a., 10/8/18.
Spong, Frederick William Edward, 2/Lt., d. of w., 2/8/17 (in Ger. hands).
Starling, Benjamin Alfred, 2/Lt., k. in a., 23/3/18.
Strange, William Frederick, 2/Lt., k. in a., 1/7/16.
Stubbs, Cecil Arthur, 2/Lt., d. of w., 2/7/16.
Sullivan, Arthur John, 2/Lt., k. in a., 15/9/16.
Thorman, Alan Marshall, 2/Lt., k. in a., 1/7/16.
Walton, Frank Arthur, 2/Lt., k. in a., 26/9/17.
Wright, John George William, 2/Lt., k. in a., 11/5/17.

3rd (City of London) Battalion The London Regiment. (Royal Fusiliers.)

Beresford, Percy William, D.S.O., Lt.-Col., d. of w., 26/10/17.
Newson, Walter Alexander, Major, died, 15/4/17.
Agius, Richard Victor Joseph Roy, Capt., k. in a., 26/10/17.
Christmas, Bernard Lovell, Capt., d. of w., 11/5/16.
Clarke, Eric Fitzgerald, Capt., k. in a., 9/4/17.
Curtis, Arthur, M.C., Capt., k. in a., 27/8/18.
Howard, Francis Stanley, Capt., k. in a., 28/11/15.
Jones, John Llewelyn Thomas, Capt., k. in a., 16/8/17.
Minshull, John Lewis, Capt., k. in a., 2/4/17.
Pulman, Harry Robert Sauve, Capt., killed, 10/3/15.
Taylor, Gilbert Leslie Frederic, Capt., d. of w., 26/8/17.
Thomas, James Leonard, Capt., killed, 28/2/17 (and R.F.C.).
Austen, Edward John, Lt., k. in a., 21-23/3/18.
Luscombe, Henry, Lt., k. in a., 11/4/17.
Mathieson, Herbert Gerard, Lt., k. in a., 10/3/15.
Jones, David William Llewellyn, Lt., d. of w., 2/7/16.
Jones, Thomas Capel, Lt., k. in a., 26/10/17.
Ring, Leslie Gordon, Lt., k. in a., 18/9/18.
Rodd, Frederick Trevor, Lt., k. in a., 16/6/17.
Stephens, John Lockhart, Lt., killed, 10/3/15.
Aberdeen, Louis Frederick, 2/Lt., k. in a., 10/9/16.
Atkins, Arthur Charles, 2/Lt., k. in a., 9/9/16.
Barton, Harry, 2/Lt., k. in a., 22/3/18.
Burgess, Harold Torrence, 2/Lt., k. in a., 2/4/17.
Burrows, William Arthur, 2/Lt., k. in a., 15/9/16.
Cahill, Alfred Gilbert, 2/Lt., k. in a., 8/10/16.
Crichton, Cyril William Alfred, 2/Lt., k. in a., 10/3/15.
Davison, Rutherford Willoughby, 2/Lt., d. of w., 10/10/16.
Ferris, Alfred William, 2/Lt., d. of w., 5/3/17.
Fraser, Charles Douglas, 2/Lt., k. in a., 22/3/18.
Gedge, Cecil Bertie, 2/Lt., k. in a., 25/9/15.
Groves, Robert Harry, M.C., 2/Lt., d. of w., 12/4/17.
Gunn, Walter Roderick Hamilton, 2/Lt., k. in a., 1/9/18.
Gunton, Reginald Oliver, 2/Lt., k. in a., 21/3/18.
Haines, Herbert Henry, 2/Lt., k. in a., 15/5/17.
Hall, Hugh Wilfred, 2/Lt., k. in a., 15/5/17.
Hard, William Thomas, 2/Lt., k. in a., 23/3/18.
Jeffree, Johnson Vivian, 2/Lt., k. in a., 10/8/18.
Jeffries, Thomas, 2/Lt., k. in a., 14/8/17.
Knight, Edgar Fredk., 2/Lt., k. in a., 28/5/16.
Knott, Stuart Wallace, 2/Lt., k. in a., 24/4/18.

Lee, C. P., 2/Lt., k. in a., 22/10/18 (att. R.A.F.).
Lidiard, Richard John Abraham, 2/Lt., k. in a., 1/7/16.
Lynch-Staunton, Eric Margrave, 2/Lt., k. in a., 9/5/17.
Mason, Charles Henry, M.C., 2/Lt., d. of w., 10/9/18.
Moorey, William Edward, 2/Lt., k. in a., 26/10/17.
Morrison, Arnold, 2/Lt., k. in a., 26/10/17.
Odell, Oliver Henry Cecil, 2/Lt., k. in a., 10/9/16.
Oldrey, Montague, 2/Lt., k. in a., 26/10/17.
Parry, William Norman Maule, 2/Lt., d. of w., 19/8/17 (in German hands).
Randall, Albert William, 2/Lt., k. in a., 8/8/18.
Scarlett, Harold Ernest, 2/Lt., k. in a., 17/9/16.
Sheffield, Ralph David, 2/Lt., k. in a., 16/6/17.
Smith, H. S., 2/Lt., k. in a., 31/7/18 (att. R.A.F.).
Smith, Raymond Alexander, 2/Lt., k. in a., 1/7/16.
Starling, Frederick Leslie, 2/Lt., k. in a., 13/9/16.
Watts, Leonard, M.M., 2/Lt., k. in a., 9/10/18.
Wharton, Christopher Willis, 2/Lt., k. in a., 26/10/17.
Whiddett, Horace, 2/Lt., d. of w., 27/8/18.
Wybrants, John Holman, 2/Lt., d. of w., 30/7/18.

4th (City of London) Battalion, The London Regiment (Royal Fusiliers).

Bottomley, Eric William, Capt., k. in a., 15/6/17.
Giles, Eric, Capt., d. of w., 16/7/16.
Goodes, George Leonard, M.C. & Bar, Capt., k. in a., 6/10/16.
Hewlett, Harold Alcester Tom, Capt., k. in a., 23/8/18.
Leake, George Ernest Arthur, D.S.O., Capt., d. of w., 2/6/17.
Monk, Ernest William, Capt., k. in a., 29/3/18 (R.F.C.).
Moore, Arthur Robert, M.C., Capt., died, 1/7/16 (in German hands).
Rix, Leslie Gordon, Capt., d. of w., 11/2/17.
Saunders, Charles Robert Edgar, Capt., d. of w., 28/4/15.
Smith, Brian Rivers, Capt., k. in a., 8/8/18.
Spicer, Eric Evan, Capt., k. in a., 28/3/18.
Stavert, Robert Elliott, Capt., k. in a., 25/8/18.
Towse, William Norman, Capt., k. in a., 15/9/16.
Webster, John Richard, Capt., k. in a., 9/9/16.
Coates, Alan David, Lt., k. in a., 27-28/4/15.
Colomb, George Lushington, Lt., k. in a., 22/11/16 (R.F.C.).
Evans, John Baynes, Lt., k. in a., 23/3/18.
Hunt, Frederick Frank, 2/Lt. (Tp. Lt.), k. in a., 27/6/15.
Jones, Harry, Lt., killed, 15/5/18.
Oldrey, Vernon Roy, Lt., k. in a., 31/8/18.
Stedman, Philip Bertram Kirk, Lt., d. of w., 19/8/16.
Vernon, William Hams, Lt., k. in a., 7/10/16.
Atterbury, Lewis John Rowley, 2/Lt., k. in a., 7/10/16.
Backler, A.M., 2/Lt., died, 25/5/18 (R.A.F.).
Blows, Cyril Sydney George, 2/Lt., k. in a., 9/9/16.
Bradford, Frederick Reith Campbell, 2/Lt., k. in a., 1/7/16.
Brodie, Colin James, 2/Lt., k. in a., 9/9/16.
Brown, Norman Algernon, 2/Lt., died, 1/3/19.
Butcher, Clarence Edward, 2/Lt., k in a., 3/5/17.
Campkin, Reginald Ernest, 2/Lt., k. in a., 28/3/18.
Carlisle, Frederick Albert, 2/Lt., k. in a., 15/9/17.
Clarke, Edward Rupert, 2/Lt., k. in a., 9/4/17.
Colomb, Mervyn William, 2/Lt., d. of w., 11/5/15 (R.F.C.).
Davey, William Henry, 2/Lt., k. in a., 9/9/16.
Davis, Harold Charles, 2/Lt., k. in a., 4/4/17.
Edkins, Charles, 2/Lt., k. in a., 29/10/18.
Elliott, John Benjamin George, 2/Lt., k. in a., 16/8/17.
Ewing, Gordon Craig, M.C., 2/Lt., k. in a., 20/9/18.
Fanghanel, Frederick Charles, 2/Lt., k. in a., 1/7/16.
Foden, Frank Joseph, 2/Lt., k. in a., 9/9/16.
Garner, Edward Harold, 2/Lt., k. in a., 27/8/18.
Geering, Sydney Cecil, 2/Lt., d. of w., 3/5/18 (P. of W.).
Gifford, William Roy, 2/Lt., k. in a., 7/10/16.
Grimsdell, Reginald Edward, 2/Lt., k. in a., 25/9/16.
Hannay, Herbert Thomas, 2/Lt., k. in a., 28/3/18.
Haycraft, Leonard Courtenay, 2/Lt., k. in a., 7/10/16.
Humphrey, William Pryn, 2/Lt., k. in a., 27/5/18.
Langton, Hugh Gordon, 2/Lt., k. in a., 26/10/17.
Lewis, Charles Edward, 2/Lt., k. in a., 9/9/16.
Mansbridge, William Kenneth Elliott, 2/Lt., k. in a., 4/10/17.
Mawby, Thomas Henry, 2/Lt., k. in a., 24/6/18.
Moody, Thomas, 2/Lt., k. in a., 1/7/16.
Mortleman, Charles Ibbetson, 2/Lt., k. in a., 9/9/16.
Osborne, William Edward, 2/Lt., d. of w., 11/9/16.
Pratt, Ernest Charles, 2/Lt., k. in a., 14/5/17.
Prince, Victor Charles, M.C., 2/Lt., k. in a., 1/9/18.
Scougall, Douglas Muir, 2/Lt., k. in a., 4/5/17.
Shaw, Thomas Charles Whitehall, 2/Lt., k. in a., 24/8/18.
Speyer, Cecil Arthur, 2/Lt., k. in a., 16/8/17.
Stoaling, Thomas, 2/Lt., k. in a., 14/5/17.
Sylvester, George Harry, 2/Lt., d. of w., 4/11/18.
Taylor, Cecil Meakin, 2/Lt., k. in a., 7/10/16.
Taylor, Herbert Berwick, 2/Lt., k. in a., 31/7/17.
Waters, Bernard Stanley, 2/Lt., k. in a., 3/5/17.
Webster, Walter Henry, D.S.O., 2/Lt., k. in a., 10/2/17.
Wheatley, Joseph Horace Lyncham, 2/Lt., k. in a., 15/6/17.
Wreford, Leslie Warren, 2/Lt., k. in a., 16/8/17.
Yeoman, B. F. L., 2/Lt., died, 11/5/18 (R.A.F.).

5th (City of London) Battalion The London Regiment (London Rifle Brigade).

Husey, Ralph Hamer, D.S.O., M.C., Brig.-Gen., d. of w., 30/5/18 (in German hands).
Bland, Bridgman Elsey, Capt., died, 26/10/17.
Butcher, William Guy Deane, Capt., k. in a., 16/8/17.
Calder, John Stewart, M.C. & Bar, Capt., k. in a., 28/3/18.
Furze, Claude, Capt., d. of w., 6/4/18.
Furze, Frederick, Capt., k. in a., 20/9/17.
Harvey, Bernard Sydney, Capt., k. in a., 1/7/16.
Hunter, Richard Jocelyn, Capt., d. of w., 25/8/18.
Kirby, Alister Graham, Capt., died, 29/3/17.
Large, Ernest L., Capt., d. of w., 21/5/15.
Morrison, Gerard H., Capt., k. in a., 31/3/15.
Rose, Eric Wollaston, Capt., k. in a., 28/3/18.
Somers-Smith, John Robert, M.C., Capt., k. in a., 1/7/16.
Welch, Vere Edward Osbaldiston, Capt., k. in a., 30/8/18.
Whitaker, George, Capt., k. in a., 20/9/17.
White, Arthur Bryan, Capt., k. in a., 16/8/17.
Bantoft, Edward Spencer, 2/Lt. (T/Lt.), d. of w., 10/9/16.
Beard, Harold Clifford, 2/Lt. (T/Lt.), k. in a., 8/10/16.
Brodie, Charles Gordon, Lt., k. in a., 23/5/17.
Clode-Baker, George Edmund, Lt., k. in a., 1/7/16.
Darrington, Clarence Philip, Lt., d. of w., 27/11/18.
Forbes, Lawrence, Lt., d. of w., 9/7/17.
Gooding, Herbert Robert Withom, Lt. k. in a. 13/5/15.
Harvest, Gordon Lindsay, M.C., Lt., d. of w., 20/6/17.
Lintott, Harry Chamen, Lt., d. of w., 22/3/18.
Maynard, Michael James, Lt., k. in a., 8/10/16.
Price, Henry Bertram, Lt., k. in a., 3/5/15.
Sedgwick, Arthur Edward, Lt., k. in a., 10/9/16.
Ticehurst, Gordon Harry, Lt., k. in a., 20/9/17.
Trenow, Geoffrey Foveaux, M.C., Lt., k. in a., 20/9/17.
Williamson, Edgar Rowe, M.C., Lt., k. in a., 10/9/16.
Williamson, Frank, Lt., k. in a., 24/3/18.
Adams, Geoffrey Julian, 2/Lt. d. of w., 27/9/18.
Baldwin, Norman Edward, 2/Lt., k. in a., 8/10/16.
Balkwill, Charles Vince, 2/Lt., k. in a., 1/7/16.
Bartleet, Henry Booth, 2/Lt., k. in a., 10/9/18.
Benns, Arthur Lionel, 2/Lt., k. in a., 1/7/16.
Carrier, John Russell, 2/Lt., k. in a., 8/10/16.
Cockerell, Donald Chessum, 2/Lt., k. in a., 6/11/18.
Cotter, George Herbert, 2/Lt., k. in a., 12/4/15.
Cross, Howard, 2/Lt., d. of w., 27/9/18.
Dewar, James Evan, 2/Lt., k. in a., 8/10/16.
Doust, Charles Bowden, 2/Lt., k. in a., 1/7/16.
Emerson, Frank, 2/Lt. k. in a., 26/8/18.
Forbes, Kenneth, 2/Lt., k. in a., 10/2/15.
Frey, Emile, 2/Lt., k. in a., 26/8/18.
Gardiner, William Edward Mansfield, 2/Lt., k. in a., 20/7/16.
Gilson, George, 2/Lt., k. in a., 1/9/18.
Gordon, Harold Eastly, 2/Lt., d. of w., 23/2/17.
Green, Cecil Ernest, 2/Lt., k. in a., 26/8/18.
Guthrie, Stuart, 2/Lt., k. in a., 4/4/18.
Harben, Kenneth Tucker, 2/Lt., k. in a., 13/8/18.
Hewitt, Humphrey St. John, 2/Lt., k. in a., 9/7/18.
Higgs, Harry Leonard, 2/Lt., k. in a., 25/3/18.
Holliday, Alfred Rowland, 2/Lt., k. in a., 20/11/17.
Hummerstone, L. G., 2/Lt., k. in a., 21/8/18 (R.A.F.).
Hunter, James Cecil, 2/Lt., d. of w., 2/9/18.
Keep, John Drummond, 2/Lt., k. in a., 13/10/18.
Lines, Sidney Martin, 2/Lt., k. in a., 13/5/15.
Lintott, Richard, 2/Lt., k. in a., 3/5/15.
Matthew, Wilfrid John, 2/Lt., k. in a., 19/5/18.
Mitchell, William Henry Lister, 2/Lt., k. in a., 20/9/17.
Newell, Francis Allister, 2/Lt., k. in a., 24/3/18.
Pocock, Beril Edmund, 2/Lt., k. in a., 13/5/15.
Pogose, Ivor Reginald, 2/Lt., k. in a., 1/7/16.
Rice, Edward Felix, 2/Lt., d. of w., 18/2/17.
Riordan, John Leonard, 2/Lt., k. in a., 8/9/18.
Sampson, Horace William, 2/Lt., k. in a., 28/5/18.
Sharman, Arthur Patrick, 2/Lt., k. in a., 20/9/17.
Slater, John Cyrus, 2/Lt., died, 6/7/17.
Smith, Horace, 2/Lt., k. in a., 8/10/16.
Stevenson, Ralph Tapley, 2/Lt., k. in a., 3/8/18.
Taylor, Frank Wilsher, 2/Lt., k. in a., 1/9/18.
Taylor, George Ossory, 2/Lt., k. in a., 8/10/16.
Thompson, Leslie Northcote, 2/Lt., k. in a., 2/12/17.
Ward, Dudley Theophilus, 2/Lt., k. in a., 20/9/17.
Warner, Archibald, 2/Lt., k. in a., 1/7/16.
Warner, Bertram, 2/Lt., k. in a., 12/4/17.
West, Leslie Gower, 2/Lt., k. in a., 24/10/18.
Young, Alan Catchpole, 2/Lt., k. in a., 24/3/18.

6th (City of London) Battalion The London Regiment (Rifles).

Collins, Robert Hayes, Major, k. in a., 20/5/17.
Maynard, John Edwin, M.C., Major, d. of w., 17/10/18.
Myer, Ernest Alex, Major, killed, 3/4/15.
Anderson, David William, M.C., Capt., k. in a., 8/8/18.
Ashby, George William, Capt., k. in a., 25/9/15.
Booth, William Leslie, Capt., d. of w., 28/5/15.
Brooke, Thomas Wickham, M.C., Capt., d. of w., 30/11/17.
Cotton, Montague Arthur Finch, Capt., k. in a., 18/5/15.
Hartley, William John, Capt., k. in a., 21/5/17.
Jones, Thomas Edward Painton, Capt., k. in a., 15/9/16.
Ordish, Henry Thomas, M.C., Capt., d. of w., 21/3/18 (in German hands).
Terry, John Norman, Capt. (Tp.), d. of w., 20/9/16.
Valentine, Guy, Capt., k. in a., 15/9/16.
Webb, Thomas Frederick, Capt., k. in a., 7/9/17.
Wiskar, Joseph William, Capt., d. of w., 7/3/17.
Andrew-Marshall, Joseph, Lt., k. in a., 20/11/17.
Faraday, Ray, Lt., k. in a., 7/6/17 (M.G.C.).
Hart, Howard Victor, M.C., Lt., killed, 23/3/19.
Keller, Francis Frederick, Lt., d. of w., 22/5/17.
McLaughlin, Edmund Coldicoate, Lt., k. in a., 18/5/15.
Smart, Edgar Herbert, Lt., k. in a., 30/11/17.
Alexander, John Rees, 2/Lt., d. of w., 4/9/18.
Allan, Henry Somerset, 2/Lt., d. of w., 2/10/16.
Beecher, Frank Alfred, 2/Lt., d. of w., 16/9/16.
Bull, Frederick John, 2/Lt., k. in a., 27/1/16.
Butler, Frederick Harold, 2/Lt., k. in a., 1/1/16.
Campbell, Stanley Frederick John, 2/Lt., k. in a., 27/8/18.
Coltman, Walter Joseph, 2/Lt., d. of w., 2/6/17.

Copping, Arthur Milton, M.M., 2/Lt., k. in a., 18/9/16.
Cropper, William, 2/Lt., k. in a., 22/8/18.
Dockree, Gilbert Arthur, 2/Lt, k. in a., 15/9/16.
Edwards, Walter, 2/Lt, k. in a., 26/4/16.
Figgins, Henry Francis, 2/Lt., k. in a., 16/9/16.
Forster, Harold Ker, 2/Lt., d. of w., 8/12/17 (in Ger. hands).
French, Robert Douglas, 2/Lt., k. in a., 15/9/16.
Fritchley, Joseph Bertram, 2/Lt., k. in a., 27/8/18.
Garrod, Ronald Percival, 2/Lt., k. in a., 22/5/15.
Gregory, John George, 2/Lt., d. of w., 8/1/16.
Gregory, Sydney Maurice, 2/Lt., k. in a., 18/5/15.
Hewson, Stanley Barton, 2/Lt., k. in a., 27/8/18.
Hill, Austen Shelbourne, 2/Lt., d. of w., 3/6/17.
Hubback, Francis William, 2/Lt., d. of w., 12/2/17.
Ker, Frederick Roxburghe, 2/Lt., k. in a., 20/9/17.
Lawrence, Harold Roy, 2/Lt., d. of w., 12/7/17.
Odam, Cecil Wilfred, 2/Lt., k. in a., 15/9/16.
Perry, Leslie Roy, 2/Lt., k. in a., 15/9/16.
Pickering, Edmund Charles, 2/Lt., k. in a., 15/9/16.
Powlesland, John Northley Julian, 2/Lt., d. of w., 20/9/16.
Quilter, Frederick Walter, 2/Lt., k. in a., 31/8/15.
Scanlan, William Jack, 2/Lt., k. in a., 1/9/17.
Soulsby, William Dobson, 2/Lt., k. in a., 31/8/18.
Spink, Dennis Boucher, 2/Lt., k. in a., 30/10/17.
Tasker, Herbert Edwin, 2/Lt., killed, 22/8/18.
Tickle, Gordon Philip, 2/Lt., d. of w., 30/9/18.
Webb, John Timms, 2/Lt., k. in a., 9/5/15.
White, William Ewart Cecil, 2/Lt., k. in a., 27/8/18.
Winslow, Benjamin Harmer, 2/Lt., k. in a., 30/11/17.
Wren, Christopher Bray, 2/Lt., k. in a., 15/9/16.

7th (City of London) Battalion, The London Regiment.

Casson, William, T.D., T/Major, k. in a., 25/9/15.
Green, Horace Salkeld, Major, k. in a., 20/9/17.
Flower, Leopold Arthur Lacon, Capt., k. in a., 7/10/16.
Halley-Jones, Percival, M.C., Capt., k. in a., 9/3/18.
Johnstone, William Joseph, Capt., d. of w., 18/12/17.
Jordon, Victor Harry, Capt., k. in a., 7/10/16.
King-Church, Cyril Edward, Capt., d. of w., 25/9/15.
Mileman, Vernon Wallace, M.C., Lt. (A/Capt.), k. in a., 16/9/17.
Rundell, Leslie Eric, M.C. & Bar, Capt., d. of w., 10/12/17.
Rushworth, Tom, Capt., k. in a., 16/9/16.
Shearman, Ambrose Augustus, Capt., d. of w., 20/4/18.
Walsh, Lionel Henry, M.C., D.C.M., A/Capt., d. of w., 29/8/18.
Bailey, Clifton Frederick, Lt., k. in a., 6/4/17.
Evershed, Philip Douglas, Lt., k. in a., 22/8/18.
Fearnside-Speed, Ronald Nelson de Dieskan, Lt., k. in a., 25/9/15.
Ferguson, Arthur Alexander, Lt., d. of w., 26/9/15.
Fletcher, John Holland Ballett, Lt., d. of w., 13/5/15.
Mantle, Alexander, Lt., k. in a., 23/5/17.
Metcalf, Cecil David, Lt., k. in a., 20/4/18.
Prince, Julius Sefton, Lt., k. in a., 25/9/15.
Roberts, Harold Owen Bodvel, M.C., Lt., d. of w., 18/11/15.
Smith, Arthur John, T/Lt., k. in a., 25/9/15.
Aitkens, Albert, Reginald Knight, 2/Lt., d. of w., 31/5/15.
Alexander, Harold John, 2/Lt., k. in a., 25/7/18.
Benstead, Harry Edwin, 2/Lt., k. in a., 14/4/17.
Bishop, John Ellis, 2/Lt., k. in a., 21/9/17.
Boag, Alfred, 2/Lt., died, 29/4/16 (and R.F.C.).
Boyer, Ernest Alexander, 2/Lt., k. in a., 5/4/18.
Brimfield, Ernest Gaskarth, 2/Lt., k. in a., 2/11/17
Coles, William Price Vivian, M.M., 2/Lt., k. in a., 7/10/16.
Constance, William Ernest, 2/Lt., k. in a., 9/8/18.
Cook, Horace Montague, 2/Lt., k. in a., 21/3/18.
Cox, George Beckett, 2/Lt., k. in a., 16/8/17.
Crosier, Vernon Swann, 2/Lt., d. of w., 6/4/18.
Cryer, Bernard Noel, 2/Lt., k. in a., 15/9/17.
Dansey, Felix Ramon Arthur, 2/Lt., k. in a., 25/7/18.
Davis, Brian Charles, 2/Lt., d. of w., 22/8/18.
Dawson, Harold, 2/Lt., killed (accid.), 14/7/17.
Donaldson, Denis Harrison, 2/Lt., k. in a., 25/9/15.
Edgar, Surrey, 2/Lt., k. in a., 7/10/16.
Edwards-Trollip, John, 2/Lt., k. in a., 27/8/18.
Feaveryear, Albert George, 2/Lt., k. in a., 5/9/18.
Fraser, Alan Cumming, M.C., 2/Lt., k. in a., 31/8/18.
Halsey, Eric Charles, 2/Lt., k. in a., 19/6/17.
Hancock, Albert Leslie 2/Lt., k. in a., 21/5/16.
Hosken, Victor Frederick, 2/Lt., k. in a., 7/10/16.
Hutton, William Wallace, 2/Lt., k. in a., 28/10/17 (and R.F.C.).
Johnstone, George Dreyer, 2/Lt., k. in a., 19/12/16.
Jury, George Rischieth, 2/Lt., k. in a., 14/9/16.
Keeler, Oscar Alan, 2/Lt., k. in a., 20/9/17.
Kirk, Ronald Leslie, 2/Lt., k. in a., 2/9/18.
Lewis, Harry Blundell, 2/Lt., k. in a., 2/12/17.
Long, Harold Dudley, 2/Lt., k. in a., 21/5/16.
Longley, Frank Arthur John, 2/Lt., k. in a., 18/6/17.
McHardy, Stewart John, 2/Lt., k. in a., 30/4/18.
McLaren, Athole, 2/Lt., k. in a., 18/9/18.
Maule-French, Eric Herbert Justus, 2/Lt., k. in a., 27/8/18.
Merchant, William John, 2/Lt., k. in a., 7/10/16.
Miller, William Edward, 2/Lt, d. of w., 17/7/16.
Montgomery, Ignatius Diego, 2/Lt., d. of w., 8/11/17.
Moore, Claude Leighton, 2/Lt., k. in a., 26/8/18.
Morgan, Fothergill Lewis, 2/Lt., d. of w., 3/12/17.
Naylor, Walter George, 2/Lt., k. in a., 31/8/18.
Neville, Stuart White, 2/Lt., k. in a., 21/9/18.
Opet, Isaac Harold, 2/Lt., d. of w., 22/3/18 (in German hands).
Polge, William Edwin, 2/Lt., k. in a., 16/8/17.
Pym, John Walter, 2/Lt., k. in a., 7/7/16.
Ralph, John Gray, 2/Lt., k. in a., 18/6/16.
Ridgway, Henry Collinson, 2/Lt., k. in a., 7/10/16.
Rinder, Charles Henry, 2/Lt., k. in a., 16/8/17.
Roberts, Francklin Allender, 2/Lt., k. in a., 8/8/18.
Roots, Percy William, 2/Lt, k. in a., 11/6/17.
Salter, Henry Albert, 2/Lt., k. in a., 7/6/17.
Sharp, Matthew, M.C., 2/Lt., d. of w., 11/2/18.
Simmons, Robert Dendney, 2/Lt., k. in a., 23/9/18.
Smith, Harold Benjamin, 2/Lt. d. of w., 20/5/17.
Solomon, John Howard, 2/Lt., d. of w., 21/4/17.
Squire, Leslie Charles Herman, 2/Lt., d. of w., 13/5/15.
Thomson, Arthur Stewart, 2/Lt., d. of w., 15/9/16.
Thurnell, William Cornelius Gibson, 2/Lt., d. of w., 16/9/16.
Tyler, William Alfred, 2/Lt., k. in a., 27/8/18.
Walker, Robert Russell, 2/Lt., k. in a., 23/3/18.
Watson, Clifford Thomas, 2/Lt., d. of w., 3/12/17.
Wilkes, George Lionel, 2/Lt., k. in a., 20/4/18
Williams, Charles Beresford, 2/Lt., k. in a., 1/9/18.
Wood, Brian Robert Philip, 2/Lt., killed (accd.), 2/7/15.

8th (City of London) Battalion, The London Regiment. (Post Office Rifles).

Alexander, George Luard, Capt. (T/Major), k. in a., 5/8/17.
Peel, Home, D.S.O., M.C., Capt. (Bde. Major), k. in a., 24/3/18.
Barnett, Edwin Bertram, Capt., k. in a., 30/10/17 (and M.G.C.).
Lanes, Ewart Reginald, M.C., Capt., k. in a., 22/3/18.
Mitchell, John Brine, M.C., Capt., k. in a., 15/9/15.
Poulton, Roy Roswell, Capt., k. in a., 8/8/18.
Russell, David Leslie, Capt., d. of w., 23/5/15.
Smith, Douglas Robert, Capt., died, 9/9/18.
Webb, Harold Oswald, Capt., k. in a., 15/9/16.
West, Lionel Reginald Everard, Capt., k. in a., 23/4/15.
Wheeldon, Frank Percy, Capt., k. in a., 30/10/17.
Blande, Arthur Frederick William, Lt., k. in a., 20/9/17.
Garrud, Owen Henry, Lt., k. in a., 24/8/18.
Hatfield, Roy Berriman, Lt., d. of w., 24/5/15.
Maclehose, Norman Crawford, Lt., k. in a., 26/5/15.
Mathieson-Macbeth, Thomas McBeth, Lt., k. in a., 5/9/17.
Miller, John Lockhart, Lt., k. in a., 21/5/16.
Newsome, Reginald Horace Arthur, M.C., Lt., d. of w., 30/8/18.
Barnes, Ralph George, 2/Lt., k. in a., 30/10/17.
Bishop, Parkyn Sydney, 2/Lt., k. in a., 30/11/17.
Brooke, William Alfred Cotterill, 2/Lt., k. in a., 14/6/15.
Cook, Philip Harry, 2/Lt., k. in a., 19/7/17.
Coote, Philip Edward, 2/Lt., k. in a., 15/9/16.
Duncan, Philip Courtnay, 2/Lt., k. in a., 30/10/17.
Edge, Edward Holden, 2/Lt., k. in a., 22-23/3/18.
Ferguson, Samuel Cranswick, 2/Lt., k. in a., 8/9/18.
Francis, Edward Griffith, 2/Lt., k. in a., 21/5/16.
Frere, Edgar, 2/Lt., d. of w., 22/5/16.
Gardner, Eric Melford, 2/Lt., k. in a., 27/9/18.
Gilman, William Harold, 2/Lt., k. in a., 14/6/18.
Graham, Hamilton Carruthers, 2/Lt., k. in a., 26/8/18.
Henderson, Eric, 2/Lt., k. in a., 7/6/17.
Hooper, Arthur James, 2/Lt., k. in a., 26/8/17.
Jenkins, Robert Henry Charles, 2/Lt., d. of w., 19/10/16.
Joyce, Walter Herbert, 2/Lt., k. in a., 22/3/18.
Kennedy, Samuel Lancelot Richard Alexander Edgar, 2/Lt., k. in a., 15/9/16.
Knell, Edward Charles, M.C., 2/Lt., k. in a., 9/8/18.
Lane, Frederick William, 2/Lt., d. of w., 19/5/17.
Lawrence, Oliver John, 2/Lt., k. in a., 26/5/15.
Leon, Edward Joseph, 2/Lt., k. in a., 7/10/16.
McAllister, Robert, 2/Lt., k. in a., 30/10/17.
MacCabe, Robert Maxwell, 2/Lt., k. in a., 23/4/15.
Mason, Arthur Edmund, 2/Lt., k. in a., 8/8/18.
Maylin, Bertram Henry, 2/Lt., k. in a., 11/4/18.
Moon, Basil Oliver, 2/Lt., k. in a., 24/5/15.
Morton, Albert Francis, 2/Lt., k. in a., 8/8/18.
Nicholls, Lionel, 2/Lt., k. in a., 26/8/16.
Nowell, Joseph Kent, 2/Lt., k. in a., 16/8/17.
Paterson, Lamont Livingstone, 2/Lt., k. in a., 1/9/18.
Potter, Frederick John, 2/Lt., k. in a., 21/5/16.
Roft, Edwin John, 2/Lt., k. in a., 25/7/18.
Sargeant, Bernard Theobald, 2/Lt., k. in a., 11/4/17.
Simpson, Alexander McGregor, 2/Lt., k. in a., 5/9/18.
Sloan, Thomas William, 2/Lt., k. in a., 20/9/17.
Smith, Thomas Edward, 2/Lt., k. in a., 5/9/18.
Stirling, George Edward, 2/Lt., k. in a., 7/10/16.
Sutcliffe, Fred Malcolm, 2/Lt., k. in a., 29/5/17.
Taylor, Richard Hayward, 2/Lt., k. in a., 20/9/17.
Titford, Claude Francis, 2/Lt., d. of w., 2/9/18.
Wakefield, Leonard John, 2/Lt., k. in a., 16/6/17.
Warren, Edgar Cecil, 2/Lt., k. in a., 3/5/17.
Watson, Oswald Halley, 2/Lt., k. in a., 9/9/17.
Weiss, Hubert Foreaux, 2/Lt., d. of w., 3/9/18.
Whitmarsh, Alec, 2/Lt., d. of w., 8/9/18.

9th (County of London) Battalion The London Regiment (Queen Victoria's Rifles).

Berry, Andrew Reginald, C.B., Lt.-Col., died, 24/3/17.
Lees, Thomas Prior, Major, k. in a., 21/4/15.
Brand, Douglas William McLeod, Capt., d. of w., 23/11/17.
Cornfoot, David Henry Harman, Capt., died, 2/5/16.
Cox, Harold Edward Leys, Capt., k. in a., 1/7/16.
Cunningham, Robert William, Capt., k. in a., 1/7/16.
Davies, Robert Finden, Capt., k. in a., 9/9/16.
Eccles, John Dennison, M.C., Capt., d. of w., 27/9/16.
Fazakerly-Westby, Gilbert Basil Joscelyn, Capt., k. in a., 21/4/15.
Flemming, Herbert Otto, Capt., d. of w., 7/5/15.
Hadden, Archibald Robert, Capt., k. in a., 25/4/18.
Griffith, Geoffrey Foster, Capt., k. in a., 26/9/17.
Holms, John Cyril, Capt., d. of w., 10/9/15.
Houghton, Philip Squarey, Capt., k. in a., 1/7/16.
Ralls, Frederic Hamilton, M.C. & Bar, Capt., d. of w., 24/8/18.
Symes, Edward Douglas, M.C., Capt., k. in a., 13/8/17.
Walker, Harold Saxon, Capt., d. of w., 12/9/17.
Woods, George, Capt. k. in a., 9/9/16.
Blackburne, Harry Devereux, Lt., k. in a., 27/9/17.

Blackwood, Henry Stear, Lt., d. of w., 1/5/17.
Brown, Sylvester Samuel, M.C., Lt., k. in a., 25/4/18 (and M.G.C.).
Easterbrook, Henry George, Lt., d. of w., 25/4/18.
Fargus, Frederick Brian Arthur, Lt., k. in a., 1/1/15.
Garside, Frank Gerald, Lt., k. in a., 27/8/18.
Lane, Edward Alfred Joseph Ardan, Lt., k. in a., 1/7/16.
Sedgley, Henry Frederick, Lt., k. in a., 22/9/18.
Astill, Ernest William Dearle, 2/Lt., k. in a., 30/3/18.
Bate, Maurice Charles Thornton, 2/Lt., k. in a., 13/8/17.
Brandram, Christopher, 2/Lt., d. of w., 1/9/18.
Bristow, Percy Henry, 2/Lt., k. in a., 23/3/18.
Browett, Reginald, 2/Lt., k. in a., 26/9/17.
Brown, John William, 2/Lt., k. in a., 16/8/17.
Caley, Pelham Russell, 2/Lt., d. of w., 14/8/17.
Cary, Richard Harry, 2/Lt., k. in a., 1/7/16.
Dowswell, Charles Victor, 2/Lt., k. in a., 8/10/16.
Fielding, Francis Willoughby, 2/Lt., k. in a., 1/7/16.
Fleetwood, Cyril Percy, 2/Lt., d. of w., 12/7/16 (in German hands).
Goundry, John Firth, 2/Lt., k. in a., 16/8/17.
Gutteridge, Richard Howard, 2/Lt., k. in a., 2/10/16.
Haselgrove, Bertram Thorpe, 2/Lt., d. of w., 3/9/18.
How, Henry James, 2/Lt., k. in a., 14/4/17.
Hunt, Louis Gordon, 2/Lt., k. in a., 22/9/18.
Hunter, Archibald Douglas, 2/Lt., k. in a., 23/4/17.
Lacey, Gordon Herbert, M.C., 2/Lt., d. of w., 29/9/18.
Leete, Frank Evelyn, 2/Lt., d. of w., 10/12/17.
Long, Arthur Glanville Holland, 2/Lt., d. of w., 13/8/17.
Ludlow, Lionel, 2/Lt., k. in a., 8/10/16.
Maddock, Owen Loftus, 2/Lt., k. in a., 7/10/16.
Mason, Overton Trollope, 2/Lt., k. in a., 1/7/16.
May, John Hayes, 2/Lt., k. in a., 20/11/17.
Meeking, Norman Arthur, 2/Lt., k. in a., 1/7/16.
Moore, Frederick Harry Bedloe, 2/Lt., k. in a., 4/11/18.
Newland, George Michael, 2/Lt., k. in a., 28/3/18.
Ord-Mackenzie, Douglas Allan, 2/Lt., k. in a., 24/9/16.
Parslow, Albert Jack, 2/Lt., d. of w., 10/10/16.
Plummer, Sidney Arthur, 2/Lt., k. in a., 24/4/18.
Prince, John Cecil Butter, 2/Lt., k. in a., 27/9/18.
Prince, W. F. J., 2/Lt., died, 30/5/18 (att. R.A.F.)
Rolason, Leslie Norton, 2/Lt., k. in a., 26/9/17.
Rumsey, Arthur Charles, 2/Lt., k. in a., 24/9/16.
Sanctuary, Cecil Reginald, 2/Lt., k. in a., 22/9/18.
Saxby, George Scrase, 2/Lt., d. of w., 22/4/17.
Sim, Norman Young, 2/Lt., k. in a., 9/9/16.
Simmonds, Percy Grabham, 2/Lt., k. in a., 1/7/16.
Smith, Horace Richard, M.C., 2/Lt., k. in a., 5/11/18.
Smith, Roy Samuel, 2/Lt., k. in a., 11/4/17.
Summerhays, Dudley Leycester, 2/Lt., k. in a., 21/4/15.
Thornton, Herbert Boucher, 2/Lt., k. in a., 9/7/17 (and M.G.C.).
Vanderlinde, Morris John Thomas, 2/Lt., k. in a., 30/8/18.
Warren, Alan Rowland, 2/Lt., k. in a., 8/10/16.
Wightwick, Sydney, 2/Lt., d. of w., 9/9/17.

10th (County of London) Battalion The London Regiment (Hackney).

Douglas, George Archibald Percy, Capt., d. of w., 30/11/15.
Farmar, Cyril Herbert Berkeley, Capt., k. in a., 19/4/17.
Holt, Leslie, Capt., k. in a., 11/3/18.
Hurrell, Colin John Richard, Capt., k. in a., 2/11/17.
Isard, Cyril Bickford, Capt., k. in a., 15/8/15.
Pattison, Robert, Capt., k. in a., 27/12/17.
Prior, Leslie Percy, Capt., d. of w., 7/6/17 (and R.F.C.).
Scrivener, Arthur William, M.C., Capt., k. in a., 2/11/17.
Solomon, Arthur Meyer, Capt., k. in a., 24/3/18.
Benzecry, Solomon, Lt., k. in a., 30/11/17.
Cranmore, George William, Lt., k. in a., 19/7/18.
Greenwood, Cecil James, Lt., k. in a., 9/8/18.
Hertslet, Warren Eccles, Lt., k. in a., 15/8/15.
Le Breton, Vivian Bertram, Lt., k. in a., 9/8/18.
Robson, Harry Stuart, Lt., k. in a., 8/8/18.
Taylor, Thomas St. Clair Gifford, Lt., k. in a., 17/3/18 (and R.F.C.).
Todman, C. V., Lt., k. in a., 3/8/18 (att. R.A.F.).
Tuffley, Victor Evelyn, D.S.O., M.C., Lt., d. of w., 7/9/18.
Arergis, Tasso Scott, 2/Lt., k. in a., 10/9/18.
Bath, Reginald Fred, 2/Lt., k. in a., 7/10/16.
Broad, Frank Cuthbert, 2/Lt., k. in a., 22/9/18.
Chubb Theodore, 2/Lt., k. in a., 17/2/17.
Croom, William Charles, 2/Lt., k. in a., 7/6/17.
Currie, James Alexander Vance, 2/Lt., k. in a., 13/3/17.
Davis, Uriah Philip, 2/Lt., k. in a., 16/4/17.
Dean, Reginald Evan, 2/Lt., k. in a., 7/6/17.
Fry, Wilfred, 2/Lt., d. of w., 3/11/18.
Glover, Cyril John, 2/Lt., d. of w., 8/10/16.
Haizelden, Benjamin, 2/Lt., d. of w., 30/8/18.
Hills, Geoffrey Wilfrid, 2/Lt., k. in a., 14/6/17.
Hoare, Henry Joseph, 2/Lt., k. in a., 15/8/15.
Hunt, H. H., 2/Lt., k. in a., 26/10/18 (att. R.A.F).
Hutchings, Edgar John. 2/Lt., died, 9/11/15.
Jackson, Arthur Frederick, 2/Lt., k. in a., 27/8/18.
Joy, Gwym, M.C., 2/Lt., d. of w., 16/7/17.
Jukes, Arthur Starr, 2/Lt., died, 6/3/17.
King, Hugh Denham, 2/Lt., k. in a., 13/3/17.
King, Hubert Weston, 2/Lt., k. in a., 10/11/18.
McNaughton, Algernon, 2/Lt., k. in a., 30/9/18.
Morbey, J. S., 2/Lt., died, 8/8/18 (att. R.A.F.).
Oakenfull, Herbert Joseph, 2/Lt., k. in a., 7/10/16.
Pakenham, John Walter Beaven, 2/Lt., k. in a., 21/9/18.
Parker, Alan, 2/Lt., k. in a., 23/9/17.
Rees, Owen George, 2/Lt., d. of w., 20/9/18.
Sheppard, Sidney, 2/Lt., k. in a., 28/4/17.
Stevenson, Hugh, 2/Lt., k. in a., 10/9/16.
Strahan, Geoffrey Bennock, 2/Lt., k. in a., 31/8/15.
Struebig, Edwin Harold, 2/Lt., k. in a., 8/8/18.
Tuite, Mark Alan Wallace, 2/Lt., d. of w., 2/12/17 (and Tanks).
Tyrrell, Oscar, 2/Lt., k. in a., 9/9/16.
Wallis, Alleyne Westaby, 2/Lt., k. in a., 7/6/17.
Whiter, Bertrand Thomas, 2/Lt., k. in a., 27/1/17.
Williams, Norman Ernest, 2/Lt., k. in a., 9/11/17 (and R.F.C.).
Williams, Richard White, 2/Lt., d. of w., 16/8/15.

11th (County of London) Battalion, The London Regiment (Finsbury Rifles).

Symonds, William Frederick John, D.S.O., Lt.-Col., d. of w., 24/4/18.
Tattersall, Philip Charles Paul, D.S.O., Capt., acc. drowned, 28/7/17.
Anderson, Peter Johnson, Lt., k. in a., 19/4/17.
Ashton, Hardric Grey, Lt., d. of w., 11/3/18 (R.F.C.).
Gibson, Harry Olivier Sumner, Lt., k. in a., 19/4/17.
Ground, Edward George, Lt., k. in a., 15/8/15.
Herbert, Reginald Strickson, Lt., k. in a., 21/5/17.
Maxwell, James, Lt., k. in a., 21/8/15.
Radloff, H., Lt., k. in a., 14/9/18 (R.A.F.).
Reid, Gerald Mortimer, Lt., k. in a., 9/5/18.
Akerman, Ralph Portland, 2/Lt., d. of w., 3/10/15.
Barry, Shiel Ronald, 2/Lt., k. in a., 7/10/16.
Clarke, Frederick Thomas Phillip, 2/Lt., k. in a., 10/4/17.
Cole, Charles Henry, 2/Lt., k. in a., 4/10/16.
Davis, Arthur George, 2/Lt., k. in a., 16/8/17.
Garner, Robert Leonard, 2/Lt., k. in a., 24/8/18.
Gibb, William Ian, 2/Lt., k. in a., 14/4/17.
Harrison, Ronald, 2/Lt., k. in a., 18/9/16.
Johnston, Alexander Francis, 2/Lt., k. in a., 10/9/16.
Matthews, Herbert Lewis Lash, 2/Lt., k. in a., 9/9/16.
Matthews, Noel Anwyl, 2/Lt., k. in a., 15/9/16.
Ritchings, Albert Arthur William, M.M., 2/Lt., k. in a., 27/9/18.
Sanderson, Gerald Stanley, 2/Lt., k. in a., 22/7/16.
Sellon, Bruce Heckford, 2/Lt., d. of w., 16/8/17.
Trounce, Frank, 2/Lt., k. in a., 4/9/18.
Unwin, Reginald William, 2/Lt., k. in a., 8/10/16.
Webster, Thomas William, 2/Lt., k. in a., 1/10/16.
Winter, Samuel Douglas, 2/Lt., died, 21/11/18.

12th (County of London) Battalion, The London Regiment (The Rangers).

Syms, Albert George Ernest, T.D., Lt.-Col., died, 22/1/18.
Foucar, James Lewis, Major, k. in a., 8/5/15.
Hoare, Vincent Robertson, Major, k. in a., 15/2/15.
Jones, Lewis Farewell, Major, k. in a., 1/7/16.
Worthington, Walter Gustavas, M.C., Major, d. of w., 27/4/18.
Arbuthnot, Ashley Herbert, Capt., d. of w., 15/5/15.
Copeland, Douglas Chatterton Bruce, M.C., Capt., d. of w., 21/6/18.
Harker, George Cuthbert Warburton, Capt., d. of w., 1/12/17.
Hoare, Richard Lennard, Capt., k. in a., 1/7/16.
Parker, John Ernest, Capt., k. in a., 8/5/15.
Simms, John Sibbald, Capt., k. in a., 26/10/17.
Studd, Lionel Fairfax, Capt., k. in a., 14/2/15.
Bailey, Douglas Ingram, Lt., died, 16/11/18.
Beeching, Geoffrey Charles, Lt., k. in a., 12/9/18.
Bradshaw, Richard Edward Kynaston, Lt., k. in a., 1/7/16.
Cohen, Solomon Maurice, Lt., k. in a., 9/9/16.
Day, G. S., Lt., k. in a., 1/10/18 (R.A.F.).
Meo, Giovanni Batista, Lt., k. in a., 10/6/16.
Rollins, Harold Victor, Lt., k. in a., 24/4/18.
Walford, Leonard Nithsdale, Lt., k. in a., 8/5/15.
Beausire, Charles Edward, 2/Lt., k. in a., 14/2/15.
Carte, Alan Simpson, 2/Lt., d. of w., 9/6/17.
Charles, Cecil Arthur, 2/Lt., d. of w., 22/9/18.
Cox, Harold, 2/Lt., d. of w., 16/4/18 (M.G.C.).
Davey, William Roy, 2/Lt., k. in a., 1/7/16.
Durston, Charles Giles, 2/Lt., k. in a., 7/10/16.
Goodall, Arthur, 2/Lt., d. of w., 20/2/18.
Griffith, William Key, 2/Lt., k. in a., 26/9/17.
Hibbard, Edmund John, 2/Lt., k. in a., 9/4/17.
Hooper, Bernard Keith, 2/Lt., k. in a., 26/9/17.
Isbister, Leonard Stanley, 2/Lt., k. in a., 9/9/16.
Jefford, William Arthur, 2/Lt., k. in a., 8/5/15.
Joseland, Frederick Osborn, 2/Lt., k. in a., 10/9/16.
Josephs, Joseph, 2/Lt., k. in a., 1/7/16.
Lawless, Barry Joseph Anthony, 2/Lt., k. in a., 17/7/17.
Legrove, Walter, 2/Lt., k. in a., 25/4/18.
Nicholson, Leonard Sampson, 2/Lt., k. in a., 2/5/15.
Peebles, Percy Norman, 2/Lt., k. in a., 9/4/17.
Phillips, Arthur Blakeway, 2/Lt., k. in a., 19/6/16.
Rose, Archibald John Gordon, 2/Lt., k. in a., 26/9/17.
Strickland, Charles John, 2/Lt., k. in a., 5/4/18.
Synyer, Richard Harold, 2/Lt., d. of w., 21/9/18.
Taplin, Albert William, 2/Lt., k. in a., 1/7/16.
Telfer, Somerville Goodman, 2/Lt., k. in a., 8/5/15.
Tucker, William Henry. 2/Lt., k. in a., 1/7/16.
Ward, Dacre Stanley, 2/Lt., k. in a., 1/7/16.
Warren, Alan John, 2/Lt., d. of w., 10/7/17.
Webb, Frank Ralph, 2/Lt., k. in a., 9/9/16.
Whitehouse, Alfred Ernest, 2/Lt., k. in a., 8/5/15.
Wildsmith, Leonard Charles, 2/Lt., k. in a., 2/3/15.
Williams, Richard James, 2/Lt., d. of w., 29/4/18.
Willis, Cyril Louis, 2/Lt., k. in a., 7/10/16.
Wood, William Edmond, 2/Lt., d. of w., 26/4/18.

13th (County of London), The London Regiment (Princess Louise's, Kensington Battalion).

Shaw, Robert Edward Fredric, M.C., Lt.-Col., k. in a., 23/8/18.
Dickens, Cedric Charles, Major, k. in a., 10/9/16.
Flower, Victor Augustine, D.S.O., Major, k. in a., 15/8/17.
Barnett, Herbert William, Capt., k. in a., 9/5/15.
Lukis, Theodore Stewart, Capt., d. of w., 15/3/15.
Perry, Henry Bernard, Capt., k. in a., 6/11/18.
Prismall, Arthur, Capt., k. in a., 14/3/15.
Rosevear, Frank Rusolph, Capt., d. of w., 23/8/18.
Ware, Francis Henry, Capt., k. in a., 1/7/16.
Baker, John Francis, Lt., k. in a., 28/8/18.
Burn, William Gladstone, Lt., k. in a., 9/5/15.
Gates, Eric Chasemore, Lt., k. in a., 14/3/15.
Hart, Ernest George, Lt., k. in a., 30/8/18.
Mitchison, Malcolm, Lt., died, 4/11/18.
Leigh-Pemberton, Thomas Edward Geoffrey, Lt., k. in a., 11/1/15.
MacGregor, Robert Murray, Lt., d. of w., 9/5/15 (in German hands).
Parnell, Leslie Reginald, Lt., k. in a., 9/10/17.
Sewell, Norman Oscar, Lt., killed, 9/5/15.
Sheppard, Reginald Thomas, Lt., k. in a., 13/5/17.
Turner, Thomas Edwin, Lt., k. in a., 9/5/15.
Walford, Leonard N., Lt., k. in a., 8/5/15.
Brooks, George Thomas, 2/Lt., k. in a., 30/11/17.
Bundle, Harry Norman, 2/Lt., k. in a., 20/9/17.
Burd, Frederick Braham, 2/Lt., k. in a., 20/9/17.
Castelli, Ernest Charles, 2/Lt., k. in a., 9/5/15.
Davis, Maurice Oliver Arthur, 2/Lt., d. of w., 1/3/18.
Dawes, Roy Samuel, 2/Lt., k. in a., 9/9/16.
Druery, Dudley Victor, 2/Lt., d. of w., 18/10/18.
Ellis, Frederick William, 2/Lt., k. in a., 3/3/18.
Goadby, John Clifton, 2/Lt., k. in a., 28/8/18.
Grosvenor, Thomas Robert, 2/Lt., k. in a., 14/8/17.
Gruselle, Henri Ernest John, 2/Lt., k. in a., 30/11/17.
Jackson, Arthur Granham, 2/Lt., k. in a., 6/10/18.
Jemmett, George Elwick, 2/Lt., d. of w., 17/12/17.
Kirk, Alfred Charles, 2/Lt., k. in a., 31/3/18.
Lawrie, Norman Ernest, 2/Lt., k. in a., 9/5/15.
Lester, Albert Edward, 2/Lt., k. in a., 8/5/18.
Lockhart, Reginald Frank, 2/Lt., d. of w., 10/7/17 (and M.G.C.).
McCallum, Edward, 2/Lt., drowned, 30/12/17.
MacKenzie, Noel Olliffe Compton, 2/Lt., k. in a., 1/7/16.
Mager, William George, 2/Lt., k. in a., 1/7/16.
Osborn, Walter, 2/Lt., k. in a., 5/11/18.
Pearce, William Henry, 2/Lt., k. in a., 19/2/18.
Peters, Arthur Stafford, 2/Lt., k. in a., 30/11/17.
Pilgrim, Henry Bastick, 2/Lt., k. in a., 1/7/16.
Posnett, William Leonard, 2/Lt., k. in a., 22/6/17.
Ranson, Charles Sherriff, 2/Lt., k. in a., 16/8/17.
Sach, Charles Burleigh, 2/Lt., k. in a., 1/7/16.
Sanders, William Alfred Thomas, 2/Lt., k. in a., 9/9/16.
Seabury, Edgar Raymond, 2/Lt., k. in a., 21/9/17.
Stern, Leonard Hermann, 2/Lt., k. in a., 9/5/15.
Stockwell, Frank Roland, 2/Lt., k. in a., 6/8/16.
Stone, Henry Reginald, 2/Lt., d. of w., 17/4/18 (in German hands).
Wilson, Richard Nelson, 2/Lt., k. in a., 23/8/18.

14th (County of London) Battalion, The London Regiment. (London Scottish).

Lindsay, Francis Howard, Major, k. in a., 1/7/16.
Bowron, Keith Stuart, D.C.M., Capt., k. in a., 8/8/18.
Douglas, Allen Grant, M.C., Capt., k. in a., 30/11/17.
Hall, George, Capt., d. of w., 23/4/18.
Hunter, Hope, Capt., died, 3/12/17.
Greig, Roy Scott, Capt., k. in a., 28/3/18.
MacGregor, Alfred Horace, Capt., k. in a., 11/9/16.
Mackie, Norman Lindsey, Capt., d. of w., 25/9/15 (and M.G.C.).
MacKinnon, William, Capt., k. in a., 11/5/17.
MacLagan, Thomas Duncan Ogilvie, M.C. & Bar, Capt., k. in a., 30/4/18.
Miller, James Cooper, Capt., d. of w., 24/11/17.
Syer, Hubert Lionel, M.C., Capt., d. of w., 18/11/16.
Thomson, Frederick Stanley, Capt., k. in a., 1/7/16 (and M.G.C.).
Thomson, James Scott, Capt., k. in a., 5/5/17.
Barthorpe, Alec Scott, Lt., k. in a., 25/4/18.
Brown-Constable, John Cecil, Lt., k. in a., 1/7/16.
Cameron, Tom Finlayson, Lt., d. of w., 30/4/18.
Farquarson, John Charles Lancelot, Lt., k. in a., 31/10-1/11/14.
Hunter, Percy Talbot Langley, Lt., died., 19/7/16.
Hyslop, James, Lt., k. in a., 5/11/18.
Lamb, Dudley William, Lt., k. in a., 22/3/18.
Baker, Frank Alexander, M.M., 2/Lt., k. in a., 1/10/18.
Bayfield, John Stanley Lucas, 2/Lt., k. in a., 29/8/18.
Bayley, Albert Clarence, 2/Lt., d. of w., 13/12/17.
Beardmore, Sydney Alfred, 2/Lt., d. of w., 1/9/18.
Brown, Ralph Adair, 2/Lt., k. in a., 1/7/16.
Brown, Robert Alexander, 2/Lt., k. in a., 16/9/18.
Browning, Ernest George, 2/Lt., d. of w., 19/7/17.
Bruce, Malcolm Ronald, 2/Lt., k. in a., 22/8/17.
Calder, Harold Joseph, 2/Lt., k. in a., 17/9/16.
Carlyle, George Pasley, 2/Lt., k. in a., 14/10/18.
Cotton, Robert Douglas, M.C., 2/Lt., died, 5/4/19.
Coxon, Herbert Archibald, 2/Lt., k. in a., 1/7/16.
Crawford, William Scott, 2/Lt., k. in a., 15/4/17.
Curror, William Edwin Forrest, 2/Lt., k. in a., 1/7/16.
Dakers, John, 2/Lt., k. in a., 12/5/17.
Duncan, David Cyril, 2/Lt., k. in a., 21/8/18.
Findlay, Edward John, 2/Lt., d. of w., 9/5/15.
Finlay, James Nelson, 2/Lt., k. in a., 28/3/18.
Fraser, Laureston Ross, 2/Lt., k. in a., 21/3/18.
Fuller, Herbert Walter, 2/Lt., k. in a., 21/8/18.
Grey, Sidney James, 2/Lt., k. in a., 1/8/18.
Hawkins, Herbert Edward, 2/Lt., k. in a., 11/5/17.
Heritage, H. A., 2/Lt., died, 28/6/18 (att. R.A.F.).
Hislop, Alec Herbert, 2/Lt., died, 24/12/17.
Ker-Gulland, Reginald Glover, 2/Lt., d. of w., 12/11/14.
Kerr, Donald, 2/Lt., k. in a., 1/7/16.
Lowe, Norman McGregor, 2/Lt., k. in a., 10/1/16.
McKenzie, William, 2/Lt., d. of w., 12/6/18.
MacLachlan, William Smith, 2/Lt., k. in a., 29/8/18.
Mello, Arnold, 2/Lt., d. of w., 17/11/15.
Morris, Reginald Martin, 2/Lt., k. in a., 17/2/17.
Petrie, Allan Strachan, 2/Lt., k. in a., 11/9/16.
Rennie, Hugh Robert, 2/Lt., d. of w., 10/7/18 (in German hands).
Roberts, Francis Watson, 2/Lt., k. in a., 14/10/15.
Roe, Sidney Charles, 2/Lt., k. in a., 5/5/17.
Silver, Edward, 2/Lt., k. in a., 1/5/18.
Struthers, Kenneth, 2/Lt., k. in a., 7/10/16.
Smith, Robert, 2/Lt., k. in a., 28/3/18.
Trollope, Cyril Harvey, 2/Lt., killed, 4/5/17 (and R.F.C.).
Wilson, Albert Cecil, 2/Lt., d. of w., 8/7/16.
Wilson, Alfred Cairns, M.C., 2/Lt., d. of w., 25/9/16.
Young, James Hill, 2/Lt., d. of w., 17/1/18 (and R.F.C.) (in German hands).

15th (County of London) Battalion, The London Regiment (Prince of Wales's Own, Civil Service Rifles).

Kemble, Henry H., D.S.O., M.C., Lt.-Col., d. of w., 7/6/17.
Davies, Leslie, Capt., k. in a., 15/9/16.
Farquhar, Hobart Brooks, Capt., k. in a., 21/5/16.
Gaze, Geoffrey Atkinson, Capt., k. in a., 15/9/16.
Hill, Frederick, D.C.M., Capt., k. in a., 8/8/18.
Ind, William Ernest, M.C., Capt., d. of w., 7/6/17.
Roberts, Arthur, Capt., k. in a., 15/9/16.
Trembath, Allen Edward, Capt., k. in a., 26/5/15.
Attwood, Stanley Albert, Lt., k. in a., 3/10/18.
Broad, Walter Victor Mantach, Lt., k. in a., 22/3/18.
Chalmers, Robert, Lt., d. of w., 25/5/15.
Hoste, George Michael, Lt., killed, 7/10/16.
Scott, Bernard, Lt., k. in a., 21/5/16.
Smith, Thomas Arthur, Lt., k. in a., 7/10/16.
Acworth, Gordon William, 2/Lt., d. of w., 7/6/17.
Aylmore, Alick Guyer Aylmer, 2/Lt., k. in a., 23/3/18.
Boyes, James Ferguson, 2/Lt., d. of w., 25/8/18.
Brantom, William Harper, D.C.M., 2/Lt., k. in a., 3/7/16.
Bullock, Alan Marlowe, 2/Lt., k. in a., 4/11/18.
Chilvers, Roland Clifford, 2/Lt., k. in a., 29/7/17.
Clark, Sidney George, 2/Lt., k. in a., 4/4/18.
Clarke, Henry Robert Ernest, 2/Lt., d. of w., 3/6/16.
Clarke, Russell Frank, 2/Lt., k. in a., 21/5/17.
Coldicott, Hubert Eric, 2/Lt., k. in a., 21/5/17.
Denny, Ernest, 2/Lt., d. of w., 4/8/17.
Fletcher, Ernest, 2/Lt., k. in a., 15/9/16.
Garrett, Maurice Humphris, 2/Lt., k. in a., 2/9/18.
Glynn, Alfred Henley, 2/Lt., d. of w., 12/2/17.
Goswell, Oliver Owen, 2/Lt., k. in a., 30/4/18.
Harris, Rowland Hanwell, 2/Lt., k. in a., 27/12/17.
Hoole, Geoffrey, 2/Lt., k. in a., 15/9/16.
Hughes, Robert Charles, 2/Lt., k. in a., 17/8/18.
Jamieson, Colin, Miller, 2/Lt., k. in a., 21/5/17.
Kearley, Harold, 2/Lt., k. in a., 3/2/18 (and R.F.C.).
Lacy, William Braithwaite, 2/Lt., d. of w., 14/12/17.
Macdonald, John Stewart, 2/Lt., killed, 5/7/18.
Marchant, Charles Victor, 2/Lt., k. in a., 30/11/17.
Northam, John McClure, 2/Lt., k. in a., 15/9/17.
Palin, Oscar Ernest, 2/Lt., k. in a., 26/10/17.
Pilcher, Alfred Mark, 2/Lt., d. of w., 6/6/18 (in German hands).
Smith, Reginald Frederick, 2/Lt., k. in a., 14/5/17.
Stoneman, William Thomas, 2/Lt., d. of w., 26/7/17.
Tatum, George Edward, 2/Lt., k. in a., 30/11/17.
Thompson, Frank Dickinson, 2/Lt., k. in a., 13/1/17.
Townsend, Eric Lever, 2/Lt., d. of w., 17/9/16.
Ware, Bertram Knight, 2/Lt., k. in a., 19/9/16.

16th (County of London) Battalion, The London Regiment (Queen's Westminster Rifles).

Glasier, Philip Mannoch, D.S.O., Lt.-Col., k. in a., 2/6/18.
Tyrwhitt, Nathaniel Bridges, Major, k. in a., 28/12/15.
Agate, Harold, Capt., k. in a., 14/4/17.
Barwell, Frederick Leycester, Capt., k. in a., 29/4/17.
Bull, Ronald John Howard, Capt., killed, 13/7/17.
Butler, Sidney, Capt., died, 22/1/19.
Caudwell, Thord, Capt. (Act.), k. in a., 30/11/17.
Cockerill, George Edward, Lt., T/Capt., d. of w., 3/7/16 (in German hands).
Dickinson, Raymond Scott, 2/Lt., T/Capt., k. in a., 2/10/15.
Gordon, Alexander John, Capt., k. in a., 27/11/17.
Green, James Archer, Capt., k. in a., 23/3/17.
Helme, Thomas Herbert, Capt., d. of w., 3/11/18.
Makins, Hugh, Capt., d. of w., 4/11/15.
Mott, Hugh Frederick, Capt., k. in a., 1/7/16.
Newcombe, Edgar, 2/Lt., A/Capt., k. in a., 15/4/18.
Shattock, Montague Mancha, Capt., k. in a., 8/1/15.
Spencer-Smith, Charles Owen, Capt., d. of w., 3/8/17.
Swainson, Francis Gibbon, Capt., k. in a., 1/7/16.
Townsend-Green, Henry Russell, Capt., d. of w., 3/3/15.
Brown, Francis Clement, Lt., k. in a., 8/12/17.
Edmonstone, Norman Stuart, Lt., d. of w., 7/11/17.
Gatfield, Reginald Alfred, Lt., d. of w., 7/6/17 (and M.G.C.).
Harrow, Leonard Phillip, D.C.M., Lt., k. in a., 28/8/18.
Hipwell, Charles Stanley, M.C., Lt., k. in a., 14/10/16.
Hoste, George Michael, Lt., k. in a., 7/10/16.
Lamaison, Wilfrid Lawrence, Lt., d. of w., 23/8/18.
Russell, Francis Wycliffe, M.C., Lt., k. in a., 27/8/18.
Sclanders, Charles Maclure, Lt., k. in a., 12/4/18

Webb, Musgrave Maitland, Lt., k. in a., 18/9/16.
Yeates, Stanley Charles, Lt., k. in a., 14/4/17.
Alexander, Alan Mansell, 2/Lt., k. in a., 8/12/17.
Baker, Thomas Sydney, 2/Lt., k. in a., 14/4/17.
Bannester, John, 2/Lt., k. in a., 4/10/18.
Basden, Maurice Duncan, 2/Lt., k. in a., 20/5/16 (and R.F.C.).
Beville, Alfred Geoffrey, 2/Lt., k. in a., 8/4/17.
Bidgood, Frank, 2/Lt., k. in a., 10/9/18.
Bovill, Edward Henry, 2/Lt., k. in a., 1/7/16.
Curwen, Gilbert Christopher, 2/Lt., k. in a., 3/6/18.
Dyson, William Hubert, 2/Lt., d. of w., 14/7/16.
Elders, John Francis, 2/Lt., k. in a., 28/10/17.
Engall, John Sherwin, 2/Lt., k. in a., 1/7/16 (and M.G.C.).
Hooper, John Hamilton Morris, 2/Lt., k. in a., 30/11/17.
Horne, James Anthony, 2/Lt., k. in a., 1/7/16.
Hutchison, Donald Herbert, 2/Lt., k. in a., 9-10/8/15.
Jacob, Henry William James, 2/Lt., k. in a., 26/10/17.
Jones, Eric Arthur Owen, 2/Lt., k. in a., 18/9/16.
Negus, Arthur George, 2/Lt., k. in a., 1/7/16.
Peter, Richard Henry, 2/Lt., k. in a., 30/4/18.
Pickworth, Arthur William, 2/Lt., k. in a., 28/9/18.
Reid, Percy Cargill, 2/Lt., k. in a., 6/5/17.
Sheppard, Charles, 2/Lt., k. in a., 27/9/18.
Spencer-Smith, Martin, 2/Lt., k. in a., 10/9/16.
Stitt, Innes d'Auvergne Stewart, 2/Lt., k. in a., 28/3/18.
Weston, John Cecil, 2/Lt., d. of w., 6/6/17.
Wright, Alfred Kyrle Terrett, 2/Lt., d. of w., 10/12/17.
Yates, Arthur Gerald Vavasour, 2/Lt., k. in a., 1/7/16.

17th (County of London) Battalion, The London Regiment (Poplar and Stepney Rifles).

Barns, Charles Stanley, Capt., died, 22/8/18 (M.G.C.).
Cain, Walter Frank, Capt., d. of w., 3/5/17.
Cotton, Brian Gordon Hamilton, Capt., d. of w., 8/11/17.
Crofts, Frederic Wilkinson, M.C., Capt., d. of w., 15/9/16.
Gibb, George Blaikie, Capt., k. in a., 1/9/18.
Thompson, Frank Samuel, Capt., k. in a., 23/3/18.
Wright, Howard Caldwell, M.C., Capt., d. of w., 2/9/17.
Carpenter, Robert Leslie, Lt., k. in a., 26/10/15.
Cave, Edward Charles, M.C., Lt., d. of w., 29/8/18 (M.G.C.).
Clarke, Harold Martin, Lt., k. in a., 26/9/15.
Gibson, Charles Leslie, M.C., Lt., d. of w., 3/9/18.
Goddard, Sydney Vernon, Lt., d. of w., 23/3/18.
Grice, Percival Samuel Henry, Lt., k. in a., 2/9/18.
Hatch, George John, Lt., k. in a., 6/4/17 (R.F.C.).
Morton, Norman Donald Rex, Lt., k. in a., 22/4/17.
Newton, Murray Edell, Lt., k. in a., 18/6/17 (R.F.C.).
Parrott, Dennis Hele, Lt., k. in a., 30/4/18.
Piercy, Wilfred Ashton, Lt., killed, 26/9/15.
Robb, Thomas Douglas, Lt., killed, 26/9/15.
Simmons, Walter John, M.C., Lt., d. of w., 27/8/18.
Whitham, Charles, Lt., k. in a., 6/10/18.
Whyte, George Herbert, Lt., k. in a., 23/12/17.
Aganoor, Aganoor John, 2/Lt., k. in a., 15/9/16.
Barnard, Lawrence Reginald, 2/Lt., k. in a., 1/10/16.
Beck, Frederick Charles, 2/Lt., k. in a., 14/9/17
Booth, Cyril Talbot, 2/Lt., k. in a., 10/6/17.
Caro, Jacob Pisa, 2/Lt., k. in a., 2/5/18.
Costello, Archibald Gordon, 2/Lt., k. in a., 15/9/16.
Crosby, Frederick Howard, 2/Lt., k. in a., 7/3/18.
Daft, Harry, 2/Lt., k. in a., 13/4/17.
Davies, Reginald Charles Spurgeon, 2/Lt., k. in a., 21/3/18.
Eaitch, Ernest, 2/Lt., d. of w., 2/11/18.
Forbes, Douglas Tulloch, 2/Lt., d. of w., 17/1/16.
Golding, Frank, 2/Lt., k. in a., 21/5/17.
Hooton, Nelson Mackrow, 2/Lt., k. in a., 16/8/17.
Idle, Wilfrid Ernest, 2/Lt., k. in a., 25/2/17.
Illingworth, Harold Locke, 2/Lt., k. in a., 23/3/18.
Kent, Walter John, 2/Lt., k. in a., 24/8/18.
King, Arthur William, 2/Lt., k. in a., 17/9/16.
Lane, Frank, 2/Lt., k. in a., 16/5/17.
Macbeth, Harold John, 2/Lt., k. in a., 15/9/16.
Ross, John Alexander, 2/Lt., k. in a., 26/10/15.
Rowland, William Ronald, 2/Lt., k. in a., 1/6/17.
Savage, Henry George, 2/Lt., k. in a., 17/10/17.
Sheppard, Hubert, 2/Lt., d. of w., 9/12/17.
Smith, Charles Alfred, 2/Lt., k. in a., 1/10/16.
Southon, John Edward, M.C., 2/Lt., k. in a., 3/12/17.
Staples, Edmund, 2/Lt., d. of w., 20/8/18.
Temple, William, 2/Lt., k. in a., 7/6/17.
Thompson, Arthur Herbert, 2/Lt., k. in a., 1/10/16.
Williams, Maxwell Henry, 2/Lt., k. in a., 19/9/17.
Wilson, Harold, 2/Lt., k. in a., 5/9/18.

18th (County of London) Battalion, The London Regiment (London Irish Rifles).

Trinder, John Robert, M.C., Major, k. in a., 15/9/16.
Curling, Frank Trevor, Capt. (Act.), k. in a., 31/8/18.
Fairley, Philip Ernest, Capt., died, 2/4/19.
Harding, Reginald William Fowler, Capt., k. in a., 7/11/17.
Houston, Kenneth D'Aguilar, Capt., k. in a., 24/3/18.
Maginn, Philip Albert Charles, M.C., Capt., k. in a., 15/9/16.
Malcolmson, James Grant, Capt., died, 22/12/14.
Standrick, Jones Harold, Capt., d. of w., 21/2/18.
Willock, Guy Charles Boileau, Capt., k. in a., 25/9/15.
Adams, Percy Lionel, Lt., d. of w., 3/10/18 (M.G.C.).
Godsill, Stanley, Lt., k. in a., 23/12/17.
Jacob, Arthur Leslie Hamilton, T/Lt., k. in a., 25/9/15.
Jones, Thomas Idwal, M.M., Lt., k. in a., 31/8/18.
Knox, John Vesey, Lt., killed, 4/1/18 (R.F.C.).
MacBeth, Stanley, Lt., k. in a., 15/9/16.
MacReight, Arthur William James, Lt., died, 23/11/15.
Miller, Howard Todd, Lt., k. in a., 21-26/3/18.
Munro, Ronald George, M.C., Lt., d. of w., 19/9/16.
Thompson, Cyril James Ockelford, Lt., d. of w., 25/12/17.
Tolson, George Henderson, Lt., d. of w., 1/12/17.
Toms, Stanley Muir, Lt., d. of w., 8/12/17.
Agate, Norman Stanford, 2/Lt., d. of w., 23/3/18.
Aird, Archibald Thomas, 2/Lt., k. in a., 30/11/17.
Barnes, Eric, 2/Lt., k. in a., 16/11/18.
Battersby, Ernest Joseph, 2/Lt., d. of w., 13/6/17.
Baxter, John Denham, 2/Lt., k. in a., 7/11/18.
Bradbrook, E. J., 2/Lt., k. in a., 20/4/18 (R.A.F.).
Brayden, Kevin, 2/Lt. k. in a., 23/12/17.
Buck, Cyril Alfred Spencer, M.M., 2/Lt., k. in a., 26/10/17.
Burke, Sydney Slaven, 2/Lt., k. in a., 22/12/17.
Butcher, John Philip Henry, 2/Lt., k. in a., 22/5/16.
Chapman, Frank Reginald, 2/Lt., d. of w., 25/9/15.
Conlan, Arthur Underhill, 2/Lt., k. in a., 22/5/16.
Cunningham, Arthur Joseph, D.C.M., 2/Lt., k. in a., 15/9/16
Downes, Benjamin, 2/Lt., k. in a., 2/6/18.
Dubois, Latimer Ridley, 2/Lt., k. in a., 7/4/17.
Gray, Cyrus Keswick, 2/Lt., k. in a., 14/4/17.
Harrison, John William, 2/Lt., k. in a., 7/6/17.
Hicks, Ernest, 2/Lt., k. in a., 9/10/16.
James, Bernard William Austin, 2/Lt., k. in a., 14/10/17.
Kennedy, James Patrick, 2/Lt., k. in a., 19/6/18 (M.G.C.).
Mitchell, John Leischman, 2/Lt., d. of w., 4/6/17.
Orr, Robert Watson, 2/Lt., k. in a., 25/9/15.
Parkes, Percy Reginald, 2/Lt., d. of w., 4/4/18 (P. of W.).
Plummer, William Francis, 2/Lt., k. in a., 15/9/16.
Pratt, Lionel Henry 2/Lt., k. in a., 25/9/15.
Richardson, Robert Harold, 2/Lt., k. in a., 6/11/17 (R.F.C.).
Richens, Richard Ivor, 2/Lt., d. of w., 14/4/17.
Sanderson, Sidney Charles, 2/Lt., k. in a., 11/10/16.
Sargeant, Harold William, 2/Lt., d. of w., 4/4/18.
Stedman, William Walter Thomas, 2/Lt., k. in a., 13/11/16.
Stokes, Leicester Henry, 2/Lt., k. in a., 31/10/17.
Thompson, Richard Seward, 2/Lt., k. in a., 16/1/17.
Willis, Thomas Ambrose, Lt., k. in a., 8/12/17.
Wilson, Harold Benjamin, 2/Lt., k. in a., 7/4/17.
Young, Samuel Kenneth, 2/Lt., k. in a., 30/11/17.

19th (County of London) Battalion, The London Regiment. (St. Pancras).

Jackson, Stanley Richardson, T/Major, d. of w., 31/12/15.
Baker, George William, Capt., d. of w., 5/12/17.
Davis, Leigh Jacob, Capt., k. in a., 15/9/16.
De Meza, Jacob, M.C., Capt., k. in a., 22/8/18.
Gauld, Alexander George, Capt., k. in a., 15/9/16.
Hanewinkel, Ernest Eberhard, Capt., k. in a., 31/8/15.
Kershaw, Henry Valder, Capt., k. in a., 15/9/16.
Pass, Joseph Albert, Capt., d. of w., 20/5/15.
Riley, Arthur Cecil, Capt., k. in a., 25/9/15.
Robson, Tom, Capt., k. in a., 22/8/18.
Schonfield, Edwin, T/Capt., k. in a., 20/9/16.
Ward, Fred, M.C., Capt., k. in a., 8/12/17.
Whitby, James Hornby, Capt., died, 16/3/16.
Bantick, Reginald Arthur Jay, Lt., k. in a., 19/5/15.
Bencher, Gilbert Alfred, Lt., d. of w., 9/12/17.
Butler, Charles Reginald, Lt., died, 28/11/18.
Carey, William Alexander, Lt., k. in a., 29/12/17.
De Fontaine, Edward Harold, Lt., d. of w., 17/11/15.
Easson, David, Lt., k. in a., 21/3/18.
Gambell, Dennis Clayton, Lt., k. in a., 30/4/18.
Gardiner, Arthur, Lt., d. of w., 26/3/18.
Hore, Kennett Scarborough, Lt., k. in a., 25/9/15.
Rickeard, William Christopher, Lt, k. in a., 30/9/15.
Smith, Frank William Howard, Lt., d. of w., 4/12/17.
Tabbener, Thomas Kemp, Lt., d. of w., 9/12/17.
Allan, George, 2/Lt., killed, 14/3/16.
Batte, Sydney, 2/Lt., d. of w., 20/1/18.
Bovey, William Bernard, 2/Lt., d. of w., 15/11/16.
Chandler, John, M.C., 2/Lt., k. in a., 2/10/16.
Clark, Charles, 2/Lt., k. in a., 24/3/18.
Cole, Humfrey Theodore Shuldham, 2/Lt., d. of w., 12/2/17.
Cooper, Alfred Lynn, 2/Lt., k. in a., 15/9/16.
Dawson, Thomas Reginald, 2/Lt., d. of w., 4/2/16.
Dawswell, George Alec, 2/Lt., k. in a., 20/3/16.
Dennis, Charles Cowley, 2/Lt., k. in a., 25/9/18 (and R.F.C.).
Eley, Ralph Corben, 2/Lt., k. in a., 24/3/18.
Evans, Albert John, 2/Lt., k. in a., 15/6/17.
Foulds, Maurice Frank, 2/Lt., k. in a., 30/10/17.
Godwin, Sidney William, 2/Lt, k. in a., 2/10/16.
Hanna, John Henry, 2/Lt., k. in a., 20/9/17.
Hendry, William. 2/Lt, k. in a., 5/3/17.
Hood, Gilbert Brackenbridge, 2/Lt., k. in a., 19/2/18.
Horne, Herbert George McMillan, 2/Lt., k. in a., 13/4/17 (and R.F.C.).
Hunt, Sidney Herman, 2/Lt., k. in a., 22/8/17.
Isaac, William Jones, 2/Lt., k. in a., 26/4/16.
Johnson, Francis Hugh, 2/Lt., k. in a., 15/9/16.
Johnson, George Arthur Moxey Tuker, 2/Lt., k. in a., 21/5/17.
Jones, Eric Irvine, 2/Lt., k. in a., 22/3/18.
Kemp, Ambrose Ernest William, 2/Lt., d. of w., 10/12/17.
Kerr, Robert, 2/Lt., d. of w., 7/6/17
Kerr, William Niven, 2/Lt., died, 26/11/18.
Macartney, Thomas Hendry, 2/Lt., k. in a., 7/6/17 (and M.G.C.)
Marr, Hugh Boyd, 2/Lt., k. in a., 16/12/16.
Morrison, Joseph McLaren, 2/Lt., d. of w., 4/12/17.
North, Stanley, 2/Lt., k. in a., 16/8/17.
Owen, Leonard Sidney, 2/Lt., k. in a., 20/9/17.
Parker, Albert Victor, 2/Lt., k. in a., 19/11/16.
Pleydell-Bouverie, Samuel Wilfred, 2/Lt., k. in a., 15/9/16.
Prince, Arthur Alec, 2/Lt., k. in a., 4/10/18.

Provand, Dixon, 2/Lt., k. in a., 15/9/16.
Robertson, James, 2/Lt., d. of w., 5/10/18.
Rowson, Tom Hollingworth, 2/Lt., k. in a., 15/9/16.
Scholefield, Arthur Hoyle, 2/Lt., k. in a., 18/5/17.
Segnitz, Hermann Ferdinand, 2/Lt., killed, 25/9/15
Sinclair, Gavin Wilson, 2/Lt., d. of w., 7/12/17.
Tyler, Gilbert Edward, M.C., 2/Lt., d. of w., 18/9/16.
Tyndall, James, 2/Lt., d. of w., 4/6/17.
Vaile, Philip Amyas, 2/Lt., d. of w., 14/10/16.
Warren, William Duncan, 2/Lt., k. in a., 20/9/17.

20th (County of London) Battalion, The London Regiment (Blackheath and Woolwich).

Brown, Angus Graham, Capt., k. in a., 1/9/18.
Burdick, F. W., M.C., T/Capt., k. in a., 29/8/18 (R.A.F.).
Edwards, Gerald John, Capt., d. of w., 9/6/17.
Griffiths, Frederick James, Capt., k. in a., 1/9/18.
Hasslacher, James Alfred Charles, Capt., k. in a., 29/12/17.
Hearn, Robert Cecil, Capt., k. in a., 30/4/18.
Jones, Reginald George, Capt., k. in a., 30/8/18.
Lane, Maurice, M.C., Lt., A/Capt., k. in a., 29/12/17.
Marchant, Charles G., Capt., killed, 3/5/15.
Rook, Reuben Victor, Capt., killed, 30/8/18.
Stanger, Philip James, Capt., k. in a., 8/11/15.
Taylor, Harold Charles Norman, Capt., k. in a., 21/5/16.
Thomas, Arthur Laurie, Capt., d. of w., 30/8/18.
Travers, Tom Stockholm, M.C., Capt., k. in a., 7/11/17.
Weston, George Primrose, M.C., Capt., k. in a., 1/10/16.
Wootton, Donald Herbert, A/Capt., d. of w., 25/8/18.
Young, Leslie Alexander, Capt., k. in a., 21/5/16.
Bennett, Robertis Charles Rudolph Busby, M.C., Lt., k. in a., 24/8/18.
Birdwood, Herbert Frederick, Lt., k. in a., 2/3/16 (and R.F.C.).
Crafter, James, M.C., Lt., died, 7/7/17 (in German hands) (R.F.C.).
Elder, William Gardner, Lt., died, 10/2/18.
Flanagan, Joseph Samuel, Lt., k. in a., 23/8/18.
Gardner, Thomas, Lt., k. in a., 22/7/16.
Hooper, Colin Holt, Lt., d. of w., 28/9/15.
Long, Leslie Paul, Lt., k. in a., 25/9/15.
Malcolm, Kenneth James, Lt., k. in a., 19/2/18.
Renton, Cyril William, Lt., died, 19/7/17.
Robertson, Ernest Cecil Leonard, Lt., k. in a., 18/10/15.
Shinn, Stanley Gilbert, Lt., died, 13/12/18.
Slaughter, Vivian, Lt., k. in a., 27/9/18.
Spencer, George, Lt., d. of w., 5/12/17.
Spurgeon, Donald Frank Parker, Lt., k. in a., 10/9/18.
Thomasset, Gurden Theodore, Lt., k. in a., 25/9/15.
Weatherley, Lawrence Edwin Martin, Lt., k. in a., 19/2/18.
Wood, Herbert, Lt., k. in a., 1/9/18.
Adams, Edward Carrington, 2/Lt., k. in a., 25/9/15.
Adamson, Duncan Francis Charles, 2/Lt., k. in a., 12/9/18.
Adkin, Arthur Wellesley, 2/Lt., k. in a., 3/6/17.
Barnes, Frank, 2/Lt., k. in a., 28/10/17.
Baylis, Thomas Forbes, 2/Lt., k. in a., 14/7/17.
Bennett, Frederick Martin, 2/Lt., k. in a., 10/9/18.
Bridle, Robert Reginald, 2/Lt., k. in a., 26/9/17.
Bulmer, Frank Stedman, 2/Lt., k. in a., 1/10/16.
Chamberlain, John Robert William, 2/Lt., k. in a., 13/9/18.
Champion, Rowland Laughton, 2/Lt., k. in a., 17/3/17.
Clarke, Edwin Alfred, 2/Lt., d. of w., 1/10/16.
Cowderoy, Horace, 2/Lt., k. in a., 15/9/16.
Crawford, James Carpenter, 2/Lt., k. in a., 1/10/16.
Denton, Arthur, 2/Lt., k. in a., 16/6/17.
Donaldson, Herbert Graham, 2/Lt., died, 16/2/18 (att. R.F.C.).
Ellen, Harry John, M.C., 2/Lt., k. in a., 14/9/18.
Fuller, Oliver Lionel, 2/Lt., died, 18/10/18 (in German hands).
Garrett, Henry William, 2/Lt., k. in a., 24/3/18.
Halford, William Stanley, 2/Lt., k. in a., 15/9/16.
Hall, Arthur James Melville, 2/Lt., k. in a., 15/9/16.
Hamilton, Robert Peyton, 2/Lt., d. of w., 25/9/15.
Hellicar, Geoffrey Theodore, 2/Lt., k. in a., 27/7/16.
Hirst, James, M.M., 2/Lt., k. in a., 14/9/18.
Hodges, Alfred John Carter, 2/Lt., k. in a., 23/8/18.
Horwood, Richard George, 2/Lt., d. of w., 8/5/18.
Japp, William Neville, 2/Lt., k. in a., 25-26/9/15.
Jewhurst, George Stanley, 2/Lt., d. of w., 19/2/18.
Jones, James Thomas, 2/Lt., d. of w., 24/8/17.
Langstone, Arthur, 2/Lt., d. of w., 19/5/17.
Lindley, Thomas Grenville, 2/Lt., d. of w., 24/9/17.
Lomas, George Archibald Colin, 2/Lt., k. in a., 22/5/16.
Ludlow, Frank Hubert Charles, 2/Lt., k. in a., 23/11/17.
McCandlish, William Ewart, 2/Lt., k. in a., 24/3/18.
Machen, Frederick James, 2/Lt., k. in a., 3/6/17.
Maxwell, Wellwood, 2/Lt., d. of w., 16/9/16.
Nelson, Harry, 2/Lt., k. in a., 15/9/16.
Newington, Francis Reginald Hayes, 2/Lt., d. of w., 3/12/17.
Prophet, Cecil, 2/Lt., k. in a., 9/10/17.
Pulleyn, Edward Henry, 2/Lt., k. in a., 25/11/17
Silvester, Reginald, 2/Lt., k. in a., 7/6/17.
Smith, John Clarence, 2/Lt., k. in a., 2/12/17
Smith, Norman Havelock, 2/Lt., k. in a., 23/3/18.
Smith, William, 2/Lt., k. in a., 1/9/18.
Spice, Ernest Robert, 2/Lt., k. in a., 30/4/18.
Stevenson, Carlos, 2/Lt., k. in a., 2/1/17.
Symons, Douglas, 2/Lt., k. in a., 1/10/16.
Thorn, Harold Lewis, 2/Lt., k. in a., 15/6/17.
Thornton, Reginald George, 2/Lt., k. in a., 5/9/17.
Tucker, Sidney, M.M., 2/Lt., d. of w., 11/8/18.
Wiggins, Alec Henry, 2/Lt., k. in a., 22/8/18.
Williams, Felix George, 2/Lt., k. in a., 21/3/18.
Williams, Sydney Mansell, 2/Lt., k. in a., 15/6/17
Young, Alan Emilius, 2/Lt., k. in a., 25/9/15.

21st (County of London) Battalion, The London Regiment (First Surrey Rifles).

Richards, Hugh Phelps, Major, k. in a., 18/5/16.
Heppell, Thomas Reginald, Capt., k. in a., 15/9/16.
Joel, Harold Walter, A/Capt., k. in a., 7/6/17.
Leman, Douglas Walter, Capt., k. in a., 28/3/18.
Messervy, Ernest Dyce, Capt., k. in a., 20/7/17 (and R.F.C.).
Perkins, Frank Arthur, Capt., d. of w., 8/6/17.
Taylor, Norman Austin, M.C. & Bar, Capt., d. of w., 26/3/18.
Aldis, Ralph Harry, Lt., k. in a., 31/10/17.
Carr, William Parsons, Lt., k. in a., 13/12/17.
Edmunds, Cecil Harry, Lt., k. in a., 23/3/18.
Hull, Lyonel Hyde Rochfort, Lt., k. in a., 25-26/5/15.
Hunt, Lawrence Herbert, Lt., k. in a., 4/12/17.
Jackson, Frederick Charles, D.C.M., Lt. & Qr.-Mr., d. of w., 11/8/17.
Martin, Cyril Basnett, Lt., k. in a., 30/3/18.
Morrison, Campbell, Lt. & Qr.-Mr., died, 20/1/17.
Reynolds, C. E., Lt., d. of w., 23/10/18 (and R.A.F.).
Richmond, Hugh Bowlin, Lt., k. in a., 9/12/17.
Savel, Harold Richard, Lt., k. in a., 25/5/15.
Walton, John Leigh, Lt., died, 22/7/18.
Aldrich, George Richard, 2/Lt., k. in a., 4/12/17.
Bradley, Hubert Mark, 2/Lt., killed, 27/5/18.
Balfour, Adrian Clive, 2/Lt., k. in a., 8/10/16.
Clare, Arthur Vernon, 2/Lt., k. in a., 15/9/16.
Cohen, Moss, 2/Lt., k. in a., 15/9/16.
Coombes, Herbert Victor, 2/Lt., k. in a., 28/3/18.
Dickson, James, 2/Lt., k. in a., 16/9/16.
Edkins, Harrison, 2/Lt., k. in a., 16/9/16.
Edmunds, Guy Victor, 2/Lt., k. in a., 23/5/16.
Eminson, George, 2/Lt., k. in a., 1/9/18.
Evans, Dennis Leslie, 2/Lt., d. of w., 15/12/17.
Frolich, John Charles Cecil, 2/Lt., k. in a., 15/9/16.
Geary, Ronald Fitzmaurice, 2/Lt., k. in a., 15/1/16.
Hodge, Frederick George, 2/Lt., k. in a., 31/10/17.
Hotchkin, Lambert Annesley, 2/Lt., k. in a., 8/10/16.
Hunter, Alexander Forbes, 2/Lt., k. in a., 23/5/16.
Jones, Frederick James, M.M., 2/Lt., k. in a., 26/10/17.
Joseph, Cyril John Gadalja, 2/Lt., died, 13/10/14.
Kendel, Benjamin, 2/Lt., k. in a., 14/6/18.
Lack, Frederick George, 2/Lt., k. in a., 30/3/18.
Lloyd, Gilbert Lewis, 2/Lt., k. in a., 30/11/17.
McCourt, Cyril Douglas, 2/Lt., k. in a., 8/10/16.
Morton, Arthur Darley, 2/Lt., k. in a., 24/8/18.
Pragnell, Archie Ernest, 2/Lt., drowned, 30/12/17.
Redway, Frank Mercer, 2/Lt., k. in a., 14/2/18.
Roberts, Charles Henry Hill, M.C., 2/Lt., k. in a., 15/9/16.
Roberts, Oscar Howard Salter, 2/Lt., d. of w., 28/9/17.
Southin, Charles Alec, M.C, 2/Lt., killed, 15/2/18 (and R.F.C.).
Ward, Cyril Bertram, 2/Lt., d. of w., 1/11/16.
Warren, Charles Gordon, 2/Lt., killed, 28/8/18.

22nd (County of London Battalion, The London Regiment (The Queen's).

Tremearne, Arthur John Newman, Major, k. in a., 25/9/15.
Baswitz, Albert, M.C., Capt., k. in a., 16/9/16.
Green, Henry Edwin, Capt., d. of w., 13/10/16.
Hodge, Lionel Bryant, Capt., d. of w., 10/11/17.
Le Chavetois, Grantley Adolphe, A/Capt., d. of w., 21/1/18.
Oakley, Christopher Herbert, M.C., Capt., d. of w., 2/9/18.
Rose, Eric Dudley, Capt., k. in a., 30/3/18.
Saumarez, Reginald Stafford, M.C., Capt., k. in a., 23/3/18.
Boosey, Noel Charles, Lt., d. of w., 22/7/15.
Cronhelm, Arthur Geoffrey, Lt., killed, 6/9/17.
Curling, Edward Thomas, Lt., killed, 15/2/18 (att. R.F.C.).
Hurst, John Julius, Lt., k. in a., 31/10/17.
Kinross, George Irvine, Lt., k. in a., 12/9/16.
Porter, Ernest James, Lt., d. of w., 22/9/16 (in German hands).
Tomlin, Charles Geoffrey, Lt., d. of w., 9/7/16.
Whicker, Frederick Paul, Lt., d. of w., 12/4/18 (in German hands).
Anderson, Joseph Henry, 2/Lt., k. in a., 9/12/17.
Arnold, Alfred Lewis, 2/Lt., k. in a., 15/8/17.
Beaumont-Edmonds, William George Beaumont, 2/Lt., k. in a., 17/9/16.
Blofeld, Dudley, M.C., 2/Lt., k. in a., 8/10/16.
Boxall, William Gratbatch, 2/Lt., d. of w., 15/4/18.
Britt, Eric John Robert, 2/Lt., k. in a., 30/3/18.
Brown, Douglas Paton McRae, 2/Lt., k. in a., 24/11/16.
Carter, Ronald John Frederick, 2/Lt., k. in a., 26/4/18.
Fry, Alfred Harold, 2/Lt., d. of w., 30/10/16.
Green, Daniel Cottle, 2/Lt, k. in a., 25/2/17 (and M.G.C.).
Hargreaves, Clifford, 2/Lt., k. in a., 22/8/18.
Hawkins, John Stephen, 2/Lt., k. in a., 23/7/17.
Healing, George William, 2/Lt., k. in a. 4/10/18.
Holdsworth, Vavasour Mervyn, 2/Lt. k. in a., 20/12/15.
King, Hamilton Boyd, 2/Lt., k. in a., 7/6/17.
Larkin, Frederick Joseph, M.C, 2/Lt., k. in a., 7/11/17.
Lawrie, Robert Rossiter, 2/Lt, d. of w., 8/4/18.
Maddox, Leonard George, M.C., 2/Lt., killed, 30/8/18.
May, William Ernest Edward Frederick, 2/Lt., k. in a., 24/11/16.
Mayes, Robert Campbell, M.C., 2/Lt, d. of w., 19/10/18.
Morgan, Frank, 2/Lt., k. in a., 22/8/18.
Moss, Charles William, 2/Lt., k. in a., 13/5/17.
Paton, Malcolm David Rutter, 2/Lt, d. of w., 12/6/17 (and R.F.C.).
Ratton, Wilfrid Holroyd, 2/Lt., died, 9/7/15.
Reid, Alexander, 2/Lt., k. in a., 15/2/17.
Rothwell, Reginald Fleetwood, 2/Lt., k. in a., 31/8/18.
Sculthorpe, William Vaughan, 2/Lt., k. in a., 8/6/17.
Stephens, Francis John, 2/Lt., k. in a., 30/1/17.
Thew, Frank Atkinson, 2/Lt., k. in a., 12/9/16.

Tomlin, Reginald Arthur, M.C., 2/Lt., k. in a., 1/9/18.
Watson-Taylor, Arthur Simon, 2/Lt., k. in a., 14/9/17.
Wright, Cecil Medwyn, 2/Lt., k. in a., 6/11/17.

23rd (County of London) Battalion, The London Regiment.

Hargreaves, Thomas Charles, D.S.O., Major, k. in a., 23/3/18.
Mabey, John Hume, Capt., d. of w., 18/11/17.
Spencer, Walter George, Capt., d. of w., 26/3/18.
Barrett, Reginald Albert Baber, Lt., k. in a., 7/11/17.
Ewen, Henry Spencer, M.C., Lt., k. in a., 5/4/18.
Mansel-Howe, Charles Iorworth, Lt., k. in a., 9/8/18.
Oppenheimer, Lehmann James, Lt., died, 8/11/16.
Quarterman, Percy Harold, Lt., k. in a., 9/10/17.
Reid, John Deighton Lewis, Lt., k. in a., 9/5/18.
Sayers, Horace George David, Lt., drowned, 2/6/17.
Wood, Keith Eric, Lt., d. of w., 27/5/15.
Ambrose, Donald, 2/Lt., k. in a., 21/3/18.
Ballard, Godfrey Adolphus, 2/Lt., k. in a., 27/9/15.
Ballard, Maurice Arnold, 2/Lt., d. of w., 29/5/15.
Chisholm, William Turner, 2/Lt., d. of w., 1/9/16.
Clarke, Algernon Percy, 2/Lt., d. of w., 24/7/15.
Clifford, Leonard Price, 2/Lt., k. in a., 7/6/17.
Davies, John Rhys, 2/Lt., d. of w., 28/11/17.
Franklyn, George William, 2/Lt., k. in a., 7/6/17.
Handley, Herbert Eustace, 2/Lt., k. in a., 25-26/5/15.
Hicks, Robert, 2/Lt., k. in a., 26/5/18.
Hunt, John Henry Sneyd, 2/Lt., k. in a., 16/9/16.
Kelsey, Leon de Barr, 2/Lt., k. in a., 16/9/16.
Lambourne, William, 2/Lt., k. in a., 9/8/18.
Mitchell, Archibald McKerrow, M.C., 2/Lt., k. in a., 6/7/17.
Phillips, Walter Ernest, M.C., 2/Lt., d. of w., 23/3/18.
Spears, Alexander George, 2/Lt., k. in a., 22/8/18.
Stevenson, Paul William John, 2/Lt., d. of w., 25/5/15.
Stone, Harold, 2/Lt., k. in a., 7/6/17.
Weeden, Charles Harold, 2/Lt., k. in a., 25/3/18.

24th (County of London) Battalion. The London Regiment (The Queens).

Figg, Donald Whiteley, D.S.O., Lt.-Col., d. of w., 5/3/17.
Garrard, Percy, Major, died, 18/9/18 (in German hands).
Nadaud, Henry Louis Fred'k. Bonnetand, Major, k. in a., 21/3/18.
Clark, Horace Arthur, Capt., k. in a., 14/9/16.
Desages, Wilfrid Roland, Capt., k. in a., 21/3/18.
Gill, Frank Malcolm, Capt., k. in a., 25-26/5/15.
Kelly, Thomas Aloysius, M.C., Capt., k. in a., 2/10/16.
Marks, Nathaniel, Capt., died, 27/7/18.
Richardson, Frank, Capt., k. in a., 7/6/17.
Wheater, Sydney, Capt., k. in a., 15/9/16.
Broderick, Herbert Thomas, Lt., d. of w., 29/12/17.
Cracknell, Charles George Raphael, Lt., d. of w., 29/12/17.
Davis, Edwin Thomas, Lt., k. in a., 27/12/17 (M.G.C.).
Goodyear, Frederick George, M.C., Lt., d. of w., 18/12/17.
Mobberley, Lionel Westwood, M.C., Lt., k. in a., 11/9/16.
Morrison, William Henry Stanley, Lt., k. in a., 26/5/15.
Smith, Eric John Garner, Lt., k. in a., 26/5/15.
Stiles, Vincent Harcourt, Lt., k. in a., 20/9/17 (M.G.C.).
Todd, Robert Victor, D.C.M., Lt., k. in a., 9/8/18.
Batchelor, Edward, 2/Lt., k. in a., 26/9/17.
Bean, Arthur Charles Stanley, 2/Lt., d. of w., 14/10/18 (in German hands).
Chance, Frank Meryon, 2/Lt., k. in a., 25-26/5/15.
Couldrey, Douglas John, 2/Lt., d. of w., 31/10/17.
Curtis, Henry Thomas, 2/Lt., d. of w., 12/2/17.
Davies, Griffith, 2/Lt., d. of w., 1/5/15.
De Jastrzebski, Hubert Stephen Slepowron, 2/Lt., d. of w., 5/4/17.
Dyke, Cyril John, 2/Lt., k. in a., 7/11/17.
Fuller, Leslie Thomas Easterbrook, 2/Lt., k. in a., 18/9/16.
Gaskell, Wallis William Penn, 2/Lt., k. in a., 25-26/5/15.
Holt, Fredk., George Bradley, 2/Lt., k. in a., 5/4/18.
Horn, Arthur Henry Harvey, 2/Lt., k. in a., 2/9/18.
Livermore, Ernest Bernard, 2/Lt., k. in a., 15/9/16.
Martin, William Harold, 2/Lt., k. in a., 14/9/16.
Pedley, Frederick Lewis, 2/Lt., d. of w., 24/8/17.
Poland, Guy Bernard, 2/Lt., k. in a., 21/3/18.
Rich, Austin Frederick, 2/Lt., k. in a., 27/12/17.
Sadler, William Harold, 2/Lt., k. in a., 24/8/18.
Snell, Herbert, 2/Lt., k. in a., 7/4/17.
Sullivan, John Duncan, 2/Lt., d. of w., 26/8/18.
Sutherland, John Alexander, 2/Lt., k. in a., 8/12/17.

25th (County of London) Cyclist Battalion The London Regiment.

Sampson, Carl Alexander, Capt., k. in a., 9/8/18.
Stapleton, Nicholas, Capt., died, 6/12/18.
Belcher, Francis Terence Julian, Lt., k. in a., 4/2/17.
Gluckman, Philip, Lt., k. in a., 8/10/16.
Grist, Percival Charles Hugh, Lt., k. in a., 18/9/18.
Homersham, Arthur Jones, Lt., k. in a., 18/2/18 (and R.F.C.).
Lascelles, Edward Rowley, Lt., k. in a., 2/9/18.
Boddington, Ralph Thomas, 2/Lt., k. in a., 2/11/17.
Boulter, Sidney Frederick, 2/Lt., d. of w., 18/2/17.
Jackson, Francis, 2/Lt., k. in a., 27/9/18.
Macrostie, Ernest James, 2/Lt., k. in a., 21/5/19.
Mather, George, 2/Lt., k. in a., 8/10/16.
Nash, Manfred Victor Johnstone, 2/Lt., k. in a., 2/11/17.
Siddall, Thomas Arthur, 2/Lt., d. of w., 17/4/17.
White, Richard Henry, M.C., 2/Lt., k. in a., 6/8/17.
Wildsmith, Raymond Charles, 2/Lt., k. in a., 7/6/17.
Woods, Richard Hartland, 2/Lt., k. in a., 4/12/17.

28th (County of London) Battalion The London Regiment (Artists' Rifles).

Laing, James Gordon, Major, k. in a., 3/10/18 (and M.G.C.).
Bare, Arnold Edwin, M.V.O., Capt., k. in a., 30/10/17.
Chetwood, Ernest Stanley, Capt., k. in a., 30/10/17.
Croft, Benjamin, Capt., k. in a., 10/11/18.
Frost, Alan, Capt., k. in a., 17/10/17 (and M.G.C.).
Job, Ernest Dalzel, Capt., k. in a., 16/7/16 (and M.G.C.).
Godfrey, Stephen Mervyn, Lt., k. in a., 30/12/17.
Haslam, James, Lt., k. in a., 30/10/17.
Groom, Cyril, Lt., k. in a., 30/12/17.
Royds, John Ilted, Lt., k. in a., 22/3/18.
Shinner, William Goodwin Blake, Lt., d. of w., 2/1/18.
Williams, Gordon, Lt., k. in a., 30/10/17.
Willis, Eric FitzGeorge, Lt., k. in a., 27/3/18.
English, Alfred Cecil, 2/Lt., k. in a., 30/12/17.
Howe, Arnold Ewart, 2/Lt., k. in a., 30/10/17.
Lightfoot, Francis Bertram, 2/Lt., k. in a., 30/12/17.
Salisbury, Walter Fred'k., 2/Lt., d. of w., 30/12/17.
Tallentire, Arthur Tom, 2/Lt., killed, 20/10/15 (and R.F.C.).

Inns of Court Officers' Training Corps.

Buller, Arthur Edward Adderley, Capt., died, 21/9/18.
Clarke, Edwin Charles Kaye, M.C., Capt., k. in a., 31/8/18.
Gabain, William George, M.C., Capt., k. in a., 24/3/17.
Pollock, Charles Thomas Anderton, Capt., k. in a., 31/3/18.

The Hertfordshire Regiment.

Page, Frank, D.S.O. & Bar, Lt.-Col., k. in a., 31/7/17.
Gough, John Bolle Tyndale, Major, k. in a., 22/3/18.
Dodgson, Guy, Capt., d. of w., 14/11/18.
Gibbons, Thomas Pilling, Capt., k. in a., 22/3/18.
Gimingham, Charles Henry, Capt., k. in a., 9/11/17 (and R.F.C.).
Lee, Edward, Capt., k. in a., 14/10/16.
Lowry, Sidney Henry, M.C., Capt., k. in a., 31/7/17.
Milne, Alexander Richard, A/Capt., k. in a., 31/7/17.
Moore, Saxon Weston, Lt. (A/Capt.), k. in a., 23/8/18.
Owen, Malcolm de Brissac, M.C., A/Capt., Lt., k. in a., 4/11/18.
Smallwood, Eric Butter, M.C., Capt., k. in a., 7/1/17.
Abbott, George, Lt., k. in a., 23/8/18.
Arnholtz, Ronald Henry Preuss, Lt., k. in a., 23/8/18.
Baker, Herbert Norman, Lt., died, 30/8/17.
Broad, John Eric, Lt., k. in a., 23/3/18.
Brown, Edward Frederick Montagu, Lt., d. of w., 8/1/18.
Cautherly, Charles Stewart, Lt., k. in a., 26/4/18.
Church, John William, Lt., d. of w., 30/3/18.
Drury, Follett McNeil, Lt., k. in a., 7/1/18.
Fryer, Christopher John Gwynne, M.C. & Bar, Lt., k. in a., 4/11/18.
Hart, Frederick Reginald, M.C., Lt., d. of w., 28/1/17.
Head, Basil William, Lt., k. in a., 31/7/17.
Hickley, Richard Trollope North, Lt., k. in a., 24/3/18.
Hurd, Angier Percy, Lt., k. in a., 30/3/18.
King, Sydney, Lt., k. in a., 31/7/17.
Lake, Frank Gilbert, Lt., k. in a., 31/7/17.
Macintosh, Eric, Lt., killed, 31/7/17.
Park, Walter Williamson, Lt., k. in a., 2/4/16.
Perry, Donovan, Lt., k. in a., 22/3/18.
Ravenscroft, Richard Birkbeck, Lt., k. in a., 16/8/17.
Snowden, Harcourt John, Lt., k. in a., 11/1/15.
Hensman, Henry John, M.C., 2/Lt., k. in a., 18/9/18.
King, Charles Leonard, 2/Lt., k. in a., 22/3/18.
Lambert, Geofrey Fontaine, 2/Lt., d. of w., 15/4/16.
Reeves, Laurence, 2/Lt., d. of w., 25/8/18.
Secretan, Reginald Herbert, 2/Lt., killed, 31/7/17.
Stonnill, Frank Roland, 2/Lt., k. in a., 24/3/18.
Taylor, Edward Algernon, 2/Lt., k. in a., 11/2/18.
V.C. Young, Frank Edward, 2/Lt., k. in a., 18/9/18.

The Herefordshire Regiment.

1 Carless, Wilfred Townsend, Major, k. in a., 12/8/15.
1 Whitehouse, Augustus George Richard, M.C., Major, k. in a., 1/8/18.
Berney, George Norman, Capt., k. in a., 6/11/17.
1 Carver, Walter Lionel, Capt., k. in a., 6/11/17.
Croft, Sir Herbert Archer (Bt.), Capt., k. in a., 11/8/15.
Holman, Arthur Vincent, Capt., died, 9/1/17.
Jordon, Leonard Owen, M.C., Capt., k. in a., 4/11/18.
1 Levason, Desmond Gee Granville, Capt., d. of w., 27/3/17.
Lloyd, Wymond Howard, Capt., died, 9/3/16.
1 Russell, Edward Stanley, M.C., Capt., k. in a., 6/11/17.
1 Sale, Richard Crawford, Capt., k. in a., 26/3/17.
1 Wilson, Alac, Capt., k. in a., 26/3/17.
1 Yeomans, Howard William, Capt., k. in a., 8/10/17.
1 Crossley, Allan Hastings, Lt., d. of w., 10/5/17.
Duff-Gordon, Cosmo Lewis, Lt., k. in a., 3/9/16 (and M.G.C.)
1 Howells, Reginald, Lt., d. of w., 30/5/18 (in Ger. hands).
1 Mitchell, Percy Maschwitz, Lt., k. in a., 6/11/17.
Pettigrew, Gilbert Thomas Richardson, Lt., killed, 12/9/17 (and R.F.C.).
Pritchett, Edward Guy, Lt., k. in a., 16/5/18.
1 Whittaker, William Robert, Lt., k. in a., 27/3/17.
1 Court, Reginald Walter Southwood, 2/Lt., k. in a., 26/3/17.
1 Jones, Ferderick Thomas Averay, 2/Lt., d. of w., 5/12/17.
1 Marshall, Ambrose, 2/Lt., k. in a., 15/4/17.
1 Reeve, Herbert Joseph, 2/Lt., died, 24/9/15.
1 Vaughan, Charles, 2/Lt., k. in a., 6/11/17.
1 Watts, John Howe, 2/Lt., k. in a., 6/11/17.
1 Wells, Norman Albert, 2/Lt., d. of w., 29/12/17.

The Northern Cyclist Battalion.

Balbour, Frank Douglas, M.C., Capt., k. in a., 23/3/18.
Brunskill, James Harold, Capt., k. in a., 29/9/17.
Hamer, Arthur Derrick, Capt., k. in a., 6/11/18.
Dixon, C., Lt., k. in a., 19/9/18 (and R.A.F.).
Ridley, Pattison Reay, Lt., k. in a., 3/5/17.
Blyth, Alick Frederick, Lt., k. in a., 22/8/17.
Pearson, Wilfred Hearne, 2/Lt., k. in a., 29/9/18 (and M.G.C.).
2/1 Sanders, George, 2/Lt., k. in a., 19/7/17.
Shimmin, Thomas Edward, 2/Lt., killed, 22/4/17 (and R.F.C.).

The Highland Cyclist Battalion.

1 Cox, John Alonzo, D.S.O., Major, k. in a., 29/9/18.
Lockhart, George Barclay, Capt., k. in a., 14/4/17 (and R.F.C.).
Bilton, E. B., Capt. (Acting), k. in a., 14/3/17.
Morrison, John, Lt., k. in a., 28/3/18.

The Kent Cyclist Battalion.

Powell, Gerald Frederick Watson, Major, k. in a., 29/7/17.

The Huntingdonshire Cyclist Battalion.

Warwick, John Douglas Barford, Major, k. in a., 10/3/17.
Hopkins, Lawrence Hilton, Capt., k. in a., 7/10/18.
Cooper, Nowell Edwin, Lt., d. of w., 16/10/18.
Crick, Cyril George, Lt., k. in a., 27/8/17.
Ebbutt, John Horace, Lt., died, 21/2/19.
Marshall, John Arthur, Lt., k. in a., 6/4/17 (and R.F.C.).
1 Darricotte, Gilbert Haley, 2/Lt., k. in a., 6/9/18.
Margerison, Thomas, 2/Lt., k. in a., 13/4/17 (and R.F.C.).
Milne, David, 2/Lt., k. in a., 21/9/18.
Slaughter, William Leonard, 2/Lt., k. in a., 6/9/18.

Royal Defence Corps.

Dewe, William Horsley, Lt.-Col., died, 31/3/18.
Hollway, James Clinton, Lt.-Col., died, 11/1/17.
MacGeorge, William Henry, Lt.-Col., died, 16/12/16.
Newnham-Davis, Nathaniel, Lt.-Col., died, 28/5/17.
Amyatt-Burney, Horace, Major, died, 8/3/19.
Belk, Charles, Major, died, 16/12/17.
Lehmann, Frederick Hope, Major, died, 3/10/17.
Sheard, Thomas William, Major, died, 29/9/17.
Spencer, Gerald Robert, Major, died, 13/5/18.
Cayley, Sir George Everard Arthur, Capt., died, 15/11/17.
Coleman, Gerald Arthur, Capt., died, 6/2/19.
Curtis, Sir William Michael (Bart.), Capt., died, 19/1/16.
8 Goater, Horace Benjamin, Capt., k. in a., 10/8/18.
Guthrie, Alexander, Capt., died, 29/12/16.
12 Kerr, John Robert, Capt., died, 7/11/17.
Scrivens, Albert, Capt., died, 11/1/19.
Barclay, F., Lt., died, 1/11/18 (R.A.F.).
Brooks, John, Lt., died, 28/10/17.
Corbitt, John Fred'k., Lt., died, 1/1/17.
De Laloubere, John Louis Claude Alfred, Lt., died, 24/9/17.
Evans, Godfrey Stanton, Lt., died, 30/6/17.
Evans, Hew Reginald, Lt., died, 15/12/16.
Hale, William Webb, Lt., died, 12/4/17.
Hollis, Walter Henry, Lt., killed, 22/7/16.
Pemberton, Charles Oliver Paget, Lt., died, 4/4/16.
Roberts, Edward Owen, Lt., died, 29/1/17.
Gilpin, Norcliffe William Bernard, 2/Lt., died, 1/6/17.
Starkey, Thomas Randle, 2/Lt., died, 13/11/16.
Gort, Albert Henry, 2/Lt., died, 6/11/18.
Jones, Harold, 2/Lt., died, 26/12/17.
O'Donoghue, Algernon Leopold, 2/Lt., died, 22/5/17.

Royal Army Service Corps (Territorial Force).

Martin, Arthur Henry, Col., died, 27/8/18.
Kearns, Reginald Arthur Ernest Holmes, C.M.G., Lt.-Col., died, 24/11/18.
Baines, Cecil Talbot, Major, d. of w., 26/4/17.
Boyle, Montgomerie, Major, died, 27/3/19.
Clough, Charles Eric, Major, died, 12/3/15.
Dixon, Robert Harrison, Major, died, 16/11/15.
Isaac, George Gower, Major, died, 31/7/16.
Booth, Robert Hutchinson, Capt., died, 1/1/16.
Brayshay, William Stead, Capt., k. in a., 6/4/17 (and R.F.C.).
Brownsword, Douglas Anderson, Capt., d. of w., 25/12/17.
Bruce, Alexander Charles Arbuthnot, Capt., k. in a., 23/4/16.
Brunskill, James Harold, Capt., k. in a., 29/9/17 (Northern Cyc. Battn.).
Cooper, J. B., Capt., died, 21/11/15.
Gemmell, Wallace Alex, Capt., died, 29/3/16.
Harrison, Edward Rainsford, Capt., died, 25/12/18.
Holt, William Parkinson, Capt., k. in a., 24/6/17 (att. R.F.C.).
Leather, John Francis, Capt., died, 16/10/18.
Lyle, John Clevendon, Capt., died, 6/12/16.
MacNaghten, Stewart Cecil, Capt., died, 9/11/18.
Mills, Robert Nickolas Fenwick, Capt., k. in a., 21/9/17 (and R.F.C.).
Robinson, Bertram Langhorn, Capt., died, 6/9/17.
Smith, Francis Geoffrey John, Lt. (A/Capt.), died, 29/7/18.
Stanley, R. B., Capt., died, 17/2/19 (and R.A.F.).
Taylor, William Wadman, Capt., k. in a., 21/3/18.
Armitage, Sidney Robert, Lt., k. in a., 11/5/17.
Beadle, George Whitmore, Lt., died, 8/3/19.
Best, Francis Behrens, Lt., k. in a., 29/7/17 (and R.F.C.).
Cairns, James, Lt., k. in a., 23/3/19.
Cameron, George Brown, Lt., d. of w., 26/8/18.
Clarke, Cyril John Digby, Lt., d. of w., 15/9/17.
Driver, Percy Scott, Lt., k. in a., 26/3/18 (and R.F.C.).
Fawcett, Geoffrey, Lt., k. in a., 14/6/18.
Gardner, Alex Young Fraser, Lt., died, 15/11/18.
Golding, Edgar, Lt., k. in a., 19/9/17 (and R.F.C.).
Goodman, Douglas, Lt., d. of w., 24/11/17.
Guest, Frederick Charles Herbert, Lt., d. of w., 3/6/17.
Hallam, Horace George Searle, Lt., k. in a., 1/12/17.
Lansdale, Ernest Conway, Lt., died, 30/9/16 (att. R.F.C.) (in German hands).
Marshall, W. E., Lt., died, 27/6/18 (and R.A.F.).
Nott, John Harley, Lt., died, 25/8/15.
Prestwich, Joseph, Lt., d. of w., 7/2/16 (and R.F.C.).
Sheringham, Hugh Valentine, Lt., died, 16/10/18.
Spankie, David Noel, Lt., died, 7/3/19.
Stonehouse, R., Lt., k. in a., 1/4/18 (and R.A.F.).
Tatlock, Robert Reginald, Lt., died, 19/6/16.
Teague, John Gooden, Lt., k. in a., 3/9/16.
Teasdale, Eric Henry Janson, Lt., drowned, 21/1/17 (and M.G.C.).
Tetlow, Cyril Lawson, Lt., k. in a., 22/8/16 (and R.F.C.).
Traylen, Norman Algernon, Lt., died, 4/11/18.
Walker, Miles, Lt., died, 3/12/18.
Warrington, Garfield, Lt., k. in a., 18/8/17.
Wood, Horace, Lt., d. of w., 24/8/18.
Armstrong, John Lewis Pasteur, 2/Lt., k. in a., 22/6/16 (and R.F.C.).

Royal Army Medical Corps.
(Territorial Force).

Barker, Arthur Edward James, Col., died, 8/4/16.
Stoneham, Charles, C.M.G., Col., died, 31/1/16.
Blandy, Francis Dawson, M.C., Lt.-Col., k. in a., 14/8/17.
Burnet, Robert, Lt.-Col., died, 28/1/15.
Chiles-Evans, David Brynmor, D.S.O., Lt.-Col., k. in a., 23/4/17.
Clarke, John Michell, Lt.-Col., died, 21/4/18.
Dauber, John Henry, Lt.-Col., drowned, 13/8/15.
Lister, Arthur Hugh, C.M.G., Lt.-Col., died, 17/7/16.
McCall, William, D.S.O., Lt.-Col., died, 27/6/18.
Ross, Alexander Aitkin, Lt.-Col., died, 24/11/15.
Pritchard, William Bridgett, Lt.-Col., d. of w., 29/6/15.
Robertson, James, Lt.-Col., k. in a., 21/3/18.
Stokes, John Wilfred, Lt.-Col., killed, 10/2/16.
Anderson, Jonas William, Major, d. of w., 26/3/18.
Benham, Charles Henry, T/Major, died, 8/11/16.
Boswell, James, Major & Q.M., died, 23/3/16.
Hawksley, Walter Linney, Major, killed, 3/4/16.
Malcolm, William Aberdein, Major, died, 3/10/15 (11th Lon. R.).
Morris, John, M.C., Major, k in a., 7/10/18.
Myles, Charles William Chester, M.C., Capt. (A/Major), died, 19/10/18.
Mowat, James, Major, drowned, 13/8/15.
Palmer, Ambrose Henry, Major, d. of w., 2/5/17.
Robinson, Henry Betham, Major, died, 31/7/18.
Robinson, H. H., M.C., Major, killed, 3/5/19 (R.A.F.).
Scott, Arthur William, Major, died, 23/9/15.
Sayres, Alexander Ward Fortescue, Major, d. of w., 10/10/17.
Taylor, James Craik, Major, d. of w., 8/6/15.
Westlake, Algernon, Major, died, 25/5/15.
Wallace, Joseph Stephen, M.C. and Bar, Capt. (A/Major), k. in a., 28/3/18.
Allan, Noel James, Capt., died, 18/10/18.
Anderson, John, Capt., died, 17/5/18.
Armitage, Frank Rhodes, D.S.O., Capt., k. in a., 30/7/17.
Atkin, Keyser, Capt., d. of w., 6/6/18.
Baird, Leonard Barron, M.C., Capt., k. in a., 20/4/17.
Begg, Henry, Capt., k. in a., 14/11/10
Beilby, Julius Henry, Capt., k. in a., 23/4/10.
Bell, Clifford Thiselton, Capt., died, 2/2/19
Beveridge, Bernard Gordon, M.C., Capt., d. of w., 21/3/18.
Blair, Edward James, M.C., Capt., k. in a., 11/4/17.
Bonser, Geoffrey Alwyn Gershom, Capt., k. in a., 29/9/18.
Brander, Bruce MacDonald, Capt., died, 30/11/18.
Brydon, John Earnsclinch, Capt., d. of w., 27/6/17.
Bull, Benjamin Allen, Capt., k. in a., 16/9/17.
Burton, Percy Herbert, Capt., k. in a., 12/5/17.
Buxton, Gurney White, Capt., died, 9/9/15.
Casey, J. P. N., Capt., died 13/12/18 (R.A.F.).
V.C. and Bar, Chavasse, Noel Godfrey, D.S.O., M.C., Capt., d. of w., 4/8/17.
Churchill, Arthur Lindsay Maury, Capt., died, 24/6/17.
Clark, Sydney, Capt., k. in a., 2/10/10
Clarke, John, Capt., k. in a., 9/9/15.
Crossman, Lionel Gordon, Capt., died, 11/12/17.
Cummings, William, Capt., k. in a., 18/5/17.
Davie, Robert Chapman, Capt., died, 4/2/19.
Douglas, James, Capt., died, 11/2/19.
Finch, George, Capt., died, 8/10/18.
Frew, Robert Dunlop Black, Capt., k. in a., 3/8/17.
Giblin, Eric Lewis, Capt., k in a., 28/9/15.
Graham, Alexander, Capt., d. of w., 19/10/15.
Green, John Leslie, Capt., k. in a., 1/7/16.
Greer, Morrice, Capt., k. in a., 16/6/17
Hardie, Frederick, Capt., d. of w., 20/9/17.
Harris, Joseph Cecil, Capt., k. in a., 16/8/17.
Harrison, Everard, Capt., k. in a., 18/4/17.
Hartnell, Edward Bush, Capt., died, 25/4/16.
Hislop, George, Capt., d. of w., 28/11/17.
Hitchin, George Robert, Capt., k. in a., 14/8/16.
Holmes, Robert Reginald John, Capt., died, 26/3/16.
Houston, Thomas Cameron, Capt., d. of w., 25/8/16.
Hunton, Frederick, Capt., k. in a., 4/5/17.
Jacobs, Robert, Capt., d. of w., 20/7/18.
Jones, Kingsmill William, D.S.O., Capt., k. in a., 2/8/18
Kellas, Arthur, Capt., k. in a., 6/8/15.
Keogh, James, Capt. & Q.M., died, 18/1/19.
Levack, George MacLeod, Capt., k. in a., 7/10/16.
Lloyd, Walter Henry, Capt., k. in a., 4/8/18.
Low, Alexander Petrie, Capt., k. in a., 14/7/16.

MacNab, Angus, Capt., k. in a., 1/11/14 (14th Lon. R.).
Marshall, Charles Bertram, Capt., drowned, 13/8/15.
Metcalfe, John Clifford, M.C., Capt., d. of w., 20/3 16.
Milne, Joseph Ellis, D.S.O., Capt., k. in a., 22/2/17.
Moysey, Lewis, Capt., drowned, 26/2/18.
Oldershaw, Leslie, Capt., d. of w., 2/10/17 (1/8th Man. R.).
Palmer, Hugh Salisbury, Capt., d. of w., 25/4/18.
Partridge, Hugh Roger M.C. & Bar, Capt., k. in a., 24/7/18.
Peters, Owen Herbert, Capt., d. of w., 5/8/16.
Rawlins, John Bromley, Capt., k. in a., 16/8/17.
Ridge, Percy Brewster Capt., died, 12/3/16.
Rielly, William Ernest, Capt., died, 28/11/15.
Roberts, Walter Rowland Southall, Capt., k. in a., 16/8/15.
V.C. Russell, John Fox, M.C., Capt., k. in a., 6/11/17.
Sells, C. P., M.C., Capt., died, 4/7/19 (and R.A.F.).
Smith, Norman McGaan, Capt., d. of w., 12/12/17.
Thompson, Arnold Bosanquet, Capt., d. of w., 25/12/15.
Townsend, Thomas Ainsworth, M.C. & Bar, Capt., k. in a., 24/3/18.
Turner, William, Capt., died, 6/4/18.
Warren, Peyton Tollemache, Capt., d. of w., 14/8/15.
Watson, George Henry, Capt., d. of w., 18/9/16.
Weaver, John James, Capt., killed, 20/4/17.
Webb, George Henry Duder, Capt., d. of w., 29/3/18.
Whitelaw, Thomas, Capt., k. in a., 7/4/18.
Wilson, James Ernest Studholme, M.C., Capt., d. of w., 23/8/17.
Wilson, William Charles Davidson, Capt., k. in a, 18/9/18.
Hayhurst, Thomas, Lt., drowned, 13/8/15.
Hislop, James Ambrose, Lt., killed, 9/9/15.
Lougher, Gwylym Robert, Lt. & Q.M., died, 21/9/17.
Monkhouse, John Arthur, Lt. & Q.M., died, 23/1/17.

Royal Army Veterinary Corps.

Blakeway, James, Major, died, 4/12/18 (T.F.).
Coe, Joseph William, Major, died, 21/10/17 (T.F.).
Anthony, Henry Leonard, Capt., k. in a., 2/5/17 (T.F.).
Clarke, Robert William, Capt., died, 10/8/16 (T.F.).
Heyes, John Peter, Capt., died, 6/7/16 (T.F.).
Stevenson, Marcus James, Lt., died, 10/9/15 (T.F.).

Territorial Force Nursing Service.

Andrews, Ellen, Sister, k. in a., 21/3/18.
Astell, Frances, Sister, died, 17/12 17.
Blacklock, A. M., S/Nurse, died, 13/8/16.
Blencowe, Mabel Edith, Sister, died, 10/3/17.
Cammack, Edith Mary, S/Nurse, died, 1/3/18.
Climie, Agnes, S/Nurse, k. in a., 1/10/17.
Goldsmith, Amy A. V., S/Nurse, died, 5/3/19.
Griffin, Lilian, Sister, died, 5/9/16.
Hills, Maud Ellen, Sister, died, 22/7/18.
Kemp, Elsie Margaret, Sister, k. in a., 20/10/17.
Lancaster, A. H., Spec. Mil. Probat., drowned, 3/6/18.
Mackinnon, Mary, S/Nurse, drowned, 26/2/18.
Milne, Mabel, Sister, d. of w., 2/10/17.
Paterson, Jessie, S/Nurse, died, 29/9/16.
Reid, Annie Campbell, S/Nurse, died, 4/3/19.
Saxon, Ethel, Sister, died, 3/9/17.
Simpson, Elizabeth, Spec. Mil. Probat., died, 11/5/17.
Trevethan, R., S/Nurse, died, 4/9/17.
Wakefield, Jessie Emily, Sister, died, 7/2/19.
Watson, Dorothy Mortimer, S/Nurse, died, 13/3/17.

General List.

Cavanagh, Bryan George, Capt. and Qr.-Mr., killed, 24/5/19 (att. Nigeria Rgt.).
Martin, Joseph Skinner, Capt. and Qr.-Mr., died, 13/2/19.
Johnson, Henry, Lt. and Qr.-Mr., k. in a., 27/5/18.

Territorial Force Reserve.

Wright, W. H., Lt.-Col., died, 8/11/15 (K.O.Y.L.I.).
Hamilton, Francis Walker Douglas, Capt., died, 24/2/19.
Nicholls, Thomas Rocliffe, Capt., k. in a., 26/9/17 (14 Hamps Rgt.).
Wilson, Robert, Capt., died, 12/4/18.
Burch, R. S., 2/Lt., k. in a., 28/6/18 (att. R.A.F.).

THE FOLLOWING NAMES ARE ADDED TO THE ROLL.

PART I.

Aitchison, Peter, 2/Lt., York. R., k. in a., 8/5/18.
Aitken, Archibald Bruce, M.C., A/Major, R.E., killed, 4/8/19.
Anderson, James, 2/Lt., Sco. Rif., k. in a., 20/8/16.
Ashton, Frederick William, Rev., R.A. Ch. D., died, 18/11/18.
Ashton, Herbert, 2/Lt., York. & Lanc. R., k. in a., 27/11/17, att. 2/5 Bn.
Auchinlech, Armar Leslie, Capt., Sco. Rif., k. in a., 17/9/16.
Bailey, Charles, Lt., R.G.A., died, 20/2/19.
Baker, Arthur Brimfield, 2/Lt., 3 S. Staff. R., d of w., 26/9/16 (att. M.G.C.).
Baxter, F. C., 2/Lt., W. York. R., k. in a., 16/4/18.
Bedale, C. H., Revd., R.A. Ch. D., died, 8/3/19.
Belloc, L., 2/Lt., R.E., k. in a., 26/8/18, att. R.A.F.
Bland, Malcolm Gordon, 2/Lt., 1 K.R. Rif. C., k. in a., 23/3/18.
Blundell, William Kennedy, T/Capt., 12 Bedf. R., died, 13/12/18.
Brown, Robert, Lt., High. L.I., died, 6/2/19.
Browne, James Lawrence, 2/Lt., 11 E. Lan. R., killed, 29/3/18, att. R.F.C.
Bruce, Jack Curtis, 2/Lt. Leic. R., k. in a., 25/3/18.
Buckle, Dudley Francis de Crespigny, A/Major, 3rd North'd Fus., died, 24/4/19.
Buckmaster, Charles Oliver Brook, T/Lt., 7th D. of Corn. L.I., died, 16/3/19.
Budibent, George, Major, R.A.S.C., died, 2/10/18.
Bush, James Cromwell, M.C., Lt., Dorset R., attd. R.F.C., 22 Sqdn., k. in a., 7/10/17.
Campbell, John, T/Capt., R.A.M.C., died, 10/2/19.
Campbell-Johnson, Patrick Seymour Campbell, Lt., R.F.A., d. of w., 30/8/19.
Carriden, William Scott, T/2/Lt., R.A.S.C., died, 12/2/19.
Chalmers, John Alexander, T/2/Lt., Labour Corps, died, 21/10/18.
Child, Henry Russell, Capt., Gen. List, k. in a., 27/3/18, att. R.F.C., 11 Sqd.
Cholmeley, Roger James, M.C., Capt., Chesh. R., drowned, 16/8/19 (in action).
Clarken, George, Capt., R.F.A., died, 3/1/19.
Colledge, Arthur Vincent, Lt., 4 Worc. R., k. in a., 10/8/19.
Coltman, Richard Lester, 2/Lt., C. Gds., k. in a., 27/11/17 (att. 2 Gd. M.G.C.).
Cope, Edward Moseley, Lt., N. Staff. R., died, 3/6/19 (att. 52 Leic. R.).
Corse-Scott, Alexander, Capt., R. Scots, died, 13/3/19.
Crowley, Cyril Raymond, 2/Lt., 1st Devon R., k. in a., 4/10/17.
Cunliffe, Robert Ellis, 2/Lt., R. Berks. R., k. in a., 9/5/15.
Dallas, George Barnes, Lt., Som. L.I., k. in a., 1/9/19 (att. M.G.C.).
Davies, Cyril Nutcombe, Lt., R.E., died, 1/3/19.
Dawson, James, 2/Lt., Bord. R., k. in a., 29/5/18 (att. 15 Durham L.I.).
De Mattos, Gerald Comber, Capt., 9th E. Lan. R., d. of w., 10/8/19.
De Moubray, Leslie St. John, Capt., R. Berks R., died, 6/9/19 (att. 5th Bn.).
Dennison, Harry Glanville, 2/Lt., R.G.A., died, 24/2/19.
Dick, Thomas Aitken, Major, R.F.A., died, 27/1/19.
Dickson, R. C., Capt., R.A.M.C., died, 16/6/19.
Driver, Harry, D.S.O., M.C., Capt., Bedf. R., k. in a., 10/8/19.
Duncan, Garnet George, Lt., W.A.F.F., k. in a., 15/12/16 (Spec. List, att. Gold Coast R.).
Dundas, Richard Charles, Lt.-Col., R. Scots, k. in a., 25/9/15.
Edwards, Reginald Howard, 2/Lt., R.F.C., 19 Sqd., k. in a., 22/9/16.
Elliker, William Harold, A/Capt., R.E., died, 19/2/19.
Elmitt, George Carleton Brooksley, 2nd Lt., 7th R. Ir. Rif., k. in a., 16/8/17.
Feurer, Sydney M., 2/Lt., R. Berks R., k. in a., 22/7/18 (att. R.A.F.).
Fielden, Norman Leyland, Lt., R.G.A., died, 22/2/19.
Fletcher, Thomas May, M.C., Lt., 20 Durh. L.I., k. in a., 1/8/17.
Forrester, Cecil James, T/Lt., R.A.S.C., died 13/1/19.
Fraser, Mackenzie Hamilton, Capt., Sea. Highrs., died, 28/6/19 (B.E. Africa).
Gauld, George, A/Lt., Rif. Brig., died, 24/6/19 (A.P.M.).
Gibbons, Charles Barry, 2/Lt., 2nd R.Ir. Regt., k. in a., 24/8-1/9/14.
Gill, Gordon Evans, Major, R.E., died, 12/3/19.
Gillies, Charles Percival, T/Lt., M.G.C., d. of w., 5/5/16.
Goodwin, John, T/Capt. & Qr.-Mr., R.A.M.C., died, 22/2/19.
Gorton, Lionel John, 2/Lt., 1 Linc. R., k. in a., 16/4/18.
Grafton-Gratton, Thomas Walter, 2/Lt., R.G.A., died, 24/2/19.
Graves, James Singleton, Lt., 6 Worc. R., k. in a., 15/6/18 (att. 2 Bn.).
Gray, Edis John William, 2/Lt., 14 Durh. L.I., k. in a., 27/9/15.
Greenfield, Benjamin, Lt., R.F.A., died, 28/11/18.
Griffith, Edward William Collisson, Capt., 10 R. Ir. Rif., d. of w., 1/2/19.
Gunning, Edward George Francis, T/Capt., R.F.A., died, 10/6/19 (att. R.A.O.C.).
Hall, Herbert John Elliott, Lt., R.F.A., died, 7/2/19.
Harris, Albert Nansen, 2/Lt., 8 R.W. Kent R., k. in a., 26/9/15.
Harrison, James Molyneux, Lt.-Col., R.A.S.C., died, 10/3/19.
Hay, Robert, T/Lt., 9 N. Lan. R., died, 7/1/19 (att. 2 Bn.).
Haynes, G. W. N. R., Capt., R. Muns. Fus., killed, 30/5/19 (att. R.A.F.).
Heard, Robert Warren, M.C., Lt., I. Gds., died, 3/3/19.
Highmore, Charles Bowver, 2/Lt., M.G.C., died, 26/2/19.
Hill, Norman Ernest Albert, 2/Lt., 14 W. York. R., died, 27/3/15.
Hill, Jesse Adolphus Henry, Capt., R.F.A., died, 1/3/19.
Hilton, Oscar, M.C., A/Capt., R.F.A., d. of w., 14/11/18.
Hirst, Leonard George, M.C., T/Lt., R.E., died, 18/10/18.
Hitch, Gerald Henry Sibbald, T/Capt., R.A.S.C., died, 10/2/19.
Hody, Edmund Hody, Major, R.A.S.C., died, 15/3/19.
Holland, Tyrrel Evelyn, M.C., Capt., Gen. List., att. 12 R.B., died, 11/1/19.
Hone, Nathaniel Frederick, Lt., 9th R. Ir. Rif., k. in a., 1/7/16.
Hooper, Charles Frederick Aubrey Albert Anderson, T/Capt., Wilts R., died, 11/11/18.
Hopkins, Frederick, Gen. List, Lt., died, 17/6/19.
Hughes, William Francis, M.C., M.M., T/2nd Lt., 17th R. Fus., d. of w., 7/9/18.

Hunt, John Goldsworth, T/Lt., R.A.S.C., d of w., 11/3/19.
Hunter-Blair, Alister, 2/Lt., Cam'n. Highrs., k. in a., 9/5/15.
Hyslop, James, T/2/Lt., R.E., died, 15/2/19.
Inglis, Arthur McCulloch, D.S.O., T/Major, Glouc. R., died, 12/5/19.
Jacob, Gwynne, Lt., E. York R., k. in a., 1/8/19.
Jacot, Edward, Lt., R.F.C., 42 Sqd., k. in a., 6/6/17.
James, R. A., Capt., 5th Midd'x R., k. in a., 16/7/18 (att. R.A.F.).
Jenkins, David, Rev., R.A.Ch.D., died, 6/3/19.
Jones, Arthur Vernon, T/Capt., Gen. List, died, 16/2/19.
Keene, Alfred, C.M.G., D.S.O., Bt.-Col., R.G.A., died, 21/4/18.
Keightley, Philip Charles Russell, Lt., R.G.A., died, 2/3/19 (262 S.B.).
Large, Ernest, T/2/Lt., R.A.S.C., died, 8/3/19.
Lees, Paul, Lt., Spec. List, died, 18/6/19 (Graves Regt.).
Leishman, Walter Algernon, Lt., Dorset R., died, 19/2/19.
Logan, William Alexander Ross, 2/Lt., M.G.C., died, 19/2/19.
Lowe, William Erl Bridson, A/Capt., 2 E. Lan. R., k. in a., 28/5/18.
McCurrach, Alexander, 2/Lt., Cam'n. Highr., k. in a., 18/10/16.
McElroy, John Oliver, A/Capt., 14 Manch. R., died, 5/3/19 (released P. of W.).
McFarland, Francis John Elliott, 2/Lt., 4 R. Ir. Fus., k. in a., 22/7/18.
McGeagh, William Morice, Lt., 3rd S. Lan. R., died, 10/2/19.
Machutchison, William Frederick, Lt., 7 R. Dub. Fus., k. in a., 26/3/18.
Macnab, Colin Lawrence, C.M.G., Brig.-Genl., died, 13/10/18.
McKinnon, C. F., Capt., Spec. List, att. 1/6 K. Afri. Rif., died, 14/6/19.
Mann, Robert Lamplough, Lt., 7 D. Gds., k. in a., 23/12/14.
Mann, Stephen William, T/2/Lt., Spec. List, k. in a., 27/3/19.
Mansel, Jestyn Llewelyn, Capt., 7 D. G., k. in a., 20/12/14.
Manship, Charles Edward, 2/Lt., 15 N. & Derby R., k. in a., 24/7/18.
Marshall, Robert Burnaby, Lt., E. Surr. R., d. of w., 14/9/19.
Mason, Derick Cecil, 2/Lt., S. Wales Bord. k. in a., 10/11/17.
Matthews, E. A., 2/Lt., 8 Som. L.I., k. in a. 2/4/18 (att. R.A.F.).
May, William Clarence, 2/Lt., North'd. Fus., k. in a., 26/10/17 (att. 1/5 Bn.).
Meade, Evelyn Augustus Kew, T/Capt., R.A.S.C., died, 13/3/19.
Meal, William, Capt., Worc. R., died, 27/5/19 (1 Gar. Bn.).
Mears, Francis Peel, T/Capt., R.A.S.C., died, 22/2/19.
Mellor, Vincent Charles Serecold, Lt., 5 K. R. Rif. C., died, 21/3/19.
Middleton, George Hilton, Lt., R.A.M.C., k. in a., 10/8/19.
Miller, George Gordon Darley, 2/Lt., R.F.A., k. in a., 15/9/19.
Moll, John Arnold, Lt., R.F.A., d. of w., 21/9/19.
Muir, John Wallace, 2/Lt., R.F.C., 46 Sqd., k. in a., 12/3/18.
Myers, Henry John, T/Capt., Gen. List, died, 19/2/19 (and R.A.S.C.).
Neville, Philip Percy, T/Lt., A.P.D., died, 27/2/10.
O'Brien, Robert Edward, 2/Lt., 2 Argyle & Suth. H., died, 20/2/19 (att. 3rd Bn.).
Parks, John Wynard, M.C., Capt., E. Lan. R., d. of w., 12/8/19.
Parish, Jesse Hugh, Lt., R.G.A., died, 22/2/19.
Peach, Francis Edward, T/2/Lt., Notts & Derby R., d. of w., 23/2/19.
Pearse, Alister Cullen, Lt., Midd'x R., d. of w., 16/9/19 (att. 45 R. Fus.).
Peel, Lawrence, Capt., York. R., k. in a., 24/10/14.
Piggot, Arthur Alfred, Lt., 13 North'd Fus., k in a., 26/9/15.
Polley, F. C., Capt., Spec. List, died, 16/4/19 (I.W.T.).
Randall, John, A/Capt., R.G.A., died, 17/2/10
Robertson, George Hawthorn Minto, T/Lt., Gen. List, died, 10/3/10 (att. Nigeria R.).
Scott, Thomas, 2/Lt., 3 Durh. L. I., k. in a., 27/5/18.
Sellars, Eric Francis, M.C., Capt., 12 Ches. R., k. in a., 18/9/18.
Settrington, Charles Henry (Lord), Lt., I. Gds., d. of w., 24/8/19.
Shaw, Alfred, 2/Lt., A. Cyclist Corps, d. of w., 8/8/19.
Shaw, Alexander Morton, Capt., York. R., k. in a., 10/4/18.
Shepherd, James Duncan, M.C., A/Major, R.E., k. in a. 8/8/19.
Shepherd, Stanley Le Fleming, M.C., Major, North'n R., k. in a., 10/8/19.
Sherrard, John Charles, T/Capt., Spec. List, died, 28/3/19.
Small, Dudley Francis, Capt., Ches. R., k. in a., 24/3/18.
Snell, Arthur Cyril Everitt, 2/Lt., 26 M.G.C., k. in a., 18/10/16.
Spedding, John Carlisle Decy, Major, A.P.D., died, 9/3/10.
Squires, Reginald Alfred, O.B.E., Capt., York. L.I., died. 25/4/10.
Stead, Horace Stuart, 2/Lt., Lan. Fus., k. in a., 26/3/18.
Steel, Robert Archibald, 2/Lt., Rif. Brig., att. R.F.C., 16 Sqd., k. in a., 27/3/18.
Stephenson, Eric Arthur, 2/Lt., York R., k. in a., 7/2/19 (att. 17 L'pool R.).
Stockham, Thomas Alan Campbell, Lt., 1 E. York. R., k. in a., 22/3/18.
Tanner, Percy Valentine, Capt., R.F.C., 79 Sqd., k. in a., 27/3/18.
Targett, Ernest, T/Lt., R.A.S.C., died, 10/2/19.
Tayler, William Ulric Chevallier, Lt., 7 R. W. Kent R., k. in a., 10/8/19.
Telfer, Henry Adam, T/Lt., Gen. List, k. in a., 1/7/16.
Thomson, David, 2/Lt., 9 Rif. Brig., died, 1/5/19.
Thomson, John, Lt., R.E., died, 25/2/10 (att. R.A.F.).
Tonson-Rye, John Reginald, Capt., R.A.S.C., died, 25/5/19.
Tutin, Guy Luntley, Lt., 3 Notts & Derby R., died, 27/1/19 (att. 2/4th R. Berks. R.).
Twentyman, Joseph Jefferson, T/2/Lt., High. L. I., died, 11/2/19.
Tytler, Robert Adam Neilson, Major, Gord. Highrs., died, 5/6/19.
Valentine, Moss, 2/Lt., 3 R. W. Surr. R., k. in a., 26/10/17.
Vanner, James Charles, D.S.O., M.C., Capt., 7th Leic. R., died, 19/3/19.
Waite, Clement William, D.S.O., T/Major, 11th E. York R., died, 31/1/19.
Walker, Howard Napier, O.B.E., M.C., Lt., Welsh R., died, 3/6/19 (and R.A.F.).
Ward, Eric Seth, Lt., Ox. & B. L. I., k. in a., 10/8/17 (with R.F.C., 32 Sqd.).
Ward, William Ernest, (late) T/Lt., Lan. Fus., died, 4/11/18.
Wardle, Joseph Frederick, T/Lt., R.E., died, 14/2/19.
Wearing, Douglas George, T/Capt., Gen. List, died, 11/11/18.
Westray, F. E., 2/Lt., Spec. List, died, 19/12/18 (Uganda Med. Ser.).
Whatford, Stuart Lumley, D.S.O., T/Lt.-Col., York. R., killed, 30/8/19.
White, Clement William, D.S.O., T/Major, 11 E. York. R., died, 31/1/19.
Wilcher, Leslie Reginald Victor, 2/Lt., R.F.A., died, 8/5/19 (att. 113 Bde.).
Williams, Oswald Morgan, 2/Lt., 16 Welsh R., k. in a., 9/4/16.
Wilson, William, A/Capt., S. Gds., died, 4/2/19.
Woods, Norman Hill, Lt., 3rd R. Innis. Fus. (att. 7th Bn.), k. in a., 16/8/17.
Young, Henry Harman, 2/Lt., R. Fus., k. in a., 24/5/15.
Zigomala, John Copeland, M.B.E., Lt., I. Gds., killed, 25/8/19.

PART II.

Adams, George Norman, Capt., 6th S. Staffs Regt., died, 20/10/18.
Alder, Thomas Gordon Edgecombe, 2/Lt., 5th East Lancs Regt., killed, 28/7/18 (att. R.A.F.).
Aizlewood, Leslie Peach, M.C., Major, 5 York. & Lan. R., k. in a., 29/9/18 (R.A.F.).
Anderson, John George, M.C., Capt., R.A.M.C., k. in a., 21/3/18.
Anderson, William Arthur, 2/Lt., 6 A. & S. High., died, 8/12/18 (R.A.F.).
Balfour, Bernard, Lt., 21st London Regt., k. in a., 16/4/18 (att. R.A.F.).
Bevis, Charles Thomas, Capt., R.E., died, 18/2/19.
Brooking, Hugh Cyril Arthur, Capt., N. Som. Yeo., died, 31/5/18.
Broomhall, Oscar Arthur, 2/Lt., 5th Liverpool Regt., d. of w., 18/4/18 (att. R.A.F.).
Brown, James Stanley, Lt., 5th East Lancs Regt., killed, 20/10/18 (att. R.A.F.).
Bruce-Clarke, William Robert, M.B.E., Capt., 14th London Regt., died, 1/12/18 (att. R.A.F.).
Bullock, Geoffrey Ernest, Lt., 5th North Staffs Regt., killed, 16/6/18 (att. R.A.F.).
Bulmer, Charles Forsyth, Lt., 10th Midd'x Regt., k. in a., 12/3/18.
Butcher, Percival Drew Pitts, Capt., R.E., died, 3-4/11/18.
Clarke, H. W., 2/Lt., 28 London R., d. of w., 2/9/18 (R.A.F.).
Clay, Arthur Joseph, T/Maj., 6th N. Staffs Regt., died, 18/2/15.
Clement, William Honeycott, Lt., 18th London Regt., died, 27/6/19.
Clydesdale, Robert Alexander Crawford, 2/Lt., Fife & Forfar Yeo., died, 27/2/19.
Coats, John Alexander Hamilton, 2/Lt., 10th R. Scots, k. in a., 8/8/16.
Cunliffe, Ernest Nicholson, Major, R.A.M.C., died, 31/3/19.
Davies, Kenneth, Lt., 6th S. Staffs Regt., died, 5/11/18.
Duff, James Mitchell, Lt., 7th Sco. Rif., died, 24/8/19.
Dunn, Robin Gaspar, Lt., 5th Lincoln Regt., killed, 19/3/19.
Evans, Arthur Frederic, Lt., 4th R. Welsh Fus., k. in a., 30-31/10/18 (att. R.A.F.).
Farran, Edmond Baker, 2/Lt., 5th R. Highrs., drowned, 8/8/15.
Fawcett, Fred, 2/Lt., D. of Lancs. Own Yeo., died, 12/11/18 (att. R.A.F.).
Ferguson, James, Major, 9th R. Scots, k. in a., 22/7/16.
Greenall, Jack Eckersley, Capt., D. of Lancs. Own Yeo., k. in a., 31/3/18 (att. R.A.F.).
Halcombe, Norman Marshall, T/Maj., R. Eng., died, 13/2/19 (att. R.A.F.).
Hall, James Henry, 2/Lt., 6th Lancs. Fus., killed, 26/7/18 (att. R.A.F.).
Hall, William Stephen, Lt., 5 So. Lan. R., drowned, 10/10/18.
Harford, Edward Bridges, Capt., 4th Som. L.I., died, 15/7/18.
Hart, Francis Henry, Lt., 10th Manch. Rgt., died, 4/7/18.
Hatch, Andrew Basil, 2/Lt., 9th Midd'x Rgt., died, 10/10/14.
Hawkswell, Lewis Bertram Lt. 6th West Yorks Rgt., d. of w., 18/9/18 (att. R.A.F.).
Hayward, Milward Cecil, Lt., R.A.M.C., died, 23/8/16.
Hepple, John, T/Maj., R.A.M.C., drowned, 30/12/16.
Hodgkinson, H. G., 2/Lt., 5th W. Rid. Rgt., d. of w., 18/10/17.
Huby, Owen Meredith, Lt., 5th R. Warwicks Rgt., killed, 23/10/18 (att. R.A.F.).
Hummerstone, Lawrence George, Lt., 5th London Rgt., k. in a., 21/8/18 (att. R.A.F.).
Hunt, G. E., 2/Lt., 5 York. L.I., killed, 21/7/18 (R.A.F.).
Hunter, Leslie Aubrey William, Lt., 4th Sea. Highrs., died, 3/11/18.
Jackson, Cecil Thomas, Lt., 12th L.N. Lan. Rgt., k. in a., 31/8/18 (att. R.A.F.).
Jacob, John Victor Reed, Lt., R.G. Arty., died, 16/3/19 (att. R.A.F.).

Jones, B. M., Lt., R.E., killed, 28/9/18 (R.A.F.).
Kennedy, Alastair McKinnon, Lt., R. Eng., died, 18/10/18.
Kershaw, Joseph Harrison, Lt., 10th Manchr. Rgt., died, 16/9/19.
Lamb, Frank Muller, Lt., 7th Notts & Derby Rgt., k. in a., 21/3/18.
Langley, Harry Gustave, Lt., R.D.C., died, 28/1/19.
Larcombe, Reginald Fred, 2/Lt., City of London Yeo., k. in a., 10/9/18.
Lawson, Robert, Lt., 7 Durh. L.I., k. in a., 27/5/18.
Leach, Fred, Lt., 8th Manchr. Rgt., killed, 16/6/18 (att. R.A.F.).
Liddell, Mathew Henry Goldie, 2/Lt., 7th Sco. Rif., died, 17/4/18 (att. R.A.F.).
Limerick, Victor, 2/Lt., R.F. Arty., died, 20/8/19 (att. R.A.F.).
Lock, Thomas Henry, Lt. & Qr.-Mr., R.N. Devon Yeo., died, 9/11/18.
Ludlow, Leonard Gordon Sutton, Lt., 4 York. L.I., k. in a., 11/8/18.
Mackinlay, James, Lt., R.D.C., died, 17/1/19.
McHardy, John, Lt., 5 Gord. High., k. in a., 24/7/18.
McPhail, Peter John Stewart, Lt., R.G. Arty., died, 26/11/18.
Marshall, Stanley, 2/Lt., 7th Lancs. Fus., d. of w., 18/4/18.
Mawson, Alan John, Lt., 5th North'd Fus., died, 4/12/18.
Melling, Harold, Lt., 5th Chesh. Regt., killed, 7/11/18 (att. R.A.F.).
Mellor, N., Lt., 4 West Rid. R., drowned, 10/10/18 (R.A.F.).
Melville, John, 2/Lt., 5th W. Rid. Regt., k. in a., 27/11/17.
Metcalfe, Francis, Capt., R.A.M.C., died, 10/7/18.
Minors, Ronald Towers, Capt., 7th Worcester Regt., killed, 27/3/19 (att. R.A.F.).
Mumford, Louis Richard, 2/Lt., 23rd London Regt., k. in a., 21/10/18 (att. R.A.F.).
Murphy, Reginald Graham, Capt., R.D.C., died, 4/10/18.
Pickard, Eugene Cuthbert Llewellyn, Capt., R.E., died, 24/11/18.
Pittom, Wenn William Pratt, 2/Lt., 4th North'n Regt., died, 10/10/14.
Pooley, Robin Mark, 2/Lt., 9th Liverpool Regt., k. in a., 12/8/16.
Poullett, William John Lydston (Earl), Capt., R.H.A., died, 11/7/18.
Powell, Cecil Henry, 2/Lt., Oxf. & Bucks L.I., k. in a., 15/6/17 (att. R.F.C.).
Reed, Allan Thomas, Lt., 17th London Regt., killed, 1/11/18 (att. R.A.F.).
Rhodes, Gerald Rudolph, Lt., 6th Cheshire Regt., died, 30/10/18.
Rigg, Samuel, A/Maj., 5th Border Regt., k. in a., 25/3/18.
Robertson, Charles Thomas Andrews, A/Maj., 5th Gord. Highrs., d. of w., 23/3/18.
Rose, Algernon Winter, M.C., Capt., Essex Yeo., died, 29/10/18 (att. R.A.F.).
Rowe, Henry Price, Capt., R.E., died, 6/11/18.
Russell, Henry Thornbury Fox, M.C., Capt., 6th R. Welsh Fus., killed, 18/11/18 (att. R.A.F.).
Russell, William, Lt., R.E., killed, 3/4/18 (R.A.F.).
Ruthven, James, M.C., Capt., 4th E. Yorks Regt., k. in a., 9/4/18.
St. Vincent-Ryan, Edmond William, Lt.-Col., R.A.M.C., died, 24/8/19.
Seneschall, George Rhodely, 2/Lt., 5th Notts & Derby Regt., died, 16/11/18.
Shepherd, Harold Ernest, Lt., R.F.A., died, 30/12/18.
Stephen, George, Lt., 4th Gord. Highrs., died, 26/10/18.
Stevenson, J., Lt., R.E., died, 15/5/18.
Strachan, Alexander Macdonald, 2/Lt., 4th R. Highrs., k. in a., 20/7/18.
Sutton, Oliver Joseph, M.C., Capt., 9th Manch. Regt., k. in a., 23/3/18.
Terry, Leslie Ryder, Lt., 5th R. Warwick Regt., died, 7/8/19.
Thomson, Robert, Lt., 10th R. Scots, d. of w., 20/9/19.
Thorburn, Walter Ernest, Capt., 8th R. Scots, died, 22/1/19.
Tower, William Claude Cecil, Capt., E. Kent Yeo., died, 30/11/18 (att. R.A.F.).
Warrington, William Barrett, Capt., R.A.M.C., died, 2/2/19.
Waterhouse, Richard Dalton, Lt-Col., 8th Lan. Fus., k. in a., 7/8/15.
Wiggins, Thomas, A/Capt., 4th Yorks. Regt., k. in a., 27/5/18.
Winstanley, Oswald Coke, 2/Lt., 5th Welsh Regt., k. in a., 10/8/15.
Wood, Ralph, Lt., 7 W. Riding R., died, 17/10/18 (R.A.F.).
Wood, Russell Elliott, Lt.-Col., R.A.M.C., died, 8/2/17
Wynn, William Alfred, Lt., 8th Midd'x Regt., died, 28/7/19.
Yorke, Frederick, Lt., 6th Cheshire Regt., killed, 13/1/19 (att. R.A.F.).

OFFICERS MISSING AND MISSING BELIEVED KILLED.

PART I.

Aikins, Joseph Russell, 2/Lt., R.F.C., 59th Sqd., 26/3/18.
Atkinson, Henry Noel, D.S.O., 2/Lt., 1/2nd Ches. R., 22/10/14.
Baldock, W. P., Capt., 6th York & Lanc. R., 22/8/15.
Bannatyne, Ninian John, Capt., 1st K. L'pool. R., 3/5/17.
Barford, Kenneth, 2/Lt., R.F.C., 2nd Sqd., 27/3/18.
Beaford, Thomas Arthur, 2/Lt., 9th W. York. R., 5/11/18.
Belfield, Eric, Capt., 4th Middx. R., 31/7/17.
Bell, Harold Stormont, 2/Lt., att. 2/8th Worc. R., 2/12/17.
Berry, John Granville, M.C., 2/Lt., 2nd W. York. R., 16/8/17.
Birch, Percy Hall, 2/Lt., R.G.A., 199th Sge. Bty., 21/3/18.
Blackledge, Ewan John, 2/Lt., K. L'pool. R., att. R.F.C., 11th Sqd., 23/11/17.
Booth, Edward Arthur, Lt., Gen. List, N.R., 23/9/19.
Brodie-Innes, Ian Stuart, 2/Lt., 8th Som. L.I., 25/9/15.
Brooksmith, John Douglas, M.C., Capt., R.F.A., 47th Bde., 21/3/18.
Brown, Frederick Charles, 2/Lt., 9th Sher. For., 7/8/15.
Brown, Sidney Wilfred, 2/Lt., att. 11th E. Lan. R., 5/9/18.
Bullock, Thomas Eben Grainger, 2/Lt., 1st E. Kent R., 24/4/17.
Bungard, Eric George, 2/Lt., 3rd, att. 6th E. Kent R., 30/11/17.
Buswell, Thomas Hubert, 2/Lt., R.F.C., 52nd Sqd., 26/3/18.
Carson, William John White, 2/Lt., 14th R. Ir. Rif., 1/7/16.
Cockett, William Arthur, 2/Lt., 3rd, att. 2nd Gord. High., 26/10/17.
Coles, Albert Edward, 2/Lt., 1st Som. L.I., att. T.M.B., 4/10/17.
Collen, John, 2/Lt., 7th R. Innis. Fus. (att. R.F.C., 7th Sqd.), 25/10/16.
Cook, Ernest Arnold Lovell, Major, R.F.A., 122nd Bde., 1/11/18.
Dawson, Cecil Hubert Thrower, Lt. & Qr.-Mr., 10 R. Ir. Rif., 24/3/18.
Deans, Albert Victor, 2/Lt., 7th (att. 12th York. R.), 11/4/18.
De Coundouroff, G., 2/Lt., Spec List, 25/7/19.
De Neufville, Eustace Charles, D.S.O., Major, R.G.A., 262nd Sge. Bty., 21/3/18.
Douglas, John Norman Turnbull, Capt., 23rd North'd Fus., 12/4/18.
Eales-White, Henry Hewlett, Capt., 6th R. Sco. Fus., 25/7/15.
Fenton, Alan Hughes, 2/Lt., R.F.C., 43rd Sqd., 4/3/17.
Fielder, Charles, Lt., 11th Welsh R., 22/9/18.
Foster, R. D., Lt., 6th Linc. R., 7/8/15.
Gifford-Wood, Leslie Keith, 2/Lt., 6th York. R., 22/8/15.
Godwin, Charles Cayley, 2/Lt., R.F.C., 1st Sqd., 17/10/16.
Gormley, Thomas, 2/Lt., 1st (att. 7/8th K.O.S.B.), 12/6/18.
Grimshawe, Charles Ronald Vaughan, Lt., 22nd Durh. L. I., 28/5/18.
Hadley, Reginald Bracebridge, Lt., 1/2nd S. Wales Bord., 31/10/14.
Hall, Arthur Ernest, Lt., 6th York. R., 22/8/15.
Harris, Herbert Brutus Aubrey, Lt., 7th R. W. Surr. R., 10/8/17.
Hatherell, Eric James, 2/Lt., 9th W. Rid. R., 25/4/17.
Hay, J. M., Lt., Ches. R. (att. R.F.C., 62nd Sqd.), 24/3/18.
Hemingway, Maurice William, M.C., Lt., R.F.A., 33rd Bde., 27/5/18.
Higgin-Birket, William, Capt., 1/2nd Lan. Fus., 2/12/14.
Holmes, James Fyfe, M.C., 2/Lt., 9th Sco. Rif., 23/3/18.
Hyatt, William Joseph, Lt., Labour C. (att. 9th Devon), 24/10/18.
Jeffrys, James Herbert, 2/Lt., 7th (att. 2nd E. Lan. R.), 27/5/18.
King, William, 2/Lt., 1st Lan. Fus., 11/4/18.
John, Hugh Graham, 2/Lt., 3rd York. & Lanc. R. (att. North'd Fus.), 16/6/15.
Joyce, Philip Solomon, Lt., R.F.C., 60th Sqd., 6/3/17.
Kirkcaldy, Ray H., 2/Lt., R.F.C., 24th Sqd., 25/3/18.
Laird, Frank, 2/Lt., 8th N. Staff. R. (att. 56th T. M. Bty.), 25/3/18.
Lewis, Leonard Geoffrey, 2/Lt., 1st Wilts R., 31/8/18.
Light, Eric, 2/Lt., M.G.C., 40th Bn., 26/3/18.
Lowth, Francis Robert Leslie, Capt., 9th Lan. Fus., 22/8/18.
Luard, Peter Dalbiac, Lt., 3rd (att. 11th Sco. Rif.), 19/9/18.
McCurry, Alexander, 2/Lt., M.G.C., 9th Bn., 25/4/18.
McDonald, John Mellis, Capt., 1st Sco. Rif., 20/7/16.
McGregor, Roderick Dear, Capt., R.A.M.C. (att. 18th Welsh R.), 9/4/18.
McKinnon, J. F., Lt., R.F.C., 65th Sqd., 28/11/17.
MacLaughlin, Alexander Wilson, Lt., R.F.C., 1st Sqd., 29/10/17.
Macnaghten, Sir Edward Harry (Bt.), 2/Lt., 1st Roy. Highs., 1/7/16.
Melling, Charles Flower, M.C., Capt., 1st Lan. Fus., 13/5/18.
Mercer, Thomas Millbourn, 2/Lt., Tank Corps, 23/11/17.
Mills, Edgar Edward, M.C., Capt., 7th S. Wales Bord. 22/9/18.
Milne, John Theobald, M.C., Capt., R.F.C., 48th Sqd., 24/10/17.
Morgan, Douglas Noel, 2/Lt., 13th R. Suss. R., 30/6/16.
Oliver, Robert, Lt., North'd Fus., 25/9/15.
Oliver, Raymond Edward Creswick, 2/Lt., 2nd Rif. Brig., 28/8/16.
Pallett, E. R., Lt., 7th Royal Fus., 6/4/18.
Pirder, Sidney Rueben, 2/Lt., R.F.C., 80th Sqd., 19/2/18.
Pine-Coffin, T. J., Lt., 3rd Devon Regt. (N.R.), 23/9/19.
Porter, Alex James, 2/Lt., 1st Norf. R., 19/4/17.
Pulling, O. L., 2/Lt., R.G.A., 25/9/15.
Reynolds, Percival, 2Lt., 10th W. York. R., 19/9/18.
Rodger, George Swan, 2/Lt., Leic. R., 2nd, 9/1/17.
St. Leger, Dennis Claude Grant, 2/Lt., R.F.A., 295th Bde., 21/3/18.
Salamonson-Sangster, Henry Pryor Saltarn, 2/Lt., 3rd K.O.S.B. (att. 14th Hamps. R.), 26/9/17.
Sayers, Keith Raymond, Lt., R. W. Kent R. (att. R.F.C , 23rd Sqd.), 9/9/17.
Setchell, Alfred Knight, 2/Lt., 9th Norf. R., 21/3/18.
Slacke, Clulow Orme, Capt., 12th E. Surr. R., 12/11/16.
Small, Walter, 2/Lt., 9th R. Sco. Fus., 30/7/16.
Smart, Edward Treloar, Lt., R.G.A. (attd. R.F.C., 2nd Sqd.), 27/3/18.
Smith, Geoffrey H., M.C., A/Capt., 1 C. Gds., 16/10/18.

Smith, George William, 2/Lt., 8th K.O.R. Lanc. R., 28/3/18.
Smith, John Selby Armstrong, 2/Lt., 3rd (attd. 10th W. Rid. R.), 25/4/17.
Steel, R. A., Lt., Rif. Brig. (attd. R.F.C., 16th Sqd.), 27/3/18.
Steele, Ben Harry, 2/Lt., 1st Worc. R., 20/11/17.
Stirling, William Aeneas, Capt., Seaf. Highrs., 14/10/16.
Storr, Leycester Benthyn, D.S.O., Major, 12th K. L'pool R. (att. 7th D. of Corn. L.I.), 29/3/18.
Streather, Edward Harry Parsons, Lt., R.F.C., 70th Sqd., 11/9/17.
Swallow, Hervey Lancelot St. George, 2/Lt., 10th York. and Lanc. R., 25/9/15.
Tayler, St. Cyprian Churchill, M.C., Capt., R. Suss. R. (att. R.F.C., 80th Sqd.), 17/3/18.
Thomson, David, M.C., 2/Lt., High. L.I., 26/11/17.
Thomson, James, M.M., 2/Lt. (att. 6th Roy. Highs.), 21/3/18.
Thomson, Wilfrid Burrell, M.C., Capt., 2nd Dorset R., 25/3/17.
Thorpe, Herbert Gordon, M.C., 2/Lt., 1st K. L'pool R., 24/3/18.
Tooley, Harold Augustus Rupert, Lt., R. Guernsey Militia (att. D.C.L.I.), 20/12/14.
Travers, Hugh Eaton Frederick, Capt., 9th Lan. Fus., 7/8/15.
Trease, Sidney Charles, 2/Lt., 3rd Sher. For. (att. 11 Sco. Rif.), 19/9/18.
Van der Hoff, Clement Lewis, Lt., R.F.C., 3rd Sqd., 29/1/18.
Vivian, Robert Trevor, Capt., R.A.M.C. (att. Devon R.), 8/3/16
Walker, Allan Dixon, Lt., 2nd Linc. R., 16/6/15.
Ware, William, 2/Lt., 2nd R. Welsh Fus., 27/10/18.
Warren, Francis Purcell, 2/Lt., 2nd S. Lan. R., 14/7/16.
Watkyn-Thomas, Alwyn, Capt., 2nd High. L.I., 13/11/16.
Weatherill, William Brown, 2/Lt., 10th (attd. 1/4th L.N. Lan. R.), 18/6/18.
Wharram, Charles Etherington, Lt., R.F.C., 52nd Sqd., 26/3/18.
White, Hill Wilson, Capt., R.A.M.C., 12/4/18.
Wilson, Alfred Clarke, 2/Lt., 3rd (att. 6th Linc. R.), 6/11/18.

PART II.

Bostock, Alfred Sidney, 2nd Lt., 8th Durham Light Infy., 27/5/18.
Bostock, Eric Norman, M.C., 2nd Lt., 4th North'n Rgt., 27/5/18.
Brown, James Cavet, 2nd Lt., 5th Arg. & Suth'd. Highrs., 24/3/18.
V.C., Buchan, John Crawford, 2/Lt., 7th Arg. & Suth'd. Highrs., 22/3/18.
Bullen, William Francis, 2nd Lt., 10th King's (L'pool Rgt.), 16/6/15.
Carbines, Henry, 2nd Lt., 8th King's (L'pool Rgt.) (att. R.F.C.), 27/3/18.
Chick, Francis William, Lt., 7th Devon Rgt., 4/10/17.
Colnett, Richard Daunteshey, Capt., 8th Essex Rgt., 13/8/18.
Davis, George Frederick, Major, 11th London Rgt., 15/8/15.
De Conway, John, Lt., Lovat's Scouts (att. R.F.C.), 15/6/17.
Field, Arthur Montague, 2nd Lt., 4th Leicester Rgt., 22/3/18.
Harvey, Austin Mozart, M.B.E., Lt., 5th Devon Rgt., 27/10/18.
Hawkins, Harold Ingleby, Capt., 2nd London Rgt., 16/6/17.
Haynes, John Lorenzo Patrick, Lt., 4th L.N. Lancs. Rgt. (att. R.F.C.), 11/3/18.
Higgerty, Frederick Charles, 2nd Lt., 8th London Rgt., 30/11/17.
Hopkinson, Edward, M.C., Lt., 8th Notts and Derby Rgt., 23/4/17.
Horrabin, Maurice Pinney, 2nd Lt., 4th E. Kent Rgt., 30/11/17.
Leadbitter, Geoffrey George, 2nd Lt., 4th North'n Rgt., 19/4/17.
Lewis, William Owen, 2nd Lt., 4th Welsh Rgt., 27/5/17.
Murray, Anthony Stoddart, 2nd Lt., 8 Arg. & Suth'd. Highrs, 22/3/18.
Pixley, Reginald George Hewett, M.C., Capt., R.F. Arty. (att. R.F.C.), 4/6/17.
Scott, James Angus, Lt., 7th North'd Fus., 26/10/17.
Smith, Albert Francis, 2nd Lt., 9th Midd'x. Rgt., 9/9/16.
Smith, Charles John, 2nd Lt., 7th Worcester Rgt., 27/5/18.
Snell, Cyril Herbert, Lt., D. of Lanc. Own Yeo., 9-10/11/17.
Street, Harvey Ferrington, 2/Lt., 7th W. Riding Rgt., 3/5/17.
Taylor, George, Lt., R. Eng., 23/3/18.

MEMORANDA.

The Ranks and Descriptions, etc., of the undermentioned Officers are as now stated.

PART I.

Addams-Williams, D.A., S.W. Bord, date 1915, not 1918.
Allbon, Bernard Charles Jeaves, Dorset R.
Aubertin, W. A., 13, not 12 Bn. R.W. Fus.
Baird, James Revd., R.A. Ch. D.
Ball, James, D. of Corn. L.I.
Ball, Thomas Henry, R.F.A.
Banks, Arthur Byers, R.G.A.
Bayness, William Henry, 1 R.W. Surr. R.
Belloc, Louis, R.E.
Bird, Henry, 1 G. Gds., att. K. Afr. Rif.
Bland, Cecil Francis Ramsden, R. Berks R.
Bower, M. Syndercombe, R.A.S.C.
Boyden, Arnold Kingsley, R.A.S.C.
Bridges, Walter, R.A.S.C.
Browning, George Stanier, Spec. List.
Burley, Ernest Sidney, Labour Corps.
Cave, Joe, W. York. R.
Child, Henry Russell, Capt., Gen. List and R.F.C.
Close, Henry Burke, R. Dub. Fus.
Daniels, Cecil William, Notts & Derby R.
Davidson, Christopher, E. Kent R.
Dorrell, H. G. Hugh, Durh. L.I.
Doyle, Christopher, R. Dub. Fus.
Edmunds, David Gwynne, Welsh R.
Ensor, J. Collen, Welsh R.
Fausset, William Willoughby Bernard, Gen. List.
Ferguson, A. C., 2/Lt., 3 R. Scots.
Finney, John, R. Innis. Fus.
Flitcroft, Joseph, R.G.A.
Forster, George Richardson, Durh. L.I.
Fuller, Gardner Henry, R.A.S.C.
Goddard, Alec, Norf. R.
Gonne, M. E., R. Fus., k. in a.
Goodeve, Thomas Edward, O.B.E., R.E.
Gough, Leo Walter, Gen. List.
Greenstreet, Ernest Henry, Midd'x. R.
Griffith, E. W. Collisson, R. Ir. Rif.
Griffith, T. Comber, L.N. Lanc. R.
Halford, Edward Frederick, R.E.
Hall, M. W. Forester, R. Innis. Fus.
Hamilton, Archibald Gilbert, R.E.
Harbord, Philip Anthony Asshelin, G. Gds.
Harrison, Alfred Herbert, R.F.A.
Herriott, John, M.G.C.
Hewitt, Sydney Rangeley, O.B.E., R.A. Ch. Dep.
Hirst, Henry Denne, E. Kent R.
Holder, Tom S., D. of Corn. L.I.
Holland, Fred, Notts & Derby R.
Hook, C. W. K., A/Capt., Manch. R.
Horsford, Thomas Herbert O'Bryan, W. York. R.
Horncastle, C. C. Schubert, R.A.
Hughes, Norman Labrey, 2/Lt., Devon R.
Hyslop, John Wallet, Gord. Highrs.
Janes, George Frederick, R.A.S.C.
Jerrard, Charles Frederick, M.C., Dorset R.
Jobling, Ernest, A. Cyclist Corps.
Judd, William Bush, R.A.S.C.
Kennefick, J. G. Hamerton, Essex R.
Kimpton, F., Lt., R.E.
Lammert, R. D., 10 Glouc. R., d. of w., 29/3/18 (P. of W.).
Lawler, L. A. B, Lt., R.A.S.C.
Le May, L. H., T/Lt., Spec. List (with K. Afr. Rif.).
Le Mesurier, Havilland, K.R. Rif. C.
Lindsay, William Horn, R. Highrs.
Lloyd, Arthur, Lt., Ches. R.
Lovett, A. C., C.B., C.B.E., Glouc. R.
Lucas, Perceval D., Border R.
Lyons, William Holmes St. John, Midd'x. R.
MacDonald, Hamish, 13 Hussars.
McDonnell, Frank Joseph, North'd. Fus.
MacDougall, Allan, R. Fus.
MacKenzie, E. J. B., Capt., R.F.A.
Makinnon, Charles Frank, Spec. List and K. Afr. Rif.
Mann, R. L., R.W. Fus., k. in a., 9/10/16, not 14.
Mann, Stephen William, Spec. List, not Gen. List.
Marsden, Harold, W. Rid. R.
Martin, Marshal, 1 Gar. Bn. Devon R.
Marshall, Claude, S. Staff. R.
Maybury, A., D.C.M., R. Berks R.
Miller, George Bell, 2/Lt., High. L.I. and R.F.C., 18 Sq. (1917), k. in a., 1/5/17.
Miller, George Blair, 2/Lt., 2 High. L.I., k. in a., 24/4/17.
Milne-Holme, David William, R.G.A.
Moscrop, William Noel Jobson, R. Fus.
Mowat, Sinclair Alexander, R.F.C. (1917).
Ninis, F. A., M.C., Temp. Capt., Ches. R.
Orgill, Philip Ronald, M.G.C.
Paterson, R. W., 2/Lt., 2 Notts & Derby R.
Peerless, Cuthbert Henry, R. Suss. R.
Philbrick, Edward Hooper, R.F.A.
Phipps, C. J., A/Major, L'pool R.
Polley, Frank Clarence, Spec. List.
Porterfield, Leonard Witherow, R.F.A.
Price, Walter Edgar, R. Suss. R.
Renwick, James Clarence, R. Ir. Rif.
Riddell, Sydney, York. & Lanc. R.
Riecke, Arnold Francis Marshall, R.F.A.
Robb-Smith, Alexander, R.A.M.C.
Rodgers, Albert Henry, R.F.A.
Rudkin, George Henry, M.G.C.
Russell, Bernard, M.C., 2/Lt., R. Berks R.
Sanders, Gordon Harry, 21 Lcrs.
Sanders, John Harry, R.A.O.C.
Sanford, W. H., Devon R., att. D. of Corn. L.I.
Savage, Tom Alixander, R.G.A.

Scales, Edward Lionel, Midd'x. R.
Sharpe, Thomas William, Labour Corps.
Shaw, John Thomas, Lan. Fus.
Shaw-Wood, Richard, 2/Lt. R.F.C. (1918), not Wood, Richard Shaw.
Smith, H. M., N. Lan. R., date of death, 2/3/17.
Solomon, Hubert, R.F.C. (1917).
Spencer, Henry Marston, E. Kent R.
Starr, D. P., Lt., C. Gds.
Steele, Benjamin Harry, Worc. R.
Stuart, John, R. Fus.
Taylor, William Berrill, Notts & Derby R.
Thorne, Charles Everard, R.E.
Tomblings, Eric Hunter Griffith, R.E.
Tuke, A. Harrington, S., North'd. Fus.
Vincent, Stanley, R.A.S.C.
Wildig, George, Shrops. L.I.
Williams, Edwin Gordon, R.W. Fus.
Willis, Frederick, A/Capt., Devon R.
Willmot, J. D., Worc. R.
Woodward, L., M.C., S. Lan. R.
Wright, Tom, Linc. R.

PART II.

Adam, Matthew, M.C., Lt., 5th R. Sco. Fus., (att. R.A.F.).
Allen, Raymond Francis, 2/Lt., 6th R. Warwick Regt., k. in a., 18/11/18 (att. R.A.F.).
Andrews, Eric Bernard, 2/Lt., R.F.Arty. (att. R.A.F.).
Ashworth, Roger William, Lt., 8th Hampshire Regt. (att. (R.A.F.).
Backler, Alfred Milne, 2/Lt., 4th London Regt. (att. R.A.F.).
Baldie, John Boyd, Lt., Fife & Forfar Yeo. (att. R.A.F.).
Barker, Frank Edward, Lt., West'd & Cum'd Yeo. (att. R.A.F.).
Barstow, John Eric Jackson, Capt., N. Somerset Yeo. (att. R.A.F.).
Binnie, William Harold, Lt., 7th R. Scots (att. R.A.F.).
Bowden, Norman, 2/Lt., 8th Notts & Derby Regt. (att. R.A.F.).
Brabrook, Edward John, Lt., 18th London Regt. (att. R.A.F.).
Bruce, James Anderson, Lt., Ayrshire Yeo. (att. R.A.F.).
Bruce, Philip John, Lt., 10th Liverpool Regt. (att. R.A.F.).
Buck, Geoffrey Sebastian, M.C., D.F.C., Capt., 1st London Regt. (att. R.A.F.).
Camm, Percy, 2/Lt., 4th East Lancs. Regt., killed, 20/10/18 (att. R.A.F.).
Claye, Charles Geoffrey, Lt., 5th Notts & Derby Regt., k. in a., 6/5/18 (att. R.A.F.).
Crombie, William Edgar, Lt., 7th R. Warwick Regt. (att. R.A.F.).
Dawson, William Ernest, Capt., R.F.Arty. (att. R.A.F.).
Day, George Samuel, Lt., 12th London Regt. (att. R.A.F.).
Duerdon, George, 2/Lt., 5th L. N. Lan. Regt., (att. R.A.F.).
Evans, Griffith William, 2/Lt., 6th R. Welsh Fus. (att. R.A.F.).
Eyre, Arthur Noel, Lt., 6th Notts & Derby Regt. (att. R.A.F.).
Gill, Kenneth Carlyle, M.C., Capt., 1st Cambs. Regt. (att. R.A.F.).
Griffin, Edward William, Lt., 6th Gloucester Regt. (att. R.A.F.).
Hepworth, Arthur Montagu, M.C., Lt., 4th R. W. Surrey Regt. (att. R.A.F.).
Herron, Kenneth Chester, Lt., Essex Yeo. (att. R.A.F.).
Hitch, George Stuart, Lt., 5th Liverpool Regt., (att. R.A.F.).
Holland, Albert, Capt., 6th R. Sussex Regt. (att. R.A.F.).
Hunt, Henry Hope, 2/Lt., 10th London Regt. (att. R.A.F.).
John, Wilbur Arnold, Lt., Sussex Yeo. (att. R.A.F.).
Keen, Stephen Whitworth, M.C., Lt., 2nd London Regt. (att. R.A.F.).
King, William Hugh, Lt., 8th Essex Regt. (att. R.A.F.).
Leake, Eric Gilbert, M.C., Capt., 7th Manch. Regt. (att. R.A.F.).
Lee, Charles Percy, 2/Lt., 3rd London Regt. (att. R.A.F.).
Limerick, Victor, 2/Lt., R.F.Arty. (att. R.A.F.).
McKerrell, William Archibald Struthers, Lt., 8th R. Scots (att. R.A.F.).
MacLean, Alfred Peter, Lt., 4th R. Scots (att. R.A.F.).
Mitchell, John, 2/Lt., 7th Sco. Rifles (att. R.A.F.).
Mogridge, Lewis, 2/Lt., 8th Liverpool Regt. (att. R.A.F.).
Mond, Francis Leopold, Capt., R.F.A. (att. R.A.F.).
Morbey, John Samuel, 2/Lt., 10th London Regt., k. in a., 1/8/18 (att. R.A.F.).
Page, Lance Stallard March, Capt., R. E. Kent Yeo. (att. R.A.F.).
Partridge, Henry Treneman, Lt., 4th R. Sussex Regt. (att. R.A.F.).
Paxton, Gerald Arthur, 2/Lt., 6th R. Sussex Regt. (att. R.A.F.).
Pearce, Sydney Martin, Major, 4th Leicester Regt., died, 7/12/18 (att. R.A.F.).
Perris, Noel Felix, 2/Lt., 2nd London Regt. (att. R.A.F.).
Proudfoot, Cyril Dallas, 2/Lt., Notts Huss. Yeo. (att. R.A.F.).
Radloff, Heinrich, Lt., 11th London Regt. (att. R.A.F.).
Reynolds, Charles Edward, Lt., 21st London Regt. (att. R.A.F.).
Robertson, James Houldsworth, Lt., R.F.C. (48 Sqd.).
Ross, George Augustus Bellair, Lt., 6th Liverpool Regt. (att. R.A.F.).
Scarborough, Edward Owen, 2/Lt., 6th Liverpool Regt. (att. R.A.F.).
Scrace, John, Lt., 5th E. Kent R., k. in a., 24/8/18 (att. R.A.F.).
Smith, Allan Bertram, M.B.E., Lt., 5th Arg. & Suth'd Hrs.
Smith, Harold Spencer, 2/Lt., 3rd London Regt. (att. R.A.F.).
Smith, John Henry, 2/Lt., 10th Middlesex Regt. (att. R.A.F.).
Smith, Ralph Eustace, Capt., North'd Yeo. (att. R.A.F.).
Smith-Grant, John Gordon Smith Cheetham, Capt., 9th R. Scots (att. R.A.F.).
South, Walter Burns Campbell, Lt., 9th Middlesex Regt.
Street, Brooks Henry, Lt., 7th Welsh Regt. (att. R.A.F.).
Sutton, Arthur Eldred Barker, Lt., 6th Liverpool Regt. (att. R.A.F.).
Todman, Charles Vincent, Lt., 10th London Regt. (att. R.A.F.).
Wells, William Lewis, M.C., Lt., 8th Middlesex Regt. (att. R.A.F.).
Whalley, Reginald Livesey, Capt., 4th East Lancs. Regt. (att. R.A.F.).
Whitfield, Nigel Bernard, Capt., R. N. Devon Yeo., (att. R.A.F.).
Williams, Frank E., M.C., Capt., 5th Welsh Regt. (att. R.A.F.).
Williams, Frederick, Lt., 7th R. Welsh Fus. (att. R.A.F.).
Williams, William Humphrey, Capt., 6th Lancs. Fus., (att. R.A.F.).
Wilson, David, 2/Lt., 5th S. Lancs. Regt., died, 12/7/18 (att. R.A.F.).
Woodhouse, Lionel Mostyn, M.C., D.F.C., Lt., Essex Yeo., k. in a., 27/9/18 (att. R.A.F.).
Wright, Walter Herbert, Lt.-Col., K.O. Yorks. L.I. (T.F.R.), died, 8/11/15.
Yeoman, Bryan Frank Lawson, Lt., 4th London Regt., k. in a., 11/5/18 (att. R.A.F.).

The following should be added to the names of the undermentioned Officers :—

C.M.G.:—
Short, W.A., Lt.-Col., R.F.A.

D.S.O.:—
Ash, W.C.C., Lt.-Col., 23rd Midd'x. R.
Blois, D. G., Lt.-Col., R.F.A.
Bull, G., Brig.-Gen., R. Ir. Fus.
Clifford, H. F. H., Brig.-Gen., Suff. R.
Jourdain, C. E. A., Lt.-Col., L.N. Lan. R.
Leigh, C., Major, K.O. Sco. Bord.
Robinson, F. W., T/Lt.-Col., R.F.A.
Rochfort-Boyd, H. C., T/Lt.-Col., R.F.A.
Taylor, B. M., M.C., A/Major, D. of Corn. L.I.
Vince, A. N., Lt.-Col., L'pool R.
Williams, H. M., Major, R.A.V.C.

M.C., M.M.:—
Place, F. C., 2nd Lt., R. Lan. R.

M.C.:—
Amery-Parkes, D. J., Major, Midd'x. R. attd. M.G. Corps.
Barclay, G. W., Major, Rif. Brig.
Bartholomew, C., Capt., S. Gds., attd. M.G. Corps.
Belcher, G., Capt., R. Berks. R.
Bell, E. I., Capt., Gen. List.
Bennett, G. W., Capt., York & Lanc. R.
Body, E. U., Major, R.F.A.
Bott, G. G. R., Lt., S. Lan. R.
Boundy, F. E., 2nd Lt., L'pool. R.
Brown, H. M., 2nd Lt., R. Berks. R.
Buck, C. B. W., Rev., R.A.Ch.D.
Burlton, G. P., Lt., Norf. R.
Campbell, C. P., 2nd Lt., R.F.A.
Carnell, F. H. W., Capt., W. Yor. R.
Carson, C. G., Capt., Essex R.
Colbourne, E. K., 2nd Lt., R. Berks. R.
Collett, C. F., T/Capt., R.F.C.
Cooke, H. E., Capt., L'pool. R.
Cooper, F. W., Lt., R.E.
Corp, B., Capt., W. York. R.
Coster, C. V., Lt., M.G. Corps.
Cowie, G. J. H., 2nd Lt., R. Fus.
Cunningham, E. M., Capt., W. Rid. R.
Dadd, E. H., Capt., R.W. Fus.
Davenport, A. A. O., Capt., E. Lan. R.
Dewar, H. E., 2nd Lt., Ches. R.
Dobie, K. S., 2nd Lt., Gord. Highrs.
Duncan, C. W., Lt., N. Staff. R.
Durlacher, E. A. O., Capt., Worc. R.
Ewan, G. T., Capt., Manch. R.
Ferguson, W., Capt., Worc. R.
Fillingham, R. J., A/Major, R.G.A.
Fletcher, T. M., Lt., Durh. L.I.
Fox, C. A. N., Lt., N. Staff. R.
Frost, R. W., Lt., R.F.A.
Gonner, E. M., Capt., K.R. Rif. C.
Harris, N. L., Capt., R.W. Fus.
Hartley, N. T., Capt., W. York. R.
Hogge, T. H., Lt., R.F.A.
Holloway, H., A/Capt., E. Lan. R.
Hoyle, J. B., Lt., S. Lan. R.
Hunnybun, G. N., Major, 9th York. R.
Hunter, G. S., Lt., R.A.S.C.
Hutcheson, A. G., Capt., Sco. Rif.
Ingrams, F. R., 2nd Lt., E. Surr. R
Jackson, T. R., Capt., 7th D. of Corn. L.I.
Johns, O. L., 2nd Lt., R.F.A.
Keefe, R. C. M., T/Capt, 19th Manch. R.
Kidd, V. N., Major, 8th W. Rid. R.
Lubbock, The Hon. E. F. P., T/Capt., R.F.C.
Miall-Smith, G. E., Lt., Norf. R. and R.F.C.
Monypenny, P. B. S. G., Lt., R.W. Kent R.
Morrison, L., Capt., L'pool R.

Pavitt, C. F., Capt., R.A.S.C.
Pengelly, E. A., Capt., R.E.
Percy, R., Capt., L'pool R.
Phillips, F. E. S., 2nd Lt., 3rd Devon. R. and R.F.C.
Rennie, J. F., 2nd Lt., R.F.A.
Round, J. M., Capt., Essex R.
Ryan, A. E., A/Capt., R.W. Surr. R.
Seale, W. H., 2nd Lt., Oxf. and Bucks L.I.
Shone, G. B., Lt., S. Staff. R. and R.F.C.
Silver, S. E., T/Capt., Essex R.
Skrine, S. H., Lt., R.F.A.
Slingsby, H. L., Capt., Yorks L.I.
Spencer-Smith, H., Capt. and Qr.-Mr., Leic. R.
Stokes, J. H., Capt., R.W. Kent R.
Strachan, A. C., Lt., R.F.A.
Stang, J. S., Capt., R. High'rs.
Stretton, J de C., 2nd Lt., R. War. R.
Summers, W. A., Capt., 18th Hussars and R.F.C.
Taylor, R. B., Capt., R.A.M.C.
Thompson, R. L., Lt., A/Major, R.F.A.
Thomson, R. G., A/Capt., Shrops. L.I.
Thorowgood, R. W. T., Lt., R. War. R.
Trevenan, S. V., Capt., R.F.A.
Vernall, A. H., 2nd Lt., Leic. R.
Vesey, J., Lt., R. Berks R.
Viner, F. H., 2nd Lt., North'd Fus.
Wanklyn, J. S., 2nd Lt., R.F.A.
Ward, E. J., 2nd Lt., R.F.A.
Wasey, C. W. C., Capt., R. War. R. and R.F.C.
Watson, J. E. M., Rev., R.A.Ch.D.
Webb, J. G., Lt., R.W. Fus.
Weston, J. S. T., Capt., R. War. R.
Whelan, H. G., Lt., R. Muns. Fus.
White, F. H., Capt., Yorks L.I.
Williams, F. L., A/Capt., Bord. R., attd. M.G. Corps.
Wilson, D. R., 2nd Lt., K.R. Rif. C.
Wilson, Ralph Aylmer, 2nd Lt., Durh. L.I.
Wood, H. S., Lt., Dorset R.
Wright, P., A/Major, R.F.A.
Young, J. L., Lt., R. High'rs.

D.C.M.:—
Hill, M., 2nd Lt., R.E.
Wallis, G. H., Capt. and Qr.-Mr., R.W. Surr. R.
Morgan, W. J., Lt., R.F.A.

M.M.:—
Robson, F. W., 2nd Lt., M.G. Corps.
West, G., 2nd Lt., Leic. R.

The following should read as under, and not as previously stated:—
Prowse, C. B., D.S.O., T/Brig.-Gen., Som L.I.
Hopwood, F. W., M.M., 2nd Lt., R. Berks R.
Stirling, G. S., M.C., Capt., K. Af. Rif.
V.C. West, R. A., D.S.O., M.C., A/Lt.-Col., Tank Corps (Capt., N. Ir. Horse).

HOSPITAL SHIPS, TRANSPORTS AND MAIL STEAMERS CONNECTED WITH THESE ROLLS WHICH HAVE BEEN SUNK OR DISABLED BY ENEMY ACTION.

FALABA, 28/3/15, Mail.
WAYFARER, 11/4/15, Transport.
ROYAL EDWARD, 13/8/15, Transport.
SOUTHLAND, 2/9/15, Transport.
RAMAZAN, 19/9/15, Transport.
MARQUETTE, 23/10/15, Transport.
MERCIAN, 3/11/15, Transport.
MOORINA, 5/11/15, Transport.
ANGLIA, 17/11/15, Hospital Ship.
PERSIA, 30/12/15, Mail.
NORSEMAN, 22/1/16, Transport.
GALEKA, 20/10/16, Hospital Ship.
MINNEWASKA, 30/11/16, Transport.
BRITANNIC, 21/11/16, Hospital Ship.
BRAEMAR, 22/11/16, Hospital Ship.
IVERNIA, 1/1/17, Transport.
PRINCESS ALBERTA, 21/2/17, Transport.
GLENART-CASTLE, 1/3/17, Hospital Ship.
GEORGIAN, 8/3/17, Transport.
ASTURIAS, 23/3/17, Hospital Ship.
GLOUCESTER-CASTLE, 30/3/17, Hospital Ship.
ARCADIAN, 15/4/17, Transport.
CAMERONIA, 15/4/17, Transport.
DONEGAL, 17/4/17, Hospital Ship.
LANFRANC, 17/4/17, Hospital Ship.
TRANSYLVANIA, 4/5/17, Transport.
HARMATTAN, 5/5/17, Transport.
DOVER-CASTLE, 25/5/17, Hospital Ship.
SALTA, 10/6/17, Hospital Ship.
CAMERONIAN, 26/6/17, Transport.
ARMADALE, 26/6/17, Transport.
GOORKHA, 17/10/17, Hospital Ship.
UMGENI, 9/11/17, Mail.
ARAGON, 30/12/17, Transport.
OSMANIEH, 31/12/17, Transport.
REWA, 4/1/18, Hospital Ship (R.N.).
ANGLO-ARCADIAN, 22/1/18, Transport.
NORMANDY, 25/1/18, Mail.
GLENART-CASTLE, 26/2/18, Hospital Ship (2nd time).
KINGSTONIAN, 11/4/18, Transport.
PANCRAS, 4/5/18, Transport.
OMRAH, 12/5/18, Transport.
LEASOWE-CASTLE, 27/5/18, Transport.
MISSIR, 30/5/18, Transport.
LLANDOVERY-CASTLE, 28/6/18, Transport.
KOSSEIR, 21/7/18, Transport.
WARILDA, 3/8/18, Transport.
GALWAY-CASTLE, 12/9/18, Transport.
LEINSTER, 10/10/18, Mail.

INDEX.

5511114R00156

Printed in Great Britain
by Amazon.co.uk, Ltd.,
Marston Gate.